The Arnold Anthology of

BRITISH AND IRISH LITERATURE

in English

The Arnold Anthology of
BRITISH AND IRISH LITERATURE
in English

Edited by
ROBERT CLARK
Senior Lecturer in English,
University of East Anglia, UK

THOMAS HEALY
Reader in Renaissance Studies,
Birkbeck College, University of London, UK

A member of the Hodder Headline Group
LONDON • SYDNEY • AUCKLAND

First published in Great Britain in 1997 by
Arnold, a member of the Hodder Headline Group,
338 Euston Road, London NW1, 3BH

© 1997 Selection and editorial matter Arnold

British Library Cataloguing in Publication Data
A catalogue record for this book is available from the British Library

ISBN 0 340 62518 X

Printed and bound by Hartnolls, Bodmin, Cornwall

Contents

Renaissance

Restoration and Eighteenth Century ───────

Romantics

Victorians

Twentieth Century

Acknowledgements

The editors and publishers would like to thank the following for permission to use copyright material in this book:

Anon: 'The Seafarer' from *The Earliest English Poems* translated by Michael Alexander (Penguin Classics 1966, Second Revised Edition 1977). Copyright © Michael Alexander, 1966, 1977.

W.H. Auden: 'Musée des Beaux Arts', and 'In Memory of W.B. Yeats' from *Collected Shorter Poems 1930–1944* by W.H. Auden. 'In Praise of Limestone' from *Nones* by W.H. Auden. 'The Shield of Achilles' by W.H. Auden. Reprinted by permission of Faber & Faber.

Samuel Beckett: 'Krapp's Last Tape' by Samuel Beckett. Copyright © Samuel Beckett 1958. Reprinted by permission of Faber & Faber. 'Dante and the Lobster' from *More Pricks Than Kicks* by Samuel Beckett, published by Calder Publications Ltd, London. Copyright © Samuel Beckett 1934, 1966, 1970, 1973 and © The Samuel Beckett Estate 1993. Reprinted by kind permission of Calder Educational Trust, London.

Angela Carter: 'The Company of Wolves' by Angela Carter (first published in *Bananas* and subsequently in *The Bloody Chamber*). Copyright © The Estate of Angela Carter 1995. Reproduced by permission of the Estate of Angela Carter, c/o Rogers, Coleridge & White Ltd., 20 Powis Mews, London, W11 1JN.

Robert Crawford: 'Rain' from *A Scottish Assembly* by Robert Crawford (Chatto & Windus, London 1990). Copyright © 1990 Robert Crawford. Reprinted by permission of Random House.

Iain Crichton Smith: 'Timoshenko', from *Iain Crichton Smith: Selected Stories* by Iain Crichton Smith. Copyright © 1990 Iain Crichton Smith. Reprinted by permission of Carcanet Press Ltd.

Douglas Dunn: 'Reading Pascal in the Lowlands' from *Elegies* by Douglas Dunn. Copyright © Douglas Dunn 1985. 'St. Kilda's Parliament', and 'A Removal from Terry Street' from *Selected Poems 1964–1983* by Douglas Dunn. Copyright © Douglas Dunn 1969 and 1979. Reprinted by permission of Faber & Faber.

C. Day Lewis: Selection from 'The Magnetic Mountain' from *The Complete Poems* by C. Day Lewis (Sinclair Stevenson, London, 1992). Copyright © 1992 in this edition the Estate of C. Day Lewis. Reprinted by permission of Reed Consumer Books Ltd.

Carol Ann Duffy: 'Stealing' from *Selling Manhattan* by Carol Ann Duffy. Copyright © Carol Ann Duffy 1987, and 'In your mind' from *The Other Country* by Carol Ann Duffy. Copyright © Carol Ann Duffy 1990. Reprinted by permission of Anvil Press Poetry Ltd.

T.S. Eliot: 'The Love Song of J. Alfred Prufrock', 'Journey of the Magi', 'Marina' and 'Little Gidding' from *Collected Poems 1909–1962* by T.S. Eliot. Copyright © T.S. Eliot 1963. Reprinted by permission of Faber & Faber.

John Fowles: Selection from *The French Lieutenant's Woman* by John Fowles (Jonathan Cape, 1969). Copyright © John Fowles 1969. Reprinted by permission of Sheil Land Associates.

Graham Greene: 'Jubilee' from *Graham Greene: Collected Stories* (The Bodley Head, London 1972). Copyright © Graham Greene 1954. Reprinted by permission of David Higham Associates Ltd.

Thomas Hardy: 'The Three Strangers' from *Complete Short Stories* by Thomas Hardy (Macmillan General Books). Reprinted by permission of Macmillan, London. 'The Darkling Thrush', 'In Time of "The Breaking of Nations"', and 'Afterwards'. Reprinted from *The Complete Poems of Thomas Hardy* (Papermac, London, 1930). Reprinted by permission of Macmillan, London.

Tony Harrison: 'A Kumquat for John Keats' from *Permanently Bard* by Tony Harrison. Copyright © 1995 Tony Harrison. Reprinted by permission of Bloodaxe Books Ltd.

Seamus Heaney: 'Tollund Man' from *Wintering Out*, by Seamus Heaney. Copyright © Seamus Heaney 1972. 'Mossbawn: Two Poems in Dedication', and 'Kinship' from *North*. Copyright © Seamus Heaney 1975. 'Clearances III' from *The Haw Lantern* by Seamus Heaney. Copyright © Seamus Heaney 1987. Station Island VII' from *Station Island*, by Seamus Heaney. Copyright © Seamus Heaney 1984. Reprinted by permission of Faber & Faber.

Geoffrey Hill: No VII (p111, 16 lines) from *Mercian Hymns*, 'Pavana Dolorosa' (p149, 14 lines) from 'Lachrimae' in *Tenebrae*, '8 Vocations' (p159, 14 lines) from 'An Apology for the Revival of Christian architecture' all from *Collected Poems* by Geoffrey Hill (Penguin Books, 1985). Copyright © Geoffrey Hill 1971, 1978, 1985, 1994.

A.E. Housman: 'On Wenlock Edge: the wood's in trouble' from *A Shropshire Lad* (XXXI). Reprinted by permission of The Society of Authors as the literary representative of the Estate of A.E. Housman.

Ted Hughes: 'The Horses', 'The Howling of Wolves', and 'That Morning' from *Selected Poems 1957–1981* by Ted Hughes. Copyright © Ted Hughes 1982. Reprinted by permission of Faber & Faber.

James Joyce: 'Araby' from *Dubliners, The Corrected Text* by James Joyce, with explanatory notes by Robert Scholes (Jonathan Cape Ltd, 1967). Chapter 7 'Aeolus' pp 112–143 from *Ulysses* by James Joyce, World's Classics Edition) by James Joyce (Oxford University Press, 1922, *World's Classics Series*). Quoted with the permission of the Estate of James Joyce. © Estate of James Joyce.

Jackie Kay: 'Pounding Rain' from *The Adoption Papers* by Jackie Kay. Copyright © 1991 Jackie Kay. Reprinted by permission of Bloodaxe Books Ltd.

Rudyard Kipling: 'Beyond the Pale' extract from *Plain Tales From the Hills*, (Macmillan London, 1920). Reprinted by permission of A. P. Watt Ltd on behalf of The National Trust for Places of Historic Interest or Natural Beauty.

Linton Kwesi Johnson: 'Inglan is a Bitch'. Reprinted from *Tings an Times: Selected Poems* by Linton Kwesi Johnson, published by Bloodaxe Books Ltd. Copyright © 1991 Linton Kwesi Johnson. Reprinted by permission of the author.

Philip Larkin: 'Church Going' by Philip Larkin from *The Less Deceived* (The Marvell Press, 1955). Copyright © 1955 Philip Larkin. Reprinted by permission of The Marvell Press, England and Australia. 'The Whitsun Weddings' and 'For Sidney Bechet' from *The Whitsun Weddings* by Philip Larkin (Faber & Faber 1964). 'Annus Mirabilis' from *High Windows* by Philip Larkin (Faber & Faber 1974). Reprinted by permission of Faber & Faber.

D.H. Lawrence: 'The Fox', from *The Short Novels of D.H. Lawrence*, and 'Snake' from *The Complete Poems of D.H. Lawrence* Edited by Vivian de Sola Pinto & Warren Roberts. Copyright © D.H. Lawrence 1964, 1971. Reprinted by permission of Laurence Pollinger Ltd and the Estate of Frieda Lawrence Ravagli.

Doris Lessing: Selection from *The Golden Notebook* by Doris Lessing (Michael Joseph, London, 1962, 1972). Copyright © Doris Lessing 1962. Reprinted by permission of Penguin Books Ltd.

Liz Lochhead: 'The Grim Sisters' from *Dreaming Frankenstein & Collected Poems*. Copyright © Liz Lochhead 1984. Reprinted by permission of the author and Polygon. 'Bagpipe Muzak, Glasgow 1990' from *Bagpipe Muzak* by Liz Lochhead. Copyright © Liz Lochhead 1991. Reprinted by permission of Penguin Books.

Derek Mahon: 'A Disused Shed in Co. Wexford' from *Poems 1962–1978* by Derek Mahon. Copyright © Derek Mahon 1979. 'Courtyards in Delft' from *The Hunt by Night* by Derek Mahon. Copyright © Derek Mahon 1982. Reprinted by permission of Oxford University Press.

Hugh MacDiarmid: 'My Quarrel with England', 'At My Father's Grave', and 'Why I became a Scottish Nationalist' from *Collected Poems of Hugh MacDiarmid*. Reprinted by permission of Carcanet Press Limited.

Louis MacNeice: 'Belfast', 'Snow', and 'Bagpipe Music' by Louis MacNeice from *Collected Poems 1925–1948* (Faber & Faber, London). Copyright © Louis MacNeice. Reprinted by permission of David Higham Associates Ltd.

John McGahern: 'High Ground' from *The Collected Stories* by John McGahern. Copyright © John McGahern 1992. Reprinted by permission of Faber & Faber.

Flann O'Brien: Selection from *At Swim-Two-Birds* by Flann O'Brien (HarperCollins, London). Copyright © Brian O'Nolan 1939 and Copyright © Evelyn O'Nolan 1967.

Sean O'Casey: 'Juno and the Paycock' from *Three Plays* by Sean O'Casey (Macmillan, London, 1957). Reprinted by permission of Macmillan.

George Orwell: 'Shooting an Elephant' from *Collected Essays* by George Orwell (Secker & Warburg, London, 1950). Copyright © The estate of the late Sonia Brownell Orwell and Martin Secker and Warburg Ltd. Reprinted by permission of A.M. Heath & Co. Ltd.

Samuel Pepys: *The Diary of Samuel Pepys* (Bell & Hyman Ltd, London, 1985). Reprinted by Permission of the Peters, Fraser & Dunlop Group Ltd.

Harold Pinter: 'The Dumb Waiter' by Harold Pinter. Copyright © Harold Pinter 1960. Reprinted by permission of Faber & Faber .

Siegfried Sassoon: 'Attack' from *Collected Poems 1908–1956* by Siegfried Sassoon (Faber, London). Reprinted by permission of George Sassoon.

Tom Stoppard: 'The Real Inspector Hound' by Tom Stoppard. Copyright © Tom Stoppard 1968, 1970. Reprinted by permission of Faber & Faber.

Dylan Thomas: 'Fern Hill', and 'A Refusal to Mourn the Death, by Fire, of a Child in London' by Dylan Thomas from *Collected Poems 1934–1953* (J. M. Dent, London 1988). Reprinted by permission of David Higham Associates Ltd.

Evelyn Waugh: Selection from 'Unconditional Surrender' by Evelyn Waugh (Chapman & Hall, 1961). Copyright © Evelyn Waugh 1961. Reprinted by permission of the Peters, Fraser & Dunlop Group Ltd.

Virginia Woolf: Selection from *Mrs Dalloway* by Virginia Woolf, and 'The Mark on the Wall', from *A Haunted House and Other Short Stories*. Reprinted by permission of The Society of Authors as the literary representative of the Estate of Virginia Woolf.

W. B. Yeats: 'Down by the Salley Gardens', 'The Lake Isle of Innisfree', 'The Secret Rose', 'The Fiddler of Dooney', 'No Second Troy', 'The Wild Swans at Coole', 'In Memory of Major Robert Gregory', 'An Irish Airman Foresees His Death', 'Easter 1916', 'The Second Coming', 'A Prayer for My Daughter', 'Sailing to Byzantium', 'Leda and the Swan', 'Among School Children', 'Byzantium', 'The Crazy Jane Poems': ('And the Bishop', 'Reproved', 'On the Day of Judgment', 'And Jack the Journeyman', 'On God', 'Talks with the Bishop), 'The Statues', 'The Circus Animals' Desertion', and 'Under Ben Bulben' from *The Collected Poems of W. B. Yeats* (Macmillan, London 1933). Reprinted by permission of A. P. Watt Ltd on behalf of Michael Yeats.

Preface

Over the last ten years this book's editors have repeatedly heard teachers in higher education voice their desire for a new one-volume anthology which would introduce students to a wide historic range of writing in English. Existing anthologies were felt to be, among other things, either too large, unwieldy and expensive, or too fragmented and limited. After considerable consultation with colleagues in Britain, Ireland, the rest of Europe, and in places as diverse as Hong Kong and South Africa, we became convinced of the viability of producing an anthology to meet the needs of current and future students either following introductory courses in literature or undertaking degrees in which literature in English was only one component. *The Arnold Anthology of British and Irish Literature in English* is the result.

We have chosen texts which have intrinsic value and are also representative of the types of writing which emerged from different periods. This is intended as a teaching anthology, not a comprehensive survey of British and Irish literature. As far as possible we have tried to provide as many full texts as we can, or, if this was not possible, to provide an extract of sufficient length for a student to be able to achieve a sense of the manner and concerns of the whole. We believe it is preferable to have one complete text rather than a collection of short excerpts by divers hands, even though this sometimes means one piece can appear to have an overly representative status for a whole genre in a period. Although such a policy has meant that some texts or authors occupy, in one sense, a disproportionately large number of pages, and that the anthology has to omit many significant works, the advantages of being able to read plays, novellas, or longer poems in their entirety significantly outweighs other factors.

A particular problem in selecting texts, however, has been the novel. It would have been too demanding on space to have included the full text of a major novel. Yet, as one of our advisers remarked about the nineteenth-century, to omit the novel would be to ignore 'the spirit of the age'. We have therefore included extracts of novels, particularly from the eighteenth and nineteenth centuries, which reflect central literary concerns of their respective periods and which, while supplying a useful extract for study, will also, we hope, entice students to read the whole.

At an early stage in this anthology's development we realised that it would be impossible to include a useful sample of all writing in English throughout the centuries and decided to focus on Britain and Ireland. Fortunately, *The Arnold Anthology of Post-Colonial Literatures in English* exists to introduce students to recent literature outside Europe and, it is hoped, a volume of

American writing will shortly appear as well. Many of the texts selected for this volume will be familiar to experienced readers because they continue to be the foundations on which we base our sense of English writing. *Lycidas*, *The Rape of the Lock* and *The Love Song of J. Alfred Prufrock*, to take but three examples, are included, however, not because they are canonical in a narrow perspective but because they continue to generate controversy and excite new readings. It is in this dynamic sense that they are touchstones of our experience of English and why they rightly need to be introduced to a new generation of readers. As well as more familiar texts, however, we have tried to include writing which is increasingly the subject of critical interest – such as women's poetry – or which reflects the diversity of regional literatures, notably in Scotland, and the different national perspective of Ireland in the Twentieth Century.

In allocating space to the various periods, we have tried to reflect the likely demands students at an early stage with English studies will make on them. Thus, there is more space given to Renaissance, nineteenth-century, and twentieth-century writing than to other periods because a majority of students' efforts tends to fall there. Although following a chronological pattern, we have not placed texts strictly according to the dates of their composition or their author's birth. Literary logic often defies chronology, so that Milton's *Paradise Lost* and Bunyan's *Pilgrim's Progress*, despite being published during the Restoration, seem more appropriately placed in the Renaissance section. Similarly, *Heart of Darkness* is in the Twentieth Century section and Hardy's poems are placed with the Victorians, though this ignores their centuries of composition. We have tried to arrange texts in a sequence which we feel is helpful for their study.

The texts in this anthology are newly edited. Rather than apply common editorial principles throughout the volume, we have largely approached the editing of texts on a case by case basis with a view, first, of ensuring that a work's integrity has not been compromised by applying modern editorial conventions of spelling or punctuation simply to make it 'an easier read', and, second, not retaining original spelling or conventions of presentation for their own sake where they would add nothing to the student's reading experience. For example, Wyatt's poetry is presented largely unpunctuated, as the manuscripts have it, because the insecurity of meaning generated by the difficulty in construing how the lines might be read appears an intrinsic part of the poetic intention: one lost by introducing modernised punctuation which attempts to force the lines into a more limited range of meanings. In contrast, the convention of contracting the spelling of most past tenses (from "ed" to "'d") in early modern drama has not been followed because either the principles of pronunciation or the shortage of 'e's in the compositor's print box no longer apply. In the case of the medieval texts, we have not sought unduly to modernise, or 'translate', the Middle English, even though we recognise that many students find this language difficult. What is even more uninviting would be reading these texts in some flat modern English version. This volume had no wish to put a writer such as Chaucer into a grey suit.

At any early stage with this project, we recognised that in order to devise a volume useful to a range of readers in differing educational environments we would need to draw extensively on the expertise of other scholars. We have been extremely fortunate in bringing together an editorial board whose advice has been crucial in helping us choose and prepare texts. Ultimately, we have not been able to take advantage of every suggestion – the responsibility for the result rests with the two editors – but the input of a team of internationally distinguished academics from varying pedagogic traditions has helped shape a distinctive anthology.

One of the key complaints about anthologies is that they are physically unattractive to use. The pleasure of reading, which is vital to the experience of literature, is considerably reduced through poor presentation. We were determined to overcome this and, with the advantages of modern technology, undertook to prepare this anthology for publication ourselves, using desktop publishing to prepare each page. The advantages of this have helped ensure textual accuracy and attractiveness of presentation.

Undertaking the preparation of camera-ready copy has entailed a closeness of co-operation with the publisher at every stage. Although we set the pages on our own computers, Arnold helped us develop our desktop skills, and we have been able to work continuously with their designers and production team selecting typefaces, discussing page layout, learning much of the mechanics of book production. Without the initial efforts of Alison Bond and, latterly, the contributions of Marianne Kirby and her production team this book would not appear as it does. The meticulous work of Alison Kelly in proof-reading has contributed greatly to the accuracy of the texts and annotation. It is with Christopher Wheeler, Director of Humanities at Arnold, however, that a good deal of the credit in producing this book rests. Christopher has been a judicious blend of visionary editor and practical negotiator: first seeing the book's potential, dealing with the complicated issues of copyright permissions, providing clear-sighted advice and encouragement at every stage, and ensuring the book was completed in a reasonable time frame.

As well as our advisory board, we are indebted to numerous individuals, and to Birkbeck College and the University of East Anglia for their assistance. Valerie Allen, Elaine Ho, Robert Miles, Tony Parr, Victor Sage, Janet Todd and Susan Wiseman made many valuable suggestions about our selections and annotation. Louise Aikman, Chris Brandon-Jones, Simon Mann, José Antonio Menor Martínez, and Mary Enna de Soissons greatly helped in the preparation and layout of texts. Marianne and Nicolas Clark and Margaret Healy were patient and supportive of this project throughout. The faults which remain are our own.

Robert Clark
Thomas Healy

April 1997

Medieval

In the ninth century, King Alfred referred to the language he spoke as 'Englisc', a tongue distinct from the Celtic, Saxon and Norse languages used by the rest of Britain's and Ireland's inhabitants. While debate continues about the relation of this and other languages to the English which developed after the Norman conquest of 1066, by the thirteenth century Alfred's Englisc was no longer understood in Britain, and compared with modern English it is a foreign language. However, Old English's literary styles, particularly its use of alliteration, exercised wide influence on medieval writing, and an example of it is included here in a translation which attempts to capture some of the poetry's sound as well as sense.

With the arrival of the Normans, England became a European country in a way which it has seldom been since: Anglo-Norman and French became the language of the court and polite society; the country was closely linked to the continent through a shared religion and the Latin culture it promoted; through conquest and inheritance, the English monarchy could lay claim to large territories in present-day France as well as Ireland and Wales. But, if in one sense more European, Britain was also less united than subsequently. Scotland throughout this period remains an independent kingdom, and, generally, regional identities are stronger and linguistically more pronounced.

This European dimension had an enormous impact on literature. With the introduction of an Anglo-Norman culture among the elite, writers turned to continental literary models emanating from France and Italy, combining these with native traditions which had their origins in Northern European oral forms. The distinctive hybridities which result are one of the strengths of this period's writing.

This is particularly noticeable in the great wealth of writing produced in the second half of the fourteenth century. Chaucer embraces the French Romance tradition, new literary ideas emerging from the Italy of Petrarch and Boccaccio, classical precedents, and a distinct ear for contemporary English. At virtually the same moment the Gawain poet draws on the alliterative techniques of Anglo-Saxon expression to articulate the culmination of a vernacular tradition, while William Langland modifies the visionary expression associated with transcendent sacred poetry and the Church's Latin scriptural heritage to a specific English setting and idiom.

Unfortunately, the civil wars which raged throughout the fifteenth century were not conducive to literature, and the enormous achievements of fourteenth-century English writing were not matched again until the sixteenth century. The fifteenth century did, however, see the emergence of a fluent 'Inglis' literature in Scotland, often openly paying homage to Chaucer and illustrating the gradual spread of the language into the lowlands. Much Scots and virtually all Irish and Welsh literature of this period, however, is in these countries' Celtic vernaculars and, as such, is beyond the scope of this anthology.

The too commonly held view that medieval writing reflects a fundamentally alien – and less developed – culture, whose feudal social order, religious devotions, and localised dialects separate it from 'modern' English and later cultural concerns, has been powerfully challenged in recent years. This writing's experimental quality; its mixing of elite and popular styles; its interest in questions of gender and the individual; its projection of often radical social visions has led us increasingly to realise a sophisticated, complex world and a highly self-conscious, controlled literature.

OLD AND MIDDLE ENGLISH LYRICS (*c.*1000–*c.*1450)

These short pieces, mostly by anonymous authors, illustrate the concerns of medieval writing. The Old English *Seafarer* characteristically merges secular preoccupations – here the exacting physical aspects of life at sea – with spiritual issues and a symbolic representation of human life. Other lyrics reflect a mixture of simple and complex expression both sacred and secular. These poems also display the period's concern with linguistic play, abounding in oxymorons, macaronic techniques, and alliteration.

The Seafarer (tenth or early eleventh century)

Translated by Michael Alexander

The tale I frame shall be found to tally:
the history is of myself.
          Sitting day-long
at an oar's end clenched against clinging sorrow,
breast-drought I have borne, and bitternesses too.
5 I have coursed my keel through care-halls without end
over furled foam, I forward in the bows
through the narrowing night, numb, watching
for the cliffs we beat along.
          Cold then
nailed my feet, frost shrank on
10 its chill clamps, cares sighed
hot about heart, hunger fed
on a mere-wearied mind.
          No man blessed
with a happy land-life is like to guess
how I, aching-hearted, on ice-cold seas
15 have wasted whole winters; the wanderer's beat,
cut off from kind . . . .
hung with hoar-frost.
          Hail flew in showers,
there was no sound there but the slam of waves
along an icy sea. The swan's blare

20　my seldom amusement; for men's laughter
there was curlew-call, there were the cries of gannets,
for mead-drinking the music of the gull.
To the storm striking the stone cliffs
gull would answer, eagle scream
25　from throats frost-feathered. No friend or brother
by to speak with the despairing mind.

This he little believes whose life has run
sweet in the burghs, no banished man,
but well-seen at wine-round, my weariness of mind
30　on the ways stretching over the salt plains.
Night thickened, and from the north snowflakes;
hail fell on the frost-bound earth,
coldest of grains.

　　　　　　There come thoughts now
knocking my heart, of the high waves,
35　clashing salt-crests, I am to cross again.
Mind-lust maddens, moves as I breathe
soul to set out, seek out the way
to a far folk-land flood-beyond.

For no man above mould is so mood-proud,
40　so thoroughly equipped, so quick to do,
so strong in his youth, or with so staunch a lord
that before faring on the sea he does not fear a little
whither the Lord shall lead him in the end.
His heart is not in harping nor in the having of rings,
45　has no delight in women nor the world's gladnesses
nor can think of any thing outside the thrash of waves,
sea-struck, is distracted, stillness lost.

The thriving of the treeland, the town's briskness,
a lightness over the leas, life gathering,
50　everything urges the eagerly mooded
man to venture on the voyage he thinks of,
the faring over flood, the far bourn.
And the cuckoo calls him in his care-laden voice,
scout of summer, sings of new griefs
55　that shall make breast-hoard bitter.
　　　　　　　　　Blithe heart cannot know,
through its happiness, what hardships they suffer
who drive the foam-furrow furthest from land.
Spirit breaks from the body's chest
to the sea's acres; over earth's breadth

---

49 leas: grasslands, generally untilled land.　　**53 cuckoo**: usually carrying happier assoications of the coming of Spring. In Welsh poetry, however, a bird of melancholy and lament, and this is the context here.

60   and whale's range roams the mind now,
        homes to the breast hungry and thirsty.

        Cuckoo's dirge drags out my heart,
        whets will to the whale's beat
        across wastes of water: far warmer to me
65   are the Lord's kindnesses than this life of death
        lent us on land.
                 I do not believe
        earthly estate is everlasting:
        three things all ways threaten a man's peace
        and one before the end shall overthrow his mind;
70   either illness or age or the edge of vengeance
        shall draw out the breath from the doom-shadowed.
        Wherefore, for earl whosoever, it is afterword,
        the praise of livers-on, that, lasting, is best:
        won in the world before wayfaring,
75   forged, framed here, in the face of enmity,
        in the Devil's spite: deeds, achievements.
        That after-speakers should respect the name
        and after them angels have honour toward it
        for always and ever. From those everlasting joys
80   the daring shall not die.
                 Days are soon over,
        on earth imperium with the earl's hand fails;
        kings are not now, kaisers are not,
        there are no gold-givers like the gone masters
        who between them framed the first deeds in the world,
85   in their lives lordly, in the lays renowned.
        That chivalry is changed, cheer is gone away,
        it is a weaker kind who wields earth now,
        sweats for its bread. Brave men are fewer,
        all excellence on earth grows old and sere
90   as now does every man over the world;
        age fares against him, his face bleaches
        and his thatch thins: had a throng of friends
        of noble houses, knows now they all
        are given to the ground. That grieves his white head.
95   Once life is going, this gristle slackens;
        nothing can pain or please flesh then,
        he cannot stir a finger, fix his thinking.

        A man may bury his brother with the dead
        and strew his grave with the golden things
100   he would have him take, treasures of all kinds,
        but gold hoarded when he here lived
        cannot allay the anger of God
        towards a soul sin-freighted.

[ll.104–24
Great is the terrible power of God, before which the earth shall turn aside; He established the firm foundations, the expanse of the earth, the heavens above. Foolish is the man who does not fear his Lord; death shall come upon him unprepared. Blessed is the man who lives in trust; grace shall come to him from the heavens. The Lord shall confrm that spirit in him, for he believes in His might. A man should manage a headstrong spirit and keep it in its place, and be true to men, fair in his dealings. He should treat every man with measure, restrain enmity towards friend and foe. He may not wish his cherished friend to be given over to the fire nor to be burnt on the pyre, yet Doom is stronger and God is mightier than any man's conception. Let us think where it is that we may find a home and then consider how we may come thither, and then indeed we may strive so that we may be able to enter into that everlasting blessedness where all life is in the Lord's love, the bliss of heaven. Thanks be to the Holy One therefore, the Prince of Glory, the everlasting Lord, that He has raised us up forever. Amen.]

Sumer is icumen in (13th century)

	Sing cuccu, nu. Sing cuccu.	now
	Sing cuccu. Sing cuccu, nu.	
	Sumer is icumen in,	
	Lhude sing cuccu.	loud
5	Groweth sed and bloweth med	flowers; meadow
	And springth the wude nu,	wood
	Sing cuccu.	
	Awe bleteth after lomb,	ewe
	Lhouth after calve cu,	
10	Bulluc sterteth, bucke verteth,	bullock; farts
	Murie sing cuccu.	
	Cuccu, cuccu,	
	Well singes thu, cuccu,	you sing well
	Ne swik thu naver nu.	

Hymn to Mary (13th century)

	Of on that is so fair and bright,	one
	Velud maris stella,	like the star of the sea
	Brighter than the dayes light,	
	Parens et puella;	parent and maid
5	Ic crye to thee, thou se to me,	

104–24: these lines are almost certainly a later scribal addition. **Sumer is:** This is a round or *rota* designed to be sung by a number of singers.

1 **cuccu:** the sound of the cuckoo, a bird associated with the arrival of Spring. **9:** The cow lows after her calf. **14:** Do not ever stop now.

Levedy, preye thy sone for me,   lady
Tam pia,   so pious
That ic mote come to thee,   may
Maria.

10 Levedy, flowr of alle thing,
Rosa sine spina,   rose without thorns
Thu bere Jesu, Hevene King,
Gratia divina.   through grace divine
Of alle thu berst the pris,   you are the most esteemed
15 Levedy, Quene of Parais   paradise
Electa;   chosen
Maide milde, moder es
Effecta.   proved

All this world was forlore
20 *Eva peccatrice,*   through the sin of Eve
Till our Lord was ibore
De te genitrice.   of you begotten
With '*Ave*' it went away,
Thuster night, and cometh the day   dark
25 *Salutis.*   of salvation
The welle springeth ut of thee   out
Virtutis.   of virtue

Well he wot he is thy sone,   knows
Ventre quem portasti;   whom you carried in your womb
30 He will nought werne thee thy bone   deny; request
Parvum quem lactasti.   whom you suckled when small
So hende and so god he is   gracious
He haveth brought ous to blis
Superni,   of heaven
35 That haveth idut the foule put   shut the foul pit
Inferni.   of hell

Of care, conseil thou ert best,
Felix fecundata;   fortunate and fruitful
Of alle wery thou ert rest.
40 *Mater honorata.*   honoured mother
Besek him with milde mod   beseech; mood
That for ous all sad his blod   shed
In cruce,   on the cross
That we moten comen till him,   may come to him
45 *In luce.*   in light

37: of troubles you are the best counsellor.

When I see on the Cross (14th century)

	Whanne ic se on rode	cross
	Jesu, my lemman	lover
	And besiden him stonden	
	Marye and Johan,	
5	And his rig iswongen	back scourged
	And his side istungen	pierced
	For the luve of man;	
	Well ou ic to wepen	ought
	And sinnes for to leten,	give up
10	Yif ic of luve can.	know
	Yif ic of luve can.	
	Yif ic of luve can.	

The Rat Poem (14th century)

	I comawnde alle the ratones that are here abowte,	command
	That non dwelle in this place, withinne ne withowte,	
	Thorgh the vertu of Iesu Crist, that Mary bare abowte,	
	That alle creatures owyn for to lowte,	
5	And thorgh the vertu of Mark, Mathew, Luke, an Jon –	
	Alle foure Awangelys corden into on –	
	Thorgh the vertu of Sent Geretrude, that mayde clene,	
	God graunte that grace	
	That non raton dwelle in the place	
10	That here namis were nemeled in;	mentioned in
	And thorgh the vertu of Sent Kasi,	
	That holy man, that prayed to God Almyty	
	For skathes that thei deden	
	Hys medyn	
15	Be dayes and be nyght,	
	God bad hem flen and gon out of euery manesse syght.	flee
	Dominus Deus Sabaot! Emanuel, the gret Godes name!	
	I betweche thes place from ratones and from alle other schame.	
	God saue this place fro alle other wykked wytes,	
20	Bothe be dayes and be nytes! *et in nomine Patris et Filtii, etc.*	

The Rat Poem 4: That all creatures ought to reverence.
6 corden: brought together. 7 Sent Geretrude: Abbess of Nivell in France (d.659), whose sign contains rats. 11 Sent Kasi: St Nicasius, celebrated as the enemy of rats. 13–14: for harm that they did to his meadow. 18: I commit [to God's protection] this place [to be free] from rats and all other harmful things. 19 wytes: intents.

I sing of a maiden (15th century)

I sing of a maiden
That is makeles;   *without equal*
King of alle kinges
To here sone she ches.   *she chose for her son*

5   He cam also stille
Ther his moder was,
As dew in Aprille
That falleth on the grass.

He cam also stille
10 To his moderes bowr,   *mother's bower*
As dew in Aprille
That falleth on the flowr.

He cam also stille
Ther his moder lay,
15 As dew in Aprille
That falleth on the spray.

Moder and maiden
Was never non but she;
Well may swich a lady   *such*
20 Godes moder be.

Adam lay in bondage (15th century)

Adam lay ibounden,
Bounden in a bond;
Foure thousand winter
Thought he not too long.
5   And all was for an apple,
And apple that he tok,
As clerkes finden   *scholars*
Wreten in here book.

Ne hadde the apple take ben,
10 The apple taken ben,
Ne hadde never our Lady
A ben Hevene Quen.   *have been Heaven's Queen*
Blissed be the time
That apple take was!
15 Therfore we moun singen,   *may*
'*Deo gracias*'.   *thanks be to God*

Adam 2 bond: sin and death as a result of the Fall.

Of his Ugly Lady (15th century)

Of my lady well me rejoise I may.
Hir golden forheed is full narw and smal;
Hir browes been lik to dim reed coral;   pale red
And as the jeet hir yen glistren ay.   black; eyes

5   Hir bowgy cheekes been as softe as clay,   baggy
With large jowes and substancial.   jaws
Hir nose a pentice is that it ne shal   over-hanging roof
Reine in hir mouth thogh she uprightes lay.   face up

Hir mouth is nothing scant with lippes gray;
10   Hir chin unnethe may be seen at al.   scarcely
Hir comly body shape as a footbal,
And she singeth full like a papejaey.   parrot

The Blacksmiths (15th century)

Swarte-smeked smethes, smatered with smoke,   smoke-blackened smiths
Drive me to deth with den of here dintes;   din; blows
Swich nois on nightes ne herd men never,
What knavene cry and clatering of knockes.
5   The cammede kongons cryen after 'Col! col!'
And blowen here bellewes that all here brain brestes.   burst
'Huf, puf,' seith that on, 'Haf, paf,' that other.
They spitten and sprawlen and spellen many spelles,   tell; tales
They gnawen and gnacchen, they grones togidere,
10   And holden hem hote with here hard hamers.
Of a bole hide ben here barm felles,
Here shankes ben shakeled for the fere flunderes.
Hevy hameres they han that hard ben handled,
Stark strokes they striken on a steled stocke.   anvil
15   'Lus, bus, las, das,' rowten by rowe.   beaten by row
Swiche dolful a dreme the Devil it todrive.
The maister longeth a litil and lasheth a lesse,
Twineth hem twein and toucheth a treble.
'Tik, tak, hic, hac, tiket, taket, tik, tak,
20   Lus, bus, lus, das'. Swich lif they leden,
Alle clothemeres, Christ hem give sorwe.
May no man for brenwateres on night han his rest.

Of his Ugly Lady: this is likely to be by Thomas Hoccleve.
Blacksmiths 5: The crooked mis-shaped creatures cry
'Coal, coal'. **11–12:** their leather aprons are made of
bull's hides, protecting their legs against fiery
sparks. **16–18:** May the Devil destroy such a troublesome noise. The master smith lengthens a little [piece of
iron] and lashes out at a smaller, turns them together
and strikes a treble [note].

21 clothemeres: literally mare-cladder, i.e. clothing horses
in armour. **22:** No man can get his rest at night on
account of burning water, i.e. the water the hot iron is
plunged into.

THE GAWAIN POET (c.1375)

A small manuscript in the British Library contains four of the most important Middle English poems (*Pearl, Cleanness, Patience* and *Sir Gawain and the Green Knight*). All are felt to be by the same author, whose identity is unknown. Written in a north-western dialect, they exemplify the continued traditions of native alliterative composition in contrast to the newer continental modes popular among poets such as Chaucer.

From Sir Gawain and the Green Knight

Gawain is the longest poem in the manuscript and illustrates the popular chivalric romance, though its ironic tone questions the exaggerated heroic qualities associated with the genre. Set in the legendary Arthurian past, the poem relates the appearance of a mysterious green knight at Arthur's court during the Christmas festivities. He proposes a beheading contest. He will allow a knight to try to cut off his head, if, a year later, the knight will submit to the same ordeal. Gawain takes up the challenge and beheads the Green Knight, only to have the knight pick up his head and depart. Concerned with honour and the development of Christian virtue, the poem details Gawain's quest to fulfil his knightly obligation in seeking the Green Knight. The following extract is the concluding section of the work. Gawain, having endured cold and monsters, comes to a castle where he has good entertainment at the year's end. His host suggests they should exchange whatever they gain during the day. Gawain agrees but keeps a girdle which his hostess gives him, one which is supposed to preserve him from death. The time then arrives for him to conclude his quest.

	Now neghes the Nw Yere and the nyght passes	nears
	The day dryves to the derk, as Dryghtyn biddes.	God bids
	Bot wylde wederes of the worlde wakned theroute;	
	Clowdes kesten kenly the colde to the erthe,	
5	Wyth nyye innoghe of the northe, the naked to tene.	
	The snawe snitered ful snart, that snayped the wylde;	
	The werbelande wynde wapped fro the hyghe	
	And drof uche dale ful of dryftes ful grete.	
	The leude lystened ful wel, that ley in his bedde;	knight
10	Thagh he lowkes his liddes, ful lyttel he slepes,	shuts
	Bi uch kok that crue he knwe wel the steuen.	
	Deliverly he dressed up er the day sprenged,	dawned
	For there was lyght of a laumpe that lemed in his chambre.	shone
	He called to his chamberlayn, that cofly hym swared,	fast replied
15	And bede hym bryng hym his bruny and his blonk sadel;	mail; horse
	That other ferkes hym up and feches hym his wedes,	bestirs; clothes
	And graythes me Sir Gawayn upon a grett wyse.	

3–7: Outside the world's wild weather awoke, clouds keenly drove cold down to the earth, a bitter north wind tormented naked flesh. Snow sleeted sharply, biting the wild animals; the whistling wind blew from the heights and filled each dale full of great drifts.

11: By each cock that crowed he knew the time. Cocks were thought to know the precise hour and believed to cry at midnight, 3 a.m. and an hour before dawn. 17: And dresses Sir Gawain in splendid style.

Fyrst he clad hym in his clothes, the colde for to were,　　keep out
And sythen his other harnays, that holdely was keped,
20　Bothe his paunce and his plates, piked ful clene,
The rynges rokked of the roust of his riche bruny;
And al was fresch as upon fyrst, and he was fayn thenne
　　To thonk.
He hade upon uche pece,　　wore
25　Wypped ful wel and wlonk;　　polished; splendid
The gayest into Grece,
The burne bede bryng his blonk

Whyle the wlonkest wedes he warp on hymselven –
His cote wyth the conysaunce of the clere werkes
30　Ennurned upon velvet, vertuus stones
Aboute beten and bounden, enbrauded semes,
And fayre furred withinne wyth fayre pelures –
Yet laft he not the lace, the ladies gifte;　　left; belt
That forgat not Gawayn, for gode of hymselven.
35　Bi he hade belted the bronde upon his balwe haunches,　　smooth
Thenn dressed he his drurye double hym aboute,
Swythe swethled umbe his swange swetely that knyght.
The gordel of the grene silke that gay wel bisemed,
Upon that ryol red clothe that ryche was to schewe.　　observe
40　Bot wered not this ilk wyye for wele this gordel,　　for its wealth
For pryde of the pendauntes, thagh polyst thay were,　　pride
And thagh the glyterande golde glent upon endes,　　glittering
Bot for to saven hymself when suffer hym byhoved,
To byde bale withoute dabate of bronde hym to were
45　　　Other knyffe.
Bi that the bolde mon boun　　was ready
Wynnes theroute bilyve;　　he came out quickly
Alle the meyny of renoun　　noble household
He thonkkes ofte ful ryve.　　abundantly

50　Thenne was Gryngolet graythe, that gret was and huge,　　ready
And hade ben sojourned saverly and in a siker wyse;
Hym lyst prik for poynt, that proude hors thenne.
The wyye wynnes hym to and wytes on his lyre,　　knight went; coat
And sayde soberly hymself and by his soth sweres,　　truth
55　'Here is a meyny in this mote that on menske thenkkes.

19–21: And then in his armour that had been carefully kept, both his abdominal armour and his plate armour, which had been kept clean, the rings of his mail-coat cleansed of rust. **22–23:** And all was as new, which he was thankful for. **26–27:** The most elegant knight fromhere to Greece now ordered his man to bring his horse. **29–32:** His coat – with the badge of bright workmanship worked on velvet with potent gems both inlaid and surrounding it, embroidered seams, and well-lined with fair furs.

30 Vertuus: gems were thought to have powers to resist evils. **36–38:** When he had doubled his love-token about him, the knight sweetly wrapping it about his waist. The green-silk girdle well became him. **44–45:** To suffer pain without resistance or defence with sword or knife. **51–52:** He had been well stabled and securely, now he was ready to gallop, that proud horse. **55:** There is a company in this castle that thinks on grace. May the man who supports them have joy; the dear lady, may love always attend her.

The mon hem maynteines, joy mot he have;
The leve lady on lyve, luf hir bityde!
Yif thay for charyte cherysen a gest,   cherish
And halden honour in her honde, the hathel hem yelde   lord; reward
60 That haldes the heven upon hyghe, and also yow alle!
And yif I myght lyf upon londe lede any quyle,
I schuld rech yow sum rewarde redyly, if I myght.'
Thenn steppes he into stirop and strydes alofte.
His schalk schewed hym his schelde; on schulder he hit laght,
65 Gordes to Gryngolet with his gilt heles,   spurs
And he startes on the ston, stod he no lenger
      To praunce.
      His hathel on hors was thenne,   man
      That bere his spere and launce
70   'This kastel to Kryst I kenne: commend
      He gef hit ay god chaunce!'   fortune

The brygge was brayde doun, and the brode yates   bridge
Unbarred and born open upon bothe halve.
The burne blessed hym bilyve, and the bredes passed;
75 Prayses the porter bifore the prynce kneled,
Gef hym God and goud day, that Gawayn he save;
And went on his way with his wyye one,   servant
That schulde teche hym to tourne to that tene place   painful
Ther the ruful race he schulde resayve.   blow
80 Thay bowen bi bonkkes ther boghes ar bare,   passed; hillsides
Thay clomben bi clyffes ther clenges the colde.
The heven was up halt, bot ugly therunder;
Mist muged on the mor, malt on the mountes,   drizzled; melted
Uch hille hade a hatte, a myst hakel huge.   mist-cap
85 Brokes byled and breke bi bonkkes aboute,
Schyre schaterande on schores ther thay doun schowved.
Wela wylle was the way ther thay bi wod schulden,
Til hit was sone sesoun that the sunne ryses
      That tyde.   at that season
90   Thay were on a hille ful hyghe,
      The quyte snaw lay bisyde;
      The burne that rod hym by   man
      Bede his mayster abide.

'For I haf wonnen yow hider, wyye, at this tyme,   brought
95 And now nar ye not fer fro that note place   designated
That ye han spied and spuryed so specially after   sought

64: His guide handed him his shield and he slung it on his shoulder. **74–76:** The knight blessed himself and passed over the boards; praised the porter who knelt before the prince, who in turn commended Gawain to God, that he would save him.

82: The clouds were high but threatening underneath. 85: Brooks boiled and broke on the hillsides, splashing brightly on the banks as the riders forced their way down. The path was wild which they took through the wood.

Bot I schal say yow for sothe, sythen I yow knowe
And ye ar a lede upon lyve that I wel lovy,   *lively knight; love*
Wolde ye worch bi my wytte, ye worthed the better.
100 The place that ye prece to ful perelous is halden;   *hasten to*
Ther wones a wyye in that waste, the worst upon erthe,   *lives*
For he is stiffe and sturne, and to strike lovies,   *strong; loves*
And more he is then any mon upon myddelerde,   *larger; earth*
And his body bigger then the best fowre
105 That ar in Arthures hous, Hestor, other other.
He cheves that chaunce at the chapel grene,   *brings it about*
Ther passes non bi that place so proude in his armes
That he ne dynges hym to dethe with dynt of his honde;   *strikes*
For he is a mon methles, and mercy non uses,   *violent*
110 For be hit chorle, other chaplayn that bi the chapel rydes,   *churl*
Monk, other masseprest, other any mon elles,
Hym thynk as queme hym to quelle as quyk go hymselven.
Forthy I say the, as sothe as ye in sadel sitte,   *as sure*
Com ye there, ye be kylled, may the knyght rede,   *has his way*
115 Trawe ye me that trwely, thagh ye had twenty lyves   *believe*
    To spende.
    He has wonyd here ful yore,   *lived; long time*
    On bent much baret bende.
    Ayayn his dyntes sore   *blows*
120   Ye may not yow defende.

'Forthy, goude Sir Gawayn, let the gome one,   *alone*
And gos away sum other gate, upon Goddes halve!   *behalf*
Cayres bi sum other kyth, ther Kryst mot yow spede.   *ride; land*
And I schal hyy me hom ayayn, and hete yow fyrre   *fire*
125 That I schal swere bi God and alle his gode halwes –   *saints*
As help me God and the halydam, and othes innoghe –
That I schal lelly yow layne, and lauce never tale
That ever ye fondet to fle for freke that I wyst.'
'Grant merci' quoth Gawayn, and gruchyng he sayde: *reluctantly*
130 'Wel worth the, wyye, that woldes my gode,   *good luck*
And that lelly me layne I leve wel thou woldes.   *desires*
Bot helde thou hit never so holde, and I here passed,   *secure*
Founded for ferde for to fie, in fourme that thou telles,
I were a knyght kowarde, I myght not be excused.
135 Bot I wyl to the chapel, for chaunce that may falle,
And talk wyth that ilk tulk the tale that me lyste,   *very knight*
Worthe hit wele other wo, as the Wyrde lykes

99: If you are led by my cleverness you will fare better.
104–105: And he is four times larger in body than any in
Arthur's house, Hestor or any other. Hestor: either
Hector of Troy or the Arthurian knight Hector de la
Mare. 112: He thinks it as pleasant to kill as to go on
living himself.

118: And has caused much strife on the battlefield.
126–28: God, the holy relic, and profuse oaths – that I
will loyally keep your secret and never tell the tale that
you were forced to flee because of any man.
133: flying because of fear in the way you suggest.
137: Whether for good or evil, as Providence decides.

Hit hafe.
Thaghe he be a sturn knape   grim knave
140   To stightel, and stad with stave,   order; armed; club
Ful wel con Dryghtyn schape   fashions it
His servauntes for to save.'

'Mary!' quoth that other mon, 'now thou so much spelles
That thou wylt thyn awen nye nyme to thyselven,
145 And the lyst lese thy lyf, the lette I ne kepe.
Haf here thi helme on thy hede, thi spere in thi honde,
And ryde me doun this ilk rake bi yon rokke syde,   path
Til thou be broght to the bothem of the brem valay.   broad
Thenne loke a littel on the launde, on thi lyfte honde,   glade
150 And thou schal se in that slade the self chapel   valley
And the borelych burne on bent that hit kepes.   huge fellow
Now fares wel, on Godes half, Gawayn the noble!
For alle the golde upon grounde I nolde go wyth the,
Ne bere the felawschip thurgh this fryth on fote fyrre.'   forest; further
155 Bi that the wyye in the wod wendes his brydel,   wood
Hit the hors with the heles as harde as he myght,
Lepes hym over the launde, and leves the knyght there   glade
Alone.
'Bi Goddes self,' quoth Gawayn,
160 'I wyl nauther grete ne grone;   weep
To Goddes wylle I am ful bayn,   obedient
And to hym I haf me tone.'   committed

Thenne gyrdes he to Gryngolet and gederes the rake,
Schowves in bi a schore at a schawe syde,
165 Rides thurgh the roghe bonk ryght to the dale.
And thenne he wayted hym aboute, and wylde hit hym thoght,
And seye no syngne of resette bisydes nowhere,   shelter
Bot hyghe bonkkes and brent upon bothe halve,   steep; sides
And rughe knokled knarres with knorned stones;   rough crags; rugged
170 The skwes of the scowtes skayned hym thoght.
Thenne he hoved and wythhylde his hors at that tyde,   halted
And ofte chaunged his cher the chapel to seche.   looked about
He sey non suche in no syde, and selly hym thoght.   peculiar
Save a lyttel on a launde, a lawe as hit were,   mound
175 A balw berw bi a bonke the brymme bysyde,
Bi a fors of a flode that ferked thare;
The borne blubred therinne as hit boyled hade.   stream
The knyght kaches his caple and com to the lawe,   horse
Lightes doun luflyly, and at a lynde taches   agilely; fastened

---

144–45: That you will take all these turmoils on yourself and look to lessen your life, I'll not try to stop you.
163: Then he spurs Gryngolet on and takes up the path,
pushing past a rock by a thicket.

170: The clouds seemed to him grazed by the jutting
rocks. 175–76: A smooth barrow by the bank of a
stream near the force of a fall that fell there.

180 The rayne and his riche with a roghe braunche.　*noble horse*
　　Thenne he bowes to the berwe, aboute hit he walkes　*comes; mound*
　　Debatande with hymself quat hit be myght.
　　Hit hade a hole on the ende and on ayther syde,　*either*
　　And overgrowen with gresse in glodes aywhere;　*patches*
185 And al was holw inwith, nobot an olde cave,
　　Or a crevisse of an olde cragge – he couthe hit noght deme
　　　　With spelle.
　　　　'We! Lorde,' quoth the gentyle knyght,
　　　　'Whether this be the grene chapelle?
190　　　Here myght aboute mydnyght
　　　　The dele his matynnes telle!　*devil*

　　'Now iwysse,' quoth Wowayn, 'wysty is here;　*desolation*
　　This oritore is ugly, with erbes overgrowen;　*oratory; weeds*
　　Wel bisemes the wyye wruxled in grene　*dressed*
195 Dele here his devocioun on the develes wyse.
　　Now I fele hit is the fende, in my fyve wyttes,　*senses*
　　That has stoken me this steven to strye me here.
　　This is a chapel of meschaunce, that chekke hit bytyde!　*bad luck*
　　Hit is the corsedest kyrk that ever I com inne.'　*most cursed*
200 With heghe helme on his hede, his launce in his honde,
　　He romes up to the roffe of tho rogh wones.　*rough dwelling*
　　Thene herde he of that hyghe hil, in a harde roche
　　Biyonde the broke, in a bonk, a wonder breme noyse.　*loud*
　　Quat! hit clatered in the clyff as hit cleve schulde,　*was about to break*
205 As one up on a gryndelston hade grounden a sythe.　*grindstone*
　　What! hit wharred and whette, as water at a mulne.　*ground; mill*
　　What! hit rusched and ronge, rawthe to here.　*terrible*
　　Thenne 'Bi Godde,' quoth Gawayn, 'that gere, as I trowe,
　　Is ryched at the reverence me, renk to mete
210　　　Bi rote.
　　　　Let God worche! "We loo" –　*[to cry] 'Alas'*
　　　　Hit helppes me not a mote
　　　　My lif thagh I forgoo,
　　　　Drede dos me no lote.'　*noise*

215 Thenne the knyght con calle ful hyghe:　*loudly*
　　'Who stightles in this sted, me steven to holde?　*commands; appointment*
　　For now is gode Gawayn goande ryght here.　*pacing*
　　If any wyye oght wyl, wynne hider fast,
　　Other now other never, his nedes to spede.'
220 'Abyde,' quoth on on the bonke aboven over his hede
　　'And thou schal haf al in hast that I the hyght ones.'　*promised once*

---

191 **matynnes:** matins begin the liturgical day, thus devil-worship reverses these.　**195:** Carries on his devotions in a devilish way.　**197:** Who has imposed this command [to meet him] to destroy me here.

208–209: 'This device I believe is arranged to honour me with ceremony in preparation for combat.　**218–19:** If any man wants anything, he should come hither quickly, now or never, to do what he must.'

Yet he rusched on that rurde rapely a throwe,
And wyth quettyng awharf, er he wolde lyght.
And sythen he keuerez bi a cragge and comes of a hole,   comes
225 Whyrlande out of a wro wyth a felle weppen,   nook; terrible
A denes ax nwe dyght, the dynt with to yelde,   return
With a borelych bytte bende by the halme,
Fyled in a fylor, fowre fote large –
Hit was no lasse, bi that lace that lemed ful bryght.   cord; gleamed
230 And the gome in the grene gered as fyrst,   arrayed
Bothe the lyre and the legges, lokkes and berde,   face
Save that fayre on his fote he foundes on the erthe,
Sette the stele to the stone and stalked bysyde.
When he wan to the watter, ther he came wade nolde,   would not
235 He hypped over on hys ax and orpedly strydes,   vaulted
Bremly brothe, on a bent that brode was aboute,
      On snawe.
    Sir Gawayn the knyght con mete,
    He ne lutte hym nothyng lowe;   bowed
240   That other sayde: 'Now, sir swete,
    Of steven mon may the trowe.

'Gawayn,' quoth that grene gome, 'God the mot loke!   guard
Iwysse thou art welcom, wyye, to my place,
And thou has tymed thi travayl as truee mon schulde.
245 And thou knowes the covenauntes kest uus bytwene:
At this tyme twelmonyth thou toke that the falled,   fell to your lot
And I schulde at this Nwe Yere yeply the quyte.   promptly; repay
And we ar in this valay verayly oure one;
Here ar no renkes us to rydde, rele as uus likes.
250 Haf thy helme of thy hede, and haf here thy pay.
Busk no more debate then I the bede thenne
When thou wypped of my hede at a wap one.'
'Nay, bi God,' quoth Gawayn, 'that me gost lante,   gave me a soul
I schal gruch the no grwe for grem that falles.
255 Bot styghtel the upon on strok, and I schal stonde stylle   limit
And warp the no wernyng to worch as the lykes,
    Nowhare.'
    He lened with the nek and lutte,   bent down
    And schewed that schyre al bare,   flesh

222–23: Yet he rapidly carried on that terrible noise for a time and turned back to his grinding before coming down.   227–28: With an enormous blade bent round the handle; sharpened on the grindstone.   232: Save that he steps elegantly on the earth.   236–37: a fierce creature against a broad snowy field.   241: 'You can be trusted to keep an arrangement.' This refers to the early parts of the poem. Gawain was allowed to behead the Green Knight as part of the contest. Gawain has now come to submit himself to the same ordeal.

249: 'Here are no men to separate us, we can be as violent as we like.' The irony reinforces Gawain's plight. He is not going to engage in traditional chivalric combat where skill, force, and virtue would prevail, but patiently receive the Green Knight's blow.   251: Offer no more resistance than I offered you [a year ago].   254: I will bear you not the slightest grudge for any harm that befalls me.   256–57: And I will not resist anything you wish to do.

260   And lette as he noght dutte;   feared
        For drede he wolde not dare.   shrink

Then the gome in the grene graythed hym swythe,   swiftly
Gederes up hys grymme tole, Gawayn to smyte;
With alle the bur in his body he ber hit on lofte,   strength
265 Munt as maghtyly as marre hym he wolde.
Hade hit dryven adoun as drey as he atled,
Ther hade ben ded of his dynt that doghty was ever.
Bot Gawayn on that giserne glyfte hym bysyde,
As hit com glydande adoun on glode hym to schende,
270 And schranke a lytel with the schulderes for the scharp yrne.
That other schalk wyth a schunt the schene wythhaldes,
And thenne repreved he the prynce with mony prowde wordes:
'Thou art not Gawayn,' quoth the gome, 'that is so goud halden,
That never arwed for no here by hylle ne be vale,   army
275 And now thou fles for ferde er thou fele harmes.
Such cowardise of that knyght cowthe I never here.   did I never see
Nawther fyked I ne flaghe, freke, quen thou myntest,
Ne kest no kavelacion in kynges hous Arthor.
My hede flaw to my fote, and yet flagh I never;
280 And thou, er any harme hent, arwes in hert.   are fearful
Wherfore the better burne me burde be called
        Therefore.'
    Quoth Gawayn: 'I schunt ones,
    And so wyl I no more;
285   Bot thagh my hede falle on the stones,
    I con not hit restore.

'Bot busk, burne, bi thi fayth, and bryng me to the poynts   quickly
Dele to me my destine and do hit out of honde,
For I schal stonde the a strok, and start no more
290 Til thyn ax have me hitte – haf here my trawthe.'   you have my word
'Haf at the thenne,' quoth that other, and heves hit alofte,
And waytes as wrothely as he wode were.
He myntes at hym maghtyly, bot not the mon rynes,   touched
Withhelde heterly his honde er hit hurt myght.
295 Gawayn graythely hit bydes and glent with no membre,
Bot stode stylle as the ston other a stubbe auther
That ratheled is in roche grounde with rotes a hundreth.
Then muryly efte con he mele, the mon in the grene: spoke
'So now thou has thi hert holle, hitte me bihoves.

265–69: Aimed a mighty blow as though to destroy him. Had it fallen, as it seem he meant, the ever bold figure would have died of the blow. But Gawain glanced askance at the axe as it glided flashing down to destroy him. 271: With a sudden movement the other withheld the blade. 277–78: I neither flinched or fled, knight, when you aimed, nor objected in King Arthur's palace.

281–82: Wherefore I should be called the better man. 292: glares at him full of wrath as though he was mad. 295–97: Gawain patiently waited, no part of him flinched, but he stood still as a stone or a stump that is entwined in rocky ground with hundred-year-old roots.

300 Halde the now the hyghe hode that Arthur the raght,
And kepe thy kanel at this kest, yif hit kever may!'
Gawayn ful gryndelly with greme thenne sayde: *fiercely; anger*
'Wy, thresch on, thou thro mon, thou thretes to longe;
I hope that thi hert arwe wyth thyn awen selven.'
305 'For sothe,' quoth that other freke, 'so felly thou spekes,
I wyl no lenger on lyte lette thin ernde   *hinder; mission*
    Right nowe.'
    Thenne tas he hym strythe to stryke   *stance*
    And frounses bothe lyppe and browe;   *puckers*
310   No mervayle thagh hym myslyke
    That hoped of no rescowe.

He lyftes lyghtly his lome and let hit doun fayre,   *weapon*
With the barbe of the bitte bi the bare nek.
Thagh he homered heterly, hurt hym no more,   *struck*
315 Bot snyrt hym on that on syde, that severed the hyde.   *clipped*
The scharp schrank to the flesche thurgh the schyre grece,
That the schene blod over his schulderes schot to the erthe.   *bright*
And quen the burne sey the blode blenk on the snawe   *gleam*
He sprit forth spenne-fote more then a spere lenthe,
320 Hent heterly his helme and on his hed cast,   *seized quickly*
Schot with his schulderes his fayre schelde under,   *jerked; down*
Braydes out a bryght sworde, and bremely he spekes –
Never syn that he was burne borne of his moder
Was he never in this worlde wyye half so blythe –   *joyful*
325 'Blynne, burne, of thy bur, bede me no mo!
I haf a stroke in this sted withoute stryf hent,
And if thow reches me any mo, I redyly schal quyte
And yelde yederly ayayn – and therto ye tryst –
    And foo.
330   Bot on stroke here me falles;
    The covenaunt schop ryght so,   *ordained*
    Festned in Arthures halles,   *arranged*
    And therfore, hende, now hoo!'   *gracious sir; cease*

The hathel heldet hym fro and on his ax   *moved away*
335 Sette the schaft upon schore and to the scharp lened,
And loked to the leude that on the launde yede,   *walked*
How that doghty, dredles, dervely ther stondes   *boldly*
Armed, ful awles; in hert hit hym lykes.   *fearless*
Thenn he meles muryly wyth a much steven,

300–301: May the noble order [of knighthood] which Arthur presented you keep you from this blow, if it can. 303–304: Why strike you terrible fellow, you threaten too long, and I think that your own heart is now in awe of you. 316: The sharp blade bit into the flesh through the shinning skin. 319: He leapt, feet together, more than a spear length. 325–26: Stop man your blows and give me no more, I have taken a stroke in this place without returning blows. 328–29: And pay them back quickly – and believe me – fiercely too. 335: Set the shaft on the ground and leaned on the blade. 339–40: Then he cheerfully spoke in a great voice and in ringing tones said to the knight.

340 And wyth a ryrskande rurde he to the renk sayde:
    'Bolde burne, on this bent be not so gryndel.   fierce
    No mon here unmanerly the mysboden habbes,   mistreated
    Ne kyd bot as covenaunde at kynges kort schaped.
    I hyght the a strok and thou hit has, halde the wel payed;
345 I relece the of the remnaunt of ryghtes alle other.
    Iif I deliver had bene, a boffet paraunter
    I couthe wrotheloker haf waret, to the haf wroght anger.
    Fyrst I mansed the muryly with a mynt one,
    And rove the wyth no rof sore, with ryght I the profered
350 For the forwarde that we fest in the fyrst nyght;   covenant
    And thou trystyly the trawthe and trwly me haldes,
    Al the gayne thow me gef, as god mon schulde.
    That other munt for the morne, mon, I the profered;
    Thou kyssedes my clere wyf, the cosses me raghtes.   gave me the kisses
355 For bothe two here I the bede bot two bare myntes   offered
            Boute scathe.   without harm
        Trwe mon trwe restore,
        Thenne thar mon drede no wathe.
        At the thrid thou fayled thore, there
360   And therfor that tappe ta the.   take

    For hit is my wede that thou weres, that ilke woven girdel;
    Myn owen wyf hit the weved, I wot wel for sothe.
    Now know I wel thy cosses and thy costes als,   contrivances
    And the wowyng of my wyf; I wroght hit myselven.
365 I sende hir to asay the, and sothly me thynkkes
    On the fautlest freke that ever on fote yede.   man; goes on foot
    As perle bi the quite pese is of prys more,   white peas
    So is Gawayn, in god fayth, bi other gay knyghtes.
    Bot here yow lakked a lyttel, sir, and lewté yow wonted;   loyalty
370 Bot that was for no wylyde werke, ne wowyng nauther,   intricate
    Bot for ye lufed your lyf – the lasse I yow blame.'
    That other stif mon in study stod a gret whyle,
    So agreved for greme he gryed withinne.   anger
    Alle the blode of his brest blende in his face,
375 That al he schrank for schome that the schalk talked.   man said
    The forme worde upon folde that the freke meled:
    'Corsed worth cowarddyse and covetyse bothe!
    In yow is vylany and vyse that vertue disstryes.'   vice; destroys
    Thenne he kaght to the knot and the kest lawses,   fastening loosened
380 Brayde brothely the belt to the burne selven: throwing angrily
    'Lo! ther the falssyng, foule mot hit falle!   bad luck befall it

---

344: I promised you a stroke and you have it, think your-self well paid.

346–49: If I had been more nimble, perhaps I could have dealt you a fiercer blow and done you harm. First I merrily threatened you with a feint and gave you no great wound, because I treated you properly.

For care of thy knokke cowardyse me taght   blow
To acorde me with covetyse, my kynde to forsake,
That is larges and lewte that longes to knyghtes.
385 Now am I fawty and falce, and ferde haf ben ever
Of trecherye and untrawthe, bothe bityde sorwe   falseness
        And care!
    I biknowe yow, knyght, here stylle,   confess; secretly
    Al fawty is my fare;
390   Letes me overtake your wylle,
    And efte I schal be ware.'

Thenn loghe that other leude and luflyly sayde: courteously
'I halde hit hardily hole, the harme that I hade;
Thou art confessed so clene, beknowen of thy mysses,   cleared
395 And has the penaunce apert of the poynt of myn egge.   weapon
I halde the polysed of that plyght and pured as clene   cleaned
As thou hades never forfeted sythen thou was fyrst borne.
And I gif the, sir, the gurdel that is golde-hemmed.
For hit is grene as my goune; Sir Gawayn, ye maye
400 Thenk upon this ilke threpe ther thou forth thrynges
Among prynces of prys, alld this a pure token
Of the chaunce of the grene chapel at chevalrous knyghtes.   exploit
And ye schal in this Nwe Yer ayayn to my wones,   come again; dwelling
And we schyn revel the remnaunt of this ryche fest
405   Ful bene.'
    Ther lathed hym fast the lorde,   invited; earnestly
    And sayde: 'With my wyf, I wene,
    We schal yow wel acorde,
    That was your enmy kene.'

410 'Nay, for sothe,' quoth the segge, and sesed hys helme   knight
And has hit of hendely, and the hathel thonkkes: courteously
'I haf sojorned sadly. Sele yow bytyde,
And he yelde hit yow yare that yarkkes al menskes!
And comaundes me to that cortays, your comlych fere,
415 Bothe that on and that other, myn honoured ladyes,
That thus hor knyght wyth hor kest han koyntly bigyleds
Bot hit is no ferly thagh a fole madde
And thurgh wyles of wymmen be wonen to sorwe.
For so was Adam in erde with one bygyled,
420 And Salamon with fele sere, and Samson eftsones –
Dalyda dalt hym hys wyrde – and Davyth therafter   fate
Was blended with Barsabe, that much bale tholed.   suffered grief

---

390–91: Let me know your command and I shall take
care in future.   393: I consider it completely amended,
the harm that I had.   400: Think upon this contest when
you are mingling with noble princes.

412: I have stayed long enough. Good fortune come to
you and may He who gives all rewards fully endow you.
416–17: That have this knight so completely misled with
their device. But it is no surprise if a silly madman . . . .

Now these were wrathed wyth her wyles, hit were a wynne huge
To luf hom wel and leve hem not, a leude that couthe.
425 For thes wer forne the freest, that folwed alle the sele
Exellently of alle thyse other under heven-ryche
      That mused;
      And alle thay were biwyled
      With wymmen that thay used.
430   Thagh I be now bigyled,
      Me think me burde be excused.   *ought to*

'Bot your gordel,' quoth Gawayn, 'God yow foryelde!   *reward*
That wyl I welde wyth guod wylle, not for the wynne golde, *wear*
Ne the saynt, ne the sylk, ne the syde pendaundes, *material*
435 For wele ne for worchyp, ne for the wlonk werkkes; *worth; rich*
Bot in syngne of my surfet I schal se hit ofte
When I ride in renoun, remorde to myselven *lament*
The faut and the fayntyse of the flesche crabbed, *perverse*
How tender hit is to entyse teches of fylthe. *promote stains*
440 And thus quen pryde schal me pryk for prowes of armes,
The loke to this luf-lace schal lethe my hert. *humble*
Bot on I wolde yow pray, displeses yow never:
Syn ye be lorde of the yonde londe ther I haf lent inne *rested*
Wyth yow wyth worschyp – the wyye hit yow yelde *being*
445 That uphaldes the heven and on hygh sittes –
How norne ye yowre ryght nome, and thenne no more?'
'That schal I telle the trwly,' quoth that other thenne,
'Bertilak de Hautdesert I hat in this londe.
Thurgh myght of Morgne la Faye, that in my hous lenges, *lives*
450 And koyntyse of clergye, bi craftes wel lerned.
The maystres of Merlyn, mony ho has taken,
For ho has dalt drwry ful dere sumtyme
With that conable klerk, that knowes alle your knyghtes
      At hame.
455   Morgne the goddes
      Therfore hit is hir name;
      Weldes non so hyghe hawtesse *pride*
      That ho ne con make ful tame.

Ho wayned me upon this wyse to your wynne halle
460 For to assay the surquidre, yif hit soth were
That rennes of the grete renoun of the Rounde Table.
Ho wayned me this wonder your wyttes to reve, *deprive*

423–27: Now they were bothered with their wiles – it is a big advantage to love them [women] but not believe them, if a man could. For these [men] were formerly the best, and excellently favoured with prosperity of all those under the rich heavens.   450–54: And who has wisdom in learned arts and is well versed in magic. She got hold of many of Merlin's mysteries, who for a time was the lover of this knowledgable scholar, as all you knights know.   **459–60:** She sent me in this disguise to your splendid hall to test your pride.

For to haf greved Gaynour and gart hir to dyye
With glopnyng of that ilke gome that gostlych speked
465 With his hede in his honde bifore the hyghe table.
That is ho that is at home, the auncian lady;
Ho is even thyn aunt, Arthures half-suster,
The duches doghter of Tyntagelle, that dere Uter after
Hade Arthur upon, that athel is nowthe.   king
470 Therfor I ethe the, hathel, to com to thy aunt,
Make myry in my hous. My meny the lovies,
And I wol the as wel, wyye, bi my faythe,
As any gome under God, for thy grete trauthe.'   integrity
And he nikked hym naye, he nolde bi no wayes.
475 Thay acolen and kyssen, bykennen ayther other   embrace; pledging
To the prynce of paradise, and parten ryght there
       On coolde.   on cold ground
     Gawayn on blonk ful bene
     To the kynges burgh buskes bolde,   hastens
480   And the knyght in the enker grene   bright
     Whiderwarde-soever he wolde

Wylde wayes in the worlde Wowen now rydes
On Gryngolet, that the grace hade geten of his lyve.
Ofte he herbered in house and ofte al theroute,   stayed; outside
485 And mony aventure in vale, and venquyst ofte,
That I ne tyght at this tyme in tale to remene.
The hurt was hole that he hade hent in his nek,
And the blykkande belt he bere theraboute,   shining
Abelef as a bauderyk, bounden bi his syde,
490 Loken under his lyfte arme, the lace, with a knot,   fastened
In tokenyng he was tane in tech of a faute.   discovered
And thus he commes to the court, knyght al in sounde.   safely
Ther wakned wele in that wone when wyst the grete
That gode Gawayn was commen; gayn hit hym thoght.   profitable
495 The kyng kysses the knyght, and the whene alce,   queen
And sythen mony syker knyght that soght hym to haylce   greet
Of his fare that hym frayned; and ferlyly he telles,
Biknowes alle the costes of care that he hade –   made known
The chaunce of the chapel, the chere of the knyght,
500 The luf of the ladi, the lace at the last.
The nirt in the nek he naked hem schewed,
That he laght for his unleute at the leudes hondes   received; faithlessness
       For blame
     He tened quen he schulde telle,   grieved

463–64: to distress Guenevere and cause her to die with fright because of a man who spoke in a ghostly manner. 474: And he [Gawain] said no to him, he would not stay on any account.

489: diagonally as a baldric strap, bound to his side. 493: There was happiness in the dwelling when the nobles heard.

505   He groned for gref and grame;   *shame*
        The blod in his face con melle,   *flowed*
        When he hit schulde schewe, for schame.

        'Lo! lorde,' quoth the leude, and the lace hondeled,
        'This is the bende of this blame I bere on my nek,   *ribbon*
510   This is the lathe and the losse that I laght have
        Of couardise and covetyse that I haf caght thare.
        This is the token of untrawthe that I am tan inne,
        And I mot nedes hit were wyle I may last.   *wear*
        For non may hyden his harme bot unhap ne may hit,
515   For ther hit ones is tachched twynne wil hit never.'
        The kyng comfortes the knyght, and alle the court als
        Laghen loude therat, and luflyly acorden   *graciously*
        That lordes and ladis that longed to the Table,
        Uche burne of the brotherhede, a bauderyk schulde have
520   A bende abelef hym aboute, of a bryght grene,
        And that, for sake of that segge, in swete to were.   *courtesy*
        For that was acorded the renoun of the Rounde Table,
        And he honoured that hit hade, evermore after,
        As hit is breved in the best boke of romaunce.
525   Thus in Arthurus day this aunter bitidde,
        The Brutus bokes therof beres wyttenesse.
        Sythen Brutus, the bolde burne, bowed hider fyrst,
        After the segge and the asaute was sesed at Troye   *seige; ceased*
            Iwysse   *certainly*
530   Mony aunteres here-biforne
        Haf fallen suche er this.
        Now that bere the croun of thorne,
        He bryng uus to his blysse! Amen.

514–15: For no one may mask what has harmed him or misfortune will occur, for where it becomes attached, it will never go away. **521 segge:** knight; here Sir Gawain. **526 Brutus bokes:** Brute, a follower of Aeneas, was the legendary founder of Britain. This suggests a mythical chronicle which relates his exploits. **532:** Now he that wore the crown of thorns.

From Pearl

Pearl is a poem which revolves around the consolation a father finds for the loss of his dead daughter, his pearl, through discovering the kingdom of heaven. Founded on the scriptural parable of the pearl (Matthew 13:45–46), it uses the popular device of a dream vision to offer an intimation of the heavenly. The following extract is the poem's opening and is about a quarter of the length of the complete work.

I

Perle, plesaunte to prynces paye	
To clanly clos in golde so clere:	
Oute of oryent, I hardyly saye,	
Ne proved I never her precios pere.	equal
5 So rounde, so reken in uche araye,	radiant; setting
So smal, so smothe her sydes were,	
Queresoever I jugged gemmes gaye,	wheresoever
I sette hyr sengeley in synglere.	uniquely
Allas! I leste hyr in on erbere;	garden
10 Thurgh gresse to grounde hit fro me yot.	fell
I dewyne, fordolked of luf-daungere	
Of that pryvy perle wythouten spot.	

Sythen in that spote hit fro me sprange,	since; darted away
Ofte haf I wayted, wyschande that wele,	
15 That wont was whyle devoyde my wrange	
And heven my happe and al my hele.	
That dos bot thrych my hert thrange,	
My breste in bale bot bolne and bele.	
Yet thoght me never so swete a sange	
20 As stylle stounde let to me stele.	quiet hour
For sothe ther fleten to me fele,	
To thenke hir color so clad in clot.	clay
O moul, thou marres a myry juele,	earth
My privy perle wythouten spotte.	

25 That spot of spyses mot nedes sprede,	
Ther such ryches to rot is runne;	
Blomes blayke and blwe and rede	
Ther schynes ful schyr agayn the sunne.	shines; brightly
Flor and fryte may not be fede	
30 Ther hit doun drof in moldes dunne;	
For uch gresse mot grow of graynes dede;	dead grains

1–2: Lovely pearl which it is a prince's pleasure to set radiantly in bright gold. 11–12: I am languishing, dangerously wounded, because of that special unblemished pearl.

14–16: Oft have I waited, longing for that precious thing that was used to drive away my sorrow and heighten my happiness and all my well being. This watching weighs heavily on my heart and my grief both swells and festers. 21: In truth there came to me many such fleeting [songs]. 30: Where it sank in the dark brown earth.

No whete were elles to wones wonne.   homes brought
Of goud uche goude is ay bygonne;
So semly a sede moght fayly not,
35   That spryngande spyces up ne sponne   would spring up
Of that precios perle wythouten spotte.

To that spot that I in speche expoun   describe
I entred in that erber grene,
In Auguste in a hygh seysoun,
40   Quen corne is corven wyth crokes kene.
On huyle ther perle hit trendeled doun   rolled
Schadowed this wortes ful schyre and schene,
Gilofre, gyngure and gromylyoun,
And pyonys powdered ay bytwene.   scattered
45   Yif hit was semly on to sene,
A fayr reflayr yet fro hit flot.   fairer fragrance
Ther wonys that worthyly, I wot and wene,
My precious perle wythouten spot.

Bifore that spot my honde I spenned   clasped
50   For care ful colde that to me caght;
A devely dele in my hert denned,   desolate anguish
Thagh resoun sette myselven saght.
I playned my perle that ther was penned
Wyth fyrce skylles that faste faght;
55   Thagh kynde of Kryst me comfort kenned,
My wreched wylle in wo ay wraghte.   will
I felle upon that floury flaght,   turf
Suche odour to my hernes schot;   head; rushed
I slode upon a slepyng-slaghte
60   On that precios perle wythouten spot.

II

Fro spot my spyryt ther sprang in space;   place
My body on balke ther bod in sweven.
My goste is gon in Godes grace
In aventure ther mervayles meven.
65   I ne wyste in this worlde quere that hit wace,   was
Bot I knew me keste ther klyfes clevell.
Towarde a foreste I bere the face,   turned
Where rych rokkes wer to dyscreven.
The lyght of hem myght no mon leven,   believe

40: When corn is reaped with curved sickles. 59: I fell into a sudden sleep. 62–64: My body stayed
42–43: The bright and radiant plants were in shadow, on the mound dreaming. My spirit went in God's grace
gillyflowers, ginger and gromwell. 47: There dwells to proceed to marvellous adventures. 66: But I know I
the precious one, I know and believe. 52–54: Although was set down at the cliff's cleave.
reason tried to make me reconcile it. I lamented my
pearl that lay imprisoned there with fierce arguments
that struggled boldly.

70 The glemande glory that of hem glent;
For wern never webbes that wyyes weven
Of half so dere adubbement.

Dubbed wern alle tho downes sydes   adorned; hill
Wyth crystal klyffes so cler of kynde.
75 Holtewodes bryght aboute hem bydes   woods
Of bolles as blwe as ble of Ynde.   trunks
As bornyst sylver the lef onslydes,
That thike con trylle on uch a tynde.
Quen glem of glodes agayns hem glydes,   clear sky
80 Wyth schymeryng schene ful schtylle thay schynde.
The gravayl that on grounde con grynde
Wern precious perles of oryente;
The sunnebemes bot blo and blynde   dark; dim
In respecte of that adubbement.   splendour
85 The adubbemente of tho downes dere
Garten my goste al greffe foryete.
So frech flavores of frytes were,
As fode hit con me fayre refete.
Fowles ther flowen in fryth in fere,   woodland; company
90 Of flaumbande hwes, bothe smale and grete.   flaming hues
Bot sytole-stryng and gyternere
Her reken myrthe moght not retrete;   repeat
For quen those bryddes her wynges bete,
Thay songen wyth a swete asent.
95 So gracios gle couthe no mon gete   joy
As here and se her adubbement.

So al was dubbet on dere asyse
That fryth ther fortwne forth me feres.
The derthe therof for to devyse
100 Nis no wyy worthe that tonge beres.
I welke ay forth in wely wyse;   happy
No bonk so byg that did me deres.   harm
The fyrre in the fryth, the feier con ryse
The playn, the plonttes, the spyse, the peres,
105 And rawes and randes and rych reveres,
As fyldor fyn her bonkes brent.
I wan to a water by schore that scheres;   meanders
Lorde, dere was hit adubbement!

71–72: For never were fabrics [tapestries] that men weave of such costly splendour.   77–78: As burnished silver the leaves slid on one another, that thickly shook on each branch.   91: But neither cithern-string nor cithern player.   97–100: So was all the wood splendidly arrayed where fortune was taking me. To try and convey its glory – there is no man who has a tongue worthy enough.   103–106: The further into the forest [I went], the fairer the meadow rose up, shrubs, spice plants, pears and hedgerows and banks of streams and rich rivers, their banks like fine gold thread.

The dubbemente of tho derworth depe   *adornment*
110 Wern bonkes bene of beryl bryght,
Swangeande swete the water con swepe,
Wyth a rownande rourde raykande aryght.
In the founce ther stonden stones stepe,   *bottom; bright*
As glente thurgh glas that glowed and glyght,   *light*
115 As stremande sternes, quen strothe-men slepe,
Staren in welkyn in wynter nyght.
For uche a pobbel in pole ther pyght
Was emerad, saffer, other gemme gente,
That alle the loghe lemed of lyght,
120 So dere was hit adubbement.

III

The dubbement dere of doun and dales,   *splendour*
Of wod and water and wlonk playnes,   *lovely meadows*
Bylde in me blys, abated my bales,
Fordidden my stresse, dystryed my paynes.   *ended*
125 Doun after a strem that dryyly hales   *flows endlessly*
I bowed in blys bredful my brayvnes.
The fyrre I folwed those floty vales,
The more strenghthe of joye myn herte straynes.
As fortune fares, ther as ho fraynes,
130 Whether solace ho sende other elles sore,
The wyy to wham her wylle ho waynes
Hyttes to have ay more and more.

More of wele was in that wyse   *well being*
Then I cowthe telle thagh I tom hade,   *opportunity*
135 For urthely herte myght not suffyse
To the tenthe dole of tho gladnes glade.   *part*
Forthy I thoght that Paradyse   *wherefore*
Was ther over gayn tho bonkes brade.   *broad*
I hoped the water were a devyse
140 Bytwene myrthes by meres made.
Byyonde the broke, by slente other slade,   *slope; valley*
I hoped that mote merked wore
Bot the water was depe, I dorst not wade,
And ever me longed ay more and more.
145 More and more, and yet wel mare,   *more*

111–12: Swirling sweetly the water swept along, flowing straight with a whispering sound.   115–18: As streaming stars, when earth men sleep, shine in the sky on a winter's night. For each pebble arrayed in the pool was an emerald, sapphire, or other noble gem. 126–27: I went in bliss, my mind overflowing [with it]. The further I followed those watery vales ....   129: As fortunes fares, just as she wishes.   131: The man to whom she sends his desire wishes to have more and more.   139–40: I hoped the water was a device (i.e. a contraption) to join the pleasurable spots made by the pools.   142: I hoped there might be a castle that I expected.

Me lyste to se the broke byyonde;
For if hit was fayr ther I con fare,
Wel loveloker was the fyrre londe.   *lovelier*
Abowte me con I stote and stare,   *halted*
150 To fynde a forthe faste con I fonde;
Bot wothes mo iwysse ther ware,
The fyrre I stalked by the stronde.
And ever me thoght I schulde not wonde
For wo ther weles so wynne wore.
155 Thenne nwe note me com on honde
That meved my mynde ay more and more.

More mervayle con my dom adaunt.   *judgement daunted*
I sey byyonde that myry mere
A crystal clyffe ful relusaunt;   *resplendent*
160 Mony ryal ray con fro hit rere   *sprang*
At the fote therof ther sete a faunt,   *sat; child*
A mayden of menske, ful debonere;   *courtesy*
Blysnande whyt was hyr bleaunt.   *glistening; mantle*
I knew hyr wel, I hade sen hyr ere
165 As glysnande golde that man con schere,
So schon that schene anunder shore
On lenghe I loked to hyr there;
The lenger, I knew hyr more and more.

The more I frayste hyr fayre face,   *examined*
170 Her fygure fyn quen I had fonte,   *discovered*
Suche gladande glory con to me glace
As lyttel byfore therto was wonte
To calle hyr lyste con me enchace,
Bot baysment gef myn hert a brunt;
175 I sey hyr in so strange a place,
Such a burre myght make myn herte blunt.   *blow*
Thenne veres ho up her fayre frount,   *raises; forehead*
Hyr vysayge whyt as playn yvore   *ivory*
That stonge myn hert ful stray atount,
180 And ever the lenger, the more and more.

IV

More then me lyste my drede aros
I stod ful stylle and dorste not calle;
Wyth yyen open and mouth ful clos

150–54: I tried hard to find a ford, but certainly there were more dangers the further I walked by the bank. And I thought I should not hesitate because of danger when there were so many joys.   165–66: As gleaming gold [thread] that a man cuts, so shone that maiden under the cliff.

171–74: Such gladdening rapture glided over me as previously it was seldom wont to do. Desire urged me on to call her but confusion gave my heart a blow.   179: This stung my heart into bewildered amazement.

I stod as hende as hawk in halle.   *still*
185 I hoped that gostly was that porpose; *spiritual; aim*
 I dred onende quat schulde byfalle,
 Lest ho me eschaped that I ther chos,
 Er I at steven hir moght stalle.
 That gracios gay wythouten galle,
190 So smothe, so smal, so seme slyght,
 Ryses up in hir araye ryalle,   *royal array*
 A precios pyece in perles pyght.

 Perles pyghte of ryal prys,
 There moght mon by grace haf sene,
195 Quen that frech as flor-de-lys
 Doun the bonke con bowe bydene.
 Al blysnande whyt was hir beau biys, *white; fine linen*
 Upon at sydes and bounden bene   *open; trimmed*
 Wyth the myryeste margarys, at my devyse, *pearls*
200 That ever I sey yet with myn yyen;
 Wyth lappes large, I wot and I wene, *wide sleeves*
 Dubbed with double perle and dyghte;
 Her cortel of self sute schene,
 Wyth precios perles al umbepyghte.

205 A pyght coroune yet wer that gyrle *decorated crown*
 Of mariorys and non other ston,   *pearls*
 Highe pynakled of cler quyt perle, *pinnacles; white*
 Wyth flurted flowres perfet upon.   *figured*
 To hed hade ho non other werle.   *circlet*
210 Her lere leke al hyr umbegon,
 Her semblaunt sade for doc other erle,
 Her ble more blaght then whalles bon. *complexion; whales*
 As schorne golde schyr her fax thenne schon, *hair*
 On schylderes that leghe unlapped lyghte. *unbound*
215 Her depe colour yet wonted non
 Of precios perle in porfyl pyghte.

 Pyght was poyned and uche a hemme *wristband; hem*
 At honde, at sydes, at overture,   *neckline*
 Wyth whyte perle and non other gemme,
220 And bornyste quyte was hyr vesture. *shining; clothing*

187–88: Lest she escape me who I there perceived, before I might stop her and arrange a meeting. 192–96: a precious person arrayed in pearls. An array of pearls of royal worth, by grace you might have seen there, when [she] as fresh as a fleur-de-lys came directly down the bank. 199 **margarys**: pearls from the Latin *margarita*, alluding to the popular girl's name, Margaret.

202: adorned and dressed with double-rows of pearls. Her shining kirtle was similar and with precious pearls arrayed. 210: Her wimple [a linen garment folded so as to envelop the head] encompassed all her face. Her semblance grave enough for a duke or earl. 215–16: Her deep [white] colour wanted nothing in comparison to the precious pearls which were arrayed in the border [of the wimple].

Bot a wonder perle wythouten wemme   flaw
Inmyddes hyr breste was sette so sure;
A mannes dom moght dryyly demme,
Er mynde moght malte in hit mesure.
225 I hope no tong moght endure
No saverly saghe say of that syght,   adequately
So was hit clene and cler and pure,
That precios perle ther hit was pyght.

Pyght in perle, that precios pyse
230 On wyther half water com doun the schore.
No gladder gome hethen into Grece
Then I, quen ho on brymme wore.
Ho was me nerre then aunte or nece;
My joy forthy was much the more.   therefore
235 Ho profered me speche, that special spyce,
Enclynande lowe in wommon lore,   bowing; fashion
Caghte of her coroun of grete tresore   removed
And haylsed me wyth a lote lyghte.   hailed; joyful cry
Wel was me that ever I was bore
240 To sware that swete in perles pyghte!   answer

V

'O perle,' quod I, 'in perles pyght,
Art thou my perle that I haf playned,
Regretted by myn one on nyghte?   on my own
Much longeyng haf I for the layned,   concealed
245 Sythen into gresse thou me aglyghte.   slipped away
Pensyf, payred, I am forpayned,   wasted
And thou in a lyf of lykyng lyghte,
In Paradys erde, of stryf unstrayned.
What wyrde has hyder my juel vayned.
250 And don me in thys del and gret daunger?   sorrow
Fro we in twynne wern towen and twayned,   severed; parted
I haf ben a joyles juelere.'

That juel thenne in gemmes gente   noble
Vered up her vyse wyth yyen graye,   raised up
255 Set on hyr coroun of perle orient,
And soberly after thenne con ho say: began
'Sir, ye haf your tale mysetente,   told incorrectly
To say your perle is al awaye,
That is in cofer so comly clente   enclosed

<hr>

223–24: A man's judgement might be utterly bewild-   230–32: When she was on the brink, where the shore
ered before the mind comprehends its measure.   comes down on the opposite side of the water, there was
no happier man than I from here to Greece.   249: What
fate has brought my jewel hither.

260 As in this gardyn gracios gaye,
Hereinne to lenge for ever and play,
Ther mys nee mornyng com never nere.   loss nor mourning
Her were a forser for the, in faye,   casket; in truth
If thou were a gentyl jueler.

265 Bot, jueler gente, if thou schal lose
Thy joy for a gemme that the was lef,   dear
Me thynk the put in a mad porpose,
And busyes the aboute a raysoun bref;
For that thou lestes was bot a rose
270 That flowred and fayled as kynde hyt gef.   allowed
Now thurgh kynde of the kyste that hyt con close
To a perle of prys hit is put in pref.
And thou has called thy Wyrde a thef,   providence
That oght of noght has mad the cler.   bright
275 Thou blames the bote of thy meschef;   remedy
Thou art no kynde jueler.'

A juel to me then was thys geste,   visitor
And jueles wern hyr gentyl sawes.   words
'Iwyse,' quod I, 'my blysfol beste,
280 My grete dystresse thou al todrawes.   dispel
To be excused I make requeste;
I trawed my perle don out of dawes.
Now haf I fonde hyt, I schal ma feste,
And wony wyth hyt in schyr wod-schawes,   dwell; bright groves
285 And love my Lorde and al his lawes,
That has me broght thys blys ner.
Now were I at yow byyonde thise wawes,
I were a joyful jueler.'

'Jueler,' sayde that gemme clene,
290 'Wy borde ye men? So madde ye be!   joke
Thre wordes has thou spoken at ene;   at once
Unavysed, for sothe, wern alle thre.
Thou ne woste in worlde quat on dos mene;
Thy worde byfore thy wytte con fle.
295 Thou says thou trawes me in this dene,   believe; valley
Bycawse thou may wyth yyen me se;
Another thou says, in thys countré
Thyself schal won wyth me ryght here
The thrydde, to passe thys water fre;
300 That may no joyfol jueler.

267–68: I think you are involved with madness, and busy yourself with little reason. 271–72: Now through the nature of the coffer which encloses it, I have been shown to be a pearl of great worth. 282: I thought my pearl done out of days (i.e. was dead). 292–94: In truth, all three were ill advised. You have not the least understanding in the world what one of them means. Your words have escaped your understanding.

I halde that jueler lyttel to prayse
That leves wel that he sez wyth yye,   *believes; eye*
And much to blame and uncortayse   *lacking courtesy*
That leves oure Lorde wolde make a lyye,
305 That lelly hyghte your lyf to rayse,   *faithfully; on high*
Thagh fortune dyd your flesch to dyye.
Ye setten Hys wordes ful westernays
That leves nothynk bot ye hit syye.
And that is a poynt o sorquydryye,   *pride*
310 That uche god mon may evel byseme,
To leve no tale be true to tryye
Bot that hys one skyl may dem.   *reason; judge*

Deme now thyself if thou con dayly
As man to God wordes schulde heve.
315 Thou says thou schal won in this bayly;   *dwell; realm*
Me thynk the burde fyrst aske leve,   *ought to*
And yet of graunt thou myghtes fayle.
Thou wylnes over thys water to weve;   *wish; pass*
Er moste thou cever to other counsayl.
320 Thy corse in clot mot calder keve.
For hit was forgarte at Paradys greve;   *forfeited; grove*
Oure yorefader hit con mysseyeme.   *neglected*
Thurgh drwry deth bos uch man dreve,
Er over thys dam hym Dryghtyn deme.'

325 'Demes thou me,' quod I, 'my swete,   *condemn*
To dol agayn, thenne I dowyne.   *grief; languish*
Now haf I fonte that I forlete,   *found; lost*
Schal I efte forgo hit er ever I fyne?
Why schal I hit bothe mysse and mete?
330 My precios perle dos me gret pyne.
What serves tresor bot gares men grete,   *causes; weeping*
When he hit schal efte wyth tenes tyne?
Now rech I never for to declyne,
Ne how fer of folde that man me fleme.
335 When I am partles of perle myne,   *deprived*
Bot durande doel what may men deme?'

'Thow demes noght bot doel-dystresse,'
Thenne sayde that wyght. 'Why dos thou so?
For dyne of doel of lures lesse

307–308: You place his words fully opposite [to their intent], believing nothing but what you see.   310: That it ill fits each good man.   313–14: Judge yourself now if your usual babble is the way man should address God.   323–24: Through cruel death must each man make his way before God judges him [as fit to come] over to this bank.   327: Shall I give it up before my end?   332–34: When he afterwards finds it ends with pain? Now I don't care if I decline, nor how far out of the man's land I am banished.   336: What can men judge that to be but lasting sorrow?   339: For crying over griefs of lesser injury.

340 Ofte mony mon forgos the mo.
   The oghte better thyselven blesse,
   And love ay God, in wele and wo,   always
   For anger gaynes the not a cresse.   straw
   Who nedes schal thole be not so thro;
345 For thogh thou daunce as any do,
   Braundysch and bray thy brathes breme,
   When thou no fyrre may, to ne fro,
   Thou moste abyde that He schal deme.

   'Deme Dryghtyn, ever Hym adyte,
350 Of the way a fote ne wyl he wrythe.
   Thy mendes mountes not a myte,   recompense
   Thagh thou for sorwe be never blythe.
   Stynt of thy strot and fyne to flyte,
   And sech Hys blythe ful swefte and swythe.
355 Thy prayer may Hys pyte byte,   pity move
   That Mercy schal hyr craftes kythe.   skill; demonstrate
   Hys comforte may thy langour lythe   assuage
   And thy lures of lyghtly fleme;
   For, marre other madde, morne and mythe,
360 Al lys in Hym to dyght and deme.'

341: They were better to bless themselves (i.e. to make the sign of the cross). 344–47: Who needs must endure [suffering], not being stubborn; for though you writhe as a doe, struggle and bray in your fierce agonies, when you can no further [go], neither to or fro. 349–50: Judge the Lord, always arraign him, and he will not turn out of his way one foot [to aid you]. 353–54: Stop your wrangling, finish striving and seek his happiness with all swiftness and quickness. 358–60: Your sorrows readily banish. For whether you lament and rave, or mourn and conceal [feelings], it all lies with him to ordain and judge.

WILLIAM LANGLAND (*c*.1330–*c*.1386)

For the Middle Ages, the stories of the Bible were a *historia,* a narrative providing a pattern, or key, through which all past, present, and future occurrences might be understood. This prompted a contemplation of the world in which the literal, symbolic and religious meanings of events were intimately combined. This perspective underlies Langland's poem, a work simultaneously presenting biting social criticism and spiritual vision, and which readily combines symbolic representations of abstract figures of virtue and vice with more naturalistic characters from contemporary England. Little is known about Langland and the poem exists in three distinct versions – the A, B and C texts. The following extract is from the B text and likely dates from the late 1370s.

From The Vision of Piers Plowman

Prologue

	In a somer seson, whan soft was the sonne,	
	I shope me into shroudes as I a sheep were,	dressed; clothes
	In habite as an heremite unholy of workes,	
	Went wyde in this world wondres to here.	
5	Ac on a May mornynge on Malverne hilles	
	Me byfel a ferly, of fairy me thoghte;	marvel; magic
	I was wery forwandred and wente me to reste	having gone astray
	Under a brode bank bi a bourne syde,	stream
	And as I lay and lened and loked on the wateres,	
10	I slombred into a slepyng, it sweyed so merye.	sounded
	Thanne gan I meten a merveillous swevene	dreamed; dream
	That I was in a wildernesse, wist I nevere where.	
	As I bihelde into the eest an heigh to the sonne,	
	I seigh a tour on a toft trielich ymaked,	
15	A deep dale bynethe, a dongeon therinne,	
	witteh depe diches and derke and dredful of sighte.	
	A fair felde ful of folk fonde I ther bytwene	
	Of alle maner of men, the mene and the riche,	
	Worchyng and wandryng as the world asketh.	working
20	Some putten hem to the plough, pleyed ful selde,	
	In settyng and sowyng swonken ful harde,	
	And wonnen that wastours with glotonye destruyeth.	
	And some putten hem to pruyde, apparailed hem therafter,	
	In contenaunce of clothyng comen disgised.	
25	In prayers and penance putten hem manye,	
	Al for the love of owre Lord lyveden ful streyte	rigorously
	In hope to have heveneriche blisse,	

---

3 **unholy:** not remaining isolated in his cell. **14:** I saw an excellent tower on a hill top. **20–22:** Some worked at ploughing, seldom taking any pleasure, planting and sowing, toiling hard, and brought in the harvest which wasters destroyed with gluttony.

As ancres and heremites that holden hem in here selles,
Coveiten noght in contree to kairen aboute
30 For no lykerous liflode here lykame to plese.
     And some chosen chaffare; they cheuen the better   trade
As it semeth to owre sight that suche men thryveth;
And some murthes to make, as mynstralles conneth,   entertainments
And geten gold with here glee giltles, I leve.
35 Ac japeres and jangelers, Judas children,   jesters; jugglers
Feynen hem fantasies, and fooles hem maketh,
And han wit at wille to worken if they sholde.
That Poul precheth of hem I nel nat preve it here:
Qui turpiloquium loquitur is Luciferes hyne.
40   Bidderes and beggeres faste aboute yede   beggers; went
Witteh her bely and her bagges of bredful ycrammed,
Fayteden for here foode, foughten at the ale.
In glotonye, God woot, gon hei to bedde,
And risen with ribaudye, tho roberdes knaves;   foul language
45 Slepe and sori sleuthe, seweth hem ever.   sloth; follow
     Pilgrymes and palmers plighted hem togidere   joined
To seke Seint James and seyntes in Rome;
Wenten forth in here wey with many wise tales,
And hadden leve to lye al here lyf after.
50 I seigh some that seiden thei hadde ysought seyntes:
To eche a tale that thei tolde here tonge was tempred to lye,
Moore than to sey soth, it semed bi here speche.   truth
     Heremites on an heep with hoked staves,   in large numbers
Wenten to Walsyngham and here wenches after;
55 Grete lobyes and longe that loth were to swynke,   louts; work
Clotheden hem in copis to ben knowen fram othere,   clerical dress
And shopen hem heremites here ese to have.
     I fond there freris, alle the foure ordres,   friars
Preched the peple for profit of hemselves,
60 Glosed the gospel as hem good lyked;
For coveitise of copis construed it as thei wolde.   coveting gowns
Manye of this maistres freris mowe clothen hem at lykyng
For here moncy and marchandise marchen togideres.
Sith Charite hath ben chapman and chief to shryve lordes

28 **ancres:** anchorites, like hermits people who withdraw from the world.   29–30: who do not desire to wander about the country [looking] for a dainty way of life to please their bodies.   34: And get gold with their innocent music, I believe.   36–37: They invent fantasies and make fools of themselves, but they have wit enough when they wish.   38 **Poul:** St Paul. 39: 'He who talks filth is Lucifer's servant.' Mixing Latin with English is characteristic of Langland.   41–42: With their bellies and their bags crammed full of bread. They dissemble to get food and fight over ale.

46 **palmers:** professional pilgrims who carry a palm branch to suggest they have been to Jerusalem. 47 **St James:** the shrine of the apostle St James the Great was at Compostella in northern Spain. 54 **Walsyngham:** Walsingham in Norfolk, one of the principal places of pilgrimage in Britain.   57: And present themselves as hermits in order to have an easy time.   58 **ordres:** The Augustines, Carmelites, Dominicans and Franciscans.   60: Interpreted the Bible as they wished.   62: Many of these master friars dress as they wish.   64: Since charity has become a trader and especially to [sell] absolution for sins to lords.

65	Manye ferlis han fallen in a fewe yeres.	marvels
	But Holy Chirche and hij holde better togideres	
	The most myschief on molde is mountyng wel faste.	the earth
	Ther preched a pardonere as he a preest were,	
	Broughte forth a bulle with bischopes seles,	seals
70	And seide that hymself myghte assoilen hem alle	absolve
	Of falshed of fastyng, of vowes ybroken.	broken fasts
	Lewed men leved him wel and lyked his wordes,	ignorant
	Comen up knelynge to kissen his bulles.	
	He bonched hem with his brevet and blered here eyes,	
75	And raughte with his ragman rynges and broches;	
	Thus they gyven here gold glotones to kepe,	
	And leveth such loseles that lecherye haunten.	good for nothings
	Were the bischop yblissed and worth bothe his eres,	
	His seel sholde nought be sent to deceyve the peple.	
80	Ac it is nought by the bischop that the boy precheth	
	For the parisshe preest and the pardoner parten the silver	divide
	That the poraille of the parissche sholde have if they nere.	
	Persones and parisch prestes pleyned hem to the bischop,	
	That here parisshes were pore sith the pestilence tyme,	
85	To have a lycence and a leve at London to dwelle,	
	And syngen ther for symonye, for silver is swete.	
	Bischopes and bachelers, bothe maistres and doctours	
	That han cure under Crist, and crounynge in tokne	
	And signe that thei sholden shryven here paroschienes,	absolve
90	Prechen and praye for hem, and the pore fede,	
	Liggen at London in Lenten an elles.	
	Some serven the King and his silver tellen,	
	In cheker and in chaucerye chalangen his dettes	
	Of wardes and of wardmotes, weyves and streyves.	
95	And some serven as servaunts lordes and ladies,	
	And in stede of stuwardes sitten and demen.	
	Here messe and here matynes and many of here oures	
	Arn doone undevoutlych; drede is at the laste	without devotion
	Lest Crist in consistorie acorse ful manye.	
100	I parceyved of the power that Peter had to kepe	
	To bynden and unbynden, as the boke telleth	

66: Unless Holy Church and they come together better.
69 **bulle**: episcopal edict. **74–75**: He knocked them with his letters of indulgence and clouded their sight. He got with his document rings and brooches. **ragman**: paper with many seals attached. **84 pestilence tyme**: Plague was rife during the 14th century. The Black death of 1348-49 killed about 1/3 of the population, making it difficult for parish priests to collect tithes because the land was untilled. **86 syngen for symonye**: singing masses for the dead, which provide indulgences for their time in Purgatory. **87 bachelers**: Church novices.

88 **crounynge in tokne**: the tonsure – the shaved upper part of the head – is a crown signifying a calling to Christ. **91**: Stay in London both at Lent and other times. **93**: In the exchequer or in chancery, collecting his dues from the property of minors, the king's wards, wives, and deceased foreigners. **96**: in the place of stewards work out costs and judges [household matters]. **97 oures**: hours; set times of day when devotions are made. **99 consistorie**: consistory courts judged ecclesiastical matters; here the last judgement. **101 the boke**: Scripture, here Matthew 16:19 where Peter is given power to bind and unbind souls.

How he it left with Love as owre Lord hight   commanded
Amonges foure vertues, the best of alle vertues,
That cardinales ben called and closynge gatis
105   There Crist is in kyngdome, to close and to shutte,
And to opne it to hem and hevene blisse shewe.
Ac of the cardinales at court that caughte of that name
And power presumed in hem a Pope to make
To han that power that Peter hadde inpugnen I nelle;
110   For in love and in letterure the eleccioun bilongcth,
Forthi I can and can naught of court speke more.
    Thanne come ther a kyng knyghthod him ladde;   knights; led
Might of the comunes made him to regne,   commons
And thanne cam kynde Witte and clerkes he made,   scholars
115   For to conseille the kyng and the comune save.
The kyng and knyghthod and clergye bothe
Casten that the comune sholde hemself fynde.
    The comune contreved of kynde Witte craftes,
And for profit of al the peple plowmen ordeygned,
120   To tilie and to travaile as trewe lif asketh.
The Kyng and the comune and kynde Witte the thridde
Shope lawe and lewte eche man to knowe his owne.   shaped; loyalty
    Thanne loked up a lunatik, a leene thyng withalle,   lean
And knelynge to the kyng clergealy he seyde,   sagely
125   'Crist kepe thee, sire kyng, and thi kyngriche,   kingdom
And leve thee lede thi lond so leute thee lovye,
And for thi rightful rewlyng be rewarded in hevene.'
    And sithen in the eyre on heigh an angel of hevene   air
Lowed to speke in Latyn for lewed men ne koude
130   Jangle ne jugge that justifie hem sholde,
But suffren and serven; forthi seide the angel:
'Sum Rex, sum Princeps neutrum fortasse deinceps;
O qui iura regis Christi specialia regis,
Hoc quod agas melius iustus es, esto pius.
135   *Nudum ius a te vestiri vult pietate.*
Qualia vis metere, talia grana sere.
Si ius nudatur, nudo de iure metatur;
Si seritur pietas, de pietate metas.'

---

104 gatis: gates. Cardinal is derived from the Latin word for hinge. **107 court:** Rome. Cardinal is the highest rank in the Roman Catholic Chruch. Cardinals elect the Pope from among themselves. **109 inpugnen I nelle:** 'I will not question.' Langland is contrasting the cardinal virtues with the princes of the Church, indirectly questioning their relation. **110 letterure:** knowledge of letters. **117:** Contrived that the commons should provide for them. **118:** The commons had generous Wit devise crafts for them. **126:** And bring you to lead your land, so that it loyally loves you.

128 angel: can mean a prophet or teacher and not necessarily a disembodied spirit. **129–30:** Came down and spoke in Latin, for ignorant men could not talk quickly and justify themselves. **132–38:** I am a king, I am a prince [you say] but after you may be neither. You who administer the high laws of Christ the king, as you would seek to do this better, be pious as well as just. Naked justice needs to be dressed by you in piety. Whatever crops you would reap, be sure to rightly sow. If justice is made naked by you, let it be similarly measured to you; if it is sown with piety, you will reap with piety.

Thanne greved him a goliardeys, a glotoun of wordes,
140 And to the angel an heigh answerde after:
'*Dum rex a regere dicatur nomen habere,*
Nomen habet sine re nisi studet iura tenere.'
And thanne gan al the comune crye in vers of Latin
To the kynges conseille construe ho-so wolde:
145 '*Precepta Regis sunt nobis vincula legis.*'
With that ran there a route of ratones at ones   rats
And smale mys myd hem mo than a thousand   mice with them
And comen to a conseille for the comune profit;
For a cat of a courte cam whan him lyked
150 And overlepe hem lyghtlich and laughte hem at his wille,   caught
And pleyde with hem perilouslych and possed hem aboute.
'For doute of dyverse dredes we dar nought wel loke
And if we grucche of his gamen he wil greve us alle   complain; game
Cracche us or clowe us and in his cloches holde,   scratch; claw
155 That us lotheth the lyf or he lete us passe.   loath; free
Mighte we with any witte his wille withstonde,
We myghte be lordes alofte and lyven at owre ese.'
A raton of renon, most renable of tonge,   eloquent
Seide for a sovereygne help to hymselve,
160 'I have ysein segges', quod he, 'in the cite of London   seen men
Beren bighes ful brighte abouten here nekkes,
And some colers of crafty work; uncoupled thei wenden
Bothe in wareine & in waste where hem leve lyketh;
And otherwhile thei aren elles-where, as I here telle.
165 Were there a belle on here beighe, bi Jesu, as me thynketh,
Men myghte wite where thei wente and awei renne.   know
And right so', quod that rat ratoun, 'reson me sheweth
To bugge a belle of bras or of brighte sylver   to buy
And knitten it on a colere for owre comune profit,   attach
170 And hangen it upon the cattes hals thanne here we mowen
Wher he ritt or rest or renneth to playe.   moving about
And if him list for to laike, thanne loke we mowen   play
And peren in his presence ther while him plaie liketh,   appear
And if him wrattheth, be ywar and his wey shonye.'   is enraged
175 Al this route of ratons to this reson thei assented.
Ac tho the belle was ybrought and on the beighe hanged

139: Then a buffoon became angry, a glutton of words.
141–42: Since a king is rightly called a king by ruling; he only has the name of king without keeping the laws. 144 **construe . . .** : let him understand it as he will. 145: The king's dictates are as binding to us as the law. 146 **ratones**: rats; this is a version of the well known fable of belling the cat. Here the rats are the important citizens, the mice the less important; the cat is likely to be John of Gaunt, whose Duchy of Lancaster was effectively a kingdom, so that he might be seen coming from a court (cf. l.149).

152: for fear of so many dangers we dare not look out. 159: offered an excellent plan of his own invention. 161 **bighes**: elaborate collars decorated in the livery of particular nobles. 162–64: And some in collars of excellent workmanship; they wander off the leash over warren and common ground, wherever they wish; and when they are not here, I'm told they are doing the same elsewhere. 170 **hals**: neck; **mowen**: may.

Ther ne was raton in al the route, for al the rewme of Fraunce,
That dorste have ybounden the belle aboute the cattis nekke,
Ne hangen it aboute the cattes hals al Engelond to wynne;
180 And helden hem unhardy and hir conseille feble, *timid*
And leten here laboure lost & al here longe studye.
 A mous that muche good couthe, as me thoughte, *shrewd*
Stroke forth sternly and stood biforn hem alle, *pushed forward*
And to the route of ratons reherced these wordes:
185 'Though we hadde culled the cat, yet sholde ther come another
To cracchy us and al owre kynde, though we crope under
  benches.
Forthi I conseille al the comune to lat the cat worthe,
And be we nevere so bolde the belle him to shewe.
For I herde my sire seyn, is seven yere ypassed, *these seven years ago*
190 "Ther the cat is a kitoun, the court is ful elyng". *miserable*
That witnesseth holy writ, whoso wile it rede
  Ve terre ubi puer rex est, &c.
For may no renk ther reste have for ratons by nyghte;
The while he caccheth conynges he coveiteth noght owre *rabbits*
  caroyne, *flesh*
But fet him al with venesoun defame we him nevere.
195 For bettre is a litel los than a long sorwe,
The mase among us alle, though we mysse a sherewe.
For many mennes malt we mys wolde destruye, *mice*
And also ye route of ratons rende mennes clothes,
Nere the cat of the court that can you overlepe; *were not*
200 For hadde ye rattes youre wille, ye couthe nought reule
  yowrselve.
I seye for me', quod the mous, 'I se so mykel after, *much*
Shal nevere the cat ne the kiton by my counseille be greved,
Ne carpynge of this coler that costed me nevere.
And though it coste me catel, biknowen it I nolde,
205 But suffre as hymself wolde to do as him lyketh
Coupled and uncoupled to cacche what thei mowe.
Forthi ech a wise wight I warne wite wel his owne.'
 What this meteles bemeneth, ye men that ben murye, *dream*
Devine ye for I ne dar, by dere God in hevene.
210 Yet hoved ther an hundred in houves of selk,
Seriauntz, it semed, that serveden atte the barre, *lawyers*
Plededen for penyes and poundes the lawe, *pleading*
And noght for love of owre Lord unlese here lippes onis.

---

177 rewme: realm. 186 cracchy: scratch. 192: Woe to the land whose king is a child. 194: So let us not defame him but let him have his venison. 196: There would be confusion among us, though we would be rid of a cursed thing.   203–207: Nor talk of this collar, though it didn't cost me anything. And if it had cost me my goods, I would not make it known. I would suffer what they wished to do, leashed or unleashed, to catch us as they may. Therefore, I think each should be wise and look out for his own. 210: Yet there swayed a hundred in coifs of silk.

Thow myghtest better mete the myste on Malverne Hilles
215   Than get a 'momme' of here mouth but money were shewed.
Barones and burgeis and bondemen als   *burgesses; peasants*
I seigh in this assemble, as ye shul here after;   *assembly*
Baxsteres and brewesteres and bocheres manye,   *bakers, brewers*
Wollewebsters and weveres of lynnen,   *wool weavers*
220   Taillours and tynkeres and tolleres in marketes,   *toll collectors*
Masons and mynours and many other craftes.
Of alkin libbyng laborers lopen forth somme,
As dykeres and delveres that doth here dedes ille
And dryven forth the longe day with '*Dieu vous save Dame
     Emme.*'
225   Cokes and here knaves crieden, 'Hote pies, hote!   *boys*
Goode gris and gees! Go we dyne, go we!'   *pigs; geese*
Taverners until hem tolde the same,
'Whit wyn of Oseye and wyn of Gascoigne,   *Portugal; Gascony*
Of the Ryne and of the Rochel, the roste to defye!'
230   Al this I seigh slepyng, and sevene sythes more.

214–15: You might more easily measure the mist on the Malvern Hills than get a breath out of their mouths until you show them money. **222–24:** All kinds of living labourers came out, some of them ditch diggers and diggers generally that do their work idly and pass the whole day singing 'God save you Dame Emme.' This is an example of the bawdy songs such types would sing. **229:** Of the Rhine and of La Rochelle [a centre for the importing of Bordeaux wines into England] and roast meat to digest.

'SIR JOHN MANDEVILLE' (c.1357)

Originally written in French, or possibly Anglo-Norman, by an anonymous author, *The Travels of Sir John Mandeville* claim to be the true account of Mandeville, who left England in 1322 on a pilgrimage to Jerusalem, but continued east, finally serving the Great Khan. In fact the author probably never left Europe. Translated into virtually every European language, the text exerted enormous influence on how Europeans imagined the east well into the Renaissance and beyond. The excerpts here are from an English version which appeared shortly after 1400. The spelling has been modernised.

From Mandeville's Travels

How men know by the idol if the sick shall die or no. Of folk of diverse shape and marvellously disfigured. And of the monks that give their relief to baboons, apes, and marmosets, and to other beasts.

From that isle [Sri Lanka] in going by sea toward the south is another great isle that is cleped Dondun [in the Andaman Islands]. In that isle be folk of diverse kinds and have evil manners, so that the father eateth the son, the son the father, the husband the wife, and the wife the husband. And if it so befall that the father or mother or any of their friends be sick, the son goeth to the priest of their law and prayeth him to ask the idol if his father or mother or friend shall die of that evil or no. And then the priest and the son go together before the idol and kneel full devoutly and ask of the idol their demand. And if the devil that is within answer that he shall live, they keep him well. And if he say that he shall die, then the priest goeth with the son or with the wife of him that is sick and they put their hands upon his mouth and stop his breath. And so they slay him.

And after that they chop all the body in small pieces and pray all his friends to come and eat of him that is dead. And they send for all the minstrels of the country and make a solemn feast. And when they have eaten the flesh, they take the bones and bury them and sing and make great melody. And all those that be of his kin or pretend them to be his friends, if they come not to that feast, they be reproved for evermore and shamed and make great dole, for never after shall they be held as friends.

And they say also that men eat their flesh for to deliver them out of pain. For if the worms of the earth eat them, the soul should suffer great pain, as they say. And namely when the flesh is tender and meagre, then say their friends that they do great sin to let them have so long languor to suffer so much pain without reason. And when they find the flesh fat, then they say that it is well done to send them soon to Paradise and that they have not suffered him to long endure in pain.

The king of this isle is a full great lord and a mighty, and hath under him fifty-four great isles that give tribute to him. And in every of these isles is a king crowned and all be obedient to that king. And he hath in those isles many diverse folk.

In one of these isles be folk of great stature as giants, and they be hideous for to look on. And they have but one eye, and that is in the middle of the front. And they eat nothing but raw flesh and raw fish.

And in another isle toward the south dwell folk of foul stature and cursed kind that have no heads. And their eyes be in their shoulders. And their mouth is crooked as an horseshoe, and that is in the midst of their breast.

And in another isle also be folk that have no heads, and their eyes and their mouth be behind in their shoulders.

And in another isle be folk that have the face all plat,[1] all plain without nose and without mouth. But they have two small holes all round instead of their eyes, and their mouth is plat also without lips.

And in another isle be folk of foul fashion and shape that have the lip above the mouth so great that when they sleep in the sun, they cover all the face with that lip.

And in another isle there be little folk as dwarfs. And they be too so much as pigmies. And they have no mouth, but instead of their mouth they have a little round hole. And when they shall eat or drink, they take through a pipe or a pen or such a thing and suck it in, for they have no tongue. And therefore they speak not but they make a manner of hissing as an adder doth. And they make signs one to another as monks do, by the which every of them understandeth other.

And in another isle be folk that have great ears and long that hang down to their knees.

And in another isle be folk that have horse feet. And they be strong and mighty and swift runners, for they take wild beasts with running and eat them.

And in another isle be folk that go upon their hands and on their feet as beasts. And they be all skinned and feathered. And they will leap as lightly into trees and from tree to tree as it were squirrels or apes.

And in another isle be folk that be both man and woman, and they have kind[2] of that one and of that other. And they have but one pap on the one side, and on that other none. And they have members of generation of man and woman, and they use both when them list, once that one and another time that other. And they get children when they use the member of man, and they bear children when they use the member of woman.

And in another be folk that go always upon their knees full marvellously, and at every pace that they go it seemeth that they would fall. And they have in every foot eight toes.

Many other diverse folk of diverse natures be there in other isles about, of the which it were too long to tell and therefore I pass over shortly.

From these isles in passing by the sea ocean toward the east by many journeys men find a great country and a great kingdom that men clepe Manzi, and that is in Ind the More [Greater India]. And it is the best land and one the fairest that may be in all the world; and the most delectable and the most plenteous of all goods that is in power of man. In that land dwell many Christian men and Saracens, for it is a good country and a great. And there be in it

---

1 **plat:** flat.   2 **kind:** sexual organs.

more than two thousand great cities and rich without other great towns, and there is more plenty of people there than in any other part of Ind for the bounty of the country.

In that country is no needy man nor none that goeth on begging. And they be full fair folk, but they be all pale. And the men have thin beards and few hairs, but they be long. But unethe[1] hath any man passing fifty hairs in his beard. And one hair sitteth here, another there as the beard of a leopard or of a cat. In that land be many fairer woman than in any other country beyond the sea, and therefore men clepe that land Albany because that the folk be white.

And the chief city of the country is Canton, and it is a journey from the sea. And it is much more than Paris. In that city is a great river bearing ships that go to all the coasts in the sea. No city of the world is so well stored of ships as is that. And all those of the city and of the country worship idols.

In that country be double sithes[2] more greater birds than be here. There be white geese red about the neck, and they have a great crest as a cock's comb upon their heads; and they be much more there than they be here. And men buy them there all quick, right great cheap. And there is great plenty of adders, of whom men make great feasts and eat them at great solemnities. And he that maketh there a feast, be it never so costly, an he have no adders he hath no thank for his travail.

Many good cities there be in that country, and men have great plenty and great cheap of all wines and victuals. In that country be many churches of religious men and of their law. And in those churches be idols as great as giants, and to these idols they give to eat at great festival days in this manner. They bring before them meat all sodden, as hot as they come from the fire, and they let the smoke go up towards the idols. And then they say that the idols have eaten, and then the religious men eat the meat afterwards.

In that country be white hens without feathers, but they bear white wool as sheep do here. In that country, women that be unmarried, they have tokens on their heads like coronals[3] to be known for unmarried.

Also in that country be beasts taught of men to go into waters, in rivers, and into deep tanks for to take fish, the which beast is but little, and men clepe them *loutres*.[4] And when men cast them into the water, anon they bring off great fish as many as men will. And if men will have more, they cast them in again and they bring up as many as men list to have.

And from that city passing many journeys is another city, one the greatest of the world, that men clepe Cassay [Hangchow], that is to say the City of Heaven. That city is well a mile about, and it is strongly inhabited with people in so much that in one house men make ten households. In that city be twelve principal gates, and before every gate a three mile or a four mile in length is a great town or a great city. That city sitteth upon a great lake on the sea as doth Venice. And in that city be more than twelve thousand bridges. And upon every bridge be strong towers and good, in the which dwell the wardens for to keep the city from the Great Khan. And on that one part of the city runneth a

---

1 **unethe**: with difficulty. 2 **sithes**: times; i.e. there are twice as many species of bird as here. 3 **coronals**: garlands; coronets. 4 *loutres*: otters.

great river all along the city. And there dwell Christian men and many merchants and other folk of diverse nations because that the land is so good and so plenteous. And there groweth full good wine that men clepe *bagni*,[1] that is full mighty and gentle in drinking. This is a city royal where the King of Manzi was wont to dwell. And there dwell many religious men as it were of the order of friars, for they be mendicants.

From that city men go by water, solacing and disporting them till they come to an abbey of monks that is fast by, that be good religious men after their faith and law. In that abbey is a great garden and a fair where be many trees of diverse manner of fruits. And in this garden is a little hill full of delectable trees. In that hill and in that garden be many diverse beasts, as of apes, marmosets, baboons, and many other diverse beasts. And every day when the convent of this abbey hath eaten, the almoner let bear the relief to the garden, and he smiteth on the garden gate with a clicket of silver that he holdeth in his hand. And anon all the beasts of the hill and of diverse places of the garden come out a three thousand or a four thousand. And they come in guise of poor men, and men give them the relief in fair vessels of silver clean overgilt. And when they have eaten, the monk smiteth eftsoons[2] on the garden gate with the clicket. And then anon all the beasts return again to their places that they come from.

And they say that these beasts be souls of worthy men that resemble in likeness of those beasts that be fair. And therefore they give them meat for the love of God. And the other beasts that be foul, they say, be souls of poor men and of rude commons. And thus they believe. And no man may put them out of this opinion. These beasts abovesaid they let take when they be young and nourish them so with alms, as many as they may find.

And I asked them if it had not been better to have given that relief to poor men rather than to those beasts. And they answered me and said that they had no poor men amongst them in that country. And though it had been so that poor men had been among them, yet were it greater alms to give it to those souls that do there their penance. Many other marvels be in that city and in the country thereabout that were too long to tell you.

From that city go men by a country a six journeys to another city that men clepe Chibense [Nanking], of the which city the walls be twenty mile about. In that city be sixty bridges of stone so fair that no man may see fairer. In that city was the first see[3] of the King of Manzi, for it is a fair city and plenteous of all goods.

After pass men overthwart a great river that men clepe Dalay [Yangtze]. And that is the greatest river of fresh water that is in the world, for there as it is most narrow it is more than four mile of breadth. And then enter men again into the land of the Great Khan.

That river goeth through the land of the Pigmies where that the folk be of little stature, that be but three span long. And they be right fair and gentle after their quantities, both the men and the women. And they marry them when they be half year of age and get children. And they live not but six year or seven at the most, and he that liveth eight year men hold him there right passing old.

---

1 **bagni**: beer.   2 **eftsoons**: a second time.   3 **see**: royal seat or throne.

These men be the best workers of gold, silver, cotton, silk, and of all such things of any other that be in the world. And they have often time war with the birds of the country that they take and eat. This little folk neither labour in lands nor in vines. But they have great men amongst them of our stature that till the land and labour amongst the vines for them. And of those men of our stature have they as great scorn as we would have among us of giants if they were amongst us. There is a good city amongst other where there is dwelling great plenty of those little folk, and it is a great city and a fair. And the men be great that dwell amongst them. But when they get any children they be as little as the pigmies. And therefore they be all for the most part all pigmies, for the nature of the land is such. The Great Khan let keep this city full well, for it is his. And albeit that the pigmies be little, yet they be full reasonable after their age and con¹ both wit and good and malice enough.

From that city go men by the country by many cities and many towns unto a city that men clepe Iamcaly [Yangchow], and it is a noble city and a rich and of great profit to the lord. And thither go men to seek merchandise of all manner of thing. That city is full much worth yearly to the lord of the country, for he hath every year to rent of that city, as they of the city say, fifty thousand *tumens* of florins of gold. For they count there all by *tumens*, and every *tumen* is ten thousand florins of gold. The king of that country is full mighty. And yet he is under the Great Khan. And the Great Khan hath under him twelve such provinces.

In that country in the good towns is a good custom. For whoso will make a feast to any of his friends, there be certain inns in every good town. And he that will make a feast will say to the hosteller, 'Array for me tomorrow a good dinner for so many folk', and telleth him the number and deviseth him the viands. And he saith also, 'Thus much I will dispend and no more.' And anon the hosteller arrayeth for him so fair and so well and so honestly that there shall lack nothing. And it shall be done sooner and with less cost than a man made it in his own house.

And a five mile from that city toward the head of the river of Dalay [Yangtze] is another city that men clepe Menk [Ningpo]. In that city is strong navy of ships, and all be white as snow of the kind that they be made off. And they be full great ships and fair and well ordained and made with halls and chambers and other easements as though it were on the land.

From thence go men by many towns and many cities through the country unto a city that men clepe Lanteryn [Linching]. And it is an eight journeys from the city above said. This city sitteth upon a fair river great and broad that men clepe Caremoran [Hwang-ho]. This river passeth throughout Cathay, and it doth often time harm and that full great when it is overgreat.

---

1 con: know.

GEOFFREY CHAUCER (c.1343–1400)

Chaucer was born in London and spent most of his life as a civil servant in the courts of Edward III and Richard II. His work took him on several missions abroad and his poetry reflects continental influences on English in contrast to the native alliterative tradition. *The Canterbury Tales* is a late work, probably begun about 1386, and is a collection of stories told by a broad social range of characters gathered together on a pilgrimage to the shrine of St Thomas Beckett. In many respects a human as opposed to a divine comedy, Chaucer's tales and their tellers reveal how the ostensibly rigid class hierarchies of the medieval world are constantly open to disruption. Asking us to consider the relation between the story and the story-teller, Chaucer's use of irony, sometimes gentle, sometimes quite savage, encourages a style which allows the tragic and frivolous, the serious and the ribald to co-exist in searching and frequently unsettling ways.

From The Canterbury Tales

The Wife of Bath's Prologue and Tale

The Prologe of the Wyves Tale of Bathe

	'Experience, though noon auctoritee	
	Were in this world, were right ynogh for me	enough
	To speke of wo that is in mariage;	
	For, lordynges, sith I twelf yeer was of age,	
5	Thonked be God, that is eterne on lyve,	eternally living
	Housbondes at chirche-dore I have had fyve –	
	For I so ofte have ywedded bee –	
	And alle were worthy men in hir degree.	in their position
	But me was toold, certeyn, nat longe agoon is,	not long ago
10	That sith that Crist ne wente nevere but onis	once
	To weddyng in the Cane of Galilee,	
	That by the same ensample, taughte he me,	
	That I ne sholde wedded be but ones.	
	Herkne eek, lo, which a sharpe word for the nones,	
15	Biside a welle Jesus, God and Man,	
	Spak in repreeve of the Samaritan.	reproof
	"Thou hast yhad fyve housbondes," quod he,	
	"And that ilke man the which that hath now thee	the same
	Is noght thyn housbonde;" thus seyde he, certeyn.	
20	What that he mente ther by, I kan nat seyn;	say
	But that I axe, why that the fifthe man	ask
	Was noon housbonde to the Samaritan?	
	How manye myghte she have in mariage?	

---

1 **noon auctoritee**: no written authority from the past.
11 **Cane**: the marriage feast at Cana, see John 2:1.
14: 'But listen to a sharp reply to my purpose'. 15: see John 4:5–42.

23 **How manye**: Church law claimed a woman could marry only once. The Wife wishes to know where the Bible puts a precise figure on the number of husbands a woman can have.

Yet herde I nevere tellen in myn age
25 Upon this nombre diffinicioun.
Men may devyne, and glosen up and doun,   speculate, interpret
But wel I woot expres withoute lye,   know expressly
God bad us for to wexe and multiplye;
That gentil text kan I wel understonde.   noble
30 Eek wel I woot, he seyde, myn housbonde   also I know well
Sholde lete fader and mooder, and take me;   leave
But of no nombre mencioun made he,
Of bigamye, or of octogamye;   marrying eight times
Why sholde men speke of it vileynye?   reproachfully
35   Lo, heere the wise kyng, daun Salomon;   Lord
I trowe he hadde wyves mo than oon.   believe
As, wolde God, it leveful were to me   would; lawful
To be refresshed half so ofte as he!
Which yifte of God hadde he for alle hise wyvys?   favour
40 No man hath swich that in this world alyve is.   such
God woot, this noble kyng, as to my wit,
The firste nyght had many a myrie fit   fling
With ech of hem, so wel was hym on lyve!
Yblessed be God, that I have wedded fyve;
45 Welcome the sixte, whan that evere he shal.
For sothe I wol nat kepe me chaast in al;
Whan myn housbonde is fro the world ygon
Som Cristen man shal wedde me anon.
For thanne th'apostle seith that I am free,
50 To wedde a Goddes half where it liketh me.   in God's name
He seith, that to be wedded is no synne,
Bet is to be wedded than to brynne.   better; burn
What rekketh me, thogh folk seye vileynye
Of shrewed Lameth and of bigamye?
55 I woot wel Abraham was an hooly man,
And Jacob eek, as ferforth as I kan,   as far as I know
And ech of hem hadde wyves mo than two,
And many another holy man also.
Wher can ye seye, in any manere age   in any era
60 That hye God defended mariage   forbade
By expres word? I pray you, telleth me,
Or where comanded he virginitee?
I woot as wel as ye, it is no drede,   there is no doubt about it
Th'apostel, whan he speketh of maydenhede,
65 He seyde, that precept therof hadde he noon.   order
Men may conseille a womman to been oon,   advise
But conseillyng is no comandement;

---

29 text: Genesis 1:28.   **43:** with each of them, so for-   **49** th'apostle: St Paul. See 1 Corinthians 7:9.   **53:** What
tunate was his life.   do I account it, though people call it scandal.

He putte it in oure owene juggement. *leaves it to*
For hadde God comanded maydenhede,
70 Thanne hadde he dampned weddyng with the dede; *damned*
And certes, if ther were no seed ysowe, *sown*
Virginitee, wherof thanne sholde it growe?
Poul dorste nat comanden, atte leeste, *at any rate*
A thyng of which his maister yaf noon heeste. *gave no command*
75 The dart is set up of virginitee;
Cacche who so may, who renneth best lat see.
  But this word is nat taken of every wight,
But ther as God lust gyve it of his myght.
I woot wel, the apostel was a mayde; *virgin*
80 But nathelees, thogh that he wroot and sayde
He wolde that every wight were swich as he,
Al nys but conseil to virginitee; *this is all nothing but*
And for to been a wyf, he yaf me leve *permission*
Of indulgence, so it is no repreve *reproach*
85 To wedde me, if that my make dye, *mate*
Withouten excepcioun of bigamye. *accusation*
Al were it good no womman for to touche,
He mente, as in his bed or in his couche;
For peril is bothe fyr and tow t'assemble;
90 Ye knowe what this ensample may resemble.
This is al and som, he heeld virginitee
Moore parfit than weddyng in freletee. *frailty*
Freletee clepe I, but if that he and she *I'll call it*
Wolde leden al hir lyf in chastitee.
95   I graunte it wel, I have noon envie,
Thogh maydenhede preferre bigamye;
Hem liketh to be clene, body and goost. *soul*
Of myn estaat I nyl nat make no boost,
For wel ye knowe, a lord in his houshold,
100 He nath nat every vessel al of gold; *wood*
Somme been of tree, and doon hir lord servyse. *various ways*
God clepeth folk to hym in sondry wyse,
And everich hath of God a propre yifte,
Som this, som that, as hym liketh shifte. *wishes to distribute them*
105 Virginitee is greet perfeccioun,
And continence eek with devocioun. *continence for spiritual devotion*
But Crist, that of perfeccioun is welle, *fountain-head*
Bad nat every wight he sholde go selle *ordered; person*
Al that he hadde, and gyve it to the poore,
110 And in swich wise folwe hym and his foore. *footsteps*

---

73 **Poul**: St Paul.   75 **dart**: probably the prize referred
to in 1 Corinthians 9:24.   76: Win it who will, let's see
who runs best.   78: but where almighty God decides
to give it.

87–89: Though it was preferable not to touch a woman,
he meant in a bed or on a couch; for it's dangerous to
mix fire and flax.

He spak to hem that wolde lyve parfitly,
And lordynges, by youre leve, that am nat I.
I wol bistowe the flour of myn age
In the actes and in fruyt of mariage.

115 Telle me also, to what conclusion
Were membres maad of generacion,   *organs*
And of so parfit wys a wight ywroght?
Trusteth right wel, they were nat maad for noght.
Glose whoso wole, and seye bothe up and doun,

120 That they were maked for purgacioun
Of urine, and oure bothe thinges smale
Were eek to knowe a femele from a male,
And for noon oother cause, – say ye no?
The experience woot wel it is noght so.

125 So that the clerkes be nat with me wrothe,   *angry*
I sey this, that they maked ben for bothe,
This is to seye, for office, and for ese   *natural function; pleasure*
Of engendrure, ther we nat God displese.
Why sholde men elles in hir bookes sette

130 That man shal yelde *to* his wyf hire dette?   *pay; what is due her*
Now wherwith sholde he make his paiement,
If he ne used his sely instrument?
Thanne were they maad upon a creature
To purge urine, and eek for engendrure.

135 But I seye noght that every wight is holde,
That hath swich harneys as I to yow tolde,   *equipment*
To goon and usen hem in engendrure.
Thanne sholde men take of chastitee no cure.   *notice*
Crist was a maide, and shapen as a man,   *virgin*

140 And many a seint, sith that the world bigan;
Yet lived they evere in parfit chastitee.
I nil envye no virgintee.
Lat hem be breed of pured whete-seed,   *bread*
And lat us wives hoten barly-breed;   *be called*

145 And yet with barly-breed, Mark telle kan,
Oure Lord Jhesu refresshed many a man.
In swich estaat as God hath cleped us
I wol persevere; I nam nat precius.
In wyfhod I wol use myn instrument

150 As frely as my Makere hath it sent.
If I be daungerous, God yeve me sorwe!   *grudging; bitterness*
Myn housbonde shal it have bothe eve and morwe,
Whan that him list come forth and paye his dette.

119: Interpret it how you like and talk it up or down.   **145 Mark:** in fact the gospel of St John 6:9 tells how
132 sely instrument: penis. sely can mean simple, happy   barley loaves fed the multitude.
and/or innocent.

An housbonde I wol have, I nyl nat lette,   *I will not give up*
155 Which shal be bothe my dettour and my thral,   *slave*
And have his tribulacioun withal
Upon his flessh whil that I am his wyf.
I have the power durynge al my lyf
Upon his propre body, and noght he.
160 Right thus the Apostel tolde it unto me,
And bad oure housbondes for to love us weel.
Al this sentence me liketh every deel – '   *every bit of it*
    Up stirte the Pardoner, and that anon,
'Now, dame,' quod he, 'by God and by Seint John,
165 Ye been a noble prechour in this cas.
I was aboute to wedde a wyf, allas!
What sholde I bye it on my flessh so deere?   *pay with my body*
Yet hadde I levere wedde no wyf to-yeere!'   *better; this year*
    'Abyde,' quod she, 'my tale is nat bigonne.
170 Nay, thou shalt drynken of another tonne,   *cask*
Er that I go, shal savoure wors than ale.   *taste*
And whan that I have toold thee forth my tale
Of tribulacioun in mariage,
Of which I am expert in al myn age,
175 (This to seyn, myself have been the whippe),
Than maystow chese wheither thou wolt sippe
Of thilke tonne that I shal abroche,   *broach*
Be war of it, er thou to ny approche   *near*
For I shal telle ensamples mo than ten.
180 Whoso that nyl be war by othere men,
By hym shul othere men corrected be.
The same wordes writeth Ptholomee;
Rede it in his Almageste, and take it there.'
    'Dame, I wolde praye yow, if youre wyl it were,'
185 Seyde this Pardoner, 'as ye bigan,
Telle forth youre tale, spareth for no man,   *refrain*
And teche us yonge men of your praktike.'
    'Gladly,' quod she, 'sith it may yow like.
But yet I praye to al this compaignye,
190 If that I speke after my fantasye,   *whim*
As taketh not agrief of that I seye,   *offence*
For myn entente nis but for to pleye.
    Now sire, now wol I telle forth my tale,
As evere moote I drynken wyn or ale,   *As I hope*
195 I shal seye sooth, tho housbondes that I hadde,   *truth*

---

156 **tribulacioun**: the 'trouble of the flesh' which St Paul speaks of.   163 **Pardoner**: a person licensed to sell indulgences granting remission of sins.   180–81: Whoever will not take heed of other men's stories will become a cautionary tale himself.   182 **Phtolomee**: Ptolomy, a Classical geographer and astronomer. *The Almageste* is his principal work but the warning the wife ascribes to it is proverbial.   184: if you would be so kind.

As thre of hem were goode, and two were badde.
The thre men were goode, and riche, and olde;
Unnethe myghte they the statut holde
In which that they were bounden unto me.

200 Ye woot wel what I meene of this, pradee!
As help me God, I laughe whan I thynke
How pitously a-nyght I made hem swynke.   sweat in labour
And by my fey, I tolde of it no stoor,
They had me yeven hir gold and hir tresoor;

205 Me neded nat do lenger diligence
To wynne hir love, or doon hem reverence,
They loved me so wel, by God above,
That I ne tolde no deyntee of hir love.   counted it no pleasure
A wys womman wol sette hire evere in oon

210 To gete hire love, ther as she hath noon.   as she has none
But sith I hadde hem hoolly in myn hond,
And sith they hadde me yeven all hir lond,
What sholde I taken heede hem for to plese,
But it were for my profit and myn ese?   comfort

215 I sette hem so a-werke, by my fey,   faith
That many a nyght they songen "weilawey."   they sang "woe is me"
The bacoun was nat fet for hem, I trowe,   fetched
That som men han in Essex at Dunmowe.
I governed hem so wel after my lawe,

220 That ech of hem ful blisful was, and fawe
To brynge me gaye thynges fro the fayre.
They were ful glad whan I spak to hem faire,
For God it woot, I chidde hem spitously.   scolded
   Now herkneth hou I baar me proprely,   conducted myself

225 Ye wise wyves, that kan understonde.
Thus shul ye speke and bere hem wrong on honde;
For half so boldely kan ther no man
Swere and lyen, as a womman kan.
I sey nat this by wyves that been wyse,

230 But if it be whan they hem mysavyse.   act unadvisedly
A wys wyf, it that she kan hir good,
Shal beren hym on hond the cow is wood,
And take witnesse of hir owene mayde,   maid
Of hir assent; but herkneth how I sayde.

235   "Sire olde kaynard, is this thyn array?
Why is my neighebores wyf so gay?
She is honoured overal ther she gooth;   everywhere

198: carry out their obligation to have intercourse.
203: And in faith, I put no store by it. 209: A shrewd
woman will always work. 217–18 bacoun: at Dunmow
a side of bacon was awarded annually to a couple who
had not fought during the year.

226: Here's how to speak and keep the upper
hand. 232: convince him that the bird is mad. Referring to a folk-tale in which a deceiving wife convinces
her husband that the bird which has told him the truth
is deluded. 235: Old dotard, is this how you carry on?

I sitte at hoom, I have no thrifty clooth.   *nothing decent to wear*
What dostow at my neighebores hous?
240 Is she so fair? artow so amorous?   *are you*
What rowne ye with oure mayde? *Benedicite,*   *whisper*
Sir olde lecchour, lat thy japes be!   *pranks*
And if I have a gossib or a freend
Withouten gilt, thou chidest as a feend
245 If that I walke or pleye unto his hous.
Thou comest hoom as dronken as a mous
And prechest on thy bench, with yvel preef!   *misfortune on you*
Thou seist to me, it is a greet meschief
To wedde a povre womman, for costage,   *because of the cost*
250 And if she be riche and of heigh parage,
Thanne seistow it is a tormentrie   *torment*
To soffre hir pride and hir malencolie.
And if she be fair, thou verray knave,
    Thou seyst that every holour wol hir have;   *lecher*
255 She may no while in chastitee abyde
That is assailled upon ech a syde.
Thou seyst, som folk desiren us for richesse,
Somme for oure shape, and somme for oure fairnesse,
And som for she kan outher synge or daunce,   *either*
260 And som for gentillesse and daliaunce,   *good upbringing; playfulness*
Som for hir handes and hir armes smale;
Thus goth al to the devel by thy tale.
Thou seyst, men may nat kepe a castel wal,
It may so longe assailled been overal.
265   And if that she be foul, thou seist that she
Coveiteth every man that she may se;   *desires*
For as a spaynel she wol on hym lepe
Til that she fynde som man hir to chepe;   *to do business with*
Ne noon so grey goos gooth ther in the lake
270 As, seistow, wol been withoute make;   *control*
And seyst, it is an hard thyng for to welde
A thyng that no man wole, his thankes, helde.
Thus seistow, lorel, whan thow goost to bedde,   *wretch*
And that no wys man nedeth for to wedde,
275 Ne no man that entendeth unto hevene,
With wilde thonderdynt and firy levene   *thunder; lightning*
Moote thy welked nekke be to-broke!   *withered*
    Thow seyst that droppyng houses, and eek smoke,   *leaking*
And chidyng wyves maken men to flee
280 Out of hir owene hous; a, *benedicitee*!

243–44 freend withouten gilt: innocent acquaintance. 269: There is not so gray a goose swimming in
the lake.

271: Something which no man would willingly keep.

What eyleth swich an old man for to chide?   ails
Thow seyst, we wyves wol oure vices hide
Til we be fast, and thanne we wol hem shewe.   secure
Wel may that be a proverbe of a shrewe!
285   Thou seist, that oxen, asses, hors, and houndes,
They been assayd at diverse stoundes;   tested; various times
Bacyns, lavours, er that men hem bye,   basins; washbowls
Spoones and stooles, and al swich housbondrye,
And so been pottes, clothes, and array;
290   But folk of wyves maken noon assay
Til they be wedded; olde dotard shrewe!
Thanne, seistow, we wol oure vices shewe.
      Thou seist also, that it displeseth me
But if that thou wolt preyse my beautee,
295   And but thou poure alwey upon my face,   gaze
And clepe me 'faire dame' in every place,
And but thou make a feeste on thilke day
That I was born, and make me fressh and gay,
And but thou do to my norice honour,   nurse
300   And to my chamberere withinne my bour,   chambermaid
And to my fadres folk and hise allyes –   relatives
Thus seistow, olde barel ful of lyes!
      And yet of oure apprentice Janekyn,
For his crisp heer, shynynge as gold so fyn,   curly
305   And for he squiereth me bothe up and doun,   escorts
Yet hastow caught a fals suspecioun.
I wol hym noght, thogh thou were deed tomorwe.
But tel me this, why hydestow, with sorwe,   hide; may you have sorrow
The keyes of my cheste awey fro me?
310   It is my good as wel as thyn, pardee;
What wenestow make an ydiot of oure dame?
Now, by that lord that called is seint Jame,
Thou shalt nat bothe, thogh that thou were wood,   enraged
Be maister of my body and of my good;
315   That oon thou shalt forgo, maugree thyne eyen.
What nedeth thee of me to enquere or spyen?
I trowe thou woldest loke me in thy chiste.
Thou sholdest seye, 'Wyf, go wher thee liste,
Taak youre disport, I wol not leve no talys,   believe
320   I knowe yow for a trewe wyf, dame Alys.'
We love no man that taketh kepe or charge
Wher that we goon, we wol ben at our large.
Of alle men yblessed moot he be,
The wise astrologien, Daun Ptholome,

311: Are you looking to have me declared insane (and   315: Despite your eyes; i.e. despite anything you can do.
thus have no rights to her property).

325 That seith this proverbe in his Almageste:
  'Of alle men his wysdom is the hyeste,
  That rekketh nevere who hath the world in honde.'
  By this proverbe thou shalt understonde,
  Have thou ynogh, what thar thee recche or care
330 How myrily that othere folkes fare?
  For, certeyn, old dotard, by youre leve,
  Ye shul have queynte right ynough at eve.   *sex*
  He is to greet a nygard, that wolde werne *miser; refuse*
  A man to lighte his candle at his lanterne;
335 He shal have never the lasse light, pardee, *less*
  Have thou ynogh, thee thar nat pleyne thee. *complain*
   Thou seyst also, that if we make us gay
  With clothyng and with precious array,
  That it is peril of oure chastitee;
340 And yet, with sorwe, thou most enforce thee,
  And seye thise wordes in the apostles name,
  'In habit, maad with chastitee and shame,
  Ye wommen shul apparaille yow,' quod he,
  'And noght in tressed heer and gay perree, *braided; jewellery*
345 As perles, ne with gold, ne clothes riche.'
  After thy text, ne after thy rubriche *interpretation*
  I wol nat wirche as muchel as a gnat!
   Thou seydest this, that I was lyk a cat;
  For whoso wolde senge a cattes skyn, *singe*
350 Thanne wolde the cat wel dwellen in his in. *house*
  And if the cattes skyn be slyk and gay,
  She wol nat dwelle in house half a day,
  But forth she wole, er any day be dawed,
  To shewe hir skyn, and goon a caterwawed. *caterwauling*
355 This is to seye, if I be gay, sire shrewe,
  I wol renne out, my borel for to shewe. *run about; clothing*
  Sire olde fool, what eyleth thee to spyen,
  Thogh thou preye Argus, with hise hundred eyen,
  To be my wardecors, as he kan best, *body-guard*
360 In feith he shal nat kepe me but me lest; *unless I wish it*
  Yet koude I make his berd, so moot I thee.
   Thou seydest eek, that ther been thynges thre,
  The whiche thynges troublen al this erthe,
  And that no wight ne may endure the ferthe.
365 O leeve sire shrewe, Jesu shorte thy lyf!

---

325 **Almageste:** see note for 182. Another proverbial saying miscredited to Ptolomy. **327:** Who takes no account of who holds the world in his hand. **329:** As long as you have enough, what do you care. **341–42:** And, I am sorry to say, you reinforce your argument by claiming St Paul's authority (1 Timothy 2:9).

347: I will take account [of your views] as much as a gnat would. **358 Argus:** figure from classical mythology with 100 eyes. **361:** If I could delude him, I might you too.

Yet prechestow and seyst an hateful wyf
Yrekened is for oon of thise meschances.   reckoned
Been ther none othere maner resemblances
That ye may likne youre parables to,
370   But if a sely wyf be oon of tho?   innocent
Thou likenest wommenes love to helle,
To bareyne lond, ther water may nat dwelle.   barren
Thou liknest it also to wilde fyr;
The moore it brenneth, the moore it hath desir
375   To consume every thyng that brent wole be.
Thou seyst, right as wormes shendeth a tree,   destroy
Right so a wyf destroyeth hir housbond.
This knowe they, that been to wyves bonde."
    Lordynges, right thus, as ye have understonde,
380   Baar I stifly myne olde housbondes on honde,
That thus they seyden in hir dronkenesse,
And al was fals, but that I took witnesse
On Janekyn and on my nece also.
O lord, the pyne I dide hem, and the wo,
385   Ful giltelees, by Goddes sweete pyne!   free of guilt; suffering
For as an hors I koude byte and whyne,
I koude pleyne, thogh I were in the gilt,
Or elles often tyme hadde I been spilt.   ruined
Who so that first to mille comth first grynt;   grinds
390   I pleyned first, so was oure werre ystynt.   strife finished
They were ful glad to excuse hem ful blyve   quickly
Of thyng of which they nevere agilte hir lyve.
Of wenches wolde I beren hym on honde,   accuse
Whan that for syk unnethes myghte he stonde,   scarcely
395   Yet tikled it his herte, for that he   tickled
Wende that I hadde of hym so greet chiertee.   affection
I swoor that al my walkynge out by nyghte
Was for tespye wenches that he dighte.   lay with
Under that colour hadde I many a myrthe;
400   For al swich thyng was yeven us in oure byrthe,
Deceite, wepyng, spynnyng, God hath yive
To wommen kyndely whil they may lyve.
And thus of o thyng I avaunte me,   boast of
Atte ende I hadde the bettre in ech degree,
405   By sleighte, or force, or by som maner thyng,
As by continueel murmure or grucchyng.   grumbling
Namely a bedde hadden they meschaunce;   particularly; misfortune
Ther wolde I chide and do hem no plesaunce,
I wolde no lenger in the bed abyde,

---

373 **wilde fyr:** Greek fire, inflammable mixture used in   380: I boldly got round my old husbands.
sea warfare.

410 If that I felte his arm over my syde
Til he had maad his raunsoun unto me;
Thanne wolde I suffre hym do his nycetee.
And therfore every man this tale I telle,
Wynne who so may, for al is for to selle.
415 With empty hand men may none haukes lure,   *hawks*
For wynnyng wolde I al his lust endure
And make me a feyned appetit;
And yet in bacoun hadde I nevere delit;   *aged meat*
That made me that evere I wolde hem chide.
420 For thogh the pope hadde seten hem biside,
I wolde nat spare hem at hir owene bord,   *table*
For by my trouthe I quitte hem word for word.   *matched*
As help me verray God omnipotent,
Though I right now sholde make my testament,
425 I ne owe hem nat a word, that it nys quit.   *nothing unpaid*
I broghte it so aboute by my wit,
That they moste yeve it up as for the beste,
Or elles hadde we nevere been in reste.
For thogh he looked as a wood leoun,   *mad lion*
430 Yet sholde he faille of his conclusioun.
    Thanne wolde I seye, "Goode lief, taak keepe,   *My darling; takenote*
How mekely looketh Wilkyn oure sheepe!
Com neer, my spouse, lat me ba thy cheke,   *kiss*
Ye sholde been al pacient and meke,
435 And han a sweete spiced conscience,
Sith ye so preche of Jobes pacience.   *Job's*
Suffreth alwey, syn ye so wel kan preche,
And but ye do, certein we shal yow teche
That it is fair to have a wyf in pees.
440 Oon of us two moste bowen, doutelees,
And sith a man is moore resonable,
Than womman is, ye moste been suffrable.   *patient*
What eyleth you to grucche thus and grone?   *grumble*
Is it for ye wolde have my queynte allone?   *sex*
445 Wy, taak it all! Lo, have it every deel!
Peter, I shrewe you, but ye love it weel;   *By St Peter I curse you*
For if I wolde selle my *bele chose*
I koude walke as fressh as is rose
But I wol kepe it for youre owene tooth   *appetite*
450 Ye be to blame, by God, I sey you sooth."
    Swiche manere wordes hadde we on honde.
Now wol I speken of my fourthe housbonde.
    My fourthe housbonde was a revelour,
This is to seyn, he hadde a paramour,

---

447 bele chose: nice thing. The wife is saying that if she was a prostitute selling her sex she could keep herself very well.

455	And I was yong and ful of ragerye,	passion
	Stibourne and strong, and joly as a pye.	magpie
	Wel koude I daunce to an harpe smale,	
	And synge, ywis, as any nyghtyngale,	
	Whan I had dronke a draughte of sweete wyn.	
460	Metellius, the foule cherl, the swyn,	
	That with a staf birafte his wyf hire lyf,	deprived
	For she drank wyn, thogh I hadde been his wyf,	
	He sholde nat han daunted me fro drynke.	scared
	And after wyn on Venus moste I thynke,	
465	For al so siker as cold engendreth hayl,	
	A likerous mouth moste han a likerous tayl.	
	In wommen vinolent is no defence,	full of wine
	This knowen lecchours by experience.	
	But, Lord Crist! whan that it remembreth me	
470	Upon my yowthe and on my jolitee,	
	It tikleth me aboute myn herte roote.	
	Unto this day it dooth myn herte boote	good
	That I have had my world, as in my tyme.	
	But age, allas, that al wole envenyme,	poison
475	Hath me biraft my beautee and my pith!	vigour
	Lat go, fare-wel, the devel go therwith!	
	The flour is goon, ther is namoore to telle,	
	The bren as I best kan, now moste I selle;	bran (husks)
	But yet to be right myrie wol I fonde.	try
480	Now wol I tellen of my fourthe housbonde.	
	I seye, I hadde in herte greet despit	
	That he of any oother had delit;	
	But he was quit, by God and by Seint Joce!	
	I made hym of the same wode a croce;	
485	Nat of my body in no foul manere,	
	But certeinly, I made folk swich cheere	
	That in his owene grece I made hym frye	
	For angre and for verray jalousye.	
	By God, in erthe I was his purgatorie,	
490	For which I hope his soule be in glorie,	
	For God it woot, he sat ful ofte and song	
	Whan that his shoo ful bitterly hym wrong!	
	Ther was no wight save God and he, that wiste	knew
	In many wise how soore I hym twiste.	tormented
495	He deyde whan I cam fro Jerusalem,	
	And lith ygrave under the roode-beem,	

---

460 Metellius: the story comes from the Roman historian Valerius Maximus.   465–66: For as sure as cold produces hail, a luxurious appetite produces a lecherous tail (i.e. a desire for sex).   483 Joce: Judocus, a saint from Brittany.

484: I made him a cross from the same wood; proverbial – I repaid him with the same troubles.   492: When his shoe (i.e. his marriage) hurt him bitterly.   496 roode-beem: a beam with a crucifix on it separating nave and chancel. To have buried him in the chancel would have been more expensive.

Al is his tombe noght so curyus   note-worthy
As was the sepulcre of hym Daryus,
Which that Appelles wroghte subtilly.
500 It nys but wast to burye hym preciously,
Lat hym fare-wel, God yeve his soule reste,
He is now in his grave, and in his cheste.   coffin
    Now of my fifthe housbonde wol I telle.
God lete his soule nevere come in helle!
505 And yet was he to me the mooste shrewe;
That feele I on my ribbes al by rewe,   in a row
And evere shal, unto myn endyng day.
But in oure bed he was ful fressh and gay,
And therwithal so wel koude he me glose   flatter
510 Whan that he solde han my *bele chose,*
That thogh he hadde me bet on every bon   beat; bone
He koude wynne agayn my love anon.
I trowe I loved hym beste, for that he
Was of his love daungerous to me.   grudging
515 We wommen han, if that I shal nat lye,
In this matere a queynte fantasye;
Wayte what thyng we may nat lightly have,
Ther-after wol we crie al day and crave.
Forbede us thyng, and that desiren we;
520 Preesse on us faste, and thanne wol we fle;
With daunger oute we al oure chaffare.
Greet prees at market maketh deere ware,   crowds
And to greet cheep is holde at litel prys;   bargin; value
This knoweth every womman that is wys.
525   My fifthe housbonde, God his soule blesse,
Which that I took for love and no richesse,
He somtyme was a clerk of Oxenford,
And hadde left scole, and wente at hom to bord
With my gossib, dwellynge in oure toun,
530 God have hir soule! hir name was Alisoun.
She knew myn herte and eek my privetee
Bet than oure parisshe preest, as moot I thee.
To hir biwreyed I my conseil al,   disclosed
For hadde myn housbonde pissed on a wal,
535 Or doon a thyng that sholde han cost his lyf,
To hir, and to another worthy wyf,
And to my nece, which that I loved weel,
I wolde han toold his conseil every deel.
And so I dide ful often, God it woot!   knows
540 That made his face ful often reed and hoot

498–99: Darius' tomb was famous; it was reputed to have   521: We grudgingly set out our wares.
been made by a Jew called Appelles.

For verray shame, and blamed hymself, for he
Had toold to me so greet a pryvetee.
   And so bifel that ones, in a Lente –
So often tymes I to my gossyb wente,
545 For evere yet I loved to be gay,
And for to walke in March, Averill, and May,
Fro hous to hous to heere sondry talys –
That Jankyn Clerk and my gossyb, dame Alys,
And I myself into the feeldes wente.
550 Myn housbonde was at London al that Lente;
I hadde the bettre leyser for to pleye,   *leisure*
And for to se, and eek for to be seye
Of lusty folk; what wiste I, wher my grace
Was shapen for to be, or in what place?
555 Therfore I made my visitaciouns
To vigilies and to processiouns,
To prechyng eek, and to thise pilgrimages,
To pleyes of myracles, and to mariages;
And wered upon my gaye scarlet gytes.   *gowns*
560 Thise wormes ne thise motthes, ne thise mytes,   *moths; mites*
Upon my peril, frete hem never a deel –
And wostow why? for they were used weel!
   Now wol I tellen forth what happed me.
I seye, that in the feeldes walked we,
565 Til trewely we hadde swich daliance,
This clerk and I, that of my purveiance   *foresight*
I spak to hym, and seyde hym, how that he,
If I were wydwe, sholde wedde me.
For certeinly, I sey for no bobance,   *boast*
570 Yet was I nevere withouten purveiance
Of mariage, n'of othere thynges eek.
I holde a mouses herte nat worth a leek
That hath but oon hole for to sterte to,
And if that faille, thanne is al ydo.
575   I bar hym on honde, he hadde enchanted me –   *I convinced him*
My dame taughte me that soutiltee.
And eek I seyde, I mette of hym al nyght,   *dreamed*
He wolde han slayn me as I lay upright,
And al my bed was ful of verray blood;
580 But yet I hope that he shal do me good,
For blood bitokeneth gold, as me was taught.
And al was fals, I dremed of it right naught,
But as I folwed ay my dames loore

553–54: How was I to know to whom and where my favours were to be given? 556 **vigilies; processions:** church vigils and ceremonial processions. 561: Upon peril of my soul, they did not consume them at all.

572–74: I don't count a mouse's life worth a thought because he has but one hole to escape to and if that goes, it's all over.

As wel of this, as of othere thynges moore.
585   But now sir, lat me se, what I shal seyn?
Aha, by God! I have my tale ageyn.
    Whan that my fourthe housbonde was on beere,   bier
I weep algate, and made sory cheere,
As wyves mooten – for it is usage –
590 And with my coverchief covered my visage;
But for that I was purveyed of a make,   provided with a mate
I wepte but smal, and that I undertake.
    To chirche was myn housbonde born amorwe   carried in the morning
With neighebores that for hym maden sorwe;
595 And Janekyn oure clerk was oon of tho.
As help me God, whan that I saugh hym go
After the beere, me thoughte he hadde a paire
Of legges and of feet so clene and faire,
That al myn herte I yaf unto his hoold.   keeping
600 He was, I trowe, a twenty wynter oold,
And I was fourty, if I shal seye sooth,
But yet I hadde alwey a coltes tooth.
Gat-tothed I was, and that bicam me weel,
I hadde the prente of Seinte Venus seel.   print
605 As help me God I was a lusty oon,
And faire, and riche, and yong, and wel bigon,   well provided for
And trewely, as myne housbondes tolde me,
I hadde the beste quonyam myghte be.   pudendum
For certes, I am al Venerien
610 In feelynge, and myn herte is Marcien.
Venus me yaf my lust, my likerousnesse,
And Mars yaf me my sturdy hardynesse.
Myn ascendent was Taur, and Mars therinne,   Taurus
Allas, allas, that evere love was synne!
615 I folwed ay myn inclinacioun
By vertu of my constellacioun;
That made me I koude noght withdrawe
My chambre of Venus from a good felawe.
Yet have I Martes mark upon my face,
620 And also in another privee place.
For God so wys be my savacioun,
I ne loved nevere by no discrecioun,   discrimination
But evere folwede myn appetit,
Al were he short, or long, or blak, or whit.
625 I took no kepe, so that he liked me,
How poore he was, ne eek of what degree.
    What sholde I seye, but at the monthes ende

---

603 **Gat-tothed:** wide gaps between the teeth, considered a mark of lasciviousness.

609–610 **Venerien, Marcien:** under the influence of the planets Venus and Mars.

	This joly clerk Jankyn, that was so hende,	comely
	Hath wedded me with greet solempnytee;	
630	And to hym yaf I al the lond and fee	property
	That evere was me yeven therbifoore;	
	But afterward repented me ful soore,	
	He nolde suffre nothyng of my list.	wants
	By God, he smoot me ones on the lyst	hit; ear
635	For that I rente out of his book a leef,	
	That of the strook myn ere wax al deef.	
	Stibourne I was as is a leonesse,	
	And of my tonge a verray jangleresse,	garrulousness
	And walke I wolde, as I had doon biforn,	
640	From hous to hous, although he had it sworn,	forbidden
	For which he often tymes wolde preche,	
	And me of olde Romayn geestes teche,	stories
	How he Symplicius Gallus lefte his wyf,	
	And hir forsook for terme of al his lyf,	
645	Noght but for open-heveded he hir say,	being bare-headed
	Lookynge out at his dore, upon a day.	
	Another Romayn tolde he me by name,	
	That for his wyf was at a someres game	midsummer festival
	Withoute his wityng, he forsook hir eke.	knowledge
650	And thanne wolde he upon his Bible seke	
	That like proverbe of Ecclesiaste,	
	Where he comandeth, and forbedeth faste,	firmly
	Man shal nat suffre his wyf go roule aboute.	
	Thanne wolde he seye right thus, withouten doute:	
655	"Who so that buyldeth his hous al of salwes,	willow
	And priketh his blynde hors over the falwes,	ploughed land
	And suffreth his wyf to go seken halwes,	shrines
	Is worthy to been hanged on the galwes!"	
	But al for noght, I sette noght an hawe	hawthorn berry
660	Of his proverbes, n'of his olde sawe,	proverbs
	Ne I wolde nat of hym corrected be.	
	I hate hym that my vices telleth me;	
	And so doo mo, God woot, of us than I!	more
	This made hym with me wood al outrely,	angry
665	I nolde noght forbere hym in no cas.	
	Now wol I seye yow sooth, by Seint Thomas,	
	Why that I rente out of his book a leef,	
	For which he smoot me so that I was deef.	
	He hadde a book that gladly, nyght and day,	
670	For his desport he wolde rede alway.	

---

642 **Romayn geestes:** Valerius Maximus, see n. for   665: In no instance would I give way to him.
1.460.   651 **Ecclesiaste:** Ecclesiastics 25:25.

He cleped it "Valerie and Theofraste,"
At whiche book he lough alwey ful faste.
And eek ther was som tyme a clerk at Rome,
A cardinal that highte Seint Jerome,
675 That made a book agayn Jovinian,
In whiche book eek ther was Tertulan,
Crisippus, Trotula, and Helowys,
That was abbesse nat fer fro Parys,
And eek the Parables of Salomon,   Proverbs
680 Ovides Art, and bookes many on,
And alle thise were bounden in o volume,
And every nyght and day was his custume
Whan he hadde leyser and vacacioun   free time
From oother worldly occupacioun,
685 To reden on this book of wikked wyves.
He knew of hem mo legendes and lyves
Than been of goode wyves in the Bible.
For trusteth wel, it is an inpossible
That any clerk wol speke good of wyves,
690 But if it be of hooly seintes lyves,
Ne noon oother womman never the mo.   in any respect
Who peyntede the leoun, tel me, who?
By God, if wommen hadde writen stories,
As clerkes han withinne hire oratories,
695 They wolde han writen of men moore wikkednesse
Than all the mark of Adam may redresse.
The children of Mercurie and Venus
Been in hir wirkyng ful contrarius,   dispositions; contrary
Mercurie loveth wysdam and science,
700 And Venus loveth ryot and dispence.   extravagance
And for hire diverse disposicioun
Ech falleth in otheres exaltacioun,   sinks; ascending
And thus, God woot, Mercurie is desolat
In Pisces, wher Venus is exaltat;
705 And Venus falleth ther Mercurie is reysed.
Therfore no womman of no clerk is preysed.
The clerk, whan he is oold and may noght do
Of Venus werkes worth his olde sho,   is worth his old shoe
Thanne sit he doun, and writ in his dotage
710 That wommen kan nat kepe hir mariage.

---

671 **Valerie and Theofraste:** Jankyn's book is a compilation of anti-feminist tracts including the *Epistola Vaerii ad Rufinum de non ducenda uxore* by Walter Map and the *Liber de Nuptiis* by Theophrastus. 675 **Jovinian:** Jovinian held that marriage was better than virginity, a view which was attacked by St Jerome. 676–78 **Tertulan:** Tertullian, early Roman writer who celebrated chastity. **Crisippus:** writer mentioned by Jerome.

Trotula: physician or possibly a midwife who wrote on women's diseases in the 11th century. **Helowys:** Heloise, nun who became passionately involved with the scholar Abelard. 680 **Ovides Art:** Ovid's *Ars Amatoria*. 692 **Who peyntede . . . :** In Avianus' fable a lion suggests that a sculpture of a lion bowing to a man must have been made by a man, for a lion sculptor would show a lion eating a man. 697 **children:** scholars and attractive women, those born under these planetary signs.

But now to purpos, why I tolde thee
That I was beten for a book, pardee.
Upon a nyght Jankyn, that was oure sire,
Redde on his book as he sat by the fire
715 Of Eva first, that for hir wikkednesse
Was al mankynde broght to wrecchednesse,
For which that Jesu Crist hymself was slayn,
That boghte us with his herte-blood agayn.
Lo, heere expres of womman may ye fynde,   expressly
720 That womman was the los of al mankynde.
Tho redde he me how Sampson loste hise heres,
Slepynge, his lemman kitte it with hir sheres,   lover
Thurgh whiche tresoun loste he bothe hise eyen.
Tho redde he me, if that I shal nat lyen,
725 Of Hercules and of his Dianyre,
That caused hym to sette hymself afyre.
No thyng forgat he the penaunce and wo
That Socrates hadde with hise wyves two,
How Xantippa caste pisse upon his heed.
730 This sely man sat stille as he were deed;   poor
He wiped his heed, namoore dorste he seyn
But, "er that thonder stynte, comth a reyn."   ceases; rain
Of Phasipha, that was the queene of Crete,
For shrewednesse hym thoughte the tale swete;
735 Fy, speke namoore! it is a grisly thyng
Of hir horrible lust and hir likyng.
Of Clitermystra for hire lecherye,
That falsly made hir housbonde for to dye,
He redde it with ful good devocioun.
740 He tolde me eek for what occasioun
Amphiorax at Thebes loste his lyf.
Myn housbonde hadde a legende of his wyf
Eriphilem, that for an ouche of gold   brooch
Hath prively unto the Grekes told
745 Wher that hir housbonde hidde hym in a place,
For which he hadde at Thebes sory grace.
Of Lyvia tolde he me, and of Lucye,
They bothe made hir housbondes for to dye,
That oon for love, that oother was for hate.
750 Lyvia hir housbonde, on an even late,

---

725 **Hercules:** Deianira, thinking to restore Hercules' love for her, gave him the shirt of Nessus, which was poisoned. 728 **Socrates:** the story of Socrates' shrewish wife Xantippa is apocryphal. 733 **Phasipha:** Pasiphae lusted after a bull and gave birth to the monstrous Minotaur. 737 **Clitermystra:** Clytemnestra, wife of the Greek hero Agamemenon, murdered her husband on his return from Troy.

741 **Amphiorax:** Amphiaraus. His wife, Eriphyle, was bribed to persuade him to take part in a war on Thebes, in which he was killed. 747 **Lyvia:** The Roman Livia was persuaded by Sejanus to poison her husband. **Lucye:** Lucilla, wife of the Roman poet Lucretius.

Empoysoned hath, for that she was his fo.
Lucia likerous loved hir housbonde so,
That for he sholde alwey upon hire thynke,
She yaf hym swich a manere love-drynke
755 That he was deed, er it were by the morwe.
And thus algates housbondes han sorw.   *in every way*
    Thanne tolde he me, how that Latumyus
Compleyned unto his felawe Arrius,   *friend*
That in his gardyn growed swich a tree,
760 On which he seyde how that hise wyves thre
Hanged hemself, for herte despitus.   *spite*
"O leeve brother," quod this Arrius,   *dear*
"Yif me a plante of thilke blissed tree,
And in my gardyn planted it shal bee."
765 Of latter date of wyves hath he red,
That somme han slayn hir housbondes in hir bed,
And lete hir lecchour dighte hir al the nyght,
Whan that the corps lay in the floor upright.
And somme han dryve nayles in hir brayn
770 Whil that they slepte, and thus they han hem slayn.
Somme han hem yeve poysoun in hir drynke.
He spak moore harm than herte may bithynke,
And therwithal he knew of mo proverbes
Than in this world ther growen gras or herbes.
775 "Bet is," quod he, "Thyn habitacioun
Be with a leoun, or a foul dragoun,
Than with a womman usynge for to chyde."   *used to scolding*
"Bet is," quod he, "hye in the roof abyde
Than with an angry wyf doun in the hous,
780 They been so wikked and contrarious
They haten that hir housbondes loveth ay."   *ever*
He seyde, "a womman cast hir shame away
Whan she cast of hir smok," and forthermo,
"A fair womman, but she be chaast also,
785 Is lyk a gold ryng in a sowes nose."
Who wolde leeve, or who wolde suppose
The wo that in myn herte was, and pyne?
    And whan I saugh he wolde nevere fyne   *finish*
To reden on this cursed book al nyght,
790 Al sodeynly thre leves have I plyght   *plucked*
Out of his book, right as he radde, and eke
I with my fest so took hym on the cheke,
That in oure fyr he fil bakward adoun.
And he up stirte as dooth a wood leoun,   *mad*
795 And with his fest he smoot me on the heed
That in the floor I lay, as I were deed.
And whan he saugh how stille that I lay,

He was agast, and wolde han fled his way,
Til atte laste out of my swogh I breyde.   swoon
800 "O, hastow slayn me, false theef," I seyde,
And for my land thus hastow mordred me?
Er I be deed, yet wol I kisse thee.
    And neer he cam and kneled faire adoun,
And seyde, "deere suster Alisoun,
805 As help me God, I shal thee nevere smyte.
That I have doon, it is thyself to wyte,
Foryeve it me, and that I thee biseke."
And yet eftsoones I hitte hym on the cheke,
And seyde, "theef, thus muchel am I wreke;   revenged
810 Now wol I dye, I may no lenger speke."
But atte laste, with muchel care and wo,
We fille acorded by us selven two.   we came to an accord
He yaf me al the bridel in myn hond,
To han the governance of hous and lond,
815 And of his tonge, and of his hond also,
And made hym brenne his book anon right tho.   burn
And whan that I hadde geten unto me
By maistrie, al the soveraynetee,
And that he seyde, "myn owene trewe wyf,
820 Do as thee lust the terme of al thy lyf,
Keepe thyn honour, and keep eek myn estaat,"
After that day we hadden never debaat.
God help me so, I was to hym as kynde
As any wyf from Denmark unto Ynde,
825 And also trewe, and so was he to me.
I prey to God, that sit in magestee,
So blesse his soule for his mercy deere.
Now wol I seye my tale, if ye wol heere.'

Biholde the wordes bitwene the Somonour and the Frere

The Frere lough whan he hadde herd al this.
830 'Now dame,' quod he, 'so have I joye or blis,
This is a long preamble of a tale.'
    And whan the Somonour herde the Frere gale,   exclaim
'Lo,' quod the Somonour, 'Goddes armes two,
A frere wol entremette hym evere-mo.   always interfere
835 Lo goode men, a flye and eek a frere
Wol falle in every dyssh and eek mateere.
What spekestow of preambulacioun?
What, amble, or trotte, or pees, or go sit doun,   pace [walk]
Thou lettest oure disport in this manere.'

---

832 **Somonour**: Summoner, a petty official who summons people to courts of law.

840 'Ye, woltow so, sire Somonour?' quod the frere,   would have it so
'Now by my feith, I shal er that I go
Telle of a Somonour swich a tale or two
That alle the folk shal laughen in this place.'
'Now elles, frere, I bishrewe thy face,'   curse
845 Quod this Somonour, 'and I bishrewe me,
But if I telle tales two or thre
Of freres, er I come to Sidyngborne,
That I shal make thyn herte for to morne,
For wel I woot thy pacience in gon.'
850 Oure Hooste cride, 'Pees, and that anon!'
And seyde, 'lat the womman telle hire tale,
Ye fare as folk that dronken were of ale.
Do, dame, telle forth youre tale, and that is best.'
'Al redy, sire,' quod she, 'right as yow lest,
855 If I have licence of this worthy frere.'
'Yis, dame,' quod he, 'tel forth, and I wol heere.'

The Tale of the Wyf of Bath

'In th'olde dayes of the Kyng Arthour,
Of which that Britons speken greet honour,
All was this land fulfild of fayerye.
860 The elf-queene, with hir joly compaignye,
Daunced ful ofte in many a grene mede;
This was the olde opinion, as I rede.
I speke of manye hundred yeres ago;
But now kan no man se none elves mo,
865 For now the grete charitee and prayeres
Of lymytours, and othere hooly freres,
That serchen every lond and every streem   visit
As thikke as motes in the sonne-beem,
Blessynge halles, chambres, kichenes, boures,   bowers
Citees, burghes, castels, hye toures,
Thropes, bernes, shipnes, dayeryes,   villages, barns, stables, dairies
This maketh that ther been no fayeryes.
For ther as wont to walken was an elf,
Ther walketh now the lymytour hymself   accustomed
875 In undermeles and in morwenynges,   afternoons; mornings
And seyth his matyns and his hooly thynges
As he gooth in his lymytacioun.
Wommen may go saufly up and doun;
In every bussh or under every tree
880 Ther is noon oother incubus but he,

---

847 **Sidyngborne:** Sittingbourne in Kent on the road to Canterbury.   866 **lymytours:** limiters, friars licensed to beg within a designated area.   880 **incubus:** male spirit who has sex with sleeping women. Here also the fairy-lover.

And he ne wol doon hem but dishonour.
And so bifel it that this kyng Arthour
Hadde in his hous a lusty bachelor,
That on a day cam ridynge fro ryver;
885 And happed that, allone as he was born,   *rode*
He saugh a mayde walkynge hym biforn,
Of whiche mayde anon, maugree hir heed,   *despite her*
By verray force he rafte hir maydenhed;
For which oppressioun was swich clamour   *wrong*
890 And swich pursute unto the kyng Arthour,   *pursuit [of justice]*
That dampned was this knyght for to be deed   *condemned*
By cours of lawe, and sholde han lost his heed,
Paraventure, swich was the statut tho,   *law*
But that the queene and othere ladyes mo
895 So longe preyeden the kyng of grace,   *begged*
Til he his lyf hym graunted in the place,
And yaf hym to the queene al at hir wille,
To chese, wheither she wolde hym save or spille.   *destroy*
The queene thanketh the kyng with al hir myght,
900 And after this thus spak she to the knyght,
Whan that she saugh hir tyme, upon a day,
"Thou standest yet," quod she, "in swich array
That of thy lyf yet hastow no suretee.   *certainty*
I grante thee lyf, if thou kanst tellen me
905 What thyng is it that wommen moost desiren.
Be war and keep thy nekke-boon from iren,   *keep your neck from the axe*
And if thou kanst nat tellen it anon,
Yet shal I yeve thee leve for to gon
A twelf-month and a day to seche and leere   *learn*
910 An answere suffisant in this mateere;
And suretee wol I han, er that thou pace,   *pledge; wander*
Thy body for to yelden in this place."
Wo was this knyght, and sorwefully he siketh,   *sighs*
But what! He may nat do al as hym liketh;
915 And at the laste he chees hym for to wende,
And come agayn right at the yeres ende,
With swich answere as God wolde hym purveye;
And taketh his leve, and wendeth forth his weye.
He seketh every hous and every place,
920 Where as he hopeth for to fynde grace
To lerne what thyng wommen loven moost;
But he ne koude arryven in no coost
Wher as he myghte fynde in this mateere
Two creatures accordynge in-feere.   *agreeing together*

881: And he [the friar] will bring them nothing but   884 **ryver**: river banks were favoured places to hawk.
dishonour.

925 Somme seyde wommen loven best richesse,
Somme seyde honour, somme seyde jolynesse,
Somme riche array, somme seyden lust abedde,
And oftetyme to be wydwe and wedde.   widowed
Somme seyde, that oure hertes been moost esed
930 Whan that we been yflatered and yplesed.
He gooth ful ny the sothe, I wol nat lye,   truth
A man shal wynne us best with flaterye;
And with attendance and with bisynesse   attention; care
Been we ylymed, bothe moore and lesse.   ensnared
935   And somme seyn, how that we loven best
For to be free, and do right as us lest,
And that no man repreve us of oure vice,
But seye that we be wise, and nothyng nyce.   foolish
For trewely, ther is noon of us alle,
940 If any wight wol clawe us on the galle,   rub; sore spot
That we nel kike; for he seith us sooth;   kick out
Assay, and he shal fynde it that so dooth.   try
For be we never so vicious withinne,
We sol been holden wise, and clene of synne.
945   And somme seyn, that greet delit han we
For to been holden stable and eke secree,   discreet
And in o purpos stedefastly to dwelle,
And nat biwerye thyng that men us telle.
But that tale is nat worth a rake stele,   rake handle
950 Pardee, we wommen konne no thyng hele.   conceal
Witnesse on Myda – wol ye heere the tale?   Midas
        Ovyde, amonges othere thynges smale,
Seyde, Myda hadde under his longe heres
Growynge upon his heed two asses eres,
955 The whiche vice he hydde, as he best myghte,
Ful subtilly from every mannes sighte;
That, save his wyf, ther wiste of it namo.
He loved hir moost and trusted hir also,
He preyede hir that to no creature
960 She sholde tellen of his disfigure.
She swoor him nay, for al this world to wynne,
She nolde do that vileynye or synne,
To make hir housbonde han so foul a name,
She nolde nat telle it for hir owene shame!
965 But nathelees, hir thoughte that she dyde,
That she so longe sholde a conseil hyde,
Hir thoughte it swal so soore aboute hir herte   swelled so sorely
That nedely som word hir moste asterte.
And sith she dorste telle it to no man,

968: That of necessity some word must force its way out.

970   Doun to a mareys faste by she ran,   marsh
       Til she came there, hir herte was afyre,
       And as a bitore bombleth in the myre,
       She leyde hir mouth unto the water doun; –
       "Biwreye me nat, thou water, with thy soun,"
975   Quod she, "to thee I telle it and namo,
       Myn housbonde hath longe asses erys two!
       Now is myn herte al hool, now is it oute,
       I myghte no lenger kepe it, out of doute."
       Heere may ye se, thogh we a tyme abyde,
980   Yet out it moot, we kan no conseil hyde.
       The remenant of the tale, if ye wol heere,
       Redeth Ovyde, and ther ye may it leere.
         This knyght, of which my tale is specially,
       Whan that he saugh he myghte nat come therby,
985   This is to seye, what wommen love moost,
       Withinne his brest ful sorweful was the goost.
       But hoom he gooth, he myghte nat sojourne;
       The day was come that homward moste he tourne,
       And in his wey it happed hym to ryde
990   In al this care under a forest syde,
       Wher as he saugh upon a daunce go
       Of ladyes foure and twenty, and yet mo;
       Toward the whiche daunce he drow ful yerne,   eagerly
       In hope that som wysdom sholde he lerne.
995   But certeinly, er he came fully there,
       Vanysshed was this daunce, he nyste where;
       No creature saugh he that bar lyf,
       Save on the grene he saugh sittynge a wyf,
       A fouler wight ther may no man devyse.
1000 Agayn the knyght this olde wyf gan ryse,
       And seyde, "Sire knyght, heerforth ne lith no wey;   through here
       Tel me what that ye seken, by your fey.   faith
       Paraventure it may the bettre be,
       Thise olde folk kan muchel thyng," quod she.   know
1005   "My leeve mooder," quod this knyght, "certeyn,   dear
       I nam but deed, but if that I kan seyn
       What thyng it is, that wommen moost desire.
       Koude ye me wisse, I wolde wel quite youre hire."
         "Plight me thy trouthe, heere in myn hand," quod she,   promise
1010 "The nexte thyng that I requere thee,
       Thou shalt it do, if it lye in thy myght,
       And I wol telle it yow, er it be nyght."
         "Have heer my trouthe," quod the knyght, "I grante."
         "Thanne," quod she, "I dar me wel avante,   boast

972: And as a bittern [a marsh bird] booms in mire.

1015 Thy lyf is sauf, for I wol stonde therby
Upon my lyf, the queene wol seye as I.
Lat se which is the proudeste of hem alle,
That wereth on a coverchief or a calle,   hairnet
That dar seye nay of that I shal thee teche.
1020 Lat us go forth withouten lenger speche."
Tho rowned she a pistel in his ere,   whispered; message
And bad hym to be glad and have no fere.
 Whan they be comen to the court, this knyght
Seyde he had holde his day, as he hadde hight,
1025 And redy was his answere, as he sayde.
Ful many a noble wyf, and many a mayde,
And many a wydwe, for that they been wise,
The queene hirself sittynge as a justise,
Assembled been, his answere for to heere;
1030 And afterward this knyght was bode appeere.   bidden
 To every wight comanded was silence,
And that the knyght sholde telle in audience
What thyng that worldly wommen loven best.
This knyght ne stood nat stille, as doth a best,   beast
1035 But to his questioun anon answerde
With manly voys, that al the court it herde,
 "My lige lady, generally," quod he,
"Wommen desiren to have sovereynetee
As wel over hir housbond as hir love,
1040 And for to been in maistrie hym above.
This is youre mooste desir, thogh ye me kille,
Dooth as yow list, I am heer at youre wille."
In al the court ne was ther wyf ne mayde
Ne wydwe that contraried that he sayde,
1045 But seyden he was worthy han his lyf.
 And with that word up stirte the olde wyf,
Which that the knyght saugh sittynge in the grene.
"Mercy," quod she, "my sovereyn lady queene,
Er that youre court departe, do me right.
1050 I taughte this answere unto the knyght,
For which he plighte me his trouthe there,
The firste thyng I wolde of hym requere,
He wolde it do, if it lay in his myght.
Bifor the court thanne preye I thee, sir knyght,"
1055 Quod she, "that thou me take unto thy wyf,
For wel thou woost that I have kept thy lyf.
If I seye fals, sey nay, upon thy fey!"
 This knyght answerde, "Allas and weylawey!
I woot right wel that swich was my biheste!
1060 For Goddes love, as chees a newe requeste,
Taak al my good, and lat my body go!"

"Nay, thanne," quod she, "I shrewe us bothe two,   curse
For thogh that I be foul and oold and poore,
I nolde for al the metal, ne for oore,   would not
1065   That under erthe is grave, or lith above,   buried
But if thy wyf I were, and eek thy love."
"My love?" quod he, "nay, my dampnacioun!
Allas, that any of my nacioun
Sholde evere so foule disparaged be!"   degraded
1070   But al for noght, the ende is this, that he
Constreyned was, he nedes moste hir wedde,
And taketh his olde wyf, and gooth to bedde.
Now wolden som men seye, paraventure,
That for my necligence I do no cure   omit
1075   To tellen yow the joye and al th'array,
That at the feeste was that ilke day;
To whiche thyng shortly answere I shal.
I seye, ther nas no joye ne feeste at al,
Ther nas but hevynesse and muche sorwe,
1080   For prively he wedde hir on a morwe,
And al day after hidde hym as an owle,
So wo was hym, his wyf looked so foule.
Greet was the wo the knyght hadde in his thoght,
Whan he was with his wyf abedde ybroght,
1085   He walweth and he turneth to and fro.
His olde wyf lay smylynge everemo,
And seyde, "O deere housbonde, *benedicitee*,
Fareth every knyght thus with his wyf, as ye?
Is this the lawe of Kyng Arthures hous?
1090   Is every knyght of his so dangerous?   stand-offish
I am youre owene love, and eek your wyf;
I am she which that saved hath youre lyf,
And certes, yet dide I yow nevere unright;
Why fare ye thus with me this firste nyght?
1095   Ye faren lyk a man had lost his wit.
What is my gilt? for Goddes love, tel it,
And it shal been amended, if I may."
"Amended," quod this knyght, "allas! nay! nay!
It wol nat been amended nevere mo;
1100   Thou art so loothly and so oold also   loathsome
And therto comen of so lough a kynde,   low class
That litel wonder is thogh I walwe and wynde.   toss and turn
So wolde God, myn herte wolde breste!"   burst
"Is this," quod she, "the cause of youre unreste?"
1105   "Ye certeinly," quod he, "no wonder is!"
"Now, sire," quod she, "I koude amende al this,
If that me liste, er it were dayes thre,
So wel ye myghte bere yow unto me.   behave

But for ye speken of swich gentillesse   nobility
1110 As is descended out of old richesse,
That therfore sholden ye be gentil men,
Swich arrogance nis nat worth an hen.
Looke who that is moost vertuous alway,
Pryvee and apert, and moost entendeth ay   privately; publicly
1115 To do the gentil dedes that he kan,
Taak hym for the grettest gentil-man.
Crist wole we clayme of hym oure gentillesse,
Nat of oure eldres for hire old richesse.   ancestors
For thogh they yeve us al hir heritage,
1120 For which we clayme to been of heigh parage,   parentage
Yet may they nat biquethe, for no thyng,
To noon of us hir vertuous lyvyng,
That made hem gentil men ycalled be,
And bad us folwen hem in swich degree.
1125   Wel kan the wise poete of Florence,
That highte Dant, speken in this sentence;
Lo in swich maner rym is Dantes tale:
'Ful selde upriseth by his branches smale   seldom
Prowesse of man, for God of his goodnesse
1130 Wole that of hym we clayme oure gentillesse.'
For of oure eldres may we no thyng clayme
But temporel thyng, that man may hurte and mayme.
   Eek every wight woot this as wel as I,
If gentillesse were planted natureelly
1135 Unto a certeyn lynage doun the lyne,
Pryvee nor apert, thanne wolde they nevere fyne   finish
To doon of gentillesse the faire office,
They myghte do no vileynye or vice.
   Taak fyr, and ber it in the derkeste hous
1140 Bitwix this and the mount of Kaukasous,   here; the Caucasuses
And lat men shette the dores and go thenne,
Yet wole the fyr as faire lye and brenne   burn
As twenty thousand men myghte it biholde;
His office natureel ay wol it holde,   function
1145 Up peril of my lyf, til that it dye.
   Heere may ye se wel, how that genterye
Is nat annexed to possessioun,
Sith folk ne doon hir operacioun   do not behave
Alwey, as dooth the fyr, lo, in his kynde.
1150 For God it woot, men may wel often fynde
A lordes sone do shame and vileynye,
And he that wole han pris of his gentrye,   praise
For he was boren of a gentil hous,
And hadde hise eldres noble and vertuous,
1155 And nel hymselven do no gentil dedis,

Ne folwen his gentil auncestre that deed is,
He nys nat gentil, be he duc or erl;
For vileyns synful dedes make a cherl.
For gentillesse nys but renomee   renown
1160 Of thyne auncestres for hire heigh bountee,
Which is a strange thyng to thy persone.   alien
Thy gentillesse cometh fro God allone,
Thanne comth oure verray gentillesse of grace,
It was no thyng biquethe us with oure place.   social rank
1165   Thenketh hou noble, as seith Valerius,
Was thilke Tullius Hostillius,
That out of poverte roos to heigh noblesse.
Reedeth Senek, and redeth eek Boece,
Ther shul ye seen expres that it no drede is,
1170 That he is gentil that dooth gentil dedis.
And therfore, leeve housbonde, I thus conclude,
Al were it that myne auncestres weren rude,
Yet may the hye God, and so hope I,
Grante me grace to lyven vertuously.
1175 Thanne am I gentil whan that I bigynne
To lyven vertuously, and weyve synne.   cast aside
   And ther as ye of poverte me repreeve,   reproach
The hye God, on whom that we bileeve
In wilful poverte chees to lyve his lyf.
1180 And certes every man, mayden or wyf,
May understonde that Jesus, hevene kyng,
Ne wolde nat chesen vicious lyvyng.
Glad poverte is an honeste thyng, certeyn,
This wole Senec and othere clerkes seyn.   wise
1185 Who so that halt hym payd of his poverte,   feels himself content
I holde hym riche, al hadde he nat a sherte.
He that coveiteth is a povre wight,   covets
For he wolde han that is nat in his myght,
But he that noght hath, ne coveiteth have,
1190 Is riche, although ye holde hym but a knave.
Verray poverte, it syngeth proprely.
Juvenal seith of poverte myrily,
The povre man, whan he goth by the weye,
Bifore the theves he may synge and pleye.
1195 Poverte is hateful good, and, as I gesse,   undesirable blessing
A ful greet bryngere out of bisynesse;   great reliever of cares
A greet amender eek of sapience   improver; wisdom

1166 Tullius Hostillius: a herdsman. He rose to rule the
Roman state.   **1168 Senek, Boece:** Roman philosophers
Seneca and Boethius. Seneca was a stoic, Boethius, whose
Consolation of Philosophy Chaucer translated, was hugely
influential in the Middle Ages.   **1192 Juvenal:** Roman satirist.

To hym that taketh it in pacience.
Poverte is this, although it seme elenge; — makes some miserable
1200 Possessioun, that no wight wol chalenge.
Poverte ful ofte, whan a man is lowe,
Maketh his God and eek hymself to knowe;
Poverte a spectacle is, as thynketh me, — glass
Thurgh which he may hise verray freendes see.
1205 And therfore, sire, syn that I noght yow greve,
Of my poverte namoore ye me repreve. — reproach
    Now sire, of elde ye repreve me, — old age
And certes, sire, thogh noon auctoritee
Were in no book, ye gentils of honour
1210 Seyn that men sholde an oold wight doon favour,
And clepe hym fader for youre gentillesse,
And auctours shal I fynden, as I gesse. — authorities
    Now, ther ye seye that I am foul and old,
Than drede you noght to been a cokewold; — cuckold
1215 For filthe and eelde, al so moot I thee, — as I hope to prosper
Been grete wardeyns upon chastitee;
But nathelees, syn I knowe youre delit,
I shal fulfille youre worldly appetit."
    "Chese now," quod she, "oon of thise thynges tweye:
1220 To han me foul and old til that I deye,
And be to yow a trewe humble wyf,
And nevere yow displese in al my lyf;
Or elles ye wol han me yong and fair,
And take youre aventure of the repair — chances; crowd
1225 That shal be to youre hous, by cause of me,
Or in som oother place may wel be.
Now chese yourselven wheither that yow liketh."
    This knyght avyseth hym and sore siketh, — considers; sighs sorrowfully
But atte laste, he seyde in this manere:
1230 "My lady and my love, and wyf so deere,
I put me in youre wise governance.
Cheseth yourself, which may be moost plesance
And moost honour to yow and me also.
I do no fors the wheither of the two, — I have no preference
1235 For, as yow liketh, it suffiseth me."
    "Thanne have I gete of yow maistrie," quod she,
"Syn I may chese and governe as me lest?"
    "Ye, certes, wyf," quod he, "I holde it best."
    "Kys me," quod she, "we be no lenger wrothe, — angry
1240 For, by my trouthe, I wol be to yow bothe!
This is to seyn, ye, bothe fair and good. — yes
I prey to God that I moote sterven wood — die mad

1200: Nobody will demand it from you if you possess it.   1205: I give you no cause for complaint.

But I to yow be al so good and trewe
As evere was wyf, syn that the world was newe.
1245 And but I be tomorn as fair to seene
As any lady, emperice or queene,
That is bitwixe the est and eke the west,
Dooth with my lyf and deth right as yow lest.
Cast up the curtyn, looke how that it is."   bed curtain
1250 And whan the knyght saugh verraily al this,
That she so fair was, and so yong therto,
For joye he hente hire in hise armes two.
His herte bathed in a bath of blisse,
A thousand tyme a-rewe he gan hir kisse,   in a row
1255 And she obeyed hym in every thyng
That myghte doon hym plesance or likyng.
    And thus they lyve unto hir lyves ende
In parfit joye; and Jesu Crist us sende
Housbondes meeke, yonge, fressh abedde,
1260 And grace t'overbyde hem that we wedde.
And eek I praye Jesu shorte hir lyves,
That nat wol be governed by hir wyves;
And olde and angry nygardes of dispence,   misers
God sende hem soone verray pestilence!'

The Nun's Priest's Prologue and Tale

The Prologue of the Nun's Priest's Tale

'Hoo!' quod the Knyght, 'good sire, namoore of this,
That ye han seyd is right ynough, ywis,   surely
And muchel moore, for litel hevynesse   much more than enough
Is right ynough to muche folk, I gesse.
5 I seye for me, it is a greet disese   discomfort
Where as men han been in greet welthe and ese,
To heeren of hir sodeyn fal, allas!
And the contrarie is joye and greet solas,
As whan a man hath been in povre estaat,   poor
10 And clymbeth up, and wexeth fortunat,
And there abideth in prosperitee.
Swich thyng is gladsom, as it thynketh me,
And of swich thyng were goodly for to telle.'
    'Ye,' quod our Hoost, 'by Seinte Poules belle,
15 Ye seye right sooth! This Monk, he clappeth lowde,   chatters
He spak, how "Fortune covered with a clowde" –

1: The Knight interrupts the Monk, who has been regaling the pilgrims with tedious stories of tragedies for nearly 800 lines.   14 Hoost: The leader of the Pilgrims is the landlord of the Tabard Inn in Southwark. Seinte Poules belle: The bells of St Paul's cathedral in London.

I noot nevere what – and als of a tragedie I know not what; besides
Right now ye herde; and pardee, no remedie
It is for to biwaille, ne compleyne bewail
20 That that is doon; and als it is a peyne,
As ye han seyd, to heere of hevynesse.
    Sire Monk, namoore of this, so God yow blesse!
Youre tale anoyeth al this compaignye;
Swich talkyng is nat worth a boterflye, butterfly
25 For therinne is ther no desport ne game. pleasure
Wherfore sir Monk, or daun Piers by youre name,
I pray yow hertely, telle us somwhat elles,
For sikerly, nere clynkyng of youre belles certainly
That on your bridel hange on every syde,
30 By hevene kyng, that for us alle dyde,
I sholde er this han fallen doun for sleepe,
Althogh the slough had never been so deepe;
Thanne hadde your tale al be toold in veyn.
For, certeinly, as that thise clerkes seyn, scholars
35 Where as a man may have noon audience,
Noght helpeth it to tellen his sentence. meaning
And wel I woot the substance is in me,
If any thyng shal wel reported be.
Sir, sey somwhat of huntyng, I yow preye.'
40   'Nay,' quod this Monk, 'I have no lust to pleye; desire
Not lat another telle as I have toold.'
Thanne spak oure Hoost, with rude speche and boold, rough
And seyde unto the Nonnes Preest anon,
'Com neer, thou preest, com hyder, thou, sir John,
45 Telle us swich thyng as may oure hertes glade;
Be blithe, though thou ryde upon a jade. an inferior horse
What thogh thyn hors be bothe foul and lene?
If he wol serve thee, rekke nat a bene! count it not a bean
Looke that thyn herte be murie everemo.'
50   'Yis sir,' quod he, 'yis, Hoost, so moot I go,
But I be myrie, ywis, I wol be blamed.' Unless; truly
And right anon his tale he hath attamed, started
And thus he seyde unto us everichon,
This sweete preest, this goodly man sir John.

The Nonnes Preestes Tale

55 'A povre wydwe, somdel stape in age, widow; somewhat advanced
Was whilom dwellyng in a narwe cotage once; small
Biside a grove, stondynge in a dale.

---

26 daun: a general title of respect from the Latin *dominus*.   **37–38:** The sense is not absolutely clear here. Probably
Monks' names are still prefixed with Dom.   'I have the capacity in me [to listen] if the thing is well
told.'

This wydwe, of which I telle yow my tale,
Syn thilke day that she was last a wyf,
60 In pacience ladde a ful symple lyf,
For litel was hir catel and hir rente.   property; income
By housbondrie, of swich as God hir sente,
She foond hirself and eek hire doghtren two.   provided for
Thre large sowes hadde she, and namo,
65 Three keen, and eek a sheep that highte Malle.   cows
Ful sooty was hir bour and eek hire halle,
In which she eet ful many a sklendre meel,   lean
Of poynaunt sauce hir neded never a deel.   pungent; not at all
No deyntee morsel passed thurgh hir throte,
70 Hir diete was accordant to hir cote.   cottage
Repleccioun ne made hir nevere sik,   surfeit
Attempree diete was al hir phisik,   temperate; medicine
And exercise, and hertes suffisaunce.   contentment
The goute lette hir nothyng for to daunce,   hindered
75 N'apoplexie shente nat hir heed.   ruin; head
No wyn ne drank she, neither whit ne reed,   white; red
Hir bord was served moost with whit and blak –
Milk and broun breed – in which she foond no lak,   fault
Seynd bacoun, and somtyme an ey or tweye,   boiled; egg
80 For she was as it were a maner deye.   kind of dairy maid
    A yeerd she hadde, enclosed al aboute
With stikkes, and a drye dych withoute,
In which she hadde a Cok, heet Chauntecleer.
In al the land of crowyng nas his peer;
85 His voys was murier than the murie orgon   organ
On messedayes, that in the chirche gon.   feast days
Wel sikerer was his crowyng in his logge,   more certain; dwelling
Than is a clokke or an abbey orlogge.   large clock
By nature he crew eche ascencioun
90 Of the equynoxial in thilke toun;
For whan degrees fiftene weren ascended,
Thanne crew he, that it myghte nat been amended.   improved
His coomb was redder than the fyn coral,   finest
And batailled, as it were a castel wal.   notched
95 His byle was blak, and as the jeet it shoon,   beak
Lyk asure were hise legges and his toon,   azure; toes
Hise nayles whiter than the lylye flour,   claws
And lyk the burned gold was his colour.
This gentil cok hadde in his governaunce   noble
100 Sevene hennes, for to doon al his plesaunce,

66: Her bedroom and dining hall were black with soot. There is irony here as this is a humble dwelling and would not have had such rooms. 83 heet Chauntecleer: called Chauntecleer, or 'clear singer'.

89–91 equynoxial: the celestial equator which is divided into 360 degrees. This is an elaborate and humorous way of saying Chauntecleer crowed each hour, implying he has great learning in astronomy.

Whiche were hise sustres and his paramours,   sisters
And wonder lyk to hym as of colours;
Of whiche the faireste hewed on hir throte
Was cleped faire damoysele Pertelote.
105   Curteys she was, discreet, and debonaire
And compaignable, and bar hyrself so faire
Syn thilke day that she was seven nyght oold,
That trewely she hath the herte in hoold
Of Chauntecleer, loken in every lith;   regarded; limb
110   He loved hir so, that wel was hym therwith.
But swiche a joye was it to here hem synge
Whan that the brighte sonne gan to sprynge,
In sweete accord, "My lief is faren in londe".
For thilke tyme, as I have understonde,   at this
115   Beestes and briddes koude speke and synge.
      And so bifel, that in the dawenynge,
As Chauntecleer among hise wyves alle,
Sat on his perche, that was in the halle,
And next hym sat this faire Pertelote,
120   This Chauntecleer gan gronen in his throte
As man that in his dreem is drecched soore.   troubled badly
And whan that Pertelote thus herde hym roore
She was agast, and seyde, "O herte deere,
What eyleth yow, to grone in this manere?
125   Ye been a verray sleper, fy for shame!"   good sleeper
And he answerde and seyde thus, "Madame,
I pray yow that ye take it nat agrief.
By God, me thoughte I was in swich meschief
Right now, that yet myn herte is soore afright.
130   Now God," quod he, "my swevene recche aright,
And kepe my body out of foul prisoun.
Me mette how that I romed up and doun   I dreamed
Withinne our yeerd, wheer as I saugh a beest
Was lyk an hound, and wolde han maad areest   taken hold of
135   Upon my body, and han had me deed.
His colour was bitwixe yelow and reed,
And tipped was his tayl and bothe hise eeris;
With blak, unlyk the remenant of hise heeris;   rest
His snowte smal, with glowynge eyen tweye.
140   Yet of his look, for feere almoost I deye!
This caused me my gronyng, doutelees."
      "Avoy!" quod she, "Fly on yow hertelees!   go on; faint heartedness
Allas," quod she, "for by that God above
Now han ye lost myn herte and al my love!

113: In sweet harmony, 'My love is gone to a far
country'.

130: 'Now God,' he said, '[Help me] my dream interpret rightly.'

145 I kan nat love a coward, by my feith,
     For certes, what so any womman seith,
     We alle desiren, if it myght bee,
     To han housbondes hardy, wise, and free,   *generous*
     And secree, and no nygard, ne no fool,   *discreet*
150 Ne hym that is agast of every tool,   *weapon*
     Ne noon avauntour; by that God above,   *boaster*
     How dorste ye seyn for shame unto youre love   *dare*
     That any thyng myghte make yow aferd?
     Have ye no mannes herte, and han a berd?   *beard*
155 Allas, and konne ye been agast of swevenys?
     No thyng, God woot, but vanitee in swevene is!   *emptiness*
     Swevenes engendren of replecciouns,   *surfeits*
     And ofte of fume and of complecciouns,   *vapours*
     Whan humours been to habundant in a wight.   *abundant; person*
160 Certes, this dreem which ye han met tonyght
     Cometh of greet superfluytee
     Of youre rede *colera*, pardee,
     Which causeth folk to dreden in hir dremes
     Of arwes, and of fyre with rede lemes,   *arrows; flames*
165 Of grete beestes, that they wol hem byte,
     Of contek, and of whelpes grete and lyte;   *strife; pups*
     Right as the humour of malencolie
     Causeth ful many a man in sleep to crie
     For feere of blake beres, or boles blake,   *bulls*
170 Or elles blake develes wole hem take.
     Of othere humours koude I telle also
     That werken many a man in sleep ful wo,
     But I wol passe as lightly as I kan.
       Lo Catoun, which that was so wys a man,
175 Seyde he nat thus, 'ne do no fors of dremes'?   *pay no attention*
     Now sire," quod she, "whan ye flee fro the bemes,   *fly*
     For goddes love as taak som laxatyf.
     Up peril of my soule, and of my lyf,   *on*
     I conseille yow the beste, I wol nat lye,
180 That bothe of colere and of malencolye
     Ye purge yow; and for ye shal nat tarie,
     Though in this toun is noon apothecarie,
     I shal myself to herbes techen yow,
     That shul been for youre hele and for youre prow.   *profit*
185 And in oure yeerd tho herbes shal I fynde,   *those*
     The whiche han of hir propretee by kynde   *nature*
     To purge yow bynethe and eek above.

---

159 humours: most medieval medicine was based on humoral theory – the combinations of fluids within the body. In the right balance they produce health, in the wrong, disease.   **162 rede *colera*:** yellow-red bile which is secreted by the liver.   **167 malencolie:** black bile.   **174 Catoun:** Cato. Cato's maxims, which date from Roman times, were set texts for young students learning Latin.

Foryet nat this, for Goddes owene love!
Ye been ful coleryk of compleccioun;
190   Ware the sonne in his ascencioun
Ne fynde yow nat repleet of humours hoote.
And if it do, I dar wel leye a grote   *bet; a four penny coin*
That ye shul have a fevere terciane,   *a fever every third day*
Or an agu that may be youre bane.   *ague [acute fever]; brain*
195   A day or two ye shul have digestyves
Of wormes, er ye take youre laxatyves
Of lawriol, centaure, and fumetere,
Or elles of ellebor that groweth there,   *hellebore*
Of katapuce, or of gaitrys beryis,   *caper-spurge; dogwood berries*
200   Of herbe yve, growyng in oure yeerd, ther mery is;
Pekke hem up right as they growe, and ete hem yn.
Be myrie, housbonde, for youre fader kyn,
Dredeth no dreem, I kan sey yow namoore!"
"Madame," quod he, "graunt mercy of youre loore,   *instruction*
205   But nathelees, as touchyng Daun Catoun,
That hath of wysdom swich a greet renoun,
Though that he bad no dremes for to drede,
By God, men may in olde bookes rede
Of many a man moore of auctorite
210   Than evere Caton was, so moot I thee,   *as I may prosper*
That al the revers seyn of this sentence,   *reverse; opinion*
And han wel founden by experience
That dremes been significaciouns
As wel of joye as of tribulaciouns
215   That folk enduren in this lif present.
Ther nedeth make of this noon argument,
The verray preeve sheweth it in dede.
Oon of the gretteste auctours that men rede
Seith thus, that whilom two felawes wente
220   On pilgrimage in a ful good entente;
And happed so, they coomen in a toun
Wher as ther was swich congregacioun
Of peple, and eek so streit of herbergage,   *limited accommodation*
That they ne founde as muche as o cotage
225   In which they bothe myghte logged bee;
Wherfore they mosten of necessitee
As for that nyght departen compaignye,
And ech of hem gooth to his hostelrye,

189–91 **coleryk of comleccioun:** your complexion is choleric, i.e. you have a peaked or reddish look to you. Therefore Chauntecleer should take care as the sun climbs in the sky – during the summer – because he is susceptible to hot humours. 197 **lawriol:** spurge laurel, an evergreen shrub. 197 **centaure:** centaury, a bitter herb. **fumetere:** fumitory or earth-smoke, another bitter herb. All were used as purges. 200 **Of herbe yve:** ivy or likely plantain. **ther mery is:** where it's pleasant. 216–17: There is no need to make a formal proof of this, the true test of it is in what actually happens.

	And took his loggyng as it wolde falle.	as chance would have it
230	That oon of hem was logged in a stalle,	
	Fer in a yeerd, with oxen of the plough;	far-off
	That oother man was logged wel ynough,	
	As was his aventure or his fortune,	
	That us governeth alle as in commune.	general
235	And so bifel, that longe er it were day	
	This man mette in his bed, ther as he lay,	dreamed
	How that his felawe gan upon hym calle	
	And seyde, 'Allas, for in an oxes stalle	
	This nyght I shal be mordred, ther I lye!	
240	Now help me, deere brother, or I dye;	
	In alle haste com to me!' he sayde.	
	This man out of his sleep for feere abrayde;	started
	But whan that he was wakened of his sleep,	
	He turned hym and took of it no keep.	account
245	Hym thoughte, his dreem nas but a vanitee.	idleness
	Thus twies in his slepyng dremed hee,	twice
	And atte thridde tyme yet his felawe	
	Cam, as hym thoughte, and seide, 'I am now slawe,	
	Bihoold my bloody woundes depe and wyde;	
250	Arys up erly in the morwe-tyde,	
	And at the west gate of the toun,' quod he,	
	'A carte ful of donge ther shaltow se,	
	In which my body is hid ful prively.	
	Do thilke carte arresten boldely;	stopped
255	My gold caused my mordre, sooth to sayn.'	truth to tell
	And tolde hym every point, how he was slayn,	
	With a ful pitous face, pale of hewe;	
	And truste wel, his dreem he foond ful trewe.	
	For on the morwe, as soone as it was day,	
260	To his felawes in he took the way,	friend's inn
	And whan that he cam to this oxes stalle,	
	After his felawe he bigan to calle.	
	The hostiler answerde hym anon,	
	And seyde, 'Sire, your felawe is agon,	
265	As soone as day he wente out of the toun.'	
	This man gan fallen in suspecioun,	
	Remembrynge on hise dremes that he mette,	
	And forth he gooth, no lenger wolde he lette,	delay
	Unto the westgate of the toun; and fond	
270	A dong carte, as it were to donge lond,	manure the land
	That was arrayed in that same wise,	decked out
	As ye han herd the dede man devyse.	describe
	And with an hardy herte he gan to crye,	
	'Vengeance and justice of this felonye;	
275	My felawe mordred is this same nyght,	

And in this carte he lith gapyng upright.
I crye out on the ministres,' quod he,
'That sholden kepe and reulen this citee.
Harrow! allas, heere lith my felawe slayn!'
280 What sholde I moore unto this tale sayn?
The peple out-sterte, and caste the cart to grounde,
And in the myddel of the dong they founde
The dede man, that mordred was al newe.
    O blisful God, that art so just and trewe!
285 Lo, howe that thou biwreyest mordre alway!   betray
Mordre wol out, that se we, day by day.
Mordre is so wlatsom and abhomynable   loathsome
To God that is so just and resonable,
That he ne wol nat suffre it heled be,   concealed
290 Though it abyde a yeer, or two, or thre.
Mordre wol out, this my conclusioun.
And right anon ministres of that toun
Han hent the carter, and so soore hym pyned,   seized; tortured
And eek the hostiler so soore engyned   racked
295 That they biknewe hire wikkednesse anon,   confessed
And were anhanged by the nekke-bon.   neck bone
Heere may men seen, that dremes been to drede!
    And certes, in the same book I rede
Right in the nexte chapitre after this –
300 I gabbe nat, so have I joye or blis –   lie not
Two men that wolde han passed over see
For certeyn cause, into a fer contree,
If that the wynd ne hadde been contrarie,
That made hem in a citee for to tarie,
305 That stood ful myrie upon an haven-syde;
But on a day, agayn the even-tyde,
The wynd gan chaunge, and blew right as hem leste. desired
Jolif and glad they wente unto hir reste,
And casten hem ful erly for to saille.   resolved
310 But herkneth, to that o man fil a greet mervaille;
That oon of hem, in slepyng as he lay,
Hym mette a wonder dreem agayn the day.
Hym thoughte a man stood by his beddes syde,
And hym comanded that he sholde abyde,
315 And seyde hym thus, 'If thou tomorwe wende   travel
Thow shalt be dreynt; my tale is at an ende.'   drowned
He wook, and tolde his felawe what he mette,   dreamed
And preyde hym his viage for to lette,   voyage; abandon
As for that day, he preyede hym to byde.
320 His felawe, that lay by his beddes syde,
Gan for to laughe and scorned him ful faste.
'No dreem,' quod he, 'may so myn herte agaste

That I wol lette for to do my thynges.
I sette nat a straw by thy dremynges,
325 For swevenes been but vanytees and japes.   follies
Men dreme al day of owles or of apes,
And eek of many a maze therwithal.   bewilderment
Men dreme of thyng that nevere was, ne shal;
But sith I see that thou wolt heere abyde
330 And thus forslewthen wilfully thy tyde,   waste by sloth; time
God woot it reweth me, and have good day.'   makes me sorry
And thus he took his leve and wente his way;
But er that he hadde half his cours yseyled,   sailed
Noot I nat why, ne what myschaunce it eyled,   ailed
335 But casuelly the shippes botme rente,   by accident; tore open
And ship and men under the water wente
In sighte of othere shippes it bisyde,   nearby
That with hem seyled at the same tyde.
And therfore, faire Pertelote so deere,
340 By swiche ensamples olde maistow leere,   learn
That no man sholde been to recchelees   careless
Of dremes, for I seye thee doutelees
That many a dreem ful soore is for to drede.   greatly
Lo, in the lyf of Seint Kenelm I rede,
345 That was Kenulphus sone, the noble kyng,
Of Mercenrike, how Kenelm mette a thyng.
A lite er he was mordred, on a day
His mordre in his avysioun he say.   vision; saw
His norice hym expowned every deel   nurse; part
350 His swevene, and bad hym for to kepe hym weel
For traisoun, but he nas but seven yeer oold,
And therfore litel tale hath he toold
Of any dreem, so hooly is his herte.
By God, I hadde levere than my sherte   dearer; shirt
355 That ye hadde rad his legende, as have I.
    Dame Pertelote, I sey yow trewely,
Macrobeus, that writ the avisioun
In Affrike of the worhty Cipioun,
Affermeth dremes, and seith that they been
360 Warnynge of thynges, that men after seen.
And forthermoore I pray yow looketh wel
In the olde testament of Daniel,
If he heeld dremes any vanitee!

---

344 Seint Kenelm: King Cenulf of Mercia died in 821 and according to legend his son, Kenelm, became king but was murdered by his aunt. He is supposed to have had a warning dream before his death. **352:** And therefore he took little account.

357: The 4th century Macrobius' commentary on Cicero's *Somnium Scipionis* [The Dream of Scipio] was a popular book in the Middle Ages. It recounts how the Roman general Scipio Africanus had a dream in which his grandfather foretold his success in the war against Carthage.

Reed eek of Joseph, and ther shul ye see
365   Wher dremes be somtyme, I sey nat alle,
Warnynge of thynges that shul after falle.
Looke of Egipte the kyng, daun Pharao,
His baker and his butiller also,
Wher they ne felte noon effect in dremes!
370   Whoso wol seken actes of sondry remes   *various realms*
May rede of dremes many a wonder thyng.
Lo Cresus, which that was of Lyde kyng,   *Croesus; Lydia*
Mette he nat that he sat upon a tree,
Which signified, he sholde anhanged bee?
375   Lo heere Adromacha, Ectores wyf,   *Hector*
That day that Ector sholde lese his lyf
She dremed on the same nyght biforn
How that the lyf of Ector sholde be lorn,   *lost*
If thilke day he wente into bataille.
380   She warned hym, but it myghte nat availle;
He wente for to fighte natheles,
But he was slayn anon of Achilles.
But thilke is al to longe for to telle,
And eek it is ny day, I may nat dwelle.
385   Shortly I seye, as for conclusioun,
That I shal han of this avisioun
Adversitee, and I seye forthermoor
That I ne telle of laxatyves no stoor,   *store*
For they been venymes, I woot it weel,   *poisonous*
390   I hem diffye, I love hem never a deel.   *defy*
Now let us speke of myrthe, and stynte al this;   *cut short*
Madame Pertelote, so have I blis,
Of o thyng God hath sent me large grace,
For whan I se the beautee of youre face,
395   Ye been so scarlet reed aboute youre eyen,
It maketh al my drede for to dyen.
For, al so siker as *In principio*   *as is certain*
Mulier est hominis confusio, –
Madame, the sentence of this Latyn is,
400   'Womman is mannes joye and al his blis.'
For whan I felle a-nyght your softe syde,   *feel*
Al be it that I may nat on yow ryde,
For that oure perche is maad so narwe, allas!   *made*
I am so ful of joye and of solas,   *comfort*
405   That I diffye bothe swevene and dreem."

---

364 Joseph: see Genesis 37–41. **365:** Whether dreams be sometimes, I am not saying always. **384:** And since it is near day, I should not linger.

397–98 In principo: Chauntecleer's translation is wrong. What the Latin says is 'In the beginning Woman is man's ruin'. In principo imitates the widely known start of the Gospel of St John, 'In the beginning was the Word'.
402 ryde: anchor; here meaning have sex.

And with that word he fly doun fro the beem,
For it was day, and eke hise hennes alle;
And with a chuk he gan hem for to calle,
For he hadde founde a corn lay in the yerd.
410 Real he was, he was namoore aferd;   regal
And fethered Pertelote twenty tyme,   caressed
And trad as ofte, er that it was pryme.
He looketh as it were a grym leoun,
And on hise toos he rometh up and doun,
415 Hym deigned nat to sette his foot to grounde.
He chukketh whan he hath a corn yfounde,
And to hym rennen thanne hise wyves alle.   run then
Thus roial as a prince is in an halle,
Leve I this Chauntecleer in his pasture,
420 And after wol I telle his aventure.
   Whan that the monthe in which the world bigan
That highte March, whan God first maked man,
Was compleet, and passed were also
Syn March bigan, thritty dayes and two,
425 Bifel that Chauntecleer in al his pryde,
Hise sevene wyves walkynge by his syde,
Caste up hise eyen to the brighte sonne,
That in the signe of Taurus hadde yronne
Twenty degrees and oon, and somwhat moore;
430 And knew by kynde, and by noon oother loore,
That it was pryme, and crew with blisful stevene.
"The sonne," he seyde, "is clomben upon hevene
Fourty degrees and oon, and moore, ywis.
Madame Pertelote, my worldes blis,
435 Herkneth thise blisful briddes how they synge,
And se the fresshe floures how they sprynge.
Ful is myn herte of revel and solas."
But sodeynly hym fil a sorweful cas,   befell; event
For evere the latter ende of joye is wo.
440 God woot that worldly joye is soone ago,
And if a rethor koude faire endite,   rhetorician; compose
He in a cronycle saufly myghte it write   safely
As for a sovereyn notabilitee.   supreme
Now every wys man, lat him herkne me;
445 This storie is al so trewe, I undertake,
As is the book of Launcelot de Lake,
That wommen holde in ful greet reverence.
Now wol I come agayn to my sentence.

412: And trod her [copulated with her] just as often   447 That: likely refers to Sir Launcelot and not the book.
before it was Prime. Prime was the first the canonical
hours appointed by the Church for Prayer. It could be
either 6 a.m. or 9 a.m.

A col-fox, ful of sly iniquitee,
450 That in the grove hadde wonned yeres three,   dwelt
By heigh ymaginacioun forncast,
The same nyght thurghout the hegges brast   through; hedge burst
Into the yerd, ther Chauntecleer the faire   where
Was wont, and eek hise wyves, to repaire;
455 And in a bed of wortes stille he lay,   plants
Til it was passed undren of the day,   midmorning
Waitynge his tyme on Chauntecleer to falle,
As gladly doon thise homycides alle   usually do; murderers
That in await liggen to mordre men.   lie
460 O false mordrour, lurkynge in thy den!
O newe Scariot! newe Genyloun!
False dissymulour, O Greek Synon
That broghtest Troye al outrely to sorwe!   utterly
O Chauntecleer, acursed be that morwe
465 That thou into that yerd flaugh fro the bemes!
Thou were ful wel ywarned by thy dremes
That thilke day was perilous to thee;
But what that God forwoot moot nedes bee,
After the opinioun of certein clerkis.
470 Witnesse on hym, that any parfit clerk is,
That in scole is greet altercacioun
In this mateere, and greet disputisoun,
And hath been of an hundred thousand men;
But I ne kan nat bulte it to the bren
475 As kan the hooly doctour Augustyn,
Or Boece or the Bisshop Bradwardyn,
Wheither that Goddes worthy forwityng   excellent foreknowledge
Streyneth me nedefully to doon a thyng,   constrains; necessarily
("Nedely" clepe I symple necessitee)
480 Or elles, if free choys be graunted me
To do that same thyng, or do it noght,
Though God forwoot it, er that it was wroght;
Or if his wityng streyneth never a deel
But by necessitee condicioneel.
485 I wel nat han to do of swich mateere;
My tale is of a cok, as ye may heere,
That took his conseil of his wyf with sorwe,

---

449 **col-fox**: coal-fox; with black markings (as Chauntecleer dreamed). 451: As ordained by Providence. **heigh ymaginacioun**: here, divine intelligence or vision. 461: O new [Judas] Iscariot, new Ganelon [a traitor in the romance *Chanson de Roland*]. 462 **Synon**: the Greek who persuaded the Trojans to take the wooden horse into the city. 471 **scole**: the faculties. The term is used to indicate the body of scholars that make up different disciplines of knowledge.

474: But I cannot shift it to the bran. i.e. I cannot sift or sort through all this. 475 **Augustyn**: St Augustine, one of the great scholars of the Church. 476 **Boece**: Boethius; a Roman writer of late antiquity whose *Consolation of Philosophy*, which Chaucer translated, was one of the great books of the Middle Ages. **Bradwardyn**: Thomas Bradwardine, a 13th century theologian. He was called the 'deep doctor'.

To walken in the yerd, upon that morwe
That he hadde met that dreem, that I of tolde.
490 Wommennes conseils been ful ofte colde;   ruinous
Wommannes conseil broghte us first to wo,
And made Adam fro Paradys to go,
Ther as he was ful myrie, and wel at ese.
But for I noot to whom it myght displese,   know not
495 If I conseil of wommen wolde blame,
Passe over, for I seye it in my game.
Rede auctours wher they trete of swich mateere,
And what they seyn of wommen ye may heere.
Thise been the cokkes wordes and nat myne,
500 I kan noon harm of no womman divyne.   divine
   Faire in the soond, to bathe hire myrily,   sand
Lith Pertelote, and alle hir sustres by,
Agayn the sonne; and Chauntecleer so free
Soony murier than the mermayde in the see;
505 For Phisiologus seith sikerly
How that they syngen wel and myrily.
And so bifel, that as he cast his eye
Among the wortes on a boterflye,
He was war of this fox that lay ful lowe.
510 Nothyng ne liste hym thanne for to crowe,
But cride anon, "cok! cok!" and up he sterte,
As man that was affrayed in his herte.
For natureelly a beest desireth flee
Fro his contrarie, if he may it see,
515 Though he never erst hadde seyn it with his eye.
   This Chauntecleer, whan he gan hym espye,
He wolde han fled, but that the fox anon
Seyde, "Gentil sire, allas, wher wol ye gon?
Be ye affrayed of me that am youre freend?
520 Now certes, I were worse than a feend
If I to yow wolde harm or vileynye.
I am nat come your conseil for t'espye,   secrets; to spy
But trewely, the cause of my comynge
Was oonly for to herkne how that ye synge.
525 For trewely, ye have as myrie a stevene   voice
As any aungel hath that is in hevene.
Therwith ye han in musyk moore feelynge
Than hadde Boece, or any that kan synge.
My lord youre fader (God his soule blesse!)
530 And eek youre mooder, of hir gentillesse
Han in myn hous ybeen, to my greet ese;   delight

---

505 Phisiologus: was the supposed Greek author of a   **528 Boece:** Boethius's *De Musica* was widely studied.
work on natural history.

And certes, sire, ful fayn wolde I yow plese.
But for men speke of syngyng, I wol seye,
So moote I brouke wel myne eyen tweye,   possess
535   Save yow I herde nevere man yet synge
As dide youre fader in the morwenynge.
Certes, it was of herte al that he song!
And for to make his voys the moore strong,
He wolde so peyne hym, that with bothe hise eyen   take such pains
540   He moste wynke, so loude he solde cryen,   shut his eyes
And stonden on his tiptoon therwithal,
And strecche forth his nekke long and smal.
And eek he was of swich discrecioun,
That ther nas no man in no regioun,
545   That hym in song or wisedom myghte passe.
I have wel rad in daun Burnel the Asse
Among hise vers, how that ther was a cok,
For that a presstes sone yaf hym a knok,
Upon his leg, whil he was yong and nyce,
550   He made hym for to lese his benefice.
But certeyn, ther nys no comparisoun
Bitwixe the wisedom and discrecioun
Of youre fader, and of his subtiltee.
Now syngeth, sire, for seinte charitee,
555   Lat se konne ye youre fader countrefete!"   imitate
This Chauntecleer hise wynges gan to bete,
As man that koude his traysoun nat espie,
So was he ravysshed with his flaterie.
Allas, ye lordes! many a fals flatour
560   Is in youre courtes, and many a losengeour,   flatterer
That plesen yow wel moore, by my feith,
Than he that soothfastnesse unto yow seith.   truthfulness
Redeth Ecclesiaste of Flaterye;
Beth war, ye lordes, of hir trecherye.
565   This Chauntecleer stood hye upon his toos,
Strecchynge his nekke, and heeld hise eyen cloos,
And gan to crowe loude for the nones,   occassion
And daun Russell the fox stirte up at ones,
And by the gargat hente Chauntecleer,   throat; seized
570   And on his bak toward the wode hym beer,
For yet ne was ther no man that hym sewed.   chased
O destinee, that mayst nat been eschewed!   avoided
Allas, that Chauntecleer fleigh fro the bemes!
Allas, his wyf ne roghte nat of dremes!   heeded
575   And on a Friday fil al this meschaunce.

---

546 **daun Burnel the Asse:** a satiric poem, *Speculum Stultorum* [Mirror of Fools], in which the main character is a donkey called Burnel. 553 **his:** the other cock in the poem. probably referring to Proverbs 29:5. 563 **Ecclesiaste:** 575 **Friday:** the Romans called the sixth day *Veneris* or Venus's day.

O Venus, that art goddesse of plesaunce!
Syn that thy servant was this Chauntecleer,
And in thy servyce dide al his poweer,
Moore for delit, than world to multiplye,
580   Why woltestow suffre hym on thy day to dye?
       O Gaufred, deere Maister soverayn!
That whan thy worthy kyng Richard was slayn
With shot, compleynedest his dccth so soore,   an arrow
Why ne hadde I now thy sentence and thy loore,   wisdom
585   The Friday for to chide, as diden ye?
(For on a Friday soothly slayn was he.)   truly
Thanne woldc I shewe yow, how that I koude pleyne
For Chauntecleres drede and for his peyne.
       Certes, swich cry, ne lamentacioun
590   Was nevere of ladyes maad, whan Ylioun   Troy
Was wonne, and Pirrus with his streite swerd,   Pyrrhus
Whan he hadde hent kyng Priam by the berd,   seized
And slayn hym, as seith us Eneydos,   as *The Aeneid* tells us
As maden alle the hennes in the clos,   yard
595   Whan they had seyn of Chauntecleer the sighte.
But sovereynly dame Pertelote shrighte   shrieked
Ful louder than dide Hasdrubales wyf,
Whan that hir housbonde hadde lost his lyf,
And that the Romayns hadde brend Cartage;   burnt
600   She was so ful of torment and of rage
That wilfully into the fyr she sterte,   leaped
And brende hirselven with a stedefast herte.
       O woful hennes, right so criden ye,
As whan that Nero brende the Citee
605   Of Rome, cryden senatoures wyves,
For that hir husbondes losten alle hir lyves,
Withouten gilt this Nero hath hem slayn.
Now I wole turne to my tale agayn.
       This sely wydwe, and eek hir doghtres two,   simple
610   Herden thise hennes crie, and maken wo,
And out at dores stirten they anon,   started up quickly
And seyn the fox toward the grove gon,
And bar upon his bak the cok away;
And cryden, "Out! harrow! and weylaway!
615   Ha! ha! the fox!" and after hym they ran,
And eek with staves many another man,   sticks
Ran Colle, oure dogge, and Talbot, and Gerland,
And Malkyn with a dystaf in hir hand,   distaff for winding wool

---

581 **Gaufred:** Geoffrey de Vinsauf, author of a treatise   597 **Hasdrubales:** Hasdrubal was the Carthaginian
on writing poetry in which he offers examples of   leader when Scipio Africanus sacked the city.
elaborate lamenting.   617: **Colle . . . :** all common names for dogs.

Ran cow and calf, and eek the verray hogges,
620 So were they fered for berkying of the dogges,
And shoutyng of the men and wommen eek,
They ronne so, hem thoughte hir herte breek;
They yolleden as feends doon in helle,
The dokes cryden as men wolde hem quelle,   ducks; kill
625 The gees for feere flowen over the trees,
Out of the hyve cam the swarm of bees,
So hydous was the noyse, a *benedicitee*!
Certes, he Jakke Straw and his meynee   company
Ne made nevere shoutes half so shrille,
630 Whan that they wolden any Flemyng kille,
As thilke day was maad upon the fox.
Of bras they broghten bemes and of box,   trumpets; boxwood
Of horn, of boon, in whiche they blewe and powped,   bone; puffed
And therwithal they skriked and they howped,   shrieked; howled
635 It seemed as that hevene sholde falle!
    Now, goode men, I pray yow, herkneth alle.
Lo, how Fortune turneth sodeynly   overturns
The hope and pryde eek of hir enemy!
This cok, that lay upon the foxes bak,
640 In al his drede unto the fox he spak,
And seyde, "Sire, if that I were as ye,
Yet wolde I seyn – as wys God helpe me –   may wise
'Turneth agayn, ye proude cherles alle,   back; fellows
A verray pestilence upon yow falle!
645 Now am I come unto the wodes syde,
Maugree youre heed, the cok shal heere abyde,   despite what you do
I wol hym ete, in feith, and that anon.'"
    The fox answerde, "In feith, it shal be don."
And as he spak that word, al sodeynly
650 This cok brak from his mouth delyverly,   nimbly
And heighe upon a tree he fleigh anon.
And whan the fox saugh that he was gon,
    "Allas!" quod he, "O Chauntecleer, allas!
I have to yow," quod he, "ydoon trespas,
655 In as muche as I maked yow aferd,
Whan I yow hente and broght into this yerd.
But, sire, I dide it of no wikke entente,
Com doun, and I shal telle yow what I mente;
I shal seye sooth to yow, God help me so."
660   "Nay, thanne," quod he, "I shrewe us bothe two,   curse
And first I shrewe myself bothe blood and bones,
If thou bigyle me ofter than ones.

---

628 Jakke Straw: Jack Straw, a leader in the Peasants' Revolt of 1381. His mob murdered many foreigners in London, especially the Flemish involved in the wool trade.

Thou shalt namoore, thurgh thy flaterye,
Do me to synge and wynke with myn eye;
665 For he that wynketh whan he sholde see,
Al wilfully, God lat him nevere thee."   let him never prosper
    "Nay," quod the fox, "but God yeve hym meschaunce,
That is so undiscreet of governaunce,
That jangleth, whan he sholde holde his pees."   chatters; peace
670   Lo, swich it is for to be recchelees,
And necligent, and truste on flaterye!
But ye that holden this tale a folye,   silly thing
As of a fox, or of a cok and hen,
Taketh the moralite, goode men;
675 For seint Paul seith, that al that writen is,
To oure doctrine it is ywrite, ywis.   teaching
Taketh the fruyt, and lat the chaf be stille.   husks
Now goode God, if that it be thy wille,
As seith my lord, so make us alle goode men,
680 And brynge us to his heighe blisse. Amen.'

Epilogue

'Sir Nonnes Preest,' our Hoste seyde anoon
'I-blessed be thy breche, and every stoon!   thighs; testicles
This was a murie tale of Chauntecleer.
But by my trouthe, if thou were seculer,   a layman
685 Thou woldest ben a tredefoul aright.   potent fowl
For if thou have corage as thou has myght,
Thee were nede of hennes, as I wene,
Ya, moo than seven tymes seventene.   more
See, which braunes has this gentil preest,   muscles
690 So gret a nekke, and swich a large breest!
He loketh as a sperhauk with his yen;   sparrowhawk
Him nedeth nat his colour for to dyen
With brasile, ne with greyn of Portyngale.
Now, sire, faire falle you for youre tale.'   may good befall

---

693 brasile: a red dye made from the wood of a tree. A similar type of tree was later found in South America and gave the name to Brazil. **greyn of Portyngale:** grain of Portugal, another red dye.

ROBERT HENRYSON (*c.*1425–*c.*1505)

Little is know about Henryson, who is thought to have taught at a school attached to the Benedictine abbey in Dunfermline, Scotland. His *Testament of Cresseid* was prompted, as the poet tells us, from a reading of Chaucer's *Troilus and Criseyde,* and illustrates how quickly Chaucer's works became known throughout Britain. In Chaucer's poem, Troilus and Criseyde become enamoured during the seige of Troy, until she is given to the Greeks and takes a new lover. Henryson continues Chaucer's tale in his own distinctive manner, concentrating on reversals in human fortune and their moral and spiritual implications. In the following excerpt, Cresseid, who has become a leper, contrasts her current condition with her previous life.

From The Testament of Cresseid

The Complaint of Cresseid

	O sop of sorrow, sonkin into cair	sunk
	O cative Cresseid, for now and ever mair,	wretched
	Gane is thy joy and all thy mirth in eird;	on earth
	Of all blyithnes now art thow blaiknit bair.	made pale and bare
5	Thair is na salve may saif the of thy sair,	wound
	Fell is thy fortoun, wickit is thy weird,	cruel; fate
	Thy blys is baneist, and thy baill on breird,	misery is increasing
	Under the eirth, God gif I gravin wer,	grant; buried
	Quhair nane of Grece nor yet of Troy micht heird.	where; hear it
10	Quhair is thy chalmer wantounlie besene	luxuriously
	With burely bed and bankouris browderit bene?	
	Spycis and wyne to thy collatioun,	refreshment
	The cowpis all of gold and silver schene	cups
	The sweit meitis, servit in plaittis clene,	plates
15	With saipheron sals of ane gude sessoun;	
	Thy gay garmentis with mony gudely goun,	
	Thy plesand lawn pinnit with goldin prene;	linen; pin
	All is areir, thy greit royall renoun.	past
	Quhair is thy garding with thir greissis gay?	garden; green plants
20	And fresche flowris, quhilk the Quene Floray	Queen Flora
	Had paintit plesandly in everie pane;	part
	Quhair thou was wont full merilye in May,	
	To walk and tak the dew be it was day,	
	And heir the merle and mawis mony ane;	blackbird; thrush
25	With ladyis fair in carrolling to gane,	go
	And se the royall rinkis in thair array	warriors

---

1 **sop:** something steeped in liquid.   11: With fine bed   15: With saffron sauce of good flavour.
and well embroidered covers.

In garmentis gay garnischit on everie grane.   decorated; detail
Thy greit triumphand fame and hie honour
Quhair thou was callit of eirdlye wichtis flour.   earthly beings
30   All is decayit, thy weird is welterit so;   overturned
Thy hie estait is turnit in darknes dour.
This lipper ludge tak for thy burelie bour,
And for thy bed tak now ane bunche of stro;
For waillit wyne, and meitis thou had tho,   choice
35   Tak mowlit breid, peirrie and ceder sour
Bot cop and clapper, now is all ago.   apart from cup; gone

My cleir voice, and courtlie carrolling,
Quhair I was wont with ladyis for to sing,
Is rawk as ruik, full hiddeous hoir and hace;
40   My plesand port all utheris precelling,   deportment; excelling
Of lustines I was hald maist conding;   worthy
Now is deformit the figour of my face,
To luik on it, na leid now lyking hes   person; liking
Sowpit in syte, I say with sair siching,
45   Ludgeit amang the lipper leid, allace.

O ladyis fair of Troy and Grece attend,
My miserie, quhilk nane may comprehend,
My frivoll fortoun, my infelicitie,   fickle fortune
My greit mischeif quhilk na man can amend,
50   Be war in tyme approchis neir the end,
And in your mynd ane mirrour mak of me;
As I am now, peraduenture that ye
For all your micht may cum to that same end,
Or ellis war, gif ony war may be.   worse

55   Nocht is your fairnes bot ane faiding flour,
Nocht is your famous laud and hie honour,   reputation
Bot wind inflat in uther mennis eiris.
Your roising reid to rotting sall retour.   rosy complexion
Exempill mak of me in your memour,
60   Quhilk of sic thingis wofull witnes beiris,
All welth in eird, away as wind it weiris;
Be war thairfor, approchis neir the hour,
Fortoun is fikkill, quhen scho beginnis and steiris.   moves

Thus chydand with hir drerie destenye,   rebuking
65   Weiping scho woik the nicht fra end to end,   kept awake
Bot all in vane; hir dule, hir cairfull cry   grief
Micht not remeid, nor yit hir murning mend.   remedy; sorrow mend

---

32: This leper's dwelling now take for your pretty bower. **35:** Take mouldy bread, perry [a cider-like drink made from pears] and sour cider. **39:** Is raucous as a rook, completely hideous, rough and hoarse. **44–45:** Immersed in sorrows, I speak with sighing wounds, living among the lepers, alas!

BALLADS

Songs which originate in oral folk traditions, ballads are difficult to date. They often exist in numerous versions and change as they are passed down through generations. Most traditional ballads express a tragic vision, their stories told with economy and impersonality. The two examples here certainly originated during the Middle Ages. 'Lord Randal' comes from the Scotish border region and probably refers to Ranulf, Earl of Chester, who is mentioned by Langland. The story of 'Little Sir Hugh' appears in another version in Chaucer's 'Prioress's Tale' and seems to have been popular with monastic communities. Its anti-semitic concern with ritual murder recalls that European folk traditions helped to propagate socially destabilising and sectarian views.

Lord Randal

'O where ha you been Lord Randal my son?
And where ha you been my handsome young man?'
'I ha been at the greenwood; mother mak my bed soon,
For I'm wearied wi hunting and fain wad lie down.'

5   'An wha met ye there Lord Randal my son?
An wha met you there, my handsome young man?'
'O I met wi my true-love; mother mak my bed soon,
For I'm wearied wi hunting and fain wad lie down.'

'And what did she give you Lord Randal my son?
10 And what did she give you my handsome young man?'
'Eels fried in a pan; mother mak my bed soon,
For I'm wearied wi hunting and fain wad lie down.'

'An wha gat your leavins Lord Randal, my son ?   left-overs
And wha gat your leavins my handsome young man?'
15 'My hawks and my hounds; mother mak my bed soon,
For I'm wearied wi hunting and fain wad lie down.'

'And what becam of them Lord Randal my son?
And what becam of them my handsome young man?'
'They stretched their legs out and died; mother mak my bed
    soon
20 For I'm wearied wi hunting and fain wad lie down.'

'O I fear you are poisoned Lord Randal my son,
I fear you are poisoned my handsome young man'
'O yes, I am poisoned; mother mak my bed soon,
For I'm wearied wi hunting and fain wad lie down.'

25 'What d'ye leave to your mother Lord Randal my son?
What d'ye leave to your mother my handsome young man?'
'Four and twenty milk kye; mother mak my bed soon,   cows
For I'm wearied wi hunting and fain wad lie down.'

'What d'ye leave to your sister Lord Randal, my son?
30   What d'ye leave to your sister, my handsome young man?'
'My gold and my silver; mother mak my bed soon,
For I'm wearied wi hunting and fain wad lie down.'

'What d'ye leave to your brother Lord Randal my son?
What d'ye leave to your brother my handsome young man?'
35   'My houses and my lands; mother mak my bed soon,
For I'm wearied wi hunting and fain wad lie down.'

'What d'ye leave to your true love Lord Randal my son?
What d'ye leave to your true love my handsome young man?'
'I leave her hell and fire; mother mak my bed soon,
40   For I'm wearied wi hunting and fain wad lie down.'

Little Sir Hugh

Four and twenty bonny boys
    Were playing at the ba   ball
And by it came him sweet Sir Hugh
    And he played o'er them all.

5   He kick'd the ba with his right foot
    And catchd it wi' his knee
And throuch and thro the Jew's window
    He gard the bonny ba flee.

He's doen him to the Jew's castell
10   And walkd it round about
And there he saw the Jew's daughter
    At the window looking out.

'Throw down the ba, ye Jew's daughter
    Throw down the ba to me.'
15   'Never a bit,' says the Jew's daughter
    'Till up to me come ye.'

'How will I come up? How can I come up?
    How can I come to thee?
For as ye did to my auld father
20   The same ye'll do to me.'

She's gane till her father's garden
    And pu'd an apple red and green   picked
'Twas a' to wyle him, sweet Sir Hugh
    And to entice him in.

25   She's led him in through ae dark door
    And sae has she thro' nine

She's laid him on a dressing-table
   And stickit him like a swine.

     And first came out the thick, thick blood
30   And syne came out the thin
     And syne came out the bonny heart's blood
     There was nae mair within.

She's row'd him in a cake o' lead   stirred him
   Bade him lie still and sleep
35   She's thrown him in Our Lady's draw-well
   Was fifty fathom deep.

When the bells were rung and mass was sung
   And a' the bairns came hame   children
When every lady gat hame her son
40   The Lady Maisry gat nane.

She's ta'en her mantle her about
   Her coffer by the hand
And she's gane out to seek her son
   And wanderd o'er the land.

45   She's doen her to the Jew's castell
     Where a' were fast asleep
'Gin ye be there my sweet Sir Hugh
   I pray you to me speak.'

She's doen her to the Jew's garden
50   Thought he had been gathering fruit
'Gin ye be there my sweet Sir Hugh
   I pray you to me speak.'

'Gae hame, gae hame, my mither dear
   Prepare my winding sheet
55 And at the back o' merry Lincoln
The morn I will you meet.'

Now Lady Maisry is gane hame
   Made him a winding sheet
And at the back o' merry Lincoln
60   The dead corpse did her meet.

And a' the bells o' merry Lincoln
   Without men's hands were rung
And a' the books o' merry Lincoln
   Were read without man's tongue
65 And ne'er was such a burial
   Sin Adam's days begun.

---

55 **Lincoln**: Lincoln cathedral. A medieval house in the city is still called the Jew's house.

SIR THOMAS MALORY (*d.*1471)

Little is know about Malory. While in prison in 1469–70 he appears to have reworked romances from French, Norman and English which dealt with the exploits of King Arthur and the Knights of the Round Table into a prose collection which reflects his views of chivalric virtues and vices. But Malory's compendium is more than a mere digest of earlier accounts. For him, Arthur is a figure both historical and legendary, a leader who embodies a distinctive British national ideal, one which is more than the parts of the islands' differing kingdoms. The following episode is from the book's conclusion. Arthur's bastard son Mordred confronts his father in open rebellion. Before the final battle Arthur has a visit from the spirit of Sir Gawayne.

From Le Morte Darthur

'Sir,' seyde Sir Gawayne, 'all thes be ladyes for whom I have foughten for whan I was man lyvynge. And all thes ar tho that I ded batayle fore in ryghteuous quarels, and God hath gyvyn hem that grace at their grete prayer, bycause I ded batayle for them for their ryght, that they shulde brynge me hydder unto you. Thus much hath gyvyn me leve God for to warne you of youre dethe. For, and ye fyght as tomorne with Sir Mordred, as ye bothe have assygned, doute ye nat ye shall be slayne, and the mhoste party of youre people on bothe partyes. And for the grete grace and goodnes that Allmyghty Jesu hath unto you, and for pyte of you and many mo other good men there shall be slayne, God hath sente me to you of Hys speciall grace to gyff you warnyng that in no wyse ye do batayle as tomorne, but that ye take a tretyse for a moneth-day. And profir[1] you largely, so that tomorne ye put in a delay. For within a moneth shall com Sir Launcelot with all hys noble knyghtes, and rescow you worshypfully, and sle Sir Mordred and all that ever wyll holde wyth hym.'

Than Sir Gawayne and all the ladyes vanysshed, and anone the Kynge called upon hys knyghtes, squyars, and yomen, and charged them wyghtly[2] to fecche hys noble lordis and wyse bysshopis unto hym. And whan they were com the Kynge tolde hem of hys avision, that Sir Gawayne had tolde hym and warned hym that, and he fought on the morn, he sholde be slayne. Than the Kynge commanded Sir Lucan the Butlere and hys brothir Sir Bedyvere the Bolde, with two bysshopis wyth hem, and charged them in ony wyse to take a tretyse for a moneth-day wyth Sir Mordred.

'And spare nat, profir hym londys and goodys as much as ye thynke resonable.'

So than they departed and cam to Sir Mordred where he had a grymme hoste of an hondred thousand, and there they entretyd Sir Mordred longe tyme. And at the laste Sir Mordred was aggreed for to have Cornwale and Kente by Kynge Arthurs dayes; and afftir that all Inglonde, after the dayes of Kynge Arthur.

Than were they condescende[3] that Kynge Arthure and Sir Mordred shulde mete betwyxte bothe their hostis, and everych of them shulde brynge fourtene persons. And so they cam wyth thys worde unto Arthur.

---

1 **profir:** offer. Make a generous offer to Mordred so he will accept the truce.   2 **wyghtly:** quickly.   3 **condescende:** agreed.

Than seyde he, 'I am glad that thys ys done,' and so he wente into the fylde.

And whan Kynge Arthur shulde departe he warned all hys hoost that and they se ony swerde drawyn, 'loke lo ye com on fyersely and sle that traytoure, Sir Mordred, for I in no wyse truste hym.' In lyke wyse Sir Mordred warned hys hoste, 'that and ye se ony maner of swerde drawyn, loke that ye com on fyersely and so sle all that ever before you stondyth, for in no wyse I woll nat truste for thys tretyse.' And in the same wyse seyde Sir Mordred unto hys hoste, 'for I know well my fadir woll be avenged upon me.'

And so they mette as their poyntemente was, and were agreed and accorded thorowly. And wyne was fette,[1] and they dranke togydir. Ryght so cam oute an addir of a lytyll hethe bushe and hit stange a knyght in the foote. And so whan the knyght felte hym so stonge, he loked downe and saw the adder, and anone he drew hys swerde to sle the addir, and thought none othir harme. And whan the hoste on bothe partyes saw that swerde drawyn, than they blewe beamys,[2] trumpettis and hornys, and shoutted grymly, and so bothe hostis dressed hem togydirs. And Kynge Arthur toke hys horse and seyde, 'Alas, this unhappy day'. And so rode to hys party, and Sir Mordred in lyke wyse.

And never syns was there never seyne a more dolefuller batayle in no Crysten londe, for there was but russhynge and rydynge, foynynge[3] and strykynge, and many a grym worde was there spokyn of aythir[4] to othir, and many a dedely stroke. But ever Kynge Arthure rode thorowoute the battayle of Sir Mordred many tymys and ded full nobely, as a noble Kynge shulde do, and at all tymes he faynted[5] never. And Sir Mordred ded hys devoure[6] that day and put hymselffe in grete perell.

And thus they fought all the longe day, and never stynted tylle the noble knyghtes were layde to the colde erthe. And ever they fought stylle tylle hit was nere nyght, and by than was there an hondred thousand leyde dede upon the erthe. Than was Kynge Arthure wode[7] wrothe oute of mesure, whan he saw hys people so slayne frome hym.

And so he loked aboute hym and cowde se no mo of all hys hoste and good knyghtes leffte, no mo on lyve but two knyghtes, the tone[8] was Sir Lucan de Buttler and hys brother, Sir Bedyvere; and yette they were full sore wounded.

'Jesu mercy,' seyde the Kynge, 'where ar all my noble knyghtes becom? Alas, that ever I shulde se thys doleful day! For now', seyde Kynge Arthur, 'I am com to myne ende. But wolde to God,' seyde he, 'that I wyste[9] now where were that traytoure Sir Mordred that hath caused all thys myschyff.'

Than Kynge Arthur loked aboute and was ware where stood Sir Mordred leanyng upon hys swerde amonge a grete hepe of dede men.

'Now, gyff me my speare,' seyde Kynge Arthure unto Sir Lucan, 'for yondir I have aspyed the traytoure that all thys woo hath wrought.'

'Sir, latte hym be,' seyde Sir Lucan, 'for he ys unhappy. And yf ye passe this unhappy day ye shall be ryght well revenged. And, good lord, remembre ye of your nyghtes dreme and what the spyryte of Sir Gawayne tolde you to nyght, and yet God of Hys grete goodnes hath preserved you hyddirto. And for Goddes

---

1 **fette:** fetched.　2 **beamys:** trumpets.　3 **foynynge:** thrusting.　4 **aythir:** either, i.e. one to another.　5 **faynted:** lacked courage.　6 **devoure:** duty.　7 **wode:** angry.　8 **tone:** one.　9 **wyste:** knew.

sake, my lorde, leve of thys, for, blyssed be God, ye have won the fylde, for yet we ben here three on lyve, and with Sir Mordred ys nat one of lyve. And therefore if ye leve of now, thys wycked day of desteny ys paste.'

'Now tyde[1] me dethe, tyde me lyff,' seyde the Kynge, 'now I se hym yondir alone, he shall never ascape myne hondes. For at a bettir avayle shall I never have hym.'

'God spyede you well.' seyde Sir Bedyvere.

Than the Kynge gate his speare in bothe hys hondis, and ran towarde Sir Mordred, cryyng and saying, 'Traytoure, now ys thy dethe-day com!'

And whan Sir Mordred saw Kynge Arthur he ran untyll hym with hys swerde drawyn in hys honde, and there Kynge Arthur smote Sir Mordred undir the shylde, with a foyne[2] of hys speare, thorowoute the body more than a fadom.[3] And whan Sir Mordred felte that he had hys dethys wounde he threste hymsclff with the myght that he had upp to the burre[4] of Kynge Arthurs speare, and ryght so he smote hys fadir, Kynge Arthure, with hys swerde holdynge in both hys hondys upon the syde of the hede, that the swerde perced the helmet and the tay[5] of the brayne. And therewith Mordred daysshed downe starke dede to the erthe.

And noble Kynge Arthure felle in a swoughe[6] to the erthe, and there he sowned oftyntymys, and Sir Lucan and Sir Bedyvere offtetymys hove hym up. And so waykly betwyxte them they lad hym to a lytyll chapell nat farre frome the sea, and whan the Kynge was there, hym thought hym resonabely eased.

Than harde they people crye in the fylde.

'Now go thou, Sir Lucan,' seyde the Kynge, 'and do me to wyte what betokyns that noyse in the fylde.'

So Sir Lucan departed, for he was grevously wounded in many placis, and so as he yode[7] he saw and harkened by the moonelyght how that pyllours and robbers were com into the fylde to pylle and to robbe many a full noble knyght of brochys and bees[8] and of many a good rynge and many a ryche juell. And who that were nat dede all oute, there they slew them for their harneys and their ryches.

Whan Sir Lucan undirstood thys warke he cam to the Kynge as sone as he myght, and tolde hym all what he had harde and seyne. 'Therefore be my rede,'[9] seyde Sir Lucan, 'hit ys beste that we brynge you to som towne.'

'I wolde hit were so,' seyde the Kynge, 'but I may nat stonde, my hede worchys[10] so. Ah, Sir Launcelot!' seyde Kynge Arthure, 'thys day have I sore myssed the. And alas, that ever I was ayenste the. For now have I my dethe, whereof Sir Gawayne me warned in my dreame.'

Than Sir Lucan toke up the Kynge the tone party, and Sir Bedyvere the othir parte, and in the lyfflyng up the Kynge sowned. And in the lyfftynge Sir Lucan felle in a sowne, that parte of hys guttis felle out of hys bodye, and therewith the noble knyght hys harte braste. And whan the Kynge awoke he behylde Sir Lucan, how he lay fomyng at the mowth and parte of his guttes lay at hys fyete.

'Alas,' seyde the Kynge, 'thys ys to me a fulle hevy syght, to se thys noble

---

1 **tyde:** befall. 2 **foyne:** thrust. 3 **fadom:** about 18 inches. 4 **burre:** ring to protect hand. 5 **tay:** outer membrane. 6 **swoughe:** swoon. 7 **yode:** went. 8 **bees:** broaches. 9 **rede:** advice. 10 **worchys:** hurts.

deuke so dye for my sake, for he wold have holpyn me that had more nede of helpe than I. Alas, that he wolde nat complayne hym, for hys harte was so sette to helpe me. Now Jesu have mercy upon hys soule.'

Than Sir Bedyvere wepte for the deth of hys brothir.

'Now leve thys mournynge and wepyng, jantyll knyght,' seyde the Kynge, 'for all thys woll nat avayle me. For wyte thou well, and I myght lyve myself, the dethe of Sir Lucan wolde greve me evermore. But my tyme passyth on faste,' seyde the Kynge. 'Therefore,' seyde Kynge Arthur unto Sir Bedyvere, 'take thou here Excaliber, my good swerde, and go wyth hit to yondir watirs syde, and whan thou commyste there, I charge the throw my swerde in that water, and com agayne and telle me what thou syeste there.'

'My Lorde,' seyde Sir Bedyvere, 'youre commaundement shall be done, and lyghtly[1] brynge you worde agayne.'

So Sir Bedyvere departed. And by the way he behylde that noble swerde, and the pomell and the hauffte was all precious stonys. And than he seyde to hymselff, 'If I throw thys ryche swerde in the water, thereof shall never com good, but harme and losse.' And than Sir Bedyvere hyd Excalyber undir a tre. And so as sone as he myght he cam agayne unto the Kynge and seyde he had bene at the watir and had throwen the swerde into the watir.

'What sawe thou there?' seyde the Kynge.

'Sir,' he seyde, I saw nothyng but wawis[2] and wyndys.'

'That ys untruly seyde of the,' seyde the Kynge. 'And therefore go thou lyghtly agayne, and do my commaundemente, as thou arte to me lyff and dere, spare nat, but throw hit in.'

Than Sir Bedyvere returned agayne and toke the swerde in hys honde; and yet hym thought synne and shame to throw away that noble swerde. And so effte[3] he hyd the swerde and returned agayne and tolde the Kynge that he had bene at the watir and done hys commaundement.

'What sawist thou there?' seyde the Kynge.

'Sir,' he seyde, 'I sy nothynge but watirs wap[4] and wawys wanne.'[5]

'Ah, traytour unto me and untrew,' seyde Kynge Arthure, 'now hast thou betrayed me twyse. Who wolde wene that thou that hast bene to me so leve and dere, and also named so noble a knyght, that thou wolde betray me for the ryches of thys swerde? But now go agayn lyghtly; for thy longe taryynge puttith me in grete jouperte of my lyff, for I have takyn colde. And but if thou do now as I bydde the, if ever I may se the, I shall sle the myne owne hondis, for thou woldist for my rych swerde se me dede.'

Than Sir Bedyvere departed and wente to the swerde and lyghtly toke hit up, and so he wente unto the watirs syde. And there he bounde the gyrdyll aboute the hyltis, and threw the swerde as farre into the watir as he myght. And there cam an arme and an honde above the watir, and toke hit and cleyght hit, and shoke hit thryse and braundysshed, and than vanysshed with the swerde into the watir.

So Sir Bedyvere cam agayne to the Kynge and tolde hym what he saw.

'Alas,' seyde the Kynge, 'helpe me hens, for I drede me I have taryed over longe.'

---

1 **lyghtly:** quickly.   2 **wawis:** waves.   3 **effte:** again.   4 **wap:** lap.   5 **wanne:** come.

Than Sir Bedyvere toke the Kynge upon hys bak and so wente with hym to the watirs syde. And whan they were there, evyn faste by the banke hoved[1] a lytyll barge wyth many fayre ladyes in hit, and amonge hem all was a quene, and all they had blak hoodis. And all they wepte and shryked whan they saw Kynge Arthur.

'Now put me into that barge,' seyde the Kynge.

And so he ded sofftely, and there receyved hym three ladyes with grete mournyng. And so they sette hem downe, and in one of their lappis Kynge Arthure layde hys hede. And than the quene sayde, 'Ah, my dere brothir. Why have ye taryed so longe frome me? Alas, thys wounde on youre hede hath caught over much coulde.' And anone they rowed fromward the londe, and Sir Bedyvere behylde all tho ladyes go frowarde hym.

Than Sir Bedyvere cryed and seyde, 'Ah, my lorde Arthur, what shall becom of me, now ye go frome me and leve me here alone amonge myne enemyes?'

'Comforte thyselff,' seyde the Kynge, 'and do as well as thou mayste, for in me ys no truste for to truste in. For I muste into the vale of Avylyon to hele me of my grevous wounde. And if thou here nevermore of me, pray for my soule.' But ever the quene and ladyes wepte and shryked, that hit was pite to hyre.

And as sone as Sir Bedyvere had loste the syght of the barge he wepte and wayled, and so toke the foreste and wente all that nyght. And in the mornyng he was ware, betwyxte two holtis hore,[2] of a chapell and an ermytage.[3]

Than was Sir Bedyvere fayne,[4] and thyder he wente, and whan he cam into the chapell he saw where lay an ermyte grovelynge on all four, faste thereby a tumbe was newe gravyn.[5] Whan the ermyte saw Sir Bedyvere he knewe hym well, for he was but lytyll tofore Bysshop of Caunturbery that Sir Mordred fleamed.[6]

'Sir,' seyde Sir Bedyvere, 'what man ys there here entyred that ye pray so faste fore?'

'Fayre sunne,' seyde the ermyte, 'I wote nar veryly but by demynge.[7] But thys same nyght, at mydnyght, here cam a numbir of ladyes and brought here a dede corse and prayde me to entyre hym. And here they offird an hondred tapers, and they gaff me a thousande besauntes.'[8]

'Alas,' seyde Sir Bedyvere, 'that was my lorde Kynge Arthur, whych lyethe here gravyn in thys chapell.'

Than Sir Bedyvere sowned, and whan he awooke he prayde the ermyte that he myght abyde with hym stylle, there to lyve with fastynge and prayers. 'For from hens woll I never go,' seyde Sir Bedyvere, 'be my wyll, but all the dayes of my lyff here to pray for my lorde Arthur.'

'Sir, ye ar wellcom to me, seyde the ermyte, 'for I know you bettir than ye wene that I do, for ye ar Sir Bedyvere the Bolde, and the full noble duke Sir Lucan de Butler was your brother.'

Than Sir Bedyvere tolde the ermyte all as ye have harde tofore, and so he belaffte[9] with the ermyte that was beforehande Bysshop of Caunturbyry.

---

1 **hoved:** was raised. 2 **holtis hore:** bare woods. 3 **ermytage:** hermitage. 4 **fayne:** lacking in courage.
5 **gravyn:** dug. 6 **fleamed:** banished. 7 **dymynge:** guessing. 8 **besauntes:** bezants. Gold coins, originally struck at Byzantium. 9 **belaffte:** remained.

And there Sir Bedyvere put upon hym poure clothys, and served the ermyte full lowly in fastyng and in prayers.

Thus of Arthur I fynde no more wrytten in bokis that bene auctorysed. Nothir more of the verry sertaynte of hys deth harde I never rede, but thus was he lad away in a shyp wherein were three quenys, that one was Kynge Arthur syster, Quene Morgan le Fay, the other was the Quene of North Galis, and the thirde was the Quene of the Waste Londis. Also there was Dame Nynyve, the chyff lady of the lake, whych had wedded Sir Pellyas, the good knyght; and thys lady had done muche for Kynge Arthure. And thys Dame Nynyve wolde never suffir Sir Pelleas to be in no place where he shulde be in daungere of hys lyff, and so he lyved unto the uttermuste of hys dayes with her in grete reste.

Now more of the deth of Kynge Arthur coude I never fynde, but that thes ladyes brought hym to hys grave, and such one was entyred there whych the ermyte bare wytnes that sometyme was Bysshop of Caunterbyry. But yet the ermyte knew nat in sertayne that he was veryly the body of Kynge Arthur. For thys tale Sir Bedyvere, a knyght of the Table Rounde, made hit to be wrytten.

Yet som men say in many partys of Inglonde that Kynge Arthur ys nat dede, but had by the wyll of oure Lorde Jesu into another place. And men say that he shall com agayne, and he shall wynne the Holy Crosse. Yet I woll nat say that hit shall be so, but rather I wolde sey, here in thys worlde he chaunged hys lyff.

And many men say that there ys wrytten upon the tumbe thys:

HIC IACET ARTHURUS, REX QUONDAM REXQUE FUTURUS[1]

And thus leve I here Sir Bedyvere with the ermyte that dwelled that tyme in a chapell besydes Glassyngbyry,[2] and there was hys ermytage. And so they lyved in prayers and fastynges and grete abstynaunce.

And whan Quene Gwenyver undirstood that Kynge Arthure was dede and all the noble knyghtes, Sir Mordred and all the remanaunte, than she stale away with fyve ladyes with her, and so she wente to Amysbyry. And there she lete make herselff a nunne, and wered whyght clothys and blak, and grete penaunce she toke upon her, as ever ded synfull woman in thys londe. And never creature coude make her myry, but ever she lyved in fastynge, prayers, and almes-dedis, that all maner of people mervayled how vertuously she was chaunged.

---

1 Hic Iacet. . . .: Here lies Arthur, King in the past and King in the future.   2 **Glassyngbyry:** Glastonbury.

EVERYMAN (c.1495)

A version of the Dutch play *Elckerlijc*, the anonymous *Everyman* is a moral drama about dying well. The development of its central message, not to trust in worldly things, illustrates how medieval drama is closely linked to sermons and devotional observations. Complexity of characterisation or plot is not sought as the play vividly seeks to deliver a relatively simple lesson. But the absence of sophisticated dramatic techniques is balanced by a liveliness of language. 'Everyman' and the figures who surround him speak a rhythmical, popular English, and despite being unmistakeably a part of late-medieval Roman Catholic culture, this play, and others like it, remained in demand with audiences for a considerable time after the Reformation.

Characters

Messenger	God	Dethe
Everyman	Felawship	Kynrede
Cosyn	Goodes	Good Dedes
Knowlege	Confessyon	Beaute
Strength	Dyscrecyon	Fyve Wyttes
Aungell	Doctour	

Here begynneth a treatyse how the hye Fader of heven sendeth Dethe to somon every creature to come and gyve acounte of theyr lyves in this worlde and is in maner of a morall playe.

[*Enter Messenger.*]
Messenger I pray you all gyve your audyence,
And here this mater with reverence,
By fygure a morall play,
The Somonynge of Everyman called it is,
5   That of our lyves and endynge shewes
How transytory we be all daye.
This mater is wonders precyous,
But the intent of it is more gracyous,
And swete to bere awaye.
10   The story sayth – Man, in the begynnynge
Loke well and take good heed to the endynge,
Be you never so gay.
Ye thynke synne in the begynnynge full swete,   sweet
Whiche in the ende causeth the soule to wepe,
15   Whan the body lyeth in claye.
Here shall you se how Felawship and Jolyte
Bothe Strength, Pleasure, and Beaute,
Wyll fade from the as floure in Maye;
For ye shall here how our Heven Kynge
20   Calleth Everyman to a generall rekenynge.
Gyve audyence, and here what he doth saye. [*Exit.*]

[*God speketh.*]

God I perceyve, here in my maieste,
How that all creatures be to me unkynde,
Lyvynge without drede in worldly prosperyte.
25 Of ghostly syght the people be so blynde   spiritual
Drowned in synne, they know me not for theyr God.
In worldely ryches is all theyr mynde;
They fere not my ryghtwysnes, the sharpe rod;
My lawe that I shewed, whan I for them dyed
30 They forgete clene, and shedynge of my blode rede.
I hanged bytwene two theves, it can not be denyed,
To gete them lyfe I suffred to be deed;
I heled theyr fete, with thornes hurt was my heed.   feet
I coude do no more than I dyde truely;
35 And nowe I se the people do clene forsake me.
They use the seven deedly synnes dampnable,
As pryde, coveytyse, wrath and lechery,
Now in the worlde be made commendable,
And thus they leve of aungelles the hevenly company.
40 Everyman lyveth so after his owne pleasure,
And yet of thery lyfe they be nothynge sure.
I se the more that I them forbere   tolerate
The worse they be fro yere to yere.
All that lyveth appayreth faste;   degenerates
45 Therfore I wyll in all the haste
Have a rekenynge of every mannes persone;
For, and I leve the people thus alone
In theyr lyfe and wycked tempestes
Veryly they will become moche worse than beestes,
50 For now one wolde by envy another up ete;   eat
Charyte they do all clene forgete.
I hoped well that every man
In my glory sholde make his mansyon,
And therto I had them all electe
55 But now I se lyke traytours dejecte
They thanke me not for the pleasure that I to them ment,
Nor yet for theyr beynge that I them have lent.
I profered the people grete multytude of mercy,
And fewe there be that asketh it hertly;
60 They be so combred with worldly ryches   encumbered
That nedes on them I must do justyce,
On every man lyvynge without fere.
Where arte thou, Deth, thou myghty messengere?
[*Enter Dethe.*]
Dethe Almyghty God, I am here at your wyll,
65 Your commaundement to fulfyll.

---

33 fete: alludes to Christ's washing of his apostles' feet, re-enacted on Maundy Thursday during Easter.

God Go thou to Everyman
And shewe hym in my name
A pylgrymage he must on hym take,
Whiche he in no wyse may escape,
70 And that he brynge with hym a sure rekenynge
Without delay or any taryenge. [*Exit.*]

Dethe Lorde, I wyll in the worlde go renne overall,   run
And cruelly out serche bothe grete and small.
Every man wyll I beset that lyveth beestly
75 Out of Goddes lawes, and dredeth not foly.
He that loveth rychesse I wyll stryke with my darte,
His syght to blynde, and fro heven to departe,
Excepte that almes be his good frende,
In Hell for to dwell, worlde with out ende.
80 Loo, yonder I se Everyman walkynge. [*Enter Everyman.*]
Full lytell he thynketh on my comynge;
His mynde is on flesshely lustes and his treasure,
And grete payne it shall cause hym to endure
Before the Lorde, Heven Kynge.
85 Everyman, stande styll! Whyder arte thou goynge
Thus gayly? Hast thou thy Maker forgete?
Everyman Why askest thou?
Woldest thou wete?   know
Dethe Ye, syr. I wyll shewe you;
90 In grete hast I am sende to the
Fro God out of his mageste.
Everyman What, sente to me?
Dethe Ye, certaynly.
Though thou have forgete hym here,
95 He thynketh on the in the hevenly spere,
As, or we departe, thou shalte knowe.
Everyman What desyreth God of me?
Dethe That shall I showe thee,
A rekenynge he wyll nedes have
100 Without only lenger respyte.
Everyman To gyve a rekenynge longer layser I crave.   leisure
This blynde mater troubleth my wytte
Dethe On the thou must take a longe journey;
Therfor thy boke of counte with the thou brynge,   account
105 For tourne agayne thou can not by no waye;
And loke thou be sure of thy rekenynge,
For before God thou shalte answere, and shewe
Thy many badde dedes, and good but a fewe;
How thou hast spente thy lyfe, and in what wyse,
110 Before the chefe Lorde of paradyse
Have ado that thou were in that waye
For, wete thou well, thou shalte make none attournay.   know; advocate

Everyman Full unredy I am suche rekenynge to gyve.
I knowe the not. What messenger art thou?

115 *Dethe* I am Dethe that no man dredeth,
For every man I reste and no man spareth;
For it is Goddes commaundement
That all to me sholde be obedyent.
Everyman Oh Deth, thou comest whan I had the leest in mynde.

120 In thy power it lyeth me to save;
Yet of my good wyl I gyve the, yf thou wyl be kynde,
Ye, a thousande pounde shalte thou have
And dyfferre this mater tyll another daye.   defer
Dethe Everyman, it may not be by no waye.

125 I set not by golde, sylver, nor rychesse,
Ne by pope, emperour, kynge, duke, ne prynces;
For, and I wolde receyve gyftes grete,
All the worlde I myght gete;
But my custome is clene contrary.

130 I gyve the no respyte. Come hens, and not tary.   hence
Everyman Alas, shall I have no lenger respyte?
I may saye Deth gyveth no warnynge.
To thynke on the, it maketh my herte seke,   sick
For all unredy is my boke of rekenynge.

135 But 12 yere and I myght have a-bydynge,   respite
My countynge-boke I wolde make so clere
That my rekenynge I sholde not nede to fere.
Wherfore, Deth, I praye the, for Goddes mercy,
Spare me tyll I be provyded of remedy.

140 *Dethe* The avayleth not to crye, wepe, and praye;
But hast the lyghtly that thou were gone that journaye,
And preve thy frendes if thou can.
For, wete thou well, the tyde abydeth no man,   know
And in the worlde eche lyvynge creature

145 For Adam's synne must dye of nature.
Everyman Dethe, if I sholde this pylgrymage take,
And my rekenynge suerly make,
Shewe me, for saynt charyte,
Sholde I not come agayne shortly?

150 *Dethe* No, Everyman; and thou be ones there,
Thou mayst never more come here,
Trust me veryly.
Everyman Oh gracyous God in the hye sete celestyall,
Have mercy on me in this moost need

155 Shall I have no company fro this vale terestryall
Of myne acqueyntaunce, that way me to lede?
Dethe Ye, if ony be so hardy   any
That wolde go with the and bere the company.

Hye the that thou were gone to Goddes magnyfycence,
160   Thy rekenynge to gyve before his presence.
What, wenest thou thy lyve is gyven the,   think
And thy worldely gooddes also?
Everyman I had wende so, veryle.
Dethe Nay, nay, it was but lende the;
165   For as soone as thou arte go,
Another a whyle shall have it, and than go therfro,
Even as thou hast done.
Everyman, thou arte mad; thou hast thy wyttes fyve
And here on erthe wyll not amende thy lyve;
170   For sodeynly I do come.
Everyman O wretched caytyfe, wheder shall I flee,   villain; whither
That I myght scape this endles sorowe?
Now, gentyll Deth, spare me tyll tomorowe,
That I may amende me
175   With good advysement.
Dethe Naye, therto I wyll not consent,
Nor man wyll I respyte
But to the herte sodeynly I shall smyte
Without ony advysement.
180   And now out of thy syght I wyll me hy.
Se thou make the redy shortely,
For thou mayst saye this is the daye
That no man lyvynge may scape a-waye. [*Exit.*]

Everyman Alas, I may well wepe with syghes depe.
185   Now have I no maner of company
To helpe me in my journey, and me to kepe;
And also my wrytynge is full unredy.
How shall I do now for to excuse me?
I wolde to God I had never be grete;   been begot
190   To my soule a full grete profyte it had be,
For now I fere paynes huge and grete.
The tyme passeth. Lorde, helpe, that all wrought;
For though I mourne, it avayleth nought.
The day passeth and is almoost ago;
195   I wote not well what for to do.
To whome were I best my complaynt to make?
What and I to Felawship therof spake
And shewed hym of this sodeyne chaunce?
For in hym is all myne affyaunce;   trust
200   We have in the worlde so many a daye
Be good frendes in sporte and playe.
I se hym yonder, certaynely.
I trust that he wyll bere me company;

---

187 **wrytynge:** the account book of his life, i.e. his sum of virtuous actions.

Therfore to hym wyll I speke to ese my sorowe.
205 Well mette, good Felawship, and good morowe.
[*Enter Felawship.*]
Felawship Everyman good morowe, by this daye!
Syr, why lokest thou so pyteously?
If ony thynge be amysse, I praye the me saye,
That I may helpe to remedy.
210 **Everyman** Ye, good Felawship, ye,
I am in greate jeoparde.
Felawship My true frende, shewe to me your mynde.
I wyll not forsake the to my lyves ende,
In the waye of good company.
215 **Everyman** That was well spoken and lovyngly.
Felawship Syr, I must nedes knowe your hevynesse.
I have pyte to se you in ony dystresse.   any
If ony have you wronged, ye shall revenged be,
Though I on the grounde be slayne for the,
220 Though that I knowe before that I sholde dye.
Everyman Veryly, Felawship, gramercy.
Felawship Tusshe, by thy thankes I set not a strawe.
Shewe me your grefe, and saye no more.
Everyman If I my herte sholde to you breke,
225 And than you to tourne your mynde fro me
And wolde not me comforte whan ye here me speke,
Than sholde I ten tymes soryer be.
Felawship Syr, I saye as I wyll do in dede.
Everyman Than be you a good frende at nede
230 I have founde you true here before.
Felawship And so ye shall evermore.
For in fayth and thou go to hell,
I wyll not forsake the by the waye.
Everyman Ye speke lyke a good frende; I byleve you well.
235 I shall deserve it, and I maye.
Felawship I speke of no deservynge, by this daye.
For he that wyll saye and nothynge do,
Is not worthy with good company to go.
Therfore shewe me the grefe of your mynde,
240 To your frende moost lovynge and kynde.
Everyman I shall shewe you how it is.
Commaunded I am to go a journaye,
A longe waye harde and daungerous,
And gyve a strayte counte, without delaye,
245 Before the hye Juge, Adonay.
Wherfore, I pray you, bere me company,
As ye have promysed, in this journaye.

245: **Adonay:** Adonai. The supreme being, the Lord.

Felawship That is mater in dede. Promyse is duty.
But, and I sholde take suche a vyage on me
250 I knowe it well, it sholde be to my payne.
Also it maketh me aferde, certayne.
But let us take counsell here as well as we can,
For your wordes wolde fere a stronge man.
Everyman Why, ye sayd yf I had nede
255 Ye wolde me never forsake, quycke ne deed,   alive or dead
Though it were to hell, truely.
Felawship So I sayd, certaynely.
But suche pleasures be set a-syde, the sothe to saye;   truth
And also, yf we toke suche a journaye
260 Whan sholde we agayne come?
Everyman Naye, never agayne tyll the daye of dome.
Felawship In fayth, than wyll not I come there
Who hath you these tydynges brought?
Everyman In dede; Deth was with me here.
265 **Felawship** Now, by God that all hathe bought,
If Deth were the messenger,
For no man that is lyvynge todaye
I wyll not go that lothe journaye,
Not for the fader that bygate me!
270 **Everyman** Ye promysed other wyse, parde.
Felawship I wote well I sayd so, truely.   know
And yet, yf thou wylte ete & drynke & make good chere,
Or haunt to women the lusty company,
I wolde not forsake you whyle the daye is clere,
275 Trust me veryly.
Everyman Ye, therto ye wolde be redy.
To go to myrthe, solas, and playe,
Your mynde wyll soner apply,
Than to bere me company in my longe journaye.
280 **Felawship** Now, in good fayth, I wyll not that waye,
But and thou wyll murder, or ony man kyll,
In that I wyll helpe the with a good wyll.
Everyman Oh, that is a symple advyse in dede.
Gentyll felawe, helpe me in my necessyte.
285 We have loved longe, and now I nede
And now, gentyll Felawship, remembre me.
Felawship Wheder ye have loved me or no,
By Saynt Johan I wyll not with the go.
Everyman Yet, I pray the, take the labour and do so moche for me
290 To brynge me forwarde, for saynt charyte
And comforte me tyll I come without the towne.
Felawship Nay, and thou wolde gyve me a newe gowne,
I wyll not a fote with the go;
But, and thou had taryed, I wolde not have lefte the so.

295 And as now God spede the in thy journaye,
 For from the I wyll departe as fast as I maye.
 Everyman Wheder awaye, Felawship? Wyll thou forsake me?
 Felawship Ye, by my faye! To God I betake the.   faith
 Everyman Farewell, good Felawship. For the my herte is sore.
300 Adewe for ever. I shall se the no more.
 Felawship In fayth, Everyman, fare well now at the endynge.
 For you I wyll remembre that partynge is mournynge. [*Exit.*]

 Everyman A-lacke, shall we thus departe in dede –
 A, Lady, helpe! – without ony more comforte?
305 Lo, Felawship forsaketh me in my moost nede.
 For helpe in this worlde wheder shall I resorte.
 Felawship here before with me wolde mery make,
 And now lytell sorowe for me dooth he take.
 It is sayd, 'In prosperyte men frendes may fynde,
310 Whiche in adversyte be full unkynde.'
 Now wheder for socoure shall I flee,
 Syth that Felawship hath forsaken me?
 To my kynnesmen I wyll, truely,
 Prayenge them to helpe me in my necessyte.
315 I byleve that they wyll do so,
 For kynde wyll crepe where it may not go.
 I wyll go saye, for yonder I se them.
 Where be ye now, my frendes and kynnesmen?
 [*Enter Kynrede and Cosyn.*]
 Kynrede Here be we now at your commaundement.
320 Cosyn, I praye you shewe us your entent
 In ony wyse, and not spare.
 Cosyn Ye, Everyman, and to us declare
 If ye be dysposed to go ony-whyder;   anywhere
 For, wete you well, we will lyve and dye to-gyder.
325 *Kynrede* In welth and wo we wyll with you holde,
 For over his kynne a man may be bolde.
 Everyman Gramercy, my frendes and kynnesmen kynde.
 Now shall I shewe you the grefe of my mynde.
 I was commaunded by a messenger,
330 That is a hye kynges chefe offycer.
 He bad me go a pylgrymage, to my payne,
 And I knowe well I shall never come agayne.
 Also I must gyve a reckenynge strayte,
 For I have a grete enemy thyat hath me in wayte,
335 Whiche entendeth me for to hynder.
 Kynrede What acounte is that whiche ye must render?
 That wolde I knowe.

---

316 crepe: crawl. The idea is that blood relations will find a way to go when they seem prevented.

Everyman Of all my workes I must shewe
How I have lyved and my dayes spent;

340 Also of yll dedes that I have used
In my tyme, syth lyfe was me lent;
And of all vertues that I have refused.
Therfore, I praye you, go thyder with me
To helpe to make myn accounte, for saynt charyte.

345 **Cosyn** What, to go thyder? Is that the mater?
Nay, Everyman, I had lever fast brede and water   rather
All this fyve yere and more.
Everyman Alas, that ever I was bore.
For now shall I never be mery,

350 If that you forsake me.
Kynrede A, syr, what ye be a mery man.
Take good herte to you, and make no mone.
But one thynge I warne you, by Saynt Anne,
As for me, ye shall go alone.

355 **Everyman** My Cosyn, wyll you not with me go?
Cosyn No, by our Lady. I have the crampe in my toe.
Trust not to me; for so God me spede,
I wyll deceyve you in your moost nede.
Kynrede It avayleth not us to tyse.   entice

360 Ye shall have my mayde with all my herte;
She loveth to go to feestes, there to be nyse,   wanton
And to daunce, and abrode to sterte.
I wyl gyve her leve to helpe you in that journey,
If that you and she may agree.

365 **Everyman** Now shewe me the very effecte of your mynde.
Wyll you go with me, or abyde behynde?
Kynrede Abyde behynde? Ye, that wyll I, and I maye!
Therfore farewell tyll another daye.
Everyman Howe sholde I be mery or gladde?

370 For fayre promyses men to me make,
But whan I have moost nede they me forsake.
I am deceyved, that maketh me sadde.
Cosyn Cosyn Everyman, farewell now,
For veryly I wyll not go with you.

375 Also of myne owne an unredy rekenyng
I have to accounte. Therfore I make taryenge.
Now God kepe the, for now I go. [*Exit Kynrede and Cosyn.*]

Everyman Ah, Jesus, is all come hereto?
Lo, fayre wordes maketh fooles fayne;   glad

380 They promyse and nothynge wyll do, certayne.
My kynnesmen promysed me faythfully
For to abyde with me stedfastly,
And now fast awaye do they flee.

Even so Felawship promysed me.
385   What frende were best me of to provyde?
I lose my tyme here longer to abyde.
Yet in my mynde a thynge there is;
All my lyfe I have loved ryches.
If that my Good now helpe me myght,
390   He wolde make my herte full lyght.
I wyll speke to hym in this dystresse.
Where arte thou, my Gooddes and ryches?
[*Enter Goodes.*]
Goodes Who calleth me? Everyman? What, hast thou haste
I lye here in corners, trussed and pyled so hye,
395   And in chestes I am locked so fast,
Also sacked in bagges. Thou mayst se with thyn eye
I can not styre; in packes lowe I lye.
What wolde ye have? Lyghtly me saye.   *quickly*
Everyman Come hyder, Good, in al the hast thou may,
400   For of counseyll I must desyre the.
Goodes Syr, and ye in the worlde have sorowe or adversyte,
That can I helpe you to remedy shortly.
Everyman It is another dysease that greveth me.
In this worlde it is not, I tell the so.
405   I am sent for, an other way to way to go,
To gyve a strayte counte generall
Before the hyest Jupyter of all.
And all my lyfe I have had joye & pleasure in the,
Therfore, I pray the, go with me.
410   For, paraventure, thou mayst before God Almyghty
My rekenyng helpe to clene and puryfy,
For it is sayd ever amonge
That money maketh all ryght that is wronge.
Goodes Nay, Everyman, I synge an other songe.
415   I folowe no man in suche vyages.
For, and I wente with the,
Thou sholdest fare moche the worse for me.
For bycause on me thou dyd set thy mynde,
Thy rekenynge I have made blotted and blynde,
420   That thyne accounte thou can not make truly,
And that hast thou for the love of me.
Everyman That wolde greve me full sore,
Whan I sholde come to that ferefull answere.
Up, let us go thyder togyder.
425   **Goodes** Nay, not so. I am to brytell, I may not endure.
I wyll folowe no man one fote, be ye sure.
Everyman Alas, I have thee loved, and had grete pleasure
All my lyfe dayes on good and treasure.

Goodes That is to thy dampnacyon, without lesynge,
430 For my love is contrary to the love everlastynge.
But if thou had me loved moderately durynge,
As to the poore gyve parte of me,
Than sholdest thou not is this dolour be,
Nor in this grete sorowe and care.
435 **Everyman** Lo, now was I deceyved or I was ware.   prepared
And all I may wyte my spendynge of tyme.   blame
Goodes What, wenest thou that I am thyne?   suppose
Everyman I had went so.
Goodes Nay Everyman, I saye no.
440 As for a whyle I was lent thee,
A season thou hast me in prosperyte.
My condycyon is mannes soule to kill.
If I save one, a thousande I do spyll.
Wenest thou that I wyll folowe the?
445 Nay, fro this worlde not, veryle.
Everyman I had wende otherwyse.
Goodes Therfore to thy soule Good is a thefe;
For whan thou arte deed, this is my gyse,
Another to deceyve in this same wyse
450 As I have done the, and all to his soules reprefe.   disgrace
Everyman Oh false Good, cursed thou be,
Thou traytour to God that hast deceyved me
And caught me in thy snare.
Goodes Mary, thou brought thy selfe in care,
455 Wherof I am gladde.
I must nedes laugh. I cannot be sadde.
Everyman A, Good, thou hast had longe my hertely love;   sincere
I gave the that whiche sholde be the Lordes above.
But wylte thou not go with me in dede?
460 I praye the trouth to saye.
Goodes No, so God me spede.
Therfore farewell, and have good daye. [*Exit.*]

Everyman Oh, to whome shall I make my mone
For to go with me in that hevy journaye?
465 Fyrst Felawship sayd he wolde with me gone.
His wordes were very pleasaunt and gaye,
But afterwarde he lefte me alone.
Than spake I to my kynnesmen, all in dyspayre,
And also they gave me wordes fayre,
470 They lacked no fayre spekynge,
But all forsake me in the endynge.
Than wente I to my Goodes that I loved best,
In hope to have comforte; but there had I leest.
For my Goodes sharpely dyd me tell

475 That he bryngeth many into hell.
Than of my selfe I was ashamed,
And so I am worthy to be blamed.
Thus may I well my selfe hate.
Of whome shall I now counseyll take?
480 I thynke that I shall never spede   prosper
Tyll that I go to my Good Dede.
But, alas, she is so weke
That she can nother go nor speke.
Yet wyll I venter on her now.
485 My Good Dedes, where be you?
[*Enter Good Dedes.*]
Good Dedes Here I lye, colde in the grounde.
Thy synnes hath me sore bounde,
That I can not stere.   stir
Everyman Oh Good Dedes, I stande in fere.
490 I must you pray of counseyll,
For helpe now sholde come ryght well.
Good Dedes Everyman, I have understandynge
That ye be somonde acount to make
Before Myssyas, of Jherusalern kynge;   Messiah
495 And you do by me that journay with you wyll I take.
Everyman Therfore I come to you my moone to make.
I praye you that ye wyll go with me.
Good Dedes I wolde full fayne, but I can not stande, veryly.   gladly
Everyman Why, is there ony thynge on you fall?
500 **Goode Dedes** Ye, syr, I may thanke you of all.
If ye had parfytely chered me,
Your boke of counte full redy had be.
Loke, the bokes of your workes and dedes eke
As how they lye under the fete,
505 To your soules hevynes.
Everyman Our Lorde Jesus helpe me.
For one letter here I cannot se.
Good Dedes There is a blynde rekenyng in tyme of dystres.
Everyman Good Dedes, I praye you helpe me in this nede,
510 Or elles I am for ever dampned in dede.
Therfore helpe me to make rekenynge
Before the Redemer of all thynge,
That Kynge is, and was, and ever shall.
Good Dedes Everyman, I am sory of your fall,
515 And fayne wolde I helpe you, and I were able.
Everyman Good Dedes, your counseyll I pray you gyve me.
Good Dedes That shall I do, veryly.
Though that on my fete I may not go,
I have a syster that shall with you also,

520 Called Knowlege, whiche shall with you abyde,
To helpe you to make that dredefull rekenynge.
[*Enter Knowlege.*]
Knowlege Everyman, I wyll go with the and be thy gyde,
In thy moost nede to go by thy syde.
Everyman In good condycyon I am now in every thynge,
525 And am hole content with this good thynge,
Thanked be God my creature.   creator
Good Dedes And whan she hath brought you there,
Where thou shalte hele the of thy smarte,
Than go you with your rekenynge and your Good Dedes togyder,
530 For to make you joyfull at herte
Before the Blessyd Trynyte.
Everyman My Good Dedes, gramercy.
I am well content, certaynly,
With your wordes swete.
535 **Knowlege** Now go we togyder lovyngly
To Confessyon, that clensynge ryvere.
Everyman For joy I wepe. I wolde we were there.
But, I pray you, gyve me cognycyon   understanding
Where dwelleth that holy man, Confessyon.
540 **Knowlege** In the hous of salvacyon.
We shall fynde hym in that place,
That shall us comforte, by Goddes grace.
[*Enter Confessyon.*]
Lo, this is Confessyon. Knele downe and aske mercy,
For he is in good conceyte with God Almyghty.
545 **Everyman** Oh gloryous fountayne, that all unclennes doth claryfy,
Wasshe fro me the spottes of vyce unclene,
That on me no synne may be sene.
I come with Knowlege for my redempcyon,
Redempte with herte and full contrycyon.   sincere
550 For I am commaunded a pylgrymage to take,
And grete accountes before God to make.
Now I praye you, Shryfte, moder of salvacyon,   Confession
Helpe my Good Dedes for my pyteous exclamacyon.
Confessyon I knowe your sorowe well, Everyman.
555 Bycause with Knowlege ye come to me,
I wyll you comforte as well as I can,
And a precyous jewell I wyll gyve the,
Called penaunce, voyder of adversyte.   remover
Therwith shall your body chastysed be,
560 With abstynence & perseveraunce in Goddes servyture.
Here shall you receyve that scourge of me,
Whiche is penaunce stronge that ye must endure,
To remembre thy Savyour was scourged for the
With sharpe scourges, and suffred it pacyently.

565 So must thou or thou scape that paynful pylgrymage.
Knowlege, kepe hym in this vyage,
And by that tyme Good Dedes wyll be with the.
But in ony wyse be seker of mercy,
For your tyme draweth fast, and ye wyll saved be.
570 Aske God mercy, and he wyll graunte truely.
Whan with the scourge of penaunce man doth hym bynde,
The oyle of forgyvenes than shall he fynde.
Everyman Thanked be God for his gracyous werke.
For now I wyll my penaunce begyn.
575 This hath rejoysed and lyghted my herte,
Though the knottes be paynful and harde within.
Knowlege Everyman, loke your penaunce that ye fulfyll,
What payne that ever it to you be.
And Knowlege shall gyve you counseyll at wyll,
580 How your accounte ye shall make clerely.
Everyman Oh eternall God, Oh Hevenly fygure,
Oh way of ryghtwysnes, Oh goodly vysyon,
Whiche dyscended downe in a vyrgyn pure
Bycause he wolde every man redeme,
585 Whiche Adam forfayted by his dysobedyence.
Oh blessyd God-heed, electe and hye devyne,
Forgyve me my grevous offence.
Here I crye the mercy in this presence.
Oh ghostly treasure, Oh raunsomer and redemer,
590 Of all the worlde hope and conduyter,   guide
Myrrour of joye, foundatour of mercy,
Whiche enlumyneth heven and erth therby,
Here my clamorous complaynt, though it late be,
Receyve my prayers unworthy in this hevy lyfe.
595 Though I be a synner moost abhomynable,
Yet let my name be wryten in Moyses table.
Oh Mary, praye to the Maker of all thynge,
Me for to helpe at my endynge.
And save me fro the power of my enemy,
600 For Deth assayleth me strongly.
And, Lady, that I may by meane of thy prayer   mediation
Of your Sones glory to be partynere,
By the meanes of his passyon, I it crave.
I beseche you helpe my soule to save.
605 Knowlege, gyve me the scourge of penaunce,
My flesshe therwith shall gyve acqueyntaunce.
I wyll now begyn, yf God gyve me grace.
Knowlege Everyman, God gyve you tyme and space.

---

596 Moyses table: During the Middle Ages, the tables of laws Moses brought down from Sinai in the Old Testament were seen as symbols of baptism and penance. Everyman hopes to escape damnation by doing penance.

Thus I bequeth you in the handes of our Savyour.
610 Now may you make your rekenynge sure.
Everyman In the name of the Holy Trynyte,
My body sore punysshed shall be.
Take this, body, for the synne of the flesshe.
Also thou delytest to go gay and fresshe,   delighted
615 And in the way of dampnacyon thou dyd me brynge.
Therfore suffre now strokes of punysshynge.
Now of penaunce I wyll wade the water clere,
To save me from Purgatory, that sharpe fyre.
Goode Dedes I thanke God, now I can walke and go,
620 And am delivered of my sykenesse and wo.
Therfore with Everyman I wyll go, and not spare
His good workes I wyll helpe hym to declare.
Knowlege Now, Everyman, be mery and glad.
Your Good Dedes cometh now, ye may not be sad.
625 Now is your Good Dedes hole and sounde,
Goynge upryght upon the grounde.
Everyman My herte is lyght, and shal be evermore.
Now wyll I smyte faster than I dyde before.   strike
Good Dedes Everyman, pylgryme, my specyall frende,
630 Blessyd be thou without ende.
For the is preparate the eternall glory.
Ye have me made hole and sounde,
Therfore I wyll byde by the in every stounde.   season
Everyman Welcome, my Good Dedes. Now I here thy voyce
635 I wepe for very swetenes of love.
Knowlege Be no more sad, but ever rejoyce.
God seeth thy lyvynge in his trone above.   throne
Put on this garment to thy behove,   advantage
Whiche is wette with your teres,
640 Or elles before God you may it mysse,
Whan ye to your journeys ende come shall.
Everyman Gentyll Knowlege, what do ye it call?
Knowlege It is a garment of sorowe,
Fro payne it wyll you borowe.
645 Contrycyon it is
That getteth forgyvenes;
He pleaseth God passynge well.
Good Dedes Everyman, wyll you were it for your hele?   salvation
Everyman Now blessyd be Jesu, Maryes sone,
650 For now have I on true contrycyon,
And lette us go now without taryenge.
Good Dedes, have we clere our rekenynge?
Good Dedes Ye, in dede, I have it here.
Everyman Than I trust we nede not fere.
655 Now, frendes, let us not parte in twayne.

Knowlege Nay, Everyman, that wyll we not, certayne.
Good Dedes Yet must thou lede with the
Thre persones of grete myght.
Everyman Who sholde they be?
660 *Good Dedes* Dyscrecyon and Strength they hyght,
And thy Beaute may not abyde behynde.
Knowlege Also ye must call to mynde
Your Fyve Wyttes as for your counseylours.
Good Dedes You must have them redy at all houres.
665 *Everyman* How shall I gette them hyder?
Knowlege You must call them all togyder,
And they wyll here you in-contynent. immediately
Everyman My frendes, come hyder and be present,
Dyscrecyon, Strength, my Fyve Wyttes, and Beaute.

[*Enter Beaute, Strength, Dyscrecyon, Fyve Wyttes.*]
670 *Beaute* Here at your wyll we be all redy.
What wyll ye that we sholde do ?
Good Dedes That ye wolde with Everyman go,
And helpe hym in his pylgrymage.
Advyse you wyll ye with him or not in that vyage?
675 *Strength* We wyll brynge hym all thyder,
To his helpe and comforte ye may byleve me.
Dyscrecyon So wyll we go with hym all togyder.
Everyman Almyghty God, loved may thou be.
I gyve the laude that I have hyder brought
680 Strength, Dyscrecyon, Beaute, & Fyve Wyttes. Lacke I nought;
And my Good Dedes with Knowlege clere,
All be in company at my wyll here.
I desyre no more to my besynes. for my purpose
Strength And I, Strength, wyll by you stande in dystres,
685 Though thou wolde in batayle fyght on the grounde.
Fyve Wyttes And though it were thrugh the worlde rounde,
We wyll not departe for swete ne soure.
Beaute No more wyll I unto dethes houre,
What so ever therof befall.
690 *Dyscrecyon* Everyman, advyse you fyrst of all.
Go with a good advysement and delyberacyon.
We all gyve you vertuous monycyon advice
That all shall be well.
Everyman My frendes, harken what I wyll tell.
695 I praye God rewarde you in his hevenly spere.
Now herken, all that be here,
For I wyll make my testament
Here before you all present.
In almes halfe my good I wyll gyve with my hande twayne
700 In the way of charyte with good entent;
And the other halfe styll shall remayne

In queth, to be retourned there it ought to be.   *legacy*
This I do in despyte of the fende of hell,
To go quyte out of his perell
705 Ever after and this daye.
    Knowlege Everyman, herken what I saye.
Go to Presthode, I you advyse,
And receyve of hym in ony wyse
The holy sacrament and oyntement togyder.
710 Than shortly se ye tourne agayne hyder;
We wyll all abyde you here.
    Fyve Wyttes Ye, Everyman, hye you that ye redy were.
There is no Emperour, Kynge, Duke, ne Baron
That of God hath commycyon   *authority*
715 As hath the leest preest in the worlde beynge.
For of the blessyd sacramentes pure and benygne   *gracious*
He bereth the keyes, and therof hath the cure
For mannes redempcyon, it is ever sure,
Whiche God for our soules medycyne
720 Gave us out of his herte with grete pyne.   *pain*
Here in this transytory lyfe, for the and me,
The blessyd sacramentes seven there be:
Baptym, confyrmacyon, with preesthode good,   *Holy Orders*
And the sacrament of Goddes precyous flesshe & blod,
725 Maryage, the holy extreme unccyon, and penaunce.
These seven be good to have in remembraunce,
Gracyous sacramentes of hye devynyte.
    Everyman Fayne wolde I receyve that holy body,   *gladly*
And mekely to my ghostly fader I wyll go.
730   **Fyve Wyttes** Everyman, that is the best that ye can do.
God wyll you to salvacyon brynge,
For preesthode excedeth all other thynge.
To us holy scrypture they do teche,
And converteth man fro synne, heven to reche.
735 God hath to them more power gyven
Than to ony aungell that is in heven.
With five wordes he may consecrate
Goddes body in flesshe and blode to make,
And handeleth his Maker bytwene his handes.
740 The preest byndeth and unbyndeth all bandes,   *fetters [of sin]*
Bothe in erthe and in heven.
Thou mynystres all the sacramentes seven.   *do administer*
Though we kysse thy fete, thou were worthy.
Thou arte surgyon that cureth synne deedly.

---

702 retourned: Everyman seems to mean a restitution of goods and property to those he took them from. **709 oyntement:** The sacrament of Extreme Unction or last rites. **715 leest preest:** lowliest priest. Since the priesthood have the power to remit sins, their spiritual authority is greater than any temporal power. **737 five wordes:** 'Hoc est enim corpus meum' [This is my body]. See Luke 22:19.

745 No remedy we fynde under God
But all onely preesthode.
Everyman, God gave preest that dygnyte,
And setteth them in his stede amonge us to be,
Thus be they above aungelles in degree. [*Exit Everyman.*]
750 **Knowlege** If preestes be good, it is so, suerly.
But whan Jesu hanged on the crosse with grete smarte,
There he gave out of his blessyd herte
The seven sacramentes in grete tourment;   torment
He solde them not to us, that Lorde omnypotent.
755 Therfore Saynt Peter the apostell dothe saye
That Jesus curse hath all they
Whiche God theyr Savyour do by or sell,
Or they for ony money do take or tell.   pay out
Synfull preestes gyveth the synners example bad.
760 Theyr chyldren sytteth by other mennes fyres, I have harde,
And some haunteth womens company
With unclene lyfe, as lustes of lechery.
These be with synne made blynde.
Fyve Wyttes I trust to God no suche may we fynde.
765 Therfore let us preesthode honour,
And folowe theyr doctryne for our soules socoure.
We be theyr shepe, and they shepeherdes be,
By whome we all be kepte in suerte.   safety
Peas! For yonder I se Everyman come,
770 Whiche hath made true satysfaccyon.
Good Dedes Me thynke it is he in dede.

[*Enter Everyman.*]
Everyman Now Jesu be your alder spede.   helper of you all
I have receyved the sacrament for my redempycon,
And than myne extreme unccyon.
775 Blessyd be all they that counseyled me to take it.
And now, frendes, let us go without longer respyte.
I thanke God that ye have taryed so longe.
Now set eche of you on this rodde your honde,   cross
And shortely folowe me.
780 I go before there I woíde be. God be our gyde.
Strength Everyman, we wyll not fro you go
Tyll ye have done this vyage longe.
Dyscrecyon I, Dyscrecyon, wyll byde by you also.
Knowlege And though this pylgrymage be never so stronge,   severe
785 I wyll never parte you fro.
Strength Everyman, I wyll be as sure by the
As ever I dyde by Judas Machabee.
Everyman Alas, I am so faynt, I may not stande.

---

787 **Judas Machabee:** leader of the Jews, he recognised the importance of godly dying.

My lymmes under me doth folde.
790 Frendes, let us not tourne agayne to this lande,
Not for all the worldes golde.
For in to this cave must I crepe
And tourne to erth, and there to slepe.
Beaute What, in to this grave? Alas.
795 *Everyman* Ye, there shall ye consume, more and lesse.
Beaute And what, sholde I smoder here?   suffocate
Everyman Ye, by my fayth, and never more appere.
In this worlde lyve no more we shall,
But in heven before the hyest Lorde of all.
800 *Beaute* I crosse out all this. Adewe, by Saynt Johan.
I take my tappe in my lappe and am gone.
Everyman What, Beaute, whyder wyll ye?
Beaute Peas! I am defe. I loke not behynde me,
Not and thou woldest gyve me all the golde in thy chest. [*Exit.*]
805 *Everyman* Alas, wherto may I truste?
Beaute gothe fast away fro me.
She promysed with me to lyve and dye.
Strength Everyman, I wyll the also forsake and denye;
Thy game lyketh me not at all.
810 *Everyman* Why than, ye wyll forsake me all?
Swete Strength, tary a lytell space.
Strength Nay, syr, by the rode of grace   cross
I wyll hye me from the fast,
Though thou wepe to thy herte to brast.
815 *Everyman* Ye wolde ever byde by me ye sayd.
Strength Ye, I have you ferre ynoughe conveyde.
Ye be olde ynoughe, I understande,
Your pylgrymage to take on hande.
I repent me that I hyder came.
820 *Everyman* Strength, you to dysplease I am to blame.
Wyll ye breke promyse that is dette?   obligation
Strength In fayth, I care not.
Thou arte but a foole to complayne.
You spende your speche and wast your brayne.
825 Go thryst the in to the grounde. [*Exit.*]
Everyman I had wende surer I sholde you have founde.   supposed
He that trusteth in his Strength,
She hym deceyveth at the length.
Bothe Strength and Beaute forsaketh me,
830 Yet they promysed me fayre and lovyngly.
Dyscrecyon Everyman, I wyll after Strength be gone.
As for me, I wyll leve you alone.
Everyman Why Dyscrecyon, wyll ye forsake me?

---

801 **tappe in my lappe**: proverbial way of saying I am going quickly.

Dyscrecyon Ye, in fayth, I wyll go fro the,
835   For whan Strength goth before
I folowe after ever more.
Everyman Yet, I pray the, for the love of the Trynyte,
Loke in my grave ones pyteously.
Dyscrecyon Nay, so nye wyll I not come.
840   Fare well, everychone. [*Exit.*]
Everyman Oh all thynge fayleth save God alone.
Beaute, Strength, and Dyscrecyon,
For whan Deth bloweth his blast,
They all renne fro me full fast.
845   **Fyve Wyttes** Everyman, my leve now of the I take.
I wyll folowe the other, for here I the forsake.
Everyman Alas, than may I wayle and wepe,
For I toke you for my best frende,
Fyve Wyttes I wyll no lenger the kepe.
850   Now fare well, and there an ende. [*Exit.*]
Everyman Oh Jesu, helpe! All hath forsaken me.
Good Dedes Nay, Everyman, I wyll byde with the.
I wyll not forsake the in dede.
Thou shalte fynde me a good frende at nede.
855   **Everyman** Gramercy, Good Dedes. Now may I true frendes se.
They have forsaken me, everychone.
I loved them better than my Good Dedes alone.
Knowlege, wyll ye forsake me also?
Knowlege Ye, Everyman, whan ye to Deth shall go.
860   But not yet, for no maner of daunger.
Everyman Gramercy, Knowlege, with all my herte.
Knowlege Nay, yet I wyll not from hens departe
Tyll I se where ye shall be come.
Everyman Me thynke, alas, that I must be gone
865   To make my rekenynge and my dettes paye,
For I se my tyme is nye spent awaye.
Take example all ye that this do here or se,
How they that I loved best do forsake me,
Excepte my Good Dedes that bydeth truely.
870   **Good Dedes** All erthly thynges is but vanyte;
Beaute, Strength, and Dyscrecyon do man forsake,
Folysshe frendes and kynnesmen that fayre spake,
All fleeth save Good Dedes, and that am I.
Everyman Have mercy on me, God moost myghty,
875   And stande by me thou moder & mayde, Holy Mary.
Good Dedes Fere not, I wyll speke for the.
Everyman Here I crye God mercy.
Good Dedes Shorte our ende and mynysshe our payne;   lessen
Let us go and never come agayne.
880   **Everyman** Into thy handes, Lorde, my soule I commende.

Receyve it, Lorde, that it be not lost.
As thou me boughtest, so me defende,
And save me from the fendes boost,   boast
That I may appere with that blessyd hoost   host
885   That shall be saved at the day of dome.
In manus tuas, of myghtes moost
For ever, *Commendo spiritum meum*. [*Exit Everyman and Good Dedes.*]
Knowlege Now hath he suffred that we all shall endure,
The Good Dedes shall make all sure.
890   Now hath he made endynge,
Me thynketh that I here aungelles synge,
And make grete joy and melody
Where Everymans soule receyved shall be. [*Exit.*]

[*Enter Aungell and Doctour.*]
The Aungell Come, excellente electe spouse, to Jesus.
895   Here above thou shalte go
Bycause of thy synguler vertue.
Now thy soule is taken thy body fro,
Thy rekenynge is crystall-clere.
Now shalte thou in to the hevenly sphere,
900   Unto the whiche all ye shall come
That lyveth well before the daye of dome.
Doctour This morall men may have in mynde.
Ye herers, take it of worth, olde and yonge,
And forsake Pryde, for he deceyveth you in the ende.
905   And remembre Beaute, Fyve Wyttes, Strength, & Dyscrecyon,
They all at the last do Everyman forsake,
Save his Good Dedes there dothe he take.
But beware, for and they be small,
Before God he hath no helpe at all,
910   None excuse may be there for Everyman.
Alas, how shall he do than?
For, after dethe, amendes may no man make,
For than mercy and pyte doth hym forsake.
If his rekenynge be not clere whan he doth come,
915   God wyll saye, '*Ite, maledicti, in ignem eternum.*'
And he that hath his accounte hole and sounde,
Hye in heven he shall be crounde.   crowned
Unto whiche place God brynge us all thyder,
That we may lyve body and soule togyder.
920   Therto helpe the Trynyte.
Amen, saye ye, for saynt charyte,

Thus endth this morall playe of Everyman.

---

885 **day of dome:** The general end of the world and Last Judgement.   **886–87 In manus . . . .:** the last words of
Christ on the cross, Luke 23:46. 'Into your hands I commend my spirit.'   **915 Ite . . . .:** Matthew 15:41. 'Go, sinner,
into eternal fire.'

Renaissance

From the fourteenth through the seventeenth centuries, the recovery of Roman and Greek writings from antiquity transformed European culture. After centuries in which the language, rhetoric, history, poetry and moral philosophy of the Classics were known in fragmentary ways, a study of the arts built on their foundations became seen as essential for understanding humanity's place in this world, and a key to fathoming human relations with the divine. A study of classical languages and literature became the central feature of an educational training which emphasised eloquence in speaking and writing, and which promoted literature as an important repository for understanding human action. Literacy grew and the establishing of printing in the mid-fifteenth century helped books to circulate widely, creating many shared cultural ideals.

While a rediscovery of classical ideas introduced a new dynamism into European thought, the Renaissance was also a period of contradictions which witnessed sinister developments, for instance the institutionalised persecution of people deemed to be witches. As Humanist writers sought to develop international links, the ideals and methods they encouraged helped to promote a questioning of previous social and religious organisations. This precipitated the division of the principal pan-European institution of the Medieval period, the Roman Catholic Church, unleashing conflicts between an increasingly Protestant north and a Catholic south. New tensions were also released as the European economy, and the social order it supported, changed from being almost wholly based on a feudal landed aristocracy to a framework increasingly dominated by the mercantile wealth of cities controlled by a growing middle class.

In fact, much of the Renaissance's intellectual vigour results from conflicts between new knowledge and old. The European discovery of the New World, greater exploration of Asia and Africa, and, through new optics, of the heavens, transformed the shape and size of the world and the cosmos. Explorations, too, of the human body in anatomy, matched with new inquiries into the conditions of their spiritual souls, offered Europeans an altered consciousness of 'who' they were and in what their identities rested, both as individuals and as communities. Even the centrality of Latin as the language of the best thought and expression competed with the development of vernacular literatures which often emphasised their integrity by using styles and genres different from classical models. Although a period celebrating the wonder of human potential, it was as much a time of scepticism and doubt.

The recovery of classical learning began in Italy and, in many respects, Britain was late participating in the European Renaissance. Little Humanist writing is undertaken here before the sixteenth century, and many continental models exert little influence until well into the seventeenth, a chronology which suggests an island culture slow to join in Renaissance trends.

Certainly, the civil wars which occupied England for much of the fifteenth century hindered the development of Renaissance culture which had seen some earlier manifestations (Chaucer's Italian contacts, for example). But British writers also appear genuinely reluctant to give up their preoccupations with chivalry and romance which had thrived during the Middle Ages. A classically based aesthetic, as developed on the continent, was never wholeheartedly embraced in Britain. Few authors during this period saw a need to emulate continental or classical models without deliberately transforming or 'Englishing' them.

For much of the sixteenth and seventeenth centuries Britain was spared the destructive wars which often plagued the continent. The advent of the Scot James VI as James I in 1603 combined England and Scotland under one rule. It was not, however, a golden age. The Reformation brought instability to the mid-sixteenth century and even Elizabeth I's reign saw threats of rebellion at home and foreign invasion – notably from Spain. In general, this period was disastrous for Ireland, which suffered under a new wave of colonial occupation by England. These changes of religion and political organisation in Britain brought new senses of national identity, but not of national harmony. The Renaissance in England culminates with a twenty-year period of civil wars (1640–1660), illustrating that the religious, social and political energies which the period generated did not work to create a kingdom at peace with itself.

SIR THOMAS MORE (1477/8–1535)

Thomas More was one of the earliest English Humanist writers to gain international recognition. *Utopia,* dating from 1515, participates in the discourse of the ideal commonwealth inaugurated by Plato's *Republic.* More coined the term utopia, deriving it from Greek so that it means both 'a good place' and 'a no place', and it is not clear how seriously we are supposed to take More's account as an illustration of a well-ordered state. The narrator describing it is Raphael Hythlodaeus (Hythloday) whose surname, also taken from Greek, means 'knowing in nonsense'. More's text reflects the classical tradition of *serio ludere* (to play seriously) where important points are made in the guise of jokes, but where it is not always clear what is serious and what a joke! *Utopia* was written in Latin. The version here is that of the first English translation made by Ralph Robinson in 1551. This excerpt is taken from The First Book where Raphael and More (himself a character in his book) are sitting in the Antwerp garden of the Humanist Peter Giles debating the question of how good advice can be given to a ruler.

From Utopia

'Well, let us proceed, then,' quoth he [Raphael Hythloday]. 'Suppose that some king and his council were together whetting[1] their wits and devising what subtle craft they might invent to enrich the king with great treasures of money. First one counselleth to raise and enhance the valuation of money when the king must pay any, and again to call down the value of coin to less than it is worth when he must receive or gather any. For thus great sums shall be paid

---

1 **whetting:** sharpening.

with a little money, and where little is due, much shall be received. Another counselleth to feign war, that when under this colour and pretence the king hath gathered great abundance of money, he may, when it shall please him, make peace with great solemnity and holy ceremonies to blind the eyes of the poor commonalty,[1] as taking pity and compassion forsooth upon man's blood like a loving and a merciful prince. Another putteth the king in remembrance of certain old and moth-eaten laws that of long time have not been put in execution, which, because no man can remember that they were made, every man hath transgressed. The fines of these laws he counselleth the king to require, for there is no way so profitable, nor more honourable, as the which hath a show and colour of justice. Another adviseth him to forbid many things under great penalties and fines, specially such things as is for the people's profit not be used,[2] and afterwards to dispense for money with them which by this prohibition sustain loss and damage. For by this means the favour of the people is won, and profit riseth two ways. First by taking forfeits[3] of them whom covetousness of gains hath brought in danger of this statute; and also by selling privileges and licences, which the better that the prince is forsooth, the dearer he selleth them, as one that is loath to grant to any private person anything that is against the profit of his people, and therefore may sell none but at an exceeding dear price.

'Another giveth the king counsel to endanger[4] unto his grace the judges of the realm that he may have them ever on his side, and that they may in every matter dispute and reason for the king's right. Yea, and further to call them into his palace and to require them there to argue and discuss his matters in his own presence. So there shall be no matter of his so openly wrong and unjust, wherein one or other of them, either because he will have something to allege and object, or that he is ashamed to say that which is said already, or else to pick a thank[5] with his prince, will not find some hole open to set a snare in, where with to take the contrary part in a trip.[6] Thus whilst the judges cannot agree amongst themselves, reasoning and arguing of that which is plain enough, and bringing the manifest truth in doubt, in the mean season[7] the king may take a fit occasion to understand the law as shall most make for his advantage, whereunto all other for shame or for fear will agree. Then the judges may be bold to pronounce on the king's side. For he that giveth sentence for the king cannot be without a good excuse. For it shall be sufficient for him to have equity[8] on his part, or the bare words of the law, or a writhen and wrested[9] understanding of the same, or else, which with good and just judges is of greater force than all laws be, the king's indisputable prerogative.

'To conclude, all the counsellors agree and consent together with the rich Crassus, that no abundance of gold can be sufficient for a prince which must keep and maintain an army;[10] furthermore that a king, though he would, can

---

1 **commonalty:** the common people (as distinct from the aristocracy). 2: things which are against the public interest. 3 **forfeits:** fines or penalties. 4 **endanger:** to make the judges subject to the king's will. 5 **pick a thank:** seek for favour. 6 **trip:** from wrestling, a move to overthrow an opponent. 7 **in the mean season:** in due course. 8 **equity:** being equal and fair. 9 **writhen and wrested:** twisted and stretched or strained. 10: adapted from Cicero's *On Moral Obligations* where the extremely rich Crassus claimed that no one could head the state unless he had enough money to maintain the army.

do nothing unjustly. For all that all men have, yea also the men themselves, be all his. And that every man hath so much of his own as the king's gentleness hath not taken from him. And that it shall be most for the king's advantage that his subjects have very little or nothing in their possession, as whose safeguard doth herein consist, that his people do not wax wanton and wealthy through riches and liberty, because where these things be, there men be not wont patiently to obey hard, unjust, and unlawful commandments; whereas, on the other part, need and poverty doth hold down and keep under stout courages, and maketh them patient perforce, taking from them bold and rebelling stomachs.

'Here, again, if I should rise up and boldly affirm that all these counsels be to the king dishonour and reproach, whose honour and safety is more and rather supported and upholden by the wealth and riches of his people than by his own treasures. And if I should declare that the commonalty chooseth their king for their own sake and not for his sake, to the intent that, through his labour and study, they might all live wealthily safe from wrongs and injuries; and that therefore the king ought to take more care for the wealth of his people than for his own wealth, even as the office and duty of a shepherd is, in that he is a shepherd, to feed his sheep rather than himself.

'For as touching this, that they think the defence and maintenance of peace to consist in the poverty of the people, the thing itself showeth that they be far out of the way. For where shall a man find more wrangling, quarrelling, brawling, and chiding, than among beggars? Who be more desirous of new mutations and alterations, than they that be not content with the present state of their life? Or, finally, who be bolder stomached to bring all in a hurly burly[1] (thereby trusting to get some windfall) than they that have now nothing to lose? And if any king were so smally regarded, and so lightly esteemed, yea, so be hated of his subjects that other ways he could not keep them in awe but only by open wrongs, by polling and shaving,[2] and by bringing them to beggary, surely it were better for him to forsake his kingdom than to hold it by this means, whereby though the name of a king be kept yet the majesty is lost. . . .

'Here if I should bring forth before them the law of the Macariens, which be not far distant from Utopia, whose king the day of his coronation is bound by a solemn oath that he shall never at any time have in his treasure above a thousand pound of gold or silver. They say a very good king, which took more care for the wealth and commodity of his country than for the enriching of himself, made this law to be a stop and a bar to kings from heaping and hoarding up so much money as might impoverish their people. For he foresaw that this sum of treasure would suffice to support the king in battle against his own people, if they should chance to rebel, and also to maintain his wars against the invasions of his foreign enemies. Again, he perceived the same stock of money to be too little and insufficient to encourage and enable him wrongfully to take away other men's goods, which was the chief cause why the law was made. Another cause was this. He thought that by this provision his people should not lack money wherewith to maintain their daily occupying and chaffer.[3] And seeing

---

1 **hurly burly:** commotion. 2 **polling and shaving:** cutting and trimming away at. 3 **chaffer:** buying and selling.

the king could not choose but lay out and bestow all that came in above the prescript sum of his stock, he thought he would seek no occasions to do his subjects injury. Such a king shall be feared of evil men and loved of good men. These, and such other informations, if I should use among men wholly inclined and given to the contrary part, how deaf hearers, think you, should I have?'

'Deaf hearers doubtless' (quoth I)[More], 'and in good faith no marvel. And to be plain with you, truly I cannot allow that such communication shall be used, or such counsel given, as you be sure shall never be regarded nor received. For how can so strange informations be profitable, or how can they be beaten into their heads, whose minds be already prevented with clean contrary persuasions? This school philosophy is not unpleasant among friends in familiar communication, but in the counsels of kings, where great matters be debated and reasoned with great authority, these things have no place.'

'That is it which I meant' (quoth he) 'when I said philosophy had no place among kings.'

'Indeed' (quoth I), 'this school philosophy hath not, which thinketh all things meet for every place. But there is another philosophy more civil, which knoweth, as ye would say, her own stage, and thereafter ordering and behaving herself in the play that she hath in hand, playeth her part accordingly with comeliness, uttering nothing out of due order and fashion. And this is the philosophy that you must use. Or else whilst a comedy of Plautus is playing, and the vile bondmen scoffing and trifling among themselves, if you should suddenly come upon the stage in a philosopher's apparel, and rehearse out of *Octavia* the place wherein Seneca disputeth with Nero,[1] had it not been better for you to have played the dumb person, than by rehearsing that which served neither for the time nor place to have made such a tragical comedy or gallimaufry?[2] For by bringing in other stuff that nothing appertaineth to the present matter, you must needs mar and pervert the play that is in hand, though the stuff that you bring be much better. What part soever you have taken upon you, play that as well as you can and make the best of it. And do not therefore disturb and bring out of order the whole matter, because that another, which is merrier and better, cometh to your remembrance.

'So the case standeth in a commonwealth, and so it is in the consultations of kings and princes. If evil opinions and naughty persuasions cannot be utterly and quite plucked out of their hearts, if you cannot, even as you would, remedy vices which use and custom hath confirmed, yet, for this cause, you must not leave and forsake the commonwealth. You must not forsake the ship in a tempest because you cannot rule and keep down the winds. No, nor you must not labour to drive into their heads new and strange informations which you know well shall be nothing regarded with them that be of clean contrary minds. But you must with a crafty wile and a subtle train study and endeavour yourself, as much as in you lieth, to handle the matter wittily and handsomely for the purpose, and that which you cannot turn to good, so to order it that it

---

1: a contrast between the ribald comedies of the Roman dramatist Plautus and the high seriousness of the tragedies of the philosopher Seneca. *Octavia*, in which Seneca appears as a character, was thought to be by Seneca at this time. Nero was the Roman emperor given to excess and debauchery. 2 **gallimaufry:** a ridiculous combination of bits and pieces.

be not very bad. For it is not possible for all things to be well, unless all men were good. Which I think will not be yet these good many years.'

'By this means' (quoth he) 'nothing else will be brought to pass, but while that I go about to remedy the madness of others, I should be even as mad as they. For if I would speak such things that be true, I must needs speak such things; but, as for to speak false things, whether that be a philosopher's part or no I cannot tell, truly it is not my part.

'Howbeit this communication of mine, though peradventure it may seem unpleasant to them, yet can I not see why it should seem strange or foolishly new-fangled. If so be that I should speak those things that Plato feigneth in his weal public,[1] or that the Utopians do in theirs, these things, though they were (as they be indeed) better, yet they might seem spoken out of place. Forasmuch as here among us, every man hath his possessions several to himself, and there all things be common. But what was in my communication contained, that might not, and ought not, in any place to be spoken? Saving that to them which have thoroughly decreed and determined with themselves to run head-long the contrary way it cannot be acceptable and pleasant, because it calleth them back and showeth them the jeopardies.[2] Verily, if all things that evil and vicious manners have caused to seem inconvenient and naught should be refused as things unmeet and reproachful, then we must among Christian people wink at the most part of all those things which Christ taught us; and so straightly forbade them to be winked at, that those things also which He whispered in the ears of His disciples He commanded to be proclaimed in open houses. And yet the most part of them are more dissident from the manners of the world nowadays than my communication was.

'But preachers, sly and wily men, following your counsel (as I suppose), because they saw men evil-willing to frame their manners to Christ's rule, they have wrested and wryed[3] his doctrine, and like a rule of lead[4] have applied it to men's manners that, by some means at the least way, they might agree together. Whereby I cannot see what good they have done, but that men may more sickerly[5] be evil. And I truly should prevail even as little in kings' councils. For either I must say otherwise than they say, and then I were as good to say nothing, or else I must say the same that they say, and (as Mitio saith in Terence)[6] help to further their madness.

'For that crafty wile and subtle train of yours, I cannot perceive to what purpose it serveth, wherewith you would have me to study and endeavour myself, if all things cannot be made good, yet to handle them wittily and hand-somely for the purpose that, as far forth as is possible, they may not be very evil. For there is no place to dissemble in, nor to wink in. Naughty counsels must be openly allowed, and very pestilent decrees must be approved. He shall be counted worse than a spy, yea, almost as evil as a traitor, that with a faint heart doth praise evil and noisome[7] decrees. Moreover, a man can have no

---

1: a characteristic playfulness by More, comparing precepts Plato created in *The Republic*'s fictional ideal state with the supposed actual practice of the Utopians. **2 jeopardies:** risks. **3 wryed:** distorted. **4:** a flexible measuring rod of lead used in architecture. Aristotle cites it as a metaphor for adaptable morality. Here, too, as opposed to a golden rule of good instruction (notably Matthew 7:12, what you would have done to you, do to others). **5 sickerly:** securely. **6:** allusion to Terence's comedy, *The Brothers*. **7 noisome:** harmful.

occasion to do good, chancing into the company of them which will sooner pervert a good man than be made good themselves, through whose evil company he shall be marred, or else, if he remain good and innocent, yet the wickedness and folly of others shall be imputed to him and laid in his neck. So that it is impossible with that crafty wile and subtle train to turn anything to better. . . .

'Howbeit, doubtless, Master More (to speak truly as my mind giveth me), where possessions be private, where money beareth all the stroke,[1] it is hard and almost impossible that there the weal public may justly be governed and prosperously flourish. Unless you think thus: that Justice is there executed where all things come into the hands of evil men; or that prosperity there flourisheth where all is divided among a few, which few nevertheless do not lead their lives very wealthily, and the residue live miserably, wretchedly, and beggarly.

'Wherefore when I consider with myself and weigh in my mind the wise and godly ordinances of the Utopians, among whom, with very few laws, all things be so well and wealthily ordered that virtue is had in prize and estimation, and, yet all things being there common, every man hath abundance of everything. Again, on the other part, when I compare with them so many nations ever making new laws, yet none of them all well and sufficiently furnished with laws, where every man calleth that he hath gotten his own proper and private goods, where so many new laws daily made be not sufficient for every man to enjoy, defend, and know from another man's that which he calleth his own; which thing the infinite controversies in the law, daily rising, never to be ended, plainly declare to be true.

'These things (I say), when I consider with myself, I hold well with Plato, and do nothing marvel that he would make no laws for them that refused those laws whereby all men should have and enjoy equal portions of wealth and commodities. For the wise man did easily foresee this to be the one and only way to the wealth of a community, if equality of all things should be brought in and established. Which I think is not possible to be observed where every man's goods be proper and peculiar to himself. For where every man under certain titles and pretences draweth and plucketh to himself as much as he can, so that a few divide among themselves all the whole riches, be there never so much abundance and store, there to the residue is left lack and poverty. And for the most part it chanceth that this latter sort is more worthy to enjoy that state of wealth than the other be, because the rich men be covetous, crafty, and unprofitable. On the other part, the poor be lowly, simple, and by their daily labour more profitable to the commonwealth than to themselves.

'Thus I do fully persuade myself that no equal and just distribution of things can be made, nor that perfect wealth shall ever be among men, unless this propriety[2] be exiled and banished. But so long as it shall continue, so long shall remain among the most and best part of men the heavy and inevitable burden of poverty and wretchedness.'

---

1 **beareth all the stroke**: is the measurement of everything.   2 **propriety**: property.

SIR THOMAS WYATT (1503–1542)

Born into an aristocratic family and educated at Cambridge, Wyatt held posts in Henry VIII's government. Diplomatic missions to France and Italy brought him into contact with the continental Renaissance and he became one of the first English poets to imitate Petrarchan forms. His intimacy with Anne Boleyn, as well as involvements with other court intrigues, caused Wyatt to be arrested a number of times, and his verse reflects the precariousness of a courtly life where there is no clear division between private and public affairs. Wyatt rarely punctuated his poems. This certainly increases their ambivalence of meaning and may reflect an author wishing to be discreet about his poetry's political intent.

[The long love that in my thought doth harbour]

The long love that in my thought doth harbour
And in mine heart doth keep his residence
Into my face presseth with bold pretence
And therein campeth spreading his banner
5   She that me learneth to love and suffer
And will that my trust and lust's negligence
Be reined by reason shame and reverence
With his hardiness taketh displeasure
Wherewithal unto the heart's forest he fleeth
10   Leaving his enterprise with pain and cry
And there him hideth and not appeareth
What may I do when my master feareth
But in the field with him to live and die
For good is the life ending faithfully

[They flee from me that sometime did me seek]

They flee from me that sometime did me seek
With naked foot stalking in my chamber
I have seen them gentle tame and meek
That now are wild and do not remember
5   That sometime they put themself in danger
To take bread at my hand and now they range
Busily seeking with a continual change

Thanked be fortune it hath been otherwise
Twenty times better but once in special
10   In thin array after a pleasant guise

The long . . . . : Wyatt's version of Petrarch's *Amor, che nel penser mio vive e regna*. 1: Wyatt personifies his love as his Soverign, moving from his heart to his face to prepare for battle. 5 me learneth: teaches me. 7 reined: held in or ruled. 8 hardiness: boldness. 12 master: Wyatt's love. They flee . . . . 2 stalking: moving quietly. 10 guise: manner, also as dress or appearance.

When her loose gown from her shoulders did fall
And she me caught in her arms long and small
Therewithal sweetly did me kiss
And softly said dear heart how like you this

15   It was no dream I lay broad waking
But all is turned thorough my gentleness
Into a strange fashion of forsaking
And I have leave to go of her goodness
And she also to use newfangleness
20   But since that I so kindly am served
I would fain know what she has deserved

[Each man me telleth I change most my device]

Each man me telleth I change most my device
And on my faith me think it good reason
To change propose like after the season
For in every case to keep still one guise
5   Is meet for them that would be taken wise
And I am not of such manner condition
But treated after a diverse fashion
And thereupon my diverseness doth rise
But you that blame this diverseness most
10   Change you no more but still after one rate
Treat ye me well and keep ye in the same state
And while with me doth dwell this wearied ghost
My word nor I shall not be variable
But always one your own both firm and stable

[Whoso list to hunt I know where is an hind]

Whoso list to hunt I know where is an hind
But as for me helas I may no more
The vain travail hath wearied me so sore
I am of them that farthest cometh behind
5   Yet may I by no means my wearied mind
Draw from the deer but as she fleeth afore
Fainting I follow I leave off therefore
Sithens in a net I seek to hold the wind
Who list her hunt I put him out of doubt
10   As well as I may spend his time in vain

---

16 **gentleness:** courtesy. 19 **newfangleness:**
novelty. 21 **fain:** gladly. **Each man . . . . 1 device:**
desire, stratagem, or emblematic or heraldic design.
3 **propose:** purpose. 4 **guise:** manner, also as dress or
appearance. 10 **rate:** consistent value.

Whoso list . . . . : the sonnet alludes to Wyatt's affair
with Anne Boleyn when Henry VIII claimed her.
1 **list:** likes. **hind:** female deer. 2 **helas:** alas.
8 **sithens:** since.

And graven with diamonds in letters plain
There is written her fair neck round about
Noli me tangere for Caesar's I am
And wild for to hold though I seem tame

[Mine own John Poyntz since ye delight to know]

Mine own John Poyntz since ye delight to know
 The cause why that homeward I me draw
 And flee the press of courts whereso they go,
Rather than to live thrall under the awe
5 Of lordly looks, wrapped within my cloak,
 To will and lust learning to set a law,
It is not for because I scorn or mock
 The power of them to whom fortune hath lent
 Charge over us, of right to strike the stroke,
10 But true it is that I have always meant
 Less to esteem them than the common sort,
 Of outward things that judge in their intent
Without regard what doth inward resort.
 I grant sometime that of glory the fire
15 Doth touch my heart, me list not to report
Blame by honour, and honour to desire,
 But how may I this honour now attain
 That cannot dye the colour black a liar?
My Poyntz I cannot frame my tongue to feign
20 To cloak the truth for praise without desert
 Of them that list all vice for to retain.
I cannot honour them that sets their part
 With Venus and Bacchus all their life long
 Nor hold my peace of them although I smart.
25 I cannot crouch nor kneel to do so great a wrong
 To worship them like God on earth alone
 That are as wolves these seely lambs among.
I cannot with my word complain and moan
 And suffer nought nor smart without complaint
30 Nor turn the word that from my mouth is gone.

---

13 *noli* . . . : 'do not touch me'; Christ's words to Mary Magdalen, also the motto on the collars of Caesar's deer.   **Caesar's I am**: Matthew 22:21, render to Caesar what is Caesar's.   **Mine Own John Poyntz** . . . . : Poyntz was one of Henry VIII's courtiers. Little is known about this friend of Wyatt.   **3 press**: crowd.   **4 thrall**: bondage, slavery.   **6**: teach myself self-control over my appetites.   **9 of right** . . . . : the right to punish.   **11 common sort**: common people, not nobles.

13 **resort**: dwell in.   **15–16**: I have no wish to speak ill of honour.   **18**: I cannot call black any other colour than black.   **20**: I cannot conceal truths about the unpraiseworthy who wish to keep their vices.   **23 Venus, Bacchus**: gods of sexual appetite and drunkenness.   **27 seely**: simple.   **28–29**: I cannot claim to be suffering when I am not suffering, nor go back on what I say.

I cannot speak and look like a saint
  Use wiles for wit and make deceit a pleasure
  And call craft counsel, for profit still to paint.
I cannot wrest the law to fill the coffer,
35   With innocent blood to feed myself fat
  And do most hurt where most help I offer.
I am not he that can allow the state
  Of him Caesar and damn Cato to die,
  That with his death did 'scape out of the gate
40 From Caesar's hands, if Livy do not lie,
  And would not live where liberty was lost
  So did his heart the common weal apply.
I am not he such eloquence to boast
  To make the crow singing as the swan
45   Nor call the lion of coward beasts the most
That cannot take a mouse as the cat can,
  And he that dieth for hunger of the gold
  Call him Alexander, and say that Pan
Passeth Apollo in music manifold,
50   Praise Sir Thopas for a noble tale
  And scorn the story that the knight told,
Praise him for counsel that is drunk of ale
  Grin when he laugheth that beareth all the sway
  Frown when he frowneth and groan when he is pale,
55 On others lust to hang both night and day.
  None of these points would ever frame in me,
  My wit is nought, I cannot learn the way,
And much the less of things that greater be
  That asken help of colours of device
60   To join the mean with each extremity,
With the nearest virtue to cloak alway the vice,
  And, as to purpose likewise it shall fall,
  To press the virtue that it may not rise.
As drunkenness good fellowship to call,
65   The friendly foe with his double face
  Say he is gentle and courteous therewithal,
And say that Favel hath a goodly grace
  In eloquence, and cruelty to name
  Zeal of justice and change in time and place,

33: I cannot call deceit good advice and colour things for my own profit. **37–40:** the Roman historian Livy records that Cato killed himself in 46 BC to avoid being captured by Caesar, exemplifying quiet resistance to tyranny. **37 allow:** approve. **47–48:** I will not say that Midas (who loved gold) is Alexander the Great, or that the god Pan's rustic music cannot be compared with the heavenly music of Apollo.

50: Chaucer's Sir Thopas in *The Canterbury Tales* tells a travesty of a tale of courtly romance. **56 frame:** appeal. **57–60:** I cannot use rhetoric to colour small things as bigger or to combine the moderate with the extreme. **61:** use one virtue to hide vices, or by some opportunity to smother virtue by calling it vice. **67 Favel:** a common personification of flattery. **68–69:** to call cruelty justice because of circumstances.

70 And he that sufferth offence without blame
    Call him pitiful, and him true and plain
    That raileth reckless to every man's shame,
Say he is rude that cannot lie and feign
    The lecher a lover, and tyranny
75 To be the right of a prince's reign.
    I cannot, I, no, no, it will not be.
        This is the cause that I could never yet
        Hang on their sleeves that weigh as thou mayst see
A chip of chance more than a pound of wit.
80   This maketh me at home to hunt and to hawk
        And in foul weather at my book to sit,
In frost and snow then with my bow to stalk,
        No man doth mark whereso I ride or go,
        In lusty leas at liberty I walk
85 And of these news I feel nor weal nor woe
        Save that a clog doth hang yet at my heel,
        No force for that, for it is ordered so
That I may leap both hedge and dike full well.
        I am not now in France to judge the wine
90   With savoury sauce the delicates to feel;
Nor yet in Spain where one must him incline,
        Rather than to be, outwardly to seem,
        I meddle not with wits that be so fine;
Nor Flanders' cheer letteth not my sight to deem
95   Of black and white nor taketh my wit away
        With beastliness, they beasts do so esteem;
Nor I am not where Christ is given in prey
        For money poison and treason at Rome,
        A common practice used night and day.
100 But here I am in Kent and Christendom
        Among the Muses where I read and rhyme,
        Where if thou list my Poyntz for to come,
Thou shalt be judge how I do spend my time.

---

84 **lusty leas:** pleasant pastures. 86 **clog:** block 94: the good food and drink of Flanders does not
attached to a prisoner's leg; Wyatt is referring to a prevent me telling black from white. **deem:** judge.
period of house arrest. 90 **delicates:** delicacies.

HENRY HOWARD, EARL OF SURREY
(1517–1547)

Surrey was the eldest son of the 3rd Duke of Norfolk and a member of one of the most powerful families in England. He held various positions in the court of Henry VIII and fought against the Scots and French. His loyalty, however, was frequently questioned and he was finally arrested and beheaded on charges of treason. Like his friend Wyatt, Surrey sought to emulate both classical and continental literary elegance. In seeking to remain true to the rhetorical and linguistic spirit of his original, Surrey introduced blank verse into English in his translation of Virgil's *Aeneid*.

[Love that doth reign and live within my thought]

Love that doth reign and live within my thought
And built his seat within my captive breast
Clad in the arms wherein with me he fought
Oft in my face he doth his banner rest
5   But she that taught me love and suffer pain
My doubtful hope and eke my hot desire
With shamefast look to shadow and refrain
Her smiling grace converteth straight to ire
And coward Love then to the heart apace
10   Taketh his flight where he doth lurk and plain
His purpose lost and dare not show his face
For my lord's guilt thus faultless bide I pain
Yet from my lord shall not my foot remove
Sweet is the death that taketh end by love

[W resteth here that quick could never rest]

W resteth here that quick could never rest,
Whose heavenly gifts encreased by disdain
And virtue sank the deeper in his breast,
Such profit he by envy could obtain.
5   A head where wisdom mysteries did frame,
Whose hammers beat still in that lively brain
As on a stithy where that some work of fame
Was daily wrought to turn to Britain's gain.
A visage stern and mild, where both did grow
10   Vice to contemn, in virtue to rejoice;
Amid great storms whom grace assured so
To live upright and smile at fortune's choice.

Love ... : a version of the same Petrarch sonnet as Wyatt's 'The Long love ...'. 6 **eke**: also. 10 **plain**: complain, lament. 12 **bide**: endure.   11 **foot remove**: military imagery: 'I will not abandon or retreat from'. **W ....**: Sir Thomas Wyatt. 1 **quick**: alive. 5 **mysteries**: deep thoughts. 7 **stithy**: anvil.

A hand that taught what might be said in rhyme,
That reft Chaucer the glory of his wit;
15 A mark the which unparfited for time,
Some may approach but never none shall hit.
A tongue that served in foreign realms his king;
Whose courteous talk to virtue did enflame
Each noble heart, a worthy guide to bring
20 Our English youth by travail unto fame.
An eye whose judgement none affect could blind,
Friends to allure and foes to reconcile,
Whose piercing look did represent a mind
With virtue fraught, reposed, void of guile.
25 A heart where dread was never so impressed
To hide the thought that might the truth advance;
In neither fortune loft nor yet repressed
To swell in wealth or yield unto mischance.
A valiant corps, where force and beauty met;
30 Happy, alas, too happy but for foes;
Lived and ran the race that nature set
Of manhood's shape where she the mould did lose.
But to the heavens that simple soul is fled,
Which left with such as covet Christ to know
35 Witness of faith that never shall be dead,
Sent for our health but not received so.
Thus, for our guilt this jewel have we lost.
The earth his bones, the heavens possess his ghost.

From Book Two of Virgil's *Aeneid*

When that I saw in Vesta's temple sit
Dame Helen, lurking in a secret place
(Such light the flame did give as I went by
While here and there I cast mine eyes about)
5 For she in dread least that the Trojans should
Revenge on her the ruin of their walls,
And of the Greeks the cruel wrekes also,
The fury eke of her forsaken make,
The common bane of Troy, and eke of Greece,
10 Hateful she sat beside the altars hid.
Then boiled my breast with flame and burning wrath
To revenge my town unto such ruin brought,
With worthy pains on her to work my will.
Thought I: 'Shall she pass to the land of Spart

---

14 **reft**: deprived. 15 **unparfited for time**: incomplete through lack of time. 21 **affect**: passion, bias. 24 **fraught**: equipped. 27 **loft**: elevated.

29 **corps**: body. *Aeneid*, Book II, ll. 744–72. 7 **wrekes**: revenge. 8 **eke**: moreover, also. **make**: gender. 9 **bane**: destroyer. 13 **pains**: punishment.

15   All safe, and see Mycene her native land,
       And like a queen return with victory
       Home to her spouse, her parents and children,
       Followed with a train of Trojan maids
       And served with a band of Phrygian slaves;
20   And Priam eke with iron murdered thus
       And Troy town consumed all with flame,
       Whose shore hath been so oft forebathed in blood?
       No, no. For though on women the revenge
       Unseemly is, such conquest hath no fame,
25   To give an end unto such mischief yet
       My just revenge shall merit worthy praise
       And quiet eke my mind, for to be wroke
       On her which was the causer of this flame,
       And satisfy the cinder of my feers.'

EDMUND SPENSER (*c.*1552–1599)

Spenser was educated in London and Cambridge. In 1580 he became secretary to Lord Grey of Wilton, Lord Deputy of Ireland, and was given lands there. He favoured a militant Protestantism both at home and abroad, and believed in the public role of poetry as a vehicle for developing a Protestant culture in England. *The Faerie Queene's* first three books were published in 1590, III to VI in 1596. Spenser describes his poem as being 'to fashion a gentleman or noble person in vertuous and gentle discipline', working by means of 'a continued allegory or darke conceit'. Although set in legendary Arthurian times, and adopting many conventions from romance, the poem draws parallels between its fictional past and the real Elizabethan present. Spenser often deliberately cultivates a linguistic archaism, part of his desire to portray a native heroic heritage for England. In this section Sir Guyon or Temperance concludes his central adventure.

From The Faerie Queene

Book II, Canto XII

> *Guyon, by Palmers gouernance,*
>   *passing through perils great,*
> *Doth ouerthrow the Bowre of blisse,*
>   *and Acrasie defeat.* *

1   Now gins this goodly frame of Temperance
       Fairely to rise, and her adorned hed
       To pricke of highest praise forth to aduance,
       Formerly grounded, and fast setteled

---

15 Mycene: Mycenae, here meaning Greece as a whole. **19 Phyrgian:** Trojan. **27 wroke:** revenged. **29 cinder of my feers:** the ashes of my companions.

* **Palmer:** a pilgrim; carrying a palm indicates a visit to the Holy Land. **Bowre:** bower, an arbour in a garden or a private room, often a bedroom. **1,1 frame:** structure. **3 pricke of:** to the position.

On firme foundation of true bountihed;
And this braue knight, that for that vertue fights,
Now comes to point of that same perilous sted,
Where Pleasure dwelles in sensuall delights,
Mongst thousand dangers, & ten thousand magick mights.

2   Two dayes now in that sea he sayled has,
Ne euer land beheld, ne liuing wight,
Ne ought saue perill, still as he did pas:
Tho when appeared the third *Morrow* bright,
Vpon the waues to spred her trembling light,
An hideous roaring farre away they heard,
That all their senses filled with affright,
And streight they saw the raging surges reard
Vp to the skyes, that them of drowning made affeard.

3   Said then the Boteman, Palmer stere aright,
And keepe an euen course; for yonder way
We needes must passe (God do vs well acquight,)
That is the *Gulfe of Greedinesse*, they say,
That deepe engorgeth all this worldes pray:
Which hauing swallowd vp excessiuely,
He soone in vomit vp againe doth lay,
And belcheth forth his superfluity,
That all the seas for feare do seeme away to fly.

4   On th'other side an hideous Rocke is pight,
Of mightie *Magnes* stone, whose craggie clift
Depending from on high, dreadfull to sight,
Ouer the waues his rugged armes doth lift,
And threatneth downe to throw his ragged rift
On who so commeth nigh; yet nigh it drawes
All passengers, that none from it can shift:
For whiles they fly that Gulfes deuouring iawes,
They on this rock are rent, and sunck in helplesse wawes.

5   Forward they passe, and strongly he them rowes,
Vntill they nigh vnto that Gulfe arriue,
Where streame more violent and greedy growes:
Then he with all his puissance doth striue
To strike his oares, and mightily doth driue
The hollow vessell through the threatfull waue,
Which gaping wide, to swallow them aliue,
In th'huge abysse of his engulfing graue,
Doth rore at them in vaine, and with great terror raue.

---

5 **bountihed:** goodness.   **2,2 wight:** creature, person.   **3,3 Gulfe of. . . .:** Charybdis of *Odyssey* Bk 12.   7 **lay:** throw.   **4,1 hideous Rocke:** Scylla of *Odyssey* Bk 12.   **pight:** placed.   **4,2 Magnes:** the magnet or loadstone, believed to attract the iron on ships.   3 **depending:** hanging down.   5 **rift:** rocks split from the cliff.   9 **wawes:** waves, also suggesting woes.   **5,4 puissance:** power.

6   They passing by, that griesly mouth did see,
      Sucking the seas into his entralles deepe,
      That seem'd more horrible then hell to bee,
      Or that darke dreadfull hole of *Tartare* steepe,
      Through which the damned ghosts doen often creepe
      Backe to the world, bad liuers to torment:
      But nought that falles into this direfull deepe,
      Ne that approcheth nigh the wide descent,
    May backe returne, but is condemned to be drent.

7   On th'other side, they saw that perilous Rocke,
      Threatning it selfe on them to ruinate,
      On whose sharpe clifts the ribs of vessels broke,
      And shiuered ships, which had bene wrecked late,
      Yet stuck, with carkasses exanimate
      Of such, as hauing all their substance spent
      In wanton ioyes, and lustes intemperate,
      Did afterwards make shipwracke violent,
    Both of their life, and fame for euer fowly blent.

8   For thy, this hight *The Rocke of vile Reproch*,
      A daungerous and detestable place,
      To which nor fish nor fowle did once approch,
      But yelling Meawes, with Seagulles hoarse and bace,
      And Cormoyrants, with birds of rauenous race,
      Which still sate waiting on that wastfull clift,
      For spoyle of wretches, whose vnhappie cace,
      After lost credite and consumed thrift,
    At last them driuen hath to this despairefull drift.

9   The Palmer seeing them in safetie past,
      Thus said; Behold th'ensamples in our sights,
      Of lustfull luxurie and thriftlesse wast:
      What now is left of miserable wights,
      Which spent their looser daies in lewd delights,
      But shame and sad reproch, here to be red,
      By these rent reliques, speaking their ill plights?
      Let all that liue, hereby be counselled,
    To shunne *Rocke of Reproch*, and it as death to dred.

10   So forth they rowed, and that *Ferryman*
      With his stiffe oares did brush the sea so strong,
      That the hoare waters from his frigot ran,
      And the light bubbles daunced all along,
      Whiles the salt brine out of the billowes sprong.

6,4 **Tartare:** Tartarus, place of punishment. 9 **drent:** drowned. 7,2 **ruinate:** bring to ruin. 4 **shiuered:** broken. 5 **exanimate:** dead. 9 **blent:** spoiled. 8,4 **Meawes:** common sea-gulls. 8,5 **Cormoyrants:** seabirds (along with gulls) used as symbols of greed. 6 **wastfull:** desolate. 9 **drift:** course. 10,3 **hoare:** white with foam. **frigot:** boat.

At last farre off they many Islands spy,
On euery side floting the floods emong:
Then said the knight, Loe I the land descry,
Therefore old Syre thy course do thereunto apply.

11   That may not be, said then the *Ferryman*
Least we vnweeting hap to be fordonne:
For those same Islands, seeming now and than,
Are not firme land, nor any certein wonne,
But straggling plots, which to and fro do ronne
In the wide waters: therefore are they hight
The *wandring Islands*. Therefore doe them shonne;
For they haue oft drawne many a wandring wight
Into most deadly daunger and distressed plight.

12   Yet well they seeme to him, that farre doth vew,
Both faire and fruitfull, and the ground dispred
With grassie greene of delectable hew,
And the tall trees with leaues apparelled,
Are deckt with blossomes dyde in white and red,
That mote the passengers thereto allure;
But whosoeuer once hath fastened
His foot thereon, may neuer it recure,
But wandreth euer more vncertein and vnsure.

13   As th'Isle of *Delos* whylome men report
Amid th'*Aegaean* sea long time did stray,
Ne made for shipping any certaine port,
Till that *Latona* traueiling that way,
Flying from *Iunoes* wrath and hard assay,
Of her faire twins was there deliuered,
Which afterwards did rule the night and day;
Thenceforth it firmely was established,
And for *Apolloes* honor highly herried.

14   They to him hearken, as beseemeth meete,
And passe on forward: so their way does ly,
That one of those same Islands, which doe fleet
In the wide sea, they needes must passen by,
Which seemd so sweet and pleasant to the eye,
That it would tempt a man to touchen there:
Vpon the banck they sitting did espy
A daintie damzell, dressing of her heare,
By whom a litle skippet floting did appeare.

11,2 **vnweeting:** unexpectedly. **fordonne:** killed.
3 **seeming:** appearing. 4 **wonne:** dwelling. 12,6 **mote:**
might or must. 8 **recure:** recover.

13,1 ***Delos:*** in Ovid a wandering island where Latona,
pregnant by Jupiter, fled to. Jupiter made the island
stand still and she gave birth to the gods Apollo
and Diana. 5 **assay:** pursuit. 9 **herried:** praised.
14,3 **fleet:** float. 9 **skippet:** a small boat.

15   She them espying, loud to them can call,
       Bidding them nigher draw vnto the shore;
       For she had cause to busie them withall;
       And therewith loudly laught: But nathemore
       Would they once turne, but kept on as afore:
       Which when she saw, she left her lockes vndight,
       And running to her boat withouten ore,
       From the departing land it launched light,
    And after them did driue with all her power and might.

16   Whom ouertaking, she in merry sort
       Them gan to bord, and purpose diuersly,
       Now faining dalliance and wanton sport,
       Now throwing forth lewd words immodestly;
       Till that the Palmer gan full bitterly
       Her to rebuke, for being loose and light:
       Which not abiding, but more scornefully
       Scoffing at him, that did her iustly wite,
    She turnd her bote about, and from them rowed quite.

17   That was the wanton *Phaedria*, which late
       Did ferry him ouer the *Idle lake*:
       Whom nought regarding, they kept on their gate,
       And all her vaine allurements did forsake,
       When them the wary Boateman thus bespake;
       Here now behoueth vs well to auyse,
       And of our safetie good heede to take;
       For here before a perlous passage lyes,
    Where many Mermayds haunt, making false melodies.

18   But by the way, there is a great Quicksand,
       And a whirlepoole of hidden ieopardy,
       Therefore, Sir Palmer, keepe an euen hand;
       For twixt them both the narrow way doth ly.
       Scarse had he said, when hard at hand they spy
       That quicksand nigh with water couered;
       But by the checked waue they did descry
       It plaine, and by the sea discoloured:
    It called was the quicksand of *Vnthriftyhed*.

19   They passing by, a goodly Ship did see,
       Laden from far with precious merchandize,
       And brauely furnished, as ship might bee,
       Which through great disauenture, or mesprize,
       Her selfe had runne into that hazardize;

15,1 can: did. 6 vndight: unadorned, in a loose state.   17,3 gate: way. 6 auyse: take thought. 18,7 checked
8 light: quickly. 16,2 bord: accost. purpose diuersly: wave: held back by the sand. 19,4 disauenture: mishap.
talk of various things. 8 wite: blame. 17,1 *Phaedria*: mesprize: mistake.
Greek meaning 'shining one'.

Whose mariners and merchants with much toyle,
Labour'd in vaine, to haue recur'd their prize,
And the rich wares to saue from pitteous spoyle,
But neither toyle nor trauell might her backe recoyle.

20   On th'other side they see that perilous Poole,
That called was the *Whirlepoole of decay*,
In which full many had with haplesse doole
Beene suncke, of whom no memorie did stay:
Whose circled waters rapt with whirling sway,
Like to a restlesse wheele, still running round,
Did couet, as they passed by that way,
To draw their boate within the vtmost bound
Of his wide *Labyrinth*, and then to haue them dround.

21   But th'heedfull Boateman strongly forth did stretch
His brawnie armes, and all his body straine,
That th'vtmost sandy breach they shortly fetch,
Whiles the dred daunger does behind remaine.
Suddeine they see from midst of all the Maine,
The surging waters like a mountaine rise,
And the great sea puft vp with proud disdaine,
To swell aboue the measure of his guise,
As threatning to deuoure all, that his powre despise.

22   The waues come rolling, and the billowes rore
Outragiously, as they enraged were,
Or wrathfull *Neptune* did them driue before
His whirling charet, for exceeding feare:
For not one puffe of wind there did appeare,
That all the three thereat woxe much afrayd,
Vnweeting, what such horrour straunge did reare.
Eftsoones they saw an hideous hoast arrayd,
Of huge Sea monsters, such as liuing sence dismayd.

23   Most vgly shapes, and horrible aspects,
Such as Dame Nature selfe mote feare to see,
Or shame, that euer should so fowle defects
From her most cunning hand escaped bee;
All dreadfull pourtraicts of deformitee:
Spring-headed *Hydraes*, and sea-shouldring Whales,
Great whirlpooles, which all fishes make to flee,
Bright Scolopendraes, arm'd with siluer scales,
Mighty *Monoceros*, with immeasured tayles.

19,7 recur'd: recovered. 9 recoyle: retrieve. 20,3 doole:
grief. 21,3 fetch: reach. 5 Maine: ocean. 22,4 charet:
chariot. 7 reare: cause. 8 Eftsoones: at once. 23,2 mote:
might.

23,6 *Hydraes*: seven-headed serpents. sea-shouldring:
lifting the sea; the whale Leviathan of Job 40:20.
7 whirlpooles: spouting whales. 8 Scolopendraes:
centipede-like fish. 9 *Monoceros*: single-horned fish.

24   The dreadfull Fish, that hath deseru'd the name
      Of Death, and like him lookes in dreadfull hew,
      The griesly Wasserman, that makes his game
      The flying ships with swiftnesse to pursew,
      The horrible Sea-satyre, that doth shew
      His fearefull face in time of greatest storme,
      Huge *Ziffius*, whom Mariners eschew
      No lesse, then rockes, (as trauellers informe,)
  And greedy *Rosmarines* with visages deforme.

25   All these, and thousand thousands many more,
      And more deformed Monsters thousand fold,
      With dreadfull noise, and hollow rombling rore,
      Came rushing in the fomy waues enrold,
      Which seem'd to fly for feare, them to behold:
      Ne wonder, if these did the knight appall;
      For all that here on earth we dreadfull hold,
      Be but as bugs to fearen babes withall,
  Compared to the creatures in the seas entrall.

26   Feare nought, (then said the Palmer well auiz'd;)
      For these same Monsters are not these in deed,
      But are into these fearefull shapes disguiz'd
      By that same wicked witch, to worke vs dreed,
      And draw from on this iourney to proceede.
      Tho lifting vp his vertuous staffe on hye,
      He smote the sea, which calmed was with speed,
      And all that dreadfull Armie fast gan flye
  Into great *Tethys* bosome, where they hidden lye.

27   Quit from that daunger, forth their course they kept,
      And as they went, they heard a ruefull cry
      Of one, that wayld and pittifully wept,
      That through the sea the resounding plaints did fly:
      At last they in an Island did espy
      A seemely Maiden, sitting by the shore,
      That with great sorrow and sad agony,
      Seemed some great misfortune to deplore,
  And lowd to them for succour called euermore.

28   Which *Guyon* hearing, streight his Palmer bad,
      To stere the boate towards that dolefull Mayd,
      That he might know, and ease her sorrow sad:
      Who him auizing better, to him sayd;
      Faire Sir, be not displeasd, if disobayd:

24,2 Death: the walrus or morse, from *mors*, the Latin for death. **3 Wasserman:** merman. **7 Ziffius:** sword-fish. **9 *Rosmarines*:** sea-horses.   **25,9 entrall:** insides, entrails.   **26,9 *Tethys*:** wife of Neputne, here the sea.   **27,9 succour:** assistance.

For ill it were to hearken to her cry;
For she is inly nothing ill apayd,
But onely womanish fine forgery,
Your stubborne hart t'affect with fraile infirmity.

29 To which when she your courage hath inclind
    Through foolish pitty, then her guilefull bayt
    She will embosome deeper in your mind,
    And for your ruine at the last awayt.
    The knight was ruled, and the Boateman strayt
    Held on his course with stayed stedfastnesse,
    Ne euer shruncke, ne euer sought to bayt
    His tyred armes for toylesome wearinesse,
But with his oares did sweepe the watry wildernesse.

30 And now they nigh approched to the sted,
    Where as those Mermayds dwelt: it was a still
    And calmy bay, on th'one side sheltered
    With the brode shadow of an hoarie hill,
    On th'other side an high rocke toured still,
    That twixt them both a pleasaunt port they made,
    And did like an halfe Theatre fulfill:
    There those fiue sisters had continuall trade,
And vsd to bath themselues in that deceiptfull shade.

31 They were faire Ladies, till they fondly striu'd
    With th'*Heliconian* maides for maistery;
    Of whom they ouer-comen, were depriu'd
    Of their proud beautie, and th'one moyity
    Transform'd to fish, for their bold surquedry,
    But th'vpper halfe their hew retained still,
    And their sweet skill in wonted melody;
    Which euer after they abusd to ill,
T'allure weake trauellers, whom gotten they did kill.

32 So now to *Guyon*, as he passed by,
    Their pleasaunt tunes they sweetly thus applide;
    O thou faire sonne of gentle Faery,
    That art in mighty armes most magnifide
    Aboue all knights, that euer battell tride,
    O turne thy rudder hither-ward a while:
    Here may thy storme-bet vessell safely ride;
    This is the Port of rest from troublous toyle,
The worlds sweet In, from paine & wearisome turmoyle.

28,7 **ill apayd**: distressed. 29,7 **shruncke**: show fear. **bayt**: abate. 30,1 **sted**: place. 4 **hoarie**: old, decaying. 5 **toured**: towered. 8 **trade**: occupation. 31,2 **maides**: the muses of Mt. Helicon. The sirens (with their alluring sensual song) compete with the high poetic song of muses. 4 **moyity**: half. 5 **surquedry**: presumption. 6 **hew**: shape. 32,2 **applide**: addressed. 7 **storme-bet**: storm-beaten.

33   With that the rolling sea resounding soft,
      In his big base them fitly answered,
      And on the rocke the waues breaking aloft,
      A solemne Meane vnto them measured,
      The whiles sweet *Zephirus* lowd whisteled
      His treble, a straunge kinde of harmony;
      Which *Guyons* senses softly tickeled,
      That he the boateman bad row easily,
    And let him heare some part of their rare melody.

34   But him the Palmer from that vanity,
      With temperate aduice discounselled,
      That they it past, and shortly gan descry
      The land, to which their course they leueled;
      When suddeinly a grosse fog ouer spred
      With his dull vapour all that desert has,
      And heauens chearefull face enueloped,
      That all things one, and one as nothing was,
    And this great Vniuerse seemd one confused mas.

35   Thereat they greatly were dismayd, ne wist
      How to direct their way in darkenesse wide,
      But feard to wander in that wastfull mist,
      For tombling into mischiefe vnespide.
      Worse is the daunger hidden, then descride.
      Suddeinly an innumerable flight
      Of harmefull fowles about them fluttering, cride,
      And with their wicked wings them oft did smight,
    And sore annoyed, groping in that griesly night.

36   Euen all the nation of vnfortunate
      And fatall birds about them flocked were,
      Such as by nature men abhorre and hate,
      The ill-faste Owle, deaths dreadfull messengere,
      The hoars Night-rauen, trump of dolefull drere,
      The lether-winged Bat, dayes enimy,
      The ruefull Strich, still waiting on the bere,
      The Whistler shrill, that who so heares, doth dy,
    The hellish Harpies, prophets of sad destiny.

37   All those, and all that else does horrour breed,
      About them flew, and fild their sayles with feare:
      Yet stayd they not, but forward did proceed,
      Whiles th'one did row, and th'other stifly steare;
      Till that at last the weather gan to cleare,

33,5 **Zephirus:** the west wind. 8 **bad:** bade.   36,5 **hoars:** old. **trump:** trumpet. **drere:** sadness.
34,2 **discounselled:** discouraged. 35,1 **wist:** knew.   7 **Strich:** screech-owl. **bere:** tomb. 37,4 **stifly:**
3 **wastfull:** desolate. 4 **vnespide:** unseen.   steadily.

And the faire land it selfe did plainly show.
Said then the Palmer, Lo where does appeare
The sacred soile, where all our perils grow;
Therefore, Sir knight, your ready armes about you throw.

38　He hearkned, and his armes about him tooke,
The whiles the nimble boate so well her sped,
That with her crooked keele the land she strooke,
Then forth the noble *Guyon* sallied,
And his sage Palmer, that him gouerned;
But th'other by his boate behind did stay.
They marched fairly forth, of nought ydred,
Both firmely armd for euery hard assay,
With constancy and care, gainst daunger and dismay.

39　Ere long they heard an hideous bellowing
Of many beasts, that roard outrageously,
As if that hungers point, or *Venus* sting
Had them enraged with fell surquedry;
Yet nought they feard, but past on hardily,
Vntill they came in vew of those wild beasts:
Who all attonce, gaping full greedily,
And rearing fiercely their vpstarting crests,
Ran towards, to deuoure those vnexpected guests.

40　But soone as they approcht with deadly threat,
The Palmer ouer them his staffe vpheld,
His mighty staffe, that could all charmes defeat:
Eftsoones their stubborne courages were queld,
And high aduaunced crests downe meekely feld,
In stead of fraying, they them selues did feare,
And trembled, as them passing they beheld:
Such wondrous powre did in that staffe appeare,
All monsters to subdew to him, that did it beare.

41　Of that same wood it fram'd was cunningly,
Of which *Caduceus* whilome was made,
Caduceus the rod of *Mercury*,
With which he wonts the *Stygian* realmes inuade,
Through ghastly horrour, and eternall shade;
Th'infernall feends with it he can asswage,
And *Orcus* tame, whom nothing can perswade,
And rule the *Furyes*, when they most do rage:
Such vertue in his staffe had eke this Palmer sage.

37,8 **sacred:** accursed.　38,7 **ydred:** in fear.　39,4 **fell surquedry:** great arrogance.　8 **crests:** combs or tufts of hair on top of head, here as head.　40,5 **feld:** fell. 6 **fraying:** frightening.　41,1 **cunningly:** skilfully.　2 *Caduceus:* the staff of the god Mercury which has power over both the dead and living.　6 **asswage:** pacify.　7 *Orcus:* Pluto, god of the underworld.

42   Thence passing forth, they shortly do arriue,
     Whereas the *Bowre of Blisse* was situate;
     A place pickt out by choice of best aliue,
     That natures worke by art can imitate:
     In which what euer in this worldly state
     Is sweet, and pleasing vnto liuing sense,
     Or that may dayntiest fantasie aggrate,
     Was poured forth with plentifull dispence,
  And made there to abound with lauish affluence.

43   Goodly it was enclosed round about,
     Aswell their entred guestes to keepe within,
     As those vnruly beasts to hold without;
     Yet was the fence thereof but weake and thin;
     Nought feard their force, that fortilage to win,
     But wisedomes powre, and temperaunces might,
     By which the mightiest things efforced bin:
     And eke the gate was wrought of substaunce light,
  Rather for pleasure, then for battery or fight.

44   Yt framed was of precious yuory,
     That seemd a worke of admirable wit;
     And therein all the famous history
     Of *Iason* and *Medaea* was ywrit;
     Her mighty charmes, her furious louing fit,
     His goodly conquest of the golden fleece,
     His falsed faith, and loue too lightly flit,
     The wondred *Argo*, which in venturous peece
  First through the Euxine seas bore all the flowr of Greece.

45   Ye might haue seene the frothy billowes fry
     Vnder the ship, as thorough them she went,
     That seemd the waues were into yuory,
     Or yuory into the waues were sent;
     And other where the snowy substaunce sprent
     With vermell, like the boyes bloud therein shed,
     A piteous spectacle did represent,
     And otherwhiles with gold besprinkeled;
  Yt seemd th'enchaunted flame, which did Creusa wed.

46   All this, and more might in that goodly gate
     Be red; that euer open stood to all,
     Which thither came: but in the Porch there sate
     A comely personage of stature tall,

42,7 aggrate: please. **43,5 fortilage:** a small fort. **44,4 Iason:** Jason sailed from Greece across the the Black Sea to capture the golden fleece. Medea, a sorceress, fell in love with him and betrayed her family. On his return, Jason abandoned her. **7 flit:** altering. **45,1 fry:** foam. **5 sprent:** sprinkled. **6 vermell:** bright red. **the boyes:** Medusa murdered her brothers. **9 Creusa:** the bride Jason abandoned Medea for. Medusa gave her a poisoned garment which burned her to death.

And semblaunce pleasing, more then naturall,
That trauellers to him seemd to entize;
His looser garment to the ground did fall,
And flew about his heeles in wanton wize,
Not fit for speedy pace, or manly exercize.

47 They in that place him *Genius* did call:
Not that celestiall powre, to whom the care
Of life, and generation of all
That liues, pertaines in charge particulare,
Who wondrous things concerning our welfare,
And straunge phantomes doth let vs oft forsee,
And oft of secret ill bids vs beware:
That is our Selfe, whom though we do not see,
Yet each doth in him selfe it well perceiue to bee.

48 Therefore a God him sage Antiquity
Did wisely make, and good *Agdistes* call:
But this same was to that quite contrary,
The foe of life, that good enuyes to all,
That secretly doth vs procure to fall,
Through guilefull semblaunts, which he makes vs see.
He of this Gardin had the gouernall,
And Pleasures porter was deuizd to bee,
Holding a staffe in hand for more formalitee.

49 With diuerse flowres he daintily was deckt,
And strowed round about, and by his side
A mighty Mazer bowle of wine was set,
As if it had to him bene sacrifide;
Wherewith all new-come guests he gratifide:
So did he eke Sir *Guyon* passing by:
But he his idle curtesie defide,
And ouerthrew his bowle disdainfully;
And broke his staffe, with which he charmed semblants sly.

50 Thus being entred, they behold around
A large and spacious plaine, on euery side
Strowed with pleasauns, whose faire grassy ground
Mantled with greene, and goodly beautifide
With all the ornaments of *Floraes* pride,
Wherewith her mother Art, as halfe in scorne
Of niggard Nature, like a pompous bride
Did decke her, and too lauishly adorne,
When forth from virgin bowre she comes in th'early morne.

46,6 **entize**: attract. 7 **looser**: too loose. 47,1 *Genius*: god of generation with two aspects, one positive called Agdistes leading to love. The negative aspect in the Bowre of Bliss leads to lust.   49,3 **Mazer bowle**: bowl associated with strong drink which bewilders or 'mazes'. 4 **sacrifide**: offered as sacrifice. 9 **charmed**: conjured. 50,5 *Floraes*: Flora, goddess of flowers. 7 **niggard**: stingy.

51   Thereto the Heauens alwayes Iouiall,
      Lookt on them louely, still in stedfast state,
      Ne suffred storme nor frost on them to fall,
      Their tender buds or leaues to violate,
      Nor scorching heat, nor cold intemperate
      T'afflict the creatures, which therein did dwell,
      But the milde air with season moderate
      Gently attempred, and disposd so well,
  That still it breathed forth sweet spirit & holesome smell.

52   More sweet and holesome, then the pleasaunt hill
      Of *Rhodope*, on which the Nimphe, that bore
      A gyaunt babe, her selfe for griefe did kill;
      Or the Thessalian *Tempe*, where of yore
      Faire *Daphne Phoebus* hart with loue did gore;
      Or *Ida*, where the Gods lou'd to repaire,
      When euer they their heauenly bowres forlore;
      Or sweet *Parnasse*, the haunt of Muses faire;
  Or *Eden* selfe, if ought with *Eden* mote compaire.

53   Much wondred *Guyon* at the faire aspect
      Of that sweet place, yet suffred no delight
      To sincke into his sence, nor mind affect,
      But passed forth, and lookt still forward right,
      Bridling his will, and maistering his might:
      Till that he came vnto another gate,
      No gate, but like one, being goodly dight
      With boughes and braunches, which did broad dilate
  Their clasping armes, in wanton wreathings intricate.

54   So fashioned a Porch with rare deuice,
      Archt ouer head with an embracing vine,
      Whose bounches hanging downe, seemed to entice
      All passers by, to tast their lushious wine,
      And did themselues into their hands incline,
      As freely offering to be gathered:
      Some deepe empurpled as the *Hyacint*,
      Some as the Rubine, laughing sweetly red,
  Some like faire Emeraudes, not yet well ripened.

55   And them amongst, some were of burnisht gold,
      So made by art, to beautifie the rest,
      Which did themselues emongst the leaues enfold,
      As lurking from the vew of couetous guest,
      That the weake bowes, with so rich load opprest,

51,1 **Iouiall**: under the beign influence of the planet Juptier (Jove). 8 **attempred**: modified in temperature. 52,2 **Rhodope**: nymph transformed to a mountain where Orpheus charmed nature. 52,4 **Tempe**: valley where Daphne was changed to a laurel to escape Apollo raping her. 7 **forlore**: left. 53,7 **dight**: made. 8 **dilate**: extend. 54,7 **Hyacint**: sapphire. 8 **Rubine**: ruby.

Did bow adowne, as ouer-burdened.
Vnder that Porch a comely dame did rest,
Clad in faire weedes, but fowle disordered,
And garments loose, that seemd vnmeet for womanhed.

56   In her left hand a Cup of gold she held,
    And with her right the riper fruit did reach,
    Whose sappy liquor, that with fulnesse sweld,
    Into her cup she scruzd, with daintie breach
    Of her fine fingers, without fowle empeach,
    That so faire wine-presse made the wine more sweet:
    Thereof she vsd to giue to drinke to each,
    Whom passing by she happened to meet:
It was her guise, all Straungers goodly so to greet.

57   So she to *Guyon* offred it to tast;
    Who taking it out of her tender hond,
    The cup to ground did violently cast,
    That all in peeces it was broken fond,
    And with the liquor stained all the lond:
    Whereat *Excesse* exceedingly was wroth,
    Yet no'te the same amend, ne yet withstond,
    But suffered him to passe, all were she loth;
Who nought regarding her displeasure forward goth.

58   There the most daintie Paradise on ground,
    It selfe doth offer to his sober eye,
    In which all pleasures plenteously abound,
    And none does others happinesse enuye:
    The painted flowres, the trees vpshooting hye,
    The dales for shade, the hilles for breathing space,
    The trembling groues, the Christall running by;
    And that, which all faire workes doth most aggrace,
The art, which all that wrought, appeared in no place.

59   One would haue thought, (so cunningly, the rude,
    And scorned parts were mingled with the fine,)
    That nature had for wantonesse ensude
    Art, and that Art at nature did repine;
    So striuing each th'other to vndermine,
    Each did the others worke more beautifie;
    So diff'ring both in willes, agreed in fine:
    So all agreed through sweete diuersitie,
This Gardin to adorne with all varietie.

56,4 **scruzd:** squeezed. **breach:** crushed. **5 empeach:** detriment. **57,4 fond:** found. **7 no'te:** could not. **58,7 Christall:** crystal-clear stream.   **58,8 aggrace:** enhance. **59,3 wantonesse:** playfulness. **ensude:** imitated. **4 repine:** complain. **7 in fine:** in the end.

60   And in the midst of all, a fountaine stood,
      Of richest substaunce, that on earth might bee,
      So pure and shiny, that the siluer flood
      Through euery channell running one might see;
      Most goodly it with curious imageree
      Was ouer-wrought, and shapes of naked boyes,
      Of which some seemd with liuely iollitee,
      To fly about, playing their wanton toyes,
    Whilest others did them selues embay in liquid ioyes.

61   And ouer all, of purest gold was spred,
      A trayle of yuie in his natiue hew:
      For the rich mettall was so coloured,
      That wight, who did not well auis'd it vew,
      Would surely deeme it to be yuie trew:
      Low his lasciuious armes adown did creepe,
      That themselues dipping in the siluer dew,
      Their fleecy flowres they tenderly did steepe,
    Which drops of Christall seemd for wantones to weepe.

62   Infinit streames continually did well
      Out of this fountaine, sweet and faire to see,
      The which into an ample lauer fell,
      And shortly grew to so great quantitie,
      That like a little lake it seemd to bee;
      Whose depth exceeded not three cubits hight,
      That through the waues one might the bottom see,
      All pau'd beneath with Iaspar shining bright,
    That seemd the fountaine in that sea did sayle vpright.

63   And all the margent round about was set,
      With shady Laurell trees, thence to defend
      The sunny beames, which on the billowes bet,
      And those which therein bathed, mote offend.
      As *Guyon* hapned by the same to wend,
      Two naked Damzelles he therein espyde,
      Which therein bathing, seemed to contend,
      And wrestle wantonly, ne car'd to hyde,
    Their dainty parts from vew of any, which them eyde.

64   Sometimes the one would lift the other quight
      Aboue the waters, and then downe againe
      Her plong, as ouer maistered by might,
      Where both awhile would couered remaine,
      And each the other from to rise restraine;

60,9 embay: bathe. 61,2 yuie: ivy. 62,3 lauer: 63,1 **margent**: border. **2 defend**: fend off. **5 to wend**:
basin. **6 three cubits**: about 1.5 metres. **8 Iaspar**:   to pass by.
green stone.

The whiles their snowy limbes, as through a vele,
So through the Christall waues appeared plaine:
Then suddeinly both would themselues vnhele,
And th'amarous sweet spoiles to greedy eyes reuele.

65 As that faire Starre, the messenger of morne,
His deawy face out of the sea doth reare:
Or as the *Cyprian* goddesse, newly borne
Of th'Oceans fruitfull froth, did first appeare:
Such seemed they, and so their yellow heare
Christalline humour dropped downe apace.
Whom such when *Guyon* saw, he drew him neare,
And somewhat gan relent his earnest pace,
His stubborne brest gan secret pleasaunce to embrace.

66 The wanton Maidens him espying, stood
Gazing a while at his vnwonted guise;
Then th'one her selfe low ducked in the flood,
Abasht, that her a straunger did avise:
But th'other rather higher did arise,
And her two lilly paps aloft displayd,
And all, that might his melting hart entise
To her delights, she vnto him bewrayd:
The rest hid vnderneath, him more desirous made.

67 With that, the other likewise vp arose,
And her faire lockes, which formerly were bownd
Vp in one knot, he low adowne did lose:
Which flowing long and thick, her cloth'd arownd,
And th'yuorie in golden mantle gownd:
So that faire spectacle from him was reft,
Yet that, which reft it, no lesse faire was fownd:
So hid in lockes and waues from lookers theft,
Nought but her louely face she for his looking left.

68 Withall she laughed, and she blusht withall,
That blushing to her laughter gaue more grace,
And laughter to her blushing, as did fall:
Now when they spide the knight to slacke his pace,
Them to behold, and in his sparkling face
The secret signes of kindled lust appeare,
Their wanton meriments they did encreace,
And to him beckned, to approch more neare,
And shewd him many sights, that courage cold could reare.

64,6 **vele:** veil. 8 **vnhele:** expose. 65,1 **Starre:**
Venus as morning star. 3 ***Cyprian:*** Venus was held
to have been born on Cyprus. 6 **humour:** moisture.
66,2 **vnwonted guise:** unfamiliar conduct.

66,4 **avise:** view. 8 **bewrayd:** exposed. 67,6 **reft:**
stolen. 68,9 **courage cold could reare:** could excite
even a frigid temperament.

69   On which when gazing him the Palmer saw,
      He much rebukt those wandring eyes of his,
      And counseld well, him forward thence did draw.
      Now are they come nigh to the *Bowre of blis*
      Of her fond fauorites so nam'd amis:
      When thus the Palmer; Now Sir, well auise;
      For here the end of all our trauell is:
      Here wonnes Acrasia, whom we must surprise,
   Else she will slip away, and all our drift despise.

70   Etfsoones they heard a most melodious sound,
      Of all that mote delight a daintie eare,
      Such as attonce might not on liuing ground,
      Saue in this Paradise, be heard elswhere:
      Right hard it was, for wight, which did it heare,
      To read, what manner musicke that mote bee:
      For all that pleasing is to liuing eare,
      Was there consorted in one harmonee,
   Birdes, voyces, instruments, windes, waters, all agree.

71   The ioyous birdes shrouded in chearefull shade,
      Their notes vnto the voyce attempred sweet;
      Th'Angelicall soft trembling voyces made
      To th'instruments diuine respondence meet:
      The siluer sounding instruments did meet
      With the base murmure of the waters fall:
      The waters fall with difference discreet,
      Now soft, now loud, vnto the wind did call:
   The gentle warbling wind low answered to all.

72   There, whence that Musick seemed heard to bee,
      Was the faire Witch her selfe now solacing,
      With a new Louer, whom through sorceree
      And witchcraft, she from farre did thither bring:
      There she had him now layd a slombering,
      In secret shade, after long wanton ioyes:
      Whilst round about them pleasauntly did sing
      Many faire Ladies, and lasciuious boyes,
   That euer mixt their song with light licentious toyes.

73   And all that while, right ouer him she hong,
      With her false eyes fast fixed in his sight,
      As seeking medicine, whence she was stong,
      Or greedily depasturing delight:

69,5 **amis:** mistakenly. 6 **auise:** consider. 9 **drift:** purpose. 70,3 **attonce:** at the same time. 71,2 **attempred:** attuned. 4 **respondence meet:** fitting response.

71,7 **difference discreet:** subtle variation. 72,9 **toyes:** sexual play, here also loose music. 73,3 **medicine:** cure. 4 **depasturing:** consuming.

And oft inclining downe with kisses light,
For feare of waking him, his lips bedewd,
And through his humid eyes did sucke his spright,
Quite molten into lust and pleasure lewd;
Wherewith she sighed soft, as if his case she rewd.

74 The whiles some one did chaunt this louely lay;
Ah see, who so faire thing doest faine to see,
In springing flowre the image of thy day;
Ah see the Virgin Rose, how sweetly shee
Doth first peepe forth with bashfull modestee,
That fairer seemes, the lesse ye see her may;
Lo see soone after, how more bold and free
Her bared bosome she doth broad display;
Loe see soone after, how she fades, and falles away.

75 So passeth, in the passing of a day,
Of mortall life the leafe, the bud, the flowre,
Ne more doth flourish after first decay,
That earst was sought to decke both bed and bowre,
Of many a Ladie, and many a Paramowre:
Gather therefore the Rose, whilest yet is prime,
For soone comes age, that will her pride deflowre:
Gather the Rose of love, whilest yet is time,
Whilest louing thou mayst loued be with equall crime.

76 He ceast, and then gan all the quire of birdes
Their diuerse notes t'attune vnto his lay,
As in approuance of his pleasing words.
The constant paire heard all, that he did say,
Yet swarued not, but kept their forward way,
Through many couert groues, and thickets close,
In which they creeping did at last display
That wanton Ladie, with her louer lose,
Whose sleepie head she in her lap did soft dispose.

77 Vpon a bed of Roses she was layd,
As faint through heat, or dight to pleasant sin,
And was arayd, or rather disarayd,
All in a vele of silke and siluer thin,
That hid no whit her alablaster skin,
But rather shewd more white, if more might bee:
More subtile web *Arachne* can not spin,
Nor the fine nets, which oft we wouen see
Of scorched deaw, do not in th'aire more lightly flee.

73,7 **spright**: soul. 9 **rewd**: pitied. 75,4 **earst**:   77, 2 **dight**: arranged. 7 ***Arachne***: famous weaver
lately.   9 **crime**: here both as sin and judgement on it.   transformed into a spider. 9 **flee**: fly.

78 Her snowy brest was bare to readie spoyle
    Of hungry eies, which n'ote therewith be fild,
    And yet through languour of her late sweet toyle,
    Few drops, more cleare then Nectar, forth distild,
    That like pure Orient perles adowne it trild,
    And her faire eyes sweet smyling in delight,
    Moystened their fierie beames, with which she thrild
    Fraile harts, yet quenched not; like starry light
Which sparckling on the silent waues, does seeme more bright.

79 The young man sleeping by her, seemd to bee
    Some goodly swayne of honorable place,
    That certes it great pittie was to see
    Him his nobilitie so foule deface;
    A sweet regard, and amiable grace,
    Mixed with manly sternnesse did appeare
    Yet sleeping, in his well proportiond face,
    And on his tender lips the downy heare
Did now but freshly spring, and silken blossomes beare.

80 His warlike armes, the idle instruments
    Of sleeping praise, were hong vpon a tree,
    And his braue shield, full of old moniments,
    Was fowly ra'st, that none the signes might see;
    Ne for them, ne for honour cared hee,
    Ne ought, that did to his aduauncement tend,
    But in lewd loues, and wastfull luxuree,
    His dayes, his goods, his bodie he did spend:
O horrible enchantment, that him so did blend.

81 The noble Elfe, and carefull Palmer drew
    So nigh them, minding nought, but lustfull game,
    That suddein forth they on them rusht, and threw
    A subtile net, which onely for the same
    The skilfull Palmer formally did frame.
    So held them vnder fast, the whiles the rest
    Fled all away for feare of fowler shame.
    The faire Enchauntresse, so vnwares opprest,
Tryde all her arts, & all her sleights, thence out to wrest.

82 And eke her louer stroue: but all in vaine;
    For that same net so cunningly was wound,
    That neither guile, nor force might it distraine.
    They tooke them both, & both them strongly bound
    In captiue bandes, which there they readie found:

78,2 **n'ote**: could not. 5 **trild**: trickled. 79,2 **swayne**: 80,9 **blend**: blind. 81,5 **formally**: expressly. 9 **wrest**: in pastoral, a courtly lover. 80,3 **moniments**: accounts twist. 82,1 **eke**: also. 3 **distraine**: break apart. of heroic deeds. 4 **ra'st**: erased.

But her in chaines of adamant he tyde;
For nothing else might keepe her safe and sound;
But *Verdant* (so he hight) he soone vntyde,
And counsell sage in steed thereof to him applyde.

83   But all those pleasant bowres and Pallace braue,
      Guyon broke downe, with rigour pittilesse;
      Ne ought their goodly workmanship might saue
      Them from the tempest of his wrathfulnesse,
      But that their blisse he turn'd to balefulnesse:
      Their groues he feld, their gardins did deface,
      Their arbers spoyle, their Cabinets suppresse,
      Their banket houses burne, their buildings race,
And of the fairest late, now made the fowlest place.

84   Then led they her away, and eke that knight
      They with them led, both sorrowfull and sad:
      The way they came, the same retourn'd they right,
      Till they arriued, where they lately had
      Charm'd those wild-beasts, that rag'd with furie mad.
      Which now awaking, fierce at them gan fly,
      As in their mistresse reskew, whom they lad;
      But them the Palmer soone did pacify.
Then *Guyon* askt, what meant those beastes, which there did ly.

85   Said he, These seeming beasts are men indeed,
      Whom this Enchauntresse hath transformed thus,
      Whylome her louers, which her lusts did feed,
      Now turned into figures hideous,
      According to their mindes like monstruous.
      Sad end (quoth he) of life intemperate,
      And mournefull meed of ioyes delicious:
      But Palmer, if it mote thee so aggrate,
Let them returned be vnto their former state.

86   Streight way he with his vertuous staffe them strooke,
      And streight of beasts they comely men became;
      Yet being men they did vnmanly looke,
      And stared ghastly, some for inward shame,
      And some for wrath, to see their captiue Dame:
      But one aboue the rest in speciall,
      That had an hog beene late, hight *Grille* by name,
      Repined greatly, and did him miscall,
That had from hoggish forme him brought to naturall.

82,6 **adamant:** very hard substance.   8 ***Verdant:*** Spring
or literally 'green-giving'.   83,5 **balefulnesse:** distress.
7 **Cabinets:** garden bowers.   8 **banket:** banquet.
race: raze.

84,7 **lad:** worshipped.   85,3 **Whylome:** formerly.
7 **meed:** reward.   8 **aggrate:** please.   86,8 **repined:**
lamented. **miscall:** regret.   9 **naturall:** natural human
form.

87 Said *Guyon*, See the mind of beastly man,
       That hath so soone forgot the excellence
       Of his creation, when he life began,
       That now he chooseth, with vile difference,
       To be a beast, and lacke intelligence.
       To whom the Palmer thus, The donghill kind
       Delights in filth and foule incontinence:
       Let *Grill* be *Grill*, and haue his hoggish mind,
     But let vs hence depart, whilest wether serues and wind.

SIR PHILIP SIDNEY (1554–1586)

Sidney is the English writer who best combined the Renaissance ideal of soldier, scholar, statesman. He travelled extensively in Europe and was promoted as the possible leader of an allied Protestant Europe against Spain. But such ambitions were not furthered by Elizabeth I and Sidney died fighting the Spanish in the Netherlands. Sidney's chief works are two versions of a pastoral romance, *The Arcadia*; *The Defence of Poetry*; and a sonnet sequence, *Astrophil and Stella*, which records a fictionalised version of his relation with Penelope Devereux, later Lady Rich. Although indebted to Petrarchan and other continental sonnet traditions, the sequence is innovative, notably in the dramatic coherence of the narrative. The numbering here indicates each sonnet's position in the sequence.

From Astrophil and Stella

Sonnet 1

               Loving in truth, and fain in verse my love to show,
               That she (dear she) might take some pleasure of my pain:
               Pleasure might cause her read, reading might make her know,
               Knowledge might pity win, and pity grace obtain,
    5   I sought fit words to paint the blackest face of woe,
               Studying inventions fine, her wits to entertain:
               Oft turning others' leaves, to see if thence would flow
               Some fresh and fruitful showers upon my sun-burn'd brain.
                 But words came halting forth, wanting Invention's stay,
    10   Invention Nature's child, fled step-dame Study's blows,
               And others' feet still seem'd but strangers in my way.
               Thus great with child to speak, and helpless in my throes,
                 Biting my truand pen, beating myself for spite,
                 Fool, said my Muse to me, look in thy heart and write.

87,4 vile difference: low preference. **Sonnet 1,6 inven-** **1,11 feet:** also in the sense of metrical measures.
tions: in rhetoric the discovery or choice of arguments **13 truand:** truant.
to use.

Sonnet 2

Not at first sight, nor with a dribbed shot,
Love gave the wound which while I breathe will bleed:
But known worth did in mine of time proceed,
Till by degrees it had full conquest got.
5   I saw, and liked; I liked, but loved not;
I loved, but straight did not what love decreed:
At length to love's decrees I, forc'd, agreed,
Yet with repining at so partial lot.
     Now even that footstep of lost liberty
10   Is gone, and now like slave-born Muscovite
I call it praise to suffer tyranny;
     And now employ the remnant of my wit
To make myself believe that all is well,
While with a feeling skill I paint my hell.

Sonnet 5

It is most true, that eyes are formed to serve
The inward light: and that the heavenly part
Ought to be king, from whose rules who do swerve,
Rebels to Nature, strive for their own smart.
5   It is most true, what we call Cupid's dart,
An image is, which for ourselves we carve;
And, fools, adore in temple of our heart,
Till that good god make church and churchmen starve.
     True, that true Beauty Virtue is indeed,
10   Whereof this beauty can be but a shade,
Which elements with mortal mixture breed:
     True, that on earth we are but pilgrims made,
And should in soul up to our country move:
True; and yet true, that I must Stella love.

Sonnet 30

Whether the Turkish new-moon minded be
To fill his horns this year on Christian coast;
How Poles' right king means, without leave of host,
To warm with ill-made fire cold Muscovy;
5   If French can yet three parts in one agree;
What now the Dutch in their full diets boast;

2,1 dribbed: random. **3 mine**: a tunnel dug underneath besieged walls. **8 partial lot**: activity which excludes others. **10**: a contemporary belief that Russians welcomed tyranny. **14 paint**: colour. **5,2 inward light**: reason. **4 smart**: feel sharp pain. **10 shade**: shadow. **5,13 our country**: heaven. **30,1 Turkish new-moon**: the crescent moon in Ottoman Turkey's flag. **3 Poles' right king**: the elected king of Poland invaded Russia in 1580. **5 three parts**: France's political factions: Protestants, Catholics and *politiques*. **6 diets**: councils.

How Holland hearts, now so good towns be lost,
   Trust in the pleasing shade of Orange tree;
      How Ulster likes of that same golden bit
10   Wherewith my father once made it half tame;
   If in the Scottish court be welt'ring yet;
   These questions busy wits to me do frame.
      I, cumbered with good manners, answer do,
      But know not how, for still I think of you.

Sonnet 35

What may words say, or what may words not say,
   Where truth itself must speak like flattery?
   Within what bounds can one his liking stay,
   Where nature doth with infinite agree?
5   What Nestor's counsel can my flames allay,
   Since Reason's self doth blow the coal in me?
   And ah, what hope that hope should once see day,
   Where Cupid is sworn page to Chastity?
      Honour is honoured, that thou dost possess
10   Him as thy slave, and now long needy Fame
   Doth even grow rich, naming my Stella's name.
      Wit learns in thee perfection to express,
   Not thou by praise, but praise in thee is rais'd;
   It is a praise to praise, when thou art prais'd.

Sonnet 37

My mouth doth water, and my breast doth swell,
   My tongue doth itch, my thoughts in labour be;
   Listen then lordings with good ear to me,
For of my life a riddle I must tell.
5   Towards Aurora's court a nymph doth dwell,
   Rich in all beauties which man's eye can see:
   Beauties so far from reach of words, that we
Abase her praise, saying she doth excel:
   Rich in the treasure of deserv'd renown,
10   Rich in the riches of a royal heart,
   Rich in those gifts that give th' eternal crown;
   Who though most rich in these and every part
      Which make the patents of true worldly bliss,
      Hath no misfortune, but that Rich she is.

30,8 **Orange:** William of Orange, the Dutch leader.
9–10: Henry Sidney, as Lord Deputy of Ireland, he
subdued Ulster, imposing a tax or 'golden bit' on it.
11 **welt'ring:** confusion.   13 **cumbered:** hampered.

35,5 **Nestor's counsel:** Greek leader in *The Iliad*
famous for politic advice.   11 **name:** Lady Rich.
37,5 **Aurora's court:** in the east. Aurora is goddess
of the dawn.   13 **make the patents:** form the titles
to possession.

Sonnet 45

Stella oft sees the very face of woe
  Painted in my beclouded stormy face;
  But cannot skill to pity my disgrace,
Not though thereof the cause herself she know:
5 Yet hearing late a fable, which did show
  Of lovers never known a grievous case,
  Pity thereof gat in her breast such place
That from that sea derived tears' spring did flow.
  Alas, if Fancy drawn by imag'd things,
10 Though false, yet with free scope more grace doth breed
  Than servant's wrack, where new doubts honour brings;
Then think my dear that you in me do read
  Of lover's ruin some sad tragedy:
  I am not I, pity the tale of me.

Sonnet 53

In martial sports I had my cunning tried,
  And yet to break more staves did me address,
  While with the people's shouts I must confess,
Youth, luck and praise even filled my veins with pride.
5 When Cupid, having me, his slave, descried
  In Mars's livery, prancing in the press:
  'What now, sir fool,' said he; 'I would no less,
Look here, I say.' I looked, and Stella spied:
  Who hard by made a window send forth light,
10 My heart then quaked, then dazzled were mine eyes,
  One hand forgot to rule, th'other to fight;
Nor trumpet's sound I heard, nor friendly cries;
  My foe came on, and beat the air for me,
  Till that her blush taught me my shame to see.

Sonnet 71

Who will in fairest book of Nature know
  How Virtue may best lodg'd in beauty be,
  Let him but learn of Love to read in thee,
Stella, those fair lines which true goodness show.
5 There shall he find all vices' overthrow,
  Not by rude force, but sweetest sovereignty
  Of reason, from whose light those night-birds fly,
That inward sun in thine eyes shineth so.

45,3 **cannot skill**: is unable. 11 **wrack**: ruin.
53,1 **martial sports**: tilting; a mock combat consisting
of two men riding at one another and breaking lances.
53,2 **staves**: tilting poles. 6 **press**: crowd. 71,7 **night-birds**: vices.

And not content to be perfection's heir
10 Thy self, dost strive all minds that way to move,
Who mark in thee what is in thee most fair;
So while thy beauty draws the heart to love,
  As fast thy virtue bends that love to good.
  But ah, desire still cries: give me some food.

Sonnet 72

Desire, though thou my old companion art,
  And oft so clings to my pure love, that I
  One from the other scarcely can descry,
While each doth blow the fire of my heart;
5 Now from thy fellowship I needs must part;
  Venus is taught with Dian's wings to fly;
  I must no more in thy sweet passions lie;
Virtue's gold now must head my Cupid's dart.
Service and honour, wonder with delight,
10 Fear to offend, will worthy to appear,
Care shining in mine eyes, faith in my sprite;
These things are left me by my only dear;
  But thou Desire because thou wouldst have all,
  Now banished art, but yet alas how shall?

Sonnet 82

Nymph of the gard'n where all beauties be:
  Beauties which do in excellency pass
  His who till death looked in a watery glass,
Or hers whom naked the Trojan boy did see.
5 Sweet gard'n nymph, which keeps the cherry tree,
  Whose fruit doth far th'Esperian taste surpass;
  Most sweet-fair, most fair-sweet, do not alas,
From coming near those cherries banish me:
For though, full of desire, empty of wit,
10 Admitted late by your best-graced grace,
I caught at one of them a hungry bit;
Pardon that fault, once more grant me the place,
  And I do swear, even by the same delight,
  I will but kiss, I never more will bite.

72,6 **Dian:** Diana, goddess of chastity. 10 **will worthy to appear:** 'wish to appear worthy'; or the Will transformed, hence it shows itself worthily. 11 **sprite:** soul.

82,3 **his:** Narcissus, who self-absorbed gazed at his own beauty in a pool. 4 **hers:** Venus, who Paris, the Trojan boy, saw naked. 6 **th'Esperian:** the golden apples of the Hesperides.

Eighth song

In a grove most rich of shade
Where birds wanton music made,
May then young his pied weeds showing,
New perfumed with flowers fresh growing,

5   Astrophil with Stella sweet
Did for mutual comfort meet,
Both within themselves oppressed,
But each in the other blessed.

Him great harms had taught much care:
10   Her fair neck a foul yoke bare,
But her sight his cares did banish,
In his sight her yoke did vanish.

Wept they had, alas the while,
But now tears themselves did smile,
15   While their eyes by love directed,
Interchangeably reflected.

Sigh they did, but now betwixt
Sighs of woes were glad sighs mixt,
With arms cross'd, yet testifying
20   Restless rest, and living dying.

Their ears hungry of each word,
Which the dear tongue would afford,
But their tongues restrain'd from walking,
Till their hearts had ended talking.

25   But when their tongues could not speak,
Love itself did silence break;
Love did set his lips asunder,
Thus to speak in love and wonder:

'Stella sovereign of my joy,
30   Fair triumpher of annoy,
Stella star of heavenly fire,
Stella lodestar of desire;

'Stella, in whose shining eyes
Are the lights of Cupid's skies,
35   Whose beams, where they once are darted,
Love therewith is straight imparted;

---

2 **wanton:** lively. 3 **pied weeds:** many coloured 32 lodestar: guiding star such as the North Star.
clothes. 19 **arms cross'd:** a symbol of melancholy, as
effigies on tombs.

'Stella, whose voice when it speaks
Senses all asunder breaks;
Stella, whose·voice when it singeth
40   Angels to acquaintance bringeth;

'Stella, in whose body is
Writ each character of bliss,
Whose face all, all beauty passeth,
Save thy mind, which yet surpasseth.

45   'Grant, O grant, but speech alas
Fails me fearing on to pass,
Grant, O me, what am I saying?
But no fault there is in praying.

'Grant, O dear, on knees I pray,
50   (Knees on ground he then did stay)
That not I but since I love you,
Time and place for me may move you.

'Never season was more fit,
Never room more apt for it;
55   Smiling air allows my reason;
These birds sing, now use the season.

'This small wind which so sweet is,
See how it the leaves doth kiss,
Each tree in his best attiring
60   Sense of love to love inspiring.

'Love makes earth the water drink,
Love to earth makes water sink;
And if dumb things be so witty,
Shall a heavenly grace want pity?'

65   There his hands in their speech fain
Would have made tongue's language plain;
But her hands his hands repelling,
Gave repulse all grace excelling.

Then she spake; her speech was such
70   As not ears but heart did touch;
While such wise she love denied,
As yet love she signified.

'Astrophil,' said she, 'my love
Cease in these effects to prove:
75   Now be still, yet still believe me,
Thy grief more than death would grieve me.

73–74: do not attempt to find a demonstration of my love in response to your efforts.

'If that any thought in me
Can taste comfort but of thee,
Let me, fed with hellish anguish,
80   Joyless, hopeless, endless languish.

'If those eyes you praised be
Half so dear as you to me,
Let me home return, stark blinded
Of those eyes, and blinder minded.

85   'If to secret of my heart,
I do any wish impart,
Where thou art not foremost placed,
Be both wish and I defaced.

'If more may be said, I say:
90   All my bliss in thee I lay;
If thou love, my love content thee,
For all love, all faith is meant thee.

'Trust me, while I thee deny,
In my self the smart I try,
95   Tyran honour thus doth use thee,
Stella's self might not refuse thee.

'Therefore, dear, this no more move,
Lest, though I leave not thy love,
Which too deep in me is framed,
100   I should blush when thou art named.'

Therewithal away she went,
Leaving him so passion-rent
With what she had done and spoken,
That therewith my song is broken.

Sonnet 90

Stella think not that I by verse seek fame,
    Who seek, who hope, who love, who live but thee;
    Thine eyes my pride, thy lips my history;
If thou praise not, all other praise is shame.
5   Nor so ambitious am I, as to frame
    A nest for my young praise in laurel tree;
    In truth I swear, I wish not there should be
Graved in mine epitaph a poet's name:
    Ne if I would, could I just title make,
10   That any laud to me thereof should grow,

Song 8,95 **Tyran:** tyrant.

90,8 **Graved:** here meaning both engraved and buried.
90,9 **ne:** nor.   10 **laud:** praise.

Without my plumes from others' wings I take.
For nothing from my wit or will doth flow,
   Since all my words thy beauty doth endite,
   And love doth hold my hand, and makes me write.

Sonnet 106

O absent presence, Stella is not here;
   False flattering hope, that with so fair a face
   Bare me in hand, that in this orphan place
Stella, I say my Stella, should appear.
5   What say'st thou now, where is that dainty cheer
   Thou told'st mine eyes should help their famished case?
   But thou art gone, now that self felt disgrace
Doth make me most to wish thy comfort near.
   But here I do store of fair ladies meet,
10   Who may with charm of conversation sweet
Make in my heavy mould new thoughts to grow:
   Sure they prevail as much with me as he
   That bade his friend, but then new maimed, to be
Merry with him, and not think of his woe.

Sonnet 108

When sorrow, using mine own fire's might,
   Melts down his lead into my boiling breast,
   Through that dark furnace to my heart opprest
There shines a joy from thee my only light;
5   But soon as thought of thee breeds my delight,
   And my young soul flutters to thee his nest,
   Most rude despair my daily unbidden guest,
Clips straight my wings, straight wraps me in his night,
   And makes me then bow down my head, and say:
10   Ah, what doth Phoebus' gold that wretch avail,
Whom iron doors do keep from use of day?'
So strangely, alas, thy works in me prevail,
   That in my woes for thee thou art my joy,
   And in my joys for thee my only annoy.

90,11 **without:** unless. 13 **endite:** indite; put into literary form. 106,3 **Bare me in hand:** led me to believe, deceived me. 106,11 **mould:** body, earthly form. 108,10 **Phoebus' gold:** light of the sun.

CHRISTOPHER MARLOWE (1564–1593)

Marlowe was born in Canterbury and educated there and at Cambridge. He adopted two unusual careers: undercover agent in the Elizabethan secret service and dramatist. Although there is a great deal of exaggeration in many depictions of Marlowe's flamboyant life, his works reveal a sceptical energy which questions orthodoxies, often in provocative manners. Marlowe's poems, plays and translations subtly rework existing genres and the Classics to excite new imaginative possibilities. Although he died young, Marlowe's drama was popular during his life and throughout the English Renaissance.

The Passionate Shepherd to his Love

Come live with me, and be my love,
And we will all the pleasures prove
That valleys, groves, hills and fields,
Woods, or steepy mountain yields.

5 And we will sit upon the rocks,
Seeing the shepherds feed their flocks
By shallow rivers, to whose falls
Melodious birds sing madrigals.

And I will make thee beds of roses,
10 And a thousand fragrant posies,
A cap of flowers, and a kirtle,
Embroider'd all with leaves of myrtle.

A gown made of the finest wool
Which from our pretty lambs we pull,
15 Fair lined slippers for the cold,
With buckles of the purest gold.

A belt of straw and ivy-buds,
With coral clasps and amber studs,
And if these pleasures may thee move,
20 Come live with me, and be my love.

The shepherd swains shall dance and sing
For thy delight each May-morning,
If these delights thy mind may move,
Then live with me, and be my love.

---

10 **posies:** bunches of flowers; collections of poetry in rhetoric.   11 **kirtle:** skirt.   21 **swains:** rustics, often country lovers.

From Hero and Leander

Marlowe's epillyon or 'brief epic' was not published until 1598 and appears unfinished. He wrote the first two books (or sestiads) and George Chapman completed these with another four, overtly moralising the work. Marlowe adopted mythology and sexual icono-clasm from the Roman poet Ovid to produce a learned, erotic verse popular in the Renaissance.

> On *Hellespont* guilty of true love's blood,
> In view and opposite two cities stood,
> Sea-borderers, disjoin'd by *Neptune's* might:
> The one *Abydos*, the other *Sestos* hight.
> 5 At *Sestos Hero* dwelt; *Hero* the fair,
> Whom young *Apollo* courted for her hair,
> And offer'd as a dower his burning throne,
> Where she should sit for men to gaze upon.
> The outside of her garments were of lawn,
> 10 The lining purple silk, with gilt stars drawn;
> Her wide sleeves green, and border'd with a grove,
> Where Venus in her naked glory strove
> To please the careless and disdainful eyes
> Of proud *Adonis* that before her lies.
> 15 Her kirtle blue, whereon was many a stain,
> Made with the blood of wretched lovers slain.
> Upon her head she ware a myrtle wreath,
> From whence her veil reach'd to the ground beneath.
> Her veil was artificial flowers and leaves,
> 20 Whose workmanship both man and beast deceives.
> Many would praise the sweet smell as she pass'd,
> When 'twas the odour which her breath forth cast;
> And there for honey bees have sought in vain,
> And beat from thence, have lighted there again.
> 25 About her neck hung chains of pebble-stone,
> Which lighten'd by her neck, like diamonds shone.
> She ware no gloves, for neither sun nor wind
> Would burn or parch her hands, but to her mind
> Or warm or cool them, for they took delight
> 30 To play upon those hands, they were so white.
> Buskins of shells all silver'd used she,
> And branch'd with blushing coral to the knee,
> Where sparrows perch'd, of hollow pearl and gold,
> Such as the world would wonder to behold:

---

1 **Hellespont**: the Dardanelles, the narrow strait of wa-ter which separates Europe from Asia. 9 **lawn**: high quality linen. 11 **border'd**: embroidered. 28 **to her mind**: as she would have it. 31 **Buskins**: short boots. 32 **branch'd**: embroidered in a branch pattern.

35 Those with sweet water oft her handmaid fills,
Which as she went would chirrup through the bills.
Some say, for her the fairest *Cupid* pin'd,
And looking in her face, was strooken blind.
But this is true, so like was one the other,
40 As he imagin'd *Hero* was his mother;
And oftentimes into her bosom flew,
About her naked neck his bare arms threw,
And laid his childish head upon her breast,
And with still panting rock'd, there took his rest.
45 So lovely fair was *Hero, Venus'* nun,
As Nature wept, thinking she was undone,
Because she took more from her than she left,
And of such wondrous beauty her bereft:
Therefore in sign her treasure suffer'd wrack,
50 Since *Hero's* time hath half the world been black.
Amorous *Leander*, beautiful and young,
(Whose tragedy divine *Musæus* sung)
Dwelt at *Abydos*; since him dwelt there none,
For whom succeeding times make greater moan.
55 His dangling tresses that were never shorn,
Had they been cut, and unto *Colchos* borne,
Would have allur'd the vent'rous youth of *Greece*
To hazard more than for the Golden Fleece.
Fair *Cynthia* wish'd his arms might be her sphere;
60 Grief makes her pale, because she moves not there.
His body was as straight as *Circe's* wand;
Jove might have sipp'd out nectar from his hand.
Even as delicious meat is to the taste,
So was his neck in touching, and surpass'd
65 The white of *Pelops'* shoulder, I could tell ye
How smooth his breast was, and how white his belly,
And whose immortal fingers did imprint
That heavenly path with many a curious dint,
That runs along his back, but my rude pen
70 Can hardly blazon forth the loves of men,
Much less of powerful gods, let it suffice
That my slack muse sings of *Leander's* eyes,
Those orient cheeks and lips, exceeding his
That leapt into the water for a kiss
75 Of his own shadow, and despising many,

40: Cupid's mother is Venus. **45** *Venus'* **nun:** often a term for priestess, but also for prostitutes. **52** *Musæus:* 5th century B.C. poet. The Elizabethans confused him with the *Aeneid's* Musæus, described as one of the first and greatest poets. **57–58:** referring to Jason and the Argonauts. **59** *Cynthia:* the moon. **sphere:** orbit. **62:** alluding to Ganymede, Jupiter's cup bearer and boy lover. **65** *Pelops'* **shoulder:** made of ivory. **68 curious dint:** elaborate indentation. **70 blazon forth:** show in public. **72 slack:** weak. **73 orient:** shining with morning radiance. **his:** Narcissus.

Died ere he could enjoy the love of any.
Had wild *Hippolytus Leander* seen,
Enamour'd of his beauty had he been,
His presence made the rudest peasant melt,
80 That in the vast uplandish country dwelt,
The barbarous *Thracian* soldier, mov'd with nought,
Was mov'd with him, and for his favour sought.
Some swore he was a maid in man's attire,
For in his looks were all that men desire,
85 A pleasant smiling cheek, a speaking eye,
A brow for love to banquet royally;
And such as knew he was a man would say,
Leander, thou art made for amorous play:
Why art thou not in love, and lov'd of all ?
90 Though thou be fair, yet be not thine own thrall.
    The men of wealthy *Sestos*, every year,
For his sake whom their goddess held so dear,
Rose-cheek'd *Adonis*, kept a solemn feast.
Thither resorted many a wand'ring guest
95 To meet their loves; such as had none at all
Came lovers home from this great festival.
For every street like to a firmament
Glistered with breathing stars, who where they went
Frighted the melancholy earth, which deem'd
100 Eternal heaven to burn, for so it seem'd,
As if another *Phaethon* had got
The guidance of the sun's rich chariot.
But far above the loveliest *Hero* shin'd,
And stole away th' enchanted gazer's mind;
105 For like sea-nymphs' inveigling harmony,
So was her beauty to the standers by.
Nor that night-wand'ring, pale and watery star
(When yawning dragons draw her thirling car
From *Latmus*' mount up to the gloomy sky,
110 Where crown'd with blazing light and majesty,
She proudly sits) more over rules the flood
Than she the hearts of those that near her stood.
Even as, when gaudy nymphs pursue the chase,
Wretched *Ixion's* shaggy-footed race,
115 Incens'd with savage heat, gallop amain
From steep pine-bearing mountains to the plain:
So ran the people forth to gaze upon her,
And all that view'd her were enamour'd on her.

---

77 **Hippolytus**: he preferred hunting to love-making. 80 **uplandish country**: poor quality, sparsely populated land. 81: Thrace was famous as a savage place. 90 **thrall**: slave. 97 **firmament**: vault of the sky. 101 **Phaethon**: dared to try and drive the sun's chariot and burned the earth. 107 **star**: the moon. 108 **thirling**: flying. 114 **race**: the half men, half horse, Centaurs.

And as in fury of a dreadful fight,
120 Their fellows being slain or put to flight,
Poor soldiers stand with fear of death dead-strooken,
So at her presence all surpris'd and tooken
Await the sentence of her scornful eyes:
He whom she favours lives, the other dies.
125 There might you see one sigh, another rage,
And some (their violent passions to assuage)
Compile sharp satires, but alas too late,
For faithful love will never turn to hate.
And many seeing great princes were denied,
130 Pin'd as they went, and thinking on her died.
On this feast day, O cursed day and hour,
Went *Hero* thorough *Sestos*, from her tower
To *Venus'* temple, where unhappily,
As after chanc'd, they did each other spy.
135 So fair a church as this, had *Venus* none:
The walls were of discolour'd jasper stone,
Wherein was *Proteus* carv'd, and o'erhead
A lively vine of green sea agate spread;
Where by one hand, light-headed *Bacchus* hung,
140 And with the other, wine from grapes outwrung.
Of crystal shining fair the pavement was,
The town of *Sestos* call'd it *Venus'* glass.
There might you see the gods in sundry shapes,
Committing heady riots, incest, rapes:
145 For know, that underneath this radiant floor
Was *Danae's* statue in a brazen tower,
Jove slyly stealing from his sister's bed,
To dally with *Idalian Ganymede*,
Or for his love *Europa* bellowing loud,
150 Or tumbling with the Rainbow in a cloud;
Blood-quaffing *Mars*, heaving the iron net
Which limping *Vulcan* and his *Cyclops* set;
Love kindling fire, to burn such towns as *Troy*;
Sylvanus weeping for the lovely boy
155 That now is turn'd into a cypress tree,
Under whose shade the wood-gods love to be.
And in the midst a silver altar stood;
There *Hero* sacrificing turtles' blood,
Vail'd to the ground, vailing her eyelids close,
160 And modestly they open'd as she rose:
Thence flew Love's arrow with the golden head,

---

137 **Proteus:** a sea god able to change his shape. 149 **Europa:** Jupiter made love to Europa as a bull.
139 **Bacchus:** god of wine. 146 **Danae:** locked in a 154 **Sylvanus:** god of woods who loved Cyparissus.
tower, Jupiter copulated with her in a shower of gold. 158 turtles': turtle doves, examples of constancy and love.

And thus *Leander* was enamoured.
Stone still he stood, and evermore he gazed,
Till with the fire that from his count'nance blazed
165 Relenting *Hero's* gentle heart was strook:
Such force and virtue hath an amorous look.
Sestiad 1 ll.1–166.

    With that, Leander stoop'd, to have embrac'd her,
But from his spreading arms away she cast her,
And thus bespake him: 'Gentle youth, forbear
To touch the sacred garments which I wear.
345 Upon a rock, and underneath a hill,
Far from the town (where all is whist and still,
Save that the sea playing on yellow sand,
Sends forth a rattling murmur to the land,
Whose sound allures the golden *Morpheus*
350 In silence of the night to visit us)
My turret stands, and there God knows I play
With Venus' swans and sparrows all the day,
A dwarfish beldam bears me company,
That hops about the chamber where I lie,
355 And spends the night (that might be better spent)
In vain discourse and apish merriment.
Come thither.' As she spake this, her tongue tripp'd,
For unawares 'Come thither' from her slipp'd,
And suddenly her former colour chang'd,
360 And here and there her eyes through anger rang'd.
And like a planet, moving several ways
At one self instant, she poor soul assays,
Loving, not to love at all, and every part
Strove to resist the motions of her heart.
365 And hands so pure, so innocent, nay such
As might have made heaven stoop to have a touch,
Did she uphold to *Venus*, and again
Vow'd spotless chastity, but all in vain.
Cupid beats down her prayers with his wings,
370 Her vows above the empty air he flings;
All deep enrag'd, his sinewy bow he bent,
And shot a shaft that burning from him went,
Wherewith she strooken, look'd so dolefully,
As made Love sigh, to see his tyranny.
375 And as she wept, her tears to pearl he turn'd,
And wound them on his arm, and for her mourn'd.
Then towards the palace of the Destinies
Laden with languishment and grief he flies,

---

346 whist: silent. 349 *Morpheus*: god of dreams.   353 beldam: aged woman. 356 apish: silly.

And to those stern nymphs humbly made request,
380 Both might enjoy each other, and be blest.
But with a ghastly dreadful countenance,
Threat'ning a thousand deaths at every glance,
They answer'd Love, nor would vouchsafe so much
As one poor word, their hate to him was such.

Sestiad 1 ll.341–84.

By this, sad *Hero*, with love unacquainted,
Viewing *Leander's* face, fell down and fainted.
He kiss'd her, and breath'd life into her lips,
Wherewith as one displeas'd, away she trips.
5 Yet as she went, full often look'd behind,
And many poor excuses did she find
To linger by the way, and once she stay'd,
And would have turn'd again, but was afraid,
In offering parley, to be counted light.
10 So on she goes, and in her idle flight,
Her painted fan of curled plumes let fall,
Thinking to train *Leander* therewithal.
He being a novice, knew not what she meant,
But stay'd, and after her a letter sent,
15 Which joyful *Hero* answer'd in such sort,
As he had hope to scale the beauteous fort
Wherein the liberal Graces lock'd their wealth,
And therefore to her tower he got by stealth.
Wide open stood the door, he need not climb,
20 And she herself before the pointed time
Had spread the board, with roses strew'd the room,
And oft look'd out, and mus'd he did not come.
At last he came, O who can tell the greeting
These greedy lovers had at their first meeting?
25 He ask'd, she gave, and nothing was denied,
Both to each other quickly were affied.
Look how their hands, so were their hearts united
And what he did she willingly requited.
(Sweet are the kisses, the embracements sweet,
30 When like desires and affections meet,
For from the earth to heaven is *Cupid* rais'd,
Where fancy is in equal balance pais'd.)
Yet she this rashness suddenly repented,
And turn'd aside, and to herself lamented,
35 As if her name and honour had been wrong'd
By being possess'd of him for whom she long'd;
Ay, and she wish'd, albeit not from her heart,

---

9 **light**: wanton. 12 **train**: entice. 20 **pointed**: appointed. 26 **affied**: betrothed. 32 **pais'd**: poised.

That he would leave her turret and depart.
The mirthful god of amorous pleasure smil'd
40 To see how he this captive nymph beguil'd.
For hitherto he did but fan the fire,
And kept it down that it might mount the higher.
Now wax'd she jealous, lest his love abated,
Fearing her own thoughts made her to be hated.
45 Therefore unto him hastily she goes,
And, like light *Salmacis*, her body throws
Upon his bosom, where with yielding eyes
She offers up herself a sacrifice,
To slake his anger, if he were displeas'd.
50 O what god would not therewith be appeas'd?
Like *Aesop's* cock, this jewel he enjoyed,
And as a brother with his sister toyed,
Supposing nothing else was to be done,
Now he her favour and good will had won.
55 But know you not that creatures wanting sense
By nature have a mutual appetence,
And wanting organs to advance a step,
Mov'd by love's force, unto each other leap?
Much more in subjects having intellect,
60 Some hidden influence breeds like effect.
Albeit *Leander*, rude in love and raw,
Long dallying with *Hero*, nothing saw
That might delight him more, yet he suspected
Some amorous rites or other were neglected.
65 Therefore unto his body hers he clung,
She, fearing on the rushes to be flung,
Striv'd with redoubled strength; the more she strived,
The more a gentle pleasing heat revived,
Which taught him all that elder lovers know,
70 And now the same gan so to scorch and glow,
As in plain terms (yet cunningly) he crav'd it;
Love always makes those eloquent that have it.
She, with a kind of granting, put him by it,
And ever as he thought himself most nigh it,
75 Like to the tree of *Tantalus* she fled,
And, seeming lavish, sav'd her maidenhead.
Ne'er king more sought to keep his diadem,
Than *Hero* this inestimable gem.
Above our life we love a steadfast friend,
80 Yet when a token of great worth we send,

---

46 **Salmacis**: wanton nymph who loved Hermaph-   56 appetence: desire.   70 gan: began.   75 *Tantalus*:
roditus.   49 slake: reduce.   51 *Aesop's* cock: rejected   in Hades he forever tries to reach a fruit which eludes
a rich jewel in favour of barley.   him.

We often kiss it, often look thereon,
And stay the messenger that would be gone:
No marvel then, though *Hero* would not yield
So soon to part from that she dearly held.

85 Jewels being lost are found again, this never,
'Tis lost but once, and once lost, lost for ever.
   Now had the Morn espied her lover's steeds,
Whereat she starts, puts on her purple weeds,
And red for anger that he stay'd so long,

90 All headlong throws herself the clouds among.
And now *Leander*, fearing to be miss'd,
Embrac'd her suddenly, took leave, and kiss'd,
Long was he taking leave, and loth to go,
And kiss'd again, as lovers use to do.

95 Sad *Hero* wrung him by the hand, and wept,
Saying, 'Let your vows and promises be kept.'
Then standing at the door, she turn'd about,
As loth to see *Leander* going out.
And now the sun, that through th' horizon peeps,

100 As pitying these lovers, downward creeps,
So that in silence of the cloudy night,
Though it was morning, did he take his flight.
But what the secret trusty night conceal'd,
Leander's amorous habit soon reveal'd:

105 With *Cupid's* myrtle was his bonnet crown'd,
About his arms the purple riband wound,
Wherewith she wreath'd her largely spreading hair,
Nor could the youth abstain, but he must wear
The sacred ring wherewith she was endow'd

110 When first religious chastity she vow'd;
Which made his love through *Sestos* to be known
And thence unto *Abydos* sooner blown
Than he could sail; for incorporeal Fame,
Whose weight consists in nothing but her name,

115 Is swifter than the wind, whose tardy plumes
Are reeking water, and dull earthly fumes.
Home when he came, he seem'd not to be there,
But like exiled air thrust from his sphere,
Set in a foreign place; and straight from thence,

120 *Alcides* like, by mighty violence,
He would have chas'd away the swelling main,
That him from her unjustly did detain.
Like as the sun in a diameter

---

88 weeds: clothes. 104 habit: dress. 106 riband: 116 reeking: vaporous. 120 *Alcides*: Hercules.
ribbon. 115 tardy: slow. 121 main: ocean.

Fires and inflames objects removed far
125 And heateth kindly, shining lat'rally,
So beauty sweetly quickens when 'tis nigh,
But being separated and removed,
Burns where it cherish'd, murders where it loved.
Therefore even as an index to a book,
130 So to his mind was young *Leander's* look.
O none but gods have power their love to hide,
Affection by the count'nance is descried.
The light of hidden fire itself discovers,
And love that is conceal'd betrays poor lovers.
135 His secret flame apparently was seen,
Leander's father knew where he had been,
And for the same mildly rebuk'd his son,
Thinking to quench the sparkles new begun.
But love resisted once, grows passionate,
140 And nothing more than counsel lovers hate.
For as a hot proud horse highly disdains
To have his head controll'd, but breaks the reins,
Spits forth the ringled bit, and with his hooves
Checks the submissive ground: so he that loves,
145 The more he is restrain'd, the worse he fares,
What is it now, but mad *Leander* dares?
'O *Hero, Hero*,' thus he cried full oft,
And then he got him to a rock aloft,
Where having spied her tower, long star'd he on't,
150 And pray'd the narrow toiling *Hellespont*
To part in twain, that he might come and go,
But still the rising billows answer'd 'No.'
With that he stripp'd him to the ivory skin,
And crying, 'Love, I come,' leapt lively in.
155 Whereat the sapphire visag'd god grew proud,
And made his capering *Triton* sound aloud,
Imagining that *Ganymede* displeas'd,
Had left the heavens, therefore on him he seiz'd.
Leander striv'd, the waves about him wound,
160 And pull'd him to the bottom, where the ground
Was strew'd with pearl, and in low coral groves
Sweet singing mermaids sported with their loves
On heaps of heavy gold, and took great pleasure
To spurn in careless sort the shipwrack treasure.
165 For here the stately azure palace stood
Where kingly *Neptune* and his train abode.

---

143 ringled: ringed. **144 checks:** hits. **150 toiling:**   **156 capering *Triton*:** merman sea-god, here frolicking
raging. **155 god:** Neptune.   or dancing. **164 spurn:** kick. **sort:** manner.

The lusty god embrac'd him, call'd him love,
And swore he never should return to *Jove*.
But when he knew it was not *Ganymede*,
170 For under water he was almost dead,
He heav'd him up, and looking on his face,
Beat down the bold waves with his triple mace,
Which mounted up, intending to have kiss'd him,
And fell in drops like tears because they miss'd him.
175 *Leander* being up, began to swim,
And, looking back, saw *Neptune* follow him;
Whereat aghast, the poor soul gan to cry,
'O let me visit *Hero* ere I die.'
The god put *Helle's* bracelet on his arm,
180 And swore the sea should never do him harm.
He clapp'd his plump cheeks, with his tresses play'd,
And smiling wantonly, his love bewray'd.
He watch'd his arms, and as they open'd wide
At every stroke, betwixt them would he slide
185 And steal a kiss, and then run out and dance,
And as he turn'd, cast many a lustful glance,
And threw him gaudy toys to please his eye,
And dive into the water, and there pry
Upon his breast, his thighs, and every limb,
190 And up again, and close beside him swim,
And talk of love. *Leander* made reply,
'You are deceiv'd, I am no woman, I.'
Thereat smil'd *Neptune*, and then told a tale,
How that a shepherd, sitting in a vale,
195 Play'd with a boy so fair and kind,
As for his love both earth and heaven pin'd,
That of the cooling river durst not drink,
Lest water-nymphs should pull him from the brink,
And when he sported in the fragrant lawns,
200 Goat-footed satyrs and up-staring fawns
Would steal him thence. Ere half this tale was done,
'Aye me,' *Leander* cried, 'th'enamour'd sun,
That now should shine on *Thetis'* glassy bower,
Descends upon my radiant *Hero's* tower.
205 O that these tardy arms of mine were wings'
And as he spake, upon the waves he springs.
Neptune was angry that he gave no ear,
And in his heart revenging malice bare:

---

179 **Helle**: drowned in the straits called Hellespont
after her. Traditionally she was saved by Neptune.
182 **bewray'd**: betrayed.

188 **pry**: look at closely. 196 **pin'd**: longed
for. 200 **fawns**: woodland gods. 203 *Thetis'* glassy
bower: the sea.

He flung at him his mace, but as it went,
210 He call'd it in, for love made him repent.
The mace returning back, his own hand hit,
As meaning to be veng'd for darting it.
When this fresh bleeding wound *Leander* view'd,
His colour went and came, as if he rued
215 The grief which *Neptune* felt. In gentle breasts
Relenting thoughts, remorse and pity rests.
And who have hard hearts and obdurate minds,
But vicious, harebrain'd, and illit'rate hinds?
The god, seeing him with pity to be moved,
220 Thereon concluded that he was beloved.
(Love is too full of faith, too credulous,
With folly and false hope deluding us.)
Wherefore *Leander's* fancy to surprise,
To the rich Ocean for gifts he flies.
225 'Tis wisdom to give much, a gift prevails,
When deep persuading oratory fails.
        By this *Leander* being near the land,
Cast down his weary feet, and felt the sand.
Breathless albeit he were, he rested not
230 Till to the solitary tower he got,
And knock'd, and call'd, at which celestial noise
The longing heart of *Hero* much more joys
Than nymphs and shepherds when the timbrel rings,
Or crooked dolphin when the sailor sings.
235 She stay'd not for her robes but straight arose,
And drunk with gladness to the door she goes,
Where seeing a naked man she screech'd for fear,
Such sights as this to tender maids are rare,
And ran into the dark herself to hide,
240 Rich jewels in the dark are soonest spied.
Unto her was he led or rather drawn,
By those white limbs which sparkled through the lawn;
The nearer that he came, the more she fled,
And seeking refuge, slipp'd into her bed.
245 Whereon *Leander* sitting, thus began,
Through numbing cold, all feeble, faint and wan:
        'If not for love, yet love, for pity sake,
Me in thy bed and maiden bosom take,
At least vouchsafe these arms some little room,
250 Who hoping to embrace thee, cheerly swum.

---

214 rued: felt remorse. **217 obdurate**: unyielding, hard. **218 harebrain'd**: having a brain like a hare, reckless, mad. **hinds**: rustics. **233 timbrel**: tambourine. **234** Arion, master of the stringed instrument the cithara, he was saved from drowning by holding onto a dolphin. **242 lawn**: transparent, fine linen. **246 wan**: pale, sickly. **250 cheerly**: gladly.

This head was beat with many a churlish billow,
And therefore let it rest upon thy pillow.'
Herewith affrighted *Hero* shrunk away,
And in her lukewarm place *Leander* lay,
255 Whose lively heat, like fire from heaven fet,
Would animate gross clay, and higher set
The drooping thoughts of base declining souls,
Than dreary *Mars* carousing nectar bowls.
His hands he cast upon her like a snare,
260 She overcome with shame and sallow fear,
Like chaste *Diana* when *Actaeon* spied her,
Being suddenly betray'd, div'd down to hide
And as her silver body downward went,
With both her hands she made the bed a tent,
265 And in her own mind thought herself secure,
O'ercast with dim and darksome coverture.
And now she lets him whisper in her ear,
Flatter, entreat, promise, protest and swear,
Yet ever as he greedily assay'd
270 To touch those dainties, she the Harpy play'd,
And every limb did as a soldier stout
Defend the fort, and keep the foeman out.
For though the rising ivory mount he scal'd,
Which is with azure circling lines empal'd,
275 Much like a globe (a globe may I term this,
By which love sails to regions full of bliss),
Yet there with *Sisyphus* he toil'd in vain,
Till gentle parley did the truce obtain.
Wherein *Leander* on her quivering breast,
280 Breathless spoke something, and sigh'd out the rest;
Which so prevail'd, as he with small ado
Enclos'd her in his arms and kiss'd her too;
And every kiss to her was as a charm,
And to *Leander* as a fresh alarm,
285 So that the truce was broke, and she alas
(Poor silly maiden) at his mercy was.
Love is not full of pity (as men say)
But deaf and cruel where he means to prey.
Even as a bird, which in our hands we wring,
290 Forth plungeth, and oft flutters with her wing,
She trembling strove; this strife of hers (like that
Which made the world) another world begat
Of unknown joy. Treason was in her thought,

---

251 churlish billow: brutal wave. **255 fet:** fetched; referring to the myth of Prometheus. **258 dreary:** bloody. **260 sallow:** yellow. **261:** The goddess Diana killed Actaeon because he accidentally saw her naked. **270 Harpy:** monstrous bird woman. **274 empal'd:** surrounded. **277 *Sisyphus*:** condemned in Hades forever to roll a block of marble uphill. **289 wring:** hold tightly.

And cunningly to yield herself she sought.
295 Seeming not won, yet won she was at length,
In such wars women use but half their strength.
Leander now, like Theban *Hercules*
Enter'd the orchard of th' *Hesperides*,
Whose fruit none rightly can describe but he
300 That pulls or shakes it from the golden tree.
And now she wish'd this night were never done,
And sigh'd to think upon th' approaching sun,
For much it griev'd her that the bright daylight
Should know the pleasure of this blessed night,
305 And them like *Mars* and *Erycine* display'd,
Both in each other's arms chain'd as they lay'd.
Again she knew not how to frame her look,
Or speak to him who in a moment took
That which so long, so charily she kept,
310 And fain by stealth away she would have crept,
And to some corner secretly have gone,
Leaving *Leander* in the bed alone.
But as her naked feet were whipping out,
He on the sudden cling'd her so about
315 That mermaid-like unto the floor she slid;
One half appear'd, the other half was hid.
Thus near the bed she blushing stood upright,
And from her countenance behold ye might
A kind of twilight break, which through the hair,
320 As from an orient cloud, glims here and there.
And round about the chamber this false morn
Brought forth the day before the day was born.
So *Hero's* ruddy cheek *Hero* betray'd,
And her all naked to his sight display'd,
325 Whence his admiring eyes more pleasure took
Than *Dis*, on heaps of gold fixing his look.
By this *Apollo's* golden harp began
To sound forth music to the ocean,
Which watchful *Hesperus* no sooner heard,
330 But he the day's bright-bearing car prepar'd,
And ran before, as harbinger of light,
And with his flaring beams mock'd ugly Night,
Till she, o'ercome with anguish, shame, and rage,
Dang'd down to hell her loathsome carriage.
Desunt nonnulla.
Sestiad 2 ll.1–332.

297–300: referring to the last labour of Hercules. **326** *Dis*: Pluto, god of the underworld. **334 Dang'd:**
305 *Erycine*: Venus. **309 charily:** carefully. **320 glims:** threw, hurled. *Desunt nonnulla*: 'something is lacking';
glimmers. printed at the end of the first edition.

Doctor Faustus

The Tragical History of Doctor Faustus was written between 1588 and 1593, most probably in 1592–93. There are records of it being regularly performed from 1594. The play was first published in 1604 in the version printed here (the A text). A different and lengthier version (the B text) was printed in 1616. Scholars now accept that neither of these early printed texts is precisely the play as Marlowe wrote it, but that both reflect the alterations and revisions which many plays of the period underwent before reaching print. Unlike most modern plays, Elizabethan plays were rarely formally divided into acts and scenes and this text largely follows the format of the 1604 edition.

Characters
The Pope
The Cardinal of Lorraine
The Emperor of Germany
The Duke and Duchess of Vanholt
A Knight, attendant on the Emperor
Doctor John Faustus, a doctor of Theology
Valdes and Cornelius, magicians
Wagner, a student and servant to Faustus
Lucifer, Prince of Hell
Mephastophilis, a devil
Alexander the Great and his Paramour, spirits
Belzabub, a devil   The Seven Deadly Sins   Good Angel
Bad Angel   Helen of Troy   An Old Man   Three Scholars
Robin and Rafe, two ostlers   A Clown   A Vinter
A Horse-Courser   Friars   Devils   Attendants

[*Enter Chorus.*]
Chorus Not marching now in fields of Thracimene,
Where Mars did mate the Carthaginians,
Nor sporting in the dalliance of love,
In courts of kings where state is overturned,
5   Nor in the pomp of proud audacious deeds,
Intends our muse to vaunt his heavenly verse.
Only this gentlemen we must perform,
The form of Faustus' fortunes good or bad.
To patient judgements we appeal our plaud,
10   And speak for Faustus in his infancy.
Now is he born, his parents base of stock,
In Germany, within a town called Rhodes.
Of riper years to Wertenberg he went,

Dramatis Personae: ostler: servant who looks after horses at inns.   Horse-courser: buyer and seller of horses.   vintner: innkeeper who sells wine.   1–2: The Carthaginian Hannibal defeated the Romans at lake Trasummenus, supposedly with the help of the god Mars.   9 our plaud: for our applause.   13 Wertenberg: Wittenberg, German university town, famous because Luther taught there.

Whereas his kinsmen chiefly brought him up.
15 So soon he profits in divinity,
The fruitful plot of scholarism graced,
That shortly he was graced with doctor's name,
Excelling all, whose sweet delight disputes
In heavenly matters of theology,
20 Till swollen with cunning, of a self conceit,
His waxen wings did mount above his reach,
And melting heavens conspired his overthrow.
For falling to a devilish exercise,
And glutted now with learning's golden gifts,
25 He surfeits upon cursed necromancy.
Nothing so sweet as magic is to him
Which he prefers before his chiefest bliss,
And this the man that in his study sits. [*Exit.*]

[*Enter Faustus in his Study.*]
Faustus Settle thy studies Faustus, and begin
30 To sound the depth of that thou wilt profess.
Having commenced, be a divine in show,
Yet level at the end of every art,
And live and die in Aristotle's works.
Sweet *Analytics* 'tis thou hast ravished me,
35 *Bene disserere est finis logices,*
Is to dispute well, logic's chiefest end,
Affords this art no greater miracle?
Then read no more, thou hast attained the end.
A greater subject fitteth Faustus' wit,
40 Bid *on kai me on* farewell, Galen come:
Seeing, *ubi desinit philosophus, ibi incipt medicus.*
Be a physician Faustus, heap up gold,
And be eternized for some wondrous cure.
Summum bonum medicinae sanitas,
45 The end of physic is our bodies' health.
Why Faustus, hast thou not attained that end?
Is not thy common talk sound aphorisms?
Are not thy bills hung up as monuments,
Whereby whole cities have escaped the plague,
50 And thousand desperate maladies been eased,
Yet art thou still but Faustus, and a man.
Wouldst thou make man to live eternally?
Or being dead, raise them to life again?
Then this profession were to be esteemed.
55 Physic farewell, where is Justinian?

---

25 necromancy: magic. **35 Bene. . . :** translated in next line. **40 on kai me on:** Greek meaning being and not being. **Galen:** famous Roman medical writer. **41 ubi. . . :** where the philosopher leaves off, the physician begins. **44 Summum:** translated next line. **48 bills:** prescriptions. **55 Justinian:** Roman emperor who ordered a compilation of law, *The Institutes*.

Si una eademque res legatur duobus,
Alter rem, alter valorem rei, etc.
A pretty case of paltry legacies:
Exhereditare filium non potest pater nisi
60 Such is the subject of the *Institute*
And universal body of the law.
His study fits a mercenary drudge,
Who aims at nothing but external trash,
Too servile and illiberal for me.
65 When all is done, divinity is best.
Jerome's Bible, Faustus, view it well.
Stipendium peccati mors est: ha, *Stipendium, etc.*
The reward of sin is death: that's hard.
Si peccasse negamus, fallimur, et nulla est in nobis veritas.
70 If we say that we have no sin,
We deceive ourselves, and there's no truth in us.
Why then belike
We must sin, and so consequently die.
Ay, we must die an everlasting death.
75 What doctrine call you this, *Che sera, sera,*
What will be, shall be? Divinity, adieu,
These metaphysics of magicians,
And necromantic books are heavenly.
Lines, circles, scenes, letters and characters:
80 Ay, these are those that Faustus most desires.
O what a world of profit and delight,
Of power, of honour, of omnipotence,
Is promised to the studious artisan?
All things that move between the quiet poles
85 Shall be at my command, emperors and kings
Are but obeyed in their several provinces,
Nor can they raise the wind, or rend the clouds.
But his dominion that exceeds in this,
Stretcheth as far as doth the mind of man.
90 A sound magician is a mighty god.
Here Faustus try thy brains to gain a deity. [*Enter Wagner.*]
Wagner, commend me to my dearest friends,
The German Valdes, and Cornelius,
Request them earnestly to visit me.
95 **Wagner** I will sir. [*Exit.*]
Faustus Their conference will be a greater help to me,
Than all my labours, plod I ne're so fast.

---

56 *Si una* . . . . : If one thing is bequeathed to two people, one shall have the thing, the other its value.
59 *Exhereditare* . . . . : a father cannot disinherit his son, except . . . .   66 **Bible**: The Vulgate, St Jerome's Latin
translation of the Bible. 67 *Stipendium.* . . : translated next line. 75 **Che** . . . . : translated next line.
69 *Si* . . . . : translated next two lines.

[*Enter good Angel and evil Angel.*]
Good Angel O Faustus, lay that damned book aside,
And gaze not on it, lest it tempt thy soul,
100 And heap God's heavy wrath upon thy head.
Read, read the scriptures, that is blasphemy.
Evil Angel Go forward Faustus in that famous art,
Wherein all nature's treasury is contained.
Be thou on earth as Jove is in the sky,
105 Lord and commander of these elements. [*Exit.*]
Faustus How am I glutted with conceit of this?
Shall I make spirits fetch me what I please,
Resolve me of all ambiguities,
Perform what desperate enterprise I will?
110 I'll have them fly to India for gold,
Ransack the ocean for orient pearl,
And search all corners of the new found world
For pleasant fruits and princely delicates.
I'll have them read me strange philosophy,
115 And tell the secrets of all foreign kings,
I'll have them wall all Germany with brass,
And make swift Rhine circle fair Wertenberg.
I'll have them fill the public schools with silk,
Wherewith the students shall be bravely clad.
120 I'll levy soldiers with the coin they bring,
And chase the Prince of Parma from our land,
And reign sole king of all our provinces.
Yea stranger engines for the brunt of war,
Then was the fiery keel at Antwerp's bridge,
125 I'll make my servile spirits to invent.
Come German Valdes and Cornelius,
And make me blest with your sage conference.
[*Enter Valdes and Cornelius.*]
Valdes, sweet Valdes, and Cornelius,
Know that your words have won me at the last,
130 To practise magic and concealed arts.
Yet not your words only, but mine own fantasy,
That will receive no object for my head,
But ruminates on necromantic skill.
Philosophy is odious and obscure,
135 Both law and physic are for petty wits,
Divinity is basest of the three,
Unpleasant, harsh, contemptible and vile,
'Tis magic, magic that hath ravished me.
Then gentle friends aid me in this attempt,

---

121 Prince of Parma: Spanish governor of the Netherlands. The context is the Protestant Dutch rebellion against the Catholic emperor Charles V.   **124 fiery keel:** fire-ship used by the Dutch against the Spanish.

140 And I that have with concise syllogisms
Gravelled the pastors of the German church,
And made the flowering pride of Wertenberg
Swarm to my problems as the infernal spirits
On sweet Musaeus when he came to hell,
145 Will be as cunning as Agrippa was,
Whose shadows made all Europe honour him.
Valdes Faustus,
These books, thy wit and our experience
Shall make all nations to canonize us,
150 As Indian Moors obey their Spanish lords,
So shall the subjects of every element
Be always serviceable to us three.
Like lions shall they guard us when we please,
Like Allmaine rutters with their horsemen's staves,
155 Or Lapland giants trotting by our sides,
Sometimes like women, or unwedded maids,
Shadowing more beauty in their airy brows,
Then has the white breasts of the Queen of Love.
From Venice shall they drag huge argosies,
160 And from America the golden fleece,
That yearly stuffs old Philip's treasury,
If learned Faustus will be resolute.
Faustus Valdes, as resolute am I in this
As thou to live, therefore object it not.
165 *Cornelius* The miracles that magic will perform,
Will make thee vow to study nothing else.
He that is grounded in astrology,
Enriched with tongues, well seen in minerals,
Hath all the principles magic doth require,
170 Then doubt not Faustus but to be renowned,
And more frequented for this mystery,
Then heretofore the Delphian oracle.
The spirits tell me they can dry the sea,
And fetch the treasure of all foreign wrecks,
175 Ay, all the wealth that our forefathers hid
Within the massy entrails of the earth.
Then tell me Faustus, what shall we three want?
Faustus Nothing, Cornelius. O this cheers my soul,
Come show me some demonstrations magical,
180 That I may conjure in some lusty grove,
And have these joys in full possession.

---

141 **gravelled:** perplexed.   144 **Musaeus:** legendary Greek poet.   145 **Agrippa:** Cornelius Agrippa, Renaissance philosopher who wrote on the occult.   150 **Indian Moors:** native Americans.   154 **Almaine rutters:** German cavalrymen.   **stave:** an iron-tipped lance.   161 **Philip:** Philip II of Spain.   168 **well . . . minerals:** knowledgeable about chemistry.   172: the god Apollo supposedly inspired the priestess at Delphi to reveal knowledge through riddles.

Valdes Then haste thee to some solitary grove,
And bear wise Bacon's and Albanus' works,
The Hebrew Psalter, and New Testament,
185　And whatsoever else is requisite
We will inform thee ere our conference cease.
Cornelius Valdes, first let him know the words of art,
And then all other ceremonies learned,
Faustus may try his cunning by himself.
190　*Valdes* First I'll instruct thee in the rudiments,
And then wilt thou be perfecter than I.
Faustus Then come and dine with me, and after meat
We'll canvass every quiddity thereof:
For ere I sleep I'll try what I can do,
195　This night I'll conjure though I die therefore. [*Exit.*]

[*Enter two scholars.*]
1st scholar I wonder what's become of Faustus, that was wont to
make our schools ring with *sic probo*.
2nd scholar That shall we know, for see here comes his boy.
[*Enter Wagner.*]
1st scholar How now sirrah, where's thy master?
200　*Wagner* God in heaven knows.
2nd scholar Why, dost not thou know?
Wagner Yes I know, but that follows not.
1st scholar Go to sirrah, leave your jesting, and tell us where he is.
Wagner That follows not necessary by force of argument, that you
205　being licentiate should stand upon't, therefore acknowledge your
error, and be attentive.
2nd scholar Why, didst thou not say thou knew'st?
Wagner Have you any witness on't?
1st scholar Yes sirrah, I heard you.
210　*Wagner* Ask my fellow if I be a thief.
2nd scholar Well, you will not tell us.
Wagner Yes sir, I will tell you, yet if you were not dunces you would
never ask me such a question, for is not he *corpus naturale*, and is not
that *mobile*? Then wherefore should you ask me such a question? but
215　that I am by nature phlegmatic, slow to wrath, and prone to lechery
(to love I would say), it were not for you to come within forty foot of
the place of execution, although I do not doubt to see you both hanged
the next sessions. Thus having triumphed over you, I will set my
countenance like a precisian, and begin to speak thus: truly my dear
220　brethren, my master is within at dinner with Valdes and Cornelius, as
this wine if it could speak, it would inform your worships, and so the

---

183: Roger Bacon and Pietro d'Abano were 13th century magicians.　193 **canvass every quiddity**: examine every
subtlety. Quiddity is a scholastic term for the essence of a thing.　197 *sic probo*: Thus I prove it.　205 **licentiate**:
a graduate of the university.　213 *corpus . . . mobile*: a body subject to change.　218 **sessions**: time when trials
take place.　219 **precisian**: a puritan.

Lord bless you, preserve you, and keep you my dear brethren, my
dear brethren. [*Exit.*]
1st scholar Nay then I fear he is fallen into that damned art, for
225 which they two are infamous through the world.
2nd scholar Were he a stranger, and not allied to me, yet should I
grieve for him: but come let us go and inform the Rector, and see if
he by his grave counsel can reclaim him.
1st scholar O but I fear me nothing can reclaim him.
230 **2nd scholar** Yet let us try what we can do. [*Exit.*]

[*Enter Faustus to conjure.*]
Faustus Now that the gloomy shadow of the earth,
Longing to view Orion's drizzling look,
Leaps from th' antartic world unto the sky,
And dims the welkin with her pitchy breath.
235 Faustus, begin thine incantations,
And try if devils will obey thy hest,
Seeing thou hast prayed and sacrificed to them.
Within this circle is Jehovah's name,
Forward and backward anagrammatized
240 The breviated names of holy saints,
Figures of every adjunct to the heavens,
And characters of signs and erring stars,
By which the spirits are enforced to rise,
Then fear not Faustus, but be resolute,
245 And try the uttermost magic can perform.
Sint mihi dei Acherontis propitii, valeat numen triplex Jehovae, ignei,
aerii, aquatani spiritus salvete, Orientis princeps Belzebub, inferni ardentis
monarcha et demogorgon, propitiamus vos, ut appareat et surgat Mephas-
tophilis: quid tu moraris? per Jehovam, Gehennam et consecratam aquam
250 *quam nunc spargo, signumque crucis quod nunc facio, et per vota nostra*
ipse nunc surgat nobis dicatus Mephastophilis. [*Enter a devil.*]
I charge thee to return and change thy shape,
Thou art too ugly to attend on me,
Go and return an old Franciscan friar,
255 That holy shape becomes a devil best. [*Exit devil.*]
I see there's virtue in my heavenly words,
Who would not be proficient in this art?
How pliant is this Mephastophilis?
Full of obedience and humility,
260 Such is the force of magic and my spells.
Now Faustus, thou art conjuror laureate

---

232 **Orion**: the constellation associated with winter storms.   234 **welkin**: sky.   239 **anagrammatized**: from the
belief that hidden meanings are found in different combination of letters.   246 ***Sint* . . . .**: Be propitious to me
spirits of Acheron! Go, threefold godhead of Jehovah. Hail spirits of fire, air, water. Belzebub, prince of the east, monarch
of fiery hell and Demogorgon, we beseech you that this Mephastophilis may arise and appear. Why do you wait? By
Jehovah, Gehenna and the consecrated water I now sprinkle, by the sign of the cross I now make, and by our vows,
my Mephastophilis now arise at our command.

That canst command great Mephastophilis,
Quin redis Mephastophilis fratris imagine.
[*Enter Mephastophilis.*]
Mephastophilis Now Faustus, what wouldst thou have me do?

265 **Faustus** I charge thee wait upon me whilst I live,
To do whatever Faustus shall command,
Be it to make the moon drop from her sphere,
Or the ocean to overwhelm the world.
Mephastophilis I am a servant to great Lucifer,

270 And may not follow thee without his leave,
No more than he commands must we perform.
Faustus Did not he charge thee to appear to me?
Mephastophilis No, I came now hither of mine own accord.
Faustus Did not my conjuring speeches raise thee? Speak.

275 **Mephastophilis** That was the cause, but yet *per accidens*,
For when we hear one rack the name of God,
Abjure the scriptures, and his saviour Christ,
We fly, in hope to get his glorious soul,
Nor will we come, unless he use such means

280 Whereby he is in danger to be damned.
Therefore the shortest cut for conjuring
Is stoutly to abjure the Trinity,
And pray devoutly to the prince of hell.
Faustus So Faustus hath

285 Already done, and holds this principle,
There is no chief but only Belzebub,
To whom Faustus doth dedicate himself,
This word damnation terrifies not him,
For he confounds hell in Elysium

290 His ghost be with the old philosophers,
But leaving these vain trifles of men's souls,
Tell me what is that Lucifer thy lord?
Mephastophilis Arch-regent and commander of all spirits.
Faustus Was not that Lucifer an angel once?

295 **Mephastophilis** Yes Faustus, and most dearly loved of God.
Faustus How comes it then that he is prince of devils?
Mephastophilis O by aspiring pride and insolence,
For which God threw him from the face of heaven.
Faustus And what are you that live with Lucifer?

300 **Mephastophilis** Unhappy spirits that fell with Lucifer,
Conspired against our God with Lucifer,
And are for ever damned with Lucifer.
Faustus Where are you damned?
Mephastophilis In hell.

---

263 Quin . . . . : return, Mephastophilis, in the image of a friar. **275 *per accidens*:** a scholastic distinction between a cause which has a necessary effect and one which provides the occasion for an effect. **276 rack:** torture. **289 Elysium:** the place of the heroic or righteous in the classical world.

305   *Faustus* How comes it then that thou art out of hell?
    Mephastophilis Why this is hell, nor am I out of it:
    Thinkst thou that I who saw the face of God,
    And tasted the eternal joys of heaven,
    Am not tormented with ten thousand hells,
310   In being deprived of everlasting bliss?
    O Faustus, leave these frivolous demands,
    Which strike a terror to my fainting soul.
    Faustus What, is great Mephastophilis so passionate,
    For being deprived of the joys of heaven?
315   Learn thou of Faustus manly fortitude,
    And scorn those joys thou never shall possess.
    Go bear those tidings to great Lucifer,
    Seeing Faustus hath incurred eternal death,
    By desperate thoughts against Jove's deity.
320   Say, he surrenders up to him his soul,
    So he will spare him 24 years,
    Letting him live in all voluptuousness,
    Having thee ever to attend on me,
    To give me whatsoever I shall ask,
325   To tell me whatsoever I demand,
    To slay mine enemies, and aid my friends,
    And always be obedient to my will.
    Go and return to mighty Lucifer,
    And meet me in my study at midnight,
330   And then resolve me of thy master's mind.
    Mephastophilis I will Faustus. [*Exit.*]
    Faustus Had I as many souls as there be stars,
    I'd give them all for Mephastophilis.
    By him I'll be great emperor of the world,
335   And make a bridge through the moving air,
    To pass the ocean with a band of men,
    I'll join the hills that bind the Afric shore,
    And make that land continent to Spain,
    And both contributory to my crown.
340   The Emperor shall not live but by my leave,
    Nor any potentate of Germany.
    Now that I have obtained what I desire,
    I'll live in speculation of this art,
    Till Mephastophilis return again. [*Exit.*]

    [*Enter Wagner and the clown.*]
345   *Wagner* Sirrah boy, come hither.
    Clown How, boy? Swowns boy, I hope you have seen many boys
    with such pickadevants as I have. Boy, quotha?

---

338 continent: join the landmass of Africa to Spain.   **346 Clown:** a rustic fool.   **Swowns:** a contraction of God's
wounds.   **347 pickadevants:** a pointed beard.

Wagner Tell me sirrah, hast thou any comings in?

Clown Ay, and goings out too, you may see else.

350 **Wagner** Alas poor slave, see how poverty jesteth in his nakedness, the villain is bare, and out of service, and so hungry, that I know he would give his soul to the devil for a shoulder of mutton, though it were blood raw.

Clown How, my soul to the devil for a shoulder of mutton though 355 'twere blood raw? Not so good friend; b'urlady I had need have it well roasted, and good sauce to it, if I pay so dear.

Wagner Well, wilt thou serve me, and I'll make thee go like *Qui mihi discipulus?*

Clown How, in verse?

360 **Wagner** No sirrah, in beaten silk and stavesacre.

Clown How, how, knavesacre? Ay, I thought that was all the land his father left him: Do ye hear, I would be sorry to rob you of your living.

Wagner Sirrah, I say in stavesacre.

365 **Clown** Oho, oho, stavesacre, why then belike, if I were your man, I should be full of vermin.

Wagner So thou shalt, whether thou beest with me, or no: but sirrah, leave your jesting, and bind your self presently unto me for seven years, or I'll turn all the lice about thee into familiars, and they shall 370 tear thee in pieces.

Clown Do you hear sir? You may save that labour, they are too familiar with me already, 'swowns they are as bold with my flesh, as if they had paid for my meat and drink.

Wagner Well, do you hear sirrah? Hold, take these guilders.

375 **Clown** Gridirons, what be they?

Wagner Why French crowns.

Clown Mass but for the name of French crowns a man were as good have as many English counters, and what should I do with these?

Wagner Why now sirrah thou art at an hour's warning whensoever 380 or wheresoever the devil shall fetch thee.

Clown No, no, here, take your gridirons again.

Wagner Truly I'll none of them.

Clown Truly but you shall.

Wagner Bear witness I gave them him.

385 **Clown** Bear witness I give them you again.

Wagner Well, I will cause two devils presently to fetch thee away. Baliol and Belcher.

Clown Let your Balio and your Belcher come here, and I'll knock them, they were never so knocked since they were devils. Say I should

---

351 **out of service:** not in the employ of anyone.   355 **b'urlady:** a contraction of by our Lady.   357 **Qui ....:** You who are my pupil.   360 **stavesacre:** a plant used to make a preparation to combat lice, also used as an emetic. 361: the clown deliberately mishears: a knave is a person of low condition, a knave's acre would be no land at all.   378 **counters:** privately issued coins with no recognised value, often referring to forged currency. The point of this exchange alludes to the debased value of French currency at the time.

390   kill one of them what would folks say? Do ye see yonder tall fellow in
the round slop, he has killed the devil: so I should be called kill-devil
all the parish over.
[*Enter two devils, and the clown runs up and down crying.*]
Wagner Baliol and Belcher, spirits away. [*Devils exit.*]
Clown What, are they gone? A vengeance on them, they have vile
395   long nails: there was a he devil and a she devil. I'll tell you how you
shall know them: all he devils has horns, and all she devils has clefts
and cloven feet.
Wagner Well sirrah follow me.
Clown But do you hear? If I should serve you, would you teach me
400   to raise up Banios and Belcheos?
Wagner I will teach thee to turn thy self to anything, to a dog, or a
cat, or a mouse, or a rat, or anything.
Clown How? A Christian fellow to a dog or a cat, a mouse or a rat?
No, no sir, if you turn me into any thing, let it be in the likeness of a
405   little pretty frisking flea, that I may be here and there and every
where. O I'll tickle the pretty wenches' plackets, I'll be amongst them
i'faith.
Wagner Well sirrah, come.
Clown But do you hear Wagner?
410   **Wagner** How Baliol and Belcher.
Clown O Lord, I pray sir, let Banio and Belcher go sleep.
Wagner Villain, call me Master Wagner, and let thy left eye be
diametarily fix't upon my right heel, with *quasi vestigias nostras
insistere.*
415   **Clown** God forgive me, he speaks Dutch fustian: well, I'll follow
him, I'll serve him, that's flat. [*Exit.*]

[*Enter Faustus in his study.*]
Faustus Now Faustus must thou needs be damned,
And canst thou not be saved?
What boots it then to think of God or heaven?
420   Away with such vain fancies and despair,
Despair in God, and trust in Belzebub.
Now go not backward. No Faustus, be resolute,
Why waverest thou? O something soundeth in mine ears:
Abjure this magic, turn to God again.
425   Ay and Faustus will turn to God again.
To God? He loves thee not,
The god thou servest is thine own appetite,
Wherein is fix't the love of Belzebub.
To him I'll build an altar and a church,
430   And offer lukewarm blood of new born babes.

---

391 **round slop**: baggy breeches.   406   **plackets**: pocket in a woman's skirt, an allusion to a woman's
genitals.   413 **diametarily**: diametrically.   *quasi* . . . : as if to follow in our footsteps.   415 **fustian**: inflated non-
sensical language.

[*Enter Good Angel and Evil Angel.*]
Good Angel Sweet Faustus, leave that execrable art.
Faustus Contrition, prayer, repentance: what of them?
Good Angel O they are means to bring thee unto heaven.
Evil Angel Rather illusions, fruits of lunacy,
435   That makes men foolish that do trust them most.
Good Angel Sweet Faustus, think of heaven, and heavenly things.
Evil Angel No Faustus, think of honour and wealth. *Exit.*
Faustus Of wealth,
    Why the signory of Emden shall be mine,
440   When Mephastophilis shall stand by me,
    What God can hurt thee Faustus? Thou art safe,
    Cast no more doubts. Come Mephastophilis,
    And bring glad tidings from great Lucifer.
    Is't not midnight? Come Mephastophilis,
445   *Veni, veni Mephastophile.* [*Enter Mephastophilis.*]
    Now tell, what says Lucifer thy lord?
Mephastophilis That I shall wait on Faustus whilst he lives,
    So he will buy my service with his soul.
Faustus Already Faustus hath hazarded that for thee.
450 **Mephastophilis** But Faustus, thou must bequeath it solemnly,
    And write a deed of gift with thine own blood,
    For that security craves great Lucifer.
    If thou deny it, I will back to hell.
Faustus Stay Mephastophilis, and tell me,
455   What good will my soul do thy lord?
Mephastophilis Enlarge his kingdom.
Faustus Is that the reason he tempts us thus?
Mephastophilis *Solamen miseris socios habuisse doloris.*
Faustus Have you any pain that tortures others?
460 **Mephastophilis** As great as have the human souls of men.
    But tell me Faustus, shall I have thy soul,
    And I will be thy slave, and wait on thee,
    And give thee more than thou hast wit to ask.
465 **Faustus** Ay, Mephastophilis, I give it thee.
Mephastophilis Then stab thine arm courageously,
    And bind thy soul, that at some certain day
    Great Lucifer may claim it as his own,
    And then be thou as great as Lucifer.
470 **Faustus** Lo, Mephastophilis, for love of thee,
    I cut mine arm, and with my proper blood
    Assure my soul to be great Lucifer's,
    Chief Lord and regent of perpetual night.
    View here the blood that trickles from mine arm,
475   And let it be propitious for my wish.

---

439 signory: rule. **Emden:** prosperous port in northwest Germany. **445 *Veni* . . . :** Come, come
Mephastophilis. **458 *Solamen* . . . :** It is a comfort to the wretched to have had company in misery.

Mephastophilis But Faustus, thou must
Write it in manner of a deed of gift.
Faustus Ay, so I will, but Mephastophilis,
My blood congeals and I can write no more.
480 **Mephastophilis** I'll fetch thee fire to dissolve it straight. [*Exit.*]
Faustus What might the staying of my blood portend?
Is it unwilling I should write this bill?
Why streams it not, that I may write afresh?
Faustus gives to thee his soul: ah there it stayed,
485 Why shouldst thou not? Is not thy soul thine own?
Then write again, Faustus gives to thee his soul.
[*Enter Mephastophilis with a chafer of coals.*]
Mephastophilis Here's fire, come Faustus, set it on.
Faustus So now the blood begins to clear again,
Now will I make an end immediately.
490 **Mephastophilis** O what will not I do to obtain his soul?
Faustus *Consummatum est*, this bill is ended,
And Faustus hath bequeathed his soul to Lucifer.
But what is this inscription on mine arm?
Homo fuge. Whither should I fly?
495 If unto God he'll throw thee down to hell,
My senses are deceived, here's nothing writ.
I see it plain, here in this place is writ,
Homo fuge. Yet shall not Faustus fly.
Mephastophilis I'll fetch him somewhat to delight his mind. [*Exit.*]
[*Enter with devils, giving crowns and rich apparel to Faustus, and dance,
and then depart.*]
500 **Faustus** Speak Mephastophilis, what means this show?
Mephastophilis Nothing Faustus, but to delight thy mind withal,
And to show thee what magic can perform.
Faustus But may I raise up spirits when I please?
Mephastophilis Ay Faustus, and do greater things then these.
505 **Faustus** Then there's enough for a thousand souls.
Here Mephastophilis receive this scroll.
A deed of gift of body and of soul:
But yet conditionally, that thou perform
All articles prescribed between us both.
510 **Mephastophilis** Faustus, I swear by hell and Lucifer
To effect all promises between us made.
Faustus Then hear me read them. On these conditions following:
First, that Faustus may be a spirit in form and substance. Secondly,
that Mephastophilis shall be his servant, and at his command. Thirdly,
515 that Mephastophilis shall do for him, and bring him whatsoever.
Fourthly, that he shall be in his chamber or house invisible. Lastly,

---

482 bill: contract. 491 *Consummatum est:* It is finished. According to John 19:30 the last words of Christ on the cross. 494 *Homo fuge:* man flee.

that he shall appear to the said John Faustus, at all times, in what
form or shape soever he please.

I, John Faustus of Wertenberg, Doctor, by these presents, do give
520   both body and soul to Lucifer prince of the East, and his minister
Mephastophilis, and furthermore grant unto them, that 24 years being expired, the articles above written inviolate, full power to fetch
or carry the said John Faustus body and soul, flesh, blood, or goods,
into their habitation wheresoever.

525   By me John Faustus.

Mephastophilis Speak Faustus, do you deliver this as your deed?

Faustus Ay, take it, and the devil give thee good on't.

Mephastophilis Now Faustus ask what thou wilt.

Faustus First will I question with thee about hell. Tell me, where is
530   the place that men call hell?

Mephastophilis Under the heavens.

Faustus Ay, but where about?

Mephastophilis Within the bowels of these elements,
Where we are tortured and remain for ever.
535   Hell hath no limits, nor is circumscribed
In one self place, for where we are is hell,
And where hell is, must we ever be:
And to conclude, when all the world dissolves,
And every creature shall be purified,
540   All places shall be hell that is not heaven.

Faustus Come, I think hell's a fable.

Mephastophilis Ay think so still, till experience change thy mind.

Faustus Why? Thinkst thou then that Faustus shall be damned?

Mephastophilis Ay, of necessity, for here's the scroll,
545   Wherein thou hast given thy soul to Lucifer.

Faustus Ay, and body too, but what of that?
Thinkst thou that Faustus is so fond to imagine
That after this life there is any pain?
Tush, these are trifles and mere old wives' tales.

550   **Mephastophilis** But Faustus, I am an instance to prove the contrary,
For I am damned, and am now in hell.

Faustus How? Now in hell? Nay and this be hell, I'll willingly be
damned here. What walking, disputing, etc. But leaving off this, let
me have a wife, the fairest maid in Germany, for I am wanton and
555   lascivious, and can not live without a wife.

Mephastophilis How, a wife? I prithee Faustus talk not of a wife.

Faustus Nay sweet Mephastophilis fetch me one, for I will have
one.

Mephastophilis Well thou wilt have one. Sit there till I come,
560   I'll fetch thee a wife in the devil's name. [*Exit.*]
[*Enter with a devil dressed like a woman, with fireworks.*]

---

519 by these presents: according to the articles in this document.   **536 self:** particular.

Mephastophilis Tell Faustus, how dost thou like thy wife?
Faustus A plague on her for a hot whore.
Mephastophilis Tut Faustus, marriage is but a ceremonial toy,
If thou lovest me, think no more of it.
565   I'll cull thee out the fairest courtesans,
And bring them every morning to thy bed.
She whom thine eye shall like, thy heart shall have,
Be she as chaste as was Penelope,
As wise as Saba, or as beautiful
570   As was bright Lucifer before his fall.
Hold, take this book, peruse it thoroughly,
The iterating of these lines brings gold,
The framing of this circle on the ground,
Brings whirlwinds, tempests, thunder, lightning.
575   Pronounce, this thrice devoutly to thyself,
And men in armour shall appear to thee,
Ready to execute what thou desir'st.
Faustus Thanks Mephastophilis, yet fain would I have a book wherein
I might behold all spells and incantations, that I might raise up spirits
580   when I please.
Mephastophilis Here they are in this book. [*There turn to them.*]
Faustus Now would I have a book where I might see all characters
and planets of the heavens, that I might know their motions and
dispositions.
585   **Mephastophilis** Here they are too. [*Turn to them.*]
Faustus Nay let me have one book more, and then I have done,
wherein I might see all plants, herbs and trees that grow upon the
earth.
Mephastophilis Here they be.
590   **Faustus** O thou art deceived.
Mephastophilis Tut I warrant thee. [*Turn to them. Exit.*]

[*Enter Robin the ostler with a book in his hand.*]
Robin O, this is admirable! Here I ha' stolen one of Doctor Faustus'
conjuring books, and i'faith I mean to search some circles for my own
use. Now will I make all the maidens in our parish dance at my pleas-
595   ure stark naked before me, and so by that means I shall see more than
ere I felt, or saw yet.
[*Enter Rafe calling Robin.*]
Rafe Robin, prithee come away, there's a gentleman tarries to have
his horse, and he would have his things rubbed and made clean: he
keeps such a chafing with my mistress about it, and she has sent me
600   to look thee out. Prithee come away.
Robin Keep out, keep out, or else you are blown up, you are
dismembred Rafe! Keep out, for I am about a roaring piece of work.

---

569 **Saba**: The Queen of Sheba, whose wisdom impressed Solomon.   591 **Tut . . . :** Come, I assure you [that this is the case].   602 **roaring**: noisy.

Rafe Come, what dost thou with that same book thou canst not
read?

605 *Robin* Yes, my master and mistress shall find that I can read, he for
his forehead, she for her private study. She's born to bear with me, or
else my art fails.

Rafe Why Robin what book is that?

Robin What book? Why the most intolerable book for conjuring that

610 ere was invented by any brimstone devil.

Rafe Canst thou conjure with it?

Robin I can do all these things easily with it. First, I can make thee
drunk with hippocras at any tavern in Europe for nothing, that's one
of my conjuring works.

615 *Rafe* Our master parson says that's nothing.

Robin True Rafe, and more Rafe, if thou hast any mind to Nan Spit,
our kitchen maid, then turn her and wind her to thy own use, as often
as thou wilt, and at midnight.

Rafe O brave Robin, shall I have Nan Spit, and to mine own use? On

620 that condition I'll feed thy devil with horse-bread as long as he lives,
of free cost.

Robin No more sweet Rafe, let's go and make clean our boots which
lie foul upon our hands, and then to our conjuring in the devil's name.
[*Exit.*]

[*Enter Faustus and Mephastophilis.*]

Faustus When I behold the heavens, then I repent,

625 And curse thee wicked Mephastophilis,
Because thou hast deprived me of those joys.

Mephastophilis Why Faustus,
Thinkst thou heaven is such a glorious thing?
I tell thee 'tis not half so fair as thou,

630 Ay, or any man that breathes on earth.

Faustus How prov'st thou that?

Mephastophilis It was made for man, therefore is man more
excellent.

Faustus If it were made for man, 'twas made for me.

635 I will renounce this magic and repent.

[*Enter good Angel and evil Angel.*]

Good Angel Faustus, repent, yet God will pity thee.

Evil Angel Thou art a spirit, God cannot pity thee.

Faustus Who buzzeth in mine ears I am a spirit?
Be I a devil, yet God may pity me,

640 Ay God will pity me, if I repent.

Evil Angel Ay, but Faustus never shall repent. [*Exit Angels.*]

Faustus My heart's so hardened I cannot repent,
Scarce can I name salvation, faith, or heaven,

606: allusions to sexual play.   613 hippocras: wine flavoured with spices.   620 horse-bread: low quality bread
often eaten by the poor as well as horses.

But fearful echoes thunders in mine ears,
645 Faustus, thou art damned, then swords and knives,
Poison, guns, halters, and envenomed steel
Are laid before me to dispatch myself,
And long ere this I should have slain myself,
Had not sweet pleasure conquered deep despair.
650 Have not I made blind Homer sing to me
Of Alexander's love, and Oenon's death,
And hath not he that built the walls of Thebes,
With ravishing sound of his melodious harp
Made music with my Mephastophilis?
655 Why should I die then, or basely despair?
I am resolved Faustus shall ne're repent.
Come Mephastophilis, let us dispute again,
And argue of divine Astrology.
Tell me, are there many heavens above the Moon?
660 Are all celestial bodies but one globe,
As is the substance of this centric earth?
Mephastophilis As are the elements, such are the spheres
Mutually folded in each other's orb,
And Faustus,
665 All jointly move upon one axle-tree,
Whose terminine is termed the world's wide pole,
Nor are the names, of Saturn, Mars, or Jupiter
Feigned but are erring stars.
Faustus But tell me, have they all one motion? Both *situ et tempore.*
670 *Mephastophilis* All jointly move from east to west in 24 hours upon
the poles of the world, but differ in their motion upon the poles of
the zodiac.
Faustus Tush, these slender trifles Wagner can decide,
Hath Mephastophilis no greater skill?
675 Who knows not the double motion of the planets?
The first is finish't in a natural day,
The second thus, as Saturn in 30 years, Jupiter in 12, Mars in 4, the
sun, Venus, and Mercury in a year,: the moon in 28 days. Tush, these
are freshmen's suppositions, but tell me, hath every sphere a
680 dominion or *intelligentia*?
Mephastophilis Ay.
Faustus How many heavens or spheres are there?
Mephastophilis Nine, the seven planets, the firmament, and the
empyreal heaven.

---

650 **Homer:** in legend Alexandros (Paris) lived with shepherds where he loved Oenone. Asked to judge the most beautiful of the goddesses, he chose Aphrodite, who rewarded him with Helen causing the Trojan war. Homer's epics do not deal with this episode: i.e. Faustus has been the first to hear Homer sing this story. **652 he that built . . . :** Amphion, whose playing of the lyre caused stones to move into their place in the wall. **666 terminine:** boundary. **669 *situ* . . . :** in place and time. **679 freshman:** first-year student at Cambridge, the university Marlowe attended. **680 dominion or intelligentia:** the belief that each planet is guided by a spiritual agent. Dominions are one of the nine orders of angels. **683 firmament:** the sphere of fixed stars.

685 **Faustus** Well, resolve me in this question, why have we not con-
junctions, oppositions, aspects, eclipses, all at one time, but in some
years we have more, in some less.
Mephastophilis *Per inaequalem motum respectu totius.*
Faustus Well, I am answered. Tell me who made the world?
690 **Mephastophilis** I will not.
Faustus Sweet Mephastophilis, tell me.
Mephastophilis Move me not, for I will not tell thee.
Faustus Villain, have I not bound thee to tell me anything?
Mephastophilis Ay, that is not against our kingdom, but this is.
695 Think thou on hell Faustus, for thou art damned.
Faustus Think Faustus upon God that made the world.
Mephastophilis Remember this. [*Exit.*]
Faustus Ay, go accursed spirit to ugly hell,
'Tis thou hast damned distressed Faustus' soul.
700 I'st not too late?
[*Enter Good Angel and Evil Angel.*]
Evil Angel Too late.
Good Angel Never too late, if Faustus can repent.
Evil Angel If thou repent, devils shall tear thee in pieces.
Good Angel Repent, and they shall never raze thy skin. [*Exit.*]
705 **Faustus** Ah Christ my saviour,
Seek to save distressed Faustus' soul.
[*Enter Lucifer, Belzebub, and Mephastophilis.*]
Lucifer Christ cannot save thy soul, for he is just,
There's none but I have interest in the same.
Faustus O who art thou that lookst so terrible?
710 **Lucifer** I am Lucifer,
And this is my companion prince in hell.
Faustus O Faustus, they are come to fetch away thy soul.
Lucifer We come to tell thee thou dost injure us.
Thou talkst of Christ, contrary to thy promise.
715 Thou shouldst not think of God, think of the devil,
And of his dam too.
Faustus Nor will I henceforth. Pardon me in this,
And Faustus vows never to look to heaven,
Never to name God, or to pray to him,
720 To burn his scriptures, slay his ministers,
And make my spirits pull his churches down.
Lucifer Do so, and we will highly gratify thee. Faustus, we are come
from hell to show thee some pastime. Sit down, and thou shalt see all
the seven deadly sins appear in their proper shapes.
725 **Faustus** That sight will be as pleasing unto me, as paradise was to
Adam, the first day of his creation.

---

688 *Per inaequalem* . . . . : Though an unequal motion with respect to the whole.   **704** raze: graze.   **716** dam:
dame, a woman of rank.

Lucifer Talk not of paradise, nor creation, but mark this show. Talk of
the devil, and nothing else: come away. [*Enter the seven deadly sins.*]
Now Faustus, examine them of their several names and dispositions.
730   ***Faustus*** What art thou? The first.
Pride I am Pride, I disdain to have any parents. I am like to Ovid's
flea, I can creep into every corner of a wench, sometimes like a periwig, I sit upon her brow, or like a fan of feathers, I kiss her lips.
Indeed I do, what do I not? But fie, what a scent is here? I'll not speak
735   another word, except the ground were perfumed and covered with
cloth of arras.
Faustus What art thou? The second.
Covetousness I am Covetousness, begotten of an old churl, in an old
leathern bag: and might I have my wish, I would desire, that this
740   house, and all the people in it were turn'd to gold, that I might lock
you up in my good chest. O my sweet gold.
Faustus What art thou? The third.
Wrath I am Wrath, I had neither father nor mother, I leapt out of a
lion's mouth, when I was scarce half an hour old, and ever since I
745   have run up and down the world, with this case of rapiers wounding
myself, when I had no body to fight withal. I was born in hell, and
look to it, for some of you shall be my father.
Faustus What art thou? The fourth.
Envy I am Envy, begotten of a chimney-sweeper and an oyster wife.
750   I cannot read, and therefore wish all books were burnt. I am lean
with seeing others eat. O that there would come a famine through
all the world, that all might die, and I live alone, then thou shouldst
see how fat I would be. But must thou sit and I stand? Come down
with a vengeance.
755   ***Faustus*** Away envious rascal. What art thou? The fifth.
Gluttony Who I sir? I am Gluttony: my parents are all dead, and the
devil a penny they have left me, but a bare pension, and that is 30
meals a day, and ten bevers, a small trifle to suffice nature. O I come
of a royal parentage, my grandfather was a gammon of bacon, my
760   grandmother a hogshead of claret-wine: My godfathers were these,
Peter Pickle-herring, and Martin Martlemas-beef. O but my godmother
she was a jolly gentlewoman, and well-beloved in every good town
and city: her name was Mistress Margery March-beer. Now Faustus,
thou hast heard all my progeny, wilt thou bid me to supper?
770   ***Faustus*** No, I'll see thee hanged, thou wilt eat up all my victuals.
Gluttony Then the devil choke thee.
Faustus Choke thy self glutton. What art thou? The sixth.
Sloth I am sloth, I was begotten on a sunny bank, where I have lain
ever since, and you have done me great injury to bring me from thence.

731–32 Ovid's flea: who goes wherever it wishes. The *Elegia de pulice*, a poem ascribed to Ovid.   **736 arras:** Arras,
a town in Flanders famous for making tapestry.   **738 churl:** a man without rank, popularly a miser.   **757 devil a
penny:** not a penny.   **758 bevers:** drinks.   **761 Martin Martlemas-beef:** cattle killed at Martinmas (11 November)
for winter, a feast at which considerable amounts were eaten.   **763 March-beer:** a strong beer brewed in March.

775 Let me be carried thither again by Gluttony and Lechery. I'll not
speak another word for a king's ransom.
Faustus What are you mistress minx, the seventh and last?
Lechery Who I sir? I am one that loves an inch of raw mutton better
then an ell of fried stock-fish, and the first letter of my name begins
780 with lechery.
Lucifer Away, to hell, to hell. [*Exit the sins.*]
Now Faustus, how dost thou like this?
Faustus O this feeds my soul.
Lucifer Tut Faustus, in hell is all manner of delight.
785 *Faustus* O might I see hell, and return again, how happy were I
then?
Lucifer Thou shalt, I will send for thee at midnight. In mean time
take this book, peruse it thoroughly, and thou shalt turn thy self into
what shape thou wilt.
790 *Faustus* Great thanks mighty Lucifer. This will I keep as chary as my
life.
Lucifer Farewell Faustus, and think on the devil.
Faustus Farewell great Lucifer. Come Mephastophilis. [*Exit all.*]

[*Enter Wagner solus.*]
Wagner Learned Faustus,
795 To know the secrets of astronomy,
Graven in the book of Jove's high firmament,
Did mount himself to scale Olympus' top,
Being seated in a chariot burning bright,
Drawn by the strength of yoky dragons' necks.
800 He now is gone to prove cosmography,
And as I guess, will first arrive at Rome,
To see the Pope, and manner of his court,
And take some part of holy Peter's feast,
That to this day is highly solemnized. [*Exit.*]
[*Enter Faustus and Mephastophilis.*]
805 *Faustus* Having now, my good Mephastophilis,
Passed with delight the stately town of Trier,
Environ'd round with airy mountain tops,
With walls of flint, and deep entrenched lakes,
Not to be won by any conquering prince.
810 From Paris next coasting the realm of France,
We saw the river Maine fall into Rhine,
Whose banks are set with groves of fruitful vines.
Then up to Naples, rich Campania,
Whose buildings fair and gorgeous to the eye,
815 The streets straight forth, and praved with finest brick,

---

777 minx: a wanton woman.   **779 ell:** a unit of measurement, similar to an inch.   **stock-fish:** dried cod, colloqui-
ally an impotent penis. All Lechery's words are sexual innuendos.   **790 chary:** carefully.   **799 yoky:** coupled by a
yoke.   **800 prove cosmography:** demonstrate if maps are correctly drawn.

Quarters the town in four equivalents.
There saw we learned Maro's golden tomb,
The way he cut an English mile in length,
Thorough a rock of stone in one night's space.
820 From thence to Venice, Padua, and the rest,
In one of which a sumptuous temple stands,
That threats the stars with her aspiring top.
Thus hitherto hath Faustus spent his time,
But tell me now, what resting place is this?
825 Hast thou as erst I did command,
Conducted me within the walls of Rome?
Mephastophilis Faustus, I have, and because we will not be
unprovided, I have taken up his Holiness' privy chamber for our use.
Faustus I hope his Holiness will bid us welcome.
830 *Mephastophilis* Tut, 'tis no matter man, we'll be bold with his good
cheer,
And now my Faustus, that thou may'st perceive
What Rome containeth to delight thee with,
Know that this city stands upon seven hills
835 That underprops the groundwork of the same,
(Just through the midst runs flowing Tiber's stream,
With winding banks that cut it in two parts,)
Over the which four stately bridges lean,
That makes safe passage to each part of Rome.
840 Upon the bridge called Ponto Angelo
Erected is a castle passing strong,
Within whose walls such store of ordnance are,
And double cannons, framed of carved brass,
As match the days within one complete year,
845 Besides the gates and high pyramids,
Which Julius Caesar brought from Africa.
Faustus Now by the kingdoms of infernal rule,
Of Styx, Acheron and the firey lake
Of ever-burning Phlegethon I swear,
850 That I do long to see the monuments
And situation of bright splendent Rome,
Come therefore, let's away.
Mephastophilis Nay Faustus stay, I know you'd fain see the Pope,
And take some part of holy Peter's feast,
855 Where thou shalt see a troupe of bald-pate friars,
Whose *summum bonum* is in belly-cheer.
Faustus Well, I am content, to compass then some sport,
And by their folly make us merriment.

---

817 **Maro's golden tomb:** Virgil, whose reputed tomb near Naples became a type of shrine.   821 St Mark's in Venice and its campanile.   848 **Styx . . . :** three of the four rivers of the underworld.   856 ***summum bonum:*** greatest good.

Then charm me that I may be invisible, to do what I please,
860 Unseen of any whilst I stay in Rome.
Mephastophilis So Faustus, now
Do what thou wilt, thou shalt not be discerned.
[*Sound a sennet. Enter the Pope and the Cardinal of Lorraine to the banquet, with friars attending.*]
Pope My lord of Lorraine, will't please you draw near.
Faustus Fall too, and the devil choke you and you spare.
865 **Pope** How now, whose that which spake? Friars look about.
Friars Here's no body, if it like your Holiness.
Pope My Lord, here is a dainty dish was sent me from the Bishop of Milan.
Faustus I thank you sir. [*Snatches it.*]
870 **Pope** How now, whose that which snatch't the meat from me? Will no man look? My Lord, this dish was sent me from the Cardinal of Florence.
Faustus You say true, I'll ha'it. [*Snatches the dish.*]
Pope What again? M'lord I'll drink to your grace.
875 **Faustus** I'll pledge your grace. [*Snatches the cup.*]
Lorraine My Lord, it may be some ghost newly crept out of Purgatory come to beg a pardon of your Holiness.
Pope It may be so. Friars prepare a dirge to lay the fury of this ghost. Once again my Lord, fall too. [*The Pope crosseth himself.*]
880 **Faustus** What, are you crossing of your self? Well use that trick no more, I would advise you. [*Cross again.*] Well, there's the second time; aware the third. I give you fair warning. [*Cross again, and Faustus hits him a box of the ear, and they all run away.*]
Come on Mephastophilis, what shall we do?
885 **Mephastophilis** Nay I know not, we shall be cursed with bell, book, and candle.
Faustus How? Bell, book, and candle; candle, book, and bell,
Forward and backward, to curse Faustus to hell.
Anon you shall hear a hog grunt, a calf bleat, and an ass bray, because
890 it is St. Peter's holy day.
[*Enter all the friars to sing the dirge.*]
Friar Come brethren, let's about our business with good devotion.
[*Sing this.*]
Cursed be he that stole away his Holiness' meat from the table.
Maledicat dominus.
Cursed be he that struck his Holiness a blow on the face.
895 *Maledicat dominus.*
Cursed be he that took Friar Sandelo a blow on the pate.
Maledicat dominus.
Cursed be he that disturbeth our holy dirge.

---

877 **pardon**: an indulgence for remission of sins.   878 **dirge**: verses from the Office of the Dead.   882 **aware**: beware.   893–99 *Maledicat dominus*: May the Lord curse him.

Maledicat dominus.

900 Cursed be he that took away his Holiness' wine.
Maledicat dominus. Et omnes sancti, Amen.
[*Mephastophilis and Faustus beat the friars, and fling fireworks among them, and so Exit.*]

[*Enter Robin and Rafe with a silver goblet.*]
Robin Come Rafe, did not I tell thee, we were for ever made by this Doctor Faustus' book? *Ecce signum*, here's a simple purchase for horse-keepers, our horses shall eat no hay as long as this lasts.
[*Enter the vintner.*]

905 **Rafe** But Robin, here comes the vintner.
Robin Hush, I'll gull him supernaturally. Drawer, I hope all is paid, God be with you. Come Rafe.
Vintner Soft sir, a word with you. I must yet have a goblet paid from you ere you go.

910 **Robin** I a goblet Rafe. I a goblet? I scorn you. And you are but a . . . I a goblet? Search me.
Vintner I mean so sir, with your favour. [*Searches Robin.*]
Robin How say you now?
Vintner I must say somewhat to your fellow. You sir.

915 **Rafe** Me sir, me sir. Search your fill. [*Vintner searches him.*]
Now sir, you may be ashamed to burden honest men with a matter of truth.
Vintner Well, one of you hath this goblet about you.
Robin You lie drawer, 'tis afore me. Sirrah you, I'll teach ye to im-

920 peach honest men. Stand by, I'll scour you for a goblet. Stand aside you had best, I charge you in the name of Belzabub. Look to the goblet Rafe.
Vintner What mean you sirrah ?
Robin I'll tell you what I mean. [*He reads.*]

925 'Sanctobulorum Periphrasticon.' Nay I'll tickle you Vintner. Look to the goblet Rafe. *He reads.*
'Polypragmos Belseboranis framanto pacostiphos tostu Mephastophilis.'
[*Enter Mephastophilis. Sets squibs at their backs, they run about.*]
Vintner O nomine Domine. What meanst thou Robin? Thou hast no goblet.

930 **Rafe** Peccatum peccatorum. Here's thy goblet, good vintner.
Robin Misericordia pro nobis. What shall I do? Good devil, forgive me now, and I'll never rob thy library more.
[*Enter to them Mephastophilis.*]
Mephastophilis Monarch of hell, under whose black survey
Great potentates do kneel with awful fear,

935 Upon whose altars thousand souls do lie,

---

901 *Et omnes sancti*: and all the saints [curse him]. 902 **made**: made rich. 903 *Ecce signum*: behold the sign. 906 **gull**: cheat. 925 *Sanctobulorum* . . .: gibberish, but effective because he names Mephastophilis. **squibs**: fireworks.

How am I vexed with these villains' charms?
From Constantinople am I hither come,
Only for pleasure of these damned slaves.
Robin How, from Constantinople? You have had a great journey,
will you take sixpence in your purse to pay for your supper, and be
gone?
Mephastophilis Well villains, for your presumption, I transform thee
into an ape, and thee into a dog, and so be gone. [*Exit.*]
Robin How, into an ape? That's brave. I'll have fine sport with the
boys. I'll get nuts and apples enow.
Rafe And I must be a dog.
Robin I'faith thy head will never be out of the potage pot. [*Exit.*]

[*Enter Chorus.*]
Chorus When Faustus had with pleasure ta'en the view
Of rarest things, and royal courts of kings,
He stayed his course, and so returned home,
Where such as bear his absence, but with grief,
I mean his friends and nearest companions,
Did gratulate his safety with kind words,
And in their conference of what befell
Touching his journey through the world and air,
They put forth questions of astrology,
Which Faustus answered with such learned skill,
As they admired and wondered at his wit.
Now is his fame spread forth in every land,
Amongst the rest the Emperor is one,
Carolus the Fifth, at whose palace now
Faustus is feasted 'mongst his noble men.
What there he did in trial of his art,
I leave untold, your eyes shall see performed. [*Exit.*]
[*Enter Emperor, Faustus, and a knight, with attendants.*]
Emperor Master Doctor Faustus, I have heard strange report of thy
knowledge in the black art, how that none in my empire, nor in the
whole world can compare with thee, for the rare effects of magic.
They say thou hast a familiar spirit, by whom thou canst accomplish
what thou list. This therefore is my request, that thou let me see
some proof of thy skill, that mine eyes may be witnesses to confirm
what mine ears have heard reported, and here I swear to thee, by the
honour of mine imperial crown, that whatever thou dost, thou shalt
be no ways prejudiced or endamaged.
Knight [*Aside*] I'faith he looks much like a conjuror.
Faustus My gracious soveraign, though I must confess myself far
inferior to the report men have published, and nothing answerable to
the honour of your imperial majesty, yet for that love and duty binds

---

961 **Carolus the Fifth:** Charles the Fifth (1500–58), Holy Roman Emperor and King of Spain.

me thereunto, I am content to do whatsoever your Majesty shall
command me.

980   *Emperor* Then Doctor Faustus, mark what I shall say.
As I was sometime solitary set,
Within my closet, sundry thoughts arose,
About the honour of mine ancestors,
How they had won by prowess such exploits,
985   Got such riches, subdued so many kingdoms,
As we that do succeed, or they that shall
Hereafter possess our throne, shall
(I fear me) never attain to that degree
Of high renown and great authority;
990   Amongst which kings is Alexander the Great,
Chief spectacle of the world's pre-eminence,
The bright shining of whose glorious acts
Lightens the world with his reflecting beams,
As when I hear but motion made of him,
995   It grieves my soul I never saw the man.
If therefore thou, by cunning of thine art,
Canst raise this man from hollow vaults below,
Where lies entombed this famous conqueror,
And bring with him his beauteous paramour,
1000   Both in their right shapes, gesture, and attire
They used to wear during their time of life,
Thou shalt both satisfy my just desire,
And give me cause to praise thee whilst I live.
   Faustus My gracious Lord, I am ready to accomplish your request,
1005 so far forth as by art and power of my spirit I am able to perform.
   Knight [*aside*] I'faith that's just nothing at all.
   Faustus But if it like your grace, it is not in my ability to present
before your eyes the true substantial bodies of those two deceased
princes which long since are consumed to dust.
1010 *Knight* [*aside*] I marry, master doctor, now there's a sign of grace in
you, when you will confess the truth.
   Faustus But such spirits as can lively resemble Alexander and his
paramour, shall appear before your Grace, in that manner that they
best lived in, in their most flourishing estate, which I doubt not shall
1015 sufficiently content your imperial Majesty.
   Emperor Go to, master doctor, let me see them presently.
   Knight Do you hear master Doctor? You bring Alexander and his
paramour before the emperor?
   Faustus How then sir?
1020 *Knight* I'faith that's as true as Diana turn'd me to a stag.
   Faustus No sir, but when Acteon died, he left the horns for you.

---

994 motion: suggestion.   1021 Acteon: The goddess Diana killed Acteon by changing him into a stag, which was
then ripped apart by Acteon's own dogs. Horns were the conventional signs of cuckoldry.

Mephastophilis be gone. [*Exit Mephastophilis.*]

Knight Nay, and you go to conjuring, I'll be gone. [*Exit Knight.*]

Faustus I'll meet with you anon for interrupting me so. Here they

1025　are, my gracious lord.

[*Enter Mephastophilis with Alexander and his paramour.*]

Emperor Master doctor, I heard this lady while she lived had a wart
or mole in her neck. How shall I know whether it be so or no?

Faustus Your highness may boldly go and see.

Emperor Sure these are no spirits, but the true substantial bodies of

1030　those two deceased princes. [*Exit Alexander and his paramour.*]

Faustus Will't please your highness now to send for the knight that
was so pleasant with me here of late?

Emperor One of you call him forth. [*Enter the knight with a pair of
horns on his head.*] How now sir knight? Why I had thought thou

1035　hadst been a bachelor, but now I see thou hast a wife that not only
gives thee horns, but makes thee wear them. Feel on thy head.

Knight Thou damned wretch, and execrable dog.
Bred in the concave of some monstrous rock.
How dar'st thou thus abuse a gentleman?

1040　Villain I say, undo what thou hast done.

Faustus O not so fast sir, there's no haste but good. Are you remembered how you crossed me in my conference with the Emperor? I
think I have met with you for it.

Emperor Good master doctor, at my entreaty release him. He hath

1045　done penance sufficient.

Faustus. My gracious lord, not so much for the injury he offered me
here in your presence, as to delight you with some mirth, hath Faustus worthily requited this injurious knight, which being all I desire, I
am content to release him of his horns. And sir knight, hereafter

1050　speak well of scholars. Mephastophilis, transform him strait. Now
my good lord having done my duty, I humbly take my leave.

Emperor Farewell master doctor, yet ere you go,
Expect from me a bounteous reward. [*Exit Emperor.*]

Faustus. Now Mephastophilis, the restless course

1055　That time doth run with calm and silent foot,
Shortening my days and thread of vital life,
Calls for the payment of my latest years,
Therefore sweet Mephastophilis, let us
Make haste to Wertenberg.

1060　**Mephastophilis** What, will you go on horse back, or on foot?

Faustus. Nay, till I am past this fair and pleasant green, I'll walk on
foot.

[*Enter a horse-courser.*]

Horse-courser I have been all this day seeking one Master Fustian.
Mass, see where he is. God save you master doctor.

1043　**met with:** even with.

1065   *Faustus* What horse-courser, you are well met.

Horse-courser Do you hear sir? I have brought you forty dollars for your horse.

Faustus I cannot sell him so. If thou lik'st him for fifty, take him.

Horse-courser Alas sir, I have no more. [*To Mephastophilis*] I pray you
1070   speak for me.

Mephastophilis I pray you let him have him. He is an honest fellow, and he has a great charge, neither wife nor child.

Faustus Well, come give me your money, my boy will deliver him to you. But I must tell you one thing before you have him, ride him not
1075   into the water at any hand.

Horse-courser Why sir, will he not drink of all waters?

Faustus O yes, he will drink of all waters, but ride him not into the water, ride him over hedge or ditch, or where thou wilt, but not into the water.

1080   *Horse-courser* Well sir, now am I made man for ever. I'll not leave my horse for forty. If he had but the quality of hey-ding-ding, hey-ding-ding, I'd make a brave living on him; he has a buttock as slick as an eel. Well God-bye sir, your boy will deliver him me. But hark ye sir, if my horse be sick, or ill at ease, if I bring his water to you, you'll
1085   tell me what it is? [*Exit horse-courser.*]

Faustus Away you villain. What, dost think I am a horse doctor?
What art thou Faustus but a man condemned to die?
Thy fatal time doth draw to final end,
Despair doth drive distrust unto my thoughts.
1090   Confound these passions with a quiet sleep.
Tush, Christ did call the thief upon the cross,
Then rest thee Faustus quiet in conceit. [*Sleeps in his chair.*]
[*Enter horse-courser all wet, crying.*]

Horse-courser Alas, alas, Doctor Fustian quotha. Mass, Doctor Lopus was never such a doctor! Has given me a purgation, has purged me of
1095   forty dollars! I shall never see them more. But yet like an ass as I was, I would not be ruled by him, for he bade me I should ride him into no water. Now I thinking my horse had had some rare quality that he would not have had me known of, I like a venturous youth, rid him into the deep pond at the town's end. I was no sooner in the middle
1100   of the pond, but my horse vanished away, and I sat upon a bottle of hay, never so near drowning in my life. But I'll seek out my doctor, and have my forty dollars again, or I'll make it the dearest horse. O yonder is his snipper-snapper. Do you hear? You, hey-pass, where's your master?

1105   *Mephastophilis* Why sir, what would you? You cannot speak with him.

1070 speak for me: speak on my behalf.   **1072**: ironically spoken as, being single, the dealer has not great expenses.   **1075 at any hand**: on any account.   **1093 Lopus**: Dr Lopez, Portuguese Jewish physician to Elizabeth I.   **1100 bottle**: bundle.   **1103 snipper-snapper**: abusive fast talker.   **hey-pass**: juggler, con artist.

Horse-courser But I will speak with him.

Mephastophilis Why he's fast asleep, come some other time.

Horse-courser I'll speak with him now, or I'll break his glass windows
1110 about his ears.

Mephastophilis I tell thee he has not slept this eight nights.

Horse-courser And he have not slept this eight weeks I'll speak with
him.

Mephastophilis See where he is fast asleep.

1115 **Horse-courser** Ay, this is he. God save ye master doctor, master doctor, Master Doctor Fustian, forty dollars, forty dollars for a bottle of
hay.

Mephastophilis Why, thou seest he hears thee not.

Horse-courser [*hallows in his ear*] So, ho, ho. So, ho, ho. No, will you
1120 not wake? I'll make you wake ere I go. [*Pulls him by the leg, and pulls it
away.*] Alas, I am undone, what shall I do?

Faustus O my leg, my leg! Help Mephastophilis! Call the officers.
My leg, my leg!

Mephastophilis Come villain to the constable.

1125 **Horse-courser** O Lord sir, let me go, and I'll give you forty dollars
more.

Mephastophilis Where be they?

Horse-courser I have none about me, come to my ostry, and I'll give
them you.

1130 **Mephastophilis** Be gone quickly. [*Horse-courser runs away.*]

Faustus What is he gone? Farewell he. Faustus has his leg again, and
the horse-courser, I take it, a bottle of hay for his labour. Well, this
trick shall cost him forty dollars more. [*Enter Wagner.*]
How now Wagner, what's the news with thee?

1135 **Wagner** Sir, the Duke of Vanholt doth earnestly entreat your
company.

Faustus The Duke of Vanholt! An honourable gentleman, to whom
I must be no niggard of my cunning. Come Mephastophilis, let's away
to him. [*Exit.*]

[*Enter to them the Duke, and the Duchess, the Duke speaks.*]

1140 **Duke** Believe me master doctor, this merriment hath much pleased
me.

Faustus My gracious lord, I am glad it contents you so well. But it
may be madam, you take no delight in this. I have heard that great-
bellied women do long for some dainties or other. What is it Madam?
1145 Tell me, and you shall have it.

Duchess Thanks, good master doctor, and for I see your courteous
intent to pleasure me, I will not hide from you the thing my heart
desires, and were it now summer, as it is January, and the dead time
of the winter, I would desire no better meat then a dish of ripe grapes.

1109 **glass windows:** spectacles.   1128 **ostry:** inn.   1143–44 **great-bellied:** pregnant.

1150   *Faustus* Alas Madam, that's nothing. Mephastophilis, be gone.
[*Exit Mephastophilis.*]
Were it a greater thing then this, so it would content you, you should
have it. [*Enter Mephastophilis with the grapes.*]
Here they be madam, will't please you taste on them?
Duke Believe me master doctor, this makes me wonder above the
1155   rest that being in the dead time of winter and in the month of January, how you should come by these grapes.
Faustus If it like your grace, the year is divided into two circles over
the whole world, that when it is here winter with us, in the contrary
circle it is summer with them, as in India, Saba, and farther countries
1160   in the east, and by means of a swift spirit that I have, I had them
brought hither, as ye see. How do you like them madam, be they
good?
  Duchess Believe me master doctor, they be the best grapes that e'er
I tasted in my life before.
1165   *Faustus* I am glad they content you so madam.
Duke Come madam let us in, where you must well reward this
learned man for the great kindness he hath showed to you.
Duchess And so I will my lord, and whilst I live,
Rest beholding for this courtesy.
1170   *Faustus*. I humbly thank your grace.
Duke Come, master doctor follow us, and receive your reward. [*Exit.*]

[*Enter Wagner solus.*]
Wagner I think my master means to die shortly,
For he hath given to me all his goods,
And yet methinks, if that death were near,
1175   He would not banquet, and carouse, and swill
Amongst the students, as even now he doth,
Who are at supper with such belly-cheer,
As Wagner ne're beheld in all his life.
See where they come: belike the feast is ended. [*Exit.*]
[*Enter Faustus with two or three scholars and Mephastophilis.*]
1180   *1st scholar* Master Doctor Faustus, since our conference about fair
ladies, which was the beautifull'st in all the world, we have determined with ourselves, that Helen of Greece was the admirablest lady
that ever lived. Therefore master doctor, if you will do us that favour,
as to let us see that peerless dame of Greece, whom all the world
1185   admires for majesty, we should think ourselves much beholding unto
you.
Faustus Gentlemen,
For that I know your friendship is unfeigned,
And Faustus' custom is not to deny
1190   The just requests of those that wish him well,

1159 **Saba:** The land of the Queen of Sheba, present-day Yemen.

You shall behold that peerless dame of Greece,
No otherways for pomp and majesty,
Then when Sir Paris crossed the seas with her,
And brought the spoils to rich Dardania.
1195 Be silent then, for danger is in words.
[*Music sounds, and Helen passeth over the stage.*]
2nd scholar Too simple is my wit to tell her praise
Whom all the world admires for majesty.
3rd scholar No marvel though the angry Greeks pursued
With ten years war the rape of such a queen,
1200 Whose heavenly beauty passeth all compare.
Since we have seen the pride of nature's works,
And only paragon of excellence, [*Enter an Old Man.*]
Let us depart, and for this glorious deed
Happy and blest be Faustus evermore.
1205 **Faustus** Gentlemen farewell, the same I wish to you. [*Exit scholars.*]
Old Man Ah Doctor Faustus, that I might prevail,
To guide thy steps unto the way of life,
By which sweet path thou may'st attain the goal
That shall conduct thee to celestial rest.
1210 Break heart, drop blood, and mingle it with tears,
Tears falling from repentant heaviness
Of thy most vile and loathsome filthiness,
The stench whereof corrupts the inward soul
With such flagitious crimes of heinous sins,
1215 As no commiseration may expel,
But mercy Faustus of thy Saviour sweet,
Whose blood alone must wash away thy guilt.
Faustus. Where art thou Faustus? Wretch what hast thou done?
Damned art thou Faustus, damned; despair and die.
1220 Hell calls for right, and with a roaring voice
Says, Faustus come, thine hour is come,
And Faustus will come to do thee right.
[*Mephastophilis gives him a dagger.*]
Old Man Ah stay good Faustus, stay thy desperate steps,
I see an angel hovers o'er thy head,
1225 And with a viol full of precious grace,
Offers to pour the same into thy soul,
Then call for mercy and avoid despair.
Faustus Ah my sweet friend, I feel
Thy words to comfort my distressed soul.
1230 Leave me a while to ponder on my sins.
Old Man I go sweet Faustus, but with heavy cheer,
Fearing the ruin of thy hopeless soul. [*Exit.*]

1194 **Dardania:** Troy. 1214 **flagitious:** atrocious. **heinous:** odious.

Faustus Accursed Faustus, where is mercy now?
I do repent, and yet I do despair:
1235 Hell strives with grace for conquest in my breast,
What shall I do to shun the snares of death?
Mephastophilis Thou traitor Faustus, I arrest thy soul
For disobedience to my soveraign lord,
Revolt, or I'll in piecemeal tear thy flesh.
1240 **Faustus** Sweet Mephastophilis, entreat thy lord,
To pardon my unjust presumption,
And with my blood again I will confirm
My former vow I made to Lucifer.
Mephastophilis Do it then quickly, with unfeigned heart,
1245 Lest greater danger do attend thy drift.
Faustus Torment sweet friend, that base and crooked age,
That durst dissuade me from thy Lucifer,
With greatest torments that our hell affords.
Mephastophilis His faith is great, I cannot touch his soul,
1250 But what I may afflict his body with,
I will attempt, which is but little worth.
Faustus One thing, good servant, let me crave of thee,
To glut the longing of my heart's desire,
That I might have unto my paramour,
1255 That heavenly Helen which I saw of late,
Whose sweet embracings may extinguish clean
These thoughts that do dissuade me from my vow,
And keep mine oath I made to Lucifer.
Mephastophilis Faustus, this, or what else thou shalt desire,
1260 Shall be performed in twinkling of an eye.
[*Enter Helen.*]
Faustus. Was this the face that launched a thousand ships?
And burnt the topless towers of Ilium?
Sweet Helen, make me immortal with a kiss.
Her lips suck forth my soul, see where it flies.
1265 Come Helen, come give me my soul again.
Here will I dwell, for heaven be in these lips,
And all is dross that is not Helena. [*Enter Old Man.*]
I will be Paris, and for love of thee,
Instead of Troy shall Wertenberg be sack'd,
1270 And I will combat with weak Menelaus,
And wear thy colours on my plumed crest:
Yea, I will wound Achilles in the heel,
And then return to Helen for a kiss.
O thou art fairer then the evening air,
1275 Clad in the beauty of a thousand stars,

1262 Ilium: Troy. 1270 Menelaus: Helen's Greek husband.

Brighter art thou then flaming Jupiter,
When he appear'd to hapless Semele,
More lovely then the monarch of the sky
In wanton Arethusa's azured arms,

1280 And none but thou shalt be my paramour. [*Exit.*]
Old Man Accursed Faustus, miserable man,
That from thy soul exclud'st the grace of heaven,
And fliest the throne of his tribunal seat. [*Enter the devils.*]
Satan begins to sift me with his pride.

1285 As in this furnace God shall try my faith,
My faith, vile hell, shall triumph over thee.
Ambitious fiends, see how the heavens smiles
At your repulse, and laughs your state to scorn.
Hence hell, for hence I fly unto my God. [*Exit.*]

[*Enter Faustus with the scholars.*]
1290 **Faustus** Ah Gentlemen!
1st scholar What ails Faustus?
Faustus Ah my sweet chamber-fellow! Had I lived with thee, then
had I lived still, but now I die eternally. Look, comes he not? Comes
he not?
1295 **2nd scholar** What means Faustus?
3rd scholar Belike he is grown into some sickness by being over
solitary.
1st scholar If it be so, we'll have physicians to cure him. 'Tis but a
surfeit, never fear man.
1300 **Faustus** A surfeit of deadly sin that hath damned both body and soul.
2nd scholar Yet Faustus, look up to heaven, remember God's
mercies are infinite.
Faustus But Faustus' offence can ne're be pardoned. The serpent
that tempted Eve may be saved, but not Faustus. Ah gentlemen, hear
1305 me with patience, and tremble not at my speeches. Though my heart
pants and quivers to remember that I have been a student here these
thirty years. O would I had never seen Wertenberg, never read book.
And what wonders I have done all Germany can witness, yea all the
world, for which Faustus hath lost both Germany and the world, yea
1310 heaven it self, heaven the seat of God, the throne of the blessed, the
kingdom of joy, and must remain in hell for ever, hell, ah hell for
ever. Sweet friends what shall become of Faustus, being in hell for
ever?
3rd scholar Yet Faustus call on God.
1315 **Faustus** On God whom Faustus hath abjured, on God, whom Faustus hath blasphemed. Ah my God, I would weep, but the devil draws
in my tears. Gush forth blood instead of tears, yea life and soul. Oh

---

1277 **Semele:** one of Jupiter's lovers, she asked that he visit her in his full splendour and was consumed by
lightning.   1279 **Arethusa:** nymph transformed into a fountain when fleeing Alpheus. Here she is characterised as
one of Jupiter's lovers.   1299 **surfeit:** excessive partaking of food and/or drink.

he stays my tongue. I would lift up my hands, but see, they hold
them, they hold them.

1320 **All** Who Faustus?

Faustus Lucifer and Mephastophilis.
Ah Gentlemen! I gave them my soul for my cunning.

All God forbid.

Faustus God forbade it indeed, but Faustus hath done it. For vain
1325 pleasure of 24 years hath Faustus lost eternal joy and felicity. I writ
them a bill with mine own blood, the date is expired, the time will
come, and he will fetch me.

1st scholar Why did not Faustus tell us of this before, that divines
might have prayed for thee?

1330 **Faustus** Oft have I thought to have done so, but the devil threatened
to tear me in pieces, if I named God, to fetch both body and soul, if
I once gave ear to divinity. And now 'tis too late. Gentlemen away,
lest you perish with me.

2nd scholar O what shall we do to Faustus?

1335 **Faustus** Talk not of me, but save your selves, and depart.

3rd scholar God will strengthen me, I will stay with Faustus.

1st scholar Tempt not God, sweet friend, but let us into the next
room, and there pray for him.

Faustus Ay, pray for me, pray for me, and what noise soever ye hear,
1340 come not unto me, for nothing can rescue me.

2nd scholar Pray thou, and we will pray that God may have mercy
upon thee.

Faustus Gentlemen farewell, if I live till morning, I'll visit you. If
not, Faustus is gone to hell.

1345 **All** Faustus, farewell. [*Exit scholars.*]
[*The clock strikes eleven.*]

Faustus Ah Faustus,
Now hast thou but one bare hour to live,
And then thou must be damned perpetually:
Stand still you ever moving spheres of heaven,
1350 That time may cease, and midnight never come.
Fair nature's eye, rise, rise again, and make
Perpetual day, or let this hour be but
A year, a month, a week, a natural day,
That Faustus may repent, and save his soul,
1355 O *lente, lente currite noctis equi.*
The stars move still, time runs, the clock will strike,
The devil will come, and Faustus must be damned.
O I'll leap up to my God. Who pulls me down?
See see where Christ's blood streams in the firmament.
1360 One drop would save my soul, half a drop, ah my Christ.
Ah rend not my heart for naming of my Christ,

1355 O *lente* . . . . : O move slowly, slowly you horses of night.

Yet will I call on him. O spare me Lucifer!
Where is it now? 'Tis gone. And see where God
Stretcheth out his arm, and bends his ireful brows.
1365 Mountains and hills, come, come, and fall on me,
And hide me from the heavy wrath of God.
No, no.
Then will I headlong run into the earth.
Earth gape. O no, it will not harbour me.
1370 You stars that reigned at my nativity,
Whose influence hath allotted death and hell,
Now draw up Faustus like a foggy mist,
Into the entrails of yon labouring cloud,
That when you vomit forth into the air,
1375 My limbs may issue from your smoky mouths,
So that my soul may but ascend to heaven.
Ah, half the hour is past. [*The watch strikes.*]
'Twill all be past anon.
Oh God,
1380 If thou wilt not have mercy on my soul,
Yet for Christ's sake, whose blood hath ransomed me,
Impose some end to my incessant pain.
Let Faustus live in hell a thousand years,
A hundred thousand, and at last be sav'd.
1385 O no end is limited to damned souls.
Why wert thou not a creature wanting soul?
Or, why is this immortal that thou hast?
Ah Pythagoras' metempsychosis, were that true,
This soul should fly from me, and I be changed
1390 Unto some brutish beast. All beasts are happy,
For when they die,
Their souls are soon dissolved in elements,
But mine must live still to be plagued in hell.
Cursed be the parents that engendered me.
1395 No Faustus, curse thy self, curse Lucifer,
That hath deprived thee of the joys of heaven.
[*The clock striketh twelve.*]
O it strikes, it strikes! Now body turn to air,
Or Lucifer will bear thee quick to hell. [*Thunder and lightning.*]
O soul, be changed into little water drops,
1400 And fall into the ocean, ne're be found.
My God, my God, look not so fierce on me. [*Enter devils.*]
Adders, and serpents, let me breath a while.
Ugly hell gape not, come not Lucifer,
I'll burn my books, ah Mephastophilis. [*Exit with him.*]

1370 **stars:** astrological belief that fate is governed by the place of the heavenly bodies at birth. 1388 **Pythagoras'**
metempsychosis: the Greek philosopher who believed in transmigration of souls.

[*Enter Chorus.*]
1405 **Chorus** Cut is the branch that might have grown full straight,
And burned is Apollo's laurel bough,
That sometime grew within this learned man.
Faustus is gone, regard his hellish fall,
Whose fiendful fortune may exhort the wise,
1410 Only to wonder at unlawful things,
Whose deepness doth entice such forward wits,
To practise more than heavenly power permits. [*Exit.*]
Terminat hora diem, terminat author opus.

SIR WALTER RALEGH (c.1552–1618)

Ralegh came from Devon and was educated at Oxford. He mixed widely in literary circles and his 'The Nymph's Reply' is a response to Marlowe's 'Passionate Shepherd'. In 1584 Elizabeth I gave Ralegh the right to take possession of 'unknown lands' in America in her name and he undertook voyages to Virginia and Guiana with a view to colonising them. The extract from his travel narratives printed here is from his first (1595) account of Guiana and reveals the combination of imaginative desire (often inherited from classical and medieval accounts of strange places) and the actual experience of travel present in many Renaissance narratives of exploration.

The Nymph's Reply

If all the world and love were young,
And truth in every shepherd's tongue,
These pretty pleasures might me move
To live with thee and be thy love.

5 Time drives the flocks from field to fold,
When rivers rage and rocks grow cold,
And Philomel becometh dumb;
The rest complains of cares to come.

The flowers do fade, and wanton fields
10 To wayward winter reckoning yields;
A honey tongue, a heart of gall,
Is fancy's spring, but sorrow's fall.

Thy gowns, thy shoes, thy beds of roses,
Thy cap, thy kirtle, and thy posies

1406 **Apollo's laurel**: referring to a capacity for virtue. Laurel was seen as difficult to burn because pure. Apollo and laurel are associated with fame and poetic success. ***Terminat . . .*** : the hour ends the day, the author ends his work.   Nymph 7 **Philomel**: the nightingale.   14 **kirtle**: skirt.   **posies**: bunches of flowers; collections of poetry.

15   Soon break, soon wither, soon forgotten,
     In folly ripe, in reason rotten.

     Thy belt of straw and ivy buds,
     The coral clasps and amber studs,
     All these in me no means can move
20   To come to thee and be thy love.

     But could youth last and love still breed,
     Had joys no date nor age no need,
     Then these delights my mind might move
     To live with thee and be thy love.

[Even such is Time which takes in trust]

     Even such is Time which takes in trust
     Our youth, our joys and what we have,
     And pays us but with earth and dust;
     Which in the dark and silent grave,
5   When we have wandered all our ways,
     Shuts up the story of our days.
         But from which earth, this grave, this dust
         The Lord shall raise me up I trust.

From The Discovery of Guiana[1]

When we were come to the tops of the first hills of the plains adjoining to the river, we beheld that wonderful breach of waters, which ran down Caroli; and might from that mountain see the river how it ran in three parts, above twenty miles off, and there appeared some ten or twelve overfalls in sight, every one as high over the other as a Church tower, which fell with that fury, that the rebound of water made it seem, as if it had been all covered over with a great shower of rain: and in some places wee took it at the first for a smoke that had risen over some great town. For mine own part I was well persuaded from thence to have returned, being a very ill footman, but the rest were all so desirous to go near the said strange thunder of waters, as they drew me on by little and little, till wee came into the next valley where we might better discern the same. I never saw a more beautiful country, nor more lively prospects, hills so raised here and there over the valleys, the river winding into divers branches, the plains adjoining without bush or stubble, all faire green grass, the ground of hard sand easy to march on, either for horse or foot, the deer crossing in every path, the birds towards the evening singing on every tree with a thousand several tunes, cranes and herons of white, crimson, and carnation perching in the river's side, the air fresh with a gentle easterly wind, and every stone that we stooped to take up, promised either gold or silver by

---

1 **Guiana:** Ralegh's Guiana, the Orinoco basin, is part of modern Venezuela. The present text modernises spelling and omits some passages from the selected pages, but retains the original place names.

his complexion. Your Lordship[1] shall see of many sorts, and I hope some of them cannot bee bettered under the sun, and yet we had no means but with our daggers and fingers to tear them out here and there, the rocks being most hard of that mineral spar aforesaid, which is like a flint, and is altogether as hard or harder, and besides the veins lie a fathom or two deep in the rock. But we wanted all things requisite save only our desires and good will to have performed more if it had pleased God. To be short, when both our companies returned, each of them brought also several sorts of stones that appeared very faire, but were such as they found loose on the ground, and were for the most part but coloured, and had not any gold fixed in them, yet such as had no judgement or experience kept all that glistered, and would not be persuaded but it was rich because of the lustre, and brought of those, and of Marquesite with all, from Trinidad, and have delivered of those stones to be tried in many places,[2] and have thereby bred an opinion that all the rest is of the same. Yet some of these stones I showed afterward to a Spaniard of the Caracas, who told me that it was El Madre del Oro, that is the mother of gold, and that the Mine was farther in the ground.

But it shall be found a weak policy in me, either to betray my self, or my country with imaginations, neither am I so far in love with that lodging, watching, care, peril, diseases, ill savours, bad fare, and many other mischiefs that accompany these voyages, as to woo my self again into any of them, were I not assured that the sun covereth not so much riches in any part of the earth. Captain Whiddon, and our surgeon Nicholas Millechap brought me a kind of stone like sapphires, what they may prove I know not. I showed them to some of the Orenoqueponi, and they promised to bring me to a mountain, that had of them very large pieces growing diamond wise. Whether it be crystal of the mountain, Bristol-Diamond,[3] or sapphire I do not yet know, but I hope the best, sure I am that the place is as likely as those from whence all the rich stones are brought, and in the same height or very near.

There is also another goodly river beyond Caroli which is called Arui, which also runs through the lake Cassipa, and falls into Orenoque farther west, making all that land between Caroli and Arui an island, which is likewise a most beautiful country. Next unto Arui there are two rivers Atoica and Caora, and on that branch which is called Caora are a nation of people whose heads appear not above their shoulders; which though it may be thought a mere fable, yet for mine own part I am resolved it is true, because every child in the provinces of Arromaia and Canuri affirms the same. They are called Ewaipanoma. They are reported to have their eyes in their shoulders, and their mouths in the middle of their breasts, and that a long train of hair grows backward between their shoulders. The son of Topiawari, which I brought with me into England told me that they are the most mighty men of all the land, and use bows, arrows, and clubs thrice as big as any of Guiana, or of the Orenoqueponi, and that one of the Iwarawakeri took a prisoner of them the year before our arrival there, and brought him into the borders of Aromaia, his

---

1 **Lordship:** Charles Howard, Lord High Admiral, or Sir Robert Cecil. The text is dedicated to both.   2: they tried to have the value assayed.   3 **Bristol-Diamond:** a gem resembling a diamond found near Bristol.

father's country. And farther when I seemed to doubt of it, he told me that it was no wonder among them, but that they were as great a nation, and as common as any other in all the provinces, and had of late years slain many hundreds of his father's people, and of other nations, their neighbours, but it was not my chance to hear of them till I was come away, and if I had but spoken one word of it while I was there, I might have brought one of them with me to put the matter out of doubt. Such a nation was written of by Mandeville, whose reports were held for fables many years, and yet since the East Indies were discovered, we find his relations true of such things as heretofore were held incredible. Whether it be true or no, the matter is not great, neither can there be any profit in the imagination; for mine own part I saw them not, but I am resolved that so many people did not all combine, or forethinke to make the report.

For the rest, which myself have seen, I will promise these things that follow, which I know to be true. Those that are desirous to discover and to see many nations, may be satisfied within this river,[1] which brings forth so many arms and branches leading to several countries and provinces, above 2000 miles east and west, and 800 miles south and north, and of these, the most either rich in gold, or in other merchandises. The common soldier shall here fight for gold, and pay himself in stead of pence, with plates of half a foot broad,[2] whereas he breaks his bones in other wars for provant[3] and penury. Those commanders and chieftains that shoot at honour and abundance, shall find there more rich and beautiful cities, more temples adorned with golden images, more sepulchres filled with treasure, then either Cortez found in Mexico, or Pizarro in Peru; and the shining glory of this conquest will eclipse all those so far extended beams of the Spanish nation. There is no country which yields more pleasure to the inhabitants, either for those common delights of hunting, hawking, fishing, fowling, or the rest, then Guiana doth. It hath so many plains, clear rivers, abundance of pheasants, partridges, quails, rails, cranes, herons, and all other fowl; deer of all sorts, porks, hares, lions, tigers, leopards, and divers other sorts of beasts, either for chase or food. It hath a kind of beast called cama or anta,[4] as big as an English beef, and in great plenty.

I conclude that both for health, good air, pleasure, and riches I am resolved it cannot be equalled by any region either in the east or west. Moreover the country is so healthful, as of an hundred persons & more (which lay without shift[5] most sluttishly, and were every day almost melted with heat in rowing and marching, and suddenly wet again with great showers, and did eat of all sorts of corrupt fruits, and made meals of fresh fish without seasoning, of tortugas,[6] of lagartos or crocodiles, and of all sorts good and bad, without either order or measure, and besides lodged in the open air every night) we lost not any one, nor had one ill disposed to my knowledge nor found any calentura,[7] or other of those pestilent diseases which dwell in all hot regions, and so near the equinoctial line.

---

1 **river**: the Orinoco. 2 **plates**: early modern England was short of coinage, so gold and silver were often held in the form of costly furnishings. 3 **provant**: rations. 4 **cama**: the tapir. 5 **shift**: without change of clothing. 6 **tortugas**: turtles. 7 **calentura**: fever which causes hallucinations.

Where there is store of gold, it is in effect needless to remember other commodities for trade. But it hath towards the south part of the river, great quantities of Brazil-wood, and diverse berries that dye a most perfect crimson and carnation. And for painting,[1] all France, Italy, or the East Indies yield none such. For the more the skin is washed, the fairer the colour appears, and with which, even those brown and tawny women spot themselves, and colour their cheeks. All places yield abundance of cotton, of silk, of balsam, and of those kinds most excellent, and never known in Europe, of all sorts of gums, of Indian pepper. And what else the countries may afford within the land we know not, neither had we time to abide the trial, and search. The soil besides is so excellent and so full of rivers, as it will carry sugar, ginger, and all those other commodities, which the West Indies have.

To conclude, Guiana is a country that hath yet her maidenhead, never sacked, turned,[2] nor wrought, the face of the earth hath not been torn, nor the virtue and salt of the soil spent by manurance,[3] the graves have not been opened for gold, the mines not broken with sledges, nor their Images pulled down out of their temples. It hath never been entered by any army of strength, and never conquered or possessed by any Christian Prince.

The West Indies were first offered her Majesty's grandfather[4] by Columbus a stranger, in whom there might be doubt of deceit, and besides it was then thought incredible that there were such and so many lands & regions never written of before. This empire is made known to her Majesty by her own vassal, and by him that oweth to her more duty then an ordinary subject, so that it shall ill sort with the many graces and benefits which I have received to abuse her Highness, either with fables or imaginations. The country is already discovered, many nations won to her Majesty's love and obedience, and those Spaniards which have latest and longest laboured about the conquest, beaten out, discouraged and disgraced, which among these nations were thought invincible. Her Majesty may in this enterprise employ all those soldiers and gentlemen that are younger brethren, and all captains and chieftains that want employment, and the charge will be only the first setting out in victualling and arming them. For after the first or second year I doubt not but to see in London a Contractation house[5] of more receipt for Guiana, then there is now in Seville for the West Indies.

---

1 **painting**: cosmetics. 2 **turned**: cultivated. 3 **manurance**: cultivation. 4 **grandfather**: Henry VII.
5 **Contraction house**: the Case de Contractacion in Seville managed all Spanish trade activities in the New World.

WILLIAM SHAKESPEARE (1564–1616)

Born in Stratford and educated at the local grammar school, Shakespeare came to London in the 1580s where he established himself as an actor, director, part-owner of a theatre company and playwright. His 154 sonnets first appeared as a collection in 1609, but it seems that Shakespeare did not prepare this edition for publication himself. Debate continues about whether these poems are a linked sequence which detail the development of two relationships (with a young man and a dark lady), an editorial arrangement of different groups of sonnets, or simply a collection of individual lyrics whose 'narrative' is constructed by the reader. The selection here indicates their number in the 1609 sequence. Shakespeare wrote nearly 40 plays, either wholly or in collaboration. *The Tempest* is one of the last of these; its first performance was probably in 1611.

From The Sonnets

Sonnet 15

When I consider every thing that grows
Holds in perfection but a little moment,
That this huge stage presenteth nought but shows
Whereon the stars in secret influence comment;
5   When I perceive that men as plants increase,
Cheered and checked even by the self-same sky,
Vaunt in their youthful sap, at height decrease,
And wear their brave state out of memory.
Then the conceit of this inconstant stay
10   Sets you most rich in youth before my sight,
Where wasteful Time debateth with Decay,
To change your day of youth to sullied night;
    And all in war with Time for love of you,
    As he takes from you, I engraft you new.

Sonnet 18

Shall I compare thee to a summer's day?
Thou art more lovely and more temperate.
Rough winds do shake the darling buds of May,
And summer's lease hath all too short a date.
5   Sometime too hot the eye of heaven shines,
And often is his gold complexion dimmed,
And every fair from fair sometime declines,
By chance or nature's changing course untrimmed.

15,6 cheered and checked: encouraged and restrained.   **18,8 untrimmed:** unprepared or unfit for change.
7 vaunt: exult.   **9:** Then the awareness of this change-
able condition.

But thy eternal summer shall not fade
10   Nor lose possession of that fair thou owest;
Nor shall Death brag thou wander'st in his shade,
When in eternal lines to time thou growest.
   So long as men can breathe or eyes can see,
   So long lives this and this gives life to thee.

Sonnet 19

Devouring Time, blunt thou the lion's paws,
And make the earth devour her own sweet brood;
Pluck the keen teeth from the fierce tiger's jaws,
And burn the long-lived phoenix in her blood;
5   Make glad and sorry seasons as thou fleets,
And do whate'er thou wilt, swift-footed Time,
To the wide world and all her fading sweets.
But I forbid thee one most heinous crime:
O, carve not with thy hours my love's fair brow,
10   Nor draw no lines there with thine antique pen;
Him in thy course untainted do allow
For beauty's pattern to succeeding men.
   Yet do thy worst, old Time: despite thy wrong,
   My love shall in my verse ever live young.

Sonnet 30

When to the sessions of sweet silent thought
I summon up remembrance of things past,
I sigh the lack of many a thing I sought,
And with old woes new wail my dear time's waste.
5   Then can I drown an eye, unused to flow,
For precious friends hid in death's dateless night,
And weep afresh love's long since cancelled woe,
And moan the expense of many a vanished sight.
Then can I grieve at grievances foregone,
10   And heavily from woe to woe tell o'er
The sad account of fore-bemoaned moan,
Which I new pay as if not paid before.
   But if the while I think on thee, dear friend,
   All losses are restored and sorrows end.

30,1 **sessions:** a time officially designated for conduct-   10 **tell o'er:** count over again.
ing meetings or judicial proceedings.

Sonnet 36

Let me confess that we two must be twain
Although our undivided loves are one;
So shall those blots that do with me remain
Without thy help by me be borne alone.
5   In our two loves there is but one respect,
Though in our lives a separable spite
Which, though it alter not love's sole effect,
Yet doth it steal sweet hours from love's delight.
I may not evermore acknowledge thee
10 Lest my bewailed guilt should do thee shame,
Nor thou with public kindness honour me
Unless thou take that honour from thy name.
   But do not so; I love thee in such sort
   As, thou being mine, mine is thy good report.

Sonnet 60

Like as the waves make towards the pebbled shore,
So do our minutes hasten to their end;
Each changing place with that which goes before,
In sequent toil all forwards do contend.
5   Nativity, once in the main of light,
Crawls to maturity, wherewith being crowned,
Crooked eclipses 'gainst his glory fight,
And Time that gave doth now his gift confound.
Time doth transfix the flourish set on youth
10 And delves the parallels in beauty's brow,
Feeds on the rarities of nature's truth,
And nothing stands but for his scythe to mow.
   And yet to times in hope my verse shall stand,
   Praising thy worth, despite his cruel hand.

Sonnet 73

That time of year thou mayst in me behold
When yellow leaves, or none, or few, do hang
Upon those boughs which shake against the cold,
Bare ruined choirs, where late the sweet birds sang.
5   In me thou seest the twilight of such day
As after sunset fadeth in the west,
Which by and by black night doth take away,
Death's second self, that seals up all in rest.

36,6 **separable spite**: a malign influence which causes separation.

60,4 **contend**: endeavour, strive. 7 **Crooked**: harmful. 10 **delves**: makes furrows in.

In me thou see'st the glowing of such fire
10   That on the ashes of his youth doth lie,
As the death-bed whereon it must expire
Consumed with that which it was nourished by.
　This thou perceivest, which makes thy love more strong,
　To love that well which thou must leave ere long.

Sonnet 94

They that have power to hurt and will do none,
That do not do the thing they most do show,
Who moving others are themselves as stone,
Unmoved, cold, and to temptation slow,
5   They rightly do inherit heaven's graces
And husband nature's riches from expense;
They are the lords and owners of their faces,
Others but stewards of their excellence.
The summer's flower is to the summer sweet,
10   Though to itself it only live and die,
But if that flower with base infection meet,
The basest weed outbraves his dignity.
　For sweetest things turn sourest by their deeds;
　Lilies that fester smell far worse than weeds.

Sonnet 116

Let me not to the marriage of true minds
Admit impediments. Love is not love
Which alters when it alteration finds,
Or bends with the remover to remove:
5   O no! it is an ever-fixed mark
That looks on tempests and is never shaken;
It is the star to every wandering bark,
Whose worth's unknown, although his height be taken.
Love's not Time's fool, though rosy lips and cheeks
10   Within his bending sickle's compass come;
Love alters not with his brief hours and weeks,
But bears it out even to the edge of doom.
　If this be error and upon me proved,
　I never writ, nor no man ever loved.

94,6: guard against excessive spending.   12 outbraves: 116,7 bark: ship.
exceeds his show.   14 fester: rot.

Sonnet 121

'Tis better to be vile than vile esteemed,
When not to be receives reproach of being,
And the just pleasure lost which is so deemed
Not by our feeling but by others' seeing.
5 For why should others' false adulterate eyes
Give salutation to my sportive blood?
Or on my frailties why are frailer spies,
Which in their wills count bad what I think good?
No, I am that I am, and they that level
10 At my abuses reckon up their own:
I may be straight, though they themselves be bevel;
By their rank thoughts my deeds must not be shown;
   Unless this general evil they maintain,
   All men are bad, and in their badness reign.

Sonnet 129

The expense of spirit in a waste of shame
Is lust in action; and till action, lust
Is perjured, murderous, bloody, full of blame,
Savage, extreme, rude, cruel, not to trust,
5 Enjoyed no sooner but despised straight,
Past reason hunted, and no sooner had
Past reason hated, as a swallowed bait
On purpose laid to make the taker mad;
Mad in pursuit and in possession so;
10 Had, having, and in quest to have, extreme;
A bliss in proof, and proved, a very woe;
Before, a joy proposed; behind, a dream.
   All this the world well knows; yet none knows well
   To shun the heaven that leads men to this hell.

Sonnet 130

My mistress' eyes are nothing like the sun;
Coral is far more red than her lips' red;
If snow be white, why then her breasts are dun;
If hairs be wires, black wires grow on her head.
5 I have seen roses damasked, red and white,
But no such roses see I in her cheeks;
And in some perfumes is there more delight
Than in the breath that from my mistress reeks.

121,6 **sportive blood**: sexually inclined desire. **9 level**: 130,3 **dun**: dusky, dingybrown colour. **5 damasked**:
aim at. **10 reckon up**: show up. **11 bevel**: oblique, variegated, as the pattern found in damask cloth.
broken.

I love to hear her speak, yet well I know
10   That music hath a far more pleasing sound;
I grant I never saw a goddess go;
My mistress, when she walks, treads on the ground.
    And yet, by heaven, I think my love as rare
    As any she belied with false compare.

Sonnet 138

When my love swears that she is made of truth
I do believe her, though I know she lies,
That she might think me some untutored youth,
Unlearned in the world's false subtleties.
5   Thus vainly thinking that she thinks me young,
Although she knows my days are past the best,
Simply I credit her false speaking tongue.
On both sides thus is simple truth suppressed.
But wherefore says she not she is unjust?
10   And wherefore say not I that I am old?
O, love's best habit is in seeming trust,
And age in love loves not to have years told.
    Therefore I lie with her and she with me,
    And in our faults by lies we flattered be.

Sonnet 144

Two loves I have, of comfort and despair,
Which like two spirits do suggest me still;
The better angel is a man right fair,
The worser spirit a woman coloured ill.
5   To win me soon to hell, my female evil
Tempteth my better angel from my side,
And would corrupt my saint to be a devil,
Wooing his purity with her foul pride.
And whether that my angel be turned fiend
10   Suspect I may, but not directly tell;
But being both from me, both to each friend,
I guess one angel in another's hell.
    Yet this shall I ne'er know, but live in doubt,
    Till my bad angel fire my good one out.

138,3 untutored: untaught.   144,2 suggest: prompt to act or think in certain ways.   **14** fire . . . out: infect with venereal disease.

Sonnet 151

Love is too young to know what conscience is,
Yet who knows not conscience is born of love?
Then, gentle cheater, urge not my amiss,
Lest guilty of my faults thy sweet self prove;
5   For, thou betraying me, I do betray
My nobler part to my gross body's treason;
My soul doth tell my body that he may
Triumph in love; flesh stays no father reason,
But, rising at thy name, doth point out thee
10   As his triumphant prize. Proud of this pride,
He is contented thy poor drudge to be,
To stand in thy affairs, fall by thy side.
    No want of conscience hold it that I call
    Her 'love' for whose dear love I rise and fall.

The Tempest

Characters

Alonso, King of Naples
Sebastian, his brother
Prospero, the right Duke of Milan
Antonio, his brother, the usurping Duke of Milan
Ferdinand, son to the King of Naples
Gonzalo, an honest old counsellor
Adrian and Francisco, lords
Caliban, a savage and deformed slave
Trinculo, a jester   Stephano, a drunken butler
Master of a Ship   Boatswain   Mariners
Miranda, daughter to Prospero
Ariel, an airy Spirit
Iris, Ceres, Juno, Nymphs, Reapers: Spirits
Other Spirits attending on Prospero

Act I, Scene i

[*A tempestuous noise of thunder and lightning heard.*
Enter a Shipmaster and a Boatswain.]
Master Boatswain!
Boatswain Here, master. What cheer?
Master Good, speak to the mariners. Fall to't, yarely, or we run
ourselves aground. Bestir, bestir. [*Exit.*]

151,3 amiss: fault.   11 drudge: one employed in
servile, mean work.

The Tempest, Boatswain: person on a ship in charge of
the sails.   Iris, Ceres, Juno: classical goddesses.   Reapers:
harvesters, those who cut grain.   3 yarely: quickly.

[*Enter Mariners.*]

5   **Boatswain** Heigh, my hearts! cheerly, cheerly, my hearts! yare, yare! Take in the topsail. Tend to the master's whistle. Blow, till thou burst thy wind, if room enough!

[*Enter Alonso, Sebastian, Antonio, Ferdinand. Gonzalo and others.*]

Alonso Good boatswain, have care. Where's the master? Play the men.

10   **Boatswain** I pray now, keep below.

Antonio Where is the master, boatswain?

Boatswain Do you not hear him? You mar our labour. Keep your cabins. You do assist the storm.

Gonzalo Nay, good, be patient.

15   **Boatswain** When the sea is. Hence! What cares these roarers for the name of king? To cabin. Silence! Trouble us not.

Gonzalo Good, yet remember whom thou hast aboard.

Boatswain None that I more love than myself. You are a counsellor; if you can command these elements to silence, and work the peace

20   of the present, we will not hand a rope more; use your authority. If you cannot, give thanks you have lived so long, and make yourself ready in your cabin for the mischance of the hour, if it so hap – Cheerly, good hearts! – Out of our way, I say. [*Exit.*]

Gonzalo I have great comfort from this fellow. Methinks he hath no

25   drowning mark upon him; his complexion is perfect gallows. Stand fast, good Fate, to his hanging. Make the rope of his destiny our cable, for our own doth little advantage. If he be not born to be hanged, our case is miserable. [*Exit.*]

[*Enter Boatswain.*]

Boatswain Down with the topmast! yare! lower, lower! Bring her to

30   try with main-course. [*A cry within.*] A plague upon this howling! They are louder than the weather or our office. [*Enter Sebastian, Antonio, and Gonzalo.*] Yet again! what do you here? Shall we give o'er and drown? Have you a mind to sink?

Sebastian A pox o' your throat, you bawling, blasphemous,

35   incharitable dog!

Boatswain Work you then.

Antonio Hang, cur! Hang, you whoreson, insolent noisemaker! We are less afraid to be drowned than thou art.

Gonzalo I'll warrant him for drowning, though the ship were no

40   stronger than a nutshell and as leaky as an unstaunched wench.

Boatswain Lay her a-hold, a-hold! Set her two courses off to sea again. Lay her off.

[*Enter Mariners wet.*]

Mariners All lost! To prayers, to prayers! All lost!

---

7 **if room enough:** if there is enough open sea.   25 **his complexion . . . :** based on proverbial phrase, he was born to be hanged not drowned.   29–30 **to try with main-course:** to lower the mainsail (course) and manoeuvre to keep away from the land.   39 **warrant him for:** guarantee him against.   40 **unstaunched:** unsatisfied.

Boatswain What, must our mouths be cold?

45   **Gonzalo** The king and prince at prayers, let's assist them,
For our case is as theirs.

  Sebastian I'm out of patience.

  Antonio We are merely cheated of our lives by drunkards.
This wide-chapped rascal – would thou mightst lie drowning
50   The washing of ten tides!

  Gonzalo He'll be hanged yet,
Though every drop of water swear against it
And gape at widest to glut him.
[*A confused noise within.*]
'Mercy on us!' – 'We split, we split!' – 'Farewell, my wife and chil-
55   dren!' – 'Farewell, brother!' – 'We split, we split, we split!'

  Antonio Let's all sink with the king.

  Sebastian Let's take leave of him. [*Exit Antonio and Sebastian.*]

  Gonzalo Now would I give a thousand furlongs of sea for an acre of
barren ground, long heath, brown furze, anything. The wills above
60   be done, but I would fain die a dry death. [*Exit.*]

Act I, Scene ii

[*The island. Before Prospero's cell. Enter Prospero and Miranda.*]

  Miranda If by your art, my dearest father, you have
Put the wild waters in this roar, allay them.
The sky, it seems, would pour down stinking pitch,
But that the sea, mounting to the welkin's cheek,
5   Dashes the fire out. O, I have suffered
With those that I saw suffer; a brave vessel,
Who had, no doubt, some noble creature in her,
Dashed all to pieces. O, the cry did knock
Against my very heart. Poor souls, they perish'd.
10   Had I been any god of power, I would
Have sunk the sea within the earth or ere
It should the good ship so have swallowed and
The fraughting souls within her.

  Prospero Be collected.
15   No more amazement. Tell your piteous heart
There's no harm done.

  Miranda O, woe the day!

  Prospero No harm.
I have done nothing but in care of thee,
20   Of thee, my dear one, thee, my daughter, who
Art ignorant of what thou art, nought knowing
Of whence I am, nor that I am more better
Than Prospero, master of a full poor cell,

---

48 merely: completely.   **49 wide-chapped:** big mouthed.   **1.2,4 welkin:** sky.   **11 or ere:** before.   **13 fraughting:** forming the cargo.

And thy no greater father.
25   **Miranda** More to know
Did never meddle with my thoughts.
Prospero 'Tis time
I should inform thee farther. Lend thy hand,
And pluck my magic garment from me. So.   [*Removes his cloak.*]
30   Lie there, my art. Wipe thou thine eyes; have comfort.
The direful spectacle of the wreck, which touched
The very virtue of compassion in thee,
I have with such provision in mine art
So safely ordered that there is no soul,
35   No, not so much perdition as an hair
Betid to any creature in the vessel
Which thou heard'st cry, which thou saw'st sink. Sit down;
For thou must now know farther.
   Miranda You have often
40   Begun to tell me what I am, but stopp'd
And left me to a bootless inquisition,
Concluding 'Stay: not yet.'
Prospero The hour's now come;
The very minute bids thee ope thine ear;
45   Obey and be attentive. Canst thou remember
A time before we came unto this cell?
I do not think thou canst, for then thou wast not
Out three years old.
   Miranda Certainly, sir, I can.
50   **Prospero** By what? By any other house or person?
Of any thing the image tell me that
Hath kept with thy remembrance.
   Miranda 'Tis far off
And rather like a dream than an assurance
55   That my remembrance warrants. Had I not
Four or five women once that tended me?
Prospero Thou hadst, and more, Miranda. But how is it
That this lives in thy mind? What seest thou else
In the dark backward and abysm of time?
60   If thou remember'st aught ere thou camest here,
How thou camest here thou mayst.
   Miranda But that I do not.
Prospero Twelve year since, Miranda, twelve year since,
Thy father was the Duke of Milan and
65   A prince of power.
   Miranda Sir, are not you my father?
Prospero Thy mother was a piece of virtue, and
She said thou wast my daughter; and thy father

---

35 perdition: loss.   **41 bootless:** without success.   **55 warrants:** guarantees.   **59 abysm:** abyss.

Was Duke of Milan; and thou his only heir
70   And princess no worse issued.
     Miranda O the heavens!
     What foul play had we, that we came from thence?
     Or blessed was't we did?
     Prospero Both, both, my girl.
75   By foul play, as thou say'st, were we heaved thence,
     But blessedly holp hither.
     Miranda O, my heart bleeds
     To think o' the teen that I have turned you to,
     Which is from my remembrance! Please you, farther.
80   **Prospero** My brother and thy uncle, call'd Antonio –
     I pray thee, mark me – that a brother should
     Be so perfidious! – he whom next thyself
     Of all the world I loved and to him put
     The manage of my state, as at that time
85   Through all the signories it was the first
     And Prospero the prime duke, being so reputed
     In dignity, and for the liberal arts
     Without a parallel; those being all my study,
     The government I cast upon my brother
90   And to my state grew stranger, being transported
     And rapt in secret studies. Thy false uncle –
     Dost thou attend me?
     Miranda Sir, most heedfully.
     Prospero Being once perfected how to grant suits,
95   How to deny them, who to advance and who
     To trash for overtopping, new created
     The creatures that were mine, I say, or changed 'em,
     Or else new formed 'em; having both the key
     Of officer and office, set all hearts i' the state
100   To what tune pleased his ear; that now he was
     The ivy which had hid my princely trunk,
     And sucked my verdure out on't. Thou attend'st not.
     Miranda O, good sir, I do.
     Prospero I pray thee, mark me.
105   I, thus neglecting worldly ends, all dedicated
     To closeness and the bettering of my mind
     With that which, but by being so retired,
     O'er-prizèd all popular rate, in my false brother
     Awaked an evil nature; and my trust,
110   Like a good parent, did beget of him

---

70 no worse issued: no less nobly born. **76 holp:** helped; from holpen, the old form of the verb. **78 teen:** trouble. **87 liberal arts:** attainments appropriate for a person of superior social position, i.e. a free as opposed to servile person. During this period: grammar, logic, rhetoric, arithmetic, geometry, music and astronomy. **94 grant suits:** answer requests. **96 overtopping:** going beyond the limits of a position. **97 creatures:** people dependent on the lord's power. **102 verdure:** sap, the image of the ivy sucking the life from the more powerful tree is a commonplace. **108 O'er prized all popular rate:** went beyond popular understanding.

A falsehood in its contrary as great
As my trust was, which had indeed no limit,
A confidence sans bound. He being thus lorded,
Not only with what my revenue yielded,
115 But what my power might else exact, like one
Who having into truth by telling of it,
Made such a sinner of his memory,
To credit his own lie, he did believe
He was indeed the duke, out o' the substitution
120 And executing the outward face of royalty,
With all prerogative. Hence his ambition growing –
Dost thou hear?
Miranda Your tale, sir, would cure deafness.
Prospero To have no screen between this part he played
125 And him he played it for, he needs will be
Absolute Milan. Me, poor man, my library
Was dukedom large enough; of temporal royalties
He thinks me now incapable; confederates –
So dry he was for sway – wi'the King of Naples
130 To give him annual tribute, do him homage,
Subject his coronet to his crown and bend
The dukedom yet unbowed – alas, poor Milan! –
To most ignoble stooping.
Miranda O the heavens!
135 *Prospero* Mark his condition and the event; then tell me
If this might be a brother.
Miranda I should sin
To think but nobly of my grandmother:
Good wombs have borne bad sons.
140 *Prospero* Now the condition.
The King of Naples, being an enemy
To me inveterate, hearkens my brother's suit;
Which was, that he, in lieu o'the premises
Of homage and I know not how much tribute,
145 Should presently extirpate me and mine
Out of the dukedom and confer fair Milan
With all the honours on my brother; whereon,
A treacherous army levied, one midnight
Fated to the purpose did Antonio open
150 The gates of Milan, and, i' the dead of darkness,
The ministers for the purpose hurried thence
Me and thy crying self.
Miranda Alack, for pity!
I, not remembering how I cried out then,

---

127 **temporal royalties**: the attributes of earthly rule.   129 **dry**: thirsty.   142 **inveterate**: of long standing.
143 **in lieu o'the premises**: in return for the conditions agreed.   145 **extirpate**: drive out.

155   Will cry it o'er again. It is a hint
That wrings mine eyes to't.
Prospero Hear a little further
And then I'll bring thee to the present business
Which now's upon's; without the which this story
160   Were most impertinent.
Miranda Wherefore did they not
That hour destroy us?
Prospero Well demanded, wench:
My tale provokes that question. Dear, they durst not,
165   So dear the love my people bore me, nor set
A mark so bloody on the business, but
With colours fairer painted their foul ends.
In few, they hurried us aboard a bark,
Bore us some leagues to sea, where they prepared
170   A rotten carcass of a butt, not rigged,
Nor tackle, sail, nor mast, the very rats
Instinctively had quit it. There they hoist us,
To cry to the sea that roared to us, to sigh
To the winds whose pity, sighing back again,
175   Did us but loving wrong.
Miranda Alack, what trouble
Was I then to you!
Prospero O, a cherubim
Thou wast that did preserve me. Thou didst smile,
180   Infused with a fortitude from heaven,
When I have decked the sea with drops full salt,
Under my burthen groaned, which raised in me
An undergoing stomach, to bear up
Against what should ensue.
185   ***Miranda*** How came we ashore?
Prospero By providence divine.
Some food we had and some fresh water that
A noble Neapolitan, Gonzalo,
Out of his charity, being then appointed
190   Master of this design, did give us, with
Rich garments, linens, stuffs and necessaries,
Which since have steaded much; so, of his gentleness,
Knowing I loved my books, he furnished me
From mine own library with volumes that
195   I prize above my dukedom.
Miranda Would I might
But ever see that man!
Prospero Now I arise.

---

155 hint: occasion.   **170 butt:** a barrel, here a small and poor boat.   **183 undergoing stomach:** put courage into me to endure.

Sit still, and hear the last of our sea-sorrow.
200 Here in this island we arrived; and here
Have I, thy schoolmaster, made thee more profit
Than other princesses can that have more time
For vainer hours and tutors not so careful.
Miranda Heavens thank you for't! And now I pray you, sir,
205 For still 'tis beating in my mind, your reason
For raising this sea-storm?
Prospero Know thus far forth.
By accident most strange, bountiful Fortune,
Now my dear lady, hath mine enemies
210 Brought to this shore; and by my prescience
I find my zenith doth depend upon
A most auspicious star, whose influence
If now I court not but omit, my fortunes
Will ever after droop. Here cease more questions;
215 Thou art inclined to sleep; 'tis a good dulness,
And give it way; I know thou canst not choose. [*Miranda sleeps.*]
Come away, servant, come. I am ready now.
Approach, my Ariel, come.
[*Enter Ariel.*]
Ariel All hail, great master! grave sir, hail! I come
220 To answer thy best pleasure; be't to fly,
To swim, to dive into the fire, to ride
On the curled clouds, to thy strong bidding task
Ariel and all his quality.
Prospero Hast thou, spirit,
225 Performed to point the tempest that I bade thee?
Ariel To every article.
I boarded the king's ship; now on the beak,
Now in the waist, the deck, in every cabin,
I flamed amazement: sometime I'd divide,
230 And burn in many places; on the topmast,
The yards and bowsprit, would I flame distinctly,
Then meet and join. Jove's lightnings, the precursors
O' the dreadful thunder-claps, more momentary
And sight-outrunning were not; the fire and cracks
235 Of sulphurous roaring the most mighty Neptune
Seem to besiege and make his bold waves tremble,
Yea, his dread trident shake.
Prospero My brave spirit!
Who was so firm, so constant, that this coil
240 Would not infect his reason?
Ariel Not a soul
But felt a fever of the mad and played

---

227 **beak**: prow. 228 **waist**: amidships. 239 **coil**: confusion.

Some tricks of desperation. All but mariners
Plunged in the foaming brine and quit the vessel,
245   Then all afire with me; the king's son, Ferdinand,
With hair up-staring – then like reeds, not hair –
Was the first man that leaped, cried, 'Hell is empty
And all the devils are here.'
Prospero Why that's my spirit!
250   But was not this nigh shore?
Ariel Close by, my master.
Prospero But are they, Ariel, safe?
Ariel Not a hair perished;
On their sustaining garments not a blemish,
255   But fresher than before; and, as thou badest me,
In troops I have dispersed them 'bout the isle.
The king's son have I landed by himself;
Whom I left cooling of the air with sighs
In an odd angle of the isle and sitting,
260   His arms in this sad knot.
Prospero Of the king's ship
The mariners say how thou hast disposed
And all the rest o' the fleet.
Ariel Safely in harbour
265   Is the king's ship; in the deep nook, where once
Thou call'dst me up at midnight to fetch dew
From the still-vexed Bermoothes, there she's hid.
The mariners all under hatches stowed;
Who, with a charm joined to their suffered labour,
270   I have left asleep; and for the rest o' the fleet
Which I dispersed, they all have met again
And are upon the Mediterranean flote,
Bound sadly home for Naples,
Supposing that they saw the king's ship wrecked
275   And his great person perish.
Prospero Ariel, thy charge
Exactly is performed; but there's more work.
What is the time o' the day?
Ariel Past the mid-season.
280   ***Prospero*** At least two glasses. The time 'twixt six and now
Must by us both be spent most preciously.
Ariel Is there more toil? Since thou dost give me pains,
Let me remember thee what thou hast promised,
Which is not yet performed me.
285   ***Prospero*** How now? Moody?
What is't thou canst demand?

---

260 sad knot: arms folded to express sorrow. **267 Bermoothes:** The Bermudas were often portrayed as an enchanted place. **272 flote:** float.

Ariel My liberty.

Prospero Before the time be out? no more!

Ariel I prithee,

290 Remember I have done thee worthy service,
Told thee no lies, made thee no mistakings, served
Without or grudge or grumblings. Thou didst promise
To bate me a full year.

Prospero Dost thou forget

295 From what a torment I did free thee?

Ariel No.

Prospero Thou dost, and think'st it much to tread the ooze
Of the salt deep,
To run upon the sharp wind of the north,

300 To do me business in the veins o' the earth
When it is baked with frost.

Ariel I do not, sir.

Prospero Thou liest, malignant thing! Hast thou forgot
The foul witch Sycorax, who with age and envy

305 Was grown into a hoop? hast thou forgot her?

Ariel No, sir.

Prospero Thou hast. Where was she born? speak, tell me.

Ariel Sir, in Argier.

Prospero O, was she so? I must

310 Once in a month recount what thou hast been,
Which thou forget'st. This damned witch Sycorax,
For mischiefs manifold and sorceries terrible
To enter human hearing, from Argier,
Thou know'st, was banished; for one thing she did

315 They would not take her life. Is not this true?

Ariel Ay, sir.

Prospero This blue-eyed hag was hither brought with child
And here was left by the sailors. Thou, my slave,
As thou report'st thyself, wast then her servant;

320 And, for thou wast a spirit too delicate
To act her earthy and abhorred commands,
Refusing her grand hests, she did confine thee,
By help of her more potent ministers
And in her most unmitigable rage,

325 Into a cloven pine; within which rift
Imprisoned thou didst painfully remain
A dozen years; within which space she died
And left thee there; where thou didst vent thy groans
As fast as mill-wheels strike. Then was this island –

330 Save for the son that she did litter here,

---

293 **bate me:** rebate me – deduct from the time Ariel agreed to serve Prospero. **308 Argier:** old name for Algiers.
322 hests: behests.

A freckled whelp hag-born – not honoured with
A human shape.
Ariel Yes, Caliban her son.
Prospero Dull thing, I say so; he, that Caliban
335 Whom now I keep in service. Thou best know'st
What torment I did find thee in; thy groans
Did make wolves howl and penetrate the breasts
Of ever angry bears: it was a torment
To lay upon the damned, which Sycorax
340 Could not again undo. It was mine art,
When I arrived and heard thee, that made gape
The pine and let thee out.
Ariel I thank thee, master.
Prospero If thou more murmur'st, I will rend an oak
345 And peg thee in his knotty entrails till
Thou hast howled away twelve winters.
Ariel Pardon, master.
I will be correspondent to command
And do my spiriting gently.
350 *Prospero* Do so, and after two days
I will discharge thee.
Ariel That's my noble master!
What shall I do? say what, what shall I do?
Prospero Go make thyself like a nymph o' the sea. Be subject
355 To no sight but thine and mine, invisible
To every eyeball else. Go take this shape
And hither come in't. Go, hence with diligence! [*Exit Ariel.*]
Awake, dear heart, awake. Thou hast slept well. Awake!
Miranda The strangeness of your story put
360 Heaviness in me.
Prospero Shake it off. Come on;
We'll visit Caliban my slave, who never
Yields us kind answer.
Miranda 'Tis a villain, sir,
365 I do not love to look on.
Prospero But, as 'tis,
We cannot miss him. He does make our fire,
Fetch in our wood and serves in offices
That profit us. What, ho! slave! Caliban!
370 Thou earth, thou! speak.
Caliban [*within*] There's wood enough within.
Prospero Come forth, I say! there's other business for thee.
Come, thou tortoise! when? [*Enter Ariel like a water-nymph.*]
Fine apparition! My quaint Ariel,
375 Hark in thine ear.

---

331 freckled: spotted.   **367 cannot miss:** cannot do without.   **374 quaint:** ingenious, odd in appearance.

Ariel My lord it shall be done. [*Exit.*]
Prospero Thou poisonous slave, got by the devil himself
Upon thy wicked dam, come forth!
[*Enter Caliban.*]
Caliban As wicked dew as e'er my mother brushed
380 With raven's feather from unwholesome fen
Drop on you both! a south-west blow on ye
And blister you all o'er!
Prospero For this, be sure, to-night thou shalt have cramps,
Side-stitches that shall pen thy breath up; urchins
385 Shall, for that vast of night that they may work,
All exercise on thee; thou shalt be pinched
As thick as honeycomb, each pinch more stinging
Than bees that made 'em.
Caliban I must eat my dinner.
390 This island's mine by Sycorax my mother,
Which thou takest from me. When thou cam'st first,
Thou strok'st me and madest much of me, wouldst give me
Water with berries in't, and teach me how
To name the bigger light and how the less,
395 That burn by day and night; and then I loved thee,
And showed thee all the qualities o' the isle,
The fresh springs, brine-pits, barren place and fertile –
Cursed be I that did so! All the charms
Of Sycorax, toads, beetles, bats, light on you!
400 For I am all the subjects that you have,
Which first was mine own king; and here you sty me
In this hard rock, whiles you do keep from me
The rest o' the island.
Prospero Thou most lying slave,
405 Whom stripes may move, not kindness! I have used thee,
Filth as thou art, with human care, and lodged thee
In mine own cell, till thou didst seek to violate
The honour of my child.
Caliban O ho, O ho! would't had been done!
410 Thou didst prevent me; I had peopled else
This isle with Calibans.
Miranda Abhorred slave,
Which any print of goodness wilt not take,
Being capable of all ill! I pitied thee,
415 Took pains to make thee speak, taught thee each hour
One thing or other; when thou didst not, savage,
Know thine own meaning, but wouldst gabble like
A thing most brutish, I endowed thy purposes
With words that made them known. But thy vile race,

---

380 raven: bird associated with witchcraft. **fen:** low-lying land, wet land.   **384 urchins:** goblins.   **401 sty:** keep me in a pen.   **413: print:** imprint.

420 Though thou didst learn, had that in't which good natures
Could not abide to be with; therefore wast thou
Deservedly confined into this rock,
Who hadst deserved more than a prison.
Caliban You taught me language, and my profit on't
425 Is I know how to curse. The red plague rid you
For learning me your language!
Prospero Hag-seed, hence!
Fetch us in fuel; and be quick, thou'rt best,
To answer other business. Shrug'st thou, malice?
430 If thou neglect'st or dost unwillingly
What I command, I'll rack thee with old cramps,
Fill all thy bones with aches, make thee roar
That beasts shall tremble at thy din.
Caliban No, pray thee.
435 [*Aside*] I must obey. His art is of such power,
It would control my dam's god, Setebos,
And make a vassal of him.
Prospero So, slave; hence! [*Exit Caliban.*]
[*Enter Ariel, invisible, playing and singing; Ferdinand following.
Ariel sings.*]
Come unto these yellow sands,
440 And then take hands;
Courtsied when you have and kissed
The wild waves whist,
Foot it featly here and there;
And, sweet sprites bear
445 The burthen. Hark, hark!
[*Burthen dispersedly.*] Bow-wow.
The watch-dogs bark!
[*Burthen dispersedly.*] Bow-wow.
Hark, hark! I hear
450 The strain of strutting chanticleer
Cry, [*Burthen dispersedly.*] Cock-a-diddle-dow.
Ferdinand Where should this music be? I' the air or the earth?
It sounds no more; and sure, it waits upon
Some god o' the island. Sitting on a bank,
455 Weeping again the king my father's wreck,
This music crept by me upon the waters,
Allaying both their fury and my passion
With its sweet air. Thence I have followed it,
Or it hath drawn me rather. But 'tis gone.
460 No, it begins again.

---

431 old cramps: the cramps of old age. **436 dam**: mother. **440 take hands**: taking hands and curtsying were usual ways of beginning a dance. **441–42 kissed the wild waves whist**: silenced the tempest. The sense suggests the dance's order as a means of calming the chaotic elements of nature. **445 burthen**: burden; here, principally, meaning the refrain or chorus of a song. **446 dispersedly**: not together at the same time. **450 chanticleer**: a commonplace name for a cock.

[*Ariel sings.*]
Full fathom five thy father lies;
Of his bones are coral made;
Those are pearls that were his eyes;
Nothing of him that doth fade
465 But doth suffer a sea-change
Into something rich and strange.
Sea-nymphs hourly ring his knell.
[*Burthen.*] Ding-dong.
Hark! now I hear them – Ding-dong, bell.
470 **Ferdinand** The ditty does remember my drowned father.
This is no mortal business, nor no sound
That the earth owes. I hear it now above me.
Prospero The fringed curtains of thine eye advance
And say what thou seest yond.
475 **Miranda** What is't? a spirit?
Lord, how it looks about! Believe me, sir,
It carries a brave form. But 'tis a spirit.
Prospero No, wench, it eats and sleeps and hath such senses
As we have such. This gallant which thou seest
480 Was in the wreck; and, but he's something stained
With grief that's beauty's canker, thou mightst call him
A goodly person. He hath lost his fellows
And strays about to find 'em.
Miranda I might call him
485 A thing divine, for nothing natural
I ever saw so noble.
Prospero [*Aside*] It goes on I see,
As my soul prompts it. Spirit, fine spirit! I'll free thee
Within two days for this.
490 **Ferdinand** Most sure, the goddess
On whom these airs attend! Vouchsafe my prayer
May know if you remain upon this island;
And that you will some good instruction give
How I may bear me here. My prime request,
495 Which I do last pronounce, is, O you wonder!,
If you be maid or no?
Miranda No wonder, sir,
But certainly a maid.
Ferdinand My language! heavens!
500 I am the best of them that speak this speech,
Were I but where 'tis spoken.
Prospero How? The best?
What wert thou if the King of Naples heard thee?

---

461 **fathom**: a measure of about 1.8 metres.   467 **knell**: solemn ringing of a bell for the dead.   481 **canker**: sore
or disease.   496 **maid**: unmarried girl.

Ferdinand A single thing, as I am now, that wonders
505 To hear thee speak of Naples. He does hear me;
And that he does I weep. Myself am Naples,
Who with mine eyes, never since at ebb, beheld
The king my father wrecked.
Miranda Alack, for mercy!
510 *Ferdinand* Yes, faith, and all his lords, the Duke of Milan
And his brave son being twain.
Prospero [*Aside*] The Duke of Milan
And his more braver daughter could control thee,
If now 'twere fit to do't. At the first sight
515 They have changed eyes. Delicate Ariel,
I'll set thee free for this. [*To Ferdinand*]
A word, good sir;
I fear you have done yourself some wrong; a word.
Miranda Why speaks my father so ungently? This
520 Is the third man that e'er I saw, the first
That e'er I sighed for. Pity move my father
To be inclined my way!
Ferdinand O, if a virgin,
And your affection not gone forth, I'll make you
525 The queen of Naples.
Prospero Soft, sir! one word more.
[*Aside*] They are both in either's powers; but this swift business
I must uneasy make, lest too light winning
Make the prize light. [*To Ferdinand*]
530 One word more; I charge thee
That thou attend me. Thou dost here usurp
The name thou owest not, and hast put thyself
Upon this island as a spy, to win it
From me, the lord on't.
535 *Ferdinand* No, as I am a man.
Miranda There's nothing ill can dwell in such a temple.
If the ill spirit have so fair a house,
Good things will strive to dwell with't.
Prospero Follow me.
540 Speak not you for him; he's a traitor. Come,
I'll manacle thy neck and feet together.
Sea-water shalt thou drink, thy food shall be
The fresh-brook muscles, withered roots and husks
Wherein the acorn cradled. Follow.
545 *Ferdinand* No,
I will resist such entertainment till
Mine enemy has more power. [*He draws, but is charmed from moving.*]

---

507 never since at ebb: continually weeping since.   **515 changed eyes:** loved at first sight.

Miranda O dear father,
Make not too rash a trial of him, for
550   He's gentle and not fearful.
Prospero What? I say,
My foot my tutor? Put thy sword up traitor;
Who makest a show but darest not strike, thy conscience
Is so possessed with guilt. Come from thy ward,
555   For I can here disarm thee with this stick
And make thy weapon drop.
Miranda Beseech you, father.
Prospero Hence! hang not on my garments.
Miranda Sir, have pity;
560   I'll be his surety.
Prospero Silence! one word more
Shall make me chide thee, if not hate thee. What!
An advocate for an imposter! Hush!
Thou think'st there is no more such shapes as he,
565   Having seen but him and Caliban. Foolish wench!
To the most of men this is a Caliban
And they to him are angels.
Miranda My affections
Are then most humble; I have no ambition
570   To see a goodlier man.
Prospero [*To Ferdinand*] Come on, obey.
Thy nerves are in their infancy again
And have no vigour in them.
Ferdinand So they are;
575   My spirits, as in a dream, are all bound up.
My father's loss, the weakness which I feel,
The wreck of all my friends, nor this man's threats,
To whom I am subdued, are but light to me,
Might I but through my prison once a day
580   Behold this maid. All corners else o' the earth
Let liberty make use of; space enough
Have I in such a prison.
Prospero [*Aside*] It works. [*To Ferdinand*] Come on.
[*To Ariel*] Thou hast done well, fine Ariel. [*To Ferdinand*] Follow me.
585   Hark what thou else shalt do me.
Miranda Be of comfort;
My father's of a better nature, sir,
Than he appears by speech. This is unwonted
Which now came from him.
590   *Prospero* [*To Ariel*] Thou shalt be free
As mountain winds; but then exactly do

---

552 my foot my tutor?: shall the lowest part rule me?   **554 ward:** defensive position.   **572 Thy nerves are in their infancy:** you are as helpless as a baby.

All points of my command.
Ariel To the syllable.
Prospero [*To Miranda*] Come, follow. Speak not for him. [*Exit.*]

Act II, Scene i

[*Another part of the island. Enter Alonso, Sebastian, Antonio, Gonzalo,
Adrian, Francisco, and others.*]
Gonzalo Beseech you, sir, be merry; you have cause,
So have we all, of joy; for our escape
Is much beyond our loss. Our hint of woe
Is common; every day some sailor's wife,
5   The masters of some merchant and the merchant
Have just our theme of woe; but for the miracle,
I mean our preservation, few in millions
Can speak like us. Then wisely, good sir, weigh
Our sorrow with our comfort.
10   **Alonso** Prithee, peace.
Sebastian [*To Antonio*] He receives comfort like cold porridge.
Antonio The visitor will not give him o'er so.
Sebastian Look he's winding up the watch of his wit; by and by it
will strike.
15   **Gonzalo** Sir,
Sebastian One, tell.
Gonzalo When every grief is entertained that's offered,
Comes to the entertainer –
Sebastian A dollar.
20   **Gonzalo** Dolour comes to him, indeed: you
have spoken truer than you purposed.
Sebastian You have taken it wiselier than I meant you should.
Gonzalo Therefore, my lord –
Antonio Fie, what a spendthrift is he of his tongue!
25   **Alonso** I prithee, spare.
Gonzalo Well, I have done; but yet –
Sebastian He will be talking.
Antonio Which, of he or Adrian, for a good wager, first begins to
crow?
30   **Sebastian** The old cock.
Antonio The cockerel.
Sebastian Done. The wager?
Antonio A laughter.
Sebastian A match!
35   **Adrian** Though this island seem to be desert –
Sebastian Ha, ha, ha! So, you're paid.

2.1,5 **masters:** owners of a ship. 12 **visitor:** a person engaged by the Church to visit the sick. 16 **tell:** counting
the hours struck by a clock. 19 **dollar:** payment. The play of words is on 'entertainer', which Sebastian uses as
performer.

Adrian Uninhabitable and almost inaccessible –
Sebastian Yet –
Adrian Yet –
40 *Antonio* He could not miss't.
Adrian It must needs be of subtle, tender and delicate temperance.
Antonio Temperance was a delicate wench.
Sebastian Ay, and a subtle; as he most learnedly delivered.
Adrian The air breathes upon us here most sweetly.
45 *Sebastian* As if it had lungs and rotten ones.
Antonio Or as 'twere perfumed by a fen.
Gonzalo Here is everything advantageous to life.
Antonio True, save means to live.
Sebastian Of that there's none, or little.
50 *Gonzalo* How lush and lusty the grass looks! how green!
Antonio The ground indeed is tawny.
Sebastian With an eye of green in't.
Antonio He misses not much.
Sebastian No, he doth but mistake the truth totally.
55 *Gonzalo* But the rarity of it is, which is indeed almost beyond
credit –
Sebastian As many vouched rarities are.
Gonzalo That our garments, being, as they were, drenched in the
sea, hold notwithstanding their freshness and glosses, being rather
60 new-dyed than stained with salt water.
Antonio If but one of his pockets could speak, would it not say he
lies?
Sebastian Ay, or very falsely pocket up his report.
Gonzalo Methinks our garments are now as fresh as when we put
65 them on first in Afric, at the marriage of the king's fair daughter
Claribel to the King of Tunis.
Sebastian 'Twas a sweet marriage, and we prosper well in our
return.
Adrian Tunis was never graced before with such a paragon to their
70 queen.
Gonzalo Not since widow Dido's time.
Antonio Widow! A pox o' that! How came that widow in? Widow
Dido!
Sebastian What if he had said 'widower Aeneas' too? Good Lord,
75 how you take it!
Adrian 'Widow Dido' said you? you make me study of that. She
was of Carthage, not of Tunis.
Gonzalo This Tunis, sir, was Carthage.
Adrian Carthage?
80 *Gonzalo* I assure you, Carthage.

---

43 subtle: here suggesting sexually skilful.   **52 eye:** tinge.   **72 widow:** Dido was a widow but this is an extremely
unusual way of referring to her.

Sebastian His word is more than the miraculous harp; he hath raised the wall and houses too.

Antonio What impossible matter will he make easy next?

Sebastian I think he will carry this island home in his pocket and
85 give it his son for an apple.

Antonio And, sowing the kernels of it in the sea, bring forth more islands.

Gonzalo Ay.

Antonio Why, in good time.

90 *Gonzalo* [*to Alonzo*] Sir, we were talking that our garments seem now as fresh as when we were at Tunis at the marriage of your daughter, who is now queen.

Antonio And the rarest that e'er came there.

Sebastian Bate, I beseech you, widow Dido.

95 *Antonio* O, widow Dido! Ay, widow Dido.

Gonzalo Is not, sir, my doublet as fresh as the first day I wore it? I mean, in a sort.

Antonio That sort was well fished for.

Gonzalo When I wore it at your daughter's marriage?

100 *Alonso* You cram these words into mine ears against
The stomach of my sense. Would I had never
Married my daughter there! For, coming thence,
My son is lost and, in my rate, she too,
Who is so far from Italy removed
105 I ne'er again shall see her. O thou mine heir
Of Naples and of Milan, what strange fish
Hath made his meal on thee?

Francisco Sir, he may live:
I saw him beat the surges under him,
110 And ride upon their backs; he trod the water,
Whose enmity he flung aside, and breasted
The surge most swoln that met him; his bold head
'Bove the contentious waves he kept, and oared
Himself with his good arms in lusty stroke
115 To the shore, that o'er his wave-worn basis bowed,
As stooping to relieve him. I not doubt
He came alive to land.

Alonso No, no, he's gone.

Sebastian Sir, you may thank yourself for this great loss,
120 That would not bless our Europe with your daughter,
But rather lose her to an African;
Where she at least is banished from your eye,
Who hath cause to wet the grief on't.

---

81 **miraculous harp**: Amphion's playing supposedly caused the stones of Thebes' wall to rise into place. Gonzalo has verbally 'rebuilt' Carthage, a city destroyed by the Romans. The city of Tunis lies near to its site. 94 **Bate**: except. 103 **rate**: in my accounting. 115 **basis**: the foot of a cliff. 123 **Who hath cause**: who has reason to grieve.

Alonso Prithee, peace.

125 *Sebastian* You were kneeled to and importuned otherwise
By all of us, and the fair soul herself
Weighed between loathness and obedience, at
Which end o' the beam should bow. We have lost your son,
I fear, for ever. Milan and Naples have
130 More widows in them of this business' making
Than we bring men to comfort them.
The fault's your own.

Alonso So is the dear'st o' the loss.

Gonzalo My lord Sebastian,
135 The truth you speak doth lack some gentleness
And time to speak it in; you rub the sore,
When you should bring the plaster.

Sebastian Very well.

Antonio And most chirurgeonly.

140 *Gonzalo* It is foul weather in us all, good sir,
When you are cloudy.

Sebastian Foul weather?

Antonio Very foul.

Gonzalo Had I plantation of this isle, my lord –
145 *Antonio* He'd sow't with nettle-seed.

Sebastian Or docks, or mallows.

Gonzalo And were the king on't, what would I do?

Sebastian 'Scape being drunk for want of wine.

Gonzalo I' the commonwealth I would by contraries
150 Execute all things; for no kind of traffic
Would I admit; no name of magistrate;
Letters should not be known; riches, poverty,
And use of service, none; contract, succession,
Bourn, bound of land, tilth, vineyard, none;
155 No use of metal, corn, or wine, or oil;
No occupation; all men idle, all;
And women too, but innocent and pure;
No sovereignty –

Sebastian Yet he would be king on't.

160 *Antonio* The latter end of his commonwealth forgets the beginning.

Gonzalo All things in common nature should produce
Without sweat or endeavour. Treason, felony,
Sword, pike, knife, gun, or need of any engine,
Would I not have; but nature should bring forth,
165 Of its own kind, all foison, all abundance,
To feed my innocent people.

---

128 **end o' the beam:** Clairbel weighed her dislike of the marriage and her obedience to her father as in an equally balanced scale. 131 **comfort:** an assumption that the king's party will return, but not the fleet. 139 **chirurgeonly:** like a surgeon. 144 **plantation:** right to colonise. 145–46 **nettle-seed, docks, mallows:** weeds. 150 **traffic:** trade. 153 **use of service:** keeping of servants. 154 **Bourn, bound of land:** boundaries. 165 **foison:** plenty.

Sebastian No marrying 'mong his subjects?
Antonio None, man; all idle, whores and knaves.
Gonzalo I would with such perfection govern, sir,
170   To excel the golden age.
Sebastian God save his majesty!
Antonio Long live Gonzalo!
Gonzalo And – do you mark me, sir?
Alonso Prithee, no more. Thou dost talk nothing to me.
175   *Gonzalo* I do well believe your highness; and did it to minister
occasion to these gentlemen, who are of such sensible and nimble
lungs that they always use to laugh at nothing.
Antonio 'Twas you we laughed at.
Gonzalo Who in this kind of merry fooling am nothing to you; so
180   you may continue and laugh at nothing still.
Antonio What a blow was there given!
Sebastian An it had not fallen flat-long.
Gonzalo You are gentlemen of brave mettle; you would lift the
moon out of her sphere, if she would continue in it five weeks with
185   out changing.
[*Enter Ariel, invisible, playing solemn music.*]
Sebastian We would so, and then go a bat-fowling.
Antonio Nay, good my lord, be not angry.
Gonzalo No, I warrant you; I will not adventure my discretion so
weakly. Will you laugh me asleep, for I am very heavy?
190   *Antonio* Go sleep, and hear us.
[*All sleep except Alonso, Sebastian, and Antonio.*]
Alonso What, all so soon asleep! I wish mine eyes
Would, with themselves, shut up my thoughts. I find
They are inclined to do so.
Sebastian Please you, sir,
195   Do not omit the heavy offer of it.
It seldom visits sorrow; when it doth,
It is a comforter.
Antonio We two, my lord,
Will guard your person while you take your rest,
200   And watch your safety.
Alonso Thank you. Wondrous heavy. [*Alonso sleeps. Exit Ariel.*]
Sebastian What a strange drowsiness possesses them!
Antonio It is the quality o' the climate.
Sebastian Why
205   Doth it not then our eyelids sink? I find not
Myself disposed to sleep.
Antonio Nor I; my spirits are nimble.
They fell together all, as by consent;

---

182 **flat-long:** on the flat of the sword, thus without harm.   186 **bat-fowling:** catching birds by night, here implying taking advantage of the foolish.

They dropped as by a thunder-stroke. What might,
210 Worthy Sebastian? O, what might? – No more –
And yet me thinks I see it in thy face,
What thou shouldst be. The occasion speaks thee, and
My strong imagination sees a crown
Dropping upon thy head.
215 *Sebastian* What, art thou waking?
Antonio Do you not hear me speak?
Sebastian I do, and surely
It is a sleepy language and thou speak'st
Out of thy sleep. What is it thou didst say?
220 This is a strange repose, to be asleep
With eyes wide open; standing, speaking, moving,
And yet so fast asleep.
Antonio Noble Sebastian,
Thou let'st thy fortune sleep – die, rather; wink'st
225 Whiles thou art waking.
Sebastian Thou dost snore distinctly;
There's meaning in thy snores.
Antonio I am more serious than my custom. You
Must be so too, if heed me; which to do
230 Trebles thee o'er.
Sebastian Well, I am standing water.
Antonio I'll teach you how to flow.
Sebastian Do so; to ebb
Hereditary sloth instructs me.
235 *Antonio* O,
If you but knew how you the purpose cherish
Whiles thus you mock it! How, in stripping it,
You more invest it! Ebbing men, indeed,
Most often do so near the bottom run
240 By their own fear or sloth.
Sebastian Prithee, say on.
The setting of thine eye and cheek proclaim
A matter from thee, and a birth indeed
Which throes thee much to yield.
245 *Antonio* Thus, sir:
Although this lord of weak remembrance, this,
Who shall be of as little memory
When he is earthed, hath here almost persuade –
For he's a spirit of persuasion, only
250 Professes to persuade – the king his son's alive,
'Tis as impossible that he's undrowned
And he that sleeps here swims.

---

230 **trebles:** makes you three times greater. 233–34 **to ebb:** I am naturally lazy because of my position as the king's younger brother. 236–37 **purpose cherish:** if only you knew how you actually want what you mock.
237–38 **stripping it:** the more you belittle it the more you make it important.

Sebastian I have no hope
That he's undrowned.

255   **Antonio** O, out of that 'no hope'
What great hope have you! no hope that way is
Another way so high a hope that even
Ambition cannot pierce a wink beyond,
But doubt discovery there. Will you grant with me

260   That Ferdinand is drowned?

Sebastian He's gone.

Antonio Then, tell me,
Who's the next heir of Naples?

Sebastian Claribel.

265   **Antonio** She that is queen of Tunis; she that dwells
Ten leagues beyond man's life; she that from Naples
Can have no note, unless the sun were post –
The man i' the moon's too slow – till new-born chins
Be rough and razorable; she that – from whom?

270   We all were sea-swallowed, though some cast again,
And by that destiny to perform an act
Whereof what's past is prologue, what to come
In yours and my discharge.

Sebastian What stuff is this! How say you?

275   'Tis true, my brother's daughter's queen of Tunis,
So is she heir of Naples, 'twixt which regions
There is some space.

Antonio A space whose every cubit
Seems to cry out, 'How shall that Claribel

280   Measure us back to Naples? Keep in Tunis,
And let Sebastian wake.' Say, this were death
That now hath seized them, why they were no worse
Than now they are. There be that can rule Naples
As well as he that sleeps, lords that can prate

285   As amply and unnecessarily
As this Gonzalo; I myself could make
A chough of as deep chat. O, that you bore
The mind that I do, what a sleep were this
For your advancement! Do you understand me?

290   **Sebastian** Methinks I do.

Antonio And how does your content
Tender your own good fortune?

Sebastian I remember
You did supplant your brother Prospero.

295   **Antonio** True.
And look how well my garments sit upon me;

---

273 **discharge**: performance. 287 **chough**: jackdaw or crow – I could teach a crow to speak as significantly.
291 **content**: liking.

Much feater than before. My brother's servants
Were then my fellows, now they are my men.
Sebastian But for your conscience?

300   **Antonio** Ay, sir, where lies that? If 'twere a kibe,
'Twould put me to my slipper; but I feel not
This deity in my bosom. Twenty consciences,
That stand 'twixt me and Milan, candied be they
And melt ere they molest! Here lies your brother,

305   No better than the earth he lies upon,
If he were that which now he's like, that's dead;
Whom I, with this obedient steel, three inches of it,
Can lay to bed for ever; whiles you, doing thus,
To the perpetual wink for aye might put

310   This ancient morsel, this Sir Prudence, who
Should not upbraid our course. For all the rest,
They'll take suggestion as a cat laps milk;
They'll tell the clock to any business that
We say befits the hour.

315   **Sebastian** Thy case, dear friend,
Shall be my precedent; as thou got'st Milan,
I'll come by Naples. Draw thy sword; one stroke
Shall free thee from the tribute which thou payest,
And I the king shall love thee.

320   **Antonio** Draw together,
And when I rear my hand do you the like,
To fall it on Gonzalo.
Sebastian O, but one word. [*They talk apart.*]
[*Enter Ariel, invisible.*]
Ariel My master through his art foresees the danger

325   That you, his friend, are in; and sends me forth –
For else his project dies – to keep them living.
[*Sings in Gonzalo's ear.*]
While you here do snoring lie,
Open-eyed conspiracy
His time doth take.

330   If of life you keep a care,
Shake off slumber, and beware.
Awake, awake!
Antonio Then let us both be sudden.
Gonzalo Now, good angels

335   Preserve the king. [*They wake.*]
Alonso Why, how now? Ho, awake! Why are you drawn?
Wherefore this ghastly looking?
Gonzalo What's the matter?

---

297 **feater:** more graceful.　**300–01 kibe. . . . :** if it were a sore on my foot it would make me wear a slipper.
303–04 candied. . . . : my conscience is frozen and would need to melt before it would bother me.　**309 perpetual
wink:** lasting sleep.

Sebastian Whiles we stood here securing your repose,
340 Even now, we heard a hollow burst of bellowing
Like bulls, or rather lions. Did't not wake you?
It struck mine ear most terribly.
Alonso I heard nothing.
Antonio O, 'twas a din to fright a monster's ear,
345 To make an earthquake! Sure, it was the roar
Of a whole herd of lions.
Alonso Heard you this, Gonzalo?
Gonzalo Upon mine honour, sir, I heard a humming,
And that a strange one too, which did awake me.
350 I shaked you, sir, and cried; as mine eyes opened,
I saw their weapons drawn. There was a noise,
That's verily. 'Tis best we stand upon our guard,
Or that we quit this place; let's draw our weapons.
Alonso Lead off this ground; and let's make further search
355 For my poor son.
Gonzalo Heavens keep him from these beasts!
For he is sure i' the island.
Alonso Lead away.
Ariel Prospero my lord shall know what I have done.
360 So, king, go safely on to seek thy son. [*Exit.*]

Act II, Scene ii

[*Another part of the island. Enter Caliban with a burden of wood. A noise of thunder heard.*]
Caliban All the infections that the sun sucks up
From bogs, fens, flats, on Prosper fall and make him
By inch-meal a disease! His spirits hear me
And yet I needs must curse. But they'll nor pinch,
5 Fright me with urchin-shows, pitch me i' the mire,
Nor lead me, like a firebrand in the dark,
Out of my way, unless he bid 'em; but
For every trifle are they set upon me;
Sometime like apes that mow and chatter at me
10 And after bite me, then like hedgehogs which
Lie tumbling in my barefoot way and mount
Their pricks at my footfall; sometime am I
All wound with adders who with cloven tongues
Do hiss me into madness. [*Enter Trinculo.*]
15 Lo, now, lo!
Here comes a spirit of his, and to torment me
For bringing wood in slowly. I'll fall flat;
Perchance he will not mind me.

2.2,3 **by inch-meal:** inch by inch. **5 urchin:** goblin. **9 mow:** grimace.

Trinculo Here's neither bush nor shrub to bear off any weather at
20 all, and another storm brewing; I hear it sing i' the wind. Yond same
black cloud, yond huge one, looks like a foul bombard that would
shed his liquor. If it should thunder as it did before I know not where
to hide my head, yond same cloud cannot choose but fall by pailfuls.
What have we here? a man or a fish? dead or alive? A fish! He smells
25 like a fish; a very ancient and fish-like smell; a kind of not of the
newest Poor-John. A strange fish! Were I in England now, as once I
was, and had but this fish painted, not a holiday fool there but would
give a piece of silver. There would this monster make a man; any
strange beast there makes a man. When they will not give a doit to
30 relieve a lame beggar, they will lazy out ten to see a dead Indian.
Legged like a man and his fins like arms! Warm o' my troth! I do
now let loose my opinion, hold it no longer: this is no fish, but an
islander that hath lately suffered by a thunderbolt. [*Thunder.*] Alas,
the storm is come again! My best way is to creep under his
35 gaberdine; there is no other shelter hereabouts. Misery acquaints a
man with strange bed-fellows. I will here shroud till the dregs of the
storm be past.
[*Enter Stephano, singing: a bottle in his hand.*]
Stephano   I shall no more to sea, to sea,
                          Here shall I die ashore –
This is a very scurvy tune to sing at a man's funeral. Well, here's my
40 comfort. [*Drinks.*]
[*Sings.*]

        The master, the swabber, the boatswain and I,
           The gunner and his mate
        Loved Mall, Meg and Marian and Margery,
           But none of us cared for Kate;
45   For she had a tongue with a tang,
           Would cry to a sailor, Go hang!
    She loved not the savour of tar nor of pitch,
    Yet a tailor might scratch her where'er she did itch.
        Then to sea, boys, and let her go hang!

50 This is a scurvy tune too; but here's my comfort. [*Drinks.*]
Caliban Do not torment me, Oh!
Stephano What's the matter? Have we devils here? Do you put
tricks upon's with savages and men of Ind, ha? I have not scaped
drowning to be afeard now of your four legs; for it hath been said: As
55 proper a man as ever went on four legs cannot make him give ground;
and it shall be said so again while Stephano breathes at' nostrils.
Caliban The spirit torments me; Oh!

---

21 bombard: cannon. **26 Poor-John:** dried fish, the food of the poor. **27 painted:** painted on a sign to advertise
it. **29 doit:** coin of small value. **35 gaberdine:** cloak. **48 Yet a tailor might. . . :** Even a tailor could have sex
with her. Tailors were associated with unmanly qualities. **53 men of Ind:** Natives of the West Indies.
54–55 As proper a man . . . : the proverbial phrase is actually 'as good a man as went on two legs'. **56 at':** at the.

Stephano This is some monster of the isle with four legs, who hath got, as I take it, an ague. Where the devil should he learn our
60   language? I will give him some relief, if it be but for that if I can recover him and keep him tame and get to Naples with him, he's a present for any emperor that ever trod on neat's leather.
Caliban: Do not torment me, prithee; I'll bring my wood home faster.
65   **Stephano** He's in his fit now and does not talk after the wisest. He shall taste of my bottle. If he have never drunk wine afore it will go near to remove his fit. If I can recover him and keep him tame, I will not take too much for him; he shall pay for him that hath him, and that soundly.
70   **Caliban** Thou dost me yet but little hurt; thou wilt anon, I know it by thy trembling. Now Prosper works upon thee.
Stephano Come on your ways, open your mouth; here is that which will give language to you, cat. Open your mouth; this will shake your shaking, I can tell you, and that soundly. You cannot tell who's
75   your friend. Open your chaps again.
Trinculo I should know that voice. It should be – but he is drowned and these are devils. O defend me!
Stephano Four legs and two voices; a most delicate monster! His forward voice now is to speak well of his friend, his backward voice
80   is to utter foul speeches and to detract. If all the wine in my bottle will recover him, I will help his ague. Come. Amen! I will pour some in thy other mouth.
Trinculo Stephano!
Stephano Doth thy other mouth call me? Mercy, mercy! This is a
85   devil, and no monster. I will leave him; I have no long spoon.
Trinculo Stephano! If thou beest Stephano, touch me and speak to me; for I am Trinculo – be not afeard – thy good friend Trinculo.
Stephano If thou beest Trinculo, come forth. I'll pull thee by the lesser legs. If any be Trinculo's legs, these are they. Thou art very
90   Trinculo indeed! How camest thou to be the siege of this moon-calf? Can he vent Trinculos?
Trinculo I took him to be killed with a thunder-stroke. But art thou not drowned, Stephano? I hope now thou art not drowned. Is the storm overblown? I hid me under the dead moon-calf's gaberdine
95   for fear of the storm. And art thou living, Stephano? O Stephano, two Neapolitans 'scaped!
Stephano Prithee, do not turn me about, my stomach is not constant.
Caliban [*Aside*] These be fine things, an if they be not sprites. That's a brave god and bears celestial liquor. I will kneel to him.
100   **Stephano** How didst thou 'scape? How camest thou hither? Swear

---

59 ague: a shaking fever.   **62 neat's-leather:** cowhide.   **67–68 I will not take.** . . : I will expect a high price for him.   **73 cat:** from the proverbial 'liquor to make a cat speak'.   **85 long spoon:** alluding to the proverb, 'he must have a long spoon who will eat with the devil'.   **90 siege:** excrement.   **moon-calf:** monster.

by this bottle how thou camest hither. I escaped upon a butt of sack
which the sailors heaved o'erboard, by this bottle, which I made of
the bark of a tree with mine own hands since I was cast ashore.

105   *Caliban* I'll swear upon that bottle to be thy true subject, for the
liquor is not earthly.

Stephano Here; swear then how thou escapedst.

Trinculo Swum ashore, man, like a duck. I can swim like a duck, I'll
be sworn.

Stephano Here, kiss the book. Though thou canst swim like a duck,
110   thou art made like a goose.

Trinculo O Stephano, hast any more of this?

Stephano The whole butt, man. My cellar is in a rock by the sea-
side where my wine is hid. How now, moon-calf! How does thine
ague?

115   *Caliban* Hast thou not dropped from heaven?

Stephano Out o' the moon, I do assure thee. I was the man i' the
moon when time was.

Caliban I have seen thee in her and I do adore thee. My mistress
showed me thee and thy dog and thy bush.

120   *Stephano* Come, swear to that; kiss the book. I will furnish it anon
with new contents. Swear.

Trinculo By this good light, this is a very shallow monster! I afeard
of him! A very weak monster! The man i' the moon! A most poor
credulous monster! Well drawn, monster, in good sooth!

125   *Caliban* I'll show thee every fertile inch o' th' island. And I will
kiss thy foot. I prithee, be my god.

Trinculo By this light, a most perfidious and drunken monster!
When's god's asleep, he'll rob his bottle.

Caliban I'll kiss thy foot; I'll swear myself thy subject.

130   *Stephano* Come on then; down, and swear.

Trinculo I shall laugh myself to death at this puppy-headed
monster. A most scurvy monster! I could find in my heart to beat
him –

Stephano Come, kiss.

135   *Trinculo* But that the poor monster's in drink; an abominable
monster!

Caliban I'll show thee the best springs; I'll pluck thee berries;
I'll fish for thee and get thee wood enough.
A plague upon the tyrant that I serve!

140   I'll bear him no more sticks, but follow thee,
Thou wondrous man.

Trinculo A most ridiculous monster, to make a wonder of a poor
drunkard!

Caliban I prithee, let me bring thee where crabs grow;

---

101 **butt of sack**: barrel holding over 500 litres of fortified wine.   122 **good light**: the sun.   144 **crabs**: either
crab apples or the crustaceans.

145 And I with my long nails will dig thee pignuts;
Show thee a jay's nest and instruct thee how
To snare the nimble marmoset; I'll bring thee
To clustering filberts and sometimes I'll get thee
Young scamels from the rock. Wilt thou go with me?

150 **Stephano** I prithee now, lead the way without any more talking.
Trinculo, the king and all our company else being drowned, we will
inherit here. Here; bear my bottle. Fellow Trinculo, we'll fill him by
and by again.

Caliban [*Sings drunkenly.*] Farewell master; farewell, farewell!

155 **Trinculo** A howling monster: a drunken monster!

Caliban   No more dams I'll make for fish
                          Nor fetch in firing
                          At requiring;
                          Nor scrape trencher, nor wash dish
160   'Ban, 'Ban, Cacaliban
                          Has a new master; get a new man.
Freedom, hey-day! Hey-day, freedom! Freedom, hey-day, freedom!

Stephano O brave monster! Lead the way.   [*Exit.*]

Act III, Scene i

[*Enter Ferdinand, bearing a log.*]

Ferdinand There be some sports are painful, and their labour
Delight in them sets off; some kinds of baseness
Are nobly undergone and most poor matters
Point to rich ends. This my mean task

5 Would be as heavy to me as odious, but
The mistress which I serve quickens what's dead
And makes my labours pleasures. O, she is
Ten times more gentle than her father's crabbed,
And he's composed of harshness. I must remove

10 Some thousands of these logs and pile them up,
Upon a sore injunction. My sweet mistress
Weeps when she sees me work, and says such baseness
Had never like executor. I forget.
But these sweet thoughts do even refresh my labours,

15 Most busy least when I do it.

[*Enter Miranda; and Prospero at a distance, unseen.*]

Miranda Alas, now pray you
Work not so hard. I would the lightning had
Burnt up those logs that you are enjoined to pile!
Pray, set it down and rest you; when this burns,

20 'Twill weep for having wearied you. My father
Is hard at study; pray now, rest yourself.

---

149 scamels: possibly a sea-bird.   **3.1,8 crabbed:** bitter.   **15 Most busy …:** I feel least busy when I am most busy.

He's safe for these three hours.
Ferdinand O most dear mistress,
The sun will set before I shall discharge
25   What I must strive to do.
Miranda If you'll sit down,
I'll bear your logs the while. Pray, give me that,
I'll carry it to the pile.
Ferdinand No, precious creature;
30   I had rather crack my sinews, break my back,
Than you should such dishonour undergo,
While I sit lazy by.
Miranda It would become me
As well as it does you; and I should do it
35   With much more ease, for my good will is to it,
And yours it is against.
Prospero Poor worm, thou art infected!
This visitation shows it.
Miranda You look wearily.
40   *Ferdinand* No, noble mistress, 'tis fresh morning with me
When you are by at night. I do beseech you –
Chiefly that I might set it in my prayers –
What is your name?
Miranda Miranda. O my father,
45   I have broke your hest to say so!
Ferdinand Admired Miranda!
Indeed the top of admiration, worth
What's dearest to the world! Full many a lady
I have eyed with best regard and many a time
50   The harmony of their tongues hath into bondage
Brought my too diligent ear. For several virtues
Have I liked several women; never any
With so full soul, but some defect in her
Did quarrel with the noblest grace she owed
55   And put it to the foil. But you, O you,
So perfect and so peerless, are created
Of every creature's best!
Miranda I do not know
One of my sex; no woman's face remember,
60   Save, from my glass, mine own; nor have I seen
More that I may call men than you, good friend,
And my dear father. How features are abroad,
I am skilless of; but, by my modesty,
The jewel in my dower, I would not wish
65   Any companion in the world but you,
Nor can imagination form a shape,

---

45 hest: command.   **51 diligent:** attentive.   **55 put it to foil:** countered it.

Besides yourself, to like of. But I prattle
Something too wildly and my father's precepts
I therein do forget.
70   *Ferdinand* I am in my condition
A prince, Miranda; I do think, a king –
I would, not so – and would no more endure
This wooden slavery than to suffer
The flesh-fly blow my mouth. I hear my soul speak,
75   The very instant that I saw you, did
My heart fly to your service; there resides
To make me slave to it; and for your sake
Am I this patient log-man.
    Miranda Do you love me?
80   *Ferdinand* O heaven, O earth, bear witness to this sound
And crown what I profess with kind event
If I speak true! If hollowly, invert
What best is boded me to mischief! I
Beyond all limit of what else i' the world
85   Do love, prize, honour you.
    Miranda I am a fool
To weep at what I am glad of.
    Prospero Fair encounter
Of two most rare affections! Heavens rain grace
90   On that which breeds between 'em!
    Ferdinand Wherefore weep you?
    Miranda At mine unworthiness that dare not offer
What I desire to give, and much less take
What I shall die to want. But this is trifling;
95   And all the more it seeks to hide itself,
The bigger bulk it shows. Hence, bashful cunning!
And prompt me, plain and holy innocence!
I am your wife, if you will marry me;
If not, I'll die your maid. To be your fellow
100   You may deny me, but I'll be your servant
Whether you will or no.
    Ferdinand My mistress, dearest;
And I thus humble ever.
    Miranda My husband, then?
105   *Ferdinand* Ay, with a heart as willing
As bondage e'er of freedom. Here's my hand.
    Miranda And mine, with my heart in't, and now farewell
Till half an hour hence.
    Ferdinand A thousand thousand! [*Exit Ferdinand and Miranda.*]
110   *Prospero* So glad of this as they I cannot be,

---

74 flesh-fly . . . : let flies lay eggs in my mouth.   **82–83 If hollowly** . . . : If I speak falsely, let any good fortune turn to ill.

Who are surprised withal; but my rejoicing
At nothing can be more. I'll to my book,
For yet ere supper-time must I perform
Much business appertaining. [*Exit.*]

Act III, Scene ii

[*Enter Caliban, Stephano, and Trinculo.*]

Stephano Tell not me; when the butt is out, we will drink water, not
a drop before. Therefore bear up, and board 'em. Servant-monster,
drink to me.

Trinculo Servant-monster! The folly of this island! They say there's
5   but five upon this isle, we are three of them; if th' other two be
brained like us, the state totters.

Stephano Drink, servant-monster, when I bid thee; thy eyes are
almost set in thy head.

Trinculo Where should they be set else? He were a brave monster
10   indeed, if they were set in his tail.

Stephano My man-monster hath drowned his tongue in sack. For
my part, the sea cannot drown me; I swam, ere I could recover the
shore, five and thirty leagues off and on. By this light, thou shalt be
my lieutenant, monster, or my standard.

15 *Trinculo* Your lieutenant, if you list; he's no standard.

Stephano We'll not run, Monsieur Monster.

Trinculo Nor go neither; but you'll lie like dogs and yet say nothing
neither.

Stephano Moon-calf, speak once in thy life, if thou beest a good
20   moon-calf.

Caliban How does thy honour? Let me lick thy shoe. I'll not serve
him, he's not valiant.

Trinculo Thou liest, most ignorant monster. I am in case to justle a
constable. Why, thou deboshed fish thou, was there ever man a
25   coward that hath drunk so much sack as I today? Wilt thou tell a
monstrous lie, being but half a fish and half a monster?

Caliban Lo, how he mocks me! wilt thou let him, my lord?

Trinculo 'Lord' quoth he! That a monster should be such a natural!

Caliban Lo, lo, again! Bite him to death, I prithee.

30 *Stephano* Trinculo, keep a good tongue in your head. If you prove a
mutineer – the next tree! The poor monster's my subject and he
shall not suffer indignity.

Caliban I thank my noble lord. Wilt thou be pleased to hearken
once again to the suit I made to thee?

35 *Stephano* Marry, will I. Kneel and repeat it; I will stand, and so shall
Trinculo.

3.2,3 **bear up . . . .**: naval terms, here meaning 'drink up'.   8 **set in thy head**: fixed drunkenly.   9 **brave**: marvellous.   13 **league**: a distance of about 5 kilometres.   14 **standard**: standard-bearer.   15 **no standard**: Caliban is too drunk to stand up properly.   23 **justle**: jostle.   24 **deboshed**: debauched.   28 **natural**: an idiot.

[*Enter Ariel, invisible.*]
Caliban As I told thee before, I am subject to a tyrant, a sorcerer,
that by his cunning hath cheated me of the island.
Ariel Thou liest.
40 **Caliban** Thou liest, thou jesting monkey, thou. I would my valiant
master would destroy thee! I do not lie.
Stephano Trinculo, if you trouble him any more in's tale, by this
hand, I will supplant some of your teeth.
Trinculo Why, I said nothing.
45 **Stephano** Mum, then, and no more. Proceed.
Caliban I say, by sorcery he got this isle;
From me he got it. If thy greatness will
Revenge it on him – for I know thou darest,
But this thing dare not –
50 **Stephano** That's most certain.
Caliban Thou shalt be lord of it and I'll serve thee.
Stephano How now shall this be compassed? Canst thou bring me
to the party?
Caliban Yea, yea, my lord. I'll yield him thee asleep, where thou
55 mayst knock a nail into his head.
Ariel Thou liest; thou canst not.
Caliban What a pied ninny's this! Thou scurvy patch!
I do beseech thy greatness, give him blows
And take his bottle from him when that's gone
60 He shall drink nought but brine; for I'll not show him
Where the quick freshes are.
Stephano Trinculo, run into no further danger; interrupt the monster one word further, and, by this hand, I'll turn my mercy out o'
doors and make a stock-fish of thee.
65 **Trinculo** Why, what did I? I did nothing. I'll go farther off.
Stephano Didst thou not say he lied?
Ariel Thou liest.
Stephano Do I so? Take thou that. [*Beats Trinculo.*] As you like this,
give me the lie another time.
70 **Trinculo** I did not give the lie. Out o' your wits and bearing too? A
pox o' your bottle! This can sack and drinking do. A murrain on your
monster, and the devil take your fingers!
Caliban Ha, ha, ha!
Stephano Now, forward with your tale. Prithee, stand farther off.
75 **Caliban** Beat him enough. After a little time, I'll beat him too.
Stephano Stand farther. Come, proceed.
Caliban Why, as I told thee, 'tis a custom with him,
I' th' afternoon to sleep. There thou mayst brain him,
Having first seized his books, or with a log

---

57 pied ninny: a fool dressed in motley, the traditional multi-coloured costume of a jester.   **patch**: jester.
64 stock-fish: pulverised dried cod.   **71 murrain**: plague.

80 Batter his skull, or paunch him with a stake,
Or cut his wezand with thy knife. Remember
First to possess his books; for without them
He's but a sot, as I am, nor hath not
One spirit to command. They all do hate him
85 As rootedly as I. Burn but his books.
He has brave utensils, for so he calls them,
Which when he has a house, he'll deck withal.
And that most deeply to consider is
The beauty of his daughter; he himself
90 Calls her a nonpareil. I never saw a woman,
But only Sycorax my dam and she;
But she as far surpasseth Sycorax
As great'st does least.
Stephano Is it so brave a lass?
95 **Caliban** Ay, lord; she will become thy bed, I warrant. And bring
thee forth brave brood.
Stephano Monster, I will kill this man. His daughter and I will be
king and queen – save our graces! And Trinculo and thyself shall be
viceroys. Dost thou like the plot, Trinculo?
100 **Trinculo** Excellent.
Stephano Give me thy hand. I am sorry I beat thee; but, while thou
livest, keep a good tongue in thy head.
Caliban Within this half hour will he be asleep. Wilt thou destroy
him then?
105 **Stephano** Ay, on mine honour.
Ariel This will I tell my master.
Caliban Thou makest me merry; I am full of pleasure;
Let us be jocund. Will you troll the catch
You taught me but while-ere?
110 **Stephano** At thy request, monster, I will do reason, any reason.
Come on, Trinculo, let us sing. [*Sings.*]
            Flout 'em and scout 'em
            And scout 'em and flout 'em
                Thought is free.
115 **Caliban** That's not the tune.
[*Ariel plays the tune on a tabor and pipe.*]
Stephano What is this same?
Trinculo This is the tune of our catch, played by the picture of
Nobody.
Stephano If thou beest a man, show thyself in thy likeness. If thou
120 beest a devil, take't as thou list.
Trinculo O, forgive me my sins!
Stephano He that dies pays all debts. I defy thee. Mercy upon us!
Caliban Art thou afeard?

---

81 **weazand**: wind-pipe.   86 **utensils**: furnishings.   90 **nonpareil**: without comparison.   115 **tabor**: a small drum.

Stephano No, monster, not I.

125 · *Caliban* Be not afeard; the isle is full of noises,
Sounds and sweet airs, that give delight and hurt not.
Sometimes a thousand twangling instruments
Will hum about mine ears, and sometime voices
That, if I then had waked after long sleep,

130 Will make me sleep again; and then, in dreaming,
The clouds methought would open and show riches
Ready to drop upon me that, when I waked,
I cried to dream again.

Stephano This will prove a brave kingdom to me, where I shall have

135 my music for nothing.

Caliban When Prospero is destroyed.

Stephano That shall be by and by. I remember the story.

Trinculo The sound is going away; let's follow it, and after do our
work.

140 *Stephano* Lead, monster, we'll follow. I would I could see this
taborer; he lays it on.

Trinculo Wilt come? I'll follow, Stephano. [*Exit.*]

Act III, Scene iii

[*Enter Alonso, Sebastian, Antonio, Gonzalo, Adrian, Francisco.*]

Gonzalo By'r lakin, I can go no further, sir;
My old bones ache. Here's a maze trod indeed
Through forth-rights and meanders! By your patience,
I needs must rest me.

5 *Alonso* Old lord, I cannot blame thee,
Who am myself attached with weariness,
To the dulling of my spirits. Sit down, and rest.
Even here I will put off my hope and keep it
No longer for my flatterer. He is drowned

10 Whom thus we stray to find, and the sea mocks
Our frustrate search on land. Well, let him go.

Antonio [*to Sebastian*] I am right glad that he's so out of hope.
Do not, for one repulse, forego the purpose
That you resolved to effect.

15 *Sebastian* The next advantage
Will we take throughly.

Antonio Let it be to-night;
For, now they are oppressed with travel, they
Will not, nor cannot, use such vigilance

20 As when they are fresh.

Sebastian I say to-night. No more.

[*Solemn and strange music.*]

3.3,1 By'r lakin: colloquial contraction of 'By our Lady'. **6 attached:** seized.

Alonso What harmony is this? My good friends, hark!
Gonzalo Marvellous sweet music!
[*Enter Prospero above, invisible. Enter several strange Shapes bringing in a banquet; they dance about it with gentle actions of salutation, and, inviting the King and the others to eat, they depart.*]
Alonso Give us kind keepers, heavens! What were these?
25 **Sebastian** A living drollery. Now I will believe
That there are unicorns, that in Arabia
There is one tree, the phoenix throne, one phoenix
At this hour reigning there.
Antonio I'll believe both;
30 And what does else want credit, come to me,
And I'll be sworn 'tis true. Travellers ne'er did lie,
Though fools at home condemn 'em.
Gonzalo If in Naples
I should report this now, would they believe me?
35 If I should say, I saw such islanders –
For, certes, these are people of the island –
Who, though they are of monstrous shape, yet, note,
Their manners are more gentle-kind than of
Our human generation you shall find
40 Many, nay, almost any.
Prospero [*Aside*] Honest lord,
Thou hast said well; for some of you there present
Are worse than devils.
Alonso I cannot too much muse
45 Such shapes, such gesture and such sound, expressing,
Although they want the use of tongue, a kind
Of excellent dumb discourse.
Prospero [*Aside*] Praise in departing.
Francisco They vanished strangely.
50 **Sebastian** No matter, since
They have left their viands behind; for we have stomachs.
Will't please you taste of what is here?
Alonso Not I.
Gonzalo Faith, sir, you need not fear. When we were boys,
55 Who would believe that there were mountaineers
Dew-lapped like bulls, whose throats had hanging at 'em
Wallets of flesh? Or that there were such men
Whose heads stood in their breasts? Which now we find
Each putter-out of five for one will bring us
60 Good warrant of.
Alonso I will stand to and feed,
Although my last. No matter, since I feel

---

25 drollery: comic entertainment, a puppet show. **30 want credit:** appears to be unbelievable. **48 Praise in departing:** Save your praise until the end. **59 Each putter out . . . . :** an early form of travel insurance. Brokers agreed to pay the traveller five times the amount he left with them, if he could prove he reached his destination.

The best is past. Brother, my lord the duke,
Stand to and do as we.
[*Thunder and lightning. Enter Ariel, like a harpy; claps his wings upon the table; and, with a quaint device, the banquet vanishes.*]

65 **Ariel** You are three men of sin, whom Destiny,
That hath to instrument this lower world
And what is in't, the never-surfeited sea
Hath caused to belch up you; and on this island
Where man doth not inhabit; you 'mongst men
70 Being most unfit to live. I have made you mad;
And even with such-like valour men hang and drown
Their proper selves. [*Alonso, Sebastian, etc. draw their swords.*]
You fools! I and my fellows
Are ministers of Fate. The elements,
75 Of whom your swords are tempered, may as well
Wound the loud winds, or with bemocked-at stabs
Kill the still-closing waters, as diminish
One dowl that's in my plume. My fellow-ministers
Are like invulnerable. If you could hurt,
80 Your swords are now too massy for your strengths
And will not be uplifted. But remember –
For that's my business to you – that you three
From Milan did supplant good Prospero;
Exposed unto the sea, which hath requit it,
85 Him and his innocent child. For which foul deed
The powers, delaying not forgetting, have
Incensed the seas and shores, yea all the creatures,
Against your peace. Thee of thy son, Alonso,
They have bereft, and do pronounce by me
90 Lingering perdition, worse than any death
Can be at once, shall step by step attend
You and your ways; whose wraths to guard you from,
Which here, in this most desolate isle, else falls
Upon your heads, is nothing but heart-sorrow
95 And a clear life ensuing.
[*He vanishes in thunder; then, to soft music enter the Shapes again, and dance, with mocks and mows, and carrying out the table.*]
Prospero Bravely the figure of this harpy hast thou
Performed, my Ariel; a grace it had, devouring.
Of my instruction hast thou nothing bated
In what thou hadst to say. So, with good life
100 And observation strange, my meaner ministers
Their several kinds have done. My high charms work
And these mine enemies are all knit up

---

64 **quaint device**: the banquet vanishes by an ingenious stage mechanism.   66 **to instrument**: uses as its instrument.   78 **dowl**: the smallest feather in a bird's plumage.   95 **mows**: mouthing mockery.   98 **bated**: omitted.

In their distractions; they now are in my power;
And in these fits I leave them, while I visit
105   Young Ferdinand, whom they suppose is drowned,
And his and mine loved darling. [*Exit.*]
Gonzalo I' the name of something holy, sir, why stand you
In this strange stare?
Alonso O, it is monstrous, monstrous.
110   Methought the billows spoke and told me of it;
The winds did sing it to me, and the thunder,
That deep and dreadful organ-pipe, pronounced
The name of Prosper. It did bass my trespass.
Therefore my son i' the ooze is bedded, and
115   I'll seek him deeper than e'er plummet sounded
And with him there lie mudded. [*Exit.*]
Sebastian But one fiend at a time,
I'll fight their legions o'er.
Antonio I'll be thy second. [*Exit Sebastian and Antonio.*]
120   **Gonzalo** All three of them are desperate. Their great guilt,
Like poison given to work a great time after,
Now 'gins to bite the spirits. I do beseech you
That are of suppler joints, follow them swiftly
And hinder them from what this ecstasy
125   May now provoke them to.
Adrian Follow, I pray you. [*Exit.*]

Act IV, Scene i

[*Enter Prospero, Ferdinand, and Miranda.*]
Prospero If I have too austerely punished you,
Your compensation makes amends, for I
Have given you here a third of mine own life,
Or that for which I live; who once again
5   I tender to thy hand. All thy vexations
Were but my trials of thy love and thou
Hast strangely stood the test. Here, afore Heaven,
I ratify this my rich gift. O Ferdinand,
Do not smile at me that I boast her off,
10   For thou shalt find she will outstrip all praise
And make it halt behind her.
Ferdinand I do believe it
Against an oracle.
Prospero Then, as my gift and thine own acquisition
15   Worthily purchased take my daughter. But
If thou dost break her virgin-knot before
All sanctimonious ceremonies may

---

113 **bass:** pronounce in a deep, serious manner.   115 **plummet sounded:** a measured weighted line used to determine the sea's depth.   **4.1,7 strangely:** wonderfully.

With full and holy rite be ministered,
No sweet aspersion shall the heavens let fall
20 To make this contract grow; but barren hate,
Sour-eyed disdain and discord shall bestrew
The union of your bed with weeds so loathly
That you shall hate it both. Therefore take heed,
As Hymen's lamps shall light you.
25 ***Ferdinand*** As I hope
For quiet days, fair issue and long life,
With such love as 'tis now, the murkiest den,
The most opportune place, the strong'st suggestion
Our worser genius can, shall never melt
30 Mine honour into lust, to take away
The edge of that day's celebration
When I shall think, or Phoebus' steeds are foundered,
Or Night kept chained below.
Prospero Fairly spoke.
35 Sit then and talk with her; she is thine own.
What, Ariel! my industrious servant, Ariel!
[*Enter Ariel.*]
Ariel What would my potent master? here I am.
Prospero Thou and thy meaner fellows your last service
Did worthily perform; and I must use you
40 In such another trick. Go bring the rabble,
O'er whom I give thee power, here to this place.
Incite them to quick motion, for I must
Bestow upon the eyes of this young couple
Some vanity of mine art. It is my promise,
45 And they expect it from me.
Ariel Presently?
Prospero Ay, with a twink.
Ariel Before you can say 'come' and 'go',
And breathe twice and cry 'so, so',
50 Each one, tripping on his toe,
Will be here with mop and mow.
Do you love me, master? No?
Prospero Dearly my delicate Ariel. Do not approach
Till thou dost hear me call.
55 ***Ariel*** Well, I conceive. [*Exit.*]
Prospero [*To Ferdinand*] Look thou be true, do not give dalliance
Too much the rein; the strongest oaths are straw
To the fire i' the blood. Be more abstemious,
Or else good night your vow!
60 ***Ferdinand*** I warrant you sir;

---

19 aspersion: sprinkling. **24 Hymen:** god of marriage. **32–33 or Phoebus' steeds . . . . :** here used to mean either that Ferdinand will think that the Sun god's horses have collapsed and cannot bring the day to an end, or that Night is being prevented from coming. **55 conceive:** understand.

The white cold virgin snow upon my heart
Abates the ardour of my liver.
Prospero Well.
Now come, my Ariel! bring a corollary,
65   Rather than want a spirit. Appear and pertly!
No tongue! All eyes! Be silent.
[*Soft music. Enter Iris.*]
Iris Ceres, most bounteous lady, thy rich leas
Of wheat, rye, barley, vetches, oats and pease;
Thy turfy mountains, where live nibbling sheep,
70   And flat meads thatched with stover them to keep;
Thy banks with pioned and twilled brims,
Which spongy April at thy hest betrims,
To make cold nymphs chaste crowns; and thy broom groves,
Whose shadow the dismissed bachelor loves,
75   Being lass-lorn. Thy pole-clipt vineyard;
And thy sea-marge, sterile and rocky-hard,
Where thou thyself dost air. The queen o' the sky,
Whose watery arch and messenger am I,
Bids thee leave these, and with her sovereign grace,
80   Here on this grass-plot, in this very place,
To come and sport. Her peacocks fly amain.
Approach, rich Ceres, her to entertain.
[*Enter Ceres.*]
Ceres Hail, many-coloured messenger, that ne'er
Dost disobey the wife of Jupiter;
85   Who with thy saffron wings upon my flowers
Diffusest honey-drops, refreshing showers,
And with each end of thy blue bow dost crown
My bosky acres and my unshrubbed down,
Rich scarf to my proud earth; why hath thy queen
90   Summoned me hither, to this short-grassed green?
Iris A contract of true love to celebrate;
And some donation freely to estate
On the blest lovers.
Ceres Tell me, heavenly bow,
95   If Venus or her son, as thou dost know,
Do now attend the queen? Since they did plot
The means that dusky Dis my daughter got,
Her and her blind boy's scandaled company
I have forsworn.
100   **Iris** Of her society
Be not afraid. I met her deity

---

64 **corollary**: an excess. 65 **pertly**: smartly. 67 **Iris**: goddess of the rainbow. **Ceres**: goddess of agriculture. **leas**: meadows. 68 **vetches**: fodder. **pease**: peas. 70 **stover**: winter food for cattle. 71 **pioned . . . :** well designed river banks. 73 **broom**: shrub considered to have amorous properties. 74 **dismissed bachelor**: rejected lover. 75 **lass-lorn**: without a girl. **pole-clipt**: pruned and well-prepared. 77 **queen o' th' sky**: the goddess Juno. 88 **bosky**: bush-covered. 92 **estate**: give. 97 **Dis**: god of the underworld. 98 **blind boy**: Cupid.

Cutting the clouds towards Paphos and her son
Dove-drawn with her. Here thought they to have done
Some wanton charm upon this man and maid,
105 Whose vows are, that no bed-right shall be paid
Till Hymen's torch be lighted. But in vain.
Mars's hot minion is returned again;
Her waspish-headed son has broke his arrows,
Swears he will shoot no more but play with sparrows
110 And be a boy right out.
     Ceres High'st queen of state,
Great Juno, comes; I know her by her gait.
[*Enter Juno.*]
Juno How does my bounteous sister? Go with me
To bless this twain, that they may prosperous be
115 And honoured in their issue.
[*They sing.*]
     Juno   Honour, riches, marriage-blessing,
             Long continuance, and increasing,
             Hourly joys be still upon you!
             Juno sings her blessings upon you.
120 **Ceres**   Earth's increase, foison plenty,
             Barns and garners never empty,
             Vines and clustering bunches growing,
             Plants with goodly burthen bowing;
             Spring come to you at the farthest
125   In the very end of harvest!
             Scarcity and want shall shun you;
             Ceres' blessing so is on you.
Ferdinand This is a most majestic vision, and
Harmonious charmingly. May I be bold
130 To think these spirits?
     Prospero Spirits, which by mine art
I have from their confines called to enact
My present fancies.
     Ferdinand Let me live here ever;
135 So rare a wondered father and a wife
Makes this place Paradise.
[*Juno and Ceres whisper, and send Iris on employment.*]
Prospero Sweet, now, silence!
Juno and Ceres whisper seriously;
There's something else to do. Hush, and be mute,
140 Or else our spell is marred.
     Iris You nymphs, call'd Naiads, of the windring brooks,
With your sedged crowns and ever-harmless looks,
Leave your crisp channels and on this green land

---

107 **Mars's hot minion**: Venus.   120 **foison**: abundance.   121 **garners**: granaries.   142 **sedged**: sedge, a river plant.

Answer your summons; Juno does command.
145 Come, temperate nymphs, and help to celebrate
A contract of true love; be not too late. [*Enter certain Nymphs.*]
You sunburnt sicklemen, of August weary,
Come hither from the furrow and be merry;
Make holiday, your rye-straw hats put on
150 And these fresh nymphs encounter every one
In country footing.
[*Enter certain Reapers, properly habited. They join with the Nymphs in a graceful dance; towards the end whereof Prospero starts suddenly, and speaks; after which, to a strange, hollow, and confused noise, they heavily vanish.*]
Prospero [*Aside*] I had forgot that foul conspiracy
Of the beast Caliban and his confederates
Against my life. The minute of their plot
155 Is almost come. [*To the Spirits*] Well done! Avoid! No more!
Ferdinand This is strange: your father's in some passion
That works him strongly.
Miranda Never till this day
Saw I him touched with anger so distempered.
160 **Prospero** You do look, my son, in a moved sort,
As if you were dismayed; be cheerful, sir.
Our revels now are ended. These our actors,
As I foretold you, were all spirits and
Are melted into air, into thin air;
165 And, like the baseless fabric of this vision,
The cloud-capped towers, the gorgeous palaces,
The solemn temples, the great globe itself,
Ye all which it inherit, shall dissolve
And, like this insubstantial pageant faded,
170 Leave not a rack behind. We are such stuff
As dreams are made on, and our little life
Is rounded with a sleep. Sir, I am vexed;
Bear with my weakness, my, brain is troubled.
Be not disturbed with my infirmity.
175 If you be pleased, retire into my cell
And there repose; a turn or two I'll walk,
To still my beating mind.
Ferdinand and **Miranda** We wish your peace. [*Exit.*]
Prospero Come with a thought – I thank thee – Ariel. Come.
[*Enter Ariel.*]
180 **Ariel** Thy thoughts I cleave to. What's thy pleasure?
Prospero Spirit,
We must prepare to meet with Caliban.
Ariel Ay, my commander! When I presented Ceres,

---

147 sicklemen: harvesters.   151 *heavily*: sorrowfully, reluctantly.

I thought to have told thee of it, but I feared
185   Lest I might anger thee.
    Prospero Say again, where didst thou leave these varlets?
    Ariel I told you, sir, they were red-hot with drinking;
  So fun of valour that they smote the air
  For breathing in their faces, beat the ground
190   For kissing of their feet, yet always bending
  Towards their project. Then I beat my tabour,
  At which, like unbacked colts, they pricked their ears,
  Advanced their eyelids, lifted up their noses
  As they smelt music. So I charmed their ears
195   That calf-like they my lowing followed through
  Toothed briers, sharp furzes, pricking goss and thorns,
  Which entered their frail shins. At last I left them
  I' the filthy-mantled pool beyond your cell,
  There dancing up to the chins, that the foul lake
200   O'erstunk their feet.
    Prospero This was well done, my bird.
  Thy shape invisible retain thou still.
  The trumpery in my house, go bring it hither,
  For stale to catch these thieves.
205   *Ariel* I go, I go. [*Exit.*]
    Prospero A devil, a born devil, on whose nature
  Nurture can never stick; on whom my pains,
  Humanely taken, all, all lost, quite lost;
  And as with age his body uglier grows,
210   So his mind cankers. I will plague them all,
  Even to roaring. [*Enter Ariel, loaden with glistering apparel, etc.*]
  Come, hang them on this line. [*Prospero and Ariel remain invisible.*
  Enter Caliban, Stephano, and Trinculo, all wet.]
    Caliban Pray you, tread softly, that the blind mole may not
  Hear a foot fall. We now are near his cell.
215   *Stephano* Monster, your fairy, which you say is a harmless fairy, has
  done little better than played the Jack with us.
    Trinculo Monster, I do smell all horse-piss, at which my nose is in
  great indignation.
    Stephano So is mine. Do you hear, monster? If I should take a
220   displeasure against you, look you –
    Trinculo Thou wert but a lost monster.
    Caliban Good my lord, give me thy favour still.
  Be patient, for the prize I'll bring thee to
  Shall hoodwink this mischance. Therefore speak softly.
225   All's hushed as midnight yet.
    Trinculo Ay, but to lose our bottles in the pool –
    Stephano There is not only disgrace and dishonour in that, monster,
  but an infinite loss.

---

192 **unbacked**: unridden.   196 **goss**: gorse.   204 **stale**: decoy.   216 **Jack**: knave.

Trinculo That's more to me than my wetting; yet this is your harm-
230 less fairy, monster.
Stephano I will fetch off my bottle, though I be o'er ears for my
labour.
Caliban Prithee, my king, be quiet. Seest thou here,
This is the mouth o' the cell; no noise, and enter.
235 Do that good mischief which may make this island
Thine own for ever, and I, thy Caliban,
For aye thy foot-licker.
Stephano Give me thy hand. I do begin to have bloody thoughts.
Trinculo O king Stephano! O peer! O worthy Stephano! Look what
240 a wardrobe here is for thee!
Caliban Let it alone, thou fool; it is but trash.
Trinculo O, ho, monster! We know what belongs to a frippery. O
king Stephano!
Stephano Put off that gown, Trinculo. By this hand, I'll have that
245 gown.
Trinculo Thy grace shall have it.
Caliban The dropsy drown this fool! What do you mean
To dote thus on such luggage? Let's alone
And do the murder first. If he awake,
250 From toe to crown he'll fill our skins with pinches,
Make us strange stuff.
Stephano Be you quiet, monster. Mistress line is not this my jerkin?
Now is the jerkin under the line. Now, jerkin, you are like to lose
your hair and prove a bald jerkin.
255 **Trinculo** Do, do. We steal by line and level, an't like your grace.
Stephano I thank thee for that jest; here's a garment for't. Wit shall
not go unrewarded while I am king of this country. 'Steal by line and
level' is an excellent pass of pate; there's another garment for't.
Trinculo Monster, come, put some lime upon your fingers, and away
260 with the rest.
Caliban I will have none on't. We shall lose our time,
And all be turned to barnacles, or to apes
With foreheads villanous low.
Stephano Monster, lay-to your fingers. Help to bear this away where
265 my hogshead of wine is, or I'll turn you out of my kingdom. Go to,
carry this.
Trinculo And this.
Stephano Ay, and this.
[*A noise of hunters heard. Enter divers Spirits, in shape of dogs and
hounds, and hunt them about, Prospero and Ariel setting them on.*]

---

242 **frippery:** second-hand clothes shop. Trinculo is saying this is not trash.   247 **dropsy:** a disease associated with
great thirst.   253 **line:** here meaning both a clothes line and the equator, where diseases which resulted in hair loss,
including sexually transmitted ones, were felt to be easily caught.   255 **line and level:** according to the
rule.   258 **pass of pate:** clever display of intelligence.   259 **lime:** sticky substance; thieves were associated with
sticky fingers.

  Prospero Hey, Mountain, hey!
270 *Ariel* Silver! There it goes, Silver!
  Prospero Fury, Fury! there, Tyrant, there! hark! hark!
  [*Caliban, Stephano, and Trinculo, are driven out.*]
  Go charge my goblins that they grind their joints
  With dry convulsions, shorten up their sinews
275 With aged cramps, and more pinch-spotted make them
  Than pard or cat o' mountain.
  Ariel Hark, they roar!
  Prospero Let them be hunted soundly. At this hour
  Lie at my mercy all mine enemies.
280 Shortly shall all my labours end, and thou
  Shalt have the air at freedom. For a little
  Follow, and do me service. [*Exit.*]

Act V, Scene i

  [*Enter Prospero in his magic robes, and Ariel.*]
  Prospero Now does my project gather to a head.
  My charms crack not, my spirits obey, and time
  Goes upright with his carriage. How's the day?
  Ariel On the sixth hour, at which time, my lord,
5 You said our work should cease.
  Prospero I did say so,
  When first I raised the tempest. Say, my spirit,
  How fares the king and's followers?
  Ariel Confined together
10 In the same fashion as you gave in charge,
  Just as you left them; all prisoners, sir,
  In the line-grove which weather-fends your cell;
  They cannot budge till your release. The king,
  His brother and yours, abide all three distracted
15 And the remainder mourning over them,
  Brimful of sorrow and dismay, but chiefly
  Him that you termed, sir, 'The good old lord Gonzalo',
  His tears run down his beard like winter's drops
  From eaves of reeds. Your charm so strongly works 'em
20 That if you now beheld them, your affections
  Would become tender.
  Prospero Dost thou think so, spirit?
  Ariel Mine would, sir, were I human.
  Prospero And mine shall.
25 Hast thou, which art but air, a touch, a feeling
  Of their afflictions, and shall not myself,

---

275 pinch-spotted: pinched black and blue. **276 pard or cat o' mountain:** the leopard or panther.
5.1,3 carriage: what Time carries, i.e. a light load at midday, so Time walks upright. **19 eaves of reeds:** thatched roofs, highly pitched so the water runs off quickly.

One of their kind, that relish all as sharply,
Passion as they, be kindlier moved than thou art?
Though with their high wrongs I am struck to the quick,
30   Yet with my nobler reason 'gainst my fury
Do I take part. The rarer action is
In virtue than in vengeance. They being penitent,
The sole drift of my purpose doth extend
Not a frown further. Go release them, Ariel.
35   My charms I'll break, their senses I'll restore,
And they shall be themselves.
Ariel I'll fetch them, sir. [*Exit.*]
Prospero Ye elves of hills, brooks, standing lakes and groves,
And ye that on the sands with printless foot
40   Do chase the ebbing Neptune and do fly him
When he comes back; you demi-puppets that
By moonshine do the green sour ringlets make,
Whereof the ewe not bites, and you whose pastime
Is to make midnight mushrooms, that rejoice
45   To hear the solemn curfew, by whose aid,
Weak masters though ye be, I have bedimmed
The noontide sun, called forth the mutinous winds,
And 'twixt the green sea and the azured vault
Set roaring war. To the dread rattling thunder
50   Have I given fire and rifted Jove's stout oak
With his own bolt; the strong-based promontory
Have I made shake and by the spurs plucked up
The pine and cedar. Graves at my command
Have waked their sleepers, oped, and let 'em forth
55   By my so potent art. But this rough magic
I here abjure, and, when I have required
Some heavenly music, which even now I do,
To work mine end upon their senses that
This airy charm is for, I'll break my staff,
60   Bury it certain fathoms in the earth,
And deeper than did ever plummet sound
I'll drown my book.
[*Solemn music. Enter Ariel before; then Alonso, with a frantic gesture,
attended by Gonzalo; Sebastian and Antonio in like manner, attended
by Adrian and Francisco. They all enter the circle which Prospero has
made, and there stand charmed; which Prospero observing, speaks.*]
A solemn air and the best comforter
To an unsettled fancy cure thy brains,
65   Now useless, boiled within thy skull! There stand,
For you are spell-stopped.

---

29 the quick: the tenderest or mortal part of a person. **42 green sour ringlets:** small circles of grass said to be formed by fairies dancing. **51 bolt:** lightning bolt.

Holy Gonzalo, honourable man,
Mine eyes, even sociable to the show of thine,
Fall fellowly drops. The charm dissolves apace,
70   And as the morning steals upon the night,
Melting the darkness, so their rising senses
Begin to chase the ignorant fumes that mantle
Their clearer reason. O good Gonzalo,
My true preserver, and a loyal sir
75   To him you follow'st! I will pay thy graces
Home both in word and deed. Most cruelly
Didst thou, Alonso, use me and my daughter.
Thy brother was a furtherer in the act.
Thou art pinched for't now, Sebastian. Flesh and blood,
80   You, brother mine, that entertained ambition,
Expelled remorse and nature; who, with Sebastian,
Whose inward pinches therefore are most strong,
Would here have killed your king; I do forgive thee,
Unnatural though thou art. Their understanding
85   Begins to swell, and the approaching tide
Will shortly fill the reasonable shore
That now lies foul and muddy. Not one of them
That yet looks on me, or would know me. Ariel,
Fetch me the hat and rapier in my cell.
90   I will discase me, and myself present
As I was sometime Milan. Quickly, spirit!
Thou shalt ere long be free.
[*Ariel sings and helps to attire him.*]
Ariel   Where the bee sucks there suck I.
In a cowslip's bell I lie;
95   There I couch when owls do cry.
On the bat's back I do fly
After summer merrily.
Merrily, merrily shall I live now
Under the blossom that hangs on the bough.
100 **Prospero** Why, that's my dainty Ariel! I shall miss thee.
But yet thou shalt have freedom. So, so, so.
To the king's ship, invisible as thou art.
There shalt thou find the mariners asleep
Under the hatches; the master and the boatswain
105 Being awake, enforce them to this place,
And presently, I prithee.
Ariel I drink the air before me, and return
Or ere your pulse twice beat. [*Exit.*]
Gonzalo All torment, trouble, wonder and amazement
110 Inhabits here. Some heavenly power guide us
Out of this fearful country!

---

90 **discase:** remove my robe.

Prospero Behold, sir king,
The wronged Duke of Milan, Prospero.
For more assurance that a living prince
115   Does now speak to thee, I embrace thy body;
And to thee and thy company I bid
A hearty welcome.
Alonso Whether thou be'st he or no,
Or some enchanted trifle to abuse me,
120   As late I have been, I not know. Thy pulse
Beats as of flesh and blood; and, since I saw thee,
The affliction of my mind amends, with which,
I fear, a madness held me. This must crave,
An if this be at all, a most strange story.
125   Thy dukedom I resign and do entreat
Thou pardon me my wrongs. But how should Prospero
Be living and be here?
Prospero First, noble friend,
Let me embrace thine age, whose honour cannot
130   Be measured or confined.
Gonzalo Whether this be
Or be not, I'll not swear.
Prospero You do yet taste
Some subtelties o' the isle, that will not let you
135   Believe things certain. Welcome, my friends all!
[*Aside to Sebastian and Antonio.*]
But you, my brace of lords, were I so minded,
I here could pluck his highness' frown upon you
And justify you traitors. At this time
I will tell no tales.
140   **Sebastian** [*Aside*] The devil speaks in him.
Prospero No.
For you, most wicked sir, whom to call brother
Would even infect my mouth, I do forgive
Thy rankest fault, all of them; and require
145   My dukedom of thee, which perforce, I know,
Thou must restore.
Alonso If thou be'st Prospero,
Give us particulars of thy preservation;
How thou hast met us here, who three hours since
150   Were wrecked upon this shore, where I have lost –
How sharp the point of this remembrance is –
My dear son Ferdinand.
Prospero I am woe for't, sir.
Alonso Irreparable is the loss, and patience
155   Says it is past her cure.

---

123 crave: call for.

Prospero I rather think
You have not sought her help, of whose soft grace
For the like loss I have her sovereign aid
And rest myself content.

160   **Alonso** You the like loss!

Prospero As great to me as late; and, supportable
To make the dear loss, have I means much weaker
Than you may call to comfort you, for I
Have lost my daughter.

165   **Alonso** A daughter?
O heavens, that they were living both in Naples,
The king and queen there! That they were, I wish
Myself were mudded in that oozy bed
Where my son lies. When did you lose your daughter?

170   **Prospero** In this last tempest. I perceive these lords
At this encounter do so much admire
That they devour their reason and scarce think
Their eyes do offices of truth, their words
Are natural breath. But, howsoe'er you have

175   Been justled from your senses, know for certain
That I am Prospero and that very duke
Which was thrust forth of Milan, who most strangely
Upon this shore, where you were wrecked, was landed,
To be the lord on't. No more yet of this;

180   For 'tis a chronicle of day by day,
Not a relation for a breakfast nor
Befitting this first meeting. Welcome, sir,
This cell's my court. Here have I few attendants
And subjects none abroad. Pray you, look in.

185   My dukedom since you have given me again,
I will requite you with as good a thing;
At least bring forth a wonder, to content ye
As much as me my dukedom.

[*Here Prospero discovers Ferdinand and Miranda playing at chess.*]

Miranda Sweet lord, you play me false.

190   **Ferdinand** No, my dear'st love,
I would not for the world.

Miranda Yes, for a score of kingdoms you should wrangle,
And I would call it fair play.

Alonso If this prove

195   A vision of the Island, one dear son
Shall I twice lose.

Sebastian A most high miracle!

Ferdinand Though the seas threaten, they are merciful;
I have cursed them without cause. [*Kneels.*]

---

175 **justled:** jostled.   192 **wrangle:** contend over.

200 **Alonso** Now all the blessings
Of a glad father compass thee about!
Arise, and say how thou camest here.
Miranda O, wonder!
How many goodly creatures are there here!
205 How beauteous mankind is! O brave new world,
That has such people in't!
Prospero 'Tis new to thee.
Alonso What is this maid with whom thou wast at play?
Your eld'st acquaintance cannot be three hours.
210 Is she the goddess that hath severed us,
And brought us thus together?
Ferdinand Sir, she is mortal;
But by immortal Providence she's mine.
I chose her when I could not ask my father
215 For his advice, nor thought I had one. She
Is daughter to this famous Duke of Milan,
Of whom so often I have heard renown,
But never saw before; of whom I have
Received a second life; and second father
220 This lady makes him to me.
Alonso I am hers.
But O, how oddly will it sound that I
Must ask my child forgiveness!
Prospero There, sir, stop.
225 Let us not burthen our remembrance with
A heaviness that's gone.
Gonzalo I have inly wept,
Or should have spoke ere this. Look down, you gods,
And on this couple drop a blessed crown!
230 For it is you that have chalked forth the way
Which brought us hither.
Alonso I say, Amen, Gonzalo!
Gonzalo Was Milan thrust from Milan, that his issue
Should become kings of Naples? O, rejoice
235 Beyond a common joy, and set it down
With gold on lasting pillars. In one voyage
Did Claribel her husband find at Tunis,
And Ferdinand, her brother, found a wife
Where he himself was lost, Prospero his dukedom
240 In a poor isle and all of us ourselves
When no man was his own.
Alonso [*To Ferdinand and Miranda*] Give me your hands.
Let grief and sorrow still embrace his heart
That doth not wish you joy!

---

230 **chalked forth:** marked the way with chalk.

245   **Gonzalo**   Be it so, Amen!
     [*Enter Ariel, with the Master and Boatswain amazedly following.*]
     O, look, sir, look, sir! Here is more of us.
     I prophesied if a gallows were on land
     This fellow could not drown. Now, blasphemy,
     That swear'st grace o'erboard, not an oath on shore?
250   Hast thou no mouth by land? What is the news?
     Boatswain   The best news is, that we have safely found
     Our king and company; the next, our ship,
     Which, but three glasses since, we gave out split,
     Is tight and yare and bravely rigged as when
255   We first put out to sea.
     Ariel   [*Aside to Prospero*]   Sir, all this service
     Have I done since I went.
     Prospero   [*Aside to Ariel*]   My tricksy spirit!
     Alonso   These are not natural events, they strengthen
260   From strange to stranger. Say, how came you hither?
     Boatswain   If I did think, sir, I were well awake,
     I'd strive to tell you. We were dead of sleep,
     And, how we know not, all clapped under hatches;
     Where but even now with strange and several noises
265   Of roaring, shrieking, howling, jingling chains,
     And more diversity of sounds all horrible,
     We were awaked; straightway at liberty,
     Where we, in all her trim, freshly beheld
     Our royal, good and gallant ship, our master
270   Capering to eye her. On a trice, so please you,
     Even in a dream, were we divided from them
     And were brought moping hither.
     Ariel   [*Aside to Prospero*]   Was't well done?
     Prospero   [*Aside to Ariel*]   Bravely, my diligence. Thou shalt be free.
275   **Alonso**   This is as strange a maze as e'er men trod,
     And there is in this business more than nature
     Was ever conduct of. Some oracle
     Must rectify our knowledge.
     Prospero   Sir, my liege,
280   Do not infest your mind with beating on
     The strangeness of this business; at picked leisure
     Which shall be shortly, single I'll resolve you,
     Which to you shall seem probable, of every
     These happened accidents; till when, be cheerful
285   And think of each thing well.
     [*Aside to Ariel*]   Come hither, spirit.
     Set Caliban and his companions free,

---

249 **swear'st grace o'erboard:** causes grace to leave the ship because of swearing.   253 **glasses:** hourglasses.   254 **yare:** seaworthy.   270 **Capering:** dancing with joy.   272 **moping:** in a bewildered state.   282 **single I'll resolve you:** I shall tell you the whole story.

Untie the spell. [*Exit Ariel.*]

How fares my gracious sir?

290   There are yet missing of your company

Some few odd lads that you remember not.

[*Enter Ariel, driving in Caliban, Stephano and Trinculo, in their stolen apparel.*]

Stephano Every man shift for all the rest, and let no man take care for himself, for all is but fortune. Coragio, bully-monster, coragio!

Trinculo If these be true spies which I wear in my head, here's a

295   goodly sight.

Caliban O Setebos, these be brave spirits indeed!

How fine my master is! I am afraid

He will chastise me.

Sebastian Ha, ha!

300   What things are these, my lord Antonio?

Will money buy 'em?

Antonio Very like; one of them

Is a plain fish and no doubt marketable.

Prospero Mark but the badges of these men, my lords,

305   Then say if they be true. This misshapen knave,

His mother was a witch, and one so strong

That could control the moon, make flows and ebbs,

And deal in her command without her power.

These three have robbed me, and this demi-devil,

310   For he's a bastard one, had plotted with them

To take my life. Two of these fellows you

Must know and own; this thing of darkness I

Acknowledge mine.

Caliban I shall be pinched to death.

315   **Alonso** Is not this Stephano, my drunken butler?

Sebastian He is drunk now. Where had he wine?

Alonso And Trinculo is reeling ripe. Where should they

Find this grand liquor that hath gilded 'em?

How camest thou in this pickle?

320   **Trinculo** I have been in such a pickle since I saw you last that, I fear me, will never out of my bones. I shall not fear fly-blowing.

Sebastian Why, how now, Stephano!

Stephano O, touch me not; I am not Stephano, but a cramp.

Prospero You'd be king o' the isle, sirrah?

325   **Stephano** I should have been a sore one then.

Alonso [*at Caliban*] This is a strange thing as e'er I looked on.

Prospero He is as disproportioned in his manners

As in his shape. Go, sirrah, to my cell,

---

293 **Coragio, bully-monster:** 'Courage, my friendly monster'. 304 **badges:** heraldic insignia. 305 **true:** honest. 308 **And deal in . . . . :** she could usurp the moon's authority without the moon being able to counter it. 321 **fear fly-blowing:** I am so pickled with drink, I will not fear maggots corrupting my body.

Take with you your companions; as you look
330 To have my pardon, trim it handsomely.
Caliban Ay, that I will; and I'll be wise hereafter
And seek for grace. What a thrice-double ass
Was I to take this drunkard for a god
And worship this dull fool!
335 *Prospero* Go to; away!
Alonso Hence, and bestow your luggage where you found it.
Sebastian Or stole it, rather. [*Exit Caliban, Stephano, and Trinculo.*]
Prospero Sir, I invite your highness and your train
To my poor cell, where you shall take your rest
340 For this one night; which, part of it, I'll waste
With such discourse as, I not doubt, shall make it
Go quick away; the story of my life
And the particular accidents gone by
Since I came to this isle; and in the morn
345 I'll bring you to your ship and so to Naples,
Where I have hope to see the nuptial
Of these our dear-beloved solemnized;
And thence retire me to my Milan, where
Every third thought shall be my grave.
350 *Alonso* I long
To hear the story of your life, which must
Take the ear strangely.
Prospero I'll deliver all;
And promise you calm seas, auspicious gales
355 And sail so expeditious that shall catch
Your royal fleet far off.
[*Aside to Ariel*] My Ariel, chick,
That is thy charge. Then to the elements
Be free, and fare thou well! Please you, draw near. [*Exit.*]

Epilogue

Prospero Now my charms are all o'erthrown,
And what strength I have's mine own,
Which is most faint. Now 'tis true
I must be here confined by you,
5 Or sent to Naples. Let me not,
Since I have my dukedom got
And pardoned the deceiver, dwell
In this bare island by your spell;
But release me from my bands
10 With the help of your good hands.
Gentle breath of yours my sails
Must fill, or else my project fails,

Which was to please. Now I want
Spirits to enforce, art to enchant,
15   And my ending is despair,
Unless I be relieved by prayer,
Which pierces so that it assaults
Mercy itself and frees all faults.
As you from crimes would pardoned be,
20   Let your indulgence set me free.

ÆMILIA LANYER (1569–1645)

Little is know about Æmilia Lanyer. Her father worked as a musician at the English court and was of Italian Jewish descent. Her one published work, a collection of poems, *Salve deus rex Judaeorum* (1611), reveals her as a devout Protestant, keen to demonstrate Christian virtue among women. *The Description of Cooke-ham*, one of the earliest country-house poems in English, celebrates Margaret, Countess of Clifford, and her daughter Anne, who became Countess of Dorset. The Cookham estate was on the river Thames in Berkshire, and Lanyer uses it as the site of an idealised world controlled by devout women.

From The Description of Cooke-ham

Farewell (sweet *Cooke-ham*) where I first obtained
Grace from that grace where perfect grace remained,
And where the muses gave their full consent,
I should have power the virtuous to content;
5   Where princely palace willed me to indite,
The sacred story of the soul's delight.
Farewell (sweet place) where virtue then did rest,
And all delights did harbour in her breast.
Never shall my sad eyes again behold
10   Those pleasures which my thoughts did then unfold.
Yet you (great Lady) mistress of that place,
From whose desires did spring this work of grace;
Vouchsafe to think upon those pleasures past,
As fleeting worldly joys that could not last;
15   Or as dim shadows of celestial pleasures,
Which are desired above all earthly treasures.
Oh how (me thought) against you thither came,
Each part did seem some new delight to frame!
The house received all ornaments to grace it,
20   And would endure no foulness to deface it.

---

5 **indite**: put into words.

The walks put on their summer liveries,
And all things else did hold like similes;
The trees with leaves, with fruits, with flowers clad,
Embraced each other, seeming to be glad,

25   Turning themselves to beauteous canopies,
To shade the bright sun from your brighter eyes;
The crystal streams with silver spangles graced,
While by the glorious sun they were embraced;
The little birds in chirping notes did sing,

30   To entertain both you and that sweet Spring.
And *Philomela* with her sundry lays,
Both you and that delightful place did praise.
Oh how me thought each plant, each flower, each tree
Set forth their beauties then to welcome thee!

35   The very hills right humbly did descend,
When you to tread upon them did intend.
And as you set your feet, they still did rise,
Glad that they could receive so rich a prize.
The gentle winds did take delight to be

40   Among those woods that were so graced by thee.
And in sad murmur uttered pleasing sound,
That pleasure in that place might more abound.
The swelling banks delivered all their pride,
When such a phœnix once they had espied.

45   Each arbor, bank, each seat, each stately tree,
Thought themselves honoured in supporting thee.
The pretty birds would oft come to attend thee,
Yet fly away for fear they should offend thee.
The little creatures in the borough by

50   Would come abroad to sport them in your eye;
Yet fearful of the bow in your fair hand,
Would run away when you did make a stand.
Now let me come unto that stately tree,
Wherein such goodly prospects you did see;

55   That oak that did in height his fellows pass,
As much as lofty trees low growing grass;
Much like a comely cedar straight and tall,
Whose beauteous stature far exceeded all;
How often did you visit this fair tree,

60   Which seeming joyful in receiving thee,
Would like a palm tree spread his arms abroad,
Desirous that you there should make abode;
Whose fair green leaves much like a comely veil,
Defended *Phebus* when he would assail;

---

21 liveries: clothes which identify the wearers as belonging to a particular household. **31 *Philomela***: the nightingale. **44 phœnix**: mythical long-living bird. At death it is consumed by fire, only to rise young again from the ashes. **64 *Phebus***: the sun god.

65 Whose pleasing boughs did yield a cool fresh air,
  Joying his happiness when you were there.
  Where being seated, you might plainly see,
  Hills, vales, and woods, as if on bended knee
  They had appeared, your honour to salute,
70 Or to prefer some strange unlooked for suit;
  All interlaced with brooks and crystal springs,
  A prospect fit to please the eyes of kings;
  And thirteen shires appeared all in your sight,
  Europe could not afford much more delight.
75 What was there then but gave you all content,
  While you the time in meditation spent,
  Of their Creator's power, which there you saw,
  In all his creatures held a perfect law;
  And in their beauties did you plain descry,
80 His beauty, wisdom, grace, love, majesty.
  In these sweet woods how often did you walk
  With Christ and his Apostles there to talk;
  Placing his holy Writ in some fair tree,
  To meditate what you therein did see;
85 With *Moses* you did mount his holy hill,
  To know his pleasure, and perform his will.
  With lovely *David* you did often sing,
  His holy hymns to Heaven's eternal King.
  And in sweet music did your soul delight,
90 To sound his praises morning, noon, and night.
  With blessed *Joseph* you did often feed
  Your pined brethren, when they stood in need.
      ll.1–92.

  And you sweet Cooke-ham, whom these Ladies leave,
  I now must tell the grief you did conceive
  At their departure; when they went away,
130 How everything retained a sad dismay;
  Nay long before, when once an inkling came,
  Me thought each thing did unto sorrow frame;
  The trees that were so glorious in our view,
  Forsook both flowers and fruit, when once they knew
135 Of your depart, their very leaves did wither,
  Changing their colours as they grew together.
  But when they saw this had no power to stay you,
  They often wept, though speechless, could not pray you;
  Letting their tears in your fair bosoms fall,
140 As if they said, Why will ye leave us all?
  This being vain, they cast their leaves away,

---

88 **hymns**: the Psalms. 91 *Joseph*: cf. Genesis 47:12.

Hoping that pity would have made you stay;
Their frozen tops, like age's hoary hairs,
Shows their disasters, languishing in fears;
145 A swarthy riveld ryne all over spread,
Their dying bodies half alive, half dead.
But your occasions called you so away,
That nothing there had power to make you stay;
Yet did I see a noble grateful mind,
150 Requiting each according to their kind;
Forgetting not to turn and take your leave
Of these sad creatures, powerless to receive
Your favour, when with grief you did depart,
Placing their former pleasures in your heart;
155 Giving great charge to noble memory,
There to preserve their love continually;
But specially the love of that fair tree,
That first and last you did vouchsafe to see:
In which it pleased you oft to take the air,
160 With noble *Dorset*, then a virgin fair;
Where many a learned book was read and scanned
To this fair tree, taking me by the hand,
You did repeat the pleasures which had past,
Seeming to grieve they could no longer last.
165 And with a chaste, yet loving kiss took leave,
Of which sweet kiss I did it soon bereave;
Scorning a senseless creature should possess
So rare a favour, so great happiness.
No other kiss it could receive from me,
170 For fear to give back what it took of thee:
So I ingrateful creature did deceive it,
Of that which you vouchsaft in love to leave it.
And though it oft had giv'n me much content,
Yet this great wrong I never could repent;
175 But of the happiest made it most forlorn,
To show that nothing's free from Fortune's scorn,
While all the rest with this most beauteous tree,
Made their sad consort sorrow's harmony.

---

145 riveld ryne: wrinkled bark due to frost.   **160 *Dorset*:** Anne Clifford married the Earl of Dorset.

SIR FRANCIS BACON (1561–1626)

Sir Francis Bacon, Baron Verulam and Viscount St Albans, was one of the foremost think-ers of the English Renaissance. He wrote a vast range of philosophical works and pursued an active public life, becoming Lord Chancellor in 1618. His *Essays,* first published in 1597 and revised and added to until the fifth edition of 1625, exemplify Bacon's moral and natural philosophical interests and his championing of the inductive method, arriv-ing at general conclusions after observation, experiment, and the accumulation and analysis of separate instances.

From The Essays

Of Death

Men fear death, as children fear to go in the dark; and, as that natural fear in children is increased with tales, so is the other. Certainly, the contemplation of death, as the wages of sin, and passage to another world, is holy and religious; but the fear of it, as a tribute due unto nature, is weak. Yet in religious medita-tions there is sometimes mixture of vanity and of superstition. You shall read in some of the friars' books of mortification that a man should think with himself what the pain is, if he have but his finger's end pressed or tortured, and thereby imagine what the pains of death are, when the whole body is corrupted and dissolved; when many times death passeth, with less pain than the torture of a limb; for the most vital parts are not the quickest of sense. And by him that spake only as a philosopher and natural man,[1] it was well said: *Pompa mortis magis terret, quam mors ipsa.*[2] Groans and convulsions, and a discoloured face, and friends weeping, and blacks[3] and obsequies, and the like, show death terrible. It is worthy the observing that there is no passion in the mind of man so weak but it mates, and masters, the fear of death; and therefore, death is no such terrible enemy, when a man hath so many attendants about him that can win the combat of him. Revenge triumphs over death; love slights it; honour aspireth to it; grief flieth to it; fear preoccupateth it; nay, we read, after Otho the emperor[4] had slain himself, pity (which is the tenderest of affections) provoked many to die out of mere compassion to their sovereign and as the truest sort of followers. Nay, Seneca adds niceness and satiety: *Cogita quamdiu eadem feceris; mori velle, non tantum fortis aut miser, sed etiam fastidiosus potest.*[5] A man would die, though he were neither valiant, nor miserable, only upon a weariness to do the same thing so oft, over and over. It is no less worthy to observe how little alteration in good spirits the approaches of death make; for they appear to be the same men till the last instant. Augustus Caesar died in a compliment: *Livia, conjugii nostri memor, vive et vale.*[6] Tiberius in dissimul-ation; as Tacitus saith of him: *Jam Tiberium vires et corpus, non dissimulatio, deserebant.*[7] Vespasian in a jest, sitting upon the stool: *Ut puto deus fio.*[8] Galba

---

1: Seneca, who wrote without benefit of divine revelation.   2: The things which belong with death are more frightening than death itself.   3: wearing mourning.   4: Roman emperor who committed suicide after losing a battle.   5: translated next sentence.   6: Farewell Livia, remember our married life as long as you live.   7: He was deserted by the strength of his body, but not his dissimulation.   8: I am cleansing myself and becoming a god.

with a sentence: *Feri, si ex re sit populi Romani,*[1] holding forth his neck. Septimius Severus in despatch: *Adeste si quid mihi restat agendum.*[2] And the like. Certainly the Stoics bestowed too much cost upon death, and by their great preparations made it appear more fearful. Better saith he: *qui finem vitae extremum inter munera ponat naturae.*[3] It is as natural to die as to be born; and to a little infant, perhaps, the one is as painful, as the other. He that dies in an earnest pursuit is like one that is wounded in hot blood, who, for the time, scarce feels the hurt; and therefore a mind fixed, and bent upon somewhat that is good, doth avert the dolors of death. But above all, believe it, the sweetest canticle is, *Nunc dimittis;*[4] when a man hath obtained worthy ends and expectations. Death hath this also; that it openeth the gate to good fame and extinguisheth envy. *Extinctus amabitur idem.*[5]

Of Plantations

Plantations[6] are amongst ancient, primitive, and heroical works. When the world was young it begat more children; but now it is old it begets fewer; for I may justly account new plantations to be the children of former kingdoms. I like a plantation in a pure soil; that is where people are not displanted, to the end to plant in others. For else it is rather an extirpation than a plantation. Planting of countries is like planting of woods; for you must make account to leese[7] almost twenty years' profit and expect your recompense in the end. For the principal thing that hath been the destruction of most plantations hath been the base and hasty drawing of profit in the first years. It is true, speedy profit is not to be neglected, as far as may stand with the good of the plant- ation, but no further. It is a shameful and unblessed thing to take the scum of people, and wicked condemned men, to be the people with whom you plant; and not only so, but it spoileth the plantation; for they will ever live like rogues and not fall to work, but be lazy and do mischief, and spend victuals, and be quickly weary, and then certify[8] over to their country to the discredit of the plantation. The people wherewith you plant ought to be gardeners, ploughmen, labourers, smiths, carpenters, joiners, fishermen, fowlers, with some few apothecaries, surgeons, cooks, and bakers. In a country of plantation, first look about what kind of victual the country yields of itself to hand: as chestnuts, walnuts, pineapples, olives, dates, plums, cherries, wild honey, and the like; and make use of them. Then consider what victual or esculent[9] things there are, which grow speedily, and within the year: as parsnips, carrots, turnips, onions, radish, artichokes of Hierusalem,[10] maize, and the like. For wheat, barley and oats, they ask too much labour; but with pease and beans you may begin, both because they ask less labour, and because they serve for meat as well as for bread. And of rice likewise cometh a great increase, and it is a kind of meat. Above all, there ought to be brought store of biscuit, oat-meal, flour, meal, and the like in the beginning, till bread may be had. For beasts or birds, take chiefly such as are

---

1: Strike, if it is needed for the good of the Roman people.   2: Come, if there is anything left for me to do.   3: Juvenal: 'who reckons the end of life one of nature's blessings.'   4: Luke 2:29: Now, let thy servant depart.   5: Horace: 'He will be loved when dead who was envied when alive.'   6: Colonies.   7: lose.   8: make claims.   9: edible.   10: Jerusalem artichokes, similar to a potato.

least subject to diseases and multiply fastest: as swine, goats, cocks, hens, turkeys, geese, house-doves, and the like. The victual in plantations ought to be expended almost as in a besieged town; that is with certain allowance. And let the main part of the ground employed to gardens or corn be to a common stock; and to be laid in, and stored up, and then delivered out in proportion; besides some spots of ground that any particular person will manure[1] for his own private. Consider likewise what commodities the soil where the plantation is doth naturally yield, that they may some way help to defray the charge of the plantation (so it be not, as was said, to the untimely prejudice of the main business, as it hath fared with tobacco in Virginia). Wood commonly aboundeth but too much; and therefore timber is fit to be one. If there be iron ore, and streams whereupon to set the mills, iron is a brave commodity where wood aboundeth. Making of bay-salt, if the climate be proper for it, would be put in experience.[2] Growing silk likewise, if any be, is a likely commodity. Pitch and tar where store of firs and pines are, will not fail. So drugs and sweet woods, where they are, cannot but yield great profit. Soap-ashes[3] likewise, and other things that may be thought of. But moil[4] not too much under ground; for the hope of mines is very uncertain, and useth to make the planters lazy in other things. For government, let it be in the hands of one assisted with some counsel; and let them have commission to exercise martial laws, with some limitation. And above all, let men make that profit of being in the wilderness, as they have God always and his service, before their eyes. Let not the government of the plantation depend upon too many counsellors and undertakers in the country that planteth, but upon a temperate number; and let those be rather noblemen and gentlemen, than merchants; for they look ever to the present gain. Let there be freedom from custom,[5] till the plantation be of strength; and not only freedom from custom, but freedom to carry their commodities where they may make their best of them, except there be some special cause of caution. Cram not in people by sending too fast company after company; but rather harken how they waste, and send supplies proportionably; but so, as the number may live well in the plantation, and not by surcharge be in penury. It hath been a great endangering to the health of some plantations that they have built along the sea and rivers, in marish[6] and unwholesome grounds. Therefore, though you begin there to avoid carriage and like discommodities, yet build still rather upwards from the streams than along. It concerneth likewise the health of the plantation that they have good store of salt with them, that they may use it in their victuals when it shall be necessary. If you plant where savages are, do not only entertain them with trifles and gingles,[7] but use them justly and graciously, with sufficient guard nevertheless; and do not win their favour, by helping them to invade their enemies, but for their defence it is not amiss; and send oft of them over to the country that plants, that they may see a better condition than their own and commend it when they return. When the plantation grows to strength, then it is time to plant with women as well as with men; that the plantation may spread into

---

1: cultivate. 2: using the heat of the sun to make salt. 3: ashes used as soap. 4: work. 5: taxes on imports and exports. 6: marshy. 7: rattles.

generations, and not be ever pieced from without. It is the sinfullest thing in the world to forsake or destitute a plantation once in forwardness; for besides the dishonour, it is the guiltiness of blood of many commiserable[1] persons.

Of Custom and Education

Men's thoughts are much according to their inclination; their discourse and speeches according to their learning and infused opinions;[2] but their deeds are after as they have been accustomed. And therefore, as Machiavel well noteth (though in an evil-favoured instance), there is no trusting to the force of nature, nor to the bravery of words, except it be corroborate by custom.[3] His instance is that for the achieving of a desperate conspiracy, a man should not rest upon the fierceness of any man's nature, or his resolute undertakings; but take such an one as hath had his hands formerly in blood. But Machiavel knew not of a Friar Clement, nor a Ravillac, nor a Jaureguy, nor a Baltazar Gerard;[4] yet his rule holdeth still: that nature, nor the engagement of words, are not so forcible as custom. Only superstition is now so well advanced that men of the first blood[5] are as firm as butchers by occupation; and votary resolution[6] is made equipollent[7] to custom even in matter of blood. In other things, the predominancy of custom is everywhere visible; insomuch as a man would wonder to hear men profess, protest, engage, give great words, and then do just as they have done before; as if they were dead images, and engines moved only by the wheels of custom. We see also the reign or tyranny of custom, what it is. The Indians (I mean the sect of their wise men) lay themselves quietly upon a stock of wood and so sacrifice themselves by fire. Nay, the wives strive to be burned with the corpses of their husbands. The lads of Sparta of ancient time were wont to be scourged upon the altar of Diana, without so much as queching.[8] I remember in the beginning of Queen Elizabeth's time of England, an Irish rebel condemned put up a petition to the deputy that he might be hanged in a withe,[9] and not in an halter, because it had been so used with former rebels. There be monks in Russia for penance that will sit a whole night in a vessel of water till they be engaged with hard ice. Many examples may be put of the force of custom, both upon mind and body. Therefore, since custom is the principal magistrate of man's life, let men by all means endeavour to obtain good customs. Certainly custom is most perfect when it beginneth in young years: this we call education, which is, in effect, but an early custom. So we see in languages, the tongue is more pliant to all expressions and sounds, the joints are more supple to all feats of activity and motions in youth than afterwards. For it is true, that late learners cannot so well take the ply; except it be in some minds that have not suffered themselves to fix, but have kept themselves open, and prepared to receive continual amendment, which is exceeding rare. But if the force of custom simple and separate, be great, the force of custom copulate

---

1: worthy of pity. 2: opinions gathered from external conditions as opposed to natural dispositions. 3: In *The Discourses*, considering the qualities of a good assassin, Machiavelli argues that experience is of the first importance. 4: Clement killed Henry III of France in 1589; Ravillac, Henry IV in 1610. Jaureguy tried to kill William the Silent, Prince of Orange in 1582; Gerard shot William in 1584. 5: killing for the first time. 6: resolution produced by a vow. 7: of equal importance. 8: twisting. 9: shackle made of twisted branches.

and conjoined and collegiate is far greater. For there example teacheth, company comforteth, emulation quickeneth, glory raiseth: so as in such places the force of custom is in his exaltation. Certainly the great multiplication of virtues upon human nature resteth upon societies well ordained and disciplined. For commonwealths and good governments do nourish virtue grown, but do not much mend the deeds. But the misery is that the most effectual means are now applied to the ends least to be desired.

JOHN DONNE (1572–1631)

Born, living, and dying in London, Donne is the most urbane of English Renaissance writers. He came from a family which had remained Roman Catholic after the Reformation, and though he ultimately found religious conviction and position within the Church of England, his writing demonstrates a preoccupation with the search for truth and anxieties about doubt. It also reveals an enormous interest in the human comedy, particularly over sexuality. Both sacred and secular writing show Donne's mastery of analogy in pursuing argument in his writing. He possesses a wide-ranging intellectual curiosity and capacity for observation. He published little of his poetry during his life and it is extremely difficult to date a great deal of his work with accuracy.

The Bait

Come live with me, and be my love,
And we will some new pleasures prove
Of golden sands, and crystal brooks,
With silken lines, and silver hooks.

5   There will the river whispering run
Warmed by thy eyes more than the sun.
And there th' inamoured fish will stay,
Begging themselves they may betray.

When thou wilt swim in that live bath,
10   Each fish, which every channel hath,
Will amorously to thee swim,
Gladder to catch thee, than thou him.

If thou, to be so seen, beest loth,
By sun or moon, thou darknest both,
15   And if myself have leave to see,
I need not their light having thee.

Let others freeze with angling reeds,
And cut their legs with shells and weeds,
Or treacherously poor fish beset,
20   With strangling snare, or windowy net.

Let coarse bold hands from slimy nest
The bedded fish in banks out-wrest,
Or curious traitors, sleavesilk flies,
Bewitch poor fishes' wand'ring eyes.

25   For thee, thou need'st no such deceit,
For thou thyself art thine own bait;
That fish, that is not catched thereby,
Alas, is wiser far than I.

The Flea

Mark but this flea, and mark in this,
How little that which thou deny'st me is;
It sucked me first, and now sucks thee,
And in this flea, our two bloods mingled be.
5   Thou know'st that this cannot be said
A sin, or shame, or loss of maidenhead,
   Yet this enjoys before it woo,
   And pampered swells with one blood made of two,
   And this, alas, is more than we would do.

10   Oh stay, three lives in one flea spare,
Where we almost, yea more than married are.
This flea is you and I, and this
Our marriage bed, and marriage temple is.
Though parents grudge, and you, w'are met,
15   And cloistered in these living walls of jet.
   Though use make you apt to kill me,
   Let not to that, self murder added be,
   And sacrilege, three sins in killing three.

Cruel and sudden, hast thou since
20   Purpled thy nail, in blood of innocence?
Wherein could this flea guilty be,
Except in that drop which it sucked from thee?
Yet thou triumph'st, and say'st that thou
Find'st not thyself, nor me the weaker now;
25   'Tis true, then learn how false, fears be.
   Just so much honour, when thou yield'st to me,
   Will waste, as this flea's death took life from thee.

The Bait, 24 sleavesilk flies: lures made from silk.

The Good-morrow

I wonder by my troth, what thou and I
Did, till we loved? Were we not weaned till then,
But sucked on country pleasures, childishly?
Or snorted we in the seven sleepers' den?
5 'Twas so; but this, all pleasures fancies be.
If ever any beauty I did see,
Which I desired, and got, 'twas but a dream of thee.

And now good morrow to our waking souls,
Which watch not one another out of fear;
10 For love, all love of other sights controls,
And makes one little room, an everywhere.
Let sea-discoverers to new worlds have gone,
Let maps to other, worlds on worlds have shown,
Let us possess one world, each hath one, and is one.

15 My face in thine eye, thine in mine appears,
And true plain hearts do in the faces rest;
Where can we find two better hemispheres,
Without sharp north, without declining west?
Whatever dies, was not mixed equally;
20 If our two loves be one, or, thou and I
Love so alike, that none do slacken, none can die.

A Nocturnal Upon St. Lucy's Day

'Tis the year's midnight, and it is the day's,
Lucy's, who scarce seven hours herself unmasks,
    The sun is spent, and now his flasks
    Send forth light squibs, no constant rays;
5   The world's whole sap is sunk;
The general balm th' hydroptic earth hath drunk,
Whither, as to the bed's feet, life is shrunk,
Dead and interred; yet all these seem to laugh,
Compared with me, who am their epitaph.

10 Study me then, you who shall lovers be
At the next world, that is, at the next spring;
    For I am every dead thing,
    In whom love wrought new alchemy.

Good-morrow, 4 den: cave where seven Christian
youths slept for two centuries to escape Roman
persecution. Nocturnal,1 year's midnight: December
12th, both the winter's solstice in the old style
calendar and the start of St. Lucy's day, a saint
associated with light.

4 squibs: firecrackers. 6 hydroptic: enormously
thirsty. 7 bed's feet: the belief that the soul retired
to the feet before death.

For his art did express
15 A quintessence even from nothingness,
From dull privations, and lean emptiness;
He ruined me, and I am re-begot
Of absence, darkness, death; things which are not.

All others, from all things, draw all that's good,
20 Life, soul, form, spirit, whence they being have;
 I, by Love's limbeck, am the grave
 Of all that's nothing. Oft a flood
 Have we two wept, and so
Drowned the whole world, us two; oft did we grow
25 To be two chaoses, when we did show
Care to aught else; and often absences
Withdrew our souls, and made us carcasses.

But I am by her death (which word wrongs her)
Of the first nothing the elixir grown;
30 Were I a man, that I were one,
 I needs must know; I should prefer,
 If I were any beast,
Some ends, some means; yea plants, yea stones detest,
And love; all, all some properties invest;
35 If I an ordinary nothing were,
As shadow, a light and body must be here.

But I am none; nor will my sun renew.
You lovers, for whose sake the lesser sun
 At this time to the Goat is run
40 To fetch new lust, and give it you,
 Enjoy your summer all;
Since she enjoys her long night's festival,
Let me prepare towards her, and let me call
This hour her vigil, and her eve, since this
45 Both the year's, and the day's deep midnight is.

A Valediction: Forbidding Mourning

As virtuous men pass mildly away,
 And whisper to their souls, to go,
Whilst some of their sad friends do say,
 'The breath goes now' and some say, 'No'.

5 So let us melt, and make no noise,
 No tear-floods, nor sigh-tempests move;

---

14 express: extract. **15 quintessence:** pure fifth element beyond earth, air, fire, water. **21 limbeck:** alembic, used in alchemy for distilling. **29 elixir:** the pure spirit. **34 properties invest:** all things have some qualities. **39 Goat:** Capricorn.

'Twere profanation of our joys
 To tell the laity our love.

Moving of th' earth brings harms and fears,
10 Men reckon what it did, and meant;
But trepidation of the spheres,
 Though greater far, is innocent.

Dull sublunary lovers' love
 (Whose soul is sense) cannot admit
15 Absence, because it doth remove
 Those things which elemented it.

But we by a love so much refined,
 That ourselves know not what it is,
Inter-assured of the mind,
20 Care less, eyes, lips, and hands to miss.

Our two souls, therefore, which are one,
 Though I must go, endure not yet
A breach, but an expansion,
 Like gold to airy thinness beat.

25 If they be two, they are two so
 As stiff twin compasses are two;
Thy soul, the fixed foot, makes no show
 To move, but doth, if th' other do.

And though it in the centre sit,
30 Yet when the other far doth roam,
It leans, and hearkens after it,
 And grows erect, as that comes home.

Such wilt thou be to me, who must
 Like th' other foot, obliquely run;
35 Thy firmness makes my circle just,
 And makes me end, where I begun.

Elegy 19: To His Mistress Going to Bed

Come, Madam, come, all rest my powers defy,
Until I labour, I in labour lie.
The foe oft-times having the foe in sight,
Is tired with standing though they never fight.
5 Off with that girdle, like heaven's zone glittering,
But a far fairer world incompassing.
Unpin that spangled breastplate which you wear,
That th' eyes of busy fools may be stopped there.

---

11 **trepidation:** trembling. 16 **elemented:** composed. 34 **obliquely:** diverging from a straight line.

Unlace yourself, for that harmonious chime
10   Tells me from you, that now 'tis your bed time.
Off with that happy busk, which I envy,
That still can be, and still can stand so nigh.
Your gown going off, such beauteous state reveals,
As when from flowery meads the hill's shadow steals.
15   Off with that wiry coronet and show
The hairy diadem which on you doth grow;
Now off with those shoes, and then safely tread
In this love's hallowed temple, this soft bed.
In such white robes heaven's angels used to be
20   Received by men; thou angel bring'st with thee
A heaven like Mahomet's paradise; and though
Ill spirits walk in white, we easily know
By this these angels from an evil sprite,
Those set our hairs, but these our flesh upright.
25   Licence my roving hands, and let them go
Before, behind, between, above, below.
O my America, my new-found-land,
My kingdom, safeliest when with one man manned,
My mine of precious stones, my empery,
30   How blessed am I in this discovering thee!
To enter in these bonds, is to be free;
Then where my hand is set, my seal shall be.
       Full nakedness! All joys are due to thee.
As souls unbodied, bodies unclothed must be,
35   To taste whole joys. Gems which you women use
Are like Atlanta's balls, cast in men's views,
That when a fool's eye lighteth on a gem,
His earthly soul may covet theirs, not them.
Like pictures, or like books' gay coverings made
40   For laymen, are all women thus arrayed;
Themselves are mystic books, which only we
Whom their imputed grace will dignify
Must see revealed. Then since I may know,
As liberally, as to a midwife, show
45   Thyself; cast all, yea, this white linen hence,
Here is no penance, much less innocence.
       To teach thee, I am naked first; why then
What needst thou have more covering than a man.

---

11 **busk**: corset. 15 **coronet**: a band for the hair. 36 **Atlanta's balls**: golden balls were thrown in front of
21 **Mahomet's paradise**: a place of sensual delights. Atlanta to delay her in a race.

From Holy Sonnets

Sonnet 5

I am a little world made cunningly
Of elements and an angelic sprite,
But black sin hath betrayed to endless night
My world's both parts, and oh both parts must die.
5   You which beyond that heaven which was most high
Have found new spheres, and of new lands can write,
Pour new seas in mine eyes, that so I might
Drown my world with my weeping earnestly,
Or wash it, if it must be drowned no more.
10   But oh it must be burnt; alas the fire
Of lust and envy have burnt it heretofore,
And made it fouler; let their flames retire,
And burn me O Lord, with a fiery zeal
Of thee and thy house, which doth in eating heal.

Sonnet 10

Death, be not proud, though some have called thee
Mighty and dreadful, for thou art not so;
For those whom thou think'st thou dost overthrow,
Die not, poor death, nor yet canst thou kill me.
5   From rest and sleep, which but thy pictures be,
Much pleasure; then from thee much more must flow,
And soonest our best men with thee do go,
Rest of their bones, and soul's delivery.
Thou art slave to fate, chance, kings, and desperate men,
10   And dost with poison, war, and sickness dwell;
And poppy or charms can make us sleep as well,
And better than thy stroke; why swell'st thou then?
One short sleep past, we wake eternally,
And death shall be no more; death, thou shalt die.

Sonnet 13

What if this present were the world's last night?
Mark in my heart, O Soul, where thou dost dwell,
The picture of Christ crucified, and tell
Whether that countenance can thee affright,
5   Tears in his eyes quench the amazing light,
Blood fills his frowns, which from his pierced head fell,
And can that tongue adjudge thee unto hell,
Which prayed forgiveness for his foes' fierce spite?

5,2 elements: earth, air, water, fire.   **sprite:** spirit.   **9 no more:** as God promised Noah.   **14:** see Psalm 69:9.

No, no; but as in my idolatry
10 I said to all my profane mistresses,
Beauty, of pity, foulness only is
A sign of rigour; so I say to thee,
To wicked spirits are horrid shapes assigned,
This beauteous form assures a piteous mind.

Sonnet 14

Batter my heart, three-personed God; for you
As yet but knock, breathe, shine, and seek to mend;
That I may rise and stand, o'erthrow me, and bend
Your force to break, blow, burn, and make me new.
5 I, like an usurped town t'another due,
Labour t'admit you, but oh, to no end,
Reason, your viceroy in me, me should defend,
But is captived, and proves weak or untrue.
Yet dearly I love you, and would be loved fain,
10 But am betrothed unto your enemy;
Divorce me, untie or break that knot again,
Take me to you, imprison me, for I,
Except you enthrall me, never shall be free,
Nor ever chaste, except you ravish me.

Sonnet 19

Oh, to vex me, contraries meet in one;
Inconstancy unnaturally hath begot
A constant habit; that when I would not
I change in vows, and in devotion.
5 As humorous is my contrition
As my profane love, and as soon forgot;
As riddlingly distempered, cold and hot,
As praying, as mute; as infinite, as none.
I durst not view heaven yesterday, and today
10 In prayers, and flattering speeches I court God;
Tomorrow I quake with true fear of his rod.
So my devout fits come and go away
Like a fantastic ague; save that here
Those are my best days, when I shake with fear.

13,11: beauty is a consequence of compassion.
14,1 **three-personed**: The Trinity.   9 **fain**: gladly.

19,5 **humorous**: a person's health was believed controlled by the humours: blood, phlegm, black bile, yellow bile.   13 **ague**: fever.

A Hymn to Christ, at the Author's last going into Germany

In what torn ship soever I embark,
That ship shall be my emblem of thy ark;
What sea soever swallow me, that flood
Shall be to me an emblem of thy blood;
5   Though thou with clouds of anger do disguise
Thy face; yet through that mask I know those eyes,
    Which, though they turn away sometimes,
      They never will despise.

I sacrifice this island unto thee,
10   And all whom I loved there, and who loved me;
When I have put our seas 'twixt them and me,
Put thou thy sea betwixt my sins and thee.
As the tree's sap doth seek the root below
In winter, in my winter now I go,
15   Where none but thee, th'eternal root
      Of true love I may know.

Nor thou nor thy religion dost control,
The amorousness of an harmonious soul,
But thou wouldst have that love thyself; as thou
20   Art jealous, Lord, so I am jealous now,
Thou lov'st not, till from loving more, thou free
My soul. Who ever gives, takes liberty;
    O, if thou car'st not whom I love
      Alas, thou lov'st not me.

25   Seal then this bill of my divorce to all,
On whom those fainter beams of love did fall;
Marry those loves, which in youth scattered be
On fame, wit, hopes (false mistresses) to thee.
Churches are best for prayer that have least light;
30   To see God only I go out of sight;
    And to 'scape stormy days, I choose
      An everlasting night.

A Hymn to God the Father

Wilt thou forgive that sin where I begun,
    Which was my sin, though it were done before?
Wilt thou forgive that sin, through which I run,
    And do run still; though still I do deplore?

Hymn to Christ, 2 ark: which saved Noah from the flood, a traditional symbol of Providence.   9 island: Britain.

5   When thou hast done, thou hast not done,
    For I have more.

   Wilt thou forgive that sin which I have won
    Others to sin? And made my sin their door?
   Wilt thou forgive that sin which I did shun
10   A year or two; but wallowed in a score?
    When thou hast done, thou hast not done,
    For I have more.

   I have a sin of fear, that when I have spun
    My last thread, I shall perish on the shore;
15   But swear by thy self, that at my death thy son
    Shall shine as he shines now, and heretofore;
    And, having done that, thou hast done,
     I fear no more.

From Devotions Upon Emergent Occasions

In 1623 Donne was seriously ill with fever. The following year his *Devotions* were published, consisting of 23 meditations on the stages of his illness which are examined as an allegory of the human passage through life into death. The following is number 19.

Oceano tandem emenso, aspicienda resurgit terra; vident, justis, medici, jam cocta mederi se posse, indiciis.
At last the physicians, after a long and stormy voyage, see land; they have so good signs of the concoction of the disease, as that they may safely proceed to purge.

Meditation

All this while the physicians themselves have been patients, patiently attending when they should see any land in this sea, any earth, any cloud, any indication of concoction in these waters. Any disorder of mine, any pretermission[1] of theirs, exalts the disease, accelerates the rages of it; no diligence accelerates the concoction, the maturity of the disease; they must stay till the season of the sickness come; and till it be ripened of itself, and then they may put to their hand to gather it before it fall off, but they cannot hasten the ripening.

 Why should we look for it in a disease, which is the disorder, the discord, the irregularity, the commotion and rebellion of the body? It were scarce a disease if it could be ordered and made obedient to our times. Why should we look for that in disorder, in a disease, when we cannot have it in nature, who is so regular and so pregnant, so forward to bring her work to perfection and to light? Yet we cannot awake the July flowers in January, nor retard the flowers of the Spring to Autumn. We cannot bid the fruits come in May, nor

---

1: omission.

the leaves to stick on in December. A woman that is weak cannot put off her ninth month to a tenth for her delivery, and say she will stay till she be stronger; nor a queen cannot hasten it to a seventh, that she may be ready for some other pleasure. Nature (if we look for durable and vigorous effects) will not admit preventions, nor anticipations, nor obligations upon her, for they are precontracts, and she will be left to her liberty.

Nature would not be spurred, nor forced to mend her pace; nor power, the power of man, greatness, loves not that kind of violence neither. There are of them that will give, that will do justice, that will pardon, but they have their own seasons for all these, and he that knows not them shall starve before that gift come, and ruin before the justice, and die before the pardon save him. Some tree bears no fruit except much dung be laid about it; and justice comes not from some till they be richly manured. Some trees require much visiting, much watering, much labour; and some men give not their fruits but upon importunity. Some trees require incision, and pruning, and lopping; some men must be intimidated and syndicated with commissions before they will deliver the fruits of justice. Some trees require the early and the often access of the sun; some men open not but upon the favours and letters of court mediation. Some trees must be housed and kept within doors; some men lock up, not only their liberality, but their justice and their compassion till the solicitation of a wife, or a son, or a friend, or a servant, turn the key. Reward is the season of one man and importunity of another; fear the season of one man and favour of another; friendship the season of one man and natural affection of another. And he that knows not their seasons, nor cannot stay them, must lose the fruits. As nature will not, so power and greatness will not be put to change their seasons. And shall we look for this indulgence in a disease, or think to shake it off before it be ripe?

All this while, therefore, we are but upon a defensive war; and that is but a doubtful state, especially where they who are besieged do know the best of their defences and do not know the worst of their enemy's power; when they cannot mend their works within and the enemy can increase his numbers without. O how many far more miserable, and far more worthy to be less miserable than I, are besieged with this sickness and lack their sentinels, their physicians, to watch; and lack their munition, their cordials, to defend; and perish before the enemy's weakness might invite them to sally, before the disease show any declination or admit any way of working upon itself? In me the siege is so far slackened as that we may come to fight and so die in the field, if I die, and not in a prison.

Expostulation

My God, my God, thou art a direct God, may I not say a literal God, a God that wouldst be understood literally and according to the plain sense of all that thou sayest. But thou art also (Lord, I intend it to thy glory, and let no profane misinterpreter abuse it to thy diminution), thou art a figurative, a

---

1: lengthy travels.

metaphorical God too; a God in whose words there is such a height of figures, such voyages, such peregrinations[1] to fetch remote and precious metaphors, such extensions, such spreadings, such curtains of allegories, such third heavens[1] of hyperboles, so harmonious elocutions, so retired and so reserved expressions, so commanding persuasions, so persuading commandments, such sinews[2] even in thy milk, and such things in thy words, as all profane authors seem of the seed of the serpent that creeps, thou art the Dove that flies. O, what words but thine can express the inexpressible texture and composition of thy word; in which, to one man, that argument that binds his faith to believe that to be the word of God is the reverent simplicity of the word, and, to another, the majesty of the word. And in which two men, equally pious, may meet, and one wonder that all should not understand it, and the other as much that any man should.

So, Lord, thou givest us the same earth to labour on and to lie in, a house and a grave of the same earth. So, Lord, thou givest us the same word for our satisfaction and for our inquisition, for our instruction and for our admiration, too. For there are places that thy servants Jerome and Augustine[3] would scarce believe (when they grew warm by mutual letters) of one another that they understood them; and yet both Jerome and Augustine call upon persons whom they knew to be far weaker than they thought one another (old women and young maids) to read the Scriptures, without confining them to these or those places.

Neither art thou thus a figurative, a metaphorical, God in thy word only, but in thy works too. The style of thy works, the phrase of thine actions, is metaphorical. The institution of thy whole worship in the Old Law[4] was a continual allegory; types and figures overspread all, and figures flowed into figures and poured themselves out into farther figures; circumcision carried a figure of baptism, and baptism carries a figure of that purity which we shall have in perfection in the New Jerusalem.[5]

Neither didst thou speak and work in this language only in the time of thy prophets; but, since thou spokest in thy Son, it is so too. How often, how much more often, doth thy Son call himself a way, and a light, and a gate, and a vine, and bread, than the Son of God or of man? How much oftener doth he exhibit a metaphorical Christ, than a real, a literal? This hath occasioned thine ancient servants, whose delight it was to write after thy copy, to proceed the same way in their expositions of the Scriptures, and in their composing both of public liturgies and of private prayers to thee; to make their accesses to thee in such a kind of language as thou wast pleased to speak to them, in a figurative, in a metaphorical language.

In which manner I am bold to call the comfort which I receive now in this sickness, in the indication of the concoction and maturity thereof in certain clouds and residences[6] which the physicians observe, a discovering of land

---

1: the highest heaven, the abode of the angels. 2: strength. 3: early Church fathers, known for intellectual powers. 4: the law of the Old Testament before Christ's coming. 5: The Bible was understood as a literal historical record and a metaphorical design where the events of The Old Testament foreshadowed the New, and where both were understood spiritually, looking forward beyond time to a heavenly state, the final New Jerusalem. 6: deposits in bodily fluids.

from sea after a long and tempestuous voyage. But wherefore, O my God, hast thou presented to us the afflictions and calamities of this life in the name of waters? So often in the name of waters, and deep waters, and seas of waters? Must we look to be drowned? Are they bottomless, are they boundless? That is not the dialect of thy language. Thou hast given a remedy against the deepest water by water, against the inundation of sin by baptism; and the first life that thou gavest to any creatures was in waters. Therefore thou dost not threaten us with an irremediableness when our affliction is a sea. It is so, if we consider ourselves. So thou callest Genezareth,[1] which was but a lake, and not salt, a sea; so thou callest the Mediterranean sea still the great sea, because the inhabitants saw no other sea. They that dwelt there thought a lake a sea, and the others thought a little sea, the greatest; and we that know not the afflictions of others call our own the heaviest.

But, O my God, that is truly great that overflows the channel, that is really a great affliction which is above my strength. But thou, O God, art my strength, and then what can be above it? *Mountains shake with the swelling of thy sea:*[2] secular mountains, men strong in power; spiritual mountains, men strong in grace, are shaken with afflictions. But *thou layest up thy sea in storehouses:*[3] even thy corrections are of thy treasure, and thou wilt not waste thy corrections. When they have done their service to humble thy patient thou wilt call them in again: *for thou givest the sea thy decree, that the waters should not pass thy commandment.*[4] All our waters shall run into Jordan, and thy servants passed Jordan dry foot. They shall run into the red sea (the sea of thy Son's blood), and the red sea, that red sea, drowns none of thine. But *they that sail on the sea tell of the danger thereof:*[5] I that am yet in this affliction owe thee the glory of speaking of it. But, as the wise man bids me, I say: *I may speak much and come short, wherefore in sum thou art all.*[6]

Since thou art so, O my God, and affliction is a sea too deep for us, what is our refuge? Thine ark, thy ship. In all other afflictions, those means which thou hast ordained in this sea, in sickness, thy ship is thy physician: *Thou hast made a way in the sea, and a safe path in the waters, showing that thou canst save from all dangers, yea, though a man went to sea without art.*[7] Yet, where I find all that, I find this added: *nevertheless thou wouldst not, that the work of thy wisdom should be idle.*[8] Thou canst save without means; but thou hast told no man that thou wilt, thou hast told every man that thou wilt not. When the centurion believed the master of the ship more than St Paul, they were all opened to a great danger.[9] This was a preferring of thy means before thee, the author of the means. But, my God, though thou beest everywhere, I have no promise of appearing to me but in thy ship. Thy blessed Son preached out of a ship; the means is preaching, he did that; and the ship was a type[10] of the church, he did it there. Thou gavest St. Paul the lives of all them that sailed with him; if they had not been in the ship with him, the gift had not extended to them. *As soon as thy Son was come out of the ship, immediately there met him, out of the tombs, a man with an unclean spirit, and*

1: Sea of Galilee. 2: Psalm 46:3. 3: Psalm 33:7. 4: Proverbs 8:29. 5: Ecclesiastes 43:24. 6: Ecclesiastes 43:27. 7: Wisdom 14:3. 8: Wisdom 14:5. 9: Acts of the Apostles 27:11. 10: figure. 11: Mark:2.

no man could hold him, no not with chains.[11] Thy Son needed no use of means; yet there we apprehend the danger to us, if we leave the ship, the means, in this case the physician.

But as they are ships to us in those seas, so is there a ship to them, too, in which they are to stay. Give me leave, O my God, to assist myself with such a construction of these words of thy servant Paul to the centurion, when the mariners would have left the ship: *except these abide in the ship, you cannot be safe.*[1] Except they who are our ships, the physicians, abide in that which is theirs and our ship, the truth and the sincere and religious worship of thee and thy gospel, we cannot promise ourselves so good safety. For though we have our ship, the physician, he hath not his ship, religion; and means are not means but in their concatenation, as they depend and are chained together. *The ships are great*, says thy apostle, *but a helm turns them;*[2] the men are learned, but their religion turns their labours to good. And, therefore, it was a heavy curse when *the third part of the ships perished;*[3] it is a heavy case where either all religion, or true religion, should forsake many of these ships whom thou hast sent to convey us over these seas.

But, O my God, my God, since I have my ship and they theirs, I have them and they have thee, why are we yet no nearer land? As soon as thy Son's disciple had taken him into the ship: *immediately the ship was at the land whither they went.*[4] Why have not they and I this dispatch? Everything is immediately done which is done when thou wouldst have it done. Thy purpose terminates every action, and what was done before that is undone yet. Shall that slacken my hope? Thy prophet from thee hath forbidden it: *It is good that a man should both hope, and quietly wait for the salvation of the Lord.*[5] Thou puttest off many judgments till the last day, and many pass this life without any; and shall not I endure the putting off thy mercy for a day? And yet, O my God, thou puttest me not to that, for the assurance of future mercy is present mercy.

But what is my assurance now? What is my seal? It is but a cloud,[6] that which my physicians call a cloud, in that which gives them their indication. But a cloud? Thy great seal to all the world, the rainbow, that secured the world for ever from drowning, was but a reflection upon a cloud. A cloud itself was a pillar which guided the church,[7] and the glory of God not only was, but appeared in, a cloud. Let me return, O my God, to the consideration of thy servant Elijah's proceeding in a time of desperate drought.[8] He bids them look towards the sea; they look and see nothing. He bids them again and again seven times; and at the seventh time they saw a little cloud rising out of the sea, and presently they had their desire of rain. Seven days, O my God, have we looked for this cloud, and now we have it. None of thy indications are frivolous. Thou makest thy signs seals, and thy seals effects, and thy effects consolation and restitution, wheresoever thou mayst receive glory by that way.

1: Acts of the Apostles 27:31. 2: James 3:4. 3: Revelations 8:9. 4: John 6:21. 5: Lamentations 3:26. 6: the condition of Donne's urine. 7: Exodus 8:21. 8: 1 Kings 18:43.

Prayer

O Eternal and most gracious God, who though thou passedst over infinite millions of generations before thou camest to a creation of this world; yet, when thou beganst, didst never intermit that work, but continuedst day to day, till thou hadst perfected all the work, and deposed it in the hands and rest of a sabbath. Though thou have been pleased to glorify thyself in a long exercise of my patience, with an expectation of thy declaration of thyself in this my sickness; yet since thou hast now of thy goodness afforded that which affords us some hope, if that be still the way of thy glory, proceed in that way and perfect that world and establish me in a sabbath and rest in thee, by this thy seal of bodily restitution.

Thy priests came up to thee by steps in the temple, thy angels came down to Jacob by steps upon the ladder;[1] we find no stair by which thou thyself camest to Adam in paradise, nor to Sodom[2] in thine anger; for thou, and thou only, art able to do all at once. But, O Lord, I am not weary of thy pace, nor weary of mine own patience. I provoke thee not with a prayer, not with a wish, not with a hope, to more haste than consists with thy purpose; nor look that any other thing should have entered into thy purpose, but thy glory. To hear thy steps coming towards me is the same comfort as to see thy face present with me; whether thou do the work of a thousand years in a day, or extend the work of a day to a thousand years, as long as thou workest, it is light and comfort. Heaven itself is but an extension of the same joy; and an extension of this mercy, to proceed at thy leisure, in the way of restitution, is a manifestation of heaven to me here upon earth.

From that people to whom thou appearedst in signs and in types, the Jews, thou art departed, because they trusted in them; but from thy church, to whom thou hast appeared in thyself, in thy Son, thou wilt never depart, because we cannot trust too much in him. Though thou have afforded me these signs of restitution, yet if I confide in them, and begin to say all was but a natural accident, and nature begins to discharge herself, and she will perfect the whole work, my hope shall vanish because it is not in thee. If thou shouldst take thy hand utterly from me and have nothing to do with me, nature alone were able to destroy me. But if thou withdraw thy helping hand, alas, how frivolous are the helps of nature, how impotent the assistances of art? As, therefore, the morning dew is a pawn of the evening fatness, so, O Lord, let this day's comfort be the earnest of tomorrow's, so far as may conform me entirely to thee, to what end, and by what way soever, thy mercy have appointed me.

1: Genesis 28:12.   2: city destroyed for its lack of religion.

BEN JONSON (1572–1637)

Educated at Westminster school, Jonson was a convinced classicist and promoted literature as a potent force for moral teaching in the public sphere. He was the first to include
English plays in his collected works (1616), presenting them as serious literature to rival
poetry. Jonson became a virtual poet laureate under James I but was less well received at
the court of Charles I.

On My First Son

> Farewell, thou child of my right hand, and joy;
>   My sin was too much hope of thee, loved boy.
> Seven years thou wert lent to me, and I thee pay,
>   Exacted by thy fate, on the just day.
> 5 O, could I lose all father now. For why
>   Will man lament the state he should envy?
> To have so soon 'scaped world's and flesh's rage,
>   And, if no other misery, yet age?
> Rest in soft peace, and, asked, say here doth lie
> 10 Ben Jonson his best piece of poetry.
> For whose sake, henceforth, all his vows be such,
>   As what he loves may never like too much.

My Picture left in Scotland

> I now think Love is rather deaf than blind,
>   For else it could not be,
>   That she,
> Whom I adore so much, should so slight me,
> 5 And cast my love behind.
> I'm sure my language to her was as sweet,
>   And every close did meet
>   In sentence of as subtle feet
>   As hath the youngest he
> 10 That sits in shadow of Apollo's tree.
> Oh, but my conscious fears,
>   That fly my thoughts between
>   Tell me that she hath seen
>   My hundreds of grey hairs,
> 15 Told seven and forty years,
> Read so much waste, as she cannot embrace
>   My mountain-belly, and my rocky face;
> And all these through her eyes have stopped her ears.

My Picture left 7 **close:** candence, end to a movement   8 **sentence:** thought.
of music.

To Penshurst

Thou art not, Penshurst, built to envious show,
    Of touch, or marble; nor canst boast a row
Of polished pillars, or a roof of gold.
    Thou hast no lantern, whereof tales are told,
5 Or stair, or courts; but stand'st an ancient pile,
    And these grudged at, art reverenced the while.
Thou joy'st in better marks, of soil, of air,
    Of wood, of water; therein thou art faire.
Thou hast thy walks for health, as well as sport;
10 Thy mount, to which the dryads do resort,
Where Pan and Bacchus their high feasts have made,
    Beneath the broad beech, and the chestnut shade;
That taller tree, which of a nut was set,
    At his great birth, where all the muses met.
15 There, in the writhed bark, are cut the names
    Of many a sylvan taken with his flames;
And there the ruddy satyrs oft provoke
    The lighter fauns to reach thy lady's oak.
Thy copse, too, named of Gamage, thou hast there,
20 That never fails to serve thee seasoned deer
When thou would'st feast, or exercise thy friends.
    The lower land, that to the river bends,
Thy sheep, thy bullocks, kine, and calves doe feed;
    The middle grounds thy mares, and horses breed.
25 Each bank doth yield thee conies; and the tops
    Fertile of wood, Ashour and Sidney's copse,
To crown thy open table, doth provide
    The purpled pheasant with the speckled side;
The painted partridge lies in every field,
30 And, for thy mess, is willing to be killed.
And if the high-swollen Medway fail thy dish,
    Thou hast thy ponds, that pay thee tribute fish,
Fat, aged carps, that run into thy net.
    And pikes, now weary their own kind to eat,
35 As loath, the second draught, or cast to stay,
    Officiously, at first, themselves betray.
Bright eels, that emulate them, and leap on land,
    Before the fisher, or into his hand.
Then hath thy orchard fruit, thy garden flowers,
40 Fresh as the air, and new as are the hours.

---

1 **Penshurst:** in Kent, the seat of the Sidney family. 2 **touch:** black marble. 4 **lantern:** a windowed turret on the top of a building. 10 **dryads:** wood nymphs. 14 **his:** Sir Philip Sidney, who reputedly had an oak planted at his birth. 18 **fauns:** woodland deities. **lady's oak:** Barbara Gamage, who became wife to Sir Robert Sidney, was reputedly wooed under an oak in the park. 19 **copse:** coppice, a small wood. 25 **conies:** rabbits.

The early cherry, with the later plum,
    Fig, grape, and quince, each in his time doth come;
The blushing apricot, and woolly peach
    Hang on thy walls, that every child may reach.
45 And though thy walls be of the country stone,
    They are reared with no man's ruin, no man's groan,
There's none, that dwell about them, wish them down;
    But all come in, the farmer and the clown;
And no one empty-handed, to salute
50   Thy lord, and lady, though they have no suit.
Some bring a capon, some a rural cake,
    Some nuts, some apples; some that think they make
The better cheeses, bring 'em; or else send
    By their ripe daughters, whom they would commend
55 This way to husbands; and whose baskets bear
    An emblem of themselves, in plum, or pear.
But what can this (more then express their love)
    Add to thy free provisions, far above
The need of such? Whose liberal board doth flow,
60   With all that hospitality doth know!
Where comes no guest, but is allowed to eat,
    Without his fear, and of thy lord's own meat;
Where the same beer and bread, and self same wine,
    That is his lordship's, shall be also mine.
65 And I not fain to sit, as some this day,
    At great men's tables, and yet dine away.
Here no man tells my cups; nor, standing by,
    A waiter, doth my gluttony envy;
But gives me what I call and lets me eat,
70   He knows, below, he shall find plenty of meat,
Thy tables hoard not up for the next day.
    Nor, when I take my lodging, need I pray
For fire, or lights, or livery; all is there;
    As if thou, then, wert mine, or I reigned here;
75 There's nothing I can wish for which I stay.
    That found King James, when hunting late this way,
With his brave son, the Prince, they saw thy fires
    Shine bright on every hearth as the desires
Of thy penates had been set on flame,
80   To entertain them; or the country came,
With all their zeal, to warm their welcome here.
    What (great, I will not say, but) sudden cheer
Did'st thou, then, make 'em! And what praise was heaped
    On thy good lady, then. Who therein reaped

---

43 **apricot, peach:** fruits difficult to grow in Britain.   67 **tells:** counts. 70 **below:** in the servant's hall.
48 **clown:** simple rustic. 50 **suit:** formal requests.   79 **penates:** household deities. 82 **sudden:** spontaneous.

85 The just reward of her high housewifery;
  To have her linen, plate, and all things nigh,
 When she was far; and not a room but dressed,
  As if it had expected such a guest.
 These, Penshurst, are thy praise, and yet not all.
90 Thy lady's noble, fruitful, chaste withal.
 His children thy great lord may call his own;
  A fortune, in this age, but rarely known.
 They are, and have been taught religion; thence
  Their gentler spirits have sucked innocence.
95 Each morn and even they are taught to pray
  With the whole household, and may everyday
 Read in their virtuous parents' noble parts
  The mysteries of manners, arms, and arts.
 Now, Penshurst, they that will proportion thee
100 With other edifices, when they see
 Those proud, ambitious heaps, and nothing else,
  May say, their lords have built, but thy lord dwells.

From Volpone or The Fox

Set in Venice – a city renowned for its mercantile wealth and and the supposed loose morals of citizens – Jonson's play attacks greed. Volpone is a rich miser without family who pretends he is old and dying so that other prominent citizens will give him presents in the hope they will be made his heir. In their determination to outdo one another, these suitors promise Volpone anything, even, in the case of Corvino, his young wife, Celia. Volpone is helped by his servant, Mosca, who is himself a parasite. Volpone was first acted in either 1605 or 1606 and first published in 1607.

Act I, Scene i

  [*Enter Volpone and Mosca.*]
  Volpone Good morning to the day; and next my gold.
  Open the shrine that I may see my saint. [*Mosca reveals a treasure.*]
  Hail the world's soul, and mine. More glad than is
  The teeming earth to see the longed-for sun
5 Peep through the horns of the celestial ram,
  Am I, to view thy splendour, darkening his;
  That lying here, amongst my other hoards,
  Showest like a flame by night; or like the day
  Struck out of chaos, when all darkness fled
10 Unto the centre. O, thou son of Sol,
  But brighter than thy father, let me kiss
  With adoration, thee, and every relic
  Of sacred treasure in this blessed room.

---

90 **fruitful**: fertile.

Well did wise poets, by thy glorious name,
15 Title that age which they would have the best;
Thou being the best of things, and far transcending
All style of joy, in children, parents, friends,
Or any other waking dream on earth.
Thy looks, when they to Venus did ascribe,
20 They should have given her twenty thousand Cupids,
Such are thy beauties, and our loves. Dear saint,
Riches, the dumb god, that giv'st all men tongues,
That canst do nought, and yet mak'st men do all things;
The price of souls; even Hell, with thee to boot,
25 Is made worth Heaven. Thou art virtue, fame,
Honour, and all things else. Who can get thee,
He shall be noble, valiant, honest, wise –
Mosca And what he will, sir. Riches are in fortune
A greater good, than wisdom is in nature.
30 *Volpone* True, my beloved Mosca. Yet, I glory
More in the cunning purchase of my wealth,
Than in the glad possession; since I gain
No common way; I use no trade, no venture;
I wound no earth with ploughshares, fat no beasts
35 To feed the shambles; have no mills for iron,
Oil, corn, or men, to grind 'em into powder;
I blow no subtle glass; expose no ships
To threatenings of the furrow-faced sea;
I turn no moneys in the public bank;
40 Nor usure private.
Mosca No, sir, nor devour
Soft prodigals. You shall ha' some will swallow
A melting heir as glibly as your Dutch
Will pills of butter, and ne'er purge for't;
45 Tear forth the fathers of poor families
Out of their beds, and coffin them, alive,
In some kind, clasping prison, where their bones
May be forthcoming, when the flesh is rotten;
But your sweet nature doth abhor these courses;
50 You loath the widow's, or the orphan's tears
Should wash your pavements, or their piteous cries
Ring in your roofs and beat the air for vengeance.
Volpone Right, Mosca, I do loath it.
Mosca And besides, sir,
55 You are not like the thresher, that doth stand
With a huge flail, watching a heap of corn,
And, hungry, dares not taste the smallest grain,

---

35 **shambles**: slaughter-house.   43 **melting**: spending freely.

But feeds on mallows, and such bitter herbs;
Nor like the merchant, who hath filled his vaults
60   With Romagnia and rich Candian wines,
Yet drinks the lees of Lombard's vinegar;
You will not lie in straw, whilst moths and worms
Feed on your sumptuous hangings and soft beds.
You know the use of riches, and dare give now,
65   From that bright heap, to me, your poor observer,
Or to your dwarf, or your hermaphrodite,
Your eunuch, or what other household trifle
Your pleasure allows maintenance.
    Volpone [*Gives Mosca money*] Hold thee, Mosca,
70   Take, of my hand; thou strik'st on truth in all;
And they are envious, term thee parasite.
Call forth my dwarf, my eunuch, and my fool,
And let 'em make me sport. [*Exit Mosca*] What should I do,
But cocker up my genius and live free
75   To all delights my fortune calls me to?
I have no wife, no parent, child, ally,
To give my substance to; but whom I make,
Must be my heir: and this makes men observe me.
This draws new clients daily to my house,
80   Women, and men of every sex and age,
That bring me presents, send me plate, coin, jewels,
With hope, that when I die (which they expect
Each greedy minute) it shall then return,
Tenfold, upon them; whilst some, covetous
85   Above the rest, seek to engross me whole,
And counter-work the one unto the other,
Contend in gifts, as they would seem, in love;
All which I suffer, playing with their hopes,
And am content to coin 'em into profit,
90   And look upon their kindness, and take more,
And look on that; still bearing them in hand,
Letting the cherry knock against their lips,
And draw it by their mouths, and back again. How now!

Act III, Scene vii

[*Enter Mosca, Corvino, Celia.*]
Mosca Death on me! You are come too soon. What meant you?
Did not I say, I would send?
Corvino Yes, but I feared
You might forget it, and then they prevent us.

---

58 mallows: coarse field plants. **60 Romagnia, Candian:** rich sweet wines from Greece and Crete. **74 cocker up:** indulge. **92 cherry:** the game of bob-cherry, in which a person attempts to bite a cherry dangling from a string.

5   *Mosca* Prevent. [*Aside*] Did e'er man haste so, for his horns?
A courtier would not ply it so for a place.
Well, now there's no helping it, stay here;
I'll presently return. [*Moves to where he has hid Bonario.*]
Corvino Where are you, Celia?
10   You know not wherefore I have brought you hither?
Celia Not well, except you told me.
Corvino Now, I will; hark hither. [*They talk together in silence.*]
Mosca [*to Bonario*] Sir, your father hath sent word,
It will be half an hour ere he come;
15   And therefore, if you please to walk the while,
Into that gallery, at the upper end,
There are some books, to entertain the time,
And I'll take care, no man shall come unto you, sir.
Bonario Yes, I will stay there. [*Aside*] I do doubt this fellow. [*Exit.*]
20   *Mosca* There, he is far enough; he can hear nothing.
And for his father, I can keep him off. *Exit.*
Corvino Nay, now, there is no starting back; and therefore
Resolve upon it; I have so decreed.
It must be done. Nor would I move't afore,
25   Because I would avoid all shifts and tricks,
That might deny me.
Celia Sir, let me beseech you,
Affect not these strange trials; if you doubt
My chastity, why lock me up forever.
30   Make me the heir of darkness. Let me live
Where I may please your fears, if not your trust.
Corvino Believe it, I have no such humour, I.
All that I speak, I mean; yet I am not mad;
Not horn-mad, see you? Go to, show yourself
35   Obedient, and a wife.
Celia O Heaven!
Corvino I say it. Do so.
Celia Was this the train?
Corvino I've told you reasons.
40   What the physicians have set down; how much,
It may concern me; what my engagements are;
My means; and the necessity of those means,
For my recovery. Wherefore, if you be
Loyal and mine, be won, respect my venture.
45   *Celia* Before your honour?
Corvino Honour? Tut, a breath;
There's no such thing, in nature, a mere term
Invented to awe fools. What is my gold

---

5 horns: a cuckold supposedly grew horns.   **6 courtier:** even someone seeking a position at court would not
so readily prostitute his wife in exchange for favours.   **34 horn-mad:** mad through being made cuckold.
41 engagements: business.

The worse, for touching? Clothes, for being looked on?
50 Why, this is no more. An old, decrepit wretch,
That has no sense, no sinew, takes his meat
With others' fingers, only knows to gape,
When you do scald his gums, a voice, a shadow;
And what can this man hurt you?
55 **Celia** Lord! What spirit is this hath entered him?
Corvino And for your fame,
That's such a jig; as if I would go tell it,
Cry it, on the piazza. Who shall know it?
But he, that cannot speak it, and this fellow,
60 Whose lips are i'my pocket; save yourself,
If you'll proclaim't, you may. I know no other,
Should come to know it.
Celia Are heaven and saints then nothing?
Will they be blind, or stupid?
65 **Corvino** How?
Celia Good sir,
Be jealous still, emulate them, and think
What hate they burn with toward every sin.
Corvino I grant you; if I thought it were a sin,
70 I would not urge you. Should I offer this
To some young Frenchman, or hot Tuscan blood,
That had read Aretine, conned all his prints,
Knew every quirk within lust's labyrinth,
And were professed critic in lechery,
75 An' I would look upon him and applaud him,
This were a sin. But here, 'tis contrary,
A pious work, mere charity, for physic,
And honest policy, to assure mine own.
Celia O Heaven! Canst thou suffer such a change?
[*Enter Volpone and Mosca.*]
80 **Volpone** [*Aside*] Thou art mine honour, Mosca, and my pride,
My joy, my tickling, my delight! Go, bring 'em.
Mosca [*to Corvino*] Please you draw near, sir.
Corvino [*to Celia*] Come on. What,
You will not be rebellious? By that light –
85 **Mosca** Sir, Signior Corvino, here, is come to see you.
Volpone [*pretending to be an invalid*] Oh.
Mosca And hearing of the consultation had,
So lately, for your health, is come to offer,
Or rather, sir, to prostitute –
90 **Corvino** Thanks, sweet Mosca.
Mosca Freely, unasked, or unentreated –
Corvino Well.

---

72 Aretine: erotic prints with verses by Aretino were a standard of Renaissance pornography.

Mosca. As the true, fervent instance of his love,
His own most fair and proper wife; the beauty,
95   Only of price, in Venice –
Corvino [*Aside*] 'Tis well urged.
Mosca To be your comfortress, and to preserve you.
Volpone Alas, I am past already. Pray you, thank him,
For his good care, and promptness; but for that,
100   'Tis a vain labour, e'en to fight 'gainst heaven;
Applying fire to a stone – uh, uh, uh, uh –
Making a dead leaf grow again. I take
His wishes gently, though; and you may tell him,
What I've done for him. Marry, my state is hopeless.
105   Will him to pray for me; and t'use his fortune,
With reverence, when he comes to't.
Mosca Do you hear, sir?
Go to him, with your wife.
Corvino Heart of my father!
110   Wilt thou persist thus? Come, I pray thee, come.
Thou see'st 'tis nothing. Celia! By this hand,
I shall grow violent. Come, do't, I say.
Celia Sir, kill me rather. I will take down poison,
Eat burning coals, do anything.
115   *Corvino* Be damned.
Heart! I will drag thee hence home by the hair;
Cry thee a strumpet through the streets; rip up
Thy mouth, unto thine ears, and slit thy nose
Like a raw rochet. Do not tempt me, come.
120   Yield, I am loath – Death! I will buy some slave,
Whom I will kill, and bind thee to him, alive;
And at my window, hang you forth, devising
Some monstrous crime, which I, in capital letters,
Will eat into thy flesh, with aquafortis,
125   And burning corrosives, on this stubborn breast.
Now, by the blood thou hast incensed, I'll do't.
Celia Sir, what you please, you may, I am your martyr.
Corvino Be not thus obstinate, I ha' not deserved it;
Think, who it is entreats you. Pray thee, sweet –
130   Good faith! – thou shalt have jewels, gowns, attires,
What thou wilt, think, and ask. Do, but, go kiss him.
Or touch him, but for my sake. At my suit.
This once. No? Not? I shall remember this.
Will you disgrace me thus? Do you thirst m'undoing?
135   *Mosca* Nay, gentle lady, be advised.
Corvino No, no.
She has watched her time. God's precious, this is scurvy,
'Tis very scurvy: and you are –

---

119 **rochet**: a fish.   124 **aquafortis**: nitric acid, used in engraving.   137 **scurvy**: skin disease; here meaning shabby.

Mosca Nay, good sir.

140 **Corvino** An arrant locust, by heaven, a locust.
Whore, crocodile, that hast thy tears prepared,
Expecting, how thou'lt bid 'em flow.

Mosca Nay, pray you, sir, she will consider.

Celia Would my life would serve to satisfy.

145 **Corvino** 'S death! If she would but speak to him,
And save my reputation, 'twere somewhat;
But spitefully to affect my utter ruin!

Mosca Ay, now you've put your fortune in her hands.
Why i'faith, it is her modesty, I must quit her;

150 If you were absent, she would be more coming
I know it, and dare undertake for her.
What woman can, before her husband? Pray you,
Let us depart, and leave her here.

Corvino Sweet Celia,

155 Thou may'st redeem all yet; I'll say no more
If not, esteem yourself as lost. Nay, stay there. [*Exit Mosca, Corvino.*]

Celia O God, and his good angels! Whither, whither,
Is shame fled human breasts? That with such ease,
Men dare put off your honours, and their own?

160 Is that, which ever was a cause of life,
Now placed beneath the basest circumstance?
And modesty an exile made, for money?

Volpone [*not as an invalid*] Ay, in Corvino, and such earth-fed minds,
That never tasted the true heaven of love.

165 Assure thee, Celia, he that would sell thee,
Only for hope of gain, and that uncertain,
He would have sold his part of paradise
For ready money, had he met a cope-man.
Why art thou 'mazed, to see me thus revived?

170 Rather applaud thy beauty's miracle;
'Tis thy great work; that hath, not now alone,
But sundry times, raised me, in several shapes,
And but this morning, like a mountebank,
To see thee at thy window. Ay, before

175 I would have left my practice for thy love,
In varying figures, I would have contended
With the blue Proteus, or the horned flood.
Now art thou welcome.

Celia Sir!

180 **Volpone** Nay, fly me not.
Nor let thy false imagination
That I was bed-rid make thee think I am so;

---

141 **crocodile:** supposedly they weep false tears. 168 **cope-man:** merchant. 173 **mountebank:** a quack doctor and performer. 177 **Proteus:** sea god capable of taking any shape. **horned flood:** the river god Achelous, who fought with Hercules in several shapes.

Thou shalt not find it. I am now as fresh,
As hot, as high, and in as jovial plight,
185 As when in that so celebrated scene,
At recitation of our comedy,
For entertainment of the great Valois,
I acted young Antinous; and attracted
The eyes and ears of all the ladies present,
190 T'admire each graceful gesture, note, and footing. [*Sings.*]
    Come, my Celia, let us prove,
    While we can, the sports of love;
    Time will not be ours, for ever,
    He, at length, our good will sever;
195   Spend not then his gifts, in vain.
    Suns that set may rise again;
    But if once we lose this light,
    'Tis with us perpetual night.
    Why should we defer our joys?
200   Fame and rumour are but toys.
    Cannot we delude the eyes
    Of a few poor household spies?
    Or his easier ears beguile,
    Thus removed by our wile?
205   'Tis no sin love's fruits to steal;
    But the sweet thefts to reveal;
    To be taken, to be seen,
    These have crimes accounted been.
Celia Some serene blast me, or dire lightning strike
210 This my offending face.
Volpone Why droops my Celia?
Thou hast in place of a base husband found
A worthy lover; use thy fortune well,
With secrecy, and pleasure. See, behold,
215 What thou art queen of; not in expectation,
As I feed others, but possessed and crowned.
See here a rope of pearl, and each, more orient
Than that the brave Egyptian queen caroused;
Dissolve, and drink 'em. See, a carbuncle,
220 May put out both the eyes of our St Mark;
A diamond, would have bought Lollia Paulina,
When she came in, like star-light, hid with jewels,
That were the spoils of provinces; take these,
And wear, and lose 'em; yet remains an ear-ring
225 To purchase them again, and this whole state.
A gem but worth a private patrimony

---

187 **Valois:** Henry III of France, who visited Venice 30 years before the time Volpone is set in. 209 **serene:** a harmful mist. 218 **queen:** Cleopatra. 219 **carbuncle:** a gem. 221 **Lollia Paulina:** wife of the decadent Roman emperor Caligula.

Is nothing, we will eat such at a meal.
The heads of parrots, tongues of nightingales,
The brains of peacocks, and of ostriches
230 Shall be our food; and could we get the phoenix,
Though nature lost her kind, she were our dish.
Celia Good sir, these things might move a mind affected
With such delights; but I whose innocence
Is all I can think wealthy, or worth th'enjoying,
235 And which once lost, I have nought to lose beyond it,
Cannot be taken with these sensual baits;
If you have conscience –
Volpone 'Tis the beggar's virtue,
If thou hast wisdom, hear me Celia.
240 Thy baths shall be the juice of July-flowers,
Spirit of roses, and of violets,
The milk of unicorns, and panthers' breath
Gathered in bags, and mixed with Cretan wines.
Our drink shall be prepared gold and amber;
245 Which we will take, until my roof whirl round
With the vertigo; and my dwarf shall dance,
My eunuch sing, my fool make up the antic;
Whilst we, in changed shapes, act Ovid's tales,
Thou, like Europa now, and I like Jove,
250 Then I like Mars, and thou like Erycine,
So, of the rest, till we have quite run through
And wearied all the fables of the gods.
Then will I have thee in more modern forms,
Attired like some sprightly dame of France,
255 Brave Tuscan lady, or proud Spanish beauty;
Sometimes, unto the Persian Sophy's wife;
Or the Grand Signior's mistress; and, for change,
To one of our most artful courtesans,
Or some quick negro, or cold Russian;
260 And I will meet thee, in as many shapes;
Where we may so transfuse our wandering souls
Out at our lips, and score up sums of pleasures,
That the curious shall not know,
How to tell them as they flow;
265 And the envious, when they find
What their number is, be pined.
Celia If you have ears that will be pierced, or eyes
That can be opened, a heart may be touched,
Or any part that yet sounds man about you;
270 If you have touch of holy saints, or heaven,

---

231 lost her kind: there is only one phoenix, so by eating it the bird would become extinct.   **248 Ovid's tales:** The Metamorphoses.   **249 Europa:** carried off and raped by Jove.   **250 Erycine:** Venus, who committed adultery with Mars.   **257 Grand Signior:** The Turkish Sultan.

Do me the grace, to let me 'scape.
If not, be bountiful, and kill me.
You do know I am a creature, hither ill betrayed
By one whose shame I would forget it were.
275 If you will deign me neither of these graces,
Yet feed your wrath, sir, rather than your lust,
It is a vice comes nearer manliness,
And punish that unhappy crime of nature,
Which you miscall my beauty; flay my face,
280 Or poison it with ointments for seducing
Your blood to this rebellion. Rub these hands,
With what may cause an eating leprosy
E'en to my bones and marrow; anything,
That may disfavour me, save in my honour.
285 And I will kneel to you, pray for you, pay down
A thousand hourly vows, sir, for your health,
Report, and think you virtuous.
Volpone Think me cold,
Frozen, and impotent, and so report me?
290 That I had Nestor's hernia thou would'st think.
I do degenerate and abuse my nation,
To play with opportunity, thus long.
I should have done the act and then have parleyed.
Yield, or I'll force thee.
295 **Celia** Oh! Just God!
Volpone In vain –
[*Enter Bonario, who has been listening from where Mosca placed him.*]
Bonario Forbear, foul ravisher, libidinous swine,
Free the forced lady or thou diest, impostor.
But that I am loath to snatch thy punishment
300 Out of the hand of justice, thou should'st yet
Be made the timely sacrifice of vengeance
Before this altar and this dross, thy idol.
Lady, let's quit the place, it is the den
Of villainy; fear nought, you have a guard;
305 And he, ere long, shall meet his just reward. [*Exit Bonario, Celia.*]
Volpone Fall on me roof, and bury me in ruin,
Become my grave, that wert my shelter. Oh!
I am unmasked, unspirited, undone,
Betrayed to beggary, to infamy.

---

290 **Nestor's hernia**: referring to impotent old age.

THOMAS MIDDLETON (1580–1627)

Middleton was a Londoner and his drama is closely connected with the city, either in its depiction of contemporary urban life in his many comedies (e.g. *A Trick to Catch the Old One, A Chaste Maid in Cheapside*), or through the promotion of London's political interests against those of the court in plays such as *A Game at Chess. The Changeling,* which is set in Spain, dates from 1622, though not published until 1653, and was jointly written with William Rowley. Such collaborations were common in the period and Rowley, who was an actor, wrote plays with a number of leading dramatists.

The Changeling

Characters
Vermandero, father to Beatrice
Tomazo de Piracquo, a noble lord
Alonzo de Piracquo, his brother, suitor to Beatrice
Alsermero, a nobleman, afterwards married to Beatrice
Jasperino, his friend
De Flores, servant to Vermandero.
Antonio, the Changeling
Pedro, friend to Antonio
Franciscus, the counterfeit madman
Alibius, a jealous doctor
Lollio, his man
Beatrice-Joanna, daughter to Vermandero
Diaphanta, her waiting-woman
Isabella, wife to Alibius
Madmen
Servants

Scene: Alicante

Act I, Scene i

[*Enter Alsemero.*]
Alsemero 'Twas in the temple where I first beheld her,
And now again the same; what omen yet
Follows of that? None but imaginary.
Why should my hopes or fate be timorous?
5   The place is holy, so is my intent.
I love her beauties to the holy purpose,
And that, methinks, admits comparison
With man's first creation, the place blest,
And is his right home back, if he achieve it.
10   The church hath first begun our interview,
And that's the place must join us into one;
So there's beginning and perfection too. [*Enter Jasperino.*]

Jasperino Oh, sir, are you here? Come, the wind's fair with you,
Y'are like to have a swift and pleasant passage.
15 *Alsemero* Sure, y'are deceived friend, 'tis contrary
In my best judgement.
Jasperino What, for Malta?
If you could buy a gale amongst the witches,
They could not serve you such a lucky pennyworth
20 As comes a' God's name.
Alsemero Even now I observed
The temple's vane to turn full in my face;
I know 'tis against me.
Jasperino Against you?
25 Then you know not where you are.
Alsemero Not well, indeed.
Jasperino Are you not well, sir?
Alsemero Yes, Jasperino, unless there be some hidden malady
Within me, that I understand not.
30 *Jasperino* And that
I begin to doubt, sir. I never knew
Your inclinations to travels at a pause
With any cause to hinder it, till now.
Ashore you were wont to call your servants up,
35 And help to trap your horses for the speed;
At sea I have seen you weigh the anchor with 'em,
Hoist sails for fear to lose the foremost breath,
Be in continual prayers for fair winds,
And have you changed your orisons?
40 *Alsemero* No friend, I keep the same church, same devotion.
Jasperino Lover I'm sure y'are none, the stoic
Was found in you long ago; your mother nor
Best friends, who have set snares of beauty,
Ay and choice ones too, could never trap you that way.
45 What might be the cause?
Alsemero Lord, how violent
Thou art ! I was but meditating of
Somewhat I heard within the temple.
Jasperino Is this violence? 'Tis but idleness
50 Compared with your haste yesterday.
Alsemero I'm all this while a-going, man. [*Enter Servants.*]
Jasperino Backwards I think, sir. Look, your servants.
1st Servant The seamen call; shall we board your trunks?
Alsemero No, not today.
55 *Jasperino* 'Tis the critical day it seems, and the sign in Aquarius.
2nd Servant [*aside*] We must not to sea today; this smoke will bring
forth fire!

---

35 trap your horses: help to harness your horses.   **39 orisons:** prayers.

Alsemero Keep all on shore; I do not know the end –
Which needs I must do – of an affair in hand
60 Ere I can go to sea.
lst Servant Well, your pleasure.
2nd Servant [*aside*] Let him e'en take his leisure too, we are safer
on land. [*Exit Servants.*]
[*Enter Beatrice, Diaphanta, servants. Alsemero greets Beatrice and kisses
her.*]
Jasperino [*aside*] How now! The laws of the Medes are changed,
65 sure; Salute a woman? He kisses too; wonderful! Where learnt he
this? And does it perfectly too; in my conscience, he ne'er rehearsed
it before. Nay, go on, this will be stranger and better news at
Valencia than if he had ransomed half Greece from the Turk.
Beatrice You are a scholar, sir?
70 **Alsemero** A weak one, lady.
Beatrice Which of the sciences is this love you speak of?
Alsemero From your tongue, I take it to be music.
Beatrice You are skilful in't, can sing at first sight.
Alsemero And I have showed you all my skill at once.
75 I want more words to express me further,
And must be forced to repetition;
I love you dearly.
Beatrice Be better advised, sir.
Our eyes are sentinels unto our judgements,
80 And should give certain judgement what they see;
But they are rash sometimes and tell us wonders
Of common things, which, when our judgements find,
They then can check the eyes and call them blind.
Alsemero But I am further, lady; yesterday
85 Was mine eyes' employment, and hither now
They brought my judgement, where are both agreed.
Both Houses then consenting, 'tis agreed;
Only there wants the confirmation
By the hand royal, that's your part, lady.
90 **Beatrice** Oh, there's one above me, sir. [*Aside*] For five days past
To be recalled! Sure, mine eyes were mistaken,
This was the man was meant me. That he should come
So near his time, and miss it!
Jasperino [*Aside*] We might have come by the carriers from
95 Valencia, I see, and saved all our sea provision; we are at
farthest, sure.
Methinks I should do something too;
I meant to be a venturer in this voyage.
Yonder's another vessel, I'll board her.
100 If she be lawful prize, down goes her topsail! [*Greets Diaphanta.*]

---

64 **laws of the Medes**: famous for unchangeable laws. 87 **Houses**: the Houses of Commons and Lords.
94 **carriers**: land transport.

[*Enter De Flores.*]
De Flores Lady, your father –
Beatrice Is in health, I hope.
De Flores Your eye shall instantly instruct you, lady.
He's coming hitherward.
105   **Beatrice** What needed then
Your duteous preface? I had rather
He had come unexpected; you must stall
A good presence with unnecessary blabbing;
And how welcome for your part you are,
110   I'm sure you know.
De Flores [*aside*] Will't never mend, this scorn,
One side nor other? Must I be enjoined
To follow still whilst she flies from me? Well,
Fates do your worst, I'll please myself with sight
115   Of her, at all opportunities,
If but to spite her anger; I know she had
Rather see me dead than living, and yet
She knows no cause for't but a peevish will.
Alsemero You seemed displeased, lady, on the sudden.
120   **Beatrice** Your pardon, sir, 'tis my infirmity;
Nor can I other reason render you,
Than his or hers, of some particular thing
They must abandon as a deadly poison,
Which to a thousand other tastes were wholesome;
125   Such to mine eyes is that same fellow there,
The same that report speaks of the basilisk.
Alsemero This is a frequent frailty in our nature;
There's scarce a man among a thousand sound,
But hath his imperfection. One distastes
130   The scent of roses, which to infinites
Most pleasing is, and odoriferous;
One oil, the enemy of poison;
Another wine, the cheerer of the heart,
And lively refresher of the countenance.
135   Indeed, this fault, if so it be, is general;
There's scarce a thing but is both loved and loathed;
Myself, I must confess, have the same frailty.
Beatrice And what may be your poison, sir? I am bold with you.
Alsemero What might be your desire, perhaps, a cherry.
140   **Beatrice** I am no enemy to any creature
My memory has, but yon gentleman.
Alsemero He does ill to tempt your sight, if he knew it.
Beatrice He cannot be ignorant of that, sir,
I have not spared to tell him so; and I want

---

126 **basilisk**: mythical creature able to kill by looking.

145 To help myself, since he's a gentleman
In good respect with my father and follows him.
Alsemero He's out of his place then now. [*They talk apart.*]
Jasperino I am a mad wag, wench.
Diaphanta So methinks, but for your comfort I can tell you we have
150 a doctor in the city that undertakes the cure of such.
Jasperino Tush, I know what physic is best for the state of mine
own body.
Diaphanta 'Tis scarce a well governed state, I believe.
Jasperino I could show thee such a thing with an ingredient that we
155 two would compound together, and if it did not tame the maddest
blood i' th' town for two hours after, I'll ne'er profess physic again.
Diaphanta A little poppy, sir, were good to cause you sleep.
Jasperino Poppy? I'll give thee a pop i' th' lips for that first, and
begin there; poppy is one simple indeed, and cuckoo – what you
160 call't – another. I'll discover no more now, another time I'll show
thee all.
Beatrice My father, sir. [*Enter Vermandero and servants.*]
Vermandero Oh, Joanna, I came to meet thee;
Your devotion's ended?
165 **Beatrice** For this time, sir.
[*Aside*] I shall change my saint, I fear me; I find
A giddy turning in me. [*to Vermandero*] Sir, this while
I am beholding to this gentleman,
Who left his own way to keep me company,
170 And in discourse I find him much desirous
To see your castle. He hath deserv'd it, sir,
If ye please to grant it.
Vermandero With all my heart, sir.
Yet there's an article between, I must know
175 Your country. We use not to give survey
Of our chief strengths to strangers. Our citadels
Are placed conspicuous to outward view,
On promonts' tops; but within are secrets.
Alsemero A Valencian, sir.
180 **Vermandero** A Valencian?
That's native, sir; of what name, I beseech you?
Alsemero Alsemero, sir.
Vermandero Alsemero? Not the son
Of John de Alsemero?
185 **Alsemero** The same, sir.
Vermandero My best love bids you welcome.
Beatrice [*aside*] He was wont
To call me so, and then he speaks a most
Unfeigned truth.

---

154 thing: sex. This banter equates medicine and sexual encounters. 159 simple: medicine from a single
plant. 159 cuckoo: the cuckoo-pint, a plant with phallic appearance.

190   **Vermandero** Oh, sir, I knew your father;
We two were in acquaintance long ago,
Before our chins were worth Iulan down,
And so continued till the stamp of time
Had coined us into silver. Well, he's gone;
195   A good soldier went with him.
    Alsemero You went together in that, sir.
    Vermandero No, by Saint Jacques, I came behind him;
Yet I have done somewhat too. An unhappy day
Swallowed him at last at Gibraltar
200   In fight with those rebellious Hollanders,
Was it not so?
    Alsemero Whose death I had revenged,
Or followed him in fate, had not the late league
Prevented me.
205   **Vermandero** Ay, ay, 'twas time to breathe.
Oh, Joanna, I should ha' told thee news,
I saw Piracquo lately.
    Beatrice [*aside*] That's ill news.
    Vermandero He's hot preparing for his day of triumph;
210   Thou must be a bride within this sevennight.
    Alsemero [*aside*] Ha!
    Beatrice Nay, good sir, be not so violent; with speed
I cannot render satisfaction
Unto the dear companion of my soul,
215   Virginity, whom I thus long have lived with,
And part with it so rude and suddenly;
Can such friends divide, never to meet again,
Without a solemn farewell?
    Vermandero Tush, tush, there's a toy.
220   **Alsemero** [*aside*] I must now part, and never meet again
With any joy on earth. [*to Vermandero*] Sir, your pardon,
My affairs call on me.
    Vermandero How, sir? By no means;
Not changed so soon, I hope. You must see my castle,
225   And her best entertainment, ere we part;
I shall think myself unkindly used else.
Come, come, let's on; I had good hope your stay
Had been a while with us in Alicant;
I might have bid you to my daughter's wedding.
230   **Alsemero** [*aside*] He means to feast me, and poisons me beforehand.
[*to Vermandero*] I should be dearly glad to be there, sir,
Did my occasions suit as I could wish.

---

192 **Iulan down**: first growth of beard. 200 **rebellious Hollanders**: the Dutch fighting for independence from Spain beat them in a naval battle at Gibraltar in 1607. 203 **league**: peace treaty signed between Spain and the Dutch in 1609.

Beatrice I shall be sorry if you be not there
When it is done, sir – but not so suddenly.
235 **Vermandero** I tell you, sir, the gentleman's complete,
A courtier and a gallant, enriched
With many fair and noble ornaments;
I would not change him for a son-in-law
For any he in Spain, the proudest he,
240 And we have great ones, that you know.
Alsemero He's much
Bound to you, sir.
Vermandero He shall be bound to me,
As fast as this tie can hold him; I'll want
245 My will else.
Beatrice [*aside*] I shall want mine if you do it.
Vermandero But come, by the way I'll tell you more of him.
Alsemero [*aside*] How shall I dare to venture in his castle
When he discharges murderers at the gate?
250 But I must on, for back I cannot go.
Beatrice [*seeing De Flores*] Not this serpent gone yet?
[*Drops her glove.*]
Vermandero Look, girl, thy glove's fall'n.
Stay, stay; De Flores, help a little. [*Exit all but Beatrice and De Flores.*]
De Flores Here, lady. [*Picks up the glove.*]
255 **Beatrice** Mischief on your officious forwardness!
Who bade you stoop? They touch my hand no more.
There. For t'other's sake I part with this; [*Drops the other glove.*]
Take 'em and draw thine own skin off with 'em. [*Exit.*]
De Flores Here's a favour come, with a mischief! Now I know
260 She had rather wear my pelt tanned in a pair
Of dancing pumps than I should thrust my fingers
Into her sockets here. I know she hates me,
Yet cannot choose but love her.
No matter; if but to vex her, I'll haunt her still;
265 Though I get nothing else, I'll have my will. [*Exit.*]

Act I, Scene ii

[*Enter Alibius and Lollio.*]
Alibius Lollio, I must trust thee with a secret; but thou must keep it.
Lollio I was ever close to a secret, sir.
Alibius The diligence that I have found in thee,
The care and industry already past,
5 Assures me of thy good continuance.
Lollio, I have a wife.
Lollio Fie, sir, 'tis too late to keep her secret, she's known to be
married all the town and country over.

---

249 murderers: small cannons.

Alibius Thou goest too fast, my Lollio. That knowledge
I allow no man can be barred it;
But there is a knowledge which is nearer,
Deeper, and sweeter, Lollio.
Lollio Well, sir, let us handle that between you and I.
Alibius 'Tis that I go about, man. Lollio,
My wife is young.
Lollio So much the worse to be kept secret, sir.
Alibius Why, now thou meet'st the substance of the point;
I am old, Lollio.
Lollio No, sir, 'tis I am old Lollio.
Alibius Yet why may not this concord and sympathize?
Old trees and young plants often grow together,
Well enough agreeing.
Lollio Ay, sir, but the old trees raise themselves higher and broader
than the young plants.
Alibius Shrewd application. There's the fear man.
I would wear my ring on my own finger;
Whilst it is borrowed it is none of mine,
But his that useth it.
Lollio You must keep it on still then; if it but lie by, one or other will
be thrusting into't.
Alibius Thou conceiv'st me, Lollio. Here thy watchful eye
Must have employment; I cannot always be
At home.
Lollio I dare swear you cannot.
Alibius I must look out.
Lollio I know't; you must look out, 'tis every man's case.
Alibius Here, I do say, must thy employment be
To watch her treadings, and in my absence
Supply my place.
Lollio I'll do my best, sir; yet surely I cannot see who you should
have cause to be jealous of.
Alibius Thy reason for that, Lollio? 'Tis a comfortable question.
Lollio We have but two sorts of people in the house, and both under
the whip, that's fools and madmen; the one has not wit enough to be
knaves, and the other not knavery enough to be fools.
Alibius Ay, those are all my patients, Lollio.
I do profess the cure of either sort;
My trade, my living 'tis, I thrive by it;
But here's the care that mixes with my thrift.
The daily visitants that come to see
My brainsick patients I would not have
To see my wife; gallants I do observe
Of quick enticing eyes, rich in habits,
Of stature and proportion very comely.
These are most shrewd temptations, Lollio.

Lollio They may be easily answered, sir; if they come to see the fools and madmen, you and I may serve the turn, and let my mistress alone, she's of neither sort.

Alibius 'Tis a good ward; indeed, come they to see

60 Our madmen or our fools, let 'em see no more
Than what they come for; by that consequent
They must not see her, I'm sure she's no fool.

Lollio And I'm sure she's no madman.

Alibius Hold that buckler fast, Lollio; my trust

65 Is on thee, and I account it firm and strong.
What hour is't, Lollio?

Lollio Towards belly-hour, sir.

Alibius Dinner time? Thou mean'st twelve o'clock?

Lollio Yes, sir, for every part has his hour. We wake at six and look

70 about us, that's eye-hour; at seven we should pray, that's knee-hour;
at eight walk, that's leg hour; at nine gather flowers and pluck a rose,
that's nose-hour; at ten we drink, that's mouth-hour; at eleven lay
about us for victuals, that's hand-hour; at twelve go to dinner, that's
belly-hour.

75 **Alibius** Profoundly, Lollio! It will be long
Ere all thy scholars learn this lesson, and
I did look to have a new one ent'red. Stay,
I think my expectation is come home.
[*Enter Pedro, and Antonio like an idiot.*]

Pedro Save you, sir; my business speaks itself,

80 This sight takes off the labour of my tongue.

Alibius Ay, ay, sir, 'tis plain enough; you mean him for my patient.

Pedro And if your pains prove but commodious, to give but some
little strength to his sick and weak part of nature in him, these are
but patterns [*Gives him money*] to show you of the whole pieces

85 that will follow to you, beside the charge of diet, washing and
other necessaries fully defrayed.

Alibius Believe it, sir, there shall no care be wanting.

Lollio Sir, an officer in this place may deserve something; the
trouble will pass through my hands.

90 **Pedro** 'Tis fit something should come to your hands then, sir.
[*Gives him money.*]

Lollio Yes, sir, 'tis I must keep him sweet, and read to him. What is
his name?

Pedro His name is Antonio; marry, we use but half to him, only
Tony.

95 **Lollio** Tony, Tony; 'tis enough, and a very good name for a fool.
What's your name, Tony?

Antonio He, he, he! Well, I thank you, cousin; he, he, he!

Lollio Good boy! Hold up your head. He can laugh; I perceive by
that he is no beast.

---

64 **buckler:** small shield.

100   **Pedro** Well, sir, If you can raise him but to any height,
Any degree of wit, might he attain,
(As I might say) to creep but on all four
Towards the chair of wit, or walk on crutches,
'Twould add an honour to your worthy pains,
105   And a great family might pray for you,
To which he should be heir, had he discretion
To claim and guide his own; assure you, sir,
He is a gentleman.
    Lollio Nay, there's nobody doubted that; at first sight I knew him
110   for a gentleman, he looks no other yet.
    Pedro Let him have good attendance and sweet lodging.
    Lollio As good as my mistress lies in, sir; and as you allow us time
and means, we can raise him to the higher degree of discretion.
    Pedro Nay, there shall no cost want, sir.
115   **Lollio** He will hardly be stretched up to the wit of a magnifico.
    Pedro Oh no, that's not to be expected, far shorter will be enough.
    Lollio I'll warrant you I make him fit to bear office in five weeks; I'll
undertake to wind him up to the wit of constable.
    Pedro If it be lower than that it might serve turn.
120   **Lollio** No, fie, to level him with a headborough, beadle, or watchman were but little better than he is; constable I'll able him. If he do
come to be a justice afterwards, let him thank the keeper. Or I'll go
further with you; say I do bring him up to my own pitch, say I make
him as wise as myself.
125   **Pedro** Why, there I would have it.
    Lollio Well, go to; either I'll be as arrant a fool as he, or he shall be
as wise as I, and then I think 'twill serve his turn.
    Pedro Nay, I do like thy wit passing well.
    Lollio Yes, you may; yet if I had not been a fool, I had had more wit
130   than I have too; remember what state you find me in.
    Pedro I will, and so leave you; your best cares, I beseech you. [*Exit.*]
    Alibius Take you none with you; leave 'em all with us.
    Antonio Oh, my cousin's gone. Cousin, cousin, oh!
    Lollio Peace, peace, Tony; you must not cry, child, you must be
135   whipped if you do. Your cousin is here still; I am your cousin, Tony.
    Antonio He, he! Then I'll not cry, if thou be'st my cousin; he, he, he!
    Lollio I were best try his wit a little, that I may know what form to
place him in.
    Alibius Ay, do, Lollio, do.
140   **Lollio** I must ask him easy questions at first. Tony, how many true
fingers has a tailor on his right hand?
    Antonio As many as on his left, cousin.
    Lollio Good; and how many on both?

---

118 constable: performed the early modern function of policeman; they were usually portrayed as stupid.
120 headborough: minor constable.   **beadle**: person who kept order in church.   **126 arrant**: notorious.

Antonio Two less than a deuce, cousin.

145 *Lollio* Very well answered. I come to you again, cousin Tony. How many fools goes to a wise man?

Antonio Forty in a day sometimes, cousin.

Lollio Forty in a day? How prove you that?

Antonio All that fall out amongst themselves, and go to a lawyer to
150 be made friends.

Lollio A parlous fool! He must sit in the fourth form at least, I perceive that. I come again, Tony. How many knaves make an honest man?

Antonio I know not that, cousin.

155 *Lollio* No, the question is too hard for you. I'll tell you, cousin, there's three knaves may make an honest man: a sergeant, a jailer, and a beadle. The sergeant catches him, the jailer holds him and the beadle lashes him; and if he be not honest then, the hangman must cure him.

160 *Antonio* Ha, ha, ha! That's fine sport, cousin.

Alibius This was too deep a question for the fool, Lollio.

Lollio Yes, this might have served yourself, though I say't. Once more, and you shall go play, Tony.

Antonio Ay, play at push-pin, cousin; ha, he!

165 *Lollio* So thou shalt. Say how many fools are here –

Antonio Two, cousin, thou and I.

Lollio Nay, y'are too forward there, Tony. Mark my question. How many fools and knaves are here? A fool before a knave, a fool behind a knave, between every two fools a knave. How many fools, how
170 many knaves?

Antonio I never learnt so far, cousin.

Alibius Thou putt'st too hard questions to him, Lollio.

Lollio I'll make him understand it easily. Cousin, stand there.

Antonio Ay, cousin.

175 *Lollio* Master, stand you next the fool.

Alibius Well, Lollio.

Lollio Here's my place. Mark now, Tony, there a fool before a knave.

Antonio That's I, cousin.

Lollio Here's a fool behind a knave, that's I; and between us two
180 fools there is a knave, that's my master; 'tis but we three, that's all.

Antonio We three, we three, cousin.

[*Madmen within.*]

1st Within Put's head i' th' pillory, the bread's too little.

2nd Within Fly, fly, and he catches the swallow.

3rd Within Give her more onion or the devil put the rope about her
185 crag.

Lollio You may hear what time of day it is, the chimes of Bedlam goes.

---

151 **parlous**: cunning. 185 **crag**: neck. 186 **Bedlam**: Bethlehem Hospital in London where the mad were confined, but widely used to mean any madhouse.

Alibius Peace, peace, or the wire comes!

3rd Within Cat whore, cat whore, her permasant, her permasant!

190 *Alibius* Peace, I say! Their hour's come, they must be fed, Lollio.

Lollio There's no hope of recovery of that Welsh madman, was undone by a mouse that spoiled him a permasant; lost his wits for't.

Alibius Go to your charge, Lollio, I'll to mine.

Lollio Go to your madmen's ward, let me alone with your fools.

195 *Alibius* And remember my last charge, Lollio. *Exit.*

Lollio Of which your patients do you think I am? Come, Tony, you must amongst your school-fellows now; there's pretty scholars amongst 'em, I can tell you, there's some of 'em at *stultus, stulta, stultum.*

200 *Antonio* I would see the madmen, cousin, if they would not bite me.

Lollio No, they shall not bite thee, Tony.

Antonio They bite when they are at dinner, do they not, coz?

Lollio They bite at dinner, indeed, Tony. Well, I hope to get credit by

205 thee; I like thee the best of all the scholars that ever I brought up, and thou shalt prove a wise man, or I'll prove a fool myself. [*Exit.*]

Act II, Scene i

[*Enter Beatrice and Jasperino.*]

Beatrice Oh sir, I'm ready now for that fair service
Which makes the name of friend sit glorious on you.
Good angels and this conduct be your guide; [*She gives him a paper.*]
Fitness of time and place is there set down, sir.

5 *Jasperino* The joy I shall return rewards my service. [*Exit.*]

Beatrice How wise is Alsemero in his friend.
It is a sign he makes his choice with judgement.
Then I appear in nothing more approved
Than making choice of him;

10 For 'tis a principle, he that can choose
That bosom well, who of his thoughts partakes,
Proves most discreet in every choice he makes.
Methinks I love now with the eyes of judgement,
And see the way to merit, clearly see it.

15 A true deserver like a diamond sparkles,
In darkness you may see him, that's in absence,
Which is the greatest darkness falls on love;
Yet he is best discerned then
With intellectual eyesight. What's Piracquo

20 My father spends his breath for? And his blessing
Is only mine as I regard his name,

189: scholars hold that this, pronounced in a stage Welsh accent, is a rebuke to a cat for failing to protect the madman's parmesan cheese.   198 *stultus* . . . : the masculine, feminine and neuter forms of the Latin for 'fool'.
2.1, 3 angels: heavenly creatures and the name of a coin.

Else it goes from me, and turns head against me,
Transformed into a curse. Some speedy way
Must be rememb'red; he's so forward too,
25   So urgent that way, scarce allows me breath
To speak to my new comforts.
    [*Enter De Flores.*]
De Flores [*aside*] Yonder's she.
Whatever ails me? Now a'late especially,
I can as well be hanged as refrain seeing her;
30   Some twenty times a day, nay, not so little,
Do I force errands, frame ways and excuses
To come into her sight, and I have small reason for't,
And less encouragement; for she baits me still
Every time worse than other, does profess herself
35   The cruellest enemy to my face in town,
At no hand can abide the sight of me,
As if danger or ill luck hung in my looks.
I must confess my face is bad enough,
But I know far worse has better fortune,
40   And not endured alone, but doted on.
And yet such pick-haired faces, chins like witches',
Here and there five hairs, whispering in a corner,
As if they grew in fear one of another,
Wrinkles like troughs, where swine-deformity swills
45   The tears of perjury that lie there like wash
Fallen from the slimy and dishonest eye;
Yet such a one plucked sweets without restraint,
And has the grace of beauty to his sweet.
Though my hard fate has thrust me out to servitude
50   I tumbled into th' world a gentleman.
She turns her blessed eye upon me now
And I'll endure all storms before I part with't.
Beatrice [*aside*] Again!
This ominous ill-faced fellow more disturbs me
55   Than all my other passions.
De Flores [*aside*] Now't begins again;
I'll stand this storm of hail though the stones pelt me.
Beatrice Thy business? What's thy business?
De Flores [*aside*] Soft and fair
60   I cannot part so soon now.
Beatrice [*aside*] The villain's fixed.
Thou standing toad-pool!
De Flores [*aside*] The shower falls amain now.
Beatrice Who sent thee? What's thy errand? Leave my sight.

---

41 **pick-haired:** prickly and sparse beard.   **45 wash:** watery discharge.

65   *De Flores* My lord your father charged me to deliver
A message to you.
Beatrice What, another since?
Do't and be hanged then, let me be rid of thee.
De Flores True service merits mercy.
70   *Beatrice* What's thy message?
De Flores Let beauty settle but in patience
You shall hear all.
Beatrice A dallying, trifling torment.
De Flores Signior Alonzo de Piracquo, lady
75   Sole brother to Tomazo de Piracquo
Beatrice Slave, when wilt make an end?
De Flores Too soon I shall.
Beatrice What all this while of him?
De Flores The said Alonzo,
80   With the foresaid Tomazo
Beatrice Yet again?
De Flores Is new alighted.
Beatrice Vengeance strike the news!
Thou thing most loathed, what cause was there in this
85   To bring thee to my sight?
De Flores My lord your father
Charged me to seek you out.
Beatrice Is there no other
To send his errand by?
90   *De Flores* It seems 'tis my luck
To be i' th' way still.
Beatrice Get thee from me.
De Flores So!
[*Aside*] Why, am not I an ass to devise ways
95   Thus to be railed at? I must see her still.
I shall have a mad qualm within this hour again,
I know't, and, like a common Garden-bull,
I do but take breath to be lugged again.
What this may bode I know not. I'll despair the less,
100   Because there's daily precedents of bad faces
Beloved beyond all reason; these foul chops
May come into favour one day 'mongst his fellows.
Wrangling has proved the mistress of good pastime.
As children cry themselves asleep, I ha' seen
105   Women have chid themselves abed to men. [*Exit.*]
Beatrice I never see this fellow, but I think
Of some harm towards me, danger's in my mind still;
I scarce leave trembling of an hour after.

---

96 **qualm:** sudden illness or attack of lust.   97   **Garden-bull:** bull used for bear-baiting in the Paris Garden in Southwark.   98 **lugged:** teased, baited.   103 **wrangling:** in oratory, the art of defending any position.

The next good mood I find my father in,
110 I'll get him quite discarded. Oh, I was
Lost in this small disturbance, and forgot
Affliction's fiercer torrent that now comes
To bear down all my comforts.
[*Enter Vermandero, Alonzo, Tomazo.*]
Vermandero Y'are both welcome,
115 But an especial one belongs to you, sir,
To whose most noble name our love presents
The addition of a son, our son Alonzo.
Alonzo The treasury of honour cannot bring forth
A title I should more rejoice in, sir.
120 *Vermandero* You have improved it well. Daughter, prepare,
The day will steal upon thee suddenly.
Beatrice [*aside*] Howe'er, I will be sure to keep the night,
If it should come so near me. [*Beatrice and Vermandero talk apart.*]
Tomazo Alonzo.
125 *Alonzo* Brother?
Tomazo In troth I see small welcome in her eye.
Alonzo Fie, you are too severe a censurer
Of love in all points, there's no bringing on you;
If lovers should mark everything a fault,
130 Affection would be like an ill-set book,
Whose faults might prove as big as half the volume.
Beatrice That's all I do entreat.
Vermandero It is but reasonable.
I'll see what my son says to't. Son Alonzo,
135 Here's a motion made but to reprieve
A maidenhead three days longer; the request
Is not far out of reason, for indeed
The former time is pinching.
Alonzo Though my joys
140 Be set back so much time as I could wish
They had been forward, yet since she desires it,
The time is set as pleasing as before; I
find no gladness wanting.
Vermandero May I ever meet it in that point still.
145 Y'are nobly welcome, sirs. [*Exit Vermandero and Beatrice.*]
Tomazo So, did you mark the dullness of her parting now?
Alonzo What dullness? Thou art so exceptious still.
Tomazo Why, let it go then; I am but a fool
To mark your harms so heedfully.
150 *Alonzo* Where's the oversight?
Tomazo Come, your faith's cozened in her, strongly cozened;
Unsettle your affection with all speed

---

122 **keep the night:** stay on guard through the night.   131 **faults:** printing errors.   147 **exceptious:** given to making objections.   151 **cozened:** cheated.

Wisdom can bring it to, your peace is ruined else.
Think what a torment 'tis to marry one
155 Whose heart is leaped into another's bosom.
If ever pleasure she receive from thee,
It comes not in thy name, or of thy gift.
She lies but with another in thine arms;
He the half-father unto all thy children
160 In the conception; if he get 'em not,
She helps to get 'em for him; and how dangerous
And shameful her restraint may go in time to,
It is not to be thought on without sufferings.
Alonzo You speak as if she loved some other, then.
165 *Tomazo* Do you apprehend so slowly?
Alonzo Nay, and that
Be your fear only, I am safe enough.
Preserve your friendship and your counsel, brother,
For times of more distress; I should depart
170 An enemy, a dangerous, deadly one,
To any but thyself that should but think
She knew the meaning of inconstancy,
Much less the use and practice; yet w'are friends.
Pray, let no more be urged; I can endure
175 Much till I meet an injury to her,
Then I am not myself. Farewell, sweet brother;
How much w'are bound to heaven to depart lovingly. [*Exit.*]
Tomazo Why, here is love's tame madness; thus a man
Quickly steals into his vexation. [*Exit.*]

Act II, Scene ii

[*Enter Diaphanta and Alsemero.*]
Diaphanta The place is my charge, you have kept your hour,
And the reward of a just meeting bless you.
I hear my lady coming; complete gentleman,
I dare not be too busy with my praises,
5 Th'are dangerous things to deal with. [*Exit.*]
Alsemero This goes well;
These women are the ladies' cabinets,
Things of most precious trust are locked into 'em.
[*Enter Beatrice.*]
Beatrice I have within mine eye all my desires;
10 Requests that holy prayers ascend heaven for,
And brings 'em down to furnish our defects,
Come not more sweet to our necessities
Than thou unto my wishes.
Alsemero W'are so like

15   In our expressions, lady, that unless I borrow
   The same words, I shall never find their equals. [*Kisses her.*]
   Beatrice How happy were this meeting, this embrace,
   If it were free from envy. This poor kiss,
   It has an enemy, a hateful one,
20   That wishes poison to't; how well were I now
   If there were none such name known as Piracquo,
   Nor no such tie as the command of parents.
   I should be but too much blessed.
   Alsemero One good service
25   Would strike off both your fears, and I'll go near it too
   Since you are so distressed; remove the cause,
   The command ceases; so there's two fears blown out
   With one and the same blast.
   Beatrice Pray, let me find you, sir.
30   What might that service be, so strangely happy?
   Alsemero The honourablest piece 'bout man, valour.
   I'll send a challenge to Piracquo instantly.
   Beatrice How? Call you that extinguishing of fear,
   When 'tis the only way to keep it flaming?
35   Are not you ventured in the action,
   That's all my joys and comforts? Pray, no more, sir.
   Say you prevailed, you're danger's and not mine then;
   The law would claim you from me, or obscurity
   Be made the grave to bury you alive.
40   I'm glad these thoughts come forth; oh, keep not one
   Of this condition, sir; here was a course
   Found to bring sorrow on her way to death;
   The tears would ne'er ha' dried till dust had choked 'em.
   [*Aside*] Blood-guiltiness becomes a fouler visage,
45   And now I think on one. I was to blame,
   I ha' marred so good a market with my scorn;
   'T had been done questionless. The ugliest creature
   Creation framed for some use, yet to see
   I could not mark so much where it should be.
50   **Alsemero** Lady –
   Beatrice [*aside*] Why, men of art make much of poison,
   Keep one to expel another; where was my art?
   Alsemero Lady, you hear not me.
   Beatrice I do especially, sir;
55   The present times are not so sure of our side
   As those hereafter may be; we must use 'em then
   As thrifty fools their wealth, sparingly now,
   Till the time opens.

---

40 one: one thought.   **45 one:** one with a foul visage.   **46 marred** . . . . : a proverbial phrase – she has ruined a good market by her insults.

Alsemero You teach wisdom, lady.
60 *Beatrice* Within there. Diaphanta!
[*Enter Diaphanta.*]
Diaphanta Do you call, madam?
Beatrice Perfect your service, and conduct this gentleman
The private way you brought him.
Diaphanta I shall, madam.
65 *Alsemero* My love's as firm as love e'er built upon.
[*Exit Diaphanta and Alsemero. Enter De Flores.*]
De Flores [*aside*] I have watched this meeting, and do wonder much
What shall become of t'other. I'm sure both
Cannot be served unless she transgress; happily
Then I'll put in for one, for if a woman
70 Fly from one point, from him she makes a husband,
She spreads and mounts then like arithmetic,
One, ten, a hundred, a thousand, ten thousand,
Proves in time sutler to an army royal.
Now do I look to be most richly railed at,
75 Yet I must see her.
Beatrice [*aside*] Why, put case I loathed him
As much as youth and beauty hates a sepulchre,
Must I needs show it? Cannot I keep that secret
And serve my turn upon him? See, he's here.
80 De Flores!
De Flores [*aside*] Ha, I shall run mad with joy!
She called me fairly by my name, De Flores,
And neither rogue nor rascal.
Beatrice What ha you done
85 To your face a'late? Y'have met with some good physician;
Y'have pruned yourself, methinks; you were not wont
To look so amorously.
De Flores [*aside*] Not I.
'Tis the same physnomy, to a hair and pimple,
90 Which she called scurvy scarce an hour ago;
How is this?
Beatrice Come hither; nearer, man.
De Flores [*aside*] I'm up to the chin in heaven!
Beatrice [*touches his face*] Turn, let me see.
95 Faugh, 'tis but the heat of the liver, I perceiv't;
I thought it had been worse.
De Flores [*aside*] Her fingers touched me!
She smells all amber.
Beatrice I'll make a water for you shall cleanse this
100 Within a fortnight.

---

73 **sutler:** supplier.   76 **put case:** allow for the fact.   86 **pruned:** preened, as a bird does to its feathers.   86 **look so amorously:** appear so attractively.   95 **liver:** traditionally the place of excessive passion.   99 **water:** wash.

De Flores With your own hands, lady?

Beatrice Yes, mine own, sir; in a work of cure
I'll trust no other.

De Flores [*aside*] 'Tis half an act of pleasure
105   To hear her talk thus to me.

Beatrice When w'are used
To a hard face, 'tis not so unpleasing;
It mends still in opinion, hourly mends,
I see it by experience.

110 **De Flores** [*aside*] I was blessed
To light upon this minute; I'll make use on't.

Beatrice Hardness becomes the visage of a man well,
It argues service, resolution, manhood,
If cause were of employment.

115 **De Flores** 'Twould be soon seen,
If e'er your ladyship had cause to use it.
I would but wish the honour of a service
So happy as that mounts to.

Beatrice We shall try you. Oh! My De Flores!

120 **De Flores** [*aside*] How's that?
She calls me hers already, 'my De Flores'.
You were about to sigh out somewhat, madam?

Beatrice No, was I? I forgot. Oh!

De Flores There tis again, the very fellow on't.

125 **Beatrice** You are too quick, sir.

De Flores There's no excuse for't now; I heard it twice, madam;
That sigh would fain have utterance, take pity on't,
And lend it a free word; 'las, how it labours
For liberty! I hear the murmur yet

130 Beat at your bosom.

Beatrice Would creation –

De Flores Ay, well said, that's it.

Beatrice Had formed me man.

De Flores Nay, that's not it.

135 **Beatrice** Oh, 'tis the soul of freedom!
I should not then be forced to marry one
I hate beyond all depths; I should have power
Then to oppose my loathings, nay, remove 'em
For ever from my sight.

140 **De Flores** [*aside*] O blest occasion!
Without change to your sex, you have your wishes.
Claim so much man in me.

Beatrice In thee, De Flores? There's small cause for that.

De Flores Put it not from me;

145 It's a service that I kneel for to you. [*Kneels.*]

Beatrice You are too violent to mean faithfully;

There's horror in my service, blood and danger;
Can those be things to sue for?
De Flores If you knew
150 How sweet it were to me to be employed
In any act of yours, you would say then
I failed, and used not reverence enough
When I receive the charge on't.
Beatrice [*aside*] This is much, methinks;
155 Belike his wants are greedy, and to such
Gold tastes like angels' food. Rise.
De Flores I'll have the work first.
Beatrice [*aside*] Possible his need is strong upon him.
There's to encourage thee; [*Gives him money.*]
160 As thou art forward and thy service dangerous,
Thy reward shall be precious.
De Flores That I have thought on;
I have assured myself of that beforehand,
And know it will be precious, the thought ravishes.
165 **Beatrice** Then take him to thy fury!
De Flores I thirst for him.
Beatrice Alonzo de Piracquo.
De Flores His end's upon him; he shall be seen no more.
Beatrice How lovely now dost thou appear to me.
170 Never was man dearlier rewarded.
De Flores I do think of that.
Beatrice Be wondrous careful in the execution.
De Flores Why, are not both our lives upon the cast?
Beatrice Then I throw all my fears upon thy service.
175 **De Flores** They ne'er shall rise to hurt you.
Beatrice When the deed's done
I'll furnish thee with all things for thy flight;
Thou may'st live bravely in another country.
De Flores Ay, ay, we'll talk of that hereafter.
180 **Beatrice** [*aside*] I shall rid myself
Of two inveterate loathings at one time,
Piracquo, and his dog-face. [*Exit.*]
De Flores Oh my blood!
Methinks I feel her in mine arms already,
185 Her wanton fingers combing out this beard,
And, being pleased, praising this bad face.
Hunger and pleasure, they'll commend sometimes
Slovenly dishes, and feed heartily on 'em,
Nay, which is stranger, refuse daintier for 'em.
190 Some women are odd feeders. I'm too loud.
Here comes the man goes supperless to bed,
Yet shall not rise tomorrow to his dinner.

---

173 **cast:** throw of dice; the assault on Piracquo.

[*Enter Alonzo.*]
Alonzo De Flores.
De Flores My kind, honourable lord.
195 **Alonzo** I am glad I ha' met with thee.
De Flores Sir?
Alonzo Thou canst show me the full strength of the castle?
De Flores That I can, sir.
Alonzo I much desire it.
200 **De Flores** And if the ways and straits
Of some of the passages be not too tedious for you,
I will assure you, worth your time and sight, my lord.
Alonzo Puh, that shall be no hindrance.
De Flores I'll be your servant then.
205 'Tis now near dinner time; 'gainst your lordship's rising
I'll have the keys about me.
Alonzo Thanks, kind De Flores.
De Flores [*aside*] He's safely thrust upon me beyond hopes. [*Exit.*]

Act III, Scene i

[*Enter Alonzo and De Flores. De Flores hides a naked rapier.*]
De Flores Yes, here are all the keys. I was afraid, my lord,
I'd wanted for the postern, this is it.
I've all, I've all, my lord; this for the sconce.
Alonzo 'Tis a most spacious and impregnable fort.
5 **De Flores** You'll tell me more, my lord. This descent
Is somewhat narrow, we shall never pass
Well with our weapons, they'll but trouble us.
Alonzo Thou say'st true. [*Takes off his sword.*]
De Flores Pray let me help your lordship.
10 **Alonzo** 'Tis done. Thanks, kind De Flores.
De Flores Here are hooks, my lord,
To hang such things on purpose. [*Hangs up the swords.*]
Alonzo Lead, I'll follow thee.
[*Exit at one door and enter at the other.*]

Act III, Scene ii

De Flores All this is nothing; you shall see anon
A place you little dream on.
Alonzo I am glad I have this leisure;
All your master's house imagine I ha' taken a gondola.
5 **De Flores** All but myself, sir; [*aside*] which makes up my safety.
My lord, I'll place you at a casement here
Will show you the full strength of all the castle.
Look, spend your eye awhile upon that object.

3.1,3 sconce: small fort.

Alonzo Here's rich variety, De Flores.
10 *De Flores* Yes, sir.
Alonzo Goodly munition.
De Flores Ay, there's ordnance, sir,
No bastard metal; will ring you a peal like bells
At great men's funerals. Keep your eye straight, my lord;
15 Take special notice of that sconce before you,
There you may dwell awhile. [*Takes out the rapier.*]
Alonzo I am upon't.
De Flores And so am I. [*Stabs him.*]
Alonzo De Flores! Oh, De Flores!
20 Whose malice hast thou put on?
De Flores Do you question
A work of secrecy? I must silence. [*Stabs him.*]
Alonzo Oh, oh, oh!
De Flores I must silence. [*Stabs him.*]
25 So here's an undertaking well accomplished.
This vault serves to good use now. Ha, what's that
Threw sparkles in my eye? Oh, 'tis a diamond
He wears upon his finger; it was well found,
This will approve the work. What, so fast on?
30 Not part in death? I'll take a speedy course then,
Finger and all shall off. [*Cuts off the finger.*] So now I'll clear
The passages from all suspect or fear. [*Exit with body.*]

Act III, Scene iii

[*Enter Isabella and Lollio.*]
Isabella Why, sirrah? Whence have you commission
To fetter the doors against me?
If you keep me in a cage, pray whistle to me,
Let me be doing something.
5 *Lollio* You shall be doing, if it please you; I'll whistle to you if you'll
pipe after.
Isabella Is it your master's pleasure or your own,
To keep me in this pinfold?
Lollio 'Tis for my master's pleasure, lest being taken in another
10 man's corn, you might be pounded in another place.
Isabella 'Tis very well, and he'll prove very wise.
Lollio He says you have company enough in the house, if you please
to be sociable, of all sorts of people.
Isabella Of all sorts? Why, here's none but fools and madmen.
15 *Lollio* Very well, and where will you find any other, if you should
go abroad? There's my master and I to boot too.

3.2,12 **ordnance**: cannons arranged in ordered ranks.   13 **bastard metal**: metal mixed with impurities.
3.3,8 **pinfold**: pen; suggesting she is kept no better than swine.

Isabella Of either sort one, a madman and a fool.

Lollio I would ev'n participate of both then, if I were as you; I know y'are half mad already, be half foolish too.

20 **Isabella** Y'are a brave, saucy rascal! Come on, sir,
Afford me then the pleasure of your bedlam;
You were commending once today to me
Your last-come lunatic; what a proper
Body there was without brains to guide it,

25 And what a pitiful delight appeared
In that defect, as if your wisdom had found
A mirth in madness. Pray, sir, let me partake,
If there be such a pleasure.

Lollio If I do not show you the handsomest, discreetest madman,

30 one that I may call the understanding madman, then say I am a fool.

Isabella Well, a match, I will say so.

Lollio When you have a taste of the madman, you shall, if you please, see Fools' College, o' th' side; I seldom lock there, 'tis but shooting a bolt or two, and you are amongst 'em. [*Exit.*]

35 [*Enter presently.*] Come on, sir, let me see how handsomely you'll behave yourself now.

[*Enter Franciscus.*]

Franciscus How sweetly she looks! Oh, but there's a wrinkle in her brow as deep as philosophy. Anacreon, drink to my mistress' health, I'll pledge it; stay, stay, there's a spider in the cup! No, 'tis but a

40 grape-stone; swallow it, fear nothing, poet; so, so, lift higher.

Isabella Alack, alack, 'tis too full of pity
To be laughed at. How fell he mad? Canst thou tell?

Lollio For love, mistress; he was a pretty poet too, and that set him forwards first; the Muses then forsook him; he ran mad for a

45 chambermaid, yet she was but a dwarf neither.

Franciscus Hail, bright Titania!
Why stand'st thou idle on these flow'ry banks?
Oberon is dancing with his Dryads;
I'll gather daisies, primrose, violets,

50 And bind them in a verse of poesy.

Lollio Not too near; you see your danger. [*Shows the whip.*]

Franciscus Oh, hold thy hand, great Diomed.
Thou feed'st thy horses well, they shall obey thee;
Get up, Bucephalus kneels. [*Kneels.*]

55 **Lollio** You see how I awe my flock; a shepherd has not his dog at more obedience.

Isabella His conscience is unquiet; sure that was
The cause of this. A proper gentleman.

Franciscus Come hither, Esculapius; hide the poison.

---

38 **Anacreon:** chocked to death on a grape-stone in a cup of wine. 46 **Titania:** Queen of Faery. 48 **Oberon:** King of Faery. **Dryads:** wood nymphs. 52 **Diomed:** king who fed his horses on human flesh. 54 **Bucephalus:** Alexander the Great's horse. 59 **Esculapius:** god of medicine.

60   **Lollio** Well, 'tis hid. [*Hides the whip. Franciscus rises.*]
     Franciscus Didst thou never hear of one Tiresias, a famous poet?
     Lollio Yes, that kept tame wild-geese.
     Franciscus That's he; I am the man.
     Lollio No!
65   **Franciscus** Yes, but make no words on't;
     I was a man seven years ago.
     Lollio A stripling I think you might.
     Franciscus Now I'm a woman, all feminine.
     Lollio I would I might see that.
70   **Franciscus** Juno struck me blind.
     Lollio I'll ne'er believe that; for a woman, they say, has an eye more
     than a man.
     Franciscus I say she struck me blind.
     Lollio And Luna made you mad; you have two trades to beg with.
75   **Franciscus** Luna is now big-bellied, and there's room
     For both of us to ride with Hecate;
     I'll drag thee up into her silver sphere,
     And there we'll kick the dog, and beat the bush,
     That barks against the witches of the night;
80   The swift lycanthropi that walks the round,
     We'll tear their wolvish skins and save the sheep. [*Tries to seize Lollio.*]
     Lollio Is't come to this? Nay then, my poison comes forth again.
     [*Shows the whip*] Mad slave, indeed, abuse your keeper!
     Isabella I prithee, hence with him, now he grows dangerous.
85   **Franciscus** [*sings*] Sweet love pity me. Give me leave to lie with
     thee.
     Lollio No, I'll see you wiser first; to your own kennel.
     Franciscus No noise, she sleeps, draw all the curtains round;
     Let no soft sound molest the pretty soul
90   But love, and love creeps in at a mouse-hole.
     Lollio I would you would get into your hole. [*Exit Franciscus.*]
     Now, mistress, I will bring you another sort, you shall be fooled
     another while; Tony, come hither, Tony; look who's yonder, Tony.
     [*Enter Antonio.*]
     Antonio Cousin, is it not my aunt?
95   **Lollio** Yes, 'tis one of 'em, Tony.
     Antonio He, he! How do you, uncle?
     Lollio Fear him not, mistress, 'tis a gentle nidget; you may play with
     him, as safely with him as with his bauble.
     Isabella How long has thou been a fool?
100   **Antonio** Ever since I came hither, cousin.
     Isabella Cousin? I'm none of thy cousins, fool.

---

61 **Tiresias:** prophet changed from a man to a woman and back again after 7 years.   74 **Luna:** the moon, a cause
of madness.   75 **big-bellied:** pregnant.   76 **Hecate:** goddess of witchcraft.   80 **lycanthropi:** people who think
themselves wolves.   97 **nidget:** contracted from an idiot.   98 **bauble:** fool's stick, with the implication of penis.

Lollio O mistress, fools have always so much wit as to claim their kindred.

Madman [*within*] Bounce, bounce, he falls, he falls!

105 **Isabella** Hark you, your scholars in the upper room are out of order.

Lollio Must I come amongst you there? Keep you the fool, mistress; I'll go up and play left-handed Orlando amongst the madmen. [*Exit.*]

Isabella Well, sir.

Antonio 'Tis opportuneful now, sweet lady! Nay,

110 Cast no amazing eye upon this change.

Isabella Ha!

Antonio This shape of folly shrouds your dearest love,
The truest servant to your powerful beauties,
Whose magic had this force thus to transform me.

115 **Isabella** You are a fine fool indeed.

Antonio Oh, 'tis not strange.
Love has an intellect that runs through all
The scrutinous sciences, and, like
A cunning poet, catches a quantity

120 Of every knowledge, yet brings all home
Into one mystery, into one secret
That he proceeds in.

Isabella Y'are a parlous fool.

Antonio No danger in me; I bring naught but love

125 And his soft-wounding shafts to strike you with.
Try but one arrow; if it hurt you,
I'll stand you twenty back in recompense.

Isabella A forward fool too!

Antonio This was love's teaching;

130 A thousand ways he fashioned out my way,
And this I found the safest and the nearest
To tread the Galaxia to my star.

Isabella Profound, withal. Certain, you dreamed of this;
Love never taught it waking.

135 **Antonio** Take no acquaintance
Of these outward follies; there is within
A gentleman that loves you.

Isabella When I see him,
I'll speak with him; so in the meantime keep

135 Your habit, it becomes you well enough.
As you are a gentleman, I'll not discover you,
That's all the favour that you must expect;
When you are weary, you may leave the school,
For all this while you have but played the fool. [*Enter Lollio.*]

140 **Antonio** And must again. He, he! I thank you cousin;
I'll be your valentine tomorrow morning.

---

107 Orlando: the hero of Ariosto's epic *Orlando Furioso*, used mockingly, hence left-handed. **132 Galaxia:** the Milky Way.

Lollio How do you like the fool, mistress?

Isabella Passing well, sir.

Lollio Is he not witty, pretty well for a fool?

145 *Isabella* If he hold on as he begins, he is like to come to something.

Lollio Ay, thank a good tutor; you may put him to't; he begins to answer pretty hard questions. Tony, how many is five times six?

Antonio Five times six is six times five.

Lollio What arithmetician could have answered better? How many

150 is one hundred and seven?

Antonio One hundred and seven is seven hundred and one, cousin.

Lollio This is no wit to speak on; will you be rid of the fool now?

Isabella By no means, let him stay a little.

Madman [*within*] Catch there, catch the last couple in hell.

155 *Lollio* Again! Must I come amongst you? Would my master were come home. I am not able to govern both these wards together. [*Exit.*]

Antonio Why should a minute of love's hour be lost?

Isabella Fie, out again! I had rather you kept

Your other posture; you become not your tongue

160 When you speak from your clothes.

Antonio How can he freeze

Lives near so sweet a warmth? Shall I alone

Walk through the orchard of the Hesperides,

And cowardly not dare to pull an apple?

165 This with the red cheeks I must venture for. [*Tries to kiss her.*]

[*Enter Lollio above.*]

Isabella Take heed, there's giants keep 'em.

Lollio [*aside*] How now, fool, are you good at that? Have you read Lipsius? He's past *Ars Amandi*; I believe I must put harder questions to him, I perceive that.

170 *Isabella* You are bold without fear too.

Antonio What should I fear,

Having all joys about me? Do you smile,

And love shall play the wanton on your lip,

Meet and retire, retire and meet again;

175 Look you but cheerfully, and in your eyes

I shall behold mine own deformity,

And dress myself up fairer; I know this shape

Becomes me not, but in those bright mirrors

I shall array me handsomely.

180 *Lollio* Cuckoo, cuckoo. [*Exit.*]

[*Enter Madmen, some as birds, other as beasts.*]

Antonio What are these?

Isabella Of fear enough to part us;

Yet they are but our schools of lunatics,

---

146 **put him to't**: test him. 163 **Hesperides**: a classic heroic quest is the sailing to the end of the earth to pick a golden apple from the garden of the Hesperides. 168 **Lipsius**: Renaissance philosopher, here invoked for the word play on lips. **past *Ars Amandi***: he has studied beyond Ovid's *Art of Love*.

That act their fantasies in any shapes
185 Suiting their present thoughts; if sad, they cry;
If mirth be their conceit, they laugh again.
Sometimes they imitate the beasts and birds,
Singing, or howling, braying, barking; all
As their wild fancies prompt 'em. [*Exit Madmen.*]
190 **Antonio** These are no fears. [*Enter Lollio.*]
Isabella But here's a large one, my man.
Antonio Ha, he! That's fine sport indeed, cousin.
Lollio I would my master were come home, 'tis too much for one
shepherd to govern two of these flocks; nor can I believe that one
195 churchman can instruct two benefices at once; there will be some
incurable mad of the one side, and very fools on the other. Come,
Tony.
Antonio Prithee, cousin, let me stay here still.
Lollio No, you must to your book now, you have played sufficiently.
200 **Isabella** Your fool is grown wondrous witty.
Lollio Well, I'll say nothing; but I do not think but he will put you
down one of these days. [*Exit Lollio and Antonio.*]
Isabella Here the restrained current might make breach,
Spite of the watchful bankers; would a woman stray,
205 She need not gad abroad to seek her sin,
It would be brought home one ways or other.
The needle's point will to the fixed north,
Such drawing arctics women's beauties are.
[*Enter Lollio.*]
Lollio How dost thou, sweet rogue?
210 **Isabella** How now?
Lollio Come, there are degrees, one fool may be better than
another.
Isabella What s the matter?
Lollio Nay, if thou giv'st thy mind to fool's flesh, have at thee!
[*Tries to kiss her.*]
215 **Isabella** You bold slave, you.
Lollio I could follow now as t'other fool did.
'What should I fear,
Having all joys about me? Do you but smile,
And love shall play the wanton on your lip,
220 Meet and retire, retire and meet again;
Look you but cheerfully, and in your eyes
I shall behold my own deformity,
And dress myself up fairer; I know this shape
Becomes me not'; and so as it follows. But is not this the more
225 foolish way? Come, sweet rogue; kiss me, my little Lacedemonian.

---

195 **benefices**: parishes.   225 **Lacedemonian**: Spartan, reference to Helen of Troy who abandoned her Spartan
husband to elope with Paris.

Let me feel how thy pulses beat; thou hast a thing about thee would
do a man pleasure, I'll lay my hand on't.
Isabella Sirrah, no more! I see you have discovered
This love's knight-errant, who hath made adventure
230   For purchase of my love; be silent, mute,
Mute as a statue, or his injunction
For me enjoying, shall be to cut thy throat.
I'll do it, though for no other purpose,
And be sure he'll not refuse it.
235   **Lollio** My share, that's all. I'll have my fool's part with you.
Isabella No more. Your master.
[*Enter Alibius.*]
Alibius Sweet, how dost thou?
Isabella Your bounden servant, sir.
Alibius Fie, fie, sweetheart, No more of that.
240   **Isabella** You were best lock me up.
Alibius In my arms and bosom, my sweet Isabella
I'll lock thee up most nearly. Lollio,
We have employment, we have task in hand;
At noble Vermandero's, our castle-captain,
245   There is a nuptial to be solemnized
(Beatrice-Joanna, his fair daughter, bride)
For which the gentleman hath bespoke our pains:
A mixture of our madmen and our fools,
To finish (as it were) and make the fag
250   Of all the revels, the third night from the first;
Only an unexpected passage over,
To make a frightful pleasure, that is all,
But not the all I aim at; could we so act it,
To teach it in a wild, distracted measure,
255   Though out of form and figure, breaking time's head,
It were no matter; 'twould be healed again
In one age or other, if not in this.
This, this, Lollio, there's a good reward begun,
And will beget a bounty, be it known.
260   **Lollio** This is easy, sir, I'll warrant you. You have about you fools and
madmen that can dance very well, and 'tis no wonder your best
dancers are not the wisest men; the reason is, with often jumping
they jolt their brains down into their feet, that their wits lie more in
their heels than in their heads.
265   **Alibius** Honest Lollio, thou giv'st me a good reason,
And a comfort in it.
Isabella Y'have a fine trade on't,
Madmen and fools are a staple commodity.

---

249 fag: conclusion.   **255 breaking time's head:** unrhythmic.

270   **Alibius** Oh, wife, we must eat, wear clothes, and live;
        Just at the lawyer's haven we arrive;
        By madmen and by fools we both do thrive. [*Exit.*]

Act III, Scene iv

[*Enter Vermandero, Alsemero, Jasperino and Beatrice.*]
Vermandero Valencia speaks so nobly of you, sir,
I wish I had a daughter now for you.
Alsemero The fellow of this creature were a partner
For a king's love.
5   **Vermandero** I had her fellow once, sir,
But Heaven has married her to joys eternal;
'Twere sin to wish her in this vale again.
Come, sir, your friend and you shall see the pleasures
Which my health chiefly joys in.
10   **Alsemero** I hear the beauty of this seat largely.
Vermandero It falls much short of that. [*Exit all but Beatrice.*]
Beatrice So, here's one step
Into my father's favour; time will fix him.
I have got him now the liberty of the house;
15   So wisdom by degrees works out her freedom,
And if that eye be darkened that offends me –
I wait but that eclipse – this gentleman
Shall soon shine glorious in my father's liking,
Through the refulgent virtue of my love.
[*Enter De Flores.*]
20   **De Flores** [*aside*] My thoughts are at a banquet; for the deed,
I feel no weight in't, 'tis but light and cheap
For the sweet recompense that I set down for't.
Beatrice De Flores.
De Flores Lady?
25   **Beatrice** Thy looks promise cheerfully.
De Flores All things are answerable: time, circumstance,
Your wishes, and my service.
Beatrice Is it done then?
De Flores Piracquo is no more.
30   **Beatrice** My joys start at mine eyes; our sweet'st delights
Are evermore born weeping.
De Flores I've a token for you.
Beatrice For me?
De Flores But it was sent somewhat unwillingly;
35   I could not get the ring without the finger. [*Shows her the finger.*]
Beatrice Bless me! What hast thou done?
De Flores Why, is that more
Than killing the whole man? I cut his heart-strings.

---

270 **lawyer's haven**: wealth, gained from fools and madmen.   **3.4,19 refulgent**: radiant.

A greedy hand thrust in a dish at court
40 In a mistake hath had as much as this.
Beatrice 'Tis the first token my father made me send him.
De Flores And I made him send it back again
For his last token; I was loath to leave it,
And I'm sure dead men have no use of jewels.
45 He was as loath to part with't, for it stuck
As if the flesh and it were both one substance.
Beatrice At the stag's fall the keeper has his fees,
'Tis soon applied; all dead men's fees are yours, sir.
I pray, bury the finger, but the stone
50 You may make use on shortly; the true value,
Take't of my truth, is near three hundred ducats.
De Flores 'Twill hardly buy a capcase for one's conscience, though,
To keep it from the worm, as fine as 'tis.
Well, being my fees, I'll take it;
55 Great men have taught me that, or else my merit
Would scorn the way on't.
Beatrice It might justly, sir;
Why, thou mistak'st, De Flores, 'tis not given
In state of recompense.
60 **De Flores** No, I hope so, lady,
You should soon witness my contempt to't then.
Beatrice Prithee, thou look'st as if thou wert offended.
De Flores That were strange, lady; 'tis not possible
My service should draw such a cause from you.
65 Offended? Could you think so? That were much
For one of my performance, and so warm
Yet in my service.
Beatrice 'Twere misery in me to give you cause, sir.
Look you, sir, here's three thousand golden florins.
70 I have not meanly thought upon thy merit.
De Flores What, salary? Now you move me!
Beatrice How De Flores?
De Flores Do you place me in the rank of verminous fellows,
To destroy things for wages? Offer gold?
75 The life blood of man! Is anything
Valued too precious for my recompense?
Beatrice I understand thee not.
De Flores I could ha' hired
A journeyman in murder at this rate,
80 And mine own conscience might have slept at ease
And have had the work brought home.
Beatrice [*aside*] I'm in a labyrinth;
What will content him? I would fain be rid of him.
I'll double the sum, sir.

---

52 capcase: travelling bag.

85   *De Flores* You take a course
To double my vexation, that's the good you do.
Beatrice [*aside*] Bless me! I am now in worse plight than I was;
I know not what will please him.
For my fear's sake, I prithee make away with all speed possible.
90   And if thou be'st so modest not to name
The sum that will content thee, paper blushes not;
Send thy demand in writing, it shall follow thee.
But prithee take thy flight.
De Flores You must fly too then.
95   *Beatrice* I?
De Flores I'll not stir a foot else.
Beatrice What's your meaning?
De Flores Why, are not you as guilty, in, I'm sure,
As deep as I? And we should stick together.
100   Come, your fears counsel you but ill; my absence
Would draw suspect upon you instantly;
There were no rescue for you.
Beatrice [*aside*] He speaks home.
De Flores Nor is it fit we two, engaged so jointly,
105   Should part and live asunder. [*Tries to kiss her.*]
Beatrice How now, sir?
This shows not well.
De Flores What makes your lip so strange?
This must not be betwixt us.
110   *Beatrice* [*aside*] The man talks wildly.
De Flores Come, kiss me with a zeal now.
Beatrice [*aside*] Heaven, I doubt him!
De Flores I will not stand so long to beg 'em shortly.
Beatrice Take heed, De Flores, of forgetfulness,
115   'Twill soon betray us.
De Flores Take you heed first;
Faith, y'are grown much forgetful, y'are to blame in't.
Beatrice [*aside*] He's bold, and I am blamed for't!
De Flores I have eased
120   You of your trouble, think on't; I'm in pain,
And must be eased of you; 'tis a charity;
Justice invites your blood to understand me.
Beatrice I dare not.
De Flores Quickly!
125   *Beatrice* Oh, I never shall!
Speak it yet further off that I may lose
What has been spoken, and no sound remain on't.
I would not hear so much offence again
For such another deed.
130   *De Flores* Soft, lady, soft;
The last is not yet paid for. Oh, this act

Has put me into spirit; I was as greedy on't
As the parched earth of moisture, when the clouds weep.
Did you not mark, I wrought myself into't,
135   Nay, sued and kneeled for't? Why was all that pains took?
You see I have thrown contempt upon your gold;
Not that I want it not, for I do piteously;
In order I will come unto't, and make use on't.
But 'twas not held so precious to begin with,
140   For I place wealth after the heels of pleasure;
And were I not resolved in my belief
That thy virginity were perfect in thee,
I should but take my recompense with grudging,
As if I had but half my hopes I agreed for.
145   **Beatrice** Why, 'tis impossible thou canst be so wicked,
Or shelter such a cunning cruelty,
To make his death the murderer of my honour!
Thy language is so bold and vicious,
I cannot see which way I can forgive it
150   With any modesty.
De Flores Push, you forget yourself!
A woman dipped in blood, and talk of modesty.
Beatrice Oh misery of sin! Would I had been bound
Perpetually unto my living hate
155   In that Piracquo, than to hear these words.
Think but upon the distance that creation
Set 'twixt thy blood and mine, and keep thee there.
De Flores Look but into your conscience, read me there,
'Tis a true book, you'll find me there your equal.
160   Push! Fly not to your birth, but settle you
In what the act has made you, y'are no more now;
You must forget your parentage to me;
Y'are the deed's creature, by that name
You lost your first condition, and I challenge you,
165   As peace and innocency has turned you out,
And made you one with me.
Beatrice With thee, foul villain?
De Flores Yes, my fair murd'ress! Do you urge me?
Though thou writ'st maid, thou whore in thy affection.
170   'Twas changed from thy first love, and that's a kind
Of whoredom in thy heart; and he's changed now,
To bring thy second on, thy Alsemero,
Whom, by all sweets that ever darkness tasted,
If I enjoy thee not, thou ne'er enjoy'st;
175   I'll blast the hopes and joys of marriage,
I'll confess all; my life I rate at nothing.
Beatrice De Flores!
De Flores I shall rest from all lovers' plagues then;

I live in pain now; that shooting eye
180 Will burn my heart to cinders.
Beatrice Oh, sir, hear me.
De Flores She that in life and love refuses me,
In death and shame my partner she shall be.
Beatrice Stay, hear me once for all; I make thee master
185 Of all the wealth I have in gold and jewels;
Let me go poor unto my bed with honour,
And I am rich in all things. [*Kneels.*]
De Flores Let this silence thee,
The wealth of all Valencia shall not buy
190 My pleasure from me;
Can you weep fate from its determined purpose?
So soon may you weep me.
Beatrice Vengeance begins;
Murder, I see, is followed by more sins.
195 Was my creation in the womb so cursed,
It must engender with a viper first?
De Flores Come, rise, and shroud your blushes in my bosom;
Silence is one of pleasure's best receipts;
Thy peace is wrought for ever in this yielding.
200 'Las, how the turtle pants! Thou'lt love anon
What thou so fear'st and faint'st to venture on.

Act IV, Scene i

[*Dumb show: Enter Gentlemen, Vermandero meeting them with action
of wonderment at the flight of Piracquo. Enter Alsemero, with Jasperino
and Gallants; Vermandero points to him, the Gentlemen seeming to
applaud the choice. Exit in procession Vermandero, Alsemero, Jasperino,
and Gentlemen; Beatrice the bride following in great state, accompanied
with Diaphanta, Isabella, and other Gentlewomen; De Flores afterall,
smiling at the accident; Alonzo's ghost appears to De Flores in the midst
of his smile, startles him, showing him the hand whose finger he had cut
off. They pass over in great solemnity. Enter Beatrice.*]
Beatrice This fellow has undone me endlessly;
Never was bride so fearfully distressed.
The more I think upon th' ensuing night,
And whom I am to cope with in embraces,
5 One who's ennobled both in blood and mind,
So clear in understanding [that's my plague now],
Before whose judgement will my fault appear
Like malefactors' crimes before tribunals,
There is no hiding on't, the more I dive
10 Into my own distress. How a wise man
Stands for a great calamity. There's no venturing

---

11 Stands for: signifies.

Into his bed – what course soe'er I light upon –
Without my shame, which may grow up to danger;
He cannot but in justice strangle me
15 As I lie by him, as a cheater use me.
'Tis a precious craft to play with a false die
Before a cunning gamester. Here's his closet,
The key left in't, and he abroad i'th' park;
Sure 'twas forgot; I'll be so bold as look in't. [*Opens the closet.*]
20 Bless me! A right physician's closet 'tis,
Set round with vials; every one her mark too.
Sure he does practise physic for his own use,
Which may be safely called your great man's wisdom.
What manuscript lies here? *The Book of Experiment,*
25 *Called Secrets in Nature.* So 'tis, 'tis so;
'How to know whether a woman be with child or no'.
I hope I am not yet. If he should try though!
Let me see, folio forty-five. Here 'tis;
The leaf tucked down upon't, the place suspicious.
30 'If you would know whether a woman be with child or not
Give her two spoonfuls of the white water in glass C.'
Where's that glass C? Oh, yonder, I see't now.
'And if she be with child she sleeps full twelve hours after; if not,
not.'
35 None of that water comes into my belly;
I'll know you from a hundred. I could break you now,
Or turn you into milk, and so beguile
The master of the mystery, but I'll look to you.
Ha! That which is next is ten times worse:
40 'How to know whether a woman be a maid or not'.
If that should be applied, what would become of me?
Belike he has a strong faith of my purity,
That never yet made proof; but this he calls
'A merry sleight, but true experiment, the author Antonius Mizaldus.
45 Give the party you suspect the quantity of a spoonful of the water in
the glass M, which, upon her that is a maid, makes three several
effects: 'twill make her incontinently gape, then fall into a sudden
sneezing, last into a violent laughing; else dull, heavy, and lumpish.'
Where had I been?
50 I fear it, yet 'tis seven hours to bedtime.
[*Enter Diaphanta.*]
Diaphanta Cuds, madam, are you here?
Beatrice [*aside*] Seeing that wench now
A trick comes in my mind; 'tis a nice piece
Gold cannot purchase. [*to Diaphanta*] I come hither, wench,
55 To look my lord.

---

16 die: dice. **44 Mizaldus:** 16th century writer whose book *De Arcanis Naturae* is being recalled.
47 incontinently: unrestrainedly. **51 Cuds:** contraction of 'God save me'.

Diaphanta Would I had such a cause to look him too!
Why, he's i' th' park, madam.
Beatrice There let him be.
Diaphanta Ay, madam, let him compass
60   Whole parks and forests, as great rangers do;
At roosting time a little lodge can hold 'em.
Earth-conquering Alexander, that thought the world
Too narrow for him, in the end had but his pit-hole.
Beatrice I fear thou art not modest, Diaphanta
65   *Diaphanta* Your thoughts are so unwilling to be known, madam;
'Tis ever the bride's fashion towards bedtime
To set light by her joys, as if she owed 'em not.
Beatrice Her joys? Her fears, thou would'st say.
Diaphanta Fear of what?
70   *Beatrice* Art thou a maid, and talk'st so to a maid?
You leave a blushing business behind,
Beshrew your heart for't!
Diaphanta Do you mean good sooth, madam?
Beatrice Well, if I'd thought upon the fear at first,
75   Man should have been unknown.
Diaphanta Is't possible?
Beatrice I will give a thousand ducats to that woman
Would try what my fear were, and tell me true
Tomorrow, when she gets from't; as she likes,
80   I might perhaps be drawn to't.
Diaphanta Are you in earnest?
Beatrice Do you get the woman, then challenge me,
And see if I'll fly from't; but I must tell you
This by the way, she must be a true maid,
85   Else there's no trial, my fears are not hers else.
Diaphanta Nay, she that I would put into your hands, madam,
Shall be a maid.
Beatrice You know I should be shamed else,
Because she lies for me.
90   *Diaphanta* 'Tis a strange humour;
But are you serious still? Would you resign
Your first night's pleasure, and give money too?
Beatrice As willingly as live; [*Aside*] alas, the gold
Is but a by-bet to wedge in the honour.
95   *Diaphanta* I do not know how the world goes abroad
For faith or honesty; there's both required in this.
Madam, what say you to me, and stray no further?
I've a good mind, in troth, to earn your money.
Beatrice Y'are too quick, I fear, to be a maid.

---

71 **blushing business behind**: you have already lost your virginity.   94 **by-bet**: side bet; to Diaphanta money is
only of secondary interest after sexual pleasure.

100   **Diaphanta** How? Not a maid? Nay, then you urge me, madam;
Your honourable self is not a truer
With all your fears upon you.
    Beatrice [*aside*] Bad enough then.
    Diaphanta Than I with all my lightsome joys about me.
105   **Beatrice** I'm glad to hear't; then you dare put your honesty
Upon an easy trial?
    Diaphanta Easy? Anything.
    Beatrice I'll come to you straight. [*Goes to the closet.*]
    Diaphanta [*aside*] She will not search me, will she,
110   Like the forewoman of a female jury?
    Beatrice Glass M; ay, this is it. Look, Diaphanta,
You take no worse than I do. [*Drinks.*]
    Diaphanta And in so doing,
I will not question what 'tis, but take it. [*Drinks.*]
115   **Beatrice** [*aside*] Now if the experiment be true, 'twill praise itself,
And give me noble ease. Begins already; [*Diaphanta gapes.*]
There's the first symptom; and what haste it makes
To fall into the second, there by this time! [*Diaphanta sneezes.*]
Most admirable secret. On the contrary,
120   It stirs me not a whit, which most concerns it.
    Diaphanta Ha, ha, ha!
    Beatrice [*aside*] Just in all things and in order,
As if 'twere circumscribed; one accident
Gives way unto another.
125   **Diaphanta** Ha, ha, ha!
    Beatrice How now, wench?
    Diaphanta Ha, ha, ha! I am so-so light
At heart – ha, ha, ha – so pleasurable.
But one swig more, sweet madam.
130   **Beatrice** Ay, tomorrow;
We shall have time to sit by't.
    Diaphanta Now I'm sad again.
    Beatrice [*aside*] It lays itself so gently, too. [*to Diaphanta*] Come,
wench,
135   Most honest Diaphanta I dare call thee now.
    Diaphanta Pray tell me, madam, what trick call you this?
    Beatrice I'll tell thee all hereafter; we must study
The carriage of this business.
    Diaphanta I shall carry't well
140   Because I love the burthen.
    Beatrice About midnight
You must not fail to steal forth gently,
That I may use the place.
    Diaphanta Oh, fear not, madam,
145   I shall be cool by that time. The bride's place,

And with a thousand ducats! I'm for a justice now,
I bring a portion with me; I scorn small fools. [*Exit.*]

Act IV, Scene ii

[*Enter Vermandero and Servant.*]
Vermandero I tell you, knave, mine honour is in question,
A thing till now free from suspicion,
Nor ever was there cause. Who of my Gentlemen
Are absent? Tell me and truly how many and who.
5 **Servant** Antonio, sir, and Franciscus.
Vermandero When did they leave the castle?
Servant Some ten days since, sir, the one intending to Briamata, th'
other for Valencia.
Vermandero The time accuses 'em. A charge of murder
10 Is brought within my castle gate, Piracquo's murder;
I dare not answer faithfully their absence.
A strict command of apprehension
Shall pursue 'em suddenly, and either wipe
The stain off clear, or openly discover it.
15 Provide me winged warrants for the purpose.
See, I am set on again. [*Exit Servant.*]
[*Enter Tomazo.*]
Tomazo I claim a brother of you.
Vermandero Y'are too hot,
Seek him not here.
20 **Tomazo** Yes, 'mongst your dearest bloods,
If my peace find no fairer satisfaction;
This is the place must yield account for him,
For here I left him, and the hasty tie
Of this snatched marriage gives strong testimony
25 Of his most certain ruin.
Vermandero Certain falsehood.
This is the place indeed; his breach of faith
Has too much marred both my abused love,
The honourable love I reserved for him,
30 And mocked my daughter's joy; the prepared morning
Blushed at his infidelity. He left
Contempt and scorn to throw upon those friends
Whose belief hurt 'em. Oh 'twas most ignoble
To take his flight so unexpectedly,
35 And throw such public wrongs on those that loved him.
Tomazo Then this is all your answer?
Vermandero 'Tis too fair
For one of his alliance; and I warn you
That this place no more see you. [*Exit.*]

---

152 **portion:** dowry which will attract a Judge.   4.2,38 **alliance:** kinship.

[*Enter De Flores.*]

40   ***Tomazo*** The best is,
There is more ground to meet a man's revenge on.
Honest De Flores?
De Flores That's my name indeed.
Saw you the bride? Good sweet sir, which way took she?

45   ***Tomazo*** I have blessed mine eyes from seeing such a false one.
De Flores [*aside*] I'd fain get off, this man's not for my company;
I smell his brother's blood when I come near him.
Tomazo Come hither, kind and true one; I remember
My brother loved thee well.

50   ***De Flores*** Oh purely, dear sir!
[*Aside*] Methinks I am now again a-killing on him,
He brings it so fresh to me.
Tomazo Thou canst guess, sirrah
(One honest friend has an instinct of jealousy),

55   At some foul guilty person?
De Flores 'Las, sir, I am so charitable I think none
Worse than myself. You did not see the bride then?
Tomazo I prithee name her not. Is she not wicked?
De Flores No, no, a pretty, easy, round-packed sinner,

60   As your most ladies are, else you might think
I flattered her; but, sir, at no hand wicked,
Till th' are so old their chins and noses meet,
And they salute witches. I am called, I think, sir.
[*Aside*] His company ev'n o'erlays my conscience. [*Exit.*]

65   ***Tomazo*** That De Flores has a wondrous honest heart;
He'll bring it out in time, I'm assured on't.
Oh, here's the glorious master of the day's joy;
'Twill not be long till he and I do reckon. [*Enter Alsemero.*]
Sir!

70   ***Alsemero*** You are most welcome.
Tomazo You may call that word back;
I do not think I am, nor wish to be.
Alsemero 'Tis strange you found the way to this house then.
Tomazo Would I'd ne'er known the cause. I'm none of those, sir,

75   That come to give you joy and swill your wine;
'Tis a more precious liquor that must lay
The fiery thirst I bring.
Alsemero Your words and you
Appear to me great strangers.

80   ***Tomazo*** Time and our swords
May make us more acquainted. This the business:
I should have a brother in your place;
How treachery and malice have disposed of him,

---

64 o'erlays: oppresses.

I'm bound to inquire of him which holds his right,
85   Which never could come fairly.
Alsemero You must look
To answer for that word, sir.
Tomazo Fear you not,
I'll have it ready drawn at our next meeting.
90   Keep your day solemn. Farewell, I disturb it not;
I'll bear the smart with patience for a time. [*Exit.*]
Alsemero 'Tis somewhat ominous this, a quarrel ent'red
Upon this day. My innocence relieves me, [*Enter Jasperino.*]
I should be wondrous sad else. Jasperino,
95   I have news to tell thee, strange news.
Jasperino I ha' some too,
I think as strange as yours; would I might keep
Mine, so my faith and friendship might be kept in't.
Faith, sir, dispense a little with my zeal,
100 And let it cool in this.
Alsemero This puts me on,
And blames thee for thy slowness.
Jasperino All may prove nothing;
Only a friendly fear that leapt from me, sir.
105 **Alsemero** No question it may prove nothing; let's partake it, though.
Jasperino 'Twas Diaphanta's chance (for to that wench
I pretend honest love, and she deserves it)
To leave me in a back part of the house,
A place we chose for private conference;
110 She was no sooner gone, but instantly
I heard your bride's voice in the next room to me;
And, lending more attention, found De Flores
Louder than she.
Alsemero De Flores? Thou art out now.
115 **Jasperino** You'll tell me more anon.
Alsemero Still I'll prevent thee.
The very sight of him is poison to her.
Jasperino That made me stagger too, but Diaphanta
At her return confirmed it.
120 **Alsemero** Diaphanta!
Jasperino Then fell we both to listen, and words passed
Like those that challenge interest in a woman.
Alsemero Peace! Quench thy zeal; 'tis dangerous to thy bosom.
Jasperino Then truth is full of peril.
125 **Alsemero** Such truths are.
Oh, were she the sole glory of the earth,
Had eyes that could shoot fire into kings' breasts,
And touched, she sleeps not here! Yet I have time,

---

101 **puts me on:** has aroused my interest.   116 **prevent:** anticipate. I will always refute the implausible.

Though night be near, to be resolved hereof;
130 And prithee, do not weigh me by my passions.
Jasperino I never weighed friend so.
Alsemero Done charitably.
That key will lead thee to a pretty secret [*Gives him a key.*]
By a Chaldean taught me, and I've made
135 My study upon some. Bring from my closet
A glass inscribed there with the letter M,
And question not my purpose.
Jasperino It shall be done, sir. [*Exit.*]
Alsemero How can this hang together? Not an hour since,
140 Her woman came pleading her lady's fears,
Delivered her for the most timorous virgin
That ever shrunk at man's name, and so modest,
She charged her weep out her request to me
That she might come obscurely to my bosom.
[*Enter Beatrice.*]
145 *Beatrice* [*aside*] All things go well. My woman's preparing yonder
For her sweet voyage, which grieves me to lose;
Necessity compels it, I lose all else.
Alsemero [*aside*] Push! Modesty's shrine is set in yonder forehead.
I cannot be too sure though. – My Joanna!
150 *Beatrice* Sir, I was bold to weep a message to you;
Pardon my modest fears.
Alsemero [*aside*] The dove's not meeker;
She's abused, questionless. [*Enter Jasperino with glass.*]
Oh, are you come, sir?
155 *Beatrice* [*aside*] The glass, upon my life! I see the letter.
Jasperino Sir, this is M.
Alsemero 'Tis it.
Beatrice [*aside*] I am suspected.
Alsemero How fitly our bride comes to partake with us.
160 *Beatrice* What is't, my lord?
Alsemero No hurt.
Beatrice Sir, pardon me,
I seldom taste of any composition.
Alsemero But this, upon my warrant, you shall venture on.
165 *Beatrice* I fear 'twill make me ill.
Alsemero Heaven forbid that!
Beatrice [*aside*] I'm put now to my cunning; th' effects I know,
If I can now but feign 'em handsomely. [*She drinks.*]
Alsemero [*to Jasperino*] It has that secret virtue, it ne'er missed, sir,
170 Upon a virgin.
Jasperino Treble qualitied? [*Beatrice gapes, then sneezes.*]
Alsemero By all that's virtuous, it takes there, proceeds!

---

134 Chaldean: soothsayer.

Jasperino This is the strangest trick to know a maid by.
Beatrice Ha, ha, ha!
175 You have given me joy of heart to drink, my lord.
Alsemero No, thou hast given me such joy of heart
That never can be blasted.
Beatrice What s the matter, sir?
Alsemero [*to Jasperino*] See, now 'tis settled in a melancholy,
180 Keeps both the time and method. My Joanna,
Chaste as the breath of Heaven, or morning's womb
That brings the day forth, thus my love encloses thee.
[*Embraces her. Exit.*]

Act IV, Scene iii

[*Enter Isabella and Lollio.*]
Isabella Oh heaven! Is this the waiting moon?
Does love turn fool, run mad, and all at once?
Sirrah, here's a madman, akin to the fool too,
A lunatic lover.
5 *Lollio* No, no, not he I brought the letter from?
Isabella Compare his inside with his out, and tell me.
[*Gives him the letter.*]
Lollio The out's mad, I'm sure of that; I had a taste on't. [*Reads the envelope.*] 'To the bright Andromeda, chief chambermaid to the Knight of the Sun, at the sign of Scorpio, in the middle region, sent by the
10 bellows-mender of Aeolus. Pay the post.' This is stark madness.
Isabella Now mark the inside. [*Reads the letter.*] 'Sweet lady, having now cast off this counterfeit cover of a madman, I appear to your best judgement a true and faithful lover of your beauty.'
Lollio He is mad still.
15 *Isabella* 'If any fault you find, chide those perfections in you which have made me imperfect; 'tis the same sun that causeth to grow and enforceth to wither –'
Lollio Oh rogue!
Isabella ' – Shapes and transshapes, destroys and builds again; I come
20 in winter to you dismantled of my proper ornaments; by the sweet splendour of your cheerful smiles, I spring and live a lover.'
Lollio Mad rascal still!
Isabella 'Tread him not under foot, that shall appear an honour to your bounties. I remain, mad till I speak with you, from whom I
25 expect my cure, Yours all, or one beside himself, Franciscus.'
Lollio You are like to have a fine time on't; my master and I may give over our professions. I do not think but you can cure fools and mad men faster than we, with little pains too.
Isabella Very likely.

4.3,10 **Aeolus**: god of winds.

30   *Lollio* One thing I must tell you, mistress: you perceive that I am
privy to your skill; if I find you minister once and set up the trade, I
put in for my thirds, I shall be mad or fool else.
Isabella The first place is thine, believe it, Lollio, if I do fall –
Lollio I fall upon you.
35   *Isabella* So.
Lollio Well, I stand to my venture.
Isabella But thy counsel now, how shall I deal with 'em?
Lollio Why, do you mean to deal with 'em?
Isabella Nay, the fair understanding, how to use 'em.
40   *Lollio* Abuse 'em! That's the way to mad the fool, and make a fool
of the madman, and then you use 'em kindly.
Isabella 'Tis easy, I'll practise; do thou observe it.
The key of thy wardrobe.
Lollio There; fit yourself for 'em, and I'll fit 'em both for you.
[*Offers a key.*]
45   *Isabella* Take thou no further notice than the outside. *Exit.*
Lollio Not an inch; I'll put you to the inside.
[*Enter Alibius.*]
Alibius Lollio, art there? Will all be perfect, think'st thou?
Tomorrow night, as if to close up the solemnity, Vermandero
expects us.
50   *Lollio* I mistrust the madmen most; the fools will do well enough, I
have taken pains with them.
Alibius Tush, they cannot miss; the more absurdity
The more commends it, so no rough behaviours
Affright the ladies, they are nice things, thou know'st.
55   *Lollio* You need not fear, sir; so long as we are there with our
commanding pizzles, they'll be as tame as the ladies themselves.
Alibius I will see them once more rehearse before they go.
Lollio I was about it, sir; look you to the madmen's morris, and let
me alone with the other. There is one or two that I mistrust their
60   fooling; I'll instruct them, and then they shall rehearse the whole
measure.
Alibius Do so; I'll see the music prepared. But Lollio,
By the way, how does my wife brook her restraint?
Does she not grudge at it?
65   *Lollio* So, so; she takes some pleasure in the house, she would abroad
else. You must allow her a little more length, she's kept too short.
Alibius She shall go along to Vermandero's with us;
That will serve her for a month's liberty.
Lollio What's that on your face, sir?
70   *Alibius* Where, Lollio? I see nothing.
Lollio Cry you mercy, sir, 'tis your nose; it showed like the trunk of
a young elephant.

---

31 trade: become a whore.   **56 pizzles:** whips made from bulls' penises.   **58 morris:** lively rural dance associated
with fertility.

Alibius Away, rascal! I'll prepare the music, Lollio. [*Exit Alibius.*]
Lollio Do, sir, and I'll dance the whilst. Tony, where art thou, Tony?
[*Enter Antonio.*]
75 *Antonio* Here, cousin; where art thou?
Lollio Come, Tony, the footmanship I taught you.
Antonio I had rather ride, cousin.
Lollio Ay, a whip take you; but I'll keep you out. Vault in; look you,
Tony: fa, la, la, la, la. [*Dances.*]
80 *Antonio* Fa, la, la, la, la. [*Dances.*]
Lollio There, an honour.
Antonio Is this an honour, cuz?
Lollio Yes, and it please your worship. [*Bows.*]
Antonio Does honour bend in the hams, cuz?
85 *Lollio* Marry, does it, as low as worship, squireship, nay, yeomandry
itself sometimes, from whence it first stiffened. There, rise, a caper.
Antonio Caper after an honour, cuz?
Lollio Very proper; for honour is but a caper, rises as fast and high,
has a knee or two, and falls to th' ground again. You can remember
90 your figure, Tony? [*Exit.*]
Antonio Yes, cousin; when I see thy figure, I can remember mine.
[*Enter Isabella like a madwoman.*]
Isabella Hey, how he treads the air! Shough, shough, t'other way!
He burns his wings else. Here's wax enough below, Icarus, more than
will be cancelled these eighteen moons. [*Antonio falls.*] He's down,
95 he's down! What a terrible fall he had!
Stand up, thou son of Cretan Dedalus,
And let us tread the lower labyrinth
I'll bring thee to the clue.
Antonio Prithee, cuz, let me alone.
100 *Isabella* Art thou now drowned?
About thy head I saw a heap of clouds,
Wrapped like a Turkish turbant; on thy back
A crooked chameleon-coloured rainbow hung
Like a tiara down unto thy hams.
105 Let me suck out those billows in thy belly;
Hark how they roar and rumble in the straits!
Bless thee from the pirates.
Antonio Pox upon you; let me alone!
Isabella Why shouldst thou mount so high as Mercury,
110 Unless thou hadst reversion of his place?
Stay in the moon with me, Endymion,

---

81 **honour:** bow. 84 **hams:** the thighs and buttocks. 85 **as low as . . . . :** the idea is that honour will be abandoned in being servile to people of even quite low rank. The language, as in this whole scene, also carries sexual
innuendos. 86 **caper:** leap. 90 **figure:** movements of the dance. 93 **Icarus:** flew too close to the sun with
wings held on by wax. The wax melted and Icarus fell to his death. 96 **Dedalus:** father of Icarus. Inventor who
made the labyrinth on Crete which held the monstrous Minotaur. He made the wings to escape. 111 **Endymion:**
youth loved by the Moon, Luna.

And we will rule these wild, rebellious waves,
That would have drowned my love.
Antonio I'll kick thee if again thou touch me,
115   Thou wild unshapen antic; I am no fool,
You bedlam!
Isabella But you are, as sure as I am, mad.
Have I put on this habit of a frantic,
With love as full of fury, to beguile
120   The nimble eye of watchful jealousy,
And am I thus rewarded? [*Removes her disguise.*]
Antonio Ha, dearest beauty!
Isabella No, I have no beauty now,
Nor never had, but what was in my garments.
125   You, a quick-sighted lover? Come not near me!
Keep your caparisons, y'are aptly clad;
I came a feigner to return stark mad. [*Exit.*]
[*Enter Lollio.*]
Antonio Stay, or I shall change condition,
And become as you are.
130   ***Lollio*** Why, Tony, whither now? Why, fool?
Antonio Whose fool, usher of idiots? You coxcomb!
I have fooled too much.
Lollio You were best be mad another while then.
Antonio So I am, stark mad; I have cause enough;
135   And I could throw the full effects on thee,
And beat thee like a fury!
Lollio Do not, do not; I shall not forbear the gentleman under the
fool, if you do; alas, I saw through your fox-skin before now. Come,
I can give you comfort; my mistress loves you, and there is as arrant
140   a madman i' th' house as you are a fool, your rival, whom she loves
not; if after the masque we can rid her of him, you earn her love, she
says, and the fool shall ride her.
Antonio May I believe thee?
Lollio Yes, or you may choose whether you will or no.
145   ***Antonio*** She's eased of him; I have a good quarrel on't.
Lollio Well, keep your old station yet, and be quiet.
Antonio Tell her I will deserve her love. [*Exit.*]
Lollio And you are like to have your desire.
[*Enter Franciscus.*]
Franciscus [*sings*] 'Down, down, down a-down a-down' and then
150   with a horse-trick,
To kick Latona's forehead, and break her bowstring.
Lollio This is t'other counterfeit; I'll put him out of his humour.
[*Takes out letter and reads*] 'Sweet lady, having now cast off this
counterfeit cover of a madman, I appear to your best judgement a

---

126 caparisons: clothes.

155 true and faithful lover of your heauty.' This is pretty well for a
madman.
Franciscus Ha! What's that?
Lollio 'Chide those perfections in you which have made me
imperfect.'
160 *Franciscus* I am discovered to the fool.
Lollio I hope to discover the fool in you, ere I have done with you.
'Yours all, or one beside himself, Franciscus.' This madman will mend
sure.
Franciscus What do you read, sirrah?
165 *Lollio* Your destiny, sir; you'll be hanged for this trick, and another
that I know.
Franciscus Art thou of counsel with thy mistress?
Lollio Next her apron strings.
Franciscus Give me thy hand.
170 *Lollio* Stay, let me put yours in my pocket first. [*Hides the letter.*]
Your hand is true, is it not? It will not pick? I partly fear it, because I
think it does lie.
Franciscus Not in a syllable.
Lollio So; if you love my mistress so well as you have handled the
175 matter here, you are like to be cured of your madness.
Franciscus And none but she can cure it.
Lollio Well, I'll give you over then, and she shall cast your water
next.
Franciscus Take for thy pains past. [*Gives him money.*]
180 *Lollio* I shall deserve more, sir, I hope; my mistress loves you, but
must have some proof of your love to her.
Franciscus There I meet my wishes.
Lollio That will not serve, you must meet her enemy and yours.
Franciscus He's dead already!
185 *Lollio* Will you tell me that, and I parted but now with him?
Franciscus Show me the man.
Lollio Ay, that's a right course now, see him before you kill him in
any case; and yet it needs not go so far neither, 'tis but a fool that
haunts the house and my mistress in the shape of an idiot. Bang but
190 his fool's coat well-favouredly, and 'tis well.
Franciscus Soundly, soundly!
Lollio Only reserve him till the masque be past; and if you find him
not now in the dance yourself, I'll show you. In, in! My master!
Franciscus He handles him like a feather. Hey! [*Exit dancing.*]
[*Enter Alibius.*]
195 *Alibius* Well said. In a readiness, Lollio?
Lollio Yes, sir.
Alibius Away then, and guide them in, Lollio;
Entreat your mistress to see this sight.

---

171 **pick:** as in pickpocket.   177 **cast your water:** diagnose your disease by examining your urine.

Hark, is there not one incurable fool
200 That might be begged? I have friends.
Lollio I have him for you, one that shall deserve it too [*Exit.*]
Alibius Good boy, Lollio.
[*Enter Isabella, then Lollio with madmen and fools. The madmen and fools dance.*]
Alibius 'Tis perfect; well, fit but once these strains,
We shall have coin and credit for our pains. [*Exit.*]

Act V, Scene i

[*Enter Beatrice. A clock strikes one.*]
Beatrice One struck, and yet she lies by't! Oh my fears!
This strumpet serves her own ends, 'tis apparent now,
Devours the pleasure with a greedy appetite,
And never minds my honour or my peace,
5 Makes havoc of my right. But she pays dearly for't –
No trusting of her life with such a secret
That cannot rule her blood to keep her promise.
Beside, I have some suspicion of her faith to me,
Because I was suspected of my lord,
10 And it must come from her. Hark! By my horrors,
Another clock strikes two. [*Strikes two.*]
[*Enter De Flores.*]
De Flores Pist! Where are you?
Beatrice De Flores?
De Flores Ay. Is she not come from him yet?
15 **Beatrice** As I am a living soul, not.
De Flores Sure the devil
Hath sowed his itch within her. Who'd trust
A waiting-woman?
Beatrice I must trust somebody.
20 **De Flores** Push, they are termagants,
Especially when they fall upon their masters
And have their ladies' first-fruits; th'are mad whelps,
You cannot stave 'em off from game royal. Then
You are so harsh and hardy, ask no counsel;
25 And I could have helped you to an apothecary's daughter,
Would have fall'n off before eleven, and thanked you too.
Beatrice Oh me, not yet? This whore forgets herself.
De Flores The rascal fares so well. Look, y'are undone,
The day-star, by this hand! See Phosphorus plain yonder.
30 **Beatrice** Advise me now to fall upon some ruin,
There is no counsel safe else.

---

200 begged: I wish to be given legal control of a madman's estate and so use its profits. **5.1,20 termagants:** savages. **30 ruin:** desperate action.

De Flores Peace, I ha't now;
For we must force a rising, there's no remedy.
Beatrice How? Take heed of that.
35 **De Flores** Tush, be you quiet,
Or else give over all.
Beatrice Prithee, I ha' done then.
De Flores This is my reach: I'll set some part a-fire
Of Diaphanta's chamber.
40 **Beatrice** How? Fire, sir?
That may endanger the whole house.
De Flores You talk of danger when your fame's on fire?
Beatrice That's true; do what thou wilt now.
De Flores Push! I aim
45 At a most rich success, strikes all dead sure.
The chimney being a-fire, and some light parcels
Of the least danger in her chamber only,
If Diaphanta should be met by chance then,
Far from her lodging [which is now suspicious],
50 It would be thought her fears and affrights then
Drove her to seek for succour; if not seen
Or met at all, as that's the likeliest,
For her own shame she'll hasten towards her lodging;
I will be ready with a piece high-charged,
55 As 'twere to cleanse the chimney. There, 'tis proper now,
But she shall be the mark.
Beatrice I'm forced to love thee now,
'Cause thou provid'st so carefully for my honour.
De Flores Slid, it concerns the safety of us both,
60 Our pleasure and continuance.
Beatrice One word now, prithee:
How for the servants?
De Flores I'll despatch them,
Some one way, some another in the hurry,
65 For buckets, hooks, ladders. Fear not you;
The deed shall find its time; and I've thought since
Upon a safe conveyance for the body too.
How this fire purifies wit! Watch you your minute.
Beatrice Fear keeps my soul upon't, I cannot stray from't.
[*Enter Alonzo's Ghost.*]
70 **De Flores** Ha! What art thou that tak'st away the light
'Twixt that star and me? I dread thee not.
'Twas but a mist of conscience; all's clear again. [*Exit.*]
Beatrice Who's that, De Flores? Bless me! It slides by! [*Exit Ghost.*]
Some ill thing haunts the house; 't has left behind it
75 A shivering sweat upon me. I'm afraid now.
This night hath been so tedious. Oh, this strumpet!
Had she a thousand lives, he should not leave her

Till he had destroyed the last. – List! Oh my terrors!
[*Clock strikes three.*]
Three struck by Saint Sebastian's!
80 **Voice within** Fire, fire, fire!
Beatrice Already? How rare is that man's speed!
How heartily he serves me. His face loathes one,
But look upon his care, who would not love him?
The east is not more beauteous than his service.
85 **Voice within** Fire, fire, fire!
[*Enter De Flores; servants pass over, a bell rings.*]
De Flores Away, despatch! Hooks, buckets, ladders! – That's well
said;
The fire-bell rings, the chimney works; my charge;
The piece is ready. [*Exit.*]
90 **Beatrice** Here's a man worth loving – [*Enter Diaphanta.*]
Oh, y'are a jewel.
Diaphanta Pardon frailty, madam;
In troth I was so well, I ev'n forgot myself.
Beatrice Y'have made trim work.
95 **Diaphanta** What?
Beatrice Hie quickly to your chamber;
Your reward follows you.
Diaphanta I never made
So sweet a bargain. [*Exit.*]
[*Enter Alsemero.*]
100 **Alsemero** O my dear Joanna
Alas, art thou risen too? I was coming,
My absolute treasure.
Beatrice When I missed you,
I could not choose but follow.
105 **Alsemero** Th'art all sweetness!
The fire is not so dangerous.
Beatrice Think you so, sir?
Alsemero I prithee tremble not; believe me, 'tis not.
[*Enter Vermandero and Jasperino.*]
Vermandero Oh bless my house and me!
110 **Alsemero** My lord your father.
[*Enter De Flores with a piece.*]
Vermandero Knave, whither goes that piece?
De Flores To scour the chimney. [*Exit.*]
Vermandero Oh, well said, well said;
That fellow's good on all occasions.
115 **Beatrice** A wondrous necessary man, my lord.
Vermandero He hath a ready wit, he's worth 'em all, sir;
Dog at a house of fire; I ha' seen him singed ere now.
[*The piece goes off.*]
Ha, there he goes.

Beatrice 'Tis done.
120   **Alsemero** Come, sweet, to bed now.
Alas, thou wilt get cold.
Beatrice Alas, the fear keeps that out;
My heart will find no quiet till I hear
How Diaphanta, my poor woman, fares;
125   It is her chamber, sir, her lodging chamber.
Vermandero How should the fire come there?
Beatrice As good a soul as ever lady countenanced,
But in her chamber negligent and heavy;
She 'scaped a mine twice.
130   **Vermandero** Twice?
Beatrice Strangely twice, sir.
Vermandero Those sleepy sluts are dangerous in a house,
And they be ne'er so good.
[*Enter De Flores.*]
De Flores O poor virginity,
135   Thou hast paid dearly for't.
Vermandero Bless us! What's that?
De Flores A thing you all knew once, Diaphanta's burnt.
Beatrice My woman, oh my woman!
De Flores Now the flames
140   Are greedy of her; burnt, burnt, burnt to death, sir!
Beatrice Oh, my presaging soul!
Alsemero Not a tear more;
I charge you by the last embrace I gave you
In bed before this raised us.
145   **Beatrice** Now you tie me;
Were it my sister, now she gets no more.
[*Enter Servant.*]
Vermandero How now?
Servant All danger's past; you may now take your rests my lords,
the fire is throughly quenched. Ah, poor gentlewoman, how soon
150   was she stifled.
Beatrice De Flores, what is left of her inter,
And we as mourners all will follow her;
I will entreat that honour to my servant,
Ev'n of my lord himself.
155   **Alsemero** Command it, sweetness.
Beatrice Which of you spied the fire first?
De Flores 'Twas I, madam.
Beatrice And took such pains in't too? A double goodness!
'Twere well he were rewarded.
160   **Vermandero** He shall be;
De Flores, call upon me.

---

129 **mine**: violent explosion.

Alsemero And upon me, sir. [*Exit. De Flores remains.*]
De Flores Rewarded? Precious! Here's a trick beyond me;
I see in all bouts both of sport and wit,
165   Always a woman strives for the last hit. [*Exit.*]

Act V, Scene ii

[*Enter Tomazo.*]
Tomazo I cannot taste the benefits of life
With the same relish I was wont to do.
Man I grow weary of, and hold his fellowship
A treacherous, bloody friendship; and because
5   I am ignorant in whom my wrath should settle,
I must think all men villains, and the next
I meet, whoe'er he be, the murderer
Of my most worthy brother. Ha! What's he?
[*Enter De Flores. Passes over the stage.*]
Oh, the fellow that some call honest De Flores;
10   But methinks honesty was hard bested
To come there for a lodging; as if a queen
Should make her palace of a pest-house.
I find a contrariety in nature
Betwixt that face and me; the least occasion
15   Would give me game upon him. Yet he's so foul
One would scarce touch him with a sword he loved
And made account of; so most deadly venomous,
He would go near to poison any weapon
That should draw blood on him, one must resolve
20   Never to use that sword again in fight,
In way of honest manhood, that strikes him;
Some river must devour't, 'twere not fit
That any man should find it. What, again? [*Enter De Flores.*]
He walks a' purpose by, sure, to choke me up,
23   To infect my blood.
De Flores My worthy noble lord.
Tomazo Dost offer to come near and breathe upon me?
[*Strikes him.*]
De Flores A blow! [*Draws his sword.*]
Tomazo Yea, are you so prepared?
30   I'll rather, like a soldier, die by th' sword. [*Draws.*]
Than like a politician by thy poison.
De Flores Hold, my lord, as you are honourable.
Tomazo All slaves that kill by poison are still cowards.
De Flores [*aside*] I cannot strike; I see his brother's wounds
35   Fresh bleeding in his eye, as in a crystal.

5.2,10 **bested:** beset 35 **crystal:** crystal ball.

I will not question this. I know y'are noble;
I take my injury with thanks given, sir,
Like a wise lawyer; and as a favour
Will wear it for the worthy hand that gave it.
40 [*Aside*] Why this from him that yesterday appeared
So strangely loving to me?
Oh, but instinct is of a subtler strain;
Guilt must not walk so near his lodge again;
He came near me now. [*Exit.*]
45 *Tomazo* All league with mankind I renounce for ever,
Till I find this murderer; not so much
As common courtesy, but I'll lock up;
For in the state of ignorance I live in,
A brother may salute his brother's murderer,
50 And wish good speed to th' villain in a greeting.
[*Enter Vermandero, Alibius and Isabella.*]
Vermandero Noble Piracquo.
Tomazo Pray keep on your way, sir,
I've nothing to say to you.
Vermandero Comforts bless you, sir.
55 *Tomazo* I have forsworn compliment, in troth I have, sir;
As you are merely man, I have not left
A good wish for you, nor any here.
Vermandero Unless you be so far in love with grief
You will not part from't upon any terms,
60 We bring that news will make a welcome for us.
Tomazo What news can that be?
Vermandero Throw no scornful smile
Upon the zeal I bring you, 'tis worth more, sir.
Two of the chiefest men I kept about me
65 I hide not from the law or your just vengeance.
Tomazo Ha!
Vermandero To give your peace more ample satisfaction,
Thank these discoverers.
Tomazo If you bring that calm,
70 Name but the manner I shall ask forgiveness in
For that contemptuous smile upon you;
I'll perfect it with reverence that belongs
Unto a sacred altar. [*Kneels.*]
Vermandero Good sir, rise;
75 Why, now you overdo as much a' this hand
As you fell short a' t'other. Speak, Alibius.
Alibius 'Twas my wife's fortune, as she is most lucky
At a discovery, to find out lately
Within our hospital of fools and madmen
80 Two counterfeits slipped into these disguises;
Their names, Franciscus and Antonio.

Vermandero Both mine, sir, and I ask no favour for 'em.
Alibius Now that which draws suspicion to their habits
   The time of their disguisings agrees justly
85   With the day of the murder.
Tomazo O blest revelation!
Vermandero Nay more, nay more, sir – I'll not spare mine own
   In way of justice – they both feigned a journey
   To Briamata, and so wrought out their leaves.
90   My love was so abused in't.
Tomazo Time's too precious
   To run in waste now; you have brought a peace
   The riches of five kingdoms could not purchase.
   Be my most happy conduct; I thirst for 'em;
95   Like subtle lightning will I wind about 'em,
   And melt their marrow in 'em. [*Exit.*]

Act V, Scene iii

[*Enter Alsemero and Jasperino.*]
Jasperino Your confidence, I'm sure, is now of proof;
   The prospect from the garden has showed
   Enough for deep suspicion.
Alsemero The black mask
5   That so continually was worn upon't
   Condemns the face for ugly ere't be seen.
   Her despite to him, and so seeming bottomless.
Jasperino Touch it home then; 'tis not a shallow probe
   Can search this ulcer soundly; I fear you'll find it
10   Full of corruption. 'Tis fit I leave you.
   She meets you opportunely from that walk;
   She took the back door at his parting with her. [*Exit Jasperino.*]
Alsemero Did my fate wait for this unhappy stroke
   At my first sight of woman? She's here.
[*Enter Beatrice.*]
15 *Beatrice* Alsemero!
Alsemero How do you?
Beatrice How do I?
   Alas! How do you? You look not well.
Alsemero You read me well enough, I am not well.
20 *Beatrice* Not well, sir? Is't in my power to better you?
Alsemero Yes.
Beatrice Nay, then y'are cured again.
Alsemero Pray resolve me one question, lady.
Beatrice If I can.
25 *Alsemero* None can so sure. Are you honest?

83 **habits:** clothes.   5.3,7 **despite:** contempt.

Beatrice Ha, ha, ha! That's a broad question, my lord.
Alsemero But that's not a modest answer, my lady.
Do you laugh? My doubts are strong upon me.
Beatrice 'Tis innocence that smiles, and no rough brow
30 Can take away the dimple in her cheek.
Say I should strain a tear to fill the vault,
Which would you give the better faith to?
Alsemero 'Twere but hypocrisy of a sadder colour,
But the same stuff. Neither your smiles nor tears
35 Shall move or flatter me from my belief:
You are a whore.
Beatrice What a horrid sound it hath!
It blasts a beauty to deformity;
Upon what face soever that breath falls,
40 It strikes it ugly. Oh, you have ruined
What you can ne'er repair again.
Alsemero I'll all demolish, and seek out truth within you,
If there be any left. Let your sweet tongue
Prevent your heart's rifling; there I'll ransack
45 And tear out my suspicion.
Beatrice You may, sir,
'Tis an easy passage. Yet, if you please,
Show me the ground whereon you lost your love;
My spotless virtue may but tread on that
50 Before I perish.
Alsemero Unanswerable!
A ground you cannot stand on; you fall down
Beneath all grace and goodness when you set
Your ticklish heel on't; there was a visor
55 O'er that cunning face, and that became you;
Now impudence in triumph rides upon't;
How comes this tender reconcilement else
'Twixt you and your despite, your rancorous loathing
De Flores? He that your eye was sore at sight of,
60 He's now become your arm's supporter, your lip's saint.
Beatrice Is there the cause?
Alsemero Worse; your lust's devil, your adultery!
Beatrice Would any but yourself say that,
'Twould turn him to a villain.
65 **Alsemero** 'Twas witnessed
By the counsel of your bosom, Diaphanta.
Beatrice Is your witness dead then?
Alsemero 'Tis to be feared
It was the wages of her knowledge, poor soul;
70 She lived not long after the discovery.

---

43 Let your . . . . : Though you may try to stop my finding you out with soothing words.

Beatrice Then hear a story of not much less horror
Than this your false suspicion is beguiled with;
To your bed's scandal I stand up innocence,
Which even the guilt of one black other deed
75 Will stand for proof of; your love has made me
A cruel murd'ress.
Alsemero Ha!
Beatrice A bloody one;
I have kissed poison for't, stroked a serpent;
80 That thing of hate, worthy in my esteem
Of no better employment, and him most worthy
To be so employed, I caused to murder
That innocent Piracquo, having no
Better means than that worst, to assure
85 Yourself to me.
Alsemero Oh, the place itself e'er since
Has crying been for vengeance, the temple
Where blood and beauty first unlawfully
Fired their devotion, and quenched the right one;
90 'Twas in my fears at first, 'twill have it now.
Oh, thou art all deformed.
Beatrice Forget not, sir,
It for your sake was done; shall greater dangers
Make the less welcome?
95 **Alsemero** Oh, thou shouldst have gone
A thousand leagues about to have avoided
This dangerous bridge of blood; here we are lost.
Beatrice Remember I am true unto your bed.
Alsemero The bed itself's a charnel, the sheets shrouds
100 For murdered carcasses. It must ask pause
What I must do in this; meantime you shall
Be my prisoner only. Enter my closet [*Exit Beatrice.*]
I'll be your keeper yet. Oh, in what part
Of this sad story shall I first begin? Ha! [*Enter De Flores.*]
105 This same fellow has put me in. De Flores!
De Flores Noble Alsemero?
Alsemero I can tell you
News, sir; my wife has her commended to you.
De Flores That's news indeed, my lord; I think she would
110 Commend me to the gallows, if she could
She ever loved me so well. I thank her.
Alsemero What's this blood upon your band, De Flores?
De Flores Blood? No, sure, 'twas washed since.
Alsemero Since when, man?
115 **De Flores** Since t'other day I got a knock
In a sword-and-dagger school. I think 'tis out.

Alsemero Yes, 'tis almost out, but 'tis perceived though.
I had forgot my message; this it is:
What price goes murder?

120   **De Flores** How sir?

Alsemero I ask you, sir;
My wife's behindhand with you, she tells me,
For a brave bloody blow you gave for her sake
Upon Piracquo.

125   **De Flores** Upon? 'Twas quite through him, sure.
Has she confessed it?

Alsemero As sure as death to both of you,
And much more than that.

De Flores It could not be much more;

130   'Twas but one thing, and that – she's a whore.

Alsemero It could not choose but follow. Oh, cunning devils!
How should blind men know you from fair-faced saints?

Beatrice [*within*] He lies, the villain does belie me!

De Flores Let me go to her, sir.

135   **Alsemero** Nay, you shall to her.
Peace, crying crocodile, your sounds are heard!
Take your prey to you, get you in to her, sir. [*Exit De Flores.*]
I'll be your pander now; rehearse again
Your scene of lust, that you may be perfect

140   When you shall come to act it to the black audience
Where howls and gnashings shall be music to you.
Clip your adult'ress freely, 'tis the pilot
Will guide you to the *Mare Mortuum*,
Where you shall sink to fathoms bottomless.
[*Enter Vermandero, Alibius, Isabella, Tomazo, Franciscus and Antonio.*]

145   **Vermandero** Oh, Alsemero, I have a wonder for you.

Alsemero No, sir, 'tis I, I have a wonder for you.

Vermandero I have suspicion near as proof itself
For Piracquo's murder.

Alsemero Sir, I have proof

150   Beyond suspicion for Piracquo's murder.

Vermandero Beseech you, hear me; these two have been disguised
E'er since the deed was done.

Alsemero I have two other
That were more close disguised than your two could be

155   E'er since the deed was done.

Vermandero You'll hear me; these mine own servants –

Alsemero Hear me; those nearer than your servants,
That shall acquit them and prove them guiltless.

Franciscus That may be done with easy truth, sir.

160   **Tomazo** How is my cause bandied through your delays!

---

136 **crocodile**: crocodiles were popularly believed to cry false tears. 143 ***Mare Mortuum***: Sea of Death.

'Tis urgent in blood and calls for haste.
Give me a brother alive or dead:
Alive, a wife with him; if dead, for both
A recompense for murder and adultery.
165 **Beatrice** [*within*] Oh, oh, oh!
Alsemero Hark, 'tis coming to you.
De Flores [*within*] Nay, I'll along for company.
Beatrice [*within*] Oh, oh!
Vermandero What horrid sounds are these?
170 **Alsemero** Come forth, you twins of mischief.
[*Enter De Flores, bringing in Beatrice wounded.*]
De Flores Here we are; if you have any more
To say to us, speak quickly, I shall not
Give you the hearing else; I am so stout yet,
And so, I think, that broken rib of mankind.
175 **Vermandero** An host of enemies ent'red my citadel
Could not amaze like this – Joanna! Beatrice-Joanna!
Beatrice Oh, come not near me, sir, I shall defile you;
I am that of your blood was taken from you
For your better health; look no more upon't,
180 But cast it to the ground regardlessly;
Let the common sewer take it from distinction.
Beneath the stars, upon yon meteor
Ever hung my fate, 'mongst things corruptible;
I ne'er could pluck it from him; my loathing
185 Was prophet to the rest, but ne'er believed;
Mine honour fell with him, and now my life.
Alsemero, I am a stranger to your bed.
Your bed was coz'ned on the nuptial night,
For which your false bride died.
190 **Alsemero** Diaphanta!
De Flores Yes, and the while I coupled with your mate
At barley-brake; now we are left in Hell.
Vermandero We are all there, it circumscribes here.
De Flores I loved this woman in spite of her heart;
195 Her love I earned out of Piracquo's murder.
Tomazo Ha! my brother's murderer?
De Flores Yes, and her honour's prize
Was my reward. I thank life for nothing
But that pleasure; it was so sweet to me
200 That I have drunk up all, left none behind
For any man to pledge me.
Vermandero Horrid villain!
Keep life in him for further tortures.

---

179 **health:** letting blood was commonly practised to cure disease. 188 **coz'ned:** defrauded by deceit.
192 **barley-brake:** a game in which couples are chased.

De Flores No.
I can prevent you; here's my penknife still;
It is but one thread more. [*Stabs himself.*] And now 'tis cut.
Make haste, Joanna, by that token to thee;
Canst not forget, so lately put in mind,
I would not go to leave thee far behind. [*Dies.*]
Beatrice Forgive me, Alsemero, all forgive;
'Tis time to die when 'tis a shame to live. [*Dies.*]
Vermandero Oh, my name is ent'red now in that record
Where till this fatal hour 'twas never read.
Alsemero Let it be blotted out; let your heart lose it,
And it can never look you in the face,
Nor tell a tale behind the back of life
To your dishonour; justice hath so right
The guilty hit that innocence is quit
By proclamation, and may joy again.
Sir, you are sensible of what truth hath done;
'Tis the best comfort that your grief can find.
Tomazo Sir, I am satisfied; my injuries
Lie dead before me. I can exact no more,
Unless my soul were loose, and could o'ertake
Those black fugitives that are fled from thence,
To take a second vengeance; but there are wraths
Deeper than mine, 'tis to be feared, about 'em.
Alsemero What an opacous body had that moon
That last changed on us. Here's beauty changed
To ugly whoredom; here, servant obedience
To a master-sin, imperious murder;
I, a supposed husband, changed embraces
With wantonness, but that was paid before;
Your change is come too, from an ignorant wrath
To knowing friendship. Are there any more on's?
Antonio Yes, sir, I was changed too, from a little ass as I was to a great
fool as I am, and had like to ha' been changed to the gallows, but
that you know my innocence always excuses me.
Franciscus I was changed from a little wit to be stark mad,
Almost for the same purpose.
Isabella [*to Alibius*] Your change is still behind,
But deserve best your transformation;
You are a jealous coxcomb, keep schools of folly,
And teach your scholars how to break your own head.
Alibius I see all apparent, wife, and will change now
Into a better husband, and never keep
Scholars that shall be wiser than myself.
Alsemero Sir, you have yet a son's duty living,

212 **record**: heaven's book of human sin.   228 **opacous**: obscure, shadowy, not reflecting light.

250   Please you accept it. Let that your sorrow,
As it goes from your eye, go from your heart;
Man and his sorrow at the grave must part.

Epilogue

Alsemero   All we can do to comfort one another,
To stay a brother's sorrow for a brother,
To dry a child from the kind father's eyes,
Is to no purpose, it rather multiplies;
5   Your only smiles have power to cause re-live
The dead again, or in their rooms to give
Brother a new brother, father a child;
If these appear, all griefs are reconciled. [*Exit all.*]

GEORGE HERBERT (1593–1632)

Born into one of the most prominent families in the country, Herbert grew up in a milieu surrounded by the arts. At Cambridge, he became Reader in Rhetoric and the University's public Orator. But in the mid-1620s Herbert abandoned the likelihood of a glittering academic, Church, or courtly career to become a country priest in the small Wiltshire village of Bemerton. Published the year after his death, the poems in Herbert's *Temple* exemplify the Anglican desire to match carefully an inner spiritual state with propriety in religion's outward display. The poems illustrate the Renaissance belief in eloquence as a means of gaining a greater intimacy with the divine.

From The Temple

The Agonie

Philosophers have measured mountains,
Fathomed the depths of seas, of states, and kings,
Walked with a staff to heav'n, and traced fountains;
   But there are two vast, spacious things,
5   The which to measure it doth more behove;
Yet few there are that sound them: Sin and Love.

Who would know Sin, let him repair
Unto Mount Olivet; there shall he see
A man so wrung with pains, that all his hair,
10   His skin, his garments bloody be.
Sin is that press and vice, which forceth pain
To hunt his cruel food through ev'ry vein.

Agonie 8 **Olivet:** mountain from which Christ ascended into heaven.   11 **press:** wine-press, imagery from the Bible alluding to the Eucharist.

Who knows not Love, let him assay
And taste that juice, which on the cross a pike
15   Did set again abroach; then let him say
If ever he did taste the like.
Love is that liquor sweet and most divine,
Which my God feels as blood; but I, as wine.

Easter-wings

Lord, who createdst man in wealth and store,
  Though foolishly he lost the same,
    Decaying more and more,
      Till he became
5   Most poor.
        With thee
      O let me rise
    As larks, harmoniously,
  And sing this day thy victories;
10 Then shall the fall further the flight in me.

My tender age in sorrow did begin;
  And still with sicknesses and shame
    Thou didst so punish sin,
      That I became
15   Most thin.
        With thee
      Let me combine
    And feel this day thy victory;
  For, if I imp my wing on thine,
20 Affliction shall advance the flight in me.

Prayer (I)

Prayer the Church's banquet, Angels' age,
God's breath in man returning to his birth,
The soul in paraphrase, heart in pilgrimage,
The Christian plummet sounding heav'n and earth;
5 Engine against th' Almighty, sinners' tower,
Reversed thunder, Christ-side-piercing spear,
The six-days' world transposing in an hour,
A kind of tune, which all things hear and fear;
Softness, and peace, and joy, and love, and bliss,
10 Exalted manna, gladness of the best,
Heaven in ordinary, man well dressed,

Easter-wings 19 **imp:** to graft feathers on to the damaged wing of a bird to improve flight. **Prayer 4 plummet:**
lead weight attached to a line to measure the sea's depth.
10 **manna:** miraculous food. 11 **ordinary:** usual
condition; also refers to the standard meal served at
inns.

The milky way, the bird of Paradise,
Church-bells beyond the stars heard, the soul's blood,
The land of spices; something understood.

Jordan (I)

Who says that fictions only and false hair
Become a verse? Is there in truth no beauty?
Is all good structure in a winding stair?
May no lines pass, except they do their duty
5   Not to a true, but painted chair?

Is it no verse, except enchanted groves
And sudden arbours shadow coarse-spun lines?
Must purling streams refresh a lover's loves?
Must all be veiled, while he that reads, divines,
10   Catching the sense at two removes?

Shepherds are honest people; let them sing;
Riddle who list, for me, and pull for prime;
I envy no man's nightingale or spring;
Nor let them punish me with loss of rhyme,
15   Who plainly say, *My God, My King.*

The H. Scriptures (II)

Oh that I knew how all thy lights combine,
And the configurations of their glory!
Seeing not only how each verse doth shine,
But all the constellations of the story.
5   This verse marks that, and both do make a motion
Unto a third, that ten leaves off doth lie.
Then as dispersed herbs do watch a potion,
These three make up some Christian's destiny.
Such are thy secrets, which my life makes good,
10   And comments on thee; for in ev'ry thing
Thy words do find me out, and parallels bring,
And in another make me understood.
Stars are poor books, and oftentimes do miss;
This book of stars lights to eternal bliss.

Jordan: river the Israelites crossed to enter the promised land. 8 purling: whirling. 12 pull for prime:
draw a winning hand in the card game Primero.

H. Scriptures 5 this verse . . . . : referring to the
practice of reading the Bible typologically, where the
events of the Old Testament foreshadow the events of
the New and provide a pattern for understanding all
history – past, present and future. 7 watch: contrive.

The Pilgrimage

I travelled on, seeing the hill, where lay
　　　　　　My expectation.
　　A long it was and weary way.
　　The gloomy cave of Desperation
5　I left on th' one, and on the other side
　　　　　　The rock of Pride.

And so I came to Fancy's meadow strowed
　　　　　　With many a flower;
　　　　Fain would I here have made abode,
10　　　　But I was quickened by my hour.
So to Care's cops I came, and there got through
　　　　　　With much ado.

That led me to the wild of Passion, which
　　　　　　Some call the wold;
15　　　　A wasted place, but sometimes rich.
　　　　Here I was robbed of all my gold,
Save one good Angel, which a friend had tied
　　　　　　Close to my side.

At length I got unto the gladsome hill,
20　　　　　　Where lay my hope,
　　Where lay my heart; and climbing still,
　　When I had gained the brow and top,
A lake of brackish waters on the ground
　　　　　　Was all I found.

25　With that abashed and struck with many a sting
　　　　　　Of swarming fears,
　　　I fell, and cried, Alas my King!
　　　Can both the way and end be tears?
Yet taking heart I rose, and then perceived
30　　　　　　I was deceived.

My hill was further; so I flung away,
　　　　　　Yet heard a cry,
　　　Just as I went, *None goes that way*
　　　And lives. If that be all, said I,
35　After so foul a journey death is fair,
　　　　　　And but a chair.

---

11 **cops:** copse, a thicket or small wood.　**14 wold:**　　17 **Angel:** a coin.　23 **brackish:** salty.
open moorland.

The Collar

I struck the board, and cried, No more.
                    I will abroad.
What? Shall I ever sigh and pine?
My lines and life are free; free as the road,
5   Loose as the wind, as large as store.
            Shall I be still in suit?
Have I no harvest but a thorn
To let me blood, and not restore
What I have lost with cordial fruit?
10   Sure there was wine
Before my sighs did dry it; there was corn
            Before my tears did drown it.
Is the year only lost to me?
        Have I no bays to crown it?
15   No flowers, no garlands gay? All blasted?
                All wasted?
Not so, my heart; but there is fruit,
            And thou hast hands.
Recover all thy sigh-blown age
20   On double pleasures; leave thy cold dispute
Of what is fit, and not. Forsake thy cage,
            Thy rope of sands,
Which petty thoughts have made, and made to thee
        Good cable, to enforce and draw,
25   And be thy law,
While thou didst wink and wouldst not see.
                Away, Take Heed;
                I will abroad,
Call in thy death's head there; tie up thy fears.
30   He that forbears
        To suit and serve his need,
            Deserves his load.
But as I raved and grew more fierce and wild
            At every word,
35   Me thoughts I heard one calling, *Child*!
                And I replied, *My Lord*.

Collar: a sign of discipline or restraint. The phrase 'to slip the collar' was proverbial. Also a pun on choler, to be angry. **5 store**: abundance, plentiful supply. **6 suit**: to be in livery or uniform; or to be pleading for favours. **14 bays**: laurel, the traditional poet's crown. **22 rope of sands**: false restraints.

The Pulley

When God at first made man,
Having a glass of blessings standing by;
Let us (said he) pour on him all we can;
Let the world's riches, which dispersed lie,
5   Contract into a span.

So strength first made a way;
Then beauty flowed, then wisdom, honour, pleasure;
When almost all was out, God made a stay,
Perceiving that alone of all his treasure
10   Rest in the bottom lay.

For if I should (said he)
Bestow this jewel also on my creature,
He would adore my gifts instead of me,
And rest in Nature, not the God of Nature;
15   So both should losers be.

Yet let him keep the rest,
But keep them with repining restlessness;
Let him be rich and weary, that at least,
If goodness lead him not, yet weariness
20   May toss him to my breast.

Love (III)

Love bade me welcome; yet my soul drew back,
        Guilty of dust and sin.
But quick-eyed Love, observing me grow slack
        From my first entrance in,
5 Drew nearer to me, sweetly questioning,
        If I lacked anything.

A guest, I answered, worthy to be here;
        Love said, You shall be he.
I the unkind, ungrateful? Ah my dear,
10   I cannot look on thee.
Love took my hand, and smiling did reply,
        Who made the eyes but I?

Truth Lord, but I have marred them; let my shame
        Go where it doth deserve.
15 And know you not, says Love, who bore the blame?
        My dear, then I will serve.
You must sit down, says Love, and taste my meat:
        So I did sit and eat.

RICHARD CRASHAW (1612–1649)

Crashaw was the son of a noted Anglican divine. At Cambridge in the 1630s he became involved in the elaborate celebration of religion favoured by the then dominant Laudian element of the English Church. Forced to go abroad in the Civil War, Crashaw became a Roman Catholic. His poetry reflects the ornamented, affective, public devotional quality favoured by Laudians and shows the influence of the continental baroque.

Prayer. An Ode, which was prefixed to a little Prayer book given to a young Gentlewoman

Lo here a little volume, but great Book!
A nest of new-born sweets;
  Whose native fires disdaining
  To ly thus folded, & complaining
5   Of these ignoble sheets,
  Affect more comely bands
  (Fair one) from thy kind hands
  And confidently look
  To find the rest
10 Of a rich binding in your BREST.
It is, in one choice handful, heaven; & all
Heavn's Royal host; incamp't thus small
To prove that true, schools use to tell,
Ten thousand Angels in one point can dwell.
15 It is love's great artillery
Which here contracts itself, & comes to ly
Close couch't in your white bosom; & from thence
As from a snowy fortress of defence,
Against your ghostly foes to take your part,
20 And fortify the hold of your chast heart.
It is an armory of light
Let constant use but keep it bright,
  You'll find it yields
To holy hands & humble hearts
25   More swords & shields
Then sin hath snares, or Hell hath darts.
  Only be sure
  The hands be pure
That hold these weapons; & the eyes
30 Those of turtles, chast & true;
  Wakeful & wise;

---

1 **Book:** The Book of Common Prayer used by the Church of England.   **13 schools:** scholastic philosophy of the Middle Ages debated issues such as how many angels might occupy the head of a pin.   **30 turtles:** turtle-doves, a symbol of grace.

Here is a friend shall fight for you,
Hold but this book before your heart
Let prayer alone to play his part,
35   But O the heart
    That studies this high ART
    Must be a sure house-keeper;
    And yet no sleeper.
    Dear soul, be strong.
40   MERCY will come e're long
And bring his bosom fraught with blessings,
Flowers of never fading graces
To make immortal dressings
For worthy souls, whose wise embraces
45 Store up themselves for HIM, who is alone
The SPOUSE of Virgins & the Virgin's son.
But if the noble BRIDEGROOM, when he come,
Shall find the loitering HEART from home;
    Leaving her chast abode
50   To gad abroad
Among the gay mates of the god of flyes;
To take her pleasure & to play
And keep the devil's holyday;
To dance ith' sunshine of some smiling
55   But beguiling
Spheres of sweet & sugared Lyes,
    Some slippery Pair
Of false, perhaps as fair,
Flattering but forswearing eyes;
60 Doubtless some other heart
    Will get the start
Meanwhile, & stepping in before
Will take possession of that sacred store
Of hidden sweets & holy joys.
65 WORDS which are not heard with EARS
(Those tumultuous shops of noise)
Effectual whispers, whose still voice
The soul it self more feels then hears;
Amorous languishments; luminous trances;
70 SIGHTS which are not seen with eyes;
Spiritual & soul-piercing glances
Whose pure & subtle lightning flyes
Home to the heart, & sets the house on fire
And melts it down in sweet desire
75   Yet does not stay

---

46 spouse: The love poetry of the Bible's Song of Song, from which much of this poem's imagery derives, was understood as a symbolic marriage of the believer to Christ.

To ask the windows leave to pass that way;
Delicious DEATHS; soft exhalations
Of soul; dear & divine annihilations;
  A thousand unknown rites
80 Of joys & rarefied delights;
A hundred thousand goods, glories, & graces,
   And many a mystic thing
   Which the divine embraces
Of the dear spouse of spirits with them will bring
85 For which it is no shame
That dull mortality must not know a name.
   Of all this store
Of blessings & ten thousand more
   (If when he come
90   He find the Heart from home)
    Doubtless he will unload
    Himself some other where,
    And pour abroad
    His pretious sweets
95 On the fair soul whom first he meets.
O fair, O fortunate! O rich, O dear!
O happy & thrice happy she
    Selected dove
    Who ere she be,
100   Whose early love
    With winged vows
Makes hast to meet her morning spouse
And close with his immortal kisses.
Happy indeed, who never misses
105 To improve that pretious hour,
    And every day
    Seize her sweet prey
All fresh & fragrant as he rises
Dropping with a balmy Shower
110 A delicious dew of spices;
O let the blissful heart hold fast
Her heavenly arm-full, she shall taste
At once ten thousand paradises;
    She shall have power
115   To rifle & deflower
The rich & roseal spring of those rare sweets
Which with a swelling bosom there she meets
    Boundless & infinite
    Bottomless treasures
120 Of pure inebriating pleasures.
Happy proof! She shall discover

> What joy, what bliss,
> How many Heav'ns at once it is
> To have her GOD become her LOVER.

ROBERT HERRICK (1591–1674)

The son of a goldsmith, Herrick entered the Church. His poetry reveals the nostalgic celebration of English rural life and pastimes characteristic of Royalist poetry during the Civil War. He excelled at the epigram, and his collected poems, *Hesperides*, published in 1648 contains over 1400 poems.

The Argument of his Book

> I sing of brooks, of blossoms, birds, and bowers,
> Of April, May, of June and July-flowers.
> I sing of May-poles, hock-carts, wassails, wakes,
> Of bridegrooms, brides and of their bridal-cakes.
> 5   I write of youth, of love and have access
> By these to sing of cleanly-wantonness.
> I sing of dews, of rains and piece by piece
> Of balm, of oil, of spice and ambergris.
> I sing of Time's trans-shifting; and I write
> 10 How roses first came red and lilies white.
> I write of groves, of twilights, and I sing
> The court of Mab and of the Fairy-King.
> I write of Hell; I sing (and ever shall)
> Of Heaven, and hope to have it after all.

Upon a Child

> Here a pretty baby lies
> Sung asleep with lullabies;
> Pray be silent, and not stir
> Th' easy earth that covers her.

To Meadows

> Ye have been fresh and green,
> Ye have been filled with flowers:
> And ye the walks have been
> Where maids have spent their hours.

Argument 3 **May-poles:** around which dances were held to celebrate Spring's fertility. **hock-carts:** brought in the last load of hay from the harvest. **wassails:** drinking health at Christmas and New Year.   3 **wakes:** annual village festival.   8 **ambergris:** secretion from whales used in cooking and to make perfume.   12 **Mab:** fairy queen who acts as a midwife to mankind's dreams.

You have beheld, how they
5   With wicker arks did come
To kiss, and bear away
The richer cowslips home.

Y'ave heard them sweetly sing,
And seen them in a round:
10   Each virgin, like a Spring,
With honeysuckles crowned.

But now, we see, none here,
Whose silv'rie feet did tread,
And with dishevelled hair,
15   Adorned this smoother mead.

Like unthrifts, having spent,
Your stock, and needy grown,
Y'are left here to lament
Your poor estates, alone.

EDMUND WALLER (1606–1687)

Waller had an active public life, serving in Parliament for many years, despite upholding Royalist values during the Civil War. His poetry is best know for its eloquent love lyrics, of which 'Go lovely Rose' is a famous example of *carpe diem* or 'seize the moment', a rhetorical persuasion to a reluctant lover.

Song: Go Lovely Rose

Go, lovely Rose,
Tell her that wastes her time and me,
That now she knows
When I resemble her to thee,
5   How sweet and fair she seems to be.

Tell her that's young,
And shuns to have her graces spied,
That hadst thou sprung
In deserts, where no men abide,
10   Thou must have uncommended died.

Small is the worth
Of beauty from the light retired;
Bid her come forth,
Suffer herself to be desired,
15   And not blush so to be admired.

Then die that she
The common fate of all things rare
May read in thee;
How small a part of time they share
20   That are so wondrous sweet and fair.

RICHARD LOVELACE (1618–1658)

A fervent Royalist, Lovelace was imprisoned for a year by Parliament during the Civil War. His poetry expresses the Royalist desire to return to a harmonious pastoral English 'golden age', presented in contrast to the conflicts of the present.

The Grasshopper

To My Noble Friend Master Charles Cotton: Ode

O thou that swing'st upon the waving hair
Of some well-filled oaten beard,
Drunk every night with a delicious tear
Dropped thee from heaven, where now th' art reared.

5   The joys of earth and air are thine entire,
That with thy feet and wings dost hop and fly;
And when thy poppy works thou dost retire
To thy carved acorn-bed to lie.

Up with the day, the sun thou welcom'st then,
10   Sport'st in the gilt-plats of his beams,
And all these merry days mak'st merry men,
Thy self, and melancholy streams.

But ah, the sickle! Golden ears are cropped;
Ceres and Bacchus bid good night;
15   Sharp frosty fingers all your flowers have topped,
And what scythes spared, winds shave off quite.

Poor verdant fool! And now green ice! Thy joys,
Large and as lasting as thy perch of grass,
Bid us lay in 'gainst winter, rain, and poise
20   Their floods with an o'erflowing glass.

Thou best of men and friends! We will create
A genuine summer in each other's breast;
And spite of this cold time and frozen fate,
Thaw us a warm seat to our rest.

Grasshopper 14 **Ceres**: goddess of the harvest. **Bacchus**: god of wine. 19 **poise**: balance.

25 Our sacred hearths shall burn eternally
As vestal flames; the North-wind, he
Shall strike his frost-stretched wings, dissolve, and fly
This Etna in epitome.

Dropping December shall come weeping in,
30 Bewailing th'usurping of his reign;
But when in showers of old Greek we begin
Shall cry, he hath his crown again.

Night as clear Hesper shall our tapers whip
From the light Casements where we play,
35 And the dark Hag from her black mantle strip,
And stick there everlasting day.

Thus richer than untempted kings are we,
That asking nothing, nothing need;
Though lord of all what seas embrace; yet he
40 That wants himself, is poor indeed.

HENRY VAUGHAN (1622–1695)

Vaughan studied in Oxford and in London before returning to his native Wales to practise medicine. A Royalist supporter during the Civil War, his poetry often registers a sense of social disintegration. Vaughan found solace in the discovery of the divine in nature and his major work, *Silex Scintillans* (1650, expanded in 1655), shows an intense combination of devotional and pastoral traditions.

Vanity of Spirit

Quite spent with thoughts I left my Cell, and lay
Where a shrill spring tuned to the early day.
　I begged here long, and groaned to know
　Who gave the clouds so brave a bow,
5 　Who bent the spheres, and circled in
　Corruption with this glorious Ring,
　What is his name, and how I might
　Descry some part of his great light.
I summoned nature; pierced through all her store,
10 Broke up some seals, which none had touched before,
　Her womb, her bosom, and her head
　Where all her secrets lay a bed
　I rifled quite, and having passed
　Through all the Creatures, came at last

---

33 **Hesper:** the evening star.　35 **mantle:** covering.　6 **Ring:** eternity; the circle signifies perfection.

15   To search myself, where I did find
        Traces, and sounds of a strange kind.
      Here of this mighty spring, I found some drills,
      With Echoes beaten from th' eternal hills;
        Weak beams, and fires flashed to my sight,
20   Like a young East, or moonshine night,
      Which showed me in a nook cast by
      A piece of much antiquity,
      With Hieroglyphics quite dismembered,
      And broken letters scarce remembered.
25   I took them up, and (much joyed) went about
      T' unite those pieces, hoping to find out
        The mystery; but this near done,
      That little light I had was gone;
      It grieved me much. At last, said I,
30   *Since in these veils my eclipsed Eye*
      May not approach thee (for at night
      Who can have commerce with the light?),
      I'll disapparel, and to buy
      But one half glance, most gladly die.

The Retreat

      Happy those early days! when I
      Shined in my angel-infancy.
      Before I understood this place
      Appointed for my second race,
5   Or taught my soul to fancy ought
      But a white, Celestial thought;
      When yet I had not walked above
      A mile or two from my first love,
      And looking back (at that short space)
10   Could see a glimpse of his bright face;
      When on some gilded Cloud or flower
      My gazing soul would dwell an hour,
      And in those weaker glories spy
      Some shadows of eternity;
15   Before I taught my tongue to wound
      My conscience with a sinful sound,
      Or had the black art to dispense,
      A sev'ral sin to ev'ry sense,
      But felt through all this fleshly dress
20   Bright shoots of everlastingness.
        O how I long to travel back,
      And tread again that ancient track.

Vanity of Spirit, 17 drills: trickles, small springs.   23 Hieroglyphics: secret figures with hidden meanings.

That I might once more reach that plain,
Where first I left my glorious train,
25 From whence th' enlightened spirit sees
That shady City of Palm trees.
But (ah!) My soul with too much stay
Is drunk, and staggers in the way.
Some men a forward motion love,
30 But I by backward steps would move,
And when this dust falls to the urn,
In that state I came, return.

SIR THOMAS BROWNE (1605–1682)

Browne spent the greater part of his life as a physician in Norfolk. His prose reveals a probing mind, curious about humanity's place in the world. But Browne's starting point is that natural experience is useful in helping to understand the divine and his work exemplifies the inseparability of early-modern scientific thought from sacred questions. The *Religio Medici* was first published in 1642.

From Religio Medici

Now for that other Virtue of Charity, without which faith is a mere notion and of no existence, I have ever endeavoured to nourish the merciful disposition and humane inclination I borrowed from my Parents, and regulate it to the written and prescribed Laws of Charity. And if I hold the true anatomy of myself, I am delineated and naturally framed to such a piece of virtue; for I am of a constitution so general that it consorts and sympathiseth with all things; I have no antipathy, or rather idiosyncrasy, in diet, humour, air, anything. I wonder not at the French for their dishes of frogs, snails, and toadstools, nor at the Jews for locusts and grasshoppers; but, being amongst them, make them my common viands; and I find they agree with my stomach as well as theirs. I could digest a salad gathered in a churchyard as well as in a garden. I cannot start at the presence of a serpent, scorpion, lizard, or salamander; at the sight of a toad or viper, I find in me no desire to take up a stone to destroy them. I feel not in myself those common antipathies that I can discover in others: those national repugnances do not touch me, nor do I behold with prejudice the French, Italian, Spaniard, or Dutch; but, where I find their actions in balance with my countrymen's, I honour, love, and embrace them, in the same degree. I was born in the eighth climate,[1] but seem to be framed and constellated unto all. I am no plant that will not prosper out of a garden. All places, all airs, make unto me one country; I am in England everywhere, and under any meridian. I have been shipwrackt, yet am not enemy with the sea or winds; I can study, play, or sleep in a tempest. In brief, I am averse from nothing; my conscience would give me the lie if I should say I absolutely detest or hate any

---

26 **City:** Jericho, where Moses died.   1 **climate:** region defined by weather.

essence, but the devil; or so at least abhor anything, but that we might come to composition. If there be any among those common objects of hatred I do contemn and laugh at, it is that great enemy of reason, virtue, and religion, the Multitude; that numerous piece of monstrosity, which taken asunder seem men, and the reasonable creatures of God, but, confused together, make but one great beast, and a monstrosity more prodigious than Hydra.[1] It is no breach of Charity to call these Fools; it is the style all holy writers have afforded them, set down by Solomon in canonical Scripture,[2] and a point of our faith to believe so. Neither in the name of Multitude do I only include the base and minor sort of people; there is a rabble even amongst the Gentry; a sort of plebeian heads, whose fancy moves with the same wheel as these, men in the same level with Mechanics,[3] though their fortunes do somewhat gild their infirmities, and their purses compound for their follies. But, as in casting account three or four men together come short in account of one man placed by himself below them,[4] so neither are a troop of these ignorant *Doradoes*[5] of that true esteem and value as many a forlorn person, whose condition doth place him below their feet. Let us speak like politicians; there is a nobility without heraldry, a natural dignity, whereby one man is ranked with another, another filed before him, according to the quality of his desert, and pre-eminence of his good parts. Though the corruption of these times, and the bias of present practice, wheel another way, thus it was in the first and primitive commonwealths, and is yet in the integrity and cradle of well ordered politics – till corruption getteth ground, ruder desires labouring after that which wiser considerations contemn, every one having a liberty to amass and heap up riches, and they a licence or faculty to do or purchase anything.

This general and indifferent temper of mine doth more nearly dispose me to this noble virtue. It is a happiness to be born and framed unto virtue, and to grow up from the seeds of nature, rather than the inoculations and forced grafts of education. Yet, if we are directed only by our particular Natures, and regulate our inclinations by no higher rule than that of our reasons, we are but Moralists; Divinity will still call us Heathens. Therefore this great work of charity must have other motives, ends, and impulsions. I give no alms to satisfy the hunger of my Brother, but to fulfil and accomplish the Will and Command of my God; I draw not my purse for his sake that demands it, but his that enjoined it; I relieve no man upon the rhetoric of his miseries, nor to content mine own commiserating disposition; for this is still but moral charity, and an act that oweth more to passion than reason. He that relieves another upon the bare suggestion and bowels of pity doth not this so much for his sake as for his own; for by compassion we make another's misery our own; and so, by reliev-ing them, we relieve ourselves also. It is as erroneous a conceit to redress other men's misfortunes upon the common considerations of merciful natures, that it may be one day our own case; for this is a sinister and politic kind of charity, whereby we seem to bespeak the pities of men in the like occasions. And truly I have observed that those professed Eleemosynaries,[6] though in a crowd or

---

1 **Hydra**: mythical beast with seven heads.   2 **Scripture**: Proverbs 1:7, 'fools despise wisdom and instruction'.
3 **Mechanics**: manual labourers.   4 referring to counting on an abacus where each bead on the top row counts as one but counts as five on the second row.   5 ***Doradoes***: gilded figures.   6 **Eleemosynaries**: beggars.

multitude, do yet direct and place their petitions on a few and selected persons; there is surely a Physiognomy,[1] which those experienced and Master Mendicants observe, whereby they instantly discover a merciful aspect, and will single out a face, wherein they spy the signatures and marks of mercy. For there are mystically in our faces certain characters which carry in them the motto of our souls, wherein he that cannot read A B C may read our natures. I hold, moreover, that there is a Phytognomy,[2] or Physiognomy, not only of men, but of plants and vegetables; and in every one of them some outward figures which hang as signs or bushes of their inward forms. The finger of God hath left an inscription upon all his works, not graphical, or composed of letters, but of their several forms, constitutions, parts, and operations, which, aptly joined together, do make one word that doth express their natures. By these letters God calls the stars by their names; and by this alphabet Adam assigned to every creature a name peculiar to its Nature. Now, there are, besides these characters in our faces, certain mystical figures in our hands, which I dare not call mere dashes, strokes *à la volée* or at random, because delineated by a pencil that never works in vain; and hereof I take more particular notice, because I carry that in mine own hand which I could never read of nor discover in another. Aristotle, I confess, in his acute and singular book of Physiognomy,[3] hath made no mention of chiromancy.[4] Yet I believe the Egyptians, who were nearer addicted to those abstruse and mystical sciences, had a knowledge therein; to which those vagabond and counterfeit Egyptians[5] did after pretend, and perhaps retained a few corrupted principles, which sometimes might verify their prognostics.

It is the common wonder of all men, how, among so many millions of faces, there should be none alike. Now, contrary, I wonder as much how there should be any. He that shall consider how many thousand several words have been carelessly and without study composed out of twenty-four letters; withal, how many hundred lines there are to be drawn in the fabric of one man, shall easily find that this variety is necessary; and it will be very hard that they shall so concur as to make one portrait like another. Let a painter carelessly limb[6] out a million of faces, and you shall find them all different; yea, let him have his copy before him, yet, after all his art, there will remain a sensible distinction; for the pattern or example of everything is the perfectest in that kind, whereof we still come short, though we transcend or go beyond it; because herein it is wide, and agrees not in all points unto its copy.[7] Nor doth the similitude of creatures disparage the variety of Nature, nor any way confound the works of God. For even in things alike there is diversity; and those that do seem to accord do manifestly disagree. And thus is Man like God; for, in the same things that we resemble him we are utterly different from him. There was never anything so like another as in all points to concur; there will ever some reserved difference slip in, to prevent the identity; without which two several things would not be alike, but the same, which is impossible.

---

1 **Physiognomy**: judging character by facial appearance. 2 **Phytognomy**: judging character of plants by their appearance. 3 **Aristotle**: a tract incorrectly attributed to Aristotle. 4 **chiromancy**: reading the character in the lines of the hand. 5 **counterfeit Egyptians**: gypsies. 6 **limb**: limn – portray, paint. 7 **copy**: every copy made by man is necessarily not an accurate reflection of the ultimate 'copy' or design of God.

JOHN MILTON (1608–1674)

Milton is the best Renaissance example in Britain of a self-fashioning writer. From early youth Milton prepared himself to write a great literary work of national importance, one that would unquestionably show England at the centre of Humanist literary culture. This endeavour became the epic *Paradise Lost* but virtually all Milton's work exemplifies the marriage of classical and Christian models to a distinct English Protestant vision. Milton did not see a separation between literary activity and social involvement. During the Civil War he became England's most articulate defender of republican ideals and held the important position of Secretary for Foreign Tongues in Cromwell's government.

From On the Morning of Christ's Nativity

This is the Month, and this the happy morn
Wherin the Son of Heaven's eternal King,
Of wedded Maid, and Virgin Mother born,
Our great redemption from above did bring;
5   For so the holy sages once did sing,
     That he our deadly forfeit should release,
And with his Father work us a perpetual peace.

That glorious Form, that Light unsufferable,
And that far-beaming blaze of Majesty,
10   Wherewith he wont at Heaven's high council-table,
To sit the midst of trinal unity,
He laid aside; and here with us to be,
Forsook the courts of everlasting Day,
And chose with us a darksome House of mortal Clay.

15   Say Heavenly Muse, shall not thy sacred vein
Afford a present to the Infant God?
Hast thou no verse, no hymn, or solemn strain,
To welcome him to this his new abode,
Now while the Heaven by the Sun's team untrod,
20   Hath took no print of the approaching light,
And all the spangled host keep watch in squadrons bright?

See how from far upon the Eastern road
The Star-led Wizards haste with odours sweet,
O run, prevent them with thy humble ode,
25   And lay it lowly at his blessed feet;
Have thou the honour first, thy Lord to greet,
And join thy voice unto the Angel Quire,
From out his secret Altar toucht with hallowed fire.

---

5 holy sages: the Hebrew prophets of the Old Testament. **6 forfeit:** sin and death, the result of Original sin inherited through Adam and Eve. **11 trinal unity:** Father, Son and Holy Spirit. **28 Altar:** In Isaiah 6:6–7 an angel touches the prophet's lips with a burning coal and he becomes inspired by God.

Lycidas

Lycidas first appeared in a 1638 collection of memorial verse on the death of Edward King – the Lycidas of the poem. King had been a Fellow of Christ's College Cambridge, which Milton also attended, but Milton does not appear to have known him intimately. As with the other poems of the volume, the death provided an opportunity to demonstrate poetic skill in elegy. Milton added the headnote below to the 1645 collection of his poems, and the text of the poem adheres to the 1645 edition.

'In this monody the author bewails a learned friend, unfortunately drowned in his passage from Chester on the Irish Seas, 1637. And by occasion foretells the ruin of our corrupted clergy then in their height.'

> Yet once more, O ye Laurels, and once more
> Ye Myrtles brown, with Ivy never sere,
> I come to pluck your berries harsh and crude,
> And with forced fingers rude,
> 5   Shatter your leaves before the mellowing year.
> Bitter constraint, and sad occasion dear,
> Compels me to disturb your season due.
> For Lycidas is dead, dead ere his prime
> Young Lycidas, and hath not left his peer.
> 10   Who would not sing for Lycidas? He knew
> Himself to sing, and build the lofty rhyme.
> He must not float upon his watery bier
> Unwept, and welter to the parching wind,
> Without the meed of some melodious tear.
> 15   Begin then, Sisters of the sacred well,
> That from beneath the seat of Jove doth spring,
> Begin, and somewhat loudly sweep the string.
> Hence with denial vain, and coy excuse,
> So may some gentle Muse
> 20   With lucky words favour my destined urn,
> And as he passes turn,
> And bid fair peace be to my sable shroud.
> For we were nurst upon the self-same hill,
> Fed the same flock, by fountain, shade, and rill.
> 25   Together both, ere the high lawns appeared
> Under the opening eye-lids of the morn,
> We drove a field, and both together heard
> What time the gray-fly winds her sultry horn,
> Batt'ning our flocks with the fresh dews of night,
> 30   Oft till the star that rose, at ev'ning bright
> Toward heaven's descent had sloped his westering wheel.

---

2 **never sere**: evergreen. 13 **welter**: tossed about. 22 **sable**: black. 24 **rill**: small stream. 25 **lawns**: glades. 14 **meed**: gift. 15 **Sisters**: the nine muses. **well**: Aganippe on Mount Helicon.

Mean while the rural ditties were not mute,
Tempered to th' oaten flute;
Rough satyrs danced, and fauns with cloven heel,
35   From the glad sound would not be absent long,
And old Damaetas loved to hear our song,
      But O the heavy change, now thou art gone,
Now thou art gone, and never must return!
Thee shepherd, thee the woods, and desert caves,
40   With wild thyme and the gadding vine o'regrown,
And all their echoes mourn.
The willows, and the hazel copses green,
Shall now no more be seen,
Fanning their joyous leaves to thy soft lays.
45   As killing as the canker to the rose,
Or taint-worm to the weanling herds that graze,
Or frost to flowers, that their gay wardrobe wear,
When first the white thorn blows;
Such, Lycidas, thy loss to shepherds ear.
50   Where were ye nymphs when the remorseless deep
Closed o're the head of your loved Lycidas?
For neither were ye playing on the steep,
Where your old bards, the famous Druids lie,
Nor on the shaggy top of Mona high,
55   Nor yet where Deva spreads her wizard stream:
Ay me, I fondly dream!
Had ye been there – for what could that have done?
What could the Muse her self that Orpheus bore,
The Muse her self, for her inchanting son
60   Whom universal nature did lament,
When by the rout that made the hideous roar,
His gory visage down the stream was sent,
Down the swift Hebrus to the Lesbian shore.
      Alas! What boots it with uncessant care
65   To tend the homely slighted shepherd's trade,
And strictly meditate the thankless muse,
Were it not better done as others use,
To sport with Amaryllis in the shade,
Or with the tangles of Neaera's hair?
70   Fame is the spur that the clear spirit doth raise
(That last infirmity of noble mind)
To scorn delights, and live laborious days;

---

33 **oaten:** made of oat reeds. 34 **fauns:** like satyrs, half man, half goat. 40 **gadding:** wandering. 46 **weanling:** weaning. 53 **Druids:** ancient British priests and soothsayers. 54 **Mona:** Anglesey in Wales. 55 **Deva:** the river Dee.

58 **Muse:** Calliope. **Orpheus:** mythological lyricist who could charm wild beasts with his song. 61 **rout that made . . . . :** Orpheus was torn to bits by savage Thracian women and his head floated to the island of Lesbos.

But the fair guerdon when we hope to find,
And think to burst out into sudden blaze,
75 Comes the blind Fury with th' abhorred shears,
And slits the thin spun life. But not the praise,
Phoebus replied, and touched my trembling ears;
Fame is no plant that grows on mortal soil,
Nor in the glistering foil
80 Set off to th' world, nor in broad rumour lies,
But lives and spreads aloft by those pure eyes,
And perfect witness of all judging Jove;
As he pronounces lastly on each deed,
Of so much fame in Heaven expect thy meed.
85   O fountain Arethuse, and thou honoured flood,
Smooth-sliding Mincius, crowned with vocal reeds,
That strain I heard was of a higher mood;
But now my Oat proceeds,
And listens to the Herald of the Sea
90 That came in Neptune's plea,
He asked the waves, and asked the felon winds,
What hard mishap hath doomed this gentle swain?
And questioned every gust of rugged wings
That blows from off each beaked promontory,
95 They knew not of his story,
And sage Hippotades their answer brings,
That not a blast was from his dungeon strayed,
The air was calm, and on the level brine,
Sleek Panope with all her sisters played.
100 It was that fatal and perfidious bark
Built in th' eclipse, and rigged with curses dark,
That sunk so low that sacred head of thine.
Next Camus, reverend sire, went footing slow,
His mantle hairy, and his bonnet sedge,
105 Inwrought with figures dim, and on the edge
Like to that sanguine flower inscribed with woe.
Ah; who hath reft (quoth he) my dearest pledge?
Last came, and last did go,
The Pilot of the Galilean lake,
110 Two massy keys he bore of metals twain,
(The golden opes, the iron shuts amain)
He shook his mitered locks, and stern bespake,

---

73 guerdon: reward. **75:** in classical mythology the Fates (not the Furies) cut the thread of life when its allotted length has been unravelled. **77 Phoebus:** Apollo, god of serious lyric poetry. **79 foil:** thin gold used in jewellery to enhance a jewel. **89 Herald:** Triton. **96 Hippotades:** Aeolus, god of the winds. **99 Panope:** sea nymph.

103 Camus, the river Cam at Cambridge, here synonymous with the University, which both King and Milton attended. **104 mantle hairy:** a fur-trimmed academic gown. **104 sedge:** rushes growing in streams. **106 flower:** the hyacinth, sprung from the blood of Hyacinth, whom his lover Apollo accidentally killed. **107 reft:** robbed. **109 Pilot:** St Peter, keeper of the keys to Heaven.

How well could I have spared for thee, young swain,
Anow of such as for their bellies sake,
115   Creep and intrude, and climb into the fold?
Of other care they little reck'ning make,
Then how to scramble at the shearers feast,
And shove away the worthy bidden guest.
Bind mouths! That scarce themselves know how to hold
120   A sheep-hook, or have learned ought else the least
That to the faithful herdman's art belongs!
What recks it them? What need they? They are sped;
And when they list, their lean and flashy songs
Grate on their scrannel pipes of wretched straw,
125   The hungry sheep look up, and are not fed,
But swollen with wind, and the rank mist they draw,
Rot inwardly, and foul contagion spread;
Besides what the grim wolf with privy paw
Daily devours apace, and nothing said,
130   But that two-handed engine at the door,
Stands ready to smite once, and smite no more.
    Return Alpheus, the dread voice is past,
That shrunk thy streams; return Sicilian Muse,
And call the vales, and bid them hither cast
135   Their bells, and flowrets of a thousand hues.
Ye valleys low where the mild whispers use,
Of shades and wanton winds, and gushing brooks,
On whose fresh lap the swart star sparely looks,
Throw hither all your quaint enamelled eyes,
140   That on the green turf suck the honied showers,
And purple all the ground with vernal flowers.
Bring the rathe primrose that forsaken dies.
The tufted crow-toe, and pale jessamine,
The white pink, and the pansy freakt with jet,
145   The glowing violet.
The musk-rose, and the well attired woodbine.
With cowslips wan that hang the pensive head,
And every flower that sad embroidery wears;
Bid amaranthus all his beauty shed,
150   And daffadillies fill their cups with tears,
To strew the laureat hearse where Lycid lies.
For so to interpose a little ease,
Let our frail thoughts dally with false surmise.

---

111 **amain:** vehemently. 114 **Anow:** enough.
122 **recks:** concerns. **sped:** satisfied. 123 **list:**
please. 124 **scrannel:** thin. 132 **Alpheus:** the
source of Arethusa's fountain: see ll. 85–88.
133 **Sicilian Muse:** the inspiration of pastoral poetry.

138 **swart star:** Sirius, associated with hot days, swart –
blackened by heat. 142 **rathe:** early. 144 **freakt with
jet:** streaked with black. 147 **wan:** pale.

Ay me! Whilst thee the shores, and sounding seas
155   Wash far away, where ere thy bones are hurled,
Whether beyond the stormy Hebrides,
Where thou perhaps under the whelming tide
Visit'st the bottom of the monstrous world;
Or whether thou to our moist vows denied,
160   Sleep'st by the fable of Bellerus old,
Where the great vision of the guarded Mount
Looks toward Namancos and Bayona's hold;
Look homeward angel now, and melt with ruth.
And, O ye dolphins, waft the hapless youth.
165   Weep no more, woeful shepherds weep no more,
For Lycidas your sorrow is not dead,
Sunk though he be beneath the watery floor,
So sinks the day-star in the ocean bed,
And yet anon repairs his drooping head,
170   And tricks his beams, and with new spangled ore,
Flames in the forehead of the morning sky.
So Lycidas sunk low, but mounted high,
Through the dear might of him that walked the waves;
Where other groves, and other streams along,
175   With nectar pure his oozy lock's he laves,
And hears the unexpressive nuptial song,
In the blest kingdoms meek of joy and love.
There entertain him all the saints above,
In solemn troops, and sweet societies
180   That sing, and singing in their glory move,
And wipe the tears for ever from his eyes.
Now Lycidas the shepherds weep no more;
Hence forth thou art the Genius of the shore,
In thy large recompense, and shalt be good
185   To all that wander in that perilous flood.
        Thus sang the uncouth swain to th' oaks and rills,
While the still morn went out with sandals gray,
He touched the tender stops of various quills,
With eager thought warbling his doric lay:
190   And now the Sun had stretched out all the hills,
And now was dropt into the western bay;
At last he rose, and twitched his mantle blew;
Tomorrow to fresh woods, and pastures new.

---

160 **Bellerus:** Milton's imaginative name for Cornwall. 161 **Mount:** Milton presents St Michael's Mount in Cornwall guarding (Protestant) Britain against (Roman Catholic) Namancos in Spain and Bayona in France. 163 **ruth:** compassion. 173 **him:** Christ. 176 **unexpressive . . . . :** the inexpressible marriage between Christ and the soul. 186 **uncouth:** unknown. 189 **doric:** a Greek form often used for pastoral.

[When I consider how my light is spent]

When I consider how my light is spent,
E're half my days, in this dark world and wide,
And that one talent which is death to hide,
Lodged with me useless, though my soul more bent
5   To serve therewith my maker, and present
My true account, least he returning chide,
Doth God exact day-labour, light denied,
I fondly ask. But patience to prevent
That murmur, soon replies, God doth not need
10   Either man's work or his own gifts, who best
Bear his mild yoak, they serve him best, his state
Is kingly. Thousands at his bidding speed
And post o're land and ocean without rest.
They also serve who only stand and wait.

[Methought I saw my late espoused saint]

Methought I saw my late espoused saint
Brought to me like Alcestis from the grave,
Whom Jove's great son to her glad husband gave,
Rescued from death by force though pale and faint.
5   Mine as whom washt from spot of child-bed taint,
Purification in the old Law did save,
And such, as yet once more I trust to have
Full sight of her in Heaven without restraint,
Came vested all in white, pure as her mind;
10   Her face was vailed, yet to my fancied sight,
Love, sweetness, goodness, in her person shined
So clear, as in no face with more delight.
But O as to embrace me she enclined
I waked, she fled, and day brought back my night.

When I consider,6 chide: scold.   Methought I 6 old Law: The Old Testament ruled that a woman was
saw,1 saint: almost certainly Milton's second wife, 'unclean' for over 2 months after the birth of a female
Katherine Woodcock. 2 Alcestis: she willingly died in child and must touch no sacred thing or come into the
place of her husband. Hercules, Jove's son, brought her temple.
back from the underworld.

From Paradise Lost, Book IV

Milton's epic poem *Paradise Lost* was first published in 1667. It charts the war in Heaven; the defeat of Satan and his rebel angels; the creation of the world and mankind; Satan's temptation of Eve and the 'fall' of humanity. It also looks forward to humanity's salvation through Messiah's (Christ's) sacrifice. In Book I Milton announces the poem's aim as justifying 'the ways of God to men', a belief in a providential order created by an ultimately benevolent God despite human sin. In part, his epic reflects what Milton saw as the tragic failure of the English to sustain a truly godly state, a commonwealth he believed should have been founded by the English Republic during the Civil War period of 1640–1660. The section below is from Book IV: Satan has travelled from Hell to the newly created Eden seeking to disrupt God's work.

O for that warning voice which he, who saw
The Apocalypse, heard cry in Heaven aloud,
Then when the Dragon, put to second rout,
Came furious down to be revenged on men,
5 *Woe to the inhabitants on earth!* that now,
While time was, our first parents had been warned
The coming of their secret foe, and scaped,
Haply so scaped his mortal snare; for now
Satan, now first inflamed with rage, came down,
10 The tempter ere the accuser of mankind,
To wreak on innocent frail man his loss
Of that first battle, and his flight to Hell;
Yet not rejoicing in his speed, though bold,
Far off and fearless, nor with cause to boast,
15 Begins his dire attempt, which nigh the birth
Now rolling, boils in his tumultuous breast,
And like a devilish engine back recoils
Upon himself; horror and doubt distract
His troubled thoughts, and from the bottom stir
20 The Hell within him; for within him Hell
He brings, and round about him, nor from Hell
One step no more than from himself can fly
By change of place; now conscience wakes despair,
That slumbered, wakes the bitter memory
25 Of what he was, what is, and what must be
Worse; of worse deeds worse sufferings must ensue.
Sometimes towards Eden which now in his view
Lay pleasant, his grieved look he fixes sad,
Sometimes towards Heaven, and the full-blazing sun,
30 Which now sat high in his meridian tower:
Then much revolving, thus in sighs began.

---

2 Apocalypse: the end of the world as foretold in the Bible's Book of Revelations.

3 the Dragon: Satan. **5 *Woe to the inhabitants* . . .** : Revelations 12:7–12.

'O thou that with surpassing glory crowned,
Look'st from thy sole dominion like the God
Of this new world, at whose sight all the stars
35 Hide their diminished heads, to thee I call,
But with no friendly voice, and add thy name
O Sun! to tell thee how I hate thy beams
That bring to my remembrance from what state
I fell, how glorious once above thy sphere;
40 Till pride and worse ambition threw me down
Warring in Heaven against Heaven's matchless King:
Ah, wherefore! he deserved no such return
From me, whom he created what I was
In that bright eminence, and with his good
45 Upbraided none; nor was his service hard.
What could be less than to afford him praise,
The easiest recompense, and pay him thanks,
How due! yet all his good proved ill in me,
And wrought but malice; lifted up so high
50 I sdeigned subjection, and thought one step higher
Would set me highest, and in a moment quit
The debt immense of endless gratitude,
So burdensome still paying, still to owe;
Forgetful what from him I still received,
55 And understood not that a grateful mind
By owing owes not, but still pays, at once
Indebted and discharged: what burden then?
O had his powerful destiny ordained
Me some inferior angel, I had stood
60 Then happy; no unbounded hope had raised
Ambition. Yet why not? Some other power
As great might have aspired, and me though mean
Drawn to his part; but other powers as great
Fell not, but stand unshaken, from within
65 Or from without to all temptations armed.
Hadst thou the same free will and power to stand?
Thou hadst; whom hast thou then or what to accuse,
But Heaven's free love dealt equally to all?
Be then his love accursed, since love or hate,
70 To me alike, it deals eternal woe.
Nay, cursed be thou; since against his thy will
Chose freely what it now so justly rues.
Me miserable! Which way shall I fly
Infinite wrath, and infinite despair?

---

50 **sdeigned**: disdained. 59 **inferior angel**: traditionally there are nine orders of angels. Lucifer/Satan
belonged to the highest.   61 **power**: recalling Powers, one of the higher orders of
angels.

75   Which way I fly is Hell; myself am Hell;
     And, in the lowest deep, a lower deep
     Still threatening to devour me opens wide,
     To which the Hell I suffer seems a Heaven.
     O, then, at last relent: is there no place
80   Left for repentance, none for pardon left?
     None left but by submission; and that word
     Disdain forbids me, and my dread of shame
     Among the Spirits beneath, whom I seduced
     With other promises and other vaunts
85   Than to submit, boasting I could subdue
     The Omnipotent. Ay me, they little know
     How dearly I abide that boast so vain,
     Under what torments inwardly I groan,
     While they adore me on the throne of Hell,
90   With diadem and sceptre high advanced,
     The lower still I fall, only supreme
     In misery: such joy ambition finds.
     But say I could repent, and could obtain,
     By act of grace, my former state; how soon
95   Would height recall high thoughts, how soon unsay
     What feigned submission swore; ease would recant
     Vows made in pain, as violent and void.
     For never can true reconcilement grow,
     Where wounds of deadly hate have pierced so deep:
100 Which would but lead me to a worse relapse
     And heavier fall: so should I purchase dear
     Short intermission bought with double smart.
     This knows my punisher; therefore as far
     From granting he, as I from begging, peace;
105 All hope excluded thus, behold in stead
     Of us outcast, exiled, his new delight,
     Mankind created, and for him this world.
     So farewell hope, and with hope, farewell fear,
     Farewell remorse; all good to me is lost;
110 Evil be thou my good; by thee at least
     Divided empire with Heaven's King I hold,
     By thee, and more than half perhaps will reign;
     As Man ere long, and this new world shall know.'
         Thus while he spake, each passion dimmed his face
115 Thrice changed with pale ire, envy, and despair,
     Which marred his borrowed visage, and betrayed
     Him counterfeit, if any eye beheld.
     For heavenly minds from such distempers foul

---

115 pale: white complexion. 120 perturbation: 126 **Assyrian mount**: mountain in the Middle East
disorder.   where the Tigris (the river of Paradise) originates.

Are ever clear. Whereof he soon aware,
120 Each perturbation smoothed with outward calm,
Artificer of fraud; and was the first
That practised falsehood under saintly show,
Deep malice to conceal, couched with revenge;
Yet not enough had practised to deceive
125 Uriel once warned; whose eye pursued him down
The way he went, and on the Assyrian mount
Saw him disfigured, more than could befall
Spirit of happy sort; his gestures fierce
He marked and mad demeanour, then alone,
130 As he supposed, all unobserved, unseen.
So on he fares, and to the border comes
Of Eden, where delicious Paradise,
Now nearer, crowns with her enclosure green,
As with a rural mound, the champaign head
135 Of a steep wilderness, whose hairy sides
With thicket overgrown, grotesque and wild,
Access denied; and overhead upgrew
Insuperable height of loftiest shade,
Cedar, and pine, and fir, and branching palm,
140 A sylvan scene, and as the ranks ascend,
Shade above shade, a woody theatre
Of stateliest view. Yet higher than their tops
The verdurous wall of Paradise upsprung;
Which to our general sire gave prospect large
145 Into his nether empire neighbouring round.
And higher than that wall a circling row
Of goodliest trees, loaden with fairest fruit,
Blossoms and fruits at once of golden hue,
Appeared, with gay enamelled colours mixed;
150 On which the sun more glad impressed his beams
Than in fair evening cloud, or humid bow,
When God hath showered the earth; so lovely seemed
That landskip; And of pure now purer air
Meets his approach, and to the heart inspires
155 Vernal delight and joy, able to drive
All sadness but despair; Now gentle gales,
Fanning their odoriferous wings, dispense
Native perfumes, and whisper whence they stole
Those balmy spoils. As when to them who fail
160 Beyond the Cape of Hope, and now are past
Mozambick, off at sea north-east winds blow

---

134 **champaign**: open, unenclosed. An issue during the English Civil War was about the right of the unpropertied to use common land. 138 **Insuperable**: unconquerable. 149 **enamelled**: smooth, lustrous surface covering. 153 **landskip**: landscape. 160 **Cape of Hope**: The Cape of Good Hope at the southern tip of Africa, the European trade route to the East. 161 **Mozambick**: Mozambique.

Sabean odours from the spicy shore
Of Araby the blest, with such delay
Well pleased they slack their course, and many a league
165   Cheered with the grateful smell old Ocean smiles:
So entertained those odorous sweets the Fiend,
Who came their bane; though with them better pleased
Than Asmodeus with the fishy fume
That drove him, though enamoured, from the spouse
170   Of Tobit's son, and with a vengeance sent
From Media post to Egypt, there fast bound.
        Now to the ascent of that steep savage hill
Satan had journeyed on, pensive and slow;
But further way found none, so thick entwined,
175   As one continued brake, the undergrowth
Of shrubs and tangling bushes had perplexed
All path of man or beast that passed that way;
One gate there only was, and that looked east
On the other side: which when the arch-felon saw,
180   Due entrance he disdained; and, in contempt,
At one flight bound high overleaped all bound
Of hill or highest wall, and sheer within
Lights on his feet. As when a prowling wolf,
Whom hunger drives to seek new haunt for prey,
185   Watching where shepherds pen their flocks at eve
In hurdled cotes amid the field secure,
Leaps o'er the fence with ease into the fold;
Or as a thief, bent to unhoard the cash
Of some rich burgher, whose substantial doors,
190   Cross-barred and bolted fast, fear no assault,
In at the window climbs, or o'er the tiles;
So clomb this first grand thief into God's fold;
So since into his church lewd hirelings climb.
Thence up he flew, and on the tree of life,
195   The middle tree and highest there that grew,
Sat like a cormorant; yet not true life
Thereby regained, but sat devising death
To them who lived; nor on the virtue thought
Of that life-giving plant, but only used
200   For prospect, what well used had been the pledge
Of immortality. So little knows
Any, but God alone, to value right
The good before him, but perverts best things

---

163 Araby the blest: the classical *Arabia Felix*, modern Yemen. Sabean is Saba, another name for Yemen. **168 Asmodeus:** to Milton a king of the Demons. ll. 168–71 are based on the Bible's apocryphal Book of Tobit.

186 hurdled cotes: enclosed shelters.   **192 clomb:** climbed.   **193 lewd hirelings:** the ignorant or wicked who work only for material gain.   **196 cormorant:** a bird noted for its greedy appetite.

To worst abuse, or to their meanest use.
205   Beneath him with new wonder now he views,
To all delight of human sense exposed,
In narrow room nature's whole wealth, yea more,
A Heaven on Earth: for blissful Paradise
Of God the garden was, by him in the east
210   Of Eden planted; Eden stretched her line
From Auran eastward to the royal towers
Of great Seleucia, built by Grecian kings,
Or where the sons of Eden long before
Dwelt in Telassar; In this pleasant soil
215   His far more pleasant garden God ordained;
Out of the fertile ground he caused to grow
All trees of noblest kind for sight, smell, taste;
And all amid them stood the tree of life,
High eminent, blooming ambrosial fruit
220   Of vegetable gold; and next to life,
Our death, the tree of knowledge grew fast by,
Knowledge of good bought dear by knowing ill.
Southward through Eden went a river large,
Nor changed his course, but through the shaggy hill
225   Passed underneath ingulfed; for God had thrown
That mountain as his garden-mould high raised
Upon the rapid current, which through veins
Of porous earth with kindly thirst up-drawn,
Rose a fresh fountain, and with many a rill
230   Watered the garden; thence united fell
Down the steep glade, and met the nether flood,
Which from his darksome passage now appears,
And now divided into four main streams,
Runs diverse, wandering many a famous realm
235   And country, whereof here needs no account;
But rather to tell how, if art could tell,
How from that sapphire fount the crisped brooks,
Rolling on orient pearl and sands of gold,
With mazy error under pendant shades
240   Ran nectar, visiting each plant, and fed
Flowers worthy of Paradise, which not nice Art
In beds and curious knots, but Nature boon
Poured forth profuse on hill and dale and plain,
Both where the morning sun first warmly smote
245   The open field, and where the unpierced shade
Embrowned the noontide bowers; thus was this place

---

211 **Auran:** Hauran, lying east of the River Jordan, an eastern boundary of Israel. 212 **great Seleucia:** city on the Tigris river built by Seleucus Nicator, a general of Alexander the Great. 214 **Telassar:** biblical land which was completely destroyed. 219 **ambrosial:** immortal. 237 **crisped:** curled. 239 **pendant:** hanging. 242 **boon:** bounteous.

A happy rural seat of various view;
Groves whose rich trees wept odorous gums and balm,
Others whose fruit, burnished with golden rind,
250 Hung amiable, Hesperian fables true,
If true, here only, and of delicious taste;
Betwixt them lawns, or level downs, and flocks
Grazing the tender herb, were interposed,
Or palmy hillock, or the flowery lap
255 Of some irriguous valley spread her store,
Flowers of all hue, and without thorn the rose;
Another side, umbrageous grots and caves
Of cool recess, o'er which the mantling vine
Lays forth her purple grape, and gently creeps
260 Luxuriant; meanwhile murmuring waters fall
Down the slope hills, dispersed, or in a lake,
That to the fringed bank with myrtle crowned
Her crystal mirror holds, unite their streams.
The birds their choir apply; airs, vernal airs,
265 Breathing the smell of field and grove, attune
The trembling leaves, while universal Pan,
Knit with the Graces and the Hours in dance,
Led on the eternal Spring. Not that fair field
Of Enna, where Proserpine gathering flowers,
270 Herself a fairer flower by gloomy Dis
Was gathered, which cost Ceres all that pain
To seek her through the world; nor that sweet grove
Of Daphne by Orontes, and the inspired
Castalian spring, might with this Paradise
275 Of Eden strive; nor that Nyseian isle
Girt with the river Triton, where old Cham,
Whom Gentiles Ammon call and Libyan Jove,
Hid Amalthea, and her florid son
Young Bacchus, from his stepdame Rhea's eye;
280 Nor where Abassin kings their issue guard,
Mount Amara, though this by some supposed
True Paradise under the Ethiop line
By Nilus' head, enclosed with shining rock,
A whole day's journey high, but wide remote
285 From this Assyrian garden, where the Fiend
Saw undelighted all delight, all kind

---

250 **Hesperian fables:** garden of golden apples guarded by three sisters: the Hesperides. 255 **irriguous:** irrigated. 257 **umbrageous:** shady. 266 **Pan:** classical deity, Renaissance symbol for universal nature. 269 **Proserpine:** daughter of Ceres, goddess of agriculture, abducted by the god of the underworld, causing the seasons to change. 273 **Daphne:** nymph changed into a laurel tree when Apollo tried to rape her. 274 **Castalian spring:** on Mt Parnassus, sacred to Apollo and the Muses. 276 **Cham:** Ham, son of Noah, identified with King Ammon of Libya and the god Jupiter. Ammon fathered Bacchus after an affair with Amalthea. 280 **Abassin:** Abyssinian. 282 **Ethiop line:** Ethiopia is on the equator or line.

Of living creatures, new to sight, and strange;
Two of far nobler shape, erect and tall,
Godlike erect, with native honour clad
290   In naked majesty seemed lords of all,
And worthy seemed; for in their looks divine
The image of their glorious Maker shone,
Truth, wisdom, sanctitude severe and pure,
Severe, but in true filial freedom placed,
295   Whence true authority in men; though both
Not equal, as their sex not equal seemed;
For contemplation he and valour formed,
For softness she and sweet attractive grace;
He for God only, she for God in him;
300   His fair large front and eye sublime declared
Absolute rule; and hyacinthine locks
Round from his parted forelock manly hung
Clustering, but not beneath his shoulders broad;
She, as a veil, down to the slender waist
305   Her unadorned golden tresses wore
Dishevelled, but in wanton ringlets waved
As the vine curls her tendrils, which implied
Subjection, but required with gentle sway,
And by her yielded, by him best received,
310   Yielded with coy submission, modest pride,
And sweet reluctant amorous delay.
Nor those mysterious parts were then concealed;
Then was not guilty shame, dishonest shame
Of nature's works, honour dishonourable,
315   Sin-bred, how have ye troubled all mankind
With shows instead, mere shows of seeming pure,
And banished from man's life his happiest life,
Simplicity and spotless innocence.
So passed they naked on, nor shunned the sight
320   Of God or angel, for they thought no ill;
So hand in hand they passed, the loveliest pair
That ever since in love's embraces met,
Adam the goodliest man of men since born
His sons, the fairest of her daughters Eve.
325   Under a tuft of shade that on a green
Stood whispering soft, by a fresh fountain side
They sat them down, and after no more toil
Of their sweet gardening labour than sufficed
To recommend cool Zephyr, and made ease
330   More easy, wholesome thirst and appetite

---

301 hyacinthine locks: recalling the beautiful youth   **329 Zephyr:** the west wind.
Hyacinth, transformed to a flower after being
accidentally killed by Apollo.

More grateful, to their supper-fruits they fell,
Nectarine fruits which the compliant boughs
Yielded them, sidelong as they sat recline
On the soft downy bank damasked with flowers;
335 The savoury pulp they chew, and in the rind
Still as they thirsted scoop the brimming stream;
Nor gentle purpose, nor endearing smiles
Wanted, nor youthful dalliance, as beseems
Fair couple linked in happy nuptial league,
340 Alone as they. About them frisking played
All beasts of the earth, since wild, and of all chase
In wood or wilderness, forest or den;
Sporting the lion ramped, and in his paw
Dandled the kid; bears, tigers, ounces, pards,
345 Gambolled before them; the unwieldy elephant,
To make them mirth, used all his might, and wreathed
His lithe proboscis; close the serpent sly,
Insinuating, wove with Gordian twine
His braided train, and of his fatal guile
350 Gave proof unheeded; others on the grass
Couched, and now filled with pasture gazing sat,
Or bedward ruminating; for the sun,
Declined, was hasting now with prone career
To the Ocean Isles, and in the ascending scale
355 Of Heaven the stars that usher evening rose;
When Satan still in gaze as first he stood,
Scarce thus at length failed speech recovered sad.
    O Hell! What do mine eyes with grief behold,
Into our room of bliss thus high advanced
360 Creatures of other mould, earth-born perhaps,
Not spirits, yet to heavenly spirits bright
Little inferior; whom my thoughts pursue
With wonder, and could love, so lively shines
In them divine resemblance, and such grace
365 The hand that formed them on their shape hath poured.
Ah gentle pair, ye little think how nigh
Your change approaches, when all these delights
Will vanish, and deliver ye to woe,
More woe, the more your taste is now of joy;
370 Happy, but for so happy ill secured
Long to continue, and this high seat your heaven
Ill fenced for heaven to keep out such a foe
As now is entered; yet no purposed foe

---

334 **damasked**: ornamented with richly-figured designs. 344 **Dandled**: petted, fondled as a child. **ounces**: lynxes or other felines. **pards**: leopards or panthers. 345 **Gambolled**: frolicked, leapt about. 348 **Gordian**: referring to a knot which could not be untied. 354 **Ocean Isles**: the Azores.

To you, whom I could pity thus forlorn,
375   Though I unpitied; league with you I seek,
And mutual amity so strait, so close,
That I with you must dwell, or you with me
Henceforth; my dwelling haply may not please,
Like this fair Paradise, your sense; yet such
380   Accept your maker's work; he gave it me,
Which I as freely give; Hell shall unfold,
To entertain you two, her widest gates,
And send forth all her kings; there will be room,
Not like these narrow limits, to receive
385   Your numerous offspring; if no better place,
Thank him who puts me loth to this revenge
On you who wrong me not for him who wronged.
And should I at your harmless innocence
Melt, as I do, yet public reason just,
390   Honour and empire with revenge enlarged,
By conquering this new world, compels me now
To do what else though damned I should abhor.
    So spake the fiend, and with necessity,
The tyrant's plea, excused his devilish deeds.
395   Then from his lofty stand on that high tree
Down he alights among the sportful herd
Of those four-footed kinds, himself now one,
Now other, as their shape served best his end
Nearer to view his prey, and unespied
400   To mark what of their state he more might learn
By word or action marked; about them round
A lion now he stalks with fiery glare;
Then as a tiger, who by chance hath spied
In some purlieu two gentle fawns at play,
405   Straight couches close, then rising changes oft
His couchant watch, as one who chose his ground,
Whence rushing, he might surest seize them both,
Gripped in each paw; when Adam first of men
To first of women Eve thus moving speech,
410   Turned him all ear to hear new utterance flow.
    Sole partner and sole part of all these joys,
Dearer thyself than all; needs must the power
That made us, and for us this ample world,
Be infinitely good, and of his good
415   As liberal and free as infinite;
That raised us from the dust, and placed us here
In all this happiness, who at his hand

---

375 **league:** to make a compact or alliance. **404 purlieu:**   **406 couchant:** lying down.
piece of land at the edge of a forest.

Have nothing merited, nor can perform
Aught whereof he hath need; he who requires
420   From us no other service than to keep
This one, this easy charge, of all the trees
In Paradise that bear delicious fruit
So various, not to taste that only tree
Of knowledge, planted by the tree of life;
425   So near grows death to life, whate'er death is,
Some dreadful thing no doubt; for well thou know'st
God hath pronounced it death to taste that tree,
The only sign of our obedience left,
Among so many signs of power and rule
430   Conferred upon us, and dominion given
Over all other creatures that possess
Earth, air, and sea. Then let us not think hard
One easy prohibition, who enjoy
Free leave so large to all things else, and choice
435   Unlimited of manifold delights;
But let us ever praise him, and extol
His bounty, following our delightful task,
To prune these growing plants, and tend these flowers,
Which were it toilsome, yet with thee were sweet.
440   To whom thus Eve replied. O thou for whom
And from whom I was formed flesh of thy flesh,
And without whom am to no end, my guide
And head, what thou hast said is just and right.
For we to him indeed all praises owe,
445   And daily thanks, I chiefly, who enjoy
So far the happier lot, enjoying thee
Pre-eminent by so much odds, while thou
Like consort to thyself canst no where find.
That day I oft remember, when from sleep
450   I first awaked, and found myself reposed
Under a shade on flowers, much wondering where
And what I was, whence thither brought, and how.
Not distant far from thence a murmuring sound
Of waters issued from a cave, and spread
455   Into a liquid plain, then stood unmoved
Pure as the expanse of Heaven; I thither went
With unexperienced thought, and laid me down
On the green bank, to look into the clear
Smooth lake, that to me seemed another sky.
460   As I bent down to look, just opposite
A shape within the watery gleam appeared,
Bending to look on me, I started back,
It started back, but pleased I soon returned,
Pleased it returned as soon with answering looks

465 Of sympathy and love; There I had fixed
Mine eyes till now, and pined with vain desire,
Had not a voice thus warned me: What thou seest,
What there thou seest, fair creature, is thyself;
With thee it came and goes; but follow me,
470 And I will bring thee where no shadow stays
Thy coming, and thy soft embraces, he
Whose image thou art; him thou shalt enjoy
Inseparably thine, to him shalt bear
Multitudes like thyself, and thence be called
475 Mother of human race. What could I do,
But follow straight, invisibly thus led?
Till I espied thee, fair indeed and tall,
Under a platan; yet methought less fair,
Less winning soft, less amiably mild,
480 Than that smooth watery image; back I turned,
Thou following cried'st aloud, Return fair Eve,
Whom fliest thou? Whom thou fliest, of him thou art,
His flesh, his bone; to give thee being I lent
Out of my side to thee, nearest my heart,
485 Substantial life, to have thee by my side
Henceforth an individual solace dear;
Part of my soul I seek thee, and thee claim
My other half; with that thy gentle hand
Seized mine, I yielded, and from that time see
490 How beauty is excelled by manly grace,
And wisdom, which alone is truly fair.
      So spake our general mother, and with eyes
Of conjugal attraction unreproved,
And meek surrender, half-embracing leaned
495 On our first father; half her swelling breast
Naked met his, under the flowing gold
Of her loose tresses hid; he in delight
Both of her beauty and submissive charms,
Smiled with superior love, as Jupiter
500 On Juno smiles when he impregns the clouds
That shed May flowers, and pressed her matron lip
With kisses pure; aside the Devil turned
For envy, yet with jealous leer malign
Eyed them askance, and to himself thus plained.
505   Sight hateful, sight tormenting! Thus these two,
Imparadised in one another's arms,
The happier Eden, shall enjoy their fill
Of bliss on bliss; while I to Hell am thrust,

---

478 platan: plane tree.   **486 individual:** inseparable.   **503 leer:** a sly look.   **504 plained:** complained, recall-
493 conjugal: married relations.   **unreproved:** innocent.   ing the literary complaint, a poem of lament or injustice.

Where neither joy nor love, but fierce desire,
510 Among our other torments not the least,
Still unfulfilled with pain of longing pines;
Yet let me not forget what I have gained
From their own mouths; all is not theirs it seems;
One fatal tree there stands of knowledge called,
515 Forbidden them to taste; knowledge forbidden?
Suspicious, reasonless. Why should their Lord
Envy them that? Can it be sin to know,
Can it be death? And do they only stand
By ignorance, is that their happy state,
520 The proof of their obedience and their faith?
O fair foundation laid whereon to build
Their ruin! Hence I will excite their minds
With more desire to know, and to reject
Envious commands, invented with design
525 To keep them low, whom knowledge might exalt
Equal with gods; aspiring to be such,
They taste and die; what likelier can ensue?
But first with narrow search I must walk round
This garden, and no corner leave unspied;
530 A chance but chance may lead where I may meet
Some wandering spirit of Heaven by fountain side,
Or in thick shade retired, from him to draw
What further would be learned. Live while ye may,
Yet happy pair; enjoy, till I return,
535 Short pleasures, for long woes are to succeed.
    So saying, his proud step he scornful turned,
But with sly circumspection, and began
Through wood, through waste, o'er hill, o'er dale, his roam.
Meanwhile in utmost longitude, where Heaven
540 With earth and ocean meets, the setting sun
Slowly descended, and with right aspect
Against the eastern gate of Paradise
Levelled his evening rays; it was a rock
Of alabaster, piled up to the clouds,
545 Conspicuous far, winding with one ascent
Accessible from earth, one entrance high;
The rest was craggy cliff, that overhung
Still as it rose, impossible to climb.
Betwixt these rocky pillars Gabriel sat,
550 Chief of the angelic guards, awaiting night;
About him exercised heroic games
The unarmed youth of Heaven, but nigh at hand

---

511 **pines**: torments. **537 circumspection**: cautious   **538 roam**: wandering.   **539 utmost longitude**: the
observation.   extreme west.

Celestial armoury, shields, helms, and spears,
Hung high with diamond flaming, and with gold.
555 Thither came Uriel, gliding through the even
On a sunbeam, swift as a shooting star
In autumn thwarts the night, when vapours fired
Impress the air, and shows the mariner
From what point of his compass to beware
560 Impetuous winds; he thus began in haste.
     Gabriel, to thee thy course by lot hath given
Charge and strict watch that to this happy place
No evil thing approach or enter in;
This day at height of noon came to my sphere
565 A spirit, zealous, as he seemed, to know
More of the almighty's works, and chiefly man,
God's latest image; I described his way
Bent all on speed, and marked his airy gait;
But in the mount that lies from Eden north,
570 Where he first lighted, soon discerned his looks
Alien from Heaven, with passions foul obscured;
Mine eye pursued him still, but under shade
Lost sight of him; one of the banished crew
I fear, hath ventured from the deep, to raise
575 New troubles; him thy care must be to find.
To whom the winged warrior thus returned:
Uriel, no wonder if thy perfect sight,
Amid the sun's bright circle where thou sit'st,
See far and wide; in at this gate none pass
580 The vigilance here placed, but such as come
Well known from Heaven; and since meridian hour
No creature thence; if Spirit of other sort,
So minded, have o'erleaped these earthly bounds
On purpose, hard thou know'st it to exclude
585 Spiritual substance with corporeal bar.
But if within the circuit of these walks,
In whatsoever shape he lurk, of whom
Thou tell'st, by morrow dawning I shall know.
     So promised he, and Uriel to his charge
590 Returned on that bright beam, whose point now raised
Bore him slope downward to the sun now fallen
Beneath the Azores; whether the prime orb,
Incredible how swift, had thither rolled
Diurnal, or this less voluble earth,
595 By shorter flight to the east, had left him there
Arraying with reflected purple and gold

---

555 **Uriel:** an archangel.   557 **thwarts:** crosses.   580 **vigilance:** guard.   594 **Diurnal:** daily. **voluble:**
568 **gait:** pace, movement.   readily rotating.

The clouds that on his western throne attend;
Now came still evening on, and twilight gray
Had in her sober livery all things clad;
600   Silence accompanied, for beast and bird,
They to their grassy couch, these to their nests
Were slunk, all but the wakeful nightingale;
She all night long her amorous descant sung;
Silence was pleased; now glowed the firmament
605   With living sapphires; Hesperus that led
The starry host, rode brightest, till the moon,
Rising in clouded majesty, at length
Apparent queen unveiled her peerless light,
And o'er the dark her silver mantle threw.
610   When Adam thus to Eve: fair consort, the hour
Of night, and all things now retired to rest,
Mind us of like repose; since God hath set
Labour and rest, as day and night, to men
Successive, and the timely dew of sleep
615   Now falling with soft slumbrous weight inclines
Our eye-lids; other creatures all day long
Rove idle unemployed, and less need rest;
Man hath his daily work of body or mind
Appointed, which declares his dignity,
620   And the regard of Heaven on all his ways;
While other animals unactive range,
And of their doings God takes no account.
Tomorrow ere fresh morning streak the east
With first approach of light, we must be risen,
625   And at our pleasant labour, to reform
Yon flowery arbours, yonder alleys green,
Our walk at noon, with branches overgrown,
That mock our scant manuring, and require
More hands than ours to lop their wanton growth;
630   Those blossoms also, and those dropping gums,
That lie bestrewn unsightly and unsmooth,
Ask riddance, if we mean to tread with ease;
Meanwhile, as nature wills, night bids us rest.
      To whom thus Eve, with perfect beauty adorned:
635   My author and disposer, what thou bid'st
Unargued I obey; so God ordains,
God is thy law, thou mine; to know no more
Is woman's happiest knowledge, and her praise.
With thee conversing I forget all time,
640   All seasons and their change, all please alike.

---

599 livery: distinctive badge or suit worn by servants.   **605 Hesperus:** the evening star.   **628 manuring:**
603 descant: melodious singing.   cultivating.

Sweet is the breath of morn, her rising sweet,
With charm of earliest birds; pleasant the sun,
When first on this delightful land he spreads
His orient beams, on herb, tree, fruit, and flower,
645   Glistering with dew; fragrant the fertile earth
After soft showers; and sweet the coming on
Of grateful evening mild; then silent night,
With this her solemn bird, and this fair moon,
And these the gems of Heaven, her starry train;
650   But neither breath of morn, when she ascends
With charm of earliest birds; nor rising sun
On this delightful land; nor herb, fruit, flower,
Glistering with dew; nor fragrance after showers;
Nor grateful evening mild; nor silent night,
655   With this her solemn bird, nor walk by moon,
Or glittering starlight, without thee is sweet.
But wherefore all night long shine these, for whom
This glorious sight, when sleep hath shut all eyes?
    To whom our general ancestor replied:
660   Daughter of God and man, accomplished Eve,
These have their course to finish round the earth
By morrow evening, and from land to land
In order, though to nations yet unborn,
Ministring light prepared, they set and rise;
665   Lest total darkness should by night regain
Her old possession, and extinguish life
In nature and all things, which these soft fires
Not only enlighten, but with kindly heat
Of various influence foment and warm,
670   Temper or nourish, or in part shed down
Their stellar virtue on all kinds that grow
On earth, made hereby apter to receive
Perfection from the sun's more potent ray.
These then, though unbeheld in deep of night,
675   Shine not in vain; nor think, though men were none,
That Heaven would want spectators, God want praise;
Millions of spiritual creatures walk the earth
Unseen, both when we wake, and when we sleep;
All these with ceaseless praise his works behold
680   Both day and night; how often from the steep
Of echoing hill or thicket have we heard
Celestial voices to the midnight air,
Sole, or responsive each to others note,
Singing their great creator; oft in bands
685   While they keep watch, or nightly rounding walk

---

669 foment: to stir up by heat.

With heavenly touch of instrumental sounds
In full harmonic number joined, their songs
Divide the night, and lift our thoughts to Heaven.
    Thus talking, hand in hand alone they passed
690 On to their blissful bower; it was a place
Chosen by the sovereign planter, when he framed
All things to man's delightful use; the roof
Of thickest covert was inwoven shade
Laurel and myrtle, and what higher grew
695 Of firm and fragrant leaf; on either side
Acanthus, and each odorous bushy shrub,
Fenced up the verdant wall; each beauteous flower,
Iris all hues, roses, and jessamine
Reared high their flourished heads between, and wrought
700 Mosaic; underfoot the violet,
Crocus, and hyacinth, with rich inlay
Broidered the ground, more coloured than with stone
Of costliest emblem; other creature here,
Bird, beast, insect, or worm durst enter none;
705 Such was their awe of Man. In shadier bower
More sacred and sequestered, though but feigned,
Pan or Sylvanus never slept, nor nymph
Nor Faunus haunted. Here in close recess
With flowers, garlands, and sweet-smelling herbs
710 Espoused Eve decked first her nuptial bed,
And heavenly choirs the hymenean sung,
What day the genial angel to our sire
Brought her in naked beauty more adorned,
More lovely than Pandora, whom the gods
715 Endowed with all their gifts, and O too like
In sad event, when to the unwiser son
Of Japhet brought by Hermes, she ensnared
Mankind with her fair looks, to be avenged
On him who had stole Jove's authentic fire.
720   Thus at their shady lodge arrived, both stood,
Both turned, and under open sky adored
The God that made both sky, air, earth and heaven
Which they beheld, the moon's resplendent globe,
And starry pole. Thou also madest the night,
725 Maker omnipotent, and thou the day,
Which we in our appointed work employed,
Have finished happy in our mutual help

---

691 **planter:** see Genesis 2:8, 'God planted a garden'; also
in the sense of founding a colony. 693 **covert:**
covering. 698 **jessamine:** jasmine. 703 **emblem:**
inlay. 707–708 **Pan, Sylvanus, Faunus:** woodland
gods. 711 **hymenean:** wedding hymn; Hymen is the god
of marriage.

714 **Pandora:** she was given by the Olympian gods to
Epimetheus (one of the sons of the Titan Japhet) to
revenge the theft of fire by his brother Prometheus.
Pandora released all evils into the world by opening a
box where they were hidden. 719 **authentic:** original.

And mutual love, the crown of all our bliss
Ordained by thee; and this delicious place
730　For us too large, where thy abundance wants
Partakers, and uncropt falls to the ground.
But thou hast promised from us two a race
To fill the earth, who shall with us extol
Thy goodness infinite, both when we wake,
735　And when we seek, as now, thy gift of sleep.
　　　　This said unanimous, and other rites
Observing none, but adoration pure
Which God likes best, into their inmost bower
Handed they went; and eased the putting off
740　These troublesome disguises which we wear,
Straight side by side were laid; nor turned, I ween,
Adam from his fair spouse, nor Eve the rites
Mysterious of connubial love refused;
Whatever hypocrites austerely talk
745　Of purity and place and innocence,
Defaming as impure what God declares
Pure, and commands to some, leaves free to all.
Our maker bids increase; who bids abstain
But our destroyer, foe to God and man?
750　Hail wedded love, mysterious law, true source
Of human offspring, sole propriety
In Paradise of all things common else.
By thee adulterous lust was driven from men
Among the bestial herds to range; by thee
755　Founded in reason, loyal, just and pure
Relations dear, and all the charities
Of father, son and brother, first were known.
Far be it that I should write thee sin or blame,
Or think thee unbefitting holiest place,
760　Perpetual fountain of domestic sweets,
Whose bed is undefiled and chaste pronounced,
Present, or past, as saints and patriarchs used.
Here Love his golden shafts employs, here lights
His constant lamp, and waves his purple wings,
765　Reigns here and revels; not in the bought smile
Of harlots, loveless, joyless, unendeared,
Casual fruition; nor in court amours,
Mixed dance, or wanton mask, or midnight ball,
Or serenade, which the starved lover sings
770　To his proud fair, best quitted with disdain.

---

741 **ween:** think.　743 **connubial:** pertaining to
marriage.　751 **propriety:** ownership.　756 **charities:**
natural affections.

763 **Love:** Cupid's golden arrows kindle love; a
Renaissance commonplace.　766 **unendeared:** without affection.

These lulled by nightingales embracing slept,
And on their naked limbs the flowery roof
Showered roses, which the morn repaired. Sleep on
Blest pair; and O yet happiest, if ye seek
775   No happier state, and know to know no more.

From Areopagitica

In 1644 Milton wrote to Parliament 'for the liberty of unlicensed printing'. Styling himself as an ancient Greek orator, he wrote as from the Areopagus, the place where the Athenian Council of State met. Milton's argument is based on the premise that liberty must be tested and its upholders must win the right to freedom, not passively follow authoritarian dictate. Beyond an argument against censorship, Milton's tract reveals some of the wider social ideals he believed revolutionary England should pursue.

I deny not, but that it is of greatest concernment in the Church and Commonwealth, to have a vigilant eye how books demean themselves as well as men; and thereafter to confine, imprison, and do sharpest justice on them as malefactors. For books are not absolutely dead things, but do contain a potency of life in them to be as active as that soul was whose progeny they are; nay, they do preserve as in a vial the purest efficacy and extraction of that living intellect that bred them. I know they as lively, and as vigorously productive, as those fabulous dragon's teeth;[1] and being sown up and down, may chance to spring up armed men. And yet, on the other hand, unless wariness be used, as good almost kill a man as kill a good book. Who kills a man kills a reasonable creature, God's image; but he who destroys a good book, kills reason itself, kills the image of God, as it were in the eye. Many a man lives a burden to the earth; but a good book is the precious lifeblood of a master spirit, embalmed and treasured up on purpose to a life beyond life. 'Tis true, no age can restore a life, whereof perhaps there is no great loss; and revolutions of ages do not oft recover the loss of a rejected truth, for the want of which whole nations fare the worse. We should be wary therefore what persecution we raise against the living labours of public men, how we spill that seasoned life of man, preserved and stored up in books, since we see a kind of homicide may be thus committed, sometimes a martyrdom, and if it extend to the whole impression, a kind of massacre; whereof the execution ends not in the slaying of an elemental life, but strikes at that ethereal and fifth essence,[2] the breath of reason itself, slays an immortality rather than a life. . . .

Lords and Commons of England, consider what nation it is whereof ye are, and whereof ye are the governors. A nation not slow and dull, but of a quick, ingenious and piercing spirit, acute to invent, subtle and sinewy to discourse, not beneath the reach of any point, the highest that human capacity can soar to. Therefore the studies of learning in her deepest sciences have been so ancient and so eminent among us, that writers of good antiquity and ablest

---

1 **dragon's teeth:** fighters who spring from the teeth of a slain dragon in Ovid's *Metamorphoses*.   2 **fifth essence:** substance which makes up heavenly bodies.

judgment have been persuaded that even the school of Pythagoras and the Persian wisdom took beginning from the old philosophy[1] of this island. And that wise and civil Roman, Julius Agricola, who governed once here for Caesar, preferred the natural wits of Britain before the laboured studies of the French. Nor is it for nothing that the grave and frugal Transylvanian[2] sends out yearly from as far as the mountainous borders of Russia, and beyond the Hercynian wilderness,[3] not their youth, but their staid men, to learn our language and our theologic arts.

Yet that which is above all this, the favour and the love of Heaven, we have great argument to think in a peculiar manner propitious and propending towards us. Why else was this nation chosen before any other, that out of her, as out of Sion, should be proclaimed and sounded forth the first tidings and trumpet of Reformation to all Europe?[4] And had it not been the obstinate perverseness of our prelates against the divine and admirable spirit of Wickliff, to suppress him as a schismatic and innovator, perhaps neither the Bohemian Huss and Jerome, no nor the name of Luther or of Calvin, had been ever known: the glory of reforming all our neighbours had been completely ours.

But now, as our obdurate clergy have with violence demeaned the matter, we are become hitherto the latest and backwardest scholars, of whom God offered to have made us the teachers. Now once again by all concurrence of signs, and by the general instinct of holy and devout men, as they daily and solemnly express their thoughts, God is decreeing to begin some new and great period in His Church, even to the reforming of Reformation itself. What does He then but reveal Himself to His servants, and as His manner is, first to His Englishmen? I say, as His manner is, first to us, though we mark not the method of His counsels, and are unworthy.

Behold now this vast city;[5] a city of refuge, the mansion house of liberty, encompassed and surrounded with His protection. The shop of war hath not there more anvils and hammers waking to fashion out the plates and instruments[6] of armed Justice in defence of beleaguered Truth, than there be pens and heads there, sitting by their studious lamps, musing, searching, revolving new notions and ideas wherewith to present, as with their homage and their fealty, the approaching Reformation. Others as fast reading, trying all things, assenting to the force of reason and convincement. What could a man require more from a nation so pliant and so prone to seek after knowledge? What wants there to such a towardly and pregnant soil, but wise and faithful labourers, to make a knowing people, a nation of prophets of sages, and of worthies? We reckon more than five months yet to harvest. There need not be five weeks; had we but eyes to lift up, the fields are white already.

Where there is much desire to learn, there of necessity will be much arguing, much writing, many opinions; for opinion in good men is but knowledge in the making. Under these fantastic terrors of sect and schism, we wrong the earnest

---

1 **old philosophy:** metempsychosis (transmigration of souls) expounded by Pythagoras and the doctrines of the Persian Zoroastrians were claimed to have originated with the Druids. 2 **Transylvania:** in Milton's time a Protestant principality. 3 **Hercynian wilderness:** vast forest of central Europe in classical times. 4: many English Protestants traced the 'reform' of their Church from the time of John Wycliffe in the 14th century. 5 **city:** London. 6 **plates and instruments:** breastplates and weapons.

and zealous thirst after knowledge and understanding which God hath stirred up in this city. What some lament of, we rather should rejoice at, should rather praise this pious forwardness among men, to reassume the ill-reputed care of their religion into their own hands again. A little generous prudence, a little forbearance of one another, and some grain of charity might win all these diligences to join, and unite in one general and brotherly search after Truth; could we but forego this prelatical tradition[1] of crowding free consciences and Christian liberties into canons and precepts of men. I doubt not, if some great and worthy stranger should come among us, wise to discern the mould and temper of a people, and how to govern it, observing the high hopes and aims, the diligent alacrity of our extended thoughts and reasonings in the pursuance of truth and freedom, but that he would cry out as Pyrrhus[2] did, admiring the Roman docility and courage: 'If such were my Epirots, I would not despair the greatest design that could be attempted, to make a Church or Kingdom happy.'

Yet these are the men cried out against for schismatics and sectaries. As if, while the temple[3] of the Lord was building, some cutting, some squaring the marble, others hewing the cedars, there should be a sort of irrational men who could not consider there must be many schisms and many dissections made in the quarry and in the timber, ere the house of God can be built. And when every stone is laid artfully together, it cannot be united into a continuity, it can but be contiguous in this world; neither can every piece of the building be of one form; nay rather the perfection consists in this, that, out of many moderate varieties and brotherly dissimilitudes that are not vastly disproportional, arises the goodly and the graceful symmetry that commends the whole pile and structure.

Let us therefore be more considerate builders, more wise in spiritual architecture, when great reformation is expected. For now the time seems come, wherein Moses the great prophet may sit in heaven rejoicing to see that memorable and glorious wish of his fulfilled, when not only our seventy elders, but all the Lord's people, are become prophets.[4] No marvel then though some men, and some good men too perhaps, but young in goodness, as Joshua then was, envy them. They fret, and out of their own weakness are in agony, lest these divisions and subdivisions will undo us. The adversary again applauds, and waits the hour. When they have branched themselves out, saith he, small enough into parties and partitions, then will be our time. Fool! He sees not the firm root out of which we all grow, though into branches; nor will be ware until he see our small divided maniples[5] cutting through at every angle of his ill-united and unwieldy brigade. And that we are to hope better of all these supposed sects and schisms, and that we shall not need that solicitude, honest perhaps though over-timorous, of them that vex in this behalf, but shall laugh in the end at those malicious applauders of our differences, I have these reasons to persuade me.

First, when a city shall be as it were besieged and blocked about, her navigable river infested, inroads and incursions round, defiance and battle oft

---

1 **prelatical tradition:** government of religion by bishops. 2 **Pyrrhus:** king of Epirus who declared he could conquer the world if he had Roman soldiers. 3 **temple:** of Solomon. 4: see Numbers 11:27–29. 5 **maniples:** company of about 150 men in the Roman army.

rumoured to be marching up even to her walls and suburb trenches, that then the people, or the greater part, more than at other times, wholly taken up with the study of highest and most important matters to be reformed, should be disputing, reasoning, reading, inventing, discoursing, even to a rarity and admiration, things not before discoursed or written of, argues first a singular goodwill, contentedness and confidence in your prudent foresight and safe government, Lords and Commons; and from thence derives itself to a gallant bravery and well-grounded contempt of their enemies, as if there were no small number of as great spirits among us, as his was, who, when Rome was nigh besieged by Hannibal, being in the city, bought that piece of ground at no cheap rate whereon Hannibal himself encamped his own regiment.

Next, it is a lively and cheerful presage of our happy success and victory. For as in a body, when the blood is fresh, the spirits pure and vigorous, not only to vital but to rational faculties, and those in the acutest and the pertest operations of wit and subtlety, it argues in what good plight and constitution the body is so when the cheerfulness of the people is so sprightly up, as that it has not only wherewith to guard well its own freedom and safety, but to spare and to bestow upon the solidest and sublimest points of controversy and new invention, it betokens us not degenerated, nor drooping to a fatal decay, but casting off the old and wrinkled skin of corruption to outlive these pangs and wax young again, entering the glorious ways of truth and prosperous virtue, destined to become great and honourable in these latter ages. Methinks I see in my mind a noble and puissant nation rousing herself like a strong man after sleep, and shaking her invincible locks. Methinks I see her as an eagle mewing[1] her mighty youth, and kindling her undazzled eyes at the full midday beam; purging and unscaling her long-abused sight at the fountain itself of heavenly radiance; while the whole noise of timorous and flocking birds, with those also that love the twilight, flutter about, amazed at what she means, and in their envious gabble would prognosticate[2] a year of sects and schisms.

What would ye do then? Should ye suppress all this flowery crop of knowledge and new light sprung up and yet springing daily in this city? Should ye set an oligarchy of twenty engrossers[3] over it, to bring a famine upon our minds again, when we shall know nothing but what is measured to us by their bushel? Believe it, Lords and Commons, they who counsel ye to such a suppressing do as good as bid ye suppress yourselves; and I will soon show how. If it be desired to know the immediate cause of all this free writing and free speaking, there cannot be assigned a truer than your own mild and free and humane government. It is the liberty, Lords and Commons, which your own valorous and happy counsels have purchased us, liberty which is the nurse of all great wits; this is that which hath rarefied and enlightened our spirits like the influence of heaven; this is that which hath enfranchised, enlarged and lifted up our apprehensions degrees above themselves.

Ye cannot make us now less capable, less knowing, less eagerly pursuing of the truth, unless ye first make yourselves, that made us so, less the lovers, less the founders of our true liberty. We can grow ignorant again, brutish, formal

---

1 **mewing**: renewing. 2 **prognosticate**: foretell. 3 **engrossers**: those holding a monopoly.

and slavish, as ye found us; but you then must first become that which ye cannot be, oppressive, arbitrary and tyrannous, as they were from whom ye have freed us. That our hearts are now more capacious, our thoughts more erected to the search and expectation of greatest and exactest things, is the issue of your own virtue propagated in us; ye cannot suppress that, unless ye reinforce an abrogated and merciless law, that fathers may despatch at will their own children. And who shall then stick closest to ye, and excite others? Not he who takes up arms for coat and conduct, and his four nobles of Danegelt.[1] Although I dispraise not the defence of just immunities, yet love my peace better, if that were all. Give me the liberty to know, to utter, and to argue freely according to conscience, above all liberties.

THOMAS HOBBES (1588–1679)

First published in 1651 and taking its title from the Book of Job where God set up Leviathan as a mighty governor, Hobbes' treatise is a defence of a government's right to claim absolute public control of matters temporal and spiritual. He considers human beings wholly governed by acquisitive self-interest, in recognition of which, our capacity for reason compels us voluntarily to surrender our freedom to an absolutist state in order to avoid chaos. Contrasting vividly with the ideals and styles promoted by Milton or Winstanley, Hobbes developed a prose around a principle of 'science': the presentation of a series of orderly, supposedly logical propositions whose argument relentlessly demonstrates the truth of its thesis.

From Leviathan or The Matter, Form & Power of a Commonwealth, Ecclesiastical and Civil

Of the Causes, Generation, and Definition of a Commonwealth

The final cause, end, or design of men, (who naturally love liberty, and dominion over others,) in the introduction of that restraint upon themselves, (in which wee see them live in commonwealths) is the foresight of their own preservation, and of a more contented life thereby; that is to say, of getting themselves out from that miserable condition of war, which is necessarily consequent to the natural passions of men, when there is no visible power to keep them in awe, and tie them by fear of punishment to the performance of their covenants,[1] and observation of the laws of Nature.

For the laws of Nature (as Justice, Equity, Modesty, Mercy, and, in sum, doing to others, as we would be done to) of themselves, without the terror of some power, to cause them to be observed, are contrary to our natural passions, that carry us to partiality, pride, revenge, and the like. And covenants, without the sword, are but words, and of no strength to secure a man at all. Therefore

---

Areopagitica 1 **nobles of Danegelt:** tribute money – a noble is a coin – paid to the Danes in the early Middle Ages but commonly used to indicate the taxes imposed by Charles I in the 1630s but which Parliament rejected. **Leviathan** 1 **covenants:** agreements.

notwithstanding the laws of Nature, (which every one hath then kept, when he has the will to keep them, when he can do it safely) if there be no power erected, or not great enough for our security; every man will and may lawfully rely on his own strength and art for caution against all other men. And in all places, where men have lived by small families, to rob and spoil one another has been a trade, and, so far from being reputed against the Law of Nature, that the greater spoils they gained, the greater was their honour; and men observed no other laws therein, but the laws of honour; that is, to abstain from cruelty, leaving to men their lives, and instruments of husbandry. And as small families did then; so now do cities and kingdoms, which are but greater families, (for their own security) enlarge their dominions, upon all pretences of danger, and fear of invasion, or assistance that may be given to invaders, endeavour as much as they can to subdue, or weaken, their neighbours by open force and secret arts, for want of other caution, justly; and are remembered for it in after ages with honour.

Nor is it the joining together of a small number of men that gives them this security; because in small numbers, small additions on the one side or the other make the advantage of strength so great as is sufficient to carry the victory; and therefore gives encouragement to an invasion. The multitude sufficient to confide in for our security is not determined by any certain number, but by comparison with the enemy we fear; and is then sufficient when the odds of the enemy is not of so visible and conspicuous moment to determine the event of war, as to move him to attempt.

And be there never so great a multitude, yet, if their actions be directed according to their particular judgements, and particular appetites, they can expect thereby no defence, nor protection, neither against a common enemy, nor against the injuries of one another. For being distracted in opinions concerning the best use and application of their strength, they do not help, but hinder one another; and reduce their strength by mutual opposition to nothing; whereby they are easily, not only subdued by a very few that agree together, but also, when there is no common enemy, they make war upon each other for their particular interests. For if we could suppose a great multitude of men to consent in the observation of justices and other laws of Nature without a common power to keep them all in awe, we might as well suppose all mankind to do the same; and then there neither would be, nor need to be any, civil government or commonwealth at all, because there would be peace without subjection.

Nor is it enough for the security, which men desire should last all the time of their life, that they be governed and directed by one judgement for a limited time, as in one battle, or one war. For, though they obtain a victory by their unanimous endeavour against a foreign enemy, yet, afterwards, when either they have no common enemy, or he that by one part is held for an enemy is by another part held for a friend, they must needs by the difference of their interests dissolve, and fall again into a war amongst themselves.

It is true that certain living creatures, as bees and ants, live sociably one with another (which are therefore by Aristotle numbered amongst political creatures) and yet have no other direction than their particular judgements and appetites; nor speech, whereby one of them can signify to another what he thinks expedient for the common benefit. And therefore some man may perhaps desire to know why mankind cannot do the same. To which I answer:

First, that men are continually in competition for honour and dignity, which these creatures are not; and consequently amongst men there ariseth, on that ground, envy and hatred, and finally war; but amongst these not so.

Secondly, that amongst these creatures the common good differeth not from the private; and being by nature inclined to their private, they procure thereby the common benefit. But man, whose joy consisteth in comparing himself with other men, can relish nothing but what is eminent.

Thirdly, that these creatures having not, as man, the use of reason, do not see, nor think they see, any fault in the administration of their common business; whereas amongst men, there are very many that think themselves wiser and abler to govern the public better than the rest. And these strive to reform and innovate, one this way, another that way, and thereby bring it into distraction and civil war.

Fourthly, that these creatures, though they have some use of voice in making known to one another their desires and other affections, yet they want that art of words by which some men can represent to others that which is good in the likeness of evil, and evil in the likeness of good; and augment or diminish the apparent greatness of good and evil, discontenting men and troubling their peace at their pleasure.

Fifthly, irrational creatures cannot distinguish between injury and damage, and, therefore, as long as they be at ease, they are not offended with their fellows; whereas man is then most troublesome when he is most at ease. For then it is that he loves to show his wisdom and control the actions of them that govern the commonwealth.

Lastly, the agreement of these creatures is natural; that of men is by covenant only, which is artificial. And, therefore, it is no wonder if there be somewhat else required (besides covenant) to make their agreement constant and lasting; which is a common power to keep them in awe, and to direct their actions to the common benefit.

The only way to erect such a common power as may be able to defend them from the invasion of foreigners and the injuries of one another (and thereby to secure them in such sort, as that by their own industry and by the fruits of the earth they may nourish themselves and live contentedly) is to confer all their power and strength upon one man, or upon one assembly of men, that may reduce all their wills by plurality of voices unto one will. Which is as much as to say to appoint one man or assembly of men to bear their person; and every one to own and acknowledge himself to be author of whatsoever he that so beareth their person shall act, or cause to be acted, in those things which concern the common peace and safety. And therein to submit their wills, every one, to his will, and their judgements to his judgement. This is more than consent or concord, it is a real unity of them all in one and the same person, made by covenant of every man with every man, in such manner, as if every man should say to every man: 'I authorise and give up my right of governing myself to this man, or to this assembly of men, on this condition – that thou give up thy right to him, and authorise all his actions in like manner.' This done, the multitude, so united in one person, is called a commonwealth, Latin *civitas*. This is the generation of that great Leviathan, or rather (to speak more reverently) of that mortal god,[1] to which we owe, under the immortal God, our peace and defence. For by this authority, given him by every particular man in the commonwealth, he hath the use of so much power and strength conferred on him, that, by terror thereof, he is enabled to form the wills of them all to peace at home and mutual aid against their enemies abroad. And in him consisteth the essence of the commonwealth; which (to define it) is one person, of whose acts a great multitude by mutual covenants, one with another, have made themselves every one the author, to the end he may use the strength and means of them all, as he shall think expedient, for their peace and common defence.

And he that carryeth this person is called Sovereign, and said to have sovereign power; and every one besides, his subject.

The attaining to this sovereign power, is by two ways. One, by natural force; as when a man maketh his children to submit themselves, and their children, to his government, as being able to destroy them if they refuse; or by war subdueth his enemies to his will, giving them their lives on that condition. The other is when men agree amongst themselves to submit to some man, or assembly of men, voluntarily, on confidence to be protected by him against all others. This later, may be called a political commonwealth or commonwealth by institution; and the former, a commonwealth by acquisition.

GERRARD WINSTANLEY (c.1609–1676)

Winstanley was born in humble origins in Wigan. In 1649 he led a band called the Diggers or 'True Levellers' which took over waste ground at St George's Hill in Surrey and formed a community based on holding all in common. This was suppressed the following year. Winstanley's combination of inner religious vision, deriving from his personal encounter with Scripture, with a programme for social reformation, and a style which eschews established rhetorical and generic norms, illustrates the enthusiastic writing which became popular outside elite social circles in Civil War England.

From Fire in the Bush: The spirit burning, not consuming but purging mankind

What the Garden of Eden is

The whole creation of fire, water, earth and air, and all the varieties of bodies made up thereof, is the clothing of God. So that all things, that is a substantial being, looked upon in the lump, is the fullness of him that fills all with himself; he is in all things and by him all things consist.

---

1 **mortal god:** the king. Hobbes' preferred model of rule is unquestionably a monarchy.

And this God or almighty ruler is universal love, strength and life; and as he begets and brings forth everything in their degree and kind, so he is the restorer of all things, from the defilement, death and sorrow which they fall into, and the alone deliverer from the oppressing power, preserving every one in peace. Therefore he is called the Lord God Almighty; for he is the only and alone living spirit, which dwells everywhere and can do what he will.

And of all those bodies that are called creatures or the clothing of God, mankind is the chief. And because the father or spirit of all things manifests himself in mankind, in life, strength and wisdom more than in any other creature, therefore mankind is made the lord of all. And the whole earth is this: the lord's.

For when all things were produced, and appeared very good in the liking and content of the creating spirit, the word of command was to whole mankind (not to one or a few single branches of mankind), 'Do thou take possession over the fish, fowl, beast; and do thou till the earth; and do thou multiply and fill the earth'. And no part or branch of mankind is shut out by him from this employment.

For as the great earth and the inferior creatures therein are as the commons,[1] forests and delights of God in the outcoasts of the creation; even so mankind, the living earth, is the very garden of Eden, wherein that spirit of love did walk and delight himself principally, as being the head and lord of all the rest.

In this garden are five rivers: hearing, seeing, tasting, smelling, feeling; which we in our age of the world call five senses. And these five water springs do refresh and preserve the whole creation, both of the outcoasts and of the garden.

In this garden, mankind, and in every branch of him, there is a tree of knowledge of good and evil, called imagination; and the tree of life, called universal love or pure knowledge in the power.

When mankind, or the living soul, feeds upon or delights himself in the fruit of that tree of good and evil, which is selfish, unwarranted and unexperienced imagination which is his weakness and disease; then he loses his honour and strength and falls from his dominion, lordship, and becomes like the beasts of the field, void of understanding. For the lord of so great and vast a body as the creation is must know all things clearly, as they be, and not by blind imagination, that leads mankind sometimes astray, as well as sometimes in the right way.

When mankind is guided by imagination, he runs a great hazard upon life and death. This power is he that calls good evil, and evil good, this knows not the creating spirit in inward feeling, but does fancy him to be sometimes one thing, sometimes another; and still dwells in the dark chamber of uncertainty.

And while mankind eats of this tree and delights himself here, he is driven out of the garden, that is, out of himself; he enjoys not himself, he knows not himself; he lives without the true God or ruler, and is like the beasts of the field, who live upon objects without them; and does not enjoy the kingdom

---

1 commons: land held in common for the use of a community. Opposing the enclosing and transfer of common land to private ownership was one of the Levellers' principal designs.

within himself, but seeks after a kingdom and peace without him, as the beasts do.

This imagination is he that fills you with fears, doubts, troubles, evil surmisings and grudges; he it is that stirs up wars and divisions; he makes you lust after every thing you see or hear of, and promises delight to you in the enjoyment, as in riches, places of government, pleasures, society of strange women; and when you have all these which you think or imagine to have content in, presently troubles follow the heels thereof; and you see your self naked and are ashamed.

So that the selfish imaginary power within you is the power of darkness, the father of lies, the deceiver, the destroyer, and the serpent that twists about everything within your self, and so leads you astray from the right way of life and peace. And the whole world of mankind generally at this day, through all the-nations of the world, is eating of this tree of knowledge of good and evil and are cast out of themselves, and know not the power that rules in them; and so are ignorant of their God. This is the fullness of the Beast's time, it is his last period;[1] all places, persons and things stink with his imaginary power of darkness in teaching and ruling. Therefore it is that fullness of time in which the restorer of all things will come, to deliver the creation from that bondage and curse, and draw up all things to live in him, who is the true life, rest and light of all things.

For in the midst of this garden likewise there is the tree of life, who is this blessing or restoring power, called universal love, or pure knowledge; which when mankind by experience begins to eat thereof, or to delight himself herein, (preferring this kingdom and law within, which is Christ, before the kingdom and law that lies in objects without, which is the devil) then man is drawn up into himself again; or new Jerusalem, which is the spirit of truth, comes down to earth, to fetch earth up to live in that life that is a life above objects; even to live in the enjoyment of Christ, the righteous spirit within himself, and to tread the earthly life, that lies in objects without, under foot. This is the life that will bring in true community and destroy murdering property. Now mankind enters into the garden of God's rest, and lives for ever, he enjoys his kingdom, and the Word within himself, he knows sin and sorrow no more; for all tears now which blind imagination brought upon him are wiped away; and man is in peace.

---

1 **last period**: widely held belief that the world's end was fast approaching.

ANDREW MARVELL (1621–1678)

Marvell was educated at Hull Grammar School and Cambridge. He supported the English Republic and Cromwell and was elected Member of Parliament for Hull in 1659. In 1660, Marvell was reconciled with the Restoration government, though he remained a trenchant critic of Charles II's court, and continued to serve as an MP until his death. Marvell's poetry is marked by great diversity of style and form. He wrote some of the most accomplished lyrics of the seventeenth century, as well as satires and occasional poems, often of considerable length. He also wrote important political and satiric prose tracts. Marvell published virtually none of his poetry during his lifetime and it is often difficult to date. His *Miscellaneous Poems* appeared in 1681.

To His Coy Mistress

Had we but world enough, and time,
This coyness Lady were no crime.
We would sit down, and think which way
To walk, and pass our long love's day.
5   Thou by the Indian Ganges side
Should'st rubies find; I by the tide
Of Humber would complain. I would
Love you ten years before the Flood;
And you should if you please refuse
10 Till the conversion of the Jews.
My vegetable love should grow
Vaster then empires, and more slow.
An hundred years should go to praise
Thine eyes, and on thy forehead gaze.
15 Two hundred to adore each breast.
But thirty thousand to the rest.
An age at least to every part,
And the last age should show your heart.
For Lady you deserve this state;
20 Nor would I love at lower rate.

But at my back I always hear
Time's winged chariot hurrying near;
And yonder all before us lye
Deserts of vast eternity.
25 Thy beauty shall no more be found;
Nor, in thy marble vault, shall sound
My echoing song. Then worms shall try
That long preserved virginity;

---

6 tide of Humber: the Humber estuary at Hull, where Marvell grew up. Tide can also mean time.
8 Flood: the Biblical flood of Genesis 6–8.

10 conversion of the Jews: according to the Bible, at the end of the world; an imminent event, many believed.

And your quaint honour turn to dust;
30 And into ashes all my lust.
The grave's a fine and private place,
But none I think do there embrace.

Now therefore, while the youthful hew
Sits on thy skin like morning dew,
35 And while thy willing soul transpires
At every pore with instant fires,
Now let us sport us while we may;
And now, like amorous birds of prey,
Rather at once our time devour,
40 Than languish in his slow-chapt power.
Let us roll all our strength, and all
Our sweetness, up into one ball:
And tear our pleasures with rough strife,
Thorough the iron gates of life.
45 Thus, though we cannot make our sun
Stand still, yet we will make him run.

The Garden

1
How vainly men themselves amaze
To win the palm, the oak, or bays;
And their uncessant labours see
Crowned from some single herb or tree,
5 Whose short and narrow verged shade
Does prudently their toils upbraid;
While all flowers and all trees do close
To weave the garlands of repose.

2
Fair Quiet, have I found thee here,
10 And Innocence thy sister dear!
Mistaken long, I sought you then
In busy companies of men.
Your sacred plants, if here below,
Only among the plants will grow.
15 Society is all but rude,
To this delicious solitude.

---

40 **chapt:** chap, an animal's jaw, used here as devouring. **5 verged:** extended. **6 upbraid:** censure. **15 rude:**
Garden 2 palm, oak, bays [laurel]: rewards for uncivilised.
military, civic and poetic success.

3

No white nor red was ever seen
So am'rous as this lovely green.
Fond lovers, cruel as their flame,
20 Cut in these trees their mistress' name.
Little, alas, they know, or heed,
How far these beauties hers exceed!
Fair trees! where s'eer you barks I wound,
No name shall but your own be found.

4

25 When we have run our passions heat,
Love hither makes his best retreat.
The gods, that mortal beauty chase,
Still in a tree did end their race.
Apollo hunted Daphne so,
30 Only that she might laurel grow.
And Pan did after Syrinx speed,
Not as a nymph, but for a reed.

5

What wondrous life is this I lead!
Ripe apples drop about my head;
35 The luscious clusters of the vine
Upon my mouth do crush their wine;
The nectaren, and curious peach,
Into my hands themselves do reach;
Stumbling on melons, as I pass,
40 Insnared with flowers, I fall on grass.

6

Meanwhile the mind, from pleasure less,
Withdraws into its happiness.
The mind, that ocean where each kind
Does straight its own resemblance find;
45 Yet it creates, transcending these,
Far other worlds, and other seas;
Annihilating all that's made
To a green thought in a green shade.

7

Here at the fountain's sliding foot,
50 Or at some fruit-tree's mossy root,
Casting the body's vest aside,
My soul into the boughs does glide.

---

23 s'eer: contraction of soever.   **29–33**: In Ovid's *Meta-*   **37** **curious**: exquisite.
morphoses the nymphs Daphne and Syrinx escape being
raped by Apollo and Pan by being transformed into a
tree and a reed.

There like a bird it sits, and sings,
Then whets, and combs its silver wings;
55   And, till prepared for longer flight,
Waves in its plumes the various light.

8

Such was that happy garden-state,
While man there walked without a mate;
After a place so pure, and sweet,
60   What other help could yet be meet!
But 'twas beyond a mortal's share
To wander solitary there;
Two paradises 'twere in one
To live in paradise alone.

9

65   How well the skilful gardner drew
Of flowers and herbs this dial new;
Where from above the milder sun
Does through a fragrant zodiac run;
And, as it works, the industrious bee
70   Computes its time as well as we.
How could such sweet and wholesome hours
Be reckoned but with herbs and flowers!

An Horatian Ode upon Cromwell's Return from Ireland

The forward youth that would appear
Must now forsake his muses dear,
        Nor in the shadows sing
        His numbers languishing.
5   'Tis time to leave the books in dust,
And oil the unused armour's rust;
        Removing from the wall
        The corslet of the hall.
So restless Cromwell could not cease
10   In the inglorious arts of peace,
        But through adventurous war
        Urged his active star.

---

54 **whets**: preens.   57 **happy garden-state**: the garden of Eden before the biblical fall of mankind.   66 **dial**: a floral sundial.

Horatian Ode. . . . : the Roman poet Horace wrote a number of odes to the Emperor Augustus. Oliver Cromwell, the commander of the English Republic's army and later Protector, or dictator, of the state, invaded Ireland in 1649 to prevent a rebellion in favour of Charles II. He returned victorious in 1650. 8 **corslet:** a piece of body armour.

And, like the three-forked lightning, first
Breaking the clouds where it was nurst,
15   Did through his own side
       His fiery way divide.
For 'tis all one to courage high
The emulous or enemy;
       And with such to enclose
20   Is more then to oppose.
Then burning through the air he went,
And palaces and temples rent;
       And Caesar's head at last
       Did through his laurels blast.
25 'Tis Madness to resist or blame
The force of angry heaven's flame:
       And, if we would speak true,
       Much to the man is due.
Who, from his private gardens, where
30 He lived reserved and austere,
       As if his highest plot
       To plant the bergamot,
Could by industrious valour climb
To ruin the great work of time,
35   And cast the kingdom old
       Into another mould.
Though justice against fate complain,
And plead the ancient rights in vain;
       But those do hold or break
40   As men are strong or weak.
Nature that hateth emptiness,
Allows of penetration less;
       And therefore must make room
       Where greater spirits come.
45 What field of all the civil wars,
Where his were not the deepest scars?
       And Hampton shows what part
       He had of wiser art.
Where, twining subtle fears with hope,
50 He wove a net of such a scope,
       That Charles himself might chase
       To Caresbrook's narrow case.
That thence the royal actor born
The tragic scaffold might adorn

---

15 **his own side:** the forces of Parliament. 23 **Caesar's head:** Cromwell's victories during the civil war of the later 1640s had resulted in King Charles I's downfall and execution. See ll. 53–66. 32 **bergamot:** a type of pear.

47–52: Charles I fled from Hampton Court to Carisbrooke castle on the Isle of Wight in 1647 but was recaptured by Parliament's forces. Many contemporary pamphlets claimed Charles' flight was managed by Cromwell to gain power. 53–64: Charles I was publicly beheaded in London in 1649.

55   While round the armed bands
     Did clap their bloody hands.
He nothing common did or mean
Upon that memorable scene;
     But with his keener eye
60   The axe's edge did try;
Nor called the gods with vulgar spite
To vindicate his helpless right,
     But bowed his comely head,
     Down as upon a bed.
65 This was that memorable hour
Which first assured the forced power.
     So when they did design
     The Capitol's first line,
A bleeding head where they begun,
70 Did fright the architects to run;
     And yet in that the state
     Foresaw it's happy fate.
And now the Irish are ashamed
To see themselves in one year tamed:
75   So much one man can do,
     That does both act and know.
They can affirm his praises best,
And have, though overcome, confest
     How good he is, how just,
80   And fit for highest trust;
Nor yet grown stiffer with command,
But still in the Republic's hand.
     How fit he is to sway
     That can so well obey.
85 He to the Commons feet presents
A kingdom, for his first year's rents;
     And, what he may, forbears
     His fame to make it theirs;
And has his sword and spoils ungirt,
90 To lay them at the public's skirt.
     So when the falcon high
     Falls heavy from the sky,
She, having killed, no more does search,
But on the next green bough to perch;
95   Where, when he first does lure,
     The falckner has her sure.

67–72: In digging the foundations of the temple of Jupiter in classical Rome a severed head was discovered. This was interpreted that Rome would be the 'head' of the world.   73–74: Cromwell suppressed largely Catholic Ireland with great savagery. 85 **Commons**: the House of Commons, Parliament. 90 **skirt**: the lower part of a gown. 96 **falckner**: falconer.

What may not then our isle presume
While victory his crest does plume!
   What may not others fear
100   If thus he crown each year!
A Caesar he ere long to Gaul,
To Italy an Hannibal,
   And to all states not free
   Shall climacteric be.
105 The Pict no shelter now shall find
Within his party-coloured mind;
   But from this valour sad
   Shrink underneath the plad:
Happy if in the tufted brake
110 The English hunter him mistake;
   Nor lay his hounds in near
   The Caledonian deer.
But thou the war's and fortune's son
March indefatigably on;
115   And for the last effect
   Still keep thy sword erect;
Besides the force it has to fright
The spirits of the shady night,
   The same arts that did gain
120   A power must it maintain.

101–104: suggesting the long standing militant Protestant desire to invade Catholic southern Europe. **Gaul:** France. **climacteric:** fatal. **105–112:** in 1650, Cromwell invaded Protestant Scotland, formerly allied with England, causing great division in Parliamentary circles over the justness of this action.

105 **Pict:** A Scot, from the Latin meaning painted and referring to the intricate body tattoos of ancient Scots; hence **party-coloured:** factional. 108 **plad:** plaid, the outer garment of Scots. 109–112: hunting imagery. **brake:** dense undergrowth. **mistake:** because of his camouflaged appearance. **lay hounds in near:** put hunting dogs on the scent. **Caledonian:** Scottish.

KATHERINE PHILIPS (1632–1664)

Although coming from a Puritan background and marrying into a Parliamentarian one during the Civil War, Katherine Philips also had considerable contacts with Royalist literary circles. Her poetry gained considerable notice after the Restoration. Her work shows how early-modern women writers began to transform male-dominated literary forms in seeking to convey a different female aesthetic, one which could be seen as challenging masculine cultural norms.

Upon the graving of her Name upon a Tree in Barnelmes Walks

Alas how barbarous are we,
Thus to reward the courteous tree,
Who its broad shade affording us,
Deserves not to be wounded thus;
5 See how the yielding bark complies
With our ungrateful injuries.
And seeing this, say how much then
Trees are more generous then men,
Who by a nobleness so pure
10 Can first oblige and then endure.

Friendship's Mystery, To My Dearest Lucasia

1
Come, my Lucasia, since we see
That miracles men's faith do move,
By wonder and by prodigy
To the dull angry world let's prove
5 There's a religion in our love.

2
For though we were designed t'agree,
That fate no liberty destroys,
But our election is as free
As angels, who with greedy choice
10 Are yet determined to their joys.

3
Our hearts are doubled by the loss,
Here mixture is addition grown;
We both diffuse, and both ingross:

Friendship's Mystery 1 Lucasia: name given to Philips 13 diffuse: spread out. ingross: condense.
friend Anne Owen. 9–10: angels naturally direct love
towards God; yet they also willingly choose this love.

And we whose minds are so much one,
15 Never, yet ever are alone.

4

We court our own captivity
Than thrones more great and innocent;
'Twere banishment to be set free,
Since we wear fetters whose intent
20 Not bondage is, but ornament.

5

Divided joys are tedious found,
And griefs united easier grow;
We are our selves but by rebound,
And all our titles shuffled so,
25 Both princes, and both subjects too.

6

Our hearts are mutual victims laid,
While they (such power in friendship lies)
Are altars, priests, and off'rings made;
And each heart which thus kindly dies,
30 Grows deathless by the sacrifice.

To my Excellent Lucasia, on our Friendship

I did not live until this time
Crowned my felicity,
When I could say without a crime,
I am not thine, but thee.

5 This carcass breathed, and walkt, and slept,
So that the world believed
There was a soul the motions kept;
But they were all deceived

For as a watch by art is wound
10 To motion, such was mine;
But never had Orinda found
A soul till she found thine;

Which now inspires, cures and supplies,
And guides my darkened breast;
15 For the art all that I can prize,
My joy, my life, my rest.

No bridegroom's nor crown-conqueror's mirth
To mine compared can be;

---

11 **Orinda:** Katherine Philips' name for herself.

>   They have but pieces of this earth,
> 20   I've all the world in thee.
>
>   Then let our flames still light and shine,
>   And no false fear control,
>   As innocent as our design,
>   Immortal as our soul.

JOHN BUNYAN (1628–1688)

Born in Bedford, Bunyan grew up in relative poverty. In 1648 he went through a religious crisis, vividly recorded in *Grace Abounding to the Chief of Sinners*. Bunyan became a preacher, and, at the Restoration, a champion of nonconformist Protestantism against the Church of England, for which he was frequently imprisoned. First published in 1678, *The Pilgrim's Progress* was instantly popular. Its simple direct style, constant echoing of the Bible and representation of the ordinary world as a spiritual battleground allowed many of its early readers to contrast its perceived 'truth' against the levity of literary fictions. Although a Restoration text, it is, in one sense, the culmination of a writing which grew out of the Reformation, but which is linked, too, to medieval dream visions, such as Langland's *Piers Plowman*. In the section from which this extract comes, Christian has been travelling with Faithful towards Heaven, constantly beset by adversaries.

From The Pilgrim's Progress

Then I saw in my dream that when they were got out of the wilderness they presently saw a town before them, and the name of that town is Vanity; and at the town there is a fair[1] kept called Vanity-Fair. It is kept all the year long; it beareth the name of Vanity-Fair, because the town where 'tis kept is lighter than vanity; and also, because all that is there sold, or that cometh thither, is vanity. As is the saying of the wise, All that cometh is vanity.

This fair is no new erected business, but a thing of ancient standing; I will show you the original of it.

Almost five thousand years agone, there were pilgrims walking to the Celestial City, as these two honest persons are; and Beelzebub, Apollyon, and Legion,[2] with their companions, perceiving by the path that the pilgrims made that their way to the City lay through this town of Vanity, they contrived here to set up a fair; a fair wherein should be sold of all sorts of vanity, and that it should last all the year long. Therefore at this fair are all such merchandise sold, as houses, lands, trades, places, honours, preferments, titles, countries, kingdoms, lusts, pleasures, and delights of all sorts, as whores, bawds, wives, husbands, children, masters, servants, lives, blood,[3] bodies, souls, silver, gold, pearls, precious stones, and what not.

---

1 **fair**: fairs where articles were bought and sold were normally held at set times of the year and were often associated with social license and sanctioned misrule, e.g. as depicted in Ben Jonson's play *Bartholomew Fair*. 2 **Beelzebub**, etc.: names of the Devil. 3 **blood**: that which excites the passions.

And moreover, at this fair there is at all times to be seen jugglings, cheats, games, plays, fools, apes, knaves, and rogues, and that of all sorts.

Here are to be seen too, and that for nothing, thefts, murders, adulteries, false-swearers, and that of a blood-red colour.

And as in other fairs of less moment there are the several rows and streets under their proper names, where such and such wares are vended; so here likewise, you have the proper places, rows, streets (viz. countries and kingdoms), where the wares of this fair are soonest to be found: here is the Britain Row, the French Row, the Italian Row, the Spanish Row, the German Row, where several sorts of vanities are to be sold. But as in other fairs, some one commodity is as the chief of all the fair, so the ware of Rome and her merchandise is greatly promoted in this fair; only our English nation, with some others, have taken a dislike thereat.

Now, as I said, the way to the Celestial City lies just through this town, where this lusty fair is kept; and he that will go to the city, and yet not go through this town, must needs go out of the world. The Prince of Princes himself,[1] when here, went through this town to his own country, and that upon a fair-day too. Yea, and as I think it was Beelzebub, the chief lord of this fair, that invited him to buy of his vanities; yea, would have made him lord of the fair, would he but have done him reverence as he went through the town. Yea, because he was such a person of honour, Beelzebub had him from street to street, and showed him all the kingdoms of the world in a little time, that he might, if possible, allure that Blessed One to cheapen and buy some of his vanities. But he had no mind to the merchandise, and therefore left the town without laying out so much as one farthing upon these vanities. This fair therefore is an ancient thing, of long standing, and a very great fair.

Now these pilgrims, as I said, must needs go through this fair. Well, so they did; but behold, even as they entered into the fair, all the people in the fair were moved, and the town itself as it were in a hubbub about them; and that for several reasons, for:

First, the pilgrims were clothed with such kind of raiment as was diverse from the raiment of any that traded in that fair. The people therefore of the fair made a great gazing upon them. Some said they were fools, some they were bedlams,[2] and some 'They are outlandish-men.'

Secondly, and as they wondered at their apparel, so they did likewise at their speech; for few could understand what they said; they naturally spoke the language of Canaan;[3] but they that kept the fair were the men of this world. So that from one end of the fair to the other, they seemed barbarians each to the other.

Thirdly, but that which did not a little amuse the merchandisers was that these pilgrims set very light by all their wares, they cared not so much as to look upon them; and if they called upon them to buy, they would put their fingers in their ears, and cry, *Turn away mine eyes from beholding vanity*; and look upwards, signifying that their trade and traffic was in Heaven.

One chanced mockingly, beholding the carriages of the men, to say unto

---

1 **Prince of Princes:** Christ. 2 **bedlams:** madmen. 3 **Canaan:** the land of promise, heaven.

them, 'What will ye buy?' But they, looking gravely upon him, said, 'We buy the truth.' At that there was an occasion taken to despise the men the more; some mocking, some taunting, some speaking reproachfully, and some mocked calling upon others to smite them. At last things came to an hubbub and great stir in the fair; insomuch that all order was confounded. Now was word presently brought to the great one of the fair, who quickly came down and deputed some of his most trusty friends to take these men into examination about whom the fair was almost overturned. So the examined men were brought to examination; and they that sat upon them asked them whence they came, whither they went, and what they did there in such an unusual garb? The men told them that they were pilgrims and strangers in the world, and that they were going to their own country, which was the heavenly Jerusalem; and that they had given none occasion to the men of the town, nor yet to the merchandisers, thus to abuse them, and to let them in their journey, except it was for that when one asked them what they would buy, they said they would buy the truth. But they that were appointed to examine them did not believe them to be any other than bedlams and mad, or else such as came to put all things into a confusion in the fair. Therefore they took them, and beat them, and besmeared them with dirt, and then put them into the cage, that they might be made a spectacle to all the men of the fair. There therefore they lay for some time, and were made the objects of any man's sport, or malice, or revenge, the great one of the fair laughing still at all that befell them. But the men being patient, and not rendering railing for railing but contrariwise blessing, and giving good words for bad, and kindness for injuries done, some men in the fair that were more observing, and less prejudiced among than the rest, began to check and blame the baser sort themselves for their continual abuses done by them to the men. They therefore in angry manner let fly at them again, counting them as bad as the men in the cage, and telling them that they seemed confederates, and should be made partakers of their misfortunes. The other replied that for aught they could see, the men were quiet, and sober, and intended nobody any harm; and that there were many that traded in their fair that were more worthy to be put into the cage, yea, and pillory too, than were the men that they had abused. Thus, after divers words had passed on both sides (the men behaving themselves all the while very wisely and soberly before them), they fell to some blows among themselves and did harm one to another. Then were these two poor men brought before their examiners again, and there charged as being guilty of the late hubbub that had been in the fair. So they beat them pitifully, and hanged irons upon them, and led them in chains up and down the fair, for an example and a terror to others, lest any should further speak in their behalf, or join themselves unto them. But Christian and Faithful behaved themselves yet more wisely, and received the ignominy and shame that was cast upon them with so much meekness and patience, that it won to their side (though but few in comparison of the rest) several of the men in the fair. This put the other party yet into a greater rage, insomuch that they concluded the death of these two men. Wherefore they threatened that the cage, nor irons, should serve their turn, but that they should die for the abuse they had done and for deluding the men of the fair.

Then were they remanded to the cage again, until further order should be taken with them. So they put them in, and made their feet fast in the stocks.

Here also they called again to mind what they had heard from their faithful friend Evangelist, and was the more confirmed in their way and sufferings by what he told them would happen to them. They also now comforted each other that whose lot it was to suffer, even he should have the best on't; therefore each man secretly wished that he might have that preferment; but committing themselves to the all wise dispose of him that ruleth all things, with much content they abode in the condition in which they were, until they should be otherwise disposed of.

Restoration and Eighteenth Century

In 1660, after 20 years of political turmoil, the Stuart monarchy was restored and until the Glorious Revolution of 1688 the crucial question would be what this restoration meant in terms of the monarch's power. The licentiousness of a king who had several public mistresses, and many more in private, set the tone for a court given to the pursuit of fashion and pleasure, but the 1680s were especially a time of crisis, as parliament tried to exclude Charles II's Catholic brother, James, from the succession. Catholicism meant absolutism, the divine right of popes and kings, a philosophy inimical to the increasingly proud and independent mercantile middle class. In 1685 James II was enthroned, but in 1688 he fled when the Dutch William of Orange and James's daughter Mary invaded at the invitation of wealthy aristocrats and merchants. William, a staunch Protestant, promised to defend the Church of England from Catholic reversion and accepted that the monarch ruled only by the permission of parliament.

The Restoration was therefore a period between revolutions. The Whigs – the very rich aristocracy and rising merchants – developed nascent manufactures and colonial trade whilst 'the town' indulged in elegant soirées, went to the theatre, and wrote cynical immoral satires or elegant reinterpretations of the classics. Whilst the ultimate question of who held political power translated into the persecution of Catholics and Nonconformists, London life was cynical, witty and perfectly rhymed. Notwithstanding Dryden's brilliant neo-classical poetry, the play was the dominant genre. There the court could gather and amuse itself as the country gent, urban 'cit', and spendthrift rake struggled to possess the person and fortune of a lovely young woman, and in the prcoess displayed the hypocrisy of prudish conventions.

After the Glorious Revolution, the play continued to prosper and became less libertine, but prose was gaining in force, drawing on the increasingly private consumption of literature, and the interest in the plain style that had been fostered by the Royal Society under Charles II and endorsed by Puritans, men of science and philosophers. The new plainness and the new science articulated a belief that the world was rational, entirely rule-governed (Newton, Locke), and tradeable (Defoe). A periodical press developed in the commercial nexus of London, the world's largest city and a great hive of exchange. Journalism became a profession, despised, then as now, for its venial ability to convince the poor reader of anything the proprietors wanted. Political control had become a business under Charles, and grew constantly more important, accompanying the rise of political parties. Defoe, Swift, Fielding, all turned their hands to political propaganda in order to secure cash, place and station.

The publication of books grew rapidly, along with the general growth in commodity exchange. Prose writers began to live entirely by money earned from their pens. Patronage or private wealth, formerly the writer's sole means of support, continued but declined. Even Pope made a fortune by marketing his translations and poems on subscription. Johnson's *Dictionary* was funded by a group of commercial publishers. The world of letters became bourgeois. Men of middle rank lined rooms with books and the 'library' and 'literature' became signs of middle-class cultivation. The novel gained in force year on year, showing the middle class how morally to behave themselves and how to focus their energies on becoming rich, and women began to figure prominently as both producers and consumers of literature.

The moral and pragmatic tendency of journalistic and novelistic prose did not have total sway. Pope's neo-classical satires and translations implied that the moderns could never be as clever and poetic as Augustan Rome, and at the same time cloaked Britain in the mantle of Greco-Roman culture. Such an inheritance nicely gave Britain imperial rights, and contained the force of new money in sanctified forms. After the middle of the century, reactions against the mechanistic appearance of neo-classical verse, and against the moral righteousness and plainness of the reasoners and entrepreneurs, gave rise to pre-Romantic cults of landscape and sensibility. Albeit the results were sometimes sentimental, the implication of such writing was that the bourgeois subject had been securely placed on the throne and could confidently elaborate his (or her) peculiar emotional sensibility.

SAMUEL PEPYS (1633–1703)

Pepys was a tailor's son who rose to become Secretary of the Admiralty. An early example of the professional bureaucrat, he was renowned for bringing honesty and efficiency to the management of the Royal Navy. His diary of the years 1660–69 (first published in 1825) provides a rich insight into the mentality of the rising middle class on the margins of the Restoration court. Coincidentally it provides an important contemporary description of the Great Plague (1665) and the Great Fire (1666) which devastated the capital. The diary as a form has links with the Puritan genre of spiritual autobiography and exemplifies the growing importance of writing about the self, an activity which gives commonplace personal experience a permanent inscription. It thus paradoxically assures the self both of its isolated significance and its social integration.

From The Diary of Samuel Pepys, June 1665

1. Up, and to the office, where sat all the morning. At noon to the Change and there did some business; and home to dinner, whither Creed comes. And after dinner I put on my new silk Camelott Sute, the best that ever I wore in my life, the suit costing me above 24*l*. In this I went with him to Goldsmiths hall to the burial of Sir Tho. Viner; which hall, and Haberdashers also, was so full of

people, that we were fain for ease and coolness to go forth to Paternoster Row to choose a silk to make me a plain ordinary suit. That done, we walked to Cornehill, and there at Mr. Cades stood in the Balcon and saw all the funerals, which was with the Bluecoat boys and old men – all the Aldermen, and Lord Mayor, &c., and the number of the company very great – the greatest I ever did see for a Taverne. Hither came up to us Dr. Allen – and then Mr. Povy and Mr. Fox. The show being over, and my discourse with Mr. Povy – I took coach and to Westminster hall, where I took the fairest flower and by coach to Tothill fields for the ayre, till it was dark. I light,[1] and in with the fairest flower to eat a cake, and there did do as much as was safe with my flower, and that was enough on my part. Broke up, and away without any notice; and after delivering the rose where it should be, I to the Temple[2] and light; and came to the middle door and there took another coach, and so home – to write letters; but very few, God knows, being (by my pleasure) made to forget everything that is. The coachman that carried [us]cannot know me again, nor the people at the house where we were. Home to bed, certain news being come that our fleet is in sight of the Dutch ships.

6. Waked in the morning at 4 a-clock with great pain to piss and great pain in pissing, by having, I think, drank too great a draught of cold drink before going to bed – but by and by to sleep again; and then rose and to the office, where very busy all the morning. And at noon to dinner with Sir G. Carteret to his house, with all our Board, where a good pasty and brave discourse. But our great fears was some fresh news of the fleet, but not from the fleet, all being said to be well and beaten the Dutch; but I do not give much belief to it, and endeed, the news came from Sir W. Batten at Harwich, and writ so simply that we all made good mirth of it. Thence to the office, where upon Sir G. Carteret's accounts, to my great vexation, there being nothing done by the Controller to right the King therein. I then to my office and wrote letters all the afternoon; and in the evening by coach to Sir P. Warwickes about my Tanger business, to get money; and so to my Lady Sandwiches, who, poor lady, expects every hour to hear of my Lord; but in the best temper, neither confident nor troubled with fear, that I ever did see in my life . . . . Thence by coach home, and to my office a little; and so, before 12 a-clock, home to bed.

7. This morning my wife and mother rose about 2 a-clock, and with Mercer, Mary, the boy and W. Hewer, as they had designed, took boat and down to refresh themselfs on the water to Gravesend. I lay till 7 a-clock; then up, and to the office upon Sir G. Carteret's accounts again – where very busy. Thence abroad and to the Change,[3] no news of certainty being yet come from the Fleete. Thence to the Dolphin Taverne, where Sir J. Mennes, Lord Brunkard, Sir Tho. Harvy and myself dined upon Sir G. Carteret's charge – and very merry we were, Sir Tho Harvy being a very drolle. Thence to the office; and meeting Creed, away with him to my Lord Treasurer's, there thinking to have met the goldsmiths, or at White-hall; but did not, and so appointed another time for my Lord to speak to them to advance us some money. Thence, it being the hottest day that ever I felt in my life, and it is confessed so by all other people the

---

1: alight. 2: Temple Bar, a city gate. 3: the Royal Exchange, meeting-place for merchants.

hottest they ever knew in England in the beginning of June – we to the New Exchange and there drunk whey, with much entreaty, getting it for our money, and [they] would not be entreated to let us have one glasse more. So took water, and to Fox hall[1] to the Spring-garden and there walked an hour or two with great pleasure, saving our minds ill at ease concerning the fleet and my Lord Sandwich, that we have no news of them, and ill reports run up and down of his being killed, but without ground. Here stayed, pleasantly walking and spending but 6*d*, till 9 at night; and then by water to White-hall, and there I stopped to hear news of the fleet, but none come, which is strange; and so by water home – where, weary with walking and with the mighty heat of the weather, and for my wife's not coming home – I staying walking in the garden till 12 at night, when it begun to Lighten[2] exceedingly through the greatness of the heat. Then, despairing of her coming home, I to bed.

This day, much against my Will, I did in Drury lane see two or three houses marked with a red cross upon the doors, and 'Lord have mercy upon us' writ there – which was a sad sight to me, being the first of that kind that to my remembrance I ever saw. It put me into an ill conception of myself and my smell, so that I was forced to buy some roll tobacco to smell to and chaw – which took away the apprehension.

8. About 5 a-clock my wife came home, it having lightened all night hard, and one great shower of rain. She came and lay upon the bed. I up, and to the office, where all the morning. I alone at home to dinner, my wife, mother, and Mercer dining at W. Joyces, I giving her a caution to go round by the Half Moone to his house, because of the plague. I to my Lord Treasurer's, by appointment of Sir Tho. Ingrams, to meet the goldsmiths – where I met with the great news, at last newly come, brought by Bab May from the Duke of Yorke,[3] that we have totally routed the Dutch. That the Duke himself, the Prince, my Lord Sandwich, and Mr. Coventry are all well. Which did put me into such a joy, that I forgot almost all other thoughts.

11. *Lords day*. Up, and expected long a new suit; but coming not, dressed myself in my late new black silk camelot suit; and when full ready, comes my new one of Colour'd Farrinden, which my wife puts me out of love with; which vexes [me], but I think it is only my not being used to wear Colours, which makes it look a little unusual upon me. To my chamber, and there spent the morning reading. At noon by invitation comes my two cousin Joyces and their wifes – my aunt James, and he-cousin Harman – his wife being ill. I had a good dinner for them, and as merry as I could be in such company. They being gone, I out of doors a little to show forsooth my new suit, and back again; and in going, saw poor Dr. Burnets[4] door shut. But he hath, I hear, gained great good-will among his neighbours; for he discovered it himself first, and caused himself to be shut up of his own accord – which was very handsome. In the evening comes Mr. Andrews and his wife and Mr. Hill, and stayed and played and sung and supped – most excellent pretty company; so pleasant, ingenious, and harmless, I cannot desire better. They gone, we to bed – my mind in great present ease.

1: Vauxhall, a pleasure garden on the south bank of the Thames where people often wore masks and behaved licentiously.   2: lightning.   3: James, Charles II's brother.   4: probably Gilbert Burnet, chaplain to the King.

12. Up, and in my yesterday's new suit to the Duke of Albemarle. And after a turn in Whitehall and thence in Westminster Hall – returned, and with my Taylor bought some gold lace for my sleeve bands at Paternoster Row. So home to dinner, and then to the office and down the River to Deptford; and then back again and to my Lord Treasurer's, and up and down to look after my Tanger business; and so home to my office, then to supper and to bed. The Duke of Yorke is sent for last night, and expected to be here tomorrow.

15. Up, and put on my new stuff suit with close knees, which becomes me most nobly as my wife says. At the office all day. At noon put on my first laced band, all lace, and to Kate Joyce's to dinner; where my mother, wife, and abundance of their friends, and good usage. Thence wife and Mercer and I to the Old Exchange and there bought two lace bands more, one of my Semstresse, whom my wife concurs with me to be a pretty woman. So down to Deptford and Woolwich, my boy and I. At Woolwich discoursed with Mr. Shelden about my bringing my wife down for a month or two to his house; which he approves of, and I think will be very convenient. So late back and to the office, wrote letters, and so home to supper and to bed. This day the News-book (upon Mr Moores showing Lestrange Captain Ferrers letter) did do my Lord Sandwich great right as to the late victory. The Duke of Yorke not yet come to town.

The town grows very sickly, and people to be afeared of it – there dying this last week of the plague 112, from 43 the week before – whereof, one in Fanchurch street and one in Broadstreete by the Treasurer's office.

20. Thanksgiving day for Victory over the Dutch. Up, and to the office, where very busy alone all the morning till church time; and there heard a mean sorry sermon of Mr. Mills. Then to the Dolphin Taverne, where all we officers of the Navy met with the Comissioners of the Ordnance by agreement and dined – where good Musique, at my direction. Our club[1] came to 34s[2] a man – nine of us. Thence after dinner I to White-hall with Sir W Berkely in his coach. And so I walked to Herberts and there spent a little time avec la mosa, sin hazer algo con ella que kiss and tocar ses mamelles, que me haza hazera la cosa a mi mismo con gran plaisir.[3] Thence by water to Fox hall, and there walked an hour alone, observing the several humours of the citizens that were there this holiday, pulling of cherries[4] and God knows what. And so home to my office, where late, my wife not being come home with my mother, who have been this day all abroad upon the water, my mother being to go out of town speedily. So I home and to supper and to bed. This day I informed myself that there died four or five at Westminster of the plague, in one alley in several houses upon Sunday last – Bell Alley, over against the Palace-gate. Yet people do think that the number will be fewer in the town then it was the last week.

1: the sum due. 2: 34 shillings, a vast amount. 3: a comic mix of poor French and Spanish; 'with the young girl, without doing more than kiss and touch her breasts, which makes me do the thing to myself with great pleasure.' 4: a sexual innuendo.

WILLIAM WYCHERLEY (1641–1715)

Of gentry origin, Wycherley was educated in France and at Oxford before enrolling as a student of law in London and flirting with military employment. Typical of his class, he aspired to be a courtier and achieved no qualifications. He became the lover of Lady Castlemaine, an ex-lover of the King, and achieved the King's admiration for his wit, before falling from favour by an injudicious marriage. His plays, *Love in A Wood, or St James's Park* (1671), *The Gentleman Dancing-Master* (1671), *The Country Wife* (1675) and *The Plain-Dealer* (1677), were esteemed for their satire on sexual hypocrisy and depiction of urbane mores. Later writers such as Pope admired them, but Johnson set the longer note in thinking them dissolute. Technically, Wycherley's use of the aside, references to staging, and play upon watchers watching the action (mirrors of the audience), provide a metatheatrical understanding of dramatic and social roles which keeps his plays in the forefront of the modern repertory.

The Country Wife

Persons

Mr Horner	Mr Harcourt
Mr Dorilant	Mr Pinchwife
Mr Sparkish	Sir Jaspar Fidget
Mrs Margery Pinchwife	Mrs Alithea
My Lady Fidget	Mrs Dainty Fidget
Mrs Squeamish	Old Lady Squeamish
A Boy	A Quack
Lucy, *Alithea's Maid*	Clasp, *a bookseller*

Waiters, Servants and Attendants, a Parson

Scene: London

Prologue

[*Spoken originally by the actor who played Horner.*]

Poets, like cudgelled bullies, never do
At first, or second blow submit to you;
But will provoke you still and ne'er have done,
Till you are weary first with laying on.
5   The late so baffled scribbler of this day,
Though he stands trembling, bids me boldly say,
What we before most plays are used to do,
For poets out of fear first draw on you;

Characters: the names provide clues to character. Those less than obvious are Horner – a maker of cuckolds, Harcourt – a gentleman, Dorilant – a smart young man (from the French for gold), Sparkish – a bit of a wit, Alithea – truth (from the Greek), Dainty – meaning choice and choosy, Squeamish – prudish, Quack – an incompetent doctor. **The Prologue 4 laying on**: hitting. **5 scribbler**: Wycherley himself.

In a fierce prologue the still pit defy,
10 And, ere you speak, like Castril give the lie.
But though our Bayeses' battles oft I've fought,
And with bruised knuckles their dear conquests bought;
Nay, never yet feared odds upon the stage,
In prologue dare not hector with the age,
15 But would take quarter from your saving hands,
Though Bayes within all yielding countermands,
Says you confederate wits no quarter give,
Therefore his play shan't ask your leave to live.
Well, let the vain rash fop, by huffing so,
20 Think to obtain the better terms of you;
But we the actors humbly will submit,
Now, and at any time, to a full pit;
Nay often we anticipate your rage,
And murder poets for you on our stage.
25 We set no guards on our tiring-room,
But when with flying colours there you come,
We patiently, you see, give up to you
Our poets, virgins, nay, our matrons too.

Act I, Scene i

[*Horner's lodging. Enter Horner, Quack following him at a distance.*]

Horner [*Aside*] A quack is as fit for a pimp as a midwife for a bawd; they are still but in their way both helpers of nature. – Well, my dear doctor, hast thou done what I desired?
Quack I have undone you for ever with the women, and
5 reported you throughout the whole town as bad as an eunuch, with as much trouble as if I had made you one in earnest.
Horner But have you told all the midwives you know, the orange wenches at the playhouses, the City husbands, and old fumbling keepers of this end of the town? – For they'll be the
10 readiest to report it.
Quack I have told all the chambermaids, waiting-women, tire-women, and old women of my acquaintance; nay, and whispered it as a secret to 'em and to the whisperers of Whitehall, so that you need not doubt 'twill spread, and you will
15 be as odious to the handsome young women as –
Horner As the smallpox. Well –

The Prologue **9 pit:** the rowdy part of the audience. **10 Castril:** see Jonson's *The Alchemist*, a boy who accuses Subtle of lying before he speaks. **11 Bayeses:** poets who seek and wear the laurel; hence Dryden, poet laureate, was mocked as Mr Bayes. **17 Bayes within:** Wycherley. **19 fop:** foolishly fashionable man. **25 tiring-room:** attiring room. **1.1, 8 orange wenches:** sellers of oranges, often of themselves. **9 keepers . . . end of town:** keepers of mistresses in the West End. **12 tire-women:** ladies' maids. **14 Whitehall:** The public rooms of the King's palace.

Quack And to the married women of this end of the town as –
Horner As the great ones – nay, as their own husbands.
Quack And to the city dames, as Aniseed Robin of filthy and
20 contemptible memory; and they will frighten their children with
your name, especially their females.
Horner And cry, 'Horner's coming, to carry you away!' I am only
afraid 'twill not be believed. You told 'em 'twas by an English-French
disaster, and an English-French surgeon, who has given me at once
25 not only a cure, but an antidote for the future against that
damned malady, and that worse distemper, love, and all other
women's evils?
Quack Your late journey into France has made it the more
credible, and your being here a fortnight before you appeared in
30 public, looks as if you apprehended the shame – which I wonder
you do not. Well, I have been hired by young gallants to belie 'em
t'other way; but you are the first would be thought a man unfit
for women.
Horner Dear Master Doctor, let vain rogues be contented only to
35 be thought abler men than they are; generally 'tis all the pleasure
they have. But mine lies another way.
Quack You take, methinks, a very preposterous way to it, and as
ridiculous as if we operators in physic should put forth bills to
disparage our medicaments, with hopes to gain customers.
40 **Horner** Doctor, there are quacks in love, as well as physic, who
get but the fewer and worse patients for their boasting. A good
name is seldom got by giving it oneself, and women no more than
honour are compassed by bragging. Come, come, doctor, the wisest
lawyer never discovers the merits of his cause till the trial; the
45 wealthiest man conceals his riches, and the cunning gamester his
play. Shy husbands and keepers, like old rooks, are not to be cheated
but by a new unpractised trick. False friendship will pass now no
more than false dice upon 'em; no, not in the city.
[*Enter Boy.*]
Boy There are two ladies and a gentleman coming up.
[*Exit Boy.*]
50 **Horner** A pox! Some unbelieving sisters of my former
acquaintance who, I am afraid, expect their sense should be
satisfied of the falsity of the report.
[*Enter Sir Jasper Fidget, Lady Fidget, and Dainty Fidget*]
No – this formal fool, and women!
Quack His wife and sister.
55 **Sir Jasper** My coach breaking just now before your door sir, I
look upon as an occasional reprimand to me sir, for not kissing
your hands sir, since your coming out of France sir. And so my

---

18 **the great ones**: the great pox, syphillis, in contrast to smallpox.   19 **Aniseed Robin**: infamous hermaphrodite who sold aniseed water in the streets of London.   25 **antidote**: he wishes to imply the surgeon has cured
him of the pox (a 'French disaster') by castration.   50 **sisters**: women of ill-repute.   56 **occasional**: timely.

disaster sir, has been my good fortune sir; and this is my wife, and sister sir.

60   **Horner** What then, sir?

Sir Jasper My lady, and sister, sir. – Wife, this is Master Horner.

Lady Fidget Master Horner, husband!

Sir Jasper My lady, my Lady Fidget, sir.

Horner So, sir.

65   **Sir Jasper** Won't you be acquainted with her sir? [*Aside*] So the report is true, I find, by his coldness or aversion to the sex. But I'll play the wag with him. – Pray salute my wife, my lady, sir.

Horner I will kiss no man's wife, sir, for him, sir. I have taken my eternal leave, sir, of the sex already, sir.

70   **Sir Jasper** [*Aside*] Ha ha ha! I'll plague him yet. – Not know my wife, sir?

Horner I do know your wife, sir, she's a woman, sir, and consequently a monster, sir, a greater monster than a husband, sir.

Sir Jasper A husband! How, sir?

75   **Horner** So, sir. [*Makes horns*] But I make no more cuckolds, sir.

Sir Jasper Ha ha ha! Mercury, Mercury!

Lady Fidget Pray, Sir Jasper, let us be gone from this rude fellow.

Dainty Fidget Who, by his breeding, would think he had ever been in France?

80   **Lady Fidget** Foh, he's but too much a French fellow, such as hate women of quality and virtue for their love to their husbands, Sir Jasper. A woman is hated by 'em as much for loving her husband, as for loving their money. But pray, let's be gone.

Horner You do well, madam, for I have nothing that you came

85   for. I have brought over not so much as a bawdy picture, new postures, nor the second part of the *École des filles*, nor –

Quack [*Apart to Horner*] Hold, for shame, sir. What d'ye mean? You'll ruin yourself for ever with the sex!

Sir Jasper Ha ha ha! He hates women perfectly, I find.

90   **Dainty Fidget** What pity 'tis he should.

Lady Fidget Ay, he's a base, rude fellow for't. But affectation makes not a woman more odious to them than virtue.

Horner Because your virtue is your greatest affectation, madam.

Lady Fidget How, you saucy fellow! Would you wrong my

95   honour?

Horner If I could.

Lady Fidget How d'ye mean, sir?

Sir Jasper Ha ha ha! No, he can't wrong your ladyship's honour, upon my honour. He, poor man – hark you in your ear – a mere

100   eunuch.

Lady Fidget Oh filthy French beast! Foh, foh! Why do we stay?

---

76 mercury: Mercury, the messenger of the Gods, wore a winged (horned) hat, represented wit and trickery, and mercury was used to treat venereal disease.   **86 bawdy . . . postures . . .** *École des filles*: pornography.

Let's be gone – I can't endure the sight of him.

Sir Jasper Stay but till the chairs come; they'll be here presently.

Lady Fidget No, no.

105 *Sir Jasper* Nor can I stay longer. 'Tis, let me see – a quarter and a half quarter of a minute past eleven. The Council will be sat; I must away. Business must be preferred always before love and ceremony with the wise, Mr Horner.

Horner And the impotent, Sir Jasper.

110 *Sir Jasper* Ay, ay, the impotent, Master Horner. Ha ha ha!

Lady Fidget What, leave us with a filthy man alone in his lodgings?

Sir Jasper He's an innocent man now, you know. Pray stay; I'll hasten the chairs to you. – Mr Horner, your servant; I should be glad to see you at my house. Pray, come and dine with me, and

115 play at cards with my wife after dinner; you are fit for women at that game yet, ha ha! [*Aside*] 'Tis as much a husband's prudence to provide innocent diversion for a wife, as to hinder her unlawful pleasures; and he had better employ her, than let her employ herself. – Farewell.

120 *Horner* Your servant, Sir Jasper.

[*Exit Sir Jasper.*]

Lady Fidget I will not stay with him, foh!

Horner Nay, madam, I beseech you stay, if it be but to see I can be as civil to ladies yet, as they would desire.

Lady Fidget No, no! Foh, you cannot be civil to ladies.

125 *Dainty Fidget* You, as civil as ladies would desire!

Lady Fidget No, no, no; foh, foh, foh!

[*Exeunt Lady Fidget and Dainty Fidget.*]

Quack Now I think I, or you yourself rather, have done your business with the women.

Horner Thou art an ass. Don't you see already, upon the report and

130 my carriage, this grave man of business leaves his wife in my lodgings, invites me to his house and wife, who before would not be acquainted with me out of jealousy.

Quack Nay, by this means you may be the more acquainted with the husbands, but the less with the wives.

135 *Horner* Let me alone. If I can but abuse the husbands, I'll soon disabuse the wives. Stay, I'll reckon you up the advantages I am like to have by my stratagem: first, I shall be rid of all my old acquaintances, the most insatiable sorts of duns that invade our lodgings in a morning; and next to the pleasure of making a new mistress, is that

140 of being rid of an old one; and of all old debts, love, when it comes to be so, is paid the most unwillingly.

Quack Well, you may be so rid of your old acquaintances – but how will you get any new ones?

---

113 **chairs**: Sedan chairs. 123 **civil**: with innuendo, implying sexually pleasing. 130 **carriage**: conduct. 135 **abuse**: deceive. 138 **duns**: creditors.

Horner Doctor, thou wilt never make a good chemist, thou art
145 so incredulous and impatient. Ask but all the young fellows of
the town, if they do not lose more time, like huntsmen, in starting
the game, than in running it down. One knows not where to find
'em, who will, or will not. Women of quality are so civil, you can
hardly distinguish love from good breeding, and a man is often
150 mistaken. But now I can be sure, she that shows an aversion to me,
loves the sport, as those women that are gone, whom I warrant to be
right. And then the next thing is, your women of honour, as you call
'em, are only chary of their reputations, not their persons, and 'tis
scandal they would avoid, not men. Now may I have, by the
155 reputation of an eunuch, the privileges of one, and be seen in a lady's
chamber in a morning, as early as her husband; kiss virgins before
their parents, or lovers; and may be, in short, the *passe-partout* of the
town. Now, doctor –
Quack Nay, now you shall be the doctor; and your process is so
160 new, that we do not know but it may succeed.
Horner Not so new neither; *probatum est*, doctor.
Quack Well, I wish you luck and many patients, whilst I go to mine.
[*Exit Quack. Enter Harcourt and Dorilant to Horner.*]
Harcourt Come, your appearance at the play yesterday has, I hope,
hardened you for the future against the women's contempt, and the
165 men's raillery; and now you'll abroad as you were wont.
Horner Did I not bear it bravely?
Dorilant With a most theatrical impudence; nay, more than the
orange wenches show there, or a drunken vizard-mask, or a great-
bellied actress – nay, or the most impudent of creatures, an ill poet;
170 or what is yet more impudent, a second-hand critic.
Horner But what say the ladies? Have they no pity?
Harcourt What ladies? The vizard-masks, you know, never pity a
man when all's gone, though in their service.
Dorilant And for the women in the boxes, you'd never pity them,
175 when 'twas in your power.
Harcourt They say 'tis pity but all that deal with common women
should be served so.
Dorilant Nay, I dare swear they won't admit you to play at cards
with them, go to plays with 'em, or do the little duties which other
180 shadows of men are wont to do for 'em.
Horner Who do you call shadows of men?
Dorilant Half-men.
Horner What, boys?
Dorilant Ay, your old boys, old *beaux garçons*, who like super-
185 annuated stallions are suffered to run, feed, and whinny with the
mares as long as they live, though they can do nothing else.

---

144 chemist: alchemist.   **152** right: ready.   **157** *passe-partout*: a master-key, or someone having leave to go everywhere.   **161** *probatum est*: it has been proved.   **168** vizard-mask: a prostitute (who sometimes wore decorative masks).   **168** great-bellied: pregnant.   **174** boxes: in the theatre, occupied by the rich.   **184** *beaux garçons*: fops.

Horner Well, a pox on love and wenching; women serve but to keep a man from better company. Though I can't enjoy them, I shall you the more. Good fellowship and friendship are lasting,

190 rational, and manly pleasures.

Harcourt For all that, give me some of those pleasures you call effeminate too; they help to relish one another.

Horner They disturb one another.

Harcourt No, mistresses are like books; if you pore upon them too

195 much, they doze you, and make you unfit for company; but if used discreetly, you are the fitter for conversation by 'em.

Dorilant A mistress should be like a little country retreat near the town, not to dwell in constantly, but only for a night and away to taste the town better when a man returns.

200 *Horner* I tell you, 'tis as hard to be a good fellow, a good friend, and a lover of women, as 'tis to be a good fellow, a good friend, and a lover of money. You cannot follow both; then choose your side. Wine gives you liberty, love takes it away.

Dorilant Gad, he's in the right on't.

205 *Horner* Wine gives you joy; love, grief and tortures, besides the surgeon's. Wine makes us witty; love, only sots. Wine makes us sleep; love breaks it.

Dorilant By the world, he has reason, Harcourt.

Horner Wine makes –

210 *Dorilant* Ay, wine makes us – makes us princes; love makes us beggars, poor rogues, egad – and wine –

Horner So, there's one converted. No, no; love and wine, oil and vinegar.

Harcourt I grant it; love will still be uppermost.

215 *Horner* Come, for my part I will have only those glorious, manly pleasures of being very drunk, and very slovenly.
[*Enter Boy.*]

Boy Mr Sparkish is below, sir
[*Exit Boy.*]

Harcourt What, my dear friend! A rogue that is fond of me only, I think, or abusing him.

220 *Dorilant* No, he can no more think the men laugh at him, than that women jilt him, his opinion of himself is so good.

Horner Well, there's another pleasure by drinking I thought not of – I shall lose his acquaintance, because he cannot drink. And you know 'tis a very hard thing to be rid of him, for he's one of those

225 nauseous offerers at wit, who, like the worst fiddlers, run themselves into all companies.

Harcourt One that by being in the company of men of sense would pass for one.

---

196 conversation: intercourse.

Horner And may so to the short-sighted world, as a false jewel
230   amongst true ones is not discerned at a distance. His company is as
    troublesome to us as a cuckold's when you have a mind to his wife's.
Harcourt No, the rogue will not let us enjoy one another, but
    ravishes our conversation, though he signifies no more to't, than
    Sir Martin Mar-all's gaping, and awkward thrumming upon the lute,
235   does to his man's voice and music.
Dorilant And to pass for a wit in town, shows himself a fool every
    night to us that are guilty of the plot.
Horner Such wits as he, are, to a company of reasonable men,
    like rooks to the gamesters, who only fill a room at the table, but
240   are so far from contributing to the play, that they only serve to spoil
    the fancy of those that do.
Dorilant Nay, they are used like rooks too: snubbed, checked, and
    abused; yet the rogues will hang on.
Horner A pox on 'em, and all that force nature, and would be still
245   what she forbids 'em. Affectation is her greatest monster.
Harcourt Most men are the contraries to that they would seem.
    Your bully, you see, is a coward with a long sword; the little, humbly
    fawning physician, with his ebony cane, is he that destroys men.
Dorilant The usurer, a poor rogue possessed of mouldy bonds, and
250   mortgages; and we they call spendthrifts are only wealthy, who lay
    out his money upon daily new purchases of pleasure.
Horner Ay, your arrantest cheat is your trustee, or executor; your
    jealous man, the greatest cuckold; your churchman, the greatest
    atheist; and your noisy pert rogue of a wit, the greatest fop, dullest
255   ass, and worst company – as you shall see; for here he comes.
    [*Enter Sparkish to them.*]
Sparkish How is't, sparks, how is't? Well, faith, Harry, I must rally
    thee a little, ha ha ha, upon the report in town of thee, ha ha ha – I
    can't hold i'faith; shall I speak?
Horner Yes, but you'll be so bitter then.
260   *Sparkish* Honest Dick and Frank here shall answer for me; I will not
    be extreme bitter, by the universe.
Harcourt We will be bound in ten thousand pound bond, he shall
    not be bitter at all.
Dorilant Nor sharp, nor sweet.
265   *Horner* What, not downright insipid?
Sparkish Nay then, since you are so brisk, and provoke me, take
    what follows. You must know, I was discoursing and rallying with
    some ladies yesterday, and they happened to talk of the fine new
    signs in town.
270   *Horner* Very fine ladies, I believe.
Sparkish Said I, 'I know where the best new sign is.' 'Where?' says

---

234 Sir Martin Mar-all: (Dryden 1668) Mar-all pretends to serenade his mistress while his hidden servant plays and
sings but mars all by failing to stop when his servant does.

one of the ladies. 'In Covent Garden,' I replied. Said another, 'In
what street?' 'In Russell Street,' answered I. 'Lord,' says another, 'I'm
sure there was ne'er a fine new sign there yesterday.' 'Yes, but there
275   was,' said I again, 'and it came out of France, and has been there a
fortnight.'
Dorilant A pox, I can hear no more, prithee.
Horner No, hear him out; let him tune his crowd a while.
Harcourt The worst music, the greatest preparation.
280   *Sparkish* Nay, faith, I'll make you laugh. 'It cannot be,' says a
third lady. 'Yes, yes,' quoth I again. Says a fourth lady –
Horner Look to't, we'll have no more ladies.
Sparkish No? – Then mark, mark now. Said I to the fourth, 'Did
you never see Mr Horner? He lodges in Russell Street, and he's a sign
285   of a man, you know, since he came out of France.' He ha he!
Horner But the devil take me, if thine be the sign of a jest.
Sparkish With that they all fell a-laughing, till they bepissed
themselves. What, but it does not move you, methinks? Well, I see
one had as good go to law without a witness, as break a jest
290   without a laugher on one's side. Come, come, sparks, but where do
we dine? I have left at Whitehall an earl, to dine with you.
Dorilant Why, I thought thou hadst loved a man with a title better
than a suit with a French trimming to't.
Harcourt Go to him again.
295   *Sparkish* No sir, a wit to me is the greatest title in the world.
Horner But go dine with your earl, sir; he may be exceptious. We are
your friends, and will not take it ill to be left, I do assure you.
Harcourt Nay, faith, he shall go to him.
Sparkish Nay, pray, gentlemen.
300   *Dorilant* We'll thrust you out if you won't. What, disappoint
anybody for us?
Sparkish Nay, dear gentlemen, hear me.
Horner No, no, sir, by no means. Pray go, sir.
Sparkish Why, dear rogues –
305   *Dorilant* No, no. [*They all thrust him out of the room.*]
All Ha ha ha!
[*Sparkish returns.*]
Sparkish But, Sparks, pray hear me. What, d'ye think I'll eat then
with gay shallow fops, and silent coxcombs? I think wit as necessary
at dinner as a glass of good wine, and that's the reason I never have
310   any stomach when I eat alone. Come, but where do we dine?
Horner Even where you will.
Sparkish At Chateline's?
Dorilant Yes, if you will.
Sparkish Or at the Cock?
315   *Dorilant* Yes, if you please.

---

278 crowd: a fiddle.   **296 exceptious**: inclined to take offence.

Sparkish Or at the Dog and Partridge?

Horner Ay, if you have a mind to't, for we shall dine at neither.

Sparkish Pshaw, with your fooling we shall lose the new play –
and I would no more miss seeing a new play the first day, than I
320 would miss sitting in the wits' row. Therefore I'll go fetch my
mistress, and away.

[*Exit Sparkish. Enter Pinchwife.*]

Horner Who have we here? Pinchwife?

Pinchwife Gentlemen, your humble servant.

Horner Well, Jack, by the long absence from the town, the grumness
325 of thy countenance, and the slovenliness of thy habit, I should give
thee joy, should I not, of marriage?

Pinchwife [*Aside*] Death, does he know I'm married too? I thought
to have concealed it from him at least. [*Aloud*] My long stay in the
country will excuse my dress, and I have a suit of law that brings me
330 up to town – that puts me out of humour. Besides, I must give
Sparkish tomorrow five thousand pound to lie with my sister.

Horner Nay, you country gentlemen, rather than not purchase, will
buy anything; and he is a cracked title, if we may quibble. Well, but
am I to give thee joy? I heard thou wert married.

335 *Pinchwife* What then?

Horner Why, the next thing that is to be heard is – thou'rt a
cuckold.

Pinchwife [*Aside*] Insupportable name.

Horner But I did not expect marriage from such a whoremaster
340 as you, one that knew the town so much, and women so well.

Pinchwife Why, I have married no London wife.

Horner Pshaw, that's all one; that grave circumspection in marrying
a country wife, is like refusing a deceitful, pampered Smithfield jade,
to go and be cheated by a friend in the country.

345 *Pinchwife* [*Aside*] A pox on him and his simile! – At least we are
a little surer of the breed there, know what her keeping has been,
whether foiled or unsound.

Horner Come, come, I have known a clap gotten in Wales; and
there are cousins, justices, clerks, and chaplains in the country –
350 I won't say coachmen. But she's handsome and young?

Pinchwife [*Aside*] I'll answer as I should do. – No, no, she has no
beauty but her youth; no attraction but her modesty; wholesome,
homely, and housewifely, that's all.

Dorilant He talks as like a grazier as he looks.

355 *Pinchwife* She's too awkward, ill-favoured, and silly to bring to town.

Horner Then methinks you should bring her, to be taught
breeding.

---

320 **wits' row:** the pit. 331 **five thousand pound:** a very large dowry. 333 **cracked title:** unsound
investment. 343 **Smithfield jade:** a worn-out horse or woman bought in Smithfield market. 347 **foiled:**
meaning injured when applied to a horse and deflowered when applied to a woman. 348 **clap:** venereal disease.

Pinchwife To be taught – ? No, sir, I thank you; good wives, and private soldiers, should be ignorant. [*Aside*] I'll keep her from
360   your instructions, I warrant you.
Harcourt [*Aside*] The rogue is as jealous as if his wife were not ignorant.
Horner Why, if she be ill-favoured, there will be less danger here for you than by leaving her in the country; we have such variety of
365   dainties that we are seldom hungry.
Dorilant But they have always coarse, constant, swingeing stomachs in the country.
Harcourt Foul feeders indeed.
Dorilant And your hospitality is great there.
370   *Harcourt* Open house, every man's welcome.
Pinchwife So, so, gentlemen.
Horner But prithee, why wouldst thou marry her? If she be ugly, ill bred, and silly, she must be rich then.
Pinchwife As rich as if she brought me twenty thousand pound out
375   of this town; for she'll be as sure not to spend her moderate portion, as a London baggage would be to spend hers, let it be what it would. So 'tis all one. Then because she's ugly, she's the likelier to be my own; and being ill-bred, she'll hate conversation; and since silly and innocent, will not know the difference betwixt a man of one-and-
380   twenty, and one of forty –
Horner Nine, to my knowledge. But if she be silly, she'll expect as much from a man of forty-nine, as from him of one-and-twenty. But methinks wit is more necessary than beauty, and I think no young woman ugly that has it, and no handsome woman agreeable
385   without it.
Pinchwife 'Tis my maxim: he's a fool that marries, but he's a greater that does not marry a fool. What is wit in a wife good for, but to make a man a cuckold?
Horner Yes, to keep it from his knowledge.
390   *Pinchwife* A fool cannot contrive to make her husband a cuckold.
Horner No, but she'll club with a man that can; and what is worse, if she cannot make her husband a cuckold, she'll make him jealous, and pass for one and then 'tis all one.
Pinchwife Well, well, I'll take care, for one; my wife shall make me
395   no cuckold, though she had your help, Mr Horner. I understand the town, sir.
Dorilant [*Aside*] His help!
Harcourt [*Aside*] He's come newly to town, it seems, and has not heard how things are with him.
400   *Horner* But tell me, has marriage cured thee of whoring, which it seldom does?
Harcourt 'Tis more than age can do.
Horner No, the word is, 'I'll marry and live honest'; but a marriage vow is like a penitent gamester's oath, and entering into bonds and

405 penalties to stint himself to such a particular small sum at play for
the future, which makes him but the more eager; and not being able
tohold out, loses his money again, and his forfeit to boot.
Dorilant Ay, ay, a gamester will be a gamester, whilst his money
lasts; and a whoremaster, whilst his vigour.
410 *Harcourt* Nay, I have known 'em, when they are broke, and can
lose no more, keep a-fumbling with the box in their hands, to fool
with only, and hinder other gamesters.
Dorilant That had wherewithal to make lusty stakes.
Pinchwife Well, gentlemen, you may laugh at me, but you shall
415 never lie with my wife; I know the town.
Horner But prithee, was not the way you were in better? Is it
keeping better than marriage?
Pinchwife A pox on't, the jades would jilt me; I could never keep a
whore to myself.
420 *Horner* So then, you only married to keep a whore to yourself. Well,
but let me tell you, women, as you say, are like soldiers, made
constant and loyal by good pay, rather than by oaths and covenants.
Therefore I'd advise my friends to keep rather than marry – since,
too, I find by your example it does not serve one's turn, for I saw you
425 yesterday in the eighteen-penny place with a pretty country wench.
Pinchwife [*Aside*] How the devil! Did he see my wife then? I sat
there that she might not be seen. But she shall never go to a play
again.
Horner What, dost thou blush, at nine-and-forty, for having been
430 seen with a wench?
Dorilant No, faith, I warrant 'twas his wife, which he seated there
out of sight – for he's a cunning rogue, and understands the town.
Harcourt He blushes; then 'twas his wife for men are now more
ashamed to be seen with them in public, than with a wench.
435 *Pinchwife* [*Aside*] Hell and damnation! I'm undone, since Horner
has seen her, and they know 'twas she.
Horner But prithee, was it thy wife? She was exceedingly pretty;
I was in love with her at that distance.
Pinchwife You are like never to be nearer to her. Your servant,
440 gentlemen. [*Offers to go.*]
Horner Nay, prithee stay.
Pinchwife I cannot; I will not.
Horner Come, you shall dine with us.
Pinchwife I have dined already.
445 *Horner* Come, I know thou hast not. I'll treat thee, dear rogue;
thou shan't spend none of thy Hampshire money today.
Pinchwife [*Aside*] Treat me! So, he uses me already like his cuckold.
Horner Nay, you shall not go.

---

411 box: dice-shaker, also by extension the vagina, an elaborate sexual pun.   **425 eighteen-penny place:** the middle gallery of the theatre, not readily visible from the pit but frequented by prostitutes.   **446 Hampshire:** near London but, to the city gallant, synonymous with the idiocy of rural life.

Pinchwife I must, I have business at home.
[*Exit Pinchwife.*]
450 **Harcourt** To beat his wife. He's as jealous of her as a Cheapside
husband of a Covent Garden wife.
Horner Why, 'tis as hard to find an old whoremaster without
jealousy and the gout, as a young one without fear or the pox.
As gout in age, from pox in youth proceeds,
455 So, wenching past, then jealousy succeeds;
The worst disease that love and wenching breeds.

[*Exeunt.*]

Act II, Scene i

[*Mrs Pinchwife's lodging. Mrs Pinchwife and Alethea; Pinchwife
peeping behind at the door.*]

Mrs Pinchwife Pray, sister, where are the host fields and woods
to walk in, in London?
Alethea A pretty question! Why, sister, Mulberry Garden, and St
James's Park; and for close walks, the New Exchange.
5 **Mrs Pinchwife** Pray, sister, tell me why my husband looks so glum
here in town? And keeps me up so close, and will not let me go
a-walking, nor let me wear my host gown yesterday?
Alethea Oh, he's jealous, sister.
Mrs Pinchwife Jealous? What's that?
10 **Alethea** He's afraid you should love another man.
Mrs Pinchwife How should he be afraid of my loving another man,
when he will not let me see any but himself.
Alethea Did he not carry you yesterday to a play?
Mrs Pinchwife Ay, but we sat amongst ugly people; he would not let
15 me come near the gentry, who sat under us, so that I could not see
'em. He told me, none but naughty women sat there, whom they
toused and moused – but I would have ventured, for all that.
Alethea But how did you like the play?
Mrs Pinchwife Indeed I was aweary of the play but I liked
20 hugeously the actors; they are the goodliest, proper'st men, sister.
Alethea Oh, but you must not like the actors, sister!
Mrs Pinchwife Ay, how should I help it, sister? Pray, sister, when
my husband comes in, will you ask leave for me to go a-walking?
Alethea [*Aside*] A-walking, ha ha! Lord, a country gentlewoman's
25 leisure is the drudgery of a foot-post, and she requires as much
airing as her husband's horses.
[*Enter Pinchwife.*]
But here comes your husband; I'll ask, though I'm sure he'll not grant it.

---

450 **Cheapside**: part of the city inhabited by clothiers, middle-class.   451 **Covent Garden**: fashionable, upper-class.   2.1, 3 **Mulberry Garden and St James's Park**: resorts for the fashionable.   25 **foot-post**: a messenger.

Mrs Pinchwife He says he won't let me go abroad, for fear of
30 catching the pox.
Alethea Fie! 'The smallpox' you should say.
Mrs Pinchwife Oh my dear, dear bud, welcome home. Why dost
thou look so froppish? Who has angered thee?
Pinchwife You're a fool.
[*Mrs Pinchwife goes aside, and cries.*]
35 *Alethea* Faith, so she is, for crying for no fault, poor, tender creature!
Pinchwife What, you would have her as impudent as yourself, as
arrant a jill-flirt, a gadder, a magpie, and – to say all – a mere
notorious town-woman?
Alethea Brother, you are my only censurer; and the honour of
40 your family shall sooner suffer in your wife there, than in me,
though I take the innocent liberty of the town.
Pinchwife Hark you, mistress, do not talk so before my wife. The
innocent liberty of the town!
Alethea Why, pray, who boasts of any intrigue with me? What
45 lampoon has made my name notorious? What ill women frequent
my lodgings? I keep no company with any women of scandalous
reputations.
Pinchwife No, you keep the men of scandalous reputations company.
50 *Alethea* Where? Would you not have me civil? Answer 'em in a box
at the plays? In the drawing-room at Whitehall? In St James's Park,
Mulberry Garden, or –
Pinchwife Hold, hold; do not teach my wife where the men are to
be found. I believe she's the worse for your town documents already.
55 I bid you keep her in ignorance, as I do.
Mrs Pinchwife Indeed, be not angry with her, bud; she will tell me
nothing of the town, though I ask her a thousand times a day.
Pinchwife Then you are very inquisitive to know, I find!
Mrs Pinchwife Not I indeed, dear; I hate London. Our placehouse
60 in the country is worth a thousand of 't; would I were there again.
Pinchwife So you shall, I warrant. But were you not talking of plays,
and players, when I came in? [*To Alethea*] You are her encourager in
such discourses.
Mrs Pinchwife No indeed, dear; she chid me just now for liking the
65 player-men.
Pinchwife [*Aside*] Nay, if she be so innocent as to own to me her
liking them, there is no hurt in't. – Come, my poor rogue; but thou
lik'st none better than me?
Mrs Pinchwife Yes, indeed, but I do; the player-men are finer folks.
70 *Pinchwife* But you love none better than me?
Mrs Pinchwife You are mine own dear bud, and I know you; I hate a stranger.

---

32 **bud**: darling.   37 **jill-flirt** etc.: a wanton, a gadabout, a chatterer (magpies were taught to speak).   45 **lampoon**:
a personal satire.   59 **placehouse**: main house on an estate, implying great wealth.

Pinchwife Ay, my dear, you must love me only, and not be like the naughty town-women, who only hate their husbands, and love every man else – love plays, visits, fine coaches, fine clothes, fiddles, balls, treats, and so lead a wicked town-life.

Mrs Pinchwife Nay, if to enjoy all these things be a town-life, London is not so bad a place, dear.

Pinchwife How! If you love me, you must hate London.

Alethea [*Aside*] The fool has forbid me discovering to her the pleasures of the town, and he is now setting her agog upon them himself.

Mrs Pinchwife But, husband, do the town-women love the player-men too?

Pinchwife Yes, I warrant you.

Mrs Pinchwife Ay, I warrant you.

Pinchwife Why, you do not, I hope?

Mrs Pinchwife No, no, bud. But why have we no player-men in the country?

Pinchwife Ha! Mistress Minx, ask me no more to go to a play.

Mrs Pinchwife Nay, why, love? I did not care for going; but when you forbid me, you make me, as 'twere, desire it.

Alethea [*Aside*] So 'twill be in other things, I warrant.

Mrs Pinchwife Pray, let me go to a play, dear.

Pinchwife Hold your peace; I won't.

Mrs Pinchwife Why, love?

Pinchwife Why? I'll tell you.

Alethea [*Aside*] Nay, if he tell her, she'll give him more cause to forbid her that place.

Mrs Pinchwife Pray, why, dear?

Pinchwife First, you like the actors, and the gallants may like you.

Mrs Pinchwife What, a homely country girl? No, bud, nobody will like me.

Pinchwife I tell you, yes, they may.

Mrs Pinchwife No, no, you jest – I won't believe you; I will go.

Pinchwife I tell you then, that one of the lewdest fellows in town, who saw you there, told me he was in love with you.

Mrs Pinchwife Indeed! Who, who, pray who was't?

Pinchwife [*Aside*] I've gone too far, and slipped before I was aware. How overjoyed she is!

Mrs Pinchwife Was it any Hampshire gallant, any of our neighbours? I promise you, I am beholding to him.

Pinchwife I promise you, you lie for he would but ruin you, as he has done hundreds. He has no other love for women but that; such as he, look upon women like basilisks, but to destroy 'em.

Mrs Pinchwife Ay, but if he loves me, why should he ruin me? Answer me to that. Methinks he should not; I would do him no harm.

---

115 basilisks: mythological serpent said to kill by looking.

Alethea Ha, Ha, Ha!

120   *Pinchwife* Tis very well – but I'll keep him from doing you any harm, or me either.

[*Enter Sparkish and Harcourt*]

But here comes company; get you in, get you in.

Mrs Pinchwife But pray, husband, is he a pretty gentleman that loves me?

125   *Pinchwife* In, baggage, in. [*Thrusts her in; shuts the door. Aside*] What, all the lewd libertines of the town brought to my lodging by this easy coxcomb! 'Sdeath, I'll not suffer it.

Sparkish Here, Harcourt, do you approve my choice? [*To Alethea*] Dear little rogue, I told you I'd bring you acquainted with all my

130   friends, the wits, and – [*Harcourt salutes her.*]

Pinchwife [*Aside*] Ay, they shall know her, as well as you yourself will, I warrant you.

Sparkish This is one of those, my pretty rogue, that are to dance at your wedding tomorrow; and him you must bid welcome ever, to

135   what you and I have.

Pinchwife [*Aside*] Monstrous!

Sparkish Harcourt, how dost thou like her, faith? – say, dear, do not look down; I should hate to have a wife of mine out of countenance at anything.

140   *Pinchwife* [*Aside*] Wonderful!

Sparkish Tell me, I say, Harcourt, how dost thou like her? Thou hast stared upon her enough to resolve me.

Harcourt So infinitely well, that I could wish I had a mistress too, that might differ from her in nothing but her love and engagement

145   to you.

Alethea Sir, Master Sparkish has often told me that his acquaintance were all wits and railleurs; and now I find it.

Sparkish No, by the universe, madam, he does not rally now; you may believe him. I do assure you, he is the honestest, worthiest,

150   true-hearted gentleman of such perfect honour, he would say nothing to a lady he does not mean.

Pinchwife [*Aside*] Praising another man to his mistress!

Harcourt Sir, you are so beyond expectation obliging, that –

Sparkish Nay, egad, I am sure you do admire her extremely; I see't

155   in your eyes. – He does admire you, madam. – By the world, don't you?

Harcourt Yes, above the world, or the most glorious part of it, her whole sex; and till now I never thought I should have envied you, or any man about to marry; but you have the best excuse for

160   marriage I ever knew.

Alethea Nay, now, sir, I'm satisfied you are of the society of the wits and railleurs, since you cannot spare your friend, even when he is but

---

162 railleurs: one who insults or defames by opprobious language (Johnson).

too civil to you. But the surest sign is, since you are an enemy to marriage – for that, I hear, you hate as much as business or
165   bad wine.
Harcourt Truly, madam, I never was an enemy to marriage till now, because marriage was never an enemy to me before.
Alethea But why, sir, is marriage an enemy to you now? Because it robs you of your friend here? For you look upon a friend married, as
170   one gone into a monastery, that is, dead to the world.
Harcourt 'Tis, indeed, because you marry him. I see, madam, you can guess my meaning. I do confess heartily and openly, I wish it were in my power to break the match; by heavens I would.
Sparkish Poor Frank!
175   *Alethea* Would you be so unkind to me?
Harcourt No, no, 'tis not because I would be unkind to you.
Sparkish Poor Frank! No, gad, 'tis only his kindness to me.
Pinchwife [*Aside*] Great kindness to you, indeed. Insensible fop, let a man make love to his wife to his face!
180   *Sparkish* Come, dear Frank, for all my wife there that shall be, thou shalt enjoy me sometimes, dear rogue. By my honour, we men of wit condole for our deceased brother in marriage, as much as for one dead in earnest. I think that was prettily said of me, ha, Harcourt? But come, Frank, be not melancholy for me.
185   *Harcourt* No, I assure you I am not melancholy for you.
Sparkish Prithee, Frank, dost think my wife that shall be, there, a fine person?
Harcourt I could gaze upon her till I became as blind as you are.
Sparkish How! As I am! How?
190   *Harcourt* Because you are a lover, and true lovers are blind, stock-blind.
Sparkish True, true. But, by the world, she has wit too, as well as beauty. Go, go with her into a corner, and try if she has wit; talk to her anything – she's bashful before me.
195   *Harcourt* Indeed, if a woman wants wit in a corner, she has it nowhere.
Alethea [*Aside to Sparkish*] Sir, you dispose of me a little before your time
Sparkish Nay, nay, madam, let me have an earnest of your
200   obedience, or – Go, go, madam. [*Harcourt courts Alethea aside.*]
Pinchwife How, sir! If you are not concerned for the honour of a wife, I am for that of a sister; he shall not debauch her. Be a pander to your own wife! Bring men to her, let 'em make love before your face, thrust 'em into a corner together, then leave 'em in private! Is this
205   your town wit and conduct?
Sparkish Ha, Ha, Ha! A silly wise rogue would make one laugh more than a stark fool, ha ha! I shall burst. Nay, you shall not disturb 'em; I'll vex thee, by the world. [*Struggles with Pinchwife to keep him from Harcourt and Alethea.*]

Alethea The writings are drawn, sir, settlements made; 'tis too late,
210   sir, and past all revocation.
Harcourt Then so is my death.
Alethea I would not be unjust to him.
Harcourt Then why to me so?
Alethea I have no obligation to you.
215 *Harcourt* My love.
Alethea I had his before.
Harcourt You never had it; he wants, you see, jealousy, the only
infallible sign of it.
Alethea Love proceeds from esteem. He cannot distrust my virtue.
220   Besides, he loves me, or he would not marry me.
Harcourt Marrying you is no more sign of his love than bribing
your woman, that he may marry you, is a sign of his generosity.
Marriage is rather a sign of interest, than love; and he that marries a
fortune, covets a mistress, not loves her. But if you take marriage for
225   a sign of love, take it from me immediately.
Alethea No, now you have put a scruple in my head. But in short, sir,
to end our dispute, I must marry him; my reputation would suffer in
the world else.
Harcourt No, if you do marry him with your pardon, madam, your
230   reputation suffers in the world, and you would be thought in
necessity for a cloak.
Alethea Nay, now you are rude, sir. – Mr Sparkish, pray come
hither; your friend here is very troublesome, and very loving.
Harcourt [*Aside to Alethea*] Hold, hold –
235 *Pinchwife* D'ye hear that?
Sparkish Why, d'ye think I'll seem to be jealous, like a country
bumpkin?
Pinchwife No, rather be a cuckold, like a credulous cit.
Harcourt Madam, you would not have been so little generous as to
240   have told him?
Alethea Yes, since you could be so little generous as to wrong him.
Harcourt Wrong him! No man can do't, he's beneath an injury –
bubble, a coward, a senseless idiot, a wretch so contemptible to
all the world but you, that –
245 *Alethea* Hold, do not rail at him, for since he is like to be my husband, I am resolved to like him. Nay, I think I am obliged to tell him
you are not his friend. – Master Sparkish, Master Sparkish!
Sparkish What, what? Now, dear rogue, has not she wit?
Harcourt [*Speaks surlily*] Not so much as I thought, and hoped, she
250   had.
Alethea Mr Sparkish, do you bring people to rail at you?
Harcourt Madam –

---

223 **interest**: self-interest.   229–31: i.e. the world would think you were pregnant.   237 **bumpkin**: a country
lout.   238 **cit**: an inhabitant of a city in a low sense, a pert, low trader (Johnson).   243 **bubble**: a dupe.

Sparkish How! No, but if he does rail at me, 'tis but in jest, I warrant – what we wits do for one another, and never take any
255   notice of it.

Alethea He spoke so scurrilously of you, I had no patience to hear him. Besides, he has been making love to me.

Harcourt [*Aside*] True, damned, tell-tale woman.

Sparkish Pshaw, to show his parts; we wits rail and make love often,
260   but to show our parts. As we have no affections, so we have no malice; we –

Alethea He said you were a wretch, below an injury.

Sparkish Pshaw.

Harcourt [*Aside*] Damned, senseless, impudent, virtuous jade! Well,
265   since she won't let me have her, she'll do as good; she'll make me hate her.

Alethea A common bubble.

Sparkish Pshaw.

Alethea A coward.

270 **Sparkish** Pshaw, pshaw!

Alethea A senseless, drivelling idiot.

Sparkish How, did he disparage my parts? Nay, then my honour's concerned. I can't put up that, sir, by the world. Brother, help me to kill him. [*Aside*] I may draw now, since we have the odds of him. 'Tis
275   a good occasion too, before my mistress.

[*Offers to draw.*]

Alethea Hold, hold.

Sparkish What, what?

Alethea [*Aside*] I must not let 'em kill the gentleman, neither, for his kindness to me. I am so far from hating him, that I wish my gallant
280   had his person and understanding. Nay, if my honour –

Sparkish I'll be thy death.

Alethea Hold, hold! Indeed, to tell the truth, the gentleman said, after all, that what he spoke was but out of friendship to you.

Sparkish How! Say I am – I am a fool, that is, no wit, out of
285   friendship to me?

Alethea Yes, to try whether I was concerned enough for you, and made love to me only to be satisfied of my virtue, for your sake.

Harcourt [*Aside*] Kind, however!

Sparkish Nay, if it were so, my dear rogue, I ask thee pardon. But
290   why would not you tell me so, faith?

Harcourt Because I did not think on't, faith.

Sparkish Come; Horner does not come. Harcourt, let's be gone to the new play – Come, madam.

Alethea I will not go, if you intend to leave me alone in the box, and
295   run into the pit, as you use to do.

Sparkish Pshaw, I'll leave Harcourt with you in the box, to entertain you, and that's as good. If I sat in the box, I should be thought no

judge but of trimmings. – Come away, Harcourt; lead her down.
[*Exeunt Sparkish, Harcourt, and Alethea.*]
Pinchwife Well, go thy ways for the flower of the true town fops,
300   such as spend their estates before they come to 'em, and are
cuckolds before they're married. But let me go look to my own
freehold – How!
[*Enter Lady Fidget, Dainty Fidget and Mistress Squeamish.*]
Lady Fidget Your servant, sir. Where is your lady? We are come to
wait upon her to the new play.
305   **Pinchwife** New play!
Lady Fidget And my husband will wait upon you presently.
Pinchwife [*Aside*] Damn your civility. – Madam, by no means; I
will not see Sir Jasper here, till I have waited upon him at home. Nor
shall my wife see you, till she has waited upon your ladyship at your
310   lodgings.
Lady Fidget Now we are here, sir –
Pinchwife No, madam.
Lady Fidget Pray, let us see her.
Mistress Squeamish We will not stir, till we see her.
315   **Pinchwife** [*Aside*] A pox on you all. [*Goes to the door, and returns.*]
She has locked the door, and is gone abroad.
Lady Fidget No, you have locked the door, and she's within.
Lady Fidget They told us below, she was here.
Pinchwife [*Aside*] Will nothing do? Well, it must out then. To tell
320   you the truth, ladies, which I was afraid to let you know before,
lest it might endanger your lives, my wife has just now the smallpox
come out upon her – do not be frightened; but pray be gone, ladies.
You shall not stay here in danger of your lives. Pray, get you gone,
ladies.
325   **Lady Fidget** No, no, we have all had 'em.
Mistress Squeamish Alack, alack!
Dainty Fidget Come, come, we must see how it goes with her; I
understand the disease.
Lady Fidget Come.
330   **Pinchwife** [*Aside*] Well, there is no being too hard for women at
their own weapon, lying; therefore I'll quit the field.
[*Exit Pinchwife.*]
Mistress Squeamish Here's an example of jealousy.
Lady Fidget Indeed, as the world goes, I wonder there are no more
jealous, since wives are so neglected.
335   **Dainty Fidget** Pshaw, as the world goes, to what end should they be
jealous?
Lady Fidget Foh, 'tis a nasty world.
Mistress Squeamish That men of parts, great acquaintance, and
quality should take up with, and spend themselves and fortunes in

---

298 trimmings: fashion.   **302 freehold:** his wife.

340 keeping, little playhouse creatures – foh!
Lady Fidget Nay, that women of understanding, great acquaintance,
and good quality should fall a-keeping too of little creatures – foh!
Mistress Squeamish Why, 'tis the men of quality's fault; they never
visit women of honour, and reputation, as they used to do, and have
345 not so much as common civility for ladies of our rank, but use us
with the same indifferency, and ill-breeding, as if we were all
married to 'em.
Lady Fidget She says true; 'tis an arrant shame women of quality
should be so slighted. Methinks birth, birth should go for something;
350 I have known men admired, courted, and followed for their
titles only.
Mistress Squeamish Ay, one would think men of honour should
not love, no more than marry, out of their own rank.
Lady Fidget Fie, fie upon 'em; they are come to think
355 cross-breeding for themselves best, as well as for their dogs and horses.
Lady Fidget They are dogs and horses for't.
Mistress Squeamish One would think, if not for love, for vanity a
little.
Lady Fidget Nay, they do satisfy their vanity upon us sometimes,
360 and are kind to us in their report – tell all the world they lie
with us.
Lady Fidget Damned rascals, that we should be only wronged by
'em! To report a man has had a person, when he has not had a
person, is the greatest wrong in the whole world, that can be done
365 to a person.
Mistress Squeamish Well, 'tis an arrant shame noble persons should
be so wronged and neglected.
Lady Fidget But still 'tis an arrant shame for a noble person to
neglect her own honour, and defame her own noble person, with
370 little inconsiderable fellows foh!
Dainty Fidget I suppose the crime against our honour is the same
with a man of quality as with another.
Lady Fidget How! No sure, the man of quality is likest one's
husband, and therefore the fault should be the less.
375 *Dainty Fidget* But then the pleasure should be the less.
Lady Fidget Fie, fie, fie, for shame, sister; whither shall we ramble?
Be continent in your discourse, or I shall hate you.
Dainty Fidget Besides, an intrigue is so much the more notorious for
the man's quality.
380 *Mistress Squeamish* 'Tis true, nobody takes notice of a private man,
and therefore with him 'tis more secret; and the crime's the less,
when 'tis not known.
Lady Fidget You say true. I'faith, I think you are in the right on't.
'Tis not an injury to a husband, till it be an injury to our honours; so

---

338–40: as King Charles had recently done with Nell Gwyn.

385 that a woman of honour loses no honour with a private person; and
to say truth –
Dainty Fidget [*Apart to Mistress Squeamish*] So the 'little fellow' is
grown a 'private person' with her.
Lady Fidget But still my dear, dear honour –
[*Enter Sir Jasper Fidget, Horner, Dorilant.*]
390 **Sir Jasper** Ay, my dear, dear of honour, thou hast still so much
honour in thy mouth
Horner [*Aside*] That she has none elsewhere.
Lady Fidget Oh, what d'ye mean, to bring in these upon us?
Lady Fidget Foh, these are as bad as wits.
395 **Mistress Squeamish** Foh!
Lady Fidget Let us leave the room.
Sir Jasper Stay, stay; faith, to tell you the naked truth –
Lady Fidget Fie, Sir Jasper, do not use that word 'naked'.
Sir Jasper Well, well; in short, I have business at Whitehall, and
400 cannot go to the play with you, therefore would have you go –
Lady Fidget With those two to a play?
Sir Jasper No, not with t'other, but with Mr Horner; there can be
no more scandal to go with him, than with Mr Tattle, or Master
Limberham.
405 **Lady Fidget** With that nasty fellow! No, no.
Sir Jasper Nay, prithee dear, hear me. [*Whispers to Lady Fidget.*]
Horner Ladies –
[*Horner, Dorilant drawing near Mistress Squeamish and Dainty Fidget.*]
Dainty Fidget Stand off.
Mistress Squeamish Do not approach us.
410 **Dainty Fidget** You herd with the wits; you are obscenity all over.
Mistress Squeamish And I would as soon look upon a picture of
Adam and Eve without fig leaves, as any of you, if I could help it;
therefore keep off, and do not make us sick.
Dorilant What a devil are these?
415 **Horner** Why, these are pretenders to honour, as critics to wit, only
by censuring others; and as every raw, peevish, out-of-humoured,
affected, dull, tea-drinking, arithmetical fop sets up for a wit by
railing at men of sense, so these for honour by railing at the court,
and ladies of as great honour as quality.
420 **Sir Jasper** Come, Mr Horner, I must desire you to go with these
ladies to the play, sir.
Horner I, sir!
Sir Jasper Ay, ay, come, sir.
Horner I must beg your pardon, sir, and theirs; I will not be seen in
425 women's company in public again, for the world.
Sir Jasper Ha, ha; strange aversion!
Mistress Squeamish No, he's for women's company in private.

---

385 **private**: untitled. 403 **Tattle…Limberham**: invented names, tattle implying gossip. 417 **arithmetical**: excessively nice.

Sir Jasper He – poor man – he!! Ha, Ha, Ha!

Dainty Fidget 'Tis a greater shame amongst lewd fellows to be
430 seen in virtuous women's company, than for the women to be seen
with them.

Horner Indeed, madam, the time was I only hated virtuous women;
but now I hate the other too – I beg your pardon, ladies.

Lady Fidget You are very obliging, sir, because we would not be
435 troubled with you.

Sir Jasper In sober sadness, he shall go.

Dorilant Nay, if he won't, I am ready to wait upon the ladies;and I
think I am the fitter man.

Sir Jasper You, sir? No, I thank you for that. Master Horner is a
440 privileged man amongst the virtuous ladies; 'twill be a great while
before you are so. He, He, He! He's my wife's gallant, He, He, He!
No, pray withdraw, sir, for, as I take it, the virtuous ladies have no
business with you.

Dorilant And I am sure he can have none with them. 'Tis strange
445 a man can't come amongst virtuous women now, but upon the
same terms as men are admitted into the Great Turk's seraglio;
but heavens keep me from being an ombre player with 'em. But
where is Pinchwife?

[*Exit Dorilant.*]

Sir Jasper Come, come, man. What, avoid the sweet society of
450 womankind? That sweet, soft, gentle, tame, noble creature woman,
made for man's companion –

Horner So is that soft, gentle, tame, and more noble creature a
spaniel, and has all their tricks – can fawn, lie down, suffer beating
and fawn the more; barks at your friends, when they come to see
455 you; makes your bed hard, gives you fleas, and the mange sometimes. And all the difference is, the spaniel's the more faithful
animal, and fawns but upon one master.

Sir Jasper He, He, He!

Mistress Squeamish Oh, the rude beast!

460 *Dainty Fidget* Insolent brute!

Lady Fidget Brute! Stinking, mortified, rotten French wether, to
dare –

Sir Jasper Hold, an't please your ladyship. – For shame, Master
Horner; your mother was a woman. [*Aside*] Now shall I never
465 reconcile 'em. Hark you, madam, take my advice in your anger. You
know you often want one to make up your drolling pack of ombre
players; and you may cheat him easily, for he's an ill gamester, and
consequently loves play. Besides, you know you have but two old
civil gentlemen (with stinking breaths too) to wait upon you abroad.
470 Take in the third into your service; the other are but crazy. And a

---

446 Great Turk's seraglio: harem of the notorious Murad IV, Sultan of Turkey, 1625–40. **447 ombre:** popular
card game for three players. **461 wether:** a castrated ram, i.e. a eunuch. **466 drolling:** ridiculous.

lady should have a supernumerary gentleman-usher, as a supernumerary coachhorse, lest sometimes you should be forced to stay at
home.

Lady Fidget But are you sure he loves play, and has money?

475 **Sir Jasper** He loves play as much as you, and has money as much
as I.

Lady Fidget Then I am contented to make him pay for his scurrility;
money makes up in a measure all other wants in men. [*Aside*] Those
whom we cannot make hold for gallants, we make fine.

480 **Sir Jasper** [*Aside*] So, so; now to mollify, to wheedle him. –
Master Horner, will you never keep civil company? Methinks 'tis
time now, since you are only fit for them. Come, come, man, you
must e'en fall to visiting our wives, eating at our tables, drinking tea
with our virtuous relations after dinner, dealing cards to 'em, reading

485 plays and gazettes to 'em, picking fleas out of their shocks for 'em,
collecting receipts, new songs, women, pages, and footmen for 'em.

Horner I hope they'll afford me better employment, sir.

Sir Jasper He, He, He! 'Tis fit you know your work before you come
into your place. And since you are unprovided of a lady to flatter,

490 and a good house to eat at, pray frequent mine, and call my wife
'mistress', and she shall call you 'gallant', according to the custom.

Horner Who, I?

Sir Jasper Faith, thou shall for my sake; come for my sake only.

Horner For your sake.

495 **Sir Jasper** Come, come, here's a gamester for you. Let him be a
little familiar sometimes – nay, what if a little rude; gamesters may
be rude with ladies, you know.

Lady Fidget Yes, losing gamesters have a privilege with women.

Horner I always thought the contrary, that the winning gamester

500 had most privilege with women, for when you have lost your money
to a man, you'll lose anything you have – all you have, they say, and
he may use you as he pleases.

Sir Jasper He, He, He! Well, win or lose, you shall have your liberty
with her.

505 **Lady Fidget** As he behaves himself; and for your sake I'll give him
admittance and freedom.

Horner All sorts of freedom, madam?

Sir Jasper Ay, ay, ay, all sorts of freedom thou canst take – and
so, go to her, begin thy new employment; wheedle her, jest with her,

510 and be better acquainted one with another.

Horner [*Aside*] I think I know her already – therefore may
venture with her, my secret for hers. [*Horner and Lady Fidget whisper.*]

Sir Jasper Sister, cuz, I have provided an innocent playfellow for
you there.

481–82: those we cannot make into gallants we make pay. **485 shocks**: poodles. **486 receipts**: recipes.
486 women: waiting women. **497 rude**: violent, stiff (sexual innuendo).

515   *Dainty Fidget* Who, he?

Mistress Squeamish There's a playfellow indeed.

Sir Jasper Yes, sure; what, he is good enough to play at cards, blind man's buff, or the fool with, sometimes.

Mistress Squeamish Foh, we'll have no such playfellows.

520   *Dainty Fidget* No, sir, you shan't choose playfellows for us, we thank you.

Sir Jasper Nay, pray hear me. [*Whispering to them.*]

Lady Fidget But, poor gentleman, could you be so generous? So truly a man of honour, as for the sakes of us women of honour, to

525   cause yourself to be reported no man? No man! And to suffer your self the greatest shame that could fall upon a man, that none might fall upon us women by your conversation. But indeed, sir, as perfectly, perfectly the same man as before your going into France, sir? As perfectly, perfectly, sir?

530   *Horner* As perfectly, perfectly, madam. Nay, I scorn you should take my word; I desire to be tried only, madam.

Lady Fidget Well, that's spoken again like a man of honour; all men of honour desire to come to the test. But indeed, generally you men report such things of yourselves, one does not know

535   how, or whom, to believe; and it is come to that pass, we dare not take your words, no more than your tailors, without some staid servant of yours be bound with you. But I have so strong a faith in your honour, dear, dear, noble sir, that I'd forfeit mine for yours at any time, dear sir.

540   *Horner* No, madam, you should not need to forfeit it for me; I have given you security already to save you harmless, my late reputation being so well known in the world, madam.

Lady Fidget But if upon any future falling out, or upon a suspicion of my taking the trust out of your hands, to employ some other, you

545   yourself should betray your trust, dear sir – I mean, if you'll give me leave to speak obscenely, you might tell, dear sir.

Horner If I did, nobody would believe me; the reputation of impotency is as hardly recovered again in the world as that of cowardice, dear madam.

550   *Lady Fidget* Nay then, as one may say, you may do your worst, dear, dear sir.

Sir Jasper Come, is your ladyship reconciled to him yet? Have you agreed on matters? – for I must begone to Whitehall.

Lady Fidget Why, indeed, Sir Jasper, Master Horner is a thousand,

555   thousand times a better man than I thought him. Cousin Squeamish, sister Dainty, I can name him now; truly, not long ago, you know, I thought his very name obscenity, and I would as soon have lain with him, as have named him.

Sir Jasper Very likely, poor madam.

---

541 **harmless:** from harm.   546 **obscenely:** probably eliding impurely with unguardedly, therefore openly.

560   *Dainty Fidget* I believe it.
    Mistress Squeamish No doubt on't.
    Sir Jasper Well, well, that your ladyship is as virtuous as any she, I
    know; and him all the town knows – He, He, He! Therefore, now you
    like him, get you gone to your business together. Go, go, to your
565   business, I say – pleasure, whilst I go to my pleasure, business.
    Lady Fidget Come then, dear gallant.
    Horner Come away, my dearest mistress.
    Sir Jasper So, so; why, 'tis as I'd have it.
    [*Exit Sir Jasper Fidget.*]
    Horner And as I'd have it.
570   **Lady Fidget** Who, for his business, from his wife will run,
    Takes the best care to have her business done.

    [*Exeunt.*]

Act III, Scene i

    [*Pinchwife's lodging. Alethea and Mrs Pinchwife.*]

    Alethea Sister, what ails you? You are grown melancholy.
    Mrs Pinchwife Would it not make anyone melancholy, to see you go
    every day fluttering about abroad, whilst I must stay at home like a
    poor lonely sullen bird in a cage?
5   **Alethea** Ay, sister, but you came young, and just from the nest, to
    your cage, so that I thought you liked it, and could be as cheerful in't
    as others that took their flight themselves early, and are hopping
    abroad in the open air.
    Mrs Pinchwife Nay, I confess I was quiet enough, till my husband
10   told me what pure lives the London ladies live abroad, with their
    dancing, meetings, and junketings, and dressed every day in their
    best gowns – and, I warrant you, play at ninepins every day of the
    week, so they do.
    [*Enter Pinchwife.*]
    Pinchwife Come, what's here to do? You are putting the town
15   pleasures in her head, and setting her a-longing.
    Alethea Yes, after ninepins! You suffer none to give her those
    longings you mean, but yourself.
    Pinchwife I tell her of the vanities of the town like a confessor.
    Alethea A confessor! Just such a confessor as he that by forbidding a
20   silly ostler to grease the horse's teeth, taught him to do't.
    Pinchwife Come, Mistress Flippant, good precepts are lost when
    bad examples are still before us. The liberty you take abroad makes
    her hanker after it, and out of humour at home, poor wretch! She
    desired not to come to London; I would bring her.

3.1, 10 pure: splendid.   **20 grease the horses' teeth:** a trick to stop the horse eating the hay its owner has paid for.

25   *Alethea* Very well.

Pinchwife She has been this week in town, and never desired, till this afternoon, to go abroad.

Alethea Was she not at a play yesterday?

Pinchwife Yes, but she ne'er asked me; I was myself the cause of

30   her going.

Alethea Then if she ask you again, you are the cause of her asking, and not my example.

Pinchwife Well, tomorrow night I shall be rid of you; and the next day, before 'tis light, she and I'll be rid of the town, and my dreadful

35   apprehensions. Come, be not melancholy, for thou shalt go into the country after tomorrow, dearest.

Alethea Great comfort.

Mrs Pinchwife Pish, what d'ye tell me of the country for?

Pinchwife How's this! What, pish at the country?

40   *Mrs Pinchwife* Let me alone, I am not well.

Pinchwife Oh, if that be all – what ails my dearest?

Mrs Pinchwife Truly, I don't know – but I have not been well since you told me there was a gallant at the play in love with me.

Pinchwife Ha!

45   *Alethea* That's by my example too.

Pinchwife Nay, if you are not well, but are so concerned because a lewd fellow chanced to lie, and say he liked you, you'll make me sick too.

Mrs Pinchwife Of what sickness?

50   *Pinchwife* Oh, of that which is worse than the plague – jealousy.

Mrs Pinchwife Pish, you jeer; I'm sure there's no such disease in our receipt-book at home.

Pinchwife No, thou never met'st with it, poor innocent. [*Aside*] Well, if thou cuckold me, 'twill be my own fault for cuckolds and

55   bastards are generally makers of their own fortune.

Mrs Pinchwife Well, but pray, bud, let's go to a play tonight.

Pinchwife 'Tis just done, she comes from it. But why are you so eager to see a play?

Mrs Pinchwife Faith, dear, not that I care one pin for their talk

60   there – but I like to look upon the player-men, and would see, if I could, the gallant you say loves me – that's all, dear bud.

Pinchwife Is that all, dear bud?

Alethea This proceeds from my example.

Mrs Pinchwife But if the play be done, let's go abroad however,

65   dear bud.

Pinchwife Come, have a little patience, and thou shalt go into the country on Friday.

Mrs Pinchwife Therefore I would see first some sights, to tell my neighbours of. Nay, I *will* go abroad, that's once.

---

57 **done:** finished, since theatre performances happened in the afternoons.   69 **that's once:** that's that.

70   *Alethea* I'm the cause of this desire, too.

   Pinchwife But now I think on't, who was the cause of Horner's coming to my lodging today? That was you.

   Alethea Not you – because you would not let him see your handsome wife out of your lodging.

75   *Mrs Pinchwife* Why! Oh Lord! Did the gentleman come hither to see me indeed?

   Pinchwife No, no. You are not cause of that damned question too, Mistress Alethea? [*Aside*] Well, she's in the right of it, he is in love with my wife, and comes after her – 'tis so. But I'll nip his love in

80   the bud, lest he should follow us into the country, and break his chariot-wheel near our house, on purpose for an excuse to come to't But I think I know the town.

   Mrs Pinchwife Come, pray, bud, let's go abroad before 'tis late. For I will go, that's flat and plain.

85   *Pinchwife* [*Aside*] So! The obstinacy already of a town wife, and I must, whilst she's here, humour her like one. – Sister, how shall we do, that she may not be seen, or known?

   Alethea Let her put on her mask.

   Pinchwife Pshaw, a mask makes people but the more inquisitive

90   and is as ridiculous a disguise as a stage beard. Her shape, stature, habit will be known. And if we should meet with Horner, he would be sure to take acquaintance with us, must wish her joy, kiss her, talk to her, leer upon her, and the devil and all. No, I'll not use her to a mask, 'tis dangerous; for masks have made more cuckolds than the

95   best faces that ever were known.

   Alethea How will you do, then?

   Mrs Pinchwife Nay, shall we go? The Exchange will be shut, and I have a mind to see that.

   Pinchwife So – I have it; I'll dress her up in the suit we are to carry

100   down to her brother, little Sir James. Nay, I understand the town tricks. Come, let's go dress her. A mask! No; a woman masked, like a covered dish, gives a man curiosity and appetite, when, it may be, uncovered, 'twould turn his stomach. No, no.

   Alethea Indeed, your comparison is something a greasy one. But I

105   had a gentle gallant used to say, 'a beauty masked, like the sun in eclipse, gathers together more gazers than if it shined out'.

[*Exeunt.*]

---

93 **use**: get her used to.   104 **greasy**: unpleasant, distasteful.

Act III, Scene ii

[*The New Exchange. Clasp and other shopkeepers. Enter Horner, Harcourt, Dorilant.*]

Dorilant Engaged to women, and not sup with us?

Horner Ay, a pox on 'em all.

Harcourt You were much a more reasonable man in the morning, and had as noble resolutions against 'em as a widower of a week's
5   liberty.

Dorilant Did I ever think to see you keep company with women in vain?

Horner In vain? No; 'tis, since I can't love 'em, to be revenged on 'em.

10   **Harcourt** Now your sting is gone, you looked, in the box amongst all those women, like a drone in the hive, all upon you; shoved and ill-used by 'em all, and thrust from one side to t'other.

Dorilant Yet he must be buzzing amongst 'em still, like other old, beetle-headed, lickerish drones. Avoid 'em, and hate 'em as they
15   hate you.

Horner Because I do hate 'em, and would hate 'em yet more, I'll frequent 'em. You may see by marriage, nothing makes a man hate a woman more, than her constant conversation. In short, I converse with 'em as you do with rich fools, to laugh at 'em, and use 'em.

20   **Dorilant** But I would no more sup with women, unless I could lie with 'em, than sup with a rich coxcomb, unless I could cheat him.

Horner Yes, I have known thee sup with a fool, for his drinking; if he could set out your hand that way only, you were satisfied; and if he were a wine-swallowing mouth, 'twas enough.

25   **Harcourt** Yes, a man drinks often with a fool, as he tosses with a marker, only to keep his hand in use – but do the ladies drink?

Horner Yes, sir, and I shall have the pleasure at least of laying 'em flat with a bottle; and bring as much scandal that way upon 'em, as formerly t'other.

30   **Harcourt** Perhaps you may prove as weak a brother amongst 'em that way as t'other.

Dorilant Foh, drinking with women is as unnatural as scolding with 'em; 'tis but a pleasure of decayed fornicators, and the basest way of quenching love.

35   **Harcourt** Nay, 'tis drowning love, instead of quenching it. But leave us for civil women too!

Dorilant Ay, when he can't be the better for 'em. We hardly pardon a man that leaves his friend for a wench – and that's a pretty lawful call.

---

14 lickerish: greedy.   **18 conversation:** company, intercourse.   **25–26 tosses with a marker:** throws dice with a scorer just to keep in practice.   **36 civil:** polite, upper-class.

40   *Horner*   Faith, I would not leave you for 'em, if they would not drink.

        Dorilant   Who would disappoint his company at Lewis's, for a gossiping?

        Harcourt   Foh, wine and women: good apart, together as nauseous as
45   sack and sugar. But hark you, sir, before you go, a little of your advice; an old, maimed general, when unfit for action, is fittest for counsel. I have other designs upon women than eating and drinking with them. I am in love with Sparkish's mistress, whom he is to marry tomorrow. Now, how shall I get her?

        [*Enter Sparkish, looking about.*]
50   *Horner*   Why, here comes one will help you to her.

        Harcourt   He! He, I tell you, is my rival, and will hinder my love.

        Horner   No, a foolish rival, and a jealous husband, assist their rival's designs; for they are sure to make their women hate them, which is the first step to their love for another man.
55   *Harcourt*   But I cannot come near his mistress but in his company.

        Horner   Still the better for you, for fools are most easily cheated when they themselves are accessories; and he is to be bubbled of his mistress, as of his money, the common mistress, by keeping him company.
60   *Sparkish*   Who is that, that is to be bubbled? Faith, let me snack, I han't met with a bubble since Christmas. Gad, I think bubbles are like their brother woodcocks – go out with the cold weather.

        Harcourt   [*Apart to Horner*] A pox, he did not hear all, I hope!

        Sparkish   Come, you bubbling rogues you, where do we sup? –
65   Oh, Harcourt, my mistress tells me you have been making fierce love to her all the play long, ha ha! But I –

        Harcourt   I make love to her?

        Sparkish   Nay, I forgive thee; for I think I know thee, and I know her, but I am sure I know myself.
70   *Harcourt*   Did she tell you so? I see all women are like these of the Exchange, who, to enhance the price of their commodities, report to their fond customers offers which were never made 'em.

        Horner   Ay, women are as apt to tell before the intrigue, as men after it, and so show themselves the vainer sex. But hast thou a mistress,
75   Sparkish? 'Tis as hard for me to believe it, as that thou ever hadst a bubble, as you bragged just now.

        Sparkish   Oh, your servant, sir. Are you at your raillery, sir? But we were some of us beforehand with you today at the play; the wits were something bold with you, sir – did you not hear us laugh?
80   *Horner*   Yes, but I thought you had gone to plays to laugh at the poet's wit, not at your own.

---

42 Lewis's: a famous London eating house.   **45 sack**: sweetened Spanish wine.   **60 bubbled**: fooled. **snack**: share.   **62 woodcocks**: dupes, stupid game birds.   **72 fond**: foolish.

Sparkish Your servant, sir. No, I thank you. Gad, I go to a play as to a country treat: I carry my own wine to one, and my own wit to t'other or else I'm sure I should not be merry at either. And the reason why we are so often louder than the players, is because we think we speak more wit, and so become the poet's rivals in his audience. For to tell you the truth, we hate the silly rogues; nay, so much that we find fault even with their bawdy upon the stage, whilst we talk nothing else in the pit as loud.

Horner But why shouldst thou hate the silly poets? Thou hast too much wit to be one, and they, like whores, are only hated by each other. And thou dost scorn writing, I'm sure.

Sparkish Yes, I'd have you to know, I scorn writing. But women, women, that make men do all foolish things, make 'em write songs too. Everybody does it. 'Tis even as common with lovers as playing with fans, and you can no more help rhyming to your Phyllis, than drinking to your Phyllis.

Harcourt Nay, poetry in love is no more to be avoided than jealousy.

Dorilant But the poets damned your songs, did they?

Sparkish Damn the poets! They turned 'em into burlesque, as they call it – that burlesque is a hocus-pocus trick they have got, which by the virtue of *hictius doctius*, topsy-turvy, they make a wise and witty man in the world a fool upon the stage, you know not how. And 'tis therefore I hate 'em too, for I know not but it may be my own case – for they'll put a man into a play for looking asquint. Their predecessors were contented to make servingmen, only, their stage fools, but these rogues must have gentlemen with a pox to 'em – nay, knights. And indeed you shall hardly see a fool upon the stage but he's a knight; and to tell you the truth, they have kept me these six years from being a knight in earnest, for fear of being knighted in a play, and dubbed a fool.

Dorilant Blame 'em not; they must follow their copy, the age.

Harcourt But why shouldst thou be afraid of being in a play, who expose yourself every day in the playhouses, and as public places?

Horner 'Tis but being on the stage, instead of standing on a bench in the pit.

Dorilant Don't you give money to painters to draw you like? And are you afraid of your pictures at length in a playhouse, where all your mistresses may see you?

Sparkish A pox! Painters don't draw the smallpox, or pimples, in one's face. Come, damn all your silly authors whatever, all books and book sellers, by the world, and all readers, courteous or uncourteous.

Harcourt But who comes here, Sparkish?

[*Enter Pinchwife, and his wife in man's clothes, Alethea, Lucy her maid.*]

Sparkish Oh hide me, there's my mistress too. [*Sparkish hides himself behind Harcourt.*]

---

96 **Phyllis**: conventional name for a lover in pastoral poetry.   102 ***hictius doctius***: nonsense term used by jugglers.

125   **Harcourt** She sees you.
      Sparkish But I will not see her. 'Tis time to go to Whitehall, and I must not fail the drawing-room.
      Harcourt Pray, first carry me and reconcile me to her.
      Sparkish Another time – faith, the king will have supped.
130   **Harcourt** Not with the worse stomach for thy absence. Thou art one of those fools that think their attendance at the king's meals as necessary as his physicians', when you are more troublesome to him than his doctors or his dogs.
      Sparkish Pshaw, I know my interest, sir; prithee hide me.
135   **Horner** Your servant, Pinchwife. – What, he knows us not!
      Pinchwife [*To his wife, aside*] Come along.
      Mrs Pinchwife [*To Clasp*] Pray, have you any ballads? Give me six pennyworth.
      Clasp We have no ballads.
140   **Mrs Pinchwife** Then give me *Covent Garden Drollery*, and a play or two – oh, here's *Tarugo's Wiles*, and *The Slighted Maiden*; I'll have them.
      Pinchwife [*Apart to her*] No, plays are not for your reading. Come along; will you discover yourself?
145   **Horner** Who is that pretty youth with him, Sparkish?
      Sparkish I believe, his wife's brother, because he's something like her – but I never saw her but once.
      Horner Extremely handsome; I have seen a face like it too. Let us follow 'em.
      [*Exeunt Pinchwife, Mrs Pinchwife; Alethea, Lucy; Horner, Dorilant following them.*]
150   **Harcourt** Come, Sparkish, your mistress saw you, and will be angry you go not to her. Besides, I would fain be reconciled to her, which none but you can do, dear friend.
      Sparkish Well, that's a better reason, dear friend. I would not go near her now, for hers or my own sake: but I can deny you nothing
155   – for though I have known thee a great while, never go, if I do not love thee as well as a new acquaintance.
      Harcourt I am obliged to you indeed, dear friend; I would be well with her, only to be well with thee still, for these ties to wives usually dissolve all ties to friends. I would be contented she should enjoy you
160   a-nights, but I would have you to myself a-days, as I have had, dear friend.
      Sparkish And thou shalt enjoy me a-days, dear, dear friend, never stir; and I'll be divorced from her, sooner than from thee. Come along.
      Harcourt [*Aside*] So, we are hard put to't, when we make our rival
165   our procurer. But neither she, nor her brother, would let me come

---

127 **fail**: fail to attend.   129 **supped**: the King's dining was a public occasion.   132 **troublesome**: of more concern.   134 **interest**: worth.   140 *Covent Garden Drollery*: compilation of songs, prologues and epilogues from plays, published 1672.   141 *Tarugo's Wiles . . . Slighted Maiden*: outmoded plays.   155 **never go**: do not worry.

near her now. When all's done, a rival is the best cloak to steal a mistress under, without suspicion; and when we have once got to her as we desire, we throw him off like other cloaks.

[*Exit Sparkish, and Harcourt following him. Re-enter Pinchwife, Mrs Pinchwife in man's clothes.*]

Pinchwife [*To Alethea*] Sister, if you will not go, we must leave you.

170 [*Aside*] The fool her gallant, and she, will muster up all the young saunterers of this place, and they will leave their dear seamstresses, to follow us. What a swarm of cuckolds and cuckold-makers are here! – Come, let's begone, Mistress Margery.

Mrs Pinchwife Don't you believe that; I ha'n't half my bellyful of
175 sights yet.

Pinchwife Then walk this way.

Mrs Pinchwife Lord, what a power of brave signs are here! Stay – the Bull's Head, the Ram's Head, and the Stag's Head, dear.

Pinchwife Nay, if every husband's proper sign here were visible, they
180 would be all alike.

Mrs Pinchwife What d'ye mean by that, bud?

Pinchwife 'Tis no matter, no matter, bud.

Mrs Pinchwife Pray tell me; nay, I will know.

Pinchwife They would be all bulls', stags', and rams' heads.

[*Exeunt Pinchwife, Mrs Pinchwife. Re-enter Sparkish, Harcourt, Alethea, Lucy at the other door.*]

185 **Sparkish** Come, dear madam, for my sake you shall be reconciled to him.

Alethea For your sake I hate him.

Harcourt That's something too cruel, madam, to hate me for his sake.

190 **Sparkish** Ay indeed, madam, too, too cruel to me, to hate my friend for my sake.

Alethea I hate him because he is your enemy – and you ought to hate him too, for making love to me, if you love me.

Sparkish That's a good one! I, hate a man for loving you? If he did
195 love you, 'tis but what he can't help, and 'tis your fault, not his, if he admires you. I, hate a man for being of my opinion? I'll ne'er do't, by the world.

Alethea Is it for your honour, or mine, to suffer a man to make love to me, who am to marry you tomorrow?

200 **Sparkish** Is it for your honour, or mine, to have me jealous? That he makes love to you is a sign you are handsome; and that I am not jealous is a sign you are virtuous that, I think, is for your honour.

Alethea But 'tis your honour too I am concerned for.

Harcourt But why, dearest madam, will you be more concerned
205 for his honour than he is himself? Let his honour alone for my sake and his; he, he has no honour.

Sparkish How's that?

Harcourt But what my dear friend can guard himself.

Sparkish Oh ho, that's right again.

210 *Harcourt* Your care of his honour argues his neglect of it, which is no honour to my dear friend here. Therefore, once more, let his honour go which way it will, dear madam.

Sparkish Ay, ay; were it for my honour to marry a woman whose virtue I suspected, and could not trust her in a friend's hands?

215 *Alethea* Are you not afraid to lose me?

Harcourt He afraid to lose you, madam! No, no – you may see how the most estimable, and most glorious creature in the world is valued by him; will you not see it?

Sparkish Right, honest Frank; I have that noble value for her, that I

220 cannot be jealous of her.

Alethea You mistake him; he means you care not for me, nor who has me.

Sparkish Lord, madam, I see you are jealous. Will you wrest a poor man's meaning from his words?

225 *Alethea* You astonish me, sir, with your want of jealousy.

Sparkish And you make me giddy, madam, with your jealousy, and fears, and virtue, and honour. Gad, I see virtue makes a woman as troublesome as a little reading or learning.

Alethea Monstrous!

230 *Lucy* [*Behind*] Well, to see what easy husbands these women of quality can meet with! A poor chambermaid can never have such ladylike luck. Besides, he's thrown away upon her – she'll make no use of her fortune, her blessing. None to a gentleman for a pure cuckold, for it requires good breeding to be a cuckold.

235 *Alethea* I tell you then plainly, he pursues me to marry me.

Sparkish Pshaw!

Harcourt Come, madam, you see you strive in vain to make him jealous of me. My dear friend is the kindest creature in the world to me.

240 *Sparkish* Poor Fellow.

Harcourt But his kindness only is not enough for me, without your favour. Your good opinion, dear madam 'tis that must perfect my happiness. Good gentleman, he believes all I say; would you would do so. Jealous of me! I would not wrong him nor you or the world.

245 *Sparkish* Look you there. [*Alethea walks carelessly to and fro.*] Hear him, hear him, and do not walk away so.

Harcourt I love you, madam, so –

Sparkish How's that? Nay, now you begin to go too far indeed.

Harcourt So much, I confess, I say I love you, that I would not have

250 you miserable, and cast yourself away upon so unworthy and inconsiderable a thing as what you see here.

[*Clapping his hand on his breast, points at Sparkish.*]

Sparkish No, faith, I believe thou wouldst not. Now his meaning is

---

223 jealous: vehement. **wrest:** divorce.

plain. But I knew before, thou wouldst not wrong me nor her.

Harcourt No, no, heavens forbid the glory of her sex should fall so
255 low as into the embraces of such a contemptible wretch, the least of
mankind! My dear friend here – I injure him?
[*Embracing Sparkish.*]

Alethea Very well.

Sparkish No, no, dear friend. – I knew it, madam; you see he will
rather wrong himself than me, in giving himself such names.

260 *Alethea* Do not you understand him yet?

Sparkish Yes, how modestly he speaks of himself, poor fellow.

Alethea Methinks he speaks impudently of yourself, since – before
yourself too, insomuch that I can no longer suffer his scurrilous
abusiveness to you, no more than his love to me. [*Offers to go.*]

265 *Sparkish* Nay, nay, madam, pray stay. His love to you? Lord, madam,
has he not spoke yet plain enough?

Alethea Yes indeed, I should think so.

Sparkish Well then, by the world, a man can't speak civilly to a
woman now, but presently she says he makes love to her. Nay, madam,
270 you shall stay, with your pardon, since you have not yet understood
him, till he has made an *eclaircissement* of his love to you that is,
what kind of love it is. [*To Harcourt*] Answer to thy catechism: friend,
do you love my mistress here?

Harcourt Yes, I wish she would not doubt it.

275 *Sparkish* But how do you love her?

Harcourt With all my soul.

Alethea I thank him; methinks he speaks plain enough now.

Sparkish [*To Alethea*] You are out still. But with what kind of love,
Harcourt?

280 *Harcourt* With the best and truest love in the world.

Sparkish Look you there, then that is, with no matrimonial love, I'm
sure.

Alethea How's that? Do you say matrimonial love is not best?

Sparkish [*Aside*] Gad, I went too far ere I was aware. – But speak
285 for thyself, Harcourt; you said you would not wrong me, nor her.

Harcourt No, no, madam, e'en take him for heaven's sake –

Sparkish Look you there, madam.

Harcourt Who should in all justice be yours; he that loves you most.
[*Claps his hand on his breast.*]

Alethea Look you there, Mr Sparkish; who's that?

290 *Sparkish* Who should it be? Go on, Harcourt.

Harcourt Who loves you more than women titles, or fortune fools.
[*Points at Sparkish.*]

Sparkish Look you there he means me still, for he points at me.

Alethea Ridiculous!

Harcourt Who can only match your faith and constancy in love.

295 *Sparkish* Ay.

Harcourt Who knows, if it be possible, how to value so much beauty and virtue.

Sparkish Ay.

Harcourt Whose love can no more be equalled in the world, than
300   that heavenly form of yours.

Sparkish No.

Harcourt Who could no more suffer a rival than your absence, and yet could no more suspect your virtue than his own constancy in his love to you.

305   *Sparkish* No.

Harcourt Who, in fine, loves you better than his eyes, that first made him love you.

Sparkish Ay. Nay, madam, faith you shan't go, till –

Sparkish But till he has saluted you, that I may be assured you are
310   friends, after his honest advice and declaration. Come, pray, madam, be friends with him.

[*Enter Pinchwife, Mrs Pinchwife.*]

Alethea You must pardon me, sir, that I am not yet so obedient to you.

Pinchwife What, invite your wife to kiss men? Monstrous! Are you
315   not ashamed? I will never forgive you.

Sparkish Are you not ashamed, that I should have more confidence in the chastity of your family than you have? You must not teach me. I am a man of honour, sir, though I am frank and free; I am frank, sir.

Pinchwife Very frank, sir, to share your wife with your friends.

320   *Sparkish* He is an humble, menial friend, such as reconciles the differences of the marriage bed. You know man and wife do not always agree; I design him for that use, therefore would have him well with my wife.

Pinchwife A menial friend! You will get a great many menial friends,
325   by showing your wife as you do.

Sparkish What then? It may be I have a pleasure in't, as I have to show fine clothes at a playhouse the first day, and count money before poor rogues.

Pinchwife He that shows his wife, or money, will be in danger of
330   having them borrowed sometimes.

Sparkish I love to be envied, and would not marry a wife that I alone could love. Loving alone is as dull as eating alone. Is it not a frank age? And I am a frank person. And to tell you the truth, it may be I love to have rivals in a wife; they make her seem to a man still
335   but as a kept mistress. And so, good night, for I must to Whitehall. Madam, I hope you are now reconciled to my friend. And so I wish you a good night, madam, and sleep if you can, for tomorrow, you know, I must visit you early with a canonical gentleman. –

---

318 frank: generous.   338 canonical gentleman: parson.

Goodnight, dear Harcourt.
[*Exit Sparkish.*]
340 *Harcourt* Madam, I hope you will not refuse my visit tomorrow, if
it should be earlier, with a canonical gentleman, than Mr Sparkish's?
Pinchwife [*Coming between Alethea and Harcourt.*] This gentle woman
is yet under my care; therefore you must yet forbear your freedom
with her, sir.
345 *Harcourt* Must, sir?
Pinchwife Yes, sir, she is my sister.
Harcourt 'Tis well she is, sir – for I must be her servant, sir.
Madam –
Pinchwife Come away, sister. We had been gone if it had not been
350 for you, and so avoided these lewd rakehells who seem to haunt us.
[*Enter Horner, Dorilant to them.*]
Horner How now, Pinchwife?
Pinchwife Your servant.
Horner What, I see a little time in the country makes a man turn
wild and unsociable, and only fit to converse with his horses, dogs,
355 and his herds.
Pinchwife I have business, sir, and must mind it. Your business is
pleasure; therefore you and I must go different ways.
Horner Well, you may go on, but this pretty young gentleman –
[*Takes hold of Mrs Pinchwife.*]
Harcourt The lady –
360 *Dorilant* And the maid –
Horner Shall stay with us, for I suppose their business is the same
with ours: pleasure.
Pinchwife [*Aside*] 'Sdeath, he knows her, she carries it so sillily; yet
if he does not, I should be more silly to discover it first.
365 *Alethea* [*To Harcourt*] Pray, let us go, sir
Pinchwife Come, come –
Horner [*To Mrs Pinchwife*] Had you not rather stay with us? –
Prithee, Pinchwife, who is this pretty young gentleman?
Pinchwife One to whom I'm a guardian. [*Aside*] I wish I could keep
370 her out of your hands.
Horner Who is he? I never saw anything so pretty in all my life.
Pinchwife Pshaw, do not look upon him so much. He's a poor bash-
ful youth; you'll put him out of countenance. Come away, brother.
[*Offers to take her away.*]
Horner Oh, your brother?
375 *Pinchwife* Yes, my wife's brother. – Come, come, she'll stay supper
for us.
Horner I thought so, for he is very like her I saw you at the play
with, whom I told you I was in love with.
Mrs Pinchwife [*Aside*] Oh Jeminy! Is this he that was in love with

---

350 **rakehells**: rakes. 356 **mind**: attend to. 364 **discover**: reveal. 379 **Jeminy**: Gemini (common expression).

380   me? I am glad on't, I vow, for he's a curious fine gentleman, and I love him already too. [*To Pinchwife*] Is this he, bud?

Pinchwife [*To his wife*] Come away, come away.

Horner Why, what haste are you in! Why won't you let me talk with him?

385 **Pinchwife** Because you'll debauch him; he's yet young and innocent, and I would not have him debauched for anything in the world. [*Aside*] How she gazes on him! The devil!

Horner Harcourt, Dorilant, look you here; this is the likeness of that dowdy he told us of, his wife. Did you ever see a lovelier

390 creature? The rogue has reason to be jealous of his wife, since she is like him, for she would make all that see her, in love with her.

Harcourt And as I remember now, she is as like him here as can be.

Dorilant She is indeed very pretty, if she be like him.

Horner 'Very pretty'? A very pretty commendation! She is a

395 glorious creature, beautiful beyond all things I ever beheld.

Pinchwife So, so.

Harcourt More beautiful than a poet's first mistress of imagination.

Horner Or another man's last mistress of flesh and blood.

Mrs Pinchwife Nay, now you jeer, sir. Pray don't jeer me.

400 **Pinchwife** Come, come. [*Aside*] By heavens, she'll discover herself.

Horner I speak of your sister, sir.

Pinchwife Ay, but saying she was handsome, if like him, made him blush. [*Aside*] I am upon a rack!

Horner Methinks he is so handsome, he should not be a man.

405 **Pinchwife** [*Aside*] Oh, there 'tis out; he has discovered her. I am not able to suffer any longer. [*To his wife*] Come, come away, I say.

Horner Nay, by your leave, sir, he shall not go yet. [*Apart to them*] Harcourt, Dorilant, let us torment this jealous rogue a little.

Harcourt, Dorilant How?

410 **Horner** I'll show you.

Pinchwife Come, pray let him go. I cannot stay fooling any longer – I tell you his sister stays supper for us.

Horner Does she? Come then, we'll all go sup with her and thee.

Pinchwife No, now I think on't – having stayed so long for us, I

415 warrant she's gone to bed. [*Aside*] I wish she and I were well out of their hands – Come, I must rise early tomorrow; come.

Horner Well then, if she be gone to bed, I wish her and you a good night. But pray, young gentleman, present my humble service to her.

Mrs Pinchwife Thank you heartily, sir.

420 **Pinchwife** [*Aside*] 'Sdeath, she will discover herself yet, in spite of me. – He is something more civil to you, for your kindness to his sister, than I am, it seems.

Horner Tell her, dear, sweet little gentleman, for all your brother

---

380 curious: remarkably.

there, that you have revived the love I had for her at first sight in
the playhouse.
Mrs Pinchwife But did you love her indeed, and indeed?
Pinchwife [*Aside*] So, so. Away, I say.
Horner Nay, stay. Yes, indeed, and indeed; pray do you tell her
so and give her this kiss from me. *Kisses her*
Pinchwife [*Aside*] Oh heavens! What do I suffer! Now 'tis too plain
he knows her, and yet –
Horner And this, and this. [*Kisses her again.*]
Mrs Pinchwife What do you kiss me for? I am no woman.
Pinchwife [*Aside*] So, there 'tis out. – Come, I cannot, nor will
stay any longer.
Horner Nay, they shall send your lady a kiss too. Here, Harcourt
Dorilant, will you not? [*They kiss her.*]
Pinchwife [*Aside*] How! Do I suffer this? Was I not accusing another
just now for this rascally patience, in permitting his wife to be
kissed before his face? Ten thousand ulcers gnaw away their lips!
Come, come.
Horner Good night, dear little gentleman. Madam, good night;
farewell, Pinchwife. [*Apart to Harcourt and Dorilant.*] Did not I tell
you I would raise his jealous gall?
[*Exeunt Horner, Harcourt, and Dorilant.*]
Pinchwife So, they are gone at last; stay, let me see first if the coach
be at this door.
[*Exit Pinchwife. Horner, Harcourt, Dorilant return.*]
Horner What, not gone yet? Will you be sure to do as I desired
you, sweet sir?
Mrs Pinchwife 'Sweet sir' – but what will you give me then?
Horner Anything; come away into the next walk.
[*Exit Horner, hauling away Mrs Pinchwife.*]
Alethea Hold, hold – what d'ye do?
Lucy Stay, stay, hold,
Harcourt Hold, madam, hold; let him present him. He'll come
presently. Nay, I will never let you go, till you answer my question.
[*Alethea, Lucy, struggling with Harcourt and Dorilant.*]
Lucy For God's sake, sir, I must follow 'em.
Dorilant No, I have something to present you with too; you shan't
follow them.
[*Pinchwife returns.*]
Pinchwife Where – ? How – ? What's become of – ? Gone!
Whither?
Lucy He's only gone with the gentleman, who will give him
something, an't please your worship.
Pinchwife Something! Give him something, with a pox! Where
are they?
Alethea In the next walk only, brother.
Pinchwife Only, only! Where, where?
[*Exit Pinchwife, and returns presently, then goes out again.*]

Harcourt What's the matter with him? Why so much concerned? But, dearest madam –

Alethea Pray let me go, sir; I have said and suffered enough already.

Harcourt Then you will not look upon, nor pity, my sufferings?

470 *Alethea* To look upon 'em, when I cannot help 'em, were cruelty, not pity, therefore I will never see you more.

Harcourt Let me then, madam, have my privilege of a banished lover: complaining or railing, and giving you but a farewell reason why, if you cannot condescend to marry me, you should not take

475 that wretch my rival.

Alethea He only, not you, since my honour is engaged so far to him, can give me a reason why I should not marry him. But if he be true, and what I think him to me, I must be so to him. Your servant, sir.

Harcourt Have women only constancy when 'tis a vice, and, like

480 fortune, only true to fools?

Dorilant [*To Lucy, who struggles to get from him*] Thou shalt not stir, thou robust creature. You see I can deal with you; therefore you should stay the rather, and be kind.

[*Enter Pinchwife.*]

Pinchwife Gone, gone, not to be found – quite gone! Ten thousand

485 plagues go with 'em. Which way went they?

Alethea But into t'other walk, brother.

Lucy Their business will be done presently, sure, an't please your worship. It can't be long in doing, I'm sure on't.

Alethea Are they not there?

490 *Pinchwife* No – you know where they are, you infamous wretch, eternal shame of your family, which you do not dishonour enough yourself, you think, but you must help her to do it too, thou legion of bawds.

Alethea Good brother!

495 *Pinchwife* Damned, damned sister!

Alethea Look you here, she's coming.

[*Enter Mrs Pinchwife in man's clothes, running, with her hat under her arm full of oranges and dried fruit, Horner following.*]

Mrs Pinchwife Oh dear bud, look you here what I have got – see.

Pinchwife [*Aside, rubbing his forehead*] And what I have got here, too, which you can't see.

500 *Mrs Pinchwife* The fine gentleman has given me better things yet.

Pinchwife Has he so? [*Aside*] Out of breath, and coloured! I must hold yet.

Horner I have only given your little brother an orange, sir.

Pinchwife [*To Horner*] Thank you, sir. [*Aside*] You have only

505 squeezed my orange, I suppose, and given it me again. Yet I must have a city patience. [*To his wife*] Come, come away

---

505 **squeezed my orange**: debauched my wife.   506 **city patience**: patience of city merchants who were reputed to be constantly cuckolded by young gallants.

Mrs Pinchwife Stay till I have put up my fine things, bud.
[*Enter Sir Jasper Fidget.*]
Sir Jasper Oh, Master Horner, come, come, the ladies stay for
you; your mistress – my wife – wonders you make not more haste
510 to her.
Horner I have stayed this half-hour for you here, and 'tis your fault
I am not now with your wife.
Sir Jasper But pray, don't let her know so much; the truth on't is, I
was advancing a certain project to his Majesty, about I'll tell you.
515 **Horner** No, let's go and hear it at your house. Good night, sweet
little gentleman. One kiss more. You'll remember me now, I hope.
[*Kisses her.*]
Dorilant What, Sir Jasper, will you separate friends? He promised to
sup with us and if you take him to your house, you'll be in danger of
our company too.
520 **Sir Jasper** Alas, gentlemen, my house is not fit for you; there are
none but civil women there, which are not for your turn. He, you
know, can bear with the society of civil women, now, Ha, Ha, Ha!
Besides, he's one of my family – he's – He, He, He!
Dorilant What is he?
525 **Sir Jasper** Faith, my eunuch, since you'll have it, He, He, He!
[*Exeunt Sir Jasper Fidget and Horner.*]
Dorilant I rather wish thou wert his, or my, cuckold. Harcourt, what
a good cuckold is lost there, for want of a man to make him one.
Thee and I cannot have Horner's privilege, who can make use of it.
Harcourt Ay, to poor Horner 'tis like coming to an estate at
530 threescore, when a man can't be the better for 't.
Pinchwife Come.
Mrs Pinchwife Presently, bud.
Dorilant Come, let us go too. [*To Alethea*] Madam, your servant.
[*To Lucy*] Good night, strapper –
535 **Harcourt** Madam, though you will not let me have a good day,
or night, I wish you one – but dare not name the other half
of my wish.
Alethea Good night, sir, for ever.
Mrs Pinchwife I don't know where to put this; here, dear bud, you
540 shall eat it. Nay, you shall have part of the fine gentleman's good
things, or treat as you call it, when we come home.
Pinchwife Indeed I deserve it, since I furnished the best part of it.
[*Strikes away the orange.*]
    The gallant treats, presents, and gives the ball
    But 'tis the absent cuckold pays for all.

Act IV, Scene i

[*In Pinchwife's house in the morning. Lucy, and Alethea
dressed in new clothes.*]

Lucy Well, madam, now have I dressed you, and set you out with so
many ornaments, and spent upon you ounces of essence and pulvilio;
and all this for no other purpose but as people adorn and perfume a
corpse for a stinking second-hand grave, such or as bad I think

5 Master Sparkish's bed.
Alethea Hold your peace.
Lucy Nay, madam, I will ask you the reason why you would banish
poor Master Harcourt for ever from your sight? How could you be
so hard-hearted?

10 **Alethea** 'Twas because I was not hard-hearted.
Lucy No, no; 'twas stark love and kindness, I warrant.
Alethea It was so. I would see him no more, because I love him.
Lucy Hey-day, a very pretty reason!
Alethea You do not understand me.

15 **Lucy** I wish you may yourself.
Alethea I was engaged to marry, you see, another man, whom my
justice will not suffer me to deceive or injure.
Lucy Can there be a greater cheat or wrong done to a man than
to give him your person without your heart? I should make a

20 conscience of it.
Alethea I'll retrieve it for him after I am married a while.
Lucy The woman that marries to love better will be as much
mistaken as the wencher that marries to live better. No, madam,
marrying to increase love is like gaming to become rich; alas, you

25 only lose what little stock you had before.
Alethea I find by your rhetoric you have been bribed to betray me.
Lucy Only by his merit, that has bribed your heart, you see, against
your word and rigid honour. But what a devil is this honour? 'Tis
sure a disease in the head, like the megrim, or falling sickness, that

30 always hurries people away to do themselves mischief. Men lose their
lives by it; women what's dearer to 'em, their love, the life of life.
Alethea Come, pray talk you no more of honour, nor Master
Harcourt. I wish the other would come, to secure my fidelity to him,
and his right in me.

35 **Lucy** You will marry him, then?
Alethea Certainly. I have given him already my word, and will my
hand too, to make it good when he comes.
Lucy Well, I wish I may never stick pin more, if he be not an arrant
natural to t'other fine gentleman.

---

2 **pulvilio:** scented powder. 29 **megrim:** migraine. 29 **falling sickness:** epilepsy. 39 **arrant natural to:**
complete simpleton compared to.

40   *Alethea* I own he wants the wit of Harcourt, which I will dispense
withal for another want he has, which is want of jealousy, which
men of wit seldom want.

    Lucy Lord, madam, what should you do with a fool to your
husband? You intend to be honest, don't you? Then that husbandly
45   virtue, credulity, is thrown away upon you.

    Alethea He only that could suspect my virtue should have cause
to do it; 'tis Sparkish's confidence in my truth that obliges me to be
so faithful to him.

    Lucy You are not sure his opinion may last.

50   *Alethea* I am satisfied 'tis impossible for him to be jealous, after the
proofs I have had of him. Jealousy in a husband – heaven defend
me from it; it begets a thousand plagues to a poor woman:
the loss of her honour, her quiet, and her –

    Lucy And her pleasure.

55   *Alethea* What d'ye mean, impertinent?

    Lucy Liberty is a great pleasure, madam.

    Alethea I say loss of her honour, her quiet, nay, her life sometimes;
and what's as bad almost, the loss of this town – that is, she is sent
into the country, which is the last ill usage of a husband to a wife,
60   I think.

    Lucy [*Aside*] Oh, does the wind lie there? – Then of necessity,
madam, you think a man must carry his wife into the country, if
he be wise. The country is as terrible, I find, to our young English
ladies, as a monastery to those abroad. And on my virginity, I think
65   they would rather marry a London jailer than a high sheriff of a
county, since neither can stir from his employment. Formerly, women
of wit married fools for a great estate, a fine seat, or the like; but now
'tis for a pretty seat only in Lincoln's Inn Fields, St James's Fields, or
the Pall Mall.

    [*Enter to them Sparkish, and Harcourt dressed like a Parson.*]

70   *Sparkish* Madam, your humble servant; a happy day to you, and to
us all.

    Harcourt Amen.

    Alethea Who have we here?

    Sparkish My chaplain, faith. Oh madam, poor Harcourt remembers
75   his humble service to you, and in obedience to your last commands,
refrains coming into your sight.

    Alethea Is not that he?

    Sparkish No, fie, no; but to show that he ne'er intended to hinder
our match, has sent his brother here to join our hands. When I get
80   me a wife, I must get her a chaplain, according to the custom. This is
his brother, and my chaplain.

    Alethea His brother?

    Lucy [*Aside*] And your chaplain, to preach in your pulpit, then.

---

83 pulpit: to cuckold you.

Alethea His brother!

85 **Sparkish** Nay, I knew you would not believe it. – I told you, sir,
she would take you for your brother Frank.

Alethea Believe it!

Lucy [*Aside*] His brother! Ha, Ha, He! He has a trick left still,
it seems.

90 **Sparkish** Come, my dearest, pray let us go to church before the
canonical hour is past.

Alethea For shame, you are abused still.

Sparkish By the world, 'tis strange now, you are so incredulous.

Alethea 'Tis strange you are so credulous .

95 **Sparkish** Dearest of my life, hear me. I tell you this is Ned Harcourt
of Cambridge, by the world; you see he has a sneaking college look.
'tis true he's something like his brother Frank, and they differ from
each other no more than in their age, for they were twins.

Lucy Ha, ha, he!

100 **Alethea** Your servant, sir; I cannot be so deceived, though you are.
But come, let's hear – how do you know what you affirm so
confidently?

Sparkish Why, I'll tell you all. Frank Harcourt coming to me this
morning, to wish me joy and present his service to you, I asked him
105 if he could help me to a parson; whereupon he told me he had a
brother in town who was in orders, and he went straight away
and sent him you see there to me.

Alethea Yes, Frank goes and puts on a black coat, then tells you
he is Ned – that's all you have for't.

110 **Sparkish** Pshaw, Pshaw, I tell you by the same token, the midwife
put her garter about Frank's neck, to know 'em asunder, they were
so like.

Alethea Frank tells you this too?

Sparkish Ay, and Ned there too, they are both in a story.

115 **Alethea** So, so; very foolish.

Sparkish Lord, if you won't believe one, you had best try him by
your chambermaid there; for chambermaids must needs know
chaplains from other men, they are so used to 'em.

Lucy Let's see. Nay, I'll be sworn he has the canonical smirk, and
120 the filthy, clammy palm of a chaplain.

Alethea Well, most reverend doctor, pray let us make an end of
this fooling.

Harcourt With all my soul, divine, heavenly creature, when you
please.

125 **Alethea** He speaks like a chaplain indeed!

Sparkish Why, was there not 'soul', 'divine', 'heavenly', in what he
said?

Alethea Once more, most impertinent blackcoat, cease your pers-

---

91 canonical hour: before noon.

ecution, and let us have a conclusion of this ridiculous love.

130 **Harcourt** [*Aside*] I had forgot; I must suit my style to my coat, or I wear it in vain.

Alethea I have no more patience left; let us make once an end of this troublesome love, I say.

Harcourt So be it, seraphic lady, when your honour shall think it
135 meet and convenient so to do.

Sparkish Gad, I'm sure none but a chaplain could speak so, I think.

Alethea Let me tell you, sir, this dull trick will not serve your turn; though you delay our marriage, you shall not hinder it.

Harcourt Far be it from me, munificent patroness, to delay your
140 marriage. I desire nothing more than to marry you presently, which I might do, if you yourself would; for my noble, good-natured, and thrice generous patron here would not hinder it.

Sparkish No, poor man, not I, faith.

Harcourt And now, madam, let me tell you plainly, nobody else
145 shall marry you, by heavens; I'll die first, for I'm sure I should die after it.

Lucy [*Aside*] How his love has made him forget his function! – As I have seen it in real parsons.

Alethea That was spoken like a chaplain too! Now you understand
150 him, I hope.

Sparkish Poor man, he takes it heinously to be refused. I can't blame him, 'tis putting an indignity upon him not to be suffered. But you'll pardon me, madam, it shan't be; he shall marry us. Come away, pray madam; 'tis late.

155 **Lucy** [*Aside*] Ha, ha, he, more ado!

Alethea Invincible stupidity! I tell you he would marry me as your rival, not as your chaplain.

Sparkish Come, come, madam. [*Pulling her away.*]

Lucy Ay, pray madam, do not refuse this reverend divine the
160 honour and satisfaction of marrying you – for I dare say he has set his heart upon't, good doctor.

Alethea [*To Harcourt*] What can you hope, or design, by this?

Harcourt [*Aside*] I could answer her, a reprieve for a day only, often revokes a hasty doom. At worst, if she will not take mercy on me,
165 and let me marry her, I have at least the lover's second pleasure, hindering my rival's enjoyment, though but for a time.

Sparkish Come madam, 'tis e'en twelve o'clock, and my mother charged me never to be married out of the canonical hours. Come, come. Lord, here's such a deal of modesty, I warrant, the first day.

170 **Lucy** Yes, an't please your worship, married women show all their modesty the first day, because married men show all their love the first day.

[*Exeunt.*]

Act IV, Scene ii

[*In Pinchwife's house: a bedchamber. Pinchwife and Mrs Pinchwife.*]

Pinchwife Come, tell me, I say.

Mrs Pinchwife Lord, ha'n't I told it an hundred times over?

Pinchwife [*Aside*] I would try if, in the repetition of the ungrateful
tale, I could find her altering it in the least circumstance; for if her
5 story be false, she is so too. – Come, how was't, baggage?

Mrs Pinchwife Lord, what pleasure you take to hear it, sure!

Pinchwife No, you take more in telling it, I find – but speak: how
was't?

Mrs Pinchwife He carried me up into the house next to the
10 Exchange.

Pinchwife So – and you two were only in the room?

Mrs Pinchwife Yes, for he sent away a youth that was there, for
some dried fruit, and China oranges.

Pinchwife Did he so? Damn him for it, and for –

15 **Mrs Pinchwife** But presently came up the gentlewoman of the
house.

Pinchwife Oh, 'twas well she did – but what did he do whilst the
fruit came?

Mrs Pinchwife He kissed me an hundred times, and told me he
20 fancied he kissed my fine sister, meaning me, you know, whom he
said he loved with all his soul, and bid me be sure to tell her so, and
to desire her to be at her window by eleven of the clock this morning, and he would walk under it at that time.

Pinchwife [*Aside*] And he was as good as his word, very punctual –
25 a pox reward him for't.

Mrs Pinchwife Well, and he said, if you were not within he would
come up to her, meaning me you know, bud, still.

Pinchwife [*Aside*] So he knew her certainly; but for this confesssion
I am obliged to her simplicity. – But what, you stood very still
30 when he kissed you?

Mrs Pinchwife Yes, I warrant you; would you have had me
discovered myself?

Pinchwife But you told me he did some beastliness to you, as you
called it. What was't?

35 **Mrs Pinchwife** Why, he put –

Pinchwife What?

Mrs Pinchwife Why, he put the tip of his tongue between my lips,
and so muzzled me – and I said I'd bite it.

Pinchwife An eternal canker seize it, for a dog.

40 **Mrs Pinchwife** Nay, you need not be so angry with him neither, for
to say truth, he has the sweetest breath I ever knew.

---

3 **ungrateful**: unpleasant. 5 **baggage**: worthless woman, so called because such women follow camps
(Johnson). 13 **China oranges**: sweet oranges, a delicacy. 39 **for a dog**: for behaving like a dog.

Pinchwife The devil! You were satisfied with it, then, and would do it again?

Mrs Pinchwife Not unless he should force me.

45 *Pinchwife* Force you, changeling! I tell you no woman can be forced.

Mrs Pinchwife Yes, but she may, sure, by such a one as he, for he's a proper, goodly, strong man; 'tis hard, let me tell you, to resist him.

Pinchwife [*Aside*] So, 'tis plain she loves him, yet she has not love enough to make her conceal it from me. But the sight of him will

50 increase her aversion for me, and love for him, and that love instruct her how to deceive me, and satisfy him, all idiot as she is. Love, 'twas he gave women first their craft, their art of deluding. Out of nature's hands they came plain, open, silly, and fit for slaves, as she and heaven intended 'em; but damned Love – Well, I must

55 strangle that little monster, whilst I can deal with him. – Go fetch pen, ink, and paper out of the next room.

Mrs Pinchwife Yes bud.

[*Exit Mrs Pinchwife.*]

Pinchwife Why should women have more invention in love than men? It can only be because they have more desires, more

60 soliciting passions, more lust, and more of the devil.

[*Mrs Pinchwife returns.*]

Come, minx, sit down and write.

Mrs Pinchwife Ay, dear bud, but I can't do't very well.

Pinchwife I wish you could not at all.

Mrs Pinchwife But what should I write for?

65 *Pinchwife* I'll have you write a letter to your lover.

Mrs Pinchwife Oh Lord, to the fine gentleman a letter!

Pinchwife Yes, to the fine gentleman.

Mrs Pinchwife Lord, you do but jeer; sure you jest.

Pinchwife I am not so merry; come, write as I bid you.

70 *Mrs Pinchwife* What, do you think I am a fool?

Pinchwife [*Aside*] She's afraid I would not dictate any love to him, therefore she's unwilling. – But you had best begin.

Mrs Pinchwife Indeed, and indeed, but I won't, so I won't.

Pinchwife Why?

75 *Mrs Pinchwife* Because he's in town; you may send for him if you will.

Pinchwife Very well; you would have him brought to you. Is it come to this? I say take the pen and write, or you'll provoke me.

Mrs Pinchwife Lord, what d'ye make a fool of me for? Don't I

80 know that letters are never writ but from the country to London, and from London into the country? Now, he's in town, and I am in town too; therefore I can't write to him, you know.

Pinchwife [*Aside*] So, I am glad it is no worse; she is innocent enough yet. – Yes, you may, when your husband bids you, write letters to

85 people that are in town.

Mrs Pinchwife Oh, may I so? Then I'm satisfied.

Pinchwife Come begin. [*Dictates.*] 'Sir –
Mrs Pinchwife Shan't I say 'Dear Sir'? You know one says always
something more than bare 'Sir'.
90 *Pinchwife* Write as I bid you, or I will write 'whore' with this
penknife in your face.
Mrs Pinchwife Nay, good bud. [*She writes.*] 'Sir'
Pinchwife 'Though I suffered last night your nauseous, loathed
kisses and embraces' – write.
95 *Mrs Pinchwife* Nay, why should I say so? You know I told you he
had a sweet breath.
Pinchwife Write.
Mrs Pinchwife Let me but put out 'loathed'.
Pinchwife Write, I say.
100 *Mrs Pinchwife* Well then. [*Writes*]
Pinchwife Let's see; what have you writ? [*Takes the paper, and reads.*]
'Though I suffered last night your kisses and embraces' – thou
impudent creature, where is 'nauseous' and 'loathed'?
Mrs Pinchwife I can't abide to write such filthy words.
105 *Pinchwife* Once more, write as I'd have you, and question it not, or
I will spoil thy writing with this [*Holds up the penknife.*] I will
stab out those eyes that cause my mischief.
Mrs Pinchwife Lord, I will. [*Writes*]
Pinchwife So . . . So . . . Let's see now. [*Reads*] 'Though I suffered
110 last night your nauseous, loathed kisses and embraces'; go on – 'yet
I would not have you presume that you shall ever repeat them.'
So . . . . [*She writes.*]
Mrs Pinchwife I have writ it.
Pinchwife On, then. 'I then concealed myself from your knowledge,
115 to avoid your insolencies.' [*She writes.*]
Mrs Pinchwife So . . .
Pinchwife 'The same reason, now I am out of your hands –
Mrs Pinchwife So . . .
Pinchwife 'Makes me own to you my unfortunate, though innocent
120 frolic, of being in man's clothes' – [*She writes.*]
Mrs Pinchwife So . . .
Pinchwife 'That you may for ever more cease to pursue her who
hates and detests you. [*She writes on.*]
Mrs Pinchwife [*Sighs*] So – Heigh!
125 *Pinchwife* What, do you sigh? 'Detests you, as much as she loves
her husband and her honour.'
Mrs Pinchwife I vow, husband, he'll ne'er believe I should write
such a letter.
Pinchwife What, he'd expect a kinder from you? Come now, your
130 name only.
Mrs Pinchwife What, shan't I say 'Your most faithful, humble
servant till death'?
Pinchwife No, tormenting fiend. [*Aside*] Her style, I find, would be

very soft. – Come, wrap it up now, whilst I go fetch wax and a
135   candle; and write on the back side 'For Mr Horner'.
[*Exit Pinchwife.*]
Mrs Pinchwife 'For Mr Horner ' – so. I am glad he has told me his
name. Dear Mr Horner – but why should I send thee such a letter,
that will vex thee, and make thee angry with me? Well, I will not
send it . . . Ay, but then my husband will kill me for I see plainly, he
140   won't let me love Mr Horner. But what care I for my husband? I
won't, so I won't, send poor Mr Horner such a letter – but then my
husband . . . But oh, what if I writ at bottom 'My husband made me
write it'? Ay, but then my husband would see't. Can one have no
shift? Ah, a London woman would have had a hundred presently.
145   Stay – what if I should write a letter, and wrap it up like this, and
write upon't too? Ay, but then my husband would see't. I don't know
what to do but yet i'vads I'll try, so I will – for – I will not send
this letter to poor Mr Horner, come what will on't.
[*She writes, and repeats what she hath writ.*]
Dear, sweet Mr Horner,' – so – 'My husband would have me send
150   you a base, rude, unmannerly letter, but I won't' – so – 'and
would have me forbid you loving me, but I won't' – so – 'and
would have me say to you, I hate you, poor Mr Horner, but I won't
tell a lie for him' – there – 'for I'm sure if you and I were in the
country at cards together' – so – 'I could not help treading on
155   your toe under the table' – so – 'or rubbing knees with you, and
staring in your face, till you saw me' – very well 'and then looking
down, and blushing for an hour together,' – so – 'but I must make
haste before my husband come; and now he has taught me to write
letters, you shall have longer ones from me, who am, dear, dear, poor
160   dear Mr Horner, your most humble friend, and servant to command
till death, Margery Pinchwife.' – Stay – I must give him a hint at
bottom – so . . . . Now wrap it up just like t'other – so. Now write
'For Mr Horner' – But oh, now what shall I do with it? For here
comes my husband.
[*Enter Pinchwife.*]
165   **Pinchwife** [*Aside*] I have been detained by a sparkish coxcomb, who
pretended a visit to me; but fear 'twas to my wife. – What, have
you done?
Mrs Pinchwife Ay, ay bud, just now.
Pinchwife Let's see't. What d'ye tremble for? What, you would not
170   have it go?
Mrs Pinchwife Here. [*Aside*] No, I must not give him that. [*He opens
and reads the first letter.*] So, I had been served if I had given him this.
Pinchwife Come, where's the wax and seal?
Mrs Pinchwife [*Aside*] Lord, what shall I do now? Nay then, I
175   have it – pray, let me see't. Lord, you think me so arrant a fool I

---

144 shift: device, plot.   **147** i'vads: in faith.

cannot seal a letter? I will do't, so I will. [*Snatches the letter from him, changes it for the other, seals it, and delivers it to him.*]
Pinchwife Nay, I believe you will learn that, and other things too, which I would not have you.
Mrs Pinchwife So, han't I done it curiously? [*Aside*] I think I have; there's my letter going to Mr Horner since he'll needs have me send letters to folks.
Pinchwife 'tis very well; but I warrant you would not have it go now?
Mrs Pinchwife Yes indeed, but I would, bud, now.
Pinchwife Well, you are a good girl then. Come, let me lock you in your chamber till I come back. And be sure you come not within three strides of the window, when I am gone – for I have a spy in the street.
[*Exit Mrs Pinchwife; Pinchwife locks the door.*]
At least 'tis fit she think so. If we do not cheat women, they'll cheat us; and fraud may be justly used with secret enemies, of which a wife is the most dangerous. And he that has a handsome one to keep, and a frontier town, must provide against treachery rather than open force. Now I have secured all within, I'll deal with the foe without with false intelligence [*Holds up the letter.*]
[*Exit Pinchwife.*]

Act IV, Scene iii

[*Horner's lodgings. Quack and Horner.*]
Quack Well sir, how fadges the new design? Have you not the luck of all your brother projectors, to deceive only yourself at last?
Horner No, good domine doctor, I deceive you, it seems, and others too; for the grave matrons and old rigid husbands think me as unfit for love as they are; but their wives, sisters and daughters know some of 'em better things already.
Quack Already!
Horner Already, I say. Last night I was drunk with half a dozen of your civil persons, as you call 'em, and people of honour, and so was made free of their society and dressingrooms for ever hereafter, and am already come to the privileges of sleeping upon their pallets, warming smocks, tying shoes and garters, and the like, doctor already, already, doctor.
Quack You have made use of your time, sir.
Horner I tell thee, I am now no more interruption to 'em, when they sing or talk bawdy, than a little squab French page who speaks no English.
Quack But do civil persons, and women of honour, drink and sing bawdy songs?

4,3. 1 **fadges**: gets on.   2 **projectors**: schemers.   3 **domine**: master.

20   *Horner* Oh, amongst friends, amongst friends; for your bigots in honour are just like those in religion: they fear the eye of the world more than the eye of heaven, and think there is no virtue but railing at vice, and no sin but giving scandal. They rail at a poor, little, kept player, and keep themselves some young, modest, pulpit comedian

25   to be privy to their sins in their closets, not to tell 'em of them in their chapels.
    Quack Nay, the truth on't is, priests amongst the women, now, have quite got the better of us lay confessors, physicians.
    Horner And they are rather their patients, but –
    [*Enter Lady Fidget, looking about her.*]

30   Now we talk of women of honour, here comes one.. Step behind the screen there, and but observe if I have not particular privileges with the women of reputation already, doctor, already.
    [*Quack conceals himself.*]
    Lady Fidget Well, Horner, am not I a woman of honour? You see I'm as good as my word.

35   *Horner* And you shall see, madam, I'll not be behindhand with you in honour – and I'll be as good as my word too, if you please but to withdraw into the next room.
    Lady Fidget But first, my dear sir, you must promise to have a care of my dear honour.

40   *Horner* If you talk a word more of your honour, you'll make me incapable to wrong it. To talk of honour in the mysteries of love, is like talking of heaven, or the deity, in an operation of witchcraft, just when you are employing the devil; it makes the charm impotent.

45   *Lady Fidget* Nay, fie, let us not be smutty. But you talk of mysteries and bewitching to me; I don't understand you.
    Horner I tell you, madam, the word 'money' in a mistress's mouth, at such a nick of time, is not a more disheartening sound to a younger brother, than that of 'honour' to an eager lover like myself.

50   *Lady Fidget* But you can't blame a lady of my reputation to be chary.
    Horner Chary! I have been chary of it already, by the report I have caused of myself.
    Lady Fidget Ay, but if you should ever let other women know that

55   dear secret, it would come out. Nay, you must have a great care of your conduct, for my acquaintance are so censorious – oh, 'tis a wicked, censorious world, Mr Horner – I say, are so censorious and detracting, that perhaps they'll talk to the prejudice of my honour, though you should not let them know the dear secret.

60   *Horner* Nay, madam, rather than they shall prejudice your honour, I'll prejudice theirs – and to serve you, I'll lie with 'em all, make the secret their own, and then they'll keep it. I am a Machiavel in love, madam.

Lady Fidget Oh no, sir, not that way.

65   *Horner* Nay, the devil take me, if censorious women are to be
silenced any other way.

Lady Fidget A secret is better kept, I hope, by a single person than a
multitude; therefore pray do not trust anybody else with it, dear,
dear Mr Horner. [*Embracing him.*]

[*Enter Sir Jasper Fidget.*]

70   *Sir Jasper* How now!

Lady Fidget [*Aside*] Oh, my husband! prevented – and what's
almost as bad, found with my arms about another man, that will
appear too much. What shall I say? Sir Jasper, come hither. I am
trying if Mr Horner were ticklish, and he's as ticklish as can be. I love

75   to torment the confounded toad. Let you and I tickle him.

Sir Jasper No, your ladyship will tickle him better without me, I
suppose. But is this your buying china? I thought you had been at
the china house.

Horner [*Aside*] China house – that's my cue; I must take it. A pox,

80   can't you keep your impertinent wives at home? Some men are
troubled with the husbands, but I with the wives. But I'd have you to
know, since I cannot be your journeyman by night, I will not be your
drudge by day, to squire your wife about, and be your man of straw,
or scarecrow, only to pies and jays that would be nibbling at your

85   forbidden fruit. I shall be shortly the hackney gentleman-usher of
the town.

Sir Jasper [*Aside*] He, He, He! poor fellow, he's in the right on't,
faith; to squire women about for other folks, is as ungrateful
an employment as to tell money for other folks. – He, He, He!

90   Ben't angry, Horner

Lady Fidget No, 'tis I have more reason to be angry, who am left
by you to go abroad indecently alone; or, what is more indecent, to
pin myself upon such ill-bred people of your acquaintance as this is.

Sir Jasper Nay, prithee what has he done?

95   *Lady Fidget* Nay, he has done nothing.

Sir Jasper But what d'ye take ill, if he has done nothing?

Lady Fidget Ha, Ha, Ha! Faith, I can't but laugh however. Why, d'ye
think, the unmannerly toad would not come down to me to the
coach; I was fain to come up to fetch him, or go without him, which

100   I was resolved not to do; for he knows china very well, and has himself very good, but will not let me see it, lest I should beg some. But
I will find it out, and have what I came for yet.

Horner [*Apart to Lady Fidget*] Lock the door, madam.

[*Exit Lady Fidget, and locks the door, followed by Horner to the door.*]

So, she has got into my chamber, and locked me out. Oh, the

105   impertinency of womankind! Well, Sir Jasper, plain dealing is a jewel:
if ever you suffer your wife to trouble me again here, she shall carry

---

85 **hackney:** hired out.   89 **tell:** count.

you home a pair of horns, by my Lord Mayor she shall. Though I
cannot furnish you myself, you are sure, yet I'll find a way.

Sir Jasper [*Aside*] Ha, Ha, He! At my first coming in, and finding
her arms about him, tickling him it seems, I was half jealous; but
now I see my folly. – He, He, He! Poor Horner.

Horner Nay, though you laugh now, 'twill be my turn ere long. Oh
women, more impertinent, more cunning, and more mischievous
than their monkeys, and to me almost as ugly. Now is she throwing
my things about, and rifling all I have, but I'll get in to her the back
way, and so rifle her for it –

Sir Jasper Ha, Ha, Ha! Poor angry Horner.

Horner Stay here a little; I'll ferret her out to you presently, I
warrant.

[*Exit Horner at the other door.*]

Sir Jasper [*Calls through the door to his wife.*] Wife, my lady Fidget,
wife, he is coming in to you the back way.

Lady Fidget [*Answers from within*] Let him come, and welcome,
which way he will.

Sir Jasper He'll catch you, and use you roughly, and be too strong
for you.

Lady Fidget Don't you trouble yourself, let him if he can.

Quack [*Behind*] This, indeed, I could not have believed from him,
nor any but my own eyes.

[*Enter Mistress Squeamish.*]

Mistress Squeamish Where's this woman-hater, this toad, this ugly,
greasy, dirty sloven?

Sir Jasper [*Aside*] So, the women all will have him ugly; methinks
he is a comely person, but his wants make his form contemptible to
'em. And 'tis e'en as my wife said yesterday, talking of him, that a
proper, handsome eunuch was as ridiculous a thing as a gigantic
coward.

Mistress Squeamish Sir Jasper, your servant; where is the odious
beast?

Sir Jasper He's within, in his chamber, with my wife; she's playing
the wag with him.

Mistress Squeamish Is she so? And he's a clownish beast, he'll give
her no quarter; he'll lay the wag with her again, let me tell you.
Come, let's go help her – what, the door's locked!

Sir Jasper Ay, my wife locked it –

Mistress Squeamish Did she so? Let us break it open then.

Sir Jasper No, no, he'll do her no hurt.

Mistress Squeamish No. [*Aside*] But is there no other way to get in
to 'em? Whither goes this? I will disturb 'em.

[*Exit Mistress Squeamish at another door. Enter Old Lady Squeamish.*]

Old Lady Squeamish Where is this harlotry, this impudent baggage,

---

116 **rifle**: plunder, pillage (sexual innuendo).

this rambling tomrig? Ah, Sir Jasper, I'm glad to see you here; did
150   you not see my vild grandchild come in hither just now?
Sir Jasper Yes.
Old Lady Squeamish Ay, but where is she, then? Where is she?
Lord, Sir Jasper, I have e'en rattled myself to pieces in pursuit of
her. But can you tell what she makes here? They say below, no
155   woman lodges here.
Sir Jasper No.
Old Lady Squeamish No? What does she here, then? Say, if it be
not a woman's lodging, what makes she here? But are you sure no
woman lodges here?
160   **Sir Jasper** No, nor no man neither; this is Mr Horner's lodging.
Old Lady Squeamish Is it so? Are you sure?
Sir Jasper Yes, yes.
Old Lady Squeamish So then, there's no hurt in't, I hope. But where
is he?
165   **Sir Jasper** He's in the next room with my wife.
Old Lady Squeamish Nay, if you trust him with your wife, I may
with my Biddy. They say he's a merry, harmless man now, e'en as
harmless a man as ever came out of Italy with a good voice, and as
pretty, harmless company for a lady as a snake without his teeth.
170   **Sir Jasper** Ay, ay, poor man.
[*Enter Mistress Squeamish.*]
Mistress Squeamish I can't find 'em. Ah, are you here, grandmother?
I followed, you must know, my Lady Fidget hither; 'tis the prettiest
lodging, and I have been staring on the prettiest pictures.
[*Enter Lady Fidget, with a piece of china in her hand, and Horner
following.*]
Lady Fidget And I have been toiling and moiling for the prettiest
175   piece of china, my dear.
Horner Nay, she has been too hard for me, do what I could.
Mistress Squeamish Oh Lord, I'll have some china too, good Mr
Horner – don't think to give other people china, and me none.
Come in with me too.
180   **Horner** Upon my honour, I have none left now.
Mistress Squeamish Nay, nay, I have known you deny your china
before now; but you shan't put me off so. Come.
Horner This lady had the last there.
Lady Fidget Yes indeed, madam; to my certain knowledge he has no
185   more left.
Mistress Squeamish Oh, but it may be he may have some you
could not find.
Lady Fidget What, d'ye think if he had had any left, I would not
have had it too? For we women of quality never think we have
190   china enough.

---

149 **tomrig**: tomboy; bold or immodest woman.   150 **vild**: vile (an antiquated form.)   168 **good voice**: a castrato.

Horner Do not take it ill; I cannot make china for you all, but I will have a roll-wagon for you too, another time.

Mistress Squeamish Thank you, dear toad.

Lady Fidget [*To Horner aside*] What do you mean by that promise?

195 **Horner** [*Apart to Lady Fidget*] Alas, she has an innocent, literal understanding.

Old Lady Squeamish Poor Mr Horner, he has enough to do to please you all, I see.

Horner Ay madam, you see how they use me.

200 **Old Lady Squeamish** Poor gentleman, I pity you.

Horner I thank you, madam; I could never find pity but from such reverend ladies as you are; the young ones will never spare a man.

Mistress Squeamish Come, come, beast, and go dine with us, for we shall want a man at ombre after dinner.

205 **Horner** That's all their use of me, madam, you see.

Mistress Squeamish Come, sloven, I'll lead you to be sure of you. [*Pulls him by the cravat.*]

Old Lady Squeamish Alas, poor man, how she tugs him. Kiss, kiss her, that's the way to make such nice women quiet.

Horner No, madam, that remedy is worse than the torment; they

210 know I dare suffer anything rather than do it.

Old Lady Squeamish Prithee kiss her, and I'll give you her picture in little, that you admired so last night; prithee do.

Horner Well, nothing but that could bribe me. I love a woman only in effigy and good painting, as much as I hate them – I'll do't, for I

215 could adore the devil well painted. [*Kisses Mistress Squeamish.*]

Mistress Squeamish Foh, you filthy toad; nay, now I've done jesting.

Old Lady Squeamish Ha ha ha, I told you so

Mistress Squeamish Foh, a kiss of his –

Sir Jasper Has no more hurt in't, than one of my spaniel's.

220 **Mistress Squeamish** Nor no more good neither.

Quack [*Behind*] I will now believe anything he tells me. [*Enter Pinchwife.*]

Lady Fidget Oh Lord, here's a man, Sir Jasper – my mask, my mask; I would not be seen here for the world.

Sir Jasper What, not when I am with you?

225 **Lady Fidget** No, no, my honour – let's be gone.

Mistress Squeamish Oh, grandmother, let us be gone; make haste, make haste, I know not how he may censure us.

Lady Fidget Be found in the lodging of anything like a man! Away! [*Exeunt Sir Jasper Fidget, Lady Fidget, Old Lady Squeamish, Mistress Squeamish.*]

Quack [*Behind*] What's here, another cuckold? He looks like one,

230 and none else sure have any business with him.

Horner Well, what brings my dear friend hither?

Pinchwife Your impertinency.

Horner My impertinency? Why, you gentlemen that have got

handsome wives think you have a privilege of saying anything to
235   your friends, and are as brutish as if you were our creditors.
    Pinchwife No, sir, I'll ne'er trust you any way.
    Horner But why not, dear Jack? Why diffide in me thou know'st
    so well?
    Pinchwife Because I do know you so well.
240   *Horner* Ha'n't I been always thy friend, honest Jack? Always ready
    to serve thee, in love, or battle, before thou wert married, and am
    so still.
    Pinchwife I believe so; you would be my second now indeed.
    Horner Well then, dear Jack, why so unkind, so grum, so strange to
245   me? Come, prithee kiss me, dear rogue. Gad, I was always, I say, and
    am still as much thy servant as –
    Pinchwife As I am yours, sir. What, you would send a kiss to my
    wife, is that it?
    Horner So there 'tis – man can't show his friendship to a married
250   man, but presently he talks of his wife to you. Prithee let thy wife
    alone, and let thee and I be all one as we were wont. What, thou art
    as shy of my kindness as a Lombard Street alderman of a courtier's
    civility at Locket's.
    Pinchwife But you are overkind to me, as kind as if I were your
255   cuckold already. Yet I must confess you ought to be kind and civil to
    me, since I am so kind, so civil to you as to bring you this; look you
    there, sir. [*Delivers him a letter.*]
    Horner What is't?
    Pinchwife Only a love letter, sir.
260   *Horner* From whom? How, this is from your wife! [*Reads.*]
    H'm . . . and h'm . . .
    Pinchwife Even from my wife, sir; am I not wondrous kind and civil
    to you now, too? [*Aside*] But you'll not think her so.
    Horner [*Aside*] Ha, is this a trick of his, or hers?
265   *Pinchwife* The gentleman's surprised, I find. What, you expected a
    kinder letter?
    Horner No faith, not I; how could I?
    Pinchwife Yes, yes, I'm sure you did; a man so well made as you are
    must needs be disappointed, if the women declare not their passion
270   at first sight or opportunity.
    Horner [*Aside*] But what should this mean? Stay, the postscript:
    [*Reads*] 'Be sure you love me whatsoever my husband says to the
    contrary, and let him not see this, lest he should come home, and
    pinch me, or kill my squirrel.' It seems he knows not what the letter
275   contains.
    Pinchwife Come, ne'er wonder at it so much.
    Horner Faith, I can't help it.

---

237 **diffide:** distrust.　**252–53 as shy . . . Locket's:** as suspicious as a city banker or moneylender of the motives of
a gallant treating him at this fashionable restaurant.

Pinchwife Now I think I have deserved your infinite friendship and kindness, and have showed myself sufficently an obliging friend and husband – am I not so, to bring a letter from my wife to her gallant?

Horner Ay, the devil take me, art thou – the most obliging, kind friend and husband in the world, ha, ha!

Pinchwife Well, you may be merry, sir, but in short I must tell you, sir, my honour will suffer no jesting.

Horner What dost thou mean?

Pinchwife Does the letter want a comment? Then know, sir, though I have been so civil a husband as to bring you a letter from my wife, to let you kiss and court her to my face, I will not be a cuckold, sir, I will not.

Horner Thou art mad with jealousy. I never saw thy wife in my life, but at the play yesterday, and I know not if it were she or no. I court her, kiss her!

Pinchwife I will not be a cuckold, I say; there will be danger in making me a cuckold.

Horner Why, wert thou not well cured of thy last clap?

Pinchhwife I wear a sword.

Horner It should be taken from thee, lest thou shouldst do thyself a mischief with it. Thou art mad, man.

Pinchwife As mad as I am, and as merry as you are, I must have more reason from you ere we part. I say again, though you kissed and courted last night my wife in man's clothes, as she confesses in her letter –

Horner [*Aside*] Ha!

Pinchwife Both she and I say you must not design it again, for you have mistaken your woman, as you have done your man.

Horner [*Aside*] Oh – I understand something now. Was that thy wife? Why wouldst thou not tell me 'twas she? Faith, my freedom with her was your fault, not mine.

Pinchwife [*Aside*] Faith, so 'twas.

Horner Fie, I'd never do't to a woman before her husband's face, sure.

Pinchwife But I had rather you should do't to my wife before my face than behind my back and that you shall never do.

Horner No – you will hinder me.

Pinchwife If I would not hinder you, you see by her letter, she would.

Horner Well, I must e'en acquiesce then, and be contented with what she writes.

Pinchwife I'll assure you, 'twas voluntarily writ; I had no hand in't, you may believe me.

Horner I do believe thee, faith.

Pinchwife And believe her too, for she's an innocent creature, has no dissembling in her. And so fare you well, sir.

Horner Pray, however, present my humble service to her, and tell

325   her I will obey her letter to a tittle, and fulfil her desires, be what
they will, or with what difficulty soever I do't; and you shall be no
more jealous of me, I warrant her, and you.

Pinchwife Well then, fare you well, and play with any man's honour
but mine, kiss any man's wife but mine, and welcome.
[*Exit Pinchwife.*]

330   *Horner* Ha, Ha, Ha! – Doctor!

Quack It seems he has not heard the report of you, or does not
believe it.

Horner Ha ha! Now doctor, what think you?

Quack Pray, let's see the letter. [*Reads the letter.*] H'm . . . 'for . . .

335   dear . . . love you.'

Horner I wonder how she could contrive it! What say'st thou to't?
'Tis an original.

Quack So are your cuckolds too, originals – or they are like no
other common cuckolds, and I will henceforth believe it not

340   impossible for you to cuckold the Grand Signior amidst his guards of
eunuchs – that I say!

Horner And I say, for the letter, 'tis the first love letter that ever was
without flames, darts, fates, destinies, lying, and dissembling in't.
[*Enter Sparkish, pulling Pinchwife.*]

Sparkish Come back; you are a pretty brother-in-law, neither go to

345   church nor to dinner with your sister bride!

Pinchwife My sister denies her marriage, and you see is gone away
from you dissatisfied.

Sparkish Pshaw, upon a foolish scruple that our parson was not in
lawful orders, and did not say all the Common Prayer; but 'tis her

350   modesty only, I believe. But let women be never so modest the first
day, they'll be sure to come to themselves by night, and I shall have
enough of her then. In the mean time, Harry Horner, you must dine
with me; I keep my wedding at my aunt's in the Piazza.

Horner Thy wedding? What stale maid has lived to despair of a

355   husband, or what young one of a gallant?

Sparkish Oh, your servant, sir. This gentleman's sister, then – no
stale maid.

Horner I'm sorry for't.

Pinchwife [*Aside*] How comes he so concerned for her?

360   *Sparkish* You sorry for't? Why, do you know any ill by her?

Horner No, I know none but by thee. 'Tis for her sakes not yours,
and another man's sake that might have hoped, I thought –

Sparkish Another man! another man? What is his name?

Horner Nay, since 'tis past he shall be nameless. [*Aside*] Poor

365   Harcourt, I am sorry thou hast missed her.

Pinchwife [*Aside*] He seems to be much troubled at the match.

---

340 **Grand Signior**: Sultan of Turkey.   353 **Piazza**: a residential area near Covent Garden, generally known for amatory meetings. See 5,3 below.

Sparkish Prithee tell me. – Nay, you shan't go, brother.
Pinchwife I must, of necessity, but I'll come to you to dinner.
[*Exit Pinchwife.*]
Sparkish But Harry – what, have I a rival in my wife already? But
370   with all my heart, for he may be of use to me hereafter, for though
my hunger is now my sauce, and I can fall on heartily without, but
the time will come when a rival will be as good sauce for a married
man to a wife, as an orange to veal.
Horner Oh, thou damned rogue, thou hast set my teeth on edge
375   with thy orange.
Sparkish Then let's to dinner – there I was with you again. Come.
Horner But who dines with thee?
Sparkish My friends and relations; my brother Pinchwife, you see,
of your acquaintance.
380   **Horner** And his wife?
Sparkish No, gad, he'll ne'er let her come amongst us good fellows;
your stingy country coxcomb keeps his wife from his friends, as he
does his little firkin of ale for his own drinking, and a gentleman
can't get a smack on't; but his servants, when his back is turned,
385   broach it at their pleasures, and dust it away, Ha, Ha, Ha! Gad, I am
witty, I think, considering I was married today, by the world. But
come –
Horner No, I will not dine with you, unless you can fetch her too.
Sparkish Pshaw, what pleasure canst thou have with women now,
390   Harry?
Horner My eyes are not gone; I love a good prospect yet, and will
not dine with you unless she does too. Go fetch her therefore, but do
not tell her husband 'tis for my sake.
Sparkish Well, I'll go try what I can do. In the meantime, come
400   away to my aunt's lodging, 'tis in the way to Pinchwife's.
Horner [*Aside to Quack*] The poor woman has called for aid, and
stretched forth her hand, doctor. I cannot but help her over the pale,
out of the briars.

[*Exeunt Sparkish, Horner, Quack.*]

Act IV, Scene iv

[*Pinchwife 's house. A table, pen, ink, and paper; Mrs Pinchwife alone
leaning on her elbow.*]

Mrs Pinchwife Well, 'tis e'en so; I have got the London disease
they call love; I am sick of my husband, and for my gallant. I have
heard this distemper called a fever, but methinks 'tis liker an ague,

---

383 firkin: cask.   402 pale: fence.   4.4, 3 ague: type of fever.

for when I think of my husband I tremble and am in a cold sweat,
and have inclinations to vomit, but when I think of my gallant, dear
Mr Horner, my hot fit comes, and I am all in a fever indeed, and as in
other fevers, my own chamber is tedious to me, and I would fain be
removed to his, and then methinks I should be well. Ah poor Mr
Horner! Well, I cannot, will not stay here, therefore I'll make an end
of my letter to him, which shall be a finer letter than my last,
because I have studied it like anything. Oh, sick, sick! [*Takes the pen
and writes. Enter Pinchwife, who, seeing her writing, steals softly behind
her, and, looking over her shoulder, snatches the paper from her.*]
Pinchwife What, writing more letters?
Mrs Pinchwife Oh Lord, bud, why d'ye fright me so? [*She offers
to run out.*]
Pinchwife How's this? Nay, you shall not stir, madam. [*He stops her,
and reads.*] 'Dear, dear, dear Mr Horner,' – very well; I have taught
you to write letters to good purpose but let's see't. 'First I am to beg
your pardon for my boldness in writing to you, which I'd have you
to know I would not have done, had not you said first you loved me
so extremely, which if you do, you will never suffer me to lie in the
arms of another man, whom I loathe, nauseate, and detest,' – Now
you can write these filthy words. But what follows? – 'Therefore I
hope you will speedily find some way to free me from this unfortunate match, which was never, I assure you, of my choice, but I'm
afraid 'tis already too far gone; however, if you love me, as I do you,
you will try what you can do, but you must help me away before
tomorrow, or else alas I shall be for ever out of your reach, for I can
defer no longer our' – [*The letter concludes.*] 'Our' – what is to
follow 'our'? Speak, what? Our 'journey into the country,' I
suppose. Oh, woman, damned woman! And Love, damned Love,
their old tempter – for this is one of his miracles. In a moment he can
make those blind that could see, and those see that were blind; those
dumb that could speak, and those prattle who were dumb before –
nay, what is more than all, make these dough-baked, senseless,
indocile animals, women, too hard for us, their politic lords and
rulers, in a moment. But make an end of your letter, and then I'll
make an end of you thus, and all my plagues together.
[*Draws his sword.*]
Mrs Pinchwife Oh Lord, Oh Lord, you are such a passionate man,
bud.
[*Enter Sparkish.*]
Sparkish How now, what's here to do?
Pinchwife This fool here now!
Sparkish What, drawn upon your wife? You should never do that
but at night in the dark, when you can't hurt her. This is my sister-in-
law, is it not? [*Pulls aside her handkerchief.*] Ay faith, e'en our country

---

33 dough-baked: inadequately cooked, or foolish. **34 politic:** shrewd.

45 Margery; one may know her. Come, she and you must go dine with me; dinner's ready, come. But where's my wife? Is she not come home yet? Where is she?

Pinchwife Making you a cuckold; 'tis that they all do, as soon as they can.

Sparkish What, the wedding day? No, a wife that designs to make a

50 cully of her husband will be sure to let him win the first stake of love, by the world. But come, they stay dinner for us. Come, I'll lead down our Margery.

Pinchwife No sir! Go; we'll follow you.

Sparkish I will not wag without you.

55 **Pinchwife** [*Aside*] This coxcomb is a sensible torment to me, amidst the greatest in the world.

Sparkish Come, come, Madam Margery.

Pinchwife No, I'll lead her my way. [*Leads her to the other door, and locks her in, and returns.*] What, would you treat your friends with

60 mine, for want of your own wife? [*Aside*] I am contented my rage should take breath.

Sparkish [*Aside*] I told Horner this.

Pinchwife Come now.

Sparkish Lord, how shy you are of your wife. But let me tell you,

65 brother, we men of wit have amongst us a saying, that cuckolding, like the smallpox, comes with a fear; and you may keep your wife as much as you will out of danger of infection, but if her constitution incline her to't, she'll have it sooner or later, by the world, say they.

Pinchwife [*Aside*] What a thing is a cuckold, that every fool can

70 make him ridiculous! – Well, sir; but let me advise you, now you are come to be concerned, because you suspect the danger, not to neglect the means to prevent it, especially when the greatest share of the malady will light upon your own head; for –

Hows'e'er the kind wife's belly comes to swell,

75 The husband breeds for her, and first is ill.

[*Exeunt.*]

Act V, Scene i

[*Pinchwife's house. A table and candle; Pinchwife and Mrs Pinchwife.*]

Pinchwife Come, take the pen and make an end of the letter, just as you intended. If you are false in a tittle I shall soon perceive it, and punish you with this as you deserve. [*Lays his hand on his sword.*] Write what was to follow. Let's see: 'You must make haste and help

---

50 **cully:** dupe, especially cuckold.   54 **wag:** go.   55 **sensible:** acutely felt.   64 **shy:** suspicious.   75 **breeds:** grows cuckold's horns.

me away before tomorrow, or else I shall be for ever out of
your reach, for I can defer no longer our – 'What follows 'our'?
Mrs Pinchwife Must all out then, bud? [*Takes the pen and writes.*]
Look you there, then.
Pinchwife Let's see. 'For I can defer no longer our – wedding,
Your slighted Alethea.' What's the meaning of this? My sister's name
to't? Speak, unriddle.
Mrs Pinchwife Yes, indeed, bud.
Pinchwife But why her name to't? Speak speak, I say.
Mrs Pinchwife Ay, but you'll tell her then again. If you would not
tell her again.
Pinchwife I will not. I am stunned, my head turns round. Speak.
Mrs Pinchwife Won't you tell her indeed, and indeed?
Pinchwife No. Speak, I say.
Mrs Pinchwife She'll be angry with me, but I had rather she should
be angry with me than you, bud. And to tell you the truth, 'twas
she made me write the letter, and taught me what I should write.
Pinchwife [*Aside*] Ha, I thought the style was somewhat better
than her own – But how could she come to you to teach you,
since I had locked you up alone?
Mrs Pinchwife Oh, through the keyhole, bud.
Pinchwife But why should she make you write a letter for her to
him, since she can write herself?
Mrs Pinchwife Why, she said because – for I was unwilling to
do it.
Pinchwife Because what? Because –
Mrs Pinchwife Because lest Mr Horner should be cruel, and refuse
her, or vain afterwards and show the letter, she might disown it, the
hand not being hers.
Pinchwife [*Aside*] How's this? Ha – then I think I shall come to
myself again. This changeling could not invent this lie; but if she
could, why should she? She might think I should soon discover it.
Stay – now I think on't too, Horner said he was sorry she had
married Sparkish, and her disowning her marriage to me, makes me
think she has evaded it for Horner's sake. Yet why should she take
this course? But men in love are fools; women may well be so. But
hark you, madam, your sister went out in the morning, and I have
not seen her within since.
Mrs Pinchwife Alackaday, she has been crying all day above, it seems,
in a corner.
Pinchwife Where is she? Let me speak with her.
Mrs Pinchwife [*Aside*] Oh Lord, then he'll discover all. Pray hold,
bud; what, d'ye mean to discover me? She'll know I have told you
then. Pray bud, let me talk with her first –
Pinchwife I must speak with her to know whether Horner ever made
her any promise; and whether she be married to Sparkish or no.

Mrs Pinchwife Pray dear bud, don't, till I have spoken with her, and told her that I have told you all, for she'll kill me else.
Pinchwife Go then, and bid her come out to me.
Mrs Pinchwife Yes, yes, bud.
55 **Pinchwife** Let me see.
Mrs Pinchwife [*Aside*] I'll go; but she is not within to come to him. I have just got time to know of Lucy her maid, who first set me on work, what lie I shall tell next, for I am e'en at my wit's end.
[*Exit Mrs Pinchwife.*]
Pinchwife Well, I resolve it: Horner shall have her. I'd rather give
60 him my sister than lend him my wife, and such an alliance will prevent his pretensions to my wife, sure – I'll make him of kin to her, and then he won't care for her.
[*Mrs Pinchwife returns.*]
Mrs Pinchwife Oh Lord, bud, I told you what anger you would make me with my sister.
65 **Pinchwife** Won't she come hither?
Mrs Pinchwife No, no, alackaday, she's ashamed to look you in the face, and she says if you go in to her, she'll run away downstairs, and shamefully go herself to Mr Horner, who has promised her marriage, she says, and she will have no other, so she won't!
70 **Pinchwife** Did he so? Promise her marriage? Then she shall have no other. Go tell her so, and if she will come and discourse with me a little concerning the means, I will about it immediately. Go!
[*Exit Mrs Pinchwife.*]
His estate is equal to Sparkish's, and his extraction as much better than his as his parts are; but my chief reason is, I'd rather be of kin to
75 him by the name of brother-in-law than that of cuckold.
[*Enter Mrs Pinchwife.*]
Well, what says she now?
Mrs Pinchwife Why, she says she would only have you lead her to Horner's lodging, with whom she first will discourse the matter before she talk with you, which yet she cannot do – for alack,
80 poor creature, she says she can't so much as look you in the face; therefore she'll come to you in a mask, and you must excuse her if she make you no answer to any question of yours, till you have brought her to Mr Horner, and if you will not chide her, nor question her, she'll come out to you immediately.
85 **Pinchwife** Let her come. I will not speak a word to her, nor require a word from her.
Mrs Pinchwife Oh, I forgot; besides, she says, she cannot look you in the face, though through a mask, therefore would desire you to put out the candle.
90 **Pinchwife** I agree to all. Let her make haste. [*Puts out the candle.*] There, 'tis out.
[*Exit Mrs Pinchwife.*]

My case is something better; I'd rather fight with Horner for not
lying with my sister, than for lying with my wife, and of the two I had
rather find my sister too forward than my wife. I expected no other
from her free education, as she calls it, and her passion for the town.
Well, wife and sister are names which make us expect love and duty,
pleasure and comfort, but we find 'em plagues and torments, and are
equally – though differently, troublesome to their keeper; for we
have as much ado to get people to lie with our sisters, as to keep 'em
from lying with our wives.
[*Enter Mrs Pinchwife, masked and in hoods and scarves, and a night
gown and petticoat of Alethea, in the dark.*]
What, are you come, sister? Let us go then – but first let me lock
up my wife. Mistress Margery, where are you?
Mrs Pinchwife Here, bud.
Pinchwife Come hither, that I may lock you up. [*Mrs Pinchwife gives
him her hand, but when he lets her go, she steals softly on the other side
of him.*] Get you in. [*Locks the door*] Come sister, where are you
now? [*Mrs Pinchwife is led away by him for his sister Alethea.*]

Act V, Scene ii

[*Horner's lodging; Quack, Horner.*]

Quack What, all alone! Not so much as one of your cuckolds
here, nor one of their wives! They use to take their turns with
you, as if they were to watch you.
Horner Yes, it often happens that a cuckold is but his wife's spy, and
is more upon family duty when he is with her gallant abroad,
hindering his pleasure, than when he is at home with her, playing the
gallant. But the hardest duty a married woman imposes upon a lover,
is keeping her husband company always.
Quack And his fondness wearies you almost as soon as hers.
Horner A pox, keeping a cuckold company after you have had his
wife, is as tiresome as the company of a country squire to a witty
fellow of the town, when he has got all his money.
Quack And as at first a man makes a friend of the husband to get
the wife, so at last you are fain to fall out with the wife to be rid of
the husband.
Horner Ay, most cuckold-makers are true courtiers; when once a
poor man has cracked his credit for 'em, they can't abide to come
near him.
Quack But at first, to draw him in, are so sweet, so kind, so dear,
just as you are to Pinchwife. But what becomes of that intrigue with
his wife?
Horner A pox, he's as surly as an alderman that has been bit, and

95

100

105

5

10

15

20

92–93 **not lying with:** refusing to marry.   106 **for:** taking her for.   **5.2, 2 use:** are accustomed to.   22 **bit:** tricked.

since he's so coy, his wife's kindness is in vain, for she's a silly innocent.

25   **Quack** Did she not send you a letter by him?

Horner Yes, but that's a riddle I have not yet solved. Allow the poor creature to be willing; she is silly too, and he keeps her up so close –

Quack Yes, so close that he makes her but the more willing, and adds but revenge to her love, which two, when met, seldom fail of

30   satisfying each other one way or other.

Horner What, here's the man we are talking of, I think.

[*Enter Pinchwife leading in his wife, masked, muffled, and in her sister's gown.*]

Pshaw!

Quack Bringing his wife to you is the next thing to bringing a love letter from her.

35   **Horner** What means this?

Pinchwife The last time, you know sir, I brought you a love letter. Now you see a mistress, I think you'll say I am a civil man to you.

Horner Ay, the devil take me, will I say thou art the civillest man I ever met with – and I have known some. I fancy I understand

40   thee now, better than I did the letter. But hark thee in thy ear –

Pinchwife What?

Horner Nothing but the usual question, man: is she sound, on thy word?

Pinchwife What! You take her for a wench, and me for a pimp?

45   **Horner** Pshaw, 'wench' and 'pimp' – paw words. I know thou art an honest fellow, and hast a great acquaintance among the ladies, and perhaps hast made love for me, rather than let me make love to thy wife.

Pinchwife Come sir; in short, I am for no fooling.

50   **Horner** Nor I neither, therefore prithee let's see her face presently. Make her show, man. Art thou sure I don't know her?

Pinchwife I am sure you do know her.

Horner A pox, why dost thou bring her to me then?

Pinchwife Because she's a relation of mine –

55   **Horner** Is she, faith, man? Then thou art still more civil and obliging, dear rogue.

Pinchwife – who desired me to bring her to you.

Horner Then she is obliging, dear rogue.

Pinchwife You'll make her welcome for my sake, I hope?

60   **Horner** I hope she is handsome enough to make herself welcome. – Prithee let her unmask.

Pinchwife Do you speak to her; she would never be ruled by me.

Horner Madam – [*Mrs Pinchwife whispers to Horner.*] She says she must speak with me in private. Withdraw, prithee

65   **Pinchwife** [*Aside*] She's unwilling, it seems, I should know all her

---

45 **paw**: obscene.

undecent conduct in this business. – Well then, I'll leave you
together, and hope when I am gone you'll agree. If not, you and I
shan't agree, sir. [*Lays his hand on his sword.*]

Horner [*Aside*] What means the fool? If she and I agree, 'tis no
70   matter what you and I do. [*Whispers to Mrs Pinchwife.*]

Pinchwife In the meantime I'll fetch a parson, and find out Sparkish
and disabuse him. You would have me fetch a parson, would you
not? [*She makes signs with her hand for him to be gone.*] Well then.
[*Aside*] Now, I think, I am rid of her, and shall have no more trouble
75   with her. Our sisters and daughters, like usurers' money, are safest
when put out; but our wives, like their writings, never safe but in our
closets, under lock and key.
[*Exit Pinchwife. Enter Boy.*]

Boy Sir Jasper Fidget, sir, is coming up.
[*Exit Boy.*]

Horner [*To Quack*] Here's the trouble of a cuckold, now, we are
80   talking of. A pox on him, has he not enough to do to hinder his
wife's sport, but he must other women's too? – Step in here, madam.
[*Exit Mrs Pinchwife. Enter Sir Jasper Fidget.*]

Sir Jasper My best and dearest friend!

Horner [*Aside to Quack*] The old style, doctor. – Well, be short, for
I am busy. What would your impertinent wife have now?

85 **Sir Jasper** Well guessed, i'faith, for I do come from her.

Horner To invite me to supper. Tell her I can't come; go.

Sir Jasper Nay, now you are out, faith, for my lady and the
whole knot of the virtuous gang, as they call themselves, are
resolved upon a frolic of coming to you tonight in a masquerade,
90   and are all dressed already.

Horner I shan't be at home.

Sir Jasper [*Aside*] Lord, how churlish he is to women! Nay, prithee
don't disappoint 'em, they'll think 'tis my fault; prithee don't. I'll
send in the banquet and the fiddles. But make no noise on't, for the
95   poor virtuous rogues would not have it known for the world that
they go a-masquerading, and they would come to no man's ball but
yours.

Horner Well, well, get you gone. And tell 'em, if they come 'twill be
at the peril of their honour and yours.

100 **Sir Jasper** He, He, He! We'll trust you for that. Farewell.
[*Exit Sir Jasper Fidget.*]

Horner Doctor, anon you too shall be my guest,
But now I'm going to a private feast.

[*Exeunt.*]

---

76 put out: invested.   **76 their writings**: the usurers' documents.   **88 gang**: group.

Act V, Scene iii

[*The Piazza of Covent Garden; Sparkish, Pinchwife.*]
Sparkish [*With the letter in his hand*] But who would have thought a woman could have been false to me? By the world, I could not have thought it.

Pinchwife You were for giving and taking liberty; she has taken it only, sir, now you find in that letter. You are a frank person, and so is she, you see there.

Sparkish Nay, if this be her hand – or I never saw it.

Pinchwife 'Tis no matter whether that be her hand or no; I am sure this hand, at her desire, led her to Mr Horner, with whom I left her just now, to go fetch a parson to 'em, at their desire too, to deprive you of her for ever – for it seems yours was but a mock marriage.

Sparkish Indeed, she would needs have it that 'twas Harcourt himself, in a parson's habit, that married us; but I'm sure he told me 'twas his brother Ned.

Pinchwife Oh, there 'tis out; and you were deceived, not she, for you are such a frank person! But I must be gone. You'll find her at Mr Horner's; go, and believe your eyes.
[*Exit Pinchwife.*]

Sparkish Nay, I'll to her, and call her as many crocodiles, sirens, harpies, and other heathenish names, as a poet would do a mistress who had refused to hear his suit – nay more, his verses on her. But stay, is not that she, following a torch at t'other end of the Piazza, and from Horner's certainly? 'tis so.
[*Enter Alethea, following a torch, and Lucy behind.*]
You are well met, madam, though you don't think so. What, you have made a short visit to Mr Horner, but I suppose you'll return to him presently, by that time the parson can be with him.

Alethea Mr Horner, and the parson, sir?

Sparkish Come, madam, no more dissembling, no more jilting, for I am no more a frank person.

Alethea How's this?

Lucy [*Aside*] So, 'twill work, I see.

Sparkish Could you find out no easy country fool to abuse? None but me, a gentleman of wit and pleasure about the town? But it was your pride to be too hard for a man of parts, unworthy, false woman. False as a friend that lends a man money to lose; false as dice, who undo those that trust all they have to 'em.

Lucy [*Aside*] He has been a great bubble by his similes, as they say.

Alethea You have been too merry, sir, at your wedding dinner, sure.

Sparkish What, d'ye mock me too?

Alethea Or you have been deluded.

Sparkish By you.

---

5 frank: generous. 27 jilting: deceiving. 36 **a great bubble by his similes:** misled by his own rhetoric.

Alethea Let me understand you.

Sparkish Have you the confidence – I should call it something else, since you know your guilt – to stand my just reproaches? You did not write an impudent letter to Mr Horner? – who I find now
45 has clubbed with you in deluding me with his aversion for women, that I might not, forsooth, suspect him for my rival.

Lucy [*Aside*] D'ye think the gentleman can be jealous now, madam?

Alethea I write a letter to Mr Horner!

Sparkish Nay madam, do not deny it; your brother showed it me
50 just now, and told me likewise he left you at Horner's lodging, to fetch a parson to marry you to him. And I wish you joy, madam, joy, joy, and to him too, much joy, and to myself more joy – for not marrying you.

Alethea [*Aside*] So, I find my brother would break off the match;
55 and I can consent to't, since I see this gentleman can be made jealous. – Oh, Lucy, by his rude usage and jealousy he makes me almost afraid I am married to him – art thou sure 'twas Harcourt himself, and no parson, that married us?

Sparkish No, madam, I thank you; I suppose that was a contrivance
60 too of Mr Horner's and yours, to make Harcourt play the parson. But I would, as little as you, have him one now, no, not for the world – for shall I tell you another truth? I never had any passion for you – till now, for now I hate you. 'Tis true, I might have married your portion, as other men of parts of the town do sometimes and so,
65 your servant. And to show my unconcernedness, I'll come to your wedding, and resign you with as much joy as I would a stale wench to a new cully, nay, with as much joy as I would after the first night, if I had been married to you. There's for you; and so, your servant, servant.

[*Exit Sparkish.*]

70 **Alethea** How was I deceived in a man!

Lucy You'll believe, then, a fool may be made jealous now? For that easiness in him that suffers him to be led by a wife, will likewise permit him to be persuaded against her by others.

Alethea But marry Mr Horner! My brother does not intend it, sure.
75 If I thought he did, I would take thy advice, and Mr Harcourt for my husband. And now I wish that if there be any over-wise woman of the town who, like me, would marry a fool for fortune, liberty, or title: first, that her husband may love play, and be a cully to all the town but her, and suffer none but fortune to be mistress of his purse.
80 Then if for liberty, that he may send her into the country under the conduct of some housewifely mother-in-law. And if for the title, may this world give 'em none but that of cuckold.

Lucy And for her greater curse, madam, may he not deserve it.

Alethea Away, impertinent. Is not this my old Lady Lanterlu's?

---

65 **your servant:** a form of leave-taking.   67 **cully:** a dupe.   68 **servant:** admirer, lover (said in irony).

85   **Lucy** Yes, Madam – [*Aside*] and here I hope we shall find Mr
       Harcourt.

       [*Exeunt.*]

Act V, Scene iv

[*Horner's lodging, a table, banquet, and bottles; Horner, Lady Fidget,
Dainty Fidget, Mistress Squeamish.*]

Horner [*Aside*] A pox, they are come too soon – before I have
sent back my new – mistress. All I have now to do, is to lock her
in, that they may not see her.
Lady Fidget That we may be sure of our welcome, we have
5   brought our entertainment with us, and are resolved to treat thee,
dear toad.
Dainty Fidget And that we may be merry to purpose, have left Sir
Jasper and my old Lady Squeamish quarrelling at home at back-
gammon.
10   **Mistress Squeamish** Therefore let us make use of our time, lest
they should chance to interrupt us.
Lady Fidget Let us sit then.
Horner First, that you may be private, let me lock this door, and
that, and I'll wait upon you presently.
15   **Lady Fidget** No sir, shut 'em only, and your lips for ever, for we
must trust you as much as our women.
Horner You know all vanity's killed in me; I have no occasion for
talking.
Lady Fidget Now ladies, supposing we had drank each of us our
20   two bottles: let us speak the truth of our hearts.
Dainty Fidget and **Mistress Squeamish** Agreed.
Lady Fidget By this brimmer, for truth is nowhere else to be found.
[*Aside to Horner*] Not in thy heart, false man.
Horner [*Aside to Lady Fidget*] You have found me a true man, I'm
25   sure.
Lady Fidget [*Aside to Horner*] Not every way. But let us sit and be
merry. [*Sings.*]

           Why should our damned tyrants oblige us to live
           On the pittance of pleasure which they only give?
30   We must not rejoice
               With wine and with noise;
           In vain we must wake in a dull bed alone,
           Whilst to our warm rival, the bottle, they're gone.
               Then lay aside charms,
35   And take up these arms.

---

35 arms: glasses.

'Tis wine only gives 'em their courage and wit;
Because we live sober, to men we submit.
  If for beauties you'd pass,
  Take a lick of the glass;
40 'Twill mend your complexions and when they are gone
The best red we have, is the red of the grape.
  Then sisters, lay't on,
  And damn a good shape.

Dainty Fidget Dear brimmer! Well, in token of our openness and
45 plain dealing, let us throw our masks over our heads.
Horner So 'twill come to the glasses anon.
Mistress Squeamish Lovely brimmer! Let me enjoy him first.
Lady Fidget No, I never part with a gallant till I've tried him.
Dear brimmer, that mak'st our husbands short-sighted. [*Drinks.*]
50 **Dainty Fidget** And our bashful gallants bold. [*Drinks.*]
Mistress Squeamish And, for want of a gallant, the butler lovely
in our eyes. [*Drinks.*] Drink, eunuch.
Lady Fidget Drink, thou representative of a husband. Damn a
husband!
55 **Dainty Fidget** And, as it were a husband, an old keeper.
Mistress Squeamish And an old grandmother.
Horner And an English bawd, and a French surgeon.
Lady Fidget Ay, we have all reason to curse 'em.
Horner For my sake, ladies.
60 **Lady Fidget** No, for our own; for the first spoils all young gallants'
industry –
Dainty Fidget And the other's art makes 'em bold only with
common women.
Mistress Squeamish And rather run the hazard of the vile
65 distemper amongst them, than of a denial amongst us.
Dainty Fidget The filthy toads choose mistresses now, as they do
stuffs, for having been fancied and worn by others.
Mistress Squeamish For being common and cheap.
Lady Fidget Whilst women of quality, like the richest stuffs, lie
70 untumbled and unasked for.
Horner Ay, neat, and cheap, and new, often they think best.
Dainty Fidget No sir, the beasts will be known by a mistress longer
than by a suit.
Mistress Squeamish And 'tis not for cheapness neither.
75 **Lady Fidget** No, for the vain fops will take up druggets, and
embroider 'em. But I wonder at the depraved appetites of witty men;
they use to be out of the common road, and hate imitation. Pray tell
me, beast, when you were a man, why you rather chose to club with

---

44 brimmer: a bowl full to the brim, but 'to brim' meant to have intercourse.   **67 stuffs:** fabrics.   **75 druggets:**
cheap woollen fabrics.

a multitude in a common house, for an entertainment, than to be
80 the only guest at a good table.
Horner Why, faith, ceremony and expectation are unsufferable
to those that are sharp bent. People always eat with the best stomach at an ordinary, where every man is snatching for the best bit.
Lady Fidget Though he get a cut over the fingers. But I have heard,
85 people eat most heartily of another man's meat, that is, what they do
not pay for.
Horner When they are sure of their welcome and freedom; for
ceremony in love and eating is as ridiculous as in fighting – falling
on briskly is all should be done in those occasions.
90 *Lady Fidget* Well then, let me tell you, sir, there is nowhere more
freedom than in our houses, and we take freedom from a young
person as a sign of good breeding, and a person may be as free as he
pleases with us, as frolic, as gamesome, as wild as he will.
Horner Ha'n't I heard you all declaim against wild men?
95 *Lady Fidget* Yes, but for all that, we think wildness in a man as
desirable a quality as in a duck, or rabbit. A tame man, foh!
Horner I know not, but your reputations frightened me, as much
as your faces invited me.
Lady Fidget Our reputation? Lord! Why should you not think that
100 we women make use of our reputation, as you men of yours, only to
deceive the world with less suspicion? Our virtue is like the statesman's religion, the Quaker's word, the gamester's oath, and the great
man's honour: but to cheat those that trust us.
Mistress Squeamish And that demureness, coyness, and modesty
105 that you see in our faces in the boxes at plays, is as much a sign of a
kind woman, as a vizard-mask in the pit.
Dainty Fidget For I assure you, women are least masked when they
have the velvet vizard on.
Lady Fidget You would have found us modest women in our
110 denials only.
Mistress Squeamish Our bashfulness is only the reflection of the
men's.
Dainty Fidget We blush when they are shamefaced.
Horner I beg your pardon, ladies, I was deceived in you devilishly.
115 But why that mighty pretence to honour?
Lady Fidget We have told you. But sometimes 'twas for the same
reason you men pretend business often: to avoid ill company,
to enjoy the better and more privately those you love.
Horner But why would you ne'er give a friend a wink, then?
120 *Lady Fidget* Faith, your reputation frightened us as much as ours
did you – you were so notoriously lewd.

---

79 **common house**: a play on conventional eating house and brothel. 88–89 **falling on**: to attack, make love, begin
to eat. 106 **kind**: promiscuous. 106 **vizard-mask**: whore's mask.

Horner And you so seemingly honest.

Lady Fidget Was that all that deterred you?

Horner And so expensive – you allow freedom, you say?

125 *Lady Fidget* Ay, ay.

Horner That I was afraid of losing my little money, as well as my little time, both which my other pleasures required.

Lady Fidget Money, foh! You talk like a little fellow now. Do such as we expect money?

130 *Horner* I beg your pardon, madam. I must confess I have heard that great ladies, like great merchants, set but the higher prices upon what they have, because they are not in necessity of taking the first offer.

Dainty Fidget Such as we, make sale of our hearts?

Mistress Squeamish We bribed for our love? Foh!

135 *Horner* With your pardon, ladies; I know, like great men in offices, you seem to exact flattery and attendance only from your followers; but you have receivers about you, and such fees to pay, a man is afraid to pass your grants. Besides, we must let you win at cards, or we lose your hearts. And if you make an assignation,

140 'tis at a goldsmith's, jeweller's, or china house, where, for your honour you deposit to him, he must pawn his to the punctual cit, and so paying for what you take up, pays for what he takes up.

Dainty Fidget Would you not have us assured of our gallant's love?

Mistress Squeamish For love is better known by liberality than by

145 jealousy.

Lady Fidget For one may be dissembled, the other not. [*Aside*] But my jealousy can be no longer dissembled, and they are telling-ripe. Come, here's to our gallants in waiting, whom we must name; and I'll begin. This is my false rogue. [*Claps him on the back.*]

150 *Mistress Squeamish* How!

Horner [*Aside*] So all will out now!

Mistress Squeamish [*Aside to Horner*] Did you not tell me, 'twas for my sake only you reported yourself no man?

Dainty Fidget [*Aside to Horner*] Oh wretch! Did you not swear to

155 me, 'twas for my love and honour you passed for that thing you do?

Horner So, so.

Lady Fidget Come, speak, ladies. This is my false villain.

Mistress Squeamish And mine too.

Dainty Fidget And mine.

160 *Horner* Well then, you are all three my false rogues too, and there's an end on't.

Lady Fidget Well then, there's no remedy. Sister sharers, let us not fall out, but have a care of our honour; though we get no presents, jewels of him, we are savers of our honour, the jewel of most value

---

122 honest: chaste.   **137 receivers:** servants who expect bribes.   **138 pass your grants:** go beyond what you grant. **141–42:** the gallant pawns his honour to the shopkeeper in return for loans to buy the expensive things you want, so he can have what he wants.

165 and use, which shines yet to the world unsuspected, though it be counterfeit.

Horner Nay, and is e'en as good as if it were true, provided the world think so. For honour, like beauty now, only depends on the opinion of others.

170 *Dainty Fidget* Well, Harry Common, I hope you can be true to three. Swear – but 'tis no purpose to require your oath, for you are as often forsworn as you swear to new women.

Horner Come, faith, madam, let us e'en pardon one another. For all the difference I find betwixt we men, and you women: we foreswear

175 ourselves at the beginning of an amour, you as long as it lasts.

[Enter Sir Jasper Fidget, and Old LadySqueamish.]

Sir Jasper Oh, my Lady Fidget, was this your cunning, to come to Mr Horner without me? But you have been nowhere else, I hope?

Lady Fidget No, Sir Jasper.

Old Lady Squeamish And you came straight hither, Biddy?

180 *Mistress Squeamish* Yes indeed, lady grandmother.

Sir Jasper 'Tis well, 'tis well; I knew when once they were throughly acquainted with poor Horner, they'd ne'er be from him. You may let her masquerade it with my wife, and Horner, and I warrant her reputation safe.

[Enter Boy.]

185 *Boy* Oh sir, here's the gentleman come, whom you bid me not suffer to come up without giving you notice – with a lady too, and other gentlemen.

Horner Do you all go in there, whilst I send 'em away –

[Exeunt Sir Jasper Fidget, Old Lady Squeamish, Lady Fidget, Dainty Fidget, Mistress Squeamish.]

And, boy, do you desire 'em to stay below till I come, which shall be

190 immediately.

Boy Yes, sir.

[Exit Boy. Exit Horner at t'other door, and returns with Pinchwife.]

Horner You would not take my advice to be gone home, before your husband came back. He'll now discover all. Yet pray, my dearest, be persuaded to go home, and leave the rest to my

195 management. I'll let you down the back way.

Mrs Pinchwife I don't know the way home, so I don't.

Horner My man shall wait upon you.

Mrs Pinchwife No. Don't you believe that I'll go at all. What, are you weary of me already?

200 *Horner* No, my life, 'tis that I may love you long; 'tis to secure my love, and your reputation with your husband – he'll never receive you again else.

Mrs Pinchwife What care I? D'ye think to frighten me with that? I

---

170 **Harry Common:** 'common' signifies prostitute, as in 'common woman'; Harry is Horner's first name. Cf. Doll Common, the prostitute in Jonson's *The Alchemist*.

don't intend to go to him again. You shall be my husband now.

205   *Horner* I cannot be your husband, dearest, since you are married to him.

Mrs Pinchwife Oh, would you make me believe that? Don't I see every day at London here, women leave their first husbands, and go and live with other men as their wives. Pish! Pshaw! You'd make me

210   angry, but that I love you so mainly.

Horner So, they are coming up – in again, in; I hear 'em.

[*Exit Mrs Pinchwife.*]

Well, a silly mistress is like a weak place: soon got, soon lost; a man has scarce time for plunder. She betrays her husband first to her gallant, and then her gallant to her husband.

[*Enter Pinchwife, Alethea, Harcourt, Sparkish, Lucy, and a parson.*]

215   *Pinchwife* Come, madam, 'tis not the sudden change of your dress, the confidence of your asseverations, and your false witness there, shall persuade me I did not bring you hither just now. Here's my witness, who cannot deny it, since you must be confronted. – Mr Horner, did not I bring this lady to you just now?

220   *Horner* [*Aside*] Now must I wrong one woman for another's sake but that's no new thing with me, for in these cases I am still on the criminal's side, against the innocent.

Alethea Pray speak, sir.

Horner [*Aside*] It must be so. I must be impudent, and try my luck;

225   impudence uses to be too hard for truth.

Pinchwife What, you are studying an evasion, or excuse for her? Speak, sir.

Horner No, faith, I am something backward only to speak in women's affairs or disputes.

230   *Pinchwife* She bids you speak.

Alethea Ay, pray sir, do; pray, satisfy him.

Horner Then, truly, you did bring that lady to me just now.

Pinchwife Oh ho! –

Alethea How, sir! –

235   *Harcourt* How, Horner!

Alethea What mean you, sir? I always took you for a man of honour.

Horner [*Aside*] Ay, so much a man of honour that I must save my mistress, I thank you, come what will on't.

Sparkish So, if I had had her, she'd have made me believe the moon

240   had been made of a Christmas pie.

Lucy [*Aside*] Now could I speak, if I durst, and solve the riddle, who am the author of it.

Alethea Oh unfortunate woman! A combination against my honour, which most concerns me now because you share in my dis-

245   grace, sir, and it is your censure, which I must now suffer, that troubles me, not theirs.

---

217 false witness: i.e. Lucy.   **225 uses to be:** is usually.

Harcourt Madam, then have no trouble. You shall now see 'tis possible for me to love too, without being jealous. I will not only believe your innocence myself, but make all the world believe it. [*Apart to Horner*] Horner, I must now be concerned for this lady's honour.

Horner And I must be concerned for a lady's honour too.

Harcourt This lady has her honour, and I will protect it.

Horner My lady has not her honour, but has given it me to keep, and I will preserve it.

Harcourt I understand you not.

Horner I would not have you.

Mrs Pinchwife [*Peeping in behind*] What's the matter with 'em all?

Pinchwife Come, come, Mr Horner, no more disputing. Here's the parson; I brought him not in vain.

Harcourt No, sir; I'll employ him, if this lady please.

Pinchwife How! What d'ye mean?

Sparkish Ay, what does he mean?

Horner Why, I have resigned your sister to him; he has my consent.

Pinchwife But he has not mine, sir. A woman's injured honour, no more than a man's, can be repaired or satisfied by any but him that first wronged it; and you shall marry her presently, or – [*Lays his hand on his sword.*]
[*Enter Mrs Pinchwife.*]

Mrs Pinchwife Oh Lord, they'll kill poor Mr Horner! Besides, he shan't marry her, whilst I stand by and look on; I'll not lose my second husband so

Pinchwife What do I see?

Alethea My sister in my clothes!

Sparkish Ha!

Mrs Pinchwife Nay, pray now don't quarrel about finding work for the parson. He shall marry me to Mr Horner, [*To Pinchwife*] for now, I believe, you have enough of me.

Horner [*Aside*] Damned, damned, loving changeling!

Mrs Pinchwife Pray sister, pardon me for telling so many lies of you.

Harcourt I suppose the riddle is plain now.

Lucy No, that must be my work. [*Kneels to Pinchwife, who stands doggedly with his hat over his eyes.*] Good sir, hear me.

Pinchwife I will never hear woman again, but make 'em all silent, thus – [*Offers to draw upon his wife.*]

Horner No, that must not be.

Pinchwife You, then, shall go first; 'tis all one to me. [*Offers to draw on Horner; stopped by Harcourt.*]

Harcourt Hold!
[*Enter Sir Jasper Fidget, Lady Fidget, Old Lady Squeamish, Dainty Fidget, Mistress Squeamish.*]

Sir Jasper What's the matter, what's the matter? Pray what's the matter, sir? I beseech you, communicate, sir.

290   **Pinchwife** Why, my wife has communicated, sir, as your wife may
have done too, sir, if she knows him, sir.
Sir Jasper Pshaw! With him? Ha, Ha, He!
Pinchwife D'ye mock me, sir? A cuckold is a kind of a wild beast;
have a care, sir!
Sir Jasper No, sure, you mock me, sir. He cuckold you? It can't be,
295   Ha, Ha, He! Why, I'll tell you, sir – [*Offers to whisper.*]
Pinchwife I tell you again, he has whored my wife, and yours too, if
he knows her, and all the women he comes near. 'Tis not his
dissembling, his hypocrisy, can wheedle me.
Sir Jasper How! Does he dissemble? Is he a hypocrite? Nay then –
300   How! – Wife, sister, is he an hypocrite?
Old Lady Squeamish An hypocrite, a dissembler? Speak, young
harlotry; speak. How!
Sir Jasper Nay, then – Oh, my head too! Oh thou libidinous lady!
Old Lady Squeamish Oh thou harloting harlotry, hast thou done't
305   then?
Sir Jasper Speak, good Horner; art thou a dissembler, a rogue?
Hast thou –
Horner Soh!
Lucy [*Apart to Homer*] I'll fetch you off, and her too, if she will but
310   hold her tongue.
Horner [*Apart to Lucy*] Canst thou? I'll give thee –
Lucy [*To Pinchwife*] Pray have but patience to hear me, sir, who am
the unfortunate cause of all this confusion. Your wife is innocent, I
only culpable. For I put her upon telling you all these lies concerning
315   my mistress, in order to the breaking off the match between Mr
Sparkish and her, to make way for Mr Harcourt.
Sparkish Did you so, eternal rotten tooth? Then it seems my
mistress was not false to me; I was only deceived by you. Brother
that should have been – now, man of conduct, who is a frank person
320   now, to bring your wife to her lover, ha?
Lucy I assure you, sir, she came not to Mr Horner out of love, for
she loves him no more.
Mrs Pinchwife Hold! I told lies for you, but you shall tell none for
me, for I do love Mr Horner with all my soul, and nobody shall say
325   me nay. Pray, don't you go to make poor Mr Horner believe to the
contrary; 'tis spitefully done of you, I'm sure.
Horner [*Aside to Mrs Pinchwife*] Peace, dear idiot.
Mrs Pinchwife Nay, I will not peace.
Pinchwife Not till I make you.
[*Enter Dorilant, Quack.*]
330   **Dorilant** Horner, your servant. I am the doctor's guest; he must
excuse our intrusion.

---

289 **communicated:** had sexual intercourse with.

Quack But what's the matter, gentlemen? For heaven's sake, what's the matter?

Horner Oh, 'tis well you are come! 'Tis a censorious world we live in; you may have brought me a reprieve, or else I had died for a crime I never committed, and these innocent ladies had suffered with me. Therefore, pray satisfy these worthy, honourable, jealous gentlemen, that – [*Whispers.*]

Quack Oh, I understand you. Is that all? – Sir Jasper, by heavens, and upon the word of a physician, sir – [*Whispers to Sir Jasper.*]

Sir Jasper Nay, I do believe you, truly. – Pardon me, my virtuous lady, and dear of honour.

Old Lady Squeamish What, then all's right again?

Sir Jasper Ay, ay, and now let us satisfy him too [*They whisper with Pinchwife.*]

Pinchwife An eunuch? Pray, no fooling with me.

Quack I'll bring half the surgeons in town to swear it.

Pinchwife They? They'll swear a man that bled to death through his wounds died of an apoplexy.

Quack Pray, hear me sir. Why, all the town has heard the report of him.

Pinchwife But does all the town believe it?

Quack Pray, enquire a little, and first, of all these.

Pinchwife I'm sure when I left the town he was the lewdest fellow in't.

Quack I tell you, sir, he has been in France since. Pray ask but these ladies and gentlemen, your friend Mr Dorilant. – Gentlemen and ladies, ha'n't you all heard the late sad report of poor Mr Horner?

All Ladies Ay, ay ay.

Dorilant Why, thou jealous fool, dost thou doubt it? He's an arrant French capon.

Mrs Pinchwife 'Tis false, sir; you shall not disparage poor Mr Horner, for to my certain knowledge –

Lucy Oh, hold!

Mistress Squeamish [*Aside to Lucy*] Stop her mouth!

Lady Fidget [*To Pinchwife*] Upon my honour, sir, 'tis as true –

Dainty Fidget D'y' think we would have been seen in his company – ?

Mistress Squeamish Trust our unspotted reputations with him!

Lady Fidget [*Aside to Horner*] This you get, and we too, by trusting your secret to a fool –

Horner Peace, madam. [*Aside to Quack*] Well, doctor, is not this a good design, that carries a man on unsuspected, and brings him off safe?

Pinchwife [*Aside*] Well, if this were true; but my wife. [*Dorilant whispers with Mrs Pinchwife.*]

---

360 **capon**: a castrated cock.

375   *Alethea* Come, brother, your wife is yet innocent, you see. But have
a care of too strong an imagination, lest like an over-concerned,
timorous gamester, by fancying an unlucky cast, it should come.
Women and fortune are truest still to those that trust 'em.
Lucy And any wild thing grows but the more fierce and hungry
380   for being kept up, and more dangerous to the keeper.
Alethea There's doctrine for all husbands, Mr Harcourt.
Harcourt I edify, madam, so much, that I am impatient till I am
one.
Dorilant And I edify so much by example, I will never be one.
385   *Sparkish* And because I will not disparage my parts I'll ne'er be one.
Horner And I, alas, can't be one.
Pinchwife But I must be one – against my will, to a country wife,
with a country murrain to me.
Mrs Pinchwife [*Aside*] And I must be a country wife still too, I find,
390   for I can't, like a city one, be rid of my musty husband and do what
I list.
Horner Now, sir, I must pronounce your wife innocent, though I
blush whilst I do it, and I am the only man by her now exposed to
shame, which I will straight drown in wine, as you shall your
395   suspicion, and the ladies' troubles we'll divert with a ballct. Doctor,
where are your maskers?
Lucy Indeed, she's innocent, sir, I am her witness. And her end of
coming out was but to see her sister's wedding, and what she has
said to your face of her love to Master Horner was but the usual
400   innocent revenge on a husband's jealousy – was it not, madam?
Speak.
Mrs Pinchwife [*Aside to Lucy and Horner*] Since you'll have me tell
more lies. – Yes, indeed, bud.
Pinchwife
    For my own sake fain I would all believe;
405   Cuckolds like lovers should themselves deceive.
    But – [*Sighs*] –
    His honour is least safe, too late I find,
    Who trusts it with a foolish wife or friend.

[*A dance of cuckolds.*]

Horner
    Vain Fops, but court, and dress, and keep a pother
410   To pass for women's men with one another;
    But he who aims by women to be prized,
    First by the men, you see, must be despised.

[*Exeunt.*]

---

408 **Dance of Cuckolds**: a number of contemporary tunes were available to signal the theme of cuckoldry to the
audience, but the dancers may equally have worn masquerade masks with horns.

Epilogue

[Spoken by the actress who plays Lady Fidget.]

Now, you the vigorous, who daily here
O'er vizard-mask in public domineer,
And what you'd do to her if in place where;
Nay, have the confidence to cry 'Come out!'
5   Yet when she says 'Lead on' you are not stout;
But to your well-dressed brother straight turn round
And cry 'Pox on her, Ned, she can't be sound!'
Then slink away, a fresh one to engage,
With so much seeming heat and loving rage,
10 You'd frighten listening actress on the stage;
Till she at last has seen you huffing come
And talk of keeping in the tiring-room,
Yet cannot be provoked to lead her home.
Next, you Falstaffs of fifty, who beset
15 Your buckram maidenheads, which your friends get;
And whilst to them you of achievements boast,
They share the booty, and laugh at your cost.
In fine, you essenced boys, both old and young,
Who would be thought so eager, brisk, and strong,
20 Yet do the ladies, not their husbands, wrong;
Whose purses for your manhood make excuse,
And keep your Flanders mares for show, not use;
Encouraged by our woman's man today,
A Horner's part may vainly think to play;
25 And may intrigues so bashfully disown
That they may doubted be by few or none;
May kiss the cards at picquet, ombre, loo,
And so be thought to kiss the lady too;
But, gallants, have a care, faith, what you do.
30 The world, which to no man his due will give,
You by experience know you can deceive,
And men may still believe you vigorous,
But then we women – there's no coz'ning us!

Epilogue **4** 'Come out!': 'Come out and fight!' **5 stout:** brave. **7 sound:** free from venereal disease. **15 buckram maidenheads:** an allusion to Shakespeare 1 Henry IV, 2.2–4, where Falstaff pretends to have valiantly opposed 'eleven buckram men' when in fact he fled at the first sight of two. **18 essenced:** perfumed. **22 Flanders mares:** mistresses. **27 kiss the cards:** i.e. make a flirtatious gesture. **33 coz'ning:** deceiving.

JOHN DRYDEN (1631–1700)

Born into a highly-placed Puritan family, Dryden was educated at Westminster and Cambridge and first employed as secretary to the Protectorate. His first mature poem was an elegy for Cromwell. Shortly after the Restoration he married into a Royalist family and thereafter espoused the Stuart cause. In the 1660s and 1670s he was the leading dramatist. In 1668 he was appointed Poet Laureate for his modern epic, *Annus Mirabilis.* Loyal to James II, he converted to Catholicism and wrote heroic satires in favour of the king, then fell into disfavour at the Glorious Revolution and spent his last decade producing some of the finest translations of Virgil and Ovid in the English language.

    Absalom and Achitophel (1681; 1031 lines) uses the biblical tale from 2 Samuel, 13–18, as an allegorical frame for a satire on the Exclusion Crisis (1678–81) in which the Earl of Shaftesbury (Achitophel) led the Whigs and dissenters in an attempt to exclude the Catholic James from acceding to his brother's throne. The Whigs supported James, Duke of Monmouth (Absalom), the attractive illegitimate son of Charles II. A key event in this crisis, referred to in the poem, was the supposed 'Popish Plot' to assassinate Charles which led to the execution of 35 people in 1681 and much anti-Catholic hysteria.

From Absalom and Achitophel

In pious times, ere priestcraft did begin,
Before polygamy was made a sin;
When man on many multiplied his kind,
Ere one to one was cursedly confined;
5   When nature prompted, and no law denied
Promiscuous use of concubine and bride;
Then Israel's monarch after heaven's own heart,
His vigorous warmth did variously impart
To wives and slaves; and, wide as his command,
10   Scattered his Maker's image through the land.
Michal, of royal blood, the crown did wear;
A soil ungrateful to the tiller's care:
Not so the rest; for several mothers bore
To godlike David several sons before.
15   But since like slaves his bed they did ascend,
No true succession could their seed attend.
Of all this numerous progeny was none
So beautiful, so brave, as Absalom:
Whether, inspired by some diviner lust,
20   His father got him with a greater gust;
Or that his conscious destiny made way,
By manly beauty, to imperial sway.
Early in foreign fields he won renown,

---

7 **Israel's monarch:** Charles II.   11 **Michal:** Catherine   14 **David:** Charles II.
of Braganza, the infertile wife of Charles II.

With kings and states allied to Israel's crown:
25 In peace the thoughts of war he could remove,
And seemed as he were only born for love.
Whate'er he did was done with so much ease,
In him alone 'twas natural to please;
His motions all accompanied with grace;
30 And paradise was opened in his face.
With secret joy indulgent David viewed
His youthful image in his son renewed:
To all his wishes nothing he denied;
And made the charming Annabel his bride.
35 What faults he had (for who from faults is free?)
His father could not, or he would not see.
Some warm excesses which the law forbore,
Were construed youth that purged by boiling o'er,
And Amnon's murder, by a specious name,
40 Was called a just revenge for injured fame.
Thus praised and loved the noble youth remained,
While David, undisturbed, in Sion reigned.
But life can never be sincerely blest;
Heaven punishes the bad, and proves the best.
45 The Jews, a headstrong, moody, murmuring race,
As ever tried the extent and stretch of grace;
God's pampered people, whom, debauched with ease,
No king could govern, nor no God could please
(Gods they had tried of every shape and size,
50 That god-smiths could produce, or priests devise);
These Adam-wits, too fortunately free,
Began to dream they wanted liberty;
And when no rule, no precedent was found,
Of men by laws less circumscribed and bound,
55 They led their wild desires to woods and caves,
And thought that all but savages were slaves.
They who, when Saul was dead, without a blow,
Made foolish Ishbosheth the crown forgo;
Who banished David did from Hebron bring,
60 And with a general shout proclaimed him king:
Those very Jews, who, at their very best,
Their humour more than loyalty expressed,
Now wondered why so long they had obeyed
An idol monarch, which their hands had made;
65 Thought they might ruin him they could create,
Or melt him to that golden calf a state.

---

34 Annabel: Monmouth's wife. **39 Amnon's murder:** probably reference to a duel. **42 Sion:** London. **45 The Jews:** the English. **57 Saul:** Oliver Cromwell. **58 Ishbosheth:** Richard Cromwell. **59 Hebron:** Scotland. Charles II was first recognised as King of Scotland in 1650.

But these were random bolts; no formed design,
Nor interest made the factious crowd to join:
The sober part of Israel, free from stain,
70   Well knew the value of a peaceful reign,
And, looking backward with a wise affright,
Saw seams of wounds, dishonest to the sight
In contemplation of whose ugly scars
They cursed the memory of civil wars.
75   The moderate sort of men, thus qualified,
Inclined the balance to the better side;
And David's mildness managed it so well,
The bad found no occasion to rebel.
But when to sin our biased nature leans,
80   The careful devil is still at hand with means;
And providently pimps for ill desires:
The Good Old Cause revived, a plot requires.
Plots, true or false, are necessary things,
To raise up commonwealths, and ruin kings.
85   The inhabitants of Old Jerusalem
Were Jebusites, the town so called from them;
And theirs the native right.
But when the chosen people grew more strong,
The rightful cause at length became the wrong;
90   And every loss the men of Jebus bore,
They still were thought God's enemies the more.
Thus worn and weakened, well or ill content,
Submit they must to David's government:
Impoverished and deprived of all command,
95   Their taxes doubled as they lost their land;
And what was harder yet to flesh and blood,
Their gods disgraced, and burnt like common wood.
This set the heathen priesthood in a flame;
For priests of all religions are the same:
100   Of whatso'er descent their godhead be,
Stock, stone, or other homely pedigree,
In his defence his servants are as bold,
As if he had been born of beaten gold.
The Jewish rabbis, though their enemies,
105   In this conclude them honest men and wise:
For 'twas their duty, all the learned think,
To espouse his cause, by whom they eat and drink.
From hence began that Plot, the nation's curse,
Bad in itself, but represented worse;

---

82 **Good Old Cause:** the Commonwealth of 1649–53. **85 Jerusalem:** London. **86 Jebusites:** Roman Catholics. 88 **the chosen people:** Protestants. 108 **that Plot:** the 'Popish plot'.

110 Raised in extremes, and in extremes decried;
With oaths affirmed, with dying vows denied;
Not weighed or winnowed by the multitude;
But swallowed in the mass, unchewed and crude.
Some truth there was, but dashed and brewed with lies,
115 To please the fools, and puzzle all the wise.
Succeeding times did equal folly call,
Believing nothing, or believing all.
The Egyptian rites the Jebusites embraced;
Where gods were recommended by their taste.
120 Such savoury deities must needs be good,
As served at once for worship and for food
By force they could not introduce these gods,
For ten to one in former days was odds;
So fraud was used (the sacrificer's trade):
125 Fools are more hard to conquer than persuade.
Their busy teachers mingled with the Jews,
And raked for converts even the court and stews:
Which Hebrew priests the more unkindly took,
Because the fleece accompanies the flock.
130 Some thought they God's anointed meant to slay
By guns, invented since full many a day:
Our author swears it not; but who can know
How far the Devil and Jebusites may go?
This Plot, which failed for want of common sense,
135 Had yet a deep and dangerous consequence:
For, as when raging fevers boil the blood,
The standing lake soon floats into a flood,
And every hostile humour, which before
Slept quiet in its channels, bubbles o'er;
140 So several factions from this first ferment
Work up to foam, and threat the government.
Some by their friends, more by themselves thought wise,
Opposed the power to which they could not rise.
Some had in courts been great, and thrown from thence,
145 Like fiends were hardened in impenitence.
Some, by their monarch's fatal mercy, grown
From pardoned rebels kinsmen to the throne,
Were raised in power and public office high;
Strong bands, if bands ungrateful men could tie.
150 Of these the false Achitophel was first,
A name to all succeeding ages cursed:
For close designs and crooked counsels fit;
Sagacious, bold, and turbulent of wit;

---

118 Egyptian: Catholic. 127 stews: brothels. 147 pardoned rebels: Shaftesbury had been a firm
129 fleece: riches. 130 God's anointed: the king. supporter of Cromwell, the architect of the Restoration.

Restless, unfixed in principles and place;
155 In power unpleased, impatient of disgrace:
A fiery soul, which, working out its way,
Fretted the pigmy body to decay,
And o'er-informed the tenement of clay.
A daring pilot in extremity;
160 Pleased with the danger, when the waves went high,
He sought the storms; but, for a calm unfit,
Would steer too nigh the sands, to boast his wit.
Great wits are sure to madness near allied,
And thin partitions do their bounds divide;
165 Else why should he, with wealth and honour blest,
Refuse his age the needful hours of rest?
Punish a body which he could not please;
Bankrupt of life, yet prodigal of ease?
And all to leave what with his toil he won,
170 To that unfeathered two-legged thing, a son,
Got, while his soul did huddled notions try;
And born a shapeless lump, like anarchy.
In friendship false, implacable in hate;
Resolved to ruin or to rule the state.
175 To compass this the triple bond he broke,
The pillars of the public safety shook;
And fitted Israel for a foreign yoke:
Then seized with fear, yet still affecting fame,
Usurped a patriot's all-atoning name.
180 So easy still it proves in factious times
With public zeal to cancel private crimes:
How safe is treason, and how sacred ill,
Where none can sin against the people's will:
Where crowds can wink, and no offence be known,
185 Since in another's guilt they find their own.
Yet fame deserved no enemy can grude:
The statesman we abhor, but praise the judge.
In Israel's courts ne'er sat an Abbethdin
With more discerning eyes, or hands more clean:
190 Unbribed, unsought, the wretched to redress,
Swift of despatch, and easy of access.
Oh, had he been content to serve the crown
With virtues only proper to the gown,
Or had the rankness of the soil been freed
195 From cockle that oppressed the noble seed,
David for him his tuneful harp had strung,
And heaven had wanted one immortal song.

---

175 **triple bond:** the alliance of England, Holland and   188 **Abbethdin:** a Jewish judge.   195 **cockle:** a weed.
Sweden against France

But wild ambition loves to slide, not stand,
And fortune's ice prefers to virtue's land.
200   Achitophel, grown weary to possess
A lawful fame and lazy happiness,
Disdained the golden fruit to gather free,
And lent the crowd his arm to shake the tree.
Now, manifest of crimes contrived long since,
205   He stood at bold defiance with his prince;
Held up the buckler of the people's cause
Against the crown, and skulked behind the laws.
The wished occasion of the Plot he takes;
Some circumstances finds, but more he makes.
210   By buzzing emissaries fills the ears
Of listening crowds with jealousies and fears
Of arbitrary counsels brought to light,
And proves the king himself a Jebusite.
Weak arguments! which yet he knew full well
215   Were strong with people easy to rebel:
For, governed by the moon, the giddy Jews
Tread the same track when she the prime renews;
And once in twenty years, their scribes record,
By natural instinct they change their lord.
220   Achitopel still wants a chief, and none
Was found so fit as warlike Absolon:
Not that he wished his greatness to create
(For politicians neither love or hate),
But for he knew his title not allowed
225   Would keep him still depending on the crowd,
That kingly power, thus ebbing out, might be
Drawn to the dregs of a democracy.

THE EARL OF ROCHESTER (1641–1680)

John Wilmot, Earl of Rochester (1641-80) was the archetypal Restoration wit and may have been the original for Horner in *The Country Wife*. Charming and intelligent, promiscuous and lewd, he died young of debauchery, probably of syphillis. The metaphysical wit of his lyric and satiric poetry was much admired by Marvel, Dryden, Swift and Pope, but his verse was later considered notorious for a degree of sexual frankness which exceeds any in English literature, and for its tendency to satirise three cardinal beliefs of modern society: Christian belief in our eventual spiritual transcendence, Englightenment belief in the power of Reason, and middle class hostility to any sexuality not bounded by matrimony. Rochester's irreligion and carnality are now very more much in phase with modern taste.

---

217 **prime:** the lunar cycle of nineteen years.

From A Satire Against Mankind

Were I, who to my cost already am
One of those strange, prodigious creatures, man,
A spirit free to choose for my own share
What sort of flesh and blood I pleased to wear,
5   I'd be a dog, a monkey, or a bear,
Or anything but that vain animal.
Who is so proud of being rational.
His senses are too gross, and he'll contrive
A sixth, to contradict the other five,
10   And before certain instinct will prefer
Reason, which fifty times for one does err.
Reason, an *ignis fatuus* of the mind,
Which leaving light of nature, sense, behind,
Pathless and dangerous wandering ways it takes,
15   Through Error's fenny bogs and thorny brakes,
Whilst the misguided follower climbs with pain
Mountains of whimseys heaped in his own brain;
Stumbling from thought to thought, falls headlong down,
Into Doubt's boundless sea where, like to drown,
20   Books bear him up awhile, and make him try
To swim with bladders of Philosophy;
In hopes still to o'ertake th'escaping light;
The vapour dances in his dazzling sight,
Till spent, it leaves him to eternal night.
25   Then Old Age and Experience, hand in hand,
Lead him to death, make him to understand,
After a search so painful, and so long,
That all his life he has been in the wrong:
Huddled in dirt the reasoning engine lies,
30   Who was so proud, so witty, and so wise.
Pride drew him in, as cheats their bubbles catch,
And made him venture to be made a wretch.
His wisdom did his happiness destroy,
Aiming to know that world he should enjoy;
35   And Wit was his vain, frivolous pretence
Of pleasing others, at his own expense.
For wits are treated just like common whores,
First they're enjoyed, and then kicked out of doors;
The pleasure past, a threatening doubt remains,
40   That frights th'enjoyer with succeeding pains:
Women and men of wit are dangerous tools,
And ever fatal to admiring fools.

---

12 *ignis fatuus*: delusion.

Upon Nothing

Nothing, thy elder brother even to Shade,
Thou hadst a being ere the world was made,
And (well fixed) art alone of ending not afraid.

Ere time and place were, Time and Place were not,
5   When primitive Nothing, Something straight begot;
Then all proceeded from the great united what.

Something, the general attribute of all,
Severed from thee, its sole original,
Into thy boundless self must undistinguished fall.

10   Yet Something did thy mighty power command
And from thy fruitful Emptiness's hand
Snatched men, beasts, birds, fire, water, air and land.

Matter, the wicked'st offspring of thy race,
By Form assisted, flew from thy embrace,
15   And rebel Light obscured thy reverend dusky face.

With Form and Matter, Time and Place did join;
Body, thy foe, with these did leagues combine
To spoil thy peaceful reign and ruin all thy line.

But turncoat Time assists the foe in vain
20   And bribed by thee destroys their short-lived reign
And to thy hungry womb drives back the slaves again.

Thy mysteries are hid from laic eyes,
And the divine alone by warrant pries
Into thy bosom, where thy truth in private lies.

25   Yet this of thee the wise may truly say,
Thou from the virtuous nothing take'st away,
And to be part of thee the wicked wisely pray.

Great Negative, how vainly would the wise
Inquire, define, distinguish, teach, devise
30   Didst thou not stand to point their dull philosophies.

Is or Is Not, the two great ends of Fate,
And True or False, the subject of debate
That perfects or destroys the vast designs of state,

When they have racked the politician's breast,
35 Within thy bosom most securely rest
And when reduced to thee are least unsafe and best.

But Nothing, why does Something still permit
That sacred monarchs should at council sit
With persons thought, at best, for nothing fit,

40 While weighty Something modestly abstains
From princes' coffers and from statesman's brains;
And nothing there like stately Nothing reigns.

Nothing, that dwells with fools in grave disguise,
For whom they reverend forms and shapes devise,
45 Lawn sleeves, and furs, and gowns, when they look wise.

French truth, Dutch prowess, British policy,
Hibernian learning, Scotch civility,
Spaniards' dispatch, Danes' wit are mainly seen in thee.

The great man's gratitude to his best friend,
50 Kings' promises, whores' vows, to thee they bend,
Flow swiftly into thee and in thee ever end.

Answer to a Paper of Verses sent to him by Lady Felton

What strange surprise to meet such words as these,
Such terms of horror were ne'er chose to please,
To meet, midst pleasures of a jovial night,
Words that can only give amaze and fright,
5 No gentler thought that does not love to invite.
Were it not better far your arms t'employ
Grasping a lover in pursuit of joy
Than handling sword and pen, weapons unfit?
Your sex gain conquest by their charms and wit.
10 Of writers slain I could with pleasure hear,
Approve of fights, o'erjoyed to cause a tear;
So slain, I mean, that she should soon revive.
Pleased in my arms to find herself alive.

APHRA BEHN (1640?–1689)

Aphra Behn was the first fully professional woman writer in English. Royalist spy against the Dutch, poet, playwright, novelist and satirist, her wit, eroticism and frank sense of female power are typical of Restoration writing but were thought shocking and unwomanly by the prurient middle class that would soon become socially dominant. Her novel *Oronooko* was published in 1688 and expresses the Glorious Revolution through a tale set in the Surniman, which Behn visited as a young woman. Oronooko, or Caesar as the Whites will call him, is an African prince of peerless valour and nobility who finds his paramour in the princess Imoinda. Their mutual felicity is blighted by Oronooko's king, who takes Imoinda as a concubine by divine right, then sells her into slavery when he discovers she still loves Oronooko. Oronooko himself is sold into slavery by a duplicitous White merchant and briefly reunited with Imoinida in Surinam. Distrusting the promise that he will be restored to Africa and kingship, Oronooko foments a slave rebellion, is captured, tortured, escapes again, and dies in the closing scene, reprinted below. The tale combines travel and ethnographic writing in an archetypal romance narrative of perfect love frustrated by the perfidy of lesser mortals. By mapping this archetype onto a Black, the tale enables a critical view of European colonialism.

From Oronooko

He considered, if he should do this deed, and die either in the attempt or after it, he left his lovely Imoinda a prey, or at best a slave to the enraged multitude; his great heart could not endure that thought. 'Perhaps,' said he, 'she may be first ravished by every brute, exposed first to their nasty lusts, and then a shameful death.' No, he could not live a moment under that apprehension, too insupportable to be borne. These were his thoughts, and his silent arguments with his heart, as he told us afterwards: so that now resolving not only to kill Byam, but all those he thought had enraged him; pleasing his great heart with the fancied slaughter he should make over the whole face of the plantation. He first resolved on a deed that (however horrid it first appeared to us all) when we had heard his reasons, we thought it brave and just. Being able to walk, and, as he believed, fit for the execution of his great design, he begged Trefry to trust him into the air, believing a walk would do him good; which was granted him, and taking Imoinda with him as he used to do in his more happy and calmer days, he led her up into a wood, where, after (with a thousand sighs, and long gazing silently on her face, while tears gushed, in spite of him, from his eyes) he told her his design, first of killing her, and then his enemies, and next himself, and the impossibility of escaping, and therefore he told her the necessity of dying. He found the heroic wife faster pleading for death than he was to propose it, when she found his fixed resolution; and, on her knees, besought him not to leave her a prey to his enemies. He (grieved to death) yet pleased at her noble resolution, took her up, and embracing her with all the passion and languishment of a dying lover, drew his knife to kill this treasure of his soul, this pleasure of his eyes. While tears trickled down his cheeks, hers were smiling with joy she should die by so noble a hand, and be sent in her own country (for that's their notion of the next world) by him she so tenderly loved, and so truly adored in this: for wives have a respect for their husbands equal to what any other people pay a deity; and when a man finds any occasion to quit his wife, if he love her, she dies by his hand; if not, he sells her, or suffers some other to kill her. It being thus, you may believe the deed was soon resolved on; and 'tis not to be doubted but the parting, the eternal leave-taking of two such lovers, so greatly born, so sensible, so beautiful, so young, and so fond, must be very moving, as the relation of it was to me afterwards.

All that love could say in such cases being ended, and all the intermitting irresolutions being adjusted, the lovely, young, and adored victim lays herself down before the sacrificer; while he, with a hand resolved, and a heart breaking within, gave the fatal stroke, first cutting her throat, and then severing her yet smiling face from that delicate body, pregnant as it was with fruits of tenderest love. As soon as he had done, he laid the body decently on leaves and flowers, of which he made a bed, and concealed it under the same coverlid of Nature; only her face he left yet bare to look on. But when he found she was dead, and past all retrieve, never more to bless him with her eyes and soft language, his grief swelled up to rage; he tore, he raved, he roared like some monster of the wood, calling on the loved name of Imoinda. A thousand times he turned the fatal knife that did the deed toward his own heart, with a resolution to go immediately after her; but dire revenge, which was now a thousand times more fierce in his soul than before, prevents him: and he would cry out, 'No, since I have sacrificed Imoinda to my revenge, shall I lose that glory which I have purchased so dear, as at the price of the fairest, dearest, softest creature that ever Nature made? No, no!' Then at her name grief would get the ascendant of rage, and he would lie down by her side, and water her face with showers of tears, which never were wont to fall from those eyes. And however bent he was on his intended slaughter, he had not power to stir from the sight of this dear object, now more beloved and more adored than ever.

He remained in this deplorable condition for two days, and never rose from the ground where he had made his sad sacrifice. At last rousing from her side, and accusing himself with living too long, now Imoinda was dead, and that the deaths of those barbarous enemies were deferred too long, he resolved now to finish the great work; but offering to rise, he found his strength so decayed that he swayed to and fro, like boughs assailed by contrary winds; so that he was forced to lie down again, and try to summon all his courage to his aid. He found his brains turn round, and his eyes were dizzy, and objects appeared not the same to him [as] they were wont to do; his breath was short, and all his limbs surprised with a faintness he had never felt before. He had not eaten in two days, which was one occasion of his feebleness, but excess of grief was the greatest; yet still he hoped he should never recover vigour to act his design, and lay expecting it yet six days longer; still mourning over the dead idol of his heart and striving every day to rise, but could not.

In all this time you may believe we were in no little affliction for Caesar and his wife. Some were of opinion he was escaped, never to return; others thought some accident had happened to him. But however, we failed not to send out a hundred people several ways, to search for him. A party of about forty went that way he took, among whom was Tuscan, who was perfectly reconciled to Byam. They had not gone very far into the wood but they smelt an unusual smell, as of a dead body; for stinks must be very noisome that can be distinguished among such a quantity of natural sweets as every inch of that land produces. So that they concluded they should find him dead, or somebody that was so. They passed on towards it, as loathsome as it was, and made such a rustling among the leaves that lie thick on the ground, by continual falling, that Caesar heard he was approached, and though he had, during the space of these eight days, endeavored to rise, but found he wanted strength, yet looking up, and seeing his pursuers, he rose, and reeled to a neighboring tree, against which he fixed his back. And being within a dozen yards of those that advanced and saw him, he called out to them, and bid them approach no nearer, if they would be safe. So that they stood still, and hardly believing their eyes, that would persuade them that it was Caesar that spoke to them, so much was he altered. They asked him what he had done with his wife, for they smelt a stink that almost struck them dead. He, pointing to the dead body, sighing, cried, 'Behold her there.' They put off the flowers that covered her, with their sticks, and found she was killed, and cried out, 'O monster! that hast murdered thy wife.' Then asking him why he did so cruel a deed; he replied he had no leisure to answer impertinent questions. 'You may go back' continued he 'and tell the faithless Governor he may thank Fortune that I am breathing my last; and that my arm is too feeble to obey my heart, in what it had designed him.' But his tongue faltering, and trembling, he could scarce end what he was saying. The English, taking advantage of his weakness, cried, 'Let us take him alive by all means.' He heard them; and, as if he had revived from a fainting, or a dream, he cried out, 'No, Gentlemen, you are deceived; you will find no more Caesars to be whipped; no more find a faith in me: feeble as you think me, I have strength yet left to secure me from a second indignity.' They swore all anew; and he only shook his head, and beheld them with scorn. Then they cried out 'Who will venture on this single man? Will nobody?' They stood all silent while Caesar replied, 'Fatal will be the attempt to the first adventurer, let him assure himself,' and at that word, held up his knife in a menacing posture. 'Look ye, ye faithless crew,' said he, ''tis not life I seek, nor am I afraid of dying,' and at that word, cut a piece of flesh from his own throat, and threw it at them, 'yet still I would live if I could, till I had perfected my revenge. But oh! it cannot be; I feel life gliding from my eyes and heart; and if I make not haste, I shall fall a victim to the shameful whip.' At that, he ripped up his own belly, and took his bowels and pulled them out, with what strength he could; while some, on their knees imploring, besought him to hold his hand. But when they saw him tottering, they cried out, 'Will none venture on him?' A bold Englishman cried, 'Yes, if he were the Devil' (taking courage when he saw him almost dead), and swearing a horrid oath for his farewell to the world, he rushed on him. Caesar with his armed hand met him so fairly as stuck him to the heart, and he fell dead at his feet. Tuscan, seeing that, cried out, 'I love thee, O Caesar! and therefore will not let thee die, if possible,' and running to him, took him in his arms: but, at the same time, warding a blow that Caesar made at his bosom, he received it quite through his arm; and Caesar having not the strength to pluck the knife forth, though he attempted it, Tuscan neither pulled it out himself, nor suffered it to be pulled out, but came down with it sticking in his arm; and the reason he gave for it was, because the air should not get into the wound. They put their hands across, and carried Caesar between six of them, fainted as he was, and they thought dead, or just dying; and they brought him to Parham, and laid him on a couch, and had the chirurgeon immediately to him, who dressed his wounds, and sewed up his belly, and used means to bring him to life, which they effected. We ran all to see him; and, if before we thought him so beautiful a sight, he was now so altered that his face was like a death's head blacked over, nothing but teeth and eye-holes. For some days we suffered nobody to speak to him, but caused cordials to be poured down his throat; which sustained his life, and in six or seven days he recovered his senses. For you must know that wounds are almost to a miracle cured in the Indies; unless wounds in the legs, which rarely ever cure.

When he was well enough to speak, we talked to him, and asked him some questions about his wife, and the reasons why he killed her. And he then told us what I have related of that resolution, and of his parting, and he besought us we would let him die, and was extremely afflicted to think it was possible he might live. He assured us, if we did not dispatch him, he would prove very fatal to a great many. We said all we could to make him live, and gave him new assurances; but he begged we would not think so poorly of him, or of his love to Imoinda, to imagine we could flatter him to life again: but the chirurgeon assured him he could not live, and therefore he need not fear. We were all (but Caesar) afflicted at this news, and the sight was ghastly. His discourse was sad; and the earthy smell about him so strong that I was persuaded to leave the place for some time (being myself but sickly, and very apt to fall into fits of dangerous illness upon any extraordinary melancholy). The servants, and Trefry, and the chirurgeons, promised all to take what possible care they could of the life of Caesar; and I, taking boat, went with other company to Colonel Martin's, about three days' journey down the river. But I was no sooner gone than the Governor, taking Trefry, about some pretended earnest business, a day's journey up the river, having communicated his design to one Banister, a wild Irishman, and one of the council, a fellow of absolute barbarity, and fit to execute any villainy, but rich. He came up to Parham, and forcibly took Caesar, and had him carried to the same post where he was whipped; and causing him to be tied to it, and a great fire made before him, he told him he should die like a dog, as he was. Caesar replied, this was the first piece of bravery that ever Banister did, and he never spoke sense till he pronounced that word; and, if he would keep it, he would declare, in the other world, that he was the only man, of all the whites, that ever he heard speak truth. And turning to the men that had bound him, he said, 'My friends, am I to die, or to be whipped?' And they cried, 'Whipped! no, you shall not escape so well.' And then he replied, smiling, 'A blessing on thee'; and assured them they need not tie him, for he would stand fixed like a rock, and endure death so as should encourage them to die; 'But, if you whip me,' said he, 'be sure you tie me fast.'

He had learned to take tobacco; and when he was assured he should die, he desired they would give him a pipe in his mouth, ready lighted; which they did. And the executioner came, and first cut off his members, and threw them into the fire; after that, with an ill-favored knife, they cut off his ears and his nose and burned them; he still smoked on, as if nothing had touched him; then they hacked off one of his arms, and still he bore up, and held his pipe; but at the cutting off the other arm, his head sunk, and his pipe dropped, and he gave up the ghost, without a groan or a reproach. My mother and sister were by him all the while, but not suffered to save him; so rude and wild were the rabble, and so inhuman were the justices who stood by to see the execution, who after paid dearly enough for their insolence. They cut Caesar in quarters, and sent them to several of the chief plantations: one quarter was sent to Colonel Martin, who refused it, and swore he had rather see the quarters of Banister, and the Governor himself, that those of Caesar, on his plantations; and that he could govern his negroes without terrifying and grieving them with frightful spectacles of a mangled king.

Thus died this great man, worthy of a better fate, and a more sublime wit than mine to write his praise. Yet, I hope, the reputation of my pen is considerable enough to make his glorious name to survive all the ages, with that of the brave, the beautiful, and the constant Imoinda.

ANNE FINCH, COUNTESS OF WINCHILSEA (1661–1720)

Anne Finch was of aristocratic birth and she and her husband were close to James II, their fortunes suffering when he fled in 1688. The Williamite years were spent on the Finches' Kent estate, but Finch returned to Court as the Lady of the Bedchamber to Queen Anne in 1711. Finch was a member of the literary circle around Pope and Swift and published in various miscellanies between 1700 and 1720. Later her reputation faded, despite the praise of Wordsworth, but it has recently been revived.

Adam Posed

> Could our first father, at his toilsome plough,
> Thorns in his path, and labour on his brow,
> Clothed only in a rude unpolished skin,
> Could he a vain, fantastic nymph have seen,
> 5   In all her airs, in all her antic graces,
> Her various fashions, and more various faces;
> How had it posed that skill, which late assigned

Just appellations to each several kind,
A right idea of the sight to frame;
10 T' have guessed from what new element she came,
T' have hit the wavering form, or given this thing a name!

A Song on the South Sea

Ombre and basset laid aside,
New games employ the fair;
And brokers all those hours divide
Which lovers used to share.

5 The court; the park, the foreign song
And harlequin's grimace,
Forlorn; amidst the city throng
Behold each blooming face.

10 Young tender virgins mix,
Of whiskers nor of beards afraid,
Nor all the cozening tricks.
With Jews and Gentiles undismayed

Bright jewels, polished once to deck
The fair one's rising breast,
15 Or sparkle round her ivory neck,
Lie pawned in iron chest.

The gayer passions of the mind
How avarice controls!
Even love does now no longer find
20 A place in female souls.

JOSEPH ADDISON (1672–1719) AND SIR RICHARD STEELE (1672–1729)

Addison and Steele were exemplary 'men of letters' whose periodical papers, the thrice weekly *Tatler* (1709–11) and daily *Spectator* (1711–12), did much to form the idea of the middle-class man as polite, leisured, intelligent and cultivated. Their tone was witty, light, moral, sensitive, providing an example of 'the literate sensibility' which is still influential. Their success had many imitators and contributed to the formation of the modern magazine article and the editorial page in newspapers. Addison also held high administrative office and had a great success with his tragedy, *Cato*. Steele edited several other papers, wrote comedies, and was a member of parliament.

The Spectator, No 4, Monday 5 March 1711

Egregii mortalem altique silenti! – Horace[1]

An author, when he first appears in the world, is very apt to believe it has nothing to think of but his performances. With a good share of this vanity in my heart, I made it my business these three days to listen after my own fame; and, as I have sometimes met with circumstances which did not displease me, I have been encountered by others which gave me as much mortification. It is incredible to think how empty I have in this time observed some part of the species to be, what mere blanks they are when they first come abroad in the morning, how utterly they are at a stand 'till they are set a going by some paragraph in a news-paper. Such persons are very acceptable to a young author, for they desire no more in any thing but to be new to be agreeable. If I found consolation among such, I was much disquieted by the incapacity of others. These are mortals who have a certain curiosity without power of reflection, and perused my papers like spectators rather than readers. But there is so little pleasure in enquiries that so nearly concern our selves (it being the worst way in the world to fame, to be too anxious about it), that upon the whole I resolved for the future to go on in my ordinary way; and without too much fear or hope about the business of reputation, to be very careful of the design of my actions, but very negligent of the consequences of them.

It is an endless and frivolous pursuit to act by any other rule than the care of satisfying our own minds in what we do. One would think a silent man, who concerned himself with no one breathing, should be very little liable to misinterpretations; and yet I remember I was once taken up for a Jesuit, for no other reason but my profound taciturnity. It is from this misfortune, that to be out of harm's way, I have ever since affected crowds. He who comes into assemblies only to gratify his curiosity, and not to make a figure, enjoys the pleasures of retirement in a more exquisite degree, than he possibly could in his closet; the lover, the ambitious, and the miser, are followed thither by a worse crowd than any they can withdraw from. To be exempt from the passions with which others are tormented, is the only pleasing solitude. I can very justly say with the ancient sage, I am *never less alone than when alone*. As I am insignificant to the company in public places, and as it is visible I do not come thither, as most do, to show my self; I gratify the vanity of all who pretend to make an appearance, and have often as kind looks from well dressed gentlemen and ladies, as a poet would bestow upon one of his audience. There are so many gratifications attend this public sort of obscurity, that some little distastes I daily receive have lost their anguish; and I did the other day, without the least displeasure, overhear one say of me, *that strange fellow*; and another answer, *I have known the fellow's face these twelve years, and so must you; but I believe you are the first ever asked who he was.* There are, I must confess, many to whom my person is as well known as that of their nearest relations, who give themselves no further trouble

---

1: outstanding among mortals and most silent!

about calling me by my name or quality, but speak of me very currently by Mr. *what-d'ye-call-him*.

To make up for these trivial disadvantages, I have the high satisfaction of beholding all nature with an unprejudiced eye; and having nothing to do with men's passions or interests, I can with the greater sagacity consider their talents, manners, failings, and merits.

It is remarkable that those who want any one sense, possess the others with greater force and vivacity. Thus my want of, or rather resignation of speech, gives me all the advantages of a dumb man. I have, methinks, a more than ordinary penetration in seeing; and flatter my self that I have looked into the highest and lowest of mankind, and make shrewd guesses, without being admitted to their conversation, at the inmost thoughts and reflections of all whom I behold. It is from hence that good or ill fortune has no manner of force towards affecting my judgement. I see men flourishing in courts, and languishing in jails, without being prejudiced from their circumstances to their favour or disadvantage, but from their inward manner of bearing their condition, often pity the prosperous and admire the unhappy.

Those who converse with the dumb, know from the turn of their eyes, and the changes of their countenance, their sentiments of the objects before them. I have indulged my silence to such an extravagance, that the few who are intimate with me, answer my smiles with concurrent sentences, and argue to the very point I shak'd my head at without my speaking. Will Honeycomb[1] was very entertaining the other night at a play to a gentleman, who sat on his right hand, while I was at his left. The gentleman believed Will was talking to himself, when upon my looking with great approbation at a young thing in a box before us, he said, 'I am quite of another opinion: she has, I will allow, a very pleasing aspect, but methinks that simplicity in her countenance is rather childish than innocent.' When I observed her a second time, he said 'I grant her dress is very becoming, but perhaps the merit of that choice is owing to her mother; for though,' continued he, 'I allow a beauty to be as much to be commended for the elegance of her dress, as a wit for that of his language; yet if she has stolen the colour of her ribbands from another, or had advice about her trimmings, I shall not allow her the praise of dress, any more than I would call a plagiary an author.' When I threw my eye towards the next woman to her, Will spoke what I looked, according to his romantick imagination, in the following manner.

'Behold, you who dare, that charming virgin. Behold the beauty of her person chastised by the innocence of her thoughts. Chastity, good-nature, and affability, are the graces that play in her countenance; she knows she is handsome, but she knows she is good. Conscious beauty adorned with conscious virtue! What a spirit is there in those eyes! What a bloom in that person! How is the whole woman expressed in her appearance! Her air has the beauty of motion, and her look the force of language.'

It was prudence to turn away my eyes from this object and therefore I turned them to the thoughtless creatures who make up the lump of that sex, and

---

1: One of the stock characters introduced in *Spectator*, No. 2, whose participation will enliven the dramatic evolution of the paper. Honeycomb is a man-about-town, a 'well bred fine gentleman.'

move a knowing eye no more than the portraitures of insignificant people by ordinary painters, which are but pictures of pictures.

Thus the working of my own mind is the general entertainment of my life; I never enter into the commerce of discourse with any but my particular friends, and not in public even with them. Such an habit has perhaps raised in me uncommon reflections; but this effect I cannot communicate but by my writings. As my pleasures are almost wholly confined to those of the sight, I take it for a peculiar happiness that I have always had an easy and familiar admittance to the fair sex. If I never praised or flattered, I never belied or contradicted them. As these compose half the world, and are by the just complaisance and gallantry of our nation the more powerful part of our people, I shall dedicate a considerable share of these my speculations to their service, and shall lead the young through all the becoming duties of virginity, marriage, and widowhood. When it is a woman's day, in my works, I shall endeavour at a style and air suitable to their understanding. When I say this, I must be understood to mean, that I shall not lower but exalt the subjects I treat upon. Discourse for their entertainment, is not to be debased but refined. A man may appear learned, without talking sentences; as in his ordinary gesture he discovers he can dance, tho' he does not cut capers. In a word, I shall take it for the greatest glory of my work, if among reasonable women this paper may furnish *tea-table talk*. In order to it, I shall treat on matters which relate to females, as they are concerned to approach or fly from the other sex, or as they are tied to them by blood, interest, or affection. Upon this occasion I think it but reasonable to declare, that whatever skill I may have in speculation, I shall never betray what the eyes of lovers say to each other in my presence. At the same time I shall not think myself obliged, by this promise, to conceal any false protestations which I observe made by glances in public assemblies; but endeavour to make both sexes appear in their conduct what they are in their hearts. By this means love, during the time of my speculations, shall be carried on with the same sincerity as any other affair of less consideration. As this is the greatest concern, men shall be from henceforth liable to the greatest reproach for misbehaviour in it. Falsehood in love shall hereafter bear a blacker aspect, than infidelity in friendship, or villainy in business. For this great and good end, all breaches against that noble passion, the cement of society, shall be severely examined. But this, and all other matters loosely hinted at now, and in my former papers, shall have their proper place in my following discourses: the present writing is only to admonish the world, that they shall not find me an idle but a very busy Spectator.

ALEXANDER POPE (1688–1744)

Alexander Pope was the son of a linen merchant forced to leave London by the expulsion of Catholics. Brought up near Windsor, a childhood illness twisted his spine and stunted his growth. Socially excluded by religion and disfigurement, he cultivated his genius and by 1713 was acknowledged as the foremost poet of his generation. His fame began with *Essay on Criticism* (1711), and was confirmed by *The Rape of the Lock* (1712–14) and *Windsor Forest* (1713), a poem which discerns in the landscape of the Thames valley Britain's inheritance of a Greco-Roman imperial mission. He became the centre of the Scriblerus group – Swift, Gay, Arbuthnot, Prior, Wortley Montagu and others – that derided the rampant commercialism of the day and satirised Enlightenment belief in progress and universal reason. He secured personal wealth through the astute marketing of his brilliant versions of the *Iliad* (1715–20) and the *Odyssey* (1725–6). His later satire, *The Dunciad* (1728–43), his *Moral Essays* (1731-5) and *Essay on Man* evidence an increasing alienation. Pope produced an intellectually sophisticated verse marked by order, antitheses, prosodic cunning and controlled satirical bathos. Like Swift, he estranges perception by dignifying the trivial and debasing the august. His writing is steeped in contemporary reference and classical learning and abounds in word play and allusive wit. In *The Rape of the Lock*, he finds burlesque comedy in the failure of contemporary experience to support an epic account, yet paradoxically he elevates the banal through the comparison. In the first-written of his *Moral Essays*, his *Epistle to Burlington,* he extols the modest refinement of his friend's translation of Palladian architectural styles. His poetry thus joins in the vogue for neo-classicism in architecture and gardens, articulates its moral aesthetics, and appropriates an antique and sanctified dress to discipline dynamic bourgeois energies.

The Rape of the Lock, An Heroi-comical Poem

Written in the Year MDCCXII, To Mrs Arabella Fermor

Madam,

It will be in vain to deny that I have some regard for this piece, since I dedicate it to you. Yet you may bear me witness, it was intended only to divert a few young ladies, who have good sense and good humour enough to laugh not only at their sex's little unguarded follies, but at their own. But as it was communicated with the air of a secret, it soon found its way into the world. An imperfect copy having been offered to a bookseller, you had the good nature for my sake to consent to the publication of one more correct: this I was forced to, before I had executed half my design, for the machinery was entirely wanting to complete it.

The machinery, Madam, is a term invented by the critics, to signify that part which the deities, angels, or daemons are made to act in a poem: for the ancient poets are in one respect like many modern ladies; let an action be never so

---

Rape of the Lock: the poem is a comic commentary upon a trivial dispute between two Catholic families known to Pope, occasioned by the theft of a lock of hair belonging to Arabella Fermor by Lord Petre.

trivial in itself, they always make it appear of the utmost importance. These machines I determined to raise on a very new and odd foundation, the Rosicrucian[1], doctrine of spirits.

I know how disagreeable it is to make use of hard words before a lady; but 'tis so much the concern of a poet to have his works understood, and particularly by your sex, that you must give me leave to explain two or three difficult terms.

The Rosicrucians are a people I must bring you acquainted with. The best account I know of them is in a French book called *Le Comte de Gabalis*,[2] which both in its title and size is so like a novel, that many of the fair sex have read it for one by mistake. According to these gentlemen, the four elements are inhabited by spirits, which they call Sylphs, gnomes, nymphs, and salamanders. The gnomes or daemons of earth delight in mischief; but the Sylphs, whose habitation is in the air, are the best conditioned creatures imaginable. For they say, any mortals may enjoy the most intimate familiarities with these gentle spirits, upon a condition very easy to all true adepts, an inviolate preservation of chastity.

As to the following cantos, all the passages of them are as fabulous, as the vision at the beginning, or the transformation at the end (except the loss of your hair, which I always mention with reverence.) The human persons are as fictitious as the airy ones; and the character of Belinda, as it is now managed, resembles you in nothing but in beauty.

If this poem had as many graces as there are in your person, or in your mind, yet I could never hope it should pass through the world half so uncensured as you have done. But let its fortune be what it will, mine is happy enough, to have given me this occasion of assuring you that I am, with the truest esteem,

Madam,

Your most obedient, humble servant,

A. Pope

Nolueram, Belinda, tuos violare capillos;
Sed juvat, hoc precibus me tribuisse tuis.

Martial[3]

Canto I

What dire offence from am'rous causes springs,
What mighty quarrels rise from trivial things,
I sing – This verse to Caryll, Muse! is due:
This, ev'n Belinda may vouchsafe to view:
5   Slight is the subject, but not so the praise,

1: a secret society founded in 1429 which purported to understand the secrets of nature by the interpretation of magical signs. 2: a light erotic fantasy (published 1670) by the Abbé de Villars which uses Rosicrucianism as its mechanism. 3: Martial, Book 2, Epigram 86: 'I had not wanted, Belinda, to violate your hair, but it pleases me to pay you this tribute.' **Canto 1.** The canto's mechanism derives from arming the hero. **3 Caryll:** a mutual friend of Pope, Lord Petre and the Fermors.

If she inspire, and he approve my lays.
Say what strange motive, Goddess! could compel
A well-bred lord t'assault a gentle belle?
Oh say what stranger cause, yet unexplored,
10   Could make a gentle belle reject a lord?
In tasks so bold, can little men engage,
And in soft bosoms dwells such mighty rage?
   Sol through white curtains shot a tim'rous ray,
And op'd those eyes that must eclipse the day:
15   Now lapdogs give themselves the rousing shake,
And sleepless lovers, just at twelve, awake:
Thrice rung the bell, the slipper knocked the ground,
And the pressed watch returned a silver sound.
Belinda still her downy pillow pressed,
20   Her guardian Sylph prolonged the balmy rest:
'Twas he had summoned to her silent bed
The morning-dream that hovered o'er her head.
A youth more glitt'ring than a birth-night beau,
(That ev'n in slumber caused her cheek to glow)
25   Seemed to her ear his winning lips to lay,
And thus in whispers said, or seemed to say:
   'Fairest of mortals, thou distinguished care
Of thousand bright inhabitants of air!
If e'er one vision touched thy infant thought,
30   Of all the nurse and all the priest have taught;
Of airy elves by moonlight shadows seen,
The silver token, and the circled green,
Or virgins visited by angel-powers,
With golden crowns and wreaths of heav'nly flowers;
35   Hear and believe! thy own importance know,
Nor bound thy narrow views to things below.
Some secret truths, from learned pride concealed,
To maids alone and children are revealed:
What though no credit doubting wits may give?
40   The fair and innocent shall still believe.
Know then, unnumbered spirits round thee fly,
The light militia of the lower sky;
These, though unseen, are ever on the wing,
Hang o'er the box, and hover round the ring:
45   Think what an equipage thou hast in air,
And view with scorn two pages and a chair.
As now your own, our beings were of old,
And once enclosed in woman's beauteous mould;
Thence, by a soft transition, we repair

---

23 **birth-night beau:** a young man splendidly dressed to
celebrate a Royal birthday.   **44 ring:** a circular carriageway in Hyde Park, like theatre boxes, a place of display.
   45 **equipage:** carrriage, horses, and footmen.   **46 chair:**
Sedan chair.

50   From earthly vehicles to these of air.
      Think not, when woman's transient breath is fled,
      That all her vanities at once are dead;
      Succeeding vanities she still regards,
      And though she plays no more, o'erlooks the cards.
55   Her joy in gilded chariots, when alive,
      And love of ombre, after death survive.
      For when the fair in all their pride expire,
      To their first elements their souls retire:
      The sprites of fiery termagants in flame
60   Mount up, and take a salamander's name.
      Soft yielding minds to water glide away,
      And sip, with nymphs, their elemental tea.
      The graver prude sinks downward to a gnome,
      In search of mischief still on earth to roam.
65   The light coquettes in Sylphs aloft repair,
      And sport and flutter in the fields of air.
         'Know farther yet; whoever fair and chaste
      Rejects mankind, is by some Sylph embraced:
      For spirits, freed from mortal laws, with ease
70   Assume what sexes and what shapes they please.
      What guards the purity of melting maids,
      In courtly balls, and midnight masquerades,
      Safe from the treach'rous friend, the daring spark,
      The glance by day, the whisper in the dark,
75   When kind occasion prompts their warm desires,
      When music softens, and when dancing fires?
      'Tis but their Sylph, the wise celestials know,
      Though honour is the word with men below.
         'Some nymphs there are, too conscious of their face,
80   For life predestined to the gnomes' embrace.
      These swell their prospects and exalt their pride,
      When offers are disdained, and love denied.
      Then gay ideas crowd the vacant brain,
      While peers and dukes, and all their sweeping train,
85   And garters, stars, and coronets appear,
      And in soft sounds, "Your Grace" salutes their ear.
      'Tis these that early taint the female soul,
      Instruct the eyes of young coquettes to roll,
      Teach infant-cheeks a bidden blush to know,
90   And little hearts to flutter at a beau.
         'Oft, when the world imagine women stray,
      The Sylphs through mystic mazes guide their way,
      Through all the giddy circle they pursue,

---

56 **Ombre:** three-handed card game that figures largely   73 **spark:** 'a lively, showy, gay man' (Johnson).   85 **garters,**
in Canto III.   **stars:** badges of aristocratic distinction.

And old impertinence expel by new.
95   What tender maid but must a victim fall
To one man's treat, but for another's ball?
When Florio speaks, what virgin could withstand,
If gentle Damon did not squeeze her hand?
With varying vanities, from every part,
100   They shift the moving toyshop of their heart;
Where wigs with wigs, with sword-knots sword-knots strive,
Beaus banish beaus, and coaches coaches drive.
This erring mortals levity may call,
Oh blind to truth! the Sylphs contrive it all.
105   'Of these am I, who thy protection claim,
A watchful sprite, and Ariel is my name.
Late, as I ranged the crystal wilds of air,
In the clear mirror of thy ruling star
I saw, alas! some dread event impend,
110   Ere to the main this morning sun descend,
But heav'n reveals not what, or how, or where:
Warned by the Sylph, oh pious maid, beware!
This to disclose is all thy guardian can:
Beware of all, but most beware of man!'
115   He said; when Shock, who thought she slept too long,
Leaped up, and waked his mistress with his tongue.
'Twas then Belinda, if report say true,
Thy eyes first opened on a billet-doux;
Wounds, charms, and ardours, were no sooner read,
120   But all the vision vanished from thy head.
        And now, unveiled, the toilet stands displayed,
Each silver vase in mystic order laid.
. First, robed in white, the nymph intent adores,
With head uncovered, the cosmetic powers.
125   A heav'nly image in the glass appears,
To that she bends, to that her eyes she rears;
The inferior priestess, at her altar's side,
Trembling, begins the sacred rites of pride.
Unnumbered treasures ope at once, and here
130   The various off'rings of the world appear;
From each she nicely culls with curious toil,
And decks the goddess with the glitt'ring spoil.
This casket India's glowing gems unlocks,
And all Arabia breathes from yonder box.
135   The tortoise here and elephant unite,
Transformed to combs, the speckled, and the white.
Here files of pins extend their shining rows,

---

98 **Florio** etc.: 'classicised' names of typical figures of   118 **billet-doux**: love letter.   121 **et seq.**: an allusion to
the town.   100 **toyshop**: shop for the sale of baubles.   the arming of the hero in epic narratives.
101 **sword-knots**: silk ornaments to the hilt of a sword.

Puffs, powders, patches, bibles, billet-doux.
Now awful beauty puts on all its arms;
140 The fair each moment rises in her charms,
Repairs her smiles, awakens every grace,
And calls forth all the wonders of her face;
Sees by degrees a purer blush arise,
And keener lightnings quicken in her eyes.
145 The busy Sylphs surround their darling care,
These set the head, and those divide the hair,
Some fold the sleeve, whilst others plait the gown;
And Betty's praised for labours not her own.

Canto II

Not with more glories, in th' ethereal plain,
The sun first rises o'er the purpled main
Than, issuing forth, the rival of his beams
Launched on the bosom of the silver Thames.
5 Fair nymphs, and well-dressed youths around her shone,
But every eye was fixed on her alone.
On her white breast a sparkling cross she wore,
Which Jews might kiss, and infidels adore.
Her lively looks a sprightly mind disclose,
10 Quick as her eyes, and as unfixed as those:
Favours to none, to all she smiles extends;
Oft she rejects, but never once offends.
Bright as the sun, her eyes the gazers strike,
And, like the sun, they shine on all alike.
15 Yet graceful ease, and sweetness void of pride
Might hide her faults, if belles had faults to hide:
If to her share some female errors fall,
Look on her face, and you'll forget 'em all.
    This nymph, to the destruction of mankind,
20 Nourished two locks, which graceful hung behind
In equal curls, and well conspired to deck
With shining ringlets the smooth iv'ry neck.
Love in these labyrinths his slaves detains,
And mighty hearts are held in slender chains.
25 With hairy springes we the birds betray,
Slight lines of hair surprise the finny prey,
Fair tresses man's imperial race ensnare,
And beauty draws us with a single hair.
    Th' adventurous Baron the bright locks admired;
30 He saw, he wished, and to the prize aspired:
Resolved to win, he meditates the way,

---

147 **Betty:** generic name for a lady's maid at this time.   **Canto II:** The canto's mechanism derives from the epic quest, especially the *Aeneid*, xii–ix. **25 springes:** traps.

By force to ravish, or by fraud betray;
For when success a lover's toil attends,
Few ask, if fraud or force attained his ends.
35   For this, ere Phoebus rose, he had implored
Propitious heav'n, and every power adored,
But chiefly love – to love an altar built,
Of twelve vast French romances, neatly gilt.
There lay three garters, half a pair of gloves;
40   And all the trophies of his former loves;
With tender billet-doux he lights the pyre,
And breathes three am'rous sighs to raise the fire.
Then prostrate falls, and begs with ardent eyes
Soon to obtain, and long possess the prize:
45   The pow'rs gave ear, and granted half his prayer,
The rest, the winds dispersed in empty air.
    But now secure the painted vessel glides,
The sunbeams trembling on the floating tides;
While melting music steals upon the sky,
50   And softened sounds along the waters die;
Smooth flow the waves, the zephyrs gently play,
Belinda smiled, and all the world was gay.
All but the Sylph – with careful thought oppressed,
Th' impending woe sate heavy on his breast.
55   He summons straight his denizens of air;
The lucid squadrons round the sails repair:
Soft o'er the shrouds aerial whispers breathe,
That seemed but zephyrs to the train beneath.
Some to the sun their insect-wings unfold,
60   Waft on the breeze, or sink in clouds of gold;
Transparent forms, too fine for mortal sight,
Their fluid bodies half dissolved in light.
Loose to the wind their airy garments flew,
Thin glittering textures of the filmy dew,
65   Dipped in the richest tincture of the skies,
Where light disports in ever-mingling dyes,
While every beam new transient colours flings,
Colours that change whene'er they wave their wings.
Amid the circle, on the gilded mast,
70   Superior by the head, was Ariel placed;
His purple pinions opening to the sun,
He raised his azure wand, and thus begun:
    'Ye Sylphs and Sylphids, to your chief give ear,
Fays, fairies, genii, elves, and daemons hear!
75   Ye know the spheres and various tasks assigned
By laws eternal, to th' aerial kind.
Some in the fields of purest ether play,
And bask and whiten in the blaze of day.

Some guide the course of wand'ring orbs on high,
80 Or roll the planets through the boundless sky.
Some less refined, beneath the moon's pale light
Pursue the stars that shoot athwart the night,
Or suck the mists in grosser air below,
Or dip their pinions in the painted bow,
85 Or brew fierce tempests on the wintry main,
Or o'er the glebe distill the kindly rain.
Others on earth o'er human race preside,
Watch all their ways, and all their actions guide:
Of these the chief the care of nations own,
90 And guard with arms divine the British throne.
  'Our humbler province is to tend the fair,
Not a less pleasing, though less glorious care;
To save the powder from too rude a gale,
Nor let th' imprisoned essences exhale;
95 To draw fresh colours from the vernal flow'rs;
To steal from rainbows e'er they drop in show'rs
A brighter wash; to curl their waving hairs,
Assist their blushes, and inspire their airs;
Nay oft, in dreams, invention we bestow,
100 To change a flounce, or add a furbelow.
  'This day, black omens threat the brightest fair
That e'er deserved a watchful spirit's care;
Some dire disaster, or by force, or slight;
But what, or where, the fates have wrapped in night.
105 Whether the nymph shall break Diana's law,
Or some frail china jar receive a flaw;
Or stain her honour, or her new brocade;
Forget her prayers, or miss a masquerade;
Or lose her heart, or necklace at a ball;
110 Or whether Heaven has doomed that Shock must fall.
Haste then, ye spirits! to your charge repair:
The flutt'ring fan be Zephyretta's care;
The drops to thee, Brillante, we consign;
And, Momentilla, let the watch be thine;
115 Do thou, Crispissa, tend her favourite lock;
Ariel himself shall be the guard of Shock.
  'To fifty chosen Sylphs, of special note,
We trust th' important charge, the petticoat:
Oft have we known that sev'nfold fence to fail,
120 Though stiff with hoops, and armed with ribs of whale;
Form a strong line about the silver bound,
And guard the wide circumference around.

---

100 furbelow: apleated fabric ornament on a gown. 112 Zephyretta: this and the following names are
105 Diana's law: chastity.   satirical portraits of imaginary types.

'Whatever spirit, careless of his charge,
His post neglects, or leaves the fair at large,
125 Shall feel sharp vengeance soon o'ertake his sins,
Be stop't in vials, or transfixed with pins;
Or plunged in lakes of bitter washes lie,
Or wedged whole ages in a bodkin's eye:
Gums and pomatums shall his flight restrain,
130 While clogged he beats his silken wings in vain;
Or alum-styptics with contracting power
Shrink his thin essence like a rivelled flower:
Or, as Ixion fixed, the wretch shall feel
The giddy motion of the whirling mill,
135 In fumes of burning chocolate shall glow,
And tremble at the sea that froths below!'
    He spoke; the spirits from the sails descend;
Some, orb in orb, around the nymph extend,
Some thread the mazy ringlets of her hair,
140 Some hang upon the pendants of her ear;
With beating hearts the dire event they wait,
Anxious, and trembling for the birth of fate.

Canto III

Close by those meads, for ever crowned with flow'rs,
Where Thames with pride surveys his rising tow'rs,
There stands a structure of majestic frame,
Which from the neighb'ring Hampton takes its name.
5 Here Britain's statesmen oft the fall foredoom
Of foreign tyrants, and of nymphs at home;
Here thou, great Anna! whom three realms obey,
Dost sometimes counsel take – and sometimes tea.
    Hither the heroes and the nymphs resort,
10 To taste awhile the pleasures of a court;
In various talk th' instructive hours they passed,
Who gave the ball, or paid the visit last:
One speaks the glory of the British Queen,
And one describes a charming Indian screen;
15 A third interprets motions, looks, and eyes;
At every word a reputation dies.
Snuff, or the fan, supply each pause of chat,
With singing, laughing, ogling, and all that.

---

127 lie: a caustic washing solution produced by leaching wood ash. **128 bodkin:** here a needle, later an ornamental pin for the hair, then a dagger. **129 pomatum:** an ointment. **131 styptics:** astringent medicines. **132 rivelled:** shrivelled. **133 Ixion:** punished by Zeus for trying to win the love of Hera by being bound everlastingly to a wheel in the underworld.

Canto III: The machinery of this canto is taken from the idea of heroic sports and feasting, here realised in the card game, ombre, and tea. **4 Hampton:** Hampton Court, the royal residence west of London. **7 Anna:** Queen Anne. **three realms:** England, Ireland, Scotland. **8 tea:** drinking tea, chocolate and coffee were new, luxurious and expensive recreations.

Mean while, declining from the noon of day,
20 The sun obliquely shoots his burning ray;
The hungry judges soon the sentence sign,
And wretches hang that jury-men may dine;
The merchant from th' Exchange returns in peace,
And the long labours of the toilet cease –
25 Belinda now, whom thirst of fame invites,
Burns to encounter two adventurous knights,
At ombre singly to decide their doom;
And swells her breast with conquests yet to come.
Straight the three bands prepare in arms to join,
30 Each band the number of the sacred nine.
Soon as she spreads her hand, th' aerial guard
Descend, and sit on each important card:
First Ariel perched upon a Matadore,
Then each, according to the rank they bore;
35 For Sylphs, yet mindful of their ancient race,
Are, as when women, wondrous fond of place.
      Behold, four Kings in majesty revered,
With hoary whiskers and a forky beard;
And four fair Queens whose hands sustain a flower,
40 Th' expressive emblem of their softer power;
Four Knaves in garbs succinct, a trusty band,
Caps on their heads, and halberds in their hand;
And particoloured troops, a shining train,
Draw forth to combat on the velvet plain.
45   The skilful nymph reviews her force with care:
'Let Spades be trumps!' she said, and trumps they were.
      Now move to war her sable Matadores,
In show like leaders of the swarthy Moors.
Spadillio first, unconquerable lord!
50 Led off two captive trumps, and swept the board.
As many more Manillio forced to yield,
And marched a victor from the verdant field.
Him Basto followed, but his fate more hard
Gained but one trump and one plebeian card.
55 With his broad sabre next, a chief in years,
The hoary Majesty of Spades appears;
Puts forth one manly leg, to sight revealed;
The rest, his many-coloured robe concealed.
The rebel-Knave, who dares his prince engage,
60 Proves the just victim of his royal rage.
Ev'n mighty Pam, that kings and queens o'erthrew,

---

23 **Exchange:** the Royal Exchange, the centre of commercial and mercantile exchange. 33 **matadore:** highest card in ombre. 36 **place:** rank, privilege.

48–53 **Spadillio, Manillio, Basto:** cards of value in the game of ombre. 61 **Pam:** a card in the game of Loo (or Lu).

And mowed down armies in the fights of Lu,
Sad chance of war! now destitute of aid,
Falls undistinguished by the victor Spade!
65   Thus far both armies to Belinda yield;
Now to the Baron fate inclines the field.
His warlike Amazon her host invades,
Th' imperial consort of the crown of Spades.
The Club's black tyrant first her victim died,
70   Spite of his haughty mien, and barbarous pride:
What boots the regal circle on his head,
His giant limbs in state unwieldy spread;
That long behind he trails his pompous robe,
And of all monarchs only grasps the globe?
75   The Baron now his Diamonds pours apace;
Th' embroidered King who shows but half his face,
And his refulgent queen, with powers combined,
Of broken troops an easy conquest find.
Clubs, Diamonds, Hearts, in wild disorder seen,
80   With throngs promiscuous strow the level green.
Thus when dispersed a routed army runs,
Of Asia's troops, and Afric's sable sons,
With like confusion different nations fly,
Of various habit and of various dye,
85   The pierced battalions dis-united fall,
In heaps on heaps; one fate o'erwhelms them all.
    The Knave of Diamonds tries his wily arts,
And wins (oh shameful chance!) the Queen of Hearts.
At this, the blood the virgin's cheek forsook,
90   A livid paleness spreads o'er all her look;
She sees, and trembles at th' approaching ill,
Just in the jaws of ruin, and Codille.
And now, (as oft in some distempered state)
On one nice trick depends the gen'ral fate.
95   An Ace of Hearts steps forth: the King unseen
Lurked in her hand, and mourned his captive Queen:
He springs to vengeance with an eager pace,
And falls like thunder on the prostrate Ace.
The nymph exulting fills with shouts the sky;
100   The walls, the woods, and long canals reply.
    Oh thoughtless mortals! ever blind to fate,
Too soon dejected, and too soon elate!
Sudden these honours shall be snatched away,
And cursed for ever this victorious day.
105   For lo! the board with cups and spoons is crowned,
The berries crackle, and the mill turns round;

---

92 codille: defeat in ombre.   106 berries: coffee beans.

On shining altars of Japan they raise
The silver lamp; the fiery spirits blaze:
From silver spouts the grateful liquors glide,
110 While China's earth receives the smoking tide.
At once they gratify their scent and taste,
And frequent cups prolong the rich repast.
Straight hover round the fair her airy band;
Some, as she sipped, the fuming liquor fanned,
115 Some o'er her lap their careful plumes displayed,
Trembling, and conscious of the rich brocade.
Coffee (which makes the politician wise,
And see through all things with his half-shut eyes)
Sent up in vapours to the Baron's brain
120 New stratagems, the radiant lock to gain.
Ah cease, rash youth! desist ere 'tis too late,
Fear the just gods, and think of Scylla's fate!
Changed to a bird, and sent to flit in air,
She dearly pays for Nisus' injured hair!
125   But when to mischief mortals bend their will,
How soon they find fit instruments of ill?
Just then, Clarissa drew with tempting grace
A two-edged weapon from her shining case:
So ladies in romance assist their knight,
130 Present the spear, and arm him for the fight.
He takes the gift with reverence, and extends
The little engine on his finger's ends;
This just behind Belinda's neck he spread,
As o'er the fragrant steams she bends her head.
135 Swift to the lock a thousand sprites repair,
A thousand wings, by turns, blow back the hair;
And thrice they twitched the diamond in her ear;
Thrice she looked back, and thrice the foe drew near.
Just in that instant, anxious Ariel sought
140 The close recesses of the virgin's thought;
As on the nosegay in her breast reclined,
He watched th' ideas rising in her mind,
Sudden he viewed, in spite of all her art,
An earthly lover lurking at her heart.
145 Amazed, confused, he found his pow'r expired,
Resigned to fate, and with a sigh retired.
    The peer now spreads the glitt'ring forfex wide,
T'enclose the lock; now joins it, to divide.
Ev'n then, before the fatal engine closed,
150 A wretched Sylph too fondly interposed;
Fate urged the sheers, and cut the Sylph in twain,

---

107 **altars of Japan:** Japanned, black lacquered tables.   122 **Scylla:** Ovid, *Metamorphoses*, 8.   147 **forfex:** scissors.

(But airy substance soon unites again)
The meeting points the sacred hair dissever
From the fair head, for ever and for ever!
155   Then flashed the living lightning from her eyes,
And screams of horror rend th' affrighted skies.
Not louder shrieks to pitying heaven are cast,
When husbands, or when lapdogs breathe their last,
Or when rich china vessels, fallen from high,
160   In glittering dust, and painted fragments lie!
    'Let wreaths of triumph now my temples twine,'
The victor cried, 'the glorious prize is mine!
While fish in streams, or birds delight in air,
Or in a coach and six the British fair,
165   As long as *Atalantis* shall be read,
Or the small pillow grace a lady's bed,
While visits shall be paid on solemn days,
When numerous wax-lights in bright order blaze,
While nymphs take treats, or assignations give,
170   So long my honour, name, and praise shall live!
    What time would spare, from steel receives its date,
And monuments, like men, submit to fate!
Steel could the labour of the Gods destroy,
And strike to dust th' imperial tow'rs of Troy;
175   Steel could the works of mortal pride confound,
And hew triumphal arches to the ground.
What wonder then, fair nymph! thy hairs should feel
The conqu'ring force of unresisted steel?

Canto IV

But anxious cares the pensive nymph oppressed,
And secret passions laboured in her breast.
Not youthful kings in battle seized alive,
Not scornful virgins who their charms survive,
5   Not ardent lovers robbed of all their bliss,
Not ancient ladies when refused a kiss,
Not tyrants fierce that unrepenting die,
Not Cynthia when her manteau's pinned awry,
E'er felt such rage, resentment, and despair,
10   As thou, sad virgin! for thy ravished hair.
    For, that sad moment, when the Sylphs withdrew,
And Ariel weeping from Belinda flew,
Umbriel, a dusky, melancholy sprite,
As ever sullied the fair face of light,

---

165 Atalantis: *The New Atalantis* by Delarivière Manley (1709), a popular scandalous novel.   **Canto IV:** Canto IV follows the journey to the underworld, especially the *Aeneid*, VI.

15   Down to the central earth, his proper scene,
Repaired to search the gloomy Cave of Spleen.
    Swift on his sooty pinions flits the gnome,
And in a vapour reached the dismal dome.
No cheerful breeze this sullen region knows,
20   The dreaded east is all the wind that blows.
Here, in a grotto, sheltered close from air,
And screened in shades from day's detested glare,
She sighs for ever on her pensive bed,
Pain at her side, and megrim at her head.
25   Two handmaids wait the throne: alike in place,
But diff'ring far in figure and in face.
Here stood ill-nature like an ancient maid,
Her wrinkled form in black and white arrayed;
With store of prayers, for mornings, nights, and noons,
30   Her hand is filled; her bosom with lampoons.
    There Affectation, with a sickly mien,
Shows in her cheek the roses of eighteen,
Practised to lisp, and hang the head aside,
Faints into airs, and languishes with pride,
35   On the rich quilt sinks with becoming woe,
Wrapped in a gown, for sickness, and for show.
The fair ones feel such maladies as these,
When each new night-dress gives a new disease.
    A constant vapour o'er the palace flies;
40   Strange phantoms rising as the mists arise;
Dreadful, as hermit's dreams in haunted shades,
Or bright as visions of expiring maids.
Now glaring fiends, and snakes on rolling spires,
Pale spectres, gaping tombs, and purple fires:
45   Now lakes of liquid gold, Elysian scenes,
And crystal domes, and angels in machines.
    Unnumbered throngs on every side are seen,
Of bodies changed to various forms by spleen.
Here living teapots stand, one arm held out,
50   One bent; the handle this, and that the spout:
A pipkin there like Homer's tripod walks;
Here sighs a jar, and there a goose-pie talks;
Men prove with child, as powerful fancy works,
And maids turned bottles, call aloud for corks.
55   Safe passed the gnome through this fantastic band,
A branch of healing spleenwort in his hand.
Then thus addressed the pow'r – 'Hail wayward Queen!
Who rule the sex to fifty from fifteen:

---

16 **Spleen**: the organ of melancholy. **18 vapour**: a   **24 megrim**: a headache. **25 wait**: await orders from.
common term for a headache or depression.   **40 et seq.**: the scene recalls contemporary pantomimes.

Parent of vapours and of female wit,
60   Who give th' hysteric or poetic fit,
On various tempers act by various ways,
Make some take physic, others scribble plays;
Who cause the proud their visits to delay,
And send the godly in a pet, to pray.
65   A nymph there is, that all thy pow'r disdains,
And thousands more in equal mirth maintains.
But oh! if e'er thy gnome could spoil a grace,
Or raise a pimple on a beauteous face,
Like citron-waters matrons' cheeks inflame,
70   Or change complexions at a losing game;
If e'er with airy horns I planted heads,
Or rumpled petticoats, or tumbled beds,
Or caused suspicion when no soul was rude,
Or discomposed the head-dress of a prude,
75   Or e'er to costive lap-dog gave disease,
Which not the tears of brightest eyes could ease:
Hear me, and touch Belinda with chagrin;
That single act gives half the world the spleen.'
    The goddess with a discontented air
80   Seems to reject him, though she grants his prayer.
A wondrous bag with both her hands she binds,
Like that where once Ulysses held the winds;
There she collects the force of female lungs,
Sighs, sobs, and passions, and the war of tongues.
85   A vial next she fills with fainting fears,
Soft sorrows, melting griefs, and flowing tears.
The gnome rejoicing bears her gifts away,
Spreads his black wings, and slowly mounts to day.
    Sunk in Thalestris' arms the nymph he found,
90   Her eyes dejected and her hair unbound.
Full o'er their heads the swelling bag he rent,
And all the furies issued at the vent.
Belinda burns with more than mortal ire,
And fierce Thalestris fans the rising fire.
95   O wretched maid!' she spread her hands, and cried,
(While Hampton's echoes, 'wretched maid!' replied)
'Was it for this you took such constant care
The bodkin, comb, and essence to prepare?
For this your locks in paper-durance bound,
100   For this with tort'ring irons wreathed around?
For this with fillets strained your tender head,

---

64 **pet:** in a sulk, a petulant mood.   69 **citron-waters:**   77 **chagrin:** melancholy.   82 **Ulysses:** *Odyssey*, X.
brandy with lemon.   72 **petticoats:** then a visible skirt,   89 **Thalestris:** Queen of the Amazons.
not an item of underwear.

And bravely bore the double loads of lead?
Gods! shall the ravisher display your hair,
While the fops envy, and the ladies stare!,
105 Honour forbid! at whose unrivalled shrine
Ease, pleasure, virtue, all, our sex resign.
Methinks already I your tears survey,
Already hear the horrid things they say,
Already see you a degraded toast,
110 And all your honour in a whisper lost!
How shall I then, your helpless fame defend?
'Twill then be infamy to seem your friend!
And shall this prize, th' inestimable prize,
Exposed through crystal to the gazing eyes,
115 And heightened by the diamond's circling rays,
On that rapacious hand for ever blaze?
Sooner shall grass in Hyde Park Circus grow,
And wits take lodgings in the sound of Bow;
Sooner let earth, air, sea, to chaos fall,
120 Men, monkeys, lap-dogs, parrots, perish all!'
       She said; then raging to Sir Plume repairs,
And bids her beau demand the precious hairs:
(Sir Plume of amber snuff-box justly vain,
And the nice conduct of a clouded cane)
125 With earnest eyes, and round unthinking face,
He first the snuff-box opened, then the case,
And thus broke out – 'My Lord, why, what the devil?
Z—ds! damn the lock! 'fore Gad, you must be civil!
Plague on't! 'tis past a jest – nay prithee, pox!
130 Give her the hair' – he spoke, and rapped his box.
       'It grieves me much,' replied the peer again,
'Who speaks so well should ever speak in vain.
But by this lock, this sacred lock I swear,
(Which never more shall join its parted hair,
135 Which never more its honours shall renew,
Clipped from the lovely head where late it grew)
That while my nostrils draw the vital air,
This hand, which won it, shall for ever wear.'
He spoke, and speaking, in proud triumph spread
140 The long-contended honours of her head.
       But Umbriel, hateful gnome! forbears not so;
He breaks the vial whence the sorrows flow.
Then see! the nymph in beauteous grief appears,
Her eyes half-languishing, half-drowned in tears;

---

102 **lead**: thin strips of lead used in hairdressing to make curls. **109 toast**: a celebrated woman to whom toasts are drunk. **118 Bow**: St Mary le Bow, i.e. in the mercantile city rather than in fashionable Westminster. **121 Sir Plume**: a man of fashion. **124 clouded cane**: an amber-headed walking-stick. **133**: this line echoes *The Iliad*, I, 309. **141 Umbriel**: spirit opposed to Ariel.

145   On her heaved bosom hung her drooping head,
Which, with a sigh, she raised, and thus she said:
   'For ever cursed be this detested day,
Which snatched my best, my fav'rite curl away!
Happy! ah ten times happy had I been,
150   If Hampton-Court these eyes had never seen!
Yet am not I the first mistaken maid,
By love of courts to num'rous ills betrayed.
Oh had I rather un-admired remained
In some lone isle, or distant northern land;
155   Where the gilt chariot never marks the way,
Where none learn ombre, none e'er taste bohea!
There kept my charms concealed from mortal eye,
Like roses that in deserts bloom and die.
What moved my mind with youthful lords to roam?
160   Oh had I stayed, and said my prayers at home!
'Twas this, the morning omens seemed to tell;
Thrice from my trembling hand the patch-box fell;
The tottering china shook without a wind,
Nay, Poll sat mute, and Shock was most unkind!
165   A Sylph too warned me of the threats of fate,
In mystic visions, now believed too late!
See the poor remnants of these slighted hairs!
My hands shall rend what ev'n thy rapine spares:
These, in two sable ringlets taught to break,
170   Once gave new beauties to the snowy neck;
The sister-lock now sits uncouth, alone,
And in its fellow's fate foresees its own;
Uncurled it hangs, the fatal sheers demands,
And tempts once more thy sacrilegious hands.
175   Oh hadst thou, cruel! been content to seize
Hairs less in sight, or any hairs but these!'

Canto V

   She said: the pitying audience melt in tears,
But Fate and Jove had stopped the Baron's ears.
In vain Thalestris with reproach assails,
For who can move when fair Belinda fails?
5   Not half so fixed the Trojan could remain,
While Anna begged and Dido raged in vain.
Then grave Clarissa graceful waved her fan;
Silence ensued, and thus the nymph began:
   Say why are beauties praised and honoured most,

147: lines 147 ff echo *The Iliad*, 18, 107 ff. **156 bohea:**   Canto V, 1–6: see *Aeneid*, IV, for Dido's tale. **7 et seq.:**
a kind of tea. **162 patch-box:** make-up box.   see Sarpendon to Glaucus, *Iliad*, XII (trans. Pope 1709).

10 The wise man's passion, and the vain man's toast?
Why decked with all that land and sea afford,
Why angels called, and angel-like adored?
Why round our coaches crowd the white-gloved beaus,
Why bows the side-box from its inmost rows?
15 How vain are all these glories, all our pains,
Unless good sense preserve what beauty gains:
That men may say, when we the front-box grace,
Behold the first in virtue, as in face!
Oh! if to dance all night, and dress all day,
20 Charmed the smallpox, or chased old age away;
Who would not scorn what huswife's cares produce,
Or who would learn one earthly thing of use?
To patch, nay ogle, might become a saint,
Nor could it sure be such a sin to paint.
25 But since, alas! frail beauty must decay,
Curled or uncurled, since locks will turn to grey;
Since painted, or not painted, all shall fade,
And she who scorns a man, must die a maid;
What then remains but well our power to use,
30 And keep good-humour still whate'er we lose?
And trust me, dear! good-humour can prevail,
When airs, and flights, and screams, and scolding fail.
Beauties in vain their pretty eyes may roll;
Charms strike the sight, but merit wins the soul.'
35 So spoke the dame, but no applause ensued;
Belinda frowned, Thalestris called her prude.
'To arms, to arms!' the fierce virago cries,
And swift as lightning to the combat flies.
All side in parties and begin th' attack;
40 Fans clap, silks rustle and tough whalebones crack;
Heroes' and heroines' shouts confusedly rise,
And bass, and treble voices strike the skies.
No common weapons in their hands are found,
Like gods they fight, nor dread a mortal wound.
45 So when bold Homer makes the gods engage,
And heavenly breasts with human passions rage;
'Gainst Pallas, Mars; Latona, Hermes arms;
And all Olympus rings with loud alarms:
Jove's thunder roars, heav'n trembles all around,
50 Blue Neptune storms, the bellowing deeps resound:
Earth shakes her nodding towers, the ground gives way,
And the pale ghosts start at the flash of day!
Triumphant Umbriel on a sconce's height
Clapped his glad wings, and sate to view the fight:

---

24 paint: make-up.   **37** virago: warrior woman.

55 Propped on their bodkin spears, the sprites survey
The growing combat, or assist the fray.
    While through the press enraged Thalestris flies,
And scatters deaths around from both her eyes,
A beau and witling perished in the throng,
60 One died in metaphor, and one in song.
'O cruel nymph! a living death I bear,'
Cried Dapperwit, and sunk beside his chair.
A mournful glance Sir Fopling upwards cast,
'Those eyes are made so killing' – was his last:
65 Thus on Maeander's flowery margin lies
Th' expiring swan, and as he sings he dies.
    When bold Sir Plume had drawn Clarissa down,
Chloe stepped in, and killed him with a frown;
She smiled to see the doughty hero slain,
70 But, at her smile, the beau revived again.
    Now Jove suspends his golden scales in air,
Weighs the men's wits against the lady's hair;
The doubtful beam long nods from side to side;
At length the wits mount up, the hairs subside.
75 See fierce Belinda on the Baron flies,
With more than usual lightning in her eyes;
Nor feared the chief th' unequal fight to try,
Who sought no more than on his foe to die.
But this bold Lord with manly strength endued,
80 She with one finger and a thumb subdued:
Just where the breath of life his nostrils drew,
A charge of snuff the wily virgin threw;
The gnomes direct, to ev'ry atom just,
The pungent grains of titillating dust.
85 Sudden, with starting tears each eye o'erflows,
And the high dome re-echoes to his nose.
    'Now meet thy fate,' the incensed Belinda cried,
And drew a deadly bodkin from her side.
(The same, his ancient personage to deck,
90 Her great great grandsire wore about his neck
In three seal-rings; which after, melted down,
Formed a vast buckle for his widow's gown:
Her infant grandame's whistle next it grew,
The bells she jingled, and the whistle blew;
95 Then in a bodkin graced her mother's hairs,
Which long she wore, and now Belinda wears.)
    'Boast not my fall,' he cried, 'insulting foe!
Thou by some other shalt be laid as low.

---

59 **witling:** a baby wit.   62 **Dapperwit:** a wit and man   63 **Sir Fopling:** Sir Fopling Flutter, the main character
of fashion in Wycherley's *Love in a Wood.*   in Etherege's popular play, *The Man of Mode.*

Nor think, to die dejects my lofty mind;
100 All that I dread is leaving you behind!
Rather than so, ah let me still survive,
And burn in Cupid's flames, – but burn alive.'
        'Restore the lock!' she cries; and all around
'Restore the lock!' the vaulted roofs rebound.
105 Not fierce Othello in so loud a strain
Roared for the handkerchief that caused his pain.
But see how oft ambitious aims are crossed,
And chiefs contend 'till all the prize is lost!
The lock, obtained with guilt, and kept with pain,
110 In every place is sought, but sought in vain:
With such a prize no mortal must be blesst,
So heav'n decrees! with heav'n who can contest?
        Some thought it mounted to the lunar sphere,
Since all things lost on earth, are treasured there.
115 There heroes' wits are kept in pond'rous vases,
And beaus' in snuff-boxes and tweezer-cases.
There broken vows, and death-bed alms are found,
And lovers' hearts with ends of ribband bound;
The courtier's promises, and sick man's prayers,
120 The smiles of harlots, and the tears of heirs,
Cages for gnats, and chains to yoke a flea;
Dried butterflies, and tomes of casuistry.
        But trust the Muse – she saw it upward rise,
Though marked by none but quick, poetic eyes:
125 (So Rome's great founder to the heavens withdrew,
To Proculus alone confessed in view.)
A sudden star, it shot through liquid air,
And drew behind a radiant trail of hair.
Not Berenice's locks first rose so bright,
130 The heavens bespangling with dishevelled light.
The Sylphs behold it kindling as it flies,
And pleased pursue its progress through the skies.
        This the *beau-monde* shall from the Mall survey,
And hail with music its propitious ray.
135 This, the blessed lover shall for Venus take,
And send up vows from Rosamonda's lake.
This Partridge soon shall view in cloudless skies,
When next he looks through Galileo's eyes;
And hence th' egregious wizard shall foredoom
140 The fate of Louis, and the fall of Rome.
        Then cease, bright nymph! to mourn thy ravished hair,
Which adds new glory to the shining sphere!

---

126 **Proculus:** the last person to see Romulus, founder of Rome.   129 **Berenice:** wife of the Egyptian Ptolemy III, a lock of whose hair became a constellation.   133 **Mall:** a fashionable walk in St James's park.   136 **Rosamunda's lake:** pond in St James's park.   138 **Galileo's eyes:** the telescope.   140 **Louis:** Louis XIV of France.

Not all the tresses that fair head can boast
Shall draw such envy as the lock you lost.
145 For, after all the murders of your eye,
When, after millions slain, yourself shall die;
When those fair suns shall set, as set they must,
And all those tresses shall be laid in dust;
This lock, the Muse shall consecrate to fame,
150 And mid'st the stars inscribe Belinda's name!

An Epistle to Richard Boyle, Earl of Burlington

Of the Use of Riches

'Tis strange, the miser should his cares employ
To gain those riches he can ne'er enjoy.
Is it less strange, the prodigal should waste
His wealth, to purchase what he ne'er can taste?
5 Not for himself he sees, or hears, or eats;
Artists must choose his pictures, music, meats:
He buys for Topham, drawings and designs,
For Pembroke statues, dirty gods, and coins;
Rare monkish manuscripts for Hearne alone,
10 And books for Mead, and butterflies for Sloane.
Think we all these are for himself? no more
Than his fine wife, alas! or finer whore.
For what has Virro painted, built, and planted?
Only to show, how many tastes he wanted.
15 What brought Sir Visto's ill got wealth to waste?
Some demon whispered, 'Visto! have a taste.'
Heaven visits with a taste the wealthy fool,
And needs no rod but Ripley with a rule.
See! sportive fate, to punish awkward pride,
20 Bids Bubo build, and sends him such a Guide:
A standing sermon, at each year's expense,
That never coxcomb reached magnificence!
    You show us, Rome was glorious, not profuse,
And pompous buildings once were things of use.
25 Yet shall (my Lord) your just, your noble rules
Fill half the land with imitating fools;
Who random drawings from your sheets shall take,
And of one beauty many blunders make;
Load some vain church with old theatric state,
30 Turn arcs of triumph to a garden-gate;

---

6 et seq.: the poem contrasts the lack of taste of many contemporary collectors, painters and architects with the good sense of the Earl of Burlington (1695–1753), Pope's friend and patron. Burlington, a prominent collector and architect, followed Inigo Jones in adapting the work of the Venetian Andrea Palladio (1508–80) to English circumstance. Palladio himself had returned to Vitruvius (*floruit* 50BC) to reinvigorate the Latin architectural tradition.

Reverse your ornaments, and hang them all
On some patched dog-hole eked with ends of wall,
Then clap four slices of pilaster on't,
That, laced with bits of rustic, makes a front:
35 Or call the winds through long arcades to roar,
Proud to catch cold at a Venetian door;
Conscious they act a true Palladian part,
And if they starve, they starve by rules of art.
  Oft have you hinted to your brother peer,
40 A certain truth, which many buy too dear:
Something there is, more needful than expense,
And something previous ev'n to taste – 'tis sense:
Good sense, which only is the gift of heaven,
And though no science, fairly worth the seven:
45 A light, which in yourself you must perceive;
Jones and Le Nôtre have it not to give.
  To build, to plant, whatever you intend,
To rear the column, or the arch to bend,
To swell the terrace, or to sink the grot;
50 In all, let nature never be forgot.
But treat the goddess like a modest fair,
Nor over-dress, nor leave her wholly bare;
Let not each beauty everywhere be spied,
Where half the skill is decently to hide.
55 He gains all points, who pleasingly confounds,
Surprises, varies, and conceals the bounds.
  Consult the genius of the place in all;
That tells the waters or to rise, or fall,
Or helps th'ambitious hill the heavens to scale,
60 Or scoops in circling theatres the vale;
Calls in the country, catches opening glades,
Joins willing woods, and varies shades from shades;
Now breaks, or now directs, th' intending lines,
Paints as you plant, and as you work, designs.
65 Still follow sense, of every art the soul,
Parts answering parts shall slide into a whole,
Spontaneous beauties all around advance,
Start ev'n from difficulty, strike from chance;
Nature shall join you; time shall make it grow
70 A work to wonder at – perhaps a Stowe.
Without it, proud Versailles! thy glory falls,
And Nero's terraces desert their walls:
The vast parterres a thousand hands shall make,

---

46 **Jones and Le Nôtre:** Inigo Jones (1573–1652), see note to line 6 above. André Le Nôtre (1613–1700) laid out the gardens at the *Palais de Versailles.*

70 **Stowe:** famous house in Buckinghamshire, seat of Lord Viscount Cobham. The gardens were a foremost example of the English landscape school of design.

Lo! Cobham comes, and floats them with a lake:
75   Or cut wide views through mountains to the plain,
You'll wish your hill or sheltered seat again.
Ev'n in an ornament its place remark,
Nor in an hermitage set Dr Clarke.
      Behold Villario's ten-years' toil complete;
80   His arbours darken, his espaliers meet;
The wood supports the plain, the parts unite,
And strength of shade contends with strength of light:
A waving glow the bloomy beds display,
Blushing in bright diversities of day,
85   With silver-quivering rills meand o'er –
Enjoy them, you! Villario can no more;
Tired of the scene parterres and fountains yield,
He finds at last he better likes a field.
      Through his young woods how pleased Sabinus strayed
90   Or sat delighted in the thickening shade,
With annual joy the reddening shoots to greet,
Or see the stretching branches long to meet.
His son's fine taste an opener vista loves,
Foe to the dryads of his father's groves,
95   One boundless green, or flourished carpet views,
With all the mournful family of yews;
The thriving plants ignoble broomsticks made,
Now sweep those alleys they were born to shade.
At Timon's villa let us pass a day,
100   Where all cry out, 'What sums are thrown away!'
So proud, so grand, of that stupendous air,
Soft and agreeable come never there.
Greatness, with Timon, dwells in such a draught
As brings all Brobdignag before your thought.
105   To compass this, his building is a town,
His pond an ocean, his parterre a down:
Who but must laugh, the master when he sees?
A puny insect, shivering at a breeze.
Lo! what huge heaps of littleness around!
110   The whole, a laboured quarry above ground.
Two cupids squirt before: a lake behind
Improves the keenness of the northern wind.
His gardens next your admiration call,
On every side you look, behold the wall!
115   No pleasing intricacies intervene,
No artful wildness to perplex the scene;
Grove nods at grove, each alley has a brother,

---

78 Dr Clarke: Samuel Clarke (1675–1729), a famous
contemporary philosopher.   **104 Brobdignag:** scene of *Gullliver's Travels*, Book 2.
The Brobignagians are giants.

And half the platform just reflects the other.
The suffering eye inverted nature sees,
120 Trees cut to statues, statues thick as trees,
With here a fountain, never to be played,
And there a summer-house, that knows no shade.
Here Amphitrite sails through myrtle bowers;
There gladiators fight, or die, in flowers;
125 Un-watered see the drooping sea-horse mourn,
And swallows roost in Nilus' dusty urn.
  My Lord advances with majestic mien,
Smit with the mighty pleasure, to be seen:
But soft – by regular approach – not yet –
130 First through the length of yon hot terrace sweat,
And when up ten steep slopes you've dragged your thighs,
Just at his study-door he'll bless your eyes.
  His study! with what authors is it stored?
In books, not authors, curious is my lord;
135 To all their dated backs he turns you round:
These Aldus printed, those Du Suëil has bound.
Lo some are vellum, and the rest as good
For all his Lordship knows, but they are wood.
For Locke or Milton 'tis in vain to look,
140 These shelves admit not any modern book.
And now the chapel's silver bell you hear,
That summons you to all the pride of prayer:
Light quirks of music, broken and uneven,
Make the soul dance upon a jig to heaven.
145 On painted ceilings you devoutly stare,
Where sprawl the saints of Verrio or Laguerre,
On gilded clouds in fair expansion lie,
And bring all paradise before your eye.
To rest, the cushion and soft dean invite,
150 Who never mentions hell to ears polite.
  But hark! the chiming clocks to dinner call;
A hundred footsteps scrape the marble hall:
The rich buffet well-coloured serpents grace,
And gaping Tritons spew to wash your face.
155 Is this a dinner? this a genial room?
No, 'tis a temple, and a hecatomb,
A solemn sacrifice, performed in state,
You drink by measure, and to minutes eat.
So quick retires each flying course, you'd swear
160 Sancho's dread doctor and his wand were there.

---

123 Amphitrite: Neptune's wife.   **126 Nilus:** the Nile.   **136 Aldus ... Du Suëil:** Aldo Manutio (1450–1515), Augustin Deseuil (1663–1721), early book makers.   **146 Verrio or Laguerre:** Antonio Verrio (1630–1707) and Louis Laguerre (1663–1721), famous ceiling painters.   **160 Sancho's:** Sancho Panza in *Don Quixote.*

Between each act the trembling salvers ring,
From soup to sweet-wine, and 'God bless the King'.
In plenty starving, tantalized in state,
And complaisantly helped to all I hate,
165   Treated, caressed, and tired, I take my leave,
Sick of his civil pride from morn to eve;
I curse such lavish cost, and little skill,
And swear no day was ever passed so ill.
     Yet hence the poor are clothed, the hungry fed;
170   Health to himself, and to his infants bread
The labourer bears: what his hard heart denies,
His charitable vanity supplies.
     Another age shall see the golden ear
Imbrown the slope, and nod on the parterre,
175   Deep harvests bury all his pride has planned,
And laughing Ceres reassume the land.
     Who then shall grace, or who improve the soil?
Who plants like Bathurst, or who builds like Boyle.
'Tis use alone that sanctifies expense,
180   And splendour borrows all her rays from sense.
     His father's acres who enjoys in peace,
Or makes his neighbours glad, if he increase;
Whose cheerful tenants bless their yearly toll,
Yet to their Lord owe more than to the soil;
185   Whose ample lawns are not ashamed to feed
The milky heifer and deserving steed;
Whose rising forests, not for pride or show,
But future buildings, future navies grow:
Let his plantations stretch from down to down,
190   First shade a country, and then raise a town.
     You too proceed! make falling arts your care,
Erect new wonders, and the old repair;
Jones and Palladio to themselves restore,
And be whate'er Vitruvius was before:
195   Till Kings call forth th' idea's of your mind,
Proud to accomplish what such hands design'd,
Bid harbors open, public ways extend,
Bid temples, worthier of the God, ascend;
Bid the broad arch the dang'rous flood contain,
200   The mole projected break the roaring main;
Back to his bounds their subject sea command,
And roll the obedient rivers thro' the land;
These honours, peace to happy Britain brings,
These are imperial works, and worthy kings.

---

176 Ceres: Greek godess of agriculture.   **178** Bathurst: Tory MP, friend of Pope and keen gardener.

LADY MARY WORTLEY MONTAGU
(1689–1762)

The oldest daughter of a Duke with literary inclinations, Mary Wortley Montagu developed her own education in her father's library. In 1712 she eloped with and married a Whig MP who served as ambassador to Turkey from 1716 to 1718. One enormous consequence was that on her return Montagu introduced small pox inoculation into England; another was her remarkable *Embassy Letters* (published 1763) which describe the private lives of Turkish women. She was celebrated in London society as a beauty and a wit and was a respected member of the Scriblerus circle which included Pope, Addison, Steele and Gay. In 1728 she was satirised in *The Dunciad*, perhaps because she did not reciprocate Pope's affections, and spent her last decades living in France and Italy. Her *Town Eclogues* were published in 1716.

From Six Town Eclogues, Saturday, The Small-Pox

Flavia

The wretched Flavia, on her couch reclined,
Thus breathed the anguish of a wounded mind.
A glass reversed in her right hand she bore,
For now she shunned the face she sought before.
5   'How am I changed! alas! how am I grown
A frightful spectre, to myself unknown!
Where's my complexion? where the radiant bloom,
That promised happiness for years to come?
Then, with what pleasure I this face surveyed!
10 To look once more, my visits oft delayed!
Charmed with the view, a fresher red would rise,
And a new life shot sparkling from my eyes!
Ah! faithless glass, my wonted bloom restore!
Alas! I rave, that bloom is now no more!
15 'The greatest good the gods on men bestow,
Ev'n youth itself, to me is useless now.
There was a time (oh! that I could forget!)
Then opera-tickets poured before my feet;
And at the Ring, where brightest beauties shine,
20 The earliest cherries of the spring were mine.
Witness, O Lillie, and thou, Motteux, tell,
How much japan these eyes have made you sell.
With what contempt ye saw me oft despise
The humble offer of the raffled prize;
25 For at each raffle still the prize I bore,

---

19 Ring: circular carriageway in Hyde Park.   **22 japan:** black lacquer-work.

With scorn rejected, or with triumph wore.
Now beauty's fled, and presents are no more.
　'For me the patriot has the House forsook,
And left debates to catch a passing look;
30　For me the soldier has soft verses writ;
For me the beau has aimed to be a wit.
For me the wit to nonsense was betrayed;
The gamester has for me his dun delayed,
And overseen the card I would have paid.
35　The bold and haughty by success made vain,
Awed by my eyes, has trembled to complain:
The bashful squire, touched with a wish unknown,
Has dared to speak with spirit not his own:
Fired by one wish, all did alike adore;
40　Now beauty's fled, and lovers are no more.
　'As round the room I turn my weeping eyes,
New unaffected scenes of sorrow rise.
Far from my sight that killing picture bear,
The face disfigure, or the canvas tear!
45　That picture, which with pride I used to show,
The lost resemblance but upbraids me now.
And thou, my toilette, where I oft have sat,
While hours unheeded passed in deep debate,
How curls should fall, or where a patch to place;
50　If blue or scarlet best became my face;
Now on some happier nymph your aid bestow;
On fairer heads, ye useless jewels, glow!
No borrowed lustre can my charms restore,
Beauty is fled, and dress is now no more.
55　'Ye meaner beauties, I permit you shine;
Go triumph in the hearts that once were mine;
But, midst your triumphs with confusion know,
'Tis to my ruin all your charms ye owe.
Would pitying heaven restore my wonted mien,
60　Ye still might move unthought of and unseen:
But oh, how vain, how wretched is the boast
Of beauty faded, and of empire lost!
What now is left but weeping to deplore
My beauty fled, and empire now no more?
65　'Ye cruel chymists, what withheld your aid?
Could no pomatums save a trembling maid?
How false and trifling is that art you boast;
No art can give me back my beauty lost!
In tears, surrounded by my friends I lay,
70　Masked o'er, and trembling at the light of day;

---

28 **House:** Parliament.　33 **dun:** bill.　　49 **patch:** a cosmetic spot.　66 **pomatums:** cosmetics.

Mirmillo came my fortune to deplore
(A golden-headed cane well carved he bore):
'Cordials', he cried, 'my spirits must restore!'
Beauty is fled, and spirit is no more!
75 Galen the grave, officious Squirt was there,
With fruitless grief and unavailing care:
Machaon too, the great Machaon, known
By his red cloak and his superior frown;
"And why," he cried, "this grief and this despair?
80 You shall again be well, again be fair;
Believe my oath" (with that an oath he swore);
False was his oath! my beauty is no more.
　'Cease, hapless maid, no more thy tale pursue,
Forsake mankind, and bid the world adieu.
85 Monarchs and beauties rule with equal sway,
All strive to serve, and glory to obey:
Alike unpitied when deposed they grow,
Men mock the idol of their former vow.
　'Adieu, ye parks – in some obscure recess,
90 Where gentle streams will weep at my distress,
Where no false friend will in my grief take part,
And mourn my ruin with a joyful heart;
There let me live in some deserted place,
There hide in shades this lost inglorious face.
95 Plays, operas, circles, I no more must view!
My toilette, patches, all the world, adieu!'

DANIEL DEFOE (1660–1731)

Defoe was raised a merchant and Dissenter in London and vigorously supported the Glorious Revolution of William III. He made huge sums in business ventures, was bankrupted and imprisoned, wrote poems and pamphlets in favour of the Williamite cause, was imprisoned and pilloried for his satire 'A Short Way with Dissenters', made to spy for the Tories, wrote an influential journal, was imprisoned yet again and made to write propaganda for the Whigs. From his mid-30s to his death he wrote thousands of pages promoting democracy, the commercial mentality, new economic institutions and the companionate marriage. He pioneered new forms of journalism (the profile, the national disaster), wrote a guide book to Britain, a ghost story, and histories of magic and of piracy. In his last years he wrote several novels, including one that became an international myth. *Robinson Crusoe* (1719) tells of a man shipwrecked on a desert island who over a period of more than twenty years converts the island into a thriving plantation by dint of his own labour. Formally Defoe's novels constitute a new achievement in prose representation, taking the lives of apparently ordinary figures and treating them with moral seriousness in a language of circumstantial description and represented speech and thought. The realist skill makes the implausibilities of the narratives almost invisible.

From Robinson Crusoe

My thoughts were now wholly employ'd about securing my self against either savages, if any should appear, or wild beasts, if any were on the island; and I had many thoughts of the method how to do this, and what kind of dwelling to make, whether I should make me a cave in the earth, or a tent upon the earth: and, in short I resolv'd upon both, the manner and description of which, it may not be improper to give an account of.

I soon found the place I was in was not for my settlement, particularly because it was upon a low moorish ground near the sea, and I beliv'd would not be wholesome, and more particularly because there was no fresh water near it, so I resolv'd to find a more healthy and more convenient spot of ground.

I consulted several things in my situation which I found would be proper for me, 1st. health and fresh water I just now mention'd, 2dly. shelter from the heat of the sun, 3dly. security from ravenous creatures, whether man or beast, 4thly. a view to the sea, that if God sent any ship in sight, I might not lose any advantage for my deliverance, of which I was not willing to banish all my expectation yet.

In search of a place proper for this, I found a little plain on the side of a rising hill; whose front towards this little plain, was steep as a house-side, so that nothing could come down upon me from the top; on the side of this rock there was a hollow place worn a little way in like the entrance or door of a cave, but there was not really any cave or way into the rock at all.

On the flat of the green, just before this hollow place, I resolv'd to pitch my tent: this plain was not above an hundred yards broad, and about twice as long, and lay like a green before my door, and at the end of it descended irregularly every way down into the low-grounds by the sea-side. It was on the N.N.W. side of the hill, so that I was shelter'd from the heat every day, till it came to a W. and by S. sun, or thereabouts, which in those countries is near the setting.

Before I set up my tent, I drew a half circle before the hollow place, which took in about ten yards in its semi-diameter from the rock, and twenty yards in its diameter, from its beginning and ending.

In this half circle I pitch'd two rows of strong stakes, driving them into the ground till they stood very firm like piles, the biggest end being out of the ground about five foot and a half, and sharpen'd on the top: The two rows did not stand above six inches from one another.

Then I took the pieces of cable which I had cut in the ship, and I laid them in rows one upon another, within the circle, between these two rows of stakes, up to the top, placing other stakes in the in-side, leaning against them, about two foot and a half high, like a spurr to a post, and this fence was so strong, that neither man or beast could get into it or over it: This cost me a great deal of time and labour, especially to cut the piles in the woods, bring them to the place, and drive them into the earth.

The entrance into this place I made to be not by a door, but by a short ladder to go over the top, which ladder, when I was in, I lifted over after me, and so I was compleatly fenc'd in, and fortify'd, as I thought, from all the world, and consequently slept secure in the night, which otherwise I could not have done, tho', as it appear'd afterward, there was no need of all this caution from the enemies that I apprehended danger from.

Into this fence or fortress, with infinite labour, I carry'd all my riches, all my provisions, ammunition and stores, of which you have the account above, and I made me a large tent, which, to preserve me from the rains that in one part of the year are very violent there, I made double, viz. One smaller tent within, and one larger tent above it, and cover'd the uppermost with a large tarpaulin which I had sav'd among the sails.

And now I lay no more for a while in the bed which I had brought on shore, but in a hammock, which was indeed a very good one, and belong'd to the mate of the ship.

Into this tent I brought all my provisions, and every thing that would spoil by the wet, and having thus enclos'd all my goods, I made up the entrance, which till now I had left open, and so pass'd and re-pass'd, as I said, by a short ladder.

When I had done this, I began to work my way into the rock, and bringing all the earth and stones that I dug down out thro' my tent, I laid 'em up within my fence in the nature of a terras, that so it rais'd the ground within about a foot and a half; and thus I made me a cave just behind my tent, which serv'd me like a cellar to my house.

It cost me much labour, and many days, before all these things were brought to perfection, and therefore I must go back to some other things which took up some of my thoughts. At the same time it happen'd after I had laid my scheme for the setting up my tent and making the cave, that a storm of rain falling from a thick dark cloud, a sudden flash of lightning happen'd, and after that a great clap of thunder, as is naturally the effect of it; I was not so much surpris'd with the lightning as I was with a thought which darted into my mind as swift as the lightning it self: O my powder! My very heart sunk within me, when I thought, that at one blast all my powder might be destroy'd, on which, not my defence only, but the providing me food, as I thought, entirely depended; I was nothing near so anxious about my own danger, tho' had the powder took fire, I had never known who had hurt me.

Such impression did this make upon me, that after the storm was over, I laid aside all my works, my building, and fortifying, and apply'd my self to make bags and boxes to separate the powder, and keep it a little and a little in a parcel, in hope, that whatever might come, it might not all take fire at once, and to keep it so apart that it should not be possible to make one part fire another: I finish'd this work in about a fortnight, and I think my powder, which in all was about 240 l. weight was divided in not less than a hundred parcels; as to the barrel that had been wet, I did not apprehend any danger from that, so I plac'd it in my new cave, which in my fancy I call'd my kitchin, and the rest I hid up and down in holes among the rocks, so that no wet might come to it, marking very carefully where I laid it.

In the interval of time while this was doing I went out once at least every day with my gun, as well to divert myself, as to see if I could kill any thing fit for food, and as near as I could to acquaint my self with what the island produc'd. The first time I went out I presently discover'd that there were goats in the island, which was a great satisfaction to me; but then it was attended with this misfortune to me, viz. That they were so shy, so subtile, and so swift of foot, that it was the difficultest thing in the world to come at them: But I was not discourag'd at this, not doubting but I might now and then shoot one, as it soon happen'd, for after I had found their haunts a little, I laid wait in this manner for them: I observ'd if they saw me in the valleys, tho' they were upon the rocks, they would run away as in a terrible fright; but if they were feeding in the valleys, and I was upon the rocks, they took no notice of me, from whence I concluded, that by the position of their opticks, their sight was so directed downward, that they did not readily see objects that were above them; so afterward I took this method, I always clim'd the rocks first to get above them, and then had frequently a fair mark. The first shot I made among these creatures, I kill'd a she-goat which had a little kid by her which she gave suck to, which griev'd me heartily; but when the old one fell, the kid stood stock still by her till I came and took her up, and not only so, but when I carry'd the old one with me upon my shoulders, the kid follow'd me quite to my enclosure, upon which I laid down the dam, and took the kid in my arms, and carry'd it over my pale, in hopes to have bred it up tame, but it would not eat, so I was forc'd to kill it and eat it my self; these two supply'd me with flesh a great while, for I eat sparingly; and sav'd my provisions (my bread especially) as much as possibly I could.

Having now fix'd my habitation, I found it absolutely necessary to provide a place to make a fire in, and fuel to burn; and what I did for that, as also how I enlarg'd my cave, and what conveniences I made, I shall give a full account of in its place: But I must first give some little account of my self, and of my thoughts about living, which it may well be suppos'd were not a few.

I had a dismal prospect of my condition, for as I was not cast away upon that island without being driven, as is said, by a violent storm quite out of the course of our intended voyage, and a great way, viz. some hundreds of leagues out of the ordinary course of the trade of mankind, I had great reason to consider it as a determination of heaven, that in this desolate place, and in this desolate manner I should end my life; the tears would run plentifully down my face when I made these reflections, and sometimes I would expostulate with my self, why providence should thus compleatly ruine its creatures, and render them so absolutely miserable, so without help abandon'd, so entirely depress'd, that it could hardly be rational to be thankful for such a life.

But something always return'd swift upon me to check these thoughts, and to reprove me; and particularly one day walking with my gun in my hand by the sea-side, I was very pensive upon the subject of my present condition, then reason as it were expostulated with me t'other way, thus: well, you are in a desolate condition 'tis true, but pray remember, where are the rest of you? Did not you come eleven of you into the boat, where are the ten? Why were not they sav'd and you lost? Why were you singled out? Is it better to be here or there? and then I pointed to the sea. All evills are to be consider'd with the good that is in them, and with what worse attends them.

Then it occurr'd to me again, how well I was furnish'd for my subsistence, and what would have been my case if it had not happen'd, which was an hundred thousand to one, that the ship floated from the place where she first struck and was driven so near to the shore that I had time to get all these things out of her: What would have been my case, if I had been to have liv'd in the condition in which I at first came on shore, without necessaries of life, or necessaries to supply and procure them? Particularly said I aloud, (tho' to my self) what should I ha' done without a gun, without ammunition, without any tools to make any thing, or to work with, without clothes, bedding, a tent, or any manner of covering, and that now I had all these to a sufficient quantity, and was in a fair way to provide my self in such a manner, as to live without my gun when my ammunition was spent; so that I had a tollerable view of subsisting without any want as long as I liv'd; for I consider'd from the beginning how I would provide for the accidents that might happen, and for the time that was to come, even not only after my ammunition should be spent, but even after my health or strength should decay.

I confess I had not entertain'd any notion of my ammunition being destroy'd at one blast, I mean my powder being blown up by lightning, and this made the thoughts of it so surprising to me when it lighten'd and thunder'd, as I observ'd just now.

And now being to enter into a melancholy relation of a scene of silent life, such perhaps as was never heard of in the world before, I shall take it from its beginning, and continue it in its order. It was, by my account, the 30th. of Sept. when, in the manner as above said, I first set foot upon this horrid island, when the sun being, to us, in its autumnal equinox, was almost just over my head, for I reckon'd my self, by observation, to be in the latitude of 9 degrees 22 minutes north of the line.

After I had been there about ten or twelve days, it came into my thoughts, that I should lose my reckoning of time for want of books and pen and ink, and should even forget the sabbath days from the working days; but to prevent this I cut it with my knife upon a large post, in capital letters, and making it into a great cross I set it up on the shore where I first landed, viz. I came on shore here on the 30th of Sept. 1659. Upon the sides of this square post I cut every day a notch with my knife, and every seventh notch was as long again as the rest, and every first day of the month as long again as that long one, and thus I kept my calander, or weekly, monthly, and yearly reckoning of time.

In the next place we are to observe, that among the many things which I brought out of the ship in the several voyages, which, as above mention'd, I made to it, I got several things of less value, but not all less useful to me, which I omitted setting down before; as in particular, pens, ink, and paper, several parcels in the captain's, mate's, gunner's, and carpenter's keeping, three or four compasses, some mathematical instruments, dials, perspectives, charts, and books of navigation, all which I huddel'd together, whether I might want them or no; also I found three very good bibles which came to me in my cargo from England, and which I had pack'd up among my things; some Portugueze books also, and among them two or three popish prayer-books, and several other books, all which I carefully secur'd. And I must not forget, that we had in the ship a dog and two cats, of whose eminent history I may have occasion to say something in its place; for I carry'd both the cats with me, and as for the dog, he jump'd out of the ship of himself and swam on shore to me the day after I went on shore with my first cargo, and was a trusty servant to me many years; I wanted nothing that he could fetch me, nor any company that he could make up to me, I only wanted to have him talk to me, but that would not do: As I observ'd before, I found pen, ink and paper, and I husbanded them to the utmost, and I shall shew, that while my ink lasted, I kept things very exact, but after that was gone I could not, for I could not make any ink by any means that I could devise.

And this put me in mind that I wanted many things, notwithstanding all that I had amass'd together, and of these, this of ink was one, as also spade, pick-axe, and shovel to dig or remove the earth, needles, pins, and thread; as for linnen, I soon learn'd to want that without much difficulty. This want of tools made every work I did go on heavily, and it was near a whole year before I had entirely finish'd my little pale or surrounded habitation: The piles or stakes, which were as heavy as I could well lift, were a long time in cutting and preparing in the woods, and more by far in bringing home, so that I spent some times two days in cutting and bringing home one of those posts, and a third day in driving it into the ground; for which purpose I got a heavy piece of wood at first, but at last bethought my self of one of the iron crows, which however tho' I found it, yet it made driving those posts or piles very laborious and tedious work.

But what need I ha' been concern'd at the tediousness of any thing I had to do, seeing I had time enough to do it in, nor had I any other employment if that had been over, at least, that I could foresee, except the ranging the island to seek for food, which I did more or less every day.

I now began to consider seriously my condition, and the circumstance I was reduc'd to, and I drew up the state of my affairs in writing, not so much to leave them to any that were to come after me, for I was like to have but few heirs, as to deliver my thoughts from daily poring upon them, and afflicting my mind; and as my reason began now to master my despondency, I began to comfort my self as well as I could, and to set the good against the evil, that I might have something to distinguish my case from worse, and I stated it very impartially, like debtor and creditor, the comforts I enjoyed against the miseries I suffered, thus:

EVIL	GOOD
I am cast upon a horrible desolate island, void of all hope of recovery.	But I am alive, and not drown'd as all my ship's company was.
I am singl'd out and separated, as it were, from all the world to be miserable.	But I am singl'd out too from all the ship's crew to be spar'd from death; and he that miraculously sav'd me from death, can deliver me from this condition.
I am divided from mankind, a solitaire, one banish'd from humane society.	But I am not starv'd and perishing on a barren place, afffording no sustenance.
I have not clothes to cover me.	But I am in a hot climate, where if I had clothes I could hardly wear them.

I am without any defence or means to resist any violence of man or beast.	But I am cast on an island, where I see no wild beasts to hurt me, as I saw on the coast of Africa: and what if I had been shipwreck'd there?
I have no soul to speak to, or relieve me.	But God wonderfully sent the ship near enough to the shore, that I have gotten out so many necessary things as will either supply my wants, or enable me to supply my self even as long as I live.

Upon the whole, here was an undoubted testimony, that there was scarce any condition in the world so miserable, but there was something negative or something positive to be thankful for in it; and let this stand as a direction from the experience of the most miserable of all conditions in this world, that we may always find in it something to comfort our selves from, and to set in the description of good and evil, on the credit side of the accompt.

Having now brought my mind a little to relish my condition, and given over looking out to sea to see if I could spy a ship, I say, giving over these things, I began to apply my self to accommodate my way of living, and to make things as easy to me as I could.

I have already describ'd my habitation, which was a tent under the side of a rock, surrounded with a strong pale of posts and cables, but I might now rather call it a wall, for I rais'd a kind of wall up against it of turfs, about two foot thick on the out-side, and after some time, I think it was a year and half, I rais'd rafters from it leaning to the rock, and thatch'd or cover'd it with bows of trees, and such things as I could get to keep out the rain, which I found at some times of the year very violent.

I have already observ'd how I brought all my goods into this pale, and into the cave which I had made behind me: But I must observe too, that at first this was a confus'd heap of goods, which as they lay in no order, so they took up all my place, I had no room to turn my self; so I set my self to enlarge my cave and works farther into the earth, for it was a loose sandy rock, which yielded easily to the labour I bestow'd on it; and so when I found I was pretty safe as to beasts of prey, I work'd side-ways to the right hand into the rock, and then turning to the right again, work'd quite out and made me a door to come out, on the outside of my pale or fortification.

This gave me not only egress and regress, as it were a back way to my tent and to my storehouse, but gave me room to stow my goods.

And now I began to apply my self to make such necessary things as I found I most wanted, as particularly a chair and a table, for without these I was not able to enjoy the few comforts I had in the world, I could not write, or eat, or do several things with so much pleasure without a table.

So I went to work; and here I must needs observe, that as reason is the substance and original of the mathematicks, so by stating and squaring every thing by reason, and by making the most rational judgment of things, every man may be in time master of every mechanick art. I had never handled a tool in my life, and yet in time by labour, application, and contrivance, I found at last that I wanted nothing but I could have made it, especially if I had had tools; however I made abundance of things, even without tools, and some with no more tools than an adze and a hatchet, which perhaps were never made that way before, and that with infinite labour: For example, if I wanted a board, I had no other way but to cut down a tree, set it on an edge before me, and hew it flat on either side with my axe, till I had brought it to be thin as a plank, and then dubb it smooth with my adze. It is true, by this method I could make but one board out of a whole tree, but this I had no remedy for but patience, any more than I had for the prodigious deal of time and labour which it took me up to make a plank or board: But my time or labour was little worth, and so it was as well employ'd one way as another.

However, I made me a table and a chair, as I observ'd above, in the first place, and this I did out of the short pieces of boards that I brought on my raft from the ship: but when I had wrought out some boards, as above, I made large shelves of the breadth of a foot and half one over another, all along one side of my cave, to lay all my tools, nails, and iron-work, and in a word, to separate every thing at large in their places, that I might come easily at them; I knock'd pieces into the wall of the rock to hang my guns and all things that would hang so that had my cave been to be seen, it look'd like a general magazine of all necessary things, and I had every thing so ready at my hand, that it was a great pleasure to me to see all my goods in such order, and especially to find my stock of all necessaries so great.

And now it was when I began to keep a journal of every day's employment, for indeed at first I was in too much hurry, and not only hurry as to labour, but in too much discomposure of mind, and my journal would ha' been full of many dull things: For example, I must have said thus. 'Sept. the 30th. After I got to shore and had escap'd drowning, instead of being thankful to God for my deliverance, having first vomited with the great quantity of salt water which was gotten into my stomach, and recovering my self a little, I ran about the shore, wringing my hands and beating my head and face, exclaiming at my misery, and crying out, I was undone, undone, till tyr'd and faint I was forc'd to lie down on the ground to repose, but durst not sleep for fear of being devour'd.'

Some days after this, and after I had been on board the ship, and got all that I could out of her, yet I could not forbear getting up to the top of a little mountain and looking out to sea in hopes of seeing a ship, then fancy at a vast distance I spy'd a sail, please my self with the hopes of it, and then after looking steadily till I was almost blind, lose it quite, and sit down and weep like a child, and thus increase my misery by my folly.

But having gotten over these things in some measure, and having settled my household stuff and habitation, made me a table and a chair, and all as handsome about me as I could, I began to keep my journal, of which I shall here give you the copy (tho' in it will be told all these particulars over again) as long as it lasted, for having no more ink I was forc'd to leave it off.

JAMES THOMSON (1700–1748)

James Thomson was a Scot and a British nationalist whose patriotic poem *Liberty* (1735–36) developed the idea (already advanced in Pope's *Windsor Forest*) that Britain had inherited from Greece and Rome an imperial mission to spread freedom. He was later the probable author of 'Rule Britannia' (1740). He first came to note with *Winter* (1726), the first poem of *The Seasons* (1726–30), an enormously popular and influential poem which, in contrast with the urban pastorals and satires of Montagu, Swift and Pope, provided dramatic and vital images of a restorative nature antithetical to the metropolis. His work became a source of inspiration for the picturesque vision which would dominate aesthetic sensibility in the last half of the century, and for the Romantic poetry, especially that of Wordsworth.

Winter

    SEE! Winter comes to rule the varied year,
Sullen and sad, with all his varied train,
Vapours, and clouds, and storms: be these my theme,
These, that exalt the soul to solemn thought,
5 And heavenly musing. Welcome, kindred glooms!
Wished, wintry horrors, hail! With frequent foot,
Pleased have I, in my cheerful morn of life,
When nursed by careless Solitude I lived,
And sung of nature with unceasing joy,
10 Pleased have I wandered through your rough domains;
Trod the pure, virgin snows, myself as pure,
Heard the winds roar, and the big torrent burst,
Or seen the deep, fermenting tempest brewed
In the red evening sky. Thus passed the time,
15 Till, through the opening chambers of the south,
Looked out the joyous Spring, looked out and smiled.
    Thee too, inspirer of the toiling swain!
Fair Autumn, yellow-robed! I'll sing of thee,
Of thy last, tempered days and sunny calms;
20 When all the golden Hours are on the wing,
Attending thy retreat and round thy wain,
Slow-rolling onward to the southern sky.
    Behold! the well-poised hornet hovering hangs,
With quivering pinions, in the genial blaze;
25 Flies off in airy circles, then returns,
And hums and dances to the beating ray:
Nor shall the man that musing walks alone,
    And heedless strays within his radiant lists,
Go unchastised away. Sometimes a fleece
30 Of clouds, wide-scattering, with a lucid veil
Soft shadow o'er th' unruffled face of heaven;

And, through their dewy sluices, shed the sun
With tempered influence down. Then is the time
For those, whom Wisdom and whom Nature charm,
35   To steal themselves from the degenerate crowd,
And soar above this little scene of things:
To tread low-thoughted Vice beneath their feet,
To lay their passions in a gentle calm,
And woo lone Quiet in her silent walks.
40   Now solitary, and in pensive guise,
Oft let me wander o'er the russet mead,
Or through the pining grove, where scarce is heard
One dying strain to cheer the woodman's toil:
Sad Philomel, perchance, pours forth her plaint
45   Far through the withering copse. Meanwhile, the leaves,
That late the forest clad with lively green,
Nipped by the drizzly night, and sallow-hued,
Fall, wavering, through the air; or shower amain,
Urged by the breeze that sobs amid the boughs.
50   Then list'ning hares forsake the rustling woods,
And, starting at the frequent noise, escape
To the rough stubble and the rushy fen.
Then woodcocks o'er the fluctuating main,
That glimmers to the glimpses of the moon
55   Stretch their long voyage to the woodland glade
Where, wheeling with uncertain flight, they mock
The nimble fouler's aim. Now Nature droops;
Languish the living herbs with pale decay,
And all the various family of flowers
60   Their sunny robes resign. The falling fruits,
Through the still night, forsake the parent-bough
That, in the first grey glances of the dawn
Looks wild, and wonders at the wintry waste.
    The year, yet pleasing but declining fast,
65   Soft o'er the secret soul, in gentle gales,
A philosophic melancholy breathes;
And bears the swelling thought aloft to heaven.
Then forming fancy rouses to conceive
What never mingled with the vulgar's dream:
70   Then wake the tender pang, the pitying tear,
The sigh for suffering worth, the wish preferred
For humankind, the joy to see them blessed
And all the social offspring of the heart!
    Oh! bear me then to high, embowering shades,
75   To twilight groves, and visionary vales

---

44 Philomel: see Ovid, *Metamorphoses*, 6, 242 ff.; Philomel is a Queen who is violated by her brother-in-law, Tereus, and then metamorphosed into a nightingale.

To weeping grottoes and to hoary caves;
Where angel-forms are seen, and voices heard
Sighed in low whispers, that abstract the soul
From outward sense, far into worlds remote.
80   Now, when the western sun withdraws the day,
And humid Evening, gliding o'er the sky,
In her chill progress checks the straggling beams,
And robs them of their gathered, vapoury prey,
Where marshes stagnate and where rivers wind,
85   Cluster the rolling fogs, and swim along
The dusky-mantled lawn: then slow descend,
Once more to mingle with their watry friends.
The vivid stars shine out in radiant files
And boundless ether glows; till the fair moon
90   Shows her broad visage in the crimsoned east;
Now, stooping, seems to kiss the passing cloud,
Now o'er the pure cerulean rides sublime.
Wide the pale deluge floats with silver waves,
O'er the skied mountain to the low-laid vale;
95   From the white rocks, with dim reflection, gleams,
And faintly glitters through the waving shades.
    All night, abundant dews unnoted fall
And, at return of morning, silver o'er
The face of mother-earth; from every branch
100   Depending, tremble the translucent gems,
And, quivering, seem to fall away, yet cling,
And sparkle in the sun, whose rising eye,
With fogs bedimmed, portends a beauteous day.
Now giddy youth, whom headlong passions fire,
105   Rouse the wild game, and stain the guiltless grove
With violence and death; yet call it sport
To scatter ruin through the realms of Love,
And Peace, that thinks no ill: but these the Muse,
Whose charity unlimited extends
110   As wide as Nature works, disdains to sing,
Returning to her nobler theme in view.
    For see! where Winter comes, himself confessed,
Striding the gloomy blast. First rains obscure
Drive through the mingling skies with tempest foul;
115   Beat on the mountain's brow, and shake the woods
That, sounding, wave below. The dreary plain
Lies overwhelmed and lost. The bellying clouds
Combine and, deepening into night, shut up
The day's fair face. The wanderers of heaven,
120   Each to his home, retire; save those that love
To take their pastime in the troubled air,
And, skimming, flutter round the dimly flood.

The cattle from th'untasted fields return,
And ask, with meaning low, their wonted stalls,
125   Or ruminate in the contiguous shade:
Thither the household, feathery people crowd,
The crested cock with all his female train,
Pensive and wet. Meanwhile, the cottage-swain
Hangs o'er th'enlivening blaze and, taleful, there
130   Recounts his simple frolic: much he talks
And much he laughs, nor recks the storm that blows
Without, and rattles on his humble roof.
    At last the muddy deluge pours along,
Resistless, roaring; dreadful down it comes
135   From the chapped mountain and the mossy wild,
Tumbling through rocks abrupt, and sounding far:
Then o'er the sanded valley, floating, spreads,
Calm, sluggish, silent; till again constrained
Betwixt two meeting hills, it bursts a way,
140   Where rocks and woods o'erhang the turbid stream.
There gathering triple force, rapid and deep,
It boils, and wheels, and foams, and thunders through.
    Nature! great parent! whose directing hand
Rolls round the seasons of the changeful year,
145   How mighty, how majestic are thy works!
With what a pleasing dread they swell the soul,
That sees, astonished! and astonished sings!
You too, ye winds! that now begin to blow
With boisterous sweep, I raise my voice to you.
150   Where are your stores, ye viewless beings! say,
Where your aerial magazines reserved,
Against the day of tempest perilous?
In what untravelled country of the air,
Hushed in still silence, sleep you when 'tis calm?
155   Late, in the louring sky, red, fiery streaks
Begin to flush about; the reeling clouds
Stagger with dizzy aim, as doubting yet
Which master to obey; while rising slow,
Sad, in the leaden-coloured east, the moon
160   Wears a bleak circle round her sullied orb.
Then issues forth the storm with loud control,
And the thin fabric of the pillared air
O'erturns at once. Prone on th'uncertain main
Descends th'ethereal force, and ploughs its waves
165   With dreadful rift: from the mid-deep appears,
Surge after surge, the rising, watry war.
Whitening, the angry billows roll immense,
And roar their terrors through the shuddering soul
Of feeble man, amidst their fury caught,

170 And dashed upon his fate. Then, o'er the cliff
Where dwells the sea-mew, unconfined they fly,
And, hurrying, swallow up the sterile shore.
The mountain growls, and all its sturdy sons
Stoop to the bottom of the rocks they shade:
175 Lone on its midnight-side, and all aghast,
The dark, wayfaring stranger, breathless, toils,
And climbs against the blast –
Low waves the rooted forest, vexed, and sheds
What of its leafy honours yet remains.
180 Thus, struggling through the dissipated grove,
The whirling tempest raves along the plain;
And, on the cottage thatched or lordly dome
Keen-fastening, shakes 'em to the solid base.
Sleep, frighted, flies; the hollow chimney howls,
185 The windows rattle, and the hinges creak.
Then too, they say, through all the burthened air
Long groans are heard, shrill sounds and distant sighs,
That, murmured by the demon of the night,
Warn the devoted wretch of woe and death!
190 Wild uproar lords it wide: the clouds commixed
With stars, swift-gliding, sweep along the sky.
All nature reels. But hark! the Almighty speaks:
Instant the chidden storm begins to pant,
And dies at once into a noiseless calm.
195 As yet 'tis midnight's reign; the weary clouds,
Slow-meeting, mingle into solid gloom.
Now, while the drowsy world lies lost in sleep,
Let me associate with the low-browed Night,
And Contemplation, her sedate compeer;
200 Let me shake off th'intrusive cares of day,
And lay the meddling senses all aside.
And now, ye lying Vanities of life!
You ever-tempting, ever-cheating train!
Where are you now? and what is your amount?
205 Vexation, disappointment and remorse.
Sad, sickening thought! and yet deluded man,
A scene of wild, disjointed visions past,
And broken slumbers, rises still resolved,
With new-flushed hopes, to run your giddy round.
210 Father of light and life! Thou Good Supreme,
O! teach me what is good! teach me thyself!
Save me from folly, vanity and vice,
From every low pursuit! and feed my soul
With knowledge, conscious peace and virtue pure,
215 Sacred, substantial, never-fading bliss!
Lo! from the livid east or piercing north,

Thick clouds ascend, in whose capacious womb
A vapoury deluge lies, to snow congealed:
Heavy, they roll their fleecy world along,
220 And the sky saddens with th'impending storm.
Through the hushed air the whitening shower descends,
At first thin-wavering; till at last the flakes
Fall broad and wide and fast, dimming the day
With a continual flow. See! sudden hoared,
225 The woods beneath the stainless burden bow;
Black'ning, along the mazy stream it melts.
Earth's universal face, deep-hid and chill,
Is all one dazzling waste. The labourer-ox
Stands covered o'er with snow, and then demands
230 The fruit of all his toil. The fowls of heaven,
Tamed by the cruel season, crowd around
The winnowing store, and claim the little boon
That Providence allows. The foodless wilds
Pour forth their brown inhabitants; the hare,
235 Though timorous of heart, and hard beset
By death in various forms, dark snares, and dogs,
And more unpitying men, the garden seeks,
Urged on by fearless want. The bleating kind
Eye the bleak heavens, and next the glistening earth,
240 With looks of dumb despair; then sad, dispersed,
Dig for the withered herb through heaps of snow.
  Now, shepherds, to your helpless charge be kind;
Baffle the raging year, and fill their pens
With food at will; lodge them below the blast,
245 And watch them strict; for from the bellowing east,
In this dire season, oft the whirlwind's wing
Sweeps up the burthen of whole wintry plains
In one fierce blast, and o'er th'unhappy flocks,
Lodged in the hollow of two neighbouring hills,
250 The billowy tempest whelms; till, upwards urged,
The valley to a shining mountain swells,
That curls its wreaths amid the freezing sky.
  Now, amid all the rigours of the year,
In the wild depth of winter, while without
255 The ceaseless winds blow keen, be my retreat
A rural, sheltered, solitary scene,
Where ruddy fire and beaming tapers join
To chase the cheerless gloom: there let me sit,
And hold high converse with the mighty dead,
260 Sages of ancient times, as gods revered,
As gods beneficent, who blessed mankind
With arts and arms, and humanised a world.
Roused at th'inspiring thought, I throw aside

The long-lived volume and, deep-musing, hail
265 The sacred shades that, slowly-rising, pass
Before my wondering eyes. First, Socrates,
Truth's early champion, martyr for his god;
Solon the next, who built his commonweal
On equity's firm base; Lycurgus then,
270 Severely good; and him of rugged Rome,
Numa, who softened her rapacious sons;
Cimon sweet-souled, and Aristides just;
Unconquered Cato, virtuous in extreme;
With that attempered hero, mild and firm,
275 Who wept the brother, while the tyrant bled;
Scipio, the humane warrior, gently brave,
Fair learning's friend, who early sought the shade,
To dwell with Innocence and Truth retired;
And, equal to the best, the Theban, he
280 Who, single, raised his country into fame.
Thousands behind, the boast of Greece and Rome,
Whom Virtue owns, the tribute of a verse
Demand, but who can count the stars of heaven?
Who sing their influence on this lower world?
285 But see who yonder comes! nor comes alone,
With sober state and of majestic mien,
The Sister-Muses in his train. 'Tis he!
Maro! the best of poets and of men!
Great Homer too appears, of daring wing!
290 Parent of song! and, equal, by his side,
The British Muse; joined hand in hand they walk,
Darkling, nor miss their way to fame's ascent.
    Society divine! Immortal minds!
Still visit thus my nights, for you reserved,
295 And mount my souring soul to deeds like yours.
Silence! thou lonely power! the door be thine:
See on the hallowed hour that none intrude,
Save Lycidas, the friend with sense refined,
Learning digested well, exalted faith,
300 Unstudied wit, and humour ever gay.
    Clear frost succeeds and, through the blue serene,
For sight too fine, th'ethereal nitre flies,
To bake the glebe and bind the slipp'ry flood.
This of the wintry season is the prime;
305 Pure are the days, and lustrous are the nights,
Brightened with starry worlds till then unseen.

266–76 Socrates et cet.: Thomson lists a series of Athenian and Roman politicians renowned from Plutarch's *Lives* for their honesty, generosity and conservatism.   288 Maro: Publius Vergilius Maro, (Virgil).   303 nitre: potassium nitrate, a fertiliser, soap and medicine.

Meanwhile the orient, darkly red, breathes forth
An icy gale that, in its mid-career,
Arrests the bickering stream. The nightly sky,
310   And all her glowing constellations, pour
Their rigid influence down. It freezes on
Till morn, late-rising, o'er the drooping world
Lifts her pale eye, unjoyous: then appears
The various labour of the silent night,
315   The pendant icicle, the frost-work fair
Where thousand figures rise, the crusted snow,
Though white, made whiter by the fining north.
On blithesome frolics bent, the youthful swains,
While every work of man is laid at rest,
320   Rush o'er the watry plains and, shuddering, view
The fearful deeps below; or with the gun
And faithful spaniel range the ravaged fields,
And, adding to the ruins of the year,
Distress the feathery or the footed game.
325   But hark! the nightly winds, with hollow voice,
Blow blustering from the south. The frost subdued
Gradual resolves into a weeping thaw.
Spotted, the mountains shine; loose sleet descends,
And floods the country round; the rivers swell,
330   Impatient for the day. Those sullen seas,
That wash th'ungenial pole, will rest no more
Beneath the shackles of the mighty north,
But, rousing all their waves, resistless heave.
And hark! the length'ning roar continuous runs
335   Athwart the rifted main; at once it bursts,
And piles a thousand mountains to the clouds!
Ill fares the bark, the wretches' last resort,
That, lost amid the floating fragments, moors
Beneath the shelter of an icy isle,
340   While night o'erwhelms the sea, and horror looks
More horrible. Can human hearts endure
Th'assembled mischiefs that besiege them round:
Unlist'ning hunger, fainting weariness,
The roar of winds and waves, the crush of ice,
345   Now ceasing, now renewed with louder rage,
And bellowing round the main? Nations remote,
Shook from their midnight-slumbers, deem they hear
Portentous thunder in the troubled sky.
More to embroil the deep, leviathan
350   And his unwieldy train, in horrid sport,
Tempest the loosened brine; while through the gloom,

---

317 fining: refining, clarifying.

Far from the dire, unhospitable shore,
The lion's rage, the wolf's sad howl is heard,
And all the fell society of night.
355 Yet Providence, that ever-waking eye,
Looks down with pity on the fruitless toil
Of mortals lost to hope, and lights them safe
Through all this dreary labyrinth of fate.
   'Tis done! Dread Winter has subdued the year,
360 And reigns tremendous o'er the desert plains!
How dead the vegetable kingdom lies!
How dumb the tuneful! Horror wide extends
His solitary empire. Now, fond Man!
Behold thy pictured life: pass some few years,
365 Thy flow'ring Spring, thy shortlived Summer's strength,
Thy sober Autumn fading into age,
And pale, concluding Winter shuts thy scene,
And shrouds thee in the grave. Where now are fled
Those dreams of greatness? Those unsolid hopes
370 Of happiness? Those longings after fame?
Those restless cares? Those busy, bustling days?
Those nights of secret guilt? Those veering thoughts,
Flutt'ring 'twixt good and ill, that shared thy life?
All now are vanished! Virtue sole survives,
375 Immortal, mankind's never-failing friend,
His guide to happiness on high. And see!
'Tis come, the glorious Morn! the second birth
Of heaven and earth! awakening Nature hears
Th'almighty trumpet's voice, and starts to life,
380 Renewed, unfading. Now th'eternal Scheme,
That dark perplexity, that mystic maze,
Which sight could never trace, nor heart conceive,
To Reason's eye refined, clears up apace.
Angels and men, astonished, pause – and dread
385 To travel through the depths of Providence,
Untried, unbounded. Ye vain learned! see,
And, prostrate in the dust, adore that Power
And Goodness, oft arraigned. See now the cause,
Why conscious worth, oppressed, in secret long
390 Mourned, unregarded; why the good man's share
In life was gall and bitterness of soul;
Why the lone widow and her orphans pined,
In starving solitude; while Luxury,
In palaces, lay prompting her low thought
395 To form unreal wants; why heaven-born Faith
And Charity, prime grace! wore the red marks
Of Persecution's scourge; why licensed Pain,
That cruel spoiler, that embosomed foe,

Imbittered all our bliss. Ye good distressed!
400 Ye noble few! that here unbending stand
Beneath life's pressures, yet a little while,
And all your woes are past. Time swiftly fleets,
And wished Eternity, approaching, brings
Life undecaying, love without allay,
405 Pure, flowing joy, and happiness sincere.

JONATHAN SWIFT (1667–1745)

Jonathan Swift was born in Dublin and educated at Trinity College. He was a cousin of Dryden, and a friend of Pope, Gay and Arbuthnot. He worked as secretary to Sir William Temple and was ordained in 1694, rising in 1713 to the office of Dean of St Patrick's in Dublin. His first notable publication was the *Tale of a Tub* and the *Battle of the Books* (1704), two satires on religious and philosophical folly. He wrote many excellent poems which were often reprinted, and many engagements in political controversy on behalf of the Whigs until 1710, thereafter for the Tories. His Tory partisanship effectively confined him to Ireland during the Whig hegemony after 1714 and he became a champion of the Irish cause against London's dominion, often accepting considerable political risk, notably for his famous *Drapier's Letters* (1724), and his *Modest Proposal* (1729), one of the most famous satires ever written. His charity and Christianty were unquestionable, but his scatalogical humour, not so scandalous to his contemporaries, later gave rise to the charge of mental disorder and misanthropy. His writing is in fact a cunning Enlightenment reflection on the limits of Enlightenment, and for that reason inimical to naive ideologies.

Gulliver's Travels, Swift's most famous single work, satirises the genres of utopia and voyage of discovery to estrange the reader from Enlightenment belief in human rationality and moral and technological progress. Highly rational in language and logic, the writing exposes the failure of reason on the rock of natural human depravity. The *Travels* are divided into four parts. In the first Gulliver encounters the minuscule Lilliputians; in the second he is minute in relation to the giant Brobdingnagians. These inversions of scale enable defamiliarising perspectives on human mores. Part Three treats a voyage to five islands which variously satirise British complacency and inhumanity, especially, in the *Voyage to Laputa*, the conceit of scientific projectors and imperialists. Part Four describes the hyper-rational utopia or dystopia of the Houyhnhnms, a race of horses that have turned filthy humans (the Yahoos) into slaves, and satirises the idea of human superiority, the repression of the body, and our savage treatment of those we call savages.

From Gulliver's Travels

From Part III, A Voyage to Laputa etc.

Chapter 2: *The Humours and Dispositions of the Laputians Described. An Account of their Learning. Of the King and his Court. The Author's Reception there.*

At my alighting I was surrounded by a crowd of people, but those who stood nearest seemed to be of better quality. They beheld me with all the marks and circumstances of wonder; neither indeed was I much in their debt; having never till then seen a race of mortals so singular in their shapes, habits, and countenances. Their heads were all reclined either to the right, or the left; one of their eyes turned inward, and the other directly up to the zenith. Their outward garments were adorned with the figures of suns, moons, and stars, interwoven with those of fiddles, flutes, harps, trumpets, guitars, harpsicords, and many more instruments of music, unknown to us in Europe. I observed here and there many in the habit of servants, with a blown bladder fastened like a flail to the end of a short stick, which they carried in their hands. In each bladder was a small quantity of dried peas, or little pebbles, (as I was afterwards informed.) With these bladders they now and then flapped the mouths and ears of those who stood near them, of which practice I could not then conceive the meaning. It seems, the minds of these people are so taken up with intense speculations, that they neither can speak, nor attend to the discourses of others, without being rouzed by some external taction[1] upon the organs of speech and hearing; for which reason, those persons who are able to afford it, always keep a *flapper*, (the original is *climenole*) in their family, as one of their domesticks; nor ever walk abroad or make visits without him. And the business of this officer is, when two or more persons are in company, gently to strike with his bladder the mouth of him who is to speak, and the right ear of him or them to whom the speaker addresseth himself. This *flapper* is likewise employed diligently to attend his master in his walks, and upon occasion to give him a soft flap on his eyes; because he is always so wrapped up in cogitation, that he is in manifest danger of falling down every precipice, and bouncing his head against every post; and in the streets, of jostling others, or being jostled himself into the kennel.[2]

It was necessary to give the reader this information, without which he would be at the same loss with me, to understand the proceedings of these people, as they conducted me up the stairs, to the top of the island, and from thence to the royal palace. While we were ascending, they forgot several times what they were about, and left me to my self, till their memories were again roused by their *flappers*; for they appeared altogether unmoved by the sight of my foreign habit and countenance, and by the shouts of the vulgar, whose thoughts and minds were more disengaged.

1: touch. 2: open sewer.

At last we entered the palace, and proceeded into the chamber of presence; where I saw the king seated on his throne, attended on each side by persons of prime quality. Before the throne, was a large table filled with globes and spheres, and mathematical instruments of all kinds. His Majesty took not the least notice of us, although our entrance were not without sufficient noise, by the concourse of all persons belonging to the court. But, he was then deep in a problem, and we attended at least an hour, before he could solve it. There stood by him on each side, a young page, with flaps in their hands; and when they saw he was at leisure, one of them gently struck his mouth, and the other his right ear; at which he started like one awaked on the sudden, and looking towards me, and the company I was in, recollected the occasion of our coming, whereof he had been informed before. He spoke some words; whereupon immediately a young man with a flap came up to my side, and flapt me gently on the right ear; but I made signs as well as I could, that I had no occasion for such an instrument; which as I afterwards found, gave his majesty and the whole court a very mean opinion of my understanding. The King, as far as I could conjecture, asked me several questions, and I addressed myself to him in all the languages I had. When it was found, that I could neither understand nor be understood, I was conducted by his order to an apartment in his palace, (this prince being distinguished above all his predecessors for his hospitality to strangers,) where two servants were appointed to attend me. My dinner was brought, and four persons of quality, whom I remembered to have seen very near the king's person, did me the honour to dine with me. We had two courses, of three dishes each. In the first course, there was a shoulder of mutton, cut into an equilateral triangle; a piece of beef into a rhomboides; and a pudding into a cycloid. The second course was two ducks, trussed up into the form of fiddles; sausages and puddings resembling flutes and haut-boys,[1] and a breast of veal in the shape of a harp. The servants cut our bread into cones, cylinders, parallelograms, and several other mathematical figures.

While we were at dinner, I made bold to ask the names of several things in their language; and those noble persons, by the assistance of their *flappers*, delighted to give me answers, hoping to raise my admiration of the great abilities, if I could be brought to converse with them. I was soon able to call for bread, and drink, or whatever else I wanted.

After dinner my company withdrew, and a person was sent to me by the king's order, attended by a *flapper*. He brought with him pen, ink, and paper, and three or four books; giving me to understand by signs, that he was sent to teach me the language. We sat together four hours, in which time I wrote down a great number of words in columns, with the translations over against them. I likewise made a shift to learn several short sentences. For my tutor would order one of my servants to fetch something, to turn about, to make a bow, to sit, or stand, or walk, and the like. Then I took down the sentence in writing. He shewed me also in one of his books, the figures of the sun, moon, and stars, the zodiack, the tropics, and polar circles, together with the denominations of many figures of planes and solids. He gave me the names and descriptions of all the

---

1: oboes.

musical instruments, and the general terms of art in playing on each of them. After he had left me, I placed all my words with their interpretations in alphabetical order. And thus in a few days, by the help of a very faithful memory, I got some insight into their language.

The word, which I interpret the *flying* or *floating island*, is in the original *laputa*;[1] whereof I could never learn the true etymology. *Lap* in the old obsolete language signifieth *high*, and *untuh* a *governor*; from which they say by corruption was derived *laputa* from *lapuntuh*. But I do not approve of this derivation, which seems to be a little strained. I ventured to offer to the learned among them a conjecture of my own, that *laputa* was *quasi lap outed*; *lap* signifying properly the dancing of the sun beams in the sea; and *outed* a wing, which however I shall not obtrude, but submit to the judicious reader.

From Part IV, A Voyage to the Country of the Houyhnhms[2]

Chapter V: The Author at his Master's Commands informs him of the State of England. The Causes of War among the Princes of Europe. The Author begins to explain the English Constitution.

The reader may please to observe, that the following extract of many conversations I had with my master, contains a summary of the most material points, which were discoursed at several times for above two years; his honour often desiring fuller satisfaction as I farther improved in the *houyhnhnm* tongue. I laid before him, as well as I could, the whole state of Europe; I discoursed of trade and manufactures, of arts and sciences; and the answers I gave to all the questions he made, as they arose upon several subjects, were a fund of conversation not to be exhausted. But I shall here only set down the substance of what passed between us concerning my own country, reducing it into order as well as I can, without any regard to time or other circumstances, while I strictly adhere to truth. My only concern is, that I shall hardly be able to do justice to my master's arguments and expressions, which must needs suffer by my want of capacity, as well as by a translation into our barbarous English.

In obedience therefore to his honour's commands, I related to him the revolution[2] under the Prince of Orange; the long war with France entered into by the said Prince, and renewed by his successor the present Queen; wherein the greatest powers of Christendom were engaged, and which still continued: I computed at his request, that about a million of *Yahoos* might have been killed in the whole progress of it; and perhaps a hundred or more cities taken, and five times as many ships burnt or sunk.

He asked me what were the usual causes or motives that made one country go to war with another. I answered, they were innumerable; but I should only mention a few of the chief. Sometimes the ambition of princes, who never think they have land or people enough to govern: sometimes the corruption of ministers, who engage their master in a war in order to stifle or divert the clamour of the subjects against their evil administration. Difference in

---

1: the island is Britain and the name may signify, from the Spanish, 'the whore'. 2: the name derives from the 'whinnying' noise made by horses.

opinions hath cost many millions of lives: for instance, whether *flesh* be *bread*, or *bread* be *flesh*: whether the juice of a certain *berry* be *blood* or *wine*: whether *whistling* be a vice or a virtue: whether it be better to *kiss a post*, or throw it into the fire: what is the best colour for a *coat*, whether *black, white, red* or *grey*; and whether it should be *long* or *short, narrow* or *wide, dirty* or *clean*; with many more. Neither are any wars so furious and bloody, or of so long continuance, as those occasioned by difference in opinion, especially if it be in things indifferent.

Sometimes the quarrel between two princes is to decide which of them shall dispossess a third of his dominions, where neither of them pretend to any right. Sometimes one prince quarrelleth with another, for fear the other should quarrel with him. Sometimes a war is entered upon, because the enemy is too *strong*, and sometimes because he is too *weak*. Sometimes our neighbours *want* the *things* which we *have*, or *have* the things which we want; and we both fight, till they take ours or give us theirs. It is a very justifiable cause of war to invade a country after the people have been wasted by famine, destroyed by pestilence, or embroiled by factions amongst themselves. It is justifiable to enter into a war against our nearest ally, when one of his towns lies convenient for us, or a territory of land, that would render our dominions round and compact. If a prince send forces into a nation, where the people are poor and ignorant, he may lawfully put half of them to death, and make slaves of the rest, in order to civilize and reduce them from their barbarous way of living. It is a very kingly, honourable, and frequent practice, when one prince desires the assistance of another to secure him against an invasion, that the assistant, when he hath driven out the invader, should seize on the dominions himself, and kill, imprison or banish the prince he came to relieve. Alliance by blood or marriage, is a sufficient cause of war between princes; and the nearer the kindred is, the greater is their disposition to quarrel: *Poor* nations are *hungry*, and *rich* nations are *proud*; and pride and hunger will ever be at variance. For these reasons, the trade of a *soldier* is held the most honourable of all others: because a *soldier* is a *Yahoo* hired to kill in cold blood as many of his own species, who have never offended him, as possibly he can.

There is likewise a kind of beggarly princes in Europe, not able to make war by themselves, who hire out their troops to richer nations for so much a day to each man; of which they keep three fourths to themselves, and it is the best part of their maintenance; such are those in many northern parts of Europe.

What you have told me, (said my master) upon the subject of war, doth indeed discover most admirably the effects of that reason you pretend to: however, it is happy that the *shame* is greater than the *danger*; and that nature hath left you utterly uncapable of doing much mischief: for your mouths lying flat with your faces, you can hardly bite each other to any purpose, unless by consent. Then, as to the claws upon your feet before and behind, they are so short and tender, that one of our *Yahoos* would drive a dozen of yours before him. And therefore in recounting the numbers of those who have been killed in battle, I cannot but think that you have *said the thing which is not*.

I could not forbear shaking my head and smiling a little at his ignorance. And, being no stranger to the art of war, I gave him a description of cannons, culverins, muskets, carabines, pistols, bullets, powder, swords, bayonets, sieges, retreats, attacks, undermines, countermines, bombardments, seafights; ships sunk with a thousand men; twenty thousand killed on each side; dying groans, limbs flying in the air; smoke, noise, confusion, trampling to death under horses feet: flight, pursuit, victory; fields strewed with carcases left for food to dogs, and wolves, and birds of prey; plundering, stripping, ravishing, burning and destroying. And, to set forth the valour of my own dear countrymen, I assured him, that I had seen them blow up a hundred enemies at once in a siege, and as many in a ship; and beheld the dead bodies drop down in pieces from the clouds, to the great diversion of all the spectators.

I was going on to more particulars, when my master commanded me silence. He said, whoever understood the nature of *Yahoos* might easily believe it possible for so vile an animal, to be capable of every action I had named, if their strength and cunning equalled their malice. But, as my discourse had increased his abhorrence of the whole species, so he found it gave him a disturbance in his mind, to which he was wholly a stranger before. He thought his ears being used to such abominable words, might by degrees admit them with less detestation. That, although he hated the *Yahoos* of this country, yet he no more blamed them for their odious qualities, than he did a *Gnnayh* (a bird of prey) for its cruelty, or a sharp stone for cutting his hoof. But, when a creature pretending to reason, could be capable of such enormities, he dreaded lest the corruption of that faculty might be worse than brutality itself. He seemed therefore confident, that instead of reason, we were only possessed of some quality fitted to increase our natural vices; as the reflection from a troubled stream returns the image of an ill-shapen body, not only larger, but more distorted.

He added, that he had heard too much upon the subject of war, both in this, and some former discourses. There was another point which a little perplexed him at present. I had said, that some of our crew left their country on account of being ruined by *law*: that I had already explained the meaning of the word; but he was at a loss how it should come to pass, that the *law* which was intended for every man's preservation, should be any man's ruin. Therefore he desired to be farther satisfied what I meant by *law*, and the dispensers thereof, according to the present practice in my own country: because he thought, nature and reason were sufficient guides for a reasonable animal, as we pretended to be, in shewing us what we ought to do, and what to avoid.

I assured his honour, that *law* was a science wherein I had not much conversed, further than by employing advocates, in vain, upon some injustices that had been done me. However, I would give him all the satisfaction I was able.

I said there was a society of men among us, bred up from their youth in the art of proving by words multiplied for the purpose, that *white* is *black*, and *black* is *white*, according as they are paid. To this society all the rest of the people are slaves.

A Modest Proposal for Preventing the Children of Poor People in Ireland from Being a Burden to their Parents or Country, and for Making them Beneficial to the Public

It is a melancholy object to those who walk through this great town[1] or travel in the country, when they see the streets, the roads, and cabin doors, crowded with beggars of the female sex, followed by three, four, or six children, all in rags and importuning every passenger for an alms. These mothers, instead of being able to work for their honest livelihood, are forced to employ all their time in strolling to beg sustenance for their helpless infants: who as they grow up either turn thieves for want of work, or leave their dear native country to fight for the Pretender in Spain, or sell themselves to the Barbadoes.

I think it is agreed by all parties that this prodigious number of children in the arms, or on the backs, or at the heels of their mothers, and frequently of their fathers, is in the present deplorable state of the kingdom a very great additional grievance; and, therefore, whoever could find out a fair, cheap, and easy method of making these children sound, useful members of the commonwealth, would deserve so well of the public as to have his statue set up for a preserver of the nation.

But my intention is very far from being confined to provide only for the children of professed beggars; it is of a much greater extent, and shall take in the whole number of infants at a certain age who are born of parents in effect as little able to support them as those who demand our charity in the streets.

As to my own part, having turned my thoughts for many years upon this important subject, and maturely weighed the several schemes of other projectors I have always found them grossly mistaken in the computation. It is true, a child just dropped from its dam may be supported by her milk for a solar year, with little other nourishment; at most not above the value of two shillings, which the mother may certainly get, or the value in scraps, by her lawful occupation of begging; and it is exactly at one year old that I propose to provide for them in such a manner as instead of being a charge upon their parents or the parish, or wanting food and raiment for the rest of their lives, they shall on the contrary contribute to the feeding, and partly to the clothing, of many thousands.

There is likewise another great advantage in my scheme, that it will prevent those voluntary abortions, and that horrid practice of women murdering their bastard children, alas! too frequent among us! sacrificing the poor innocent babes I doubt more to avoid the expense than the shame, which would move tears and pity in the most savage and inhuman breast.

The number of souls in this kingdom being usually reckoned one million and a half, of these I calculate there may be about two hundred thousand couple whose wives are breeders; from which number I subtract thirty thousand couples who are able to maintain their own children, although I apprehend there

---

1: i.e. Dublin.

cannot be so many, under the present distresses of the kingdom; but this being granted, there will remain an hundred and seventy thousand breeders. I again subtract fifty thousand for those women who miscarry, or whose children die by accident or disease within the year. There only remains one hundred and twenty thousand children of poor parents annually born. The question therefore is, how this number shall be reared and provided for, which, as I have already said, under the present situation of affairs, is utterly impossible by all the methods hitherto proposed. For we can neither employ them in handicraft or agriculture; we neither build houses (I mean in the country) nor cultivate land: they can very seldom pick up a livelihood by stealing, till they arrive at six years old, except where they are of towardly parts,[1] although I confess they learn the rudiments much earlier, during which time, they can however be properly looked upon only as probationers, as I have been informed by a principal gentleman in the county of Cavan, who protested to me that he never knew above one or two instances under the age of six, even in a part of the kingdom so renowned for the quickest proficiency in that art.

I am assured by our merchants, that a boy or a girl before twelve years old is no saleable commodity; and even when they come to this age they will not yield above three pounds, or three pounds and half-a-crown at most on the exchange; which cannot turn to account either to the parents or kingdom, the charge of nutriment and rags having been at least four times that value.

I shall now therefore humbly propose my own thoughts, which I hope will not be liable to the least objection.

I have been assured by a very knowing American of my acquaintance in London, that a young healthy child well nursed is at a year old a most delicious, nourishing, and wholesome food, whether stewed, roasted, baked, or boiled; and I make no doubt that it will equally serve in a fricassee or a ragout.

I do therefore humbly offer it to public consideration that of the hundred and twenty thousand children already computed, twenty thousand may be reserved for breed, whereof only one-fourth part to be males; which is more than we allow to sheep, black cattle or swine; and my reason is, that these children are seldom the fruits of marriage, a circumstance not much regarded by our savages, therefore one male will be sufficient to serve four females. That the remaining hundred thousand may, at a year old, be offered in the sale to the persons of quality and fortune through the kingdom; always advising the mother to let them suck plentifully in the last month, so as to render them plump and fat for a good table. A child will make two dishes at an entertainment for friends; and when the family dines alone, the fore or hind quarter will make a reasonable dish, and seasoned with a little pepper or salt will be very good boiled on the fourth day, especially in winter.

I have reckoned upon a medium that a child just born will weigh 12 pounds, and in a solar year, if tolerably nursed, increaseth to 28 pounds.

I grant this food will be somewhat dear, and therefore very proper for landlords, who, as they have already devoured most of the parents, seem to have the best title to the children.

1: promising abilities.

Infant's flesh will be in season throughout the year, but more plentiful in March, and a little before and after; for we are told by a grave author, an eminent French physician,[1] that fish being a prolific diet, there are more children born in Roman Catholic countries about nine months after Lent than at any other season; therefore, reckoning a year after Lent, the markets will be more glutted than usual, because the number of popish infants is at least three to one in this kingdom: and therefore it will have one other collateral advantage, by lessening the number of papists among us.

I have already computed the charge of nursing a beggar's child (in which list I reckon all cottagers, laborers, and four-fifths of the farmers) to be about two shillings per annum, rags included, and I believe no gentleman would repine to give ten shillings for the carcass of a good fat child, which, as I have said, will make four dishes of excellent nutritive meat, when he hath only some particular friend, or his own family to dine with him. Thus the squire will learn to be a good landlord, and grow popular among his tenants; the mother will have eight shillings net profit, and be fit for work till she produces another child.

Those who are more thrifty (as I must confess the times require) may flay the carcass; the skin of which artificially dressed will make admirable gloves for ladies, and summer boots for fine gentlemen.

As to our city of Dublin, shambles[2] may be appointed for this purpose in the most convenient parts of it, and butchers we may be assured will not be wanting; although I rather recommend buying the children alive, and dressing them hot from the knife, as we do roasting pigs. A very worthy person, a true lover of his country, and whose virtues I highly esteem, was lately pleased in discoursing on this matter to offer a refinement upon my scheme. He said that many gentlemen of this kingdom, having of late destroyed their deer, he conceived that the want of venison might be well supplied by the bodies of young lads and maidens, not exceeding fourteen years of age nor under twelve; so great a number of both sexes in every country being now ready to starve for want of work and service; and these to be disposed of by their parents, if alive, or otherwise by their nearest relations.

But with due deference to so excellent a friend and so deserving a patriot, I cannot be altogether in his sentiments; for as to the males, my American acquaintance assured me, from frequent experience, that their flesh was generally tough and lean, like that of our schoolboys by continual exercise, and their taste disagreeable; and to fatten them would not answer the charge. Then as to the females, it would, I think, with humble submission be a loss to the public, because they soon would become breeders themselves; and besides, it is not improbable that some scrupulous people might be apt to censure such a practice (although indeed very unjustly), as a little bordering upon cruelty; which, I confess, hath always been with me the strongest objection against any project, however so well intended. But in order to justify my friend, he confessed that this expedient was put into his head by the famous Psalmanazar,[3] a native of

---

1: François Rabelais (c. 1494–1553), a humorist and a satirist, by no means grave. 2: slaughterhouses. 3: (1679–1763), a famous imposter. A Frenchman, he imposed himself on English noblemen as a native of Formosa, and wrote an entirely fictitious account of this country, describing human sacrifices and cannibalism.

the island Formosa, who came from thence to London above twenty years ago, and in conversation told my friend, that in his country when any young person happened to be put to death, the executioner sold the carcass to persons of quality as a prime dainty; and that in his time the body of a plump girl of fifteen, who was crucified for an attempt to poison the emperor, was sold to his imperial majesty's prime minister of state, and other great mandarins of the court, in joints from the gibbet, at four hundred crowns. Neither indeed can I deny, that if the same use were made of several plump young girls in this town, who without one single groat to their fortunes cannot stir abroad without a chair, and appear at playhouse and assemblies in foreign fineries which they never will pay for, the kingdom would not be the worse.

Some persons of a desponding spirit are in great concern about that vast number of poor people, who are aged, diseased, or maimed, and I have been desired to employ my thoughts what course may be taken to ease the nation of so grievous an encumbrance. But I am not in the least pain upon that matter, because it is very well known that they are every day dying and rotting by cold and famine, and filth and vermin, as fast as can be reasonably expected. And as to the young laborers, they are now in as hopeful a condition; they cannot get work, and consequently pine away for want of nourishment, to a degree that if at any time they are accidentally hired to common labor, they have not strength to perform it; and thus the country and themselves are happily delivered from the evils to come.

I have too long digressed, and therefore shall return to my subject. I think the advantages by the proposal which I have made are obvious and many, as well as of the highest importance.

For first, as I have already observed, it would greatly lessen the number of papists, with whom we are yearly overrun, being the principal breeders of the nation as well as our most dangerous enemies; and who stay at home on purpose with a design to deliver the kingdom to the Pretender, hoping to take their advantage by the absence of so many good protestants, who have chosen rather to leave their country than stay at home and pay tithes against their conscience to an episcopal curate.

Secondly, the poorer tenants will have something valuable of their own, which by law may be made liable to distress and help to pay their landlord's rent, their corn and cattle being already seized, and money a thing unknown.

Thirdly, Whereas the maintenance of an hundred thousand children, from two years old and upward, cannot be computed at less than ten shillings apiece per annum, the nation's stock will be thereby increased fifty thousand pounds per annum, beside the profit of a new dish introduced to the tables of all gentlemen of fortune in the kingdom who have any refinement in taste. And the money will circulate among ourselves, the goods being entirely of our own growth and manufacture.

Fourthly, the constant breeders, beside the gain of eight shillings sterling per annum by the sale of their children, will be rid of the charge of maintaining them after the first year.

Fifthly, this food would likewise bring great custom to taverns; where the vintners will certainly be so prudent as to procure the best receipts for dressing it to perfection, and consequently have their houses frequented by all the fine gentlemen, who justly value themselves upon their knowledge in good eating: and a skilful cook, who understands how to oblige his guests, will contrive to make it as expensive as they please.

Sixthly, this would be a great inducement to marriage, which all wise nations have either encouraged by rewards or enforced by laws and penalties. It would increase the care and tenderness of mothers toward their children, when they were sure of a settlement for life to the poor babes, provided in some sort by the public, to their annual profit instead of expense. We should see an honest emulation among the married women, which of them could bring the fattest child to the market. Men would become as fond of their wives during the time of their pregnancy as they are now of their mares in foal, their cows in calf, their sows when they are ready to farrow; nor offer to beat or kick them (as is too frequent a practice) for fear of a miscarriage.

Many other advantages might be enumerated. For instance, the addition of some thousand carcasses in our exportation of barrelled beef, the propagation of swine's flesh, and improvement in the art of making good bacon, so much wanted among us by the great destruction of pigs, too frequent at our tables; which are no way comparable in taste or magnificence to a well-grown, fat, yearling child, which roasted whole will make a considerable figure at a lord mayor's feast or any other public entertainment. But this and many others I omit, being studious of brevity.

Supposing that one thousand families in this city, would be constant customers for infant's flesh, besides others who might have it at merry-meetings, particularly weddings and christenings, I compute that Dublin would take off annually about twenty thousand carcasses, and the rest of the kingdom (where probably they will be sold somewhat cheaper) the remaining eighty thousand.

I can think of no one objection that will possibly be raised against this proposal, unless it should be argued that the number of people will be thereby much lessened in the kingdom. This I freely own, and it was indeed one principal design in offering it to the world. I desire the reader will observe, that I calculate my remedy for this one individual Kingdom of Ireland, and for no other that ever was, is, or I think, ever can be upon earth. Therefore let no man talk to me of other expedients: Of taxing our absentees at five shillings a pound: Of using neither clothes, nor household furniture, except what is of our own growth and manufacture: Of utterly rejecting the materials and instruments that promote foreign luxury: Of curing the expensiveness of pride, vanity, idleness, and gaming in our women: Of introducing a vein of parsimony, prudence and temperance: Of learning to love our Country, wherein we differ even from Laplanders and the inhabitants of Topinambo:[1] Of quitting our animosities and factions, nor act any longer like the Jews, who were murdering one another at the very moment their city was taken:[2] Of being a little cautious not to sell our country and our consciences for nothing: Of teaching landlords to have at least one degree of mercy towards their tenants. Lastly of putting a spirit of honesty, industry and skill into our shopkeepers, who, if a resolution could now

---

1: a Brazilian tribe.   2: during the siege of Jerusalem by Titus (AD 70).

be taken to buy only our native goods, would immediately untie to cheat and exact upon us in the price, the measure and the goodness, nor could ever yet be bought to make one fair proposal of just dealing, though often and earnestly invited to it.

Therefore I repeat, let no man talk to me of these and the like expedients, till he hath at least some glimpse of hope that there will ever be some hearty and sincere attempt to put them in practice.

But as to myself, having been wearied out for many years with offering vain, idle and visionary thoughts, and at length utterly despairing of success, I fortunately fell upon this proposal, which as it is wholly new, so it hath something solid and real, of no expense and little trouble, full in our own power, and whereby we can incur no danger in disobliging England. For this kind of commodity will not bear exportation, the flesh being of too tender a consistence to admit a long continuance in salt, although perhaps I could name a country which would be glad to eat up our whole nation without it.

After all, I am not so violently bent upon my own opinion as to reject any offer proposed by wise men, which shall be found equally innocent, cheap, easy, and effectual. But before something of that kind shall be advanced in contradiction to my scheme, and offering a better, I desire the author or authors will be pleased maturely to consider two points. First, as things now stand, how they will be able to find food and raiment for an hundred thousand useless mouths and backs. And secondly, there being a round million of creatures in human figure throughout this kingdom, whose whole subsistence put into a common stock would leave them in debt two millions of pounds sterling, adding those who are beggars by profession to the bulk of farmers, cottagers, and laborers, with their wives and children who are beggars in effect: I desire those politicians who dislike my overture, and may perhaps be so bold as to attempt an answer, that they will first ask the parents of these mortals, whether they would not at this day think it a great happiness to have been sold for food, at a year old in the manner I prescribe, and thereby have avoided such a perpetual scene of misfortunes as they have since gone through by the oppression of landlords, the impossibility of paying rent without money or trade, the want of common sustenance, with neither house nor clothes to cover them from the inclemencies of the weather, and the most inevitable prospect of entailing the like or greater miseries upon their breed for ever.

I profess, in the sincerity of my heart, that I have not the least personal interest in endeavoring to promote this necessary work, having no other motive than the public good of my country, by advancing our trade, providing for infants, relieving the poor, and giving some pleasure to the rich. I have no children by which I can propose to get a single penny; the youngest being nine years old, and my wife past child-bearing.

The Lady's Dressing Room

Five hours, (and who can do it less in?)
By haughty Celia spent in dressing;
The goddess from her chamber issues,
Arrayed in lace, brocade and tissues:
5   Strephon, who found the room was void
And Betty otherwise employed,
Stole in, and took a strict survey,
Of all the litter as it lay:
Whereof, to make the matter clear,
10   An inventory follows here.
     And first, a dirty smock appeared,
Beneath the arm-pits well besmeared;
Strephon, the rogue, displayed it wide,
And turned it round on every side.
15   On such a point few words are best,
And Strephon bids us guess the rest;
But swears how damnably the men lie,
In calling Celia sweet and cleanly.
Now listen while he next produces
20   The various combs for various uses,
Filled up with dirt so closely fixt,
No brush could force a way betwixt;
A paste of composition rare,
Sweat, dandruff, powder, lead and hair,
25   A forehead cloth with oil upon't
To smooth the wrinkles on her front;
Here alum flower to stop the steams,
Exhaled from sour unsavoury streams;
There night-gloves made of Tripsy's hide,
30   Bequeathed by Tripsy when she died;
With puppy water, beauty's help,
Distilled from Tripsy's darling whelp.
Here gallipots and vials placed,
Some filled with washes, some with paste;
35   Some with pomatum, paints and slops,
And ointments good for scabby chops
Hard by a filthy basin stands,
Fouled with the scouring of her hands;
The basin takes whatever comes,
40   The scrapings of her teeth and gums,
A nasty compound of all hues,

---

5 **Strephon:** conventional name for a rustic lover   31 **puppy water:** a quack cosmetic made from a dog's
deriving from Sir Philip Sydney's *Arcadia*.   27 **alum**   innards.   33 **gallipots:** ointment pots.
flower: a medicinal salt.

For here she spits, and here she spews.
But oh! it turned poor Strephon's bowels,
When he beheld and smelled the towels;
45 Begummed, bemattered, and beslimed;
With dirt, and sweat, and earwax grimed.
No object Strephon's eye escapes,
Here, petticoats in frowzy heaps;
Nor be the handkerchiefs forgot,
50 All varnished o'er with snuff and snot.
The stockings why should I expose,
Stained with the moisture of her toes;
Or greasy coifs and pinners reeking,
Which Celia slept at least a week in?
55 A pair of tweezers next he found
To pluck her brows in arches round,
Or hairs that sink the forehead low,
Or on her chin like bristles grow.
    The virtues we must not let pass,
60 Of Celia's magnifying glass;
When frighted Strephon cast his eye on't,
It showed visage of a giant:
A glass that can to sight disclose
The smallest worm in Celia's nose,
65 And faithfully direct her nail
To squeeze it out from head to tail;
For catch it nicely by the head,
It must come out alive or dead.
    Why, Strephon, will you tell the rest?
70 And must you needs describe the chest?
That careless wench! no creature warn her
To move it out from yonder corner,
But leave it standing full in sight,
For you to exercise your spite.
75 In vain the workman showed his wit
With rings and hinges counterfeit
To make it seem in this disguise,
A cabinet to vulgar eyes;
For Strephon ventured to look in,
80 Resolved to go through thick and thin;
He lifts the lid: there need no more,
He smelt it all the time before.
As, from within Pandora's box,
When Epimethus oped the locks,

---

48 **frowzy**: unkempt.   83 **Pandora**: Pandora had all the gifts of the gods and kept the evils stored in a jar. Prometheus's simple brother, Epimethus, the 'after-thinker', married her and opened the box, letting out all the evils of the world, only hope remaining.

85   A sudden universal crew
      Of human evils upward flew;
      He still was comforted to find
      That hope at last remained behind.
      So, Strephon, lifting up the lid,
90   To view what in the chest was hid,
      The vapours flew from out the vent,
      But Strephon cautious never meant
      The bottom of the pan to grope,
      And foul his hands in search of hope.
95   O never may such vile machine
      Be once in Celia's chamber seen!
      O may she better learn to keep
      'Those secrets of the hoary deep.'
        As mutton cutlets, prime of meat,
100   Which though with art you salt and beat,
      As laws of cookery require,
      And roast them at the clearest fire;
      If from adown the hopeful chops
      The fat upon a cinder drops,
105   To stinking smoke it turns the flame
      Poisoning the flesh from whence it came;
      And up exhales a greasy stench,
      For which you curse the careless wench:
      So things which must not be expressed,
110   When plumped into the reeking chest,
      Send up an excremental smell
      To taint the parts from which they fell:
      The petticoats and gown perfume,
      And waft a stink round every room.
115   Thus finishing his grand survey,
      Disgusted Strephon stole away,
      Repeating in his amorous fits,
      'Oh! Celia, Celia, Celia shits!'
        But Vengeance, goddess never sleeping,
120   Soon punished Strephon for his peeping.
      His foul imagination links
      Each dame he sees with all her stinks:
      And, if unsavoury odours fly,
      Conceives a lady standing by:
125   All women his description fits,
      And both ideas jump like wits,
      By vicious fancy coupled fast,
      And still appearing in contrast.
      I pity wretched Strephon, blind
130   To all the charms of womankind;

Should I the queen of love refuse,
Because she rose from stinking ooze?
To him that looks behind the scene,
Statira's but some pocky quean.
135　When Celia in her glory shows,
If Strephon would but stop his nose,
(Who now so impiously blasphemes
Her ointments, daubs, and paints and creams;
Her washes, slops, and every clout,
140　With which he makes so foul a rout,
He soon would learn to think like me,
And bless his ravished eyes to see
Such order from confusion sprung,
Such gaudy tulips raised from dung.

A Beautiful Young Nymph Going to Bed

Written For The Honour Of The Fair Sex

Corinna, pride of Drury Lane,
For whom no shepherd sighs in vain,
Never did Covent Garden boast
So bright a battered, strolling toast;
5　No drunken rake to pick her up,
No cellar where on tick to sup;
Returning at the midnight hour;
Four storeys climbing to her bower;
Then, seated on a three-legged chair,
10　Takes off her artificial hair:
Now, picking out a crystal eye,
She wipes it clean, and lays it by.
Her eyebrows from a mouse's hide,
Stuck on with art on either side,
15　Pulls off with care, and first displays 'em,
Then in a play-book smoothly lays 'em
Now dexterously her plumpers draws,
That serve to fill her hollow jaws.
Untwists a wire; and from her gums
20　A set of teeth completely comes.
Pulls out the rags contrived to prop
Her flabby dugs, and down they drop.
Proceeding on, the lovely goddess
Unlaces next her steel-ribbed bodice;
25　Which by the operator's skill,

---

134 **Statira**: heroine of Lee's play *Rival Queens* (1677). **quean**: a strumpet (Johnson), a whore.　3 **Covent Garden:** an area known for its theatres and brothels.　6 **on tick:** on credit.　17 **plumpers:** a cosmetic device used to fill out cheeks made hollow by disease.

Press down the lumps, the hollows fill.
Up goes her hand, and off she slips
The bolsters that supply her hips.
With gentlest touch, she next explores
30 Her shankers, issues, running sores;
Effects of many a sad disaster,
And then to each applies a plaster.
But must, before she goes to bed,
Rub off the daubs of white and red.
35 And smooth the furrows in her front,
With greasy paper stuck upon't.
She takes a bolus e'er she sleeps;
And then between two blankets creeps.
With pains of love tormented lies;
40 Or if she chance to close her eyes,
Of Bridewell and the compter dreams,
And feels the lash, and faintly screams.
Or, by a faithless bully drawn,
At some hedge-tavern lies in pawn
45 Or to Jamaica seems transported,
Alone, and by no planter courted;
Or, near Fleet Ditch's oozy brinks,
Surrounded with a hundred stinks,
Belated, seems on watch to lie,
50 And snap some cully passing by;
Or, struck with fear, her fancy runs
On watchmen, constables and duns,
From whom she meets with frequent rubs;
But, never from religious clubs;
55 Whose favour she is sure to find,
Because she pays them all in kind.
Corinna wakes. A dreadful sight!
Behold the ruins of the night!
A wicked rat her plaster stole,
60 Half ate, and dragged it to his hole.
The crystal eye, alas, was missed;
And Puss had on her plumpers pissed.
A pigeon picked her issue-peas,
And Shock her tresses filled with fleas.
65   The nymph, though in this mangled plight,
Must every morn her limbs unite.
But how shall I describe her arts

---

30 **shankers:** sores, presumably veneral. **35 front:** forehead. **41 Bridewell . . . compter:** city prisons. **43 bully:** pimp. **44 hedge-tavern:** cheap inn.   **47 Fleet Ditch:** the Fleet river, a noisome open sewer forming the Western margin to the City. **50 cully:** someone easily fooled. **54 religious clubs:** societies for the reformation of manners.

To recollect the scattered parts?
Or show the anguish, toil, and pain,
70 Of gathering up herself again?
The bashful muse will never bear
In such a scene to interfere.
Corinna in the morning dizened,
Who sees, will spew; who smells, be poisoned.

SAMUEL RICHARDSON (1689–1761)

Samuel Richardson was the son of a Derbyshire joiner and served apprenticeship as a printer before setting up his own business as a printer and publisher in 1721. Through intelligence and hard work he became one of the most highly reputed printer-publishers in the country, having the contract to print for the House of Commons and being called upon to advise on the reform of Oxford University Press. In 1739 he began a volume of exemplary letters which evolved into the novel *Pamela* (1740) and met with critical acclaim and enormous popular success, especially with women. A second part was added to *Pamela* in 1741, and in 1747–48 he published one of the longest novels in the English language, *Clarissa*. This attracted international praise and spawned numerous imitations. Richardson's novels were all epistolary, a genre to which he brought an unprecedented vivacity and psychological subtlety. *Pamela*, like *Clarissa*, is a story of a woman held against her will and threatened with rape by a man of superior social class. Pamela is a servant whose good looks first attract Mr B., her employer, but as the novel develops he becomes more and more taken by her letters and in the following scene demands that she hand them over to him. In the end they will marry, his manners reformed by both her literary style and her exemplary conduct.

From Pamela

About nine o'clock he [Mr. B.] sent for me down into the parlour. I went a little fearfully, and he held the papers in his hand, and said, 'Now, Pamela, you come upon your trial.' Said I, 'I hope I have a *just* judge to hear my cause.' – 'Aye,' said he, 'and you may hope for a merciful one too, or else I know not what will become of you.'

'I expect,' continued he, 'that you will answer me directly, and plainly, to every question I shall ask you. In the first place, here are several love-letters between you and Williams.'

'Love-letters? Sir,' said I. – 'Well, call them what you will,' said he, 'I don't entirely like them, I'll assure you, with all the allowances you desired me to make for you.' – 'Do you find, Sir,' said I, 'that I encouraged his proposals?' Why,' said he, 'you discourage his address in appearance; but no otherwise than all your cunning sex do to ours, to make us more eager in pursuing you.'

'Well, Sir,' said I, 'that is your comment; but it does not appear so in the text.' – 'Smartly said!' says he: 'where a d—l gottest thou, at these years, all this knowledge? And then thou hast a memory, as I see by your papers, that nothing escapes.' – 'Alas! Sir,' said I, 'what poor abilities I have serve only to make me more miserable! I have no pleasure in my memory which impresses things upon me, that I could be glad never *were*, or everlastingly to *forget*.'

'Well,' said he, 'but where are the accounts (since you have kept so exact a journal of all that has befallen you) *previous* to these in my hand?' – 'My father has them, Sir,' said I. 'By whose means?' said he. 'By Mr. Williams's,' said I. 'Well answered,' said he. 'But cannot you contrive to get me a sight of them?' – 'That would be pretty!' said I. 'I wish I could have contrived to have kept those you have from your sight.' Said he, 'I *must* see them, Pamela, or I shall never be easy; for I must know how this correspondence between you and Williams began: and if I *can* see them it shall be better for you, if they answer what these give me hope they will.'

'I can tell you, Sir, very faithfully,' said I, 'what the beginning was; for I was bold enough to be the *beginner*.' – 'That won't do,' said he; 'for though this may appear a punctilio to *you*, to *me* it is of high importance.' – 'Sir,' said I, 'if you please to let me go to my father, I will send them to you by any messenger you shall send for them.' – 'Will you so? But I dare say, if you will write for them, they will send them to you, without the trouble of such a journey to yourself: and I beg you will.'

'I think Sir,' said I, 'as you have seen all my *former* letters through John's baseness, and now *these*, through your faithful housekeeper's officious watchfulness, you *might* see *all the rest*; but I hope you will not desire it, till I can see how much my pleasing you in this particular will be of use to myself.'

'You must trust to my honour for that. But tell me, Pamela,' said the sly gentleman, 'since I have seen *these* would you have voluntarily shown me *those*, had they been in your possession?'

I was not aware of this inference, and said, 'Yes, truly, Sir, I think I should, if you commanded it.' 'Well, then, Pamela,' said he, 'as I am sure you have found means to continue your journal, I desire, till the *former part* can come, that you will show me the *succeeding*.' 'O Sir,' said I, 'have you caught me so? But indeed you must excuse me there.'

'Why,' said he, 'tell me truly, have you not continued your account till now?' – 'Don't ask me, Sir,' said I. 'But I insist upon your answer,' replied he. – 'Why, then, Sir, I will not tell an untruth; I have.' – 'That's my good girl!' said he; 'I love sincerity at my heart' – 'In *another*, Sir,' said I, 'I presume you mean!' – 'Well,' said he, 'I'll allow you to be a little witty upon me; because it is *in you*, and you cannot help it; but you will greatly oblige me, to show me voluntarily what you have written. I long to see the particulars of your plot, and your disappointment, where your papers leave off: for you have so beautiful a manner that it is partly that, and partly my love for you, that has made me desirous of reading all you write; though a great deal of it is against myself; for which you must expect to suffer a little; and as I have furnished you with the subject I have a title to see the fruit of your pen. Besides,' said he, 'there is such a pretty air of romance in *your* plots, and *my* plots, that I shall be better directed in what manner to wind up the catastrophe of the pretty novel.'

'If I was your equal, Sir,' said I, 'I should say, this is a very provoking way of jeering at the misfortunes you have brought upon me.'

'O' said he, 'the liberties you have taken with my character in your letters set us upon a par, at least, in that respect.' – ' Sir, I could not have taken those liberties if you had not given me the cause: and the cause, Sir, you know, is before the *effect*.'

'True, Pamela,' said he; 'you chop logic very prettily. What the deuce do we men go to school for? If our wits were equal to women's we might spare much time and pains in our education, for nature teaches your sex what, in a long course of nature and study, ours can hardly attain to. But indeed every lady is not a Pamela.'

'You delight to banter your poor servant,' said I. ' Nay,' continued he, 'I believe I must assume to myself half the merit of your wit too; for the innocent exercises you have had for it from me have certainly sharpened your invention.'

'Sir,' said I, 'could I have been without those *innocent* exercises, as you are pleased to call them, I should have been glad to have been as dull as a beetle.' – 'But then, Pamela,' said he, 'I should not have loved you so well.' – 'But then, Sir, I should have been safe, easy, and happy.' – 'Aye, maybe so, and maybe not; and the wife too of some clouterly plough-boy.' – 'But then, Sir, I should have been content and innocent; and that's better than being a princess, and not so.' – 'Maybe not,' said he; 'for with that pretty face, some of us keen fox-hunters should have found you out; and, in spite of your romantic notions (which then, perhaps, would not have had so strong a place in your mind), might have been more happy with the ploughman's wife, than I have been with my mother's Pamela.' – ' I hope, Sir,' said I, 'God would have given me more grace.'

'Well, but,' resumed he, 'as to these writings of yours, that follow your fine plot, I must see them.' – 'Indeed, Sir, you must not, if I can help it.' – 'Nothing,' said he, 'pleases me better than that in all your arts and stratagems, you have a great regard to truth; and, in all your little pieces of deceit told a very few *wilful* fibs. Now I expect you'll continue this laudable rule in your conversation with me. Let me know where you have found supplies of pen, ink, and paper, when Mrs. Jewkes was so vigilant, and gave you but two sheets at a time? – Tell me the truth.'

'Why, Sir, little did I think I should have such occasion for them; but when I went away from your house I begged some of each of good Mr. Longman, who gave me plenty.' – 'Yes, yes,' said he, 'it must be *good* Mr. Longman! All your confederates are good, every one of them; but such of my servants as have done their duty, and obeyed my orders, are painted by you as black as devils; so am I too, I dare say.'

'Sir,' said I, 'I hope you won't be angry; but, saving yourself, do you think they are painted worse than they deserve?'

'You say, saving myself, Pamela; but is not that saving a mere compliment to me because I am present, and you are in my hands?' – 'Good Sir, excuse me; but I fancy I might ask you, why you should think so, if there was not a little bit of conscience that told you there was but too much reason for it?'

He kissed me, and said 'I must either do this, or be angry with you; for you are very saucy, Pamela. But with your bewitching chit-chat, and pretty impertinence, I will not lose my question. Where did you hide your paper, pens, and ink?'

'Some, Sir, in one place, some in another; that I might have some left, if others should be found.' – 'That's a good girl!' said he, 'I love you for your sweet veracity. Now tell me where it is you hide your written papers, your saucy journal!' – 'I must beg your excuse for that, Sir,' said I. – 'But' answered he, 'you will not have it: for I *will* know, and *see* them.' – 'That is very hard, Sir,' said I; 'but I must say you shall not, if I can help it.'

We were standing most of the time, but he then sat down, and took me by both my hands, and said, – 'Well said, my pretty Pamela, *if you can help it!* But I will not let you help it. Tell me, are they in your pocket?' – 'No, Sir,' said I; my heart up at my mouth. Said he 'I know you won't tell a downright *fib* for the world; but for *equivocation!* no Jesuit ever went beyond you. Answer me, are they in neither of your pockets?' – 'No, Sir,' said I. – 'Are they not,' said he, 'about your stays?' – 'No, Sir,' replied I: 'but pray, no more questions; for ask me ever so much, I will not tell you.'

'O,' said he, 'I have a way for that. I can do as they do abroad, when the criminals won't confess; torture them till they do.' – 'But pray, Sir,' said I, 'is this fair or honest? I am no criminal; and I won't confess.'

'O, my girl!' said he, 'many an innocent person has been put to the torture. But let me know where they are, and you shall escape the *question*, as they call it abroad.'

'Sir,' said I, 'the torture is not used in England; and I hope you won't bring it up.' – 'Admirably said!' replied he. 'But I can tell you of as good a punishment. If a criminal won't plead with us here in England, we press him to death, or till he does plead. And so, Pamela, that is a punishment that shall certainly be yours, if you won't tell without.'

Tears stood in my eyes, and I said, 'This, Sir is very cruel and barbarous.' 'No matter,' said he; 'it is but like your *Lucifer*, you know, in my shape! And after I have done so many heinous things by you, as *you* think, you have no great reason to judge so hardly of this; or, at least, it must be of a piece with the rest.'

'But, Sir,' said I (dreadfully afraid he had some notion they were about me), 'if you will be obeyed in this unreasonable manner – though it is sad tyranny, to be sure – let me go up to them, and read them over again, and you shall see so far as to the end of the sad story that follows those you have.'

'I'll see them all,' said he, 'down to this time, if you have written so far, or, at least, till within this week.' – 'Then let me go up to see them,' said I, 'and see what I have written, and to what day, to show them to you, for you won't desire to see every thing.' – 'But I will,' replied he. 'But say, Pamela, tell me truth, are they *above*?' I was much affrighted. He saw my confusion. 'Tell me truth,' said he. 'Why, Sir,' answered I, 'I have sometimes hid them under the dry mould in the garden; sometimes in one place, sometimes in another; and those in your hand were several days under a rose-bush in the garden.' – 'Artful slut!' said he, 'what's this to my queen? Are they not *about* you?' – 'If,' said I, 'I must pluck them from my hiding-place behind the wainscot, won't you see me?' – 'Still more and more artful,' said he. 'Is this an answer to my question? I have searched every place above, and in your closet for them, and cannot find them; so I *will* know where they are. Now,' said he, 'it is my opinion they are about you; and I never undressed a girl in my life; but I will now begin to strip my pretty Pamela; and I hope I shall not go far before I find them.'

I fell a crying, and said – 'I will not be used in this manner! Pray, Sir,' said I (for he began to unpin my handkerchief), 'consider! Pray, Sir, do!' – 'Pray,' said he, 'do *you* consider; for I will see these papers. But, maybe,' said he, 'they are tied about your knees with your garters;' and stooped. Was ever any thing so vile and wicked? I fell on my knees, and said, 'What *can* I do? If you'll let me go up, I'll fetch them.' – 'Will you,' said he, 'on your honour, let me see them all, and not offer to conceal a single paper?' – 'I will, Sir.' – 'On your honour?' – 'Yes, Sir.' And so he let me go up stairs, crying sadly for vexation to be so used. Sure nobody was ever so served as I am!

I went to my closet, and sat down. I could not bear the thoughts of giving up my papers. Besides I must almost undress me to untack them. – So I writ thus:

'Sir, –
'To expostulate with such an arbitrary gentleman, I know will signify nothing; most hardly do you use the power you so wickedly have got over me. I have heart enough, Sir, to do a deed that would make you regret using me thus: I can hardly bear it, and what I am further to undergo. But a superior consideration withholds me; thank God it does! I will, however, keep my word, if you insist upon it when you have read this; but, Sir, let me beg of you to give me time till tomorrow morning, that I may just run them over, and see what I put into your hands against me: I will then give my papers to you, without the least alteration; but I should beg still to be excused, if you please; but if not, spare them to me till tomorrow morning: and this, so hardly am I used, shall be thought a favour, which I shall be very thankful for.'

I guessed it would not be long before I heard from him: and he accordingly sent up Mrs. Jewkes for what I had promised. So I gave her this note to carry to him. He sent word that I must keep my promise, and he would give me till morning but that I must bring them to him without his asking again.

So I took off my undercoat, and with great trouble unsewed them. There is a vast quantity. I will slightly touch upon the subjects, because I may not, perhaps, get them again for you to see.

Letter to Sophia Westcomb, 1746

Most eighteenth-century novels presented themselves in the form of daily journals or exchanges of letters because these cultural practices were of growing importance for an increasingly literate population. In addition to writing epistolary novels, Richardson was an assiduous correspondent and the following letter, first published by Laetitia Barbauld in 1804, offers an example of the genre as well as important reflections on the art and purpose of the letter.

What charming advantages, what high delights, my dear, good, and condescending Miss Westcomb, flow from the familiar correspondences of friendly and undesigning hearts! – Surprising! that the generality of young ladies, delicate by sex, by education; and polite as delicate; their imaginations likewise so happily qualifying them for these mental employments, should be so little sensible of them as they are! – When styles differ, too, as much as faces, and are indicative, generally beyond the power of disguise, of the mind of the writer! – Who would not choose, when necessary absence, when the demands of an indulgent parent, deprive her of the person of her charming friend, to have a delight in retiring to her closet, and there, by pen and ink, continue, and, as I may say, perpetuate, the ever agreeable and innocent pleasures that flow from social love, from hearts united by the same laudable ties?

I make no scruple to aver, that a correspondence by letters, written on occasions of necessary absence, and which leaves a higher joy still in hope, which presence takes away, gives the most desirable opportunities of displaying the force of friendship, that can be wished for by a friendly heart. This correspondence is, indeed, the cement of friendship: it is friendship avowed under hand and seal: friendship upon bond, as I may say: more pure, yet more ardent, and less broken in upon, than personal conversation can be even amongst the most pure, because of the deliberation it allows, from the very preparation to, and action of writing.

A proof of this appears in the letter before me! – Every line of it flowing with that artless freedom, that noble consciousness of honourable meaning, which shine in every feature, in every sentiment, in every expression of the fair writer!

While I read it, I have you before me in person: I converse with you, and your dear Anna, as arm-in-arm you traverse the happy terrace: kept myself at humble distance, more by my own true respect for you both, than by your swimming robes: I would say hoops, but that I love not the mechanic word! – I see you, I sit with you, I talk with you, I read to you, I stop to hear your sentiments, in the summer-house: your smiling obligingness, your polite and easy expression, even your undue diffidence, are all in my eye and my ear as I read. Who then shall decline the converse of the pen? The pen that makes distance, presence; and brings back to sweet remembrance all the delights of presence; which makes even presence but body, while absence becomes the soul; and leaves no room for the intrusion of breakfast-calls, or dinner or supper direction, which often broke in upon us.

Not that these cares, neither, are to be neglected; nor, indeed, any of the least duties of that economy which falls properly under a lady's inspection: I have taken care to make my Clarissa, whom you obligingly three times in your letter take notice of, inculcate this doctrine, – that all the intellectual pleasures a lady can give herself, not neglecting the necessary employments that shall make her shine in her domestic duties, should be given; but otherwise that she should prefer the useful to all theoretic knowledge. But this is one of the felicities that give a preference to familiar correspondencies – that they may be carried on, and best carried on, at the retired hour, either morning or evening, before needful avocations take place, or after they have been answered. For the pen is jealous of company. It expects, as I may say, to engross the writer's whole self; every body allows the writer to withdraw: it disdains company; and will have the entire attention.

Writing to your own sex I would principally recommend; since ours is hardly ever void of design, and makes a correspondence dangerous:— Except protected by times as in my case, by general character, by choice already filled up; where is the man that deserves to be favoured? – And were there the least room to suspect that there was any thing less than paternal in my views, I would not dare to urge the favour, or take the liberty.

But it is the diffidence I wish to banish: the diffidence! which, in the right place, is so great a beauty in the charming sex; – but why the diffidence to such a one as I am! – a plain writer: a sincere well-wisher: an undesigning scribbler; who admire none but the natural and easy beauties of the pen: no carper: and one who has so just an opinion of the sex, that he knows, in an hundred instances, that the ladies who love the pen are qualified by genius and imagination to excell in the beauties of this sort of writing: and that bashfulness, or diffidence of a person's own merits, are but other words for undoubted worthiness; and that such a lady cannot set pen to paper but a beauty must follow it; yet herself the last person that knows it.

But do not, dear Madam, in the future favours you bid me hope for, make apologies for length. The person who sits down, designing brevity, writing to a friend, on subjects of conversation and friendship, hastening, as I have known some visibly do, in their first line to the last, must, if leisure allow a larger letter, intend a slight. For what friendly heart can want a subject on such an occasion; when it must be sensible, that the goings-out, the comings-in, the visit either meditated, paid, or received, the visitors, the reading or musical subjects, the morning meditation, the mid-day bower, the evening walk: what she hopes, what she wishes, what she fears, are proper topics for the pen; and what friendship cannot be indifferent to. For what one thing is there, that a friend does, or is concerned in, or for, which can be too slight a subject to a friend?

I am, dear Miss Westcomb,
   Your most obliged correspondent,
      S. Richardson.

EDWARD YOUNG (1683–1765)

Well-connected but not rich, Edward Young achieved a doctorate in law at Oxford and in the 1720s used poetry to find aristocratic, political and royal preferment. In this he had more financial than literary success, being the author of much bombast and flatness. He then took holy orders, became rector of Welwyn to the north of London in 1730 and married. In 1741 his wife died and in 1742–45 he published his poetic meditations on the death of his wife, stepdaughter and her husband as *Night Thoughts,* a work which became widely influential throughout Europe, bequeathing many sayings to the English language. The work, which reached nine volumes, is exemplary of the 'graveyard school', a flourishing genre in the mid-eighteenth century which offered melancholy reflections on change, death, vicissitude, mortality and immortality.

From The Complaint, or Night Thoughts on Life, Death and Immortality

Night I

Tired Nature's sweet restorer, balmy sleep!
He, like the world, his ready visit pays
Where fortune smiles; the wretched he forsakes;
Swift on his downy pinion flies from woe,
5   And lights on lids unsullied with a tear.
   From short (as usual) and disturbed repose,
I wake: how happy they, who wake no more!
Yet that were vain, if dreams infest the grave.
I wake, emerging from a sea of dreams
10 Tumultuous; where my wrecked desponding thought,
From wave to wave of fancied misery,
At random drove, her helm of reason lost.
Though now restored, 'tis only change of pain,
(A bitter change!) severer for severe.
15 The day too short for my distress; and night,
Even in the zenith of her dark domain,
Is sunshine to the colour of my fate.
   Night, sable goddess! from her ebon throne,
In rayless majesty, now stretches forth
20 Her leaden sceptre o'er a slumb'ring world.
Silence, how dead! and darkness, how profound!
Nor eye, nor listening ear, an object finds;
Creation sleeps. 'Tis as the general pulse
Of life stood still, and nature made a pause;
25 An awful pause! prophetic of her sad end.
And let her prophecy be soon fulfill'd;
Fate! drop the curtain; I can lose no more.
   Silence and darkness! solemn sisters! twins
From ancient night, who nurse the tender thought
30 To reason, and on reason build resolve,
(That column of true majesty in man)
Assist me: I will thank you in the grave;
The grave, your kingdom: there is this frame shall fall
A victim sacred to your dreary shrine.
35 But what are ye? —
   Thou, who didst put to flight
Primeval silence, when the morning stars,
Exulting, shouted o'er the rising ball;
Thou, whose word from solid darkness struck
40 That spark, the sun; strike wisdom from my soul;

My soul, which flies to Thee, her trust, her treasure,
As misers to their gold, while others rest.
   Through this opaque of nature, and of soul,
This double night, transmit one pitying ray,
45 To lighten and to cheer. O lead my mind,
(A mind that fain would wander from its woe)
Lead it through various scenes of life and death;
And from each scene, the noblest truths inspire.
Nor less inspire my conduct, than my song;
50 Teach my best reason, reason; my best will
Teach rectitude; and fix my firm resolve
Wisdom to wed, and pay her long arrear:
Nor let the phial of thy vengeance, pour'd
On this devoted head, be pour'd in vain.
55   The bell strikes one. We take no note of time
But from its loss. To give it then a tongue
Is wise in man. As if an angel spoke,
I feel the solemn sound. If heard aright,
It is the knell of my departed hours:
60 Where are they? With the years beyond the flood.
It is the signal that demands dispatch:
How much is to be done? My hopes and fears
Start up alarmed, and o'er life's narrow verge
Look down. – On what? a fathomless abyss;
65 A dread eternity! how surely mine!
And can eternity belong to me,
Poor pensioner on the bounties of an hour?
   How poor, how rich, how abject, how august,
How complicate, how wonderful, is man!
70 How passing wonder He, who made him such!
Who centred in our make such strange extremes!
From different natures marvellously mixt,
Connection exquisite of different worlds!
Distinguish'd link in being's endless chain!
75 Midway from nothing to the deity!
A beam ethereal, sullied, and absorbed!
Though sullied, and dishonoured still divine!
Dim miniature of greatness absolute!
An heir of glory! a frail child of dust!
80 Helpless immortal! insect infinite!
A worm! a god! – I tremble at myself,
And in myself am lost! at home a stranger,
Thought wanders up and down, surprised, aghast
And wondering at her own: how reason reels!
85 O what a miracle to man is man,
Triumphantly distressed! what joy, what dread!
Alternately transported, and alarmed!

What can preserve my life? or what destroy!
An angel's arm can't snatch me from the grave;
90   Legions of angels can't confine me there.
'Tis past conjecture; all things rise in proof:
While o'er my limbs sleep's soft dominion spread:
What though my soul fantastic measures trod
O'er fairy fields; or mourned along the gloom
95   Of pathless woods; or down the craggy steep
Hurled headlong, swam with pain the mantled pool;
Or scaled the cliff; or danced on hollow winds,
With antic shapes, wild natives of the brain?
Her ceaseless flight, though devious, speaks her nature
100 Of subtler essence than the trodden clod;
Active, aerial, towering, unconfined,
Unfettered with her gross companion's fall.
Even silent night proclaims my soul immortal:
Even silent night proclaims eternal day.

WILLIAM COLLINS (1721–1759)

William Collins had a precocious and melancholic talent and died relatively young. Educated at Winchester and Oxford, he knew Joseph Warton, James Thomson and Samuel Johnson. His *Persian Eclogues* (1742) and *Odes on Several Descriptive and Allegoric Subjects* (1746) had slight impact in his own lifetime. However, the publication of Edmund Burke's *A Philosophical Enquiry into the Origin of our Ideas of the Sublime and the Beautiful* in 1757, and Joseph Warton's *Essay on the Writings and Genius of Pope* in 1756, marked a shift in aesthetic dominance from the neo-classical emphasis on wit and satire to an emphasis on nature, inspiration and the sublime. This new poetic shared Collins's idea of the poet as a sublime visionary and his work became very influential for pre-Romantic and Romantic writers.

Ode to Evening

If aught of oaten stop, or pastoral song,
May hope, chaste Eve, to soothe thy modest ear
Like thy own solemn springs,
Thy springs, and dying gales,
5   O nymph reserved, while now the bright-haired sun
Sits in yon western tent, whose cloudy skirts
With brede ethereal wove,
O'erhang his wavy bed:
Now air is hushed, save where the weak-eyed bat

---

1 **oaten stop:** the hole in a shepherd's pipe   7 **brede:** braid.
(from Milton, *Comus*, l. 345).

10   With short shrill shriek flits by on leathern wing,
       Or where the beetle winds
       His small but sullen horn,
       As oft he rises 'midst the twilight path,
       Against the pilgrim born in heedless hum:
15   Now teach me, maid composed,
       To breathe some softened strain,
       Whose numbers, stealing through thy darkening vale,
       May not unseemly with its stillness suit,
       As, musing slow, I hail
20   Thy genial loved return!
       For when thy folding-star arising shows
       His paly circlet, at his warning lamp
       The fragrant Hours, and elves
       Who slept in flowers the day,
25   And many a nymph who wreathes her brows with sedge,
       And sheds the freshening dew, and, lovelier still,
       The pensive pleasures sweet,
       Prepare thy shadowy car.
       Then lead, calm vot'ress, where some sheety lake
30   Cheers the lone heath, or some time-hallowed pile,
       Or upland fallows grey,
       Reflect its last cool gleam.
       But when chill blustering winds, or driving rain,
       Forbid my willing feet, be mine the hut,
35   That from the mountain's side
       Views wilds, and swelling floods,
       And hamlets brown, and dim-discovered spires,
       And hears their simple bell, and marks o'er all
       Thy dewy fingers draw
40   The gradual dusky veil.
       While Spring shall pour his showers, as oft he wont,
       And bathe thy breathing tresses, meekest Eve!
       While Summer loves to sport
       Beneath thy lingering light;
45   While sallow Autumn fills thy lap with leaves,
       Or Winter, yelling through the troublous air,
       Affrights thy shrinking train,
       And rudely rends thy robes;
       So long, sure-found beneath the sylvan shed,
50   Shall Fancy, Friendship, Science, rose-lipped Health
       Thy gentlest influence own,
       And hymn thy favorite name!

---

11 winds: sounds.   **21 folding-star:** evening star (from Milton, *Comus*, l. 93).   **29 sheety:** like a sheet (a coined word).   **42 breathing:** scented.

HENRY FIELDING (1707–1754)

Henry Fielding was born into a Somerset gentry family and educated at Eton. Encouraged by his cousin, Mary Wortley Montagu, he had early success as a dramatist, writing 25 plays between 1729 and 1737 when his satirical attacks on the government of Robert Walpole – along with those of his friend John Gay – precipitated a state censorship of the theatres which was to last until 1968. Fielding then read for the bar and in 1748 became a crusading Justice of the Peace for Westminster. With his half-brother Sir John Fielding he laid the basis for the modern police force, militated against corruption in the judiciary, and set an unparalleled example for honesty and fairness. The publication of Richardson's *Pamela* (1740) led Fielding to respond with a parody, *Shamela* (1741), and then to extend the joke with a history of Pamela's brother in *Joseph Andrews* (1742). His *History of Tom Jones, A Foundling* (1749) attracted the criticism of Richardson and Johnson (see *The Rambler*, 4, pp. 639–43 below) and enduring fame. His 'comic epic poem in prose' brought a neo-classical interest in form and literary allusion into ironic counterpoint with a picaresque tale and a range of characters from the vulgar to the aristocratic. It established the possibility of writing as 'an author' (rather than through a persona), and demonstrated the aesthetic pleasure that could be achieved by playing between the author, the reader, the character and the plot. *Tom Jones* established the form for nineteenth-century fiction, notably that of Scott, Thackeray, Dickens and Eliot.

    Tom Jones is a picaresque romance focused on the courtship of Sophia Western by Tom Jones, a foundling child who has been raised in Somersetshire by Squire Allworthy. Sophia is the daughter of a neighbouring squire, so the marriage would unify two estates. Allworthy's nephew, the sanctimonious and hypocritical Mr Blifil, succeeds in having the rumbustious but warm-hearted Tom driven from Allworthy's house. Tom then sets off to make his fortune in London. Sophia soon flees in the same direction rather than be forced into wedlock with Blifil. (In this and in many ways the novel takes the measure of Richardson's *Clarissa*.) After many adventures which bring Tom into many different beds and finally near to death by hanging, Tom is discovered to be Allworthy's nephew, is united with Sophia, and Blifil gets his just deserts.

From The History of Tom Jones, A Foundling

Book II, Chapter 1

Showing what kind of a history this is; what it is like, and what it is not like.

Though we have properly enough entitled this our work, a history, and not a life; nor an apology for a life, as is more in fashion; yet we intend in it rather to pursue the method of those writers, who profess to disclose the revolutions of countries, than to imitate the painful and voluminous historian, who, to preserve the regularity of his series, thinks himself obliged to fill up as much paper with the detail of months and years in which nothing remarkable happened, as he employs upon those notable eras when the greatest scenes have been transacted on the human stage.

    Such histories as these do, in reality, very much resemble a newspaper, which consists of just the same number of words, whether there be any news in it or not. They may likewise be compared to a stage coach, which performs constantly the same course, empty as well as full. The writer, indeed, seems to think himself obliged to keep even pace with time, whose amanuensis he is; and, like his master, travels as slowly through centuries of monkish dulness, when the world seems to have been asleep, as through that bright and busy age so nobly distinguished by the excellent Latin poet.

> *Ad confligendum venientibus undique poenis,*
> *Omnia cum belli trepido concussa tumultu*
> *Horrida contremuere sub altis aetheris auris;*
> *In dubioque fuit sub utrorum regna cadendum*
> *Omnibus humanis esset, terraque marique.*

Of which we wish we could give our readers a more adequate translation than that by Mr. Creech,[1]

> When dreadful Carthage frighted Rome with arms,
> And all the world was shook with fierce alarms;
> Whilst undecided yet, which part should fall,
> Which nation rise the glorious lord of all.

Now it is our purpose, in the ensuing pages, to pursue a contrary method. When any extraordinary scene presents itself (as we trust will often be the case), we shall spare no pains nor paper to open it at large to our reader; but if whole years should pass without producing any thing worthy his notice, we shall not be afraid of a chasm in our history; but shall hasten on to matters of consequence, and leave such periods of time totally unobserved.

These are indeed to be considered as blanks in the grand lottery of time. We therefore, who are the registers of that lottery, shall imitate those sagacious persons who deal in that which is drawn at Guildhall,[2] and who never trouble the public with the many blanks they dispose of; but when a great prize happens to be drawn, the newspapers are presently filled with it, and the world is sure to be informed at whose office it was sold: indeed, commonly two or three different offices lay claim to the honour of having disposed of it; by which, I suppose, the adventurers are given to understand that certain brokers are in the secrets of Fortune, and indeed of her cabinet council.

My reader then is not to be surprised, if, in the course of this work, he shall find some chapters very short, and others altogether as long; some that contain only the time of a single day, and others that comprise years; in a word, if my history sometimes seems to stand still, and sometimes to fly. For all which I shall not look on myself as accountable to any court of critical jurisdiction whatever: for as I am, in reality, the founder of a new province of writing, so I am at liberty to make what laws I please therein. And these laws, my readers, whom I consider as my subjects, are bound to believe in and to obey; with which that they may readily and cheerfully comply, I do hereby assure them that I shall principally regard their ease and advantage in all such institutions:

1: Thomas Creech (1659–1700) popular and widely quoted translator, here of Lucretius, *De Rerum Naturam*, iii, 833–37.   2: a state lottery, often abused by fraudsters dealing in false tickets.

for I do not, like a *jure divino*[1] tyrant, imagine that they are my slaves, or my commodity. I am, indeed, set over them for their own good only, and was created for their use, and not they for mine. Nor do I doubt, while I make their interest the great rule of my writings, they will unanimously concur in supporting my dignity, and in rendering me all the honour I shall deserve or desire.

Book V, Chapter 10

Showing the truth of many observations of Ovid, and of other more grave writers, who have proved beyond contradiction, that wine is often the forerunner of incontinency.

Jones retired from the company, in which we have seen him engaged, into the fields, where he intended to cool himself by a walk in the open air before he attended Mr. Allworthy. There, whilst he renewed those meditations on his dear Sophia, which the dangerous illness of his friend and benefactor had for some time interrupted, an accident happened, which with sorrow we relate, and with sorrow doubtless will it be read; however, that historic truth to which we profess so inviolable an attachment, obliges us to communicate it to posterity.

It was now a pleasant evening in the latter end of June, when our hero was walking in a most delicious grove, where the gentle breezes fanning the leaves, together with the sweet trilling of a murmuring stream, and the melodious notes of nightingales, formed altogether the most enchanting harmony. In this scene, so sweetly accommodated to love, he meditated on his dear Sophia. While his wanton fancy roamed unbounded over all her beauties, and his lively imagination painted the charming maid in various ravishing forms, his warm heart melted with tenderness; and at length, throwing himself on the ground, by the side of a gently murmuring brook, he broke forth into the following ejaculation:

'O Sophia, would Heaven give thee to my arms, how blest would be my condition! Cursed be that fortune which sets a distance between us. Was I but possessed of thee, one only suit of rags thy whole estate, is there a man on earth whom I would envy! How contemptible would the brightest Circassian beauty, dressed in all the jewels of the Indies, appear to my eyes! But why do I mention another woman? Could I think my eyes capable of looking at any other with tenderness, these hands should tear them from my head. No, my Sophia, if cruel fortune separates us for ever, my soul shall dote on thee alone. The chastest constancy will I ever preserve to thy image. Though I should never have possession of thy charming person, still shalt thou alone have possession of my thoughts, my love, my soul. Oh! my fond heart is so wrapped in that tender bosom, that the brightest beauties would for me have no charms, nor would a hermit be colder in their embraces. Sophia, Sophia alone shall be mine. What raptures are in that name! I will engrave it on every tree.'

1: the doctrine of absolutist monarchy that the king rules by divine right, attacked by Locke in *Two Treatises on Government* (1690) and effectively abolished in Britain at the Glorious Revolution.

At these words he started up, and beheld – not his Sophia – no, nor a Circassian maid richly and elegantly attired for the grand Signior's seraglio. No; without a gown, in a shift that was somewhat of the coarsest, and none of the cleanest, bedewed likewise with some odoriferous effluvia, the produce of the day's labour, with a pitchfork in her hand, Molly Seagrim approached. Our hero had his penknife in his hand, which he had drawn for the before-mentioned purpose of carving on the bark; when the girl coming near him, cried out with a smile, 'You don't intend to kill me, squire, I hope!' 'Why should you think I would kill you?' answered Jones. 'Nay,' replied she, 'after your cruel usage of me when I saw you last, killing me would, perhaps, be too great kindness for me to expect.'

Here ensued a parley, which, as I do not think myself obliged to relate, I shall omit. It is sufficient that it lasted a full quarter of an hour, at the conclusion of which they retired into the thickest part of the grove.

Some of my readers may be inclined to think this event unnatural. However, the fact is true; and perhaps may be sufficiently accounted for by suggesting, that Jones probably thought one woman better than none, and Molly as probably imagined two men to be better than one. Besides the before-mentioned motive assigned to the present behaviour of Jones, the reader will be likewise pleased to recollect in his favour, that he was not at this time perfect master of that wonderful power of reason, which so well enables grave and wise men to subdue their unruly passions, and to decline any of these prohibited amusements. Wine now had totally subdued this power in Jones. He was, indeed, in a condition, in which, if reason had interposed, though only to advise, she might have received the answer which one Cleostratus gave many years ago to a silly fellow, who asked him, if he was not ashamed to be drunk? 'Are not you,' said Cleostratus, 'ashamed to admonish a drunken man?' – To say the truth, in a court of justice drunkenness must not be an excuse, yet in a court of conscience it is greatly so; and therefore Aristotle, who commends the laws of Pittacus, by which drunken men received double punishment for their crimes, allows there is more of policy than justice in that law. Now, if there are any transgressions pardonable from drunkenness, they are certainly such as Mr. Jones was at present guilty of; on which head I could pour forth a vast profusion of learning, if I imagined it would either entertain my reader, or teach him anything more than he knows already. For his sake therefore I shall keep my learning to myself, and return to my history.

It hath been observed, that Fortune seldom doth things by halves. To say truth, there is no end to her freaks whenever she is disposed to gratify or displease. No sooner had our hero retired with his Dido, but

Speluncam Blifil dux et divinus eandem Deveniunt[1]

the parson and the young squire, who were taking a serious walk, arrived at the stile which leads into the grove, and the latter caught a view of the lovers just as they were sinking out of sight.

1: A parody of the *Aeneid*, iv., 165–6. Dido and Aeneas shelter from the rain in a cave and consummate their love.

Blifil knew Jones very well, though he was at above a hundred yards' distance, and he was as positive to the sex of his companion, though not to the individual person. He started, blessed himself, and uttered a very solemn ejaculation.

Thwackum expressed some surprise at these sudden emotions, and asked the reason of them. To which Blifil answered, 'He was certain he had seen a fellow and wench retire together among the bushes, which he doubted not was with some wicked purpose.' As to the name of Jones, he thought proper to conceal it, and why he did so must be left to the judgment of the sagacious reader; for we never choose to assign motives to the actions of men, when there is any possibility of our being mistaken.

The parson, who was not only strictly chaste in his own person, but a great enemy to the opposite vice in all others, fired at this information. He desired Mr. Blifil to conduct him immediately to the place, which as he approached he breathed forth vengeance mixed with lamentations; nor did he refrain from casting some oblique reflections on Mr. Allworthy; insinuating that the wickedness of the country was principally owing to the encouragement he had given to vice, by having exerted such kindness to a bastard, and by having mitigated that just and wholesome rigour of the law which allots a very severe punishment to loose wenches.

The way through which our hunters were to pass in pursuit of their game was so beset with briars, that it greatly obstructed their walk, and caused besides such a rustling, that Jones had sufficient warning of their arrival before they could surprise him; nay, indeed, so incapable was Thwackum of concealing his indignation, and such vengeance did he utter forth every step he took, that this alone must have abundantly satisfied Jones that he was (to use the language of sportsmen) found sitting.

Book VIII, Chapter 8

Jones arrives at Gloucester, and goes to the Bell; the character of that house, and of a petty-fogger which he there meets with.

Mr. Jones and Partridge, or Little Benjamin (which epithet of Little was perhaps given him ironically, he being in reality near six feet high), having left their last quarters in the manner before described, travelled on to Gloucester without meeting any adventure worth relating.

Being arrived here, they chose for their house of entertainment the sign of the Bell, an excellent house indeed, and which I do most seriously recommend to every reader who shall visit this ancient city. The master of it is brother to the great preacher Whitefield; but is absolutely untainted with the pernicious principles of Methodism, or of any other heretical sect. He is indeed a very honest plain man, and, in my opinion, not likely to create any disturbance either in church or state. His wife hath, I believe, had much pretension to beauty, and is still a very fine woman. Her person and deportment might have made a shining figure in the politest assemblies; but though she must be conscious of this and many other perfections, she seems perfectly contented with, and resigned to, that state of life to which she is called; and this resignation is entirely owing to the prudence and wisdom of her temper; for she is at present as free from any Methodistical notions as her husband: I say at present; for she freely confesses that her brother's documents made at first some impression upon her, and that she had put herself to the expense of a long hood, in order to attend the extraordinary emotions of the Spirit; but having found, during an experiment of three weeks, no emotions, she says, worth a farthing, she very wisely laid by her hood, and abandoned the sect. To be concise, she is a very friendly good-natured woman; and so industrious to oblige, that the guests must be of very morose disposition who are not extremely well satisfied in her house.

Mrs. Whitefield happened to be in the yard when Jones and his attendant marched in. Her sagacity soon discovered in the air of our hero something which distinguished him from the vulgar. She ordered her servants, therefore, immediately to show him into a room, and presently afterwards invited him to dinner with herself; which invitation he very thankfully accepted; for indeed much less agreeable company than that of Mrs. Whitefield, and a much worse entertainment than she had provided, would have been welcome after so long fasting and so long a walk.

Besides Mr. Jones and the good governess of the mansion, there sat down at table an attorney of Salisbury, indeed the very same who had brought the news of Mrs. Blifil's death to Mr. Allworthy, and whose name, which I think we did not before mention, was Dowling: there was likewise present another person, who styled himself a lawyer, and who lived somewhere near Lidlinch, in Somersetshire. This fellow, I say, styled himself a lawyer, but was indeed a most vile petty-fogger, without sense or knowledge of any kind; one of those who may be termed train-bearers to the law; a sort of supernumeraries in the profession, who are the hackneys of attorneys, and will ride more miles for half-a-crown than a postboy.

During the time of dinner, the Somersetshire lawyer recollected the face of Jones, which he had seen at Mr. Allworthy's; for he had often visited in that gentleman's kitchen. He therefore took occasion to enquire after the good family there with that familiarity which would have become an intimate friend or acquaintance of Mr. Allworthy; and indeed he did all in his power to insinuate himself to be such, though he had never had the honour of speaking to any person in that family higher than the butler. Jones answered all his questions with much civility, though he never remembered to have seen the petty-fogger before; and though he concluded, from the outward appearance and behaviour of the man, that he usurped a freedom with his betters, to which he was by no means entitled.

As the conversation of fellows of this kind is of all others the most detestable to men of any sense, the cloth was no sooner removed than Mr. Jones withdrew, and a little barbarously left poor Mrs. Whitefield to do a penance, which I have often heard Mr. Timothy Harris, and other publicans of good taste, lament, as the severest lot annexed to their calling, namely, that of being obliged to keep company with their guests.

Jones had no sooner quitted the room, than the petty-fogger, in a whispering tone, asked Mrs. Whitefield, 'If she knew who that fine spark was?' She answered, 'She had never seen the gentleman before.' 'The gentleman, indeed!' replied the petty-fogger; 'a pretty gentleman, truly! Why, he's the bastard of a fellow who was hanged for horse-stealing. He was dropped at Squire Allworthy's door, where one of the servants found him in a box so full of rainwater, that he would certainly have been drowned, had he not been reserved for another fate.' 'Ay, ay, you need not mention it, I protest: we understand what that fate is very well,' cries Dowling, with a most facetious grin. 'Well,' continued the other, 'the squire ordered him to be taken in; for he is a timbersome man every body knows, and was afraid of drawing himself into a scrape; and there the bastard was bred up, and fed, and cloathified all to the world like any gentleman; and there he got one of the servant-maids with child, and persuaded her to swear it to the squire himself; and afterwards he broke the arm of one Mr. Thwackum a clergyman, only because he reprimanded him for following whores; and afterwards he snapped a pistol at Mr. Blifil behind his back; and once, when Squire Allworthy was sick, he got a drum, and beat it all over the house to prevent him from sleeping; and twenty other pranks he hath played, for all which, about four or five days ago, just before I left the country, the squire stripped him stark naked, and turned him out of doors.'

'And very justly too, I protest,' cries Dowling; 'I would turn my own son out of doors, if he was guilty of half as much. And pray what is the name of this pretty gentleman?'

'The name o' un?' answered Petty-fogger; 'why, he is called Thomas Jones.'

'Jones!' answered Dowling a little eagerly; 'what, Mr. Jones that lived at Mr. Allworthy's! was that the gentleman that dined with us?' 'The very same,' said the other. 'I have heard of the gentleman,' cries Dowling, 'often; but I never heard any ill character of him.' 'And I am sure,' says Mrs. Whitefield, 'if half what this gentleman hath said be true, Mr. Jones hath the most deceitful countenance I ever saw; for sure his looks promise something very different; and I must say, for the little I have seen of him, he is as civil a well-bred man as you would wish to converse with.'

Petty-fogger calling to mind that he had not been sworn, as he usually was, before he gave his evidence, now bound what he had declared with so many oaths and imprecations that the landlady's ears were shocked, and she put a stop to his swearing, by assuring him of her belief. Upon which he said, 'I hope, madam, you imagine I would scorn to tell such things of any man, unless I knew them to be true. What interest have I in taking away the reputation of a man who never injured me? I promise you every syllable of what I have said is fact, and the whole country knows it.'

As Mrs. Whitefield had no reason to suspect that the petty-fogger had any motive or temptation to abuse Jones, the reader cannot blame her for believing what he so confidently affirmed with many oaths. She accordingly gave up her skill in physiognomy, and henceforwards conceived so ill an opinion of her guest, that she heartily wished him out of her house.

This dislike was now farther increased by a report which Mr. Whitefield made from the kitchen, where Partridge had informed the company, 'that though he carried the knapsack, and contented himself with staying among servants, while Tom Jones (as he called him) was regaling in the parlour, he was not his servant, but only a friend and companion, and as good a gentleman as Mr. Jones himself.'

Dowling sat all this while silent, biting his fingers, making faces, grinning, and looking wonderfully arch; at last he opened his lips, and protested that the gentleman looked like another sort of man. He then called for his bill with the utmost haste, declared he must be at Hereford that evening, lamented his great hurry of business, and wished he could divide himself into twenty pieces, in order to be at once in twenty places.

The petty-fogger now likewise departed, and then Jones desired the favour of Mrs. Whitefield's company to drink tea with him; but she refused, and with a manner so different from that with which she had received him at dinner, that it a little surprised him. And now he soon perceived her behaviour totally changed; for instead of that natural affability which we have before celebrated, she wore a constrained severity on her countenance, which was so disagreeable to Mr. Jones, that he resolved, however late, to quit the house that evening.

He did indeed account somewhat unfairly for this sudden change; for besides some hard and unjust surmises concerning female fickleness and mutability, he began to suspect that he owed this want of civility to his want of horses; a sort of animals which, as they dirty no sheets, are thought in inns to pay better for their beds than their riders, and are therefore considered as the more desirable company; but Mrs. Whitefield, to do her justice, had a much more liberal way of thinking. She was perfectly well-bred, and could be very civil to a gentleman, though he walked on foot. In reality, she looked on our hero as a sorry scoundrel, and therefore treated him as such, for which not even Jones himself, had he known as much as the reader, could have blamed her; nay, on the contrary, he must have approved her conduct, and have esteemed her the more for the disrespect shown towards himself. This is indeed a most aggravating circumstance, which attends depriving men unjustly of their reputation; for a man who is conscious of having an ill character, cannot justly be angry with those who neglect and slight him; but ought rather to despise such as affect his conversation, unless where a perfect intimacy must have convinced them that their friend's character hath been falsely and injuriously aspersed.

This was not, however, the case of Jones; for as he was a perfect stranger to the truth, so he was with good reason offended at the treatment he received. He therefore paid his reckoning and departed, highly against the will of Mr. Partridge, who having remonstrated much against it to no purpose, at last condescended to take up his knapsack and to attend his friend.

From Book XVII, Chapter 1

Containing a portion of introductory writing

When a comic writer hath made his principal characters as happy as he can; or when a tragic writer hath brought them to the highest pitch of human misery, they both conclude their business to be done, and that their work is come to a period.

Had we been of the tragic complexion, the reader must allow we were now very nearly arrived at this period, since it would be difficult for the devil, or any of his representatives on earth, to have contrived much greater torments for poor Jones, than those in which we left him in the last chapter; and as for Sophia, a good-natured woman would hardly wish more uneasiness to a rival, than what she must at present be supposed to feel. What then remains to complete the tragedy but a murder or two, and a few moral sentences.

But to bring our favourites out of their present anguish and distress, and to land them at last on the shore of happiness, seems a much harder task; a task indeed so hard that we do not undertake to execute it. In regard to Sophia, it is more than probable, that we shall somewhere or other provide a good husband for her in the end, either Blifil, or my lord, or somebody else; but as to poor Jones, such are the calamities in which he is at present involved, owing to his imprudence by which if a man doth not become a felon to the world, he is at least a *felo de se*;[1] so destitute is he now of friends, and so persecuted by enemies, that we almost despair of bringing him to any good; and if our reader delights in seeing executions, I think he ought not to lose any time in taking a first row at Tyburn.[2]

This I faithfully promise, that notwithstanding any affection, which we may be supposed to have for this rogue, whom we have unfortunately made our hero, we will lend him none of that supernatural assistance with which we are entrusted, upon condition that we use it only on very important occasions. If he doth not therefore find some natural means of fairly extricating himself from all his distresses, we will do no violence to the truth and dignity of history for his sake; for we had rather relate that he was hanged at Tyburn (which may very probably be the case) than forfeit our integrity, or shock the faith of our reader.

In this the ancients had a great advantage over the moderns. Their mythology, which was at that time more firmly believed by the vulgar than any religion is at present, gave them always an opportunity of delivering a favourite hero. Their deities were always ready at the writer's elbow, to execute any of his purposes; and the more extraordinary the intervention was, the greater was the surprise and delight of the credulous leader. Those writers could with greater ease have conveyed a hero from one country to another, nay from one world to another, and have brought him back again, than a poor circumscribed modern can deliver him from a gaol.

The Arabians and Persians had an equal advantage in writing their tales from the genii and fairies, which they believe in as an article of their faith, upon the authority of the Koran itself. But we have none of these helps. To natural means alone are we confined; let us try therefore what by these means may be done for poor Jones; though, to confess the truth, something whispers me in the ear, that he doth not yet know the worst of his fortune; and that a more shocking piece of news than any he hath yet heard, remains for him in the unopened leaves of fate.

1: legal Latin; felons to themselves, i.e. suicides.   2: London's place of public execution.

THOMAS GRAY (1716–1761)

Thomas Gray was the son of a London scrivener. Educated at Eton, he went up to Cambridge and spent most of his adult life there as a solitary scholar, departing in the summer for the Lakes or Scotland in pursuit of the sublime and picturesque. He was at first a competent Latin poet, and later a skilled writer of odes who sought and achieved perfection of thought and phrase. His poetry has a consequent lucidity which looks back to classical and neo-classical traditions, yet his habitual tone of melancholy and concern with human mortality links his work with the contemporary idea of the poet as the antithesis of the thrusting reasoner and man of the world. His *Elegy Written in a Country Churchyard*, one of the best known of all English poems, reminds an ambitious age that not everyone fulfils their dreams or their potential, and that all share the same ultimate fate.

Elegy Written in A Country Churchyard

The curfew tolls the knell of parting day,
The lowing herd wind slowly o'er the lea,
The ploughman homeward plods his weary way,
And leaves the world to darkness and to me.

5   Now fades the glimmering landscape on the sight,
And all the air a solemn stillness holds,
Save where the beetle wheels his droning flight,
And drowsy tinklings lull the distant folds;

Save that from yonder ivy-mantled tower
10 The moping owl does to the moon complain
Of such as, wandering near her secret bower,
Molest her ancient solitary reign.

Beneath those rugged elms, that yew-tree's shade,
Where heaves the turf in many a mouldering heap,
15 Each in his narrow cell for ever laid,
The rude forefathers of the hamlet sleep.

The breezy call of incense-breathing Morn,
The swallow twittering from the straw-built shed,
The cock's shrill clarion, or the echoing horn,
20 No more shall rouse them from their lowly bed.

For them no more the blazing hearth shall burn,
Or busy housewife ply her evening care;
No children run to lisp their sire's return,
Or climb his knees the envied kiss to share,

---

16 **rude:** ignorant, untaught (Johnson); humble.

25   Oft did the harvest to their sickle yield,
    Their furrow oft the stubborn glebe has broke;
    How jocund did they drive their team afield!
    How bowed the woods beneath their sturdy stroke!

    Let not Ambition mock their useful toil,
30   Their homely joys, and destiny obscure;
    Nor Grandeur hear with a disdainful smile,
    The short and simple annals of the poor.

    The boast of heraldry, the pomp of power,
    And all that beauty, all that wealth e'er gave,
35   Awaits alike the inevitable hour.
    The paths of glory lead but to the grave.

    Nor you, ye Proud, impute to these the fault
    If Memory o'er their tomb no trophies raise,
    Where through the long-drawn aisle and fretted vault
40   The pealing anthem swells the note of praise.

    Can storied urn or animated bust
    Back to its mansion call the fleeting breath?
    Can Honour's voice provoke the silent dust,
    Or Flattery soothe the dull cold ear of Death?

45   Perhaps in this neglected spot is laid
    Some heart once pregnant with celestial fire;
    Hands, that the rod of empire might have swayed,
    Or waked to ecstasy the living lyre.

    But Knowledge to their eyes her ample page
50   Rich with the spoils of time, did ne'er unroll;
    Chill Penury repressed their noble rage,
    And froze the genial current of the soul.

    Full many a gem of purest ray serene
    The dark unfathomed caves of ocean bear:
55   Full many a flower is born to blush unseen,
    And waste its sweetness on the desert air.

    Some village Hampden, that with dauntless breast
    The little tyrant of his fields withstood,
    Some mute inglorious Milton here may rest,
60   Some Cromwell, guiltless of his country's blood.

---

26 glebe: ground, turf.   **57 Hampden:** John Hampden (1594–1643), a vigorous parliamentarian who opposed Charles I. His arrest was one of the events that precipitated the Civil War.   **60 Cromwell:** Oliver Cromwell (1599–1658), Puritan politician, soldier and leader during the Civil War.

The applause of listening senates to command,
The threats of pain and ruin to despise,
To scatter plenty o'er a smiling land,
And read their history in a nation's eyes,

65 Their lot forbad: nor circumscribed alone
Their growing virtues, but their crimes confined;
Forbad to wade through slaughter to a throne,
And shut the gates of mercy on mankind,

The struggling pangs of conscious truth to hide,
70 To quench the blushes of ingenuous shame,
Or heap the shrine of Luxury and Pride
With incense kindled at the Muse's flame.

Far from the madding crowd's ignoble strife,
Their sober wishes never learned to stray;
75 Along the cool sequestered vale of life
They kept the noiseless tenor of their way.

Yet even these bones from insult to protect
Some frail memorial still erected nigh,
With uncouth rhymes and shapeless sculpture decked,
80 Implores the passing tribute of a sigh.

Their name, their years, spelt by the unlettered Muse,
The place of fame and elegy supply:
And many a holy text around she strews,
That teach the rustic moralist to die.

85 For who to dumb Forgetfulness a prey,
This pleasing anxious being e'er resign'd,
Let the warm precincts of the cheerful day,
Nor cast one longing lingering look behind?

On some fond breast the parting soul relies,
90 Some pious drops the closing eye requires;
Even from the tomb the voice of Nature cries,
Even in our ashes live their wonted fires.

For thee, who, mindful of the unhonoured dead,
Dost in these lines their artless tale relate;
95 If chance, by lonely contemplation led,
Some kindred spirit shall inquire thy fate,

Haply some hoary-headed swain may say,
'Oft have we seen him at the peep of dawn
Brushing with hasty steps the dews away,
100 To meet the sun upon the upland lawn.

'There at the foot of yonder nodding beech
That wreathes its old fantastic roots so high,
His listless length at moontide would he stretch
And pore upon the brook that babbles by.

105 'Hard by yon wood, now smiling as in scorn,
Muttering his wayward fancies he would rove;
Now drooping, woeful wan, like one forlorn,
Or crazed with care, or crossed in hopeless love.

'One morn I missed him on the customed hill,
110 Along the heath, and near his favourite tree;
Another came; nor yet beside the rill,
Nor up the lawn, nor at the wood was he;

'The next with dirges due in sad array
Slow through the churchway path we saw him borne.
115 Approach and read (for thou canst read) the lay
Graved on the stone beneath yon aged thorn.'

THE EPITAPH

Here rests his head upon the lap of Earth
A Youth, to Fortune and to Fame unknown;
Fair Science frowned not on his humble birth,
120 *And Melancholy marked him for her own.*

Large was his bounty, and his soul sincere;
Heaven did a recompense as largely send:
He gave to Misery all he had, a tear,
He gain'd from Heaven, ('twas all he wished) a friend.

125 *No farther seek his merits to disclose,*
Or draw his frailties from their dread abode,
(There they alike in trembling hope repose,)
The bosom of his Father and his God.

Ode on the Death of a Favourite Cat

Drowned in a Tub of Gold Fishes

'Twas on a lofty vase's side,
Where China's gayest art had dyed
  The azure flowers that blow;
Demurest of the tabby kind,
5 The pensive Selima reclined,
  Gazed on the lake below.

---

119 Science: learning.   **3** blow: bloom.

Her conscious tail her joy declared;
The fair round face, the snowy beard,
   The velvet of her paws,
10   Her coat that with the tortoise vies,
Her ears of jet and emerald eyes,
   She saw; and purred applause.

Still had she gazed; but 'midst the tide
Two angel forms were seen to glide,
15   The genii of the stream:
Their scaly armour's Tyrian hue
Through richest purple to the view
   Betrayed a golden gleam.

The hapless nymph with wonder saw:
20   A whisker first and then a claw,
   With many an ardent wish,
She stretched in vain to reach the prize.
What female heart can gold despise?
   What cat's averse to fish?

25   Presumptuous maid! with looks intent
Again she stretched, again she bent,
   Nor knew the gulf between.
(Malignant Fate sat by and smiled)
The slippery verge her feet beguiled,
30   She tumbled headlong in.

Eight times emerging from the flood
She mewed to every watry god,
   Some speedy aid to send.
No dolphin came, no Nereid stirred:
35   Nor cruel Tom nor Susan heard.
   A favourite has no friend!

From hence, ye beauties, undeceived,
Know, one false step is ne'er retrieved,
   And be with caution bold.
40   Not all that tempts your wandering eyes
And heedless hearts is lawful prize;
   Nor all that glisters gold.

---

16 **Tyrian**: a purple dye made in Tyre.   34 **Nereid**: sea nymph, daughter of the sea god Nereus.

LAURENCE STERNE (1713–1768)

Laurence Sterne was born in Clonmel, Ireland, and spent his early years in military camps as his father, though well-connected, had married beneath him and was without prospects. It was only through the patronage of a relative, the Archbishop of York, that Sterne was able to study at Cambridge, take holy orders and find a living in a Yorkshire parish. His sermons in York Minster were popular, and he became a Justice of the Peace and lived a typical gentry life, eating well, dabbling in learning and the arts, flirting. Well into middle age, he published the first two volumes of *The Life and Opinions of Tristram Shandy* in 1759 and was soon famous. Four more volumes were added in 1761, two more in 1765, and the final volume in 1767. In 1766 he published his *Sentimental Journey through France and Italy*, a sequence of sketches written on a tour in 1765.

The appeal of Sterne's work was and remains many-faceted. At the formal level *Tristram Shandy* is a parody of the novelistic conventions which were already settling into shape, especially the authority of the single point of view, the assumption of the direct reflection of experience in transparent prose, and the linear developmental narrative. *Tristram Shandy* offers short chapters, blank pages, diagrams and typological jokes, anti-linear narrative, endless digressions, lewd puns, and learned allusions, many of them evidently faked. This formal and intellectual playfulness is complemented by a profound understanding of how the mind establishes personal associations which subvert 'normal' sense, and how the new technologies of clock time, dictionaries and novelistic representation betray the richness of experience into tidy and false abstractions. Judged too odd to survive long by Dr Johnson, *Tristram Shandy* has proved an endlessly vital resource for novelists in the twentieth century.

From The Life and Opinions of Tristram Shandy

Volume One, Chapter One

I wish either my father or my mother, or indeed both of them, as they were in duty both equally bound to it, had minded what they were about when they begot me; had they duly considered how much depended upon what they were then doing; that not only the production of a rational Being was concerned in it, but that possibly the happy formation and temperature of his body, perhaps his genius and the very cast of his mind; and, for aught they knew to the contrary, even the fortunes of his whole house might take their turn from the humours and dispositions which were then uppermost: – Had they duly weighed and considered all this, and proceeded accordingly, I am verily persuaded I should have made a quite different figure in the world, from that, in which the reader is likely to see me. – Believe me, good folks, this is not so inconsiderable a thing as many of you may think it; – you have all, I dare say, heard of the animal spirits, as how they are transfused from father to son &c. &c. – and a great deal to that purpose:– Well, you may take my word, that nine parts in ten of a man's sense or his nonsense, his successes and miscarriages in this world depend upon their motions and activity, and the different tracts and trains you put them into, so that when they are once set a-going, whether right or wrong, 'tis not a halfpenny matter, – away they go cluttering like hey-go-mad; and by treading the same steps over and over again, they presently make a road of it, as plain and as smooth as a garden-walk, which, when they are once used to, the Devil himself sometimes shall not be able to drive them off it.

Pray, my dear, quoth my mother, *have you not forgot to wind up the clock?* Good G—! cried my father, making an exclamation, but taking care to moderate his voice at the same time, – *Did ever woman, since the creation of the world, interrupt a man with such a silly question?* Pray, what was your father saying?– Nothing.

Chapter Two

– Then, positively, there is nothing in the question, that I can see, either good or bad. – Then let me tell you, Sir, it was a very unseasonable question at least, because it scattered and dispersed the animal spirits, whose business it was to have escorted and gone hand-in-hand with the *HOMUNCULUS*,[1] and conducted him safe to the place destined for his reception.

The HOMUNCULUS, Sir, in however low and ludicrous a light he may appear, in this age of levity, to the eye of folly or prejudice:– to the eye of reason in scientific research, he stands confessed – a BEING guarded and circumscribed with rights: – The minutest philosophers, who, by the bye, have the most enlarged understandings, (their souls being inversely as their enquiries) shew us incontestably, That the HOMUNUCLUS is created by the same hand, – engendered in the same course of nature,– endowed with the same locomotive powers and faculties with us: – That he consists as we do, of skin, hair, fat, flesh, veins, arteries, ligaments, nerves, cartilages, bones, marrow, brains, glands, genitals, humours, and articulations; – is a Being of as much activity, – and, in all senses of the word, as much and as truly our fellow-creature as my Lord Chancellor of England.[2] He may be benefited, he may be injured, – he may obtain redress; – in a word, he has all the claims and rights of humanity, which Tully, Puffendorff,[3] or the best ethic writers allow to arise out of that state and relation.

Now, dear Sir, what if any accident had befallen him in his way alone? – or that, through terror of it, natural to so young a traveller, my little gentleman had got to his journey's end miserably spent; his muscular strength and virility worn down to a thread; his own animal spirits ruffled beyond description, and that in this sad disordered state of nerves, he had laid down a prey to sudden starts, or a series of melancholy dreams and fancies for nine long, long months together. I tremble to think what a foundation had been laid for a thousand weaknesses both of body and mind, which no skill of the physician or the philosopher could ever afterwards have set thoroughly to rights.

1: literally 'little man'. The passage plays with the idea that the male seed contains a little man whose animal spirits are predetermined at the moment of conception. Tristram, and his book, will be rendered eternally 'shandean', i.e. crack brained, by this disorder.   2: the highest legal officer in the state.   3: Marcus Tullius Cicero (106–43BC), Samuel Puffendorff (1632–94), noted jurists.

Chapter Three

To my uncle Mr Toby Shandy do I stand indebted for the preceding anecdote, to whom my father, who was an excellent natural philosopher, and much given to close reasoning upon the smallest matters, had oft, and heavily, complained of the injury; but once more particularly, as my uncle Toby well remembered, upon his observing a most unaccountable obliquity (as he called it) in my manner of setting up my top, and justifying the principles upon which I had done it, the old gentleman shook his head, and in a tone more expressive by half of sorrow than reproach, he said his heart all along foreboded, and he saw it verified in this, and from a thousand other observations he had made upon me, That I should neither think nor act like any other man's child: – *But alas!* continued he, shaking his head a second time, and wiping away a tear which was trickling down his cheeks, *My Tristram's misfortunes began nine months before ever he came into the world.*

My mother, who was sitting by, looked up, but she knew no more than her backside what my father meant, but my uncle, Mr Toby Shandy, who had been often informed of the affair, understood him very well.

Chapter Four

I know there are readers in the world, as well as many other good people in it, who are no readers at all, – who find themselves ill at ease, unless they are let into the whole secret from first to last, of everything which concerns you.

It is in pure compliance with this humour of theirs, and from a backwardness in my nature to disappoint any one soul living, that I have been so very particular already. As my life and opinions are likely to make some noise in the world, and, if I conjecture right, will take in all ranks, professions, and denominations of men whatever, – be no less read than the *Pilgrim's Progress* itself and, in the end, prove the very thing which Montaigne dreaded his essays should turn out, that is, a book for a parlour-window; I find it necessary to consult every one a little in his turn; and therefore must beg pardon for going on a little further in the same way: For which cause, right glad I am, that I have begun the history of myself in the way I have done; and that I am able to go on tracing every thing in it, as Horace says, *ab Ovo*.[1]

Horace, I know does not recommend this fashion altogether: But that gentleman is speaking only of an epic poem or a tragedy; – (I forget which) – besides, if it was not so, I should beg Mr Horace's pardon; – for in writing what I have set about, I shall confine myself neither to his rules, nor to any man's rules that ever lived.

To such, however, as do not choose to go so far back into these things, I can give no better advice, than that they skip over the remaining part of this chapter; for I declare beforehand, 'tis wrote only for the curious and inquisitive.

– – – – – – – – Shut the door – – – – – – – –

1: from the egg. Horace had praised Homer for beginning 'in the midst', not from Leda's egg, from which Helen was born. Sterne therefore jokingly reverses classical precedent by starting with Tristram's conception.

I was begot in the night, betwixt the first Sunday and the first Monday in the month of March, in the year of our Lord one thousand seven hundred and eighteen. I am positive I was. – But how I came to be so very particular in my account of a thing which happened before I was born, is owing to another small anecdote known only in our own family, but now made public for the better clearing up this point.

My father, you must know, who was originally a Turkey[1] merchant, but had left off business for some years, in order to retire to, and die upon, his paternal estate in the county of – , was, I believe, one of the most regular men in everything he did, whether 'twas matter of business, or matter of amusement, that ever lived. As a small specimen of this extreme exactness of his, to which he was in truth a slave, – he had made it a rule for many years of his life, – on the first Sunday night of every month throughout the whole year, as certain as ever the Sunday night came, – to wind up a large house-clock, which we had standing upon the backstairs head, with his own hands: – And being somewhere between fifty and sixty years of age, at the time I have been speaking of, he had likewise gradually brought some other little family concernments to the same period, in order, as he would often say to my uncle Toby, to get them all out of the way at one time, and be no more plagued and pestered with them the rest of the month.

It was attended with but one misfortune, which, in a great measure, fell upon myself, and the effects of which I fear I shall carry with me to my grave; namely, that from an unhappy association of ideas which have no connection in nature, it so fell out at length, that my poor mother could never hear the said clock wound up, – but the thoughts of some other things unavoidably popped into her head – & vice versa: which strange combination of ideas, the sagacious Locke,[2] who certainly understood the nature of these things better than most men, affirms to have produced more wry actions than all other sources of prejudice whatsoever.

But this by the bye.

Now it appears by a memorandum in my father's pocket-book, which now lies upon the table, 'That on Lady-Day which was on the 25th of the same month in which I date my geniture, – my father set out upon his journey to London with my eldest brother Bobby, to fix him at Westminster school;' and, as it appears from the same authority 'That he did not get down to his wife and family till the second week in May following,' – it brings the thing almost to a certainty. However, what follows in the beginning of the next chapter puts it beyond all possibility of doubt.

But pray, Sir, What was your father doing all December, January, and February? Why, Madam, he was all that time afflicted with a Sciatica.

1: merchant trading in Turkish goods.   2: John Locke (1632–1704) whose *Essay Concerning Human Understanding* (1690) founded the analytic philosophy of mind and deeply influenced Sterne, especially his thoughts on the association of ideas and the way one idea entrains another.

Chapter Five

On the fifth day of November, 1718, which to the era fixed on, was as near nine calendar months as any husband could in reason have expected, – was I, Tristram Shandy, Gentleman, brought forth into this scurvy and disastrous world of ours. I wish I had been born in the Moon, or in any of the planets, (except Jupiter or Saturn, because I never could bear cold weather) for it could not well have fared worse with me in any of them (though I will not answer for Venus) than it has in this vile, dirty planet of ours, – which, o' my conscience, with reverence be it spoken, I take to be made up of the shreds and clippings of the rest; not but the planet is well enough, provided a man could be born in it to a great title or to a great estate; or could any how contrive to be called up to public charges, and employments of dignity or power; – but that is not my case; – and therefore every man will speak of the fair as his own market has gone in it, – for which cause I affirm it over again to be one of the vilest worlds that ever was made; for I can truly say, that from the first hour I drew my breath in it, to this, that I can now scarce draw it at all, for an asthma I got in skating against the wind in Flanders; – I have been the continual sport of what the world calls fortune; and though I will not wrong her by saying, She has ever made me feel the weight of any great or signal evil; – yet with all the good temper in the world, I affirm it of her, that in every stage of my life, and at every turn and corner where she could get fairly at me, the ungracious Duchess has pelted me with a set of as pitiful misadventures and cross accidents as ever small HERO sustained.

From Chapter Six

In the beginnings of the last chapter, I informed you exactly when I was born; but I did not inform you *how*. No; that particular was reserved entirely for a chapter by itself; – besides, Sir, as you and I are in a manner perfect strangers to each other, it would not have been proper to have let you into too many circumstances relating to myself all at once. – You must have a little patience. I have undertaken, you see, to write not only my life, but my opinions also; hoping and expecting that your knowledge of my character, and of what kind of a mortal I am, by the one, would give you a better relish for the other: As you proceed further with me, the slight acquaintance which is now beginning betwixt us, will grow into familiarity; and that, unless one of us is in fault, will terminate in friendship. – O *diem praeclarum!*[1] – then nothing which has touched me will be thought trifling in its nature, or tedious in its telling. Therefore, my dear friend and companion, if you should think me somewhat sparing of my narrative on my first setting out, bear with me, and let me go on, and tell my story my own way: – or, if I should seem now and then to trifle upon the road, – or should sometimes put on a fool's cap with a bell to it, for a moment or two as we pass along, – don't fly off, but rather courteously give me credit for a little more wisdom than appears upon my outside; and as we jog on, either laugh with me, or at me, or in short do any thing,– only keep your temper. –

1: O splendid day!

From Volume 2, Chapter Six

What can they be doing, brother? said my father. – I think, replied my uncle Toby, taking, as I told you, his pipe from his mouth, and striking the ashes out of it as he began his sentence; I think, replied he, – it would not be amiss, brother, if we rung the bell.

Pray, what's all that racket over our heads, Obadiah? – quoth my father; my brother and I can scarce hear ourselves speak.

Sir, answered Obadiah, making a bow towards his left shoulder, my Mistress is taken very badly; and where's Susannah running down the garden there, as if they were going to ravish her? Sir, she is running the shortest cut into the town, replied Obadiah, to fetch the old midwife. – Then saddle a horse, quoth my father, and do you go directly for Dr Slop, the man-midwife with all our services,[1] – and let him know your Mistress is fallen into labour – and that I desire he will return with you with all speed.

It is very strange, says my father, addressing himself to my uncle Toby, as Obadiah shut the door, as there is so expert an operator as Dr Slop so near that my wife should persist to the very last in this obstinate humour of hers, in trusting the life of my child, who has had one misfortune already, to the ignorance of an old woman; and not only the life of my child, brother – but her own life, and with it the lives of all the children I might, peradventure, have begot out of her hereafter.

Mayhap, brother, replied my uncle Toby, my sister does it to save the expence: – A pudding's end,[2] replied my father, the doctor must be paid the same for inaction as action, – if not better, – to keep him in temper.

Then it can be out of nothing in the whole world, quoth my uncle Toby, in the simplicity of his heart, but MODESTY: – My sister, I dare say, added he, does not care to let a man come so near her ····. I will not say whether my uncle Toby had completed the sentence or not; – 'tis for his advantage to suppose he had, as, I think, he could have added no ONE WORD which would have improved it.

If, on the contrary, my uncle Toby had not fully arrived at the period's end, – then the world stands indebted to the sudden snapping of my father's tobacco-pipe, for one of the neatest examples of that ornamental figure in oratory, which Rhetoricians stile the *Aposiopesis*.[3] – Just heaven! how does the *Poco piu*[4] and the *Poco meno* of the Italian artists; – the insensible MORE or LESS, determine the precise line of beauty in the sentence, as well as in the statue! How do the slight touches of the chisel, the pencil, the pen, the fiddlestick, *et caetera*, give the true swell, which gives the true pleasure! O my countrymen! – be nice; be cautious of your language; – and never, O! never let it be forgotten upon what small particles your eloquence and your fame depend.

– 'My sister, mayhap,' quoth my uncle Toby 'does not choose to let a man come so near her ····.' Make this dash, – 'tis an Aposiopesis. Take the dash away, and write *Backside*, – 'tis Bawdy. Scratch Backside out, and put *Covered way* in, 'tis a Metaphor; and, I dare say, as fortification ran so much in my uncle Toby's

---

1: professions of respect (Johnson). 2: end of a meat sausage, therefore a phallic reference. 3: a sudden breaking off in mid-sentence as if unwilling to continue. 4: musical notation; a little more, a little less.

head, that if he had been left to have added one word to the sentence, that word was it.

But whether that was the case or not the case; – or whether the snapping of my father's tobacco-pipe so critically, happened through accident or anger – will be seen in due time.

Chapter Seven

Though my father was a good natural philosopher, yet he was something of a moral philosopher too; for which reason, when his tobacco-pipe snapped short in the middle, – he had nothing to do, as such, but to have taken hold of the two piecces, and thrown them gently upon the back of the fire. – He did no such thing; – he threw them with all the violence in the world; and, to give the action still more emphasis, he started up upon both his legs to do it.

This looked something like heat; – and the manner of his reply to what my uncle Toby was saying, proved it was so. – 'Not choose,' quoth my father, (repeating my uncle Toby's words) 'to let a man come so near her.' – By heaven, brother Toby! you would try the patience of a Job; – and I think I have the plagues of one already without it. Why? – Where ? – Wherein?– Wherefore? – Upon what account? replied my uncle Toby, in the utmost astonishment. – To think, said my father, of a man living to your age, brother, and knowing so little about women! I know nothing at all about them, replied my uncle Toby; and I think, continued he, that the shock I received the year after the demolition of Dunkirk, in my affair with widow Wadman; – which shock you know I should not have received, but from my total ignorance of the sex, – has given me just cause to say, That I neither know, nor do pretend to know, any thing about 'em or their concerns either. – Methinks, brother, replied my father, you might, at least, know so much as the right end of a woman from the wrong. – It is said in *Aristotle's Master-Piece*, 'That when a man doth think of any thing which is past, he looketh down upon the ground; but that when he thinketh of something that is to come, he looketh up towards the heavens.'

My uncle Toby, I suppose, thought of neither, for he looked horizontally. Right end, quoth my uncle Toby, muttering the two words low to himself, and fixing his two eyes insensibly as he muttered them, upon a small crevice, formed by a bad joint in the chimney-piece. Right end of a woman! I declare, quoth my uncle, I know no more which it is, than the man in the moon; – and if I was to think, continued my uncle Toby, (keeping his eye still fixed upon the bad joint) this month together, I am sure I should not be able to find it out.

Then, brother Toby, replied my father, I will tell you. – Every thing in this world, continued my father (filling a fresh pipe) – every thing in this earthly world, my dear brother Toby, has two handles. Not always, quoth my uncle Toby. At least, replied my father, every one has two hands, which comes to the same thing. Now, if a man was to sit down coolly, and consider within himself the make, the shape, the construction, come-at-ability, and convenience of all the parts which constitute the whole of that animal, called Woman, and compare them analogically. – I never understood rightly the meaning of that word, – quoth my uncle Toby. ANALOGY, replied my father, is the certain relation and agreement, which different – Here a devil of a rap at the door snapped my father's definition (like his tobacco-pipe) in two, and, at the same time, crushed the head of as notable and curious a dissertation as ever was engendered in the womb of speculation; – it was some months before my father could get an opportunity to be safely delivered of it: And, at this hour, it is a thing full as problematical as the subject of the dissertation itself, – (considering the confusion and distresses of our domestic misadventures, which are now coming thick one upon the back of another) whether I shall be able to find a place for it in the third volume or not.

Chapter Eight

It is about an hour and a half's tolerable good reading since my uncle Toby rung the bell, when Obadiah was ordered to saddle a horse, and go for Dr Slop, the man-midwife; so that no one can say, with reason, that I have not allowed Obadiah time enough, poetically speaking, and considering the emergency too, both to go and come; though, morally and truly speaking, the man, perhaps, has scarce had time to get on his boots.

If the hypercritic will go upon this; and is resolved after all to take a pendulum, and measure the true distance betwixt the ringing of the bell, and the rap at the door; – and, after finding it to be no more than two minutes, thirteen seconds, and three fifths, – should take upon him to insult over me for such a breach in the unity, or rather probability, of time; – I would remind him, that the idea of duration and of its simple modes, is got merely from the train and succession of our ideas, and is the true scholastic pendulum, – and by which, as a scholar, I will be tried in this matter, – abjuring and detesting the jurisdiction of all other pendulums whatever.

I would, therefore, desire him to consider that it is but poor eight miles from Shandy Hall to Dr Slop, the man-midwife's house; and that whilst Obadiah has been going those said miles and back, I have brought my uncle Toby from Namur, quite across all Flanders, into England: – That I have had him ill upon my hands near four years; – and have since travelled him and Corporal Trim in a chariot and four, a journey of near two hundred miles down into Yorkshire; all which put together, must have prepared the reader's imagination for the entrance of Dr Slop upon the stage, – as much, at least (I hope) as a dance, a song, or a concerto between the acts.

If my hypercritic is intractable, alleging, that two minutes and thirteen seconds are no more than two minutes and thirteen seconds, when I have said all I can about them; and that this plea, though it might save me dramatically, will damn me biographically, rendering my book from this very moment, a professed Romance, which, before, was a book apocryphal: If I am thus pressed – I then put an end to the whole objection and controversy about it all at once, by acquainting him, that Obadiah had not got above three-score yards from the stable-yard before he met with Dr Slop; and indeed he gave a dirty proof that he had met with him, and was within an ace of giving a tragical one too.

Imagine to yourself; but this had better begin a new chapter.

Chapter Nine

Imagine to yourself a little squat, uncourtly figure of a Doctor Slop, of about four feet and a half perpendicular height, with a breadth of back, and a sesquipedality[1] of belly, which might have done honour to a serjeant in the horse-guards.

Such were the outlines of Dr Slop's figure, which, if you have read Hogarth's analysis of beauty, and if you have not, I wish you would; you must know, may as certainly be caricatured, and conveyed to the mind by three strokes as three hundred.

Imagine such a one, for such, I say, were the outlines of Dr Slop's figure, coming slowly along, foot by foot, waddling through the dirt upon the vertebrae of a little diminutive pony, of a pretty colour; but of strength, – alack! scarce able to have made an amble of it, under such a fardel,[2] had the roads been in an ambling condition.

– They were not. Imagine to yourself, Obadiah mounted upon a strong monster of a coach-horse, pricked into a full gallop, and making all practicable speed the adverse way.

Pray, Sir, let me interest you a moment in this description.

Had Dr Slop beheld Obadiah a mile off, posting in a narrow lane directly towards him, at that monstrous rate, – splashing and plunging like a devil through thick and thin, as he approached, would not such a phenomenon, with such a vortex of mud and water moving along with it, round its axis, – have been a subject of juster apprehension to Dr Slop in his situation, than the *worst* of Whiston's comets? To say nothing of the Nucleus; that is, of Obadiah and the coach-horse. – In my idea, the vortex alone of 'em was enough to have involved and carried, if not the doctor, at least the doctor's pony, quite away with it. What then do you think must the terror and hydrophobia of Dr Slop have been, when you read (which you are just going to do) that he was advancing thus warily along towards Shandy Hall, and had approached to within sixty yards of it, and within five yards of a sudden turn, made by an acute angle of the garden wall, – and in the dirtiest part of a dirty lane, when Obadiah and his coach-horse turned the corner, rapid, furious, – pop, – full upon him! Nothing, I think, in nature, can be supposed more terrible than such a Rencounter – so imprompt! so ill prepared to stand the shock of it as Dr Slop was!

What could Dr Slop do? He crossed himself + – Pugh! but the doctor, Sir, was a Papist. – No matter; he had better have kept hold of the pummel. – He had so; nay as it happened, he had better have done nothing at all; – for in crossing himself he let go his whip, – and in attempting to save his whip betwixt his knee and his saddle's skirt, as it slipped, he lost his stirrup, in losing which, he lost his seat; and in the multitude of all these losses (which, by the bye, shews what little advantages there is in crossing) the unfortunate doctor lost his presence of mind. So that, without waiting for Obadiah's onset, he left his pony to its destiny, tumbling off it diagonally, something in the style and manner of a pack of wool, and without any other consequence from the fall, save that of

---

1: from Horace, *Ars Poetica*, a foot and a half.   2: a bundle, a little pack (Johnson).

being left (as it would have been) with the broadest part of him sunk about twelve inches deep in the mire.

Obadiah pulled off his cap twice to Dr Slop; once as he was falling, and then again when he saw him seated. – Ill-timed complaisance! had not the fellow better have stopped his horse, and got off and helped him? – Sir, he did: all that his situation would allow; but the MOMENTUM of the coach-horse was so great, that Obadiah could not do it all at once; he rode in a circle three times round Dr Slop, before he could fully accomplish it any how; and at the last, when he did stop his beast, 'twas done with such an explosion of mud, that Obadiah had better been a league off. In short, never was a Dr Slop so beluted,[1] and so transsubstantiated, since that affair came into fashion.

From A Sentimental Journey through France and Italy

A Sentimental Journey begins *in medias res* and relates the sentimental adventures of Parson Yorick from *Tristram Shandy* as he travels as far as Lyons, then ends in mid-sentence. It is told through discontinuous scenes, each a gentle epiphany that displays the charm and sensibility of its author, and passes ironic comment on the factual tone and chauvinist presumption usual to contemporary travel narratives. The work was influential in disseminating the cult of sensibility that dominated the late eighteenth century and spawned many contemporary sequences of illustrations.

Montriul[2]

When all is ready, and every article is disputed and paid for in the inn, unless you are a little sour'd by the adventure, there is always a matter to compound at the door, before you can get into your chaise, and that is with the sons and daughters of poverty, who surround you. Let no man say, 'Let them go to the devil!' – 'tis a cruel journey to send a few miserables, and they have had sufferings enow without it: I always think it better to take a few sous out in my hand; and I would counsel every gentle traveller to do so likewise; he need not be so exact in setting down his motives for giving them: – They will be register'd elsewhere.

For my own part, there is no man gives so little as I do; for few, that I know, have so little to give: but as this was the first public act of my charity in France, I took the more notice of it.

– A well-a-way! said I, I have but eight sous in the word, showing them in my hand, and there are eight poor men and eight poor women for 'em.

A poor tatter'd soul, without a shirt on, instantly withdrew his claim, by retiring two steps out of the circle, and making a disqualifying bow on his part. Had the whole *parterre* cried out, *Place aux dames*, with one voice, it would not have conveyed the sentiment of a deference for the sex with half the effect.

1: bespattered with mud.   2: probably Montreuil.

Just Heaven! for what wise reasons hast thou ordered it, that beggary and urbanity, which are at such variance in other countries, should find a way to be at unity in this?

I insisted upon presenting him with a single sous, merely for his *politesse*.

A poor little dwarfish, brisk fellow, who stood over against me in the circle, putting something first under his arm, which had once been a hat, took his snuff-box out of his pocket, and generously offer'd a pinch on both sides of him: it was a gift of consequence, and modestly declined. The poor little fellow press'd it upon them with a nod of welcomeness – *Prenez-en – prenez*, said he, looking another way; so they each took a pinch.– Pity thy box should ever want one, said I to myself; so I put a couple of sous into it – taking a small pinch out of his box, to enhance their value, as I did it.– He felt the weight of the second obligation more than of the first – 'twas doing him an honour – the other was only doing him a charity – and he made me a bow down to the ground for it.

– Here! said I to an old soldier with one hand, who had been campaign'd and worn out to death in the service – here's a couple of sous for thee. – *Vive le Roi!* said the old soldier.

I had then but three sous left: so I gave one, simply *pour l'amour de Dieu*, which was the footing on which it was begg'd – The poor woman had a dislocated hip; so it could not well be upon any other motive.

Mon cher et très charitable Monsieur – There's no opposing this, said I.

My Lord Anglois! – the very sound was worth the money; so I gave *my last sous for it*. But in the eagerness of giving, I had overlooked *pauvre honteux*, who had no one to ask a sous for him, and who, I believed, would have perished ere he could have ask'd one for himself; he stood by the chaise, a little without the circle, and wiped a tear from a face which I thought had seen better days.

– Good God! said I, and I have not one single sous left to give him – But you have a thousand! cried all the powers of Nature, stirring within me – so I gave him – no matter what – I am ashamed to say *how much*, now – and was ashamed to think how little, then; so if the reader can form any conjecture of my disposition, as these two fixed points are given him, he may judge within a livre or two what was the precise sum.

I could afford nothing for the rest, but '*Dieu vous bénisse*'– Et *le bon Dieu vous bénisse encore* – said the old soldier, the dwarf, &c. The *pauvre honteux* could say nothing – he pull'd out a little handkerchief, and wiped his face as he turned away – and I thought he thanked me more than them all.

The Pulse. Paris

Hail ye small sweet courtesies of life, for smooth do ye make the road of it! like grace and beauty which beget inclinations to love at first sight: 'tis ye who open this door and let the stranger in.

– Pray, Madame, said I, have the goodness to tell me which way I must turn to go to the *Opéra-comique*: . . . Most willingly, Monsieur, said she, laying aside her work –

I had given a cast with my eye into half a dozen shops as I came along in search of a face not likely to be disordered by such an interruption; till at last, this hitting my fancy, I had walked in.

She was working a pair of ruffles as she sat in a low chair on the far side of the shop facing the door.

... *Très voluntiers*; most willingly, said she, laying her work down upon a chair next her, and rising up from the low chair she was sitting in, with so cheerful a movement and so cheerful a look, that had I been laying out fifty *louis d'ors* with her, I should have said – 'This woman is grateful.'

You must turn, Monsieur, said she, going with me to the door of the shop, and pointing the way down the street I was to take – you must turn first to your left hand – *mais prenez garde* – there are two turns; and be so good as to take the second – then go down a little way and you'll see a church, and when you are past it, give yourself the trouble to turn directly to the right, and that will lead you to the foot of the Pont-Neuf, which you must cross – and there any one will do himself the pleasure to shew you.

She repeated her instructions three times over to me, with the same good-natur'd patience the third time as the first; – and if tones and manners have a meaning, which certainly they have, unless to hearts which shut them out – she seemed really interested, that I should not lose myself.

I will not suppose it was the woman's beauty, notwithstanding she was the handsomest *grisette*,[1] I think, I ever saw, which had much to do with the sense I had of her courtesy; only I remember, when I told her how much I was obliged to her, that I looked very full in her eyes, – and that I repeated my thanks as often as she had done her instructions.

I had not got ten paces from the door, before I found I had forgot every tittle of what she had said – so looking back, and seeing her still standing in the door of the shop as if to look whether I went right or not – I returned back, to ask her whether the first turn was to my right or left – for that I had absolutely forgot. – Is it possible? said she, half laughing. – 'Tis very possible, replied I, when a man is thinking more of a woman, than of her good advice.

As this was the real truth – she took it, as every woman takes a matter of right, with a slight courtesy.

– *Attendez*, said she, laying her hand upon my arm to detain me, whilst she called a lad out of the back-shop to get ready a parcel of gloves. I am just going to send him, said she, with a packet into that quarter, and if you will have the complaisance to step in, it will be ready in a moment, and he shall attend you to the place. – So I walk'd in with her to the far side of the shop, and taking up the ruffle in my hand which she laid upon the chair, as if I had a mind to sit, she sat down herself in her low chair, and I instantly sat myself down beside her.

– He will be ready, Monsieur, said she, in a moment ... And in that moment, replied I, most willingly would I say something very civil to you for all these courtesies. Any one may do a casual act of good-nature, but a continuation of them shews it is a part of the temperature; and certainly, added I, if it is the same blood which comes from the heart, which descends to the extremes (touching her wrist), I am sure you must have one of the best pulses of any

---

1: a flirtatious French working-class girl (from the colour of grey flannel).

woman in the world – Feel it, said she, holding out her arm. So laying down my hat, I took hold of her fingers in one hand, and applied the two fore-fingers of my other to the artery –

– Would to heaven! my dear Eugenius,[1] thou hadst passed by, and beheld me sitting in my black coat, and in my lack-a-day-sical manner, counting the throbs of it, one by one, with as much true devotion as if I had been watching the critical ebb or flow of her fever – How wouldst thou have laugh'd and moralised upon my new profession! – and thou shouldst have laugh'd and moralised on – Trust me, my dear Eugenius, I should have said, 'there are worse occupations in this world *than feeling a woman's pulse.'*– But a *grissette's*! thou wouldst have said – and in an open shop, Yorick! –

– So much the better: for when my views are direct, Eugenius, I care not if all the world saw me feel it.

SAMUEL JOHNSON (1709–1784)

Born to a prominent bookseller in Lichfield, Johnson studied at Lichfield Grammar and briefly at Pembroke College, Oxford, then worked as a school master with little success. He moved to London and worked as a professional writer – a new form of employment – contributing to the development of parliamentary reporting and to the art of critical biography, notably with *An Account of the Life of Mr Richard Savage* (1744). He also wrote poetry, notably *The Vanity of Human Wishes* (1749), tragedies, a novel *Rasselas* (1759) and two influential and successful papers, *The Rambler* (1750–52) and *The Idler* (1758–60), and contributed to the *Universal Chronicle*. His *Dictionary of the English Language* (1755) was not the first English dictionary, but its systematic preparation and comprehensiveness gave it the appearance of priority over all others and confirmed Johnson in the role of prime arbiter of public meanings which he would enjoy for the rest of his life. His edition of *The Plays of William Shakespeare* (1765) was again not the first, but it established new criteria for editorial exactness, and his *Lives of the English Poets* (1779–81) did much to give method and authority to the new genre of literary criticism which developed in response to the new importance given to contemporary letters. Others had lived by turning their pens to such various needs before, notably Daniel Defoe, but they had not escaped the charge of 'hack' writing (in other words being available, like a hackney carriage, for hire, therefore insincere). Johnson combined writing for money with the expression of high principle. His characteristic mode was to phrase his critical opinions as common-sensical aphorisms about human nature, and thus make literary commentary a philosophical and moral commentary on life as well as on representation. His life's achievement was to secure for the critic and the 'man of letters' the professional esteem and cultural significance which we now take for granted.

1: a minor character from *Tristram Shandy*, believed to represent Hall-Stevenson, a life-long friend of Sterne.

The Rambler, Number 4, Saturday 31 March 1750

Simul et jucunda et idenea discere Vitae.
Horace[1]

And join both profit and delight in one.
Creech[2]

The works of fiction, with which the present generation seems more particularly delighted, are such as exhibit life in its true state, diversified only by accidents that daily happen in the world, and influenced by passions and qualities which are really to be found in conversing with mankind.

This kind of writing may be termed not improperly the comedy of romance, and is to be conducted nearly by the rules of comic poetry. Its province is to bring about natural events by easy means, and to keep up curiosity without the help of wonder; it is therefore precluded from the machines and expedients of the heroic romance, and can neither employ giants to snatch away a lady from the nuptial rites, nor knights to bring her back from captivity; it can neither bewilder its personages in deserts, nor lodge them in imaginary castles.

I remember a remark made by Scaliger upon Pontanus,[3] that all his writings are filled with the same images; and that if you take from him his lilies and his roses, his satyrs and his dryads, he will have nothing left that can be called poetry. In like manner, almost all the fictions of the last age will vanish, if you deprive them of a hermit and a wood, a battle and a shipwreck.

Why this wild strain of imagination found reception so long, in polite and learned ages, it is not easy to conceive; but we cannot wonder that while readers could be procured, the authors were willing to continue it; for when a man had by practice gained some fluency of language, he had no farther care than to retire to his closet, let loose his invention, and heat his mind with incredibilities; a book was thus produced without fear of criticism, without the toil of study, without knowledge of nature, or acquaintance with life.

The task of our present writers is very different; it requires, together with that learning which is to be gained from books, that experience which can never be attained by solitary diligence, but must arise from general converse and accurate observation of the living world. Their performances have, as Horace expresses it, *plus oneris, quanto veniae minus*, little indulgence, and therefore more difficulty.[4] There are engaged in portraits of which every one knows the original, and can detect any deviation from exactness of resemblance. Other writings are safe, except from the malice of learning, but these are in danger from every common reader; as the slipper ill executed was censured by a shoemaker who happened to stop in his way at the Venus of Apelles.[5]

But the fear of not being approved as just copiers of human manners, is not the most important concern that an author of this sort ought to have before

---

1: Horace, *Ars Poetica*, 334.   2: Thomas Creech (1659–1700) a popular translator.   3: Julius Scaliger (1484–1558) criticising Giovanni Pontanus (1425–1503) in his *Poetics* (*ante* 1581), in sum, a grand display of empty erudition.   4: Horace, *Epistulae* 2, I, 170.   5: Apelles (fourth century BC) was the most famous painter of ancient Greece. Pliny, 35, 10, relates that a shoemaker rightly criticised his depiction of a sandal in the painting of Venus arising from the waves, then presumed to criticise the leg. This led to the expression, 'let the shoemaker stick to his last.'

him. These books are written chiefly to the young, the ignorant, and the idle, to whom they serve as lectures of conduct, and introductions into life. They are the entertainment of minds unfurnished with ideas, and therefore easily susceptible of impressions; not fixed by principles, and therefore easily following the current of fancy; not informed by experience, and consequently open to every false suggestion and partial account.

That the highest degree of reverence should be paid to youth, and that nothing indecent should be suffered to approach their eyes or ears, are precepts extorted by sense and virtue from an ancient writer, by no means eminent for chastity of thought.[1] The same kind, though not the same degree of caution, is required in every thing which is laid before them, to secure them from unjust prejudices, perverse opinions and incongruous combinations of images.

In the romances formerly written, every transaction and sentiment was so remote from all that passes among men that the reader was in very little danger of making any applications to himself; the virtues and crimes were equally beyond his sphere of activity; and he amused himself with heroes and with traitors, deliverers and persecutors, as with beings of another species, whose actions were regulated upon motives of their own, and who had neither faults nor excellences in common with himself.

But when an adventurer is levelled with the rest of the world, and acts in such scenes of the universal drama, as may be the lot of any other man, young spectators fix their eyes upon him with closer attention, and hope, by observing his behaviour and success, to regulate their own practices, when they shall be engaged in the like part.

For this reason these familiar histories may perhaps be made of greater use than the solemnities of professed morality, and convey the knowledge of vice and virtue with more efficacy than axioms and definitions. But if the power of example is so great as to take possession of the memory by a kind of violence, and produce effects almost without the intervention of the will, care ought to be taken that, when the choice is unrestrained, the best examples only should be exhibited; and that which is likely to operate so strongly should not be mischievous or uncertain in its effects.

The chief advantage which these fictions have over real life is that their authors are at liberty, though not to invent, yet to select objects, and to cull from the mass of mankind, those individuals upon which the attention ought most to be employed; as a diamond, though it cannot be made, may be polished by art, and placed in such a situation as to display that lustre which before was buried among common stones.

It is justly considered as the greatest excellency of art to imitate nature; but it is necessary to distinguish those parts of nature, which are most proper for imitation: greater care is still required in representing life, which is so often discoloured by passion, or deformed by wickedness. If the world be promiscuously[1] described, I cannot see of what use it can be to read the account; or why it may not be as safe to turn the eye immediately upon mankind

---

1: Juvenal, *Satires*, xiv., 1-58.

as upon a mirror which shows all that presents itself without discrimination.

It is therefore not a sufficient vindication of a character, that it is drawn as it appears, for many characters ought never to be drawn; nor of a narrative, that the train of events is agreeable to observation and experience, for that observation which is called knowledge of the world will be found much more frequently to make men cunning than good. The purpose of these writings is surely not only to show mankind, but to provide that they may be seen hereafter with less hazard; to teach the means of avoiding the snares which are laid by Treachery for Innocence, without infusing any wish for that superiority with which the betrayer flatters his vanity; to give the power of counteracting fraud, without the temptation to practise it; to initiate youth by mock encounters in the art of necessary defence, and to increase prudence without impairing virtue.

Many writers, for the sake of following nature, so mingle good and bad qualities in their principal personages, that they are both equally conspicuous; and as we accompany them through their adventures with delight, and are led by degrees to interest ourselves in their favour, we lose the abhorrence of their faults, because they do not hinder our pleasure, or, perhaps, regard them with some kindness for being united with so much merit.

There have been men indeed splendidly wicked, whose endowments threw a brightness on their crimes, and whom scarce any villainy made perfectly detestable, because they never could be wholly divested of their excellencies; but such have been in all ages the great corrupters of the world, and their resemblance ought no more to be preserved, than the art of murdering without pain.

Some have advanced, without due attention to the consequences of this notion, that certain virtues have their correspondent faults, and therefore that to exhibit either part is to deviate from probability. Thus men are observed by Swift to be 'grateful in the same degree as they are resentful.' This principle, with others of the same kind, supposes man to act from a brute impulse, and pursue a certain degree of inclination, without any choice of the object; for, otherwise, though it should be allowed that gratitude and resentment arise from the same constitution of the passions, it follows not that they will be equally indulged when reason is consulted; yet unless that consequence be admitted, this sagacious maxim becomes an empty sound, without any relation to practice or to life.

Nor is it evident, that even the first motions to these effects are always in the same proportion. For pride, which produces quickness of resentment, will obstruct gratitude, by unwillingness to admit that inferiority which obligation implies; and it is very unlikely, that he who cannot think he receives a favour, will acknowledge or repay it.

It is of the utmost importance to mankind, that positions of this tendency should be laid open and confuted; for while men consider good and evil as springing from the same root, they will spare the one for the sake of the other, and in judging, if not of others at least of themselves, will be apt to estimate their virtues by their vices. To this fatal error all those will contribute, who

---

1: indiscriminately.

confound the colours of right and wrong, and instead of helping to settle their boundaries, mix them with so much art, that no common mind is able to disunite them.

In narratives, where historical veracity has no place, I cannot discover why there should not be exhibited the most perfect idea of virtue; of virtue not angelical, nor above probability, for what we cannot credit we shall never imitate, but the highest and purest that humanity can reach, which, exercised in such trials as the various revolution of things shall bring upon it, may, by conquering some calamities, and enduring others, teach us what we may hope, and what we can perform. Vice, for vice is necessary to be shown, should always disgust; nor should the graces of gaiety, or the dignity of courage, be so united with it, as to reconcile it to the mind: wherever it appears, it should raise hatred by the malignity of its practices, and contempt by the meanness of its stratagems: for while it is supported by either parts or spirit, it will be seldom heartily abhorred. The Roman tyrant was content to be hated, if he was but feared; and there are thousands of the readers of romances willing to be thought wicked, if they may be allowed to be wits. It is therefore to be steadily inculcated, that virtue is the highest proof of understanding, and the only solid basis of greatness; and that vice is the natural consequence of narrow thoughts; that it begins in mistake, and ends in ignominy.

From The Preface to the Plays of William Shakespeare

As among the works of nature no man can properly call a river deep or a mountain high, without the knowledge of many mountains and many rivers; so in the productions of genius, nothing can be styled excellent till it has been compared with other works of the same kind. Demonstration immediately displays its power, and has nothing to hope or fear from the flux of years; but works tentative and experimental must be estimated by their proportion to the general and collective ability of man, as it is discovered in a long succession of endeavours. Of the first building that was raised, it might be with certainty determined that it was round or square, but whether it was spacious or lofty must have been referred to time. The Pythagorean scale of numbers was at once discovered to be perfect;[1] but the poems of Homer we yet know not to transcend the common limits of human intelligence, but by remarking, that nation after nation, and century after century, has been able to do little more than transpose his incidents, new name his characters, and paraphrase his sentiments.

The reverence due to writings that have long subsisted arises therefore not from any credulous confidence in the superior wisdom of past ages, or gloomy persuasion of the degeneracy of mankind, but is the consequence of acknowledged and indubitable positions, that what has been longest known has been most considered, and what is most considered is best understood.

The poet, of whose works I have undertaken the revision, may now begin to assume the dignity of an ancient, and claim the privilege of established fame

---

1: Pythagoras discovered that the main intervals of the musical scale correspond to numerical ratios.

and prescriptive veneration. He has long outlived his century, the term commonly fixed as the test of literary merit. Whatever advantages he might once derive from personal allusions, local customs, or temporary opinions, have for many years been lost; and every topic of merriment or motive of sorrow, which the modes of artificial life afforded him, now only obscure the scenes which they once illuminated. The effects of favour and competition are at an end; the tradition of his friendships and his enmities has perished; his works support no opinion with arguments, nor supply any faction with invectives; they can neither indulge vanity nor gratify malignity, but are read without any other reason than the desire of pleasure, and are therefore praised only as pleasure is obtained; yet, thus unassisted by interest or passion, they have passed through variations of taste and changes of manners, and, as they devolved from one generation to another, have received new honours at every transmission.

But because human judgment, though it be gradually gaining upon certainty, never becomes infallible; and approbation, though long continued, may yet be only the approbation of prejudice or fashion; it is proper to inquire, by what peculiarities of excellence Shakespeare has gained and kept the favour of his countrymen.

Nothing can please many, and please long, but just representations of general nature. Particular manners can be known to few, and therefore few only can judge how nearly they are copied. The irregular combinations of fanciful invention may delight awhile, by that novelty of which the common satiety of life sends us all in quest; but the pleasures of sudden wonder are soon exhausted, and the mind can only repose on the stability of truth.

Shakespeare is above all writers, at least above all modern writers, the poet of nature; the poet that holds up to his readers a faithful mirror of manners and of life. His characters are not modified by the customs of particular places, unpractised by the rest of the world; by the peculiarities of studies or professions, which can operate but upon small numbers; or by the accidents of transient fashions or temporary opinions: they are the genuine progeny of common humanity, such as the world will always supply, and observation will always find. His persons act and speak by the influence of those general passions and principles by which all minds are agitated, and the whole system of life is continued in motion. In the writings of other poets a character is too often an individual; in those of Shakespeare it is commonly a species.

It is from this wide extension of design that so much instruction is derived. It is this which fills the plays of Shakespeare with practical axioms and domestic wisdom. It was said of Euripides, that every verse was a precept; and it may be said of Shakespeare, that from his works may be collected a system of civil and economical prudence. Yet his real power is not shown in the splendour of particular passages, but by the progress of his fable, and the tenor of his dialogue; and he that tries to recommend him by select quotations, will succeed like the pedant in Hierocles, who, when he offered his house to sale, carried a brick in his pocket as a specimen.

It will not easily be imagined how much Shakespeare excels in accommodating his sentiments to real life, but by comparing him with other authors. It was observed of the ancient schools of declamation, that the more diligently they were frequented, the more was the student disqualified for the world, because he found nothing there which he should ever meet in any other place. The same remark may be applied to every stage but that of Shakespeare. The theatre, when it is under any other direction, is peopled by such characters as were never seen, conversing in a language which was never heard, upon topics which will never arise in the commerce of mankind. But the dialogue of this author is often so evidently determined by the incident which produces it, and is pursued with so much ease and simplicity, that it seems scarcely to claim the merit of fiction, but to have been gleaned by diligent selection out of common conversation, and common occurrences.

Upon every other stage the universal agent is love, by whose power all good and evil is distributed, and every action quickened or retarded. To bring a lover, a lady and a rival into the fable; to entangle them in contradictory obligations, perplex them with oppositions of interest, and harass them with violence of desires inconsistent with each other; to make them meet in rapture and part in agony; to fill their mouths with hyperbolical joy and outrageous sorrow; to distress them as nothing human ever was distressed; to deliver them as nothing human ever was delivered, is the business of a modern dramatist. For this, probability is violated, life is misrepresented, and language is depraved. But love is only one of many passions, and as it has no great influence upon the sum of life, it has little operation in the dramas of a poet, who caught his ideas from the living world, and exhibited only what he saw before him. He knew, that any other passion, as it was regular or exorbitant, was a cause of happiness or calamity.

Characters thus ample and general were not easily discriminated and preserved, yet perhaps no poet ever kept his personages more distinct from each other. I will not say with Pope that every speech may be assigned to the proper speaker, becaause many speeches there are which have nothing characteristical; but, perhaps, though some may be equally adapted to every person, it will be difficult to find any that can be properly transferred from the present possessor to another claimant. The choice is right, when there is reason for choice.

Other dramatists can only gain attention by hyperbolical or aggravated characters, by fabulous and unexampled excellence or depravity, as the writers of barbarous romances invigorated the reader by a giant and a dwarf; and he that should form his expectations of human affairs from the play, or from the tale, would be equally deceived. Shakespeare has no heroes; his scenes are occuped only by men, who act and speak as the reader thinks that he should himself have spoken or acted on the same occasion. Even where the agency is supernatural, the dialogue is level with life. Other writers disguise the most natural passions and most frequent incidents, so that he who contemplates them in the book will not know them in the world. Shakespeare approximates[1] the remote and familiarises the wonderful; the event which he represents will not happen but, if it were possible, its effects would probably be such as he has assigned; and it may be said that he has not only shown human nature as it acts in real exigences, but as it would be found in trials to which it cannot be exposed.

1: brings near.

OLIVER GOLDSMITH (1730–1774)

Born in Ireland and educated at Trinity College, Dublin, Oliver Goldsmith studied medicine at Edinburgh but did not graduate, travelled extensively in Europe and then settled to practise medicine in London without success. He became a hack, contributed essays to numerous periodicals, was befriended by Edmund Burke and Samuel Johnson, and became wealthy through his skill with the pen. He knew some success with his poem *The Traveller* (1762), and his novel *The Vicar of Wakefield* (1764) was to remain popular well into the twentieth century, as was *The Deserted Village* (1770). His robust anti-sentimental comedy, *She Stoops to Conquer* (1773), is still produced for the modern stage. Goldsmith had written critically of the vogue for sentimental declamation, but his own work, through its very discipline and detachment, represents a higher and more enduring form of the emotional sensibility that lies at the heart of sentimental writing. *The Deserted Village* is a response to the wholesale depopulation of the countryside that resulted when capitalist attitudes transformed agiruculture into a profit-oriented business, and to the parallel vogue for surrounding country houses with landscaped gardens to signal the tasteful and natural relationship of their owners to the land. (Cf. Alexander Pope, *Epistle to Burlington*; and Jane Austen, *Mansfield Park*). The poem contrasts a luxurious and parasitic landowning class bent more on pleasure than profit with a rural poor whose lives are grandly idealised but whose destitution is none the less deeply felt. Its easy grace belies its considerable skill.

The Deserted Village

Sweet Auburn, loveliest village of the plain,
Where health and plenty cheered the labouring swain,
Where smiling spring its earliest visit paid,
And parting summer's lingering blooms delayed:
5   Dear lovely bowers of innocence and ease,
Seats of my youth, when every sport could please,
How often have I loitered o'er thy green,
Where humble happiness endeared each scene;
How often have I paused on every charm,
10   The sheltered cot, the cultivated farm,
The never-failing brook, the busy mill,
The decent church that topped the neighbouring hill,
The hawthorn bush, with seats beneath the shade,
For talking age and whispering lovers made.
15   How often have I blessed the coming day,
When toil remitting lent its turn to play,
And all the village train, from labour free,
Led up their sports beneath the spreading tree,
While many a pastime circled in the shade,
20   The young contending as the old surveyed;
And many a gambol frolicked o'er the ground,
And sleights of art and feats of strength went round.

And still as each repeated pleasure tired,
Succeeding sports the mirthful band inspired;
25   The dancing pair that simply sought renown,
By holding out to tire each other down;
The swain mistrustless of his smutted face,
While secret laughter tittered round the place;
The bashful virgin's sidelong looks of love,
30   The matron's glance that would those looks reprove.
These were thy charms, sweet village; sports like these,
With sweet succession, taught even toil to please;
These round thy bowers their cheerful influence shed,
These were thy charms – but all these charms are fled.

35   Sweet smiling village, loveliest of the lawn,
Thy sports are fled and all thy charms withdrawn;
Amidst thy bowers the tyrant's hand is seen,
And desolation saddens all thy green:
One only master grasps the whole domain,
40   And half a tillage stints thy smiling plain:
No more thy glassy brook reflects the day,
But, choked with sedges, works its weedy way.
Along thy glades, a solitary guest,
The hollow-sounding bittern guards its nest;
45   Amidst thy desert walks the lapwing flies,
And tires their echoes with unvaried cries.
Sunk are thy bowers in shapeless ruin all,
And the long grass o'ertops the mouldering wall;
And trembling, shrinking from the spoiler's hand,
50   Far, far away, thy children leave the land.

Ill fares the land, to hastening ills a prey,
Where wealth accumulates and men decay:
Princes and lords may flourish or may fade;
A breath can make them, as a breath has made;
55   But a bold peasantry, their country's pride,
When once destroyed, can never be supplied.

A time there was, ere England's griefs began,
When every rood of ground maintained its man;
For him light labour spread her wholesome store,
60   Just gave what life required, but gave no more:
His best companions, innocence and health;
And his best riches, ignorance of wealth.

But times are altered; trade's unfeeling train
Usurp the land and dispossess the swain;
65   Along the lawn, where scattered hamlets rose,

Unwieldy wealth and cumbrous pomp repose;
And every want to opulence allied,
And every pang that folly pays to pride.
These gentle hours that plenty bade to bloom,
70   Those calm desires that asked but little room,
Those healthful sports that graced the peaceful scene,
Lived in each look and brightened all the green;
These, far departing, seek a kinder shore,
And rural mirth and manners are no more.

75   Sweet Auburn! parent of the blissful hour,
Thy glades forlorn confess the tyrant's power.
Here as I take my solitary rounds,
Amidst thy tangling walks and ruined grounds,
And, many a year elapsed, return to view
80   Where once the cottage stood, the hawthorn grew,
Remembrance wakes with all her busy train,
Swells at my breast and turns the past to pain.

In all my wanderings round this world of care,
In all my griefs – and God has given my share –
85   I still had hopes my latest hours to crown,
Amidst these humble bowers to lay me down;
To husband out life's taper at the close
And keep the flame from wasting by repose.
I still had hopes, for pride attends us still,
90   Amidst the swains to show my book-learned skill,
Around my fire an evening group to draw,
And tell of all I felt and all I saw;
And, as a hare, whom hounds and horns pursue,
Pants to the place from whence at first she flew,
95   I still had hopes, my long vexations past,
Here to return – and die at home at last.

O blest retirement, friend to life's decline,
Retreats from care that never must be mine,
How happy he who crowns in shades like these
100 A youth of labour with an age of ease;
Who quits a world where strong temptations try,
And, since 'tis hard to combat, learns to fly.
For him no wretches, born to work and weep,
Explore the mine or tempt the dangerous deep;
105 No surly porter stands in guilty state
To spurn imploring famine from the gate;
But on he moves to meet his latter end,
Angels around befriending virtue's friend;
Bends to the grave with unperceived decay,

110 While resignation gently slopes the way;
And, all his prospects brightening to the last,
His heaven commences ere the world be past

Sweet was the sound, when oft at evening's close
Up yonder hill the village murmur rose;
115 There, as I passed with careless steps and slow,
The mingling notes came softened from below;
The swain responsive as the milkmaid sung,
The sober herd that lowed to meet their young;
The noisy geese that gabbled o'er the pool,
120 The playful children just let loose from school;
The watchdog's voice that bayed the whispering wind,
And the loud laugh that spoke the vacant mind;
These all in sweet confusion sought the shade,
And filled each pause the nightingale had made.
125 But now the sounds of population fail,
No cheerful murmurs fluctuate in the gale,
No busy steps the grassgrown foot-way tread,
For all the bloomy flush of life is fled.
All but yon widowed, solitary thing
130 That feebly bends beside the plashy spring;
She, wretched matron, forced, in age, for bread,
To strip the brook with mantling cresses spread,
To pick her wintry faggot from the thorn,
To seek her nightly shed and weep till morn;
135 She only left of all the harmless train,
The sad historian of the pensive plain.

Near yonder copse, where once the garden smiled,
And still where many a garden flower grows wild;
There where a few torn shrubs the place disclose,
140 The village preacher's modest mansion rose.
A man he was to all the country dear,
And passing rich with forty pounds a year;
Remote from towns he ran his godly race,
Nor e'er had changed, nor wished to change, his place;
145 Unpractised he to fawn, or seek for power,
By doctrines fashioned to the varying hour;
Far other aims his heart had learned to prize,
More skilled to raise the wretched than to rise.
His house was known to all the vagrant train,
150 He chid their wanderings, but relieved their pain;
The long-remembered beggar was his guest,
Whose beard descending swept his aged breast;
The ruined spendthrift, now no longer proud,
Claimed kindred there and had his claims allowed;

155 The broken soldier, kindly bade to stay,
Sat by his fire and talked the night away;
Wept o'er his wounds or tales of sorrow done,
Shouldered his crutch and showed how fields were won.
Pleased with his guests, the good man learned to glow,
160 And quite forgot their vices in their woe;
Careless their merits or their faults to scan,
His pity gave ere charity began.

Thus to relieve the wretched was his pride,
And even his failings leaned to virtue's side;
165 But in his duty prompt at every call,
He watched and wept, he prayed and felt, for all.
And, as a bird each fond endearment tries
To tempt its new-fledged offspring to the skies,
He tried each art, reproved each dull delay,
170 Allured to brighter worlds, and led the way.

Beside the bed where parting life was laid,
And sorrow, guilt, and pain by turns dismayed,
The reverend champion stood. At his control,
Despair and anguish fled the struggling soul;
175 Comfort came down the trembling wretch to raise,
And his last faltering accents whispered praise.
At church, with meek and unaffected grace,
His looks adorned the venerable place;
Truth from his lips prevailed with double sway,
180 And fools, who came to scoff, remained to pray.
The service past, around the pious man,
With steady zeal each honest rustic ran;
Even children followed with endearing while,
And plucked his gown, to share the good man's smile.
185 His ready smile a parent's warmth expressed,
Their welfare pleased him and their cares distressed;
To them his heart, his love, his griefs were given,
But all his serious thoughts had rest in heaven.
As some tall cliff, that lifts its awful form,
190 Swells from the vale and midway leaves the storm,
Though round its breast the rolling clouds are spread,
Eternal sunshine settles on its head.

Beside yon straggling fence that skirts the way,
With blossomed furze unprofitably gay,
195 There, in his noisy mansion, skilled to rule,
The village master taught his little school;
A man severe he was and stern to view;
I knew him well, and every truant knew;

Well had the boding tremblers learned to trace
200　The day's disasters in his morning face;
Full well they laughed, with counterfeited glee,
At all his jokes, for many a joke had he;
Full well the busy whisper, circling round,
Conveyed the dismal tidings when he frowned;
205　Yet he was kind, or, if severe in aught,
The love he bore to learning was in fault;
The village all declared how much he knew;
'Twas certain he could write and cipher too;
Lands he could measure, terms and tides presage,
210　And even the story ran that he could gauge.
In arguing too, the parson owned his skill,
For even though vanquished, he could argue still;
While words of learned length and thundering sound
Amazed the gazing rustics ranged around,
215　And still they gazed, and still the wonder grew,
That one small head could carry all he knew.

But past is all his fame. The very spot,
Where many a time he triumphed, is forgot.
Near yonder thorn, that lifts its head on high,
220　Where once the signpost caught the passing eye,
Low lies that house where nutbrown draughts inspired,
Where greybeard mirth and smiling toil retired,
Where village statesmen talked with looks profound,
And news much older than their ale went round.
225　Imagination fondly stoops to trace
The parlour splendours of that festive place;
The white-washed wall, the nicely sanded floor,
The varnished clock that clicked behind the door;
The chest contrived a double debt to pay,
230　A bed by night, a chest of drawers by day;
The pictures placed for ornament and use,
The twelve good rules, the royal game of goose;
The hearth, except when winter chilled the day,
With aspen boughs and flowers and fennel gay;
235　While broken teacups, wisely kept for show,
Ranged o'er the chimney, glistened in a row.

Vain, transitory splendours! Could not all
Reprieve the tottering mansion from its fall!
Obscure it sinks, nor shall it more impart
240　An hour's importance to the poor man's heart;
Thither no more the peasant shall repair
To sweet oblivion of his daily care;
No more the farmer's news, the barber's tale,

No more the woodman's ballad shall prevail;
245 No more the smith his dusky brow shall clear
Relax his ponderous strength and lean to hear
The host himself no longer shall be found
Careful to see the mantling bliss go round;
Nor the coy maid, half willing to be pressed,
250 Shall kiss the cup to pass it to the rest.

Yes! let the rich deride, the proud disdain
These simple blessings of the lowly train;
To me more dear, congenial to my heart,
One native charm than all the gloss of art;
255 Spontaneous joys, where nature has its play,
The soul adopts and owns their firstborn sway;
Lightly they frolic o'er the vacant mind,
Unenvied, unmolested, unconfined:
But the long pomp, the midnight masquerade
260 With all the freaks of wanton wealth arrayed,
In these, ere triflers half their wish obtain,
The toiling pleasure sickens into pain;
And, even while fashion's brightest arts decoy
The heart distrusting asks, if this be joy.

265 Ye friends to truth, ye statesmen, who survey
The rich man's joys increase, the poor's decay,
'Tis yours to judge how wide the limits stand
Between a splendid and an happy land.
Proud swells the tide with loads of freighted ore,
270 And shouting Folly hails them from her shore;
Hoards, even beyond the miser's wish, abound,
And rich men flock from all the world around.
Yet count our gains. This wealth is but a name
That leaves our useful products still the same.
275 Not so the loss. The man of wealth and pride
Takes up a space that many poor supplied;
Space for his lake, his park's extended bounds
Space for his horses, equipage and hounds;
The robe that wraps his limbs in silken sloth
280 Has robbed the neighbouring fields of half their growth;
His seat, where solitary sports are seen,
Indignant spurns the cottage from the green;
Around the world each needful product flies
For all the luxuries the world supplies:
285 While thus the land, adorned for pleasure all,
In barren splendour feebly waits the fall.

As some fair female unadorned and plain,
Secure to please while youth confirms her reign,
Slights every borrowed charm that dress supplies,
290 Nor shares with art the triumph of her eyes;
But when those charms are passed, for charms are frail,
When time advances and when lovers fail,
She then shines forth, solicitous to bless,
In all the glaring impotence of dress:
295 Thus fares the land, by luxury betrayed,
In nature's simplest charms at first arrayed;
But verging to decline, its splendours rise,
Its vistas strike, its palaces surprise;
While scourged by famine from the smiling land,
300 The mournful peasant leads his humble band;
And while he sinks, without one arm to save,
The country blooms – a garden and a grave.

Where then, ah where, shall poverty reside,
To 'scape the pressure of contiguous pride?
305 If to some common's fenceless limits strayed,
He drives his flock to pick the scanty blade,
Those fenceless fields the sons of wealth divide,
And even the bare-worn common is denied.

If to the city sped – what waits him there?
310 To see profusion that he must not share;
To see ten thousand baneful arts combined
To pamper luxury and thin mankind;
To see those joys the sons of pleasure know
Extorted from his fellow-creature's woe.
315 Here, while the courtier glitters in brocade,
There the pale artist plies the sickly trade;
Here, while the proud their long-drawn pomps display,
There the black gibbet glooms beside the way.
The dome where Pleasure holds her midnight reign
320 Here, richly decked, admits the gorgeous train;
Tumultuous grandeur crowds the blazing square,
The rattling chariots clash, the torches glare.
Sure scenes like these no troubles e'er annoy!
Sure these denote one universal joy!
325 Are these thy serious thoughts? – Ah, turn thine eyes
Where the poor, houseless, shivering female lies.
She once, perhaps, in village plenty blessed,
Has wept at tales of innocence distressed;
Her modest looks the cottage might adorn,
330 Sweet as the primrose peeps beneath the thorn;

Now lost to all; her friends, her virtue fled,
Near her betrayer's door she lays her head,
And, pinched with cold and shrinking from the shower,
With heavy heart deplores that luckless hour,
335   When idly first, ambitious of the town,
She left her wheel and robes of country brown.

Do thine, sweet Auburn, thine, the loveliest train,
Do thy fair tribes participate her pain?
Even now, perhaps, by cold and hunger led,
340   At proud men's doors they ask a little bread!

Ah, no. To distant climes, a dreary scene,
Where half the convex world intrudes between,
Through torrid tracts with fainting steps they go,
Where wild Altama murmurs to their woe.
345   Far different there from all that charmed before
The various terrors of that horrid shore:
Those blazing suns that dart a downward ray,
And fiercely shed intolerable day,
Those matted woods where birds forget to sing,
350   But silent bats in drowsy clusters cling;
Those poisonous fields with rank luxuriance crowned,
Where the dark scorpion gathers death around;
Where at each step the stranger fears to wake
The rattling terrors of the vengeful snake;
355   Where crouching tigers wait their hapless prey,
And savage men more murderous still than they;
While oft in whirls the mad tornado flies,
Mingling the ravaged landscape with the skies.
Far different these from every former scene,
360   The cooling brook, the grassy-vested green,
The breezy covert of the warbling grove,
That only sheltered thefts of harmless love.

Good heaven! what sorrows gloomed that parting day,
That called them from their native walks away;
365   When the poor exiles, every pleasure past,
Hung round their bowers and fondly looked their last,
And took a long farewell, and wished in vain
For seats like these beyond the western main;
And shuddering still to face the distant deep,
370   Returned and wept, and still returned to weep.
The good old sire the first prepared to go
To new-found worlds, and wept for others' woe;

---

344 **Altama**: the Altamaha river in the state of Georgia, USA.

But for himself, in conscious virtue brave,
He only wished for worlds beyond the grave.
375 His lovely daughter, lovelier in her tears,
The fond companion of his helpless years,
Silent went next, neglectful of her charms,
And left a lover's for a father's arms.
With louder plaints the mother spoke her woes,
380 And blessed the cot where every pleasure rose;
And kissed her thoughtless babes with many a tear,
And clasped them close, in sorrow doubly dear;
Whilst her fond husband strove to lend relief
In all the silent manliness of grief.

385   O luxury! thou cursed by heaven's decree,
How ill exchanged are things like these for thee!
How do thy potions with insidious joy
Diffuse their pleasures only to destroy!
Kingdoms, by thee to sickly greatness grown,
390 Boast of a florid vigour not their own.
At every draught more large and large they grow,
A bloated mass of rank unwieldy woe;
Till sapped their strength and every part unsound,
Down, down they sink and spread a ruin round.

395   Even now the devastation is begun,
And half the business of destruction done;
Even now, methinks, as pondering here I stand,
I see the rural virtues leave the land.
Down where yon anchoring vessel spreads the sail,
400 That idly waiting flaps with every gale,
Downward they move, a melancholy band,
Pass from the shore and darken all the strand.
Contented toil and hospitable care,
And kind connubial tenderness are there;
405 And piety, with wishes placed above,
And steady loyalty and faithful love.
And thou, sweet Poetry, thou loveliest maid,
Still first to fly where sensual joys invade;
Unfit, in these degenerate times of shame,
410 To catch the heart or strike for honest fame;
Dear charming nymph, neglected and decried,
My shame in crowds, my solitary pride;
Thou source of all my bliss and all my woe,
That found'st me poor at first and keep'st me so;
415 Thou guide by which the nobler arts excel,
Thou nurse of every virtue, fare thee well!
Farewell, and oh, where'er thy voice be tried,

On Torno's cliffs or Pambamarca's side,
Whether where equinoctial fervours glow,
420   Or winter wraps the polar world in snow,
Still let thy voice, prevailing over time,
Redress the rigours of the inclement clime;
Aid slighted truth; with thy persuasive strain
Teach erring man to spurn the rage of gain;
425   Teach him that states of native strength possessed,
Though very poor, may still be very blest;
That trade's proud empire hastes to swift decay,
As ocean sweeps the laboured mole away;
While self-dependent power can time defy,
430   As rocks resist the billows and the sky.

WILLIAM COWPER (1731–1800)

William Cowper was the son of a Hertfordshire rector, educated at Westminster School and trained for the law. His character was painfully emotional, melancholic, suicidal. He sought consolation in evangelical Christianity and in 1779 published *Olney Hymns*, including many that became national standards. His poem in six books, *The Task* (1785), extolling the virtues of a retired life, was very popular, admired by Robert Burns and Jane Austen, and influential on Wordsworth. 'The Castaway', one of his last and most famous poems, was written in 1799 and published in 1803.

The Castaway

Obscurest night involved the sky,
    The Atlantic billows roared,
When such a destined wretch as I,
    Washed headlong from on board,
5   Of friends, of hope, of all bereft,
His floating home for ever left.

No braver chief could Albion boast
    Than he with whom he went,
Nor ever ship left Albion's coast
10   With warmer wishes sent.
He loved them both, but both in vain,
Nor him beheld, nor her again.
Not long beneath the whelming brine,
    Expert to swim, he lay;

---

418 Torno...Pambamarca: the River Torne in Sweden, and a mountain in Ecuador. Both had been the subject of recent scientific expeditions.

7 chief: George, Lord Anson. The story comes from his *Voyage Around the World* (1748).

15   Nor soon he felt his strength decline,
    Or courage die away;
  But waged with death a lasting strife,
  Supported by despair of life.

  He shouted; nor his friends had failed
20   To check the vessel's course,
  But so the furious blast prevailed,
    That, pitiless perforce,
  They left their outcast mate behind,
  And scudded still before the wind.

25   Some succour yet they could afford;
    And, such as storms allow,
  The cask, the coop, the floated cord,
    Delayed not to bestow.
  But he (they knew) nor ship nor shore,
30   Whate'er they gave, should visit more.

  Nor, cruel as it seemed, could he
    Their haste himself condemn,
  Aware that flight, in such a sea,
    Alone could rescue them;
35   Yet bitter felt it still to die
  Deserted, and his friends so nigh.

  He long survives, who lives an hour
    In ocean, self-upheld;
  And so long he, with unspent power,
40   His destiny repelled;
  And ever, as the minutes flew,
  Entreated help, or cried 'Adieu!'

  At length, his transient respite past,
    His comrades, who before
45   Had heard his voice in every blast,
    Could catch the sound no more.
  For then, by toil subdued, he drank
  The stifling wave, and then he sank.

  No poet wept him: but the page
50   Of narrative sincere,
  That tells his name, his worth, his age,
    Is wet with Anson's tear.
  And tears by bards or heroes shed
  Alike immortalise the dead.

55   I therefore purpose not, or dream,
        Descanting on his fate,
    To give the melancholy theme
        A more enduring date:
    But misery still delights to trace
60   Its semblance in another's case.

    No voice divine the storm allayed,
        No light propitious shone,
    When, snatched from all effectual aid,
        We perished, each alone:
65   But I beneath a rougher sea,
    And whelmed in deeper gulfs than he.

Romantics

Throughout the eighteenth century, European powers, and especially Britain and France, fought for the domination of world trade through the control of colonial resources and markets. In 1763 Britain forced the French to cede control of North America, but, ill-led by George III (who reigned 1760–1820), Britain itself was forced to cede independence to the American revolutionaries in 1783. The American Revolution inspired others: in 1789 the people of France revolted against the *ancien régime*, and by 1792 were offering to export the revolution to any countries that needed their help. In response Britain, Prussia, Austria, Spain and Portugal attacked France and unleashed a pan-European war that would last until 1815, by which time revolutionary idealism had passed through the Terror (1793–94) into the slaughter of millions on the bench of Napoleon's imperial ambitions (1804–15).

The cause of the ferment was the growth of capital, the opportunities it created and the resistances it encountered in established classes and ways of life. For Britain especially, success in dominating global trade provided money for investment in new manufacturing technologies, especially in textiles, potteries, ironworks and communications. The invention of the steam engine in 1765, and then of new machines to apply its force, led to the concentration of labour in factory towns, especially in the textile trades, and the end of a long tradition of cottage industry that had balanced domestic accounts for many rural workers. Simultaneously the new 'scientific agriculture' encouraged landowners to maximise cash returns by greater investment and rationality in use. The long historical process of 'the enclosures' – taking common land into private hands and hedging it so that fields could be rotated between pasture and crops – entered a last hectic phase, depopulating the countryside, augmenting the cities, reducing yet further the costs of labour but increasing the demand for trade in goods and services. Women and young children led lives of near-slavery in coal mines and iron foundries. Taking their tune from the laissez-faire doctrines of Adam Smith's *An Inquiry into the Nature and Causes of the Wealth of Nations* (1776), the wealthy proposed that their enrichment would soon trickle down to the benefit of all. Especially under the Regency (1811–20), when George III's madness placed authority in the hands of the Prince of Wales, later George IV, they enjoyed ever more comfortable and gaudy consumption and the centres of London, Bath and many spa towns received elegant new assembly rooms, colonnades, terraces and shopping streets which are enjoyed to this day.

In the first heady years a new spirit was abroad. The French Revolution signalled that people could transform history; that class, money and gender were not unchangeable prescriptions on human rights; that a world could be founded on the universal equality of the human spirit. Convention, tradition and rules no longer seemed the appropriate guides to social or aesthetic conduct; the reinvention of forms, even of our concept of 'man', was the pressing task. Such ideas were not universally welcome. Edmund Burke, an MP and political philosopher with a long history of supporting libertarian causes, inveighed against the dire implications in his *Reflections on the Revolution in France* (1790). More enthusiastic responses were offered in Mary Wollstonecraft's *Vindication of the Rights of Man* (1790) and *Vindication of the Rights of Woman* (1792), Thomas Paine's *The Rights of Man* (1791, 1792), and William Godwin's *An Enquiry concerning Political Justice* (1793). Immediate effects of such enthusiasm were the arrest or exile of the most prominent radicals, show trials and increased police surveillance.

All the poets which later generations would group under the label 'romantic' were sympathetic to the libertarian cause, although in many cases the excesses of the Terror in France and the climate of opinion in Britain would change radicals into Tories by the end of the century. But even when formal political endorsement was withdrawn, the trace of these events is evident in every aspect of literature – in the quest for new forms, the quest for a new poetic language, and for a condition of spiritual beatitude which lies as the telos to a contradictory path through the melancholy loss of innocence and the passionate struggle for the truth. Where the eighteenth-century poet had often seen his task as satirical moral correction, or as description of fixed conditions within relatively fixed genres, the romantic poet defined poetry as the search of the poetic mind for transcendent knowledge. The poet was a spiritual pathfinder, necessarily outside social mores and conventions, exploring an interior condition which was the mirror of cosmic conditions. The emphasis was on vision, feeling, intuition, spontaneity, on re-seeing the seen, more than on wit and logic. The history of the modern existential intellectual, rhapsodic in his alienation, begins at this point.

For other literary genres, the repressive politics of the time, augmented by the fear of riots at public gatherings and the fact that only two theatres in London had official licences, allowed little chance for new developments. What original dramatic energy there was went into verse dramas intended to be read rather than performed – Byron's *Manfred*, Coleridge's *Remorse*, Shelley's *Prometheus Unbound* and *The Cenci*. The novel, which was to become so brilliant at the end of this period, seems at first to find contemporary experience too problematic to approach directly: the most interesting work is done in the Gothic where dark and mysterious forces are sometimes probed with startling intuitive sense, but are mostly contained (and dulled) into clichéd threats and portents. Inverting the disposition of poetry, the Gothic novel tends to take a black view of human nature and the irrational, emphasising humans' ability to derive pleasure from the suffering of others. It is only with Jane Austen's *Sense and Sensibility* (1811) and Walter Scott's *Waverely* (1814), in both cases published after a long gestation, that a new technique for the novel is forged, and it is then discovered to be of a kind that will take over the world: clever at tracing history in the smallest inflection of manners, authoritative, ironic, founding itself in actual historical conditions, realistic, discriminating, moral. In many ways intentionally the apparent antithesis of romantic passion, the realist novel will in fact harness its energies to a more gradual and less inspiring vision of progress. As it appears, so the last torch carriers of a more demanding vision – Byron and Shelley – will emigrate and die.

WILLIAM BLAKE (1757–1827)

William Blake was raised in London in radical Protestant circles and earned his living as an engraver, illustrating many of his own works, the chief of which were *Songs of Innocence* (1789), *The Book of Thel* (1789), *The Marriage of Heaven and Hell* (1790–93), *Visions of the Daughters of Albion* (1793), *Songs of Innocence and of Experience* (1794) *The Book of Urizen* (1794), *The Four Zoas* (1797–1804), *Jerusalem* (1804–20) and *Milton* (1804–08). In his lifetime he knew little success as either poet or illustrator, but from the 1860s a critical following developed among the Pre-Raphaelites and he came to be seen as an artist of considerable significance in both domains. The original form of the *Songs*, for example, was as a book of hand-coloured etchings in which the words of each poem are woven with other symbols into a visual allegory of complex beauty. Such was the labour involved in producing these etchings that only 28 copies are known to exist. Blake welcomed the French Revolution as a cleansing apocalypse and evolved in his poetry an elaborate philosophical critique of Enlightenment rationalism and materialism. He saw a world dominated by narrow conceptualisations of reason and progress which he traced back to Newton and Locke and saw as supported by the Anglican church and British establishment (notably Dryden, Pope, Johnson, Reynolds, Burke). Against this tradition he counterposed a personal mythology in which the ability of the imagination to regain a unity lost in dialectical strife is seen as the central humanising faculty, and in which political rebellion against tyranny and restrictive moral codes is a constant necessity. His *Songs of Innocence and of Experience* propose and question the dialectical relationship between these two fundamental conditions, which cannot be situated along a progressive historical axis and which betoken further questions about morality, desire, restraint and repression.

From Songs of Innocence

The Ecchoing Green

      The sun does arise,
      And make happy the skies.
      The merry bells ring,
      To welcome the spring.
5   The skylark and thrush,
      The birds of the bush,
      Sing louder around,
      To the bell's cheerful sound,
      While our sports shall be seen
10   On the Ecchoing Green.

      Old John with white hair,
      Does laugh away care,
      Sitting under the oak,
      Among the old folk.
15   They laugh at our play,

And soon they all say,
Such, such were the joys,
When we all, girls and boys,
In our youth time were seen,
20 On the Ecchoing Green.

Till the little ones weary
No more can be merry
The sun does descend.
And our sports have an end:
25 Round the laps of their mothers
Many sisters and brothers,
Like birds in their nest,
Are ready for rest:
And sport no more seen,
30 On the darkening Green.

The Lamb

Little Lamb who made thee
Dost thou know who made thee
Gave thee life & bid thee feed,
By the stream & o'er the mead;
5 Gave thee clothing of delight,
Softest clothing wooly bright;
Gave thee such a tender voice,
Making all the vales rejoice:
Little Lamb who made thee
10 Dost thou know who made thee

Little Lamb I'll tell thee,
Little Lamb I'll tell thee;
He is called by thy name,
For he calls himself a Lamb:
15 He is meek & he is mild,
He became a little child:
I a child & thou a lamb,
We are called by his name.
Little Lamb God bless thee,
20 Little Lamb God bless thee.

The Chimney Sweeper

When my mother died I was very young,
And my father sold me while yet my tongue,
Could scarcely cry weep weep weep weep.
So your chimneys I sweep & in soot I sleep.

5 Theres little Tom Dacre, who cried when his head
 That curl'd like a lambs back, was shav'd, so I said
 Hush Tom never mind it, for when your head's bare,
 You know that the soot cannot spoil your white hair.

 And so he was quiet, & that very night,
10 As Tom was a sleeping he had such a sight
 That thousands of sweepers, Dick, Joe, Ned & Jack
 Were all of them lock'd up in coffins of black,

 And by came an Angel who had a bright key
 And he open'd the coffins & set them all free.
15 Then down a green plain leaping and laughing they run
 And wash in a river and shine in the Sun.

 Then naked & white, all their bags left behind,
 They rise upon clouds, and sport in the wind.
 And the Angel told Tom, if he'd be a good boy
20 He'd have God for his father & never want joy.

 And so Tom awoke and we rose in the dark
 And got with our bags & our brushes to work.
 Tho' the morning was cold, Tom was happy & warm
 So if all do their duty, they need not fear harm.

From Songs of Experience

The Clod and the Pebble

 Love seeketh not Itself to please,
 Nor for itself hath any care;
 But for another gives its ease,
 And builds a Heaven in Hells despair.

5 So sang a little Clod of Clay
 Trodden with the cattles feet;
 But a Pebble of the brook
 Warbled out these metres meet:

 Love seeketh only Self to please,
10 To bind another to Its delight;
 Joys in anothers loss of ease,
 And builds a Hell in Heavens despite.

Holy Thursday

Is this a holy thing to see,
In a rich and fruitful land,
Babes reducd to misery,
Fed with cold and usurous hand?

5   Is that trembling cry a song?
Can it be a song of joy?
And so many children poor?
It is a land of poverty!

And their sun does never shine.
10   And their fields are bleak & bare.
And their ways are fill'd with thorns
It is eternal winter there.

For where-e'er the sun does shine,
And where-e'er the rain does fall:
15   Babe can never hunger there,
Nor poverty the mind appall.

The Chimney Sweeper

A little black thing among the snow:
Crying weep, weep, in notes of woe!
Where are thy father & mother? say?
They are both gone up to the church to pray.

5   Because I was happy upon the heath,
And smil'd among the winters snow:
They clothed me in the clothes of death,
And taught me to sing the notes of woe.

And because I am happy, & dance & sing,
10   They think they have done me no injury:
And are gone to praise God & his Priest & King
Who make up a heaven for our misery.

The Sick Rose

O Rose thou art sick.
The invisible worm,
That flies in the night
In the howling storm:

5   Has found out thy bed
       Of crimson joy:
       And his dark secret love
       Does thy life destroy.

The Tyger

       Tyger Tyger, burning bright,
       In the forests of the night;
       What immortal hand or eye,
       Could frame thy fearful symmetry?

5   In what distant deeps or skies,
       Burnt the fire of thine eyes?
       On what wings dare he aspire?
       What the hand, dare sieze the fire?

       And what shoulder, & what art,
10   Could twist the sinews of thy heart?
       And when thy heart began to beat,
       What dread hand? & what dread feet?

       What the hammer? what the chain,
       In what furnace was thy brain?
15   What the anvil? what dread grasp,
       Dare its deadly terrors clasp?

       When the stars threw down their spears,
       And water'd heaven with their tears:
       Did he smile his work to see?
20   Did he who made the Lamb make thee?

       Tyger Tyger burning bright
       In the forests of the night:
       What immortal hand or eye,
       Dare frame thy fearful symmetry?

The Garden of Love

       I went to the Garden of Love.
       And saw what I never had seen:
       A Chapel was built in the midst,
       Where I used to play on the green.

5   And the gates of this Chapel were shut,
     And Thou shalt not, writ over the door;
     So I turn'd to the Garden of Love,
     That so many sweet flowers bore,

     And I saw it was filled with graves,
10   And tomb-stones where flowers should be:
     And Priests in black gowns, were walking their rounds,
     And binding with briars, my joys & desires.

London

     I wander thro' each charter'd street,
     Near where the charter'd Thames does flow
     And mark in every face I meet
     Marks of weakness, marks of woe.

5   In every cry of every Man,
     In every Infants cry of fear.
     In every voice; in every ban,
     The mind-forg'd manacles I hear

     How the Chimney-sweepers cry
10   Every blackning Church appalls
     And the hapless Soldiers sigh
     Runs in blood down Palace walls

     But most thro' midnight streets I hear
     How the youthful Harlots curse
15   Blasts the new-born Infants tear
     And blights with plagues the Marriage hearse.

Infant Sorrow

     My mother groand! my father wept.
     Into the dangerous world I leapt:
     Helpless, naked, piping loud:
     Like a fiend hid in a cloud.

5   Struggling in my fathers hands:
     Striving against my swadling bands;
     Bound and weary I thought best
     To sulk upon my mothers breast.

A Poison Tree

I was angry with my friend:
I told my wrath, my wrath did end.
I was angry with my foe:
I told it not, my wrath did grow.

5   And I waterd it in fears,
Night & morning with my tears:
And I sunned it with smiles,
And with soft deceitful wiles.

And it grew both day and night,
10   Till it bore an apple bright.
And my foe beheld it shine,
And he knew that it was mine.

And into my garden stole,
When the night had veild the pole;
15   In the morning glad I see,
My foe outstretchd beneath the tree.

MARY WOLLSTONECRAFT (1759–1797)

Mary Wollstonecraft's father was a wealthy, wife-beating drunk who wasted a large inheritance. She suffered the fate of many educated and penniless women, being employed as a lady's companion and governess. She set up a school in Newington Green in 1783 and made friends in London radical and dissenting circles. Joseph Johnson, a famous radical bookseller, published her *Thoughts on the Education of Daughters* in 1783 and she thereafter published with him *Mary, a Fiction* (1788), *Original Stories from Real Life* (1788 – a subsequent edition was illustrated by Willliam Blake), and *The Female Reader* (1789). She taught herself French and German, moved in radical intellectual circles with Godwin, Price and Paine, and worked for Johnson as reader and translator. In 1790 she responded to the conservative Emund Burke's *Reflections on a Revolution in France* with *A Vindication of the Rights of Men* and followed this in 1792 with *A Vindication of the Rights of Woman*. At the end of 1792 she went to observe the revolution in Paris and lived there through the Terror with an American, William Imlay, with whom she had a daughter, Fanny. She then returned to London, eventually living with William Godwin, the most prominent radical of those times and author of *Inquiry Concerning Political Justice* (1793). In 1797 she died giving birth to their daughter Mary, who was to become the author of *Frankenstein*. Wollstonecraft's *Vindication* is remarkable for its utter lucidity of thought about long-obfuscated and deeply invested issues, and for its clear sense of how social conditions give rise to the gendering and classing of human mentalities. It is a triumph of Reason, a faculty women were then generally considered not to possess.

From A Vindication of the Rights of Woman[1]

In the middle rank of life ... men, in their youth, are prepared for professions, and marriage is not considered as the grand feature in their lives; whilst women, have no other scheme to sharpen their faculties. It is not business, extensive plans, or any of the excursive flights of ambition, that engross their attention; no, their thoughts are not employed in rearing such noble structures. To rise in the world, and have the liberty of running from pleasure to pleasure, they must marry advantageously, and to this object their time is sacrificed, and their persons often legally prostituted. A man when he enters any profession has his eye steadily fixed on some future advantage (and the mind gains great strength by having all its efforts directed to one point), and, full of his business, pleasure is considered as mere relaxation; whilst women seek for pleasure as the main purpose of existence. In fact, from the education which they receive from society, the love of pleasure may be said to govern them all; but does this prove that there is a sex in souls? It would seem just as rational to declare that the courtiers in France, when a destructive system of despotism had formed their characters, were not men, because liberty, virtue and humanity, were sacrificed to pleasure and vanity. – Fatal passions, which have ever domineered over the whole race!

The same love of pleasure, fostered by the whole tendency of their education, gives a trifling turn to the conduct of women in most circumstances: for instance, they are ever anxious about secondary things; and on the watch for adventures, instead of being occupied by duties.

A man, when he undertakes a journey, has, in general, the end in view, a woman thinks more of the incidental occurrences, the strange things that may possibly occur on the road; the impression that she may make on her fellow travellers; and, above all, she is anxiously intent on the care of the finery that she carries with her, which is more than ever a part of herself, when going to figure on a new scene; when, to use an apt French turn of expression, she is going to produce a sensation. – Can dignity of mind exist with such trivial cares?

In short, women, in general, as well as the rich of both sexes, have acquired all the follies and vices of civilisation, and missed the useful fruit. It is not necessary for me always to premise, that I speak of the condition of the whole sex, leaving exceptions out of the question. Their senses are inflamed, and their understandings neglected, consequently they become the prey of their senses, delicately termed sensibility, and are blown about by every momentary gust of feeling. Civilised women are, therefore, so weakened by false refinement, that, respecting morals, their condition is much below what it would be were they left in a state nearer to nature. Ever restless and anxious, their over exercised sensibility not only renders them uncomfortable themselves, but troublesome, to use a soft phrase, to others. All their thoughts turn on things calculated to excite emotion; and feeling, when they should reason, their conduct is unstable, and their opinions wavering – not the wavering produced by a deliberation or progressive views, but by contradictory emotions. By fits and starts

---

1: From Chapter 4, 'Observations on the State of Degradation to which Woman is reduced by Various Causes'.

they are warm in many pursuits; yet this warmth, never concentrated into perseverance, soon exhausts itself; exhaled by its own heat, or meeting with some other fleeting passion, to which reason has never given any specific gravity, neutrality ensues. Miserable, indeed, must be that being whose cultivation of mind has only tended to inflame its passions! A distinction should be made between inflaming and strengthening them. The passions thus pampered, whilst judgement is left unformed, what can be expected to ensue? – Undoubtedly, a mixture of madness and folly!

This observation should not be confined to the fair sex; however, at present, I only mean to apply it to them.

Novels, music, poetry, and gallantry, all tend to make women the creatures of sensation, and their character is thus formed in the mould of folly during the time they are acquiring accomplishments, the only improvement they are expected, by their station in society, to acquire. This overstretched sensibility naturally relaxes the other powers of the mind, and prevents intellect from attaining that sovereignty which it ought to attain to render a rational creature useful to others, and content with its own station: for the exercise of the understanding, as life advances, is the only method pointed out by nature to calm the passions.

Satiety has a very different effect, and I have often been forcibly struck by an emphatical description of damnation: – when the spirit is represented as continually hovering with abortive eagerness round the defiled body, unable to enjoy any thing without the organs of sense. Yet, to their senses, are women made slaves, because it is by their sensibility that they obtain present power.

And will moralists pretend to assert, that this is the condition in which one half of the human race should be encouraged to remain with listless inactivity and stupid acquiescence? Kind instructors! What were we created for? To a remain, it may be said, innocent; they mean in a state of childhood. – We might as well never have been born, unless it were necessary that we should be created to enable man to acquire the noble privilege of reason, the power of discerning good from evil, whilst we lie down in the dust from whence we were taken, never to rise again. –

It would be an endless task to trace the variety of meannesses, cares, and sorrows, into which women are plunged by the prevailing opinion, that they were created rather to feel than to reason, and that all the power they obtain, must be obtained by their charms and weakness:

Fine by defect, and amiably weak![1]

And, made by this amiable weakness entirely dependent, excepting what they gain by illicit sway, on man, not only for protection, but advice, is it surprising that, neglecting the duties that reason alone points out, and shrinking from trials calculated to strengthen their minds, they only exert themselves to give their defects a graceful covering, which may serve to heighten their charms in the eye of the voluptuary, though it sink them below the scale of moral excellence?

1: cf. Alexander Pope: 'Fine by defect and delicately weak'. *Moral Essays* II: 'Epistle to a Lady,' l. 44.

ANN RADCLIFFE (1764–1823)

Ann Radcliffe was raised in Bath and London, her father a shopkeeper. In 1787 she married a prominent London journalist, William Radcliffe. She published her first novel, a romance entitled *The Castles of Athlin and Dunbayne*, in 1789; then followed *The Sicilian Romance* (1790), *The Romance of the Forest* (1791), *The Mysteries of Udolpho* (1794) and *The Italian* (1797), the last three novels taking their measure from Horace Walpole's pioneering Gothic novel, *The Castle of Otranto: a Gothic Story* (1764). These works sold in large numbers, earned unprecedented advances and became widely influential, their typical motifs, techniques and scenes being adopted by other Gothic writers such as Matthew Lewis, Charles Maturin and William Beckford and also influencing the Romantic poets and many later novelists. Radcliffe synthesised the late-eighteenth-century interest in death, graveyards, melancholy sensibility and the picturesque landscape into a narrative which could sustain dramatic tension and readers' interest. Her agents were stock characters (the damsel in distress, the lover, the villain, the wicked sibling/parent, the misunderstood) and the drama relied upon having her women imprisoned in foreign castles, convents or monasteries by tyrannical parents and binding them in often implausible inheritance plots. The location of at least part of each story in Catholic Italy invoked nationalist and Protestant suspicions of the European 'other'. The various components, rather like the monster in *Frankenstein,* never quite lose their lines of suture, but the works are able to tap into the rich preconscious reservoir of modern fear and desire. The following is a typical scene (from Volume 1, chapter 8) in which the heroine, Ellena, has been kidnapped by mysterious men, then imprisoned in a convent on the orders of her lover's mother who opposes the match, an experience which in those days was not entirely imaginary.

From The Italian

On the following evening Ellena was again permitted to attend vespers, and, on the way to the chapel, the hope of seeing her interesting favourite reanimated her spirits. In the same part of the gallery, as on the preceding night, she again appeared, and kneeling, as before, beneath the lamp, in private orison, for the service was not begun.

Ellena endeavoured to subdue the impatience she felt to express her regard, and to be noticed by the holy sister, till she should have finished. When the nun rose, and observed Ellena, she lifted her veil, and, fixing her with the same enquiring eye, her countenance brightened into a smile so full of compassion and intelligence, that Ellena, forgetting the decorums of the place, left her seat to approach her; it seemed as if the soul, which beamed forth in that smile, had been long acquainted with hers. As she advanced, the nun dropped her veil, a reproof she immediately understood, and she withdrew to her seat; but her attention remained fixed on the nun during the whole service.

At the conclusion, when they left the chapel, and she saw Olivia pass without noticing her, Ellena could scarcely restrain her tears; she returned in deep dejection to her room. The regard of this nun was not only delightful, but seemed necessary to her heart, and she dwelt, with fond perseverance, on the smile that had expressed so much, and which threw one gleam of comfort, even through the bars of her prison.

Her reverie was soon interrupted by a light step, that approached her cell, and in the next moment the door was unlocked, and Olivia herself appeared. Ellena rose with emotion to meet her; the nun held forth her hand to receive hers.

'You are unused to confinement,' said she, curtsying mournfully, and placing on the table a little basket containing refreshment, 'and our hard fare' –

'I understand you,' said Ellena, with a look expressive of her gratitude; 'you have a heart that can pity, though you inhabit these walls; – you have suffered too, and know the delicate generosity of softening the sorrows of others, by any attention that may tell them your sympathy. Oh! if I could express how much the sense of this affects me!'

Tears interrupted her. Olivia pressed her hand, looked steadily upon her face, and was somewhat agitated, but she soon recovered apparent tranquillity, and said, with a serious smile, 'You judge rightly, my sister, respecting my sentiments, however you may do concerning my sufferings. My heart is not insensible to pity, nor to you, my child. You were designed for happier days than you can hope to find within these cloisters!'

She checked herself as if she had allowed too much, and then added, 'But you may, perhaps, be peaceful; and since it consoles you to know that you have a friend near you, believe me that friend – but believe it in silence. I will visit you when I am permitted – but do not enquire for me; and if my visits are short, do not press me to lengthen them.'

'How good this is!' said Ellena, in a faltering voice. 'How sweet too it is! you will visit me, and I am pitied by you!'

'Hush!' said the nun, expressively; 'no more; I may be observed. Good night, my sister; may your slumbers be light!'

Ellena's heart sunk. She had not spirits to say 'Good night!' but her eyes, covered with tears, said more. The nun turned her own away suddenly, and, pressing her hand in silence, left the cell. Ellena, firm and tranquil under the insults of the abbess, was now melted into tears by the kindness of a friend. These gentle tears were refreshing to her long-oppressed spirits, and she indulged them. Of Vivaldi[1] she thought with more composure than she had done since she left the villa Altieri; and something like hope began to revive in her heart, though reflection offered nothing to support it.

On the following morning, she perceived that the door of the cell had not been closed. She rose impatiently, and, not without a hope of liberty, immediately passed it. The cell, opening upon a short passage, which communicated with the main building, and which was shut up by a door, was secluded, and almost insulated from every other chamber; and this door being now secured, Ellena was as truly a prisoner as before. It appeared then, that the nun had omitted to fasten the cell only for the purpose of allowing her more space to walk in the passage, and she was grateful for the attention. Still more

---

1: Her lover.

she was so, when, having traversed it, she perceived one extremity terminate in a narrow stair-case, that appeared to lead to other chambers.

She ascended the winding steps hastily, and found they led only to a door, opening into a small room, where nothing remarkable appeared, till she approached the windows, and beheld thence an horizon, and a landscape spread below, whose grandeur awakened all her heart. The consciousness of her prison was lost, while her eyes ranged over the wide and freely-sublime scene without. She perceived that this chamber was within a small turret, projecting from an angle of the convent over the walls, and suspended, as in air, above the vast precipices of granite, that formed part of the mountain. These precipices were broken into cliffs, which, in some places, impended far above their base, and, in others, rose, in nearly perpendicular lines, to the walls of the monastery, which they supported. Ellena, with a dreadful pleasure, looked down them, shagged as they were with larch, and frequently darkened by lines of gigantic pine bending along the rocky ledges, till her eye rested on the thick chestnut woods that extended over their winding base, and which, softening to the plains, seemed to form a gradation between the variegated cultivation there, and the awful wildness of the rocks above. Round these extensive plains were tumbled the mountains, of various shape and attitude, which Ellena had admired on her approach to San Stefano; some shaded with forests of olive and almond trees, but the greater part abandoned to the flocks, which, in summer, feed on their aromatic herbage, and on the approach of winter, descend to the sheltered plains of the *Tavogliere di Puglia*.[1]

On the left opened the dreadful pass which she had traversed, and the thunder of whose waters now murmured at a distance. The accumulation of overtopping points, which the mountains of this dark perspective exhibited, presented an image of grandeur superior to any thing she had seen while within the pass itself.

To Ellena, whose mind was capable of being highly elevated, or sweetly soothed, by scenes of nature, the discovery of this little turret was an important circumstance. Hither she could come, and her soul, refreshed by the views it afforded, would acquire strength to bear her, with equanimity, through the persecutions that might await her. Here, gazing upon the stupendous imagery around her, looking, as it were, beyond the awful veil which obscures the features of the Deity, and conceals Him from the eyes of His creatures, dwelling as with a present God in the midst of his sublime works; with a mind thus elevated, how insignificant would appear to her the transactions, and the sufferings of this world! How poor the boasted power of man, when the fall of a single cliff from these mountains would with ease destroy thousands of his race assembled on the plains below! How would it avail them, that they were accoutred for battle, armed with all the instruments of destruction that human invention ever fashioned? Thus man, the giant who now held her in captivity, would shrink to the diminutiveness of a fairy; and she would experience, that his utmost force was unable to enchain her soul, or compel her to fear him, while he was destitute of virtue.

1: The Apulian tableland in the heel of Italy, then renowned for its backwardness.

Ellena's attention was recalled from the scene without by a sound from within the gallery, and she then heard a key turning in the door of the passage. Fearing that it was sister Margaritone who approached, and who, informed by her absence of the consolatory turret she had discovered, would perhaps debar her from ever returning to it, Ellena descended with a palpitating heart, and found that nun in the cell. Surprise and severity were in her countenance, when she enquired by what means Ellena had unclosed the door, and whither she had been.

WILLIAM WORDSWORTH (1770–1850)

Wordsworth was born at Cockermouth, Cumbria, on the edge of the Lake District. His mother died when he was 8, his father, an attorney and land agent, died when he was 13. He studied at Cambridge, then walked through France, Italy and the Alps before residing in Paris where he was inspired by the Revolution and conceived a child with his lover, Annette Vallon. At the end of 1792 he returned to England and was then prevented from return by the outbreak of war. In 1795 he met Coleridge and began a friendship of great importance. In 1796 he settled with his sister Dorothy in Somerset, near to the Coleridges, and together the poets worked on what was to become *Lyrical Ballads, with a few Other Poems* (1798, reissued with a preface 1801, 1802), the landmark work in English romanticism. In 1798–99 he studied in Germany, partly with Coleridge, then returned to live at Grasmere in the Lake District. He married Mary Hutchinson in 1802 and with her had five children. In middle age he became a conservative establishment figure and in 1813 was appointed Stamp Distributor for Westmoreland, patronage by sinecure. His major publications were *Poems in Two Volumes* (1807), *The Excursion* (1814), *Miscellaneous Poems* (1815), and *The Prelude* (written as two volumes in 1799, extensively revised in 1805, then revised intermittently until his death and published posthumously in 1850). From 1807 his poetic achievement declined. The radical new poetic announced in *Lyrical Ballads* returned poetry to ordinary speech and to the sensations of ordinary country people, making the consciousness of the individual into a sufficient subject in itself and defenestrating the tradition of inherently 'poetic' subjects and pregiven dictions, genres and forms. The 'egotism' which interested Wordsworth was an acute meditation on our alienation from nature and our former innocent and enthusiastic selves, a meditation which often succeeded in a quasi-religious reintegration of the soul with the natural being from which society and history necessarily estranges.

From The Preface to Lyrical Ballads

The principal object ... which I proposed to myself in these pages was to choose incidents and situations from common life, and to relate or describe them, throughout, as far as was possible, in a selection of language really used by men; and, at the same time, to throw over them a certain colouring of imagination, whereby ordinary things should be presented to the mind in an unusual way;

and, further, and above all, to make these incidents and situations interesting by tracing in them, truly though not ostentatiously, the primary laws of our nature: chiefly, as far as regards the manner in which we associate ideas in a state of excitement. Low and rustic life was generally chosen, because in that condition, the essential passions of the heart find a better soil in which they can attain their maturity, are less under restraint, and speak a plainer and more emphatic language; because in that condition of life our elementary feelings coexist in a state of greater simplicity, and, consequently, may be more accurately contemplated, and more forcibly communicated; because the manners of rural life germinate from those elementary feelings; and, are more durable; and lastly, because in that condition the passions of men are incorporated with the beautiful and permanent forms of nature. The language, too, of these men is adopted (and purified indeed from what appear to be its real defects, from all lasting and rational causes of dislike or disgust) because such men hourly communicate with the best objects from which the best part of language is originally derived; and because, from their rank in society and the sameness and narrow circle of their intercourse, being less under the influence of social vanity they convey their feelings and notions in simple and unelaborate expressions. Accordingly, such a language, arising out of repeated experience and regular feelings, is a more permanent and a far more philosophical language, than that which is frequently substituted for it by poets, who think that they are conferring honour upon themselves and their art, in proportion as they separate themselves from the sympathies of men, and indulge in arbitrary and capricious habits of expression, in order to furnish food for fickle tastes, and fickle appetites, of their own creation.

I cannot, however, be insensible of the present outcry against the triviality and meanness both of thought and language, which some of my contemporaries have occasionally introduced into their metrical compositions; and I acknowledge that this defect, where it exists, is more dishonourable to the writer's own character than false refinement or arbitrary innovation, though I should contend at the same time that it is far less pernicious in the sum of its consequences. From such verses the poems in these volumes will be found distinguished at least by one mark of difference, that each of them has a worthy *purpose*. Not that I mean to say, that I always began to write with a distinct purpose formally conceived; but I believe that my habits of meditation have so formed my feelings, as that my descriptions of such objects as strongly excite those feelings, will be found to carry along with them a *purpose*. If in this opinion I am mistaken, I can have little right to the name of a poet. For all good poetry is the spontaneous overflow of powerful feelings; but though this be true, poems to which any value can be attached, were never produced on any variety of subjects but by a man who, being possessed of more than usual organic sensibility, had also thought long and deeply. For our continued influxes of feeling are modified and directed by our thoughts, which are indeed the representatives of all our past feelings, and as by contemplating the relation of these general representatives to each other we discover what is really important to men, so, by the repetition and continuance of this act, our feelings will be connected with important subjects, till at length, if we be originally possessed of much sensibility, such habits of mind will be produced, that, by obeying blindly and mechanically the impulses of those habits, we shall describe objects, and utter sentiments, of such a nature and in such connection with each other, that the understanding of the being to whom we address ourselves, if he be in a healthful state of association, must necessarily be in some degree enlightened, his taste exalted, and his affections ameliorated.

Having dwelt thus long on the subjects and aims of these poems, I shall request the reader's permission to apprise him of a few circumstances related to their *style*, in order, among other reasons, that I may not be censured for not having performed what I never attempted. The reader will find that personifications of abstract ideas rarely occur in these volumes, and are utterly rejected as an ordinary device to elevate the style, and raise it above prose. I have proposed to myself to imitate, and as far as possible to adopt, the very language of men, and assuredly such personifcations do not make any natural or regular part of that language. They are, indeed, a figure of speech occasionally prompted by passion, and I have made use of them as such; but I have endeavoured utterly to reject them as a mechanical device of style, or as a family language which writers in metre seem to lay claim to by prescription. I have wished to keep my reader in the company of flesh and blood, persuaded that by so doing I shall interest him. I am, however, well aware, that others who pursue a different track may interest him likewise; I do not interfere with their claim, I only wish to prefer a different claim of my own. There will also be found in these volumes little of what is usually called poetic diction; I have taken as much pains to avoid it as others ordinarily take to produce it; this I have done for the reason already alleged, to bring my language near to the language of men, and further, because the pleasure which I have proposed to myself to impart is of a kind very different from that which is supposed by many persons to be the proper object of poetry. I do not know how, without being culpably particular, I can give my reader a more exact notion of the style in which I wished these poems to be written than by informing him that I have at all times endeavoured to look steadily at my subject, consequently, I hope that there is in these poems little falsehood of description, and that my ideas are expressed in language fitted to their respective importance. Something I must have gained by this practice, as is friendly to one property of all good poetry, namely good sense; but it has necessarily cut me off from a large portion of phrases and figures of speech which from father to son have long been regarded as the common inheritance of poets. I have also thought it expedient to restrict myself still further, having abstained from the use of many expressions, in themselves proper and beautiful, but which have been foolishly repeated by bad poets, till such feelings of disgust are connected with them as it is scarcely possible by any art of association to overpower.

If in a poem there should be found a series of lines, or even a single line, in which the language, though naturally arranged and according to the strict laws of metre, does not differ from that of prose, there is a numerous class of critics, who, when they stumble upon these prosaisms as they call them, imagine that they have made a notable discovery, and exult over the poet as over a man ignorant of his own profession. Now these men would establish a canon of criticism which the reader will conclude he must utterly reject if he wishes to be pleased with these volumes. And it would be a most easy task to prove to him, that not only the language of a large portion of every good poem, even of the most elevated character, must necessarily, except with reference to the metre, in no respect differ from that of good prose, but likewise that some of the most interesting parts of the best poems will be bound to be strictly the language of prose, when the prose is well written.

[The Mind of the Poet]

[The poet] considers man and nature as essentially adapted to each other, and the mind of man as naturally the mirror of the fairest and most interesting qualities of nature. And thus the poet, prompted by this feeling of pleasure which accompanies him through the whole course of his studies, converses with general nature with affections akin to those, which, through labour and length of time, the man of science has raised up in himself, by conversing with those particular parts of nature which are the objects of his studies. The knowledge both of the poet and the man of science is a pleasure; but the knowledge of the one cleaves to us as a necessary part of our existence, our natural and inalienable inheritance; the other is a personal and individual acquisition, slow to come to us, and by no habitual and direct sympathy connecting us with our fellow beings. The man of science seeks truth as a remote and unknown benefactor; he cherishes and loves it in his solitude: the poet, singing a song in which all human beings join him, rejoices in the presence of truth as our visible friend and hourly companion. Poetry is the breath and finer spirit of all knowledge; it is the impassioned expression which is in the countenance of all science. Emphatically may it be said of the poet, as Shakespeare hath said of man, 'that he looks before and after.' He is the rock of defence of human nature; an upholder and preserver, carrying everywhere with him relationship and love. In spite of difference of soil and climate, of language and manners, of laws and customs, in spite of things silently gone out of mind and things violently destroyed, the poet binds together by passion and knowledge the vast empire of human society, as it is spread over the whole earth, and over all time. The objects of the poet's thoughts are everywhere; though the eyes and sense of man are, it is true, his favourite guides, yet he will follow wheresoever he can find an atmosphere of sensation in which to move his wings. Poetry is the first and last of all knowledge – it is as immortal as the heart of man. If the labours of men of science should ever create any material revolution, direct or indirect, in our condition, and in the impressions which we habitually receive, the poet will sleep then no more than at present, but he will be ready to follow the steps of the man of science, not only in those general indirect effects, but he will be at this side, carrying sensation into the mist of the objects of the science itself. The remotest discoveries of the chemist, the botanist, the mineralogist, will be as proper objects of the poet's art as any upon which it can be employed, if the relations under which they are contemplated by the followers of these respective sciences shall be manifestly and palpably material to us as enjoying and suffering beings. If the time should ever come when what is now called science, thus familiarised to men, shall be ready to put on, as it were, a form of flesh and blood, the poet will lend his divine spirit to aid the transfiguration, and will welcome the being thus produced, as a dear and genuine inmate of the household of man.

Lines Composed a Few Miles above Tintern Abbey, on Revisiting the Banks of the Wye during a Tour, July 13, 1798

Five years have past; five summers, with the length
Of five long winters! and again I hear
These waters, rolling from their mountain-springs
With a sweet inland murmur. – Once again
5   Do I behold these steep and lofty cliffs,
Which on a wild secluded scene impress
Thoughts of more deep seclusion; and connect
The landscape with the quiet of the sky.
The day is come when I again repose
10   Here, under this dark sycamore, and view
These plots of cottage-ground, these orchard-tufts,
Which, at this season, with their unripe fruits,
Are clad in one green hue, and lose themselves,
'Mid groves and copses. Once again I see
15   These hedge-rows, hardly hedge-rows, little lines
Of sportive wood run wild; these pastoral farms
Green to the very door; and wreaths of smoke
Sent up, in silence, from among the trees,
With some uncertain notice, as might seem,
20   Of vagrant dwellers in the houseless woods,
Or of some hermit's cave, where by his fire
The hermit sits alone.

              These beauteous forms,
Through a long absence, have not been to me,
As is a landscape to a blind man's eye:
25   But oft, in lonely rooms, and 'mid the din
Of towns and cities, I have owed to them
In hours of weariness, sensations sweet,
Felt in the blood, and felt along the heart,
And passing even into my purer mind
30   With tranquil restoration: – feelings too
Of unremembered pleasure; such, perhaps,
As may have had no slight or trivial influence

On that best portion of a good man's life;
His little, nameless, unremembered acts
35 Of kindness and of love. Nor less, I trust,
To them I may have owed another gift,
Of aspect more sublime; that blessed mood,
In which the burthen of the mystery,
In which the heavy and the weary weight
40 Of all this unintelligible world,
Is lightened: – that serene and blessed mood,
In which the affections gently lead us on, –
Until, the breath of this corporeal frame
And even the motion of our human blood
45 Almost suspended, we are laid asleep
In body, and become a living soul:
While with an eye made quiet by the power
Of harmony, and the deep power of joy,
We see into the life of things.

                                 If this
50 Be but a vain belief, yet, oh! how oft –
In darkness, and amid the many shapes
Of joyless daylight; when the fretful stir
Unprofitable, and the fever of the world,
Have hung upon the beatings of my heart –
55 How oft, in spirit, have I turned to thee
O sylvan Wye! Thou wanderer through the woods,
How often has my spirit turned to thee!

And now, with gleams of half-extinguished thought,
With many recognitions dim and faint,
60 And somewhat of a sad perplexity,
The picture of the mind revives again:
While here I stand, not only with the sense
Of present pleasure, but with pleasing thoughts
That in this moment there is life and food
65 For future years. And so I dare to hope
Though changed, no doubt, from what I was, when first
I came among these hills; when like a roe
I bounded o'er the mountains, by the sides
Of the deep rivers, and the lonely streams,
70 Wherever nature led; more like a man
Flying from something that he dreads, than one
Who sought the thing he loved. For nature then
(The coarser pleasures of my boyish days,
And their glad animal movements all gone by)
75 To me was all in all. – I cannot paint

What then I was. The sounding cataract
Haunted me like a passion: the tall rock,
The mountain, and the deep and gloomy wood,
Their colours and their forms, were then to me
80   An appetite: a feeling and a love,
That had no need of a remoter charm,
By thought supplied, nor any interest
Unborrowed from the eye. – That time is past,
And all its aching joys are now no more,
85   And all its dizzy raptures. Not for this
Faint I, nor mourn nor murmur; other gifts
Have followed, for such loss, I would believe,
Abundant recompense. For I have learned
To look on nature, not as in the hour
90   Of thoughtless youth, but hearing oftentimes
The still, sad music of humanity,
Nor harsh nor grating, though of ample power
To chasten and subdue. And I have felt
A presence that disturbs me with the joy
95   Of elevated thoughts; a sense sublime
Of something far more deeply interfused,
Whose dwelling is the light of setting suns,
And the round ocean, and the living air,
And the blue sky, and in the mind of man,
100   A motion and a spirit, that impels
All thinking things, all objects of all thought,
And rolls through all things. Therefore am I still
A lover of the meadows and the woods,
And mountains; and of all that we behold
105   From this green earth; of all the mighty world
Of eye and ear, both what they half create,
And what perceive; well pleased to recognise
In nature and the language of the sense,
'The anchor of my purest thoughts, the nurse,
110   The guide, the guardian of my heart, and soul
Of all my moral being.

                 Nor, perchance,
If I were not thus taught, should I the more
Suffer my genial spirits to decay:
For thou art with me, here, upon the banks
115   Of this fair river; thou, my dearest Friend,
My dear, dear Friend, and in thy voice I catch
The language of my former heart, and read
My former pleasures in the shooting lights
Of thy wild eyes. Oh! yet a little while

120   May I behold in thee what I was once,
My dear, dear Sister! And this prayer I make,
Knowing that Nature never did betray
The heart that loved her; 'tis her privilege,
Through all the years of this our life, to lead
125   From joy to joy: for she can so inform
The mind that is within us, so impress
With quietness and beauty, and so feed
With lofty thoughts, that neither evil tongues,
Rash judgments, nor the sneers of selfish men,
130   Nor greetings where no kindness is, nor all
The dreary intercourse of daily life,
Shall e'er prevail against us, or disturb
Our cheerful faith that all which we behold
Is full of blessings. Therefore let the moon
135   Shine on thee in thy solitary walk;
And let the misty mountain winds be free
To blow against thee: and in after years,
When these wild ecstasies shall be matured
Into a sober pleasure, when thy mind
140   Shall be a mansion for all lovely forms,
Thy memory be as a dwelling-place
For all sweet sounds and harmonies; oh! then,
If solitude, or fear, or pain, or grief,
Should be thy portion, with what healing thoughts
145   Of tender joy wilt thou remember me,
And these my exhortations! Nor, perchance –
If I should be, where I no more can hear
Thy voice, nor catch from thy wild eyes these gleams
Of past existence – wilt thou then forget
150   That on the banks of this delightful stream
We stood together; and that I, so long
A worshipper of Nature, hither came,
Unwearied in that service: rather say
With warmer love, – oh! with far deeper zeal
155   Of holier love. Nor wilt thou then forget,
That after many wanderings, many years
Of absence, these steep woods and lofty cliffs,
And this green pastoral landscape, were to me
More dear, both for themselves, and for thy sake!

Strange fits of passion have I known

Strange fits of passion have I known,
And I will dare to tell,
But in the Lover's ear alone,
What once to me befel.

5   When she I loved looked every day
Fresh as a rose in June,
I to her cottage bent my way,
Beneath an evening moon.

Upon the moon I fixed my eye,
10   All over the wide lea;
With quickening pace my horse drew nigh
Those paths so dear to me.

And now we reached the orchard plot,
And, as we climbed the hill,
15   The sinking moon to Lucy's cot
Came near, and nearer still.

In one of those kind dreams I slept,
Kind Nature's gentlest boon!
And all the while my eyes I kept
20   On the descending moon.

My horse moved on, hoof after hoof
He raised and never stopped:
When down behind the cottage roof
At once the bright moon dropped.

25   What fond and wayward thoughts will slide
Into a Lover's head –
'Oh mercy!' to myself I cried,
'If Lucy should be dead!'

Composed Upon Westminster Bridge, September 3, 1802

Earth has not any thing to show more fair:
Dull would he be of soul who could pass by
A sight so touching in its majesty:
This City now doth like a garment wear
5   The beauty of the morning; silent, bare,
Ships, towers, domes, theatres, and temples lie

Open unto the fields, and to the sky,
All bright and glittering in the smokeless air.
Never did sun more beautifully steep
10   In his first splendour, valley, rock, or hill;
Ne'er saw I, never felt, a calm so deep!
The river glideth at his own sweet will:
Dear God! the very houses seem asleep;
And all that mighty heart is lying still!

From The Prelude

From Book I. Introduction, Childhood and School-Time

Fair seed-time had my soul, and I grew up
Fostered alike by beauty and by fear:
Much favoured in my birthplace, and no less
In that beloved Vale to which erelong
305   We were transplanted – there were we let loose
For sports of wider range. Ere I had told
Ten birth-days, when among the mountain-slopes
Frost, and the breath of frosty wind, had snapped
The last autumnal crocus, 'twas my joy
310   With store of springes o'er my shoulder hung
To range the open heights where woodcocks run
Among the smooth green turf. Through half the night,
Scudding away from snare to snare, I plied
That anxious visitation; – moon and stars
315   Were shining o'er my head. I was alone,
And seemed to be a trouble to the peace
That dwelt among them. Sometimes it befell
In these night wanderings, that a strong desire
O'erpowered my better reason, and the bird
320   Which was the captive of another's toil
Became my prey; and when the deed was done
I heard among the solitary hills
Low breathings coming after me, and sounds
Of undistinguishable motion, steps
325   Almost as silent as the turf they trod.

Nor less when spring had warmed the cultured Vale,
Moved we as plunderers where the mother-bird
Had in high places built her lodge; though mean
Our object and inglorious, yet the end
330   Was not ignoble. Oh! when I have hung
Above the raven's nest, by knots of grass

---

310 **springes**: snares.

And half-inch fissures in the slippery rock
But ill sustained, and almost (so it seemed)
Suspended by the blast that blew amain,
335 Shouldering the naked crag, oh, at that time
While on the perilous ridge I hung alone,
With what strange utterance did the loud dry wind
Blow through my ear! the sky seemed not a sky
Of earth – and with what motion moved the clouds!

340   Dust as we are, the immortal spirit grows
Like harmony in music; there is a dark
Inscrutable workmanship that reconciles
Discordant elements, makes them cling together
In one society. How strange that all
345 The terrors, pains, and early miseries,
Regrets, vexations, lassitudes interfused
Within my mind, should e'er have borne a part,
And that a needful part, in making up
The calm existence that is mine when I
350 Am worthy of myself! Praise to the end!
Thanks to the means which Nature deigned to employ;
Whether her fearless visitings, or those
That came with soft alarm, like hurtless light
Opening the peaceful clouds; or she may use
355 Severer interventions, ministry
More palpable, as best might suit her aim.

One summer evening (led by her) I found
A little boat tied to a willow tree
Within a rocky cave, its usual home.
360 Straight I unloosed her chain, and stepping in
Pushed from the shore. It was an act of stealth
And troubled pleasure, nor without the voice
Of mountain-echoes did my boat move on;
Leaving behind her still, on either side,
365 Small circles glittering idly in the moon,
Until they melted all into one track
Of sparkling light. But now, like one who rows,
Proud of his skill, to reach a chosen point
With an unswerving line, I fixed my view
370 Upon the summit of a craggy ridge,
The horizon's utmost boundary; far above
Was nothing but the stars and the grey sky.
She was an elfin pinnace; lustily
I dipped my oars into the silent lake,
375 And, as I rose upon the stroke, my boat
Went heaving through the water like a swan;

When, from behind that craggy steep till then
The horizon's bound, a huge peak, black and huge,
As if with voluntary power instinct
380 Upreared its head. I struck and struck again,
And growing still in stature the grim shape
Towered up between me and the stars, and still,
For so it seemed, with purpose of its own
And measured motion like a living thing,
385 Strode after me. With trembling oars I turned,
And through the silent water stole my way
Back to the covert of the willow tree;
There in her mooring-place I left my bark, –
And through the meadows homeward went, in grave
390 And serious mood; but after I had seen
That spectacle, for many days, my brain
Worked with a dim and undetermined sense
Of unknown modes of being; o'er my thoughts
There hung a darkness, call it solitude
395 Or blank desertion. No familiar shapes
Remained, no pleasant images of trees,
Of sea or sky, no colours of green fields;
But huge and mighty forms, that do not live
Like living men, moved slowly through the mind
400 By day, and were a trouble to my dreams.

Wisdom and Spirit of the universe!
Thou Soul that art the eternity of thought
That givest to forms and images a breath
And everlasting motion, not in vain
405 By day or star-light thus from my first dawn
Of childhood didst thou intertwine for me
The passions that build up our human soul;
Not with the mean and vulgar works of man,
But with high objects, with enduring things –
410 With life and nature – purifying thus
The elements of feeling and of thought,
And sanctifying, by such discipline,
Both pain and fear, until we recognise
A grandeur in the beatings of the heart.
415 Nor was this fellowship vouchsafed to me
With stinted kindness. In November days,
When vapours rolling down the valley make
A lonely scene more lonesome, among woods,
At noon and 'mid the calm of summer nights,
420 When, by the margin of the trembling lake,
Beneath the gloomy hills homeward I went
In solitude, such intercourse was mine;

Mine was it in the fields both day and night,
And by the waters, all the summer long.

425   And in the frosty season, when the sun
Was set, and visible for many a mile
The cottage windows blazed through twilight gloom,
I heeded not their summons: happy time
It was indeed for all of us – for me
430   It was a time of rapture! Clear and loud
The village clock tolled six, – I wheeled about
Proud and exulting like an untired horse
That cares not for his home. All shod with steel,
We hissed along the polished ice in games
435   Confederate, imitative of the chase
And woodland pleasures, the resounding horn,
The pack loud chiming, and the hunted hare.
So through the darkness and the cold we flew,
And not a voice was idle; with the din
440   Smitten, the precipices rang aloud;
The leafless trees and every icy crag
Tinkled like iron; while far distant hills
Into the tumult sent an alien sound
Of melancholy not unnoticed, while the stars
445   Eastward were sparkling clear, and in the west
The orange sky of evening died away.
Not seldom from the uproar I retired
Into a silent bay, or sportively
Glanced sideway, leaving the tumultuous throng,
450   To cut across the reflex of a star
That fled, and, flying still before me, gleamed
Upon the glassy plain; and oftentimes,
When we had given our bodies to the wind,
And all the shadowy banks on either side
455   Came sweeping through the darkness, spinning still
The rapid line of motion, then at once
Have I, reclining back upon my heels,
Stopped short; yet still the solitary cliffs
Wheeled by me – even as if the earth had rolled
460   With visible motion her diurnal round!
Behind me did they stretch in solemn train,
Feebler and feebler, and I stood and watched
Till all was tranquil as a dreamless sleep.

Ye Presences of Nature in the sky
465   And on the earth! Ye Visions of the hills!

---

450 reflex: reflection.

And Souls of lonely places! can I think
A vulgar hope was yours when ye employed
Such ministry, when ye through many a year
Haunting me thus among my boyish sports,
470 On caves and trees, upon the woods and hills,
Impressed upon all forms the characters
Of danger or desire; and thus did make
The surface of the universal earth
With triumph and delight, with hope and fear,
475 Work like a sea?

From Book IV. Summer Vacation

As one who hangs down-bending from the side
Of a slow-moving boat, upon the breast
Of a still water, solacing himself
With such discoveries as his eye can make
260 Beneath him in the bottom of the deep,
Sees many beauteous sights – weeds, fishes, flowers,
Grots, pebbles, roots of trees, and fancies more,
Yet often is perplexed and cannot part
The shadow from the substance, rocks and sky,
265 Mountains and clouds, reflected in the depth
Of the clear flood, from things which there abide
In their true dwelling; now is crossed by gleam
Of his own image, by a sunbeam now,
And wavering motions sent he knows not whence,
270 Impediments that make his task more sweet;
Such pleasant office have we long pursued
Incumbent o'er the surface of past time
With like success, nor often have appeared
Shapes fairer or less doubtfully discerned
275 Than these to which the Tale, indulgent Friend!
Would now direct thy notice. Yet in spite
Of pleasure won, and knowledge not withheld,
There was an inner falling off – I loved,
Loved deeply all that had been loved before,
280 More deeply even than ever: but a swarm
Of heady schemes jostling each other, gawds,
And feast and dance, and public revelry,
And sports and games (too grateful in themselves,
Yet in themselves less grateful, I believe,
285 Than as they were a badge glossy and fresh
Of manliness and freedom) all conspired
To lure my mind from firm habitual quest

---

275 **Friend:** Samuel Taylor Coleridge.   281 **gawds:** gauds, trinkets, cheap finery.

Of feeding pleasures, to depress the zeal
And damp those yearnings which had once been mine –
290 A wild, unwordly-minded youth, given up
To his own eager thoughts. It would demand
Some skill, and longer time than may be spared,
To paint these vanities, and how they wrought
In haunts where they, till now, had been unknown.
295 It seemed the very garments that I wore
Preyed on my strength, and stopped the quiet stream
Of self-forgetfulness.

From Book VII. Residence in London

O' wondrous power of words, by simple faith
120 Licensed to take the meaning that we love!
Vauxhall and Ranelagh! I then had heard
Of your green groves, and wilderness of lamps
Dimming the stars, and fireworks magical,
And gorgeous ladies, under splendid domes,
125 Floating in dance, or warbling high in air
The songs of spirits! Nor had Fancy fed
With less delight upon that other class
Of marvels, broad-day wonders permanent:
The River proudly bridged; the dizzy top
130 And Whispering Gallery of St Paul's; the tombs
Of Westminster; the Giants of Guildhall;
Bedlam, and those carved maniacs at the gates,
Perpetually recumbent; Statues – man,
And the horse under him – in gilded pomp
135 Adorning flowery gardens, 'mid vast squares;
The Monument, and that Chamber of the Tower
Where England's sovereigns sit in long array,
Their steeds bestriding, – every mimic shape
Cased in the gleaming mail the monarch wore,
140 Whether for gorgeous tournaments addressed,
Or life or death upon the battle-field.
Those bold imaginations in due time
Had vanished, leaving others in their stead:
And now I looked upon the living scene;
145 Familiarly perused it; oftentimes,
In spite of strongest disappointment, pleased
Through courteous self-submission, as a tax
Paid to the object by prescriptive right.
Rise up, thou monstrous ant-hill on the plain
150 Of a too busy world! Before me flow,
Thou endless stream of men and moving things!
Thy every-day appearance, as it strikes –

With wonder heightened, or sublimed by awe –
On strangers of all ages; the quick dance
155 Of colours, lights, and forms; the deafening din;
The comers and the goers face to face,
Face after face; the string of dazzling wares,
Shop after shop, with symbols, blazoned names,
And all the tradesman's honours overhead:
160 Here, fronts of houses, like a title-page,
With letters huge inscribed from top to toe,
Stationed above the door, like guardian saints;
There, allegoric shapes, female or male,
Or physiognomies of real men,
165 Land-warriors, kings, or admirals of the sea,
Boyle, Shakespeare, Newton, or the attractive head
Of some quack-doctor, famous in his day.

Meanwhile the roar continues, till at length,
Escaped as from an enemy, we turn
170 Abruptly into some sequestered nook,
Still as a sheltered place when winds blow loud!
At leisure, thence, through tracts of thin resort,
And sights and sounds that come at intervals,
We take our way. A raree-show is here,
175 With children gathered round; another street
Presents a company of dancing dogs,
Or dromedary, with an antic pair
Of monkeys on his back; a minstrel band
Of Savoyards; or, single and alone,
180 An English ballad-singer. Private courts,
Gloomy as coffins, and unsightly lanes
Thrilled by some female vendor's scream, belike
The very shrillest of all London cries,
May then entangle our impatient steps;
185 Conducted through those labyrinths, unawares,
To privileged regions and inviolate,
Where from their airy lodges studious lawyers
Look out on waters, walks, and gardens green.

Thence back into the throng, until we reach,
190 Following the tide that slackens by degrees,
Some half-frequented scene, where wider streets
Bring straggling breezes of suburban air.
Here files of ballads dangle from dead walls;
Advertisements, of giant-size, from high
195 Press forward, in all colours, on the sight;

---

174 raree-show: a street show or carnival, a peepshow.

These, bold in conscious merit, lower down;
That, fronted with a most imposing word,
Is, peradventure, one in masquerade.
As on the broadening causeway we advance,
200 Behold, turned upwards, a face hard and strong
In lineaments, and red with over-toil.
'Tis one encountered here and everywhere;
A travelling cripple, by the trunk cut short,
And stumping on his arms. In sailor's garb
205 Another lies at length, beside a range
Of well-formed characters, with chalk inscribed
Upon the smooth flat stones: the Nurse is here,
The Bachelor, that loves to sun himself,
The military Idler, and the Dame,
210 That field-ward takes her walk with decent steps.

 Now homeward through the thickening hubbub, where
See, among less distinguishable shapes,
The begging scavenger, with hat in hand;
The Italian, as he thrids his way with care,
215 Steadying, far-seen, a frame of images
Upon his head; with basket at his breast
The Jew; the stately and slow-moving Turk,
With freight of slippers piled beneath his arm!

 Enough; – the mighty concourse I surveyed
220 With no unthinking mind, well pleased to note
Among the crowd all specimens of man,
Through all the colours which the sun bestows,
And every character of form and face:
The Swede, the Russian; from the genial south,
225 The Frenchman and the Spaniard; from remote
America, the Hunter-Indian; Moors,
Malays, Lascars, the Tartar, the Chinese,
And Negro Ladies in white muslin gowns.

* * * *

 As the black storm upon the mountain-top
620 Sets off the sunbeam in the valley, so
That huge fermenting mass of humankind
Serves as a solemn background, or relief,
To single forms and objects, whence they draw,
For feeling and contemplative regard,
625 More than inherent liveliness and power.
How oft, amid those overflowing streets,
Have I gone forward with the crowd, and said
Unto myself, 'The face of every one

That passes by me is a mystery!'
630 Thus have I looked, nor ceased to look, oppressed
By thoughts of what and wither, when and how,
Until the shapes before my eyes became
A second-sight procession, such as glides
Over still mountains, or appears in dreams;
635 And once, far-travelled in such mood, beyond
The reach of common indication, lost
Amid the moving pageant, I was smitten
Abruptly, with the view (a sight not rare)
Of a blind Beggar, who, with upright face,
640 Stood, propped against a wall, upon his chest
Wearing a written paper, to explain
His story, whence he came, and who he was.
Caught by the spectacle my mind turned round
As with the might of waters; an apt type
645 This label seemed of the utmost we can know,
Both of ourselves and of the universe;
And, on the shape of that unmoving man,
His steadfast face and sightless eyes, I gazed,
As if admonished from another world.

From Book IX. Residence in France

And when we chanced
510 One day to meet a hunger-bitten girl,
Who crept along fitting her languid gait
Unto a heifer's motion, by a cord
Tied to her arm, and picking thus from the lane
Its sustenance, while the girl with pallid hands
515 Was busy knitting in a heartless mood
Of solitude, and at the sight my friend
In agitation said, 'Tis against *that*
That we are fighting,' I with him believed
That a benignant spirit was abroad
520 Which might not be withstood, that poverty
Abject as this would in a little time
Be found no more, that we should see the earth
Unthwarted in her wish to recompense
The meek, the lowly, patient child of toil,
525 All institutes for ever blotted out
That legalised exclusion, empty pomp
Abolished, sensual state and cruel power,
Whether by edict of the one or few;
And finally, as sum and crown of all,
530 Should see the people having a strong hand

In framing their own laws; whence better days
To all mankind.

From Book X. Residence in France and French Revolution

Cheered with this hope, to Paris I returned,
And ranged, with ardour heretofore unfelt,
50   The spacious city, and in progress passed
The prison where the unhappy Monarch lay,
Associate with his children and his wife
In bondage; and the palace, lately stormed
With roar of cannon by a furious host.
55   I crossed the square (an empty area then!)
Of the Carrousel, where so late had lain
The dead, upon the dying heaped, and gazed
On this and other spots, as doth a man
Upon a volume whose contents he knows
60   Are memorable, but from him locked up,
Being written in a tongue he cannot read,
So that he questions the mute leaves with pain,
And half upbraids their silence. But that night
I felt most deeply in what world I was,
65   What ground I trod on, and what air I breathed.
High was my room and lonely, near the roof
Of a large mansion or hotel, a lodge
That would have pleased me in more quiet times:
Nor was it wholly without pleasure then.
70   With unextinguished taper, I kept watch,
Reading at intervals; the fear gone by
Pressed on me almost like a fear to come.
I thought of those September massacres,
Divided from me by one little month,
75   Saw them and touched: the rest was conjured up
From tragic fictions or true history,
Remembrances and dim admonishments.
The horse is taught his manage, and no star
Of wildest course but treads back his own steps;
80   For the spent hurricane the air provides
As fierce a successor; the tide retreats
But to return out of its hiding-place
In the great deep; all things have second birth;
The earthquake is not satisfied at once;
85   And in this way I wrought upon myself,
Until I seemed to hear a voice that cried,
To the whole city, 'Sleep no more.' The trance

---

56 **Carrousel:** Place du Carrousel.   78 **manage:** management.

Fled with the voice to which it had given birth;
But vainly comments of a calmer mind
90 Promised soft peace and sweet forgetfulness.
The place, all hushed and silent as it was,
Appeared unfit for the repose of night,
Defenceless as a wood where tigers roam.

[Wordsworth returns to England]

                    Twice had the trees let fall
Their leaves, as often Winter had put on
His hoary crown, since I had seen the surge
Beat against Albion's shore, since ear of mine
240 Had caught the accents of my native speech
Upon our native country's sacred ground.
A patriot of the world, how could I glide
Into communion with her sylvan shades,
Erewhile my tuneful haunt? It pleased me more
245 To abide in the great City, where I found
The general air still busy with the stir
Of that first memorable onset made
By a strong levy of humanity
Upon the traffickers in Negro blood;
250 Effort which, though defeated, had recalled
To notice old forgotten principles,
And through the nation spread a novel heat
Of virtuous feeling. For myself, I own
That this particular strife had wanted power
255 To rivet my affections; nor did now
Its unsuccessful issue much excite
My sorrow; for I brought with me the faith
That, if France prospered, good men would not long
Pay fruitless worship to humanity,
260 And this most rotten branch of human shame,
Object, so seemed it, of superfluous pains,
Would fall together with its parent tree.
What, then, were my emotions, when in arms
Britain put forth her freeborn strength in league,
265 Oh, pity and shame! with those confederate Powers!
Not in my single self alone I found,
But in the minds of all ingenuous youth,
Change and subversion from that hour. No shock
Given to my moral nature had I known
270 Down to that very moment; neither lapse

---

247 **onset**: the abolitionist movement.   265 **Powers**: Austria, Prussia, Spain, Portugal.

Nor turn of sentiment that might be named
A revolution, save at this one time;
All else was progress on the self-same path
On which, with a diversity of pace,
275 I had been travelling: this a stride at once
Into another region. As a light
And pliant harebell, swinging in the breeze
On some grey rock – its birthplace – so had I
Wantoned, fast rooted on the ancient tower
280 Of my beloved country, wishing not
A happier fortune than to wither there:
Now was I from that pleasant station torn
And tossed about in whirlwind. I rejoiced,
Yea, afterwards – truth most painful to record! –
285 Exulted, in the triumph of my soul,
When Englishmen by thousands were o'erthrown,
Left without glory on the field, or driven,
Brave hearts! to shameful flight. It was a grief, –
Grief call it not, 'twas anything but that, –
290 A conflict of sensations without name,
Of which *he* only, who may love the sight
Of a village steeple, as I do, can judge,
When, in the congregation bending all
To their great Father, prayers were offered up,
295 Or praises for our country's victories;
And, 'mid the simple worshippers, perchance
I only, like an uninvited guest
Whom no one owned, sate silent, shall I add,
Fed on the day of vengeance yet to come.

* * * *

In France, the men, who, for their desperate ends,
Had plucked up mercy by the roots, were glad
Of this new enemy. Tyrants, strong before
335 In wicked pleas, were strong as demons now;
And thus, on every side beset with foes,
The goaded land waxed mad; the crimes of few
Spread into the madness of the many; blasts
From hell cam sanctified like airs from heaven.

* * * *

Domestic carnage now filled the whole year
With feast-days; old men from the chimney-nook,
The maiden from the bosom of her love,

---

286 **o'erthrown:** the British were driven from Toulon.

The mother from the cradle of her babe,
360 The warrior from the field – all perished, all –
Friends, enemies, of all parties, ages, ranks,
Head after head, and never heads enough
For those that bade them fall. They found their joy,
They made it proudly, eager as a child,
365 (If like desires of innocent little ones
May with such heinous appetites be compared),
Pleased in some open field to exercise
A toy that mimics with revolving wings
The motion of a wind-mill; though the air
370 Do of itself blow fresh, and make the vanes
Spin in his eyesight, *that* contents him not,
But, with the plaything at arm's length, he sets
His front against the blast, and runs amain,
That it may whirl the faster.
                                                    Amid the depth
375 Of those enormities, even thinking minds
Forgot, at seasons, whence they had their being;
Forgot that such a sound was ever heard
As Liberty upon earth: yet all beneath
Her innocent authority was wrought,
380 Nor could have been, without her blessed name.
The illustrious wife of Roland, in the hour
Of her composure, felt that agony,
And gave it vent in her last words. O Friend!
It was a lamentable time for man,
385 Whether a hope had e'er been his or not;
A woeful time for them whose hopes survived
The shock; most woeful for those few who still
Were flattered, and had trust in human kind:
They had the deepest feeling of the grief.
390 Meanwhile the Invaders fared as they deserved:
The Herculean Commonwealth had put forth her arms,
And throttled with an infant godhead's might
The snakes about her cradle; that was well,
And as it should be; yet no cure for them
395 Whose souls were sick with pain of what would be
Hereafter brought in charge against mankind.
Most melancholy at that time, O Friend!
Were my day-thoughts, – my nights were miserable;
Through months, through years, long after the last beat
400 Of those atrocities, the hour of sleep

---

381 **Roland:** On her way to the guillotine in November 1793, Madame Roland famously called out, 'O Liberty, what things are done in thy name!'

To me came rarely charged with natural gifts,
Such ghastly visions had I of despair
And tyranny, and implements of death;
And innocent victims sinking under fear,
405   And momentary hope, and worn-out prayer,
Each in his separate cell, or penned in crowds
For sacrifice, and struggling with fond mirth
And levity in dungeons, where the dust
Was laid with tears. Then suddenly the scene
410   Changed, and the unbroken dream entangled me
In long orations, which I strove to plead
Before unjust tribunals, – with a voice
Labouring, a brain confounded, and a sense,
Death-like, of treacherous desertion, felt
415   In the last place of refuge – my own soul.

SAMUEL TAYLOR COLERIDGE (1772–1834)

Coleridge was the youngest son of the vicar of Ottery St Mary in Devon. A precocious scholar, he was educated in London at Christ's Hospital and at Cambridge. He sympathised with the French Revolution. He planned to found a 'Pantisocracy', a utopian colony in the United States, with the then radical (later Tory) poet Robert Southey, but they lacked the practical skills. In 1795 he met Wordsworth and began a deeply creative friendship which was to last until they quarrelled in 1810. (They were reconciled in 1828.) In 1798–99 he studied Kantian philosophy in Germany and in 1800 moved to the Lake District with Wordsworth. The medical prescription of opium led to a deepening addiction, contributing to bouts of depression in the early 1800s and later to severe breakdowns. His poetry after *Lyrical Ballads* was less distinguished and he gave much of his energy to philosophical and critical works in which he translated Kantian idealism to British and American interests and evolved a conservative Christian cultural theory which was long influential. These later works were *Lectures on Poetry and Drama* (1808), *The Friend* (1809–10), *Christabel and Other Poems* (1816), *Sybilline Leaves* (1817), *Lay Sermons* (1816, 1817); *Biographia Literaria* (1817), *Aids to Reflection* (1825), and *Church and State* (1830). His speculative work is by turns sophisticated and brilliant, and fragmentary and derived, because whilst a brilliant talker he lacked sustained application. The poems he contributed to *Lyrical Ballads* were of two kinds, the 'daemonic' or Gothic dream poems such as 'The Rime of the Ancient Mariner', and the 'conversation' poems exemplified in 'Frost at Midnight' in which the poet's self-conscious meditations lead to a sense of spiritual reconciliation. The method in these conversational poems was quickly absorbed by Wordsworth and became a much-used resource for later poets.

The Eolian Harp

Composed August 20th, 1795 At Clevedon, Somersetshire

My pensive Sara! thy soft cheek reclined
Thus on mine arm, most soothing sweet it is
To sit beside our Cot, our Cot o'ergrown
With white-flower'd Jasmin, and the broad-leaved Myrtle,
5   (Meet emblems they of Innocence and Love!)
And watch the clouds, that late were rich with light,
Slow saddenning round, and mark the star of eve
Serenely brilliant (such should Wisdom be)
Shine opposite! How exquisite the scents
10   Snatched from yon bean-field! and the world so hushed!
The stilly murmur of the distant Sea
Tells us of silence.
                       And that simplest Lute,
Placed length-ways in the clasping casement, hark!
How by the desultory breeze caressed,
15   Like some coy maid half-yielding to her lover,
It pours such sweet upbraiding, as must needs
Tempt to repeat the wrong! And now, its strings
Boldlier swept, the long sequacious notes
Over delicious surges sink and rise,
20   Such a soft floating witchery of sound
As twilight Elfins make, when they at eve
Voyage on gentle gales from Fairy-Land,
Where Melodies round honey-dropping flowers,
Footless and wild, like birds of Paradise,
25   Nor pause, nor perch, hovering on untamed wing!
O! the one Life within us and abroad,
Which meets all motion and becomes its soul,
A light in sound, a sound-like power in light,
Rhythm in all thought, and joyance every where –
30   Methinks, it should have been impossible
Not to love all things in a world so fill'd;
Where the breeze warbles, and the mute still air
Is Music slumbering on her instrument.

    And thus, my Love! as on the midway slope
35   Of yonder hill I stretch my limbs at noon,
Whilst through my half-closed eye-lids I behold
The sunbeams dance, like diamonds, on the main,
And tranquil muse upon tranquillity:

Eolian Harp: written for Sara Fricker, whom Coleridge married on 4 October 1795.

12 Lute: The Aeolian harp, named after Aeolus, god of the winds, makes music when wind passes over its strings.
18 sequacious: in sequence.

Full many a thought uncalled and undetain'd,
40 And many idle flitting phantasies,
Traverse my indolent and passive brain,
As wild and various, as the random gales
That swell and flutter on this subject Lute!
    And what if all of animated nature
45 Be but organic Harps diversly framed,
That tremble into thought, as o'er them sweeps
Plastic and vast, one intellectual breeze,
At once the Soul of each, and God of all ?

    But thy more serious eye a mild reproof
50 Darts, O belovèd Woman! nor such thoughts
Dim and unhallowed dost thou not reject,
And biddest me walk humbly with my God.
Meek Daughter in the Family of Christ!
Well hast thou said and holily dispraised
55 These shapings of the unregenerate mind;
Bubbles that glitter as they rise and break
On vain Philosophy's aye-babbling spring.
For never guiltless may I speak of him,
The Incomprehensible! save when with awe
60 I praise him, and with Faith that inly *feels*;
Who with his saving mercies healèd me,
A sinful and most miserable man,
Wildered and dark, and gave me to possess
Peace, and this Cot, and thee, heart-honoured Maid!

This Lime-Tree Bower My Prison

[Addressed to Charles Lamb, of the India House, London]

Well, they are gone, and here must I remain,
This lime-tree bower my prison! I have lost
Beauties and feelings, such as would have been
Most sweet to my remembrance even when age
5 Had dimm'd mine eyes to blindness! They, meanwhile,
Friends, whom I never more may meet again,
On springy heath, along the hill-top edge,
Wander in gladness, and wind down, perchance,
    To that still roaring dell, of which I told;
10 The roaring dell, o'erwooded, narrow, deep,
And only speckled by the mid-day sun;
Where its slim trunk the ash from rock to rock
Flings arching like a bridge; – that branchless ash,

Lime-Tree Bower: In July 1797, Coleridge could not join the Wordsworths and Lamb on a walk because of a slight injury.   **Charles Lamb (1775–1834):** a school friend of Coleridge, a prominent essayist, critic and occasional poet.

Unsunned and damp, whose few poor yellow leaves
15   Ne'er tremble in the gale, yet tremble still,
Fann'd by the water-fall! and there my friends
Behold the dark green file of long lank weeds,
That all at once (a most fantastic sight!)
Still nod and drip beneath the dripping edge
20   Of the blue clay-stone.
                  Now, my friends emerge
Beneath the wide wide Heaven – and view again
The many-steepled tract magnificent
Of hilly fields and meadows, and the sea,
With some fair bark, perhaps, whose sails light up
25   The slip of smooth clear blue betwixt two Isles
Of purple shadow! Yes! they wander on
In gladness all; but thou, methinks, most glad,
My gentle-hearted Charles! for thou hast pined
And hungered after Nature, many a year,
30   In the great City pent, winning thy way
With sad yet patient soul, through evil and pain
And strange calamity! Ah! slowly sink
Behind the western ridge, thou glorious Sun!
Shine in the slant beams of the sinking orb,
35   Ye purple heath-flowers! richlier burn, ye clouds!
Live in the yellow light, ye distant groves!
And kindle, thou blue Ocean! So my friend
Struck with deep joy may stand, as I have stood,
Silent with swimming sense; yea, gazing round
40   On the wide landscape, gaze till all doth seem
Less gross than bodily; and of such hues
As veil the Almighty Spirit, when yet he makes
Spirits perceive his presence.
                       A delight
Comes sudden on my heart, and I am glad
45   As I myself were there! Nor in this bower,
This little lime-tree bower, have I not marked
Much that has sooth'd me. Pale beneath the blaze
Hung the transparent foliage; and I watch'd
Some broad and sunny leaf, and loved to see
50   The shadow of the leaf and stem above
Dappling its sunshine! And that walnut-tree
Was richly ting'd, and a deep radiance lay
Full on the ancient ivy, which usurps
Those fronting elms, and now, with blackest mass
55   Makes their dark branches gleam a lighter hue
Through the late twilight: and though now the bat

---

32 calamity: his sister had stabbed their mother to death.

Wheels silent by, and not a swallow twitters,
Yet still the solitary humble bee
Sings in the bean-flower! Henceforth I shall know
60   That Nature ne'er deserts the wise and pure;
No plot so narrow, be but Nature there,
No waste so vacant, but may well employ
Each faculty of sense, and keep the heart
Awake to Love and Beauty! and sometimes
65   'Tis well to be bereft of promis'd good,
That we may lift the soul, and contemplate
With lively joy the joys we cannot share.
My gentle-hearted Charles! when the last rook
Beat its straight path across the dusky air
70   Homewards, I blessed it! deeming its black wing
(Now a dim speck, now vanishing in light)
Had crossed the mighty Orb's dilated glory,
While thou stood'st gazing; or, when all was still,
Flew creeking o'er thy head, and had a charm
75   For thee, my gentle-hearted Charles, to whom
No sound is dissonant which tells of Life.

The Rime of the Ancient Mariner[1]

In Seven Parts

*Facile credo, plures esse Naturas invisibiles quam visibiles in rerum universitate.
Sed horum omnium familiam quis nobis enarrabit? et gradus et cognationes et
discrimina et singulorum munera? Quid agunt? quae loca habitant? Harum rerum
notitiam semper ambivit ingenium humanum, nunquam attigit. Juvat, interea, non
diffiteor, quandoque in animo, tanquam in tabul, majoris et melioris mundi imaginem
contemplari: ne mens assuefacta hodiernae vitae minutiis se contrahat nimis, et tota
subsidat in pusillas cogitationes. Sed veritati interea invigilandum est, modusque
servandus, ut certa ab incertis, diem a nocte, distinguamus.* – T. Burnet[2]

Argument

How a Ship having passed the Line was driven by storms to the cold Country
towards the South Pole; and how from thence she made her course to the
tropical Latitude of the Great Pacific Ocean; and of the strange things that
befell; and in what manner the Ancyent Marinere came back to his own
Country.

1: First published in *Lyrical Ballads*, the marginal glosses were added by Coleridge in 1816.   **2:** Thomas Burnet
(1635?–1715), English divine, author of *The Theory of the Earth* (1684–90), a mythological cosmogony. The epigraph reads, 'I readily believe there are more invisible than visible beings in the universe. But who will explain to us
the families of all these, and their ranks and relations and differences and functions? What do they do? Where do
they live? The human mind has always sought knowledge of these things, but has never attained it. But I do not deny
that it is beneficial sometimes to contemplate in thought, as in a picture, the image of a greater and better world;
otherwise the mind, habituated to the petty matters of daily life, narrow itself and sink entirely into trivial thoughts.
But it is important to be vigilant for truth, and keep proportion, that we may distiguish the certain from the
uncertain, day from night.'

Part I

An ancient Mariner meeteth three Gallants bidden to a wedding-feast, and detaineth one.

It is an ancient Mariner,
And he stoppeth one of three.
'By thy long beard and glittering eye,
Now wherefore stopp'st thou me?

5   The Bridegroom's doors are opened wide,
And I am next of kin;
The guests are met, the feast is set:
May'st hear the merry din.'

He holds him with his skinny hand,
10   'There was a ship,' quoth he.
'Hold off ! unhand me, greybeard loon!'
Eftsoons his hand dropt he.

The Wedding-Guest is spellbound by the eye of the old seafaring man, and constrained to hear his tale.

He holds him with his glittering eye –
The Wedding-Guest stood still,
15   And listens like a three years' child:
The Mariner hath his will.

The Wedding-Guest sat on a stone:
He cannot choose but hear;
And thus spake on that ancient man,
20   The bright-eyed Mariner.

'The ship was cheered, the harbour cleared,
Merrily did we drop
Below the kirk, below the hill,
Below the lighthouse top.

The Mariner tells how the ship sailed southward with a good wind and fair weather, till it reached the Line.

25   The Sun came up upon the left,
Out of the sea came he!
And he shone bright, and on the right
Went down into the sea.

Higher and higher every day,
30   Till over the mast at noon – '
The Wedding-Guest here beat his breast,
For he heard the loud bassoon.

The Wedding-Guest heareth the bridal music; but the Mariner continueth his tale.

The bride hath paced into the hall,
Red as a rose is she;

---

23 **kirk**: church.

35 Nodding their heads before her goes
The merry minstrelsy.

The Wedding-Guest he beat his breast,
Yet he cannot choose but hear;
And thus spake on that ancient man,
40 The bright-eyed Mariner.

The ship driven by a storm
toward the south pole.

'And now the STORM-BLAST came, and he
Was tyrannous and strong:
He struck with his o'ertaking wings,
And chased us south along.

45 With sloping masts and dipping prow,
As who pursued with yell and blow
Still treads the shadow of his foe,
And forward bends his head,
The ship drove fast, loud roared the blast,
50 The southward aye we fled.

The land of ice, and of fearful
sounds where no living thing
was to be seen.

And now there came both mist and snow,
And it grew wondrous cold:
And ice, mast-high, came floating by,
As green as emerald.

55 And through the drifts the snowy clifts
Did send a dismal sheen:
Nor shapes of men nor beasts we ken –
The ice was all between.

The ice was here, the ice was there,
60 The ice was all around:
It cracked and growled, and roared and howled,
Like noises in a swound!

Till a great sea bird, called the
Albatross, came through the
snow-fog, and was received
with great joy and hospitality.

At length did cross an Albatross,
Thorough the fog it came;
65 As if it had been a Christian soul,
We hailed it in God's name.

It ate the food it ne'er had eat,
And round and round it flew.
The ice did split with a thunder-fit;
70 The helmsman steered us through!

---

62 swound: swoon.

And lo! the Albatross proveth
a bird of good omen, and
followeth the ship as it
returned northward through
fog and floating ice.

And a good south wind sprung up behind;
The Albatross did follow,
And every day, for food or play,
Came to the mariners' hollo!

75 In mist or cloud, on mast or shroud,
It perched for vespers nine;
Whiles all the night, through fog-smoke white,
Glimmered the white Moon-shine.'

The ancient Mariner
inhospitably killeth the pious
bird of good omen.

'God save thee, ancient Mariner!
80 From the fiends, that plague thee thus! –
Why look'st thou so?' – With my crossbow
I shot the ALBATROSS.

PART II

The Sun now rose upon the right:
Out of the sea came he,
85 Still hid in mist, and on the left
Went down into the sea.

And the good south wind still blew behind,
But no sweet bird did follow,
Nor any day, for food or play
90 Came to the mariners' hollo!

His shipmates cry out against
the ancient Mariner, for killing
the bird of good luck.

And I had done an hellish thing,
And it would work 'em woe:
For all averred, I had killed the bird
That made the breeze to blow.
95 Ah wretch! said they, the bird to slay,
That made the breeze to blow!

But when the fog cleared off,
they justify the same, and thus
make themselves accomplices
in the crime.

Nor dim nor red, like God's own head,
The glorious Sun uprist:
Then all averred, I had killed the bird
100 That brought the fog and mist.
'Twas right, said they, such birds to slay,
That bring the fog and mist.

The fair breeze continues; the
ship enters the Pacific Ocean,
and sails northward, even till it
reaches the Line.

The fair breeze blew, the white foam flew,
The furrow followed free;
105 We were the first that ever burst
Into that silent sea.

*The ship hath been suddenly
becalmed.*

Down dropt the breeze, the sails dropt down,
'Twas sad as sad could be;
And we did speak only to break
110 The silence of the sea!

All in a hot and copper sky,
The bloody Sun, at noon,
Right up above the mast did stand,
No bigger than the Moon.

115 Day after day, day after day,
We stuck, nor breath nor motion;
As idle as a painted ship
Upon a painted ocean.

*And the Albatross begins to be
avenged.*

Water, water, everywhere,
120 And all the boards did shrink;
Water, water, everywhere,
Nor any drop to drink.

The very deep did rot: O Christ!
That ever this should be!
125 Yea, slimy things did crawl with legs
Upon the slimy sea.

About, about, in reel and rout
The death-fires danced at night;
The water, like a witch's oils,
130 Burnt green, and blue and white.

*A Spirit had followed them;
one of the invisible inhabitants
of this planet, neither departed
souls nor angels; concerning
whom the learned Jew,
Josephus, and the Platonic
Constantinopolitan, Michael
Psellus, may be consulted.
They are very numerous, and
there is no climate or element
without one or more.*

And some in dreams assurèd were
Of the Spirit that plagued us so;
Nine fathom deep he had followed us
From the land of mist and snow.

135 And every tongue, through utter drought,
Was withered at the root;
We could not speak, no more than if
We had been choked with soot.

*The shipmates, in their sore
distress, would fain throw the
whole guilt on the ancient
Mariner: in sign whereof they
hang the dead sea bird round
his neck.*

Ah! well a-day! what evil looks
140 Had I from old and young!
Instead of the cross, the Albatross
About my neck was hung.

PART III

There passed a weary time. Each throat
Was parched, and glazed each eye.

145   A weary time! a weary time!
How glazed each weary eye,

The ancient Mariner beholdeth
a sign in the element afar off.

When looking westward, I beheld
A something in the sky.

At first it seemed a little speck,

150   And then it seemed a mist;
It moved and moved, and took at last
A certain shape, I wist.

A speck, a mist, a shape, I wist!
And still it neared and neared:

155   As if it dodged a water-sprite,
It plunged and tacked and veered.

At its nearer approach, it
seemeth him to be a ship; and
at a dear ransom he freeth his
speech from the bonds of
thirst.

With throats unslaked, with black lips baked,
We could nor laugh nor wail;
Through utter drought all dumb we stood!

160   I bit my arm, I sucked the blood,
And cried, A sail! a sail!

With throats unslaked, with black lips baked,
Agape they heard me call:

A flash of joy;

Gramercy! they for joy did grin,

165   And all at once their breath drew in,
As they were drinking all.

And horror follows. For can it
be a ship that comes onward
without wind or tide.

See! see! (I cried) she tacks no more!
Hither to work us weal;
Without a breeze, without a tide,

170   She steadies with upright keel!

The western wave was all aflame.
The day was well nigh done!
Almost upon the western wave
Rested the broad bright Sun;

175   When that strange shape drove suddenly
Betwixt us and the Sun.

It seemeth him but the
skeleton of a ship.

And straight the Sun was flecked with bars,
(Heaven's Mother send us grace!)

---

164 Gramercy: 'great thanks', from *'grand merci'*.   **168 weal:** good.

As if through a dungeon grate he peered
180 With broad and burning face.

Alas! (thought I, and my heart beat loud)
How fast she nears and nears!
Are those *her* sails that glance in the Sun,
Like restless gossameres?

185 Are those *her* ribs through which the Sun
Did peer, as through a grate?
And is that Woman all her crew?
Is that a DEATH? and are there two?
Is DEATH that woman's mate?

190 *Her* lips were red, *her* looks were free,
Her locks were yellow as gold:
Her skin was as white as leprosy,
The Nightmare LIFE-IN-DEATH was she,
Who thicks man's blood with cold.

195 The naked hulk alongside came,
And the twain were casting dice;
'The game is done! I've won! I've won!'
Quoth she, and whistles thrice.

The Sun's rim dips; the stars rush out:
200 At one stride comes the dark;
With far-heard whisper, o'er the sea,
Off shot the spectre-bark.

We listened and looked sideways up!
Fear at my heart, as at a cup,
205 My life-blood seemed to sip!
The stars were dim, and thick the night,
The steerman's face by his lamp gleamed white;
From the sails the dew did drip –
Till clomb above the eastern bar
210 The hornèd Moon, with one bright star
Within the nether tip.

One after one, by the star-dogged Moon,
Too quick for groan or sigh,
Each turned his face with a ghastly pang,
215 And cursed me with his eye.

And its ribs are seen as bars on the face of the setting Sun.

The Spectre-Woman and her Deathmate, and no other on board the skeleton ship.

Like vessel, like crew!

Death and Life-in-Death have diced for the ship's crew, and she (the latter) winneth the ancient Mariner.

No twilight within the courts of the Sun.

At the rising of the Moon,

One after another,

His shipmates drop down dead.

Four times fifty living men,
(And I heard nor sigh nor groan)
With heavy thump, a lifeless lump,
They dropped down one by one.

But Life-in-Death begins her work on the ancient Mariner.

220 The souls did from their bodies fly, –
They fled to bliss or woe!
And every soul, it passed me by,
Like the whizz of my cross-bow!

PART IV

The Wedding-Guest feareth that a Spirit is talking to him;

'I fear thee, ancient Mariner!
225 I fear thy skinny hand!
And thou art long, and lank, and brown,
As is the ribbed sea-sand.

I fear thee and thy glittering eye,
And thy skinny hand, so brown.' –

But the ancient Mariner assureth him of his bodily life, and proceedeth to relate his horrible penance.

230 Fear not, fear not, thou Wedding-Guest!
This body dropt not down.

Alone, alone, all, all alone,
Alone on a wide wide sea!
And never a saint took pity on
235 My soul in agony.

He despiseth the creatures of the calm,

The many men, so beautiful!
And they all dead did lie:
And a thousand thousand slimy things
Lived on; and so did I.

And envieth that they should live, and so many lie dead.

240 I looked upon the rotting sea,
And drew my eyes away;
I looked upon the rotting deck,
And there the dead men lay.

I looked to heaven, and tried to pray;
245 But or ever a prayer had gusht,
A wicked whisper came, and made
My heart as dry as dust.

I closed my lids, and kept them close,
And the balls like pulses beat,
250 For the sky and the sea, and the sea and the sky
Lay like a load on my weary eye,
And the dead were at my feet.

But the curse liveth for him in the eye of the dead men.

The cold sweat melted from their limbs,
Nor rot nor reek did they:
255 The look with which they looked on me
Had never passed away.

An orphan's curse would drag to hell
A spirit from on high;
But oh! more horrible than that
260 Is the curse in a dead man's eye!
Seven days, seven nights, I saw that curse,
And yet I could not die.

In his loneliness and fixedness he yearneth towards the journeying Moon, and the stars that still sojourn, yet still move onward; and every where the blue sky belongs to them, and is their appointed rest, and their native country and their own natural homes, which they enter unannounced, as lords that are certainly expected and yet there is a silent joy at their arrival.

The moving Moon went up the sky,
And no where did abide:
265 Softly she was going up,
And a star or two beside –

Her beams bemocked the sultry main,
Like April hoar-frost spread;
But where the ship's huge shadow lay,
270 The charmèd water burnt alway
A still and awful red.

By the light of the Moon he beholdeth God's creatures of the great calm.

Beyond the shadow of the ship,
I watched the water-snakes:
They moved in tracks of shining white,
275 And when they reared, the elfish light
Fell off in hoary flakes.

Within the shadow of the ship
I watched their rich attire:
Blue, glossy green, and velvet black,
280 They coiled and swam; and every track
Was a flash of golden fire.

Their beauty and their happiness.

O happy living things! no tongue
Their beauty might declare:
A spring of love gushed from my heart,

He blesseth them in his heart.

285 And I blessed them unaware:
Sure my kind saint took pity on me,
And I blessed them unaware.

The spell begins to break.

The self-same moment I could pray;
And from my neck so free
290 The Albatross fell off, and sank
Like lead into the sea.

PART V

Oh sleep! it is a gentle thing,
Beloved from pole to pole!
To Mary Queen the praise be given!
295 She sent the gentle sleep from Heaven,
That slid into my soul.

By grace of the holy Mother,
the ancient Mariner is refreshed
with rain.

The silly buckets on the deck,
That had so long remained,
I dreamt that they were filled with dew;
300 And when I awoke, it rained.

My lips were wet, my throat was cold,
My garments all were dank;
Sure I had drunken in my dreams,
And still my body drank.

305 I moved, and could not feel my limbs:
I was so light – almost
I thought that I had died in sleep,
And was a blessèd ghost.

He heareth sounds and seeth
strange sights and
commotions in the sky and
the element.

And soon I heard a roaring wind:
310 It did not come anear;
But with its sound it shook the sails,
That were so thin and sere.

The upper air burst into life!
And a hundred fire-flags sheen,
315 To and fro they were hurried about!
And to and fro, and in and out,
The wan stars danced between.

And the coming wind did roar more loud,
And the sails did sigh like sedge;
320 And the rain poured down from one black cloud;
The Moon was at its edge.

The thick black cloud was cleft, and still
The Moon was at its side:
Like waters shot from some high crag,
325 The lightning fell with never a jag,
A river steep and wide.

---

297 **silly**: humble.   314 **sheen**: gleam.   319 **sedge**: tall coarse marsh grass.

The loud wind never reached the ship,
Yet now the ship moved on!
Beneath the lightning and the Moon
330 The dead men gave a groan.

They groaned, they stirred, they all uprose,
Nor spake, nor moved their eyes;
It had been strange, even in a dream,
To have seen those dead men rise.

335 The helmsman steered, the ship moved on;
Yet never a breeze up-blew;
The mariners all 'gan work the ropes,
Where they were wont to do;
They raised their limbs like lifeless tools –
340 We were a ghastly crew.

The body of my brother's son
Stood by me, knee to knee:
The body and I pulled at one rope,
But he said nought to me.

345 'I fear thee, ancient Mariner!'
Be calm, thou Wedding-Guest!
'Twas not those souls that fled in pain,
Which to their corses came again,
But a troop of spirits blest:

350 For when it dawned – they dropped their arms,
And clustered round the mast;
Sweet sounds rose slowly through their mouths,
And from their bodies passed.

Around, around, flew each sweet sound,
355 Then darted to the Sun;
Slowly the sounds came back again,
Now mixed, now one by one.

Sometimes a-dropping from the sky
I heard the sky-lark sing;
360 Sometimes all little birds that are,
How they seemed to fill the sea and air
With their sweet jargoning!

---

362 jargoning: warbling (Middle English).

And now 'twas like all instruments,
Now like a lonely flute;
365 And now it is an angel's song,
That makes the heavens be mute.

It ceased; yet still the sails made on
A pleasant noise till noon,
A noise like of a hidden brook
370 In the leafy month of June,
That to the sleeping woods all night
Singeth a quiet tune.

Till noon we quietly sailed on,
Yet never a breeze did breathe:
375 Slowly and smoothly went the ship,
Moved onward from beneath.

The lonesome Spirit from the South Pole carries on the ship as far as the Line, in obedience to the angelic troop, but still requireth vengeance.

Under the keel nine fathom deep,
From the land of mist and snow,
The spirit slid: and it was he
380 That made the ship to go.
The sails at noon left off their tune,
And the ship stood still also.

The Sun, right up above the mast,
Had fixed her to the ocean:
385 But in a minute she 'gan stir,
With a short uneasy motion –
Backwards and forwards half her length
With a short uneasy motion.

Then like a pawing horse let go,
390 She made a sudden bound:
It flung the blood into my head,
And I fell down in a swound.

The Polar Spirit's fellow demons, the invisible inhabitants of the element, take part in his wrong; and two of them relate, one to the other, that penance long and heavy for the ancient Mariner hath been accorded to the Polar Spirit, who returneth southward.

How long in that same fit I lay,
I have not to declare;
395 But ere my living life returned,
I heard and in my soul discerned
Two voices in the air.

'Is it he?' quoth one, 'Is this the man?
By him who died on cross,
400 With his cruel bow he laid full low
The harmless Albatross.

The spirit who bideth by himself
In the land of mist and snow,
He loved the bird that loved the man
405 Who shot him with his bow.'

The other was a softer voice,
As soft as honey-dew:
Quoth he, 'The man hath penance done,
And penance more will do.'

PART VI

FIRST VOICE

410 'But tell me, tell me! speak again,
Thy soft response renewing –
What makes that ship drive on so fast?
What is the ocean doing?'

SECOND VOICE

'Still as a slave before his lord,
415 The ocean hath no blast;
His great bright eye most silently
Up to the Moon is cast –

If he may know which way to go;
For she guides him smooth or grim.
420 See, brother, see! how graciously
She looketh down on him.'

FIRST VOICE

The Mariner hath been cast into a trance; for the angelic power causeth the vessel to drive northward faster than human life could endure.

'But why drives on that ship so fast,
Without or wave or wind?'

SECOND VOICE

'The air is cut away before,
425 And closes from behind.

Fly, brother, fly! more high, more high!
Or we shall be belated:
For slow and slow that ship will go,
When the Mariner's trance is abated.'

The supernatural motion is retarded; the Mariner awakes, and his penance begins anew.

430 I woke, and we were sailing on
As in a gentle weather:
'Twas night, calm night, the moon was high;
The dead men stood together.

All stood together on the deck,
435 For a charnel-dungeon fitter:
All fixed on me their stony eyes,
That in the Moon did glitter.

The pang, the curse, with which they died,
Had never passed away:
440 I could not draw my eyes from theirs,
Nor turn them up to pray.

The curse is finally expiated.   And now this spell was snapt: once more
I viewed the ocean green,
And looked far forth, yet little saw
445 Of what had else been seen –

Like one, that on a lonesome road
Doth walk in fear and dread,
And having once turned round walks on,
And turns no more his head;
450 Because he knows, a frightful fiend
Doth close behind him tread.

But soon there breathed a wind on me,
Nor sound nor motion made:
Its path was not upon the sea,
455 In ripple or in shade.

It raised my hair, it fanned my cheek
Like a meadow-gale of spring –
It mingled strangely with my fears,
Yet it felt like a welcoming.

460 Swiftly, swiftly flew the ship,
Yet she sailed softly too:
Sweetly, sweetly blew the breeze –
On me alone it blew.

And the ancient Mariner   Oh! dream of joy! is this indeed
beholdeth his native country.
465 The lighthouse top I see?
Is this the hill? is this the kirk?
Is this mine own countree?

We drifted o'er the harbour-bar,
And I with sobs did pray –

---

435 charnel-dungeon: burial vault.   **457 meadow-gale:** summer breeze.

470 O let me be awake, my God!
  Or let me sleep alway.

  The harbour-bay was clear as glass,
  So smoothly it was strewn!
  And on the bay the moonlight lay,
475 And the shadow of the Moon.

  The rock shone bright, the kirk no less,
  That stands above the rock:
  The moonlight steeped in silentness
  The steady weathercock.

480 And the bay was white with silent light,
  Till rising from the same,
The angelic spirits leave the   Full many shapes, that shadows were,
dead bodies,   In crimson colours came.

  A little distance from the prow
And appear in their own forms 485 Those crimson shadows were:
of light.   I turned my eyes upon the deck –
  Oh, Christ! what saw I there!

  Each corse lay flat, lifeless and flat,
  And, by the holy rood!
490 A man all light, a seraph-man,
  On every corse there stood.

  This seraph-band, each waved his hand:
  It was a heavenly sight!
  They stood as signals to the land,
495 Each one a lovely light;

  This seraph-band, each waved his hand,
  No voice did they impart –
  No voice; but oh! the silence sank
  Like music on my heart.

500 But soon I heard the dash of oars,
  I heard the Pilot's cheer;
  My head was turned perforce away
  And I saw a boat appear.

  The Pilot and the Pilot's boy,
505 I heard them coming fast:
  Dear Lord in Heaven! it was a joy
  The dead men could not blast.

I saw a third – I heard his voice:
It is the Hermit good!
510   He singeth loud his godly hymns
That he makes in the wood.
He'll shrieve my soul, he'll wash away
The Albatross's blood.

PART VII

The Hermit of the Wood,
This Hermit good lives in that wood
515   Which slopes down to the sea.
How loudly his sweet voice he rears!
He loves to talk with marineres
That come from a far countree.

He kneels at morn, and noon, and eve –
520   He hath a cushion plump:
It is the moss that wholly hides
The rotted old oak-stump.

The skiff-boat neared: I heard them talk,
'Why, this is strange, I trow!
525   Where are those lights so many and fair,
That signal made but now?'

*Approacheth the ship with
wonder.*
'Strange, by my faith!' the Hermit said –
'And they answered not our cheer!
The planks looked warped! and see those sails,
530   How thin they are and sere!
I never saw aught like to them,
Unless perchance it were

Brown skeletons of leaves that lag
My forest-brook along;
535   When the ivy tod is heavy with snow,
And the owlet whoops to the wolf below,
That eats the she-wolf's young.'

'Dear Lord! it hath a fiendish look –
The Pilot made reply,
540   I am a-feared' – 'Push on, push on!'
Said the Hermit cheerily.

The boat came closer to the ship,
But I nor spake nor stirred;
The boat came close beneath the ship,
545   And straight a sound was heard.

---

535 **ivy tod**: a tuft or clump of ivy.

The ship suddenly sinketh.

Under the water it rumbled on,
Still louder and more dread:
It reached the ship, it split the bay;
The ship went down like lead.

*The ancient Mariner is saved
in the Pilot's boat.*

550 Stunned by that loud and dreadful sound,
Which sky and ocean smote,
Like one that hath been seven days drowned
My body lay afloat;
But swift as dreams, myself I found
555 Within the Pilot's boat.

Upon the whirl, where sank the ship,
The boat spun round and round;
And all was still, save that the hill
Was telling of the sound.

560 I moved my lips – the Pilot shrieked
And fell down in a fit;
The holy Hermit raised his eyes,
And prayed where he did sit.

I took the oars: the Pilot's boy,
565 Who now doth crazy go,
Laughed loud and long, and all the while
His eyes went to and fro.
'Ha! ha!' quoth he, 'full plain I see,
The Devil knows how to row.'

570 And now, all in my own countree,
I stood on the firm land!
The Hermit stepped forth from the boat,
And scarcely he could stand.

*The ancient Mariner earnestly
entreateth the Hermit to
shrieve him; and the penance
of life falls on him.*

'O shrieve me, shrieve me, holy man!'
575 The Hermit crossed his brow.
'Say quick,' quoth he, 'I bid thee say –
What manner of man art thou?'

Forthwith this frame of mine was wrenched
With a woful agony,
580 Which forced me to begin my tale;
And then it left me free.

*And ever and anon through
out his future life an agony
constraineth him to travel from
land to land;*

Since then, at an uncertain hour,
That agony returns:

---

574 shrieve me: confess me, and grant absolution.

And till my ghastly tale is told,
585   This heart within me burns.

I pass, like night, from land to land;
I have strange power of speech;
That moment that his face I see,
I know the man that must hear me:
590   To him my tale I teach.

What loud uproar bursts from that door!
The wedding guests are there:
But in the garden-bower the bride
And bridemaids singing are:
595   And hark the little vesper bell,
Which biddeth me to prayer!

O Wedding-Guest! this soul hath been
Alone on a wide wide sea:
So lonely 'twas, that God himself
600   Scarce seemèd there to be.

O sweeter than the marriage feast,
'Tis sweeter far to me,
To walk together to the kirk
With a goodly company! –

605   To walk together to the kirk,
And all together pray,
While each to his great Father bends,
Old men, and babes, and loving friends
And youths and maidens gay!

And to teach, by his own
example, love and reverence
to al things that God made and
loveth.

610   Farewell, farewell! but this I tell
To thee, thou Wedding-Guest!
He prayeth well, who loveth well
Both man and bird and beast.

He prayeth best, who loveth best
615   All things both great and small;
For the dear God who loveth us,
He made and loveth all.

The Mariner, whose eye is bright,
Whose beard with age is hoar,
620   Is gone: and now the Wedding-Guest
Turned from the bridegroom's door.

He went like one that hath been stunned,
And is of sense forlorn:
A sadder and a wiser man,
625   He rose the morrow morn.

Kubla Khan

Or, A Vision In A Dream. A Fragment

In Xanadu did Kubla Khan
A stately pleasure-dome decree:
Where Alph, the sacred river, ran
Through caverns measureless to man
5   Down to a sunless sea.
So twice five miles of fertile ground
With walls and towers were girdled round:
And there were gardens bright with sinuous rills,
Where blossomed many an incense-bearing tree;
10   And here were forests ancient as the hills,
Enfolding sunny spots of greenery.
But oh! that deep romantic chasm which slanted
Down the green hill athwart a cedarn cover!
A savage place! as holy and enchanted
15   As e'er beneath a waning moon was haunted
By woman wailing for her demon-lover!
And from this chasm, with ceaseless turmoil seething,
As if this earth in fast thick pants were breathing,
A mighty fountain momently was forced:
20   Amid whose swift half-intermitted burst
Huge fragments vaulted like rebounding hail,
Or chaffy grain beneath the thresher's flail:
And 'mid these dancing rocks at once and ever
It flung up momently the sacred river.
25   Five miles meandering with a mazy motion
Through wood and dale the sacred river ran,
Then reached the caverns measureless to man,
And sank in tumult to a lifeless ocean:
And 'mid this tumult Kubla heard from far
30   Ancestral voices prophesying war!
    The shadow of the dome of pleasure
    Floated midway on the waves;
    Where was heard the mingled measure
    From the fountain and the caves.
35   It was a miracle of rare device,
A sunny pleasure-dome with caves of ice!
    A damsel with a dulcimer

In a vision once I saw:
It was an Abyssinian maid,
40 And on her dulcimer she played,
Singing of Mount Abora.
Could I revive within me
Her symphony and song,
To such a deep delight 'twould win me,
45 That with music loud and long,
I would build that dome in air,
That sunny dome! those caves of ice!
And all who heard should see them there,
And all should cry, Beware! Beware!
50 His flashing eyes, his floating hair!
Weave a circle round him thrice,
And close your eyes with holy dread,
For he on honey-dew hath fed,
And drunk the milk of Paradise.

Frost at Midnight

The Frost performs its secret ministry,
Unhelped by any wind. The owlet's cry
Came loud – and hark, again! loud as before.
The inmates of my cottage, all at rest,
5 Have left me to that solitude, which suits
Abstruser musings: save that at my side
My cradled infant slumbers peacefully.
'Tis calm indeed! so calm, that it disturbs
And vexes meditation with its strange
10 And extreme silentness. Sea, hill, and wood,
This populous village! Sea, and hill, and wood,
With all the numberless goings-on of life,
Inaudible as dreams! the thin blue flame
Lies on my low-burnt fire, and quivers not;
15 Only that film, which fluttered on the grate,
Still flutters there, the sole unquiet thing.
Methinks, its motion in this hush of nature
Gives it dim sympathies with me who live,
Making it a companionable form,
20 Whose puny flaps and freaks the idling Spirit
By its own moods interprets, everywhere
Echo or mirror seeking of itself,
And makes a toy of Thought.

---

7 **infant:** Hartley Coleridge, then 17 months old.   15 **film:** a leaf of soot. Coleridge noted 'these films are called *strangers* and supposed to portend the arrival of some absent friend.'

But O! how oft,
How oft, at school, with most believing mind,
25   Presageful, have I gazed upon the bars,
To watch that fluttering *stranger*! and as oft
With unclosed lids, already had I dreamt
Of my sweet birthplace, and the old church tower,
Whose bells, the poor man's only music, rang
30   From morn to evening, all the hot Fair-day,
So sweetly, that they stirred and haunted me
With a wild pleasure, falling on mine ear
Most like articulate sounds of things to come!
So gazed I, till the soothing things, I dreamt,
35   Lulled me to sleep, and sleep prolonged my dreams!
And so I brooded all the following morn,
Awed by the stern preceptor's face, mine eye
Fixed with mock study on my swimming book:
Save if the door half opened, and I snatched
40   A hasty glance, and still my heart leaped up,
For still I hoped to see the *stranger's* face,
Townsman, or aunt, or sister more beloved,
My play-mate when we both were clothed alike !

      Dear Babe, that sleepest cradled by my side,
45   Whose gentle breathings, heard in this deep calm,
Fill up the interspersèd vacancies
And momentary pauses of the thought!
My babe so beautiful! it thrills my heart
With tender gladness, thus to look at thee,
50   And think that thou shalt learn far other lore,
And in far other scenes! For I was reared
In the great city, pent 'mid cloisters dim,
And saw nought lovely but the sky and stars.
But *thou*, my babe! shalt wander like a breeze
55   By lakes and sandy shores, beneath the crags
Of ancient mountain, and beneath the clouds,
Which image in their bulk both lakes and shores
And mountain crags: so shalt thou see and hear
The lovely shapes and sounds intelligible
60   Of that eternal language, which thy God
Utters, who from eternity doth teach
Himself in all, and all things in himself.
Great universal Teacher! he shall mould
Thy spirit, and by giving make it ask.

65   Therefore all seasons shall be sweet to thee,
Whether the summer clothe the general earth
With greenness, or the redbreast sit and sing

Betwixt the tufts of snow on the bare branch
Of mossy apple tree, while the nigh thatch
70 Smokes in the sun-thaw; whether the eave-drops fall
Heard only in the trances of the blast,
Or if the secret ministry of frost
Shall hang them up in silent icicles,
Quietly shining to the quiet Moon.

JANE AUSTEN (1775–1817)

Jane Austen's father was a cultivated clergyman, then rector at Steventon, Hampshire, who educated his own daughters alongside his paying tutees. Well-read and intelligent, she displayed a precocious talent for elegant and witty writing, especially when describing family acquaintance. As her father had little capital, the family was dependent for preferment and entertainment on the favour of their more wealthy connections in the landed gentry. Her experience was only of the restricted world represented in her novels – occasional visits to London, Bath and Lyme Regis, dining at the great house, country walks. Her first novels were epistolary, the style then dominant, and had to be revised several times before they could find a publisher. *Sense and Sensibility* (1811) was written in 1795–96 as *Elinor and Marianne*; *Pride and Prejudice* (1812) was written in 1797 as *First Impressions*. She then wrote a parody of the Gothic, *Northanger Abbey*, which was published posthumously with *Persuasion* in 1818. The revision of the early works into the eventually published form involved perfecting a new narrative technique, ironic narration by an omniscient, impersonal authority. This form of narration is seen at its best and most complex in the novels written after success had come, *Mansfield Park* (1814) and *Emma* (1816). Austen's narratives are romances of young love and marriage; but her ability to trace out the moral seriousness of small things, her insight into consciousness and set characters in play with each other, and her ironic fascination with the moral duplicities of representation give her work a range of pleasures that have never in this genre been surpassed. Acknowledged by Sir Walter Scott as a master, Austen's work experienced some contemporary esteem, but since Henry James converted the novel from a moral and representational medium into a self-sustaining art form, her reputation has been on a plane with that of Shakespeare.

From Pride and Prejudice

Chapter 1

It is a truth universally acknowledged, that a single man in possession of a good fortune must be in want of a wife.

However little known the feelings or views of such a man may be on his first entering a neighbourhood, this truth is so well fixed in the minds of the surrounding families, that he is considered as the rightful property of some one or other of their daughters.

'My dear Mr. Bennet,' said his lady to him one day, 'have you heard that Netherfield Park is let at last?'

Mr. Bennet replied that he had not.

'But it is,' returned she; 'for Mrs. Long has just been here, and she told me all about it.'

Mr. Bennet made no answer.

'Do not you want to know who has taken it?' cried his wife impatiently.

'*You* want to tell me, and I have no objection to hearing it.'

This was invitation enough.

'Why, my dear, you must know, Mrs. Long says that Netherfield is taken by a young man of large fortune from the north of England; that he came down on Monday in a chaise and four to see the place, and was so much delighted with it that he agreed with Mr. Morris immediately; that he is to take possession before Michaelmas, and some of his servants are to be in the house by the end of next week.'

'What is his name?'

'Bingley.'

'Is he married or single?'

'Oh! single, my dear, to be sure! A single man of large fortune; four or five thousand a year. What a fine thing for our girls!'

'How so? How can it affect them?'

'My dear Mr. Bennet,' replied his wife, 'how can you be so tiresome! You must know that I am thinking of his marrying one of them.'

'Is that his design in settling here?'

'Design! nonsense, how can you talk so! But it is very likely that he *may* fall in love with one of them, and therefore you must visit him as soon as he comes.'

'I see no occasion for that. You and the girls may go, or you may send them by themselves, which perhaps will be still better; for, as you are as handsome as any of them, Mr. Bingley might like you the best of the party.'

'My dear, you flatter me. I certainly *have* had my share of beauty, but I do not pretend to be any thing extraordinary now. When a woman has five grown up daughters, she ought to give over thinking of her own beauty.'

'In such cases, a woman has not often much beauty to think of.'

'But, my dear, you must indeed *go* and *see* Mr. Bingley when he comes into the neighbourhood.'

'It is more than I engage for, I assure you.'

'But consider your daughters. Only think what an establishment it would be for one of them. Sir William and Lady Lucas are determined to go, merely on that account, for in general, you know they visit no new comers. Indeed you must go, for it will be impossible for *us* to visit him, if you do not.'

'You are over scrupulous, surely. I dare say Mr. Bingley will be very glad to see you; and I will send a few lines by you to assure him of my hearty consent to his marrying which ever he chuses of the girls; though I must throw in a good word for my little Lizzy.'

'I desire you will do no such thing. Lizzy is not a bit better than the others; and I am sure she is not half so handsome as Jane, nor half so good humoured as Lydia. But you are always giving *her* the preference.'

'They have none of them much to recommend them,' replied he; 'they are all silly and ignorant like other girls; but Lizzy has something more of quickness than her sisters.'

'Mr. Bennet, how can you abuse your own children in such a way? You take delight in vexing me. You have no compassion on my poor nerves.'

'You mistake me, my dear. I have a high respect for your nerves. They are my old friends. I have heard you mention them with consideration these twenty years at least.'

'Ah! you do not know what I suffer.'

'But I hope you will get over it, and live to see many young men of four thousand a year come into the neighbourhood.'

'It will be no use to us if twenty such should come, since you will not visit them.'

'Depend upon it, my dear, that when there are twenty I will visit them all.'

Mr. Bennet was so odd a mixture of quick parts, sarcastic humour, reserve, and caprice, that the experience of three and twenty years had been insufficient to make his wife understand his character. *Her* mind was less difficult to develop. She was a woman of mean understanding, little information, and uncertain temper. When she was discontented, she fancied herself nervous. The business of her life was to get her daughters married; its solace was visiting and news.

Chapter 2

Mr. Bennet was among the earliest of those who waited on Mr. Bingley. He had always intended to visit him, though to the last always assuring his wife that he should not go; and till the evening after the visit was paid, she had no knowledge of it. It was then disclosed in the following manner. Observing his second daughter employed in trimming a hat, he suddenly addressed her with,

'I hope Mr. Bingley will like it, Lizzy.'

'We are not in a way to know *what* Mr. Bingley likes,' said her mother resentfully, 'since we are not to visit.'

'But you forget, mama,' said Elizabeth, 'that we shall meet him at the assemblies, and that Mrs. Long has promised to introduce him.'

'I do not believe Mrs. Long will do any such thing. She has two nieces of her own. She is a selfish, hypocritical woman, and I have no opinion of her.'

'No more have I,' said Mr. Bennet; 'and I am glad to find that you do not depend on her serving you.'

Mrs. Bennet deigned not to make any reply; but unable to contain herself, began scolding one of her daughters.

'Don't keep coughing so, Kitty, for heaven's sake! Have a little compassion on my nerves. You tear them to pieces.'

'Kitty has no discretion in her coughs,' said her father; 'she times them ill.'

'I do not cough for my own amusement,' replied Kitty fretfully.

'When is your next ball to be, Lizzy?'

'To-morrow fortnight.'

'Aye, so it is,' cried her mother, 'and Mrs. Long does not come back till the day before; so it will be impossible for her to introduce him, for she will not know him herself.'

'Then, my dear, you may have the advantage of your friend, and introduce Mr. Bingley to *her*.'

'Impossible, Mr. Bennet, impossible, when I am not acquainted with him myself; how can you be so teasing?'

'I honour your circumspection. A fortnight's acquaintance is certainly very little. One cannot know what a man really is by the end of a fortnight. But if *we* do not venture, somebody else will; and after all, Mrs. Long and her nieces must stand their chance; and therefore, as she will think it an act of kindness, if you decline the office, I will take it on myself.'

The girls stared at their father. Mrs. Bennet said only, 'Nonsense, nonsense!'

'What can be the meaning of that emphatic exclamation?' cried he. 'Do you consider the forms of introduction, and the stress that is laid on them, as nonsense? I cannot quite agree with you *there*. What say you, Mary? for you are a young lady of deep reflection I know, and read great books, and make extracts.'

Mary wished to say something very sensible, but knew not how.

'While Mary is adjusting her ideas,' he continued, 'let us return to Mr. Bingley.'

'I am sick of Mr. Bingley,' cried his wife.

'I am sorry to hear *that*; but why did not you tell me so before? If I had known as much this morning, I certainly would not have called on him. It is very unlucky; but as I have actually paid the visit, we cannot escape the acquaintance now.'

The astonishment of the ladies was just what he wished; that of Mrs. Bennet perhaps surpassing the rest; though when the first tumult of joy was over, she began to declare that it was what she had expected all the while.

'How good it was in you, my dear Mr. Bennet! But I knew I should persuade you at last. I was sure you loved your girls too well to neglect such an acquaintance. Well, how pleased I am! and it is such a good joke, too, that you should have gone this morning, and never said a word about it till now.'

'Now, Kitty, you may cough as much as you chuse,' said Mr. Bennet; and, as he spoke, he left the room, fatigued with the raptures of his wife.

'What an excellent father you have, girls,' said she, when the door was shut. 'I do not know how you will ever make him amends for his kindness; or me either, for that matter. At our time of life, it is not so pleasant I can tell you, to be making new acquaintance every day; but for your sakes, we would do any thing. Lydia, my love, though you are the youngest, I dare say Mr. Bingley will dance with you at the next ball.'

'Oh!' said Lydia stoutly, 'I am not afraid; for though I *am* the youngest, I'm the tallest.'

The rest of the evening was spent in conjecturing how soon he would return Mr. Bennet's visit, and determining when they should ask him to dinner.

Chapter 3

Not all that Mrs. Bennet, however, with the assistance of her five daughters, could ask on the subject was sufficient to draw from her husband any satisfactory description of Mr. Bingley. They attacked him in various ways; with barefaced questions, ingenious suppositions, and distant surmises; but he eluded the skill of them all; and they were at last obliged to accept the second-hand intelligence of their neighbour Lady Lucas. Her report was highly favourable. Sir William had been delighted with him. He was quite young, wonderfully handsome, extremely agreeable, and, to crown the whole, he meant to be at the next assembly with a large party. Nothing could be more delightful! To be fond of dancing was a certain step towards falling in love; and very lively hopes of Mr. Bingley's heart were entertained.

'If I can but see one of my daughters happily settled at Netherfield,' said Mrs. Bennet to her husband, 'and all the others equally well married, I shall have nothing to wish for.'

In a few days Mr. Bingley returned Mr. Bennet's visit, and sat about ten minutes with him in his library. He had entertained hopes of being admitted to a sight of the young ladies, of whose beauty he had heard much; but he saw only the father. The ladies were somewhat more fortunate, for they had the advantage of ascertaining, from an upper window, that he wore a blue coat and rode a black horse.

An invitation to dinner was soon afterwards dispatched; and already had Mrs. Bennet planned the courses that were to do credit to her housekeeping, when an answer arrived which deferred it all. Mr. Bingley was obliged to be in town the following day, and consequently unable to accept the honour of their invitation, &c. Mrs. Bennet was quite disconcerted. She could not imagine what business he could have in town so soon after his arrival in Hertfordshire; and she began to fear that he might be always flying about from one place to another, and never settled at Netherfield as he ought to be. Lady Lucas quieted her fears a little by starting the idea of his being gone to London only to get a large party for the ball; and a report soon followed that Mr. Bingley was to bring twelve ladies and seven gentlemen with him to the assembly. The girls grieved over such a large number of ladies; but were comforted the day before the ball by hearing that, instead of twelve, he had brought only six with him from London, his five sisters and a cousin. And when the party entered the assembly room, it consisted of only five altogether; Mr. Bingley, his two sisters, the husband of the oldest, and another young man.

Mr. Bingley was good looking and gentlemanlike; he had a pleasant countenance, and easy, unaffected manners. His brother-in-law, Mr. Hurst, merely looked the gentleman; but his friend Mr. Darcy soon drew the attention of the room by his fine, tall person, handsome features, noble mien; and the report which was in general circulation within five minutes after his entrance, of his having ten thousand a year. The gentlemen pronounced him to be a fine figure of a man, the ladies declared he was much handsomer than Mr. Bingley, and he was looked at with great admiration for about half the evening, till his manners gave a disgust which turned the tide of his popularity; for he was discovered to be proud, to be above his company, and above being pleased; and not all his large estate in Derbyshire could then save him from having a most forbidding, disagreeable countenance, and being unworthy to be compared with his friend.

Mr. Bingley had soon made himself acquainted with all the principal people in the room; he was lively and unreserved, danced every dance, was angry that the ball closed so early, and talked of giving one himself at Netherfield. Such amiable qualities must speak for themselves. What a contrast between him and his friend! Mr. Darcy danced only once with Mrs. Hurst and once with Miss Bingley, declined being introduced to any other lady, and spent the rest of the evening in walking about the room, speaking occasionally to one of his own party. His character was decided. He was the proudest, most disagreeable man in the world, and every body hoped that he would never come there again. Amongst the most violent against him was Mrs. Bennet, whose dislike of his general behaviour was sharpened into particular resentment by his having slighted one of her daughters.

Elizabeth Bennet had been obliged, by the scarcity of gentlemen, to sit down for two dances; and during part of that time, Mr. Darcy had been standing near enough for her to overhear a conversation between him and Mr. Bingley, who came from the dance for a few minutes to press his friend to join it.

'Come, Darcy,' said he, 'I must have you dance. I hate to see you standing about by yourself in this stupid manner. You had much better dance.'

'I certainly shall not. You know how I detest it, unless I am particularly acquainted with my partner. At such an assembly as this, it would be insupportable. Your sisters are engaged, and there is not another woman in the room whom it would not be a punishment to me to stand up with.'

'I would not be so fastidious as you are,' cried Bingley, 'for a kingdom! Upon my honour I never met with so many pleasant girls in my life, as I have this evening; and there are several of them, you see, uncommonly pretty.'

'*You* are dancing with the only handsome girl in the room,' said Mr. Darcy, looking at the eldest Miss Bennet.

'Oh! she is the most beautiful creature I ever beheld! But there is one of her sisters sitting down just behind you, who is very pretty, and I dare say very agreeable. Do let me ask my partner to introduce you.'

'Which do you mean?' and turning round, he looked for a moment at Elizabeth, till catching her eye, he withdrew his own and coldly said, 'She is tolerable; but not handsome enough to tempt *me*; and I am in no humour at present to give consequence to young ladies who are slighted by other men. You had better return to your partner and enjoy her smiles, for you are wasting your time with me.'

Mr. Bingley followed his advice. Mr. Darcy walked off; and Elizabeth remained with no very cordial feelings towards him. She told the story however with great spirit among her friends; for she had a lively, playful disposition, which delighted in any thing ridiculous.

The evening altogether passed off pleasantly to the whole family. Mrs. Bennet had seen her eldest daughter much admired by the Netherfield party. Mr. Bingley had danced with her twice, and she had been distinguished by his sisters. Jane was as much gratified by this as her mother could be, though in a quieter way. Elizabeth felt Jane's pleasure. Mary had heard herself mentioned to Miss Bingley as the most accomplished girl in the neighbourhood; and Catherine and Lydia had been fortunate enough to be never without partners, which was all that they had yet learnt to care for at a ball. They returned therefore, in good spirits to Longbourn, the village where they lived, and of which they were the principal inhabitants. They found Mr. Bennet still up. With a book, he was regardless of time; and on the present occasion he had a good deal of curiosity as to the event of an evening which had raised such splendid expectations. He had rather hoped that all his wife's views on the stranger would be disappointed; but he soon found that he had a very different story to hear.

'Oh! my dear Mr. Bennet,' as she entered the room, 'we have had a most delightful evening, a most excellent ball. I wish you had been there. Jane was so admired, nothing could be like it. Every body said how well she looked; and Mr. Bingley thought her quite beautiful, and danced with her twice. Only think of *that* my dear; he actually danced with her twice; and she was the only creature in the room that he asked a second time. First of all, he asked Miss Lucas. I was so vexed to see him stand up with her; but, however, he did not admire her at all: indeed, nobody can, you know; and he seemed quite struck with Jane as she was going down the dance. So, he enquired who she was, and got introduced, and asked her for the two next. Then, the two third he danced with Miss King, and the two fourth with Maria Lucas, and the two fifth with Jane again, and the two sixth with Lizzy, and the Boulanger –'

'If he had had any compassion for *me*,' cried her husband impatiently, 'he would not have danced half so much! For God's sake, say no more of his partners. Oh! that he had sprained his ankle in the first dance!'

'Oh! my dear,' continued Mrs. Bennet, 'I am quite delighted with him. He is so excessively handsome! and his sisters are charming women. I never in my life saw any thing more elegant than their dresses. I dare say the lace upon Mrs. Hurst's gown –'

Here she was interrupted again. Mr. Bennet protested against any description of finery. She was therefore obliged to seek another branch of the subject, and related, with much bitterness of spirit and some exaggeration, the shocking rudeness of Mr. Darcy.

'But I can assure you,' she added, 'that Lizzy does not lose much by not suiting *his* fancy; for he is a most disagreeable, horrid man, not at all worth pleasing. So high and so conceited that there was no enduring him! He walked here, and he walked there, fancying himself so very great! Not handsome enough to dance with! I wish you had been there, my dear, to have given him one of your set downs. I quite detest the man.'

Chapter 4

When Jane and Elizabeth were alone, the former, who had been cautious in her praise of Mr. Bingley before, expressed to her sister how very much she admired him.

'He is just what a young man ought to be,' said she, 'sensible, good humoured, lively; and I never saw such happy manners! – so much ease, with such perfect good breeding!'

'He is also handsome,' replied Elizabeth, 'which a young man ought likewise to be, if he possibly can. His character is thereby complete.'

'I was very much flattered by his asking me to dance a second time. I did not expect such a compliment.'

'Did not you? *I* did for you. But that is one great difference between us. Compliments always take *you* by surprise, and *me* never. What could be more natural than his asking you again? He could not help seeing that you were about five times as pretty as every other woman in the room. No thanks to his gallantry for that. Well, he certainly is very agreeable, and I give you leave to like him. You have liked many a stupider person.'

'Dear Lizzy!'

'Oh! you are a great deal too apt you know, to like people in general. You never see a fault in any body. All the world are good and agreeable in your eyes. I never heard you speak ill of a human being in my life.'

'I would wish not to be hasty in censuring any one; but I always speak what I think.'

'I know you do; and it is *that* which makes the wonder. With *your* good sense, to be honestly blind to the follies and nonsense of others! Affectation of candour is common enough; – one meets it every where. But to be candid without ostentation or design – to take the good of every body's character and make it still better, and say nothing of the bad – belongs to you alone. And so, you like this man's sisters too, do you? Their manners are not equal to his.'

'Certainly not; at first. But they are very pleasing women when you converse with them. Miss Bingley is to live with her brother and keep his house; and I am much mistaken if we shall not find a very charming neighbour in her.'

Elizabeth listened in silence, but was not convinced. Their behaviour at the assembly had not been calculated to please in general; and with more quickness of observation and less pliancy of temper than her sister, and with a judgment, too, unassailed by any attention to herself, she was very little disposed to approve them. They were in fact very fine ladies, not deficient in good humour when they were pleased, nor in the power of being agreeable where they chose it; but proud and conceited. They were rather handsome, had been educated in one of the first private seminaries in town, had a fortune of twenty thousand pounds, were in the habit of spending more than they ought, and of associating with people of rank; and were therefore in every respect entitled to think well of themselves, and meanly of others. They were of a respectable family in the north of England; a circumstance more deeply impressed on their memories than that their brother's fortune and their own had been acquired by trade.

Mr. Bingley inherited property to the amount of nearly an hundred thousand pounds from his father, who had intended to purchase an estate, but did not live to do it. – Mr. Bingley intended it likewise, and sometimes made choice of his county; but as he was now provided with a good house and the liberty of a manor, it was doubtful to many of those who best knew the easiness of his temper, whether he might not spend the remainder of his days at Netherfield, and leave the next generation to purchase.

His sisters were very anxious for his having an estate of his own; but though he was now established only as a tenant, Miss Bingley was by no means unwilling to preside at his table, nor was Mrs. Hurst, who had married a man of more fashion than fortune, less disposed to consider his house as her home when it suited her. Mr. Bingley had not been of age two years, when he was tempted by an accidental recommendation to look at Netherfield House. He did look at it and into it for half an hour, was pleased with the situation and the principal rooms, satisfied with what the owner said in its praise, and took it immediately.

Between him and Darcy there was a very steady friendship, in spite of a great opposition of character. – Bingley was endeared to Darcy by the easiness, openness, ductility of his temper, though no disposition could offer a greater contrast to his own, and though with his own he never appeared dissatisfied. On the strength of Darcy's regard Bingley had the firmest reliance, and of his judgment the highest opinion. In understanding, Darcy was the superior. Bingley was by no means deficient, but Darcy was clever. He was at the same time haughty, reserved, and fastidious, and his manners, though well bred, were not inviting. In that respect his friend had greatly the advantage. Bingley was sure of being liked wherever he appeared; Darcy was continually giving offence.

The manner in which they spoke of the Meryton assembly was sufficiently characteristic. Bingley had never met with pleasanter people or prettier girls in his life; every body had been most kind and attentive to him, there had been no formality, no stiffness; he had soon felt acquainted with all the room; and as to Miss Bennet, he could not conceive an angel more beautiful. Darcy, on the contrary, had seen a collection of people in whom there was little beauty and no fashion, for none of whom he had felt the smallest interest, and from none received either attention or pleasure. Miss Bennet he acknowledged to be pretty, but she smiled too much.

Mrs. Hurst and her sister allowed it to be so – but still they admired her and liked her, and pronounced her to be a sweet girl, and one whom they should not object to know more of. Miss Bennet was therefore established as a sweet girl, and their brother felt authorised by such commendation to think of her as he chose.

GEORGE GORDON, LORD BYRON
(1788–1824)

Byron's father was a wastrel who ruined two wealthy wives and died in debt in 1791. His child, George Gordon, inherited the title 'sixth baron Byron' through the unexpected demise of those more directly in line. He attended Harrow and Cambridge and accumulated enormous debts. His first volume of poetry, *Hours of Idleness* (1807) was generally thought facile. In 1809–11 he travelled extensively in the war-torn Mediterranean countries, notably Albania and Greece, then under Turkish rule. The highly successful first two cantos of *Childe Harold's Pilgrimage* (1812), based on this experience, launched Byron into society which he then outraged with scandalous affairs. His reputation of being notoriously bad fed the appetite of the age. His poetry sold in unprecedented quantities but ostracism and debt forced him to leave England in 1816. He lived in Italy and wrote Cantos III and IV of *Childe Harold, Don Juan* (17 Cantos, 1819–24) and other poems. In 1824 he supported the Greek uprising against Turkish dominion but died of fever before seeing action. His poetry was often derided as immoral but was hugely successful throughout Europe and America and inspired numerous imitations and repetitions in all the arts. 'The Byronic' became a universal topos, the work deriving from the life and constructing a persona and a voice, adventurous, gallant, charming, intolerant of hypocrisy, led by desire.

She Walks in Beauty

    She walks in beauty, like the night
    Of cloudless climes and starry skies;
    And all that's best of dark and bright
    Meet in her aspect and her eyes:
5   Thus mellow'd to that tender light
    Which heaven to gaudy day denies.

    On shade the more, one ray the less,
    Had half impair'd the nameless grace
    Which waves in every raven tress,
10   Or softly lightens o'er her face;
    Where thoughts serenely sweet express
    How pure, how dear their dwelling place.

    And on that cheek, and o'er that brow,
    So soft, so calm, yet eloquent,
15   The smiles that win, the tints that glow,
    But tell of days in goodness spent,
    A mind at peace with all below,
    A heart whose love is innocent!

From Don Juan, Canto I

I want a hero, an uncommon want,
When every year and month sends forth a new one,
Till after cloying the gazettes with cant,
The age discovers he is not the true one.
Of such as these I should not care to vaunt;
I'll therefore take our ancient friend Don Juan.
We all have seen him in the pantomime
Sent to the devil somewhat ere his time.

* * * *

6

Most epic poets plunge in *medias res*
(Horace makes this the heroic turnpike road),
And then your hero tells whene'er you please
What went before by way of episode,
While seated after dinner at his ease
Beside his mistress in some soft abode,
Palace or garden, paradise or cavern,
Which serves the happy couple for a tavern.

7

That is the usual method, but not mine;
My way is to begin with the beginning.
The regularity of my design
Forbids all wandering as the worst of sinning,
And therefore I shall open with a line
(Although it cost me half an hour in spinning)
Narrating somewhat of Don Juan's father
And also of his mother, if you'd rather.

8

In Seville was he born, a pleasant city,
Famous for oranges and women. He
Who has not seen it will be much to pity;
So says the proverb, and I quite agree.
Of all the Spanish towns is none more pretty;
Cadiz perhaps, but that you soon may see.
Don Juan's parents lived beside the river,
A noble stream, and called the Guadalquivir.

9

His father's name was Jóse – Don, of course.
A true hidalgo, free from every strain
Of Moor or Hebrew blood, he traced his source
Through the most Gothic gentlemen of Spain.

A better cavalier ne'er mounted horse,
Or being mounted e'er got down again,
Than Jóse, who begot our hero, who
Begot – but that's to come. Well, to renew:

10

His mother was a learnèd lady, famed
For every branch of every science known,
In every Christian language ever named,
With virtues equalled by her wit alone.
She made the cleverest people quite ashamed,
And even the good with inward envy groan,
Finding themselves so very much exceeded
In their own way by all the things that she did.

* * * *

38

Sagest of women, even of widows, she
Resolved that Juan should be quite a paragon,
And worthy of the noblest pedigree
(His sire was of Castile, his dam from Arragon).
Then for accomplishments of chivalry,
In case our lord the king should go to war again,
He learned the arts of riding, fencing, gunnery,
And how to scale a fortress – or a nunnery.

39

But that which Donna Inez most desired
And saw into herself each day before all
The learnèd tutors whom for him she hired
Was that his breeding should be strictly moral.
Much into all his studies she inquired,
And so they were submitted first to her, all
Arts, sciences; no branch was made a mystery
To Juan's eyes, excepting natural history.

40

The languages, especially the dead,
The sciences, and most of all the abstruse,
The arts, at least all such as could be said
To be the most remote from common use,
In all these he was much and deeply read,
But not a page of anything that's loose
Or hints continuation of the species
Was ever suffered, lest he should grow vicious.

* * * *

44

Juan was taught from out the best edition,
Expurgated by learnèd men, who place
Judiciously from out the schoolboy's vision
The grosser parts, but fearful to deface
Too much their modest bard by this omission
And pitying sore his mutilated case,
They only add them all in an appendix,
Which saves in fact the trouble of an index,

45

For there we have them all at one fell swoop,
Instead of being scattered through the pages.
They stand forth marshalled in a handsome troop
To meet the ingenuous youth of future ages,
Till some less rigid editor shall stoop
To call them back into their separate cages,
Instead of standing staring altogether
Like garden gods – and not so decent either.

46

The missal too (it was the family missal)
Was ornamented in a sort of way
Which ancient mass-books often are, and this all
Kinds of grotesques illumined; and how they
Who saw those figures on the margin kiss all
Could turn their optics to the text and pray
Is more than I know, but Don Juan's mother
Kept this herself and gave her son another.

* * * *

54

Young Juan now was sixteen years of age,
Tall, handsome, slender, but well knit; he seemed
Active, though not so sprightly as a page,
And everybody but his mother deemed
Him almost man, but she flew in a rage
And bit her lips (for else she might have screamed),
If any said so, for to be precocious
Was in her eyes a thing the most atrocious.

55

Amongst her numerous acquaintance, all
Selected for discretion and devotion,
There was the Donna Julia, whom to call
Pretty were but to give a feeble notion

Of many charms in her as natural
As sweetness to the flower or salt to ocean,
Her zone to Venus or his bow to Cupid,
But this last simile is trite and stupid.

56
The darkness of her oriental eye
Accorded with her Moorish origin.
Her blood was not all Spanish, by the by;
In Spain, you know, this is a sort of sin.
When proud Grenada fell, and forced to fly,
Boabdil wept, of Donna Julia's kin
Some went to Africa, some stayed in Spain.
Her great-great-grandmamma chose to remain.

* * * *

69
Juan she saw and as a pretty child,
Caressed him often. Such a thing might be
Quite innocently done and harmless styled
When she had twenty years, and thirteen he;
But I am not so sure I should have smiled
When he was sixteen, Julia twenty-three.
These few short years make wondrous alterations,
Particularly amongst sunburnt nations.

70
Whate'er the cause might be, they had become
Changed, for the dame grew distant, the youth shy,
Their looks cast down, their greetings almost dumb,
And much embarrassment in either eye.
There surely will be little doubt with some
That Donna Julia knew the reason why,
But as for Juan, he had no more notion
Than he who never saw the sea of ocean.

71
Yet Julia's very coldness still was kind,
And tremulously gentle her small hand
Withdrew itself from his, but left behind
A little pressure, thrilling and so bland
And slight, so very slight that to the mind
'Twas but a doubt; but ne'er magician's wand
Wrought change with all Armida's fairy art
Like what this light touch left on Juan's heart.

56, 6 **Boabdil**: last Moorish king of Granada.

71, 7 **Armida**: benign sorceress in the epic poem *Jerusalem Delivered* (1580–81) by Torquato Tasso (1544–95) who leads the hero to forget his crusader's vows.

72

And if she met him, though she smiled no more,
She looked a sadness sweeter than her smile,
As if her heart had deeper thoughts in store
She must not own, but cherished more the while,
For that compression in its burning core.
Even innocence itself has many a wile
And will not dare to trust itself with truth,
And love is taught hypocrisy from youth.

73

But passion most dissembles yet betrays
Even by its darkness; as the blackest sky
Foretells the heaviest tempest, it displays
Its workings through the vainly guarded eye,
And in whatever aspect it arrays
Itself, 'tis still the same hypocrisy.
Coldness or anger, even disdain or hate
Are masks it often wears, and still too late.

74

Then there were sighs, the deeper for suppression,
And stolen glances, sweeter for the theft,
And burning blushes, though for no transgression,
Tremblings when met and restlessness when left.
All these are little preludes to possession,
Of which young passion cannot be bereft,
And merely tend to show how greatly love is
Embarrassed at first starting with a novice.

75

Poor Julia's heart was in an awkward state;
She felt it going and resolved to make
The noblest efforts for herself and mate,
For honour's, pride's, religion's, virtue's sake.
Her resolutions were most truly great
And almost might have made a Tarquin quake.
She prayed the Virgin Mary for her grace,
As being the best judge of a lady's case.

76

She vowed she never would see Juan more
And next day paid a visit to his mother
And looked extremely at the opening door,
Which by the Virgin's grace, let in another.

Grateful she was and yet a little sore.
Again it opens, it can be no other,
'Tis surely Juan now. No, I'm afraid
That night the Virgin was no further prayed.

* * * *

86

So much for Julia; now we'll turn to Juan.
Poor little fellow, he had no idea
Of his own case and never hit the true one.
In feelings quick as Ovid's Miss Medea,
He puzzled over what he found, a new one,
But not as yet imagined it could be a
Thing quite in course and not at all alarming,
Which with a little patience might grow charming.

87

Silent and pensive, idle, restless, slow,
His home deserted for the lonely wood,
Tormented with a wound he could not know,
His, like all deep grief, plunged in solitude.
I'm fond myself of solitude or so,
But then I beg it may be understood;
By solitude I mean a sultan's, not
A hermit's, with a harem for a grot.

* * * *

90

Young Juan wandered by the glassy brooks
Thinking unutterable things. He threw
Himself at length within the leafy nooks
Where the wild branch of the cork forest grew.
There poets find materials for their books,
And every now and then we read them through,
So that their plan and prosody are eligible,
Unless like Wordsworth they prove unintelligible.

91

He, Juan (and not Wordsworth), so pursued
His self-communion with his own high soul
Until his mighty heart in its great mood
Had mitigated part, though not the whole
Of its disease. He did the best he could
With things not very subject to control
And turned, without perceiving his condition,
Like Coleridge into a metaphysician.

92

He thought about himself and the whole earth,
Of man the wonderful and of the stars
And how the deuce they ever could have birth,
And then he thought of earthquakes and of wars,
How many miles the moon might have in girth,
Of air balloons and of the many bars
To perfect knowledge of the boundless skies.
And then he thought of Donna Julia's eyes.

93

In thoughts like these true wisdom may discern
Longings sublime and aspirations high,
Which some are born with, but the most part learn
To plague themselves withal, they know not why.
'Twas strange that one so young should thus concern
His brain about the action of the sky.
If you think 'twas philosophy that this did,
I can't help thinking puberty assisted.

94

He pored upon the leaves and on the flowers
And heard a voice in all the winds; and then
He thought of wood nymphs and immortal bowers,
And how the goddesses came down to men.
He missed the pathway, he forgot the hours,
And when he looked upon his watch again,
He found how much old Time had been a winner.
He also found that he had lost his dinner.

* * * *

103

'Twas on a summer's day, the sixth of June –
I like to be particular in dates,
Not only of the age and year, but moon.
They are a sort of post-house, where the Fates
Change horses, making history change its tune,
Then spur away o'er empires and o'er states,
Leaving at last not much besides chronology,
Excepting the post-obits of theology.

104

'Twas on the sixth of June about the hour
Of half-past six, perhaps still nearer seven,
When Julia sate within as pretty a bower
As e'er held houri in that heathenish heaven

104, 4 houri: in Muslim belief, a nymph of paradise.

Described by Mahomet and Anacreon Moore,
To whom the lyre and laurels have been given
With all the trophies of triumphant song.
He won them well, and may he wear them long!

      * * * *

106

How beautiful she looked! Her conscious heart
Glowed in her cheek, and yet she felt no wrong.
Oh Love, how perfect is thy mystic art,
Strengthening the weak and trampling on the strong.
How self-deceitful is the sagest part
Of mortals whom thy lure hath led along.
The precipice she stood on was immense,
So was her creed in her own innocence.

107

She thought of her own strength and Juan's youth
And of the folly of all prudish fears,
Victorious virtue and domestic truth,
And then of Don Alfonso's fifty years.
I wish these last had not occurred in sooth,
Because that number rarely much endears
And through all climes, the snowy and the sunny,
Sounds ill in love, whate'er it may in money.

      * * * *

109

Julia had honour, virtue, truth, and love
For Don Alfonso, and she inly swore
By all the vows below to powers above,
She never would disgrace the ring she wore
Nor leave a wish which wisdom might reprove.
And while she pondered this, besides much more,
One hand on Juan's carelessly was thrown,
Quite by mistake – she thought it was her own.

110

Unconsciously she leaned upon the other,
Which played within the tangles of her hair.
And to contend with thoughts she could not smother,
She seemed by the distraction of her air.
'Twas surely very wrong in Juan's mother
To leave together this imprudent pair,
She who for many years had watched her son so.
I'm very certain mine would not have done so.

104, 5 Moore: Thomas Moore (1779–1852), a friend of   **107, 4 Don Alfonso:** Julia's husband.
Byron who translated the *Odes* of Anacreon.

111

The hand which still held Juan's, by degrees
Gently but palpably confirmed its grasp,
As if it said, 'Detain me, if you please.'
Yet there's no doubt she only meant to clasp
His fingers with a pure Platonic squeeze.
She would have shrunk as from a toad or asp,
Had she imagined such a thing could rouse
A feeling dangerous to a prudent spouse.

112

I cannot know what Juan thought of this,
But what he did is much what you would do.
His young lip thanked it with a grateful kiss
And then abashed at its own joy, withdrew
In deep despair, lest he had done amiss.
Love is so very timid when 'tis new.
She blushed and frowned not, but she strove to speak
And held her tongue, her voice was grown so weak.

* * * *

116

Oh Plato, Plato, you have paved the way
With your confounded fantasies to more
Immoral conduct by the fancied sway
Your system feigns o'er the controlless core
Of human hearts than all the long array
Of poets and romancers. You're a bore,
A charlatan, a coxcomb, and have been
At best no better than a go-between.

117

And Julia's voice was lost, except in sighs,
Until too late for useful conversation.
The tears were gushing from her gentle eyes;
I wish indeed they had not had occasion,
But who, alas, can love and then be wise?
Not that remorse did not oppose temptation;
A little still she strove and much repented,
And whispering, 'I will ne'er consent' – consented.

* * * *

120

Here my chaste Muse a liberty must take.
Start not, still chaster reader, she'll be nice hence –
Forward, and there is no great cause to quake.
This liberty is a poetic licence,

Which some irregularity may make
In the design, and as I have a high sense
Of Aristotle and the rules, 'tis fit
To beg his pardon when I err a bit.

121

This licence is to hope the reader will
Suppose from June the sixth (the fatal day,
Without whose epoch my poetic skill
For want of facts would all be thrown away),
But keeping Julia and Don Juan still
In sight, that several months have passed. We'll say
'Twas in November, but I'm not so sure
About the day; the era's more obscure.

* * * *

135

'Twas, as the watchmen say, a cloudy night,
No moon, no stars; the wind was low or loud
By gusts. And many a sparkling hearth was bright
With the piled wood, round which the family crowd.
There's something cheerful in that sort of light,
Even as a summer's sky's without a cloud.
I'm fond of fire and crickets and all that,
A lobster salad and champagne and chat.

136

'Twas midnight, Donna Julia was in bed,
Sleeping, most probably, when at her door
Arose a clatter might awake the dead,
If they had never been awoke before,
And that they have been so we all have read,
And are to be so, at the least, once more.
The door was fastened, but with voice and fist
First knocks were heard, then 'Madam – Madam – hist!

137

'For God's sake, Madam – Madam – here's my master
With more than half the city at his back.
Was ever heard of such a curst disaster!
'Tis not my fault – I kept good watch – alack!
Do, pray undo the bolt a little faster.
They're on the stair just now and in a crack
Will all be here. Perhaps he yet may fly.
Surely the window's not so very high!'

138

By this time Don Alfonso was arrived
With torches, friends, and servants in great number.
The major part of them had long been wived
And therefore paused not to disturb the slumber
Of any wicked woman, who contrived
By stealth her husband's temples to encumber.
Examples of this kind are so contagious,
Were one not punished, all would be outrageous.

139

I can't tell how or why or what suspicion
Could enter into Don Alfonso's head,
But for a cavalier of his condition
It surely was exceedingly ill-bred,
Without a word of previous admonition,
To hold a levee round his lady's bed
And summon lackeys, armed with fire and sword,
To prove himself the thing he most abhorred.

140

Poor Donna Julia, starting as from sleep
(Mind – that I do not say she had not slept),
Began at once to scream and yawn and weep.
Her maid Antonia, who was an adept,
Contrived to fling the bedclothes in a heap,
As if she had just now from out them crept.
I can't tell why she should take all this trouble
To prove her mistress had been sleeping double.

141

But Julia mistress and Antonia maid
Appeared like two poor harmless women, who
Of goblins, but still more of men afraid,
Had thought one man might be deterred by two,
And therefore side by side were gently laid,
Until the hours of absence should run through,
And truant husband should return and say,
'My dear, I was the first who came away.'

142

Now Julia found at length a voice and cried,
'In heaven's name, Don Alfonso, what d'ye mean?
Has madness seized you? Would that I had died
Ere such a monster's victim I had been!

What may this midnight violence betide,
A sudden fit of drunkenness or spleen?
Dare you suspect me, whom the thought would kill?
Search then the room!' Alfonso said, 'I will.'

143

He searched, they searched and rummaged everywhere,
Closet and clothespress, chest and window seat,
And found much linen, lace, and several pair
Of stockings, slippers, brushes, combs, complete
With other articles of ladies fair,
To keep them beautiful or leave them neat.
Arras they pricked and curtains with their swords
And wounded several shutters and some boards.

144

Under the bed they searched and there they found –
No matter what; it was not that they sought.
They opened windows, gazing if the ground
Had signs or footmarks, but the earth said nought;
And then they stared each others' faces round.
'Tis odd, not one of all these seekers thought,
And seems to me almost a sort of blunder,
Of looking in the bed as well as under.

145

During this inquisition Julia's tongue
Was not asleep. 'Yes, search and search,' she cried,
'Insult on insult heap, and wrong on wrong!
It was for this that I became a bride!
For this in silence I have suffered long
A husband like Alfonso at my side,
But now I'll bear no more nor here remain,
If there be law or lawyers in all Spain.

146

'Yes, Don Alfonso, husband now no more,
If ever you indeed deserved the name,
Is't worthy of your years? You have threescore,
Fifty or sixty – it is all the same.
Is't wise or fitting causeless to explore
For facts against a virtuous woman's fame?
Ungrateful, perjured, barbarous Don Alfonso,
How dare you think your lady would go on so?

* * * *

159

The Señor Don Alfonso stood confused.
Antonia bustled round the ransacked room
And turning up her nose, with looks abused
Her master and his myrmidons, of whom
Not one, except the attorney, was amused.
He, like Achates faithful to the tomb,
So there were quarrels, cared not for the cause,
Knowing they must be settled by the laws.

160

With prying snub-nose and small eyes, he stood,
Following Antonia's motions here and there,
With much suspicion in his attitude.
For reputations he had little care,
So that a suit or action were made good.
Small pity had he for the young and fair
And ne'er believed in negatives, till these
Were proved by competent false witnesses.

161

But Don Alfonso stood with downcast looks,
And truth to say he made a foolish figure.
When after searching in five hundred nooks
And treating a young wife with so much rigour,
He gained no point, except some self-rebukes,
Added to those his lady with such vigour
Had poured upon him for the last half-hour,
Quick, thick, and heavy as a thunder-shower.

162

At first he tried to hammer an excuse,
To which the sole reply were tears and sobs
And indications of hysterics, whose
Prologue is always certain throes and throbs,
Gasps and whatever else the owners choose.
Alfonso saw his wife and thought of Job's.
He saw too in perspective her relations,
And then he tried to muster all his patience.

163

He stood in act to speak or rather stammer,
But sage Antonia cut him short before
The anvil of his speech received the hammer,
With 'Pray sir, leave the room and say no more,

159, 6 Achates: faithful companion of Aeneas.

Or madam dies.' Alfonso muttered, 'Damn her,'
But nothing else. The time of words was o'er.
He cast a rueful look or two and did,
He knew not wherefore, that which he was bid.

164
With him retired his *posse comitatus,*
The attorney last, who lingered near the door
Reluctantly, still tarrying there as late as
Antonia let him, not a little sore
At this most strange and unexplained hiatus
In Don Alfonso's facts, which just now wore
An awkward look. As he revolved the case,
The door was fastened in his legal face.

165
No sooner was it bolted than – oh shame,
Oh sin, oh sorrow, and oh womankind!
How can you do such things and keep your fame,
Unless this world and t'other too be blind?
Nothing so dear as an unfilched good name.
But to proceed, for there is more behind.
With much heartfelt reluctance be it said,
Young Juan slipped, half-smothered, from the bed.

* * * *

169
What's to be done? Alfonso will be back
The moment he has sent his fools away.
Antonia's skill was put upon the rack,
But no device could be brought into play.
And how to parry the renewed attack?
Besides it wanted but few hours of day.
Antonia puzzled; Julia did not speak,
But pressed her bloodless lip to Juan's cheek.

170
He turned his lip to hers and with his hand
Called back the tangles of her wandering hair.
Even then their love they could not all command
And half forgot their danger and despair.
Antonia's patience now was at a stand;
'Come, come, 'tis no time now for fooling there,'
She whispered in great wrath. 'I must deposit
This pretty gentleman within the closet.'

* * * *

173

Now Don Alfonso entering, but alone,
Closed the oration of the trusty maid.
She loitered, and he told her to be gone,
An order somewhat sullenly obeyed.
However, present remedy was none,
And no great good seemed answered if she stayed.
Regarding both with slow and sidelong view,
She snuffed the candle, curtsied, and withdrew.

174

Alfonso paused a minute, then begun
Some strange excuses for his late proceeding.
He would not justify what he had done;
To say the best, it was extreme ill-breeding,
But there were ample reasons for it, none
Of which he specified in this his pleading.
His speech was a fine sample, on the whole,
Of rhetoric, which the learn'd call rigmarole.

175

Julia said nought, though all the while there rose
A ready answer, which at once enables
A matron who her husband's foible knows,
By a few timely words to turn the tables,
Which if it does not silence still must pose,
Even if it should comprise a pack of fables:
'Tis to retort with firmness and when he
Suspects with one, do you reproach with three.

* * * *

180

Alfonso closed his speech and begged her pardon,
Which Julia half withheld and then half granted
And laid conditions, he thought, very hard on,
Denying several little things he wanted.
He stood like Adam lingering near his garden,
With useless penitence perplexed and haunted,
Beseeching she no further would refuse,
When lo! he stumbled o'er a pair of shoes.

181

A pair of shoes. What then? Not much, if they
Are such as fit with ladies' feet, but these
(No one can tell how much I grieve to say)
Were masculine. To see them and to seize

Was but a moment's act. Ah, well-a-day,
My teeth begin to chatter, my veins freeze.
Alfonso first examined well their fashion
And then flew out into another passion.

182

He left the room for his relinquished sword,
And Julia instant to the closet flew.
'Fly, Juan, fly! For heaven's sake, not a word!
The door is open. You may yet slip through
The passage you so often have explored.
Here is the garden key. Fly – fly – adieu!
Haste – haste! I hear Alfonso's hurrying feet.
Day has not broke, there's no one in the street.'

183

None can say that this was not good advice;
The only mischief was it came too late.
Of all experience 'tis the usual price,
A sort of income tax laid on by fate.
Juan had reached the room door in a trice
And might have done so by the garden gate,
But met Alfonso in his dressing gown,
Who threatened death – so Juan knocked him down.

184

Dire was the scuffle and out went the light.
Antonia cried out 'Rape!' and Julia 'Fire!'
But not a servant stirred to aid the fight.
Alfonso, pommelled to his heart's desire,
Swore lustily he'd be revenged this night;
And Juan too blasphemed an octave higher.
His blood was up; though young, he was a Tartar
And not at all disposed to prove a martyr.

185

Alfonso's sword had dropped ere he could draw it,
And they continued battling hand to hand,
For Juan very luckily ne'er saw it.
His temper not being under great command,
If at that moment he had chanced to claw it,
Alfonso's days had not been in the land
Much longer. Think of husbands', lovers' lives,
And how ye may be doubly widows – wives!

186

Alfonso grappled to detain the foe,
And Juan throttled him to get away,
And blood ('twas from the nose) began to flow.
At last as they more faintly wrestling lay,
Juan contrived to give an awkward blow,
And then his only garment quite gave way.
He fled, like Joseph, leaving it, but there
I doubt, all likeness ends between the pair.

187

Lights came at length, and men and maids, who found
An awkward spectacle their eyes before.
Antonia in hysterics, Julia swooned,
Alfonso leaning breathless by the door,
Some half-torn drapery scattered on the ground,
Some blood and several footsteps, but no more.
Juan the gate gained, turned the key about,
And liking not the inside, locked the out.

188

Here ends this canto. Need I sing or say
How Juan naked, favoured by the night,
Who favours what she should not, found his way
And reached his home in an unseemly plight?
The pleasant scandal which arose next day,
The nine days' wonder which was brought to light,
And how Alfonso sued for a divorce
Were in the English newspapers, of course.

* * * *

199

This was Don Juan's earliest scrape; but whether
I shall proceed with his adventures is
Dependent on the public altogether.
We'll see, however, what they say to this;
Their favour in an author's cap's a feather,
And no great mischief's done by their caprice,
And if their approbation we experience,
Perhaps they'll have some more about a year hence.

200

My poem's epic and is meant to be
Divided in twelve books, each book containing,
With love and war, a heavy gale at sea,
A list of ships and captains and kings reigning,

New characters; the episodes are three.
A panoramic view of hell's in training,
After the style of Virgil and of Homer,
So that my name of epic's no misnomer.

201

All these things will be specified in time
With strict regard to Aristotle's rules,
The *vade mecum* of the true sublime,
Which makes so many poets and some fools.
Prose poets like blank verse; I'm fond of rhyme.
Good workmen never quarrel with their tools.
I've got new mythological machinery
And very handsome supernatural scenery.

202

There's only one slight difference between
Me and my epic brethren gone before,
And here the advantage is my own, I ween
(Not that I have not several merits more,
But this will more peculiarly be seen).
They so embellish that 'tis quite a bore
Their labyrinth of fables to thread through,
Whereas this story's actually true.

203

If any person doubt it, I appeal
To history, tradition, and to facts,
To newspapers, whose truth all know and feel,
To plays in five, and operas in three acts.
All these confirm my statement a good deal,
But that which more completely faith exacts
Is that myself and several now in Seville
Saw Juan's last elopement with the devil.

* * * *

216

My days of love are over, me no more
The charms of maid, wife, and still less of widow
Can make the fool of which they made before;
In short, I must not lead the life I did do.
The credulous hope of mutual minds is o'er,
The copious use of claret is forbid too,
So for a good old-gentlemanly vice,
I think I must take up with avarice.

201, 3 *vade mecum*: a handbook.

PERCY BYSSHE SHELLEY (1792–1822)

Percy Bysshe Shelley was the son of a wealthy MP for Sussex of aristocratic descent, and was educated at Eton and Oxford where he read Godwin and Paine with enthusiasm. He was expelled in 1811 for atheism. His first publications were Gothic stories and verses. He married unwisely and engaged in radical politics. In 1813 he published his first major work, *Queen Mab*, a prophetic and allegorical poem which offered a Godwinian denunciation of Regency society and proposed a communist utopia. In 1814 he abandoned his wife and eloped to France with Wollstonecraft and Godwin's daughter, Mary, scandalising family, friends and society. In the following years he lived a wandering existence in London and Italy. In 1819–20 he experienced an *annus mirabilis* in which he completed *Prometheus Unbound* (1820), wrote a satire on Wordsworth, *Peter Bell the Third*, the brilliant political poems *The Mask of Anarchy* and 'To Liberty', as well as his 'Ode to the West Wind', many fine lyrics, and the verse tragedy *The Cenci*. In the following year he wrote *A Defence of Poetry*, *Epipsychidon*, *Adonais* on the death of Keats, and a drama, *Hellas*, concerning the Greek struggle for emancipation. In 1822 he drowned when sailing across the bay of Lerici. He was the most political and most radical of all the romantic poets, a passionate advocate of liberty and a brilliant critic of the half-truths that are used to enslave. He was widely read and could deploy different verse forms with extraordinary fluency.

Mont Blanc

Lines Written In The Vale Of Chamouni

I

The everlasting universe of things
Flows through the mind, and rolls its rapid waves,
Now dark – now glittering – now reflecting gloom –
Now lending splendour, where from secret springs
5 The source of human thought its tribute brings
Of waters, – with a sound but half its own,
Such as a feeble brook will oft assume
In the wild woods, among the mountains lone,
Where waterfalls around it leap forever,
10 Where woods and winds contend, and a vast river
Over its rocks ceaselessly bursts and raves.

II

Thus thou, Ravine of Arve – dark, deep Ravine –
Thou many-coloured many-voiced vale,
Over whose pines and crags and caverns sail
15 Fast cloud shadows and sunbeams; awful scene,
Where Power in likeness of the Arve comes down
From the ice gulfs that gird his secret throne,

Bursting through these dark mountains like the flame
Of lightning through the tempest; – thou dost lie,
20 Thy giant brood of pines around thee clinging,
Children of elder time, in whose devotion
The chainless winds still come and ever came
To drink their odours, and their mighty swinging
To hear, an old and solemn harmony;
25 Thine earthly rainbows stretched across the sweep
Of the etherial waterfall, whose veil
Robes some unsculptured image; the strange sleep
Which, when the voices of the desert fail,
Wraps all in its own deep eternity;
30 Thy caverns echoing to the Arve's commotion
A loud lone sound no other sound can tame.
Thou art pervaded with that ceaseless motion
Thou art the path of that unresting sound,
Dizzy Ravine! And, when I gaze on thee,
35 I seem, as in a trance sublime and strange,
To muse on my own separate fantasy,
My own, my human mind, which passively
Now renders and receives fast influencings,
Holding an unremitting interchange
40 With the clear universe of Things around;
One legion of wild thoughts, whose wandering wings
Now float above thy darkness, and now rest
Where that or thou art no unbidden guest,
In the still cave of the witch Poesy, –
45 Seeking among the shadows that pass by,
Ghosts of all things that are, some shade of thee,
Some phantom, some faint image. Till the breast
From which they fled recalls them, thou art there!

III

Some say that gleams of a remoter world
50 Visit the soul in sleep, – that death is slumber,
And that its shapes the busy thoughts outnumber
Of those who wake and live. I look on high;
Has some unknown omnipotence unfurled
The veil of life and death? Or do I lie
55 In dream, and does the mightier world of sleep
Spread far around and inaccessibly
Its circles? For the very spirit fails,
Driven like a homeless cloud from steep to steep
That vanishes among the viewless gales!
60 Far, far above, piercing the infinite sky,
Mont Blanc appears – still, snowy, and serene.

Its subject mountains their unearthly forms
Pile around it, ice and rock; broad vales between
Of frozen floods, unfathomable deeps,
65 Blue as the overhanging heaven, that spread
And wind among the accumulated steeps;
A desert peopled by the storms alone,
Save when the eagle brings some hunter's bone,
And the wolf tracks her there. How hideously
70 Its shapes are heaped around! rude, bare, and high,
Ghastly and scarred and riven. – Is this the scene
Where the old Earthquake-daemon taught her young
Ruin? Were these their toys? or did a sea
Of fire envelop once this silent snow?
75 None can reply – all seems eternal now.
The wilderness has a mysterious tongue
Which teaches awful doubt, or faith so mild,
So solemn, so serene, that man may be
But for such faith, with nature reconciled;
80 Thou hast a voice, great Mountain, to repeal
Large codes of fraud and woe; not understood
By all, but which the wise and great and good
Interpret, or make felt, or deeply feel.

IV

The fields, the lakes, the forests, and the streams,
85 Ocean, and all the living things that dwell
Within the daedal earth, lightning and rain,
Earthquake and fiery flood and hurricane,
The torpor of the year when feeble dreams
Visit the hidden buds, or dreamless sleep
90 Holds every future leaf and flower, the bound
With which from that detested trance they leap,
The works and ways of man, their death and birth,
And that of him, and all that his may be,
All things that move and breathe, with toil and sound
95 Are born and die, revolve, subside, and swell.
Power dwells apart in its tranquillity,
Remote, serene, and inaccessible:
And this the naked countenance of earth
On which I gaze, even these primaeval mountains,
100 Teach the adverting mind. The glaciers creep,
Like snakes that watch their prey, from their far fountains,
Slow rolling on; there, many a precipice
Frost and the Sun in scorn of mortal power
Have piled: dome, pyramid, and pinnacle,

---

86 **daedal**: from Daedalus, maker of labyrinths.

105 A city of death, distinct with many a tower
And wall impregnable of beaming ice.
Yet not a city, but a flood of ruin,
Is there, that from the boundaries of the sky
Rolls its perpetual stream; vast pines are strewing
110 Its destined path, or in the mangled soil
Branchless and shattered stand; the rocks, drawn down
From yon remotest waste, have overthrown
The limits of the dead and living world,
Never to be reclaimed. The dwelling-place
115 Of insects, beasts, and birds, becomes its spoil;
Their food and their retreat for ever gone,
So much of life and joy is lost. The race
Of man flies far in dread; his work and dwelling
Vanish, like smoke before the tempest's stream,
120 And their place is not known. Below, vast caves
Shine in the rushing torrents' restless gleam,
Which, from those secret chasms in tumult welling,
Meet in the Vale; and one majestic River,
The breath and blood of distant lands, for ever
125 Rolls its loud waters to the ocean waves,
Breathes its swift vapours to the circling air.

V

Mont Blanc yet gleams on high: the power is there,
The still and solemn power, of many sights
And many sounds, and much of life and death.
130 In the calm darkness of the moonless nights,
In the lone glare of day, the snows descend
Upon that Mountain; none beholds them there,
Nor when the flakes burn in the sinking sun,
Or the star-beams dart through them. Winds contend
135 Silently there, and heap the snow, with breath
Rapid and strong, but silently. Its home
The voiceless lightning in these solitudes
Keeps innocently, and like vapour broods
Over the snow. The secret strength of things,
140 Which governs thought, and to the infinite dome
Of heaven is as a law, inhabits thee!
And what were thou and earth and stars and sea,
If to the human mind's imaginings
Silence and solitude were vacancy?

Ozymandias

I met a traveller from an antique land
Who said: 'Two vast and trunkless legs of stone
Stand in the desert. Near them on the sand,
Half sunk, a shattered visage lies, whose frown
5   And wrinkled lip and sneer of cold command,
Tell that its sculptor well those passions read
Which yet survive, stamped on these lifeless things
The hand that mocked them and the heart that fed.
And on the pedestal these words appear:
10   "My name is Ozymandias, King of Kings:
Look on my Works, ye Mighty, and despair."
Nothing beside remains. Round the decay
Of that colossal Wreck, boundless and bare,
The lone and level sands stretch far away.'

England in 1819

An old, mad, blind, despised, and dying King,
Princes, the dregs of their dull race, who flow
Through public scorn, mud from a muddy spring
Rulers who neither see nor feel nor know,
5   But leechlike to their fainting country cling,
Till they drop, blind in blood, without a blow,
A people starved and stabbed in the untilled field
An army which liberticide and prey
Make as a two-edged sword to all who wield;
10   Golden and sanguine laws which tempt and slay
Religion Christless, Godless – a book sealed,
A senate, Time's worst statute unrepealed –
Are graves from which a glorious Phantom may
Burst to illumine our tempestuous day.

The Cloud

I bring fresh showers for the thirsting flowers,
From the seas and the streams;
I bear light shade for the leaves when laid
In their noonday dreams.
5   From my wings are shaken the dews that waken

Ozymandias: the Pharaoah Rameses II, whose tomb at
Thebes is in the shape of a sphinx.   England in 1819:
The king was George III, long dying of a debilitating
illness, the country ruled meanwhile by the Regent, his
son, the Prince of Wales.

England in 1819   7 field: St Peter's Field, Manchester;
the poem was occasioned by the Peterloo massacre when
drunken troops charged a peaceful demonstation in favour of Parliamentary reform.   12 unrepealed: the law
barring Dissenters and Catholics from public
office, long a subject of reformist demands.

The sweet buds every one,
When rocked to rest on their mother's breast,
As she dances about the Sun.
I wield the flail of the lashing hail,
10 And whiten the green plains under;
And then again I dissolve it in rain,
And laugh as I pass in thunder.

I sift the snow on the mountains below,
And their great pines groan aghast;
15 And all the night 'tis my pillow white,
While I sleep in the arms of the blast.
Sublime on the towers of my skiey bowers
Lightning my pilot sits;
In a cavern under is fettered the thunder,
20 It struggles and howls at fits;
Over earth and ocean with gentle motion
This pilot is guiding me,
Lured by the love of the genii that move
In the depths of the purple sea;
25 Over the rills and the crags and the hills,
Over the lakes and the plains,
Wherever he dream under mountain or stream
The Spirit he loves remains;
And I all the while bask in heaven's blue smile,
30 Whilst he is dissolving in rains.

The sanguine Sunrise, with his meteor eyes,
And his burning plumes outspread,
Leaps on the back of my sailing rack,
When the morning star shines dead:
35 As on the jag of a mountain crag
Which an earthquake rocks and swings
An eagle alit one moment may sit
In the light of its golden wings.
And, when Sunset may breathe, from the lit sea beneath,
40 Its ardours of rest and of love,
And the crimson pall of eve may fall
From the depth of heaven above,
With wings folded I rest on mine airy nest,
As still as a brooding dove.

45 That orbed maiden with white fire laden
Whom mortals call the Moon

---

20 at fits: fitfully. **33 rack:** probably as in wrack, **41 pall:** cloth covering a coffin.
the remnant of a storm.

Glides glimmering o'er my fleece-like floor
By the midnight breezes strewn;
And wherever the beat of her unseen feet,
50   Which only the angels hear,
May have broken the woof of my tent's thin roof,
The stars peep behind her and peer.
And I laugh to see them whirl and flee
Like a swarm of golden bees,
55   When I widen the rent in my wind-built tent,
Till the calm rivers, lakes, and seas,
Like strips of the sky fallen through me on high,
Are each paved with the moon and these.

I bind the Sun's throne with a burning zone,
60   And the Moon's with a girdle of pearl;
The volcanoes are dim, and the Stars reel and swim,
When the whirlwinds my banner unfurl.
From cape to cape, with a bridge-like shape,
Over a torrent sea,
65   Sunbeam-proof, I hang like a roof;
The mountains its columns be!
The triumphal arch through which I march,
With hurricane, fire, and snow,
When the Powers of the air are chained to my chair,
70   Is the million-coloured bow;
The sphere-fire above its soft colours wove,
While the moist Earth was laughing below.

I am the daughter of Earth and Water,
And the nursling of the Sky:
75   I pass through the pores of the ocean and shores;
I change, but I cannot die,
For after the rain, when with never a stain
The pavilion of heaven is bare,
And the winds and sunbeams with their convex gleams
80   Build up the blue dome of air,
I silently laugh at my own cenotaph, –
And out of the caverns of rain,
Like a child from the womb,
Like a ghost from the tomb,
85   I arise, and unbuild it again.

Ode to the West Wind

I

O wild West Wind, thou breath of Autumn's being,
Thou, from whose unseen presence the leaves dead
Are driven, like ghosts from an enchanter fleeing,

Yellow, and black, and pale, and hectic red,
5   Pestilence-stricken multitudes: O Thou,
Who chariotest to their dark wintry bed

The wingèd seeds, where they lie cold and low,
Each like a corpse within its grave, until
Thine azure sister of the Spring shall blow

10   Her clarion o'er the dreaming earth, and fill
(Driving sweet buds like flocks to feed in air)
With living hues and odors plain and hill:

Wild Spirit, which art moving everywhere;
Destroyer and preserver; hear, oh, hear!

II

15   Thou on whose stream, 'mid the steep sky's commotion,
Loose clouds like earth's decaying leaves are shed,
Shook from the tangled boughs of Heaven and Ocean,

Angels of rain and lightning: there are spread
On the blue surface of thine aery surge,
20   Like the bright hair uplifted from the head

Of some fierce Maenad, even from the dim verge
Of the horizon to the zenith's height,
The locks of the approaching storm. Thou dirge

Of the dying year, to which this closing night
25   Will be the dome of a vast sepulchre,
Vaulted with all thy congregated might

Of vapors, from whose solid atmosphere
Black rain, and fire, and hail will burst: oh, hear!

III

Thou who didst waken from his summer dreams
30   The blue Mediterranean, where he lay,
Lulled by the coil of his crystalline streams,

---

21 **Maenad:** a dancer in the temple of Dionysus (Bacchus), god of wine, harvests, fertility.

Beside a pumice isle in Baiae's bay,
And saw in sleep old palaces and towers
Quivering within the wave's intenser day,

35 All overgrown with azure moss and flowers
So sweet, the sense faints picturing them! Thou
For whose path the Atlantic's level powers

Cleave themselves into chasms, while far below
The sea-blooms and the oozy woods which wear
40 The sapless foliage of the ocean, know

Thy voice, and suddenly grow gray with fear,
And tremble and despoil themselves: oh, hear!

IV

If I were a dead leaf thou mightest bear;
If I were a swift cloud to fly with thee;
45 A wave to pant beneath thy power, and share

The impulse of thy strength, only less free
Than thou, O uncontrollable! If even
I were as in my boyhood, and could be

The comrade of thy wanderings over Heaven,
50 As then, when to outstrip thy skiey speed
Scarce seemed a vision; I would ne'er have striven

As thus with thee in prayer in my sore need.
Oh, lift me as a wave, a leaf, a cloud!
I fall upon the thorns of life! I bleed!

55 A heavy weight of hours has chained and bowed
One too like thee: tameless, and swift, and proud.

V

Make me thy lyre, even as the forest is:
What if my leaves are falling like its own!
The tumult of thy mighty harmonies

60 Will take from both a deep, autumnal tone,
Sweet though in sadness. Be thou, Spirit fierce,
My spirit! Be thou me, impetuous one!

---

32 **Baiae:** Terme di Baia, near Naples, Greek colony in Roman times, now splendid ruins.

Drive my dead thoughts over the universe
Like withered leaves to quicken a new birth!
65   And, by the incantation of this verse,

Scatter, as from an unextinguished hearth
Ashes and sparks, my words among mankind!
Be through my lips to unawakened earth

The trumpet of a prophecy! O Wind,
70   If Winter comes, can Spring be far behind?

To a Skylark

Hail to thee, blithe Spirit!
Bird thou never wert,
That from Heaven, or near it,
Pourest thy full heart
5   In profuse strains of unpremeditated art.

Higher still and higher
From the earth thou springest
Like a cloud of fire;
The blue deep thou wingest,
10   And singing still dost soar, and soaring ever singest.

In the golden lightning
Of the sunken sun
O'er which clouds are brightning,
Thou dost float and run,
15   Like an unbodied joy whose race is just begun.

The pale purple even
Melts around thy flight;
Like a star of Heaven
In the broad daylight
20   Thou art unseen, but yet I hear thy shrill delight,

Keen as are the arrows
Of that silver sphere,
Whose intense lamp narrows
In the white dawn clear
25   Until we hardly see – we feel that it is there.

All the earth and air
With thy voice is loud.
As, when night is bare,
From one lonely cloud
30   The moon rains out her beams, and heaven is overflowed.

What thou art we know not;
What is most like thee?
From rainbow clouds there flow not
Drops so bright to see
35   As from thy presence showers a rain of melody.

Like a poet hidden
In the light of thought,
Singing hymns unbidden,
Till the world is wrought
40   To sympathy with hopes and fears it heeded not:

Like a high-born maiden
In a palace tower,
Soothing her love-laden
Soul in secret hour
45   With music sweet as love, which overflows her bower:

Like a glow-worm golden
In a dell of dew,
Scattering unbeholden
Its aerial hue
50   Among the flowers and grass, which screen it from the view:

Like a rose embowered
In its own green leaves,
By warm winds deflowered,
Till the scent it gives
55   Makes faint with too much sweet these heavy-winged thieves.

Sound of vernal showers
On the twinkling grass,
Rain-awakened flowers,
All that ever was
60   Joyous, and clear, and fresh, thy music doth surpass.

Teach us, sprite or bird,
What sweet thoughts are thine:
I have never heard
Praise of love or wine
65   That panted forth a flood of rapture so divine.

Chorus hymeneal
Or triumphal chaunt
Matched with thine, would be all
But an empty vaunt –
70   A thing wherein we feel there is some hidden want.

What objects are the fountains
Of thy happy strain?
What fields, or waves, or mountains?
What shapes of sky or plain?
75   What love of thine own kind? what ignorance of pain?

With thy clear keen joyance
Languor cannot be:
Shadow of annoyance
Never came near thee:
80   Thou lovest, but ne'er knew love's sad satiety.

Waking or asleep,
Thou of death must deem
Things more true and deep
Than we mortals dream,
85   Or how could thy notes flow in such a crystal stream?

We look before and after,
And pine for what is not:
Our sincerest laughter
With some pain is fraught;
90   Our sweetest songs are those that tell of saddest thought.

Yet if we could scorn
Hate, and pride, and fear;
If we were things born
Not to shed a tear,
95   I know not how thy joy we ever should come near.

Better than all measures
Of delightful sound,
Better than all treasures
That in books are found,
100   Thy skill to poet were, thou scorner of the ground!

Teach me half the gladness
That thy brain must know,
Such harmonious madness
From my lips would flow
105   The world should listen then, as I am listening now!

JOHN KEATS (1795–1821)

John Keats's father was born poor but rose to manage a London livery stable. He died when John was 8. His mother died when he was 14 of the tuberculosis that would kill his brother in 1818 and Keats himself in 1821. Although financially provided for and a keen student of the arts, Keats was apprenticed by his guardian to a surgeon-apothecary in 1810. He qualified in 1816 and immediately abandoned this secure career for the uncertain life of a poet, encouraged by Leigh Hunt who published 'O Solitude' and 'On First Looking into Chapman's Homer' in *The Examiner*. Hunt introduced Keats to Hazlitt, Lamb and Shelley, who provided an encouraging auditory. In 1817 he published his first volume, *Poems*, and wrote the 4000-line epic *Endymion*, an allegory of the quest for the ideal woman which was savaged by conservative critics as indicative of the 'Cockney school', partly because it was published under the aegis of Hunt. Keats however saw *Endymion* as mere 'prentice-work' for his Miltonic epic, *Hyperion*, which was eventually published as *The Fall of Hyperion* in *Lamia, The Eve of St Agnes, and other poems* (1820), a volume which collected the extraordinary fruit of the year 1819 when Keats, inspired by his love for Fanny Brawne, produced one assured masterpiece after another. Early in 1820 he found he was dying of tuberculosis; one year later he was dead. In a letter of 12–27 December 1817, Keats famously remarked that he sought in his poetry the quality which 'Shakespeare possessed – I mean Negative Capability, that is when man is capable of being in uncertainties, mysteries, doubts, without any irritable reaching after fact and reason.'

On First Looking into Chapman's Homer

> Much have I travell'd in the realms of gold,
> And many goodly states and kingdoms seen;
> Round many western islands have I been
> Which bards in fealty to Apollo hold.
> 5 Oft of one wide expanse had I been told
> That deep-brow'd Homer ruled as his demesne;
> Yet did I never breathe its pure serene
> Till I heard Chapman speak out loud and bold:
> Then felt I like some watcher of the skies
> 10 When a new planet swims into his ken;
> Or like stout Cortez when with eagle eyes
> He star'd at the Pacific – and all his men
> Look'd at each other with a wild surmise –
> Silent, upon a peak in Darien.

Chapman's Homer: The poem was written in a few hours in 1816 just after Keats had read the translation of Homer published in 1616 by George Chapman (1559–1634).   **4 fealty:** loyalty.   **14 Darien:** Cortez sounds smoother, but it was Vasco Núñez de Balboa who first saw the Pacific from the heights of Darien (now in Panama) in 1513.

La Belle Dame Sans Merci: A Ballad

I

O what can ail thee, knight-at-arms,
Alone and palely loitering?
The sedge has wither'd from the lake,
And no birds sing.

II

5   O what can ail thee, knight at arms!
So haggard and so woe-begone?
The squirrel's granary is full,
And the harvest's done.

III

I see a lily on thy brow
10   With anguish moist and fever dew,
And on thy cheeks a fading rose
Fast withereth too.

IV

I met a lady in the meads,
Full beautiful – a faery's child,
15   Her hair was long, her foot was light,
And her eyes were wild.

V

I made a garland for her head,
And bracelets too, and fragrant zone;
She look'd at me as she did love,
20   And made sweet moan.

VI

I set her on my pacing steed,
And nothing else saw all day long,
For sidelong would she bend, and sing
A faery's song.

VII

25   She found me roots of relish sweet,
And honey wild, and manna dew,
And sure in language strange she said –
'I love thee true.'

VIII

She took me to her elfin grot,
30   And there she wept, and sigh'd full sore,

La Belle Dame Sans Merci: 'The Lovely Lady without   **18 zone**: a belt of flowers.
Pity'; the story is frequent in medieval folk tales.

And there I shut her wild wild eyes
With kisses four.

IX

And there she lulled me asleep,
And there I dream'd – Ah! woe betide!
35 The latest dream I ever dream'd
On the cold hill's side.

X

I saw pale kings and princes too,
Pale warriors, death pale were they all;
They cried – 'La Belle Dame sans Merci
40 Hath thee in thrall!'

XI

I saw their starved lips in the gloam,
With horrid warning gaped wide,
And I awoke and found me here,
On the cold hill's side.

XII

45 And this is why I sojourn here,
Alone and palely loitering,
Though the sedge is wither'd from the lake,
And no birds sing.

Ode to a Nightingale

I

My heart aches, and a drowsy numbness pains
My sense, as though of hemlock I had drunk,
Or emptied some dull opiate to the drains
One minute past, and Lethe-wards had sunk:
5 'Tis not through envy of thy happy lot,
But being too happy in thine happiness, –
That thou, light-winged Dryad of the trees,
In some melodious plot
Of beechen green, and shadows numberless,
10 Singest of summer in full-throated ease.

II

O, for a draught of vintage! that hath been
Cool'd a long age in the deep-delved earth,
Tasting of Flora and the country green,
Dance, and Provençal song, and sunburnt mirth!

---

2 **hemlock:** poisonous herb.   4 **Lethe-wards:** toward
Lethe, the Greek river of forgetfulness in Hades.   13 **Flora:** Goddess of flowers.   14 **Provençal song:**
troubadour song, typically of love.

15   O for a beaker full of the warm South,
     Full of the true, the blushful Hippocrene,
     With beaded bubbles winking at the brim,
     And purple-stained mouth;
     That I might drink, and leave the world unseen,
20   And with thee fade away into the forest dim:

III

     Fade far away, dissolve, and quite forget
     What thou among the leaves hast never known,
     The weariness, the fever, and the fret
     Here, where men sit and hear each other groan;
25   Where palsy shakes a few, sad, last gray hairs,
     Where youth grows pale, and spectre-thin, and dies;
     Where but to think is to be full of sorrow
     And leaden-eyed despairs,
     Where Beauty cannot keep her lustrous eyes,
30   Or new Love pine at them beyond to-morrow.

IV

     Away! away! for I will fly to thee,
     Not charioted by Bacchus and his pards,
     But on the viewless wings of Poesy,
     Though the dull brain perplexes and retards:
35   Already with thee! tender is the night,
     And haply the Queen-Moon is on her throne,
     Cluster'd around by all her starry Fays;
     But here there is no light,
     Save what from heaven is with the breezes blown
40   Through verdurous glooms and winding mossy ways.

V

     I cannot see what flowers are at my feet,
     Nor what soft incense hangs upon the boughs,
     But, in embalmed darkness, guess each sweet
     Wherewith the seasonable month endows
45   The grass, the thicket, and the fruit-tree wild;
     White hawthorn, and the pastoral eglantine;
     Fast fading violets cover'd up in leaves;
     And mid-May's eldest child,
     The coming musk-rose, full of dewy wine,
50   The murmurous haunt of flies on summer eves.

---

16 **Hippocrene:** wine.   26 **dies:** Keats's brother, Tom,   33 **viewless:** invisible.   37 **Fays:** fairies.   46 **eglantine:** had just died of tuberculosis.   32 **pards:** leopards, some-   honeysuckle. times represented drawing the chariot of Bacchus.

VI

Darkling I listen; and, for many a time
I have been half in love with easeful Death,
Call'd him soft names in many a mused rhyme,
To take into the air my quiet breath;
55 Now more than ever seems it rich to die,
To cease upon the midnight with no pain,
While thou art pouring forth thy soul abroad
In such an ecstasy!
Still wouldst thou sing, and I have ears in vain –
60 To thy high requiem become a sod.

VII

Thou wast not born for death, immortal Bird!
No hungry generations tread thee down;
The voice I hear this passing night was heard
In ancient days by emperor and clown:
65 Perhaps the self-same song that found a path
Through the sad heart of Ruth, when, sick for home,
She stood in tears amid the alien corn;
The same that oft-times hath
Charm'd magic casements, opening on the foam
70 Of perilous seas, in faery lands forlorn.

VIII

Forlorn! the very word is like a bell
To toil me back from thee to my sole self!
Adieu! the fancy cannot cheat so well
As she is fam'd to do, deceiving elf.
75 Adieu! adieu! thy plaintive anthem fades
Past the near meadows, over the still stream,
Up the hill-side; and now 'tis buried deep
In the next valley-glades:
Was it a vision, or a waking dream?
80 Fled is that music: – Do I wake or sleep?

Ode on a Grecian Urn

I

Thou still unravish'd bride of quietness,
Thou foster-child of silence and slow time,
Sylvan historian, who canst thus express
A flowery tale more sweetly than our rhyme:
5 What leaf-fring'd legend haunts about thy shape

---

51 **darkling:** in the dark, or darkening.   3 **Sylvan:** of the wood, idyllically rustic.

Of deities or mortals, or of both,
In Tempe or the dales of Arcady?
What men or gods are these? What maidens loth?
What mad pursuit? What struggle to escape?
10 What pipes and timbrels? What wild ecstasy?

II

Heard melodies are sweet, but those unheard
Are sweeter; therefore, ye soft pipes, play on;
Not to the sensual ear, but, more endear'd,
Pipe to the spirit ditties of no tone:
15 Fair youth, beneath the trees, thou canst not leave
Thy song, nor ever can those trees be bare;
Bold Lover, never, never canst thou kiss,
Though winning near the goal – yet, do not grieve;
She cannot fade, though thou hast not thy bliss,
20 For ever wilt thou love, and she be fair!

III

Ah, happy, happy boughs! that cannot shed
Your leaves, nor ever bid the Spring adieu;
And, happy melodist, unwearied,
For ever piping songs for ever new;
25 More happy love! more happy, happy love!
For ever warm and still to be enjoy'd,
For ever panting, and for ever young;
All breathing human passion far above,
That leaves a heart high-sorrowful and cloy'd,
30 A burning forehead, and a parching tongue.

IV

Who are these coming to the sacrifice?
To what green altar, O mysterious priest,
Lead'st thou that heifer lowing at the skies,
And all her silken flanks with garlands drest?
35 What little town by river or sea shore,
Or mountain-built with peaceful citadel,
Is emptied of this folk, this pious morn?
And, little town, thy streets for evermore
Will silent be; and not a soul to tell
40 Why thou art desolate, can e'er return.

V

O Attic shape! Fair attitude! with brede
Of marble men and maidens overwrought

---

7 **Tempe ... Arcady:** sites of the pastoral ideal.   42 **overwrought:** overlaid with a braid (brede) or orna-
41 **Attic:** Attica, the region of Greece around Athens.   mental band.

With forest branches and the trodden weed;
Thou, silent form, dost tease us out of thought
45   As doth eternity: Cold Pastoral!
When old age shall this generation waste,
Thou shalt remain, in midst of other woe
Than ours, a friend to man, to whom thou say'st,
'Beauty is truth, truth beauty' – that is all
50   Ye know on earth, and all ye need to know.

Ode on Melancholy

I

No, no! go not to Lethe, neither twist
Wolf's-bane, tight-rooted, for its poisonous wine;
Nor suffer thy pale forehead to be kissed
By nightshade, ruby grape of Proserpine;
5   Make not your rosary of yew-berries,
Nor let the beetle nor the death-moth be
Your mournful Psyche, nor the downy owl
A partner in your sorrow's mysteries;
For shade to shade will come too drowsily,
10   And drown the wakeful anguish of the soul.

II

But when the melancholy fit shall fall
Sudden from heaven like a weeping cloud,
That fosters the droop-headed flowers all,
And hides the green hill in an April shroud;
15   Then glut thy sorrow on a morning rose,
Or on the rainbow of the salt sand-wave,
Or on the wealth of globed peonies;
Or if thy mistress some rich anger shows,
Emprison her soft hand, and let her rave,
20   And feed deep, deep upon her peerless eyes.

III

She dwells with Beauty – Beauty that must die;
And Joy, whose hand is ever at his lips
Bidding adieu; and aching Pleasure nigh,
Turning to poison while the bee-mouth sips;
25   Ay, in the very temple of delight
Veiled Melancholy has her sovran shrine,

---

1 **Lethe:** the river of forgetfulness in Hades. **2 wolf's bane:** a poisonous plant. **4 nightshade:** a poisonous plant. **Proserpine:** Queen of the Underworld. **5 yew-berries:** poisonous and symbolic of midwinter and death. **6 beetle and death-moth:** emblems of death since both resemble skulls, especially the scarab. **7 Psyche:** the soul. **8 mysteries:** secret religious rites.

Though seen of none save him whose strenuous tongue
Can burst Joy's grape against his palate fine;
His soul shall taste the sadness of her might,
30   And be among her cloudy trophies hung.

Ode to Autumn

I

Season of mists and mellow fruitfulness,
Close bosom-friend of the maturing sun;
Conspiring with him how to load and bless
With fruit the vines that round the thatch-eaves run;
5   To bend with apples the mossed cottage-trees,
And fill all fruit with ripeness to the core;
To swell the gourd, and plump the hazel shells
With a sweet kernel; to set budding more,
And still more, later flowers for the bees,
10   Until they think warm days will never cease,
For Summer has o'er-brimmed their clammy cells.

II

Who hath not seen thee oft amid thy store?
Sometimes whoever seeks abroad may find
Thee sitting careless on a granary floor,
15   Thy hair soft-lifted by the winnowing wind;
Or on a half-reaped furrow sound asleep,
Drowsed with the fume of poppies, while thy hook
Spares the next swath and all its twined flowers;
And sometimes like a gleaner thou dost keep
20   Steady thy laden head across a brook;
Or by a cider-press, with patient look,
Thou watchest the last oozings, hours by hours.

III

Where are the songs of Spring? Ay, where are they?
Think not of them, thou hast thy music too –
25   While barred clouds bloom the soft-dying day,
And touch the stubble-plains with rosy hue;
Then in a wailful choir, the small gnats mourn
Among the river sallows, borne aloft
Or sinking as the light wind lives or dies;
30   And full-grown lambs loud bleat from hilly bourn;
Hedge crickets sing; and now with treble soft
The redbreast whistles from a garden-croft,
And gathering swallows twitter in the skies.

---

17 **hook:** scythe.   28 **sallows:** willows.   32 **garden-croft:** garden plot next to a cottage.

SIR WALTER SCOTT (1771–1832)

Born in Edinburgh, the son of a lawyer, Scott trained to be a barrister. He shared the contemporary interest in ballads and folklore, collected (and often 'improved') *The Minstrelsy of the Scottish Border* (1802–03) and wrote three very popular verse romances in the same strain, *The Lay of the Last Minstrel* (1805), *Marmion* (1808) and *The Lady of the Lake* (1810). He founded the influential Tory *Quarterly Review* and was a highly successful publisher and editor. He wrote or contributed to numerous historical works. In 1814 he published his first novel, *Waverley,* which was a phenomenal success in Britain and internationally. In the next 17 years he wrote more than 30 *Waverley Novels* which rank amongst the most influential artistic productions of all time: he established the genre of the historical novel, developed the technique of authoritative omniscient narration and the serious representation of rural characters. His characteristic method, pioneered in *Waverley,* is to place his characters astride a crucial historical transition where they must decide between an heroic, aristocratic past and a more sober but more reasonable future. Like Byron he was admired internationally. His example was imitated explicitly by Balzac in *La Comédie Humaine* and Fenimore Cooper in *The Leather-Stocking Tales,* as well as by Tolstoy and George Eliot, and implicitly by all subsequent novelists. *The Heart of Midlothian* was published in 1818. The 'Heart' is an ironic name for Edinburgh's main prison, the Tolbooth, and in the opening chapters Scott focuses on the famous historical incident of the Porteus riot of 1736.

From The Heart of Mid-Lothian

Chapter III

> And thou, great god of aqua-vitæ!
> Wha sways the empire of this city
> (When fou we're sometimes capernoity),
>   Be thou prepared,
> To save us frae that black banditti,
>   The City Guard!
>
> Ferguson's Daft Days

Captain John Porteous, a name memorable in the traditions of Edinburgh, as well as in the records of criminal jurisprudence, was the son of a citizen of Edinburgh, who endeavoured to breed him up to his own mechanical trade of a tailor. The youth, however, had a wild and irreclaimable propensity to dissipation, which finally sent him to serve in the corps long maintained in the service of the States of Holland, and called the Scotch Dutch. Here he learned military discipline; and, returning afterwards, in the course of an idle and wandering life, to his native city, his services were required by the magistrates of Edinburgh in the disturbed year 1715, for disciplining their City Guard, in which he shortly afterwards received a captain's commission. It was only by his military skill and an alert and resolute character as an officer of police, that he merited this promotion, for he is said to have been a man of profligate habits, an unnatural son, and a brutal husband. He was, however, useful in his station, and his harsh and fierce habits rendered him formidable to rioters or disturbers of the public peace.

The corps in which he held his command is, or perhaps we should rather say *was*, a body of about one hundred and twenty soldiers divided into three companies, and regularly armed, clothed, and embodied. They were chiefly veterans who enlisted in this corps, having the benefit of working at their trades when they were off duty. These men had the charge of preserving public order, repressing riots and street robberies, acting, in short, as an armed police, and attending on all public occasions where confusion or popular disturbance might be expected. Poor Ferguson, whose irregularities sometimes led him into unpleasant rencontres with these military conservators of public order, and who mentions them so often that he may be termed their poet laureate, thus admonishes his readers, warned doubtless by his own experience: –

> 'Gude folk, as ye come frae the fair,
>   Bide yont frae this black squad;
> There's nae sic savages elsewhere
>   Allow'd to wear cockad.'

In fact, the soldiers of the City Guard, being, as we have said, in general discharged veterans, who had strength enough remaining for this municipal duty, and being, moreover, for the greater part, Highlanders, were neither by birth, education, nor former habits, trained to endure with much patience the insults of the rabble, or the provoking petulance of truant schoolboys, and idle debauches of all descriptions, with whom their occupation brought them into contact. On the contrary, the tempers of the poor old fellows were soured by the indignities with which the mob distinguished them on many occasions, and frequently might have required the soothing strains of the poet we have just quoted: –

> 'O soldiers! for your ain dear sakes,
> For Scotland's love, the Land o' Cakes,
> Gie not her bairns sic deadly paiks,
>   Nor be sae rude,
> Wi' firelock or Lochaber-axe,
>   As spill their bluid!'

On all occasions when a holyday licensed some riot and irregularity, a skirmish with these veterans was a favourite recreation with the rabble of Edinburgh. These pages may perhaps see the light when many have in fresh recollection such onsets as we allude to. But the venerable corps, with whom the contention was held, may now be considered as totally extinct. Of late the gradual diminution of these civic soldiers reminds one of the abatement of King Lear's hundred knights. The edicts of each succeeding set of magistrates have, like those of Goneril and Regan, diminished this venerable band with the similar question, 'What need we five-and-twenty? – ten? – or five?' And it is now nearly come to, 'What need one?' A spectre may indeed here and there still be seen, of an old grey-headed and grey-bearded Highlander, with war-worn features, but bent double by age; dressed in an old fashioned cocked-hat, bound with white tape instead of silver lace; and in coat, waistcoat, and breeches, of a muddy-coloured red, bearing in his withered hand an ancient weapon, called a Lochaber-axe; a long pole, namely, with an axe at the extremity, and a hook at the back of the hatchet. Such a phantom of former days still creeps, I have been informed, round the statue of Charles the Second, in the Parliament Square, as if the image of a Stuart were the last refuge for any memorial of our ancient manners; and one or two others are supposed to glide around the door of the guardhouse assigned to them in the Luckenbooths, when their ancient refuge in the High Street was laid low. But the fate of manuscripts bequeathed to friends and executors is so uncertain, that the narrative containing these frail memorials of the old Town Guard of Edinburgh, who, with their grim and valiant corporal, John Dhu (the fiercest-looking fellow I ever saw), were, in my boyhood, the alternate terror and derision of the petulant brood of the High School, may, perhaps, only come to light when all memory of the institution has faded away, and then serve as an illustration of Kay's caricatures, who has preserved the features of some of their heroes. In the preceding generation, when there was a perpetual alarm for the plots and activity of the Jacobites, some pains were taken by the magistrates of Edinburgh to keep this corps, though composed always of such materials as we have noticed, in a more effective state than was afterwards judged necessary, when their most dangerous service was to skirmish with the rabble on the king's birthday. They were, therefore, more the objects of hatred, and less that of scorn, than they were afterwards accounted.

To Captain John Porteous, the honour of his command and of his corps seems to have been a matter of high interest and importance. He was exceedingly incensed against Wilson for the affront which he construed him to have put upon his soldiers, in the effort he made for the liberation of his companion, and expressed himself most ardently on the subject. He was no less indignant at the report, that there was an intention to rescue Wilson himself from the gallows, and uttered many threats and imprecations upon that subject, which were afterwards remembered to his disadvantage. In fact, if a good deal of determination and promptitude rendered Porteous, in one respect, fit to command guards designed to suppress popular commotion, he seems, on the other, to have been disqualified for a charge so delicate, by a hot and surly temper, always too ready to come to blows and violence; a character void of principle; and a disposition to regard the rabble, who seldom failed to regale him and his soldiers with some marks of their displeasure, as declared enemies, upon whom it was natural and justifiable that he should seek opportunities of vengeance. Being, however, the most active and trustworthy among the captains of the City Guard, he was the person to whom the magistrates confided the command of the soldiers appointed to keep the peace at the time of Wilson's execution. He was ordered to guard the gallows and scaffold, with about eighty men, all the disposable force that could be spared for that duty.

But the magistrates took farther precautions, which affected Porteous's pride very deeply. They requested the assistance of part of a regular infantry regiment, not to attend upon the execution, but to remain drawn up on the principal street of the city, during the time that it went forward, in order to intimidate the multitude, in case they should be disposed to be unruly, with a display of force which could not be resisted without desperation. It may sound ridiculous in our ears, considering the fallen state of this ancient civic corps, that its officer should have felt punctiliously jealous of its honour. Yet so it was. Captain Porteous resented, as an indignity, the introducing the Welsh Fusileers within the city, and drawing them up in the street where no drums but his own were allowed to be sounded without the special command or permission of the magistrates. As he could not show his ill-humour to his patrons the magistrates, it increased his indignation and his desire to be revenged on the unfortunate criminal Wilson, and all who favoured him. These internal emotions of jealousy and rage wrought a change on the man's mien and bearing, visible to all who saw him on the fatal morning when Wilson was appointed to suffer. Porteous's ordinary appearance was rather favourable. He was about the middle size, stout, and well made, having a military air, and yet rather a gentle and mild countenance. His complexion was brown, his face somewhat fretted with the scars of the smallpox, his eyes rather languid than keen or fierce. On the present occasion, however, it seemed to those who saw him as if he were agitated by some evil demon. His step was irregular, his voice hollow and broken, his countenance pale, his eyes staring and wild, his speech imperfect and confused, and his whole appearance so disordered, that many remarked he seemed to be *fey*, a Scottish expression, meaning the state of those who are driven on to their impending fate by the strong impulse of some irresistible necessity.

One part of his conduct was truly diabolical, if indeed it has not been exaggerated by the general prejudice entertained against his memory. When Wilson, the unhappy criminal, was delivered to him by the keeper of the prison, in order that he might be conducted to the place of execution, Porteous, not satisfied with the usual precautions to prevent escape, ordered him to be manacled. This might be justifiable from the character and bodily strength of the malefactor, as well as from the apprehensions so generally entertained of an expected rescue. But the handcuffs which were produced being found too small for the wrists of a man so big-boned as Wilson, Porteous proceeded with his own hands, and by great exertion of strength, to force them till they clasped together, to the exquisite torture of the unhappy criminal. Wilson remonstrated against such barbarous usage, declaring that the pain distracted his thoughts from the subjects of meditation proper to his unhappy condition.

'It signifies little,' replied Captain Porteous; 'your pain will soon be at an end.'

'Your cruelty is great,' answered the sufferer. 'You know not how soon you yourself may have occasion to ask the mercy which you are now refusing to a fellow-creature. May God forgive you!'

These words, long afterwards quoted and remembered, were all that passed between Porteous and his prisoner; but as they took air, and became known to the people, they greatly increased the popular compassion for Wilson, and excited a proportionate degree of indignation against Porteous; against whom, as strict, and even violent in the discharge of his unpopular office, the common people had some real, and many imaginary causes of complaint.

When the painful procession was completed, and Wilson, with the escort, had arrived at the scaffold in the Grassmarket, there appeared no signs of that attempt to rescue him which had occasioned such precautions. The multitude, in general, looked on with deeper interest than at ordinary executions; and there might be seen, on the countenances of many, a stern and indignant expression, like that with which the ancient Cameronians might be supposed to witness the execution of their brethren, who glorified the Covenant on the same occasion, and at the same spot. But there was no attempt at violence. Wilson himself seemed disposed to hasten over the space that divided time from eternity. The devotions proper and usual on such occasions were no sooner finished than he submitted to his fate, and the sentence of the law was fulfilled.

He had been suspended on the gibbet so long as to be totally deprived of life, when at once, as if occasioned by some newly received impulse, there arose a tumult among the multitude. Many stones were thrown at Porteous and his guards; some mischief was done; and the mob continued to press forward with whoops, shrieks, howls, and exclamations. A young fellow, with a sailor's cap slouched over his face, sprung on the scaffold, and cut the rope by which the criminal was suspended. Others approached to carry off the body, either to secure for it a decent grave, or to try, perhaps, some means of resuscitation. Captain Porteous was wrought, by this appearance of insurrection against his authority, into a rage so headlong as made him forget, that, the sentence having been fully executed, it was his duty not to engage in hostilities with the misguided multitude, but to draw off his men as fast as possible. He sprung from the scaffold, snatched a musket from one of his soldiers, commanded the party to give fire, and, as several eye-witnesses concurred in swearing, set them the example, by discharging his piece, and shooting a man dead on the spot. Several soldiers obeyed his command or followed his example; six or seven persons were slain, and a great many were hurt and wounded.

After this act of violence, the Captain proceeded to withdraw his men towards their guard-house in the High Street. The mob were not so much intimidated as incensed by what had been done. They pursued the soldiers with execrations, accompanied by volleys of stones. As they pressed on them, the rearmost soldiers turned, and again fired with fatal aim and execution. It is not accurately known whether Porteous commanded this second act of violence; but of course the odium of the whole transactions of the fatal day attached to him, and to him alone. He arrived at the guard-house, dismissed his soldiers, and went to make his report to the magistrates concerning the unfortunate events of the day.

Apparently by this time Captain Porteous had began to doubt the propriety of his own conduct, and the reception he met with from the magistrates was such as to make him still more anxious to gloss it over. He denied that he had given orders to fire; he denied he had fired with his own hand; he even produced the fusee which he carried as an officer for examination; it was found still loaded. Of three cartridges which he was seen to put in his pouch that morning, two were still there; a white handkerchief was thrust into the muzzle of the piece, and returned unsoiled or blackened. To the defence founded on these circumstances it was answered, that Porteous had not used his own piece, but had been seen to take one from a soldier. Among the many who had been killed and wounded by the unhappy fire, there were several of better rank; for even the humanity of such soldiers as fired over the heads of the mere rabble around the scaffold, proved in some instances fatal to persons who were stationed in windows, or observed the melancholy scene from a distance. The voice of public indignation was loud and general; and, ere men's tempers had time to cool, the trial of Captain Porteous took place before the High Court of Justiciary. After a long and patient hearing, the jury had the difficult duty of balancing the positive evidence of many persons, and those of respectability, who deposed positively to the prisoner's commanding his soldiers to fire, and himself firing his piece, of which some swore that they saw the smoke and flash, and beheld a man drop at whom it was pointed, with the negative testimony of others, who, though well stationed for seeing what had passed, neither heard Porteous give orders to fire, nor saw him fire himself; but, on the contrary, averred that the first shot was fired by a soldier who stood close by him. A great part of his defence was also founded on the turbulence of the mob, which witnesses, according to their feelings, their predilections, and their opportunities of observation, represented differently; some describing as a formidable riot, what others represented as a trifling disturbance such as always used to take place on the like occasions, when the executioner of the law, and the men commissioned to protect him in his task, were generally exposed to some indignities. The verdict of the jury sufficiently shows how the evidence preponderated in their minds. It declared that John Porteous fired a gun among the people assembled at the execution; that he gave orders to his soldiers to fire, by which many persons were killed and wounded; but, at the same time, that the prisoner and his guard had been wounded and beaten, by stones thrown at them by the multitude. Upon this verdict, the Lords of Justiciary passed sentence of death against Captain John Porteous, adjudging him, in the common form, to be hanged on a gibbet at the common place of execution, on Wednesday, 8th September 1736, and all his movable property to be forfeited to the king's use, according to the Scottish law in cases of wilful murder.

Chapter IV

> 'The hour's come, but not the man.'
>
> Kelpie

On the day when the unhappy Porteous was expected to suffer the sentence of the law, the place of execution, extensive as it is, was crowded almost to suffocation. There was not a window in all the lofty tenements around it, or in the steep and crooked street called the Bow, by which the fatal procession was to descend from the High Street, that was not absolutely filled with spectators. The uncommon height and antique appearance of these houses, some of which were formerly the property of the Knights Templars, and the Knights of St. John, and still exhibit on their fronts and gables the iron cross of these orders, gave additional effect to a scene in itself so striking. The area of the Grassmarket resembled a huge dark lake or sea of human heads, in the centre of which arose the fatal tree, tall, black, and ominous, from which dangled the deadly halter. Every object takes interest from its uses and associations, and the erect beam and empty noose, things so simple in themselves, became, on such an occasion, objects of terror and of solemn interest.

Amid so numerous an assembly there was scarcely a word spoken, save in whispers. The thirst of vengeance was in some degree allayed by its supposed certainty; and even the populace, with deeper feeling than they are wont to entertain, suppressed all clamorous exultation, and prepared to enjoy the scene of retaliation in triumph, silent and decent, though stern and relentless. It seemed as if the depth of their hatred to the unfortunate criminal scorned to display itself in anything resembling the more noisy current of their ordinary feelings. Had a stranger consulted only the evidence of his ears, he might have supposed that so vast a multitude were assembled for some purpose which affected them with the deepest sorrow, and stilled those noises which, on all ordinary occasions, arise from such a concourse; but if he had gazed upon their faces, he would have been instantly undeceived. The compressed lip, the bent brow, the stern and flashing eye of almost everyone on whom he looked, conveyed the expression of men come to glut their sight with triumphant revenge. It is probable that the appearance of the criminal might have somewhat changed the temper of the populace in his favour, and that they might in the moment of death have forgiven the man against whom their resentment had been so fiercely heated. It had, however, been destined, that the mutability of their sentiments was not to be exposed to this trial.

The usual hour for producing the criminal had been past for many minutes, yet the spectators observed no symptom of his appearance. 'Would they venture to defraud public justice?' was the question which men began anxiously to ask at each other. The first answer in every case was bold and positive, – 'They dare not.' But when the point was further canvassed, other opinions were entertained, and various causes of doubt were suggested. Porteous had been a favourite officer of the magistracy of the city, which, being a numerous and fluctuating body, requires for its support a degree of energy in its functionaries, which the individuals who compose it cannot at all times alike be supposed to possess in their own persons. It was remembered, that in the Information for Porteous (the paper, namely, in which his case was stated to the Judges of the criminal court), he had been described by his counsel as the person on whom the magistrates chiefly relied in all emergencies of uncommon difficulty. It was argued, too, that his conduct, on the unhappy occasion of Wilson's execution, was capable of being attributed to an imprudent excess of zeal in the execution of his duty, a motive for which those under whose authority he acted might be supposed to have great sympathy. And as these considerations might move the magistrates to make a favourable representation of Porteous's case, there were not wanting others in the higher departments of Government, which would make such suggestions favourably listened to.

The mob of Edinburgh, when thoroughly excited, had been at all times one of the fiercest which could be found in Europe; and of late years they had risen repeatedly against the Government, and sometimes not without temporary success. They were conscious, therefore, that they were no favourites with the rulers of the period, and that, if Captain Porteous's violence was not altogether regarded as good service, it might certainly be thought, that to visit it with a capital punishment would render it both delicate and dangerous for future officers, in the same circumstances, to act with effect in repressing tumults. There is also a natural feeling, on the part of all members of Government, for the general maintenance of authority; and it seemed not unlikely, that what to the relatives of the sufferers appeared a wanton and unprovoked massacre, should be otherwise viewed in the cabinet of St. James's. It might be there supposed, that upon the whole matter, Captain Porteous was in the exercise of a trust delegated to him by the lawful civil authority; that he had been assaulted by the populace, and several of his men hurt; and that, in finally repelling force by force, his conduct could be fairly imputed to no other motive than self-defence in the discharge of his duty.

These considerations, of themselves very powerful, induced the spectators to apprehend the possibility of a reprieve; and to the various causes which might interest the rulers in his favour, the lower part of the rabble added one which was peculiarly well adapted to their comprehension. It was averred, in order to increase the odium against Porteous, that while he repressed with the utmost severity the slightest excesses of the poor, he not only overlooked the license of the young nobles and gentry, but was very willing to lend them the countenance of his official authority, in execution of such loose pranks as it was chiefly his duty to have restrained. This suspicion, which was perhaps much exaggerated, made a deep impression on the minds of the populace; and when several of the higher rank joined in a petition, recommending Porteous to the mercy of the Crown, it was generally supposed he owed their favour not to any conviction of the hardship of his case, but to the fear of losing a convenient accomplice in their debaucheries. It is scarcely necessary to say how much this suspicion augmented the people's detestation of this obnoxious criminal, as well as their fear of his escaping the sentence pronounced against him.

While these arguments were stated and replied to, and canvassed and supported, the hitherto silent expectation of the people became changed into that deep and agitating murmur, which is sent forth by the ocean before the tempest begins to howl. The crowded populace, as if their motions had corresponded with the unsettled state of their minds, fluctuated to and fro without any visible cause of impulse, like the agitation of the waters, called by sailors the ground-swell. The news, which the magistrates had almost hesitated to communicate to them, were at length announced, and spread among the spectators with a rapidity like lightning. A reprieve from the Secretary of State's office, under the hand of his Grace the Duke of Newcastle, had arrived, intimating the pleasure of Queen Caroline (regent of the kingdom during the absence of George II on the Continent), that the execution of the sentence of death pronounced against John Porteous, late Captain-Lieutenant of the City Guard of Edinburgh, present prisoner in the Tolbooth of that city, be respited for six weeks from the time appointed for his execution.

The assembled spectators of almost all degrees, whose minds had been wound up to the pitch which we have described, uttered a groan, or rather a roar of indignation and disappointed revenge, similar to that of a tiger from whom his meal has been rent by his keeper when he was just about to devour it. This fierce exclamation seemed to forbode some immediate explosion of popular resentment, and, in fact, such had been expected by the magistrates, and the necessary measures had been taken to repress it. But the shout was not repeated, nor did any sudden tumult ensue, such as it appeared to announce. The populace seemed to be ashamed of having expressed their disappointment in a vain clamour, and the sound changed, not into the silence which had preceded the arrival of these stunning news, but into stifled mutterings, which each group maintained among themselves, and which were blended into one deep and hoarse murmur which floated above the assembly.

Yet still, though all expectation of the execution was over, the mob remained assembled, stationary, as it were, through very resentment, gazing on the preparations for death, which had now been made in vain, and stimulating their feelings, by recalling the various claims which Wilson might have had on royal mercy, from the mistaken motives on which he acted, as well as from the generosity he had displayed towards his accomplice. 'This man,' they said, – 'the brave, the resolute, the generous, was executed to death without mercy for stealing a purse of gold, which in some sense he might consider as a fair reprisal; while the profligate satellite, who took advantage of a trifling tumult, inseparable from such occasions, to shed the blood of twenty of his fellow-citizens, is deemed a fitting object for the exercise of the royal prerogative of mercy. Is this to be borne? – would our fathers have borne it? Are not we, like them, Scotsmen and burghers of Edinburgh?'

The officers of justice began now to remove the scaffold, and other preparations which had been made for the execution, in hopes, by doing so, to accelerate the dispersion of the multitude. The measure had the desired effect; for no sooner had the fatal tree been unfixed from the large stone pedestal or socket in which it was secured, and sunk slowly down upon the wain intended to remove it to the place where it was usually deposited, than the populace, after giving vent to their feelings in a second shout of rage and mortification, began slowly to disperse to their usual abodes and occupations.

The windows were in like manner gradually deserted, and groups of the more decent class of citizens formed themselves, as if waiting to return homewards when the streets should be cleared of the rabble. Contrary to what is frequently the case, this description of persons agreed in general with the sentiments of their inferiors, and considered the cause as common to all ranks. Indeed, as we have already noticed, it was by no means amongst the lowest class of the spectators, or those most likely to be engaged in the riot at Wilson's execution, that the fatal fire of Porteous's soldiers had taken effect. Several persons were killed who were looking out at windows at the scene, who could not of course belong to the rioters, and were persons of decent rank and condition. The burghers, therefore, resenting the loss which had fallen on their own body, and proud and tenacious of their rights, as the citizens of Edinburgh have at all times been, were greatly exasperated at the unexpected respite of Captain Porteous.

It was noticed at the time, and afterwards more particularly remembered, that, while the mob were in the act of dispersing, several individuals were seen busily passing from one place and one group of people to another, remaining long with none, but whispering for a little time with those who appeared to be declaiming most violently against the conduct of Government. These active agents had the appearance of men from the country, and were generally supposed to be old friends and confederates of Wilson, whose minds were of course highly excited against Porteous.

If, however, it was the intention of these men to stir the multitude to any sudden act of mutiny, it seemed for the time to be fruitless. The rabble, as well as the more decent part of the assembly, dispersed, and went home peaceably; and it was only by observing the moody discontent on their brows, or catching the tenor of the conversation they held with each other, that a stranger could estimate the state of their minds. We will give the reader this advantage, by associating ourselves with one of the numerous groups who were painfully ascending the steep declivity of the West Bow, to return to their dwellings in the Lawnmarket.

'An unco thing this, Mrs Howden,' said old Peter Plumdamas to his neighbour the rouping-wife, or saleswoman, as he offered her his arm to assist her in the toilsome ascent, 'to see the grit folk at Lunnon set their face against law and gospel, and let loose sic a reprobate as Porteous upon a peaceable town!'

'And to think o' the weary walk they hae gien us,' answered Mrs Howden, with a groan; 'and sic a comfortable window as I had gotten, too, just within a penny-stane-cast of the scaffold – I could hae heard every word the minister said – and to pay twalpennies for my stand, and a' for naething!'

'I am judging,' said Mr Plumdamas, 'that this reprieve wadna stand gude in the auld Scots law, when the kingdom *was* a kingdom.'

'I dinna ken muckle about the law,' answered Mrs Howden; 'but I ken, when we had a king, and a chancellor, and parliament men o' our ain, we could aye peeble them wi' stanes when they werena gude bairns – But naebody's nails can reach the length o' Lunnon.'

'Weary on Lunnon, and a' that e'er came out o't!' said Miss Grizel Damahoy, an ancient seamstress; 'they hae taen awa our parliament, and they hae oppressed our trade. Our gentles will hardly allow that a Scots needle can sew ruffles on a sark, or lace on an owerlay.'

'Ye may say that, Miss Damahoy, and I ken o' them that hae gotten raisins frae Lunnon by forpits at ance,' responded Plumdamas; 'and then sic an host of idle English gaugers and excisemen as hae come down to vex and torment us, that an honest man canna fetch sae muckle as a bit anker o' brandy frae Leith to the Lawnmarket, but he's like to be rubbit o' the very gudes he's bought and paid for. – Weel, I winna justify Andrew Wilson for pitting hands on what wasna his; but if he took nae mair than his ain, there's an awfu' difference between that and the fact this man stands for.'

'If ye speak about the law,' said Mrs Howden, 'here comes Mr Saddletree, that can settle it as weel as ony on the bench.'

The party she mentioned, a grave elderly person, with a superb periwig, dressed in a decent suit of sad-coloured clothes, came up as she spoke, and courteously gave his arm to Miss Grizel Damahoy.

It may be necessary to mention, that Mr Bartoline Saddletree kept an excellent and highly esteemed shop for harness, saddles, &c. &c. at the sign of the Golden Nag, at the head of Bess Wynd. His genius, however (as he himself and most of his neighbours conceived), lay towards the weightier matters of the law, and he failed not to give frequent attendance upon the pleadings and arguments of the lawyers and judges in the neighbouring square, where, to say the truth, he was oftener to be found than would have consisted with his own emolument; but that his wife, an active painstaking person, could, in his absence, make an admirable shift to please the customers and scold the journeymen. This good lady was in the habit of letting her husband take his way, and go on improving his stock of legal knowledge without interruption; but, as if in requital, she insisted upon having her own will in the domestic and commercial departments which he abandoned to her. Now, as Bartoline Saddletree had a considerable gift of words, which he mistook for eloquence, and conferred more liberally upon the society in which he lived than was at all times gracious and acceptable, there went forth a saying, with which wags used sometimes to interrupt his rhetoric, that, as he had a golden nag at his door, so he had a grey mare in his shop. This reproach induced Mr Saddletree, on all occasions, to assume rather a haughty and stately tone towards his good woman, a circumstance by which she seemed very little affected, unless he attempted to exercise any real authority, when she never failed to fly into open rebellion. But such extremes Bartoline seldom provoked; for, like the gentle King Jamie, he was fonder of talking of authority than really exercising it. This turn of mind was, on the whole, lucky for him; since his substance was increased without any trouble on his part, or any interruption of his favourite studies.

This word in explanation has been thrown in to the reader, while Saddletree was laying down, with great precision, the law upon Porteous's case, by which he arrived at this conclusion, that, if Porteous had fired five minutes sooner, before Wilson was cut down, he would have been *versans in licito*; engaged, that is, in a lawful act, and only liable to be punished *propter excessum*, or for lack of discretion, which might have mitigated the punishment to *pœna ordinaria*.

'Discretion!' echoed Mrs Howden, on whom, it may well be supposed, the fineness of this distinction was entirely thrown away, – 'whan had Jock Porteous either grace, discretion, or gude manners? – I mind when his father – '

'But, Mrs Howden,' said Saddletree.

'And I,' said Miss Damahoy, 'mind when his mother – '

'Miss Damahoy,' entreated the interrupted orator.

'And I,' said Plumdamas, 'mind when his wife – '

'Mr Plumdamas – Mrs Howden – Miss Damahoy,' again implored the orator, 'Mind the distinction, as Counsellor Crossmyloof says – "I," says he, "take a distinction." Now, the body of the criminal being cut down, and the execution ended, Porteous was no longer official; the act which he came to protect and guard, being done and ended, he was no better than *cuivis ex populo*.'

'*Quivis* – *quivis*, Mr Saddletree, craving your pardon,' said (with a prolonged emphasis on the first syllable) Mr Butler, the deputy schoolmaster of a parish near Edinburgh, who at that moment came up behind them as the false Latin was uttered.

'What signifies interrupting me, Mr Butler? – but I am glad to see ye notwithstanding – I speak after Counsellor Crossmyloof, and he said *cuivis*.'

'If Counsellor Crossmyloof used the dative for the nominative, I would have crossed *his* loof with a tight leathern strap, Mr Saddletree; there is not a boy on the booby form but should have been scourged for such a solecism in grammar.'

'I speak Latin like a lawyer, Mr Butler, and not like a schoolmaster,' retorted Saddletree.

'Scarce like a schoolboy, I think,' rejoined Butler.

'It matters little,' said Bartoline; 'all I mean to say is, that Porteous has become liable to the *pœna extra ordinem*, or capital punishment, which is to say, in plain Scotch, the gallows, simply because he did not fire when he was in office, but waited till the body was cut down, the execution whilk he had in charge to guard implemented, and he himself exonered of the public trust imposed on him.'

'But, Mr Saddletree,' said Plumdamas, 'do ye really think John Porteous's case wad hae been better if he had begun firing before ony stanes were flung at a'?'

'Indeed do I, neighbour Plumdamas,' replied Bartoline, confidently, 'he being then in point of trust and in point of power, the execution being but inchoat, or, at least, not implemented, or finally ended; but after Wilson was cut down it was a' ower – he was clean exauctorate, and had nae mair ado but to get awa wi' his guard up this West Bow as fast as if there had been a caption after him – And this is law, for I heard it laid down by Lord Vincovincentem.'

'Vincovincentem? – Is he a lord of state, or a lord of seat?' inquired Mrs Howden.

'A lord of seat – a lord of session. – I fash mysell little wi' lords o' state; they vex me wi' a wheen idle questions about their saddles, and curpels, and holsters and horse-furniture, and what they'll cost, and whan they'll be ready – a wheen galloping geese – my wife may serve the like o' them.'

'And so might she, in her day, hae served the best lord in the land, for as little as ye think o' her, Mr Saddletree,' said Mrs Howden, somewhat indignant at the contemptuous way in which her gossip was mentioned; 'when she and I were twa gilpies, we little thought to hae sitten doun wi' the like o' my auld Davie Howden, or you either, Mr Saddletree.'

While Saddletree, who was not bright at a reply, was cudgelling his brains for an answer to this home-thrust, Miss Damahoy broke in on him.

'And as for the lords of state,' said Miss Damahoy, 'ye suld mind the riding o' the parliament, Mr Saddletree, in the gude auld time before the Union, – a year's rent o' mony a gude estate gaed for horse-graith and harnessing, forby broidered robes and foot-mantles, that wad hae stude by their lane wi' gold brocade, and that were muckle in my ain line.'

'Ay, and then the lusty banqueting, with sweetmeats and comfits wet and dry, and dried fruits of divers sorts,' said Plumdamas. 'But Scotland was Scotland in these days.'

'I'll tell ye what it is, neighbours,' said Mrs Howden, 'I'll ne'er believe Scotland is Scotland ony mair, if our kindly Scots sit doun with the affront they hae gien us this day. It's not only the blude that *is* shed, but the blude that might hae been shed, that's required at our hands; there was my daughter's wean, little

Eppie Daidle – my oe, ye ken, Miss Grizel – had played the truant frae the school, as bairns will do, ye ken, Mr Butler – '

'And for which,' interjected Mr Butler, 'they should be soundly scourged by their well-wishers.'

'And had just cruppen to the gallows' foot to see the hanging, as was natural for a wean; and what for mightna she hae been shot as weel as the rest o' them, and where wad we a' hae been then? I wonder how Queen Carline (if her name be Carline) wad hae liked to hae had ane o' her ain bairns in sic a venture?'

'Report says,' answered Butler, 'that such a circumstance would not have distressed her majesty beyond endurance.'

'Aweel,' said Mrs Howden, 'the sum o' the matter is, that, were I a man, I wad hae amends o' Jock Porteous, be the upshot what like o't, if a' the carles and carlines in England had sworn to the nay-say.'

'I would claw down the Tolbooth door wi' my nails,' said Miss Grizel, 'but I wad be at him.'

'Ye may be very right, ladies,' said Butler, 'but I would not advise you to speak so loud.'

'Speak!' exclaimed both the ladies together, 'there will be naething else spoken about frae the Weigh-house to the Water-gate, till this is either ended or mended.'

The females now departed to their respective places of abode. Plumdamas joined the other two gentlemen in drinking their *meridian* (a bumper-dram of brandy), as they passed the well-known low-browed shop in the Lawnmarket, where they were wont to take that refreshment. Mr Plumdamas then departed towards his shop, and Mr Butler, who happened to have some particular occasion for the rein of an old bridle (the truants of that busy day could have anticipated its application), walked down the Lawnmarket with Mr Saddletree, each talking as he could get a word thrust in, the one on the laws of Scotland, the other on those of syntax, and neither listening to a word which his companion uttered.

MARY SHELLEY (1797–1851)

Mary Shelley was the daughter of William Godwin and Mary Wollstonecraft, two of the most important radical intellectuals of the revolutionary period. Her mother died of puerperal fever a few days after Mary's birth. In 1814 Mary Godwin eloped with Percy Bysshe Shelley, who was a friend of her father. In 1815 she had a premature baby which died. In 1816 Mary had a son, William, and they moved to Geneva. It was there whilst Byron was visiting that they began for amusement to invent Gothic tales and the story of Frankenstein was conceived. Towards the close of 1816, as Mary was working on her tale, both Mary's half-sister, Fanny Imlay, and Harriet Shelley committed suicide. Mary's tale drew deeply on her recent traumatic experiences and extensive reading and attracted considerable notice when it was published in 1818. Whilst the story in some obvious respects belongs to the Gothic tradition, it transcends them in the seriousness of its concerns, and in its complex narrative method. The questions posed by *Frankenstein* about men, reason, science, society, alienation and nature have grown more rather than less pressing in the ensuing years. In 1822 Percy Shelley was drowned, leaving Mary impoverished, and she returned to England and lived as a woman of letters, writing five novels, of which only the science-fiction tale *The Last Man* (1826) is well-regarded.

From Frankenstein, or The Modern Prometheus

From Chapter 3

The next morning I delivered my letters of introduction, and paid a visit to some of the principal professors. Chance – or rather the evil influence, the Angel of Destruction, which asserted omnipotent sway over me from the moment I turned my reluctant steps from my father's door – led me first to M. Krempe, professor of natural philosophy. He was an uncouth man, but deeply embued in the secrets of his science. He asked me several questions concerning my progress in the different branches of science appertaining to natural philosophy. I replied carelessly; and, partly in contempt, mentioned the names of my alchemists as the principal authors I had studied. The professor stared: 'Have you,' he said, 'really spent your time in studying such nonsense?'

I replied in the affirmative. 'Every minute,' continued M. Krempe with warmth, 'every instant that you have wasted on those books is utterly and entirely lost. You have burdened your memory with exploded systems and useless names. Good God! in what desert land have you lived, where no one was kind enough to inform you that these fancies, which you have so greedily imbibed, are a thousand years old, and as musty as they are ancient? I little expected, in this enlightened and scientific age, to find a disciple of Albertus Magnus and Paracelsus.[1] My dear sir, you must begin your studies entirely anew.'

So saying, he stepped aside, and wrote down a list of several books treating of natural philosophy, which he desired me to procure; and dismissed me, after mentioning that in the beginning of the following week he intended to

---

1: Albertus Magnus (1193–1280), Dominican monk who studied the brain; Paracelsus (1493–1541), Swiss doctor, alchemist and serious medical researcher.

commence a course of lectures upon natural philosophy in its general relations, and that M. Waldman, a fellow-professor, would lecture upon chemistry the alternate days that he omitted.

I returned home, not disappointed, for I have said that I had long considered those authors useless whom the professor reprobated; but I returned, not at all the more inclined to recur to these studies in any shape. M. Krempe was a little, squat man, with a gruff voice and a repulsive countenance; the teacher, therefore, did not prepossess me in favour of his pursuits. In rather too philosophical and connected a strain, perhaps, I have given an account of the conclusions I had come to concerning them in my early years. As a child, I had not been content with the results promised by the modern professors of natural science. With a confusion of ideas only to be accounted for by my extreme youth, and my want of a guide on such matters, I had retrod the steps of knowledge along the paths of time, and exchanged the discoveries of recent enquirers for the dreams of forgotten alchemists. Besides, I had a contempt for the uses of modern natural philosophy. It was very different, when the masters of the science sought immortality and power; such views, although futile, were grand: but now the scene was changed. The ambition of the enquirer seemed to limit itself to the annihilation of those visions on which my interest in science was chiefly founded. I was required to exchange chimeras of boundless grandeur for realities of little worth.

Such were my reflections during the first two or three days of my residence at Ingolstadt, which were chiefly spent in becoming acquainted with the localities, and the principal residents in my new abode. But as the ensuing week commenced, I thought of the information which M. Krempe had given me concerning the lectures. And although I could not consent to go and hear that little conceited fellow deliver sentences out of a pulpit, I recollected what he had said of M. Waldman, whom I had never seen, as he had hitherto been out of town.

Partly from curiosity, and partly from idleness, I went into the lecturing room, which M. Waldman entered shortly after. This professor was very unlike his colleague. He appeared about fifty years of age, but with an aspect expressive of the greatest benevolence; a few grey hairs covered his temples, but those at the back of his head were nearly black. His person was short, but remarkably erect; and his voice the sweetest I had ever heard. He began his lecture by a recapitulation of the history of chemistry, and the various improvements made by different men of learning, pronouncing with fervour the names of the most distinguished discoverers. He then took a cursory view of the present state of the science, and explained many of its elementary terms. After having made a few preparatory experiments, he concluded with a panegyric upon modern chemistry, the terms of which I shall never forget: –

'The ancient teachers of this science,' said he, 'promised impossibilities, and performed nothing. The modern masters promise very little; they know that metals cannot be transmuted, and that the elixir of life is a chimera. But these philosophers, whose hands seem only made to dabble in dirt, and their eyes to pore over the microscope or crucible, have indeed performed miracles. They penetrate into the recesses of nature, and show how she works in her hiding places. They ascend into the heavens: they have discovered how the blood circulates, and the nature of the air we breathe. They have acquired new and almost unlimited powers; they can command the thunders of heaven, mimic the earthquake, and even mock the invisible world with its own shadows.'

Such were the professor's words – rather let me say such the words of fate, enounced to destroy me. As he went on, I felt as if my soul were grappling with a palpable enemy; one by one the various keys were touched which formed the mechanism of my being: chord after chord was sounded, and soon my mind was filled with one thought, one conception, one purpose. So much has been done, exclaimed the soul of Frankenstein, – more, far more, will I achieve: treading in the steps already marked, I will pioneer a new way, explore unknown powers, and unfold to the world the deepest mysteries of creation.

I closed not my eyes that night. My internal being was in a state of insurrection and turmoil; I felt that order would thence arise, but I had no power to produce it. By degrees, after the morning's dawn, sleep came. I awoke, and my yesternight's thoughts were as a dream. There only remained a resolution to return to my ancient studies, and to devote myself to a science for which I believed myself to possess a natural talent. On the same day, I paid M. Waldman a visit. His manners in private were even more mild and attractive than in public; for there was a certain dignity in his mien during his lecture, which in his own house was replaced by the greatest affability and kindness. I gave him pretty nearly the same account of my former pursuits as I had given to his fellow-professor. He heard with attention the little narration concerning my studies, and smiled at the names of Cornelius Agrippa[1] and Paracelsus, but without the contempt that M. Krempe had exhibited. He said, that 'these were men to whose indefatigable zeal modern philosophers were indebted for most of the foundations of their knowledge. They had left to us, as an easier task, to give new names, and arrange in connected classifications, the facts which they in a great degree had been the instruments of bringing to light. The labours of men of genius, however erroneously directed, scarcely ever fail in ultimately turning to the solid advantage of mankind.' I listened to his statement, which was delivered without any presumption or affectation; and then added, that his lecture had removed my prejudices against modern chemists; I expressed myself in measured terms, with the modesty and deference due from a youth to his instructor, without letting escape (inexperience in life would have made me ashamed) any of the enthusiasm which stimulated my intended labours. I requested his advice concerning the books I ought to procure.

'I am happy,' said M. Waldman, 'to have gained a disciple; and if your application equals your ability, I have no doubt of your success. Chemistry is that branch of natural philosophy[2] in which the greatest improvements have been and may be made: it is on that account that I have made it my peculiar study; but at the same time I have not neglected the other branches of science. A man would make but a very sorry chemist if he attended to that department of human knowledge alone. If your wish is to become really a man of science,

---

1: Agrippa (1486–1535), German author of works on the occult. 2: Natural philosophy was a discipline embracing all branches of the physical sciences.

and not merely a petty experimentalist, I should advise you to apply to every branch of natural philosophy, including mathematics.'

He then took me into his laboratory, and explained to me the uses of his various machines; instructing me as to what I ought to procure, and promising me the use of his own when I should have advanced far enough in the science not to derange their mechanism. He also gave me the list of books which I had requested; and I took my leave.

Thus ended a day memorable to me: it decided my future destiny.

Chapter 4

From this day natural philosophy, and particularly chemistry, in the most comprehensive sense of the term, became nearly my sole occupation. I read with ardour those works, so full of genius and discrimination, which modern enquirers have written on these subjects. I attended the lectures, and cultivated the acquaintance, of the men of science of the university; and I found even in M. Krempe a great deal of sound sense and real information, combined, it is true, with a repulsive physiognomy and manners, but not on that account the less valuable. In M. Waldman I found a true friend. His gentleness was never tinged by dogmatism; and his instructions were given with an air of frankness and good nature, that banished every idea of pedantry. In a thousand ways he smoothed for me the path of knowledge, and made the most abstruse enquiries clear and facile to my apprehension. My application was at first fluctuating and uncertain; it gained strength as I proceeded, and soon became so ardent and eager, that the stars often disappeared in the light of morning whilst I was yet engaged in my laboratory.

As I applied so closely, it may be easily conceived that my progress was rapid. My ardour was indeed the astonishment of the students, and my proficiency that of the masters. Professor Krempe often asked me, with a sly smile, how Cornelius Agrippa went on? whilst M. Waldman expressed the most heartfelt exultation in my progress. Two years passed in this manner, during which I paid no visit to Geneva,[1] but was engaged, heart and soul, in the pursuit of some discoveries, which I hoped to make. None but those who have experienced them can conceive of the enticements of science. In other studies you go as far as others have gone before you, and there is nothing more to know; but in a scientific pursuit there is continual food for discovery and wonder. A mind of moderate capacity, which closely pursues one study, must infallibly arrive at great proficiency in that study; and I, who continually sought the attainment of one object of pursuit, and was solely wrapt up in this, improved so rapidly, that, at the end of two years, I made some discoveries in the improvement of some chemical instruments, which procured me great esteem and admiration at the university. When I had arrived at this point, and had become as well acquainted with the theory and practice of natural philosophy as depended on the lessons of any of the professors at Ingolstadt, my residence there being no longer conducive to my improvements, I thought of returning to my friends and my

---

1: Frankenstein comes from Geneva and his family and fiancée still live there.

native town, when an incident happened that protracted my stay.

One of the phenomena which had peculiarly attracted my attention was the structure of the human frame, and, indeed, any animal endued with life. Whence, I often asked myself, did the principle of life proceed? It was a bold question, and one which has ever been considered as a mystery; yet with how many things are we upon the brink of becoming acquainted, if cowardice or carelessness did not restrain our enquiries. I revolved these circumstances in my mind, and determined thenceforth to apply myself more particularly to those branches of natural philosophy which relate to physiology. Unless I had been animated by an almost supernatural enthusiasm, my application to this study would have been irksome, and almost intolerable. To examine the causes of life, we must first have recourse to death. I became acquainted with the science of anatomy: but this was not sufficient; I must also observe the natural decay and corruption of the human body. In my education my father had taken the greatest precautions that my mind should be impressed with no supernatural horrors. I do not ever remember to have trembled at a tale of superstition, or to have feared the apparition of a spirit. Darkness had no effect upon my fancy; and a churchyard was to me merely the receptacle of bodies deprived of life, which, from being the seat of beauty and strength, had become food for the worm. Now I was led to examine the cause and progress of this decay, and forced to spend days and nights in vaults and charnel-houses. My attention was fixed upon every object the most insupportable to the delicacy of the human feelings. I saw how the fine form of man was degraded and wasted; I beheld the corruption of death succeed to the blooming cheek of life; I saw how the worm inherited the wonders of the eye and brain. I paused, examining and analysing all the minutiae of causation, as exemplified in the change from life to death, and death to life, until from the midst of this darkness a sudden light broke in upon me – a light so brilliant and wondrous, yet so simple, that while I became dizzy with the immensity of the prospect which it illustrated, I was surprised, that among so many men of genius who had directed their enquiries towards the same science, I alone should be reserved to discover so astonishing a secret.

Remember, I am not recording the vision of a madman. The sun does not more certainly shine in the heavens, than that which I now affirm is true. Some miracle might have produced it, yet the stages of the discovery were distinct and probable. After days and nights of incredible labour and fatigue, I succeeded in discovering the cause of generation and life; nay, more, I became myself capable of bestowing animation upon lifeless matter.

The astonishment which I had at first experienced on this discovery soon gave place to delight and rapture. After so much time spent in painful labour, to arrive at once at the summit of my desires, was the most gratifying consummation of my toils. But this discovery was so great and overwhelming, that all the steps by which I had been progressively led to it were obliterated, and I beheld only the result. What had been the study and desire of the wisest men since the creation of the world was now within my grasp. Not that, like a magic scene, it all opened upon me at once: the information I had obtained was of a nature rather to direct my endeavours so soon as I should point them towards the object of my search, than to exhibit that object already accomplished.

I was like the Arabian who had been buried with the dead, and found a passage to life, aided only by one glimmering, and seemingly ineffectual, light.

I see by your[1] eagerness, and the wonder and hope which your eyes express, my friend, that you expect to be informed of the secret with which I am acquainted; that cannot be: listen patiently until the end of my story, and you will easily perceive why I am reserved upon that subject. I will not lead you on, unguarded and ardent as I then was, to your destruction and infallible misery. Learn from me, if not by my precepts, at least by my example, how dangerous is the acquirement of knowledge, and how much happier that man is who believes his native town to be the world, than he who aspires to become greater than his nature will allow.

When I found so astonishing a power placed within my hands, I hesitated a long time concerning the manner in which I should employ it. Although I possessed the capacity of bestowing animation, yet to prepare a frame for the reception of it, with all its intricacies of fibres, muscles, and veins, still remained a work of inconceivable difficulty and labour. I doubted at first whether I should attempt the creation of a being like myself, or one of simpler organization; but my imagination was too much exalted by my first success to permit me to doubt of my ability to give life to an animal as complex and wonderful as man. The materials at present within my command hardly appeared adequate to so arduous an undertaking; but I doubted not that I should ultimately succeed. I prepared myself for a multitude of reverses; my operations might be incessantly baffled, and at last my work be imperfect: yet, when I considered the improvement which every day takes place in science and mechanics, I was encouraged to hope my present attempts would at least lay the foundations of future success. Nor could I consider the magnitude and complexity of my plan as any argument of its impracticability. It was with these feelings that I began the creation of a human being. As the minuteness of the parts formed a great hindrance to my speed, I resolved, contrary to my first intention, to make the being of a gigantic stature; that is to say, about eight feet in height, and proportionably large. After having formed this determination, and having spent some months in successfully collecting and arranging my materials, I began.

No one can conceive the variety of feelings which bore me onwards, like a hurricane, in the first enthusiasm of success. Life and death appeared to me ideal bounds, which I should first break through, and pour a torrent of light into our dark world. A new species would bless me as its creator and source; many happy and excellent natures would owe their being to me. No father could claim the gratitude of his child so completely as I should deserve theirs. Pursuing these reflections, I thought, that if I could bestow animation upon lifeless matter, I might in process of time (although I now found it impossible) renew life where death had apparently devoted the body to corruption.

These thoughts supported my spirits, while I pursued my undertaking with unremitting ardour. My cheek had grown pale with study, and my person had

---

1: The story begins with four letters from Robert Walton, who is making a voyage to find the North Pole. (He is another scientist who puts ego before heart.) The letters are sent to his sister, Mrs Saville, explaining how he has picked up a distraught man from the ice. The man is Frankenstein, and he tells his story to Walton.

become emaciated with confinement. Sometimes, on the very brink of certainty, I failed; yet still I clung to the hope which the next day or the next hour might realise. One secret which I alone possessed was the hope to which I had dedicated myself; and the moon gazed on my midnight labours, while, with unrelaxed and breathless eagerness, I pursued nature to her hiding-places. Who shall conceive the horrors of my secret toil, as I dabbled among the unhallowed damps of the grave, or tortured the living animal to animate the lifeless clay? My limbs now tremble, and my eyes swim with the remembrance; but then a resistless, and almost frantic, impulse, urged me forward; I seemed to have lost all soul or sensation but for this one pursuit. It was indeed but a passing trance, that only made me feel with renewed acuteness so soon as, the unnatural stimulus ceasing to operate, I had returned to my old habits. I collected bones from charnel-houses; and disturbed, with profane fingers, the tremendous secrets of the human frame. In a solitary chamber, or rather cell, at the top of the house, and separated from all the other apartments by a gallery and staircase, I kept my workshop of filthy creation: my eye-balls were starting from their sockets in attending to the details of my employment. The dissecting room and the slaughter-house furnished many of my materials; and often did my human nature turn with loathing from my occupation, whilst, still urged on by an eagerness which perpetually increased, I brought my work near to a conclusion.

The summer months passed while I was thus engaged, heart and soul, in one pursuit. It was a most beautiful season; never did the fields bestow a more plentiful harvest, or the vines yield a more luxuriant vintage: but my eyes were insensible to the charms of nature. And the same feelings which made me neglect the scenes around me caused me also to forget those friends who were so many miles absent, and whom I had not seen for so long a time. I knew my silence disquieted them; and I well remembered the words of my father: 'I know that while you are pleased with yourself, you will think of us with affection, and we shall hear regularly from you. You must pardon me if I regard any interruption in your correspondence as a proof that your other duties are equally neglected.'

I knew well therefore what would be my father's feelings; but I could not tear my thoughts from my employment, loathsome in itself, but which had taken an irresistible hold of my imagination. I wished, as it were, to procrastinate all that related to my feelings of affection until the great object, which swallowed up every habit of my nature, should be completed.

I then thought that my father would be unjust if he ascribed my neglect to vice, or faultiness on my part; but I am now convinced that he was justified in conceiving that I should not be altogether free from blame. A human being in perfection ought always to preserve a calm and peaceful mind, and never to allow passion or a transitory desire to disturb his tranquillity. I do not think that the pursuit of knowledge is an exception to this rule. If the study to which you apply yourself has a tendency to weaken your affections, and to destroy your taste for those simple pleasures in which no alloy can possibly mix, then that study is certainly unlawful, that is to say, not befitting the human mind. If this rule were always observed; if no man allowed any pursuit whatsoever to interfere with the tranquillity of his domestic affections, Greece had not been enslaved; Caesar would have spared his country; America would have been discovered more gradually; and the empires of Mexico and Peru had not been destroyed.

But I forget that I am moralising in the most interesting part of my tale; and your looks remind me to proceed.

My father made no reproach in his letters, and only took notice of my silence by enquiring into my occupations more particularly than before. Winter, spring, and summer passed away during my labours; but I did not watch the blossom or the expanding leaves – sights which before always yielded my supreme delight – so deeply was I engrossed in my occupation. The leaves of that year had withered before my work drew near to a close; and now every day showed me more plainly how well I had succeeded. But my enthusiasm was checked by my anxiety, and I appeared rather like one doomed by slavery to toil in the mines, or any other unwholesome trade, than an artist occupied by his favourite employment. Every night I was oppressed by a slow fever, and I became nervous to a most painful degree; the fall of a leaf startled me, and I shunned my fellow-creatures as if I had been guilty of a crime. Sometimes I grew alarmed at the wreck I perceived that I had become; the energy of my purpose alone sustained me: my labours would soon end, and I believed that exercise and amusement would then drive away incipient disease; and I promised myself both of these when my creation should be complete.

Chapter 5

It was on a dreary night of November, that I beheld the accomplishment of my toils. With an anxiety that almost amounted to agony, I collected the instruments of life around me, that I might infuse a spark of being into the lifeless thing that lay at my feet. It was already one in the morning; the rain pattered dismally against the panes, and my candle was nearly burnt out, when, by the glimmer of the half-extinguished light, I saw the dull yellow eye of the creature open; it breathed hard, and a convulsive motion agitated its limbs.

How can I describe my emotions at this catastrophe, or how delineate the wretch whom with such infinite pains and care I had endeavoured to form? His limbs were in proportion, and I had selected his features as beautiful. Beautiful! – Great God! His yellow skin scarcely covered the work of muscles and arteries beneath; his hair was of a lustrous black, and flowing; his teeth of a pearly whiteness; but these luxuriances only formed a more horrid contrast with his watery eyes, that seemed almost of the same colour as the dun white sockets in which they were set, his shrivelled complexion and straight black lips.

The different accidents of life are not so changeable as the feelings of human nature. I had worked hard for nearly two years, for the sole purpose of infusing life into an inanimate body. For this I had deprived myself of rest and health. I had desired it with an ardour that far exceeded moderation; but now that I had finished, the beauty of the dream vanished, and breathless horror and disgust filled my heart. Unable to endure the aspect of the being I had created, I rushed out of the room, and continued a long time traversing my bedchamber, unable to compose my mind to sleep. At length lassitude succeeded to the tumult I had before endured; and I threw myself on the bed in my clothes, endeavouring to seek a few moments of forgetfulness. But it was in vain; I slept, indeed, but I was disturbed by the wildest dreams. I thought I saw Elizabeth,[1] in the bloom of health, walking in the streets of Ingolstadt. Delighted and surprised, I embraced her; but as I imprinted the first kiss on her lips, they became livid with the hue of death; her features appeared to change, and I thought that I held the corpse of my dead mother in my arms; a shroud enveloped her form, and I saw the graveworms crawling in the folds of the flannel. I started from my sleep with horror; a cold dew covered my forehead, my teeth chattered, and every limb became convulsed; when, by the dim and yellow light of the moon, as it forced its way through the window shutters, I beheld the wretch – the miserable monster whom I had created. He held up the curtain of the bed; and his eyes, if eyes they may be called, were fixed on me. His jaws opened, and he muttered some inarticulate sounds, while a grin wrinkled his cheeks. He might have spoken, but I did not hear; one hand was stretched out, seemingly to detain me, but I escaped, and rushed down stairs. I took refuge in the courtyard belonging to the house which I inhabited; where I remained during the rest of the night, walking up and down in the greatest agitation, listening attentively, catching and fearing each sound as if it were to announce the approach of the demoniacal corpse to which I had so miserably given life.

Oh! no mortal could support the horror of that countenance. A mummy again endued with animation could not be so hideous as that wretch. I had gazed on him while unfinished; he was ugly then; but when those muscles and joints were rendered capable of motion, it became a thing such as even Dante could not have conceived.

I passed the night wretchedly. Sometimes my pulse beat so quickly and hardly, that I felt the palpitation of every artery; at others, I nearly sank to the ground through languor and extreme weakness. Mingled with this horror, I felt the bitterness of disappointment; dreams that had been my food and pleasant rest for so long a space were now become a hell to me; and the change was so rapid, the overthrow so complete!

Morning, dismal and wet, at length dawned, and discovered to my sleepless and aching eyes the church of Ingolstadt, its white steeple and clock, which indicated the sixth hour. The porter opened the gates of the court, which had that night been my asylum, and I issued into the streets, pacing them with quick steps, as if I sought to avoid the wretch whom I feared every turning of the street would present to my view. I did not dare return to the apartment which I inhabited, but felt impelled to hurry on, although drenched by the rain which poured from a black and comfortless sky.

I continued walking in this manner for some time, endeavouring, by bodily exercise, to ease the load that weighed upon my mind. I traversed the streets, without any clear conception of where I was, or what I was doing. My heart palpitated in the sickness of fear; and I hurried on with irregular steps, not daring to look about me: –

1: Elizabeth is Frankenstein's cousin and fiancée.

> Like one who, on a lonely road,
>   Doth walk in fear and dread,
>   And, having once turned round, walks on,
>   And turns no more his head;
>   Because he knows a frightful fiend
>   Doth close behind him tread.[1]

Continuing thus, I came at length opposite to the inn at which the various diligences and carriages usually stopped. Here I paused, I knew not why; but I remained some minutes with my eyes fixed on a coach that was coming towards me from the other end of the street. As it drew nearer, I observed that it was the Swiss diligence: it stopped just where I was standing; and, on the door being opened, I perceived Henry Clerval,[2] who, on seeing me, instantly sprung out. 'My dear Frankenstein,' exclaimed he, 'how glad I am to see you! how fortunate that you should be here at the very moment of my alighting!'

Nothing could equal my delight on seeing Clerval; his presence brought back to my thoughts my father, Elizabeth, and all those scenes of home so dear to my recollection. I grasped his hand, and in a moment forgot my horror and misfortune; I felt suddenly, and for the first time during many months, calm and serene joy. I welcomed my friend, therefore, in the most cordial manner, and we walked towards my college. Clerval continued talking for some time about our mutual friends, and his own good fortune in being permitted to come to Ingolstadt. 'You may easily believe,' said he, 'how great was the difficulty to persuade my father that all necessary knowledge was not comprised in the noble art of book-keeping; and, indeed, I believe I left him incredulous to the last, for his constant answer to my unwearied entreaties was the same as that of the Dutch schoolmaster in the Vicar of Wakefield: – "I have ten thousand florins a year without Greek, I eat heartily without Greek."[3] But his affection for me at length overcame his dislike of learning, and he has permitted me to undertake a voyage of discovery to the land of knowledge.'

'It gives me the greatest delight to see you; but tell me how you left my father, brothers, and Elizabeth.'

'Very well, and very happy, only a little uneasy that they hear from you so seldom. By the by, I mean to lecture you a little upon their account myself. – But, my dear Frankenstein,' continued he, stopping short, and gazing full in my face, 'I did not before remark how very ill you appear; so thin and pale; you look as if you had been watching for several nights.'

'You have guessed right; I have lately been so deeply engaged in one occupation, that I have not allowed myself sufficient rest, as you see; but I hope, I sincerely hope, that all these employments are now at an end, and that I am at length free.'

I trembled excessively; I could not endure to think of, and far less to allude to, the occurrences of the preceding night. I walked with a quick pace, and we soon arrived at my college. I then reflected, and the thought made me shiver,

---

1: Coleridge, *The Rime of the Ancient Mariner*, ll. 446–51. 2: Frankenstein's oldest friend. 3: Oliver Goldsmith (1730–74), *The Vicar of Wakefield* (1764), Ch. 20.

that the creature whom I had left in my apartment might still be there, alive, and walking about. I dreaded to behold this monster; but I feared still more that Henry should see him. Entreating him, therefore, to remain a few minutes at the bottom of the stairs, I darted up towards my own room. My hand was already on the lock of the door before I recollected myself. I then paused; and a cold shivering came over me. I threw the door forcibly open, as children are accustomed to do when they expect a spectre to stand in waiting for them on the other side; but nothing appeared. I stepped fearfully in: the apartment was empty; and my bedroom was also freed from its hideous guest. I could hardly believe that so great a good fortune could have befallen me; but when I became assured that my enemy had indeed fled, I clapped my hands for joy, and ran down to Clerval.

We ascended into my room, and the servant presently brought breakfast; but I was unable to contain myself. It was not joy only that possessed me; I felt my flesh tingle with excess of sensitiveness, and my pulse beat rapidly. I was unable to remain for a single instant in the same place; I jumped over the chairs, clapped my hands, and laughed aloud. Clerval at first attributed my unusual spirits to joy on his arrival; but when he observed me more attentively, he saw a wildness in my eyes for which he could not account; and my loud, unrestrained, heartless laughter, frightened and astonished him.

'My dear Victor,' cried he, 'what, for God's sake, is the matter? Do not laugh in that manner. How ill you are! What is the cause of all this?'

'Do not ask me,' cried I, putting my hands before my eyes, for I thought I saw the dreaded spectre glide into the room; '*he* can tell. – Oh, save me! save me!' I imagined that the monster seized me; I struggled furiously, and fell down in a fit.

Poor Clerval! what must have been his feelings? A meeting, which he anticipated with such joy, so strangely turned to bitterness. But I was not the witness of his grief; for I was lifeless, and did not recover my senses for a long, long time.

[The escaped monster takes refuge in the outhouse of a rural cottage and learns about language and human culture by secretly observing the occupants. He is soon able to read Milton, Plutarch and Goethe. His attempt to befriend the cottagers is repulsed. He travels, finds himself despised everywhere, and returns to Frankenstein to demand he make him a mate so that he can end his solitude. Frankenstein promises to do so, but defers the act, travelling to England, then to the Orkneys where the monster catches up with him. Frankenstein decides to destroy the mate rather than have the monsters procreate. In revenge, the monster sets about destroying all those whom Frankenstein loves.]

From Chapter 22

Sweet and beloved Elizabeth! I read and re-read her letter, and some softened feelings stole into my heart, and dared to whisper paradisiacal dreams of hope and joy; but the apple was already eaten, and the angel's arm bared to drive me from all hope. Yet I would die to make her happy. If the monster executed his threat, death was inevitable; yet, again, I considered whether my marriage would hasten my fate. My destruction might indeed arrive a few months sooner; but if my torturer should suspect that I postponed it, influenced by his menaces, he would surely find other, and perhaps more dreadful means of revenge. He had vowed *to be with me on my wedding-night*, yet he did not consider that threat as binding him to peace in the mean time; for, as if to show me that he was not yet satiated with blood, he had murdered Clerval immediately after the enunciation of his threats. I resolved, therefore, that if my immediate union with my cousin would conduce either to hers or my father's happiness, my adversary's designs against my life should not retard it a single hour.

In this state of mind I wrote to Elizabeth. My letter was calm and affectionate. 'I fear, my beloved girl,' I said, 'little happiness remains for us on earth; yet all that I may one day enjoy is centred in you. Chase away your idle fears; to you alone do I consecrate my life, and my endeavours for contentment. I have one secret, Elizabeth, a dreadful one; when revealed to you, it will chill your frame with horror, and then, far from being surprised at my misery, you will only wonder that I survive what I have endured. I will confide this tale of misery and terror to you the day after our marriage shall take place; for, my sweet cousin, there must be perfect confidence between us. But until then, I conjure you, do not mention or allude to it. This I most earnestly entreat, and I know you will comply.'

In about a week after the arrival of Elizabeth's letter, we returned to Geneva. The sweet girl welcomed me with warm affection; yet tears were in her eyes, as she beheld my emaciated frame and feverish cheeks. I saw a change in her also. She was thinner, and had lost much of that heavenly vivacity that had before charmed me; but her gentleness, and soft looks of compassion, made her a more fit companion for one blasted and miserable as I was.

The tranquillity which I now enjoyed did not endure. Memory brought madness with it; and when I thought of what had passed, a real insanity possessed me; sometimes I was furious, and burnt with rage, sometimes low and despondent. I neither spoke, nor looked at any one, but sat motionless, bewildered by the multitude of miseries that overcame me.

Elizabeth alone had the power to draw me from these fits; her gentle voice would soothe me when transported by passion, and inspire me with human feelings when sunk in torpor. She wept with me, and for me. When reason returned, she would remonstrate, and endeavour to inspire me with resignation. Ah! it is well for the unfortunate to be resigned, but for the guilty there is no peace. The agonies of remorse poison the luxury there is otherwise sometimes found in indulging the excess of grief.

Soon after my arrival, my father spoke of my immediate marriage with Elizabeth. I remained silent.

'Have you, then, some other attachment?'

'None on earth. I love Elizabeth and look forward to our union with delight. Let the day therefore be fixed; and on it I will consecrate myself, in life or death, to the happiness of my cousin.'

'My dear Victor, do not speak thus. Heavy misfortunes have befallen us; but let us cling closer to what remains, and transfer our love for those whom we have lost, to those who yet live. Our circle will be small, but bound close by the ties of affection and mutual misfortune. And when time shall have softened your despair, new and dear objects of care will be born to replace those of whom we have been so cruelly deprived.'

Such were the lessons of my father. But to me the remembrance of the threat returned: nor can you wonder, that, omnipotent as the fiend had yet been in his deeds of blood, I should almost regard him as invincible; and that when he had pronounced the words 'I shall be with you on your wedding night,' I should regard the threatened fate as unavoidable. But death was no evil to me, if the loss of Elizabeth were balanced with it; and I therefore, with a contented and even cheerful countenance, agreed with my father, that if my cousin would consent, the ceremony should take place in ten days, and thus put, as I imagined, the seal to my fate.

Great God! if for one instant I had thought what might be the hellish intention of my fiendish adversary, I would rather have banished myself forever from my native country, and wandered a friendless outcast over the earth, than have consented to this miserable marriage. But, as if possessed of magic powers, the monster had blinded me to his real intentions; and when I thought that I had prepared only my own death, I hastened that of a far dearer victim.

As the period fixed for our marriage drew near, whether from cowardice or a prophetic feeling, I felt my heart sink within me. But I concealed my feelings by an appearance of hilarity that brought smiles and joy to the countenance of my father, but hardly deceived the ever-watchful and nicer eye of Elizabeth. She looked forward to our union with placid contentment, not unmingled with a little fear, which past misfortunes had impressed, that what now appeared certain and tangible happiness, might soon dissipate into an airy dream, and leave no trace but deep and everlasting regret.

Preparations were made for the event; congratulatory visits were received; and all wore a smiling appearance. I shut up, as well as I could, in my own heart the anxiety that preyed there, and entered with seeing earnestness into the plans of my father, although they might only serve as the decorations of my tragedy. Through my father's exertions, a part of the inheritance of Elizabeth had been restored to her by the Austrian government. A small possession on the shores of Como belonged to her. It was agreed that, immediately after our union we should proceed to the Villa Lavenza and spend our first days of happiness beside the beautiful lake near which it stood.

In the mean time I took every precaution to defend my person, in case the fiend should openly attack me. I carried pistols and a dagger constantly about me, and was ever on the watch to prevent artifice; and by these means gained a greater degree of tranquillity. Indeed, as the period approached, the threat appeared more as a delusion, not to be regarded as worthy to disturb my peace, while the happiness I hoped for in my marriage wore a greater appearance of certainty, as the day fixed for its solemnisation drew nearer, and I heard it continually spoken of as an occurrence which no accident could possibly prevent.

Elizabeth seemed happy; my tranquil demeanour contributed greatly to calm her mind. But on the day that was to fulfil my wishes and my destiny, she was melancholy, and a presentiment of evil pervaded her; and perhaps also she thought of the dreadful secret which I had promised to reveal to her on the following day. My father was in the mean time overjoyed, and, in the bustle of preparation, only recognised in the melancholy of his niece the diffidence of a bride.

After the ceremony was performed, a large party assembled at my father's; but it was agreed that Elizabeth and I should commence our journey by water, sleeping that night at Evian, and continuing our voyage on the following day. The day was fair, the wind favourable, all smiled on our nuptial embarkation.

Those were the last moments of my life during which I enjoyed the feeling of happiness. We passed rapidly along: the sun was hot, but we were sheltered from its rays by a kind of canopy, while we enjoyed the beauty of the scene, sometimes on one side of the lake, where we saw Mont Salêve, the pleasant banks of the Montalègre, and at a distance, surmounting all, the beautiful Mont Blanc, and the assemblage of snowy mountains that in vain endeavour to emulate her; sometimes coasting the opposite banks, we saw the mighty Jura opposing its dark side to the ambition that would quit its native country, and an almost insurmountable barrier to the invader who should wish to enslave it.

I took the hand of Elizabeth: 'You are sorrowful, my love. Ah! If you knew what I have suffered, and what I may yet endure, you would endeavour to let me taste the quiet and freedom from despair, that this one day at least permits me to enjoy.'

'Be happy, my dear Victor,' replied Elizabeth; 'there is, I hope, nothing to distress you; and be assured that if a lively joy is not painted in my face, my heart is contented. Something whispers to me not to depend too much upon the prospect of what is opened before us; but I will not listen to such a sinister voice. Observe how fast we move along, and how the clouds, which sometimes obscure and sometimes rise above the dome of Mont Blanc, render this scene of beauty still more interesting. Look also at the innumerable fish that are swimming in the clear waters, where we can distinguish every pebble that lies at the bottom. What a divine day! how happy and serene all nature appears!'

Thus Elizabeth endeavoured to divert her thoughts and mine from all reflection upon melancholy subjects. But her temper was fluctuating; joy for a few instants shone in her eyes, but it continually gave place to distraction and reverie.

The sun sunk lower in the heavens; we passed the river Drance, and observed its path through the chasms of the higher, and the glens of the lower hills. The Alps here come close to the lake, and we approached the amphitheatre of mountains which forms its eastern boundary. The spire of Evian shone under the woods that surrounded it, and the range of mountain above mountain by which it was overhung.

The wind, which had hitherto carried us along with amazing rapidity, sunk at sunset to a light breeze; the soft air just ruffled the water, and caused a pleasant motion among the trees as we approached the shore, from which it wafted the most delightful scent of flowers and hay. The sun sunk beneath the horizon as we landed; and as I touched the shore, I felt those cares and fears revive, which soon were to clasp me, and cling to me forever.

Chapter 23

It was eight o'clock when we landed; we walked for a short time on the shore, enjoying the transitory light, and then retired to the inn, and contemplated the lovely scene of waters, woods, and mountains, obscured in darkness, yet displaying their black outlines.

The wind, which had fallen in the south, now rose with great violence in the west. The moon had reached her summit in the heavens, and was beginning to descend: the clouds swept across it swifter than the flight of the vulture, and dimmed her rays, while the lake reflected the scene of the busy heavens, rendered still busier by the restless waves that were beginning to rise. Suddenly a heavy storm of rain descended.

I had been calm during the day; but so soon as night obscured the shapes of objects, a thousand fears arose in my mind. I was anxious and watchful, while my right hand grasped a pistol which was hidden in my bosom; every sound terrified me; but I resolved that I would sell my life dearly, and not shrink from the conflict until my own life, or that of my adversary, was extinguished.

Elizabeth observed my agitation for some time in timid and fearful silence; but there was something in my glance which communicated terror to her, and trembling she asked, 'What is it that agitates you, my dear Victor? What is it you fear?'

'Oh! peace, peace, my love,' replied I; 'this night, and all will be safe: but this night is dreadful, very dreadful.'

I passed an hour in this state of mind, when suddenly I reflected how fearful the combat which I momentarily expected would be to my wife, and I earnestly entreated her to retire, resolving not to join her until I had obtained some knowledge as to the situation of my enemy.

She left me, and I continued some time, walking up and down the passages of the house, and inspecting every corner that might afford a retreat to my adversary. But I discovered no trace of him, and was beginning to conjecture that some fortunate chance had intervened to prevent the execution of his menaces; when suddenly I heard a shrill and dreadful scream. It came from the room into which Elizabeth had retired. As I heard it, the whole truth rushed into my mind, my arms dropped, the motion of every muscle and fibre was suspended; I could feel the blood trickling in my veins, and tingling in the extremities of my limbs. This state lasted but for an instant; the scream was repeated, and I rushed into the room.

Great God! why did I not then expire! Why am I here to relate the destruction of the best hope, and the purest creature of earth? She was there, lifeless and inanimate, thrown across the bed, her head hanging down, and her pale and distorted features half covered by her hair. Every where I turn I see the same figure – her bloodless arms and relaxed form flung by the murderer on its bridal bier. Could I behold this, and live? Alas! life is obstinate, and clings closest where it is most hated. For a moment only did I lose recollection; I fell senseless on the ground.

When I recovered, I found myself surrounded by the people of the inn; their countenances expressed a breathless terror: but the horror of others appeared only as a mockery, a shadow of the feelings that oppressed me. I escaped from them to the room where lay the body of Elizabeth, my love, my wife, so lately living, so dear, so worthy. She had been moved from the position in which I had first beheld her; and now, as she lay, her head upon her arm, and a handkerchief thrown across her face and neck, I might have supposed her asleep. I rushed towards her, and embraced her with ardour; but the deadly languor and coldness of the limbs told me, that what I now held in my arms had ceased to be the Elizabeth whom I had loved and cherished. The murderous mark of the fiend's grasp was on her neck, and the breath had ceased to issue from her lips.

While I still hung over her in the agony of despair, I happened to look up. The windows of the room had before been darkened; and I felt a kind of panic on seeing the pale yellow light of the moon illuminate the chamber. The shutters had been thrown back; and, with a sensation of horror not to be described, I saw at the open window a figure the most hideous and abhorred. A grin was on the face of the monster; he seemed to jeer, as with a fiendish finger he pointed towards the corpse of my wife. I rushed towards the window, and drawing a pistol from my bosom, fired; but he eluded me, leaped from his station, and, running with the swiftness of lightning, plunged into the lake.

The report of the pistol brought the crowd into the room. I pointed to the spot where he had disappeared, and we followed the track with boats; nets were cast, but in vain. After passing several hours, we returned hopeless, most of my companions believing it to have been a form conjured up by my fancy. After having landed, they proceeded to search the country, parties going in different directions among the woods and vines.

I attempted to accompany them, and proceeded a short distance from the house; but my head whirled round, my steps were like those of a drunken man, I fell at last in a state of utter exhaustion; a film covered my eyes, and my skin was parched with the heat of fever. In this state I was carried back, and placed on a bed, hardly conscious of what had happened; my eyes wandered around the room, as if to seek something that I had lost.

After an interval, I arose, and, as if by instinct, crawled into the room where the corpse of my beloved lay. There were women weeping around – I hung over it, and joined my sad tears to theirs – all this time no distinct idea presented itself to my mind; but my thoughts rambled to various subjects, reflecting confusedly on my misfortunes, and their cause. I was bewildered in a cloud of wonder and horror. The death of William, the execution of Justine, the murder of Clerval, and lastly of my wife; even at that moment I knew not that my only remaining friends were safe from the malignity of the fiend; my father even now might be writhing under his grasp, and Ernest might be dead at his feet. The idea made me shudder, and recalled me to action. I started up, and resolved to return to Geneva with all possible speed.

There were no horses to be procured, and I must return by the lake; but the wind was unfavourable, and the rain fell in torrents. However, it was hardly morning, and I might reasonably hope to arrive by night, I hired men to row, and took an oar myself; for I had always experienced relief from mental torment in bodily exercise. But the overflowing misery I now felt, and the excess of agitation that I endured, rendered me incapable of any exertion. I threw down the oar; and leaning my head upon my hands, gave way to every gloomy idea that arose. If I looked up, I saw the scenes which were familiar to me in my happier time, and which I had contemplated but the day before in the company of her who was now but a shadow and a recollection. Tears streamed from my eyes. The rain ceased for a moment, and I saw the fish play in the waters as they had done a few hours before; they had then been observed by Elizabeth. Nothing is so painful to the human mind as a great and sudden change. The sun might shine, or the clouds might lower: but nothing could appear to me as it had done the day before. A fiend had snatched from me every hope of future happiness: no creature had ever been so miserable as I was; so frightful an event is single in the history of man.

But why should I dwell upon the incidents that followed this last overwhelming event? Mine has been a tale of horrors; I have reached their *acme*, and what I must now relate can but be tedious to you. Know that, one by one, my friends were snatched away; I was left desolate. My own strength is exhausted; and I must tell, in a few words, what remains of my hideous narration.

I arrived at Geneva. My father and Ernest yet lived; but the former sunk under the tidings that I bore. I see him now, excellent and venerable old man! his eyes wandered in vacancy, for they had lost their charm and their delight – his Elizabeth, his more than daughter, whom he doted on with all the affection which a man feels, who in the decline of life, having few affections, clings more earnestly to those that remain. Cursed, cursed be the fiend that brought misery on his grey hairs, and doomed him to waste in wretchedness! He could not live under the horrors that were accumulated around him; the springs of his existence suddenly gave way: he was unable to rise from his bed, and in a few days he died in my arms.

What then became of me? I know not; I lost sensation, and chains and darkness were the only objects that pressed upon me. Sometimes, indeed, I dreamt that I wandered in flowery meadows and pleasant vales with the friends of my youth; but I awoke, and found myself in a dungeon. Melancholy followed, but by degrees I gained a clear conception of my miseries and situation, and was then released from my prison. For they had called me mad; and during many months, as I understood, a solitary cell had been my habitation.

CHARLES MATURIN (1782–1824)

Charles Robert Maturin was raised as a strict Calvinist, educated at Trinity College Dublin and took orders in the Church of Ireland. He published *The Fatal Revenge* (1807), *The Wild Irish Boy* (1808) and *The Milesian Chief* (1811). But it was with *Melmoth the Wanderer* (1820) that he knew his greatest success. *Melmoth* was among the last and most effective Gothic novels and was very popular, partly because, like Matthew Lewis's *The Monk* (1796), it was prepared to indulge, almost to a point of indecency, the Gothic propensity to excess. Faust-like, Melmoth offers relief to suffering and a long life to anyone who will take his place in a pact with the devil. The device enables Melmoth to recite tales of depravity and suffering which cumulatively prove the wickedness of human nature, and therefore the folly of Enlightenment and emancipatory hopes. Such works remind us that this was also the age of the Marquis de Sade. The addressee in the following episode is Melmoth.

From Melmoth the Wanderer

'I remember,' said he, 'an extraordinary circumstance connected with this vault. I wondered how I felt so familiar with this door, this arch, at first. – I did not recollect immediately, so many strange thoughts have crossed my mind every day, that events which would make a life-lasting impression on others, pass like shadows before me, while thoughts appear like substances. *Emotions are my events* – you know what brought me to this cursed convent – well, don't shiver or look *paler* – you were pale before. However it was, I found myself in the convent, and I was obliged to susbscribe to its discipline. A part of it was, that extraordinary criminals should undergo what they called extraordinary penance; that is, not only submit to every ignominy and rigour of conventual life, (which, unfortunately for its penitents, is never wanting in such amusing resources), but act the part of executioner whenever any distinguished punishment was to be inflicted or witnessed. They did me the honour to believe me particularly qualified for this species of recreation, and perhaps they did not flatter me, I had all the humility of a saint on trial; but still I had a kind of confidence in my talents of this description, provided they were put to a proper test; and the monks had the goodness to assure me, that I never could long be without one in a convent. This was a very tempting picture of my situation, but I found these worthy people had not in the least exaggerated. An instance occurred a few days after I had the happiness to become a member of this amiable community, of whose merits you are doubtless sensible. I was desired to attach myself to a young monk of a distinguished family, who had lately taken the vows, and who had performed his duties with that heartless punctuality that intimated to the community that his heart was elsewhere. I was soon put in possession of the business; from their ordering me to *attach* myself to him, I instantly conceived I was bound to the most deadly hostility against him. The friendship of convents is always a treacherous league – we watch, suspect, and torment each other, for the love of God. This young monk's only crime was that he was suspected of cherishing an earthly passion. He was, in fact, as I have stated, the son of a distinguished family, who (from the fear of his contracting what is called a degrading marriage, i.e. of marrying a woman of inferior rank whom he loved, and who would have made him happy, as fools, that is, half mankind, estimate happiness) forced him to take the vows. He appeared at times broken-hearted, but at times there was a light of hope in his eye, that looked somewhat ominous in the eyes of the community. It is certain, that hope not being an indigenous plant in the parterre of a convent, must excite suspicion with regard both to its origin and its growth.

'Some time after, a young novice entered the convent. From the moment he did so, a change the most striking took place in the young monk. He and the novice became inseparable companions – there was something suspicious in that. My eyes were on the watch in a moment. Eyes are particularly sharpened in discovering misery when they can hope to aggravate it. The attachment between the young monk and the novice went on. They were for ever in the garden together – they inhaled the odours of the flowers – they cultivated the same cluster of carnations – they entwined themselves as they walked together – when they were in the choir, their voices were like mixed incense. Friendship is often carried to excess in conventual life, but this friendship was too like love. For instance, the psalms sung in the choir sometimes breathe a certain language; at these words, the young monk and the novice would direct their voices to each other in sounds that could not be misunderstood. If the least correction was inflicted, one would intreat to undergo it for the other. If a day of relaxation was allowed, whatever presents were sent to the cell of one, were sure to be found in the cell of the other. This was enough for me. I saw that secret of mysterious happiness, which is the greatest misery to those who never can share it. My vigilance was redoubled, and it was rewarded by the discovery of a secret – a secret that I had to communicate and raise my consequence by. You cannot guess the importance attached to the discovery of a secret in a convent, (particularly when the remission of our own offences depends on the discovery of those of others.)

'One evening as the young monk and his darling novice were in the garden, the former plucked a peach, which he immediately offered to his favourite; the latter accepted it with a movement I thought rather awkward – it seemed like what I imagined would be the reverence of a female. The young monk divided the peach with a knife; in doing so, the knife grazed the finger of the novice, and the monk, in agitation inexpressible, tore his habit to bind up the wound. I saw it all – my mind was made up on the business – I went to the Superior that very night. The result may be conceived. They were watched, but cautiously at first. They were probably on their guard; for, for some time it defied even my vigilance to make the slightest discovery. It is a situation incomparably tantalizing, when suspicion is satisfied of her own suggestions, as of the truth of the gospel, but still wants the *little fact* to make them credible to others. One night that I had, by direction of the Superior, taken my station in the gallery, (where I was contented to remain hour after hour, and night after night, amid solitude, darkness, and cold, for the chance of the power of retaliating on others the misery inflicted on myself) – One night, I thought I heard a step in the gallery – I have told you that I was in the dark – a light step passed me. I could hear the broken and palpitating respiration of the person. A few moments after, I heard a door open, and knew it to be the door of the young monk. I knew it; for by long watching in the dark, and accustoming myself to number the cells, by the groan from one, the prayer from another, the faint shriek of restless dreams from a third, my ear had become so finely graduated, that I could instantly distinguish the opening of *that door*, from which (to my sorrow) no sound had ever before issued. I was provided with a small chain, by which I fastened the handle of the door to a contiguous one, in such a manner, that it was impossible to open either of them from the inside. I then hastened to the Superior, with a pride of which none but the successful tracer of a guilty secret in convents, can have any conception. I believe the Superior was himself agitated by the luxury of the same feelings, for he was awake and up in his apartment, attended by *four monks*, whom you may remember.' I shuddered at the remembrance. 'I communicated my intelligence with a voluble eagerness, not only unsuited to the respect I owed these persons, but which must have rendered me almost unintelligible, yet they were good enough not only to over-look this violation of decorum, which would in any other case have been severely punished, but even to supply certain pauses in my narrative, with a condescension and facility truly miraculous. I felt what it was to acquire impor-tance in the eyes of a Superior, and glorified in all the dignified depravity of an informer. We set out without losing a moment, – we arrived at the door of the cell, and I pointed out with triumph the chain unremoved, though a slight vibration, perceptible at our approach, showed the wretches within were already apprised of their danger. I unfastened the door, – how they must have shuddered! The Superior and his satellites burst into the cell, and *I* held the light. You tremble, – why? I was guilty, and I wished to witness guilt that palliated mine, at least in the opinion of the convent. I had only violated the laws of nature, but they had outraged the decorum of a convent, and, of course, in the creed of a convent, there was no proportion between our offences. Besides, I was anxious to witness misery that might perhaps equal or exceed my own, and this is a curiosity not easily satisfied. It is actually possible to become *amateurs in suffering.* I have heard of men who have travelled into countries where horrible executions were to be daily witnessed, for the sake of that excitement which the sight of suffering never fails to give, from the spectacle of a tragedy, or an *auto da fe*, down to the writhings of the meanest reptile on whom you can inflict torture, and feel that torture is the result of your own power. It is a species of feeling of which we never can divest ourselves, – a triumph over those whose sufferings have placed them below us, and no wonder, – suffering is always an indication of weakness, – we glory in our impenetrability. *I* did, as we burst into the cell. The wretched husband and wife were locked in each others arms. You may imagine the scene that followed. Here I must do the Superior reluctant justice. He was a man (of course from his coventual feelings) who had no more idea of the intercourse between the sexes, than between two beings of a different species. The scene that he beheld could not have revolted him more, than if he had seen the horrible loves of the baboons and the Hottentot women, at the Cape of Good Hope; or those still more loathsome unions between the serpents of South

America and their human victims, *(note)* when they can catch them, and twine round them in folds of unnatural and ineffable union. He really stood as much astonished and appalled, to see two human beings of different sexes, who dared to love each other in spite of monastic ties, as if he had witnessed the horrible conjunctions I have alluded to. Had he seen vipers engendering in that frightful knot which seems the pledge of mortal hostility, instead of love, he could not have testified more horror, – and I do him the justice to believe he felt all he testified. Whatever affectation he might employ on points of conventual austerity, there was none here. Love was a thing he always believed connected with sin, even though consecrated by the name of a sacrament, and called marriage, as it is in our church. But, love in a convent! – Oh, there is no conceiving his rage; still less is it possible to conceive the majestic and overwhelming extent of that rage, when strengthened by principle, and sanctified by religion. I enjoyed the scene beyond all power of description. I saw those wretches, who had triumphed over me, reduced to my level in a moment, – their passions all displayed, and the display placing me a hero triumphant above all. I had crawled to the shelter of their walls, a wretched degraded outcast, and what was my crime? Well, – you shudder, I have done with that. I can only say want drove me to it. And here were beings whom, a few months before, I would have knelt to as to the images round the shrine, – to whom, in the moments of my desperate penitence, I would have clung as to the "horns of the altar," all brought as low, and lower than myself. "Sons of the morning," as I deemed them in the agonies of my humiliation, "how were they fallen!" I feasted on the degradation of the apostate monk and novice, – I enjoyed, to the core of my ulcerated heart, the passion of the Superior, – I felt that they were all men like myself. Angels, as I had thought them, they had all proved themselves mortal; and, by watching their motions, and flattering their passions, and promoting their interest, or setting up my own in opposition to them all, while I made them believe it was only theirs I was intent on, I might make shift to contrive as much misery to others, and to carve out as much occupation to myself, as if I were actually living in the world. Cutting my father's throat was a noble feat certainly, (I ask your pardon, I did not mean to extort that groan from you), but here were hearts to be cut, – and to the core, every day, and all day long, so I never could want employment.'

Here he wiped his hard brow, drew his breath for a moment, and then said, 'I do not quite like to go through the details by which this wretched pair were deluded into the hope of effecting their escape from the convent. It is enough that I was the principal agent, – that the Superior connived at it, – that I led them through the very passages you have traversed to-night, they trembling and blessing me at every step, – that –' 'Stop,' I cried; 'wretch! you are tracing my course this night step by step.' – 'What?' he retorted, with a ferocious laugh, 'you think I am betraying you, then; and if it were true, what good would your suspicions do you, – you are in my power? My voice might summon half the convent to seize you this moment, – my arm might fasten you to that wall, till those dogs of death, that wait but my whistle, plunged their fangs into your very vitals. I fancy you would not find their bite less keen, from their tusks being so long sharpened by an immersion in holy water.' Another laugh, that seemed to issue from the lungs of a demon, concluded this sentence. 'I know I am in your power,' I answered; 'and were I to trust to that, or to your heart, I had better dash out my brains at once against these walls of rock, which I believe are not harder than the latter. But I know your interests to be some way or other connected with my escape, and therefore I trust you, – because I must. Though my blood, chilled as it is by famine and fatigue, seems frozen in every drop while I listen to you, yet listen I must, and trust my life and liberation to you. I speak to you with the horrid confidence our situation has taught me, – I hate, – I dread you. If we were to meet in life, I would shrink from you with loathings of unspeakable abhorrence, but here mutual misery has mixed the most repugnant substances in unnatural coalition. The force of that alchemy must cease at the moment of my escape from the convent and from you; yet, for these miserable hours, my life is as much dependent on your exertions and presence, as my power of supporting them is on the continuance of your horrible tale, – go on, then. Let us struggle through this dreadful day. *Day!* a name unknown *here*, where noon and night shake hands that never unlock. Let us struggle through it, "hateful and hating one another," and when it has passed, let us curse and part.'

As I uttered these words, Sir, I felt that terrible *confidence of hostility* which the worst beings are driven to in the worst of circumstances, and I question whether there is a more horrible situation than that in which we cling to each other's hate, instead of each other's love, – in which, at every step of our progress, we hold a dagger to our companion's breast, and say, 'If you falter for a moment, this is in your heart. I hate, – I fear, but I must bear with you.' It was singular to me, though it would not be so to those who investigate human nature, that, in proportion as my situation inspired me with a ferocity quite unsuited to our comparative situations, and which must have been the result of the madness of despair and famine, my companion's respect for me appeared to increase. After a long pause, he asked, might he continue his story? I could not speak, for, after the slightest exertion, the sickness of deadly hunger returned on me, and I could only signify, by a feeble motion of my hand, that he might go on.

'They were conducted here,' he continued; 'I had suggested the plan, and the Superior consented to it. He would not be present, but his dumb nod was enough. I was the conductor of their (intended) escape; they believed they were departing with the connivance of the Superior. I led them through those very passages that you and I have trod. I had a map of this subterranean region, but my blood ran cold as I traversed it; and it was not at all inclined to resume its usual temperament, as I felt what was to be the destination of my attendants. Once I turned the lamp, on pretence of trimming it, to catch a glimpse of the devoted wretches. They were embracing each other, – the light of joy trembled in their eyes. They were whispering to each other hopes of liberation and happiness, and blending my name in the interval they could spare from their prayers for each other. That sight extinguished the last remains of compunction with which my horrible task had inspired me. They dared to be happy in the sight of one who must be for ever miserable, – could there be a greater insult? I resolved to punish it on the spot. This very apartment was near, – I knew it, and the map of their wanderings no longer trembled in my hand. I urged them to enter this recess, (the door was then entire), while I went to examine the passage. They entered it, thanking me for my precaution, – they knew not they were never to quit it alive. But what were their lives for the agony their happiness cost me? The moment they were inclosed, and clasping each other, (a sight that made me grind my teeth), I closed and locked the door. This movement gave them no immediate uneasiness, – they thought it a friendly precaution. The moment they were secured, I hastened to the Superior, who was on fire at the insult offered to the sanctity of his convent, and still more to the purity of his penetration, on which the worthy Superior piqued himself as much as if it had ever been possible for him to acquire the smallest share of it. He descended with me to the passage, – the monks followed with eyes on fire. In the agitation of their rage, it was with difficulty they could discover the door after I had repeatedly pointed it out to them. The Superior, with his own hands, tafeffectually joined it to the staple, *never to be disjoined;* and every blow he gave, doubtless he felt as if it was a reminiscence to the accusing angel, to strike out a sin from the catalogue of his accusations. The work was soon done, – the work never to be undone. At the first sound of steps in the passage, and blows on the door, the victims uttered a shriek of terror. They imagined they were detected, and that an incensed party of monks were breaking open the door. These terrors were soon exchanged for others, – and worse, – as they heard the door nailed up, and listened to our departing steps. They uttered another shriek, but O how different was the accent of its despair! – they knew their doom.

* * * *

'It was my penance (no, – my delight) to watch at the door, under the pretence of precluding the possibility of their escape, (of which they knew there was no possibility); but, in reality, not only to inflict on me the indignity of being the convent gaoler, but of teaching me that callosity of heart, and induration of nerve, and stubbornness of eye, and apathy of ear, that were best suited to my office. But they might have saved themselves the trouble, – I had them all before ever I entered the convent. Had I been the Superior of the community, I should have undertaken the office of watching the door. You will call this cruelty, I call it curiosity, – that curiosity that brings thousands to witness a tragedy, and makes the most delicate female feast on groans and agonies. I had an advantage over them, – the groan, the agony I feasted on, were real. I took my station at *the door* – that door which, like that of Dante's hell, might have borne the inscription, "Here is no hope," – with a face of mock penitence, and genuine – cordial delectation. I could hear every word that transpired. For the first hours they tried to comfort each other, – they suggested to each other hopes of liberation, – and as my shadow, crossing the threshold, darkened or restored the light, they said, "That is he;" – then, when this occurred repeatedly, without any effect, they said, "No, – no, it is not he," and swallowed down the sick sob of despair, to hide it from each other. Towards night a monk came to take my place, and to offer me food. I would not have quitted my place for worlds; but I talked to the monk in his own language, and told him I would make a merit with God of my sacrifices, and was resolved to remain there all night, with the permission of the Superior. The monk was glad of having a substitute on such easy terms, and I was glad of the food he left me, for I was hungry now, but I reserved the appetite of my soul for richer luxuries. I heard them talking within. While I was eating, I actually lived on the famine that was devouring them, but of which they did not dare to say a word to each other. They debated, deliberated, and, as misery grows ingenious in its own defence, they at last assured each other that it was impossible the Superior had locked them in there to perish by hunger. At these words I could not help laughing. This laugh reached their ears, and they became silent in a moment. All that night, however, I heard their groans, – those groans of physical suffering, that laugh to scorn all the sentimental sighs that are exhaled from the hearts of the most intoxicated lovers that ever breathed. I heard them all that night. I had read French romances, and all their unimaginable nonsense. Madame Sevigné herself says she would have been tired of her daughter in a long *tête-à-tête* journey, but clap me two lovers into a dungeon, without food, light, or hope, and I will be damned (that I am already, by the bye) if they do not grow sick of each other within the first twelve hours. The second day hunger and darkness had their usual influence. They shrieked for liberation, and knocked loud and long at their dungeon door. They exclaimed they were ready to submit to any punishment; and the approach of the monks, which they would have dreaded so much the preceding night, they now solicited on their knees. What a jest, after all, are the most awful vicissitudes of human life! – they supplicated now for what they would have sacrificed their souls to avert four-and-twenty hours before. Then the agony of hunger increased, they shrunk from the door, and grovelled apart from each other. *Apart!* – how I watched that. They were rapidly becoming objects of hostility to each other, – oh what a feast to me! They could not disguise from each other the revolting circumstances of their mutual sufferings. It is one thing for lovers to sit down to a feast magnificently spread, and another for lovers to couch in darkness and famine, – to exchange that appetite which cannot be supported without dainties and flattery, for that which would barter a descended Venus for a morsel of food. The second night they raved and groaned, (as occurred); and, amid their agonies, (I must do justice to women, whom I hate as well as men), the man often accused the female as the cause of all his sufferings, but the woman never, – never reproached him. Her groans might indeed have reproached him bitterly, but she never uttered a word that could have caused him pain. There was a change which I well could mark, however, in their physical feelings. The first day they clung together, and every movement I felt was like that of one person. The next the man alone struggled, and the woman moaned in helplessness. The third night, – how shall I tell it? – but you have bid me go on. All the horrible and loathsome excruciations of famine had been undergone; the disunion of every tie of the heart, of passion, of nature, had commenced. In the agonies of their famished sickness they loathed each other, – they could have cursed each other, if they had had breath to curse. It was on the fourth night that I heard the shriek of that wretched female, – her lover, in the agony of hunger, had fastened his teeth in her shoulder; – that bosom on which he had so often luxuriated, became a meal to him now.'

* * * *

'Monster! and you laugh?' – 'Yes, I laugh at all mankind, and the imposition they dare to practise when they talk of hearts. I laugh at human passions and human cares, – vice and virtue, religion and impiety; they are all the result of petty localities, and artificial situation. One physical want, one severe and abrupt lesson from the tintless and shrivelled lip of necessity, is worth all the logic of the empty wretches who have presumed to prate it, from Zeno down to Burgersdicius. Oh! it silences in a second all the feeble sophistry of *coventional* life, and ascititious passion. Here were a pair who would not have believed all the world on their knees, even though angels had descended to join in the attestation, that it was possible for them to exist without the other. They had risked every thing, trampled on every thing human and divine, to be in each others sight and arms. One hour of hunger undeceived them. A trivial and ordinary want, whose claims at another time they would have regarded as a vulgar interruption of their spiritualised intercourse, not only, by its natural operation, sundered it for ever, but, before it ceased, converted that intercourse into a source of torment and hostility inconceivable, except among cannibals. The bitterest enemies on earth could not have regarded each other with more abhorrence than *these lovers*. Deluded wretches! you boasted of having hearts, I boast I have none, and which of us gained most by the vaunt, let life decide. My story is nearly finished, and so I hope is the day. When I was last here I had something to excite me; – talking of those things is poor employment to one who has been a witness to them. On the *sixth* day all was still. The door was unnailed, we entered, – they were no more. They lay far from each other, farther than on that voluptuous couch into which their passion had converted the mat of a convent bed. She lay contracted in a heap, a lock of her long hair in her mouth. There was a slight scar on her shoulder, – the rabid despair of famine had produced no farther outrage. He lay extended at his length, – his hand was between his lips; it seemed as if he had not strength to execute the purpose for which he had brought it there. The bodies were brought out for interment. As we removed them into the light, the long hair of the female, falling over a face no longer disguised by the novice's dress, recalled a likeness I thought I could remember. I looked closer, she was my own sister, – my only one, – and I had heard her own voice grow fainter and fainter. I had heard –' and his own voice grew fainter – it ceased.

JOHN CLARE (1793–1864)

John Clare was the son of a Northamptonshire agricultural worker who ensured his modest education. He worked in a variety of labouring employments, read widely and wrote continuously. In 1820 his *Poems Descriptive of Rural Life and Scenery* were published to considerable critical acclaim. There then followed *The Village Minstrel* (1821), *The Shepherd's Calendar* (1827) and *The Rural Muse* (1835). In 1837 he was declared insane and placed in Northampton General Asylum for the rest of his life. He was well-treated and given liberty to write and to wander into Northampton, but the taste for 'ploughman poets' had passed and his 'Asylum' poems remained unpublished until the early years of this century.

I Am

I am – yet what I am, none cares or knows
My friends forsake me like a memory lost
I am the self-consumer of my woes –
They rise and vanish in oblivious host
5 Like shadows in love's frenzied stifled throes
And yet I am, and live like vapours tossed

Into the nothingness of scorn and noise
Into the living sea of waking dreams
Where there is neither sense of life or joys
10 But the vast shipwreck of my life's esteems
And e'en the dearest – that I love the best –
Are strange – nay, rather stranger than the rest

I long for scenes where man hath never trod
A place where woman never smiled or wept
15 There to abide with my Creator God
And sleep as I in childhood sweetly slept
Untroubling and untroubled where I lie
The grass below – above the vaulted sky.

Clock a Clay

In the cowslips peeps I lie
Hidden from the buzzing fly
While green grass beneath me lies
Pearled wi' dew like fishes' eyes
5 Here I lie a Clock a clay
Waiting for the time o'day

Clock a Clay: the Clock a Clay is a ladybird. The poem recalls Ariel's song in Shakespeare's *Tempest*, Act 5: 'Where the bee sucks, there suck I, In a cowslip's bell I lie.' The cowslip flower has many small tubular florets, or 'peeps'.

Wile grassy forest quake surprise
                And the wild wind sobs and sighs
                My gold home rocks as like to fall
10   On its pillar green and tall
                When the pattering rain drives by
                Clock a Clay keeps warm and dry

                Day by day and night by night
                All the week I hide from sight
15   In the cowslips peeps I lie
                In rain and dew still warm and dry
                Day and night and night and day
                Red black spotted clock a clay

                My home it shakes in wind and showers
20   Pale green pillar hopped wi' flowers
                Bending at the wild wind's breath
                Here still I live lone clock a clay
                Watching for the time of day

Song

                I hid my love when young while I
                Couldn't bear the buzzing of a fly
                I hid my love to my despite
                Till I could not bear to look at light
5   I dare not gaze upon her face
                But left her memory in each place
                Where ere I saw a wild flower lie
                I kissed and bade my love goodbye

                I met her in the greenest dells
10   Where dew drops pearl the wood bluebells
                The lost breexe kissed her bright blue eyue
                The bee kissed and went singing by
                A sunbeam found a passage there
                A gold chain round her neck so fair
15   As secret as the wild bee's song
                She lay there all the summer long

                I hid my love in field and town
                Till e'en the breeze would knock me down
                The bees seemed singing ballades o'er
20   The fly's buss turned a Lion's roar
                And even silence found a tongue

Song, 20 buss: to kiss.

To haunt me all the summer long
The riddle nature could not prove
Was nothing else but secret love

Summer Winds

The wind waves o'er the meadows green
    And shakes my own wild flowers
And shifts about the moving scene
    Like the life of summer hours
5   The little bents with reedy head
    The scarce seen shapes of flowers
All kink about like skeins of thread
    In these wind-shaken hours

All stir and strife and life and bustle
10   In everything around one sees
The rushes whistle, sedges rustle
    The grass is buzzing round like bees
The butterflies are tossed about
    Like skiffs upon a stormy sea
15   The bees are lost amid the rout
    And drop in perplexity

Wilt thou be mine thou bonny lass
    Thy drapery floats so gracefully
We'll walk along the meadow grass
20   We'll stand beneath the willow tree
We'll mark the little reeling bee
    Along the grassy ocean rove
Tossed like a little boat at sea
    And interchange our vows of love

---

26 rove: wander.

Victorians

The reign of Queen Victoria (1837–1901) was long and very profitable, driven by coal, iron and steam: the years 1830–50 saw a mania of railway-promoting, fortune-making and bankruptcy, that would interconnect all parts of the island in a network of rapid commercial exchanges, and give it regular clock time and a vast, uniformed, regulated workforce. This communications revolution responded to and developed the growth of factory towns and ports, and the ever greater expansion of London into a vast sprawling metropolis. It was also replicated around the world as the British armies and merchants knitted together an empire which would by the end of the century bring one quarter of the world under the British flag. After the end of the Civil War in the United States (1864), and Bismarck's unification of Germany (1871), British manufacturers and gun-boats would meet increasingly stiff competition, and squabbles about how to divide world resources would lay the seeds for global conflict between imperialist powers, but at the end of Victoria's reign there was no doubt that Britain was the workshop of a world whose waves it ruled, along with its insurance, engineering and banking.

The benefits of this expansion accrued primarily to middle-class capitalists who progressively took political control of the State. Having benefited from a series of compromises with the landed interests in the eighteenth century, Britain did not experi-ence either the positive or negative effects of a French-style revolution. British history could be represented as immemorially continuous and calm, and the actual antagonism of bourgeois and aristocrat constantly elided. In 1830 the Tories, in power since 1783, finally yielded to the Whigs who, in the 1832 Reform Bill, extended the vote to nearly all middle- and lower-middle-class men and reformed constituencies so that the new manu-facturing towns at last had representation proportionate to their populations. The 1840s proved the wisdom of these changes when a series of poor harvests and the potato blight produced high food costs and global economic recession. Faced with widespread unrest, and starvation in Ireland, Peel repealed the Corn Laws and the Navigation Acts which had maintained artificial markets to the benefit of the landed interests, thereby inaugurating a period of Free Trade. The Chartists urgently and unsuccessfully demanded the extension of the franchise to working men, but Britain rode the political storms without the bloodshed which convulsed every major European country in 1848.

Not that conditions for the working class were good: they were appalling, as the novels of Gaskell, Kingsley, Dickens and Disraeli revealed, and the status of women in general was as bad or worse since they were usually figured as mental and physical weaklings and were treated as the legal property of fathers or husbands. Prostitution was as much an industry as fulminating about the innocence of women and the need to preserve family values. But in Britain there were secure patterns of deference, there was the cushioning income from the colonies, and there were practical measures to relieve the conditions of the poor. Acts of Parliament placed responsibility on an expanding local government administration to limit the hours of work, ensure sanitation and adequate housing, and even, by the 1880s, ensure minimal literacy; and there were hard-fought improvements to the condition of women. This regulation of private life by the State was another aspect of industrialisation, a new social technology.

In the general ideology, these processes are reflected as an opposition between Utilitarianism and – such was Utilitarianism's force – an anti-Utilitarianism which at times was no stronger than whimsy. Jeremy Bentham (1772–1832), the begetter of Utilitarianism, argued that all laws and acts could be evaluated by a minute calculation of the benefits to society, thereby providing a scientific basis for all human conduct. He also held that people were deeply self-interested and could only be coerced into taking the interests of others into account. John Mill, the father of John Stuart Mill, was his disciple, and Gradgrind in Dickens's *Hard Times* (1854) the richest comic portrayal of his philosophy. Whilst Bentham was a staunch democrat and reformer of judicial abuses, he saw imaginative literature as merely a lie. There was no place in Utilitarianism for philanthropy, or for God or the soul, which were deemed old superstitions. Such a stark creed could not explain the whole personality so it was countered both by a High Church Christianity led by John Henry Newman and deeply influenced by Coleridge, and by a Low Church evangelical Christianity that propagated Puritanical self-repression but did much to alleviate the sufferings of the poor. The High Church tendency had a marked influence on intellectuals, notably upon Matthew Arnold. Christian militancy, however, could only militate against the predominant tendency of an age in which science and engineering daily proved its effective dominance, and in which geology and the new textual scholarship of the Bible (the 'Higher Criticism', as it was called) constructed a secular history that saw human existence as bereft of Divine intention. Darwin's reflections in *On the Origin of Species* (1859) led to the doctrine of natural selection and the idea that man was kin to the apes (*The Descent of Man*, 1871). The late-nineteenth century viewed life an unremitting struggle to survive that pitted individual against individual and tended to see culture was a thin veneer over fundamental savagery. Apart from Christian piety, only the new socialist movements inspired by the works of Karl Marx (*The Communist Manifesto*, 1848, *Capital*, 1867, 1885, 1895) and Friedrich Engels (*The Condition of the Working Class in England*, 1845) offered a progressive and optimistic account of historical experience, and this account had implications which were not to everyone's taste.

Britain's prosperity in the late-nineteenth century was astounding, but there was a growing sense of intractable difficulties in the conflicts between men of property and their 'hands', and, as the empire expanded, so there was growing resistance to British dominion from the Irish, the Indians, the Zulu, the Ashanti, and the Boers, to name but some of those who responded with violence to British rule. It may be that such historical resistance caused many writers at the end of the century to set aside the realistic representation of historical experience, and attend rather to the aesthetic nature of the art work. Or it may be that it is the evolutionary nature of technologies to become ever more sophisticated, so as an art matures it becomes more interested in the nature of its own processes. Or it may be that as society turned into a department store, so art objects were subject to the general law of commodities and sought more and more specialised niches. Probably all three factors led later-Victorian writing towards the Modernist belief that the aesthetic experience is both an antidote to rampant commercialisation and a token of the values of a middle-class culture that makes its pursuit possible.

ALFRED, LORD TENNYSON (1809–1892)

Alfred Tennyson's father was an extremely learned, alcoholic and violent Lincolnshire rector. He was inclined to melancholy, tutored his sons at home, and drove one son mad and another to opium. After this difficult start in life, Alfred Tennyson went up to Cambridge where he won a poetry prize. By the age of 21 he had already published two volumes of verse, *Poems, Chiefly Lyrical* (1830) being savaged by the critics. In 1832 he travelled the Continent with his friend Hallam, who died in 1833. Tennyson then began to compose *In Memoriam* to his memory, a chain of brooding meditations on love, mortality and redemption which profoundly expresses the sense of loss that haunted the most dynamic century in human history. The poem was eventually published to considerable esteem in 1850, the year in which Tennyson succeeded Wordsworth as poet laureate. It was in this capacity that he wrote such state-occasion and newspaper verse as 'The Charge of the Light Brigade' (1854). His *Poems* (1832) included many enduring verses, including 'The Lady of Shalott' and 'The Lotos Eaters' which were considerably revised and improved for his *Poems* (1842). The later volume added such notable works as the 'Morte d'Arthur', 'Locksely Hall' and 'Ulysses'. In 1855 he published *Maud and Other Poems*, *Maud* itself being a long and successful monologue in the style being developed by Browning. In these years, Tennyson's work was as popular as that of Dickens, and his income resembled that of a modern mass-culture idol. *Idylls of the Kings* (12 vols,1855–88) developed the Arthurian strain and mythology of the earlier 'Morte d'Arthur', secured Tennyson's role as ideologist of the age, and earned him both a peerage (in 1884) and a reputation for empty versification.

The Lady of Shalott

I

On either side the river lie
Long fields of barley and of rye,
That clothe the wold and meet the sky;
And through the field the road runs by
5   To many-towered Camelot;
And up and down the people go,
Gazing where the lilies blow
Round an island there below,
    The island of Shalott.

10   Willows whiten, aspens quiver,
Little breezes dusk and shiver
Through the wave that runs for ever
By the island in the river
    Flowing down to Camelot.

---

3 **wold:** weald, open countryside, usually upland.   7 **blow:** bloom.
5 **Camelot:** legendary site of King Arthur's court.

15 Four grey walls, and four grey towers,
 Overlook a space of flowers,
 And the silent isle imbowers
  The Lady of Shalott.

 By the margin, willow-veiled,
20 Slide the heavy barges trailed
 By slow horses; and unhailed
 The shallop flitteth silken-sailed
  Skimming down to Camelot:
 But who hath seen her wave her hand?
25 Or at the casement seen her stand?
 Or is she known in all the land,
  The Lady of Shalott?

 Only reapers, reaping early,
 In among the bearded barley,
30 Hear a song that echoes cheerly
 From the river winding clearly;
  Down to towered Camelot;
 And by the moon the reaper weary,
 Piling sheaves in uplands airy,
35 Listening, whispers, ''Tis the fairy
  Lady of Shalott.'

     II
 There she weaves by night and day
 A magic web with colours gay.
 She has heard a whisper say,
40 A curse is on her if she stay
  To look down to Camelot.
 She knows not what the curse may be,
 And so she weaveth steadily,
 And little other care hath she,
45 The Lady of Shalott.

 And moving through a mirror clear
 That hangs before her all the year,
 Shadows of the world appear.
 There she sees the highway near
50 Winding down to Camelot;
 There the river eddy whirls,
 And there the surly village churls,
 And the red cloaks of market girls
  Pass onward from Shalott.

---

22 shallop: a light rowing boat.

55   Sometimes a troop of damsels glad,
An abbot on an ambling pad,
Sometimes a curly shepherd lad,
Or long-haired page in crimson clad
   Goes by to towered Camelot;
60   And sometimes through the mirror blue
The knights come riding two and two.
She hath no loyal Knight and true,
   The Lady of Shalott.

But in her web she still delights
65   To weave the mirror's magic sights,
For often through the silent nights
A funeral, with plumes and lights
   And music, went to Camelot;
Or when the moon was overhead,
70   Came two young lovers lately wed.
'I am half sick of shadows,' said
   The Lady of Shalott.

III

A bowshot from her bower eaves,
He rode between the barley sheaves,
75   The sun came dazzling through the leaves,
And flamed upon the brazen greaves
   Of bold Sir Lancelot.
A red-cross knight for ever kneeled
To a lady in his shield,
80   That sparkled on the yellow field,
   Beside remote Shalott.

The gemmy bridle glittered free,
Like to some branch of stars we see
Hung in the golden Galaxy.
85   The bridle bells rang merrily
   As he rode down to Camelot:
And from his blazoned baldric slung
A mighty silver bugle hung,
And as he rode his armour rung
90   Beside remote Shalott.

All in the blue unclouded weather
Thick-jeweled shone the saddle leather,

---

56 **pad:** horse.   76 **greaves:** armour for the lower leg.   87 **baldric:** shoulder sash for the support of a sword.
78 **red-cross:** the heraldic device on his shield.

The helmet and the helmet-feather
Burned like one burning flame together,
95   As he rode down to Camelot.
As often through the purple night,
Below the starry clusters bright,
Some bearded meteor, burning bright,
Moves over still Shalott.

100   His broad clear brow in sunlight glowed;
On burnished hooves his war horse trode;
From underneath his helmet flowed
His coal-black curls as on he rode,
    As he rode down to Camelot.
105   From the bank and from the river
He flashed into the crystal mirror,
'Tirra lirra,' by the river
    Sang Sir Lancelot.

She left the web, she left the loom,
110   She made three paces through the room,
She saw the water lily bloom,
She saw the helmet and the plume,
    She looked down to Camelot.
Out flew the web and floated wide;
115   The mirror cracked from side to side;
'The curse is come upon me,' cried
    The Lady of Shalott.

IV
In the stormy east wind straining,
The pale yellow woods were waning,
120   The broad stream in his banks complaining.
Heavily the low sky raining
    Over towered Camelot;
Down she came and found a boat
Beneath a willow left afloat,
125   And round about the prow she wrote
    The Lady of Shalott.

And down the river's dim expanse
Like some bold seer in a trance,
Seeing all his own mischance –
130   With a glassy countenance
    Did she look to Camelot.

And at the closing of the day
She loosed the chain, and down she lay;
The broad stream bore her far away,
135   The Lady of Shalott.

Lying, robed in snowy white
That loosely flew to left and right –
The leaves upon her falling light –
Through the noises of the night,
140   She floated down to Camelot:
And as the boat-head wound along
The willowy hills and fields among,
They heard her singing her last song,
    The Lady of Shalott.

145 Heard a carol, mournful, holy,
Chanted loudly, chanted lowly,
Till her blood was frozen slowly,
And her eyes were darkened wholly,
    Turned to towered Camelot.
150 For ere she reached upon the tide
The first house by the waterside,
Singing in her song she died,
    The Lady of Shalott.

Under tower and balcony,
155 By garden wall and gallery,
A gleaming shape she floated by,
Dead-pale between the houses high,
    Silent into Camelot.
Out upon the wharfs they came,
160 Knight and burgher, lord and dame,
And round the prow they read her name,
    The Lady of Shalott.

Who is this? And what is here?
And in the lighted palace near
165 Died the sound of royal cheer;
And they crossed themselves for fear,
    All the knights at Camelot;
But Lancelot mused a little space
He said, 'She has a lovely face;
170 God in his mercy lend her grace,
    The Lady of Shalott.'

Ulysses

It little profits that an idle king,
By this still hearth, among these barren crags,
Matched with an aged wife, I mete and dole
Unequal laws unto a savage race,
5   That hoard, and sleep, and feed, and know not me.
     I cannot rest from travel; I will drink
Life to the lees. All times I have enjoyed
Greatly, have suffered greatly, both with those
That loved me, and alone; on shore, and when
10   Through scudding drifts the rainy Hyades
Vexed the dim sea. I am become a name;
For always roaming with a hungry heart
Much have I seen and known, – cities of men
And manners, climates, councils, governments,
15   Myself not least, but honored of them all, –
And drunk delight of battle with my peers,
Far on the ringing plains of windy Troy.
I am a part of all that I have met;
Yet all experience is an arch wherethrough
20   Gleams that untraveled world whose margin fades
Forever and forever when I move.
How dull it is to pause, to make an end,
To rust unburnished, not to shine in use!
As though to breathe were life! Life piled on life
25   Were all too little, and of one to me
Little remains; but every hour is saved
From that eternal silence, something more,
A bringer of new things; and vile it were
For some three suns to store and hoard myself,
30   And this gray spirit yearning in desire
To follow knowledge like a sinking star,
Beyond the utmost bound of human thought.

     This is my son, mine own Telemachus,
to whom I leave the sceptre and the isle –
35   Well-loved of me, discerning to fulfill
This labor, by slow prudence to make mild
A rugged people, and through soft degrees
Subdue them to the useful and the good.
Most blameless is he, centred in the sphere

Ulysses: The poem was begun a few days after Arthur
Hallam's death. It represents Ulysses' thoughts when he
is required to go on a last voyage after killing the suitors
for Penelope's hand. See *Odyssey* 11, ll. 100–137.

4 Unequal laws: suited to situation.   10 Hyades: seven
nymphs, daughters of Atlas, who were placed by Zeus
among the stars. Because of their tears, their appearance
near dawn presages rain.

40 Of common duties, decent not to fail
In offices of tenderness, and pay
Meet adoration to my household gods,
When I am gone. He works his work, I mine.

There lies the port; the vessel puffs her sail;
45 There gloom the dark, broad seas. My mariners,
Souls that have toiled, and wrought, and thought with me –
That ever with a frolic welcome took
The thunder and the sunshine, and opposed
Free hearts, free foreheads – you and I are old;
50 Old age hath yet his honor and his toil.
Death closes all; but something ere the end,
Some work of noble note, may yet be done,
Not unbecoming men that strove with Gods.
The lights begin to twinkle from the rocks;
55 The long day wanes; the slow moon climbs; the deep
Moans round with many voices. Come, my friends.
'Tis not too late to seek a newer world.
Push off, and sitting well in order smite
The sounding furrows; for my purpose holds
60 To sail beyond the sunset, and the baths
Of all the western stars, until I die.
It may be that the gulfs will wash us down;
It may be we shall touch the Happy Isles,
And see the great Achilles, whom we knew.
65 Though much is taken, much abides; and though
We are not now that strength which in old days
Moved earth and heaven, that which we are, we are, –
One equal temper of heroic hearts,
Made weak by time and fate, but strong in will
70 To strive, to seek, to find, and not to yield.

The Eagle: A Fragment

He clasps the crag with crooked hands;
Close to the sun in lonely lands,
Ringed with the azure world, he stands.

The wrinkled sea beneath him crawls;
5 He watches from his mountain walls,
And like a thunderbolt he falls.

From In Memoriam

2

Old yew, which graspest at the stones
  That name the underlying dead,
  Thy fibres net the dreamless head,
Thy roots are wrapped about the bones.

5   The seasons bring the flower again,
  And bring the firstling to the flock;
  And in the dusk of thee the clock
Beats out the little lives of men.

O, not for thee the glow, the bloom,
10   Who changest not in any gale,
  Nor branding summer suns avail
To touch thy thousand years of gloom;

And gazing on thee, sullen tree,
  Sick for thy stubborn hardihood,
15   I seem to fail from out my blood
And grow incorporate into thee.

3

O Sorrow, cruel fellowship,
  O Priestess in the vaults of Death,
  O sweet and bitter in a breath,
What whispers from thy lying lip?

5   'The stars,' she whispers, 'blindly run;
  A web is woven across the sky;
  From out waste places comes a cry,
And murmurs from the dying sun;

'And all the phantom, Nature, stands –
10   With all the music in her tone,
  A hollow echo of my own –
A hollow form with empty hands.'

And shall I take a thing so blind,
  Embrace her as my natural good;
15   Or crush her, like a vice of blood,
Upon the threshold of the mind?

4

To Sleep I give my powers away;
  My will is bondsman to the dark;
  I sit within a helmless bark,
And with my heart I muse and say:

5 O heart, how fares it with thee now,
  That thou should fail from thy desire,
  Who scarcely darest to inquire,
'What is it makes me beat so low?'

Something it is which thou hast lost,
10 Some pleasure from thine early years.
  Break thou deep vase of chilling tears,
That grief hath shaken into frost!

Such clouds of nameless trouble cross
  All night below the darkened eyes;
15 With morning wakes the will, and cries,
'Thou shalt not be the fool of loss.'

5

I sometimes hold it half a sin
  To put in words the grief I feel;
  For words, like Nature, half reveal
And half conceal the Soul within.

5 But, for the unquiet heart and brain,
  A use in measured language lies;
  The sad mechanic exercise,
Like dull narcotics, numbing pain.

In words, like weeds, I'll wrap me o'er,
10 Like coarsest clothes against the cold;
  But that large grief which these enfold
Is given in outline and no more.

9

Fair ship, that from the Italian shore
  Sailest the placid ocean-plains
  With my lost Arthur's loved remains,
Spread thy full wings, and waft him o'er.

5, 9 **weeds:** clothing, usually as 'widows' weeds'.

5 So draw him home to those that mourn
  In vain; a favourable speed
  Ruffle thy mirrored mast, and lead
 Through prosperous floods his holy urn.

 All night no ruder air perplex
10 Thy sliding keel, till Phosphor, bright
  As our pure love, through early light
 Shall glimmer on the dewey decks.

 Sphere all your lights around, above;
  Sleep, gentle heavens, before the prow;
15 Sleep, gentle winds, as he sleeps now,
 My friend, the brother of my love;

 My Arthur, whom I shall not see
  Till all my widowed race be run;
  Dear as the mother to the son,
20 More than my brothers are to me.

11

 Calm is the morn without a sound,
  Calm as to suit a calmer grief,
  And only through the faded leaf
 The chestnut pattering to the ground;

5 Calm and deep peace on this high wold,
  And on these dews that drench the furze,
  And all the silvery gossamers
 That twinkle into green and gold;

 Calm and still light on yon great plain
10 That sweeps with all its autumn bowers,
  And crowded farms and lessening towers,
 To mingle with the bounding main;

 Calm and deep peace in this wide air,
  These leaves that redden to the fall,
15 And in my heart, if calm at all,
 If any calm, a calm despair;

 Calm on the seas, and silver sleep,
  And waves that sway themselves in rest,
  And dead calm in that noble breast
20 Which heaves but with the heaving deep.

35

Yet if some voice that man could trust
  Should murmur from the narrow house,
  'The cheeks drop in, the body bows;
Man dies, nor is there hope in dust;'

5   Might I not say? 'Yet even here,
  But for one hour, O Love, I strive
  To keep so sweet a thing alive.'
But I should turn mine ears and hear

The moanings of the homeless sea,
10   The sound of streams that swift or slow
  Draw down Aeonian hills, and sow
The dust of continents to be;

And Love would answer with a sigh,
  'The sound of that forgetful shore
15   Will change my sweetness more and more,
Half-dead to know that I shall die.'

O me, what profits it to put
  An idle case? If Death were seen
  At first as Death, Love had not been,
20   Or been in narrowest working shut,

Mere fellowship of sluggish moods,
  Or, in his coarsest Satyr-shape
  Had bruised the herb and crushed the grape,
And basked and battened in the woods.

50

Be near me when my light is low,
  When the blood creeps, and the nerves prick
  And tingle; and the heart is sick,
And all the wheels of being slow.

5   Be near me when the sensuous frame
  Is racked with pangs that conquer trust;
  And Time, a maniac scattering dust,
And Life, a Fury slinging flame.

35, 11 **Aeonian**: everlasting.   35, 24 **basked and battened**: to laze about and thrive.

Be near me when my faith is dry,
10   And men the flies of latter spring,
        That lay their eggs, and sting and sing
And weave their petty cells and die.

Be near me when I fade away,
        To point the term of human strife,
15   And on the low dark verge of life
The twilight of eternal day.

57

Peace; come away: the song of woe
        Is after all an earthly song.
        Peace; come away: we do him wrong
To sing so wildly: let us go.

5   Come; let us go: your cheeks are pale;
        But half my life I leave behind.
        Methinks my friend is richly shrined;
But I shall pass, my work will fail.

Yet in these ears, till hearing dies,
10   One set slow bell will seem to toll
        The passing of the sweetest soul
That ever looked with human eyes.

I hear it now, and o'er and o'er,
        Eternal greetings to the dead;
15   And 'Ave, Ave, Ave,' said,
'Adieu, adieu,' for evermore.

58

In those sad words I took farewell.
        Like echoes in sepulchral halls,
        As drop by drop the water falls
In vaults and catacombs, they fell;

5   And, falling, idly broke the peace
        Of hearts that beat from day to day.
        Half-conscious of their dying clay,
And those cold crypts where they shall cease.

The high Muse answered: 'Wherefore grieve
10   Thy brethen with a fruitless tear?
        Abide a little longer here,
And thou shalt take a nobler leave.'

59

O Sorrow, wilt thou live with me
  No casual mistress, but a wife,
  My bosom friend and half of life;
As I confess it needs must be?

5 O Sorrow, wilt thou rule my blood,
  Be sometimes lovely like a bride,
  And put thy harsher moods aside,
If thou wilt have me wise and good?

My centred passion cannot move,
10 Nor will it lessen from today;
  But I'll have leave at times to play
As with the creature of my love;

And set thee forth, for thou art mine,
  With so much hope for years to come,
15 That, howsoe'er I know thee, some
Could hardly tell what name were thine.

106

Ring out, wild bells, to the wild sky,
  The flying cloud, the frosty light:
  The year is dying in the night;
Ring out, wild bells, and let him die.

5 Ring out the old, ring in the new,
  Ring, happy bells, across the snow:
  The year is going, let him go;
Ring out the false, ring in the true.

Ring out the grief that saps the mind,
10 For those that here we see no more;
  Ring out the feud of rich and poor,
Ring in redress to all mankind.

Ring out a slowly dying cause,
  And ancient forms of party strife;
15 Ring in the nobler modes of life,
With sweeter manners, purer laws.

Ring out the want, the care, the sin,
  The faithless coldness of the times:
  Ring out, ring out my mournful rhymes,
20 But ring the fuller minstrel in.

Ring out false pride in place and blood,
    The civic slander and the spite;
    Ring in the love of truth and right,
Ring in the common love of good.

25 Ring out old shapes of foul disease;
    Ring out the narrowing lust of gold;
    Ring out the thousand wars of old,
Ring in the thousand years of peace.

Ring in the valiant man and free,
30   The larger heart, the kindlier hand;
    Ring out the darkness of the land,
Ring in the Christ that is to be.

115

Now fades the long streak of snow,
    Now burgeons every maze of quick
    About the flowering squares, and thick
By ashen roots the violets blow.

5 Now rings the woodland loud and long,
    The distance takes a lovelier hue,
    And drowned in yonder living blue
The lark becomes a sightless song.

Now dance the lights on lawn and lea,
10   The flocks are whiter down the vale,
    And milkier every milky sail
On winding stream or distant sea;

Where now the seamew pipes, or dives
    In yonder greening gleam, and fly
15   The happy birds, that change their sky
To build and brood, that live their lives

From land to land; and in my breast
    Spring wakens too, and my regret
    Becomes an April violet,
20 And buds and blossoms like the rest.

The Charge of the Light Brigade

Half a league, half a league,
Half a league onward,
All in the valley of Death
Rode the six hundred.
5 'Forward, the Light Brigade!
Charge for the guns!' he said:
Into the valley of Death
Rode the six hundred.

'Forward, the Light Brigade!'
10 Was there a man dismayed?
Not though the soldier knew
Some one had blunder'd:
Their's not to make reply,
Their's not to reason why,
15 Their's but to do and die:
Into the valley of Death
Rode the six hundred.

Cannon to right of them,
Cannon to left of them,
20 Cannon in front of them
Volleyed and thundered;
Stormed at with shot and shell,
Boldly they rode and well,
Into the jaws of Death,
25 Into the mouth of Hell
Rode the six hundred.

Flashed all their sabres bare,
Flashed as they turned in air
Sab'ring the gunners there,
30 Charging an army, while
All the world wondered:
Plunged in the battery smoke
Right through the line they broke;
Cossack and Russian
35 Reeled from the sabre stroke
Shattered and sundered.
Then they rode back, but not
Not the six hundred.

Cannon to right of them,
40 Cannon to left of them,
Cannon behind them
Volleyed and thundered;
Stormed at with shot and shell,
While horse and hero fell,
45 They that had fought so well
Came through the jaws of Death,
Back from the mouth of hell,
All that was left of them,
Left of six hundred.

50 When can their glory fade?
O the wild charge they made!
All the world wondered.
Honor the charge they made!
Honor the Light Brigade,
55 Noble six hundred!

Crossing the Bar

Sunset and evening star,
And one clear call for me!
And may there be no moaning of the bar,
When I put out to sea,

5 But such a tide as moving seems asleep,
Too full for sound and foam,
When that which drew from out the boundless deep
Turns again home.

Twilight and evening bell,
10 And after that the dark!
And may there be no sadness of farewell,
When I embark;

For tho' from out our bourne of Time and Place
The flood may bear me far,
15 I hope to see my Pilot face to face
When I have crossed the bar.

Crossing the Bar: Tennyson asked that this poem, writ-   **13 bourne:** stream or spring.
ten in 1889, appear last in collections of his work. The
'bar' is the line of demarcation between the waters of a
harbour or river and the waters of the sea, often marked
by a bank of sand or shingle.

ROBERT BROWNING (1812–1889)

Robert Browning's father was a clerk in the Bank of England. Browning was educated mainly at home in his father's extensive library where he read avidly: Byron, Keats and Shelley. His first publication, *Pauline* (1833), was an imitation of Shelley, and the next, *Paracelsus* (1835), was quite well received, but *Sordello* (1840), seven years in the making, was deemed an obscure failure (although it is now critically appreciated). From the mid-1830s to mid-1840s Browning tried writing for the theatre, but whilst this taught him valuable skills deployed in *Dramatic Lyrics* (1842), success still eluded him. In 1845 he began to court the most famous woman poet of the day, Elizabeth Barrett, whose *Poems* (1844) he had admired. Their courtship was difficult (see Elizabeth Barrett Browning) and in 1846 they eloped to live happily together in Pisa and Florence until she died in 1861. Browning's *Men and Women* (1855) reflects this happiness and began to bring him recognition which was confirmed by *Dramatis Personae* (1864), and his retelling (in 12 volumes) of a seventeenth-century murder story, *The Ring and the Book* (1868–69). This rich and novel-like work assured Browning of many admirers. Browning's particular achievement was to establish the dramatic monologue as a poetic form, and in this he was so successful that he was imitated not only by many contemporaries, notably Tennyson and Augusta Webster, but by many more recent poets, notably T. S. Eliot (see 'Prufrock'), Ezra Pound and Robert Lowell.

Soliloquy of the Spanish Cloister

Gr-r-r – there go, my heart's abhorrence!
 Water your damned flower-pots, do!
If hate killed men, Brother Lawrence,
 God's blood, would not mine kill you!
5 What? your myrtle bush wants trimming?
 Oh, that rose has prior claims –
Needs its leaden vase filled brimming?
 Hell dry you up with its flames

II
At the meal we sit together:
10 *Salve tibi!* I must hear
Wise talk of the kind of weather,
 Sort of season, time of year:
Not a plenteous cork crop: scarcely
 Dare we hope oak-galls, I doubt:
15 *What's the Latin name for 'parsley'?*
 What's the Greek name for Swine's Snout?

---

10 *Salve tibi!*: 'Greetings to you!' 14 galls: growths on 16 Swine's Snout: dandelion.
oak bark used in tanning.

III

Whew! We'll have our platter burnished,
    Laid with care on our own shelf!
With a fire-new spoon we're furnished,
20   And a goblet for ourself,
Rinsed like something sacrificial
    Ere 'tis fit to touch our chaps –
Marked with L. for our initial!
    (He-he! There his lily snaps!)

IV

25   *Saint*, forsooth! While brown Dolores
    Squats outside the Convent bank
With Sanchicha, telling stories,
    Steeping tresses in the tank,
Blue-black, lustrous, thick like horsehairs,
30   – Can't I see his dead eye glow,
Bright as 'twere a Barbary corsair's?
    (That is, if he'd let it show!)

V

When he finishes refection,
    Knife and fork he never lays
35   Cross-wise, to my recollection,
    As do I, in Jesu's praise.
I the Trinity illustrate,
    Drinking watered orange pulp –
In three sips the Arian frustrate;
40   While he drains his at one gulp.

VI

Oh, those melons? If he's able
    We're to have a feast! so nice!
One goes to the Abbot's table,
    All of us get each a slice.
45   How go on your flowers? None double?
    Not one fruit-sort can you spy?
Strange! – And I, too, at such trouble,
    Keep them close-nipped on the sly!

VII

There's a great text in Galatians,
50   Once you trip on it, entails

---

22 chaps: jaws. 31 corsair: pirate. 33 refection: eating. 39 Arian: a heretic who denied the Trinity.

49 Galatians: *Galatians,* 5, ll. 15–23 in which Paul lists the crimes of the flesh that lead to damnation.

Twenty-nine distinct damnations,
One sure, if another fails:
If I trip him just a-dying,
Sure of heaven as sure can be,
55 Spin him round and send him flying
Off to hell, a Manichee?

VIII

Or, my scrofulous French novel
On grey paper with blunt type!
Simply glance at it, you grovel
60 Hand and foot in Belial's gripe:
If I double down its pages
At the woeful sixteenth print,
When he gathers his greengages,
Ope a sieve and slip it in't?

IX

65 Or, there's Satan! – one might venture
Pledge one's soul to him, yet leave
Such a flaw in the indenture
As he'd miss till, past retrieve,
Blasted lay that rose-acacia
70 We're so proud of ! *Hy, Zy, Hine* . . .
'St, there's Vespers! *Plena gratia*
Ave, Virgo! Gr-r-r – you swine!

My Last Duchess

Ferrara

That's my last Duchess painted on the wall,
Looking as if she were alive. I call
That piece a wonder, now: Frà Pandolf's hands
Worked busily a day, and there she stands.
5 Will't please you sit and look at her? I said
'Frà Pandolf' by design, for never read
Strangers like you that pictured countenance,
The depth and passion of its earnest glance,
But to myself they turned (since none puts by
10 The curtain I have drawn for you, but I)
And seemed as they would ask me, if they durst,

---

56 Manichee: a heretical follower of Mani. **57 scrofu-**
lous: tubercular. **71–2 *Virgo*:** the interlocutor has
muddled his prayer 'Ave Maria, gratia plena': Behold
Mary, full of Grace.

My Last Duchess: The poem is spoken by Alfonso II,
Duke of Ferrara, whose first wife died in 1561 and who
sought a new one from the Count of Tirol. **3 Frà**
Pandolf: an imaginary painter and a friar.

How such a glance came there; so, not the first
Are you to turn and ask thus. Sir, 'twas not
Her husband's presence only, called that spot
15 Of joy into the Duchess' cheek: perhaps
Frà Pandolf chanced to say 'Her mantle laps
Over my lady's wrist too much,' or 'Paint
Must never hope to reproduce the faint
Half-flush that dies along her throat': such stuff
20 Was courtesy, she thought, and cause enough
For calling up that spot of joy. She had
A heart – how shall I say? – too soon made glad,
Too easily impressed; she liked whate'er
She looked on, and her looks went everywhere.
25 Sir, 'twas all one! My favour at her breast,
The dropping of the daylight in the West,
The bough of cherries some officious fool
Broke in the orchard for her, the white mule
She rode with round the terrace – all and each
30 Would draw from her alike the approving speech,
Or blush, at least. She thanked men, – good! but thanked
Somehow – I know not how – as if she ranked
My gift of a nine-hundred-years-old name
With anybody's gift. Who'd stoop to blame
35 This sort of trifling? Even had you skill
In speech – (which I have not) – to make your will
Quite clear to such an one, and say, 'Just this
Or that in you disgusts me; here you miss,
Or there exceed the mark' – and if she let
40 Herself be lessoned so, nor plainly set
Her wits to yours, forsooth, and made excuse,
– E'en then would be some stooping; and I choose
Never to stoop. Oh sir, she smiled, no doubt,
Whene'er I passed her; but who passed without
45 Much the same smile? This grew; I gave commands;
Then all smiles stopped together. There she stands
As if alive. Will't please you rise? We'll meet
The company below, then. I repeat,
The Count your master's known munificence
50 Is ample warrant that no just pretense
Of mine for dowry will be disallowed;
Though his fair daughter's self, as I avowed
At starting, is my object. Nay, we'll go
Together down, sir. Notice Neptune, though,
55 Taming a sea-horse, thought a rarity,
Which Claus of Innsbruck cast in bronze for me.

Frà Lippo Lippi

I am poor brother Lippo, by your leave!
You need not clap your torches to my face.
Zooks, what's to blame? you think you see a monk!
What, 'tis past midnight, and you go the rounds,
5   And here you catch me at an alley's end
Where sportive ladies leave their doors ajar?
The Carmine's my cloister: hunt it up,
Do, – harry out, if you must show your zeal,
Whatever rat, there, haps on his wrong hole,
10   And nip each softling of a wee white mouse,
Weke, weke, that's crept to keep him company!
Aha, you know your betters! Then, you'll take
Your hand away that's fiddling on my throat,
And please to know me likewise. Who am I?
15   Why, one, sir, who is lodging with a friend
Three streets off – he's a certain . . . how d'ye call?
Master – a . . . Cosimo of the Medici,
I' the house that caps the corner. Boh! you were best!
Remember and tell me, the day you're hanged,
20   How you affected such a gullet's gripe!
But you, sir, it concerns you that your knaves
Pick up a manner nor discredit you:
Zooks, are we pilchards, that they sweep the streets
And count fair price what comes into their net?
25   He's Judas to a tittle, that man is!
Just such a face! Why, sir, you make amends.
Lord, I'm not angry! Bid your hangdogs go
Drink out this quarter-florin to the health
Of the munificent House that harbors me
30   (And many more beside, lads! more beside!)
And all's come square again. I'd like his face –
His, elbowing on his comrade in the door
With the pike and lantern – for the slave that holds
John Baptist's head a-dangle by the hair
35   With one hand ('Look you, now,' as who should say)
And his weapon in the other, yet unwiped!
It's not your chance to have a bit of chalk,
A wood-coal or the like? or you should see!
Yes, I'm the painter, since you style me so.
40   What, brother Lippo's doings, up and down,

Frà Lippo Lippi: (1406–69), Florentine friar and painter. **3 Zooks:** gadzooks, corruption of 'God's hooks' (nails of the cross). **7 Carmine:** Santa Maria del Carmine, Florence, centre of the Carmelite order.

17 Cosimo of the Medici: (1519–74) duke of Florence and first grand duke of Tuscany (1569–74), Lippi's patron.

You know them and they take you? like enough!
I saw the proper twinkle in your eye –
'Tell you, I liked your looks at very first.
Let's sit and set things straight now, hip to haunch.

45   Here's spring come, and the nights one makes up bands
To roam the town and sing out carnival,
And I've been three weeks shut within my mew,
A-painting for the great man, saints and saints
And saints again. I could not paint all night –

50   Ouf! I leaned out of window for fresh air.
There came a hurry of feet and little feet,
A sweep of lute strings, laughs, and whifts of song, –
Flower o' the broom,
Take away love, and our earth is a tomb!

55   *Flower o' the quince,*
I let Lisa go, and what good is life since?
Flower o' the thyme – and so on. Round they went.
Scarce had they turned the corner when a titter
Like the skipping of rabbits by moonlight, – three slim shapes,

60   And a face that looked up ... zooks, sir, flesh and blood,
That's all I'm made of! Into shreds it went,
Curtain and counterpane and coverlet,
All the bed-furniture – a dozen knots,
There was a ladder! Down I let myself,

65   Hands and feet, scrambling somehow, and so dropped,
And after them. I came up with the fun
Hard by Saint Laurence, hail fellow, well met, –
Flower o' the rose,
If I've been merry, what matter who knows?

70   And so as I was stealing back again
To get to bed and have a bit of sleep
Ere I rise up to-morrow and go work
On Jerome knocking at his poor old breast
With his great round stone to subdue the flesh,

75   You snap me of the sudden. Ah, I see!
Though your eye twinkles still, you shake your head –
Mine's shaved – a monk, you say – the sting's in that!
If Master Cosimo announced himself,
Mum's the word naturally; but a monk!

80   Come, what am I a beast for? tell us, now!
I was a baby when my mother died
And father died and left me in the street.
I starved there, God knows how, a year or two
On fig skins, melon parings, rinds and shucks,

85   Refuse and rubbish. One fine frosty day,

My stomach being empty as your hat,
The wind doubled me up and down I went.
Old Aunt Lapaccia trussed me with one hand,
(Its fellow was a stinger as I knew)
90 And so along the wall, over the bridge,
By the straight cut to the convent. Six words there,
While I stood munching my first bread that month:
'So, boy, you're minded,' quoth the good fat father
Wiping his own mouth, 'twas refection time, –
95 'To quit this very miserable world?
Will you renounce' . . . 'the mouthful of bread?' thought I;
By no means! Brief, they made a monk of me;
I did renounce the world, its pride and greed,
Palace, farm, villa, shop, and banking house,
100 Trash, such as these poor devils of Medici
Have given their hearts to – all at eight years old.
Well, sir, I found in time, you may be sure,
'Twas not for nothing – the good bellyful,
The warm serge and the rope that goes all round,
105 And day-long blessed idleness beside!
'Let's see what the urchin's fit for' – that came next.
Not overmuch their way, I must confess.
Such a to-do! They tried me with their books:
Lord, they'd have taught me Latin in pure waste!
110 *Flower o' the clove.*
All the Latin I construe is, 'amo' I love!
But, mind you, when a boy starves in the streets
Eight years together, as my fortune was,
Watching folk's faces to know who will fling
115 The bit of half-stripped grape bunch he desires,
And who will curse or kick him for his pains, –
Which gentleman processional and fine,
Holding a candle to the Sacrament,
Will wink and let him lift a plate and catch
120 The droppings of the wax to sell again,
Or holla for the Eight and have him whipped, –
How say I? – nay, which dog bites, which lets drop
His bone from the heap of offal in the street, –
Why, soul and sense of him grow sharp alike,
125 He learns the look of things, and none the less
For admonition from the hunger-pinch.
I had a store of such remarks, be sure,
Which, after I found leisure, turned to use.
I drew men's faces on my copy-books,
130 Scrawled them within the antiphonary's marge,

---

121 **Eight**: the magistrates of Florence. 130 **antiphonary marge**: margin of a psalter.

Joined legs and arms to the long music-notes,
Found eyes and nose and chin for A's and B's,
And made a string of pictures of the world
Betwixt the ins and outs of verb and noun,
135   On the wall, the bench, the door. The monks looked black.
'Nay,' quoth the Prior, 'turn him out, d'ye say?
In no wise. Lose a crow and catch a lark.
What if at last we get our man of parts,
We Carmelites, like those Camaldolese
140   And Preaching Friars, to do our church up fine
And put the front on it that ought to be!'
And hereupon he bade me daub away.
Thank you! my head being crammed, the walls a blank,
Never was such prompt disemburdening.
145   First, every sort of monk, the black and white,
I drew them, fat and lean: then, folk at church,
From good old gossips waiting to confess
Their cribs of barrel droppings, candle ends, –
To the breathless fellow at the altar-foot,
150   Fresh from his murder, safe and sitting there
With the little children round him in a row
Of admiration, half for his beard and half
For that white anger of his victim's son
Shaking a fist at him with one fierce arm,
155   Signing himself with the other because of Christ
(Whose sad face on the cross sees only this
After the passion of a thousand years)
Till some poor girl, her apron o'er her head,
(Which the intense eyes looked through) came at eve
160   On tiptoe, said a word, dropped in a loaf,
Her pair of earrings and a bunch of flowers
(The brute took growling), prayed, and so was gone.
I painted all, then cried "Tis ask and have;
Choose, for more's ready!' – laid the ladder flat,
165   And showed my covered bit of cloister wall.
The monks closed in a circle and praised loud
Till checked, taught what to see and not to see,
Being simple bodies, – 'That's the very man!
Look at the boy who stoops to pat the dog!
170   That woman's like the Prior's niece who comes
To care about his asthma: it's the life!'
But there my triumph's straw-fire flared and funked;
Their betters took their turn to see and say:
The Prior and the learned pulled a face
175   And stopped all that in no time. 'How? what's here?

---

140 **Preaching friars**: the Benedictines and Dominicans.   172 **funked**: defeated.

Quite from the mark of painting, bless us all!
Faces, arms, legs, and bodies like the true
As much as pea and pea! it's devil's-game!
Your business is not to catch men with show,
180   With homage to the perishable clay,
But lift them over it, ignore it all,
Make them forget there's such a thing as flesh.
Your business is to paint the souls of men –
Man's soul, and it's a fire, smoke . . . no, it's not . . .
185   It's vapour done up like a newborn babe –
(In that shape when you die it leaves your mouth)
It's . . . well, what matters talking, it's the soul!
Give us no more of body than shows soul!
Here's Giotto, with his Saint a-praising God,
190   That sets us praising – why not stop with him?
Why put all thoughts of praise out of our head
With wonder at lines, colours, and what not?
Paint the soul, never mind the legs and arms!
Rub all out, try at it a second time.
195   Oh, that white smallish female with the breasts,
She's just my niece . . . Herodias, I would say, –
Who went and danced and got men's heads cut off!
Have it all out!' Now, is this sense, I ask?
A fine way to paint soul, by painting body
200   So ill, the eye can't stop there, must go further
And can't fare worse! Thus, yellow does for white
When what you put for yellow's simply black,
And any sort of meaning looks intense
When all beside itself means and looks naught.
205   Why can't a painter lift each foot in turn,
Left foot and right foot, go a double step,
Make his flesh liker and his soul more like,
Both in their order? Take the prettiest face,
The Prior's niece . . . patron-saint – is it so pretty
210   You can't discover if it means hope, fear,
Sorrow or joy? won't beauty go with these?
Suppose I've made her eyes all right and blue,
Can't I take breath and try to add life's flash,
And then add soul and heighten them threefold?
215   Or say there's beauty with no soul at all –
(I never saw it – put the case the same –)
If you get simple beauty and naught else,
You get about the best thing God invents:

---

189 Giotto: Giotto di Bondone (?1267–1337), Florentine painter who developed the naturalistic style characteristic of the Renaissance. **196 Herodias:** wife of Herod Antipas who asked for John the Baptist's head.

That's somewhat: and you'll find the soul you have missed,
220 Within yourself, when you return him thanks.
'Rub all out!' Well, well, there's my life, in short,
And so the thing has gone on ever since.
I'm grown a man no doubt, I've broken bounds:
You should not take a fellow eight years old
225 And make him swear to never kiss the girls.
I'm my own master, paint now as I please –
Having a friend, you see, in the Corner-house!
Lord, it's fast holding by the rings in front –
Those great rings serve more purposes than just
230 To plant a flag in, or tie up a horse!
And yet the old schooling sticks, the old grave eyes
Are peeping o'er my shoulder as I work,
The heads shake still – 'It's art's decline, my son!
You're not of the true painters, great and old;
235 Brother Angelico's the man, you'll find;
Brother Lorenzo stands his single peer:
Fag on at flesh, you'll never make the third!'
Flower o' the pine,
You keep your mistr . . . manners, and I'll stick to mine!
240 I'm not the third, then: bless us, they must know!
Don't you think they're the likeliest to know,
They with their Latin? So, I swallow my rage,
Clench my teeth, suck my lips in tight, and paint
To please them – sometimes do and sometimes don't;
245 For, doing most, there's pretty sure to come
A turn, some warm eve finds me at my saints –
A laugh, a cry, the business of the world –
(*Flower o' the peach*
Death for us all, and his own life for each!)
250 And my whole soul revolves, the cup runs over,
The world and life's too big to pass for a dream,
And I do these wild things in sheer despite,
And play the fooleries you catch me at,
In pure rage! The old mill-horse, out at grass
255 After hard years, throws up his stiff heels so,
Although the miller does not preach to him
The only good of grass is to make chaff.
What would men have? Do they like grass or no –
May they or mayn't they? all I want's the thing
260 Settled forever one way. As it is,
You tell too many lies and hurt yourself:
You don't like what you only like too much,
You do like what, if given you at your word,

---

257 chaff: fine straw.

You find abundantly detestable.
265 For me, I think I speak as I was taught;
I always see the garden and God there
A-making man's wife: and, my lesson learned,
The value and significance of flesh,
I can't unlearn ten minutes afterwards.

270 You understand me: I'm a beast, I know.
But see, now – why, I see as certainly
As that the morning star's about to shine,
What will hap some day. We've a youngster here
Comes to our convent, studies what I do,
275 Slouches and stares and lets no atom drop:
His name is Guidi – he'll not mind the monks –
They call him Hulking Tom, he lets them talk –
He picks my practice up – he'll paint apace.
I hope so – though I never live so long,
280 I know what's sure to follow. You be judge!
You speak no Latin more than I, belike;
However, you're my man, you've seen the world
– The beauty and the wonder and the power,
The shapes of things, their colours, lights and shades,
285 Changes, surprises, – and God made it all!
– For what? Do you feel thankful, ay or no,
For this fair town's face, yonder river's line,
The mountain round it and the sky above,
Much more the figures of man, woman, child,
290 These are the frame to? What's it all about?
To be passed over, despised? or dwelt upon,
Wondered at? oh, this last of course! – you say.
But why not do as well as say, – paint these
Just as they are, careless what comes of it?
295 God's works – paint any one, and count it crime
To let a truth slip. Don't object, 'His works
Are here already; nature is complete:
Suppose you reproduce her – (which you can't)
There's no advantage! you must beat her, then.'
300 For, don't you mark? we're made so that we love
First when we see them painted, things we have passed
Perhaps a hundred times nor cared to see;
And so they are better, painted – better to us,
Which is the same thing. Art was given for that;
305 God uses us to help each other so,
Lending our minds out. Have you noticed, now,

---

276 Guidi: Tommaso Guidi (1401–28), also known as Masaccio; Florentine painter, early pioneer of the laws of perspective whose frescoes are in the church of Sta. Maria del Carmine, Florence. See note to line 7 above.

Your cullion's hanging face? A bit of chalk,
And trust me but you should, though! How much more,
If I drew higher things with the same truth!
310   That were to take the Prior's pulpit-place,
Interpret God to all of you! Oh, oh,
It makes me mad to see what men shall do
And we in our graves! This world's no blot for us,
Nor blank; it means intensely, and means good:
315   To find its meaning is my meat and drink.
'Ay, but you don't so instigate to prayer!'
Strikes in the Prior: 'when your meaning's plain
It does not say to folk – remember matins,
Or, mind you fast next Friday!' Why, for this
320   What need of art at all? A skull and bones,
Two bits of stick nailed crosswise, or, what's best,
A bell to chime the hour with, does as well.
I painted a Saint Laurence six months since
At Prato, splashed the fresco in fine style:
325   'How looks my painting, now the scaffold's down?'
I ask a brother: 'Hugely,' he returns –
'Already not one phiz of your three slaves
Who turn the Deacon off his toasted side,
But it's scratched and prodded to our heart's content,
330   The pious people have so eased their own
With coming to say prayers there in a rage:
We get on fast to see the bricks beneath.
Expect another job this time next year,
For pity and religion grow i' the crowd –
335   Your painting serves its purpose!' Hang the fools!

– That is – you'll not mistake an idle word
Spoke in a huff by a poor monk, God wot,
Tasting the air this spicy night which turns
The unaccustomed head like Chianti wine!
340   Oh, the church knows! don't misreport me, now!
It's natural a poor monk out of bounds
Should have his apt word to excuse himself:
And hearken how I plot to make amends.
I have bethought me: I shall paint a piece
345   . . . There's for you! Give me six months, then go, see
Something in Sant' Ambrogio's! Bless the nuns!
They want a cast o' my office. I shall paint
God in the midst, Madonna and her babe,
Ringed by a bowery, flowery angel brood,

---

307 **cullion's**: knave's. 323–24: I painted a fresco of the 347 **a cast**: an example of my work.
martyrdom of San Lorenzo in the town of Prato.

350 Lilies and vestments and white faces, sweet
As puff on puff of grated orris-root
When ladies crowd to Church at midsummer.
And then i' the front, of course a saint or two –
Saint John, because he saves the Florentines,
355 Saint Ambrose, who puts down in black and white
The convent's friends and gives them a long day,
And Job, I must have him there past mistake,
The man of Uz (and Us without the z,
Painters who need his patience). Well, all these
360 Secured at their devotion, up shall come
Out of a corner when you least expect,
As one by a dark stair into a great light,
Music and talking, who but Lippo! I! –
Mazed, motionless, and moonstruck – I'm the man!
365 Back I shrink – what is this I see and hear?
I, caught up with my monk's things by mistake,
My old serge gown and rope that goes all round,
I, in this presence, this pure company!
Where's a hole, where's a corner for escape?
370 Then steps a sweet angelic slip of a thing
Forward, puts out a soft palm – 'Not so fast!'
– Addresses the celestial presence, 'nay –
He made you and devised you, after all,
Though he's none of you! Could Saint John there draw –
375 His camel-hair make up a painting brush?
We come to brother Lippo for all that,
Iste perfecit opus!' So, all smile –
I shuffle sideways with my blushing face
Under the cover of a hundred wings
380 Thrown like a spread of kirtles when you're gay
And play hot cockles, all the doors being shut,
Till, wholly unexpected, in there pops
The hothead husband! Thus I scuttle off
To some safe bench behind, not letting go
385 The palm of her, the little lily thing
That spoke the good word for me in the nick,
Like the Prior's niece . . . Saint Lucy, I would say.
And so all's saved for me, and for the church
A pretty picture gained. Go, six months hence!
390 Your hand, sir, and good-bye: no lights, no lights!
The street's hushed, and I know my own way back,
Don't fear me! There's the grey beginning. Zooks!

---

351 **puff . . . orris-root:** perfume made from iris root.   380 **kirtles:** skirts.   381 **cockles:** a game like blind-man's
377 ***Iste perfecit opus:*** this man made the work.   buff.

THOMAS CARLYLE (1795–1881)

Thomas Carlyle was born in Dumfriesshire into a staunch Calvinist family. His father, a peasant stonemason and farmer, intended him for the ministry and sent him to Edinburgh University, but there Carlyle gave up his faith and decided on a life of letters. He published a life of Schiller (1825), and then translations of Goethe, by whom he was deeply influenced. He married in 1826 and moved to a remote farmhouse where he wrote *Sartor Resartus* (1833–34), an eccentric mélange of German philosophy, strange humour and searching social criticism which would only later find a readership. In 1834 he moved to Chelsea and set to work on his *History of the French Revolution* (1837) which, with *Chartism* (1839), would secure his reputation as a historian and polemicist. His lectures of 1840 were attended by glittering crowds and were immensely successful when published as *Heroes and Hero-Worship* (1841). His *Past and Present* (1843) and *Latter-Day Pamphlets* (1850) gave him pre-eminent stature among Victorian intellectuals. Carlyle's style is pugnacious, unsystematic, obnoxious and purgative. He denounced what he called 'Mammonism' – a society where 'cash payment has become the sole nexus of man to man'. He scorned both incompetent administration and democracy (since not all electors are competent to judge), and argued the need in all ages for strong men (heroes) who could inspire (and force) the crowd to follow the right path. He was a racist and proto-fascist whose immense popularity and influence on nearly all writers stems from his willingness to address central issues of the age with a forthright energy. He believed the analytic mind was overvalued and expressed in his own style and ideas a belief in instinct, mystery, vitalism and idiosyncratic energy.

From Past and Present

From Book III. The Modern Worker: Democracy

Truly they are strange results to which this leaving all to 'Cash'; of quietly shutting up the God's Temple, and gradually opening wide-open the Mammon's Temple, with 'Laissez-faire, and Every man for himself,' – have led us in these days! We have Upper, speaking Classes, who indeed do 'speak' as never man spake before; the withered flimsiness, godless baseness and barrenness of whose Speech might of itself indicate what kind of Doing and practical Governing went on under it! For Speech is the gaseous element out of which most kinds of Practice and Performance, especially all kinds of moral Performance, condense themselves, and take shape; as the one is, so will the other be. Descending, accordingly, into the Dumb Class in its Stockport Cellars and Poor-Law Bastilles,[1] have we not to announce that they are hitherto unexampled in the History of Adam's Posterity?

Life was never a May-game for men: in all times the lot of the dumb millions born to toil was defaced with manifold sufferings, injustices, heavy burdens, avoidable and unavoidable; not play at all, but hard work that made the sinews sore and the heart sore. As bond-slaves, *villani, bordorii, sochemanni,* nay indeed

---

1: workhouses for the poor.

as dukes, earls and kings, men were oftentimes made weary of their life; and had to say, in the sweat of their brow and of their soul, Behold, it is not sport, it is grim earnest, and our back can bear no more! Who knows not what massacrings and harryings there have been; grinding, long-continuing, unbearable injustices, – till the heart had to rise in madness, and some '*Eu Sachsen, nimith euer sachses,* You Saxons, out with your gully-knives, then!' You Saxons, some 'arrestment,' partial 'arrestment of the Knaves and Dastards' has become indispensable! – The page of Dryasdust[1] is heavy with such details.

And yet I will venture to believe that in no time, since the beginnings of Society, was the lot of those same dumb millions of toilers so entirely unbearable as it is even in the days now passing over us. It is not to die, or even to die of hunger, that makes a man wretched; many men have died; all men must die, – the last exit of us all is in a Fire-Chariot of Pain. But it is to live miserable we know not why; to work sore and yet gain nothing; to be heart-worn, weary, yet isolated, unrelated, girt-in with a cold universal Laissez-faire: it is to die slowly all our life long, imprisoned in a deaf, dead, Infinite Injustice, as in the accursed iron belly of a Phalaris' Bull![2] This is and remains for ever intolerable to all men whom God has made. Do we wonder at French Revolutions, Chartisms, Revolts of Three Days? The times, if we will consider them, are really unexampled.

*   *   *

Liberty? The true liberty of a man, you would say, consisted in his finding out, or being forced to find out, the right path, and to walk thereon. To learn, or to be taught, what work he actually was able for; and then by permission, persuasion, and even compulsion, to set about doing of the same! That is his true blessedness, honour, 'liberty' and maximum of wellbeing: if liberty be not that, I for one have small care about liberty. You do not allow a palpable madman to leap over precipices; you violate his liberty, you that are wise; and keep him, were it in strait-waistcoats, away from the precipices! Every stupid, every cowardly and foolish man is but a less palpable madman: his true liberty were that a wiser man, that any and every wiser man, could, by brass collars, or in whatever milder or sharper way, lay hold of him when he was going wrong, and order and compel him to go a little righter. O, if thou really art my *Senior,* Seigneur, my *Elder,* Presbyter or Priest, – if thou art in very deed my *Wiser,* may a beneficent instinct lead and impel thee to 'conquer' me, to command me! If thou do know better than I what is good and right, I conjure thee in the name of God, force me to do it; were it by never such brass collars, whips and handcuffs, leave me not to walk over precipices! That I have been called, by all the Newspapers, a 'free man' will avail me little, if my pilgrimage have ended in death and wreck. O that the Newspapers had called me slave, coward, fool, or what it pleased their sweet voices to name me, and I had attained not death, but life! – Liberty requires new definitions.

A conscious abhorrence and intolerance of Folly, of Baseness, Stupidity, Poltroonery and all that brood of things, dwells deep in some men: still deeper

---

1: a dull historian invented by Sir Walter Scott and made a stock figure by Carlyle. 2: Phalaris was a legendary tyrant who roasted his enemies inside a brass bull.

in others an *un*conscious abhorrence and intolerance, clothed moreover by the beneficent Supreme Powers in what stout appetites, energies, egoisms so-called, are suitable to it; – these latter are your Conquerors, Romans, Normans, Russians, Indo-English; Founders of what we call Aristocracies. Which indeed have they not the most 'divine right' to found; – being themselves very truly?*Aristoi*, BRAVEST, BEST; and conquering generally a confused rabble of WORST, or at lowest, clearly enough, of WORSE? I think their divine right, tried, with affirmatory verdict, in the greatest Law-Court known to me, was good! A class of men who are dreadfully exclaimed against by Dryasdust; of whom nevertheless beneficent Nature has oftentimes had need; and may, alas, again have need.

From Book IV. Horoscope. Captains of Industry

If I believed that Mammonism with its adjuncts was to continue henceforth the one serious principle of our existence, I should reckon it idle to solicit remedial measures from any Government, the disease being insusceptible of remedy. Government can do much, but it can in no wise do all. Government, as the most conspicuous object in Society, is called upon to give signal of what shall be done; and, in many ways, to preside over, further, and command the doing of it. But the Government cannot do, by all its signalling and commanding, what the Society is radically indisposed to do. In the long-run every Government is the exact symbol of its People, with their wisdom and unwisdom; we have to say, Like People like Government. – The main substance of this immense Problem of Organising Labour, and first of all of Managing the Working Classes, will, it is very clear, have to be solved by those who stand practically in the middle of it; by those who themselves work and preside over work. Of all that can be enacted by any Parliament in regard to it, the germs must already lie potentially extant in those two Classes, who are to obey such enactment. A Human Chaos *in* which there is no light, you vainly attempt to irradiate by light shed *on* it: order never can arise there.

But it is my firm conviction that the 'Hell of England' will *cease* to be that of 'not making money'; that we shall get a nobler Hell and a nobler Heaven! I anticipate light *in* the Human Chaos, glimmering, shining more and more; under manifold true signals from without That light shall shine. Our deity no longer being Mammon, – O Heavens, each man will then say to himself: 'Why such deadly haste to make money? I shall not go to Hell, even if I do not make money! There is another Hell, I am told!' Competition, at railway-speed, in all branches of commerce and work will then abate: – good felt-hats for the head, in every sense, instead of seven-feet lath-and-plaster hats on wheels, will then be discoverable! Bubble-periods,[1] with their panics and commercial crises, will again become infrequent; steady modest industry will take the place of gambling speculation. To be a noble Master, among noble Workers, will again be the first ambition with some few; to be a rich Master only the second. How the Inventive Genius of England, with the whirr of its bobbins and billy-rollers[2] shoved somewhat into the backgrounds of the brain, will contrive and devise,

---

1: speculative financial booms, leading to crashes.   2: parts of spinning machines.

not cheaper produce exclusively, but fairer distribution of the produce at its present cheapness! By degrees, we shall again have a Society with something of Heroism in it, something of Heaven's Blessing on it; we shall again have, as my German friend[1] asserts, 'instead of Mammon-Feudalism with unsold cotton-shirts and Preservation of the Game, noble just Industrialism and Government by the Wisest!'

It is with the hope of awakening here and there a British man to know himself for a man and divine soul, that a few words of parting admonition, to all persons to whom the Heavenly Powers have lent power of any kind in this land, may now be addressed. And first to those same Master-Workers, Leaders of Industry; who stand nearest, and in fact powerfullest, though not most prominent, being as yet in too many senses a Virtuality rather than an Actuality.

The Leaders of Industry, if Industry is ever to be led, are virtually the Captains of the World; if there be no nobleness in them, there will never be an Aristocracy more. But let the Captains of Industry consider: once again, are they born of other clay than the old Captains of Slaughter; doomed for ever to be not Chivalry, but a mere gold-plated *Doggery*, – what the French well name *Canaille*,[2] 'Doggery' with more or less gold carrion at its disposal? Captains of Industry are the true Fighters, henceforth recognisable as the only true ones: Fighters against Chaos, Necessity and the Devils and Jötuns;[3] and lead on Mankind in that great, and alone true, and universal warfare; the stars in their courses fighting for them, and all Heaven and all Earth saying audibly, Well done! Let the Captains of Industry retire into their own hearts, and ask solemnly, If there is nothing but vulturous hunger for fine wines, valet reputation and gilt carriages, discoverable there? Of hearts made by the Almighty God I will not believe such a thing. Deep-hidden under wretchedest god-forgetting Cants, Epicurisms, Dead-SeaApisms; forgotten as under foullest fat Lethe mud and weeds, there is yet, in all hearts born into this God's-World, a spark of the Godlike slumbering. Awake, O nightmare sleepers; awake, arise, or be for ever fallen! This is not playhouse poetry; it is sober fact. Our England, our world cannot live as it is. It will connect itself with a God again, or go down with nameless throes and fire-consummation to the Devils. Thou who feelest aught of such a Godlike stirring in thee, any faintest intimation of it as through heavy-laden dreams, follow *it*, I conjure thee. Arise, save thyself, be one of those that save thy country.

Bucaniers, Chactaw Indians, whose supreme aim in fighting is that they may get the scalps, the money, that they may amass scalps and money; out of such came no Chivalry, and never will! Out of such came only gore and wreck, infernal rage and misery; desperation quenched in annihilation. Behold it, I bid thee, behold there, and consider! What is it that thou have a hundred thousand-pound bills laid up in thy strong-room, a hundred scalps hung up in thy wigwam? I value not them or thee. Thy scalps and thy thousand-pound bills are as yet nothing, if no nobleness from within irradiate them; if no Chivalry, in action, or in embryo ever struggling towards birth and action, be there.

1: Baron Teufelsdröck in *Sartor Resartus*.   2: the rabble.   3: giants in the Norse myths.

Love of men cannot be bought by cash-payment; and without love, men cannot endure to be together. You cannot lead a Fighting World without having it regimented, chivalried: the thing, in a day, becomes impossible; all men in it, the highest at first, the very lowest at last, discern consciously, or by a noble instinct, this necessity. And can you any more continue to lead a Working World unregimented, anarchic? I answer, and the Heavens and Earth are now answering, No! The thing becomes not 'in a day' impossible; but in some two generations it does. Yes, when fathers and mothers, in Stockport hunger-cellars, begin to eat their children, and Irish widows have to prove their relationship by dying of typhus-fever; and amid Governing 'Corporations of the Best and Bravest,' busy to preserve their game by 'bushing,' dark millions of God's human creatures start up in mad Chartisms,[1] impracticable Sacred Months, and Manchester Insurrections;[2] – and there is a virtual Industrial Aristocracy as yet only half-alive, spell-bound amid money-bags and ledgers; and an actual Idle Aristocracy seemingly near dead in somnolent delusions, in trespasses and double-barrels;[3] 'sliding,' as on inclined-planes, which every new year they *soap* with new Hansard's-jargon[4] under God's sky, and so are 'sliding' ever faster, towards a 'scale' and balance-scale whereon is written *Thou art found Wanting:*– in such days, after a generation or two, I say, it does become, even to the low and simple, very palpably impossible! No Working World, any more than a Fighting World, can be led on without a noble Chivalry of Work, and laws and fixed rules which follow out of that, – far nobler than any Chivalry of Fighting was. As an anarchic multitude on mere Supply-and-demand, it is becoming inevitable that we dwindle in horrid suicidal convulsion, and self-abrasion, frightful to the imagination, into thousand-pound bills; with savagery, depopulation, chaotic desolation! Good Heavens, will not one French Revolution and Reign of Terror suffice us, but must there be two? There will be two if needed; there will be twenty if needed; there will be precisely as many as are needed. The Laws of Nature will have themselves fulfilled. That is a thing certain to me.

Your gallant battle-hosts and work-hosts, as the others did, will need to be made loyally yours; they must and will be regulated, methodically secured in their just share of conquest under you; – joined with you in veritable brother-hood, sonhood, by quite other and deeper ties than those of temporary day's wages! How would mere red-coated regiments, to say nothing of chivalries, fight for you, if you could discharge them on the evening of the battle, on payment of the stipulated shillings, – Chelsea Hospitals,[5] pensions, promotions, rigorous lasting covenant on the one side and on the other, are indispensable even for a hired fighter. The Feudal Baron, much more, – how could he subsist with mere temporary mercenaries round him, at sixpence a day; ready to go over to the other side, if seven pence were offered? He could not have subsisted; – and his noble instinct saved him from the necessity of even trying! The Feudal Baron had a Man's Soul in him!

1: the movement for Parliamentary reform. 2: see note to Shelley's 'England in 1819'. 3: a two-part hyphenated surname, supposed sign of aristocratic status. 4: Hansard is the official record of parliamentary debates. 5: Chelsea Hospital was a home for old and invalid soldiers.

CHARLOTTE BRONTË (1816–1855)

Charlotte Brontë was the third daughter of Patrick Brontë, curate of Haworth, Yorkshire, and elder sister of Emily, Anne and Branwell Brontë. Their mother died in 1821 and the four older daughters were sent to a boarding school where the eldest two died of consumption. Thereafter the children were educated in their remote home, read extensively in Byron and Scott, and invented imaginary worlds to people their solitude. From 1835 Charlotte Brontë worked as a teacher and governess, and in 1842–43, thinking to establish a school in Haworth, she went to study languages in Brussels. There she fell in love with her teacher, M. Heger. In 1846 she published with her sisters *Poems of Currer, Ellis and Acton Bell,* but the work was poorly promoted and did not sell. Her first novel, *The Professor,* could not find a publisher (although it was eventually published in 1857), but *Jane Eyre: An Autobiography* by Currer Bell (1847) was a considerable success. Between 1848 and 1849, Branwell, Emily and Anne died of consumption; nevertheless Charlotte continued to work on *Shirley* (1849), a robust tale about the Luddite riots (1811–12) and a woman who has more financial and intellectual power than most men. *Villette* (1853), a sometimes uncertain and Gothic tale based on her love for M. Heger, was to be her last novel. She married her father's curate in 1854 and died the next year of complications in pregnancy. Although Charlotte Brontë's last three novels were popular, their intensity of feeling and thought, and treatment of sexual repression, perturbed male critics who liked their women to be angels in the house.

Passion

Some have won a wild delight,
  By daring wilder sorrow;
Could I gain thy love to-night,
  I'd hazard death to-morrow.

5 Could the battle-struggle earn
  One kind glance from thine eye,
How this withering heart would burn,
  The heady fight to try!

Welcome nights of broken sleep,
10 And days of carnage cold,
Could I deem that thou wouldst weep
  To hear my perils told.

Tell me, if with wandering bands
  I roam full far away,
15 Wilt thou, to those distant lands,
  In spirit ever stray?

Wild, long, a trumpet sounds afar;
   Bid me – bid me go
Where Sheik and Briton meet in war,
20   On Indian Sutlej's flow.

Blood has dyed the Sutlej's waves
With scarlet stain, I know;
Indus' borders yawn with graves,
Yet, command me go!

25   Though rank and high the holocaust
   Of nations, steams to heaven,
Glad I'd join the death-doomed host,
   Were but the mandate given.

Passion's strength should nerve my arm,
30   Its ardour stir my life,
Till human force to that dread charm
Should yield and sink in wild alarm,
Like trees to tempest-strife.

If, hot from war, I seek thy love,
35   Darest thou turn aside?
Darest thou, then, my fire reprove,
   By scorn, and maddening pride?

No – my will shall yet control
   Thy will, so high and free,
40   And love shall tame that haughty soul –
   Yes – tenderest love for me.

I'll read my triumph in thine eyes,
   Behold, and prove the change;
Then leave, perchance, my noble prize,
45   Once more in arms to range.

I'd die when all the foam is up,
   The bright wine sparkling high;
Nor wait till in the exhausted cup
   Life's dull dregs only lie.

50   Then Love thus crowned with sweet reward,
   Hope blest with fulness large,
I'd mount the saddle, draw the sword,
   And perish in the charge !

---

20 **Sutlej . . . Indus:** both rivers flow across the Punjab, sites of conflict with the British imperial forces.

From Jane Eyre: An Autobiography

[The novel opens with Jane Eyre living at Gateshead Hall, where she is made to feel inferior to her peers, Eliza, John, and Georgiana Reed, and is tyrannised by Mrs Reed.]

From Volume I, Chapter 1

'You have no business to take our books; you are a dependant, mama says, you have no money; your father left you none; you ought to beg, and not to live here with gentlemen's children like us, and eat the same meals we do, and wear clothes at our mama's expense. Now, I'll teach you to rummage my book-shelves: for they *are* mine; all the house belongs to me, or will do in a few years. Go and stand by the door, out of the way of the mirror and the windows.'

I did so, not at first aware what was his intention; but when I saw him lift and poise the book and stand in act to hurl it, I instinctively started aside with a cry of alarm: not soon enough, however; the volume was flung, it hit me, and I fell, striking my head against the door and cutting it. The cut bled, the pain was sharp: my terror had passed its climax; other feelings succeeded.

'Wicked and cruel boy!' I said. 'You are like a murderer – you are like a slave-driver – you are like the Roman emperors!'

I had read Goldsmith's *History of Rome*, and had formed my opinion of Nero, Caligula, &c.[1] Also I had drawn parallels in silence, which I never thought thus to have declared aloud.

'What! what!' he cried. 'Did she say that to me? Did you hear her, Eliza and Georgiana? Won't I tell mama? but first –'

He ran headlong at me: I felt him grasp my hair and shoulder; he had closed with a desperate thing. I really saw him a tyrant: a murderer. I felt a drop or two of blood from my head trickle down my neck, and was sensible of somewhat pungent suffering: these sensations for the time predominated over fear, and I received him in frantic sort. I don't very well know what I did with my hands, but he called me 'Rat! rat!' and bellowed out aloud. Aid was near him: Eliza and Georgiana had run for Mrs Reed, who was gone upstairs; she now came upon the scene, followed by Bessie and her maid Abbot. We were parted: I heard the words: –

'Dear! dear! what a fury to fly at Master John!'

'Did ever anybody see such a picture of passion?'

Then Mrs Reed subjoined: –

'Take her away to the red-room, and lock her in there.' Four hands were immediately laid upon me, and I was borne up stairs.

Volume I, Chapter 2

I resisted all the way: a new thing for me, and a circumstance which greatly strengthened the bad opinion Bessie and Miss Abbot were disposed to entertain of me. The fact is, I was a trifle beside myself, or rather *out* of myself, as the

---

1: Oliver Goldsmith (1730–74), the poet and novelist, whose *Roman History* (1769) was hack-work but widely used as a school primer. His attitude to the tyrants Nero and Caligula was one of contempt.

French would say: I was conscious that a moment's mutiny had already rendered me liable to strange penalties, and like any other rebel slave, I felt resolved in my desperation, to go all lengths.

'Hold her arms, Miss Abbot, she's like a mad cat.'

'For shame!, for shame!' cried the lady's-maid. 'What shocking conduct, Miss Eyre, to strike a young gentleman, your benefactress's son! Your young master!'

'Master? How is he my master? Am I a servant?'

'No; you are less than a servant for you do nothing for your keep. There, sit down, and think over your wickedness.'

They had got me by this time into the apartment indicated by Mrs Reed, and had thrust me upon a stool: my impulse was to rise from it like a spring; their two pairs of hands arrested me instantly.

'If you don't sit still, you must be tied down,' said Bessie. 'Miss Abbot, lend me your garters; she would break mine directly.'

Miss Abbot turned to divest a stout leg of the necessary ligature. This preparation for bonds, and the additional ignominy it inferred, took a little of the excitement out of me.

'Don't take them off,' I cried; 'I will not stir.'

In guarantee whereof, I attached myself to my seat by my hands.

'Mind you don't,' said Bessie; and when she had ascertained that I was really subsiding, she loosened her hold of me, then she and Miss Abbot stood with folded arms, looking darkly and doubtfully on my face, as incredulous of my sanity.

'She never did so before,' at last said Bessie, turning to the Abigail.[1]

'But it was always in her,' was the reply. 'I've told Missis often my opinion about the child, and Missis agreed with me. She is an underhand little thing: I never saw a girl of her age with so much cover.'[2]

Bessie answered not; but ere long, addressing me, she said, –

'You ought to know, Miss, that you are under obligations to Mrs Reed; she keeps you: if she were to turn you off, you would have to go to the poor-house.'

I had nothing to say to these words: they were not new to me: my very first recollections of existence included hints of the same kind. This reproach of my dependence had become a vague singsong in my ear; very painful and crushing, but only half intelligible. Miss Abbot joined in: –

'And you ought not to think yourself on an equality with the Misses Reed and Master Reed, because Missis kindly allows you to be brought up with them. They will have a great deal of money and you will have none: it is your place to be humble, and to try to make yourself agreeable to them.'

'What we tell you, is for your good,' added Bessie, in no harsh voice: 'You should try to be useful and pleasant, then, perhaps, you would have a home here; but if you become passionate and rude, Missis will send you away, I am sure.'

'Besides,' said Miss Abbot, 'God will punish her: he might strike her dead in the midst of her tantrums, and then where would she go? Come, Bessie, we will leave her: I wouldn't have her heart for anything. Say your prayers, Miss Eyre,

---

1: a generic name for a lady's maid. 2: such a thick skin, so much cheek.

when you are by yourself; for if you don't repent, something bad might be permitted to come down the chimney, and fetch you away.'

They went, shutting the door, and locking it behind them.

The red-room was a spare chamber, very seldom slept in; I might say never, indeed; unless when a chance influx of visitors at Gateshead Hall rendered it necessary to turn to account all the accommodation it contained: yet it was one of the largest and stateliest chambers in the mansion. A bed supported on massive pillars of mahogany, hung with curtains of deep-red damask, stood out like a tabernacle in the centre; the two large windows, with their blinds always drawn down, were half shrouded in festoons and falls of similar drapery; the carpet was red; the table at the foot of the bed was covered with a crimson cloth; the walls were a soft fawn colour, with a blush of pink in it; the wardrobe, the toilet-table, the chairs were of darkly polished old mahogany. Out of these deep surrounding shades rose high, and glared white, the piled-up mattresses and pillows of the bed, spread with a snowy Marseilles counterpane. Scarcely less prominent was an ample, cushioned easy-chair near the head of the bed, also white, with a footstool before it; and looking, as I thought, like a pale throne.

This room was chill, because it seldom had a fire; it was silent, because remote from the nursery and kitchens; solemn, because it was known to be so seldom entered. The house-maid alone came here on Saturdays, to wipe from the mirrors and the furniture a week's quiet dust: and Mrs Reed herself, at far intervals, visited it to review the contents of a certain secret drawer in the wardrobe, where were stored divers parchments, her jewel-casket, and a miniature of her deceased husband; and in those last words lies the secret of the red-room: the spell which kept it so lonely in spite of its grandeur.

Mr Reed had been dead nine years: it was in this chamber he breathed his last; here he lay in state; hence his coffin was borne by the undertaker's men; and, since that day, a sense of dreary consecration had guarded it from frequent intrusion.

My seat, to which Bessie and the bitter Mrs Abbot had left me riveted, was a low ottoman near the marble chimney-piece; the bed rose before me; to my right hand there was the high, dark wardrobe, with subdued, broken reflections varying the gloss of its panels; to my left were the muffled windows; a great looking glass between them repeated the vacant majesty of the bed and room. I was not quite sure whether they had locked the door; and, when I dared move, I got up, and went to see. Alas! yes: no jail was ever more secure. Returning, I had to cross before the looking-glass; my fascinated glance involuntarily explored the depth it revealed. All looked colder and darker in that visionary hollow than in reality: and the strange little figure there gazing at me, with a white face and arms specking the gloom, and glittering eyes of fear moving where all else was still, had the effect of a real spirit: I thought it like one of the tiny phantoms, half fairy, half imp, Bessie's evening stories represented as coming out of lone, ferny dells in moors, and appearing before the eyes of belated travellers. I returned to my stool.

Superstition was with me at that moment; but it was not yet her hour for complete victory: my blood was still warm; the mood of the revolted slave was still bracing me with its bitter vigour; I had to stem a rapid rush of retrospective thought before I quailed to the dismal present.

All John Reed's violent tyrannies, all his sisters' proud indifference, all my mother's aversion, all the servants' partiality, turned up in my disturbed mind like a dark deposit in a turbid well. Why was I always suffering, always brow-beaten, always accused, for ever condemned? Why could I never please? Why was it useless to try to win any one's favour? Eliza, who was headstrong and selfish, was respected. Georgiana, who had a spoiled temper, a very acrid spite, a captious and insolent carriage, was universally indulged. Her beauty, her pink cheeks and golden curls, seemed to give delight to all who looked at her, and to purchase indemnity for every fault. John, no one thwarted, much less punished; though he twisted the necks of the pigeons, killed the little pea-chicks, set the dogs at the sheep, stripped the hothouse vines of their fruit, and broke the buds off the choicest plants in the conservatory: he called his mother 'old girl', too; sometimes reviled her for her dark skin, similar to his own; bluntly disregarded her wishes; not infrequently tore and spoiled her silk attire; and he was still 'her own darling.' I dared commit no fault: I strove to fulfil every duty; and I was termed naughty and tiresome, sullen and sneaking, from morning to noon, and from noon to night.

My head still ached and bled with the blow I had received: no one had reproved John for wantonly striking me; and because I had turned against him to avert farther irrational violence, I was loaded with general opprobrium.

'Unjust! – unjust!' said my reason, forced by the agonising stimulus into precocious though transitory power; and Resolve, equally wrought up, instigated some strange expedient to achieve escape from insupportable oppression – as running away, or, if that could not be effected, never eating or drinking more and letting myself die.

What a consternation of soul was mine that dreary afternoon! How all my brain was in tumult, and all my heart in insurrection! Yet in what darkness, what dense ignorance, was the mental battle fought! I could not answer the ceaseless inward question – *why* I thus suffered; now, at the distance of – I will not say how many years, I see it clearly.

I was a discord in Gateshead Hall; I was like nobody there; I had nothing in harmony with Mrs Reed or her children, or her chosen vassalage. If they did not love me, in fact, as little did I love them. They were not bound to regard with affection a thing that could not sympathise with one amongst them; heteroge-neous thing, opposed to them, in temperament, in capacity, in propensities, a useless thing, incapable of serving their interest, or adding to their pleasure, a noxious thing, cherishing the germs of indignation at their treatment, of contempt of their judgement. I know that had I been a sanguine, brilliant, care-less, exacting, handsome, romping child – though equally dependent and friendless – Mrs Reed would have endured my presence more complacently; her children would have entertained for me more of the cordiality of fellow-feeling; the servants would have been less prone to make me the scape-goat of the nursery.

Daylight began to forsake the red-room; it was past four o'clock, and the beclouded afternoon was tending to drear twilight. I heard the rain still beating continuously on the staircase window, and the wind howling in the grove behind the hall; I grew by degrees cold as a stone; and then my courage sank. My habitual mood of humiliation, self-doubt, forlorn depression, fell damp on the embers of my decaying ire. All said I was wicked, and perhaps I might be so: what thought had I been but just conceiving of starving myself to death? That certainly was a crime: and was I fit to die? Or was the vault under the chancel of Gateshead church an inviting bourne? In such vault I had been told did Mr Reed lie buried; and led by this thought to recall his idea, I dwelt on it with gathering dread. I could not remember him; but I knew he was my own uncle – my mother's brother – that he had taken me when a parentless infant to his house; and that in his last moments he had required a promise of Mrs Reed that she would rear and maintain me as one of her own children. Mrs Reed probably considered she had kept this promise; and so she had, I dare say, as well as her nature would permit her; but how could she really like an inter-loper not of her race, and unconnected with her, after her husband's death, by any tie? It must have been most irksome to find herself bound by a hard-wrung pledge to stand in the stead of a parent to a strange child she could not love, and to see an uncongenial alien permanently intruded on her own family group.

A singular notion dawned upon me. I doubted not – never doubted – that if Mr Reed had been alive he would have treated me kindly; and now, as I sat looking at the white bed and overshadowed walls – occasionally also turning a fascinated eye towards the dimly gleaming mirror – I began to recall what I had heard of dead men, troubled in their graves by the violation of their last wishes, revisiting the earth to punish the perjured and avenge the oppressed; and I thought Mr Reed's spirit, harassed by the wrongs of his sister's child, might quit his abode – whether in the church vault or in the unknown world of the departed – and rise before me in this chamber. I wiped my tears and hushed my sobs; fearful lest any sign of violent grief might waken a preternatural voice to comfort me, or elicit from the gloom some haloed face, bending over me with strange pity. This idea, consolatory in theory, I felt would be terrible if realised: with all my might I endeavoured to stifle it – I endeavoured to be firm. Shaking my hair from my eyes, I lifted my head and tried to look boldly round the dark room: at this moment a light gleamed on the wall. Was it, I asked myself, a ray from the moon penetrating some aperture in the blind? No; moonlight was still, and this stirred; while I gazed, it glided up to the ceiling and quivered over my head. I can now conjecture readily that this streak of light was, in all likeli-hood, a gleam from a lantern, carried by some one across the lawn: but then, prepared as my mind was for horror, shaken as my nerves were by agitation, I thought the swift-darting beam was a herald of some coming vision from another world. My heart beat thick, my head grew hot; a sound filled my ears, which I deemed the rushing of wings: something seemed near me; I was oppressed, suffocated: endurance broke down – I uttered a wild involuntary cry[1] –

1: Michael Mason has recently noted that this sentence was missed in the manuscript of Jane Eyre and left out of all printed editions before the Penguin edition of 1996. Without the sentence, a perturbing Gothic implication derived from the unexplained nature of the cry.

I rushed to the door and shook the lock in desperate effort. Steps came running along the outer passage; the key turned, Bessie and Abbot entered.

'Miss Eyre, are you ill?' said Bessie.

'What a dreadful noise! it went quite through me!' exclaimed Abbot.

'Take me out! Let me go into the nursery!' was my cry.

'What for? Are you hurt? Have you seen something?' again demanded Bessie.

'Oh! I saw a light, and I thought a ghost would come.' I had now got hold of Bessie's hand, and she did not snatch it from me.

'She has screamed out on purpose,' declared Abbot, in some disgust. 'And what a scream! If she had been in great pain one would have excused it, but she only wanted to bring us all here: I know her naughty tricks.'

'What is all this?' demanded another voice, peremptorily; and Mrs Reed came along the corridor, her cap flying wide, her gown rustling stormily. 'Abbot and Bessie, I believe I gave orders that Jane Eyre should be left in the red-room till I came to her myself.'

'Miss Jane screamed so loud, ma'am,' pleaded Bessie.

'Let her go,' was the only answer. 'Loose Bessie's hand, child: you cannot succeed in getting out by these means, be assured. I abhor artifice, particularly in children; it is my duty to show that tricks will not answer: you will now stay here an hour longer, and it is only on condition of perfect submission and stillness that I shall liberate you then.'

'Oh aunt, have pity! Forgive me! I cannot endure it – let me be punished some other way! I shall be killed if – '

'Silence! This violence is almost repulsive;' and so, no doubt, she felt it. I was a precocious actress in her eyes: she sincerely looked on me as a compound of virulent passions, mean spirit, and dangerous duplicity.

Bessie and Abbot having retreated, Mrs Reed, impatient of my now frantic anguish and wild sobs, abruptly thrust me back and locked me in, without farther parley. I heard her sweeping away; and soon after she was gone, I suppose I had a species of fit: unconsciousness closed the scene.

[The Reeds' efforts to drive out Jane Eyre culminate in her being sent to boarding school, Lowood, a cruel place where the children are ill-fed, cold, uncared for. The only redemption is the loving relationships Jane establishes with a fellow pupil, Helen Burns, and the superintendent, Miss Temple. Typhus fever sweeps through the school and Helen Burns dies in Jane's arms. Jane stays another eight years and rises to be a pupil teacher but when Miss Temple marries and leaves, the school is no longer the same to her and she advertises for a place as a governess. A Mrs Fairfax at Thornfield Hall offers her a place as governess for a young girl. Once there Jane discovers that the girl is called Adela (or Adèle) Varens, is French, and is the ward of the master of the house, Mr Rochester, who travels a great deal. She also encounters Grace Poole, a woman with an hysterical laugh who lives on the third floor. October passes to January, then one early evening Jane takes a stroll.]

From Volume I, Chapter 12

I was a mile from Thornfield, in a lane noted for wild roses in summer, for nuts and blackberries in autumn, and even now possessing a few coral treasures in hips and haws; but whose best winter delight lay in its utter solitude and leafless repose. If a breath of air stirred, it made no sound here; for there was not a holly, not an evergreen to rustle and the stripped hawthorn and hazel bushes were as still as the white, worn stones which causewayed the middle of the path. Far and wide, on each side, there were only fields, where no cattle now browsed; and the little brown birds which stirred occasionally in the hedge, looked like single russet leaves that had forgotten to drop.

On the hill-top above me sat the rising moon; pale yet as a cloud, but brightening momently: she looked over Hay, which, half lost in trees, sent up a blue smoke from its few chimneys; it was yet a mile distant, but in the absolute hush I could hear plainly its thin murmurs of life. My ear too felt the flow of currents; in what dales and depths I could not tell: but there were many hills beyond Hay, and doubtless many becks threading their passes. That evening calm betrayed alike the tinkle of the nearest streams, the sough of the most remote.

A rude noise broke on these fine ripplings and whisperings, at once so far away and so clear: a positive tramp, tramp; a metallic clatter, which effaced the soft wave-wanderings; as, in a picture, the solid mass of a crag, or the rough boles of a great oak, drawn in dark and strong on the foreground, efface the aerial distance of azure hill, sunny horizon and blended clouds, where tint melts into tint.

The din was on the causeway: a horse was coming; the windings of the lane yet hid it, but it approached. I was just leaving the stile; yet, as the path was narrow, I sat still to let it go by. In those days I was young, and all sorts of fancies bright and dark tenanted my mind: the memories of nursery stories were there amongst other rubbish; and when they recurred, maturing youth added to them a vigour and vividness beyond what childhood could give. As this horse approached, and as I watched for it to appear through the dusk, I remembered certain of Bessie's tales wherein figured a North-of-England spirit, called a 'Gytrash'; which, in the form of horse, mule and large dog, haunted solitary ways, and sometimes came upon belated travellers, as this horse was now coming upon me.

It was very near, but not yet in sight; when, in addition to the tramp, tramp, I heard a rush under the hedge, and close down by the hazel stems glided a great dog, whose black and white colour made him a distinct object against the trees. It was exactly one mask of Bessie's Gytrash, – a lion-like creature with long hair and a huge head: it passed me, however, quietly enough; not staying to look up, with strange pretercanine eyes, in my face, as I half expected it would. The horse followed, – a tall steed, and on its back a rider. The man, the human being, broke the spell at once. Nothing ever rode the Gytrash: it was always alone; and goblins, to my notions, though they might tenant the dumb carcasses of beasts, could scarce covet shelter in the common-place human form. No Gytrash was this, – only a traveller taking the short cut to Millcote.

He passed, and I went on; a few steps, and I turned: a sliding sound and an exclamation of 'What the deuce is to do now?' and a clattering tumble, arrested my attention. Man and horse were down; they had slipped on the sheet of ice which glazed the causeway. The dog came bounding back, and seeing his master in a predicament, and hearing the horse groan, barked till the evening hills echoed the sound; which was deep in proportion to his magnitude. He snuffed round the prostrate group, and then he ran up to me, it was all he could do, – there was no other to help at hand to summon. I obeyed him, and walked down to the traveller, by this time struggling himself free of his steed. His efforts were so vigorous, I thought he could not be much hurt; but I asked him the question: –

'Are you injured, sir?'

I think he was swearing, but am not certain; however, he was pronouncing some formula which prevented him from replying to me directly.

'Can I do anything?' I asked again.

'You must just stand on the side,' he answered as he rose, first to his knees, and then to his feet. I did; whereupon began a heaving, stamping, clattering process, accompanied by a barking and baying which removed me effectually some yards distance; but I would not be driven quite away till I saw the event. This was finally fortunate; the horse re-established, and the dog was silenced with a 'Down, Pilot!' The traveller now, stooping, felt his foot and leg, as if trying whether they were sound; apparently something ailed them, for he halted at the stile whence I had just risen, and sat down.

I was in the mood for being useful, or at least officious, I think, for I now drew near him again.

'If you are hurt, and want help, sir, I can fetch some one, either from Thornfield Hall or from Hay.'

'Thank you; I shall do: I have no broken bones, – only a sprain;' and again he stood up and tried his foot, but the result extorted an involuntary 'Ugh!'

Something of daylight still lingered, and the moon was waxing bright: I could see him plainly. His figure was enveloped in a riding cloak, fur collared, and steel clasped; its details were not apparent, but I traced the general points of middle height, and considerable breadth of chest. He had a dark face, with stern features and a heavy brow; his eyes and gathered eyebrows looked ireful and thwarted just now; he was past youth, but had not reached middle age; perhaps he might be thirty-five. I felt no fear of him, and but little shyness. Had he been a handsome, heroic-looking young gentleman, I should not have dared to stand thus questioning him against his will, and offering my services unasked. I had hardly ever seen a handsome youth; never in my life spoken to one. I had a theoretical reverence and homage for beauty, elegance, gallantry, fascination; but had I met those qualities incarnate in masculine shape, I should have known instinctively that they neither had nor could have sympathy with anything in me, and should have shunned them as one would fire, lightning, or anything else that is bright but antipathetic.

If even this stranger had smiled and been good-humoured to me when I addressed him; if he had put off my offer of assistance gaily and with thanks, I should have gone on my way and not felt any vocation to renew inquiries: but the frown, the roughness of the traveller set me at my ease: I retained my station when he waved to me to go, and announced: –

'I can not think of leaving you, sir, at so late hour, in this solitary lane, till I see you are fit to mount your horse.'

He looked at me when I said this: he had hardly turned his eyes in my direction before.

'I should think that you ought to be at home yourself,' said he, 'if you have a home in this neighbourhood: where do you come from?'

'From just below; and I am not at all afraid of being out late when it is moon-light: I will run over to Hay for you with pleasure, if you wish it – indeed, I am going there to post a letter.'

'You live just below – do you mean at that house with the battlements?' pointing to Thornfield Hall, on which the moon cast a hoary gleam, bringing it out distinct and pale from the woods, that, by contrast with the western sky, now seemed one mass of shadow.

'Yes, sir.'

'Whose house is it?'

'Mr Rochester's.'

'Do you know Mr Rochester?'

'No, I have never seen him.'

'He is not resident then?'

'No.'

'Can you tell me where he is?'

'I cannot.'

'You are not a servant at the hall, of course. You are – ' He stopped, ran his eye over my dress, which, as usual, was quite simple: a black merino cloak, a black beaver bonnet; neither of them half fine enough for a lady's-maid. He seemed puzzled to decide what I was: I helped him.

'I am the governess.'

'Ah, the governess!' he repeated; 'deuce take me, if I had not forgotten! The governess!' and again my raiment underwent scrutiny. In two minutes he rose from the stile: his face expressed pain when he tried to move.

'I cannot commission you to fetch help,' he said: 'but you may help me a little yourself, if you will be so kind.'

'Yes, sir.'

'You have not an umbrella that I can use as a stick?'

'No.'

'Try to get hold of my horse's bridle and lead him to me: you are not afraid?'

I should have been afraid to touch a horse when alone, but when told to do it, I was disposed to obey. I put down my muff on the stile, and went up to the tall steed; I endeavoured to catch the bridle, but it was a spirited thing, and would not let me come near its head; I made effort on effort, though in vain: meantime, I was mortally afraid of its trampling fore feet. The traveller waited and watched for some time, and at last he laughed.

'I see,' he said, 'the mountain will never be brought to Mahomet, so all you can do is to aid Mahomet to go to the mountain; I must beg of you to come here.'

I came – 'Excuse me,' he continued: 'necessity compels me to make you useful.' He laid a heavy hand on my shoulder, and leaning on me with some stress, limped to his horse. Having once caught the bridle, he mastered it directly, and sprang to his saddle; grimacing grimly as he made the effort, for it wrenched his sprain.

'Now,' said he, releasing his under lip from a hard bite, 'just hand me my whip; it lies there under the hedge.'

I sought it and found it.

'Thank you; now make haste with the letter to Hay, and return as fast as you can.'

A touch of a spurred heel made his horse first start and rear, and then bound away; the dog rushed in his traces: all three vanished

> 'Like heath that in the wilderness
> The wild wind whirls away.'

I took up my muff and walked on. The incident had occurred and was gone for me: it *was* an incident of no moment, no romance, no interest in a sense; yet it marked with change one single hour of a monotonous life. My help had been needed and claimed; I had given it: I was pleased to have done something; trivial, transitory though the deed was, it was yet an active thing, and I was weary of an existence all passive. The new face, too, was like a new picture introduced to the gallery of memory; and it was dissimilar to all the others hanging there; firstly, because it was masculine; and secondly, because it was dark, strong, and stern. I had it still before me when I entered Hay, and slipped the letter into the post-office; I saw it as I walked fast down the hill all the way home. When I came to the stile I stopped a minute, looked round and listened; with an idea that a horse's hoofs might ring on the causeway again, and that a rider in a cloak, a Gytrash-like Newfoundland dog, might be again apparent: I saw only the hedge and a pollard willow before me, rising up still and straight to meet the moonbeams; I heard only the faintest waft of wind, roaming fitful among the trees round Thornfield, a mile distant; and when I glanced down in the direction of the murmur, my eye, traversing the hall-front, caught a light kindling in a window: it reminded me that I was late and I hurried on.

I did not like re-entering Thornfield. To pass its threshold was to return to stagnation: to cross the silent hall, to ascend the darksome staircase, to seek my own lonely little room, and then to meet tranquil Mrs Fairfax, and spend the long winter evening with her, and her only, was to quell wholly the faint excitement wakened by my walk, – to slip again over my faculties the viewless fetters of a uniform and too still existence; of an existence whose very privileges of security and ease I was becoming incapable of appreciating. What good it would have done me at that time to have been tossed in the storms of an uncertain struggling life, and to have been taught by rough and bitter experience to long for the calm amidst which I now repined! Yes, just as much good as it would do a man tired of sitting still in a 'too easy chair' to take a long walk: and just as natural was the wish to stir, under my circumstances, as it would be under his.

I lingered at the gates; I lingered on the lawn; I paced backwards and forwards on the pavement. The shutters of the glass door were closed; I could not see into the interior; and both my eyes and spirit seemed drawn from the gloomy house – from the grey hollow filled with rayless cells, as it appeared to me – to that sky expanded before me, – a blue sea absolved from taint of cloud; the moon ascending it in solemn march; her orb seeming to look up as she left the hill tops, from behind which she had come, far and farther below her, and aspired to the zenith, midnight-dark to its fathomless depth and measureless distance: and for those trembling stars that followed her course, they made my heart tremble, my veins glow when I viewed them. Little things recall us to earth: the clock struck in the hall; that sufficed; I turned from moon and stars, opened a side-door, and went in.

The hall was not dark, nor yet was it lit only by the high-hung bronze lamp: a warm glow suffused both it and the lower steps of the oak staircase. This ruddy shine issued from the great dining-room, whose two-leaved door stood open, and showed a genial fire in the grate, glancing on marble hearth and brass fire-irons, and revealing purple draperies and polished furniture, in the most pleasant radiance. It revealed, too, a group near the mantelpiece: I had scarcely caught it, and scarcely become aware of a cheerful mingling of voices, amongst which I seemed to distinguish the tones of Adèle, when the door closed.

I hastened to Mrs Fairfax's room: there was a fire, there, too; but no candle, and no Mrs Fairfax. Instead, all alone, sitting upright on the rug, and gazing with gravity at the blaze, I beheld a great black and white long-haired dog, just like the Gytrash of the lane. It was so like that I went forward and said, –

'Pilot,' and the thing got up and came to me and snuffed me. I caressed him, and he wagged his great tail: but he looked an eerie creature to be alone with, and I could not tell whence he had come. I rang the bell, for I wanted a candle; and I wanted, too, to get an account of this visitant. Leah entered.

'What dog is this?'

'He came with the master.'

'With whom?'

'With master – Mr Rochester – he is just arrived.'

'Indeed! and is Mrs Fairfax with him?'

'Yes, and Miss Adèle; they are in the dining-room, and John is gone for a surgeon: for master has had an accident; his horse fell and his ankle is sprained.'

'Did the horse fall in Hay Lane?'

'Yes, coming down hill; it slipped on some ice.'

'Ah! Bring me a candle, will you, Leah?'

Leah brought it; she entered, followed by Mrs Fairfax, who repeated the news; adding that Mr Carter the surgeon was come and was now with Mr Rochester: then she hurried out to give orders about tea, and I went up stairs to take off my things.

[Jane begins to understand and like Mr Rochester, despite his forbidding manner.]

From Volume I, Chapter 15

And was Mr Rochester now ugly in my eyes? No, reader: gratitude and many associations, all pleasurable and genial, made his face the object I best liked to see; his presence in a room was more cheering than the brightest fire. Yet I had not forgotten his faults; indeed, I could not, for he brought them frequently before me. He was proud, sardonic, harsh to inferiority of every description: in my secret soul I knew that his greater kindness to me was balanced by unjust severity to many others. He was moody, too, unaccountably so; I more than once, when sent for to read to him, found him sitting in his library alone, with his head bent on his folded arms; and, when he looked up, a morose, almost a malignant scowl blackened his features. But I believed that his moodiness, his harshness, and his former faults of morality (I say former, for now he seemed corrected of them) had their source in some cruel cross of fate. I believed he was naturally a man of better tendencies, higher principles, and purer tastes than such as circumstances had developed, education instilled, or destiny encouraged. I thought there were exellent materials in him; though for the present they hung togther somewhat spoiled and tangled. I cannot deny that I grieved for his grief, whatever that was, and would have given much to assuage it.

Though I had now extinguished my candle and was laid down in bed, I could not sleep for thinking of his look when he paused in the avenue, and told how his destiny had risen up before him, and dared him to be happy at Thornfield.

'Why not?' I asked myself. 'What alienates him from the house? Will he leave it again soon? Mrs Fairfax said he seldom stayed here longer than a fortnight at a time; and he has now been resident eight weeks. If he does go, the change will be doleful. Suppose he should be absent spring, summer and autumn: how joyless sunshine and fine days will seem!'

I hardly know whether I had slept or not after this musing, at any rate I started wide awake on hearing a vague murmur, peculiar and lugubrious, which sounded, I thought, just above me. I wished I had kept my candle burning: the night was drearily dark; my spirits were depressed. I rose and I sat up in bed, listening. The sound was hushed.

I tried again to sleep; but my heart beat anxiously: my inward tranquility was broken. The clock, far down in the hall, struck two. Just then it seemed my chamber-door was touched; as if fingers had swept the panels in groping a way along the dark gallery outside. I said, 'Who is there?' Nothing answered, I was chilled with fear.

All at once I remembered that it might be Pilot: who, when the kitchen-door chanced to be left open, not unfrequently found his way up to the threshold of Mr Rochester's chamber: I had seen him lying there myself, in the mornings. The idea calmed me somewhat: I lay down. Silence composes the nerves; and as an unbroken hush now reigned again through the whole house, I began to feel the return of slumber. But it was not fated that I should sleep that night. A dream had scarcely approached my ear, when it fled affrighted, scared by a marrow-freezing incident enough.

This was a demoniac laugh – low, suppressed, and deep – uttered, as it seemed, at the very key-hole of my chamber-door. The head of my bed was near the door, and I thought at first the goblin-laugher stood at my bedside – or rather crouched by my pillow: but I rose, looked round, and could see nothing; while, as I still gazed, the unnatural sound was reiterated: and I knew it came from behind the panels. My first impulse was to rise and fasten the bolt; my next, again to cry out, 'Who is there?'

Something gurgled and moaned. Ere long, steps retreated up the gallery towards the third storey staircase: a door had lately been made to shut in that staircase; I heard it open and close, and all was still.

'Was that Grace Poole? and is she possessed with a devil?' thought I. Impossible now to remain longer by myself: I must go to Mrs Fairfax. I hurried on my frock and a shawl; I withdrew the bolt and opened the door with a trembling hand. There was a candle burning just outside, left on the matting in the gallery. I was surprised at this circumstance; but still more was I amazed to perceive the air quite dim, as if filled with smoke; and, while looking to the right hand and left, to find whence these blue wreaths issued, I became further aware of a strong smell of burning.

Something creaked: it was a door ajar; and that door was Mr Rochester's, and the smoke rushed in a cloud from thence. I thought no more of Mrs Fairfax; I thought no more of Grace Poole or the laugh: in an instant, I was within the chamber. Tongues of flame darted round the bed: the curtains were on fire. In the midst of blaze and vapour, Mr Rochester lay stretched motionless, in deep sleep.

'Wake! wake!' I cried – I shook him, but he only murmured and turned: the smoke had stupefied him. Not a moment could be lost: the very sheets were kindling. I rushed to his basin and ewer; fortunately, one was wide and the other deep, and both were filled with water. I heaved them up, deluged the bed and its occupant, flew back to my own room, brought my own water-jug, baptised the couch afresh, and by God's aid, succeeded in extinguishing the flames which were devouring it.

The hiss of the quenched element, the breakage of a pitcher which I flung from my hand when I had emptied it, and above all, the splash of the shower-bath I had liberally bestowed, roused Mr Rochester at last. Though it was now dark, I knew he was awake, because I heard him fulminating strange anathemas at finding himself lying in a pool of water.

'Is there a flood?' he cried.

'No, sir,' I answered; 'but there has been a fire: get up, do, you are quenched now, I will fetch you a candle.'

'In the name of all the elves in Christendom, is that Jane Eyre?' he demanded. 'What have you done with me, witch, sorceress? Who is in the room besides you? Have you plotted to drown me?'

'I will fetch you a candle, sir; and in Heaven's name, get up. Somebody has plotted something: you cannot too soon find out who and what it is.'

[The next morning, Mr Rochester departs early on a social visit, returning with a party of house guests several weeks later.]

From Volume II, Chapter 4

'Are you aware, Mr Rochester, thate a stranger has arrived here since you left this morning?'

'A stranger! – no; who can it be? I expected no one; has he gone?'

'No; he said he had known you long, and that he could take the liberty of installing himself here till you returned.'

'The devil he did! Did he give his name?'

'His name is Mason, sir; and he comes from the West Indies; from Spanish Town, in Jamaica, I think.'

Mr Rochester was standing near me; he had taken my hand, as if to lead me to a chair. As I spoke, he gave my wrist a compulsive grip; the smile on his lips froze; apparently a spasm caught his breath.

'Mason! – the West Indies!' he said, in the tone one might fancy a speaking automaton to enounce its single words; 'Mason! – the West Indies!' he reiterated; and he went over the syllables three times, growing, in the intervals of speaking, whiter than ashes: he hardly seemed to know what he was doing.

'Do you feel ill, sir?' I inquired.

'Jane, I've got a blow; – I've got a blow, Jane!' He staggered.

'Oh! – lean on me, sir.'

'Jane, you offered me your shoulder once before, let me have it now.'

'Yes, sir, yes; and my arm.'

He sat down, and made me sit beside him. Holding my arm in both his own, he chafed it; gazing on me, at the same time, with the most troubled and dreary look.

'My little friend!' said he, 'I wish I were in a quiet island with only you; and trouble, and danger, and hideous recollections removed from me.'

'Can I help you, sir? – I'd give my life to serve you.'

'Jane, if aid is wanted, I'll seek it at your hands; I promise you that.'

'Thank you, sir; tell me what to do, – I'll try at least to do it.'

'Fetch me now, Jane, a glass of wine from the dining-room; they will be at supper there; and tell me if Mason is with them, and what is he doing.'

I went. I found all the party in the dining-room at supper, as Mr Rochester had said; they were not seated at table, – the supper was arranged on sideboards; each had taken what he chose, and they stood about here and there in groups, their plates and glasses in their hands. Every one seemed in high glee; laughter and conversation were general and animated. Mr Mason stood near the fire, talking to Colonel and Mrs Dent, and appeared as merry as one of them. I filled a wine-glass (I saw Miss Ingram watch me frowningly as I did so: she thought I was taking a liberty, I dare say), and I returned to the library.

Mr Rochester's extreme pallor had disappeared, and he looked once more firm and stern. He took the glass from my hand.

'Here is to your health, ministrant spirit!' he said: he swallowed the contents and returned it to me. 'What are they doing, Jane?'

'Laughing and talking, sir.'

'They don't look grave and mysterious, as if they had heard something strange?'

'Not at all: – they are full of jests and gaiety.'

'And Mason?'

'He is laughing too.'

'If all these people came in a body and spat at me, what would you do, Jane?'

'Turn them out of the room, sir, if I could.'

He half smiled. 'But if I were to go to them, and they only looked at me coldly, and whispered sneeringly amongst each other, and then dropt off and left me one by one, what then? Would you go with them?'

'I rather think not, sir: I should have more pleasure in staying with you.'

'To comfort me?

'Yes, sir, to comfort you, as well as I could.'

'And if they laid you under a ban for adhering to me?'

'I, probably, should know nothing about their ban; and if I did, I should care nothing about it.'

'Then, you could dare censure for my sake?'

'I could dare it for the sake of any friend who deserved my adherence; as you, I am sure, do.'

'Go back now into the room; step quietly up to Mason, and whisper in his ear that Mr Rochester is come and wishes to see him: show him in here, and then leave me.'

'Yes, sir.'

I did his behest. The company all stared at me as I passed straight among them. I sought Mr Mason, delivered the message, and preceded him from the room: I ushered him into the library, and then I went up stairs.

At a late hour after I had been in bed some time, I heard the visitors repair to their chambers: I distinguished Mr Rochester's voice, and heard him say, 'This way, Mason; this is your room.'

He spoke cheerfully: the gay tones set my heart at ease. I was soon asleep.

Volume II, Chapter 5

I had forgotten to draw my curtain, which I usually did; and also to let down my window-blind. The consequence was, that when the moon, which was full and bright (for the night was fine), came in her course to that space in the sky opposite to my casement, and looked in at me through the unveiled panes, her glorious gaze roused me. Awaking in the dead of night, I opened my eyes on her disk – silver-white and crystal-clear. It was beautiful, but too solemn: I half rose, and stretched my arm to draw the curtain.

Good God! What a cry!

The night – its silence – its rest, was rent in twain by a savage, a sharp, a shrill sound that ran from end to end of Thornfield Hall.

My pulse stopped: my heart stood still; my stretched arm was paralysed. The cry died, and was not renewed. Indeed, whatever being uttered that fearful shriek could not soon repeat it: not the widest-winged condor on the Andes could, twice in succession, send out such a yell from the cloud shrouding his eyrie. The thing delivering such utterance must rest ere it could repeat the effort.

It came out of the third storey; for it passed overhead. And overhead –
yes, in the room just above my chamber-ceiling – I now heard a struggle: a
deadly one it seemed from the noise; and a half-smothered voice shouted –
'Help! help! help!' three times rapidly.

'Will no one come?' it cried; and then, while the staggering and stamping
went on wildly, I distinguished through plank and plaster: –

'Rochester, Rochester! for God's sake, come!'

A chamber-door opened: some one ran, or rushed, along the gallery. Another
step stamped on the flooring above, and something fell; and there was silence.

I had put on some clothes, though horror shook all my limbs: I issued from
my apartment. The sleepers were all aroused: ejaculations, terrified murmurs,
sounded in every room; door after door unclosed; one looked out and another
looked out; the gallery filled. Gentlemen and ladies alike had quitted their
beds; and 'Oh! what is it?' – 'Who is hurt?' – 'What has happened?' – 'Fetch a
light!' – 'Is it fire?' – 'Are there robbers?' – 'Where shall we run?' was
demanded confusedly on all hands. But for the moon-light they would have
been in complete darkness. They ran to and fro; they crowded together: some
sobbed, some stumbled: the confusion was inextricable.

'Where the devil is Rochester?' cried Colonel Dent. 'I cannot find him in his
bed.'

'Here! here!' was shouted in return. 'Be composed, all of you: I'm coming.'

And the door at the end of the gallery opened, and Mr Rochester advanced
with a candle: he had just descended from the upper storey. One of the ladies
ran to him directly; she seized his arm: it was Miss Ingram.

'What awful event has taken place?' said she. 'Speak! let us know the worst at
once!'

'But don't pull me down or strangle me,' he replied: for the Misses Eshton
were clinging about him now; and the two dowagers, in vast white wrappers,
were bearing down on him like ships in full sail.

'All's right! – all's right!' he cried. 'It is a mere rehearsal of *Much Ado About
Nothing*. Ladies, keep off; or I shall wax dangerous.'

And dangerous he looked: his black eyes darted sparks. Calming himself by
an effort, he added: –

'A servant has had a nightmare; that is all. She's an excitable, nervous person:
she construed her dream into an apparition, or something of that sort, no doubt;
and has taken a fit with fright. Now, then, I must see you all back into your
rooms; for, till the house is settled, she cannot be looked after. Gentlemen, have
the goodness to set the ladies the example. Miss Ingram, I am sure you will not
fail in evincing superiority to idle terrors. Amy and Louisa, return to your nests
like a pair of doves, as you are. Mesdames,' (to the dowagers), 'you will take
cold to a dead certainty, if you stay in this chill gallery any longer.'

And so, by dint of alternate coaxing and commanding, he contrived to get
them all once more enclosed in their separate dormitories. I did not wait to be
ordered back to mine; but retreated unnoticed: as unnoticed I had left it.

Not, however, to go to bed: on the contrary, I began and dressed myself carefully. The sounds I had heard after the scream, and the words that had been

uttered, had probably been heard only by me; from they had proceeded from the room above mine; but they assured me that it was not a servant's dream which had thus struck horror through the house; and that the explanation Mr Rochester had given was merely an invention framed to pacify his guests. I dressed, then, to be ready for emergencies. When dressed, I sat a long time by the window, looking out over the silent grounds and silvered fields, and waiting for I knew not what. It seemed to me that some event must follow the strange cry, struggle and call.

No; stillness returned: each murmur and movement ceased gradually, and in about an hour Thornfield Hall was again as hushed as a desert. It seemed that sleep and night had resumed their empire. Meantime the moon declined: she was about to set. Not liking to sit in the cold and darkness, I thought I would lie down on my bed, dressed as I was. I left the window, and moved with little noise across the carpet; as I stooped to take off my shoes, a cautious hand tapped low at my door.

'Am I wanted?' I asked.

'Are you up?' asked the voice I expected to hear, viz., my master's.

'Yes, sir.'

'And dressed?'

'Yes.'

'Come out, then, quietly.'

I obeyed. Mr Rochester stood in the gallery, holding a light.

'I want you,' he said: 'come this way: take your time, and make no noise.'

My slippers were thin: I could walk the matted floor as softly as a cat. He glided up the gallery and up the stairs, and stopped in the dark, low corridor of the third storey; I had followed and stood at his side.

'Have you a sponge in your room?' he asked in a whisper.

'Yes, sir.'

'Have you any salts – volatile salts?'

'Yes.'

'Go back and fetch both.'

I returned, sought the sponge in the washstand, the salts in the drawer, and once more retraced my steps. He still waited, he held a key in his hand: approaching one of the small, black doors, he put it in the lock and addressed me again.

'You don't turn sick at the sight of blood?'

'I think I shall not: I have never been tried yet.'

I felt a thrill while I answered him, but no coldness, and no faintness.

'Just give me your hand,' he said; 'It will not do to risk a fainting fit.'

I put my fingers into his. 'Warm and steady,' was his remark: he turned the key and opened the door.

I saw a room I remembered to have seen before; the day Mrs Fairfax showed me over the house: it was hung with tapestry; but the tapestry was now looped up in one part, and there was a door apparent, which had then been concealed. This door was open; a light shone out of the room within: I heard thence a snarling, snatching sound, almost like a dog quarrelling. Mr Rochester, putting down his candle, said to me, 'wait a minute,' and he went forward to the inner apartment. A shout of laughter greeted his entrance; noisy at first, and terminating in Grace Poole's own goblin ha! ha! *She* then was there. He made some sort of arrangement, without speaking: though I heard a low voice address him: he came out and closed the door behind him.

'Here, Jane!' he said; and walked round to the other side of a large bed, which with its drawn curtains concealed a considerable portion of the chamber. An easy-chair was near the bed-head; a man sat in it, dressed with the exception of his coat; he was still, his head leant back; his eyes were closed. Mr Rochester held the candle over him, I recognised in his pale and seemingly lifeless face – the stranger, Mason: I saw too that his linen on one side, and one arm, was almost soaked in blood.

'Hold the candle,' said Mr Rochester, and I took it; he fetched a basin of water from the wash-stand: 'Hold that,' said he. I obeyed. He took the sponge, dipped it in and moistened the corpse-like face: he asked for the smelling-bottle, and applied it to the nostrils. Mr Mason shortly unclosed his eyes, he groaned. Mr Rochester opened the shirt of the wounded man, whose arm and shoulder were bandaged: he sponged away blood, trickling fast down.

'Is there immediate danger?' murmured Mr Mason.

'Pooh! No – a mere scratch. Don't be so overcome, man; bear up! I'll fetch a surgeon for you now, myself: you'll be able to be removed by morning, I hope. Jane – ' he continued.

'Sir?'

'I shall have to leave you in this room with this gentleman, for an hour, or perhaps two hours; you will sponge the blood as I do when it returns; if he feels faint, you will put the glass of water on that stand to his lips, and your salts to his nose. You will not speak to him on any pretext – and – Richard – it will be at the peril of your life if you speak to her: open your lips – agitate yourself – and I'll not answer for the consequences.'

Again the poor man groaned; he looked as if he dare not move: fear, either of death or something else, appeared almost to paralyse him. Mr Rochester put the now bloody sponge into my hand, and I proceeded to use it as he had done. He watched me a second, then saying, 'Remember! – No conversation,' he left the room. I experienced a strange feeling as the key grated in the lock, and the sound of his retreating step ceased to be heard.

Here then I was in the third storey, fastened into one of its mystic cells; night around me; a pale and bloody spectacle under my eyes and hands; a murderess hardly separated from me by a single door, yes – that was appalling – the rest I could bear, but I shuddered at the thought of Grace Poole bursting out upon me.

I must keep to my post, however. I must watch this ghastly countenance – these blue, still lips forbidden to unclose – these eyes now shut, now opening, now wandering through the room, now fixing on me, and even glazed with the dullness of horror. I must dip my hand again and again in the basin of blood and water, and wipe away the trickling gore. I must see the light of the unsnuffed candle wane on my employment; the shadows darken on the wrought, antique tapestry round me, and grow black under the hangings of the vast old bed, and quiver strangely over the doors of a great cabinet opposite – whose front, divided into twelve panels, bore in grim design, the heads of the twelve apostles, each inclosed in its separate panel as in a frame; while above them at the top rose an ebony crucifix and a dying Christ.

According as the shifting obscurity and flickering gleam hovered here or glanced there, it was now the bearded physician, Luke, that bent his brow; now Saint John's long hair that waved; and anon the devilish face of Judas, that grew out of the panel, and seemed gathering life and threatening a revelation of the arch-traitor – of Satan himself – in his subordinate's form.

Amidst all this, I had to listen, as well as watch: to listen for the movements of the wild beast or the fiend in yonder side den. But since Mr Rochester's visit it seemed spellbound: all the night I heard but three sounds at three long intervals, – a step creak, a momentary renewal of the snarling, canine noise, and a deep human groan.

Then my own thoughts worried me. What crime was this, that lived incarnated in this sequestered mansion, and could neither be expelled nor subdued by the owner? – What mystery, that broke out, now in fire now in blood, at the deadest hours of night? – What creature was it, that, masked in an ordinary woman's face and shape, uttered the voice, now of a mocking demon, and anon of a carrion-seeking bird of prey?

And this man I bent over – this commonplace, quiet stranger – how had he become involved in the web of horror? and why had the Fury flown at him? What made him seek this quarter of the house at an untimely season, when he should have been asleep in bed? I had heard Mr Rochester assign him an apartment below – what brought him here? And, why, now, was he so tame under the violence or treachery done him? Why did he so quietly submit to the concealment Mr Rochester enforced? Why *did* Mr Rochester enforce this concealment? His guest had been outraged, his own life on a former occasion had been hideously plotted against; and both attempts he smothered in secrecy and sank in oblivion! Lastly, I saw Mr Mason was submissive to Mr Rochester; that the impetuous will of the latter held complete sway over the inertness of the former: the few words which had passed between them assured me of this. It was evident that in their former intercourse, the passive disposition of the one had been habitually influenced by the active energy of the other: whence then had arisen Mr Rochester's dismay when he heard of Mr Mason's arrival? Why had the mere name of this unresisting individual – whom his word was now sufficient to control like a child – fallen on him, a few hours since, as a thunderbolt might fall on an oak?

Oh! I could not forget his look and his paleness when he whispered: 'Jane, I have got a blow – I have got a blow, Jane.' I could not forget how the arm had trembled which he rested on my shoulder: and it was not light matter which could thus bow the resolute spirit and thrill the vigorous frame of Fairfax Rochester.

'When will he come? When will he come?' I cried inwardly, as the night lingered and lingered – as my bleeding patient drooped, moaned, sickened: and neither day nor aid arrived. I had, again and again, held the water to Mason's white lips; again and again offered him the stimulating salts; my efforts seemed ineffectual: either bodily or mental suffering, or loss of blood, or all three combined, were fast prostrating his strength. He moaned so, and looked so weak, wild, and lost, I feared he was dying; and I might not even speak to him!

The candle, wasted at last, went out; as it expired, I perceived streaks of grey light edging the window curtains: dawn was then approaching. Presently I heard Pilot bark far below, out of his distant kennel in the courtyard: hope revived. Nor was it unwarranted: in five minutes more the grating key, the yielding lock, warned me my watch was relieved. It could not have lasted more than two hours: many a week has seemed shorter.

Mr Rochester entered, and with him the surgeon he had been to fetch.

'Now, Carter, be on alert,' he said to this last: 'I give you but half an hour for dressing the wound, fastening the bandages, getting the patient down stairs and all.'

'But is he fit to move, sir?'

'No doubt of it; it is nothing serious: he is nervous, his spirits must be kept up. Come, set to work.'

Mr Rochester drew back the thick curtain, drew up the Holland blind, let in all the daylight he could; and I was surprised and cheered to see how far dawn was advanced: what rosy streaks were beginning to brighten the east. Then he approached Mason, whom the surgeon was already handling.

'Now, my good fellow, how are you?' he asked.

'She's done for me, I fear,' was the faint reply.

'Not a whit! – courage! This day fortnight you'll hardly be a pin the worse of it: you've lost a little blood; that's all. Carter, assure him there's no danger.'

'I can do that conscientiously,' said Carter, who had now undone the bandages; 'only I wish I could have got here sooner: he would not have bled so much – but how is this? The flesh on the shoulder is torn as well as cut. This wound was not done with a knife: there have been teeth here!'

'She bit me,' he murmured. 'She worried me like a tigress, when Rochester got the knife from her.'

'You should not have yielded: you should not have grappled with her at once,' said Mr Rochester.

'But under such circumstances, what could one do?' returned Mason. 'Oh it was frightful!' he added, shuddering. 'And I did not expect it: she looked so quiet at first.'

'I warned you,' was his friend's answer; 'I said – be on your guard when you go near her. Besides, you might have waited till to-morrow, and had me with you: it was mere folly to attempt the interview tonight, and alone.'

'I thought I could have done some good.'

'You thought! you thought! Yes; it makes me impatient to hear you: but, however, you have suffered, and are likely to suffer enough for not taking my advice; so I'll say no more. Carter – hurry! – hurry! The sun will soon rise, and I must have him off.'

'Directly, sir. The shoulder is just bandaged. I must look to this other wound in the arm: she has had her teeth here too, I think.'

'She sucked the blood, she said she'd drain my heart,' said Mason.

I saw Mr Rochester shudder: a singularly marked expression of disgust, horror, hatred, warped his countenance almost to distortion; but he only said: –

'Come, be silent, Richard, and never mind her gibberish: don't repeat it.'

'I wish I could forget it,' was the answer.

'You will when you are out of the country: when you get back to Spanish Town, you may think of her as dead and buried – or rather, you need not think of her at all.'

[The relationship of Jane and Rochester grows ever closer, until . . .]

From Volume II, Chapter 8

'Must I move on, sir?' I asked. 'Must I leave Thornfield?'

'I believe you must, Jane. I am sorry, Janet, but I believe indeed you must.'

This was a blow: but I did not let it prostrate me.

'Well, sir, I shall be ready when the order to march comes.'

'It is come now – I must give it to-night.'

'Then you are going to be married, sir?'

'Ex-act-ly – pre-ci-se-ly: with your usual acuteness, you have hit the nail straight on the head.'

'Soon, sir?'

'Very soon, my – that is, Miss Eyre: and you'll remember, Jane, the first time I, or Rumour, plainly intimated to you that it was my intention to put my old bachelor's neck into the sacred noose, to enter into the holy estate of matrimony – to take Miss Ingram to my bosom, in short (she's an extensive armful: but that's not the point – one can't have too much of such a very excellent thing as my beautiful Blanche): well, as I was saying – listen to me, Jane! you're not turning your head to look after more moths, are you? That was only a lady-clock, child, "flying away home".[1] I wish to remind you that it was you who first said to me, with that discretion I respect in you – with that foresight, prudence and humility which befit your responsible and dependent position – that in case I married Miss Ingram – both you and little Adèle had better trot forthwith. I pass over the sort of slur conveyed in this suggestion on the character of my beloved; indeed, when you are far away, Janet, I'll try to forget it: I shall notice only its wisdom; which is such that I have made it my law of action. Adèle must go to school; and you, Miss Eyre, must get a new situation.'

'Yes, sir, I will advertise immediately: and meantime, I suppose –?' I was going to say 'I suppose I may stay here, till I find another shelter to betake myself to?' but I stopped, feeling it would not do to risk a long sentence, for my voice was not quite under command.

'In about a month I hope to be a bride-groom,' continued Mr Rochester: 'and in the interim, I shall myself look out for employment and an asylum for you.'

'Thank you, sir; I am sorry to give –?'

1: a lady bird (cf. John Clare's 'Clock a Clay'). The reference is to a children's rhyme, one version of which is 'Lady bird, lady bird, fly away home, your house is on fire and your children are home.'

'Oh, no need to apologise! I consider that when a dependant does her duty as well as you have done yours, she has a sort of claim upon her employer for any little assistance he can conveniently render her; indeed I have already, through my future mother-in-law, heard of a place that I think will suit: it is to undertake the education of the five daughters of Mrs Dionysius O'Gall of Bitternutt Lodge, Connaught, Ireland. You'll like Ireland, I think; they're such a warm-hearted people there, they say.'

'It is a long way off, sir.'

'No matter – a girl of your sense will not object to the voyage or the distance.'

'Not the voyage, but the distance: and then the sea is a barrier – ?'

'From what, Jane?'

'From England and Thornfield: and – ?'

'Well?'

'From *you*, sir.'

I said this involuntarily; and with as little sanction of free will, my tears gushed out. I did not cry so as to be heard, however, I avoided sobbing. The thought of Mrs O'Gall and Bitternutt Lodge struck cold to my heart; and colder the thought of all the brine and foam, destined, as it seemed, to rush between me and the master at whose side I now walked; and colder the remembrance of the wider ocean – wealth, caste, custom intervened between me and what I naturally and inevitably loved.

'It is a long way?' I again said.

'It is to be sure; and when you get to Bitternutt Lodge, Connaught, Ireland, I shall never see you again, Jane: that's morally certain. I never go over to Ireland, not having myself much of a fancy for the country. We have been good friends, Jane, have we not?'

'Yes, sir.'

'And when friends are on the eve of separation, they like to spend the little time that remains to them close to each other. Come – we'll talk over the voyage and the parting quietly, half an hour or so, while the stars enter into their shining life up in heaven yonder: here is the chestnut tree; here is the bench at its old roots. Come, we will sit there in peace tonight, though we should never more be destined to sit there together.'

He seated me and himself.

'It is a long way to Ireland, Janet, and I am sorry to send my little friend on such weary travels: but I can't do better, how is it to be helped? Are you anything akin to me, do you think, Jane?'

I could risk no sort of answer by this time: my heart was full.

'Because?' he said, 'I sometimes have a queer feeling with regard to you – especially when you are near me, as now: it is as if I had a string somewhere under my left ribs, tightly and inextricably knotted to a similar string situated in the corresponding quarter of your little frame. And if that boisterous channel, and two hundred miles or so of land come broad between us, I am afraid that cord of communion will be snapt; and then I've a nervous notion I should take to bleeding inwardly. As for you, – you'd forget me.'

'That I *never* should, sir: you know – ' impossible to proceed.

'Jane, do you hear that nightingale singing in the wood? Listen!'

In listening, I sobbed convulsively; for I could repress what I endured no longer; I was obliged to yield, and I was shaken from head to foot with acute distress. When I did speak, it was only to express an impetuous wish that I had never been born, or never come to Thornfield.

'Because you are sorry to leave it?'

The vehemence of emotion, stirred by grief and love within me, was claiming mastery, and struggling for full sway; and asserting a right to predominate; to overcome, to live, rise, and reign at last; yes, – and to speak.

'I grieve to leave Thornfield: I love Thornfield: – I love it, because I have lived in it a full and delightful life, – momentarily at least. I have not been trampled on. I have not been petrified. I have not been buried with inferior minds, and excluded from glimpse of communion with what is bright and energetic, and high. I have talked, face to face, with what I reverence; with what I delight in, – with an original, a vigorous, an expanded mind. I have known you, Mr Rochester; and it strikes me with terror and anguish to feel I absolutely must be torn from you for ever. I see the necessity of departure; and it is like looking on the necessity of death.'

'Where do you see the necessity?' he asked suddenly.

'Where? You, sir, have placed it before me.'

'In what shape?'

'In the shape of Miss Ingram; a noble and beautiful woman, – your bride.'

'My bride! What bride? I have no bride!'

'But you will have.'

'Yes; I will! I will!' He set his teeth.

'Then I must go: – you have said it yourself.'

'No: you must stay, I swear it – and the oath shall be kept.'

'I tell you I must go!' I retorted, roused to something like passion. 'Do you think I can stay to become nothing to you? Do you think I am an automaton? – a machine without feelings? and can bear to have my morsel of bread snatched from my lips, and my drop of living water dashed from my cup? Do you think, because I am poor, obscure, plain, and little, I am soulless and heartless? – You think wrong! – I have as much soul as you, – and full as much heart! And if God had gifted me with some beauty, and much wealth, I should have made it as hard for you to leave me, as it is now for me to leave you. I am not talking to you now through the medium of custom, conventionalities, nor even of mortal flesh: – it is my spirit that addresses your spirit; just as if both have passed through the grave, and we stood at God's feet, equal – as we are!'

'As we are!' repeated Mr Rochester – 'so,' he added, enclosing me in his arms, gathering me to his breast, pressing his lips on my lips: 'so, Jane!'

'Yes, so, sir,' I rejoined: 'and yet not so; for you are a married man – or as good as a married man, and wed to no one inferior to you – to one with whom you have no sympathy – whom I do not believe you truly love; for I have seen and heard you sneer at her. I would scorn such a union: therefore I am better than you – let me go!'

'Where, Jane? To Ireland?'

'Yes – to Ireland. I have spoken my mind and can go anywhere now.'

'Jane, be still; don't struggle so, like a wild, frantic bird that is rending its own plumage in its desperation.'

'I am no bird; and no net ensnares me; I am a free human being with an independent will; which I now exert to leave you.'

Another effort set me at liberty, and I stood erect before him.

'And your will shall decide your destiny,' he said: 'I offer you my hand, my heart, and a share of all my possessions.'

'You play a farce which I merely laugh at.'

'I ask you to pass through life at my side – to be my second self, and best earthly companion.'

'For that fate you have already made your choice, and must abide by it.'

'Jane, be still a few moments; you are over-excited: I will be still too.'

A waft of wind came sweeping down the laurel-walk, and trembled through the boughs of the chestnut: it wandered away – away – to an indefinite distance – it died. The nightingale's song was then the only voice of the hour: in listening to it, I again wept. Mr Rochester sat quiet, looking at me gently and seriously. Some time passed before he spoke, he at last said: –

'Come to my side, Jane, and let us explain and understand one another.'

'I will never again come to your side: I am torn away now, and cannot return.'

'But, Jane, I summon you as my wife: it is only you I intend to marry.'

I was silent, I thought he mocked me.

'Come, Jane – come hither.'

'Your bride stands between us.'

He rose, and with a stride reached me.

'My bride is here,' he said, again drawing me to him, 'because my equal is here, and my likeness. Jane, will you marry me?'

Still I did not answer, and still I writhed myself from his grasp; for I was still incredulous.

'Do you doubt me, Jane?'

'Entirely.'

'You have no faith in me?'

'Not a whit.'

'Am I a liar to your eyes?' he asked passionately. 'Little sceptic, you *shall* be convinced. What love have I for Miss Ingram? None; and that you know. What love has she for me? None: as I have taken pains to prove: I caused a rumour to reach her that my fortune was not a third of what was supposed, and after that I presented myself to see the result; it was coldness both from her and her mother. I would not – I could not – marry Miss Ingram. You – you strange – you almost unearthly thing! – I love as my own flesh. You – poor and obscure, and small and plain as you are – I entreat to accept me as your husband.'

'What, me!' I ejaculated: beginning in his earnestness – and especially in his incivility – to credit his sincerity: 'me who have not a friend in the world but you – if you are my friend: not a shilling but what you have given me?'

'You, Jane. I must have you for my own – entirely my own. Will you be mine? Say yes, quickly.'

'Mr Rochester, let me look at your face: turn to the moonlight.'

'Why?'

'Because I want to read your countenance: turn!'

'There you will find it scarcely more legible than a crumpled, scratched page. Read on: only make haste, for I suffer.'

His face was very much agitated, and very much flushed, and there were strong workings in the features, and strange gleams in the eyes.

'Oh, Jane, you torture me!' he exclaimed. 'With that searching and yet faithful and generous look, you torture me!'

'How can I do that? If you are true, and your offer real, my only feelings to you must be gratitude and devotion – they cannot torture.'

'Gratitude!' he ejaculated; and added wildly – 'Jane, accept me quickly. Say Edward – give me my name – Edward – I will marry you.'

'Are you in earnest? – Do you truly love me? – Do you sincerely desire me to be your wife?'

'I do; and if an oath is necessary to satisfy you, I swear it.'

'Then, sir, I will marry you.'

'Edward – my little wife!'

'Dear Edward!'

'Come to me – come to me entirely now,' said he: and added, in his deepest tone, speaking in my ear, as his cheek was laid on mine, 'Make my happiness – I will make yours.'

'God pardon me!' he subjoined ere long; 'and man meddle not with me: I have her, and will hold her.'

'There is no one to meddle, sir. I have no kindred to interfere.'

'No – that is the best of it,' he said. And if I had loved him less I should have thought his accent and look of exultation savage: but sitting by him, roused from the nightmare of parting – called to the paradise of union – I thought only of the bliss given me to drink in so abundant a flow. Again and again he said, 'Are you happy, Jane?' and again and again I answered, 'Yes.' After which he murmured, 'It will atone – it will atone. Have I not found her friendless, and cold, and comfortless? Will I not guard, and cherish, and solace her? Is there no love in my heart, and constancy in my resolves? It will expiate at God's tribunal. I know my Maker sanctions what I do. For the world's judgement – I wash my hands thereof. For man's opinion – I defy it.'

But what had befallen the night? The moon was not yet set, and we were all in shadow. I could scarcely see my master's face, near as I was. And what ailed the chestnut tree? it writhed and groaned; while wind roared in the laurel walk, and came sweeping over us.

'We must go in,' said Mr Rochester: 'the weather changes. I could have sat with thee till morning, Jane.'

'And so,' thought I, 'could I with you.' I should have said so, perhaps, but a livid, vivid spark leapt out of a cloud at which I was looking, and there was a crack, a crash and a close rattling peal; and I thought only of hiding my dazzled eyes against Mr Rochester's shoulder.

The rain rushed down. He hurried me up to the walk, through the grounds, and into the house; but we were quite wet before we could pass the threshold. He was taking off my shawl in the hall, and shaking the water out of my loosened hair, when Mrs Fairfax emerged from her room. I did not observe her at first, nor did Mr Rochester. The lamp was lit. The clock was on the stroke of twelve.

'Hasten to take off your wet things,' said he: 'and before you go, good-night – good-night my darling!'

He kissed me repeatedly. When I looked up, on leaving his arms, there stood the widow, pale, grave and amazed. I only smiled at her, and ran upstairs, 'Explanation will do for another time,' thought I. Still, when I reached my chamber, I felt a pang at the idea she should even temporarily misconstrue what she had seen. But joy soon effaced every other feeling; and loud as the wind blew, near and deep as the thunder crashed, fierce and frequent as the lightning gleamed, cataract-like as the rain fell during a storm of two hours' duration, I experienced no fear, and little awe. Mr Rochester came thrice to my door in the course of it, to ask if I was safe and tranquil: and that was comfort, that was strength for anything.

Before I left my bed in the morning, little Adèle came running in to tell me that the great horse-chestnut, at the bottom of the orchard had been struck by lightning in the night, and half of it split away.

[Preparations for their marriage continue.]

From Volume II, Chapter 11

'I require and charge you both (as ye will answer at the dreadful day of judgement, when the secrets of all hearts shall be disclosed), that if either of you know any impediment why ye may not lawfully be joined together in matrimony, ye do now confess it; for be ye well assured that so many as are coupled together otherwise than God's Word doth allow, are not joined together by God, neither is their matrimony lawful.'

He paused, as the custom is. When is the pause after that sentence ever broken by reply? Not, perhaps, once in a hundred years. And the clergyman, who had not lifted his eyes from his book, and had held his breath but for a moment, was proceeding: his hand was already stretched towards Mr Rochester, as his lips unclosed to ask, 'Wilt thou have this woman for thy wedded wife?' – when a distinct and near voice said: –

'The marriage can not go on: I declare the existence of an impediment.'

The clergyman looked up at the speaker, and stood mute; the clerk did the same; Mr Rochester moved slightly, as if an earthquake had rolled under his feet: taking a firmer footing, and not turning his head or eyes, he said, 'Proceed.'

Profound silence fell when he had uttered that word, with deep but low intonation. Presently Mr Wood said: –

'I cannot proceed without some investigation into what has been asserted, and evidence of its truth or falsehood.'

'The ceremony is quite broken off,' subjoined the voice behind us. 'I am in a condition to prove my allegation: an insuperable impediment to this marriage exists.'

Mr Rochester heard, but heeded not: he stood stubborn and rigid: making no movement, but to possess himself of my hand. What a hot and strong grasp he had! – and how like quarried marble was his pale, firm, massive front at this moment! How his eye shone, still, watchful, and yet wild beneath!

Mr Wood seemed at a loss. 'What is the nature of the impediment?' he asked. 'Perhaps it may be got over – explained away?'

'Hardly,' was the answer: 'I have called it insuperable, and I speak advisedly.'

The speaker came forwards, and leaned on the rails. He continued, uttering each word distinctly, calmly, steadily, but not loudly.

'It simply consists in the existence of a previous marriage: Mr Rochester has a wife now living.'

My nerves vibrated to those low-spoken words as they had never vibrated to thunder – my blood felt their subtle violence as it had never felt frost or fire: but I was collected, and in no danger of swooning. I looked at Mr Rochester: I made him look at me. His whole face was colourless rock: his eye was both spark and flint. He disavowed nothing: he seemed as if he would defy all things. Without speaking, without smiling; without seeming to recognise in me a human being he only twined my waist with his arm, and riveted me to his side.

'My name is Briggs – a solicitor of — Street, London.'

'And you would thrust on me a wife?'

'I would remind you of your lady's existence, sir; which the law recognises, if you do not.'

'Favour me with an account of her – with her name, her parentage, her place of abode.'

'Certainly,' Mr Briggs calmly took a paper from his pocket, and read out in a sort of official, nasal voice: –

'"I affirm and can prove that on the 20th of October, AD —, (a date of fifteen years back) Edward Fairfax Rochester of Thornfield Hall, in the country of —, and of Ferndean Manor, in —shire, England, was married to my sister, Bertha Antoinetta Mason, daughter of Jonas Mason, merchant, and of Antoinetta his wife, a Creole[1] – at — church, Spanish-Town, Jamaica. The record of the marriage will be found in the register of that church – a copy of it is now in my possession. Signed, Richard Mason."'

'That, if a genuine document, may prove I have been married, but it does not prove that the woman mentioned therein as my wife is still living.'

'She was living three months ago,' returned the lawyer.

'How do you know?'

'I have a witness to the fact; whose testimony even you, sir, will scarcely controvert.'

'Produce him – or go to hell.'

'I will produce him first – he is on the spot: Mr Mason, have the goodness to step forward.'

Mr Rochester, on hearing the name, set his teeth; he experienced, too, a sort of strong convulsive quiver; near to him as I was, I felt the spasmodic

---

1: either a person of West Indian birth but of European origin, or a person of mixed European and Negro ancestry who speaks French or Spanish. In this case, the implication is of mixed blood.

movement of fury or despair run through his frame. The second stranger, who had hitherto lingered in the background, now drew near; a pale face looked over the solicitor's shoulder – yes, it was Mason himself. Mr Rochester turned and glared at him. His eye, as I have often said, was a black eye: it had now a tawny, nay a bloody light in its gloom; and his face flushed – olive cheek, and hueless forehead received a glow, as from spreading, ascending heart-fire: and he stirred, lifted his strong arm – he could have struck Mason – dashed him on the church-floor – shocked by ruthless blow the breath from his body – but Mason shrank away, and cried faintly, 'Good God!' Contempt fell cool on Mr Rochester – his passion died as if a blight had shrivelled it up: he only asked, 'What have *you* to say?'

An inaudible reply escaped Mason's white lips.

'The devil is in it if you cannot answer distinctly. I again demand, what have *you* to say?'

'Sir – sir –' interrupted the clergyman, 'do not forget you are in a sacred place.' Then addressing Mason, he inquired gently, 'Are you aware, sir, whether or not this gentleman's wife is still living?'

'Courage,' urged the lawyer, – 'speak out.'

'She is now living at Thornfield Hall;' said Mason, in more articulate tones: 'I saw her there last April. I am her brother.'

* * * *

The morning had been a quiet morning enough – all except the brief scene with the lunatic: the transaction in the church had not been noisy; there was no explosion of passion, no loud altercation, no dispute, no defiance or challenge, no tears, no sobs: a few words had been spoken, a calmly pronounced objection to the marriage made; some stern, short questions put by Mr Rochester; answers, explanations given, evidence adduced; an open admission of the truth had been uttered by my master; then the living proof had been seen; the intruders were gone, and all was over.

I was in my own room as usual – just myself, without obvious change: nothing had smitten me, or scathed me, or maimed me. And yet, where was the Jane Eyre of yesterday? – where was her life? – where were her prospects?

Jane Eyre, who had been an ardent, expectant woman – almost a bride – was a cold, solitary girl again: her life was pale, her prospects were desolate. A Christmas frost had come at midsummer; a white December storm had whirled over June; ice glazed the ripe apples, drifts crushed the blowing roses; on hay-field and corn-field lay a frozen shroud: lanes which last night blushed full of flowers, to-day were pathless with untrodden snow; and the woods, which twelve hours since waved leafy and fragrant as groves between the tropics, now spread, waste, wild, and white as pine-forests in wintry Norway. My hopes were all dead – struck with a subtle doom, such as, in one night, fell on all the first-born in the land of Egypt. I looked on my cherished wishes, yesterday so blooming and glowing; they lay stark chill, livid corpses that could never revive. I looked at my love: that feeling which was my master's – which he had created; it shivered in my heart, like a suffering child in a cold cradle; sickness and anguish had seized it; it could not seek Mr Rochester's arms – it could not derive warmth from his breast. Oh, never more could it turn to him; for faith was blighted – confidence destroyed! Mr Rochester was not to me what he had been; for he was not what I had thought him. I would not ascribe vice to him; I would not say that he had betrayed me: but the attribute of stainless truth was gone from his idea; and from his presence I must go: *that* I perceived well. When – how – whither, I could not discern; but he himself, I doubted not, would hurry me from Thornfield. Real affection, it seemed, he could not have for me; it had been only fitful passion: that was balked; he would want me no more. I should fear even to cross his path now: my view must be hateful to him. Oh, how blind had been my eyes! How weak my conduct!

My eyes were covered and closed: eddying darkness seemed to swim round me, and reflection came in as black and confused a flow. Self-abandoned, relaxed and effortless, I seemed to have laid me down in the dried-up bed of a great river; I heard a flood loosened in remote mountains, and felt the torrent come: to rise I had no will, to flee I had no strength. I lay faint; longing to be dead. One idea only still throbbed life-like within me – a remembrance of God: it begot an uttered prayer: these words went wandering up and down in my rayless mind, as something that should be whispered; but no energy was found to express them: –

'Be not far from me, for trouble is near: there is none to help.'

It was near: and as I had lifted no petition to Heaven to avert it – as I had neither joined my hands, nor bent my knees, nor moved my lips – it came: in full, heavy swing the torrent poured over me. The whole consciousness of my life lorn, my love lost, my hope quenched, my faith death-struck, swayed full and mighty above me in one sullen mass. That bitter hour cannot be described: in truth, 'the waters came into my soul; I sank in deep mire: I felt no standing; I came into deep waters; the floods overflowed me.'[1]

[Volume III begins with Jane resolving to leave Thornfield and Mr Rochester explaining how his father had given all the family wealth to his brother and set him up as a West India planter with Mr Mason, who had a handsome daughter. Only when Mr Rochester had married the daughter did he discover that the mother he had thought dead was in fact insane. The death of Rochester's father and elder brother left him a rich man, encumbered with a Creole wife whose madness was increasing. Because Jane cannot fulfill her love for Rochester in marriage, she leaves, taking with her no more than she possessed on her arrival. She wanders the heath in the rain and catches a fever. She is rescued by Mary, Diana and St John Rivers who nurse her to health and find her work in a local school. It later transpires that these kind people are her cousins, and that all four together are beneficiaries of the estate of an uncle. St John Rivers is going to India as a missionary and invites Jane to go as his wife to help him. She is prepared to go as a missionary, but scorns his dispassionate and duty-laden understanding of love. Jane feels summoned by Rochester. She goes to see him but finds Thornfield burned to the ground. Bertha Mason died in the fire; Rochester was cruelly injured in trying to save her. Jane hurries to his side at Ferndean Manor.]

1: Psalm 69, v. 2.

From Volume III, Chapter 11

'Can there be life here?' I asked.

Yes: life of some kind there was, for I heard a movement – that narrow front-door was unclosing, and some shape was about to issue from the grange.

It opened slowly: a figure came out into the twilight and stood on the step; a man without a hat: he stretched forth his hand as if to feel whether it rained. Dusk as it was, I had recognised him – it was my master, Edward Fairfax Rochester, and no other.

I stayed my step, almost my breath, and stood to watch him – to him, myself unseen, and alas! to him invisible. It was a sudden meeting, and one in which rapture was kept well in check by pain. I had no difficulty in restraining my voice from exclamation, my step from hasty advance.

His form was of the same strong and saltward[1] contour as ever: his port was still erect, his hair was still raven-black; nor were his features altered or sunk: not in one year's space, by any sorrow, could his athletic strength be quelled, or his vigorous prime blighted. But in his countenance, I saw a change: that looked desperate and brooding – that reminded me of some wronged and fettered wild beast or bird, dangerous to approach in his sullen woe. The caged eagle, whose gold-ringed eyes cruelty has extinguished, might look as looked that sightless Samson.

And, reader, do you think I feared him in his blind ferocity? – if you do, you little know me. A soft hope blent with my sorrow that soon I should dare to drop a kiss on that brow of rock, and on those lids so sternly sealed beneath it: but not yet. I would not accost him yet.

He descended one step, and advanced slowly and gropingly towards the grass-plat.[2] Where was his daring stride now? Then he paused, as if he knew not which way to turn. He lifted his head and opened his eyelids, gazed blank and with a straining effort, on the sky and towards the amphitheatre of trees: one saw that all to him was void darkness. He stretched his right hand (the left arm, the mutilated one, he kept hidden in his bosom); he seemed to wish by touch to gain an idea of what lay around him: he met but vacancy still; for the trees were some yards off where he stood. He relinquished the endeavour, folded his arms, and stood quiet and mute in the rain, now falling fast on his uncovered head. At this moment, John approached him from some quarter.

'Will you take my arm, sir?' he said; 'there is a heavy shower coming on: had you not better go in?'

'Let me alone,' was the answer.

John withdrew, without having observed me. Mr Rochester now tried to walk about, vainly, – all was too uncertain. He groped his way back to the house, and, re-entering it, closed the door.

I now drew near and knocked: John's wife opened for me. 'Mary,' I said; 'how are you?'

She started as if she had seen a ghost: I calmed her. To her hurried 'It is really you, Miss, come at this late hour to this lonely place?' I answered by taking her

---

1: seaman-like. 2: a plot of grass-covered ground.

hand; and then I followed her into the kitchen, where John now sat by a good fire. I explained to them, in few words, that I had heard all which had happened since I left Thornfield, and that I was come to see Mr Rochester. I asked John to go down to the turnpike-house, where I had dismissed the chaise, and bring my trunk, which I had left there: and then, when I removed my bonnet and shawl, I questioned Mary as to whether I could be accommodated at the Manor House for the night; and finding that arrangements to that effect, though difficult, would not be impossible, I informed her I should stay. Just at this moment the parlour-bell rang.

'When you go in,' said I, 'tell your master that a person wishes to speak to him, but do not give my name.'

'I don't think he will see you,' she answered; 'he refuses everybody.'

When she returned, I inquired what he had said.

'You are to send in your name and your business,' she replied. She then proceeded to fill a glass with water, and place it on a tray, together with candles.

'Is it what he rang for?' I asked.

'Yes: he always has candles brought in at dark, though he is blind.'

'Give the tray to me, I will carry it in.'

I took it from her hand, she pointed me out the parlour door. The tray shook as I held it; the water spilt from the glass; my heart struck my ribs loud and fast. Mary opened the door for me, and shut it behind me.

This parlour looked gloomy: a neglected handful of fire burnt low in the grate; and, leaning over it, with his head supported against the high, old-fashioned mantel-piece, appeared the blind tenant of the room. His old dog, Pilot, lay on one side, removed out of the way, and coiled up as if afraid of being inadvertently trodden upon. Pilot pricked up his ears when I came in; then he jumped up with a yelp and a whine, and bounded towards me: he almost knocked the tray from my hands. I set it on the table, then patted him, and said softly, 'Lie down!' Mr Rochester turned mechanically to *see* what the commotion was; but as he *saw* nothing, he returned and sighed.

'Give me the water, Mary,' he said.

I approached him with the now half-filled glass, Pilot followed me, still excited.

'What's the matter?' he enquired.

'Down Pilot!' I again said. He checked the water on the way to his lips, and seemed to listen: he drank and put the glass down. 'This is you, Mary, is it not?'

'Mary is in the kitchen,' I answered.

He put out his hand with a quick gesture, but not seeing where I stood, he did not touch me. 'Who is this? Who is this?' he demanded, trying, as it seemed, to *see* with those sightless eyes – unavailing and distressing attempt! 'Answer me – speak again!' he ordered imperiously and aloud.

'Will you have a little more water, sir? I split half of what was in the glass,' I said.

'*Who* is this? *What* is it? Who speaks?'

'Pilot knows me, and John and Mary know I am here. I came only this evening,' I answered.

'Great God! – what a delusion has come over me? What sweet madness has seized me?'

'No delusion – no madness: your mind, sir, is too strong for delusion, your health too sound for frenzy.'

'And where is the speaker? Is it only a voice? Oh! I *cannot* see, but I must feel or my heart will stop and my brain burst. Whatever – whoever you are – be perceptible to the touch, or I cannot live!'

He groped: I arrested his wandering hand, and prisoned it in both mine.

'Her very fingers!' he cried; 'her small slight fingers! If so, there must be more of her.'

The muscular hand broke from my custody; my arm was seized, my shoulder – neck – waist – I was entwined and gathered to him.

'Is it Jane? *What* is it? This is her shape – this is her size – '

'And this, her voice,' I added. 'She is all here: her heart, too. God bless you, sir! I am glad to be so near you again.'

'Jane Eyre! – Jane Eyre!' was all he said.

'My dear master,' I answered, 'I am Jane Eyre: I have found you out – I am come back to you.'

'In truth? – in the flesh? My living Jane?'

'You touch me, sir, – you hold me, and fast enough: I am not cold like a corpse, nor vacant like air, am I?'

'My living darling! These are certainly her limbs, and these her features: but I cannot be so blest after all my misery. It is a dream: such dreams as I have had a night when I have clasped her once more to my heart, as I do now; and kissed her, as thus – and felt that she loved me, and trusted that she would not leave me.'

'Which I never will, sir, from this day.'

'Never will, says the vision? but I always awoke and found it an empty mockery; and I was desolate and abandoned – my life dark; lonely, hopeless – my soul athirst and forbidden to drink – my heart famished and never to be fed. Gentle, soft dream, nestling in my arms now, you will fly too; as your sisters have fled before you but kiss me before you go – embrace me, Jane.'

'There sir - and there!'

I pressed my lips to his once brilliant and now rayless eyes – I swept his hair from his brow, and kissed that too. He suddenly seemed to rouse himself: the conviction of the reality of all this seized him.

'It is you – is it Jane? You are come back to me then.'

'I am.'

[Volume III, Chapter 12, the final chapter, begins, 'Reader, I married him.']

EMILY BRONTË (1818–1848)

Emily Brontë was the fourth daughter of Patrick Brontë, curate of Haworth, Yorkshire, and elder sister of Anne and Branwell Brontë. Their mother died in 1821 and the four eldest daughters were sent to a boarding school where the two eldest of them died. Thereafter the children were educated by their father in their remote home on the Yorkshire moors and read extensively in contemporary literature. Emily and Anne invented "Gondal', an imaginary realm loosely inspired by Scott and Byron in which Emily set many of her poems. Emily Brontë worked as a governess from 1837, and spent 1842 in Brussels with Charlotte studying languages, but was the most reclusive of the sisters and returned to Haworth and the landscape she loved. Her poems were published with those of her sisters in *Poems, by Currer, Ellis and Acton Bell* (1846), the pseudonyms being adopted to evade prejudice against authoresses. The volume received hardly any attention. Emily Brontë's *Wuthering Heights* by Ellis Bell and Anne Brontë's *Agnes Grey* by Acton Bell were published together on a half-costs basis in 1847 just before Emily died of tuberculosis. Reviewers considered *Wuthering Heights* "disagreeable', "painful', "rugged', "malign', "baffling', "troublesome' and "morose'. It has now become one of the most famous novels of all time.

The Philosopher

'Enough of thought, philosopher!
  Too long hast thou been dreaming
Unlightened, in this chamber drear,
  While summer's sun is beaming!
5 Space-sweeping soul, what sad refrain
Concludes thy musings once again?

Oh, for the time when I shall sleep
  Without identity,
And never care how rain may steep,
10 Or snow may cover me!
No promised heaven, these wild desires,
Could all, or half fulfil;
No threatened hell, with quenchless fires,
Subdue this quenchless will!'

15 'So said I, and still say the same;
  Still, to my death, will say –
Three gods, within this little frame,
  Are warring night and day;
Heaven could not hold them all, and yet
20 They all are held in me;

And must be mine till I forget
  My present entity!
Oh, for the time, when in my breast
  Their struggles will be o'er!
25 Oh, for the day, when I shall rest,
  And never suffer more!'

'I saw a spirit, standing, man,
  Where thou dost stand – an hour ago,
And round his feet three rivers ran,
30 Of equal depth, and equal flow –
A golden stream – and one like blood;
  And one like sapphire seemed to be;
But, where they joined their triple flood
  It tumbled in an inky sea.
35 The spirit sent his dazzling gaze
  Down through that ocean's gloomy night
Then, kindling all, with sudden blaze,
  The glad deep sparkled wide and bright –
White as the sun, far, far more fair
40 Than its divided sources were!'

'And even for that spirit, seer,
  I've watched and sought my life-time long;
Sought him in heaven, hell, earth, and air –
  An endless search, and always wrong!
45 Had I but seen his glorious eye
  Once light the clouds that wilder me,
I ne'er had raised this coward cry
  To cease to think, and cease to be;
I ne'er had called oblivion blest,
50 Nor, stretching eager hands to death,
  Implored to change for senseless rest
This sentient soul, this living breath –
  Oh, let me die – that power and will
Their cruel strife may close;
55 And conquered good, and conquering ill
Be lost in one repose!'

Remembrance

Cold in the earth, and the deep snow piled above thee,
Far, far removed, cold in the dreary grave!
Have I forgot, my only Love, to love thee,
Severed at last by Time's all-severing wave?

5   Now, when alone, do my thoughts no longer hover
Over the mountains, on that northern shore,
Resting their wings where heath and fern-leaves cover
That noble heart for ever, ever more?

Cold in the earth – and fifteen wild Decembers,
10   From these brown hills have melted into spring.
Faithful indeed is the spirit that remembers
After such years of change and suffering!

Sweet Love of youth, forgive if I forget thee,
While the world's tide is bearing me along;
15   Other desires and other hopes beset me,
Hopes which obscure, but cannot do thee wrong!

No later light has lightened up my heaven,
No second morn has ever shone for me;
All my life's bliss from thy dear life was given,
20   All my life's bliss is in the grave with thee.

But, when the days of golden dreams had perished,
And even Despair was powerless to destroy;
Then did I learn how existence could be cherished,
Strengthened, and fed without the aid of joy.

25   Then did I check the tears of useless passion –
Weaned my young soul from yearning after thine;
Sternly denied its burning wish to hasten
Down to that tomb already more than mine.

And, even yet, I dare not let it languish,
30   Dare not indulge in memory's rapturous pain;
Once drinking deep of that divinest anguish,
How could I seek the empty world again?

From Wuthering Heights

[Mr Lockwood, seeking refreshment from an ennervating London social life, takes a tenancy of Thrushcross Grange in Yorkshire. He calls at Wuthering Heights, the home of his landlord, Mr Heathcliff, which creates a rather Gothic impression. He is not welcome, but he imposes, and again the next day, and is then trapped by a snow storm and a nose bleed into staying the night. Zillah, the cook, shows him to his bedroom.]

Chapter 3

While leading the way upstairs, she recommended that I should hide the candle, and not make a noise; for her master had an odd notion about the chamber she would put me in, and never let anybody lodge there willingly.

I asked the reason.

She did not know, she answered; she had only lived there a year or two; and they had so many queer goings on, she could not begin to be curious.

Too stupified to be curious myself, I fastened my door and glanced round for the bed. The whole furniture consisted of a chair, a clothes-press, and a large oak case, with squares cut out near the top resembling coach windows.

Having approached this structure, I looked inside, and perceived it to be a singular sort of old-fashioned couch, very conveniently designed to obviate the necessity for every member of the family having a room to himself. In fact, it formed a little closet, and the ledge of a window, which it enclosed, served as a table.

I slid back the panelled sides, got in with my light, pulled them together again, and felt secure against the vigilance of Heathcliff, and every one else.

The ledge, where I placed my candle, had a few mildewed books piled up in one corner; and it was covered with writing scratched on the paint. This writing, however, was nothing but a name repeated in all kinds of characters, large and small – *Catherine Earnshaw*, here and there varied to *Catherine Heathcliff* and then again to *Catherine Linton*.

In vapid listlessness I leant my head against the window, and continued spelling over Catherine Earnshaw – Heathcliff – Linton, till my eyes closed. But they had not rested five minutes when a glare of white letters started from the dark as vivid as spectres – the air swarmed with Catherines; and rousing myself to dispel the obtrusive name, I discovered my candle-wick reclining on one of the antique volumes, and perfuming the place with an odour of roasted calf-skin.

I snuffed it off, and, very ill at ease under the influence of cold and lingering nausea, sat up and spread open the injured tome on my knee. It was a Testament, in lean type, and smelling dreadfully musty. A fly-leaf bore the inscription, "Catherine Earnshaw, her book,' and a date some quarter of a century back.

I shut it, and took up another, and another, till I had examined all. Catherine's library was select, and its state of dilapidation proved it to have been well used, though not altogether for a legitimate purpose. Scarcely one chapter had escaped a pen and ink commentary – at least, the appearance of one – covering every morsel of blank that the printer had left.

Some were detached sentences; other parts took the form of a regular diary, scrawled in an unformed, childish hand. At the top of an extra page, quite a treasure, probably, when first lighted on, I was greatly amused to behold an excellent caricature of my friend Joseph, rudely yet powerfully sketched.

An immediate interest kindled within me for the unknown Catherine, and I began forthwith to decipher her faded hieroglyphics.

'An awful Sunday!' commenced the paragraph beneath. 'I wish my father were back again. Hindley is a detestable substitute – his conduct to Heathcliff is atrocious – H. and I are going to rebel – we took our initiatory step this evening.'

'All day had been flooding with rain. We could not go to church, so Joseph must needs get up a congregation in the garret; and while Hindley and his wife basked downstairs before a comfortable fire – doing anything but reading their Bibles, I'll answer for it – Heathcliff, myself, and the unhappy plough-boy were commanded to take our Prayer-books and mount. We were ranged in a row on a sack of corn, groaning and shivering, and hoping that Joseph would shiver too, so that he might give us a short homily for his own sake. A vain idea! The service lasted precisely three hours; and yet my brother had the face to exclaim, when he saw us descending,

"What! done already?"

On Sunday evenings we used to be permitted to play, if we did not make much noise; now a mere titter is sufficient to send us into corners!

"You forget you have a master here," says the tyrant. "I'll demolish the first who puts me out of temper! I insist on perfect sobriety and silence. Oh boy! was that you? – Frances darling, pull his hair as you go by. I heard him snap his fingers."

Frances pulled his hair heartily, and then went and seated herself on her husband's knee; and there they were, like two babies, kissing and talking nonsense by the hour – foolish palaver that we should be ashamed of.

We made ourselves as snug as our means allowed in the arch of the dresser. I had just fastened our pinafores together, and hung them up for a curtain, when in comes Joseph on an errand from the stables. He tears down my handywork, boxes my ears, and croaks:

"T' maister nobbut just buried, and Sabbath no oe'red, und t' sahnd uh't gospel still i' yer lugs, and ye darr be laiking! shame on ye! sit ye dahn, ill childer! they's good books eneugh if ye'll read 'em; sit ye dahn, and think uh yer sowls!"

Saying this, he compelled us so to square our positions that we might receive from the far-off fire a dull ray to show us the text of the lumber he thrust upon us.

I could not bear the employment. I took my dingy volume by the scroop,[1] and hurled it into the dog-kennel, vowing I hated a good book.

Heathcliff kicked his to the same place.

Then there was a hubbub!

"Maister Hindley!" shouted our chaplain. "Maister, coom hither! Miss Cathy's riven th' back off 'Th' Helmet uh Salvation,' un' Heathcliff's pawsed his fit

---

1: dialect word, presumably the cover.

intuh t' first part uh 'T' Broad Way to Destruction!' It's fair flaysome ut yah, let 'em goa on this gait. Ech! th' owd man ud uh laced 'em properly – bud he's goan!"

Hindley hurried up from his paradise on the hearth, and seizing one of us by the collar, and the other by the arm, hurled both into the back-kitchen, where, Joseph asseverated, "owd Nick"[1] would fetch us as sure as we were living; and, so comforted, we each sought a separate nook to await his advent.

I reached this book, and a pot of ink from a shelf, and pushed the house-door ajar to give me light, and I have got the time on with writing for twenty minutes; but my companion is impatient and proposes that we should appropriate the dairy woman's cloak, and have a scamper on the moors, under its shelter. A pleasant suggestion – and then, if the surly old man come in, he may believe his prophecy verified – we cannot be damper, or colder, in the rain than we are here.'

I suppose Catherine fulfilled her project, for the next sentence took up another subject; she waxed lachrymose.

'How little did I dream that Hindley would ever make me cry so!' she wrote. 'My head aches, till I cannot keep it on the pillow; and still I can't give over. Poor Heathcliff! Hindley calls him a vagabond, and won't let him sit with us, nor eat with us any more; and he says, he and I must not play together, and threatens to turn him out of the house if we break his orders.

He has been blaming our father (how dared he?) for treating H. too liberally; and swears he will reduce him to his right place – '

I began to nod drowsily over the dim page; my eye wandered from manuscript to print. I saw a red ornamented title – 'Seventy Times Seven, and the First of the Seventy-First. A Pious Discourse delivered by the Reverend Jabes Branderham, in the Chapel of Gimmerden Sough.' And while I was, half consciously, worrying my brain to guess what Jabes Branderham would make of his subject, I sank back in bed, and fell asleep.

Alas, for the effects of bad tea and bad temper! what else could it be that made me pass such a terrible night? I don't remember another that I can at all compare with it since I was capable of suffering.

I began to dream, almost before I ceased to be sensible of my locality. I thought it was morning, and I had set out on my way home, with Joseph for a guide. The snow lay yards deep in our road; and, as we floundered on, my companion wearied me with constant reproaches that I had not brought a pilgrim's staff, telling me I could never get into the house without one, and boastfully flourishing a heavy-headed cudgel, which I understood to be so denominated.

For a moment I considered it absurd that I should need such a weapon to gain admittance into my own residence. Then, a new idea flashed across me. I was not going there. We were journeying to hear the famous Jabes Branderham preach from the text, 'Seventy Times Seven,' and either Joseph, the preacher, or I had committed the 'First of the Seventy-First,' and were to be publicly exposed and excommunicated.

1: the Devil.

We came to the chapel. I have passed it really in my walks twice or thrice. It lies in a hollow between two hills – an elevated hollow, near a swamp, whose peaty moisture is said to answer all the purposes of embalming on the few corpses deposited there. The roof has been kept whole hitherto; but as the clergyman's stipend is only twenty pounds per annum, and a house with two rooms, threatening speedily to determine into one, no clergyman will undertake the duties of pastor, especially as it is currently reported that his flock would rather let him starve than increase the living by one penny from their own pockets. However, in my dream, Jabes had a full and attentive congregation, and he preached – good God! what a sermon, divided into *four hundred and ninety parts*, each fully equal to an ordinary address from the pulpit, and each discussing a separate sin! Where he searched for them, I cannot tell. He had his private manner of interpreting the phrase, and it seemed necessary the brother should sin different sins on every occasion.

They were of the most curious character – odd transgressions that I never imagined previously.

Oh, how weary I grew! How I writhed, and yawned, and nodded, and revived! How I pinched, and pricked myself, and rubbed my eyes, and stood up, and sat down again, and nudged Joseph to inform me if he would *ever* have done!

I was condemned to hear all out. Finally, he reached the '*First of the Seventy-First.*' At that crisis, a sudden inspiration descended on me. I was moved to rise and denounce Jabes Branderham as the sinner of the sin that no Christian need pardon.

'Sir,' I exclaimed, 'sitting here within these four walls, at one stretch, I have endured and forgiven the four hundred and ninety heads of your discourse. Seventy times seven times have I plucked up my hat and been about to depart; seventy times seven times have you preposterously forced me to resume my seat. The four hundred and ninety first is too much. – Fellow-martyrs, have at him! Drag him down, and crush him to atoms, that the place which knows him may know him no more!'

'*Thou art the Man!*' cried Jabes, after a solemn pause, leaning over his cushion. 'Seventy times seven times didst thou gapingly contort thy visage; seventy times seven did I take counsel with my soul. Lo, this is human weakness; this also may be absolved! The First of the Seventy-First is come. Brethren, execute upon him the judgment written! Such honour have all His saints!'

With that concluding word, the whole assembly, exalting their pilgrim's staves, rushed round me in a body; and I, having no weapon to raise in self-defence, commenced grappling with Joseph, my nearest and most ferocious assailant, for his. In the confluence of the multitude several clubs crossed; blows aimed at me fell on other sconces. Presently the whole chapel resounded with rappings and counter-rappings. Every man's hand was against his neighbour; and Branderham, unwilling to remain idle, poured forth his zeal in a shower of loud taps on the boards of the pulpit, which responded so smartly that at last, to my unspeakable relief, they woke me.

And what was it that had suggested the tremendous tumult? What had played

Jabes's part in the row? Merely the branch of a fir-tree that touched my lattice, as the blast wailed by, and rattled its dry cones against the panes!

I listened doubtingly an instant, detected the disturber, then turned and dozed, and dreamt again; if possible, still more disagreeably than before.

This time I remembered I was lying in the oak closet, and I heard distinctly the gusty wind and the driving of the snow. I heard also the fir-bough repeat its teasing sound, and ascribed it to the right cause. But it annoyed me so much that I resolved to silence it, if possible; and I thought I rose and endeavoured to unhasp the casement. The hook was soldered into the staple – a circumstance observed by me when awake, but forgotten.

'I must stop it, nevertheless!' I muttered, knocking my knuckles through the glass, and stretching an arm out to seize the importunate branch; instead of which, my fingers closed on the fingers of a little, ice-cold hand!

The intense horror of nightmare came over me. I tried to draw back my arm, but the hand clung to it, and a most melancholy voice sobbed,

'Let me in – let me in!'

'Who are you?' I asked, struggling, meanwhile, to disengage myself.

'Catherine Linton,' it replied shiveringly (why did I think of *Linton*? I had read *Earnshaw* twenty times for Linton.) 'I'm come home. I'd lost my way on the moor!'

As it spoke, I discerned, obscurely, a child's face looking through the window. Terror made me cruel; and finding it useless to attempt shaking the creature off, I pulled its wrist on to the broken pane, and rubbed it to and fro till the blood ran down and soaked the bedclothes. Still it wailed, 'Let me in!' and maintained its tenacious gripe, almost maddening me with fear.

'How can I?' I said at length. 'Let *me* go, if you want me to let you in!'

The fingers relaxed; I snatched mine through the hole, hurriedly piled the books up in a pyramid against it, and stopped my ears to exclude the lamentable prayer.

I seemed to keep them closed above a quarter of an hour; yet the instant I listened again, there was the doleful cry moaning on!

'Begone!' I shouted; 'I'll never let you in – not if you beg for twenty years.'

'It is twenty years,' mourned the voice – 'twenty years. I've been a waif for twenty years!'

Thereat began a feeble scratching outside, and the pile of books moved as if thrust forward.

I tried to jump up, but could not stir a limb, and so yelled aloud in a frenzy of fright.

To my confusion, I discovered the yell was not ideal. Hasty footsteps approached my chamber door; somebody pushed it open with a vigorous hand, and a light glimmered through the squares at the top of the bed. I sat shuddering yet, and wiping the perspiration from my forehead. The intruder appeared to hesitate, and muttered to himself.

At last he said in a half-whisper, plainly not expecting an answer,

'Is any one here?'

I considered it best to confess my presence, for I knew Heathcliff's accents, and feared he might search further if I kept quiet.

With this intention I turned and opened the panels. I shall not soon forget the effect my action produced.

Heathcliff stood near the entrance, in his shirt and trousers, with a candle dripping over his fingers, and his face as white as the wall behind him. The first creak of the oak startled him like an electric shock. The light leaped from his hold to a distance of some feet, and his agitation was so extreme that he could hardly pick it up.

'It is only your guest, sir,' I called out, desirous to spare him the humiliation of exposing his cowardice further. 'I had the misfortune to scream in my sleep, owing to a frightful nightmare. I'm sorry I disturbed you.'

'Oh, God confound you, Mr Lockwood! I wish you were at the – ' commenced my host, setting the candle on a chair, because he found it impossible to hold it steady.

'And who showed you up into this room?' he continued, crushing his nails into his palms and grinding his teeth to subdue the maxillary convulsions. 'Who was it? I've a good mind to turn them out of the house this moment.'

'It was your servant Zillah,' I replied, flinging myself on to the floor, and rapidly resuming my garments. 'I should not care if you did, Mr Heathcliff; she richly deserves it. I suppose that she wanted to get another proof that the place was haunted, at my expense. Well, it is – swarming with ghosts and goblins! You have reason in shutting it up, I assure you. No one will thank you for a doze in such a den!'

'What do you mean?' asked Heathcliff, 'and what are you doing? Lie down and finish out the night, since you *are* here; but, for Heaven's sake, don't repeat that horrid noise. Nothing could excuse it, unless you were having your throat cut!'

'If the little fiend had got in at the window, she probably would have strangled me!' I returned. 'I'm not going to endure the persecutions of your hospitable ancestors again. Was not the Reverend Jabes Branderham akin to you on the mother's side? And that minx, Catherine Linton, or Earnshaw, or however she was called, she must have been a changeling – wicked little soul! She told me she had been walking the earth these twenty years – a just punishment for her mortal transgressions, I've no doubt!'

Scarcely were these words uttered, when I recollected the association of Heathcliff's with Catherine's name in the book, which had completely slipped from my memory, till thus awakened. I blushed at my inconsideration; but without showing further consciousness of the offence, I hastened to add,

'The truth is, sir, I passed the first part of the night – ' Here I stopped afresh. I was about to say 'perusing those old volumes,' then it would have revealed my knowledge of their written, as well as their printed contents; so, correcting myself, I went on, 'In spelling over the name scratched on that window-ledge. A monotonous occupation, calculated to set me asleep, like counting, or – '

'What *can* you mean by talking in this way to *me*?' thundered Heathcliff, with savage vehemence. 'How – how *dare* you, under my roof? – God, he's mad to speak so!' And he struck his forehead with rage.

I did not know whether to resent this language or pursue my explanation; but he seemed so powerfully affected that I took pity and proceeded with my dreams, affirming I had never heard the appellation of "Catherine Linton' before, but reading it often over produced an impression which personified itself when I had no longer my imagination under control.

Heathcliff gradually fell back into the shelter of the bed as I spoke, finally sitting down almost concealed behind it. I guessed, however, by his irregular and intercepted breathing, that he struggled to vanquish an access of violent emotion.

Not liking to show him that I had heard the conflict, I continued my toilette rather noisily, looked at my watch, and soliloquized on the length of the night.

'Not three o'clock yet! I could have taken oath it had been six. Time stagnates here. We must surely have retired to rest at eight!'

'Always at nine in winter, and rise at four,' said my host, suppressing a groan, and, as I fancied, by the motion of his arm's shadow, dashing a tear from his eyes.

'Mr Lockwood,' he added, 'you may go into my room. You'll only be in the way, coming downstairs so early; and your childish outcry has sent sleep to the devil for me.'

'And for me too,' I replied. 'I'll walk in the yard till daylight, and then I'll be off; and you need not dread a repetition of my intrusion. I'm now quite cured of seeking pleasure in society, be it country or town. A sensible man ought to find sufficient company in himself.'

'Delightful company!' muttered Heathcliff. 'Take the candle, and go where you please. I shall join you directly. Keep out of the yard, though – the dogs are unchained; and the house – Juno mounts sentinel there, and – nay, you can only ramble about the steps and passages. But away with you! I'll come in two minutes!'

I obeyed, so far as to quit the chamber; when, ignorant where the narrow lobbies led, I stood still, and was witness, involuntarily, to a piece of superstition on the part of my landlord which belied oddly his apparent sense.

He got on to the bed and wrenched open the lattice, bursting, as he pulled at it, into an uncontrollable passion of tears.

'Come in! come in!' he sobbed. 'Cathy, do come! Oh, do – *once* more! Oh! my heart's darling! hear me *this* time, Catherine, at last!'

The spectre showed a spectre's ordinary caprice. It gave no sign of being; but the snow and wind whirled wildly through, even reaching my station, and blowing out the light.

There was such anguish in the gush of grief that accompanied this raving that my compassion made me overlook its folly, and I drew off, half angry to have listened at all, and vexed at having related my ridiculous nightmare, since it produced that agony; though *why* was beyond my comprehension.

I descended cautiously to the lower regions, and landed in the back-kitchen, where a gleam of fire, raked compactly together, enabled me to rekindle my candle.

Nothing was stirring except a brindled, gray cat, which crept from the ashes, and saluted me with a querulous mew.

Two benches, shaped in sections of a circle, nearly enclosed the hearth. On one of these I stretched myself, and Grimalkin mounted the other. We were both of us nodding, ere any one invaded our retreat, and then it was Joseph, shuffling down a wooden ladder that vanished in the roof, through a trap, the ascent to his garret, I suppose.

He cast a sinister look at the little flame which I had enticed to play between the ribs, swept the cat from its elevation, and bestowing himself in the vacancy, commenced the operation of stuffing a three-inch pipe with tobacco. My presence in his sanctum was evidently esteemed a piece of impudence too shameful for remark. He silently applied the tube to his lips, folded his arms, and puffed away.

I let him enjoy the luxury unannoyed; and after sucking out his last wreath, and heaving a profound sigh, he got up, and departed as solemnly as he came.

A more elastic footstep entered next; and now I opened my mouth for a 'good morning,' but closed it again, the salutation unachieved, for Hareton Earnshaw was performing his orisons, *sotto voce*, in a series of curses directed against every object he touched, while he rummaged a corner for a spade or shovel to dig through the drifts. He glanced over the back of the bench, dilating his nostrils, and thought as little of exchanging civilities with me as with my companion the cat.

I guessed by his preparations that egress was allowed, and leaving my hard couch, made a movement to follow him. He noticed this, and thrust at an inner door with the end of his spade, intimating by an inarticulate sound that there was the place where I must go if I changed my locality.

It opened into the house, where the females were already astir, Zillah urging flakes of flame up the chimney with a colossal bellows; and Mrs Heathcliff, kneeling on the hearth, reading a book by the aid of the blaze.

She held her hand interposed between the furnace-heat and her eyes, and seemed absorbed in her occupation; desisting from it only to chide the servant for covering her with sparks, or to push away a dog, now and then, that snoozled its nose over-forwardly into her face.

I was surprised to see Heathcliff there also. He stood by the fire, his back towards me, just finishing a stormy scene to poor Zillah, who ever and anon interrupted her labour to pluck up the corner of her apron and heave an indignant groan.

'And you, you worthless – ' he broke out as I entered, turning to his daughter-in-law, and employing an epithet as harmless as duck or sheep, but generally represented by a dash.

'There you are at your idle tricks again! The rest of them do earn their bread; you live on my charity! Put your trash away, and find something to do. You shall pay me for the plague of having you eternally in my sight. Do you hear, damnable jade?'

'I'll put my trash away, because you can make me if I refuse,' answered the young lady, closing her book and throwing it on a chair. "But I'll not do anything, though you should swear your tongue out, except what I please!'

Heathcliff lifted his hand, and the speaker sprang to a safer distance, obviously acquainted with its weight.

Having no desire to be entertained by a cat and dog combat, I stepped forward briskly, as if eager to partake the warmth of the hearth, and innocent of any knowledge of the interrupted dispute. Each had enough decorum to suspend further hostilities. Heathcliff placed his fists, out of temptation, in his pockets; Mrs Heathcliff curled her lip, and walked to a seat far off, where she kept her word by playing the part of a statue during the remainder of my stay.

That was not long. I declined joining their breakfast, and at the first gleam of dawn took an opportunity of escaping into the free air, now clear, and still, and cold as impalpable ice.

My landlord hallooed for me to stop ere I reached the bottom of the garden, and offered to accompany me across the moor. It was well he did, for the whole hill-back was one billowy, white ocean, the swells and falls not indicating corresponding rises and depressions in the ground. Many pits, at least, were filled to a level, and entire ranges of mounds, the refuse of the quarries, blotted out from the chart which my yesterday's walk left pictured in my mind.

I had remarked on one side of the road, at intervals of six or seven yards, a line of upright stones, continued through the whole length of the barren. These were erected and daubed with lime on purpose to serve as guides in the dark, and also when a fall, like the present, confounded the deep swamps on either hand with the firmer path; but, excepting a dirty dot pointing up here and there, all traces of their existence had vanished, and my companion found it necessary to warn me frequently to steer to the right or left, when I imagined I was following correctly the windings of the road.

We exchanged little conversation, and he halted at the entrance of Thrushcross Park, saying I could make no error there. Our adieux were limited to a hasty bow, and then I pushed forward, trusting to my own resources, for the porter's lodge is untenanted as yet.

The distance from the gate to the Grange is two miles; I believe I managed to make it four, what with losing myself among the trees, and sinking up to the neck in snow, a predicament which only those who have experienced it can appreciate. At any rate, whatever were my wanderings, the clock chimed twelve as I entered the house, and that gave exactly an hour for every mile of the usual way from Wuthering Heights.

My human fixture and her satellites rushed to welcome me, exclaiming tumultuously they had completely given me up. Everybody conjectured that I perished last night, and they were wondering how they must set about the search for my remains.

I bid them be quiet, now that they saw me returned, and, benumbed to my very heart, I dragged upstairs; whence, after putting on dry clothes, and pacing to and fro thirty or forty minutes, to restore the animal heat, I am adjourned to my study, feeble as a kitten, almost too much so to enjoy the cheerful fire and smoking coffee which the servant has prepared for my refreshment.

[Chapter 4: Over breakfast the next morning, Mr Lockwood begis to learn the history of the Earnshaws of Wuthering Heights and the Lintons of Thrushcross Grange, and how years ago old Mr Earnshaw had returned from a business trip to Liverpool with a waif he had picked up on the streets. The waif was Heathcliff, and he soon struck up a close relationship with Catherine Earnshaw, the daughter of the house, and an equally hostile relationship with Hindley Earnshaw, the son.]

Chapter 5

[Mrs Deans tells Mr Lockwood.]

'In the course of time, Mr Earnshaw began to fail. He had been active and healthy, yet his strength left him suddenly; and when he was confined to the chimney-corner he grew grievously irritable. A nothing vexed him, and suspected slights of his authority nearly threw him into fits.

This was especially to be remarked if any one attempted to impose upon, or domineer over, his favourite: he was painfully jealous lest a word should be spoken amiss to him, seeming to have got into his head the notion that, because he liked Heathcliff, all hated, and longed to do him an ill-turn.

It was a disadvantage to the lad, for the kinder among us did not wish to fret the master, so we humoured his partiality; and that humouring was rich nourishment to the child's pride and black tempers. Still it became in a manner necessary; twice, or thrice, Hindley's manifestations of scorn, while his father was near, roused the old man to a fury. He seized his stick to strike him, and shook with rage that he could not do it.

At last, our curate (we had a curate then who made the living answer by teaching the little Lintons and Earnshaws, and farming his bit of land himself), he advised that the young man should be sent to college, and Mr Earnshaw agreed, though with a heavy spirit, for he said –

"Hindley was naught, and would never thrive as where he wandered."

I hoped heartily we should have peace now. It hurt me to think the master should be made uncomfortable by his own good deed. I fancied the discontent of age and disease arose from his family disagreements, as he would have it that it did. Really, you know, sir, it was in his sinking frame.

We might have got on tolerably, notwithstanding, but for two people, Miss Cathy and Joseph the servant. You saw him, I dare say, up yonder. He was, and is yet most likely, the wearisomest self-righteous pharisee that ever ransacked a Bible to rake the promises to himself and fling the curses on his neighbours. By his knack of sermonizing and pious discoursing he contrived to make a great impression on Mr Earnshaw; and the more feeble the master became, the more influence he gained.

He was relentless in worrying him about his soul's concerns, and about ruling his children rigidly. He encouraged him to regard Hindley as a reprobate; and night after night he regularly grumbled out a long string of tales against Heathcliff and Catherine, always minding to flatter Earnshaw's weakness by heaping the heaviest blame on the latter.

Certainly she had ways with her such as I never saw a child take up before; and she put all of us past our patience fifty times and oftener in a day. From the hour she came downstairs till the hour she went to bed we had not a moment's security that she wouldn't be in mischief. Her spirits were always at high-water mark, her tongue always going – singing, laughing, and plaguing everybody who would not do the same. A wild, wicked slip she was; but she had the bonniest eye, and sweetest smile, and lightest foot in the parish. And, after all, I believe she meant no harm; for when once she made you cry in good earnest, it seldom happened that she would not keep you company, and oblige you to be quiet, that you might comfort her.

She was much too fond of Heathcliff. The greatest punishment we could invent for her was to keep her separate from him; yet she got chided more than any of us on his account.

In play she liked exceedingly to act the little mistress, using her hands freely, and commanding her companions. She did so to me, but I would not bear slapping and ordering, and so I let her know.

Now, Mr Earnshaw did not understand jokes from his children. He had always been strict and grave with them; and Catherine, on her part, had no idea why her father should be crosser and less patient in his ailing condition, than he was in his prime.

His peevish reproofs wakened in her a naughty delight to provoke him. She was never so happy as when we were all scolding her at once, and she defying us with her bold, saucy look and her ready words, turning Joseph's religious curses into ridicule, baiting me, and doing just what her father hated most, showing how her pretended insolence, which he thought real, had more power over Heathcliff than his kindness; how the boy would do *her* bidding in anything, and *his* only when it suited his own inclination.

After behaving as badly as possible all day, she sometimes came fondling to make it up at night.

"Nay, Cathy," the old man would say, "I cannot love thee; thou'rt worse than thy brother. Go say thy prayers, child, and ask God's pardon. I doubt thy mother and I must rue that we ever reared thee!"

That made her cry at first; and then being repulsed continually hardened her, and she laughed if I told her to say she was sorry for her faults, and beg to be forgiven.

But the hour came at last that ended Mr Earnshaw's troubles on earth. He died quietly in his chair one October evening, seated by the fireside.

A high wind blustered round the house and roared in the chimney. It sounded wild and stormy, yet it was not cold, and we were all together – I, a little removed from the hearth, busy at my knitting, and Joseph reading his Bible near the table (for the servants generally sat in the house then, after their work was done). Miss Cathy had been sick, and that made her still. She leant against her father's knee, and Heathcliff was lying on the floor with his head in her lap.

I remember the master, before he fell into a doze, stroking her bonny hair – it pleased him rarely to see her gentle – and saying –

"Why canst thou not always be a good lass, Cathy?"

And she turned her face up to his, and laughed, and answered –

"Why cannot you always be a good man, father?"

But as soon as she saw him vexed again, she kissed his hand, and said she would sing him to sleep. She began singing very low, till his fingers dropped from hers, and his head sank on his breast. Then I told her to hush, and not stir, for fear she should wake him. We all kept as mute as mice a full half hour, and should have done longer, only Joseph, having finished his chapter, got up and said that he must rouse the master for prayers and bed. He stepped forward, and called him by name, and touched his shoulder, but he would not move – so he took the candle and looked at him.

I thought there was something wrong as he set down the light; and seizing the children each by an arm, whispered them to "frame upstairs,[1] and make little din – they might pray alone that evening – he had summut to do."

"I shall bid father good-night first," said Catherine, putting her arms round his neck, before we could hinder her.

The poor thing discovered her loss directly – she screamed out –

"Oh, he's dead, Heathcliff! he's dead!"

And they both set up a heart-breaking cry.

I joined my wail to theirs, loud and bitter; but Joseph asked what we could be thinking of to roar in that way over a saint in heaven.

He told me to put on my cloak and run to Gimmerton for the doctor and the parson. I could not guess the use that either would be of, then. However, I went, through wind and rain, and brought one, the doctor, back with me; the other said he would come in the morning.

Leaving Joseph to explain matters, I ran to the children's room; their door was ajar, I saw they had never laid down, though it was past midnight; but they were calmer, and did not need me to console them. The little souls were comforting each other with better thoughts than I could have hit on; no parson in the world ever pictured heaven so beautifully as they did, in their innocent talk; and, while I sobbed and listened, I could not help wishing we were all there safe together.'

[Hindley returns for his father's funeral with a wife, an empty-headed woman. He banishes Heathcliff from the house, returning him to his 'proper' station as a labourer. The affection between Catherine and Heathcliff intensifies, although both are wild spirits. One night, Cathy and Heathcliff are peering through the windows of Thrushcross Grange at an adult party when they are attacked by a dog. Catherine is bitten on the ankle and taken indoors. Heathcliff runs home.]

Chapter 7

'Cathy stayed at Thrushcross Grange five weeks, till Christmas. By that time her ankle was thoroughly cured, and her manners much improved. The mistress visited her often, in the interval, and commenced her plan of reform by trying to raise her self-respect with fine clothes and flattery, which she took readily: so that, instead of a wild, hatless little savage jumping into the house, and rushing to squeeze us all breathless, there lighted from a handsome black pony a very dignified person, with brown ringlets falling from the cover of a feathered beaver, and a long cloth habit which she was obliged to hold up with both hands that she might sail in.

Hindley lifted her from her horse, exclaiming delightedly,

"Why, Cathy, you are quite a beauty! I should scarcely have known you – you look like a lady now – Isabella Linton is not to be compared with her, is she, Frances?"

1: dialectal usage, to make an effort, in this sense 'to go'.

"Isabella has not her natural advantages," replied his wife, "but she must mind and not grow wild again here. Ellen, help Miss Catherine off with her things – Stay, dear, you will disarrange your curls – let me untie your hat."

I removed the habit, and there shone forth beneath, a grand plaid silk frock, white trousers, and burnished shoes; and, while her eyes sparkled joyfully when the dogs came bounding up to welcome her, she dare hardly touch them lest they should fawn upon her splendid garments.

She kissed me gently, I was all flour making the Christmas cake, and it would not have done to give me a hug; and then she looked round for Heathcliff. Mr and Mrs Earnshaw watched anxiously their meeting, thinking it would enable them to judge, in some measure, what grounds they had for hoping to succeed in separating the two friends.

Heathcliff was hard to discover at first. If he were careless and uncared for before Catherine's absence, he had been ten times more so since.

Nobody but I even did him the kindness to call him a dirty boy, and bid him wash himself, once a week; and children of his age seldom have a natural pleasure in soap and water. Therefore, not to mention his clothes, which had seen three months' service in mire and dust, and his thick uncombed hair, the surface of his face and hands was dismally beclouded. He might well skulk behind the settle, on beholding such a bright, graceful damsel enter the house, instead of a rough-headed counterpart to himself, as he expected.

"Is Heathcliff not here?" she demanded, pulling off her gloves, and displaying fingers wonderfully whitened with doing nothing and staying indoors.

"Heathcliff, you may come forward," cried Mr Hindley, enjoying his discomfiture, and gratified to see what a forbidding young blackguard he would be compelled to present himself. "You may come and wish Miss Catherine welcome, like the other servants."

Cathy, catching a glimpse of her friend in his concealment, flew to embrace him. She bestowed seven or eight kisses on his cheek within the second, and then stopped, and drawing back, burst into a laugh, exclaiming,

"Why, how very black and cross you look! and how – how funny and grim! But that's because I'm used to Edgar and Isabella Linton. Well, Heathcliff, have you forgotten me?"

She had some reason to put the question, for shame and pride threw double gloom over his countenance, and kept him immovable.

"Shake hands, Heathcliff," said Mr Earnshaw, condescendingly; "once in a way, that is permitted."

"I shall not," replied the boy, finding his tongue at last; "I shall not stand to be laughed at, I shall not bear it."

And he would have broken from the circle, but Miss Cathy seized him again.

"I did not mean to laugh at you," she said; "I could not hinder myself. Heathcliff, shake hands at least! What are you sulky for? It was only that you looked odd. If you wash your face and brush your hair it will be all right; but you are so dirty!"

She gazed concernedly at the dusky fingers she held in her own, and also at her dress, which she feared had gained no embellishment from its contact with his.

"You needn't have touched me," he answered, following her eye and snatching away his hand. "I shall be as dirty as I please; and I like to be dirty, and I will be dirty."

With that he dashed head foremost out of the room, amid the merriment of the master and mistress, and to the serious disturbance of Catherine, who could not comprehend how her remarks should have produced such an exhibition of bad temper.

After playing lady's maid to the new comer, and putting my cakes in the oven, and making the house and kitchen cheerful with great fires, befitting Christmas Eve, I prepared to sit down and amuse myself by singing carols all alone, regardless of Joseph's affirmations that he considered the merry tunes I chose as next door to songs.

He had retired to private prayer in his chamber, and Mr and Mrs Earnshaw were engaging Missy's attention by sundry gay trifles bought for her to present to the little Lintons, as an acknowledgment of their kindness.

They had invited them to spend the morrow at Wuthering Heights, and the invitation had been accepted, on one condition. Mrs Linton begged that her darlings might be kept carefully apart from that "naughty, swearing boy."

Under these circumstances I remained solitary. I smelt the rich scent of the heating spices, and admired the shining kitchen utensils, the polished clock, decked in holly, the silver mugs ranged on a tray ready to be filled with mulled ale for supper, and, above all, the speckless purity of my particular care – the scoured and well-swept floor.

I gave due inward applause to every object, and then I remembered how old Earnshaw used to come in when all was tidied, and call me a cant lass, and slip a shilling into my hand as a Christmas box; and from that I went on to think of his fondness for Heathcliff, and his dread lest he should suffer neglect after death had removed him; and that naturally led me to consider the poor lad's situation now, and from singing I changed my mind to crying. It struck me soon, however, there would be more sense in endeavouring to repair some of his wrongs than shedding tears over them. I got up and walked into the court to seek him.

He was not far. I found him smoothing the glossy coat of the new pony in the stable, and feeding the other beasts, according to custom.

"Make haste, Heathcliff!" I said; "the kitchen is so comfortable, and Joseph is upstairs. Make haste, and let me dress you smart before Miss Cathy comes out, and then you can sit together, with the whole hearth to yourselves, and have a long chatter till bedtime."

He proceeded with his task, and never turned his head towards me.

"Come – are you coming?" I continued. "There's a little cake for each of you, nearly enough; and you'll need half an hour's donning."

I waited five minutes, but getting no answer left him . . . . Catherine supped with her brother and sister-in-law. Joseph and I joined at an unsociable meal, seasoned with reproofs on one side and sauciness on the other. His cake and cheese remained on the table all night for the fairies. He managed to continue work till nine o'clock, and then marched dumb and dour to his chamber.

Cathy sat up late, having a world of things to order for the reception of her new friends. She came into the kitchen once to speak to her old one; but he was gone, and she only stayed to ask what was the matter with him, and then went back.

In the morning he rose early; and as it was a holiday carried his ill-humour on to the moors, not reappearing till the family were departed for church. Fasting and reflection seemed to have brought him to a better spirit. He hung about me for a while, and having screwed up his courage, exclaimed abruptly,

"Nelly, make me decent; I'm going to be good."

"High time, Heathcliff," I said; "you have grieved Catherine. She's sorry she ever came home, I dare say. It looks as if you envied her because she is more thought of than you."

The notion of *envying* Catherine was incomprehensible to him, but the notion of grieving her he understood clearly enough.

"Did she say she was grieved?" he inquired, looking very serious.

"She cried when I told her you were off again this morning."

"Well, *I* cried last night," he returned, "and I had more reason to cry than she."

"Yes, you had the reason of going to bed with a proud heart and an empty stomach," said I. "Proud people breed sad sorrows for themselves. But, if you be ashamed of your touchiness, you must ask pardon, mind, when she comes in. You must go up and offer to kiss her, and say – you know best what to say; only do it heartily, and not as if you thought her converted into a stranger by her grand dress. And now, though I have dinner to get ready, I'll steal time to arrange you so that Edgar Linton shall look quite a doll beside you; and that he does. You are younger, and yet, I'll be bound, you are taller and twice as broad across the shoulders. You could knock him down in a twinkling. Don't you feel that you could?"

Heathcliff's face brightened a moment; then it was overcast afresh, and he sighed.

"But, Nelly, if I knocked him down twenty times, that wouldn't make him less handsome or me more so. I wish I had light hair and a fair skin, and was dressed and behaved as well, and had a chance of being as rich as he will be!"

"And cried for mamma at every turn," I added, "and trembled if a country lad heaved his fist against you, and sat at home all day for a shower of rain. Oh, Heathcliff, you are showing a poor spirit! Come to the glass, and I'll let you see what you should wish. Do you mark those two lines between your eyes; and those thick brows that, instead of rising arched, sink in the middle; and that couple of black fiends, so deeply buried, who never open their windows boldly, but lurk glinting under them, like devil's spies? Wish and learn to smooth away the surly wrinkles, to raise your lids frankly, and change the fiends to confident, innocent angels, suspecting and doubting nothing, and always seeing friends where they are not sure of foes. Don't get the expression of a vicious cur that appears to know the kicks it gets are its desert, and yet hates all the world as well as the kicker for what it suffers."

"In other words, I must wish for Edgar Linton's great blue eyes and even forehead," he replied. "I do, and that won't help me to them."

"A good heart will help you to a bonny face, my lad," I continued, "if you were a regular black; and a bad one will turn the bonniest into something worse than ugly. And now that we've done washing, and combing, and sulking, tell me whether you don't think yourself rather handsome? I'll tell you I do. You're fit for a prince in disguise. Who knows but your father was Emperor of China, and your mother an Indian queen, each of them able to buy up, with one week's income, Wuthering Heights and Thrushcross Grange together? And you were kidnapped by wicked sailors and brought to England. Were I in your place, I would frame high notions of my birth; and the thoughts of what I was should give me courage and dignity to support the oppressions of a little farmer!"

So I chattered on; and Heathcliff gradually lost his frown and began to look quite pleasant; when all at once our conversation was interrupted by a rumbling sound moving up the road and entering the court. He ran to the window and I to the door, just in time to behold the two Lintons descend from the family carriage, smothered in cloaks and furs, and the Earnshaws dismount from their horses. They often rode to church in winter. Catherine took a hand of each of the children, and brought them into the house and set them before the fire, which quickly put colour into their white faces.

I urged my companion to hasten now and show his amiable humour, and he willingly obeyed; but ill luck would have it that, as he opened the door leading from the kitchen on one side, Hindley opened it on the other. They met, and the master, irritated at seeing him clean and cheerful, or, perhaps, eager to keep his promise to Mrs Linton, shoved him back with a sudden thrust, and angrily bade Joseph "keep the fellow out of the room; send him into the garret till dinner is over. He'll be cramming his fingers in the tarts and stealing the fruit, if left alone with them a minute."

"Nay, sir," I could not avoid answering; "he'll touch nothing – not he; and I suppose he must have his share of the dainties as well as we."

"He shall have his share of my hand if I catch him downstairs again till dark," cried Hindley –"Begone, you vagabond! What! you are attempting the coxcomb, are you? Wait till I get hold of those elegant locks; see if I won't pull them a bit longer."

"They are long enough already," observed Master Linton, peeping from the doorway; "I wonder they don't make his head ache. It's like a colt's mane over his eyes."

He ventured this remark without any intention to insult; but Heathcliff's violent nature was not prepared to endure the appearance of impertinence from one whom he seemed to hate, even then, as a rival. He seized a tureen of hot apple sauce – the first thing that came under his gripe – and dashed it full against the speaker's face and neck, who instantly commenced a lament that brought Isabella and Catherine hurrying to the place.

Mr Earnshaw snatched up the culprit directly, and conveyed him to his chamber, where, doubtless, he administered a rough remedy to cool the fit of passion, for he appeared red and breathless. I got the dish-cloth, and rather spitefully scrubbed Edgar's nose and mouth, affirming it served him right for meddling. His sister began weeping to go home, and Cathy stood by confounded, blushing for all.

"You should not have spoken to him!" she expostulated with Master Linton. "He was in a bad temper; and now you've spoilt your visit, and he'll be flogged.

I hate him to be flogged. I can't eat my dinner. Why did you speak to him, Edgar?"

"I didn't," sobbed the youth, escaping from my hands and finishing the remainder of the purification with his cambric pocket-handkerchief. "I promised mamma that I wouldn't say one word to him, and I didn't."

"Well, don't cry," replied Catherine contemptuously; "you're not killed. Don't make more mischief. My brother is coming; be quiet! – Hush, Isabella! Has anybody hurt *you*?"

"There, there, children – to your seats," cried Hindley, bustling in. "That brute of a lad has warmed me nicely. Next time, Master Edgar, take the law into your own fists; it will give you an appetite!"

The little party recovered its equanimity at sight of the fragrant feast. They were hungry after their ride, and easily consoled, since no real harm had befallen them.

Mr Earnshaw carved bountiful platefuls, and the mistress made them merry with lively talk. I waited behind her chair, and was pained to behold Catherine, with dry eyes and an indifferent air, commence cutting up the wing of a goose before her.

"An unfeeling child," I thought to myself; "how lightly she dismisses her old playmate's troubles! I could not have imagined her to be so selfish."

She lifted a mouthful to her lips, then she set it down again; her cheeks flushed, and the tears gushed over them. She slipped her fork to the floor, and hastily dived under the cloth to conceal her emotion. I did not call her unfeeling long, for I perceived she was in purgatory throughout the day, and wearying to find an opportunity of getting by herself, or paying a visit to Heathcliff, who had been locked up by the master, as I discovered, on endeavouring to introduce to him a private mess of victuals.

In the evening we had a dance. Cathy begged that he might be liberated then, as Isabella Linton had no partner. Her entreaties were vain, and I was appointed to supply the deficiency.

We got rid of all gloom in the excitement of the exercise, and our pleasure was increased by the arrival of the Gimmerton band, mustering fifteen strong – a trumpet, a trombone, clarionets, bassoons, French horns, and a bass viol, besides singers. They go the rounds of all the respectable houses, and receive contributions every Christmas, and we esteemed it a first-rate treat to hear them.

After the usual carols had been sung, we set them to songs and glees. Mrs Earnshaw loved the music, and so they gave us plenty.

Catherine loved it too, but she said it sounded sweetest at the top of the steps, and she went up in the dark; I followed. They shut the house door below, never noting our absence, it was so full of people. She made no stay at the stairs' head, but mounted farther to the garret where Heathcliff was confined, and called him. He stubbornly declined answering for a while; she persevered, and finally persuaded him to hold communion with her through the boards.

I let the poor things converse unmolested, till I supposed the songs were going to cease, and the singers to get some refreshment; then I clambered up the ladder to warn her.

Instead of finding her outside, I heard her voice within. The little monkey had crept by the skylight of one garret, along the roof, into the skylight of the other, and it was with the utmost difficulty I could coax her out again.

When she did come, Heathcliff came with her, and she insisted that I should take him into the kitchen, as my fellow-servant had gone to a neighbour's to be removed from the sound of our "devil's psalmody," as it pleased him to call it. I told them I intended by no means to encourage their tricks, but as the prisoner had never broken his fast since yesterday's dinner, I would wink at his cheating Mr Hindley that once.

He went down; I set him a stool by the fire, and offered him a quantity of good things; but he was sick, and could eat little, and my attempts to entertain him were thrown away. He leant his two elbows on his knees, and his chin on his hands, and remained wrapt in dumb meditation.

On my inquiring the subject of his thoughts he answered gravely, –

"I'm trying to settle how I shall pay Hindley back. I don't care how long I wait, if I can only do it at last. I hope he will not die before I do!"

"For shame, Heathcliff!" said I. "It is for God to punish wicked people; we should learn to forgive."

"No; God won't have the satisfaction that I shall," he returned. "I only wish I knew the best way! Let me alone, and I'll plan it out; while I'm thinking of that I don't feel pain."

But, Mr Lockwood, I forget these tales cannot divert you. I'm annoyed how I should dream of chattering on at such a rate, and your gruel cold, and you nodding for bed! I could have told Heathcliff's history – all that you need hear – in half a dozen words.'

Thus interrupting herself, the housekeeper rose and proceeded to lay aside her sewing; but I felt incapable of moving from the hearth, and I was very far from nodding.

'Sit still, Mrs Dean,' I cried, 'do sit still another half hour! You've done just right to tell the story leisurely – that is the method I like; and you must finish it in the same style. I am interested in every character you have mentioned, more or less.'

'The clock is on the stroke of eleven, sir.'

'No matter. I'm not accustomed to go to bed in the long hours. One or two is early enough for a person who lies till ten.'

'You shouldn't lie till ten. There's the very prime of the morning gone long before that time. A person who has not done one half his day's work by ten o'clock, runs a chance of leaving the other half undone.'

'Nevertheless, Mrs Dean, resume your chair, because to-morrow I intend lengthening the night till afternoon. I prognosticate for myself an obstinate cold, at least.'

'I hope not, sir. Well, you must allow me to leap over some three years. During that space Mrs Earnshaw – '

'No, no; I'll allow nothing of the sort! Are you acquainted with the mood of mind in which, if you were seated alone, and the cat licking its kitten on the rug before you, you would watch the operation so intently that puss's neglect of one ear would put you seriously out of temper?'

'A terribly lazy mood, I should say.'

'On the contrary, a tiresomely active one. It is mine at present; and, therefore, continue minutely. I perceive that people in these regions acquire over people in towns the value that a spider in a dungeon does over a spider in a cottage, to their various occupants; and yet the deepened attraction is not entirely owing to the situation of the looker-on. They *do* live more in earnest, more in themselves, and less in surface, change, and frivolous external things. I could fancy a love for life here almost possible; and I was a fixed unbeliever in any love of a year's standing. One state resembles setting a hungry man down to a single dish, on which he may concentrate his entire appetite and do it justice; the other, introducing him to a table laid out by French cooks. He can perhaps extract as much enjoyment from the whole, but each part is a mere atom in his regard and remembrance.'

'Oh, here we are the same as anywhere else, when you get to know us,' observed Mrs Dean, somewhat puzzled at my speech.

'Excuse me,' I responded. 'You, my good friend, are a striking evidence against that assertion. Excepting a few provincialisms of slight consequence, you have no marks of the manners which I am habituated to consider as peculiar to your class. I am sure you have thought a great deal more than the generality of servants think. You have been compelled to cultivate your reflective faculties, for want of occasions for frittering your life away in silly trifles.'

Mrs Dean laughed.

'I certainly esteem myself a steady, reasonable kind of body,' she said, 'not exactly from living among the hills and seeing one set of faces and one series of actions from year's end to year's end, but I have undergone sharp discipline, which has taught me wisdom; and then, I have read more than you would fancy, Mr Lockwood. You could not open a book in this library that I have not looked into, and got something out of also – unless it be that range of Greek and Latin, and that of French; and those I know one from another. It is as much as you can expect of a poor man's daughter.

'However, if I am to follow my story in true gossip's fashion, I had better go on; and instead of leaping three years, I will be content to pass to the next summer – the summer of 1778; that is nearly twenty-three years ago.'

[Hindley Earnshaw's wife, Frances, gives birth to a son, Hareton, and dies of consumption. Heathcliff overhears Catherine telling Nelly that she could not marry him because it would degrade her and leaves too soon to hear her confess her passion for him. In his absence, Catherine marries Edgar Linton, a dullard. Hindley's irascible and dissolute temperament worsens and he becomes a drunken gambler. After three years, Heathcliff returns, having miraculously enriched himself in the colonies, and marries Isabella Linton, Edgar's sister, as the first step in a campaign to wreak vengeance on all the Lintons and Earnshaws. Catherine is torn by her love for him, his unkindness, and the cold manners of her dull husband. As she gives birth to a daughter, Catherine, she dies of a fever induced by these strains. Heathcliff has a son, Linton. He progressively destroys Hindley and Edgar, brings all the children under his control, brutalises Hareton to pay back his father's crimes and marries Catherine to his son Linton to secure all the property. Young Linton then dies, leaving Heathcliff with Catherine and Hareton whom she is trying to educate.]

Chapter 33

'On the morrow of that Monday, Earnshaw being still unable to follow his ordinary employments, and, therefore, remaining about the house, I speedily found it would be impracticable to retain my charge beside me, as heretofore.

She got downstairs before me, and out into the garden, where she had seen her cousin performing some easy work; and when I went to bid them come to breakfast, I saw she had persuaded him to clear a large space of ground from currant and gooseberry bushes, and they were busy planning together an importation of plants from the Grange.

I was terrified at the devastation which had been accomplished in a brief half hour; the black currant trees were the apple of Joseph's eye, and she had just fixed her choice of a flower bed in the midst of them!

"There! That will be all shewn to the master," I exclaimed, "the minute it is discovered. And what excuse have you to offer for taking such liberties with the garden? We shall have a fine explosion on the head of it: see if we don't! Mr Hareton, I wonder you should have no more wit, than to go and make that mess at her bidding!"

"I'd forgotten they were Joseph's," answered Earnshaw, rather puzzled, "but I'll tell him I did it."

We always ate our meals with Mr Heathcliff. I held the mistress's post in making tea and carving; so I was indispensable at table. Catherine usually sat by me; but to-day she stole nearer to Hareton, and I presently saw she would have no more discretion in her friendship, than she had in her hostility.

"Now, mind you don't talk with and notice your cousin too much," were my whispered instructions as we entered the room.

"It will certainly annoy Mr Heathcliff, and he'll be mad at you both."

"I'm not going to," she answered.

The minute after, she had sidled to him, and was sticking primroses in his plate of porridge.

He dared not speak to her there; he dared hardly look; and yet she went on teasing, till he was twice on the point of being provoked to laugh. I frowned, and then she glanced toward the master, whose mind was occupied on other subjects than his company, as his countenance evinced; and she grew serious for an instant, scrutinising him with deep gravity. Afterwards she turned and recommenced her nonsense. At last Hareton uttered a smothered laugh.

Mr Heathcliff started; his eye rapidly surveyed our faces. Catherine met it with her accustomed look of nervousness and yet defiance, which he abhorred.

"It is well you are out of my reach," he exclaimed. "What fiend possesses you to stare back at me continually with those infernal eyes? Down with them! and don't remind me of your existence again. I thought I had cured you of laughing."

"It was me," muttered Hareton.

"What do you say?" demanded the master.

Hareton looked at his plate, and did not repeat the confession. Mr Heathcliff looked at him a bit, and then silently resumed his breakfast and his interrupted musing.

We had nearly finished, and the two young people prudently shifted wider asunder, so I anticipated no further disturbance during that sitting; when Joseph appeared at the door, revealing by his quivering lip and furious eyes that the outrage committed on his precious shrubs was detected.

He must have seen Cathy and her cousin about the spot before he examined it, for while his jaws worked like those of a cow chewing its cud, and rendered his speech difficult to understand, he began:

"I mun hev my wage, and I mun goa! I *hed* aimed to dee wheare I'd sarved fur sixty years, and I thowt I'd lug my books up into t' garret, and all my bits o' stuff, and they sud hev t' kitchen to theirseln, for t' sake o' quietness. It wur hard to gie up my awn hearthstun, but I thowt I *could* do that. But nah; shoo's taan my garden fro' me, and by th' heart, maister, I cannot stand it. Yah may bend to th' yoak, and ye will; *I* noan used to't, and an old man doesn't sooin get used to new barthens. I'd rayther arn my bite an' my sup wi' a hammer in th' road!"

"Now, now, idiot," interrupted Heathcliff, "cut it short! What's your grievance? I'll interfere in no quarrels between you and Nelly. She may thrust you into the coal-hole for anything I care."

"It's noan Nelly," answered Joseph. "I sudn't shift for Nelly, nasty ill nowt as shoo is. Thank God! *shoo* cannot stale t' sowl o' nob'dy! Shoo wer niver soa handsome but what a body mud look at her 'bout winking. It's yon flaysome, graceless quean that's witched our lad wi' her bold een and her forrard ways – till – Nay, it fair brusts my heart! He's forgotten all I've done for him, and made on him, and goan and riven up a whole row o' t' grandest currant trees i' t' garden!" And here he lamented outright, unmanned by a sense of his bitter injuries and Earnshaw's ingratitude and dangerous condition.

"Is the fool drunk?" asked Mr Heathcliff. – "Hareton, is it you he's finding fault with?"

"I've pulled up two or three bushes," replied the young man, "but I'm going to set 'em again."

"And why have you pulled them up?" said the master.

Catherine wisely put in her tongue.

"We wanted to plant some flowers there," she cried. "I'm the only person to blame, for I wished him to do it."

"And who the devil gave *you* leave to touch a stick about the place?" demanded her father-in-law, much surprised – "And who ordered *you* to obey her?" he added, turning to Hareton.

The latter was speechless. His cousin replied, –

"You shouldn't grudge a few yards of earth for me to ornament, when you have taken all my land!"

"Your land, insolent slut! You never had any," said Heathcliff.

"And my money," she continued, returning his angry glare, and meantime biting a piece of crust, the remnant of her breakfast.

"Silence!" he exclaimed. "Get done, and begone!"

"And Hareton's land, and his money," pursued the reckless thing. "Hareton and I are friends now, and I shall tell him all about you!"

The master seemed confounded a moment. He grew pale and rose up, eyeing her all the while with an expression of mortal hate.

"If you strike me, Hareton will strike you," she said, "so you may as well sit down."

"If Hareton does not turn you out of the room I'll strike him to hell," thundered Heathcliff. "Damnable witch! dare you pretend to rouse him against me? – Off with her! Do you hear? Fling her into the kitchen! – I'll kill her, Ellen Dean, if you let her come into my sight again!"

Hareton tried, under his breath, to persuade her to go.

"Drag her away!" he cried savagely. "Are you staying to talk?" And he approached to execute his own command.

"He'll not obey you, wicked man, any more!" said Catherine, "and he'll soon detest you as much as I do!"

"Wisht! wisht!" muttered the young man reproachfully. "I will not hear you speak so to him. Have done."

"But you won't let him strike me?" she cried.

"Come, then," he whispered earnestly.

It was too late. Heathcliff had caught hold of her.

"Now, *you* go!" he said to Earnshaw. "Accursed witch! this time she has provoked me when I could not bear it, and I'll make her repent it for ever!"

He had his hand in her hair. Hareton attempted to release her locks, entreating him not to hurt her that once. Heathcliff's black eyes flashed – he seemed ready to tear Catherine in pieces; and I was just worked up to risk coming to the rescue, when of a sudden his fingers relaxed; he shifted his grasp from her head to her arm, and gazed intently in her face. Then he drew his hand over her eyes, stood a moment to collect himself apparently, and turning anew to Catherine, said with assumed calmness,

"You must learn to avoid putting me in a passion, or I shall really murder you some time! Go with Mrs Dean, and keep with her, and confine your insolence to her ears. As to Hareton Earnshaw, if I see him listen to you I'll send him seeking his bread where he can get it! Your love will make him an outcast and a beggar. – Nelly, take her; and leave me, all of you! – leave me!"

I led my young lady out. She was too glad of her escape to resist. The other followed, and Mr Heathcliff had the room to himself till dinner.

I had counselled Catherine to get hers upstairs, but as soon as he perceived her vacant seat he sent me to call her. He spoke to none of us, ate very little, and went out directly afterwards, intimating that he should not return before evening.

The two friends established themselves in the house during his absence, when I heard Hareton sternly check his cousin on her offering a revelation of her father-in-law's conduct to his father.

He said he wouldn't suffer a word to be uttered in his disparagement; if he were the devil, it didn't signify – he would stand by him; and he'd rather she would abuse himself, as she used to, than begin on Mr Heathcliff.

Catherine was waxing cross at this; but he found means to make her hold her tongue by asking how she would like *him* to speak ill of her father? Then she comprehended that Earnshaw took the master's reputation home to himself, and was attached by ties stronger than reason could break – chains forged by habit, which it would be cruel to attempt to loosen.

She showed a good heart, thenceforth, in avoiding both complaints and expressions of antipathy concerning Heathcliff; and confessed to me her sorrow that she had endeavoured to raise a bad spirit between him and Hareton. Indeed, I don't believe she has ever breathed a syllable, in the latter's hearing, against her oppressor since.

When this slight disagreement was over, they were thick again, and as busy as possible in their several occupations of pupil and teacher. I came in to sit with them after I had done my work, and I felt so soothed and comforted to watch them that I did not notice how time got on. You know they both appeared in a measure my children. I had long been proud of one, and now I was sure the other would be a source of equal satisfaction. His honest, warm, and intelligent nature shook off rapidly the clouds of ignorance and degradation in which it had been bred; and Catherine's sincere commendations acted as a spur to his industry. His brightening mind brightened his features, and added spirit and nobility to their aspect. I could hardly fancy it the same individual I had beheld on the day I discovered my little lady at Wuthering Heights, after her expedition to the Crags.

While I admired and they laboured, dusk grew on, and with it returned the master. He came upon us quite unexpectedly, entering by the front way, and had a full view of the whole three ere we could raise our heads to glance at him.

Well, I reflected, there was never a pleasanter or more harmless sight, and it will be a burning shame to scold them. The red firelight glowed on their two bonny heads, and revealed their faces animated with the eager interest of children; for though he was twenty-three and she eighteen, each had so much of novelty to feel and learn that neither experienced nor evinced the sentiments of sober, disenchanted maturity.

They lifted their eyes together, to encounter Mr Heathcliff. Perhaps you have never remarked that their eyes are precisely similar, and they are those of Catherine Earnshaw. The present Catherine has no other likeness to her, except a breadth of forehead and a certain arch of the nostril that makes her appear rather haughty, whether she will or not. With Hareton the resemblance is carried further. It is singular at all times; then it was particularly striking, because his senses were alert, and his mental faculties wakened to unwonted activity.

I suppose this resemblance disarmed Mr Heathcliff. He walked to the hearth in evident agitation, but it quickly subsided as he looked at the young man; or, I should say, altered its character, for it was there yet.

He took the book from his hand and glanced at the open page, then returned it without any observation, merely signing Catherine away. Her companion lingered very little behind her; and I was about to depart also, but he bade me sit still.

"It is a poor conclusion, is it not?" he observed, having brooded a while on the scene he had just witnessed – "an absurd termination to my violent exertions? I get levers and mattocks to demolish the two houses, and train myself to be capable of working like Hercules, and when everything is ready and in my power I find the will to lift a slate of either roof has vanished! My old enemies have not beaten me. Now would be the precise time to revenge myself on their representatives. I could do it, and none could hinder me. But where is the use? I don't care for striking; I can't take the trouble to raise my hand. That sounds as if I had been labouring the whole time only to exhibit a fine trait of magnanimity. It is far from being the case. I have lost the faculty of enjoying their destruction, and I am too idle to destroy for nothing."

"Nelly, there is a strange change approaching; I'm in its shadow at present. I take so little interest in my daily life that I hardly remember to eat and drink. Those two who have left the room are the only objects which retain a distinct material appearance to me; and that appearance causes me pain, amounting to agony. About *her* I won't speak, and I don't desire to think, but I earnestly wish she were invisible. Her presence invokes only maddening sensations. *He* moves me differently; and yet if I could do it without seeming insane, I'd never see him again! You'll perhaps think me rather inclined to become so," he added, making an effort to smile, "if I try to describe the thousand forms of past associations and ideas he awakens or embodies. But you'll not talk of what I tell you; and my mind is so eternally secluded in itself, it is tempting at last to turn it out to another."

"Five minutes ago Hareton seemed a personification of my youth, not a human being. I felt to him in such a variety of ways that it would have been impossible to have accosted him rationally."

"In the first place, his startling likeness to Catherine connected him fearfully with her. That, however, which you may suppose the most potent to arrest my imagination, is actually the least; for what is not connected with her to me? and what does not recall her? I cannot look down to this floor but her features are shaped on the flags. In every cloud, in every tree – filling the air at night, and caught by glimpses in every object by day – I am surrounded with her image. The most ordinary faces of men and women – my own features – mock me with a resemblance. The entire world is a dreadful collection of memoranda that she did exist, and that I have lost her."

"Well, Hareton's aspect was the ghost of my immortal love, of my wild endeavours to hold my right, my degradation, my pride, my happiness, and my anguish – "

"But it is frenzy to repeat these thoughts to you; only it will let you know why, with a reluctance to be always alone, his society is no benefit, rather an aggravation of the constant torment I suffer; and it partly contributes to render me regardless how he and his cousin go on together. I can give them no attention any more."

"But what do you mean by a *change*, Mr Heathcliff?" I said, alarmed at his manner, though he was neither in danger of losing his senses nor dying, according to my judgement. He was quite strong and healthy; and as to his reason, from childhood he had a delight in dwelling on dark things and entertaining odd fancies. He might have had a monomania on the subject of his departed idol, but on every other point his wits were as sound as mine.

"I shall not know that till it comes," he said, "I'm only half conscious of it now."

"You have no feeling of illness, have you?" I asked.

"No, Nelly, I have not," he answered.

"Then you are not afraid of death?" I pursued.

"Afraid? No!" he replied. "I have neither a fear, nor a presentiment, nor a hope of death. Why should I? With my hard constitution, and temperate mode of living, and unperilous occupations, I ought to, and probably *shall*, remain above ground till there is scarcely a black hair on my head. And yet I cannot continue in this condition! I have to remind myself to breathe, almost to remind my heart to beat! And it is like bending back a stiff spring; it is by compulsion that I do the slightest act not prompted by one thought, and by compulsion that I notice anything alive or dead which is not associated with one universal idea. I have a single wish, and my whole being and faculties are yearning to attain it. They have yearned towards it so long and so unwaveringly that I'm convinced it *will* be reached – and *soon* – because it has devoured my existence. I am swallowed in the anticipation of its fulfilment."

"My confessions have not relieved me, but they may account for some otherwise unaccountable phases of humour which I show. – O God! it is a long fight, I wish it were over!"

He began to pace the room, muttering terrible things to himself, till I was inclined to believe, as he said Joseph did, that conscience had turned his heart to an earthly hell. I wondered greatly how it would end.

Though he seldom before had revealed his state of mind, even by looks, it was his habitual mood, I had no doubt. He asserted it himself; but not a soul, from his general bearing, would have conjectured the fact. You did not when you saw him, Mr Lockwood; and at the period of which I speak he was just the same as then, only fonder of continued solitude, and perhaps still more laconic in company.'

WILLIAM MAKEPEACE THACKERAY
(1811–1863)

Thackeray was born in Calcutta where his father worked for the East India Company. His father died when he was three and he was sent to school in England at the age of six, thence to Charterhouse and Cambridge. He spent time in France and Germany, studied art, dabbled in the law, gambled and wasted his inheritance. By the late 1830s he was writing critical essays and comic pieces for a variety of London magazines. In 1844 he published serially *The Luck of Barry Lyndon* (revised as *The Memoirs of Barry Lyndon*, 1852), a novel set in the eighteenth century, and in 1847–48 produced his masterpiece, *Vanity Fair*, a comic novel of Regency rogues. It was followed by *The History of Pendennis* (1848–50). In 1851 he gave a series of lectures published as *English Humourists of the Eighteenth Century*, and in the next year he published *The History of Henry Esmond* (1852), a historical novel set in the time of Queen Ann. There followed *The Newcomes* (1853–55) and *The Virginians* (1857–59). Thackeray learned his satirical techniques from Henry Fielding and added a particularly Victorian delight in debunking humbug, and an almost too-modern playfulness about the status of the text. He delighted in having editors in his books whose attempts to tie meaning down inevitably called the truth into question, as he also delighted in characters like Becky Sharpe in *Vanity Fair* whose lives are a sequence of deceptions, and whose trajectory through society proves that what distinguishes the scoundrel from the saint is the intelligence and honesty of the former. The following chapter is typical of the comic vignettes much admired by Victorian readers.

From Vanity Fair

Chapter 9. Family Portraits

Sir Pitt Crawley was a philosopher with a taste for what is called low life. His first marriage with the daughter of the noble Binkie had been made under the auspices of his parents; and as he often told Lady Crawley in her lifetime she was such a confounded quarrelsome high-bred jade that when she died he was hanged if he would ever take another of her sort, and at her ladyship's demise he kept his promise, and selected for a second wife Miss Rose Dawson, daughter of Mr John Thomas Dawson, ironmonger, of Mudbury. What a happy woman was Rose to be my Lady Crawley!

Let us set down the items of her happiness. In the first place, she gave up Peter Butt, a young man who kept company with her, and in consequence of his disappointment in love, took to smuggling, poaching, and a thousand other bad courses. Then she quarrelled, as in duty bound, with all her friends and intimates of her youth, who, of course, could not be received by my Lady at Queen's Crawley – nor did she find in her new rank and abode any persons who were willing to welcome her. Who ever did? Sir Huddleston Fuddleston had three daughters who all hoped to be Lady Crawley. Sir Giles Wapshot's family were insulted that one of the Wapshot girls had not the preference in the marriage, and the remaining baronets of the county were indignant at their comrade's misalliance. Never mind the commoners, whom we will leave to grumble anonymously.

Sir Pitt did not care, as he said, a brass farden for any one of them. He had his pretty Rose, and what more need a man require than to please himself? So he used to get drunk every night; to beat his pretty Rose sometimes: to leave her in Hampshire when he went to London for the parliamentary session, without a single friend in the wide world. Even Mrs Bute Crawley, the Rector's wife, refused to visit her, as she said she would never give the *pas* to a tradesman's daughter.

As the only endowments with which Nature had gifted Lady Crawley were those of pink cheeks and a white skin, and as she had no sort of character, nor talents, nor opinions, nor occupations, nor amusements, nor that vigour of soul and ferocity of temper which often falls to the lot of entirely foolish women, her hold upon Sir Pitt's affections was not very great. Her roses faded out of her cheeks, and the pretty freshness left her figure after the birth of a couple of children, and she became a mere machine in her husband's house, of no more use than the late Lady Crawley's grand piano. Being a light-complexioned woman, she wore light clothes, as most blondes will, and appeared, in preference, in draggled sea-green, or slatternly sky-blue. She worked that worsted day and night, or other pieces like it. She had counterpanes in the course of a few years to all the beds in Crawley. She had a small flower-garden, for which she had rather an affection; but beyond this no other like or disliking. When her husband was rude to her she was apathetic: whenever he struck her she cried. She had not character enough to take to drinking, and moaned about, slipshod and in curl-papers, all day. O Vanity Fair – Vanity Fair! This might have been, but for you, a cheery lass: Peter Butt and Rose a happy man and wife, in a snug farm, with a hearty family; and an honest portion of pleasures, cares, hopes, and struggles: but a title and a coach and four are toys more precious than happiness in Vanity Fair: and if Harry the Eighth or Bluebeard were alive now, and wanted a tenth wife, do you suppose he could not get the prettiest girl that shall be presented this season.

The languid dulness of their mamma did not, as it may be supposed, awaken much affection in her little daughters, but they were very happy in the servants' hall and in the stables; and the Scotch gardener having luckily a good wife and some good children, they got a little wholesome society and instruction in his lodge, which was the only education bestowed upon them until Miss Sharp came.

Her engagement was owing to the remonstrances of Mr Pitt Crawley, the only friend or protector Lady Crawley ever had, and the only person, besides her children, for whom she entertained a little feeble attachment. Mr Pitt took after the noble Binkies, from whom he was descended, and was a very polite and proper gentleman. When he grew to man's estate, and came back from Christchurch, he began to reform the slackened discipline of the hall, in spite of his father, who stood in awe of him. He was a man of such rigid refinement, that he would have starved rather than have dined without a white neckcloth.

Once, when just from college, and when Horrocks the butler brought him a letter without placing it previously on a tray, he gave that domestic a look, and administered to him a speech so cutting, that Horrocks ever after trembled before him; the whole household bowed to him: Lady Crawley's curl-papers came off earlier when he was at home: Sir Pitt's muddy gaiters disappeared; and if that incorrigible old man still adhered to other old habits, he never fuddled himself with rum-and-water in his son's presence, and only talked to his servants in a very reserved and polite manner; and those persons remarked that Sir Pitt never swore at Lady Crawley while his son was in the room.

It was he who taught the butler to say, 'My lady is served,' and who insisted on handing her ladyship in to dinner. He seldom spoke to her, but when he did it was with the most powerful respect; and he never let her quit the apartment without rising in the most stately manner to open the door, and making an elegant bow at her egress.

At Eton he was called Miss Crawley; and there, I am sorry to say, his younger brother Rawdon used to lick him violently. But though his parts were not brilliant, he made up for his lack of talent by meritorious industry, and was never known, during eight years at school, to be subject to that punishment which it is generally thought none but a cherub can escape.

At college his career was of course highly creditable. And here he prepared himself for public life, into which he was to be introduced by the patronage of his grandfather, Lord Binkie, by studying the ancient and modern orators with great assiduity, and by speaking unceasingly at the debating societies. But though he had a fine flux of words, and delivered his little voice with great pomposity and pleasure to himself, and never advanced any sentiment or opinion which was not perfectly trite and stale, and supported by a Latin quotation; yet he failed somehow, in spite of a mediocrity which ought to have insured any man a success. He did not even get the prize poem, which all his friends said he was sure of.

After leaving college he became Private Secretary to Lord Binkie, and was then appointed Attaché to the Legation at Pumpernickel, which post he filled with perfect honour, and brought home despatches, consisting of Strasburg pie, to the Foreign Minister of the day. After remaining ten years Attaché (several years after the lamented Lord Binkie's demise), and finding the advancement slow, he at length gave up the diplomatic service in some disgust, and began to turn country gentleman.

He wrote a pamphlet on Malt on returning to England (for he was an ambitious man, and always liked to be before the public), and took a strong part in the Negro Emancipation question. Then he became a friend of Mr Wilberforce's,[1] whose politics he admired, and had that famous correspondence with the Reverend Silas Hornblower, on the Ashantee[2] Mission. He was in London, if not for the Parliament session, at least in May, for the religious meetings. In the country he was a magistrate, and an active visitor and speaker among those destitute of religious instruction. He was said to be paying his addresses to Lady Jane Sheepshanks, Lord Southdown's third daughter, and whose sister,

---

1: the leading anti-slavery campaigner. 2: an African civilisation which violently opposed British colonialism.

Lady Emily, wrote those sweet tracts, 'The Sailor's True Binnacle', and 'The Applewoman of Finchley Common'.

Miss Sharp's accounts of his employment at Queen's Crawley were not caricatures. He subjected the servants there to the devotional exercises before mentioned, in which (and so much the better) he brought his father to join. He patronized an Independent meeting-house in Crawley parish, much to the indignation of his uncle the Rector, and to the consequent delight of Sir Pitt, who was induced to go himself once or twice, which occasioned some violent sermons at Crawley parish church, directed point-blank at the Baronet's old Gothic pew there. Honest Sir Pitt, however, did not feel the force of these discourses, as he always took his nap during sermon-time.

Mr Crawley was very earnest, for the good of the nation and of the Christian world, that the old gentleman should yield him up his place in Parliament; but this the elder constantly refused to do. Both were of course too prudent to give up the fifteen hundred a year which was brought in by the second seat (at this period filled by Mr Quadroon, with carte-blanche on the Slave question); indeed the family estate was much embarrassed, and the income drawn from the borough was of great use to the house of Queen's Crawley.

It had never recovered the heavy fine imposed upon Walpole Crawley, first baronet, for peculation in the Tape and Sealing-Wax Office. Sir Walpole was a jolly fellow, eager to seize and spend money ('alieni appetens, sui profusus,'[1] as Mr Crawley would remark with a sigh), and in his day beloved by all the county for the constant drunkenness and hospitality which was maintained at Queen's Crawley. The cellars were filled with Burgundy then, the kennels with hounds, and the stables with gallant hunters; now, such horses as Queen's Crawley possessed went to plough, or ran in the Trafalgar Coach; and it was with a team of these very horses, on an off-day, that Miss Sharp was brought to the Hall; for boor as he was, Sir Pitt was a stickler for his dignity while at home, and seldom drove out but with four horses, and though he dined off boiled mutton, had always three footmen to serve it.

If mere parsimony could have made a man rich, Sir Pitt Crawley might have become very wealthy – if he had been an attorney in a country town, with no capital but his brains, it is very possible that he would have turned them to good account and might have achieved for himself a very considerable influence and competency. But he was unluckily endowed with a good name and a large though encumbered estate, both of which went rather to injure than to advance him. He had a taste for law, which cost him many thousands yearly; and being a great deal too clever to be robbed, as he said, by any single agent, allowed his affairs to be mismanaged by a dozen, whom he all equally mistrusted. He was such a sharp landlord, that he could hardly find any but bankrupt tenants; and such a close farmer, as to grudge almost the seed to the ground, whereupon revengeful Nature grudged him the crops which she granted to more liberal husbandmen. He speculated in every possible way; he worked mines; bought canal-shares; horsed coaches; took government contracts, and was the busiest man and magistrate of his county. As he would not pay honest

---

1: 'envious of others' property, prodigal with his own.' Sallust, *Catiline*, 5, 4.

agents at his granite quarry, he had the satisfaction of finding that four overseers ran away, and took fortunes with them to America. For want of proper precautions, his coal-mines filled with water: the government flung his contract of damaged beef upon his hands: and for his coach-horses, every mail proprietor in the kingdom knew that he lost more horses than any man in the country, from underfeeding and buying cheap. In disposition he was sociable, and far from being proud; nay, he rather preferred the society of a farmer or a horse-dealer to that of a gentleman, like my lord, his son: he was fond of drink, of swearing, of joking with the farmers' daughters: he was never known to give away a shilling or to do a good action, but was of a pleasant, sly, laughing mood, and would cut his joke and drink his glass with a tenant and sell him up the next day; or have his laugh with the poacher he was transporting with equal good humour. His politeness for the fair sex has already been hinted at by Miss Rebecca Sharp – in a word, the whole baronetage, peerage, commonage of England, did not contain a more cunning, mean, selfish, foolish, disreputable old man. That blood-red hand of Sir Pitt Crawley's would be in anybody's pocket except his own; and it is with grief and pain, that, as admirers of the British aristocracy, we find ourselves obliged to admit the existence of so many ill qualities in a person whose name is in Debrett.

One great cause why Mr Crawley had such a hold over the affections of his father, resulted from money arrangements. The Baronet owed his son a sum of money out of the jointure of his mother, which he did not find it convenient to pay; indeed he had an almost invincible repugnance to paying anybody, and could only be brought by force to discharge his debts. Miss Sharp calculated (for she became, as we shall hear speedily, inducted into most of the secrets of the family) that the mere payment of his creditors cost the honourable Baronet several hundreds yearly; but this was a delight he could not forego; he had a savage pleasure in making the poor wretches wait, and in shifting from court to court and from term to term the period of satisfaction. What's the good of being in Parliament, he said, if you must pay your debts? Hence, indeed, his position as a senator was not a little useful to him.

Vanity Fair – Vanity Fair! Here was a man, who could not spell, and did not care to read – who had the habits and the cunning of a boor: whose aim in life was pettifogging: who never had a taste, or emotion, or enjoyment, but what was sordid and foul; and yet he had rank, and honours, and power, somehow: and was a dignitary of the land, and a pillar of the state. He was a high sheriff, and rode in a golden coach. Great ministers and statesmen courted him; and in Vanity Fair he had a higher place than the most brilliant genius or spotless virtue.

Sir Pitt had an unmarried half-sister who inherited her mother's large fortune, and though the Baronet proposed to borrow this money of her on mortgage, Miss Crawley declined the offer, and preferred the security of her funds. She had signified, however, her intention of leaving her inheritance between Sir Pitt's second son and the family at the Rectory and had once or twice paid the debts of Rawdon Crawley in his career at college and in the army. Miss Crawley was, in consequence, an object of great respect when she came to Queen's Crawley, for she had a balance at her banker's which would have made her beloved anywhere.

What a dignity it gives an old lady, that balance at the bankers! How tenderly we look at her faults if she is a relative (and may every reader have a score of such), what a kind good-natured old creature we find her! How the junior partner of Hobbs and Dobbs leads her smiling to the carriage with the lozenge upon it, and the fat wheezy coachman! How, when she comes to pay us a visit, we generally find an opportunity to let our friends know her station in the world! We say (and with perfect truth) I wish I had Miss MacWhirter's signature to a cheque for five thousand pounds. She wouldn't miss it, says your wife. She is my aunt, say you, in an easy careless way, when your friend asks if Miss MacWhirter is any relative. Your wife is perpetually sending her little testimonies of affection, your little girls work endless worsted baskets, cushions, and footstools for her. What a good fire there is in her room when she comes to pay you a visit, although your wife laces her stays without one! The house during her stay assumes a festive, neat, warm, jovial, snug appearance not visible at other seasons. You yourself, dear sir, forget to go to sleep after dinner, and find yourself all of a sudden (though you invariably lose) very fond of a rubber. What good dinners you have – game every day, Malmsey-Madeira, and no end of fish from London. Even the servants in the kitchen share in the general prosperity; and, somehow, during the stay of Miss MacWhirter's fat coachman, the beer is grown much stronger, and the consumption of tea and sugar in the nursery (where her maid takes her meals) is not regarded in the least. Is it so, or is it not so? I appeal to the middle classes. Ah, gracious powers! I wish you would send me an old aunt – a maiden aunt – an aunt with a lozenge on her carriage, and a front of light coffee-coloured hair – how my children should work workbags for her, and my Julia and I would make her comfortable! Sweet – sweet vision! Foolish – foolish dream!

ELIZABETH GASKELL (1810–1865)

Elizabeth Gaskell (née Stevenson) was born in the village of Knutsford, Cheshire, the daughter of a Unitarian minister and in 1832 married William Gaskell of Manchester, also a Unitarian minister. Manchester was a booming mill town, and was to be cruelly afflicted by the long recession of 1837–50. Mrs Gaskell's experiences in that decade led her to write *Mary Barton* (1848) which contains some of the most vivid evocations of the conditions of the urban working class, as well as some of the most penetrating insights into class mentality. It was also a masterpiece of plotting and suspense. The novel was denounced by the Tory party and the mill owners, but admired by Carlyle and by Dickens who invited Gaskell to contribute to his new periodical, *Household Words*. Elizabeth Gaskell wrote a complementary analysis of the relations of capital and labour in *North and South* (1855) in which she tried to reform the attitudes of factory owners, and she also wrote *Cranford* (1853), *Ruth* (1853), *Sylvia's Lovers* (1863) and *Wives and Daughters* (1866). She also wrote a biography of her friend Charlotte Brontë (1857).

From Mary Barton

Chapter 2

> Polly, put the kettle on,
> And let's have tea!
> Polly, put the kettle on,
> And we'll all have tea.

'Here we are, wife; didst thou think thou'd lost us?' quoth the hearty-voiced Wilson, as the two women rose and shook themselves in preparation for their homeward walk. Mrs Barton was evidently soothed, if not cheered, by the unburdening of her fears and thoughts to her friend; and her approving look went far to second her husband's invitation that the whole party should adjourn from Green Heys Fields to tea, at the Bartons' house. The only faint opposition was raised by Mrs Wilson, on account of the lateness of the hour at which they would probably return, which she feared on her babies' account.

'Now, hold your tongue, missus, will you?' said her husband, good-temperedly. 'Don't you know them brats never goes to sleep till long past ten? and haven't you a shawl, under which you can tuck one lad's head, as safe as a bird's under its wing? And as for t'other one, I'll put it in my pocket rather than not stay, now we are this far away from Ancoats.'

'Or I can lend you another shawl,' suggested Mrs Barton.

'Ay, any thing rather than not stay.'

The matter being decided, the party proceeded home, through many half-finished streets, all so like one another that you might have easily been bewildered and lost your way. Not a step, however, did our friends lose; down this entry, cutting off that corner, until they turned out of one of these innumerable streets into a little paved court, having the backs of houses at the end opposite to the opening, and a gutter running through the middle to carry off household slops, washing suds, &c. The women who lived in the court were busy taking in strings of caps, frocks, and various articles of linen, which hung from side to side, dangling so low, that if our friends had been a few minutes sooner, they would have had to stoop very much, or else the half-wet clothes would have flapped in their faces; but although the evening seemed yet early when they were in the open fields – among the pent-up houses, night, with its mists, and its darkness, had already begun to fall.

Many greetings were given and exchanged between the Wilsons and these women, for not long ago they had also dwelt in this court.

Two rude lads, standing at a disorderly looking house-door, exclaimed, as Mary Barton (the daughter) passed, 'Eh, look! Polly Barton's gotten a sweetheart.'

Of course this referred to young Wilson, who stole a look to see how Mary took the idea. He saw her assume the air of a young fury, and to his next speech she answered not a word.

Mrs Barton produced the key of the door from her pocket; and on entering the house-place it seemed as if they were in total darkness, except one bright spot, which might be a cat's eye, or might be, what it was, a red-hot fire, smouldering under a large piece of coal, which John Barton immediately applied himself to break up, and the effect instantly produced was warm and glowing light in every corner of the room. To add to this (although the coarse yellow glare seemed lost in the ruddy glow from the fire), Mrs Barton lighted a dip by sticking it in the fire, and having placed it satisfactorily in a tin candlestick, began to look further about her, on hospitable thoughts intent. The room was tolerably large, and possessed many conveniences. On the right of the door, as you entered, was a longish window, with a broad ledge. On each side of this, hung blue-and-white check curtains, which were now drawn, to shut in the friends met to enjoy themselves. Two geraniums, unpruned and leafy, which stood on the sill, formed a further defence from out-door pryers. In the corner between the window and the fire-side was a cupboard, apparently full of plates and dishes, cups and saucers, and some more non-descript articles, for which one would have fancied their possessors could find no use – such as triangular pieces of glass to save carving knives and forks from dirtying table-cloths. However, it was evident Mrs Barton was proud of her crockery and glass, for she left her cupboard door open, with a glance round of satisfaction and pleasure. On the opposite side to the door and window was the staircase, and two doors; one of which (the nearest to the fire), led into a sort of little back kitchen, where dirty work, such as washing up dishes, might be done, and whose shelves served as larder, and pantry, and storeroom, and all. The other door, which was considerably lower, opened into the coalhole – the slanting closet under the stairs; from which, to the fire-place, there was a gay-coloured piece of oil-cloth laid. The place seemed almost crammed with furniture (sure sign of good times among the mills). Beneath the window was a dresser with three deep drawers. Opposite the fire-place was a table, which I should call a Pembroke, only that it was made of deal, and I cannot tell how far such a name may be applied to such humble material. On it, resting against the wall, was a bright green japanned tea-tray, having a couple of scarlet lovers embracing in the middle. The fire-light danced merrily on this, and really (setting all taste but that of a child's aside) it gave a richness of colouring to that side of the room. It was in some measure propped up by a crimson tea-caddy, also of japan ware. A round table on one branching leg ready for use, stood in the corresponding corner to the cupboard; and, if you can picture all this with a washy, but clean stencilled pattern on the walls, you can form some idea of John Barton's home.

The tray was soon hoisted down, and before the merry chatter of cups and saucers began, the women disburdened themselves of their out-of-door things, and sent Mary up stairs with them. Then came a long whispering, and chinking of money, to which Mr and Mrs Wilson were too polite to attend; knowing, as they did full well, that it all related to the preparations for hospitality; hospitality that, in their turn, they should have such pleasure in offering. So they tried to be busily occupied with the children, and not to hear Mrs Barton's directions to Mary.

'Run, Mary dear, just round the corner, and get some fresh eggs at Tipping's (you may get one a-piece, that will be fivepence), and see if he has any nice ham cut, that he would let us have a pound of.'

'Say two pounds, missis, and don't be stingy,' chimed in the husband.

'Well, a pound and a half, Mary. And get it Cumberland ham, for Wilson comes from there-away, and it will have a sort of relish of home with it he'll like, – and Mary' (seeing the lassie fain to be off), 'you must get a pennyworth of milk and a loaf of bread – mind you get it fresh and new – and, and – that's all, Mary.'

'No, it's not all,' said her husband. 'Thou must get sixpennyworth of rum, to warm the tea; thou'll get it at the "Grapes". And thou just go to Alice Wilson; he says she lives just right round the corner, under 14, Barber Street' (this was addressed to his wife), 'and tell her to come and take her tea with us; she'll like to see her brother, I'll be bound, let alone Jane and the twins.'

'If she comes she must bring a tea-cup and saucer, for we have but half-a-dozen, and here's six of us,' said Mrs Barton.

'Pooh! pooh! Jem and Mary can drink out of one, surely.'

But Mary secretly determined to take care that Alice brought her tea-cup and saucer, if the alternative was to be her sharing any thing with Jem.

Alice Wilson had but just come in. She had been out all day in the fields, gathering wild herbs for drinks and medicine, for in addition to her invaluable qualities as a sick nurse and her wordly occupation as a washerwoman, she added a considerable knowledge of hedge and field simples; and on fine days, when no more profitable occupation offered itself, she used to ramble off into the lanes and meadows as far as her legs would carry her. This evening she had returned loaded with nettles, and her first object was to light a candle and see to hang them up in bunches in every available place in her cellar room. It was the perfection of cleanliness: in one corner stood the modest-looking bed, with a check curtain at the head, the whitewashed wall filling up the place where the corresponding one should have been. The floor was bricked, and scrupulously clean, although so damp that it seemed as if the last washing would never dry up. As the cellar window looked into an area in the street, down which boys might throw stones, it was protected by an outside shelter, and was oddly festooned with all manner of hedge-row, ditch, and field plants, which we are accustomed to call valueless, but which have a powerful effect either for good or for evil, and are consequently much used among the poor. The room was strewed, hung, and darkened with these bunches, which emitted no very fragrant odour in their process of drying. In one corner was a sort of broad hanging shelf, made of old planks, where some old hoards of Alice's were kept. Her little bit of crockery ware was ranged on the mantelpiece, where also stood her candlestick and box of matches. A small cupboard contained at the bottom coals, and at the top her bread and basin of oatmeal, her frying pan, teapot, and a small tin saucepan, which served as a bottle, as well as for cooking the delicate little messes of broth which Alice sometimes was able to manufacture for a sick neighbour.

After her walk she felt chilly and weary, and was busy trying to light her fire with the damp coals, and half green sticks, when Mary knocked.

'Come in,' said Alice, remembering, however, that she had barred the door for the night, and hastening to make it possible for any one to come in.

'Is that you, Mary Barton?' exclaimed she, as the light from her candle streamed on the girl's face. 'How you are grown since I used to see you at my brother's! Come in, lass, come in.'

'Please,' said Mary, almost breathless, 'mother says you're to come to tea, and bring your cup and saucer, for George and Jane Wilson is with us, and the twins, and Jem. And you're to make haste, please.'

'I'm sure it's very neighbourly and kind in your mother, and I'll come, with many thanks. Stay, Mary, has your mother got any nettles for spring drink? If she hasn't I'll take her some.'

'No, I don't think she has.'

Mary ran off like a hare to fulfil what, to a girl of thirteen, fond of power, was the more interesting part of her errand – the money-spending part. And well and ably did she perform her business, returning home with a little bottle of rum, and the eggs in one hand, while her other was filled with some excellent red-and-white smoke-flavoured, Cumberland ham, wrapped up in paper.

She was at home, and frying ham, before Alice had chosen her nettles, put out her candle, locked her door, and walked in a very foot-sore manner as far as John Barton's. What an aspect of comfort did his houseplace present, after her humble cellar. She did not think of comparing; but for all that she felt the delicious glow of the fire, the bright light that revelled in every corner of the room, the savoury smells, the comfortable sounds of a boiling kettle, and the hissing, frizzling ham. With a little old-fashioned curtsey she shut the door, and replied with a loving heart to the boisterous and surprised greeting of her brother.

And now all preparations being made, the party sat down. Mrs Wilson in the post of honour, the rocking chair on the right hand side of the fire, nursing her baby, while its father, in an opposite arm-chair, tried vainly to quieten the other with bread soaked in milk.

Mrs Barton knew manners too well to do any thing but sit at the tea-table and make tea, though in her heart she longed to be able to superintend the frying of the ham, and cast many an anxious look at Mary as she broke the eggs and turned the ham, with a very comfortable portion of confidence in her own culinary powers. Jem stood awkwardly leaning against the dresser, replying rather gruffly to his aunt's speeches, which gave him, he thought, the air of being a little boy; whereas he considered himself as a young man, and not so very young neither, as in two months he would be eighteen. Barton vibrated between the fire and the tea-table, his only drawback being a fancy that every now and then his wife's face flushed and contracted as if in pain.

At length the business actually began. Knives and forks, cups and saucers made a noise, but human voices were still, for human beings were hungry, and had no time to speak. Alice first broke silence; holding her tea-cup with the manner of one proposing a toast, she said, 'Here's to absent friends. Friends may meet, but mountains never.'

It was an unlucky toast or sentiment, as she instantly felt. Every one thought of Esther, the absent Esther; and Mrs Barton put down her food, and could not hide the fast dropping tears. Alice could have bitten her tongue out.

It was a wet blanket to the evening; for though all had been said and suggested in the fields that could be said or suggested, every one had a wish to say something in the way of comfort to poor Mrs Barton, and a dislike to talk about any thing else while her tears fell fast and scalding. So George Wilson, his wife and children, set off early home not before (in spite of *mal-à-propos* speeches) they had expressed a wish that such meetings might often take place, and not before John Barton had given his hearty consent; and declared that as soon as ever his wife was well again they would have just such another evening.

'I will take care not to come and spoil it,' thought poor Alice; and going up to Mrs Barton she took her hand almost humbly, and said, 'You don't know how sorry I am I said it.'

To her surprise, a surprise that brought tears of joy into her eyes, Mary Barton put her arms round her neck, and kissed the self-reproaching Alice. 'You didn't mean any harm, and it was me as was so foolish; only this work about Esther, and not knowing where she is, lies so heavy on my heart. Good night, and never think no more about it. God bless you, Alice.'

Many and many a time, as Alice reviewed that evening in her after life, did she bless Mary Barton for these kind and thoughtful words. But just then all she could say was, 'Good night, Mary, and may God bless *you*.'

Chapter 3

> But when the morn came dim and sad,
> And chill with early showers,
> Her quiet eyelids closed – she had
> Another morn than ours!
>   Hood

In the middle of that same night a neighbour of the Bartons was roused from her sound, well-earned sleep, by a knocking, which had at first made part of her dream; but starting up, as soon as she became convinced of its reality, she opened the window, and asked who was there?

'Me, John Barton,' answered he, in a voice tremulous with agitation. 'My missus is in labour, and, for the love of God, step in while I run for th'doctor, for she's fearful bad.'

While the woman hastily dressed herself, leaving the window still open, she heard cries of agony, which resounded in the little court in the stillness of the night. In less than five minutes she was standing by Mrs Barton's bed-side, relieving the terrified Mary, who went about, where she was told, like an automaton; her eyes tearless, her face calm, though deadly pale, and uttering no sound, except when her teeth chattered for very nervousness.

The cries grew worse.

The doctor was very long in hearing the repeated rings at his night-bell, and still longer in understanding who it was that made this sudden call upon his services; and then he begged Barton just to wait while he dressed himself, in order that no time might be lost in finding the court and house. Barton absolutely stamped with impatience, outside the doctor's door, before he came down; and walked so fast homewards, that the medical man several times asked him to go slower.

'Is she so very bad?' asked he.

'Worse, much worser than ever I saw her before,' replied John.

No! she was not – she was at peace. The cries were still for ever. John had no time for listening. He opened the latched door, stayed not to light a candle for the mere ceremony of showing his companion up the stairs, so well known to himself; but, in two minutes was in the room, where lay the dead wife, whom he had loved with all the power of his strong heart. The doctor stumbled up the stairs by the fire-light, and met the awe-struck look of the neighbour, which at once told him the state of things. The room was still, as he, with habitual tip-toe step, approached the poor frail body, whom nothing now could more disturb. Her daughter knelt by the bed-side, her face buried in the clothes, which were almost crammed into her mouth, to keep down the choking sobs. The husband stood like one stupified. The doctor questioned the neighbour in whispers, and then approaching Barton, said, 'You must go down stairs. This is a great shock, but bear it like a man. Go down.'

He went mechanically and sat down on the first chair. He had no hope. The look of death was too clear upon her face. Still, when he heard one or two unusual noises, the thought burst on him that it might only be a trance, a fit, a – he did not well know what, – but not death! Oh, not death! And he was starting up to go up stairs again, when the doctor's heavy cautious creaking footstep was heard on the stairs. Then he knew what it really was in the chamber above.

'Nothing could have saved her – there has been some shock to the system – ' and so he went on; but, to unheeding ears, which yet retained his words to ponder on; words not for immediate use in conveying sense, but to be laid by, in the store-house of memory, for a more convenient season. The doctor seeing the state of the case, grieved for the man; and, very sleepy, thought it best to go, and accordingly wished him good-night – but there was no answer, so he let himself out; and Barton sat on, like a stock or a stone, so rigid, so still. He heard the sounds above too, and knew what they meant. He heard the stiff, unseasoned drawer, in which his wife kept her clothes, pulled open. He saw the neighbour come down, and blunder about in search of soap and water. He knew well what she wanted, and *why* she wanted them, but he did not speak, nor offer to help. At last she went, with some kindly-meant words (a text of comfort, which fell upon a deafened ear), and something about 'Mary', but which Mary he could not tell, in his bewildered state.

He tried to realise it, to think it possible. And then his mind wandered off to other days, to far different times. He thought of their courtship; of his first seeing her, an awkward, beautiful rustic, far too shiftless for the delicate factory work to which she was apprenticed; of his first gift to her, a bead necklace, which had long ago been put by, in one of the deep drawers of the dresser, to be kept for Mary. He wondered if it was there yet, and with a strange curiosity he got up to feel for it; for the fire by this time was well-nigh out, and candle he had none. His groping hand fell on the piled-up tea things, which at his desire she had left unwashed till morning – they were all so tired. He was reminded of one of the daily little actions, which acquire such power when they have been performed for the last time, by one we love. He began to think over his wife's daily round of duties; and something in the remembrance that these would never more be done by her, touched the source of tears, and he cried aloud. Poor Mary, meanwhile, had mechanically helped the neighbour in all the last attentions to the dead; and when she was kissed, and spoken to soothingly, tears stole quietly down her cheeks; but she reserved the luxury of a full burst of grief till she should be alone. She shut the chamber-door softly, after the neighbour had gone, and then shook the bed by which she knelt, with her agony of sorrow. She repeated, over and over again, the same words; the same vain, unanswered address to her who was no more. 'Oh, mother! mother, are you really dead! Oh, mother, mother!'

At last she stopped, because it flashed across her mind that her violence of grief might disturb her father. All was still below. She looked on the face so changed, and yet so strangely like. She bent down to kiss it. The cold, unyielding flesh struck a shudder to her heart, and, hastily obeying her impulse, she grasped the candle, and opened the door. Then she heard the sobs of her father's grief; and quickly, quietly, stealing down the steps, she knelt by him, and kissed his hand. He took no notice at first, for his burst of grief would not be controlled. But when her shriller sobs, her terrified cries (which she could not repress), rose upon his ear, he checked himself.

'Child, we must be all to one another, now *she* is gone,' whispered he.

'Oh, father, what can I do for you? Do tell me! I'll do any thing.'

'I know thou wilt. Thou must not fret thyself ill, that's the first thing I ask. Thou must leave me, and go to bed now, like a good girl as thou art.'

'Leave you, father! oh, don't say so.'

'Ah, but thou must! thou must go to bed, and try and sleep; thou'lt have enough to do and to bear, poor wench, to-morrow.'

Mary got up, kissed her father, and sadly went up stairs to the little closet, where she slept. She thought it was of no use undressing, for that she could never, never sleep, so threw herself on her bed in her clothes, and before ten minutes had passed away, the passionate grief of youth had subsided into sleep.

Barton had been roused by his daughter's entrance, both from his stupor and from his uncontrollable sorrow. He could think on what was to be done, could plan for the funeral, could calculate the necessity of soon returning to his work, as the extravagance of the past night would leave them short of money, if he long remained away from the mill. He was in a club, so that money was provided for the burial. These things settled in his own mind, he recalled the doctor's words, and bitterly thought of the shock his poor wife had so recently had, in the mysterious disappearance of her cherished sister. His feelings towards Esther almost amounted to curses. It was she who had brought on all this sorrow. Her giddiness, her lightness of conduct, had wrought this woe. His previous thoughts about her had been tinged with wonder and pity, but now he hardened his heart against her for ever.

One of the good influences over John Barton's life had departed that night.

One of the ties which bound him down to the gentle humanites of earth was loosened, and henceforward the neighbours all remarked he was a changed man. His gloom and his sternness became habitual instead of occasional. He was more obstinate. But never to Mary. Between the father and the daughter there existed in full force that mysterious bond which unites those who have been loved by one who is now dead and gone. While he was harsh and silent to others, he humoured Mary with tender love; she had more of her own way than is common in any rank with girls of her age. Part of this was the necessity of the case; for, of course, all the money went through her hands, and the household arrangements were guided by her will and pleasure. But part was her father's indulgence, for he left her, with full trust in her unusual sense and spirit, to choose her own associates, and her own times for seeing her associates.

With all this, Mary had not her father's confidence in the matters which now began to occupy him, heart and soul; she was aware that he had joined clubs, and become an active member of a trades' union, but it was hardly likely that a girl of Mary's age (even when two or three years had elapsed since her mother's death) should care much for the differences between the employers and the employed, – an eternal subject for agitation in the manufacturing districts, which, however it may be lulled for a time, is sure to break forth again with fresh violence at any depression of trade, showing that in its apparent quiet, the ashes had still smouldered in the breasts of a few.

Among these few was John Barton. At all times it is a bewildering thing to the poor weaver to see his employer removing from house to house, each one grander than the last, till he ends in building one more magnificent than all, or withdraws his money from the concern, or sells his mill to buy an estate in the country, while all the time the weaver, who thinks he and his fellows are the real makers of this wealth, is struggling on for bread for their children, through the vicissitudes of lowered wages, short hours, fewer hands employed, &c. And when he knows trade is bad, and could understand (at least partially) that there are not buyers enough in the market to purchase the goods already made, and consequently that there is no demand for more; when he would bear and endure much without complaining, could he also see that his employers were bearing their share; he is, I say, bewildered and (to use his own word) 'aggravated' to see that all goes on just as usual with the mill-owners. Large houses are still occupied, while spinners' and weavers' cottages stand empty, because the families that once occupied them are obliged to live in rooms or cellars. Carriages still roll along the streets, concerts are still crowded by subscribers, the shops for expensive luxuries still find daily customers, while the workman loiters away his unemployed time in watching these things, and thinking of the pale, uncomplaining wife at home, and the wailing children asking in vain for enough of food, of the sinking health, of the dying life of those near and dear to him. The contrast is too great. Why should he alone suffer from bad times?

I know that this is not really the case; and I know what is the truth in such matters: but what I wish to impress is what the workman feels and thinks. True, that with child-like improvidence, good times will often dissipate his grumbling, and make him forget all prudence and foresight.

But there are earnest men among these people, men who have endured wrongs without complaining, but without ever forgetting or forgiving those whom (they believe) have caused all this woe.

Among these was John Barton. His parents had suffered, his mother had died from absolute want of the necessaries of life. He himself was a good, steady workman, and, as such, pretty certain of steady employment. But he spent all he got with the confidence (you may also call it improvidence) of one who was willing, and believed himself able, to supply all his wants by his own exertions. And when his master suddenly failed, and all hands in that mill were turned back, one Tuesday morning, with the news that Mr Hunter had stopped, Barton had only a few shillings to rely on; but he had good heart of being employed at some other mill, and accordingly, before returning home, he spent some hours in going from factory to factory, asking for work. But at every mill was some sign of depression of trade; some were working short hours, some were turning off hands, and for weeks Barton was out of work, living on credit. It was during this time his little son, the apple of his eye, the cynosure of all his strong power of love, fell ill of the scarlet fever. They dragged him through the crisis, but his life hung on a gossamer thread. Every thing, the doctor said, depended on good nourishment, on generous living, to keep up the little fellow's strength, in the prostration in which the fever had left him. Mocking words! when the commonest food in the house would not furnish one little meal. Barton tried credit; but it was worn out at the little provision shops, which were now suffering in their turn. He thought it would be no sin to steal, and would have stolen; but he could not get the opportunity in the few days the child lingered. Hungry himself, almost to an animal pitch of ravenousness, but with the bodily pain swallowed up in anxiety for his little sinking lad, he stood at one of the shop windows where all edible luxuries are displayed; haunches of venison, Stilton cheeses, moulds of jelly – all appetising sights to the common passer by. And out of this shop came Mrs Hunter! She crossed to her carriage, followed by the shopman loaded with purchases for a party. The door was quickly slammed to, and she drove away; and Barton returned home with a bitter spirit of wrath in his heart, to see his only boy a corpse!

You can fancy, now, the hoards of vengeance in his heart against the employers. For there are never wanting those who, either in speech or in print, find it their interest to cherish such feelings in the working classes; who know how and when to rouse the dangerous power at their command; and who use their knowledge with unrelenting purpose to either party.

So while Mary took her own way, growing more spirited every day, and growing in her beauty too, her father was chairman at many a trades' union meeting; a friend of delegates, and ambitious of being a delegate himself; a Chartist,[1] and ready to do any thing for his order.

But now times were good; and all these feelings were theoretical, not practical. His most practical thought was getting Mary apprenticed to a

---

1: The People's Charter was published in May 1837 and demanded universal adult male suffrage, secret ballots, no property qualifications for parliamentary candidates, payment for MPs and consituencies of equal size. Mass meetings led to the presentation of a mass petition to Parliament in 1839 which Parliament refused to admit. It was represented in 1842, and again in 1848, and always refused, after which the movement declined.

dressmaker; for he had never left off disliking a factory for a girl, on more accounts than one.

Mary must do something. The factories being, as I said, out of the question, there were two things open – going out to service, and the dressmaking business; and against the first of these, Mary set herself with all the force of her strong will. What that will might have been able to achieve had her father been against her, I cannot tell; but he disliked the idea of parting with her, who was the light of his hearth, the voice of his otherwise silent home. Besides, with his ideas and feelings towards the higher classes, he considered domestic servitude as a species of slavery; a pampering of artificial wants on the one side, a giving-up of every right of leisure by day and quiet rest by night on the other. How far his strong exaggerated feelings had any foundation in truth, it is for you to judge. I am afraid that Mary's determination not to go to service arose from far less sensible thoughts on the subject than her father's. Three years of independence of action (since her mother's death such a time had now elapsed) had little inclined her to submit to rules as to hours and associates, to regulate her dress by a mistress's ideas of propriety, to lose the dear feminine privileges of gossiping with a merry neighbour, and working night and day to help one who was sorrowful. Besides all this, the sayings of her absent, her mysterious aunt, Esther, had an unacknowledged influence over Mary. She knew she was very pretty; the factory people as they poured from the mills, and in their freedom told the truth (whatever it might be) to every passer-by, had early let Mary into the secret of her beauty. If their remarks had fallen on an unheeding ear, there were always young men enough, in a different rank from her own, who were willing to compliment the pretty weaver's daughter as they met her in the streets. Besides, trust a girl of sixteen for knowing well if she is pretty; concerning her plainness she may be ignorant. So with this consciousness she had early determined that her beauty should make her a lady; the rank she coveted the more for her father's abuse; the rank to which she firmly believed her lost Aunt Esther had arrived. Now, while a servant must often drudge and be dirty, must be known as a servant by all who visited at her master's house, a dressmaker's apprentice must (or so Mary thought) be always dressed with a certain regard to appearance; must never soil her hands, and need never redden or dirty her face with hard labour. Before my telling you so truly what folly Mary felt or thought, injures her without redemption in your opinion, think what are the silly fancies of sixteen years of age in every class, and under all circumstances. The end of all the thoughts of father and daughter was, as I said before, Mary was to be a dressmaker; and her ambition prompted her unwilling father to apply at all the first establishments, to know on what terms of painstaking and zeal his daughter might be admitted into ever so humble a workwoman's situation. But high premiums were asked at all; poor man! he might have known that without giving up a day's work to ascertain the fact. He would have been indignant, indeed, had he known that if Mary had accompanied him, the case might have been rather different, as her beauty would have made her desirable as a show-woman. Then he tried second-rate places; at all the payment of a sum of money was necessary, and money he had none. Disheartened and angry he went home at night, declaring it was time lost; that dressmaking was at all events a toilsome business, and not worth learning. Mary saw that the grapes were sour, and the next day set out herself, as her father could not afford to lose another day's work; and before night (as yesterday's experience had considerably lowered her ideas) she had engaged herself as apprentice (so called, though there were no deeds or indentures to the bond) to a certain Miss Simmonds, milliner and dressmaker, in a respectable little street leading off Ardwick Green, where her business was duly announced in gold letters on a black ground, enclosed in a bird's-eye maple frame, and stuck in the front parlour window; where the workwomen were called 'her young ladies'; and where Mary was to work for two years without any remuneration, on consideration of being taught the business; and where afterwards she was to dine and have tea, with a small quarterly salary (paid quarterly, because so much more genteel than by week), a *very* small one, divisible into a minute weekly pittance. In summer she was to be there by six, bringing her day's meals during the first two years; in winter she was not to come till after breakfast. Her time for returning home at night must always depend upon the quantity of work Miss Simmonds had to do.

And Mary was satisfied; and seeing this, her father was contented too, although his words were grumbling and morose; but Mary knew his ways, and coaxed and planned for the future so cheerily, that both went to bed with easy if not happy hearts.

CHARLES DICKENS (1812–1870)

Charles Dickens's father was a clerk in the navy pay office. He was born in Portsmouth and raised in Chatham. When his father was briefly imprisoned in the Marshalsea for debt, Charles was sent to work in a blacking warehouse and the experience of being déclassé gave him an insight into the social structure which was to underlie all his later work. Dickens then went to work in an office, became reporter of parliamentary debates for the *Morning Chronicle* and discovered a talent for humorous sketches, collected in his first book publication, *Sketches by Boz*. He was then commissioned to write *Pickwick Papers* (1836–37) which became immensely popular. *Oliver Twist* (1837–38) and *Nicholas Nickleby* (1838–39) confirmed his ability as a novelist and in the next 33 years he would write at least ten novels which would then and now exert global appeal, and many shorter works. These novels included *The Old Curiosity Shop* (1840–41), *Barnaby Rudge* (1841), *Martin Chuzzlewhit* (1843–44), *Dombey and Son* (1848), *David Copperfield* (1849–50), *Bleak House* (1852–53), *Hard Times* (1854), *Little Dorrit* (1855–57), *A Tale of Two Cities* (1859), *Great Expectations* (1860–61), *Our Mutual Friend* (1864–65). *The Mystery of Edwin Drood* (1870) was unfinished at his death. He would also attempt to establish a daily paper, *The Daily News* (1846), and more successfully founded and edited two magazines, *Household Words* and *All the Year Round*. He made a considerable fortune, led a full social life, undertook philanthropic crusades, gave too many public readings of his works, and survived private scandal when in middle age he left his wife for a young actress. The appeal of Dickens's works was phenomenal and international. Nearly all were at first serialised in weekly or monthly parts and their following was such that when the last issue of *The Old Curiosity Shop* arrived in the United States, thousands of fans besieged the port in pursuit of copies. The roots of this appeal are various and deep: a sincere but sometimes theatricalised social and moral concern, a broad streak of sentimentality, an ability to alternate tragedy with comedy, characterisation that is at once specifically realised and archetypal, a fascination with the corruptions of law and the anarchic appeal of creative energy. Perhaps most important was his acute ear for the rhythms of everyday speech and consciousness of his methods. Together these make every sentence at least twice-told, advancing the plot or story and making a ironic comment about the technique of telling a story.

From David Copperfield

Chapter 11. I Begin Life On My Own Account, and Don't Like It

I know enough of the world now, to have almost lost the capacity of being much surprised by anything; but it is a matter of some surprise to me, even now, that I can have been so easily thrown away at such an age. A child of excellent abilities, and with strong powers of observation, quick, eager, delicate, and soon hurt bodily or mentally, it seems wonderful to me that nobody should have made any sign in my behalf. But none was made; and I became, at ten years old, a little laboring hind in the service of Murdstone and Grinby.

Murdstone and Grinby's warehouse was at the waterside. It was down in Blackfriars. Modern improvements have altered the place; but it was the last house at the bottom of a narrow street, curving down hill to the river, with some stairs at the end, where people took boat. It was a crazy old house with a wharf of its own, abutting on the water when the tide was in, and on the mud when the tide was out, and literally overrun with rats. Its panelled rooms, discolored with the dirt and smoke of a hundred years, I dare say; its decaying floors and staircase; the squeaking and scuffling of the old grey rats down in the cellars; and the dirt and rottenness of the place; are things, not of many years ago, in my mind, but of the present instant. They are all before me, just as they were in the evil hour when I went among them for the first time, with my trembling hand in Mr Quinion's.

Murdstone and Grinby's trade was among a good many kinds of people, but an important branch of it was the supply of wines and spirits to certain packet ships. I forget now where they chiefly went, but I think there were some among them that made voyages both to the East and West Indies. I know that a great many empty bottles were one of the consequences of this traffic, and that certain men and boys were employed to examine them against the light, and reject those that were flawed, and to rinse and wash them. When the empty bottles ran short, there were labels to be pasted on full ones, or corks to be fitted to them, or seals to be put upon the corks, or finished bottles to be packed in casks. All this work was my work, and of the boys employed upon it I was one.

There were three or four of us, counting me. My working place was established in a corner of the warehouse, where Mr Quinion could see me, when he chose to stand up on the bottom rail of his stool in the counting-house, and look at me through a window above the desk. Hither, on the first morning of my so auspiciously beginning life on my own account, the oldest of the regular boys was summoned to show me my business. His name was Mick Walker, and he wore a ragged apron and a paper cap. He informed me that his father was a bargeman, and walked, in a black velvet head-dress, in the Lord Mayor's Show. He also informed me that our principal associate would be another boy whom he introduced by the – to me – extraordinary name of Mealy Potatoes. I discovered, however, that this youth had not been christened by that name, but that it had been bestowed upon him in the warehouse, on account of his complexion, which was pale or mealy. Mealy's father was a waterman, who had the additional distinction of being a fireman, and was engaged as such at one of the large theatres; where some young relation of Mealy's – I think his little sister – did Imps in the Pantomimes.

No words can express the secret agony of my soul as I sunk into this companionship; compared these henceforth everyday associates with those of my happier childhood – not to say with Steerforth, Traddles, and the rest of those boys; and felt my hopes of growing up to be a learned and distinguished man, crushed in my bosom. The deep remembrance of the sense I had, of being utterly without hope now; of the shame I felt in my position; of the misery it was to my young heart to believe that day by day, what I had learned, and thought, and delighted in, and raised my fancy and my emulation up by, would pass away from me, little by little, never to be brought back any more; cannot be written. As often as Mick Walker went away in the course of that forenoon, I mingled my tears with the water in which I was washing the bottles; and sobbed as if there were a flaw in my own breast, and it were in danger of bursting.

The counting-house clock was at half-past twelve, and there was general preparation for going away to dinner, when Mr Quinion tapped at the counting-house window, and beckoned to me to go in. I went in, and found there a stoutish, middle-aged person, in a brown surtout and black tights and shoes, with no more hair upon his head (which was a large one, and very shining) than there is upon an egg, and with a very extensive face, which he turned full upon me. His clothes were shabby, but he had an imposing shirt-collar on. He carried a jaunty sort of a stick, with a large pair of rusty tassels to it; and a quizzing-glass hung outside his coat, – for ornament, I afterwards found, as he very seldom looked through it, and couldn't see anything when he did.

'This,' said Mr Quinion, in allusion to myself; 'is he.'

'This,' said the stranger, with a certain condescending roll in his voice and a certain indescribable air of doing something genteel, which impressed me very much, 'is Master Copperfield. I hope I see you well, sir?'

I said I was very well, and hoped he was. I was sufficiently ill at ease, Heaven knows; but it was not in my nature to complain much at that time of my life, so I said I was very well, and hoped he was.

'I am,' said the stranger, 'thank Heaven, quite well. I have received a letter from Mr Murdstone, in which he mentions that he would desire me to receive into an apartment in the rear of my house, which is at present unoccupied – and is, in short, to be let as a – in short,' said the stranger, with a smile and in a burst of confidence, 'as a bedroom – the young beginner whom I have now the pleasure to –' and the stranger waved his hand, and settled his chin in his shirt-collar.

'This is Mr Micawber,' said Mr Quinion to me.

'Ahem!' said the stranger, 'that is my name.'

'Mr Micawber,' said Mr Quinion, 'is known to Mr Murdstone. He takes orders for us on commission, when he can get any. He has been written to by Mr Murdstone, on the subject of your lodgings, and he will receive you as a lodger.'

'My address,' said Mr Micawber, 'is Windsor Terrace, City Road. I – in short,' said Mr Micawber, with the same genteel air, and in another burst of confidence – 'I live there.'

I made him a bow.

'Under the impression,' said Mr Micawber, 'that your peregrinations in this metropolis have not as yet been extensive, and that you might have some difficulty in penetrating the arcana of the Modern Babylon in the direction of the City Road – in short,' said Mr Micawber, in another burst of confidence, 'that you might lose yourself – I shall be happy to call this evening, and install you in the knowledge of the nearest way.'

I thanked him with all my heart, for it was friendly in him to offer to take that trouble.

'At what hour,' said Mr Micawber, 'shall I –'

'At about eight,' said Mr Quinion.

'At about eight,' said Mr Micawber. 'I beg to wish you good day, Mr Quinion. I will intrude no longer.'

So he put on his hat, and went out with his cane under his arm: very upright, and humming a tune when he was clear of the counting-house.

Mr Quinion then formally engaged me to be as useful as I could in the warehouse of Murdstone and Grinby, at a salary, I think, of six shillings a week. I am not clear whether it was six or seven. I am inclined to believe, from my uncertainty on this head, that it was six at first and seven afterwards. He paid me a week down (from his own pocket, I believe), and I gave Mealy sixpence out of it to get my trunk carried to Windsor Terrace that night: it being too heavy for my strength, small as it was. I paid sixpence more for my dinner, which was a meat pie and a turn at a neighbouring pump; and passed the hour which was allowed for that meal, in walking about the streets.

At the appointed time in the evening, Mr Micawber reappeared. I washed my hands and face, to do the greater honor to his gentility, and we walked to our house, as I suppose I must now call it, together; Mr Micawber impressing the names of streets, and the shapes of corner houses upon me, as we went along, that I might find my way back, easily, in the morning.

Arrived at his house in Windsor Terrace (which I noticed was shabby like himself, but also, like himself, made all the show it could), he presented me to Mrs Micawber, a thin and faded lady, not at all young, who was sitting in the parlor (the first floor was altogether unfurnished, and the blinds were kept down to delude the neighbours), with a baby at her breast. This baby was one of twins; and I may remark here that I hardly ever, in all my experience of the family, saw both the twins detached from Mrs Micawber at the same time. One of them was always taking refreshment.

There were two other children; Master Micawber, aged about four, and Miss Micawber, aged about three. These, and a dark-complexioned young woman, with a habit of snorting, who was servant to the family, and informed me, before half an hour had expired, that she was 'a Orfling,' and came from Saint Luke's workhouse, in the neighbourhood, completed the establishment. My room was at the top of the house at the back: a close chamber; stencilled all over with an ornament which my young imagination represented as a blue muffin, and very scantily furnished.

'I never thought,' said Mrs Micawber, when she came up, twin and all, to show me the apartment, and sat down to take breath, 'before I was married, when I lived with papa and mama, that I should ever find it necessary to take a lodger. But Mr Micawber being in difficulties, all considerations of private feeling must give way.'

I said: 'Yes, ma'am.'

'Mr Micawber's difficulties are almost overwhelming just at present,' said Mrs Micawber; 'and whether it is possible to bring him through them, I don't know. When I lived at home with papa and mama, I really should have hardly understood what the word meant, in the sense in which I now employ it, but experientia does it – as papa used to say.'

I cannot satisfy myself whether she told me that Mr Micawber had been an officer in the Marines, or whether I have imagined it. I only know that I believe to this hour that he *was* in the Marines once upon a time, without knowing why. He was a sort of town traveller for a number of miscellaneous houses, now; but made little or nothing of it, I am afraid.

'If Mr Micawber's creditors *will not* give him time,' said Mrs Micawber, 'they must take the consequences; and the sooner they bring it to an issue the better. Blood cannot be obtained from a stone, neither can anything on account be obtained at present (not to mention law expenses) from Mr Micawber.'

I never can quite understand whether my precocious self-dependence confused Mrs Micawber in reference to my age, or whether she was so full of the subject that she would have talked about it to the very twins if there had been nobody else to communicate with, but this was the strain in which she began, and she went on accordingly all the time I knew her.

Poor Mrs Micawber! She said she had tried to exert herself; and so, I have no doubt, she had. The centre of the street door was perfectly covered with a great brass-plate, on which was engraved 'Mrs Micawber's Boarding Establishment for Young Ladies': but I never found that any young lady had ever been to school there; or that any young lady ever came, or proposed to come; or that the least preparation was ever made to receive any young lady. The only visitors I ever saw or heard of, were creditors. *They* used to come at all hours, and some of them were quite ferocious. One dirty-faced man, I think he was a boot-maker, used to edge himself into the passage as early as seven o'clock in the morning, and call up the stairs to Mr Micawber – 'Come! You ain't out yet, you know. Pay us, will you? Don't hide, you know; that's mean. I wouldn't be mean if I was you. Pay us, will you? You just pay us, d'ye hear? Come!'

Receiving no answer to these taunts, he would mount in his wrath to the words 'swindlers' and 'robbers;' and these being ineffectual too, would sometimes go to the extremity of crossing the street, and roaring up at the windows of the second floor, where he knew Mr Micawber was. At these times, Mr Micawber would be transported with grief and mortification, even to the length (as I was once made aware by a scream from his wife) of making motions at himself with a razor; but within half an hour afterwards he would polish up his shoes with extraordinary pains, and go out, humming a tune with a greater air of gentility than ever. Mrs Micawber was quite as elastic. I have known her to be thrown into fainting fits by the king's taxes at three o'clock, and to eat lamb-chops, breaded, and drink warm ale (paid for with two teaspoons that had gone to the pawnbroker's) at four. On one occasion, when an execution had just been put in, coming home through some chance as early as six o'clock, I saw her lying (of course with a twin) under the grate in a swoon, with her hair all torn about her face; but I never knew her more cheerful than she was, that very same night, over a veal cutlet before the kitchen fire, telling me stories about her papa and mama, and the company they used to keep.

In this house, and with this family, I passed my leisure time. My own exclusive breakfast of a penny loaf and a pennyworth of milk, I provided myself. I kept another small loaf, and a modicum of cheese, on a particular shelf of a particular cupboard, to make my supper on when I came back at night. This made a hole in the six or seven shillings, I know well; and I was out at the warehouse all day, and had to support myself on that money all the week. From Monday morning until Saturday night, I had no advice, no counsel, no encouragement, no consolation, no assistance, no support, of any kind, from anyone, that I can call to mind, as I hope to go to heaven!

I was so young and childish, and so little qualified – how could I be otherwise? – to undertake the whole charge of my own existence, that often, in going to Murdstone and Grinby's, of a morning, I could not resist the stale pastry put out for sale at half-price at the pastrycook's doors, and spent in that, the money I should have kept for my dinner. Then, I went without my dinner, or bought a roll or a slice of pudding. I remember two pudding shops, between which I was divided, according to my finances. One was in a court close to St. Martin's Church – at the back of the church – which is now removed altogether. The pudding at that shop was made of currants, and was rather a special pudding, but was dear, twopennyworth not being larger than a pennyworth of more ordinary pudding. A good shop for the latter was in the Strand – somewhere in that part which has been rebuilt since. It was a stout pale pudding, heavy and flabby, and with great flat raisins in it, stuck in whole at wide distances apart. It came up hot at about my time every day, and many a day did I dine off it. When I dined regularly and handsomely, I had a saveloy and a penny-loaf, or a fourpenny plate of red beef from a cook's shop; or a plate of bread and cheese and a glass of beer, from a miserable old public-house opposite our place of business, called the Lion, or the Lion and something else that I have forgotten. Once, I remember carrying my own bread (which I had brought from home in the morning) under my arm, wrapped in a piece of paper, like a book, and going to a famous alamode beef-house near Drury Lane, and ordering a 'small plate' of that delicacy to eat with it. What the waiter thought of such a strange little apparition coming in all alone, I don't know; but I can see him now, staring at me as I ate my dinner, and bringing up the other waiter to look. I gave him a halfpenny for himself, and I wish he hadn't taken it.

We had half an hour, I think, for tea. When I had money enough, I used to get half-a-pint of ready-made coffee and a slice of bread and butter. When I had none, I used to look at a venison shop in Fleet Street; or I have strolled, at such a time, as far as Covent Garden Market, and stared at the pineapples. I was fond of wandering about the Adelphi, because it was a mysterious place, with those dark arches. I see myself emerging one evening from some of these arches, on a little public-house close to the river, with an open space before it, where some coal-heavers were dancing; to look at whom I sat down upon a bench. I wonder what they thought of me!

I was such a child, and so little, that frequently when I went into the bar of a strange public-house for a glass of ale or porter, to moisten what I had had for dinner, they were afraid to give it me. I remember one hot evening I went into the bar of a public-house, and said to the landlord:

'What is your best – your *very best* – ale a glass?' For it was a special occasion. I don't know what. It may have been my birthday.

'Twopence-halfpenny,' says the landlord, 'is the price of the Genuine Stunning ale.'

'Then,' says I, producing the money, 'just draw me a glass of the Genuine Stunning, if you please, with a good head to it.'

The landlord looked at me in return over the bar, from head to foot, with a strange smile on his face; and instead of drawing the beer, looked round the screen and said something to his wife. She came out from behind it, with her work in her hand, and joined him in surveying me. Here we stand, all three, before me now. The landlord in his shirt-sleeves, leaning against the bar window-frame; his wife looking over the little half-door; and I, in some confusion, looking up at them from outside the partition. They asked me a good many questions; as, what my name was, how old I was, where I lived, how I was employed, and how I came there. To all of which, that I might commit nobody, I invented, I am afraid, appropriate answers. They served me with the ale, though I suspect it was not the Genuine Stunning; and the landlord's wife, opening the little half-door of the bar, and bending down, gave me my money back, and gave me a kiss that was half admiring and half compassionate, but all womanly and good, I am sure.

I know I do not exaggerate, unconsciously and unintentionally, the scantiness of my resources or the difficulties of my life. I know that if a shilling were given me by Mr Quinion at any time, I spent it in a dinner or a tea. I know that I worked, from morning until night, with common men and boys, a shabby child. I know that I lounged about the streets, insufficiently and unsatisfactorily fed. I know that, but for the mercy of God, I might easily have been, for any care that was taken of me, a little robber or a little vagabond.

Yet I held some station at Murdstone and Grinby's too. Besides that Mr Quinion did what a careless man so occupied, and dealing with a thing so anomalous, could, to treat me as one upon a different footing from the rest, I never said, to man or boy, how it was that I came to be there, or gave the least indication of being sorry that I was there. That I suffered in secret, and that I suffered exquisitely, no one ever knew but I. How much I suffered, it is, as I have said already, utterly beyond my power to tell. But I kept my own counsel, and I did my work. I knew from the first, that, if I could not do my work as well as any of the rest, I could not hold myself above slight and contempt. I soon became at least as expeditious and as skilful as either of the other boys. Though perfectly familiar with them, my conduct and manner were different enough from theirs to place a space between us. They and the men generally spoke of me as 'the little gent,' or 'the young Suffolker.' A certain man named Gregory, who was foreman of the packers, and another named Tipp, who was the carman, and wore a red jacket, used to address me sometimes as 'David:' but I think it was mostly when we were very confidential, and when I had made some efforts to entertain them, over our work, with some results of the old readings; which were fast perishing out of my remembrance. Mealy Potatoes uprose once, and rebelled against my being so distinguished; but Mick Walker settled him in no time.

My rescue from this kind of existence I considered quite hopeless, and abandoned, as such, altogether. I am solemnly convinced that I never for one hour was reconciled to it, or was otherwise than miserably unhappy; but I bore it; and even to Peggotty, partly for the love of her and partly for shame, never in any letter (though many passed between us) revealed the truth.

Mr Micawber's difficulties were an addition to the distressed state of my mind. In my forlorn state I became quite attached to the family, and used to walk about, busy with Mrs Micawber's calculations of ways and means, and heavy with the weight of Mr Micawber's debts. On a Saturday night, which was my grand treat, – partly because it was a great thing to walk home with six or seven shillings in my pocket, looking into the shops and thinking what such a sum would buy, and partly because I went home early, – Mrs Micawber would make the most heart-rending confidences to me; also on a Sunday morning, when I mixed the portion of tea or coffee I had bought over-night, in a little shaving-pot, and sat late at my breakfast. It was nothing at all unusual for Mr Micawber to sob violently at the beginning of one of these Saturday night conversations, and sing about Jack's delight being his lovely Nan, towards the end of it. I have known him come home to supper with a flood of tears, and a declaration that nothing was now left but a jail; and go to bed making a calculation of the expense of putting bow-windows to the house, 'in case anything turned up,' which was his favourite expression. And, Mrs Micawber was just the same.

A curious equality of friendship, originating, I suppose, in our respective circumstances, sprung up between me and these people, notwithstanding the ludicrous disparity in our years. But I never allowed myself to be prevailed upon to accept any invitation to eat and drink with them out of their stock (knowing that they got on badly with the butcher and baker, and had often not too much for themselves), until Mrs Micawber took me into her entire confidence. This she did one evening as follows:

'Master Copperfield,' said Mrs Micawber, 'I make no stranger of you, and therefore do not hesitate to say that Mr Micawber's difficulties are coming to a crisis.'

It made me very miserable to hear it, and I looked at Mrs Micawber's red eyes with the utmost sympathy.

'With the exception of the heel of a Dutch cheese – which is not adapted to the wants of a young family' – said Mrs Micawber, 'there is really not a scrap of anything in the larder. I was accustomed to speak of the larder when I lived with papa and mama, and I use the word almost unconsciously. What I mean to express, is, that there is nothing to eat in the house.'

'Dear me!' I said, in great concern.

I had two or three shillings of my week's money in my pocket – from which I presume that it must have been on a Wednesday night when we held this conversation – and I hastily produced them, and with heartfelt emotion begged Mrs Micawber to accept of them as a loan. But that lady, kissing me, and making me put them back in my pocket, replied that she couldn't think of it.

'No, my dear Master Copperfield,' said she, 'far be it from my thoughts! But you have a discretion beyond your years, and can render me another kind of service, if you will; and a service I will thankfully accept of.'

I begged Mrs Micawber to name it.

'I have parted with the plate myself,' said Mrs Micawber. 'Six tea, two salt, and a pair of sugars, I have at different times borrowed money on, in secret, with my own hands. But the twins are a great tie; and to me, with my recollections of papa and mama, these transactions are very painful. There are still a few trifles that we could part with. Mr Micawber's feelings would never allow *him* to dispose of them; and Clickett' – this was the girl from the workhouse –'being of a vulgar mind, would take painful liberties if so much confidence was reposed in her. Master Copperfield, if I might ask you' –

I understood Mrs Micawber now, and begged her to make use of me to any extent. I began to dispose of the more portable articles of property that very evening; and went out on a similar expedition almost every morning, before I went to Murdstone and Grinby's.

Mr Micawber had a few books on a little chiffonier, which he called the library; and those went first. I carried them, one after another, to a bookstall in the City Road – one part of which, near our house, was almost all bookstalls and bird-shops then – and sold them for whatever they would bring. The keeper of this bookstall, who lived in a little house behind it, used to get tipsy every night, and to be violently scolded by his wife every morning. More than once, when I went there early, I had audience of him in a turn-up bedstead, with a cut in his forehead or a black eye, bearing witness to his excesses over-night (I am afraid he was quarrelsome in his drink), and he, with a shaking hand, endeavouring to find the needful shillings in one or other of the pockets of his clothes, which lay upon the floor, while his wife, with a baby in her arms and her shoes down at heel, never left off rating him. Sometimes he had lost his money, and then he would ask me to call again; but his wife had always got some – had taken his, I dare say, while he was drunk – and secretly completed the bargain on the stairs, as we went down together.

At the pawnbroker's shop, too, I began to be very well known. The principal gentleman who officiated behind the counter, took a good deal of notice of me; and often got me, I recollect, to decline a Latin noun or adjective, or to conjugate a Latin verb, in his ear, while he transacted my business. After all these occasions Mrs Micawber made a little treat, which was generally a supper; and there was a peculiar relish in these meals which I well remember.

At last Mr Micawber's difficulties came to a crisis, and he was arrested early one morning, and carried over to the King's Bench Prison in the Borough. He told me, as he went out of the house, that the God of day had now gone down upon him – and I really thought his heart was broken and mine too. But I heard, afterwards, that he was seen to play a lively game at skittles, before noon.

On the first Sunday after he was taken there, I was to go and see him, and have dinner with him. I was to ask my way to such a place, and just short of that place I should see such another place, and just short of that I should see a yard, which I was to cross, and keep straight on until I saw a turnkey. All this I did; and when at last I did see a turnkey (poor little fellow that I was!), and thought how, when Roderick Random was in a debtors' prison, there was a man there with nothing on him but an old rug, the turnkey swam before my dimmed eyes and my beating heart.

Mr Micawber was waiting for me within the gate, and we went up to his room (top story but one), and cried very much. He solemnly conjured me, I remember, to take warning by his fate; and to observe that if a man had twenty pounds a-year for his income, and spent nineteen pounds nineteen shillings and sixpence, he would be happy, but that if he spent twenty pounds one he would be miserable. After which he borrowed a shilling of me for porter, gave me a written order on Mrs Micawber for the amount, and put away his pocket-handkerchief, and cheered up.

We sat before a little fire, with two bricks put within the rusted grate, one on each side, to prevent its burning too many coals; until another debtor, who shared the room with Mr Micawber, came in from the bakehouse with the loin of mutton which was our joint-stock repast. Then I was sent up to 'Captain Hopkins' in the room overhead, with Mr Micawber's compliments, and I was his young friend, and would Captain Hopkins lend me a knife and fork.

Captain Hopkins lent me the knife and fork, with his compliments to Mr Micawber. There was a very dirty lady in his little room, and two wan girls, his daughters, with shock heads of hair. I thought it was better to borrow Captain Hopkins's knife and fork, than Captain Hopkins's comb. The Captain himself was in the last extremity of shabbiness, with large whiskers, and an old, old brown great-coat with no other coat below it. I saw his bed rolled up in a corner; and what plates and dishes and pots he had, on a shelf; and I divined (God knows how) that though the two girls with the shock heads of hair were Captain Hopkins's children, the dirty lady was not married to Captain Hopkins. My timid station on his threshhold was not occupied more than a couple of minutes at most; but I came down again with all this in my knowledge, as surely as the knife and fork were in my hand.

There was something gipsy-like and agreeable in the dinner, after all. I took back Captain Hopkins's knife and fork early in the afternoon, and went home to comfort Mrs Micawber with an account of my visit. She fainted when she saw me return, and made a little jug of egg-hot afterwards to console us while we talked it over.

I don't know how the household furniture came to be sold for the family benefit, or who sold it, except that *I* did not. Sold it was, however, and carried away in a van; except the bed, a few chairs, and the kitchen table. With these possessions we encamped, as it were, in the two parlours of the emptied house in Windsor Terrace; Mrs Micawber, the children, the Orfling, and myself; and lived in those rooms night and day. I have no idea for how long, though it seems to me for a long time. At last Mrs Micawber resolved to move into the prison, where Mr Micawber had now secured a room to himself. So I took the key of the house to the landlord, who was very glad to get it; and the beds were sent over to the King's Bench, except mine, for which a little room was hired outside the walls in the neighbourhood of that Institution, very much to my satisfaction, since the Micawbers and I had become too used to one another, in our troubles, to part. The Orfling was likewise accommodated with an inexpensive lodging in the same neighbourhood. Mine was a quiet back-garret with a sloping roof, commanding a pleasant prospect of a timberyard; and when I took possession of it, with the reflection that Mr Micawber's troubles had come to a crisis at last, I thought it quite a paradise.

All this time I was working at Murdstone and Grinby's in the same common way, and with the same common companions, and with the same sense of unmerited degradation as at first. But I never, happily for me no doubt, made a single acquaintance, or spoke to any of the many boys whom I saw daily in going to the warehouse, in coming from it, and in prowling about the streets at meal-times. I led the same secretly unhappy life; but I led it in the same lonely, self-reliant manner. The only changes I am conscious of are, firstly, that I had grown more shabby, and secondly, that I was now relieved of much of the weight of Mr and Mrs Micawber's cares; for some relatives or friends had engaged to help them at their present pass, and they lived more comfortably in the prison than they had lived for a long while out of it. I used to breakfast with them now, in virtue of some arrangement, of which I have forgotten the details. I forget, too, at what hour the gates were opened in the morning, admitting of my going in; but I know that I was often up at six o'clock, and that my favorite lounging-place in the interval was old London Bridge, where I was wont to sit in one of the stone recesses, watching the people going by, or to look over the balustrades at the sun shining in the water, and lighting up the golden flame on the top of the Monument. The Orfling met me here sometimes, to be told some astonishing fictions respecting the wharves and the Tower; of which I can say no more than that I hope I believed them myself. In the evening I used to go back to the prison, and walk up and down the parade with Mr Micawber; or play casino with Mrs Micawber, and hear reminiscences of her papa and mama. Whether Mr Murdstone knew where I was, I am unable to say. I never told them at Murdstone and Grinby's.

Mr Micawber's affairs, although past their crisis, were very much involved by reason of a certain 'Deed,' of which I used to hear a great deal, and which I suppose, now, to have been some former composition with his creditors, though

I was so far from being clear about it then, that I am conscious of having confounded it with those demoniacal parchments which are held to have, once upon a time, obtained to a great extent in Germany. At last this document appeared to be got out of the way, somehow; at all events it ceased to be the rock ahead it had been; and Mrs Micawber informed me that 'her family' had decided that Mr Micawber should apply for his release under the Insolvent Debtors Act, which would set him free, she expected, in about six weeks.

'And then,' said Mr Micawber, who was present, 'I have no doubt I shall, please Heaven, begin to be beforehand with the world, and to live in a perfectly new manner, if – in short, if anything turns up.'

By way of going in for anything that might be on the cards, I call to mind that Mr Micawber, about this time, composed a petition to the House of Commons, praying for an alteration in the law of imprisonment for debt. I set down this remembrance here, because it is an instance to myself of the manner in which I fitted my old books to my altered life, and made stories for myself, out of the streets, and out of men and women; and how some main points in the character I shall unconsciously develop, I suppose, in writing my life, were gradually forming all this while.

There was a club in the prison, in which Mr Micawber, as a gentleman, was a great authority. Mr Micawber had stated his idea of this petition to the club, and the club had strongly approved of the same. Wherefore Mr Micawber (who was a thoroughly good-natured man, and as active a creature about everything but his own affairs as ever existed, and never so happy as when he was busy about something that could never be of any profit to him) set to work at the petition, invented it, engrossed it on an immense sheet of paper, spread it out on a table, and appointed a time for all the club, and all within the walls if they chose, to come up to his room and sign it.

When I heard of this approaching ceremony, I was so anxious to see them all come in, one after another, though I knew the greater part of them already, and they me, that I got an hour's leave of absence from Murdstone and Grinby's, and established myself in a corner for that purpose. As many of the principal members of the club as could be got into the small room without filling it, supported Mr Micawber in front of the petition, while my old friend Captain Hopkins (who had washed himself, to do honor to so solemn an occasion) stationed himself close to it, to read it to all who were unacquainted with its contents. The door was then thrown open and the general population began to come in, in a long file: several waiting outside, while one entered, affixed his signature, and went out. To everybody in succession, Captain Hopkins said: 'Have you read it?'–'No.'–'Would you like to hear it read?' If he weakly showed the least disposition to hear it, Captain Hopkins, in a loud sonorous voice, gave him every word of it. The Captain would have read it twenty thousand times, if twenty thousand people would have heard him, one by one. I remember a certain luscious roll he gave to such phrases as 'The people's representatives in Parliament assembled,' 'Your petitioners therefore humbly approach your honorable house,' 'His gracious Majesty's unfortunate subjects,' as if the words were something real in his mouth, and delicious to taste; Mr Micawber, meanwhile, listening with a little of an author's vanity, and contemplating (not severely) the spikes on the opposite wall.

As I walked to and fro daily between Southwark and Blackfriars, and lounged about at meal-times in obscure streets, the stones of which may, for anything I know, be worn at this moment by my childish feet, I wonder how many of these people were wanting in the crowd that used to come filing before me in review again, to the echo of Captain Hopkins's voice! When my thoughts go back, now, to that slow agony of my youth, I wonder how much of the histories I invented for such people hangs like a mist of fancy over well-remembered facts! When I tread the old ground, I do not wonder that I seem to see and pity, going on before me, an innocent romantic boy, making his imaginative world out of such strange experiences and sordid things!

Chapter 12. Liking Life On My Own Account No Better, I Form a Great Resolution

In due time, Mr Micawber's petition was ripe for hearing; and that gentleman was ordered to be discharged under the Act, to my great joy. His creditors were not implacable; and Mrs Micawber informed me that even the revengeful bootmaker had declared in open court that he bore him no malice, but that when money was owing to him he liked to be paid. He said he thought it was human nature.

Mr Micawber returned to the King's Bench when his case was over, as some fees were to be settled, and some formalities observed, before he could be actually released. The club received him with transport, and held an harmonic meeting that evening in his honor; while Mrs Micawber and I had a lamb's fry in private, surrounded by the sleeping family.

'On such an occasion I will give you, Master Copperfield,' said Mrs Micawber, 'in a little more flip,' for we had been having some already, 'the memory of my papa and mama.'

'Are they dead, ma'am?' I enquired, after drinking the toast in a wineglass.

'My mama departed this life,' said Mrs Micawber, 'before Mr Micawber's difficulties commenced, or at least before they became pressing. My papa lived to bail Mr Micawber several times, and then expired, regretted by a numerous circle.'

Mrs Micawber shook her head, and dropped a pious tear upon the twin who happened to be in hand.

As I could hardly hope for a more favourable opportunity of putting a question in which I had a near interest, I said to Mrs Micawber:

'May I ask, ma'am, what you and Mr Micawber intend to do, now that Mr Micawber is out of his difficulties, and at liberty? Have you settled yet?'

'My family,' said Mrs Micawber, who always said those two words with an air, though I never could discover who came under the denomination, 'my family are of opinion that Mr Micawber should quit London and exert his talents in the country. Mr Micawber is a man of great talent, Master Copperfield.'

I said I was sure of that.

'Of great talent,' repeated Mrs Micawber. 'My family are of opinion that, with a little interest; something might be done for a man of his ability in the Custom House. The influence of my family being local, it is their wish that Mr Micawber should go down to Plymouth. They think it indispensable that he should be upon the spot.'

'That he may be ready?' I suggested.

'Exactly,' returned Mrs Micawber. 'That he may be ready – in case of anything turning up.'

'And do you go too, ma'am?'

The events of the day, in combination with the twins, if not with the flip, had made Mrs Micawber hysterical, and she shed tears as she replied:

'I never will desert Mr Micawber. Mr Micawber may have concealed his difficulties from me in the first instance, but his sanguine temper may have led him to expect that he would overcome them. The pearl necklace and bracelets which I inherited from mama, have been disposed of for less than half their value; and the set of coral, which was the wedding gift of my papa, has been actually thrown away for nothing. But I never will desert Mr Micawber. No!' cried Mrs Micawber, more affected than before, 'I never will do it! It's of no use asking me!'

I felt quite uncomfortable – as if Mrs Micawber supposed I had asked her to do anything of the sort! – and sat looking at her in alarm.

'Mr Micawber has his faults. I do not deny that he is improvident. I do not deny that he has kept me in the dark as to his resources and his liabilities both,' she went on, looking at the wall: 'but I never will desert Mr Micawber!'

Mrs Micawber having now raised her voice into a perfect scream, I was so frightened that I ran off to the club-room, and disturbed Mr Micawber in the act of presiding at a long table, and leading the chorus of

Gee up, Dobbin,
Gee ho, Dobbin,
Gee up, Dobbin,
Gee up, and gee ho–o–o!

– with the tidings that Mrs Micawber was in an alarming state, upon which he immediately burst into tears, and came away with me with his waistcoat full of the heads and tails of shrimps, of which he had been partaking.

'Emma, my angel!' cried Mr Micawber, running into the room; 'what is the matter?'

'I never will desert you, Micawber!' she exclaimed.

'My life!' said Mr Micawber, taking her in his arms. 'I am perfectly aware of it.'

'He is the parent of my children! He is the father of my twins! He is the husband of my affections,' cried Mrs Micawber, struggling; 'and I ne–ver–will– desert Mr Micawber!'

Mr Micawber was so deeply affected by this proof of her devotion (as to me, I was dissolved in tears), that he hung over her in a passionate manner, imploring her to look up, and to be calm. But the more he asked Mrs Micawber to look up, the more she fixed her eyes on nothing; and the more he asked her to compose herself, the more she wouldn't. Consequently Mr Micawber was soon so overcome, that he mingled his tears with hers and mine; until he begged me to do him the favour of taking a chair on the staircase, while he got her into bed. I would have taken my leave for the night, but he would not hear of my doing that until the strangers' bell should ring. So I sat at the staircase-window, until he came out with another chair and joined me.

'How is Mrs Micawber now, sir?' I said.

'Very low,' said Mr Micawber, shaking his head; 'reaction. Ah this has been a dreadful day! We stand alone now – everything is gone from us!'

Mr Micawber pressed my hand, and groaned, and afterwards shed tears. I was greatly touched, and disappointed too, for I had expected that we should be quite gay on this happy and long-looked-for occasion. But Mr and Mrs Micawber were so used to their old difficulties, I think, that they felt quite shipwrecked when they came to consider that they were released from them. All their elasticity was departed, and I never saw them half so wretched as on this night; insomuch that when the bell rang, and Mr Micawber walked with me to the lodge, and parted from me there with a blessing, I felt quite afraid to leave him by himself, he was so profoundly miserable.

But through all the confusion and lowness of spirits in which we had been, so unexpectedly to me, involved, I plainly discerned that Mr and Mrs Micawber and their family were going away from London, and that a parting between us was near at hand. It was in my walk home that night, and in the sleepless hours which followed when I lay in bed, that the thought first occurred to me – though I don't know how it came into my head – which afterwards shaped itself into a settled resolution.

I had grown to be so accustomed to the Micawbers, and had been so intimate with them in their distresses, and was so utterly friendless without them, that the prospect of being thrown upon some new shift for a lodging, and going once more among unknown people, was like being that moment turned adrift into my present life, with such a knowledge of it ready made, as experience had given me. All the sensitive feelings it wounded so cruelly, all the shame and misery it kept alive within my breast, became more poignant as I thought of this; and I determined that the life was unendurable.

That there was no hope of escape from it, unless the escape was my own act, I knew quite well. I rarely heard from Miss Murdstone, and never from Mr Murdstone: but two or three parcels of made or mended clothes had come up for me, consigned to Mr Quinion, and in each there was a scrap of paper to the effect that J. M. trusted D. C. was applying himself to business, and devoting himself wholly to his duties – not the least hint of my ever being anything else than the common drudge into which I was fast settling down.

The very next day showed me, while my mind was in the first agitation of what it had conceived, that Mrs Micawber had not spoken of their going away without warrant. They took a lodging in the house where I lived, for a week; at the expiration of which time they were to start for Plymouth. Mr Micawber himself came down to the counting-house, in the afternoon, to tell Mr Quinion that he must relinquish me on the day of his departure, and to give me a high character, which I am sure I deserved. And Mr Quinion, calling in Tipp the carman, who was a married man, and had a room to let, quartered me prospectively on him – by our mutual consent, as he had every reason to think; for I said nothing, though my resolution was now taken.

I passed my evenings with Mr and Mrs Micawber, during the remaining term of our residence under the same roof; and I think we became fonder of one another as the time went on. On the last Sunday, they invited me to dinner; and we had a loin of pork and apple sauce, and a pudding. I had bought a spotted wooden horse over-night as a parting gift to little Wilkins Micawber – that was the boy – and a doll for little Emma. I had also bestowed a shilling on the Orfling, who was about to be disbanded.

We had a very pleasant day, though we were all in a tender state about our approaching separation.

'I shall never, Master Copperfield,' said Mrs Micawber, 'revert to the period when Mr Micawber was in difficulties, without thinking of you. Your conduct has always been of the most delicate and obliging description. You have never been a lodger. You have been a friend.'

'My dear,' said Mr Micawber; 'Copperfield,' for so he had been accustomed to call me, of late, 'has a heart to feel for the distresses of his fellow creatures when they are behind a cloud, and a head to plan, and a hand to – in short, a general ability to dispose of such available property as could be made away with.'

I expressed my sense of this commendation, and said I was very sorry we were going to lose one another.

'My dear young friend,' said Mr Micawber, 'I am older than you; man of some experience in life, and – and of some experience, in short, in difficulties, generally speaking. At present, and until something turns up (which I am, I may say, hourly expecting), I have nothing to bestow but advice. Still my advice is so far worth taking, that – in short, that I have never taken it myself, and am the'– here Mr Micawber, who had been beaming and smiling, all over his head and face, up to the present moment, checked himself and frowned – 'the miserable wretch you behold.'

'My dear Micawber!' urged his wife.

'I say,' returned Mr Micawber, quite forgetting himself, and smiling again, 'the miserable wretch you behold. My advice is, never do tomorrow what you can do today. Procrastination is the thief of time. Collar him!'

'My poor papa's maxim,' Mrs Micawber observed.

'My dear,' said Mr Micawber, 'your papa was very well in his way, and Heaven forbid that I should disparage him. Take him for all in all, we never shall – in short, make the acquaintance, probably, of anybody else possessing, at his time of life, the same legs for gaiters, and able to read the same description of print, without spectacles. But he applied that maxim to our marriage, my dear; and that was so far prematurely entered into, in consequence, that I never recovered the expense.'

Mr Micawber looked aside at Mrs Micawber, and added: 'Not that I am sorry for it. Quite the contrary, my love.' After which, he was grave for a minute or so.

'My other piece of advice, Copperfield,' said Mr Micawber, 'you know. Annual income twenty pounds, annual expenditure nineteen nineteen and six, result happiness. Annual income twenty pounds, annual expenditure twenty pounds ought and six, result misery. The blossom is blighted, the leaf is withered, the God of day goes down upon the dreary scene, and – and in short you are for ever floored. As I am!'

To make his example the more impressive, Mr Micawber drank a glass of punch with an air of great enjoyment and satisfaction, and whistled the College Hornpipe.

I did not fail to assure him that I would store these precepts in my mind, though indeed I had no need to say so, for, at the time, they affected me visibly. Next morning I met the whole family at the coach office, and saw them, with a desolate heart, take their places outside, at the back.

'Master Copperfield,' said Mrs Micawber, 'God bless you! I never can forget all that, you know, and I never would if I could.'

'Copperfield,' said Mr Micawber, 'farewell! Every happiness and prosperity! If, in the progress of revolving years, I could persuade myself that my blighted destiny had been a warning to you, I should feel that I had not occupied another man's place in existence altogether in vain. In case of anything turning up (of which I am rather confident), I shall be extremely happy if it should lie in my power to improve your prospects.'

I think, as Mrs Micawber sat at the back of the coach, with the children, and I stood in the road looking wistfully at them, a mist cleared from her eyes, and she saw what a little creature I really was. I think so, because she beckoned to me to climb up, with quite a new and motherly expression in her face, and put her arm round my neck, and gave me just such a kiss as she might have given to her own boy. I had barely time to get down again before the coach started, and I could hardly see the family for the handkerchiefs they waved. It was gone in a minute. The Orfling and I stood looking vacantly at each other in the middle of the road, and then shook hands and said good bye; she going back, I suppose, to Saint Luke's workhouse, as I went to begin my weary day at Murdstone and Grinby's.

But with no intention of passing many more weary days there. No. I had resolved to run away. – To go, by some means or other, down into the country, to the only relation I had in the world, and tell my story to my aunt, Miss Betsey.

I have already observed that I don't know how this desperate idea came into my brain. But, once there, it remained there; and hardened into a purpose than which I have never entertained a more determined purpose in my life. I am far from sure that I believed there was anything hopeful in it, but my mind was thoroughly made up that it must be carried into execution.

Again, and again, and a hundred times again, since the night when the thought had first occurred to me and banished sleep, I had gone over that old story of my poor mother's about my birth, which it had been one of my great delights in the old time to hear her tell, and which I knew by heart. My aunt walked into that story, and walked out of it, a dread and awful personage; but there was one little trait in her behaviour which I liked to dwell on, and which gave me some faint shadow of encouragement. I could not forget how my mother had thought that she felt her touch her pretty hair with no ungentle hand; and though it might have been altogether my mother's fancy, and might have had no foundation whatever in fact, I made a little picture, out of it, of my terrible aunt relenting towards the girlish beauty that I recollected so well and loved so much, which softened the whole narrative. It is very possible that it had been in my mind a long time, and had gradually engendered my determination.

As I did not even know where Miss Betsey lived, I wrote a long letter to Peggotty, and asked her, incidentally, if she remembered; pretending that I had heard of such a lady living at a certain place I named at random, and had a curiosity to know if it were the same. In the course of that letter, I told Peggotty that I had a particular occasion for half a guinea; and that if she could lend me that sum until I could repay it, I should be very much obliged to her, and would tell her afterwards what I had wanted it for.

Peggotty's answer soon arrived, and was, as usual, full of affectionate devotion. She enclosed the half-guinea (I was afraid she must have had a world of trouble to get it out of Mr Barkis's box), and told me that Miss Betsey lived near Dover, but whether at Dover itself, at Hythe, Sandgate, or Folkestone, she could not say. One of our men, however, informing me on my asking him about these places, that they were all close together, I deemed this enough for my object, and resolved to set out at the end of that week.

Being a very honest little creature, and unwilling to disgrace the memory I was going to leave behind me at Murdstone and Grinby's, I considered myself bound to remain until Saturday night; and, as I had been paid a week's wages in advance when I first came there, not to present myself in the counting-house at the usual hour, to receive my stipend. For this express reason, I had borrowed the half-guinea, that I might not be without a fund for my travelling-expenses. Accordingly, when the Saturday night came, and we were all waiting in the warehouse to be paid, and Tipp the carman, who always took precedence, went in first to draw his money, I shook Mick Walker by the hand; asked him when it came to his turn to be paid, to say to Mr Quinion that I had gone to move my box to Tipp's; and, bidding a last good night to Mealy Potatoes, ran away.

My box was at my old lodging, over the water, and I had written a direction for it on the back of one of our address cards that we nailed on the casks: 'Master David, to be left till called for, at the Coach Office, Dover.' This I had in my pocket ready to put on the box, after I should have got it out of the house; and as I went towards my lodging, I looked about me for someone who would help me to carry it to the booking-office.

There was a long-legged young man with a very little empty donkeycart, standing near the Obelisk, in the Blackfriars Road, whose eye I caught as I was going by, and who, addressing me as 'Sixpenn'orth of bad ha'pence,' hoped 'I should know him agin to swear to' – in allusion, I have no doubt, to my staring at him. I stopped to assure him that I had not done so in bad manners, but uncertain whether he might or might not like a job.

'Wot job?' said the long-legged young man.

'To move a box,' I answered.

'Wot box?' said the long-legged young man.

I told him mine, which was down that street there, and which I wanted him to take to the Dover coach-office for sixpence.

'Done with you for a tanner!' said the long-legged young man, and directly got upon his cart, which was nothing but a large wooden tray on wheels, and rattled away at such a rate, that it was as much as I could do to keep pace with the donkey.

There was a defiant manner about this young man, and particularly about the way in which he chewed straw as he spoke to me, that I did not much like; as the bargain was made, however, I took him upstairs to the room I was leaving, and we brought the box down, and put it on his cart. Now, I was unwilling to put the direction-card on there, lest any of my landlord's family should fathom what I was doing, and detain me; so I said to the young man that I would be glad if he would stop for a minute, when he came to the dead-wall of the King's Bench prison. The words were no sooner out of my mouth, than he rattled away as if he, my box, the cart, and, the donkey, were all equally mad; and I was quite out of breath with running and calling after him, when I caught him at the place appointed.

Being much flushed and excited, I tumbled my half-guinea out of my pocket in pulling the card out. I put it in my mouth for safety, and though my hands trembled a good deal, had just tied the card on very much to my satisfaction, when I felt myself violently chucked under the chin by the long-legged young man, and saw my half-guinea fly out of my mouth into his hand.

'Wot!' said the young man, seizing me by my jacket-collar, with a frightful grin. 'This is a pollis case, is it? You're a-going to bolt, are you? Come to the pollis, you young warmin, come to the pollis!'[1]

'You give me my money back, if you please,' said I, very much frightened; 'and leave me alone.'

'Come to the pollis!' said the young man. 'You shall prove it yourn to the pollis.'

'Give me my box and money, will you,' I cried, bursting into tears.

The young man still replied: 'Come to the pollis!' and was dragging me against the donkey in a violent manner, as if there were an affinity between that animal and a magistrate, when he changed his mind, jumped into the cart, sat upon my box, and, exclaiming that he would drive to the pollis straight, rattled away harder than ever.

I ran after him as fast as I could, but I had no breath to call out with, and should not have dared to call out, now, if I had. I narrowly escaped being run over, twenty times at least, in half a mile. Now I lost him, now I saw him, now I lost him, now I was cut at with a whip, now shouted at, now down in the mud, now up again, now running into somebody's arms, now running headlong at a post. At length, confused by fright and heat, and doubting whether half London might not by this time be turning out for my apprehensions I left the young man to go where he would with my box and money; and, panting and crying, but never stopping, faced about for Greenwich, which I had understood was on the Dover Road: taking very little more out of the world, towards the retreat of my aunt, Miss Betsey, than I had brought into it, on the night when my arrival gave her so much umbrage.

1: 'you young varmint (vermin), come to the police!'

From Little Dorrit

Chapter 14. Little Dorrit's Party

Arthur Clennam rose hastily, and saw her standing at the door. This history must sometimes see with Little Dorrit's eyes and shall begin that course by seeing him.

Little Dorrit looked into a dim room, which seemed a spacious one to her, and grandly furnished. Courtly ideas of Covent Garden, as a place with famous coffee-houses, where gentlemen wearing gold-laced coats and swords had quarrelled and fought duels; costly ideas of Covent Garden, as a place where there were flowers in winter at guineas a-piece, pine-apples at guineas a pound, and peas at guineas a pint; picturesque ideas of Covent Garden, as a place where there was a mighty theatre, showing wonderful and beautiful sights to richly-dressed ladies and gentlemen, and which was for ever far beyond the reach of poor Fanny or poor uncle; desolate ideas of Covent Garden, as having those arches in it, where the miserable children in rags among whom she had just now passed, like young rats, slunk and hid, fed on offal, huddled together for warmth, and were hunted about (look to the rats young and old, and ye Barnacles, for before God they are eating away our foundations, and will bring the roofs on our heads!); teeming ideas of Covent Garden, as a place of past and present mystery, romance, abundance, want, beauty, ugliness, fair country gardens, and foul street gutters; all confused together – made the room dimmer than it was in Little Dorrit's eyes, as they timidly saw it from the door.

At first in the chair before the gone-out fire, and then turned round wondering to see her, was the gentleman whom she sought. The brown, grave gentleman, who smiled so pleasantly, who was so frank and considerate in his manner, and yet in whose earnestness there was something that reminded her of his mother, with the great difference that she was earnest in asperity and he in gentleness. Now he regarded her with that attentive and inquiring look before which Little Dorrit's eyes had always fallen, and before which they fell still.

'My poor child! Here at midnight?'

'I said Little Dorrit, sir, on purpose to prepare you. I knew you must be very much surprised.'

'Are you alone?'

'No sir, I have got Maggy with me.'

Considering her entrance sufficiently prepared for by this mention of her name, Maggy appeared from the landing outside, on the broad grin. She instantly suppressed that manifestation, however, and became fixedly solemn.

'And I have no fire,' said Clennam. 'And you are –' He was hoping to say so lightly clad, but stopped himself in what would have been a reference to her poverty, saying instead, 'And it is so cold.'

Putting the chair from which he had risen nearer to the grate, he made her sit down in it; and hurriedly bringing wood and coal, heaped them together and got a blaze.

'Your foot is like marble, my child;' he had happened to touch it, while stooping on one knee at his work of kindling the fire; 'put it nearer the warmth.' Little

Dorrit thanked him hastily. It was quite warm, it was very warm! It smote upon his heart to see that shed hid her thin, worn shoe.

Little Dorrit was not ashamed of her poor shoes. He knew her story, and it was not that. Little Dorrit had a misgiving that he might blame her father, if he saw them; that he might think, 'why did he dine to-day, and leave this little creature to the mercy of the cold stones!' She had no belief that it would have been a just reflection; she simply knew, by experience, that such delusions did sometimes present themselves to people. It was a part of her father's misfortunes that they did.

'Before I say anything else,' Little Dorrit began, sitting before the pale fire, and raising her eyes again to the face which in its harmonious look of interest, and pity, and protection, she felt to be a mystery far above her in degree, and almost removed beyond her guessing at; 'may I tell you something sir?'

'Yes my child.'

A slight shade of distress fell upon her, at this so often calling her a child. She was surprised that he should see it, or think of such a slight thing; but he said directly:

'I wanted a tender word, and could think of no other. As you just now gave yourself the name they give you at my mother's, and as that is the name by which I always think of you, let me call you Little Dorrit.'

'Thank you, sir, I should like it better than my name.'

'Little Dorrit.'

'Little mother,' Maggy (who had been falling asleep) put in, as a correction.

'It's all the same, Maggy,' returned Little Dorrit, 'all the same.'

'Is it all the same, mother?'

'Just the same.'

Maggy laughed, and immediately snored. In Little Dorrit's eyes and ears, the uncouth figure and the uncouth sound were as pleasant as could be. There was a glow of pride in her big child, overspreading her face, when it again met the eyes of the grave brown gentleman. She wondered what he was thinking of, as he looked at Maggy and her. She thought what a good father he would be. How, with some such look, he would counsel and cherish his daughter.

'What I was going to tell you, sir,' said Little Dorrit, 'is, that my brother is at large.'

Arthur was rejoiced to hear it, and hoped he would do well.

'And what I was going to tell you, sir,' said Little Dorrit, trembling in all her little figure and in her voice, 'is, that I am not to know whose generosity released him – am never to ask, and am never to be told, and am never to thank that gentleman with all my grateful heart!'

He would probably need no thanks, Clennam said. Very likely he would be thankful himself (and with reason), that he had had the means and chance of doing a little service to her, who well deserved a great one.

'And what I was going to say, sir, is,' said Little Dorrit, trembling more and more, 'that if I knew him, and I might, I would tell him that he can never, never know how I feel his goodness, and how my good father would feel it. And what I was going to say, sir, is, that if I knew him, and I might – but I don't know him and I must not – I know that! – I would tell him that I shall never any more lie down to sleep without having prayed to heaven to bless him and reward him.

And if I knew him, and I might, I would go down on my knees to him, and take his hand and kiss it and ask him not to draw it away, but to leave it – O to leave it for a moment – and let my thankful tears fall on it; for I have no other thanks to give him!'

Little Dorrit had put his hand to her lips, and would have kneeled to him, but he gently prevented her, and replaced her in her chair. Her eyes, and the tones of her voice, had thanked him far better than she thought. He was not able to say, quite as completely as usual, 'There, Little Dorrit, there, there, there! We will suppose that you did know this person, and that you might do all this, and that it was all done. And now tell me, who am quite another person – who am nothing more than the friend who begged you to trust him – why you are out at midnight, and what it is that brings you so far through the streets at this late hour, my slight, delicate,' child was on his lips again, 'Little Dorrit!'

'Maggy and I have been to-night', she answered, subduing herself with the quiet effort that had long been natural to her, 'to the theatre where my sister is engaged.'

'And oh ain't it an Ev'nly place,' suddenly interrupted Maggy, who seemed to have the power of going to sleep and waking up whenever she chose. 'Almost as good as a hospital. Only there ain't no Chicking in it.'

Here she shook herself, and fell asleep again.

'We went there,' said Little Dorrit, glancing at her charge, 'because I like sometimes to know, of my own knowledge, that my sister is doing well; and like to see her there, with my own eyes, when neither she nor Uncle is aware. It is very seldom indeed that I can do that, because when I am not out at work, I am with my father, and even when I am out at work, I hurry home to him. But I pretend to-night that I am at a party'.

As she made the confession, timidly hesitating, she raised her eyes to the face, and read its expression so plainly that she answered it.

'Oh no, certainly! I never was at a party in my life.'

She paused a little under his attentive look, and then said, 'I hope there is no harm in it. I could never have been of any use, if I had not pretended a little.'

She feared that he was blaming her in his mind for so devising to contrive for them, think for them, and watch over them, without their knowledge or gratitude; perhaps even with their reproaches for supposed neglect. But what was really in his mind was the weak figure with its strong purpose, the thin worn shoes, the insufficient dress, and the pretence of recreation and enjoyment. He asked where the suppositious party was? At a place where she worked, answered Little Dorrit, blushing. She had said very little about it; only a few words to make her father easy. Her father did not believe it to be a grand party – indeed he might suppose that. And she glanced for an instant at the shawl she wore.

'It is the first night,' said Little Dorrit, 'that I have ever been away from home. And London looks so large, so barren, and so wild.' In Little Dorrit's eyes, its vastness under the black sky was awful; a tremor passed over her as she said the words.

'But this is not,' she added, with the quiet effort again, 'what I have come to trouble you with sir. My sister's having found a friend, a lady she has told me of and made me rather anxious about was the first cause of my coming away from home. And being away and coming (on purpose) round by where you lived and seeing a light in the window – '

Not for the first time. No, not for the first time. In Little Dorrit's eyes, the outside of that window had been a distant star on other nights than this. She had toiled out of her way, tired and troubled, to look up at it, and wonder about the grave, brown gentleman from so far off, who had spoken to her as a friend and protector.

'There were three things,' said Little Dorrit, 'that I thought I would like to say, if you were alone and I might come up-stairs. First, what I would have tried to say, but never can – never shall – '

'Hush, hush! That is done with, and disposed of. Let us pass to the second,' said Clennam, smiling her agitation away, making the blaze shine upon her, and putting wine and cake and fruit towards her on the table.

'I think,' said Little Dorrit – 'this is the second thing, sir – I think Mrs Clennam must have found out my secret, and must know where I come from and where I go to. Where I live, I mean.'

'Indeed!' returned Clennam quickly. He asked her, after short consideration, why she supposed so.

'I think,' replied Little Dorrit, 'that Mr Flintwinch must have watched me.'

And why, Clennam asked, as he turned his eyes upon the fire, bent his brows, and considered again; why did she suppose that?

'I have met him twice. Both times near home. Both times at night, when I was going back. Both times I thought (though that may easily be a mistake), that he hardly looked as if he had met me by accident.'

'Did he say anything?'

'No; he only nodded and put his head on one side.'

'The devil take his head!' mused Clennam, still looking at the fire; 'it's always on one side.'

He roused himself to persuade her to put some wine to her lips, and to touch something to eat – it was very difficult, she was so timid and shy – and then said, musing again:

'Is my mother at all changed to you?'

'Oh, not at all. She is just the same. I wondered whether I had better tell her my history. I wondered whether I might – I mean, whether you would like me to tell her. I wondered,' said Little Dorrit, looking at him in a suppliant way, and gradually withdrawing her eyes as he looked at her, 'whether you would advise me what I ought to do.'

'Little Dorrit,' said Clennam; and the phrase had already begun, between these two, to stand for a hundred gentle phrases, according to the varying tone and connection in which it was used; 'do nothing. I will have some talk with my old friend, Mrs Affery. Do nothing, Little Dorrit – except refresh yourself with such means as there are here. I entreat you to do that.'

'Thank you, I am not hungry. Nor,' said Little Dorrit, as he softly put her glass towards her, 'nor thirsty. – I think Maggy might like something, perhaps.'

'We will make her find pockets presently for all there is here,' said Clennam: 'but before we awake her, there was a third thing to say.'

'Yes. You will not be offended, sir?'

'I promise that, unreservedly.'

'It will sound strange. I hardly know how to say it. Don't think it unreasonable or ungrateful in me,' said Little Dorrit, with returning and increasing agitation.

'No, no, no. I am sure it will be natural and right. I am not afraid that I shall put a wrong construction on it, whatever it is.'

'Thank you. You are coming back to see my father again?'

'Yes.'

'You have been so good and thoughtful as to write him a note saying that you are coming to-morrow?'

'Oh that was nothing! Yes.'

'Can you guess,' said Little Dorrit, folding her small hands tight in one another, and looking at him with all the earnestness of her soul looking steadily out of her eyes, 'what I am going to ask you not to do?'

'I think I can. But I may be wrong.'

'No, you are not wrong,' said Little Dorrit, shaking her head. 'If we should want it so very, very badly that we cannot do without it, let *me* ask you for it.'

'I will, – I will.'

'Don't encourage him to ask. Don't understand him if he does ask. Don't give it to him. Save him and spare him that, and you will be able to think better of him!'

Clennam said – not very plainly, seeing those tears glistening in her anxious eyes – that her wish should be sacred with him.

'You don't know what he is,' she said; 'you don't know what he really is. How can you, seeing him there all at once, dear love, and not gradually, as I have done! You have been so good to us, so delicately and truly good, that I want him to be better in your eyes than in anybody's. And I cannot bear to think,' cried Little Dorrit, covering her tears with her hands, 'I cannot bear to think that you of all the world should see him in his only moments of degradation.'

'Pray,' said Clennam, 'do not be so distressed. Pray, pray, Little Dorrit! This is quite understood now.'

'Thank you, sir. Thank you! I have tried very much to keep myself from saying this'; I have thought about it, days and nights, but when I knew for certain you were coming again, I made up my mind to speak to you. Not because I am ashamed of him,' she dried her tears quickly, 'but because I know him better than any ones does, and love him, and am proud of him.'

Relieved of this weight, Little Dorrit was nervously anxious to be gone. Maggy being broad awake, and in the act of distantly gloating over the fruit and cakes with chuckles of anticipation, Clennam made the best diversion in his power by pouring her out a glass of wine, which she drank in a series of loud smacks; putting her hand upon her windpipe after every one, and saying, breathing, with her eyes in a prominent state, 'Oh, ain't it d'licious! Ain't it hospitality!' When she had finished the wine and these encomiums, he charged her to load her basket (she was never without her basket) with every eatable thing upon the table, and to take especial care to leave no scrap behind. Maggy's pleasure in doing this and her little mother's pleasure in seeing Maggy pleased, was as good a turn as circumstances could have given to the late conversation.

'But the gates will have been locked long ago,' said Clennam, suddenly remembering it. 'Where are you going?'

'I am going to Maggy's lodging,' answered Little Dorrit. 'I shall be quite safe, quite well taken care of.'

'I must accompany you there,' said Clennam, 'I cannot let you go alone.'

'Yes, pray leave us to go there by ourselves. Pray do!' begged Little Dorrit.

She was so earnest in the petition, that Clennam felt a delicacy in obtruding himself upon her: the rather, because he could well understand that Maggy's lodging was of the obscurest sort. 'Come Maggy,' said Little Dorrit cheerily, 'we shall do very well; we know the way by this time, Maggy?'

'Yes, yes, little mother; we know the way,' chuckled Maggy. And away they went. Little Dorrit turned at the door to say, 'God bless you!' She said it very softly, but perhaps she may have been audible above – who knows! – as a whole cathedral choir.

Arthur Clennam suffered them to pass the corner of the street before he followed at a distance; not with any idea of encroaching a second time on Little Dorrit's privacy, but to satisfy his mind by seeing her secure in the neighbourhood to which she was accustomed. So diminutive she looked, so fragile and defenceless against the bleak damp weather, flitting along in the shuffling shadow of her charge, that he felt, in his compassion, and in his habit of considering her a child apart from the rest of the rough world, as if he would have been glad to Etake her up in his arms and carry her to her journey's end.

In course of time she came into the leading thoroughfare where the Marshalsea was, and then he saw them slacken their pace, and soon turn down a by-street. He stopped, felt that he had now right to go further, and slowly left them. He had no suspicion that they ran any risk of being houseless until morning; had no idea of the truth until long, long afterwards.

But, said Little Dorrit, when they stopped at a poor dwelling all in darkness, and heard no sound on listening at the door, 'Now, this is a good lodging for you, Maggy, and we must not give offence. Consequently, we will only knock twice, and not very loud; and if we cannot wake them so, we must walk about till day.'

Once, Little Dorrit knocked with a careful hand, and listened. Twice, Little Dorrit knocked with a careful hand, and listened. All was close and still. 'Maggy, we must do the best we can, my dear. We must be patient, and wait for day.'

It was a chill dark night, with a damp wind blowing, when they came out into the leading street again, and heard clocks strike half-past one. 'In only five hours and a half,' said Little Dorrit, 'we shall be able to go home.' To speak of home, and to go and look at it, it being so near, was a natural sequence. They went to the closed gate, and peeped through into the court-yard. 'I hope he is sound asleep,' said Little Dorrit, kissing one of the bars, 'and does not miss me.'

The gate was so familiar, and so like a companion, that they put down Maggy's basket in a corner to serve for a seat, and keeping close together, rested there for some time. While the street was empty and silent, Little Dorrit was not afraid; but when she heard a footstep at a distance, or saw a moving shadow among the street lamps, she was startled, and whispered, 'Maggy, I see some one. Come away!' Maggy would then wake up more or less fretfully, and they would wander about a little and come back again.

As long as eating was a novelty and an amusement, Maggy kept up pretty well. But that period going by, she became querulous about the cold, and shivered and whimpered. 'It will soon be over, dear,' said Little Dorrit patiently. 'Oh it's all very fine for you, little mother,' returned Maggy, 'but I'm a poor thing, only ten years old.' At last, in the dead of the night, when the street was very still indeed, Little Dorrit laid the heavy head upon her bosom, and soothed her to sleep. And thus she sat at the gate, as it were alone; looking up at the stars, and seeing the clouds pass over them in their wild flight – which was the dance at Little Dorrit's party.

'If it really was a party!' she thought once, as she sat there, 'If it was light and warm and beautiful, and it was our house, and my father dear was its master, and had never been inside these walls. And if Mr Clennam was one of our visitors, and we were dancing to delightful music, and were all as gay and light-hearted as ever we could be! I wonder – ' Such a vista of wonder opened out before her, that she sat looking up at the stars, quite lost, until Maggy was querulous again, and wanted to get up and walk.

Three o'clock, and half-past three, and they had passed over London Bridge. They had heard the rush of the tide against obstacles; and looked down, awed, through the dark vapour on the river; had seen little spots of lighted water where the bridge lamps were reflected, shining like demon eyes, with a terrible fascination in them for guilt and misery. They had shrunk past homeless people, lying coiled up in nooks. They had run from drunkards. They had started from slinking men, whistling and signing to one another at bye corners, or running away at full speed. Though everywhere the leader and the guide, Little Dorrit, happy for once in her youthful appearance, feigned to cling to and rely upon Maggy. And more than once some voice, from among a knot of brawling or prowling figures in their path, had called out to the rest to 'let the woman and the child go by!'

So, the woman and the child had gone by, and gone on, and five had sounded from the steeples. They were walking slowly towards the east, already looking for the first pale streak of day, when a woman came after them.

'What are you doing with the child?' she said to Maggy.

She was young – far too young to be there, Heaven knows! – and neither ugly nor wicked-looking. She spoke coarsely, but with no naturally coarse voice; there was even something musical in its sound.

'What are you doing with yourself?' retorted Maggy, for want of a better answer.

'Can't you see, without my telling you?'

'I don't know as I can,' said Maggy.

'Killing myself. Now I have answered you, answer me. What are you doing with the child?'

The supposed child kept her head drooped down, and kept her form close at Maggy's side.

'Poor thing!' said the woman. 'Have you no feeling, that you keep her out in the cruel streets at such a time as this? Have you no eyes, that you don't see how delicate and slender she is? Have you no sense (you don't look as if you had much) that you don't take pity on this cold and trembling little hand?'

She had stepped across to that side, and held the hand between her own two, chafing it. 'Kiss a poor lost creature, dear,' she said bending her face, 'and tell me where's she taking you.'

Little Dorrit turned towards her.

'Why, my God!' she said, recoiling, 'you're a woman!'

'Don't mind that!' said Little Dorrit, clasping one of her hands that had suddenly released hers. 'I am not afraid of you.'

'Then you had better be,' she answered. 'Have you no mother?'

'No.'

'No father?'

'Yes, a very dear one.'

'Go home to him, and be afraid of me. Let me go. Good night!'

'I must thank you first; let me speak to you as if I really was a child.'

'You can't do it,' said the woman. 'You are kind and innocent; but you can't look at me out of a child's eyes. I never should have touched you, but I thought that you were a child.'

And with a strange, wild, cry, she went away.

No day yet in the sky, but there was day in the resounding stones of the streets; in the waggons, carts, and coaches; in the workers going to various occupations; in the opening of early shops; in the traffic at markets; in the stir of the riverside. There was coming day in the flaring lights, with a feebler colour in them than they would have had at another time; coming day in the increased sharpness of the air, and the ghastly dying of the night.

They went back again to the gate, intending to wait there now until it should be opened; but the air was so raw and cold that Little Dorrit, leading Maggy about in her sleep, kept in motion. Going round by the Church, she saw lights there, and the door open; and went up the steps and looked in.

'Who's that?' cried a stout old man, who was putting on a nightcap as if he were going to bed in a vault.

'It's no one particular, sir,' said Little Dorrit.

'Stop!' cried the man. 'Let's have a look at you!'

This caused her to turn back again in the act of going out, and to present herself and her charge before him.

'I thought so!' said he. 'I know *you*.'

'We have often seen each other,' said Little Dorrit, recognising the sexton, or the beadle, or the verger, or whatever he was, 'when I have been at church here.'

'More than that, we've got your birth in our Register, you know; you're one of our curiosities.'

'Indeed!' said Little Dorrit.

'To be sure. As the child of the – by-the-bye, how did you get out so early?'

'We were shut out last night, and are waiting to get in.'

'You don't mean it? And there's another hour good yet! Come into the vestry. You'll find a fire in the vestry, on account of the painters. I'm waiting for the painters, or I shouldn't be here, you may depend upon it. One of our curiosities mustn't be cold when we have it in our power to warm her up comfortable. Come along.'

He was a very good old fellow, in his familiar way; and having stirred the vestry fire, he looked round the shelves of registers for a particular volume. 'Here you are, you see,' he said, taking it down and turning the leaves. 'Here you'll find yourself, as large as life. Amy, daughter of William and Fanny Dorrit. Born, Marshalsea Prison, Parish of St George. And we tell people that you have lived there, without so much as a day's or night's absence, ever since. It is true?'

'Quite true, till last night.'

'Lord!' But his surveying her with an admiring gaze suggested something else to him, to wit: 'I am sorry to see, though, that you are faint and tired. Stay a bit. I'll get some cushions out of the church, and you and your friend shall lie down before the fire. Don't be afraid of not going in to join your father when the gate opens. *I'll* call you.'

He soon brought in the cushions, and strewed them on the ground.

'There you are, you see. Again as large as life. Oh, never mind thanking. I've daughters of my own. And though they weren't born in the Marshalsea Prison, they might have been, if I had been, in my ways of carrying on, of your father's breed. Stop a bit. I must put something under the cushion for your head. Here's a burial volume. Just the thing! We have got Mrs Bangham in this book. But what makes these books interesting to most people is – not who's in 'em, but who isn't – who's coming, you know, and when. That's the interesting question.'

Commendingly looking back at the pillow he had improvised, he left them to their hour's repose. Maggy was snoring already and Little Dorrit was soon fast asleep with her head resting on the sealed book of Fate, untroubled by its mysterious blank leaves.

This was Little Dorrit's party. The shame, desertion, wretchedness, and exposure of the great capital; the wet, the cold, the slow hours, and the swift clouds of the dismal night. This was the party from which Little Dorrit went home, jaded, in the first grey mist of a rainy morning.

Chapter 15. Mrs Flintwinch Has Another Dream

The debilitated old house in the city, wrapped in its mantle of soot, and leaning heavily on the crutches that had partaken of its decay and worn out with it, never knew a healthy or a cheerful interval, let what would betide. If the sun ever touched it, it was but with a ray, and that was gone in half an hour; if the moonlight ever fell upon it, it was only to put a few patches on its doleful cloak, and make it look more wretched. The stars, to be sure, coldly watched it when the nights and the smoke were clear enough; and all bad weather stood by it with a rare fidelity. You should alike find rain, hail, frost, and thaw lingering in that dismal enclosure when they had vanished from other places; and as to snow, you should see it there for weeks, long after it had changed from yellow to black, slowly weeping away its grimy life. The place had no other adherents. As to street noises, the rumbling of wheels in the lane merely rushed in at the gateway in going past, and rushed out again: making the listening Mistress Affery feel as if she were deaf, and recovered the sense of hearing by instantaneous flashes. So with whistling, singing, talking, laughing, and all pleasant human sounds. They leaped the gap in a moment, and went upon their way.

The varying light of fire and candle in Mrs Clennam's room made the greatest change that ever broke the dead monotony of the spot. In her two long narrow windows, the fire shone sullenly all day, and sullenly all night. On rare occasions it flashed up passionately, as she did; but for the most part it was suppressed, like her, and preyed upon itself evenly and slowly. During many hours of the short winter days, however, when it was dusk there early in the afternoon, changing distortions of herself in her wheeled chair, of Mr Flintwinch with his wry neck, of Mistress Affery coming and going, would be thrown upon the house wall that was over the gateway, and would hover there like shadows from a great magic lantern. As the room-ridden invalid settled for the night, these would gradually disappear: Mistress Affery's magnified shadow always flitting about, last, until it finally glided away into the air, as though she were off upon a witch excursion. Then the solitary light would burn unchangingly, until it burned pale before the dawn, and at last died under the breath of Mrs Affery, as her shadow descended on it from the witch-region of sleep.

Strange, if the little sick-room fire were in effect a beacon fire, summoning some one, and that the most unlikely some one in the world, to the spot that *must* be come to. Strange, if the little sick-room light were in effect a watch-light, burning in that place very light until an appointed event should be watched out! Which of the vast multitude of travellers, under the sun and the stars, climbing the dusty hills and toiling along the weary plains, journeying by land and journeying by sea, coming and going so strangely, to meet and to act and react on one another; which of the host may with no suspicion of the journey's end, be travelling surely hither?

Time shall show us. The post of honour and the post of shame, the general's station and the drummer's, a peer's statue in Westminster Abbey and a seaman's hammock in the bosom of the deep, the mitre and the workhouse, the woolsack and the gallows, the throne and the guillotine – the travellers to all are on the great high road, but it has wonderful divergencies, and only Time shall show us whither each traveller is bound.

ELIZABETH BARRETT BROWNING
(1806–1861)

Elizabeth Barrett was born and brought up in Herefordshire, largely educating herself by borrowing her brother's tutor and studying such Latin and Greek, history and philosophy, that she was later able to publish translations of ancient Greek poetry. She early developed her own poetic talents and became the most prominent woman poet of the age, much better known than Robert Browning whom she married after eloping to Italy with him in 1846, an act made necessary by her tyrannical father who had forbidden all his children to marry and was in the process of turning Elizabeth into an hysterical invalid. Once in Italy, she rapidly became fully healthy and bore a son. Elizabeth Barrett Browning's poetry was typically didactic and moral, related to the alleviation of such miseries as child poverty and slavery (from which her own family wealth derived). It was for *The Seraphim and Other Poems* (1838) and *Poems* (1844) that she was best known, the latter volume being ranked on a par with Wordsworth. Her *Sonnets from the Portuguese* which issue from her romance with Robert Browning constitue some of the most passionate sonnets in the English language and have survived the disinterest which has befallen her polemical verse. Her verse novel about the development of a woman writer, *Aurora Leigh* (1857), had fervent admirers in her own time and has been recently re-discovered as a female parallel to Wordsworth's *The Prelude*.

To George Sand

  Thou large-brained woman and large-hearted man,
  Self-called George Sand! whose soul, amid the lions
  Of thy tumultous senses, moans defiance
  And answers roar for roar, as spirits can:
5 I would some mild miraculous thunder ran
  Above the applauded circus, in appliance
  Of thine own nobler nature's strength and science,
  Drawing two pinions, white as wings of swan,
  From thy strong shoulders, to amaze the place
10 With holier light! that thou to woman's claim
  And man's, mightst join beside the angel's grace
  Of a pure genius sanctified from blame,
  Till child and maiden pressed to thine embrace
  To kiss upon thy lips a stainless fame.

From Sonnets from the Portuguese

21

  Say over again, and yet once over again,
  That thou dost love me. Though the word repeated
  Should seem 'a cuckoo song,' as thou dost treat it,
  Remember, never to the hill or plain,

5   Valley and wood, without her cuckoo strain
Comes the fresh Spring in all her green completed.
Beloved, I, amid the darkness greeted
By a doubtful spirit voice, in that doubt's pain
Cry, 'Speak once more – thou lovest!' Who can fear
10 Too many stars, though each in heaven shall roll,
Too many flowers, though each shall crown the year?
Say thou dost love me, love me, love me – toll
The silver iterance! – only mind, Dear,
To love me also in silence with thy soul.

22

When our two souls stand up erect and strong,
Face to face, silent, drawing nigh and nigher,
Until the lengthening wings break into fire
At either curved point – what bitter wrong
5   Can the earth do to us, that we should not long
Be here contented? Think. In mounting higher,
The angels would press on us and aspire
To drop some golden orb of perfect song
Into our deep, dear silence. Let us stay
10 Rather on earth, Beloved, – where the unfit
Contrarious moods of men recoil away
And isolate pure spirits, and permit a
A place to stand and love in for a day,
With darkness and the death-hour rounding it.

43

How do I love thee? Let me count the ways.
I love thee to the length and breadth and height
My soul can reach, when feeling out of sight
For the ends of Being and ideal Grace.
5   I love thee to the level of everyday's
Most quiet need, by sun and candlelight.
I love thee freely, as men strive for Right;
I love thee purely, as they turn from Praise.
I love thee with the passion put to use
10 In my old griefs, and with my childhood's faith.
I love thee with a love I seemed to lose
With my lost saints – I love thee with the breath,
Smiles, tears, of all my life! and, if God choose,
I shall but love thee better after death.

MATTHEW ARNOLD (1822–1888)

Matthew Arnold was the son of Thomas Arnold, headmaster of Rugby and a prominent educational reformer who promoted the liberal idea of training the whole personality. Arnold was educated at Rugby, Winchester and Oxford where he played the fop, won a poetry prize and became a fellow. From 1857–67 he held the professorship of poetry at Oxford and his lectures were published as *Essays in Criticism* (First Series, 1861; Second Series, 1888), prefaced by the essay 'The Function of Criticism at the Present Time' in which we find a very modern sense of how a culture preconditions the work of individual writers. From 1851 he was an Inspector of Schools, and in 1859 and 1865 he studied education in France and Germany. These experiences reinforced his conviction that Britain needed a more self-conscious and emphatic theory of culture, and needed radical educational reform in order to reduce chauvinism and stimulate independent intellectual activity. His poetry was written mainly in the late 1840s and 1850s and collected in *The Strayed Reveller, and Other Poems* (1849), *Empedocles on Etna, and Other Poems* (1852), *Poems, Second Series* (1855), and *New Poems* (1867). The latter volume included 'Dover Beach', his most widely appreciated poem, which was begun as early as 1851 during his honeymoon. In the 1860s Arnold's critical dissatisfaction with his poetic achievements led his energies almost exclusively to literary, religious and educational criticism where he argued that as Christianity became less and less credible, so literature, and more particularly poetry, had to provide people with a sense of their spiritual selves. These views were given forceful expression in *Culture and Anarchy* (1869).

The Scholar Gypsy

Go, for they call you, shepherd, from the hill;
  Go shepherd, and untie the wattled cotes!
   No longer leave thy wistful flock unfed,
  Nor let thy bawling fellows rack their throats,
5   Nor the cropped herbage shoot another head.
    But when the fields are still,
  And the tired men and dogs all gone to rest,
    And only the white sheep are sometimes seen
    Cross and recross the strips of moon-blanched green,
10 Come, shepherd, and again begin the quest!

  Here, where the reaper was at work of late –
   In this high field's dark corner, where he leaves
    His coat, his basket, and his earthen cruse,
  And in the sun all morning binds the sheaves,
15   Then here, at noon, comes back his stores to use –
    Here will I sit and wait,

---

2 **cotes:** sheep folds.   13 **cruse:** jug.

While to my ear from uplands far away
 The bleating of the folded flocks is borne,
  With distant cries of reapers in the corn –
20 All the live murmur of a summer's day.

Screened is this nook o'er the high, half-reaped field,
 And here till sundown, shepherd! will I be.
  Through the thick corn the scarlet poppies peep,
And round green roots and yellowing stalks I see
25 Pale pink convolvulus in tendrils creep;
   And air-swept lindens yield
Their scent, and rustle down their perfumed showers
 Of bloom on the bent grass where I am laid,
 And bower me from the August sun with shade;
30 And the eye travels down to Oxford's towers.

And near me on the grass lies Glanvill's book –
 Come, let me read the oft-read tale again!
  The story of the Oxford scholar poor,
Of pregnant parts and quick inventive brain,
35 Who, tired of knocking at preferment's door,
   One summer morn forsook
His friends, and went to learn the gypsy lore,
 And roamed the world with that wild brotherhood,
 And came, as most men deemed, to little good,
40 But came to Oxford and his friends no more.

But once, years after, in the country lanes,
 Two scholars, whom at college erst he knew,
  Met him, and of his way of life inquired;
Whereat he answered, that the gypsy crew,
45 His mates, had arts to rule as they desired
   The workings of men's brains,
And they can bind them to what thoughts they will.
 'And I,' he said, 'the secret of their art,
 When fully learned, will to the world impart;
50 But it needs heaven-sent moments for this skill.'

This said, he left them, and returned no more. –
 But rumors hung about the countryside,
  That the lost Scholar long was seen to stray,
Seen by rare glimpses, pensive and tongue-tied,
55 In hat of antique shape, and cloak of grey,

---

18 **folded:** penned. 31 **Glanvill:** Joseph Glanvill, *The Vanity of Dogmatizing* (1661), from which the original anecdote is taken. 34 **pregnant parts:** full of ideas.

The same the gypsies wore.
    Shepherds had met him on the Hurst in spring;
        At some lone alehouse in the Berkshire moors,
        On the warm ingle-bench, the smock-frocked boors
60 Had found him seated at their entering,

But 'mid their drink and clatter, he would fly.
    And I myself seem half to know thy looks,
        And put the shepherds, wanderer! on thy trace;
    And boys who in lone wheatfields scare the rooks
65   I ask if thou hast passed their quiet place;
        Or in my boat I lie
    Moored to the cool bank in the summer heats,
        'Mid wide grass meadows which the sunshine fills,
        And watch the warm, green-muffled Cumner hills,
70 And wonder if thou haunt'st their shy retreats.

For most, I know, thou lov'st retired ground!
    Thee at the ferry Oxford riders blithe,
        Returning home on summer nights, have met
    Crossing the stripling Thames at Bab-lock-hithe,
75   Trailing in the cool stream thy fingers wet,
        As the punt's rope chops round;
    And leaning backward in a pensive dream,
        And fostering in thy lap a heap of flowers
        Plucked in shy fields and distant Wychwood bowers,
80 And thine eyes resting on the moonlit stream.

And then they land, and thou art seen no more! –
    Maidens, who from the distant hamlets come
        To dance around the Fyfield elm in May,
    Oft through the darkening fields have seen thee roam,
85   Or cross a stile into the public way.
        Oft thou hast given them store
    Of flowers – the frail-leafed, white anemone,
        Dark bluebells drenched with dews of summer eves,
        And purple orchises with spotted leaves –
90 But none hath words she can report of thee.

And, above Godstow Bridge, when hay time's here
    In June, and many a scythe in sunshine flames,
        Men who through those wide fields of breezy grass
    Where black-winged swallows haunt the glittering Thames,
95   To bathe in the abandoned lasher pass,

---

57 Hurst: a hill outside Oxford.   **59 boors:** rustics.   **76 punt:** flat-bottomed boat.   **95 pass:** weir.

Have often passed thee near
Sitting upon the river bank o'ergrown;
  Marked thine outlandish garb, thy figure spare,
  Thy dark vague eyes, and soft abstracted air –
100 But, when they came from bathing, thou wast gone!

At some lone homestead in the Cumner hills,
  Where at her open door the housewife darns,
    Thou hast been seen, or hanging on a gate
To watch the threshers in the mossy barns.
105   Children, who early range these slopes and late
    For cresses from the rills,
Have known thee eying, all an April day,
  The springing pastures and the feeding kine;
  And marked thee, when the stars come out and shine,
110 Through the long dewy grass move slow away.

In autumn, on the skirts of Bagley Wood –
  Where most the gypsies by the turf-edged way
    Pitch their smoked tents, and every bush you see
With scarlet patches tagged and shreds of grey,
115   Above the forest ground called Thessaly –
    The blackbird, picking food,
Sees thee, nor stops his meal, nor fears at all;
  So often has he known thee past him stray,
  Rapt, twirling in thy hand a withered spray,
120 And waiting for the spark from heaven to fall.

And once, in winter, on the causeway chill
  Where home through flooded fields foot-travelers go,
    Have I not passed thee on a wooden bridge,
Wrapped in thy cloak and battling with the snow,
125   Thy face tow'rd Hinksey and its wintry ridge?
    And thou hast climbed the hill,
And gained the white brow of the Cumner range;
  Turned once to watch, while thick the snowflakes fall,
  The line of festal light in Christ Church hall –
130 Then sought thy straw in some sequestered grange.

But what – I dream! Two hundred years are flown
  Since first thy story ran through Oxford halls,
    And the grave Glanvill did the tale inscribe
That thou wert wandered from the studious walls
135   To learn strange arts, and join a gypsy tribe;
    And thou from earth art gone
Long since, and in some quiet churchyard laid –

Some country nook, where o'er thy unknown grave
Tall grasses and white flowering nettles wave,
140 Under a dark, red-fruited yew tree's shade.

– No, no, thou hast not felt the lapse of hours!
For what wears out the life of mortal men?
'Tis that from change to change their being rolls;
'Tis that repeated shocks, again, again,
145 Exhaust the energy of strongest souls
And numb the elastic powers.
Till having used our nerves with bliss and teen,
And tired upon a thousand schemes our wit,
To the just-pausing Genius we remit
150 Our worn-out life, and are – what we have been.

Thou hast not lived, why should'st thou perish, so?
Thou hadst *one* aim, *one* business, *one* desire;
Else wert thou long since numbered with the dead!
Else hadst thou spent, like other men, thy fire!
155 The generations of thy peers are fled,
And we ourselves shall go;
But thou possessest an immortal lot,
And we imagine thee exempt from age
And living as thou liv'st on Glanvill's page,
160 Because thou hadst – what we, alas! have not.

For early didst thou leave the world, with powers
Fresh, undiverted to the world without,
Firm to their mark, not spent on other things;
Free from the sick fatigue, the languid doubt,
165 Which much to have tried, in much been baffled, brings.
O life unlike to ours!
Who fluctuate idly without term or scope,
Of whom each strives, nor knows for what he strives,
And each half lives a hundred different lives;
170 Who wait like thee, but not, like thee, in hope.

Thou waitest for the spark from heaven! and we,
Light half-believers of our casual creeds,
Who never deeply felt, nor clearly willed,
Whose insight never has borne fruit in deeds,
175 Whose vague resolves never have been fulfilled;
For whom each year we see
Breeds new beginnings, disappointments new;

---

147 teen: woe.

Who hesitate and falter life away,
    And lose tomorrow the ground won today –
180 Ah! do not we, wanderer! await it too?

Yes, we await it! – but it still delays,
    And then we suffer! and amongst us one,
      Who most has suffered, takes dejectedly
His seat upon the intellectual throne;
185   And all his store of sad experience he
      Lays bare of wretched days;
Tells us his misery's birth and growth and signs,
    And how the dying spark of hope was fed,
    And how the breast was soothed, and how the head,
190 And all his hourly varied anodynes.

This for our wisest! and we others pine,
    And wish the long unhappy dream would end,
      And waive all claim to bliss, and try to bear;
With close-lipped patience for our only friend,
195   Sad patience, too near neighbour to despair –
      But none has hope like thine!
Thou through the fields and through the woods dost stray,
    Roaming the countryside, a truant boy,
    Nursing thy project in unclouded joy,
200 And every doubt long blown by time away.

O born in days when wits were fresh and clear,
    And life ran gaily as the sparkling Thames;
      Before this strange disease of modern life,
With its sick hurry, its divided aims,
205   Its heads o'ertaxed, its palsied hearts, was rife –
      Fly hence, our contact fear!
Still fly, plunge deeper in the bowering wood!
    Averse, as Dido did with gesture stern
    From her false friend's approach in Hades turn,
210 Waves us away, and keep thy solitude!

Still nursing the unconquerable hope,
    Still clutching the inviolable shade,
      With a free, onward impulse brushing through,
By night, the silvered branches of the glade –
215   Far on the forest skirts, where none pursue.
      On some mild pastoral slope
Emerge, and resting on the moonlit pales

---

208 Dido: when Aeneas spurned her, she killed herself, and when Aeneas sought her in Hades, she turned away.

Freshen thy flowers as in former years
With dew, or listen with enchanted ears,
220　From the dark dingles, to the nightingales!

But fly our paths, our feverish contact fly!
For strong the infection of our mental strife,
Which, though it gives no bliss, yet spoils for rest;
And we should win thee from thy own fair life,
225　Like us distracted, and like us unblest.
Soon, soon thy cheer would die,
Thy hopes grow timorous, and unfixed thy powers,
And thy clear aims be cross and shifting made;
And then thy glad perennial youth would fade,
230　Fade, and grow old at last, and die like ours.

Then fly our greetings, fly our speech and smiles!
– As some grave Tyrian trader, from the sea,
Decried at sunrise an emerging prow
Lifting the cool-haired creepers stealthily,
235　The fringes of a southward-facing brow
Among the Aegean isles;
And saw the merry Grecian coaster come,
Freighted with amber grapes, and Chian wine,
Green, bursting figs, and tunnies steeped in brine –
240　And knew the intruders on his ancient home,

The young lighthearted masters of the waves –
And snatched his rudder, and shook out more sail;
And day and night held on indignantly
O'er the blue Midland waters with the gale,
245　Betwixt the Syrtes and soft Sicily,
To where the Atlantic raves
Outside the western straits; and unbent sails
There, where down cloudy cliffs, through sheets of foam,
Shy traffickers, the dark Iberians come;
250　And on the beach undid his corded bales.

Dover Beach

The sea is calm tonight.
The tide is full, the moon lies fair
Upon the straits – on the French coast the light
Gleams and is gone; the cliffs of England stand,

---

220 dingles: small valleys. **239 tunnies:** tuna. **249 Iberians:** Spanish gypsies.
245 Syrtes: point on the African coast facing Sicily.

5   Glimmering and vast, out in the tranquil bay.
Come to the window, sweet is the night air!
Only, from the long line of spray
Where the sea meets the moon-blanched land,
Listen! you hear the grating roar
10   Of pebbles which the waves draw back, and fling,
At their return, up the high strand,
Begin, and cease, and then again begin,
With tremulous cadence slow, and bring
The eternal note of sadness in.

15   Sophocles long ago
Heard it on the Aegean, and it brought
Into his mind the turbid ebb and flow
Of human misery; we
Find also in the sound a thought,
20   Hearing it by this distant northern sea.

The Sea of Faith
Was once, too, at the full, and round earth's shore
Lay like the folds of a bright girdle furled.
But now I only hear
25   Its melancholy, long, withdrawing roar,
Retreating, to the breath
Of the night wind, down the vast edges drear
And naked shingles of the world.

Ah, love, let us be true
30   To one another! for the world, which seems
To lie before us like a land of dreams,
So various, so beautiful, so new,
Hath really neither joy, nor love, nor light,
Nor certitude, nor peace, nor help for pain;
35   And we are here as on a darkling plain
Swept with confused alarms of struggle and flight,
Where ignorant armies clash by night.

From The Function of Criticism at the Present Time

The critical power is of lower rank than the creative. True; but in assenting to this proposition, one or two things are to be kept in mind. It is undeniable that the exercise of a creative power, that a free creative activity, is the highest function of man; it is proved to be so by man's finding in it his true happiness. But it is undeniable, also, that men may have the sense of exercising this free creative activity in other ways than in producing great works of literature or art; if it were not so, all but a very few men would be shut out from the true happiness of all men. They may have it in well-doing, they may have it in learning, they may have it even in criticising. This is the one thing to be kept in mind. Another is, that the exercise of the creative power in the production of great works of literature or art, however high this exercise of it may rank, is not at all epochs and under all conditions possible; and that therefore labour may be vainly spent in attempting it, which might with more fruit be used in preparing for it, in rendering it possible. This creative power works with elements, with materials; what if it has not those materials, those elements, ready for its use? In that case it must surely wait till they are ready. Now, in literature – I will limit myself to literature, for it is about literature that the question arises –the elements with which the creative power works are ideas; the best ideas on every matter which literature touches, current at the time. At any rate we may lay it down as certain that in modern literature no manifestation of the creative power not working with these can be very important or fruitful. And I say *current* at the time, not merely accessible at the time; for creative literary genius is a work of synthesis and exposition, not of analysis and discovery; its gift lies in the faculty of being happily inspired by a certain intellectual and spiritual atmosphere, by a certain order of ideas, when it finds itself in them; of dealing divinely with these ideas, presenting them in the most effective and attractive combination – making beautiful works with them, in short. But it must have the atmosphere, it must find itself amidst the order of ideas, in order to work freely; and these it is not so easy to command. This is why great creative epochs in literature are so rare, this is why there is so much that is unsatisfactory in the productions of many men of real genius; because, for the creation of a masterwork of literature two powers must concur, the power of the man and the power of the moment, and the man is not enough without the moment; the creative power has, for its happy exercise, appointed elements, and those elements are not in its own control.

Nay, they are more within the control of the critical power. It is the business of the critical power, as I said in the words already quoted, 'in all branches of knowledge, theology, philosophy, history, art, science, to see the object as in itself it really is.' Thus it tends, at last, to make an intellectual situation of which the creative power can profitably avail itself. It tends to establish an order of ideas, if not absolutely true, yet true by comparison with that which it displaces; to make the best ideas prevail. Presently these new ideas reach society, the touch of truth is the touch of life, and there is a stir and growth everywhere; out of this stir and growth come the creative epochs of literature.

Or, to narrow our range, and quit these considerations of the general march of genius and of society – considerations which are apt to become too abstract and impalpable – everyone can see that a poet, for instance, ought to know life and the world before dealing with them in poetry; and life and the world being in modern times very complex things, the creation of a modern poet, to be worth much, implies a great critical effort behind it; else it must be a comparatively poor, barren, and short-lived affair. This is why Byron's poetry had so little endurance in it, and Goethe's so much; both Byron and Goethe had a great productive power, but Goethe's was nourished by a great critical effort providing the true materials for it, and Byron's was not; Goethe knew life and the world, the poet's necessary subjects, much more comprehensively and thoroughly than Byron. He knew a great deal more of them, and he knew them much more as they really are.

It has long seemed to me that the burst of creative activity in our literature, through the first quarter of this century, had about it in fact something premature; and that from this cause its productions are doomed, most of them, in spite of the sanguine hopes which accompanied and do still accompany them, to prove hardly more lasting than the productions of far less splendid epochs. And this prematureness comes from its having proceeded without having its proper data, without sufficient materials to work with. In other words, the English poetry of the first quarter of this century, with plenty of energy, plenty of creative force, did not know enough. This makes Byron so empty of matter, Shelley so incoherent, Wordsworth even, profound as he is, yet so wanting in completeness and variety. Wordsworth cared little for books, and disparaged Goethe. I admire Wordsworth, as he is, so much that I cannot wish him different; and it is vain, no doubt, to imagine such a man different from what he is, to suppose that he *could* have been different. But surely the one thing wanting to make Wordsworth an even greater poet than he is – his thought richer, and his influence of wider application – was that he should have read more books, among them, no doubt, those of that Goethe whom he disparaged without reading him.

But to speak of books and reading may easily lead to a misunderstanding here. It was not really books and reading that lacked to our poetry at this epoch: Shelley had plenty of reading, Coleridge had immense reading. Pindar and Sophocles – as we all say so glibly, and often with so little discernment of the real import of what we are saying – had not many books; Shakespeare was no deep reader. True; but in the Greece of Pindar and Sophocles, in the England of Shakespeare, the poet lived in a current of ideas in the highest degree animating and nourishing to the creative power; society was in the fullest measure, permeated by fresh thought, intelligent and alive. And this state of things is the true basis for the creative power's exercise, in this it finds its data, its materials, truly ready for its hand; all the books and reading in the world are only valuable as they are helps to this. Even when this does not actually exist, books and reading may enable a man to construct a kind of semblance of it in his own mind, a world of knowledge and intelligence in which he may live and work. This is by no means an equivalent to the artist for the nationally diffused life and thought of the epochs of Sophocles or Shakespeare; but, besides that it may be a means of preparation for such epochs, it does really constitute, if many share in it, a quickening and sustaining atmosphere of great value. Such an atmosphere the many-sided learning and the long and widely combined critical effort of Germany formed for Goethe, when he lived and worked. There was no national glow of life and thought there as in the Athens of Pericles or the England of Elizabeth. That was the poet's weakness. But there was a sort of equivalent for it in the complete culture and unfettered thinking of a large body of Germans. That was his strength. In the England of the first quarter of this century there was neither a national glow of life and thought, such as we had in the age of Elizabeth, nor yet a culture and a force of learning and criticism such as were to be found in Germany. Therefore the creative power of poetry wanted, for success in the higher sense, materials and a basis; a thorough interpretation of the world was necessarily denied to it.

*   *   *

It is the fashion to treat Burke's writings on the French Revolution as superannuated and conquered by the event; as the eloquent but unphilosophical tirades of bigotry and prejudice. I will not deny that they are often disfigured by the violence and passion of the moment, and that in some directions Burke's view was bounded, and his observation therefore at fault. But on the whole, and for those who can make the needful corrections, what distinguishes these writings is their profound, permanent, fruitful, philosophical truth. They contain the true philosophy of an epoch of concentration, dissipate the heavy atmosphere which its own nature is apt to engender round it, and make its resistance rational instead of mechanical.

But Burke is so great because, almost alone in England, he brings thought to bear upon politics, he saturates politics with thought. It is his accident that his ideas were at the service of an epoch of concentration, not of an epoch of expansion; it is his characteristic that he so lived by ideas, and had such a source of them welling up within him, that he could float even an epoch of concentration and English Tory politics with them. It does not hurt him that Dr Price[1] and the Liberals were enraged with him; it does not even hurt him that George the Third and the Tories were enchanted with him. His greatness is that he lived in a world which neither English Liberalism nor English Toryism is apt to enter – the world of ideas, not the world of catchwords and party habits. So far is it from being really true of him that he 'to party gave up what was meant for mankind,' that at the very end of his fierce struggle with the French Revolution, after all his invectives against its false pretensions, hollowness, and madness, with his sincere convictions of its mischievousness, he can close a memorandum on the best means of combating it, some of the last pages he ever wrote – the *Thoughts on French Affairs*, in December 1791 – with these striking words:

> 'The evil is stated, in my opinion, as it exists. The remedy must be where power, wisdom, and information, I hope, are more united with good intentions than they can be with me. I have done with this subject, I believe, forever. It has given me many anxious moments for the last two years. *If a great change is to be made in human affairs, the minds of men will be fitted to it; the general opinions and feelings will draw that way. Every fear, every hope will forward it; and then they who persist in opposing this mighty current in human affairs, will appear rather to resist the decrees of Providence itself, than the mere designs of men. They will not be resolute and firm, but perverse and obstinate.*'

1: Richard Price (1723–91), dissenting minister, influenced Mary Wollstonecraft, supported the American revolutions and gave a sermon in support of the French Revolution that precipitated Burke's *Reflections*.

That return of Burke upon himself has always seemed to me one of the finest things in English literature, or indeed in any literature. That is what I call living by ideas: when one side of a question has long had your earnest support, when all your feelings are engaged, when you hear all round you no language but one, when your party talks this language like a steam engine and can imagine no other – still to be able to think, still to be irresistibly carried, if so it be, by the current of thought to the opposite side of the question, and, like Balaam,[1] to be unable to speak anything *but what the Lord has put in your mouth*. I know nothing more striking, and I must add that I know nothing more un-English.

For the Englishman in general is like my friend the Member of Parliament, and believes, point-blank, that for a thing to be an anomaly is absolutely no objection to it whatever. He is like the Lord Auckland of Burke's day, who, in a memorandum on the French Revolution, talks of certain 'miscreants, assuming the name of philosophers, who have presumed themselves capable of establishing a new system of society.' The Englishman has been called a political animal, and he values what is political and practical so much that ideas easily become objects of dislike in his eyes, and thinkers, 'miscreants,' because ideas and thinkers have rashly meddled with politics and practice. This would be all very well if the dislike and neglect confined themselves to ideas transported out of their own sphere, and meddling rashly with practice, but they are inevitably extended to ideas as such, and to the whole life of intelligence; practice is everything, a free play of the mind is nothing. The notion of the free play of the mind upon all subjects being a pleasure in itself, being an object of desire, being an essential provider of elements without which a nation's spirit, whatever compensations it may have for them, must, in the long run, die of inanition, hardly enters into an Englishman's thoughts. It is noticeable that the word *curiosity*, which in other languages is used in a good sense, to mean, as a high and fine quality of man's nature, just this disinterested love of a free play of the mind on all subjects, for its own sake – it is noticeable, I say, that this word has in our language no sense of the kind, no sense but a rather bad and disparaging one. But criticism, real criticism, is essentially the exercise of this very quality. It obeys an instinct prompting it to try to know the best that is known and thought in the world, irrespectively of practice, politics, and everything of the kind; and to value knowledge and thought as they approach this best, without the intrusion of any other considerations whatever. This is an instinct for which there is, I think, little original sympathy in the practical English nature, and what there was of it has undergone a long benumbing period of blight and suppression in the epoch of concentration which followed the French Revolution.

But epochs of concentration cannot well endure forever; epochs of expansion, the due course of things, follow them. Such an epoch of expansion seems to be opening in this country. In the first place all danger of a hostile forcible pressure of foreign ideas upon our practice has long disappeared; like the traveller in the fable, therefore, we begin to wear our cloak a little more loosely. Then, with a long peace, the ideas of Europe steal gradually and

---

1: A Mesopotamian diviner who was summoned to curse the Israelites but was reproached by his ass and prophesied future glories for them instead. (*Numbers*, 22–23).

amicably in, and mingle, though in infinitesimally small quantities at a time, with our own notions. Then, too, in spite of all that is said about the absorbing and brutalising influence of our passionate material progress, it seems to me indisputable that this progress is likely, though not certain, to lead in the end to an apparition of intellectual life; and that man, after he has made himself perfectly comfortable and has now to determine what to do with himself next, may begin to remember that he has a mind, and that the mind may be made the source of great pleasure. I grant this is mainly the privilege of faith, at present, to discern this end to our railways, our business, and our fortune-making; but we shall see if, here as elsewhere, faith is not in the end a true prophet. Our ease, our travelling, and our unbounded liberty to hold just as hard and securely as we please to the practice to which our notions have given birth, all tend to beget an inclination to deal a little more freely with these notions themselves, to canvass them a little, to penetrate a little into their real nature. Flutterings of curiosity, in the foreign sense of the word, appear among us, and it is in these that criticism must look to find its account. Criticism first; a time of true creative activity, perhaps – which, as I have said, must inevitably be preceded among us by a time of criticism – hereafter, when criticism has done its work.

It is of the last importance that English criticism should clearly discern what rule for its course, in order to avail itself of the field now opening to it, and to produce fruit for the future, it ought to take. The rule may be summed up in one word – *disinterestedness.* And how is criticism to show disinterestedness? By keeping aloof from what is called 'the practical view of things'; by resolutely following the law of its own nature, which is to be a free play of the mind on all subjects which it touches. By steadily refusing to lend itself to any of those ulterior, political, practical considerations about ideas, which plenty of people will be sure to attach to them, which perhaps ought to be attached to them, which in this country at any rate are certain to be attached to them quite sufficiently, but which criticism has really nothing to do with. Its business is, as I have said, simply to know the best that is known and thought in the world, and by in its turn making this known, to create a current of true and fresh ideas. Its business is to do this with inflexible honesty, with due ability; but its business is to do no more, and to leave alone all questions of practical consequences and applications, questions which will never fail to have due prominence given to them. Else criticism, besides being really false to its own nature, merely continues in the old rut which it has hitherto followed in this country, and will certainly miss the chance now given to it. For what is at present the bane of criticism in this country? It is that practical considerations cling to it and stifle it. It subserves interests not its own. Our organs of criticism are organs of men and parties having practical ends to serve, and with them those practical ends are the first thing and the play of mind the second; so much play of mind as is compatible with the prosecution of those practical ends is all that is wanted. An organ like the *Revue des Deux Mondes*,[1] having for its main function to understand and utter the best that is known and thought in the world, existing, it may be said, as just an organ for a free play of the mind,

---

1: French review of literature, the arts and politics.

we have not. But we have the *Edinburgh Review*,[1] existing as an organ of the old Whigs, and for as much play of mind as may suit its being that; we have the *Quarterly Review*,[2] existing as an organ of the Tories, and for as much play of mind as may suit its being that; we have the *British Quarterly Review*, existing as an organ of the political Dissenters, and for as much play of mind as may suit its being that; we have the *Times*, existing as an organ of the common, satisfied, well-to-do Englishman, and for as much play of mind as may suit its being that. And so on through all the various fractions, political and religious, of our society; every fraction has, as such, its organ of criticism, but the notion of combining all fractions in the common pleasure of a free disinterested play of mind meets with no favour. Directly this play of mind wants to have more scope, and to forget the pressure of practical considerations a little, it is checked, it is made to feel the chain.

From Culture and Anarchy

We have not the notion, so familiar on the Continent and to antiquity, of *the State* – the nation in its collective and corporate character, entrusted with stringent powers for the general advantage, and controlling individual wills in the name of an interest wider than that of individuals. We say, what is very true, that this notion is often made instrumental to tyranny; we say that a State is in reality made up of the individuals who compose it, and that every individual is the best judge of his own interests. Our leading class is an aristocracy, and no aristocracy likes the notion of a State-authority greater than itself, with a stringent administrative machinery superseding the decorative inutilities of lord-lieutenancy, deputy-lieutenancy, and the *posse comitatûs*,[3] which are all in its own hands. Our middle class, the great representative of trade and Dissent, with its maxims of every man for himself in business, every man for himself in religion, dreads a powerful administration which might somehow interfere with it; and besides, it has its own decorative inutilities of vestrymanship and guardianship, which are to this class what lord-lieutenancy and the country magistracy are to the aristocratic class, and a stringent administration might either take these functions out of its hands, or prevent its exercising them in its own comfortable, independent manner, as at present.

Then as to our working class. This class, pressed constantly by the hard daily compulsion of material wants, is naturally the very centre and stronghold of our national idea, that it is man's ideal right and felicity to do as he likes. I think I have somewhere related how M. Michelet[4] said to me of the people of France, that it was 'a nation of barbarians civilised by the conscription.' He meant that through their military service the idea of public duty and of discipline was brought to the mind of these masses, in other respects so raw and uncultivated. Our masses are quite as raw and uncultivated as the French; and so far from their having the idea of public duty and of discipline, superior to the individual's

1: The major quarterly expressing Whig and Reform sentiments (1802–1929).   2: The major Tory quarterly founded by John Murray and Walter Scott in opposition to the *Edinburgh* (1809–1967).   3: A group of men sworn in by a Sheriff to uphold the law.   4: Jules Michelet, republican historian, author of *La révolution française* (1847–53).

self-will, brought to their mind by a universal obligation of military service, such as that of the conscription, – so far from their having this, the very idea of a conscription is so at variance with our English notion of the prime right and blessedness of doing as one likes, that I remember the manager of the Clay Cross works in Derbyshire told me during the Crimean war,[1] when our want of soldiers was much felt and some people were talking of a conscription, that sooner than submit to a conscription the population of that district would flee to the mines, and lead a sort of Robin Hood life under ground.

For a long time, as I have said, the strong feudal habits of subordination and deference continued to tell upon the working class. The modern spirit has now almost entirely dissolved those habits, and the anarchical tendency of our worship of freedom in and for itself, of our superstitious faith, as I say, in machinery, is becoming very manifest. More and more, because of this our blind faith in machinery, because of our want of light to enable us to look beyond machinery to the end for which machinery is valuable, this and that man, and this and that body of men, all over the country, are beginning to assert and put in practice an Englishman's right to do what he likes; his right to march where he likes, meet where he likes, enter where he likes, hoot as he likes, threaten as he likes, smash as he likes. All this, I say, tends to anarchy; and though a number of excellent people, and particularly my friends of the Liberal or progressive party, as they call themselves, are kind enough to reassure us by saying that these are trifles, that a few transient outbreaks of rowdyism signify nothing, that our system of liberty is one which itself cures all the evils which it works, that the educated and intelligent classes stand in overwhelming strength and majestic repose, ready, like our military force in riots, to act at a moment's notice, – yet one finds that one's Liberal friends generally say this because they have such faith in themselves and their nostrums, when they shall return, as the public welfare requires, to place and power. But this faith of theirs one cannot exactly share, when one has so long had them and their nostrums at work, and sees that they have not prevented our coming to our present embarrassed condition. And one finds, also, that the outbreaks of rowdyism tend to become less and less of trifles, to become more frequent rather than less frequent; and that meanwhile our educated and intelligent classes remain in their majestic repose, and somehow or other, whatever happens, their overwhelming strength, like our military force in riots, never does act . . . .

Having, I say, at the bottom of our English hearts a very strong belief in freedom, and a very weak belief in right reason, we are soon silenced when a man pleads the prime right to do as he likes, because this is the prime right for ourselves too; and even if we attempt now and then to mumble something about reason, yet we have ourselves thought so little about this and so much about liberty, that we are in conscience forced, when our brother Philistine with whom we are meddling turns boldly round upon us and asks: *Have you any light?* – to shake our heads ruefully, and to let him go his own way after all.

There are many things to be said on behalf of this exclusive attention of ours to liberty, and of the relaxed habits of government which it has engendered. It

---

1: The Crimean War (1853–56) pitted Russia against an alliance of Turkey, Sardinia, France, and Britain.

is very easy to mistake or exaggerate the sort of anarchy from which we are in danger through them. We are not in danger from Fenianism,[1] fierce and turbulent as it may show itself; for against this our conscience is free enough to let us act resolutely and put forth our overwhelming strength the moment there is any real need for it. In the first place, it never was any part of our creed that the great right and blessedness of an Irishman, or, indeed, of anybody on earth except an Englishman, is to do as he likes; and we can have no scruple at all about abridging, if necessary, a non-Englishman's assertion of personal liberty. The British Constitution, its checks, and its prime virtues, are for Englishmen. We may extend them to others out of love and kindness; but we find no real divine law written on our hearts constraining us so to extend them. And then the difference between an Irish Fenian and an English rough is so immense, and the case, in dealing with the Fenian, so much more clear! He is so evidently desperate and dangerous, a man of a conquered race, a Papist, with centuries of ill-usage to inflame him against us, with an alien religion established in his country by us at his expense, with no admiration of our institutions, no love of our virtues, no talents for our business, no turn for our comfort! Show him our symbolical Truss Manufactory on the finest site in Europe, and tell him that British industrialism and individualism can bring a Man to that, and he remains cold! Evidently, if we deal tenderly with a sentimentalist like this, it is out of pure philanthropy.

But with the Hyde Park rioter[2] how different! He is our own flesh and blood; he is a Protestant; he is framed by nature to do as we do, hate as we hate, love what we love; he is capable of feeling the symbolical force of the Truss Manufactory; the question of questions, for him, is a wages question. That beautiful sentence Sir Daniel Gooch quoted to the Swindon workmen, and which I reassure as Mrs Gooch's Golden Rule, or the Divine Injunction 'Be ye Perfect' done into British, – the sentence Sir Daniel Gooch's mother repeated to him every morning when he was a boy going to work: '*Ever remember, my dear Dan, that you should look forward to being some day manager of that concern!*' – this fruitful maxim is perfectly fitted to shine forth in the heart of the Hyde Park rough also, and to be his guiding-star through life. He has no visionary schemes of revolution and transformation, though of course he would like his class to rule, as the aristocratic class like their class to rule, and the middle class theirs. But meanwhile our social machine is a little out of order; there are a good many people in our paradisiacal centres of industrialism and individualism taking the bread out of one another's mouths. The rough has not yet quite found his groove and settled down to his work, and so he is just asserting his personal liberty a little, going where he likes, assembling where he likes, bawling as he likes, hustling as he likes. Just as the rest of us, – as the country squires in the aristocratic class, as the political dissenters in the middle class, – he has no idea of a *State*, of the nation in its collective and corporate character

---

1: A terrorist movement formed to drive the English out of Ireland, very active in the years 1865–70. In 1867 they had blown up part of Clerkenwell gaol and killed 12 people and there were many violent Fenian demonstrations. The emancipation of the Irish had long commanded influential support in Britain. Edmund Burke, for example, had spoken powerfully in favour.   2: Gladstone introduced a Reform Bill in 1866 which aimed to extend the franchise. When this was defeated in June, a meeting held by the Reform League in Hyde Park led to riots.

controlling, as government, the free swing of this or that one of its members in the name of the higher reason of all of them, his own as well as that of others. He sees the rich, the aristocratic class, in occupation of the executive government, and so if he is stopped from making Hyde Park a bear-garden or the streets impassable, he says he is being butchered by the aristocracy.

His apparition is somewhat embarrassing, because too many cooks spoil the broth; because, while the aristocratic and middle classes have long been doing as they like with great vigour, he has been too undeveloped and submissive hitherto to join in the game; and now, when he does come, he comes in immense numbers, and is rather raw and rough. But he does not break many laws, or not many at one time; and, as our laws were made for very different circumstances from our present (but always with an eye to Englishmen doing as they like), and as the clear letter of the law must be against our Englishman who does as he likes and not only the spirit of the law and public policy, and as Government must neither have any discretionary power nor act resolutely on its own interpretation of the law if any one disputes it, it is evident our laws give our playful giant, in doing as he likes, considerable advantage. Besides, even if he can be clearly proved to commit an illegality in doing as he likes, there is always the resource of not putting the law in force, or of abolishing it. So he has his way, and if he has his way he is soon satisfied for the time. However, he falls into the habit of taking it oftener and oftener, and at last begins to create by his operations a confusion of which mischievous people can take advantage, and which at any rate, by troubling the common course of business throughout the country, tends to cause distress, and so to increase the sort of anarchy and social disintegration which had previously commenced. And thus that profound sense of settled order and security, without which a society like ours cannot live and grow at all, sometimes seems to be beginning to threaten us with taking its departure.

Now, if culture, which simply means trying to perfect oneself, and one's mind as part of oneself, brings us light, and if light shows us that there is nothing so very blessed in merely doing as one likes, that the worship of the mere freedom to do as one likes is worship of machinery, that the really blessed thing is to like what right reason ordains, and to follow her authority, then we have got a practical benefit out of culture. We have got a much wanted principle, a principle of authority, to counteract the tendency to anarchy which seems to be threatening us.

But how to organise this authority, or to what hands to entrust the wielding of it? How to get your *State*, summing up the right reason of the community, and giving effect to it, as circumstances may require, with vigour? And here I think I see my enemies waiting for me with a hungry joy in their eyes. But I shall elude them.

The *State*, the power most representing the right reason of the nation, and most worthy, therefore, of ruling, – of exercising, when circumstances require it, authority over us all, – is for Mr. Carlyle the aristocracy. For Mr. Lowe, it is the middle class with its incomparable Parliament. For the Reform League, it is the working class, the class with 'the brightest powers of sympathy and readiest powers of action.' Now, culture, with its disinterested pursuit of perfection, culture, simply trying to see things as they are, in order to seize on the best and to make it prevail, is surely well fitted to help us to judge rightly, by all the aids of observing, reading, and thinking, the qualifications and titles to our confidence of these three candidates for authority, and can thus render us a practical service of no mean value.

So when Mr. Carlyle, a man of genius to whom we have all at one time or other been indebted for refreshment and stimulus, says we should give rule to the aristocracy, mainly because of its dignity and politeness, surely culture is useful in reminding us, that in our idea of perfection the characters of beauty and intelligence are both of them present, and sweetness and light, the two noblest of things, are united. Allowing, therefore, with Mr. Carlyle, the aristocratic class to possess sweetness, culture insists on the necessity of light also, and shows us that aristocracies, being by the very nature of things inaccessible to ideas, unapt to see how the world is going, must be somewhat wanting in light, and must therefore be, at a moment when light is our great requisite, inadequate to our needs. Aristocracies, those children of the established fact, are for epochs of concentration. In epochs of expansion, epochs such as that in which we now live, epochs when always the warning voice is again heard: *Now is the judgement of this world* – in such epochs aristocracies with their natural clinging to the established fact, their want of sense for the flux of things, for the inevitable transitoriness of all human institutions, are bewildered and helpless. Their serenity, their high spirit, their power of haughty resistance, – the great qualities of an aristocracy, and the secret of its distinguished manners and dignity, – these very qualities, in an epoch of expansion, turn against their possessors. Again and again I have said how the refinement of an aristocracy may be precious and educative to a raw nation as a kind of shadow of true refinement; how its serenity and dignified freedom from petty cares may serve as a useful foil to set off the vulgarity and hideousness of that type of life which a hard middle class tends to establish, and to help people to see this vulgarity and hideousness in their true colours. From such an ignoble spectacle as that of poor Mrs. Lincoln, – a spectacle to vulgarise a whole nation, – aristocracies undoubtedly preserve us. But the true grace and serenity is that of which Greece and Greek art suggest the admirable ideals of perfection, – a serenity which comes from having made order among ideas and harmonised them; whereas the serenity of aristocracies, at least the peculiar serenity of aristocracies of Teutonic origin, appears to come from their never having had any ideas to trouble them. And so, in a time of expansion like the present, a time for ideas, one gets, perhaps, in regarding an aristocracy, even more than the idea of serenity, the idea of futility and sterility.

One has often wondered whether upon the whole earth there is anything so unintelligent, so unapt to perceive how the world is really going, as an ordinary young Englishman of our upper class. Ideas he has not, and neither has he that seriousness of our middle class which is, as I have often said, the great strength of this class, and may become its salvation. Why, a man may hear of a young Dives of the aristocratic class, when the whim takes him to sing the praises of wealth and material comfort, sing them with a cynicism from which the conscience of the veriest Philistine of our industrial middle class would recoil in affright. And when, with the natural sympathy of aristocracies for firm dealing with the multitude, and his uneasiness at our feeble dealing with it at home, an unvarnished young Englishman of our aristocratic class applauds the absolute rulers on the Continent, he in general manages completely to miss the grounds of reason and intelligence which alone can give any colour of justification, any possibility of existence, to those rulers, and applauds them on grounds which it would make their own hair stand on end to listen to.

And all this time we are in an epoch of expansion; and the essence of an epoch of expansion is a movement of ideas, and the one salvation of an epoch of expansion is a harmony of ideas. The very principle of the authority which we are seeking as a defence against anarchy is right reason, ideas, light. The more, therefore, an aristocracy calls to its aid its innate forces, – its impenetrability, its high spirit, its power of haughty resistance, – to deal with an epoch of expansion, the graver is the danger, the greater the certainty of explosion, the surer the aristocracy's defeat; for it is trying to do violence to nature instead of working along with it. The best powers shown by the best men of an aristocracy at such an epoch are, it will be observed, non-aristocratical powers, powers of industry, powers of intelligence; and these powers, thus exhibited, tend really not to strengthen the aristocracy, but to take their owners out of it, to expose them to the dissolving agencies of thought and change, to make them men of the modern spirit and of the future. If, as sometimes happens, they add to their non-aristocratical qualities of labour and thought, a strong dose of aristocratical qualities also, – of pride, defiance, turn for resistance – this truly aristocratical side of them, so far from adding any strength to them, really neutralises their force and makes them impracticable and ineffective . . . .

Surely, now, it is no inconsiderable boon which culture confers upon us, if in embarrassed times like the present it enables us to look at the ins and the outs of things in this way, without hatred and without partiality, and with a disposition to see the good in everybody all round. And I try to follow just the same course with our middle class as with our aristocracy. Mr. Lowe talks to us of this strong middle part of the nation, of the unrivalled deeds of our Liberal middle-class Parliament, of the noble, the heroic work it has performed in the last thirty years; and I begin to ask myself if we shall not, then, find in our middle class the principle of authority we want, and if we had not better take administration as well as legislation away from the weak extreme which now administers for us, and commit both to the strong middle part. I observe, too, that the heroes of middle-class Liberalism, such as we have hitherto known it, speak with a kind of prophetic anticipation of the great destiny which awaits them, and as if the future was clearly theirs. The advanced party, the progressive party, the party in alliance with the future, are the names they like to give themselves. 'The principles which will obtain recognition in the future,' says Mr. Miall, a personage of deserved eminence among the political Dissenters, as they are called, who have been the backbone of middle-class Liberalism – 'the principles which will obtain recognition in the future are the principles for which I have long and zealously laboured. I qualified myself for joining in the work of harvest by doing to the best of my ability the duties of seed time.' These duties, if one is to gather them from the works of the great Liberal party in the last thirty years, are, as I have elsewhere summed them up, the advocacy of free-trade, of parliamentary reform, of abolition of church-rates, of voluntaryism in religion and education, of non-interference of the State between employers and employed, and of marriage with one's deceased wife's sister.

Now I know, when I object that all this is machinery, the great Liberal middle class has by this time grown cunning enough to answer that it always meant more by these things than meets the eye; that it has had that within which passes show, and that we are soon going to see, in a Free Church and all manner of good things, what it was. But I have learned from Bishop Wilson (if Mr. Frederic Harrison will forgive my again quoting that poor old hierophant of a decayed superstition): 'If we would really know our heart let us impartially view our action;' and I cannot help thinking that if our Liberals had had so much sweetness and light in their inner minds as they allege, more of it must have come out in their saying and doings.

An American friend of the English Liberals says, indeed, that their Dissidence of Dissent has been a mere instrument of the political Dissenters for making reason and the will of God prevail (and no doubt he would say the same of marriage with one's deceased wife's sister); and that the abolition of a State Church is merely the Dissenter's means to this end, just as culture is mine. Another American defender of theirs says just the same of their industrialism and free-trade; indeed, this gentleman, taking the bull by the horns, proposes that we should for the future call industrialism culture, and the industrialists the men of culture, and then of course there can be no longer any misapprehension about their true character; and besides the pleasure of being wealthy and comfortable, they will have authentic recognition as vessels of sweetness and light.

All this is undoubtedly specious; but I must remark that the culture of which I talked was an endeavour to come at reason and the will of God by means of reading, observing, and thinking; and that whoever calls anything else culture, may, indeed, call it so if he likes, but then he talks of something quite different from what I talked of. And, again, as culture's way of working for reason and the will of God is by directly trying to know more about them, while the Dissidence of Dissent is evidently in itself an effort of this kind, nor is its Free Church, in fact, a church with worthier conceptions of God and the ordering of the world than the State Church professes, but with mainly the same conceptions of these as the State Church has, only that every man is to comport himself as he likes in professing them, – this being so, I cannot at once accept the Non-conformity any more than the industrialism and the other great works of our Liberal middle-class as proof positive that this class is in possession of light, and that here is the true seat of authority for which we are in search; but I must try a little further, and seek for other indications which may enable me to make up my mind.

Why should we not do with the middle class as we have done with the aristocratic class, – find in it some representative men who may stand for the virtuous mean of this class, for the perfection of its present qualities and mode of being, and also for the excess of them. Such men must clearly not be men of genius like Mr. Bright;[1] for, as I have formerly said, so far as a man has genius he tends to take himself out of the category of class altogether, and to become simply a man. Mr. Bright's brother, Mr. Jacob Bright, would, perhaps, be more to the purpose; he seems to sum up very well in himself, without disturbing influences, the general liberal force of the middle class, the force by which it has done its great works of free-trade, parliamentary reform, voluntaryism, and so on, and the spirit in which it has done them. Now it is clear, from what has been already said, that there has been at least an apparent want of light in the force and spirit through which these great works have been done, and that the works have worn in consequence too much a look of machinery. But this will be clearer still if we take, as the happy mean of the middle class, not Mr. Jacob Bright, but his colleague in the representation of Manchester, Mr. Bazley. Mr. Bazley sums up for us, in general, the middle class, its spirit and its works, at least as well as Mr. Jacob Bright; and he has given us, moreover, a famous sentence, which bears directly on the resolution of our present question, – whether there is light enough in our middle class to make it the proper seat of the authority we wish to establish. When there was a talk some little while ago about the state of middle-class education, Mr. Bazley, as the representative of that class, spoke some memorable words: – 'There had been a cry that middle class education ought to receive more attention. He confessed himself very much surprised by the clamour that was raised. He did not think that class need excite the sympathy either of the legislature or the public.' Now this satisfaction of Mr. Bazley with the mental state of the middle class was truly representative, and makes good his claim to stand as the beautiful and virtuous mean of that class. But it is obviously at variance with our definition of culture, or the pursuit of light and perfection, which made light and perfection consist, not in resting and being, but in growing and becoming, in a perpetual advance in beauty and wisdom. So the middle class is by its essence, as one may say, by its incomparable self-satisfaction decisively expressed through its beautiful and virtuous mean, self-excluded from wielding an authority of which light is to be the very soul . . . .

I conclude, therefore – what, indeed, few of those who do me the honour to read this disquisition are likely to dispute, – that we can as little find in the working class as in the aristocratic or in the middle class our much-wanted source of authority, as culture suggests it to us.

Well, then, what if we tried to rise above the idea of class to the idea of the whole community, *the State*, and to find our centre of light and authority there? Every one of us has the idea of country, as a sentiment; hardly any one of us has the idea of *the State*, as a working power. And why? Because we habitually live in our ordinary selves, which do not carry us beyond the ideas and wishes of the

---

1: John Bright (1811–89), prominent agitator for full adult male suffrage and amelioration of the lot of the working man; fought for the 1832 reforms, the repeal of the corn laws, and the 1869 reforms.

class to which we happen to belong. And we are all afraid of giving to the State too much power, because we only conceive of the State as something equivalent to the class in occupation of the executive government, and are afraid of that class abusing power to its own purposes. If we strengthen the State with the aristocratic class in occupation of the executive government, we imagine we are delivering ourselves up captive to the ideas and wishes of our fierce aristocratical baronet Sir Thomas Bateson; if with the middle class in occupation of the executive government, to those of our truculent middle-class Dissenting minister, the Rev. W. Cattle; if with the working class, to those of its notorious tribune, Mr. Bradlaugh. And with much justice; owing to the exaggerated notion which we English, as I have said, entertain of the right and blessedness of the mere doing as one likes, of the affirming oneself, and oneself just as it is. People of the aristocratic class want to affirm their ordinary selves, their likings and dislikings; people of the middle class the same, people of the working class the same. By our every-day selves, however, we are separate, personal, at war; we are only safe from one another's tyranny when no one has any power; and this safety, in its turn, cannot save us from anarchy. And when, therefore, anarchy presents itself as a danger to us, we know not where to turn.

But by our *best self* we are united, impersonal, at harmony. We are in no peril from giving authority to this, because it is the truest friend we all of us can have; and when anarchy is a danger to us, to this authority we may turn with Tafperfection, seeks to develop in us; at the expense of our old untransformed self, taking pleasure only in doing what it likes or is used to do, and exposing us to the risk of clashing with every one else who is doing the same! So that our poor culture, which is flouted as so unpractical, leads us to the very ideas capable of meeting the great want of our present embarrassed times! We want an authority, and we find nothing but jealous classes, checks, and a deadlock; culture suggests the idea of *the State*. We find no basis for a firm State-power in our ordinary selves; culture suggests one to us in our *best self.*

It cannot but acutely try a tender conscience to be accused, in a practical country like ours, of keeping aloof from the work and hope of a multitude of earnest-hearted men, and of merely toying with poetry and aesthetics. So it is with no little sense of relief that I find myself thus in the position of one who makes a contribution in aid of the practical necessities of our times. The great thing, it will be observed, is to find our *best* self, and to seek to affirm nothing but that; not, – as we English with our over-value for merely being free and busy have been so accustomed to do, – resting satisfied with a self which comes uppermost long before our best self, and affirming that with blind energy. In short, – to go back yet once more to Bishop Wilson, – of these two excellent rules of Bishop Wilson's for a man's guidance: 'Firstly, never go against the best light you have; secondly, take care that your light be not darkness,' we English have followed with praiseworthy zeal the first rule, but we have not given so much heed to the second.

ADELAIDE ANNE PROCTER (1825–1864)

Adelaide Procter's father was a London solicitor, a poet, and a friend of Charles Dickens. Dickens admired Adelaide Procter's early work and published it in *Household Words* and *All the Year Round*. Procter's poetry was collected in *Legends and Lyrics* (1858; 1861). She was a forceful feminist, helped to found the *English Women's Journal* (1858) and contributed poetry to its pages, and worked tirelessly to alleviate the condition of poor women and improve their employment prospects. Her poetry was very popular and was admired by Tennyson and Thackeray. Her life was cut short when she died of consumption. 'A Lost Chord' was her best-known lyric and had the distinction of being set to music by Sir Arthur Sullivan.

Envy

He was the first always: Fortune
    Shone bright in his face.
I fought for years; with no effort
    He conquered the place:
5 We ran; my feet were all bleeding,
    But he won the race.

Spite of his many successes
    Men loved him the same;
My one pale ray of good fortune
10   Met scoffing and blame.
When we erred, they gave him pity,
    But me – only shame.

My home was still in the shadow,
    His lay in the sun:
15 I longed in vain: what he asked for
    It straightway was done.
Once I staked all my heart's treasure,
    We played – and he won.

Yes; and just now I have seen him,
20   Cold, smiling, and blest,
Laid in his coffin. God help me!
    While he is at rest,
I am cursed still to live: – even
    Death loved him the best.

A Lost Chord

Seated one day at the Organ,
I was weary and ill at ease,
And my fingers wandered idly
Over the noisy keys.

5   I do not know what I was playing,
   Or what I was dreaming then;
But I struck one chord of music,
   Like the sound of a great Amen.

It flooded the crimson twilight
10   Like the close of an Angel's Psalm,
And it lay on my fevered spirit
   With a touch of infinite calm.

It quieted pain and sorrow,
   Like love overcoming strife;
15   It seemed the harmonious echo
   From our discordant life.

It linked all perplexèd meanings
   Into one perfect peace,
And trembled away into silence
20   As it were loth to cease.

I have sought, but I seek it vainly,
   That one lost chord divine,
Which came from the soul of the Organ,
   And entered into mine.

25   It may be that Death's bright angel
   Will speak that chord again, –
It may be that only in Heaven
   I shall hear that grand Amen.

CHRISTINA ROSSETTI (1830–1894)

Christina Rossetti's father, Gabriele Rossetti, was professor of Italian at King's College, London, and a poet and political refugee. Her mother was Frances Polidori, daughter of the novelist and physician Dr John Polidori who helped to edit *Lyrical Ballads*. Her brother, Dante Gabriele Rossetti, was to become a leading painter of the Pre-Raphaelite movement and a minor poet; her brother William became a leading art critic. Christina

Rossetti was a precocious poet in English and Italian and published her first volume in 1847 at the age of 16. Financial difficulties in the 1850s reduced her to teaching in a school established with her mother but this was not successful. She made her reputation with *Goblin Market and Other Poems* (1862), and followed this with *Prince's Progress and Other Poems* (1866), *Sing-Song: A Nursery Rhyme Book* (1872), and *A Pageant and Other Poems* (1881). She was deeply religious, beginning in the evangelical persuasion but gravitating towards Anglo-Catholicism, and she devoted much energy to helping fallen women. In later life she wrote several volumes of devotional prose. She also wrote the beautiful Christmas carol, 'In the bleak midwinter', which has become internationally famous.

My Secret

I tell my secret? No indeed, not I:
Perhaps some day, who knows?
But not today; it froze, and blows and snows,
And you're too curious: fie!
5   You want to hear it? well:
Only my secret's mine, and I won't tell.

   Or, after all, perhaps there's none:
Suppose there is no secret after all,
But only just my fun.
10   Today's a nipping day, a biting day;
In which one wants a shawl,
A veil, a cloak, and other wraps:
I cannot ope to every one who taps,
And let the draughts come whistling thro' my hall;
15   Come bounding and surrounding me,
Come buffeting, astounding me,
Nipping and clipping thro' my wraps and all.
I wear my mask for warmth: who ever shows
His nose to Russian snows
20   To be pecked at by every wind that blows?
You would not peck? I thank you for good will,
Believe, but leave that truth untested still.

   Spring's an expansive time: yet I don't trust
March with its peck of dust,
25   Nor April with its rainbow-crowned brief showers,
Nor even May, whose flowers
One frost may wither thro' the sunless hours.

   Perhaps some languid summer day,
When drowsy birds sing less and less,
30   And golden fruit is ripening to excess,

If there's not too much sun nor too much cloud,
And the warm wind is neither still nor loud,
Perhaps my secret I may say,
Or you may guess.

Cobwebs

It is a land with neither night nor day,
Nor heat nor cold, nor any wind, nor rain,
Nor hills nor valleys; but one even plain
Stretches thro' long unbroken miles away:
5   While thro' the sluggish air a twilight grey
Broodeth; no moons or seasons wax and wane,
No ebb and flow are there along the main,
No bud-time no leaf-falling, there for aye:–
No ripple on the sea, no shifting sand,
10   No beat of wings to stir the stagnant space,
No pulse of life thro' all the loveless land:
And loveless sea; no trace of days before,
No guarded home, no toil-won resting place,
No future hope no fear for evermore.

Goblin Market

Morning and evening
Maids heard the goblins cry:
'Come buy our orchard fruits,
Come buy, come buy:
5   Apples and quinces,
Lemons and oranges,
Plump unpecked cherries,
Melons and raspberries,
Bloom-down-cheeked peaches,
10   Swart-headed mulberries,
Wild free-born cranberries,
Crabapples, dewberries,
Pineapples, blackberries,
Apricots, strawberries; –
15   All ripe together
In summer weather, –
Morns that pass by,
Fair eyes that fly;
Come buy, come buy:
20   Our grapes fresh from the vine,
Pomegranates full and fine,
Dates and sharp bullaces,

Rare pears and greengages,
Damsons and bilberries,
25   Taste them and try:
Currents and gooseberries,
Bright-fire-like barberries,
Figs to fill your mouth,
Citrons from the South,
30   Sweet to tongue and sound to eye;
Come buy, come buy.'

Evening by evening
Among the brookside rushes,
Laura bowed her head to hear,
35   Lizzie veiled her blushes:
Crouching close together
In the cooling weather,
With clasping arms and cautioning lips,
With tingling cheeks and finger tips.
40   'Lie close,' Laura said,
Pricking up her golden head:
'We must not look at goblin men,
We must not buy their fruits:
Who knows upon what soil they fed
45   Their hungry thirsty roots?'
'Come buy,' call the goblins
Hobbling down the glen.
'Oh,' cried Lizzie, 'Laura, Laura,
You should not peep at goblin men.'
50   Lizzie covered up her eyes,
Covered close lest they should look;
Laura reared her glossy head,
And whispered like the restless brook:
'Look, Lizzie, look, Lizzie,
55   Down the glen tramp little men.
One hauls a basket,
One bears a plate,
One lugs a golden dish
Of many pounds' weight.
60   How fair the vine must grow
Whose grapes are so luscious;
How warm the wind must blow
Through those fruit bushes.'
'No,' said Lizzie: 'No, no, no;
65   Their offers should not charm us,
Their evil gifts would harm us.'
She thrust a dimpled finger

In each ear, shut eyes and ran:
Curious Laura chose to linger
70   Wondering at each merchant man.
One had a cat's face,
One whisked a tail,
One tramped at a rat's pace,
One crawled like a snail,
75   One like a wombat prowled obtuse and furry,
One like a ratel tumbled hurry skurry.
She heard a voice like voices of doves
Cooing all together:
They sounded kind and full of loves
80   In the pleasant weather.

Laura stretched her gleaming neck
Like a rush-imbedded swan,
Like a lily from the beck,
Like a moonlit poplar branch,
85   Like a vessel at the launch
When its last restraint is gone.

Backwards up the mossy glen
Turned and trooped the goblin men,
With their shrill repeated cry,
90   'Come buy, come buy.'
When they reached where Laura was
They stood stock still upon the moss,
Leering at each other,
Brother with queer brother;
95   Signaling each other,
Brother with sly brother,
One set his basket down,
One reared his plate;
One began to weave a crown
100   Of tendrils, leaves, and rough nuts brown
(Men sell not such in any town):
One heaved the golden weight
Of dish and fruit to offer her:
'Come buy, come buy,' was still their cry.
105   Laura stared but did not stir,
Longed but had no money.
The whisk-tailed merchant bade her taste
In tones as smooth as honey,
The cat-faced purr'd,
110   The rat-paced spoke a word

---

76 **ratel:** the South African honey badger.   83 **beck:** a swiftly flowing stream.

Of welcome, and the snail-paced even was heard;
One parrot-voiced and jolly
Cried 'Pretty Goblin' still for 'Pretty Polly':
One whistled like a bird.

115 But sweet-tooth Laura spoke in haste:
'Good Folk, I have no coin;
To take were to purloin:
I have no copper in my purse,
I have no silver either,
120 And all my gold is on the furze
That shakes in windy weather
Above the rusty heather.'
'You have much gold upon your head,'
They answered all together:
125 'Buy from us with a golden curl.'
She clipped a precious golden lock,
She dropped a tear more rare than pearl,
Then sucked their fruit globes fair or red.
Sweeter than honey from the rock,
130 Stronger than man-rejoicing wine,
Clearer than water flowed that juice;
She never tasted such before,
How should it cloy with length of use?
She sucked and sucked and sucked the more
135 Fruits which that unknown orchard bore;
She sucked until her lips were sore;
Then flung the emptied rinds away
But gathered up one kernel stone,
And knew not was it night or day
140 As she turned home alone.

Lizzie met her at the gate
Full of wise upbraidings:
'Dear, you should not stay so late,
Twilight is not good for maidens;
145 Should not loiter in the glen
In the haunts of goblin men.
Do you not remember Jeanie,
How she met them in the moonlight,
Took their gifts both choice and many,
150 Ate their fruits and wove their flowers
Plucked from bowers
Where summer ripens at all hours?
But ever in the noonlight
She pined and pined away;

155 Sought them by night and day,
Found them no more, but dwindled and grew gray;
Then fell with the first snow,
While to this day no grass will grow
Where she lies low:
160 I planted daisies there a year ago
That never blow.
You should not loiter so.'
'Nay, hush,' said Laura:
'Nay, hush, my sister:
165 I ate and ate my fill,
Yet my mouth waters still:
Tomorrow night I will
Buy more'; and kissed her.
'Have done with sorrow;
170 I'll bring you plums tomorrow
Fresh on their mother twigs,
Cherries worth getting;
You cannot think what figs
My teeth have met in,
175 What melons icy-cold
Piled on a dish of gold
Too huge for me to hold,
What peaches with a velvet nap,
Pellucid grapes without one seed:
180 Odorous indeed must be the mead
Whereon they grow, and pure the wave they drink
With lilies at the brink,
And sugar-sweet their sap.'

Golden head by golden head,
185 Like two pigeons in one nest
Folded in each other's wings,
They lay down in their curtained bed:
Like two blossoms on one stem,
Like two flakes of new-fallen snow,
190 Like two wands of ivory
Tipped with gold for awful kings.
Moon and stars gazed in at them,
Winds sang to them lullaby,
Lumbering owls forebore to fly,
195 Not a bat flapped to and fro
Round their nest:
Cheek to cheek and breast to breast
Locked together in one nest.

---

191 **awful**: inspiring awe.

Early in the morning
200 When the first cock crowed his warning.
Neat like bees, as sweet and busy,
Laura rose with Lizzie:
Fetched in honey, milked the cows,
Aired and set to rights the house,
205 Kneaded cakes of whitest wheat,
Cakes for dainty mouths to eat,
Next churned butter, whipped up cream,
Fed their poultry, sat and sewed;
Talked as modest maidens should:
210 Lizzie with an open heart,
Laura in an absent dream,
One content, one sick in part;
One warbling for the mere bright day's delight,
One longing for the night.

215 At length slow evening came:
They went with pitchers to the reedy brook:
Lizzie most placid in her look,
Laura most like a leaping flame,
They drew the gurgling water from its deep.
220 Lizzie plucked purple and rich golden flags,
Then turning homewards said: 'The sunset flushes
Those furthest loftiest crags;
Come, Laura, not another maiden lags.
No willful squirrel wags,
225 The beasts and birds are fast asleep.'
But Laura loitered still among the rushes.
And said the bank was steep.

And said the hour was early still,
The dew not fallen, the wind not chill;
230 Listening ever, but not catching
The customary cry,
'Come buy, come buy,'
With its iterated jingle
Of sugar-baited words:
235 Not for all her watching
Once discerning even one goblin
Racing, whisking, tumbling, hobbling –
Let alone the herds
That used to tramp along the glen,
240 In groups or single,
Of brisk fruit-merchant men.
Till Lizzie urged, 'O Laura, come;'
I hear the fruit-call, but I dare not look:

You should not loiter longer at this brook:
245 Come with me home.
The stars rise, the moon bends her arc,
Each glow-worm winks her spark,
Let us get home before the night grows dark:
For clouds may gather
250 Though this is summer weather,
Put out the lights and drench us through;
Then if we lost our way what should we do?

Laura turned cold as stone
To find her sister heard that cry alone,
255 That goblin cry,
'Come buy our fruits, come buy.'
Must she then buy no more such dainty fruit?
Must she no more such succous pasture find,
Gone deaf and blind?
260 Her tree of life dropped from the root:
She said not one word in her heart's sore ache:
But peering through the dimness, nought discerning,
Trudged home, her pitcher dripping all the way;
So crept to bed, and lay
265 Silent till Lizzie slept;
Then sat up in a passionate yearning.
And gnashed her teeth for balked desire, and wept
As if her heart would break.

Day after day, night after night,
270 Laura kept watch in vain
In sullen silence of exceeding pain.
She never caught again the goblin cry,
'Come buy, come buy;' –
She never spied the goblin men
275 Hawking their fruits along the glen:
But when the noon waxed bright
Her hair grew thin and gray;
She dwindled, as the fair full moon doth turn
To swift decay and burn
280 Her fire away.

One day remembering her kernelstone
She set it by a wall that faced the south;
Dewed it with tears, hoped for a root,
Watched for a waxing shoot,
285 But there came none.

---

258 **succous**: succulent, sweet.

It never saw the sun,
It never felt the trickling moisture run:
While with sunk eyes and faded mouth
She dreamed of melons, as a traveler sees
290   False waves in desert drouth
With shade of leaf-crowned trees,
And burns the thirstier in the sandful breeze.

She no more swept the house,
Tended the fowls or cows,
295   Fetched honey, kneaded cakes of wheat,
Brought water from the brook:
But sat down listless in the chimneynook
And would not eat.

Tender Lizzie could not bear
300   To watch her sister's cankerous care,
Yet not to share.
She night and morning
Caught the goblins' cry:
'Come buy our orchard fruits,
305   Come buy, come buy:' –
Beside the brook, along the glen,
She heard the tramp of goblin men,
The voice and stir
Poor Laura could not hear;
310   Longed to buy fruit to comfort her,
But feared to pay too dear.
She thought of Jeanie in her grave,
Who should have been a bride;
But who for joys brides hope to have
315   Fell sick and died
In her gay prime,
In earliest Winter time,
With the first glazing rime,
With the first snow-fall of crisp Winter time.

320   Till Laura dwindling
Seemed knocking at Death's door.
Then Lizzie weighed no more
Better and worse;
But put a silver penny in her purse,
325   Kissed Laura, crossed the heath with clumps of furze
At twilight, halted by the brook:
And for the first time in her life
Began to listen and look.
Laughed every goblin

330 When they spied her peeping:
Came towards her hobbling,
Flying, running, leaping,
Puffing and blowing,
Chuckling, clapping, crowing,
335 Clucking and gobbling,
Mopping and mowing,
Full of airs and graces,
Pulling wry faces,
Demure grimaces,
340 Cat-like and rat-like,
Ratel- and wombat-like,
Snail-paced in a hurry,
Parrot-voiced and whistler,
Helter skelter, hurry skurry,
345 Chattering like magpies,
Fluttering like pigeons,
Gliding like fishes, –
Hugged her and kissed her:
Squeezed and caressed her:
350 Stretched up their dishes,
Panniers, and plates:
'Look at our apples
Russet and dun,
Bob at our cherries,
355 Bite at our peaches,
Citrons and dates,
Grapes for the asking,
Pears red with basking
Out in the sun,
360 Plums on their twigs;
Pluck them and suck them, –
Pomegranates, figs.'

'Good folk,' said Lizzie,
Mindful of Jeanie:
365 'Give me much and many': –
Held out her apron,
Tossed them her penny
'Nay, take a seat with us,
Honor and eat with us,'
370 They answered grinning:
'Our feast is but beginning.
Night yet is early,
Warm and dew-pearly,
Wakeful and starry:
375 Such fruits as these

No man can carry;
Half their bloom would fly,
Half their dew would dry,
Half their flavor would pass by.
380 Sit down and feast with us,
Be welcome guest with us,
Cheer you and rest with us.' –
'Thank you,' said Lizzie: 'But one waits
At home alone for me:
385 So without further parleying,
If you will not sell me any
Of your fruits though much and many,
Give me back my silver penny
I tossed you for a fee.' –
390 They began to scratch their pates,
No longer wagging, purring,
But visibly demurring,
Grunting and snarling.
One called her proud,
395 Cross-grained, uncivil;
Their tones waxed loud,
Their looks were evil.
Lashing their tails
They trod and hustled her,
400 Elbowed and jostled her,
Clawed with their nails,
Barking, mewing, hissing, mocking,
Tore her gown and soiled her stocking,
Twitched her hair out by the roots,
405 Stamped upon her tender feet,
Held her hands and squeezed their fruits
Against her mouth to make her eat.

White and golden Lizzie stood,
Like a lily in a flood, –
410 Like a rock of blue-veined stone
Lashed by tides obstreperously, –
Like a beacon left alone
In a hoary roaring sea,
Sending up a golden fire, –
415 Like a fruit crowned orange-tree
White with blossoms honey-sweet
Sore beset by wasp and bee, –
Like a royal virgin town
Topped with gilded dome and spire
420 Close beleaguered by a fleet
Mad to tug her standard down.

One may lead a horse to water,
Twenty cannot make him drink,
Though the goblins cuffed and caught her,
425 Coaxed and fought her,
Bullied and besought her,
Scratched her, pinched her black as ink,
Kicked and knocked her,
Mauled and mocked her,
430 Lizzie uttered not a word;
Would not open lip from lip
Lest they should cram a mouthful in:
But laughed in heart to feel the drip
Of juice that syruped all her face,
435 And lodged in dimples of her chin,
And streaked her neck which quaked like curd.
At last the evil people,
Worn out by her resistance,
Flung back her penny, kicked their fruit
440 Along whichever road they took,
Not leaving root or stone or shoot;
Some writhed into the ground,
Some dived into the brook
With ring and ripple,
445 Some scudded on the gale without a sound,
Some vanished in the distance.

In a smart, ache, tingle,
Lizzie went her way;
Knew not was it night or day;
450 Sprang up the bank, tore through the furze,
Threaded copse and dingle,
And heard her penny jingle
Bouncing in her purse,
Its bounce was music to her ear.
455 She ran and ran
As if she feared some goblin man
Dogged her with gibe or curse
Or something worse:
But not one goblin skurried after,
460 Nor was she pricked by fear;
The kind heart made her windy-paced
That urged her home quite out of breath with haste
And inward laughter.

She cried, 'Laura,' up the garden,
465 'Did you miss me?
Come and kiss me.

Never mind my bruises,
Hug me, kiss me, suck my juices
Squeezed from goblin fruits for you,
470 Goblin pulp and goblin dew.
Eat me, drink me, love me;
Laura, make much of me;
For your sake I have braved the glen
And had to do with goblin merchant men.'

475 Laura started from her chair,
Flung her arms up in the air,
Clutched her hair:
'Lizzie, Lizzie, have you tasted
For my sake the fruit forbidden?
480 Must your light like mine be hidden,
Your young life like mine be wasted,
Undone in mine undoing,
And ruined in my ruin,
Thirsty, cankered, goblin-ridden?' –
485 She clung about her sister,
Kissed and kissed and kissed her:
Tears once again
Refreshed her shrunken eyes,
Dropping like rain
490 After long sultry drouth;
Shaking with anguish, fear, and pain,
She kissed and kissed her with a hungry mouth.

Her lips began to scorch,
That juice was wormwood to her tongue,
495 She loathed the feast:
Writhing as one possessed she leaped and sung,
Rent all her robe, and wrung
Her hands in lamentable haste,
And beat her breast,
500 Her locks streamed like the torch
Borne by a racer at full speed,
Or like the mane of horses in their flight,
Or like an eagle when she stems the light
Straight toward the sun,
505 Or like a caged thing freed,
Or like a flying flag when armies run.

Swift fire spread through her veins, knocked at her heart,
Met the fire smoldering there

---

503 **stems:** to make headway against the wind.

And overbore its lesser flame;
510 She gorged on bitterness without a name:
Ah! fool, to choose such part
Of soul-consuming care!
Sense failed in the mortal strife:
Like the watch-tower of a town
515 Which an earthquake shatters down,
Like a lightning-stricken mast,
Like a wind-uprooted tree
Spun about,
Like a foam-topped waterspout
520 Cast down headlong in the sea,
She fell at last;
Pleasure past and anguish past,
Is it death or is it life?

Life out of death.
525 That night long Lizzie watched by her,
Counted her pulse's flagging stir,
Felt for her breath,
Held water to her lips, and cooled her face
With tears and fanning leaves.
530 But when the first birds chirped about their eaves,
And early reapers plodded to the place
Of golden sheaves,
And dew-wet grass
Bowed in the morning winds so brisk to pass,
535 And new buds with new day
Opened of cup-like lilies on the stream,
Laura awoke as from a dream,
Laughed in the innocent old way,
Hugged Lizzie but not twice or thrice;
540 Her gleaming locks showed not one thread of gray,
Her breath was sweet as May,
And light danced in her eyes.

Days, weeks, months, years
Afterwards, when both were wives
545 With children of their own;
Their mother-hearts beset with fears,
Their lives bound up in tender lives;
Laura would call the little ones
And tell them of her early prime,
550 Those pleasant days long gone
Of not-returning time:
Would talk about the haunted glen,
The wicked quaint fruit-merchant men,

Their fruits like honey to the throat
555 But poison in the blood
(Men sell not such in any town):
Would tell them how her sister stood
In deadly peril to do her good,
And win the fiery antidote:
560 Then joining hands to little hands
Would bid them cling together,
'For there is no friend like a sister
In calm or stormy weather;
To cheer one on the tedious way,
565 To fetch one if one goes astray,
To lift one if one totters down,
To strengthen whilst one stands.'

DORA GREENWELL (1821–1882)

Dora Greenwell was born at Greenwell Ford, County Durham, where her father was a prominent country gentleman. Educated by governesses, she was inspired by Tennyson and Elizabeth Barrett Browning and published *Poems* (1848) and *Stories that Might be True, with Other Poems* (1850), *Poems* (1865, 1867), *Carmina Crucis* (1869), *Songs of Salvation* (1873), *The Soul's Legend* (1873) and *Camera Obscura* (1876). She became a friend of Christina Rossetti, with whose work hers was often linked. Like her, she was deeply religious and a campaigner against all forms of social injustice, notably the slave trade, the incarceration of the insane and economic discrimination against women. She also actively campaigned for women's suffrage and was a close friend of the prominent feminist, Josephine Butler.

A Scherzo (A Shy Person's Wishes)

With the wasp at the innermost heart of a peach,
On a sunny wall out of tip-toe reach,
With the trout in the darkest summer pool,
With the fern-seed clinging behind its cool
5 Smooth frond, in the chink of an aged tree,
In the woodbine's horn with the drunken bee,
With the mouse in its nest in a furrow old,
With the chrysalis wrapt in its gauzy fold;
With things that are hidden, and safe, and bold,
10 With things that are timid, and shy, and free,
Wishing to be;
With the nut in its shell, with the seed in its pod,
With the corn as it sprouts in the kindly clod,
Far down where the secret of beauty shows

15   In the bulb of the tulip, before it blows;
With things that are rooted, and firm, and deep,
Quiet to lie, and dreamless to sleep;
With things that are chainless, and tameless, and proud,
With the fire in the jagged thunder-cloud,
20   With the wind in its sleep, with the wind in its waking,
With the drops that go to the rainbow's making,
Wishing to be with the light leaves shaking,
Or stones on some desolate highway breaking;
Far up on the hills, where no fool surprises
25   The dew as it falls, or the dust as it rises;
To be couched with the beast in its torrid lair,
Or drifting on ice with the polar bear,
With the weaver at work at his quiet loom;
Anywhere, anywhere, out of this room!

AUGUSTA WEBSTER (1837–1894)

Augusta Webster's father was a Vice-Admiral and she was raised in Dorset, Scotland and Cambridge, where she studied art. She married Thomas Webster, a lecturer in law and solicitor. As 'Cecil Home', she published *Blanche Lisle and Other Poems* (1860) and *Lilian Gray* (1864), but her major volumes were published under her own name; *Dramatic Studies* (1866), *A Woman Sold and Other Poems* (1867), and *Portraits* (1870). She was a considerable linguist and published translations of Aeschylus and Euripides. In her later years she wrote verse dramas, notably *The Sentence* (1887) which Rossetti considered a masterpiece. In her verse collections Webster adopted the Brownings' method of dramatic monologue, often using it to give powerful voice to women's concerns, as in *The Castaway* which is spoken by a prostitute.

From A Castaway

Poor little diary, with its simple thoughts,
Its good resolves, its 'Studied French an hour,'
'Read Modern History,' 'Trimmed up my grey hat,'
'Darned stockings,' 'Tatted,' 'Practised my new song,'
5   'Went to the daily service,' 'Took Bess soup,'
'Went out to tea.' Poor simple diary!
And did *I* write it? Was I this good girl,
This budding colourless young rose of home?
Did I so live content in such a life,
10   Seeing no larger scope, nor asking it,
Than this small constant round – old clothes to mend,
New clothes to make, then go and say my prayers,
Or carry soup, or take a little walk

And pick the ragged-robins in the hedge?
15 Then, for ambition, (was there ever life
That could forego that?) to improve my mind
And know French better and sing harder songs;
For gaiety, to go, in my best white
Well washed and starched and freshened with new bows,
20 And take tea out to meet the clergyman.
No wishes and no cares, almost no hopes,
Only the young girl's hazed and golden dreams
That veil the Future from her.
                                    So long since:
And now it seems a jest to talk of me
25 As if I could be one with her, of me
Who am . . . me.
                        And what is that? My looking-glass
Answers it passably; a woman sure,
No fiend, no slimy thing out of the pools,
A woman with a ripe and smiling lip
30 That has no venom in its touch I think,
With a white brow on which there is no brand;
A woman none dare call not beautiful,
Not womanly in every woman's grace.

Aye, let me feed upon my beauty thus,
35 Be glad in it like painters when they see
At last the face they dreamed but could not find
Look from their canvas on them, triumph in it,
The dearest thing I have. Why, 'tis my all,
Let me make much of it: is it not this,
40 This beauty, my own curse at once and tool
To snare men's souls, (I know what the good say
Of beauty in such creatures) is it not this
That makes me feel myself a woman still,
With still some little pride, some little –
                                                Stop!
45 'Some little pride, some little' – Here's a jest!
What word will fit the sense but modesty?
A wanton I, but modest!
                            Modest, true;
I'm not drunk in the streets, ply not for hire
At infamous corners with my likenesses
50 Of the humbler kind; yes, modesty's my word –
'Twould shape my mouth well too, I think I'll try:
'Sir, Mr What-you-will, Lord Who-knows-what,
My present lover or my next to come,
Value me at my worth, fill your purse full,

55   For I am modest; yes, and honour me
     As though your schoolgirl sister or your wife
     Could let her skirts brush mine or talk of me;
     For I am modest.'
                      Well, I flout myself:
     But yet, but yet –
                  Fie, poor fantastic fool,
60   Why do I play the hypocrite alone,
     Who am no hypocrite with others by?
     Where should be my 'But yet'? I am that thing
     Called half a dozen dainty names, and none
     Dainty enough to serve the turn and hide
65   The one coarse English worst that lurks beneath:
     Just that, no worse, no better.
                     And, for me,
     I say let no one be above her trade;
     I own my kindredship with any drab
     Who sells herself as I, although she crouch
70   In fetid garrets and I have a home
     All velvet and marqueterie and pastilles,
     Although she hide her skeleton in rags
     And I set fashions and wear cobweb lace:
     The difference lies but in my choicer ware,
75   That I sell beauty and she ugliness;
     Our traffic's one – I'm no sweet slaver-tongue
     To gloze upon it and explain myself
     A sort of fractious angel misconceived –
     Our traffic's one: I own it. And what then?
80   I know of worse that are called honourable.
     Our lawyers, who with noble eloquence
     And virtuous outbursts lie to hang a man,
     Or lie to save him, which way goes the fee:
     Our preachers, gloating on your future hell
85   For not believing what they doubt themselves:
     Our doctors, who sort poisons out by chance
     And wonder how they'll answer, and grow rich:
     Our journalists, whose business is to fib
     And juggle truths and falsehoods to and fro:
90   Our tradesmen, who must keep unspotted names
     And cheat the least like stealing that they can:
     Our – all of them, the virtuous worthy men
     Who feed on the world's follies, vices, wants,
     And do their businesses of lies and shams
95   Honestly, reputably, while the world
     Claps hands and cries 'good luck,' which of their trades,
     Their honourable trades, barefaced like mine,

All secrets brazened out, would shew more white?
   And whom do I hurt more than they? as much?
100 The wives? Poor fools, what do I take from them
Worth crying for or keeping? If they knew
What their fine husbands look like seen by eyes
That may perceive there are more men than one!
But, if they can, let them just take the pains
105 To keep them: 'tis not such a mighty task
To pin an idiot to your apron-string;
And wives have an advantage over us,
(The good and blind ones have) the smile or pout
Leaves them no secret nausea at odd times.
110 Oh, they could keep their husbands if they cared,
But 'tis an easier life to let them go,
And whimper at it for morality.

* * * *

Why, if the worthy men who think all's done
280 If we'll but come where we can hear them preach,
Could bring us all, or any half of us,
Into their fold, teach all us wandering sheep,
Or only half of us, to stand in rows
And baa them hymns and moral songs, good lack,
285 What would they do with us? what could they do?
Just think! with were't but half of us on hand
To find work for . . . or husbands. Would they try
To ship us to the colonies for wives?

Well, well, I know the wise ones talk and talk:
290 'Here's cause, here's cure:' 'No, here it is, and here:'
And find society to blame, or law,
The Church, the men, the women, too few schools,
Too many schools, too much, too little taught:
Somewhere or somehow someone is to blame:
295 But I say all the fault's with God himself
Who puts too many women in the world.
We ought to die off reasonably and leave
As many as the men want, none to waste.
Here's cause; the woman's superfluity:
300 And for the cure, why, if it were the law,
Say, every year, in due percentages,
Balancing them with males as the times need,
To kill off female infants, 'twould make room;
And some of us would not have lost too much,
305 Losing life ere we know what it *can* mean.

The other day I saw a woman weep
Beside her dead child's bed: the little thing
Lay smiling, and the mother wailed half mad,
Shrieking to God to give it back again.
310   I could have laughed aloud: the little girl
Living had but her mother's life to live;
There she lay smiling, and her mother wept
To know her gone!

                  My mother would have wept.
Oh, mother, mother, did you ever dream,
315   You good grave simple mother, you pure soul
No evil could come nigh, did you once dream
In all your dying cares for your lone girl
Left to fight out her fortune helplessly
That there would be *this* danger? – for *your* girl,
320   Taught by you, lapped in a sweet ignorance,
Scarcely more wise of what things sin could be
Than some young child a summer six months old,
Where in the north the summer makes a day,
Of what is darkness . . . darkness that will come
325   To-morrow suddenly. Thank God at least
For this much of my life, that when you died,
That when you kissed me dying, not a thought
Of this made sorrow for you, that I too
Was pure of even fear.
330   Oh yes, I thought,
Still new in my insipid treadmill life,
(My father so late dead), and hopeful still,
There might be something pleasant somewhere in it,
Some sudden fairy come, no doubt, to turn
My pumpkin to a chariot, I thought then
335   That I might plod and plod and drum the sounds
Of useless facts into unwilling ears,
Tease children with dull questions half the day
Then con dull answers in my room at night
Ready for next day's questions, mend quill pens
340   And cut my fingers, add up sums done wrong
And never get them right; teach, teach, and teach –
What I half knew, or not at all – teach, teach
For years, a lifetime – *I!*

                 And yet, who knows?
It might have been, for I was patient once,
345   And willing, and meant well; it might have been
Had I but still clung on in my first place –
A safe dull place, where mostly there were smiles
But never merry-makings; where all days

Jogged on sedately busy, with no haste;
350 Where all seemed measured out, but margins broad:
A dull home but a peaceful, where I felt
My pupils would be dear young sisters soon,
And felt their mother take me to her heart,
Motherly to all lonely harmless things.
355 But I must have a conscience, must blurt out
My great discovery of my ignorance!
And who required it of me? And who gained?
What did it matter for a more or less
The girls learnt in their schoolbooks, to forget
360 In their first season? We did well together:
They loved me and I them: but I went off
To housemaid's pay, six crossgrained brats to teach,
Wrangles and jangles, doubts, disgrace . . . then this;
And they had a perfection found for them,
365 Who has all ladies' learning in her head
Abridged and scheduled, speaks five languages,
Knows botany and conchology and globes,
Draws, paints, plays, sings, embroiders, teaches all
On a patent method never known to fail:
370 And now they're finished and, I hear, poor things,
Are the worst dancers and worst dressers out.
And where's their profit of those prison years
All gone to make them wise in lesson-books?
Who wants his wife to know weeds' Latin names?
375 Who ever chose a girl for saying dates?
Or asked if she had learned to trace a map?

Well, well, the silly rules this silly world
Makes about women! This is one of them.
Why must there be pretence of teaching them
380 What no one ever cares that they should know,
What, grown out to the schoolroom, they cast off
Like the schoolroom pinafore, no better fit
For any use of real grown-up life,
For any use to her who seeks or waits
385 The husband and the home, for any use,
For any shallowest pretence of use,
To her who had them? Do I not know this,
I, like my betters, that a woman's life,
Her natural life, her good life, her one life,
390 Is in her husband, God on earth to her,
And what she knows and what she can and is
Is only good as it brings good to him?

Oh God, do I not know it? I the thing
Of shame and rottenness, the animal
395   That feed men's lusts and prey on them, I, I,
Who should not dare to take the name of wife
On my polluted lips, who in the word
Hear but my own reviling, I know that.
I could have lived by that rule, how content:
400   My pleasure to make him some pleasure, pride
To be as he would have me, duty, care,
To fit all to his taste, rule my small sphere
To his intention; then to lean on him,
Be guided, tutored, loved – no not that word,
405   That *loved* which between men and women means
All selfishness, all cloying talk, all lust,
All vanity, all idiocy – not loved,
But cared for. I've been loved myself, I think,
Some once or twice since my poor mother died,
410   But *cared for*, never: – that's a word for homes,
Kind homes, good homes, where simple children come
And ask their mother is this right or wrong,
Because they know she's perfect, cannot err;
Their father told them so, and he knows all,
415   Being so wise and good and wonderful,
Even enough to scold even her at times
And tell her everything she does not know.
Ah the sweet nursery logic!

                      Fool! Thrice fool!
Do I hanker after that too? Fancy me
420   Infallible nursery saint, live code of law!
Me preaching! teaching innocence to be good! –
A mother!

               Yet the baby thing that woke
And wailed an hour or two, and then was dead,
Was mine, and had he lived . . . why then my name
425   Would have been mother. But 'twas well he died:
I could have been no mother, I, lost then
Beyond his saving. Had he come before
And lived, come to me in the doubtful days
When shame and boldness had not grown one sense,
430   For his sake, with the courage come of him,
I might have struggled back.

                  But how? But how?
His father would not then have let me go:

His time had not yet come to make an end
Of my 'for ever' with a hireling's fee
435 And civil light dismissal. None but him
To claim a bit of bread of if I went,
Child or no child: would he have given it to me?
He! no; he had not done with me. No help,
No help, no help. Some ways can be trodden back,
440 But never our way, we who one wild day
Have given goodbye to what in our deep hearts
The lowest woman still holds best in life,
Good name – good name though given by the world
That mouths and garbles with its decent prate,
445 And wraps it in respectable grave shams,
And patches conscience partly by the rule
Of what one's neighbour thinks, but something more
By what his eyes are sharp enough to see.
How I could scorn it with its Pharisees,
450 If it could not scorn me: but yet, but yet –
Oh God, if I could look it in the face!

Oh I am wild, am ill, I think, to-night:
Will no one come and laugh with me? No feast,
No merriment to-night. So long alone!
455 Will no one come?

                  At least there's a new dress
To try, and grumble at – they never fit
To one's ideal. Yes, a new rich dress,
With lace like this too, that's a soothing balm
For any fretting woman, cannot fail;
460 I've heard men say it . . . and they know so well
What's in all women's hearts, especially
Women like me.

GEORGE ELIOT (1819–1880)

Mary Anne Evans's father was a land agent in Derbyshire and Warwickshire. She was educated in local schools in the Midlands, notably at a boarding school in Coventry, but when her mother died in 1836 she kept her father's house and took private lessons in Italian, German, Latin and Greek. She also read widely in philosophy, theology, German and romantic literature, especially Scott and Wordsworth. During these years she lost her passionate evangelical faith and became a free-thinker, but the need for love and duty, and the problems of moral failure, would remain important concerns in her work. Her first publication was a translation of David Friedrich Strauss's *Life of Jesus, Critically Examined* (1846), a pioneer work in the 'Higher Criticism' that treated the gospels as a mythologised record of actual events rather than as allegorical revelations of divine mystery. This translation introduced Evans to free-thinking intellectual circles, and in 1850 she moved to London to work on the *Westminster Review*. Her next publication, a translation of Ludwig Feuerbach's *Essence of Christianity* (1854), argued that the religious impulse is a culturally valuable projection of human self-interest; Feuerbach's opinion was adopted by many intellectuals, notably Matthew Arnold, but was none the less heterodox. Evans became a scandalous woman when she entered a 'common law' marriage with George Henry Lewes, a prominent intellectual who encouraged her writing. In 1858 she published to acclaim *Scenes from Clerical Life* under the name of George Eliot. There followed three very successful rural novels, *Adam Bede* (1859), *The Mill on the Floss* (1860), and *Silas Marner* (1861). Her next novel, *Romola* (1863), was a historical novel set in fifteenth-century Florence. Responding to the agitation that led to the 1867 Reform Bill, she then wrote a novel about working-class unrest, *Felix Holt, the Radical* (1866). In 1871–72 she produced her greatest work, *Middlemarch: A Story of Provincial Life*, set in the earlier Reform period (1832). *Daniel Deronda* (1876) was set in her own time and concerned with the Jewish cause for a national home. George Eliot was recognised as the leading novelist of the 1870s. She was acutely aware of how complex consciousness can be, how people live both within historical time and in intersubjective space with others but sadly fail to understand their own identities and needs. What contemporaries most admired was the power and wit of the philosophical generalisations which provide the moral underpinning for many paragraphs but which also appear to be derived from the life being narrated. Moral realism may have no finer exemplar.

From Middlemarch: A Study of Provincial Life

Prelude

Who cares much to know the history of man, and how the mysterious mixture behaves under the varying experiments of Time, has not dwelt, at least briefly, on the life of Saint Teresa,[1] has not smiled with some gentleness at the thought of the little girl walking forth one morning hand-in-hand with her still smaller brother, to go and seek martyrdom in the country of the Moors? Out they

---

1: Saint Teresa of Avila (1515–82), a Spanish mystic who wrote a spiritual autobiography, *The Way to Perfection*.

toddled from a rugged Avila, wide-eyed and helpless looking as two fawns, but with human hearts, already beating to a national idea; until domestic reality met them in the shape of uncles, and turned them back from their great resolve. That child-pilgrimage was a fit beginning. Theresa's passionate, ideal nature demanded an epic life: what were many-volumed romances of chivalry and the social conquests of a brilliant girl to her? Her flame quickly burned up that light fuel; and, fed from within, soared after some illimitable satisfaction, some object which would never justify weariness, which would reconcile self-despair with the rapturous consciousness of life beyond self. She found her epos in the reform of a religious order.

That Spanish woman who lived three hundred years ago was certainly not the last of her kind. Many Theresas have been born who found themselves no epic life wherein there was a constant unfolding of far-resonant action; perhaps only a life of mistakes, the offspring of a certain spiritual grandeur ill-matched with the meanness of opportunity; perhaps a tragic failure which found no sacred poet and sank unwept into oblivion. With dim lights and tangled circumstance they tried to shape their thought and deed in noble agreement; but after all, to common eyes their struggles seemed mere inconsistency and formlessness; for these late-born Theresas were helped by no coherent social faith and order which could perform the function of knowledge for the ardently willing soul. Their ardour alternated between a vague ideal and the common yearning of womanhood; so that the one was disapproved as extravagance, and the other condemned as a lapse.

Some have felt that these blundering lives are due to the inconvenient indefiniteness with which the supreme power has fashioned the natures of women: if there were one level of feminine incompetence as strict as the ability to count three and no more, the social lot of women might be treated with scientific certitude. Meanwhile the indefiniteness remains, and the limits of variation are really much wider than any one would imagine from the sameness of women's coiffure and the favourite love-stories in prose and verse. Here and there a cygnet is reared uneasily among the ducklings in the brown pond, and never finds the living stream in fellowship with its own oary-footed kind. Here and there is born a Saint Theresa, foundress of nothing, whose loving heart-beats and sobs after an unattained goodness tremble off and are dispersed among hindrances, instead of centering in some long-recognisable deed.

Book One. Miss Brooke

Chapter 1

> Since I can do no good because a woman,
> Reach constantly at something that is near it.
> > *The Maid's Tragedy*, Beaumont and Fletcher[1]

Miss Brooke had that kind of beauty which seems to be thrown into relief by poor dress. Her hand and wrist were so finely formed that she could wear

---

1: *The Maid's Tragedy*, IV, i, 253–54, written 1610–11.

sleeves not less bare of style than those in which the Blessed Virgin appeared to Italian painters; and her profile as well as her stature and bearing seemed to gain the more dignity from her plain garments, which by the side of provincial fashion gave her the impressiveness of a fine quotation from the Bible, – or from one of our elder poets, – in a paragraph of to-day's newspaper. She was usually spoken of as being remarkably clever, but with the addition that her sister Celia had more common-sense. Nevertheless, Celia wore scarcely more trimmings; and it was only to close observers that her dress differed from her sister's, and had a shade of coquetry in its arrangements; for Miss Brooke's plain dressing was due to mixed conditions, in most of which her sister shared. The pride of being ladies had something to do with it: the Brooke connections, though not exactly aristocratic, were unquestionably 'good': if you inquired backward for a generation or two, you would not find any yard-measuring or parcel-tying forefathers – anything lower than an admiral or a clergyman; and there was even an ancestor discernible as a Puritan gentleman who served under Cromwell, but afterwards conformed,[1] and managed to come out of all political troubles as the proprietor of a respectable family estate. Young women of such birth, living in a quiet country-house, and attending a village church hardly larger than a parlour, naturally regarded frippery[2] as the ambition of a huckster's daughter. Then there was well-bred economy, which in those days made show in dress the first item to be deducted from, when any margin was required for expenses more distinctive of rank. Such reasons would have been enough to account for plain dress, quite apart from religious feeling; but in Miss Brooke's case, religion alone would have determined it; and Celia mildly acquiesced in all her sister's sentiments, only infusing them with that common-sense which is able to accept momentous doctrines without any eccentric agitation. Dorothea knew many passages of Pascal's *Pensées* and of Jeremy Taylor[3] by heart; and to her the destinies of mankind, seen by the light of Christianity, made the solicitudes of feminine fashion appear an occupation for Bedlam.[4] She could not reconcile the anxieties of a spiritual life involving eternal consequences, with a keen interest in guimp[5] and artificial protusions of drapery. Her mind was theoretic, and yearned by its nature after some lofty conception of the world which might frankly include the parish of Tipton and her own rule of conduct there; she was enamoured of intensity and greatness, and rash in embracing whatever seemed to her to have those aspects; likely to seek martyrdom, to make retractions, and then to incur martyrdom after all in a quarter where she had not sought it. Certainly such elements in the character of a marriageable girl tended to interfere with her lot, and hinder it from being decided according to custom, by good looks, vanity, and merely canine affection. With all this, she, the elder of the sisters, was not yet twenty, and they had both been educated, since they were about twelve years old and had lost their parents, on plans at once narrow and promiscuous, first in an English

---

1: Oliver Cromwell (1599–1658), leader of the Parliamentary and Puritan side in the Civil War who often 'conformed' to the Church of England when Charles II was restored to the throne. 2: trivial ornamentation. 3: Blaise Pascal (1623–62) whose *Pensées* (1670) justified Christian belief. Jeremy Taylor (1613–67), theologian who advocated religious toleration. 4: the Bethlehem Hospital for the insane in London, popularly contracted to 'Bedlam'. 5: a short blouse.

family and afterwards in a Swiss family at Lausanne, their bachelor uncle and guardian trying in this way to remedy the disadvantages of their orphaned condition.

It was hardly a year since they had come to live at Tipton Grange with their uncle, a man nearly sixty, of acquiescent temper, miscellaneous opinions, and uncertain vote. He had travelled in his younger years, and was held in this part of the county to have contracted a too rambling habit of mind. Mr Brooke's conclusions were as difficult to predict as the weather: it was only safe to say that he would act with benevolent intentions, and that he would spend as little money as possible in carrying them out. For the most glutinously indefinite minds enclose some hard grains of habit; and a man has been seen lax about all his own interests except the retention of his snuff-box, concerning which he was watchful, suspicious, and greedy of clutch.

In Mr Brooke the hereditary strain of Puritan energy was clearly in abeyance; but in his niece Dorothea it glowed alike through faults and virtues, turning sometimes into impatience of her uncle's talk or his way of 'letting things be' on his estate, and making her long all the more for the time when she would be of age and have some command of money for generous schemes. She was regarded as an heiress, for not only had the sisters seven hundred a-year – each from their parents, but if Dorothea married and had a son, that son would inherit Mr Brooke's estate, presumably worth about three thousand a-year – a rental which seemed wealth to provincial families, still discussing Mr Peel's late conduct on the Catholic Question,[1] innocent of future gold-fields, and of that gorgeous plutocracy which has so nobly exalted the necessities of genteel life.

And how should Dorothea not marry? – a girl so handsome and with such prospects? Nothing could hinder it but her love of extremes, and her insistence on regulating life according to notions which might cause a wary man to hesitate before he made her an offer, or even might lead her at last to refuse all offers. A young lady of some birth and fortune, who knelt suddenly down on a brick floor by the side of a sick labourer and prayed fervidly as if she thought herself living in the time of the Apostles – who had strange whims of fasting like a Papist, and of sitting up at night to read old theological books! Such a wife might awaken you some fine morning with a new scheme for the application of her income which would interfere with political economy and the keeping of saddle-horses: a man would naturally think twice before he risked himself in such fellowship. Women were expected to have weak opinions; but the great safeguard of society and of domestic life was, that opinions were not acted on. Sane people did what their neighbours did, so that if any lunatics were at large, one might know and avoid them.

The rural opinion about the new young ladies, even among the cottagers, was generally in favour of Celia, as being so amiable and innocent-looking, while Miss Brooke's large eyes seemed, like her religion, too unusual and striking. Poor Dorothea! compared with her, the innocent-looking Celia was knowing and worldly-wise; so much subtler is a human mind than the outside tissues which make a sort of blazonry or clock-face for it.

1: Robert Peel (1788–1850), Home Secretary, was elected as an opponent of Catholic emancipation but then obliged to speak in its favour in 1829.

Yet those who approached Dorothea, though prejudiced against her by this alarming hearsay, found that she had a charm unaccountably reconcilable with it. Most men thought her bewitching when she was on horseback. She loved the fresh air and the various aspects of the country, and when her eyes and cheeks glowed with mingled pleasure she looked very little like a devotee. Riding was an indulgence which she allowed herself in spite of conscientious qualms; she felt that she enjoyed it in a pagan sensuous way, and always looked forward to renouncing it.

She was open, ardent, and not in the least self-admiring; indeed, it was pretty to see how her imagination adorned her sister Celia with attractions altogether superior to her own, and if any gentleman appeared to come to the Grange from some other motive than that of seeing Mr Brooke, she concluded that he must be in love with Celia: Sir James Chettam, for example, whom she constantly considered from Celia's point of view, inwardly debating whether it would be good for Celia to accept him. That he should be regarded as a suitor to herself would have seemed to her a ridiculous irrelevance. Dorothea, with all her eagerness to know the truths of life, retained very childlike ideas about marriage. She felt sure that she would have accepted the judicious Hooker[1], if she had been born in time to save him from that wretched mistake he made in matrimony; or John Milton when his blindness had come on; or any of the other great men whose odd habits it would have been glorious piety to endure; but an amiable handsome baronet, who said 'Exactly' to her remarks even when she expressed uncertainty, – how could he affect her as a lover? The really delightful marriage must be that where your husband was a sort of father, and could teach you even Hebrew, if you wished it.

These peculiarities of Dorothea's character caused Mr Brooke to be all the more blamed in neighbouring families for not securing some middle-aged lady as guide and companion to his nieces. But he himself dreaded so much the sort of superior woman likely to be available for such a position, that he allowed himself to be dissuaded by Dorothea's objections, and was in this case brave enough to defy the world – that is to say, Mrs Cadwallader the Rector's wife, and the small group of gentry with whom he visited in the north-east corner of Loamshire.[2] So Miss Brooke presided in her uncle's household, and did not at all dislike her new authority, with the homage that belonged to it.

Sir James Chettam was going to dine at the Grange to-day with another gentleman whom the girls had never seen, and about whom Dorothea felt some venerating expectation. This was the Reverend Edward Casaubon,[3] noted in the county as a man of profound learning, understood for many years to be engaged on a great work concerning religious history; also as a man of wealth enough to give lustre to his piety, and having views of his own which were to be more clearly ascertained on the publication of his book. His very name carried an impressiveness hardly to be measured without a precise chronology of scholarship.

1: Richard Hooker (1554–1600) a theologian who was unhappily married.   2: a fictitious county-name first coined in *Adam Bede*.   3: Casaubon's namesake, Isaac Casaubon (1559–1614), published commentaries on ancient Greek authors and planned a major history of the church but finished only the first volume.

Early in the day Dorothea had returned from the infant school which she had set going in the village, and was taking her usual place in the pretty sitting-room which divided the bedrooms of the sisters, bent on finishing a plan for some buildings (a kind of work which she delighted in), when Celia, who had been watching her with a hesitating desire to propose something, said –

'Dorothea dear, if you don't mind – if you are not very busy – suppose we looked at mamma's jewels to-day, and divided them? It is exactly six months to-day since uncle gave them to you, and you have not looked at them yet.'

Celia's face had the shadow of a pouting expression in it, the full presence of the pout being kept back by an habitual awe of Dorothea and principle; two associated facts which might show a mysterious electricity if you touched them incautiously. To her relief, Dorothea's eyes were full of laughter as she looked up.

'What a wonderful little almanac you are, Celia! Is it six calendar or six lunar months?'

'It is the last day of September now, and it was the first of April when uncle gave them to you. You know, he said that he had forgotten them till then. I believe you have never thought of them since you locked them up in the cabinet here.'

'Well, dear, we should never wear them, you know.' Dorothea spoke in a full cordial tone, half caressing, half explanatory. She had her pencil in her hand, and was making tiny side-plans on a margin.

Celia coloured, and looked very grave. 'I think, dear, we are wanting in respect to mamma's memory, to put them by and take no notice of them. And,' she added, after hesitating a little, with a rising sob of mortification, 'necklaces are quite usual now; and Madame Poinçon, who was stricter in some things even than you are, used to wear ornaments. And Christians generally – surely there are women in heaven now who wore jewels.' Celia was conscious of some mental strength when she really applied herself to argument.

'You would like to wear them?' exclaimed Dorothea, an air of astonished discovery animating her whole person with a dramatic action which she had caught from that very Madame Poinçon who wore the ornaments. 'Of course, then, let us have them out. Why did you not tell me before? But the keys, the keys!' She pressed her hands against the sides of her head and seemed to despair of her memory.

'They are here,' said Celia, with whom this explanation had been long meditated and prearranged.

'Pray open the large drawer of the cabinet and get out the jewel-box.'

The casket was soon open before them, and the various jewels spread out, making a bright parterre on the table. It was no great collection, but a few of the ornaments were really of remarkable beauty, the finest that was obvious at first being a necklace of purple amethysts set in exquisite gold-work, and a pearl cross with five brilliants in it. Dorothea immediately took up the necklace and fastened it round her sister's neck, where it fitted almost as closely as a bracelet; but the circle suited the Henrietta-Maria[1] style of Celia's head and neck, and she could see that it did, in the pier-glass opposite.

1: Henrietta-Maria, wife of Charles I, often portrayed wearing a pearl choker necklace.

'There, Celia! you can wear that with your Indian muslin. But this cross you must wear with your dark dresses.'

Celia was trying not to smile with pleasure. 'O, Dodo, you must keep the cross yourself.'

'No, no, dear, no,' said Dorothea, putting up her hand with careless deprecation.

'Yes, indeed you must; it would suit you – in your black dress, now,' said Celia, insistingly. 'You *might* wear that.'

'Not for the world, not for the world. A cross is the last thing I would wear as a trinket.' Dorothea shuddered slightly.

'Then you will think it wicked in me to wear it,' said Celia, uneasily.

'No, dear, no,' said Dorothea, stroking her sister's cheek. 'Souls have complexions too: what will suit one will not suit another.'

'But you might like to keep it for mamma's sake.'

'No, I have other things of mamma's – her sandal-wood box, which I am so fond of – plenty of things. In fact, they are all yours, dear. We need discuss them no longer. There – take away your property.'

Celia felt a little hurt. There was a strong assumption of superiority in this Puritanic toleration, hardly less trying to the blond flesh of an unenthusiastic sister than a Puritanic persecution.

'But how can I wear ornaments if you, who are the elder sister, will never wear them?'

'Nay, Celia, that is too much to ask, that I should wear trinkets to keep you in countenance. If I were to put on such a necklace as that, I should feel as if I had been pirouetting. The world would go round with me, and I should not know how to walk.'

Celia had unclasped the necklace and drawn it off. 'It would be a little tight for your neck; something to lie down and hang would suit you better,' she said, with some satisfaction. The complete unfitness of the necklace from all points of view for Dorothea, made Celia happier in taking it. She was opening some ring-boxes, which disclosed a fine emerald with diamonds, and just then the sun passing beyond a cloud sent a bright gleam over the table.

'How very beautiful these gems are!' said Dorothea, under a new current of feeling, as sudden as the gleam. 'It is strange how deeply colours seem to penetrate one, like scent. I suppose that is the reason why gems are used as spiritual emblems in the Revelation of St John. They look like fragments of heaven. I think that emerald is more beautiful than any of them.'

'And there is a bracelet to match it,' said Celia. 'We did not notice this at first.'

'They are lovely,' said Dorothea, slipping the ring and bracelet on her finely-turned finger and wrist, and holding them towards the window on a level with her eyes. All the while her thought was trying to justify her delight in the colours by merging them in her mystic religious joy.

'You *would* like those, Dorothea,' said Celia, rather falteringly, beginning to think with wonder that her sister showed some weakness, and also that emeralds would suit her own complexion even better than purple amethysts.

'You must keep that ring and bracelet – if nothing else. But see, these agates are very pretty – and quiet.'

'Yes! I will keep these – this ring and bracelet,' said Dorothea. Then, letting her hand fall on the table, she said in another tone – 'Yet what miserable men find such things, and work at them, and sell them!' She paused again, and Celia thought that her sister was going to renounce the ornaments, as in consistency she ought to do.

'Yes, dear, I will keep these,' said Dorothea, decidedly. 'But take all the rest away, and the casket.'

She took up her pencil without removing the jewels, and still looking at them. She thought of often having them by her, to feed her eye at these little fountains of pure colour.

'Shall you wear them in company?' said Celia, who was watching her with real curiosity as to what she would do.

Dorothea glanced quickly at her sister. Across all her imaginative adornment of those whom she loved, there darted now and then a keen discernment, which was not without a scorching quality. If Miss Brooke ever attained perfect meekness, it would not be for lack of inward fire.

'Perhaps,' she said, rather haughtily. 'I cannot tell to what level I may sink.'

Celia blushed, and was unhappy; she saw that she had offended her sister, and dared not say even anything pretty about the gift of the ornaments which she put back into the box and carried away. Dorothea too was unhappy, as she went on with her plan-drawing, questioning the purity of her own feeling and speech in the scene which had ended with that little explosion.

Celia's consciousness told her that she had not been at all in the wrong: it was quite natural and justifiable that she should have asked that question, and she repeated to herself that Dorothea was inconsistent: either she should have taken her full share of the jewels, or, after what she had said, she should have renounced them altogether.

'I am sure – at least, I trust,' thought Celia, 'that the wearing of a necklace will not interfere with my prayers. And I do not see that I should be bound by Dorothea's opinions now we are going into society, though of course she herself ought to be bound by them. But Dorothea is not always consistent.'

Thus Celia, mutely bending over her tapestry, until she heard her sister calling her.

'Here, Kitty, come and look at my plan; I shall think I am a great architect, if I have not got incompatible stairs and fireplaces.'

As Celia bent over the paper, Dorothea put her cheek against her sister's arm caressingly. Celia understood the action. Dorothea saw that she had been in the wrong, and Celia pardoned her. Since they could remember, there had been a mixture of criticism and awe in the attitude of Celia's mind towards her elder sister. The younger had always worn a yoke: but is there any yoked creature without its private opinions?

Chapter 2

'Dime; no ves aquel caballero que hacia nosotros viene sobre un caballo rucio rodado que trae puesto en la cabeza un yelmo de oro?' 'Lo que veo y columbro,' respondió Sancho, 'no es sino un hombre sobre un asno pardo como el mio, que trae sobre la cabeza una cosa que relumbra.' 'Pues ese es el yelmo de Mambrino,' dijo Don Quijote.

Cervantes

'Seest thou not yon cavalier who cometh toward us on a dapple-grey steed, and weareth a golden helmet?' 'What I see,' answered Sancho, 'is nothing but a man on a grey ass like my own, who carries something shiny on his head.' 'Just so,' answered Don Quixote: 'and that resplendent object is the helmet of Mambrino.'

'Sir Humphry Davy?'[1] said Mr Brooke, over the soup, in his easy smiling way, taking up Sir James Chettam's remark that he was studying Davy's *Agricultural Chemistry*. 'Well, now, Sir Humphry Davy: I dined with him years ago at Cartwright's, and Wordsworth was there too – the poet Wordsworth, you know. Now there was something singular. I was at Cambridge when Wordsworth was there, and I never met him – and I dined with him twenty years afterwards at Cartwright's. There's an oddity in things, now. But Davy was there: he was a poet too. Or, as I may say, Wordsworth was poet one, and Davy was poet two. That was true in every sense, you know.'

Dorothea felt a little more uneasy than usual. In the beginning of dinner, the party being small and the room still, these motes[2] from the mass of a magistrate's mind fell too noticeably. She wondered how a man like Mr Casaubon would support such triviality. His manners, she thought, were very dignified; the set of his iron-grey hair and his deep eye-sockets made him resemble the portrait of Locke. He had the spare form and the pale complexion which became a student; as different as possible from the blooming Englishman of the red-whiskered type represented by Sir James Chettam.

'I am reading the *Agricultural Chemistry*,' said this excellent baronet, 'because I am going to take one of the farms into my own hands, and see if something cannot be done in setting a good pattern of farming among my tenants. Do you approve of that, Miss Brooke?'

'A great mistake, Chettam,' interposed Mr. Brooke, 'going into electrifying your land and that kind of thing, and making a parlour of your cow-house. It won't do. I went into science a great deal myself at one time; but I saw it would not do. It leads to everything; you can let nothing alone. No, no – see that your tenants don't sell their straw, and that kind of thing; and give them draining-tiles, you know. But your fancy-farming will not do – the most expensive sort of whistle you can buy; you may as well keep a pack of hounds.'

'Surely,' said Dorothea, 'it is better to spend money in finding out how men can make the most of the land which supports them all, than in keeping dogs

---

1: Sir Humphry Davy (1778–1829), a brilliant chemist who discovered the electrical nature of chemical combination and a proponent of the new scientific improvement of agriculture. He invented the miner's saftey lamp, was a friend of Wordsworth, helped correct the proofs of *Lyrical Ballads*, and was a minor poet.   2: tiny speck of dust.

and horses only to gallop over it. It is not a sin to make yourself poor in performing experiments for the good of all.'

She spoke with more energy than is expected of so young a lady, but Sir James had appealed to her. He was accustomed to do so, and she had often thought that she could urge him to many good actions when he was her brother-in-law.

Mr Casaubon turned his eyes very markedly on Dorothea while she was speaking, and seemed to observe her newly.

'Young ladies don't understand political economy, you know,' said Mr Brooke, smiling towards Mr Casaubon. 'I remember when we were all reading Adam Smith.[1] *There* is a book, now. I took in all the new ideas at one time – human perfectibility, now. But some say, history moves in circles; and that may be very well argued; I have argued it myself. The fact is, human reason may carry you a little too far – over the hedge, in fact. It carried me a good way at one time; but I saw it would not do. I pulled up; I pulled up in time. But not too hard. I have always been in favour of a little theory: we must have Thought; else we shall be landed back in the dark ages. But talking of books, there is Southey's *Peninsular War*.[2] I am reading that of a morning. You know Southey?'

'No,' said Mr Casaubon, not keeping pace with Mr Brooke's impetuous reason, and thinking of the book only. 'I have little leisure for such literature just now. I have been using up my eyesight on old characters lately; the fact is, I want a reader for my evenings; but I am fastidious in voices, and I cannot endure listening to an imperfect reader. It is a misfortune, in some senses: I feed too much on the inward sources; I live too much with the dead. My mind is something like the ghost of an ancient, wandering about the world and trying mentally to construct it as it used to be, in spite or ruin and confusing changes. But I find it necessary to use the utmost caution about my eyesight.'

This was the first time that Mr Casaubon had spoken at any length. He delivered himself with precision, as if he had been called upon to make a public statement; and the balanced singsong neatness of his speech, occasionally corresponded to by a movement of his head, was the more conspicuous from its contrast with good Mr Brooke's scrappy slovenliness. Dorothea said to herself that Mr Casaubon was the most interesting man she had ever seen, not excepting even Monsieur Liret,[3] the Vaudois clergyman who had given conferences on the history of the Waldenses. To reconstruct a past world, doubtless with a view to the highest purposes of truth – what a work to be in any way present at, to assist in, though only as a lamp-holder! This elevating thought lifted her above her annoyance at being twitted with her ignorance of political economy, that never-explained science which was thrust as an extinguisher over all her lights.

'But you are fond of riding, Miss Brooke,' Sir James presently took an opportunity of saying. 'I should have thought you would enter a little into the pleasures of hunting. I wish you would let me send over a chesnut horse for you

---

1: Adam Smith (1723–90), apostle of *laissez-faire* economics in *An Inquiry into the Naure and Causes of the Wealth of Nations* (1776).   2: Robert Southey (1774–1843) a friend of Coleridge, radical romantic poet who turned Tory and became poet laureate, biographer and historian. His *History of the Peninsular War* (1823–32) told of Wellington's campaigns in the Iberian peninsular.   3: a reformist, therefore heretical, Catholic sect.

to try. It has been trained for a lady. I saw you on Saturday cantering over the hill on a nag not worthy of you. My groom shall bring Corydon[1] for you every day, if you will only mention the time.'

'Thank you, you are very good. I mean to give up riding. I shall not ride any more,' said Dorothea, urged to this brusque resolution by a little annoyance that Sir James would be soliciting her attention when she wanted to give it all to Mr Casaubon.

'No, that is too hard,' said Sir James, in a tone of reproach that showed strong interest. 'Your sister is given to self-mortification, is she not?' he continued, turning to Celia, who sat at his right hand.

'I think she is,' said Celia, feeling afraid lest she should say something that would not please her sister, and blushing as prettily as possible above her necklace. 'She likes giving up.'

'If that were true, Celia, my giving up would be self-indulgence, not self-mortification. But there may be good reasons for choosing not to do what is very agreeable,' said Dorothea.

Mr Brooke was speaking at the same time, but it was evident that Mr Casaubon was observing Dorothea, and she was aware of it.

'Exactly,' said Sir James. 'You give up from some high, generous motive.'

'No, indeed, not exactly. I did not say that of myself,' answered Dorothea, reddening. Unlike Celia, she rarely blushed, and only from high delight or anger. At this moment she felt angry with the perverse Sir James. Why did he not pay attention to Celia, and leave her to listen to Mr Casaubon? – if that learned man would only talk, instead of allowing himself to be talked to by Mr Brooke, who was just then informing him that the Reformation either meant something or it did not, that he himself was a Protestant to the core, but that Catholicism was a fact; and as to refusing an acre of your ground for a Romanist chapel, all men needed the bridle of religion, which, properly speaking, was the dread of a Hereafter.

'I made a great study of theology at one time,' said Mr Brooke, as if to explain the insight just manifested. 'I know something of all schools. I knew Wilberforce[2] in his best days. Do you know Wilberforce?[2]

Mr Casaubon said, 'No.'

'Well, Wilberforce was perhaps not enough of a thinker; but if I went into Parliament, as I have been asked to do, I should sit on the independent bench, as Wilberforce did, and work at philanthropy.'

Mr Casaubon bowed, and observed that it was a wide field.

'Yes,' said Mr Brooke, with an easy smile, 'but I have documents. I began a long while ago to collect documents. They want arranging, but when a question has struck me, I have written to somebody and got an answer. I have documents at my back. But now, how do you arrange your documents?'

'In pigeon-holes partly,' said Mr Casaubon, with rather a startled air of effort.

'Ah, pigeon-holes will not do. I have tried pigeon-holes, but everything gets mixed in pigeon-holes: I never know whether a paper is in A or Z.'

1: learned wit – Corydon is a shepherd in Virgil's *Eclogues* and a stock figure in pastoral poetry.   2: William Wilberforce (1759–1833), leading evangelical who campaigned for the abolition of slavery, achieved in 1833.

'I wish you would let me sort your papers for you, uncle,' said Dorothea. 'I would letter them all, and then make a list of subjects under each letter.'

Mr Casaubon gravely smiled approval, and said to Mr Brooke, 'You have an excellent secretary at hand, you perceive.'

'No, no,' said Mr Brooke, shaking his head; 'I cannot let young ladies meddle with my documents. Young ladies are too flighty.'

Dorothea felt hurt. Mr Casaubon would think that her uncle had some special reason for delivering this opinion, whereas the remark lay in his mind as lightly as the broken wing of an insect among all the other fragments there, and a chance current had sent it alighting on *her*.

When the two girls were in the drawing-room alone, Celia said –

'How very ugly Mr Casaubon is!'

'Celia! He is one of the most distinguished-looking men I ever saw. He is remarkably like the portrait of Locke. He has the same deep eye-sockets.'

'Had Locke those two white moles with hairs on them?'

'Oh, I daresay! when people of a certain sort looked at him,' said Dorothea, walking away a little.

'Mr Casaubon is so sallow.'

'All the better. I suppose you admire a man with the complexion of a *cochon de lait*.'

'Dodo!' exclaimed Celia, looking after her in surprise. 'I never heard you make such a comparison before.'

'Why should I make it before the occasion came? It is a good comparison: the match is perfect.'

Miss Brooke was clearly forgetting herself, and Celia thought so.

'I wonder you show temper, Dorothea.'

'It is so painful in you, Celia, that you will look at human beings as if they were merely animals with a toilette, and never see the great soul in a man's face.'

'Has Mr Casaubon a great soul?' Celia was not without a touch of naïve malice.

'Yes, I believe he has,' said Dorothea, with the full voice of decision. 'Everything I see in him corresponds to his pamphlet on Biblical Cosmology.'

'He talks very little,' said Celia.

'There is no one for him to talk to.'

Celia thought privately, 'Dorothea quite despises Sir James Chettam; I believe she would not accept him.' Celia felt that this was a pity. She had never been deceived as to the object of the baronet's interest. Sometimes, indeed, she had reflected that Dodo would perhaps not make a husband happy who had not her way of looking at things; and stifled in the depths of her heart was the feeling that her sister was too religious for family comfort. Notions and scruples were like spilt needles, making one afraid of treading, or sitting down, or even eating.

When Miss Brooke was at the tea-table, Sir James came to sit down by her, not having felt her mode of answering him at all offensive. Why should he? He thought it probable that Miss Brooke liked him, and manners must be very marked indeed before they cease to be interpreted by preconceptions either confident or distrustful. She was thoroughly charming to him, but of course he theorized a little about his attachment. He was made of excellent human dough, and had the rare merit of knowing that his talents, even if let loose, would not set the smallest stream in the county on fire: hence he liked the prospect of a wife to whom he could say, 'What shall we do?' about this or that; who could help her husband out with reasons, and would also have the property qualification for doing so. As to the excessive religiousness alleged against Miss Brooke, he had a very indefinite notion of what it consisted in, and thought that it would die out with marriage. In short, he felt himself to be in love in the right place, and was ready to endure a great deal of predominance, which, after all, a man could always put down when he liked. Sir James had no idea that he should ever like to put down the predominance of this handsome girl, in whose cleverness he delighted. Why not? A man's mind – what there is of it – has always the advantage of being masculine – as the smallest birch-tree is of a higher kind than the most soaring palm – and even his ignorance is of a sounder quality. Sir James might not have originated this estimate; but a kind Providence furnishes the limpest personality with a little gum or starch in the form of tradition.

'Let me hope that you will rescind that resolution about the horse, Miss Brooke,' said the persevering admirer. 'I assure you, riding is the most healthy of exercises.'

'I am aware of it,' said Dorothea, coldly. 'I think it would do Celia good – if she would take to it.'

'But you are such a perfect horsewoman.'

'Excuse me; I have had very little practice, and I should be easily thrown.'

'Then that is a reason for more practice. Every lady ought to be a perfect horsewoman, that she may accompany her husband.'

'You see how widely we differ, Sir James. I have made up my mind that I ought not to be a perfect horsewoman, and so I should never correspond to your pattern of a lady,' Dorothea looked straight before her, and spoke with cold brusquerie, very much with the air of a handsome boy, in amusing contrast with the solicitous amiability of her admirer.

'I should like to know your reasons for this cruel resolution. It is not possible that you should think horsemanship wrong.'

'It is quite possible that I should think it wrong for me.'

'Oh, why?' said Sir James, in a tender tone of remonstrance.

Mr Casaubon had come up to the table, tea-cup in hand, and was listening.

'We must not inquire too curiously into motives,' he interposed, in his measured way. 'Miss Brooke knows that they are apt to become feeble in the utterance: the aroma is mixed with the grosser air. We must keep the germinating grain away from the light.'

Dorothea coloured with pleasure, and looked up gratefully to the speaker. Here was a man who could understand the higher inward life, and with whom there could be some spiritual communion; nay, who could illuminate principle with the widest knowledge: a man whose learning almost amounted to a proof of whatever he believed!

Dorothea's inferences may seem large; but really life could never have gone on at any period but for this liberal allowance of conclusion, which has facilitated marriage under the difficulties of civilization. Has anyone ever pinched into its pilulous smallness the cobweb of pre-matrimonial acquaintanceship?

'Certainly,' said good Sir James. 'Miss Brooke shall not be urged to tell reasons she would rather be silent upon. I am sure her reasons would do her honour.'

He was not in the least jealous of the interest with which Dorothea had looked up at Mr Casaubon: it never occurred to him that a girl to whom he was meditating an offer of marriage could care for a dried bookworm towards fifty, except, indeed, in a religious sort of way, as for a clergyman of some distinction.

However, since Miss Brooke had become engaged in a conversation with Mr Casaubon about the Vaudois clergy, Sir James betook himself to Celia, and talked to her about her sister; spoke of a house in town, and asked whether Miss Brooke disliked London. Away from her sister, Celia talked quite easily, and Sir James said to himself that the second Miss Brooke was certainly very agreeable as well as pretty, though not, as some people pretended, more clever and sensible than the elder sister. He felt that he had chosen the one who was in all respects the superior; and a man naturally likes to look forward to having the best. He would be the very Mawworm[1] of bachelors who pretended not to expect it.

Chapter 3

> Say, goddess, what ensued, when Raphael,
> The affable archangel . . .
>
> > > Eve
> The story heard attentive, and was filled
> With admiration, and deep muse, to hear
> Of things so high and strange.
>
> *Paradise Lost*, Bk. vii

If it had really occurred to Mr Casaubon to think of Miss Brooke as a suitable wife for him, the reasons that might induce her to accept him were already planted in her mind, and by the evening of the next day the reasons had budded and bloomed. For they had had a long conversation in the morning, while Celia, who did not like the company of Mr Casaubon's moles and sallowness, had escaped to the vicarage to play with the curate's ill-shod but merry children.

Dorothea by this time had looked deep into the ungauged reservoir of Mr Casaubon's mind, seeing reflected there in vague labyrinthine extension every quality she herself brought; had opened much of her own experience to him, and had understood from him the scope of his great work, also of attractively labyrinthine extent. For he had been as instructive as Milton's 'affable archangel;' and with something of the archangelic manner he told her how he had undertaken to show (what indeed had been attempted before, but not with that thoroughness, justice of comparison, and effectiveness of arrangement at which Mr Casaubon aimed) that all the mythical systems or

---

1: Mawworm, pious hypocrite in Isaac Bickerstaafe's *The Hypocrite* (1769).

erratic mythical fragments in the world were corruptions of a tradition originally revealed. Having once mastered the true position and taken a firm footing there, the vast field of mythical constructions became intelligible, nay, luminous with the reflected light of correspondences. But to gather in this great harvest of truth was no light or speedy work. His notes already made a formidable range of volumes, but the crowning task would be to condense these voluminous still-accumulating results and bring them, like the earlier vintage of Hippocratic books,[1] to fit a little shelf. In explaining this to Dorothea, Mr Casaubon expressed himself nearly as he would have done to a fellow-student, for he had not two styles of talking at command: it is true that when he used a Greek or Latin phrase he always gave the English with scrupulous care, but he would probably have done this in any case. A learned provincial clergyman is accustomed to think of his acquaintances as of 'lords, knyghtes, and other noble and worthi men, that conne Latyn but lytille'.[2]

Dorothea was altogether captivated by the wide embrace of this conception. Here was something beyond the shallows of ladies'-school literature: here was a living Bossuet,[3] whose work would reconcile complete knowledge with devoted piety; here was a modern Augustine[4] who united the glories of doctor and saint.

The sanctity seemed no less clearly marked than the learning, for when Dorothea was impelled to open her mind on certain themes which she could speak of to no one whom she had before seen at Tipton, especially on the secondary importance of ecclesiastical forms and articles of belief compared with that spiritual religion, that submergence of self in communion with Divine perfection which seemed to her to be expressed in the best Christian books of widely-distant ages, she found in Mr Casaubon a listener who understood her at once, who could assure her of his own agreement with that view when duly tempered with wise conformity, and could mention historical examples before unknown to her.

'He thinks with me,' said Dorothea to herself, 'or rather, he thinks a whole world of which my thought is but a poor two-penny mirror. And his feelings too, his whole experience – what a lake compared with my little pool!'

Miss Brooke argued from words and dispositions not less unhesitatingly than other young ladies of her age. Signs are small measurable things, but interpretations are illimitable, and in girls of sweet, ardent nature, every sign is apt to conjure up wonder, hope, belief, vast as a sky, and coloured by a diffused thimbleful of matter in the shape of knowledge. They are not always too grossly deceived; for Sinbad himself may have fallen by good luck on a true description, and wrong reasoning sometimes lands poor mortals in right conclusions: starting a long way off the true point, and proceeding by loops and zigzags, we now and then arrive just where we ought to be. Because Miss Brooke was hasty in her trust, it is not therefore clear that Mr Casaubon was unworthy of it.

1: from Hippocrates (?460–?377 BC), Greek physician and founder of modern medicine.   2: from *Prologue to the Voiage and Travaile of Sir John Mandeville* (1366).   3: Jacques Bénigne Bossuet (1627–1704), French bishop who strove for reconciliation of the Protestants and Catholics.   4: Augustine of Hippo (354–430), saint, foremost theologian of the early church.

He stayed a little longer than he had intended, on a slight pressure of invitation from Mr Brooke, who offered no bait except his own documents on machine-breaking and rick-burning.[1] Mr Casaubon was called into the library to look at these in a heap, while his host picked up first one and then the other to read aloud from in a skipping and uncertain way, passing from one unfinished passage to another with a 'Yes, now, but here!' and finally pushing them all aside to open the journal of his youthful Continental travels.

'Look here – here is all about Greece, Rhamnus, the ruins of Rhamnus – you are a great Grecian, now. I don't know whether you have given much study to the topography. I spent no end of time in making out these things – Helicon, now. Here, now! – We started the next morning for Parnassus, the double-peaked Parnassus.[2] All this volume is about Greece, you know,' Mr Brooke wound up, rubbing his thumb transversely along the edges of the leaves as he held the book forward.

Mr Casaubon made a dignified though somewhat sad audience; bowed in the right place, and avoided looking at anything documentary as far as possible, without showing disregard or impatience; mindful that this desultoriness was associated with the institutions of the country, and that the man who took him on this severe mental scamper was not only an amiable host, but a landholder and *custos rotulorum*.[3] Was his endurance aided also by the reflection that Mr Brooke was the uncle of Dorothea?

Certainly he seemed more and more bent on making her talk to him, on drawing her out, as Celia remarked to herself; and in looking at her, his face was often lit up by a smile like pale wintry sunshine. Before he left the next morning, while taking a pleasant walk with Miss Brooke along the gravelled terrace, he had mentioned to her that he felt the disadvantage of loneliness, the need of that cheerful companionship with which the presence of youth can lighten or vary the serious toils of maturity. And he delivered this statement with as much careful precision as if he had been a diplomatic envoy whose words would be attended with results. Indeed, Mr Casaubon was not used to expect that he should have to repeat or revise his communications of a practical or personal kind. The inclinations which he had deliberately stated on the 2nd of October he would think it enough to refer to by the mention of that date; judging by the standard of his own memory, which was a volume where a *vide supra* could serve instead of repetitions, and not the ordinary long-used blotting-book which only tells of forgotten writing. But in this case Mr Casaubon's confidence was not likely to be falsified, for Dorothea heard and retained what he said with the eager interest of a fresh young nature to which every variety in experience is an epoch.

It was three o'clock in the beautiful breezy autumn day when Mr Casaubon drove off to his Rectory at Lowick, only five miles from Tipton; and Dorothea, who had on her bonnet and shawl, hurried along the shrubbery and across the park that she might wander through the bordering wood with no other visible companionship than that of Monk, the Great St Bernard dog, who always took

---

1: common forms of agricultural protest in the lean years after the end of the Napoleonic wars. 2: Helicon and Parnassus, Greek mountains which were the homes of the muses and of poetry. 3: keeper of public records.

care of the young ladies in their walks. There had risen before her the girl's vision of a possible future for herself to which she looked forward with trembling hope, and she wanted to wander on in that visionary future without interruption. She walked briskly in the brisk air, the colour rose in her cheeks, and her straw-bonnet (which our contemporaries might look at with conjectural curiosity as at an obsolete form of basket) fell a little backward. She would perhaps be hardly characterized enough if it were omitted that she wore her brown hair flatly braided and coiled behind so as to expose the outline of her head in a daring manner at a time when public feeling required the meagreness of nature to be dissimulated by tall barricades of frizzed curls and bows, never surpassed by any great race except the Feejeean. This was a trait of Miss Brooke's asceticism. But there was nothing of an ascetic's expression in her bright full eyes, as she looked before her, not consciously seeing, but absorbing into the intensity of her mood, the solemn glory of the afternoon with its long swathes of light between the far-off rows of limes, whose shadows touched each other.

All people, young or old (that is, all people in those ante-reform times), would have thought her an interesting object if they had referred the glow in her eyes and cheeks to the newly-awakened ordinary images of young love: the illusions of Chloe about Strephon[1] have been sufficiently consecrated in poetry, as the pathetic loveliness of all spontaneous trust ought to be. Miss Pippin adoring young Pumpkin and dreaming along endless vistas of unwearying companionship, was a little drama which never tired our fathers and mothers, and had been put into all costumes. Let but Pumpkin have a figure which would sustain the disadvantages of the short-waisted swallow-tail, and everybody felt it not only natural but necessary to the perfection of womanhood, that a sweet girl should be at once convinced of his virtue, his exceptional ability, and above all, his perfect sincerity. But perhaps no persons then living – certainly none in the neighbourhood of Tipton – would have had a sympathetic understanding for the dreams of a girl whose notions about marriage took their colour entirely from an exalted enthusiasm about the ends of life, an enthusiasm which was lit chiefly by its own fire, and included neither the niceties of the *trousseau*,[2] the pattern of plate, nor even the honours and sweet joys of the blooming matron.

It had now entered Dorothea's mind that Mr Casaubon might wish to make her his wife, and the idea that he would do so touched her with a sort of reverential gratitude. How good of him – nay, it would be almost as if a winged messenger had suddenly stood beside her path and held out his hand towards her! For a long while she had been oppressed by the indefiniteness which hung in her mind, like a thick summer haze, over all her desire to make her life greatly effective. What could she do, what ought she to do? – she, hardly more than a budding woman, but yet with an active conscience and a great mental need, not to be satisfied by a girlish instruction comparable to the nibblings and judgments of a discursive mouse. With some endowment of stupidity and conceit, she might have thought that a Christian young lady of fortune should find her ideal of life in village charities, patronage of the humbler clergy, the

---

1: Chloe and Strephon were stock figures in pastoral from the time of Sir Philip Sidney's *Arcadia* (1590).
2: trousseau: clothes and linen collected by a bride for her marriage.

perusal of *Female Scripture Characters*,[1] unfolding the private experience of Sara under the Old Dispensation, and Dorcas under the New, and the care of her soul over her embroidery in her own boudoir – with a background of prospective marriage to a man who, if less strict than herself as being involved in affairs religiously inexplicable, might be prayed for and seasonably exhorted. From such contentment poor Dorothea was shut out. The intensity of her religious disposition, the coercion it exercised over her life, was but one aspect of a nature altogether ardent, theoretic, and intellectually consequent: and with such a nature, struggling in the bands of a narrow teaching, hemmed in by a social life which seemed nothing but a labyrinth of petty courses, a walled-in maze of small paths that led no whither, the outcome was sure to strike others as at once exaggeration and inconsistency. The thing which seemed to her best, she wanted to justify by the completest knowledge; and not to live in a pretended admission of rules which were never acted on. Into this soul-hunger as yet all her youthful passion was poured; the union which attracted her was one that would deliver her from her girlish subjection to her own ignorance, and give her the freedom of voluntary submission to a guide who would take her along the grandest path.

'I should learn everything then,' she said to herself, still walking quickly along the bridle road through the wood. 'It would be my duty to study that I might help him the better in his great works. There would be nothing trivial about our lives. Everyday-things with us would mean the greatest things. It would be like marrying Pascal. I should learn to see the truth by the same light as great men have seen it by. And then I should know what to do, when I got older: I should see how it was possible to lead a grand life here – now – in England. I don't feel sure about doing good in any way now: everything seems like going on a mission to a people whose language I don't know; – unless it were building good cottages – there can be no doubt about that. Oh, I hope I should be able to get the people well housed in Lowick! I will draw plenty of plans while I have time.'

Dorothea checked herself suddenly with self-rebuke for the presumptuous way in which she was reckoning on uncertain events, but she was spared any inward effort to change the direction of her thoughts by the appearance of a cantering horseman round a turning of the road. The well-groomed chestnut horse and two beautiful setters could leave no doubt that the rider was Sir James Chettam. He discerned Dorothea, jumped off his horse at once, and, having delivered it to his groom, advanced towards her with something white on his arm, at which the two setters were barking in an excited manner.

'How delightful to meet you, Miss Brooke,' he said, raising his hat and showing his sleekly-waving blond hair. 'It has hastened the pleasure I was looking forward to.'

Miss Brooke was annoyed at the interruption. This amiable baronet, really a suitable husband for Celia, exaggerated the necessity of making himself agreeable to the elder sister. Even a prospective brother-in-law may be an

---

1: a work by Frances Elizabeth King published in 1813. Sara bore a son to Abraham when 90 years old (*Genesis*, 16-18, 21); St Peter brought Dorcas, a good woman, back to life (*Acts*, 9: 36–43).

oppression if he will always be presupposing too good an understanding with you, and agreeing with you even when you contradict him. The thought that he had made the mistake of paying his addresses to herself could not take shape: all her mental activity was used up in persuasions of another kind. But he was positively obtrusive at this moment, and his dimpled hands were quite disagreeable. Her roused temper made her colour deeply, as she returned his greeting with some haughtiness.

Sir James interpreted the heightened colour in the way most gratifying to himself, and thought he never saw Miss Brooke looking so handsome.

'I have brought a little petitioner,' he said, 'or rather I have brought him to see if he will be approved before his petition is offered.' He showed the white object under his arm, which was a tiny Maltese puppy, one of nature's most naïve toys.

'It is painful to me to see these creatures that are bred merely as pets,' said Dorothea, whose opinion was forming itself that very moment (as opinions will) under the heat of irritation.

'Oh, why?' said Sir James, as they walked forward.

'I believe all the petting that is given them does not make them happy. They are too helpless: their lives are too frail. A weasel or a mouse that gets its own living is more interesting. I like to think that the animals about us have souls something like our own, and either carry on their own little affairs or can be companions to us, like Monk here. Those creatures are parasitic.'

'I am so glad I know that you do not like them,' said good Sir James. 'I should never keep them for myself, but ladies usually are fond of these Maltese dogs. Here, John, take this dog, will you?'

The objectionable puppy, whose nose and eyes were equally black and expressive, was thus got rid of, since Miss Brooke decided that it had better not have been born. But she felt it necessary to explain.

'You must not judge of Celia's feeling from mine. I think she likes these small pets. She had a tiny terrier once, which she was very fond of. It made me unhappy, because I was afraid of treading on it. I am rather short-sighted.'

'You have your own opinion about everything, Miss Brooke, and it is always a good opinion.'

What answer was possible to such stupid complimenting?

'Do you know, I envy you that,' Sir James said, as they continued walking at the rather brisk pace set by Dorothea.

'I don't quite understand what you mean.'

'Your power of forming an opinion. I can form an opinion of persons. I know when I like people. But about other matters, do you know, I have often a difficulty in deciding. One hears very sensible things said on opposite sides.'

'Or that seem sensible. Perhaps we don't always discriminate between sense and nonsense.'

Dorothea felt that she was rather rude.

'Exactly,' said Sir James. 'But you seem to have the power of discrimination.'

'On the contrary, I am often unable to decide. But that is from ignorance. The right conclusion is there all the same, though I am unable to see it.'

'I think there are few who would see it more readily. Do you know, Lovegood was telling me yesterday that you had the best notion in the world of a plan for cottages – quite wonderful for a young lady, he thought. You had a real *genius*, to use his expression. He said you wanted Mr Brooke to build a new set of cottages, but he seemed to think it hardly probable that your uncle would consent. Do you know, that is one of the things I wish to do – I mean, on my own estate? I should be so glad to carry out that plan of yours, if you would let me see it. Of course, it is sinking money; that is why people object to it. Labourers can never pay rent to make it answer. But, after all, it is worth doing.'

'Worth doing! yes, indeed,' said Dorothea, energetically, forgetting her previous small vexations. 'I think we deserve to be beaten out of our beautiful houses with a scourge of small cords – all of us who let tenants live in such sties as we see round us. Life in cottages might be happier than ours, if they were real houses fit for human beings from whom we expect duties and affections.'

'Will you show me your plan?'

'Yes, certainly. I daresay it is very faulty. But I have been examining all the plans for cottages in Loudon's book,[1] and picked out what seem the best things. Oh what a happiness it would be to set the pattern about here! I think, instead of Lazarus at the gate, we should put the pig-sty cottages outside the park gate.'

Dorothea was in the best temper now. Sir James, as brother-in-law, building model cottages on his estate, and then, perhaps, others being built at Lowick, and more and more elsewhere in imitation – it would be as if the spirit of Oberlin[2] had passed over the parishes to make the life of poverty beautiful!

Sir James saw all the plans, and took one away to consult upon with Lovegood. He also took away a complacent sense that he was making great progress in Miss Brooke's good opinion. The Maltese puppy was not offered to Celia; an omission which Dorothea afterwards thought of with surprise; but she blamed herself for it. She had been engrossing Sir James. After all, it was a relief that there was no puppy to tread upon.

Celia was present while the plans were being examined, and observed Sir James's illusion. 'He thinks that Dodo cares about him, and she only cares about her plans. Yet I am not certain that she would refuse him if she thought he would let her manage everything and carry out all her notions. And how very uncomfortable Sir James would be! I cannot bear notions.'

It was Celia's private luxury to indulge in this dislike. She dared not confess it to her sister in any direct statement, for that would be laying herself open to a demonstration that she was somehow or other at war with all goodness. But on safe opportunities, she had an indirect mode of making her negative wisdom tell upon Dorothea, and calling her down from her rhapsodic mood by reminding her that people were staring, not listening. Celia was not impulsive: what she had to say could wait, and came from her always with the same quiet, staccato evenness. When people talked with energy and emphasis she watched their faces and features merely. She never could understand how well-bred persons consented to

---

1: John Claudius Loudon, *Observations on Laying out Farms* (1821), a work promoting the new agriculture.
2: Johann Friedrich Oberlin (1740–1826), Alsatian Protestant pastor.

sing and open their mouths in the ridiculous manner requisite for that vocal exercise.

It was not many days before Mr Casaubon paid a morning visit, on which he was invited again for the following week to dine and stay the night. Thus Dorothea had three more conversations with him, and was convinced that her first impressions had been just. He was all she had at first imagined him to be: almost everything he had said seemed like a specimen from a mine, or the inscription on the door of a museum which might open on the treasures of past ages; and this trust in mental wealth was all the deeper and more effective on her inclination because it was now obvious that his visits were made for her sake. This accomplished man condescended to think of a young girl, and take the pains to talk to her, not with absurd compliment, but with an appeal to her understanding, and sometimes with instructive correction. What delightful companionship! Mr Casaubon seemed even unconscious that trivialities existed, and never handed round that small-talk of heavy men which is as acceptable as stale bride-cake brought forth with an odour of cupboard. He talked of what he was interested in, or else he was silent and bowed with sad civility. To Dorothea this was adorable genuineness, and religious abstinence from that artificiality which uses up the soul in the efforts of pretence. For she looked as reverently at Mr Casaubon's religious elevation above herself as she did at his intellect and learning. He assented to her expressions of devout feeling, and usually with an appropriate quotation; he allowed himself to say that he had gone through some spiritual conflicts in his youth; in short, Dorothea saw that here she might reckon on understanding sympathy and guidance. On one – only one – of her favourite themes she was disappointed. Mr Casaubon apparently did not care about building cottages, and diverted the talk to the extremely narrow accommodation which was to be had in the dwellings of the ancient Egyptians, as if to check a too high standard. After he was gone, Dorothea dwelt with some agitation on this indifference of his; and her mind was much exercised with arguments drawn from the varying conditions of climate which modify human needs, and from the admitted wickedness of pagan despots. Should she not urge these arguments on Mr Casaubon when he came again? But further reflection told her that she was presumptuous in demanding his attention to such a subject; he would not disapprove of her occupying herself with it in leisure moments, as other women expected to occupy themselves with their dress and embroidery – would not forbid it when – Dorothea felt rather ashamed as she detected herself in these speculations. But her uncle had been invited to go to Lowick to stay a couple of days: was it reasonable to suppose that Mr Casaubon delighted in Mr Brooke's society for its own sake, either with or without documents?

Meanwhile that little disappointment made her delight the more in Sir James Chettam's readiness to set on foot the desired improvements. He came much oftener than Mr Casaubon, and Dorothea ceased to find him disagreeable since he showed himself so entirely in earnest; for he had already entered with much practical ability into Lovegood's estimates, and was charmingly docile. She proposed to build a couple of cottages, and transfer two families from their old cabins, which could then be pulled down, so that new ones could be built on the old sites. Sir James said, 'Exactly,' and she bore the word remarkably well.

Certainly these men who had so few spontaneous ideas might be very useful members of society under good feminine direction, if they were fortunate in choosing their sisters-in-law! It is difficult to say whether there was or was not a little wilfulness in her continuing blind to the possibility that another sort of choice was in question in relation to her. But her life was just now full of hope and action: she was not only thinking of her plans, but getting down learned books from the library and reading many things hastily (that she might be a little less ignorant in talking to Mr Casaubon), all the while being visited with conscientious questionings whether she were not exalting these poor doings above measure and contemplating them with that self-satisfaction which was the last doom of ignorance and folly.

[Chapter 4: Mr Brooke reveals to Dorothea that both Chettam and Casaubon wish to marry her. Dorothea declares antipathy to Chettam and interest in Casaubon. She is given his letter.]

Chapter 5

> Hard students are commonly troubled with gowts, catarrhs, rheums, cachexia, bradypepsia, bad eyes, stone, and collick, crudities, oppilations, vertigo, winds, consumptions, and all such diseases as come by over-much sitting: they are most part lean, dry, ill-coloured . . . and all through immoderate pains and extraordinary studies. If you will not believe the truth of this, look upon great Tostatus and Thomas Aquainas' works; and tell me whether those men took pains.
>
> Burton's *Anatomy of Melancholy*, p.1, S.2.[1]

This was Mr Casaubon's letter.

> My dear Miss Brooke, – I have your guardian's permission to address you on a subject than which I have none more at heart. I am not, I trust, mistaken in the recognition of some deeper correspondence than that of date in the fact that a consciousness of need in my own life had arisen contemporaneously with the possibility of my becoming acquainted with you. For in the first hour of meeting you, I had an impression of your eminent and perhaps exclusive fitness to supply that need (connected, I may say, with such activity of the affections as even the preoccupations of a work too special to be abdicated could not uninterruptedly dissimulate); and each succeeding opportunity for observation has given the impression an added depth by convincing me more emphatically of that fitness which I had preconceived, and thus evoking more decisively those affections to which I have but now referred. Our conversations have, I think, made sufficiently clear to you the tenor of my life and purposes: a tenor unsuited, I am aware, to the commoner order of minds. But I have discerned in you an elevation of thought and a capability of devotedness, which I had hitherto not conceived to be compatible either with the early bloom of youth or with those graces of sex that may be said at once to win and to confer distinction

---

1: published in 1621, an erudite satire on the futility of learning by physician Robert Burton (1577–1640).

when combined, as they notably are in you, with the mental qualities above indicated. It was, I confess, beyond my hope to meet with this rare combination of elements both solid and attractive, adapted to supply aid in graver labours and to cast a charm over vacant hours; and but for the event of my introduction to you (which, let me again say, I trust not to be superficially coincident with foreshadowing needs, but providentially related thereto as stages towards the completion of a life's plan), I should presumably have gone on to the last without any attempt to lighten my solitariness by a matrimonial union.

Such, my dear Miss Brooke, is the accurate statement of my feelings; and I rely on your kind indulgence in venturing now to ask you how far your own are of a nature to confirm my happy presentiment. To be accepted by you as your husband and the earthly guardian of your welfare, I should regard as the highest of providential gifts. In return I can at least offer you an affection hitherto unwasted, and the faithful consecration of a life which, however short in the sequel, has no backward pages whereon, if you choose to turn them, you will find records such as might justly cause you either bitterness or shame. I await the expression of your sentiments with an anxiety which it would be the part of wisdom (were it possible) to divert by a more arduous labour than usual. But in this order of experience I am still young, and in looking forward to an unfavourable possibility I cannot but feel that resignation to solitude will be more difficult after the temporary illumination of hope. In any case, I shall remain, yours with sincere devotion,

Edward Casaubon

Dorothea trembled while she read this letter; then she fell on her knees, buried her face, and sobbed. She could not pray under the rush of solemn emotion in which thoughts became vague and images floated uncertainly, she could but cast herself, with a childlike sense of reclining in the lap of a divine consciousness which sustained her own. She remained in that attitude till it was time to dress for dinner.

How could it occur to her to examine the letter, to look at it critically as a profession of love? Her whole soul was possessed by the fact that a fuller life was opening before her: she was a neophyte about to enter on a higher grade of initiation. She was going to have room for the energies which stirred uneasily under the dimness and pressure of her own ignorance and the petty peremptoriness of the world's habits.

Now she would be able to devote herself to large yet definite duties; now she would be allowed to live continually in the light of a mind that she could reverence. This hope was not unmixed with the glow of proud delight – the joyous maiden surprise that she was chosen by the man whom her admiration had chosen. All Dorothea's passion was transfused through a mind struggling towards an ideal life; the radiance of her transfigured girlhood fell on the first object that came within its level. The impetus with which inclination became resolution was heightened by those little events of the day which had roused her discontent with the actual conditions of her life.

After dinner, when Celia was playing an 'air, with variations', a small kind of tinkling which symbolized the aesthetic part of the young ladies' education,

Dorothea went up to her room to answer Mr Casaubon's letter. Why should she defer the answer? She wrote it over three times, not because she wished to change the wording, but because her hand was unusually uncertain, and she could not bear that Mr Casaubon should think her handwriting bad and illegible. She piqued herself on writing a hand in which each letter was distinguishable without any large range of conjecture, and she meant to make much use of this accomplishment, to save Mr Casaubon's eyes. Three times she wrote.

> My dear Mr Casaubon, – I am very grateful to you for loving me, and thinking me worthy to be your wife. I can look forward to no better happiness than that which would be one with yours. If I said more, it would only be the same thing written out at greater length, for I cannot now dwell on any other thought than that I may be through life, yours devotedly,
>
> Dorothea Brooke

Later in the evening she followed her uncle into the library to give him the letter, that he might send it in the morning. He was surprised, but his surprise only issued in a few moments' silence, during which he pushed about various objects on his writing-table, and finally stood with his back to the fire, his glasses on his nose, looking at the address of Dorothea's letter.

'Have you thought enough about this, my dear?' he said at last.

'There was no need to think long, uncle. I know of nothing to make me vacillate. If I changed my mind, it must be because of something important and entirely new to me.'

'Ah! – then you have accepted him? Then Chettam has no chance? Has Chettam offended you – offended you, you know? What is it you don't like in Chettam?'

'There is nothing that I like in him,' said Dorothea, rather impetuously.

Mr Brooke threw his head and shoulders backward as if some one had thrown a light missile at him. Dorothea immediately felt some self-rebuke, and said –

'I mean in the light of a husband. He is very kind, I think – really very good about the cottages. A well-meaning man.'

'But you must have a scholar, and that sort of thing? Well, it lies a little in our family. I had it myself – that love of knowledge, and going into everything – a little too much – it took me too far; though that sort of thing doesn't often run in the female line; or it runs underground like the rivers in Greece, you know – it comes out in the sons. Clever sons, clever mothers. I went a good deal into that, at one time. However, my dear, I have always said that people should do as they like in these things up to a certain point. I couldn't, as your guardian, have consented to a bad match. But Casaubon stands well: his position is good. I am afraid Chettam will be hurt, though, and Mrs. Cadwallader will blame me.'

That evening, of course, Celia knew nothing of what had happened. She attributed Dorothea's abstracted manner, and the evidence of further crying since they had got home, to the temper she had been in about Sir James Chettam and the buildings, and was careful not to give further offence: having once said what she wanted to say, Celia had no disposition to recur to disagreeable subjects. It had been her nature when a child never to quarrel with anyone – only to observe with wonder that they quarrelled with her, and looked like turkey-cocks; whereupon she was ready to play at cat's cradle with them whenever they recovered themselves. And as to Dorothea, it had always been her way to find something wrong in her sister's words, though Celia inwardly protested that she always said just how things were, and nothing else: she never did and never could put words together out of her own head. But the best of Dodo was, that she did not keep angry for long together. Now, though they had hardly spoken to each other all the evening, yet when Celia put by her work, intending to go to bed, a proceeding in which she was always much the earlier, Dorothea, who was seated on a low stool, unable to occupy herself except in meditation, said, with the musical intonation which in moments of deep but quiet feeling made her speech like a fine bit of recitative –

'Celia, dear, come and kiss me,' holding her arms open as she spoke.

Celia knelt down to get the right level and gave her a little butterfly kiss, while Dorothea encircled her with gentle arms and pressed her lips gravely on each cheek in turn.

'Don't sit up, Dodo, you are so pale tonight: go to bed soon,' said Celia, in a comfortable way, without any touch of pathos.

'No, dear, I am very, very happy,' said Dorothea, fervently.

'So much the better,' thought Celia. 'But how strangely Dodo goes from one extreme to the other.'

The next day, at luncheon, the butler, handing something to Mr Brooke, said, 'Jonas is come back, sir, and has brought this letter.'

Mr Brooke read the letter, and then, nodding toward Dorothea, said, 'Casaubon, my dear: he will be here to dinner; he didn't wait to write more – didn't wait, you know.'

It could not seem remarkable to Celia that a dinner guest should be announced to her sister beforehand, but her eyes following the same direction as her uncle's, she was struck with the peculiar effect of the announcement on Dorothea. It seemed as if something like the reflection of a white sunlit wing had passed across her features, ending in one of her rare blushes. For the first time it entered into Celia's mind that there might be something more between Mr Casaubon and her sister than his delight in bookish talk and her delight in listening. Hitherto she had classed the admiration for this 'ugly' and learned acquaintance with the admiration for Monsieur Liret at Lausanne, also ugly and learned. Dorothea had never been tired of listening to old Monsieur Liret when Celia's feet were as cold as possible, and when it had really become dreadful to see the skin of his bald head moving about. Why then should her enthusiasm not extend to Mr Casaubon simply in the same way as to Monsieur Liret? And it seemed probable that all learned men had a sort of schoolmaster's view of young people.

But now Celia was really startled at the suspicion which had darted into her mind. She was seldom taken by surprise in this way, her marvellous quickness in observing a certain order of signs generally preparing her to expect such outward events as she had an interest in. Not that she now imagined Mr Casaubon to be already an accepted lover: she had only begun to feel disgust at the possibility that anything in Dorothea's mind could tend toward such an issue. Here was something really to vex her about Dodo: it was all very well not to accept Sir James Chettam, but the idea of marrying Mr Casaubon! Celia felt a sort of shame mingled with a sense of the ludicrous. But perhaps Dodo, if she were really bordering on such an extravagance, might be turned away from it: experience had often shown that her impressibility might be calculated on. The day was damp, and they were not going to walk out, so they both went up to their sitting-room; and there Celia observed that Dorothea, instead of settling down with her usually diligent interest to some occupation, simply leaned her elbow on an open book and looked out of the window at the great cedar silvered with the damp. She herself had taken up the making of a toy for the curate's children, and was not going to enter on any subject too precipitately.

Dorothea was in fact thinking that it was desirable for Celia to know of the momentous change in Mr Casaubon's position since he had last been in the house: it did not seem fair to leave her in ignorance of what would necessarily affect her attitude towards him; but it was impossible not to shrink from telling her. Dorothea accused herself of some meanness in this timidity: it was always odious to her to have any small fears or contrivances about her actions, but at this moment she was seeking the highest aid possible that she might not dread the corrosiveness of Celia's pretty carnally minded prose. Her reverie was broken, and the difficulty of decision banished, by Celia's small and rather guttural voice speaking in its usual tone, of a remark aside or a 'by the by'.

'Is any one else coming to dine besides Mr Casaubon?'

'Not that I know of.'

'I hope there is some one else. Then I shall not hear him eat his soup so.'

'What is there remarkable about his soup-eating?'

'Really, Dodo, can't you hear how he scrapes his spoon? And he always blinks before he speaks. I don't know whether Locke blinked, but I'm sure I am sorry for those who sat opposite to him, if he did.'

'Celia,' said Dorothea, with emphatic gravity, 'pray don't make any more observations of that kind.'

'Why not? They are quite true,' returned Celia, who had her reasons for persevering, though she was beginning to be a little afraid.

'Many things are true which only the commonest minds observe.'

'Then I think the commonest minds must be rather useful. I think it is a pity Mr Casaubon's mother had not a commoner mind: she might have taught him better.' Celia was inwardly frightened, and ready to run away, now she had hurled this light javelin.

Dorothea's feelings had gathered to an avalanche, and there could be no further preparation.

'It is right to tell you, Celia, that I am engaged to marry Mr Casaubon.'

Perhaps Celia had never turned so pale before. The paper man she was making would have had his leg injured, but for her habitual care of whatever she held in her hands. She laid the fragile figure down at once, and sat perfectly still for a few moments. When she spoke there was a tear gathering.

'O Dodo, I hope you will be happy.' Her sisterly tenderness could not but surmount other feelings at this moment, and her fears were the fears of affection.

Dorothea was still hurt and agitated.

'It is quite decided, then?' said Celia, in an awed undertone. 'And uncle knows?'

'I have accepted Mr Casaubon's offer. My uncle brought me the letter that contained it; he knew about it beforehand.'

'I beg your pardon, if I have said anything to hurt you, Dodo,' said Celia, with a slight sob. She never could have thought that she should feel as she did. There was something funereal in the whole affair, and Mr Casaubon seemed to be the officiating clergyman, about whom it would be indecent to make remarks.

'Never mind, Kitty, do not grieve. We should never admire the same people. I often offend in something of the same way; I am apt to speak too strongly of those who don't please me.'

In spite of this magnanimity Dorothea was still smarting: perhaps as much from Celia's subdued astonishment as from her small criticisms. Of course all the world round Tipton would be out of sympathy with this marriage. Dorothea knew of no one who thought as she did about life and its best objects.

Nevertheless before the evening was at an end she was very happy. In an hour's *tête-à-tête* with Mr Casaubon she talked to him with more freedom than she had ever felt before, even pouring out her joy at the thought of devoting herself to him, and of learning how she might best share and further all his great ends. Mr Casaubon was touched with an unknown delight (what man would not have been?) at this childlike unrestrained ardour: he was not surprised (what lover would have been?) that he should be the object of it.

'My dear young lady – Miss Brooke – Dorothea!' he said, pressing her hand between his hands, 'this is a happiness greater than I had ever imagined to be in reserve for me. That I should ever meet with a mind and person so rich in the mingled graces which could render marriage desirable, was far indeed from my conception. You have all – nay, more than all – those qualities which I have ever regarded as the characteristic excellences of womanhood. The great charm of your sex is its capability of an ardent self-sacrificing affection, and herein we see its fitness to round and complete the existence of our own. Hitherto I have known few pleasures save of the severer kind: my satisfactions have been those of the solitary student. I have been little disposed to gather flowers that would wither in my hand, but now I shall pluck them with eagerness, to place them in your bosom.'

No speech could have been more thoroughly honest in its intention: the frigid rhetoric at the end was as sincere as the bark of a dog, or the cawing of an amorous rook. Would it not be rash to conclude that there was no passion behind those sonnets to Delia[1] which strike us as the thin music of a mandolin?

Dorothea's faith supplied all that Mr Casaubon's words seemed to leave unsaid: what believer sees a disturbing omission or infelicity? The text, whether of prophet or of poet, expands for whatever we can put into it, and even his bad grammar is sublime.

'I am very ignorant – you will quite wonder at my ignorance,' said Dorothea. 'I have so many thoughts that may be quite mistaken; and now I shall be able to tell them all to you, and ask you about them. But,' she added, with rapid imagination of Mr Casaubon's probable feeling, 'I will not trouble you too

---

1: Samuel Daniel (1563–1619), *Sonnets to Delia* (1592), admired by Lamb, Wordsworth and Coleridge.

much; only when you are inclined to listen to me. You must often be weary with the pursuit of subjects in your own track. I shall gain enough if you will take me with you there.'

'How should I be able now to persevere in any path without your companionship?' said Mr Casaubon, kissing her candid brow, and feeling that heaven had vouchsafed him a blessing in every way suited to his peculiar wants. He was being unconsciously wrought upon by the charms of a nature which was entirely without hidden calculations either for immediate effects or for remoter ends. It was this which made Dorothea so childlike, and according to some judges, so stupid, with all her reputed cleverness; as, for example, in the present case of throwing herself, metaphorically speaking, at Mr Casaubon's feet, and kissing his unfashionable shoe-ties as if he were a Protestant Pope. She was not in the least teaching Mr Casaubon to ask if he were good enough for her, but merely asking herself anxiously how she could be good enough for Mr Casaubon. Before he left the next day it had been decided that the marriage should take place within six weeks. Why not? Mr Casaubon's house was ready. It was not a parsonage, but a considerable mansion, with much land attached to it. The parsonage was inhabited by the curate, who did all the duty except preaching the morning sermon.

LEWIS CARROLL (1832–1898)

Charles Lutwidge Dodgson was educated at Rugby and Christ Church, Oxford, where he then became a fellow in mathematics, a subject to which he contributed elementary introductions. He was a sincere Christian, and was ordained a Deacon, but never took holy orders. He enjoyed inventing mathematical and word puzzles, and performing conjuring tricks, and was 'fond of children (not boys),' especially delighting in drawing them or photgraphing them – he was a pioneer of the art – in the nude. In an age which idealised the purity and innocence of children, and especially young girls, such a fixation was less striking than it would be today. It was for the most adored of these young girls – Alice Liddell, also adored by John Ruskin – that Dodgson wrote *Alice's Adventures in Wonderland* (1865) and *Through the Looking Glass and What Alice Found There* (1871), works which see the world as the frightening, baffling and magical place it must seem through the eyes of a five-year-old. His *The Hunting of the Snark* (1876) sustains brilliant poetical nonsense for the whole of a book. His long, fantastic novel *Sylvie and Bruno* (1889–93) proves that without verse to sustain the whimsy, bathos results.

Jabberwocky

'Twas brillig, and the slithy toves
Did gyre and gimble in the wabe;
All mimsy were the borogoves,
And the mome raths outgrabe.

⁵ 'Beware the Jabberwock, my son!
The jaws that bite, the claws that catch!
Beware the Jubjub bird, and shun
The frumious Bandersnatch!'

He took his vorpal sword in hand;
¹⁰ Long time the manxome foe he sought –
So rested he by the Tumtum tree,
And stood awhile in thought.

And, as in uffish thought he stood,
The Jabberwock, with eyes of flame,
¹⁵ Came whiffling through the tulgey wood,
And burbled as it came!

One, two! One, two! And through and through
The vorpal blade went snicker-snack!
He left it dead, and with its head
²⁰ He went galumphing back.

'And hast thou slain the Jabberwock?
Come to my arms, my beamish boy!
O frabjous day! Callooh! Callay!'
He chortled in his joy.

²⁵ 'Twas brillig, and the slithy toves
Did gyre and gimble in the wabe;
All mimsy were the borogoves,
And the mome raths outgrabe.

GERARD MANLEY HOPKINS (1844–1889)

Hopkins was born in Essex to a large, prosperous middle-class family with High Anglican leanings. He was influenced by Keats and aestheticism, went up to Oxford where Matthew Arnold was then professor of poetry and was tutored by Walter Pater. Following the lead of John Henry Newman, Hopkins converted to Roman Catholicism on his graduation in 1866 and eventually became a Jesuit priest. He renounced poetry as incompatible with his religious calling until, encouraged by his superiors in the church, he wrote *The Wreck of Deutschland* (1876), commemorating a shipwreck in which five Franciscan nuns lost their lives. In the remaining years of his life, and especially in 1877, he wrote some of the most remarkable English poems, most of which were considered too difficult by his contemporaries and not published until 1918. To reconcile his art to his religion, Hopkins elaborated a creed of the poetic and religious calling which was to recognise the *inscape* or characteristic indwelling energy of a person or thing. This *inscape* is sustained by an *instress* which flows into those who acutely attend. His poetry enshrines this process, notably using assonance, alliteration, compound and coined words, ellipsis, puns and repetition in order to express the impacted and epiphanic revelation of God's rhymes and reasons. Hopkins also used a radical new concept of rhythm, *sprung rhythm*, breaking with the traditional (usually iambic) foot. He maintained that the true metre of English verse, found in common speech and pre-Renaissance verse, used a variable foot of stressed and unstressed syllables which, like Greek and Anglo-Saxon poetry, as well as much twentieth-century lyric, highbrow and popular, achieves regularity through associating a regular beat within the line with key semantic or phonemic parallels.

God's Grandeur

The world is charged with the grandeur of God.
　It will flame out, like shining from shook foil;
　It gathers to a greatness, like the ooze of oil
Crushed. Why do men then now not reck his rod?
5　Generations have trod, have trod, have trod;
　And all is seared with trade; bleared, smeared with toil;
　And wears man's smudge and shares man's smell: the soil
Is bare now, nor can foot feel, being shod.

And for all this, nature is never spent;
10　There lives the dearest freshness deep down things;
And though the last lights off the black West went
　Oh, morning, at the brown brink eastward, springs –
Because the Holy Ghost over the bent
　World broods with warm breast and with ah! bright wings.

---

2 foil: gold leaf.　　　　　**4 crushed:** i.e. from crushed olives.

As Kingfishers Catch Fire

As kingfishers catch fire, dragonflies draw flame;
    As tumbled over rim in roundy wells
    Stones ring; like each tucked string tells, each hung bell's
Bow swung finds tongue to fling out broad its name;
5 Each mortal thing does one thing and the same:
    Deals out that being indoors each one dwells;
    Selves – goes itself; *myself* it speaks and spells;
Crying *What I do is me: for that I came.*

I say more: the just man justices;
10   Keeps grace: that keeps all his goings graces;
Acts in God's eye what in God's eye he is –
    Christ. For Christ plays in ten thousand places,
Lovely in limbs, and lovely in eyes not his
    To the Father through the features of men's faces.

The Windhover

To Christ our Lord

I caught this morning morning's minion, king-
    dom of daylight's dauphin, dapple-dawn-drawn Falcon, in his riding
Of the rolling level underneath him steady air, and striding
High there, how he rung upon the rein of a wimpling wing
5 In his ecstasy! then off, off, forth on swing,
    As a skate's heel sweeps smooth on a bow-bend: the hurl and gliding
Rebuffed the big wind. My heart in hiding
Stirred for a bird, the achieve of, the mastery of the thing!

Brute beauty and valour and act, oh, air, pride, plume, here
10 Buckle! AND the fire that breaks from thee then, a billion
Times told lovelier, more dangerous, O my chevalier!

No wonder of it: sheer plod makes plough down sillion
Shine, and blue-bleak embers, ah my dear,
    Fall, gall themselves, and gash gold-vermilion.

The Windhover: a small falcon. **1 minion:** a favourite dependant. **2 dauphin:** the heir to the French throne. **4 wimpling:** to lay in pleats, to ripple.   **11 chevalier:** knight. **12 sillion:** ridge between the furrows of a ploughed field. **14 gall:** make sore by chafing, irritate, annoy, vex.

HENRY JAMES (1843–1916)

Henry James was born in New York, the second son of Henry James, Sr., a very wealthy Swedenborgian philosopher of considerable standing. He was a friend of Ralph Waldo Emerson and Thomas Carlyle. Henry's elder brother William was to become the most prominent American philosopher of the nineteenth century. The James children were educated rather variously amongst the wealthy American expatriate community in Switzerland, France and Germany where Henry James experienced the truth of the then dominant American belief that Europe was all culture, history and aristocracy, whilst America was all brash and cash. He settled in London in 1877 and lived in England until his death, travelling often on the continent, and living a refined social life amongst those whose earnings came from dividends and whose mores are the stuff of his fictions. His early novels gave the 'international theme' of Europe vs. America a moral and philosophical richness which it had never seen. *Roderick Hudson* (1876), *The American* (1877), *The Europeans* (1878), and his most famous novella 'Daisy Miller' (1879), ironically explore how a naive American fails to fathom the sophistications of European society. His masterpiece, *The Portrait of a Lady* (1881), explores this theme on its most ambitious scale. The next 20 years of James's writing were less certain: for economic reasons he adapted his earlier stories for the stage, and attempted new plays, without conspicuous success, but at the same time wrote many stories and novellas which are now considered remarkable. He also approached contemporary political themes and wrote *The Bostonians*, a satire on female emancipation, and *The Princess Casamassima* about anarchists and aristocrats in London. The years 1897–1904 saw an extraordinary flourishing of his talents in a sequence of novels which ironically comprehend and enjoy the stifling aestheticism and base motives of the *rentier* class: *The Spoils of Poynton*, *What Maisie Knew* (1897), *The Turn of the Screw* (1898), *The Awkward Age* (1899), *The Sacred Fount* (1901), *The Wings of the Dove* (1902), *The Ambassadors* (1903), and *The Golden Bowl* (1904). The stylistic elaboration of these later works defeats many readers but is a logical development of James's fundamental interest in the novel as an aesthetic object that communicates through a progression of sophisticated points of view. James's critical essays and his prefaces to the New York edition of his novels (1907–09) are major contributions to criticism.

Daisy Miller

1

At the little town of Vevey, in Switzerland, there is a particularly comfortable hotel. There are, indeed, many hotels; for the entertainment of tourists is the business of the place, which as many travellers will remember, is seated upon the edge of a remarkably blue lake – a lake that it behoves every tourist to visit.[1] The shore of the lake presents an unbroken array of establishments of this order, of every category, from the 'grand hotel' of the newest fashion, with a chalk-white front, a hundred balconies, and a dozen flags flying from its roof, to the little Swiss *pension*[2] of an elder day, with its name inscribed in

---

1: Lake Geneva. 2: a small hotel.

German-looking lettering upon a pink or yellow wall, and an awkward summer-house in the angle of the garden. One of the hotels at Vevey, however, is famous, even classical, being distinguished from many of its upstart neighbours by an air both of luxury and of maturity. In this region, in the month of June, American travellers are extremely numerous; it may be said, indeed, that Vevey assumes at this period some of the characteristics of an American watering-place. There are sights and sounds which evoke a vision, an echo, of Newport and Saratoga.[1] There is a flitting hither and thither of 'stylish' young girls, a rustling of muslin flounces, a rattle of dance-music in the morning hours, a sound of high-pitched voices at all times. You receive an impression of these things at the excellent inn of the *Trois Couronnes*, and are transported in fancy to the Ocean House or to Congress Hall. But at the *Trois Couronnes*, it must be added, there are other features that are much at variance with these suggestions: neat German waiters, who look like secretaries of legation; Russian princesses sitting in the garden; little Polish boys walking about, held by the hand, with their governors; a view of the snowy crest of the Dent du Midi and the picturesque towers of the Castle of Chillon.[2]

I hardly know whether it was the analogies or the differences that were uppermost in the mind of a young American, who, two or three years ago, sat in the garden of the *Trois Couronnes*, looking about him, rather idly, at some of the graceful objects I have mentioned. It was a beautiful summer morning, and in whatever fashion the young American looked at things, they must have seemed to him charming. He had come from Geneva the day before, by the little steamer, to see his aunt, who was staying at the hotel – Geneva having been for a long time his place of residence. But his aunt had a headache – his aunt had almost always a headache – and now she was shut up in her room, smelling camphor, so that he was at liberty to wander about. He was some seven-and-twenty years of age; when his friends spoke of him, they usually said that he was at Geneva, 'studying'. When his enemies spoke of him they said – but, after all, he had no enemies; he was an extremely amiable fellow, and universally liked. What I should say is, simply, that when certain persons spoke of him they affirmed that the reason of his spending so much time at Geneva was that he was extremely devoted to a lady who lived there – a foreign lady – a person older than himself. Very few Americans – indeed I think none – had ever seen this lady, about whom there were some singular stories. But Winterbourne had an old attachment for the little metropolis of Calvinism; he had been put to school there as a boy, and he had afterwards gone to college there – circumstances which had led to his forming a great many youthful friendships. Many of these he had kept, and they were a source of great satisfaction to him.

After knocking at his aunt's door and learning that she was indisposed, he had taken a walk about the town, and then he had come in to his breakfast. He had now finished his breakfast, but he was drinking a small cup of coffee, which had been served to him on a little table in the garden by one of the waiters who

---

1: Newport, Rhode Island, and Saratoga Springs, NY, fashionable resorts for wealthy Americans. 2: The castle was made famous for English readers by one of Byron's most popular poems, 'The Prisoner of Chillon' (1816).

looked like an attaché. At last he finished his coffee and lit a cigarette. Presently a small boy came walking along the path – an urchin of nine or ten. The child, who was diminutive for his years, had an aged expression of countenance, a pale complexion, and sharp little features. He was dressed in knickerbockers, with red stockings, which displayed his poor little spindleshanks; he also wore a brilliant red cravat. He carried in his hand a long alpenstock, the sharp point of which he thrust into everything that he approached – the flowerbeds, the garden-benches, the trains of the ladies' dresses. In front of Winterbourne he paused, looking at him with a pair of bright, penetrating little eyes.

'Will you give me a lump of sugar?' he asked, in a sharp, hard little voice – a voice immature, and yet, somehow, not young.

Winterbourne glanced at the small table near him, on which his coffee-service rested, and saw that several morsels of sugar remained. 'Yes, you may take one,' he answered; 'but I don't think sugar is good for little boys.'

This little boy stepped forward and carefully selected three of the coveted fragments, two of which he buried in the pocket of his knickerbockers, depositing the other as promptly in another place. He poked his alpenstock, lance-fashion, into Winterbourne's bench, and tried to crack the lump of sugar with his teeth.

'Oh, blazes; it's har-r-d!' he exclaimed, pronouncing the adjective in a peculiar manner.

Winterbourne had immediately perceived that he might have the honour of claiming him as a fellow-countryman. 'Take care you don't hurt your teeth,' he said, paternally.

'I haven't got any teeth to hurt. They have all come out. I have only got seven teeth. My mother counted them last night, and one came out right afterwards. She said she'd slap me if any more came out. I can't help it. It's this old Europe. It's the climate that makes them come out. In America they didn't come out. It's these hotels.'

Winterbourne was much amused. 'If you eat three lumps of sugar, you mother will certainly slap you,' he said.

'She's got to give me some candy, then,' rejoined his young interlocutor. 'I can't get any candy here – any American candy. American candy's the best candy.'

'And are American little boys the best little boys?' asked Winterbourne.

'I don't know. I'm an American boy,' said the child.

'I see you are one of the best!' laughed Winterbourne.

'Are you an American man?' pursued the vivacious infant.

And then, on Winterbourne's affirmative reply – 'American men are the best,' he declared.

His companion thanked him for the compliment; and the child, who had now got astride of his alpenstock, stood looking about him, while he attacked a second lump of sugar. Winterbourne wondered if he himself had been like this in his infancy, for he had been brought to Europe at about this age.

'Here comes my sister!' cried the child, in a moment. 'She's an American girl.'

Winterbourne looked along the path and saw a beautiful young lady advancing. 'American girls are the best girls,' he said, cheerfully, to his young companion.

'My sister ain't the best!' the child declared. 'She's always blowing at me.'

'I imagine that is your fault, not hers,' said Winterbourne. The young lady meanwhile had drawn near. She was dressed in white muslin, with a hundred frills and flounces, and knots of pale-coloured ribbon. She was bare-headed; but she balanced in her hand a large parasol, with a deep border of embroidery; and she was strikingly, admirably pretty. 'How pretty they are!' thought Winterbourne, straightening himself in his seat, as if he was prepared to rise.

The young lady paused in front of his bench, near the parapet of the garden, which overlooked the lake. The little boy had now converted his alpenstock into a vaulting-pole, by the aid of which he was springing about in the gravel, and kicking it up not a little.

'Randolph,' said the young lady, 'what *are* you doing?'

'I'm going up the Alps,' replied Randolph. 'This is the way!' And he gave another little jump, scattering the pebbles about Winterbourne's ears.

'That's the way they come down,' said Winterbourne.

'He's an American man!' cried Randolph, in his little hard voice.

The young lady gave no heed to this announcement, but looked straight at her brother. 'Well, I guess you had better be quiet,' she simply observed.

It seemed to Winterbourne that he had been in a manner presented. He got up and stepped slowly toward the young girl, throwing away his cigarette. 'This little boy and I have made acquaintance,' he said, with great civility. In Geneva, as he had been perfectly aware, a young man was not at liberty to speak to a young unmarried lady except under certain rarely occurring conditions; but here, at Vevey, what conditions could be better than these? – a pretty young American girl coming and standing in front of you in a garden. This pretty American girl, however, on hearing Winterbourne's observation, simply glanced at him; she then turned her head and looked over the parapet, at the lake and the opposite mountains. He wondered whether he had gone too far; but he decided that he must advance farther rather than retreat. While he was thinking of something else to say, the young lady turned to the little boy again.

'I should like to know where you got that pole,' she said.

'I bought it!' responded Randolph.

'You don't mean to say you're going to take it to Italy!'

'Yes, I am going to take it to Italy!' the child declared.

The young girl glanced over the front of her dress, and smoothed out a knot or two of ribbon. Then she rested her eyes upon the prospect again. 'Well, I guess you had better leave it somewhere,' she said, after a moment.

'Are you going to Italy?' Winterbourne inquired, in a tone of great respect.

The young lady glanced at him again. 'Yes, sir,' she replied. And she said nothing more.

'Are you – a – going over the Simplon?' Winterbourne pursued, a little embarrassed.

'I don't know,' she said. 'I suppose it's some mountain. Randolph, what mountain are we going over?'

'Going where?' the child demanded.

'To Italy,' Winterbourne explained.

'I don't know,' said Randolph. 'I don't want to go to Italy. I want to go to America.'

'Oh Italy is a beautiful place!' rejoined the young man.

'Can you get candy there?' Randolph loudly inquired.

'I hope not,' said his sister. 'I guess you have had enough candy, and mother thinks so too.'

'I haven't had any for ever so long – for a hundred weeks!' cried the boy, still jumping about.

The young lady inspected her flounces and smoothed her ribbons again; and Winterbourne presently risked an observation upon the beauty of the view. He was ceasing to be embarrassed, for he had begun to perceive that she was not in the least embarrassed herself. There had not been the slightest alteration in her charming complexion; she was evidently neither offended nor fluttered. If she looked another way when he spoke to her, and seemed not particularly to hear him, this was simply her habit, her manner. Yet, as he talked a little more, and pointed out some of the objects of interest in the view, with which she appeared quite unacquainted, she gradually gave him more of the benefit of her glance; and then he saw that this glance was perfectly direct and unshrinking. It was not, however, what would have been called an immodest glance, for the young girl's eyes were singularly honest and fresh. They were wonderfully pretty eyes; and, indeed, Winterbourne had not seen for a long time anything prettier than his fair countrywoman's various features – her complexion, her nose, her ears, her teeth. He had a great relish for feminine beauty; he was addicted to observing and analysing it; and as regards this young lady's face he made several observations. It was not at all insipid, but it was not exactly expressive; and thought it was eminently delicate, Winterbourne mentally accused it – very forgivingly – of a want of finish. He thought it very possible that master Randolph's sister was a coquette; he was sure she had a spirit of her own; but in her bright, sweet, superficial little visage there was no mockery, no irony. Before long it became obvious that she was much disposed towards conversation. She told him that they were going to Rome for the winter – she and her mother and Randolph. She asked him if he was a 'real American'; she wouldn't have taken him for one; he seemed more like a German – this was said after a little hesitation, especially when he spoke. Winterbourne, laughing, answered that he had met Germans who spoke like Americans; but that he had not, so far as he remembered, met an American who spoke like a German. Then he asked her if she would not be more comfortable in sitting upon the bench which he had just quitted. She answered that she liked standing up and walking about; but she presently sat down. She told him she was from New York State – 'if you know where that is'. Winterbourne learned more about her by catching hold of her small, slippery brother and making him stand a few minutes by his side.

'Tell me your name, my boy,' he said.

'Randolph C. Miller,' said the boy, sharply. 'And I'll tell you her name'; and he levelled his alpenstock at his sister.

'You had better wait until you are asked!' said this young lady, calmly.

'I should very much like to know your name,' said Winterbourne.

'Her name is Daisy Miller!' cried the child. 'But that isn't her real name; that isn't her name on the cards.'

'It's a pity you haven't got one of my cards!' said Miss Miller.

'Her real name is Annie P. Miller,' the boy went on.

'Ask him *his* name,' said his sister, indicating Winterbourne.

But on this point Randolph seemed perfectly indifferent; he continued to supply information with regard to his own family. 'My father's name is Ezra B. Miller,' he announced. 'My father ain't in Europe; my father's in a better place than Europe.'

Winterbourne imagined for a moment that this was the manner in which the child had been taught to intimate that Mr Miller had been removed to the sphere of celestial rewards. But Randolph immediately added, 'My father's in Schenectady.[1] He's got a big business. My father's rich, you bet.'

'Well!' ejaculated Miss Miller, lowering her parasol and looking at the embroidered border. Winterbourne presently released the child, who departed, dragging his alpenstock along the path. 'He doesn't like Europe,' said the young girl. 'He wants to go back.'

'To Schenectady, you mean?'

'Yes; he wants to go right home. He hasn't got any boys here. There is one boy here, but he always goes round with a teacher; they won't let him play.'

'And your brother hasn't any teacher?' Winterbourne inquired.

'Mother thought of getting him one, to travel round with us. There was a lady told her of a very good teacher; an American lady – perhaps you know her – Mrs Sanders. I think she came from Boston. She told her of this teacher, and we thought of getting him to travel round with us. But Randolph said he didn't want a teacher travelling round with us. He said he wouldn't have lessons when he was in the cars.[2] And we *are* in the cars about half the time. There was an English lady we met in the cars – I think her name was Miss Featherstone; perhaps you know her. She wanted to know why I didn't give Randolph lessons – give him "instruction", she called it. I guess he could give me more instruction than I could give him. He's very smart.'

'Yes,' said Winterbourne; 'he seems very smart.'

'Mother's going to get a teacher for him as soon as we get to Italy. Can you get good teachers in Italy?'

'Very good, I should think,' said Winterbourne.

'Or else she's going to find some school. He ought to learn some more. He's only nine. He's going to college.' And in this way Miss Miller continued to converse upon the affairs of her family, and upon other topics. She sat there with her extremely pretty hands, ornamented with very brilliant rings, folded in her lap, and with her pretty eyes now resting upon those of Winterbourne, now wandering over the garden, the people who passed by, and the beautiful view. She talked to Winterbourne as if she had known him a long time. He found it very pleasant. It was many years since he had heard a young girl talk so much. It might have been said of this unknown young lady, who had come and sat down beside him upon a bench, that she chattered. She was very quiet, she

---

1: a commercial town on the Mohawk River in Upper New York State.   2: railway carriages.

sat in a charming tranquil attitude; but her lips and her eyes were constantly moving. She had a soft, slender, agreeable voice, and her tone was decidedly sociable. She gave Winterbourne a history of her movements and intentions, and those of her mother and brother, in Europe, and enumerated, in particular, the various hotels at which they had stopped. 'That English lady in the cars,' she said – 'Miss Featherstone – asked me if we didn't all live in hotels in America. I told her I had never been in so many hotels in my life as since I came to Europe. I have never seen so many – it's nothing but hotels.' But Miss Miller did not make this remark in a querulous accent; she appeared to be in the best humour with everything. She declared that the hotels were very good, when once you got used to their ways, and that Europe was perfectly sweet. She was not disappointed – not a bit. Perhaps it was because she had heard so much about it before. She had ever so many intimate friends that had been there ever so many times. And then she had had ever so many dresses and things from Paris. Whenever she put on a Paris dress she felt as if she were in Europe.

'It was a kind of wishing-cap,' said Winterbourne.

'Yes,' said Miss Miller, without examining this analogy; 'it always made me wish I was here. But I needn't have done that for dresses. I am sure they send all the pretty ones to America; you see the most frightful things here. The only thing I don't like,' she proceeded, 'is the society. There isn't any society; or, if there is, I don't know where it keeps itself. Do you? I suppose there is some society somewhere, but I haven't seen anything of it. I'm very fond of society, and I have always had a great deal of it. I don't mean only in Schenectady, but in New York. I used to go to New York every winter. In New York I had lots of society. Last winter I had seventeen dinners given me; and three of them were by gentlemen,' added Daisy Miller. 'I have more friends in New York than in Schenectady – more gentlemen friends; and more young lady friends too,' she resumed in a moment. She paused again for an instant; she was looking at Winterbourne with all her prettiness in her lively eyes and in her light, slightly monotonous smile. 'I have always had,' she said, 'a great deal of gentlemen's society.'

Poor Winterbourne was amused, perplexed, and decidedly charmed. He had never yet heard a young girl express herself in just this fashion; never, at least, save in cases where to say such things seemed a kind of demonstrative evidence of a certain laxity of deportment. And yet was he to accuse Miss Daisy Miller of actual or potential *inconduite*,[1] as they said at Geneva? He felt that he had lived in Geneva so long that he had lost a good deal; he had become dishabituated to the American tone. Never indeed, since he had grown old enough to appreciate things, had he encountered a young American girl of so pronounced a type as this. Certainly she was very charming; but how deucedly sociable! Was she simply a pretty girl from New York State – were they all like that, the pretty girls who had a good deal of gentlemen's society? Or was she also a designing, an audacious, an unscrupulous young person? Winterbourne had lost his instinct in this matter, and his reason could not help him. Miss Daisy Miller looked extremely innocent. Some people had told him that, after all, American girls

---

1: social misconduct, breach of etiquette.

were exceedingly innocent; and others had told him that, after all, they were not. He was inclined to think Miss Daisy Miller was a flirt – a pretty American flirt. He had never, as yet, had any relations with young ladies of this category. He had known, here in Europe, two or three women – persons older than Miss Daisy Miller, and provided for respectability's sake, with husbands – who were great coquettes – dangerous, terrible women, with whom one's relations were liable to take a serious turn. But this young girl was not a coquette in that sense; she was very unsophisticated; she was only a pretty American flirt. Winterbourne was almost grateful for having found the formula that applied to Miss Daisy Miller. He leaned back in his seat; he remarked to himself that she had the most charming nose he had ever seen; he wondered what were the regular conditions and limitations of one's intercourse with a pretty American flirt. It presently became apparent that he was on the way to learn.

'Have you been to that old castle?' asked the young girl, pointing with her parasol to the far-gleaming walls of the Château de Chillon.

'Yes, formerly, more than once,' said Winterbourne. 'You too, I suppose, have seen it?'

'No; we haven't been there. I want to go there dreadfully. Of course I mean to go there. I wouldn't go away from here without having seen that old castle.'

'It's a very pretty excursion,' said Winterbourne, 'and very easy to make. You can drive, you know, or you can go by the little steamer.'

'You can go in the cars,' said Miss Miller.

'Yes, you can go in the cars,' Winterbourne assented.

'Our courier says they take you right up to the castle,' the young girl continued. 'We were going last week; but my mother gave out. She suffers dreadfully from dyspepsia. She said she couldn't go. Randolph wouldn't go either; he says he doesn't think much of old castles. But I guess we'll go this week, if we can get Randolph.'

'Your brother is not interested in ancient monuments?' Winterbourne inquired, smiling.

'He says he don't care much about old castles. He's only nine. He wants to stay at the hotel. Mother's afraid to leave him alone, and the courier won't stay with him; so we haven't been to many places. But it will be too bad if we don't go up there.' And Miss Miller pointed again at the Château de Chillon.

'I should think it might be arranged,' said Winterbourne. 'Couldn't you get someone to stay – for the afternoon – with Randolph?'

Miss Miller looked at him a moment; and then, very placidly – 'I wish *you* would stay with him!' she said.

Winterbourne hesitated a moment. 'I would much rather go to Chillon with you.'

'With me?' asked the young girl, with the same placidity. She didn't rise, blushing, as a young girl at Geneva would have done; and yet Winterbourne, conscious that he had been very bold, thought it possible she was offended.

'With your mother,' he answered very respectfully.

But it seemed that both his audacity and his respect were lost upon Miss Daisy Miller. 'I guess my mother won't go, after all,' she said. 'She don't like to ride round in the afternoon. But did you really mean what you said just now; that you would like to go up there?'

'Most earnestly,' Winterbourne declared.

'Then we may arrange it. If mother will stay with Randolph, I guess Eugenio will.'

'Eugenio?' the young man inquired.

'Eugenio's our courier. He doesn't like to stay with Randolph; he's the most fastidious man I ever saw. But he's a splendid courier. I guess he'll stay at home with Randolph if mother does, and then we can go to the castle.'

Winterbourne reflected for an instant as lucidly as possible – 'we' could only mean Miss Daisy Miller and himself. This programme seemed almost too agreeable for credence; he felt as if he ought to kiss the young lady's hand. Possibly he would have done so – and quite spoiled the project; but at this moment another person – presumably Eugenio – appeared. A tall, handsome man, with superb whiskers, wearing a velvet morning-coat and a brilliant watch-chain, approached Miss Miller, looking sharply at her companion. 'Oh, Eugenio!' said Miss Miller, with the friendliest accent.

Eugenio had looked at Winterbourne from head to foot; he now bowed gravely to the young lady. 'I have the honour to inform mademoiselle that luncheon is upon the table.'

Miss Miller slowly rose. 'See here, Eugenio,' she said. 'I'm going to that old castle, anyway.'

'To the Château de Chillon, mademoiselle?' the courier inquired. 'Mademoiselle has made arrangements?' he added, in a tone which struck Winterbourne as very impertinent.

Eugenio's tone apparently threw, even to Miss Miller's own apprehension, a slightly ironical light upon the young girl's situation. She turned to Winterbourne, blushing a little – a very little. 'You won't back out?' she said.

'I shall not be happy till we go!' he protested.

'And you are staying in this hotel?' she went on. 'And you are really an American?'

The courier stood looking at Winterbourne, offensively. The young man, at least, thought his manner of looking an offence to Miss Miller; it conveyed an imputation that she 'picked up' acquaintances. 'I shall have the honour of presenting to you a person who will tell you all about me,' he said smiling, and referring to his aunt.

'Oh well, we'll go some day,' said Miss Miller. And she gave him a smile and turned away. She put up her parasol and walked back to the inn beside Eugenio. Winterbourne stood looking after her; and as she moved away, drawing her muslin furbelows[1] over the gravel, said to himself that she had the *tournure*[2] of a princess.

1: flounces, ornamental trim.   2: turnout and general appearance.

2

He had, however, engaged to do more than proved feasible, in promising to present his aunt, Mrs Costello, to Miss Daisy Miller. As soon as the former lady had got better of her headache he waited upon her in her apartment; and, after the proper inquiries in regard to her health, he asked her if she had observed in the hotel, an American family – a mamma, a daughter, and a little boy.

'And a courier?' said Mrs Costello. 'Oh, yes, I have observed them. Seen them – heard them – and kept out of their way.' Mrs Costello was a widow with a fortune; a person of much distinction, who frequently intimated that, if she were not so dreadfully liable to sick-headaches, she would probably have left a deeper impress upon her time. She had a long pale face, a high nose, and a great deal of very striking white hair, which she wore in large puffs and *rouleaux* over the top of her head. She had two sons married in New York, and another who was now in Europe. This young man was amusing himself at Homburg, and, though he was on his travels, was rarely perceived to visit any particular city at the moment selected by his mother for her own appearance there. Her nephew, who had come up to Vevey expressly to see her, was therefore more attentive than those who, as she said, were nearer to her. He had imbibed at Geneva the idea that one must always be attentive to one's aunt. Mrs Costello had not seen him for many years, and she was greatly pleased with him, manifesting her approbation by initiating him into many of the secrets of that social sway which, as she gave him to understand, she exerted in the American capital. She admitted that she was very exclusive; but, if he were acquainted with New York, he would see that one had to be. And her picture of the minutely hierarchical constitution of the society of that city, which she presented to him in many different lights, was, to Winterbourne's imagination, almost oppressively striking.

He immediately perceived, from her tone, that Miss Daisy Miller's place in the social scale was low. 'I'm afraid you don't approve of them,' he said.

'They are very common,' Mrs Costello declared. 'They are the sort of Americans that one does one's duty by not – not accepting.'

'Ah, you don't accept them?' said the young man.

'I can't, my dear Frederick. I would if I could, but I can't.'

'The young girl is very pretty,' said Winterbourne, in a moment.

'Of course she's pretty. But she is very common.'

'I see what you mean, of course,' said Winterbourne, after another pause.

'She has that charming look that they all have,' his aunt resumed. 'I can't think where they pick it up; and she dresses in perfection – no, you don't know how well she dresses. I can't think where they get their taste.'

'But, my dear aunt, she is not, after all, a Comanche savage.'

'She is a young lady,' said Mrs Costello, 'who has an intimacy with her mamma's courier.'

'An intimacy with the courier?' the young man demanded.

'Oh, the mother is just as bad! They treat the courier like a familiar friend – like a gentleman. I shouldn't wonder if he dines with them. Very likely they have never seen a man with such good manners, such fine clothes, so like a gentleman. He probably corresponds to the young lady's idea of a Count. He sits with them in the garden, in the evening. I think he smokes.'

Winterbourne listened with interest to these disclosures; they helped him to make up his mind about Miss Daisy. Evidently she was rather wild. 'Well', he said, 'I am not a courier, and yet she was very charming to me.'

'You had better have said at first,' said Mrs Costello with dignity, 'that you had made her acquaintance.'

'We simply met in the garden, and we talked a bit.'

'*Tout bonnement!* And pray what did you say?'

'I said I should take the liberty of introducing her to my admirable aunt.'

'I am much obliged to you.'

'It was to guarantee my respectability,' said Winterbourne.

'And pray who is to guarantee hers?'

'Ah, you are cruel!' said the young man. 'She's a very nice girl.'

'You don't say that as if you believed it,' Mrs Costello observed.

'She is completely uncultivated,' Winterbourne went on. 'But she is wonderfully pretty, and, in short, she is very nice. To prove that I believe it, I am going to take her to the Château de Chillon.'

'You two are going off there together? I should say it proved just the contrary. How long had you known her, may I ask, when this interesting project was formed? You haven't been twenty-four hours in the house.'

'I had known her half an hour!' said Winterbourne, smiling.

'Dear me!' cried Mrs Costello. 'What a dreadful girl!'

Her nephew was silent for some moments. 'You really think, then,' he began earnestly, and with a desire for trustworthy information – 'you really think that – ' But he paused again.

'Think what, sir,' said his aunt.

'That she is the sort of young lady who expects a man – sooner or later – to carry her off?'

'I haven't the least idea what such young ladies expect a man to do. But I really think that you had better not meddle with little American girls that are uncultivated, as you call them. You have lived too long out of the country. You will be sure to make some great mistake. You are too innocent.'

'My dear aunt, I am not so innocent,' said Winterbourne, smiling and curling his moustache.

'You are too guilty, then?'

Winterbourne continued to curl his moustache, meditatively. 'You won't let the poor girl know you then?' he asked at last.

'Is it literally true that she is going to the Château de Chillon with you?'

'I think that she fully intends it.'

'Then, my dear Frederick,' said Mrs Costello, 'I must decline the honour of her acquaintance. I am an old woman, but I am not too old – thank Heaven – to be shocked!'

'But don't they all do these things – the young girls in America?' Winterbourne inquired.

Mrs Costello stared a moment. 'I should like to see my granddaughters do them!' she declared, grimly.

This seemed to throw some light upon the matter, for Winterbourne remembered to have heard that his pretty cousins in New York were 'tremendous flirts'. If, therefore, Miss Daisy Miller exceeded the liberal licence allowed to these young ladies, it was probable that anything might be expected of her. Winterbourne was impatient to see her again, and he was vexed with himself that, by instinct, he should not appreciate her justly.

Though he was impatient to see her, he hardly knew what he should say to her about his aunt's refusal to become acquainted with her; but he discovered, promptly enough, that with Miss Daisy Miller there was no great need of walking on tiptoe. He found her that evening in the garden, wandering about in the warm starlight, like an indolent sylph, and swinging to and fro the largest fan he had ever beheld. It was ten o'clock. He had dined with his aunt, had been sitting with her since dinner, and had just taken leave of her till the morrow. Miss Daisy Miller seemed very glad to see him; she declared it was the longest evening she had ever passed.

'Have you been all alone?' he asked.

'I have been walking round with mother. But mother gets tired walking round,' she answered.

'Has she gone to bed?'

'No; she doesn't like to go to bed,' said the young girl. 'She doesn't sleep – not three hours. She says she doesn't know how she lives. She's dreadfully nervous. I guess she sleeps more than she thinks. She's gone somewhere after Randolph; she wants to try to get him to go to bed. He doesn't like to go to bed.'

'Let us hope she will persuade him,' observed Winterbourne.

'She will talk to him all she can; but he doesn't like her to talk to him,' said Miss Daisy, opening her fan. 'She's going to try to get Eugenio to talk to him. But he isn't afraid of Eugenio. Eugenio's a splendid courier, but he can't make much impression on Randolph! I don't believe he'll go to bed before eleven.' It appeared that Randolph's vigil was in fact triumphantly prolonged, for Winterbourne strolled about with the young girl for some time without meeting her mother. 'I have been looking round for that lady you want to introduce me to,' his companion resumed. 'She's your aunt.' Then, on Winterbourne's admitting the fact, and expressing some curiosity as to how she had learned it, she said she had heard all about Mrs Costello from the chambermaid. She was very quiet and very *comme il faut*; she wore white puffs; she spoke to no one, and she never dined at the *table d'hôte*. Every two days she had a headache. 'I think that's a lovely description, headache and all!' said Miss Daisy, chattering along in her thin, gay voice. 'I want to know her ever so much. I know just what *your* aunt would be; I know I should like her. She would be very exclusive. I like a lady to be exclusive; I'm dying to be exclusive myself. Well, we *are* exclusive, mother and I. We don't speak to everyone – or they don't speak to us. I suppose it's about the same thing. Anyway, I shall be ever so glad to know your aunt.'

Winterbourne was embarrassed. 'She would be most happy,' he said, 'but I am afraid those headaches will interfere.'

The young girl looked at him through the dusk. 'But I suppose she doesn't have a headache every day,' she said, sympathetically.

Winterbourne was silent a moment. 'She tells me she does,' he answered at last – not knowing what to say.

Miss Daisy Miller stopped and stood looking at him. Her prettiness was still visible in the darkness; she was opening and closing her enormous fan. 'She doesn't want to know me!' she said suddenly. 'Why don't you say so? You needn't be afraid. I'm not afraid!' And she gave a little laugh.

Winterbourne fancied there was a tremor in her voice; he was touched, shocked, mortified by it. 'My dear young lady,' he protested, 'she knows no one. It's her wretched health.'

The young girl walked on a few steps, laughing still. 'You needn't be afraid,' she repeated. 'Why should she want to know me?' Then she paused again; she was close to the parapet of the garden, and in front of her was the starlit lake. There was a vague sheen upon its surface, and in the distance were dimly seen mountain forms. Daisy Miller looked out upon the mysterious prospect, and then she gave another little laugh. 'Gracious! She *is* exclusive!' she said. Winterbourne wondered whether she was seriously wounded, and for a moment almost wished that her sense of injury might be such as to make it becoming in him to attempt to reassure and comfort her. He had a pleasant sense that she would be very approachable for consolatory purposes. He felt then, for the instant, quite ready to sacrifice his aunt, conversationally; to admit that she was a proud, rude woman, and to declare that they needn't mind her. But before he had time to commit himself to this perilous mixture of gallantry and impiety, the young lady, resuming her walk, gave an exclamation in quite another tone. 'Well; here's mother! I guess she hasn't got Randolph to go to bed.' The figure of a lady appeared, at a distance, very indistinct in the darkness, and advancing with a slow and wavering movement. Suddenly it seemed to pause.

'Are you sure it is your mother? Can you distinguish her in this thick dusk?' Winterbourne asked.

'Well!' cried Miss Daisy Miller, with a laugh, 'I guess I know my own mother. And when she has got on my shawl, too! She is always wearing my things.'

The lady in question, ceasing to advance, hovered vaguely about the spot at which she had checked her steps.

'I am afraid your mother doesn't see you,' said Winterbourne. 'Or perhaps,' he added – thinking, with Miss Miller, the joke permissible – 'perhaps she feels guilty about your shawl.'

'Oh, it's a fearful old thing!' the young girl replied, serenely. 'I told her she could wear it. She won't come here, because she sees you.'

'Ah, then,' said Winterbourne, 'I had better leave you.'

'Oh, no; come on!' urged Miss Daisy Miller.

'I'm afraid your mother doesn't approve of my walking with you.'

Miss Miller gave him a serious glance. 'It isn't for me; it's for you – that is, it's for *her*. Well; I don't know who it's for! But mother doesn't like any of my gentlemen friends. She's right down timid. She always makes a fuss if I introduce a gentleman. But I *do* introduce them – almost always. If I didn't introduce my gentlemen friends to mother,' the young girl added, in her little soft, flat monotone, 'I shouldn't think I was natural.'

'To introduce me,' said Winterbourne, 'you must know my name.' And he proceeded to pronounce it.

'Oh dear; I can't say all that!' said his companion, with a laugh. But by this time they had come up to Mrs Miller, who, as they drew near, walked to the parapet of the garden and leaned upon it, looking intently at the lake and turning her back upon them. 'Mother!' said the young girl, in a tone of decision. Upon this the elder lady turned round. 'Mr Winterbourne,' said Miss Daisy Miller, introducing the young man very frankly and prettily. 'Common' she was, as Mrs Costello had pronounced her; yet it was a wonder to Winterbourne that, with her commonness, she had a singularly delicate grace.

Her mother was a small, spare, light person, with a wandering eye, a very exiguous nose, and a large forehead, decorated with a certain amount of thin, much-frizzled hair. Like her daughter, Mrs Miller was dressed with extreme elegance; she had enormous diamonds in her ears. So far as Winterbourne could observe, she gave him no greeting – she certainly was not looking at him. Daisy was near her, pulling her shawl straight. 'What are you doing, poking round here?' this young lady inquired; but by no means with that harshness of accent which her choice of words may imply.

'I don't know,' said her mother, turning toward the lake again.

'I shouldn't think you'd want that shawl!' Daisy exclaimed.

'Well – I do!' her mother answered, with a little laugh.

'Did you get Randolph to go to bed?' asked the young girl.

'No; I couldn't induce him,' said Mrs Miller, very gently. 'He wants to talk to the waiter. He likes to talk to that waiter.'

'I was telling Mr Winterbourne,' the young girl went on; and to the young man's ear her tone might have indicated that she had been uttering his name all her life.

'Oh, yes!' said Winterbourne; 'I have the pleasure of knowing your son.'

Randolph's mamma was silent; she turned her attention to the lake. But at last she spoke. 'Well, I don't see how he lives!'

'Anyhow, it isn't so bad as it was at Dover,' said Daisy Miller.

'And what occurred at Dover?' Winterbourne asked.

'He wouldn't go to bed at all. I guess he sat up all night – in the public parlour. He wasn't in bed at twelve o'clock: I know that.'

'It was half past twelve,' declared Mrs Miller, with mild emphasis.

'Does he sleep much during the day?' Winterbourne demanded.

'I guess he doesn't sleep much,' Daisy rejoined.

'I wish he would!' said her mother. 'It seems as if he couldn't.'

'I think he's real tiresome,' Daisy pursued.

Then, for some moments, there was silence. 'Well, Daisy Miller,' said the elder lady, presently, 'I shouldn't think you'd want to talk against your own brother!'

'Well, he *is* tiresome, mother,' said Daisy, quite without the asperity of a retort.

'He's only nine,' urged Mrs Miller.

'Well, he wouldn't go to that castle,' said the young girl. 'I'm going there with Mr Winterbourne.'

To this announcement, very placidly made, Daisy's mamma offered no response. Winterbourne took for granted that she deeply disapproved of the projected excursion; but he said to himself that she was a simple, easily managed person, and that a few deferential protestations would take the edge from her displeasure. 'Yes,' he began; 'your daughter has kindly allowed me the honour of being her guide.'

Mrs Miller's wandering eyes attached themselves, with a sort of appealing air, to Daisy, who, however, strolled a few steps farther, gently humming to herself. 'I presume you will go in the cars,' said her mother.

'Yes; or in the boat,' said Winterbourne.

'Well, of course, I don't know,' Mrs Miller rejoined. 'I have never been to that castle.'

'It's a pity you shouldn't go,' said Winterbourne, beginning to feel reassured as to her opposition. And yet he was quite prepared to find that, as a matter of course, she meant to accompany her daughter.

'We've been thinking ever so much about going,' she pursued; 'but it seems as if we couldn't. Of course Daisy – she wants to go round. But there's a lady here – I don't know her name – she says she shouldn't think we'd want to go to see castles *here*; she should think we'd want to wait until we got to Italy. It seems as if there would be so many there,' continued Mrs Miller, with an air of increasing confidence. 'Of course, we only want to see the principal ones. We visited several in England,' she presently added.

'Ah, yes! In England there are beautiful castles,' said Winterbourne. 'But Chillon, here, is very well worth seeing.'

'Well, if Daisy feels up to it – ,' said Mrs Miller, in a tone impregnated with a sense of magnitude of the enterprise. 'It seems as if there was nothing she wouldn't undertake.'

'Oh, I think she'll enjoy it!' Winterbourne declared. And he desired more and more to make it a certainty that he was to have the privilege of the *tête-à-tête* with the young lady, who was still strolling along in front of them, softly vocalizing. 'You are not disposed, madam,' he inquired, 'to undertake it yourself?'

Daisy's mother looked at him, an instant, askance, and then walked forward in silence. Then – 'I guess she had better go alone,' she said, simply.

Winterbourne observed to himself that this was a very different type of maternity from that of the vigilant matrons who massed themselves in the forefront of social intercourse in the dark old city at the other end of the lake. But his meditations were interrupted by hearing his name very distinctly pronounced by Mrs Miller's unprotected daughter.

'Mr Winterbourne!' murmured Daisy.

'Mademoiselle!' said the young man.

'Don't you want to take me out in a boat?'

'At present?' he asked.

'Of course!' said Daisy.

'Well, Annie Miller!' exclaimed her mother.

'I beg you, madam, to let her go,' said Winterbourne, ardently; for he had never yet enjoyed the sensation of guiding through the summer starlight a skiff freighted with a fresh and beautiful young girl.

'I shouldn't think she'd want to,' said her mother. 'I should think she'd rather go indoors.'

'I'm sure Mr Winterbourne wants to take me,' Daisy declared. 'He's so awfully devoted!'

'I will row you over to Chillon, in the starlight.'

'I don't believe it!' said Daisy.

'Well!' ejaculated the elder lady again.

'You haven't spoken to me for half an hour,' her daughter went on.

'I have been having some very pleasant conversation with your mother,' said Winterbourne.

'Well; I want you to take me out in a boat!' Daisy repeated. They had all stopped, and she turned round and was looking at Winterbourne. Her face wore a charming smile, her pretty eyes were gleaming, she was swinging her great fan about. No; it's impossible to be prettier than that, thought Winterbourne.

'There are half a dozen boats moored at the landing-place,' he said, pointing to certain steps which descended from the garden to the lake. 'If you will do me the honour to accept my arm, we will go and select one of them.'

Daisy stood there smiling; she threw back her head and gave a little light laugh. 'I like gentlemen to be formal!' she declared.

'I assure you it's a formal offer.'

'I was bound I would make you say something,' Daisy went on.

'You see it's not very difficult,' said Winterbourne. 'But I am afraid you are chaffing me.'

'I think not, sir,' remarked Mrs Miller, very gently.

'Do, then, let me give you a row,' he said to the young girl.

'It's quite lovely, the way you say that!' cried Daisy.

'It will be still more lovely to do it.'

'Yes, it would be lovely!' said Daisy. But she made no movement to accompany him; she only stood there laughing.

'I should think you had better find out what time it is,' interposed her mother.

'It is eleven o'clock, madam,' said a voice, with a foreign accent, out of the neighbouring darkness; and Winterbourne, turning, perceived the florid personage who was in attendance upon the two ladies. He had apparently just approached.

'Oh, Eugenio,' said Daisy, 'I am going out in a boat!'

Eugenio bowed. 'At eleven o'clock, mademoiselle?'

'I am going with Mr Winterbourne. This very minute.'

'Do tell her she can't,' said Mrs Miller to the courier.

'I think you had better not go out in a boat, mademoiselle,' Eugenio declared.

Winterbourne wished to Heaven this pretty girl were not so familiar with her courier; but he said nothing.

'I suppose you don't think it's proper!' Daisy exclaimed, ''Eugenio doesn't think anything's proper.'

'I am at your service,' said Winterbourne.

'Does mademoiselle propose to go alone?' asked Eugenio of Mrs Miller.

'Oh, no; with this gentleman!' answered Daisy's mamma.

The courier looked for a moment at Winterbourne – the latter thought he was smiling – and then, solemnly, with a bow, 'As mademoiselle pleases!' he said.

'Oh, I hoped you would make a fuss!' said Daisy. 'I don't care to go now.'

'I myself shall make a fuss if you don't go,' said Winterbourne.

'That's all I want – a little fuss!' And the young girl began to laugh again.

'Mr Randolph has gone to bed!' the courier announced, frigidly.

'Oh, Daisy; now we can go!' said Mrs Miller.

Daisy turned away from Winterbourne, looking at him, smiling and fanning herself. 'Good night,' she said; 'I hope you are disappointed, or disgusted, or something!'

He looked at her, taking the hand she offered him. 'I am puzzled,' he answered.

'Well; I hope it won't keep you awake!' she said, very smartly; and, under the escort of the privileged Eugenio, the two ladies passed towards the house.

Winterbourne stood looking after them; he was indeed puzzled. He lingered beside the lake for a quarter of an hour, turning over the mystery of the young girl's sudden familiarities and caprices. But the only very definite conclusion he came to was that he should enjoy deucedly 'going off' with her somewhere.

Two days afterwards he went off with her to the Castle of Chillon. He waited for her in the large hall of the hotel, where the couriers, the servants, the foreign tourists were lounging about and staring. It was not the place he would have chosen, but she had appointed it. She came tripping downstairs, buttoning her long gloves, squeezing her folded parasol against her pretty figure, dressed in the perfection of a soberly elegant travelling costume. Winterbourne was a man of imagination and, as our ancestors used to say, of sensibility; as he looked at her dress and, on the great staircase, her little rapid, confiding step, he felt as if there were something romantic going forward. He could have believed he was going to elope with her. He passed out with her among all the idle people that were assembled there; they were all looking at her very hard; she had begun to chatter as soon as she joined him. Winterbourne's preference had been that they should be conveyed to Chillon in a carriage; but she expressed a lively wish to go in the little steamer; she declared that she had a passion for steamboats. There was always such a lovely breeze upon the water, and you saw such lots of people. The sail was not long, but Winterbourne's companion found time to say a great many things. To the young man himself their little excursion was so much of an escapade – an adventure – that, even allowing for her habitual sense of freedom, he had some expectation of seeing her regard it in the same way. But it must be confessed that, in this particular, he was disappointed. Daisy Miller was extremely animated, she was in charming spirits; but she was apparently not at all excited; she was not fluttered; she avoided neither his eyes nor those of anyone else; she blushed neither when she looked at him nor when she saw that people were looking at her. People continued to look at her a great deal, and Winterbourne took much satisfaction in his pretty companion's distinguished air. He had been a little afraid that she would talk loud, laugh overmuch, and even, perhaps, desire to move about the boat a good deal. But he quite forgot his fears; he sat smiling, with his eyes upon her face, while without moving from her place, she delivered herself of a great number of original reflections. It was the most charming garrulity he had ever heard. He had assented to the idea that she was 'common'; but was she so, after all, or was he simply getting used to her commonness? Her conversation was chiefly of what metaphysicians term the objective cast; but every now and then it took a subjective turn.

'What on *earth* are you so grave about?' she suddenly demanded, fixing her agreeable eyes upon Winterbourne's.

'Am I grave?' he asked. 'I had an idea I was grinning from ear to ear.'

'You look as if you were taking me to a funeral. If that's a grin, your ears are very near together.'

'Should you like me to dance a hornpipe on the deck?'

'Pray do, and I'll carry round your hat. It will pay the expenses of our journey.'

'I never was better pleased in my life,' murmured Winterbourne.

She looked at him a moment, and then burst into a little laugh. 'I like to make you say those things! You're a queer mixture!'

In the castle, after they had landed, the subjective element decidedly prevailed. Daisy tripped about the vaulted chambers, rustled her skirts in the corkscrew staircases, flirted back with a pretty little cry and a shudder from the edge of the *oubliettes*,[1] and turned a singularly well-shaped ear to everything that Winterbourne told her about the place. But he saw that she cared very little for feudal antiquities, and that the dusky traditions of Chillon made but a slight impression upon her. They had the good fortune to have been able to walk about without other companionship than that of the custodian; and Winterbourne arranged with this functionary that they should not be hurried – that they should linger and pause wherever they chose. The custodian inter- preted the bargain generously – Winterbourne, on his side, had been generous – and ended by leaving them quite to themselves. Miss Miller's observations were not remarkable for logical consistency; for anything she wanted to say she was sure to find a pretext. She found a great many pretexts in the rugged embrasures of Chillon for asking Winterbourne sudden questions about himself – his family, his previous history, his tastes, his habits, his intentions – and for supplying information upon corresponding points in her own personality. Of her own tastes, habits, and intentions Miss Miller was prepared to give the most definite, and indeed the most favourable, account.

'Well; I hope you know enough!' she said to her companion, after he had told her the history of the unhappy Bonivard.[2] 'I never saw a man that knew so much!' The history of Bonivard had evidently, as they say, gone into one ear and out of the other. But Daisy went on to say that she wished Winterbourne would travel with them and 'go round' with them; they might know something in that case. 'Don't you want to come and teach Randolph?' she asked. Winterbourne said that nothing could possibly please him so much; but that he

---

1: dungeons whose only entrance is through the top – where you place people to forget about them.   2: François de Bonnivard (1496–1570), subject of Byron's poem 'The Prisoner of Chillon', a famous democrat and Genevese priest kept in solitary confinement in the *oubliette*.

had unfortunately other occupations. 'Other occupations? I don't believe it!' said Miss Daisy. 'What do you mean? You are not in business.' The young man admitted that he was not in business; but he had engagements which, even within a day or two, would force him to go back to Geneva. 'Oh, bother!' she said, 'I don't believe it!' and she began to talk about something else. But a few moments later, when he was pointing out to her the pretty design of an antique fireplace, she broke out irrelevantly, 'You don't mean to say you are going back to Geneva?'

'It is a melancholy fact that I shall have to return to Geneva tomorrow.'

'Well, Mr Winterbourne,' said Daisy; 'I think you're horrid!'

'Oh, don't say such dreadful things!' said Winterbourne, 'just at the last.'

'The last!' cried the young girl; 'I call it the first. I have half a mind to leave you here and go straight back to the hotel alone.' And for the next ten minutes she did nothing but call him horrid. Poor Winterbourne was fairly bewildered; no young lady had as yet done him the honour to be so agitated by the announcement of his movements. His companion, after this, ceased to pay any attention to the curiosities of Chillon or the beauties of the lake; she opened fire upon the mysterious charmer in Geneva, whom she appeared to have instantly taken it for granted that he was hurrying back to see. How did Miss Daisy Miller know that there was a charmer in Geneva? Winterbourne, who denied the existence of such a person, was quite unable to discover; and he was divided between amazement at the rapidity of her induction and amusement at the frankness of her *persiflage*.² She seemed to him, in all this, an extraordinary mixture of innocence and crudity. 'Does she never allow you more than three days a time?' asked Daisy, ironically. 'Doesn't she give you a vacation in summer? There's no one so hard worked but they can get leave to go off somewhere at this season. I suppose, if you stay another day, she'll come after you in the boat. Do wait over till Friday, and I will go down to the landing to see her arrive!'

Winterbourne began to think he had been wrong to feel disappointed in the temper in which the young lady had embarked. If he had missed the personal accent, the personal accent was now making its appearance. It sounded very distinctly, at last, in her telling him she would stop 'teasing' him if he would promise her solemnly to come down to Rome in the winter.

'That's not a difficult promise to make,' said Winterbourne. 'My aunt has taken an apartment in Rome for the winter, and has already asked me to come and see her.'

'I don't want you to come for your aunt,' said Daisy; 'I want you to come for me.' And this was the only allusion that the young man was ever to hear her make to his invidious kinswoman. He declared, that, at any rate, he would certainly come. After this Daisy stopped teasing. Winterbourne took a carriage, and they drove back to Vevey in the dusk; the young girl was very quiet.

In the evening Winterbourne mentioned to Mrs Costello that he had spent the afternoon at Chillon, with Miss Daisy Miller.

'The Americans – of the courier?' asked this lady.

1: lightly mocking banter.

'Ah, happily,' said Winterbourne, 'the courier stayed at home.'

'She went with you all alone?'

'All alone.'

Mrs Costello sniffed a little at her smelling-bottle. 'And that,' she exclaimed, 'is the young person you wanted me to know!'

3

Winterbourne, who had returned to Geneva the day after his excursion to Chillon, went to Rome towards the end of January. His aunt had been established there for several weeks, and he had received a couple of letters from her. 'Those people you were so devoted to last summer at Vevey have turned up here, courier and all,' she wrote. 'They seem to have made several acquaintances, but the courier continues to be the most *intime*. The young lady, however, is also very intimate with some third-rate Italians, with whom she rackets about in a way that makes much talk. Bring me that pretty novel of Cherbuliex's – *Paule Méré* – and don't come later than the 23rd.'

In the natural course of events, Winterbourne, on arriving in Rome, would presently have ascertained Mrs Miller's address at the American banker's and have gone to pay his compliments to Miss Daisy. 'After what happened at Vevey I certainly think I may call upon them,' he said to Mrs Costello.

'If, after what happens – at Vevey and everywhere – you desire to keep up the acquaintance, you are very welcome. Of course a man may know everyone. Men are welcome to the privilege!'

'Pray what is it that happens – here, for instance?' Winterbourne demanded.

'The girl goes about along with her foreigners. As to what happens further, you must apply elsewhere for information. She has picked up half a dozen of the regular Roman fortune-hunters; and she takes them about to people's houses. When she comes to a party she brings with her a gentleman with a good deal of manner and a wonderful moustache.'

'And where is the mother?'

'I haven't the least idea. They are very dreadful people.'

Winterbourne meditated for a moment. 'They are very ignorant – very innocent only. Depend upon it they are not bad.'

'They are hopelessly vulgar,' said Mrs Costello. 'Whether or no being hopelessly vulgar is being "bad" is a question for the metaphysicians. They are bad enough to dislike, at any rate; and for this short life that is quite enough.'

The news that Daisy Miller was surrounded by half a dozen wonderful moustaches checked Winterbourne's impulse to go straightaway to see her. He had perhaps not definitely flattered himself that he had made an ineffaceable impression upon her heart, but he was annoyed at hearing of a state of affairs so little in harmony with an image that had lately flitted in and out of his own meditations; the image of a very pretty girl looking out of an old Roman window and asking herself urgently when Mr Winterbourne would arrive. If, however, he determined to wait a little before reminding Miss Miller of his claims to her consideration, he went very soon to call upon two or three other friends. One of these friends was an American lady who had spent several winters at

Geneva, where she had placed her children at school. She was a very accomplished woman and she lived in the Via Gregoriana. Winterbourne found her in a little crimson drawing-room, on a third floor; the room was filled with southern sunshine. He had not been there ten minutes when the servant came in, announcing 'Madam Mila!' This announcement was presently followed by the entrance of little Randolph Miller, who stopped in the middle of the room and stood staring at Winterbourne. An instant later his pretty sister crossed the threshold; and then, after a considerable interval, Mrs Miller slowly advanced.

'I know you!' said Randolph.

'I'm sure you know a great many things,' exclaimed Winterbourne, taking him by the hand. 'How is your education coming on?'

Daisy was exchanging greetings very prettily with her hostess; but when she heard Winterbourne's voice she quickly turned her head. 'Well, I declare!' she said.

'I told you I should come, you know,' Winterbourne rejoined, smiling.

'Well – I didn't believe it,' said Miss Daisy.

'I am much obliged to you,' laughed the young man.

'You might have come to see me!' said Daisy.

'I arrived only yesterday.'

'I don't believe that!' the young girl declared.

Winterbourne turned with a protesting smile to her mother; but this lady evaded his glance, and seating herself, fixed her eyes upon her son. 'We've got a bigger place than this,' said Randolph. 'It's all gold on the walls.'

Mrs Miller turned uneasily in her chair. 'I told you if I were to bring you, you would say something!' she murmured.

'I told *you*!' Randolph exclaimed. 'I tell *you*, sir!' he added jocosely, giving Winterbourne a thump on the knee. 'It *is* bigger, too!'

Daisy had entered upon a lively conversation with her hostess; Winterbourne judged it becoming to address a few words to her mother. 'I hope you have been well since we parted at Vevey,' he said.

Mrs Miller now certainly looked at him – at his chin. 'Not very well, sir,' she answered.

'She's got the dyspepsia,' said Randolph. 'I've got it too. Father's got it. I've got it worst!'

This announcement, instead of embarrassing Mrs Miller, seemed to relieve her. 'I suffer from the liver,' she said. 'I think it's this climate; it's less bracing than Schenectady, especially in the winter season. I don't know whether you know we reside at Schenectady. I was saying to Daisy that I certainly hadn't found anyone like Dr Davis, and I didn't believe I should. Oh, at Schenectady, he stands first; they think everything of him. He has so much to do, and yet there was nothing he wouldn't do for me. He said he never saw anything like my dyspepsia, but he was bound to cure it. I'm sure there was nothing he wouldn't try. He was just going to try something new when we came off. Mr Miller wanted Daisy to see Europe for herself. But I wrote to Mr Miller that it seems as if I couldn't get on without Dr Davis. At Schenectady he stands at the very top; and there's a great deal of sickness there, too. It affects my sleep.'

Winterbourne had a good deal of pathological gossip with Dr Davis's patient, during which Daisy chattered unremittingly to her own companion. The young man asked Mrs Miller how she was pleased with Rome. 'Well, I must say I am disappointed,' she answered. 'We had heard so much about it; I suppose we had heard too much. But we couldn't help that. We had been led to expect something different.'

'Ah, wait a little, and you will become very fond of it,' said Winterbourne.

'I hate it worse and worse every day!' cried Randolph.

'You are like the infant Hannibal,' said Winterbourne.

'No I ain't!' Randolph declared, at a venture.

'You are not much like an infant,' said his mother. 'But we have seen places,' she resumed, 'that I should put a long way before Rome.' And in reply to Winterbourne's interrogation, 'There's Zürich,' she observed; 'I think Zürich is lovely; and we hadn't heard half so much about it.'

'The best place we've seen is the *City of Richmond*!' said Randolph.

'He means the ship,' his mother explained. 'We crossed in that ship. Randolph had a good time on the *City of Richmond*.'

'It's the best place I've seen,' the child repeated. 'Only it was turned the wrong way.'

'Well, we've got to turn the right way some time,' said Mrs Miller, with a little laugh. Winterbourne expressed the hope that her daughter at least found some gratification in Rome, and she declared that Daisy was quite carried away. 'It's on account of the society – the society's splendid. She goes round everywhere; she has made a great number of acquaintances. Of course she goes round more than I do. I must say they have been sociable; they have taken her right in. And then she knows a great many gentlemen. Oh, she thinks there's nothing like Rome. Of course, it's a great deal pleasanter for a young lady if she knows plenty of gentlemen.'

By this time Daisy had turned her attention again to Winterbourne. 'I've been telling Mrs Walker how mean you were!' the young girl announced.

'And what is the evidence you have offered?' asked Winterbourne, rather annoyed at Miss Miller's want of appreciation of the zeal of an admirer who on his way down to Rome had stopped neither at Bologna nor at Florence, simply because of a certain sentimental impatience. He remembered that a cynical compatriot had once told him that American women – the pretty ones, and this gave a largeness to the axiom – were at once the most exacting in the world and the least endowed with a sense of indebtedness.

'Why, you were awfully mean at Vevey,' said Daisy, 'you wouldn't do anything. You wouldn't stay there when I asked you.'

'My dearest young lady,' cried Winterbourne, with eloquence, 'have I come all the way to Rome to encounter your reproaches?'

'Just hear him say that!' said Daisy to her hostess, giving a twist to a bow on this lady's dress. 'Did you ever hear anything so quaint?'

'So quaint, my dear?' murmured Mrs Walker, in the tone of a partisan of Winterbourne.

'Well, I don't know,' said Daisy, fingering Mrs Walker's ribbons. 'Mrs Walker, I want to tell you something.'

'Motherr,' interposed Randolph, with his rough ends to his words, 'I tell you you've got to go. Eugenio'll raise something!'

'I'm not afraid of Eugenio,' said Daisy, with a toss of her head. 'Look here, Mrs Walker,' she went on, ' you know I'm coming to your party.'

'I am delighted to hear it.'

'I've got a lovely dress.'

'I am very sure of that.'

'But I want to ask a favour – permission to bring a friend.'

'I shall be happy to see any of your friends,' said Mrs Walker, turning with a smile to Mrs Miller.

'Oh, they are not my friends,' answered Daisy's mamma, smiling shyly, in her own fashion. 'I never spoke to them!'

'It's an intimate friend of mine – Mr Giovanelli,' said Daisy, without a tremor in her clear little voice or a shadow in her brilliant little face.

Mrs Walker was silent a moment, she gave a rapid glance at Winterbourne. 'I shall be glad to see Mr Giovanelli,' she then said.

'He's an Italian,' Daisy pursued, with the prettiest serenity. 'He's a great friend of mine – he's the handsomest man in the world – except Mr Winterbourne! He knows plenty of Italians, but he wants to know some Americans. He thinks ever so much of Americans. He's tremendously clever. He's perfectly lovely!'

It was settled that this brilliant personage should be brought to Mrs Walker's party, and then Mrs Miller prepared to take her leave. 'I guess we'll go back to the hotel,' she said.

'You may go back to the hotel, mother, but I'm going to take a walk,' said Daisy.

'She's going to walk with Mr Giovanelli,' Randolph proclaimed.

'I am going to the Pincio,'[1] said Daisy, smiling.

'Alone, my dear – at this hour?' Mrs Walker asked. The afternoon was drawing to a close – it was the hour for the throng of carriages and of contemplative pedestrians. 'I don't think it's safe, my dear,' said Mrs Walker.

'Neither do I,' subjoined Mrs Miller. 'You'll get the fever as sure as you live. Remember what Dr Davis told you!'

'Give her some medicine before she goes,' said Randolph.

The company had risen to its feet; Daisy, still showing her pretty teeth, bent over and kissed her hostess. 'Mrs Walker, you are too perfect,' she said. 'I'm not going alone; I am going to meet a friend.'

'Your friend won't keep you from getting the fever,' Mrs Miller observed.

'Is it Mr Giovanelli?' asked the hostess.

Winterbourne was watching the young girl; at this question his attention quickened. She stood there smiling and smoothing her bonnet-ribbons; she glanced at Winterbourne. Then, while she glanced and smiled, she answered without a shade of hesitation, 'Mr Giovanelli – the beautiful Giovanelli.'

'My dear young friend,' said Mrs Walker, taking her hand, pleadingly, 'don't walk off to the Pincio at this hour to meet a beautiful Italian.'

'Well, he speaks English,' said Mrs Miller.

1: the public gardens in central Rome, a fashionable place to walk or drive.

'Gracious me!' Daisy exclaimed, 'I don't want to do anything improper. There's a way to settle it.' She continued to glance at Winterbourne. 'The Pincio is only a hundred yards distant, and if Mr Winterbourne were as polite as he pretends he would offer to walk with me!'

Winterbourne's politeness hastened to affirm himself, and the young girl gave him gracious leave to accompany her. They passed downstairs before her mother, and at the door Winterbourne perceived Mrs Miller's carriage drawn up, with the ornamental courier whose acquaintance he had made at Vevey seated within. 'Good-bye, Eugenio!' cried Daisy, 'I'm going to take a walk.' The distance from the Via Gregoriana to the beautiful garden at the other end of the Pincian Hill is, in fact, rapidly traversed. As the day was splendid, however, and the concourse of vehicles, walkers, and loungers numerous, the young Americans found their progress much delayed. This fact was highly agreeable to Winterbourne, in spite of his consciousness of his singular situation. The slow-moving, idly gazing Roman crowd bestowed much attention upon the extremely pretty young foreign lady who was passing through it upon his arm; and he wondered what on earth had been in Daisy's mind when she proposed to expose herself unattended, to its appreciation. His own mission, to her sense, apparently, was to consign her to the hands of Mr Giovanelli; but Winterbourne, at once annoyed and gratified, resolved that he would do no such thing.

'Why haven't you been to see me?' asked Daisy. 'You can't get out of that.'

'I have had the honour of telling you that I have only just stepped out of the train.'

'You must have stayed in the train a good while after it stopped!' cried the young girl, with her little laugh. 'I suppose you were asleep. You have had time to go to see Mrs Walker.'

'I knew Mrs Walker – ' Winterbourne began to explain.

'I knew you knew her. You knew her at Geneva. She told me so. Well, you knew me at Vevey. That's just as good. So you ought to have come.' She asked him no other question than this; she began to prattle about her own affairs. 'We've got splendid rooms at the hotel; Eugenio says they're the best rooms in Rome. We are going to stay all winter – if we don't die of the fever; and I guess we'll stay then. It's a great deal nicer than I thought; I thought it would be fearfully quiet; I was sure it would be awfully poky. I was sure we should be going round all the time with one of those dreadful old men that explain about the pictures and things. But we only had about a week of that, and now I'm enjoying myself. I know ever so many people, and they are all so charming. The society's extremely select. There are all kinds – English, and Germans, and Italians. I think I like the English best. I like their style of conversation. But there are some lovely Americans. I never saw anything so hospitable. There's something or other every day. There's not much dancing; but I must say I never thought dancing was everything. I was always fond of conversation. I guess I shall have plenty at Mrs Walker's – her rooms are so small.' When they had passed the gate of the Pincian Gardens, Miss Miller began to wonder where Mr Giovanelli might be. 'We had better go straight to that place in front,' she said, 'where you look at the view.'

'I certainly shall not help you to find him,' Winterbourne declared.

'Then I shall find him without you,' said Miss Daisy.

'You certainly won't leave me!' cried Winterbourne.

She burst into her little laugh. 'Are you afraid you'll get lost – or run over? But there's Giovanelli, leaning against that tree. He's staring at the women in the carriages: did you ever see anything so cool?'

Winterbourne perceived at some distance a little man standing with folded arms, nursing his cane. He had a handsome face, an artfully poised hat, a glass in one eye, and a nosegay in his button-hole. Winterbourne looked at him a moment and then said, 'Do you mean to speak to that man?'

'Do I mean to speak to him? Why, you don't suppose I mean to communicate by signs?'

'Pray understand, then,' said Winterbourne, 'that I intend to remain with you.'

Daisy stopped and looked at him, without a sign of troubled consciousness in her face; with nothing but the presence of her charming eyes and her happy dimples. 'Well, she's a cool one!' thought the young man.

'I don't like the way you say that,' said Daisy. 'It's too imperious.'

'I beg your pardon if I say it wrong. The main point is to give you an idea of my meaning.'

The young girl looked at him more gravely, but with eyes that were prettier than ever. 'I have never allowed a gentleman to dictate to me, or to interfere with anything I do.'

'I think you have made a mistake,' said Winterbourne. 'You should sometimes listen to a gentleman – the right one.'

Daisy began to laugh again, 'I do nothing but listen to gentlemen!' she exclaimed. 'Tell me if Mr Giovanelli is the right one?'

The gentleman with the nosegay in his bosom had now perceived our two friends, and was approaching the young girl with obsequious rapidity. He bowed to Winterbourne as well as to the latter's companion; he had a brilliant smile, an intelligent eye; Winterbourne thought him not a bad-looking fellow. But he nevertheless said to Daisy – 'No, he's not the right one.'

Daisy evidently had a natural talent for performing introductions; she mentioned the name of each of her companions to the other. She strolled along with one of them on each side of her; Mr Giovanelli, who spoke English very cleverly – Winterbourne afterwards learned that he had practised the idiom upon a great many American heiresses – addressed to her a great deal of very polite nonsense; he was extremely urbane, and the young American, who said nothing, reflected upon that profundity of Italian cleverness which enables people to appear more gracious in proportion as they are more acutely disappointed. Giovanelli, of course, had counted upon something more intimate; he had not bargained for a party of three. But he kept his temper in a manner which suggested far-stretching intentions. Winterbourne flattered himself that he had taken his measure. 'He is not a gentleman,' said the young American; 'he is only a clever imitation of one. He is a music-master, or a penny-a-liner, or a third-rate artist. Damm his good looks!' Mr Giovanelli had certainly a very pretty face; but Winterbourne felt a superior indignation at his own lovely fellow-countrywoman's not knowing the difference between a spurious gentleman and a real one. Giovanelli chattered and jested and made himself wonderfully agreeable. It was true that if he was an imitation the imitation was very skilful. 'Nevertheless,' Winterbourne said to himself, 'a nice girl ought to know!' And then he came back to the question whether this was in fact a nice girl. Would a nice girl – even allowing for her being a little American flirt – make a rendezvous with a presumably low-lived foreigner? The rendezvous in this case, indeed, had been in broad daylight, and in the most crowded corner of Rome; but was it not impossible to regard the choice of these circumstances as a proof of extreme cynicism? Singular though it may seem, Winterbourne was vexed that the young girl, in joining her *amoroso*, should not appear more impatient of his own company, and he was vexed because of his inclination. It was impossible to regard her as a perfectly well-conducted young lady; she was wanting in a certain indispensable delicacy. It would therefore simplify matters greatly to be able to treat her as the object of one of those sentiments which are called by romancers 'lawless passions'. That she should seem to wish to get rid of him would help him to think more lightly of her, and to be able to think more lightly of her would make her much less perplexing. But Daisy, on this occasion, continued to present herself as an inscrutable combination of audacity and innocence.

She had been walking some quarter of an hour, attended by her two cavaliers, and responding in a tone of very childish gaiety, as it seemed to Winterbourne, to the pretty speeches of Mr Giovanelli, when a carriage that had detached itself from the revolving train drew up beside the path. At the same moment Winterbourne perceived that his friend Mrs Walker – the lady whose house he had lately left – was seated in the vehicle and was beckoning to him. Leaving Miss Miller's side, he hastened to obey her summons. Mrs Walker was flushed; she wore an excited air. 'It is really too dreadful,' she said. 'That girl must not do this sort of thing. She must not walk here with you two men. Fifty people have noticed her.'

Winterbourne raised his eyebrows. 'I think it's a pity to make too much fuss of it.'

'It's a pity to let the girl ruin herself!'

'She is very innocent,' said Winterbourne.

'She's very crazy!' cried Mrs Walker. 'Did you ever see anything so imbecile as her mother? After you had all left me, just now, I could not sit still for thinking of it. It seemed too pitiful, not even to attempt to save her. I ordered the carriage and put on my bonnet, and came here as quickly as possible. Thank heaven I have found you!'

'What do you propose to do with us?' asked Winterbourne, smiling.

'To ask her to get in, to drive her about here for half an hour, so that the world may see she is not running absolutely wild, and then to take her safely home.'

'I don't think it's a very happy thought,' said Winterbourne; 'but you can try.'

Mrs Walker tried. The young man went in pursuit of Miss Miller, who had simply nodded and smiled at his interlocutrix in the carriage and had gone her way with her own companion. Daisy, on learning that Mrs Walker wished to speak to her, retraced her steps in a perfect good grace and with Mr Giovanelli at her side. She declared that she was delighted to have a chance to present this gentleman to Mrs Walker. She immediately achieved the introduction, and declared that she had never in her life seen anything so lovely as Mrs Walker's carriage-rug.

'I am glad you admire it,' said this lady, smiling sweetly. 'Will you get in and let me put it over you?'

'Oh, no, thank you,' said Daisy. 'I shall admire it much more as I see you driving round with it.'

'Do get in and drive with me,' said Mrs Walker.

'That would be charming, but it's so enchanting just as I am!' and Daisy gave a brilliant glance at the gentlemen on either side of her.

'It may be enchanting, dear child, but it is not the custom here,' urged Mrs Walker, learning forward in her victoria with her hands devoutly clasped.

'Well it ought to be, then!' said Daisy. 'If I didn't walk I should expire.'

'You should walk with your mother, dear,' cried the lady from Geneva, losing patience.

'With my mother dear!' exclaimed the young girl. Winterbourne saw that she scented interference. 'My mother never walked ten steps in her life. And then, you know,' she added with a laugh, 'I am more than five years old.'

'You are old enough to be more reasonable. You are old enough, dear Miss Miller, to be talked about.'

Daisy looked at Mrs Walker, smiling intensely. 'Talked about? What do you mean!'

'Come into my carriage and I will tell you.'

Daisy turned her quickened glance again from one of the gentlemen beside her to the other. Mr Giovanelli was bowing to and fro, rubbing down his gloves and laughing very agreeably; Winterbourne thought it a most unpleasant scene. 'I don't think I want to know what you mean,' said Daisy presently. 'I don't think I should like it.'

Winterbourne wished that Mrs Walker would tuck in her carriage-rug and drive away; but this lady did not enjoy being defied, as she afterwards told him. 'Should you prefer being thought a very reckless girl?' she demanded.

'Gracious me!' exclaimed Daisy. She looked again at Mr Giovanelli, then she turned to Winterbourne. There was a little pink flush in her cheek; she was tremendously pretty. 'Does Mr Winterbourne think,' she asked slowly, smiling, throwing back her head and glancing at him from head to foot, 'that – to save my reputation – I ought to get into the carriage?'

Winterbourne coloured; for an instant he hesitated greatly. It seemed so strange to hear her speak that way of her 'reputation'. But he himself, in fact, must speak in accordance with gallantry. The finest gallantry, here, was simply to tell her the truth; and the truth, for Winterbourne, as the few indications I have been able to give had made him known to the reader, was that Daisy Miller should take Mrs Walker's advice. He looked at her exquisite prettiness; and then he said very gently, 'I think you should get into the carriage.'

Daisy gave a violent laugh. 'I never heard anything so stiff! If this is improper, Mrs Walker,' she pursued, 'then I am all improper, and you must give me up. Good-bye; I hope you'll have a lovely ride!' and, with Mr Giovanelli, who made a triumphantly obsequious salute, she turned away.

Mrs Walker sat looking after her, and there were tears in Mrs Walker's eyes. 'Get in here, sir,' she said to Winterbourne, indicating the place beside her. The young man answered that he felt bound to accompany Miss Miller; whereupon Mrs Walker declared that if he refused her this favour she would never speak to him again. She was evidently in earnest. Winterbourne overtook Daisy and her companion and, offering the young girl his hand, told her that Mrs Walker had made an imperious claim upon his society. He expected that in answer she would say something rather free, something to commit herself still farther to that 'recklessness' from which Mrs Walker had so charitably endeavoured to dissuade her. But she only shook his hand, hardly looking at him, while Mr Giovanelli bade him farewell with a too emphatic flourish of the hat.

Winterbourne was not in the best possible humour as he took his seat in Mrs Walker's victoria. 'That was not clever of you,' he said candidly, while the vehicle mingled again with the throng of carriages.

'In such a case,' his companion answered, 'I don't wish to be clever, I wish to be *earnest*!'

'Well, your earnestness has only offended her and put her off.'

'It has happened very well,' said Mrs Walker. 'If she is so perfectly determined to compromise herself, the sooner one knows it the better; one can act accordingly.'

'I suspect she meant no harm,' Winterbourne rejoined.

'So I thought a month ago. But she has been going too far.'

'What has she been doing?'

'Everything that is not done here. Flirting with any man she could pick up; sitting in corners with mysterious Italians; dancing all the evening with the same partners; receiving visitors at eleven o'clock at night. Her mother goes away when visitors come.'

'But her brother,' said Winterbourne, laughing, 'sits up till midnight.'

'He must be edified by what he sees. I'm told that at their hotel everyone is talking about her, and that a smile goes round among the servants when a gentleman comes and asks for Miss Miller.'

'The servants should be hanged!' said Winterbourne angrily. 'The poor girl's only fault,' he presently added, 'is that she is very uncultivated.'

'She is naturally indelicate,' Mrs Walker declared. 'Take that example this morning. How long had you known her at Vevey?'

'A couple of days.'

'Fancy, then, her making it a personal matter that you should have left the place!'

Winterbourne was silent for some moments; then he said, 'I suspect, Mrs Walker, that you and I have lived too long at Geneva!' And he added a request that she should inform him with what particular design she had made him enter her carriage.

'I wished to beg you to cease your relations with Miss Miller – not to flirt with her – to give her no further opportunity to expose herself – to let her alone, in short.'

'I'm afraid I can't do that,' said Winterbourne. 'I like her extremely.'

'All the more reason that you shouldn't help her to make a scandal.'

'There shall be nothing scandalous in my attentions to her.'

'There certainly will be in the way she takes them. But I have said what I had on my conscience.' Mrs Walker pursued. 'If you wish to rejoin the young lady I will put you down. Here, by the way, you have a chance.'

The carriage was traversing that part of the Pincian Garden which overhangs the wall of Rome and overlooks the beautiful Villa Borghese. It is bordered by a large parapet, near which there are several seats. One of the seats, at a distance, was occupied by a gentleman and a lady, towards whom Mrs Walker gave a toss of her head. At the same moment these persons rose and walked towards the parapet. Winterbourne had asked the coachman to stop; he now descended from the carriage. His companion looked at him a moment in silence; then, while he raised his hat, she drove majestically away. Winterbourne stood there; he had turned his eyes towards Daisy and her cavalier. They evidently saw no one; they were too deeply occupied with each other. When they reached the low garden-wall they stood a moment looking off at the great flat-topped pine-clusters of the Villa Borghese; then Giovanelli seated himself familiarly upon the broad edge of the wall. The western sun in the opposite sky sent out a brilliant shaft through a couple of cloud-bars; whereupon Daisy's companion took her parasol out of her hands and opened it. She came a little nearer and he held the parasol over her; then, still holding it, he let it rest upon her shoulder, so that both their heads were hidden from Winterbourne. This young man lingered a moment, then he began to walk. But he walked – not towards the couple with the parasol; towards the residence of his aunt, Mrs Costello.

4

He flattered himself on the following day that there was no smiling among the servants when he, at least, asked for Mrs Miller at her hotel. This lady and her daughter, however, were not at home; and on the next day, after repeating his visit, Winterbourne again had the misfortune not to find them. Mrs Walker's party took place on the evening of the third day, and in spite of the frigidity of his last interview with the hostess, Winterbourne was among the guests. Mrs Walker was one of those American ladies who, while residing abroad, makes a point, in their own phrase, of studying European society; and she had on this occasion collected several specimens of her diversely born fellow-mortals to serve, as it were, as text-books. When Winterbourne arrived, Daisy Miller was not there; but in a few moments he saw her mother come in alone, very shyly and ruefully. Mrs Miller's hair, above her exposed-looking temples, was more frizzed than ever. As she approached Mrs Walker, Winterbourne also drew near.

'You see I've come all alone,' said poor Mrs Miller. 'I'm so frightened; I don't know what to do; it's the first time I've ever been to a party alone – especially in this country. I wanted to bring Randolph or Eugenio, or someone, but Daisy just pushed me off by myself. I ain't used to going round alone.'

'And does not your daughter intend to favour us with her society?' demanded Mrs Walker, impressively.

'Well, Daisy's all dressed,' said Mrs Miller, with that accent of the dispassionate, if not of the philosophic, historian with which she always recorded the current incidents of her daughter's career. 'She's got dressed on purpose before dinner. But she's got a friend of hers there; that gentleman – the Italian – that she wanted to bring. They've got going at the piano; it seems as if they couldn't leave off. Mr Giovanelli sings splendidly. But I guess they'll come before very long,' concluded Mrs Miller hopefully.

'I'm sorry she should come – in that way,' said Mrs Walker.

'Well, I told her that there was no use in her getting dressed before dinner if she was going to wait three hours,' responded Daisy's mamma. 'I didn't see the use of her putting on such a dress as that to sit round with Mr Giovanelli.'

'That is most horrible!' said Mrs Walker, turning away and addressing herself to Winterbourne. '*Elle s'affiche.*[1] It's her revenge for my having ventured to remonstrate with her. When she comes I shall not speak to her.'

Daisy came after eleven o'clock, but she was not, on such an occasion, a young lady to wait to be spoken to. She rustled forward in radiant loveliness, smiling and chattering, carrying a large bouquet and attended by Mr Giovanelli. Everyone stopped talking and turned and looked at her. She came straight to Mrs Walker. 'I'm afraid you thought I never was coming, so I sent my mother off to tell you. I wanted to make Mr Giovanelli practise some things before he came; you know he sings beautifully, and I want you to ask him to sing. This is Mr Giovanelli; you know I introduced him to you; he's got the most lovely voice and he knows the most charming set of songs. I made him go over them this evening, on purpose; we had the greatest time at the hotel.' Of all this Daisy delivered herself with the sweetest, brightest audibleness, looking now at her hostess and now round the room, while she gave a series of little pats, round her shoulders, to the edges of her dress. 'Is there anyone I know?' she asked.

'I think everyone knows you!' said Mrs Walker pregnantly, and she gave a very cursory greeting to Mr Giovanelli. This gentleman bore himself gallantly. He smiled and bowed and showed his white teeth, he curled his moustaches and rolled his eyes, and performed all the proper functions of a handsome Italian at an evening party. He sang, very prettily, half a dozen songs, though Mrs Walker afterwards declared that she had been quite unable to find out who asked him. It was apparently not Daisy who had given him his orders. Daisy sat at a distance from the piano, and though she had publicly, as it were, professed a high admiration for his singing, talked, not inaudibly, while it was going on.

'It's a pity these rooms are so small; we can't dance,' she said to Winterbourne, as if she had seen him five minutes before.

'I am not sorry we can't dance,' Winterbourne answered; 'I don't dance.'

1: to show off, and to seek notoriety.

'Of course you don't dance; you're too stiff,' said Miss Daisy. 'I hope you enjoyed your drive with Mrs Walker.'

'No I didn't enjoy it; I preferred walking with you.'

'We paired off, that was much better,' said Daisy. 'But did you ever hear anything so cool as Mrs Walker's wanting me to get into her carriage and drop poor Mr Giovanelli; and under the pretext that it was proper? People have different ideas! It would have been most unkind; he had been talking about that walk for ten days.'

'He should not have talked about it at all,' said Winterbourne; 'he would never have proposed to a young lady of this country to walk about the streets with him.'

'About the streets?' cried Daisy, with her pretty stare. 'Where then would he have proposed to her to walk? The Pincio is not the streets, either; and I, thank goodness, am not a young lady of this country. The young ladies of this country have a dreadfully poky time of it, so far as I can learn; I don't see why I should change my habits for *them*.'

'I am afraid your habits are those of a flirt,' said Winterbourne gravely.

'Of course they are,' she cried, giving him her little smiling stare again. 'I'm a fearful, frightful flirt! Did you ever hear of a nice girl that was not? But I suppose you will tell me now that I am not a nice girl.'

'You're a very nice girl, but I wish you would flirt with me, and me only,' said Winterbourne.

'Ah! Thank you, thank you very much; you are the last man I should think of flirting with. As I have had the pleasure of informing you, you are too stiff.'

'You say that too often,' said Winterbourne.

Daisy gave a delighted laugh. 'If I could have the sweet hope of making you angry, I would say it again.'

'Don't do that; when I am angry I'm stiffer than ever. But if you won't flirt with me, do cease at least to flirt with your friend at the piano; they don't understand that sort of thing here.'

'I thought they understood nothing else!' exclaimed Daisy.

'Not in young unmarried women.'

'It seems to me much more proper in young unmarried women than in old married ones,' Daisy declared.

'Well,' said Winterbourne, 'when you deal with natives you must go by the custom of the place. Flirting is a purely American custom; it doesn't exist here. So when you show yourself in public with Mr Giovanelli and without your mother – '

'Gracious! Poor mother!' interposed Daisy.

'Though you may be flirting, Mr Giovanelli is not; he means something else.'

'He isn't preaching, at any rate,' said Daisy with vivacity. 'And if you want very much to know, we are neither of us flirting; we are too good friends for that; we are very intimate friends.'

'Ah,' rejoined Winterbourne, 'if you are in love with each other it is another affair.'

She had allowed him up to this point to talk so frankly that he had no expectation of shocking her by this ejaculation; but she immediately got up, blushing visibly, and leaving him to exclaim mentally that little American flirts were the queerest creatures in the world. 'Mr Giovanelli, at least,' she said, giving her interlocutor a single glance, 'never says such very disagreeable things to me.'

Winterbourne was bewildered; he stood staring. Mr Giovanelli had finished singing; he left the piano and came over to Daisy. 'Won't you come into the other room and have some tea?' he asked, bending before her with his decorative smile.

Daisy turned to Winterbourne, beginning to smile again. He was still more perplexed, for this inconsequent smile made nothing clear, though it seemed to prove, indeed, that she had a sweetness and softness that reverted instinctively to the pardon of offences. 'It has never occurred to Mr Winterbourne to offer me any tea,' she said, with her little tormenting manner.

'I have offered you advice,' Winterbourne rejoined.

'I prefer weak tea!' cried Daisy, and she went off with the brilliant Giovanelli. She sat with him in the adjoining room, in the embrasure of the window, for the rest of the evening. There was an interesting performance at the piano, but neither of these young people gave heed to it. When Daisy came to take leave of Mrs Walker, this lady conscientiously repaired the weakness of which she had been guilty at the moment of the young girl's arrival. She turned her back straight upon Miss Miller and left her to depart with what grace she might. Winterbourne was standing near the door; he saw it all. Daisy turned very pale and looked at her mother, but Mrs Miller was humbly unconscious of any violation of the usual social forms. She appeared, indeed, to have felt an incongruous impulse to draw attention to her own striking observance of them. 'Goodnight, Mrs Walker,' she said; 'we've had a beautiful evening. You see if I let Daisy come to parties without me. I don't want her to go away without me.' Daisy turned away, looking with a pale, grave face at the circle near the door; Winterbourne saw that, for the first moment, she was too much shocked and puzzled even for indignation. He on his side was greatly touched.

'That was very cruel,' he said to Mrs Walker.

'She never enters my drawing-room again,' replied his hostess.

Since Winterbourne was not to meet her in Mrs Walker's drawing-room, he went as often as possible to Mrs Miller's hotel. The ladies were rarely at home, but when he found them the devoted Giovanelli was always present. Very often the polished little Roman was in the drawing-room with Daisy alone, Mrs Miller being apparently constantly of the opinion that discretion is the better part of surveillance. Winterbourne noted, at first with surprise, that Daisy on these occasions was never embarrassed or annoyed by his own entrance; but he very presently began to feel that she had no more surprises for him; the unexpected in her behaviour was the only thing to expect. She showed no displeasure in her *tête-à-tête* with Giovanelli being interrupted; she could chatter as freshly and freely with two gentlemen as with one; there was always, in her conversation, the same odd mixture of audacity and puerility. Winterbourne remarked to himself that if she was seriously interested in Giovanelli it was very singular that she should not take more trouble to preserve the sanctity of their interviews, and he liked her the more for her innocent-looking indifference and her apparently inexhaustible good humour. He could hardly have said why, but she seemed to him a girl who would never be jealous. At the risk of exciting a somewhat derisive smile on the reader's part, I may affirm that with regard to the women who had hitherto interested him it very often seemed to Winterbourne among the possibilities that, given certain contingencies, he should be afraid – literally afraid – of these ladies. He had a pleasant sense that he should never be afraid of Daisy Miller. It must be added that this sentiment was not altogether flattering to Daisy; it was part of his conviction, or rather his apprehension, that she would prove a very light young person.

But she was evidently very much interested in Giovanelli. She looked at him whenever he spoke; she was perpetually telling him to do this and to do that; she was constantly 'chaffing' and abusing him. She appeared completely to have forgotten that Winterbourne had said anything to displease her at Mrs Walker's little party. One Sunday afternoon, having gone to St Peter's with his aunt, Winterbourne perceived Daisy strolling about the great church in company with the inevitable Giovanelli. Presently he pointed out the young girl and her cavalier to Mrs Costello. This lady looked at them a moment through her eyeglass, and then she said:

'That's what makes you so pensive in these days, eh?'

'I had not the least idea I was pensive,' said the young man.

'You are very preoccupied, you are thinking of something.'

'And what is it,' he asked, 'that you accuse me of thinking of?'

'Of that young lady's, Miss Baker's, Miss Chandler's – what's her name? – Miss Miller's intrigue with that little barber's block.'

'Do you call it an intrigue,' Winterbourne asked – 'an affair that goes on with such peculiar publicity?'

'That's their folly,' said Mrs Costello, 'it's not their merit.'

'No,' rejoined Winterbourne, with something of that pensiveness to which his aunt had alluded. 'I don't believe that there is anything to be called an intrigue.'

'I have heard a dozen people speak of it; they say she is quite carried away by him.'

'They are certainly very intimate,' said Winterbourne.

Mrs Costello inspected the young couple again with her optical instrument. 'He is very handsome. One easily sees how it is. She thinks him the most elegant man in the world, the finest gentleman. She has never seen anything like him; he is better even than the courier. It was the courier probably who introduced him, and if he succeeds in marrying the young lady, the courier will come in for a magnificent commission.'

'I don't believe she thinks of marrying him,' said Winterbourne, 'and I don't believe he hopes to marry her.'

'You may be very sure she thinks of nothing. She goes on from day to day, from hour to hour, as they did in the Golden Age. I can imagine nothing more vulgar. And at the same time,' added Mrs Costello, 'depend upon it that she may tell you any moment that she is "engaged".'

'I think that is more than Giovanelli expects,' said Winterbourne.

'Who is Giovanelli?'

'The little Italian. I have asked questions about him and learned something. He is apparently a perfectly respectable little man. I believe he is in a small way a *cavaliere avvocato*.[1] But he doesn't move in what are called the first circles. I think it is really not absolutely impossible that the courier introduced him. He is evidently immensely charmed with Miss Miller. If she thinks him the finest gentleman in the world, he, on his side, has never found himself in personal contact with such splendour, such opulence, such expensiveness, as this young lady's. And then she must seem to him wonderfully pretty and interesting. I rather doubt whether he dreams of marrying her. That must appear to him too impossible a piece of luck. He has nothing but his handsome face to offer, and there is a substantial Mr Miller in that mysterious land of dollars. Giovanelli knows that he hasn't a title to offer. If he were only a count or a *marchese*! He must wonder at his luck at the way they have taken him up.'

'He accounts for it by his handsome face, and thinks Miss Miller a young lady *qui se passe ses fantaisies*!'[2] said Mrs Costello.

'It is very true,' Winterbourne pursued, 'that Daisy and her mamma have not yet risen to that stage of – what shall I call it? – of culture, at which the idea of catching a count or a *marchese* begins. I believe that they are intellectually incapable of the conception.'

'Ah! But the *cavaliere* can't believe it,' said Mrs Costello.

Of the observation excited by Daisy's 'intrigue', Winterbourne gathered that day at St Peter's sufficient evidence. A dozen of the American colonists in Rome came to talk with Mrs Costello, who sat on a little portable stool at the base of one of the great pilasters. The vesper-service was going forward in splendid chants and organ-tones in the adjacent choir, and meanwhile, between Mrs Costello and her friends, there was a great deal said about poor little Miss Miller's going really 'too far'. Winterbourne was not pleased with what he heard; but when, coming out upon the great steps of the church, he saw Daisy, who had emerged before him, get into an open cab with her accomplice and roll away through the cynical streets of Rome, he could not deny himself that she was going very far indeed. He felt very sorry for her – not exactly that he believed that she had completely lost her head, but because it was painful to hear so much that was pretty and undefended and natural assigned to a vulgar place among the categories of disorder. He made an attempt after this to give a hint to Mrs Miller. He met one day in the Corso a friend – a tourist like himself – who had just come out of the Doria Palace, where he had been walking through the beautiful gallery. His friend talked for a moment about the superb portrait of Innocent X by Velazquez, which hangs in one of the cabinets of the palace, and then said, 'And in the same cabinet, by the way, I had the pleasure of contemplating a picture of a different kind – that pretty American girl whom you pointed out to me last week.' In answer to Winterbourne's inquiries, his friend narrated that the pretty American girl – prettier than ever – was seated with a companion in the secluded nook in which the great papal portrait is enshrined.

'Who was her companion?' asked Winterbourne.

1: a gentleman lawyer.   2: she indulges her fantasies.

'A little Italian with a bouquet in his buttonhole. The girl is delightfully pretty, but I thought I understood from you the other day that she was a young lady *du meilleur monde.*'

'So she is!' answered Winterbourne; and having assured himself that his informant had seen Daisy and her companion but five minutes before, he jumped into a cab and went to call on Mrs Miller. She was at home; but she apologised to him for receiving him in Daisy's absence.

'She's gone out somewhere with Mr Giovanelli,' said Mrs Miller. 'She's always going round with Mr Giovanelli.'

'I have noticed that they are very intimate,' Winterbourne observed.

'Oh! It seems as if they couldn't live without each other!' said Mrs Miller. 'Well, he's a real gentleman, anyhow. I keep telling Daisy she's engaged!'

'And what does Daisy say?'

'Oh, she says she isn't engaged. But she might as well be!' this impartial parent resumed. 'She goes on as if she was. But I've made Mr Giovanelli promise to tell me, if *she* doesn't. I should want to write to Mr Miller about it – shouldn't you?'

Winterbourne replied that he certainly should; and the state of mind of Daisy's mamma struck him as so unprecedented in the annals of parental vigilance that he gave up as utterly irrelevant the attempt to place her upon her guard.

After this Daisy was never at home, and Winterbourne cased to meet her at the houses of their common acquaintances, because, as he perceived, these shrewd people had quite made up their minds that she was going too far. They ceased to invite her, and they intimated that they desired to express to observant Europeans the great truth that, though Miss Daisy Miller was a young American lady, her behaviour was not representative – was regarded by her compatriots as abnormal. Winterbourne wondered how she felt about all the cold shoulders that were turned towards her, and sometimes it annoyed him to suspect that she did not feel at all. He said to himself that she was too light and childish, too uncultivated and unreasoning, too provincial, to have reflected upon her ostracism or even to have perceived it. Then at other moments he believed that she carried about in her elegant and irresponsible little organism a defiant, passionate, perfectly observant consciousness of the impression she produced. He asked himself whether Daisy's defiance came from the consciousness of innocence or from her being, essentially, a young person of the reckless class. It must be admitted that holding oneself to a belief in Daisy's 'innocence' came to seem to Winterbourne more and more a matter of fine-spun gallantry. As I have already had occasion to relate, he was angry at finding himself reduced to chopping logic about this young lady; he was vexed at his want of instinctive certitude as to how far her eccentricities were generic, national, and how far they were personal. From either view of them he had somehow missed her, and now it was too late. She was 'carried away' by Mr Giovanelli.

A few days after his brief interview with her mother, he encountered her in that beautiful abode of flowering desolation known as the Palace of the Caesars. The early Roman spring had filled the air with bloom and perfume, and the rugged surface of the Palantine was muffled with tender verdure. Daisy was strolling along the top of one of those great mounds of ruin that are embanked with mossy marble and paved with monumental inscriptions. It seemed to him that Rome had never been so lovely as just then. He stood looking off at the enchanting harmony of line and colour that remotely encircles the city, inhaling the softly humid odours and feeling the freshness of the year and the antiquity of the palace reaffirm themselves in mysterious interfusion. It seemed to him also that Daisy had never looked so pretty; but this had been an observation of his whenever he met her. Giovanelli was at her side, and Giovanelli, too, wore an aspect of even unwonted brilliancy.

'Well,' said Daisy, 'I should think you would be lonesome!'

'Lonesome?' asked Winterbourne.

'You are always going round by yourself. Can't you get anyone to walk with you?'

'I am not so fortunate,' said Winterbourne, 'as your companion.'

Giovanelli, from the first, had treated Winterbourne with distinguished politeness; he listened with a deferential air to his remarks; he laughed, punctiliously, at his pleasantries; he seemed disposed to testify to his belief that Winterbourne was a superior young man. He carried himself in no degree like a jealous wooer; he had obviously a great deal of tact; he had no objection to your expecting a little humility of him. It even seemed to Winterbourne at times that Giovanelli would find a certain mental relief in being able to have a private understanding with him – to say to him, as an intelligent man, that, bless you, *he* knew how extraordinary was this young lady, and didn't flatter himself with delusive – or at least *too* delusive – hopes of matrimony and dollars. On this occasion he strolled away from his companion to pluck a sprig of almond blossom, which he carefully arranged in his buttonhole.

'I know why you say that,' said Daisy, watching Giovanelli. 'Because you think I go round too much with *him*!' And she nodded at her attendant.

'Everyone thinks so – if you care to know,' said Winterbourne.

'Of course I care to know!' Daisy exclaimed seriously. 'But I don't believe it. They are only pretending to be shocked. They don't really care a straw what I do. Besides, I don't go round so much.'

'I think you will find they do care. They will show it – disagreeably.'

Daisy looked at him a moment. 'How – disagreeably?'

'Haven't you noticed anything?' Winterbourne asked.

'I have noticed you. But I noticed you were as stiff as an umbrella the first time I saw you.'

'You will find I am not so stiff as several others,' said Winterbourne, smiling.

'How shall I find it?'

'By going to see the others.'

'What will they do to me?'

'They will give you the cold shoulder. Do you know what that means?'

Daisy was looking at him intently; she began to colour. 'Do you mean as Mrs Walker did the other night?'

'Exactly!' said Winterbourne.

She looked away at Giovanelli, who was decorating himself with his almond blossom. Then looking back at Winterbourne – 'I shouldn't think you would let people be so unkind!' she said.

'How can I help it?' he asked.

'I should think you would say something.'

'I do say something'; and he paused a moment. 'I say that your mother tells me that she believes you are engaged.'

'Well, she does,' said Daisy very simply.

Winterbourne began to laugh. 'And does Randolph believe it?' he asked.

'I guess Randolph doesn't believe anything.' said Daisy. Randolph's scepticism excited Winterbourne to further hilarity, and he observed that Giovanelli was coming back to them. Daisy, observing it too, addressed herself to her countryman. 'Since you have mentioned it,' she said, 'I *am* engaged.' ... Winterbourne looked at her; he had stopped laughing. 'You don't believe it!' she added.

He was silent a moment; and then, 'Yes, I believe it!' he said.

'Oh, no, you don't,' she answered. 'Well, then – I am not!'

The young girl and her cicerone[1] were on their way to the gate of the enclosure, so that Winterbourne, who had but lately entered, presently took leave of them. A week afterwards he went to dine at a beautiful villa on the Caelian Hill, and, on arriving, dismissed his hired vehicle. The evening was charming, and he promised himself the satisfaction of walking home beneath the Arch of Constantine and past the vaguely lighted monuments of the Forum. There was a waning moon in the sky, and her radiance was not brilliant, but she was veiled in a thin cloud-curtain which seemed to diffuse and equalize it. When, on his return from the villa (it was eleven o'clock), Winterbourne approached the dusky circle of the Colosseum, it occurred to him, as a lover of the picturesque, that the interior, in the pale moonshine, would be well worth a glance. He turned aside and walked to one of the empty arches, near which, as he observed, an open carriage – one of the little Roman street-cabs – was stationed. Then he passed in among the cavernous shadows of the great structure, and emerged upon the clear and silent arena. The place had never seemed to him more impressive. One half of the gigantic circus was in deep shade; the other was sleeping in the luminous dusk. As he stood there he began to murmur Byron's famous lines, out of *Manfred*;[2] but before he had finished his quotation he remembered that if nocturnal meditations in the Colosseum are recommended by the poets, they are deprecated by the doctors. The historic atmosphere was there, certainly; but the historic atmosphere, scientifically considered, was no better than a villainous miasma.[3] Winterbourne walked to the middle of the arena, to take a more general glance, intending thereafter to make a hasty retreat. The great cross in the centre was covered with shadow; it was only as he drew near it that he made it out distinctly. Then he saw that two persons were stationed upon the low steps which formed its base. One of these was a woman, seated; her companion was standing in front of her.

1: a guide to sightseers, by ironic reference to the fabled erudition of the historian Cicero. 2: *Manfred*, III, iv, 10–40; in which Manfred recollects the Colosseum seen by moonlight. 3: an unwholesome atmosphere.

Presently the sound of the woman's voice came to him distinctly in the warm night air. 'Well, he looks at us as one of the old lions or tigers may have looked at the Christian martyrs!' These were the words he heard, in the familiar accent of Miss Daisy Miller.

'Let us hope he is not very hungry,' responded the ingenious Giovanelli. 'He will have to take me first; you will serve for dessert!'

Winterbourne stopped, with a sort of horror; and it must be added, with a sort of relief. It was as if a sudden illumination had been flashed upon the ambiguity of Daisy's behaviour and the riddle had become easy to read. She was a young lady whom a gentleman need no longer be at pains to respect. He stood there looking at her – looking at her companion, and not reflecting that though he saw them vaguely, he himself must have been more brightly visible. He felt angry with himself that he had bothered so much about the right way of regarding Miss Daisy Miller. Then, as he was going to advance again, he checked himself; not from the fear that he was doing her injustice, but from a sense of danger of appearing unbecomingly exhilarated by this sudden revulsion from cautious criticism. He turned away towards the entrance of the place; but as he did so he heard Daisy speak again.

'Why, it was Mr Winterbourne! He saw me – and he cuts me!'

What a clever little reprobate she was, and how smartly she played an injured innocence! But he wouldn't cut her. Winterbourne came forward again, and went towards the great cross. Daisy had got up; Giovanelli lifted his hat. Winterbourne had now begun to think simply of the craziness, from a sanitary point of view, of a delicate young girl lounging away the evening in this nest of malaria. What if she *were* a clever little reprobate? That was no reason for her dying of the *perniciosa*.[1] 'How long have you been here?' he asked, almost brutally.

Daisy, lovely in the flattering moonlight, looked at him a moment. Then – 'All the evening,' she answered gently. . . . 'I never saw anything so pretty.'

'I am afraid,' said Winterbourne, 'that you will not think Roman fever very pretty. This is the way people catch it. I wonder,' he added, turning to Giovanelli, 'that you, a native Roman, should countenance such a terrible indiscretion.'

'Ah,' said the handsome native, 'for myself, I am not afraid.'

'Neither am I – for you! I am speaking for this young lady.'

Giovanelli lifted his well-shaped eyebrows and showed his brilliant teeth. But he took Winterbourne's rebuke with docility. 'I told the Signorina it was a grave indiscretion; but when was the Signorina ever prudent?'

'I never was sick, and I don't mean to be!' the Signorina declared. 'I don't look like much, but I'm healthy! I was bound to see the Colosseum by moonlight; I shouldn't have wanted to go home without that; and we have had the most beautiful time, haven't we, Mr Giovanelli! If there has been any danger, Eugenio can give me some pills. He has got some splendid pills.'

'I should advise you,' said Winterbourne, 'to drive home as fast as possible and take one!'

'What you say is very wise,' Giovanelli rejoined. 'I will go and make sure the carriage is at hand.' And he went forward rapidly.

1: Roman fever.

Daisy followed with Winterbourne. He kept looking at her; she seemed not in the least embarrassed. Winterbourne said nothing; Daisy chattered about the beauty of the place. 'Well, I *have* seen the Colosseum by moonlight!' she exclaimed. 'That's one good thing.' Then, noticing Winterbourne's silence, she asked him why he didn't speak. He made no answer; he only began to laugh. They passed under one of the dark archways; Giovanelli was in front with the carriage. Here Daisy stopped a moment, looking at the young American, '*Did* you believe I was engaged the other day?' she asked.

'It doesn't matter what I believed the other day,' said Winterbourne, still laughing.

'Well, what do you believe now?'

'I believe that it makes very little difference whether you are engaged or not!'

He felt the young girl's pretty eyes fixed upon him through the thick gloom of the archway; she was apparently going to answer. But Giovanelli hurried her forward. 'Quick, quick,' he said; 'if we get in by midnight we are quite safe.'

Daisy took her seat in the carriage, and the fortunate Italian placed himself beside her. 'Don't forget Eugenio's pills!' said Winterbourne, as he lifted his hat.

'I don't care,' said Daisy, in a little strange tone, 'whether I have Roman fever or not!' Upon this the cab-driver cracked his whip, and they rolled away over the desultory patches of the antique pavement.

Winterbourne – to do him justice, as it were – mentioned to no one that he had encountered Miss Miller, at midnight, in the Colosseum with a gentleman; but nevertheless, a couple of days later, the fact of her having been there under these circumstances was known to every member of the little American circle, and commented accordingly. Winterbourne reflected that they had of course known it at the hotel, and that, after Daisy's return, there had been an exchange of jokes between the porter and the cab-driver. But the young man was conscious at the same moment that it had ceased to be a matter of serious regret to him that the little American flirt should be 'talked about' by low-minded menials. These people, a day or two later, had serious information to give: the little American flirt was alarmingly ill. Winterbourne, when the rumour came to him, immediately went to the hotel for more news. He found that two or three charitable friends had preceded him, and that they were being entertained in Mrs Miller's salon by Randolph.

'It's going round at night,' said Randolph – 'that's what made her sick. She's always going round at night. I shouldn't think she'd want to – it's so plaguey dark. You can't see anything here at night, except when there's a moon. In America there's always a moon!' Mrs Miller was invisible; she was now, at least, giving her daughter the advantage of her society. It was evident that Daisy was dangerously ill.

Winterbourne went often to ask for news of her, and once he saw Mrs Miller, who, though deeply alarmed, was – rather to his surprise – perfectly composed, and, as it appeared, a most efficient and judicious nurse. She talked a good deal about Dr Davis, but Winterbourne paid her the compliment of saying to himself that she was not, after all, such a monstrous goose. 'Daisy spoke of you the other day,' she said to him. 'Half the time she doesn't know what she's saying, but that time I think she did. She gave me a message; she told me to tell you. She told me to tell you that she never was engaged to that handsome Italian. I am sure I am very glad; Mr Giovanelli hasn't been near us since she was taken ill. I thought he was so much of a gentleman; but I don't call that very polite! A lady told me that he was afraid I was angry with him for taking Daisy round at night. Well, so I am; but I suppose he knows I'm a lady. I would scorn to scold him. Anyway, she says she's not engaged. I don't know why she wanted you to know; but she said to me three times – "Mind you tell Mr Winterbourne." And then she told me to ask if you remembered the time you went to that castle, in Switzerland. But I said I wouldn't give any such messages as that. Only, if she is not engaged, I'm sure I'm glad to know it.'

But, as Winterbourne had said, it mattered very little. A week after this the poor girl died; it had been a terrible case of the fever. Daisy's grave was in the little Protestant cemetery, in an angle of the wall of imperial Rome, beneath the cypresses and the thick spring flowers. Winterbourne stood there beside it, with a number of other mourners; a number larger than the scandal excited by the young lady's career would have led you to expect. Near him stood Giovanelli, who came nearer still before Winterbourne turned away. Giovanelli was very pale; on this occasion he had no flower in his buttonhole; he seemed to wish to say something. At last he said, 'She was the most beautiful young lady I ever saw, and the most amiable.' And then he added in a moment, 'And she was the most innocent.'

Winterbourne looked at him, and presently repeated his words, 'And the most innocent?'

'The most innocent!'

Winterbourne felt sore and angry. 'Why the devil,' he asked, 'did you take her to that fatal place?'

Mr Giovanelli's urbanity was apparently imperturbable. He looked on the ground a moment, and then he said, 'For myself, I had no fear; and she wanted to go.'

'That was no reason!' Winterbourne declared.

The subtle Roman again dropped his eyes. 'If she had lived, I should have got nothing. She would never have married me, I am sure.'

'She would never had married you?'

'For a moment I hoped so. But no, I am sure.'

Winterbourne listened to him; he stood staring at the raw protuberance among the April daisies. When he turned away again Mr Giovanelli, with his light slow step, had retired.

Winterbourne almost immediately left Rome; but the following summer he again met his aunt, Mrs Costello, at Vevey. Mrs Costello was fond of Vevey. In the interval Winterbourne had often thought of Daisy Miller and her mystifying manners. One day he spoke of her to his aunt – said it was on his conscience that he had done her injustice.

'I am sure I don't know,' said Mrs Costello. 'How did your injustice affect her?'

'She sent me a message before her death which I didn't understand at the time. But I have understood it since. She would have appreciated one's esteem.'

'Is that a modest way,' asked Mrs Costello, 'of saying that she would have reciprocated one's affection?'

Winterbourne offered no answer to this question; but he presently said, 'You were right in that remark that you made last summer. I was booked to make a mistake. I have lived too long in foreign parts.'

Nevertheless, he went back to Geneva, whence there continue to come the most contradictory accounts of his motives of sojourn: a report that he is 'studying' hard – an intimation that he is much interested in a very clever foreign lady.

AMY LEVY (1861–1889)

Amy Levy was born in Clapham, South London; her parents were Jewish intellectuals. She studied at Newnham College, Cambridge, which had recently been established to enable the university education of women. Whilst at Cambridge she published a forceful feminist collection of poems, *Xantippe and Other Verse* (1881), in which, like Augusta Webster, she used the genre of dramatic monologue developed by Robert Browning. In the next eight years she published two more collections and three novels, one, *Reuben Sachs* (1888), becoming notorious for its negative representation of London Jewish life. She took her own life in 1889.

Magdalen

All things I can endure, save one.
The bare, blank room where there is no sun;
The parcelled hours; the pallet hard;
The dreary faces here within;
5   The outer women's cold regard;
The Pastor's iterated 'sin'; –
These things could I endure, and count
No overstrain'd, unjust amount;
No undue payment for such bliss –
10 Yea, all things bear, save only this:
That you, who knew what thing would be,
Have wrought this evil unto me.
It is so strange to think on still –
That you, that *you* should do me ill!
15 Not as one ignorant or blind,
But seeing clearly in your mind
How this must be which now has been,
Nothing aghast at what was seen.

Now that the tale is told and done,
20 It is so strange to think upon.

You were so tender with me, too!
One summer's night a cold blast blew,
Closer about my throat you drew
The half-slipt shawl of dusky blue.
25 And once my hand, on a summer's morn,
I stretched to pluck a rose; a thorn
Struck through the flesh and made it bleed
(A little drop of blood indeed!)
Pale grew your cheek; you stoopt and bound
30 Your handkerchief about the wound;
Your voice came with a broken sound;
With the deep breath your breast was riven;
I wonder, did God laugh in Heaven?
How strange, that *you* should work my woe!
35 How strange! I wonder, do you know
How gladly, gladly I had died
(And life was very sweet that tide)
To save you from the least, light ill?
How gladly I had borne your pain.
40 With one great pulse we seem'd to thrill, –
Nay, but we thrill'd with pulses twain.

Even if one had told me this,
'A poison lurks within your kiss,
Gall that shall turn to night his day':
45 Thereon I straight had turned away –
Ay, tho' my heart had crack'd with pain –
And never kiss'd your lips again.

At night, or when the daylight nears,
I hear the other women weep;
50 My own heart's anguish lies too deep
For the soft rain and pain of tears.
I think my heart has turn'd to stone,
A dull, dead weight that hurts my breast;
Here, on my pallet-bed alone,
55 I keep apart from all the rest.
Wide-eyed I lie upon my bed,
I often cannot sleep all night;
The future and the past are dead,
There is no thought can bring delight.
60 All night I lie and think and think;

If my heart were not made of stone,
But flesh and blood, it needs must shrink
Before such thoughts. Was ever known
A woman with a heart of stone?

65 The doctor says that I shall die.
It may be so, yet what care I?
Endless reposing from the strife?
Death do I trust no more than life.
For one thing is like one arrayed,
70 And there is neither false nor true;
But in a hideous masquerade
All things dance on, the ages through.
And good is evil, evil good;
Nothing is known or understood
75 Save only Pain. I have no faith
In God or Devil, Life or Death.

The doctor says that I shall die.
You, that I knew in days gone by,
I fain would see your face once more,
80 Con well its features o'er and o'er;
And touch your hand and feel your kiss,
Look in your eyes and tell you this:
That all is done, that I am free;
That you, through all eternity,
85 Have neither part nor lot in me.

THOMAS HARDY (1840–1928)

Thomas Hardy was born near Dorchester in Dorset, the son of a stonemason, educated in Dorchester and trained as an architect. He specialised in refashioning churches into the Gothic style, then much in vogue. His first published novel was *Desperate Remedies* (1871). In his second, *Under the Greenwood Tree* (1872), he began to discover his characteristic method, the serious and unsentimental depiction of a rural life. This novel was followed by *A Pair of Blue Eyes* (1873), loosely based on his courtship of Emma Gifford in Cornwall, then by *Far from the Madding Crowd* (1874) which was his first conspicuous success and enabled him to marry and devote himself to writing. In the next 24 years Hardy published three collections of short stories and 14 novels, including *The Return of the Native* (1878), *Tess of the D'Urbervilles* (1891) and *Jude the Obscure* (1896). He gave up writing novels after *Jude* to devote himself to what he considered to be the superior art of poetry, publishing eight volumes in the remaining years of his life. Hardy's best-known novels and stories are those which mediated a vanishing rural world to an urban readership that found the manners and compulsions of his rural characters entrancing and perturbing. His brooding sense that history was not universal amelioration, despite the official optimism of the times, but rather a Darwinian struggle of the individual against nature or a malign fate, was very much of its historical moment, even though it outraged the orthodox. The frankness about sexuality in his works had the same effect. The novels he set outside of 'Wessex' – his fictionalised Dorset – were often uncomfortably aware of a class-ridden and snobbish society. He was much honoured in later life, but always felt, like his hero Jude, excluded from polite society and official culture.

The Three Strangers

Among the few features of agricultural England which retain an appearance but little modified by the lapse of centuries, may be reckoned the long, grassy and furzy[1] downs, coombs,[2] or ewe-leases, as they are called according to their kind, that fill a large area of certain counties in the south and south-west. If any mark of human occupation is met with hereon, it usually takes the form of the solitary cottage of some shepherd.

Fifty years ago such a lonely cottage stood on such a down, and may possibly be standing there now. In spite of its loneliness, however, the spot, by actual measurement, was not three miles from a county-town. Yet that affected it little. Three miles of irregular upland, during the long inimical seasons, with their sleets, snows, rains, and mists, afford withdrawing space enough to isolate a Timon or a Nebuchadnezzar;[3] much less, in fair weather, to please that less repellent tribe, the poets, philosophers, artists, and others who 'conceive and meditate of pleasant things.'

Some old earthen camp or barrow, some clump of trees, at least some starved

---

1: gorse-covered. 2: short, deep valleys or hollows. 3: Timon wasted his substance in generous parties and when refused help by those he had fed, retreated to a cave to live on roots. Nebuchadnezzar destroyed Jerusalem and exiled the Jews to Babylon (II Kings, 24–25).

fragment of ancient hedge is usually taken advantage of in the erection of these forlorn dwellings. But, in the present case, such a kind of shelter had been disregarded. Higher Crowstairs, as the house was called, stood quite detached and undefended. The only reason for its precise situation seemed to be the crossing of two footpaths at right angles hard by, which may have crossed there and thus for a good five hundred years. Hence the house was exposed to the elements on all sides. But, though the wind up here blew unmistakably when it did blow, and the rain hit hard whenever it fell, the various weathers of the winter season were not quite so formidable on the down as they were imagined to be by dwellers on low ground. The raw rimes were not so pernicious as in the hollows, and the frosts were scarcely so severe. When the shepherd and his family who tenanted the house were pitied for their sufferings from the exposure, they said that upon the whole they were less inconvenienced by 'wuzzes and flames' (hoarses and phlegms) than when they had lived by the stream of a snug neighbouring valley.

The night of March 28, 182–, was precisely one of the nights that were wont to call forth these expressions of commiseration. The level rainstorm smote walls, slopes, and hedges like the clothyard shafts of Senlac and Crecy.[1] Such sheep and outdoor animals as had no shelter stood with their buttocks to the winds; while the tails of little birds trying to roost on some scraggy thorn were blown inside-out like umbrellas. The gable-end of the cottage was stained with wet, and the eavesdroppings[2] flapped against the wall. Yet never was commiseration for the shepherd more misplaced. For that cheerful rustic was entertaining a large party in glorification of the christening of his second girl.

The guests had arrived before the rain began to fall, and they were all now assembled in the chief or living room of the dwelling. A glance into the apartment at eight o'clock on this eventful evening would have resulted in the opinion that it was as cosy and comfortable a nook as could be wished for in boisterous weather. The calling of its inhabitant was proclaimed by a number of highly-polished sheep-crooks[3] without stems that were hung ornamentally over the fireplace, the curl of each shining crook varying from the antiquated type engraved in the patriarchal pictures of old family Bibles to the most approved fashion of the last local sheep-fair. The room was lighted by half-a-dozen candles, having wicks only a trifle smaller than the grease which enveloped them, in candlesticks that were never used but at high-days, holy-days, and family feasts. The lights were scattered about the room, two of them standing on the chimney-piece. This position of candles was in itself significant. Candles on the chimney-piece always meant a party.

On the hearth, in front of a back-brand to give substance, blazed a fire of thorns, that crackled 'like the laughter of the fool.'

Nineteen persons were gathered here. Of these, five women, wearing gowns of various bright hues, sat in chairs along the wall; girls shy and not shy filled the window-bench; four men, including Charley Jake the hedge-carpenter, Elijah New the parish-clerk, and John Pitcher, a neighbouring dairyman, the

---

1: arrows; Senlac was the hill on which the Battle of Hastings was fought in 1066. Crecy: battle where the English defeated the French in 1346.   2: water dripping from the eaves.   3: a shepherd's staff with a hooked end.

shepherd's father-in-law, lolled in the settle; a young man and maid, who were blushing over tentative *pourparlers*[1] on a life-companionship, sat beneath the corner-cupboard; and an elderly engaged man of fifty or upward moved restlessly about from spots where his betrothed was not to the spot where she was. Enjoyment was pretty general, and so much the more prevailed in being unhampered by conventional restrictions. Absolute confidence in each other's good opinion begat perfect ease, while the finishing stroke of manner, amounting to a truly princely serenity, was lent to the majority by the absence of any expression or trait denoting that they wished to get on in the world, enlarge their minds, or do any eclipsing thing whatever – which nowadays so generally nips the bloom and *bonhomie*[2] of all except the two extremes of the social scale.

Shepherd Fennel had married well, his wife being a dairyman's daughter from a vale at a distance, who brought fifty guineas in her pocket – and kept them there, till they should be required for ministering to the needs of a coming family. This frugal woman had been somewhat exercised as to the character that should be given to the gathering. A sit-still party had its advantages; but an undisturbed position of ease in chairs and settles was apt to lead on the men to such an unconscionable deal of toping[3] that they would sometimes fairly drink the house dry. A dancing-party was the alternative; but this, while avoiding the foregoing objection on the score of good drink, had a counterbalancing disadvantage in the matter of good victuals, the ravenous appetites engendered by the exercise causing immense havoc in the buttery. Shepherdess Fennel fell back upon the intermediate plan of mingling short dances with short periods of talk and singing, so as to hinder any ungovernable rage in either. But this scheme was entirely confined to her own gentle mind: the shepherd himself was in the mood to exhibit the most reckless phases of hospitality.

The fiddler was a boy of those parts, about twelve years of age, who had a wonderful dexterity in jigs and reels, though his fingers were so small and short as to necessitate a constant shifting for the high notes, from which he scrambled back to the first position with sounds not of unmixed purity of tone. At seven the shrill tweedle-dee of this youngster had begun, accompanied by a booming ground-bass from Elijah New, the parish-clerk, who had thoughtfully brought with him his favourite musical instrument, the serpent.[4] Dancing was instant-aneous, Mrs Fennel privately enjoining the players on no account to let the dance exceed the length of a quarter of an hour.

But Elijah and the boy in the excitement of their position quite forgot the injunction. Moreover, Oliver Giles, a man of seventeen, one of the dancers, who was enamoured of his partner, a fair girl of thirty-three rolling years, had recklessly handed a new crownpiece to the musicians, as a bribe to keep going as long as they had muscle and wind. Mrs Fennel, seeing the steam begin to generate on the countenances of her guests, crossed over and touched the fiddler's elbow and put her hand on the serpent's mouth. But they took no notice, and fearing she might lose her character of genial hostess if she were to interfere too markedly, she retired and sat down helpless. And so the dance

---

1: preliminary conference.   2: exuberant friendliness.   3: drinking.   4: deep-toned woodwind instrument.

whizzed on with cumulative fury, the performers moving in their planet-like courses, direct and retrograde, from apogee to perigee,[1] till the hand of the well-kicked clock at the bottom of the room had travelled over the circumference of an hour.

While these cheerful events were in course of enactment within Fennel's pastoral dwelling an incident having considerable bearing on the party had occurred in the gloomy night without. Mrs Fennel's concern about the growing fierceness of the dance corresponded in point of time with the ascent of a human figure to the solitary hill of Higher Crowstairs from the direction of the distant town. This personage strode on through the rain without a pause, following the little-worn path which, further on in its course, skirted the shepherd's cottage.

It was nearly the time of full moon, and on this account, though the sky was lined with a uniform sheet of dripping cloud, ordinary objects out of doors were readily visible. The sad wan light revealed the lonely pedestrian to be a man of supple frame; his gait suggested that he had somewhat passed the period of perfect and instinctive agility, though not so far as to be otherwise than rapid of motion when occasion required. At a rough guess, he might have been about forty years of age. He appeared tall, but a recruiting sergeant, or other person accustomed to the judging of men's heights by the eye, would have discerned that this was chiefly owing to his gauntness, and that he was not more than five-feet-eight or nine.

Notwithstanding the regularity of his tread there was caution in it, as in that of one who mentally feels his way; and despite the fact that it was not a black coat nor a dark garment of any sort that he wore, there was something about him which suggested that he naturally belonged to the black-coated tribes of men. His clothes were of fustian, and his boots hobnailed, yet in his progress he showed not the mud-accustomed bearing of hobnailed and fustianed peasantry.

By the time that he had arrived abreast of the shepherd's premises the rain came down, or rather came along, with yet more determined violence. The outskirts of the little settlement partially broke the force of wind and rain, and this induced him to stand still. The most salient of the shepherd's domestic erections was an empty sty at the forward corner of his hedgeless garden, for in these latitudes the principle of masking the homelier features of your establishment by a conventional frontage was unknown. The traveller's eye was attracted to this small building by the pallid shine of the wet slates that covered it. He turned aside, and, finding it empty, stood under the pent-roof for shelter.

While he stood the boom of the serpent within the adjacent house, and the lesser strains of the fiddler, reached the spot as an accompaniment to the surging hiss of the flying rain on the sod, its louder beating on the cabbage-leaves of the garden, on the straw hackles of eight or ten beehives just discernible by the path, and its dripping from the eaves into a row of buckets and pans that had been placed under the walls of the cottage. For at Higher Crowstairs, as at all such elevated domiciles, the grand difficulty of housekeeping was an insufficiency

---

1: the points when the earth is furthest from and then nearest to the sun.

of water – and a casual rainfall was utilized by turning out, as catchers, every utensil that the house contained. Some queer stories might be told of the contrivances for economy in suds and dish-waters that are absolutely necessitated in upland habitations during the droughts of summer. But at this season there were no such exigencies; a mere acceptance of what the skies bestowed was sufficient for an abundant store.

At last the notes of the serpent ceased and the house was silent. This cessation of activity aroused the solitary pedestrian from the reverie into which he had lapsed, and, emerging from the shed, with an apparently new intention, he walked up the path to the house-door. Arrived here, his first act was to kneel down on a large stone beside the row of vessels, and to drink a copious draught from one of them. Having quenched his thirst he rose and lifted his hand to knock, but paused with his eye upon the panel. Since the dark surface of the wood revealed absolutely nothing, it was evident that he must be mentally looking through the door, as if he wished to measure thereby all the possibilities that a house of this sort might include, and how they might bear upon the question of his entry.

In his indecision he turned and surveyed the scene around. Not a soul was anywhere visible. The garden path stretched downward from his feet, gleaming like the track of a snail; the roof of the little well (mostly dry), the well-cover, the top rail of the garden gate, were varnished with the same dull liquid glaze; while, far away in the vale, a faint whiteness of more than usual extent showed that the rivers were high in the meads. Beyond all this winked a few bleared lamplights through the beating drops – lights that denoted the situation of the county-town from which he had appeared to come. The absence of all notes of life in that direction seemed to clinch his intentions, and he knocked at the door.

Within, a desultory chat had taken the place of movement and musical sound. The hedge-carpenter was suggesting a song to the company, which nobody just then was inclined to undertake, so that the knock afforded a not unwelcome diversion.

'Walk in!' said the shepherd promptly.

The latch clicked upward, and out of the night our pedestrian appeared upon the door-mat. The shepherd arose, snuffed two of the nearest candles, and turned to look at him.

Their light disclosed that the stranger was dark in complexion and not unprepossessing as to feature. His hat, which for a moment he did not remove, hung low over his eyes, without concealing that they were large, open, and determined, moving with a flash rather than a glance round the room. He seemed pleased with his survey, and, baring his shaggy head, said, in a rich deep voice, 'The rain is so heavy, friends, that I ask leave to come in and rest awhile.'

'To be sure, stranger,' said the shepherd. 'And faith, you've been lucky in choosing your time, for we are having a bit of a fling[1] for a glad cause – though, to be sure, a man could hardly wish that glad cause to happen more than once a year.'

1: a party.

'Nor less,' spoke up a woman. 'For 'tis best to get your family over and done with, as soon as you can, so as to be all the earlier out of the fag[1] o't.'

'And what may be this glad cause?' asked the stranger.

'A birth and christening,' said the shepherd.

The stranger hoped his host might not be made unhappy either by too many or too few of such episodes, and being invited by a gesture to a pull at the mug, he readily acquiesced. His manner, which, before entering, had been so dubious, was now altogether that of a careless and candid man.

'Late to be traipsing[2] athwart this coomb – hey?' said the engaged man of fifty.

'Late it is, master, as you say. – I'll take a seat in the chimney-corner, if you have nothing to urge against it, ma'am; for I am a little moist on the side that was next the rain.'

Mrs Shepherd Fennel assented, and made room for the self-invited comer, who, having got completely inside the chimney-corner, stretched out his legs and his arms with the expansiveness of a person quite at home.

'Yes, I am rather cracked in the vamp,' he said freely, seeing that the eyes of the shepherd's wife fell upon his boots, 'and I am not well fitted either. I have had some rough times lately, and have been forced to pick up what I can get in the way of wearing, but I must find a suit better fit for working-days when I reach home.'

'One of hereabouts?' she inquired.

'Not quite that – further up the country.'

'I thought so. And so be I; and by your tongue you come from my neighbourhood.'

'But you would hardly have heard of me,' he said quickly. 'My time would be long before yours, ma'am, you see.'

This testimony to the youthfulness of his hostess had the effect of stopping her cross-examination.

'There is only one thing more wanted to make me happy,' continued the new-comer. 'And that is a little baccy, which I am sorry to say I am out of.'

'I'll fill your pipe,' said the shepherd.

'I must ask you to lend me a pipe likewise.'

'A smoker, and no pipe about 'ee?'

'I have dropped it somewhere on the road.'

The shepherd filled and handed him a new clay pipe, saying, as he did so, 'Hand me your baccy-box – I'll fill that too, now I am about it.'

The man went through the movement of searching his pockets.

'Lost that too?' said his entertainer, with some surprise.

'I am afraid so,' said the man with some confusion. 'Give it to me in a screw of paper.' Lighting his pipe at the candle with a suction that drew the whole flame into the bowl, he resettled himself in the corner and bent his looks upon the faint steam from his damp legs, as if he wished to say no more.

Meanwhile the general body of guests had been taking little notice of this visitor by reason of an absorbing discussion in which they were engaged with

---

1: tiredness.   2: to walk heavily, with tiredness.

the band about a tune for the next dance. The matter being settled, they were about to stand up when an interruption came in the shape of another knock at the door.

At sound of the same the man in the chimney-corner took up the poker and began stirring the brands as if doing it thoroughly were the one aim of his existence; and a second time the shepherd said, 'Walk in!' In a moment another man stood upon the straw-woven door-mat. He too was a stranger.

This individual was one of a type radically different from the first. There was more of the commonplace in his manner, and a certain jovial cosmopolitanism sat upon his features. He was several years older than the first arrival, his hair being slightly frosted, his eyebrows bristly, and his whiskers cut back from his cheeks. His face was rather full and flabby, and yet it was not altogether a face without power. A few grog-blossoms[1] marked the neighbourhood of his nose. He flung back his long drab greatcoat, revealing that beneath it he wore a suit of cinder-gray shade throughout, large heavy seals, of some metal or other that would take a polish, dangling from his fob as his only personal ornament. Shaking the water-drops from his low-crowned glazed hat, he said, 'I must ask for a few minutes' shelter, comrades, or I shall be wetted to my skin before I get to Casterbridge.'

'Make yourself at home, master,' said the shepherd, perhaps a trifle less heartily than on the first occasion. Not that Fennel had the least tinge of niggardliness in his composition; but the room was far from large, spare chairs were not numerous, and damp companions were not altogether desirable at close quarters for the women and girls in their bright-coloured gowns.

However, the second comer, after taking off his greatcoat, and hanging his hat on a nail in one of the ceiling-beams as if he had been specially invited to put it there, advanced and sat down at the table. This had been pushed so closely into the chimney-corner, to give all available room to the dancers, that its inner edge grazed the elbow of the man who had ensconced himself by the fire; and thus the two strangers were brought into close companionship. They nodded to each other by way of breaking the ice of unacquaintance, and the first stranger handed his neighbour the family mug – a huge vessel of brown ware, having its upper edge worn away like a threshold by the rub of whole generations of thirsty lips that had gone the way of all flesh, and bearing the following inscription burnt upon its rotund side in yellow letters: –

> THERE IS NO FUN
> UNTILL I CUM

The other man, nothing loth, raised the mug to his lips, and drank on, and on, and on – till a curious blueness overspread the countenance of the shepherd's wife, who had regarded with no little surprise the first stranger's free offer to the second of what did not belong to him to dispense.

'I knew it!' said the toper[2] to the shepherd with much satisfaction. 'When I walked up your garden before coming in, and saw the hives all of a row, I said to myself, "Where there's bees there's honey, and where there's honey there's

---

1: grog is rum, hence 2: habitual drinker.

mead." But mead of such a truly comfortable sort as this I really didn't expect to meet in my older days.' He took yet another pull at the mug, till it assumed an ominous elevation.

'Glad you enjoy it!' said the shepherd warmly.

'It is goodish mead,' assented Mrs Fennel, with an absence of enthusiasm which seemed to say that it was possible to buy praise for one's cellar at too heavy a price. 'It is trouble enough to make – and really I hardly think we shall make any more. For honey sells well, and we ourselves can make shift with a drop o' small mead and metheglin¹ for common use from the comb-washings.'

'O, but you'll never have the heart!' reproachfully cried the stranger in cinder-gray, after taking up the mug a third time and setting it down empty. 'I love mead, when 'tis old like this, as I love to go to church o' Sundays, or to relieve the needy any day of the week.'

'Ha, ha, ha!' said the man in the chimney-corner, who, in spite of the taciturnity induced by the pipe of tobacco, could not or would not refrain from this slight testimony to his comrade's humour.

Now the old mead of those days, brewed of the purest first-year or maiden honey, four pounds to the gallon – with its due complement of white of eggs, cinnamon, ginger, cloves, mace, rosemary, yeast, and processes of working, bottling, and cellaring – tasted remarkably strong; but it did not taste so strong as it actually was. Hence, presently, the stranger in cinder-gray at the table, moved by its creeping influence, unbuttoned his waistcoat, threw himself back in his chair, spread his legs, and made his presence felt in various ways.

'Well, well, as I say,' he resumed, 'I am going to Casterbridge, and to Casterbridge I must go. I should have been almost there by this time; but the rain drove me into your dwelling, and I'm not sorry for it.'

'You don't live in Casterbridge?' said the shepherd.

'Not as yet; though I shortly mean to move there.'

'Going to set up in trade, perhaps?'

'No, no,' said the shepherd's wife. 'It is easy to see that the gentleman is rich, and don't want to work at anything.'

The cinder-gray stranger paused, as if to consider whether he would accept that definition of himself. He presently rejected it by answering, 'Rich is not quite the word for me, dame. I do work, and I must work. And even if I only get to Casterbridge by midnight I must begin work there at eight to-morrow morning. Yes, het² or wet, blow or snow, famine or sword, my day's work to-morrow must be done.'

'Poor man! Then, in spite o' seeming, you be worse off than we?' replied the shepherd's wife.

''Tis the nature of my trade, men and maidens. 'Tis the nature of my trade more than my poverty. . . . But really and truly I must up and off, or I shan't get a lodging in the town.' However, the speaker did not move, and directly added, 'There's time for one more draught of friendship before I go; and I'd perform it at once if the mug were not dry.'

1: medicated mead.   2: heat.

'Here's a mug o' small,' said Mrs Fennel. 'Small, we call it, though to be sure 'tis only the first wash o' the combs.'

'No,' said the stranger disdainfully. 'I won't spoil your first kindness by partaking o' your second.'

'Certainly not,' broke in Fennel. 'We don't increase and multiply every day, and I'll fill the mug again.' He went away to the dark place under the stairs where the barrel stood. The shepherdess followed him.

'Why should you do this?' she said reproachfully, as soon as they were alone. 'He's emptied it once, though it held enough for ten people; and now he's not contented wi' the small, but must needs call for more o' the strong! And a stranger unbeknown to any of us. For my part, I don't like the look o' the man at all.'

'But he's in the house, my honey; and 'tis a wet night, and a christening. Daze it,[1] what's a cup of mead more or less? There'll be plenty more next bee-burning.'

'Very well – this time, then,' she answered, looking wistfully at the barrel. 'But what is the man's calling, and where is he one of, that he should come in and join us like this?'

'I don't know. I'll ask him again.'

The catastrophe of having the mug drained dry at one pull by the stranger in cinder-gray was effectually guarded against this time by Mrs Fennel. She poured out his allowance in a small cup, keeping the large one at a discreet distance from him. When he had tossed off his portion the shepherd renewed his inquiry about the stranger's occupation.

The latter did not immediately reply, and the man in the chimney-corner, with sudden demonstrativeness, said, 'Anybody may know my trade – I'm a wheelwright.'

'A very good trade for these parts,' said the shepherd.

'And anybody may know mine – if they've the sense to find it out,' said the stranger in cinder-gray.

'You may generally tell what a man is by his claws,' observed the hedge-carpenter, looking at his own hands. 'My fingers be as full of thorns as an old pin-cushion is of pins.'

The hands of the man in the chimney-corner instinctively sought the shade, and he gazed into the fire as he resumed his pipe. The man at the table took up the hedge-carpenter's remark, and added smartly, 'True; but the oddity of my trade is that, instead of setting a mark upon me, it sets a mark upon my customers.'

No observation being offered by anybody in elucidation of this enigma the shepherd's wife once more called for a song. The same obstacles presented themselves as at the former time – one had no voice, another had forgotten the first verse. The stranger at the table, whose soul had now risen to a good working temperature, relieved the difficulty by exclaiming that, to start the company, he would sing himself. Thrusting one thumb into the arm-hole of his waistcoat, he waved the other hand in the air, and, with an extemporizing gaze at the shining sheepcrooks above the mantlepiece, began: –

1: daze means to stun, thus 'I'll be stunned.'

> 'O my trade it is the rarest one,
>   Simple shepherds all –
>   My trade is a sight to see;
> For my customers I tie, and take them up on high,
>   And waft 'em to a far countree!'

The room was silent when he had finished the verse – with one exception, that of the man in the chimney-corner, who, at the singer's word, 'Chorus!' joined him in a deep bass voice of musical relish –

> 'And waft 'em to a far countree!'

Oliver Giles, John Pitcher the dairyman, the parish-clerk, the engaged man of fifty, the row of young women against the wall, seemed lost in thought not of the gayest kind. The shepherd looked meditatively on the ground, the shepherdess gazed keenly at the singer, and with some suspicion; she was doubting whether this stranger were merely singing an old song from recollection, or was composing one there and then for the occasion. All were as perplexed at the obscure revelation as the guests at Belshazzar's Feast,[1] except the man in the chimney-corner, who quietly said, 'Second verse, stranger,' and smoked on.

The singer thoroughly moistened himself from his lips inwards, and went on with the next stanza as requested: –

> 'My tools are but common ones,
>   Simple shepherds all –
>   My tools are no sight to see:
> A little hempen string, and a post whereon to swing,
>   Are implements enough for me!'

Shepherd Fennel glanced round. There was no longer any doubt that the stranger was answering his question rhythmically. The guests one and all started back with suppressed exclamations. The young woman engaged to the man of fifty fainted half-way, and would have proceeded, but finding him wanting in alacrity for catching her she sat down trembling.

'O, he's the – !' whispered the people in the background, mentioning the name of an ominous public officer. 'He's come to do it! 'Tis to be at Casterbridge jail to-morrow – the man for sheepstealing – the poor clock-maker we heard of, who used to live away at Shottsford and had no work to do – Timothy Summers, whose family were a-starving, and so he went out of Shottsford by the high-road and took a sheep in open daylight, defying the farmer and the farmer's wife and the farmer's lad, and every man jack among 'em. He' (and they nodded towards the stranger of the deadly trade) 'is come from up the country to do it because there's not enough to do in his own county-town, and he's got the place here now our own county man's dead; he's going to live in the same cottage under the prison wall.'

1: Belshazzar, son of Nebuchadnezzar (Daniel 5:1, 17; 8:1), received a divine message of doom written on a wall at a banquet.

The stranger in cinder-gray took no notice of this whispered string of observations, but again wetted his lips. Seeing that his friend in the chimney-corner was the only one who reciprocated his joviality in any way, he held out his cup towards that appreciative comrade, who also held out his own. They clinked together, the eyes of the rest of the room hanging upon the singer's actions. He parted his lips for the third verse; but at that moment another knock was audible upon the door. This time the knock was faint and hesitating.

The company seemed scared; the shepherd looked with consternation towards the entrance, and it was with some effort that he resisted his alarmed wife's deprecatory glance, and uttered for the third time the welcoming words, 'Walk in!'

The door was gently opened, and another man stood upon the mat. He, like those who had preceded him, was a stranger. This time it was a short, small personage, of fair complexion, and dressed in a decent suit of dark clothes.

'Can you tell me the way to – ?' he began: when, gazing round the room to observe the nature of the company amongst whom he had fallen, his eyes lighted on the stranger in cinder-gray. It was just at the instant when the latter, who had thrown his mind into his song with such a will that he scarcely heeded the interruption, silenced all whispers and inquiries by bursting into his third verse: –

> 'To-morrow is my working day,
>   Simple shepherds all –
>   To-morrow is a working day for me:
> For the farmer's sheep is slain, and the lad who did it ta'en,
>   And on his soul may God ha' merc-y!'

The stranger in the chimney-corner, waving cups with the singer so heartily that his mead splashed over on the hearth, repeated in his bass voice as before: –

> 'And on his soul may God ha' merc-y!'

All this time the third stranger had been standing in the doorway. Finding now that he did not come forward or go on speaking, the guests particularly regarded him. They noticed to their surprise that he stood before them the picture of abject terror – his knees trembling, his hand shaking so violently that the door-latch by which he supported himself rattled audibly: his white lips were parted, and his eyes fixed on the merry officer of justice in the middle of the room. A moment more and he had turned, closed the door, and fled.

'What a man can it be?' said the shepherd.

The rest, between the awfulness of their late discovery and the odd conduct of this third visitor, looked as if they knew not what to think, and said nothing. Instinctively they withdrew further and further from the grim gentleman in their midst, whom some of them seemed to take for the Prince of Darkness himself, till they formed a remote circle, an empty space of floor being left between them and him –

> '. . . *circulus, cujus centrum diabolus.*'[1]

1: a circle, of which the centre is the devil.

The room was so silent – though there were more than twenty people in it – that nothing could be heard but the patter of the rain against the window-shutters, accompanied by the occasional hiss of a stray drop that fell down the chimney into the fire, and the steady puffing of the man in the corner, who had now resumed his pipe of long clay.

The stillness was unexpectedly broken. The distant sound of a gun reverberated through the air – apparently from the direction of the county-town.

'Be jiggered!' cried the stranger who had sung the song, jumping up.

'What does that mean?' asked several.

'A prisoner escaped from the jail – that's what it means.'

All listened. The sound was repeated, and none of them spoke but the man in the chimney-corner, who said quietly, 'I've often been told that in this county they fire a gun at such times; but I never heard it till now.'

'I wonder if it is *my* man?' murmured the personage in cinder-gray.

'Surely it is!' said the shepherd involuntarily. 'And surely we've zeed him! That little man who looked in at the door by now, and quivered like a leaf when he zeed ye and heard your song!'

'His teeth chattered, and the breath went out of his body,' said the dairyman.

'And his heart seemed to sink within him like a stone,' said Oliver Giles.

'And he bolted as if he'd been shot at,' said the hedge-carpenter.

'True – his teeth chattered, and his heart seemed to sink; and he bolted as if he'd been shot at,' slowly summed up the man in the chimney-corner.

'I didn't notice it,' remarked the hangman.

'We were all a-wondering what made him run off in such a fright,' faltered one of the women against the wall, 'and now 'tis explained!'

The firing of the alarm-gun went on at intervals, low and sullenly, and their suspicions became a certainty. The sinister gentleman in cinder-gray roused himself. 'Is there a constable here?' he asked, in thick tones. 'If so, let him step forward.'

The engaged man of fifty stepped quavering out from the wall, his betrothed beginning to sob on the back of the chair.

'You are a sworn constable?'

'I be, sir.'

'Then pursue the criminal at once, with assistance, and bring him back here. He can't have gone far.'

'I will, sir, I will – when I've got my staff. I'll go home and get it, and come sharp here, and start in a body.'

'Staff! – never mind your staff; the man'll be gone!'

'But I can't do nothing without my staff – can I, William, and John, and Charles Jake? No; for there's the king's royal crown a painted on en in yaller and gold, and the lion and the unicorn, so as when I raise en up and hit my prisoner, 'tis made a lawful blow thereby. I wouldn't 'tempt to take up a man without my staff – no, not I. If I hadn't the law to gie me courage, why, instead o' my taking up him he might take up me!'

'Now, I'm a king's man myself, and can give you authority enough for this,' said the formidable officer in gray. 'Now then, all of ye, be ready. Have ye any lanterns?'

'Yes – have ye any lanterns? – I demand it!' said the constable.

'And the rest of you able-bodied – '

'Able-bodied men – yes – the rest of ye!' said the constable.

'Have you some good stout staves and pitchforks – '

'Staves and pitchforks – in the name o' the law! And take 'em in yer hands and go in quest, and do as we in authority tell ye!'

Thus aroused, the men prepared to give chase. The evidence was, indeed, though circumstantial, so convincing, that but little argument was needed to show the shepherd's guests that after what they had seen it would look very much like connivance if they did not instantly pursue the unhappy third stranger, who could not as yet have gone more than a few hundred yards over such uneven country.

A shepherd is always well provided with lanterns; and, lighting these hastily, and with hurdle-staves in their hands, they poured out of the door, taking a direction along the crest of the hill, away from the town, the rain having fortunately a little abated.

Disturbed by the noise, or possibly by unpleasant dreams of her baptism, the child who had been christened began to cry heart-brokenly in the room over-head. These notes of grief came down through the chinks of the floor to the ears of the women below, who jumped up one by one, and seemed glad of the excuse to ascend and comfort the baby, for the incidents of the last half-hour greatly oppressed them. Thus in the space of two or three minutes the room on the ground-floor was deserted quite.

But it was not for long. Hardly had the sound of footsteps died away when a man returned round the corner of the house from the direction the pursuers had taken. Peeping in at the door, and seeing nobody there, he entered leisurely. It was the stranger of the chimney-corner, who had gone out with the rest. The motive of his return was shown by his helping himself to a cut piece of skimmer-cake that lay on a ledge beside where he had sat, and which he had apparently forgotten to take with him. He also poured out half a cup more mead from the quantity that remained, ravenously eating and drinking these as he stood. He had not finished when another figure came in just as quietly – his friend in cinder-gray.

'O – you here?' said the latter, smiling. 'I thought you had gone to help in the capture.' And this speaker also revealed the object of his return by looking solicitously round for the fascinating mug of old mead.

'And I thought you had gone,' said the other, continuing his skimmer-cake with some effort.

'Well, on second thoughts, I felt there were enough without me,' said the first confidentially, 'and such a night as it is, too. Besides, 'tis the business o' the Government to take care of its criminals – not mine.'

'True; so it is. And I felt as you did, that there were enough without me.'

'I don't want to break my limbs running over the humps and hollows of this wild country.'

'Nor I neither, between you and me.'

'These shepherd-people are used to it – simple-minded souls, you know, stirred up to anything in a moment. They'll have him ready for me before the morning, and no trouble to me at all.'

'They'll have him, and we shall have saved ourselves all labour in the matter.'

'True, true. Well, my way is to Casterbridge; and 'tis as much as my legs will do to take me that far. Going the same way?'

'No, I am sorry to say I have to get home over there' (he nodded indefinitely to the right), 'and I feel as you do, that it is quite enough for my legs to do before bedtime.'

The other had by this time finished the mead in the mug, after which, shaking hands heartily at the door, and wishing each other well, they went their several ways.

In the meantime the company of pursuers had reached the end of the hog's-back elevation which dominated this part of the down. They had decided on no particular plan of action; and, finding that the man of the baleful trade was no longer in their company, they seemed quite unable to form any such plan now. They descended in all directions down the hill, and straightway several of the party fell into the snare set by Nature for all misguided midnight ramblers over this part of the cretaceous formation. The 'lanchets,' or flint slopes, which belted the escarpment at intervals of a dozen yards, took the less cautious ones unawares, and losing their footing on the rubbly steep they slid sharply downwards, the lanterns rolling from their hands to the bottom, and there lying on their sides till the horn was scorched through.

When they had again gathered themselves together the shepherd, as the man who knew the country best, took the lead, and guided them round these treacherous inclines. The lanterns, which seemed rather to dazzle their eyes and warn the fugitive than to assist them in the exploration, were extinguished, due silence was observed; and in this more rational order they plunged into the vale. It was a grassy, briery, moist defile, affording some shelter to any person who had sought it; but the party perambulated it in vain, and ascended on the other side. Here they wandered apart, and after an interval closed together again to report progress. At the second time of closing in they found themselves near a lonely ash, the single tree on this part of the coomb, probably sown there by a passing bird some fifty years before. And here, standing a little to one side of the trunk, as motionless as the trunk itself, appeared the man they were in quest of, his outline being well defined against the sky beyond. The band noiselessly drew up and faced him.

'Your money or your life!' said the constable sternly to the still figure.

'No, no,' whispered John Pitcher. ''Tisn't our side ought to say that. That's the doctrine of vagabonds like him, and we be on the side of the law.'

'Well, well,' replied the constable impatiently; 'I must say something, mustn't I? and if you had all the weight o' this undertaking upon your mind, perhaps you'd say the wrong thing too! – Prisoner at the bar, surrender, in the name of the Father – the Crown, I mane!'

The man under the tree seemed now to notice them for the first time, and, giving them no opportunity whatever for exhibiting their courage, he strolled slowly towards them. He was, indeed, the little man, the third stranger; but his trepidation had in a great measure gone.

'Well, travellers,' he said, 'did I hear ye speak to me?'

'You did: you've got to come and be our prisoner at once!' said the constable.

'We arrest 'ee on the charge of not biding[1] in Casterbridge jail in a decent proper manner to be hung to-morrow morning. Neighbours, do your duty, and seize the culpet!'[2]

On hearing the charge the man seemed enlightened, and, saying not another word, resigned himself with preternatural civility to the search-party, who, with their staves in their hands, surrounded him on all sides, and marched him back towards the shepherd's cottage.

It was eleven o'clock by the time they arrived. The light shining from the open door, a sound of men's voices within, proclaimed to them as they approached the house that some new events had arisen in their absence. On entering they discovered the shepherd's living room to be invaded by two officers from Casterbridge jail, and a well-known magistrate who lived at the nearest country-seat, intelligence of the escape having become generally circulated.

'Gentlemen,' said the constable. 'I have brought back your man – not without risk and danger; but every one must do his duty! He is inside this circle of able-bodied persons, who have lent me useful aid, considering their ignorance of Crown work.[3] Men, bring forward your prisoner!' And the third stranger was led to the light.

'Who is this?' said one of the officials.

'The man,' said the constable.

'Certainly not,' said the turnkey; and the first corroborated his statement.

'But how can it be otherwise?' asked the constable. 'Or why was he so terrified at sight o' the singing instrument of the law who sat there?' Here he related the strange behaviour of the third stranger on entering the house during the hangman's song.

'Can't understand it,' said the officer coolly. 'All I know is that it is not the condemned man. He's quite a different character from this one; a gauntish fellow, with dark hair and eyes, rather good-looking, and with a musical bass voice that if you heard it once you'd never mistake as long as you lived.'

'Why, souls – 'twas the man in the chimney-corner!'

'Hey – what?' said the magistrate, coming forward after inquiring particulars from the shepherd in the background. 'Haven't you got the man after all?'

'Well, sir,' said the constable, 'he's the man we were in search of, that's true; and yet he's not the man we were in search of. For the man we were in search of was not the man we wanted, sir, if you understand my every-day way; for 'twas the man in the chimney-corner!'

'A pretty kettle of fish altogether!' said the magistrate. 'You had better start for the other man at once.'

The prisoner now spoke for the first time. The mention of the man in the chimney-corner seemed to have moved him as nothing else could do. 'Sir,' he said, stepping forward to the magistrate, 'take no more trouble about me. The time is come when I may as well speak. I have done nothing; my crime is that the condemned man is my brother. Early this afternoon I left home at Shottsford to tramp it all the way to Casterbridge jail to bid him farewell. I was benighted,

---

1: staying. 2: culprit. 3: Government work.

and called here to rest and ask the way. When I opened the door I saw before me the very man, my brother, that I thought to see in the condemned cell at Casterbridge. He was in this chimney-corner; and jammed close to him, so that he could not have got out if he had tried, was the executioner who'd come to take his life, singing a song about it and not knowing that it was his victim who was close by, joining in to save appearances. My brother threw a glance of agony at me, and I knew he meant, "Don't reveal what you see; my life depends on it." I was so terror-struck that I could hardly stand, and, not knowing what I did, I turned and hurried away.'

The narrator's manner and tone had the stamp of truth, and his story made a great impression on all around. 'And do you know where your brother is at the present time?' asked the magistrate.

'I do not. I have never seen him since I closed this door.'

'I can testify to that, for we've been between ye ever since,' said the constable.

'Where does he think to fly to? – what is his occupation?'

'He's a watch-and-clock-maker, sir.'

' 'A said 'a was a wheelwright – a wicked rogue,' said the constable.

'The wheels of clocks and watches he meant, no doubt,' said Shepherd Fennel. 'I thought his hands were palish for's trade.'

'Well, it appears to me that nothing can be gained by retaining this poor man in custody,' said the magistrate; 'your business lies with the other, unquestionably.'

And so the little man was released off-hand; but he looked nothing the less sad on that account, it being beyond the power of magistrate or constable to raze out the written troubles in his brain, for they concerned another whom he regarded with more solicitude than himself. When this was done, and the man had gone his way, the night was found to be so far advanced that it was deemed useless to renew the search before the next morning.

Next day, accordingly, the quest for the clever sheep-stealer became general and keen, to all appearance at least. But the intended punishment was cruelly disproportioned to the transgression, and the sympathy of a great many country-folk in that district was strongly on the side of the fugitive. Moreover, his marvellous coolness and daring in hob-and-nobbing with the hangman, under the unprecedented circumstances of the shepherd's party, won their admiration. So that it may be questioned if all those who ostensibly made themselves so busy in exploring woods and fields and lanes were quite so thorough when it came to the private examination of their own lofts and out-houses. Stories were afloat of a mysterious figure being occasionally seen in some old over-grown trackway or other, remote from turnpike roads; but when a search was instituted in any of these suspected quarters nobody was found. Thus the days and weeks passed without tidings.

In brief, the bass-voiced man of the chimney-corner was never recaptured. Some said that he went across the sea, others that he did not, but buried himself in the depths of a populous city. At any rate, the gentleman in cinder-gray never did his morning's work at Casterbridge, nor met anywhere at all, for business purposes, the genial comrade with whom he had passed an hour of relaxation in the lonely house on the slope of the coomb.

The grass has long been green on the graves of Shepherd Fennel and his frugal wife; the guests who made up the christening party have mainly followed their entertainers to the tomb; the baby in whose honour they all had met is a matron in the sere[1] and yellow leaf. But the arrival of the three strangers at the shepherd's that night, and the details connected therewith, is a story as well known as ever in the country about Higher Crowstairs.

The Darkling Thrush

I leant upon a coppice gate
　When Frost was spectre-gray,
And Winter's dregs made desolate
　The weakening eye of day.
5　The tangled bine-stems scored the sky
　Like strings of broken lyres,
And all mankind that haunted nigh
　Had sought their household fires.

The land's sharp features seemed to be
10　The Century's corpse outleant,
His crypt the cloudy canopy,
　The wind his death-lament.
The ancient pulse of germ and birth
　Was shrunken hard and dry,
15　And every spirit upon earth
　Seemed fervourless as I.

At once a voice arose among
　The bleak twigs overhead
In a full-hearted evensong
20　Of joy illimited;
An aged thrush, frail, gaunt, and small,
　In blast-beruffled plume,
Had chosen thus to fling his soul
　Upon the growing gloom.

25　So little cause for carolings
　Of such ecstatic sound
Was written on terrestrial things
　Afar or nigh around,

1: dried up.　　　　　　　10 **outleant**: leant outwards, beyond (a coined word).

That I could think there trembled through
30   His happy good-night air
Some blessed Hope, whereof he knew
    And I was unaware.

The Going

Why did you give no hint that night
That quickly after the morrow's dawn,
And calmly, as if indifferent quite,
You would close your term here, up and be gone
5   Where I could not follow
    With wing of swallow
To gain one glimpse of you ever anon!

    Never to bid good-bye,
    Or lip me the softest call,
10 Or utter a wish for a word, while I
Saw morning harden upon the wall,
    Unmoved, unknowing
    That your great going
Had place that moment, and altered all.

15 Why do you make me leave the house
And think for a breath it is you I see
At the end of the alley of bending boughs
Where so often at dusk you used to be;
    Till in darkening dankness
20   The yawning blankness
Of the perspective sickens me!

    You were she who abode
    By those red-veined rocks far West.
You were the swan-necked one who rode
25 Along the beetling Beeny Crest,
    And, reining nigh me,
    Would muse and eye me,
While Life unrolled us its very best

Why, then, latterly did we not speak,
30 Did we not think of those days long dead,
And ere your vanishing strive to seek
That time's renewal? We might have said
    'In this bright spring weather
    We'll visit together
35 Those places that once we visited.'

Well, well! All's past amend,
Unchangeable. It must go.
I seem but a dead man held on end
To sink down soon. . . . O you could not know
40   That such swift fleeing
No soul foreseeing –
Not even I – would undo me so!

In Time of 'The Breaking of Nations'

I
Only a man harrowing clods
In a slow silent walk
With an old horse that stumbles and nods
Half asleep as they stalk.

II
5   Only thin smoke without flame
From the heaps of couch-grass:
Yet this will go onward the same
Though Dynasties pass.

III
Yonder a maid and her wight
10   Come whispering by:
War's annals will cloud into night
Ere their story die.

Afterwards

When the Present has latched its postern behind my tremulous stay,
  And the May month flaps its glad green leaves like wings,
Delicate-filmed as new-spun silk, will the neighbours say,
  'He was a man who used to notice such things'?

5 If it be in the dusk when, like an eyelid's soundless blink,
  The dewfall-hawk comes crossing the shades to alight
Upon the wind-warped upland thorn, a gazer may think,
  'To him this must have been a familiar sight.'

If I pass during some nocturnal blackness, mothy and warm,
10 When the hedgehog travels furtively over the lawn,

The Breaking of Nations: The reference is to *Jeremiah*, 51. 20. 'Thou art my battle axe and weapon of war: for with thee I will break in pieces the nations.' The poem was composed in 1915. **9 wight:** her lover.

One may say, 'He strove that such innocent creatures should come
to no harm,
But he could do little for them; and now he is gone.'

If, when hearing that I have been stilled at last, they stand at the door,
Watching the full-starred heavens that winter sees,
15 Will this thought rise on those who will meet my face no more,
'He was one who had an eye for such mysteries'?

And will any say when my bell of quittance is heard in the gloom,
And a crossing breeze cuts a pause in its outrollings,
Till they rise again, as they were a new bell's boom,
20 'He hears it not now, but used to notice such things'?

RUDYARD KIPLING (1865–1936)

Rudyard Kipling was born in Bombay; his mother was the sister-in-law of Edward Burne-Jones, the Pre-Raphaelite painter. He was sent to boarding school in England – an experience later transmuted into *Stalky and Co* – and he then worked as a journalist in India where his stories and poems were published in newspapers. These were collected in *Plain Tales from the Hills* (1888, including the story 'Beyond the Pale'), *Soldiers Three* (1890), *Wee Willie Winkie* (1890) and *Barrack-Room Ballads* (1892). As a poet Kipling was seen as the voice of imperialism and was as much praised at its highwater mark around 1900 as he was derided thereafter. Both responses failed to note ambiguities in his writing which today make his position much less easy to ascertain, and much more interesting. Unlike most imperial writers, he knew his subject intimately and did not betray its quality by turning it into simple romance. He married an American, Caroline Balestier, in 1892 and thereafter lived in Vermont and in Sussex where he wrote his famous children's stories, *The Jungle Book* (1894), *Stalky and Co* (1899), *Kim* (1901) – a tale of a boy-spy in India which is his most searching and impressive work – the *Just So Stories* (1902), *Puck of Pook's Hill* (1906), and *Rewards and Fairies* (1910). He was the first British writer to be awarded the Nobel prize (in 1907).

Beyond the Pale

> *Love heeds not caste, nor sleep a broken bed.*
> *I went in search of love and lost myself.*
>
> Hindu Proverb

A man should, whatever happens, keep to his own caste, race, and breed. Let the White go to the White and the Black to the Black. Then, whatever trouble falls is in the ordinary course of things – neither sudden, alien, nor unexpected.

This is the story of a man who wilfully stepped beyond the safe limits of decent everyday society, and paid for it heavily.

He knew too much in the first instance; and he saw too much in the second. He took too deep an interest in native life; but he will never do so again.

Deep away in the heart of the City, behind Jitha Megji's *bustee*,[1] lies Amir Nath's Gully,[2] which ends in a dead-wall pierced by one grated window. At the head of the Gully is a big cowbyre, and the walls on either side of the Gully are without windows. Neither Suchet Singh nor Gaur Chand approve of their women-folk looking into the world. If Durga Charan had been of their opinion, he would have been a happier man today, and little Bisesa would have been able to knead her own bread. Her room looked out through the grated window into the narrow dark Gully where the sun never came and where the buffaloes wallowed in the blue slime. She was a widow, about fifteen years old, and she prayed the Gods, day and night, to send her a lover; for she did not approve of living alone.

One day, the man – Trejago his name was – came into Amir Nath's Gully on an aimless wandering; and, after he had passed the buffaloes, stumbled over a big heap of cattle-food.

Then he saw that the Gully ended in a trap, and heard a little laugh from behind the grated window. It was a pretty little laugh, and Trejago, knowing that, for all practical purposes, the old *Arabian Nights* are good guides, went forward to the window, and whispered that verse of 'The Love Song of Har Dyal' which begins: –

Can a man stand upright in the face of the naked Sun; or a Lover in the Presence of his Beloved?
If my feet fail me, O Heart of my Heart, am I to blame, being blinded by the glimpse of your beauty?

There came the faint *tchink* of a woman's bracelets from behind the grating, and a little voice went on with the song at the fifth verse: –

Alas! alas! Can the Moon tell the Lotus of her love when the Gate of Heaven is shut and the clouds gather for the rains?
They have taken my Beloved, and driven her with the pack-horses to the North.
There are iron chains on the feet that were set on my heart.
Call to the bowmen to make ready –

The voice stopped suddenly, and Trejago walked out of Amir Nath's Gully, wondering who in the world could have capped 'The Love Song of Har Dyal' so neatly.

Next morning, as he was driving to office, an old woman threw a packet into his dogcart. In the packet was the half of a broken glass-bangle, one flower of the blood-red *dhak*,[3] a pinch of *bhusa* or cattle-food, and eleven cardamoms. That packet was a letter – not a clumsy compromising letter, but an innocent unintelligible lover's epistle.

Trejago knew far too much about these things, as I have said. No Englishman should be able to translate object-letters. But Trejago spread all the trifles on the lid of his office-box and began to puzzle them out.

1: quarter.   2: from the French *goulet*, the neck of a bottle.   3: 'The Flame of the Forest' flower.

A broken glass-bangle stands for a Hindu widow all India over; because, when her husband dies, a woman's bracelets are broken on her wrists. Trejago saw the meaning of the little bit of glass. The flower of the *dhak* means diversely 'desire,' 'come,' 'write,' or 'danger,' according to the other things with it. One cardamom means 'jealousy;' but when any article is duplicated in an object-letter, it loses its symbolic meaning and stands merely for one of a number indicating time, or, if incense, curds, or saffron be sent also, place. The message ran then – 'A widow – *dhak* flower and *bhusa* – at eleven o'clock.' The pinch of *bhusa* enlightened Trejago. He saw – this kind of letter leaves much to instinctive knowledge – that the *bhusa* referred to the big heap of cattle-food over which he had fallen in Amir Nath's Gully, and that the message must come from the person behind the grating; she being a widow. So the message ran then – 'A widow, in the Gully in which is the heap of *bhusa*, desires you to come at eleven o'clock.'

Trejago threw all the rubbish into the fireplace and laughed. He knew that men in the East do not make love under windows at eleven in the forenoon, nor do women fix appointments a week in advance. So he went, that very night at eleven, into Amir Nath's Gully, clad in a *boorka*,[1] which cloaks a man as well as a woman. Directly the gongs of the City made the hour, the little voice behind the grating took up 'The Love Song of Har Dyal' at the verse where the Pathan girl calls upon Har Dyal to return. The song is really pretty in the Vernacular. In English you miss the wail of it. It runs something like this: –

> Alone upon the housetops, to the North
>   I turn and watch the lightning in the sky, –
> The glamour of thy footsteps in the North,
>   *Come back to me, Beloved, or I die!*
>
> Below my feet the still bazar is laid
>   Far, far, below the weary camels lie, –
> The camels and the captives of thy raid.
>   *Come back to me, Beloved, or I die!*
>
> My father's wife is old and harsh with years,
>   And drudge of all my father's house am I. –
> My bread is sorrow and my drink is tears,
>   *Come back to me, Beloved, or I die!*

As the song stopped, Trejago stepped up under the grating and whispered 'I am here.'

Bisesa was good to look upon.

That night was the beginning of many strange things, and of a double life so wild that Trejago today sometimes wonders if it were not all a dream. Bisesa, or her old handmaiden who had thrown the object-letter, had detached the heavy grating from the brick-work of the wall; so that the window slid inside, leaving only a square of raw masonry into which an active man might climb.

1: as head-to-toe robe worn by Muslim women.

In the day-time, Trejago drove through his routine of office-work, or put on his calling-clothes and called on the ladies of the Station; wondering how long they would know him if they knew of poor little Bisesa. At night, when all the City was still, came the walk under the evil-smelling *boorka*, the patrol through Jitha Megji's *bustee*, the quick turn into Amir Nath's Gully between the sleeping cattle and the dead walls, and then, last of all, Bisesa, and the deep, even breathing of the old woman who slept outside the door of the bare little room that Durga Charan allotted to his sister's daughter. Who or what Durga Charan was, Trejago never inquired; and why in the world he was not discovered and knifed never occurred to him till his madness was over, and Bisesa. . . . But this comes later.

Bisesa was an endless delight to Trejago. She was as ignorant as a bird; and her distorted versions of the rumours from the outside world that had reached her in her room, amused Trejago almost as much as her lisping attempts to pronounce his name – 'Christopher.' The first syllable was always more than she could manage, and she made funny little gestures with her roseleaf hands, as one throwing the name away, and then, kneeling before Trejago, asked him, exactly as an Englishwoman would do, if he were sure he loved her. Trejago swore that he loved her more than anyone else in the world. Which was true.

After a month of this folly, the exigencies of his other life compelled Trejago to be especially attentive to a lady of his acquaintance. You may take it for a fact that anything of this kind is not only noticed and discussed by a man's own race but by some hundred and fifty natives as well. Trejago had to walk with this lady and talk to her at the bandstand, and once or twice to drive with her; never for an instant dreaming that this would affect his dearer, out-of-the-way life. But the news flew, in the usual mysterious fashion, from mouth to mouth, till Bisesa's duenna heard of it and told Bisesa. The child was so troubled that she did the household work evilly, and was beaten by Durga Charan's wife in consequence.

A week later Bisesa taxed Trejago with the flirtation. She understood no gradations and spoke openly. Trejago laughed and Bisesa stamped her little feet – little feet, light as marigold flowers, that could lie in the palm of a man's one hand.

Much that is written about Oriental passion and impulsiveness is exaggerated and compiled at secondhand, but a little of it is true; and when an Englishman finds that little, it is quite as startling as any passion in his own proper life. Bisesa raged and stormed, and finally threatened to kill herself if Trejago did not at once drop the alien *Memsahib* who had come between them. Trejago tried to explain, and to show her that she did not understand these things from a Western standpoint. Bisesa drew herself up, and said simply –

'I do not. I know only this – it is not good that I should have made you dearer than my own heart to me, *Sahib*. You are an Englishman. I am only a black girl' – she was fairer than bar-gold in the Mint, – 'and the widow of a black man.'

Then she sobbed and said – 'But on my soul and my Mother's soul, I love you. There shall no harm come to you, whatever happens to me.'

Trejago argued with the child, and tried to soothe her, but she seemed quite unreasonably disturbed. Nothing would satisfy her save that all relations between them should end. He was to go away at once. And he went. As he dropped out of the window she kissed his forehead twice, and he walked home wondering.

A week, and then three weeks, passed without a sign from Bisesa. Trejago, thinking that the rupture had lasted quite long enough, went down to Amir Nath's Gully for the fifth time in the three weeks, hoping that his rap at the sill of the shifting grating would be answered. He was not disappointed.

There was a young moon, and one stream of light fell down into Amir Nath's Gully, and struck the grating which was drawn away as he knocked. From the black dark, Bisesa held out her arms into the moonlight. Both hands had been cut off at the wrists, and the stumps were nearly healed.

Then, as Bisesa bowed her head between her arms and sobbed, someone in the room grunted like a wild beast, and something sharp – knife, sword, or spear,– thrust at Trejago in his *boorka*. The stroke missed his body, but cut into one of the muscles of the groin, and he limped slightly from the wound for the rest of his days.

The grating went into its place. There was no sign whatever from inside the house – nothing but the moonlight strip on the high wall, and the blackness of Amir Nath's Gully behind.

The next thing Trejago remembers, after raging and shouting like a madman between those pitiless walls, is that he found himself near the river as the dawn was breaking, threw away his *boorka* and went home bareheaded.

What was the tragedy – whether Bisesa had, in a fit of causeless despair, told everything, or the intrigue had been discovered and she tortured to tell; whether Durga Charan knew his name and what became of Bisesa – Trejago does not know to this day. Something horrible had happened, and the thought of what it must have been comes upon Trejago in the night now and again, and keeps him company till the morning. One special feature of the case is that he does not know where lies the front of Durga Charan's house. It may open on to a court-yard common to two or more houses, or it may lie behind any one of the gates of Jitha Megji's *bustee*. Trejago cannot tell. He cannot get Bisesa – poor little Bisesa – back again. He has lost her in the City where each man's house is as guarded and as unknowable as the grave; and the grating that opens into Amir Nath's Gully has been walled up.

But Trejago pays his calls regularly, and is reckoned a very decent sort of man.

There is nothing peculiar about him, except a slight stiffness, caused by a riding-strain, in the right leg.

MATHILDE BLIND (1841–1896)

Mathilde Blind was born Mathilde Cohen in Mannheim, Germany. Her father, a banker, died, and her mother married Karl Blind, a leader of the 1848 insurrections. Because of Blind's political activity the family was expelled from France and moved to London where they associated with the many European intellectuals who found asylum in a relatively liberal Britain. The Italian republicans and patriots Mazzini and Garibaldi were family friends. Mathilde's brother Ferdinand committed suicide after he failed to assassinate Bismarck. Mathilde herself was expelled from school for supporting the new geological theory of the earth's formation in opposition to the creationist orthodoxy. Her mature life was lived as a woman of letters. She wrote biographies of George Eliot (1883) and Madame Roland (1886), edited Shelley (1872) and Byron (1886), and followed in George Eliot's footsteps by translating David Friedrich Strauss's *The Old Faith and the New* (1873), a work in the German 'Higher Criticism' of the Bible. Most of her poetry was published late in her life, notably *The Heather on Fire* (1886) about the Highland clearances, *The Ascent of Man* (1889) responding to Darwin's *The Descent of Man* (1871), *Dramas in Miniature* (1891), *Songs and Sonnets* (1893) and *Birds of Passage* (1895).

On a Torso of Cupid

    Peach trees and Judas trees,
    Poppies and roses,
    Purple anemones
    In garden closes!
5   Lost in the limpid sky,
    Shrills a gay lark on high;
    Lost in the covert's hush,
    Gurgles a wooing thrush.

    Look, where the ivy weaves,
10   Closely embracing,
    Tendrils of clinging leaves
    Round him enlacing,
    With Nature's sacredness
    Clothing the nakedness,
15   Clothing the marble of
    This poor, dismembered love.

    Gone are the hands whose skill
    Aimed the light arrow,
    Strong once to cure or kill,
20   Pierce to the marrow;

Gone are the lips whose kiss
Held hives of honeyed bliss;
Gone too the little feet,
Overfond, overfleet.

25 O helpless god of old,
Maimed mid the tender
Blossoming white and gold
Of April splendour!
Shall we not make thy grave
30 Where the long grasses wave;
Hide thee, O headless god,
Deep in the daisied sod?

Here thou mayst rest at last
After life's fever;
35 After love's fret is past
Rest thee for ever.
Nay, broken God of Love,
Still must thou bide above
While left for woe or weal
40 Thou hast a heart to feel.

OSCAR WILDE (1854–1900)

Oscar Wilde was born in Dublin, the son of Sir William Wilde, a surgeon, and Jane
Elgee, a well-known writer and literary hostess. Wilde was educated at Trinity College,
Dublin, then at Oxford where he appeared as a dandy and a devotee of Pater's
aestheticism. His early literary output was various, extending from *Poems* (1881) to fairy
stories, *The Happy Prince and other Tales* (1888), and a novel, *The Picture of Dorian
Gray* (1890), his aesthete's version of the theme of the double. It was in his plays of the
early 1890s – *Lady Windermere's Fan* (1892), *A Woman of No Importance* (1893), *An
Ideal Husband* (1895) and *The Importance of Being Earnest* (1895) – that he discovered
his most appropriate genre, a brilliant comedy of manners where his epigrammatic wit
could both satirise and summarise the investment of his society in mere form. His most
subversive play, *Salomé*, explored the erotic tension between Salomé, her father King
Herod, and John the Baptist. It was refused performance in England but played in Paris in
1896 where it created a *succès de scandale* and later inspired both a libretto by Richard
Strauss and a famous series of illustrations by Aubrey Beardsley. Wilde was imprisoned for
homosexuality in 1895 and after his release went to live in France where he wrote *The
Ballad of Reading Gaol* descanting on his experience.

The Importance of Being Earnest

Persons of the play

John Worthing, J.P.	Cecily Cardew
Lady Bracknell	Miss Prism, Governess
Algernon Moncrieff	Lane, Manservant
Hon. Gwendolen Fairfax	Merriman, Butler
Rev. Canon Chasuble, D.D.	

Act I

[*Scene: Morning room*[1] *in Algernon's flat in Half-Moon Street. The room is luxuriously and artistically furnished. The sound of a piano is heard in the adjoining room. Lane is arranging afternoon tea on the table, and after the music has ceased, Algernon enters.*]

Algernon Did you hear what I was playing, Lane?

Lane I didn't think it polite to listen, sir.

Algernon I'm sorry for that, for your sake. I don't play accurately – anyone can play accurately – but I play with wonderful expression. As far as the piano is concerned, sentiment is my forte. I keep science for life.

Lane Yes, sir.

Algernon And, speaking of the science of life, have you got the cucumber sandwiches cut for Lady Bracknell?

Lane Yes, sir. [*Hands them on a salver.*]

Algernon [*Inspects them, takes two, and sits down on the sofa.*] Oh! . . . by the way, Lane, I see from your book that on Thursday night, when Lord Shoreman and Mr Worthing were dining with me, eight bottles of champagne are entered as having been consumed.

Lane Yes, sir; eight bottles and a pint.

Algernon Why is it that at a bachelor's establishment the servants invariably drink the champagne? I ask merely for information.

Lane I attribute it to the superior quality of the wine, sir. I have often observed that in married households the champagne is rarely of a first-rate brand.

Algernon Good Heavens! Is marriage so demoralising as that?

Lane I believe it *is* a very pleasant state, sir. I have had very little experience of it myself up to the present. I have only been married once. That was in consequence of a misunderstanding between myself and a young person.

Algernon [*Languidly*] I don't know that I am much interested in your family life, Lane.

Lane No, sir; it is not a very interesting subject. I never think of it myself.

Algernon Very natural, I am sure. That will do, Lane, thank you.

Lane Thank you, sir. [*Lane goes out.*]

Algernon Lane's views on marriage seem somewhat lax. Really, if the lower

---

1: A semi-formal room for the reception of friends, and for taking one's ease, as opposed to a drawing room, which was grander and was used in the evenings.

orders don't set us a good example, what on earth is the use of them? They seem, as a class, to have absolutely no sense of moral responsibility.
[*Enter Lane.*]
Lane Mr Ernest Worthing.
[*Enter Jack. Lane goes out.*]
Algernon How are you, my dear Ernest? What brings you up to town?
Jack Oh, pleasure, pleasure! What else should bring one anywhere? Eating as usual, I see, Algy!
Algernon [*Stiffly*] I believe it is customary in good society to take some slight refreshment at five o'clock. Where have you been since last Thursday?
Jack [*Sitting down on the sofa*] In the country.
Algernon What on earth do you do there?
Jack [*Pulling off his gloves*] When one is in town one amuses oneself. When one is in the country one amuses other people. It is excessively boring.
Algernon And who are the people you amuse?
Jack [*Airily*] Oh, neighbours, neighbours.
Algernon Got nice neighbours in your part of Shropshire?
Jack Perfectly horrid! Never speak to one of them.
Algernon How immensely you must amuse them! [*Goes over and takes sandwich.*] By the way, Shropshire is your county, is it not?
Jack Eh? Shropshire? Yes, of course. Hallo! Why all these cups? Why cucumber sandwiches? Why such reckless extravagance in one so young? Who is coming to tea?
Algernon Oh! merely Aunt Augusta and Gwendolen.
Jack How perfectly delightful!
Algernon Yes, that is all very well; but I am afraid Aunt Augusta won't quite approve of your being here.
Jack May I ask why?
Algernon My dear fellow, the way you flirt with Gwendolen is perfectly disgraceful. It is almost as bad as the way Gwendolen flirts with you.
Jack I am in love with Gwendolen. I have come up to town expressly to propose to her.
Algernon I thought you had come up for pleasure? . . . I call that business.
Jack How utterly unromantic you are!
Algernon I really don't see anything romantic about proposing. It is very romantic to be in love. But there is nothing romantic about a definite proposal. Why, one may be accepted. One usually is, I believe. Then the excitement is all over. The very essence of romance is uncertainty. If ever I get married, I'll certainly try to forget the fact.
Jack I have no doubt about that, dear Algy. The Divorce Court was specially invented for people whose memories are so curiously constituted.
Algernon Oh! there is no use speculating on that subject. Divorces are made in Heaven. – [*Jack puts out his hand to take a sandwich. Algernon at once interferes.*] Please don't touch the cucumber sandwiches. They are ordered specially for Aunt Augusta. [*Takes one and eats it.*]
Jack Well, you have been eating them all the time.
Algernon That is quite a different matter. She is my aunt. [*Takes plate from*

below.] Have some bread and butter. The bread and butter is for Gwendolen. Gwendolen is devoted to bread and butter.

Jack [*Advancing to table and helping himself*] And very good bread and butter it is too.

Algernon Well, my dear fellow, you need not eat as if you were going to eat it all. You behave as if you were married to her already. You are not married to her already, and I don't think you ever will be.

Jack Why on earth do you say that?

Algernon Well, in the first place girls never marry the men they flirt with. Girls don't think it right.

Jack Oh, that is nonsense!

Algernon It isn't. It is a great truth. It accounts for the extraordinary number of bachelors that one sees all over the place. In the second place, I don't give my consent.

Jack Your consent!

Algernon My dear fellow, Gwendolen is my first cousin. And before I allow you to marry her, you will have to clear up the whole question of Cecily. [*Rings bell.*]

Jack Cecily! What on earth do you mean? What do you mean, Algy, by Cecily? I don't know anyone of the name of Cecily.

[*Enter Lane.*]

Algernon Bring me that cigarette case Mr Worthing left in the smoking room the last time he dined here.

Lane Yes, sir. [*Lane goes out.*]

Jack Do you mean to say you have had my cigarette case all this time? I wish to goodness you had let me know. I have been writing frantic letters to Scotland Yard about it. I was very nearly offering a large reward.

Algernon Well, I wish you would offer one. I happen to be more than usually hard up.

Jack There is no good offering a large reward now that the thing is found.

[*Enter Lane with the cigarette case on a salver. Algernon takes it at once. Lane goes out.*]

Algernon I think that is rather mean of you, Ernest, I must say. [*Opens case and examines it.*] However, it makes no matter, for, now that I look at the inscription inside, I find that the thing isn't yours after all.

Jack Of course it's mine. [*Moving to him*] You have seen me with it a hundred times, and you have no right whatsoever to read what is written inside. It is a very ungentlemanly thing to read a private cigarette case.

Algernon Oh! it is absurd to have a hard and fast rule about what one should read and what one shouldn't. More than half of modern culture depends on what one shouldn't read.

Jack I am quite aware of the fact, and I don't propose to discuss modern culture. It isn't the sort of thing one should talk of in private. I simply want my cigarette case back.

Algernon Yes; but this isn't your cigarette case. This cigarette case is a present from someone of the name of Cecily, and you said you didn't know anyone of that name.

Jack Well, if you want to know, Cecily happens to be my aunt.

Algernon Your aunt!

Jack Yes. Charming old lady she is, too. Lives at Tunbridge Wells. Just give it back to me, Algy.

Algernon [*Retreating to back of sofa*] But why does she call herself little Cecily if she is your aunt and lives at Tunbridge Wells? [*Reading*] 'From little Cecily with her fondest love.'

Jack [*Moving to sofa and kneeling upon it*] My dear fellow, what on earth is there in that? Some aunts are tall, some aunts are not tall. That is a matter that surely an aunt may be allowed to decide for herself. You seem to think that every aunt should be exactly like your aunt! That is absurd! For Heaven's sake give me back my cigarette case. [*Follows Algernon round the room.*]

Algernon Yes. But why does your aunt call you her uncle? 'From little Cecily, with her fondest love to her dear Uncle Jack.' There is no objection, I admit, to an aunt being a small aunt, but why an aunt, no matter what her size may be, should call her own nephew her uncle, I can't quite make out. Besides, your name isn't Jack at all; it is Ernest.

Jack It isn't Ernest; it's Jack.

Algernon You have always told me it was Ernest. I have introduced you to everyone as Ernest. You answer to the name of Ernest. You look as if your name was Ernest. You are the most earnest looking person I ever saw in my life. It is perfectly absurd your saying that your name isn't Ernest. It's on your cards. Here is one of them. [*Taking it from case*] 'Mr Ernest Worthing, B. 4, The Albany.' I'll keep this as a proof that your name is Ernest if ever you attempt to deny it to me, or to Gwendolen, or to anyone else. [*Puts the card in his pocket.*]

Jack Well, my name is Ernest in town and Jack in the country, and the cigarette case was given to me in the country.

Algernon Yes, but that does not account for the fact that your small Aunt Cecily, who lives at Tunbridge Wells, calls you her dear uncle. Come, old boy, you had much better have the thing out at once.

Jack My dear Algy, you talk exactly as if you were a dentist. It is very vulgar to talk like a dentist when one isn't a dentist. It produces a false impression.

Algernon Well, that is exactly what dentists always do. Now, go on! Tell me the whole thing. I may mention that I have always suspected you of being a confirmed and secret Bunburyist; and I am quite sure of it now.

Jack Bunburyist? What on earth do you mean by a Bunburyist?

Algernon I'll reveal to you the meaning of that incomparable expression as soon as you are kind enough to inform me why you are Ernest in town and Jack in the country.

Jack Well, produce my cigarette case first.

Algernon Here it is. [*Hands cigarette case.*] Now produce your explanation, and pray make it improbable. [*Sits on sofa.*]

Jack My dear fellow, there is nothing improbable about my explanation at all. In fact it's perfectly ordinary. Old Mr Thomas Cardew, who adopted me when I was a little boy, made me in his will guardian to his granddaughter, Miss Cecily Cardew. Cecily, who addresses me as her uncle from motives of respect that you could not possibly appreciate, lives at my place in the country under the charge of her admirable governess, Miss Prism.

Algernon Where is that place in the country, by the way?

Jack That is nothing to you, dear boy. You are not going to be invited . . . I may tell you candidly that the place is not in Shropshire.

Algernon I suspected that, my dear fellow! I have Bunburyed all over Shropshire on two separate occasions. Now, go on. Why are you Ernest in town and Jack in the country?

Jack My dear Algy, I don't know whether you will be able to understand my real motives. You are hardly serious enough. When one is placed in the position of guardian, one has to adopt a very high moral tone on all subjects. It's one's duty to do so. And as a high moral tone can hardly be said to conduce very much to either one's health or one's happiness, in order to get up to town I have always pretended to have a younger brother of the name of Ernest, who lives in the Albany, and gets into the most dreadful scrapes. That, my dear Algy, is the whole truth pure and simple.

Algernon The truth is rarely pure and never simple. Modern life would be very tedious if it were either, and modern literature a complete impossibility!

Jack That wouldn't be at all a bad thing.

Algernon Literary criticism is not your forte, my dear fellow. Don't try it. You should leave that to people who haven't been at a University. They do it so well in the daily papers. What you really are is a Bunburyist. I was quite right in saying you were a Bunburyist. You are one of the most advanced Bunburyists I know.

Jack What on earth do you mean?

Algernon You have invented a very useful young brother called Ernest, in order that you may be able to come up to town as often as you like. I have invented an invaluable permanent invalid called Bunbury, in order that I may be able to go down into the country whenever I choose. Bunbury is perfectly invaluable. If it wasn't for Bunbury's extraordinary bad health, for instance, I wouldn't be able to dine with you at Willis's tonight, for I have been really engaged to Aunt Augusta for more than a week.

Jack I haven't asked you to dine with me anywhere tonight.

Algernon I know. You are absurdly careless about sending out invitations. It is very foolish of you. Nothing annoys people so much as not receiving invitations.

Jack You had much better dine with your Aunt Augusta.

Algernon I haven't the smallest intention of doing anything of the kind. To begin with I dined there on Monday, and once a week is quite enough to dine with one's own relations. In the second place, whenever I do dine there I am always treated as a member of the family, and sent down with either no woman at all, or two. In the third place, I know perfectly well whom she will place me next to, tonight. She will place me next Mary Farquhar, who always flirts with her own husband across the dinner-table. That is not very pleasant. Indeed, it is not even decent . . . and that sort of thing is enormously on the increase. The amount of women in London who flirt with their own husbands is perfectly scandalous. It looks so bad. It is simply washing one's clean linen in public. Besides, now that I know you to be a confirmed Bunburyist, I naturally want to talk to you about Bunburying. I want to tell you the rules.

Jack I'm not a Bunburyist at all. If Gwendolen accepts me, I am going to kill my brother, indeed I think I'll kill him in any case. Cecily is a little too much interested in him. It is rather a bore. So I am going to get rid of Ernest. And I strongly advise you to do the same with Mr ... with your invalid friend who has the absurd name.

Algernon Nothing will induce me to part with Bunbury, and if you ever get married, which seems to me extremely problematic, you will be very glad to know Bunbury. A man who marries without knowing Bunbury has a very tedious time of it.

Jack That is nonsense. If I marry a charming girl like Gwendolen, and she is the only girl I ever saw in my life that I would marry, I certainly won't want to know Bunbury.

Algernon Then your wife will. You don't seem to realise, that in married life three is company and two is none.

Jack [*Sententiously*] That, my dear young friend, is the theory that the corrupt French Drama has been propounding for the last fifty years.

Algernon Yes; and that the happy English home has proved in half the time.

Jack For heaven's sake, don't try to be cynical. It's perfectly easy to be cynical.

Algernon My dear fellow, it isn't easy to be anything nowadays. There's such a lot of beastly competition about. [*The sound of an electric bell is heard.*] Ah! that must be Aunt Augusta. Only relatives, or creditors, ever ring in that Wagnerian manner. Now, if I get her out of the way for ten minutes, so that you can have an opportunity for proposing to Gwendolen, may I dine with you tonight at Willis's?

Jack I suppose so, if you want to.

Algernon Yes, but you must be serious about it. I hate people who are not serious about meals. It is so shallow of them.

[*Enter Lane.*]

Lane Lady Bracknell and Miss Fairfax.

[*Algernon goes forward to meet them. Enter Lady Bracknell and Gwendolen.*]

Lady Bracknell Good afternoon, dear Algernon, I hope you are behaving very well.

Algernon I'm feeling very well, Aunt Augusta.

Lady Bracknell That's not quite the same thing. In fact the two things rarely go together. [*Sees Jack and bows to him with icy coldness.*]

Algernon [*To Gwendolen*] Dear me, you are smart!

Gwendolen I am always smart! Aren't I, Mr Worthing?

Jack You're quite perfect, Miss Fairfax.

Gwendolen Oh! I hope I am not that. It would leave no room for developments, and I intend to develop in many directions.

[*Gwendolen and Jack sit down together in the corner.*]

Lady Bracknell I'm sorry if we are a little late, Algernon, but I was obliged to call on dear Lady Harbury. I hadn't been there since her poor husband's death. I never saw a woman so altered; she looks quite twenty years younger. And now I'll have a cup of tea, and one of those nice cucumber sandwiches you promised me.

Algernon Certainly, Aunt Augusta. [*Goes over to tea-table.*]

Lady Bracknell Won't you come and sit here, Gwendolen?

Gwendolen Thanks, Mamma, I'm quite comfortable where I am.

Algernon [*Picking up empty plate in horror*] Good heavens! Lane! Why are there no cucumber sandwiches? I ordered them specially.

Lane [*Gravely*] There were no cucumbers in the market this morning, sir. I went down twice.

Algernon No cucumbers!

Lane No, sir. Not even for ready money.

Algernon That will do, Lane, thank you.

Lane Thank you, sir. [*Lane goes out.*]

Algernon I am greatly distressed, Aunt Augusta, about there being no cucumbers, not even for ready money.

Lady Bracknell It really makes no matter, Algernon. I had some crumpets with Lady Harbury, who seems to me to be living entirely for pleasure now.

Algernon I hear her hair has turned quite gold from grief.

Lady Bracknell It certainly has changed its colour. From what cause I, of course, cannot say. [*Algernon crosses and hands tea.*] Thank you. I've quite a treat for you tonight, Algernon. I am going to send you down with Mary Farquhar. She is such a nice woman, and so attentive to her husband. It's delightful to watch them.

Algernon I am afraid, Aunt Augusta, I shall have to give up the pleasure of dining with you tonight after all.

Lady Bracknell [*Frowning*] I hope not, Algernon. It would put my table completely out. Your uncle would have to dine upstairs. Fortunately he is accustomed to that.

Algernon It is a great bore, and, I need hardly say, a terrible disappointment to me, but the fact is I have just had a telegram to say that my poor friend Bunbury is very ill again. [*Exchanges glances with Jack.*] They seem to think I should be with him.

Lady Bracknell It is very strange. This Mr Bunbury seems to suffer from curiously bad health.

Algernon Yes; poor Bunbury is a dreadful invalid.

Lady Bracknell Well, I must say, Algernon, that I think it is high time that Mr Bunbury made up his mind whether he was going to live or to die. This shilly-shallying with the question is absurd. Nor do I in any way approve of the modern sympathy with invalids. I consider it morbid. Illness of any kind is hardly a thing to be encouraged in others. Health is the primary duty of life. I am always telling that to your poor uncle, but he never seems to take much notice . . . as far as any improvement in his ailments goes. I should be obliged if you would ask Mr Bunbury, from me, to be kind enough not to have a relapse on Saturday, for I rely on you to arrange my music for me. It is my last reception, and one wants something that will encourage conversation, particularly at the end of the season when everyone has practically said whatever they had to say, which, in most cases, was probably not much.

Algernon I'll speak to Bunbury, Aunt Augusta, if he is still conscious, and I think I can promise you he'll be all right by Saturday. Of course the music is a great difficulty. You see, if one plays good music, people don't listen, and if one plays bad music, people don't talk. But I'll run over the programme I've drawn out, if you will kindly come into the next room for a moment.

Lady Bracknell Thank you, Algernon. It is very thoughtful of you. [*Rising, and following Algernon*] I'm sure the programme will be delightful, after a few expurgations. French songs I cannot possibly allow. People always seem to think that they are improper, and either look shocked, which is vulgar, or laugh, which is worse. But German sounds a thoroughly respectable language, and indeed, I believe it is so. Gwendolen, you will accompany me.

Gwendolen Certainly, mamma.

[*Lady Bracknell and Algernon go into the music-room, Gwendolen remains behind.*]

Jack Charming day it has been, Miss Fairfax.

Gwendolen Pray don't talk to me about the weather, Mr Worthing. Whenever people talk to me about the weather, I always feel quite certain that they mean something else. And that makes me so nervous.

Jack I do mean something else.

Gwendolen I thought so. In fact, I am never wrong.

Jack And I would like to be allowed to take advantage of Lady Bracknell's temporary absence . . .

Gwendolen I would certainly advise you to do so. Mamma has a way of coming back suddenly into a room that I have often had to speak to her about.

Jack [*Nervously*] Miss Fairfax, ever since I met you I have admired you more than any girl . . . I have ever met since . . . I met you.

Gwendolen Yes, I am quite aware of the fact. And I often wish that in public, at any rate, you had been more demonstrative. For me you have always had an irresistible fascination. Even before I met you I was far from indifferent to you. [*Jack looks at her in amazement.*] We live, as I hope you know, Mr Worthing, in an age of ideals. The fact is constantly mentioned in the more expensive monthly magazines, and has reached the provincial pulpits I am told: and my ideal has always been to love someone of the name of Ernest. There is something in that name that inspires absolute confidence. The moment Algernon first mentioned to me that he had a friend called Ernest, I knew I was destined to love you.

Jack You really love me, Gwendolen?

Gwendolen Passionately!

Jack Darling! You don't know how happy you've made me.

Gwendolen My own Ernest!

Jack But you don't really mean to say that you couldn't love me if my name wasn't Ernest?

Gwendolen But your name is Ernest.

Jack Yes, I know it is. But supposing it was something else? Do you mean to say you couldn't love me then?

Gwendolen [*Glibly*] Ah! that is clearly a metaphysical speculation, and like most metaphysical speculations has very little reference at all to the actual facts of real life, as we know them.

Jack Personally, darling, to speak quite candidly, I don't much care about the name of Ernest . . . I don't think the name suits me at all.

Gwendolen It suits you perfectly. It is a divine name. It has a music of its own. It produces vibrations.

Jack Well, really, Gwendolen, I must say that I think there are lots of other much nicer names. I think Jack, for instance, a charming name.

Gwendolen Jack? . . . No, there is very little music in the name Jack, if any at all, indeed. It does not thrill. It produces absolutely no vibrations . . . I have known several Jacks, and they all, without exception, were more than usually plain. Besides, Jack is a notorious domesticity for John! And I pity any woman who is married to a man called John. She would probably never be allowed to know the entrancing pleasure of a single moment's solitude. The only really safe name is Ernest.

Jack Gwendolen, I must get christened at once. I mean we must get married at once. There is no time to be lost.

Gwendolen Married, Mr Worthing?

Jack [*Astounded*] Well . . . surely. You know that I love you, and you led me to believe, Miss Fairfax, that you were not absolutely indifferent to me.

Gwendolen I adore you. But you haven't proposed to me yet. Nothing has been said at all about marriage. The subject has not even been touched on.

Jack Well . . . may I propose to you now?

Gwendolen I think it would be an admirable opportunity. And to spare you any possible disappointment, Mr Worthing, I think it only fair to tell you quite frankly beforehand that I am fully determined to accept you.

Jack Gwendolen!

Gwendolen Yes, Mr Worthing, what have you got to say to me?

Jack You know what I have got to say to you.

Gwendolen Yes, but you don't say it.

Jack Gwendolen, will you marry me? [*Goes on his knees.*]

Gwendolen Of course I will, darling. How long you have been about it! I am afraid you have had very little experience in how to propose.

Jack My own one, I have never loved anyone in the world but you.

Gwendolen Yes, but men often propose for practice. I know my brother Gerald does. All my girl-friends tell me so. What wonderfully blue eyes you have, Ernest! They are quite, quite blue. I hope you will always look at me just like that, especially when there are other people present.

[*Enter Lady Bracknell.*]

Lady Bracknell Mr Worthing! Rise, sir, from this semi-recumbent posture. It is most indecorous.

Gwendolen Mamma! [*He tries to rise; she restrains him.*] I must beg you to retire. This is no place for you. Besides, Mr Worthing has not quite finished yet.

Lady Bracknell Finished what, may I ask?

Gwendolen I am engaged to Mr Worthing, mamma. [*They rise together.*]

Lady Bracknell Pardon me, you are not engaged to anyone. When you do become engaged to someone, I, or your father, should his health permit him, will inform you of the fact. An engagement should come on a young girl as a surprise, pleasant or unpleasant, as the case may be. It is hardly a matter that she could be allowed to arrange for herself. . . . And now I have a few questions to put to you, Mr Worthing. While I am making these inquiries, you, Gwendolen, will wait for me below in the carriage.

Gwendolen [*Reproachfully*] Mamma!

Lady Bracknell In the carriage, Gwendolen! [*Gwendolen goes to the door. She and Jack blow kisses to each other behind Lady Bracknell's back. Lady Bracknell looks vaguely about as if she could not understand what the noise was. Finally turns round.*] Gwendolen, the carriage!

Gwendolen Yes, mamma. [*Goes out, looking back at Jack.*]

Lady Bracknell [*Sitting down*] You can take a seat, Mr Worthing.

[*Looks in her pocket for note-book and pencil.*]

Jack Thank you, Lady Bracknell, I prefer standing.

Lady Bracknell [*Pencil and note-book in hand*] I feel bound to tell you that you are not down on my list of eligible young men, although I have the same list as the dear Duchess of Bolton has. We work together, in fact. However, I am quite ready to enter your name, should your answers be what a really affectionate mother requires. Do you smoke?

Jack Well, yes, I must admit I smoke.

Lady Bracknell I am glad to hear it. A man should always have an occupation of some kind. There are far too many idle men in London as it is. How old are you?

Jack Twenty-nine.

Lady Bracknell A very good age to be married at. I have always been of the opinion that a man who desires to get married should know either everything or nothing. Which do you know?

Jack [*After some hesitation*] I know nothing, Lady Bracknell.

Lady Bracknell I am pleased to hear it. I do not approve of anything that tampers with natural ignorance. Ignorance is like a delicate exotic fruit; touch it and the bloom is gone. The whole theory of modern education is radically unsound. Fortunately in England, at any rate, education produces no effect whatsoever. If it did, it would prove a serious danger to the upper classes, and probably lead to acts of violence in Grosvenor Square. What is your income?

Jack Between seven and eight thousand a year.

Lady Bracknell [*Makes a note in her book.*] In land, or in investments?

Jack In investments, chiefly.

Lady Bracknell That is satisfactory. What between the duties expected of one during one's lifetime, and the duties exacted from one after one's death, land has ceased to be either a profit or a pleasure. It gives one position, and prevents one from keeping it up. That's all that can be said about land.

Jack I have a country house with some land, of course, attached to it, about fifteen hundred acres, I believe; but I don't depend on that for my real income. In fact, as far as I can make out, the poachers are the only people who make anything out of it.

Lady Bracknell A country house! How many bedrooms? Well, that point can be cleared up afterwards. You have a town house, I hope? A girl with a simple, unspoiled nature, like Gwendolen, could hardly be expected to reside in the country.

Jack Well, I own a house in Belgrave Square, but it is let by the year to Lady Bloxham. Of course, I can get it back whenever I like, at six months' notice.
Lady Bracknell Lady Bloxham? I don't know her.
Jack Oh, she goes about very little. She is a lady considerably advanced in years.
Lady Bracknell Ah, nowadays that is no guarantee of respectability of character. What number in Belgrave Square?
Jack 149.
Lady Bracknell [*Shaking her head*] The unfashionable side.¹ I thought there was something. However, that could easily be altered.
Jack Do you mean the fashion, or the side?
Lady Bracknell [*Sternly*] Both, if necessary, I presume. What are your politics?
Jack Well, I am afraid I really have none. I am a Liberal Unionist.
Lady Bracknell Oh, they count as Tories. They dine with us. Or come in the evening, at any rate. Now to minor matters. Are your parents living?
Jack I have lost both my parents.
Lady Bracknell To lose one parent, Mr Worthing, may be regarded as a misfortune; to lose both looks like carelessness. Who was your father? He was evidently a man of some wealth. Was he born in what the Radical papers call the purple of commerce, or did he rise from the ranks of aristocracy?
Jack I am afraid I really don't know. The fact is, Lady Bracknell, I said I had lost my parents. It would be nearer the truth to say that my parents seem to have lost me.... I don't actually know who I am by birth. I was ... well, I was found.
Lady Bracknell Found!
Jack The late Mr Thomas Cardew, an old gentleman of a very charitable and kindly disposition, found me, and gave me the name of Worthing, because he happened to have a first-class ticket for Worthing in his pocket at the time. Worthing is a place in Sussex. It is a seaside resort.
Lady Bracknell Where did the charitable gentleman who had a first-class ticket for this seaside resort find you?
Jack [*Gravely*] In a handbag.
Lady Bracknell A handbag?
Jack [*Very seriously*] Yes, Lady Bracknell. I was in a handbag – a somewhat large, black leather handbag, with handles to it – an ordinary handbag, in fact.
Lady Bracknell In what locality did this Mr James, or Thomas, Cardew come across this ordinary handbag?
Jack In the cloakroom at Victoria Station. It was given to him in mistake for his own.
Lady Bracknell The cloakroom at Victoria Station?
Jack Yes. The Brighton Line.
Lady Bracknell The line is immaterial. Mr Worthing, I confess I feel somewhat bewildered by what you have just told me. To be born, or at any rate, bred in a handbag, whether it had handles or not, seems to me to display a contempt for the ordinary decencies of family life that reminds one of the worst excesses of the French Revolution. And I presume you know what that unfortunate movement led to? As for the particular locality in which the handbag was found, a cloakroom at a railway station might serve to conceal a social indiscretion – has

---

1: Belgrave Square is so fashionable that such a distinction is recondite.

probably, indeed, been used for that purpose before now – but it could hardly be regarded as an assured basis for a recognised position in good society.

Jack May I ask you then what you would advise me to do? I need hardly say I would do anything in the world to ensure Gwendolen's happiness.

Lady Bracknell I would strongly advise you, Mr Worthing, to try and acquire some relations as soon as possible, and to make a definite effort to produce at any rate one parent, of either sex, before the season is quite over.

Jack Well, I don't see how I could possibly manage to do that. I can produce the handbag at any moment. It is in my dressingroom at home. I really think that should satisfy you, Lady Bracknell.

Lady Bracknell Me, sir! What has it to do with me? You can hardly imagine that I and Lord Bracknell would dream of allowing our only daughter – a girl brought up with the utmost care – to marry into a cloakroom, and form an alliance with a parcel? Good morning, Mr Worthing!

[*Lady Bracknell sweeps out in majestic indignation.*]

Jack Good morning! [*Algernon, from the other room, strikes up the Wedding March. Jack looks perfectly furious, and goes to the door.*] For goodness' sake don't play that ghastly tune, Algy! How idiotic you are!

[*The music stops, and Algernon enters cheerily.*]

Algernon Didn't it go off all right, old boy? You don't mean to say Gwendolen refused you? I know it is a way she has. She is always refusing people. I think it is most ill-natured of her.

Jack Oh, Gwendolen is as right as a trivet.[1] As far as she is concerned, we are engaged. Her mother is perfectly unbearable. Never met such a gorgon . . . I don't really know what a gorgon[2] is like, but I am quite sure that Lady Bracknell is one. In any case, she is a monster, without being a myth, which is rather unfair . . . I beg your pardon, Algy, I suppose I shouldn't talk about your own aunt in that way before you.

Algernon My dear boy, I love hearing my relations abused. It is the only thing that makes me put up with them at all. Relations are simply a tedious pack of people who haven't got the remotest knowledge of how to live, nor the smallest instinct about when to die.

Jack Oh, that is nonsense!

Algernon It isn't!

Jack Well, I won't argue about the matter. You always want to argue about things.

Algernon That is exactly what things were originally made for.

Jack Upon my word, if I thought that, I'd shoot myself. . . . [*A pause*] You don't think there is any chance of Gwendolen becoming like her mother in about a hundred and fifty years, do you, Algy?

Algernon All women become like their mothers. That is their tragedy. No man does. That's his.

Jack Is that clever?

Algernon It is perfectly phrased! and quite as true as any observation in civilized life should be.

1: in perfect health.   2: three monstrous Greek sisters who had snakes in their hair and could turn men to stone by looking at them.

Jack I am sick to death of cleverness. Everybody is clever nowadays. You can't go anywhere without meeting clever people. The thing has become an absolute public nuisance. I wish to goodness we had a few fools left.

Algernon We have.

Jack I should extremely like to meet them. What do they talk about?

Algernon The fools! Oh! about the clever people, of course.

Jack What fools!

Algernon By the way, did you tell Gwendolen the truth about your being Ernest in town, and Jack in the country?

Jack [*In a very patronizing manner*] My dear fellow, the truth isn't quite the sort of thing one tells to a nice sweet refined girl. What extraordinary ideas you have about the way to behave to a woman!

Algernon The only way to behave to a woman is to make love to her, if she is pretty, and to someone else if she is plain.

Jack Oh, that is nonsense.

Algeron What about your brother? What about the profligate Ernest?

Jack Oh, before the end of the week I shall have got rid of him. I'll say he died in Paris of apoplexy. Lots of people die of apoplexy, quite suddenly, don't they?

Algernon Yes, but it's hereditary, my dear fellow. It's a sort of thing that runs in families. You had much better say a severe chill.

Jack You are sure that a severe chill isn't hereditary, or anything of that kind?

Algernon Of course it isn't!

Jack Very well, then. My poor brother Ernest is carried off suddenly in Paris, by a severe chill. That gets rid of him.

Algernon But I thought you said that . . . Miss Cardew was a little too much interested in your poor brother Ernest? Won't she feel his loss a good deal?

Jack Oh, that is all right. Cecily is not a silly romantic girl, I am glad to say. She has got a capital appetite, goes long walks, and pays no attention at all to her lessons.

Algernon I would rather like to see Cecily.

Jack I will take very good care you never do. She is excessively pretty, and she is only just eighteen.

Algernon Have you told Gwendolen yet that you have an excessively pretty ward who is only just eighteen?

Jack Oh! one doesn't blurt these things out to people. Cecily and Gwendolen are perfectly certain to be extremely great friends. I'll bet you anything you like that half an hour after they have met, they will be calling each other sister.

Algernon Women only do that when they have called each other a lot of other things first. Now, my dear boy, if we want to get a good table at Willis's, we really must go and dress. Do you know it is nearly seven?

Jack [*Irritably*] Oh! it always is nearly seven.

Algernon Well, I'm hungry.

Jack I never knew you when you weren't . . .

Algernon What shall we do after dinner? Go to the theatre?

Jack Oh no! I loathe listening.

Algernon Well, let us go to the club?

Jack Oh, no! I hate talking.

Algernon Well, we might trot round to the Empire at ten?

Jack Oh no! I can't bear looking at things. It is so silly.

Algernon Well, what shall we do?

Jack Nothing!

Algernon It is awfully hard work doing nothing. However, I don't mind hard work where there is no definite object of any kind.

[*Enter Lane.*]

Lane Miss Fairfax.

[*Enter Gwendolen. Lane goes out.*]

Algernon Gwendolen, upon my word!

Gwendolen Algy, kindly turn your back. I have something very particular to say to Mr Worthing.

Algernon Really, Gwendolen, I don't think I can allow this at all.

Gwendolen Algy, you always adopt a strictly immoral attitude towards life. You are not quite old enough to do that. [*Algernon retires to the fireplace.*]

Jack My own darling!

Gwendolen Ernest, we may never be married. From the expression on mamma's face I fear we never shall. Few parents nowadays pay any regard to what their children say to them. The old-fashioned respect for the young is fast dying out. Whatever influence I ever had over mamma, I lost at the age of three. But although she may prevent us from becoming man and wife, and I may marry someone else, and marry often, nothing that she can possibly do can alter my eternal devotion to you.

Jack Dear Gwendolen!

Gwendolen The story of your romantic origin, as related to me by Mamma, with unpleasing comments, has naturally stirred the deeper fibres of my nature. Your Christian name has an irresistible fascination. The simplicity of your character makes you exquisitely incomprehensible to me. Your town address at the Albany I have. What is your address in the country?

Jack The Manor House, Woolton, Hertfordshire.

[*Algernon, who has been carefully listening, smiles to himself, and writes the address on his shirt-cuff. Then picks up the Railway Guide.*]

Gwendolen There is a good postal service, I suppose? It may be necessary to do something desperate. That of course will require serious consideration. I will communicate with you daily.

Jack My own one!

Gwendolen How long do you remain in town?

Jack Till Monday.

Gwendolen Good! Algy, you may turn round now.

Algernon Thanks, I've turned round already.

Gwendolen You may also ring the bell.

Jack You will let me see you to your carriage, my own darling?

Gwendolen Certainly.

Jack [*To Lane, who now enters*] I will see Miss Fairfax out.

Lane Yes, sir. [*Jack and Gwendolen go off.*]

[*Lane presents several letters on a salver to Algernon. It is to be surmised that they are bills, as Algernon after looking at the envelopes, tears them up.*]

Algernon A glass of sherry, Lane.

Lane Yes, sir.

Algernon Tomorrow, Lane, I'm going Bunburying.

Lane Yes, sir.

Algernon I shall probably not be back till Monday. You can put up my dress clothes, my smoking jacket, and all the Bunbury suits . . .

Lane Yes, sir. [*Handing sherry.*]

Algernon I hope tomorrow will be a fine day, Lane.

Lane It never is, sir.

Algernon Lane, you're a perfect pessimist.

Lane I do my best to give satisfaction, sir. [*Enter Jack. Lane goes off.*]

Jack There's a sensible, intellectual girl! The only girl I ever cared for in my life. [*Algernon is laughing immoderately.*] What on earth are you so amused at?

Algernon Oh, I'm a little anxious about poor Bunbury, that is all.

Jack If you don't take care, your friend Bunbury will get you into a serious scrape some day.

Algernon I love scrapes. They are the only things that are never serious.

Jack Oh, that's nonsense, Algy. You never talk anything but nonsense.

Algernon Nobody ever does.

[*Jack looks indignantly at him, and leaves the room. Algernon lights a cigarette, reads his shirt-cuff, and smiles.*]

[Act Drop]

Act II

[*Scene: Garden at the Manor House. A flight of grey stone steps leads up to the house. The garden, an old-fashioned one, full of roses. Time of year, July. Basket chairs, and a table covered with books, are set under a large yew tree. Miss Prism discovered seated at the table. Cecily is at the back watering flowers.*]

Miss Prism [*Calling*] Cecily, Cecily! Surely such a utilitarian occupation as the watering of flowers is rather Moulton's duty than yours? Especially at a moment when intellectual pleasures await you. Your German grammar is on the table. Pray open it at page fifteen. We will repeat yesterday's lesson.

Cecily [*Coming over very slowly*] But I don't like German. It isn't at all a becoming language. I know perfectly well that I look quite plain after my German lesson.

Miss Prism Child, you know how anxious your guardian is that you should improve yourself in every way. He laid particular stress on your German, as he was leaving for town yesterday. Indeed, he always lays stress on your German when he is leaving for town.

Cecily Dear Uncle Jack is so very serious! Sometimes he is so serious that I think he cannot be quite well.

Miss Prism [*Drawing herself up*] Your guardian enjoys the best of health, and his gravity of demeanour is especially to be commended in one so comparatively young as he is. I know no one who has a higher sense of duty and responsibility.

Cecily I suppose that is why he often looks a little bored when we three are together.

Miss Prism Cecily! I am surprised at you. Mr Worthing has many troubles in his life. Idle merriment and triviality would be out of place in his conversation. You must remember his constant anxiety about that unfortunate young man his brother.

Cecily I wish Uncle Jack would allow that unfortunate young man, his brother, to come down here sometimes. We might have a good influence over him, Miss Prism. I am sure you certainly would. You know German, and geology, and things of that kind influence a man very much. [*Cecily begins to write in her diary.*]

Miss Prism [*Shaking her head*] I do not think that even I could produce any effect on a character that according to his own brother's admission is irretrievably weak and vacillating. Indeed I am not sure that I would desire to reclaim him. I am not in favour of this modern mania for turning bad people into good people at a moment's notice. As a man sows so let him reap. You must put away your diary, Cecily. I really don't see why you should keep a diary at all.

Cecily I keep a diary in order to enter the wonderful secrets of my life. If I didn't write them down I should probably forget all about them.

Miss Prism Memory, my dear Cecily, is the diary that we all carry about with us.

Cecily Yes, but it usually chronicles the things that have never happened, and couldn't possibly have happened. I believe that memory is responsible for nearly all the three-volume novels that Mudie[1] sends us.

Miss Prism Do not speak slightingly of the three-volume novel, Cecily. I wrote one myself in earlier days.

Cecily Did you really, Miss Prism? How wonderfully clever you are! I hope it did not end happily? I don't like novels that end happily. They depress me so much.

Miss Prism The good ended happily, and the bad unhappily. That is what fiction means.

Cecily I suppose so. But it seems so very unfair. And was your novel ever published?

Miss Prism Alas! no. The manuscript unfortunately was abandoned. I use the word in the sense of lost or mislaid. To your work, child, these speculations are profitless.

Cecily [*Smiling*] But I see dear Dr Chasuble coming up through the garden.

Miss Prism [*Rising and advancing*] Dr Chasuble! This is indeed a pleasure. [*Enter Canon Chasuble.*]

Chasuble And how are we this morning? Miss Prism, you are, I trust, well?

Cecily Miss Prism has just been complaining of a slight headache. I think it would do her so much good to have a short stroll with you in the Park, Dr Chasuble.

1: Mudie's Circulating Library, a nineteenth-century institution that rented out books by the week.

Miss Prism Cecily, I have not mentioned anything about a headache.

Cecily No, dear Miss Prism, I know that, but I felt instinctively that you had a headache. Indeed I was thinking about that, and not about my German lesson, when the Rector came in.

Chasuble I hope, Cecily, you are not inattentive.

Cecily Oh, I am afraid I am.

Chasuble That is strange. Were I fortunate enough to be Miss Prism's pupil, I would hang upon her lips. [*Miss Prism glares.*] I spoke metaphorically. My metaphor was drawn from bees.[1] Ahem! Mr Worthing, I suppose, has not returned from town yet?

Miss Prism We do not expect him till Monday afternoon.

Chasuble Ah yes, he usually likes to spend his Sunday in London. He is not one of those whose sole aim is enjoyment, as, by all accounts, that unfortunate young man his brother seems to be. But I must not disturb Egeria[2] and her pupil any longer.

Miss Prism Egeria? My name is Lætitia, Doctor.

Chasuble [*Bowing*] A classical allusion merely, drawn from the pagan authors. I shall see you both no doubt at Evensong?[3]

Miss Prism I think, dear Doctor, I will have a stroll with you. I find I have a headache after all, and a walk might do it good.

Chasuble With pleasure, Miss Prism, with pleasure. We might go as far as the schools and back.

Miss Prism That would be delightful. Cecily, you will read your Political Economy in my absence. The chapter on the Fall of the Rupee you may omit. It is somewhat too sensational. Even these metallic problems have their melodramatic side.

[*Goes down the garden with Dr Chasuble.*]

Cecily [*Picks up books and throws them back on table.*] Horrid Political Economy! Horrid geography! Horrid, horrid German!

[*Enter Merriman with a card on a salver.*]

Merriman Mr Ernest Worthing has just driven over from the station. He has brought his luggage with him.

Cecily [*Takes the card and reads it.*] 'Mr Ernest Worthing, B. 4, The Albany, W.' Uncle Jack's brother! Did you tell him Mr Worthing was in town?

Merriman Yes, Miss. He seemed very much disappointed. I mentioned that you and Miss Prism were in the garden. He said he was anxious to speak to you privately for a moment.

Cecily Ask Mr Ernest Worthing to come here. I suppose you had better talk to the housekeeper about a room for him.

Merriman Yes, Miss. [*Merriman goes off.*]

Cecily I have never met any really wicked person before. I feel rather frightened. I am so afraid he will look just like everyone else.

[*Enter Algernon, very gay and debonair.*]

He does!

1: the reference is to the phrase 'to hang upon her every word', but the relation to bees is obscure. 2: mythical female adviser to Numa Pompilius, king of Rome. 3: a church service held in the late afternoon.

Algernon [*Raising his hat*] You are my little cousin Cecily, I'm sure.

Cecily You are under some strange mistake. I am not little. In fact, I believe I am more than usually tall for my age. [*Algernon is rather taken aback.*] But I am your cousin Cecily. You, I see from your card, are Uncle Jack's brother, my cousin Ernest, my wicked cousin Ernest.

Algernon Oh! I am not really wicked at all, cousin Cecily. You mustn't think that I am wicked.

Cecily If you are not, then you have certainly been deceiving us all in a very inexcusable manner. I hope you have not been leading a double life, pretending to be wicked and being really good all the time. That would be hypocrisy.

Algeron [*Looks at her in amazement.*] Oh! Of course I have been rather reckless.

Cecily I am glad to hear it.

Algernon In fact, now you mention the subject, I have been very bad in my own small way.

Cecily I don't think you should be so proud of that, though I am sure it must have been very pleasant.

Algernon It is much pleasanter being here with you.

Cecily I can't understand how you are here at all. Uncle Jack won't be back till Monday afternoon.

Algernon That is a great disappointment. I am obliged to go up by the first train on Monday morning. I have a business appointment that I am anxious . . . to miss.

Cecily Couldn't you miss it anywhere but in London?

Algernon No; the appointment is in London.

Cecily Well, I know, of course, how important it is not to keep a business engagement, if one wants to retain any sense of the beauty of life, but still I think you had better wait till Uncle Jack arrives. I know he wants to speak to you about your emigrating.

Algernon About my what?

Cecily Your emigrating. He has gone up to buy your outfit.

Algernon I certainly wouldn't let Jack buy my outfit. He has no taste in neckties at all.

Cecily I don't think you will require neckties. Uncle Jack is sending you to Australia.

Algernon Australia! I'd sooner die.

Cecily Well, he said at dinner on Wednesday night, that you would have to choose between this world, the next world, and Australia.

Algernon Oh, well! The accounts I have received of Australia and the next world are not particularly encouraging. This world is good enough for me, cousin Cecily.

Cecily Yes, but are you good enough for it?

Algernon I'm afraid I'm not that. That is why I want you to reform me. You might make that your mission, if you don't mind, cousin Cecily.

Cecily I'm afraid I've no time, this afternoon.

Algernon Well, would you mind my reforming myself this afternoon?

Cecily It is rather quixotic of you. But I think you should try.

Algernon I will. I feel better already.

Cecily You are looking a little worse.

Algernon That is because I am hungry.

Cecily How thoughtless of me. I should have remembered that when one is going to lead an entirely new life, one requires regular and wholesome meals. Won't you come in?

Algernon Thank you. Might I have a buttonhole first? I never have any appetite unless I have a buttonhole first.

Cecily A Maréchal Niel?[1] [*Picks up scissors.*]

Algernon No, I'd sooner have a pink rose.

Cecily Why? [*Cuts a flower.*]

Algernon Because you are like a pink rose, cousin Cecily.

Cecily I don't think it can be right for you to talk to me like that. Miss Prism never says such things to me.

Algernon Then Miss Prism is a short-sighted old lady. [*Cecily puts the rose in his buttonhole.*] You are the prettiest girl I ever saw.

Cecily Miss Prism says that all good looks are a snare.

Algernon They are a snare that every sensible man would like to be caught in.

Cecily Oh! I don't think I would care to catch a sensible man. I shouldn't know what to talk to him about.

[*They pass into the house. Miss Prism and Dr Chasuble return.*]

Miss Prism You are too much alone, dear Dr Chasuble. You should be married. A misanthrope I can understand – a womanthrope, never!

Chasuble [*With a scholar's shudder*] Believe me, I do not deserve so neologistic a phrase. The precept as well as the practice of the Primitive Church was distinctly against matrimony.

Miss Prism [*Sententiously*] That is obviously the reason why the Primitive Church has not lasted up to the present day. And do you not seem to realise, dear Doctor, that by persistently remaining single, a man converts himself into a permanent public temptation. Men should be more careful; this very celibacy leads weaker vessels astray.

Chasuble But is a man not equally attractive when married?

Miss Prism No married man is ever attractive except to his wife.

Chasuble And often, I've been told, not even to her.

Miss Prism That depends on the intellectual sympathies of the woman. Maturity can always be depended on. Ripeness can be trusted. Young women are green. [*Dr Chasuble starts.*] I spoke horticulturally. My metaphor was drawn from fruits. But where is Cecily?

Chasuble Perhaps she followed us to the schools.

[*Enter Jack slowly from the back of the garden. He is dressed in the deepest mourning, with crape hatband and black gloves.*]

Miss Prism Mr Worthing!

Chasuble Mr Worthing?

Miss Prism This is indeed a surprise. We did not look for you till Monday afternoon.

1: a yellow rose.

Jack [*Shakes Miss Prism's hand in a tragic manner.*] I have returned sooner than I expected. Dr Chasuble, I hope you are well?

Chasuble Dear Mr Worthing, I trust this garb of woe does not betoken some terrible calamity?

Jack My brother.

Miss Prism More shameful debts and extravagance?

Chasuble Still leading his life of pleasure?

Jack [*Shaking his head*] Dead!

Chasuble Your brother Ernest dead?

Jack Quite dead.

Miss Prism What a lesson for him! I trust he will profit by it.

Chasuble Mr Worthing, I offer you my sincere condolence. You have at least the consolation of knowing that you were always the most generous and forgiving of brothers.

Jack Poor Ernest! He had many faults, but it is a sad, sad blow.

Chasuble Very sad indeed. Were you with him at the end?

Jack No. He died abroad; in Paris, in fact. I had a telegram last night from the manager of the Grand Hotel.

Chasuble Was the cause of death mentioned?

Jack A severe chill, it seems.

Miss Prism As a man sows, so shall he reap.

Chasuble [*Raising his hand*] Charity, dear Miss Prism, charity! None of us are perfect. I myself am peculiarly susceptible to draughts. Will the interment take place here?

Jack No. He seemed to have expressed a desire to be buried in Paris.

Chasuble In Paris! [*Shakes his head.*] I fear that hardly points to any very serious state of mind at the last. You would no doubt wish me to make some slight allusion to this tragic domestic affliction next Sunday. [*Jack presses his hand convulsively.*] My sermon on the meaning of the manna in the wilderness can be adapted to almost any occasion, joyful, or, as in the present case, distressing. [*All sigh.*] I have preached it at harvest celebrations, christenings, confirmations, on days of humiliation and festal days. The last time I delivered it was in the Cathedral, as a charity sermon on behalf of the Society for the Prevention of Discontent among the Upper Orders. The Bishop, who was present, was much struck by some of the analogies I drew.

Jack Ah! that reminds me, you mentioned christenings, I think, Dr Chasuble? I suppose you know how to christen all right? [*Dr Chasuble looks astounded.*] I mean, of course, you are continually christening, aren't you?

Miss Prism It is, I regret to say, one of the Rector's most constant duties in this parish. I have often spoken to the poorer classes on the subject. But they don't seem to know what thrift is.

Chasuble But is there any particular infant in whom you are interested, Mr Worthing? Your brother was, I believe, unmarried, was he not?

Jack Oh yes.

Miss Prism [*Bitterly*] People who live entirely for pleasure usually are.

Jack But it is not for any child, dear Doctor. I am very fond of children. No! the fact is, I would like to be christened myself, this afternoon, if you have nothing better to do.

Chasuble But surely, Mr Worthing, you have been christened already?

Jack I don't remember anything about it.

Chasuble But have you any grave doubts on the subject?

Jack I certainly intend to have. Of course I don't know if the thing would bother you in any way, or if you think I am a little too old now.

Chasuble Not at all. The sprinkling, and, indeed, the immersion of adults is a perfectly canonical practice.

Jack Immersion!

Chasuble You need have no apprehensions. Sprinkling is all that is necessary, or indeed I think advisable. Our weather is so changeable. At what hour would you wish the ceremony performed?

Jack Oh, I might trot round about five if that would suit you.

Chasuble Perfectly, perfectly! In fact I have two similar ceremonies to perform at that time. A case of twins that occurred recently in one of the outlying cottages on your own estate. Poor Jenkins the carter, a most hard-working man.

Jack Oh! I don't see much fun in being christened along with other babies. It would be childish. Would half-past five do?

Chasuble Admirably! Admirably! [*Takes out watch.*] And now, dear Mr Worthing, I will not intrude any longer into a house of sorrow. I would merely beg you not to be too much bowed down by grief. What seems to us bitter trials are often blessings in disguise.

Miss Prism This seems to me a blessing of an extremely obvious kind.

[*Enter Cecily from the house.*]

Cecily Uncle Jack! Oh, I am pleased to see you back. But what horrid clothes you have got on! Do go and change them.

Miss Prism Cecily!

Chasuble My child! my child! [*Cecily goes towards Jack; he kisses her brow in a melancholy manner.*]

Cecily What is the matter, Uncle Jack? Do look happy! You look as if you had toothache, and I have got such a surprise for you. Who do you think is in the dining-room? Your brother!

Jack Who?

Cecily Your brother Ernest. He arrived about half an hour ago.

Jack What nonsense! I haven't got a brother!

Cecily Oh, don't say that. However badly he may have behaved to you in the past he is still your brother. You couldn't be so heartless as to disown him. I'll tell him to come out. And you will shake hands with him, won't you, Uncle Jack? [*Runs back into the house.*]

Chasuble These are very joyful tidings.

Miss Prism After we had all been resigned to his loss, his sudden return seems to me peculiarly distressing.

Jack My brother is in the dining-room? I don't know what it all means. I think it is perfectly absurd.

[*Enter Algernon and Cecily hand in hand. They come slowly up to Jack.*]

Jack Good heavens! [*Motions Algernon away.*]

Algernon Brother John, I have come down from town to tell you that I am very sorry for all the trouble I have given you, and that I intend to lead a better life in the future. [*Jack glares at him and does not take his hand.*]

Cecily Uncle Jack, you are not going to refuse your own brother's hand?

Jack Nothing will induce me to take his hand. I think his coming down here disgraceful. He knows perfectly well why.

Cecily Uncle Jack, do be nice. There is some good in everyone. Ernest has just been telling me about his poor invalid friend Mr Bunbury whom he goes to visit so often. And surely there must be much good in one who is kind to an invalid, and leaves the pleasures of London to sit by a bed of pain.

Jack Oh! he has been talking about Bunbury, has he?

Cecily Yes, he has told me all about poor Mr Bunbury, and his terrible state of health.

Jack Bunbury! Well, I won't have him talk to you about Bunbury or about anything else. It is enough to drive one perfectly frantic.

Algernon Of course I admit that the faults were all on my side. But I must say that I think that Brother John's coldness to me is peculiarly painful. I expected a more enthusiastic welcome, especially considering it is the first time I have come here.

Cecily Uncle Jack, if you don't shake hands with Ernest, I will never forgive you.

Jack Never forgive me?

Cecily Never, never, never!

Jack Well, this is the last time I shall ever do it. [*Shakes hands with Algernon and glares.*]

Chasuble It's pleasant, is it not, to see so perfect a reconciliation? I think we might leave the two brothers together.

Miss Prism Cecily, you will come with us.

Cecily Certainly, Miss Prism. My little task of reconciliation is over.

Chasuble You have done a beautiful action today, dear child.

Miss Prism We must not be premature in our judgments.

Cecily I feel very happy. [*They all go off except Jack and Algernon.*]

Jack You young scoundrel, Algy, you must get out of this place as soon as possible. I don't allow any Bunburying here.

[*Enter Merriman.*]

Merriman I have put Mr Ernest's things in the room next to yours, sir. I suppose that is all right?

Jack What?

Merriman Mr Ernest's luggage, sir. I have unpacked it and put it in the room next to your own.

Jack His luggage?

Merriman Yes, sir. Three portmanteaus, a dressing-case, two hat boxes, and a large luncheon-basket.

Algernon I am afraid I can't stay more than a week this time.

Jack Merriman, order the dog-cart at once. Mr Ernest has been suddenly called back to town.

Merriman Yes, sir. [*Goes back into the house.*]

Algernon What a fearful liar you are, Jack. I have not been called back to town at all.

Jack Yes, you have.

Algernon I haven't heard anyone call me.

Jack Your duty as a gentleman calls you back.

Algernon My duty as a gentleman has never interfered with my pleasures in the smallest degree.

Jack I can quite understand that.

Algernon Well, Cecily is a darling.

Jack You are not to talk of Miss Cardew like that. I don't like it.

Algernon Well, I don't like your clothes. You look perfectly ridiculous in them. Why on earth don't you go up and change? It is perfectly childish to be in deep mourning for a man who is actually staying for a whole week with you in your house as a guest. I call it grotesque.

Jack You are certainly not staying with me for a whole week as a guest or anything else. You have got to leave . . . by the four-five train.

Algernon I certainly won't leave you so long as you are in mourning. It would be most unfriendly. If I were in mourning you would stay with me, I suppose. I should think it very unkind if you didn't.

Jack Well, will you go if I change my clothes?

Algernon Yes, if you are not too long. I never saw anybody take so long to dress, and with such little result.

Jack Well, at any rate, that is better than being always overdressed as you are.

Algernon If I am occasionally a little overdressed, I make up for it by being always immensely over-educated.

Jack Your vanity is ridiculous, your conduct an outrage, and your presence in my garden utterly absurd. However, you have got to catch the four-five, and I hope you will have a pleasant journey back to town. This Bunburying, as you call it, has not been a great success for you. [*Goes into the house.*]

Algernon I think it has been a great success. I'm in love with Cecily, and that is everything.

[*Enter Cecily at the back of the garden. She picks up the can and begins to water the flowers.*]

But I must see her before I go, and make arrangements for another Bunbury. Ah, there she is.

Cecily Oh, I merely came back to water the roses. I thought you were with Uncle Jack.

Algernon He's gone to order the dog-cart for me.

Cecily Oh, is he going to take you for a nice drive?

Algernon He's going to send me away.

Cecily Then have we got to part?

Algernon I am afraid so. It's a very painful parting.

Cecily It is always painful to part from people whom one has known for a very brief space of time. The absence of old friends one can endure with equanimity. But even a momentary separation from anyone to whom one has just been introduced is almost unbearable.

Algernon Thank you.

[*Enter Merriman.*]

Merriman The dog-cart is at the door, sir.

[*Algernon looks appealingly at Cecily.*]

Cecily It can wait, Merriman . . . for . . . five minutes.

Merriman Yes, Miss. [*Exit Merriman.*]

Algernon I hope, Cecily, I shall not offend you if I state quite frankly and openly that you seem to me to be in every way the visible personification of absolute perfection.

Cecily I think your frankness does you great credit, Ernest. If you will allow me I will copy your remarks into my diary. [*Goes over to table and begins writing in diary.*]

Algernon Do you really keep a diary? I'd give anything to look at it.

Cecily Oh no. [*Puts her hand over it*] You see, it is simply a very young girl's record of her own thoughts and impressions, and consequently meant for publication. When it appears in volume form I hope you will order a copy. But pray, Ernest, don't stop. I delight in taking down from dictation. I have reached 'absolute perfection.' You can go on. I am quite ready for more.

Algernon [*Somewhat taken aback*] Ahem! Ahem!

Cecily Oh, don't cough, Ernest. When one is dictating one should speak fluently and not cough. Besides, I don't know how to spell a cough.

Algernon [*Speaking very rapidly*] Cecily, ever since I first looked upon your wonderful and incomparable beauty, I have dared to love you wildly, passionately, devotedly, hopelessly.

Cecily I don't think that you should tell me that you love me wildly, passionately, devotedly, hopelessly. Hopelessly doesn't seem to make much sense, does it?

Algernon Cecily!

[*Enter Merriman.*]

Merriman The dog-cart is waiting, sir.

Algernon Tell it to come round next week, at the same hour.

Merriman [*Looks at Cecily, who makes no sign.*] Yes, sir.

[*Merriman retires.*]

Cecily Uncle Jack would be very much annoyed if he knew you were staying on till next week, at the same hour.

Algernon Oh, I don't care about Jack. I don't care for anybody in the whole world but you. I love you, Cecily. You will marry me, won't you?

Cecily You silly boy! Of course. Why, we have been engaged for the last three months.

Algernon For the last three months?

Cecily Yes, it will be exactly three months on Thursday.

Algernon But how did we become engaged?

Cecily Well, ever since dear Uncle Jack first confessed to us that he had a younger brother who was very wicked and bad, you of course have formed the chief topic of conversation between my self and Miss Prism. And of course a man who is much talked about is always very attractive. One feels there must be something in him after all. I daresay it was foolish of me, but I fell in love with you, Ernest.

Algernon Darling! And when was the engagement actually settled?

Cecily On the 14th of February last. Worn out by your entire ignorance of my existence, I determined to end the matter one way or the other, and after a long struggle with myself I accepted you under this dear old tree here. The next day I bought this little ring in your name, and this is the little bangle with the true lovers' knot I promised you always to wear.

Algernon Did I give you this? It's very pretty, isn't it?

Cecily Yes, you've wonderfully good taste, Ernest. It's the excuse I've always given for your leading such a bad life. And this is the box in which I keep all your dear letters. [*Kneels at table, opens box, and produces letters tied up with blue ribbon.*]

Algernon My letters! But my own sweet Cecily, I have never written you any letters.

Cecily You need hardly remind me of that, Ernest. I remember only too well that I was forced to write your letters for you. I always wrote three times a week, and sometimes oftener.

Algernon Oh, do let me read them, Cecily.

Cecily Oh, I couldn't possibly. They would make you far too conceited. [*Replaces box.*] The three you wrote me after I had broken off the engagement are so beautiful, and so badly spelled, that even now I can hardly read them without crying a little.

Algernon But was our engagement ever broken off?

Cecily Of course it was. On the 22nd of last March. You can see the entry if you like. [*Shows diary.*] 'Today I broke off my engagement with Ernest. I feel it is better to do so. The weather still continues charming.'

Algernon But why on earth did you break it off? What had I done? I had done nothing at all. Cecily, I am very much hurt indeed to hear you broke it off. Particularly when the weather was so charming.

Cecily It would hardly have been a really serious engagement if it hadn't been broken off at least once. But I forgave you before the week was out.

Algernon [*Crossing to her, and kneeling*] What a perfect angel you are, Cecily.

Cecily You dear romantic boy. [*He kisses her, she puts her fingers through his hair.*] I hope your hair curls naturally, does it?

Algernon Yes, darling, with a little help from others.

Cecily I am so glad.

Algernon You'll never break off our engagement again, Cecily?

Cecily I don't think I could break it off now that I have actually met you. Besides, of course, there is the question of your name.

Algernon [*Nervously*] Yes, of course.

Cecily You must not laugh at me, darling, but it had always been a girlish dream of mine to love someone whose name was Ernest. [*Algernon rises, Cecily also.*] There is something in that name that seems to inspire absolute confidence. I pity any poor married woman whose husband is not called Ernest.

Algeron But, my dear child, do you mean to say you could not love me if I had some other name?

Cecily But what name?

Algernon Oh, any name you like – Algernon for instance . . .

Cecily But I don't like the name of Algernon.

Algernon Well, my own dear, sweet, loving little darling, I really can't see why you should object to the name of Algernon. It is not at all a bad name. In fact, it is rather an aristocratic name. Half of the chaps who get into the Bankruptcy Court are called Algernon. But seriously, Cecily [*Moving to her*] . . . if my name was Algy, couldn't you love me?

Cecily [*Rising*] I might respect you, Ernest, I might admire your character, but I fear that I should not be able to give you my undivided attention.

Algernon Ahem! Cecily! [*Picking up hat*] Your Rector here is, I suppose, thoroughly experienced in the practice of all the rites and ceremonials of the Church?

Cecily Oh, yes. Dr Chasuble is a most learned man. He has never written a single book, so you can imagine how much he knows.

Algernon I must see him at once on a most important christening – I mean on most important business.

Cecily Oh!

Algernon I shan't be away more than half an hour.

Cecily Considering that we have been engaged since February 14th, and that I only met you today for the first time, I think it is rather hard that you should leave me for so long a period as half an hour. Couldn't you make it twenty minutes?

Algernon I'll be back in no time. [*Kisses her and rushes down the garden.*]

Cecily What an impetuous boy he is! I like his hair so much. I must enter his proposal in my diary.

[*Enter Merriman.*]

Merriman A Miss Fairfax has just called to see Mr Worthing. On very important business Miss Fairfax states.

Cecily Isn't Mr Worthing in his library?

Merriman Mr Worthing went over in the direction of the Rectory some time ago.

Cecily Pray ask the lady to come out here; Mr Worthing is sure to be back soon. And you can bring tea.

Merriman Yes, Miss. [*Goes out.*]

Cecily Miss Fairfax! I suppose one of the many good elderly women who are associated with Uncle Jack in some of his philanthropic work in London. I don't quite like women who are interested in philanthropic work. I think it is so forward of them.

[*Enter Merriman.*]

Merriman Miss Fairfax.

[*Enter Gwendolen. Exit Merriman.*]

Cecily [*Advancing to meet her*] Pray let me introduce myself to you. My name is Cecily Cardew.

Gwendolen Cecily Cardew? [*Moving to her and shaking hands*] What a very sweet name! Something tells me that we are going to be great friends. I like you already more than I can say. My first impressions of people are never wrong.

Cecily How nice of you to like me so much after we have known each other such a comparatively short time. Pray sit down.

Gwendolen [*Still standing up*] I may call you Cecily, may I not?

Cecily With pleasure!

Gwendolen And you will always call me Gwendolen, won't you?

Cecily If you wish.

Gwendolen Then that is all quite settled, is it not?

Cecily I hope so. [*A pause. They both sit down together.*]

Gwendolen Perhaps this might be a favourable opportunity for my mentioning who I am. My father is Lord Bracknell. You have never heard of papa, I suppose?

Cecily I don't think so.

Gwendolen Outside the family circle, papa, I am glad to say, is entirely unknown. I think that is quite as it should be. The home seems to me to be the proper sphere for the man. And certainly once a man begins to neglect his domestic duties he becomes painfully effeminate, does he not? And I don't like that. It makes men so very attractive. Cecily, mamma, whose views on education are remarkably strict, has brought me up to be extremely short-sighted; it is part of her system; so do you mind my looking at you through my glasses?

Cecily Oh! not at all, Gwendolen. I am very fond of being looked at.

Gwendolen [*After examining Cecily carefully through a lorgnette[1]*] You are here on a short visit I suppose.

Cecily Oh no! I live here.

Gwendolen [*Severely*] Really? Your mother, no doubt, or some female relative of advanced years, resides here also?

Cecily Oh no! I have no mother, nor, in fact, any relations.

Gwendolen Indeed?

Cecily My dear guardian, with the assistance of Miss Prism, has the arduous task of looking after me.

Gwendolen Your guardian?

Cecily Yes, I am Mr Worthing's ward.

Gwendolen Oh! It is strange he never mentioned to me that he had a ward. How secretive of him! He grows more interesting hourly. I am not sure, however, that the news inspires me with feelings of unmixed delight. [*Rising and going to her.*] I am very fond of you, Cecily; I have liked you ever since I met you! But I am bound to state that now that I know that you are Mr Worthing's ward, I cannot help expressing a wish you were – well just a little older than you seem to be – and not quite so very alluring in appearance. In fact, if I may speak candidly –

Cecily Pray do! I think that whenever one has anything unpleasant to say, one should always be quite candid.

Gwendolen Well, to speak with perfect candour, Cecily, I wish that you were fully forty-two, and more than usually plain for your age. Ernest has a strong upright nature. He is the very soul of truth and honour. Disloyalty would be as impossible to him as deception. But even men of the noblest possible moral character are extremely susceptible to the influence of the physical charms of others. Modern, no less than ancient history, supplies us with many most painful

---

1: pair of spectacles or opera glasses mounted on a handle.

examples of what I refer to. If it were not so, indeed, history would be quite unreadable.

Cecily I beg your pardon, Gwendolen, did you say Ernest?

Gwendolen Yes.

Cecily Oh, but it is not Mr Ernest Worthing who is my guardian. It is his brother – his elder brother.

Gwendolen [*Sitting down again*] Ernest never mentioned to me that he had a brother.

Cecily I am sorry to say they have not been on good terms for a long time.

Gwendolen Ah! that accounts for it. And now that I think of it I have never heard any man mention his brother. The subject seems distasteful to most men. Cecily, you have lifted a load from my mind. I was growing almost anxious. It would have been terrible if any cloud had come across a friendship like ours, would it not? Of course you are quite, quite sure that it is not Mr Ernest Worthing who is your guardian?

Cecily Quite sure. [*A pause*] In fact, I am going to be his.

Gwendolen [*Inquiringly*] I beg your pardon?

Cecily [*Rather shy and confidingly*] Dearest Gwendolen, there is no reason why I should make a secret of it to you. Our little county newspaper is sure to chronicle the fact next week. Mr Ernest Worthing and I are engaged to be married.

Gwendolen [*Quite politely, rising*] My darling Cecily, I think there must be some slight error. Mr Ernest Worthing is engaged to me. The announcement will appear in the *Morning Post* on Saturday at the latest.

Cecily [*Very politely, rising*] I am afraid you must be under some misconception. Ernest proposed to me exactly ten minutes ago. [*Shows diary.*]

Gwendolen [*Examines diary through her lorgnette carefully.*] It is certainly very curious, for he asked me to be his wife yesterday afternoon at 5:30. If you would care to verify the incident, pray do so. [*Produces diary of her own.*] I never travel without my diary. One should always have something sensational to read in the train. I am so sorry, dear Cecily, if it is any disappointment to you, but I am afraid I have the prior claim.

Cecily It would distress me more than I can tell you, dear Gwendolen, if it caused you any mental or physical anguish, but I feel bound to point out that since Ernest proposed to you he clearly has changed his mind.

Gwendolen [*Meditatively*] If the poor fellow has been entrapped into any foolish promise I shall consider it my duty to rescue him at once, and with a firm hand.

Cecily [*Thoughtfully and sadly*] Whatever unfortunate entanglement my dear boy may have got into, I will never reproach him with it after we are married.

Gwendolen Do you allude to me, Miss Cardew, as an entanglement? You are presumptuous. On an occasion of this kind it becomes more than a moral duty to speak one's mind. It becomes a pleasure.

Cecily Do you suggest, Miss Fairfax, that I entrapped Ernest into an engagement? How dare you? This is no time for wearing the shallow mask of manner. When I see a spade I call it a spade.

Gwendolen [*Satirically*] I am glad to say that I have never seen a spade. It is obvious that our social spheres have been widely different.
[*Enter Merriman, followed by the footman. He carries a salver, tablecloth, and plate stand. Cecily is about to retort. The presence of the servants exercises a restraining influence, under which both girls chafe.*]
Merriman Shall I lay tea here as usual, Miss?
Cecily [*Sternly, in a calm voice*] Yes, as usual. [*Merriman begins to clear table and lay cloth. A long pause. Cecily and Gwendolen glare at each other.*]
Gwendolen Are there many interesting walks in the vicinity, Miss Cardew?
Cecily Oh! yes! a great many. From the top of one of the hills quite close one can see five counties.
Gwendolen Five counties! I don't think I should like that. I hate crowds.
Cecily [*Sweetly*] I suppose that is why you live in town? [*Gwendolen bites her lip, and beats her foot nervously with her parasol.*]
Gwendolen [*Looking round*] Quite a well-kept garden this is, Miss Cardew.
Cecily So glad you like it, Miss Fairfax.
Gwendolen I had no idea there were any flowers in the country.
Cecily Oh, flowers are as common here, Miss Fairfax, as people are in London.
Gwendolen Personally I cannot understand how anybody manages to exist in the country, if anybody who is anybody does. The country always bores me to death.
Cecily Ah! This is what the newspapers call agricultural depression, is it not? I believe the aristocracy are suffering very much from it just at present. It is almost an epidemic amongst them, I have been told. May I offer you some tea, Miss Fairfax?
Gwendolen [*With elaborate politeness*] Thank you. [*Aside*] Detestable girl! But I require tea!
Cecily [*Sweetly*] Sugar?
Gwendolen [*Superciliously*] No, thank you. Sugar is not fashionable any more. [*Cecily looks angrily at her, takes up the tongs and puts four lumps of sugar into the cup.*]
Cecily [*Severely*] Cake or bread and butter?
Gwendolen [*In a bored manner*] Bread and butter, please. Cake is rarely seen at the best houses nowadays.
Cecily [*Cuts a very large slice of cake, and puts it on the tray.*] Hand that to Miss Fairfax.
[*Merriman does so, and goes out with footman. Gwendolen drinks the tea and makes a grimace. Puts down cup at once, reaches out her hand to the bread and butter, looks at it, and finds it is cake. Rises in indignation.*]
Gwendolen You have filled my tea with lumps of sugar, and though I asked most distinctly for bread and butter, you have given me cake. I am known for the gentleness of my disposition, and the extraordinary sweetness of my nature, but I warn you, Miss Cardew, you may go too far.
Cecily [*Rising.*] To save my poor, innocent, trusting boy from the machinations of any other girl there are no lengths to which I would not go.
Gwendolen From the moment I saw you I distrusted you. I felt that you were

false and deceitful. I am never deceived in such matters. My first impressions of people are invariably right.

Cecily It seems to me, Miss Fairfax, that I am trespassing on your valuable time. No doubt you have many other calls of a similar character to make in the neighbourhood.

[*Enter Jack.*]

Gwendolen [*Catching sight of him*] Ernest! My own Ernest!

Jack Gwendolen! Darling! [*Offers to kiss her.*]

Gwendolen [*Drawing back*] A moment! May I ask if you are engaged to be married to this young lady? [*Points to Cecily.*]

Jack To dear little Cecily! Of course not! What could have put such an idea into your pretty little head?

Gwendolen Thank you. You may! [*Offers her cheek.*]

Cecily [*Very sweetly*] I knew there must be some misunderstanding, Miss Fairfax. The gentleman whose arm is at present round your waist is my dear guardian, Mr John Worthing.

Gwendolen I beg your pardon?

Cecily This is Uncle Jack.

Gwendolen [*Receding*] Jack! Oh!

[*Enter Algernon.*]

Cecily Here is Ernest.

Algernon [*Goes straight over to Cecily without noticing anyone else.*] My own love! [*Offers to kiss her.*]

Cecily [*Drawing back*] A moment, Ernest! May I ask you – are you engaged to be married to this young lady?

Algernon [*Looking round*] To what young lady? Good heavens! Gwendolen!

Cecily Yes! to good heavens, Gwendolen, I mean to Gwendolen.

Algernon [*Laughing*] Of course not! What could have put such an idea into your pretty little head?

Cecily Thank you. [*Presenting her cheek to be kissed*] You may. [*Algernon kisses her.*]

Gwendolen I felt there was some slight error, Miss Cardew. The gentleman who is now embracing you is my cousin, Mr Algernon Moncrieff.

Cecily [*Breaking away from Algernon*] Algernon Moncrieff! Oh! [*The two girls move towards each other and put their arms round each other's waists as if for protection.*]

Cecily Are you called Algernon?

Algernon I cannot deny it.

Cecily Oh!

Gwendolen Is your name really John?

Jack [*Standing rather proudly*] I could deny it if I liked. I could deny anything if I liked. But my name certainly is John. It has been John for years.

Cecily [*To Gwendolen*] A gross deception has been practised on both of us.

Gwendolen My poor wounded Cecily!

Cecily My sweet wronged Gwendolen!

Gwendolen [*Slowly and seriously*] You will call me sister, will you not? [*They embrace. Jack and Algernon groan and walk up and down.*]

Cecily [*Rather brightly*] There is just one question I would like to be allowed to ask my guardian.

Gwendolen An admirable idea! Mr Worthing, there is just one question I would like to be permitted to put to you. Where is your brother Ernest? We are both engaged to be married to your brother Ernest, so it is a matter of some importance to us to know where your brother Ernest is at present.

Jack [*Slowly and hesitatingly*] Gwendolen – Cecily – it is very painful for me to be forced to speak the truth. It is the first time in my life that I have ever been reduced to such a painful position, and I am really quite inexperienced in doing anything of the kind. However I will tell you quite frankly that I have no brother Ernest. I have no brother at all. I never had a brother in my life, and I certainly have not the smallest intention of ever having one in the future.

Cecily [*Surprised*] No brother at all?

Jack [*Cheerily*] None!

Gwendolen [*Severely*] Had you never a brother of any kind?

Jack [*Pleasantly*] Never. Not even of any kind.

Gwendolen I am afraid it is quite clear, Cecily, that neither of us is engaged to be married to anyone.

Cecily It is not a very pleasant position for a young girl suddenly to find herself in. Is it?

Gwendolen Let us go into the house. They will hardly venture to come after us there.

Cecily No, men are so cowardly, aren't they?

[*They retire into the house with scornful looks.*]

Jack This ghastly state of things is what you call Bunburying, I suppose?

Algernon Yes, and a perfectly wonderful Bunbury it is. The most wonderful Bunbury I have ever had in my life.

Jack Well, you've no right whatsoever to Bunbury here.

Algernon That is absurd. One has a right to Bunbury anywhere one chooses. Every serious Bunburyist knows that.

Jack Serious Bunburyist! Good heavens!

Algernon Well, one must be serious about something, if one wants to have any amusement in life. I happen to be serious about Bunburying. What on earth you are serious about I haven't got the remotest idea. About everything, I should fancy. You have such an absolutely trivial nature.

Jack Well, the only small satisfaction I have in the whole of this wretched business is that your friend Bunbury is quite exploded. You won't be able to run down to the country quite so often as you used to do, dear Algy. And a very good thing too.

Algernon Your brother is a little off colour, isn't he, dear Jack? You won't be able to disappear to London quite so frequently as your wicked custom was. And not a bad thing either.

Jack As for your conduct towards Miss Cardew, I must say that your taking in a sweet, simple, innocent girl like that is quite inexcusable. To say nothing of the fact that she is my ward.

Algernon I can see no possible defence at all for your deceiving a brilliant, clever, thoroughly experienced young lady like Miss Fairfax. To say nothing of the fact that she is my cousin.

Jack I wanted to be engaged to Gwendolen, that is all. I love her.

Algernon Well, I simply wanted to be engaged to Cecily. I adore her.

Jack There is certainly no chance of your marrying Miss Cardew.

Algernon I don't think there is much likelihood, Jack, of you and Miss Fairfax being united.

Jack Well, that is no business of yours.

Algernon If it was my business, I wouldn't talk about it. [*Begins to eat muffins.*] It is very vulgar to talk about one's business. Only people like stockbrokers do that, and then merely at dinner parties.

Jack How you can sit there, calmly eating muffins when we are in this horrible trouble, I can't make out. You seem to me to be perfectly heartless.

Algernon Well, I can't eat muffins in an agitated manner. The butter would probably get on my cuffs. One should always eat muffins quite calmly. It is the only way to eat them.

Jack I say it's perfectly heartless your eating muffins at all, under the circumstances.

Algernon When I am in trouble, eating is the only thing that consoles me. Indeed, when I am in really great trouble, as anyone who knows me intimately will tell you, I refuse everything except food and drink. At the present moment I am eating muffins because I am unhappy. Besides, I am particularly fond of muffins. [*Rising.*]

Jack [*Rising*] Well, that is no reason why you should eat them all in that greedy way. [*Takes muffins from Algernon.*]

Algernon [*Offering tea-cake.*] I wish you would have tea-cake instead. I don't like tea-cake.

Jack Good heavens! I suppose a man may eat his own muffins in his own garden.

Algernon But you have just said it was perfectly heartless to eat muffins.

Jack I said it was perfectly heartless of you, under the circumstances. That is a very different thing.

Algernon That may be. But the muffins are the same. [*He seizes the muffin-dish from Jack.*]

Jack Algy, I wish to goodness you would go.

Algeron You can't possibly ask me to go without having some dinner. It's absurd. I never go without my dinner. No one ever does, except vegetarians and people like that. Besides I have just made arrangements with Dr Chasuble to be christened at a quarter to six under the name of Ernest.

Jack My dear fellow, the sooner you give up that nonsense the better. I made arrangements this morning with Dr Chasuble to be christened myself at 5:30, and I naturally will take the name of Ernest. Gwendolen would wish it. We can't both be christened Ernest. It's absurd. Besides, I have a perfect right to be christened if I like. There is no evidence at all that I ever have been christened by anybody. I should think it extremely probable that I never was, and so does Dr Chasuble. It is entirely different in your case. You have been christened already.

Algernon Yes, but I have not been christened for years.

Jack Yes, but you have been christened. That is the important thing.

Algernon Quite so. So I know my constitution can stand it. If you are not quite sure about your ever having been christened, I must say I think it rather dangerous your venturing on it now. It might make you very unwell. You can hardly have forgotten that some one very closely connected with you was very nearly carried off this week in Paris by a severe chill.

Jack Yes, but you said yourself that a severe chill was not hereditary.

Algernon It usen't to be, I know – but I daresay it is now. Science is always making wonderful improvements in things.

Jack [*Picking up the muffin-dish*] Oh, that is nonsense; you are always talking nonsense.

Algernon Jack, you are at the muffins again! I wish you wouldn't. There are only two left. [*Takes them.*] I told you I was particularly fond of muffins.

Jack But I hate tea-cake.

Algernon Why on earth then do you allow tea-cake to be served up for your guests? What ideas you have of hospitality!

Jack Algernon! I have already told you to go. I don't want you here. Why don't you go!

Algernon I haven't quite finished my tea yet! and there is still one muffin left. [*Jack groans, and sinks into a chair, Algernon still continues eating.*]

[*Act Drop*]

Act III

[*Scene. Morning-room at the Manor House. Gwendolen and Cecily are at the window, looking out into the garden.*]

Gwendolen The fact that they did not follow us at once into the house, as anyone else would have done, seems to me to show that they have some sense of shame left.

Cecily They have been eating muffins. That looks like repentance.

Gwendolen [*After a pause*] They don't seem to notice us at all. Couldn't you cough?

Cecily But I haven't got a cough!

Gwendolen They're looking at us. What effrontery!

Cecily They're approaching. That's very forward of them.

Gwendolen Let us preserve a dignified silence.

Cecily Certainly. It's the only thing to do now.

[*Enter Jack followed by Algernon. They whistle some dreadful popular air from a British opera.*]

Gwendolen This dignified silence seems to produce an unpleasant effect.

Cecily A most distasteful one.

Gwendolen But we will not be the first to speak.

Cecily Certainly not.

Gwendolen Mr Worthing, I have something very particular to ask you. Much depends on your reply.

Cecily Gwendolen, your common sense is invaluable. Mr Moncrieff, kindly answer me the following question. Why did you pretend to be my guardian's brother?

Algernon In order that I might have an opportunity of meeting you.

Cecily [*To Gwendolen*] That certainly seems a satisfactory explanation, does it not?

Gwendolen Yes, dear, if you can believe him.

Cecily I don't. But that does not affect the wonderful beauty of this answer.

Gwendolen True. In matters of grave importance, style, not sincerity is the vital thing. Mr Worthing, what explanation can you offer to me for pretending to have a brother? Was it in order that you might have an opportunity of coming up to town to see me as often as possible?

Jack Can you doubt it, Miss Fairfax?

Gwendolen I have the gravest doubts upon the subject. But I intend to crush them. This is not the moment for German scepticism. [*Moving to Cecily*] Their explanations appear to be quite satisfactory, especially Mr Worthing's. That seems to me to have the stamp of truth upon it.

Cecily I am more than content with what Mr Moncrieff said. His voice alone inspires one with absolute credulity.

Gwendolen Then you think we should forgive them?

Cecily Yes. I mean no.

Gwendolen True! I had forgotten. There are principles at stake that one cannot surrender. Which of us should tell them? The task is not a pleasant one.

Cecily Could we not both speak at the same time?

Gwendolen An excellent idea! I nearly always speak at the same time as other people. Will you take the time from me?

Cecily Certainly. [*Gwendolen beats time with uplifted finger.*]

Gwendolen and Cecily [*Speaking together*] Your Christian names are still an insuperable barrier. That is all!

Jack and Algernon [*Speaking together*] Our Christian names! Is that all? But we are going to be christened this afternoon.

Gwendolen [*To Jack*] For my sake you are prepared to do this terrible thing?

Jack I am.

Cecily [*To Algernon*] To please me you are ready to face this fearful ordeal?

Algernon I am!

Gwendolen How absurd to talk of the equality of the sexes! Where questions of self-sacrifice are concerned, men are infinitely beyond us.

Jack We are. [*Clasps hands with Algernon.*]

Cecily They have moments of physical courage of which we women know absolutely nothing.

Gwendolen [*To Jack*] Darling!

Algernon [*To Cecily*] Darling! [*They fall into each other's arms. Enter Merriman. When he enters he coughs loudly, seeing the situation.*]

Merriman Ahem! Ahem! Lady Bracknell!

Jack Good heavens!

[*Enter Lady Bracknell. The couples separate in alarm. Exit Merriman.*]

Lady Bracknell Gwendolen! What does this mean?

Gwendolen Merely that I am engaged to be married to Mr Worthing, mamma.

Lady Bracknell Come here. Sit down. Sit down immediately. Hesitation of any kind is a sign of mental decay in the young, of physical weakness in the old. [*Turns to Jack.*] Apprised, sir, of my daughter's sudden flight by her trusty maid, whose confidence I purchased by means of a small coin, I followed her at once by a luggage train. Her unhappy father is, I am glad to say, under the impression that she is attending a more than usually lengthy lecture by the University Extension Scheme on the influence of a permanent income on thought. I do not propose to undeceive him. Indeed I have never undeceived him on any question. I would consider it wrong. But of course, you will clearly understand that all communication between yourself and my daughter must cease immediately from this moment. On this point, as indeed on all points, I am firm.

Jack I am engaged to be married to Gwendolen, Lady Bracknell!

Lady Bracknell You are nothing of the kind, sir. And now, as regards Algernon! . . . Algernon!

Algernon Yes, Aunt Augusta.

Lady Bracknell May I ask if it is in this house that your invalid friend Mr Bunbury resides?

Algernon [*Stammering*] Oh! No! Bunbury doesn't live here. Bunbury is somewhere else at present. In fact, Bunbury is dead.

Lady Bracknell Dead! When did Mr Bunbury die? His death must have been extremely sudden.

Algernon [*Airily*] Oh! I killed Bunbury this afternoon. I mean poor Bunbury died this afternoon.

Lady Bracknell What did he die of?

Algernon Bunbury? Oh, he was quite exploded.

Lady Bracknell Exploded! Was he the victim of a revolutionary outrage? I was not aware that Mr Bunbury was interested in social legislation. If so, he is well punished for his morbidity.

Algernon My dear Aunt Augusta, I mean he was found out! The doctors found out that Bunbury could not live, that is what I mean – so Bunbury died.

Lady Bracknell He seems to have had great confidence in the opinion of his physicians. I am glad, however, that he made up his mind at the last to some definite course of action, and acted under proper medical advice. And now that we have finally got rid of this Mr Bunbury, may I ask, Mr Worthing, who is that young person whose hand my nephew Algernon is now holding in what seems to me a peculiarly unnecessary manner?

Jack That lady is Miss Cecily Cardew, my ward. [*Lady Bracknell bows coldly to Cecily.*]

Algernon I am engaged to be married to Cecily, Aunt Augusta.

Lady Bracknell I beg your pardon?

Cecily Mr Moncrieff and I are engaged to be married, Lady Bracknell.

Lady Bracknell [*With a shiver, crossing to the sofa and sitting down*] I do not know whether there is anything peculiarly exciting in the air of this particular part of Hertfordshire, but the number of engagements that go on seems to me considerably above the proper average that statistics have laid down for our guidance. I think some preliminary enquiry on my part would not be out of place. Mr Worthing, is Miss Cardew at all connected with any of the larger railway stations in London? I merely desire information. Until yesterday I had no idea that there were any families or persons whose origin was a Terminus. [*Jack looks perfectly furious, but restrains himself.*]

Jack [*In a clear, cold voice*] Miss Cardew is the granddaughter of the late Mr Thomas Cardew of 149, Belgrave Square, S.W.; Gervase Park, Dorking, Surrey; and the Sporran, Fifeshire, N.B.

Lady Bracknell That sounds not unsatisfactory. Three addresses always inspire confidence, even in tradesmen. But what proof have I of their authenticity?

Jack I have carefully preserved the Court Guides of the period. They are open to your inspection, Lady Bracknell.

Lady Bracknell [*Grimly*] I have known strange errors in that publication.

Jack Miss Cardew's family solicitors are Messrs. Markby, Markby, and Markby.

Lady Bracknell Markby, Markby, and Markby? A firm of the very highest position in their profession. Indeed I am told that one of the Mr Markbys is occasionally to be seen at dinner parties. So far I am satisfied.

Jack [*Very irritably*] How extremely kind of you, Lady Bracknell! I have also in my possession, you will be pleased to hear, certificates of Miss Cardew's birth, baptism, whooping cough, registration, vaccination, confirmation, and the measles; both the German and the English variety.

Lady Bracknell Ah! A life crowded with incident, I see; though perhaps somewhat too exciting for a young girl. I am not myself in favour of premature experiences. [*Rises, looks at her watch.*] Gwendolen! the time approaches for our departure. We have not a moment to lose. As a matter of form, Mr Worthing, I had better ask you if Miss Cardew has any little fortune?

Jack Oh! about a hundred and thirty thousand pounds in the Funds.[1] That is all. Good-bye, Lady Bracknell. So pleased to have seen you.

Lady Bracknell [*Sitting down again*] A moment, Mr Worthing. A hundred and thirty thousand pounds! And in the Funds! Miss Cardew seems to me a most attractive young lady, now that I look at her. Few girls of the present day have any really solid qualities, any of the qualities that last, and improve with time. We live, I regret to say, in an age of surfaces. [*To Cecily*] Come over here, dear. [*Cecily goes across.*] Pretty child! your dress is sadly simple, and your hair seems almost as nature might have left it. But we can soon alter all that. A thoroughly experienced French maid produces a really marvellous result in a very brief space of time. I remember recommending one to young Lady Lancing, and after three months her own husband did not know her.

Jack And after six months nobody knew her.[2]

Lady Bracknell [*Glares at Jack for a few moments. Then bends, with a practised smile, to Cecily.*] Kindly turn round, sweet child. [*Cecily turns completely round.*] No, the side view is what I want. [*Cecily presents her profile.*] Yes, quite as I expected. There are distinct social possibilities in your profile. The two weak points in our age are its want of principle and its want of profile. The chin a

---

1: government loan stock.   2: meaning that she had become a scandalous woman.

little higher, dear. Style largely depends on the way the chin is worn. They are worn very high, just at present. Algernon!

Algernon Yes, Aunt Augusta!

Lady Bracknell There are distinct social possibilities in Miss Cardew's profile.

Algernon Cecily is the sweetest, dearest, prettiest girl in the whole world. And I don't care twopence about social possibilities.

Lady Bracknell Never speak disrespectfully of Society, Algernon. Only people who can't get into it do that. [*To Cecily*] Dear child, of course you know that Algernon has nothing but his debts to depend upon. But I do not approve of mercenary marriages. When I married Lord Bracknell I had no fortune of any kind. But I never dreamed for a moment of allowing that to stand in my way. Well, I suppose I must give my consent.

Algernon Thank you, Aunt Augusta.

Lady Bracknell Cecily, you may kiss me!

Cecily [*Kisses her.*] Thank you, Lady Bracknell.

Lady Bracknell You may also address me as Aunt Augusta for the future.

Cecily Thank you, Aunt Augusta.

Lady Bracknell The marriage, I think, had better take place quite soon.

Algernon Thank you, Aunt Augusta.

Cecily Thank you, Aunt Augusta.

Lady Bracknell To speak frankly, I am not in favour of long engagements. They give people the opportunity of finding out each other's character before marriage, which I think is never advisable.

Jack I beg your pardon for interrupting you, Lady Bracknell, but this engagement is quite out of the question. I am Miss Cardew's guardian, and she cannot marry without my consent until she comes of age. That consent I absolutely decline to give.

Lady Bracknell Upon what grounds may I ask? Algernon is an extremely, I may almost say an ostentatiously, eligible young man. He has nothing, but he looks everything. What more can one desire?

Jack It pains me very much to have to speak frankly to you, Lady Bracknell, about your nephew, but the fact is that I do not approve at all of his moral character. I suspect him of being untruthful. [*Algernon and Cecily look at him in indignant amazement.*]

Lady Bracknell Untruthful! My nephew Algernon? Impossible! He is an Oxonian.[1]

Jack I fear there can be no possible doubt about the matter. This afternoon, during my temporary absence in London on an important question of romance, he obtained admission to my house by means of the false pretence of being my brother. Under an assumed name he drank, I've just been informed by my butler, an entire pint bottle of my Perrier-Jouet, Brut, '89; wine I was specially reserving for myself. Continuing his disgraceful deception, he succeeded in the course of the afternoon in alienating the affections of my only ward. He subsequently stayed to tea, and devoured every single muffin. And what makes his conduct all the more heartless is, that he was perfectly well aware from the

---

1: someone who has studied at Oxford University.

first that I have no brother, that I never had a brother, and that I don't intend to have a brother, not even of any kind. I distinctly told him so myself yesterday afternoon.

Lady Bracknell Ahem! Mr Worthing, after careful consideration I have decided entirely to overlook my nephew's conduct to you.

Jack That is very generous of you, Lady Bracknell. My own decision, however, is unalterable. I decline to give my consent.

Lady Bracknell [*To Cecily*] Come here, sweet child. [*Cecily goes over.*] How old are you, dear?

Cecily Well, I am really only eighteen, but I always admit to twenty when I go to evening parties.

Lady Bracknell You are perfectly right in making some slight alteration. Indeed, no woman should ever be quite accurate about her age. It looks so calculating . . . [*In a meditative manner*] Eighteen, but admitting to twenty at evening parties. Well, it will not be very long before you are of age and free from the restraints of tutelage. So I don't think your guardian's consent is, after all, a matter of any importance.

Jack Pray excuse me, Lady Bracknell, for interrupting you again, but it is only fair to tell you that according to the terms of her grandfather's will Miss Cardew does not come legally of age till she is thirty-five.

Lady Bracknell That does not seem to me to be a grave objection. Thirty-five is a very attractive age. London society is full of women of the very highest birth who have, of their own free choice, remained thirty-five for years. Lady Dumbleton is an instance in point. To my own knowledge she has been thirty-five ever since she arrived at the age of forty, which was many years ago now. I see no reason why our dear Cecily should not be even still more attractive at the age you mention than she is at present. There will be a large accumulation of property.

Cecily Algy, could you wait for me till I was thirty-five?

Algernon Of course I could, Cecily. You know I could.

Cecily Yes, I felt it instinctively, but I couldn't wait all that time. I hate waiting even five minutes for anybody. It always makes me rather cross. I am not punctual myself, I know, but I do like punctuality in others, and waiting, even to be married, is quite out of the question.

Algernon Then what is to be done, Cecily?

Cecily I don't know, Mr Moncrieff.

Lady Bracknell My dear Mr Worthing, as Miss Cardew states positively that she cannot wait till she is thirty-five – a remark which I am bound to say seems to me to show a somewhat impatient nature – I would beg of you to reconsider your decision.

Jack But my dear Lady Bracknell, the matter is entirely in your own hands. The moment you consent to my marriage with Gwendolen, I will most gladly allow your nephew to form an alliance with my ward.

Lady Bracknell [*Rising and drawing herself up*] You must be quite aware that what you propose is out of the question.

Jack Then a passionate celibacy is all that any of us can look forward to.

Lady Bracknell That is the destiny I propose for Gwendolen. Algernon, of course, can choose for himself. [*Pulls out her watch.*] Come, dear; [*Gwendolen rises.*] we have already missed five, if not six, trains. To miss any more might expose us to comment on the platform.
[*Enter Dr Chasuble.*]
Chasuble Everything is quite ready for the christenings.
Lady Bracknell The christenings, sir! Is not that somewhat premature?
Chasuble [*Looking rather puzzled, and pointing to Jack and Algernon*] Both these gentlemen have expressed a desire for immediate baptism.
Lady Bracknell At their age? The idea is grotesque and irreligious! Algernon, I forbid you to be baptized. I will not hear of such excesses. Lord Bracknell would be highly displeased if he learned that that was the way in which you wasted your time and money.
Chasuble Am I to understand then that there are to be no christenings at all this afternoon?
Jack I don't think that, as things are now, it would be of much practical value to either of us, Dr Chasuble.
Chasuble I am grieved to hear such sentiments from you, Mr Worthing. They savour of the heretical views of the Anabaptists, views that I have completely refuted in four of my unpublished sermons. However, as your present mood seems to be one peculiarly secular, I will return to the church at once. Indeed, I have just been informed by the pew-opener that for the last hour and a half Miss Prism has been waiting for me in the vestry.
Lady Bracknell [*Starting*] Miss Prism! Did I hear you mention a Miss Prism?
Chasuble Yes, Lady Bracknell. I am on my way to join her.
Lady Bracknell Pray allow me to detain you for a moment. This matter may prove to be one of vital importance to Lord Bracknell and myself. Is this Miss Prism a female of repellent aspect, remotely connected with education?
Chasuble [*Somewhat indignantly*] She is the most cultivated of ladies, and the very picture of respectability.
Lady Bracknell It is obviously the same person. May I ask what position she holds in your household?
Chasuble [*Severely*] I am a celibate, madam.
Jack [*Interposing*] Miss Prism, Lady Bracknell, has been for the last three years Miss Cardew's esteemed governess and valued companion.
Lady Bracknell In spite of what I hear of her, I must see her at once. Let her be sent for.
Chasuble [*Looking off*] She approaches; she is nigh.
[*Enter Miss Prism hurriedly.*]
Miss Prism I was told you expected me in the vestry, dear Canon. I have been waiting for you there for an hour and three quarters. [*Catches sight of Lady Bracknell who has fixed her with a stony glare. Miss Prism grows pale and quails. She looks anxiously round as if desirous to escape.*]
Lady Bracknell [*In a severe, judicial voice*] Prism! [*Miss Prism bows her head in shame.*] Come here, Prism! [*Miss Prism approaches in a humble manner.*] Prism! Where is that baby? [*General consternation. The Canon starts back in horror.*

Algernon and Jack pretend to be anxious to shield Cecily and Gwendolen from hearing the details of a terrible public scandal.] Twenty-eight years ago, Prism, you left Lord Bracknell's house, Number 104, Upper Grosvenor Street, in charge of a perambulator that contained a baby, of the male sex. You never returned. A few weeks later, through the elaborate investigations of the Metropolitan police, the perambulator was discovered at midnight, standing by itself in a remote corner of Bayswater. It contained the manuscript of a three-volume novel of more than usually revolting sentimentality. [*Miss Prism starts in involuntary indignation.*] But the baby was not there! [*Everyone looks at Miss Prism.*] Prism! Where is that baby? [*A pause.*]

Miss Prism Lady Bracknell, I admit with shame that I do not know. I only wish I did. The plain facts of the case are these. On the morning of the day you mention, a day that is for ever branded on my memory, I prepared as usual to take the baby out in its perambulator. I had also with me a somewhat old, but capacious handbag, in which I had intended to place the manuscript of a work of fiction that I had written during my few unoccupied hours. In a moment of mental abstraction, for which I never can forgive myself, I deposited the manuscript in the basinette, and placed the baby in the handbag.

Jack [*Who has been listening attentively*] But where did you deposit the handbag?

Miss Prism Do not ask me, Mr Worthing.

Jack Miss Prism, this is a matter of no small importance to me. I insist on knowing where you deposited the handbag that contained that infant.

Miss Prism I left it in the cloakroom of one of the larger railway stations in London.

Jack What railway station?

Miss Prism [*Quite crushed*] Victoria. The Brighton line. [*Sinks into a chair.*]

Jack I must retire to my room for a moment. Gwendolen, wait here for me.

Gwendolen If you are not too long, I will wait here for you all my life.

[*Exit Jack in great excitement.*]

Chasuble What do you think this means, Lady Bracknell?

Lady Bracknell I dare not even suspect, Dr Chasuble. I need hardly tell you that in families of high position strange coincidences are not supposed to occur. They are hardly considered the thing.

[*Noises are heard overhead as if someone was throwing trunks about. Everyone looks up.*]

Cecily Uncle Jack seems strangely agitated.

Chasuble Your guardian has a very emotional nature.

Lady Bracknell This noise is extremely unpleasant. It sounds as if he was having an argument. I dislike arguments of any kind. They are always vulgar, and often convincing.

Chasuble [*Looking up*] It has stopped now. [*The noise is redoubled.*]

Lady Bracknell I wish he would arrive at some conclusion.

Gwendolen The suspense is terrible. I hope it will last.

[*Enter Jack with a handbag of black leather in his hand.*]

Jack [*Rushing over to Miss Prism.*] Is this the handbag, Miss Prism? Examine it carefully before you speak. The happiness of more than one life depends on your answer.

Miss Prism [*Calmly*] It seems to be mine. Yes, here is the injury it received through the upsetting of a Gower Street omnibus in younger and happier days. Here is the stain on the lining caused by the explosion of a temperance beverage, an incident that occurred at Leamington. And here, on the lock, are my initials. I had forgotten that in an extravagant mood I had had them placed there. The bag is undoubtedly mine. I am delighted to have it so unexpectedly restored to me. It has been a great inconvenience being without it all these years.

Jack [*In a pathetic voice.*] Miss Prism, more is restored to you than this handbag. I was the baby you placed in it.

Miss Prism [*Amazed*] You?

Jack [*Embracing her*] Yes . . . mother!

Miss Prism [*Recoiling in indignant astonishment*] Mr Worthing! I am unmarried!

Jack Unmarried! I do not deny that is a serious blow. But after all, who has the right to cast a stone against one who has suffered? Cannot repentance wipe out an act of folly? Why should there be one law for men, and another for women? Mother, I forgive you. [*Tries to embrace her again.*]

Miss Prism [*Still more indignant*] Mr Worthing, there is some error. [*Pointing to Lady Bracknell.*] There is the lady who can tell you who you really are.

Jack [*After a pause*] Lady Bracknell, I hate to seem inquisitive, but would you kindly inform me who I am?

Lady Bracknell I am afraid that the news I have to give you will not altogether please you. You are the son of my poor sister, Mrs Moncrieff, and consequently Algernon's elder brother.

Jack Algy's elder brother! Then I have a brother after all. I knew I had a brother! I always said I had a brother! Cecily, how could you have ever doubted that I had a brother? [*Seizes hold of Algernon*] Dr Chasuble, my unfortunate brother. Miss Prism, my unfortunate brother. Gwendolen, my unfortunate brother. Algy, you young scoundrel, you will have to treat me with more respect in the future. You have never behaved to me like a brother in all your life.

Algernon Well, not till today, old boy, I admit. I did my best, however, though I was out of practice. [*Shakes hands.*]

Gwendolen [*To Jack*] My own! But what own are you? What is your Christian name, now that you have become someone else?

Jack Good heavens! . . . I had quite forgotten that point. Your decision on the subject of my name is irrevocable, I suppose?

Gwendolen I never change, except in my affections.

Cecily What a noble nature you have, Gwendolen!

Jack Then the question had better be cleared up at once. Aunt Augusta, a moment. At the time when Miss Prism left me in the handbag, had I been christened already?

Lady Bracknell Every luxury that money could buy, including christening, had been lavished on you by your fond and doting parents.

Jack Then I was christened! That is settled. Now, what name was I given? Let me know the worst.

Lady Bracknell Being the eldest son you were naturally christened after your father.

Jack [*Irritably*] Yes, but what was my father's Christian name?

Lady Bracknell [*Meditatively*] I cannot at the present moment recall what the General's Christian name was. But I have no doubt he had one. He was eccentric, I admit. But only in later years. And that was the result of the Indian climate, and marriage, and indigestion, and other things of that kind.

Jack Algy! Can't you recollect what our father's Christian name was?

Algernon My dear boy, we were never even on speaking terms. He died before I was a year old.

Jack His name would appear in the Army Lists of the period, I suppose, Aunt Augusta.

Lady Bracknell The General was essentially a man of peace, except in his domestic life. But I have no doubt his name would appear in any military directory.

Jack The Army Lists of the last forty years are here. These delightful records should have been my constant study. [*Rushes to bookcase and tears the books out.*] M. Generals . . . Mallam, Maxbohm, Magley, what ghastly names they have Markby, Migsby, Mobbs, Moncrieff! Lieutenant 1840, Captain, Lieutenant-Colonel, Colonel, General 1869, Christian names, Ernest John. [*Puts book very quietly down and speaks quite calmly.*] I always told you, Gwendolen, my name was Ernest, didn't I? Well, it is Ernest after all. I mean it naturally is Ernest.

Lady Bracknell Yes, I remember now that the General was called Ernest. I knew I had some particular reason for disliking the name.

Gwendolen Ernest! My own Ernest! I felt from the first that you could have no other name!

Jack Gwendolen, it is a terrible thing for a man to find out suddenly that all his life he has been speaking nothing but the truth. Can you forgive me?

Gwendolen I can. For I feel that you are sure to change.

Jack My own one!

Chasuble [*To Miss Prism*] Lætitia! [*Embraces her.*]

Miss Prism [*Enthusiastically*] Frederick! At last!

Algernon Cecily! [*Embraces her*] At last!

Jack Gwendolen! [*Embraces her*] At last!

Lady Bracknell My nephew, you seem to be displaying signs of triviality.

Jack On the contrary, Aunt Augusta, I've now realised for the first time in my life the vital Importance of Being Earnest.

[Curtain]

Twentieth Century

This last century has seen profound changes in the way Europeans understand and write about themselves. At the start of the century, many of the continent's inhabitants confidently imagined that 'civilisation' and 'European' were virtually synonymous and this appeared confirmed by the area's commercial, technological and military pre-eminence which allowed its domination of the world. At the end of the century, after two great destructive wars, extraordinary shifts of economic and technological power outside Europe, and a renewal of the question of what 'Europe' is – geographically, socially, economically – Europeans no longer rest secure with easy cultural self-definitions.

In fact questions of identity lie behind much of the century's literature, as writers have sought new language and forms which would allow them to grapple with fundamental reconfigurations in the ways people now imagined themselves; not simply because of changed geopolitical issues, but through new ideas about 'the self': its psychology, biology and gender. There have also been wide-ranging transformations in social consciousness. The determination among those previously marginalised by class, sex, and race within Europe to claim their legitimate place within societies no longer exclusively defined by an elite ruling caste has often led to an attitude of 'goodbye to all that', where previous cultural standards are constantly questioned or even abandoned. Nothing is automatically taken for granted. Language as a vehicle in expressing the self and as a means of communication with others has been closely scrutinised, even to posing the question: 'what can be said?'

For Britain and Ireland, the twentieth century has seen extraordinary change. From being the world's most powerful nation in control of a vast empire at the century's start, Britain has constantly had to confront shrinking resources and a much diminished role in the world. That it has done so without large-scale violence from internal social upheaval or from foreign occupation may owe as much to good fortune as to the nation's character, but part of contemporary British experience is that it seems to accommodate contradictions, albeit uneasily. A nation which often appears to outsiders as either reverently steeped in, or fatally tied to, tradition, it is also a country of immigrants. At the end of the century, London is frequently cited as the most cosmopolitan city on earth (where one London school authority recognises 39 different languages among its pupils). At the same time, Britain can appear xenophobic to its European Union partners and condescendingly 'colonial' to those from its former territories. While many Britons like to imagine the country coming together in times of need, most famously during the First and Second World Wars, this has also been a century of social and geographical fragmentation. The changes in traditional industries have had pervasive, and often tragic, consequences for many communities, while the gap between the affluent and the poor, which was wide at the century's start, but which contracted in the mid-century, has again grown wider at the century's conclusion. In Scotland particularly, recent times have witnessed a growing number of people favouring greater independence from 'Westminister', the English-dominated seat of government.

This century is also the first in which the state began to take its national literature seriously. After the First World War, English and English literature became seen as a means of social cohesiveness, the central plank of an educational policy designed to give all citizens a sense of investment in their heritage. From being almost non-existent as a subject in universities, English literary study is now one of the most popular courses pursued in higher education, and English (with science and technology) is at the centre of British educational policy. However, rather than a promoting a sense of national wholeness, debates about English – how it should be spoken and written, the place of dialect, what literary texts should be studied – produce no easy consensus. Often appearing obsessed with English as an issue of national identity, Britain has also frequently been slow to recognise that English is not somehow its special preserve and that other people who speak English as their mother tongue (e.g. in North America, parts of the Caribbean, South Africa, Australia) as well as those who use it widely as a second language (e.g. Indians, Africans, increasingly continental Europeans) do not necessarily see Britain as the centre of English language or literature.

It is significant, though, that this century is the first in which a number of the most important 'British' writers come from elsewhere: Conrad from Poland, Mansfield from New Zealand, Eliot from the United States, Stoppard from Czechoslovakia, Lessing from East Africa. In addition, Britain has been the home for writers in English who remain associated with other regions (e.g. Naipaul and Rushdie: see *The Arnold Anthology of Post-Colonial Literatures*). But if this vitality from outside Britain has joined forces with native talent (and one of the strongest features of British literature at the century's close is the growth of regional voices among Scots, Welsh, and English writers), other writers have sounded a note of decay, either gentle or strident, suggesting, at best, the maintenance of some individual integrity in confronting a new barbarism.

For Ireland, this past century has been equally dramatic. If at the start of the twentieth century, Joyce's vision of Dublin as an important European capital seemed fanciful, this is an identity many would naturally acknowledge at the century's close. After seven centuries, Ireland gained its independence from Britain and the cultural forces which urged the development of a distinctive identity also provoked a literary output of astonishing quality for this small country. Indeed, partly because of the role of literature in articulating national aspirations, writing has a centrality in Irish culture which is not so immediately obvious in Britain. Far more than Britain, too, Ireland has sought to consolidate its place in Europe: it is notable that two of its greatest writers, Joyce and Beckett, lived most of their lives on the continent. Yet, for Ireland this century has also embraced many contradictions. Although most Irish have rural origins, it is increasingly an urban country with almost half the population living in and around Dublin. Despite independence, economics have meant that the Irish still frequently find themselves working and living abroad, particularly in Britain and the United States. Nor did self-government give Ireland peace. The question of Northern Ireland helped spark off a bitter civil war in the 1920s, and Ulster has remained an unresolved Irish and British dilemma.

JOSEPH CONRAD (1857–1924)

Conrad was born in Poland and did not learn English until he was an adult. He had a desire to go to sea and joined first the French, and then the British, merchant navy, undertaking voyages to all parts of the earth, which subsequently provided him with a great deal of the material for his fiction. He began to write seriously in 1894 and within 15 years had produced a number of novels, novellas and short stories of astonishingly quality such as *Lord Jim, Nostromo, The Secret Agent,* and *Under Western Eyes*. First published in 1899, *Heart of Darkness* deals with the issue of European imperial exploitation of Africa, exploring questions of savagery, civilisation, and the nature of evil. Although Conrad depicts Africa from the a European perspective as 'the Dark Continent', his novella shows that it is Europeans who are responsible for his story's barbarousness.

Heart of Darkness

I

The Nellie, a cruising yawl, swung to her anchor without a flutter of the sails, and was at rest. The flood had made, the wind was nearly calm, and being bound down the river, the only thing for it was to come to and wait for the turn of the tide.

The sea-reach of the Thames stretched before us like the beginning of an interminable waterway. In the offing the sea and the sky were welded together without a joint, and in the luminous space the tanned sails of the barges drifting up with the tide seemed to stand still in red clusters of canvas sharply peaked, with gleams of varnished spirits. A haze rested on the low shores that ran out to sea in vanishing flatness. The air was dark above Gravesend, and farther back still seemed condensed into a mournful gloom, brooding motionless over the biggest, and the greatest, town on earth.

The Director of Companies was our captain and our host. We four affectionately watched his back as he stood in the bows looking to seaward. On the whole river there was nothing that looked half so nautical. He resembled a pilot, which to a seaman is trustworthiness personified. It was difficult to realize his work was not out there in the luminous estuary, but behind him, within the brooding gloom. Between us there was, as I have already said somewhere, the bond of the sea. Besides holding our hearts together through long periods of separation, it had the effect of making us tolerant of each other's yarns – and even convictions. The Lawyer – the best of old fellows – had, because of his many years and many virtues, the only cushion on deck, and was lying on the only rug. The Accountant had brought out already a box of dominoes, and was toying architecturally with the bones. Marlow sat cross-legged right aft, leaning against the mizzenmast. He had sunken cheeks, a yellow complexion, a straight back, an ascetic aspect, and, with his arms dropped, the palms of hands outwards, resembled an idol. The Director, satisfied the anchor had good hold, made his way aft and sat down amongst us. We exchanged a few words lazily. Afterwards there was silence on board the yacht. For some reason or other we did not begin that game of dominoes. We felt meditative, and fit for nothing but placid staring. The day was ending in a serenity of still and exquisite brilliance. The water shone pacifically; the sky, without a speck, was a benign immensity of unstained light; the very mist on the Essex marsh was like a gauzy and radiant fabric, hung from the wooded rises inland, and draping the low shores in diaphanous folds. Only the gloom to the west, brooding over the upper reaches, became more sombre every minute, as if angered by the approach of the sun. And at last, in its curved and imperceptible fall, the sun sank low, and from glowing white changed to a dull red without rays and without heat, as if about to go out suddenly, stricken to death by the touch of that gloom brooding over a crowd of men. Forthwith a change came over the waters, and the serenity became less brilliant but more profound. The old river in its broad reach rested unruffled at the decline of day, after ages of good service done to the race that peopled its banks, spread out in the tranquil dignity of a waterway leading to the uttermost ends of the earth. We looked at the venerable stream not in the vivid flush of a short day that comes and departs for ever, but in the august light of abiding memories. And indeed nothing is easier for a man who has, as the phrase goes, 'followed the sea' with reverence and affection, than to evoke the great spirit of the past upon the lower reaches of the Thames. The tidal current runs to and fro in its unceasing service, crowded with memories of men and ships it had borne to the rest of home or to the battles of the sea. It had known and served all the men of whom the nation is proud, from Sir Francis Drake to Sir John Franklin, knights all, titled and untitled – the great knights-errant of the sea.[1] It had borne all the ships whose names are like jewels flashing in the night of time, from the Golden Hind returning with her round flanks full of treasure, to be visited by the Queen's Highness and thus pass out of the gigantic tale, to the *Erebus* and *Terror*, bound on other conquests – and that never returned. It had known the ships and the men. They had sailed from Deptford, from Greenwich, from Erith – the adventurers and the settlers; kings' ships and the ships of men on 'Change';[2] captains, admirals, the dark 'interlopers' of the Eastern trade, and the commissioned 'generals' of East India fleets. Hunters for gold or pursuers of fame, they all had gone out on that stream, bearing the sword, and often the torch, messengers of the might within the land, bearers of a spark from the sacred fire. What greatness had not floated on the ebb of that river into the mystery of an unknown earth! . . . The dreams of men, the seed of commonwealths, the germs of empires. The sun set; the dusk fell on the stream, and lights began to appear along the shore. The Chapman lighthouse, a three-legged thing erect on a mud-flat, shone strongly. Lights of ships moved in the fairway – a great stir of lights going up and going down. And farther west on the upper reaches the place of the monstrous town was still marked ominously on the sky, a brooding gloom in sunshine, a lurid glare under the stars.

'And this also,' said Marlow suddenly, 'has been one of the dark places of the earth.' He was the only man of us who still 'followed the sea.' The worst that

---

1: Drake circumnavigated the globe in *The Golden Hind* during the 16th century. Franklin was an 18th century explorer of the Arctic who commanded *Erebus* and *Terror* which were lost while searching for the North-West Passage. 2 **Change**: merchant business.

could be said of him was that he did not represent his class. He was a seaman, but he was a wanderer, too, while most seamen lead, if one may so express it, a sedentary life. Their minds are of the stay-at-home order, and their home is always with them – the ship; and so is their country – the sea.

One ship is very much like another, and the sea is always the same. In the immutability of their surroundings the foreign shores, the foreign faces, the changing immensity of life, glide past, veiled not by a sense of mystery but by a slightly disdainful ignorance; for there is nothing mysterious to a seaman unless it be the sea itself, which is the mistress of his existence and as inscrutable as Destiny. For the rest, after his hours of work, a casual stroll or a casual spree on shore suffices to unfold for him the secret of a whole continent, and generally he finds the secret not worth knowing. The yarns of seamen have a direct simplicity, the whole meaning of which lies within the shell of a cracked nut. But Marlow was not typical (if his propensity to spin yarns be excepted), and to him the meaning of an episode was not inside like a kernel but outside, enveloping the tale which brought it out only as a glow brings out a haze, in the likeness of one of these misty halos that sometimes are made visible by the spectral illumination of moonshine. His remark did not seem at all surprising. It was just like Marlow. It was accepted in silence. No one took the trouble to grunt even; and presently he said, very slow – 'I was thinking of very old times, when the Romans first came here, nineteen hundred years ago – the other day. . . . Light came out of this river since – you say Knights? Yes; but it is like a running blaze on a plain, like a flash of lightning in the clouds. We live in the flicker – may it last as long as the old earth keeps rolling! But darkness was here yesterday. Imagine the feelings of a commander of a fine – what d'ye call 'em? – trireme in the Mediterranean, ordered suddenly to the north run overland across the Gauls in a hurry; put in charge of one of these craft the legionaries – a wonderful lot of handy men they must have been, too – used to build, apparently by the hundred, in a month or two, if we may believe what we read. Imagine him here – the very end of the world, a sea the colour of lead, a sky the colour of smoke, a kind of ship about as rigid as a concertina – and going up this river with stores, or orders, or what you like. Sand-banks, marshes, forests, savages, – precious little to eat fit for a civilized man, nothing but Thames water to drink. No Falernian wine here, no going ashore. Here and there a military camp lost in a wilderness, like a needle in a bundle of hay – cold, fog, tempests, disease, exile, and death – death skulking in the air, in the water, in the bush. They must have been dying like flies here. Oh, yes – he did it. Did it very well, too, no doubt, and without thinking much about it either, except afterwards to brag of what he had gone through in his time, perhaps. They were men enough to face the darkness. And perhaps he was cheered by keeping his eye on a chance of promotion to the fleet at Ravenna by and by, if he had good friends in Rome and survived the awful climate. Or think of a decent young citizen in a toga – perhaps too much dice, you know – coming out here in the train of some prefect, or tax-gatherer, or trader even, to mend his fortunes. Land in a swamp, march through the woods, and in some inland post feel the savagery, the utter savagery, had closed round him – all that mysterious life of the wilderness that stirs in the forest, in the jungles, in the hearts of wild men.

There's no initiation either into such mysteries. He has to live in the midst of the incomprehensible, which is also detestable. And it has a fascination, too, that goes to work upon him. The fascination of the abomination – you know, imagine the growing regrets, the longing to escape, the powerless disgust, the surrender, the hate.'

He paused.

'Mind,' he began again, lifting one arm from the elbow, the palm of the hand outwards, so that, with his legs folded before him, he had the pose of a Buddha preaching in European clothes and without a lotus-flower – 'Mind, none of us would feel exactly like this. What saves us is efficiency – the devotion to efficiency. But these chaps were not much account, really. They were no colonists; their administration was merely a squeeze, and nothing more, I suspect. They were conquerors, and for that you want only brute force – nothing to boast of, when you have it, since your strength is just an accident arising from the weakness of others. They grabbed what they could get for the sake of what was to be got. It was just robbery with violence, aggravated murder on a great scale, and men going at it blind – as is very proper for those who tackle a darkness. The conquest of the earth, which mostly means the taking it away from those who have a different complexion or slightly flatter noses than ourselves, is not a pretty thing when you look into it too much. What redeems it is the idea only. An idea at the back of it; not a sentimental pretence but an idea; and an unselfish belief in the idea – something you can set up, and bow down before, and offer a sacrifice to . . . '

He broke off. Flames glided in the river, small green flames, red flames, white flames, pursuing, overtaking, joining, crossing each other – then separating slowly or hastily. The traffic of the great city went on in the deepening night upon the sleepless river. We looked on, waiting patiently – there was nothing else to do till the end of the flood; but it was only after a long silence, when he said, in a hesitating voice, 'I suppose you fellows remember I did once turn fresh water sailor for a bit,' that we knew we were fated, before the ebb began to run, to hear about one of Marlow's inconclusive experiences.

'I don't want to bother you much with what happened to me personally,' he began, showing in this remark the weakness of many tellers of tales who seem so often unaware of what their audience would best like to hear; 'yet to understand the effect of it on me you ought to know how I got out there, what I saw, how I went up that river to the place where I first met the poor chap. It was the farthest point of navigation and the culminating point of my experience. It seemed somehow to throw a kind of light on everything about me – and into my thoughts. It was sombre enough, too – and pitiful – not extraordinary in any way – not very clear either. No, not very clear. And yet it seemed to throw a kind of light.

'I had then, as you remember, just returned to London after a lot of Indian Ocean, Pacific, China Seas, a regular dose of the East – six years or so, and I was loafing about, hindering you fellows in your work and invading your homes, just as though I had got a heavenly mission to civilize you. It was very fine for a time, but after a bit I did get tired of resting. Then I began to look for a ship –

I should think the hardest work on earth. But the ships wouldn't even look at me. And I got tired of that game, too.

'Now when I was a little chap I had a passion for maps. I would look for hours at South America, or Africa, or Australia, and lose myself in all the glories of exploration. At that time there were many blank spaces on the earth, and when I saw one that looked particularly inviting on a map (but they all look that) I would put my finger on it and say, "When I grow up I will go there." The North Pole was one of these places, I remember. Well, I haven't been there yet, and shall not try now. The glamour's off. Other places were scattered about the Equator, and in every sort of latitude all over the two hemispheres. I have been in some of them, and . . . well, we won't talk about that. But there was one yet – the biggest, the most blank, so to speak – that I had a hankering after.

'True, by this time it was not a blank space any more. It had got filled since my boyhood with rivers and lakes and names. It had ceased to be a blank space of delightful mystery – a white patch for a boy to dream gloriously over. It had become a place of darkness. But there was in it one river especially, a mighty big river, that you could see on the map, resembling an immense snake uncoiled, with its head in the sea, its body at rest curving afar over a vast country, and its tail lost in the depths of the land. And as I looked at the map of it in a shop-window, it fascinated me as a snake would a bird – a silly little bird. Then I remembered there was a big concern, a Company for trade on that river. Dash it all! I thought to myself, they can't trade without using some kind of craft on that lot of fresh water – steamboats! Why shouldn't I try to get charge of one? I went on along Fleet Street, but could not shake off the idea. The snake had charmed me.

'You understand it was a Continental concern, that Trading society;[1] but I have a lot of relations living on the Continent, because it's cheap and not so nasty as it looks, they say.

'I am sorry to own I began to worry them. This was already a fresh departure for me. I was not used to get things that way, you know. I always went my own road and on my own legs where I had a mind to go. I wouldn't have believed it of myself; but, then – you see – I felt somehow I must get there by hook or by crook. So I worried them. The men said "My dear fellow," and did nothing. Then – would you believe it? – I tried the women. I, Charlie Marlow, set the women to work – to get a job. Heavens! Well, you see, the notion drove me. I had an aunt, a dear enthusiastic soul. She wrote: "It will be delightful. I am ready to do anything, anything for you. It is a glorious idea. I know the wife of a very high personage in the Administration, and also a man who has lots of influence with," etc., etc. She was determined to make no end of fuss to get me appointed skipper of a river steamboat, if such was my fancy.

'I got my appointment – of course; and I got it very quick. It appears the Company had received news that one of their captains had been killed in a scuffle with the natives. This was my chance, and it made me the more anxious to go. It was only months and months afterwards, when I made the attempt to recover what was left of the body, that I heard the original quarrel arose from a

---

1: the Société Belge pour le Commerce du Haut Congo.

misunderstanding about some hens. Yes, two black hens. Fresleven – that was the fellow's name, a Dane – thought himself wronged somehow in the bargain, so he went ashore and started to hammer the chief of the village with a stick. Oh, it didn't surprise me in the least to hear this, and at the same time to be told that Fresleven was the gentlest, quietest creature that ever walked on two legs. No doubt he was; but he had been a couple of years already out there engaged in the noble cause, you know, and he probably felt the need at last of asserting his self-respect in some way. Therefore he whacked the old nigger mercilessly, while a big crowd of his people watched him, thunderstruck, till some man – I was told the chief's son – in desperation at hearing the old chap yell, made a tentative jab with a spear at the white man – and of course it went quite easy between the shoulder-blades. Then the whole population cleared into the forest, expecting all kinds of calamities to happen, while, on the other hand, the steamer Fresleven commanded left also in a bad panic, in charge of the engineer, I believe. Afterwards nobody seemed to trouble much about Fresleven's remains, till I got out and stepped into his shoes. I couldn't let it rest, though; but when an opportunity offered at last to meet my predecessor, the grass growing through his ribs was tall enough to hide his bones. They were all there. The supernatural being had not been touched after he fell. And the village was deserted, the huts gaped black, rotting, all askew within the fallen enclosures. A calamity had come to it, sure enough. The people had vanished. Mad terror had scattered them, men, women, and children, through the bush, and they had never returned. What became of the hens I don't know either. I should think the cause of progress got them, anyhow. However, through this glorious affair I got my appointment, before I had fairly begun to hope for it.

'I flew around like mad to get ready, and before forty-eight hours I was crossing the Channel to show myself to my employers, and sign the contract. In a very few hours I arrived in a city that always makes me think of a whited sepulchre. Prejudice no doubt. I had no difficulty in finding the Company's offices. It was the biggest thing in the town, and everybody I met was full of it. They were going to run an oversea empire, and make no end of coin by trade.

'A narrow and deserted street in deep shadow, high houses, innumerable windows with venetian blinds, a dead silence, grass sprouting between the stones, imposing carriage archways right and left, immense double doors standing ponderously ajar. I slipped through one of these cracks, went up a swept and ungarnished staircase, as arid as a desert, and opened the first door I came to. Two women, one fat and the other slim, sat on straw-bottomed chairs, knitting black wool. The slim one got up and walked straight at me – still knitting with downcast eyes – and only just as I began to think of getting out of her way, as you would for a somnambulist, stood still, and looked up. Her dress was as plain as an umbrella-cover, and she turned round without a word and preceded me into a waiting-room. I gave my name, and looked about. Deal table in the middle, plain chairs all round the walls, on one end a large shining map, marked with all the colours of a rainbow. There was a vast amount of red – good to see at any time, because one knows that some real work is done in there, a deuce of a lot of blue, a little green, smears of orange, and, on the East Coast, a purple patch, to show where the jolly pioneers of progress drink the jolly lager-beer.

However, I wasn't going into any of these. I was going into the yellow. Dead in the centre. And the river was there – fascinating – deadly – like a snake. Ough! A door opened, a white-haired secretarial head, but wearing a compassionate expression, appeared, and a skinny forefinger beckoned me into the sanctuary. Its light was dim, and a heavy writing-desk squatted in the middle. From behind that structure came out an impression of pale plumpness in a frock-coat. The great man himself. He was five feet six, I should judge, and had his grip on the handle-end of ever so many millions. He shook hands, I fancy, murmured vaguely, was satisfied with my French. *Bon voyage.*

'In about forty-five seconds I found myself again in the waiting-room with the compassionate secretary, who, full of desolation and sympathy, made me sign some document. I believe I undertook amongst other things not to disclose any trade secrets. Well, I am not going to.

'I began to feel slightly uneasy. You know I am not used to such ceremonies, and there was something ominous in the atmosphere. It was just as though I had been let into some conspiracy – I don't know – something not quite right; and I was glad to get out. In the outer room the two women knitted black wool feverishly. People were arriving, and the younger one was walking back and forth introducing them. The old one sat on her chair. Her flat cloth slippers were propped up on a foot-warmer, and a cat reposed on her lap. She wore a starched white affair on her head, had a wart on one cheek, and silver-rimmed spectacles hung on the tip of her nose. She glanced at me above the glasses. The swift and indifferent placidity of that look troubled me. Two youths with foolish and cheery countenances were being piloted over, and she threw at them the same quick glance of unconcerned wisdom. She seemed to know all about them and about me, too. An eerie feeling came over me. She seemed uncanny and fateful. Often far away there I thought of these two, guarding the door of Darkness, knitting black wool as for a warm pall, one introducing, introducing continuously to the unknown, the other scrutinizing the cheery and foolish faces with unconcerned old eyes. *Ave*! Old knitter of black wool. *Morituri te salutant.*[1] Not many of those she looked at ever saw her again – not half, by a long way.

'There was yet a visit to the doctor. "A simple formality," assured me the secretary, with an air of taking an immense part in all my sorrows. Accordingly a young chap wearing his hat over the left eyebrow, some clerk I suppose – there must have been clerks in the business, though the house was as still as a house in a city of the dead – came from somewhere up-stairs, and led me forth. He was shabby and careless, with inkstains on the sleeves of his jacket, and his cravat was large and billowy, under a chin shaped like the toe of an old boot. It was a little too early for the doctor, so I proposed a drink, and thereupon he developed a vein of joviality. As we sat over our vermouths he glorified the Company's business, and by and by I expressed casually my surprise at him not going out there. He became very cool and collected all at once. "I am not such a fool as I look, quoth Plato to his disciples," he said sententiously, emptied his glass with great resolution, and we rose.

---

1 Morituri . . . : 'We who are about to die salute you'. The gladiators' greeting to the Roman emperor in the arena.

'The old doctor felt my pulse, evidently thinking of something else the while. "Good, good for there," he mumbled, and then with a certain eagerness asked me whether I would let him measure my head. Rather surprised, I said Yes, when he produced a thing like calipers and got the dimensions back and front and every way, taking notes carefully. He was an unshaven little man in a threadbare coat like a gaberdine, with his feet in slippers, and I thought him a harmless fool. "I always ask leave, in the interests of science, to measure the crania of those going out there," he said. "And when they come back, too?" I asked. "Oh, I never see them," he remarked; "and, moreover, the changes take place inside, you know." He smiled, as if at some quiet joke. "So you are going out there. Famous. Interesting, too." He gave me a searching glance, and made another note. "Ever any madness in your family?" he asked, in a matter-of-fact tone. I felt very annoyed. "Is that question in the interests of science, too?" "It would be," he said, without taking notice of my irritation, "interesting for science to watch the mental changes of individuals, on the spot, but . . ." "Are you an alienist?"[1] I interrupted. "Every doctor should be – a little," answered that original, imperturbably. "I have a little theory which you messieurs who go out there must help me to prove. This is my share in the advantages my country shall reap from the possession of such a magnificent dependency. The mere wealth I leave to others. Pardon my questions, but you are the first Englishman coming under my observation . . . ." I hastened to assure him I was not in the least typical. "If I were," said I, "I wouldn't be talking like this with you." "What you say is rather profound, and probably erroneous," he said, with a laugh. "Avoid irritation more than exposure to the sun. Adieu. How do you English say, eh? Good-bye. Ah! Good-bye. Adieu. In the tropics one must before everything keep calm." . . . He lifted a warning forefinger . . . "*Du calme, du calme, Adieu.*"

'One thing more remained to do – say good-bye to my excellent aunt. I found her triumphant. I had a cup of tea – the last decent cup of tea for many days – and in a room that most soothingly looked just as you would expect a lady's drawing-room to look, we had a long quiet chat by the fireside. In the course of these confidences it became quite plain to me I had been represented to the wife of the high dignitary, and goodness knows to how many more people besides, as an exceptional and gifted creature – a piece of good fortune for the Company – a man you don't get hold of every day. Good heavens! and I was going to take charge of a two-penny-half-penny river-steamboat with a penny whistle attached! It appeared, however, I was also one of the Workers, with a capital – you know. Something like an emissary of light, something like a lower sort of apostle. There had been a lot of such rot let loose in print and talk just about that time, and the excellent woman, living right in the rush of all that humbug, got carried off her feet. She talked about "weaning those ignorant millions from their horrid ways," till, upon my word, she made me quite uncomfortable. I ventured to hint that the Company was run for profit.

' "You forget, dear Charlie, that the labourer is worthy of his hire," she said, brightly. It's queer how out of touch with truth women are. They live in a

---

1 alienist: someone who treats mental diseases.

world of their own, and there has never been anything like it, and never can be. It is too beautiful altogether, and if they were to set it up it would go to pieces before the first sunset. Some confounded fact we men have been living contentedly with ever since the day of creation would start up and knock the whole thing over.

'After this I got embraced, told to wear flannel, be sure to write often, and so on – and I left. In the street – I don't know why – a queer feeling came to me that I was an impostor. Odd thing that I, who used to clear out for any part of the world at twenty-four hours' notice, with less thought than most men give to the crossing of a street, had a moment – I won't say of hesitation, but of startled pause, before this commonplace affair. The best way I can explain it to you is by saying that, for a second or two, I felt as though, instead of going to the centre of a continent, I were about to set off for the centre of the earth.

'I left in a French steamer, and she called in every blamed port they have out there, for, as far as I could see, the sole purpose of landing soldiers and custom-house officers. I watched the coast. Watching a coast as it slips by the ship is like thinking about an enigma. There it is before you – smiling, frowning, inviting, grand, mean, insipid, or savage, and always mute with an air of whispering, "Come and find out." This one was almost featureless, as if still in the making, with an aspect of monotonous grimness. The edge of a colossal jungle, so dark-green as to be almost black, fringed with white surf, ran straight, like a ruled line, far, far away along a blue sea whose glitter was blurred by a creeping mist. The sun was fierce, the land seemed to glisten and drip with steam. Here and there greyish-whitish specks showed up clustered inside the white surf, with a flag flying above them perhaps. Settlements some centuries old, and still no bigger than pinheads on the untouched expanse of their background. We pounded along, stopped, landed soldiers; went on, landed custom-house clerks to levy toll in what looked like a God-forsaken wilderness, with a tin shed and a flag-pole lost in it; landed more soldiers to take care of the custom-house clerks, presumably. Some, I heard, got drowned in the surf; but whether they did or not, nobody seemed particularly to care. They were just flung out there, and on we went. Every day the coast looked the same, as though we had not moved; but we passed various places – trading places with names like Gran' Bassam, Little Popo; names that seemed to belong to some sordid farce acted in front of a sinister back-cloth. The idleness of a passenger, my isolation amongst all these men with whom I had no point of contact, the oily and languid sea, the uniform sombreness of the coast, seemed to keep me away from the truth of things, within the toil of a mournful and senseless delusion. The voice of the surf heard now and then was a positive pleasure, like the speech of a brother. It was something natural, that had its reason, that had a meaning. Now and then a boat from the shore gave one a momentary contact with reality. It was paddled by black fellows. You could see from afar the white of their eyeballs glistening. They shouted, sang; their bodies streamed with perspiration; they had faces like grotesque masks – these chaps; but they had bone, muscle, a wild vitality, an intense energy of movement, that was as natural and true as the surf along their coast. They wanted no excuse for being there. They were a great comfort to look at. For a time I would feel I belonged still to a world of straightforward facts; but the feeling would not last long. Something would turn up to scare it away. Once, I remember, we came upon a man-of-war anchored off the coast. There wasn't even a shed there, and she was shelling the bush. It appears the French had one of their wars going on thereabouts. Her ensign dropped limp like a rag; the muzzles of the long six-inch guns stuck out all over the low hull; the greasy, slimy swell swung her up lazily and let her down, swaying her thin masts. In the empty immensity of earth, sky, and water, there she was, incomprehensible, firing into a continent. Pop, would go one of the six-inch guns; a small flame would dart and vanish, a little white smoke would disappear, a tiny projectile would give a feeble screech – and nothing happened. Nothing could happen. There was a touch of insanity in the proceeding, a sense of lugubrious drollery in the sight; and it was not dissipated by somebody on board assuring me earnestly there was a camp of natives – he called them enemies! – hidden out of sight somewhere.

'We gave her her letters (I heard the men in that lonely ship were dying of fever at the rate of three a day) and went on. We called at some more places with farcical names, where the merry dance of death and trade goes on in a still and earthy atmosphere as of an overheated catacomb; all along the formless coast bordered by dangerous surf, as if Nature herself had tried to ward off intruders; in and out of rivers, streams of death in life, whose banks were rotting into mud, whose waters, thickened into slime, invaded the contorted mangroves, that seemed to writhe at us in the extremity of an impotent despair. Nowhere did we stop long enough to get a particularized impression, but the general sense of vague and oppressive wonder grew upon me. It was like a weary pilgrimage amongst hints for nightmares.

'It was upward of thirty days before I saw the mouth of the big river. We anchored off the seat of the government. But my work would not begin till some two hundred miles farther on. So as soon as I could I made a start for a place thirty miles higher up.

'I had my passage on a little sea-going steamer. Her captain was a Swede, and knowing me for a seaman, invited me on the bridge. He was a young man, lean, fair, and morose, with lanky hair and a shuffling gait. As we left the miserable little wharf, he tossed his head contemptuously at the shore. "Been living there?" he asked. I said, "Yes." "Fine lot these government chaps – are they not?" he went on, speaking English with great precision and considerable bitterness. "It is funny what some people will do for a few francs a month. I wonder what becomes of that kind when it goes up country?" I said to him I expected to see that soon. "So-o-o!" he exclaimed. He shuffled athwart, keeping one eye ahead vigilantly. "Don't be too sure," he continued. "The other day I took up a man who hanged himself on the road. He was a Swede, too." "Hanged himself! Why, in God's name?" I cried. He kept on looking out watchfully. "Who knows? The sun too much for him, or the country perhaps."

'At last we opened a reach. A rocky cliff appeared, mounds of turned-up earth by the shore, houses on a hill, others with iron roofs, amongst a waste of excavations, or hanging to the declivity. A continuous noise of the rapids above hovered over this scene of inhabited devastation. A lot of people, mostly black and naked, moved about like ants. A jetty projected into the river. A blinding sunlight drowned all this at times in a sudden recrudescence of glare. "There's your Company's station," said the Swede, pointing to three wooden barrack-like structures on the rocky slope. "I will send your things up. Four boxes did you say? So. Farewell."

'I came upon a boiler wallowing in the grass, then found a path leading up the hill. It turned aside for the boulders, and also for an undersized railway-truck lying there on its back with its wheels in the air. One was off. The thing looked as dead as the carcass of some animal. I came upon more pieces of decaying machinery, a stack of rusty rails. To the left a clump of trees made a shady spot, where dark things seemed to stir feebly. I blinked, the path was steep. A horn tooted to the right, and I saw the black people run. A heavy and dull detonation shook the ground, a puff of smoke came out of the cliff, and that was all. No change appeared on the face of the rock. They were building a railway. The cliff was not in the way or anything; but this objectless blasting was all the work going on.

'A slight clinking behind me made me turn my head. Six black men advanced in a file, toiling up the path. They walked erect and slow, balancing small baskets full of earth on their heads, and the clink kept time with their footsteps. Black rags were wound round their loins, and the short ends behind waggled to and fro like tails. I could see every rib, the joints of their limbs were like knots in a rope; each had an iron collar on his neck, and all were connected together with a chain whose bights swung between them, rhythmically clinking. Another report from the cliff made me think suddenly of that ship of war I had seen firing into a continent. It was the same kind of ominous voice; but these men could by no stretch of imagination be called enemies. They were called criminals, and the outraged law, like the bursting shells, had come to them, an insoluble mystery from the sea. All their meagre breasts panted together, the violently dilated nostrils quivered, the eyes stared stonily uphill. They passed me within six inches, without a glance, with that complete, death-like indifference of unhappy savages. Behind this raw matter one of the reclaimed, the product of the new forces at work, strolled despondently, carrying a rifle by its middle. He had a uniform jacket with one button off, and seeing a white man on the path, hoisted his weapon to his shoulder with alacrity. This was simple prudence, white men being so much alike at a distance that he could not tell who I might be. He was speedily reassured, and with a large, white, rascally grin, and a glance at his charge, seemed to take me into partnership in his exalted trust. After all, I also was a part of the great cause of these high and just proceedings.

'Instead of going up, I turned and descended to the left. My idea was to let that chain-gang get out of sight before I climbed the hill. You know I am not particularly tender; I've had to strike and to fend off. I've had to resist and to attack sometimes – that's only one way of resisting – without counting the exact cost, according to the demands of such sort of life as I had blundered into. I've seen the devil of violence, and the devil of greed, and the devil of hot desire; but, by all the stars! these were strong, lusty, red-eyed devils, that swayed and drove men – men, I tell you. But as I stood on this hillside, I foresaw that in the blinding sunshine of that land I would become acquainted with a flabby, pretending, weak-eyed devil of a rapacious and pitiless folly. How insidious he could be, too, I was only to find out several months later and a thousand miles farther. For a moment I stood appalled, as though by a warning. Finally I descended the hill, obliquely, towards the trees I had seen.

'I avoided a vast artificial hole somebody had been digging on the slope, the purpose of which I found it impossible to divine. It wasn't a quarry or a sand-pit, anyhow. It was just a hole. It might have been connected with the philanthropic desire of giving the criminals something to do. I don't know. Then I nearly fell into a very narrow ravine, almost no more than a scar in the hillside. I discovered that a lot of imported drainage-pipes for the settlement had been tumbled in there. There wasn't one that was not broken. It was a wanton smash-up. At last I got under the trees. My purpose was to stroll into the shade for a moment; but no sooner within than it seemed to me I had stepped into the gloomy circle of some Inferno. The rapids were near, and an uninter-rupted, uniform, headlong, rushing noise filled the mournful stillness of the grove, where not a breath stirred, not a leaf moved, with a mysterious sound – as though the tearing pace of the launched earth had suddenly become audible.

'Black shapes crouched, lay, sat between the trees leaning against the trunks, clinging to the earth, half coming out, half effaced within the dim light, in all the attitudes of pain, abandonment, and despair. Another mine on the cliff went off, followed by a slight shudder of the soil under my feet. The work was going on. The work! And this was the place where some of the helpers had withdrawn to die.

'They were dying slowly – it was very clear. They were not enemies, they were not criminals, they were nothing earthly now – nothing but black shadows of disease and starvation, lying confusedly in the greenish gloom. Brought from all the recesses of the coast in all the legality of time contracts, lost in uncongenial surroundings, fed on unfamiliar food, they sickened, became inefficient, and were then allowed to crawl away and rest. These mori-bund shapes were free as air – and nearly as thin. I began to distinguish the gleam of the eyes under the trees. Then, glancing down, I saw a face near my hand. The black bones reclined at full length with one shoulder against the tree, and slowly the eyelids rose and the sunken eyes looked up at me, enormous and vacant, a kind of blind, white flicker in the depths of the orbs, which died out slowly. The man seemed young – almost a boy – but you know with them it's hard to tell. I found nothing else to do but to offer him one of my good Swede's ship's biscuits I had in my pocket. The fingers closed slowly on it and held – there was no other movement and no other glance. He had tied a bit of white worsted round his neck – Why? Where did he get it? Was it a badge – an ornament – charm – a propitiatory act? Was there any idea at all connected with it? It looked startling round his black neck, this bit of white thread from beyond the seas.

'Near the same tree two more bundles of acute angles sat with their legs drawn up. One, with his chin propped on his knees, stared at nothing, in an intolerable and appalling manner: his brother phantom rested its forehead, as if overcome with a great weariness; and all about others were scattered in every pose of contorted collapse, as in some picture of a massacre or a pestilence.

While I stood horrorstruck, one of these creatures rose to his hands and knees, and went off on all-fours towards the river to drink. He lapped out of his hand, then sat up in the sunlight, crossing his shins in front of him, and after a time let his woolly head fall on his breastbone.

'I didn't want any more loitering in the shade, and I made haste towards the station. When near the buildings I met a white man, in such an unexpected elegance of getup that in the first moment I took him for a sort of vision. I saw a high starched collar, white cuffs, a light alpaca jacket, snowy trousers, a clean necktie, and varnished boots. No hat. Hair parted, brushed, oiled, under a green-lined parasol held in a big white hand. He was amazing, and had a penholder behind his ear.

'I shook hands with this miracle, and I learned he was the Company's chief accountant, and that all the bookkeeping was done at this station. He had come out for a moment, he said, "to get a breath of fresh air." The expression sounded wonderfully odd, with its suggestion of sedentary desk-life. I wouldn't have mentioned the fellow to you at all, only it was from his lips that I first heard the name of the man who is so indissolubly connected with the memories of that time. Moreover, I respected the fellow. Yes; I respected his collars, his vast cuffs, his brushed hair. His appearance was certainly that of a hairdresser's dummy; but in the great demoralization of the land he kept up his appearance. That's backbone. His starched collars and got-up shirt-fronts were achievements of character. He had been out nearly three years; and later, I could not help asking him how he managed to sport such linen. He had just the faintest blush, and said modestly, "I've been teaching one of the native women about the station. It was difficult. She had a distaste for the work." Thus this man had verily accomplished something. And he was devoted to his books, which were in apple-pie order.

'Everything else in the station was in a muddle – heads, things, buildings. Strings of dusty niggers with splay feet arrived and departed; a stream of manu-factured goods, rubbishy cottons, beads, and brasswire set into the depths of darkness, and in return came a precious trickle of ivory.

'I had to wait in the station for ten days – an eternity. I lived in a hut in the yard, but to be out of the chaos I would sometimes get into the accountant's office. It was built of horizontal planks, and so badly put together that, as he bent over his high desk, he was barred from neck to heels with narrow strips of sunlight. There was no need to open the big shutter to see. It was hot there, too; big flies buzzed fiendishly, and did not sting, but stabbed. I sat generally on the floor, while, of faultless appearance (and even slightly scented), perching on a high stool, he wrote, he wrote. Sometimes he stood up for exercise. When a trucklebed with a sick man (some invalid agent from upcountry) was put in there, he exhibited a gentle annoyance. "The groans of this sick person," he said, "distract my attention. And without that it is extremely difficult to guard against clerical errors in this climate."

'One day he remarked, without lifting his head, "In the interior you will no doubt meet Mr Kurtz." On my asking who Mr Kurtz was, he said he was a first-class agent; and seeing my disappointment at this information, he added slowly, laying down his pen, "He is a very remarkable person." Further questions elicited from him that Mr Kurtz was at present in charge of a trading-post, a very important one, in the true ivory-country, at "the very bottom of there. Sends in as much ivory as all the others put together . . ." He began to write again. The sick man was too ill to groan. The flies buzzed in a great peace.

'Suddenly there was a growing murmur of voices and a great tramping of feet. A caravan had come in. A violent babble of uncouth sounds burst out on the other side of the planks. All the carriers were speaking together, and in the midst of the uproar the lamentable voice of the chief agent was heard "giving it up" tearfully for the twentieth time that day. . . . He rose slowly. "What a frightful row," he said. He crossed the room gently to look at the sick man, and returning, said to me, "He does not hear." "What! Dead?" I asked, startled. "No, not yet," he answered, with great composure. Then, alluding with a toss of the head to the tumult in the station-yard, "When one has got to make correct entries, one comes to hate those savages – hate them to the death." He remained thoughtful for a moment. "When you see Mr Kurtz," he went on, "tell him from me that everything here" – he glanced at the deck – "is very satisfactory. I don't like to write to him – with those messengers of ours you never know who may get hold of your letter – at that Central Station." He stared at me for a moment with his mild, bulging eyes. "O ho, he will go far, very far," he began again. "He will be a somebody in the Administration before long. They, above – the Council in Europe, you know – mean him to be."

'He turned to his work. The noise outside had ceased, and presently in going out I stopped at the door. In the steady buzz of flies the homeward-bound agent was lying flushed and insensible; the other, bent over his books, was making correct entries of perfectly correct transactions; and fifty feet below the doorstep I could see the still treetops of the grove of death.

'Next day I left that station at last, with a caravan of sixty men, for a two-hundred-mile tramp.

'No use telling you much about that. Paths, paths, everywhere; a stamped-in network of paths spreading over the empty land, through the long grass, through burnt grass, through thickets, down and up chilly ravines, up and down stony hills ablaze with heat; and a solitude, a solitude, nobody, not a hut. The population had cleared out a long time ago. Well, if a lot of mysterious niggers armed with all kinds of fearful weapons suddenly took to travelling on the road between Deal and Gravesend, catching the yokels right and left to carry heavy loads for them, I fancy every farm and cottage thereabouts would get empty very soon. Only here the dwellings were gone, too. Still I passed through several abandoned villages. There's something pathetically childish in the ruins of grass walls. Day after day, with the stamp and shuffle of sixty pair of bare feet behind me, each pair under a 60-lb. load. Camp, cook, sleep, strike camp, march. Now and then a carrier dead in harness, at rest in the long grass near the path, with an empty water-gourd and his long staff lying by his side. A great silence around and above. Perhaps on some quiet night the tremor of far-off drums, sinking, swelling, a tremor vast, faint; a sound weird, appealing, suggestive, and wild – and perhaps with as profound a meaning as the sound of bells in a Christian country. Once a white man in an unbuttoned uniform, camping on the path with an armed escort of lank Zanzibaris, very hospitable and festive – not to say drunk. Was looking after the upkeep of the road, he declared. Can't say I saw any road or any upkeep, unless the body of a middle-aged negro, with a bullet-hole in the forehead, upon which I absolutely stumbled three miles farther on, may be considered as a permanent improvement. I had a white companion, too, not a bad chap, but rather too fleshy and with the exasperating habit of fainting on the hot hillsides, miles away from the least bit of shade and water. Annoying, you know, to hold your own coat like a parasol over a man's head while he is coming to. I couldn't help asking him once what he meant by coming there at all. "To make money, of course. What do you think?" he said, scornfully. Then he got fever, and had to be carried in a hammock slung under a pole. As he weighed sixteen stone I had no end of rows with the carriers. They jibbed, ran away, sneaked off with their loads in the night – quite a mutiny. So, one evening, I made a speech in English with gestures, not one of which was lost to the sixty pairs of eyes before me, and the next morning I started the hammock off in front all right. An hour afterwards I came upon the whole concern wrecked in a bush – man, hammock, groans, blankets, horrors. The heavy pole had skinned his poor nose. He was very anxious for me to kill somebody, but there wasn't the shadow of a carrier near. I remembered the old doctor – "It would be interesting for science to watch the mental changes of individuals, on the spot." I felt I was becoming scientifically interesting. However, all that is to no purpose. On the fifteenth day I came in sight of the big river again, and hobbled into the Central Station. It was on a back water surrounded by scrub and forest, with a pretty border of smelly mud on one side, and on the three others enclosed by a crazy fence of rushes. A neglected gap was all the gate it had, and the first glance at the place was enough to let you see the flabby devil was running that show. White men with long staves in their hands appeared languidly from amongst the buildings, strolling up to take a look at me, and then retired out of sight somewhere. One of them, a stout, excitable chap with black moustaches, informed me with great volubility and many digressions, as soon as I told him who I was, that my steamer was at the bottom of the river. I was thunderstruck. What, how, why? Oh, it was "all right." The "manager himself" was there. All quite correct. "Everybody had behaved splendidly! splendidly!" – "you must," he said in agitation, "go and see the general manager at once. He is waiting!"

'I did not see the real significance of that wreck at once. I fancy I see it now, but I am not sure not at all. Certainly the affair was too stupid – when I think of it – to be altogether natural. Still . . . But at the moment it presented itself simply as a confounded nuisance. The steamer was sunk. They had started two days before in a sudden hurry up the river with the manager on board, in charge of some volunteer skipper, and before they had been out three hours they tore the bottom out of her on stones, and she sank near the south bank. I asked myself what I was to do there, now my boat was lost. As a matter of fact, I had plenty to do in fishing my command out of the river. I had to set about it the very next day. That, and the repairs when I brought the pieces to the station, took some months.

'My first interview with the manager was curious. He did not ask me to sit down after my twenty-mile walk that morning. He was commonplace in complexion, in feature, in manners, and in voice. He was of middle size and of ordinary build. His eyes, of the usual blue, were perhaps remarkably cold, and he certainly could make his glance fall on one as trenchant and heavy as an axe. But even at these times the rest of his person seemed to disclaim the intention. Otherwise there was only an indefinable, faint expression of his lips, something stealthy – a smile – not a smile – I remember it, but I can't explain. It was unconscious, this smile was, though just after he had said something it got intensified for an instant. It came at the end of his speeches like a seal applied on the words to make the meaning of the commonest phrase appear absolutely inscrutable. He was a common trader, from his youth up employed in these parts – nothing more. He was obeyed, yet he inspired neither love nor fear, nor even respect. He inspired uneasiness. That was it! Uneasiness. Not a definite mistrust – just uneasiness – nothing more. You have no idea how effective such a . . . a . . . faculty can be. He had no genius for organizing, for initiative, or for order even. That was evident in such things as the deplorable state of the station. He had no learning, and no intelligence. His position had come to him – why? Perhaps because he was never ill . . . He had served three terms of three years out there . . . Because triumphant health in the general rout of constitutions is a kind of power in itself. When he went home on leave he rioted on a large scale – pompously. Jack ashore – with a difference – in externals only. This one could gather from his casual talk. He originated nothing, he could keep the routine going – that's all. But he was great. He was great by this little thing that it was impossible to tell what could control such a man. He never gave that secret away. Perhaps there was nothing within him. Such a suspicion made one pause – for out there there were no external checks. Once when various tropical diseases had laid low almost every "agent" in the station, he was heard to say, "Men who come out here should have no entrails." He sealed the utterance with that smile of his, as though it had been a door opening into a darkness he had in his keeping. You fancied you had seen things – but the seal was on. When annoyed at mealtimes by the constant quarrels of the white men about precedence, he ordered an immense round table to be made, for which a special house had to be built. This was the station's mess-room. Where he sat was the first place – the rest were nowhere. One felt this to be his unalterable conviction. He was neither civil nor uncivil. He was quiet. He allowed his 'boy' – an overfed young negro from the coast – to treat the white men, under his very eyes, with provoking insolence.

'He began to speak as soon as he saw me. I had been very long on the road. He could not wait. Had to start without me. The up-river stations had to be relieved. There had been so many delays already that he did not know who was dead and who was alive, and how they got on – and so on, and so on. He paid no attention to my explanation, and, playing with a stick of sealing-wax, repeated several times that the situation was "very grave, very grave." There were rumours that a very important station was in jeopardy, and its chief, Mr Kurtz, was ill. Hoped it was not true. Mr Kurtz was . . . I felt weary and irritable. Hang Kurtz, I thought. I interrupted him by saying I had heard of Mr Kurtz on the coast. "Ah! So they talk of him down there," he murmured to himself. Then he began again, assuring me Mr Kurtz was the best agent he had, an exceptional man, of the greatest importance to the Company; therefore I could understand his anxiety. He was, he said, "very, very uneasy." Certainly he fidgeted on his chair a good deal, exclaimed, "Ah, Mr Kurtz!" broke the stick of sealingwax and seemed dumfounded by the accident. Next thing he wanted to know "how long it would take to" . . . I interrupted him again. Being hungry, you know, and kept on my feet too, I was getting savage. "How can I tell?" I said. "I haven't even seen the wreck yet – some months, no doubt." All this talk seemed to me so futile. "Some months," he said. "Well, let us say three months before we can make a start. Yes. That ought to do the affair." I flung out of his hut (he lived all alone in a clay hut with a sort of verandah) muttering to myself my opinion of him. He was a chattering idiot. Afterwards I took it back when it was borne in upon me startlingly with what extreme nicety he had estimated the time requisite for the "affair."

'I went to work the next day, turning, so to speak, my back on that station. In that way only it seemed to me I could keep my hold on the redeeming facts of life. Still, one must look about sometimes; and then I saw this station, these men strolling aimlessly about in the sunshine of the yard. I asked myself sometimes what it all meant. They wandered here and there with their absurd long staves in their hands, like a lot of faithless pilgrims bewitched inside a rotten fence. The word "ivory" rang in the air, was whispered, was sighed. You would think they were praying to it. A taint of imbecile rapacity blew through it all, like a whiff from some corpse. By Jove! I've never seen anything so unreal in my life. And outside, the silent wilderness surrounding this cleared speck on the earth struck me as something great and invincible, like evil or truth, waiting patiently for the passing away of this fantastic invasion.

'Oh, these months! Well, never mind. Various things happened. One evening a grass shed full of calico, cotton prints, beads, and I don't know what else, burst into a blaze so suddenly that you would have thought the earth had opened to let an avenging fire consume all that trash. I was smoking my pipe quietly by my dismantled steamer, and saw them all cutting capers in the light, with their arms lifted high, when the stout man with moustaches came tearing down to the river, a tin pail in his hand, assured me that everybody was "behaving splendidly, splendidly," dipped about a quart of water and tore back again. I noticed there was a hole in the bottom of his pail.

'I strolled up. There was no hurry. You see the thing had gone off like a box of matches. It had been hopeless from the very first. The flame had leaped high, driven everybody back, lighted up everything – and collapsed. The shed was already a heap of embers glowing fiercely. A nigger was being beaten near by. They said he had caused the fire in some way; be that as it may, he was screeching most horribly. I saw him, after, for several days, sitting in a bit of shade looking very sick and trying to recover himself: afterwards he arose and went out – and the wilderness without a sound took him into its bosom again. As I approached the glow from the dark I found myself at the back of two men, talking. I heard the name of Kurtz pronounced, then the words, "take advantage of this unfortunate accident." One of the men was the manager. I wished him a good evening. "Did you ever see anything like it – eh? it is incredible," he said, and walked off. The other man remained. He was a first-class agent, young, gentlemanly, a bit reserved, with a forked little beard and a hooked nose. He was stand-offish with the other agents, and they on their side said he was the manager's spy upon them. As to me, I had hardly ever spoken to him before. We got into talk, and by and by we strolled away from the hissing ruins. Then he asked me to his room, which was in the main building of the station. He struck a match, and I perceived that this young aristocrat had not only a silver-mounted dressing-case but also a whole candle all to himself. Just at that time the manager was the only man supposed to have any right to candles. Native mats covered the clay walls; a collection of spears, assegais, shields, knives was hung up in trophies. The business intrusted to this fellow was the making of bricks – so I had been informed; but there wasn't a fragment of a brick anywhere in the station, and he could not make bricks without something, I don't know what – straw maybe. Anyway, it could not be found there and as it was not likely to be sent from Europe, it did not appear clear to me what he was waiting for. An act of special creation perhaps. However, they were all waiting – all the sixteen or twenty pilgrims of them – for something; and upon my word it did not seem an uncongenial occupation, from the way they took it, though the only thing that ever came to them was disease – as far as I could see. They beguiled the time by backbiting and intriguing against each other in a foolish kind of way. There was an air of plotting about that station, but nothing came of it, of course. It was as unreal as everything else – as the philanthropic pretence of the whole concern, as their talk, as their government, as their show of work. The only real feeling was a desire to get appointed to a trading-post where ivory was to be had, so that they could earn percentages. They intrigued and slandered and hated each other only on that account – but as to effectually lifting a little finger – oh, no. By heavens! there is something after all in the world allowing one man to steal a horse while another must not look at a halter. Steal a horse straight out. Very well. He has done it. Perhaps he can ride. But there is a way of looking at a halter that would provoke the most charitable of saints into a kick.

'I had no idea why he wanted to be sociable, but as we chatted in there it suddenly occurred to me the fellow was trying to get at something – in fact, pumping me. He alluded constantly to Europe, to the people I was supposed to know there – putting leading questions as to my acquaintances in the sepulchral city, and so on. His little eyes glittered like mica discs – with curiosity – though he tried to keep up a bit of superciliousness. At first I was astonished, but very soon I became awfully curious to see what he would find out from me. I couldn't possibly imagine what I had in me to make it worth his while. It was very pretty to see how he baffled himself, for in truth my body was full only of chills, and my head had nothing in it but that wretched steamboat business. It was evident he took me for a perfectly shameless prevaricator. At last he got angry, and, to conceal a movement of furious annoyance, he yawned. I rose. Then I noticed a small sketch in oils, on a panel, representing a woman, draped and blindfolded, carrying a lighted torch. The background was sombre – almost black. The movement of the woman was stately, and the effect of the torchlight on the face was sinister.

'It arrested me, and he stood by civilly, holding an empty half-pint champagne bottle (medical comforts) with the candle stuck in it. To my question he said Mr Kurtz had painted this – in this very station more than a year ago – while waiting for means to go to his trading-post. "Tell me, pray," said I, "who is this Mr Kurtz?"

' "The chief of the Inner Station," he answered in a short tone, looking away. "Much obliged," I said, laughing. "And you are the brickmaker of the Central Station. Every one knows that." He was silent for a while. "He is a prodigy," he said at last. "He is an emissary of pity and science and progress, and devil knows what else. We want," he began to declaim suddenly, "for the guidance of the cause intrusted to us by Europe, so to speak, higher intelligence, wide sym-pathies, a singleness of purpose." "Who says that?" I asked. "Lots of them," he replied. "Some even write that; and so he comes here, a special being, as you ought to know." "Why ought I to know?" I interrupted, really surprised. He paid no attention. "Yes. Today he is chief of the best station, next year he will be assistant-manager, two years more and . . . but I daresay you know what he will be in two years' time. You are of the new gang – the gang of virtue. The same people who sent him specially also recommended you. Oh, don't say no. I've my own eyes to trust." Light dawned upon me. My dear aunt's influential acquaintances were producing an unexpected effect upon that young man. I nearly burst into a laugh. "Do you read the Company's confidential correspond-ence?" I asked. He hadn't a word to say. It was great fun. "When Mr Kurtz," I continued, severely, "is General Manager, you won't have the opportunity."

'He blew the candle out suddenly, and we went outside. The moon had risen. Black figures strolled about listlessly, pouring water on the glow, whence proceeded a sound of hissing; steam ascended in the moonlight, the beaten nigger groaned somewhere. "What a row the brute makes!" said the indefat-igable man with the moustaches, appearing near us. "Serve him right. Transgression – punishment – bang! Pitiless, pitiless. That's the only way. This will prevent all conflagrations for the future. I was just telling the manager . . ." He noticed my companion, and became crestfallen all at once. "Not in bed yet," he said, with a kind of servile heartiness; "it's so natural. Ha! Danger – agitation." He vanished. I went on to the riverside, and the other followed me. I heard a scathing murmur at my ear, "Heap of muffs – go to." The pilgrims could be seen in knots gesticulating, discussing. Several had still their staves in their hands. I verily believe they took these sticks to bed with them. Beyond the fence the forest stood up spectrally in the moonlight, and through the dim stir, through the faint sounds of that lamentable courtyard, the silence of the land went home to one's very heart – its mystery, its greatness, the amazing reality of its concealed life. The hurt nigger moaned feebly somewhere near by, and then fetched a deep sigh that made me mend my pace away from there. I felt a hand introducing itself under my arm. "My dear sir," said the fellow, "I don't want to be misunderstood, and especially by you, who will see Mr Kurtz long before I can have that pleasure. I wouldn't like him to get a false idea of my disposition . . . ."

'I let him run on, this papier-mache Mephistopheles, and it seemed to me that if I tried I could poke my forefinger through him, and would find nothing inside but a little loose dirt, maybe. He, don't you see, had been planning to be assistant-manager by and by under the present man, and I could see that the coming of that Kurtz had upset them both not a little. He talked precipitately, and I did not try to stop him. I had my shoulders against the wreck of my steamer, hauled up on the slope like a carcass of some big river animal. The smell of mud, of primeval mud, by Jove! was in my nostrils, the high stillness of primeval forest was before my eyes; there were shiny patches on the black creek. The moon had spread over everything a thin layer of silver – over the rank grass, over the mud, upon the wall of matted vegetation standing higher than the wall of a temple, over the great river I could see through a sombre gap glittering, glittering, as it flowed broadly by without a murmur. All this was great, expectant, mute, while the man jabbered about himself. I wondered whether the stillness on the face of the immensity looking at us two were meant as an appeal or as a menace. What were we who had strayed in here? Could we handle that dumb thing, or would it handle us? I felt how big, how confoundedly big, was that thing that couldn't talk, and perhaps was deaf as well. What was in there? I could see a little ivory coming out from there, and I had heard Mr Kurtz was in there. I had heard enough about it, too – God knows! Yet somehow it didn't bring any image with it – no more than if I had been told an angel or a fiend was in there. I believed it in the same way one of you might believe there are inhabitants in the planet Mars. I knew once a Scotch sailmaker who was certain, dead sure, there were people in Mars. If you asked him for some idea how they looked and behaved, he would get shy and mutter something about "walking on all-fours." If you as much as smiled, he would – though a man of sixty – offer to fight you. I would not have gone so far as to fight for Kurtz, but I went for him near enough to lie. You know I hate, detest, and can't bear a lie, not because I am straighter than the rest of us, but simply because it appals me. There is a taint of death, a flavour of mortality in lies which is exactly what I hate and detest in the world – what I want to forget. It makes me miserable and sick, like biting something rotten would do. Temperament, I suppose. Well, I went near enough to it by letting the young fool there believe anything he liked to imagine as to my influence in Europe. I became in an instant as much of a pretence as the rest of the bewitched pilgrims. This simply because I had a notion it somehow would be of help to that Kurtz, whom at the time I did not see, you understand. He was just a word for me. I did not see the man in the name any more than you do. Do you see him? Do you see the story? Do you see anything? It seems to me I am trying to tell you a dream – making a vain attempt, because no relation of a dream can convey the dream-sensation, that commingling of absurdity, surprise, and bewilderment in a tremor of struggling revolt, that notion of being captured by the incredible which is of the very essence of dreams. . . .'

He was silent for a while.

'. . . No, it is impossible; it is impossible to convey the life-sensation of any given epoch of one's existence – that which makes its truth, its meaning its subtle and penetrating essence. It is impossible. We live, as we dream, alone . . . .'

He paused again if reflecting, then added:

'Of course in this you fellows see more than I could then. You see me, whom you know. . . .'

It had become so pitch dark that we listeners could hardly see one another. For a long time already he, sitting apart, had been no more to us than a voice. There was not a word from anybody. The others might have been asleep, but I was awake. I listened, I listened on the watch for the sentence, for the word, that would give me the clue to the faint uneasiness inspired by this narrative that seemed to shape itself without human lips in the heavy night-air of the river.

'. . . Yes – I let him run on,' Marlow began again, 'and think what he pleased about the powers that were behind me. I did! And there was nothing behind me! There was nothing but that wretched, old, mangled steamboat I was leaning against, while he talked fluently about "the necessity for every man to get on." "And when one comes out here, you conceive, it is not to gaze at the moon." Mr Kurtz was a "universal genius," but even a genius would find it easier to work with "adequate tools – intelligent men." He did not make bricks – why, there was a physical impossibility in the way – as I was well aware; and if he did secretarial work for the manager, it was because "no sensible man rejects wantonly the confidence of his superiors." Did I see it? I saw it. What more did I want? What I really wanted was rivets, by heaven! Rivets. To get on with the work – to stop the hole. Rivets I wanted. There were cases of them down at the coast cases piled up – burst – split! You kicked a loose rivet at every second step in that station-yard on the hillside. Rivets had rolled into the grove of death. You could fill your pockets with rivets for the trouble of stooping down – and there wasn't one rivet to be found where it was wanted. We had plates that would do, but nothing to fasten them with. And every week the messenger, a lone negro, letterbag on shoulder and staff in hand, left our station for the coast. And several times a week a coast caravan came in with trade goods – ghastly glazed calico that made you shudder only to look at it, glass beads value about a penny a quart, confounded spotted cotton handkerchiefs. And no rivets. Three carriers could have brought all that was wanted to set that steamboat afloat.

'He was becoming confidential now, but I fancy my unresponsive attitude must have exasperated him at last, for he judged it necessary to inform me he feared neither God nor devil, let alone any mere man. I said I could see that very well, but what I wanted was a certain quantity of rivets – and rivets were what really Mr Kurtz wanted, if he had only known it. Now letters went to the coast every week. . . . "My dear sir," he cried, "I write from dictation." I demanded rivets. There was a way – for an intelligent man. He changed his manner; became very cold, and suddenly began to talk about a hippopotamus; wondered whether sleeping on board the steamer (I stuck to my salvage night and day) I wasn't disturbed. There was an old hippo that had the bad habit of getting out on the bank and roaming at night over the station grounds. The pilgrims used to turn out in a body and empty every rifle they could lay hands on at him. Some even had sat up o' nights for him. All this energy was wasted, though. "That animal has a charmed life," he said; "but you can say this only of brutes in this country. No man – you apprehend me? no man here bears a charmed life." He stood there for a moment in the moonlight with his delicate hooked nose set a little askew, and his mica eyes glittering without a wink, then, with a curt Goodnight, he strode off. I could see he was disturbed and considerably puzzled, which made me feel more hopeful than I had been for days. It was a great comfort to turn from that chap to my influential friend, the battered, twisted, ruined, tin-pot steamboat. I clambered on board. She rang under my feet like an empty Huntley & Palmer biscuit-tin kicked along a gutter; she was nothing so solid in make, and rather less pretty in shape, but I had expended enough hard work on her to make me love her. No influential friend would have served me better. She had given me a chance to come out a bit – to find out what I could do. No, I don't like work. I had rather laze about and think of all the fine things that can be done. I don't like work – no man does – but I like what is in the work – the chance to find yourself. Your own reality – for yourself, not for others – what no other man can ever know. They can only see the mere show, and never can tell what it really means.

'I was not surprised to see somebody sitting aft, on the deck, with his legs dangling over the mud. You see I rather chummed with the few mechanics there were in that station, whom the other pilgrims naturally despised – on account of their imperfect manners, I suppose. This was the foreman – a boiler-maker by trade – a good worker. He was a lank, bony, yellowfaced man, with big intense eyes. His aspect was worried, and his head was as bald as the palm of my hand; but his hair in falling seemed to have stuck to his chin, and had prospered in the new locality, for his beard hung down to his waist. He was a widower with six young children (he had left them in charge of a sister of his to come out there), and the passion of his life was pigeon-flying. He was an enthusiast and a connoisseur. He would rave about pigeons. After work hours he used sometimes to come over from his hut for a talk about his children and his pigeons; at work, when he had to crawl in the mud under the bottom of the steamboat, he would tie up that beard of his in a kind of white serviette he brought for the purpose. It had loops to go over his ears. In the evening he could be seen squatted on the bank rinsing that wrapper in the creek with great care, then spreading it solemnly on a bush to dry.

'I slapped him on the back and shouted, "We shall have rivets!" He scrambled to his feet exclaiming, "No! Rivets!" as though he couldn't believe his ears. Then in a low voice, "You . . . eh?" I don't know why we behaved like lunatics. I put my finger to the side of my nose and nodded mysteriously. "Good for you!" he cried, snapped his fingers above his head, lifting one foot. I tried a jig. We capered on the iron deck. A frightful clatter came out of that hulk, and the virgin forest on the other bank of the creek sent it back in a thundering roll upon the sleeping station. It must have made some of the pilgrims sit up in their hovels. A dark figure obscured the lighted doorway of the manager's hut, vanished, then, a second or so after, the doorway itself vanished, too. We stopped, and the silence driven away by the stamping of our feet flowed back again from the recesses of the land. The great wall of vegetation, an exuberant and entangled mass of trunks, branches, leaves, boughs, festoons, motionless in the moonlight, was like a rioting invasion of soundless life, a rolling wave of plants, piled up, crested, ready to topple over the creek, to sweep every little man of us out of his little existence. And it moved not. A deadened burst of mighty splashes and snorts reached us from afar, as though an ichthyosaurus had been taking a bath of glitter in the great river. "After all," said the boiler-maker in a reasonable tone, "why shouldn't we get the rivets?" Why not, indeed! I did not know of any reason why we shouldn't. "They'll come in three weeks," I said, confidently.

'But they didn't. Instead of rivets there came an invasion, an infliction, a visitation. It came in sections during the next three weeks, each section headed by a donkey carrying a white man in new clothes and tan shoes, bowing from that elevation right and left to the impressed pilgrims. A quarrelsome band of footsore sulky niggers trod on the heels of the donkey; a lot of tents, campstools, tin boxes, white cases, brown bales would be shot down in the court-yard, and the air of mystery would deepen a little over the muddle of the station. Five such instalments came, with their absurd air of disorderly flight with the loot of innumerable outfit shops and provision stores, that, one would think, they were lugging, after a raid, into the wilderness for equitable division. It was an inextricable mess of things decent in themselves but that human folly made look like the spoils of thieving.

'This devoted band called itself the Eldorado Exploring Expedition, and I believe they were sworn to secrecy. Their talk, however, was the talk of sordid buccaneers: it was reckless without hardihood, greedy without audacity, and cruel without courage; there was not an atom of foresight or of serious intention in the whole batch of them, and they did not seem aware these things are wanted for the work of the world. To tear treasure out of the bowels of the land was their desire, with no more moral purpose at the back of it than there is in burglars breaking into a safe. Who paid the expenses of the noble enterprise I don't know; but the uncle of our manager was leader of that lot.

'In exterior he resembled a butcher in a poor neighbourhood, and his eyes had a look of sleepy cunning. He carried his fat paunch with ostentation on his short legs, and during the time his gang infested the station spoke to no one but his nephew. You could see these two roaming about all day long with their heads close together in an everlasting confab.

'I had given up worrying myself about the rivets. One's capacity for that kind of folly is more limited than you would suppose. I said Hang! – and let things slide. I had plenty of time for meditation, and now and then I would give some thought to Kurtz. I wasn't very interested in him. No. Still, I was curious to see whether this man, who had come out equipped with moral ideas of some sort, would climb to the top after all and how he would set about his work when there.'

II

'One evening as I was lying flat on the deck of my steamboat, I heard voices approaching – and there were the nephew and the uncle strolling along the bank. I laid my head on my arm again, and had nearly lost myself in a doze, when somebody said in my ear, as it were: "I am as harmless as a little child, but I don't like to be dictated to. Am I the manager – or am I not? I was ordered to send him there. It's incredible.". . . . I became aware that the two were standing on the shore alongside the forepart of the steamboat, just below my head. I did not move; it did not occur to me to move: I was sleepy. "It is unpleasant," grunted the uncle. "He has asked the Administration to be sent there," said the other, "with the idea of showing what he could do; and I was instructed accordingly. Look at the influence that man must have. Is it not frightful?" They both agreed it was frightful, then made several bizarre remarks: "Make rain and fine weather – one man – the Council – by the nose" – bits of absurd sentences that got the better of my drowsiness, so that I had pretty near the whole of my wits about me when the uncle said, "The climate may do away with this difficulty for you. Is he alone there?" "Yes," answered the manager; "he sent his assistant down the river with a note to me in these terms: 'Clear this poor devil out of the country, and don't bother sending more of that sort. I had rather be alone than have the kind of men you can dispose of with me.' It was more than a year ago. Can you imagine such impudence!" "Anything since then?" asked the other hoarsely. "Ivory," jerked the nephew; "lots of it – prime sort – lots – most annoying, from him." "And with that?" questioned the heavy rumble. "Invoice," was the reply fired out, so to speak. Then silence. They had been talking about Kurtz.

'I was broad awake by this time, but, lying perfectly at ease, remained still, having no inducement to change my position. "How did that ivory come all this way?" growled the elder man, who seemed very vexed. The other explained that it had come with a fleet of canoes in charge of an English half-caste clerk Kurtz had with him; that Kurtz had apparently intended to return himself, the station being by that time bare of goods and stores, but after coming three hundred miles, had suddenly decided to go back, which he started to do alone in a small dugout with four paddlers, leaving the half-caste to continue down the river with the ivory. The two fellows there seemed astounded at anybody attempting such a thing. They were at a loss for an adequate motive. As to me, I seemed to see Kurtz for the first time. It was a distinct glimpse: the dugout, four paddling savages, and the lone white man turning his back suddenly on the headquarters, on relief, on thoughts of home – perhaps; setting his face towards the depths of the wilderness, towards his empty and desolate station. I did not know the motive. Perhaps he was just simply a fine fellow who stuck to his work for its own sake. His name, you understand, had not been pronounced once. He was "that man." The half caste, who, as far as I could see, had conducted a difficult trip with great prudence and pluck, was invariably alluded to as "that scoundrel." The "scoundrel" had reported that the "man" had been very ill – had recovered imperfectly. . . . The two below me moved away then a few paces, and strolled back and forth at some little distance. I heard: "Military post – doctor – two hundred miles – quite alone now – unavoidable delays – nine months – no news – strange rumours." They approached again, just as the manager was saying, "No one, as far as I know, unless a species of wandering trader – a pestilential fellow, snapping ivory from the natives." Who was it they were talking about now? I gathered in snatches that this was some man supposed to be in Kurtz's district, and of whom the manager did not approve. "We will not be free from unfair competition till one of these fellows is hanged for an example," he said. "Certainly," grunted the other; "get him hanged! Why not? Anything – anything can be done in this country. That's what I say; nobody here, you understand, here, can endanger your position. And why? You stand the climate – you outlast them all. The danger is in Europe; but there before I left I took care to – " They moved off and whispered, then their voices rose again. "The extraordinary series of delays is not my fault. I did my best." The fat man sighed. "Very sad." "And the pestiferous absurdity of his talk," continued the other; "he bothered me enough when he was here. 'Each station should be like a beacon on the road towards better things, a centre for trade of course, but also for humanizing, improving, instructing.' Conceive you – that ass! And he wants to be manager! No, it's – " Here he got choked by excessive indignation, and I lifted my head the least bit. I was surprised to see how near they were – right under me. I could have spat upon their hats. They were looking on the ground, absorbed in thought. The manager was switching his leg with a slender twig: his sagacious relative lifted his head. "You have been well since you came out this time?" he asked. The other gave a start. "Who? I? Oh! Like a charm – like a charm. But the rest – oh, my goodness! All sick. They die so quick, too, that I haven't the time to send them out of the country – it's incredible!" "H'm. Just so," grunted the uncle. "Ah! my boy, trust to this – I say, trust to this." I saw him extend his short flipper of an arm for a gesture that took in the forest, the creek, the mud, the river – seemed to beckon with a dishonouring flourish before the sunlit face of the land a treacherous appeal to the lurking death, to the hidden evil, to the profound darkness of its heart. It was so startling that I leaped to my feet and looked back at the edge of the forest, as though I had expected an answer of some sort to that black display of confidence. You know the foolish notions that come to one sometimes. The high stillness confronted these two figures with its ominous patience, waiting for the passing away of a fantastic invasion.

'They swore aloud together – out of sheer fright, I believe – then pretending not to know anything of my existence, turned back to the station. The sun was low; and leaning forward side by side, they seemed to be tugging painfully uphill their two ridiculous shadows of unequal length, that trailed behind them slowly over the tall grass without bending a single blade.

'In a few days the Eldorado Expedition went into the patient wilderness, that closed upon it as the sea closes over a diver. Long afterwards the news came that all the donkeys were dead. I know nothing as to the fate of the less valuable animals. They, no doubt, like the rest of us, found what they deserved. I did not inquire. I was then rather excited at the prospect of meeting Kurtz very soon. When I say very soon I mean it comparatively. It was just two months from the day we left the creek when we came to the bank below Kurtz's station.

'Going up that river was like travelling back to the earliest beginnings of the world, when vegetation rioted on the earth and the big trees were kings. An empty stream, a great silence, an impenetrable forest. The air was warm, thick, heavy, sluggish. There was no joy in the brilliance of sunshine. The long stretches of the waterway ran on, deserted, into the gloom of over-shadowed distances. On silvery sandbanks hippos and alligators sunned themselves side by side. The broadening waters flowed through a mob of wooded islands; you lost your way on that river as you would in a desert, and butted all day long against shoals, trying to find the channel, till you thought yourself bewitched and cut off for ever from everything you had known once – somewhere – far away – in another existence perhaps. There were moments when one's past came back to one, as it will sometimes when you have not a moment to spare to yourself; but it came in the shape of an unrestful and noisy dream, remembered with wonder amongst the overwhelming realities of this strange world of plants, and water, and silence. And this stillness of life did not in the least resemble a peace. It was the stillness of an implacable force brooding over an inscrutable intention. It looked at you with a vengeful aspect. I got used to it afterwards; I did not see it any more; I had no time. I had to keep guessing at the channel; I had to discern, mostly by inspiration, the signs of hidden banks; I watched for sunken stones; I was learning to clap my teeth smartly before my heart flew out, when I shaved by a fluke some infernal sly old snag that would have ripped the life out of the tin-pot steamboat and drowned all the pilgrims; I had to keep a lookout for the signs of dead wood we could cut up in the night for next day's steaming. When you have to attend to things of that sort, to the mere incidents of the surface, the reality – the reality, I tell you – fades. The inner truth is hidden – luckily, luckily. But I felt it all the same; I felt often its mysterious stillness watching me at my monkey tricks, just as it watches you fellows performing on your respective tight-ropes for – what is it? half-a-crown a tumble –'

'Try to be civil, Marlow,' growled a voice, and I knew there was at least one listener awake besides myself.

'I beg your pardon. I forgot the heartache which makes up the rest of the price. And indeed what does the price matter, if the trick be well done? You do your tricks very well. And I didn't do badly either, since I managed not to sink that steamboat on my first trip. It's a wonder to me yet. Imagine a blindfolded man set to drive a van over a bad road. I sweated and shivered over that business considerably, I can tell you. After all, for a seaman, to scrape the bottom of the thing that's supposed to float all the time under his care is the unpardonable sin. No one may know of it, but you never forget the thump – eh? A blow on the very heart. You remember it, you dream of it, you wake up at night and think of it – years after – and go hot and cold all over. I don't pretend to say that steamboat floated all the time. More than once she had to wade for a bit, with twenty cannibals splashing around and pushing. We had enlisted some of these chaps on the way for a crew. Fine fellows – cannibals – in their place. They were men one could work with, and I am grateful to them. And, after all, they did not eat each other before my face: they had brought along a provision of hippo-meat which went rotten, and made the mystery of the wilderness stink in my nostrils. Phoo! I can sniff it now. I had the manager on board and three or four pilgrims with their staves – all complete. Sometimes we came upon a station close by the bank, clinging to the skirts of the unknown, and the white men rushing out of a tumbledown hovel, with great gestures of joy and surprise and welcome, seemed very strange – had the appearance of being held there captive by a spell. The word ivory would ring in the air for a while – and on we went again into the silence, along empty reaches, round the still bends, between the high walls of our winding way, reverberating in hollow claps the ponderous beat of the stern-wheel. Trees, trees, millions of trees, massive, immense, running up high; and at their foot, hugging the bank against the stream, crept the little begrimed steamboat, like a sluggish beetle crawling on the floor of a lofty portico. It made you feel very small, very lost, and yet it was not altogether depressing, that feeling. After all, if you were small, the grimy beetle crawled on – which was just what you wanted it to do. Where the pilgrims imagined it crawled to I don't know. To some place where they expected to get something. I bet! For me it crawled towards Kurtz – exclusively; but when the steam-pipes started leaking we crawled very slow. The reaches opened before us and closed behind, as if the forest had stepped leisurely across the water to bar the way for our return. We penetrated deeper and deeper into the heart of darkness. It was very quiet there. At night sometimes the roll of drums behind the curtain of trees would run up the river and remain sustained faintly, as if hovering in the air high over our heads, till the first break of day. Whether it meant war, peace, or prayer we could not tell. The dawns were heralded by the descent of a chill stillness; the wood-cutters slept, their fires burned low; the snapping of a twig would make you start. We were wanderers on a prehistoric earth, on an earth that wore the aspect of an unknown planet. We could have fancied ourselves the first of men taking possession of an accursed inheritance, to be subdued at the cost of profound anguish and of excessive toil. But suddenly, as we struggled round a bend, there would be a glimpse of rush walls, of peaked grass-roofs, a burst of yells, a whirl of black limbs, a mass of hands clapping, of feet stamping, of bodies swaying, of eyes rolling, under the droop of heavy and motionless foliage. The steamer toiled along slowly on the edge of a black and incomprehensible frenzy. The prehistoric man was cursing us, praying to us, welcoming us – who could tell? We were cut off from the comprehension of our surroundings; we glided past like phantoms, wondering and secretly appalled, as sane men would be before an enthusiastic outbreak in a madhouse. We could not understand because we were too far and could not remember because we were ravelling in the night of first ages, of those ages that are gone, leaving hardly a sign – and no memories.

'The earth seemed unearthly. We are accustomed to look upon the shackled form of a conquered monster, but there – there you could look at a thing monstrous and free. It was unearthly, and the men were – No, they were not inhuman. Well, you know, that was the worst of it – this suspicion of their not being inhuman. It would come slowly to one. They howled and leaped, and spun, and made horrid faces; but what thrilled you was just the thought of their humanity – like yours– the thought of your remote kinship with this wild and passionate uproar. Ugly. Yes, it was ugly enough; but if you were man enough you would admit to yourself that there was in you just the faintest trace of a response to the terrible frankness of that noise, a dim suspicion of there being a meaning in it which you – so remote from the night of first ages – could comprehend. And why not? The mind of man is capable of anything – because everything is in it, all the past as well as all the future. What was there after all? Joy, fear, sorrow, devotion, valour, rage – who can tell? – but truth – truth stripped of its cloak of time. Let the fool gape and shudder – the man knows, and can look on without a wink. But he must at least be as much of a man as these on the shore. He must meet that truth with his own true stuff – with his own inborn strength. Principles won't do. Acquisitions, clothes, pretty rags – rags that would fly off at the first good shake. No; you want a deliberate belief. An appeal to me in this fiendish row – is there? Very well; I hear; I admit, but I have a voice, too, and for good or evil mine is the speech that cannot be silenced. Of course, a fool, what with sheer fright and fine sentiments, is always safe. Who's that grunting? You wonder I didn't go ashore for a howl and a dance? Well, no – I didn't. Fine sentiments, you say? Fine sentiments, be hanged! I had no time. I had to mess about with white-lead and strips of woolen blanket helping to put bandages on those leaky steampipes – I tell you. I had to watch the steering, and circumvent those snags, and get the tin-pot along by hook or by crook. There was surface truth enough in these things to save a wiser man. And between whiles I had to look after the savage who was fireman. He was an improved specimen; he could fire up a vertical boiler. He was there below me, and, upon my word, to look at him was as edifying as seeing a dog in a parody of breeches and a feather hat, walking on his hindlegs. A few months of training had done for that really fine chap. He squinted at the steam-gauge and at the water-guage with an evident effort of intrepidity – and he had filed teeth, too, the poor devil, and the wool of his pate shaved into queer patterns, and three ornamental scars on each of his cheeks. He ought to have been clapping his hands and stamping his feet on the bank, instead of which he was hard at work, a thrall to strange witchcraft, full of improving knowledge. He was useful because he had been instructed; and what he knew was this – that should the water in that transparent thing disappear, the evil spirit inside the boiler would get angry through the greatness of his thirst, and take a terrible vengeance. So he sweated and watched the glass fearfully (with an impromptu charm, made of rags, tied to his arm, and a piece of polished bone, as big as a watch, stuck flatways through his lower lip), while the wooded banks slipped past us slowly, the short noise was left behind, the interminable miles of silence – and we crept on, towards Kurtz. But the snags were thick, the water was treacherous and shallow, the boiler seemed indeed to have a sulky devil in it, and thus neither that fireman nor I had any time to peer into our creepy thoughts.

'Some fifty miles below the Inner Station we came upon a hut of reeds, an inclined and melancholy pole, with the unrecognizable tatters of what had been a flag of some sort flying from it, and a neatly stacked woodpile. This was unexpected. We came to the bank, and on the stack of firewood found a flat piece of board with some faded pencil-writing on it. When deciphered it said: "Wood for you. Hurry up. Approach cautiously." There was a signature, but it was illegible – not Kurtz – a much longer word. "Hurry up." Where? Up the river? "Approach cautiously." We had not done so. But the warning could not have been meant for the place where it could be only found after approach. Something was wrong above. But what – and how much? That was the question. We commented adversely upon the imbecility of that telegraphic style. The bush around said nothing, and would not let us look very far either. A torn curtain of red twill hung in the doorway of the hut, and flapped sadly in our faces. The dwelling was dismantled; but we could see a white man had lived there not very long ago. There remained a rude table – a plank on two posts; a heap of rubbish reposed in a dark corner, and by the door I picked up a book. It had lost its covers, and the pages had been thumbed into a state of extremely dirty softness; but the back had been lovingly stitched afresh with white cotton thread, which looked clean yet. It was an extraordinary find. Its title was, *An Inquiry into some Points of Seamanship*, by a man Towser, Towson – some such name – Master in his Majesty's Navy. The matter looked dreary reading enough, with illustrative diagrams and repulsive tables of figures, and the copy was sixty years old. I handled this amazing antiquity with the greatest possible tenderness, lest it should dissolve in my hands. Within, Towson or Towser was inquiring earnestly into the breaking strain of ships' chains and tackle, and other such matters. Not a very enthralling book; but at the first glance you could see there a singleness of intention, an honest concern for the right way of going to work, which made these humble pages, thought out so many years ago, luminous with another than a professional light. The simple old sailor, with his talk of chains and purchases, made me forget the jungle and the pilgrims in a delicious sensation of having come upon something unmistakably real. Such a book being there was wonderful enough but still more astounding were the notes pencilled in the margin, and plainly referring to the text. I couldn't believe my eyes! They were in cipher! Yes, it looked like cipher. Fancy a man lugging with him a book of that description into this nowhere and study-ing it – and making notes – in cipher at that! It was an extravagant mystery.

'I had been dimly aware for some time of a worrying noise, and when I lifted my eyes I saw the woodpile was gone, and the manager, aided by all the pilgrims, was shouting at me from the riverside. I slipped the book into my pocket. I assure you to leave off reading was like tearing myself away from the shelter of an old and solid friendship.

'I started the lame engine ahead. "It must be this miserable trader – this intruder," exclaimed the manager, looking back malevolently at the place we had left. "He must be English," I said. "It will not save him from getting into trouble if he is not careful," muttered the manager darkly. I observed with assumed innocence that no man was safe from trouble in this world.

'The current was more rapid now, the steamer seemed at her last gasp, the stern-wheel flopped languidly, and I caught myself listening on tiptoe for the next beat of the boat, for in sober truth I expected the wretched thing to give up every moment. It was like watching the last flickers of a life. But still we crawled. Sometimes I would pick out a tree a little way ahead to measure our progress towards Kurtz by, but I lost it invariably before we got abreast. To keep the eyes so long on one thing was too much for human patience. The manager displayed a beautiful resignation. I fretted and fumed and took to arguing with myself whether or no I would talk openly with Kurtz; but before I could come to any conclusion it occurred to me that my speech or my silence, indeed any action of mine, would be a mere futility. What did it matter what any one knew or ignored? What did it matter who was manager? One gets sometimes such a flash of insight. The essentials of this affair lay deep under the surface, beyond my reach, and beyond my power of meddling.

'Towards the evening of the second day we judged ourselves about eight miles from Kurtz's station. I wanted to push on; but the manager looked grave, and told me the navigation up there was so dangerous that it would be advisable, the sun being very low already, to wait where we were till next morning. Moreover, he pointed out that if the warning to approach cautiously were to be followed, we must approach in daylight – not at dusk or in the dark. This was sensible enough. Eight miles meant nearly three hours' steaming for us, and I could also see suspicious ripples at the upper end of the reach. Nevertheless, I was annoyed beyond expression at the delay, and most unreasonably, too, since one night more could not matter much after so many months. As we had plenty of wood, and caution was the word, I brought up in the middle of the stream. The reach was narrow, straight, with high sides like a railway cutting. The dusk came gliding into it long before the sun had set. The current ran smooth and swift, but a dumb immobility sat on the banks. The living trees, lashed together by the creepers and every living bush of the undergrowth, might have been changed into stone, even to the slenderest twig, to the lightest leaf. It was not sleep – it seemed unnatural, like a state of trance. Not the faintest sound of any kind could be heard. You looked on amazed, and began to suspect yourself of being deaf – then the night came suddenly, and struck you blind as well. About three in the morning some large fish leaped, and the loud splash made me jump as though a gun had been fired. When the sun rose there was a white fog, very warm and clammy, and more blinding than the night. It did not shift or drive; it was just there, standing all round you like something solid. At eight or nine, perhaps, it lifted as a shutter lifts. We had a glimpse of the towering multitude of trees, of the immense matted jungle, with the blazing little ball of the sun hanging over it – all perfectly still – and then the white shutter came down again, smoothly, as if sliding in greased grooves. I ordered the chain, which we had begun to heave in, to be paid out again. Before it stopped running with a muffled rattle, a cry, a very loud cry, as of infinite desolation, soared slowly in the opaque air. It ceased. A complaining clamour, modulated in savage discords, filled our ears. The sheer unexpectedness of it made my hair stir under my cap. I don't know how it struck the others: to me it seemed as though the mist itself had screamed, so suddenly, and apparently from all sides at once, did this tumultuous and mournful uproar arise. It culminated in a hurried outbreak of almost intolerably excessive shrieking, which stopped short, leaving us stiffened in a variety of silly attitudes, and obstinately listening to the nearly as appalling and excessive silence. "Good God! What is the meaning –" stammered at my elbow one of the pilgrims – a little fat man, with sandy hair and red whiskers, who wore sidespring boots, and pink pyjamas tucked into his socks. Two others remained open-mouthed a whole minute, then dashed into the little cabin, to rush out incontinently and stand darting scared glances, with Winchesters at 'ready' in their hands. What we could see was just the steamer we were on, her outlines blurred as though she had been on the point of dissolving, and a misty strip of water, perhaps two feet broad, around her – and that was all. The rest of the world was nowhere, as far as our eyes and ears were concerned. Just nowhere. Gone, disappeared; swept off without leaving a whisper or a shadow behind.

'I went forward, and ordered the chain to be hauled in short, so as to be ready to trip the anchor and move the steamboat at once if necessary. "Will they attack?" whispered an awed voice. "We will all be butchered in this fog," murmured another. The faces twitched with the strain, the hands trembled slightly, the eyes forgot to wink. It was very curious to see the contrast of expressions of the white men and of the black fellows of our crew, who were as much strangers to that part of the river as we, though their homes were only eight hundred miles away. The whites, of course greatly discomposed, had besides a curious look of being painfully shocked by such an outrageous row. The others had an alert, naturally interested expression; but their faces were essentially quiet, even those of the one or two who grinned as they hauled at the chain. Several exchanged short, grunting phrases, which seemed to settle the matter to their satisfaction. Their headman, a young, broadchested black, severely draped in darkblue fringed cloths, with fierce nostrils and his hair all done up artfully in oily ringlets, stood near me. "Aha!" I said, just for good fellowship's sake. "Catch 'im," he snapped, with a bloodshot widening of his eyes and a flash of sharp teeth – "catch 'im. Give 'im to us." "To you, eh?" I asked; "what would you do with them?" "Eat 'im!" he said curtly, and, leaning his elbow on the rail, looked out into the fog in a dignified and profoundly pensive attitude. I would no doubt have been properly horrified, had it not occurred to me that he and his chaps must be very hungry: that they must have been growing increasingly hungry for at least this month past. They had been engaged for six months (I don't think a single one of them had any clear idea of time, as we at the end of countless ages have. They still belonged to the beginnings of time – had no inherited experience to teach them as it were), and of course, as long as there was a piece of paper written over in accordance with some farcical law or other made down the river, it didn't enter anybody's head to trouble how they would live. Certainly they had brought with them some rotten hippo-meat, which couldn't have lasted very long, anyway, even if the pilgrims hadn't, in the midst of a shocking hullabaloo, thrown a considerable quantity of it overboard. It looked like a high-handed proceeding; but it was really a case of legitimate self-defence. You can't breathe dead hippo waking, sleeping, and eating, and at the same time keep your precarious grip on existence. Besides that, they had given them every week three pieces of brass wire, each about nine inches long; and the theory was they were to buy their provisions with that currency in riverside villages. You can see how that worked. There were either no villages, or the people were hostile, or the director, who like the rest of us fed out of tins, with an occasional old he-goat thrown in, didn't want to stop the steamer for some more or less recondite reason. So, unless they swallowed the wire itself, or made loops of it to snare the fishes with, I don't see what good their extravagant salary could be to them. I must say it was paid with a regularity worthy of a large and honourable trading Company. For the rest, the only thing to eat – though it didn't look eatable in the least – I saw in their possession was a few lumps of some stuff like half-cooked dough, of a dirty lavender colour, they kept wrapped in leaves, and now and then swallowed a piece of, but so small that it seemed done more for the looks of the thing than for any serious purpose of sustenance. Why in the name of all the gnawing devils of hunger they didn't go for us – they were thirty to five – and have a good tuck-in for once, amazes me now when I think of it. They were big powerful men, with not much capacity to weigh the consequences, with courage, with strength, even yet, though their skins were no longer glossy and their muscles no longer hard. And I saw that something restraining, one of those human secrets that baffle probability, had come into play there. I looked at them with a swift quickening of interest – not because it occurred to me I might be eaten by them before very long, though I own to you that just then I perceived – in a new light, as it were – how unwholesome the pilgrims looked, and I hoped, yes, I positively hoped, that my aspect was not so – what shall I say? – so – unappetizing: a touch of fantastic vanity which fitted well with the dream-sensation that pervaded all my days at that time. Perhaps I had a little fever, too. One can't live with one's finger everlastingly on one's pulse. I had often "a little fever," or a little touch of other things – the playful paw-strokes of the wilderness, the preliminary trifling before the more serious onslaught which came in due course. Yes; I looked at them as you would on any human being, with a curiosity of their impulses, motives, capacities, weaknesses, when brought to the test of an inexorable physical necessity. Restraint! What possible restraint? Was it superstition, disgust, patience, fear – or some kind of primitive honour? No fear can stand up to hunger, no patience can wear it out, disgust simply does not exist where hunger is; and as to superstition, beliefs, and what you may call principles, they are less than chaff in a breeze. Don't you know the devilry of lingering starvation, its exasperating torment, its black thoughts, its sombre and brooding ferocity? Well, I do. It takes a man all his inborn strength to fight hunger properly. It's really easier to face bereavement, dishonour, and the perdition of one's soul – than this kind of prolonged hunger. Sad, but true. And these chaps, too, had no earthly reason for any kind of scruple. Restraint! I would just as soon have expected restraint from a hyena prowling amongst the corpses of a battlefield. But there was the act facing me – the fact dazzling, to be seen, like the foam on the depths of the sea, like a ripple on an unfathomable enigma, a mystery greater – when I thought of it – than the curious, inexplicable note of desperate grief in this savage clamour that had swept by us on the river-bank, behind the blind whiteness of the fog.

'Two pilgrims were quarrelling in hurried whispers as to which bank. "Left." "No, no; how can you? Right, right, of course." "It is very serious," said the manager's voice behind me; "I would be desolated if anything should happen to Mr Kurtz before we came up." I looked at him, and had not the slightest doubt he was sincere. He was just the kind of man who would wish to preserve appearances. That was his restraint. But when he muttered something about going on at once, I did not even take the trouble to answer him. I knew, and he knew, that it was impossible. Were we to let go our hold of the bottom, we would be absolutely in the air – in space. We wouldn't be able to tell where we were going to – whether up or down stream, or across – till we fetched against one bank or the other – and then we wouldn't know at first which it was. Of course I made no move. I had no mind for a smash-up. You couldn't imagine a more deadly place for a shipwreck. Whether drowned at once or not, we were sure to perish speedily in one way or another. "I authorize you to take all the risks," he said, after a short silence. "I refuse to take any," I said shortly; which was just the answer he expected, though its tone might have surprised him. "Well, I must defer to your judgment. You are captain," he said with marked civility. I turned my shoulder to him in sign of my appreciation, and looked into the fog. How long would it last? It was the most hopeless lookout. The approach to this Kurtz grubbing for ivory in the wretched bush was beset by as many dangers as though he had been an enchanted princess sleeping in a fabulous castle. "Will they attack, do you think?" asked the manager, in a confidential tone.

'I did not think they would attack, for several obvious reasons. The thick fog was one. If they left the bank in their canoes they would get lost in it, as we would be if we attempted to move. Still, I had also judged the jungle of both banks quite impenetrable – and yet eyes were in it, eyes that had seen us. The riverside bushes were certainly very thick; but the undergrowth behind was evidently penetrable. However, during the short lift I had seen no canoes any-where in the reach – certainly not abreast of the steamer. But what made the idea of attack inconceivable to me was the nature of the noise – of the cries we had heard. They had not the fierce character boding immediate hostile inten-tion. Unexpected, wild, and violent as they had been, they had given me an irresistible impression of sorrow. The glimpse of the steamboat had for some reason filled those savages with unrestrained grief. The danger, if any, I expounded, was from our proximity to a great human passion let loose. Even extreme grief may ultimately vent itself in violence – but more generally takes the form of apathy. . . .

'You should have seen the pilgrims stare! They had no heart to grin, or even to revile me: but I believe they thought me gone mad – with fright, maybe. I delivered a regular lecture. My dear boys, it was no good bothering. Keep a lookout? Well, you may guess I watched the fog for the signs of lifting as a cat watches a mouse; but for anything else our eyes were of no more use to us than if we had been buried miles deep in a heap of cotton-wool. It felt like it, too – choking, warm, stifling. Besides, all I said, though it sounded extravagant, was absolutely true to fact. What we afterwards alluded to as an attack was really an attempt at repulse. The action was very far from being aggressive – it was not even defensive, in the usual sense: it was undertaken under the stress of desperation, and in its essence was purely protective.

'It developed itself, I should say, two hours after the fog lifted, and its commencement was at a spot, roughly speaking, about a mile and a half below Kurtz's station. We had just floundered and flopped round a bend, when I saw an islet, a mere grassy hummock of bright green, in the middle of the stream. It was the only thing of the kind; but as we opened the reach more, I perceived it was the head of a long sand-bank, or rather of a chain of shallow patches stretching down the middle of the river. They were discoloured, just awash, and the whole lot was seen just under the water, exactly as a man's backbone is seen running down the middle of his back under the skin. Now, as far as I did see, I could go to the right or to the left of this. I didn't know either channel, of course. The banks looked pretty well alike, the depth appeared the same; but as I had been informed the station was on the west side, I naturally headed for the western passage.

'No sooner had we fairly entered it than I became aware it was much narrower than I had supposed. To the left of us there was the long uninterrupted shoal, and to the right a high, steep bank heavily overgrown with bushes. Above the bush the trees stood in serried ranks. The twigs overhung the current thickly, and from distance to distance a large limb of some tree projected rigidly over the stream. It was then well on in the afternoon, the face of the forest was gloomy, and a broad strip of shadow had already fallen on the water. In this shadow we steamed up – very slowly, as you may imagine. I steered her well inshore – the water being deepest near the bank, as the sounding-pole informed me.

'One of my hungry and forbearing friends was sounding in the bows just below me. This steamboat was exactly like a decked scow. On the deck, there were two little teakwood houses, with doors and windows. The boiler was in the fore-end, and the machinery right astern. Over the whole there was a light roof, supported on stanchions. The funnel projected through that roof, and in front of the funnel a small cabin built of light planks served for a pilot-house. It contained a couch, two camp-stools, a loaded Martini-Henry leaning in one corner, a tiny table, and the steering-wheel. It had a wide door in front and a broad shutter at each side. All these were always thrown open, of course. I spent my days perched up there on the extreme fore-end of that roof, before the door. At night I slept, or tried to, on the couch. An athletic black belonging to some coast tribe and educated by my poor predecessor, was the helmsman. He sported a pair of brass earrings, wore a blue cloth wrapper from the waist to the ankles, and thought all the world of himself. He was the most unstable kind of fool I had ever seen. He steered with no end of a swagger while you were by; but if he lost sight of you, he became instantly the prey of an abject funk, and would let that cripple of a steamboat get the upper hand of him in a minute.

'I was looking down at the sounding-pole, and feeling much annoyed to see at each try a little more of it stick out of that river, when I saw my poleman give up the business suddenly, and stretch himself flat on the deck, without even taking the trouble to haul his pole in. He kept hold on it though, and it trailed in the water. At the same time the fireman, whom I could also see below me, sat down abruptly before his furnace and ducked his head. I was amazed. Then I had to look at the river mighty quick, because there was a snag in the fairway. Sticks, little sticks, were flying about – thick: they were whizzing before my nose, dropping below me, striking behind me against my pilot-house. All this time the river, the shore, the woods, were very quiet – perfectly quiet. I could only hear the heavy splashing thump of the stern-wheel and the patter of these things. We cleared the snag clumsily. Arrows, by Jove! We were being shot at! I stepped in quickly to close the shutter on the landside. That fool-helmsman, his hands on the spokes, was lifting his knees high, stamping his feet, champing his mouth, like a reined-in horse. Confound him! And we were staggering within ten feet of the bank. I had to lean right out to swing the heavy shutter, and I saw a face amongst the leaves on the level with my own, looking at me very fierce and steady; and then suddenly, as though a veil had been removed from my eyes, I made out, deep in the tangled gloom, naked breasts, arms, legs, glaring eyes – the bush was swarming with human limbs in movement, glistening, of bronze colour. The twigs shook, swayed, and rustled, the arrows flew out of them, and then the shutter came to. "Steer her straight," I said to the helmsman. He held his head rigid, face forward; but his eyes rolled, he kept on lifting and setting down his feet gently, his mouth foamed a little. "Keep quiet!" I said in a fury. I might just as well have ordered a tree not to sway in the wind. I darted out. Below me there was a great scuffle of feet on the iron deck; confused exclamations; a voice screamed, "Can you turn back?" I caught sight of a V-shaped ripple on the water ahead. What? Another snag! A fusillade burst out under my feet. The pilgrims had opened with their Winchesters, and were simply squirting lead into that bush. A deuce of a lot of smoke came up and drove slowly forward. I swore at it. Now I couldn't see the ripple or the snag either. I stood in the doorway, peering, and the arrows came in swarms. They might have been poisoned, but they looked as though they wouldn't kill a cat. The bush began to howl. Our wood-cutters raised a warlike whoop; the report of a rifle just at my back deafened me. I glanced over my shoulder, and the pilot-house was yet full of noise and smoke when I made a dash at the wheel. The fool-nigger had dropped everything, to throw the shutter open and let off that Martini-Henry. He stood before the wide opening, glaring, and I yelled at him to come back, while I straightened the sudden twist out of that steamboat. There was no room to turn even if I had wanted to, the snag was somewhere very near ahead in that confounded smoke, there was no time to lose, so I just crowded her into the bank – right into the bank, where I knew the water was deep.

'We tore slowly along the overhanging bushes in a whirl of broken twigs and flying leaves. The fusillade below stopped short, as I had foreseen it would when the squirts got empty. I threw my head back to a glinting whizz that traversed the pilot-house, in at one shutter-hole and out at the other. Looking past that mad helmsman, who was shaking the empty rifle and yelling at the shore, I saw vague forms of men running bent double, leaping, gliding, distinct, incomplete, evanescent. Something big appeared in the air before the shutter, the rifle went overboard, and the man stepped back swiftly, looked at me over his shoulder in an extraordinary, profound, familiar manner, and fell upon my feet. The side of his head hit the wheel twice, and the end of what appeared a long cane clattered round and knocked over a little campstool. It looked as though after wrenching that thing from somebody ashore he had lost his balance in the effort. The thin smoke had blown away, we were clear of the snag, and looking ahead I could see that in another hundred yards or so I would be free to sheer off, away from the bank; but my feet felt so very warm and wet that I had to look down. The man had rolled on his back and stared straight up at me; both his hands clutched that cane. It was the shaft of a spear that, either thrown or lunged through the opening, had caught him in the side just below the ribs; the blade had gone in out of sight, after making a frightful gash; my shoes were full; a pool of blood lay very still, gleaming dark-red under the wheel; his eyes shone with an amazing lustre. The fusillade burst out again. He looked at me anxiously, gripping the spear like something precious, with an air of being afraid I would try to take it away from him. I had to make an effort to free my eyes from his gaze and attend to the steering. With one hand I felt above my head for the line of the steam whistle, and jerked out screech after screech hurriedly. The tumult of angry and warlike yells was checked instantly, and then from the depths of the woods went out such a tremulous and prolonged wail of mournful fear and utter despair as may be imagined to follow the flight of the last hope from the earth. There was a great commotion in the bush; the shower of arrows stopped, a few dropping shots rang out sharply – then silence, in which the languid beat of the stern-wheel came plainly to my ears. I put the helm hard a-starboard at the moment when the pilgrim in pink pyjamas, very hot and agitated, appeared in the doorway. "The manager sends me –" he began in an official tone, and stopped short. "Good God!" he said, glaring at the wounded man.

'We two whites stood over him, and his lustrous and inquiring glance enveloped us both. I declare it looked as though he would presently put to us some question in an understandable language; but he died without uttering a sound, without moving a limb, without twitching a muscle. Only in the very last moment, as though in response to some sign we could not see, to some whisper we could not hear, he frowned heavily, and that frown gave to his black death-mask an inconceivably sombre, brooding, and menacing expression. The lustre of inquiring glance faded swiftly into vacant glassiness. "Can you steer?" I asked the agent eagerly. He looked very dubious; but I made a grab at his arm, and he understood at once I meant him to steer whether or no. To tell you the truth, I was morbidly anxious to change my shoes and socks. "He is dead," murmured the fellow, immensely impressed. "No doubt about it," said I, tugging like mad at the shoe laces. "And by the way, I suppose Mr Kurtz is dead as well by this time."

'For the moment that was the dominant thought. There was a sense of extreme disappointment, as though I had found out I had been striving after something altogether without a substance. I couldn't have been more disgusted if I had travelled all this way for the sole purpose of talking with Mr Kurtz. Talking with . . . I flung one shoe overboard, and became aware that that was exactly what I had been looking forward to – a talk with Kurtz. I made the strange discovery that I had never imagined him as doing, you know, but as discoursing. I didn't say to myself, "Now I will never see him," or "Now I will never shake him by the hand," but, "Now I will never hear him." The man presented himself as a voice. Not of course that I did not connect him with some sort of action. Hadn't I been told in all the tones of jealousy and admiration that he had collected, bartered, swindled, or stolen more ivory than all the other agents together? That was not the point. The point was in his being a gifted creature, and that of all his gifts the one that stood out pre-eminently, that carried with it a sense of real presence, was his ability to talk, his words – the gift of expression, the bewildering, the illuminating, the most exalted and the most contemptible, the pulsating stream of light, or the deceitful flow from the heart of an impenetrable darkness.

'The other shoe went flying unto the devil-god of that river. I thought, "By Jove! it's all over. We are too late; he has vanished – the gift has vanished, by means of some spear, arrow, or club. I will never hear that chap speak after all" – and my sorrow had a startling extravagance of emotion, even such as I had noticed in the howling sorrow of these savages in the bush. I couldn't have felt more of lonely desolation somehow, had I been robbed of a belief or had missed my destiny in life . . . . Why do you sigh in this beastly way, somebody? Absurd? Well, absurd. Good Lord! mustn't a man ever – Here, give me some tobacco.'. . .

There was a pause of profound stillness, then a match flared, and Marlow's lean face appeared, worn, hollow, with downward folds and dropped eyelids, with an aspect of concentrated attention; and as he took vigorous draws at his pipe, it seemed to retreat and advance out of the night in the regular flicker of tiny flame. The match went out.

'Absurd!' he cried. 'This is the worst of trying to tell. . . . Here you all are, each moored with two good addresses, like a hulk with two anchors, a butcher round one corner, a policeman round another, excellent appetites, and temperature normal – you hear – normal from year's end to year's end. And you say, Absurd! Absurd be – exploded! Absurd! My dear boys, what can you expect from a man who out of sheer nervousness had just flung overboard a pair of new shoes! Now I think of it, it is amazing I did not shed tears. I am, upon the whole, proud of my fortitude. I was cut to the quick at the idea of having lost the inestimable privilege of listening to the gifted Kurtz. Of course I was wrong. The privilege was waiting for me. Oh, yes, I heard more than enough. And I was right, too. A voice. He was very little more than a voice. And I heard – him – it – this voice – other voices – all of them were so little more than voices – and the memory of that time itself lingers around me, impalpable, like a dying vibration of one immense jabber, silly, atrocious, sordid, savage, or simply mean, without any kind of sense. Voices, voices – even the girl herself – now –'

He was silent for a long time.

'I laid the ghost of his gifts at last with a lie,' he began, suddenly. 'Girl! What? Did I mention a girl? Oh, she is out of it – completely. They – the women I mean – are out of it – should be out of it. We must help them to stay in that beautiful world of their own, lest ours gets worse. Oh, she had to be out of it. You should have heard the disinterred body of Mr Kurtz saying, "My Intended." You would have perceived directly then how completely she was out of it. And the lofty frontal bone of Mr Kurtz! They say the hair goes on growing some-times, but this – ah – specimen, was impressively bald. The wilderness had patted him on the head, and, behold, it was like a ball – an ivory ball; it had caressed him, and – lo! – he had withered; it had taken him, loved him, embraced him, got into his veins, consumed his flesh, and sealed his soul to its own by the inconceivable ceremonies of some devilish initiation. He was its spoiled and pampered favourite. Ivory? I should think so. Heaps of it, stacks of it. The old mud shanty was bursting with it. You would think there was not a single tusk left either above or below the ground in the whole country. "Mostly fossil," the manager had remarked, disparagingly. It was no more fossil than I am; but they call it fossil when it is dug up. It appears these niggers do bury the tusks sometimes – but evidently they couldn't bury this parcel deep enough to save the gifted Mr Kurtz from his fate. We filled the steamboat with it, and had to pile a lot on the deck. Thus he could see and enjoy as long as he could see, because the appreciation of this favour had remained with him to the last. You should have heard him say, "My ivory." Oh, yes, I heard him. "My Intended, my ivory, my station, my river, my –" everything belonged to him. It made me hold

my breath in expectation of hearing the wilderness burst into a prodigious peal
of laughter that would shake the fixed stars in their places. Everything
belonged to him – but that was a trifle. The thing was to know what he
belonged to, how many powers of darkness claimed him for their own. That
was the reflection that made you creepy all over. It was impossible – it was not
good for one either – trying to imagine. He had taken a high seat amongst the
devils of the land – I mean literally. You can't understand. How could you? –
With solid pavement under your feet, surrounded by kind neighbours ready to
cheer you or to fall on you, stepping delicately between the butcher and the
policeman, in the holy terror of scandal and gallows and lunatic asylums – how
can you imagine what particular region of the first ages a man's untrammelled
feet may take him into by the way of solitude – utter solitude without a
policeman – by the way of silence – utter silence, where no warning voice of a
kind neighbour can be heard whispering of public opinion? These little things
make all the great difference. When they are gone you must fall back upon
your own innate strength, upon your own capacity for faithfulness. Of course
you may be too much of a fool to go wrong – too dull even to know you are
being assaulted by the powers of darkness. I take it, no fool ever made a bargain
for his soul with the devil; the fool is too much of a fool, or the devil too much
of a devil – I don't know which. Or you may be such a thunderingly exalted
creature as to be altogether deaf and blind to anything but heavenly sights and
sounds. Then the earth for you is only a standing place – and whether to be like
this is your loss or your gain I won't pretend to say. But most of us are neither
one nor the other. The earth for us is a place to live in, where we must put up
with sights, with sounds, with smells, too, by Jove! – breathe dead hippo, so to
speak, and not be contaminated. And there, don't you see? Your strength comes
in, the faith in your ability for the digging of unostentatious holes to bury the
stuff in – your power of devotion, not to yourself, but to an obscure back-
breaking business. And that's difficult enough. Mind, I am not trying to excuse
or even explain – I am trying to account to myself for – for – Mr Kurtz – for the
shade of Mr Kurtz. This initiated wraith from the back of Nowhere honoured
me with its amazing confidence before it vanished altogether. This was because
it could speak English to me. The original Kurtz had been educated partly in
England, and – as he was good enough to say himself – his sympathies were in
the right place. His mother was half-English, his father was half-French. All
Europe   contributed to the making of Kurtz; and by and by I learned that,
most appropriately, the International Society for the Suppression of Savage
Customs had intrusted him with the making of a report, for its future guidance. And he had written it, too. I've seen it. I've read it. It was eloquent,
vibrating with eloquence, but too high-strung, I think. Seventeen pages of close
writing he had found time for! But this must have been before his – let us say –
nerves, went wrong, and caused him to preside at certain midnight dances
ending with unspeakable rites, which – as far as I reluctantly gathered from
what I heard at various times – were offered up to him – do you understand? –
to Mr Kurtz himself. But it was a beautiful piece of writing. The opening
paragraph, however, in the light of later information, strikes me now as
ominous. He began with the argument that we whites, from the point of

development we had arrived at, "must necessarily appear to them [savages] in the nature of supernatural beings – we approach them with the might as of a deity," and so on, and so on. "By the simple exercise of our will we can exert a power for good practically unbounded," etc., etc. From that point he soared and took me with him. The peroration was magnificent, though difficult to remember, you know. It gave me the notion of an exotic Immensity ruled by an august Benevolence. It made me tingle with enthusiasm. This was the unbounded power of eloquence – of words – of burning noble words. There were no practical hints to interrupt the magic current of phrases, unless a kind of note at the foot of the last page, scrawled evidently much later, in an unsteady hand, may be regarded as the exposition of a method. It was very simple, and at the end of that moving appeal to every altruistic sentiment it blazed at you, luminous and terrifying, like a flash of lightning in a serene sky: "Exterminate all the brutes!" The curious part was that he had apparently forgotten all about that valuable postscriptum, because, later on, when he in a sense came to himself, he repeatedly entreated me to take good care of "my pamphlet" (he called it), as it was sure to have in the future a good influence upon his career. I had full inform-ation about all these things, and, besides, as it turned out, I was to have the care of his memory. I've done enough for it to give me the indisput-able right to lay it, if I choose, for an everlasting rest in the dust-bin of progress, amongst all the sweepings and, figuratively speaking, all the dead cats of civilization. But then, you see, I can't choose. He won't be forgotten. Whatever he was, he was not common. He had the power to charm or frighten rudiment-ary souls into an aggravated witch-dance in his honour; he could also fill the small souls of the pilgrims with bitter misgivings: he had one devoted friend at least, and he had conquered one soul in the world that was neither rudiment-ary nor tainted with self-seeking. No; I can't forget him, though I am not prepared to affirm the fellow was exactly worth the life we lost in getting to him. I missed my late helmsman awfully – I missed him even while his body was still lying in the pilot-house. Perhaps you will think it passing strange this regret for a savage who was no more account than a grain of sand in a black Sahara. Well, don't you see, he had done something, he had steered; for months I had him at my back – a help – an instrument. It was a kind of partnership. He steered for me – I had to look after him, I worried about his deficiencies, and thus a subtle bond had been created, of which I only became aware when it was suddenly broken. And the intimate profundity of that look he gave me when he received his hurt remains to this day in my memory – like a claim of distant kinship affirmed in a supreme moment.

'Poor fool! If he had only left that shutter alone. He had no restraint, no restraint – just like Kurtz – a tree swayed by the wind. As soon as I had put on a dry pair of slippers, I dragged him out, after first jerking the spear out of his side, which operation I confess I performed with my eyes shut tight. His heels leaped together over the little doorstep; his shoulders were pressed to my breast; I hugged him from behind desperately. Oh! he was heavy, heavy; heavier than any man on earth, I should imagine. Then without more ado I tipped him overboard. The current snatched him as though he had been a wisp of grass, and I saw the body roll over twice before I lost sight of it for ever. All the pilgrims and the manager were then congregated on the awning-deck about the pilot-house, chattering at each other like a flock of excited magpies, and there was a scandalized murmur at my heartless promptitude. What they wanted to keep that body hanging about for I can't guess. Embalm it, maybe. But I had also heard another, and a very ominous, murmur on the deck below. My friends the woodcutters were likewise scandalized, and with a better show of reason – though I admit that the reason itself was quite inadmissible. Oh, quite! I had made up my mind that if my late helmsman was to be eaten, the fishes alone should have him. He had been a very second-rate helmsman while alive, but now he was dead he might have become a first-class temptation, and possibly cause some startling trouble. Besides, I was anxious to take the wheel, the man in pink pyjamas showing himself a hopeless duffer at the business.

'This I did directly the simple funeral was over. We were going half-speed, keeping right in the middle of the stream, and I listened to the talk about me. They had given up Kurtz, they had given up the station; Kurtz was dead, and the station had been burnt – and so on – and so on. The red-haired pilgrim was beside himself with the thought that at least this poor Kurtz had been properly avenged. "Say! We must have made a glorious slaughter of them in the bush. Eh? What do you think? Say?" He positively danced, the bloodthirsty little gingery beggar. And he had nearly fainted when he saw the wounded man! I could not help saying, "You made a glorious lot of smoke, anyhow." I had seen, from the way the tops of the bushes rustled and flew, that almost all the shots had gone too high. You can't hit anything unless you take aim and fire from the shoulder; but these chaps fired from the hip with their eyes shut. The retreat, I maintained – and I was right – was caused by the screeching of the steam whistle. Upon this they forgot Kurtz, and began to howl at me with indignant protests.

'The manager stood by the wheel murmuring confidentially about the necessity of getting well away down the river before dark at all events, when I saw in the distance a clearing on the riverside and the outlines of some sort of building. "What's this?" I asked. He clapped his hands in wonder. "The station!" he cried. I edged in at once, still going half-speed.

'Through my glasses I saw the slope of a hill interspersed with rare trees and perfectly free from undergrowth. A long decaying building on the summit was half buried in the high grass; the large holes in the peaked roof gaped black from afar; the jungle and the woods made a background. There was no enclosure or fence of any kind; but there had been one apparently, for near the house half-a-dozen slim posts remained in a row, roughly trimmed, and with their upper ends ornamented with round carved balls. The rails, or whatever there had been between, had disappeared. Of course the forest surrounded all that. The river-bank was clear, and on the waterside I saw a white man under a hat like a cartwheel beckoning persistently with his whole arm. Examining the edge of the forest above and below, I was almost certain I could see movements – human forms gliding here and there. I steamed past prudently, then stopped the engines and let her drift down. The man on the shore began to shout, urging us to land. "We have been attacked," screamed the manager. "I know – I know. It's all right," yelled back the other, as cheerful as you please. "Come along. It's all right. I am glad."

'His aspect reminded me of something I had seen – something funny I had seen somewhere. As I manoeuvred to get alongside, I was asking myself, "What does this fellow look like?" Suddenly I got it. He looked like a harlequin. His clothes had been made of some stuff that was brown holland probably, but it was covered with patches all over, with bright patches, blue, red, and yellow – patches on the back, patches on the front, patches on elbows, on knees; coloured binding around his jacket, scarlet edging at the bottom of his trousers; and the sunshine made him look extremely gay and wonderfully neat withal, because you could see how beautifully all this patching had been done. A beard-less, boyish face, very fair, no features to speak of, nose peeling, little blue eyes, smiles and frowns chasing each other over that open countenance like sunshine and shadow on a windswept plain. "Look out, captain!" he cried; "there's a snag lodged in here last night." What! Another snag? I confess I swore shame-fully. I had nearly holed my cripple, to finish off that charming trip. The harlequin on the bank turned his little pug-nose up to me. "You English?" he asked, all smiles. "Are you?" I shouted from the wheel. The smiles vanished, and he shook his head as if sorry for my disappointment. Then he brightened up. "Never mind!" he cried encouragingly. "Are we in time?" I asked. "He is up there," he replied, with a toss of the head up the hill, and becoming gloomy all of a sudden. His face was like the autumn sky, overcast one moment and bright the next.

'When the manager, escorted by the pilgrims, all of them armed to the teeth, had gone to the house this chap came on board. "I say, I don't like this. These natives are in the bush," I said. He assured me earnestly it was all right. "They are simple people," he added; "well, I am glad you came. It took me all my time to keep them off." "But you said it was all right," I cried. "Oh, they meant no harm," he said; and as I stared he corrected himself, "Not exactly." Then vivaciously, "My faith, your pilot-house wants a clean-up!" In the next breath he advised me to keep enough steam on the boiler to blow the whistle in case of any trouble. "One good screech will do more for you than all your rifles. They are simple people," he repeated. He rattled away at such a rate he quite overwhelmed me. He seemed to be trying to make up for lots of silence, and actually hinted, laughing, that such was the case. "Don't you talk with Mr Kurtz?" I said. "You don't talk with that man – you listen to him," he exclaimed with severe exaltation. "But now –" He waved his arm, and in the twinkling of an eye was in the uttermost depths of despondency. In a moment he came up again with a jump, possessed himself of both my hands, shook them continu-ously, while he gabbled: "Brother sailor . . . honour . . . pleasure . . . delight . . . introduce myself . . . Russian . . . son of an arch-priest . . . Government of Tambov . . . What? Tobacco! English tobacco; the excellent English tobacco! Now, that's brotherly. Smoke? Where's a sailor that does not smoke?"

'The pipe soothed him, and gradually I made out he had run away from school, had gone to sea in a Russian ship; ran away again; served some time in English ships; was now reconciled with the archpriest. He made a point of that. "But when one is young one must see things, gather experience, ideas;

enlarge the mind." "Here!" I interrupted. "You can never tell! Here I met Mr Kurtz," he said, youthfully solemn and reproachful. I held my tongue after that. It appears he had persuaded a Dutch tradinghouse on the coast to fit him out with stores and goods, and had started for the interior with a light heart and no more idea of what would happen to him than a baby. He had been wandering about that river for nearly two years alone, cut off from everybody and everything. "I am not so young as I look. I am twenty-five," he said. "At first old Van Shuyten would tell me to go to the devil," he narrated with keen enjoyment; "but I stuck to him, and talked and talked, till at last he got afraid I would talk the hind-leg off his favourite dog, so he gave me some cheap things and a few guns, and told me he hoped he would never see my face again. Good old Dutchman, Van Shuyten. I've sent him one small lot of ivory a year ago, so that he can't call me a little thief when I get back. I hope he got it. And for the rest I don't care. I had some wood stacked for you. That was my old house. Did you see?"

'I gave him Towson's book. He made as though he would kiss me, but restrained himself. "The only book I had left, and I thought I had lost it," he said, looking at it ecstatically. "So many accidents happen to a man going about alone, you know. Canoes get upset sometimes – and sometimes you've got to clear out so quick when the people get angry." He thumbed the pages. "You made notes in Russian?" I asked. He nodded. "I thought they were written in cipher," I said. He laughed, then became serious. "I had lots of trouble to keep these people off," he said. "Did they want to kill you?" I asked. "Oh, no!" he cried, and checked himself. "Why did they attack us?" I pursued. He hesitated, then said shamefacedly, "They don't want him to go." "Don't they?" I said curiously. He nodded a nod full of mystery and wisdom. "I tell you," he cried, "this man has enlarged my mind." He opened his arms wide, staring at me with his little blue eyes that were perfectly round.'

III

'I looked at him, lost in astonishment. There he was before me, in motley, as though he had absconded from a troupe of mimes, enthusiastic, fabulous. His very existence was improbable, inexplicable, and altogether bewildering. He was an insoluble problem. It was inconceivable how he had existed, how he had succeeded in getting so far, how he had managed to remain – why he did not instantly disappear. "I went a little farther," he said, "then still a little farther – till I had gone so far that I don't know how I'll ever get back. Never mind. Plenty time. I can manage. You take Kurtz away quick – quick – I tell you." The glamour of youth enveloped his parti-coloured rags, his destitution, his loneliness, the essential desolation of his futile wanderings. For months – for years – his life hadn't been worth a day's purchase; and there he was gallantly, thoughtlessly alive, to all appearance indestructible solely by the virtue of his few years and of his unreflecting audacity. I was seduced into something like admiration – like envy. Glamour urged him on, glamour kept him unscathed. He surely wanted nothing from the wilderness but space to breathe in and to push on through. His need was to exist, and to move onwards at the greatest possible risk, and with a maximum of privation. If the absolutely pure, uncalculating, unpractical spirit of adventure had ever ruled a human being, it ruled this bepatched youth. I almost envied him the possession of this modest and clear flame. It seemed to have consumed all thought of self so completely, that even while he was talking to you, you forgot that it was he – the man before your eyes – who had gone through these things. I did not envy him his devotion to Kurtz, though. He had not meditated over it. It came to him, and he accepted it with a sort of eager fatalism. I must say that to me it appeared about the most dangerous thing in every way he had come upon so far.

'They had come together unavoidably, like two ships becalmed near each other, and lay rubbing sides at last. I suppose Kurtz wanted an audience, because on a certain occasion, when encamped in the forest, they had talked all night, or more probably Kurtz had talked. "We talked of everything," he said, quite transported at the recollection. "I forgot there was such a thing as sleep. The night did not seem to last an hour. Everything! Everything! . . . Of love, too." "Ah, he talked to you of love!' I said, much amused. "It isn't what you think," he cried, almost passionately. "It was in general. He made me see things – things.'

'He threw his arms up. We were on deck at the time, and the headman of my wood cutters, lounging near by, turned upon him his heavy and glittering eyes. I looked around, and I don't know why, but I assure you that never, never before, did this land, this river, this jungle, the very arch of this blazing sky, appear to me so hopeless and so dark, so impenetrable to human thought, so pitiless to human weakness. "And, ever since, you have been with him, of course?" I said.

'On the contrary. It appears their intercourse had been very much broken by various causes. He had, as he informed me proudly, managed to nurse Kurtz through two illnesses (he alluded to it as you would to some risky feat), but as a rule Kurtz wandered alone, far in the depths of the forest. "Very often coming to this station, I had to wait days and days before he would turn up," he said. "Ah, it was worth waiting for! – sometimes." "What was he doing? exploring or what?" I asked. "Oh, yes, of course", he had discovered lots of villages, a lake, too – he did not know exactly in what direction; it was dangerous to inquire too much – but mostly his expeditions had been for ivory. "But he had no goods to trade with by that time," I objected. "There's a good lot of cartridges left even yet," he answered, looking away. "To speak plainly, he raided the country," I said. He nodded. "Not alone, surely!" He muttered something about the villages round that lake. "Kurtz got the tribe to follow him, did he?" I suggested. He fidgeted a little. "They adored him," he said. The tone of these words was so extraordinary that I looked at him searchingly. It was curious to see his mingled eagerness and reluctance to speak of Kurtz. The man filled his life, occupied his thoughts, swayed his emotions. "What can you expect?" he burst out; "he came to them with thunder and lightning, you know – and they had never seen anything like it– and very terrible. He could be very terrible. You can't judge Mr Kurtz as you would an ordinary man. No, no, no! Now – just to give you an idea – I don't mind telling you, he wanted to shoot me, too, one day – but I don't judge him." "Shoot you!" I cried "What for?" "Well, I had a small lot of ivory the chief of that village near my house gave me. You see I used to shoot game for them. Well, he wanted it, and wouldn't hear reason. He declared he would shoot me unless I gave him the ivory and then cleared out of the country, because he could do so, and had a fancy for it, and there was nothing on earth to prevent him killing whom he jolly well pleased. And it was true, too. I gave him the ivory. What did I care! But I didn't clear out. No, no. I couldn't leave him. I had to be careful, of course, till we got friendly again for a time. He had his second illness then. Afterwards I had to keep out of the way; but I didn't mind. He was living for the most part in those villages on the lake. When he came down to the river, sometimes he would take to me, and sometimes it was better for me to be careful. This man suffered too much. He hated all this, and somehow he couldn't get away. When I had a chance I begged him to try and leave while there was time; I offered to go back with him. And he would say yes, and then he would remain; go off on another ivory hunt; disappear for weeks; forget himself amongst these people – forget himself – you know." "Why! he's mad," I said. He protested indignantly. Mr Kurtz couldn't be mad. If I had heard him talk, only two days ago, I wouldn't dare hint at such a thing. . . . I had taken up my binoculars while we talked, and was looking at the shore, sweeping the limit of the forest at each side and at the back of the house. The consciousness of there being people in that bush, so silent, so quiet – as silent and quiet as the ruined house on the hill – made me uneasy. There was no sign on the face of nature of this amazing tale that was not so much told as suggested to me in desolate exclamations, completed by shrugs, in interrupted phrases, in hints ending in deep sighs. The woods were unmoved, like a mask – heavy, like the closed door of a prison – they looked with their air of hidden knowledge, of patient expectation, of unapproachable silence. The Russian was explaining to me that it was only lately that Mr Kurtz had come down to the river, bringing along with him all the fighting men of that lake tribe. He had been absent for several months – getting himself adored, I suppose – and had come down unexpectedly, with the intention to all appearance of making a raid either across the river or down stream. Evidently the appetite for more ivory had got the better of the – what shall I say? – less material aspirations. However he had got much worse suddenly. "I heard he was lying helpless, and so I came up – took my chance," said the Russian. "Oh, he is bad, very bad." I directed my glass to the house. There were no signs of life, but there was the ruined roof, the long mud wall peeping above the grass, with three little square window-holes, no two of the same size; all this brought within reach of my hand, as it were. And then I made a brusque movement, and one of the remaining posts of that vanished fence leaped up in the field of my glass. You remember I told you I had been struck at the distance by certain attempts at ornamentation, rather remarkable in the ruinous aspect of the place. Now I had suddenly a nearer view, and its first result was to make me throw my head back as if before a blow. Then I went carefully from post to post with my glass, and I saw my mistake. These round knobs were not ornamental but symbolic; they were expressive and puzzling, striking and disturbing – food for thought and also for vultures if there had been any looking down from the sky; but at all events for such ants as were industrious enough to ascend the pole. They would have been even more impressive, those heads on the stakes, if their faces had not been turned to the house. Only one, the first I had made out, was facing my way. I was not so shocked as you may think. The start back I had given was really nothing but a movement of surprise. I had expected to see a knob of wood there, you know. I returned deliberately to the first I had seen – and there it was, black, dried, sunken, with closed eyelids – a head that seemed to sleep at the top of that pole, and, with the shrunken dry lips showing a narrow white line of the teeth, was smiling, too, smiling continuously at some endless and jocose dream of that eternal slumber.

'I am not disclosing any trade secrets. In fact, the manager said afterwards that Mr Kurtz's methods had ruined the district. I have no opinion on that point, but I want you clearly to understand that there was nothing exactly profitable in these heads being there. They only showed that Mr Kurtz lacked restraint in the gratification of his various lusts, that there was something wanting in him – some small matter which, when the pressing need arose, could not be found under his magnificent eloquence. Whether he knew of his deficiency himself I can't say. I think the knowledge came to him at last – only at the very last. But the wilderness had found him out early, and had taken on him a terrible vengeance for the fantastic invasion. I think it had whispered to him things about himself which he did not know, things of which he had no conception till he took counsel with this great solitude – and the whisper had proved irresistibly fascinating. It echoed loudly within him because he was hollow at the core. . . . I put down the glass, and the head that had appeared near enough to be spoken to seemed at once to have leaped away from me into inaccessible distance.

'The admirer of Mr Kurtz was a bit crestfallen. In a hurried, indistinct voice he began to assure me he had not dared to take these – say, symbols – down. He was not afraid of the natives; they would not stir till Mr Kurtz gave the word. His ascendancy was extraordinary. The camps of the people surrounded the place, and the chiefs came every day to see him. They would crawl. . . . "I don't want to know anything of the ceremonies used when approaching Mr Kurtz," I shouted. Curious, this feeling that came over me that such details would be more intolerable than those heads drying on the stakes under Mr Kurtz's windows. After all, that was only a savage sight, while I seemed at one bound to have been transported into some lightless region of subtle horrors, where pure, uncomplicated savagery was a positive relief, being something that had a right to exist – obviously – in the sunshine. The young man looked at me with surprise. I suppose it did not occur to him that Mr Kurtz was no idol of mine. He forgot I hadn't heard any of these splendid monologues on, what was it? on love, justice, conduct of life – or what not. If it had come to crawling before Mr Kurtz, he crawled as much as the veriest savage of them all. I had no idea of the conditions, he said: these heads were the heads of rebels. I shocked him excessively by laughing. Rebels! What would be the next definition I was to hear? There had been enemies, criminals, workers – and these were rebels. Those rebellious heads looked very subdued to me on their sticks. "You don't know how such a life tries a man like Kurtz," cried Kurtz's last disciple. "Well, and you?" I said. "I! I! I am a simple man. I have no great thoughts. I want nothing from anybody. How can you compare me to . . . ?" His feelings were too much for speech, and suddenly he broke down. "I don't understand," he groaned.

"I've been doing my best to keep him alive, and that's enough. I had no hand in all this. I have no abilities. There hasn't been a drop of medicine or a mouthful of invalid food for months here. He was shamefully abandoned. A man like this, with such ideas. Shamefully! Shamefully! I – I – haven't slept for the last ten nights . . ."

'His voice lost itself in the calm of the evening. The long shadows of the forest had slipped downhill while we talked, had gone far beyond the ruined hovel, beyond the symbolic row of stakes. All this was in the gloom, while we down there were yet in the sunshine, and the stretch of the river abreast of the clearing glittered in a still and dazzling splendour, with a murky and over-shadowed bend above and below. Not a living soul was seen on the shore. The bushes did not rustle.

'Suddenly round the corner of the house a group of men appeared, as though they had come up from the ground. They waded waist-deep in the grass, in a compact body, bearing an improvised stretcher in their midst. Instantly, in the emptiness of the landscape, a cry arose whose shrillness pierced the still air like a sharp arrow flying straight to the very heart of the land; and, as if by enchant-ment, streams of human beings – of naked human beings – with spears in their hands, with bows, with shields, with wild glances and savage movements, were poured into the clearing by the dark-faced and pensive forest. The bushes shook, the grass swayed for a time, and then everything stood still in attentive immobility.

' "Now, if he does not say the right thing to them we are all done for," said the Russian at my elbow. The knot of men with the stretcher had stopped, too, halfway to the steamer, as if petrified. I saw the man on the stretcher sit up, lank and with an uplifted arm, above the shoulders of the bearers. "Let us hope that the man who can talk so well of love in general will find some particular reason to spare us this time," I said. I resented bitterly the absurd danger of our situation, as if to be at the mercy of that atrocious phantom had been a dishon-ouring necessity. I could not hear a sound, but through my glasses I saw the thin arm extended commandingly, the lower jaw moving, the eyes of that apparition shining darkly far in its bony head that nodded with grotesque jerks. Kurtz – Kurtz – that means short in German – don't it? Well, the name was as true as everything else in his life – and death. He looked at least seven feet long. His covering had fallen off, and his body emerged from it pitiful and appalling as from a winding-sheet. I could see the cage of his ribs all astir, the bones of his arm waving. It was as though an animated image of death carved out of old ivory had been shaking its hand with menaces at a motionless crowd of men made of dark and glittering bronze. I saw him open his mouth wide – it gave him a weirdly voracious aspect, as though he had wanted to swallow all the air, all the earth, all the men before him. A deep voice reached me faintly. He must have been shouting. He fell back suddenly. The stretcher shook as the bearers staggered forward again, and almost at the same time I noticed that the crowd of savages was vanishing without any perceptible movement of retreat, as if the forest that had ejected these beings so suddenly had drawn them in again as the breath is drawn in a long aspiration.

'Some of the pilgrims behind the stretcher carried his arms – two shot-guns, a heavy rifle, and a light revolver-carbine – the thunderbolts of that pitiful

Jupiter. The manager bent over him murmuring as he walked beside his head. They laid him down in one of the little cabins – just a room for a bed place and a camp-stool or two, you know. We had brought his belated correspondence, and a lot of torn envelopes and open letters littered his bed. His hand roamed feebly amongst these papers. I was struck by the fire of his eyes and the composed languor of his expression. It was not so much the exhaustion of disease. He did not seem in pain. This shadow looked satiated and calm, as though for the moment it had had its fill of all the emotions.

'He rustled one of the letters, and looking straight in my face said, "I am glad." Somebody had been writing to him about me. These special recommen-dations were turning up again. The volume of tone he emitted without effort, almost without the trouble of moving his lips, amazed me. A voice! a voice! It was grave, profound, vibrating, while the man did not seem capable of a whisper. However, he had enough strength in him – factitious no doubt – to very nearly make an end of us, as you shall hear directly.

'The manager appeared silently in the doorway; I stepped out at once and he drew the curtain after me. The Russian, eyed curiously by the pilgrims, was staring at the shore. I followed the direction of his glance.

'Dark human shapes could be made out in the distance, flitting indistinctly against the gloomy border of the forest, and near the river two bronze figures, leaning on tall spears, stood in the sunlight under fantastic head-dresses of spotted skins, warlike and still in statuesque repose. And from right to left along the lighted shore moved a wild and gorgeous apparition of a woman.

'She walked with measured steps, draped in striped and fringed clothes, tread-ing the earth proudly, with a slight jingle and flash of barbarous ornaments. She carried her head high; her hair was done in the shape of a helmet; she had brass leggings to the knee, brass wire gauntlets to the elbow, a crimson spot on her tawny cheek, innumerable necklaces of glass beads on her neck; bizarre things, charms, gifts of witch-men, that hung about her, glittered and trembled at every step. She must have had the value of several elephant tusks upon her. She was savage and superb, wild-eyed and magnificent; there was something ominous and stately in her deliberate progress. And in the hush that had fallen suddenly upon the whole sorrowful land, the immense wilderness, the colossal body of the fecund and mysterious life seemed to look at her, pensive, as though it had been looking at the image of its own tenebrous and passionate soul.

'She came abreast of the steamer, stood still, and faced us. Her long shadow fell to the water's edge. Her face had a tragic and fierce aspect of wild sorrow and of dumb pain mingled with the fear of some struggling, half-shaped resolve. She stood looking at us without a stir, and like the wilderness itself, with an air of brooding over an inscrutable purpose. A whole minute passed, and then she made a step forward. There was a low jingle, a glint of yellow metal, a sway of fringed draperies, and she stopped as if her heart had failed her. The young fellow by my side growled. The pilgrims murmured at my back. She looked at us all as if her life had depended upon the unswerving steadiness of her glance. Suddenly she opened her bared arms and threw them up rigid above her head, as though in an uncontrollable desire to touch the sky, and at the same time the swift shadows darted out on the earth, swept around on the river, gathering the steamer into a shadowy embrace. A formidable silence hung over the scene.

'She turned away slowly, walked on, following the bank, and passed into the bushes to the left. Once only her eyes gleamed back at us in the dusk of the thickets before she disappeared.

' "If she had offered to come aboard I really think I would have tried to shoot her," said the man of patches, nervously. "I have been risking my life every day for the last fortnight to keep her out of the house. She got in one day and kicked up a row about those miserable rags I picked up in the storeroom to mend my clothes with. I wasn't decent. At least it must have been that, for she talked like a fury to Kurtz for an hour, pointing at me now and then. I don't understand the dialect of this tribe. Luckily for me, I fancy Kurtz felt too ill that day to care, or there would have been mischief. I don't understand. . . . No – it's too much for me. Ah, well, it's all over now."

'At this moment I heard Kurtz's deep voice behind the curtain: 'Save me! – save the ivory, you mean. Don't tell me. Save me! Why, I've had to save you. You are interrupting my plans now. Sick! Sick! Not so sick as you would like to believe. Never mind. I'll carry my ideas out yet – I will return. I'll show you what can be done. You with your little peddling notions – you are interfering with me. I will return. I . . ."

'The manager came out. He did me the honour to take me under the arm and lead me aside. "He is very low, very low," he said. He considered it necessary to sigh, but neglected to be consistently sorrowful. "We have done all we could for him – haven't we? But there is no disguising the fact, Mr Kurtz has done more harm than good to the Company. He did not see the time was not ripe for vigorous action. Cautiously, cautiously – that's my principle. We must be cautious yet. The district is closed to us for a time. Deplorable! Upon the whole, the trade will suffer. I don't deny there is a remarkable quantity of ivory – mostly fossil. We must save it, at all events – but look how precarious the position is – and why? Because the method is unsound." "Do you," said I, looking at the shore, "call it 'unsound method?' " "Without doubt," he exclaimed hotly. "Don't you?". . . "No method at all," I murmured after a while. "Exactly," he exulted. "I anticipated this. Shows a complete want of judgment. It is my duty to point it out in the proper quarter." "Oh," said I, "that fellow – what's his name? – the brickmaker, will make a readable report for you." He appeared confounded for a moment. It seemed to me I had never breathed an atmosphere so vile, and I turned mentally to Kurtz for relief – positively for relief. "Nevertheless I think Mr Kurtz is a remarkable man," I said with emphasis. He started, dropped on me a cold heavy glance, said very quietly, "He *was*," and turned his back on me. My hour of favour was over; I found myself lumped along with Kurtz as a partisan of methods for which the time was not ripe: I was unsound! Ah! but it was something to have at least a choice of nightmares.

'I had turned to the wilderness really, not to Mr Kurtz, who, I was ready to admit, was as good as buried. And for a moment it seemed to me as if I also were buried in a vast grave full of unspeakable secrets. I felt an intolerable weight oppressing my breast, the smell of the damp earth, the unseen presence of victorious corruption, the darkness of an impenetrable night. . . . The Russian tapped me on the shoulder. I heard him mumbling and stammering something about "brother seaman – couldn't conceal – knowledge of matters that would affect Mr Kurtz's reputation." I waited. For him evidently Mr Kurtz was not in his grave; I suspect that for him Mr Kurtz was one of the immortals. "Well!" said I at last, "speak out. As it happens, I am Mr Kurtz's friend – in a way."

'He stated with a good deal of formality that had we not been "of the same profession," he would have kept the matter to himself without regard to consequences. He suspected there was an active ill will towards him on the part of these white men that – "You are right," I said, remembering a certain conversation I had overheard. "The manager thinks you ought to be hanged." He showed a concern at this intelligence which amused me at first. "I had better get out of the way quietly," he said earnestly. "I can do no more for Kurtz now, and they would soon find some excuse. What's to stop them? There's a military post three hundred miles from here." "Well, upon my word," said I, "perhaps you had better go if you have any friends amongst the savages near by." "Plenty," he said. "They are simple people – and I want nothing, you know." He stood biting his lip, then: "I didn't want any harm to happen to these whites here, but of course I was thinking of Mr Kurtz's reputation – but you are a brother seaman and – " "All right," said I, after a time. "Mr Kurtz's reputation is safe with me." I did not know how truly I spoke.

'He informed me, lowering his voice, that it was Kurtz who had ordered the attack to be made on the steamer. "He hated sometimes the idea of being taken away – and then again. . . . But I don't understand these matters. I am a simple man. He thought it would scare you away – that you would give it up, thinking him dead. I could not stop him. Oh, I had an awful time of it this last month." "Very well," I said. "He is all right now." "Ye-e-es," he muttered, not very convinced apparently. "Thanks," said I; "I shall keep my eyes open." "But quiet – eh?" he urged anxiously. "It would be awful for his reputation if anybody here –" I promised a complete discretion with great gravity. "I have a canoe and three black fellows waiting not very far. I am off. Could you give me a few Martini-Henry cartridges?" I could, and did, with proper secrecy. He helped himself, with a wink at me, to a handful of my tobacco. "Between sailors – you know – good English tobacco." At the door of the pilot-house he turned round – "I say, haven't you a pair of shoes you could spare?" He raised one leg. "Look" The soles were tied with knotted strings sandal-wise under his bare feet. I rooted out an old pair, at which he looked with admiration before tucking it under his left arm. One of his pockets (bright red) was bulging with cartridges, from the other (dark blue) peeped 'Towson's Inquiry,' etc., etc. He seemed to think himself excellently well equipped for a renewed encounter with the wilderness. "Ah! I'll never, never meet such a man again. You ought to have heard him recite poetry – his own, too, it was, he told me. Poetry!" He rolled his eyes at the recollection of these delights. "Oh, he enlarged my mind!" "Goodbye," said I. He shook hands and vanished in the night. Sometimes I ask myself whether I had ever really seen him – whether it was possible to meet such a phenomenon! . . .

'When I woke up shortly after midnight his warning came to my mind with its hint of danger that seemed, in the starred darkness, real enough to make me get up for the purpose of having a look round. On the hill a big fire burned, illuminating fitfully a crooked corner of the station-house. One of the agents with a picket of a few of our blacks, armed for the purpose, was keeping guard over the ivory; but deep within the forest, red gleams that wavered, that seemed to sink and rise from the ground amongst confused columnar shapes of intense blackness, showed the exact position of the camp where Mr Kurtz's adorers were keeping their uneasy vigil. The monotonous beating of a big drum filled the air with muffled shocks and a lingering vibration. A steady droning sound of many men chanting each to himself some weird incantation came out from the black, flat wall of the woods as the humming of bees comes out of a hive, and had a strange narcotic effect upon my half-awake senses. I believe I dozed off leaning over the rail, till an abrupt burst of yells, an overwhelming outbreak of a pent-up and mysterious frenzy, woke me up in a bewildered wonder. It was cut short all at once, and the low droning went on with an effect of audible and soothing silence. I glanced casually into the little cabin. A light was burning within, but Mr Kurtz was not there.

'I think I would have raised an outcry if I had believed my eyes. But I didn't believe them at first – the thing seemed so impossible. The fact is I was completely unnerved by a sheer blank fright, pure abstract terror, unconnected with any distinct shape of physical danger. What made this emotion so over-powering was – how shall I define it? – the moral shock I received, as if something altogether monstrous, intolerable to thought and odious to the soul, had been thrust upon me unexpectedly. This lasted of course the merest fraction of a second, and then the usual sense of commonplace, deadly danger, the possibil-ity of a sudden onslaught and massacre, or something of the kind, which I saw impending, was positively welcome and composing. It pacified me, in fact, so much that I did not raise an alarm.

'There was an agent buttoned up inside an ulster and sleeping on a chair on deck within three feet of me. The yells had not awakened him; he snored very slightly; I left him to his slumbers and leaped ashore. I did not betray Mr Kurtz – it was ordered I should never betray him – it was written I should be loyal to the nightmare of my choice. I was anxious to deal with this shadow by myself alone – and to this day I don't know why I was so jealous of sharing with any one the peculiar blackness of that experience.

'As soon as I got on the bank I saw a trail – a broad trail through the grass. I remember the exultation with which I said to myself, "He can't walk – he is crawling on all-fours – I've got him." The grass was wet with dew. I strode rapidly with clenched fists. I fancy I had some vague notion of falling upon him and giving him a drubbing. I don't know. I had some imbecile thoughts. The knitting old woman with the cat obtruded herself upon my memory as a most improper person to be sitting at the other end of such an affair. I saw a row of pilgrims squirting lead in the air out of Winchesters held to the hip. I thought I would never get back to the steamer, and imagined myself living alone and unarmed in the woods to an advanced age. Such silly things – you know. And I remember I confounded the beat of the drum with the beating of my heart, and was pleased at its calm regularity.

'I kept to the track though – then stopped to listen. The night was very clear; a dark blue space, sparkling with dew and starlight, in which black things stood very still. I thought I could see a kind of motion ahead of me. I was strangely cocksure of everything that night. I actually left the track and ran in a wide semicircle (I verily believe chuckling to myself) so as to get in front of that stir, of that motion I had seen – if indeed I had seen anything. I was circumventing Kurtz as though it had been a boyish game.

'I came upon him, and, if he had not heard me coming, I would have fallen over him, too, but he got up in time. He rose, unsteady, long, pale, indistinct, like a vapour exhaled by the earth, and swayed slightly, misty and silent before me; while at my back the fires loomed between the trees, and the murmur of many voices issued from the forest. I had cut him off cleverly; but when actually confronting him I seemed to come to my senses, I saw the danger in its right proportion. It was by no means over yet. Suppose he began to shout? Though he could hardly stand, there was still plenty of vigour in his voice. "Go away – hide yourself," he said, in that profound tone. It was very awful. I glanced back. We were within thirty yards from the nearest fire. A black figure stood up, strode on long black legs, waving long black arms, across the glow. It had horns – antelope horns, I think – on its head. Some sorcerer, some witch-man, no doubt: it looked fiendlike enough. "Do you know what you are doing?" I whispered. "Perfectly," he answered, raising his voice for that single word: it sounded to me far off and yet loud, like a hail through a speaking-trumpet. "If he makes a row we are lost," I thought to myself. This clearly was not a case for fisticuffs, even apart from the very natural aversion I had to beat that Shadow – this wandering and tormented thing. "You will be lost," I said – "utterly lost." One gets sometimes such a flash of inspiration, you know. I did say the right thing, though indeed he could not have been more irretrievably lost than he was at this very moment, when the foundations of our intimacy were being laid – to endure – to endure – even to the end – even beyond.

' "I had immense plans," he muttered irresolutely. "Yes," said I; "but if you try to shout I'll smash your head with –" There was not a stick or a stone near. "I will throttle you for good," I corrected myself. "I was on the threshold of great things," he pleaded, in a voice of longing, with a wistfulness of tone that made my blood run cold. "And now for this stupid scoundrel –" "Your success in Europe is assured in any case," I affirmed steadily. I did not want to have the throttling of him, you understand – and indeed it would have been very little use for any practical purpose. I tried to break the spell – the heavy, mute spell of the wilderness – that seemed to draw him to its pitiless breast by the awakening of forgotten and brutal instincts, by the memory of gratified and monstrous passions. This alone, I was convinced, had driven him out to the edge of the forest, to the bush, towards the gleam of fires, the throb of drums, the drone of weird incantations; this alone had beguiled his unlawful soul beyond the bounds of permitted aspirations. And, don't you see, the terror of the position was not in being knocked on the head – though I had a very lively sense of that danger, too – but in this, that I had to deal with a being to whom I could not appeal in the name of anything high or low. I had, even like the niggers, to invoke him – himself – his own exalted and incredible degradation. There was nothing either above or below him, and I knew it. He had kicked himself loose of the earth. Confound the man! he had kicked the very earth to pieces. He was alone, and

I before him did not know whether I stood on the ground or floated in the air. I've been telling you what we said – repeating the phrases we pronounced – but what's the good? They were common everyday words – the familiar, vague sounds exchanged on every waking day of life. But what of that? They had behind them, to my mind, the terrific suggestiveness of words heard in dreams, of phrases spoken in nightmares. Soul! If anybody ever struggled with a soul, I am the man. And I wasn't arguing with a lunatic either. Believe me or not, his intelligence was perfectly clear – concentrated, it is true, upon himself with horrible intensity, yet clear; and therein was my only chance – barring, of course, the killing him there and then, which wasn't so good, on account of unavoidable noise. But his soul was mad. Being alone in the wilderness, it had looked within itself, and, by heavens! I tell you, it had gone mad. I had – for my sins, I suppose – to go through the ordeal of looking into it myself. No eloquence could have been so withering to one's belief in mankind as his final burst of sincerity. He struggled with himself, too. I saw it – I heard it. I saw the inconceivable mystery of a soul that knew no restraint, no faith, and no fear, yet struggling blindly with itself. I kept my head pretty well; but when I had him at last stretched on the couch, I wiped my forehead, while my legs shook under me as though I had carried half a ton on my back down that hill. And yet I had only supported him, his bony arm clasped round my neck – and he was not much heavier than a child.

'When next day we left at noon, the crowd, of whose presence behind the curtain of trees I had been acutely conscious all the time, flowed out of the woods again, filled the clearing, covered the slope with a mass of naked, breathing, quivering, bronze bodies. I steamed up a bit, then swung down stream, and two thousand eyes followed the evolutions of the splashing, thumping, fierce river-demon beating the water with its terrible tail and breathing black smoke into the air. In front of the first rank, along the river, three men, plastered with bright red earth from head to foot, strutted to and fro restlessly. When we came abreast again, they faced the river, stamped their feet, nodded their horned heads, swayed their scarlet bodies; they shook towards the fierce river-demon a bunch of black feathers, a mangy skin with a pendent tail – something that looked like a dried gourd; they shouted periodically together strings of amazing words that resembled no sounds of human language; and the deep murmurs of the crowd, interrupted suddenly, were like the responses of some satanic litany.

'We had carried Kurtz into the pilot-house: there was more air there. Lying on the couch, he stared through the open shutter. There was an eddy in the mass of human bodies, and the woman with helmeted head and tawny cheeks rushed out to the very brink of the stream. She put out her hands, shouted something, and all that wild mob took up the shout in a roaring chorus of articulated, rapid, breathless utterance.

' "Do you understand this?" I asked.

'He kept on looking out past me with fiery, longing eyes, with a mingled expression of wistfulness and hate. He made no answer, but I saw a smile, a smile of indefinable meaning, appearing on his colourless lips that a moment after twitched convulsively. "Do I not?" he said slowly, gasping, as if the words had been torn out of him by a supernatural power.

'I pulled the string of the whistle, and I did this because I saw the pilgrims on deck getting out their rifles with an air of anticipating a jolly lark. At the sudden screech there was a movement of abject terror through that wedged mass of bodies. "Don't! don't you frighten them away," cried some one on deck disconsolately. I pulled the string time after time. They broke and ran, they leaped, they crouched, they swerved, they dodged the flying terror of the sound. The three red chaps had fallen flat, face down on the shore, as though they had been shot dead. Only the barbarous and superb woman did not so much as flinch, and stretched tragically her bare arms after us over the sombre and glittering river.

'And then that imbecile crowd down on the deck started their little fun, and I could see nothing more for smoke.

'The brown current ran swiftly out of the heart of darkness, bearing us down towards the sea with twice the speed of our upward progress; and Kurtz's life was running swiftly, too, ebbing, ebbing out of his heart into the sea of inexorable time. The manager was very placid, he had no vital anxieties now, he took us both in with a comprehensive and satisfied glance: the "affair" had come off as well as could be wished. I saw the time approaching when I would be left alone of the party of "unsound method." The pilgrims looked upon me with disfavour. I was, so to speak, numbered with the dead. It is strange how I accepted this unforeseen partnership, this choice of nightmares forced upon me in the tenebrous land invaded by these mean and greedy phantoms.

'Kurtz discoursed. A voice! a voice! It rang deep to the very last. It survived his strength to hide in the magnificent folds of eloquence the barren darkness of his heart. Oh, he struggled! he struggled! The wastes of his weary brain were haunted by shadowy images now – images of wealth and fame revolving obsequiously round his unextinguishable gift of noble and lofty expression. My Intended, my station, my career, my ideas – these were the subjects for the occasional utterances of elevated sentiments. The shade of the original Kurtz frequented the bedside of the hollow sham, whose fate it was to be buried presently in the mould of primeval earth. But both the diabolic love and the unearthly hate of the mysteries it had penetrated fought for the possession of that soul satiated with primitive emotions, avid of lying fame, of sham distinction, of all the appearances of success and power.

'Sometimes he was contemptibly childish. He desired to have kings meet him at railway-stations on his return from some ghastly Nowhere, where he intended to accomplish great things. "You show them you have in you something that is really profitable, and then there will be no limits to the recognition of your ability," he would say. "Of course you must take care of the motives – right motives – always." The long reaches that were like one and the same reach, monotonous bends that were exactly alike, slipped past the steamer with their multitude of secular trees looking patiently after this grimy fragment of another world, the forerunner of change, of conquest, of trade, of massacres, of blessings. I looked ahead – piloting. "Close the shutter," said Kurtz suddenly one day; "I can't bear to look at this." I did so. There was a silence. "Oh, but I will wring your heart yet!" he cried at the invisible wilderness.

'We broke down – as I had expected – and had to lie up for repairs at the head of an island. This delay was the first thing that shook Kurtz's confidence. One morning he gave me a packet of papers and a photograph – the lot tied together with a shoe-string. "Keep this for me," he said. "This noxious fool" (meaning the manager) "is capable of prying into my boxes when I am not looking." In the afternoon I saw him. He was lying on his back with closed eyes, and I withdrew quietly, but I heard him mutter, "Live rightly, die, die . . ." I listened. There was nothing more. Was he rehearsing some speech in his sleep, or was it a fragment of a phrase from some newspaper article? He had been writing for the papers and meant to do so again, "for the furthering of my ideas. It's a duty."

'His was an impenetrable darkness. I looked at him as you peer down at a man who is lying at the bottom of a precipice where the sun never shines. But I had not much time to give him, because I was helping the engine-driver to take to pieces the leaky cylinders, to straighten a bent connecting-rod, and in other such matters. I lived in an infernal mess of rust, filings, nuts, bolts, spanners, hammers, ratchet drills – things I abominate, because I don't get on with them. I tended the little forge we fortunately had aboard; I toiled wearily in a wretched scrap-heap – unless I had the shakes too bad to stand.

'One evening coming in with a candle I was startled to hear him say a little tremulously, "I am lying here in the dark waiting for death." The light was within a foot of his eyes. I forced myself to murmur, "Oh, nonsense!" and stood over him as if transfixed.

'Anything approaching the change that came over his features I have never seen before, and hope never to see again. Oh, I wasn't touched. I was fascinated. It was as though a veil had been rent. I saw on that ivory face the expression of sombre pride, of ruthless power, of craven terror – of an intense and hopeless despair. Did he live his life again in every detail of desire, temptation, and surrender during that supreme moment of complete knowledge? He cried in a whisper at some image, at some vision – he cried out twice, a cry that was no more than a breath:

' "The horror! The horror!"

'I blew the candle out and left the cabin. The pilgrims were dining in the mess-room, and I took my place opposite the manager, who lifted his eyes to give me a questioning glance, which I successfully ignored. He leaned back, serene, with that peculiar smile of his sealing the unexpressed depths of his meanness. A continuous shower of small flies streamed upon the lamp, upon the cloth, upon our hands and faces. Suddenly the manager's boy put his insolent black head in the doorway, and said in a tone of scathing contempt:

' "Mistah Kurtz – he dead."

'All the pilgrims rushed out to see. I remained, and went on with my dinner. I believe that I was considered brutally callous. However, I did not eat much. There was a lamp in there – light, don't you know – and outside it was so beastly, beastly dark. I went no more near the remarkable man who had pronounced a judgment upon the adventures of his soul on this earth. The voice was gone. What else had been there? But I am of course aware that next day the pilgrims buried something in a muddy hole.

'And then they very nearly buried me.

'However, as you see, I did not go to join Kurtz there and then. I did not. I remained to dream the nightmare out to the end, and to show my loyalty to Kurtz once more. Destiny. My destiny! Droll thing life is – that mysterious arrangement of merciless logic for a futile purpose. The most you can hope from it is some knowledge of yourself – that comes too late – a crop of unextinguishable regrets. I have wrestled with death. It is the most unexciting contest you can imagine. It takes place in an impalpable greyness, with nothing underfoot, with nothing around, without spectators, without clamour, without glory, without the great desire of victory, without the great fear of defeat, in a sickly atmosphere of tepid scepticism, without much belief in your own right, and still less in that of your adversary. If such is the form of ultimate wisdom, then life is a greater riddle than some of us think it to be. I was within a hair's breadth of the last opportunity for pronouncement, and I found with humiliation that probably I would have nothing to say. This is the reason why I affirm that Kurtz was a remarkable man. He had something to say. He said it. Since I had peeped over the edge myself, I understand better the meaning of his stare, that could not see the flame of the candle, but was wide enough to embrace the whole universe, piercing enough to penetrate all the hearts that beat in the darkness. He had summed up – he had judged. "The horror!" He was a remarkable man. After all, this was the expression of some sort of belief; it had candour, it had conviction, it had a vibrating note of revolt in its whisper, it had the appalling face of a glimpsed truth – the strange commingling of desire and hate. And it is not my own extremity I remember best – a vision of greyness without form filled with physical pain, and a careless contempt for the evanescence of all things – even of this pain itself. No! It is his extremity that I seem to have lived through. True, he had made that last stride, he had stepped over the edge, while I had been permitted to draw back my hesitating foot. And perhaps in this is the whole difference; perhaps all the wisdom, and all truth, and all sincerity, are just compressed into that inappreciable moment of time in which we step over the threshold of the invisible. Perhaps! I like to think my summing-up would not have been a word of careless contempt. Better his cry – much better. It was an affirmation, a moral victory paid for by innumerable defeats, by abominable terrors, by abominable satisfactions. But it was a victory! That is why I have remained loyal to Kurtz to the last, and even beyond, when a long time after I heard once more, not his own voice, but the echo of his magnificent eloquence thrown to me from a soul as translucently pure as a cliff of crystal.

'No, they did not bury me, though there is a period of time which I remember mistily, with a shuddering wonder, like a passage through some inconceivable world that had no hope in it and no desire. I found myself back in the sepulchral city resenting the sight of people hurrying through the streets to filch a little money from each other, to devour their infamous cookery, to gulp their unwholesome beer, to dream their insignificant and silly dreams. They trespassed upon my thoughts. They were intruders whose knowledge of life was to me an irritating pretence, because I felt so sure they could not possibly know the things I knew. Their bearing, which was simply the bearing of commonplace individuals going about their business in the assurance of perfect safety, was offensive to me like the outrageous flauntings of folly in the face of a danger it is unable to comprehend. I had no particular desire to enlighten them, but I had some difficulty in restraining myself from laughing in their faces so full of stupid importance. I daresay I was not very well at that time. I tottered about the streets – there were various affairs to settle – grinning bitterly at perfectly respectable persons. I admit my behaviour was inexcusable, but then my temperature was seldom normal in these days. My dear aunt's endeavours to "nurse up my strength" seemed altogether beside the mark. It was not my strength that wanted nursing, it was my imagination that wanted soothing. I kept the bundle of papers given me by Kurtz, not knowing exactly what to do with it. His mother had died lately, watched over, as I was told, by his Intended. A cleanshaved man, with an official manner and wearing gold-rimmed spectacles, called on me one day and made inquiries, at first circuitous, afterwards suavely pressing, about what he was pleased to denominate certain "documents." I was not surprised, because I had had two rows with the manager on the subject out there. I had refused to give up the smallest scrap out of that package, and I took the same attitude with the spectacled man. He became darkly menacing at last, and with much heat argued that the Company had the right to every bit of information about its "territories." And said he, "Mr Kurtz's knowledge of unexplored regions must have been necessarily extensive and peculiar – owing to his great abilities and to the deplorable circumstances in which he had been placed: therefore – " I assured him Mr Kurtz's knowledge, however extensive, did not bear upon the problems of commerce or administration. He invoked then the name of science. "It would be an incalculable loss if," etc., etc. I offered him the report on the "Suppression of Savage Customs," with the postscriptum torn off. He took it up eagerly, but ended by sniffing at it with an air of contempt. "This is not what we had a right to expect," he remarked. "Expect nothing else," I said. "There are only private letters." He withdrew upon some threat of legal proceedings, and I saw him no more; but another fellow, calling himself Kurtz's cousin, appeared two days later, and was anxious to hear all the details about his dear relative's last moments. Incidentally he gave me to understand that Kurtz had been essentially a great musician. "There was the making of an immense success," said the man, who was an organist, I believe, with lank grey hair flowing over a greasy coat-collar. I had no reason to doubt his statement, and to this day I am unable to say what was Kurtz's profession, whether he ever had any – which was the greatest of his talents. I had taken him for a painter who wrote for the papers, or else for a journalist who could paint – but even the cousin (who took snuff during the interview) could not tell me what he had been – exactly. He was a universal genius – on that point I agreed with the old chap, who thereupon blew his nose noisily into a large cotton handkerchief and withdrew in senile agitation, bearing off some family letters and memoranda without importance. Ultimately a journalist anxious to know something of the fate of his "dear colleague" turned up. This visitor informed me Kurtz's proper sphere ought to have been politics "on the popular side." He had furry straight eye-brows, bristly hair cropped short, an eyeglass on a broad ribbon, and, becoming expansive, confessed his opinion that Kurtz really couldn't write a bit – "but heavens! how that man could talk. He electrified large meetings. He had faith – don't you see? – he had the faith. He could get himself to believe anything – anything. He would have been a splendid leader of an extreme party." "What party?" I asked. "Any party," answered the other. "He was an – an – extremist." Did I not think so? I assented. Did I know, he asked, with a sudden flash of curiosity, "what it was that had induced him to go out there?" "Yes," said I, and forthwith handed him the famous Report for publication, if he thought fit. He glanced through it hurriedly, mumbling all the time, judged "it would do," and took himself off with this plunder.

'Thus I was left at last with a slim packet of letters and the girl's portrait. She struck me as beautiful – I mean she had a beautiful expression. I know that the sunlight can be made to lie, too, yet one felt that no manipulation of light and pose could have conveyed the delicate shade of truthfulness upon those features. She seemed ready to listen without mental reservation, without suspicion, without a thought for herself. I concluded I would go and give her back her portrait and those letters myself. Curiosity? Yes; and also some other feeling perhaps. All that had been Kurtz's had passed out of my hands: his soul, his body, his station, his plans, his ivory, his career. There remained only his memory and his Intended – and I wanted to give that up, too, to the past, in a way – to surrender personally all that remained of him with me to that oblivion which is the last word of our common fate. I don't defend myself. I had no clear perception of what it was I really wanted. Perhaps it was an impulse of uncon-scious loyalty, or the fulfilment of one of those ironic necessities that lurk in the facts of human existence. I don't know. I can't tell. But I went.

'I thought his memory was like the other memories of the dead that accumu-late in every man's life – a vague impress on the brain of shadows that had fallen on it in their swift and final passage; but before the high and ponderous door, between the tall houses of a street as still and decorous as a well-kept alley in a cemetery, I had a vision of him on the stretcher, opening his mouth voraciously, as if to devour all the earth with all its mankind. He lived then before me; he lived as much as he had ever lived – a shadow insatiable of splendid appearances, of frightful realities; a shadow darker than the shadow of the night, and draped nobly in the folds of a gorgeous eloquence. The vision seemed to enter the house with me – the stretcher, the phantom-bearers, the wild crowd of obedient worshippers, the gloom of the forests, the glitter of the reach between the murky bends, the beat of the drum, regular and muffled like the beating of a heart – the heart of a conquering darkness. It was a moment of triumph for the wilderness, an invading and vengeful rush which, it seemed to me, I would have to keep back alone for the salvation of another soul. And the memory of what I had heard him say afar there, with the horned shapes stirring at my back, in the glow of fires, within the patient woods, those broken phrases came back to me, were heard again in their ominous and terrifying simplicity. I remembered his abject pleading, his abject threats, the colossal scale of his vile desires, the meanness, the torment, the tempestuous anguish of his soul. And later on I seemed to see his collected languid manner, when he said one day, "This lot of ivory now is really mine. The Company did not pay for it. I collected it myself at a very great personal risk. I am afraid they will try to claim it as theirs though. H'm. It is a difficult case. What do you think I ought to do – resist? Eh? I want no more than justice." . . . He wanted no more than justice– no more than justice. I rang the bell before a mahogany door on the first floor, and while I waited he seemed to stare at me out of the glassy panel – stare with that wide and immense stare embracing, condemning, loathing all the universe. I seemed to hear the whispered cry, "The horror! The horror!"

'The dusk was falling. I had to wait in a lofty drawing room with three long windows from floor to ceiling that were like three luminous and bedraped columns. The bent gilt legs and backs of the furniture shone in indistinct curves. The tall marble fireplace had a cold and monumental whiteness. A grand piano stood massively in a corner; with dark gleams on the flat surfaces like a sombre and polished sarcophagus. A high door opened – closed. I rose.

'She came forward, all in black, with a pale head, floating towards me in the dusk. She was in mourning. It was more than a year since his death, more than a year since the news came; she seemed as though she would remember and mourn forever. She took both my hands in hers and murmured, "I had heard you were coming." I noticed she was not very young – I mean not girlish. She had a mature capacity for fidelity, for belief, for suffering. The room seemed to have grown darker, as if all the sad light of the cloudy evening had taken refuge on her forehead. This fair hair, this pale visage, this pure brow, seemed surrounded by an ashy halo from which the dark eyes looked out at me. Their glance was guileless, profound, confident, and trustful. She carried her sorrowful head as though she were proud of that sorrow, as though she would say, "I – I alone know how to mourn for him as he deserves." But while we were still shaking hands, such a look of awful desolation came upon her face that I perceived she was one of those creatures that are not the playthings of Time. For her he had died only yesterday. And, by Jove! the impression was so powerful that for me, too, he seemed to have died only yesterday – nay, this very minute. I saw her and him in the same instant of time – his death and her sorrow – I saw her sorrow in the very moment of his death. Do you understand? I saw them together – I heard them together. She had said, with a deep catch of the breath, "I have survived" while my strained ears seemed to hear distinctly, mingled with her tone of despairing regret, the summing up whisper of his eternal condemnation. I asked myself what I was doing there, with a sensation of panic in my heart as though I had blundered into a place of cruel and absurd mysteries not fit for a human being to behold. She motioned me to a chair. We sat down. I laid the packet gently on the little table, and she put her hand over it. . . . "You knew him well," she murmured, after a moment of mourning silence.

"'Intimacy grows quickly out there," I said. "I knew him as well as it is possible for one man to know another."

"'And you admired him," she said. "It was impossible to know him and not to admire him. Was it?"

"'He was a remarkable man," I said, unsteadily. Then before the appealing fixity of her gaze, that seemed to watch for more words on my lips, I went on, "It was impossible not to –"

"'Love him,' she finished eagerly, silencing me into an appalled dumbness. "How true! how true! But when you think that no one knew him so well as I! I had all his noble confidence. I knew him best."

"'You knew him best,' I repeated. And perhaps she did. But with every word spoken the room was growing darker, and only her forehead, smooth and white, remained illumined by the unextinguishable light of belief and love.

"'You were his friend,' she went on. "His friend," she repeated, a little louder. "You must have been, if he had given you this, and sent you to me. I feel I can speak to you – and oh! I must speak. I want you – you who have heard his last words – to know I have been worthy of him. . . . It is not pride. . . . Yes! I am proud to know I understood him better than any one on earth – he told me so himself. And since his mother died I have had no one – no one – to – to –"

'I listened. The darkness deepened. I was not even sure whether he had given me the right bundle. I rather suspect he wanted me to take care of another batch of his papers which, after his death, I saw the manager examining under the lamp. And the girl talked, easing her pain in the certitude of my sympathy; she talked as thirsty men drink. I had heard that her engagement with Kurtz had been disapproved by her people. He wasn't rich enough or something. And indeed I don't know whether he had not been a pauper all his life. He had given me some reason to infer that it was his impatience of comparative poverty that drove him out there.

"'. . . Who was not his friend who had heard him speak once?" she was saying. "He drew men towards him by what was best in them." She looked at me with intensity. "It is the gift of the great," she went on, and the sound of her low voice seemed to have the accompaniment of all the other sounds, full of mystery, desolation, and sorrow, I had ever heard – the ripple of the river, the soughing of the trees swayed by the wind, the murmurs of the crowds, the faint ring of incomprehensible words cried from afar, the whisper of a voice speaking from beyond the threshold of an eternal darkness. "But you have heard him! You know!" she cried.

"'Yes, I know,' I said with something like despair in my heart, but bowing my head before the faith that was in her, before that great and saving illusion that shone with an unearthly glow in the darkness, in the triumphant darkness from which I could not have defended her – from which I could not even defend myself.

"'What a loss to me – to us!' – she corrected herself with beautiful generosity; then added in a murmur, "To the world." By the last gleams of twilight I could see the glitter of her eyes, full of tears – of tears that would not fall.

"'I have been very happy – very fortunate – very proud,' she went on. "Too fortunate. Too happy for a little while. And now I am unhappy for – for life."

'She stood up; her fair hair seemed to catch all the remaining light in a glimmer of gold. I rose, too.

"'And of all this,' she went on mournfully, "of all his promise, and of all his greatness, of his generous mind, of his noble heart, nothing remains – nothing but a memory. You and I –"

"'We shall always remember him," I said hastily.

"'No!' she cried. "It is impossible that all this should be lost – that such a life should be sacrificed to leave nothing – but sorrow. You know what vast plans he had. I knew of them, too – I could not perhaps understand – but others knew of them. Something must remain. His words, at least, have not died."

"'His words will remain," I said.

"'And his example," she whispered to herself. "Men looked up to him – his goodness shone in every act. His example –"

"'True," I said; "his example, too. Yes, his example. I forgot that."

"'But I do not. I cannot – I cannot believe – not yet. I cannot believe that I shall never see him again, that nobody will see him again, never, never, never."

'She put out her arms as if after a retreating figure, stretching them back and with clasped pale hands across the fading and narrow sheen of the window. Never see him! I saw him clearly enough then. I shall see this eloquent phantom as long as I live, and I shall see her, too, a tragic and familiar Shade, resembling in this gesture another one, tragic also, and bedecked with power-less charms, stretching bare brown arms over the glitter of the infernal stream, the stream of darkness. She said suddenly very low, "He died as he lived."

"'His end," said I, with dull anger stirring in me, "was in every way worthy of his life."

"'And I was not with him," she murmured. My anger subsided before a feel-ing of infinite pity.

"'Everything that could be done – " I mumbled.

"'Ah, but I believed in him more than any one on earth – more than his own mother, more than – himself. He needed me! Me! I would have treasured every sigh, every word, every sign, every glance."

'I felt like a chill grip on my chest. "Don't," I said, in a muffled voice.

' "Forgive me. I – I have mourned so long in silence – in silence. . . . You were with him – to the last? I think of his loneliness. Nobody near to understand him as I would have understood. Perhaps no one to hear. . . ."

"'To the very end," I said, shakily. "I heard his very last words. . . ." I stopped in a fright.

"'Repeat them," she murmured in a heart-broken tone. "I want – I want – something – something – to – to live with."

'I was on the point of crying at her, "Don't you hear them?" The dusk was repeating them in a persistent whisper all around us, in a whisper that seemed to swell menacingly like the first whisper of a rising wind. "The horror! The horror!"

' "His last word – to live with," she insisted. "Don't you understand I loved him – I loved him – I loved him!'

'I pulled myself together and spoke slowly.

"'The last word he pronounced was – your name."

'I heard a light sigh and then my heart stood still, stopped dead short by an exulting and terrible cry, by the cry of inconceivable triumph and of unspeak-able pain. "I knew it – I was sure!" . . . She knew. She was sure. I heard her weeping; she had hidden her face in her hands. It seemed to me that the house would collapse before I could escape, that the heavens would fall upon my head. But nothing happened. The heavens do not fall for such a trifle. Would they have fallen, I wonder, if I had rendered Kurtz that justice which was his due? Hadn't he said he wanted only justice? But I couldn't. I could not tell her. It would have been too dark – too dark altogether. . . ."

Marlow ceased, and sat apart, indistinct and silent, in the pose of a meditating Buddha. Nobody moved for a time. 'We have lost the first of the ebb,' said the Director suddenly. I raised my head. The offing was barred by a black bank of clouds, and the tranquil waterway leading to the uttermost ends of the earth flowed sombre under an overcast sky – seemed to lead into the heart of an immense darkness.

J.M. SYNGE (1871–1911)

Born in Dublin, John Millington Synge was a key figure in the Irish literary revival and the Abbey Theatre. *Riders to the Sea* is set on the Aran Islands off Ireland's west coast, a place where Irish was, and is, still spoken, and illustrates Synge's attempt to translate a Gaelic idiom to English.

Riders to the Sea

Characters

Maurya, an old woman	Bartley, her son
Cathleen, her daughter	Nora, a younger daughter
Men And Women	

Scene: An Island off the West of Ireland

[*Cottage kitchen, with nets, oilskins, spinning-wheel, some new boards standing by the wall, etc. Cathleen, a girl of about twenty, finishes kneading cake, and puts it down in the pot-oven by the fire; then wipes her hands, and begins to spin at the wheel. Nora, a young girl, puts her head in at the door.*]

Nora [*In a low voice.*] Where is she?
Cathleen She's lying down, God help her, and maybe sleeping, – if she's able.
[*Nora comes in softly, and takes a bundle from under her shawl.*]
Cathleen [*Spinning the wheel rapidly.*] What is it you have?
Nora The young priest is after bringing them. It's a shirt and a plain stocking were got off a drowned man in Donegal.
[*Cathleen stops her wheel with a sudden movement, and leans out to listen.*]
Nora We're to find out if it's Michael's they are, some time herself will be down looking by the sea.
Cathleen How would they be Michael's, Nora? How would he go the length of that way to the far north ?
Nora The young priest says he's known the like of it. 'If it's Michael's they are,' says he, 'you can tell herself he's got a clean burial, by the grace of

God; and if they're not his, let no one say a word about them, for she'll be getting her death,' says he, 'with crying and lamenting.'
[*The door which Nora half closed is blown open by a gust of wind.*]
Cathleen [*Looking out anxiously.*] Did you ask him would he stop Bartley going this day with the horses to the Galway fair?
Nora 'I won't stop him,' says he; 'but let you not be afraid. Herself does be saying prayers half through the night, and the Almighty God won't leave her destitute,' says he, 'with no son living.'
Cathleen Is the sea bad by the white rocks, Nora?
Nora Middling bad, God help us. There's a great roaring in the west, and it's worse it'll be getting when the tide's turned to the wind. [*She goes over to the table with the bundle.*] Shall I open it now?
Cathleen Maybe she'd wake up on us, and come in before we'd done. [*Coming to the table.*] It's a long time we'll be, and the two of us crying.
Nora [*Goes to the inner door and listens.*] She's moving about on the bed. She'll be coming in a minute.
Cathleen Give me the ladder, and I'll put them up in the turf loft,[1] the way she won't know of them at all, and maybe when the tide turns she'll be going down to see would he be floating from the east.
[*They put the ladder against the gable of the chimney; Cathleen goes up a few steps and hides the bundle in the turf loft. Maurya comes from the inner room.*]
Maurya [*Looking up at Cathleen and speaking querulously.*] Isn't it turf enough you have for this day and evening?
Cathleen There's a cake baking at the fire for a short space [*throwing down the turf*] and Bartley will want it when the tide turns if he goes to Connemara. [*Nora picks up the turf and puts it round the pot-oven.*]
Maurya [*Sitting down on a stool at the fire.*] He won't go this day with the wind rising from the south and west. He won't go this day, for the young priest will stop him surely.
Nora He'll not stop him, mother; and I heard Eamon Simon and Stephen Pheety and Colum Shawn saying he would go.
Maurya Where is he itself?
Nora He went down to see would there be another boat sailing in the week, and I'm thinking it won't be long till he's here now, for the tide's turning at the green head,[2] and the hooker's[3] tacking from the east.
Cathleen I hear someone passing the big stones.
Nora [*Looking out.*] He's coming now, and he in a hurry.
Bartley [*Comes in and looks round the room, speaking sadly and quietly.*] Where is the bit of new rope, Cathleen, was bought in Connemara?
Cathleen [*Coming down.*] Give it to him, Nora; it's on a nail by the white boards. I hung it up this morning, for the pig with the black feet was eating it.
Nora [*Giving him a rope.*] Is that it, Bartley?
Maurya You'd do right to leave that rope, Bartley, hanging by the boards. [*Bartley takes the rope.*] It will be wanting in this place, I'm telling you, if

---

1 **turf:** peat, cut and dried as bricks, formed the staple heating source in the west of Ireland.   2 **green head:** grassy headland.   3 **hooker:** heavily built boat used in costal trade.

Michael is washed up tomorrow morning, or the next morning, or any morning in the week; for it's a deep grave we'll make him, by the grace of God.

Bartley [*Beginning to work with the rope.*] I've no halter the way I can ride down on the mare, and I must go now quickly. This is the one boat going for two weeks or beyond it, and the fair will be a good fair for horses, I heard them saying below.

Maurya It's a hard thing they'll be saying below if the body is washed up and there's no man in it to make the coffin, and I after giving a big price for the finest white boards you'd find in Connemara.

[*She looks round at the boards.*]

Bartley How would it be washed up, and we after looking each day for nine days, and a strong wind blowing a while back from the west and south?

Maurya If it isn't found itself, that wind is raising the sea, and there was a star up against the moon, and it rising in the night. If it was a hundred horses, or a thousand horses you had itself, what is the price of a thousand horses against a son where there is one son only?

Bartley [*Working at the halter, to Cathleen.*] Let you go down each day, and see the sheep aren't jumping in on the rye, and if the jobber comes you can sell the pig with the black feet if there is a good price going.

Maurya How would the like of her get a good price for a pig?

Bartley [*To Cathleen.*] If the west winds holds with the last bit of the moon let you and Nora get up weed[1] enough for another cock for the kelp.[2] It's hard set we'll be from this day with no one in it but one man to work.

Maurya It's hard set we'll be surely the day you're drowned with the rest. What way will I live and the girls with me, and I an old woman looking for the grave?

[*Bartley lays down the halter, takes off his old coat, and puts on a newer one of the same flannel.*]

Bartley [*To Nora.*] Is she coming to the pier?

Nora [*Looking out.*] She's passing the green head and letting fall her sails.

Bartley [*Getting his purse and tobacco.*] I'll have half an hour to go down, and you'll see me coming again in two days, or in three days, or maybe in four days if the wind is bad.

Maurya [*Turning round to the fire, and putting her shawl over her head.*] Isn't it a hard and cruel man won't hear a word from an old woman, and she holding him from the sea?

Cathleen It's the life of a young man to be going on the sea, and who would listen to an old woman with one thing and she saying it over?

Bartley [*Taking the halter.*] I must go now quickly. I'll ride down on the red mare, and the grey pony'ill run behind me. . . . The blessing of God on you.

[*He goes out.*]

Maurya [*Crying out as he is in the door.*] He's gone now, God spare us, and we'll not see him again. He's gone now, and when the black night is falling I'll have no son left me in the world.

---

1 **weed**: seaweed gathered from the rocks and used to fertilise the poor land.   2 **cock for the kelp**: conical shaped mound of seaweed, rather like a dung heap.

Cathleen Why wouldn't you give him your blessing and he looking round in the door? Isn't it sorrow enough is on every one in this house without your sending him out with an unlucky word behind him, and a hard word in his ear?

[*Maurya takes up the tongs and begins raking the fire aimlessly without looking round.*]

Nora [*Turning towards her.*] You're taking away the turf from the cake.[1]

Cathleen [*Crying out.*] The Son of God forgive us, Nora, we're after forgetting his bit of bread.

[*She comes over to the fire.*]

Nora And it's destroyed he'll be going till dark night, and he after eating nothing since the sun went up.

Cathleen [*Turning the cake out of the oven.*] It's destroyed he'll be surely. There's no sense left on any person in a house where an old woman will be talking for ever. [*Maurya sways herself on her stool.*]

Cathleen [*Cutting off some of the bread and rolling it in a cloth; to Maurya.*] Let you go down now to the spring well and give him this and he passing. You'll see him then and the dark word will be broken, and you can say 'God speed you,' the way he'll be easy in his mind

Maurya [*Taking the bread.*] Will I be in it as soon as himself?

Cathleen If you go now quickly.

Maurya [*Standing up unsteadily.*] It's hard set I am to walk.

Cathleen [*Looking at her anxiously.*] Give her the stick, Nora, or maybe she'll slip on the big stones

Nora What stick?

Cathleen The stick Michael brought from Connemara.

Maurya [*Taking a stick Nora gives her.*] In the big world the old people do be leaving things after them for their sons and children, but in this place it is the young men do be leaving things behind for them that do be old.

[*She goes out slowly. Nora goes over to the ladder.*]

Cathleen Wait, Nora, maybe she'd turn back quickly. She's that sorry, God help her, you wouldn't know the thing she'd do.

Nora Is she gone round by the bush?

Cathleen [*Looking out.*] She's gone now. Throw it down quickly, for the Lord knows when she'll be out of it again.

Nora [*Getting the bundle from the loft.*] The young priest said he'd be passing to-morrow, and we might go down and speak to him below if it's Michael's they are surely.

Cathleen [*Taking the bundle.*] Did he say what way they were found?

Nora [*Coming down.*] 'There were two men,' said he, 'and they rowing round with poteen[2] before the cocks crowed, and the oar of one of them caught the body, and they passing the black cliffs of the north.'

Cathleen [*Trying to open the bundle.*] Give me a knife, Nora; the string's

---

1 **turf from the cake**: soda-bread cooked in heavy pots over which glowing turf is piled. 2 **poteen**: illegally distilled whiskey, often of great alcoholic strength.

perished with the salt water, and there's a black knot on it you wouldn't loosen in a week.

Nora [*Giving her a knife.*] I've heard tell it was a long way to Donegal.

Cathleen [*Cutting the string.*] It is surely. There was a man in here a while ago – the man sold us that knife – and he said if you set off walking from the rocks beyond, it would be in seven days you'd be in Donegal.

Nora And what time would a man take, and he floating?

[*Cathleen opens the bundle and takes out a bit of a shirt and a stocking. They look at them eagerly.*]

Cathleen [*In a low voice.*] The Lord spare us, Nora! isn't it a queer hard thing to say if it's his they are surely?

Nora I'll get his shirt off the hook the way we can put the one flannel on the other. [*She looks through some clothes hanging in the corner.*] It's not with them, Cathleen, and where will it be?

Cathleen I'm thinking Bartley put it on him in the morning, for his own shirt was heavy with the salt in it. [*Pointing to the corner.*] There's a bit of a sleeve was of the same stuff. Give me that and it will do.

[*Nora brings it to her and they compare the flannel.*]

Cathleen It's the same stuff, Nora; but if it is itself, aren't there great rolls of it in the shops of Galway, and isn't it many another man may have a shirt of it as well as Michael himself?

Nora [*Who has taken up the stocking and counted the stitches, crying out.*] It's Michael, Cathleen, it's Michael; God spare his soul, and what will herself say when she hears this story, and Bartley on the sea?

Cathleen [*Taking the stocking.*] It's a plain stocking.

Nora It's the second one of the third pair I knitted, and I put up three-score stitches, and I dropped four of them.

Cathleen [*Counts the stitches.*] It's that number is in it. [*Crying out.*] Ah, Nora, isn't it a bitter thing to think of him floating that way to the far north, and no one to keen[1] him but the black hags[2] that do be flying on the sea?

Nora [*Swinging herself half round, and throwing out her arms on the clothes.*] And isn't it a pitiful thing when there is nothing left of a man who was a great rower and fisher but a bit of an old shirt and a plain stocking?

Cathleen [*After an instant.*] Tell me is herself coming, Nora? I hear a little sound on the path.

Nora [*Looking out.*] She is, Cathleen. She's coming up to the door.

Cathleen Put these things away before she'll come in. Maybe it's easier she'll be after giving her blessing to Bartley, and we won't let on we've heard anything the time he's on the sea.

Nora [*Helping Cathleen to close the bundle.*] We'll put them here in the corner.

[*They put them into a hole in the chimney corner. Cathleen goes back to the spinning-wheel.*]

Nora Will she see it was crying I was?

---

1 **keen:** ritual wail for the dead. 2 **black hags:** shags or cormorants, black birds.

Cathleen Keep your back to the door the way the light'll not be on you.
[*Nora sits down at the chimney corner, with her back to the door. Maurya comes in very slowly, without looking at the girls, and goes over to her stool at the other side of the fire. The cloth with the bread is still in her hand. The girls look at each other, and Nora points to the bundle of bread.*]
Cathleen [*After spinning for a moment.*] You didn't give him his bit of bread?
[*Maurya begins to keen softly, without turning round.*]
Cathleen Did you see him riding down?
[*Maurya goes on keening.*]
Cathleen [*A little impatiently.*] God forgive you; isn't it a better thing to raise your voice and tell what you seen, than to be making lamentation for a thing that's done? Did you see Bartley, I'm saying to you?
Maurya [*With a weak voice.*] My heart's broken from this day.
Cathleen [*As before.*] Did you see Bartley?
Maurya I seen the fearfullest thing.
Cathleen [*Leaves her wheel and looks out.*] God forgive you; he's riding the mare now over the green head, and the grey pony behind him.
Maurya [*Starts so that her shawl falls back from her head and shows her white tossed hair. With a frightened voice.*] The grey pony behind him. . . .
Cathleen [*Coming to the fire.*] What is it ails you at all?
Maurya [*Speaking very slowly.*] I've seen the fearfullest thing any person has seen since the day Bride Dara seen the dead man with the child in his arms.
Cathleen and Nora Uah.
[*They crouch down in front of the old woman at the fire.*]
Nora Tell us what it is you seen?
Maurya I went down to the spring well, and I stood there saying a prayer to myself. Then Bartley came along, and he riding on the red mare with the grey pony behind him. [*She puts up her hands, as if to hide something from her eyes.*] The Son of God spare us, Nora!
Cathleen What is it you seen?
Maurya I seen Michael himself.
Cathleen [*Speaking softly.*] You did not, mother. It wasn't Michael you seen, for his body is after being found in the far north, and he's got a clean burial, by the grace of God.
Maurya [*A little defiantly.*] I'm after seeing him this day, and he riding and galloping. Bartley came first on the red mare, and I tried to say 'God speed you,' but something choked the words in my throat. He went by quickly; and 'The blessing of God on you,' says he, and I could say nothing. I looked up then, and I crying, at the grey pony, and there was Michael upon it – with fine clothes on him, and new shoes on his feet.
Cathleen [*Begins to keen.*] It's destroyed we are from this day. It's destroyed, surely.
Nora Didn't the young priest say the Almighty God won't leave her destitute with no son living?
Maurya [*In a low voice, but clearly.*] It's little the like of him knows of the sea. . . . Bartley will be lost now, and let you call in Eamon and make me a

good coffin out of the white boards, for I won't live after them. I've had a husband, and a husband's father, and six sons in this house – six fine men, though it was a hard birth I had with every one of them and they coming into the world – and some of them were found and some of them were not found, but they're gone now the lot of them. . . . There were Stephen and Shawn were lost in the great wind, and found after in the Bay of Gregory of the Golden Mouth, and carried up the two of them on one plank, and in by that door.

[*She pauses for a moment, the girls start as if they heard something through the door that was half open behind them.*]

Nora [*In a whisper.*] Did you hear that, Cathleen? Did you hear a noise in the north-east?

Cathleen [*In a whisper.*] There's someone after crying out by the seashore.

Maurya [*Continues without hearing anything.*] There was Sheamus and his father, and his own father again, were lost in a dark night, and not a stick or sign was seen of them when the sun went up. There was Patch after was drowned out of a curragh[1] that turned over. I was sitting here with Bartley, and he a baby lying on my two knees, and I seen two women, and three women, and four women coming in, and they crossing themselves and not saying a word. I looked out then, and there were men coming after them, and they holding a thing in the half of a red sail, and water dripping out of it – it was a dry day, Nora – and leaving a track to the door.

[*She pauses again with her hand stretched out towards the door. It opens softly and old women begin to come in, crossing themselves on the threshold, and kneeling down in front of the stage with red petticoats over their heads.*]

Maurya [*Half in a dream, to Cathleen.*] Is it Patch, or Michael, or what is it at all?

Cathleen Michael is after being found in the far north, and when he is found there how could he be here in this place?

Maurya There does be a power of young men floating round in the sea, and what way would they know if it was Michael they had, or another man like him, for when a man is nine days in the sea, and the wind blowing, it's hard set his own mother would be to say what man was in it.

Cathleen It's Michael, God spare him, for they're after sending us a bit of his clothes from the far north.

[*She reaches out and hands Maurya the clothes that belonged to Michael. Maurya stands up slowly, and takes them in her hands. Nora looks out.*]

Nora They're carrying a thing among them, and there's water dripping out of it and leaving a track by the big stones.

Cathleen [*In a whisper to the women who have come in.*] Is it Bartley it is?

One of the Women It is, surely, God rest his soul.

[*Two younger women come in and pull out the table. Then men carry in the body of Bartley, laid on a plank, with a bit of a sail over it, and lay it on the table.*]

Cathleen [*To the women as they are doing so.*] What way was he drowned?

---

1 **curragh:** long boat made of canvass and lath, a common boat in the west of Ireland.

One of the Women The grey pony knocked him over into the sea, and he was washed out where there is a great surf on the white rocks.

[*Maurya has gone over and knelt down at the head of the table. The women are keening softly and swaying themselves with a slow movement. Cathleen and Nora kneel at the other end of the table. The men kneel near the door.*]

Maurya [*Raising her head and speaking as if she did not see the people around her.*] They're all gone now, and there isn't anything more the sea can do to me. . . . I'll have no call now to be up crying and praying when the wind breaks from the south, and you can hear the surf is in the east, and the surf is in the west, making a great stir with the two noises, and they hitting one on the other. I'll have no call now to be going down and getting Holy Water in the dark nights after Samhain,[1] and I won't care what way the sea is when the other women will be keening. [*To Nora.*] Give me the Holy Water, Nora; there's a small sup still on the dresser. [*Nora gives it to her.*]

Maurya [*Drops Michael's clothes across Bartley's feet, and sprinkles the Holy Water over him.*] It isn't that I haven't prayed for you, Bartley, to the Almighty God. It isn't that I haven't said prayers in the dark night till you wouldn't know what I'd be saying; but it's a great rest I'll have now, and it's time, surely. It's a great rest I'll have now, and great sleeping in the long nights after Samhain, if it's only a bit of wet flour we do have to eat, and maybe a fish that would be stinking.

[*She kneels down again, crossing herself, and saying prayers under her breath.*]

Cathleen [*To an old man.*] Maybe yourself and Eamon would make a coffin when the sun rises. We have fine white boards herself bought, God help her, thinking Michael would be found, and I have a new cake you can eat while you'll be working.

The old man [*Looking at the boards.*] Are there nails with them?

Cathleen There are not, Colum; we didn't think of the nails.

Another man It's a great wonder she wouldn't think of the nails, and all the coffins she's seen made already.

Cathleen It s getting old she is, and broken.

[*Maurya stands up again very slowly and spreads out the pieces of Michael's clothes beside the body, sprinkling them with the last of the Holy Water.*]

Nora [*In a whisper to Cathleen.*] She's quiet now and easy; but the day Michael was drowned you could hear her crying out from this to the spring well. It's fonder she was of Michael, and would any one have thought that?

Cathleen [*Slowly and clearly.*] An old woman will be soon tired with anything she will do, and isn't it nine days herself is after crying and keening, and making great sorrow in the house?

Maurya [*Puts the empty cup mouth downwards on the table, and lays her hands together on Bartley's feet.*] They're all together this time, and the end is come. May the Almighty God have mercy on Bartley's soul, and on Michael's soul, and on the souls of Sheamus and Patch, and Stephen and Shawn; [*bending her head.*] and may He have mercy on my soul, Nora, and on the soul of every one is left living in the world.

---

1 **Samhain:** (pronounced Sowin), the 1st of November, the Feast of All Souls and the day of the dead in pagan times.

[*She pauses, and the keen rises a little more loudly from the women, then sinks away.*]
Maurya [*Continuing.*] Michael has a clean burial in the far north, by the grace of the Almighty God. Bartley will have a fine coffin out of the white boards, and a deep grave surely. What more can we want than that? No man at all can be living for ever, and we must be satisfied.
[*She kneels down again and the curtain falls slowly.*]

WILLIAM BUTLER YEATS (1865–1939)

Yeats' career is marked by his passionate advocacy of an Irish literary and national revival. Though a political figure – he eventually became a senator of the Irish Republic – Yeats largely saw the world through poetic eyes, and much of his work expresses a mysterious visionary quality, reflecting his constant interest in esoteric and occult knowledge. Like many involved with Ireland's literary revival at the end of the nineteenth century, Yeats' early ideal of Ireland is based on a romanticised Celtic past, a land of dreams and minstrelsy which challenges the materialism of the modern world. But the nationalist uprising during the First World War, and the severity of the British response to it, provoked Yeats into taking a more active stance in favour of Irish independence, and this period also sees his development of a more direct poetic idiom. Despite his nationalism, however, Yeats deplored the erosion of the values of the socially elite Anglo-Irish, particularly those associated with the world of the country-house. In later years Yeats' writing reveals his fascination for the local and the global. A richly symbolic poetry is his vehicle to articulate a deterministic vision of human history. The following selection of poems is arranged chronologically.

Down by the Salley Gardens

Down by the salley gardens my love and I did meet;
She passed the salley gardens with little snow-white feet.
She bid me take love easy, as the leaves grow on the tree;
But I, being young and foolish, with her would not agree.
In a field by the river my love and I did stand,
And on my leaning shoulder she laid her snow-white hand.
She bid me take life easy, as the grass grows on the weirs;
But I was young and foolish, and now am full of tears.

The Lake Isle of Innisfree

I will arise and go now, and go to Innisfree,
And a small cabin build there, of clay and wattles made:
Nine bean-rows will I have there, a hive for the honeybee,
And live alone in the bee-loud glade.

Salley: willow.

5   And I shall have some peace there, for peace comes dropping
       slow,
    Dropping from the veils of the morning to where the cricket
       sings;
    There midnight's all a glimmer, and noon a purple glow,
    And evening full of the linnet's wings.

    I will arise and go now, for always night and day
10   I hear lake water lapping with low sounds by the shore;
    While I stand on the roadway, or on the pavements grey,
    I hear it in the deep heart's core.

The Secret Rose

    Far-off, most secret, and inviolate Rose,
    Enfold me in my hour of hours; where those
    Who sought thee in the Holy Sepulchre,
    Or in the wine-vat, dwell beyond the stir
5   And tumult of defeated dreams; and deep
    Among pale eyelids, heavy with the sleep
    Men have named beauty. Thy great leaves enfold
    The ancient beards, the helms of ruby and gold
    Of the crowned Magi; and the king whose eyes
10   Saw the pierced Hands and Rood of elder rise
    In Druid vapour and make the torches dim;
    Till vain frenzy awoke and he died; and him
    Who met Fand walking among flaming dew
    By a grey shore where the wind never blew,
15   And lost the world and Emer for a kiss;
    And him who drove the gods out of their liss,
    And till a hundred morns had flowered red
    Feasted, and wept the barrows of his dead;
    And the proud dreaming king who flung the crown
20   And sorrow away, and calling bard and clown
    Dwelt among wine-stained wanderers in deep woods;
    And him who sold tillage, and house, and goods,
    And sought through lands and islands numberless years,
    Until he found, with laughter and with tears,
25   A woman of so shining loveliness
    That men threshed corn at midnight by a tress,
    A little stolen tress. I, too, await
    The hour of thy great wind of love and hate.
    When shall the stars be blown about the sky,

Secret Rose 9 **Magi:** the three kings or wise men who came from the east to attend the Christ child in the manger. 10 **Rood:** cross. 13 **Fand:** Celtic god of the sea. 15 **Emer:** wife of the great legendary hero Cuchulain. 16 **liss:** (in Irish lios), a supernatural enclosed space.

30   Like the sparks blown out of a smithy, and die?
     Surely thine hour has come, thy great wind blows,
     Far-off, most secret, and inviolate Rose?

The Fiddler of Dooney

When I play on my fiddle in Dooney.
Folk dance like a wave of the sea;
My cousin is priest in Kilvarnet,
My brother in Mocharabuiee.

5   I passed my brother and cousin:
    They read in their books of prayer;
    I read in my book of songs
    I bought at the Sligo fair.

When we come at the end of time
10   To Peter sitting in state,
     He will smile on the three old spirits,
     But call me first through the gate;

For the good are always the merry,
Save by an evil chance,
15   And the merry love the fiddle,
     And the merry love to dance:

And when the folk there spy me,
They will all come up to me,
With 'Here is the fiddler of Dooney!'
20   And dance like a wave of the sea.

No Second Troy

Why should I blame her that she filled my days
With misery, or that she would of late
Have taught to ignorant men most violent ways,
Or hurled the little streets upon the great.
5   Had they but courage equal to desire?
    What could have made her peaceful with a mind
    That nobleness made simple as a fire,
    With beauty like a tightened bow, a kind
    That is not natural in an age like this,
10   Being high and solitary and most stern?
     Why, what could she have done, being what she is?
     Was there another Troy for her to burn?

Fiddler **4 Mocharabuiee:** pronounced Mockrabwee.

The Wild Swans at Coole

The trees are in their autumn beauty,
The woodland paths are dry,
Under the October twilight the water
Mirrors a still sky;
5   Upon the brimming water among the stones
Are nine-and-fifty swans.

The nineteenth autumn has come upon me
Since I first made my count;
I saw, before I had well finished,
10   All suddenly mount
And scatter wheeling in great broken rings
Upon their clamorous wings.

I have looked upon those brilliant creatures,
And now my heart is sore.
15   All's changed since I, hearing at twilight,
The first time on this shore,
The bell-beat of their wings above my head,
Trod with a lighter tread.

Unwearied still, lover by lover,
20   They paddle in the cold
Companionable streams or climb the air;
Their hearts have not grown old;
Passion or conquest, wander where they will,
Attend upon them still.

25   But now they drift on the still water,
Mysterious, beautiful;
Among what rushes will they build,
By what lake's edge or pool
Delight men's eyes when I awake some day
30   To find they have flown away?

In Memory of Major Robert Gregory

I

Now that we're almost settled in our house
I'll name the friends that cannot sup with us
Beside a fire of turf in th' ancient tower,
And having talked to some late hour
5   Climb up the narrow winding stair to bed:
Discoverers of forgotten truth

Major Robert Gregory: only son of Lady Gregory, who helped build the Abbey Theatre. A representative of the affluent, Anglo-Irish world Yeats identified with. He was killed in action in 1918.

Or mere companions of my youth,
All, all are in my thoughts to-night being dead.

II

Always we'd have the new friend meet the old
10   And we are hurt if either friend seem cold,
And there is salt to lengthen out the smart
In the affections of our heart,
And quarrels are blown up upon that head;
But not a friend that I would bring
15   This night can set us quarrelling,
For all that come into my mind are dead.

III

Lionel Johnson comes the first to mind,
That loved his learning better than mankind.
Though courteous to the worst; much falling he
20   Brooded upon sanctity
Till all his Greek and Latin learning seemed
A long blast upon the horn that brought
A little nearer to his thought
A measureless consummation that he dreamed.

IV

25   And that enquiring man John Synge comes next,
That dying chose the living world for text
And never could have rested in the tomb
But that, long travelling, he had come
Towards nightfall upon certain set apart
30   In a most desolate stony place,
Towards nightfall upon a race
Passionate and simple like his heart.

V

And then I think of old George Pollexfen,
In muscular youth well known to Mayo men
35   For horsemanship at meets or at racecourses,
That could have shown how pure-bred horses
And solid men, for all their passion, live
But as the outrageous stars incline
By opposition, square and trine;
40   Having grown sluggish and contemplative.

---

17 **Lionel Johnson:** poet and member of the Rhymers   33 **George Pollexfen:** Yeats' uncle, who was interested
Club whom Yeats knew in London. 25 **Synge:** J.M.   in astrology and the cabbala.
Synge: close friend of Yeats, who also developed the
Abbey Theatre.

VI

They were my close companions many a year.
A portion of my mind and life, as it were,
And now their breathless faces seem to look
Out of some old picture-book;
45   I am accustomed to their lack of breath,
But not that my dear friend's dear son,
Our Sidney and our perfect man,
Could share in that discourtesy of death.

VII

For all things the delighted eye now sees
50   Were loved by him: the old storm-broken trees
That cast their shadows upon road and bridge;
The tower set on the stream's edge;
The ford where drinking cattle make a stir
Nightly, and startled by that sound
55   The water-hen must change her ground;
He might have been your heartiest welcomer.

VIII

When with the Galway foxhounds he would ride
From Castle Taylor to the Roxborough side
Or Esserkelly plain, few kept his pace;
60   At Mooneen he had leaped a place
So perilous that half the astonished meet
Had shut their eyes; and where was it
He rode a race without a bit?
And yet his mind outran the horses' feet.

IX

65   We dreamed that a great painter had been born
To cold Clare rock and Galway rock and thorn,
To that stern colour and that delicate line
That are our secret discipline
Wherein the gazing heart doubles her might.
70   Soldier, scholar, horseman, he,
And yet he had the intensity
To have published all to be a world's delight.

X

What other could so well have counselled us
In all lovely intricacies of a house
75   As he that practised or that understood
All work in metal or in wood,
In moulded plaster or in carven stone?

---

47 **Our Sidney:** Sir Philip Sidney, the Elizabethan poet, soldier, statesman.

Soldier, scholar, horseman, he,
And all he did done perfectly
80 As though he had but that one trade alone.

XI
Some burn dam faggots, others may consume
The entire combustible world in one small room
As though dried straw, and if we turn about
The bare chimney is gone black out
85 Because the work had finished in that flare.
Soldier, scholar, horseman, he,
As 'twere all life's epitome.
What made us dream that he could comb grey hair?

XII
I had thought, seeing how bitter is that wind
90 That shakes the shutter, to have brought to mind
All those that manhood tried, or childhood loved
Or boyish intellect approved,
With some appropriate commentary on each;
Until imagination brought
95 A fitter welcome; but a thought
Of that late death took all my heart for speech.

An Irish Airman Foresees his Death

I know that I shall meet my fate
Somewhere among the clouds above;
Those that I fight I do not hate,
Those that I guard I do not love;
5 My county is Kiltartan Cross,
My countrymen Kiltartan's poor,
No likely end could bring them loss
Or leave them happier than before.
Nor law, nor duty bade me fight,
10 Nor public men, nor cheering crowds,
A lonely impulse of delight
Drove to this tumult in the clouds;
The years to come seemed waste of breath,
A waste of breath the years behind
15 In balance with this life, this death.

Easter 1916

I have met them at close of day
Coming with vivid faces
From counter or desk among grey
Eighteenth-century houses.
5 I have passed with a nod of the head
Or polite meaningless words,
Or have lingered awhile and said
Polite meaningless words,
And thought before I had done
10 Of a mocking tale or a gibe
To please a companion
Around the fire at the club,
Being certain that they and I
But lived where motley is worn:
15 All changed, changed utterly:
A terrible beauty is born.

That woman's days were spent
In ignorant good-will,
Her nights in argument
20 Until her voice grew shrill.
What voice more sweet than hers
When, young and beautiful,
She rode to harriers?
This man had kept a school
25 And rode our winged horse;
This other his helper and friend
Was coming into his force;
He might have won fame in the end,
So sensitive his nature seemed,
30 So daring and sweet his thought.
This other man I had dreamed
A drunken, vainglorious lout.
He had done most bitter wrong
To some who are near my heart,
35 Yet I number him in the song;
He, too, has resigned his part
In the casual comedy;

Easter 1916: On Easter Monday, 24 April 1916, the Irish Republic was proclaimed and the centre of Dublin occupied by the Irish Volunteers. They held out against British troops until 29 April. Within two weeks, 15 of their leaders were executed. **17 That woman:** Constance Gore Booth. She took part in the rising but her death sentence was commuted.

24 This man: Patrick Pearse, founded St Enda's School, President of the provisional Irish Government during the Easter uprising. He was executed. **26 This other:** Thomas MacDonagh, poet and dramatist. He taught at University College, Dublin. **31 This other man:** John MacBride, husband of Maud Gonne with whom Yeats was in love.

He, too, has been changed in his turn,
Transformed utterly:
40   A terrible beauty is born.

Hearts with one purpose alone
Through summer and winter seem
Enchanted to a stone
To trouble the living stream.
45   The horse that comes from the road.
The rider, the birds that range
From cloud to tumbling cloud,
Minute by minute they change;
A shadow of cloud on the stream
50   Changes minute by minute;
A horse-hoof slides on the brim,
And a horse plashes within it;
The long-legged moor-hens dive,
And hens to moor-cocks call;
55   Minute by minute they live:
The stone's in the midst of all.

Too long a sacrifice
Can make a stone of the heart.
O when may it suffice?
60   That is Heaven's part, our part
To murmur name upon name,
As a mother names her child
When sleep at last has come
On limbs that had run wild.
65   What is it but nightfall?
No, no, not night but death;
Was it needless death after all?
For England may keep faith
For all that is done and said.
70   We know their dream; enough
To know they dreamed and are dead;
And what if excess of love
Bewildered them till they died?
I write it out in a verse –
75   MacDonagh and MacBride
And Connolly and Pearse
Now and in time to be,
Wherever green is worn,
Are changed, changed utterly:
80   A terrible beauty is born.

---

76 **Connolly:** James Connolly, military commander of the Republican forces in Dublin, executed on May 12.

The Second Coming

Turning and turning in the widening gyre
The falcon cannot hear the falconer;
Things fall apart; the centre cannot hold;
Mere anarchy is loosed upon the world,
5 The blood-dimmed tide is loosed, and everywhere
The ceremony of innocence is drowned;
The best lack all conviction, while the worst
Are full of passionate intensity.

Surely some revelation is at hand;
10 Surely the Second Coming is at hand.
The Second Coming! Hardly are those words out
When a vast image out of *Spiritus Mundi*
Troubles my sight: somewhere in sands of the desert
A shape with lion body and the head of a man,
15 A gaze blank and pitiless as the sun,
Is moving its slow thighs, while all about it
Reel shadows of the indignant desert birds.
The darkness drops again; but now I know
That twenty centuries of stony sleep
20 Were vexed to nightmare by a rocking cradle,
And what rough beast, its hour come round at last,
Slouches towards Bethlehem to be born?

A Prayer for my Daughter

Once more the storm is howling, and half hid
Under this cradle-hood and coverlid
My child sleeps on. There is no obstacle
But Gregory's wood and one bare hill
5 Whereby the haystack- and roof-levelling wind,
Bred on the Atlantic, can be stayed;
And for an hour I have walked and prayed
Because of the great gloom that is in my mind.

I have walked and prayed for this young child an hour
10 And heard the sea-wind scream upon the tower,
And under the arches of the bridge, and scream
In the elms above the flooded stream;
Imagining in excited reverie
That the future years had come,

Second Coming: a mixture of Christ's predicted second
coming and the advent of the beast of the Apocalypse
in Revelations. 1 gyre: a revolving vortex. In Yeats a
cone-shaped structure whose mystical significance he developed in *A Vision*.

12 *Spiritus Mundi*: 'The World Soul', for Yeats a vast
storehouse of images which are in a general cultural
domain.

15   Dancing to a frenzied drum,
    Out of the murderous innocence of the sea.

    May she be granted beauty and yet not
    Beauty to make a stranger's eye distraught,
    Or hers before a looking-glass, for such,
20   Being made beautiful overmuch,
    Consider beauty a sufficient end,
    Lose natural kindness and maybe
    The heart-revealing intimacy
    That chooses right, and never find a friend.

25   Helen being chosen found life flat and dull
    And later had much trouble from a fool,
    While that great Queen, that rose out of the spray,
    Being fatherless could have her way
    Yet chose a bandy-legged smith for man.
30   It's certain that fine women eat
    A crazy salad with their meat
    Whereby the Horn of Plenty is undone.

    In courtesy I'd have her chiefly learned;
    Hearts are not had as a gift but hearts are earned
35   By those that are not entirely beautiful;
    Yet many, that have played the fool
    For beauty's very self, has charm made wise.
    And many a poor man that has roved,
    Loved and thought himself beloved,
40   From a glad kindness cannot take his eyes.

    May she become a flourishing hidden tree
    That all her thoughts may like the linnet be,
    And have no business but dispensing round
    Their magnanimities of sound,
45   Nor but in merriment begin a chase,
    Nor but in merriment a quarrel.
    O may she live like some green laurel
    Rooted in one dear perpetual place.

    My mind, because the minds that I have loved,
50   The sort of beauty that I have approved,
    Prosper but little, has dried up of late,
    Yet knows that to be choked with hate
    May well be of all evil chances chief.
    If there's no hatred in a mind
55   Assault and battery of the wind
    Can never tear the linnet from the leaf.

---

25 **Helen:** Helen of Troy.

27 **Queen:** Aphrodite, the goddess of Love. She married Hephaestus, the blacksmith of the gods.

An intellectual hatred is the worst,
So let her think opinions are accursed.
Have I not seen the loveliest woman born
60   Out of the mouth of plenty's horn,
Because of her opinionated mind
Barter that horn and every good
By quiet natures understood
For an old bellows full of angry wind?

65   Considering that, all hatred driven hence,
The soul recovers radical innocence
And learns at last that it is self-delighting,
Self-appeasing, self-affrighting,
And that its own sweet will is Heaven's will;
70   She can, though every face should scowl
And every windy quarter howl
Or every bellows burst, be happy still.

And may her bridegroom bring her to a house
Where all's accustomed, ceremonious;
75   For arrogance and hatred are the wares
Peddled in the thoroughfares.
How but in custom and in ceremony
Are innocence and beauty born?
Ceremony's a name for the rich horn,
80   And custom for the spreading laurel tree.

Sailing to Byzantium

I

That is no country for old men. The young
In one another's arms, birds in the trees
– Those dying generations – at their song,
The salmon-falls, the mackerel-crowded seas,
5   Fish, flesh, or fowl commend all summer long
Whatever is begotten, born, and dies.
Caught in that sensual music all neglect
Monuments of unaging intellect.

II

An aged man is but a paltry thing,
10   A tattered coat upon a stick, unless
Soul clap its hands and sing, and louder sing
For every tatter in its mortal dress,
Nor is there singing school but studying
Monuments of its own magnificence;

Byzantium: ancient Greek city, rebuilt by Constantine as Constantinople.

15 And therefore I have sailed the seas and come
To the holy city of Byzantium.

III

O sages standing in God's holy fire
As in the gold mosaic of a wall,
Come from the holy fire, perne in a gyre,
20 And be the singing-masters of my soul.
Consume my heart away; sick with desire
And fastened to a dying animal
It knows not what it is; and gather me
Into the artifice of eternity.

IV

25 Once out of nature I shall never take
My bodily form from any natural thing,
But such a form as Grecian goldsmiths make
Of a hammered gold and gold enamelling
To keep a drowsy Emperor awake;
30 Or set upon a golden bough to sing
To the lords and ladies of Byzantium
Of what is past, or passing, or to come.

Leda and the Swan

A sudden blow: the great wings beating still
Above the staggering girl, her thighs caressed
By the dark webs, her nape caught in his bill,
He holds her helpless breast upon his breast.

5 How can those terrified vague fingers push
The feathered glory from her loosening thighs?
And how can body, laid in that white rush,
But feel the strange heart beating where it lies?

A shudder in the loins engenders there
10 The broken wall, the burning roof and tower
And Agamemnon dead.
                                    Being so caught up,
So mastered by the brute blood of the air,
Did she put on his knowledge with his power
Before the indifferent beak could let her drop?

Leda: she was raped by Zeus while he was disguised as a
swan. Leda produced two 'eggs' which each bore twins:
Castor and Pollux and Helen and Clytaemnestra.

11 **Agamemnon:** leader of the Greeks at Troy. He was
murdered by his wife Clytaemnestra on his return.

Among School Children

I

I walk through the long schoolroom questioning;
A kind old nun in a white hood replies;
The children learn to cipher and to sing,
To study reading-books and histories,
5   To cut and sew, be neat in everything
In the best modern way – the children's eyes
In momentary wonder stare upon
A sixty-year-old smiling public man.

II

I dream of a Ledaean body, bent
10   Above a sinking fire. A tale that she
Told of a harsh reproof, or trivial event
That changed some childish day to tragedy –
Told, and it seemed that our two natures blent
Into a sphere from youthful sympathy,
15   Or else, to alter Plato's parable,
Into the yolk and white of the one shell.

III

And thinking of that fit of grief or rage
I look upon one child or t'other there
And wonder if she stood so at that age –
20   For even daughters of the swan can share
Something of every paddler's heritage –
And had that colour upon cheek or hair,
And thereupon my heart is driven wild:
She stands before me as a living child.

IV

25   Her present image floats into the mind –
Did Quattrocento finger fashion it
Hollow of cheek as though it drank the wind
And took a mess of shadows for its meat?
And I though never of Ledaean kind
30   Had pretty plumage once – enough of that,
Better to smile on all that smile, and show
There is a comfortable kind of old scarecrow.

V

What youthful mother, a shape upon her lap
Honey of generation had betrayed,

---

15 Plato's parable: in the *Symposium*, it is argued that humanity was originally 'doubled' in a spherical shape, but became divided in two and, thus, we are constantly seeking our lost unity.

26 Quattrocento: 14th century Italian art. Yeats appears to have been thinking specifically of Leonardo da Vinci.

35 And that must sleep, shriek, struggle to escape
As recollection or the drug decide,
Would think her Son, did she but see that shape
With sixty or more winters on its head,
A compensation for the pang of his birth,
40 Or the uncertainty of his setting forth?

VI
Plato thought nature but a spume that plays
Upon a ghostly paradigm of things;
Solider Aristotle played the taws
Upon the bottom of a king of kings;
45 World-famous golden-thighed Pythagoras
Fingered upon a fiddle-stick or strings
What a star sang and careless Muses heard:
Old clothes upon old sticks to scare a bird.

VII
Both nuns and mothers worship images,
50 But those the candles light are not as those
That animate a mother's reveries,
But keep a marble or a bronze repose.
And yet they too break hearts – O presences
That passion, piety or affection knows,
55 And that all heavenly glory symbolise –
O self-born mockers of man's enterprise;

VIII
Labour is blossoming or dancing where
The body is not bruised to pleasure soul.
Nor beauty born out of its own despair,
60 Nor blear-eyed wisdom out of midnight oil.
O chestnut-tree, great-rooted blossomer,
Are you the leaf, the blossom or the bole?
O body swayed to music, O brightening glance,
How can we know the dancer from the dance?

Byzantium

The unpurged images of day recede;
The Emperor's drunken soldiery are abed;
Night resonance recedes, night walkers' song
After great cathedral gong;
5 A starlit or a moonlit dome disdains

---

43 **Soldier Aristotle**: the philosopher who tutored Alexander the Great. **taws**: a strap, divided into strips at its end.

45 **gold-thighed Pythagoras**: Greek philosopher who expounded the doctrine of transmigration of souls; golden-thighed comes from Iamblichus' life of Phythagoras.

All that man is,
All mere complexities,
The fury and the mire of human veins.

Before me floats an image, man or shade,
10 Shade more than man, more image than a shade;
For Hades' bobbin bound in mummy-cloth
May unwind the winding path;
A mouth that has no moisture and no breath
Breathless mouths may summon;
15 I hail the superhuman;
I call it death-in-life and life-in-death.

Miracle, bird or golden handiwork,
More miracle than bird or handiwork,
Planted on the star-lit golden bough,
20 Can like the cocks of Hades crow,
Or, by the moon embittered, scorn aloud
In glory of changeless metal
Common bird or petal
And all complexities of mire or blood.

25 At midnight on the Emperor's pavement flit
Flames that no faggot feeds, nor steel has lit,
Nor storm disturbs, flames begotten of flame,
Where blood-begotten spirits come
And all complexities of fury leave,
30 Dying into a dance,
An agony of trance,
An agony of flame that cannot singe a sleeve.

Astraddle on the dolphin's mire and blood,
Spirit after Spirit! The smithies break the flood.
35 The golden smithies of the Emperor!
Marbles of the dancing floor
Break bitter furies of complexity,
Those images that yet
Fresh images beget,
40 That dolphin-torn, that gong-tormented sea.

Crazy Jane and the Bishop

Bring me to the blasted oak
That I, midnight upon the stroke,
(*All find safety in the tomb.*)
May call down curses on his head
5 Because of my dear Jack that's dead.

Coxcomb was the least he said
The solid man and the coxcomb.

Nor was he Bishop when his ban
Banished Jack the Journeyman,
10   (*All find safety in the tomb.*)
Nor so much as parish priest,
Yet he, an old book in his fist,
Cried that we lived like beast and beast:
The solid man and the coxcomb.

15   The Bishop has a skin, God knows,
Wrinkled like the foot of a goose,
(*All find safety in the tomb.*)
Nor can he hide in holy black
The heron's hunch upon his back,
20   But a birch-tree stood my Jack
The solid man and the coxcomb.

Jack had my virginity,
And bids me to the oak, for he
(*All find safety in the tomb.*)
25   Wanders out into the night
And there is shelter under it,
But should that other come, I spit:
The solid man and the coxcomb.

Crazy Jane Reproved

I care not what the sailors say:
All those dreadful thunder-stones,
All that storm that blots the day
Can but show that Heaven yawns;
5   Great Europa played the fool
That changed a lover for a bull
Fol de rol, fol de rol.

To round that shell's elaborate whorl,
Adorning every secret track
10   With the delicate mother-of-pearl,
Made the joints of Heaven crack:
So never hang your heart upon
A roaring, ranting journeyman
Fol de rol, fol de rol.

Crazy Jane and the Bishop 6 coxcomb: a fool, named
for a cap which resembles a cock's comb worn by jesters.
9 Jack the Journeyman: a tramp, the name of character
in a Yeats play.

Crazy Jane Reproved 5 Europa: Zeus changed into a
bull and carried her off to Crete, where he raped her.

Crazy Jane on the Day of Judgment

'Love is all
Unsatisfied
That cannot take the whole
Body and soul';
5   *And that is what Jane said.*

'Take the sour
If you take me,
I can scoff and lour
And scold for an hour.'
10   *'That's certainly the case,' said he.*

'Naked I lay,
The grass my bed;
Naked and hidden away,
That black day';
15   *And that is what Jane said.*

'What can be shown?
What true love be?
All could be known or shown
If Time were but gone.'
20   *'That's certainly the case,' said he.*

Crazy Jane and Jack the Journeyman

I know, although when looks meet
I tremble to the bone,
The more I leave the door unlatched
The sooner love is gone,
5   For love is but a skein unwound
Between the dark and dawn.

A lonely ghost the ghost is
That to God shall come;
I – love's skein upon the ground,
10   My body in the tomb –
Shall leap into the light lost
In my mother's womb.

But were I left to lie alone
In an empty bed,
15   The skein so bound us ghost to ghost
When he turned his head
Passing on the road that night,
Mine must walk when dead.

Crazy Jane on God

That lover of a night
Came when he would,
Went in the dawning light
Whether I would or no;
5   Men come, men go;
All things remain in God.

Banners choke the sky;
Men-at-arms tread;
Armoured horses neigh
10   Where the great battle was
In the narrow pass:
All things remain in God.

Before their eyes a house
That from childhood stood
15   Uninhabited, ruinous,
Suddenly lit up
From door to top:
All things remain in God.

I had wild Jack for a lover;
20   Though like a road
That men pass over
My body makes no moan
But sings on:
All things remain in God.

Crazy Jane Talks with the Bishop

I met the Bishop on the road
And much said he and I.
'Those breasts are flat and fallen now,
Those veins must soon be dry;
5   Live in a heavenly mansion,
Not in some foul sty.'

'Fair and foul are near of kin,
And fair needs foul,' I cried.
'My friends are gone, but that's a truth
10   Nor grave nor bed denied,
Learned in bodily lowliness
And in the heart's pride.

'A woman can be proud and stiff
When on love intent;

15 But Love has pitched his mansion in
    The place of excrement;
    For nothing can be sole or whole
    That has not been rent.'

The Statues

Pythagoras planned it. Why did the people stare?
His numbers, though they moved or seemed to move
In marble or in bronze, lacked character.
But boys and girls, pale from the imagined love
5   Of solitary beds, knew what they were,
That passion could bring character enough,
And pressed at midnight in some public place
Live lips upon a plummet-measured face.

No! Greater than Pythagoras, for the men
10 That with a mallet or a chisel modelled these
Calculations that look but casual flesh, put down
All Asiatic vague immensities,
And not the banks of oars that swam upon
The many-headed foam at Salamis.
15 Europe put off that foam when Phidias
Gave women dreams and dreams their looking-glass.

One image crossed the many-headed, sat
Under the tropic shade, grew round and slow,
No Hamlet thin from eating flies, a fat
20 Dreamer of the Middle Ages. Empty eyeballs knew
That knowledge increases unreality, that
Mirror on mirror mirrored is all the show.
When gong and conch declare the hour to bless
Grimalkin crawls to Buddha's emptiness.

25 When Pearse summoned Cuchulain to his side.
What stalked through the Post Office? What intellect,
What calculation, number, measurement, replied?
We Irish, born into that ancient sect
But thrown upon this filthy modern tide
30 And by its formless spawning fury wrecked,
Climb to our proper dark, that we may trace
The lineaments of a plummet-measured face.

Statues 1 **Pythagoras:** doctrine of numbers by which all things are harmoniously related, or not, according to a system of exact measurements. 14 **Salamis:** Greek island where a famous victory over the Persians was won. 15 **Phidias:** famous Greek sculptor, known for creating life-like statues. 24 **Grimalkin:** a cat. 25 **Cuchulain:** legendary Irish warrior of great strength. **Pearse:** President of the Irish Republicans.

The Circus Animals' Desertion

I

I sought a theme and sought for it in vain,
I sought it daily for six weeks or so.
Maybe at last, being but a broken man,
I must be satisfied with my heart, although
5   Winter and summer till old age began
My circus animals were all on show,
Those stilted boys, that burnished chariot,
Lion and woman and the Lord knows what.

II

What can I but enumerate old themes?
10   First that sea-rider Oisin led by the nose
Through three enchanted islands, allegorical dreams,
Vain gaiety, vain battle, vain repose,
Themes of the embittered heart, or so it seems,
That might adorn old songs or courtly shows;
15   But what cared I that set him on to ride,
I, starved for the bosom of his faery bride?

And then a counter-truth filled out its play,
The Countess Cathleen was the name I gave it;
She, pity-crazed, had given her soul away,
20   But masterful Heaven had intervened to save it.
I thought my dear must her own soul destroy,
So did fanaticism and hate enslave it,
And this brought forth a dream and soon enough
This dream itself had all my thought and love.

25   And when the Fool and Blind Man stole the bread
Cuchulain fought the ungovernable sea;
Heart-mysteries there, and yet when all is said
It was the dream itself enchanted me:
Character isolated by a deed
30   To engross the present and dominate memory.
Players and painted stage took all my love,
And not those things that they were emblems of.

III

Those masterful images because complete
Grew in pure mind, but out of what began?
35   A mound of refuse or the sweepings of a street,
Old kettles, old bottles, and a broken can,
Old iron, old bones, old rags, that raving slut

---

10 Oisin: long-lived poet of Irish legend.   **18** *The Countess Cathleen*: Yeats play, which he wrote for Maud Gonne.

Who keeps the till. Now that my ladder's gone,
I must lie down where all the ladders start
40   In the foul rag-and-bone shop of the heart.

Under Ben Bulben

I

Swear by what the sages spoke
Round the Mareotic Lake
That the Witch of Atlas knew,
Spoke and set the cocks a-crow.

5   Swear by those horsemen, by those women
Complexion and form prove superhuman,
That pale, long-visaged company
That air in immortality
Completeness of their passions won;
10   Now they ride the wintry dawn
Where Ben Bulben sets the scene.

Here's the gist of what they mean.

II

Many times man lives and dies
Between his two eternities,
15   That of race and that of soul,
And ancient Ireland knew it all.
Whether man die in his bed
Or the rifle knocks him dead,
A brief parting from those dear
20   Is the worst man has to fear.
Though grave-diggers' toil is long,
Sharp their spades, their muscles strong.
They but thrust their buried men
Back in the human mind again.

III

25   You that Mitchel's prayer have heard,
'Send war in our time, O Lord!'
Know that when all words are said
And a man is fighting mad,
Something drops from eyes long blind,
30   He completes his partial mind,
For an instant stands at ease,

Ben Bulben: mountain north of Sligo where Yeats lived. **2 Mareotic Lake:** or sea, wilderness know for monasticism in the 4th century. **3 Witch of Atlas:** symbolised beauty in Shelley poem of this name.   **25 Mitchel:** John Mitchel, 19th century Irish patriot whose prayer was 'Give us war in our time, O Lord'.

Laughs aloud, his heart at peace.
Even the wisest man grows tense
With some sort of violence
35 Before he can accomplish fate,
Know his work or choose his mate.

IV

Poet and sculptor, do the work,
Nor let the modish painter shirk
What his great forefathers did.
40 Bring the soul of man to God,
Make him fill the cradles right.

Measurement began our might:
Forms a stark Egyptian thought,
Forms that gentler Phidias wrought.
45 Michael Angelo left a proof
On the Sistine Chapel roof,
Where but half-awakened Adam
Can disturb globe-trotting Madam
Till her bowels are in heat,
50 Proof that there's a purpose set
Before the secret working mind:
Profane perfection of mankind.

Quattrocento put in paint
On backgrounds for a God or Saint
55 Gardens where a soul's at ease;
Where everything that meets the eye,
Flowers and grass and cloudless sky,
Resemble forms that are or seem
When sleepers wake and yet still dream.
60 And when it's vanished still declare,
With only bed and bedstead there,
That heavens had opened.
                              Gyres run on;
When that greater dream had gone
Calvert and Wilson, Blake and Claude,
65 Prepared a rest for the people of God,
Palmer's phrase, but after that
Confusion fell upon our thought.

V

Irish poets, earn your trade,
Sing whatever is well made,

---

64 **Calvert:** probably Edward Calvert, 19th century English visionary artist. **Wilson:** probably Richard Wilson, 18th century landscape painter. 64 **Claude:** Claude Lorrain, French artist famous for his views of Italy. 66 **Palmer:** Samuel Palmer, 19th century English painter of visionary landscapes.

70 Scorn the sort now growing up
All out of shape from toe to top,
Their unremembering hearts and heads
Base-born products of base beds.
Sing the peasantry, and then
75 Hard-riding country gentlemen,
The holiness of monks, and after
Porter-drinkers' randy laughter;
Sing the lords and ladies gay
That were beaten into the clay
80 Through seven heroic centuries;
Cast your mind on other days
That we in coming days may be
Still the indomitable Irishry.

VI

Under bare Ben Bulben's head
85 In Drumcliff churchyard Yeats is laid.
An ancestor was rector there
Long years ago, a church stands near,
By the road an ancient cross.
No marble, no conventional phrase;
90 On limestone quarried near the spot
By his command these words are cut:
Cast a cold eye
On life, on death.
Horseman, pass by!

RURALISTS AND WAR POETS

The horror of the First World War (1914–18) prompted many to look back to the period immediately before the conflict as an idyll. A nostalgia for a bucolic poetry, often based on a classical idiom, which celebrated the English countryside, was confronted with the carnage of the battlefields. The well-educated, affluent, refined young gentlemen who read and wrote pastoral in the first decade of the twentieth century were destroyed in the trenches of western France. The following selection attempts to show the contrasting nature of the poetry produced in peace and war.

A.E. HOUSMAN (1859–1936)

A celebrated Classicist, Housman's collection of lyrics *A Shropshire Lad* (1896) was widely read as a celebration of a vanishing England and became particularly popular during the First World War. Wenlock Edge is a ridge in Shropshire near to which stood the Roman town of Uricon.

---

85 **Drumcliff**: small country churchyard where during the early 19th century, John Yeats had been rector.

On Wenlock Edge

On Wenlock Edge the wood's in trouble;
His forest fleece the Wrekin heaves;
The gale, it plies the saplings double,
And thick on Severn snow the leaves.

5   'Twould blow like this through holt and hanger
When Uricon the city stood:
'Tis the old wind in the old anger,
But then it threshed another wood.

Then, 'twas before my time, the Roman
10   At yonder heaving hill would stare:
The blood that warms an English yeoman,
The thoughts that hurt him, they were there.

There, like the wind through woods in riot,
Through him the gale of life blew high;
15   The tree of man was never quiet:
Then 'twas the Roman, now 'tis I.

The gale, it plies the saplings double,
It blows so hard, 'twill soon be gone:
To-day the Roman and his trouble
20   Are ashes under Uricon.

EDWARD THOMAS (1878–1917)

A dedicated observer of landscape and its history, Thomas wrote substantial prose and journalism about nature, attempting to convey the spirit of the English countryside. An encounter with the American poet Robert Frost in 1914 prompted him to employ his rhythmical but plain diction in the writing of poetry.

Adlestrop

Yes. I remember Adlestrop –
The name, because one afternoon
Of heat the express train drew up there
Unwontedly. It was late June.

5   The steam hissed. Someone cleared his throat.
No one left and no one came
On the bare platform. What I saw
Was Adlestrop – only the name

And willows, willow-herb, and grass,
10   And meadowsweet; and haycocks dry,

No whit less still and lonely fair
Than the high cloudlets in the sky.

And for that minute a blackbird sang
Close by, and round him, mistier,
15 Farther and farther, all the birds
Of Oxfordshire and Gloucestershire.

SIEGFRIED SASSOON (1886–1967)

As a soldier, Sassoon became disillusioned with an establishment he felt was deliberately prolonging the war. His poetry attempts to convey the sense of waste in the trenches.

Attack

At dawn the ridge emerges massed and dun
In the wild purple of the glow'ring sun,
Smouldering through spouts of drifting smoke that shroud
The menacing scarred slope; and, one by one,
5 Tanks creep and topple forward to the wire.
The barrage roars and lifts. Then, clumsily bowed
With bombs and guns and shovels and battle-gear,
Men jostle and climb to meet the bristling fire.
Lines of grey, muttering faces, masked with fear,
10 They leave their trenches, going over the top,
While time ticks blank and busy on their wrists,
And hope, with furtive eyes and grappling fists,
Flounders in mud. O Jesus, make it stop!

ISAAC ROSENBERG (1890–1918)

Rosenberg's unadorned verse often has a detached and fragmented quality about it which foreshadows styles developed by modernists such as T.S. Eliot in the 1920s.

Break of Day in the Trenches

The darkness crumbles away –
It is the same old druid Time as ever.
Only a live thing leaps my hand –
A queer sardonic rat –
5 As I pull the parapet's poppy
To stick behind my ear.
Droll rat, they would shoot you if they knew
Your cosmopolitan sympathies.

Now you have touched this English hand
10 You will do the same to a German –
Soon, no doubt, if it be your pleasure
To cross the sleeping green between.
It seems you inwardly grin as you pass
Strong eyes, fine limbs, haughty athletes
15 Less chanced than you for life,
Bonds to the whims of murder,
Sprawled in the bowels of the earth,
The torn fields of France.
What do you see in our eyes
20 At the shrieking iron and flame
Hurled through still heavens?
What quaver – what heart aghast?
Poppies whose roots are in man's veins
Drop, and are ever dropping;
25 But mine in my ear is safe,
Just a little white with the dust.

WILFRED OWEN (1893–1918)

Owen's early verse reveals a Romanticism which initially attracted many of the War Poets. His later poetry, composed shortly before his death in battle, shows less exuberance and an angrier, more bitter tone. Indeed, it was to further a poetry he described as 'in no sense consolatory' that, after a period of injury in 1918, he requested to return to the trenches. He was killed one week before the armistice. His best poetry vividly conveys the meaningless destruction of an entire generation.

Anthem for Doomed Youth

What passing-bells for these who die as cattle?
    Only the monstrous anger of the guns.
    Only the stuttering rifles' rapid rattle
Can patter out their hasty orisons.
5 No mockeries for them from prayers or bells,
    Nor any voice of mourning save the choirs, –
The shrill, demented choirs of wailing shells;
    And bugles calling for them from sad shires.

What candles may be held to speed them all?
10 Not in the hands of boys, but in their eyes
Shall shine the holy glimmers of good-byes.
    The pallor of girls' brows shall be their pall;
Their flowers the tenderness of silent minds,
And each slow dusk a drawing-down of blinds.

Dulce et Decorum Est

Bent double, like old beggars under sacks,
Knock-kneed, coughing like hags, we cursed through sludge,
Till on the haunting flares we turned our backs
And towards our distant rest began to trudge.
5   Men marched asleep. Many had lost their boots
But limped on, blood-shod. All went lame; all blind;
Drunk with fatigue; deaf even to the hoots
Of tired, outstripped Five-Nines that dropped behind.

Gas! Gas! Quick, boys! – An ecstasy of fumbling,
10 Fitting the clumsy helmets just in time;
But someone still was yelling out and stumbling
And flound'ring like a man in fire or lime . . .
Dim, through the misty panes and thick green light,
As under a green sea, I saw him drowning.

15 In all my dreams, before my helpless sight,
He plunges at me, guttering, choking, drowning.

If in some smothering dreams you too could pace
Behind the wagon that we flung him in,
And watch the white eyes writhing in his face,
20 His hanging face, like a devil's sick of sin;
If you could hear, at every jolt, the blood
Come gargling from the froth-corrupted lungs,
Obscene as cancer, bitter as the cud
Of vile, incurable sores on innocent tongues, –
25 My friend, you would not tell with such high zest
To children ardent for some desperate glory,
The old Lie: *Dulce et decorum est*
Pro patria mori.

Strange Meeting

It seemed that out of battle I escaped
Down some profound dull tunnel, long since scooped
Through granites which titanic wars had groined.
Yet also there encumbered sleepers groaned,
5 Too fast in thought or death to be bestirred.
Then, as I probed them, one sprang up, and stared
With piteous recognition in fixed eyes,
Lifting distressful hands as if to bless.
And by his smile, I knew that sullen hall,

Dulce . . . : 'It is sweet and proper to die for the homeland'. Roman sentiment, illustrating the type of patriotism taught as an ideal to young gentlemen.

10   By his dead smile I knew we stood in Hell.
       With a thousand pains that vision's face was grained;
       Yet no blood reached there from the upper ground,
       And no guns thumped, or down the flues made moan.
       'Strange friend,' I said, 'here is no cause to mourn.'
15   'None,' said that other, 'save the undone years,
       The hopelessness. Whatever hope is yours,
       Was my life also; I went hunting wild
       After the wildest beauty in the world,
       Which lies not calm in eyes, or braided hair,
20   But mocks the steady running of the hour,
       And if it grieves, grieves richlier than here.
       For of my glee might many men have laughed,
       And of my weeping something had been left,
       Which must die now. I mean the truth untold,
25   The pity of war, the pity war distilled.
       Now men will go content with what we spoiled,
       Or, discontent, boil bloody, and be spilled.
       They will be swift with swiftness of the tigress.
       None will break ranks, though nations trek from progress.
30   Courage was mine, and I had mystery,
       Wisdom was mine, and I had mastery:
       To miss the march of this retreating world
       Into vain citadels that are not walled.
       Then, when much blood had clogged their chariot-wheels,
35   I would go up and wash them from sweet wells,
       Even with truths that lie too deep for taint.
       I would have poured my spirit without stint
       But not through wounds; not on the cess of war.
       Foreheads of men have bled where no wounds were.
40   I am the enemy you killed, my friend.
       I knew you in this dark: for so you frowned
       Yesterday through me as you jabbed and killed.
       I parried; but my hands were loath and cold.
       Let us sleep now. . . .'

JAMES JOYCE (1882–1941)

Joyce is the Irish and European writer who catapulted Ireland out of a British provincialism and who, with Yeats, helped demonstrate that this small country was capable of producing a distinctive world-class literature. At the core of Joyce's writing is his relation with Dublin, the city where he was born, and from which he became a voluntary exile. To write, not only the consciousness, but the unconsciousness of its inhabitants, each of his four major works – *Dubliners*, *A Portrait of the Artist as a Young Man*, *Ulysses* and *Finnegans Wake* – shows Joyce developing ever more complex stylistic and narrative techniques.

From Dubliners

Dubliners is a collection of short stories through which Joyce wished to present Dublin to the world. Joyce's Dubliners inhabit a city of slender economic means and, though frequently articulate, are rarely capable of realising their potentials. In these stories Joyce developed his idea of the epiphany, the sudden moment of realisation which dispels illusion, though rarely bringing any comfort.

Araby

North Richmond Street, being blind, was a quiet street except at the hour when the Christian Brothers' School set the boys free. An uninhabited house of two stories stood at the blind end, detached from its neighbours in a square ground. The other houses of the street, conscious of decent lives within them, gazed at one another with brown imperturbable faces.

The former tenant of our house, a priest, had died in the back drawing-room. Air, musty from having been long enclosed, hung in all the rooms, and the waste room behind the kitchen was littered with old useless papers. Among these I found a few paper-covered books, the pages of which were curled and damp: *The Abbot*, by Walter Scott, *The Devout Communicant* and *The Memoirs of Vidocq*. I liked the last best because its leaves were yellow. The wild garden behind the house contained a central apple-tree and a few straggling bushes, under one of which I found the late tenant's rusty bicycle-pump. He had been a very charitable priest; in his will he had left all his money to institutions and the furniture of his house to his sister.

When the short days of winter came, dusk fell before we had well eaten our dinners. When we met in the street the houses had grown sombre. The space of sky above us was the colour of ever-changing violet and towards it the lamps of the street lifted their feeble lanterns. The cold air stung us and we played till our bodies glowed. Our shouts echoed in the silent street. The career of our play brought us through the dark muddy lanes behind the houses, where we ran the gauntlet of the rough tribes from the cottages, to the back doors of the dark dripping gardens where odours arose from the ashpits, to the dark odorous stables where a coachman smoothed and combed the horse or shook music from the buckled harness. When we returned to the street, light from the kitchen windows had filled the areas. If my uncle was seen turning the corner we hid in the shadow until we had seen him safely housed. Or if Mangan's sister came out on the doorstep to call her brother in to his tea, we watched her from our shadow peer up and down the street. We waited to see whether she would remain or go in and, if she remained, we left our shadow and walked up to Mangan's steps resignedly. She was waiting for us, her figure defined by the light from the half-opened door. Her brother always teased her before he obeyed, and I stood by the railings looking at her. Her dress swung as she moved her body, and the soft rope of her hair tossed from side to side.

Every morning I lay on the floor in the front parlour watching her door. The blind was pulled down to within an inch of the sash so that I could not be seen. When she came out on the doorstep my heart leaped. I ran to the hall, seized my books and followed her. I kept her brown figure always in my eye and, when we came near the point at which our ways diverged, I quickened my pace and passed her. This happened morning after morning. I had never spoken to her, except for a few casual words, and yet her name was like a summons to all my foolish blood.

Her image accompanied me even in places the most hostile to romance. On Saturday evenings when my aunt went marketing I had to go to carry some of the parcels. We walked through the flaring streets, jostled by drunken men and bargaining women, amid the curses of labourers, the shrill litanies of shop-boys who stood on guard by the barrels of pigs' cheeks, the nasal chanting of street-singers, who sang a *come-all-you* about O' Donovan Rossa, or a ballad about the troubles in our native land. These noises converged in a single sensation of life for me: I imagined that I bore my chalice safely through a throng of foes. Her name sprang to my lips at moments in strange prayers and praises which I myself did not understand. My eyes were often full of tears (I could not tell why) and at times a flood from my heart seemed to pour itself out into my bosom. I thought little of the future. I did not know whether I would ever speak to her or not or, if I spoke to her, how I could tell her of my confused adoration. But my body was like a harp and her words and gestures were like fingers running upon the wires.

One evening I went into the back drawing-room in which the priest had died. It was a dark rainy evening and there was no sound in the house. Through one of the broken panes I heard the rain impinge upon the earth, the fine incessant needles of water playing in the sodden beds. Some distant lamp or lighted window gleamed below me. I was thankful that I could see so little. All my senses seemed to desire to veil themselves and, feeling that I was about to slip from them, I pressed the palms of my hands together until they trembled, murmuring: 'O *love* O *love!*' many times.

At last she spoke to me. When she addressed the first words to me I was so confused that I did not know what to answer. She asked me was I going to Araby. I forgot whether I answered yes or no. It would be a splendid bazaar; she said she would love to go.

'And why can't you?' I asked.

While she spoke she turned a silver bracelet round and round her wrist. She could not go, she said, because there would be a retreat that week in her convent. Her brother and two other boys were fighting for their caps, and I was alone at the railings. She held one of the spikes, bowing her head towards me. The light from the lamp opposite our door caught the white curve of her neck, lit up her hair that rested there and, falling, lit up the hand upon the railing. It fell over one side of her dress and caught the white border of a petticoat, just visible as she stood at ease.

'It's well for you,' she said.

'If I go,' I said, 'I will bring you something.'

What innumerable follies laid waste my waking and sleeping thoughts after that evening! I wished to annihilate the tedious intervening days. I chafed against the work of school. At night in my bedroom and by day in the class room her image came between me and the page I strove to read. The syllables of the word Araby were called to me through the silence in which my soul luxuriated and cast an Eastern enchantment over me. I asked for leave to go to the bazaar on Saturday night. My aunt was surprised, and hoped it was not some Freemason affair. I answered few questions in class. I watched my master's face pass from amiability to sternness; he hoped I was not beginning to idle. I could not call my wandering thoughts together. I had hardly any patience with the serious work of life which, now that it stood between me and my desire, seemed to me child's play, ugly monotonous child's play.

On Saturday morning I reminded my uncle that I wished to go to the bazaar in the evening. He was fussing at the hallstand, looking for the hat-brush, and answered me curtly: 'Yes, boy, I know.'

As he was in the hall I could not go into the front parlour and lie at the window. I felt the house in bad humour and walked slowly towards the school. The air was pitilessly raw and already my heart misgave me.

When I came home to dinner my uncle had not yet been home. Still it was early. I sat staring at the clock for some time and, when its ticking began to irritate me, I left the room. I mounted the staircase and gained the upper part of the house. The high, cold, empty, gloomy rooms liberated me and I went from room to room singing. From the front window I saw my companions playing below in the street. Their cries reached me weakened and indistinct and, leaning my forehead against the cool glass, I looked over at the dark house where she lived. I may have stood there for an hour, seeing nothing but the brown-clad figure cast by my imagination, touched discreetly by the lamplight at the curved neck, at the hand upon the railings and at the border below the dress.

When I came down stairs again I found Mrs. Mercer sitting at the fire. She was an old, garrulous woman, a pawnbroker's widow, who collected used stamps for some pious purpose. I had to endure the gossip of the tea-table. The meal was prolonged beyond an hour and still my uncle did not come. Mrs. Mercer stood up to go: she was sorry she couldn't wait any longer, but it was after eight o'clock and she did not like to be out late, as the night air was bad for her. When she had gone I began to walk up and down the room, clenching my fists. My aunt said:

'I'm afraid you may put off your bazaar for this night of Our Lord.'

At nine o'clock I heard my uncle's latchkey in the hall door. I heard him talking to himself and heard the hallstand rocking when it had received the weight of his overcoat. I could interpret these signs. When he was midway through his dinner I asked him to give me the money to go to the bazaar. He had forgotten.

'The people are in bed and after their first sleep now,' he said.

I did not smile. My aunt said to him energetically:

'Can't you give him the money and let him go? You've kept him late enough as it is.'

My uncle said he was very sorry he had forgotten. He said he believed in the old saying: 'All work and no play makes Jack a dull boy.' He asked me where I was going and, when I had told him a second time, he asked me did I know *The Arab's Farewell to his Steed*. When I left the kitchen he was about to recite the opening lines of the piece to my aunt.

I held a florin tightly in my hand as I strode down Buckingham Street towards the station. The sight of the streets thronged with buyers and glaring with gas recalled to me the purpose of my journey. I took my seat in a third-class carriage of a deserted train. After an intolerable delay the train moved out of the station slowly. It crept onward among ruinous houses and over the twinkling river. At Westland Row Station a crowd of people pressed to the carriage doors; but the porters moved them back, saying that it was a special train for the bazaar. I remained alone in the bare carriage. In a few minutes the train drew up beside an improvised wooden platform. I passed out on to the road and saw by the lighted dial of a clock that it was ten minutes to ten. In front of me was a large building which displayed the magical name.

I could not find any sixpenny entrance and, fearing that the bazaar would be closed, I passed in quickly through a turnstile, handing a shilling to a weary-looking man. I found myself in a big hall girded at half its height by a gallery. Nearly all the stalls were closed and the greater part of the hall was in darkness. I recognized a silence like that which pervades a church after a service. I walked into the centre of the bazaar timidly. A few people were gathered about the stalls which were still open. Before a curtain, over which the words *Cafe Chantant* were written in coloured lamps, two men were counting money on a salver. I listened to the fall of the coins.

Remembering with difficulty why I had come, I went over to one of the stalls and examined porcelain vases and flowered tea-sets. At the door of the stall a young lady was talking and laughing with two young gentlemen. I remarked their English accents and listened vaguely to their conversation.

'O, I never said such a thing!'

'O, but you did!'

'O, but I didn't!'

'Didn't she say that?'

'Yes. I heard her.'

'O, there's a . . . fib!'

Observing me, the young lady came over and asked me did I wish to buy anything. The tone of her voice was not encouraging; she seemed to have spoken to me out of a sense of duty. I looked humbly at the great jars that stood like eastern guards at either side of the dark entrance to the stall and murmured:

'No, thank you.'

The young lady changed the position of one of the vases and went back to the two young men. They began to talk of the same subject. Once or twice the young lady glanced at me over her shoulder.

I lingered before her stall, though I knew my stay was useless, to make my interest in her wares seem the more real. Then I turned away slowly and walked down the middle of the bazaar. I allowed the two pennies to fall against the sixpence in my pocket. I heard a voice call from one end of the gallery that the light was out. The upper part of the hall was now completely dark.

Gazing up into the darkness I saw myself as a creature driven and derided by vanity; and my eyes burned with anguish and anger.

From Ulysses

Written between 1914 and 1921 in three cities – Trieste, Zurich, Paris – *Ulysses* is a voyage around Dublin, presenting the life of the city on a single day, 16 June 1904. *Ulysses'* sections are loosely structured on *The Odyssey*; its title is the Latin form of Odysseus, the Greek hero of Homer's epic who spends 10 years after the Trojan wars attempting to return home. Joyce's hero is Leopold Bloom, a Dublin Jew, and one of the concerns of the book is Bloom's attempt to rebuild a family around his unfaithful wife, Molly, and Stephen Dedalus, the character based on Joyce himself, who has returned from exile to his native city. But in a wider sense, *Ulysses* offers, in all its fragmented and random experience, the consciousness of the city at a particular historic moment. The following episode, 'Aeolus' in Joyce's Odyssey model, is set around newspaper offices and considers, among other things, issues of Irish nationalism in a city whose centre is presided over by Nelson's column, the visible symbol of British rule. Joyce set out to defy the usual narrative expectations of the novel, and this is well illustrated in this section by his mimicking of a popular newspaper's propensity to seek exaggerated headlines which have, at best, only an incidental relation to the story. Here it is as though a demented editor has played havoc with the flow and structure of the narrative by generating as many spurious headlines as he can.

IN THE HEART OF THE HIBERNIAN METROPOLIS

Before Nelson's pillar trams slowed, shunted, changed trolley, started for Blackrock, Kingstown and Dalkey, Clonskea, Rathgar and Terenure, Palmerston Park and upper Rathmines, Sandymount Green, Rathmines, Ringsend and Sandymount Tower, Harold's Cross. The hoarse Dublin United Tramway Company's timekeeper bawled them off:

– Rathgar and Terenure!

– Come on, Sandymount Green!

Right and left parallel clanging ringing a doubledecker and a singledeck moved from their railheads, swerved to the down line, glided parallel.

– Start, Palmerston Park!

THE WEARER OF THE CROWN

Under the porch of the general post office shoeblacks called and polished. Parked in North Prince's street His Majesty's vermilion mailcars, bearing on their sides the royal initials, E. R., received loudly flung sacks of letters, postcards, lettercards, parcels, insured and paid, for local, provincial, British and overseas delivery.

GENTLEMEN OF THE PRESS

Grossbooted draymen rolled barrels dullthudding out of Prince's stores and bumped them up on the brewery float. On the brewery float bumped dullthudding barrels rolled by grossbooted draymen out of Prince's stores.

– There it is, Red Murray said. Alexander Keyes.

– Just cut it out, will you? Mr Bloom said, and I'll take it round to the *Telegraph* office.

The door of Ruttledge's office creaked again. Davy Stephens, minute in a large capecoat, a small felt hat crowning his ringlets, passed out with a roll of papers under his cape, a king's courier.

Red Murray's long shears sliced out the advertisement from the newspaper in four clean strokes. Scissors and paste.

– I'll go through the printing works, Mr Bloom said, taking the cut square.

– Of course, if he wants a par, Red Murray said earnestly, a pen behind his ear, we can do him one.

– Right, Mr Bloom said with a nod. I'll rub that in.

We.

WILLIAM BRAYDEN, ESQUIRE, OF OAKLANDS, SANDYMOUNT

Red Murray touched Mr Bloom's arm with the shears and whispered:

– Brayden.

Mr Bloom turned and saw the liveried porter raise his lettered cap as a stately figure entered between the newsboards of the *Weekly Freeman and National Press* and the *Freeman's Journal and National Press*. Dullthudding Guinness's barrels. It passed statelily up the staircase, steered by an umbrella, a solemn beardframed face. The broadcloth back ascended each step: back. All his brains are in the nape of his neck, Simon Dedalus says. Welts of flesh behind on him. Fat folds of neck, fat, neck, fat, neck.

– Don't you think his face is like Our Saviour? Red Murray whispered.

The door of Ruttledge's office whispered: ee: cree. They always build one door opposite another for the wind to. Way in. Way out.

Our Saviour: beardframed oval face: talking in the dusk. Mary, Martha. Steered by an umbrella sword to the footlights: Mario the tenor.

– Or like Mario, Mr Bloom said.

– Yes, Red Murray agreed. But Mario was said to be the picture of Our Saviour.

Jesusmario with rougy cheeks, doublet and spindle legs. Hand on his heart. In *Martha*.

> Co-ome thou lost one,
> Co-ome thou dear one!

THE CROZIER AND THE PEN

– His grace phoned down twice this morning, Red Murray said gravely. They watched the knees, legs, boots vanish. Neck.

A telegram boy stepped in nimbly, threw an envelope on the counter and stepped off posthaste with a word:

– *Freeman*!

Mr Bloom said slowly:

– Well, he is one of our saviours also.

A meek smile accompanied him as he lifted the counterflap, as he passed in through a sidedoor and along the warm dark stairs and passage, along the now reverberating boards. But will he save the circulation? Thumping. Thumping.

He pushed in the glass swingdoor and entered, stepping over strewn packing paper. Through a lane of clanking drums he made his way towards Nannetti's reading closet.

WITH UNFEIGNED REGRET IT IS WE ANNOUNCE THE DISSOLUTION OF A MOST RESPECTED DUBLIN BURGESS

Hynes here too: account of the funeral probably. Thumping. Thump. This morning the remains of the late Mr Patrick Dignam. Machines. Smash a man to atoms if they got him caught. Rule the world today. His machineries are pegging away too. Like these, got out of hand: fermenting. Working away, tearing away. And that old grey rat tearing to get in.

HOW A GREAT DAILY ORGAN IS TURNED OUT

Mr Bloom halted behind the foreman's spare body, admiring a glossy crown.

Strange he never saw his real country. Ireland my country. Member for College green. He boomed that workaday worker tack for all it was worth. It's the ads and side features sell a weekly, not the stale news in the official gazette. Queen Anne is dead. Published by authority in the year one thousand and. Demesne situate in the townland of Rosenallis, barony of Tinnahinch. To all whom it may concern schedule pursuant to statute showing return of number of mules and jennets exported from Ballina. Nature notes. Cartoons. Phil Blake's weekly Pat and Bull story. Uncle Toby's page for tiny tots. Country bumpkin's queries. Dear Mr Editor, what is a good cure for flatulence? I'd like that part. Learn a lot teaching others. The personal note. M. A. P. Mainly all pictures. Shapely bathers on golden strand. World's biggest balloon. Double marriage of sisters celebrated. Two bridegrooms laughing heartily at each other. Cuprani too, printer. More Irish than the Irish.

The machines clanked in threefour time. Thump, thump, thump. Now if he got paralysed there and no-one knew how to stop them they'd clank on and on the same, print it over and over and up and back. Monkeydoodle the whole thing. Want a cool head.

– Well, get it into the evening edition, councillor, Hynes said.

Soon be calling him my lord mayor. Long John is backing him, they say.

The foreman, without answering, scribbled press on a corner of the sheet and made a sign to a typesetter. He handed the sheet silently over the dirty glass screen.

– Right: thanks, Hynes said moving off.

Mr Bloom stood in his way.

– If you want to draw the cashier is just going to lunch, he said, pointing backward with his thumb.

– Did you? Hynes asked.

– Mm, Mr Bloom said. Look sharp and you'll catch him.

– Thanks, old man, Hynes said. I'll tap him too.

He hurried on eagerly towards the *Freeman's Journal* office.

Three bob I lent him in Meagher's. Three weeks. Third hint.

WE SEE THE CANVASSER AT WORK

Mr Bloom laid his cutting on Mr Nannetti's desk.

– Excuse me, councillor, he said. This ad, you see. Keyes, you remember?

Mr Nannetti considered the cutting awhile and nodded.

– He wants it in for July, Mr Bloom said. The foreman moved his pencil towards it.

– But wait, Mr Bloom said. He wants it changed. Keyes, you see. He wants two keys at the top.

Hell of a racket they make. He doesn't hear it. Nannan. Iron nerves. Maybe he understands what I.

The foreman turned round to hear patiently and, lifting an elbow, began to scratch slowly in the armpit of his alpaca jacket.

– Like that, Mr Bloom said, crossing his forefingers at the top.

Let him take that in first.

Mr Bloom, glancing sideways up from the cross he had made, saw the foreman's sallow face, think he has a touch of jaundice, and beyond the obedient reels feeding in huge webs of paper. Clank it. Clank it. Miles of it unreeled. What becomes of it after? O, wrap up meat, parcels: various uses, thousand and one things.

Slipping his words deftly into the pauses of the clanking he drew swiftly on the scarred woodwork.

HOUSE OF KEY(E)S

– Like that, see. Two crossed keys here. A circle. Then here the name. Alexander Keyes, tea, wine and spirit merchant. So on.

Better not teach him his own business.

– You know yourself, councillor, just what he wants. Then round the top in leaded: the house of keys. You see? Do you think that's a good idea?

The foreman moved his scratching hand to his lower ribs and scratched there quietly.

– The idea, Mr Bloom said, is the house of keys. You know, councillor, the Manx parliament. Innuendo of home rule. Tourists, you know, from the isle of Man. Catches the eye, you see. Can you do that?

I could ask him perhaps about how to pronounce that *voglio*. But then if he didn't know only make it awkward for him. Better not.

– We can do that, the foreman said. Have you the design?

– I can get it, Mr Bloom said. It was in a Kilkenny paper. He has a house there too. I'll just run out and ask him. Well, you can do that and just a little par calling attention. You know the usual. Highclass licensed premises. Longfelt want. So on.

The foreman thought for an instant.

– We can do that, he said. Let him give us a three months' renewal.

A typesetter brought him a limp galleypage. He began to check it silently. Mr Bloom stood by, hearing the loud throbs of cranks, watching the silent typesetters at their cases.

ORTHOGRAPHICAL

Want to be sure of his spelling. Proof fever. Martin Cunningham forgot to give us his spellingbee conundrum this morning. It is amusing to view the unpar one ar alleled embarra two ars is it? double ess ment of a harassed pedlar while gauging au the symmetry of a peeled pear under a cemetery wall. Silly, isn't it? Cemetery put in of course on account of the symmetry.

I should have said when he clapped on his topper. Thank you. I ought to have said something about an old hat or something. No. I could have said. Looks as good as new now. See his phiz then.

Sllt. The nethermost deck of the first machine jogged forward its flyboard with sllt the first batch of quirefolded papers. Sllt. Almost human the way it sllt to call attention. Doing its level best to speak. That door too sllt creaking, asking to be shut. Everything speaks in its own way. Sllt.

NOTED CHURCHMAN AN OCCASIONAL CONTRIBUTOR

The foreman handed back the galleypage suddenly, saying:

– Wait. Where's the archbishop's letter? It's to be repeated in the *Telegraph*. Where's what's his name?

He looked about him round his loud unanswering machines.

– Monks, sir? a voice asked from the castingbox.

– Ay. Where's Monks?

– Monks!

Mr Bloom took up his cutting. Time to get out.

– Then I'll get the design, Mr Nannetti, he said, and you'll give it a good place I know.

– Monks!

– Yes, sir.

Three months' renewal. Want to get some wind off my chest first. Try it anyhow. Rub in August: good idea: horseshow month. Ballsbridge. Tourists over for the show.

A DAYFATHER

He walked on through the caseroom passing an old man, bowed, spectacled, aproned. Old Monks, the dayfather. Queer lot of stuff he must have put through his hands in his time: obituary notices, pubs' ads, speeches, divorce suits, found drowned. Nearing the end of his tether now. Sober serious man with a bit in the savingsbank I'd say. Wife a good cook and washer. Daughter working the machine in the parlour. Plain Jane, no damn nonsense.

AND IT WAS THE FEAST OF THE PASSOVER

He stayed in his walk to watch a typesetter neatly distributing type. Reads it backwards first. Quickly he does it. Must require some practice that. mangiD kcirtaP. Poor papa with his hagadah book, reading backwards with his finger to me. Pessach. Next year in Jerusalem. Dear, O dear! All that long business about that brought us out of the land of Egypt and into the house of bondage *alleluia*. *Shema Israel Adonai Elohenu*. No, that's the other. Then the twelve brothers, Jacob's sons. And then the lamb and the cat and the dog and the stick and the water and the butcher. And then the angel of death kills the butcher and he kills the ox and the dog kills the cat. Sounds a bit silly till you come to look into it well. Justice it means but it's everybody eating everyone else. That's what life is after all. How quickly he does that job. Practice makes perfect. Seems to see with his fingers.

Mr Bloom passed on out of the clanking noises through the gallery on to the landing. Now am I going to tram it out all the way and then catch him out perhaps. Better phone him up first. Number? Yes. Same as Citron's house. Twentyeight. Twentyeight double four.

ONLY ONCE MORE THAT SOAP

He went down the house staircase. Who the deuce scrawled all over those walls with matches? Looks as if they did it for a bet. Heavy greasy smell there always is in those works. Lukewarm glue in Thom's next door when I was there.

He took out his handkerchief to dab his nose. Citronlemon? Ah, the soap I put there. Lose it out of that pocket. Putting back his handkerchief he took out the soap and stowed it away, buttoned, into the hip pocket of his trousers.

What perfume does your wife use? I could go home still: tram: something I forgot. Just to see: before: dressing. No. Here. No.

A sudden screech of laughter came from the *Evening Telegraph* office. Know who that is. What's up? Pop in a minute to phone. Ned Lambert it is.

He entered softly.

ERIN, GREEN GEM OF THE SILVER SEA

– The ghost walks, professor MacHugh murmured softly, biscuitfully to the dusty windowpane.

Mr Dedalus, staring from the empty fireplace at Ned Lambert's quizzing face, asked of it sourly:

– Agonising Christ, wouldn't it give you a heartburn on your arse?

Ned Lambert, seated on the table, read on:

– *Or again, note the meanderings of some purling rill as it babbles on its way, tho' quarrelling with the stony obstacles, to the tumbling waters of Neptune's blue domain, 'mid mossy banks, fanned by gentlest zephyrs, played on by the glorious sunlight or 'neath the shadows cast o'er its pensive bosom by the overarching leafage of the giants of the forest.* What about that, Simon? he asked over the fringe of his newspaper. How's that for high?

– Changing his drink, Mr Dedalus said.

Ned Lambert, laughing, struck the newspaper on his knees, repeating:

– *The pensive bosom and the overarsing leafage.* O boys! O boys!

– And Xenophon looked upon Marathon, Mr Dedalus said, looking again on the fireplace and to the window, and Marathon looked on the sea.

– That will do, professor MacHugh cried from the window. I don't want to hear any more of the stuff.

He ate off the crescent of water biscuit he had been nibbling and, hungered, made ready to nibble the biscuit in his other hand.

High falutin stuff. Bladderbags. Ned Lambert is taking a day off I see. Rather upsets a man's day, a funeral does. He has influence they say. Old Chatterton, the vicechancellor, is his granduncle or his greatgranduncle. Close on ninety they say. Subleader for his death written this long time perhaps. Living to spite them. Might go first himself. Johnny, make room for your uncle. The right honourable Hedges Eyre Chatterton. Daresay he writes him an odd shaky cheque or two on gale days. Windfall when he kicks out. Alleluia.

– Just another spasm, Ned Lambert said.

– What is it? Mr Bloom asked.

– A recently discovered fragment of Cicero, professor MacHugh answered with pomp of tone. *Our lovely land.*

SHORT BUT TO THE POINT

– Whose land? Mr Bloom said simply.

– Most pertinent question, the professor said between his chews. With an accent on the whose.

– Dan Dawson's land Mr Dedalus said.

– Is it his speech last night? Mr Bloom asked.

Ned Lambert nodded.

– But listen to this, he said.

The doorknob hit Mr Bloom in the small of the back as the door was pushed in.

– Excuse me, J. J. O'Molloy said, entering.

Mr Bloom moved nimbly aside.

– I beg yours, he said.

– Good day, Jack.

– Come in. Come in.

– Good day.

– How are you, Dedalus?

– Well. And yourself? J. J. O'Molloy shook his head.

SAD

Cleverest fellow at the junior bar he used to be. Decline, poor chap. That hectic flush spells finis for a man. Touch and go with him. What's in the wind, I wonder. Money worry.

– *Or again if we but climb the serried mountain peaks.*

– You're looking extra.

– Is the editor to be seen? J. J. O'Molloy asked, looking towards the inner door.

– Very much so, professor MacHugh said. To be seen and heard. He's in his sanctum with Lenehan.

J. J. O'Molloy strolled to the sloping desk and began to turn back the pink pages of the file.

Practice dwindling. A mighthavebeen. Losing heart. Gambling. Debts of honour. Reaping the whirlwind. Used to get good retainers from D. and T. Fitzgerald. Their wigs to show the grey matter. Brains on their sleeve like the statue in Glasnevin. Believe he does some literary work for the *Express* with Gabriel Conroy. Wellread fellow. Myles Crawford began on the *Independent*. Funny the way those newspaper men veer about when they get wind of a new opening. Weathercocks. Hot and cold in the same breath. Wouldn't know which to believe. One story good till you hear the next. Go for one another baldheaded in the papers and then all blows over. Hailfellow well met the next moment.

– Ah, listen to this for God' sake, Ned Lambert pleaded. *Or again if we but climb the serried mountain peaks . . .*

– Bombast! the professor broke in testily. Enough of the inflated windbag!

– *Peaks*, Ned Lambert went on, *towering high on high, to bathe our souls, as it were . . .*

– Bathe his lips, Mr Dedalus said. Blessed and eternal God! Yes? Is he taking anything for it?

– *As 'twere, in the peerless panorama of Ireland's portfolio, unmatched, despite their wellpraised prototypes in other vaunted prize regions, for very beauty, of bosky grove and undulating plain and luscious pastureland of vernal green, steeped in the transcendent translucent glow of our mild mysterious Irish twilight . . .*

HIS NATIVE DORIC

– The moon, professor MacHugh said. He forgot Hamlet.

– *That mantles the vista far and wide and wait till the glowing orb of the moon shine forth to irradiate her silver effulgence . . .*

– O! Mr Dedalus cried, giving vent to a hopeless groan. Shite and onions! That'll do, Ned. Life is too short.

He took off his silk hat and, blowing out impatiently his bushy moustache, welshcombed his hair with raking fingers.

Ned Lambert tossed the newspaper aside, chuckling with delight. An instant after a hoarse bark of laughter burst over professor MacHugh's unshaven blackspectacled face.

– Doughy Daw! he cried.

WHAT WETHERUP SAID

All very fine to jeer at it now in cold print but it goes down like hot cake that stuff. He was in the bakery line too, wasn't he? Why they call him Doughy Daw. Feathered his nest well anyhow. Daughter engaged to that chap in the inland revenue office with the motor. Hooked that nicely. Entertainments. Open house. Big blowout. Wetherup always said that. Get a grip of them by the stomach.

The inner door was opened violently and a scarlet beaked face, crested by a comb of feathery hair, thrust itself in. The bold blue eyes stared about them and the harsh voice asked:

– What is it?

– And here comes the sham squire himself! professor MacHugh said grandly.

– Getonouthat, you bloody old pedagogue! the editor said in recognition.

– Come, Ned, Mr Dedalus said, putting on his hat. I must get a drink after that.

– Drink! the editor cried. No drinks served before mass.

– Quite right too, Mr Dedalus said, going out. Come on, Ned. Ned Lambert sidled down from the table. The editor's blue eyes roved towards Mr Bloom's face, shadowed by a smile.

– Will you join us, Myles? Ned Lambert asked.

MEMORABLE BATTLES RECALLED

– North Cork militia! the editor cried, striding to the mantelpiece. We won every time! North Cork and Spanish officers!

– Where was that, Myles? Ned Lambert asked with a reflective glance at his toecaps.

– In Ohio! the editor shouted.

– So it was, begad, Ned Lambert agreed. Passing out he whispered to J. J. O'Molloy:

– Incipient jigs. Sad case.

– Ohio! the editor crowed in high treble from his uplifted scarlet face. My Ohio!

– A perfect cretic! the professor said. Long, short and long.

O, HARP EOLIAN!

He took a reel of dental floss from his waistcoat pocket and, breaking off a piece, twanged it smartly between two and two of his resonant unwashed teeth.

– Bingbang, bangbang.

Mr Bloom, seeing the coast clear, made for the inner door.

– Just a moment, Mr Crawford, he said. I just want to phone about an ad.
He went in.

– What about that leader this evening? professor MacHugh asked, coming to
the editor and laying a firm hand on his shoulder.

– That'll be all right, Myles Crawford said more calmly. Never you fret. Hello,
Jack. That's all right.

– Good day, Myles, J. J. O'Molloy said, letting the pages he held slip limply
back on the file. Is that Canada swindle case on today?

The telephone whirred inside.

– Twentyeight . . . No, twenty . . . Double four . . . Yes.

SPOT THE WINNER

Lenehan came out of the inner office with *Sport's* tissues.

– Who wants a dead cert for the Gold cup? he asked. Sceptre with O.
Madden up.

He tossed the tissues on to the table.

Screams of newsboys barefoot in the hall rushed near and the door was flung
open.

– Hush, Lenehan said. I hear feetstoops.

Professor MacHugh strode across the room and seized the cringing urchin by
the collar as the others scampered out of the hall and down the steps. The
tissues rustled up in the draught, floated softly in the air blue scrawls and under
the table came to earth.

– It wasn't me, sir. It was the big fellow shoved me, sir.

– Throw him out and shut the door, the editor said. There's a hurricane
blowing.

Lenehan began to paw the tissues up from the floor, grunting as he stooped
twice.

– Waiting for the racing special, sir, the newsboy said. It was Pat Farrell shoved
me, sir.

He pointed to two faces peering in round the doorframe.

– Him, sir.

– Out of this with you, professor MacHugh said gruffly.

He hustled the boy out and banged the door to.

J. J. O'Molloy turned the files cracklingly over, murmuring, seeking:

– Continued on page six, column four.

– Yes, *Evening Telegraph* here, Mr Bloom phoned from the inner office. Is the
boss . . . ? Yes, *Telegraph* . . . To where?. . . Aha! Which auction rooms?. . . Aha!
I see . . . Right. I'll catch him.

A COLLISION ENSUES

The bell whirred again as he rang off. He came in quickly and bumped against
Lenehan who was struggling up with the second tissue.

— *Pardon, monsieur*, Lenehan said, clutching him for an instant and making a grimace.

— My fault, Mr Bloom said, suffering his grip. Are you hurt? I'm in a hurry.

— Knee, Lenehan said.

He made a comic face and whined, rubbing his knee:

— The accumulation of the *anno Domini*.

— Sorry, Mr Bloom said.

He went to the door and, holding it ajar, paused. J. J. O'Molloy slapped the heavy pages over. The noise of two shrill voices, a mouthorgan, echoed in the bare hallway from the newsboys squatted on the doorsteps:

> *We are the boys of Wexford*
> *Who fought with heart and hand.*

EXIT BLOOM

— I'm just running round to Bachelor's walk, Mr Bloom said, about this ad of Keyes's. Want to fix it up. They tell me he's round there in Dillon's.

He looked indecisively for a moment at their faces. The editor who, leaning against the mantelshelf, had propped his head on his hand, suddenly stretched forth an arm amply.

— Begone! he said. The world is before you.

— Back in no time, Mr Bloom said, hurrying out.

J. J. O'Molloy took the tissues from Lenehan's hand and read them, blowing them apart gently, without comment.

— He'll get that advertisement, the professor said, staring through his black-rimmed spectacles over the crossblind. Look at the young scamps after him.

— Show. Where? Lenehan cried, running to the window.

A STREET CORTEGE

Both smiled over the crossblind at the file of capering newsboys in Mr Bloom's wake, the last zigzagging white on the breeze a mocking kite, a tail of white bowknots.

— Look at the young guttersnipe behind him hue and cry, Lenehan said, and you'll kick. O, my rib risible! Taking off his flat spaugs and the walk. Small nines. Steal upon larks.

He began to mazurka in swift caricature across the floor on sliding feet past the fireplace to J. J. O'Molloy who placed the tissues in his receiving hands.

— What's that? Myles Crawford said with a start. Where are the other two gone?

— Who? the professor said, turning. They're gone round to the Oval for a drink. Paddy Hooper is there with Jack Hall. Came over last night.

— Come on then, Myles Crawford said. Where's my hat?

He walked jerkily into the office behind, parting the vent of his jacket, jingling his keys in his back pocket. They jingled then in the air and against the wood as he locked his desk drawer.

— He's pretty well on, professor MacHugh said in a low voice.

– Seems to be, J. J. O'Molloy said, taking out a cigarettecase in murmuring meditation, but it is not always as it seems. Who has the most matches?

THE CALUMET OF PEACE

He offered a cigarette to the professor and took one himself. Lenehan promptly struck a match for them and lit their cigarettes in turn. J. J. O'Molloy opened his case again and offered it.

– *Thanky vous*, Lenehan said, helping himself. The editor came from the inner office, a straw hat awry on his brow. He declaimed in song, pointing sternly at professor MacHugh:

> *'Twas rank and fame that tempted thee,*
> *'Twas empire charmed thy heart.*

The professor grinned, locking his long lips.

– Eh? You bloody old Roman empire? Myles Crawford said.

He took a cigarette from the open case. Lenehan, lighting it for him with quick grace, said:

– Silence for my brandnew riddle!

– *Imperium romanum*, J. J. O'Molloy said gently. It sounds nobler than British or Brixton. The word reminds one somehow of fat in the fire.

Myles Crawford blew his first puff violently towards the ceiling.

– That's it, he said. We are the fat. You and I are the fat in the fire. We haven't got the chance of a snowball in hell.

THE GRANDEUR THAT WAS ROME

– Wait a moment, professor MacHugh said, raising two quiet claws. We mustn't be led away by words, by sounds of words. We think of Rome, imperial, imperious, imperative.

He extended elocutionary arms from frayed stained shirtcuffs, pausing:

– What was their civilisation? Vast, I allow: but vile. Cloacae: sewers. The jews in the wilderness and on the mountaintop said: *It is meet to be here. Let us build an altar to Jehovah.* The Roman, like the Englishman who follows in his footsteps, brought to every new shore on which he set his foot (on our shore he never set it) only his cloacal obsession. He gazed about him in his toga and he said: *It is meet to be here. Let us construct a watercloset.*

– Which they accordingly did do, Lenehan said. Our old ancient ancestors, as we read in the first chapter of Guinness's, were partial to the running stream.

– They were nature's gentlemen, J. J. O'Molloy murmured. But we have also Roman law.

– And Pontius Pilate is its prophet, professor MacHugh responded.

– Do you know that story about chief baron Palles? J. J. O'Molloy asked. It was at the royal university dinner. Everything was going swimmingly . . .

– First my riddle, Lenehan said. Are you ready?

Mr O'Madden Burke, tall in copious grey of Donegal tweed, came in from the hallway. Stephen Dedalus, behind him, uncovered as he entered.

– *Entrez, mes enfants!* Lenehan cried.

– I escort a suppliant, Mr O'Madden Burke said melodiously. Youth led by Experience visits Notoriety.

– How do you do? the editor said, holding out a hand. Come in. Your governor is just gone.

? ? ?

Lenehan said to all:

– Silence! What opera resembles a railwayline? Reflect, ponder, excogitate, reply.

Stephen handed over the typed sheets, pointing to the title and signature.

– Who? the editor asked.

Bit torn off.

– Mr Garrett Deasy, Stephen said.

– That old pelters, the editor said. Who tore it? Was he short taken?

> *On swift sail flaming*
> *From storm and south*
> *He comes, pale vampire,*
> *Mouth to my mouth.*

– Good day, Stephen, the professor said, coming to peer over their shoulders. Foot and mouth? Are you turned . . . ?

Bullockbefriending bard.

SHINDY IN WELLKNOWN RESTAURANT

– Good day, sir, Stephen answered blushing. The letter is not mine. Mr Garrett Deasy asked me to . . .

– O, I know him, Myles Crawford said, and I knew his wife too. The bloodiest old tartar God ever made. By Jesus, she had the foot and mouth disease and no mistake! The night she threw the soup in the waiter's face in the Star and Garter. Oho!

A woman brought sin into the world. For Helen, the runaway wife of Menelaus, ten years the Greeks. O'Rourke, prince of Breffni.

– Is he a widower? Stephen asked.

– Ay, a grass one, Myles Crawford said, his eye running down the typescript. Emperor's horses. Habsburg. An Irishman saved his life on the ramparts of Vienna. Don't you forget! Maximilian Karl O'Donnell, graf von Tirconnell in Ireland. Sent his heir over to make the king an Austrian fieldmarshal now. Going to be trouble there one day. Wild geese. O yes, every time. Don't you forget that!

– The moot point is did he forget it, J. J. O'Molloy said quietly, turning a horseshoe paperweight. Saving princes is a thankyou job.

Professor MacHugh turned on him.

– And if not? he said.

– I'll tell you how it was, Myles Crawford began. A Hungarian it was one day . . .

LOST CAUSES
NOBLE MARQUESS MENTIONED

– We were always loyal to lost causes, the professor said. Success for us is the death of the intellect and of the imagination. We were never loyal to the successful. We serve them. I teach the blatant Latin language. I speak the tongue of a race the acme of whose mentality is the maxim: time is money. Material domination. Domine! Lord! Where is the spirituality? Lord Jesus? Lord Salisbury? A sofa in a westend club. But the Greek!

KYRIE ELEISON!

A smile of light brightened his darkrimmed eyes, lengthened his long lips.
– The Greek! he said again. *Kyrios!* Shining word! The vowels the Semite and the Saxon know not. *Kyrie!* The radiance of the intellect. I ought to profess Greek, the language of the mind. *Kyrie eleison!* The closetmaker and the cloacamaker will never be lords of our spirit. We are liege subjects of the catholic chivalry of Europe that foundered at Trafalgar and of the empire of the spirit, not an *imperium*, that went under with the Athenian fleets at Aegospotami. Yes, yes. They went under. Pyrrhus, misled by an oracle, made a last attempt to retrieve the fortunes of Greece. Loyal to a lost cause.
He strode away from them towards the window.
– They went forth to battle, Mr O'Madden Burke said greyly, but they always fell.
– Boohoo! Lenehan wept with a little noise. Owing to a brick received in the latter half of the matinée. Poor, poor, poor Pyrrhus!
He whispered then near Stephen's ear:

LENEHAN'S LIMERICK

There's a ponderous pundit MacHugh
Who wears goggles of ebony hue.
As he mostly sees double
To wear them why trouble?
I can't see the Joe Miller. Can you?

In mourning for Sallust, Mulligan says. Whose mother is beastly dead Myles Crawford crammed the sheets into a sidepocket.
– That'll be all right, he said. I'll read the rest after. That'll be all right.
Lenehan extended his hands in protest.
– But my riddle! he said. What opera is like a railwayline?
– Opera? Mr O'Madden Burke's sphinx face reriddled.
Lenehan announced gladly:
– *The Rose of Castile.* See the wheeze? Rows of cast steel. Gee!
He poked Mr O'Madden Burke mildly in the spleen. Mr O'Madden Burke fell back with grace on his umbrella, feigning a gasp.
– Help! he sighed. I feel a strong weakness.
Lenehan, rising to tiptoe, fanned his face rapidly with the rustling tissues.

The professor, returning by way of the files, swept his hand across Stephen's and Mr O'Madden Burke's loose ties.

– Paris, past and present, he said. You look like communards.

– Like fellows who had blown up the Bastile, J. J. O'Molloy said in quiet mockery. Or was it you shot the lord lieutenant of Finland between you? You look as though you had done the deed. General Bobrikoff.

– We were only thinking about it, Stephen said.

OMNIUM GATHERUM

– All the talents, Myles Crawford said. Law, the classics . . .

– The turf, Lenehan put in.

– Literature, the press.

– If Bloom were here, the professor said. The gentle art of advertisement.

– And Madam Bloom, Mr O'Madden Burke added. The vocal muse. Dublin's prime favourite.

Lenehan gave a loud cough.

– Ahem! he said very softly. O, for a fresh of breath air! I caught a cold in the park. The gate was open.

"YOU CAN DO IT!"

The editor laid a nervous hand on Stephen's shoulder.

– I want you to write something for me, he said. Something with a bite in it. You can do it. I see it in your face. *In the lexicon of youth* . . .

See it in your face. See it in your eye. Lazy idle little schemer.

– Foot and mouth disease! the editor cried in scornful invective. Great nationalist meeting in Borris-in-Ossory. All balls! Bulldosing the public! Give them something with a bite in it. Put us all into it, damn its soul. Father, Son and Holy Ghost and Jakes M'Carthy.

– We can all supply mental pabulum, Mr O'Madden Burke said. Stephen raised his eyes to the bold unheeding stare.

– He wants you for the pressgang, J. J. O'Molloy said.

THE GREAT GALLAHER

– You can do it, Myles Crawford repeated, clenching his hand in emphasis. Wait a minute. We'll paralyse Europe as Ignatius Gallaher used to say when he was on the shaughraun, doing billiardmarking in the Clarence. Gallaher, that was a pressman for you. That was a pen. You know how he made his mark? I'll tell you. That was the smartest piece of journalism ever known. That was in eightyone, sixth of May, time of the invincibles, murder in the Phoenix park, before you were born, I suppose. I'll show you.

He pushed past them to the files.

– Look at here, he said turning. *The New York World* cabled for a special. Remember that time?

Professor MacHugh nodded.

– *New York World*, the editor said, excitedly pushing back his straw hat. Where it took place. Tim Kelly, or Kavanagh I mean. Joe Brady and the rest of them. Where Skin-the-Goat drove the car. Whole route, see?

– Skin-the-Goat, Mr O'Madden Burke said. Fitzharris. He has that cabman's shelter, they say, down there at Butt bridge. Holohan told me. You know Holohan?

– Hop and carry one, is it? Myles Crawford said.

– And poor Gumley is down there too, so he told me, minding stones for the corporation. A night watchman.

Stephen turned in surprise.

– Gumley? he said. You don't say so? A friend of my father's, is it?

– Never mind Gumley, Myles Crawford cried angrily. Let Gumley mind the stones, see they don't run away. Look at here. What did Ignatius Gallaher do? I'll tell you. Inspiration of genius. Cabled right away. Have you *Weekly Freeman* of 17 March? Right. Have you got that?

He flung back pages of the files and stuck his finger on a point.

– Take page four, advertisement for Bransome's coffee, let us say. Have you got that? Right.

The telephone whirred.

A DISTANT VOICE

– I'll answer it, the professor said, going.

– B is parkgate. Good.

His finger leaped and struck point after point, vibrating.

– T is viceregal lodge. C is where murder took place. K is Knockmaroon gate.

The loose flesh of his neck shook like a cock's wattles. An illstarched dicky jutted up and with a rude gesture he thrust it back into his waistcoat.

– Hello? *Evening Telegraph* here. Hello? . . . Who's there? . . . Yes . . . Yes . . . Yes . . .

– F to P is the route Skin-the-Goat drove the car for an alibi, Inchicore, Roundtown, Windy Arbour, Palmerston Park, Ranelagh. F. A. B. P. Got that? X is Davy's publichouse in upper Leeson street.

The professor came to the inner door.

– Bloom is at the telephone, he said.

– Tell him go to hell, the editor said promptly. X is Davy's publichouse, see?

CLEVER, VERY

– Clever, Lenehan said. Very.

– Gave it to them on a hot plate, Myles Crawford said, the whole bloody history. Nightmare from which you will never awake.

– I saw it, the editor said proudly. I was present. Dick Adams, the besthearted bloody Corkman the Lord ever put the breath of life in, and myself. Lenehan bowed to a shape of air, announcing:

– Madam, I'm Adam. And Able was I ere I saw Elba.

– History! Myles Crawford cried. The Old Woman of Prince's street was there first. There was weeping and gnashing of teeth over that. Out of an advertisement. Gregor Grey made the design for it. That gave him the leg up. Then Paddy Hooper worked Tay Pay who took him on to the *Star*. Now he's got in with Blumenfeld. That's press. That's talent. Pyatt! He was all their daddies!

– The father of scare journalism, Lenehan confirmed, and the brother-in-law of Chris Callinan.

– Hello? Are you there? Yes, he's here still. Come across yourself.

– Where do you find a pressman like that now, eh? the editor cried. He flung the pages down.

– Clamn dever, Lenehan said to Mr O'Madden Burke.

– Very smart, Mr O'Madden Burke said. Professor MacHugh came from the inner office.

– Talking about the invincibles, he said, did you see that some hawkers were up before the recorder.

– O yes, J. J. O'Molloy said eagerly. Lady Dudley was walking home through the park to see all the trees that were blown down by that cyclone last year and thought she'd buy a view of Dublin. And it turned out to be a commemoration postcard of Joe Brady or Number One or Skin-the-Goat. Right outside the viceregal lodge, imagine!

– They're only in the hook and eye department, Myles Crawford said. Psha! Press and the bar! Where have you a man now at the bar like those fellows, like Whiteside, like Isaac Butt, like silvertongued O'Hagan. Eh? Ah, bloody nonsense. Only in the halfpenny place!

His mouth continued to twitch unspeaking in nervous curls of disdain.

Would anyone wish that mouth for her kiss? How do you know? Why did you write it then?

RHYMES AND REASONS

Mouth, south. Is the mouth south someway? Or the south a mouth? Must be some. South, pout, out, shout, drouth. Rhymes: two men dressed the same, looking the same, two by two.

.... *la tua pace*
. . . . *che parlar ti piace*
. . . *mentreche il vento, come fa, si tace.*

He saw them three by three, approaching girls, in green, in rose, in russet, entwining, *per l'aer perso*, in mauve, in purple, *quella pacifica oriafiamma*, gold of oriflamme, *di rimirar fe piu ardenti*. But I old men, penitent, leadenfooted, underdarkneath the night: mouth south: tomb womb.

– Speak up for yourself, Mr O'Madden Burke said.

SUFFICIENT FOR THE DAY . . .

J. J. O'Molloy, smiling palely, took up the gage.

– My dear Myles, he said, flinging his cigarette aside, you put a false construction on my words. I hold no brief, as at present advised, for the third profession qua profession but your Cork legs are running away with you. Why not bring in Henry Grattan and Flood and Demosthenes and Edmund Burke? Ignatius Gallaher we all know and his Chapelizod boss, Harmsworth of the farthing press, and his American cousin of the Bowery guttersheet not to mention *Paddy Kelly's Budget, Pue's Occurrences* and our watchful friend *The Skibereen Eagle*. Why bring in a master of forensic eloquence like Whiteside? Sufficient for the day is the newspaper thereof.

LINKS WITH BYGONE DAYS OF YORE

– Grattan and Flood wrote for this very paper, the editor cried in his face. Irish volunteers. Where are you now? Established 1763. Dr Lucas. Who have you now like John Philpot Curran? Psha!

– Well, J. J. O'Molloy said, Bushe K. C., for example.

– Bushe? the editor said. Well, yes: Bushe, yes. He has a strain of it in his blood. Kendal Bushe or I mean Seymour Bushe.

– He would have been on the bench long ago, the professor said, only for . . . But no matter.

J. J. O'Molloy turned to Stephen and said quietly and slowly:

– One of the most polished periods I think I ever listened to in my life fell from the lips of Seymour Bushe. It was in that case of fratricide, the Childs murder case. Bushe defended him.

And in the porches of mine ear did pour.

By the way how did he find that out? He died in his sleep. Or the other story, beast with two backs?

– What was that? the professor asked.

ITALIA, MAGISTRA ARTIUM

– He spoke on the law of evidence, J. J. O'Molloy said, of Roman justice as contrasted with the earlier Mosaic code, the *lex talionis*. And he cited the Moses of Michelangelo in the Vatican.

– Ha.

– A few wellchosen words, Lenehan prefaced. Silence! Pause. J. J. O'Molloy took out his cigarettecase.

False lull. Something quite ordinary. Messenger took out his matchbox thoughtfully and lit his cigar. I have often thought since on looking back over that strange time that it was that small act, trivial in itself, that striking of that match, that determined the whole aftercourse of both our lives.

A POLISHED PERIOD

J. J. O'Molloy resumed, moulding his words:

– He said of it: *that stony effigy in frozen music, horned and terrible, of the human form divine, that eternal symbol of wisdom and of prophecy which, if aught that the imagination or the hand of sculptor has wrought in marble of soultransfigured and of soultransfiguring deserves to live, deserves to live.*

His slim hand with a wave graced echo and fall.

– Fine! Myles Crawford said at once.

– The divine afflatus, Mr O'Madden Burke said.

– You like it? J. J. O'Molloy asked Stephen. Stephen, his blood wooed by grace of language and gesture, blushed. He took a cigarette from the case. J. J. O'Molloy offered his case to Myles Crawford. Lenehan lit their cigarettes as before and took his trophy, saying:

– Muchibus thankibus.

A MAN OF HIGH MORALE

– Professor Magennis was speaking to me about you, J. J. O'Molloy said to Stephen. What do you think really of that hermetic crowd, the opal hush poets: A. E. the mastermystic? That Blavatsky woman started it. She was a nice old bag of tricks. A. E. has been telling some yankee interviewer that you came to him in the small hours of the morning to ask him about planes of consciousness. Magennis thinks you must have been pulling A. E.'s leg. He is a man of the very highest morale, Magennis.

Speaking about me. What did he say? What did he say? What did he say about me? Don't ask.

– No, thanks, professor MacHugh said, waving the cigarettecase aside. Wait a moment. Let me say one thing. The finest display of oratory I ever heard was a speech made by John F. Taylor at the college historical society. Mr Justice Fitzgibbon, the present lord justice of appeal, had spoken and the paper under debate was an essay (new for those days), advocating the revival of the Irish tongue.

He turned towards Myles Crawford and said:

– You know Gerald Fitzgibbon. Then you can imagine the style of his discourse.

– He is sitting with T. Healy, J. J. O'Molloy said, rumour has it, on the Trinity college estates commission.

– He is sitting with a sweet thing, Myles Crawford said, in a child's frock. Go on. Well?

– It was the speech, mark you, the professor said, of a finished orator, full of courteous haughtiness and pouring in chastened diction I will not say the vials of his wrath but pouring the proud man's contumely upon the new movement. It was then a new movement. We were weak, therefore worthless.

He closed his long thin lips an instant but, eager to be on, raised an outspanned hand to his spectacles and, with trembling thumb and ringfinger touching lightly the black rims, steadied them to a new focus.

IMPROMPTU

In ferial tone he addressed J. J. O'Molloy:

– Taylor had come there, you must know, from a sickbed. That he had prepared his speech I do not believe for there was not even one shorthandwriter in the hall. His dark lean face had a growth of shaggy beard round it. He wore a loose white silk neckcloth and altogether he looked (though he was not) a dying man.

His gaze turned at once but slowly from J. J. O'Molloy's towards Stephen's face and then bent at once to the ground, seeking. His unglazed linen collar appeared behind his bent head, soiled by his withering hair. Still seeking, he said:

– When Fitzgibbon's speech had ended John F Taylor rose to reply. Briefly, as well as I can bring them to mind, his words were these.

He raised his head firmly. His eyes bethought themselves once more. Witless shellfish swam in the gross lenses to and fro, seeking outlet.

He began:

– *Mr chairman, ladies and gentlemen: Great was my admiration in listening to the remarks addressed to the youth of Ireland a moment since by my learned friend. It seemed to me that I had been transported into a country faraway from this country, into an age remote from this age, that I stood in ancient Egypt and that I was listening to the speech of some highpriest of that land addressed to the youthful Moses.*

His listeners held their cigarettes poised to hear, their smokes ascending in frail stalks that flowered with his speech. *And let our crooked smokes.* Noble words coming. Look out. Could you try your hand at it yourself?

– *And it seemed to me that I heard the voice of that Egyptian highpriest raised in a tone of like haughtiness and like pride. I heard his words and their meaning was revealed to me.*

FROM THE FATHERS

It was revealed to me that those things are good which yet are corrupted which neither if they were supremely good nor unless they were good could be corrupted. Ah, curse you! That's saint Augustine.

– Why will you jews not accept our culture, our religion and our language? You are a tribe of nomad herdsmen: we are a mighty people. You have no cities nor no wealth: our cities are hives of humanity and our galleys, trireme and quadrireme, laden with all manner merchandise furrow the waters of the known globe. You have but emerged from primitive conditions: we have a literature, a priesthood, an agelong history and a polity.

Nile.

Child, man, effigy.

By the Nilebank the babemaries kneel, cradle of bulrushes: a man supple in combat: stonehorned, stonebearded, heart of stone.

– *You pray to a local and obscure idol: our temples, majestic and mysterious, are the abodes of Isis and Osiris, of Horus and Ammon Ra. Yours serfdom, awe and humbleness: ours thunder and the seas. Israel is weak and few are her children: Egypt is an host and terrible are her arms. Vagrants and daylabourers are you called: the world trembles at our name.*

A dumb belch of hunger cleft his speech. He lifted his voice above it boldly:

– *But, ladies and gentlemen, had the youthful Moses listened to and accepted that view of life, had he bowed his head and bowed his will and bowed his spirit before that arrogant admonition he would never have brought the chosen people out of their house of bondage, nor followed the pillar of the cloud by day. He would never*

have spoken with the Eternal amid lightnings on Sinai's mountaintop nor ever have
come down with the light of inspiration shining in his countenance and bearing in
his arms the tables of the law, graven in the language of the outlaw.

He ceased and looked at them, enjoying a silence.

OMINOUS – FOR HIM!

J. J. O'Molloy said not without regret:

– And yet he died without having entered the land of promise.

– A sudden-at-the-moment-though-from-lingering-illness-often-previously-expectorated- demise, Lenehan added. And with a great future behind him.

The troop of bare feet was heard rushing along the hallway and pattering up the staircase.

– That is oratory, the professor said uncontradicted.

Gone with the wind. Hosts at Mullaghmast and Tara of the kings. Miles of ears of porches. The tribune's words, howled and scattered to the four winds. A people sheltered within his voice. Dead noise. Akasic records of all that ever anywhere wherever was. Love and laud him: me no more.

I have money.

– Gentlemen, Stephen said. As the next motion on the agenda paper may I suggest that the house do now adjourn?

– You take my breath away. It is not perchance a French compliment? Mr O'Madden Burke asked. 'Tis the hour, methinks, when the winejug, metaphorically speaking, is most grateful in Ye ancient hostelry.

– That it be and hereby is resolutely resolved. All that are in favour say ay, Lenehan announced. The contrary no. I declare it carried. To which particular boosingshed . . . ? My casting vote is: Mooney's!

He led the way, admonishing:

– We will sternly refuse to partake of strong waters, will we not? Yes, we will not. By no manner of means.

Mr O'Madden Burke, following close, said with an ally's lunge of his umbrella:

– Lay on, Macduff!

– Chip of the old block! the editor cried, clapping Stephen on the shoulder. Let us go. Where are those blasted keys?

He fumbled in his pocket, pulling out the crushed typesheets.

– Foot and mouth. I know. That'll be all right. That'll go in. Where are they? That's all right.

He thrust the sheets back and went into the inner office.

LET US HOPE

J. J. O'Molloy, about to follow him in, said quietly to Stephen:

– I hope you will live to see it published. Myles, one moment.

He went into the inner office, closing the door behind him.

– Come along, Stephen, the professor said. That is fine, isn't it? It has the prophetic vision. *Fuit Ilium!* The sack of windy Troy. Kingdoms of this world. The masters of the Mediterranean are fellaheen today.

The first newsboy came pattering down the stairs at their heels and rushed out into the street, yelling:

– Racing special! Dublin. I have much, much to learn. They turned to the left along Abbey street.

– I have a vision too, Stephen said.

– Yes? the professor said, skipping to get into step. Crawford will follow. Another newsboy shot past them, yelling as he ran:

– Racing special!

DEAR DIRTY DUBLIN

Dubliners.

– Two Dublin vestals, Stephen said, elderly and pious, have lived fifty and fiftythree years in Fumbally's lane.

– Where is that? the professor asked.

– Off Blackpitts, Stephen said. Damp night reeking of hungry dough. Against the wall. Face glistering tallow under her fustian shawl. Frantic hearts. Akasic records. Quicker, darlint!

On now. Dare it. Let there be life.

– They want to see the views of Dublin from the top of Nelson's pillar. They save up three and tenpence in a red tin letterbox moneybox. They shake out the threepenny bits and sixpences and coax out the pennies with the blade of a knife. Two and three in silver and one and seven in coppers. They put on their bonnets and best clothes and take their umbrellas for fear it may come on to rain.

– Wise virgins, professor MacHugh said.

LIFE ON THE RAW

– They buy one and fourpenceworth of brawn and four slices of panloaf at the north city diningrooms in Marlborough street from Miss Kate Collins, proprietress. They purchase four and twenty ripe plums from a girl at the foot of Nelson's pillar to take off the thirst of the brawn. They give two threepenny bits to the gentleman at the turnstile and begin to waddle slowly up the winding staircase, grunting, encouraging each other, afraid of the dark, panting, one asking the other have you the brawn, praising God and the Blessed Virgin, threatening to come down, peeping at the airslits. Glory be to God. They had no idea it was that high. Their names are Anne Kearns and Florence MacCabe. Anne Kearns has the lumbago for which she rubs on Lourdes water, given her by a lady who got a bottleful from a passionist father. Florence MacCabe takes a crubeen and a bottle of double X for supper every Saturday.

– Antithesis, the professor said nodding twice. Vestal virgins. I can see them. What's keeping our friend?

He turned.

A bevy of scampering newsboys rushed down the steps, scattering in all directions, yelling, their white papers fluttering. Hard after them Myles Crawford appeared on the steps, his hat aureoling his scarlet face, talking with J. J. O'Molloy.

– Come along, the professor cried, waving his arm.

He set off again to walk by Stephen's side.

– Yes, he said. I see them.

RETURN OF BLOOM

Mr Bloom, breathless, caught in a whirl of wild newsboys near the offices of the *Irish Catholic* and *Dublin Penny Journal*, called:

– Mr Crawford! A moment!

– *Telegraph*! Racing special!

– What is it? Myles Crawford said, falling back a pace.

A newsboy cried in Mr Bloom's face:

– Terrible tragedy in Rathmines! A child bit by a bellows!

INTERVIEW WITH THE EDITOR

– Just this ad, Mr Bloom said, pushing through towards the steps, puffing, and taking the cutting from his pocket. I spoke with Mr Keyes just now. He'll give a renewal for two months, he says. After he'll see. But he wants a par to call attention in the *Telegraph* too, the Saturday pink. And he wants it copied if it's not too late I told councillor Nannetti from the *Kilkenny People*. I can have access to it in the national library. House of keys, don't you see? His name is Keyes. It's a play on the name. But he practically promised he'd give the renewal. But he wants just a little puff. What will I tell him, Mr Crawford?

K. M. A.

– Will you tell him he can kiss my arse? Myles Crawford said throwing out his arm for emphasis. Tell him that straight from the stable.

A bit nervy. Look out for squalls. All off for a drink. Arm in arm. Lenehan's yachting cap on the cadge beyond. Usual blarney. Wonder is that young Dedalus the moving spirit. Has a good pair of boots on him today. Last time I saw him he had his heels on view. Been walking in muck somewhere. Careless chap. What was he doing in Irishtown?

– Well, Mr Bloom said, his eyes returning, if I can get the design I suppose it's worth a short par. He'd give the ad, I think. I'll tell him . . .

K. M. R. I. A.

– He can kiss my royal Irish arse, Myles Crawford cried loudly over his shoulder. Any time he likes, tell him.

While Mr Bloom stood weighing the point and about to smile he strode on jerkily.

RAISING THE WIND

– *Nulla bona*, Jack, he said, raising his hand to his chin. I'm up to here. I've been through the hoop myself. I was looking for a fellow to back a bill for me

no later than last week. Sorry, Jack. You must take the will for the deed. With a
heart and a half if I could raise the wind anyhow.

J. J. O'Molloy pulled a long face and walked on silently. They caught up on
the others and walked abreast.

– When they have eaten the brawn and the bread and wiped their twenty
fingers in the paper the bread was wrapped in they go nearer to the railings.

– Something for you, the professor explained to Myles Crawford. Two old
Dublin women on the top of Nelson's pillar.

SOME COLUMN! – THAT'S
WHAT WADDLER ONE SAID

– That's new, Myles Crawford said. That's copy. Out for the waxies Dargle.
Two old trickies, what?

– But they are afraid the pillar will fall, Stephen went on. They see the roofs
and argue about where the different churches are: Rathmines' blue dome, Adam
and Eve's, saint Laurence O'Toole's. But it makes them giddy to look so they
pull up their skirts . . .

THOSE SLIGHTLY RAMBUNCTIOUS FEMALES

– Easy all, Myles Crawford said. No poetic licence. We're in the archdiocese
here.

– And settle down on their striped petticoats, peering up at the statue of the
onehandled adulterer.

– Onehandled adulterer! the professor cried. I like that. I see the idea. I see
what you mean.

DAMES DONATE DUBLIN'S CITS
SPEEDPILLS VELOCITOUS AEROLITHS, BELIEF

– It gives them a crick in their necks, Stephen said, and they are too tired to
look up or down or to speak. They put the bag of plums between them and eat
the plums out of it, one after another, wiping off with their handkerchiefs the
plumjuice that dribbles out of their mouths and spitting the plumstones slowly
out between the railings.

He gave a sudden loud young laugh as a close. Lenehan and Mr O'Madden
Burke, hearing, turned, beckoned and led on across towards Mooney's.

– Finished? Myles Crawford said. So long as they do no worse.

SOPHIST WALLOPS HAUGHTY
HELEN SQUARE ON PROBOSCIS. SPARTANS GNASH
MOLARS. ITHACANS VOW PEN IS CHAMP.

– You remind me of Antisthenes, the professor said, a disciple of Gorgias, the
sophist. It is said of him that none could tell if he were bitterer against others or
against himself. He was the son of a noble and a bondwoman. And he wrote a

book in which he took away the palm of beauty from Argive Helen and handed it to poor Penelope.

Poor Penelope. Penelope Rich.

They made ready to cross O'Connell street.

HELLO THERE, CENTRAL!

At various points along the eight lines tramcars with motionless trolleys stood in their tracks, bound for or from Rathmines, Rathfarnham, Blackrock, Kingstown and Dalkey, Sandymount Green, Ringsend and Sandymount Tower, Donnybrook, Palmerston Park and Upper Rathmines, all still, becalmed in short circuit. Hackney cars, cabs, delivery waggons, mailvans, private broughams, aerated mineral water floats with rattling crates of bottles, rattled, rolled, horsedrawn, rapidly.

WHAT? – AND LIKEWISE – WHERE?

– But what do you call it? Myles Crawford asked. Where did they get the plums?

VIRGILLIAN, SAYS PEDAGOGUE. SOPHOMORE PLUMPS FOR OLD MAN MOSES

– Call it, wait, the professor said, opening his long lips wide to reflect. Call it, let me see. Call it: *deus nobis haec otia fecit.*

– No, Stephen said. I call it *A Pisgah Sight of Palestine or The Parable of The Plums.*

– I see, the professor said.

He laughed richly.

– I see, he said again with new pleasure. Moses and the promised land. We gave him that idea, he added to J. J. O'Molloy.

HORATIO IS CYNOSURE THIS FAIR JUNE DAY

J. J. O'Molloy sent a weary sidelong glance towards the statue and held his peace.

– I see, the professor said.

He halted on sir John Gray's pavement island and peered aloft at Nelson through the meshes of his wry smile.

DIMINISHED DIGITS PROVE TOO TITILLATING FOR FRISKY FRUMPS. ANNE WIMBLES, FLO WANGLES – YET CAN YOU BLAME THEM?

– Onehandled adulterer, he said smiling grimly. That tickles me, I must say.

– Tickled the old ones too, Myles Crawford said, if the God Almighty's truth was known.

D.H. LAWRENCE (1885–1930)

Born a miner's son in a working-class environment, Lawrence became a passionate prophetic figure, using fiction to address an England he felt was in danger of losing its vitality through emotional paralysis. In his many stories and novels (notably *Sons and Lovers, The Rainbow, Women in Love, Lady Chatterley's Lover*), his characters may be found seeking a heightened sense of 'Life', one opposed to the narrow, constraining social forces of industrial England. Lawrence believed that fiction was a key human achievement and a force for moral improvement. But he opposed the experimental narrative techniques of Joyce and other modernists, believing them too self-conscious, and developed a distinctive style, both direct and symbolically charged.

The Fox

The two girls were usually known by their surnames, Banford and March. They had taken the farm together, intending to work it all by themselves: that is, they were going to rear chickens, make a living by poultry, and add to this by keeping a cow, and raising one or two young beasts. Unfortunately, things did not turn out well.

Banford was a small, thin, delicate thing with spectacles. She, however, was the principal investor, for March had little or no money. Banford's father, who was a tradesman in Islington, gave his daughter the start, for her health's sake, and because he loved her, and because it did not look as if she would marry. March was more robust. She had learned carpentry and joinery at the evening classes in Islington. She would be the man about the place. They had, moreover, Banford's old grandfather living with them at the start. He had been a farmer. But unfortunately the old man died after he had been at Bailey Farm for a year. Then the two girls were left alone.

They were neither of them young: that is, they were near thirty. But they certainly were not old. They set out quite gallantly with their enterprise. They had numbers of chickens, black Leghorns and white Leghorns, Plymouths and Wyandottes; also some ducks; also two heifers in the fields. One heifer, unfortunately, refused absolutely to stay in the Bailey Farm closes. No matter how March made up the fences, the heifer was out, wild in the woods, or trespassing on the neighbouring pasture, and March and Banford were away, flying after her, with more haste than success. So this heifer they sold in despair. Then, just before the other beast was expecting her first calf, the old man died, and the girls, afraid of the coming event, sold her in a panic, and limited their attentions to fowls and ducks.

In spite of a little chagrin, it was a relief to have no more cattle on hand. Life was not made merely to be slaved away. Both girls agreed in this. The fowls were quite enough trouble. March had set up her carpenter's bench at the end of the open shed. Here she worked, making coops and doors and other appurtenances. The fowls were housed in the bigger building which had served as barn and cowshed in old days. They had a beautiful home, and should have been perfectly content. Indeed, they looked well enough. But the girls were disgusted at their tendency to strange illnesses, at their exacting way of life, and at their refusal, obstinate refusal to lay eggs.

March did most of the outdoor work. When she was out and about, in her puttees and breeches, her belted coat and her loose cap, she looked almost like some graceful, loose-balanced young man, for her shoulders were straight, and her movements easy and confident, even tinged with a little indifference, or irony. But her face was not a man's face, ever. The wisps of her crisp dark hair blew about her as she stooped, her eyes were big and wide and dark, when she looked up again, strange, startled, shy and sardonic at once. Her mouth, too, was almost pinched as if in pain and irony. There was something odd and unexplained about her. She would stand balanced on one hip, looking at the fowls pattering about in the obnoxious fine mud of the sloping yard, and calling to her favourite white hen, which came in answer to her name. But there was an almost satirical flicker in March's big, dark eyes as she looked at her three-toed flock pottering about under her gaze, and the same slight dangerous satire in her voice as she spoke to the favoured Patty, who pecked at March's boot by way of friendly demonstration.

Fowls did not flourish at Bailey Farm, in spite of all that March did for them. When she provided hot food for them in the morning, according to rule, she noticed that it made them heavy and dozy for hours. She expected to see them lean against the pillars of the shed in their languid processes of digestion. And she knew quite well that they ought to be busily scratching and foraging about, if they were to come to any good. So she decided to give them their hot food at night, and let them sleep on it. Which she did. But it made no difference.

War conditions, again, were very unfavourable to poultry keeping. Food was scarce and bad. And when the Daylight Saving Bill was passed, the fowls obstinately refused to go to bed as usual, about nine o'clock in the summer-time. That was late enough, indeed, for there was no peace till they were shut up and asleep. Now they cheerfully walked around, without so much as glancing at the barn, until ten o'clock or later. Both Banford and March disbelieved in living for work alone. They wanted to read or take a cycle-ride in the evening, or perhaps March wished to paint curvilinear swans on porcelain, with green background, or else make a marvellous fire-screen by processes of elaborate cabinet work. For she was a creature of odd whims and unsatisfied tendencies. But from all these things she was prevented by the stupid fowls.

One evil there was greater than any other. Bailey Farm was a little homestead, with ancient wooden barn and low-gabled farmhouse, lying just one field removed from the edge of the wood. Since the war the fox was a demon. He carried off the hens under the very noses of March and Banford. Banford would start and stare through her big spectacles with all her eyes, as another squawk and flutter took place at her heels. Too late! Another white Leghorn gone. It was disheartening.

They did what they could to remedy it. When it became permitted to shoot foxes, they stood sentinel with their guns, the two of them, at the favoured hours. But it was no good. The fox was too quick for them. So another year passed, and another, and they were living on their losses, as Banford said. They let their farmhouse one summer, and retired to live in a railway-carriage that was deposited as a sort of out-house in a corner of the field. This amused them, and helped their finances. None the less, things looked dark.

Although they were usually the best of friends, because Banford, though nervous and delicate, was a warm, generous soul, and March, though so odd and absent in herself, had a strange magnanimity, yet, in the long solitude, they were apt to become a little irritable with one another, tired of one another. March had four-fifths of the work to do, and though she did not mind, there seemed no relief, and it made her eyes flash curiously sometimes. Then Banford, feeling more nerveworn than ever, would become despondent, and March would speak sharply to her. They seemed to be losing ground, somehow, losing hope as the months went by. There alone in the fields by the wood, with the wide country stretching hollow and dim to the round hills of the White Horse, in the far distance, they seemed to have to live too much off themselves. There was nothing to keep them up – and no hope.

The fox really exasperated them both. As soon as they had let the fowls out, in the early summer mornings, they had to take their guns and keep guard: and then again, as soon as evening began to mellow, they must go once more. And he was so sly. He slid along in the deep grass; he was difficult as a serpent to see. And he seemed to circumvent the girls deliberately. Once or twice March had caught sight of the white tip of his brush, or the ruddy shadow of him in the deep grass, and she had let fire at him. But he made no account of this.

One evening March was standing with her back to the sunset, her gun under her arm, her hair pushed under her cap. She was half watching, half musing. It was her constant state. Her eyes were keen and observant, but her inner mind took no notice of what she saw. She was always lapsing into this odd, rapt state, her mouth rather screwed up. It was a question whether she was there, actually conscious present, or not.

The trees on the wood-edge were a darkish, brownish green in the full light – for it was the end of August. Beyond, the naked, copper-like shafts and limbs of the pine-trees shone in the air. Nearer the rough grass, with its long brownish stalks all agleam, was full of light. The fowls were round about – the ducks were still swimming on the pond under the pine-trees. March looked at it all, saw it all, and did not see it. She heard Banford speaking to the fowls in the distance – and she did not hear. What was she thinking about? Heaven knows. Her consciousness was, as it were, held back.

She lowered her eyes, and suddenly saw the fox. He was looking up at her. His chin was pressed down, and his eyes were looking up. They met her eyes. And he knew her. She was spellbound – she knew he knew her. So he looked into her eyes, and her soul failed her. He knew her, he was not daunted.

She struggled, confusedly she came to herself, and saw him making off, with slow leaps over some fallen boughs, slow, impudent jumps. Then he glanced over his shoulder, and ran smoothly away. She saw his brush held smooth like a feather, she saw his white buttocks twinkle. And he was gone, softly, soft as the wind.

She put her gun to her shoulder, but even then pursed her mouth, knowing it was nonsense to pretend to fire. So she began to walk slowly after him, in the direction he had gone, slowly, pertinaciously. She expected to find him. In her heart she was determined to find him. What she would do when she saw him again she did not consider. But she was determined to find him. So she walked abstractedly about on the edge of the wood, with wide, vivid dark eyes, and a faint flush in her cheeks. She did not think. In strange mindlessness she walked hither and thither.

At last she became aware that Banford was calling her. She made an effort of attention, turned, and gave some sort of screaming call in answer. Then again she was striding off towards the homestead. The red sun was setting, the fowls were retiring towards their roost. She watched them, white creatures, black creatures, gathering to the barn. She watched them spellbound, without seeing them. But her automatic intelligence told her when it was time to shut the door.

She went indoors to supper, which Banford had set on the table. Banford chatted easily. March seemed to listen, in her distant, manly way. She answered a brief word now and then. But all the time she was as if spellbound. And as soon as supper was over, she rose again to go out, without saying why.

She took her gun again and went to look for the fox. For he had lifted his eyes upon her, and his knowing look seemed to have entered her brain. She did not so much think of him: she was possessed by him. She saw his dark, shrewd, unabashed eye looking into her, knowing her. She felt him invisibly master her spirit. She knew the way he lowered his chin as he looked up, she knew his muzzle, the golden brown, and the greyish white. And again, she saw him glance over his shoulder at her, half inviting, half contemptuous, and cunning. So she went, with her great startled eyes glowing, her gun under her arm, along the wood edge. Meanwhile the night fell, and a great moon rose above the pine-trees. And again Banford was calling.

So she went indoors. She was silent and busy. She examined her gun, and cleaned it, musing abstractedly by the lamplight. Then she went out again, under the great moon, to see if everything was right. When she saw the dark crests of the pine-trees against the blood-red sky, again her heart beat to the fox, the fox. She wanted to follow him, with her gun.

It was some days before she mentioned the affair to Banford. Then suddenly one evening she said:

'The fox was right at my feet on Saturday night.'

'Where?' said Banford, her eyes opening behind her spectacles.

'When I stood just above the pond.'

'Did you fire?' cried Banford

'No, I didn't.'

'Why not?'

'Why, I was too much surprised, I suppose.'

It was the same old, slow, laconic way of speech March always had. Banford stared at her friend for a few moments.

'You saw him?' she cried.

'Oh yes! He was looking up at me, cool as anything.'

'I tell you,' cried Banford – 'the cheek! They're not afraid of us, Nellie.'

'Oh no,' said March.

'Pity you didn't get a shot at him,' said Banford.

'Isn't it a pity! I've been looking for him ever since. But I don't suppose he'll come so near again.'

'I don't suppose he will,' said Banford.

And she proceeded to forget about it, except that she was more indignant than ever at the impudence of the beggar. March also was not conscious that she thought of the fox. But whenever she fell into her half-musing, when she was half rapt and half intelligently aware of what passed under her vision, then it was the fox which somehow dominated her unconsciousness, possessed the blank half of her musing. And so it was for weeks, and months. No matter whether she had been climbing the trees for the apples, or beating down the last of the damsons, or whether she had been digging out the ditch from the duck-pond, or clearing out the barn, when she had finished, or when she straightened herself, and pushed the wisps of hair away again from her forehead, and pursed up her mouth again in an odd, screwed fashion, much too old for her years, there was sure to come over her mind the old spell of the fox, as it came when he was looking at her. It was as if she could smell him at these times. And it always recurred, at unexpected moments, just as she was going to sleep at night, or just as she was pouring the water into the teapot to make tea – it was the fox, it came over her like a spell.

So the months passed. She still looked for him unconsciously when she went towards the wood. He had become a settled effect in her spirit, a state permanently established, not continuous, but always recurring. She did not know what she felt or thought: only the state came over her, as when he looked at her.

The months passed, the dark evenings came, heavy, dark November, when March went about in high boots, ankle deep in mud, when the night began to fall at four o'clock, and the day never properly dawned. Both girls dreaded these times. They dreaded the almost continuous darkness that enveloped them on their desolate little farm near the wood. Banford was physically afraid. She was afraid of tramps, afraid lest someone should come prowling round. March was not so much afraid as uncomfortable, and disturbed. She felt discomfort and gloom in all her physique.

Usually the two girls had tea in the sitting-room. March lighted a fire at dusk, and put on the wood she had chopped and sawed during the day. Then the long evening was in front, dark, sodden, black outside, lonely and rather oppressive inside, a little dismal. March was content not to talk, but Banford could not keep still. Merely listening to the wind in the pines outside, or the drip of water, was too much for her.

One evening the girls had washed up the tea-things in the kitchen, and March had put on her house-shoes, and taken up a roll of crochet-work, which she worked at slowly from time to time. So she lapsed into silence. Banford stared at the red fire, which, being of wood, needed constant attention. She was afraid to begin to read too early, because her eyes would not bear any strain. So she sat staring at the fire, listening to the distant sounds, sound of cattle lowing, of a dull, heavy, moist wind, of the rattle of the evening train on the little railway not far off. She was almost fascinated by the red glow of the fire.

Suddenly both girls started, and lifted their heads. They heard a footstep – distinctly a footstep. Banford recoiled in fear. March stood listening. Then rapidly she approached the door that led into the kitchen. At the same time they heard the footsteps approach the back door. They waited a second. The back door opened softly. Banford gave a loud cry. A man's voice said softly:

'Hello!'

March recoiled, and took a gun from a corner.

'What do you want?' she cried, in a sharp voice.

Again the soft, softly vibrating man's voice said:

'Hello! What's wrong?'

'I shall shoot!' cried March. 'What do you want?'

'Why, what's wrong? What's wrong?' came the soft, wondering, rather scared voice: and a young soldier, with his heavy kit on his back, advanced into the dim light.

'Why,' he said, 'who lives here then?'

'We live here,' said March. 'What do you want?'

'Oh!' came the long, melodious, wonder-note from the young soldier. 'Doesn't William Grenfel live here then?'

'No – you know he doesn't.'

'Do I? Do I? I don't, you see. He did live here, because he was my grandfather, and I lived here myself five years ago. What's become of him then?'

The young man – or youth, for he would not be more than twenty – now advanced and stood in the inner doorway. March, already under the influence of his strange, soft, modulated voice, stared at him spellbound. He had a ruddy, roundish face, with fairish hair, rather long, flattened to his forehead with sweat. His eyes were blue, and very bright and sharp. On his cheeks, on the fresh ruddy skin were fine, fair hairs, like a down, but sharper. It gave him a slightly glistening look. Having his heavy sack on his shoulders, he stooped, thrusting his head forward. His hat was loose in one hand. He stared brightly, very keenly from girl to girl, particularly at March, who stood pale, with great dilated eyes, in her belted coat and puttees, her hair knotted in a big crisp knot behind. She still had the gun in her hand. Behind her, Banford, clinging to the sofa-arm, was shrinking away, with half-averted head.

'I thought my grandfather still lived here? I wonder if he's dead.'

'We've been here for three years,' said Banford, who was beginning to recover her wits, seeing something boyish in the round head with its rather long sweaty hair.

'Three years! You don't say so! And you don't know who was here before you?'

'I know it was an old man, who lived by himself.'

'Ay! Yes, that's him! And what became of him then?'

'He died. I know he died.'

'Ay! He's dead then!'

The youth stared at them without changing colour or expression. If he had any expression, beside a slight baffled look of wonder, it was one of sharp curiosity concerning the two girls; sharp, impersonal curiosity, the curiosity of that round young head.

But to March he was the fox. Whether it was the thrusting forward of his head, or the glisten of fine whitish hairs on the ruddy cheek-bones, or the bright, keen eyes, that can never be said: but the boy was to her the fox, and she could not see him otherwise.

'How is it you didn't know if your grandfather was alive or dead?' asked Banford, recovering her natural sharpness.

'Ay, that's it,' replied the softly-breathing youth. 'You see I joined up in Canada, and I hadn't heard for three or four years. I ran away to Canada.'

'And now have you just come from France?'

'Well – from Salonika really.'

There was a pause, nobody knowing quite what to say.

'So you've nowhere to go now?' said Banford rather lamely.

'Oh, I know some people in the village. Anyhow, I can go to the Swan.'

'You came on the train, I suppose. Would you like to sit down a bit?'

'Well – I don't mind.'

He gave an odd little groan as he swung off his kit. Banford looked at March.

'Put the gun down,' she said. 'We'll make a cup of tea.'

'Ay,' said the youth. 'We've seen enough of rifles.'

He sat down rather tired on the sofa, leaning forward.

March recovered her presence of mind, and went into the kitchen. There she heard the soft young voice musing:

'Well, to think I should come back and find it like this!' He did not seem sad, not at all – only rather interestedly surprised.

'And what a difference in the place, eh?' he continued, looking round the room.

'You see a difference, do you?' said Banford.

'Yes – don't I?'

His eyes were unnaturally clear and bright, though it was the brightness of abundant health.

March was busy in the kitchen preparing another meal. It was about seven o'clock. All the time, while she was active, she was attending to the youth in the sitting-room, not so much listening to what he said as feeling the soft run of his voice. She primmed up her mouth tighter and tighter, puckering it as if it were sewed, in her effort to keep her will uppermost. Yet her large eyes dilated and glowed in spite of her; she lost herself. Rapidly and carelessly she prepared the meal, cutting large chunks of bread and margarine – for there was no butter. She racked her brain to think of something else to put on the tray – she had only bread, margarine, and jam, and the larder was bare. Unable to conjure anything up, she went into the sitting-room with her tray.

She did not want to be noticed. Above all, she did not want him to look at her. But when she came in, and was busy setting the table just behind him, he pulled himself up from his sprawling, and turned and looked over his shoulder. She became pale and wan.

The youth watched her as she bent over the table, looked at her slim, well-shapen legs, at the belted coat dropping around her thighs, at the knot of dark hair, and his curiosity, vivid and widely alert, was again arrested by her.

The lamp was shaded with a dark-green shade, so that the light was thrown downwards and the upper half of the room was dim. His face moved bright under the light, but March loomed shadowy in the distance.

She turned round, but kept her eyes sideways, dropping and lifting her dark lashes. Her mouth unpuckered as she said to Banford:

'Will you pour out?'

Then she went into the kitchen again.

'Have your tea where you are, will you?' said Banford to the youth – 'unless you'd rather come to the table.'

'Well,' said he, 'I'm nice and comfortable here, aren't I? I will have it here, if you don't mind.'

'There's nothing but bread and jam,' she said. And she put his plate on a stool by him. She was very happy now, waiting on him. For she loved company. And now she was no more afraid of him than if he were her own younger brother. He was such a boy.

'Nellie,' she called. 'I've poured you a cup out.'

March appeared in the doorway, took her cup, and sat down in a corner, as far from the light as possible. She was very sensitive in her knees. Having no skirts to cover them, and being forced to sit with them boldly exposed, she suffered. She shrank and shrank, trying not to be seen. And the youth, sprawling low on the couch, glanced up at her, with long, steady, penetrating looks, till she was almost ready to disappear. Yet she held her cup balanced, she drank her tea, screwed up her mouth and held her head averted. Her desire to be invisible was so strong that it quite baffled the youth. He felt he could not see her distinctly. She seemed like a shadow within the shadow. And ever his eyes came back to her, searching, unremitting, with unconscious fixed attention.

Meanwhile he was talking softly and smoothly to Banford, who loved nothing so much as gossip, and who was full of perky interest, like a bird. Also he ate largely and quickly and voraciously, so that March had to cut more chunks of bread and margarine, for the roughness of which Banford apologized.

'Oh well,' said March, suddenly speaking, 'if there's no butter to put on it, it's no good trying to make dainty pieces.'

Again the youth watched her, and he laughed, with a sudden, quick laugh, showing his teeth and wrinkling his nose.

'It isn't, is it,' he answered, in his soft, near voice.

It appeared he was Cornish by birth and upbringing. When he was twelve years old he had come to Bailey Farm with his grandfather, with whom he had never agreed very well. So he had run away to Canada, and worked far away in the West. Now he was here – and that was the end of it.

He was very curious about the girls, to find out exactly what they were doing. His questions were those of a farm youth; acute, practical, a little mocking. He was very much amused by their attitude to their losses: for they were amusing on the score of heifers and fowls.

'Oh well,' broke in March, 'we don't believe in living for nothing but work.'

'Don't you?' he answered. And again the quick young laugh came over his face. He kept his eyes steadily on the obscure woman in the corner.

'But what will you do when you've used up all your capital?' he said.

'Oh, I don't know,' answered March laconically. 'Hire ourselves out for land-workers, I suppose.'

'Yes, but there won't be any demand for women landworkers now the war's over,' said the youth.

'Oh, we'll see. We shall hold on a bit longer yet,' said March, with a plangent, half-sad, half-ironical indifference.

'There wants a man about the place,' said the youth softly.

Banford burst out laughing.

'Take care what you say,' she interrupted. 'We consider ourselves quite efficient.'

'Oh,' came March's slow plangent voice, 'it isn't a case of efficiency, I'm afraid. If you're going to do farming you must be at it from morning till night, and you might as well be a beast yourself.'

'Yes, that's it,' said the youth. 'You aren't willing to put yourselves into it.'

'We aren't,' said March, 'and we know it.'

'We want some of our time for ourselves,' said Banford.

The youth threw himself back on the sofa, his face tight with laughter, and laughed silently but thoroughly. The calm scorn of the girls tickled him tremendously.

'Yes,' he said, 'but why did you begin then?'

'Oh,' said March, 'we had a better opinion of the nature of fowls then than we have now.'

'Of Nature altogether, I'm afraid,' said Banford. 'Don't talk to me about Nature.'

Again the face of the youth tightened with delighted laughter.

'You haven't a very high opinion of fowls and cattle, haven't you?' he said.

'Oh no – quite a low one,' said March.

He laughed out.

'Neither fowls nor heifers,' said Banford, 'nor goats nor the weather.'

The youth broke into a sharp yap of laughter, delighted. The girls began to laugh too, March turning aside her face and wrinkling her mouth in amusement.

'Oh, well,' said Banford, 'we don't mind, do we, Nellie?'

'No,' said March, 'we don't mind.'

The youth was very pleased. He had eaten and drunk his fill. Banford began to question him. His name was Henry Grenfel – no, he was not called Harry, always Henry. He continued to answer with courteous simplicity, grave and charming. March, who was not included, cast long, slow glances at him from her recess, as he sat there on the sofa, his hands clasping his knees, his face under the lamp bright and alert, turned to Banford. She became almost peaceful at last. He was identified with the fox – and he was here in full presence. She need not go after him any more. There in the shadow of her corner she gave herself up to a warm, relaxed peace, almost like sleep, accepting the spell that was on her. But she wished to remain hidden. She was only fully at peace whilst he forgot her, talking to Banford. Hidden in the shadow of the corner, she need not any more be divided in herself trying to keep up two planes of consciousness. She could at last lapse into the odour of the fox.

For the youth, sitting before the fire in his uniform, sent a faint but distinct odour into the room, indefinable, but something like a wild creature. March no longer tried to reserve herself from it. She was still and soft in her corner like a passive creature in its cave.

At last the talk dwindled. The youth relaxed his clasp of his knees, pulled himself together a little, and looked round. Again he became aware of the silent, half-invisible woman in the corner.

'Well,' he said, unwillingly, 'I suppose I'd better be going, or they'll be in bed at the Swan.'

'I'm afraid they're in bed anyhow,' said Banford. 'They've all got this influenza.'

'Have they!' he exclaimed. And he pondered. 'Well,' he continued, 'I shall find a place somewhere.'

'I'd say you could stay here, only – ' Banford began.

He turned and watched her, holding his head forward.

'What?' he asked.

'Oh, well,' she said, 'propriety, I suppose.' She was rather confused.

'It wouldn't be improper, would it?' he said, gently surprised.

'Not as far as we're concerned,' said Banford.

'And not as far as I'm concerned,' he said, with grave *naïveté*. 'After all, it's my own home, in a way.'

Banford smiled at this.

'It's what the village will have to say,' she said.

There was a moment's blank pause.

'What do you say, Nellie?' asked Banford.

'I don't mind,' said March, in her distinct tone. 'The village doesn't matter to me, anyhow.'

'No,' said the youth, quick and soft. 'Why should it? I mean, what should they say?'

'Oh, well,' came March's laconic voice, 'they'll easily find something to say. But it makes no difference what they say. We can look after ourselves.'

'Of coarse you can,' said the youth.

'Well, then, stop if you like,' said Banford. 'The spare room is quite ready.'

His face shone with pleasure.

'If you're quite sure it isn't troubling you too much,' he said, with that soft courtesy which distinguished him.

'Oh, it's no trouble,' they both said.

He looked, smiling with delight, from one to another.

'It's awfully nice not to have to turn out again, isn't it?' he said gratefully.

'I suppose it is,' said Banford.

March disappeared to attend to the room. Banford was as pleased and thought-ful as if she had her own young brother home from France. It gave her just the same kind of gratification to attend on him, to get out the bath for him, and everything. Her natural warmth and kindliness had now an outlet.

And the youth luxuriated in her sisterly attention. But it puzzled him slightly to know that March was silently working for him too. She was so curiously silent and obliterated. It seemed to him he had not really seen her. He felt he should not know her if he met her in the road.

That night March dreamed vividly. She dreamed she heard a singing outside which she could not understand, a singing that roamed round the house, in the fields, and in the darkness. It moved her so that she felt she must weep. She went out, and suddenly she knew it was the fox singing. He was very yellow and bright, like corn. She went nearer to him, but he ran away and ceased singing. He seemed near, and she wanted to touch him. She stretched out her hand, but suddenly he bit her wrist, and at the same instant, as she drew back, the fox, turning round to bound away, whisked his brush across her face, and it seemed his brush was on fire, for it seared and burned her mouth with a great pain. She awoke with the pain of it, and lay trembling as if she were really seared.

In the morning, however, she only remembered it as a distant memory. She arose and was busy preparing the house and attending to the fowls. Banford flew into the village on her bicycle to try and buy food. She was a hospitable soul. But alas, in the year 1918 there was not much food to buy. The youth came downstairs in his shirt-sleeves. He was young and fresh, but he walked with his head thrust forward, so that his shoulders seemed raised and rounded, as if he had a slight curvature of the spine. It must have been only a manner of bearing himself, for he was young and vigorous. He washed himself and went outside, while the women were preparing breakfast.

He saw everything, and examined everything. His curiosity was quick and insatiable. He compared the state of things with that which he remembered before, and cast over in his mind the effect of the changes. He watched the fowls and the ducks, to see their condition; he noticed the flight of woodpigeons overhead: they were very numerous; he saw the few apples high up, which March had not been able to reach; he remarked that they had borrowed a draw-pump, presumably to empty the big soft-water cistern which was on the north side of the house.

'It's a funny, dilapidated old place,' he said to the girls as he sat at breakfast.

His eyes were wise and childish, with thinking about things. He did not say much, but ate largely. March kept her face averted. She, too, in the early morning could not be aware of him, though something about the glint of his khaki reminded her of the brilliance of her dream-fox.

During the day the girls went about their business. In the morning he attended to the guns, shot a rabbit and a wild duck that was flying high towards the wood. That was a great addition to the empty larder. The girls felt that already he had earned his keep. He said nothing about leaving, however. In the afternoon he went to the village. He came back at tea-time. He had the same alert, forward-reaching look on his roundish face. He hung his hat on a peg with a little swinging gesture. He was thinking about something.

'Well,' he said to the girls, as he sat at table. 'What am I going to do?'

'How do you mean – what are you going to do?' said Banford.

'Where am I going to find a place in the village to stay?' he said.

'I don't know,' said Banford. 'Where do you think of staying?'

'Well' – he hesitated – 'at the Swan they've got this flu, and at the Plough and Harrow they've got the soldiers who are collecting the hay for the army; besides, in the private houses, there's ten men and a corporal altogether billeted in the village, they tell me. I'm not sure where I could get a bed.'

He left the matter to them. He was rather calm about it. March sat with her elbows on the table, her two hands supporting her chin, looking at him unconsciously. Suddenly he lifted his clouded blue eyes, and unthinking looked straight into March's eyes. He was startled as well as she. He, too, recoiled a little. March felt the same sly, taunting, knowing spark leap out of his eyes, as he turned his head aside, and fall into her soul, as it had fallen from the dark eyes of the fox. She pursed her mouth as if in pain, as if asleep too.

'Well, I don't know,' Banford was saying. She seemed reluctant, as if she were afraid of being imposed upon. She looked at March. But, with her weak, troubled sight, she only saw the usual semi-abstraction on her friend's face. 'Why don't you speak, Nellie?' she said.

But March was wide-eyed and silent, and the youth, as if fascinated, was watching her without moving his eyes.

'Go on – answer something,' said Banford. And March turned her head slightly aside, as if coming to consciousness, or trying to come to consciousness.

'What do you expect me to say?' she asked automatically.

'Say what you think,' said Banford.

'It's all the same to me,' said March.

And again there was silence. A pointed light seemed to be on the boy's eyes, penetrating like a needle.

'So it is to me,' said Banford. 'You can stop on here if you like.'

A smile like a cunning little flame came over his face, suddenly and involuntarily. He dropped his head quickly to hide it, and remained with his head dropped, his face hidden.

'You can stop on here if you like. You can please yourself, Henry,' Banford concluded.

Still he did not reply, but remained with his head dropped. Then he lifted his face. It was bright with a curious light, as if exultant, and his eyes were strangely clear as he watched March. She turned her face aside, her mouth suffering as if wounded, and her consciousness dim.

Banford became a little puzzled. She watched the steady pellucid gaze of the youth's eyes as he looked at March, with the invisible smile gleaming on his face. She did not know how he was smiling, for no feature moved. It seemed only in the gleam, almost the glitter of the fine hairs on his cheeks. Then he looked with quite a changed look at Banford.

'I'm sure,' he said in his soft, courteous voice, 'you're awfully good. You're too good. You don't want to be bothered with me, I'm sure.'

'But a bit of bread, Nellie,' said Banford uneasily, adding: 'It's no bother, if you like to stay. It's like having my own brother here for a few days. He's a boy like you are.'

'That's awfully kind of you,' the lad repeated. 'I should like to stay ever so much, if you're sure I'm not a trouble to you .'

'No, of course you're no trouble. I tell you, it's a pleasure to have somebody in the house besides ourselves,' said warm-hearted Banford.

'But Miss March?' he said in his soft voice, looking at her.

'Oh, it's quite all right as far as I'm concerned,' said March vaguely.

His face beamed, and he almost rubbed his hands with pleasure.

'Well then,' he said, 'I should love it, if you'd let me pay my board and help with the work.'

'You've no need to talk about board,' said Banford.

One or two days went by, and the youth stayed on at the farm. Banford was quite charmed by him. He was so soft and courteous in speech, not wanting to say much himself, preferring to hear what she had to say, and to laugh in his quick, half-mocking way. He helped readily with the work – but not too much. He loved to be out alone with the gun in his hands, to watch, to see. For his sharp-eyed, impersonal curiosity was insatiable, and he was most free when he was quite alone, half-hidden, watching.

Particularly he watched March. She was a strange character to him. Her figure, like a graceful young man's, piqued him. Her dark eyes made something rise in his soul, with a curious elate excitement, when he looked into them, an excitement he was afraid to let be seen, it was so keen and secret. And then her odd, shrewd speech made him laugh outright. He felt he must go further, he was inevitably impelled. But he put away the thought of her and went off towards the wood's edge with the gun.

The dusk was falling as he came home, and with the dusk, a fine, late November rain. He saw the fire-light leaping in the window of the sitting-room, a leaping light in the little cluster of the dark buildings. And he thought to himself it would be a good thing to have this place for his own. And then the thought entered him shrewdly: why not marry March? He stood still in the middle of the field for some moments, the dead rabbit hanging still in his hand, arrested by this thought. His mind waited in amazement – it seemed to calculate – and then he smiled curiously to himself in acquiescence. Why not? Why not indeed? It was a good idea. What if it was rather ridiculous? What did it matter? What if she was older than he? It didn't matter. When he thought of her dark, startled, vulnerable eyes he smiled subtly to himself. He was older than she, really. He was master of her.

He scarcely admitted his intention even to himself. He kept it as a secret even from himself. It was all too uncertain as yet. He would have to see how things went. Yes, he would have to see how things went. If he wasn't careful, she would just simply mock at the idea. He knew, sly and subtle as he was, that if he went to her plainly and said: 'Miss March, I love you and want you to marry me,' her inevitable answer would be: 'Get out. I don't want any of that tomfoolery.' This was her attitude to men and their 'tomfoolery.' If he was not careful, she would turn round on him with her savage, sardonic ridicule, and dismiss him from the farm and from her own mind for ever. He would have to go gently. He would have to catch her as you catch a deer or a woodcock when you go out shooting. It's no good walking out into the forest and saying to the deer: 'Please fall to my gun.' No, it is a slow, subtle, battle. When you really go out to get a deer, you gather yourself together, you coil yourself inside yourself, and you advance secretly, before dawn, into the mountains. It is not so much what you do, when you go out hunting, as how you feel. You have to be subtle and cunning and absolutely fatally ready. It becomes like a fate. Your own fate overtakes and determines the fate of the deer you are hunting. First of all, even before you come in sight of your quarry, there is a strange battle, like mesmerism. Your own soul, as a hunter, has gone out to fasten on the soul of the deer, even before you see any deer. And the soul of the deer fights to escape. Even before the deer has any wind of you, it is so. It is a subtle, profound battle of wills which takes place in the invisible. And it is a battle never finished till your bullet goes home. When you are really worked up to the true pitch, and you come at last into range, you don't then aim as you do when you are firing at a bottle. It is your own will which carries the bullet into the heart of your quarry. The bullet's flight home is a sheer projection of your own fate into the fate of the deer. It happens like a supreme wish, a supreme act of volition, not as a dodge of cleverness.

He was a huntsman in spirit, not a farmer, and not a soldier stuck in a regiment. And it was as a young hunter that he wanted to bring down March as his quarry, to make her his wife. So he gathered himself subtly together, seemed to withdraw into a kind of invisibility. He was not quite sure how he would go on. And March was suspicious as a hare. So he remained in appearance just the nice, odd stranger-youth, staying for a fortnight on the place.

He had been sawing logs for the fire in the afternoon. Darkness came very early. It was still a cold, raw mist. It was getting almost too dark to see. A pile of short-sawed logs lay beside the trestle. March came to carry them indoors, or into the shed, as he was busy sawing the last log. He was working in his shirt-sleeves, and did not notice her approach; she came unwillingly, as if shy. He saw her stooping to the bright-ended logs, and he stopped sawing. A fire like lightning flew down his legs in the nerves.

'March?' he said, in his quiet, young voice.

She looked up from the logs she was piling.

'Yes!' she said.

He looked down on her in the dusk. He could see her not too distinctly.

'I wanted to ask you something,' he said.

'Did you? What was it?' she said. Already the fright was in her voice. But she was too much mistress of herself.

'Why' – his voice seemed to draw out soft and subtle, it penetrated her nerves – 'why, what do you think it is?'

She stood up, placed her hands on her hips, and stood looking at him trans-fixed, without answering. Again he burned with a sudden power.

'Well,' he said, and his voice was so soft it seemed rather like a subtle touch, like the merest touch of a cat's paw, a feeling rather than a sound. 'Well – I wanted to ask you to marry me.'

March felt rather than heard him. She was trying in vain to turn aside her face. A great relaxation seemed to have come over her. She stood silent, her head slightly on one side. He seemed to be bending towards her, invisibly smiling. It seemed to her fine sparks came out of him.

Then very suddenly she said:

'Don't try any of your tomfoolery on me.'

A quiver went over his nerves. He had missed. He waited a moment to collect himself again. Then he said, putting all the strange softness into his voice, as if he were imperceptibly stroking her:

'Why, it's not tomfoolery. It's not tomfoolery. I mean it. I mean it. What makes you disbelieve me?'

He sounded hurt. And his voice had such a curious power over her; making her feel loose and relaxed. She struggled somewhere for her own power. She felt for a moment that she was lost – lost – lost. The word seemed to rock in her as if she were dying. Suddenly again she spoke.

'You don't know what you are talking about,' she said, in a brief and transient stroke of scorn. 'What nonsense! I'm old enough to be your mother.'

'Yes, I do know what I'm talking about. Yes, I do,' he persisted softly, as if he were producing his voice in her blood. 'I know quite well what I'm talking about. You're not old enough to be my mother. That isn't true. And what does it matter even if it was. You can marry me whatever age we are. What is age to me? And what is age to you! Age is nothing.'

A swoon went over her as he concluded. He spoke rapidly – in the rapid Cornish fashion – and his voice seemed to sound in her somewhere where she was helpless against it. 'Age is nothing!' The soft, heavy insistence of it made her sway dimly out there in the darkness. She could not answer.

A great exultance leaped like fire over his limbs. He felt he had won.

'I want to marry you, you see. Why shouldn't I?' he proceeded, soft and rapid. He waited for her to answer. In the dusk he saw her almost phosphorescent. Her eyelids were dropped, her face half-averted and unconscious. She seemed to be in his power. But he waited, watchful. He dared not yet touch her.

'Say then,' he said, 'say then you'll marry me. Say – say!' He was softly insistent.

'What?' she asked, faint, from a distance, like one in pain. His voice was now unthinkably near and soft. He drew very near to her.

'Say yes.'

'Oh, I can't,' she wailed helplessly, half-articulate, as if semi-conscious, and as if in pain, like one who dies. 'How can I?'

'You can,' he said softly, laying his hand gently on her shoulder as she stood with her head averted and dropped, dazed. 'You can. Yes, you can. What makes you say you can't. You can. You can.' And with awful softness he bent forward and just touched her neck with his mouth and his chin.

'Don't!' she cried, with a faint mad cry like hysteria, starting away and facing round on him. 'What do you mean?' But she had no breath to speak with. It was as if she was killed.

'I mean what I say,' he persisted softly and cruelly. 'I want you to marry me. I want you to marry me. You know that, now, don't you? You know that, now? Don't you? Don't you?'

'What?' she said.

'Know,' he replied.

'Yes,' she said. 'I know you say so.'

'And you know I mean it, don't you?'

'I know you say so.'

'You believe me?' he said.

She was silent for some time. Then she pursed her lips.

'I don't know what I believe,' she said.

'Are you out there?' came Banford's voice, calling from the house.

'Yes, we're bringing in the logs,' he answered.

'I thought you'd gone lost,' said Banford disconsolately. 'Hurry up, do, and come and let's have tea. The kettle's boiling.'

He stooped at once, to take an armful of little logs and carry them into the kitchen, where they were piled in a corner. March also helped, filling her arms and carrying the logs on her breast as if they were some heavy child. The night had fallen cold.

When the logs were all in, the two cleaned their boots noisily on the scraper outside, then rubbed them on the mat. March shut the door and took off her old felt hat – her farmgirl hat. Her thick, crisp black hair was loose, her face was pale and strained. She pushed back her hair vaguely, and washed her hands. Banford came hurrying into the dimly lighted kitchen, to take from the oven the scones she was keeping hot.

'Whatever have you been doing all this time?' she asked fretfully. 'I thought you were never coming in. And it's ages since you stopped sawing. What were you doing out there?'

'Well,' said Henry, 'we had to stop that hole in the barn, to keep the rats out.'

'Why, I could see you standing there in the shed. I could see your shirt-sleeves,' challenged Banford.

'Yes, I was just putting the saw away.'

They went in to tea. March was quite mute. Her face was pale and strained and vague. The youth, who always had the same ruddy, self-contained look on his face, as though he were keeping himself to himself, had come to tea in his shirt-sleeves as if he were at home. He bent over his plate as he ate his food.

'Aren't you cold?' said Banford spitefully. 'In your shirtsleeves.'

He looked up at her, with his chin near his plate, and his eyes very clear, pellucid, and unwavering as he watched her.

'No, I'm not cold,' he said with his usual soft courtesy. 'It's much warmer in here than it is outside, you see.'

'I hope it is,' said Banford, feeling nettled by him. He had a strange suave assurance, and a wide-eyed bright look that got on her nerves this evening.

'But perhaps,' he said softly and courteously, 'you don't like me coming to tea without my coat. I forgot that.'

'Oh, I don't mind,' said Banford; although she did.

'I'll go and get it, shall I?' he said.

March's dark eyes turned slowly down to him.

'No, don't you bother,' she said in her queer, twanging tone. 'If you feel all right as you are, stop as you are.' She spoke with a crude authority.

'Yes,' said he, 'I feel all right, if I'm not rude.'

'It's usually considered rude,' said Banford. 'But we don't mind.'

'Go along, "considered rude," ' ejaculated March. 'Who considers it rude?'

'Why you do, Nellie, in anybody else,' said Banford, bridling a little behind her spectacles, and feeling her food stick in her throat.

But March had again gone vague and unheeding, chewing her food as if she did not know she was eating at all. And the youth looked from one to another, with bright, watchful eyes.

Banford was offended. For all his suave courtesy and soft voice, the youth seemed to her impudent. She did not like to look at him. She did not like to meet his clear, watchful eyes, she did not like to see the strange glow in his face, his cheeks with their delicate fine hair, and his ruddy skin that was quite dull and yet which seemed to burn with a curious heat of life. It made her feel a little ill to look at him: the quality of his physical presence was too penetrating, too hot.

After tea the evening was very quiet. The youth rarely went into the village. As a rule he read: he was a great reader, in his own hours. That is, when he did begin, he read absorbedly. But he was not very eager to begin. Often he walked about the fields and along the hedges alone in the dark at night, prowling with a queer instinct for the night, and listening to the wild sounds.

To-night, however, he took a Captain Mayne Reid book from Banford's shelf and sat down with knees wide apart and immersed himself in his story. His brownish fair hair was long, and lay on his head like a thick cap, combed sideways. He was still in his shirt-sleeves, and bending forward under the lamp-light, with his knees stuck wide apart and the book in his hand and his whole figure absorbed in the rather strenuous business of reading, he gave Banford's sitting-room the look of a lumber-camp. She resented this. For on her sitting-room floor she had a red Turkey rug and dark stain round, the fire-place had fashionable green tiles, the piano stood open with the latest dance-music – she played quite well: and on the walls were March's hand-painted swans and water-lilies. Moreover, with the logs nicely, tremulously burning in the grate, the thick curtains drawn, the doors all shut, and the pine-trees hissing and shuddering in the wind outside, it was cosy, it was refined and nice. She resented the big, raw, longlegged youth sticking his khaki knees out and sitting there with his soldier's shirt-cuffs buttoned on his thick red wrists. From time to time he turned a page, and from time to time he gave a sharp look at the fire, settling the logs. Then he immersed himself again in the intense and isolated business of reading.

March, on the far side of the table, was spasmodically crocheting. Her mouth was pursed in an odd way, as when she had dreamed the fox's brush turned it, her beautiful, crisp black hair strayed in wisps. But her whole figure was absorbed in its bearing, as if she herself was miles away. In a sort of semi-dream she seemed to be hearing the fox singing round the house in the wind, singing wildly and sweetly and like a madness. With red but well-shaped hands she slowly crocheted the white cotton, very slowly, awkwardly.

Banford was also trying to read, sitting in her low chair. But between those two she felt fidgety. She kept moving and looking round and listening to the wind, and glancing secretly from one to the other of her companions. March, seated on a straight chair, with her knees in their close breeches crossed, and slowly, laboriously crocheting, was also a trial.

'Oh dear!' said Banford. 'My eyes are bad to-night.' And she pressed her fingers on her eyes.

The youth looked up at her with his clear, bright look, but did not speak.

'Are they, Jill?' said March absently.

Then the youth began to read again, and Banford perforce returned to her book. But she could not keep still. After a while she looked up at March, and a queer, almost malignant little smile was on her thin face.

'A penny for them, Nell,' she said suddenly.

March looked round with big, startled black eyes, and went pale as if with terror. She had been listening to the fox singing so tenderly, so tenderly, as he wandered round the house.

'What?' she said vaguely.

'A penny for them,' said Banford sarcastically. 'Or twopence, if they're as deep as all that.'

The youth was watching with bright, clear eyes from beneath the lamp.

'Why,' came March's vague voice, 'what do you want to waste your money for?'

'I thought it would be well spent,' said Banford.

'I wasn't thinking of anything except the way the wind was blowing,' said March.

'Oh dear,' replied Banford, 'I could have had as original thoughts as that myself. I'm afraid I have wasted my money this time.'

'Well, you needn't pay,' said March.

The youth suddenly laughed. Both women looked at him: March rather surprised-looking, as if she had hardly known he was there.

'Why, do you ever pay up on these occasions?' he asked.

'Oh yes,' said Banford. 'We always do. I've sometimes had to pass a shilling a week to Nellie, in the winter-time. It costs much less in summer.'

'What, paying for each other's thoughts?' he laughed.

'Yes, when we've absolutely come to the end of everything else.'

He laughed quickly, wrinkling his nose sharply like a puppy and laughing with quick pleasure, his eyes shining.

'It's the first time I ever heard of that,' he said.

'I guess you'd hear of it often enough if you stayed a winter on Bailey Farm,' said Banford lamentably.

'Do you get so tired, then?' he asked.

'So bored,' said Banford.

'Oh!' he said gravely. 'But why should you be bored?'

'Who wouldn't be bored?' said Banford.

'I'm sorry to hear that,' he said gravely.

'You must be, if you were hoping to have a lively time here,' said Banford.

He looked at her long and gravely.

'Well,' he said, with his odd, young seriousness, 'it's quite lively enough for me.'

'I'm glad to hear it,' said Banford.

And she returned to her book. In her thin, frail hair were already many threads of grey, though she was not yet thirty. The boy did not look down, but turned his eyes to March, who was sitting with pursed mouth laboriously crocheting, her eyes wide and absent. She had a warm, pale, fine skin, and a delicate nose. Her pursed mouth looked shrewish. But the shrewish look was contradicted by the curious lifted arch of her dark brows, and the wideness of her eyes; a look of startled wonder and vagueness. She was listening again for the fox, who seemed to have wandered farther off into the night.

From under the edge of the lamp-light the boy sat with his face looking up, watching her silently, his eyes round and very clear and intent. Banford, biting her fingers irritably, was glancing at him under her hair. He sat there perfectly still, his ruddy face tilted up from the low level under the light, on the edge of the dimness, and watching with perfect abstract intentness. March suddenly lifted her great, dark eyes from her crocheting, and saw him. She started, giving a little exclamation.

'There he is!' she cried, involuntarily, as if terribly startled.

Banford looked around in amazement, sitting up straight.

'Whatever has got you, Nellie?' she cried.

But March, her face a flushed delicate rose colour, was looking away to the door.

'Nothing! Nothing!' she said crossly. 'Can't one speak?'

'Yes, if you speak sensibly,' said Banford. 'Whatever did you mean?'

'I don't know what I meant,' cried March testily.

'Oh, Nellie, I hope you aren't going jumpy and nervy. I feel I can't stand another thing! Whoever did you mean? Did you mean Henry?' cried poor, frightened Banford.

'Yes. I suppose so,' said March laconically. She would never confess to the fox.

'Oh dear, my nerves are all gone for to-night,' wailed Banford.

At nine o'clock March brought in a tray with bread and cheese and tea – Henry had confessed that he liked a cup of tea. Banford drank a glass of milk, and ate a little bread. And soon she said:

'I'm going to bed, Nellie. I'm all nerves to-night. Are you coming?'

'Yes, I'm coming the minute I've taken the tray away,' said March.

'Don't be long then,' said Banford fretfully. 'Good night, Henry. You'll see the fire is safe, if you come up last, won't you.'

'Yes, Miss Banford, I'll see it's safe,' he replied in his reassuring way.

March was lighting the candle to go to the kitchen. Banford took her candle and went upstairs. When March came back to the fire, she said to him:

'I suppose we can trust you to put out the fire and everything?' She stood there with her hand on her hip, and one knee loose, her head averted shyly, as if she could not look at him. He had his face lifted, watching her.

'Come and sit down a minute,' he said softly.

'No, I'll be going. Jill will be waiting, and she'll get upset if I don't come.'

'What made you jump like that this evening?' he asked.

'When did I jump?' she retorted, looking at him.

'Why, just now you did,' he said. 'When you cried out.'

'Oh!' she said. 'Then! Why, I thought you were the fox!' And her face screwed into a queer smile, half-ironic.

'The fox! Why the fox?' he asked softly.

'Why, one evening last summer when I was out with the gun I saw the fox in the grass nearly at my feet, looking straight up at me. I don't know – I suppose he made an impression on me.' She turned aside her head again, and let one foot stray loose, self-consciously.

'And did you shoot him?' asked the boy.

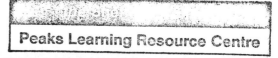

'No, he gave me such a start, staring straight at me as he did, and then stopping to look back at me over his shoulder with a laugh on his face.'

'A laugh on his face!' repeated Henry, also laughing. 'He frightened you, did he?'

'No, he didn't frighten me. He made an impression on me, that's all.'

'And you thought I was the fox, did you?' he laughed, with the same queer, quick little laugh, like a puppy wrinkling its nose.

'Yes, I did, for the moment,' she said. 'Perhaps he'd been in my mind without my knowing.'

'Perhaps you think I've come to steal your chickens or something,' he said, with the same young laugh.

But she only looked at him with a wide, dark, vacant eye. 'It's the first time,' he said, 'that I've ever been taken for a fox. Won't you sit down for a minute?' His voice was very soft and cajoling.

'No,' she said. 'Jill will be waiting.' But still she did not go, but stood with one foot loose and her face turned aside, just outside the circle of light.

'But won't you answer my question?' he said, lowering his voice still more.

'I don't know what question you mean.'

'Yes, you do. Of course you do. I mean the question of you marrying me.'

'No, I shan't answer that question,' she said flatly.

'Won't you?' The queer, young laugh came on his nose again. 'Is it because I'm like the fox? Is that why?' And still he laughed.

She turned and looked at him with a long, slow look.

'I wouldn't let that put you against me,' he said. 'Let me turn the lamp low, and come and sit down a minute.'

He put his red hand under the glow of the lamp, and suddenly made the light very dim. March stood there in the dimness quite shadowy, but unmoving. He rose silently to his feet, on his long legs. And now his voice was extraordinarily soft and suggestive, hardly audible.

'You'll stay a moment,' he said. 'Just a moment.' And he put his hand on her shoulder. She turned her face from him. 'I'm sure you don't really think I'm like the fox,' he said, with the same softness and with a suggestion of laughter in his tone, a subtle mockery. 'Do you now?' And he drew her gently towards him and kissed her neck, softly. She winced and trembled and hung away. But his strong, young arm held her, and he kissed her softly again, still on the neck, for her face was averted.

'Won't you answer my question? Won't you now?' came his soft, lingering voice. He was trying to draw her near to kiss her face. And he kissed her cheek softly, near the ear.

At that moment Banford's voice was heard calling fretfully, crossly from upstairs.

'There's Jill!' cried March, starting and drawing erect.

And as she did so, quick as lightning he kissed her on the mouth, with a quick brushing kiss. It seemed to burn through her every fibre. She gave a queer little cry.

'You will, won't you? You will?' he insisted softly.

'Nellie! Nellie! Whatever are you so long for?' came Banford's faint cry from the outer darkness.

But he held her fast, and was murmuring with that intolerable softness and insistency:

'You will, won't you? Say yes! Say yes!'

March, who felt as if the fire had gone through her and scathed her, and as if she could do no more, murmured:

'Yes! Yes! Anything you like! Anything you like! Only let me go! Only let me go! Jill's calling.'

'You know you've promised,' he said insidiously.

'Yes! Yes! I do!' Her voice suddenly rose into a shrill cry. 'All right, Jill, I'm coming.'

Startled, he let her go, and she went straight upstairs.

In the morning at breakfast, after he had looked round the place and attended to the stock and thought to himself that one could live easily enough here, he said to Banford:

'Do you know what, Miss Banford?'

'Well, what?' said the good-natured, nervy Banford.

He looked at March, who was spreading jam on her bread.

'Shall I tell?' he said to her.

She looked up at him, and a deep pink colour flushed over her face.

'Yes, if you mean Jill,' she said. 'I hope you won't go talking all over the village, that's all.' And she swallowed her dry bread with difficulty.

'Whatever's coming?' said Banford, looking up with wide, tired, slightly reddened eyes. She was a thin, frail little thing, and her hair, which was delicate and thin, was bobbed, so it hung softly by her worn face in its faded brown and grey.

'Why, what do you think?' he said, smiling like one who has a secret.

'How do I know!' said Banford.

'Can't you guess?' he said, making bright eyes, and smiling, pleased with himself.

'I'm sure I can't. What's more, I'm not going to try.'

'Nellie and I are going to be married.'

Banford put down her knife out of her thin, delicate fingers, as if she would never take it up to eat any more. She stared with blank, reddened eyes.

'You what?' she exclaimed.

'We're going to get married. Aren't we, Nellie?' and he turned to March.

'You say so, anyway,' said March laconically. But again she flushed with an agonized flush. She, too, could swallow no more.

Banford looked at her like a bird that has been shot: a poor, little sick bird. She gazed at her with all her wounded soul in her face, at the deep-flushed March.

'Never!' she exclaimed, helpless.

'It's quite right,' said the bright and gloating youth.

Banford turned aside her face, as if the sight of the food on the table made her sick. She sat like this for some moments, as if she were sick. Then, with one hand on the edge of the table, she rose to her feet.

'I'll *never* believe it, Nellie,' she cried. 'It's absolutely impossible!'

Her plaintive, fretful voice had a thread of hot anger and despair.

'Why? Why shouldn't you believe it?' asked the youth, with all his soft, velvety impertinence in his voice.

Banford looked at him from her wide, vague eyes, as if he were some creature in a museum.

'Oh,' she said languidly, 'because she can never be such a fool. She can't lose her self-respect to such an extent.' Her voice was cold and plaintive, drifting.

'In what way will she lose her self-respect?' asked the boy.

Banford looked at him with vague fixity from behind her spectacles.

'If she hasn't lost it already,' she said.

He became very red, vermilion, under the slow, vague stare from behind the spectacles.

'I don't see it at all,' he said.

'Probably you don't. I shouldn't expect you would,' said Banford, with that straying mild tone of remoteness which made her words even more insulting.

He sat stiff in his chair, staring with hot, blue eyes from his scarlet face. An ugly look had come on his brow.

'My word, she doesn't know what she's letting herself in for,' said Banford, in her plaintive, drifting, insulting voice.

'What has it got to do with you, anyway?' said the youth, in a temper.

'More than it has to do with you, probably,' she replied, plaintive and venomous.

'Oh, has it! I don't see that at all,' he jerked out.

'No, you wouldn't,' she answered, drifting.

'Anyhow,' said March, pushing back her chair and rising uncouthly. 'It's no good arguing about it.' And she seized the bread and the teapot, and strode away to the kitchen.

Banford let her fingers stray across her brow and along her hair, like one bemused. Then she turned and went away upstairs.

Henry sat stiff and sulky in his chair, with his face and his eyes on fire. March came and went, clearing the table. But Henry sat on, stiff with temper. He took no notice of her. She had regained her composure and her soft, even, creamy complexion. But her mouth was pursed up. She glanced at him each time as she came to take things from the table glanced from her large, curious eyes, more in curiosity than anything. Such a long, red-faced, sulky boy! That was all he was. He seemed as remote from her as if his red face were a red chimney-pot on a cottage across the fields, and she looked at him just as objectively, as remotely.

At length he got up and stalked out into the fields with the gun.

He came in only at dinner-time, with the devil still in his face, but his manners quite polite. Nobody said anything particular; they sat each one at the sharp corner of a triangle, in obstinate remoteness. In the afternoon he went out again at once with the gun. He came in at nightfall with a rabbit and a pigeon. He stayed in all the evening, but hardly opened his mouth. He was in the devil of a temper, feeling he had been insulted.

Banford's eyes were red, she had evidently been crying. But her manner was more remote and supercilious than ever; the way she turned her head if he spoke at all, as if he were some tramp or inferior intruder of that sort, made his blue eyes go almost black with rage. His face looked sulkier. But he never forgot his polite intonation, if he opened his mouth to speak.

March seemed to flourish in this atmosphere. She seemed to sit between the two antagonists with a little wicked smile on her face, enjoying herself. There was even a sort of complacency in the way she laboriously crocheted this evening.

When he was in bed, the youth could hear the two women talking and arguing in their room. He sat up in bed and strained his ears to hear what they said. But he could hear nothing, it was too far off. Yet he could hear the soft, plaintive drip of Banford's voice, and March's deeper note.

The night was quiet, frosty. Big stars were snapping outside, beyond the ridge-tops of the pine-trees. He listened and listened. In the distance he heard a fox yelping: and the dogs from the farms barking in answer. But it was not that he wanted to hear. It was what the two women were saying.

He got stealthily out of bed, and stood by his door. He could hear no more than before. Very, very carefully he began to lift the door latch. After quite a time he had his door open. Then he stepped stealthily out into the passage. The old oak planks were cold under his feet, and they creaked preposterously. He crept very, very gently up the one step, and along by the wall, till he stood outside their door. And there he held his breath and listened. Banford's voice:

'No, I simply couldn't stand it. I should be dead in a month. Which is just what he would be aiming at, of course. That would just be his game, to see me in the churchyard. No, Nellie, if you were to do such a thing as to marry him, you could never stop here. I couldn't, I couldn't live in the same house with him. Oh–h! I feel quite sick with the smell of his clothes. And his red face simply turns me over. I can't eat my food when he's at the table. What a fool I was ever to let him stop. One ought never to try to do a kind action. It always flies back in your face like a boomerang.'

'Well, he's only got two more days,' said March.

'Yes, thank heaven. And when he's gone he'll never come in this house again. I feel so bad while he's here. And I know, I know he's only counting what he can get out of you. I know that's all it is. He's just a good-for-nothing, who doesn't want to work, and who thinks he'll live on us. But he won't live on me. If you're such a fool, then it's your own look-out. Mrs. Burgess knew him all the time he was here. And the old man could never get him to do any steady work. He was off with the gun on every occasion, just as he is now. Nothing but the gun! Oh, I do hate it. You don't know what you're doing. Nellie, you don't. If you marry him he'll just make a fool of you. He'll go off and leave you stranded. I know he will, if he can't get Bailey Farm out of us – and he's not going to, while I live. While I live he's never going to set foot here. I know what it would be. He'd soon think he was master of both of us as he thinks he's master of you already.'

'But he isn't,' said Nellie.

'He thinks he is, anyway. And that's what he wants: to come and be master here. Yes, imagine it! That's what we've got the place together for, is it, to be bossed and bullied by a hateful red-faced boy, a beastly labourer. Oh, we *did*

make a mistake when we let him stop. We ought never to have lowered ourselves. And I've had such a fight with all the people here, not to be pulled down
to their level. No, he's not coming here. And then you see – if he can't have the
place, he'll run off to Canada or somewhere again, as if he'd never known you.
And here you'll be, absolutely ruined and made a fool of. I know I shall never
have any peace of mind again.'

'We'll tell him he can't come here. We'll tell him that,' said March.

'Oh, don't you bother; I'm going to tell him that, and other things as well,
before he goes. He's not going to have all his own way while I've got the strength
left to speak. Oh, Nellie, he'll despise you, he'll despise you, like the awful
little beast he is, if you give way to him. I'd no more trust him than I'd trust a
cat not to steal. He's deep, he's deep, and he's bossy, and he's selfish through
and through, as cold as ice. All he wants is to make use of you. And when
you're no more use to him, then I pity you.'

'I don't think he's as bad as all that,' said March.

'No, because he's been playing up to you. But you'll find out, if you see
much more of him. Oh, Nellie, I can't bear to think of it.'

'Well, it won't hurt you, Jill, darling.'

'Won't it! Won't it! I shall never know a moment's peace again while I live,
nor a moment's happiness. No, Nellie – ' and Banford began to weep bitterly.

The boy outside could hear the stifled sound of the woman's sobbing, and
could hear March's soft, deep, tender voice comforting, with wonderful
gentleness and tenderness, the weeping woman.

His eyes were so round and wide that he seemed to see the whole night, and
his ears were almost jumping off his head. He was frozen stiff. He crept back to
bed, but felt as if the top of his head were coming off. He could not sleep. He
could not keep still. He rose, quietly dressed himself, and crept out on to the
landing once more. The women were silent. He went softly downstairs and out
to the kitchen.

Then he put on his boots and his overcoat, and took the gun. He did not
think to go away from the farm. No, he only took the gun. As softly as possible
he unfastened the door and went out into the frosty December night. The air
was still, the stars bright, the pine-trees seemed to bristle audibly in the sky. He
went stealthily away down a fenceside, looking for something to shoot. At the
same time he remembered that he ought not to shoot and frighten the women.
So he prowled round the edge of the gorse cover, and through the grove of tall
old hollies, to the woodside. There he skirted the fence, peering through the
darkness with dilated eyes that seemed to be able to grow black and full of sight
in the dark, like a cat's. An owl was slowly and mournfully whooing round a great
oak-tree. He stepped stealthily with his gun, listening, listening, watching.

As he stood under the oaks of the wood-edge he heard the dogs from the
neighbouring cottage up the hill yelling suddenly and startlingly, and the
wakened dogs from the farms around barking answer. And suddenly, it seemed
to him England was little and tight, he felt the landscape was constricted even
in the dark, and that there were too many dogs in the night, making a noise like
a fence of sound, like the network of English hedges netting the view. He felt

the fox didn't have a chance. For it must be the fox that had started all this hullabaloo.

Why not watch for him, anyhow! He would, no doubt, be coming sniffing round. The lad walked downhill to where the farmstead with its few pine-trees crouched blackly. In the angle of the long shed in the black dark, he crouched down. He knew the fox would be coming. It seemed to him it would be the last of the foxes in this loudly barking, thick-voiced England, tight with innumerable little houses.

He sat a long time with his eyes fixed unchanging upon the open gateway, where a little light seemed to fall from the stars or from the horizon, who knows. He was sitting on a log in a dark corner with the gun across his knees. The pine-trees snapped. Once a chicken fell off its perch in the barn with a loud crawk and cackle and commotion that startled him, and he stood up, watching with all his eyes, thinking it might be a rat. But he felt it was nothing. So he sat down again with the gun on his knees and his hands tucked in to keep them warm, and his eyes fixed unblinking on the pale reach of the open gateway. He felt he could smell the hot, sickly, rich smell of live chickens on the cold air.

And then – a shadow. A sliding shadow in the gateway. He gathered all his vision into a concentrated spark, and saw the shadow of the fox, the fox creeping on his belly through the gate. There he went, on his belly like a snake. The boy smiled to himself and brought the gun to his shoulder. He knew quite well what would happen. He knew the fox would go to where the fowl-door was boarded up, and sniff there. He knew he would lie there for a minute, sniffing the fowls within. And then he would start again prowling under the edge of the old barn, waiting to get in.

The fowl-door was at the top of a slight incline. Soft, soft as a shadow the fox slid up this incline, and crouched with his nose to the boards. And at the same moment there was the awful crash of a gun reverberating between the old buildings, as if all the night had gone smash. But the boy watched keenly. He saw even the white belly of the fox as the beast beat his paws in death. So he went forward.

There was a commotion everywhere. The fowls were scuffling and crawking, the ducks were quark-quarking, the pony had stamped wildly to his feet. But the fox was on his side, struggling in his last tremors. The boy bent over him and smelt his foxy smell.

There was a sound of a window opening upstairs, then March's voice calling: 'Who is it?'

'It's me,' said Henry; 'I've shot the fox.'

'Oh, goodness! You nearly frightened us to death.'

'Did I? I'm awfully sorry.'

'Whatever made you get up?'

'I heard him about.'

'And have you shot him?'

'Yes, he's here,' and the boy stood in the yard holding up the warm, dead brute. 'You can't see, can you? Wait a minute.' And he took his flashlight from his pocket, and flashed it on to the dead animal. He was holding it by the brush. March saw, in the middle of the darkness, just the reddish fleece and the white belly and the white underneath of the pointed chin, and the queer, dangling paws. She did not know what to say.

'He's a beauty,' he said. 'He will make you a lovely fur.'

'You don't catch me wearing a fox fur,' she replied.

'Oh!' he said. And he switched off the light.

'Well, I should think you'll come in and go to bed again now,' she said.

'Probably I shall. What time is it?'

'What time is it, Jill?' called March's voice. It was a quarter to one.

That night March had another dream. She dreamed that Banford was dead, and that she, March, was sobbing her heart out. Then she had to put Banford into her coffin. And the coffin was the rough wood-box in which the bits of chopped wood were kept in the kitchen, by the fire. This was the coffin, and there was no other, and March was in agony and dazed bewilderment, looking for something to line the box with, something to make it soft with, something to cover up the poor, dead darling. Because she couldn't lay her in there just in her white, thin nightdress, in the horrible wood-box. So she hunted and hunted, and picked up thing after thing, and threw it aside in the agony of dream-frustration. And in her dream despair all she could find that would do was a fox-skin. She knew that it wasn't right, that this was not what she should have. But it was all she could find. And so she folded the brush of the fox, and laid her darling Jill's head on this, and she brought round the skin of the fox and laid it on the top of the body, so that it seemed to make a whole ruddy, fiery coverlet, and she cried and cried, and woke to find the tears streaming down her face.

The first thing that both she and Banford did in the morning was to go out to see the fox. Henry had hung it up by the heels in the shed, with its poor brush falling backwards. It was a lovely dog-fox in its prime, with a handsome, thick, winter coat: a lovely golden-red colour, with grey as it passed to the belly, and belly all white, and a great full brush with a delicate black and grey and pure white tip.

'Poor brute!' said Banford. 'If it wasn't such a thieving wretch, you'd feel sorry for it.'

March said nothing, but stood with her foot trailing aside, one hip out; her face was pale and her eyes big and black, watching the dead animal that was suspended upside down. White and soft as snow his belly: white and soft as snow. She passed her hand softly down it. And his wonderful blackglinted brush was full and frictional, wonderful. She passed her hand down this also, and quivered. Time after time, she took the full fur of that thick tail between her fingers, and passed her hand slowly downwards. Wonderful, sharp, thick, splendour of a tail. And he was dead! She pursed her lips, and her eyes went black and vacant. Then she took the head in her hand.

Henry was sauntering up, so Banford walked rather pointedly away. March stood there bemused, with the head of the fox in her hand. She was wondering, wondering, wondering over his long fine muzzle. For some reason it reminded her of a spoon or a spatula. She felt she could not understand it. The beast was a strange beast to her, incomprehensible, out of her range. Wonderful silver whiskers he had, like ice-threads. And pricked ears with hair inside. But that long, long, slender spoon of a nose! – and the marvellous white teeth beneath! It was to thrust forward and bite with, deep, deep into the living prey, to bite and bite the blood.

'He's a beauty, isn't he?' said Henry, standing by.

'Oh yes, he's a fine big fox. I wonder how many chickens he's responsible for,' she replied.

'A good many. Do you think he's the same one you saw in the summer?'

'I should think very likely he is,' she replied.

He watched her, but he could make nothing of her. Partly she was so shy and virgin, and partly she was so grim, matter-of-fact, shrewish. What she said seemed to him so different from the look of her big, queer, dark eyes.

'Are you going to skin him?' she asked.

'Yes, when I've had breakfast, and got a board to peg him on.'

'My word, what a strong smell he's got! Pooo! It'll take some washing off one's hands. I don't know why I was so silly as to handle him.' And she looked at her right hand, that had passed down his belly and along his tail, and had even got a tiny streak of blood from one dark place in his fur.

'Have you seen the chickens when they smell him, how frightened they are?' he said.

'Yes, aren't they!'

'You must mind you don't get some of his fleas.'

'Oh, fleas!' she replied, nonchalant.

Later in the day she saw the fox's skin nailed flat on a board, as if crucified. It gave her an uneasy feeling.

The boy was angry. He went about with his mouth shut, as if he had swallowed part of his chin. But in behaviour he was polite and affable. He did not say anything about his intention. And he left March alone.

That evening they sat in the dining-room. Banford wouldn't have him in her sitting-room any more. There was a very big log on the fire. And everybody was busy. Banford had letters to write. March was sewing a dress, and he was mending some little contrivance.

Banford stopped her letter-writing from time to time to look round and rest her eyes. The boy had his head down, his face hidden over his job.

'Let's see,' said Banford. 'What train do you go by, Henry ?'

He looked up straight at her.

'The morning train. In the morning,' he said.

'What, the eight-ten or the eleven-twenty?'

'The eleven-twenty, I suppose,' he said.

'That is the day after to-morrow?' said Banford.

'Yes, the day after to-morrow.'

'Mm!" murmured Banford, and she returned to her writing. But as she was licking her envelope, she asked:

'And what plans have you made for the future, if I may ask?'

'Plans?' he said, his face very bright and angry.

'I mean about you and Nellie, if you are going on with this business. When do you expect the wedding to come off?' She spoke in a jeering tone.

'Oh, the wedding!' he replied. 'I don't know.'

'Don't you know anything?' said Banford. 'Are you going to clear out on Friday and leave things no more settled than they are?'

'Well, why shouldn't I? We can always write letters.'

'Yes, of course you can. But I wanted to know because of this place. If Nellie is going to get married all of a sudden, I shall have to be looking round for a new partner.'

'Couldn't she stay on here if she were married?' he said. He knew quite well what was coming.

'Oh,' said Banford, 'this is no place for a married couple. There's not enough work to keep a man going, for one thing. And there's no money to be made. It's quite useless your thinking of staying on here if you marry. Absolutely!'

'Yes, but I wasn't thinking of staying on here,' he said.

'Well, that's what I want to know. And what about Nellie, then? How long is she going to be here with me, in that case.'

The two antagonists looked at one another.

'That I can't say,' he answered.

'Oh, go along,' she cried petulantly. 'You must have some idea what you are going to do, if you ask a woman to marry you. Unless it's all a hoax.'

'Why should it be a hoax? I am going back to Canada.'

'And taking her with you?'

'Yes, certainly.'

'You hear that, Nellie?' said Banford.

March, who had had her head bent over her sewing, now looked up with a sharp, pink blush on her face, and a queer, sardonic laugh in her eyes and on her twisted mouth.

'That's the first time I've heard that I was going to Canada,' she said.

'Well, you have to hear it for the first time, haven't you?' said the boy.

'Yes, I suppose I have,' she said nonchalantly. And she went back to her sewing.

'You're quite ready, are you, to go to Canada? Are you, Nellie?' asked Banford.

March looked up again. She let her shoulders go slack, and let her hand that held the needle lie loose in her lap.

'It depends on how I'm going,' she said. 'I don't think I want to go jammed up in the steerage, as a soldier's wife. I'm afraid I'm not used to that way.'

The boy watched her with bright eyes.

'Would you rather stay over here while I go first?' he asked.

'I would, if that's the only alternative,' she replied.

'That's much the wisest. Don't make it any fixed engagement,' said Banford. 'Leave yourself free to go or not after he's got back and found you a place, Nellie. Anything else is madness, madness.'

'Don't you think,' said the youth, 'we ought to get married before I go – and then go together, or separate, according to how it happens?'

'I think it's a terrible idea,' cried Banford.

But the boy was watching March.

'What do you think?' he asked her.

She let her eyes stray vaguely into space.

'Well, I don't know,' she said. 'I shall have to think about it.'

'Why?' he asked, pertinently.

'Why?' She repeated his question in a mocking way, and looked at him laughing, though her face was pink again. 'I should think there's plenty of reasons why.'

He watched her in silence. She seemed to have escaped him. She had got into league with Banford against him. There was again the queer sardonic look about her; she would mock stoically at everything he said or which life offered.

'Of course,' he said, 'I don't want to press you to do anything you don't wish to do.'

'I should think not, indeed,' cried Banford indignantly.

At bedtime Banford said plaintively to March:

'You take my hot bottle up for me, Nellie, will you.'

'Yes, I'll do it,' said March, with the kind of willing unwillingness she so often showed towards her beloved but uncertain Jill.

The two women went upstairs. After a time March called from the top of the stairs: 'Good night, Henry. I shan't be coming down. You'll see to the lamp and the fire, won't you?'

The next day Henry went about with the cloud on his brow and his young cub's face shut up tight. He was cogitating all the time. He had wanted March to marry him and go back to Canada with him. And he had been sure she would do it. Why he wanted her he didn't know. But he did want her. He had set his mind on her. And he was convulsed with a youth's fury at being thwarted. To be thwarted, to be thwarted! It made him so furious inside that he did not know what to do with himself. But he kept himself in hand. Because even now things might turn out differently. She might come over to him. Of course she might. It was her business to do so.

Things drew to a tension again towards evening. He and Banford had avoided each other all day. In fact, Banford went in to the little town by the 11.20 train. It was market day. She arrived back on the 4.25. Just as the night was falling Henry saw her little figure in a dark-blue coat and a dark blue tam-o'shanter hat crossing the first meadow from the station. He stood under one of the wild pear-trees, with the old dead leaves round his feet. And he watched the little blue figure advancing persistently over the rough winter-ragged meadow. She had her arms full of parcels, and advanced slowly, frail thing she was, but with that devilish little certainty which he so detested in her. He stood invisible under the pear-tree, watching her every step. And if looks could have affected her, she would have felt a log of iron on each of her ankles as she made her way forward. 'You're a nasty little thing, you are,' he was saying softly, across the distance. 'You're a nasty little thing. I hope you'll be paid back for all the harm you've done me for nothing. I hope you will – you nasty little thing. I hope you'll have to pay for it. You will, if wishes are anything. You nasty little creature that you are.'

She was toiling slowly up the slope. But if she had been slipping back at every step towards the Bottomless Pit, he would not have gone to help her with her parcels. Aha, there went March, striding with her long, land stride in her breeches and her short tunic! Striding downhill at a great pace, and even running a few steps now and then, in her great solicitude and desire to come to the rescue of the little Banford. The boy watched her with rage in his heart. See her leap a ditch, and run, run as if a house was on fire, just to get to that creeping, dark little object down there! So, the Banford just stood still and waited. And March strode up and took all the parcels except a bunch of yellow chrysanthemums. These the Banford still carried – yellow chrysanthemums!

'Yes, you look well, don't you,' he said softly into the dusk air. 'You look well, pottering up there with a bunch of flowers, you do. I'd make you eat them for your tea, if you hug them so tight. And I'd give them you for breakfast again, I would. I'd give you flowers. Nothing but flowers.'

He watched the progress of the two women. He could hear their voices: March always outspoken and rather scolding in her tenderness, Banford murmuring rather vaguely. They were evidently good friends. He could not hear what they said till they came to the fence of the home meadow, which they must climb. Then he saw March manfully climbing over the bars with all her packages in her arms, and on the still air he heard Banford's fretful:

'Why don't you let me help you with the parcels?' She had a queer, plaintive hitch in her voice. Then came March's robust and reckless:

'Oh, I can manage. Don't you bother about me. You've all you can do to get yourself over.'

'Yes, that's all very well,' said Banford fretfully. 'You say, *Don't you bother about me*, and then all the while you feel injured because nobody thinks of you.'

'When do I feel injured?' said March.

'Always. You always feel injured. Now you're feeling injured because I won't have that boy to come and live on the farm.'

'I'm not feeling injured at all,' said March.

'I know you are. When he's gone you'll sulk over it. I know you will.'

'Shall I?' said March. 'We'll see.'

'Yes, we shall see, unfortunately. I can't think how you can make yourself so cheap. I can't imagine how you can lower yourself like it.'

'I haven't lowered myself,' said March.

'I don't know what you call it, then. Letting a boy like that come so cheeky and impudent and make a mug of you. I don't know what you think of yourself. How much respect do you think he's going to have for you afterwards? My word, I wouldn't be in your shoes, if you married him.'

'Of course you wouldn't. My boots are a good bit too big for you, and not half dainty enough,' said March, with rather a miss-fire sarcasm.

'I thought you had too much pride, really I did. A woman's got to hold herself high, especially with a youth like that. Why, he's impudent. Even the way he forced himself on us at the start.'

'We asked him to stay,' said March.

'Not till he'd almost forced us to. And then he's so cocky and self-assured. My word, he puts my back up. I simply can't imagine how you can let him treat you so cheaply.'

'I don't let him treat me cheaply,' said March. 'Don't you worry yourself, nobody's going to treat me cheaply. And even you aren't, either.' She had a tender defiance, and a certain fire in her voice.

'Yes, it's sure to come back to me,' said Banford bitterly. 'That's always the end of it. I believe you only do it to spite me.'

They went now in silence up the steep, grassy slope and over the brow, through the gorse-bushes. On the other side of the hedge the boy followed in the dusk, at some little distance. Now and then, through the huge ancient hedge of hawthorn, risen into trees, he saw the two dark figures creeping up the hill. As he came to the top of the slope he saw the homestead dark in the twilight, with a huge old pear-tree leaning from the near gable, and a little yellow light twinkling in the small side windows of the kitchen. He heard the clink of the latch and saw the kitchen door open into light as the two women went indoors. So, they were at home.

And so! – this was what they thought of him. It was rather in his nature to be a listener, so he was not at all surprised whatever he heard. The things people said about him always missed him personally. He was only rather surprised at the women's way with one another. And he disliked the Banford with an acid dislike. And he felt drawn to the March again. He felt again irresistibly drawn to her. He felt there was a secret bond, a secret thread between him and her, something very exclusive, which shut out everybody else and made him and her possess each other in secret.

He hoped again that she would have him. He hoped with his blood suddenly firing up that she would agree to marry him quite quickly: at Christmas, very likely. Christmas was not far off. He wanted, whatever else happened, to snatch her into a hasty marriage and a consummation with him. Then for the future, they could arrange later. But he hoped it would happen as he wanted it. He hoped that to-night she would stay a little while with him, after Banford had gone upstairs. He hoped he could touch her soft, creamy cheek, her strange, frightened face. He hoped he could look into her dilated, frightened dark eyes, quite near. He hoped he might even put his hand on her bosom and feel her soft breasts under her tunic. His heart beat deep and powerful as he thought of that. He wanted very much to do so. He wanted to make sure of her soft woman's breasts under her tunic. She always kept the brown linen coat buttoned so close up to her throat. It seemed to him like some perilous secret, that her soft woman's breasts must be buttoned up in that uniform. It seemed to him, moreover, that they were so much softer, tenderer, more lovely and lovable, shut up in that tunic, than were the Banford's breasts, under her soft blouses and chiffon dresses. The Banford would have little iron breasts, he said to himself. For all her frailty and fretfulness and delicacy, she would have tiny iron breasts. But March, under her crude, fast, workman's tunic, would have soft, white breasts, white and unseen. So he told himself, and his blood burned.

When he went in to tea, he had a surprise. He appeared at the inner door, his face very ruddy and vivid and his blue eyes shining, dropping his head forward as he came in, in his usual way, and hesitating in the doorway, to watch the inside of the room, keenly and cautiously, before he entered. He was wearing a long-sleeved waistcoat. His face seemed extraordinarily like a piece of the out-of-doors come indoors: as holly-berries do. In his second of pause in the doorway he took in the two women sitting at table, at opposite ends, saw them sharply. And to his amazement March was dressed in a dress of dull, green silk crape.

His mouth came open in surprise. If she had suddenly grown a moustache he could not have been more surprised.

'Why,' he said, 'do you wear a dress, then?'

She looked up, flushing a deep rose colour, and twisting her mouth with a smile, said:

'Of course I do. What else do you expect me to wear, but a dress ?'

'A land-girl's uniform, of course,' said he.

'Oh,' she cried, nonchalant, 'that's only for this dirty, mucky work about here.'

'Isn't it your proper dress, then?' he said.

'No, not indoors it isn't,' she said. But she was blushing all the time as she poured out his tea. He sat down in his chair at table, unable to take his eyes off her. Her dress was a perfectly simple slip of bluey-green crape, with a line of gold stitching round the top and round the sleeves, which came to the elbow. It was cut just plain and round at the top, and showed her white, soft throat. Her arms he knew, strong and firm-muscled, for he had often seen her with her sleeves rolled up. But he looked her up and down, up and down.

Banford, at the other end of the table, said not a word, but jiggled with the sardine on her plate. He had forgotten her existence. He just simply stared at March, while he ate his bread and margarine in huge mouthfuls, forgetting even his tea

'Well, I never knew anything make such a difference!' he murmured, across his mouthfuls.

'Oh goodness!' cried March, blushing still more. 'I might be a pink monkey!'

And she rose quickly to her feet and took the teapot to the fire, to the kettle. And as she crouched on the hearth with her green slip about her, the boy stared more wide-eyed than ever. Through the crape her woman's form seemed soft and womanly. And when she stood up and walked he saw her legs move soft within her modernly short skirt. She had on black silk stockings, and small patent shoes with little gold buckles.

No, she was another being. She was something quite different. Seeing her always in the hard-cloth breeches, wide on the hips, buttoned on the knee, strong as armour, and in the brown puttees and thick boots, it had never oc-curred to him that she had a woman's legs and feet. Now it came upon him. She had a woman's soft, skirted legs, and she was accessible. He blushed to the roots of his hair, shoved his nose in his teacup and drank his tea with a little noise that made Banford simply squirm: and strangely, suddenly he felt a man, no longer a youth. He felt a man, with all a man's grave weight of responsibil-ity. A curious quietness and gravity came over his soul. He felt a man, quiet, with a little of the heaviness of male destiny upon him.

She was soft and accessible in her dress. The thought went home in him like an everlasting responsibility.

'Oh, for goodness' sake, say something, somebody,' cried Banford fretfully. 'It might be a funeral.' The boy looked at her, and she could not bear his face.

'A funeral!' said March, with a twisted smile. 'Why, that breaks my dream.'

Suddenly she had thought of Banford in the wood-box for a coffin.

'What, have you been dreaming of a wedding?' said Banford sarcastically.

'Must have been,' said March.

'Whose wedding?' asked the boy.

'I can't remember,' said March.

She was shy and rather awkward that evening in spite of the fact that, wearing a dress, her bearing was much more subdued than in her uniform. She felt unpeeled and rather exposed. She felt almost improper.

They talked desultorily about Henry's departure next morning, and made the trivial arrangement. But of the matter on their minds, none of them spoke. They were rather quiet and friendly this evening; Banford had practically nothing to say. But inside herself she seemed still, perhaps kindly.

At nine o'clock March brought in the tray with the everlasting tea and a little cold meat which Banford had managed to procure. It was the last supper, so Banford did not want to be disagreeable. She felt a bit sorry for the boy, and felt she must be as nice as she could.

He wanted her to go to bed. She was usually the first. But she sat on in her chair under the lamp, glancing at her book now and then, and staring into the fire. A deep silence had come into the room. It was broken by March asking, in a rather small tone:

'What time is it, Jill?'

'Five past ten,' said Banford, looking at her wrist.

And then not a sound. The boy had looked up from the book he was holding between his knees. His rather wide, catshaped face had its obstinate look, his eyes were watchful.

'What about bed?' said March at last.

'I'm ready when you are,' said Banford.

'Oh, very well,' said March. 'I'll fill your bottle.'

She was as good as her word. When the hot-water bottle was ready, she lit a candle and went upstairs with it. Banford remained in her chair, listening acutely. March came downstairs again.

'There you are, then,' she said. 'Are you going up?'

'Yes, in a minute,' said Banford. But the minute passed, and she sat on in her chair under the lamp.

Henry, whose eyes were shining like a cat's as he watched from under his brows, and whose face seemed wider, more chubbed and cat-like with unalterable obstinacy, now rose to his feet to try his throw.

'I think I'll go and look if I can see the she-fox,' he said. 'She may be creeping round. Won't you come as well for a minute, Nellie, and see if we see anything?'

'Me!' cried March, looking up with her startled wondering face.

'Yes. Come on,' he said. It was wonderful how soft and warm and coaxing his voice could be, how near. The very sound of it made Banford's blood boil. 'Come on for a minute,' he said, looking down into her uplifted, unsure face.

And she rose to her feet as if drawn up by his young, ruddy face that was looking down on her.

'I should think you're never going out at this time of night, Nellie!' cried Banford.

'Yes, just for a minute,' said the boy, looking round on her and speaking with an odd, sharp yelp in his voice.

March looked from one to the other, as if confused, vague. Banford rose to her feet for battle

'Why, it's ridiculous. It's bitter cold. You'll catch your death in that thin frock. And in those slippers. You're not going to do any such thing.'

There was a moment's pause. Banford turtled up like a little fighting cock, facing March and the boy.

'Oh, I don't think you need worry yourself,' he replied. 'A moment under the stars won't do anybody any damage. I'll get the rug off the sofa in the dining-room. You're coming, Nellie.'

His voice had so much anger and contempt and fury in it as he spoke to Banford: and as much tenderness and proud authority as he spoke to March, that the latter answered:

'Yes, I'm coming.'

And she turned with him to the door.

Banford, standing there in the middle of the room, suddenly burst into a long wail and a spasm of sobs. She covered her face with her poor, thin hands, and her thin shoulders shook in an agony of weeping. March looked back from the door.

'Jill!' she cried in a frantic tone, like someone just coming awake. And she seemed to start towards her darling.

But the boy had March's arm in his grip, and she could not move. She did not know why she could not move. It was as in a dream when the heart strains and the body cannot stir.

'Never mind,' said the boy softly. 'Let her cry. Let her cry. She will have to cry sooner or later. And the tears will relieve her feelings. They will do her good.'

So he drew March slowly through the doorway. But her last look was back to the poor little figure which stood in the middle of the room with covered face and thin shoulders shaken with bitter weeping.

In the dining-room he picked up the rug and said:

'Wrap yourself up in this.'

She obeyed – and they reached the kitchen door, he holding her soft and firm by the arm, though she did not know it. When she saw the night outside she started back.

'I must go back to Jill,' she said. 'I must! Oh yes, I must.'

Her tone sounded final. The boy let go of her and she turned indoors. But he seized her again and arrested her.

'Wait a minute,' he said. 'Wait a minute. Even if you go, you're not going yet.'

'Leave go! Leave go!' she cried. 'My place is at Jill's side. Poor little thing, she's sobbing her heart out.'

'Yes,' said the boy bitterly. 'And your heart too, and mine as well.'

'Your heart?' said March. He still gripped her and detained her.

'Isn't it as good as her heart?' he said. 'Or do you think it's not?'

'Your heart?' she said again, incredulous.

'Yes, mine! Mine! Do you think I haven't got a heart?'

And with his hot grasp he took her hand and pressed it under his left breast. 'There's my heart,' he said, 'if you don't believe in it.'

It was wonder which made her attend. And then she felt the deep, heavy, powerful stroke of his heart, terrible, like something from beyond. It was like something from beyond, something awful from outside, signalling to her. And the signal paralysed her. It beat upon her very soul, and made her helpless. She forgot Jill. She could not think of Jill any more. She could not think of her. That terrible signalling from outside!

The boy put his arm round her waist.

'Come with me,' he said gently. 'Come and let us say what we've got to say.'

And he drew her outside, closed the door. And she went with him darkly down the garden path. That he should have a beating heart! And that he should have his arm round her, outside the blanket! She was too confused to think who he was or what he was.

He took her to a dark corner of the shed, where there was a tool-box with a lid, long and low.

'We'll sit here a minute,' he said.

And obediently she sat down by his side.

'Give me your hand,' he said.

She gave him both her hands, and he held them between his own. He was young, and it made him tremble.

'You'll marry me. You'll marry me before I go back, won't you?' he pleaded.

'Why, aren't we both a pair of fools?' she said.

He had put her in the corner, so that she should not look out and see the lighted window of the house, across the dark yard and garden. He tried to keep her all there inside the shed with him.

'In what way a pair of fools?' he said. 'If you go back to Canada with me, I've got a job and a good wage waiting for me, and it's a nice place, near the mountains. Why shouldn't you marry me? Why shouldn't we marry? I should like to have you there with me. I should like to feel I'd got somebody there, at the back of me, all my life.'

'You'd easily find somebody else who'd suit you better,' she said.

'Yes, I might easily find another girl. I know I could. But not one I really wanted. I've never met one I really wanted, for good. You see, I'm thinking of all my life. If I marry, I want to feel it's for all my life. Other girls: well, they're just girls, nice enough to go a walk with now and then. Nice enough for a bit of play. But when I think of my life, then I should be very sorry to have to marry one of them, I should indeed.'

'You mean they wouldn't make you a good wife.'

'Yes, I mean that. But I don't mean they wouldn't do their duty by me. I mean – I don't know what I mean. Only when I think of my life, and of you, then the two things go together.'

'And what if they didn't?' she said, with her odd, sardonic touch.

'Well, I think they would.'

They sat for some time silent. He held her hands in his, but he did not make love to her. Since he had realized that she was a woman, and vulnerable, accessible, a certain heaviness had possessed his soul. He did not want to make love to her. He shrank from any such performance, almost with fear. She was a woman, and vulnerable, accessible to him finally, and he held back from that which was ahead, almost with dread. It was a kind of darkness he knew he would enter finally, but of which he did not want as yet even to think. She was the woman, and he was responsible for the strange vulnerability he had suddenly realized in her.

'No,' she said at last, 'I'm a fool. I know I'm a fool.'

'What for?' he asked.

'To go on with this business.'

'Do you mean me?' he asked.

'No, I mean myself. I'm making a fool of myself, and a big one.'

'Why, because you don't want to marry me, really?'

'Oh, I don't know whether I'm against it, as a matter of fact. That's just it. I don't know.'

He looked at her in the darkness, puzzled. He did not in the least know what she meant.

'And don't you know whether you like to sit here with me this minute, or not?' he asked.

'No, I don't really. I don't know whether I wish I was somewhere else, or whether I like being here. I don't know, really.'

'Do you wish you were with Miss Banford? Do you wish you'd gone to bed with her?' he asked, as a challenge.

She waited a long time before she answered:

'No,' she said at last. 'I don't wish that.'

'And do you think you would spend all your life with her – when your hair goes white, and you are old?' he said

'No,' she said, without much hesitation. 'I don't see Jill and me two old women together.'

'And don't you think, when I'm an old man and you're an old woman, we might be together still, as we are now?' he said.

'Well, not as we are now,' she replied. 'But I could imagine – no, I can't. I can't imagine you an old man. Besides, it's dreadful!'

'What, to be an old man?'

'Yes, of course.'

'Not when the time comes,' he said. 'But it hasn't come. Only it will. And when it does, I should like to think you'd be there as well.'

'Sort of old age pensions,' she said drily.

Her kind of witless humour always startled him. He never knew what she meant. Probably she didn't quite know herself.

'No,' he said, hurt.

'I don't know why you harp on old age,' she said. 'I'm not ninety.'

'Did anybody ever say you were?' he asked, offended.

They were silent for some time, pulling different ways in the silence.

'I don't want you to make fun of me,' he said.

'Don't you?' she replied, enigmatic.

'No, because just this minute I'm serious. And when I'm serious, I believe in not making fun of it.'

'You mean nobody else must make fun of you,' she replied.

'Yes, I mean that. And I mean I don't believe in making fun of it myself. When it comes over me so that I'm serious, then – there it is, I don't want it to be laughed at.'

She was silent for some time. Then she said, in a vague, almost pained voice: 'No, I'm not laughing at you.'

A hot wave rose in his heart.

'You believe me, do you?' he asked.

'Yes, I believe you,' she replied, with a twang of her old tired nonchalance, as if she gave in because she was tired. But he didn't care. His heart was hot and clamorous.

'So you agree to marry me before I go? – perhaps at Christmas?'

'Yes, I agree.'

'There!' he exclaimed. 'That's settled it.'

And he sat silent, unconscious, with all the blood burning in all his veins, like fire in all the branches and twigs of him. He only pressed her two hands to his chest, without knowing. When the curious passion began to die down, he seemed to come awake to the world.

'We'll go in, shall we?' he said: as if he realized it was cold.

She rose without answering.

'Kiss me before we go, now you've said it,' he said.

And he kissed her gently on the mouth, with a young, frightened kiss. It made her feel so young, too, and frightened, and wondering: and tired, tired, as if she were going to sleep.

They went indoors. And in the sitting-room, there, crouched by the fire like a queer little witch, was Banford. She looked round with reddened eyes as they entered, but did not rise. He thought she looked frightening, unnatural, crouching there and looking round at them. Evil he thought her look was, and he crossed his fingers.

Banford saw the ruddy, elate face of the youth: he seemed strangely tall and bright and looming. And March had a delicate look on her face; she wanted to hide her face, to screen it, to let it not be seen.

'You've come at last,' said Banford uglily.

'Yes, we've come,' said he.

'You've been long enough for anything,' she said

'Yes, we have. We've settled it. We shall marry as soon as possible,' he replied.

'Oh, you've settled it, have you! Well, I hope you won't live to repent it,' said Banford.

'I hope so too,' he replied.

'Are you going to bed now, Nellie?' said Banford.

'Yes, I'm going now.'

'Then for goodness' sake come along.'

March looked at the boy. He was glancing with his very bright eyes at her and at Banford. March looked at him wistfully. She wished she could stay with him. She wished she had married him already, and it was all over. For oh, she felt suddenly so safe with him. She felt so strangely safe and peaceful in his presence. If only she could sleep in his shelter and not with Jill. She felt afraid of Jill. In her dim, tender state, it was agony to have to go with Jill and sleep with her. She wanted the boy to save her. She looked again at him.

And he, watching with bright eyes, divined something of what she felt. It puzzled and distressed him that she must go with Jill.

'I shan't forget what you've promised,' he said, looking clear into her eyes, right into her eyes, so that he seemed to occupy all her self with his queer, bright look.

She smiled to him, faintly, gently. She felt safe again – safe with him.

But in spite of all the boy's precautions, he had a set-back. The morning he was leaving the farm he got March to accompany him to the market-town, about six miles away, where they went to the registrar and had their names stuck up as two people who were going to marry. He was to come at Christmas, and the wedding was to take place then. He hoped in the spring to be able to take March back to Canada with him, now the war was really over. Though he was so young, he had saved some money.

'You never have to be without some money at the back of you, if you can help it,' he said.

So she saw him off in the train that was going West: his camp was on Salisbury Plain. And with big, dark eyes she watched him go, and it seemed as if everything real in life was retreating as the train retreated with his queer, chubby, ruddy face, that seemed so broad across the cheeks, and which never seemed to change its expression, save when a cloud of sulky anger hung on the brow, or the bright eyes fixed themselves in their stare. This was what happened now. He leaned there out of the carriage window as the train drew off, saying good-bye and staring back at her, but his face quite unchanged. There was no emotion on his face. Only his eyes tightened and became fixed and intent in their watching like a cat's when suddenly she sees something and stares. So the boy's eyes stared fixedly as the train drew away, and she was left feeling intensely forlorn. Failing his physical presence, she seemed to have nothing of him. And she had nothing of anything. Only his face was fixed in her mind: the full, ruddy, unchanging cheeks, and the straight snout of a nose, and the two eyes staring above. All she could remember was how he suddenly wrinkled his nose when he laughed, as a puppy does when he is playfully growling. But him, himself, and what he was – she knew nothing, she had nothing of him when he left her.

On the ninth day after he had left her he received this letter.

'Dear Henry,

I have been over it all again in my mind, this business of me and you, and it seems to me impossible. When you aren't there I see what a fool I am. When you are there you seem to blind me to things as they actually are. You make me see things all unreal, and I don't know what. Then when I am alone again with Jill I seem to come to my own senses and realize what a fool I am making of myself, and how I am treating you unfairly. Because it must be unfair to you for me to go on with this affair when I can't feel in my heart that I really love you. I know people talk a lot of stuff and nonsense about love, and I don't want to do that. I want to keep to plain facts and act in a sensible way. And that seems to me what I'm not doing. I don't see on what grounds I am going to marry you. I know I am not head over heels in love with you, as I have fancied myself to be with fellows when I was a young fool of a girl. You are an absolute stranger to me, and it seems to me you will always be one. So on what grounds am I going to marry you ? When I think of Jill, she is ten times more real to me. I know her and I'm awfully fond of her, and I hate myself for a beast if I ever hurt her little finger. We have a life together. And even if it can't last for ever, it is a life while it does last. And it might last as long as either of us lives. Who knows how long we've got to live? She is a delicate little thing, perhaps nobody but me knows how delicate. And as for me, I feel I might fall down the well any day. What I don't seem to see at all is you. When I think of what I've been and what I've done with you, I'm afraid I am a few screws loose. I should be sorry to think that softening of the brain is setting in so soon, but that is what it seems like. You are such an absolute stranger, and so different from what I'm used to, and we don't seem to have a thing in common. As for love, the very word seems impossible. I know what love means even in Jill's case and I know that in this affair with you it's an absolute impossibility. And then going to Canada. I'm sure I must have been clean off my chump when I promised such a thing. It makes me feel fairly frightened of myself. I feel I might do something really silly, that I wasn't responsible for – and end my days in a lunatic asylum. You may think that's all I'm fit for after the way I've gone on, but it isn't a very nice thought for me. Thank goodness Jill is here, and her being here makes me feel sane again, else I don't know what I might do; I might have an accident with the gun one evening. I love Jill, and she makes me feel safe and sane, with her loving anger against me for being such a fool. Well, what I want to say is, won't you let us cry the whole thing off? I can't marry you, and really, I won't do such a thing if it seems to me wrong. It is all a great mistake. I've made a complete fool of myself, and all I can do is to apologize to you and ask you please to forget it, and please to take no further notice of me. Your fox skin is nearly ready, and seems all right. I will post it to you if you will let me know if this address is still right, and if you will accept my apology for the awful and lunatic way I have behaved with you, and then let the matter rest.

Jill sends her kindest regards. Her mother and father are staying with us over Christmas.

Yours very sincerely,

Ellen March.'

The boy read this letter in camp as he was cleaning his kit. He set his teeth, and for a moment went almost pale, yellow round the eyes with fury. He said nothing and saw nothing and felt nothing but a livid rage that was quite unreasoning. Balked! Balked again! Balked! He wanted the woman, he had fixed like doom upon having her. He felt that was his doom, his destiny, and his reward, to have this woman. She was his heaven and hell on earth, and he would have none elsewhere. Sightless with rage and thwarted madness he got through the morning. Save that in his mind he was lurking and scheming towards an issue, he would have committed some insane act. Deep in himself he felt like roaring and howling and gnashing his teeth and breaking things. But he was too intelligent. He knew society was on top of him, and he must scheme. So with his teeth bitten together, and his nose curiously slightly lifted, like some creature that is vicious, and his eyes fixed and staring, he went through the morning's affairs drunk with anger and suppression. In his mind was one thing – Banford. He took no heed of all March's outpouring: none. One thorn rankled, stuck in his mind. Banford. In his mind, in his soul, in his whole being, one thorn rankling to insanity. And he would have to get it out. He would have to get the thorn of Banford out of his life, if he died for it.

With this one fixed idea in his mind, he went to ask for twenty-four hours' leave of absence. He knew it was not due to him. His consciousness was supernaturally keen. He knew where he must go – he must go to the captain. But how could he get at the captain? In that great camp of wooden huts and tents he had no idea where his captain was. But he went to the officers' canteen. There was his captain standing talking with three other officers. Henry stood in the doorway at attention.

'May I speak to Captain Berryman?' The captain was Cornish like himself.

'What do you want?' called the captain.

'May I speak to you, Captain?'

'What do you want?' replied the captain, not stirring from among his group of fellow-officers.

Henry watched his superior for a minute without speaking.

'You won't refuse me, sir, will you?' he asked gravely.

'It depends what it is.'

'Can I have twenty-four hours' leave?'

'No, you've no business to ask.'

'I know I haven't. But I must ask you.'

'You've had your answer.'

'Don't send me away, Captain.'

There was something strange about the boy as he stood there so everlasting in the doorway. The Cornish captain felt the strangeness at once, and eyed him shrewdly.

'Why, what's afoot?' he said, curious.

'I'm in trouble about something. I must go to Blewbury,' said the boy.

'Blewbury, eh? After the girls?'

'Yes, it is a woman, Captain.' And the boy, as he stood there with his head reaching forward a little, went suddenly terribly pale, or yellow, and his lips seemed to give off pain. The captain saw and paled a little also. He turned aside.

'Go on, then,' he said. 'But for God's sake don't cause any trouble of any sort.'

'I won't, Captain, thank you.'

He was gone. The captain, upset, took a gin and bitters. Henry managed to hire a bicycle. It was twelve o'clock when he left the camp. He had sixty miles of wet and muddy crossroads to ride. But he was in the saddle and down the road without a thought of food.

At the farm, March was busy with a work she had had some time in hand. A bunch of Scotch fir-trees stood at the end of the open shed, on a little bank where ran the fence between two of the gorse-shaggy meadows. The furthest of these trees was dead – it had died in the summer, and stood with all its needles brown and sere in the air. It was not a very big tree. And it was absolutely dead. So March determined to have it, although they were not allowed to cut any of the timber. But it would make such splendid firing, in these days of scarce fuel.

She had been giving a few stealthy chops at the trunk for a week or more, every now and then hacking away for five minutes, low down, near the ground, so no one should notice. She had not tried the saw, it was such hard work, alone. Now the tree stood with a great yawning gap in his base, perched as it were on one sinew, and ready to fall. But he did not fall.

It was late in the damp December afternoon, with cold mists creeping out of the woods and up the hollows, and darkness waiting to sink in from above. There was a bit of yellowness where the sun was fading away beyond the low woods of the distance. March took her axe and went to the tree. The small thud-thud of her blows resounded rather ineffectual about the wintry homestead. Banford came out wearing her thick coat, but with no hat on her head, so that her thin, bobbed hair blew on the uneasy wind that sounded in the pines and in the wood.

'What I'm afraid of,' said Banford, 'is that it will fall on the shed and we sh'll have another job repairing that.'

'Oh, I don't think so,' said March, straightening herself, and wiping her arm over her hot brow. She was flushed red, her eyes were very wide-open and queer, her upper lip lifted away from her two white, front teeth with a curious, almost rabbit-look.

A little stout man in a black overcoat and a bowler hat came pottering across the yard. He had a pink face and a white beard and smallish pale-blue eyes. He was not very old, but nervy, and he walked with little short steps.

'What do you think, father?' said Banford. 'Don't you think it might hit the shed in falling?'

'Shed, no!' said the old man. 'Can't hit the shed. Might as well say the fence.'

'The fence doesn't matter,' said March in her high voice.

'Wrong as usual, am I?' said Banford, wiping her straying hair from her eyes.

The tree stood as it were on one spelch of itself, leaning, and creaking in the wind. It grew on the bank of a little dry ditch between the two meadows. On the top of the bank straggled one fence, running to the bushes uphill. Several trees clustered there in the corner of the field near the shed and near the gate which led into the yard. Towards this gate, horizontal across the weary meadows, came the grassy, rutted approach from the high road. There trailed another rickety fence, long split poles joining the short, thick, wide-apart uprights. The three people stood at the back of the tree, in the corner of the shed meadow, just above the yard gate. The house, with its two gables and its porch, stood tidy in a little grassed garden across the yard. A little, stout, rosy-faced woman in a little red woollen shoulder shawl had come and taken her stand in the porch.

'Isn't it down yet?' she cried, in a high little voice.

'Just thinking about it,' called her husband. His tone towards the two girls was always rather mocking and satirical. March did not want to go on with her hitting while he was there. As for him, he wouldn't lift a stick from the ground if he could help it, complaining, like his daughter, of rheumatics in his shoulder. So the three stood there a moment silent in the cold afternoon, in the bottom corner near the yard.

They heard the far-off taps of a gate, and craned to look. Away across, on the green horizontal approach, a figure was just swinging on to a bicycle again, and lurching up and down over the grass, approaching.

'Why, it's one of our boys – it's Jack,' said the old man.

'Can't be,' said Banford.

March craned her head to look. She alone recognized the khaki figure. She flushed, but said nothing.

'No, it isn't Jack, I don't think,' said the old man, staring with little round blue eyes under his white lashes. In another moment the bicycle lurched into sight, and the rider dropped off at the gate. It was Henry, his face wet and red and spotted with mud. He was altogether a muddy sight.

'Oh!' cried Banford, as if afraid. 'Why, it's Henry!'

'What!' muttered the old man. He had a thick, rapid, muttering way of speaking, and was slightly deaf. 'What? What? Who is it? Who is it, do you say? That young fellow? That young fellow of Nellie's? Oh! Oh!' And the satiric smile came on his pink face and white eyelashes.

Henry, pushing the wet hair off his steaming brow, had caught sight of them and heard what the old man said. His hot, young face seemed to flame in the cold light.

'Oh, are you all there!' he said, giving his sudden, puppy's little laugh. He was so hot and dazed with cycling he hardly knew where he was. He leaned the bicycle against the fence and climbed over into the corner on to the bank, without going into the yard.

'Well, I must say, we weren't expecting you,' said Banford laconically.

'No, I suppose not,' said he, looking at March.

She stood aside, slack, with one knee drooped and the axe resting its head loosely on the ground. Her eyes were wide and vacant, and her upper lip lifted from her teeth in that helpless, fascinated rabbit-look. The moment she saw his glowing, red face it was all over with her. She was as helpless as if she had been bound. The moment she saw the way his head seemed to reach forward.

'Well, who is it? Who is it, anyway?' asked the smiling, satiric old man in his muttering voice.

'Why, Mr. Grenfel, whom you've heard us tell about, father,' said Banford coldly.

'Heard you tell about, I should think so. Heard of nothing else practically,' muttered the elderly man, with his queer little jeering smile on his face. 'How do you do,' he added, suddenly reaching out his hand to Henry.

The boy shook hands just as startled. Then the two men fell apart.

'Cycled over from Salisbury Plain, have you?' asked the old man.

'Yes.'

'Hm! Longish ride. How long d'it take you, eh? Some time, eh? Several hours, I suppose.'

'About four.'

'Eh? Four! Yes, I should have thought so. When are you going back, then?'

'I've got till to-morrow evening.'

'Till to-morrow evening, eh? Yes. Hm! Girls weren't expecting you, were they?'

And the old man turned his pale-blue, round little eyes under their white lashes mockingly towards the girls. Henry also looked round. He had become a little awkward. He looked at March, who was still staring away into the distance as if to see where the cattle were. Her hand was on the pommel of the axe, whose head rested loosely on the ground.

'What were you doing there?' he asked in his soft, courteous voice. 'Cutting a tree down?'

March seemed not to hear, as if in a trance.

'Yes,' said Banford. 'We've been at it for over a week.'

'Oh! And have you done it all by yourselves then?'

'Nellie's done it all, I've done nothing,' said Banford.

'Really! You must have worked quite hard,' he said, addressing himself in a curious gentle tone direct to March. She did not answer, but remained half averted, staring away towards the woods above as if in a trance.

'Nellie!' cried Banford sharply. 'Can't you answer?'

'What – me?' cried March, starting round, and looking from one to the other. 'Did anyone speak to me?'

'Dreaming!' muttered the old man, turning aside to smile. 'Must be in love, eh, dreaming in the day-time!'

'Did you say anything to me?' said March, looking at the boy as from a strange distance, her eyes wide and doubtful, her face delicately flushed.

'I said you must have worked hard at the tree,' he replied courteously.

'Oh that! Bit by bit. I thought it would have come down by now.'

'I'm thankful it hasn't come down in the night, to frighten us to death,' said Banford.

'Let me just finish it for you, shall I ?' said the boy.

March slanted the axe-shaft in his direction.

'Would you like to?' she said.

'Yes, if you wish it,' he said.

'Oh, I'm thankful when the thing's down, that's all,' she replied, nonchalant.

'Which way is it going to fall?' said Banford. 'Will it hit the shed?'

'No, it won't hit the shed,' he said. 'I should think it will fall there – quite clear. Though it might give a twist and catch the fence.'

'Catch the fence!' cried the old man. 'What, catch the fence! When it's leaning at the angle? Why, it's further off than the shed. It won't catch the fence.'

'No,' said Henry, 'I don't suppose it will. It has plenty of room to fall quite clear, and I suppose it will fall clear.'

'Won't tumble backwards on top of us, will it?' asked the old man, sarcastic.

'No, it won't do that,' said Henry, taking off his short overcoat and his tunic. 'Ducks! Ducks! Go back!'

A line of four brown-speckled ducks led by a brown-and-green drake were stemming away downhill from the upper meadow, coming like boats running on a ruffled sea, cockling their way top speed downwards towards the fence and towards the little group of people, and cackling as excitedly as if they brought news of the Spanish Armada.

'Silly things! Silly things!' cried Banford, going forward to turn them off. But they came eagerly towards her, opening their yellow-green beaks and quacking as if they were so excited to say something.

'There's no food. There's nothing here. You must wait a bit,' said Banford to them. 'Go away. Go away. Go round to the yard.'

They didn't go, so she climbed the fence to swerve them round under the gate and into the yard. So off they waggled in an excited string once more, wagging their rumps like the sterns of little gondolas, ducking under the bar of the gate. Banford stood on the top of the bank, just over the fence, looking down on the other three.

Henry looked up at her, and met her queer, round-pupilled, weak eyes staring behind her spectacles. He was perfectly still. He looked away, up at the weak, leaning tree. And as he looked into the sky, like a huntsman who is watching a flying bird, he thought to himself: 'If the tree falls in just such a way, and spins just so much as it falls, then the branch there will strike her exactly as she stands on top of that bank.'

He looked at her again. She was wiping the hair from her brow again, with that perpetual gesture. In his heart he had decided her death. A terrible still force seemed in him, and a power that was just his. If he turned even a hair's breadth in the wrong direction, he would lose the power.

'Mind yourself, Miss Banford,' he said. And his heart held perfectly still, in the terrible pure will that she should not move.

'Who, me, mind myself?' she cried, her father's jeering tone in her voice. 'Why, do you think you might hit me with the axe?'

'No, it's just possible the tree might, though,' he answered soberly. But the tone of his voice seemed to her to imply that he was only being falsely solicitous, and trying to make her move because it was his will to move her.

'Absolutely impossible,' she said.

He heard her. But he held himself icy still, lest he should lose his power.

'No, it's just possible. You'd better come down this way.'

'Oh, all right. Let us see some crack Canadian tree-felling,' she retorted.

'Ready, then,' he said, taking the axe, looking round to see he was clear.

There was a moment of pure, motionless suspense, when the world seemed to stand still. Then suddenly his form seemed to flash up enormously tall and fearful, he gave two swift, flashing blows, in immediate succession, the tree was severed, turning slowly, spinning strangely in the air and coming down like a sudden darkness on the earth. No one saw what was happening except himself. No one heard the strange little cry which the Banford gave as the dark end of the bough swooped down, down on her. No one saw her crouch a little and receive the blow on the back of the neck. No one saw her flung outwards and laid, a little twitching heap, at the foot of the fence. No one except the boy. And he watched with intense bright eyes, as he would watch a wild goose he had shot. Was it winged, or dead? Dead!

Immediately he gave a loud cry. Immediately March gave a wild shriek that went far, far down the afternoon. And the father started a strange bellowing sound.

The boy leapt the fence and ran to the figure. The back of the neck and head was a mass of blood, of horror. He turned it over. The body was quivering with little convulsions. But she was dead really. He knew it, that it was so. He knew it in his soul and his blood. The inner necessity of his life was fulfilling itself, it was he who was to live. The thorn was drawn out of his bowels. So he put her down gently. She was dead.

He stood up. March was standing there petrified and absolutely motionless.

Her face was dead white, her eyes big black pools. The old man was scrambling horribly over the fence.

'I'm afraid it's killed her,' said the boy.

The old man was making curious, blubbering noises as he huddled over the fence. 'What!' cried March, starting electric.

'Yes, I'm afraid,' repeated the boy.

March was coming forward. The boy was over the fence before she reached it.

'What do you say, killed her?' she asked in a sharp voice.

'I'm afraid so,' he answered softly.

She went still whiter, fearful. The two stood facing one another. Her black eyes gazed on him with the last look of resistance. And then in a last agonized failure she began to grizzle, to cry in a shivery little fashion of a child that doesn't want to cry, but which is beaten from within, and gives that little first shudder of sobbing which is not yet weeping, dry and fearful.

He had won. She stood there absolutely helpless, shuddering her dry sobs and her mouth trembling rapidly. And then, as in a child, with a little crash came the tears and the blind agony of sightless weeping. She sank down on the grass, and sat there with her hands on her breast and her face lifted in sightless, convulsed weeping. He stood above her, looking down on her, mute, pale, and everlasting seeming. He never moved, but looked down on her. And among all the torture of the scene, the torture of his own heart and bowels, he was glad, he had won.

After a long time he stooped to her and took her hands.

'Don't cry,' he said softly. 'Don't cry.'

She looked up at him with tears running from her eyes, a senseless look of helplessness and submission. So she gazed on him as if sightless, yet looking up to him. She would never leave him again. He had won her. And he knew it and was glad, because he wanted her for his life. His life must have her. And now he had won her. It was what his life must have.

But if he had won her, he had not yet got her. They were married at Christmas as he had planned, and he got again ten days' leave. They went to Cornwall, to his own village, on the sea. He realized that it was awful for her to be at the farm any more.

But though she belonged to him, though she lived in his shadow, as if she could not be away from him, she was not happy. She did not want to leave him: and yet she did not feel free with him. Everything around her seemed to watch her, seemed to press on her. He had won her, he had her with him, she was his wife. And she – she belonged to him, she knew it. But she was not glad. And he was still foiled. He realized that though he was married to her and possessed her in every possible way, apparently, and though she *wanted* him to possess her, she wanted it, she wanted nothing else, now, still he did not quite succeed.

Something was missing. Instead of her soul swaying with new life, it seemed to droop, to bleed, as if it were wounded. She would sit for a long time with her hand in his, looking away at the sea. And in her dark, vacant eyes was a sort of wound, and her face looked a little peaked. If he spoke to her, she would turn to him with a faint new smile, the strange, quivering little smile of a woman who has died in the old way of love, and can't quite rise to the new way. She still felt she ought to *do* something, to strain herself in some direction. And there was nothing to do, and no direction in which to strain herself. And she could not quite accept the submergence which his new love put upon her. If she was in love, she ought to herself, in some way, loving. She felt the weary need of our day to *exert* herself in love. But she knew that in fact she must no more exert herself in love. He would not have the love which exerted itself towards him. It made his brow go black. No, he wouldn't let her exert her love towards him. No, she had to be passive, to acquiesce, and to be submerged under the surface of love. She had to be like the seaweeds she saw as she peered down from the boat, swaying forever delicately under water, with all their delicate fibrils put tenderly out upon the flood, sensitive, utterly sensitive and receptive within the shadowy sea, and never, never rising and looking forth above water while they lived. Never. Never looking forth from the water until they died, only then washing, corpses, upon the surface. But while they lived, always submerged, always beneath the wave. Beneath the wave they might have powerful roots, stronger than iron; they might be tenacious and dangerous in their soft waving within the flood. Beneath the water they might be stronger, more indestructible than resistant oak trees are on land. But it was always under-water, always under-water. And she, being a woman, must be like that.

And she had been so used to the very opposite. She had had to take all the thought for love and for life, and all the responsibility. Day after day she had been responsible for the coming day, for the coming year; for her dear Jill's health and happiness and well-being. Verily, in her own small way, she had felt herself responsible for the well-being of the world. And this had been her great stimulant, this grand feeling that, in her own small sphere, she was responsible for the well-being of the world.

And she had failed. She knew that, even in her small way, she had failed. She had failed to satisfy her own feeling of responsibility. It was so difficult. It seemed so grand and easy at first. And the more you tried, the more difficult it became. It had seemed so easy to make one beloved creature happy. And the more you tried, the worse the failure. It was terrible. She had been all her life reaching, reaching, and what she reached for seemed so near, until she had stretched to her utmost limit. And then it was always beyond her.

Always beyond her, vaguely, unrealizably beyond her, and she was left with nothingness at last. The life she reached for, the happiness she reached for, the well-being she reached for all slipped back, became unreal, the further she stretched her hand. She wanted some goal, some finality – and there was none. Always this ghastly reaching, reaching, striving for something that might be just beyond. Even to make Jill happy. She was glad Jill was dead. For she had realized that she could never make her happy. Jill would always be fretting herself thinner and thinner, weaker and weaker. Her pains grew worse instead of less. It would be so for ever. She was glad she was dead.

And if Jill had married a man it would have been just the same. The woman striving, striving to make the man happy, striving within her own limits for the well-being of her world. And always achieving failure. Little, foolish successes in money or in ambition. But at the very point where she most wanted success, in the anguished effort to make some one beloved human being happy and perfect, there the failure was almost catastrophic. You wanted to make your beloved happy, and his happiness seemed always achievable. If only you did just this, that, and the other. And you did this, that, and the other, in all good faith, and every time the failure became a little more ghastly. You could love yourself to ribbons, and strive and strain yourself to the bone, and things would go from bad to worse, bad to worse, as far as happiness went. The awful mistake of happiness.

Poor March, in her goodwill and her responsibility, she had strained herself till it seemed to her that the whole of life and everything was only a horrible abyss of nothingness. The more you reached after the fatal flower of happiness, which trembles so blue and lovely in a crevice just beyond your grasp, the more fearfully you become aware of the ghastly and awful gulf of the precipice below you, into which you will inevitably plunge, as into the bottomless pit, if you reach any further. You pluck flower after flower – it is never the flower. The flower itself – its calyx is a horrible gulf, it is the bottomless pit.

That is the whole history of the search for happiness, whether it be your own or somebody else's that you want to win. It ends, and it always ends, in the ghastly sense of the bottomless nothingness into which you will inevitably fall if you strain any further.

And women? What goal can any woman conceive, except happiness? Just happiness, for herself and the whole world. That and nothing else. And so, she assumes the responsibility, and sets off towards her goal. She can see it there, at the foot of the rainbow. Or she can see it a little way beyond, in the blue distance. Not far, not far.

But the end of the rainbow is a bottomless gulf down which you can fall forever without arriving, and the blue distance is a void pit which can swallow you and all your efforts into its emptiness, and still be no emptier. You and all your efforts. So, the illusion of attainable happiness!

Poor March, she had set off so wonderfully towards the blue goal. And the further and further she had gone, the more fearful had become the realization of emptiness. An agony, an insanity at last.

She was glad it was over. She was glad to sit on the shore and look westwards over the sea, and know the great strain had ended. She would never strain for love and happiness any more. And Jill was safely dead. Poor Jill, poor Jill. It must be sweet to be dead.

For her own part, death was not her destiny. She would have to leave her destiny to the boy. But then, the boy. He wanted more than that. He wanted her to give herself without defences, to sink and become submerged in him. And she – she wanted to sit still, like a woman on the last milestone, and watch. She wanted to see, to know, to understand. She wanted to be alone: with him at her side.

And he! He did not want her to watch any more, to see any more, to understand any more. He wanted to veil her woman's spirit, as Orientals veil the woman's face. He wanted her to commit herself to him, and to put her independent spirit to sleep. He wanted to take away from her all her effort, all that seemed her very *raison d'être*. He wanted to make her submit, yield, blindly pass away out of all her strenuous consciousness. He wanted to take away her consciousness, and make her just his woman. Just his woman.

And she was so tired, so tired, like a child that wants to go to sleep, but which fights against sleep, as if sleep were death. She seemed to stretch her eyes wider in the obstinate effort and tension of keeping awake. She *would* keep awake. She *would* know. She *would* consider and judge and decide. She *would* have the reins of her own life between her own hands. She *would* be an independent woman, to the last. But she was so tired, so tired of everything. And sleep seemed near. And there was such rest in the boy.

Yet there, sitting in a niche of the high, wild cliffs of West Cornwall, looking over the westward sea, she stretched her eyes wider and wider. Away to the West, Canada, America. She would know and she *would* see what was ahead. And the boy, sitting beside her, staring down at the gulls, had a cloud between his brows and the strain of discontent in his eyes. He wanted her asleep, at peace in him. He wanted her at peace, asleep in him. And *there* she was, dying with the strain of her own wakefulness. Yet she would not sleep: no, never. Sometimes he thought bitterly that he ought to have left her. He ought never to have killed Banford: He should have left Banford and March to kill one another.

But that was only impatience: and he knew it. He was waiting, waiting to go west. He was aching almost in torment to leave England, to go west, to take March away. To leave this shore! He believed that as they crossed the seas, as they left this England which he so hated, because in some way it seemed to have stung him with poison, she would go to sleep. She would close her eyes at last, and give in to him.

And then he would have her, and he would have his own life at last. He chafed, feeling he hadn't got his own life. He would never have it till she yielded and slept in him. Then he would have all his own life as a young man and a male, and she would have all her own life as a woman and a female. There would be no more of this awful straining. She would not be a man any more, an independent woman with a man's responsibility. Nay, even the responsibility for her own soul she would have to commit to him. He knew it was so, and obstinately held out against her, waiting for the surrender.

'You'll feel better when once we get over the seas to Canada over there,' he said to her as they sat among the rocks on the cliff.

She looked away to the sea's horizon, as if it were not real. Then she looked round at him, with the strained, strange look of a child that is struggling against sleep.

'Shall I?' she said.

'Yes,' he answered quietly.

And her eyelids dropped with the *slow* motion, sleep weighing them unconscious. But she pulled them open again to say:

'Yes, I may. I can't tell. I can't tell what it will be like over there.'

'If only we could go soon!' he said, with pain in his voice.

Snake

A snake came to my water-trough
On a hot, hot day, and I in pyjamas for the heat,
to drink there.

In the deep, strange-scented shade of the great dark carob tree
5   I came down the steps with my pitcher
And must wait, must stand and wait, for there he was at the
    trough before me.

He reached down from a fissure in the earth-wall in the gloom
And trailed his yellow-brown slackness soft-bellied down, over
    the edge of the stone trough
And rested his throat upon the stone bottom
10   And where the water had dripped from the tap, in a small
    clearness,
He sipped with his straight mouth,
Softy drank through his straight gums, into his slack long body,
Silently.

Someone was before me at my water-trough,
15   And I, like a second-comer, waiting.

He lifted his head from his drinking, as cattle do,
And looked at me vaguely, as drinking cattle do,
And flickered his two-forked tongue from his lips, and mused a
    moment,
And stooped and drank a little more,
20   Being earth-brown, earth-golden from the burning bowels of the
    earth
On the day of Sicilian July, with Etna smoking.

The voice of my education said to me
He must be killed,
For in Sicily the black, black snakes are innocent, the gold are
    venomous.

25   And voices in me said, If you were a man
You would take a stick and break him now, and finish him off.

But must I confess how I liked him,
How glad I was he had come like a guest in quiet, to drink at my
    water-trough
And depart peaceful, pacified, and thankless,
30   Into the burning bowels of this earth?

Was it cowardice, that I dared not kill him?
Was it perversity, that I longed to talk to him?
Was it humility, to feel so honoured?
I felt so honoured.

35   And yet those voices:
      If you were not afraid, you would kill him!

      And truly I was afraid, I was most afraid,
      But even so, honoured still more
      That he should seek my hospitality
40   From out the dark door of the secret earth.

      He drank enough
      And lifted his head dreamily, as one who has drunken,
      And flickered his tongue like a forked night on the air, so black,
      Seeming to lick his lips,
45   And looked around like a god, unseeing, into the air,
      And slowly turned his head,
      And slowly, very slowly, as if thrice a dream,
      Proceeded to draw his slow length curving round
      And climb again the broken bank of my wall-face.

50   And as he put his head into that dreadful hole,
      And as he slowly drew up, snake-easing his shoulders, and
            entered farther,
      A sort of horror, a sort of protest against his withdrawing into
            that horrid black hole,
      Deliberately going into the blackness, and slowly drawing
            himself after,
      Overcame me now his back was turned.

55   I looked round, I put down my pitcher,
      I picked up a clumsy log
      And threw it at the water-trough with a clatter.

      I think it did not hit him,
      But suddenly that part of him that was left behind convulsed in
            undignified haste,
60   Writhed like lightning, and was gone
      Into the black hole, the earth-lipped fissure in the wallfront,
      At which, in the intense still noon, I stared with fascination.

      And immediately I regretted it.
      I thought how paltry, how vulgar, what a mean act.
65   I despised myself and the voices of my accursed human education.
      And I thought of the albatross,
      And I wished he would come back, my snake.
      For he seemed to me again like a king,
      Like a king in exile, uncrowned in the underworld,
70   Now due to be crowned again.

      And so, I missed my chance with one of the lords
      Of life.
      And I have something to expiate:
      A pettiness.

VIRGINIA WOOLF (1882–1941)

Woolf was one of the twentieth century's writers most determined to free herself from the novel's established conventions. As she characterised it, life was a 'luminous halo', and her novels and stories attempt to use the coherence and structure offered by fictional forms in ways which do not misrepresent the impressionistic, insecure quality of experience. Pioneering techniques such as stream of consciousness, or, as in the example below, interior monologue, Woolf's fiction is marked by experimentation. She championed the role of the woman writer, and, as part of the Bloomsbury circle, challenged a wide range of accepted social norms, though with the advantage of working in an affluent, privileged environment.

From Mrs. Dalloway

Mrs. Dalloway said she would buy the flowers herself.

For Lucy had her work cut out for her. The doors would be taken off their hinges; Rumpelmayer's men were coming. And then, thought Clarissa Dalloway, what a morning – fresh as if issued to children on a beach.

What a lark! What a plunge! For so it had always seemed to her when, with a little squeak of the hinges, which she could hear now, she had burst open the French windows and plunged at Bourton into the open air. How fresh, how calm, stiller than this of course, the air was in the early morning; like the flap of a wave; the kiss of a wave; chill and sharp and yet (for a girl of eighteen as she then was) solemn, feeling as she did, standing there at the open window, that something awful was about to happen; looking at the flowers, at the trees with the smoke winding off them and the rooks rising, falling; standing and looking until Peter Walsh said, 'Musing among the vegetables?' – was that it? – 'I prefer men to cauliflowers' – was that it? He must have said it at breakfast one morning when she had gone out on to the terrace – Peter Walsh. He would be back from India one of these days, June or July, she forgot which, for his letters were awfully dull; it was his sayings one remembered; his eyes, his pocket-knife, his smile, his grumpiness and, when millions of things had utterly vanished – how strange it was! – a few sayings like this about cabbages.

She stiffened a little on the kerb, waiting for Durtnall's van to pass. A charming woman, Scrope Purvis thought her (knowing her as one does know people who live next door to one in Westminster); a touch of the bird about her, of the jay, blue-green, light, vivacious, though she was over fifty, and grown very white since her illness. There she perched, never seeing him, waiting to cross, very upright.

For having lived in Westminster – how many years now? over twenty, – one feels even in the midst of the traffic, or waking at night, Clarissa was positive, a particular hush, or solemnity; an indescribable pause; a suspense (but that might be her heart, affected, they said, by influenza) before Big Ben strikes. There! Out it boomed. First a warning, musical; then the hour, irrevocable. The leaden circles dissolved in the air. Such fools we are, she thought, crossing Victoria Street. For Heaven only knows why one loves it so, how one sees it so, making it up, building it round one, tumbling it, creating it every moment afresh; but the veriest frumps, the most dejected of miseries sitting on doorsteps (drink their downfall) do the same; can't be dealt with, she felt positive, by Acts of Parliament for that very reason: they love life. In people's eyes, in the swing, tramp, and trudge; in the bellow and the uproar; the carriages, motor cars, omnibuses, vans, sandwich men shuffling and swinging; brass bands; barrel organs; in the triumph and the jingle and the strange high singing of some aeroplane overhead was what she loved; life; London; this moment of June.

For it was the middle of June. The War was over, except for some one like Mrs. Foxcroft at the Embassy last night eating her heart out because that nice boy was killed and now the old Manor House must go to a cousin; or Lady Bexborough who opened a bazaar, they said, with the telegram in her hand, John, her favourite, killed; but it was over; thank Heaven – over. It was June. The King and Queen were at the Palace. And everywhere, though it was still so early, there was a beating, a stirring of galloping ponies, tapping of cricket bats; Lords, Ascot, Ranelagh and all the rest of it; wrapped in the soft mesh of the grey-blue morning air, which, as the day wore on, would unwind them, and set down on their lawns and pitches the bouncing ponies, whose forefeet just struck the ground and up they sprung, the whirling young men, and laughing girls in their transparent muslins who, even now, after dancing all night, were taking their absurd woolly dogs for a run; and even now, at this hour, discreet old dowagers were shooting out in their motor cars on errands of mystery; and the shopkeepers were fidgeting in their windows with their paste and diamonds, their lovely old sea-green brooches in eighteenth-century settings to tempt Americans (but one must economise, not buy things rashly for Elizabeth), and she, too, loving it as she did with an absurd and faithful passion, being part of it, since her people were courtiers once in the time of the Georges, she, too, was going that very night to kindle and illuminate; to give her party. But how strange, on entering the Park, the silence; the mist; the hum; the slow-swimming happy ducks; the pouched birds waddling; and who should be coming along with his back against the Government buildings, most appropriately, carrying a des-patch box stamped with the Royal Arms, who but Hugh Whitbread; her old friend Hugh – the admirable Hugh!

'Good-morning to you, Clarissa!' said Hugh, rather extravagantly, for they had known each other as children. 'Where are you off to?'

'I love walking in London,' said Mrs. Dalloway. 'Really, it's better than walk-ing in the country.'

They had just come up – unfortunately – to see doctors. Other people came to see pictures; go to the opera; take their daughters out; the Whitbreads came 'to see doctors.' Times without number Clarissa had visited Evelyn Whitbread in a nursing home. Was Evelyn ill again? Evelyn was a good deal out of sorts, said Hugh, intimating by a kind of pout or swell of his very well-covered, manly, extremely handsome, perfectly upholstered body (he was almost too well dressed always, but presumably had to be, with his little job at Court) that his wife had some internal ailment, nothing serious? which, as an old friend, Clarissa Dalloway would quite understand without requiring him to specify. Ah yes, she did of course; what a nuisance; and felt very sisterly and oddly conscious at the same time of her hat. Not the right hat for the early morning, was that it? For Hugh always made her feel, as he bustled on, raising his hat rather extravagantly and assuring her that she might be a girl of eighteen, and of course he was coming to her party to-night, Evelyn absolutely insisted, only a little late he might be after the party at the Palace to which he had to take one of Jim's boys, – she always felt a little skimpy beside Hugh; schoolgirlish; but attached to him, partly from having known him always, but she did think him a good sort in his own way, though Richard was nearly driven mad by him, and as for Peter Walsh, he had never to this day forgiven her for liking him.

She could remember scene after scene at Bourton – Peter furious; Hugh not, of course, his match in any way, but still not a positive imbecile as Peter made out; not a mere barber's block. When his old mother wanted him to give up shooting or to take her to Bath he did it, without a word; he was really unselfish, and as for saying, as Peter did, that he had no heart, no brain, nothing but the manners and breeding of an English gentleman, that was only her dear Peter at his worst; and he could be intolerable; he could be impossible; but adorable to walk with on a morning like this.

(June had drawn out every leaf on the trees. The mothers of Pimlico gave suck to their young. Messages were passing from the Fleet to the Admiralty. Arlington Street and Piccadilly seemed to chafe the very air in the Park and lift its leaves hotly, brilliantly, on waves of that divine vitality which Clarissa loved. To dance, to ride, she had adored all that.)

For they might be parted for hundreds of years, she and Peter; she never wrote a letter and his were dry sticks; but suddenly it would come over her, if he were with me now what would he say?– some days, some sights bringing him back to her calmly, without the old bitterness; which perhaps was the reward of having cared for people; they came back in the middle of St. James's Park on a fine morning – indeed they did. But Peter – however beautiful the day might be, and the trees and the grass, and the little girl in pink – Peter never saw a thing of all that. He would put on his spectacles, if she told him to; he would look. It was the state of the world that interested him; Wagner, Pope's poetry, people's characters eternally, and the defects of her own soul. How he scolded her! How they argued! She would marry a Prime Minister and stand at the top of a staircase; the perfect hostess he called her (she had cried over it in her bedroom), she had the makings of the perfect hostess, he said.

So she would still find herself arguing in St. James's Park, still making out that she had been right – and she had too – not to marry him. For in marriage a little licence, a little independence there must be between people living together day in day out in the same house; which Richard gave her, and she him. (Where was he this morning, for instance? Some committee, she never asked what.) But with Peter everything had to be shared; everything gone into. And it was intolerable, and when it came to that scene in the little garden by the fountain, she had to break with him or they would have been destroyed, both of them ruined, she was convinced; though she had borne about her for years like an arrow sticking in her heart the grief, the anguish: and then the horror of the moment when some one told her at a concert that he had married a woman met on the boat going to India! Never should she forget all that.

Cold, heartless, a prude, he called her. Never could she understand how he cared. But those Indian women did presumably – silly, pretty, flimsy nincompoops. And she wasted her pity. For he was quite happy, he assured her – perfectly happy, though he had never done a thing that they talked of; his whole life had been a failure. It made her angry still.

She had reached the Park gates. She stood for a moment, looking at the omnibuses in Piccadilly.

She would not say of any one in the world now that they were this or were that. She felt very young; at the same time unspeakably aged. She sliced like a knife through everything; at the same time was outside, looking on. She had a perpetual sense, as she watched the taxicabs, of being out, out, far out to sea and alone; she always had the feeling that it was very, very dangerous to live even one day. Not that she thought herself clever, or much out of the ordinary. How she had got through life on the few twigs of knowledge Fraulein Daniels gave them she could not think. She knew nothing; no language, no history; she scarcely read a book now, except memoirs in bed; and yet to her it was absolutely absorbing; all this; the cabs passing; and she would not say of Peter, she would not say of herself, I am this, I am that.

Her only gift was knowing people almost by instinct, she thought, walking on. If you put her in a room with some one, up went her back like a cat's; or she purred. Devonshire House, Bath House, the house with the china cockatoo, she had seen them all lit up once; and remembered Sylvia, Fred, Sally Seton – such hosts of people; and dancing all night; and the waggons plodding past to market; and driving home across the Park. She remembered once throwing a shilling into the Serpentine. But every one remembered; what she loved was this, here, now, in front of her; the fat lady in the cab. Did it matter then, she asked herself, walking towards Bond Street, did it matter that she must inevitably cease completely; all this must go on without her; did she resent it; or did it not become consoling to believe that death ended absolutely? but that somehow in the streets of London, on the ebb and flow of things, here, there, she survived, Peter survived, lived in each other, she being part, she was positive, of the trees at home; of the house there, ugly, rambling all to bits and pieces as it was; part of people she had never met; being laid out like a mist between the people she knew best, who lifted her on their branches as she had seen the trees lift the mist, but it spread ever so far, her life, herself. But what was she dreaming as she looked into Hatchards' shop window? What was she trying to recover? What image of white dawn in the country, as she read in the book spread open:

> Fear no more the heat o' the sun
> Nor the furious winter's rages.

This late age of world's experience had bred in them all, all men and women, a well of tears. Tears and sorrows; courage and endurance; a perfectly upright and stoical bearing. Think, for example, of the woman she admired most, Lady Bexborough, opening the bazaar.

There were Jorrocks' *Jaunts and Jollities;* there were *Soapy Sponge* and Mrs. Asquith's *Memoirs* and *Big Game Shooting in Nigeria,* all spread open. Ever so many books there were; but none that seemed exactly right to take to Evelyn

Whitbread in her nursing home. Nothing that would serve to amuse her and make that indescribably dried-up little woman look, as Clarissa came in, just for a moment cordial; before they settled down for the usual interminable talk of women's ailments. How much she wanted it – that people should look pleased as she came in, Clarissa thought and turned and walked back towards Bond Street, annoyed, because it was silly to have other reasons for doing things. Much rather would she have been one of those people like Richard who did things for themselves, whereas, she thought, waiting to cross, half the time she did things not simply, not for themselves; but to make people think this or that; perfect idiocy she knew (and now the policeman held up his hand) for no one was ever for a second taken in. Oh if she could have had her life over again! she thought, stepping on to the pavement, could have looked even differently!

She would have been, in the first place, dark like Lady Bexborough, with a skin of crumpled leather and beautiful eyes. She would have been, like Lady Bexborough, slow and stately; rather large; interested in politics like a man; with a country house; very dignified, very sincere. Instead of which she had a narrow pea-stick figure; a ridiculous little face, beaked like a bird's. That she held herself well was true; and had nice hands and feet; and dressed well, considering that she spent little. But often now this body she wore (she stopped to look at a Dutch picture), this body, with all its capacities, seemed nothing – nothing at all. She had the oddest sense of being herself invisible; unseen; unknown; there being no more marrying, no more having of children now, but only this astonishing and rather solemn progress with the rest of them, up Bond Street, this being Mrs. Dalloway; not even Clarissa any more; this being Mrs. Richard Dalloway.

Bond Street fascinated her; Bond Street early in the morning in the season; its flags flying; its shops; no splash; no glitter; one roll of tweed in the shop where her father had bought his suits for fifty years; a few pearls; salmon on an iceblock.

'That is all,' she said, looking at the fishmonger's. 'That is all,' she repeated, pausing for a moment at the window of a glove shop where, before the War, you could buy almost perfect gloves. And her old Uncle William used to say a lady is known by her shoes and her gloves. He had turned on his bed one morning in the middle of the War. He had said, 'I have had enough.' Gloves and shoes; she had a passion for gloves; but her own daughter, her Elizabeth, cared not a straw for either of them.

Not a straw, she thought, going on up Bond Street to a shop where they kept flowers for her when she gave a party. Elizabeth really cared for her dog most of all. The whole house this morning smelt of tar. Still, better poor Grizzle than Miss Kilman; better distemper and tar and all the rest of it than sitting mewed in a stuffy bedroom with a prayer book! Better anything, she was inclined to say. But it might be only a phase, as Richard said, such as all girls go through. It might be falling in love. But why with Miss Kilman? who had been badly treated of course; one must make allowances for that, and Richard said she was very able, had a really historical mind. Anyhow they were inseparable, and Elizabeth, her own daughter, went to Communion; and how she dressed, how she treated people who came to lunch she did not care a bit, it being her experience that the religious ecstasy made people callous (so did causes); dulled their feelings, for Miss Kilman would do anything for the Russians, starved herself for the Austrians, but in private inflicted positive torture, so insensitive was she, dressed in a green mackintosh coat. Year in year out she wore that coat; she perspired; she was never in the room five minutes without making you feel her superiority, your inferiority; how poor she was; how rich you were; how she lived in a slum without a cushion or a bed or a rug or whatever it might be, all her soul rusted with that grievance sticking in it, her dismissal from school during the War – poor, embittered, unfortunate creature! For it was not her one hated but the idea of her, which undoubtedly had gathered in to itself a great deal that was not Miss Kilman; had become one of those spectres with which one battles in the night; one of those spectres who stand astride us and suck up half our life-blood, dominators and tyrants; for no doubt with another throw of the dice, had the black been uppermost and not the white, she would have loved Miss Kilman! But not in this world. No.

It rasped her, though, to have stirring about in her this brutal monster! to hear twigs cracking and feel hooves planted down in the depths of that leaf-encumbered forest, the soul; never to be content quite, or quite secure, for at any moment the brute would be stirring, this hatred, which, especially since her illness, had power to make her feel scraped, hurt in her spine; gave her physical pain, and made all pleasure in beauty, in friendship, in being well, in being loved and making her home delightful, rock, quiver, and bend as if indeed there were a monster grubbing at the roots, as if the whole panoply of content were nothing but self love! this hatred!

Nonsense, nonsense! she cried to herself, pushing through the swing doors of Mulberry's the florists.

She advanced, light, tall, very upright, to be greeted at once by button-faced Miss Pym, whose hands were always bright red, as if they had been stood in cold water with the flowers.

There were flowers: delphiniums, sweet peas, bunches of lilac; and carnations, masses of carnations. There were roses; there were irises. Ah yes – so she breathed in the earthy-garden sweet smell as she stood talking to Miss Pym who owed her help, and thought her kind, for kind she had been years ago; very kind, but she looked older, this year, turning her head from side to side among the irises and roses and nodding tufts of lilac with her eyes half closed, snuffing in, after the street uproar the delicious scent, the exquisite coolness. And then, opening her eyes, how fresh, like frilled linen clean from a laundry laid in wicker trays, the roses looked; and dark and prim the red carnations, holding their heads up; and all the sweet peas spreading in their bowls, tinged violet, snow white, pale – as if it were the evening and girls in muslin frocks came out to pick sweet peas and roses after the superb summer's day, with its almost blue-black sky, its delphiniums, its carnations, its arum lilies, was over; and it was the moment between six and seven when every flower – roses, carnations, irises, lilac – glows; white, violet, red, deep orange; every flower seems to burn by itself, softly, purely in the misty beds; and how she loved the grey white moths spinning in and out, over the cherry pie, over the evening primroses!

And as she began to go with Miss Pym from jar to jar, choosing, nonsense, nonsense, she said to herself, more and more gently, as if this beauty, this scent, this colour, and Miss Pym liking her, trusting her, were a wave which she let flow over her and surmount that hatred, that monster, surmount it all; and it lifted her up and up when – oh! a pistol shot in the street outside!

'Dear, those motor cars,' said Miss Pym, going to the window to look, and corning back and smiling apologetically with her hands full of sweet peas, as if those motor cars, those tyres of motor cars, were all her fault.

The violent explosion which made Mrs. Dalloway jump and Miss Pym go to the window and apologise came from a motor car which had drawn to the side of the pavement precisely opposite Mulberry's shop window. Passers-by, who, of course, stopped and stared, had just time to see a face of the very greatest importance against the dove-grey upholstery, before a male hand drew the blind and there was nothing to be seen except a square of dove grey.

Yet rumours were at once in circulation from the middle of Bond Street to Oxford Street on one side, to Atkinson's scent shop on the other, passing invisibly, inaudibly, like a cloud, swift, veil-like upon hills, falling indeed with something of a cloud's sudden sobriety and stillness upon faces which a second before had been utterly disorderly. But now mystery had brushed them with her wing; they had heard the voice of authority; the spirit of religion was abroad with her eyes bandaged tight and her lips gaping wide. But nobody knew whose face had been seen. Was it the Prince of Wales's, the Queen's, the Prime Minister's? Whose face was it? Nobody knew.

Edgar J. Watkiss, with his roll of lead piping round his arm, said audibly, humorously of course: 'The Proime Minister's kyar.'

Septimus Warren Smith, who found himself unable to pass, heard him.

Septimus Warren Smith, aged about thirty, palefaced, beak-nosed, wearing brown shoes and a shabby overcoat, with hazel eyes which had that look of apprehension in them which makes complete strangers apprehensive too. The world has raised its whip; where will it descend?

Everything had come to a standstill. The throb of the motor engines sounded like a pulse irregularly drumming through an entire body. The sun became extraordinarily hot because the motor car had stopped outside Mulberry's shop window; old ladies on the tops of omnibuses spread their black parasols; here a green, here a red parasol opened with a little pop. Mrs. Dalloway, coming to the window with her arms full of sweet peas, looked out with her little pink face pursed in inquiry. Every one looked at the motor car. Septimus looked. Boys on bicycles sprang off. Traffic accumulated. And there the motor car stood, with drawn blinds, and upon them a curious pattern like a tree Septimus thought, and this gradual drawing together of everything to one centre before his eyes, as if some horror had come almost to the surface and was about to burst into flames, terrified him. The world wavered and quivered and threatened to burst into flames. It is I who am blocking the way, he thought. Was he not being looked at and pointed at; was he not weighted there, rooted to the pavement, for a purpose? But for what purpose?

'Let us go on, Septimus,' said his wife, a little woman, with large eyes in a sallow pointed face; an Italian girl.

But Lucrezia herself could not help looking at the motor car and the tree pattern on the blinds. Was it the Queen in there – the Queen going shopping?

The chauffeur, who had been opening something, turning something, shutting something, got on to the box.

'Come on,' said Lucrezia.

But her husband, for they had been married four, five years now, jumped, started, and said, 'All right!' angrily, as if she had interrupted him.

People must notice; people must see. People, she thought, looking at the crowd staring at the motor car; the English people, with their children and their horses and their clothes, which she admired in a way; but they were 'people' now, because Septimus had said, 'I will kill myself'; an awful thing to say. Suppose they had heard him? She looked at the crowd. Help, help! she wanted to cry out to butchers' boys and women. Help! Only last autumn she and Septimus had stood on the Embankment wrapped in the same cloak and, Septimus reading a paper instead of talking, she had snatched it from him and laughed in the old man's face who saw them! But failure one conceals. She must take him away into some park.

'Now we will cross,' she said.

She had a right to his arm, though it was without feeling. He would give her, who was so simple, so impulsive, only twenty-four, without friends in England, who had left Italy for his sake, a piece of bone.

The motor car with its blinds drawn and an air of inscrutable reserve proceeded towards Piccadilly, still gazed at, still ruffling the faces on both sides of the street with the same dark breath of veneration whether for Queen, Prince, or Prime Minister nobody knew. The face itself had been seen only once by three people for a few seconds. Even the sex was now in dispute. But there could be no doubt that greatness was seated within; greatness was passing, hidden, down Bond Street, removed only by a hand's-breadth from ordinary people who might now, for the first time and last, be within speaking distance of the majesty of England, of the enduring symbol of the state which will be known to curious antiquaries, sifting the ruins of time, when London is a grass-grown path and all those hurrying along the pavement this Wednesday morning are but bones with a few wedding rings mixed up in their dust and the gold stoppings of innumerable decayed teeth. The face in the motor car will then be known.

It is probably the Queen, thought Mrs. Dalloway, coming out of Mulberry's with her flowers: the Queen. And for a second she wore a look of extreme dignity standing by the flower shop in the sunlight while the car passed at a foot's pace, with its blinds drawn. The Queen going to some hospital; the Queen opening some bazaar, thought Clarissa.

The crush was terrific for the time of day. Lords, Ascot, Hurlingham, what was it? she wondered, for the street was blocked. The British middle classes sitting sideways on the tops of omnibuses with parcels and umbrellas, yes, even furs on a day like this, were, she thought, more ridiculous, more unlike anything there has ever been than one could conceive; and the Queen herself held up; the Queen herself unable to pass. Clarissa was suspended on one side of Brook Street; Sir John Buckhurst, the old Judge, on the other, with the car between them (Sir John had laid down the law for years and liked a well-dressed woman) when the chauffeur, leaning ever so slightly, said or showed something to the policeman, who saluted and raised his arm and jerked his head and moved the omnibus to the side and the car passed through. Slowly and very silently it took its way.

Clarissa guessed; Clarissa knew of course; she had seen something white, magical, circular, in the footman's hand, a disc inscribed with a name, – the Queen's, the Prince of Wales's, the Prime Minister's? – which by force of its own lustre, burnt its way through (Clarissa saw the car diminishing, disappearing), to blaze among candelabras, glittering stars, breasts stiff with oak leaves, Hugh Whitbread and all his colleagues, the gentlemen of England, that night in Buckingham Palace. And Clarissa, too, gave a party. She stiffened a little; so she would stand at the top of her stairs.

The car had gone, but it had left a slight ripple which flowed through glove shops and hat shops and tailors' shops on both sides of Bond Street. For thirty seconds all heads were inclined the same way – to the window. Choosing a pair of gloves – should they be to the elbow or above it, lemon or pale grey? – ladies stopped; when the sentence was finished something had happened. Something so trifling in single instances that no mathematical instrument, though capable of transmitting shocks in China, could register the vibration; yet in its fullness rather formidable and in its common appeal emotional; for in all the hat shops and tailors' shops strangers looked at each other and thought of the dead; of the flag; of Empire. In a public-house in a back street a Colonial insulted the House of Windsor, which led to words, broken beer glasses, and a general shindy, which echoed strangely across the way in the ears of girls buying white underlinen threaded with pure white ribbon for their weddings. For the surface agitation of the passing car as it sunk grazed something very profound.

Gliding across Piccadilly, the car turned down St. James's Street. Tall men, men of robust physique, well-dressed men with their tail-coats and their white slips and their hair raked back, who, for reasons difficult to discriminate, were standing in the bow window of White's with their hands behind the tails of their coats, looking out, perceived instinctively that greatness was passing, and the pale light of the immortal presence fell upon them as it had fallen upon Clarissa Dalloway. At once they stood even straighter, and removed their hands, and seemed ready to attend their Sovereign, if need be, to the cannon's mouth, as their ancestors had done before them. The white busts and the little tables in the background covered with copies of the *Tatler* and bottles of soda water seemed to approve; seemed to indicate the flowing corn and the manor houses of England; and to return the frail hum of the motor wheels as the walls of a whispering gallery return a single voice expanded and made sonorous by the might of a whole cathedral. Shawled Moll Pratt with her flowers on the pavement wished the dear boy well (it was the Prince of Wales for certain) and would have tossed the price of a pot of beer – a bunch of roses – into St. James's Street out of sheer light-heartedness and contempt of poverty had she not seen the constable's eye upon her, discouraging an old Irishwoman's loyalty. The sentries at St. James's saluted; Queen Alexandra's policeman approved.

A small crowd, meanwhile, had gathered at the gates of Buckingham Palace. Listlessly, yet confidently, poor people all of them, they waited; looked at the Palace itself with the flag flying; at Victoria, billowing on her mound, admired her shelves of running water, her geraniums; singled out from the motor cars in the Mall first this one, then that; bestowed emotion, vainly, upon commoners out for a drive; recalled their tribute to keep it unspent while this car passed and that; and all the time let rumour accumulate in their veins and thrill the nerves in their thighs at the thought of Royalty looking at them; the Queen bowing; the Prince saluting; at the thought of the heavenly life divinely bestowed upon Kings; of the equerries and deep curtsies; of the Queen's old doll's house; of Princess Mary married to an Englishman, and the Prince – ah! the Prince! who took wonderfully, they said, after old King Edward, but was ever so much slimmer. The Prince lived at St. James's; but he might come along in the morning to visit his mother.

So Sarah Bletchley said with her baby in her arms, tipping her foot up and down as though she were by her own fender in Pimlico, but keeping her eyes on the Mall, while Emily Coates ranged over the Palace windows and thought of the housemaids, the innumerable housemaids, the bedrooms, the innumerable bedrooms. Joined by an elderly gentleman with an Aberdeen terrier, by men without occupation, the crowd increased. Little Mr. Bowley, who had rooms in the Albany and was sealed with wax over the deeper sources of life, but could be unsealed suddenly, inappropriately, sentimentally, by this sort of thing – poor women waiting to see the Queen go past – poor women, nice little children, orphans, widows, the War – tut-tut – actually had tears in his eyes. A breeze flaunting ever so warmly down the Mall through the thin trees, past the bronze heroes, lifted some flag flying in the British breast of Mr. Bowley and he raised his hat as the car turned into the Mall and held it high as the car approached and let the poor mothers of Pimlico press close to him, and stood very upright. The car came on.

Suddenly Mrs. Coates looked up into the sky. The sound of an aeroplane bored ominously into the ears of the crowd. There it was coming over the trees, letting out white smoke from behind, which curled and twisted, actually writing something! making letters in the sky! Every one looked up.

Dropping dead down, the aeroplane soared straight up, curved in a loop, raced, sank, rose, and whatever it did, wherever it went, out fluttered behind it a thick ruffled bar of white smoke which curled and wreathed upon the sky in letters. But what letters? A C was it? an E, then an L? Only for a moment did they lie still; then they moved and melted and were rubbed out up in the sky, and the aeroplane shot further away and again, in a fresh space of sky, began writing a K, an E, a Y perhaps?

'Blaxo,' said Mrs. Coates in a strained, awestricken voice, gazing straight up, and her baby, lying stiff and white in her arms, gazed straight up.

'Kreemo,' murmured Mrs. Bletchley, like a sleepwalker. With his hat held out perfectly still in his hand, Mr. Bowley gazed straight up. All down the Mall people were standing and looking up into the sky. As they looked the whole world became perfectly silent, and a flight of gulls crossed the sky, first one gull leading, then another, and in this extraordinary silence and peace, in this pallor, in this purity, bells struck eleven times, the sound fading up there among gulls. The aeroplane turned and raced and swooped exactly where it liked, swiftly, freely, like a skater –

'That's an E,' said Mrs. Bletchley –

or a dancer –

'It's toffee,' murmured Mr. Bowley –

(and the car went in at the gates and nobody looked at it), and shutting off the smoke, away and away it rushed, and the smoke faded and assembled itself round the broad white shapes of the clouds.

The Mark on the Wall

Perhaps it was the middle of January in the present year that I first looked up and saw the mark on the wall. In order to fix a date it is necessary to remember what one saw. So now I think of the fire; the steady film of yellow light upon the page of my book; the three chrysanthemums in the round glass bowl on the mantelpiece. Yes, it must have been the winter time, and we had just finished our tea, for I remember that I was smoking a cigarette when I looked up and saw the mark on the wall for the first time. I looked up through the smoke of my cigarette and my eye lodged for a moment upon the burning coals, and that old fancy of the crimson flag flapping from the castle tower came into my mind, and I thought of the cavalcade of red knights riding up the side of the black rock. Rather to my relief the sight of the mark interrupted the fancy, for it is an old fancy, an automatic fancy, made as a child perhaps. The mark was a small round mark, black upon the white wall, about six or seven inches above the mantelpiece.

How readily our thoughts swarm upon a new object, lifting it a little way, as ants carry a blade of straw so feverishly, and then leave it . . . If that mark was made by a nail, it can't have been for a picture, it must have been for a miniature – the miniature of a lady with white powdered curls, powder-dusted cheeks, and lips like red carnations. A fraud of course, for the people who had this house before us would have chosen pictures in that way – an old picture for an old room. That is the sort of people they were – very interesting people, and I think of them so often, in such queer places, because one will never see them again, never know what happened next. They wanted to leave this house because they wanted to change their style of furniture, so he said, and he was in process of saying that in his opinion art should have ideas behind it when we were torn asunder, as one is torn from the old lady about to pour out tea and the young man about to hit the tennis ball in the back garden of the suburban villa as one rushes past in the train.

But for that mark, I'm not sure about it; I don't believe it was made by a nail after all; it's too big, too round, for that. I might get up, but if I got up and looked at it, ten to one I shouldn't be able to say for certain; because once a thing's done, no one ever knows how it happened. Oh! dear me, the mystery of life: the inaccuracy of thought! The ignorance of humanity! To show how very little control of our possessions we have – what an accidental affair this living is after all our civilization – let me just count over a few of the things lost in one lifetime, beginning, for that seems always the most mysterious of losses – what cat would gnaw what rat would nibble – three pale blue canisters of bookbinding tools? Then there were the bird cages, the iron hoops, the steel skates, the Queen Anne coal-scuttle, the bagatelle board, the hand organ – all gone, and jewels, too. Opals and emeralds, they lie about the roots of turnips. What a scraping paring affair it is to be sure! The wonder is that I've any clothes on my back, that I sit surrounded by solid furniture at this moment. Why, if one wants to compare life to anything, one must liken it to being blown through the Tube at fifty miles an hour – landing at the other end without a single hairpin in one's hair! Shot out at the feet of God entirely naked! Tumbling head over heels in the asphodel meadows like brown paper parcels pitched down a shoot in the post office! With one's hair flying back like the tail of a race-horse. Yes, that seems to express the rapidity of life, the perpetual waste and repair; all so casual, all so haphazard . . .

But after life. The slow pulling down of thick green stalks so that the cup of the flower, as it turns over, deluges one with purple and red light. Why, after all, should one not be born there as one is born here, helpless, speechless, unable to focus one's eyesight, groping at the roots of the grass, at the toes of the Giants? As for saying which are trees, and which are men and women, or whether there are such things, that one won't be in a condition to do for fifty years or so. There will be nothing but spaces of light and dark, intersected by thick stalks, and rather higher up perhaps, rose-shaped blots of an indistinct colour – dim pinks and blues – which will, as time goes on, become more definite, become – I don't know what . . .

And yet that mark on the wall is not a hole at all. It may even be caused by some round black substance, such as a small rose leaf, left over from the summer, and I, not being a very vigilant housekeeper – look at the dust on the mantelpiece, for example, the dust which, so they say, buried Troy three times over, only fragments of pots utterly refusing annihilation, as one can believe.

The tree outside the window taps very gently on the pane . . . I want to think quietly, calmly, spaciously, never to be interrupted, never to have to rise from my chair, to slip easily from one thing to another, without any sense of hostility, or obstacle. I want to sink deeper and deeper, away from the surface, with its hard separate facts. To steady myself, let me catch hold of the first idea that passes . . . Shakespeare . . . Well, he will do as well as another. A man who sat himself solidly in an arm-chair, and looked into the fire, so – A shower of ideas fell perpetually from some very high Heaven down through his mind. He leant his forehead on his hand, and people, looking in through the open door for this scene is supposed to take place on a summer's evening – But how dull this is, this historical fiction! It doesn't interest me at all. I wish I could hit upon a pleasant track of thought, a track indirectly reflecting credit upon myself for those are the pleasantest thoughts, and very frequent even in the minds of modest mouse-coloured people, who believe genuinely that they dislike to hear their own praises. They are not thoughts directly praising oneself – that is the beauty of them; they are thoughts like this:

'And then I came into the room. They were discussing botany. I said how I'd seen a flower growing on a dust heap on the site of an old house in Kingsway.

The seed, I said, must have been sown in the reign of Charles the First. What flowers grew in the rein of Charles the First?' I asked – (but I don't remember the answer). Tall flowers with purple tassels to them perhaps. And so it goes on. All the time I'm dressing up the figure of myself in my own mind, lovingly, stealthily, not openly adoring it, for if I did that, I should catch myself out, and stretch my hand at once for a book in self-protection. Indeed, it is curious how instinctively one protects the image of oneself from idolatry or any other handling that could make it ridiculous, or too unlike the original to be believed in any longer. Or is it not so very curious after all? It is a matter of great importance. Supposing the looking-glass smashes, the image disappears, and the romantic figure with the green of forest depths all about it is there no longer, but only that shell of a person which is seen by other people – what an airless, shallow, bald, prominent world it becomes! A world not to be lived in. As we face each other in omnibuses and underground railways we are looking into the mirror; that accounts for the vagueness, the gleam of glassiness, in our eyes. And the novelists in future will realize more and more the importance of these reflections, for of course there is not one reflection but an almost infinite number; those are the depths they will explore, those the phantoms they will pursue, leaving the description of reality more and more out of their stories, taking a knowledge of it for granted, as the Greeks did and Shakespeare perhaps – but these generalizations are very worthless. The military sound of the word is enough. It recalls leading articles, cabinet ministers – a whole class of things indeed which, as a child, one thought the thing itself, the standard thing, the real thing, from which one could not depart save at the risk of nameless damnation. Generalizations bring back somehow Sunday in London, Sunday afternoon walks, Sunday luncheons, and also ways of speaking of the dead, clothes, and habits – like the habit of sitting all together in one room until a certain hour, although nobody liked it. There was a rule for everything. The rule for tablecloths at that particular period was that they should be made of tapestry with little yellow compartments marked upon them, such as you may see in photographs of the carpets in the corridors of the royal palaces. Tablecloths of a different kind were not real tablecloths. How shocking, and yet how wonderful it was to discover that these real things, Sunday luncheons, Sunday walks, country houses, and tablecloths were not entirely real, were indeed half phantoms, and the damnation which visited the disbeliever in them was only a sense of illegitimate freedom. What now takes the place of those things I wonder, those real standard things? Men perhaps, should you be a woman; the masculine point of view which governs our lives, which sets the standard, which established Whitaker's Table of Precedency, which has become, I suppose, since the war, half a phantom to many men and women, which soon, one may hope, will be laughed into the dustbin where the phantoms go, the mahogany sideboards and the Landseer prints, Gods and Devils, Hell, and so forth, leaving us all with an intoxicating sense of illegitimate freedom – if freedom exists . . .

In certain lights that mark on the wall seems actually to project from the wall. Nor is it entirely circular. I cannot be sure, but it seems to cast a perceptible shadow, suggesting that if I ran my finger down that strip of the wall it would at a certain point, mount and descend a small tumulus, a smooth tumulus like those barrows on the South Downs which are, they say, either tombs or camps. Of the two I should prefer them to be tombs, desiring melancholy like most English people, and finding it natural at the end of a walk to think of the bones stretched beneath the turf . . . There must be some book about it. Some antiquary must have dug up those bones and given them a name . . . What sort of a man is an antiquary, I wonder? Retired Colonels for the most part, I dare say, leading parties of aged labourers to the top here, examining clods of earth and stone, and getting into correspondence with the neighbouring clergy, which, being opened at breakfast time, gives them a feeling of importance, and the comparison of arrowheads necessitates cross-country journeys to the county towns, an agreeable necessity both to them and to their elderly wives, who wish to make plum jam or to clean out the study, and have every reason for keeping that great question of the camp or the tomb in perpetual suspension while the Colonel himself feels agreeably philosophic in accumulating evidence on both sides of the question. It is true that he does finally incline to believe in the camp; and, being opposed, indites a pamphlet which he is about to read at the quarterly meeting of the local society when a stroke lays him low, and his last conscious thoughts are not of wife or child, but of the camp and that arrow-head there, which is now in the case at the local museum, together with the foot of a Chinese murderess, a handful of Elizabethan nails, a great many Tudor clay pipes, a piece of Roman pottery, and the wineglass that Nelson drank out of – proving I really don't know what.

No, no, nothing is proved, nothing is known. And if I were to get up at this very moment and ascertain that the mark on the wall is really – what shall we say? – the head of a gigantic old nail, driven in two hundred years ago, which has now, owing to the patient attrition of many generations of housemaids, revealed its head above the coat of paint, and is taking its first view of modern life in the sight of a white-walled fire-lit room, what should I gain? Knowledge? Matter for further speculation? I can think sitting still as well as standing up. And what is knowledge? What are our learned men save the descendants of witches and hermits who crouched in caves and in woods brewing herbs, interrogating shrew-mice and writing down the language of the stars? And the less we honour them as our superstitions dwindle and our respect for beauty and health of mind increases . . . Yes, one could imagine a very pleasant world. A quiet, spacious world, with the flowers so red and blue in the open fields. A world without professors or specialists or house-keepers with the profiles of policemen, a world which one could slice with one's thought as a fish slices the water with his fin, grazing the stems of the water-lilies, hanging suspended over nests of white sea eggs . . . How peaceful it is down here, rooted in the centre of the world and gazing up through the grey waters, with their sudden gleams of light, and their reflections – if it were not for Whitaker's Almanack – if it were not for the Table of Precedency!

I must jump up and see for myself what that mark on the wall really is – a nail, a rose-leaf, a crack in the wood ?

Here is nature once more at her old game of self-preservation. This train of thought, she perceives, is threatening mere waste of energy, even some collision with reality for who will ever be able to lift a finger against Whitaker's

Table of Precedency? The Archbishop of Canterbury is followed by the Lord High Chancellor; the Lord High Chancellor is followed by the Archbishop of York. Everybody follows somebody, such is the philosophy of Whitaker, and the great thing is to know who follows whom. Whitaker knows, and let that, so Nature counsels, comfort you, instead of enraging you; and if you can't be comforted, if you must shatter this hour of peace, think of the mark on the wall.

I understand Nature's game – her prompting to take action as a way of ending any thought that threatens to excite or to pain. Hence. I suppose, comes our slight contempt for men of action – men, we assume, who don't think. Still, there's no harm in putting a full stop to one's disagreeable thoughts by looking at a mark on the wall.

Indeed, now that I have fixed my eyes upon it, I feel that I have grasped a plank in the sea; I feel a satisfying sense of reality which at once turns the two Archbishops and Lord High Chancellor to the shadows of shades. Here is something definite, something real. Thus, waking from a midnight dream of horror, one hastily turns on the light and lies quiescent, worshipping the chest of drawers, worshipping solidity, worshipping reality, worshipping the impersonal world which is a proof of some existence other than ours. That is what one wants to be sure of . . . Wood is a pleasant thing to think about. It comes from a tree; and trees grow, and we don't know how they grow. For years and years they grow, without paying any attention to us, in meadows, in forests, and by the side of rivers – all things one likes to think about. The cows swish their tails beneath them on hot afternoons; they paint rivers so green that when a moorhen dives one expects to see its feathers all green when it comes up again. I like to think of the fish balanced against the stream like flags blown out; and of water-beetles slowly raising domes of mud upon the bed of the river. I like to think of the tree itself: first the close dry sensation of being wood; then the grinding of the storm; then the slow, delicious ooze of sap. I like to think of it, too, on winter's nights standing in the empty field with all leaves close-furled, nothing tender exposed to the iron bullets of the moon, a naked mast upon an earth that goes tumbling, tumbling, all night long. The song of birds must sound very loud and strange in June; and how cold the feet of insects must feel upon it, as they make laborious progresses up the creases of the bark, or sun themselves upon the thin green awning of the leaves, and look straight in front of them with diamond-cut red eyes . . . One by one the fibres snap beneath the immense cold pressure of the earth, then the last storm comes and, falling, the highest branches drive deep into the ground again. Even so, life isn't done with; there are a million patient, watchful lives still for a tree, all over the world, in bedrooms, in ships, on the pavement, lining rooms, where men and women sit after tea, smoking cigarettes. It is full of peaceful thoughts, happy thoughts, this tree. I should like to take each one separately – but something is getting in the way . . . Where was I? What has it all been about? A tree? A river? The Downs? Whitaker's Almanack? The fields of asphodel? I can't remember a thing. Everything's moving, falling, slipping, vanishing . . . There is a vast upheaval of matter. Someone is standing over me and saying:

'I'm going out to buy a newspaper.'

'Yes?'

'Though it's no good buying newspapers . . . Nothing ever happens. Curse this war; God damn this war! . . . All the same, I don't see why we should have a snail on our wall.'

Ah, the mark on the wall! It was a snail.

KATHERINE MANSFIELD (1888–1923)

Born Kathleen Mansfield Beauchamp in New Zealand, Katherine Mansfield was partly educated in England. In 1908, she return to London intent on a literary career and began to write for journals, creating a distinctive feminine perspective in short stories which are wonderfully lyrical and technically masterful. In 1917 she contracted tuberculosis and wrote under increasing difficulties arising from ill health. *Bliss* is taken from her second collection of stories and was first published in 1920.

Bliss

Although Bertha Young was thirty she still had moments like this when she wanted to run instead of walk, to take dancing steps on and off the pavement, to bowl a hoop, to throw something up in the air and catch it again, or to stand still and laugh at – nothing – at nothing, simply.

What can you do if you are thirty and, turning the corner of your own street, you are overcome, suddenly, by a feeling of bliss – absolute bliss! – as though you'd suddenly swallowed a bright piece of that late afternoon sun and it burned in your bosom, sending out a little shower of sparks into every particle, into every finger and toe? . . .

Oh, is there no way you can express it without being 'drunk and disorderly'? How idiotic civilization is! Why be given a body if you have to keep it shut up in a case like a rare, rare fiddle?

'No, that about the fiddle is not quite what I mean,' she thought, running up the steps and feeling in her bag for the key – she'd forgotten it, as usual – and rattling the letterbox. 'It's not what I mean, because – Thank you, Mary' – she went into the hall. 'Is nurse back?'

'Yes, M'm.'

'And has the fruit come?'

'Yes, M'm. Everything's come.'

'Bring the fruit up to the dining-room, will you? I'll arrange it before I go upstairs.'

It was dusky in the dining-room and quite chilly. But all the same Bertha threw off her coat; she could not bear the tight clasp of it another moment, and the cold air fell on her arms.

But in her bosom there was still that bright glowing place – that shower of little sparks coming from it. It was almost unbearable. She hardly dared to breathe for fear of fanning it higher, and yet she breathed deeply, deeply. She hardly dared to look into the cold mirror – but she did look, and it gave her back a woman, radiant, with smiling, trembling lips, with big, dark eyes and an air of listening, waiting for something . . . divine to happen . . . that she knew must happen . . . infallibly.

Mary brought in the fruit on a tray and with it a glass bowl, and a blue dish, very lovely, with a strange sheen on it as though it had been dipped in milk.

'Shall I turn on the light, M'm?'

'No, thank you. I can see quite well.'

There were tangerines and apples stained with strawberry pink. Some yellow pears, smooth as silk, some white grapes covered with a silver bloom and a big cluster of purple ones. These last she had bought to tone in with the new dining-room carpet. Yes, that did sound rather far-fetched and absurd, but it was really why she had bought them. She had thought in the shop: 'I must have some purple ones to bring the carpet up to the table.' And it had seemed quite sense at the time.

When she had finished with them and had made two pyramids of these bright round shapes, she stood away from the table to get the effect – and it really was most curious. For the dark table seemed to melt into the dusky light and the glass dish and the blue bowl to float in the air. This, of course in her present mood, was so incredibly beautiful. . . . She began to laugh.

'No, no. I'm getting hysterical.' And she seized her bag and coat and ran upstairs to the nursery.

Nurse sat at a low table giving Little B her supper after her bath. The baby had on a white flannel gown and a blue woollen jacket, and her dark, fine hair was brushed up into a funny little peak. She looked up when she saw her mother and began to jump.

'Now, my lovey, eat it up like a good girl,' said Nurse, setting her lips in a way that Bertha knew, and that meant she had come into the nursery at another wrong moment.

'Has she been good, Nanny?'

'She's been a little sweet all the afternoon,' whispered Nanny. 'We went to the park and I sat down on a chair and took her out of the pram and a big dog came along and put its head on my knee and she clutched its ear, tugged it. Oh, you should have seen her.'

Bertha wanted to ask if it wasn't rather dangerous to let her clutch at a strange dog's ear. But she did not dare to. She stood watching them, her hands by her side, like the poor little girl in front of the rich little girl with the doll.

The baby looked up at her again, stared, and then smiled so charmingly that Bertha couldn't help crying:

'Oh, Nanny, do let me finish giving her her supper while you put the bath things away.'

'Well, M'm, she oughtn't to be changed hands while she's eating,' said Nanny, still whispering. 'It unsettles her; it's very likely to upset her.'

How absurd it was. Why have a baby if it has to be kept – not in a case like a rare, rare fiddle – but in another woman's arms?

'Oh, I must!' said she.

Very offended, Nanny handed her over.

'Now, don't excite her after her supper. You know you do, M'm. And I have such a time with her after!'

Thank heaven! Nanny went out of the room with the bath towels.

'Now I've got you to myself, my little precious,' said Bertha, as the baby leaned against her.

She ate delightfully, holding up her lips for the spoon and then waving her hands. Sometimes she wouldn't let the spoon go; and sometimes, just as Bertha had filled it, she waved it away to the four winds.

When the soup was finished Bertha turned round to the fire.

'You're nice – you're very nice!' said she, kissing her warm baby. 'I'm fond of you. I like you.'

And, indeed, she loved Little B so much – her neck as she bent forward, her exquisite toes as they shone transparent in the firelight – that all her feeling of bliss came back again, and again she didn't know how to express it – what to do with it.

'You're wanted on the telephone,' said Nanny, coming back in triumph and seizing *her* Little B.

Down she flew. It was Harry.

'Oh, is that you, Ber? Look here. I'll be late. I'll take a taxi and come along as quickly as I can, but get dinner put back ten minutes – will you? All right?'

'Yes, perfectly. Oh, Harry!'

'Yes?'

What had she to say? She'd nothing to say. She only wanted to get in touch with him for a moment. She couldn't absurdly cry: 'Hasn't it been a divine day!'

'What is it?' rapped out the little voice.

'Nothing. *Entendu*,' said Bertha, and hung up the receiver, thinking how more than idiotic civilization was.

They had people coming to dinner. The Norman Knights – a very sound couple – he was about to start a theatre, and she was awfully keen on interior decoration, a young man, Eddie Warren, who had just published a little book of poems and whom everybody was asking to dine, and a 'find' of Bertha's called Pearl Fulton. What Miss Fulton did, Bertha didn't know. They had met at the club and Bertha had fallen in love with her, as she always did fall in love with beautiful women who had something strange about them.

The provoking thing was that, though they had been about together and met a number of times and really talked, Bertha couldn't yet make her out. Up to a certain point Miss Fulton was rarely, wonderfully frank, but the certain point was there, and beyond that she would not go.

Was there anything beyond it? Harry said 'No.' Voted her dullish, and 'cold like all blonde women, with a touch, perhaps, of anaemia of the brain'. But Bertha wouldn't agree with him; not yet, at any rate.

'No, the way she has of sitting with her head a little on one side, and smiling, has something behind it, Harry, and I must find out what that something is.'

'Most likely it's a good stomach,' answered Harry.

He made a point of catching Bertha's heels with replies of that kind . . . 'liver frozen, my dear girl', or 'pure flatulence', or 'kidney disease', . . . and so on. For some strange reason Bertha liked this, and almost admired it in him very much.

She went into the drawing-room and lighted the fire; then picking up the cushions, one by one, that Mary had disposed so carefully, she threw them back on to the chairs and the couches. That made all the difference; the room came alive at once. As she was about to throw the last one she surprised herself by suddenly hugging it to her, passionately, passionately. But it did not put out the fire in her bosom. Oh, on the contrary!

The windows of the drawing-room opened on to a balcony overlooking the garden. At the far end, against the wall, there was a tall, slender pear tree in fullest, richest bloom; it stood perfect, as though becalmed against the jade-green sky. Bertha couldn't help feeling, even from this distance, that it had not a single bud or a faded petal. Down below, in the garden beds, the red and yellow tulips, heavy with flowers, seemed to lean upon the dusk. A grey cat, dragging its belly, crept across the lawn, and a black one, its shadow, trailed after. The sight of them, so intent and so quick, gave Bertha a curious shiver.

'What creepy things cats are!' she stammered, and she turned away from the window and began walking up and down. . . .

How strong the jonquils smelled in the warm room. Too strong? Oh, no. And yet, as though overcome, she flung down on a couch and pressed her hands to her eyes.

'I'm too happy – too happy!' she murmured.

And she seemed to see on her eyelids the lovely pear tree with its wide open blossoms as a symbol of her own life.

Really – really – she had everything. She was young. Harry and she were as much in love as ever, and they got on together splendidly and were really good pals. She had an adorable baby. They didn't have to worry about money. They had this absolutely satisfactory house and garden. And friends – modern, thrilling friends, writers and painters and poets or people keen on social questions – just the kind of friends they wanted. And then there were books, and there was music, and she had found a wonderful little dressmaker, and they were going abroad in the summer, and their new cook made the most superb omelettes. . . .

'I'm absurd. Absurd!' She sat up; but she felt quite dizzy, quite drunk. It must have been the spring.

Yes, it was the spring. Now she was so tired she could not drag herself upstairs to dress.

A white dress, a string of jade beads, green shoes and stockings. It wasn't intentional. She had thought of this scheme hours before she stood at the drawing-room window.

Her petals rustled softly into the hall, and she kissed Mrs Norman Knight, who was taking off the most amusing orange coat with a procession of black monkeys round the hem and up the fronts.

'. . . Why! Why! Why is the middle-class so stodgy – so utterly without a sense of humour! My dear, it's only by a fluke that I am here at all – Norman being the protective fluke. For my darling monkeys so upset the train that it rose to a man and simply ate me with its eyes. Didn't laugh – wasn't amused – that I should have loved. No, just stared – and bored me through and through.'

'But the cream of it was,' said Norman, pressing a large tortoiseshell-rimmed monocle into his eye, 'you don't mind me telling this, Face, do you?' (In their home and among their friends they called each other Face and Mug.) 'The cream of it was when she, being full fed, turned to the woman beside her and said: " Haven't you ever seen a monkey before ?"'

'Oh, yes!' Mrs Norman Knight joined in the laughter. 'Wasn't that too absolutely creamy?'

And a funnier thing still was that now her coat was off she did look like a very intelligent monkey – who had even made that yellow silk dress out of scraped banana skins. And her amber ear-rings; they were like little dangling nuts.

'This is a sad, sad fall!' said Mug, pausing in front of Little B's perambulator. 'When the perambulator comes into the hall – ' and he waved the rest of the quotation away.

The bell rang. It was lean, pale Eddie Warren (as usual) in a state of acute distress.

'It *is* the right house, *isn't* it?' he pleaded.

'Oh, I think so – I hope so,' said Bertha brightly.

'I have had such a *dreadful* experience with a taxi-man; he was *most* sinister. I couldn't get him to *stop*. The *more* I knocked and called the *faster* he went. And *in* the moonlight this *bizarre* figure with the *flattened* head *crouching* over the *little* wheel. . . .'

He shuddered, taking off an immense white silk scarf. Bertha noticed that his socks were white, too – most charming.

'But how dreadful!' she cried.

'Yes, it really was,' said Eddie, following her into the drawing-room. 'I saw myself *driving* through Eternity in a *timeless taxi.*'

He knew the Norman Knights. In fact, he was going to write a play for N. K. when the theatre scheme came off.

'Well, Warren, how's the play?' said Norman Knight, dropping his monocle and giving his eye a moment in which to rise to the surface before it was screwed down again.

And Mrs Norman Knight: 'Oh, Mr. Warren, what happy socks?'

'*I am so* glad you like them,' said he, staring at his feet. 'They seem to have got so *much* whiter since the moon rose.' And he turned his lean sorrowful young face to Bertha. 'There is a moon, you know.'

She wanted to cry: 'I am sure there is – often – often!'

He really was a most attractive person. But so was Face, crouched before the fire in her banana skins, and so was Mug, smoking a cigarette and saying as he flicked the ash: 'Why doth the bridegroom tarry?'

'There he is, now.'

Bang went the front door open and shut. Harry shouted: 'Hullo, you people. Down in five minutes.' And they heard him swarm up the stairs. Bertha couldn't help smiling; she knew how he loved doing things at high pressure. What, after all, did an extra five minutes matter? But he would pretend to himself that they mattered beyond measure. And then he would make a great point of coming into the drawing-room, extravagantly cool and collected.

Harry had such a zest for life. Oh, how she appreciated it in him. And his passion for fighting – for seeking in everything that came up against him another test of his power and of his courage – that, too, she understood. Even when it made him just occasionally, to other people, who didn't know him well, a little ridiculous perhaps. . . . For there were moments when he rushed into battle where no battle was. . . . She talked and laughed and positively forgot until he had come in (just as she had imagined) that Pearl Fulton had not turned up.

'I wonder if Miss Fulton has forgotten?'

'I expect so,' said Harry. 'Is she on the phone?'

'Ah! There's a taxi, now.' And Bertha smiled with that little air of proprietorship that she always assumed while her women finds were new and mysterious. 'She lives in taxis.'

'She'll run to fat if she does,' said Harry coolly, ringing the bell for dinner. 'Frightful danger for blonde women.'

'Harry – don't,' warned Bertha, laughing up at him.

Came another tiny moment, while they waited, laughing and talking, just a trifle too much at their ease, a trifle too unaware. And then Miss Fulton, all in silver, with a silver fillet binding her pale blonde hair, came in smiling, her head a little on one side.

'Am I late?'

'No, not at all,' said Bertha. 'Come along.' And she took her arm and they moved into the dining-room.

What was there in the touch of that cool arm that could fan – fan – start blazing – blazing – the fire of bliss that Bertha did not know what to do with?

Miss Fulton did not look at her; but then she seldom did look at people directly. Her heavy eyelids lay upon her eyes and the strange half smile came and went upon her lips as though she lived by listening rather than seeing. But Bertha knew, suddenly, as if the longest, most intimate look had passed between them – as if they had said to each other: 'You, too?' – that Pearl Fulton, stirring the beautiful red soup in the grey plate, was feeling just what she was feeling.

And the others? Face and Mug, Eddie and Harry, their spoons rising and falling – dabbing their lips with their napkins, crumbling bread, fiddling with the forks and glasses and talking.

'I met her at the Alpha show – the weirdest little person. She'd not only cut off her hair, but she seemed to have taken a dreadfully good snip off her legs and arms and her neck and her poor little nose as well.'

'Isn't she very *liée* with Michael Oat?'

'The man who wrote *Love in False Teeth*?'

'He wants to write a play for me. One act. One man. Decides to commit suicide. Gives all the reasons why he should and why he shouldn't. And just as he has made up his mind either to do it or not to do it – curtain. Not half a bad idea.'

'What's he going to call it – "Stomach Trouble"?'

'I *think* I've come across the *same* idea in a lit-tle French review, *quite* unknown in England.'

No, they didn't share it. They were dears – dears – and she loved having them there, at her table, and giving them delicious food and wine. In fact, she longed to tell them how delightful they were, and what a decorative group they made, how they seemed to set one another off and how they reminded her of a play by Chekhov.

Harry was enjoying his dinner. It was part of his – well, not his nature, exactly, and certainly not his pose – his something or other – to talk about food and to glory in his 'shameless passion for the white flesh of the lobster' and 'the green of pistachio ices – green and cold like the eyelids of Egyptian dancers'.

When he looked up at her and said: 'Bertha, this is a very admirable *soufflé*!' she almost could have wept with childlike pleasure.

Oh, why did she feel so tender towards the whole world tonight? Everything was good – was right. All that happened seemed to fill again her brimming cup of bliss.

And still, in the back of her mind, there was the pear tree. It would be silver now, in the light of poor dear Eddie's moon, silver as Miss Fulton, who sat there turning a tangerine in her slender fingers that were so pale a light seemed to come from them.

What she simply couldn't make out – what was miraculous – was how she should have guessed Miss Fulton's mood so exactly and so instantly. For she never doubted for a moment that she was right, and yet what had she to go on? Less than nothing.

'I believe this does happen very, very rarely between women. Never between men,' thought Bertha. 'But while I am making the coffee in the drawing-room perhaps she will "give a sign".'

What she meant by that she did not know, and what would happen after that she could not imagine.

While she thought like this she saw herself talking and laughing. She had to talk because of her desire to laugh.

'I must laugh or die.'

But when she noticed Face's funny little habit of tucking something down the front of her bodice – as if she kept a tiny, secret hoard of nuts there, too – Bertha had to dig her nails into her hands – so as not to laugh too much.

It was over at last. And: 'Come and see my new coffee machine,' said Bertha.

'We only have a new coffee machine once a fortnight,' said Harry. Face took her arm this time; Miss Fulton bent her head and followed after.

The fire had died down in the drawing-room to a red, flickering 'nest of baby phoenixes', said Face.

'Don't turn up the light for a moment. It is so lovely.'

And down she crouched by the fire again. She was always cold . . . 'without her little red flannel jacket, of course,' thought Bertha.

At that moment Miss Fulton 'gave the sign'.

'Have you a garden?' said the cool, sleepy voice.

This was so exquisite on her part that all Bertha could do was to obey. She crossed the room, pulled the curtains apart, and opened those long windows.

'There!' she breathed.

And the two women stood side by side looking at the slender, flowering tree. Although it was so still it seemed, like the flame of a candle, to stretch up, to point, to quiver in the bright air, to grow taller as they gazed – almost to touch the rim of the round, silver moon.

How long did they stand there? Both, as it were, caught in that circle of unearthly light, understanding each other perfectly, creatures of another world, and wondering what they were to do in this one with all this blissful treasure that burned in their bosoms and dropped, in silver flowers, from their hair and hands?

For ever – for a moment? And did Miss Fulton murmur: 'Yes. Just *that*.' Or did Bertha dream it?

Then the light was snapped on and Face made the coffee and Harry said: 'My dear Mrs Knight, don't ask me about my baby. I never see her. I shan't feel the slightest interest in her until she has a lover,' and Mug took his eye out of the conservatory for a moment and then put it under glass again and Eddie Warren drank his coffee and set down the cup with a face of anguish as though he had drunk and seen the spider.

'What I want to do is to give the young men a show. I believe London is simply teeming with first-chop, unwritten plays. What I want to say to 'em is: "Here's the theatre. Fire ahead."'

'You know, my dear, I am going to decorate a room for the Jacob Nathans. Oh, I am so tempted to do a fried-fish scheme, with the backs of the chairs shaped like frying pans and lovely chip potatoes embroidered all over the curtains.'

'The trouble with our young writing men is that they are still too romantic. You can't put out to sea without being seasick and wanting a basin. Well, why won't they have the courage of those basins?'

'A *dreadful* poem about a *girl* who was *violated* by a beggar *without* a nose in a lit-tle wood. . . .'

Miss Fulton sank into the lowest, deepest chair and Harry handed round the cigarettes.

From the way he stood in front of her shaking the silver box and saying abruptly: 'Egyptian? Turkish? Virginian? They're all mixed up,' Bertha realized that she not only bored him; he really disliked her. And she decided from the way Miss Fulton said: 'No, thank you, I won't smoke,' that she felt it, too, and was hurt.

'Oh, Harry, don't dislike her. You are quite wrong about her. She's wonderful, wonderful. And, besides, how can you feel so differently about someone who means so much to me. I shall try to tell you when we are in bed tonight what has been happening. What she and I have shared.'

At those last words something strange and almost terrifying darted into Bertha's mind. And this something blind and smiling whispered to her: 'Soon these people will go. The house will be quiet – quiet. The lights will be out. And you and he will be alone together in the dark room – the warm bed. . . .'

She jumped from her chair and ran over to the piano.

'What a pity someone does not play!' she cried. 'What a pity somebody does not play.'

For the first time in her life Bertha Young desired her husband.

Oh, she'd loved him – she'd been in love with him, of course, in every other way, but just not in that way. And, equally, of course, she'd understood that he was different. They'd discussed it so often. It had worried her dreadfully at first to find that she was so cold, but after a time it had not seemed to matter. They were so frank with each other – such good pals. That was the best of being modern.

But now – ardently! ardently! The word ached in her ardent body! Was this what that feeling of bliss had been leading up to? But then –

'My dear,' said Mrs Norman Knight, 'you know our shame. We are victims of time and train. We live in Hampstead. It's been so nice.'

'I'll come with you into the hall,' said Bertha. 'I loved having you. But you must not miss the last train. That's so awful, isn't it?'

'Have a whisky, Knight, before you go?' called Harry.

'No thanks, old chap.'

Bertha squeezed his hand for that as she shook it.

'Good night, good-bye,' she cried from the top step, feeling that this self of hers was taking leave of them for ever.

When she got back into the drawing-room the others were on the move.

'. . . Then you can come part of the way in my taxi.'

'I shall be *so* thankful *not* to have to face *another* drive *alone* after my *dreadful* experience.'

'You can get a taxi at the rank just at the end of the street. You won't have to walk more than a few yards.'

'That's a comfort. I'll go and put on my coat.'

Miss Fulton moved towards the hall and Bertha was following when Harry almost pushed past.

'Let me help you.'

Bertha knew that he was repenting his rudeness – she let him go. What a boy he was in some ways – so impulsive – so – simple.

And Eddie and she were left by the fire.

'*I wonder* if you have seen Bilks' *new* poem called *Table d'Hôte*,' said Eddie softly. 'It's *so* wonderful. In the last anthology. Have you got a copy? I'd *so* like to *show* it to you. It begins with an *incredibly* beautiful line: "Why must it always be tomato soup?"'

'Yes,' said Bertha. And she moved noiselessly to a table opposite the drawing-room door and Eddie glided noiselessly after her. She picked up the little book and gave it to him; they had not made a sound.

While he looked it up she turned her head towards the hall. And she saw . . . Harry with Miss Fulton's coat in his arms and Miss Fulton with her back turned to him and her head bent. He tossed the coat away, put his hands on her shoulders, and turned her violently to him. His lips said: 'I adore you,' and Miss Fulton laid her moonbeam fingers on his cheeks and smiled her sleepy smile. Harry's nostrils quivered; his lips curled back in a hideous grin while he whispered: 'Tomorrow,' and with her eyelids Miss Fulton said: 'Yes.'

'Here it is,' said Eddie. '"Why must it always be tomato soup?" It's so *deeply* true, don't you feel? Tomato soup is *so dreadfully* eternal.'

'If you prefer,' said Harry's voice, very loud, from the hall, 'I can phone you a cab to come to the door.'

'Oh, no. It's not necessary,' said Miss Fulton, and she came up to Bertha and gave her the slender fingers to hold.

'Good-bye. Thank you so much.'

'Good-bye,' said Bertha.

Miss Fulton held her hand a moment longer.

'Your lovely pear tree!' she murmured.

And then she was gone, with Eddie following, like the black cat following the grey cat.

'I'll shut up shop,' said Harry, extravagantly cool and collected.

'Your lovely pear tree – pear tree – pear tree!'

Bertha simply ran over to the long windows.

'Oh, what is going to happen now?' she cried.

But the pear tree was as lovely as ever and as full of flower and as still.

T.S. ELIOT (1888–1965)

Born in the United States, Eliot settled in London and in 1927 became a British citizen. Like that of his fellow American, Ezra Pound, Eliot's work constantly stresses the importance of tradition. But it is tradition made new, reformed in distinctive, idiosyncratic, and even apparently fragmented ways, through which the writer creates his vision. Although he fashioned himself as a quintessential Englishman, Eliot's writing reflects his cosmopolitan outlook: nineteenth-century French symbolists and Dante are as potent influences as seventeenth-century English poets. Eliot's early work is marked by the sense of a civilisation in decline (e.g. *The Waste Land*). Increasingly, though, his later work finds spiritual solace and *The Four Quartets,* despite being written amidst the destruction of the Second World War, suggest the possibilities of salvation.

The Love Song of J. Alfred Prufrock

> *S'io credessi che mia risposta fosse*
> *a persona che mai tornasse al mondo,*
> *questa fiamma staria senza più scosse*
> *Ma per ciò che giammai di questo fondo*
> *non tornò vivo alcun, s'i'odo il vero,*
> *senza tema d'infamia ti rispondo.*

Let us go then, you and I,
When the evening is spread out against the sky
Like a patient etherised upon a table;
Let us go, through certain half-deserted streets,
5   The muttering retreats

S'io credessi: The epigraph is from Dante's *Inferno* (xxvii, 66-71) where the soul of Guido tells Dante: 'If I believed my reply was to one who could return to the world, this flame would speak no longer. But since no one from this depth has ever returned alive, if what I hear is true, I will reply to you without fear of infamy.'

Of restless nights in one-night cheap hotels
And sawdust restaurants with oyster-shells:
Streets that follow like a tedious argument
Of insidious intent
10   To lead you to an overwhelming question . . .
Oh, do not ask, 'What is it?'
Let us go and make our visit.

In the room the women come and go
Talking of Michelangelo.

15   The yellow fog that rubs its back upon the window-panes,
The yellow smoke that rubs its muzzle on the window-panes,
Licked its tongue into the corners of the evening,
Lingered upon the pools that stand in drains,
Let fall upon its back the soot that falls from chimneys,
20   Slipped by the terrace, made a sudden leap,
And seeing that it was a soft October night,
Curled once about the house, and fell asleep.

And indeed there will be time
For the yellow smoke that slides along the street
25   Rubbing its back upon the window-panes;
There will be time, there will be time
To prepare a face to meet the faces that you meet;
There will be time to murder and create,
And time for all the works and days of hands
30   That lift and drop a question on your plate;
Time for you and time for me,
And time yet for a hundred indecisions,
And for a hundred visions and revisions,
Before the taking of a toast and tea.

35   In the room the women come and go
Talking of Michelangelo.

And indeed there will be time
To wonder, 'Do I dare?' and, 'Do I dare?'
Time to turn back and descend the stair,
40   With a bald spot in the middle of my hair –
(They will say: 'How his hair is growing thin!')
My morning coat, my collar mounting firmly to the chin,
My necktie rich and modest, but asserted by a simple pin –
(They will say: 'But how his arms and legs are thin!')
45   Do I dare
Disturb the universe?
In a minute there is time
For decisions and revisions which a minute will reverse.

For I have known them all already, known them all –
50 Have known the evenings, mornings, afternoons,
I have measured out my life with coffee spoons;
I know the voices dying with a dying fall
Beneath the music from a farther room.
        So how should I presume?

55 And I have known the eyes already, known them all –
The eyes that fix you in a formulated phrase,
And when I am formulated, sprawling on a pin,
When I am pinned and wriggling on the wall,
Then how should I begin
60 To spit out all the butt-ends of my days and ways?
        And how should I presume?

And I have known the arms already, known them all –
Arms that are braceleted and white and bare
(But in the lamplight, downed with light brown hair!)
65 Is it perfume from a dress
That makes me so digress?
Arms that lie along a table, or wrap about a shawl.
        And should I then presume?
        And how should I begin?
                    .   .   .   .   .
70   Shall I say, I have gone at dusk through narrow streets
And watched the smoke that rises from the pipes
Of lonely men in shirt-sleeves, leaning out of windows? . . .

    I should have been a pair of ragged claws
Scuttling across the floors of silent seas.
                    .   .   .   .   .
75   And the afternoon, the evening, sleeps so peacefully!
Smoothed by long fingers,
Asleep . . . tired . . . or it malingers,
Stretched on the floor, here beside you and me.
Should I, after tea and cakes and ices,
80 Have the strength to force the moment to its crisis?
But though I have wept and fasted, wept and prayed,
Though I have seen my head (grown slightly bald) brought in
        upon a platter,
I am no prophet – and here's no great matter;
I have seen the moment of my greatness flicker,
85 And I have seen the eternal Footman hold my coat, and snicker,
And in short, I was afraid.

    And would it have been worth it, after all,
After the cups, the marmalade, the tea,
Among the porcelain, among some talk of you and me,
90 Would it have been worth while,

To have bitten off the matter with a smile,
To have squeezed the universe into a ball
To roll it towards some overwhelming question,
To say: 'I am Lazarus, come from the dead,
95   Come back to tell you all, I shall tell you all' –
If one, settling a pillow by her head,
        Should say: 'That is not what I meant at all.
        That is not it, at all.'

        And would it have been worth it, after all,
100   Would it have been worth while,
After the sunsets and the dooryards and the sprinkled streets,
After the novels, after the teacups, after the skirts that trail along
        the floor –
And this, and so much more? –
It is impossible to say just what I mean!
105   But as if a magic lantern threw the nerves in patterns on a
        screen:
Would it have been worth while
If one, settling a pillow or throwing off a shawl,
And turning toward the window, should say:
        'That is not it at all,
110   That is not what I meant, at all.'

                .   .   .   .   .

        No! I am not Prince Hamlet, nor was meant to be;
Am an attendant lord, one that will do
To swell a progress, start a scene or two,
Advise the prince; no doubt, an easy tool,
115   Deferential, glad to be of use,
Politic, cautious, and meticulous;
Full of high sentence, but a bit obtuse;
At times, indeed, almost ridiculous –
Almost, at times, the Fool.

120   I grow old . . . I grow old . . .
I shall wear the bottoms of my trousers rolled.

        Shall I part my hair behind? Do I dare to eat a peach?
I shall wear white flannel trousers, and walk upon the beach.
I have heard the mermaids singing, each to each.

125   I do not think that they will sing to me.

I have seen them riding seaward on the waves
Combing the white hair of the waves blown back
When the wind blows the water white and black.

We have lingered in the chambers of the sea
130   By sea-girls wreathed with seaweed red and brown
Till human voices wake us, and we drown.

Journey of the Magi

'A cold coming we had of it,
Just the worst time of the year
For a journey, and such a long journey:
The ways deep and the weather sharp,
5   The very dead of winter.'
And the camels galled, sore-footed, refractory,
Lying down in the melting snow.
There were times we regretted
The summer palaces on slopes, the terraces,
10   And the silken girls bringing sherbet.
Then the camel men cursing and grumbling
And running away, and wanting their liquor and women,
And the night-fires going out, and the lack of shelters,
And the cities hostile and the towns unfriendly
15   And the villages dirty and charging high prices:
A hard time we had of it.
At the end we preferred to travel all night,
Sleeping in snatches,
With the voices singing in our ears, saying
20   That this was all folly.

Then at dawn we came down to a temperate valley,
Wet, below the snow line, smelling of vegetation,
With a running stream and a water-mill beating the darkness,
And three trees on the low sky.
25   And an old white horse galloped away in the meadow.
Then we came to a tavern with vine-leaves over the lintel,
Six hands at an open door dicing for pieces of silver,
And feet kicking the empty wine-skins.
But there was no information, and so we continued
30   And arrived at evening, not a moment too soon
Finding the place; it was (you may say) satisfactory.

All this was a long time ago, I remember,
And I would do it again, but set down
This set down
35   This: were we led all that way for
Birth or Death? There was a Birth, certainly,
We had evidence and no doubt. I had seen birth and death,
But had thought they were different; this Birth was
Hard and bitter agony for us, like Death, our death.
40   We returned to our places, these Kingdoms,
But no longer at ease here, in the old dispensation,
With an alien people clutching their gods.
I should be glad of another death.

Marina

Quis hic locus, quae regio,
quae mundi plaga?

What seas what shores what grey rocks and what islands
What water lapping the bow
And scent of pine and the woodthrush singing through the fog
What images return
5   O my daughter.

Those who sharpen the tooth of the dog, meaning
Death
Those who glitter with the glory of the hummingbird, meaning
Death
10   Those who sit in the sty of contentment, meaning
Death
Those who suffer the ecstasy of the animals, meaning
Death

Are become unsubstantial, reduced by a wind,
15   A breath of pine, and the woodsong fog
By this grace dissolved in place

What is this face, less clear and clearer
The pulse in the arm, less strong and stronger –
Given or lent? more distant than stars and nearer than the eye

20   Whispers and small laughter between leaves and hurrying feet
Under sleep, where all the waters meet.
Bowsprit cracked with ice and paint cracked with heat.
I made this, I have forgotten
And remember.
25   The rigging weak and the canvas rotten
Between one June and another September.
Made this unknowing, half conscious, unknown, my own.
The garboard strake leaks, the seams need caulking.
This form, this face, this life
30   Living to live in a world of time beyond me; let me
Resign my life for this life, my speech for that unspoken,
The awakened, lips parted, the hope, the new ships.

What seas what shores what granite islands towards my
    timbers
And woodthrush calling through the fog
35   My daughter.

Marina: the lost daughter of Pericles in Shakespeare's   28 garboard strake: planks laid near a ship's keel.
Pericles. **Quis hic** . . . : epigraph from Seneca's *Hecules*
Furens, 'What place is this? What region, what part of
the world?'

From Four Quartets

Little Gidding

I

Midwinter spring is its own season
Sempiternal though sodden towards sundown,
Suspended in time, between pole and tropic.
When the short day is brightest, with frost and fire,
5   The brief sun flames the ice, on pond and ditches,
In windless cold that is the heart's heat,
Reflecting in a watery mirror
A glare that is blindness in the early afternoon.
And glow more intense than blaze of branch, or brazier,
10   Stirs the dumb spirit: no wind, but pentecostal fire
In the dark time of the year. Between melting and freezing
The soul's sap quivers. There is no earth smell
Or smell of living thing. This is the spring time
15   But not in time's covenant. Now the hedgerow
Is blanched for an hour with transitory blossom
Of snow, a bloom more sudden
Than that of summer, neither budding nor fading,
Not in the scheme of generation.
20   Where is the summer, the unimaginable
Zero summer?

     If you came this way,
Taking the route you would be likely to take
From the place you would be likely to come from,
25   If you came this way in may time, you would find the hedges
White again, in May, with voluptuary sweetness.
It would be the same at the end of the journey,
If you came at night like a broken king,
If you came by day not knowing what you came for,
30   It would be the same, when you leave the rough road
And turn behind the pig-sty to the dull façade
And the tombstone. And what you thought you came for
Is only a shell, a husk of meaning
From which the purpose breaks only when it is fulfilled
35   If at all. Either you had no purpose
Or the purpose is beyond the end you figured
And is altered in fulfilment. There are other places
Which also are the world's end, some at the sea jaws,

Little Gidding: Anglican religious community founded   2 sempiternal: everlasting.
during the 17th century and visited by George Herbert
and Richard Crashaw.

Or over a dark lake, in a desert or a city –
40 But this is the nearest, in place and time,
Now and in England.

     If you came this way,
Taking any route, starting from anywhere,
At any time or at any season,
45 It would always be the same: you would have to put off
Sense and notion. You are not here to verify,
Instruct yourself, or inform curiosity
Or carry report. You are here to kneel
Where prayer has been valid. And prayer is more
50 Than an order of words, the conscious occupation
Of the praying mind, or the sound of the voice praying.
And what the dead had no speech for, when living,
They can tell you, being dead: the communication
Of the dead is tongued with fire beyond the language of the living.
55 Here, the intersection of the timeless moment
Is England and nowhere. Never and always.

II

Ash on an old man's sleeve
Is all the ash the burnt roses leave.
Dust in the air suspended
60 Marks the place where a story ended.
Dust inbreathed was a house –
The wall, the wainscot and the mouse.
The death of hope and despair,
    This is the death of air.

65 There are flood and drouth
Over the eyes and in the mouth,
Dead water and dead sand
Contending for the upper hand.
The parched eviscerate soil
70 Gapes at the vanity of toil,
Laughs without mirth.
    This is the death of earth.

Water and fire succeed
The town, the pasture and the weed.
75 Water and fire deride
The sacrifice that we denied.
Water and fire shall rot
The marred foundations we forgot,
Of sanctuary and choir.
80   This is the death of water and fire.

In the uncertain hour before the morning
  Near the ending of interminable night
  At the recurrent end of the unending
After the dark dove with the flickering tongue
85   Had passed below the horizon of his homing
  While the dead leaves still rattled on like tin
Over the asphalt where no other sound was
  Between three districts whence the smoke arose
  I met one walking, loitering and hurried
90 As if blown towards me like the metal leaves
  Before the urban dawn wind unresisting.
  And as I fixed upon the down-turned face
That pointed scrutiny with which we challenge
  The first-met stranger in the waning dusk
95   I caught the sudden look of some dead master
Whom I had known, forgotten, half recalled
  Both one and many; in the brown baked features
  The eyes of a familiar compound ghost
Both intimate and unidentifiable.
100 So I assumed a double part, and cried
  And heard another's voice cry: 'What! are *you* here?'
Although we were not. I was still the same,
  Knowing myself yet being someone other –
  And he a face still forming; yet the words sufficed
105 To compel the recognition they preceded.
  And so, compliant to the common wind,
  Too strange to each other for misunderstanding,
In concord at this intersection time
  Of meeting nowhere, no before and after,
110 We trod the pavement in a dead patrol.
I said: 'The wonder that I feel is easy,
  Yet ease is cause of wonder. Therefore speak:
  I may not comprehend, may not remember.'
And he: 'I am not eager to rehearse
115 My thoughts and theory which you have forgotten.
  These things have served their purpose: let them be.
So with your own, and pray they be forgiven
  By others, as I pray you to forgive
  Both bad and good. Last season's fruit is eaten
120 And the fullfed beast shall kick the empty pail.
  For last year's words belong to last year's language
  And next year's words await another voice.
But, as the passage now presents no hindrance
  To the spirit unappeased and peregrine
125 Between two worlds become much like each other,

So I find words I never thought to speak
In streets I never thought I should revisit
When I left my body on a distant shore.
Since our concern was speech, and speech impelled us
130   To purify the dialect of the tribe
And urge the mind to aftersight and foresight,
Let me disclose the gifts reserved for age
To set a crown upon your lifetime's effort.
First, the cold friction of expiring sense
135 Without enchantment, offering no promise
But bitter tastelessness of shadow fruit
As body and soul begin to fall asunder.
Second, the conscious impotence of rage
At human folly, and the laceration
140   Of laughter at what ceases to amuse.
And last, the rending pain of re-enactment
Of all that you have done, and been; the shame
Of motives late revealed, and the awareness
Of things ill done and done to others' harm
145   Which once you took for exercise of virtue.
Then fools' approval stings, and honour stains.
From wrong to wrong the exasperated spirit
Proceeds, unless restored by that refining fire
Where you must move in measure, like a dancer.'
150 The day was breaking. In the disfigured street
He left me, with a kind of valediction,
And faded on the blowing of the horn.

III

There are three conditions which often look alike
Yet differ completely, flourish in the same hedgerow:
155 Attachment to self and to things and to persons, detachment
From self and from things and from persons; and, growing
    between them, indifference
Which resembles the others as death resembles life,
Being between two lives – unflowering, between
The live and the dead nettle. This is the use of memory:
160 For liberation – not less of love but expanding
Of love beyond desire; and so liberation
From the future as well as the past. Thus, love of a country
Begins as attachment to our own field of action
And comes to find that action of little importance
165 Though never indifferent. History may be servitude,
History may be freedom. See, now they vanish,
The faces and places, with the self which, as it could, loved them,
To become renewed, transfigured, in another pattern.

Sin is Behovely, but
170 All shall be well, and
All manner of thing shall be well.
If I think, again, of this place,
And of people, not wholly commendable,
Of no immediate kin or kindness,
175 But some of peculiar genius,
All touched by a common genius,
United in the strife which divided them;
If I think of a king at nightfall,
Of three men, and more, on the scaffold
180 And a few who died forgotten
In other places, here and abroad,
And of one who died blind and quiet,
Why should we celebrate
These dead men more than the dying?
185 It is not to ring the bell backward
Nor is it an incantation
To summon the spectre of a Rose.
We cannot revive old factions
We cannot restore old policies
190 Or follow an antique drum.
These men, and those who opposed them
And those whom they opposed
Accept the constitution of silence
And are folded in a single party.
195 Whatever we inherit from the fortunate
We have taken from the defeated
What they had to leave us – a symbol:
A symbol perfected in death.
And all shall be well and
200 All manner of thing shall be well
By the purification of the motive
In the ground of our beseeching.

IV

The dove descending breaks the air
With flame of incandescent terror
205 Of which the tongues declare
The one discharge from sin and error.
The only hope, or else despair
 Lies in the choice of pyre or pyre –
 To be redeemed from fire by fire.

---

169 Behovely: incumbent. A quote from the medieval mystic Julian of Norwich.

210 Who then devised the torment? Love.
Love is the unfamiliar Name
Behind the hands that wove
The intolerable shirt of flame
Which human power cannot remove.
215   We only live, only suspire
    Consumed by either fire or fire.

V

What we call the beginning is often the end
And to make an end is to make a beginning.
The end is where we start from. And every phrase
220 And sentence that is right (where every word is at home,
Taking its place to support the others,
The word neither diffident nor ostentatious,
An easy commerce of the old and the new,
The common word exact without vulgarity,
225 The formal word precise but not pedantic,
The complete consort dancing together)
Every phrase and every sentence is an end and a beginning,
Every poem an epitaph. And any action
Is a step to the block, to the fire, down the sea's throat
230 Or to an illegible stone: and that is where we start.
We die with the dying:
See, they depart, and we go with them.
We are born with the dead:
See, they return, and bring us with them.
235 The moment of the rose and the moment of the yew-tree
Are of equal duration. A people without history
Is not redeemed from time, for history is a pattern
Of timeless moments. So, while the light fails
On a winter's afternoon, in a secluded chapel
240 History is now and England.

With the drawing of this Love and the voice of this Calling

We shall not cease from exploration
And the end of all our exploring
Will be to arrive where we started
245 And know the place for the first time.
Through the unknown, remembered gate
When the last of earth left to discover
Is that which was the beginning;
At the source of the longest river
250 The voice of the hidden waterfall
And the children in the apple-tree
Not known, because not looked for
But heard, half-heard, in the stillness

Between two waves of the sea.
255 Quick now, here, now, always –
A condition of complete simplicity
(Costing not less than everything)
And all shall be well and
All manner of thing shall be well
260 When the tongues of flame are in-folded
Into the crowned knot of fire
And the fire and the rose are one.

SEAN O'CASEY (1880–1965)

Born into a poor Dublin family, O'Casey came to prominence with a series of plays performed at Dublin's Abbey Theatre in the 1920s. Although nationalist in his sympathies, O'Casey's Ireland is not a romanticised place and his drama centres on the lives of the poor in working-class Dublin caught up in 'The Troubles', the Irish struggle for independence from Britain and the subsequent Civil War.

Juno and the Paycock

Characters

'Captain' Jack Boyle	Juno Boyle, *his wife*	Johnny Boyle
Mary Boyle	Joxer Daly	Mrs. Maisie Madigan
Needle Nugent, *a tailor*	Charles Bentham, *a school teacher*	
Mrs. Tancred	Jerry Devine	Two Irregulars[1]
An Irregular Mobilizer	A Sewing Machine Man	A Coal-Block Vendor
Two Neighbours	Two Furniture Removal Men	

Scene

Act I. The living apartment of a two-roomed tenancy of the Boyle family, in a tenement house in Dublin.

Act II. The same.

Act III. The same.

A few days elapse between Acts I and II, and two months between Acts II and III.

During Act III the curtain is lowered for a few minutes to denote the lapse of one hour.

Period of the play, 1922.[2]

---

1 **Irregulars:** rebel soldiers who refused to accept the authority of the Government of the Irish Free State.
2 **1922:** the period of the Irish Civil War.

Act I

The living-room of a two-room tenancy occupied by the Boyle family in a tenement house in Dublin. Left, a door leading to another part of the house; left of door a window looking into the street; at back a dresser; farther to right at back, a window looking into the back of the house. Between the window and the dresser is a picture of the Virgin; below the picture, on a bracket, is a crimson bowl in which a floating votive light is burning. Farther to the right is a small bed partly concealed by cretonne hangings strung on a twine. To the right is the fireplace; near the fireplace is a door leading to the other room. Beside the fireplace is a box containing coal. On the mantelshelf is an alarm clock lying on its face. In a corner near the window looking into the back is a galvanized bath. A table and some chairs. On the table are breakfast things for one. A teapot is on the hob and a frying-pan stands inside the fender. There are a few books on the dresser and one on the table. Leaning against the dresser is a long-handled shovel – the kind invariably used by labourers when turning concrete or mixing mortar. Johnny Boyle is sitting crouched beside the fire. Mary with her jumper off – it is lying on the back of a chair – is arranging her hair before a tiny mirror perched on the table. Beside the mirror is stretched out the morning paper, which she looks at when she isn't gazing into the mirror. She is a well-made and good-looking girl of twenty-two. Two forces are working in her mind – one, through the circumstances of her life, pulling her back; the other, through the influence of books she has read, pushing her forward. The opposing forces are apparent in her speech and her manners, both of which are degraded by her environment, and improved by her acquaintance – slight though it be – with literature. The time is early forenoon.

Mary [*looking at the paper*] On a little by-road, out beyant Finglas, he was found.
[*Mrs. Boyle enters by door on right; she has been shopping and carries a small parcel in her hand. She is forty-five years of age, and twenty years ago she must have been a pretty woman; but her face has now assumed that look which ultimately settles down upon the faces of the women of the working-class; a look of listless monotony and harassed anxiety, blending with an expression of mechanical resistance. Were circumstances favourable, she would probably be a handsome, active and clever woman.*]
Mrs Boyle Isn't he come in yet?
Mary No, mother.
Mrs Boyle Oh, he'll come in when he likes; struttin' a-bout the town like a paycock with Joxer, I suppose. I hear all about Mrs. Tancred's son is in this mornin's paper.
Mary The full details are in it this mornin'; seven wounds he had – one entherin' the neck, with an exit wound beneath the left shoulder-blade; another in the left breast penethratin' the heart, an' . . .
Johnny [*springing up from the fire*] Oh, quit that readin' for God's sake! Are yous losin' all your feelin's? It'll soon be that none of you'll read anythin' that's not about butcherin'!
[*He goes quickly into the room on left.*]

Mary He's gettin' very sensitive, all of a sudden!

Mrs Boyle I'll read it myself, Mary, by an' by, when I come home. Everybody's sayin' that he was a Diehard – thanks be to God that Johnny had nothin' to do with him this long time. . . . [*Opening the parcel and taking out some sausages, which she places on a plate*] Ah, then, if that father o' yours doesn't come in soon for his breakfast, he may go without any; I'll not wait much longer for him.

Mary Can't you let him get it himself when he comes in?

Mrs Boyle Yes, an' let him bring in Joxer Daly along with him? Ay, that's what he'd like an' that's what he's waitin' for – till he thinks I'm gone to work, an' then sail in with the boul' Joxer, to burn all the coal an' dhrink all the tea in the place, to show them what a good Samaritan he is! But I'll stop here till he comes in, if I have to wait till tomorrow mornin'.

Voice of Johnny inside Mother!

Mrs Boyle Yis?

Voice of Johnny Bring us in a dhrink o' wather.

Mrs Boyle Bring in that fella a dhrink o' wather, for God's sake, Mary.

Mary Isn't he big an' able enough to come out an' get it himself?

Mrs Boyle If you weren't well yourself you'd like somebody to bring you in a dhrink o' wather.

[*She brings in drink and returns.*]

Mrs Boyle Isn't it terrible to have to be waitin' this way! You'd think he was bringin' twenty poun's a week into the house the way he's going on. He wore out the Health Insurance long ago, he's afther wearin' out the unemployment dole, an', now, he's thryin' to wear out me! An' constantly singin', no less, when he ought always to be on his knees offerin' up a Novena for a job!

Mary [*trying a ribbon fillet-wise around her head*] I don't like this ribbon, ma; I think I'll wear the green – it looks betther than the blue.

Mrs Boyle Ah, wear whatever ribbon you like, girl, only don't be botherin' me. I don't know what a girl on strike wants to be wearin' a ribbon round her head for, or silk stockin's on her legs either; it's wearin' them things that make the employers think they're givin' yous too much money.

Mary The hour is past now when we'll ask the employers' permission to wear what we like.

Mrs Boyle I don't know why you wanted to walk out for Jennie Claffey; up to this you never had a good word for her.

Mary What's the use of belongin' to a Trades Union if you won't stand up for your principles? Why did they sack her? It was a clear case of victimization. We couldn't let her walk the streets, could we?

Mrs Boyle No, of course yous couldn't – yous wanted to keep her company. Wan victim wasn't enough. When the employers sacrifice wan victim, the Trades Unions go wan betther be sacrificin' a hundred.

Mary It doesn't matther what you say, ma – principle's a principle.

---

1 Diehard: In 1922, Ireland became an independent country except for the six counties of Ulster, which remained part of Britain. Because a united Ireland had been the aim of the Republicans this compromise arrangement split the movement and caused civil war to break out between those who backed the Government of the Free State and the 'Diehards' who favoured continued struggle for a united Ireland.

Mrs Boyle Yis; an' when I go into oul' Murphy's tomorrow, an' he gets to know that, instead o' payin' all, I'm goin' to borry more, what'll he say when I tell him a principle's a principle? What'll we do if he refuses to give us any more on tick?

Mary He daren't refuse – if he does, can't you tell him he's paid?

Mrs Boyle It's lookin' as if he was paid, whether he refuses or no.

[*Johnny appears at the door on left. He can be plainly seen now; he is a thin, delicate fellow, something younger than Mary. He has evidently gone through a rough time. His face is pale and drawn; there is a tremulous look of indefinite fear in his eyes. The left sleeve of his coat is empty, and he walks with a slight halt.*]

Johnny I was lyin' down; I thought yous were gone. Oul' Simon Mackay is thrampin' about like a horse over me head, an' I can't sleep with him – they're like thunder-claps in me brain! The curse o' – God forgive me for goin' to curse!

Mrs Boyle There, now; go back an' lie down again an' I'll bring you in a nice cup o' tay.

Johnny Tay, tay, tay! You're always thinkin' o' tay. If a man was dyin', you'd thry to make him swally a cup o' tay! [*He goes back.*]

Mrs Boyle I don't know what's goin' to be done with him. The bullet he got in the hip in Easter Week[1] was bad enough; but the bomb that shatthered his arm in the fight in O'Connell Street put the finishin' touch on him. I knew he was makin' a fool of himself. God knows I went down on me bended knees to him not to go agen the Free State.

Mary He stuck to his principles, an', no matther how you may argue, ma, a principle's a principle.

Voice of Johnny Is Mary goin' to stay here?

Mary No, I'm not goin' to stay here; you can't expect me to be always at your beck an' call, can you?

Voice of Johnny I won't stop here be meself!

Mrs Boyle Amn't I nicely handicapped with the whole o' yous! I don't know what any o' yous ud do without your ma. [*To Johnny*] Your father'll be here in a minute, an' if you want anythin,' he'll get it for you.

Johnny I hate assin' him for anythin' . . . He hates to be assed to stir. . . . Is the light lightin' before the picture o' the Virgin?

Mrs Boyle Yis, yis! The wan inside to St. Anthony isn't enough, but he must have another wan to the Virgin here!

[*Jerry Devine enters hastily. He is about twenty-five, well set, active and earnest. He is a type, becoming very common now in the Labour Movement, of a mind knowing enough to make the mass of his associates, who know less, a power, and too little to broaden that power for the benefit of all. Mary seizes her jumper and runs hastily into room left.*]

Jerry [*breathless*] Where's the Captain, Mrs. Boyle, where's the Captain?

Mrs Boyle You may well ass a body that: he's wherever Joxer Daly is – dhrinkin' in some snug or another.

Jerry Father Farrell is just afther stoppin' to tell me to run up an' get him to go

---

1 **Easter Week:** On Easter Monday, 24 April 1916, the Irish Republic was proclaimed and the centre of Dublin occupied by the Irish Volunteers. They held out against British troops until 29 April. Within two weeks, 15 of their leaders were executed.

to the new job that's goin' on in Rathmines; his cousin is foreman o' the job, an' Father Farrell was speakin' to him about poor Johnny an' his father bein' idle so long, an' the foreman told Father Farrell to send the Captain up an' he'd give him a start – I wondher where I'd find him?

Mrs Boyle You'll find he's ayther in Ryan's or Foley's.

Jerry I'll run round to Ryan's – I know it's a great house o' Joxer's.

[*He rushes out.*]

Mrs Boyle [*piteously*] There now, he'll miss that job, or I know for what! If he gets win' o' the word, he'll not come back till evenin', so that it'll be too late. There'll never be any good got out o' him so long as he goes with that shouldher-shruggin' Joxer. I killin' meself workin', an' he shruttin' about from mornin' till night like a paycock!

[*The steps of two persons are heard coming up a flight of stairs. They are the footsteps of Captain Boyle and Joxer. Captain Boyle is singing in a deep, sonorous, self-honouring voice.*]

The Captain Sweet Spirit, hear me prayer! Hear . . . Oh . . . hear . . . me prayer . . . hear, oh, hear . . . Oh, he . . . ar . . . oh, he . . . ar . . . me . . . pray . . . er!

Joxer [*outside*] Ah, that's a darlin' song, a daaarlin' song!

Mrs Boyle [*viciously*] Sweet spirit hear his prayer! Ah, then, I'll take me solemn affeydavey, it's not for a job he's prayin'!

[*She sits down on the bed so that the cretonne hangings hide her from the view of those entering.*

The Captain comes in. He is a man of about sixty; stout, grey-haired and stocky. His neck is short, and his head looks like a stone ball that one sometimes sees on top of a gate-post. His cheeks, reddish-purple, are puffed out, as if he were always repressing an almost irrepressible ejaculation. On his upper lip is a crisp, tightly cropped moustache; he carries himself with the upper part of his body slightly thrown back, and his stomach slightly thrust forward. His walk is a slow, consequential strut. His clothes are dingy, and he wears a faded seaman's cap with a glazed peak.]

Boyle [*to Joxer, who is still outside*] Come on, come on in, Joxer; she's gone out long ago, man. If there's nothing else to be got, we'll furrage out a cup o' tay, anyway. It's the only bit I get in comfort when she's away. 'Tisn't Juno should be her pet name at all, but Deirdre of the Sorras, for she's always grousin'.

[*Joxer steps cautiously into the room. He may be younger than the Captain but he looks a lot older. His face is like a bundle of crinkled paper; his eyes have a cunning twinkle; he is spare and loosely built; he has a habit of constantly shrugging his shoulders with a peculiar twitching movement, meant to be ingratiating. His face is invariably ornamented with a grin.*]

Joxer It's a terrible thing to be tied to a woman that's always grousin'. I don't know how you stick it – it ud put years on me. It's a good job she has to be so ofen away, for [*with a shrug*] when the cat's away, the mice can play!

Boyle [*with a commanding and complacent gesture*] Pull over to the fire, Joxer, an' we'll have a cup o' tay in a minute.

Joxer Ah, a cup o' tay's a darlin' thing, a daaarlin' thing – the cup that cheers but doesn't . . .

[*Joxer's rhapsody is cut short by the sight of Juno coming forward and confronting the two cronies. Both are stupefied.*]

Mrs Boyle [*with sweet irony– poking the fire, and turning her head to glare at Joxer*]. Pull over to the fire, Joxer Daly, an' we'll have a cup o' tay in a minute! Are you sure, now, you wouldn't like an egg?

Joxer I can't stop, Mrs. Boyle; I'm in a desperate hurry, a desperate hurry.

Mrs Boyle Pull over to the fire, Joxer Daly; people is always far more comfortabler here than they are in their own place.

[*Joxer makes hastily for the door. Boyle stirs to follow him; thinks of something to relieve the situation – stops, and says suddenly*]

Joxer!

Joxer [*at door ready to bolt*] Yis?

Boyle You know the foreman o' that job that's goin' on down in Killesther, don't you, Joxer?

Joxer [*puzzled*] Foreman – Killesther?

Boyle [*with a meaning look*] He's a butty o' yours, isn't he?

Joxer [*the truth dawning on him*] The foreman at Killesther – oh yis, yis. He's an oul' butty o' mine – oh, he's a darlin' man, a daarlin' man.

Boyle Oh, then, it's a sure thing. It's a pity we didn't go down at breakfast first thing this mornin' – we might ha' been working now; but you didn't know it then.

Joxer [*with a shrug*] It's betther late than never.

Boyle It's nearly time we got a start, anyhow; I'm fed up knockin' round, doin' nothin'. He promised you – gave you the straight tip?

Joxer Yis. 'Come down on the blow o' dinner,' says he, 'an' I'll start you, an' any friend you like to brin' with you.' 'Ah,' says I, 'you're a darlin' man, a daaarlin' man.'

Boyle Well, it couldn't come at a betther time – we're a long time waitin' for it.

Joxer Indeed we were; but it's a long lane that has no turnin'.

Boyle The blow up for dinner is at one – wait till I see what time it 'tis.

[*He goes over to the mantelpiece, and gingerly lifts the clock.*]

Mrs Boyle Min' now, how you go on fiddlin' with that clock – you know the least little thing sets it asthray.

Boyle The job couldn't come at a betther time; I'm feelin' in great fettle, Joxer. I'd hardly believe I ever had a pain in me legs, an' last week I was nearly crippled with them.

Joxer That's betther an' betther; ah, God never shut wan door but He opened another!

Boyle It's only eleven o'clock; we've lashin's o' time. I'll slip on me oul' mole-skins after breakfast, an' we can saunter down at our ayse. [*Putting his hand on the shovel*] I think, Joxer, we'd betther bring our shovels?

Joxer Yis, Captain, yis; it's betther to go fully prepared an' ready for all even-tualities. You bring your long-tailed shovel, an' I'll bring me navvy. We mighten' want them, an', then agen, we might: for want of a nail the shoe was lost, for want of a shoe the horse was lost, an' for want of a horse the man was lost – aw, that's a darlin' proverb, a daarlin' . . .

[*As Joxer is finishing his sentence, Mrs. Boyle approaches the door and Joxer retreats hurriedly. She shuts the door with a bang.*]

Boyle [*suggestively*] We won't be long pullin' ourselves together agen when I'm working for a few weeks.

[*Mrs. Boyle takes no notice.*]

Boyle The foreman on the job is an oul' butty o' Joxer's; I have an idea that I know him meself. [*Silence*] . . . There's a button off the back o' me moleskin trousers. . . . If you leave out a needle an' thread I'll sew it on meself. . . . Thanks be to God, the pains in me legs is gone, anyhow!

Mrs Boyle [*with a burst*] Look here, Mr. Jacky Boyle, them yarns won't go down with Juno. I know you an' Joxer Daly of an oul' date, an' if you think you're able to come it over me with them fairy tales, you're in the wrong shop.

Boyle [*coughing subduedly to relieve the tenseness of the situation*] U-u-u-ugh!

Mrs Boyle Butty o' Joxer's! Oh, you'll do a lot o' good as long as you continue to be a butty o' Joxer's!

Boyle U-u-u-ugh !

Mrs Boyle Shovel! Ah, then, me boyo, you'd do far more work with a knife an' fork than ever you'll do with a shovel! If there was e'er a genuine job goin' you'd be dh'other way about – not able to lift your arms with the pains in your legs! Your poor wife slavin' to keep the bit in your mouth, an' you gallivantin' about all the day like a paycock!

Boyle It ud be betther for a man to be dead, betther for a man to be dead.

Mrs Boyle [*ignoring the interruption*] Everybody callin' you 'Captain', an' you only wanst on the wather, in an oul' collier from here to Liverpool, when anybody, to listen or look at you, ud take you for a second Christo For Columbus!

Boyle Are you never goin' to give us a rest?

Mrs Boyle Oh, you're never tired o' lookin' for a rest.

Boyle D'ye want to dhrive me out o' the house?

Mrs Boyle It ud be easier to dhrive you out o' the house than to dhrive you into a job. Here, sit down an' take your breakfast – it may be the last you'll get, for I don't know where the next is goin' to come from.

Boyle If I get this job we'll be all right.

Mrs Boyle Did ye see Jerry Devine?

Boyle [*testily*] No, I didn't see him.

Mrs Boyle No, but you seen Joxer. Well, he was here lookin' for you.

Boyle Well, let him look!

Mrs Boyle Oh, indeed, he may well look, for it ud be hard for him to see you, an' you stuck in Ryan's snug.

Boyle I wasn't in Ryan's snug – I don't go into Ryan's.

Mrs Boyle Oh, is there a mad dog there? Well, if you weren't in Ryan's you were in Foley's.

Boyle I'm telling you for the last three weeks I haven't tasted a dhrop of intoxicatin' liquor. I wasn't in ayther wan snug or dh'other – I could swear that on a prayer-book – I'm as innocent as the child unborn!

Mrs Boyle Well, if you'd been in for your breakfast you'd ha' seen him.

Boyle [*suspiciously*] What does he want me for?

Mrs Boyle He'll be back any minute an' then you'll soon know.

Boyle I'll dhrop out an' see if I can meet him.

Mrs Boyle You'll sit down an' take your breakfast, an' let me go to me work, for I'm an hour late already waitin' for you.

Boyle You needn't ha' waited, for I'll take no breakfast – I've a little spirit left in me still!

Mrs Boyle Are you goin' to have your breakfast – yes or no?

Boyle [*too proud to yield*] I'll have no breakfast – yous can keep your breakfast. [*Plaintively*] I'll knock out a bit somewhere, never fear.

Mrs Boyle Nobody's goin' to coax you – don't think that.

[*She vigorously replaces the pan and the sausages in the press.*]

Boyle I've a little spirit left in me still.

[*Jerry Devine enters hastily.*]

Jerry Oh, here you are at last! I've been searchin' for you everywhere. The foreman in Foley's told me you hadn't left the snug with Joxer ten minutes before I went in.

Mrs Boyle An' he swearin' on the holy prayer-book that he wasn't in no snug!

Boyle [*to Jerry*] What business is it o' yours whether I was in a snug or no? What do you want to be gallopin' about afther me for? Is a man not to be allowed to leave his house for a minute without havin' a pack o' spies, pimps an' informers cantherin' at his heels?

Jerry Oh, you're takin' a wrong view of it, Mr. Boyle; I simply was anxious to do you a good turn. I have a message for you from Father Farrell: He says that if you go to the job that's on in Rathmines, an' ask for Foreman Managan, you'll get a start.

Boyle That's all right, but I don't want the motions of me body to be watched the way an asthronomer ud watch a star. If you're folleyin' Mary aself, you've no pereeogative to be folleyin' me. [*Suddenly catching his thigh*] U-ugh, I'm afther gettin' a terrible twinge in me right leg !

Mrs Boyle Oh, it won't be very long now till it travels into your left wan. It's miraculous that whenever he scents a job in front of him, his legs begin to fail him! Then, me bucko, if you lose this chance, you may go an' furrage for yourself!

Jerry This job'll last for some time too, Captain, an' as soon as the foundations are in, it'll be cushy enough.

Boyle Won't it be a climbin' job? How d'ye expect me to be able to go up a ladder with these legs? An', if I get up aself, how am I goin' to get down agen?

Mrs Boyle [*viciously*] Get wan o' the labourers to carry you down in a hod! You can't climb a laddher but you can skip like a goat into a snug!

Jerry I wouldn't let myself be let down that easy, Mr. Boyle; a little exercise, now, might do you all the good in the world.

Boyle It's a docthor you should have been, Devine – maybe you know more about the pains in me legs than meself that has them?

Jerry [*irritated*] Oh, I know nothin' about the pains in your legs; I've brought the message that Father Farrell gave me, an' that's all I can do.

Mrs Boyle Here, sit down an' take your breakfast, an' go an' get ready; an' don't be actin' as if you couldn't pull a wing out of a dead bee.

Boyle I want no breakfast, I tell you; it ud choke me afther all that's been said. I've a little spirit left in me still.

Mrs Boyle Well, let's see your spirit, then, an' go in at wanst an' put on your moleskin trousers!

Boyle [*moving towards the door on left*] It ud be betther for a man to be dead! U-ugh! There's another twinge in me other leg! Nobody but meself knows the sufferin' I'm goin' through with the pains in these legs o' mine!

[*He goes into the room on left as Mary comes out with her hat in her hand.*]

Mrs Boyle I'll have to push off now, for I'm terrible late already, but I was determined to stay an' hunt that Joxer this time.

[*She goes off.*]

Jerry Are you going out, Mary?

Mary It looks like it when I'm putting on my hat, doesn't it?

Jerry The bitther word agen, Mary.

Mary You won't allow me to be friendly with you; if I thry, you deliberately misundherstand it.

Jerry I didn't always misundherstand it; you were often delighted to have the arms of Jerry around you.

Mary If you go on talkin' like this, Jerry Devine, you'll make me hate you!

Jerry Well, let it be either a weddin' or a wake! Listen, Mary, I'm standin' for the Secretaryship of our Union. There's only one opposin' me; I'm popular with all the men, an' a good speaker – all are sayin' that I'll get elected.

Mary Well ?

Jerry The job's worth three hundred an' fifty pounds a year, Mary. You an' I could live nice an' cosily on that; it would lift you out o' this place an' . . .

Mary I haven't time to listen to you now – I have to go.

[*She is going out, when Jerry bars the way.*]

Jerry [*appealingly*] Mary, what's come over you with me for the last few weeks? You hardly speak to me, an' then only a word with a face o' bitherness on it. Have you forgotten, Mary, all the happy evenin's that were as sweet as the scented hawthorn that sheltered the sides o' the road as we saunthered through the country?

Mary That's all over now. When you get your new job, Jerry, you won't be long findin' a girl far betther than I am for your sweetheart.

Jerry Never, never, Mary! No matther what happens, you'll always be the same to me.

Mary I must be off; please let me go, Jerry.

Jerry I'll go a bit o' the way with you.

Mary You needn't, thanks; I want to be by meself.

Jerry [*catching her arm*] You're goin' to meet another fella; you've clicked with someone else, me lady!

Mary That's no concern o' yours, Jerry Devine; let me go!

Jerry I saw yous comin' out o' the Cornflower Dance Class, an' you hangin' on his arm – a thin, lanky strip of a Micky Dazzler, with a walkin' stick and gloves!

Voice of Johnny [*loudly*] What are you doin' there – pullin' about everything!

Voice of Boyle [*loudly and viciously*] I'm puttin' on me moleskin trousers!

Mary You're hurtin' me arm! Let me go, or I'll scream, an' then you'll have the oul' fella out on top of us!

Jerry Don't be so hard on a fella, Mary, don't be so hard.

Boyle [*appearing at the door*] What's the meanin' of all this hillabaloo?

Mary Let me go, let me go!

Boyle D'ye hear me – what's all this hillabaloo about?

Jerry [*plaintively*] Will you not give us one kind word, one kind word, Mary?

Boyle D'ye hear me talkin' to yous? What's all this hillabaloo for?

Jerry Let me kiss your hand, your little, tiny, white hand!

Boyle Your little, tiny, white hand – are you takin' leave o' your senses, man?

[*Mary breaks away and rushes out.*]

Boyle This is nice goin's on in front of her father!

Jerry Ah, dhry up, for God's sake! [*He follows Mary.*]

Boyle Chiselurs don't care a damn now about their parents, they're bringin' their fathers' grey hairs down with sorra to the grave, an' laughin' at it, laughin' at it. Ah, I suppose it's just the same everywhere – the whole worl's in a state o' chassis! [*He sits by the fire.*] Breakfast! Well, they can keep their breakfast for me. Not if they went down on their bended knees would I take it – I'll show them I've a little spirit left in me still! [*He goes over to the press, takes out a plate and looks at it.*] Sassige! Well, let her keep her sassige. [*He returns to the fire, takes up the teapot and gives it a gentle shake.*] The tea's wet right enough.

[*A pause; he rises, goes to the press, takes out the sausage, puts it on the pan, and puts both on the fire. He attends the sausage with a fork.*]

Boyle [*singing*]:

  When the robins nest agen,

  And the flowers are in bloom,

  When the Springtime's sunny smile seems to banish all sorrow an' gloom;

  Then me bonny blue-ey'd lad, if me heart be true till then –

  He's promised he'll come back to me,

  When the robins nest agen!

[*He lifts his head at the high note, and then drops his eyes to the pan.*]

Boyle [*singing*] When the . . .

[*Steps are heard approaching; he whips the pan off the fire and puts it under the bed, then sits down at the fire. The door opens and a bearded man looking in says:*] You don't happen to want a sewin' machine?

Boyle [*furiously*] No, I don't want e'er a sewin' machine!

[*He returns the pan to the fire, and commences to sing again.*]

Boyle [*singing*]:

  When the robins nest agen,

  And the flowers they are in bloom,

  He's . . .

[*A thundering knock is heard at the street door.*]

Boyle There's a terrible tatheraraa – that's a stranger – that's nobody belongin' to the house.

[*Another loud knock.*]

Joxer [*sticking his head in al the door*] Did ye hear them tatherarahs?

Boyle Well, Joxer, I'm not deaf.

Johnny [*appearing in his shirt and trousers at the door on left; his face is anxious and his voice is tremulous*] Who's that at the door; who's that at the door? Who gave that knock – d'ye yous hear me – are yous deaf or dhrunk or what?

Boyle [*to Johnny*] How the hell do I know who 'tis? Joxer, stick your head out o' the window an' see.

Joxer An' mebbe get a bullet in the kisser? Ah, none o' them thricks for Joxer! It's betther to lie a coward than a corpse!

Boyle [*looking cautiously out of the window*] It's a fella in a trench coat.

Johnny Holy Mary, Mother o' God, I . . .

Boyle He's goin' away – he must ha' got tired knockin'.

[*Johnny returns to the room on left.*]

Boyle Sit down an' have a cup o' tay, Joxer.

Joxer I'm afraid the missus ud pop in on us agen before we'd know where we are. Somethin's tellin' me to go at wanst.

Boyle Don't be superstitious, man; we're Dublin men, an' not boyos that's only afther comin' up from the bog o' Allen – though if she did come in, right enough, we'd be caught like rats in a thrap.

Joxer An' you know the sort she is – she wouldn't listen to reason – an' wanse bitten twice shy.

Boyle [*going over to the window at back*] If the worst came to the worst, you could dart out here, Joxer; it's only a dhrop of a few feet to the roof of the return room, an' the first minute she goes into dh'other room I'll give you the bend, an' you can slip in an' away.

Joxer [*yielding to the temptation*] Ah, I won't stop very long anyhow [*Picking up a book from the table*] Whose is the buk?

Boyle Aw, one o' Mary's; she's always readin' lately – nothin' but thrash, too. There's one I was lookin' at dh'other day: three stories, *The Doll's House, Ghosts,* an' *The Wild Duck*[1] – buks only fit for chiselurs!

Joxer Didja ever rade *Elizabeth, or Th' Exile o' Sibayria?* Ah, it's a darlin' story, a daarlin story!

Boyle You eat your sassige, an' never min' *Th' Exile o' Sibayria.*

[*Both sit down; Boyle fills out tea, pours gravy on Joxer's plate, and keeps the sausage for himself.*]

Joxer What are you wearin' your moleskin trousers for?

Boyle I have to go to a job, Joxer. Just afther you'd gone, Devine kem runnin' in to tell us that Father Farrell said if I went down to the job that's goin' on in Rathmines I'd get a start.

Joxer Be the holy, that's good news!

Boyle How is it good news? I wondher if you were in my condition, would you call it good news?

Joxer I thought . . .

Boyle You thought! You think too sudden sometimes, Joxer. D'ye know, I'm hardly able to crawl with the pains in me legs!

Joxer Yis, yis; I forgot the pains in your legs. I know you can do nothin' while they're at you.

Boyle You forgot; I don't think any of yous realize the state I'm in with the pains in my legs. What ud happen if I had to carry a bag o' cement?

Joxer Ah, any man havin' the like of them pains id be down an' out, down an' out.

---

1 The Doll's House . . . : three plays by Henrick Ibsen.

Boyle I wouldn't mind if he had said it to meself; but, no, oh no, he rushes in an' shouts it out in front o' Juno, an' you know what Juno is, Joxer. We all know Devine knows a little more than the rest of us, but he doesn't act as if he did; he's a good boy, sober, able to talk an' all that, but still . . .

Joxer Oh ay; able to argufy, but still . . .

Boyle If he's runnin' afther Mary, aself; he's not goin' to be runnin' afther me. Captain Boyle's able to take care of himself. Afther all, I'm not gettin' brought up on Virol. I never heard him usin' a curse; I don't believe he was ever dhrunk in his life – sure he's not like a Christian at all!

Joxer You're afther takin' the word out o' me mouth – afther all, a Christian's natural, but he's unnatural.

Boyle His oul' fella was just the same – a Wicklow man.

Joxer A Wicklow man! That explains the whole thing. I've met many a Wicklow man in me time, but I never met wan that was any good.

Boyle 'Father Farrell,' says he, 'sent me down to tell you.' Father Farrell! . . . D'ye know, Joxer, I never like to be beholden to any o' the clergy.

Joxer It's dangerous, right enough.

Boyle If they do anything for you, they'd want you to be livin' in the Chapel. . . . I'm goin' to tell you somethin', Joxer, that I wouldn't tell to anybody else – the clergy always had too much power over the people in this unfortunate country.

Joxer You could sing that if you had an air to it!

Boyle [*becoming enthusiastic*] Didn't they prevent the people in '47 from seizin' the corn, an' they starvin'; didn't they down Parnell; didn't they say that hell wasn't hot enough nor eternity long enough to punish the Fenians?[1] We don't forget, we don't forget them things, Joxer. If they've taken everything else from us, Joxer, they've left us our memory.

Joxer [*emotionally*] For mem'ry's the only friend that grief can call its own, that grief . . . can . . . call . . . its own!

Boyle Father Farrell's beginnin' to take a great intherest in Captain Boyle; because of what Johnny did for his country, says he to me wan day. It's a curious way to reward Johnny be makin' his poor oul' father work. But that's what the clergy want, Joxer – work, work, work for me an' you; havin' us mulin' from mornin' till night, so that they may be in betther fettle when they come hoppin' round for their dues! Job! Well, let him give his job to wan of his hymn-singin', prayer-spoutin', craw-thumpin' Confraternity men!

[*The voice of a coal-block vendor is heard chanting in the street.*]

Voice of Coal Vendor Blocks . . . coal-blocks! Blocks coal-blocks!

Joxer God be with the young days when you were steppin' the deck of a manly ship, with the win' blowin' a hurricane through the masts, an' the only sound you'd hear was, 'Port your helm!' an' the only answer, 'Port it is, sir!'

Boyle Them was days, Joxer, them was days. Nothin' was too hot or too heavy for me then. Sailin' from the Gulf o' Mexico to the Antanartic Ocean. I seen

---

1 **prevent the people . . . . :** the references all suggest that the clergy sided with the (British) establishment against the Irish. The famines of the mid-nineteenth-century drastically reduced the population of Ireland through death and forced emigration. Parnell tried to achieve home rule for Ireland but was condemned by the clergy because of an extramarital affair. The Fenians were (sometimes violent) nationalists.

things; I seen things, Joxer, that no mortal man should speak about that knows his Catechism. Ofen, an' ofen, when I was fixed to the wheel with a marlin-spike, an' the win's blowin' fierce an' the waves lashin' an' lashin', till you'd think every minute was goin' to be your last, an' it blowed, an' blowed – blew is the right word, Joxer, but blowed is what the sailors use. . . .

Joxer Aw, it's a darlin' word, a daarlin' word.

Boyle An', as it blowed an' blowed, I ofen looked up at the sky an' assed meself the question – what is the stars, what is the stars?

Voice of Coal Vendor Any blocks, coal-blocks; blocks, coal-blocks!

Joxer Ah, that's the question, that's the question – what is the stars?

Boyle An' then, I'd have another look, an' I'd ass meself – what is the moon?

Joxer Ah, that's the question – what is the moon, what is the moon?

[*Rapid steps are heard coming towards the door. Boyle makes desperate efforts to hide everything; Joxer rushes to the window in a frantic effort to get out; Boyle begins to innocently lilt 'Oh, me darlin' Jennie, I will be thrue to thee', when the door is opened, and the black face of the Coal Vendor appears.*]

The Coal Vendor D'yez want any blocks?

Boyle [*with a roar*] No, we don't want any blocks!

Joxer [*coming back with a sigh of relief*] That's afther puttin' the heart across me – I could ha' sworn it was Juno. I'd betther be goin', Captain; you couldn't tell the minute Juno'd hop in on us.

Boyle Let her hop in; we may as well have it out first as at last. I've made up me mind – I'm not goin' to do only what she damn well likes.

Joxer Them sentiments does you credit, Captain; I don't like to say anything as between man an' wife, but I say as a butty, as a butty, Captain, that you've stuck it too long, an' that it's about time you showed a little spunk.

How can a man die betther than facin' fearful odds,

For th' ashes of his fathers an' the temples of his gods?

Boyle She has her rights – there's no one denyin' it, but haven't I me rights too?

Joxer Of course you have – the sacred rights o' man!

Boyle Today, Joxer, there's goin' to be issued a proclamation be me, establishin' an independent Republic, an' Juno'll have to take an oath of allegiance.

Joxer Be firm, be firm, Captain; the first few minutes'll be the worst: if you gently touch a nettle it'll sting you for your pains; grasp it like a lad of mettle, an' as soft as silk remains!

Voice of Juno outside Can't stop, Mrs. Madigan – I haven't a minute!

Joxer [*flying out of the window*] Holy God, here she is!

Boyle [*packing the things away with a rush in the press*] I knew that fella ud stop till she was in on top of us!

[*He sits down by the fire Juno enters hastily; she is flurried and excited.*]

Juno Oh, you're in – you must have been only afther comin' in?

Boyle No, I never went out.

Juno It's curious, then, you never heard the knockin'.

She puts her coat and hat on bed.

Boyle Knockin'? Of course I heard the knockin'.

Juno An' why didn't you open the door, then? I suppose you were so busy with Joxer that you hadn't time.

Boyle I haven't seen Joxer since I seen him before. Joxer! What ud bring Joxer here?

Juno D'ye mean to tell me that the pair of yous wasn't collogin' together here when me back was turned?

Boyle What ud we be collogin' together about? I have somethin' else to think of besides collogin' with Joxer. I can swear on all the holy prayer-books . . .

Mrs Boyle That you weren't in no snug! Go on in at wanst now, an' take off that moleskin trousers o' yours, an' put on a collar an' tie to smarten yourself up a bit. There's a visitor comin' with Mary in a minute, an' he has great news for you.

Boyle A job, I suppose; let us get wan first before we start lookin' for another.

Mrs Boyle That's the thing that's able to put the win' up you. Well, it's no job, but news that'll give you the chance o' your life.

Boyle What's a'l the mystery about?

Mrs Boyle G'win an' take off the moleskin trousers when you're told!

[*Boyle goes into room on left.*]

[*Mrs. Boyle tidies up the room, puts the shovel under the bed, and goes to the press.*]

Mrs Boyle Oh, God bless us, looka the way everything's thrun about! Oh, Joxer was here, Joxer was here!

[*Mary enters with Charlie Bentham; he is a young man of twenty-five, tall, good-looking, with a very high opinion of himself generally. He is dressed in a brown coat, brown knee-breeches, grey stockings, a brown sweater, with a deep blue tie; he carries gloves and a walking-stick.*]

Mrs Boyle [*fussing round*] Come in, Mr. Bentham; sit down, Mr. Bentham, in this chair; it's more comfortabler than that, Mr. Bentham. Himself'll be here in a minute; he's just takin' off his trousers.

Mary Mother!

Bentham Please don't put yourself to any trouble, Mrs. Boyle – I'm quite all right here, thank you.

Mrs Boyle An' to think of you knowin' Mary, an' she knowin' the news you had for us, an' wouldn't let on; but it's all the more welcomer now, for we were on our last lap!

Voice of Johnny inside What are you kickin' up all the racket for?

Boyle [*roughly*] I'm takin' off me moleskin trousers!

Johnny Can't you do it, then, without lettin' th' whole house know you're takin' off your trousers? What d'ye want puttin' them on an' takin' them off again?

Boyle Will you let me alone, will you let me alone? Am I never goin' to be done thryin' to please th' whole o' yous?

Mrs Boyle [*to Bentham*] You must excuse th' state o' th' place, Mr. Bentham; th' minute I turn me back that man o' mine always makes a litther o' th' place, a litther o' th' place.

Bentham Don't worry, Mrs. Boyle; it's all right, I assure . . .

Boyle [*inside*] Where's me braces; where in th' name o' God did I leave me braces? . . . Ay, did you see where I put me braces?

Johnny [*inside, calling out*] Ma, will you come in here an' take da away ou' o' this or he'll dhrive me mad.

Mrs Boyle [*going towards the door*] Dear, dear, dear, that man'll be lookin' for somethin' on th' day o' Judgement. [*Looking into room and calling to Boyle*] Look at your braces, man, hangin' round your neck!

Boyle [*inside*] Aw, Holy God!

Mrs Boyle [*calling*] Johnny, Johnny, come out here for a minute.

Johnny Ah, leave Johnny alone, an' don't be annoyin' him!

Mrs Boyle Come on, Johnny, till I inthroduce you to Mr. Bentham. [*To Bentham*] My son, Mr. Bentham; he's afther goin' through the mill. He was only a chiselur of a Boy Scout in Easter Week, when he got hit in the hip; and his arm was blew off in the fight in O'Connell Street. [*Johnny comes in*] Here he is, Mr. Bentham; Mr. Bentham, Johnny. None can deny he done his bit for Irelan', if that's goin' to do him any good.

Johnny [*boastfully*] I'd do it agen, ma, I'd do it agen; for a principle's a principle.

Mrs Boyle Ah, you lost your best principle, me boy, when you lost your arm; them's the only sort o' principles that's any good to a workin' man.

Johnny Ireland only half free'll never be at peace while she has a son left to pull a trigger.

Mrs Boyle To be sure, to be sure – no bread's a lot betther than half a loaf. [*Calling loudly in to Boyle*] Will you hurry up there?

[*Boyle enters in his best trousers, which aren't too good, and looks very uncomfortable in his collar and tie.*]

Mrs Boyle This is my husband; Mr. Boyle, Mr. Bentham.

Bentham Ah, very glad to know you, Mr. Boyle. How are you?

Boyle Ah, I'm not too well at all; I suffer terrible with pains in me legs. Juno can tell you there what . . .

Mrs Boyle You won't have many pains in your legs when you hear what Mr. Bentham has to tell you.

Bentham Juno! What an interesting name! It reminds one of Homer's glorious story of ancient gods and heroes.

Boyle Yis, doesn't it? You see, Juno was born an' christened in June; I met her in June; we were married in June, an' Johnny was born in June, so wan day I says to her, 'You should ha' been called Juno,' an' the name stuck to her ever since.

Mrs Boyle Here, we can talk o' them things agen; let Mr. Bentham say what he has to say now.

Bentham Well, Mr. Boyle, I suppose you'll remember a Mr. Ellison of Santry – he's a relative of yours, I think.

Boyle [*viciously*] Is it that prognosticator an' procrastinator! Of course I remember him.

Bentham Well, he's dead, Mr. Boyle . . .

Boyle Sorra many'll go into mournin' for him.

Mrs Boyle Wait till you hear what Mr. Bentham has to say, an' then, maybe, you'll change your opinion.

Bentham A week before he died he sent for me to write his will for him. He told me that there were two only that he wished to leave his property to: his second cousin, Michael Finnegan of Santry, and John Boyle, his first cousin, of Dublin.

Boyle [*excitedly*] Me, is it me, me?

Bentham You, Mr. Boyle; I'll read a copy of the will that I have here with me, which has been duly filed in the Court of Probate.

[*He takes a paper from his pocket and reads:*]

6th February 1922

This is the last Will and Testament of William Ellison, of Santry, in the County of Dublin. I hereby order and wish my property to be sold and divided as follows: –

£20 to the St. Vincent de Paul Society.

£60 for Masses for the repose of my soul [5s. for each Mass].

The rest of my property to be divided between my first and second cousins.

I hereby appoint Timothy Buckly, of Santry, and Hugh Brierly, of Coolock, to be my Executors.

> (Signed)
> William Ellison
> Hugh Brierly
> Timothy Buckly
> Charles Bentham, N.T.

Boyle [*eagerly*] An' how much'll be comin' out of it, Mr. Bentham?

Bentham The Executors told me that half of the property would be anything between £1500 and £2000.

Mary A fortune, father, a fortune!

Johnny We'll be able to get out o' this place now, an' go somewhere we're not known.

Mrs Boyle You won't have to trouble about a job for awhile, Jack.

Boyle [*fervently*] I'll never doubt the goodness o' God agen.

Bentham I congratulate you, Mr. Boyle.

[*They shake hands.*]

Boyle An' now, Mr. Bentham, you'll have to have a wet.

Bentham A wet?

Boyle A wet – a jar – a boul!

Mrs Boyle Jack, you're speakin' to Mr. Bentham, and not to Joxer.

Boyle [*solemnly*] Juno . . . Mary . . . Johnny . . . we'll have to go into mournin' at wanst. . . . I never expected that poor Bill ud die so sudden. . . . Well, we all have to die some day . . . you, Juno, to-day . . . an' me, maybe, to-morrow. . . . It's sad, but it can't be helped. . . . Requiescat in pace . . . or, usin' our oul' tongue like St. Patrick or St. Bridget, Guh sayeree jeea ayera!

Mary Oh, father, that's not Rest in Peace; that's God save Ireland.

Boyle U-u-ugh, it's all the same – isn't it a prayer? . . . Juno, I'm done with Joxer; he's nothin' but a prognosticator an' a . . .

Joxer [*climbing angrily through the window and bounding into the room*] You're done with Joxer, are you? Maybe you thought I'd stop on the roof all the night for you! Joxer out on the roof with the win' blowin' through him was nothin' to you an' your friend with the collar an' tie!

Mrs Boyle What in the name o' God brought you out on the roof; what were you doin' there?

Joxer [*ironically*] I was dhreamin' I was standin' on the bridge of a ship, an' she sailin' the Antartic Ocean, an' it blowed, an' blowed, an' I lookin' up at the sky an' sayin', what is the stars, what is the stars?

Mrs Boyle [*opening the door and standing at it*] Here, get ou' o' this, Joxer Daly; I was always thinkin' you had a slate off.

Joxer [*moving to the door*] I have to laugh every time I look at the deep-sea sailor; an' a row on a river ud make him seasick!

Boyle Get ou' o' this before I take the law into me own hands!

Joxer [*going out*] Say aw rewaeawr, but not good-bye. Lookin' for work, an' prayin' to God he won't get it!

[*He goes.*]

Mrs Boyle I'm tired tellin' you what Joxer was; maybe now you see yourself the kind he is.

Boyle He'll never blow the froth off a pint o' mine agen, that's a sure thing. Johnny . . . Mary . . . you're to keep yourselves to yourselves for the future. Juno, I'm done with Joxer. . . . I'm a new man from this out. . . .

[*Clasping Juno's hand, and singing emotionally:*]

O, me darlin' Juno, I will be thrue to thee;
Me own, me darlin' Juno, you're all the world to me.

[*Curtain*]

Act II

[*The same, but the furniture is more plentiful, and of a vulgar nature. A glaringly upholstered armchair and lounge; cheap pictures and photos everywhere. Every available spot is ornamented with huge vases filled with artificial flowers. Crossed festoons of coloured paper chains stretch from end to end of ceiling. On the table is an old attaché case. It is about six in the evening, and two days after the First Act. Boyle, in his shirt-sleeves, is voluptuously stretched on the sofa; he is smoking a clay pipe. He is half asleep. A lamp is lighting on the table. After a few moments' pause the voice of Joxer is heard singing softly outside at the door – 'Me pipe I'll smoke, as I dhrive me moke – are you there, Mor . . . ee . . . ar . . . i . . . teee!'*]

Boyle [*leaping up, takes a pen in his hand and busies himself with papers*] Come along, Joxer, me son, come along.

Joxer [*putting his head in*] Are you be yourself?

Boyle Come on, come on; that doesn't matther; I'm masther now, an' I'm goin' to remain masther.

[*Joxer comes in.*]

Joxer How d'ye feel now, as a man o' money?

Boyle [*solemnly*] It's a responsibility, Joxer, a great responsibility.

Joxer I suppose 'tis now, though you wouldn't think it.

Boyle Joxer, han' me over that attackey case on the table there. [*Joxer hands the case.*] Ever since the Will was passed I've run hundreds o' dockyments through me han's – I tell you, you have to keep your wits about you.

[*He busies himself with papers.*]

Joxer Well, I won't disturb you; I'll dhrop in when . . .

Boyle [*hastily*] It's all right, Joxer, this is the last one to be signed to-day. [*He signs a paper, puts it into the case, which he shuts with a snap, and sits back pompously in the chair.*] Now, Joxer, you want to see me; I'm at your service – what can I do for you, me man?

Joxer I've just dhropped in with the £3:5s. that Mrs. Madigan riz on the blankets an' table for you, an' she says you're to be in no hurry payin' it back.

Boyle She won't be long without it; I expect the first cheque for a couple o' hundhred any day. There's the five bob for yourself – go on, take it, man; it'll not be the last you'll get from the Captain. Now an' agen we have our differ, but we're there together all the time.

Joxer Me for you, an' you for me, like the two Musketeers.

Boyle Father Farrell stopped me to-day an' tole me how glad he was I fell in for the money.

Joxer He'll be stoppin' you ofen enough now; I suppose it was 'Mr.' Boyle with him?

Boyle He shuk me be the han' . . .

Joxer [*ironically*] I met with Napper Tandy, an' he shuk me be the han'!

Boyle You're seldom asthray, Joxer, but you're wrong shipped this time. What you're sayin' of Father Farrell is very near to blasfeemey. I don't like any one to talk disrespectful of Father Farrell.

Joxer You're takin' me up wrong, Captain; I wouldn't let a word be said agen Father Farrell – the heart o' the rowl, that's what he is; I always said he was a darlin' man, a daarlin' man.

Boyle Comin' up the stairs who did I meet but that bummer, Nugent. 'I seen you talkin' to Father Farrell,' says he, with a grin on him. 'He'll be folleyin' you,' says he, 'like a Guardian Angel from this out' – all the time the oul' grin on him, Joxer.

Joxer I never seen him yet but he had that oul' grin on him!

Boyle 'Mr. Nugent,' says I, 'Father Farrell is a man o' the people, an', as far as I know the History o' me country, the priests was always in the van of the fight for Irelan's freedom.

Joxer [*fervently*]:

　　Who was it led the van, Soggart Aroon?

　　Since the fight first began, Soggart Aroon?

Boyle 'Who are you tellin'? says he. 'Didn't they let down the Fenians, an' didn't they do in Parnell? An' now . . .' 'You ought to be ashamed o' yourself,' says I interruptin' him, 'not to know the History o' your country.' An' I left him gawkin' where he was.

Joxer Where ignorance 's bliss 'tis folly to be wise; I wondher did he ever read the Story o' Irelan'.

Boyle Be J. L. Sullivan? Don't you know he didn't.

Joxer Ah, it's a darlin' buk, a daarlin' buk!

Boyle You'd betther be goin', now, Joxer; his Majesty, Bentham, 'll be here any minute, now.

Joxer Be the way things is lookin', it'll be a match between him an' Mary. She's thrun over Jerry altogether. Well, I hope it will, for he's a darlin' man.

Boyle I'm glad you think so – I don't. [*Irritably*] What's darlin' about him?

Joxer [*nonplussed*] I only seen him twiced; if you want to know me, come an' live with me.

Boyle He's too dignified for me – to hear him talk you'd think he knew as much as a Boney's Oraculum. He's given up his job as teacher, an' is goin' to become a solicitor in Dublin – he's been studyin' law. I suppose he thinks I'll set him up, but he's wrong shipped. An' th' other fella – Jerry's as bad. The two o' them ud give you a pain in your face, listenin to them; Jerry believin' in nothin', an' Bentham believin' in everythin'. One that says all is God an' no man; an' th' other that says all is man an' no God!

Joxer Well, I'll be off now.

Boyle Don't forget to dhrop down afther awhile; we'll have a quiet jar, an' a song or two.

Joxer Never fear.

Boyle An' tell Mrs. Madigan that I hope we'll have the pleasure of her organization at our little enthertainment.

Joxer Righto; we'll come down together.

[*He goes out.*]

[*Johnny comes from room on left, and sits down moodily at the fire. Boyle looks at him for a few moments, and shakes his head. He fills his pipe.*]

Voice of Juno at the door Open the door, Jack; this thing has me nearly kilt with the weight.

[*Boyle opens the door. Juno enters carrying the box of a gramophone, followed by Mary carrying the horn and some parcels. Juno leaves the box on the table and flops into a chair.*]

Juno Carryin' that from Henry Street was no joke.

Boyle U-u-ugh, that's a grand-lookin' insthrument – how much was it?

Juno Pound down, an' five to be paid at two shillin's a week.

Boyle That's reasonable enough.

Juno I'm afraid we're runnin' into too much debt; first the furniture, an' now this.

Boyle The whole lot won't be much out of £2000.

Mary I don't know what you wanted a gramophone for – I know Charlie hates them; he says they're destructive of real music.

Boyle Desthructive of music – that fella ud give you a pain in your face. All a gramophone wants is to be properly played; its thrue wondher is only felt when everythin's quiet – what a gramophone wants is dead silence!

Mary But, father, Jerry says the same; afther all, you can only appreciate music when your ear is properly trained.

Boyle That's another fella ud give you a pain in your face. Properly thrained! I suppose you couldn't appreciate football unless your fut was properly thrained.

Mrs Boyle [*to Mary*] Go on in ower that an' dress, or Charlie'll be in on you, an' tea nor nothin'll be ready.

[*Mary goes into room left.*]

Mrs Boyle [*arranging table for tea*] You didn't look at our new gramophone, Johnny?

Johnny 'Tisn't gramophones I'm thinking of.

Mrs Boyle An' what is it you're thinkin' of, allanna?

Johnny Nothin', nothin', nothin'.

Mrs Boyle Sure, you must be thinkin' of somethin'; it's yourself that has yourself the way y'are; sleepin' wan night in me sisther's, an' the nex' in your father's brother's – you'll get no rest goin' on that way.

Johnny I can rest nowhere, nowhere, nowhere.

Mrs Boyle Sure, you're not thryin' to rest anywhere.

Johnny Let me alone, let me alone, let me alone, for God's sake.

[*A knock at street door.*]

Mrs Boyle [*in a flutter*] Here he is; here's Mr. Bentham!

Boyle Well, there's room for him; it's a pity there's not a brass band to play him in.

Mrs Boyle We'll han' the tea round, an' not be clusthered round the table, as if we never seen nothin'.

[*Steps are heard approaching, and Juno opening the door, allows Bentham to enter.*]

Juno Give your hat an' stick to Jack, there . . . sit down, Mr. Bentham . . . no, not there . . . in th' easy chair be the fire . . . there, that's betther. Mary'll be out to you in a minute.

Boyle [*solemnly*] I seen be the paper this mornin' that Consols was down half per cent. That's serious, min' you, an' shows the whole counthry's in a state o' chassis.

Mrs Boyle What's Consols, Jack?

Boyle Consols? Oh, Consols is – oh, there's no use tellin' women what Consols is – th' wouldn't undherstand.

Bentham It's just as you were saying, Mr. Boyle . . .

[*Mary enters, charmingly dressed.*]

Bentham Oh, good evening, Mary; how pretty you're looking!

Mary [*archly*] Am I?

Boyle We were just talkin' when you kem in, Mary; I was tellin' Mr. Bentham that the whole counthry's in a state o' chassis.

Mary [*to Bentham*] Would you prefer the green or the blue ribbon round me hair, Charlie?

Mrs Boyle Mary, your father's speakin'.

Boyle [*rapidly*] I was jus' tellin' Mr. Bentham that the whole counthry's in a state o' chassis.

Mary I'm sure you're frettin', da, whether it is or no.

Mrs Boyle With all our churches an' religions, the worl's not a bit the betther.

Boyle [*with a commanding gesture*] Tay!

[*Mary and Mrs. Boyle dispense the tea.*]

Mrs Boyle An' Irelan's takin' a leaf out o' the worl's buk; when we got the makin' of our own laws I thought we'd never stop to look behind us, but instead of that we never stopped to look before us! If the people ud folley up their religion betther there'd be a betther chance for us – what do you think, Mr. Bentham?

Bentham I'm afraid I can't venture to express an opinion on that point, Mrs. Boyle; dogma has no attraction for me.

Mrs Boyle I forgot you didn't hold with us: what's this you said you were?

Bentham A Theosophist, Mrs. Boyle.

Mrs Boyle An' what in the name o' God's a Theosophist?

Boyle A Theosophist, Juno, 's a – tell her, Mr. Bentham. Tell her.

Bentham It's hard to explain in a few words: Theosophy's founded on The Vedas, the religious books of the East. Its central theme is the existence of an all-pervading Spirit – the Life-Breath. Nothing really exists but this one Universal Life-Breath. And whatever even seems to exist separately from this Life-Breath, doesn't really exist at all. It is all vital force in man, in all animals, and in all vegetation. This Life-Breath is called the Prawna.

Mrs Boyle The Prawna! What a comical name !

Boyle Prawna; yis, the Prawna. [*Blowing gently through his lips*] That's the Prawna!

Mrs Boyle Whist, whist, Jack.

Bentham The happiness of man depends upon his sympathy with this Spirit. Men who have reached a high state of excellence are called Yogi. Some men become Yogi in a short time, it may take others millions of years.

Boyle Yogi! I seen hundhreds of them in the streets o' San Francisco.

Bentham It is said by these Yogi that if we practise certain mental exercises we would have powers denied to others – for instance, the faculty of seeing things that happen miles and miles away.

Mrs Boyle I wouldn't care to meddle with that sort o' belief; it's a very curious religion, altogether.

Boyle What's curious about it? Isn't all religions curious? – if they weren't, you wouldn't get any one to believe them. But religions is passin' away – they've had their day like everything else. Take the real Dublin people, f'rinstance: they know more about Charlie Chaplin an' Tommy Mix[1] than they do about SS. Peter an' Paul!

Mrs Boyle You don't believe in ghosts, Mr. Bentham?

Mary Don't you know he doesn't, mother?

Bentham I don't know that, Mary. Scientists are beginning to think that what we call ghosts are sometimes seen by person of a certain nature. They say that sensational actions, such as the killing of a person, demand great energy, and that energy lingers in the place where the action occurred. People may live in the place and see nothing, when someone may come along whose personality has some peculiar connection with the energy of the place, and, in a flash, the person sees the whole affair.

Johnny [*rising swiftly, pale and affected*] What sort o' talk is this to be goin' on with? Is there nothin' betther to be talkin' about but the killin' o' people? My God, isn't it bad enough for these things to happen without talkin' about them! [*He hurriedly goes into the room on left.*]

Bentham Oh, I'm very sorry, Mrs. Boyle; I never thought . . .

Mrs Boyle [*apologetically*] Never mind, Mr. Bentham, he's very touchy.

[*A frightened scream is heard from Johnny inside.*]

Mrs Boyle Mother of God, what's that?

[*He rushes out again, his face pale, his lips twitching, his limbs trembling.*]

---

1 Charlie Chaplin, Tommy Mix: popular stars of the early cinema, one a comedian, the other a cowboy.

Johnny Shut the door, shut the door, quick, for God's sake! Great God, have mercy on me! Blessed Mother o' God, shelter me, shelther your son!

Mrs Boyle [*catching him in her arms*] What's wrong with you? What ails you? Sit down, sit down, here, on the bed . . . there now . . . there now.

Mary Johnny, Johnny, what ails you?

Johnny I seen him, I seen him . . . kneelin' in front o' the statue . . . merciful Jesus, have pity on me !

Mrs Boyle [*to Boyle*] Get him a glass o' whisky . . . quick, man, an' don't stand gawkin'.

[*Boyle gets the whisky.*]

Johnny Sit here, sit here, mother . . . between me an' the door.

Mrs Boyle I'll sit beside you as long as you like, only tell me what was it came across you at all?

Johnny [*after taking some drink*] I seen him. . . . I seen Robbie Tancred kneelin' down before the statue . . . an' the red light shinin' on him . . . an' when I went in . . . he turned an' looked at me . . . an' I seen the woun's bleedin' in his breast. . . . Oh, why did he look at me like that? . . . it wasn't my fault that he was done in. . . . Mother o' God, keep him away from me!

Mrs Boyle There, there, child, you've imagined it all. There was nothin' there at all – it was the red light you seen, an' the talk we had put all the rest into your head. Here, dhrink more o' this – it'll do you good. . . . An', now, stretch yourself down on the bed for a little. [*To Boyle*] Go in, Jack, an' show him it was only in his own head it was.

Boyle [*making no move*] E-e-e-e-eh; it's all nonsense; it was only a shadda he saw.

Mary Mother o' God, he made me heart lep!

Bentham It was simply due to an overwrought imagination – we all get that way at times.

Mrs Boyle There, dear, lie down in the bed, an' I'll put the quilt across you . . . e-e-e-eh, that's it . . . you'll be as right as the mail in a few minutes.

Johnny Mother, go into the room an' see if the light's lightin' before the statue.

Mrs Boyle [*to Boyle*] Jack, run in an' see if the light's lightin' before the statue.

Boyle [*to Mary*] Mary, slip in an' see if the light's lightin' before the statue.

[*Mary hesitates to go in.*]

Bentham It's all right; Mary, I'll go.

[*He goes into the room; remains for a few moments, and returns.*]

Bentham Everything's just as it was – the light burning bravely before the statue.

Boyle Of course; I knew it was all nonsense.

[*A knock at the door.*]

Boyle [*going to open the door*] E-e-e-e-eh.

[*He opens it, and Joxer, followed by Mrs. Madigan, enters. Mrs. Madigan is a strong, dapper little woman of about forty-five; her face is almost always a wide-spread smile of complacency. She is a woman who, in manner at least, can mourn with them that mourn, and rejoice with them that do rejoice. When she is feeling comfortable, she is inclined to be reminiscent; when others say anything, or following a statement made by herself, she has a habit of putting her head a little to one side, and nodding it rapidly several times in succession, like a bird pecking at a hard*] *berry. Indeed, she has a good deal of the bird in her, but the bird instinct is by no means a melodious one. She is ignorant, vulgar and forward, but her heart is generous withal. For instance, she would help a neighbour's sick child; she would probably kill the child, but her intention would be to cure it; she would be more at home helping a drayman to lift a fallen horse. She is dressed in a rather soiled grey dress and a vivid purple blouse; in her hair is a huge comb, ornamented with huge coloured beads. She enters with a gliding step, beaming smile and nodding head. Boyle receives them effusively.*]

Boyle Come on in, Mrs. Madigan; come on in; I was afraid you weren't comin'.... [*Slyly*] There's some people able to dhress, ay, Joxer?

Joxer Fair as the blossoms that bloom in the May, an' sweet as the scent of the new-mown hay. . . . Ah, well she may wear them.

Mrs. Madigan [*looking at Mary*] I know some as are as sweet as the blossoms that bloom in the May – oh, no names, no pack dhrill!

Boyle An' now I'll inthroduce the pair o' yous to Mary's intended: Mr. Bentham, this is Mrs. Madigan, an oul' back-parlour neighbour, that, if she could help it at all, ud never see a body shuk!

Bentham [*rising, and tentatively shaking the hand of Mrs. Madigan*] I'm sure, it's a great pleasure to know you, Mrs. Madigan.

Mrs. Madigan An' I'm goin' to tell you, Mr. Bentham, you're goin' to get as nice a bit o' skirt in Mary, there, as ever you seen in your puff. Not like some of the dhressedup dolls that's knockin' about lookin' for men when it's a skelpin' they want. I remember, as well as I remember yesterday, the day she was born – of a Tuesday, the 25th o' June, in the year 1901, at thirty-three minutes past wan in the day be Foley's clock, the pub at the corner o' the street. A cowld day it was too, for the season o' the year, an' I remember sayin' to Joxer, there, who I met comin' up th' stairs, that the new arrival in Boyle's ud grow up a hardy chiselur if it lived, an' that she'd be somethin' one o' these days that nobody suspected, an' so signs on it, here she is to-day, goin' to be married to a young man lookin' as if he'd be fit to commensurate in any position in life it ud please God to call him!

Boyle [*effusively*] Sit down, Mrs. Madigan, sit down, me oul' sport. [*To Bentham*] This is Joxer Daly, Past Chief Ranger of the Dear Little Shamrock Branch of the Irish National Foresters, an oul' front-top neighbour, that never despaired, even in the darkest days of Ireland's sorra.

Joxer Nil desperandum, Captain, nil desperandum.

Boyle Sit down, Joxer, sit down. The two of us was ofen in a tight corner.

Mrs. Boyle Ay, in Foley's snug!

Joxer An' we kem out of it flyin', we kem out of it flyin', Captain.

Boyle An' now for a dhrink – I know yous won't refuse an oul' friend.

Mrs. Madigan [*to Juno*] Is Johnny not well, Mrs. . . .

Mrs. Boyle [*warningly*] S-s-s-sh.

Mrs. Madigan Oh, the poor darlin'.

Boyle Well, Mrs. Madigan, is it tea or what?

Mrs. Madigan Well, speakin' for meself, I jus' had me tea a minute ago, an' I'm afraid to dhrink any more – I'm never the same when I dhrink too much tay. Thanks all the same, Mr. Boyle.

Boyle Well, what about a bottle o' stout or a dhrop o' whisky?

Mrs Madigan A bottle o' stout ud be a little too heavy for me stummock afther me tay. . . . A-a-ah, I'll thry the ball o' malt.

[*Boyle prepares the whisky.*]

Mrs Madigan There's nothin' like a ball o' malt occasional like – too much of it isn't good. [*To Boyle, who is adding water*] Ah, God, Johnny, don't put too much wather on it! [*She drinks*] I suppose yous'll be lavin' this place.

Boyle I'm looking for a place near the sea; I'd like the place that you might say was me cradle, to be me grave as well. The sea is always callin' me.

Joxer She is callin', callin', callin', in the win' an' on the sea.

Boyle Another dhrop o' whisky, Mrs. Madigan?

Mrs Madigan Well, now, it ud be hard to refuse seein' the suspicious times that's in it.

Boyle [*with a commanding gesture*] Song! . . . Juno . . . Mary . . . 'Home to Our Mountains'!

Mrs Madigan [*enthusiastically*] Hear, hear!

Joxer Oh, tha's a darlin' song, a daarlin' song!

Mary [*bashfully*] Ah no, da; I'm not in a singin' humour.

Mrs Madigan Gawn with you, child, an' you only goin' to be marrid; I remember as well as I remember yestherday, – it was on a lovely August evenin', exactly, accordin' to date, fifteen years ago, come the Tuesday folleyin' the nex' that's comin' on, when me own man – the Lord be good to him – an' me was sittin' shy together in a doty little nook on a counthry road, adjacent to The Stiles. 'That'll scratch your lovely, little white neck,' says he, ketchin' hould of a danglin' bramble branch, holdin' clusters of the loveliest flowers you ever seen, an' breakin' it off, so that his arm fell, accidental like, roun' me waist, an' as I felt it tightenin', an' tightenin', an' tightenin', I thought me buzzom was every minute goin' to burst out into a roystherin' song about

'The little green leaves that were shakin' on the threes,
The gallivantin' buttherflies, an' buzzin' o' the bees!'

Boyle Ordher for the song!

Juno Come on, Mary – we'll do our best.

[*Juno and Mary stand up, and choosing a suitable position, sing simply 'Home to Our Mountains'.*]

[*They bow to the company, and return to their places.*]

Boyle [*emotionally, at the end of song*] Lull . . . me . . . to . . . rest!

Joxer [*clapping his hands*] Bravo, bravo! Darlin' girulls, darlin' girulls!

Mrs Madigan Juno, I never seen you in betther form.

Bentham Very nicely rendered indeed.

Mrs Madigan A noble call, a noble call!

Mrs Boyle What about yourself, Mrs. Madigan?

[*After some coaxing, Mrs. Madigan rises, and in a quavering voice sings the following verse:*]

If I were a blackbird I'd whistle and sing;
I'd follow the ship that my thrue love was in;
An' on the top riggin', I'd there build me nest,
An' at night I would sleep on me Willie's white breast!

[*Becoming husky, amid applause, she sits down.*]

Mrs Madigan Ah, me voice is too husky now, Juno; though I remember the time when Maisie Madigan could sing like a nightingale at matin' time. I remember as well as I remember yesterday, at a party given to celebrate the comin' of the first chiselur to Annie an' Benny Jimeson – who was the barber, yous may remember, in Henrietta Street, that, afther Easter Week, hung out a green, white an' orange pole, an' then, when the Tans started their Jazz dancin', whipped it in agen, an' stuck out a red, white an' blue wan instead, givin' as an excuse that a barber's pole was strictly non-political singin' 'An' You'll Remember Me' with the top notes quiverin' in a dead hush of pethrified attention, folleyed be a clappin' o' han's that shuk the tumblers on the table, an' capped by Jimeson, the barber, sayin' that it was the best rendherin' of ' You'll Remember Me' he ever heard in his natural!

Boyle [*peremptorily*] Ordher for Joxer's song!

Joxer Ah no, I couldn't; don't ass me, Captain.

Boyle Joxer's song, Joxer's song – give us wan of your shut-eyed wans.

[*Joxer settles himself in his chair; takes a drink; clears his throat; solemnly closes his eyes, and begins to sing in a very querulous voice:*]

　　She is far from the lan' where her young hero sleeps,
　　An' lovers around her are sighing

[*He hesitates.*]

　　An' lovers around her are sighin' . . . sighin' . . . sighin' . . .

[*A pause.*]

Boyle [*imitating Joxer*]:

　　And lovers around her are sighing!

What's the use of you thryin' to sing the song if you don't know it?

Mary Thry another one, Mr. Daly – maybe you'd be more fortunate.

Mrs Madigan Gawn, Joxer; thry another wan.

Joxer [*starting again*]:

　　I have heard the mavis singin' his love song to the morn;
　　I have seen the dew-dhrop clingin' to the rose jus' newly born; but . . .

but . . . [*frantically*] To the rose jus' newly born . . . newly born . . . born.

Johnny Mother, put on the gramophone, for God's sake, an' stop Joxer's bawlin'.

Boyle [*commandingly*] Gramophone! . . . I hate to see fellas thryin' to do what they're not able to do.

[*Boyle arranges the gramophone, and is about to start it, when voices are heard of persons descending the stairs.*]

Mrs Boyle [*warningly*] Whisht, Jack, don't put it on, don't put it on yet; this must be poor Mrs. Tancred comin' down to go to the hospital – I forgot all about them bringin' the body to the church to-night. Open the door, Mary, an' give them a bit o' light.

[*Mary opens the door, and Mrs. Tancred – a very old woman, obviously shaken by the death of her son – appears, accompanied by several neighbours. The first few phrases are spoken before they appear.*]

First Neighbour It's a sad journey we're goin' on, but God's good, an' the Republicans won't be always down.

Mrs Tancred Ah, what good is that to me now? Whether they're up or down –
it won't bring me darlin' boy from the grave.

Mrs Boyle Come in an' have a hot cup o' tay, Mrs. Tancred, before you go.

Mrs Tancred Ah, I can take nothin' now Mrs. Boyle – I won't be long afther
him.

First Neighbour Still an' all, he died a noble death, an' we'll bury him like a king.

Mrs Tancred An' I'll go on livin' like a pauper. Ah, what's the pains I suffered
bringin' him into the world to carry him to his cradle, to the pains I'm sufferin'
now, carryin' him out o' the world to bring him to his grave!

Mary It would be better for you not to go at all, Mrs. Tancred, but to stay at
home beside the fire with some o' the neighbours.

Mrs Tancred I seen the first of him, an' I'll see the last of him.

Mrs Boyle You'd want a shawl, Mrs. Tancred, it's a cowld night, an' the win's
blowin' sharp.

Mrs Madigan [*rushing out*] I've a shawl above.

Mrs Tancred Me home is gone now; he was me only child, an' to think that he
was lyin' for a whole night stretched out on the side of a lonely counthry lane,
with his head, his darlin' head, that I ofen kissed an' fondled, half hidden in the
wather of a runnin' brook. An' I'm told he was the leadher of the ambush
where me nex' door neighbour, Mrs. Mannin', lost her Free State soldier son.
An' now here's the two of us oul' women, standin' one on each side of a scales
o' sorra, balanced be the bodies of our two dead darlin' sons. [*Mrs. Madigan
returns, and wraps a shawl around her.*] God bless you, Mrs. Madigan. . . . [*She
moves slowly towards the door*] Mother o' God, Mother o' God, have pity on
the pair of us! . . . O Blessed Virgin, where were you when me darlin' son was
riddled with bullets, when me darlin' son was riddled with bullets! . . . Sacred
Heart of the Crucified Jesus, take away our hearts o' stone . . . an' give us hearts
o' flesh! . . . Take away this murdherin' hate . . . an' give us Thine own eternal
love!

[*They pass out of the room.*]

Mrs Boyle [*explanatorily to Bentham*] That was Mrs. Tancred of the two-pair
back; her son was found, e'er yestherday, lyin' out beyant Finglas riddled with
bullets. A Diehard he was, be all accounts. He was a nice quiet boy, but lattherly
he went to hell, with his Republic first, an' Republic last an' Republic over all.
He often took tea with us here, in the oul' days, an' Johnny, there, an' him used
to be always together.

Johnny Am I always to be havin' to tell you that he was no friend o' mine? I
never cared for him, an' he could never stick me. It's not because he was Commandant of the Battalion that I was Quarther-Masther of, that we were friends.

Mrs Boyle He's gone now – the Lord be good to him! God help his poor oul'
creature of a mother, for no matther whose friend or enemy he was, he was her
poor son.

Bentham The whole thing is terrible, Mrs. Boyle; but the only way to deal with
a mad dog is to destroy him.

Mrs Boyle An' to think of me forgettin' about him bein' brought to the church
to-night, an' we singin' an' all, but it was well we hadn't the gramophone goin',
anyhow.

Boyle Even if we had aself. We've nothin' to do with these things, one way or t'other. That's the Government's business, an' let them do what we're payin' them for doin'.

Mrs Boyle I'd like to know how a body's not to mind these things; look at the way they're afther leavin' the people in this very house. Hasn't the whole house, nearly, been massacreed? There's young Dougherty's husband with his leg off; Mrs. Travers that had her son blew up be a mine in Inchegeela, in Co. Cork; Mrs. Mannin' that lost wan of her sons in an ambush a few weeks ago, an' now, poor Mrs. Tancred's only child gone west with his body made a collandher of. Sure, if it's not our business, I don't know whose business it is.

Boyle Here, there, that's enough about them things, they don't affect us, an' we needn't give a damn. If they want a wake, well, let them have a wake. When I was a sailor, I was always resigned to meet with a wathery grave an' if they want to be soldiers, well, there's no use o' them squealin' when they meet a soldier's fate.

Joxer Let me like a soldier fall – me breast expandin' to th' ball!

Mrs Boyle In wan way, she deserves all she got; for lately, she let th' Diehards make an open house of th' place an' for th' last couple of months, either when th' sun was risin' or when th' sun was settin', you had C.I.D.[1] men burstin' into your room, assin' you where were you born, where were you christened, where were you married, an' where would you be buried!

Johnny For God's sake, let us have no more o' this talk.

Mrs Madigan What about Mr. Boyle's song before we start th' gramophone?

Mary [*getting her hat, and putting it on*] Mother, Charlie and I are goin' out for a little sthroll.

Mrs Boyle All right, darlin'.

Bentham [*going out with Mary*] We won't be long away, Mrs. Boyle.

Mrs Madigan Gwan, Captain, gwan.

Boyle E-e-e-e-eh, I'd want to have a few more jars in me, before I'd be in fettle for singin'.

Joxer Give us that poem you writ t'other day. [*To the rest*] Aw, it's a darlin' poem, a daarlin' poem.

Mrs Boyle God bless us, is he startin' to write poetry!

Boyle [*rising to his feet*] E-e-e-e-eh.

[*He recites in an emotional, consequential manner the following verses:*]
> Shawn an' I were friends, sir, to me he was all in all.
> His work was very heavy and his wages were very small.
> None bewther on th' beach as Docker, I'll go bail,
> 'Tis now I'm feelin' lonely, for to-day he lies in jail.
> He was not what some call pious – seldom at church or prayer;
> For the greatest scoundrels I know, sir, goes every Sunday there.
> Fond of his pint – well, rather, but hated the Boss by creed
> But never refused a copper to comfort a pal in need.

E-e-e-e-eh.

[*He sits down.*]

---

1 C.I.D.: Criminal Investigation Division, part of the police.

Mrs Madigan Grand, grand; you should folly that up, you should folly that up.
Joxer It's a daarlin' poem!
Boyle [*delightedly*] E-e-e-e-eh.
Johnny Are yous goin' to put on th' gramophone to-night, or are yous not?
Mrs Boyle Gwan, Jack, put on a record.
Mrs Madigan Gwan, Captain, gw-an.
Boyle Well, yous'll want to keep a dead silence.
[*He sets a record, starts the machine, and it begins to play 'If you're Irish, come into the Parlour'. As the tune is in full blare, the door is suddenly opened by a brisk, little bald-headed man, dressed circumspectly in a black suit; he glares fiercely at all in the room; he is 'Needle Nugent', a tailor. He carries his hat in his hand.*]
Nugent [*Loudly, above the noise of the gramophone*] Are yous goin' to have that thing bawlin' an' the funeral of Mrs. Tancred's son passin' the house? Have none of yous any respect for the Irish people's National regard for the dead?
[*Boyle stops the gramophone.*]
Mrs Boyle Maybe, Needle Nugent, it's nearly time we had a little less respect for the dead, an' a little more regard for the livin'.
Mrs Madigan We don't want you, Mr. Nugent, to teach us what we learned at our mother's knee. You don't look yourself as if you were dyin' of grief; if y'ass Maisie Madigan anything, I'd call you a real thrue Diehard an' livesoft Republican, attendin' Republican funerals in the day, an' stoppin' up half the night makin' suits for the Civic Guards!
[*Persons are heard running down to the street, some saying, 'Here it is, here it is'. Nugent withdraws, and the rest, except Johnny, go to the window looking into the street, and look out. Sounds of a crowd coming nearer are heard; portion are singing:*]
> To Jesus' Heart all burning
> With fervent love for men,
> My heart with fondest yearning
> Shall raise its joyful strain.
> While ages course along,
> Blest be with loudest song
> The Sacred Heart of Jesus
> By every heart and tongue.

Mrs Boyle Here's the hearse, here's the hearse!
Boyle There's t'oul' mother walkin' behin' the coffin.
Mrs Madigan You can hardly see the coffin with the wreaths.
Joxer Oh, it's a darlin' funeral, a daarlin' funeral!
Mrs Madigan W'd have a betther view from the street.
Boyle Yes – this place ud give you a crick in your neck.
[*They leave the room, and go down. Johnny sits moodily by the fire. A young man enters; he looks at Johnny for a moment.*]
The Young Man Quarther-Masther Boyle.
Johnny [*with a start*] The Mobilizer !
The Young Man You're not at the funeral?
Johnny I'm not well.
The Young Man I'm glad I've found you; you were stoppin' at your aunt's; I

called there but you'd gone. I've to give you an ordher to attend a Battalion Staff meetin' the night afther to-morrow.
Johnny Where?
The Young Man I don't know; you're to meet me at the Pillar at eight o'clock; then we're to go to a place I'll be told of to-night; there we'll meet a mothor that'll bring us to the meeting. They think you might be able to know somethin' about them that gave the bend where Commandant Tancred was shelterin'.
Johnny I'm not goin', then. I know nothing about Tancred.
The Young Man [*at the door*] You'd betther come for your own sake – remember your oath.
Johnny [*passionately*] I won't go! Haven't I done enough for Ireland! I've lost me arm, an' me hip's desthroyed so that I'll never be able to walk right agen! Good God, haven't I done enough for Ireland?
The Young Man Boyle, no man can do enough for Ireland!
[*He goes.*]
[*Faintly in the distance the crowd is heard saying:*]
   Hail, Mary, full of grace, the Lord is with Thee;
   Blessed art Thou amongst women, and blessed, etc.

                        [*Curtain*]

Act III

[*The same as Act II. It is about half-past six on a November evening; a bright fire burns in the grate; Mary, dressed to go out, is sitting on a chair by the fire, leaning forward, her hands under her chin, her elbows on her knees. A look of dejection, mingled with uncertain anxiety, is on her face. A lamp, turned low, is lighting on the table. The votive light under the picture of the Virgin gleams more redly than ever. Mrs. Boyle is putting on her hat and coat. It is two months later.*]
Mrs Boyle An' has Bentham never even written to you since – not one line for the past month?
Mary [*tonelessly*] Not even a line, mother.
Mrs Boyle That's very curious. . . . What came between the two of yous at all? To leave you so sudden, an' yous so great together. . . . To go away t' England, an' not to even leave you his address. . . . The way he was always bringin' you to dances, I thought he was mad afther you. Are you sure you said nothin' to him?
Mary No, mother – at least nothing that could possibly explain his givin me up.
Mrs Boyle You know you're a bit hasty at times, Mary, an' say things you shouldn't say.
Mary I never said to him what I shouldn't say, I'm sure of that.
Mrs Boyle How are you sure of it?
Mary Because I love him with all my heart and soul, mother. Why, I don't know; I often thought to myself that he wasn't the man poor Jerry was, but I couldn't help loving him, all the same.
Mrs Boyle But you shouldn't be frettin' the way you are; when a woman loses a man, she never knows what she's afther losin', to be sure, but, then, she never knows what she's afther gainin', either. You're not the one girl of a month ago –

you look like one pinin' away. It's long ago I had a right to bring you to the doctor, instead of waitin' till to-night.

Mary There's no necessity, really, mother, to go to the doctor; nothing serious is wrong with me – I'm run down and disappointed, that's all.

Mrs Boyle I'll not wait another minute; I don't like the look of you at all . . . I'm afraid we made a mistake in throwin' over poor Jerry. . . . He'd have been betther for you than that Bentham.

Mary Mother, the best man for a woman is the one for whom she has the most love, and Charlie had it all.

Mrs Boyle Well, there's one thing to be said for him – he couldn't have been thinkin' of the money, or he wouldn't ha' left you . . . it must ha' been somethin' else.

Mary [*wearily*] I don't know . . . I don't know, mother . . . only I think . . .

Mrs Boyle What d'ye think?

Mary I imagine . . . he thought . . . we weren't . . . good enough for him.

Mrs Boyle An' what was he himself, only a school teacher? Though I don't blame him for fightin' shy of people like that Joxer fella an' that oul' Madigan wan – nice sort o' people for your father to inthroduce to a man like Mr. Bentham. You might have told me all about this before now, Mary; I don't know why you like to hide everything from your mother; you knew Bentham, an' I'd ha' known nothin' about it if it hadn't bin for the Will; an' it was only to-day, afther long coaxin', that you let out that he's left you.

Mary It would have been useless to tell you – you wouldn't understand.

Mrs Boyle [*hurt*] Maybe not. . . . Maybe I wouldn't understand. . . . Well, we'll be off now.

[*She goes over to door left, and speaks to Boyle inside.*]

Mrs Boyle We're goin' now to the doctor's. Are you goin' to get up this evenin'?

Boyle [*from inside*] The pains in me legs is terrible! It's me should be poppin' off to the doctor instead o' Mary, the way I feel.

Mrs Boyle Sorra mend you! A nice way you were in last night – carried in in a frog's march, dead to the world. If that's the way you'll go on when you get the money it'll be the grave for you, an asylum for me and the Poorhouse for Johnny.

Boyle I thought you were goin'?

Mrs Boyle That's what has you as you are – you can't bear to be spoken to. Knowin' the way we are, up to our ears in debt, it's a wondher you wouldn't ha' got up to go to th' solicitor's an' see if we could ha' gotten a little o' the money even.

Boyle [*shouting*] I can't be goin' up there night, noon an' mornin', can I? He can't give the money till he gets it, can he? I can't get blood out of a turnip, can I?

Mrs Boyle It's nearly two months since we heard of the Will, an' the money seems as far off as ever. . . . I suppose you know we owe twenty pouns to oul' Murphy?

Boyle I've a faint recollection of you tellin' me that before.

Mrs Boyle Well, you'll go over to the shop yourself for the things in future – I'll face him no more.

Boyle I thought you said you were goin'?

Mrs Boyle I'm goin' now; come on, Mary.

Boyle Ey, Juno, ey!

Mrs Boyle Well, what d'ye want now?

Boyle Is there e'er a bottle o' stout left?

Mrs Boyle There's two o' them here still.

Boyle Show us in one o' them an' leave t'other there till I get up. An' throw us in the paper that's on the table, an' the bottle o' Sloan's Liniment that's in th' drawer.

Mrs Boyle [*getting the liniment and the stout*] What paper is it you want – the *Messenger*?

Boyle *Messenger*! The *News o' the World*!

[*Mrs. Boyle brings in the things asked for, and comes out again.*]

Mrs Boyle [*at door*] Mind the candle, now, an' don't burn the house over our heads. I left t'other bottle o' stout on the table.

[*She puts bottle of stout on table. She goes out with Mary. A cork is heard popping inside.*]

[*A pause; then outside the door is heard the voice of Joxer lilting softly: 'Me pipe I'll smoke, as I dhrive me moke ....are you ...there ... Mor ... ee ... ar ... i ... teee!' A gentle knock is heard, and after a pause the door opens, and Joxer, followed by Nugent, enters.*]

Joxer Be God, they must be all out; I was thinkin' there was somethin' up when he didn't answer the signal. We seen Juno an' Mary goin', but I didn't see him, an' it's very seldom he escapes me.

Nugent He's not goin' to escape me – he's not goin' to be let go to the fair altogether.

Joxer Sure, the house couldn't hould them lately; an' he goin' about like a mastherpiece of the Free State counthry; forgettin' their friends; forgettin' God – wouldn't even lift his hat passin' a chapel! Sure they were bound to get a dhrop! An' you really think there's no money comin' to him afther all?

Nugent Not as much as a red rex, man; I've been a bit anxious this long time over me money, an' I went up to the solicitor's to find out all I could – ah, man, they were goin' to throw me down the stairs. They toul' me that the oul' cock himself had the stairs worn away comin' up afther it, an' they black in the face tellin' him he'd get nothin'. Some way or another that the Will is writ he won't be entitled to get as much as a make!

Joxer Ah, I thought there was somethin' curious about the whole thing; I've bin havin' sthrange dhreams for the last couple o' weeks. An' I notice that that Bentham fella doesn't be comin' here now – there must be somethin' on the mat there too. Anyhow, who, in the name o' God, ud leave anythin' to that oul' bummer? Sure it ud be unnatural. An' the way Juno an' him's been throwin' their weight about for the last few months! Ah, him that goes a borrowin' goes a sorrowin'!

Nugent Well, he's not goin' to throw his weight about in the suit I made for him much longer. I'm tellin' you seven pouns aren't to be found growin' on the bushes these days.

Joxer An' there isn't hardly a neighbour in the whole street that hasn't lent him money on the strength of what he was goin' to get, but they're after backing the wrong horse. Wasn't it a mercy o' God that I'd nothin' to give him! The softy I am, you know, I'd ha' lent him me last juice! I must have had somebody's good prayers. Ah, afther all, an honest man's the noblest work o' God!

[*Boyle coughs inside.*]

Joxer Whisht, damn it, he must be inside in bed.

Nugent Inside o' bed or outside of it, he's goin' to pay me for that suit, or give it back – he'll not climb up my back as easily as he thinks.

Joxer Gwan in at wanst, man, an' get it off him, an' don't be a fool.

Nugent [*going to door left, opening it and looking in*] Ah, don't disturb yourself, Mr. Boyle; I hope you're not sick?

Boyle Th' oul' legs, Mr. Nugent, the oul' legs.

Nugent I just called over to see if you could let me have anything off the suit?

Boyle E-e-e-eh, how much is this it is?

Nugent It's the same as it was at the start – seven pouns.

Boyle I'm glad you kem, Mr. Nugent; I want a good heavy top-coat – Irish frieze, if you have it. How much would a top-coat like that be, now?

Nugent About six pouns.

Boyle Six pouns – six an' seven, six an' seven is thirteen – that'll be thirteen pouns I'll owe you.

[*Joxer slips the bottle of stout that is on the table into his pocket. Nugent rushes into the room, and returns with suit on his arm; he pauses at the door.*]

Nugent You'll owe me no thirteen pouns. Maybe you think you're betther able to owe it than pay it!

Boyle [*frantically*] Here, come back to hell ower that – where're you goin' with them clothes o' mine?

Nugent Where am I goin' with them clothes o' yours? Well, I like your damn cheek!

Boyle Here, what am I goin' to dhress meself in when I'm goin' out?

Nugent What do I care what you dhress yourself in! You can put yourself in a bolsther cover, if you like.

[*He goes towards the other door, followed by Joxer.*]

Joxer What'll he dhress himself in! Gentleman Jack an' his frieze coat!

[*They go out.*]

Boyle [*inside*] Ey, Nugent; ey, Mr. Nugent, Mr. Nugent!

[*After a pause Boyle enters hastily, buttoning the braces of his moleskin trousers; his coat and vest are on his arm; he throws these on a chair and hurries to the door on right.*]

Boyle Ey, Mr. Nugent, Mr. Nugent!

Joxer [*meeting him at the door*] What's up, what's wrong, Captain?

Boyle Nugent's been here an' took away me suit – the only things I had to go out in!

Joxer Tuk your suit – for God's sake! An' what were you doin' while he was takin' them?

Boyle I was in bed when he stole in like a thief in the night, an' before I knew even what he was thinkin' of, he whipped them from the chair an' was off like a redshank!

Joxer An' what, in the name o' God, did he do that for?

Boyle What did he do it for? How the hell do I know what he done it for? – jealousy an' spite, I suppose.

Joxer Did he not say what he done it for?

Boyle Amn't I afther tellin' you that he had them whipped up an' was gone before I could open me mouth?

Joxer That was a very sudden thing to do; there mus' be somethin' bellin' it. Did he hear anythin', I wondher?

Boyle Did he hear anythin'? – you talk very queer, Joxer – what could he hear?

Joxer About you not gettin' the money, in some way or t'other?

Boyle An' what ud prevent me from gettin' th' money?

Joxer That's jus' what I was thinkin' – what ud prevent you from gettin' the money – nothin', as far as I can see.

Boyle [*looking round for bottle of stout, with an exclamation*] Aw, holy God!

Joxer What's up, Jack?

Boyle He must have afther lifted the bottle o' stout that Juno left on the table!

Joxer [*horrified*] Ah no, ah no; he wouldn't be afther doin' that now.

Boyle An' who done it then? Juno left a bottle o' stout here, an' it's gone – it didn't walk, did it?

Joxer Oh, that's shockin'; ah, man's inhumanity to man makes countless thousands mourn!

Mrs Madigan [*appearing at the door*] I hope I'm not disturbin' you in any discussion on your forthcomin' legacy – if I may use the word – an' that you'll let me have a barny for a minute or two with you, Mr. Boyle.

Boyle [*uneasily*] To be sure, Mrs. Madigan – an oul' friend's always welcome.

Joxer Come in the evenin', come in th' mornin'; come when you're assed, or come without warnin', Mrs. Madigan.

Boyle Sit down, Mrs. Madigan.

Mrs Madigan [*ominously*] Th' few words I have to say can be said standin'. Puttin' aside all formularies, I suppose you remember me lendin' you some time ago three pouns that I raised on blankets an' furniture in me uncle's?

Boyle I remember it well. I have it recorded in me book – three pouns five shillings from Maisie Madigan, raised on articles pawned; an', item: fourpence, given to make up the price of a pint, on th' principle that no bird ever flew on wan wing; all to be repaid at par, when the ship comes home.

Mrs Madigan Well, ever since I shoved in the blankets I've been perishing with th' cowld, an' I've decided, if I'll be too hot in th' next' world aself, I'm not goin' to be too cowld in this wan; an' consequently, I want me three pouns, if you please.

Boyle This is a very sudden demand, Mrs. Madigan, an' can't be met; but I'm willin' to give you a receipt in full, in full.

Mrs Madigan Come on, out with th' money, an' don't be jack-actin'.

Boyle You can't get blood out of a turnip, can you?

Mrs Madigan [*rushing over and shaking him*] Gimme me money, y'oul' reprobate, or I'll shake the worth of it out of you!

Boyle Ey, houl' on, there; houl' on, there! You'll wait for your money now, me lassie!

Mrs Madigan [*looking around the room and seeing the gramophone*] I'll wait for it, will I? Well, I'll not wait long; if I can't get th' cash I'll get th' worth of it. [*She catches up the gramophone.*]

Boyle Ey, ey, there, wher'r you goin' with that?

Mrs Madigan I'm goin' to th' pawn to get me three quid five shillins; I'll brin' you th' ticket, an' then you can do what you like, me bucko.

Boyle You can't touch that, you can't touch that! It's not my property, an' it's not ped for yet!

Mrs Madigan So much th' better. It'll be an ayse to me conscience, for I'm takin' what doesn't belong to you. You're not goin' to be swankin' it like a paycock with Maisie Madigan's money – I'll pull some o' tll' gorgeous feathers out o' your tail!

[*She goes out with the gramophone.*]

Boyle What's th' world comin' to at all? I ass you, Joxer Daly, is there any morality left anywhere?

Joxer I wouldn't ha' believed it, only I seen it with me own two eyes. I didn't think Maisie Madigan was that sort of woman; she has either a sup taken, or she's heard somethin'.

Boyle Heard somethin' – about what, if it's not any harm to ass you?

Joxer She must ha' heard some rumour or other that you weren't goin' to get th' money.

Boyle Who says I'm not goin' to get th' money?

Joxer Sure, I don't know – I was only sayin'.

Boyle Only sayin' what?

Joxer Nothin'.

Boyle You were goin' to say somethin' – don't be a twisther.

Joxer [*angrily*] Who's a twisther?

Boyle Why don't you speak your mind, then?

Joxer You never twisted yourself – no, you wouldn't know how!

Boyle Did you ever know me to twist; did you ever know me to twist?

Joxer [*fiercely*] Did you ever do anythin' else! Sure, you can't believe a word that comes out o' your mouth.

Boyle Here, get out, ower o' this; I always knew you were a prognosticator an' a procrastinator!

Joxer [*going out as Johnny comes in*] The anchor's weighed, farewell, ree . . . mem . . . ber . . . me. Jacky Boyle, Esquire, infernal rogue an' damned liar.

Johnny Joxer an' you at it agen? – when are you goin' to have a little respect for yourself, an' not be always makin' a show of us all?

Boyle Are you goin' to lecture me now?

Johnny Is mother back from the doctor yet, with Mary?

[*Mrs. Boyle enters; it is apparent from the serious look on her face that something has happened. She takes off her hat and coat without a word and puts them by. She then sits down near the fire, and there is a few moments' pause.*]

Boyle Well, what did the doctor say about Mary?

Mrs Boyle [*in an earnest manner and with suppressed agitation*] Sit down here, Jack; I've something to say to you . . . about Mary.

Boyle [*awed by her manner*] About . . . Mary?

Mrs Boyle Close that door there and sit down here.

Boyle [*closing the door*] More throuble in our native land, is it? [*She sits down*] Well, what is it?

Mrs Boyle It's about Mary.

Boyle Well, what about Mary – there's nothin' wrong with her, is there?

Mrs Boyle I'm sorry to say there's a gradle wrong with her.

Boyle A gradle wrong with her! [*Peevishly*] First Johnny an' now Mary; is the whole house goin' to become an hospital! It's not consumption, is it?

Mrs Boyle No . . . it's not consumption . . . it's worse.

Johnny Worse! Well, we'll have to get her into some place ower this, there's no one here to mind her.

Mrs Boyle We'll all have to mind her now. You might as well know now, Johnny, as another time. [*To Boyle*] D'ye know what the doctor said to me about her, Jack?

Boyle How ud I know – I wasn't there, was I?

Mrs Boyle He told me to get her married at wanst.

Boyle Married at wanst! An' why did he say the like o' that?

Mrs Boyle Because Mary's goin' to have a baby in a short time.

Boyle Goin' to have a baby! – my God, what'll Bentham say when he hears that?

Mrs Boyle Are you blind, man, that you can't see that it was Bentham that has done this wrong to her?

Boyle [*passionately*] Then he'll marry her, he'll have to marry her!

Mrs Boyle You know he's gone to England, an' God knows where he is now.

Boyle I'll folly him, I'll folly him, an' bring him back, an' make him do her justice. The scoundrel, I might ha' known what he was, with his yogees an' his prawna!

Mrs Boyle We'll have to keep it quiet till we see what we can do.

Boyle Oh, isn't this a nice thing to come on top o' me, an' the state I'm in! A pretty show I'll be to Joxer an' to that oul' wan, Madigan! Amn't I afther goin' through enough without havin' to go through this!

Mrs Boyle What you an' I'll have to go through'll be nothin' to what poor Mary'll have to go through; for you an' me is middlin' old, an' most of our years is spent; but Mary'll have maybe forty years to face an' handle, an' every wan of them'll be tainted with a bitther memory.

Boyle Where is she? Where is she till I tell her off? I'm tellin' you when I'm done with her she'll be a sorry girl!

Mrs Boyle I left her in me sister's till I came to speak to you. You'll say nothin' to her, Jack; ever since she left school she's earned her livin', an' your fatherly care never throubled the poor girl.

Boyle Gwan, take her part agen her father! But I'll let you see whether I'll say nothin' to her or no! Her an' her readin'! That's more o' th' blasted nonsense that has the house fallin' down on top of us! What did th' likes of her, born in a tenement house, want with readin'? Her readin's afther bringin' her to a nice pass – oh, it's madnin', madnin', madnin'!

Mrs Boyle When she comes back say nothin' to her, Jack, or she'll leave this place.

Boyle Leave this place! Ay, she'll leave this place, an' quick too!

Mrs Boyle If Mary goes, I'll go with her.

Boyle Well, go with her! Well, go, th' pair o' yous! I lived before I seen yous, an' I can live when yous are gone. Isn't this a nice thing to come rollin' in on top o' me afther all your prayin' to St. Anthony an' The Little Flower! An' she's a Child o' Mary, too – I wonder what'll the nuns think of her now? An' it'll be bellows'd all over th' disthrict before you could say Jack Robinson; an' whenever I'm seen they'll whisper, 'That's th' father of Mary Boyle that had th' kid be th' swank she used to go with; d'ye know, d'ye know?' To be sure they'll know – more about it than I will meself!

Johnny She should be dhriven out o' th' house she's brought disgrace on!

Mrs Boyle Hush, you, Johnny. We needn't let it be bellows'd all over the place; all we've got to do is to leave this place quietly an' go somewhere where we're not known an' nobody'll be th' wiser.

Boyle You're talkin' like a two-year-oul', woman. Where'll we get a place ou' o' this? – places aren't that easily got.

Mrs Boyle But, Jack, when we get the money . . .

Boyle Money – what money?

Mrs Boyle Why, oul' Ellison's money, of course.

Boyle There's no money comin' from oul' Ellison, or any one else. Since you've heard of wan throuble, you might as well hear of another. There's no money comin' to us at all – the Will's a wash-out !

Mrs Boyle What are you sayin', man – no money?

Johnny How could it be a wash-out?

Boyle The boyo that's afther doin' it to Mary done it to me as well. The thick made out the Will wrong; he said in th' Will, only first cousin an' second cousin, instead of mentionin' our names, an' now any one that thinks he's a first cousin or second cousin t'oul' Ellison can claim the money as well as me, an' they're springin' up in hundreds, an' comin' from America an' Australia, thinkin' to get their whack out of it, while all the time the lawyers is gobblin' it up, till there's not as much as ud buy a stockin' for your lovely daughter's baby!

Mrs Boyle I don't believe it, I don't believe it, I don't believe it!

Johnny Why did you say nothin' about this before?

Mrs Boyle You're not serious, Jack; you're not serious!

Boyle I'm tellin' you the scholar, Bentham, made a banjax o' th' Will; instead o' sayin', 'th' rest o' me property to be divided between me first cousin, Jack Boyle, an' me second cousin, Mick Finnegan, o' Santhry', he writ down only, 'me first an' second cousins', an' the world an' his wife are afther th' property now.

Mrs Boyle Now I know why Bentham left poor Mary in th' lurch; I can see it all now – oh, is there not even a middlin' honest man left in th' world?

Johnny [*to Boyle*] An' you let us run into debt, an' you borreyed money from everybody to fill yourself with beer! An' now you tell us the whole thing's a washout! Oh, if it's thrue, I'm done with you, for you're worse than me sisther Mary!

Boyle You hole your tongue, d'ye hear? I'll not take any lip from you. Go an' get Bentham if you want satisfaction for all that's afther happenin' us.

Johnny I won't hole me tongue, I won't hole me tongue! I'll tell you what I think of you, father an' all as you are . . . you . . .

Mrs Boyle Johnny, Johnny, Johnny, for God's sake, be quiet!

Johnny I'll not be quiet, I'll not be quiet; he's a nice father, isn't he? Is it any wondher Mary went asthray, when . . .

Mrs Boyle Johnny, Johnny, for my sake be quiet – for your mother's sake!

Boyle I'm goin' out now to have a few dhrinks with th' last few makes I have, an' tell that lassie o' yours not to be here when I come back; for if I lay me eyes on her, I'll lay me hans on her, an' if I lay me hans on her, I won't be account-able for me actions!

Johnny Take care somebody doesn't lay his hans on you – y'oul'. . .

Mrs Boyle Johnny, Johnny!

Boyle [*at door, about to go out*] Oh, a nice son, an' a nicer daughter, I have. [*Calling loudly upstairs*] Joxer, Joxer, are you there?

Joxer [*from a distance*] I'm here, More . . . ee . . . aar . . . i . . . tee!

Boyle I'm goin' down to Foley's – are you comin'?

Joxer Come with you? With that sweet call me heart is stirred; I'm only wait-ing for the word, an' I'll be with you, like a bird!

[*Boyle and Joxer pass the door going out.*]

Johnny [*throwing himself on the bed*] I've a nice sisther, an' a nice father, there's no bettin' on it. I wish to God a bullet or a bomb had whipped me ou' o' this long ago! Not one o' yous, not one o' yous, have any thought for me!

Mrs Boyle [*with passionate remonstrance*] If you don't whisht, Johnny, you'll drive me mad. Who has kep' th' home together for the past few years – only me? An' who'll have to bear th' biggest part o' this throuble but me?– but whinin' an' whingin' isn't goin' to do any good.

Johnny You're to blame yourself for a gradle of it – givin' him his own way in everything, an' never assin' to check him, no matther what he done. Why didn't you look afther th' money? Why . . .

[*There is a knock at the door; Mrs. Boyle opens it; Johnny rises on his elbow to look and listen; two men enter.*]

First Man We've been sent up be th' Manager of the Hibernian Furnishing Co., Mrs. Boyle, to take back the furniture that was got a while ago.

Mrs Boyle Yous'll touch nothin' here – how do I know who yous are?

First Man [*showing a paper*] There's the ordher, ma'am. [*Reading*] A chest o' drawers, a table, wan easy an' two ordinary chairs; wan mirror; wan chestherfield divan, an' a wardrobe an' two vases. [*To his comrade*] Come on, Bill, it's afther knockin'-off time already.

Johnny For God's sake, mother, run down to Foley's an' bring father back, or we'll be left without a stick.

[*The men carry out the table.*]

Mrs Boyle What good would it be? – you heard what he said before he went out.

Johnny Can't you thry? He ought to be here, an' the like of this goin' on.

[*Mrs. Boyle puts a shawl around her, as Mary enters.*]

Mary What's up, mother? I met men carryin' away the table, an' everybody's talking about us not gettin' the money after all.

Mrs Boyle Everythin's gone wrong, Mary, everythin'. We're not gettin' a penny out o' the Will, not a penny – I'll tell you all when I come back; I'm goin' for your father.
[*She runs out.*]
Johnny [*to Mary, who has sat down by the fire*] It's a wondher you're not ashamed to show your face here, afther what has happened.
[*Jerry enters slowly; there is a look of earnest hope on his face. He looks at Mary for a few moments.*]
Jerry [*softly*] Mary!
[*Mary does not answer.*]
Jerry Mary, I want to speak to you for a few moments, may I?
[*Mary remains silent; Johnny goes slowly into room on left.*]
Jerry Your mother has told me everything, Mary, and I have come to you. . . . I have come to tell you, Mary, that my love for you is greater and deeper than ever. . . .
Mary [*with a sob*] Oh, Jerry, Jerry, say no more; all that is over now; anything like that is impossible now!
Jerry Impossible? Why do you talk like that, Mary?
Mary After all that has happened.
Jerry What does it matter what has happened? We are young enough to be able to forget all those things. [*He catches her hand.*] Mary, Mary, I am pleading for your love. With Labour, Mary, humanity is above everything; we are the Leaders in the fight for a new life. I want to forget Bentham, I want to forget that you left me – even for a while.
Mary Oh, Jerry, Jerry, you haven't the bitter word of scorn for me after all.
Jerry [*passionately*] Scorn! I love you, love you, Mary!
Mary [*rising, and looking him in the eyes*] Even though . . .
Jerry Even though you threw me over for another man; even though you gave me many a bitter word!
Mary Yes, yes, I know; but you love me, even though . . . even though . . . I'm . . . goin' . . . goin' . . . [*He looks at her questioningly, and fear gathers in his eyes.*] Ah, I was thinkin' so. . . . You don't know everything!
Jerry [*poignantly*] Surely to God, Mary, you don't mean that . . . that . . . that . . .
Mary Now you know all, Jerry; now you know all.
Jerry My God, Mary, have you fallen as low as that?
Mary Yes, Jerry, as you say, I have fallen as low as that.
Jerry I didn't mean it that way, Mary . . . it came on me so sudden, that I didn't mind what I was sayin'. . . . I never expected this – your mother never told me. . . . I'm sorry . . . God knows, I'm sorry for you, Mary.
Mary Let us say no more, Jerry; I don't blame you for thinkin' it's terrible. . . . I suppose it is. . . . Everybody'll think the same . . . it's only as I expected – your humanity is just as narrow as the humanity of the others.
Jerry I'm sorry, all the same. . . . I shouldn't have troubled you. . . . I wouldn't if I'd known. . . . If I can do anything for you . . . Mary . . . I will.
[*He turns to go, and halts at the door.*]

Mary Do you remember, Jerry, the verses you read when you gave the lecture in the Socialist Rooms some time ago, on Humanity's Strife with Nature?
Jerry The verses – no; I don't remember them.
Mary I do. They're runnin' in me head now –

> An' we felt the power that fashion'd
> All the lovely things we saw,
> That created all the murmur
> Of an everlasting law,
> Was a hand of force an' beauty,
> With an eagle's tearin' claw.
>
> Then we saw our globe of beauty
> Was an ugly thing as well,
> A hymn divine whose chorus
> Was an agonizin' yell;
> Like the story of a demon,
> That an angel had to tell;
>
> Like a glowin' picture by a
> Hand unsteady, brought to ruin;
> Like her craters, if their deadness
> Could give life unto the moon;
> Like the agonizing horror
> Of a violin out of tune.

[*There is a pause, and Devine goes slowly out.*]
Johnny [*returning*] Is he gone?
Mary Yes.
[*The two men re-enter.*]
First Man We can't wait any longer for t'oul' fella – sorry, Miss, but we have to live as well as th' nex' man.
[*They carry out some things.*]
Johnny Oh, isn't this terrible! . . . I suppose you told him everything . . . couldn't you have waited for a few days? . . . he'd have stopped th' takin' of the things, if you'd kep' your mouth shut. Are you burnin' to tell every one of the shame you've brought on us?
Mary [*snatching up her hat and coat*] Oh, this is unbearable!
[*She rushes out.*]
First Man [*re-entering*] We'll take the chest o' drawers next – it's the heaviest.
[*The votive light flickers for a moment, and goes out.*]
Johnny [*in a cry of fear*] Mother o' God, the light's after goin' out!
First Man You put the win' up me the way you bawled that time. The oil's all gone, that's all.
Johnny [*with an agonizing cry*] Mother o' God, there's a shot I'm after gettin'!
First Man What's wrong with you, man? Is it a fit you're takin'?
Johnny I'm after feelin' a pain in me breast, like the tearin' by of a bullet!
First Man He's goin' mad – it's a wondher they'd leave a chap like that here by himself.

[*Two Irregulars enter swiftly; they carry revolvers; one goes over to Johnny; the other covers the two furniture men.*]

First Irregular [*to the men, quietly and incisively*] Who are you? – What are yous doin' here? – quick!

First Man Removin' furniture that's not paid for.

Irregular Get over to the other end of the room an' turn your faces to the wall – quick!

[*The two men turn their faces to the wall, with their hands up.*]

Second Irregular [*to Johnny*] Come on, Sean Boyle, you're wanted; some of us have a word to say to you.

Johnny I'm sick, I can't – what do you want with me?

Second Irregular Come on, come on; we've a distance to go, an' haven't much time – come on.

Johnny I'm an oul' comrade – yous wouldn't shoot an oul' comrade.

Second Irregular Poor Tancred was an oul' comrade o' yours, but you didn't think o' that when you gave him away to the gang that sent him to his grave. But we've no time to waste; come on – here, Dermot, ketch his arm. [*To Johnny*] Have you your beads?

Johnny Me beads! Why do you ass me that, why do you ass me that?

Second Irregular Go on, go on, march!

Johnny Are yous goin' to do in a comrade? – Look at me arm, I lost it for Ireland.

Second Irregular Commandant Tancred lost his life for Ireland.

Johnny Sacred Heart of Jesus, have mercy on me! Mother o' God, pray for me – be with me now in the agonies o' death! . . . Hail, Mary, full o' grace . . . the Lord is . . . with Thee.

[*They drag out Johnny Boyle, and the curtain falls. When it rises again the most of the furniture is gone. Mary and Mrs. Boyle, one on each side, are sitting in a darkened room, by the fire; it is an hour later.*]

Mrs Boyle I'll not wait much longer . . . what did they bring him away in the mothor for? Nugent says he thinks they had guns . . . is me throubles never goin' to be over? If anything ud happen to poor Johnny, I think I'd lose me mind. . . . I'll go to the Police Station, surely they ought to be able to do somethin'.

[*Below is heard the sound of voices.*]

Mrs Boyle Whisht, is that something? Maybe, it's your father, though when I left him in Foley's he was hardly able to lift his head. Whisht!

[*A knock at the door.*]

The voice of Mrs. Madigan [*speaking very softly*] Mrs. Boyle, Mrs. Boyle.

[*Mrs. Boyle opens the door.*]

Mrs Madigan Oh, Mrs. Boyle, God an' His Blessed Mother be with you this night!

Mrs Boyle [*calmly*] What is it, Mrs. Madigan? It's Johnny – something about Johnny.

Mrs Madigan God send it's not, God send it's not Johnny!

Mrs Boyle Don't keep me waitin', Mrs. Madigan; I've gone through so much lately that I feel able for anything.

Mrs Madigan Two polismen below wantin' you.

Mrs Boyle Wantin' me; an' why do they want me?

Mrs Madigan Some poor fella's been found, an' they think it's, it's . . .

Mrs Boyle Johnny, Johnny!

Mary [*with her arms round her mother*] Oh, mother, mother, me poor, darlin' mother.

Mrs Boyle Hush, hush, darlin'; you'll shortly have your own throuble to bear. [*To Mrs. Madigan*] An' why do the polis think it's Johnny, Mrs. Madigan?

Mrs Madigan Because one o' the doctors knew him when he was attendin' with his poor arm.

Mrs Boyle Oh, it's thrue, then; it's Johnny, it's me son, me own son!

Mary Oh, it's thrue, it's thrue what Jerry Devine says – there isn't a God, there isn't a God; if there was He wouldn't let these things happen!

Mrs Boyle Mary, you mustn't say them things. We'll want all the help we can get from God an' His Blessed Mother now! These things have nothin' to do with the Will o' God. Ah, what can God do agen the stupidity o' men!

Mrs Madigan The polis want you to go with them to the hospital to see the poor body – they're waitin' below.

Mrs Boyle We'll go. Come, Mary, an' we'll never come back here agen. Let your father furrage for himself now; I've done all I could an' it was all no use – he'll be hopeless till the end of his days. I've got a little room in me sisther's where we'll stop till your throuble is over, an' then we'll work together for the sake of the baby.

Mary My poor little child that'll have no father!

Mrs Boyle It'll have what's far betther – it'll have two mothers.

A rough voice [*shouting from below*] Are yous goin' to keep us waitin' for yous all night?

Mrs Madigan [*going to the door, and shouting down*] Take your hour, there, take your hour! If yous are in such a hurry, skip off, then, for nobody wants you here – if they did yous wouldn't be found. For you're the same as yous were undher the British Government – never where yous are wanted! As far as I can see, the Polis as Polis, in this city, is Null an' Void!

Mrs Boyle We'll go, Mary, we'll go; you to see your poor dead brother, an' me to see me poor dead son!

Mary I dhread it, mother, I dhread it!

Mrs Boyle I forgot, Mary, I forgot; your poor oul' selfish mother was only thinkin' of herself. No, no, you mustn't come – it wouldn't be good for you. You go on to me sisther's an' I'll face th' ordeal meself. Maybe I didn't feel sorry enough for Mrs. Tancred when her poor son was found as Johnny's been found now – because he was a Diehard! Ah, why didn't I remember that then he wasn't a Diehard or a Stater, but only a poor dead son! It's well I remember all that she said – an' it's my turn to say it now: What was the pain I suffered, Johnny, bringin' you into the world to carry you to your cradle, to the pains I'll suffer carryin' you out o' the world to bring you to your grave! Mother o' God, Mother o' God, have pity on us all! Blessed Virgin, where were you when me darlin' son was riddled with bullets, when me darlin' son was riddled with bullets? Sacred Heart o' Jesus, take away our hearts o' stone, and give us hearts o' flesh! Take away this murdherin' hate, an' give us Thine own eternal love! [*They all go slowly out.*]

[*There is a pause; then a sound of shuffling steps on the stairs outside. The door opens and Boyle and Joxer, both of them very drunk, enter.*]

Boyle I'm able to go no farther.... Two polis, ey ... what were they doin' here, I wondher?... Up to no good, anyhow ... an' Juno an' that lovely daughter o' mine with them. [*Taking a sixpence from his pocket and looking at it*] Wan single, solitary tanner left out of all I borreyed.... [*He lets it fall*] The last o' the Mohicans.... The blinds is down, Joxer, the blinds is down!

Joxer [*walking unsteadily across the room, and anchoring at the bed*] Put all ... your throubles ... in your oul' kit-bag ... an' smile ... smile ... smile!

Boyle The counthry'll have to steady itself ... it's goin' ... to hell.... Where'r all ... the chairs ... gone to ... steady itself, Joxer.... Chairs'll ... have to ... steady themselves.... No matther ... what any one may ... say.... Irelan' sober ... is Irelan' ... free.

Joxer [*stretching himself on the bed*] Chains ... an' ... slaveree ... that's a darlin' motto ... a daaarlin' ... motto!

Boyle If th' worst comes ... to th' worse ... I can join a ... flyin' ... column. ... I done ... me bit ... in Easther Week ... had no business ... to ... be ... there ... but Captain Boyle's Captain Boyle!

Joxer Breathes there a man with soul ... so ... de ... ad ... this ... me ... o ... wn, me nat ... ive ... I ... an'!

Boyle [*subsiding into a sitting posture on the floor*] Commandant Kelly died... in them ... arms ... Joxer.... Tell me Volunteer Butties ... says he ... that ... I died for Irelan'!

Joxer D'jever rade Willie ... Reilly ... an' his own ... Colleen ... Bawn? It's a darlin' story, a daarlin' story!

Boyle I'm telling you ... Joxer ... th' whole worl's ... in a terr ... ible state o' ... chassis!

[*Curtain*]

W.H. AUDEN (1907–1973)

In the late 1920s and 1930s, Auden was part of a group of writers, including Christopher Isherwood and Stephen Spender, committed to a Marxist social vision. A supporter of the Republican cause in the Spanish Civil War, by the beginning of Second World War Auden began to turn away from active political engagement in his poetry. Developing a philosophy of individualism, Auden's later work uses language with enormous craft, precision and lyricism.

Musée des Beaux Arts

About suffering they were never wrong,
The Old Masters: how well they understood
Its human position; how it takes place
While someone else is eating or opening a window or just
    walking dully along;
5   How, when the aged are reverently, passionately waiting
For the miraculous birth, there always must be
Children who did not specially want it to happen, skating
On a pond at the edge of the wood: They never forgot
That even the dreadful martyrdom must run its course
10   Anyhow in a corner, some untidy spot
Where the dogs go on with their doggy life and the torturer's
    horse
Scratches its innocent behind on a tree.

In Brueghel's *Icarus*, for instance: how everything turns away
Quite leisurely from the disaster; the ploughman may
15   Have heard the splash, the forsaken cry,
But for him it was not an important failure; the sun shone
As it had to on the white legs disappearing into the green
Water; and the expensive delicate ship that must have seen
Something amazing, a boy falling out of the sky,
20   Had somewhere to get to and sailed calmly on.

In Memory of W. B. Yeats (d.Jan. 1939)

I

He disappeared in the dead of winter:
The brooks were frozen, the airports almost deserted,
And snow disfigured the public statues;
The mercury sank in the mouth of the dying day.
5   What instruments we have agree
The day of his death was a dark cold day.

Far from his illness
The wolves ran on through the evergreen forests,

The peasant river was untempted by the fashionable quays;
10   By mourning tongues
The death of the poet was kept from his poems.

But for him it was his last afternoon as himself,
An afternoon of nurses and rumours;
The provinces of his body revolted,
15   The squares of his mind were empty,
Silence invaded the suburbs,
The current of his feeling failed; he became his admirers.

Now he is scattered among a hundred cities
And wholly given over to unfamiliar affections,
20   To find his happiness in another kind of wood
And be punished under a foreign code of conscience.
The words of a dead man
Are modified in the guts of the living.

But in the importance and noise of to-morrow
25   When the brokers are roaring like beasts on the floor of the
        Bourse,
And the poor have the sufferings to which they are fairly
        accustomed,
And each in the cell of himself is almost convinced of his
        freedom,
A few thousand will think of this day
As one thinks of a day when one did something slightly unusual.
30   What instruments we have agree
The day of his death was a dark cold day.

II
You were silly like us; your gift survived all:
The parish of rich women, physical decay,
Yourself. Mad Ireland hurt you into poetry.
35   Now Ireland has her madness and her weather still,
For poetry makes nothing happen: it survives
In the valley of its making where executives
Would never want to tamper, flows on south
From ranches of isolation and the busy griefs,
40   Raw towns that we believe and die in; it survives,
A way of happening, a mouth.

III
Earth, receive an honoured guest:
William Yeats is laid to rest.
Let the Irish vessel lie
45   Emptied of its poetry.

In the nightmare of the dark
All the dogs of Europe bark,
And the living nations wait,
Each sequestered in its hate;

50 Intellectual disgrace
Stares from every human face,
And the seas of pity lie
Locked and frozen in each eye.

Follow, poet, follow right
55 To the bottom of the night,
With your unconstraining voice
Still persuade us to rejoice;

With the farming of a verse
Make a vineyard of the curse,
60 Sing of human unsuccess
In a rapture of distress;

In the deserts of the heart
Let the healing fountain start,
In the prison of his days
65 Teach the free man how to praise.

In Praise of Limestone

If it form the one landscape that we, the inconstant ones,
    Are consistently homesick for, this is chiefly
Because it dissolves in water. Mark these rounded slopes
    With their surface fragrance of thyme and, beneath,
5   A secret system of caves and conduits; hear the springs
        That spurt out everywhere with a chuckle,
    Each filling a private pool for its fish and carving
        Its own little ravine whose cliffs entertain
    The butterfly and the lizard; examine this region
10   Of short distances and definite places:
    What could be more like Mother or a fitter background
        For her son, the flirtatious male who lounges
    Against a rock in the sunlight, never doubting
        That for all his faults he is loved; whose works are but
15 Extensions of his power to charm? From weathered outcrop
        To hill-top temple, from appearing waters to
    Conspicuous fountains, from a wild to a formal vineyard,
        Are ingenious but short steps that a child's wish
    To receive more attention than his brothers, whether
20   By pleasing or teasing, can easily take.

Watch, then, the band of rivals as they climb up and down
    Their steep stone gennels in twos and threes, at times
Arm in arm, but never, thank God, in step; or engaged
    On the shady side of a square at midday in
25   Voluble discourse, knowing each other too well to think
    There are any important secrets, unable
To conceive a god whose temper-tantrums are moral
    And not to be pacified by a clever line
Or a good lay: for, accustomed to a stone that responds,
30   They have never had to veil their faces in awe
Of a crater whose blazing fury could not be fixed;
    Adjusted to the local needs of valleys
Where everything can be touched or reached by walking,
    Their eyes have never looked into infinite space
35   Through the lattice-work of a nomad's comb; born lucky,
    Their legs have never encountered the fungi
And insects of the jungle, the monstrous forms and lives
    With which we have nothing, we like to hope, in common.
So, when one of them goes to the bad, the way his mind works
40   Remains comprehensible: to become a pimp
Or deal in fake jewellery or ruin a fine tenor voice
    For effects that bring down the house, could happen to all
But the best and the worst of us . . .
                   That is why, I suppose,
    The best and worst never stayed here long but sought
45   Immoderate soils where the beauty was not so external,
    The light less public and the meaning of life
Something more than a mad camp. 'Come!' cried the granite
        wastes,
    'How evasive is your humour, how accidental
Your kindest kiss, how permanent is death.' (Saints-to-be
50   Slipped away sighing.) 'Come!' purred the clays and gravels.
'On our plains there is room for armies to drill; rivers
    Wait to be tamed and slaves to construct you a tomb
In the grand manner: soft as the earth is mankind and both
    Need to be altered.' (Intendant Caesars rose and
55   Left, slamming the door.) But the really reckless were fetched
    By an older colder voice, the oceanic whisper:
'I am the solitude that asks and promises nothing;
    That is how I shall set you free. There is no love;
There are only the various envies, all of them sad.'
60   They were right, my dear, all those voices were right
And still are; this land is not the sweet home that it looks,
    Nor its peace the historical calm of a site
Where something was settled once and for all: A backward
    And dilapidated province, connected
65   To the big busy world by a tunnel, with a certain

Seedy appeal, is that all it is now? Not quite:
It has a worldly duty which in spite of itself
  It does not neglect, but calls into question
All the Great Powers assume; it disturbs our rights. The poet,
70   Admired for his earnest habit of calling
The sun the sun, his mind Puzzle, is made uneasy
  By these marble statues which so obviously doubt
His antimythological myth; and these gamins,
  Pursuing the scientist down the tiled colonnade
75 With such lively offers, rebuke his concern for Nature's
  Remotest aspects: I, too, am reproached, for what
And how much you know. Not to lose time, not to get caught,
  Not to be left behind, not, please! to resemble
The beasts who repeat themselves, or a thing like water
80   Or stone whose conduct can be predicted, these
Are our Common Prayer, whose greatest comfort is music
  Which can be made anywhere, is invisible,
And does not smell. In so far as we have to look forward
  To death as a fact, no doubt we are right: But if
85 Sins can be forgiven, if bodies rise from the dead,
  These modifications of matter into
Innocent athletes and gesticulating fountains,
  Made solely for pleasure, make a further point:
The blessed will not care what angle they are regarded from,
90   Having nothing to hide. Dear, I know nothing of
Either, but when I try to imagine a faultless love
  Or the life to come, what I hear is the murmur
Of underground streams, what I see is a limestone landscape.

The Shield of Achilles

She looked over his shoulder
  For vines and olive trees,
Marble well-governed cities
  And ships upon untamed seas,
5   But there on the shining metal
  His hands had put instead
An artificial wilderness
  And a sky like lead.

A plain without a feature, bare and brown,
10   No blade of grass, no sign of neighbourhood,
Nothing to eat and nowhere to sit down,
  Yet, congregated on its blankness, stood

Shield of Achilles: In Homer's *Iliad*, the god of metal work, Hephaestos, makes a shield for Achilles at the request of his mother, Thetis. On the shield is portrayed the earth and, particularly, two cities: one at peace, the other at war.

An unintelligible multitude,
A million eyes, a million boots in line,
15   Without expression, waiting for a sign.

Out of the air a voice without a face
   Proved by statistics that some cause was just
In tones as dry and level as the place:
   No one was cheered and nothing was discussed;
20   Column by column in a cloud of dust
They marched away enduring a belief
Whose logic brought them, somewhere else, to grief

She looked over his shoulder
    For ritual pieties,
25   White flower-garlanded heifers,
    Libation and sacrifice,
But there on the shining metal
    Where the altar should have been,
She saw by his flickering forge-light
30   Quite another scene.

Barbed wire enclosed an arbitrary spot
   Where bored officials lounged (one cracked a joke)
And sentries sweated for the day was hot:
   A crowd of ordinary decent folk
35   Watched from without and neither moved nor spoke
As three pale figures were led forth and bound
To three posts driven upright in the ground.

The mass and majesty of this world, all
   That carries weight and always weighs the same
40   Lay in the hands of others; they were small
   And could not hope for help and no help came:
    What their foes liked to do was done, their shame
Was all the worst could wish; they lost their pride
And died as men before their bodies died.

45   She looked over his shoulder
    For athletes at their games,
Men and women in a dance
    Moving their sweet limbs
Quick, quick, to music,
50   But there on the shining shield
His hands had set no dancing-floor
    But a weed-choked field.

A ragged urchin, aimless and alone,
   Loitered about that vacancy, a bird
55   Flew up to safety from his well-aimed stone:

That girls are raped, that two boys knife a third,
Were axioms to him, who'd never heard
Of any world where promises were kept,
Or one could weep because another wept.

60   The thin-lipped armourer,
      Hephaestos hobbled away,
    Thetis of the shining breasts
      Cried out in dismay
    At what the god had wrought
65   To please her son, the strong
    Iron-hearted man-slaying Achilles
    Who would not live long.

SAMUEL BECKETT (1906–1989)

Born and educated in Dublin, Beckett spent most of his working life in Paris and wrote in both French and English. Although best known for his plays, Beckett also wrote novels and stories. His writing reflects the fragments, memories (usually disrupted and imperfect), and miscellaneous cultural inheritances which make up experience, and which lead to no conclusion. The two selections here are an early story (first published, 1934) and one of his mature short plays (1960).

From More Pricks than Kicks

Dante and the Lobster

It was morning and Belacqua was stuck in the first of the canti in the moon. He was so bogged that he could move neither backward nor forward. Blissful Beatrice was there, Dante also, and she explained the spots on the moon to him.[1] She showed him in the first place where he was at fault, then she put up her own explanation. She had it from God, therefore he could rely on its being accurate in every particular. All he had to do was to follow her step by step. Part one, the refutation, was plain sailing. She made her point clearly, she said what she had to say without fuss or loss of time. But part two, the demonstration, was so dense that Belacqua could not make head or tail of it. The disproof, the reproof, that was patent. But then came the proof, a rapid shorthand of the real facts, and Belacqua was bogged indeed. Bored also, impatient to get on to Piccarda. Still he pored over the enigma, he would not concede himself conquered, he would understand at least the meanings of the words, the order in which they were spoken and the nature of the satisfaction that they conferred on the misinformed poet, so that when they were ended he was refreshed and could raise his heavy head, intending to return thanks and make formal retraction of his old opinion.

---

1 **Beatrice**: Dante's beloved in *The Divine Comedy*. She helps guide the poet through Paradise.

He was still running his brain against this impenetrable passage when he heard midday strike. At once he switched his mind off its task. He scooped his fingers under the book and shovelled it back till it lay wholly on his palms. The Divine Comedy face upward on the lectern of his palms. Thus disposed he raised it under his nose and there he slammed it shut. He held it aloft for a time, squinting at it angrily, pressing the boards inwards with the heels of his hands. Then he laid it aside.

He leaned back in his chair to feel his mind subside and the itch of this mean quodlibet[1] die down. Nothing could be done until his mind got better and was still, which gradually it did. Then he ventured to consider what he had to do next. There was always something that one had to do next. Three large obligations presented themselves. First lunch, then the lobster, then the Italian lesson. That would do to be going on with. After the Italian lesson he had no very clear idea. No doubt some niggling curriculum had been drawn up by someone for the late afternoon and evening, but he did not know what. In any case it did not matter. What did matter was: one, lunch; two, the lobster; three, the Italian lesson. That was more than enough to be going on with.

Lunch, to come off at all, was a very nice affair. If his lunch was to be enjoyable, and it could be very enjoyable indeed, he must be left in absolute tranquillity to prepare it. But if he were disturbed now, if some brisk tattler were to come bouncing in now with a big idea or a petition, he might just as well not eat at all, for the food would turn to bitterness on his palate or, worse again, taste of nothing. He must be left strictly alone, he must have complete quiet and privacy, to prepare the food for his lunch.

The first thing to do was to lock the door. Now nobody could come at him. He deployed an old Herald[2] and smoothed it out on the table. The rather handsome face of McCabe the assassin stared up at him. Then he lit the gas-ring and unhooked the square flat toaster, asbestos grill, from its nail and set it precisely on the flame. He found he had to lower the flame. Toast must not on any account be done too rapidly. For bread to be toasted as it ought, through and through, it must be done on a mild steady flame. Otherwise you only charred the outsides and left the pith as sodden as before. If there was one thing he abominated more than another it was to feel his teeth meet in a bathos of pith and dough. And it was so easy to do the thing properly. So, he thought, having regulated the flow and adjusted the grill, by the time I have the bread cut that will be just right. Now the long barrel-loaf came out of its biscuit-tin and had its end evened off on the face of McCabe. Two inexorable drives with the bread-saw and a pair of neat rounds of raw bread, the main elements of his meal, lay before him, awaiting his pleasure. The stump of the loaf went back into prison, the crumbs, as though there were no such thing as a sparrow in the wide world, were swept in a fever away, and the slices snatched up and carried to the grill. All these preliminaries were very hasty and impersonal.

It was now that real skill began to be required, it was at this point that the average person began to make a hash of the entire proceedings. He laid his cheek against the soft of the bread, it was spongy and warm, alive. But he

---

1 **quodlibet**: a question for debate in philosophy.   2 **Herald**: Dublin newspaper.

would very soon take that plush feel off it, by God but he would very quickly take that fat white look off its face. He lowered the gas a suspicion and plaqued one flabby slab plump down on the glowing fabric, but very pat and precise, so that the whole resembled the Japanese flag. Then on top, there not being room for the two to do evenly side by side, and if you did not do them evenly you might just as well save yourself the trouble of doing them at all, the other round was set to warm. When the first candidate was done, which was only when it was black through and through, it changed places with its comrade, so that now it in its turn lay on top, done to a dead end, black and smoking, waiting till as much could be said of the other.

For the tiller of the field the thing was simple, he had it from his mother. The spots were Cain with his truss of thorns, dispossessed, cursed from the earth, fugitive and vagabond.[1] The moon was that countenance fallen and branded, seared with the first stigma[2] of God's pity, that an outcast might not die quickly. It was a mix-up in the mind of the tiller, but that did not matter. It had been good enough for his mother, it was good enough for him.

Belacqua on his knees before the flame, poring over the grill, controlled every phase of the broiling. It took time, but if a thing was worth doing at all it was worth doing well, that was a true saying. Long before the end the room was full of smoke and the reek of burning. He switched off the gas, when all that human care and skill could do had been done, and restored the toaster to its nail. This was an act of dilapidation, for it seared a great weal in the paper. This was hooliganism pure and simple. What the hell did he care? Was it his wall? The same hopeless paper had been there fifty years. It was livid with age. It could not be disimproved.

Next a thick paste of Savora, salt and Cayenne on each round, well worked in while the pores were still open with the heat. No butter, God forbid, just a good forment of mustard and salt and pepper on each round. Butter was a blunder, it made the toast soggy. Buttered toast was all right for Senior Fellows and Salvationists, for such as had nothing but false teeth in their heads. It was no good at all to a fairly strong young rose like Belacqua. This meal that he was at such pains to make ready, he would devour it with a sense of rapture and victory, it would be like smiting the sledded Polacks on the ice.[3] He would snap at it with closed eyes, he would gnash it into a pulp, he would vanquish it utterly with his fangs. Then the anguish of pungency, the pang of the spices, as each mouthful died, scorching his palate, bringing tears.

But he was not yet all set, there was yet much to be done. He had burnt his offering, he had not fully dressed it. Yes, he had put the horse behind the tumbrel.[4]

He clapped the toasted rounds together, he brought them smartly together like cymbals, they clave the one to the other on the viscid salve of Savora. Then he wrapped them up for the time being in any old sheet of paper. Then he made himself ready for the road.

---

1 **Cain:** In Genesis, Cain is condemned to wander the earth for the murder of his brother Abel.   2 **stigma:** a mark; also signs on the body resembling the wounds of the crucified Christ.   3 **sledded Polacks:** in *Hamlet*, Fortinbras leads his army against the Poles to the admiration of Hamlet.   4 **tumbrel:** cart.

Now the great thing was to avoid being accosted. To be stopped at this stage and have conversational nuisance committed all over him would be a disaster. His whole being was straining forward towards the joy in store. If he were accosted now he might just as well fling his lunch into the gutter and walk straight back home. Sometimes his hunger, more of mind, I need scarcely say, than of body, for this meal amounted to such a frenzy that he would not have hesitated to strike any man rash enough to buttonhole and baulk him, he would have shouldered him out of his path without ceremony. Woe betide the meddler who crossed him when his mind was really set on this meal.

He threaded his way rapidly, his head bowed, through a familiar labyrinth of lanes and suddenly dived into a little family grocery. In the shop they were not surprised. Most days, about this hour, he shot in off the street in this way.

The slab of cheese was prepared. Separated since morning from the piece, it was only waiting for Belacqua to call and take it. Gorgonzola cheese. He knew a man who came from Gorgonzola, his name was Angelo. He had been born in Nice but all his youth had been spent in Gorgonzola. He knew where to look for it. Every day it was there, in the same corner, waiting to be called for. They were very decent obliging people.

He looked sceptically at the cut of cheese. He turned it over on its back to see was the other side any better. The other side was worse. They had laid it better side up, they had practised that little deception. Who shall blame them? He rubbed it. It was sweating. That was something. He stooped and smelt it. A faint fragrance of corruption. What good was that? He didn't want fragrance, he wasn't a bloody gourmet, he wanted a good stench. What he wanted was a good green stenching rotten lump of Gorgonzola cheese, alive, and by God he would have it.

He looked fiercely at the grocer.

'What's that?' he demanded.

The grocer writhed.

'Well?' demanded Belacqua, he was without fear when roused, 'is that the best you can do?'

'In the length and breadth of Dublin,' said the grocer, 'you won't find a rottener bit this minute.'

Belacqua was furious. The impudent dogsbody, for two pins he would assault him.

'It won't do,' he cried, 'do you hear me, it won't do at all. I won't have it.' He ground his teeth.

The grocer, instead of simply washing his hands like Pilate, flung out his arms in a wild crucified gesture of supplication. Sullenly Belacqua undid his packet and slipped the cadaverous tablet of cheese between the hard cold black boards of the toast. He stumped to the door where he whirled round however.

'You heard me?' he cried.

'Sir,' said the grocer. This was not a question, nor yet an expression of acquiescence. The tone in which it was let fall made it quite impossible to know what was in the man's mind. It was a most ingenious riposte.

'I tell you,' said Belacqua with great heat, 'this won't do at all. If you can't do better than this,' he raised the hand that held the packet, 'I shall be obliged to go for my cheese elsewhere. Do you mark me?'

'Sir,' said the grocer.

He came to the threshold of his store and watched the indignant customer hobble away. Belacqua had a spavined[1] gait, his feet were in ruins, he suffered with them almost continuously. Even in the night they took over from the corns and hammer-toes, and carried on. So that he would press the fringes of his feet desperately against the end-rail of the bed or better again, reach down with his hand and drag them up and back towards the instep. Skill and patience could disperse the pain, but there it was, complicating his night's rest.

The grocer, without closing his eyes or taking them off the receding figure, blew his nose in the skirt of his apron. Being a warmhearted human man he felt sympathy and pity for this queer customer who always looked ill and dejected. But at the same time he was a small tradesman, don't forget that, with a small tradesman's sense of personal dignity and what was what. Thruppence, he cast it up, thruppence worth of cheese per day, one and a tanner per week. No, he would fawn on no man for that, no, not on the best in the land. He had his pride.

Stumbling along by devious ways towards the lowly public where he was expected, in the sense that the entry of his grotesque person would provoke no comment or laughter, Belacqua gradually got the upper hand of his choler. Now that lunch was as good as a fait accompli, because the incontinent bosthoons of his own class, itching to pass on a big idea or inflict an appointment, were seldom at large in this shabby quarter of the city, he was free to consider items two and three, the lobster and the lesson, in closer detail.

At a quarter to three he was due at the School. Say five to three. The public closed, the fishmonger reopened, at half-past two. Assuming then that his lousy old bitch of an aunt had given her order in good time that morning, with strict injunctions that it should be ready and waiting so that her blackguard boy should on no account be delayed when he called for it first thing in the afternoon, it would be time enough if he left the public as it closed, he could remain on till the last moment. Benissimo. He had half-a-crown. That was two pints of draught anyway and perhaps a bottle to wind up with. Their bottled stout was particularly excellent and well up. And he would still be left with enough coppers to buy a Herald and take a tram if he felt tired or was pinched for time. Always assuming, of course, that the lobster was all ready to be handed over. God damn these tradesmen, he thought, you can never rely on them. He had not done an exercise but that did not matter. His Professoressa was so charming and remarkable. Signorina Adriana Ottolenghi! He did not believe it possible for a woman to be more intelligent or better informed than the little Ottolenghi. So he had set her on a pedestal in his mind, apart from other women. She had said last day that they would read Il Cinque Maggio together. But she would not mind if he told her, as he proposed to, in Italian, he would frame a shining phrase on his way from the public, that he would prefer to postpone the Cinque Maggio to another occasion. Manzoni was an old woman, Napoleon was another. Napoleone di mezza calzetta, fa l'amore a Giacominetta. Why did he

---

1 spavined: limping.

think of Manzoni as an old woman? Why did he do him that injustice? Pellico
was another. They were all old maids, suffragettes. He must ask his Signorina
where he could have received that impression, that the nineteenth century in
Italy was full of old hens trying to cluck like Pindar. Carducci was another. Also
about the spots on the moon. If she could not tell him there and then she
would make it up, only too gladly, against the next time. Everything was all set
now and in order. Bating,[1] of course, the lobster, which had to remain an
incalculable factor. He must just hope for the best. And expect the worst, he
thought gaily, diving into the public, as usual.

Belacqua drew near to the school, quite happy, for all had gone swimmingly.
The lunch had been a noticeable success, it would abide as a standard in his
mind. Indeed he could not imagine its ever being superseded. And such a pale
soapy piece of cheese to prove so strong! He must only conclude that he had
been abusing himself all these years in relating the strength of cheese directly
to its greenness. We live and learn, that was a true saying. Also his teeth and
jaws had been in heaven, splinters of vanquished toast spraying forth at each
gnash. It was like eating glass. His mouth burned and ached with the exploit.
Then the food had been further spiced by the intelligence, transmitted in a low
tragic voice across the counter by Oliver the improver, that the Malahide
murderer's petition for mercy, signed by half the land, having been rejected,
the man must swing at dawn in Mountjoy and nothing could save him. Ellis the
hangman was even now on his way. Belacqua, tearing at the sandwich and
swilling the precious stout, pondered on McCabe in his cell.
  The lobster was ready after all, the man handed it over instanter, and with
such a pleasant smile. Really a little bit of courtesy and goodwill went a long
way in this world. A smile and a cheerful word from a common working-man
and the face of the world was brightened. And it was so easy, a mere question
of muscular control.
  'Lepping,' he said cheerfully, handing it over.
  'Lepping?' said Belacqua. What on earth was that?
  'Lepping fresh, sir,' said the man, 'fresh in this morning.'
  Now Belacqua, on the analogy of mackerel and other fish that he had heard
described as lepping fresh when they had been taken but an hour or two previously, supposed the man to mean that the lobster had very recently been killed.
  Signorina Adriana Ottolenghi was waiting in the little front room off the
hall, which Belacqua was naturally inclined to think of rather as the vestibule.
That was her room, the Italian room. On the same side, but at the back, was
the French room. God knows where the German room was. Who cared about
the German room anyway?
  He hung up his coat and hat, laid the long knobby brown-paper parcel on
the hall-table, and went prestly[2] in to the Ottolenghi.
  After about half-an-hour of this and that obiter, she complimented him on
his grasp of the language.
  'You make rapid progress,' she said in her ruined voice.

---

1 **Bating:** leaving out of account.   2 **prestly:** quickly.

There subsisted as much of the Ottolenghi as might be expected to the person of a lady of a certain age who had found being young and beautiful and pure more of a bore than anything else.

Belacqua, dissembling his great pleasure, laid open the moon enigma.

'Yes,' she said, 'I know the passage. It is a famous teaser. Off-hand I cannot tell you, but I will look it up when I get home.'

The sweet creature! She would look it up in her big Dante when she got home. What a woman!

'It occurred to me,' she said, 'apropos of I don't know what, that you might do worse than make up Dante's rare movements of compassion in Hell. That used to be' – her past tenses were always sorrowful – 'a favourite question.'

He assumed an expression of profundity.

'In that connexion,' he said, 'I recall one superb pun anyway: "qui vive la pieta quando e ben morta . . ."'

She said nothing.

'Is it not a great phrase?' he gushed.

She said nothing.

'Now,' he said like a fool, 'I wonder how you could translate that?'

Still she said nothing. Then:

'Do you think', she murmured, 'it is absolutely necessary to translate it?'

Sounds as of conflict were borne in from the hall. Then silence. A knuckle tambourined on the door, it flew open and lo it was Mlle Glain, the French instructress, clutching her cat, her eyes out on stalks, in a state of the greatest agitation.

'Oh,' she gasped, 'forgive me. I intrude, but what was in the bag?'

'The bag?' said the Ottolenghi.

Mlle Glain took a French step forward.

'The parcel,' she buried her face in the cat, 'the parcel in the hall.'

Belacqua spoke up composedly.

'Mine', he said, 'a fish.'

He did not know the French for lobster. Fish would do very well. Fish had been good enough for Jesus Christ, Son of God, Saviour. It was good enough for Mlle Glain.

'Oh,' said Mlle Glain, inexpressibly relieved, 'I caught him in the nick of time.' She administered a tap to the cat. 'He would have tore it to flitters.'

Belacqua began to feel a little anxious.

'Did he actually get at it?' he said.

'No no,' said Mlle Glain, 'I caught him just in time. But I did not know' – with a bluestocking snigger – 'what it might be, so I thought I had better come and ask.'

Base prying bitch.

The Ottolenghi was faintly amused.

'Puisqu'il n'y a pas de mal . . . ' she said with great fatigue and elegance.

'Heureusement' – it was clear at once that Mlle Glain was devout – 'heureusement.'

Chastening the cat with little skelps she took herself off. The grey hairs of her maidenhead screamed at Belacqua. A devout, virginal bluestocking, honing after a penny's worth of scandal.

'Where were we?' said Belacqua.

But Neapolitan patience has its limits.

'Where are we ever?' cried the Ottolenghi, 'where we were, as we were.'

Belacqua drew near to the house of his aunt. Let us call it Winter, that dusk may fall now and a moon rise. At the corner of the street a horse was down and a man sat on its head. I know, thought Belacqua, that that is considered the right thing to do. But why? A lamplighter flew by on his bike, tilting with his pole at the standards, jousting a little yellow light into the evening. A poorly-dressed couple stood in the bay of a pretentious gateway, she sagging against the railings, her head lowered, he standing facing her. He stood up close to her, his hands dangled by his sides. Where we were, thought Belacqua, as we were. He walked on, gripping his parcel. Why not piety and pity both, even down below? Why not mercy and Godliness together? A little mercy in the stress of sacrifice, a little mercy to rejoice against judgment. He thought of Jonah and the gourd and the pity of a jealous God on Nineveh. And poor McCabe, he would get it in the neck at dawn. What was he doing now, how was he feeling? He would relish one more meal, one more night.

His aunt was in the garden, tending whatever flowers die at that time of year. She embraced him and together they went down into the bowels of the earth, into the kitchen in the basement. She took the parcel and undid it and abruptly the lobster was on the table, on the oilcloth, discovered.

'They assured me it was fresh,' said Belacqua.

Suddenly he saw the creature move, this neuter creature. Definitely it changed its position. His hand flew to his mouth.

'Christ!' he said, 'it's alive.'

His aunt looked at the lobster. It moved again. It made a faint nervous act of life on the oilcloth. They stood above it, looking down on it, exposed cruciform on the oilcloth. It shuddered again. Belacqua felt he would be sick.

'My God,' he whined, 'it's alive, what'll we do?'

The aunt simply had to laugh. She bustled off to the pantry to fetch her smart apron, leaving him goggling down at the lobster, and came back with it on and her sleeves rolled up, all business.

'Well,' she said, 'it is to be hoped so, indeed.'

'All this time', muttered Belacqua. Then, suddenly aware of her hideous equipment: 'What are you going to do?' he cried.

'Boil the beast,' she said, 'what else?'

'But it's not dead', protested Belacqua, 'you can't boil it like that.'

She looked at him in astonishment. Had he taken leave of his senses?

'Have sense', she said sharply, 'lobsters are always boiled alive. They must be.' She caught up the lobster and laid it on its back. It trembled. 'They feel nothing,' she said.

In the depths of the sea it had crept into the cruel pot. For hours, in the midst of its enemies, it had breathed secretly. It had survived the Frenchwoman's cat

and his witless clutch. Now it was going alive into scalding water. It had to.
Take into the air my quiet breath.

Belacqua looked at the old parchment of her face, grey in the dim kitchen.

'You make a fuss,' she said angrily, 'and upset me and then lash into it for
your dinner.'

She lifted the lobster clear of the table. It had about thirty seconds to live.

Well, thought Belacqua, it's a quick death, God help us all.

It is not.

Krapp's Last Tape

A late evening in the future.
Krapp's den.
Front centre a small table, the two drawers of which open towards the audience.
Sitting at the table, facing front, i.e. across from the drawers, a wearish old man:
Krapp.
Rusty black narrow trousers too short for him. Rusty black sleeveless waistcoat,
four capacious pockets. Heavy silver watch and chain. Grimy white shirt open at
neck, no collar. Surprising pair of dirty white boots, size ten at least, very narrow
and pointed.
White face. Purple nose. Disordered grey hair. Unshaven.
Very near-sighted (but unspectacled). Hard of hearing.
Cracked voice. Distinctive intonation.
Laborious walk.
On the table a tape-recorder with microphone and a number of cardboard boxes
containing reels of recorded tapes.
Table and immediately adjacent area in strong white light. Rest of stage in
darkness.

[*Krapp remains a moment motionless, heaves a great sigh, looks at his watch,*
fumbles in his pockets, takes out an envelope, puts it back, fumbles, takes out a
small bunch of keys, raises it to his eyes, chooses a key, gets up and moves to front of
table. He stoops, unlocks first drawer, peers into it, feels about inside it, takes out a
reel of tape, peers at it, puts it back, locks drawer, unlocks second drawer, peers into
it, feels about inside it, takes out a large banana, peers at it, locks drawer, puts keys
back in his pocket. He turns, advances to edge of stage, halts, strokes banana, peels
it, drops skin at his feet, puts end of banana in his mouth and remains motionless,
staring vacuously before him. Finally he bites off the end, turns aside and begins
pacing to and fro at edge of stage, in the light, i.e. not more than four or five paces
either way, meditatively eating banana. He treads on skin, slips, nearly falls, recov-
ers himself, stoops and peers at skin and finally pushes it, still stooping, with his foot
over edge of stage into pit. He resumes his pacing, finishes banana, returns to table,
sits down, remains a moment motionless, heaves a great sigh, takes keys from his
pockets, raises them to his eyes, chooses key, gets up and moves to front of table,
unlocks second drawer, takes out a second large banana, peers at it, locks drawer,
puts back keys in his pocket, turns, advances to edge of stage, halts, strokes banana,
peels it, tosses skin into pit, puts end of banana in his mouth and remains

motionless, staring vacuously before him. Finally he has an idea, puts banana in his waistcoat pocket, the end emerging, and goes with all the speed he can muster backstage into darkness. Ten seconds. Loud pop of cork. Fifteen seconds. He comes back into light carrying an old ledger and sits down at table. He lays ledger on table, wipes his mouth, wipes his hands on the front of his waistcoat, brings them smartly together and rubs them.]

Krapp [*briskly*] Ah! [*He bends over ledger, turns the pages, finds the entry he wants, reads*] Box . . . thrree . . . spool . . . five. [*He raises his head and stares front. With relish*] Spool! [*Pause.*] Spooool! [*Happy smile. Pause. He bends over table, starts peering and poking at the boxes*] Box . . . thrree . . . thrree . . . four . . . two . . . [*with surprise*] nine! good God! . . . seven . . . ah! the little rascal! [*He takes up box, peers at it*] Box thrree. [*He lays it on table, opens it and peers at spools inside*] Spool . . . [*he peers at ledger*] . . . five . . . [*he peers at spools*] . . . five . . . five . . . ah! the little scoundrel! [*He takes out a spool, peers at it*] Spool five. [*He lays it on table, closes box three, puts it back with the others, takes up the spool*] Box thrree, spool five. [*He bends over the machine, looks up. With relish*] Spooool! [*Happy smile. He bends, loads spool on machine, rubs his hands*] Ah! [*He peers at ledger, reads entry at foot of page*] Mother at rest at last. . . . Hm. . . . The black ball. . . . [*He raises his head, stares blankly front. Puzzled*] Black ball? . . . [*He peers again at ledger, reads*] The dark nurse. . . . [*He raises his head, broods, peers again at ledgers, reads*] Slight improvement in bowel condition. . . . Hm. . . . Memorable . . . *what?* [*He peers closer*] Equinox, memorable equinox. [*He raises his head, stares blankly front. Puzzled*] Memorable equinox? . . . [*Pause. He shrugs his shoulders, peers again at ledger, reads.*] Farewell to [*he turns page*] – love.

[*He raises his head, broods, bends over machine, switches on and assumes listening posture, i.e. leaning forward, elbows on table, hand cupping ear towards machine, face front.*]

Tape [*strong voice, rather pompous, clearly Krapp's at a much earlier time*] Thirty-nine today, sound as a [*Settling himself more comfortably he knocks one of the boxes off the table, curses, switches off, sweeps boxes and ledger violently to the ground, winds tape back to beginning, switches on, resumes posture*] Thirty-nine today, sound as a bell, apart from my old weakness, and intellectually I have now every reason to suspect at the . . . [*hesitates*] . . . crest of the wave or thereabouts. Celebrated the awful occasion, as in recent years, quietly at the Winehouse. Not a soul. Sat before the fire with closed eyes, separating the grain from the husks. Jotted down a few notes, on the back of an envelope. Good to be back in my den, in my old rags. Have just eaten I regret to say three bananas and only with difficulty refrained from a fourth. Fatal things for a man with my condition. [*Vehemently*] Cut 'em out! [*Pause*] The new light above my table is a great improvement. With all this darkness round me I feel less alone. [*Pause*] In a way. [*Pause*] I love to get up and move about in it, then back here to . . . [*hesitates*] . . . me. [*Pause*] Krapp.

[*Pause.*]

The grain, now what I wonder do I mean by that, I mean . . . [*hesitates*] . . . I suppose I mean those things worth having when all the dust has – when all my dust has settled. I close my eyes and try and imagine them.

[*Pause. Krapp closes his eyes briefly.*]

Extraordinary silence this evening, I strain my ears and do not hear a sound. Old Miss McGlome always sings at this hour. But not tonight. Songs of her girlhood, she says. Hard to think of her as a girl. Wonderful woman though. Connaught, I fancy. [*Pause*] Shall I sing when I am her age, if I ever am? No. [*Pause*] Did I sing as a boy? No. [*Pause*] Did I ever sing? No.

[*Pause.*]

Just been listening to an old year, passages at random. I did not check in the book, but it must be at least ten or twelve years ago. At that time I think I was still living on and off with Bianca in Kedar Street. Well out of that, Jesus yes! Hopeless business. [*Pause*] Not much about her, apart from a tribute to her eyes. Very warm. I suddenly saw them again. [*Pause*] Incomparable! [*Pause*] Ah well. . . . [*Pause*] These old P.M.s are gruesome, but I often find them – [*Krapp switches off, broods, switches on*] – a help before embarking on a new . . . [*hesitates*] . . . retrospect. Hard to believe I was ever that young whelp. The voice! Jesus! And the aspirations! [*Brief laugh in which Krapp joins*] And the resolutions! [*Brief laugh in which Krapp joins*] To drink less, in particular. [*Brief laugh of Krapp alone*] Statistics. Seventeen hundred hours, out of the preceding eight thousand odd, consumed on licensed premises alone. More than 20 per cent, say 40 per cent of his waking life. [*Pause*] Plans for a less . . . [*hesitates*] . . . engrossing sexual life. Last illness of his father. Flagging pursuit of happiness. Unattainable laxation. Sneers at what he calls his youth and thanks to God that it's over. [*Pause*] False ring there. [*Pause*] Shadows of the opus . . . magnum. Closing with a – [*brief laugh*] – yelp to Providence. [*Prolonged laugh in which Krapp joins*] What remains of all that misery? A girl in a shabby green coat, on a railway-station platform? No?

[*Pause.*]

When I look –

[*Krapp switches off, broods, looks at his watch, gets up, goes backstage into darkness. Ten seconds. Pop of cork. Ten seconds. Second cork. Ten seconds. Third cork. Ten seconds. Brief burst of quavering song.*]

Krapp [*sings*]   Now the day is over,
                      Night is drawing nigh-igh,
                      Shadows –

[*Fit of coughing. He comes back into light, sits down, wipes his mouth, switches on, resumes his listening posture.*]

Tape – back on the year that is gone, with what I hope is perhaps a glint of the old eye to come, there is of course the house on the canal where mother lay a-dying, in the late autumn, after her long viduity [*Krapp gives a start*] and the – [*Krapp switches off, winds back tape a little, bends his ear closer to machine, switches on*] – a-dying, after her long viduity, and the –

[*Krapp switches off, raises his head, stares blankly before him. His lips move in the syllables of 'viduity'. No sound. He gets up, goes backstage into darkness, comes back with an enormous dictionary, lays it on table, sits down and looks up the word.*]

Krapp [*reading from dictionary*] State – or condition – of being – or remain-ing – a widow – or widower. [*Looks up. Puzzled*] Being – or remaining? . . . [*Pause. He peers again at dictionary. Reading*] 'Deep weeds of viduity.' . . . Also of an animal, especially a bird . . . the vidua or weaver-bird. . . . Black plumage of male . . . . [*He looks up. With relish*] The vidua-bird!

[*Pause. He closes dictionary, switches on, resumes listening posture.*]

Tape – bench by the weir from where I could see her window. There I sat, in the biting wind, wishing she were gone. [*Pause*] Hardly a soul, just a few regulars, nursemaids, infants, old men, dogs, I got to know them quite well – oh by appearance of course I mean! One dark young beauty I recollect particu-larly, all white and starch, incomparable bosom, with a big black hooded perambulator, most funereal thing. Whenever I looked in her direction she had her eyes on me. And yet when I was bold enough to speak to her not having been introduced she threatened to call a policeman. As if I had designs on her virtue! [*Laugh. Pause*] The face she had! The eyes! Like . . . [*hesitates*] . . . chrysolite! [*Pause*] Ah well. . . . [*Pause*] I was there when – [*Krapp switches off, broods, switches on again*] – the blind went down, one of those dirty brown roller affairs, throwing a ball for a little white dog as chance would have it. I happened to look up and there it was. All over and done with, at last. I sat on for a few moments with the ball in my hand and the dog yelping and pawing at me. [*Pause*] Moments. Her moments, my moments. [*Pause*] The dog's moments. [*Pause*] In the end I held it out to him and he took it in his mouth, gently, gently. A small, old, black, hard, solid rubber ball. [*Pause*] I shall feel it, in my hand, until my dying day. [*Pause*] I might have kept it. [*Pause*] But I gave it to the dog.

[*Pause.*]

Ah well . . . .

[*Pause.*]

Spiritually a year of profound gloom and indigence until that memorable night in March, at the end of the jetty, in the howling wind, never to be forgotten, when suddenly I saw the whole thing. The vision at last. This I fancy is what I have chiefly to record this evening, against the day when my work will be done and perhaps no place left in my memory, warm or cold, for the miracle that . . . [*hesitates*] . . . for the fire that set it alight. What I suddenly saw then was this, that the belief I had been going on all my life, namely – [*Krapp switches off impatiently, winds tape forward, switches on again*] – great granite rocks the foam flying up in the light of the lighthouse and the wind-gauge spinning like a propeller, clear to me at last that the dark I have always struggled to keep under is in reality my most – [*Krapp curses, switches off, winds tape forward, switches on again*] – unshatterable association until my dissolution of storm and night with the light of the understanding and the fire – [*Krapp curses louder, switches off, winds Tape forward, switches on again*] – my face in her breasts and my hand on her. We lay there without moving. But under us all moved, and moved us, gently, up and down, and from side to side.

[*Pause.*]

Past midnight. Never knew such silence. The earth might be uninhabited.

[*Pause.*]

Here I end –

[*Krapp switches off, winds tape back, switches on again*] – upper lake, with the punt, bathed off the bank, then pushed out into the stream and drifted. She lay stretched out on the floorboards with her hands under her head and her eyes closed. Sun blazing down, bit of a breeze, water nice and lively. I noticed a scratch on her thigh and asked her how she came by it. Picking gooseberries, she said. I said again I thought it was hopeless and no good going on and she agreed, without opening her eyes. [*Pause*] I asked her to look at me and after a few moments – [*pause*] – after a few moments she did, but the eyes just slits, because of the glare. I bent over her to get them in the shadow and they opened. [*Pause. Low*] Let me in. [*Pause*] We drifted in among the flags and stuck. The way they went down, sighing, before the stem! [*Pause*] I lay down across her with my face in her breasts and my hand on her. We lay there without moving. But under us all moved, and moved us, gently, up and down, and from side to side.

[*Pause.*]

Past midnight. Never knew –

[*Krapp switches off, broods. Finally he fumbles in his pockets, encounters the banana, takes it out, peers at it, puts it back, fumbles, brings out envelope, fumbles, puts back envelope, looks at his watch, gets up and goes backstage into darkness. Ten seconds. Sound of bottle against glass, then brief siphon. Ten seconds. Bottle against glass alone. Ten seconds. He comes back a little unsteadily into light, goes to front of table, takes out keys, raises them to his eyes, chooses key, unlocks first drawer, peers into it, feels about inside, takes out reel, peers at it, locks drawer, puts keys back in his pocket, goes and sits down, takes reel off machine, lays it on dictionary, loads virgin reel on machine, takes envelope from his pocket, consults back of it, lays it on table, switches on, clears his throat and begins to record.*]

Krapp Just been listening to that stupid bastard I took myself for thirty years ago, hard to believe I was ever as bad as that. Thank God that's all done with anyway. [*Pause*] The eyes she had! [*Broods, realizes he is recording silence,* *switches off, broods. Finally*] Everything there, everything, all the – [*Realizes this is not being recorded, switches off*] Everything there, everything on this old muckball, all the light and dark and famine and feasting of . . . [*hesitates*] . . . the ages! [*In a shout*] Yes! [*Pause*] Let that go! Jesus! Take his mind off his homework! Jesus! [*Pause. Weary*] Ah well, maybe he was right. [*Pause*] Maybe he was right. [*Broods. Realizes. Switches off. Consults envelope*] Pah! [*Crumples it and throws it away. Broods. Switches on*] Nothing to say, not a squeak. What's a year now? The sour cud and the iron stool. [*Pause*] Revelled in the word spool. [*With relish*] Spooool! Happiest moment of the past half million. [*Pause.*] Seventeen copies sold, of which eleven at trade price to free circulating libraries beyond the seas. Getting known. [*Pause*] One pound six and something, eight I have little doubt. [*Pause*] Crawled out once or twice, before the summer was cold. Sat shivering in the park, drowned in dreams and burning to be gone. Not a soul. [*Pause*] Last fancies. [*Vehemently*] Keep 'em under! [*Pause*] Scalded the eyes out of me reading *Effie* again, a page a day, with tears again. Effie . . . . [*Pause*] Could have been happy with her, up there on the Baltic, and the pines, and the dunes. [*Pause*] Could I? [*Pause*] And she? [*Pause*] Pah! [*Pause*] Fanny came in a couple of times. Bony old ghost of a whore. Couldn't do much, but I suppose better than a kick in the crutch. The last time wasn't so bad. How do you manage it, she said, at your age? I told her I'd been saving up for her all my life. [*Pause*] Went to Vespers once, like when I was in short trousers. [*Pause. Sings*]

> Now the day is over,
> Night is drawing nigh-igh,
> Shadows – [*coughing, then almost inaudible*] – of the evening
> Steal across the sky.

[*Gasping*] Went to sleep and fell off the pew. [*Pause*] Sometimes wondered in the night if a last effort mightn't – [*Pause*] Ah finish your booze now and get to your bed. Go on with this drivel in the morning. Or leave it at that. [*Pause*] Leave it at that. [*Pause*] Lie propped up in the dark and wander. Be again in the dingle[1] on a Christmas Eve, gathering holly, the red-berried. [*Pause*] Be again on Croghan on a Sunday morning, in the haze, with the bitch, stop and listen to the bells. [*Pause*] And so on. [*Pause*] Be again, be again. [*Pause*] All that old misery. [*Pause*] Once wasn't enough for you. [*Pause*] Lie down across her.

[*Long pause. He suddenly bends over machine, switches off, wrenches off tape, throws it away, puts on the other, winds it forward to the passage he wants, switches on, listens staring front.*]

Tape – gooseberries, she said. I said again I thought it was hopeless and no good going on and she agreed, without opening her eyes. [*Pause*] I asked her to look at me and after a few moments – [*pause*] – after a few moments she did, but the eyes just slits, because of the glare. I bent over her to get them in the shadow and they opened. [*Pause. Low*] Let me in. [*Pause*] We drifted in

---

1 **dingle:** hollow.

among the flags and stuck. The way they went down, sighing, before the stem! [*Pause*] I lay down across her with my face in her breasts and my hand on her. We lay there without moving. But under us all moved, and moved us, gently, up and down, and from side to side.

[*Pause. Krapp's lips move. No sound.*]

Past midnight. Never knew such silence. The earth might be uninhabited.

[*Pause.*]

Here I end this reel. Box – [*pause*] – three, spool – [*pause*] – five. [*Pause*] Perhaps my best years are gone. When there was a chance of happiness. But I wouldn't want them back. Not with the fire in me now. No, I wouldn't want them back.

[*Krapp motionless staring before him. The Tape runs on in silence.*]

FLANN O'BRIEN (1911–1966)

Novelist, journalist and humorist, Flann O'Brien was born Brian O'Nolan and studied at University College, Dublin. For many he years he wrote a column for *The Irish Times* as Myles n Gopaleen. A nationalist, O'Brien disliked the romaticised view of a sentimental rural Ireland. His novel *At Swim-Two-Birds*, first published in 1939, is an extraordinary portrait of Dublin life, mixing legendary exploit, realism and comic fantasy.

From At Swim-Two-Birds

Substance of reminiscence by Mr Shanahan, the comments of his hearers being embodied parenthetically in the text; with relevant excerpts from the public Press: Do you know what I am going to tell you, there was a rare life in Dublin in the old days. (There was certainly.) That was the day of the great O'Callaghan, the day of Baskin, the day of Tracy that brought cowboys to Ringsend. I knew them all, man.

   Relevant excerpt from the Press: We regret to announce the passing of Mr William Tracy, the eminent novelist, which occurred yesterday under painful circumstances at his home in Grace Park Gardens. Early in the afternoon, deceased was knocked down in Weavers' Square by a tandem cycle proceeding towards the city. He got up unaided, however, laughed heartily, treated the accident as a joke in the jolly way that was peculiarly his own and made his way home on a tram. When he had smoked six after-dinner pipes, he went to ascend the stairs and dropped dead on the landing. A man of culture and old-world courtesy, his passing will be regretted by all without distinction of creed or class and in particular by the world of letters, which he adorned with distinction for many years. He was the first man in Europe to exhibit twenty-nine lions in a cage at the same time and the only writer to demonstrate that cowpunching could be economically carried on in Ringsend. His best-known works were *Red Flanagan's Last Throw, Flower o' the Prairie,* and *Jake's Last Ride.* Deceased was fifty-nine. Conclusion of excerpt.

One day Tracy sent for me and gave me my orders and said it was one of his own cowboy books. Two days later I was cow-punching down by the river in Ringsend with Shorty Andrews and Slug Willard, the toughest pair of boyos you'd meet in a day's walk. Rounding up steers, you know, and branding, and breaking in colts in the corral with lassoes on our saddle-horns and pistols at our hips. (O the real thing; Was there any drink to be had?) There certainly was. At night we would gather in the bunkhouse with our porter and all our orders, cigarettes and plenty there on the chiffonier to be taken and no questions asked, school-marms and saloon-girls and little black maids skivvy-ing there in the galley. (That was the place to be, now.) After a while be damned but in would walk a musicianer with a fiddle or a pipes in the hollow of his arm and there he would sit and play A*ve Maria* to bring the tears to your eyes. Then the boys would take up an old come-all-ye, the real old stuff, you know, *Phil the Fluter's Ball* or the *Darling Girl from Clare,* a bloody lovely thing. (That was very nice certainly.) O we had the right time of it. One morning Slug and Shorty and myself and a few of the boys got the wire to saddle and ride up to Drumcondra to see my nabs Mr Tracy to get our orders for the day. Up we went on our horses, cantering up Mountjoy Square with our hats tilted back on our heads and the sun in our eyes and our gun-butts swinging at our holsters. When we got the length, go to God but wasn't it a false alarm. (A false alarm! Lord save us! What brought that about now?) Wait till I tell you. Get back to hell, says Tracy, I never sent any message. Get back to hell to your prairies, says he, you pack of lousers that can be taken in by any fly-be-night with a fine story. I'm telling you that we were small men when we took the trail again for home. When we got the length, be damned but wasn't the half of our steers rustled across the border in Irishtown by Red Kiersay's gang of thieving ruffians. (Well that was a kick for you where-you-know.) Certainly it was. Red Kiersay, you understand, was working for another man by the name of Henderson that was writing another book about cattledealers and jobbing and shipping bullocks to Liverpool. (Likely it was he sent you the false message?) Do you mind the cuteness of it? Get yourselves fed, says I to Shorty and Slug, we're goin' ridin' tonight. Where? says Slug. Right over to them thar rustlers' roost, says I, before Tracy finds out and skins us. Where's the nigger skivvies? says Shorty. Now go to God, says I, don't tell me they have taken the lot with them. (And had they?) Every one.

Relevant excerpt from the Press: An examination of the galley and servants' sleep-ing-quarters revealed no trace of the negro maids. They had been offered lucrative inducements to come from the United States and had at no time expressed themselves as being dissatisfied with their conditions of service. Detective-Officer Snodgrass found a pearl-handled shooting-iron under the pillow in the bed of Liza Roberts, the youngest of the maids. No great importance is attached by the police to this discovery, however, as ownership has been traced to Peter (Shorty) Andrews, a cowboy, who states that though at a loss to explain the presence of his property in the maid's bed, it is possible that she appropriated the article in order to clean it in her spare time in bed (she was an industrious girl) or in order to play a joke. It is stated that the former explanation is the more likely of the two as there is no intercourse of a social character between the men and the scullerymaids. A number of minor clues have been found and an arrest is expected in the near future. Conclusion of excerpt.

I'm not what you call fussy when it comes to women but damn it all I draw the line when it comes to carrying off a bunch of black niggers – human beings, you must remember – and a couple of thousand steers, by God. So when the moon had raised her lamp o'er the prairie grasses, out flies the bunch of us, Slug, Shorty and myself on a buckboard making like hell for Irishtown with our ears back and the butts of our six-guns streaming out behind us in the wind. (You were out to get your own?) We were out to get our own. I tell you we were travelling in great style. Shorty drew out and gave the horses an unmerciful skelp across the where-you-know and away with us like the wind and us roaring and cursing out of us like men that were lit with whisky, our steel-studded holsters swaying at our hips and the sheep-fur on our leg-chaps lying down like corn before a spring-wind. Be damned to the lot of us, I roared, flaying the nags and bashing the buckboard across the prairie, passing out lorries and trams and sending poor so-and-so's on bicycles scuttling down side-lanes with nothing showing but the whites of their eyes. (By God you were travelling all right.) Certainly, going like the hammers of hell. I smell cattle, says Slug and sure enough there was the ranch of Red Kiersay the length of a turkey trot ahead of us sitting on the moonlit prairie as peaceful as you please.

Relevant excerpt from the Press: The Circle N is reputed to be the most venerable of Dublin's older ranches. The main building is a gothic structure of red sandstone timbered in the Elizabethan style and supported by corinthian pillars at the posterior. Added as a lean-to at the south gable is the wooden bunk-house, one of the most up to date of its kind in the country. It contains three holster-racks, ten gas fires and a spacious dormitory fitted with an ingenious apparatus worked by compressed air by which all verminous beds can be fumigated instantaneously by the mere pressing of a button, the operation occupying only the space of forty seconds. The old Dublin custom of utilizing imported negroid labour for operating the fine electrically equipped cooking-galley is still observed in this time-hallowed house. On the land adjacent, grazing is available for 10000 steers and 2000 horses, thanks to the public spirit of Mr William Tracy, the indefatigable novelist, who had 8912 dangerous houses demolished in the environs of Irishtown and Sandymount to make the enterprise possible. Visitors can readily reach the ranch by taking the Number 3 tram. The exquisitely laid out gardens of the ranch are open for inspection on Thursdays and Fridays, the nominal admission fee of one and sixpence being devoted to the cause of the Jubilee Nurses' Fund. Conclusion of excerpt.

Down we got offa the buckboard to our hands and knees and up with us towards the doss-house on our bellies, our silver-mounted gun-butts jiggling at our hips, our eyes narrowed into slits and our jaws set and stern like be damned. (By God you weren't a party to meet on a dark night.) Don't make a sound, says I *viva voce* to the boys, or it's kiss my hand to taking these lousers by surprise. On we slithered with as much sound out of us as an eel in a barrel of tripes, right up to the bunkhouse on the flat of our three bellies. (Don't tell me you were seen?) Go to hell but a lad pulls a gun on us from behind and tells us to get on our feet and no delay or monkeywork. Be damned but wasn't it Red Kiersay himself, the so-and-so, standing there with an iron in each hand and a Lucifer leer on his beery face. What are you at, you swine, he asks in a real snotty voice. Don't come it, Kiersay, says I, we're here for our own and damn the bloody thing else. (You were in the right, of course. What was the upshot?) Come across, Kiersay, says I, come across with our steers and our black girls or down I go straight to Lad Lane and get the police up. Keep your hands up or I'll paste your guts on that tree, says he, you swine. You can't cow the like of us with your big gun, says Slug, and don't think it my boyo. (O trust Slug.) You dirty dog, says I between my teeth, you dirty swine you, Kiersay, you bastard. My God I was in the right temper and that's a fact. (You had good reason to be. If I was there I don't know what I'd do.) Well the upshot was that he gave us three minutes to go home and home we went like boys because Kiersay would think nothing of shooting the lights out of us and that's the God's truth. (You had a right to go for the police.) That's the very thing we done. Out we crept to the buggy and down Londonbridge Road and across the town to Lad Lane. It was good gas all right. The station sergeant was with us from the start and gave us over to the superintendent, a Clohessy from Tipp. Nothing would do him but give us a whole detachment of the D.M.P. to see fair play and justice done, and the fire-brigade there for the calling. (Well that was very decent of him now.) Do you know what it is, says Slug, Tracy is writing another book too and has a crowd of Red Indians up in the Phoenix Park, squaws and wigwams and warpaint an' all, the real stuff all right, believe me. A couple of bob to the right man there and the lot are ours for the asking, says he. Go to hell, says I, you don't tell me. As sure as God, says he. Right, says I, let yourself go for the Indians, let Shorty here go back for our own boys and let myself stop where I am with the police. Let the lot of us meet at Kiersay's at a quarter past eight. (Fair enough, fair enough.) Off went the two at a half-canter on the buckboard and the super and myself got stuck into a dozen stout in the back room. After a while, the policemen were rounded up and marched across the prairies to the Circle N, as fine a body of men as you'd hope to see, myself and the super as proud as be damned at the head of them. (Well that was a sight to see.) When we got the length, there was Slug with his Red Indians, Shorty and his cow-boys, the whole shooting gallery waiting for the word. The super and myself put our heads together and in no time we had everything arranged. In behind the buckboard and food wagons with the policemen and the cowboys to wait for the sweet foe. Away with the Red Indians around the ranch-house in circles, the braves galloping like red hell on their Arab ponies, screaming and shrieking and waving their bloody scalp-hatchets and firing flaming rods into the house from their little bows. (Boys-a-dear.) I'm telling you it was the business. The whole place was burning like billyo in no time and out came Red with a shot-gun in his hand and followed by his men, prepared if you please to make a last stand for king and country. The Indians got windy and flew back to us behind the buckboards and go to God if Red doesn't hold up a passing tram and take cover behind it, firing all the people out with a stream of dirty filthy language. (Well dirty language is thing I don't like. He deserved all he got.) Lord save us but it was the right hard battle. I fired off my six bullets without stopping. A big sheet of plate-glass crashed from the tram to the roadway. Then with a terrible scutter of oaths, the boys began to get busy. We broke every pane of glass in that tram, raked the roadway with a death-dealing rain of six-gun shrapnel and took the tip off an enemy cowboy's ear, by God. In no time wasn't there a crowd around the battlefield and them cheering and calling and asking every man of us to do his duty. (O you'll always get those boys to gather. Sneeze in the street and they're all around you.) The bloody Indians started squealing at the back and slapping their horses on the belly, the policemen were firing of their six-guns and their batons in the air and Shorty and myself behind a sack of potatoes picking off the snipers like be damned. On raged the scrap for a half an hour, the lot of us giving back more than we got and never thinking of the terrible danger we were in, every man jack of us, loading and shooting off our pistols like divils from below. Be damned but the enemy was weakening. Now is your chance, says I to the super, now is your chance to lead your men over the top, says I, and capture the enemy's stronghold for good and all. Right you are, says he. Over the top with my brave bobbies, muttered oaths flying all over the place, as bold as brass with their batons in their hands. The crowd gave a big cheer and the Indians shrieked and flayed the bellies offa their horses with their hands. (Well did the dodge work?) Certainly. The battle was over before you could count your fingers and here were my brave men handcuffed hand-and-foot and marched down to Lad Lane like a bunch of orphans out for a Sunday walk. Did you get Red? says I to the super. Didn't see him at all at all, says he. As sure as God, says I, he's doing the Brian Boru in his bloody tent. (What, at the prayers?) Round I searched till I found the tent and here was my bold man inside on his two knees and him praying there for further orders. Where's our girls, Red, says I. Gone home, says he. Take yourself out of here, says he, and bring your steers with you, says he, can't you see I'm at my prayers. Do you mind the cuteness of it? I could do nothing, of course, him there in front of me on his two knees praying. There wasn't a thing left for me to do but go off again and choke down my rising dander. Come on away with me, says I to Slug and Shorty till we get our stolen steers. Next day didn't the super bring the enemy punchers up before the bench and got every man of them presented free with seven days' hard without option. Cool them down, says Slug.

Relevant excerpt from the Press: A number of men, stated to be labourers, were arraigned before Mr Lamphall in the District Court yesterday morning on charges of riotous assembly and malicious damage. Accused were described by Superintendent Clohessy as a gang of corner-boys whose horse-play in the streets was the curse of the Ringsend district. They were pests and public nuisances whose antics were not infrequently attended by damage to property. Complaints as to their conduct were frequently being received from residents in the area. On the occasion of the last escapade, two windows were broken in a tram-car the property of the Dublin United Tramway Company. Inspector Quin of the Company stated that the damage to the vehicle amounted to £2

11s. 0d. Remarking that no civilized community could tolerate organized hooliganism of this kind, the justice sentenced the accused to seven days' hard labour without the option of a fine, and hoped that it would be a lesson to them and to other playboys of the boulevards. Conclusion of excerpt.

GEORGE ORWELL (1903–1950)

Orwell is the pseudonym of Eric Arthur Blair, novelist, essayist and journalist. Closely associated with the British Left, Orwell attempted to show a self-satisfied, imperialist England its darker and less savoury social underclass in works such as *Down and Out in Paris and London* and *The Road to Wigan Pier*. A champion of Republican Spain, he served as a volunteer with Republican forces during the Spanish Civil War, an experience vividly recounted in *Homage to Catalonia*. Although committed to socialism, Orwell readily recognised the Stalinism of Russia as no model for the West. His masterful *1984* shows a Stalinist-style state ruling Britain. Orwell's first career was with the Imperial Police in Burma, and it is from experiences there that the following essay derives.

Shooting an Elephant

In Moulmein, in Lower Burma, I was hated by large numbers of people – the only time in my life that I have been important enough for this to happen to me. I was subdivisional police officer of the town, and in an aimless, petty kind of way anti-European feeling was very bitter. No one had the guts to raise a riot, but if a European woman went through the bazaars alone somebody would probably spit betel juice over her dress. As a police officer I was an obvious target and was baited whenever it seemed safe to do so. When a nimble Burman tripped me up on the football field and the referee (another Burman) looked the other way, the crowd yelled with hideous laughter. This happened more than once. In the end the sneering yellow faces of young men that met me everywhere, the insults hooted after me when I was at a safe distance, got badly on my nerves. The young Buddhist priests were the worst of all. There were several thousands of them in the town and none of them seemed to have anything to do except stand on street corners and jeer at Europeans.

All this was perplexing and upsetting. For at that time I had already made up my mind that imperialism was an evil thing and the sooner I chucked up my job and got out of it the better. Theoretically – and secretly, of course – I was all for the Burmese and all against their oppressors, the British. As for the job I was doing, I hated it more bitterly than I can perhaps make clear. In a job like that you see the dirty work of Empire at close quarters. The wretched prisoners huddling in the stinking cages of the lock-ups, the grey, cowed faces of the long-term convicts, the scarred buttocks of the men who had been flogged with bamboos – all these oppressed me with an intolerable sense of guilt. But I could get nothing into perspective. I was young and ill-educated and I had had to think out my problems in the utter silence that is imposed on every Englishman in the East. I did not even know that the British Empire is dying, still less did I know that it is a great deal better than the younger empires that are going to supplant it. All I knew was that I was stuck between my hatred of the empire I served and my rage against the evil-spirited little beasts who tried to make my job impossible. With one part of my mind I thought of the British Raj as an unbreakable tyranny, as something clamped down, in *saecula saeculorum*,[1] upon the will of prostrate peoples; with another part I thought that the greatest joy in the world would be to drive a bayonet into a Buddhist priest's guts. Feelings like these are the normal by-products of imperialism; ask any Anglo-Indian official, if you can catch him off duty.

One day something happened which in a roundabout way was enlightening. It was a tiny incident in itself, but it gave me a better glimpse than I had had before of the real nature of imperialism – the real motives for which despotic governments act. Early one morning the sub-inspector at a police station the other end of the town rang me up on the phone and said that an elephant was ravaging the bazaar. Would I please come and do something about it? I did not know what I could do, but I wanted to see what was happening and I got on to a pony and started out. I took my rifle, an old .44 Winchester and much too small to kill an elephant, but I thought the noise might be useful *in terrorem*. Various Burmans stopped me on the way and told me about the elephant's doings. It was not, of course, a wild elephant, but a tame one which had gone 'must'. It had been chained up, as tame elephants always are when their attack of 'must' is due, but on the previous night it had broken its chain and escaped. Its mahout, the only person who could manage it when it was in that state, had set out in pursuit, but had taken the wrong direction and was now twelve hours' journey away, and in the morning the elephant had suddenly reappeared in the town. The Burmese population had no weapons and were quite helpless against it. It had already destroyed somebody's bamboo hut, killed a cow and raided some fruit-stalls and devoured the stock; also it had met the municipal rubbish van, and, when the driver jumped out and took to his heels, had turned the van over and inflicted violences upon it.

The Burmese sub-inspector and some Indian constables were waiting for me in the quarter where the elephant had been seen. It was a very poor quarter, a labyrinth of squalid bamboo huts, thatched with palm-leaf, winding all over a steep hillside. I remember that it was a cloudy, stuffy morning at the beginning of the rains. We began questioning the people as to where the elephant had gone, and, as usual failed to get any definite information. That is invariably the case in the East; a story always sounds clear enough at a distance, but the nearer you get to the scene of events the vaguer it becomes. Some of the people said that the elephant had gone in one direction, some said that he had gone in another, some professed not even to have heard of any elephant. I had almost made up my mind that the whole story was a pack of lies, when we heard yells a little distance away. There was a loud, scandalized cry of 'Go away child! Go away this instant!' and an old woman with a switch in her hand came round the corner of a hut, violently shooing away a crowd of naked children. Some more women followed, clicking their tongues and exclaiming. Evidently

---

1 **saecula** . . . . : forever and ever.

there was something that the children ought not to have seen. I rounded the hut and saw a man's dead body sprawling in the mud. He was an Indian, a black Dravidian coolie, almost naked, and he could not have been dead many minutes. The people said that the elephant had come suddenly upon him round the corner of the hut, caught him with its trunk, put its foot on his back and ground him into the earth. This was the rainy season and the ground was soft, and his face had scored a trench a foot deep and a couple of yards long. He was lying on his belly with arms crucified and head sharply twisted to one side. His face was coated with mud, the eyes wide open, the teeth bared and grinning with an expression of unendurable agony. (Never tell me, by the way, that the dead look peaceful. Most of the corpses I have seen looked devilish.) The friction of the great beast's foot had stripped the skin from his back as neatly as one skins a rabbit. As soon as I saw the dead man I sent an orderly to a friend's house nearby to borrow an elephant rifle. I had already sent back the pony, not wanting it to go mad with fright and throw me if it smelt the elephant.

The orderly came back in a few minutes with a rifle and five cartridges, and meanwhile some Burmans had arrived and told us that the elephant was in the paddy fields below, only a few hundred yards away. As I started forward practically the whole population of the quarter flocked out of the houses and followed me. They had seen the rifle and were all shouting excitedly that I was going to shoot the elephant. They had not shown much interest in the elephant when he was merely ravaging their homes, but it was different now that he was going to be shot. It was a bit of fun to them, as it would be to an English crowd; besides they wanted the meat. It made me vaguely uneasy. I had no intention of shooting the elephant – I had merely sent for the rifle to defend myself if necessary – and it is always unnerving to have a crowd following you. I marched down the hill, looking and feeling a fool, with the rifle over my shoulder and an ever-growing army of people jostling at my heels. At the bottom, when you got away from the huts, there was a metalled road and beyond that a miry waste of paddy fields a thousand yards across, not yet ploughed but soggy from the first rains and dotted with coarse grass. The elephant was standing eight yards from the road, his left side towards us. He took not the slightest notice of the crowd's approach. He was tearing up bunches of grass, beating them against his knees to clean them and stuffing them into his mouth.

I had halted on the road. As soon as I saw the elephant I knew with perfect certainty that I ought not to shoot him. It is a serious matter to shoot a working elephant – it is comparable to destroying a huge and costly piece of machinery – and obviously one ought not to do it if it can possibly be avoided. And at that distance, peacefully eating the elephant looked no more dangerous than a cow. I thought then and I think now that his attack of 'must' was already passing off; in which case he would merely wander harmlessly about until the mahout came back and caught him. Moreover, I did not in the least want to shoot him. I decided that I would watch him for a little while to make sure that he did not turn savage again, and then go home.

But at that moment I glanced round at the crowd that had followed me. It was an immense crowd, two thousand at the least and growing every minute. It blocked the road for a long distance on either side. I looked at the sea of yellow faces above the garish clothes – faces all happy and excited over this bit of fun, all certain that the elephant was going to be shot. They were watching me as they would watch a conjurer about to perform a trick. They did not like me, but with the magical rifle in my hands I was momentarily worth watching. And suddenly I realized that I should have to shoot the elephant after all. The people expected it of me and I had got to do it; I could feel their two thousand wills pressing me forward, irresistibly. And it was at this moment, as I stood there with the rifle in my hands, that I first grasped the hollowness, the futility of the white man's dominion in the East. Here was I, the white man with his gun, standing in front of the unarmed native crowd – seemingly the leading actor of the piece; but in reality I was only an absurd puppet pushed to and fro by the will of those yellow faces behind. I perceived in this moment that when the white man turns tyrant it is his own freedom that he destroys. He becomes a sort of hollow, posing dummy, the conventionalized figure of a sahib. For it is the condition of his rule that he shall spend his life in trying to impress the 'natives', and so in every crisis he has got to do what the 'natives' expect of him. He wears a mask, and his face grows to fit it. I had got to shoot the elephant. I had committed myself to doing it when I sent for the rifle. A sahib has got to act like a sahib; he has got to appear resolute, to know his own mind and do definite things. To come all that way, rifle in hand, with two thousand people marching at my heels, and then to trail feebly away, having done nothing – no, that was impossible. The crowd would laugh at me. And my whole life, every white man's life in the East, was one long struggle not to be laughed at.

But I did not want to shoot the elephant. I watched him beating his bunch of grass against his knees, with that preoccupied grandmotherly air that elephants have. It seemed to me that it would be murder to shoot him. At that age I was not squeamish about killing animals, but I had never shot an elephant and never wanted to. (Somehow it always seems worse to kill a *large* animal.) Besides, there was the beast's owner to be considered. Alive, the elephant was worth at least a hundred pounds; dead, he would only be worth the value of his tusks, five pounds, possibly. But I had got to act quickly. I turned to some experienced-looking Burmans who had been there when we arrived, and asked them how the elephant had been behaving. They all said the same thing: he took no notice of you if you left him alone, but he might charge if you went too close to him.

It was perfectly clear to me what I ought to do. I ought to walk up to within, say, twenty-five yards of the elephant and test his behaviour. If he charged I could shoot, if he took no notice of me it would be safe to leave him until the mahout came back. But also I knew that I was going to do no such thing. I was a poor shot with a rifle and the ground was soft mud into which one would sink at every step. If the elephant charged and I missed him, I should have about as much chance as a toad under a steam-roller. But even then I was not thinking particularly of my own skin, only of the watchful yellow faces behind. For at that moment, with the crowd watching me, I was not afraid in the ordinary sense, as I would have been if I had been alone. A white man mustn't be frightened in front of 'natives'; and so, in general, he isn't frightened. The sole thought in my mind was that if anything went wrong those two thousand Burmans would see me pursued, caught, trampled on and reduced to a grinning corpse like that Indian up the hill. And if that happened it was quite probable that some of them would laugh. That would never do. There was only one alternative. I shoved the cartridges into the magazine and lay down on the road to get a better aim.

The crowd grew very still, and a deep, low, happy sigh, as of people who see the theatre curtain go up at last breathed from innumerable throats. They were going to have their bit of fun after all. The rifle was a beautiful German thing with cross-hair sights. I did not then know that in shooting an elephant one should shoot to cut an imaginary bar running from ear-hole to ear-hole. I ought therefore, as the elephant was sideways on, to have aimed straight at his ear-hole; actually I aimed several inches in front of this, thinking the brain would be further forward.

When I pulled the trigger I did not hear the bang or feel the kick – one never does when a shot goes home – but I heard the devilish roar of glee that went up from the crowd. In that instant, in too short a time, one would have thought, even for the bullet to get there, a mysterious, terrible change had come over the elephant. He neither stirred nor fell, but every line of his body had altered. He looked suddenly stricken, shrunken, immensely old, as though the frightful impact of the bullet had paralysed him without knocking him down. At last, after what seemed a long time – it might have been five seconds, I dare say – he sagged flabbily to his knees. His mouth slobbered. An enormous senility seemed to have settled upon him. One could have imagined him thousands of years old. I fired again into the same spot. At the second shot he did not collapse but climbed with desperate slowness to his feet and stood weakly upright, with legs sagging and head drooping. I fired a third time. That was the shot that did for him. You could see the agony of it jolt his whole body and knock the last remnant of strength from his legs. But in falling he seemed for a moment to rise, for as his hind legs collapsed beneath him he seemed to tower upwards like a huge rock toppling, his trunk reaching skywards like a tree. He trumpeted, for the first and only time. And then down he came, his belly towards me, with a crash that seemed to shake the ground even where I lay.

I got up. The Burmans were already racing past me across the mud. It was obvious that the elephant would never rise again, but he was not dead. He was breathing very rhythmically with long rattling gasps, his great mound of a side painfully rising and falling. His mouth was wide open – I could see far down into caverns of pale pink throat. I waited a long time for him to die, but his breathing did not weaken. Finally I fired my two remaining shots into the spot where I thought his heart must be. The thick blood welled out of him like red velvet, but still he did not die. His body did not even jerk when the shots hit him, the tortured breathing continued without a pause. He was dying, very slowly and in great agony, but in some world remote from me where not even a bullet could damage him further. I felt that I had got to put an end to that dreadful noise. It seemed dreadful to see the great beast lying there, powerless to move and yet powerless to die, and not even to be able to finish him. I sent back for my small rifle and poured shot after shot into his heart and down his throat. They seemed to make no impression. The tortured gasps continued as steadily as the ticking of a dock.

In the end I could not stand it any longer and went away. I heard later that it took him half an hour to die. Burmans were bringing dahs and baskets even before I left, and I was told they had stripped his body almost to the bones by the afternoon.

Afterwards, of course, there were endless discussions about the shooting of the elephant. The owner was furious, but he was only an Indian and could do nothing. Besides, legally I had done the right thing, for a mad elephant has to be killed, like a mad dog, if its owner fails to control it. Among the Europeans opinion was divided. The older men said I was right, the younger men said it was a damn shame to shoot an elephant for killing a coolie, because an elephant was worth more than any damn Coringhee coolie. And afterwards I was very glad that the coolie had been killed; it put me legally in the right and it gave me a sufficient pretext for shooting the elephant. I often wondered whether any of the others grasped that I had done it solely to avoid looking a fool.

GRAHAM GREENE (1904–1991)

Novelist, short-story writer and playwright, Greene was educated at Oxford. He became popular during the 1930s writing thrillers – often dealing with the world of espionage – and works he termed 'entertainments', usually sceptically exposing the absurdity of imperial pretension. His devout Roman Catholicism marked his more serious fiction, notably *Brighton Rock, The Heart of the Matter* and *The Power and the Glory*. His story 'Jubilee' appeared in 1936. Its title refers to the celebrations to mark the 25 years of George V's reign in 1935.

Jubilee

Mr Chalfont ironed his trousers and his tie. Then he folded up his ironing-board and put it away. He was tall and he had preserved his figure; he looked distinguished even in his pants in the small furnished bed-sitting-room he kept off Shepherd's Market. He was fifty, but he didn't look more than forty-five; he was stony broke, but he remained unquestionably Mayfair.[1]

He examined his collar with anxiety; he hadn't been out of doors for more than a week, except to the public-house at the corner to eat his morning and evening ham roll, and then he always wore an overcoat and a soiled collar. He decided that it wouldn't damage the effect if he wore it once more; he didn't believe in economizing too rigidly over his laundry, you had to spend money in order to earn money, but there was no point in being extravagant. And somehow he didn't believe in his luck this cocktail time; he was going out for the good of his morale, because after a week away from the restaurants it would

---

1 **Mayfair**: fashionable district in London's West End.

have been so easy to let everything slide, to confine himself to his room and his twice daily visit to the public-house.

The Jubilee decorations were still out in the cold windy May. Soiled by showers and soot the streamers blew up across Piccadilly, draughty with desolation. They were the reminder of a good time Mr Chalfont hadn't shared; he hadn't blown whistles or thrown paper ribbons; he certainly hadn't danced to any harmoniums. His neat figure was like a symbol of Good Taste as he waited with folded umbrella for the traffic lights to go green; he had learned to hold his hand so that one frayed patch on his sleeve didn't show, and the rather exclusive club tie, freshly ironed, might have been bought that morning. It wasn't lack of patriotism or loyalty which had kept Mr Chalfont indoors all through Jubilee week. Nobody drank the toast of the King more sincerely than Mr Chalfont so long as someone else was standing the drink, but an instinct deeper than good form had warned him not to be about. Too many people whom he had once known (so he explained it) were coming up from the country; they might want to look him up, and a fellow just couldn't ask them back to a room like this. That explained his discretion; it didn't explain his sense of oppression while he waited for the Jubilee to be over.

Now he was back at the old game.

He called it that himself, smoothing his neat grey military moustache. The old game. Somebody going rapidly round the corner into Berkeley Street nudged him playfully and said, 'Hullo, you old devil,' and was gone again, leaving the memory of many playful nudges in the old days, of Merdy and the Boob. For he couldn't disguise the fact that he was after the ladies. He didn't want to disguise it. It made his whole profession appear even to himself rather gallant and carefree. It disguised the fact that the ladies were not so young as they might be and that it was the ladies (God bless them!) who paid. It disguised the fact that Merdy and the Boob had long ago vanished from his knowledge. The list of his acquaintances included a great many women but hardly a single man; no one was more qualified by a long grimy experience to tell smoking-room stories, but the smoking-room in which Mr Chalfont was welcome did not nowadays exist.

Mr Chalfont crossed the road. It wasn't an easy life, it exhausted him nervously and physically, he needed a great many sherries to keep going. The first sherry he had always to pay for himself; that was the thirty pounds he marked as expenses on his income tax-return. He dived through the entrance, not looking either way, for it would never do for the porter to think that he was soliciting any of the women who moved heavily like seals through the dim aquarium light of the lounge. But his usual seat was occupied.

He turned away to look for another chair where he could exhibit himself discreetly: the select tie, the tan, the grey distinguished hair, the strong elegant figure, the air of a retired Governor from the Colonies. He studied the woman who sat in his chair covertly: he thought he'd seen her somewhere, the mink coat, the overblown figure, the expensive dress. Her face was familiar but unnoted, like that of someone you pass every day at the same place. She was vulgar, she was cheerful, she was undoubtedly rich. He couldn't think where he had met her.

She caught Mr Chalfont's eye and winked. He blushed, he was horrified, nothing of this sort had ever happened to him before; the porter was watching and Mr Chalfont felt scandal at his elbow, robbing him of his familiar restaurant, his last hunting ground, turning him perhaps out of Mayfair altogether into some bleak Paddington parlour where he couldn't keep up the least appearance of gallantry. Am I so obvious, he thought, so obvious? He went hastily across to her before she could wink again. 'Excuse me,' he said, 'you must remember me. What a long time . . . '

'Your face is familiar, dear,' she said. 'Have a cocktail.'

'Well,' Mr Chalfont said, 'I should certainly not mind a sherry, Mrs – Mrs – I've quite forgotten your surname.'

'You're a sport,' the woman said, 'but Amy will do.'

'Ah,' Mr Chalfont said, 'you are looking very well, Amy. It gives me much pleasure to see you sitting there again after all these – months – why, years it must be. The last time we met . . .'

'I don't remember you clearly, dear, though of course when I saw you looking at me. . . . I suppose it was in Jermyn Street.'

'Jermyn Street,' Mr Chalfont said. 'Surely not Jermyn Street. I've never. . . . Surely it must have been when I had my flat in Curzon Street. Delectable evenings one had there. I've moved since then to a rather humbler abode where I wouldn't dream of inviting you. . . . But perhaps we could slip away to some little nest of your own. Your health, my dear. You look younger than ever.'

'Happy days,' Amy said. Mr Chalfont winced. She fingered her mink coat. 'But you know – I've retired.'

'Ah, lost money, eh,' Mr Chalfont said. 'Dear lady, I've suffered in that way too. We must console each other a little. I suppose business is bad. Your husband – I seem to recall a trying man who did his best to interfere with our idyll. It was quite an idyll, wasn't it, those evenings in Curzon Street?'

'You've got it wrong, dear. I never was in Curzon Street. But if you date back to the time I tried that husband racket, why that goes years back, to the mews off Bond Street. Fancy your remembering. It was wrong of me. I can see that now. And it never really worked. I don't think he looked like a husband. But now I've retired. Oh, no,' she said, leaning forward until he could smell the brandy on her plump little lips, 'I haven't lost money; I've made it.'

'You're lucky,' Mr Chalfont said.

'It was all the Jubilee,' Amy explained.

'I was confined to my bed during the Jubilee,' Mr Chalfont said. 'I understand it all went off very well.'

'It was lovely,' Amy said. 'Why, I said to myself, everyone ought to do something to make it a success. So I cleaned up the streets.'

'I don't quite understand,' Mr Chalfont said. 'You mean the decorations?'

'No, no,' Amy said, 'that wasn't it at all. But it didn't seem to me nice, when all these Colonials were in London, for them to see the girls in Bond Street and Wardour Street and all over the place. I'm proud of London, and it didn't seem right to me that we should get a reputation.'

'People must live.'

'Of course they must live. Wasn't I in the business myself, dear?'

'Oh,' Mr Chalfont said, 'you were in the business?' It was quite a shock to him; he looked quickly this way and that, fearing that he might have been observed.

'So you see I opened a House and split with the girls. I took all the risk, and then of course I had my other expenses. I had to advertise.'

'How did you – how did you get it known?' He couldn't help having a kind of professional interest.

'Easy, dear. I opened a tourist bureau. Trips to the London underworld. Limehouse and all that. But there was always an old fellow who wanted the guide to show him something privately afterwards.'

'Very ingenious,' Mr Chalfont said.

'And loyal too, dear. It cleaned up the streets properly. Though of course I only took the best. I was very select. Some of them jibbed, because they said they did all the work, but as I said to them, it was My Idea.'

'So now you're retired?'

'I made five thousand pounds, dear. It was really my jubilee as well, though you mightn't think it to look at me. I always had the makings of a business woman, and I saw, you see, how I could extend the business. I opened at Brighton too. I cleaned up England in a way of speaking. It was ever so much nicer for the Colonials. There's been a lot of money in the country these last weeks. Have another sherry, dear, you are looking poorly.'

'Really, really you know I ought to be going.'

'Oh, come on. It's Jubilee, isn't it? Celebrate. Be a sport.'

'I think I see a friend.'

He looked helplessly around: a friend: he couldn't even think of a friend's name. He wilted before a personality stronger than his own. She bloomed there like a great dressy autumn flower. He felt old: my jubilee. His frayed cuffs showed; he had forgotten to arrange his hand. He said, 'Perhaps. Just one. It ought really to be on me,' and as he watched her bang for the waiter in the dim genteel place and dominate his disapproval when he came, Mr Chalfont couldn't help wondering at the unfairness of her confidence and her health. He had a touch of neuritis, but she was carnival; she really seemed to belong to the banners and drinks and plumes and processions. He said quite humbly, 'I should like to have seen the procession, but I wasn't up to it. My rheumatism,' he excused himself. His little withered sense of good taste could not stand the bright plebeian spontaneity. He was a fine dancer, but they'd have outdanced him on the pavements; he made love attractively in his formal well-bred way, but they'd have outloved him, blind and drunk and crazy and happy in the park. He had known that he would be out of place, he'd kept away; but it was humiliating to realize that Amy had missed nothing.

'You look properly done, dear,' Amy said. 'Let me lend you a couple of quid.'

'No, no,' Mr Chalfont said. 'Really I couldn't.'

'I expect you've given me plenty in your time.'

But had he? He couldn't remember her; it was such a long time since he'd been with a woman except in the way of business. He said, 'I couldn't. I really couldn't.' He tried to explain his attitude while she fumbled in her bag.

'I never take money – except, you know, from friends,' he admitted desperately, 'or except in business.' But he couldn't take his eyes away. He was broke and it was cruel of her to show him a five-pound note. 'No. Really.' It was a long time since his market price had been as high as five pounds.

'I know how it is, dear,' Amy said, 'I've been in the business myself, and I know just how you feel. Sometimes a gentleman would come home with me, give me a quid and run away as if he was scared. It was insulting. I never did like taking money for nothing.'

'But you're quite wrong,' Mr Chalfont said. 'That's not it at all. Not it at all.'

'Why, I could tell almost as soon as you spoke to me. You don't need to keep up pretences with me, dear,' Amy went inexorably on, while Mayfair faded from his manner, until there remained only the bed-sitting-room, the ham rolls, the iron heating on the stove. 'You don't need to be proud. But if you'd rather (it's all the same to me, it doesn't mean a thing to me) we'll go home, and let you do your stuff. It's all the same to me, dear, but if you'd rather – I know how you feel,' and presently they went out together arm-in-arm into the decorated desolate street.

'Cheer up, dear,' Amy said, as the wind picked up the ribbons and tore them from the poles and lifted the dust and made the banners flap, 'a girl likes a cheerful face.' And suddenly she became raucous and merry, slapping Mr Chalfont on his back, pinching his arm, saying, 'Let's have a little Jubilee spirit, dear,' taking her revenge for a world of uncongenial partners on old Mr Chalfont. You couldn't call him anything else now but old Mr Chalfont.

HUGH MACDIARMID (1892–1978)

Born Christopher Murray Grieve, MacDiarmid wrote in both Scots and English and was a central figure in the revival of Scots as a modern literary language. A nationalist, he was a founder member of the Scottish National Party, though he subsequently joined the Communist Party.

My Quarrel with England

And let me pit in guid set terms
My quarrel wi' th'owre sonsy rose,
That roond about its devotees
A fair fat cast o' aureole throws
5   That blinds them, in its mirlygoes,
To the necessity o' foes.

Upon their King and system I
Glower as on things that whiles in pairt
I may admire (at least for them),
10   But wi' nae claim upon my hert,
While a' their pleasure and their pride

Ootside me lies – and there maun bide.
Ootside me lies – and mair than that,
For I stand still for forces which
15   Were subjugated to mak' way
For England's poo'er, and to enrich
The kinds o' English, and o' Scots,
The least congenial to my thoughts

Hauf his soul a Scot maun use
20   Indulgin' in illusions,
And hauf in gettin' rid o' them
And comin' to conclusions
Wi' the demoralisin' dearth
O' onything worth while on Earth. . . .

Why I Became a Scottish Nationalist

Gi'e me Scots-room in life and love
And set me then my smeddum to prove
In scenes like these. Like Pushkin I
My time for flichty conquests by,
5   Valuing nae mair some quick-fire cratur'
Wha hurries up the ways o' natur',
Am happy, when after lang and sair
Pursuit you yield yoursel' to me,
But wi' nae raptur, cauldly there,
10   Open but glowerin' callously,
Yet slow but surely heat until
You catch my flame against your will
And the mureburn tak's the hill.

At My Father's Grave

The sunlicht still on me, you row'd in clood,
We look upon each ither noo like hills
Across a valley. I'm nae mair your son.
It is my mind, nae son o yours, that looks,
5   And the great darkness o' your death comes up
And equals it across the way.
A livin' man upon a deid man thinks
And ony sma'er thocht's impossible.

LOUIS MACNEICE (1907–1963)

Born in Northern Ireland, MacNeice spent most of his life in England, and Ireland's and England's often conflicting cultures can be readily witnessed in his work. He taught Classics for a time, but in 1941 joined the BBC where he created a distinctive radio drama. Like many poets of the 'Auden Generation', MacNeice supported left-wing causes, notably Republican Spain, during the 1930s.

Belfast

The hard cold fire of the northerner
Frozen into his blood from the fire in his basalt
Glares from behind the mica of his eyes
And the salt carrion water brings him wealth.

5   Down there at the end of the melancholy lough
Against the lurid sky over the stained water
Where hammers clang murderously on the girders
Like crucifixes the gantries stand.

And in the marble stores rubber gloves like polyps
10   Cluster; celluloid, painted ware, glaring
Metal patents, parchment lampshades, harsh
Attempts at buyable beauty.

In the porch of the chapel before the garish Virgin
A shawled factory-woman as if shipwrecked there
15   Lies a bunch of limbs glimpsed in the cave of gloom
By us who walk in the street so buoyantly and glib.

Over which country of cowled and haunted faces
The sun goes down with a banging of Orange drums
While the male kind murders each its woman
20   To whose prayer for oblivion answers no Madonna.

Snow

The room was suddenly rich and the great bay-window was
Spawning snow and pink roses against it
Soundlessly collateral and incompatible:
World is suddener than we fancy it.

5   World is crazier and more of it than we think,
Incorrigibly plural. I peel and portion
A tangerine and spit the pips and feel
The drunkenness of things being various.

And the fire flames with a bubbling sound for world
10   Is more spiteful and gay than one supposes –

On the tongue on the eyes on the ears in the palms of one's
 hands –
There is more than glass between the snow and the huge roses.

Bagpipe Music

It's no go the merrygoround, it's no go the rickshaw,
All we want is a limousine and a ticket for the peepshow.
Their knickers are made of crêpe-de-chine, their shoes are made
 of python,
Their halls are lined with tiger rugs and their walls with heads of
 bison.

5 John MacDonald found a corpse, put it under the sofa,
Waited till it came to life and hit it with a poker,
Sold its eyes for souvenirs, sold its blood for whisky,
Kept its bones for dumb-bells to use when he was fifty.

It's no go the Yogi-Man, it's no go Blavatsky,
10 All we want is a bank balance and a bit of skirt in a taxi.

Annie MacDougall went to milk, caught her foot in the heather,
Woke to hear a dance record playing of Old Vienna.
It's no go your maidenheads, it's no go your culture,
All we want is a Dunlop tyre and the devil mend the puncture.

15 The Laird o' Phelps spent Hogmanay declaring he was sober,
Counted his feet to prove the fact and found he had one foot
 over.
Mrs. Carmichael had her fifth, looked at the job with repulsion,
Said to the midwife 'Take it away; I'm through with over-
 production'.

It's no go the gossip column, it's no go the Ceilidh,
20 All we want is a mother's help and a sugar-stick for the baby.

Willie Murray cut his thumb, couldn't count the damage,
Took the hide of an Ayrshire cow and used it for a bandage.
His brother caught three hundred cran when the seas were
 lavish,
Threw the bleeders back in the sea and went upon the parish.

25 It's no go the Herring Board, it's no go the Bible,
All we want is a packet of fags when our hands are idle.
It's no go the picture palace, it's no go the stadium,
It's no go the country cot with a pot of pink geraniums,

---

9 **Yogi-Man; Blavatsky**: interest in theosophy and mysticism of Yeats and others of the Anglo-Irish elite, particularly as promoted by Mme Blvatsky. 15 **Hogmanay**: New Year. 19 **Ceilidh**: festival of Celtic singing and dancing. 28 **cot**: cottage.

It's no go the Government grants, it's no go the elections,
30   Sit on your arse for fifty years and hang your hat on a pension.

It's no go my honey love, it's no go my poppet;
Work your hands from day to day, the winds will blow the
        profit.
The glass is falling hour by hour, the glass will fall for ever,
But if you break the bloody glass you won't hold up the weather.

C. DAY LEWIS (1904–1972)

Like MacNeice, Cecil Day Lewis was of Anglo-Irish extraction, a Classicist, and a supporter of the Left during the 1930s. More influenced by Romanticism than MacNeice or Auden, his later career was principally as a translator, notably of Virgil. This lyric comes from his 1933 collection, *The Magnetic Mountain*.

[You that love England]

You that love England, who have an ear for her music,
The slow movement of clouds in benediction,
Clear arias of light thrilling over her uplands,
Over the chords of summer sustained peacefully;
5   Ceaseless the leaves' counterpoint in a west wind lively,
Blossom and river rippling loveliest allegro,
And the storms of wood strings brass at year's finale:
Listen. Can you not hear the entrance of a new theme?

You who go out alone, on tandem or on pillion,
10   Down arterial roads riding in April,
Or sad beside lakes where hill-slopes are reflected
Making fires of leaves, your high hopes fallen:
Cyclists and hikers in company, day excursionists,
Refugees from cursed towns and devastated areas;
15   Know you seek a new world, a saviour to establish
Long-lost kinship and restore the blood's fulfilment.

You who like peace, good sorts, happy in a small way
Watching; birds or playing cricket with schoolboys,
Who pay for drinks all round, whom disaster chose not;
20   Yet passing derelict mills and barns roof-rent
Where despair has burnt itself out– hearts at a standstill,
Who suffer loss, aware of lowered vitality;
We can tell you a secret, offer a tonic; only
Submit to the visiting angel, the strange new healer.

---

31 **poppet**: term of endearment.

25 You above all who have come to the far end, victims
    Of a run-down machine, who can bear it no longer;
    Whether in easy chairs chafing at impotence
    Or against hunger, bullies and spies preserving
    The nerve for action, the spark of indignation –
30 Need fight in the dark no more, you know your enemies.
    You shall be leaders when zero hour is signalled,
    Wielders of power and welders of a new world.

DYLAN THOMAS (1914–1953)

Born in Wales, Thomas spent his adulthood mostly in London. His individual, highly rhetorical, emotionally extravagant poetry was popular during his lifetime and he was much in demand as a reader. Although most frequently recalled as a lyrical, nostalgic writer about Wales, Thomas is also an interesting war poet.

Fern Hill

Now as I was young and easy under the apple boughs
About the lilting house and happy as the grass was green,
    The night above the dingle starry,
        Time let me hail and climb
5   Golden in the heydays of his eyes,
And honoured among wagons I was prince of the apple towns
And once below a time I lordly had the trees and leaves
        Trail with daisies and barley
    Down the rivers of the windfall light.

10 And as I was green and carefree, famous among the barns
About the happy yard and singing as the farm was home,
    In the sun that is young once only,
        Time let me play and be
        Golden in the mercy of his means,
15 And green and golden I was huntsman and herdsman, the calves
Sang to my horn, the foxes on the hills barked clear and cold,
        And the sabbath rang slowly
    In the pebbles of the holy streams.

All the sun long it was running, it was lovely, the hay
20 Fields high as the house, the tunes from the chimneys, it was air
        And playing, lovely and watery
            And fire green as grass.
        And nightly under the simple stars
As I rode to sleep the owls were bearing the farm away,

---

3 **dingle**: hollow.

25   All the moon long I heard, blessed among stables, the nightjars
        Flying with the ricks, and the horses
            Flashing into the dark.

        And then to awake, and the farm, like a wanderer white
        With the dew, come back, the cock on his shoulder: it was all
30   Shining, it was Adam and maiden,
            The sky gathered again
        And the sun grew round that very day.
        So it must have been after the birth of the simple light
        In the first, spinning place, the spellbound horses walking warm
35   Out of the whinnying green stable
            On to the fields of praise.

        And honoured among foxes and pheasants by the gay house
        Under the new made clouds and happy as the heart was long,
           In the sun born over and over
40   I ran my heedless ways,
           My wishes raced through the house high hay
        And nothing I cared, at my sky blue trades, that time allows
        In all his tuneful turning so few and such morning songs
           Before the children green and golden
45   Follow him out of grace,

        Nothing I cared, in the lamb white days, that time would take me
        Up to the swallow thronged loft by the shadow of my hand,
           In the moon that is always rising,
             Nor that riding to sleep
50   I should hear him fly with the high fields
        And wake to the farm forever fled from the childless land.
        Oh as I was young and easy in the mercy of his means,
           Time held me green and dying
        Though I sang in my chains like the sea.

A Refusal to Mourn the Death, by Fire, of a Child in London

        Never until the mankind making
        Bird beast and flower
        Fathering and all humbling darkness
        Tells with silence the last light breaking
5   And the still hour
        Is come of the sea tumbling in harness

        And I must enter again the round
        Zion of the water bead
        And the synagogue of the ear of corn
10   Shall I let pray the shadow of a sound

Or sow my salt seed
In the least valley of sackcloth to mourn

The majesty and burning of the child's death.
I shall not murder
15   The mankind of her going with a grave truth
Nor blaspheme down the stations of the breath
With any further
Elegy of innocence and youth.

Deep with the first dead lies London's daughter,
20   Robed in the long friends,
The grains beyond age, the dark veins of her mother,
Secret by the unmourning water
Of the riding Thames.
After the first death, there is no other.

EVELYN WAUGH (1902–1966)

Waugh emerged as a leading satirical novelist in the 1930s, exposing with bitter irony a Britain he believed in social and moral decline. Like Graham Greene, a Catholic convert, his postwar fiction, notably *Brideshead Revisited*, explores the maintenance of civilised decency, personal integrity and spiritual growth in an increasingly ugly world. This was also the case with the three novels written in the 1950s which make up the *Sword of Honour* trilogy, of which *Unconditional Surrender* is the last. Loosely based on Waugh's own wartime experiences, the novels follow the attempts of the Catholic aristocrat Guy Crouchback to keep some code of honour in the, often comic, insanity of the Second World War. In the following excerpt, a military mission has been sent to German-held Yugoslavia, where Guy is based. It includes his correspondent friend Ian, the war photographer Sneiffel, and various important military men, including the eccentric British General, Ritchie-Hook.

From Unconditional Surrender

The aeroplane flew high over the Adriatic and the lightless enemy-held coast of Dalmatia. All the passengers were sleeping when at last the little lights went up and the American General who had been travelling in the cockpit returned to his place in the tail saying: 'All right, fellows. We're there.' Everyone began groping for equipment. The photographer next to Ian tenderly nursed his camera. Ian heard the change of speed in the engines and felt the rapid descent, the list as they banked, then straightened for the run-in. Then unexpectedly the engines burst up in full throat; the machine suddenly rose precipitously, throwing the passengers hard back in their seats – then as suddenly dived, throwing them violently forward. The last thing Ian heard was a yelp of alarm from Sneiffel. Then a great door slammed in his mind.

He was standing in the open beside a fire. London, he thought; Turtle's Club going up in flames. But why was maize growing in St James's Street? Other figures were moving around him, unrecognizable against the fierce light. One seemed familiar. 'Loot,' he said, 'what are you doing here?' and then added: 'Job says the gutters are running with wine.'

Always polite Lieutenant Padfield said: 'Is that so?'

A more distinctly American, more authoritative voice was shouting: 'Is everyone out?'

Another familiar figure came close to him. A single eye glittered terribly in the flames. 'You there,' said Ritchie-Hook, 'were you driving that thing?'

As though coming round from gas in the dentist's chair Ian saw that 'that thing' was an aeroplane, shorn of its under-carriage, part buried in the great furrow it had ploughed for itself, burning furiously in the bows, with flames trickling back along the fuselage like the wines of Turtle's. Ian remembered he had left Bari in an aeroplane and that he had been bound for Jugoslavia.

Then he was aware of the gaunt figure confronting him and of a single eye which caught the blaze. 'Are you the pilot?' demanded Ritchie-Hook. 'Pure bad driving. Why can't you look where you're going?' The concussion which had dazed his companions had momentarily awakened Ritchie-Hook. 'You're under arrest,' he roared above the sound of the fire.

'Who's missing?' demanded the American General.

Ian then saw a man leave the group and trot to the pyre and deliberately climb back through the escape-hatch.

'What the devil does that idiot think he's doing?' cried Ritchie-Hook. 'Come back. You're under arrest.'

Ian's senses were clearer now. He still seemed to be in a dream but in a very vivid one. 'It's like the croquet match in *Alice in Wonderland*,' he heard himself say to Lieutenant Padfield.

'That's a very, very gallant act,' said the Lieutenant.

The figure emerged again in the aperture, jumped, and dragged out behind him not, as first appeared, an insensible fellow passenger but, it transpired, a bulky cylindrical object; he staggered clear with it and then proceeded to roll on the ground.

'Good God, it's Dawkins,' said Ritchie-Hook. 'What the devil are you doing?'

'Trousers on fire, sir,' said Dawkins. 'Permission to take them off, sir?' Without waiting for orders he did so, pulling them down, then with difficulty unfastening his anklets and kicking the smouldering garment clear of his burden. He stood thus in shirt, tunic, and boots gazing curiously at his bare legs. 'Fair roasted,' he said.

The American General asked: 'Were there any men left inside?'

'Yes, sir. I think there was, sir. They didn't look like moving. Too hot to stay and talk. Had to get the General's valise out.'

'Are you hurt.'

'Yes, sir. I think so, sir. But I don't seem to feel it.'

'Shock,' said the General. 'You will later.'

The flames had now taken hold of the tail. 'No one is to attempt any further rescue operations.' No one had shown any inclination to do so. 'Who's missing?' he said to his aide. 'Count and find out.'

'I don't see Almeric,' said Lieutenant Padfield.

'How did any of us get out?' Ian asked.

'The General, our General Spitz. He got both the hatches open before anyone else moved.'

'Something to be said for technological training.'

Gilpin was loudly complaining of burned fingers. No one heeded him. The little group was behaving in an orderly, mechanical manner. They spoke at random and did not listen. Each seemed alone, isolated by his recent shock. Someone said: 'I wonder where the hell we are.' No one answered. Ritchie-Hook said to Ian: 'You are not in any way responsible for that intolerable exhibition of incompetence?'

'I'm a press-officer, sir.'

'Oh, I thought you were the pilot. You need not consider yourself under arrest. But be careful in future. This is the second time this has happened to me. They tried it on before in Africa.'

The two generals stood side by side. 'Neat trick of yours that,' Ritchie-Hook conceded, 'getting the door open. I was slow off the mark. Didn't really know what was happening for a moment. Might have been in there still.'

The aide came to report to General Spitz: 'All the crew are missing.'

'Ha,' said Ritchie-Hook. 'The dog it was that died.'

'And six from the rest of the party. I'm afraid Sneiffel is one of them.'

'Too bad, too bad,' said General Spitz; 'he was a fine boy.'

'And the civilian musician.'

'Too bad.'

'And the French liaison officer.'

General Spitz was not listening to the casualty list. An epoch seemed to have passed since the disaster. General Spitz looked at his watch. 'Eight minutes,' he said. 'Someone ought to be here soon.'

The place where the aeroplane had fallen was pasture. The maize field lay astern of it, tall, ripe for reaping, glowing golden in the firelight. These stalks now parted and through them came running the first of the reception party from the airfield, partisans and the British Mission. There were greetings and anxious inquiries. Ian lost all interest in the scene. He found himself uncontrollably yawning and sat on the ground with his head on his knees while behind him the chatter of solicitude and translation faded to silence.

Another great space of time, two minutes by a watch, was broken by someone saying: 'Are you hurt?'

'I don't think so.'

'Can you walk?'

'I suppose so. I'd sooner stay here.'

'Come on, it's not far.'

Someone helped him to his feet. He noticed without surprise that it was Guy. Guy, he remembered, was an inhabitant of this strange land. There was something he ought to say to Guy. It came to him. 'Very sorry about Virginia,' he said.

'Thank you. Have you got any belongings?'

'Burned. Damn fool thing to have happened. I never trusted the Air Force ever since they accepted me. Must be something wrong with people who'd accept me.'

'Are you sure nothing hit you on the head in that crash?' said Guy.

'Not sure. I think I'm just sleepy.'

A partisan doctor went round the survivors. No one except Halberdier Dawkins and Gilpin had any visible injuries; the doctor made light of Gilpin's burnt fingers. Dawkins was suffering from surface burns which had rapidly swelled into enormous blisters covering his legs and thighs. He prodded them with detached curiosity. 'It's a rum go,' he said; 'spill a kettle on your toe and you're fair dancing. Boil you in oil like a heathen and you don't feel a thing.'

The doctor gave him morphia and two partisan girls bore him off on a stretcher.

The unsteady little procession followed the path the rescuers had trodden through the maize. The flames cast deep shadows before their feet. At the edge of the field grew a big chestnut. 'Do you see what I see?' said Ian. Something like a monkey was perched in the branches gibbering at them. It was Sneiffel with his camera.

'Lovely pictures,' he said. 'Sensational if they come out.'

When Ian woke next morning it was as though from a debauch; all the symptoms of alcoholic hangover, such as he had not experienced since adolescence, overwhelmed him. As in those days, he had no memory of going to bed. As in those days, he received an early call from the man who had put him there.

'How are you?' asked Guy.

'Awful.'

'There's a doctor going the rounds. Do you want to see him?'

'No.'

'Do you want any breakfast?'

'No.'

He was left alone. The room was shuttered. The only light came in narrow strips between the hinges. Outside poultry was cackling. Ian lay still. The door opened again; someone stamped into the room and opened shutters and windows revealing herself, in the brief moment before Ian shut his eyes and turned them from the light, as a female in man's uniform, wearing a red cross brassard and carrying a box of objects which clinked and rattled. She began stripping Ian of his blanket and pulling at his arm.

'What the devil are you doing?'

The woman flourished a syringe.

'Get out,' cried Ian.

She jabbed at him. He knocked the instrument from her hand. She called: 'Bakic. Bakic,' and was joined by a man to whom she talked excitedly in a foreign tongue. 'She's de nurse,' said Bakic. 'She's got an injection for you.'

'What on earth for?'

'She says tetanus. She says she always injects tetanus for everyone.'

'Tell her to get out.'

'She says are you frightened of a needle? She says partisans are never frightened.'

'Turn her out.'

So far as anything so feminine could be ascribed to this visitant, she exhibited pique. So far as it was possible to flounce in tight battle-dress, she flounced as she left her patient. Guy returned.

'I say I'm sorry about that. I've been keeping her out all the morning. She got through while I was with the General.'

'Did you put me to bed last night?'

'I helped. You seemed all right. In fact in fine form.'

'It's worn off,' said Ian.

'You'd just like to be left alone?'

'Yes.'

But it was not to be. He had closed his eyes and lapsed into a state approaching sleep when something not very heavy depressed his feet, as though a dog or a cat had landed there. He looked and saw Sneiffel.

'Well, well, well, so you're a newspaper man? My, but you've got a story. I've been down to the wreck. It's still too hot to get near it. They reckon there's five stiffs in there besides the crew. Lieutenant Padfield is het up about some British musician he's lost. What the Hell? There isn't going to be any concert now. So what? There'll be an elegant funeral when they get the bodies out. Everyone seems kinda het up today. Not me though. Maybe it's being light I don't shock so easy. The partisans were for putting off the battle but General Spitz works to a schedule. He's got to have the battle on the day it was planned and then get out his report and I've got to have the pictures to go with it. So the battle's tomorrow as per schedule. What say you come round with me and talk to some of these partisans? I've got the General's interpreter. He's not feeling too bright this morning but I reckon he can still hear and speak.'

So Ian gingerly set foot to the floor, dressed and began his work as a war correspondent.

No one could give a technical explanation of the night's mishap. Guy had stood at his usual post on the edge of the airfield. He had heard the Squadron Leader talking his peculiar jargon into his wireless set, had seen the girls run from tar-barrel to barrel lighting the path for the incoming aeroplane, had watched it come down as he had watched many others, had seen it overrun its objective, rocket suddenly up like a driven pheasant and fall as though shot half a mile away. He had heard de Souza say: 'That's the end of them,' had seen the flames kindle and spread and then had seen one after another a few dark, unrecognizable, apparently quite lethargic figures emerge from the hatches and stand near the wreck. He had joined in the rush to the scene. After that he had been busy with his duties as host in getting the survivors to their beds and finding in the store replacements for their lost equipment.

The partisans were inured to disaster. They had a certain relish for it. They did not neglect to mention that this was an entirely Anglo-American failure, but they did so with a rare cordiality. They had never been convinced that the allies were taking the war seriously. This unsolicited burnt offering seemed in some way to appease them.

De Souza was very busy with his tear-off cipher-pads and it devolved on Guy to arrange the day of the newcomers. General Spitz's aide had been struck with a delayed stammer by his fall and complained of pains in his back. Gilpin now had both hands bandaged and useless. The two generals were the fittest of the party; General Spitz brisk and business-like, Ritchie-Hook reanimated. Guy had not seen him in his decline. He was now as he had always been in Guy's experience.

Halberdier Dawkins said: 'It's been a fair treat for the General. He's his old self. Come in this morning and gave me rocket for disobeying orders getting his gear out.'

Dawkins was a stretcher case, and after arduous years in Ritchie-Hook's service not sorry to be honourably at ease. He submitted without complaint to his tetanus injections and basked in the hospitality of the Mission sergeant who brought him whisky and cigarettes and gossip.

The former Minister of the Interior reluctantly cancelled the *Vin d'Honneur* and the concert but there were sociable meetings between the general staff and their guests, the observers, at which the plans for the little battle were discussed. It was after one of these that Ritchie-Hook took Guy aside and said: 'I'd like you to arrange for me to have a quiet talk with the fellow whose name ends in "itch".'

'All their names end like that, sir.'

'I mean the decent young fellow. They call him a brigadier. The fellow who's going to lead the assault.'

Guy identified him as a ferocious young Montenegran who had a certain affinity to Ritchie-Hook in that he, too, lacked an eye and a large part of one hand.

Guy arranged a meeting and left the two warriors with the Commissar's interpreter. Ritchie-Hook returned in high good humour. 'Rattling good fellow that Itch,' he said. 'No flannel or ormolu[1] about him. D'you suppose all his stories are true?'

'No, sir.'

'Nor do I. I pulled his leg a bit but I am not sure that interpreter quite twigged. Anyway, we had a perfectly foul drink together – *that* ended in Itch too – extraordinary language – and we parted friends. I've attached myself to him for tomorrow. Don't tell the others. Itch hasn't room for more than one tourist in his car. We're driving out tonight to make a recce[2] and get the men in place for the attack.'

'You know, sir,' Guy said, 'there's a certain amount of humbug about this attack. It's being laid on for General Spitz.'

'Don't try and teach your grandmother to suck eggs,' said Ritchie-Hook 'Of course I twigged all that from the word "go". Itch and I understand one another. It's a demonstration. Sort of thing we did in training. But we enjoyed that, didn't we?'

Guy thought of those long chilly exercises in 'biffing' at Southsands, Penkirk, and Hoy. 'Yes, sir,' he said, 'those were good days.'

'And between you and me I reckon it's the last chance I have of hearing a shot fired in anger. If there's any fun going, Itch will be in it.'

---

1 flannel; ormolu: prevarication; deceit, falsity.   2 recce: reconnaissance.

At eight next morning General Spitz, and his aide, the British Mission, the partisan general staff, Ian and Sneiffel assembled beside the line of miscell-aneous cars which the Jugoslavs had all the summer kept secreted, with so much else, in the forest. Guy made Ritchie-Hook's excuses to General Spitz who merely said: 'Well, there's plenty of us without him.'

The convoy set out through a terrain of rustic enchantment, as through a water-colour painting of the last century. Strings of brilliant peppers hung from the eaves of the cottages. The women at work in the fields sometimes waved a greeting, sometimes hid their faces. There was no visible difference between 'liberated' territory and that groaning under foreign oppression. Ian was unaware when they passed the vague frontier.

'It's like driving to a meet,' he said, 'when the horses have gone on ahead.'

In less than an hour they were in sight of the block-house. A place had been chosen 500 yards from it, well screened by foliage, where the observers could await events in comfort and safety. The partisans had moved out in the darkness and should have been in position surrounding their objective in the nearest cover.

'I'm going down to look for them,' said Sneiffel.

'I shall stay here,' said Ian. He was still feeling debauched by shock.

General Spitz studied the scene through very large binoculars. 'Blockhouse' had been a slightly deceptive term. What he saw was a very solid little fort built more than a century earlier, part of the defensive line of Christendom against the Turk. 'I appreciate now why they want air support,' said General Spitz. 'Can't see anyone moving. Anyway we've achieved surprise.'

'As a matter of fact,' said de Souza aside to Guy, 'things have not gone quite right. One of the brigades lost its way in the approach-march. They may turn up in time. Don't let on to our allies.'

'You'd think there would be more sign of life from a German post,' said General Spitz. 'Everyone seems asleep.'

'These are *domobrans*,' said the Commissar's interpreter. 'They are lazy people.'

'How's that again?'

'Fascist collaborators.'

'Oh. I got the idea in Bari we were going to fight Germans. I suppose it's all the same thing.'

The sun rose high but it was cool in the shade of the observation post. The air support was timed to begin at ten o'clock. That was to be the signal for the infantry to come into the open.

At half-past nine rifle-fire broke out below them. The partisan general looked vexed.

'What are they up to?' asked General Spitz.

A partisan runner was sent down to inquire. Before he returned the firing ceased. When he reported, the interpreter said to General Spitz, 'It is nothing, it was a mistake.'

'It's lost us surprise.'

De Souza, who had heard and understood the runner's report, said to Guy: 'That was the second brigade turning up. The first thought they were enemy and started pooping off. No one's been hit but, as our ally remarks, we have "lost surprise".'

There was no longer peace in the valley. For the next quarter of an hour occasional shots came, at random it seemed, some from the parapet of the block-house, some from the surrounding cover; then sharp at ten, just as on General Spitz's elaborate watch the minute hand touched its zenith, there came screaming out of the blue sky the two aeroplanes. They swooped down one behind the other. The first fired simultaneously two rockets which just missed their target and exploded in the woods beyond, where part of the attacking force was now grouped. The second shot straighter. Both his rockets landed square on the masonry, raising a cloud of flying rubble. Then the machines climbed and circled. Guy, remembering the dive-bombers in Crete relentlessly tracking and pounding the troops on the ground, waited for their return. Instead they dwindled from sight and hearing.

The airman who had been sent to observe them, stood near. 'Lovely job,' he said, 'right on time, right on target.'

'Is that all?' asked Guy.

'That's all. Now the soldiers can do some work.'

Silence had fallen in the valley. Everyone, friend and enemy alike, expected the return of the aeroplanes. The dust cleared revealing to those on the hillside equipped with binoculars two distinct patches of dilapidation in the massive walls of the block-house. Some of the partisans began discharging their weapons. None came into view. The Air Force observer began to explain to General Spitz the complexity of the task which he had seen successfully executed. The Commissar and the partisan General spoke earnestly and crossly in their own language. A runner from below came to report to them. 'It appears,' the interpreter explained to General Spitz, 'that the attack must be postponed. A German armoured column has been warned and is on its way here.'

'What do your men do about that?'

'Before a German armoured column they disperse. That is the secret of our great and many victories.'

'Well, uncle,' said de Souza to Guy, 'we had better begin thinking of luncheon for our visitors. They've seen all the sport we have to offer here.'

But he was wrong. Just as the observers were turning towards their cars, Ian said: 'Look.'

Two figures had emerged from the scrub near the block-house walls and were advancing across the open ground. Guy remembered the precept of his musketry instructor: 'At 200 yards all parts of the body are distinctly seen. At 300 the outline of the face is blurred. At 400 no face. At 600 the head is a dot and the body tapers.' He raised his binoculars and recognized the incongruous pair; the first was Ritchie-Hook. He was signalling fiercely, summoning to the advance the men behind him, who were already slinking away; he went forward at a slow and clumsy trot towards the place where the rocket-bombs had disturbed the stones. He did not look back to see if he was being followed. He did not know that he was followed, by one man, Sneiffel, who like a terrier, like the pet dwarf privileged to tumble about the heels of a prince of the

Renaissance, was gambolling round him with his camera, crouching and skipping, so small and agile as to elude the snipers on the walls. A first bullet hit Ritchie-Hook when he was some 20 yards from the walls. He spun completely round, then fell forwards on his knees, rose again and limped slowly on. He was touching the walls, feeling for a handhold, when a volley from above caught him and flung him down dead. Sneiffel paused long enough to record his last posture, then bolted, and the defenders were so much surprised by the whole incident that they withheld their fire until he had plunged into the ranks of the retreating partisans.

The German patrol – not, as the partisan scouts had reported, an armoured column, but two scout cars summoned by telephone when the first shots were fired – arrived at the block-house to find the scars of the rocket and the body of Ritchie-Hook. They did not move from the road. A section of *domobrans* investigated the wood where the first aeroplane had misplaced its missiles. They found some smouldering timber and the bodies of four partisans. A puzzled German captain composed his report of the incident which circulated through appropriate files of the Intelligence Service attracting incredulous minutes as long as the Balkan branch continued to function. The single-handed attack on a fortified position by a British major-general, attended in one account by a small boy, in another by a midget, had no precedent in Clausewitz. There must be some deep underlying motive, German Intelligence agreed, which was obscure to them. Perhaps the body was not really Ritchie-Hook's – they had his full biography – but that of a sacrificial victim. Ritchie-Hook was being preserved for some secret enterprise. Warning orders were issued throughout the whole 'Fortress of Europe' to be vigilant for one-eyed men.

PHILIP LARKIN (1922–1985)

Larkin published two novels in the 1940s after leaving Oxford but it is as a poet that he is rightly best known. His work captures the often unexpected preoccupations of middle-England after the war, jazz and sex lying just under the fatigued propriety of provincial gentility. Larkin often figures himself as the outsider, and his work indicates the social accommodations and divisions of contemporary Britain.

For Sidney Bechet

That note you hold, narrowing and rising, shakes
Like New Orleans reflected on the water,
And in all ears appropriate falsehood wakes,

Building for some a legendary Quarter
5   Of balconies, flower-baskets and quadrilles,
Everyone making love and going shares –
Oh, play that thing! Mute glorious Storyvilles

Sidney Bechet: famous jazz trumpeter.   4 **Quarter:** The French Quarter in New Orleans.

Others may license, grouping round their chairs
Sporting-house girls like circus tigers (priced

10   Far above rubies) to pretend their fads,
While scholars *manqués* nod around unnoticed
Wrapped up in personnels like old plaids.

On me your voice falls as they say love should,
Like an enormous yes. My Crescent City
15   Is where your speech alone is understood,

And greeted as the natural noise of good,
Scattering long-haired grief and scored pity.

Church Going

Once I am sure there's nothing going on
I step inside, letting the door thud shut.
Another church: matting, seats, and stone,
And little books; sprawlings of flowers, cut
5   For Sunday, brownish now; some brass and stuff
Up at the holy end; the small neat organ;
And a tense, musty, unignorable silence,
Brewed God knows how long. Hatless, I take off
My cycle-clips in awkward reverence,

10   Move forward, run my hand around the font.
From where I stand, the roof looks almost new –
Cleaned, or restored? Someone would know: I don't.
Mounting the lectern, I peruse a few
Hectoring large-scale verses, and pronounce
15   'Here endeth' much more loudly than I'd meant.
The echoes snigger briefly. Back at the door
I sign the book, donate an Irish sixpence,
Reflect the place was not worth stopping for.

Yet stop I did: in fact I often do,
20   And always end much at a loss like this,
Wondering what to look for; wondering, too,
When churches fall completely out of use
What we shall turn them into, if we shall keep
A few cathedrals chronically on show,
25   Their parchment, plate and pyx in locked cases,
And let the rest rent-free to rain and sheep.
Shall we avoid them as unlucky places?

Or, after dark, will dubious women come
To make their children touch a particular stone;

---

25 pyx: case containing the Holy Sacrament.

30   Pick simples for a cancer; or on some
       Advised night see walking a dead one?
       Power of some sort or other will go on
       In games, in riddles, seemingly at random;
       But superstition, like belief, must die,
35   And what remains when disbelief has gone?
       Grass, weedy pavement, brambles, buttress, sky,

       A shape less recognisable each week,
       A purpose more obscure. I wonder who
       Will be the last, the very last, to seek
40   This place for what it was; one of the crew
       That tap and jot and know what rood-lofts were?
       Some ruin-bibber, randy for antique,
       Or Christmas-addict, counting on a whiff
       Of gown-and-bands and organ-pipes and myrrh?
45   Or will he be my representative,

       Bored, uninformed, knowing the ghostly silt
       Dispersed, yet tending to this cross of ground
       Through suburb scrub because it held unspilt
       So long and equably what since is found
50   Only in separation – marriage, and birth,
       And death, and thoughts of these – for which was built
       This special shell? For, though I've no idea
       What this accoutred frowsty barn is worth,
       It pleases me to stand in silence here;

55   A serious house on serious earth it is,
       In whose blent air all our compulsions meet,
       Are recognised, and robed as destinies.
       And that much never can be obsolete,
       Since someone will forever be surprising
60   A hunger in himself to be more serious,
       And gravitating with it to this ground,
       Which, he once heard, was proper to grow wise in,
       If only that so many dead lie round.

The Whitsun Weddings

       That Whitsun, I was late getting away:
         Not till about
       One-twenty on the sunlit Saturday
       Did my three-quarters-empty train pull out,
5   All windows down, all cushions hot, all sense

---

30 simples: medicines composed of single element, often a herb. **53 frowsty:** stale smelling, musty.   **Whitsun:** Whitsuntide; the days surrounding the seventh Sunday after Easter.

Of being in a hurry gone. We ran
Behind the backs of houses, crossed a street
Of blinding windscreens, smelt the fish-dock; thence
The river's level drifting breadth began,
10 Where sky and Lincolnshire and water meet.

All afternoon, through the tall heat that slept
　　For miles inland,
A slow and stopping curve southwards we kept.
Wide farms went by, short-shadowed cattle, and
15 Canals with floatings of industrial froth;
A hothouse flashed uniquely: hedges dipped
And rose: and now and then a smell of grass
Displaced the reek of buttoned carriage-cloth
Until the next town, new and nondescript,
20 Approached with acres of dismantled cars.

At first, I didn't notice what a noise
　　The weddings made
Each station that we stopped at: sun destroys
The interest of what's happening in the shade,
25 And down the long cool platforms whoops and skirls
I took for porters larking with the mails,
And went on reading. Once we started, though,
We passed them, grinning and pomaded, girls
In parodies of fashion, heels and veils,
30 All posed irresolutely, watching us go,

As if out on the end of an event
　　Waving goodbye
To something that survived it. Struck, I leant
More promptly out next time, more curiously,
35 And saw it all again in different terms:
The fathers with broad belts under their suits
And seamy foreheads; mothers loud and fat;
An uncle shouting smut; and then the perms,
The nylon gloves and jewellery-substitutes,
40 The lemons, mauves, and olive-ochres that

Marked off the girls unreally from the rest.
　　Yes, from cafes
And banquet-halls up yards, and bunting-dressed
Coach-party annexes, the wedding-days
45 Were coming to an end. All down the line
Fresh couples climbed aboard: the rest stood round;
The last confetti and advice were thrown,
And, as we moved, each face seemed to define

---

25 skirls: shrill scream.　　　　　**28 pomaded:** scented.

Just what it saw departing: children frowned
50   At something dull; fathers had never known

Success so huge and wholly farcical;
    The women shared
The secret like a happy funeral;
    While girls, gripping their handbags tighter, stared
55   At a religious wounding. Free at last,
And loaded with the sum of all they saw,
We hurried towards London, shuffling gouts of steam.
Now fields were building-plots, and poplars cast
Long shadows over major roads, and for
60   Some fifty minutes, that in time would seem

Just long enough to settle hats and say
    I nearly died,
A dozen marriages got under way.
They watched the landscape, sitting side by side
65   – An Odeon went past, a cooling tower,
And someone running up to bowl – and none
Thought of the others they would never meet
Or how their lives would all contain this hour.
I thought of London spread out in the sun,
70   Its postal districts packed like squares of wheat:

There we were aimed. And as we raced across
    Bright knots of rail
Past standing Pullmans, walls of blackened moss
Came close, and it was nearly done, this frail
75   Travelling coincidence; and what it held
Stood ready to be loosed with all the power
That being changed can give. We slowed again,
And as the tightened brakes took hold, there swelled
A sense of falling, like an arrow-shower
80   Sent out of sight, somewhere becoming rain.

Annus Mirabilis

Sexual intercourse began
In nineteen sixty-three
(Which was rather late for me) –
Between the end of the *Chatterley* ban
5   And the Beatles' first LP.

Up till then there'd only been
A sort of bargaining,

Annus Mirabilis: Miraculous year.

4 *Chatterley* ban: D.H. Lawrence's *Lady Chatterley's Lover* was banned as an obscene publication for many years.

A wrangle for a ring,
A shame that started at sixteen
10 And spread to everything.

Then all at once the quarrel sank:
Everyone felt the same,
And every life became
A brilliant breaking of the bank,
15 A quite unlosable game.

So life was never better than
In nineteen sixty-three
(Though just too late for me) –
Between the end of the *Chatterley* ban
20 And the Beatles' first LP.

TED HUGHES (1930–)

Ted Hughes was raised in West Yorkshire and his poetry shows a strong affinity for its dialect, one which he felt reached back to Middle English traditions. Hughes' poetry of the 1950s and 1960s is marked by a strong elemental feeling and he often uses the perspective of animals in articulating a physical, frequently violent, lyric expression.

The Horses

I climbed through woods in the hour-before-dawn dark.
Evil air, a frost-making stillness,

Not a leaf, not a bird, –
A world cast in frost. I came out above the wood

5 Where my breath left tortuous statues in the iron light.
But the valleys were draining the darkness

Till the moorline – blackening dregs of the brightening grey
Halved the sky ahead. And I saw the horses:

Huge in the dense grey – ten together
10 Megalith-still. They breathed, making no move,

With draped manes and tilted hind-hooves,
Making no sound.

I passed: not one snorted or jerked its head.
Grey silent fragments

15 Of a grey silent world.

---

10 **Megalith:** a great stone usually used in the construction of ancient monuments such as Stonehenge.

I listened in emptiness on the moor-ridge.
The curlew's tear turned its edge on the silence.

Slowly detail leafed from the darkness. Then the sun
Orange, red, red erupted.

20   Silently, and splitting to its core tore and flung cloud,
Shook the gulf open, showed blue,

And the big planets hanging –
I turned

Stumbling in the fever of a dream, down towards
25   The dark woods, from the kindling tops,

And came to the horses.
                              There, still they stood,
But now steaming and glistening under the flow of light,

Their draped stone manes, their tilted hind-hooves
Stirring under a thaw while all around them

30   The frost showed its fires. But still they made no sound.
Not one snorted or stamped,

Their hung heads patient as the horizons
High over valleys, in the red levelling rays

In din of the crowded streets, going among the years, the faces,
35   May I still meet my memory in so lonely a place

Between the streams and the red clouds, hearing curlews,
Hearing the horizons endure.

The Howling of Wolves

Is without world.

What are they dragging up and out on their long leashes of
        sound
That dissolve in the mid-air silence?

Then crying of a baby, in this forest of starving silences,
5   Brings the wolves running.
Tuning of a viola, in this forest delicate as an owl's ear,
Brings the wolves running – brings the steel traps clashing and
        slavering,
The steel furred to keep it from cracking in the cold,
The eyes that never learn how it has come about
10   That they must live like this,

---

17 **curlew:** bird with sharp cry.

That they must live

Innocence crept into minerals.

The wind sweeps through and the hunched wolf shivers.
It howls you cannot say whether out of agony or joy.

15 The earth is under its tongue,
A dead weight of darkness, trying to see through its eyes.
The wolf is living for the earth.
But the wolf is small, it comprehends little.

It goes to and fro, trailing its haunches and whimpering horribly.

20 It must feed its fur.

The night snows stars and the earth creaks.

That Morning

We came where the salmon were so many
So steady, so spaced, so far-aimed
On their inner map, England could add

Only the sooty twilight of South Yorkshire
5 Hung with the drumming drift of Lancasters
Till the world had seemed capsizing slowly.

Solemn to stand there in the pollen light
Waist-deep in wild salmon swaying massed
As from the hand of God. There the body

10 Separated, golden and imperishable,
From its doubting thought – a spirit-beacon
Lit by the power of the salmon

That came on, came on, and kept on coming
As if we flew slowly, their formations
15 Lifting us toward some dazzle of blessing

One wrong thought might darken. As if the fallen
World and salmon were over. As if these
Were the imperishable fish

That had let the world pass away –

20 There, in a mauve light of drifted lupins,
They hung in the cupped hands of mountains

Made of tingling atoms. It had happened.
Then for a sign that we were where we were
Two gold bears came down and swam like men

---

5 Lancasters: British heavy bomber in Second World War.

25

Beside us. And dived like children.
And stood in deep water as on a throne
Eating pierced salmon off their talons.

So we found the end of our journey.

So we stood, alive in the river of light
30   Among the creatures of light, creatures of light.

HAROLD PINTER (1930–)

Pinter was one of the first British playwrights to learn from Samuel Beckett that silence is often more eloquent than speech and that language often acts as a mask, better at hiding than revealing characters' thoughts and identities. In plays written in the late 1950s, notably *The Birthday Party*, *The Caretaker* and *The Dumb Waiter*, Pinter mixed comic absurdity and menace, creating a strange but recognisable British landscape, often with ominous political undercurrents. *The Dumb Waiter* was first performed in 1960.

The Dumb Waiter

Cast: Ben, Gus.

Scene: A basement room. Two beds, flat against the back wall. A serving hatch, closed, between the beds. A door to the kitchen and lavatory, left. A door to a passage, right.

[*Ben is lying on a bed, left, reading a paper. Gus is sitting on a bed, right, tying his shoelaces, with difficulty. Both are dressed in shirts, trousers and braces.*
Silence.
Gus ties his laces, rises, yawns and begins to walk slowly to the door, left. He stops, looks down, and shakes his foot.
Ben lowers his paper and watches him. Gus kneels and unties his shoe-lace and slowly takes off the shoe. He looks inside it and brings out a flattened matchbox. He shakes it and examines it. Their eyes meet. Ben rattles his paper and reads. Gus puts the matchbox in his pocket and bends down to put on his shoe. He ties his lace, with difficulty. Ben lowers his paper and watches him. Gus walks to the door, left, stops, and shakes the other foot. He kneels, unties his shoe-lace, and slowly takes off the shoe. He looks inside it and brings out a flattened cigarette packet. He shakes it and examines it. Their eyes meet. Ben rattles his paper and reads. Gus puts the packet in his pocket, bends down, puts on his shoe and ties the lace.
He wanders off, left.
Ben slams the paper down on the bed and glares after him. He picks up the paper and lies on his back, reading.
Silence.
A lavatory chain is pulled twice off, left, but the lavatory does not flush.
Silence.

Gus re-enters, left, and halts at the door, scratching his head.
Ben slams down the paper.]

Ben Kaw!
[*He picks up the paper.*]
What about this? Listen to this!
[*He refers to the paper.*]
A man of eighty-seven wanted to cross the road. But there was a lot of traffic, see? He couldn't see how he was going to squeeze through. So he crawled under a lorry.
Gus He what?
Ben He crawled under a lorry. A stationary lorry.
Gus No?
Ben The lorry started and ran over him.
Gus Go on!
Ben That's what it says here.
Gus Get away.
Ben Its enough to make you want to puke, isn't it?
Gus Who advised him to do a thing like that?
Ben A man of eighty-seven crawling under a lorry!
Gus It's unbelievable.
Ben It's down here in black and white.
Gus Incredible.

[*Silence.*
Gus shakes his head and exits.
Ben lies back and reads. The lavatory chain is pulled once off left, but the lavatory does not flush.
Ben whistles at an item in the paper.
Gus re-enters.]
I want to ask you something.
Ben What are you doing out there?
Gus Well, I was just –
Ben What about the tea?
Gus I'm just going to make it.
Ben Well, go on, make it.
Gus Yes, I will. [*He sits in a chair. Ruminatively*] He's laid on some very nice crockery this time, I'll say that. It's sort of striped. There's a white stripe.
[*Ben reads.*]
It's very nice. I'll say that.
[*Ben turns the page.*]
You know, sort of round the cup. Round the rim. All the rest of it's black, you see. Then the saucer's black, except for right in the middle, where the cup goes, where it's white.
[*Ben reads.*]
Then the plates are the same, you see. Only they've got a black stripe – the plates – right across the middle. Yes, I'm quite taken with the crockery.

Ben [*still reading*] What do you want plates for? You're not going to eat.
Gus I've brought a few biscuits.
Ben Well, you'd better eat them quick.
Gus I always bring a few biscuits. Or a pie. You know I can't drink tea without anything to eat.
Ben Well, make the tea then, will you? Time's getting on.
[*Gus brings out the flattened cigarette packet and examines it.*]
Gus You got any cigarettes? I think I've run out.
[*He throws the packet high up and leans forward to catch it.*]
I hope it won't be a long job, this one.
[*Aiming carefully, he flips the packet under his bed.*]
Oh, I wanted to ask you something.
Ben [*slamming his paper down*] Kaw!
Gus What's that?
Ben A child of eight killed a cat
Gus Get away.
Ben It's a fact. What about that, eh? A child of eight killing a cat!
Gus How did he do it?
Ben It was a girl.
Gus How did she do it?
Ben She –
[*He picks up the paper and studies it.*]
It doesn't say.
Gus Why not?
Ben Wait a minute. It just says her brother, aged eleven, viewed the incident from the toolshed.
Gus Go on!
Ben That's bloody ridiculous.
[*Pause.*]
Gus I bet he did it.
Ben Who?
Gus The brother.
Ben I think you're right.
[*Pause.*]
[*Slamming down the paper.*] What about that, eh? A kid of eleven killing a cat and blaming it on his little sister of eight! It's enough to –
[*He breaks off in disgust and seizes the paper. Gus rises.*]
Gus What time is he getting in touch?
[*Ben reads.*]
What time is he getting in touch?
Ben What's the matter with you? It could be any time. Any time.
Gus [*moves to the foot of Ben's bed*] Well, I was going to ask you something.
Ben What?
Gus Have you noticed the time that tank takes to fill?
Ben What tank?
Gus In the lavatory.

Ben No. Does it?

Gus Terrible.

Ben Well, what about it?

Gus What do you think's the matter with it?

Ben Nothing.

Gus Nothing?

Ben It's got a deficient ballcock, that's all.

Gus A deficient what?

Ben Ballcock.

Gus No? Really?

Ben That's what I should say.

Gus Go on! That didn't occur to me.

[*Gus wanders to his bed and presses the mattress.*]

I didn't have a very restful sleep today, did you? It's not much of a bed. I could have done with another blanket too. [*He catches sight of a picture on the wall.*] Hello, what's this? [*Peering at it*] 'The First Eleven.' Cricketers. You seen this, Ben?

Ben [*reading*] What?

Gus The first eleven.

Ben What?

Gus There's a photo here of the first eleven.

Ben What first eleven?

Gus [*studying the photo*] It doesn't say.

Ben What about that tea?

Gus They all look a bit old to me.

[*Gus wanders downstage, looks out front, then all about the room.*]

I wouldn't like to live in this dump. I wouldn't mind if you had a window, you could see what it looked like outside.

Ben What do you want a window for?

Gus Well, I like to have a bit of a view, *Ben*. It whiles away the time.

[*He walks about the room.*]

I mean, you come into a place when it's still dark, you come into a room you've never seen before, you sleep all day, you do your job, and then you go away in the night again.

[*Pause.*]

I like to get a look at the scenery. You never get the chance in this job.

Ben You get your holidays, don't you?

Gus Only a fortnight.

Ben [*lowering the paper*] You kill me. Anyone would think you're working every day. How often do we do a job? Once a week? What are you complaining about?

Gus Yes, but we've got to be on tap though, haven't we? You can't move out of the house in case a call comes.

Ben You know what your trouble is?

Gus What?

Ben You haven't got any interests.

Gus I've got interests.
Ben What? Tell me one of your interests.
[*Pause.*]
Gus I've got interests.
Ben Look at me. What have I got?
Gus I don't know. What?
Ben I've got my woodwork. I've got my model boats. Have you ever seen me idle? I'm never idle. I know how to occupy my time, to its best advantage. Then when a call comes, I'm ready.
Gus Don't you ever get a bit fed up?
Ben Fed up? What with?

[*Silence.*
Ben reads. Gus feels in the pocket of his jacket, which hangs on the bed.]
Gus You got any cigarettes? I've run out.
[*The lavatory flushes off left.*]
There she goes.
[*Gus sits on his bed.*]
No, I mean, I say the crockery's good. It is. It's very nice. But that's about all I can say for this place. It's worse than the last one. Remember that last place we were in? Last time, where was it? At least there was a wireless there. No, honest. He doesn't seem to bother much about our comfort these days.
Ben When are you going to stop jabbering?
Gus You'd get rheumatism in a place like this, if you stay long.
Ben We're not staying long. Make the tea, will you? We'll be on the job in a minute.
[*Gus picks up a small bag by his bed and brings out a packet of tea. He examines it and looks up.*]
Gus Eh, I've been meaning to ask you.
Ben What the hell is it now?
Gus Why did you stop the car this morning, in the middle of that road?
Ben [*lowering the paper*] I thought you were asleep.
Gus I was, but I woke up when you stopped. You did stop, didn't you?
[*Pause.*]
In the middle of that road. It was still dark, don't you remember? I looked out. It was all misty. I thought perhaps you wanted to kip,[1] but you were sitting up dead straight, like you were waiting for something.
Ben I wasn't waiting for anything.
Gus I must have fallen asleep again. What was all that about then? Why did you stop?
Ben [*picking up the paper*] We were too early.
Gus Early? [*He rises*] What do you mean? We got the call, didn't we, saying we were to start right away. We did. We shoved out on the dot. So how could we be too early?
Ben [*quietly*] Who took the call, me or you?
Gus You.

---

1 kip: sleep.

Ben We were too early.

Gus Too early for what?

[*Pause.*]

You mean someone had to get out before we got in?

[*He examines the bedclothes.*]

I thought these sheets didn't look too bright. I thought they ponged a bit. I was too tired to notice when I got in this morning. Eh, that's taking a bit of a liberty, isn't it? I don't want to share my bed-sheets. I told you things were going down the drain. I mean, we've always had clean sheets laid on up till now. I've noticed it.

Ben How do you know those sheets weren't clean?

Gus What do you mean?

Ben How do you know they weren't clean? You've spent the whole day in them, haven't you?

Gus What, you mean it might be my pong? [*He sniffs sheets.*] Yes. [*He sits slowly on bed.*] It could be my pong, I suppose. It's difficult to tell. I don't really know what I pong like, that's the trouble.

Ben [*referring to the paper*] Kaw!

Gus Eh, Ben.

Ben Kaw!

Gus Ben.

Ben What?

Gus What town are we in? I've forgotten.

Ben I've told you. Birmingham.

Gus Go on!

[*He looks with interest about the room.*]

That's in the Midlands. The second biggest city in Great Britain. I'd never have guessed.

[*He snaps his fingers.*]

Eh, it's Friday today, isn't it? It'll be Saturday tomorrow.

Ben What about it?

Gus [*excited*] We could go and watch the Villa.[1]

Ben They're playing away.

Gus No, are they? Caarr! What a pity.

Ben Anyway there's no time. We've got to get straight back.

Gus Well, we have done in the past, haven't we? Stayed over and watched a game, haven't we? For a bit of relaxation.

Ben Things have tightened up, mate. They've tightened up.

[*Gus chuckles to himself.*]

Gus I saw the Villa get beat in a cup-tie once. Who was it against now? White shirts. It was one-all at half-time. I'll never forget it. Their opponents won by a penalty. talk about drama. Yes, it was a disputed penalty. Disputed. They got beat two-one, anyway, because of it. You were there yourself.

Ben Not me.

Gus Yes, you were there. Don't you remember that disputed penalty?

---

1 Villa: Aston Villa Football Club.

Ben No.

Gus He went down just inside the area. Then they said he was just acting. I didn't think the other bloke touched him myself. But the referee had the ball on the spot.

Ben Didn't touch him! What are you talking about? He laid him out flat!

Gus Not the Villa. The Villa don't play that sort of game.

Ben Get out of it.

[*Pause.*]

Gus Eh, that must have been here, in Birmingham.

Ben What must?

Gus The Villa. That must have been here.

Ben They were playing away.

Gus Because you know who the other team was? It was the Spurs. It was Tottenham Hotspur.

Ben Well, what about it?

Gus We've never done a job in Tottenham

Ben How do you know?

Gus I'd remember Tottenham.

[*Ben turns on his bed to look at him.*]

Ben Don't make me laugh, will you?

[*Ben turns back and reads. Gus yawns and speaks through his yawn.*]

Gus When's he going to get in touch?

[*Pause.*]

Yes, I'd like to see another football match. I've always been an ardent football fan. Here, what about coming to see the Spurs tomorrow?

Ben [*tonelessly*] They're playing away.

Gus Who are?

Ben The Spurs.

Gus Then they might be playing here.

Ben Don't be silly.

Gus If they're playing away they might be playing here. They might be playing the Villa.

Ben [*tonelessly*] But the Villa are playing away.

[*Pause. An envelope slides under the door, right. Gus sees it. He stands, looking at it.*]

Ben Away. They're all playing away.

Gus Ben, look here.

Ben What?

Gus Look.

[*Ben turns his head and sees the envelope. He stands.*]

Ben What's that?

Gus I don't know.

Ben Where did it come from?

Gus Under the door.

Ben Well, what is it?

Gus I don't know.

[*They stare at it.*]

Ben Pick it up.
Gus What do you mean?
Ben Pick it up!
[*Gus slowly moves towards it, bends and picks it up.*]
What is it?
Gus An envelope.
Ben Is there anything on it?
Gus No.
Ben Is it sealed?
Gus Yes.
Ben Open it.
Gus What?
Ben Open it!
[*Gus opens it and looks inside.*]
What's in it?
[*Gus empties twelve matches into his hand.*]
Gus Matches.
Ben Matches?
Gus Yes.
Ben Show it to me.
[*Gus passes the envelope. Ben examines it.*]
Nothing on it. Not a word.
Gus That's funny, isn't it ?
Ben It came under the door?
Gus Must have done.
Ben Well, go on
Gus Go on where?
Ben Open the door and see if you can catch anyone outside.
Gus Who, me?
Ben Go on!
[*Gus stares at him, puts the matches in his pocket, goes to his bed and brings a revolver from under the pillow. He goes to the door, opens it, looks out and shuts it.*]
Gus No one.
[*He replaces the revolver.*]
Ben What did you see?
Gus Nothing.
Ben They must have been pretty quick.
[*Gus takes the matches from his pocket and looks at them.*]
Gus Well, they'll come in handy.
Ben Yes.
Gus Won't they?
Ben Yes, you're always running out, aren't you?
Gus All the time.
Ben Well, they'll come in handy then.
Gus Yes.
Ben Won't they?

Gus Yes, I could do with them. I could do with them too.
Ben You could, eh?
Gus Yes.
Ben Why?
Gus We haven't got any.
Ben Well, you've got some now, haven't you?
Gus I can light the kettle now.
Ben Yes, you're always cadging matches. How many have you got there?
Gus About a dozen.
Ben Well, don't lose them. Red too. You don't even need a box.
[*Gus probes his ear with a match.*]
[*Slapping his hand*] Don't waste them! Go on, go and light it.
Gus Eh?
Ben Go and light it.
Gus Light what?
Ben The kettle.
Gus You mean the gas.
Ben Who does?
Gus You do.
Ben [*his eyes narrowing*] What do you mean, I mean the gas?
Gus Well, that's what you mean, don't you? The gas.
Ben [*powerfully*] If I say go and light the kettle I mean go and light the kettle.
Gus How can you light a kettle?
Ben It's a figure of speech! Light the kettle. It's a figure of speech!
Gus I've never heard it.
Ben Light the kettle! It's common usage!
Gus I think you've got it wrong.
Ben [*menacing*] What do you mean?
Gus They say put on the kettle.
Ben [*taut*] Who says?
[*They stare at each other, breathing hard.*]
[*Deliberately*] I have never in all my life heard anyone say put on the kettle.
Gus I bet my mother used to say it.
Ben Your mother? When did you last see your mother?
Gus I don't know, about
Ben Well, what are you talking about your mother for?
[*They stare.*]
Gus, I'm not trying to be unreasonable. I'm just trying to point out something to you.
Gus Yes, but –
Ben Who's the senior partner here, me or you?
Gus You.
Ben I'm only looking after your interests, Gus. You've got to learn, mate.
Gus Yes, but I've never heard –
Ben [*vehemently*] Nobody says light the gas! What does the gas light?
Gus What does the gas – ?

Ben [*grabbing him with two hands by the throat, at arm's length*] THE KETTLE, YOU FOOL!
[*Gus takes the hands from his throat.*]
Gus All right, all right.
[*Pause.*]
Ben Well, what are you waiting for?
Gus I want to see if they light.
Ben What?
Gus The matches.
[*He takes out the flattened box and tries to strike.*]
No.
[*He throws the box under the bed. Ben stares at him.*
Gus raises his foot.]
Shall I try it on here?
[*Ben stares.*
Gus strikes a match on his shoe. It lights.]
Here we are.
Ben [*wearily*] Put on the bloody kettle, for Christ's sake.
[*Ben goes to his bed, but realising what he has said, stops and half turns. They look at each other. Gus slowly exits, left. Ben slams his paper down on the bed and sits on it, head in hands.*]
Gus [*entering*] It's going.
Ben What?
Gus The stove.
Gus [*goes to his bed and sits*] I wonder who it'll be tonight.

[*Silence.*]
Eh, I've been wanting to ask you something.
Ben [*putting his legs on the bed*] Oh, for Christ's sake.
Gus No. I was going to ask you something.
[*He rises and sits on Ben's bed.*]
Ben What are you sitting on my bed for?
[*Gus sits.*]
What's the matter with you? You're always asking me questions. What's the matter with you?
Gus Nothing.
Ben You never used to ask me so many damn questions. What's come over you?
Gus No, I was just wondering.
Ben Stop wondering. You've got a job to do. Why don't you just do it and shut up?
Gus That's what I was wondering about.
Ben What?
Gus The job.
Ben What job?
Gus [*tentatively*] I thought perhaps you might know something.
[*Ben looks at him.*]

I thought perhaps you – I mean – have you got any idea who it's going to be tonight?
Ben Who what's going to be?
[*They look at each other.*]
Gus [*at length*] Who it's going to be.

[*Silence.*]
Ben Are you feeling all right?
Gus Sure.
Ben Go and make the tea.
Gus Yes, sure.
[*Gus exits, left, Ben looks after him. He then takes his revolver from under the pillow and checks it for ammunition. Gus re-enters.*]
The gas has gone out.
Ben Well, what about it?
Gus There's a meter.
Ben I haven't got any money.
Gus Nor have I.
Ben You'll have to wait.
Gus What for?
Ben For Wilson.
Gus He might not come. He might just send a message. He doesn't always come.
Ben Well, you'll have to do without it, won't you?
Gus Blimey.
Ben You'll have a cup of tea afterwards. What's the matter with you?
Gus I like to have one before.
[*Ben holds the revolver up to the light and polishes it.*]
Ben You'd better get ready anyway.
Gus Well, I don't know, that's a bit much, you know, for my money.
[*He picks up a packet of tea from the bed and throws it into the bag.*]
I hope he's got a shilling, anyway, if he comes. He's entitled to have. After all, it's his place, he could have seen there was enough gas for a cup of tea.
Ben What do you mean, it's his place?
Gus Well, isn't it?
Ben He's probably only rented it. It doesn't have to be his place.
Gus I know it's his place. I bet the whole house is. He's not even laying on any gas now either.
[*Gus sits on his bed.*]
It's his place all right. Look at all the other places. You go to this address, there's a key there, there's a teapot, there's never a soul in sight – [*He pauses.*] Eh, nobody ever hears a thing, have you ever thought of that? We never get any complaints, do we, too much noise or anything like that? You never see a soul, do you? – except the bloke who comes. You ever noticed that? I wonder if the walls are sound-proof [*He touches the wall above his bed.*] Can't tell. All you do is wait, eh? Half the time he doesn't even bother to put in an appearance, Wilson.

Ben Why should he? He's a busy man.
Gus [*thoughtfully*] I find him hard to talk to, Wilson. Do you know that, Ben?
Ben Scrub round it, will you?
[*Pause.*]
Gus There are a number of things I want to ask him. But I can never get round to it, when I see him.
[*Pause.*]
I've been thinking about the last one.
Ben What last one?
Gus That girl.
[*Ben grabs the paper, which he reads.*]
[*Rising, looking down at Ben*] How many times have you read that paper?
[*Ben slams the paper down and rises.*]
Ben [*angrily*] What do you mean?
Gus I was just wondering how many times you'd –
Ben What are you doing, criticising me?
Gus No, I was just –
Ben You'll get a swipe round your earhole if you don't watch your step.
Gus Now look here, Ben
Ben I'm not looking anywhere! [*He addresses the room.*] How many times have I– ! A bloody liberty!
Gus I didn't mean that.
Ben You just get on with it, mate. Get on with it, that's all.
[*Ben gets back on the bed.*]
Gus I was just thinking about that girl, that's all.
[*Gus sits on his bed.*]
She wasn't much to look at, I know, but still. It was a mess though, wasn't it? What a mess. Honest, I can't remember a mess like that one. They don't seem to hold together like men, women. A looser texture, like. Didn't she spread, eh? She didn't half spread. Kaw! But I've been meaning to ask you
[*Ben sits up and clenches his eyes.*]
Who clears up after we're gone? I'm curious about that. Who does the clearing up? Maybe they don't clear up. Maybe they just leave them there, eh? What do you think? How many jobs have we done? Blimey, I can't count them.
Ben [*pityingly*] You mutt. Do you think we're the only branch of this organisation? Have a bit of common.[1] They got departments for everything.
Gus What cleaners and all?
Ben You birk.
Gus No, it was that girl made me start to think –

[*There is a loud clatter and racket in the bulge of wall between the beds, of something descending. They grab their revolvers, jump up and face the wall. The noise comes to a stop. Silence. They look at each other. Ben gestures sharply towards the wall. Gus approaches the wall slowly. He bangs it with his revolver. It is hollow. Ben moves to the heard of his bed, his revolver cocked. Gus puts his revolver on his bed*

---

1 **common**: common sense.

and pats along the bottom of the centre panel. He finds a rim. He lifts the panel. Disclosed is a serving hatch, a 'dumb waiter'. A wide box is held by pulleys. Gus peers into the box. He brings out a piece of paper.]

Ben What is it?

Gus You have a look at it.

Ben Read it

Gus [*reading*] Two braised steak and chips. Two sago puddings. Two teas without sugar.

Ben Let me see that [*He takes the paper.*]

Gus [*to himself*] Two teas without sugar.

Ben Mmnn.

Gus What do you think of that?

Ben Well –

[*The box goes up. Ben levels his revolver.*]

Gus Give us a chance! They're in a hurry, aren't they?

[*Ben re-reads the note. Gus looks over his shoulder.*]

That's a bit – that's a bit funny, isn't it?

Ben [*quickly*] No. It's not funny. It probably used to be a cafe here, that's all. Upstairs. These places change hands very quickly.

Gus A cafe?

Ben Yes.

Gus What, you mean this was the kitchen, down here?

Ben Yes, they change hands overnight, these places. Go into liquidation. The people who run it, you know, they don't find it a going concern, they move out.

Gus You mean the people who ran this place didn't find it a going concern and moved out?

Ben Sure.

Gus WELL, WHO'S GOT IT NOW?

[*Silence.*]

Ben What do you mean, who's got it now?

Gus Who's got it now? If they moved out, who moved in?

Ben Well, that all depends –

[*The box descends with a clatter and bang. Ben levels his revolver. Gus goes to the box and brings out a piece of paper.*]

Gus [*reading*] Soup of the day. Liver and onions. Jam tart.

[*A pause. Gus looks at Ben. Ben takes the note and reads it. He walks slowly to the hatch. Gus follows. Ben looks into the hatch but not up it. Gus puts his hand on Ben's shoulder. Ben throws it off. Gus puts his finger to his mouth. He leans on the hatch and swiftly looks up it. Ben flings him away in alarm. Ben looks at the note. He throws his revolver on the bed and speaks with decision.*]

Ben We'd better send something up.

Gus Eh?

Ben We'd better send something up.

Gus Oh! Yes. Yes. Maybe you're right.

[*They are both relieved at the decision.*]

Ben [*purposefully*] Quick! What have you got in that bag?
Gus Not much.
[*Gus goes to the hatch and shouts up it.*]
Wait a minute!
Ben Don't do that!
[*Gus examines the contents of the bag and brings them out, one by one.*]
Gus Biscuits. A bar of chocolate. Half a pint of milk.
Ben That all?
Gus Packet of tea.
Ben Good.
Gus We can't send the tea. That's all the tea we've got.
Ben Well, there's no gas. You can't do anything with it, can you?
Gus Maybe they can send us down a bob.
Ben What else is there?
Gus [*reaching into bag*] One Eccles cake.
Ben One Eccles cake?
Gus Yes.
Ben You never told me you had an Eccles cake.
Gus Didn't I?
Ben Why only one? Didn't you bring one for me?
Gus I didn't think you'd be keen.
Ben Well, you can't send up one Eccles cake, anyway.
Gus Why not?
Ben Fetch one of those plates.
Gus All right.
[*Gus goes towards the door, left, and stops.*]
Do you mean I can keep the Eccles cake then?
Ben Keep it?
Gus Well, they don't know we've got it, do they?
Ben That's not the point.
Gus Can't I keep it?
Ben No, you can't. Get the plate.
[*Gus exits, left. Ben looks in the bag. He brings out a packet of crisps. Enter Gus with a plate.*]
[*Accusingly, holding up the crisps*] Where did these come from?
Gus What?
Ben Where did these crisps come from?
Gus Where did you find them?
Ben [*hitting him on the shoulder*] You're playing a dirty game, my lad!
Gus I only eat those with beer!
Ben Well, where were you going to get the beer?
Gus I was saving them till I did.
Ben I'll remember this. Put everything on the plate.
[*They pile everything on to the plate. The box goes up without the plate.*]
Wait a minute!
[*They stand.*]

Gus Its gone up.
Ben Its all your stupid fault, playing about!
Gus What do we do now?
Ben We'll have to wait till it comes down.
[*Ben puts the plate on the bed, puts on his shoulder holster, and starts to put on his tie.*]
You'd better get ready.
[*Gus goes to his bed, puts on his tie, and starts to fix his holster.*]
Gus Hey, Ben.
Ben What?
Gus What's going on here?
[*Pause.*]
Ben What do you mean?
Gus How can this be a cafe?
Ben It used to be a cafe.
Gus Have you seen the gas stove?
Ben What about it?
Gus It's only got three rings.
Ben So what?
Gus Well, you couldn't cook much on three rings, not for a busy place like this.
Ben [*irritably*] That's why the service is slow!
[*Ben puts on his waistcoat.*]
Gus Yes, but what happens when we're not here? What do they do then? All these menus coming down and nothing going up. It might have been going on like this for years.
[*Ben brushes his jacket.*]
What happens when we go?
[*Ben puts on his jacket.*]
They can't do much business.
[*The box descends. They turn about. Gus goes to the hatch and brings out a note.*]
Gus [*reading*] Macaroni Pastitsio. Ormitha Macarounada.
Ben What was that?
Gus Macaroni Pastitsio. Ormitha Macarounada.
Ben Greek dishes.
Gus No.
Ben That's right.
Gus That's pretty high class.
Ben Quick before it goes up.
[*Gus puts the plate in the box.*]
Gus [*calling up the hatch*] Three McVitie and Price! One Lyons Red Label! One Smith's Crisps! One Eccles cake! One Fruit and Nut!
Ben Cadbury's.
Gus [*Up the hatch*] Cadbury's!
Ben [*handing the milk*] One bottle of milk.
Gus [*Up the hatch*] One bottle of milk! Half a pint! [*He looks at the label.*] Express Dairy! [*He puts the bottle in the box.*]

[*The box goes up.*]
Just did it.
Ben You shouldn't shout like that.
Gus Why not?
Ben It isn't done.
[*Ben goes to his bed.*]
Well, that should be all right, anyway, for the time being.
Gus You think so, eh?
Ben Get dressed, will you? It'll be any minute now.
[*Gus puts on his waistcoat.*
Ben lies down and looks up at the ceiling.]
Gus This is some place. No tea and no biscuits.
Ben Eating makes you lazy, mate. You're getting lazy, you know that? You don't want to get slack on your job.
Gus Who me?
Ben Slack, mate, slack.
Gus Who me? Slack?
Ben Have you checked your gun? You haven't even checked your gun. It looks disgraceful, anyway. Why don't you ever polish it?
[*Gus rubs his revolver on the sheet. Ben takes out a pocket mirror and straightens his tie.*]
Gus I wonder where the cook is. They must have had a few, to cope with that. Maybe they had a few more gas stoves. Eh! Maybe there's another kitchen along the passage.
Ben Of course there is! Do you know what it takes to make an Ormitha Macarounada?
Gus No, what?
Ben An Ormitha – ! Buck your ideas up, will you?
Gus Takes a few cooks, eh?
[*Gus puts his revolver in its holster.*]
The sooner we're out of this place the better.
[*He puts on his jacket.*]
Why doesn't he get in touch? I feel like I've been here years. [*He takes his revolver out of its holster to check the ammunition.*] We've never let him down though, have we? We've never let him down. I was thinking only the other day, Ben. We're reliable, aren't we?
[*He puts his revolver back in its holster.*]
Still, I'll be glad when it's over tonight.
[*He brushes his jacket.*]
I hope the bloke's not going to get excited tonight, or anything. I'm feeling a bit off. I've got a splitting headache.

[*Silence.*
The box descends. Ben jumps up. Gus collects the note.]
[*Reading*] One Bamboo Shoots, Water Chestnuts and Chicken. One Char Siu and Beansprouts.
Ben Beansprouts?

Gus Yes.
Ben Blimey.
Gus I wouldn't know where to begin.
[*He looks back at the box. The packet of tea is inside it. He picks it up.*]
They've sent back the tea.
Ben [*anxious*] What'd they do that for?
Gus Maybe it isn't tea-time.

[*The box goes up. Silence.*]
Ben [*throwing the tea on the bed, and speaking urgently*] Look here. We'd better
tell them.
Gus Tell them what?
Ben That we can't do it, we haven't got it.
Gus All right then.
Ben Lend us your pencil. We'll write a note.
[*Gus, turning for a pencil, suddenly discovers the speaking-tube which hangs on the
right wall of the hatch facing his bed.*]
Gus What's this?
Ben What?
Gus This.
Ben [*examining it*] This? It's a speaking-tube.
Gus How long has that been there?
Ben Just the job. We should have used it before, instead of shouting up there.
Gus Funny I never noticed it before.
Ben Well, come on.
Gus What do you do?
Ben See that? That's a whistle.
Gus What, this?
Ben Yes, take it out. Pull it out.
[*Gus does so.*]
That's it.
Gus What do we do now?
Ben Blow into it.
Gus Blow?
Ben It whistles up there if you blow. Then they know you want to speak. Blow.

[*Gus blows. Silence.*]
Gus [*tube at mouth*] I can't hear a thing.
Ben Now you speak! Speak into it!
[*Gus looks at Ben, then speaks into the tube.*]
Gus The larder's bare!
Ben Give me that!
[*He grabs the tube and puts it to his mouth.*]
[*Speaking with great deference*] Good evening. I'm sorry to bother you, but we
just thought we'd better let you know that we haven't got anything left. We
sent up all we had. There's no more food down here.
[*He brings the tube slowly to his ear.*]

What?
[*To mouth.*]
What?
[*To ear. He listens. To mouth.*]
No, all we had we sent up.
[*To ear. He listens. To mouth.*]
Oh, I'm very sorry to hear that.
[*To ear. He listens. To Gus.*]
The Eccles cake was stale.
[*He listens. To Gus.*]
The chocolate was melted.
[*He listens. To Gus.*]
The milk was sour.
Gus What about the crisps?
Ben [*listening*] The biscuits were mouldy.
[*He glares at Gus. Tube to mouth.*]
Well, we're very sorry about that
[*Tube to ear.*]
What?
[*To mouth.*]
What?
[*To ear.*]
Yes. Yes.
[*To mouth.*]
Yes certainly. Certainly. Right away.
[*To ear. The voice has ceased. He hangs up the tube.*]
[*Excitedly*] Did you hear that?
Gus That?
Ben You know what he sad? Light the kettle! Not put on the kettle! Not light the gas! But light the kettle!
Gus How can we light the kettle?
Ben What do you mean?
Gus There's no gas.
Ben [*clapping hand to head*] Now what do we do?
Gus What did he want us to light the kettle for?
Ben For tea. He wanted a cup of tea.
Gus *He* wanted a cup of tea! What about me? I've been wanting a cup of tea all night!
Ben [*despairingly*] What do we do now?
Gus What are we supposed to drink?
[*Ben sits on his bed, staring.*]
What about us?
[*Ben sits.*]
I'm thirsty too. I'm starving. And he wants a cup of tea. That beats the band, that does.
[*Ben lets his head sink on to his chest.*]

I could do with a bit of sustenance myself. What about you? You look as if you could do with something too.

[*Gus sits on his bed.*]

We send him up all we've got and he's not satisfied. No, honest, it's enough to make the cat laugh. Why did you send him up all that stuff? [*Thoughtfully*] Why did I send it up?

[*Pause.*]

Who knows what he's got upstairs? He's probably got a salad bowl. They must have something up there. They won't get much from down here. You notice they didn't ask for any salads? They've probably got a salad bowl up there. Cold meat, radishes, cucumbers. Watercress. Roll mops.

[*Pause.*]

Hardboiled eggs.

[*Pause.*]

The lot. They've probably got a crate of beer too. Probably eating my crisps with a pint of beer now. Didn't have anything to say about those crisps, did he? They do all right, don't worry about that. You don't think they're just going to sit there and wait for stuff to come up from down here, do you? That'll get them nowhere.

[*Pause.*]

They do all right.

[*Pause.*]

And he wants a cup of tea.

[*Pause.*]

That's past a joke, in my opinion.

[*He looks over at Ben, rises, and goes to him.*]

What's the matter with you? You don't look too bright. I feel like an Alka-Seltzer[1] myself.

[*Ben sits up.*]

Ben [*in a low voice*] Time's getting on.

Gus I know. I don't like doing a job on an empty stomach.

Ben [*wearily*] Be quiet a minute. Let me give you your instructions.

Gus What for? We always do it the same way, don't we?

Ben Let me give you your instructions.

[*Gus sighs and sits next to Ben on the bed. The instructions are stated and repeated automatically.*]

When we get the call, you go over and stand behind the door.

Gus Stand behind the door.

Ben If there's a knock on the door you don't answer it.

Gus If there's a knock on the door I don't answer it.

Ben But there won't be a knock on the door.

Gus So I won't answer it.

Ben When the bloke comes in

Gus When the bloke comes in

Ben Shut the door behind him.

---

1 **Alka-Seltzer**: popular medicine to settle the stomach.

Gus Shut the door behind him.
Ben Without divulging your presence.
Gus Without divulging my presence.
Ben He'll see me and come towards me.
Gus He'll see you and come towards you.
Ben He won't see you.
Gus [*absently*] Eh?
Ben He won't see you.
Gus He won't see me.
Ben But he'll see me.
Gus He'll see you.
Ben He won't know you're there.
Gus He won't know you're there.
Ben He won't know *you're* there.
Gus He won't know I'm there.
Ben I take out my gun.
Gus You take out your gun.
Ben He stops in his tracks.
Gus He stops in his tracks.
Ben If he turns round –
Gus If he turns round
Ben You're there.
Gus I'm here.
[*Ben frowns and presses his forehead.*]
You've missed something out.
Ben I know. What?
Gus I haven't taken my gun out, according to you.
Ben You take your gun out
Gus After I've closed the door.
Ben After you've closed the door.
Gus You've never missed that out before, you know that?
Ben When he sees you behind him
Gus Me behind him
Ben And me in front of him
Gus And you in front of him
Ben He'll feel uncertain –
Gus Uneasy.
Ben He won't know what to do.
Gus So what will he do?
Ben He'll look at me and he'll look at you.
Gus We won't say a word.
Ben We'll look at him.
Gus He won't say a word.
Ben He'll look at us.
Gus And we'll look at him.
Ben Nobody says a word.
[*Pause.*]

Gus What do we do if it's a girl?
Ben We do the same.
Gus Exactly the same?
Ben Exactly.
[*Pause.*]
Gus We don't do anything different?
Ben We do exactly the same.
Gus Oh.
[*Gus rises, and shivers.*]
Excuse me.
[*He exits through the door on the left. Ben remains sitting on the bed, still. The lavatory chain is pulled once off left, but the lavatory does not flush.*]

[*Silence.*
Gus re-enters and stops inside the door, deep in thought. He looks at Ben, then walks slowly across to his own bed. He is troubled. He stands, thinking. He turns and looks at Ben He moves a few paces towards him.*]
[*Slowly in a low tense voice*] Why did he send us matches if he knew there was no gas?

[*Silence.*
Ben stares in front of him. Gus crosses to the left side of Ben to the foot of his bed, to get to his other ear.*]
Ben, Why did he send us matches if he knew there was no gas?
[*Ben looks up.*]
Why did he do that?
Ben Who?
Gus Who sent us those matches?
Ben What are you talking about?
[*Gus stares down at him.*]
Gus [*thickly*] Who is it upstairs?
Ben [*nervously*] What's one thing to do with another?
Gus Who is it, though?
Ben What's one thing to do with another?
[*Ben fumbles for his paper on the bed.*]
Gus I asked you a question.
Ben Enough!
Gus [*with growing agitation*] I asked you before. Who moved in? I asked you. You said the people who had it before moved out. Well, who moved in?
Ben [*hunched*] Shut up.
Gus I told you, didn't I?
Ben [*standing*] Shut up!
Gus [*feverishly*] I told you before who owned this place, didn't I? I told you.
[*Ben hits him viciously on the shoulder.*]
I told you who ran this place, didn't I?
[*Ben hits him viciously on the shoulder.*]
[*Violently*] Well, what's he playing all these games for? That's what I want to know. What's he doing it for?

Ben What games?

Gus [*passionately, advancing*] What's he doing it for? We've been through our tests, haven't we? We got right through our tests, years ago, didn't we? We took them together, don't you remember, didn't we? We've proved ourselves before now, haven't we? We've always done our job. What's he doing all this for? What's the idea? What's he playing these games for?

[*The box in the shaft comes down behind them. The noise is this time accompanied by a shrill whistle, as it falls Gus rushes to the hatch and seizes the note.*]

[*Reading*] Scampi!

[*He crumples the note, picks up the tube, takes out the whistle, blows and speaks.*]

WE'VE GOT NOTHING LEFT! NOTHING! DO YOU UNDERSTAND?

[*Ben seizes the tube and flings Gus away. He follows Gus and slaps him hard, back-handed, across the chest.*]

Ben Stop it! You maniac!

Gus But you heard!

Ben [*savagely*] That's enough! I'm warning you!

[*Silence.*

Ben hangs the tube. He goes to his bed and lies down. He picks up his paper and reads.]

[*Silence.*

The box goes up.

They turn quickly, their eyes meet. Ben turns to his paper. Slowly Gus goes back to his bed, and sits.]

[*Silence.*

The hatch falls back into place.

They turn quickly, their eyes meet. Ben turns back to his paper.]

[*Silence.*

Ben throws his paper down.]

Ben Kaw!

[*He picks up the paper and looks at it.*]

Listen to this !

[*Pause.*]

What about that eh?

[*Pause.*]

Kaw!

[*Pause.*]

Have you ever heard such a thing?

Gus [*dully*] Go on!

Ben It's true.

Gus Get away.

Ben It's down here in black and white.

Gus [*very low*] Is it a fact?

Ben Can you imagine it.

Gus It's unbelievable.

Ben It's enough to make you want to puke, isn't it?

Gus [*almost inaudible*] Incredible.

[*Ben shakes his head. He puts the paper down and rises. He fixes the revolver in his holster.*

Gus stands up. He goes towards the door on the left.]

Ben Where are you going?

Gus I'm going to have a glass of water.

[*He exits. Ben brushes dust off his clothes and shoes. The whistle in the speaking-tube blows. He goes to it, takes the whistle out and puts the tube to his ear. He listens. He puts it to his mouth.*]

Ben Yes.

[*To ear. He listens. To mouth.*]

Straight away. Right.

[*To ear. He listens. To mouth.*]

Sure we're ready.

[*To ear. He listens. To mouth.*]

Understood. Repeat. He has arrived and will be coming in straight away. The normal method to be employed. Understood.

[*To ear. He listens. To mouth.*]

Sure we're ready.

[*To ear. He listens. To mouth.*]

Right.

[*He hangs the tube up.*]

Gus!

[*He takes out a comb and combs his hair, adjusts his jacket to diminish the bulge of the revolver. The lavatory flushes off left. Ben goes quickly to the door, left.*]

Gus!

[*The door right opens sharply. Ben turns, his revolver levelled at the door.*

Gus stumbles in.

He is stripped of his jacket, waistcoat, tie, holster and revolver.

He stops, body stooping, his arms at his sides.

He raises his head and looks at Ben.

A long silence.

They stare at each other.]

[*Curtain.*]

DORIS LESSING (1919–)

Lessing grew up in East Africa and settled in Britain in 1949. A highly politicised writer, her 1962 novel, *The Golden Notebook,* articulates the dilemmas of forging new forms of female social realisation within the context of more traditional radical politics, particularly communism, which is nevertheless dominated by paternalistic attitudes. Through a series of different-coloured notebooks kept by the central protagonist, Anna Wulf, Lessing shows how public and private spheres merge as Anna attempts to find a means of narrating female experience in a convincing, accurate manner.

From The Golden Notebook

[The blue notebook continued.]

15th September, 1954

Last night Michael said (I had not seen him for a week): 'Well, Anna, and so our great love affair is coming to an end?' Characteristic of him that it is a question mark: he is bringing it to an end, but talks as if I am. I said, smiling but ironical in spite of myself: 'But at least it has been a great love affair?' He, then: 'Ah, Anna, you make up stories about life and tell them to yourself, and you don't know what is true and what isn't.' 'And so we haven't had a great love affair?' This was breathless and pleading; though I had not meant it. I felt a terrible dismay and coldness at his words, as if he were denying my existence. He said, whimsically: 'If you say we have, then we have. And if you say not, then not.' 'So what you feel doesn't count?' 'Me? But Anna, why should I count?' (This was bitter, mocking, but affectionate.) Afterwards I fought with a feeling that always takes hold of me after one of these exchanges: unreality, as if the substance of my self were thinning and dissolving. And then I thought how ironical it was that in order to recover myself I had to use precisely that Anna which Michael dislikes most; the critical and thinking Anna. Very well then; he says I make up stories about our life together. I shall write down, as truthfully as I can, every stage of a day. Tomorrow. When tomorrow ends I shall sit down and write.

17th September, 1954

I could not write last night because I was too unhappy. And now of course, I am wondering if the fact that I chose to be very conscious of everything that happened yesterday changed the shape of the day. That just because I was conscious I made it a special day? However, I shall write it and see how it looks. I woke early, about five, tensed, because I thought I heard Janet move in the room through the wall. But she must have moved and gone to sleep again. A grey stream of water on the windowpane. The light grey. The shapes of furniture enormous in the vague light. Michael and I were lying facing the window, I with my arms around him under his pyjama jacket, my knees tucked into the angle of his knees. A fierce healing warmth from him to me. I thought: Very soon now he won't come back. Perhaps I'll know it is the last time, perhaps not. Perhaps this is the last time? But it seemed impossible to associate the two feelings: Michael warm in my arms, asleep; and knowing that soon he would not be there. I moved my hand up and the hair on his breast was slippery yet rough against my palm. It gave me intense delight. He started up, feeling me awake, and said sharply: 'Anna, what is it?' His voice came out of a dream, it was frightened and angry. He turned on his back, and was asleep again. I looked at his face to see the shadow of the dream on it; his face was clenched up. Once he said, waking abrupt and frightened out of a dream: 'My dear Anna, if you insist on sleeping with a man who is the history of Europe over the last twenty years you mustn't complain if he has uneasy dreams.' This was resentful: the resentment was because I wasn't part of that history. Yet I know that one of the reasons he is with me is that I wasn't part of it and I haven't had something destroyed in me. This morning I looked at the tight sleeping face and again tried to imagine it, so that it was part of my own experience, what it would mean: 'Seven of my family, including my mother and father, were murdered in the gas chambers. Most of my close friends are dead: communists murdered by communists. The survivors are mostly refugees in strange countries. I shall live for the rest of my life in a country which will never really be my home.' But as usual, I failed to imagine it. The light was thick and heavy because of the rain outside. His face unclenched, relaxed. It was now broad, calm, assured. Calm sealed lids, and above them the lightly-marked, glossy brows. I could see him as a child, fearless, cocky, with a clear, candid, alert smile. And I could see him old: he will be an irascible, intelligent, energetic old man, locked in a bitter intelligent loneliness. I was filled with an emotion one has, women have, about children: a feeling of fierce triumph: that against all odds, against the weight of death, this human being exists, here, a miracle of breathing flesh. I shored this feeling up, strengthened it, against the other one, that he would soon be leaving me. He must have felt it in his sleep, because he stirred and said: 'Go to sleep, Anna.' He smiled, his eyes shut. The smile was strong and warm; out of another world than the one where he says: But Anna, why should I count? I felt 'nonsense', of course he won't leave me; he can't smile at me, like that, and mean to leave me. I lay down beside him, on my back. I was careful not to sleep, because very soon Janet would wake. The light in the room was like thin greyish water, moving, because of the streaming wet on the panes. The panes shook slightly. On windy nights they batter and shake, but I don't wake. Yet I wake if Janet turns over in bed.

It must be about six o'clock. My knees are tense. I realise that what I used to refer to, to Mother Sugar, as 'the housewife's disease' has taken hold of me. The tension in me, so that peace has already gone away from me, is because the current has been switched on: I must-dress-Janet-get-her-breakfast-send-her-off-to-school-get-Michael's-breakfast-don't-forget-I'm-out-of-tea-etc.-etc. With this useless but apparently unavoidable tension resentment is also switched on. Resentment against what? An unfairness. That I should have to spend so much of my time worrying over details. The resentment focuses itself on Michael; although I know with my intelligence it has nothing to do with Michael. And yet I do resent him, because he will spend his day, served by secretaries, nurses, women in all kinds of capacities, who will take this weight off him. I try to relax myself, to switch off the current. But my limbs have started to ache, and

I must turn over. There is another movement from beyond the wall – Janet is waking. Simultaneously, Michael stirs and I feel him growing big against my buttocks. The resentment takes the form: Of course he chooses now, when I am unrelaxed and listening for Janet. But the anger is not related to him. Long ago, in the course of the sessions with Mother Sugar, I learned that the resentment, the anger, is impersonal. It is the disease of women in our time. I can see it in women's faces, their voices, every day, or in the letters that come to the office. The woman's emotion: resentment against injustice, an impersonal poison. The unlucky ones who do not know it is impersonal, turn it against their men. The lucky ones like me fight it. It is a tiring fight. Michael takes me from behind, half asleep, fierce and close. He is taking me impersonally, and so I do not respond as I do when he is loving Anna. And besides with one half of my mind I am thinking how, if I hear Janet's soft feet outside I must be up and across the room to stop her coming in. She never comes in until seven; that is the rule; I do not expect her to come in; yet I have to be alert. While Michael grips me and fills me the noises next door continue, and I know he hears them too, and that part of the pleasure, for him, is to take me in hazard; that Janet, the little girl, the eight-year-old, represents for him partly women – other women, whom he betrays to sleep with me; and partly, child; the essence of child, against whom he is asserting his rights to live. He never speaks of his own children without a small, half-affectionate, half-aggressive laugh – his heirs, and his assassins. My child, a few feet away through the wall, he will not allow to cheat him of his freedom. When we are finished, he says: 'And now, Anna, I suppose you are going to desert me for Janet?' And he sounds like a child who feels himself slighted for a younger brother or sister. I laugh and kiss him; although the resentment is suddenly so strong I clench my teeth against it. I control it, as always, by thinking: If I were a man I'd be the same. The control and discipline of being a mother came so hard to me, that I can't delude myself that if I'd been a man, and not forced into self-control, I'd have been any different. And yet for the few moments it takes for me to put on the wrap to go into Janet, the resentment is like a raging poison. Before I go into Janet I wash myself quickly between the legs so that the smell of sex may not disturb her, even though she doesn't yet know what it is. I like the smell, and hate to wash it off so quickly; and the fact that I must adds to my bad temper. (I remember thinking that the fact I was deliberately watching all my reactions was exacerbating them; normally they would not be so strong.) Yet when I close Janet's door behind me, and see her sitting up in bed, her black hair wild, in elf-locks, her small pale face (mine) smiling, the resentment vanishes under the habit of discipline, and almost at once becomes affection. It is six-thirty and the little room is very cold. Janet's window is also streaming with grey wet. I light the gas fire, while she sits up in bed, surrounded by bright patches of colour from her comics, watching me to see if I do everything as usual, and reading at the same time. I shrink, in affection, to Janet's size, and become Janet. The enormous yellow fire like a great eye; the window, enormous, through which anything can enter; a grey and ominous light which waits for the sun, a devil or an angel, which will shake away the rain. Then I make myself be Anna: I see Janet, a small child in a big bed. A train passes, and the walls shake slightly. I go over to kiss her, and smell the good smell of warm flesh, and hair, and the stuff of her pyjamas, heated by sleep. While her room warms I go into the kitchen and prepare her breakfast – cereal, fried eggs and tea, on a tray. I take the tray back into her room, and she eats her breakfast sitting up in bed, and I drink tea and smoke. The house is dead still – Molly will be asleep for another two or three hours. Tommy came in late with a girl; they'll be asleep too. Through the wall, a baby is crying. It gives me a feeling of continuity, of rest, the baby crying, as Janet once cried. It is the contented half-sleepy cry of a baby who has been fed and will be asleep in a moment. Janet says: 'Why don't we have another baby?' She says this often. And I say: 'Because I haven't got a husband and you must have a husband to get a baby.' She asks this question partly because she would like me to have a baby; and partly to be reassured about the role of Michael. Then she asks: 'Is Michael here?' 'Yes he is, and he is asleep,' I say firmly. My firmness reassures her; and she goes on with her breakfast. Now the room is warm, and she gets out of bed in her white sleeping suit, looking fragile and vulnerable. She puts her arms around my neck and swings on it, back and forth, singing: Rockabye baby. I swing her and sing – babying her, she has become the baby next door, the baby I won't have. Then, abruptly, she lets me go, so that I feel myself spring up like a tree that has been bent over by a weight. She dresses herself, crooning, still half-drowsy, still peaceful. I think that she will retain the peace for years, until the pressure comes on her, and she must start thinking. In half an hour I must remember to cook the potatoes and then I must write a list for the grocer and then I must remember to change the collar on my dress and then . . . I want very much to protect her from the pressure, to postpone it; then I tell myself I must protect her from nothing, this need is really Anna wanting to protect Anna. She dresses slowly, chattering a little, humming; she has the lazy bumbling movements of a bee in the sun. She wears a short red pleated skirt and a dark blue jersey and long dark blue socks. A pretty little girl. Janet. Anna. The baby is asleep next door; there is the silence of content from the baby. Everyone asleep save me and Janet. It is a feeling of intimacy and exclusiveness – a feeling that began when she was born, when she and I were awake together at times when the city slept around us. It is a warm, lazy, intimate gaiety. She seems to me so fragile, that I want to put out my hand to save her from a wrong step, or a careless movement; and at the same time so strong that she is immortal. I feel what I felt with sleeping Michael, a need to laugh out in triumph, because of this marvellous, precarious, immortal human being, in spite of the weight of death.

Now it is nearly eight o'clock and another pressure starts; this is Michael's day for going to the hospital in South London, so he must wake at eight to be in time. He prefers Janet to have left for school before he wakes. And I prefer it, because it divides me. The two personalities – Janet's mother, Michael's mistress, are happier separated. It is a strain having to be both at once. It is no longer raining. I wipe the fog of condensed breath and night-sweat from the window-pane, and see it is a cool, damp, but clear day. Janet's school is close, a short walk. I say: 'You must take your raincoat.' Instantly her voice raises into protest: 'Oh no, mummy, I hate my raincoat, I want my duffle coat.' I say, calm and firm: 'No. Your raincoat. It's been raining all night.' 'How do you know when you were asleep?' This triumphant retort puts her into a good humour. She will now take the raincoat and put on her gum-boots without any further fuss. 'Are you going to fetch me from school this afternoon?' 'Yes, I think so, but if I'm not there, then come back, and Molly will be here.' 'Or Tommy.' 'No, not Tommy.' 'Why not?' 'Tommy's grown-up now, and he's got a girl-friend.' I say this on purpose because she has shown-signs of jealousy of Tommy's girl. She says, calmly: 'Tommy will always like me best.' And adds: 'If you're not there to pick me up, I'll go and play at Barbara's house.' 'Well, if you do I'll come and fetch you at six.' She rushes off down the stairs, making a terrific din. It sounds like an avalanche sliding down the centre of the house. I am afraid Molly might wake. I stand at the head of the stairs, listening, until, ten minutes later, the front door slams; and I make myself shut out all thoughts of Janet until the proper time. I go back into the bedroom. Michael is a dark hump under the bedclothes. I draw the curtains right back, and sit on the bed and kiss Michael awake. He grips me and says: 'Come back to bed.' I say: 'It's eight o'clock. After.' He puts his hands on my breasts. My nipples begin to burn, and I control my response to him and say: 'It's eight o'clock.' 'Oh, Anna, but you're always so efficient and practical in the morning.' 'It's just I as well I am,' I say, lightly, but I can hear the annoyance in my voice. 'Where is Janet?' 'Gone to school.' He lets his hands fall from my breasts, and now I feel disappoint-ment – perversely – because we won't make love. Also relief; because if we did he would be late, and short-tempered with me. And of course, the resentment: my affliction, my burden, and my cross. The resentment is because he said: 'You are always so efficient and practical,' when it is precisely my efficiency and practicality that gains him an extra two hours in bed.

He gets up and washes and shaves and I make his breakfast. We always eat it on a low table by the bed, whose covers have been hastily pulled up. Now we have coffee and fruit and toast; and he is already the professional man, smooth-suited, clear-eyed, calm. He is watching me. I know this is because he plans to tell me something. Is today the day he will break it off? I remember this is the first morning together for a week. I don't want to think about this because it is unlikely that Michael, feeling confined and unhappy in his home, as he does, has been with his wife for the last six days. Where then? My feeling is not so much of jealousy, as of a dull heavy pain, the pain of loss. But I smile, pass him the toast, offer him the newspapers. He takes the papers, glances at them, and remarks: 'If you can put up with me two nights running – I have to be at the hospital down the road this evening to give a lecture.' I smile; for a moment we exchange irony, because of the years we have spent night after night together. Then he slides off into sentimentality, but parodying it at the same time: 'Ah, Anna, but look how it has worn thin for you.' I merely smile again, because there's no point in saying anything, and then he says, this time gaily, in the parody of a rake's manner: 'You get more and more practical with every day that dawns. Every man with sense knows that when a woman gets all efficient on him, the time has come to part.' Suddenly it's too painful for me to play this game, and I say: 'Well, anyway, I'll love you to come this evening. Do you want to eat here?' He says: 'It's not likely I should refuse to eat with you when you're such a cook, now is it?' 'I shall look forward to it,' I say.

He says: 'If you can get dressed quickly, I can give you a lift to your office.' I hesitate, because I am thinking: If I have to cook this evening, then I must buy food before I go to work. He says quickly, because of the hesitation: 'But if you'd rather not, then I'll be off.' He kisses me; and the kiss is a continuation of all the love we've had together. He says, cancelling the moment of intimacy, for his words continue the other theme: 'If we have nothing else in common, we have sex.' Whenever he says this, and it is only recently he has been saying it, I feel the pit of my stomach go cold; it is the total rejection of me, or so I feel it; and there is a great distance between us. Across the distance I say ironically: 'Is that all we have together?' and he says: '*All*? But my dear Anna, my dear Anna – but I must go, I'll be late.' And he goes, with the bitter rueful smile of a rejected man.

And now I must hurry. I wash again and dress. I choose a black and white wool dress with a small white collar, because Michael likes it, and there mightn't be time to change before this evening. Then I run down to the grocer and the butcher. It is a great pleasure, buying food I will cook for Michael; a sensuous pleasure, like the act of cooking itself. I imagine the meat in its coat of crumbs and egg; the mushrooms, simmering in sour cream and onions, the clear strong, amber-coloured soup. Imagining it I create the meal, the movements I will use, checking ingredients, heat, textures. I take the provisions up and put them on the table; then I remember the veal must be beaten and I must do it now, because later it will wake Janet. So I beat the veal flat and fold the tissues of meat in paper and leave them. It is now nine o'clock. I'm short of money so I must go by bus, not taxi. I have fifteen minutes in hand. I hastily sweep the room and make the bed, changing the undersheet which is stained from last night. As I push the stained sheet into the linen-basket I notice a stain of blood. But surely it's not time yet for my period? I hastily check dates, and realise yes, it's today. Suddenly I feel tired and irritable, because these feelings accompany my periods. (I wondered if it would be better not to choose today to write down everything I felt; then decided to go ahead. It was not planned; I had forgotten about the period. I decided that the instinctive feeling of shame and modesty was dishonest: no emotion for a writer.) I stuff my vagina with the tampon of cotton wool, and am already on my way downstairs, when I remember I've forgotten to take a supply of tampons with me. I am late. I roll tampons into my handbag, concealing them under a handkerchief, feeling more and more irritable. At the same time I am telling myself that if I had not noticed my period had started, I would not be feeling nearly so irritable. But all the same, I must control myself now, before leaving for work, or I'll find myself cracking into bad temper in the office. I might as well take a taxi after all – that way I'll have ten minutes in hand. I sit down and try to relax in the big chair. But I am too tense. I look for ways to relax tension. There are half a dozen pots of creeper on the window sill, a greenish-grey wandering plant I don't know the name of. I take the six earthenware pots to the kitchen and submerge them, one after another, in a basin of water, watching the bubbles rise as the water sinks down and drives up the air. The leaves sparkle with water. The dark earth smells of damp growth. I feel better. I put the pots of growth back on the window sill where they can catch the sun, if there is any. Then I snatch up my coat and run downstairs, passing Molly, sleepy in her housecoat. 'What are you in such a hurry for?' she asks; and I shout back: 'I'm late,' hearing the contrast between her loud, lazy, unhurried voice, and mine, tense. There isn't a taxi before I reach the bus-stop, and a bus comes along so I get on, just as the rain comes down. My stockings are slightly splashed; I must remember to change them tonight; Michael notices this sort of detail. Now, sitting on the bus, I feel the dull drag at my lower belly. Not bad at all. Good, if this first pang is slight, then it will all be over in a couple of days. Why am I so ungrateful when I suffer so little compared to other women? – Molly, for instance, groaning and complaining in enjoyable suffering for five or six days. I find my mind is on the practical treadmill again, the things I have to do today, this time in connection with the office. Simultaneously I am worrying about this business of being conscious of everything so as to write it down, particularly in connection with my having a period. Because, whereas to me, the fact I am having a period is no more than an entrance into an emotional state, recurring regularly, that is of no particular importance; I know that as soon as I write the word 'blood', it will be giving a wrong emphasis, and even to me when I come to read what I've written. And so I begin to doubt the value of a day's recording before I've started to record it. I am thinking, I realise, about a major problem of literary style, of tact. For instance, when James Joyce described his man in the act of defecating, it was a shock, shocking. Though it was his intention to rob words of their power to shock. And I read recently in some review, a man said he would be revolted by the description of a woman defecating. I resented this; because of course, what he meant was, he would not like to have that romantic image, a woman, made less romantic. But he was right, for all that. I realise it's not basically a literary problem at all. For instance, when Molly said to me, with her loud jolly laugh: I've got the curse; I have instantly to suppress distaste, even though we are both women; and I begin to be conscious of the possibility of bad smells. Thinking of my reaction to Molly, I forget about my problems of being truthful in writing, (which is being truthful about oneself) and I begin to worry: Am I smelling? It is the only smell I know of that I dislike. I don't mind my own immediate lavatory smells; I like the smell of sex, of sweat, of skin, or hair. But the faintly dubious, essentially stale smell of menstrual blood, I hate. And resent. It is a smell that I feel as strange even to me, an imposition from outside. Not from me. Yet for two days I have to deal with this thing from outside – a bad smell, emanating from me. I realise that all these thoughts would not have been in my head at all had I not set myself to be conscious. A period is something I deal with, without thinking about it particularly, or rather I think of it with a part of my mind that deals with routine problems. It is the same part of my mind that deals with the problem of routine cleanliness. But the idea that I will have to write it down is changing the balance, destroying the truth; so I shut the thoughts of my period out of my mind; making, however, a mental note that as soon as I get to the office I must go to the washroom to make sure there is no smell. I ought really to be thinking over the coming encounter with Comrade Butte. I call him comrade ironically; as he calls me, ironically, Comrade Anna. Last week I said to him, furious about something: 'Comrade Butte, do you realise that if by some chance we had both been Russian communists, you would have had me shot years ago?' 'Yes, Comrade Anna, that seems to me more than likely.' (This particular joke is characteristic of the Party in this period.) Meanwhile, Jack sat and smiled at us both behind his round spectacles. He enjoys my fights with Comrade Butte. After John Butte had left, Jack said: 'There's one thing you don't take into account, and that you might very well have been the one to order the shooting of John Butte.' This remark came close to my private nightmare, and to exorcise it I joked: 'My dear Jack, the essence of my position is that I am essentially the one to be shot – this is, traditionally, my role.' 'Don't be too sure, if you'd known John Butte in the 'thirties you wouldn't be so ready to cast him in the role of a bureaucratic executioner.' 'And anyway, that isn't the point.' 'Which is?' 'Stalin's been dead nearly a year, and nothing has changed.' 'A great deal has changed.' 'They're letting people out of prison; nothing is being done to change the attitudes that put them there.' 'They're considering changing the law.' 'The legal system's being changed this way and that way'll do nothing to change the spirit I'm talking about.' After a moment he nodded. 'Quite possibly, but we don't know.' He was examining me, mildly. I've often wondered if this mildness, this detachment, which makes it possible for us to have these conversations, is a sign of a broken personality; the sell-out most people make at some time or another; or whether it is a self-effacing strength. I don't know. I do know that Jack is the only person in the Party with whom I can have this kind of discussion. Some weeks ago I told him I was thinking of leaving the Party, and he replied in jest: 'I've been in the Party thirty years, and sometimes I think I and John Butte will be the only people, of the thousands I've known, who will remain in it.' 'Is that a criticism of the Party or of the thousands who have left?' 'Of the thousands who have left, naturally,' he said, laughing. Yesterday he said: 'Well, Anna, if you are going to leave the Party, please give me the usual month's notice, because you're very useful and I shall need time to replace you.'

TOM STOPPARD (1937–)

Stoppard was born in Czechoslovakia and came to Britain via Singapore. His drama of the 1960s and 1970s, of which *The Real Inspector Hound* (1968) is a good example, shows a marvellous ability to parody well-known conventions of theatre and other literary institutions. Stoppard, though, is also a playwright of ideas: philosophic and scientific concepts are readily mixed with the humour and pace of traditional farce.

The Real Inspector Hound

Characters

Moon	Birdboot	Mrs Drudge
Simon	Felicity	Cynthia
Magnus	Inspector Hound	

The first thing is that the audience appear to be confronted by their own reflection in a huge mirror. Impossible. However, back there in the gloom – not at the footlights – a bank of plush seats and pale smudges of faces. The total effect having been established, it can be progressively faded out as the play goes on, until the front row remains to remind us of the rest and then, finally, merely two seats in that row – one of which is now occupied by Moon. Between Moon and the auditorium is an acting area which represents, in as realistic an idiom as possible, the drawing-room of Muldoon Manor. French windows at one side. A telephone fairly well upstage (i.e. towards Moon). The body of a man lies sprawled face down on the floor in front of a large settee. This settee must be of a size and design to allow it to be wheeled over the body, hiding it completely.

Silence. The room. The body. Moon.

Moon stares blankly ahead. He turns his head to one side then the other, then up, then down – waiting. He picks up his programme and reads the front cover. He turns over the page and reads.

He turns over the page and reads.
He turns over the page and reads.
He turns over the page and reads.
He looks at the back cover and reads.

He puts it down and crosses his legs and looks about. He stares front. Behind him and to one side, barely visible, a man enters and sits down: Birdboot.

Pause. Moon picks up his programme, glances at the front cover and puts it down impatiently. Pause. . . . Behind him there is the crackle of a chocolate-box, absurdly loud. Moon looks round. He and Birdboot see each other. They are clearly known to each other. They acknowledge each other with constrained waves. Moon looks straight ahead. Birdboot comes down to join him.

Note: Almost always, Moon and Birdboot converse in tones suitable for an auditorium, sometimes a whisper. However good the acoustics might be, they will have to have microphones where they are sitting. The effect must be not of sound picked up, amplified and flung out at the audience, but of sound picked up, carried and gently dispersed around the auditorium.

Anyway, Birdboot, with a box of Black Magic, makes his way down to join Moon and plumps himself down next to him, plumpish middle-aged Birdboot and younger taller, less-relaxed Moon.

Birdboot [*sitting down; conspiratorially*] Me and the lads have had a meeting in the bar and decided it's first-class family entertainment but if it goes on beyond half-past ten it's self-indulgent – pass it on . . . [*and laughs jovially*] I'm on my own tonight, don't mind if I join you?

Moon Hello, Birdboot.

Birdboot Where's Higgs?

Moon I'm standing in.

Moon and Birdboot Where's Higgs?

Moon Every time.

Birdboot What?

Moon It is as if we only existed one at a time, combining to achieve continuity. I keep space warm for Higgs. My presence defines his absence, his absence confirms my presence, his presence precludes mine. . . . When Higgs and I walk down this aisle together to claim our common seat, the oceans will fall into the sky and the trees will hang with fishes.

Birdboot [*he has not been paying attention, looking around vaguely, now catches up*] Where's Higgs?

Moon The very sight of me with a complimentary ticket is enough. The streets are impassable tonight, the country is rising and the cry goes up from hill to hill – Where – is – Higgs? [*Small pause*] Perhaps he's dead at last, or trapped in a lift somewhere, or succumbed to amnesia, wandering the land with his turn-ups stuffed with ticket-stubs.

[*Birdboot regards him doubtfully for a moment.*]

Birdboot Yes. . . . Yes, well I didn't bring Myrtle tonight – not exactly her cup of tea, I thought, tonight.

Moon Over her head, you mean?

Birdboot Well, no – I mean it's a sort of a *thriller*, isn't it?

Moon Is it?

Birdboot That's what I heard. Who killed thing? – no one will leave the house.

Moon I suppose so. Underneath.

Birdboot Underneath?!? It's a whodunnit, man! – Look at it!

[*They look at it. The room. The body. Silence.*]

Has it started yet?

Moon Yes.

[*Pause. They look at it.*]

Birdboot Are you sure?

Moon It's a pause.

Birdboot You can't start with a *pause*! If you want my opinion there's total panic back there. [*Laughs and subsides*] Where's Higgs tonight, then?

Moon It will follow me to the grave and become my epitaph – Here lies Moon the second string: where's Higgs? . . . Sometimes I dream of revolution, a bloody *coup d'etat* by the second rank – troupes of actors slaughtered by their under-studies, magicians sawn in half by indefatigably smiling glamour girls, cricket teams wiped out by marauding bands of twelfth men – I dream of champions chopped down by rabbit-punching sparring partners while eternal bridesmaids turn and rape the bridegrooms over the sausage rolls and parliamentary private secretaries plant bombs in the Minister's Humber –[1] comedians die on provincial stages, robbed of their feeds by mutely triumphant stooges – and – march – an army of assistants and deputies, the seconds-in command, the runners-up, the right-hand men – storming the palace gates wherein the second son has already mounted the throne having committed regicide with a croquet-mallet – stand-ins of the world stand up! –

[*Beat*] Sometimes I dream of Higgs.

[*Pause. Birdboot regards him doubtfully. He is at a loss, and grasps reality in the form of his box of chocolates.*]

Birdboot [*Chewing into mike*] Have a chocolate!

Moon What kind?

Birdboot [*Chewing into mike*] Black Magic.

Moon No thanks.

[*Chewing stops dead.*]

Of such tiny victories and defeats . . . .

Birdboot I'll give you a tip, then. Watch the girl.

Moon You think she did it?

Birdboot No, no – the *girl*, watch her.

Moon What girl ?

Birdboot You won't know her, I'll give you a nudge.

Moon You know her, do you?

Birdboot [*suspiciously, bridling*] What's *that* supposed to mean?

Moon I beg your pardon?

Birdboot I'm trying to tip you a wink – give you a nudge as good as a tip – for God's sake, Moon, what's the matter with you? – you could do yourself some good, spotting her first time out – she's new, from the provinces, going straight to the top. I don't want to put words into your mouth but a word from us and we could make her.

Moon I suppose you've made dozens of them, like that.

Birdboot [*instantly outraged*] I'll have you know I'm a family man devoted to my homely but good-natured wife, and if you're suggesting –

Moon No, no –

Birdboot – A man of my scrupulous morality –

Moon I'm sorry.

Birdboot – falsely besmirched.

Moon Is that her ?

[*For Mrs Drudge has entered.*]

Birdboot – don't be absurd, wouldn't be seen dead with the old – ah.

[*Mrs Drudge is the char, middle-aged, turbanned. She heads straight for the radio, dusting on the trot.*]

---

1 Humber: make of car.

Moon [*reading his programme*] Mrs Drudge the Help.

Radio [*without preamble, having been switched on by Mrs Drudge*] We inter-rupt our programme for a special police message. [*Mrs Drudge stops to listen.*] The search still goes on for the escaped madman who is on the run in Essex.

Mrs Drudge [*fear and dismay*] Essex!

Radio County police led by Inspector Hound have received a report that the man has been seen in the desolate marshes around Muldoon Manor.

[*Fearful gasp from Mrs Drudge.*]

The man is wearing a darkish suit with a lightish shirt. He is of medium height and build and youngish. Anyone seeing a man answering to this description and acting suspiciously, is advised to phone the nearest police station.

[*A man answering this description has appeared behind Mrs Drudge. He is acting suspiciously. He creeps in. He creeps out. Mrs Drudge does not see him. He does not see the body.*]

That is the end of the police message.

[*Mrs Drudge turns off the radio and resumes her cleaning. She does not see the body. Quite fortuitously, her view of the body is always blocked, and when it isn't she has her back to it. However, she is dusting and polishing her way towards it.*]

Birdboot So that's what they say about me, is it?

Moon What?

Birdboot Oh, I know what goes on behind my back – sniggers – slanders – hole-in-corner innuendo – What have you heard?

Moon Nothing.

Birdboot [*urbanely*] Tittle tattle. Tittle, my dear fellow, tattle. I take no notice of it – the sly envy of scandal mongers – I can afford to ignore them, I'm a respectable married man –

Moon Incidentally –

Birdboot Water off a duck's back, I assure you.

Moon Who was that Lady I saw you with last night?

Birdboot [*unexpectedly stung into fury*] How dare you! [*More quietly*] How dare you. Don't you come here with your slimy insinuations! My wife Myrtle understands perfectly well that a man of my critical standing is obliged occa-sionally to mingle with the world of the footlights, simply by way of keeping *au fait* with the latest –

Moon I'm sorry –

Birdboot That a critic of my scrupulous integrity should be vilified and pillo-ried in the stocks of common gossip –

Moon Ssssh –

Birdboot I have nothing to hide! – why, if this should reach the ears of my beloved Myrtle –

Moon Can I have a chocolate?

Birdboot What? Oh [*Mollified*] Oh yes – my dear fellow– yes, let's have a chocolate. No point in – yes, good show. [*Pops chocolate into his mouth and chews*] Which one do you fancy? – Cherry? Strawberry? Coffee cream? Turk-ish delight?

Moon I'll have montelimar.

[*Chewing stops.*]

Birdboot Ah. Sorry. Just missed that one.

Moon Gooseberry fondue?

Birdboot No.

Moon Pistacchio fudge? Nectarine cluster? Hickory nut praline? Chateau Neuf du Pape '55 cracknell?

Birdboot I'm afraid not. . . . Caramel?

Moon Yes, all right.

Birdboot Thanks very much. [*He gives Moon a chocolate. Pause.*] Incidentally, old chap, I'd be grateful if you didn't mention – I mean, you know how these misunderstandings get about . . . .

Moon What?

Birdboot The fact is, Myrtle simply doesn't *like* the theatre . . . .

[*He tails off hopelessly. Mrs Drudge, whose discovery of the body has been imminent, now – by way of tidying the room – slides the couch over the corpse, hiding it completely. She resumes dusting and humming.*]

Moon By the way, congratulations, Birdboot.

Birdboot What?

Moon At the Theatre Royal. Your entire review reproduced in neon!

Birdboot [*pleased*] Oh . . . that old thing.

Moon You've seen it, of course.

Birdboot [*vaguely*] Well, I was passing. . . .

Moon I definitely intend to take a second look when it has settled down.

Birdboot As a matter of fact I have a few colour transparencies – I don't know whether you'd care to . . . ?

Moon Please, please, love to, love to.

[*Birdboot hands over a few colour slides and a battery powered viewer which Moon holds up to his eyes as he speaks.*]

Yes . . . yes . . . lovely . . . awfully sound. It has scale, it has colour, it is, in the best sense of the word, electric. Large as it is, it is a small masterpiece – I would go so far as to say – kinetic without being pop, and having said that, I think it must be said that here we have a review that adds a new dimension to the critical scene. I urge you to make haste to the Theatre Royal, for this is the stuff of life itself.

[*Handing back the slides, morosely*] All I ever got was 'Unforgettable' on the posters for . . . What was it?

Birdboot Oh – yes – I know. . . . Was that you? I thought it was Higgs.

[*The phone rings. Mrs Drudge seems to have been waiting for it to do so and for the last few seconds has been dusting it with an intense concentration. She snatches it up.*]

Mrs Drudge [*into phone*] Hello, the drawing-room of Lady Muldoon's country residence one morning in early spring?. . . Hello! – the draw – Who? Who did you wish to speak to? I'm afraid there is no one of that name here, this is all very mysterious and I'm sure it's leading up to something, I hope nothing is amiss for we, that is Lady Muldoon and her houseguests, are here cut off from the world, including Magnus, the wheelchair-ridden half-brother of her Ladyship's husband Lord Albert Muldoon who ten years ago went out for a walk on the cliffs and was never seen again – and all alone, for they had no children.

Moon Derivative, of course.

Birdboot But quite sound.

Mrs Drudge Should a stranger enter our midst, which I very much doubt, I will tell him you called. Good-bye.

[*She puts down the phone and catches sight of the previously seen suspicious character who has now entered again, more suspiciously than ever, through the French windows. He senses her stare, freezes, and straightens up.*]

Simon Ah! – hello there! I'm Simon Gascoyne, I hope you don't mind, the door was open so I wandered in. I'm a friend of Lady Muldoon, the Lady of the house, having made her acquaintance through a mutual friend, Felicity Cunningham, shortly after moving into this neighbourhood just the other day.

Mrs Drudge I'm Mrs Drudge. I don't live in but I pop in on my bicycle when the weather allows to help in the running of charming though somewhat isolated Muldoon Manor. Judging by the time [*she glances at the clock*] you did well to get here before high water cut us off for all practical purposes from the outside world.

Simon I took the short cut over the cliffs and followed one of the old smugglers' paths through the treacherous swamps that surround this strangely inaccessible house.

Mrs Drudge Yes, many visitors have remarked on the topographical quirk in the local strata whereby there are no roads leading from the Manor, though there *are* ways of getting to it, weather allowing.

Simon Yes, well I must say it's a lovely day so far.

Mrs Drudge Ah, but now that the cuckoo-beard is in bud there'll be fog before the sun hits Foster's Ridge.

Simon I say, it's wonderful how you country people really know weather.

Mrs Drudge [*suspiciously*] Know whether what?

Simon [*glancing out of the window*] Yes, it does seem to be coming on a bit foggy.

Mrs Drudge The fog is very treacherous around here – it rolls off the sea without warning, shrouding the cliffs in a deadly mantle of blind man's buff.

Simon Yes, I've heard it said.

Mrs Drudge I've known whole week-ends when Muldoon Manor, as this lovely old Queen Anne House is called, might as well have been floating on the pack ice for all the good it would have done phoning the police. It was on such a week-end as this that Lord Muldoon who had lately brought his beautiful bride back to the home of his ancestors, walked out of this house ten years ago, and his body was never found.

Simon Yes, indeed, poor Cynthia.

Mrs Drudge His name was Albert.

Simon Yes indeed, poor Albert. But tell me, is Lady Muldoon about?

Mrs Drudge I believe she is playing tennis on the lawn with Felicity Cunningham.

Simon [*startled*] Felicity Cunningham?

Mrs Drudge A mutual friend, I believe you said. A happy chance. I will tell them you are here.

Simon Well, I can't really stay as a matter of fact – please don't disturb them – I really should be off.

Mrs Drudge They would be very disappointed. It is some time since we have had a four for pontoon bridge at the Manor, and I don't play cards myself.

Simon There is another guest, then?

Mrs Drudge Major Magnus, the crippled half-brother of Lord Muldoon who turned up out of the blue from Canada just the other day, completes the house-party.

[*Mrs Drudge leaves on this, Simon is undecided.*]

Moon [*ruminating quietly*] I think I must be waiting for Higgs to die.

Birdboot What?

Moon Half afraid that I will vanish when he does.

[*The phone rings. Simon picks it up.*]

Simon Hello?

Moon I wonder if it's the same for Puckeridge?

Birdboot and Simon [*together*] Who?

Moon Third string.

Birdboot Your stand-in?

Moon Does he wait for Higgs and I to write each other's obituary – does he dream?

Simon To whom did you wish to speak?

Birdboot What's he like?

Moon Bitter.

Simon There is no one of that name here.

Birdboot No – as a critic, what's Puckeridge like as a critic?

Moon [*laughs poisonously*] Nobody knows.

Simon You must have got the wrong number!

Moon – there's always been me and Higgs.

[*Simon replaces the phone and paces nervously. Pause. Birdboot consults his programme.*]

Birdboot Simon Gascoyne. It's not him, of course.

Moon What?

Birdboot I said it's not him.

Moon Who is it, then?

Birdboot My guess is Magnus.

Moon In disguise, you mean?

Birdboot What?

Moon You think he's Magnus in disguise?

Birdboot I don't think you're concentrating, Moon.

Moon I thought you said –

Birdboot You keep chattering on about Higgs and Puckeridge – what's the matter with you?

Moon [*thoughtfully*] I wonder if they talk about me . . . ?

[*A strange impulse makes Simon turn on the radio.*]

Radio Here is another police message. Essex county police are still searching in vain for the madman who is at large in the deadly marshes of the coastal region. Inspector Hound who is masterminding the operation, is not available for comment but it is widely believed that he has a secret plan. . . . Meanwhile police and volunteers are combing the swamps with loud-hailers, shouting,

'Don't be a madman, give yourself up.' That is the end of the police message. [*Simon turns off the radio. He is clearly nervous. Moon and Birdboot are on separate tracks.*]

Birdboot [*knowingly*] Oh yes. . . .

Moon Yes, I should think my name is seldom off Puckeridge's lips . . . sad, really. I mean, it's no life at all, a stand-in's stand-in.

Birdboot Yes . . . yes . . .

Moon Higgs never gives me a second thought. I can tell by the way he nods.

Birdboot Revenge, of course.

Moon What?

Birdboot Jealousy.

Moon Nonsense – there's nothing *personal* in it –

Birdboot The paranoid grudge –

Moon [*sharply first, then starting to career . . .*] It is merely that it is not enough to wax at another's wane, to be held in reserve, to be on hand, on call, to step in or not at all, the substitute the near offer – the temporary-acting – for I am Moon, continuous Moon, in my own shoes, Moon in June, April, September and no member of the human race keeps warm my bit of space – yes, I can tell by the way he nods.

Birdboot Quite mad, of course.

Moon What?

Birdboot The answer lies out there in the swamps.

Moon Oh.

Birdboot The skeleton in the cupboard is coming home to roost.

Moon Oh yes. [*He clears his throat . . . for both he and Birdboot have a 'public' voice, a critic voice which they turn on for sustained pronouncements of opinion.*] Already in the opening stages we note the classic impact of the catalystic figure – the outsider – plunging through to the centre of an ordered world and setting up the disruptions – the shock waves which unless I am much mistaken, will strip these comfortable people – these crustaceans in the rock pool of society – strip them of their shells and leave them exposed as the trembling raw meat which, at heart, is all of us. But there is more to it than that –

Birdboot I agree – keep your eye on Magnus.

[*A tennis ball bounces through the French windows, closely followed by Felicity, who is in her 20's. She wears a pretty tennis outfit, and carries a racket.*]

Felicity [*calling behind her*] Out!

[*It takes her a moment to notice Simon who is standing shiftily to one side. Moon is stirred by a memory.*]

Moon I say, Birdboot . . .

Birdboot That's the one.

Felicity [*catching sight of Simon*] You!

[*Felicity's manner at the moment is one of great surprise but some pleasure.*]

Simon [*nervously*] Er, yes – hello again.

Felicity What are you doing here?

Simon Well, I . . .

Moon She's –

Birdboot Sssh. . . .

Simon No doubt you're surprised to see me.

Felicity Honestly, darling, you really are extraordinary.

Simon Yes, well, here I am.

Felicity You must have been desperate to see me – I mean, I'm *flattered*, but couldn't it wait till I got back?

Simon [*bravely*] There is something you don't know.

Felicity What is it?

Simon Look, about the things I said – it may be that I got carried away a little – we both did –

Felicity [*stiffly*] What are you trying to say?

Simon I love another!

Felicity I see.

Simon I didn't make any promises – I merely –

Felicity You don't have to say any more –

Simon Oh, I didn't want to hurt you –

Felicity Of all the nerve!

Simon Well, I –

Felicity You philandering coward.

Simon Let me explain –

Felicity This is hardly the time and place – you think you can barge in any-where, whatever I happen to be doing –

Simon But I want you to know that my admiration for you is sincere – I don't want you to think that I didn't mean those things I said –

Felicity I'll kill you for this, Simon Gascoyne!

[*She leaves in tears, passing Mrs Drudge who has entered in time to overhear her last remark.*]

Moon It was her.

Birdboot I told you – straight to the top –

Moon No, no –

Birdboot Sssh. . . .

Simon [*to Mrs Drudge*] Yes, what is it?

Mrs Drudge I have come to set up the card table, sir.

Simon I don't think I can stay.

Mrs Drudge Oh, Lady Muldoon will be disappointed.

Simon Does she know I'm here?

Mrs Drudge Oh yes, sir, I just told her and it put her in quite a tizzy.

Simon Really . . . Well, I suppose now that I've cleared the I air. . . . Quite a tizzy, you say . . . really . . . really . . .

[*He and Mrs Drudge start setting up for card game. Mrs Drudge leaves when this is done.*]

Moon Felicity! – she's the one.

Birdboot Nonsense – red herring.

Moon I mean, it was *her*!

Birdboot [*exasperated*] *What* was?

Moon That Lady I saw you with last night!

Birdboot [*inhales with fury*] Are you suggesting that a man of my scrupulous integrity would trade his pen for a mess of potage?! Simply because in the course of my profession I happen to have struck up an acquaintance – to have, that is, a warm regard, if you like, for a fellow toiler in the vineyard of grease-paint – I find it simply intolerable to be pillified and villoried –

Moon I never implied –

Birdboot – to find myself the object of uninformed malice, the petty slanders of little men –

Moon I'm sorry –

Birdboot – to suggest that my good opinion in a journal of unimpeachable integrity is at the disposal of the first coquette who gives me what I want –

Moon Sssssh –

Birdboot A ladies' man! . . . Why, Myrtle and I have been together now for – Christ! – who's *that*?

[*Enter Lady Cynthia Muldoon through French windows. A beautiful woman in her thirties. She wears a cocktail dress, is formally coiffured, and carries a tennis racket. Her effect on Birdboot is also impressive. He half rises and sinks back agape.*]

Cynthia [*entering*] Simon!

[*A dramatic freeze between her and Simon.*]

Moon Lady Muldoon.

Birdboot No, I mean – who is she?

Simon [*coming forward*] Cynthia!

Cynthia Don't say anything for a moment – just hold me.

[*He seizes her and glues his lips to hers, as they say. While their lips are glued*]

Birdboot She's *beautiful* – a vision of eternal grace, a poem . . .

Moon I think she's got her mouth open.

[*Cynthia breaks away dramatically.*]

Cynthia We can't go on meeting like this!

Simon We have nothing to be ashamed of!

Cynthia But darling, this is madness!

Simon Yes! – I am mad with love for you!

Cynthia Please remember where we are!

Simon Cynthia, I love you!

Cynthia Don't – I love Albert!

Simon He's dead! [*Shaking her*] Do you understand me – Albert's dead!

Cynthia No – I'll never give up hope! Let me go! We are not free!

Simon I don't care, we were meant for each other – had we but met in time.

Cynthia You're a cad, Simon. You will use me and cast me aside as you have cast aside so many others.

Simon No, Cynthia! – you can make me a better person!

Cynthia You're ruthless – so strong, so cruel –

[*Ruthlessly he kisses her.*]

Moon The son she never had, now projected in this handsome stranger and transformed into lover – youth, vigour, the animal, the athlete as aesthete – breaking down the barriers at the deepest level of desire.

Birdboot By Jove, I think you're right. Her mouth is open.

[*Cynthia breaks away. Mrs Drudge has entered.*]

Cynthia Stop, can't you see you're making a fool of yourself!

Simon I'll kill anyone who comes between us!

Cynthia Yes, what is it, Mrs Drudge?

Mrs Drudge Should I close the windows, my Lady? The fog is beginning to roll off the sea like a – deadly –

Cynthia Yes, you'd better. It looks as if we're in for one of those days. Are the cards ready?

Mrs Drudge Yes, my Lady.

Cynthia Would you tell Miss Cunningham we are waiting.

Mrs Drudge Yes, my Lady.

Cynthia And fetch the Major down.

Mrs Drudge I think I hear him coming downstairs now [*as she leaves*].

[*She does: the sound of a wheelchair approaching down several flights of stairs with landings in between. It arrives bearing Magnus at about 15 m.p.h., knocking Simon over violently.*]

Cynthia Simon!

Magnus [*roaring*] Never had a chance! Ran under the wheels!

Cynthia Darling, are you all right?

Magnus I have witnesses!

Cynthia Oh, Simon say something!

Simon [*sitting up suddenly*] I'm most frightfully sorry.

Magnus [*shouting yet*] How long have you been a pedestrian?

Simon Ever since I could walk.

Cynthia Can you walk now . . . ?

[*Simon rises and walks.*]

Thank God! Magnus, this is Simon Gascoyne.

Magnus What's he doing here?

Cynthia He just turned up.

Magnus Really? How do you like it here?

Simon [*to Cynthia*] I could stay for ever. [*Felicity enters.*]

Felicity So – you're still here.

Cynthia Of course he's still here. We're going to play cards. There's no need to introduce you two, is there, for I recall now that you, Simon, met me through Felicity, our mutual friend.

Felicity Yes, Simon is an old friend, though not as old as you, Cynthia dear.

Simon Yes, I haven't seen Felicity since –

Felicity Last night.

Cynthia Indeed? Well, you deal, Felicity. Simon, you help me with the sofa. Will you partner Felicity, Magnus, against Simon and me?

Magnus [*aside*] Will Simon and you always be partnered against me, Cynthia?

Cynthia What do you mean, Magnus?

Magnus You are a damned attractive woman, Cynthia.

Cynthia Please! Please! Remember Albert!

Magnus Albert's dead, Cynthia – and you are still young. I'm sure he would have wished that you and I –

Cynthia No, Magnus, this is not to be!

Magnus It's Gascoyne, isn't it? I'll kill him if he comes between us!

Cynthia [*calling*] Simon!

[*The sofa is shoved towards the card table, once more revealing the corpse, though not to the players.*]

Birdboot Simon's for the chop all right.

Cynthia Right! Who starts ?

Magnus I do. No bid.

Cynthia Did I hear you say you saw Felicity last night, Simon?

Simon Did I? – Ah yes, yes, quite – your turn, Felicity.

Felicity I've had my turn, haven't I, Simon? – now, it seems, it's Cynthia's turn.

Cynthia That's my trick, Felicity dear.

Felicity Hell hath no fury like a woman scorned, Simon.

Simon Yes, I've heard it said.

Felicity So I hope you have not been cheating, Simon.

Simon [*standing up and throwing down his cards*] No, Felicity, it's just that I hold the cards!

Cynthia Well done, Simon!

[*Magnus pays Simon, while Cynthia deals.*]

Felicity Strange how Simon appeared in the neighbourhood from nowhere. We know so little about him.

Simon It doesn't always pay to show your hand!

Cynthia Right! Simon, it's your opening on the minor bid.

[*Simon plays.*]

Cynthia Hm, let's see. . . . [*Plays.*]

Felicity I hear there's a dangerous madman on the loose.

Cynthia Simon?

Simon Yes – yes – sorry. [*Plays.*]

Cynthia I meld.[1]

Felicity Yes – personally, I think he's been hiding out in the deserted cottage [*plays*] on the cliffs.

Simon Flush!

Cynthia No! Simon – your luck's in tonight!

Felicity We shall see – the night is not over yet, Simon Gascoyne! [*She exits.*]

[*Magnus pays Simon again.*]

Simon [*to Magnus*] So you're the crippled half-brother of Lord Muldoon who turned up out of the blue from Canada just the other day, are you? It's taken you a long time to get here. What did you do – walk? Oh, I say, I'm most frightfully sorry!

Magnus Care for a spin round the rose garden, Cynthia?

Cynthia No, Magnus, I must talk to Simon.

Simon My round, I think, Major.

Magnus You think so?

Simon Yes, Major – I do.

Magnus There's an old Canadian proverb handed down from the Bladfoot Indians, which says: He who laughs last laughs longest.

Simon Yes, I've heard it said.

[*Simon turns away to Cynthia.*]

---

1 **meld**: declare a hand at cards.

Magnus Well, I think I'll go and oil my gun. [*He exits.*]

Cynthia I think Magnus suspects something. And Felicity . . . Simon, was there anything between you and Felicity?

Simon No, no – it's over between her and me, Cynthia – it was a mere passing fleeting thing we had – but now that I have found you –

Cynthia If I find that you have been untrue to me – if I find that you have falsely seduced me from my dear husband Albert – I will kill you, Simon Gascoyne!

[*Mrs Drudge has entered silently to witness this. On this tableau, pregnant with significance, the act ends, the body still undiscovered. Perfunctory applause.*]

[*Moon and Birdboot seem to be completely preoccupied, becoming audible, as it were.*]

Moon Camps it around the Old Vic in his opera cloak and passes me the tat.

Birdboot Do you believe in love at first sight?

Moon It's not that I think I'm a better critic –

Birdboot I feel my whole life changing

Moon I am but it's not that.

Birdboot Oh, the world will laugh at me, I know . . .

Moon It is not that they are much in the way of shoes to step into . . .

Birdboot . . . call me an infatuated old fool . . .

Moon . . . They are not.

Birdboot . . . condemn me . . .

Moon He is standing in my light, that is all.

Birdboot . . . betrayer of my class . . .

Moon . . . an almost continuous eclipse, interrupted by the phenomenon of moonlight.

Birdboot I don't care, I'm a gonner.

Moon And I dream . . .

Birdboot The Blue Angel all over again.

Moon . . . of the day his temperature climbs through the top of his head . . .

Birdboot Ah, the sweet madness of love . . .

Moon . . . of the spasm on the stairs . . .

Birdboot Myrtle, farewell . . .

Moon . . . dreaming of the stair he'll never reach –

Birdboot . . . for I only live but once . . .

Moon Sometimes I dream that I've killed him.

Birdboot What?

Moon What?

[*They pull themselves together.*]

Birdboot Yes . . . yes . . . . A beautiful performance, a collector's piece. I shall say so.

Moon A very promising debut. I'll put in a good word.

Birdboot It would be as hypocritical of me to withhold praise on grounds of personal feelings, as to withhold censure.

Moon You're right. Courageous.

Birdboot Oh, I know what people will say. There goes Birdboot buttering up his latest –

Moon Ignore them –

Birdboot But I rise above that. The fact is I genuinely believe her performance to be one of the summits in the range of contemporary theatre.

Moon Trim-buttocked, that's the word for her.

Birdboot – the radiance, the inner sadness –

Moon Does she actually come across with it?

Birdboot The part as written is a mere cypher but she manages to make Cynthia a real person –

Moon Cynthia?

Birdboot And should she, as a result, care to meet me over a drink, simply by way of er – thanking me, as it were –

Moon Well, you fickle old bastard!

Birdboot [*aggressively*] Are you suggesting . . . ?

[*Birdboot shudders to a halt and clears his throat.*]

Birdboot Well now – shaping up quite nicely, wouldn't you say?

Moon Oh yes, yes. A nice trichotomy of forces. One must reserve judgement of course, until the confrontation, but I think it's pretty clear where we're heading.

Birdboot I agree. It's Magnus a mile off.

[*Small pause.*]

Moon What's Magnus a mile off?

Birdboot If we knew that we wouldn't be here.

Moon [*clears throat*] Let me at once say that it has *élan* while at the same time avoiding *éclat*. Having said that, and I think it must be said, I am bound to ask – does this play know where it is going?

Birdboot Well, it seems open and shut to me, Moon – Magnus is not what he pretends to be and he's got his next victim marked down –

Moon Does it, I repeat, declare its affiliations? There are moments, and I would not begrudge it this, when the play, if we can call it that, and I think on balance we can, aligns itself uncompromisingly on the side of life. *Je suis*, it seems to be saying, *ergo sum*. But is that enough? I think we are entitled to ask. For what in fact is this play concerned with? It is my belief that here we are concerned with what I have referred to elsewhere as the nature of identity. I think we are entitled to ask – and here one is irresistibly reminded of Voltaire's cry, '*Voila!*' – I think we are entitled to ask – *Where is God?*

Birdboot [*stunned*] Who?

Moon Go-od.

Birdboot [*peeping furtively into his programme*] God?

Moon I think we are entitled to ask.

[*The phone rings.*]

[*The set re-illumines to reveal Cynthia, Felicity and Magnus about to take coffee, which is being taken round by Mrs Drudge. Simon is missing. The body lies in position.*]

Mrs Drudge [*into phone*] The same, half an hour later? . . . No, I'm sorry – there's no one of that name here. [*She replaces phone and goes round with coffee. To Cynthia*] Black or white, my Lady?

Cynthia White please.
[*Mrs Drudge pours.*]
Mrs Drudge [*to Felicity*] Black or white, miss?
Felicity White please.
[*Mrs Drudge pours*]
Mrs Drudge [*to Magnus*] Black or white, Major?
Magnus White please. [*Ditto.*]
Mrs Drudge [*to Cynthia*] Sugar, my Lady?
Cynthia Yes please. [*Puts sugar in.*]
Mrs Drudge [*to Felicity*] Sugar, miss?
Felicity Yes please. [*Ditto.*]
Mrs Drudge [*to Magnus*] Sugar, Major?
Magnus Yes please. [*Ditto.*]
Mrs Drudge [*to Cynthia*] Biscuit, my Lady?
Cynthia No thank you.
Birdboot [*writing elaborately in his notebook*] The second act, however, fails to fulfil the promise . . .
Felicity If you ask me, there's something funny going on.
[*Mrs Drudge's approach to Felicity makes Felicity jump to her feet in impatience. She goes to the radio while Magnus declines his biscuit, and Mrs Drudge leaves.*]
Radio We interrupt our programme for a special police message. The search for the dangerous madman who is on the loose in Essex has now narrowed to the immediate vicinity of Muldoon Manor. Police are hampered by the deadly swamps and the fog, but believe that the madman spent last night in a deserted cottage on the cliffs. The public is advised to stick together and make sure none of their number is missing. That is the end of the police message. [*Felicity turns off the radio nervously. Pause.*]
Cynthia Where's Simon?
Felicity Who?
Cynthia Simon. Have you seen him?
Felicity No.
Cynthia Have you, Magnus?
Magnus No.
Cynthia Oh.
Felicity Yes, there's something foreboding in the air, it is as if one of us –
Cynthia Oh, Felicity, the house is locked up tight – no one can get in – and the police are practically on the doorstep.
Felicity I don't know – it's just a feeling.
Cynthia It's only the fog.
Magnus Hound will never get through on a day like this.
Cynthia [*shouting at him*] Fog!
Felicity He means the Inspector.
Cynthia Is he bringing a dog?
Felicity Not that I know of.
Magnus – never get through the swamps. Yes, I'm afraid the madman can show his hand in safety now.
[*A mournful baying hooting is heard in the distance, scary.*]

Cynthia What's that?!
Felicity [*tensely*] It sounded like the cry of a gigantic hound!
Magnus Poor devil!
Cynthia Ssssh!
[*They listen. The sound is repeated, nearer.*]
Felicity There it is again!
Cynthia It's coming this way– it's right outside the house!
[*Mrs Drudge enters.*]
Mrs Drudge Inspector Hound!
Cynthia A police dog?
[*Enter Inspector Hound. On his feet are his swamp boots. These are two inflatable – and inflated – pontoons with flat bottoms about two feet across. He carries a foghorn.*]
Hound Lady Muldoon?
Cynthia Yes.
Hound I came as soon as I could. Where shall I put my foghorn and my swamp boots?
Cynthia Mrs Drudge will take them out. Be prepared, as the Force's motto has it, eh, Inspector? How very resourceful!
Hound [*divesting himself of boots and foghorn*] It takes more than a bit of weather to keep a policeman from his duty.
[*Mrs Drudge leaves with chattels. A pause.*]
Cynthia Oh er, Inspector Hound – Felicity Cunningham, Major Magnus Muldoon.
Hound Good evening.
[*He and Cynthia continue to look expectantly at each other.*]
Cynthia and Hound [*together*] Well? – Sorry –
Cynthia No, do go on.
Hound Thank you. Well, tell me about it in your own words – take your time, begin at the beginning and don't leave anything out.
Cynthia I beg your pardon?
Hound Fear nothing. You are in safe hands now. I hope you haven't touched anything.
Cynthia I'm afraid I don't understand.
Hound I'm Inspector Hound.
Cynthia Yes.
Hound Well, what's it all about?
Cynthia I really have no idea.
Hound How did it begin?
Cynthia What?
Hound The . . . thing.
Cynthia What thing ?
Hound [*rapidly losing confidence but exasperated*] The trouble!
Cynthia There hasn't been any trouble!
Hound Didn't you phone the police?
Cynthia No.
Felicity I didn't.

Magnus What for?
Hound I see. [*Pause.*] This puts me in a very difficult position. [*A steady pause*] Well, I'll be getting along, then. [*He moves towards the door.*]
Cynthia I'm terribly sorry.
Hound [*stiffly*] That's perfectly all right.
Cynthia Thank you so much for coming.
Hound Not at all. You never know, there might have been a serious matter.
Cynthia Drink?
Hound More serious than that, even.
Cynthia [*correcting*] Drink before you go?
Hound No thank you. [*Leaves.*]
Cynthia [*through the door*] I do hope you find him.
Hound [*reappearing at once*] Find who, Madam? – out with it!
Cynthia I thought you were looking for the lunatic.
Hound And what do you know about that?
Cynthia It was on the radio.
Hound Was it, indeed? Well, that's what I'm here about, really. I didn't want to mention it because I didn't know how much you knew. No point in causing unnecessary panic, even with a murderer in our midst.
Felicity Murderer, did you say?
Hound Ah – so that was not on the radio?
Cynthia Whom has he murdered, Inspector?
Hound Perhaps no one – yet. Let us hope we are in time.
Magnus You believe he is in our midst, Inspector?
Hound I do. If anyone of you have recently encountered a youngish good-looking fellow in a smart suit, white shirt, hatless, well-spoken – someone possibly claiming to have just moved into the neighbourhood, someone who on the surface seems as sane as you or I, then now is the time to speak!
Felicity I –
Hound Don't interrupt!
Felicity Inspector –
Hound Very well.
Cynthia No. Felicity!
Hound Please, Lady Cynthia, we are all in this together. I must ask you to put yourself completely in my hands.
Cynthia Don't, Inspector. I love Albert.
Hound I don't think you quite grasp my meaning.
Magnus Is one of us in danger, Inspector?
Hound Didn't it strike you as odd that on his escape the madman made a beeline for Muldoon Manor? It is my guess that he bears a deep-seated grudge against someone in this very house! Lady Muldoon – where is your husband?
Cynthia My husband ?– you don't mean –?
Hound I don't know – but I have a reason to believe that one of you is the real McCoy!
Felicity The real what?
Hound William Herbert McCoy who as a young man, meeting the madman in the street and being solicited for sixpence for a cup of tea, replied, 'Why don't

you do a decent day's work, you shifty old bag of horse manure,' in Canada all those many years ago and went on to make his fortune. [*He starts to pace intensely.*] The madman was a mere boy at the time but he never forgot that moment, and thenceforth carried in his heart the promise of revenge! [*At which point he finds himself standing on top of the corpse. He looks down carefully.*]

Hound Is there anything you have forgotten to tell me ?

[*They all see the corpse for the first time.*]

Felicity So the madman has struck!

Cynthia Oh – it's horrible – horrible –

Hound Yes, just as I feared. Now you see the sort of man you are protecting.

Cynthia I can't believe it!

Felicity I'll have to tell him, Cynthia – Inspector, a stranger of that description has indeed appeared in our midst – Simon Gascoyne. Oh, he had charm, I'll give you that, and he took me in completely. I'm afraid I made a fool of myself over him, and so did Cynthia.

Hound Where is he now?

Magnus He must be around the house – he couldn't get away in these conditions.

Hound You're right. Fear naught, Lady Muldoon – I shall apprehend the man who killed your husband.

Cynthia My husband? I don't understand.

Hound Everything points to Gascoyne.

Cynthia But who's that? [*The corpse.*]

Hound Your husband.

Cynthia No, it's not.

Hound Yes, it is.

Cynthia I tell you it's not.

Hound I'm in charge of this case!

Cynthia But that's not my husband.

Hound Are you sure?

Cynthia For goodness sake!

Hound Then who is it?

Cynthia I don't know.

Hound Anybody?

Felicity I've never seen him before.

Magnus Quite unlike anybody I've ever met.

Hound This case is becoming an utter shambles.

Cynthia But what are we going to do?

Hound [*snatching the phone*] I'll phone the police!

Cynthia But you are the police!

Hound Thank God I'm here – the lines have been cut!

Cynthia You mean?

Hound Yes! – we're on our own, cut off from the world and in grave danger!

Felicity You mean?

Hound Yes! – I think the killer will strike again!

Magnus You mean?

Hound Yes! One of us ordinary mortals thrown together by fate and cut off by the elements, is the murderer! He must be found – search the house!
[*All depart speedily in different directions leaving a momentarily empty stage. Simon strolls on.*]
Simon [*entering, calling*] Anyone about? – funny . . .
[*He notices the corpse and is surprised. He approaches it and turns it over. He stands up and looks about in alarm.*]
Birdboot This is where Simon gets the chop.
[*There is a shot. Simon falls dead.*]
[*Inspector Hound runs on and crouches down by Simon's body. Cynthia appears at the French windows. She stops there and stares.*]
Cynthia What happened, Inspector?!
[*Hound turns to face her.*]
Hound He's dead. . . . Simon Gascoyne, I presume. Rough justice even for a killer – unless – unless – We assumed that the body could not have been lying there before Simon Gascoyne entered the house . . . but . . . [*he slides the sofa over the body*] there's your answer. And now – who killed Simon Gascoyne? And why?
[*Curtain, freeze, applause, exeunt.*]
Moon Why not ?
Birdboot Exactly. Good riddance.
Moon Yes, getting away with murder must be quite easy provided that one's motive is sufficiently inscrutable.
Birdboot Fickle young pup! He was deceiving her right, left and centre.
Moon [*thoughtfully*] Of course. I'd still have Puckeridge behind me –
Birdboot She needs someone steadier, more mature –
Moon – And if I could, so could he –
Birdboot Yes, I know of this rather nice hotel, very discreet, run by a man of the world –
Moon Uneasy lies the head that wears the crown.
Birdboot Breakfast served in one's room and no questions asked.
Moon Does Puckeridge dream of me?
Birdboot [*pause*] Hello – what's happened?
Moon What? Oh yes – what do you make of it, so far?
Birdboot [*clears throat*] It is at this point that the play for me comes alive. The groundwork has been well and truly laid, and the author has taken the trouble to learn from the masters of the genre. He has created a real situation, and few will doubt his ability to resolve it with a startling denouement. Certainly that is what it so far lacks, but it has a beginning, a middle and I have no doubt it will prove to have an end. For this let us give thanks, and double thanks for a good clean show without a trace of smut. But perhaps even all this would be for nothing were it not for a performance which I consider to be one of the summits in the range of contemporary theatre. In what is possibly the finest Cynthia since the war –
Moon If we examine this more closely, and I think close examination is the least tribute that this play deserves, I think we will find that within the austere framework of what is seen to be on one level a country-house week-end, and

what a useful symbol that is, the author has given us – yes, I will go so far – he has given us the human condition –

Birdboot More talent in her little finger –

Moon An uncanny ear that might belonged to a Van Gogh –

Birdboot – a public scandal that the Birthday Honours to date have neglected –

Moon Faced as we are with such ubiquitous obliquity, it is hard, it is hard indeed, and therefore I will not attempt, to refrain from invoking the names of Kafka, Sartre, Shakespeare, St. Paul, Beckett, Birkett, Pinero, Pirandello, Dante and Dorothy L. Sayers.

Birdboot A rattling good evening out. I was held.

[*The phone starts to ring on the empty stage. Moon tries to ignore it.*]

Moon Harder still – Harder still if possible – Harder still if it is – possible to be – Neither do I find it easy Dante and Dorothy L. Sayers. Harder still –

Birdboot Others taking part included – Moon!

[*For Moon has lost patience and is bearing down on the ringing phone. He is frankly irritated.*]

Moon [*picking up phone, barks*] Hel-lo! [*Pause, turns to Birdboot, quietly.*] It's for you. [*Pause.*]

[*Birdboot gets up. He approaches cautiously. Moon gives him the phone and moves back to his seat. Birdboot watches him go. He looks round and smiles weakly, expiating himself.*]

Birdboot [*into phone*] Hello . . . [*Explosion*] Oh, for God's sake, Myrtle! – I've told you never to phone me at work! [*He is naturally embarrassed, looking about with surreptitious fury.*] What? Last night? Good God, woman, this is hardly the time to – I assure you, Myrtle, there is absolutely nothing going on between me and – I took her to dinner simply by way of keeping *au fait* with the world of the paint and the motley – Yes, I promise – Yes, I do. Yes, I said yes – I do – and you are mine too, Myrtle – darling – I can't – [*whispers*] I'm not alone – [*up*]. No, she's not! – [*he looks around furtively, licks his lips and mumbles*] All right! I love your little pink ears and you are my own fluffy bunny-boo. Now for God's sake. Good-bye, Myrtle – [*puts down phone*].

[*Birdboot mops his brow with his handkerchief. As he turns, a tennis ball bounces into through the French windows, followed by Felicity, as before, in tennis outfit. The lighting is as it was. Everything is as it was. It is, let us say, the same moment of time.*]

Felicity [*calling*] Out! [*She catches sight of Birdboot and is amazed.*] You!

Birdboot Er, yes – hello again.

Felicity What are you doing here?!

Birdboot Well, I . . .

Felicity Honestly, darling, you really are extraordinary –

Birdboot Yes, well, here I am. [*He looks round sheepishly.*]

Felicity You must have been desperate to see me – I mean, I'm flattered, but couldn't it wait till I got back?

Birdboot No, no, you've got it all wrong.

Felicity What is it?

Birdboot And about last night – perhaps I gave you the wrong impression – got carried away a bit, perhaps

Felicity [*stiffly*] What are you trying to say?

Birdboot I want to call it off.

Felicity I see.

Birdboot I didn't promise anything – and the fact is, I have my reputation – people do talk.

Felicity You don't have to say any more –

Birdboot And my wife, too – I don't know how she got to hear of it, but –

Felicity Of all the nerve! To march in here and –

Birdboot I'm sorry you had to find out like this – the fact is I didn't mean it this way –

Felicity You philandering coward!

Birdboot I'm sorry – but I want you to know that I meant those things I said – oh yes – shows brilliant promise – I shall say so –

Felicity I'll kill you for this, Simon Gascoyne!

[*She leaves in tears, passing Mrs Drudge who has entered in time to overhear her last remark.*]

Birdboot [*wide-eyed*] Good God. . . .

Mrs Drudge I have come to set up the card table, sir.

Birdboot [*wildly*] I can't stay for a game of cards!

Mrs Drudge Oh, Lady Muldoon will be disappointed.

Birdboot You mean . . . you mean, she wants to meet me . . . ?

Mrs Drudge Oh yes, sir, I just told her and it put her in quite a tizzy.

Birdboot Really? Yes, well, a man of my influence is not to be I sneezed at – I think I have some small name for the making of reputations – mmm, yes, quite a tizzy, you say?

[*Mrs Drudge is busied with the card table. Birdboot stands marooned and bemused for a moment.*]

Moon [*from his seat*] Birdboot [*a tense whisper*] Birdboot [*Birdboot looks round vaguely*] What the hell are you doing?

Birdboot Nothing.

Moon Stop making an ass of yourself. Come back.

Birdboot Oh, I know what you're thinking – but the fact is I genuinely consider her performance to be one of the summits –

[*Cynthia enters as before. Mrs Drudge has gone.*]

Cynthia Darling!

Birdboot Ah, good evening – may I say that I genuinely consider

Cynthia Don't say anything for a moment – just hold me. [*She falls into his arms.*]

Birdboot All right! [*They kiss*] My God! – she does have her mouth open! Dear Lady, from the first moment I saw you, I felt my whole life changing –

Cynthia [*breaking free*] We can't go on meeting like this!

Birdboot I am not ashamed to proclaim nightly my love for you! – but fortunately that will not be necessary – I know of a very good hotel, discreet – run by a man of the world –

Cynthia But darling, this is madness!

Birdboot Yes! I am mad with love.

Cynthia Please! – remember where we are!

Birdboot I don't care! Let them think what they like, I love you!

Cynthia Don't – I love Albert!

Birdboot He's dead. [*Shaking her*] Do you understand me – Albert's dead!

Cynthia No – I'll never give up hope! Let me go! We are not free!

Birdboot You mean Myrtle? She means nothing to me – nothing! – she's all cocoa and blue nylon fur slippers – not a spark of creative genius in her whole slumping kneelength-knickered body –

Cynthia You're a cad, Simon! You will use me and cast me aside as you have cast aside so many others!

Birdboot No, Cynthia, now that I have found you –

Cynthia You're ruthless – so strong – so cruel –

[*Birdboot seizes her in an embrace, during which Mrs Drudge enters, and Moon's fevered voice is heard.*]

Moon Have you taken leave of your tiny mind? [*Cynthia breaks free.*]

Cynthia Stop – can't you see you're making a fool of yourself!

Moon She's right.

Birdboot [*to Moon*] You keep out of this.

Cynthia Yes, what is it, Mrs Drudge?

Mrs Drudge Should I close the windows, my Lady? The fog –

Cynthia Yes, you'd better.

Moon Look, they've got your number –

Birdboot I'll leave in my own time, thank you very much.

Moon It's the finish of you, I suppose you know that –

Birdboot I don't need your twopenny Grubb Street prognostications – I have found something bigger and finer –

Moon [*bemused, to himself*] If only it were Higgs . . .

Cynthia . . . And fetch the Major down.

Mrs Drudge I think I hear him coming down stairs now.

[*She leaves. The sound of a wheelchair's approach as before. Birdboot prudently keeps out of the chair's former path but it enters from the next wing down and knocks him flying. A babble of anguish and protestation.*]

Cynthia Simon – say something!

Birdboot That reckless bastard – [*as he sits up*].

Cynthia Thank God! –

Magnus What's he doing here?

Cynthia He just turned up.

Magnus Really? How do you like it here?

Birdboot I couldn't take it night after night.

[*Felicity enters.*]

Felicity So – you're still here.

Cynthia Of course he's still here. We're going to play cards. There is no need to introduce you two, is there, for I recall now that you, Simon, met me through Felicity, our mutual friend.

Felicity Yes, Simon is an old friend –

Birdboot Ah – yes – well, I like to give young up and comers the benefit of my er – Of course, she lacks technique as yet –

Felicity Last night.

Birdboot I'm not talking about last night!

Cynthia Indeed? Well, you deal, Felicity. Simon, you help me with the sofa.

Birdboot [*to Moon*] Did you see that? Tried to kill me. I told you it was Magnus – not that it is Magnus.

Moon Who did it, you mean?

Birdboot What?

Moon You think it's not Magnus who did it?

Birdboot Get a grip on yourself, Moon – the facts are staring you in the face. He's after Cynthia for one thing.

Magnus It's Gascoyne, isn't it?

Birdboot Over my dead body!

Magnus If he comes between us . . .

Moon [*angrily*] For God's sake sit down!

Cynthia Simon!

Birdboot She needs me, Moon. I've got to make up a four.

[*Cynthia and Birdboot move the sofa as before, and they all sit at the table.*]

Cynthia Right! Who starts?

Magnus I do. I'll dummy for a no-bid ruff and double my holding on South's queen. [*While he moves cards.*]

Cynthia Did I hear you say you saw Felicity last night, Simon?

Birdboot Er – er –

Felicity Pay twenty-ones or trump my contract. [*discards*] Cynthia's turn.

Cynthia I'll trump your contract with five dummy no-trumps there, [*discards*] and I'll move West's rook for the re-bid with a banker ruff on his second trick there. [*discards*] Simon?

Birdboot Would you mind doing that again?

Cynthia And I'll ruff your dummy with five no-bid trumps there, [*discards*] and I support your re-bid with a banker for the solo ruff in the dummy trick there. [*discards*]

Birdboot [*standing up and throwing down his cards*] And I call your bluff!

Cynthia Well done, Simon!

[*Magnus pays Birdboot while Cynthia deals.*]

Felicity Strange how Simon appeared in the neighbourhood from nowhere, we know so little about him.

Cynthia Right, Simon, it's your opening on the minor bid. Hmm. Let's see. I think I'll overbid the spade convention with two no-trumps and King's gambit offered there – [*discards*] and West's dummy split double to Queen's Bishop four there!

Magnus [*as he plays cards*] Faites vos jeux. Rien ne va plus. Rouge et noir. Zero.

Cynthia Simon?

Birdboot [*triumphant, leaping to his feet*] And I call your bluff!

Cynthia [*imperturbably*] I meld.

Felicity I huff.

Magnus I ruff.

Birdboot I bluff.

Cynthia Twist.

Felicity Bust.

Magnus. Check.

Birdboot Snap.

Cynthia How's that?

Felicity Not out.

Magnus Double top.

Birdboot Bingo!

Cynthia No! Simon – your luck's in tonight.

Felicity We shall see – the night is not over yet, Simon Gascoyne!

[*She quickly exits.*]

Birdboot [*looking after Felicity*] Red herring – smell it a mile off. [*To Magnus.*] Oh, yes, she's as clean as a whistle, I've seen it a thousand times. And I've seen you before too, haven't I? Strange – there's something about you –

Magnus Care for a spin round the rose garden, Cynthia?

Cynthia No, Magnus, I must talk to Simon.

Birdboot There's nothing for you there, you know.

Magnus You think so?

Birdboot Oh, yes, she knows which side her bread is buttered. I am a man not without a certain influence among those who would reap the limelight – she's not going to throw me over for a heavily disguised cripple.

Magnus There's an old Canadian proverb –

Birdboot Don't give me that – I tumbled to you right from the start – oh, yes, you chaps are not as clever as you think. . . . Sooner or later you make your mistake. . . . Incidentally, where was it I saw you?. . . . I've definitely –

Magnus [*leaving*] Well, I think I'll go and oil my gun. [*Exit.*]

Birdboot [*after Magnus*] Double bluff! – [*to Cynthia*] I've seen it a thousand times.

Cynthia I think Magnus suspects something. And Felicity? Simon, was there anything between you and Felicity?

Birdboot No, no – that's all over now. I merely flattered her a little over a – drink, told her she'd go far, that sort of thing. Dear me, the fuss that's been made over a simple flirtation –

Cynthia [*as Mrs Drudge enters behind*] If I find you have falsely seduced me from my dear husband Albert, I will kill you, Simon Gascoyne!

[*The Curtain as before. Mrs Drudge and Cynthia leave. Birdboot starts to follow them.*]

Moon Birdboot!

[*Birdboot stops.*]

Moon For God's sake pull yourself together.

Birdboot I can t help it.

Moon What do you think you're doing? You're turning it into a complete farce!

Birdboot I know, I know – but I can't live without her. [*He is making erratic neurotic journeys about the stage.*] I shall resign my position, of course. I don't care I'm a gonner, I tell you – [*He has arrived at the body. He looks at it in surprise, hesitates, bends and turns it over.*]

Moon Birdboot, think of your family, your friends – your high standing in the world of letters – I say, what are you doing?

[*Birdboot is staring at the body's face.*]

Birdboot . . . leave it alone. Come and sit down – what's the matter with you?

Birdboot [*dead-voiced*] It's Higgs.

Moon What?

Birdboot It's Higgs.

[*Pause.*]

Moon Don't be silly.

Birdboot I tell you it s Higgs!

[*Moon half rises. Bewildered.*]

I don't understand. . . . He's dead.

Moon Dead?

Birdboot Who would want to . . . ?

Moon He must have been lying there all the time . . .

Birdboot . . . kill Higgs?

Moon But what's he doing here? I was standing in tonight . . .

Birdboot [*turning*] Moon? . . .

Moon [*in wonder, quietly*] So it's me and Puckeridge now.

Birdboot Moon . . . ?

Moon [*faltering*] But I swear I . . .

Birdboot I've got it –

Moon But I didn't –

Birdboot [*quietly*] My God . . . O that was it. . . . [*Up*] Moon – now I see –

Moon – I swear I didn't –

Birdboot Now – finally – I see it all –

[*There is a shot and Birdboot falls dead.*]

Moon Birdboot!

[*He runs on, to Birdboot's body*]

[*Cynthia appears at the French windows. She stops and stares. All as before.*]

Cynthia Oh my God – what happened, Inspector?

Moon [*almost to himself*] He's dead . . . [*He rises*] That's a bit rough, isn't it? – A bit extreme! – He may have had his faults – I admit he was a fickle old . . . Who did this, and why?

[*Moon turns to face her. He stands up and makes swiftly for his seat. Before he gets there he is stopped by the sound of voices.*]

[*Simon and Hound are occupying the critics' seats.*]

[*Moon freezes.*]

Simon To say that it is without pace, point, focus, interest, drama, wit or originality is to say simply that it does not happen to be my cup of tea. One has only to compare this ragbag with the masters of the genre to see that here we have a trifle that is not my cup of tea at all.

Hound I'm sorry to be blunt but there is no getting away from it. It lacks pace. A complete ragbag.

Simon I will go further. Those of you who were fortunate enough to be at the

Comédie Française on Wednesday last, will not need to be reminded that hysterics are no substitute for *éclat*.

Hound It lacks *élan*.

Simon Some of the cast seem to have given up acting altogether, apparently aghast, with every reason, at finding themselves involved in an evening that would, and indeed will, make the angels weep.

Hound I am not a prude but I fail to see any reason for the shower of filth and sexual allusion foisted on to an unsuspecting public in the guise of modernity at all costs . . .

[*Behind Moon, Felicity, Magnus and Mrs Drudge have made their entrances, so that he turns to face their semicircle.*]

Magnus [*pointing to Birdboot's body*] Well, Inspector, is this your man?

Moon [*warily*] . . . Yes . . . Yes . . .

Cynthia It's Simon . . .

Moon Yes . . . yes . . . poor . . . [*Up*] Is this some kind of a joke?

Magnus If it is, Inspector, it's in very poor taste.

[*Moon pulls himself together and becomes galvanic, a little wild, in grief for Birdboot.*]

Moon All right! I'm going to find out who did this! I want everyone to go to the positions they occupied when the was fired – [*they move; hysterically*] No one will leave house! [*They move back.*]

Magnus I think we all had the opportunity to fire the shot, Inspector –

Moon [*furious*] I am not –

Magnus – but which of us would want to?

Moon Perhaps you, Major Magnus!

Magnus Why should I want to kill him?

Moon Because he was on to you – yes, he tumbled you right the start – and you shot him just when he was about to reveal that you killed – [*Moon points, pauses and then crosses to Higgs's body and falters*] – killed – [*he turns Higgs over*] this . . . chap.

Magnus But what motive would there be for killing him? [*Pause*] Who is this chap? [*Pause*] Inspector?

Moon [*rising*] I don't know. Quite unlike anyone I've ever met [*Long pause*] Well . . . now . . .

Mrs Drudge Inspector?

Moon [*eagerly*] Yes? Yes, what is it, dear Lady?

Mrs Drudge Happening to enter this room earlier in the day to close the windows, I chanced to overhear a remark made by the deceased Simon Gascoyne to her Ladyship, viz. – 'I kill anyone who comes between us.'

Moon Ah – yes – well, that's it, then. This . . . chap . . . [*pointing*] was obviously killed by [*pointing*] er . . . by [*pause*] Simon.

Cynthia But he didn't come between us!

Magnus And who, then, killed Simon?

Mrs Drudge Subsequent to that reported remark, I also happened to be in earshot of a remark made by Lady Muldoon to the deceased, to the effect, 'I will kill you, Simon Gascoyne!' I hope you don't mind my mentioning it.

Moon Not at all. I'm glad you did. It is from these chance remarks that we in the force build up our complete picture before moving in to make the arrest. It

will not be long now, I fancy, and I must warn you, Lady Muldoon that anything you say –

Cynthia Yes! – I hated Simon Gascoyne, for he had me in his power! – But I
didn't kill him!

Mrs Drudge Prior to that, Inspector, I also chanced to overhear a remark made
by Miss Cunningham, no doubt in the heat of the moment, but it stuck in my
mind as these things do, viz., 'I will kill you for this, Simon Gascoyne!'

Moon Ah! The final piece of the jigsaw! I think I am now in a position to reveal
the mystery. This man [*the corpse*] was, of course, McCoy, the Canadian who,
as we heard, meeting Gascoyne in the street and being solicited for sixpence
for a toffee apple, smacked him across the ear, with the cry, 'How's that for a
grudge to harbour, you sniffling little workshy!' all those many years ago.
Gascoyne bided his time, but in due course tracked McCoy down to this house,
having, on the way, met, in the neighbourhood, a simple ambitious girl from
the provinces. He was charming; persuasive – told her, I have no doubt, that
she would go straight to the top – and she, flattered by his sophistication, taken
in by his promises to see her all right on the night, gave in to his simple desires.
Perhaps she loved him. We shall never know. But in the very hour of her
promised triumph, his eye fell on another – yes, I refer to Lady Cynthia Muldoon.
From the moment he caught sight of her there was no other woman for him –
he was in her spell, willing to sacrifice anything, even you, Felicity Cunningham.
It was only today – unexpectedly finding him here – that you learned the truth.
There was a bitter argument which ended with your promise to kill him – a
promise that you carried out in this very room at your first opportunity! And I
must warn you that anything you say –

Felicity But it doesn't make sense!

Moon Not at first glance, perhaps.

Magnus Could not Simon have been killed by the same person who killed
McCoy?

Felicity But why should any of us want to kill a perfect stranger Magnus?

Magnus Perhaps he was not a stranger to *one* of us.

Moon [*faltering*] But Simon was the madman, wasn't he ?

Magnus We only have your word for that, Inspector. We only have your word
for a lot of things. For instance – McCoy Who is he? Is his name McCoy? Is
there any truth in the fantastic and implausible tale of the insult inflicted in the
Canadian streets? Or is there something else, something quite unknown to us,
behind all this? Suppose for a moment that the madman, having killed this
unknown stranger for private and inscrutable reasons of his own, was disturbed
before he could dispose of the body, so having cut the telephone wires he
decided to return to the scene of the crime, masquerading as – Police Inspector
Hound!

Moon But . . . I'm not mad . . . I'm almost sure I'm not mad . . .

Magnus . . . only to discover that in the house was a man, Simon Gascoyne,
who recognised the corpse as a man against whom you had held a deep-seated
grudge – !

Moon But I didn't kill – I'm almost sure I –

Magnus I put it to you! – are you the real Inspector Hound?!

Moon You know damn well I'm not! What's it all about?
Magnus I thought as much.
Moon I only dreamed . . . sometimes I dreamed –
Cynthia So it was you!
Mrs Drudge The madman!
Felicity The killer!
Cynthia Oh, it's horrible, horrible.
Mrs Drudge The stranger in our midst!
Magnus Yes, we had a shrewd suspicion he would turn up here – and he walked into the trap!
Moon What *trap*?
Magnus I am not the real Magnus Muldoon! – It was a mere subterfuge! – and [*standing up and removing his moustaches*] I now reveal myself as –
Cynthia You mean?
Magnus Yes! – I am the real Inspector Hound!
Moon [*pause*] Puckeridge!
Magnus [*with pistol*] Stand where you are, or I shoot!
Moon [*backing*] Puckeridge! You killed Higgs – and Birdboot tried to tell me –
Magnus Stop in the name of the law!
[*Moon turns to run. Magnus fires. Moon drops to his knees.*]
I have waited a long time for this moment.
Cynthia So you are the real Inspector Hound.
Magnus Not only that! – I have been leading a double life – at *least*!
Cynthia You mean – ?
Magnus Yes! – It's been ten long years, but don't you know me?
Cynthia You mean?
Magnus Yes! – it is me, Albert! – who lost his memory and joined the force, rising by merit to the rank of Inspector, his past blotted out – until fate cast him back into the home he left behind, back to the beautiful woman he had brought here as his girlish bride in short, my darling, my memory has returned and your long wait is over!
Cynthia Oh, Albert! [*They embrace.*]
Moon [*with a trace of admiration*] Puckeridge . . . you cunning bastard.
[*Moon dies.*]

THE END

JOHN FOWLES (1926–)

An interesting development in the fiction of the last 30 years has been the creation of a pastiche of earlier writing styles, matched with the novelist's own self-conscious interrogation about the way narratives and the past are constructed. Fowles' 1969 novel *The French Lieutenant's Woman* is, in one respect, an exploration of Victorian mores and current perceptions of them through the story of Sarah Woodruff, a supposedly fallen woman, and Charles Smithson, an affluent gentleman and collector of fossils who becomes obsessed with her. But the novel also demonstrates the writer's own obsession with his act of contrivance. The following two chapters illustrate how Fowles juxtaposes his fictional incidences, here Charles' sighting of the mysterious Sarah in a wood near Lyme Regis in Dorset, with his own meta-narrative on them.

From The French Lieutenant's Woman

Chapter 12

> In what does the alienation of labour consist? First, that the work
> is external to the worker, that it is not a part of his nature, that
> consequently he does not fulfil himself in his work but denies
> himself, has a feeling of misery, not of well-being . . . The worker
> therefore feels himself at home only during his leisure, whereas
> at work he feels homeless.
> Marx, *Economic and Political Manuscripts* (1844)

> And was the day of my delight
> As pure and perfect as I say?
> Tennyson, *In Memoriam* (1850)

Charles put his best foot forward, and thoughts of the mysterious woman behind him, through the woods of Ware Commons. He walked for a mile or more, until he came simultaneously to a break in the trees and the first outpost of civilization. This was a long thatched cottage, which stood slightly below his path. There were two or three meadows round it, running down to the cliffs; and just as Charles came out of the woodlands he saw a man hoying a herd of cows away from a low byre beside the cottage. There slipped into his mind an image: a deliciously cool bowl of milk. He had eaten nothing since the double dose of muffins. Tea and tenderness at Mrs Tranter's called, but the bowl of milk shrieked . . . and was much closer at hand. He went down a steep grass slope and knocked on the back door of the cottage.

It was opened by a small barrel of a woman, her fat arms shiny with suds. Yes, he was welcome to as much milk as he could drink. The name of the place? The Dairy, it seemed, was all it was called. Charles followed her into the slant-roofed room that ran the length of the rear of the cottage. It was dark, shadowy, very cool; a slate-floor; and heavy with the smell of ripening cheese. A line of scalding bowls, great copper pans on wooden trestles, each with its golden crust of cream, were ranged under the cheese, which sat roundly, like squadrons of reserve moons, on the open rafters above. Charles remembered then to have heard of the place. Its cream and butter had a local reputation; Aunt Tranter had spoken of it. He mentioned her name, and the woman who ladled the rich milk from a churn by the door into just what he had imagined, a simple blue-and-white china bowl, glanced at him with a smile. He was less strange and more welcome.

As he was talking, or being talked to, by the woman on the grass outside the Dairy, her husband came back driving out his cows. He was a bald, vast-bearded man with a distinctly saturnine cast to his face; a Jeremiah. He gave his wife a stern look. She promptly forwent her chatter and returned indoors to her copper. The husband was evidently a taciturn man, though he spoke quietly enough when Charles asked him how much he owed for the bowl of excellent milk. A penny, one of those charming heads of the young Victoria that still occasionally turn up in one's change, with all but that graceful head worn away by the century's use, passed hands.

Charles was about to climb back to the path. But he had hardly taken a step back when a black figure appeared out of the trees above the two men. It was the girl. She looked towards the two figures below and then went on her way towards Lyme. Charles glanced back at the dairyman, who continued to give the figure above a dooming stare. He plainly did not allow delicacy to stand in the way of prophetic judgment.

'Do you know that Lady?'

'Aye.'

'Does she come this way often?'

'Often enough.' The dairyman continued to stare. Then he said, 'And she been't no Lady. She be the French Loot'n'nt's Hoer.'

Some moments passed before Charles grasped the meaning of that last word. And he threw an angry look at the bearded dairyman, who was a Methodist and therefore fond of calling a spade a spade, especially when the spade was somebody else's sin. He seemed to Charles to incarnate all the hypocritical gossip – and gossips – of Lyme. Charles could have believed many things of that sleeping face; but never that its owner was a whore.

A few seconds later he was himself on the cart-track back to Lyme. Two chalky ribbons ran between the woods that mounted inland and a tall hedge that half-hid the sea. Ahead moved the black and now bonneted figure of the girl; she walked not quickly, but with an even pace, without feminine affectation, like one used to covering long distances. Charles set out to catch her up, and after a hundred yards or so he came close behind her. She must have heard the sound of his nailed boots on the flint that had worn through the chalk, but she did not turn. He perceived that the coat was a little too large for her, and that the heels of her shoes were mudstained. He hesitated a moment then; but the memory of the surly look on the dissenting dairyman's face kept Charles to his original chivalrous intention: to show the poor woman that not everybody in her world was a barbarian.

'Madam!'

She turned, to see him hatless, smiling; and although her expression was one of now ordinary enough surprise, once again that face had an extraordinary effect on him. It was as if after each sight of it, he could not believe its effect, and had to see it again. It seemed to both envelop and reject him; as if she was a figure in a dream, both standing still and yet always receding.

'I owe you two apologies. I did not know yesterday that you were Mrs Poulteney's secretary. I fear I addressed you in a most impolite manner.'

She stared down at the ground. 'It's no matter, sir.'

'And just now when I seemed . . . I was afraid lest you had been taken ill.'

Still without looking at him, she inclined her head and turned to walk on.

'May I not accompany you? Since we walk in the same direction?'

She stopped, but did not turn. 'I prefer to walk alone.'

'It was Mrs Tranter who made me aware of my error. I am – '

'I know who you are, sir.'

He smiled at her timid abruptness. 'Then . . .'

Her eyes were suddenly on his, and with a kind of despair beneath the timidity.

'Kindly allow me to go on my way alone.' His smile faltered. He bowed and stepped back. But instead of continuing on her way, she stared at the ground a moment. 'And please tell no one you have seen me in this place.'

Then, without looking at him again, she did turn and go on, almost as if she knew her request was in vain and she regretted it as soon as uttered. Standing in the centre of the road, Charles watched her black back recede. All he was left with was the after-image of those eyes – they were abnormally large, as if able to see more and suffer more. And their directness of look – he did not know it, but it was the tract-delivery look he had received – contained a most peculiar element of rebuffal. Do not come near me, they said. *Noli me tangere.*[1]

He looked round, trying to imagine why she should not wish it known that she came among these innocent woods. A man perhaps; some assignation? But then he remembered her story.

When Charles finally arrived in Broad Street, he decided to call at Mrs Tranter's on his way to the White Lion to explain that as soon as he had bathed and changed into decent clothes he would . . .

The door was opened by Mary; but Mrs Tranter chanced to pass through the hall – to be exact, deliberately came out into the hall – and insisted that he must not stand upon ceremony; and were not his clothes the best proof of his excuses? So Mary smilingly took his ashplant and his rucksack, and he was ushered into the little back drawing-room, then shot with the last rays of the setting sun, where the invalid lay in a charmingly elaborate state of carmine-and-grey *déshabille*.

'I feel like an Irish navigator transported into a queen's boudoir,' complained Charles, as he kissed Ernestina's fingers in a way that showed he would in fact have made a very poor Irish navvy.

She took her hand away. 'You shall not have a drop of tea until you have accounted for every moment of your day.'

He accordingly described everything that had happened to him; or almost

---

1 *Noli me tangere*: 'Do not touch me'. The words of the dead Christ to Mary Magdalen at his tomb.

everything, for Ernestina had now twice made it clear that the subject of the French Lieutenant's Woman was distasteful to her – once on the Cobb,[1] and then again later at lunch afterwards when Aunt Tranter had given Charles very much the same information as the vicar of Lyme had given Mrs Poulteney twelve months before. But Ernestina had reprimanded her nurse-aunt for boring Charles with dull tittle-tattle, and the poor woman – too often summonsed for provinciality not to be alert to it – had humbly obeyed.

Charles produced the piece of ammonitiferous rock he had brought for Ernestina, who put down her fireshield and attempted to hold it, and could not, and forgave Charles everything for such a labour of Hercules, and then was mock-angry with him for endangering life and limb.

'It is a most fascinating wilderness, the Undercliff. I had no idea such places existed in England. I was reminded of some of the maritime sceneries of Northern Portugal.'

'Why, the man is tranced,' cried Ernestina. 'Now confess, Charles, you haven't been beheading poor innocent rocks – but dallying with the wood-nymphs.'

Charles showed here an unaccountable moment of embarrassment, which he covered with a smile. It was on the tip of his tongue to tell them about the girl; a facetious way of describing how he had come upon her entered his mind; and yet seemed a sort of treachery, both to the girl's real sorrow and to himself. He knew he would have been lying if he had dismissed those two encounters lightly; and silence seemed finally less a falsehood in that trivial room.

It remains to be explained why Ware Commons had appeared to evoke Sodom and Gomorrah in Mrs Poulteney's face a fortnight before.

One needs no further explanation, in truth, than that it was the nearest place to Lyme where people could go and not be spied on. The area had an obscure, long and mischievous legal history. It had always been considered common land until the enclosure acts; then it was encroached on, as the names of the fields of the Dairy, which were all stolen from it, still attest. A gentleman in one of the great houses that lie behind the Undercliff performed a quiet *Anschluss*[2] – with, as usual in history, the approval of his fellows in society. It is true that the more republican citizens of Lyme rose in arms – if an axe is an arm. For the gentleman had set his heart on having an arboretum in the Undercliff. It came to law, and then to a compromise: a right of way was granted, and the rare trees stayed unmolested. But the commonage was done for.

Yet there had remained locally a feeling that Ware Commons was public property. Poachers slinked in less guiltily than elsewhere after the pheasants and rabbits; one day it was discovered, horror of horrors, that a gang of gipsies had been living there, encamped in a hidden dell, for nobody knew how many months. These outcasts were promptly cast out; but the memory of their presence remained, and became entangled with that of a child who had disappeared about the same time from a near-by village. It was – forgive the pun – common knowledge that the gipsies had taken her, and thrown her into a rabbit stew, and buried her bones. Gipsies were not English; and therefore almost certain to be cannibals.

---

1 Cobb: the stone sea break at Lyme harbour. 2 *Anschluss*: the annexation of Austria by Nazi Germany in 1938.

But the most serious accusation against Ware Commons had to do with far worse infamy: though it never bore that familiar rural name, the cart-track to the Dairy and beyond to the wooded common was a *de facto* Lover's Lane. It drew courting couples every summer. There was the pretext of a bowl of milk at the Dairy; and many inviting little paths, as one returned, led up into the shielding bracken and hawthorn coverts.

That running sore was bad enough; a deeper darkness still existed. There was an antediluvian tradition (much older than Shakespeare) that on Midsummer's Night young people should go with lanterns, and a fiddler, and a keg or two of cider, to a patch of turf known as Donkey's Green in the heart of the woods and there celebrate the solstice with dancing. Some said that after midnight more reeling than dancing took place; and the more draconian claimed that there was very little of either, but a great deal of something else.

Scientific agriculture, in the form of myxomatosis, has only very recently lost us the Green for ever, but the custom itself lapsed in relation to the lapse in sexual mores. It is many years since anything but fox or badger cubs tumbled over Donkey's Green on Midsummer's Night. But it was not so in 1867.

Indeed, only a year before, a committee of ladies, generalled by Mrs Poulteney, had pressed the civic authorities to have the track gated, fenced and closed. But more democratic voices prevailed. The public right of way must be left sacrosanct; and there were even some disgusting sensualists among the Councillors who argued that a walk to the Dairy was an innocent pleasure; and the Donkey's Green Ball no more than an annual jape. But it is sufficient to say that among the more respectable townsfolk one had only to speak of a boy or a girl as 'one of the Ware Commons kind' to tar them for life. The boy must thenceforth be a satyr; and the girl, a hedge-prostitute.

Sarah therefore found Mrs Poulteney sitting in wait for her when she returned from her walk on the evening Mrs Fairley had so nobly forced herself to do her duty. I said 'in wait'; but 'in state' would have been a more appropriate term. Sarah appeared in the private drawing-room for the evening Bible-reading, and found herself as if faced with the muzzle of a cannon. It was very clear that any moment Mrs Poulteney might go off, and with a very loud bang indeed.

Sarah went towards the lectern in the corner of the room where the large 'family' Bible – not what you may think of as a family Bible, but one from which certain inexplicable errors of taste in the Holy Writ (such as the Song of Solomon) had been piously excised – lay in its off-duty hours. But she saw that all was not well.

'Is something wrong, Mrs Poulteney?'

'Something is very wrong,' said the abbess. 'I have been told something I can hardly believe.'

'To do with me?'

'I should never have listened to the doctor. I should have listened to the dictates of my own common sense.'

'What have I done?'

'I do not think you are mad at all. You are a cunning, wicked creature. You know very well what you have done.'

'I will swear on the Bible –'

But Mrs Poulteney gave her a look of indignation. 'You will do nothing of the sort! That is blasphemy.'

Sarah came forward, and stood in front of her mistress. 'I must insist on knowing of what I am accused.' Mrs Poulteney told her.

To her amazement Sarah showed not the least sign of shame.

'But what is the sin in walking on Ware Commons?'

'The sin! You, a young woman, alone, in such a place!'

'But ma'm, it is nothing but a large wood.'

'I know very well what it is. And what goes on there. And the sort of person who frequents it.'

'No one frequents it. That is why I go there – to be alone.'

'Do you contradict me, miss! Am I not to know what I speak of?'

The first simple fact was that Mrs Poulteney had never set eyes on Ware Commons, even from a distance, since it was out of sight of any carriage road. The second simple fact is that she was an opium-addict – but before you think I am wildly sacrificing plausibility to sensation, let me quickly add that she did not know it. What we call opium she called laudanum. A shrewd, if blasphemous, doctor of the time called it Our-Lordanum, since many a nine-teenth-century Lady – and less, for the medicine was cheap enough (in the form of Godfrey's Cordial) to help all classes get through that black night of womankind – sipped it a good deal more frequently than Communion wine. It was, in short, a very near equivalent of our own age's sedative pills. Why Mrs Poulteney should have been an inhabitant of the Victorian valley of the dolls we need not inquire, but it is to the point that laudanum, as Coleridge once discovered, gives vivid dreams.

I cannot imagine what Bosch-like picture of Ware Commons Mrs Poulteney had built up over the years; what satanic orgies she divined behind every tree, what French abominations under every leaf. But I think we may safely say that it had become the objective correlative[1] of all that went on in her own subcon-scious.

Her outburst reduced both herself and Sarah to silence. Having discharged, Mrs Poulteney began to change her tack.

'You have distressed me deeply.'

'But how was I to tell? I am not to go to the sea. Very well, I don't go to the sea. I wish for solitude. That is all. That is not a sin. I will not be called a sinner for that.'

'Have you never heard speak of Ware Commons?'

'As a place of the kind you imply – never.'

Mrs Poulteney looked somewhat abashed then before the girl's indignation. She recalled that Sarah had not lived in Lyme until recently; and that she could therefore, just conceivably, be ignorant of the obloquy she was inviting.

'Very well. But let it be plainly understood. I permit no one in my employ to go or to be seen near that place. You will confine your walks to where it is seemly. Do I make myself clear?'

---

1 **objective correlative**: expressing emotion in the form of art; an object or set of objects which are the formula for a particular emotion, so that when it is evoked, the emotion is evoked. The concept was popularised by T.S. Eliot.

'Yes. I am to walk in the paths of righteousness.' For one appalling moment Mrs Poulteney thought she had been the subject of a sarcasm; but Sarah's eyes were solemnly down, as if she had been pronouncing sentence on herself; and righteousness were synonymous with suffering.

'Then let us hear no more of this foolishness. I do this for your own good.' Sarah murmured, 'I know.' Then, 'I thank you, ma'm.'

No more was said. She turned to the Bible and read the passage Mrs Poulteney had marked. It was the same one as she had chosen for that first interview – Psalm 119: 'Blessed are the undefiled in the way, who walk in the law of the Lord.' Sarah read in a very subdued voice, seemingly without emotion. The old woman sat facing the dark shadows at the far end of the room; like some pagan idol she looked, oblivious of the blood sacrifice her pitiless stone face demanded.

Later that night Sarah might have been seen – though I cannot think by whom, unless a passing owl – standing at the open window of her unlit bedroom. The house was silent, and the town as well, for people went to bed by nine in those days before electricity and television. It was now one o'clock. Sarah was in her nightgown, with her hair loose; and she was staring out to sea. A distant lantern winked faintly on the black waters out towards Portland Bill, where some ship sailed towards Bridport. Sarah had seen the tiny point of light; and not given it a second thought.

If you had gone closer still, you would have seen that her face was wet with silent tears. She was not standing at her window as part of her mysterious vigil for Satan's sails; but as a preliminary to jumping from it.

I will not make her teeter on the window-sill; or sway forward, and then collapse sobbing back on to the worn carpet of her room. We know she was alive a fortnight after this incident, and therefore she did not jump. Nor were hers the sobbing, hysterical sort of tears that presage violent action; but those produced by a profound conditional, rather than emotional, misery – slow-welling, unstoppable, creeping like blood through a bandage.

Who is Sarah?

Out of what shadows does she come?

Chapter Thirteen

> For the drift of the Maker is dark, an Isis hid by the veil . . .
> Tennyson, *Maud* (1855)

I do not know. This story I am telling is all imagination. These characters I create never existed outside my own mind. If I have pretended until now to know my characters' minds and innermost thoughts, it is because I am writing in (just as I have assumed some of the vocabulary and 'voice' of) a convention universally accepted at the time of my story: that the novelist stands next to God. He may not know all, yet he tries to pretend that he does. But I live in the age of Alain Robbe-Grillet and Roland Barthes; if this is a novel, it cannot be a novel in the modern sense of the word.

So perhaps I am writing a transposed autobiography; perhaps I now live in one of the houses I have brought into the fiction; perhaps Charles is myself disguised. Perhaps it is only a game. Modern women like Sarah exist, and I have never understood them. Or perhaps I am trying to pass off a concealed book of essays on you. Instead of chapter headings, perhaps I should have written 'On the Horizontality of Existence', 'The Illusions of Progress', 'The History of the Novel Form', 'The Aetiology of Freedom', 'Some Forgotten Aspects of the Victorian Age' . . . what you will.

Perhaps you suppose that a novelist has only to pull the right strings and his puppets will behave in a lifelike manner; and produce on request a thorough analysis of their motives and intentions. Certainly I intended at this stage (*Chap. Thirteen – unfolding of Sarah's true state of mind*) to tell all – or all that matters. But I find myself suddenly like a man in the sharp spring night, watching from the lawn beneath that dim upper window in Marlborough House; I know in the context of my book's reality that Sarah would never have brushed away her tears and leant down and delivered a chapter of revelation. She would instantly have turned, had she seen me there just as the old moon rose, and disappeared into the interior shadows.

But I am a novelist, not a man in a garden – I can follow her where I like. But possibility is not permissibility. Husbands could often murder their wives – and the reverse – and get away with it. But they don't.

You may think novelists always have fixed plans to which they work, so that the future predicted by Chapter One is always inexorably the actuality of Chapter Thirteen. But novelists write for countless different reasons: for money, for fame, for reviewers, for parents, for friends, for loved ones; for vanity, for pride, for curiosity, for amusement: as skilled furniture-makers enjoy making furniture, as drunkards like drinking, as judges like judging, as Sicilians like emptying a shotgun into an enemy's back. I could fill a book with reasons, and they would all be true, though not true of all. Only one same reason is shared by all of us: *we wish to create worlds as real as, but other than the world that is.* Or was. This is why we cannot plan. We know a world is an organism, not a machine. We also know that a genuinely created world must be independent of its creator; a planned world (a world that fully reveals its planning) is a dead world. It is only when our characters and events begin to disobey us that they begin to live. When Charles left Sarah on her cliff-edge, I ordered him to walk straight back to Lyme Regis. But he did not; he gratuitously turned and went down to the Dairy.

Oh, but you say, come on – what I really mean is that the idea crossed my mind as I wrote that it might be more clever to have him stop and drink milk . . . and meet Sarah again. That is certainly one explanation of what happened; but I can only report – and I am the most reliable witness – that the idea seemed to me to come clearly from Charles, not myself. It is not only that he has begun to gain an autonomy; I must respect it, and disrespect all my quasi-divine plans for him, if I wish him to be real.

In other words, to be free myself, I must give him, and Tina, and Sarah, even the abominable Mrs Poulteney, their freedoms as well. There is only one good definition of God: the freedom that allows other freedoms to exist. And I must conform to that definition.

The novelist is still a god, since he creates (and not even the most aleatory[1] avant-garde modern novel has managed to extirpate its author completely); what has changed is that we are no longer the gods of the Victorian image, omniscient and decreeing; but in the new theological image, with freedom our first principle, not authority.

I have disgracefully broken the illusion? No. My characters still exist, and in a reality no less, or no more, real than the one I have just broken. Fiction is woven into all, as a Greek observed some two and a half thousand years ago. I find this new reality (or unreality) more valid; and I would have you share my own sense that I do not fully control these creatures of my mind, any more than you control – however hard you try, however much of a latter-day Mrs Poulteney you may be – your children, colleagues, friends or even yourself.

But this is preposterous? A character is either 'real' or 'imaginary'? If you think that, *hypocrite lecteur*, I can only smile. You do not even think of your own past as quite real; you dress it up, you gild it or blacken it, censor it, tinker with it . . . fictionalize it, in a word, and put it away on a shelf – your book, your romanced autobiography. We are all in flight from the real reality. That is a basic definition of *Homo sapiens*.

So if you think all this unlucky (but it is Chapter Thirteen) digression has nothing to do with your Time, Progress, Society, Evolution and all those other capitalized ghosts in the night that are rattling their chains behind the scenes of this book . . . I will not argue. But I shall suspect you.

I report, then, only the outward facts: that Sarah cried in the darkness, but did not kill herself; that she continued, in spite of the express prohibition, to haunt Ware Commons. In a way, therefore, she had indeed jumped; and was living in a kind of long fall, since sooner or later the news must inevitably come to Mrs Poulteney of the sinner's compounding of her sin. It is true Sarah went less often to the woods than she had become accustomed to, a deprivation at first made easy for her by the wetness of the weather those following two weeks. It is true also that she took some minimal precautions of a military kind. The cart-track eventually ran out into a small lane, little better than a superior cart-track itself, which curved down a broad combe called Ware Valley until it joined, on the outskirts of Lyme, the main carriage road to Sidmouth and Exeter. There was a small scatter of respectable houses in Ware Valley, and it was therefore a seemly place to walk. Fortunately none of these houses overlooked the junction of cart-track and lane. Once there, Sarah had merely to look round to see if she was alone. One day she set out with the intention of walking into the woods. But as in the lane she came to the track to the Dairy she saw two people come round a higher bend. She walked straight on towards them, and once round the bend, watched to make sure that the couple did not themselves take the Dairy track; then retraced her footsteps and entered her sanctuary unobserved.

She risked meeting other promenaders on the track itself; and might always have risked the dairyman and his family's eyes. But this latter danger she avoided

---

1 **aleatory**: dependent on the throw of a dice; more generally dependent on arbitrary contingencies.

by discovering for herself that one of the inviting paths into the bracken above the track led round, out of sight of the Dairy, on to the path through the woods. This path she had invariably taken, until that afternoon when she recklessly – as we can now realize – emerged in full view of the two men.

The reason was simple. She had overslept, and she knew she was late for her reading. Mrs Poulteney was to dine at Lady Cotton's that evening; and the usual hour had been put forward to allow her to prepare for what was always in essence, if not appearance, a thunderous clash of two brontosauri; with black velvet taking the place of iron cartilage, and quotations from the Bible the angry raging teeth; but no less dour and relentless a battle.

Also, Charles's down-staring face had shocked her; she felt the speed of her fall accelerate; when the cruel ground rushes up, when the fall is from such a height, what use are precautions?

SEAMUS HEANEY (1939–)

Born in Northern Ireland, Heaney's poetry engages with Ulster. Its distinctive geography and troubled politics, and the poet's own sense of location between Ireland and Britain, lie at the centre of much of his writing.

Mossbawn: Two Poems In Dedication
For Mary Heaney

1. Sunlight

There was a sunlit absence.
The helmeted pump in the yard
heated its iron,
water honeyed

5   in the slung bucket
and the sun stood
like a griddle cooling
against the wall

of each long afternoon.
10   So, her hands scuffled
over the bakeboard,
the reddening stove

sent its plaque of heat
against her where she stood
15   in a floury apron
by the window.

Now she dusts the board
with a goose's wing,
now sits, broad-lapped,
20   with whitened nails

and measling shins:
here is a space
again, the scone rising
to the tick of two clocks.

25   And here is love
like a tinsmith's scoop
sunk past its gleam
in the meal-bin.

2. The Seed Cutters

They seem hundreds of years away. Breughel,
You'll know them if I can get them true.
They kneel under the hedge in a half-circle
Behind a windbreak wind is breaking through.
5   They are the seed cutters. The tuck and frill
Of leaf-sprout is on the seed potatoes
Buried under that straw. With time to kill
They are taking their time. Each sharp knife goes
Lazily halving each root that falls apart
10   In the palm of the hand: a milky gleam,
And, at the centre, a dark watermark.
O calendar customs! Under the broom
Yellowing over them, compose the frieze
With all of us there, our anonymities.

Kinship

I

Kinned by hieroglyphic
peat on a spreadfield
to the strangled victim,
the love-nest in the bracken,

5   I step through origins
like a dog turning
its memories of wilderness
on the kitchen mat:

Kinship 3 strangled: Heaney is fascinated by sacrificial victims of ancient times who were buried and often preserved in peat.

the bog floor shakes,
10   water cheeps and lisps
as I walk down
rushes and heather.

I love this turf-face,
its black incisions,
15   the cooped secrets
of process and ritual;

I love the spring
off the ground,
each bank a gallows drop,
20   each open pool

the unstopped mouth
of an urn, a moon-drinker,
not to be sounded
by the naked eye.

II

25   Quagmire, swampland, morass:
the slime kingdoms,
domains of the cold-blooded,
of mud pads and dirtied eggs.

But *bog*
30   meaning soft,
the fall of windless rain,
pupil of amber.

Ruminant ground,
digestion of mollusc
35   and seed-pod,
deep pollen bin.

Earth-pantry, bone-vault,
sun-bank, enbalmer
of votive goods
40   and sabred fugitives.

Insatiable bride
Sword-swallower,
casket, midden,
floe of history.

45   Ground that will strip
its dark side,

---

43 **midden**: dung heap.

nesting ground,
outback of my mind.

III

I found a turf-spade
50 hidden under bracken,
laid flat, and overgrown
with a green fog.

As I raised it
the soft lips of the growth
55 muttered and split,
a tawny rut

opening at my feet
like a shed skin,
the shaft wettish
60 as I sank it upright

and beginning to
steam in the sun.
And now they have twinned
that obelisk:

65 among the stones,
under a bearded cairn
a love-nest is disturbed,
catkin and bog-cotton tremble

as they raise up
70 the cloven oak-limb.
I stand at the edge of centuries
facing a goddess.

IV

This centre holds
and spreads,
75 sump and seedbed,
a bag of waters

and a melting grave.
The mothers of autumn
sour and sink,
80 ferments of husk and leaf

deepen their ochres.
Mosses come to a head,
heather unseeds,
brackens deposit

85 their bronze.
This is the vowel of earth
dreaming its root
in flowers and snow,

mutation of weathers
90 and seasons,
a windfall composing
the floor it rots into.

I grew out of all this
like a weeping willow
95 inclined to
the appetites of gravity.

V

The hand carved felloes
of the turf-cart wheels
buried in a litter
100 of turf mould,

the cupid's bow
of the tail-board,
the socketed lips
of the cribs:

105 I deified the man
who rode there,
god of the waggon,
the hearth-feeder.

I was his privileged
110 attendant, a bearer
of bread and drink,
the squire of his circuits.

When summer died
and wives forsook the fields
115 we were abroad,
saluted, given right-of-way.

Watch our progress
down the haw-lit hedges,
my manly pride
120 when he speaks to me.

---

97 **felloes**: wheel rims.   118 **haw-lit**: dyed with the hawthorne fruit.

VI

And you, Tacitus,
observe how I make my grove
on an old crannog
piled by the fearful dead:

125   a desolate peace.
Our mother ground
is sour with the blood
of her faithful,

they lie gargling
130   in her sacred heart
as the legions stare
from the ramparts.

Come back to this
'island of the ocean'
135   where nothing will suffice.
Read the inhumed faces

of casualty and victim;
report us fairly,
how we slaughter
140   for the common good

and shave the heads
of the notorious,
how the goddess swallows
our love and terror.

Tollund Man

I

Some day I will go to Aarhus
To see his peat-brown head,
The mild pods of his eye-lids,
His pointed skin cap.

5   In the flat country nearby
Where they dug him out,
His last gruel of winter seeds
Caked in his stomach,

Naked except for
10   The cap, noose and girdle,

---

121 **Tacitus:** Roman Historian who wrote about Britain. The Romans did not invade Ireland.   123 **crannog:** ancient lake dwelling.   134 **island. . . . :** the Roman name for Ireland.   136 **inhumed:** buried.   **Tollund:** place in Denmark where bodies of ancient sacrifical victims preserved in peat were found.

I will stand a long time.
Bridegroom to the goddess,

She tightened her torc on him
And opened her fen,
15 Those dark juices working
Him to a saint's kept body,

Trove of the turfcutters'
Honeycombed workings.
Now his stained face
20 Reposes at Aarhus.

II
I could risk blasphemy,
Consecrate the cauldron bog
Our holy ground and pray
Him to make germinate

25 The scattered, ambushed
Flesh of labourers,
Stockinged corpses
Laid out in the farmyards,

Tell-tale skin and teeth
30 Flecking the sleepers
Of four young brothers, trailed
For miles along the lines.

III
Something of his sad freedom
As he rode the tumbril
35 Should come to me, driving,
Saying the names

Tollund, Grabaulle, Nebelgard,
Watching the pointing hands
Of country people,
40 Not knowing their tongue.

Out there in Jutland
In the old man-killing parishes
I will feel lost,
45 Unhappy and at home.

---

13 **torc**: collar or necklace of twisted bands.

Clearances III

When all the others were away at Mass
I was all hers as we peeled potatoes.
They broke the silence, let fall one by one
Like solder weeping off the soldering iron:
5   Cold comforts set between us, things to share
Gleaming in a bucket of clean water.
And again let fall. Little pleasant splashes
From each other's work would bring us to our senses.

So while the parish priest at her bedside
10   Went hammer and tongs at the prayers for the dying
And some were responding and some crying
I remembered her head bent towards my head,
Her breath in mine, our fluent dipping knives –
Never closer the whole rest of our lives.

From Station Island

VII

I had come to the edge of the water,
soothed by just looking, idling over it
as if it were a clear barometer

or a mirror, when his reflection
5   did not appear but I sensed a presence
entering into my concentration

on not being concentrated as he spoke
my name. And though I was reluctant
I turned to meet his face and the shock

10 is still in me at what I saw. His brow
was blown open above the eye and blood
had dried on his neck and cheek. 'Easy now,'

he said, 'it's only me. You've seen men as raw
after a football match . . . What time it was
15 when I was wakened up I still don't know

but I heard this knocking, knocking, and it
scared me, like the phone in the small hours,
so I had the sense not to put on the light

but looked out from behind the curtain.
20 I saw two customers on the doorstep
and an old landrover with the doors open

parked on the street so I let the curtain drop;
but they must have been waiting for it to move
for they shouted to come down into the shop.

25   She started to cry then and roll round the bed,
lamenting and lamenting to herself,
not even asking who it was. "Is your head

astray, or what's come over you?" I roared, more
to bring myself to my senses
30   than out of any real anger at her

for the knocking shook me, the way they kept it up,
and her whingeing and half-screeching made it worse.
All the time they were shouting, "Shop!

Shop!" so I pulled on my shoes and a sportscoat
35   and went back to the window and called out,
"What do you want? Could you quieten the racket

or I'll not come down at all." "There's a child not well.
Open up and see what you have got – pills
or a powder or something in a bottle,"

40   one of them said. He stepped back off the footpath
so I could see his face in the street lamp
and when the other moved I knew them both.

But bad and all as the knocking was, the quiet
hit me worse. She was quiet herself now,
45   lying dead still, whispering to watch out.

At the bedroom door I switched on the light.
"It's odd they didn't look for a chemist.
Who are they anyway at this time of the night?"

she asked me, with the eyes standing in her head.
50   "I know them to see," I said, but something
made me reach and squeeze her hand across the bed

before I went downstairs into the aisle
of the shop. I stood there, going weak
in the legs. I remember the stale smell

55   of cooked meat or something coming through
as I went to open up. From then on
you know as much about it as I do.'

'Did they say nothing?' 'Nothing. What would they say?'
'Were they in uniform? Not masked in any way?'
60   'They were barefaced as they would be in the day,

shites thinking they were the be-all and the end-all.'
'Not that it is any consolation, but they were caught,'
I told him, 'and got jail.'

Big-limbed, decent, open-faced, he stood
65 forgetful of everything now except
whatever was welling up in his spoiled head,

beginning to smile. 'You've put on weight
since you did your courting in that big Austin
you got the loan of on a Sunday night.'

70 Through life and death he had hardly aged.
There always was an athlete's cleanliness
shining off him and except for the ravaged

forehead and the blood, he was still that same
rangy midfielder in a blue jersey and starched pants,
75 the one stylist on the team,

the perfect, clean, unthinkable victim.
'Forgive the way I have lived indifferent –
forgive my timid circumspect involvement,'

I surprised myself by saying. 'Forgive
80 my eye,' he said, 'all that's above my head.'
And then a stun of pain seemed to go through him

and he trembled like a heatwave and faded.

GEOFFREY HILL (1932–)

Born in Worcestershire, Hill became an academic in English studies, teaching for many years at the University of Leeds. His poetry can be at once intellectually complex and resonantly lyrical, disciplined and linguistically playful. Integrating past and present, his work shows an enormous fascination for the language and manner of Medieval and Renaissance verse, often merging these forms with a decisive, even jarring, sense of modernity.

From The Kingdom of Offa

VII

Gasholders, russet among fields. Milldams, marlpools
that lay unstirring. Eel-swarms. Coagulations of
frogs; once, with branches and half-bricks, he
battered a ditchful; then sidled away from the
stillness and silence.

Kingdom of Offa sidled: to move sideways in a furtive manner

Ceolred was his friend and remained so, even after
the day of the lost fighter: a biplane, already
obsolete and irreplaceable, two inches of heavy
snub silver. Ceolred let it spin through a hole
in the classroom-floorboards, softly, into the
rat-droppings and coins.

After school he lured Ceolred, who was sniggering
with fright, down to the old quarries, and flayed
him. Then, leaving Ceolred, he journeyed for hours,
calm and alone, in his private derelict sandlorry
named *Albion.*

Pavana Dolorosa

Loves I allow and passions I approve:
Ash-Wednesday feasts, ascetic opulence,
the wincing lute, so real in its pretence,
itself a passion amorous of love.

5   Self-wounding martyrdom, what joys you have,
true-torn among this fictive consonance,
music's creation of the moveless dance,
the decreation to which all must move.

Self-seeking hunter of forms, there is no end
10   to such pursuits. None can revoke your cry.
Your silence is an ecstasy of sound

and your nocturnals blaze upon the day.
I founder in desire for things unfound.
I stay amid the things that will not stay.

Vocations

While friends defected, you stayed and were sure,
fervent in reason, watchful of each name:
a signet-seal's unostentatious gem
gleams against walnut on the escritoire,

5   focus of reckoning and judicious prayer.
This is the durable covenant, a room
quietly furnished with stuff of martyrdom,
lit by the flowers and moths from your own shire,

by silvery vistas frothed with convolvulus,
10   radiance of dreams hardly to be denied.
The twittering pipistrelle, so strange and close,

Pavana Doloroso: a stately slow and elaborate dance.   Vocations 11 pipistrelle: a small bat.

plucks its curt flight through the moist eventide;
the children thread among old avenues
of snowberries, clear-calling as they fade.

TONY HARRISON (1937–)

Born into a working-class environment in Leeds, educated on scholarships at Leeds Grammar School and studying Classics at university, Harrison is acutely aware of the class implications of language and education. A writer of dramatic verse, he is one of few contemporary poets to engage with occasional verse, addressing current issues such as the Salman Rushdie affair or the Gulf War in lengthy works. He is also distinctive in his devotion to rhyme and his employment of rhyming couplets.

A Kumquat for John Keats

Today I found the right fruit for my prime,
not orange, not tangelo, and not lime,
nor moon-like globes of grapefruit that now hang
outside our bedroom, nor tart lemon's tang
5   (though last year full of bile and self-defeat
I wanted to believe no life was sweet)
nor the tangible sunshine of the tangerine,
and no incongruous citrus ever seen
at greengrocers' in Newcastle or Leeds
10   mis-spelt by the spuds and mud-caked swedes,
a fruit an older poet might substitute
for the grape John Keats thought fit to be Joy's fruit,
when, two years before he died, he tried to write
how Melancholy dwelled inside Delight,
15   and if he'd known the citrus that I mean
that's not orange, lemon, lime or tangerine,
I'm pretty sure that Keats, though he had heard
'of candied apple, quince and plum and gourd'
instead of 'grape against the palate fine'
20   would have, if he'd known it, plumped for mine,
this Eastern citrus scarcely cherry size
he'd bite just once and then apostrophize
and pen one stanza how the fruit had all
the qualities of fruit before the Fall,
25   but in the next few lines be forced to write
how Eve's apple tasted at the second bite,
and if John Keats had only lived to be,
because of extra years, in need like me,

12–14 Keat's . . . . : 'The Ode to Melancholy'.

at 42 he'd help me celebrate
30 that Micanopy kumquat that I ate
whole, straight off the tree, sweet pulp and sour skin
or was it sweet outside, and sour within?
For however many kumquats that I eat
I'm not sure if it's flesh or rind that's sweet,
35 and being a man of doubt at life's mid-way
I'd offer Keats some kumquats and I'd say:
You'll find that one part's sweet and one part's tart:
say where the sweetness or the sourness start.

I find I can't, as if one couldn't say
40 exactly where the night became the day,
which makes for me the kumquat taken whole
best fruit, and metaphor, to fit the soul
of one in Florida at 42 with Keats
crunching kumquats, thinking, as he eats
45 the flesh, the juice, the pith, the pips, the peel,
that this is how a full life ought to feel,
its perishable relish prick the tongue,
when the man who savours life 's no longer young,
the fruits that were his futures far behind.
50 Then it's the kumquat fruit expresses best
how days have darkness round them like a rind,
life has a skin of death that keeps its zest.

History, a life, the heart, the brain
flow to the taste buds and flow back again.
55 That decade or more past Keats's span
makes me an older not a wiser man,
who knows that it's too late for dying young,
but since youth leaves some sweetnesses unsung,
he's granted days and kumquats to express
60 Man's Being ripened by his Nothingness.
And it isn't just the gap of sixteen years,
a bigger crop of terrors, hopes and fears,
but a century of history on this earth
between John Keats's death and my own birth –
65 years like an open crater, gory, grim,
with bloody bubbles leering at the rim;
a thing no bigger than an urn explodes
and ravishes all silence, and all odes,
Flora asphyxiated by foul air
70 unknown to either Keats or Lemprière,
dehydrated Naiads, Dryad amputees

---

70 **Lemprière:** compiler of large and popular Classical   71 **Naiad; Dryad:** minor classical deities.
Dictionary, first published 1788.

dragging themselves through slagscapes with no trees,
a shirt of Nessus fire that gnaws and eats
children half the age of dying Keats . . .

75 Now were you twenty five or six years old
when that fevered brow at last grew cold?
I've got no books to hand to check the dates.
My grudging but glad spirit celebrates
that all I've got to hand 's the kumquats, John,
80 the fruit I'd love to have your verdict on,
but dead men don't eat kumquats, or drink wine,
they shiver in the arms of Proserpine,
not warm in bed beside their Fanny Brawne,
nor watch her pick ripe grapefruit in the dawn
85 as I did, waking, when I saw her twist,
with one deft movement of a sunburnt wrist,
the moon, that feebly lit our last night's walk
past alligator swampland, off its stalk.
I thought of moon-juice juleps when I saw,
90 as if I'd never seen the moon before,
the planet glow among the fruit, and its pale light
make each citrus on the tree its satellite.

Each evening when I reach to draw the blind
stars seem the light zest squeezed through night's black rind;
95 the night's peeled fruit the sun, juiced of its rays,
first stains, then streaks, then floods the world with days,
days, when the very sunlight made me weep,
days, spent like the nights in deep, drugged sleep,
days in Newcastle by my daughter's bed,
100 wondering if she, or I, weren't better dead,
days in Leeds, grey days, my first dark suit,
my mother's wreaths stacked next to Christmas fruit,
and days, like this in Micanopy. Days!

As strong sun burns away the dawn's grey haze
105 I pick a kumquat and the branches spray
cold dew in my face to start the day.
The dawn's molasses make the citrus gleam
still in the orchards of the groves of dream.

The limes, like Galway after weeks of rain,
110 glow with a greenness that is close to pain,
the dew-cooled surfaces of fruit that spent
all last night flaming in the firmament.
The new day dawns. O days! My spirit greets

---

73 **shirt of Nessus:** poisoned garment which killed   83 **Fanny Brawne:** fiancée of John Keats.
Hercules.   82 **Proserpine:** Queen of the Underworld.

the kumquat with the spirit of John Keats.
115   O kumquat, comfort for not dying young,
both sweet and bitter, bless the poet's tongue!
I burst the whole fruit chilled by morning dew
against my palate. Fine, for 42!

I search for buzzards as the air grows clear
120   and see them ride fresh thermals overhead.
Their bleak cries were the first sound I could hear
when I stepped at the start of sunrise out of doors,
and a noise like last night's bedsprings on our bed
from Mr Fowler sharpening farmers' saws.

DOUGLAS DUNN (1942–)

Dunn was born and raised near Glasgow. After studying English at the University of Hull in the 1960s, he remained there until 1984 and his early writing shows the influence of Philip Larkin with whom he worked in the University library. Dunn's poetry engages with contemporary Scotland. His work is built around precise observation of a wide variety of moods and facets of life, often focused on 'common' experience, but revealing an emotional lyrical engagement which lifts his observations above the ordinary. He is also an accomplished writer of short stories.

A Removal from Terry Street

On a squeaking cart, they push the usual stuff,
A mattress, bed ends, cups, carpets, chairs,
Four paperback westerns. Two whistling youths
In surplus US Army battle-jackets
5   Remove their sister's goods. Her husband
Follows, carrying on his shoulders the son
Whose mischief we are glad to see removed,
And pushing, of all things, a lawnmower.
There is no grass in Terry Street. The worms
10   Come up cracks in concrete yards in moonlight.
That man, I wish him well. I wish him grass.

St. Kilda's Parliament: 1879–1979

The photographer revisits his picture

On either side of a rock-paved lane,
Two files of men are standing barefooted,
Bearded, waistcoated, each with a tam-o'-shanter

St Kilda: the outermost of the Hebrides off Scotland's west coast, it maintained a small, isolated community until the remaining islanders opted to leave in the 1930s.

On his head, and most with a set half-smile
5   That comes from their companionship with rock,
With soft mists, with rain, with roaring gales.
And from a diet of solan goose and eggs,
A diet of dulse and sloke and sea-tangle,
And ignorance of what a pig, a bee, a rat,
10   Or rabbit look like, although they remember
The three apples brought here by a traveller
Five years ago, and have discussed them since.
And there are several dogs doing nothing
Who seem contemptuous of my camera,
15   And a woman who might not believe it
If she were told of the populous mainland.
A man sits on a bank by the door of his house,
Staring out to sea and at a small craft
Bobbing there, the little boat that brought me here,
20   Whose carpentry was slowly shaped by waves,
By a history of these northern waters.
Wise men or simpletons – it is hard to tell
But in that way they almost look alike
You also see how each is individual,
25   Proud of his shyness and of his small life
On this outcast of the Hebrides
With his eyes full of weather and seabirds,
Fish, and whatever morsel he grows here.
Clear, too, is manhood, and how each man looks
30   Secure in the love of a woman who
Also knows the wisdom of the sun rising,
Of weather in the eyes like landmarks.
Fifty years before depopulation
Before the boats came at their own request
35   To ease them from their dying babies
It was easy, even then, to imagine
St Kilda return to its naked self,
Its archaeology of hazelraw
And footprints stratified beneath the lichen.
40   See, how simple it all is, these toes
Playfully clutching the edge of a boulder.
It is a remote democracy, where men,
In manacles of place, outstare a sea
That rattes back its manacles of salt,
45   The moody jailer of the wild Atlantic.
     Traveller, tourist with your mind set on
Romantic Staffas and materials for
Winter conversations, if you should go there,

---

8 **dulse; sloke; sea-tangle:** edible sea-weeds.

Landing at sunrise on its difficult shores,
50 On St Kilda you will surely hear Gaelic
Spoken softly like a poetry of ghosts
By those who never were contorted by
Hierarchies of cuisine and literacy.
You need only look at the faces of these men
55 Standing there like everybody's ancestors,
This flick of time I shuttered on a face.
Look at their sly, assuring mockery.
They are aware of what we are up to
With our internal explorations, our
60 Designs of affluence and education.
They know us so well, and are not jealous,
Whose be-all and end-all was an eternal
Casual husbandry upon a toehold
Of Europe, which, when failing, was not their fault.
65 You can see they have already prophesied
A day when survivors look across the stern
Of a departing vessel for the last time
At their gannet-shrouded cliffs, and the farewells
Of the St Kilda mouse and St Kilda wren
70 As they fall into the texts of specialists,
Ornithological visitors at the prow
Of a sullenly managed boat from the future.
They pose for ever outside their parliament,
Looking at me, as if they have grown from
75 Affection scattered across my own eyes.
And it is because of this that I, who took
This photograph in a year of many events –
The Zulu massacres, Tchaikovsky's opera –
Return to tell you this, and that after
80 My many photographs of distressed cities,
My portraits of successive elegants,
Of the emaciated dead, the lost empires,
Exploded fleets, and of the writhing flesh
Of dead civilians and commercial copulations.
85 That after so much of that larger franchise
It is to this island that I return.
Here I whittle time, like a dry stick,
From sunrise to sunset, among the groans
And sighings of a tongue I cannot speak,
90 Outside a parliament, looking at them,
As they, too, must always look at me
Looking through my apparatus at them
Looking. Benevolent, or malign? But who,
At this late stage, could tell, or think it worth it?
95 For I was there, and am, and I forget.

Reading Pascal in the Lowlands

His aunt has gone astray in her concern
And the boy's mum leans across his wheelchair
To talk to him. She points to the river.
An aged angler and a boy they know
5   Cast lazily into the rippled sun.
They go there, into the dappled grass, shadows
Bickering and falling from the shaken leaves.

His father keeps apart from them, walking
On the beautiful grass that is bright green
10   In the sunlight of July at 7 p.m.
He sits on the bench beside me, saying
It is a lovely evening, and I rise
From my sorrows, agreeing with him.
His large hand picks tobacco from a tin;

15   His smile falls at my feet, on the baked earth
Shoes have shuffled over and ungrassed.
It is discourteous to ask about
Accidents, or of the sick, the unfortunate.
I do not need to, for he says "Leukaemia".
20   We look at the river, his son holding a rod,
The line going downstream in a cloud of flies.

I close my book, the *Pensées* of Pascal
I am light with meditation, religiose
And mystic with a day of solitude.
25   I do not tell him of my own sorrows.
He is bored with misery and premonition.
He has seen the limits of time, asking "Why?"
Nature is silent on that question.

A swing squeaks in the distance. Runners jog
30   Round the perimeter. He is indiscreet.
His son is eight years old, with months to live.
His right hand trembles on his cigarette.
He sees my book, and then he looks at me,
Knowing me for a stranger. I have said
35   I am sorry. What more is there to say?

He is called over to the riverbank.
I go away, leaving the Park, walking through
The Golf Course, and then a wood, climbing,
And then bracken and gorse, sheep pasturage.
40   From a panoptic hill I look down on
A little town, its estuary, its bridge,
Its houses, churches, its undramatic streets.

IAIN CRICHTON SMITH (1928–)

Poet, novelist and short-story writer, Crichton Smith was born on the island of Lewis in the Hebrides and has been a champion of Scots Gaelic culture, both as a writer in Gaelic and as a translator. His English work is marked by a direct, plain style, and is usually focused on life in the Scottish Highlands and Islands.

Timoshenko

When I went into the thatched house as I always did at nine o'clock at night, he was lying on the floor stabbed with a bread knife, his usually brick-red face pale and his ginger moustache a dark wedge under his nose. His eyes were wide open like blue marbles. I wondered where she was. The radio was still on and I went over and switched it off. At that moment she came down from the other room and sat on the bench. There was no point in going for a doctor; he was obviously dead: even I could tell that. She sat like a child, her knees close together, her hands folded in her lap.

I had regarded the two of them as children. He had a very bad limp and sat day after day at the earthen wall which bordered the road, his glassy hands resting on his stick, talking to the passers-by. Sometimes he would blow on his fingers, his cheeks red and globular. She on the other hand sat in the house most of the time, perhaps cooking a meal or washing clothes. Of the two I considered her the simpler, though she had been away from the island a few times, in her youth, at the fishing, but had to be looked after by the other girls in case she did something silly.

'Did you do that?' I said, pointing to the body which seemed more eloquent than either of us. She nodded wordlessly. As a matter of fact I hadn't liked him very much. He was always asking me riddles to which I did not know the answer, and when I was bewildered he would nod his head and say, 'I don't understand what they are teaching at these schools nowadays.' He had an absolutely bald head which shone in the light, and a sarcastic way of speaking. He would call his sister Timoshenko or Voroshilov, because the Russians at that time were driving the Germans out of their country and these generals were always in the news. 'Timoshenko will know about it,' he would say and she would stand there smiling, a teapot in her hands.

But of course I never thought what it was like for the two of them when I wasn't there. Perhaps he persecuted her. Perhaps his sarcasm was a perpetual wound. Perhaps, lame as he was, sitting at the wall all day, he was petrified by boredom and his tiny mind squirmed like the snail-like meat inside a whelk. He had never left the island in his whole life and I didn't know what had caused his limp which was so serious that he had to drag himself along by means of two sticks.

The blood had stopped flowing and the body lay on the floor like a log. The fire was out and the dishes on the dresser were clean and colourful rising in tier after tier. The floor which was made of clay seemed to undulate slightly. I felt unreal as if at any moment the body would rise from the floor like a question mark and ask me another riddle, the moustache twitching like an antenna. But this didn't happen. It stayed there solid and heavy, the knife sticking from its breast.

I knew that soon I would have to get someone, perhaps the policeman or a doctor or perhaps a neighbour. But I was so fascinated by the woman that I stayed, wondering why she had done it. Girlishly she sat on the bench, her hands in her lap, not even twisting them nervously.

Suddenly she said, 'I don't know why but I took the knife and I . . . I don't know why.'

She looked past me, then added, 'I can't remember why I did it. I don't understand.'

I waited for her to talk and after a while she went on.

'Many years ago,' she said, 'I was going to be married. He made fun of me when Norman came into the house. He said I couldn't cook and I couldn't wash, and that was wrong. That must have been twenty years ago. He was limping then too. He told Norman I was a bit daft. That was many years ago. But that wasn't it. Anyway, he told Norman I was silly. Norman had put on his best suit when he came to the house. He wasn't rich or anything like that. You didn't know him. Anyway he's dead now. He died last week in the next village. He was on his own and they found him in the house dead. He had been dead for a week; of course he was quite old. He was older than me then. Anyway he came into the house and he was wearing his best suit and he had polished his shoes and I thought that he looked very handsome. Well, Donald said that I wasn't any good at cooking and that I was silly. He made fun of me and all the time he made fun of me Norman looked at me, as if he wanted me to say something. I remember he had a white handkerchief in his pocket and it looked very clean. Norman didn't have much to say for himself. In those days he worked a croft, and he was building a house. I was thirty years old then and he was forty-two. I was wearing a long brown skirt which I had got at the fishing and I was sitting as I am sitting now with my hands in my lap as my mother taught me. Donald said that I smoked when I was away from home. That was wicked of him. Of course to him it was a joke but it wasn't true. I think Norman believed him and he didn't like women smoking. My brother, you see, would make jokes all the time, they were like knives in my body, and my mind wasn't quick enough to say something back to him. Norman maybe didn't love me but we would have been happy together. Donald believed that his jokes were very funny, that people looked up to him, and that he was a clever man. But of course he . . . Maybe if it hadn't been for his limp he might have carried on in school, so he said anyway. I left school at twelve. I had to look after him even when my parents were alive.

'It didn't matter what I did, it was wrong. The tea was too hot or too cold. The potatoes weren't cooked right or the herring wasn't salt enough. "Who would marry you?" he would say to me. But I think Norman would have married me. Norman was a big man but he was slow and honest. He wasn't sarcastic at all and he couldn't think like my brother.

"She was in Yarmouth," Donald told him, "but they won't have her back, she's too stupid. Aren't you, Mary?" he asked me. That wasn't true. The reason

I couldn't go to Yarmouth was because I had to stay at home and look after him. I was going to go but he made me stop. He got very ill the night before I was due to leave and I had to stay behind. Anyway Norman went away that night and he never came back. I can still see him going out the door in his new suit back to the new house he was building. I found out afterwards that my brother had seen him and told him that I used to have fits at the time of the new moon, and that wasn't true.

'So I never married, and Donald would say to me, if I did something that he didn't like, "That's why Norman never married you, you're too stupid. And you shouldn't be going about with your stockings hanging down to your ankles. It doesn't look ladylike."'

I remembered how I used to come and listen to the news in this very house and it would tell of the German armies being inexorably strangled by the Russians. I would have visions of myself like Timoshenko standing up in my tank with dark goggles over my eyes as the Germans cowered in the snow and the rope of cold was drawn tighter and tighter. And he would say to me, 'Now then, tell me how many mackerel there are in a barrel. Go on now, tell me that.' And he would put his bald head on one side and look at me, his ginger moustache bristling. Or he would say, 'Tell me, then, what is the Gaelic for a compass. Eh? The proper Gaelic, I mean. Timoshenko will tell you that. Won't you, Timoshenko? She was at the fishing, weren't you, Timoshenko?'

And he would shift his aching legs, sighing heavily, his face becoming redder and redder.

'He thought I knew nothing,' she said. 'Other times he would threaten to put me out of the house because it belongs to him, you see.' She looked down at the body as if he were still alive and he were liable to stand up and throw her out of the house, crowing like a cockerel, his red cheeks inflated, and his red wings beating.

'He would say, "I'll get a housekeeper in. There's plenty who would make a good housekeeper. You're so stupid you don't know anything. And you leave everything so dirty. Look at this shirt you're supposed to have washed!"'

Was all this really true, I wondered. Had this woman lived in this village for so many years without anyone knowing anything about her suffering? It seemed so strange and unreal. All the time we had thought of the two as likeable comedians and one was cruel and vicious and the other was tormented and resentful. We had thought of them as nice, pleasant people, characters in the village. We didn't think of them as people at all, human beings who were locked in a death struggle. When people talked about her she became a sunny figure out of a comic, blundering about in a strange English world when she left the island, but happy all the same. We hadn't imagined that she was suffering like this in her dim world. And when we saw him sitting by the wall we thought of him as a fixture and we would shout greetings to him and he would shout back some quaint witticism. How odd it all was.

'But I knew what was going on all the time,' she continued. 'I could follow the news too. I knew what the Germans were doing, and the Russians. But he made me out to be a fool. And the thing was even after I heard of Norman's death I didn't say anything, though he said a few things himself. He told me one day, "You should have been his housekeeper and he wouldn't have been found dead like that on his own. But you weren't good enough for him. Poor man." And he would look at me with those small eyes of his. They had found Norman, you see, by the fire. He had fallen into it, he was ill and old. He hadn't been well for years. I often thought of taking him food but Donald wouldn't let me. After all we're all human and a little food wouldn't have been missed. I used to think of when we were young so many years ago. And when I was young I wasn't ugly. I wasn't beautiful but I wasn't ugly. I used to go to the dances when I was young, like the others. And of course I was at Yarmouth. He had never been out of the island though he was a man and I was only a woman and we used to bring presents home at the end of the season. I bought him a pipe once and another time I got him a melodeon but he wouldn't play it. So you see, there was that.'

There was another longish silence. Outside, it was pitch black and there was ice on the roads. In fact coming over from my own house I nearly slipped and fell but I had a torch so that was all right.

I wasn't at all afraid of her. I was in a strange way enjoying our conversation or rather her monologue. It was as if I was listening to an important story about life, a warning and a disaster. I remembered how as children we would be frightened by her brother waving his sticks from the wall where he was sitting. And we would run away full tilt as if we were running away from a monster. Our parents would say, 'It's only his joking,' and think how kind he was to go out of his way to entertain the children, but I wondered now whether in fact it might not be that he hated children and it wasn't acting at all, that cockerel clapping his sticks at us as we scattered across the moor.

Maybe too he had been more in pain than we had thought.

The trouble was that we didn't visit the two of them much at all. I did so, but only because I wished to listen to their radio to hear the news. Also, I was a quiet, reserved person who was happier in the company of people older than myself. But I hadn't actually looked at either of them with a clear hard look. To me she was a simple creature who smiled when her brother made some joke about Timoshenko, for his jokes tended to be remorselessly repetitive. It didn't occur to me that she was perhaps being pierced to the core by his primitive witticisms and it didn't occur to me either that they were meant to be cruel and were in fact outcrops from a perpetual war.

Suddenly she said to me, 'Would you like a cup of tea?' Without thinking I said 'Yes,' as if it was the most natural remark in the world while the body lay on the floor between us. I was amazed at how calmly I had accepted the presence of the body, though I had always thought of myself as sensitive and delicate. But on the other hand it was as if the body was not real, as if, as I have said, it would get to its feet, place its sticks under its arms, and walk towards me asking me riddles. Naturally however this didn't happen. And so we drank the tea out of neat cups with thin blue stripes at the rim.

'I had to give him all my saccharins,' she said, 'because he liked sweet things. It's a long time since I've had such a sweet cup of tea.' I noticed then that she had put saccharins in my tea and I realized that this was the first time that I had had tea in her house. She was in a strange way savouring her transient freedom.

'I remember now,' she said. 'It was the Germans and Timoshenko. The Germans had been trying to destroy Russia. I knew that, I'm not daft. And now the Russians were killing them. I heard that on the six o'clock news. And Timoshenko, he was doing that, he was winning. It was then that I . . . ' She stopped then, the cup at her lips. 'I remember now. It was when it said about Timoshenko and he said the tea wasn't sweet enough. That was when I . . . I must have been cutting bread. I must . . . '

She looked at me in amazement as if it was just at that moment that she realized she had killed him. As she began to tremble I took the cup from her hands – it was spilling over – and put my arm around her and comforted her while she cried.

ANGELA CARTER (1940–1992)

Born in Sussex, Carter studied English at university. Novelist, short-story writer and essayist, her work uses conventions taken from theatre, music-hall, fairy-tale and fantasy to create a provocative fiction which challenges conventional ideas of sexuality, of age, and of male–female relations. She has become one of the most widely studied of contemporary English writers. The following fairy-tale retold for adults is from her 1979 collection *The Bloody Chamber*.

The Company of Wolves

One beast and only one howls in the woods by night.

The wolf is carnivore incarnate and he's as cunning as he is ferocious; once he's had a taste of flesh then nothing else will do.

At night, the eyes of wolves shine like candle flames, yellowish, reddish, but that is because the pupils of their eyes fatten on darkness and catch the light from your lantern to flash it back to you – red for danger; if a wolf's eyes reflect only moonlight, then they gleam a cold and unnatural green, a mineral, a piercing colour. If the benighted traveller spies those luminous, terrible sequins stitched suddenly on the black thickets, then he knows he must run, if fear has not struck him stock-still.

But those eyes are all you will be able to glimpse of the forest assassins as they cluster invisibly round your smell of meat as you go through the wood unwisely late. They will be like shadows, they will be like wraiths, grey members of a congregation of nightmare; hark! his long, wavering howl . . . an aria of fear made audible.

The wolfsong is the sound of the rending you will suffer, in itself a murdering.

It is winter and cold weather. In this region of mountain and forest, there is now nothing for the wolves to eat. Goats and sheep are locked up in the byre, the deer departed for the remaining pasturage on the southern slopes – wolves grow lean and famished. There is so little flesh on them that you could count the starveling ribs through their pelts, if they gave you time before they pounced.

Those slavering jaws; the lolling tongue; the rime of saliva on the grizzled chops – of all the teeming perils of the night and the forest, ghosts, hobgoblins, ogres that grill babies upon gridirons, witches that fatten their captives in cages for cannibal tables, the wolf is worst for he cannot listen to reason.

You are always in danger in the forest, where no people are. Step between the portals of the great pines where the shaggy branches tangle about you, trapping the unwary traveller in nets as if the vegetation itself were in a plot with the wolves who live there, as though the wicked trees go fishing on behalf of their friends – step between the gateposts of the forest with the greatest trepidation and infinite precautions; for if you stray from the path for one instant, the wolves will eat you. They are grey as famine, they are as unkind as plague.

The grave-eyed children of the sparse villages always carry knives with them when they go to tend the little flocks of goats that provide the homesteads with acrid milk and rank, maggoty cheese. Their knives are half as big as they are, the blades are sharpened daily.

But the wolves have ways of arriving at your own hearthside. We try and try but sometimes we cannot keep them out. There is no winter's night the cottager does not fear to see a lean, grey, famished snout questing under the door, and there was a woman once bitten in her own kitchen as she was straining the macaroni.

Fear and flee the wolf; for, worst of all, the wolf may be more than he seems.

There was a hunter once, near here, that trapped a wolf in a pit. This wolf had massacred the sheep and goats; eaten up a mad old man who used to live by himself in a hut halfway up the mountain and sing to Jesus all day; pounced on a girl looking after the sheep, but she made such a commotion that men came with rifles and scared him away and tried to track him to the forest but he was cunning and easily gave them the slip. So this hunter dug a pit and put a duck in it, for bait, all alive-oh; and he covered the pit with straw smeared with wolf dung. Quack, quack! went the duck and a wolf came slinking out of the forest, a big one, a heavy one, he weighed as much as a grown man and the straw gave way beneath him – into the pit he tumbled. The hunter jumped down after him, slit his throat, cut off all his paws for a trophy.

And then no wolf at all lay in front of the hunter but the bloody trunk of a man, headless, footless, dying, dead.

A witch from up the valley once turned an entire wedding party into wolves because the groom had settled on another girl. She use to order them to visit her, at night, from spite, and they would sit and howl around her cottage for her, serenading her with their misery.

Not so very long ago, a young woman in our village married a man who vanished clean away on her wedding night. The bed was made with new sheets and the bride lay down in it; the groom said, he was going out to relieve himself, insisted on it, for the sake of decency, and she drew the coverlet up to her chin and lay there. And she waited and she waited and then she waited again – surely he's been gone a long time? Until she jumps up in bed and shrieks to hear a howling, coming on the wind from the forest.

That long-drawn, wavering howl has, for all its fearful resonance, some inherent sadness in it, as if the beasts would love to be less beastly if only they knew how and never cease to mourn their own condition. There is a vast melancholy in the canticles of the wolves, melancholy infinite as the forest, endless as these long nights of winter and yet that ghastly sadness, that mourning for their own, irremediable appetites, can never move the heart for not one phrase in it hints at the possibility of redemption; grace could not come to the wolf from its own despair, only through some external mediator, so that, sometimes, the beast will look as if he half welcomes the knife that dispatches him.

The young woman's brothers searched the outhouses and the haystacks but never found any remains so the sensible girl dried her eyes and found herself another husband not too shy to piss into a pot who spent the nights indoors. She gave him a pair of bonny babies and all went right as a trivet until, one freezing night, the night of the solstice, the hinge of the year when things do not fit together as well as they should, the longest night, her first good man came home again.

A great thump on the door announced him as she was stirring the soup for the father of her children and she knew him the moment she lifted the latch to him although it was years since she'd worn black for him and now he was in rags and his hair hung down his back and never saw a comb, alive with lice.

'Here I am again, missus,' he said. 'Get me my bowl of cabbage and be quick about it.'

Then her second husband came in with wood for the fire and when the first one saw she'd slept with another man and, worse, clapped his red eyes on her little children who'd crept into the kitchen to see what all the din was about, he shouted: 'I wish I were a wolf again, to teach this whore a lesson!' So a wolf he instantly became and tore off the eldest boy's left foot before he was chopped by the hatchet they used for chopping logs. But when the wolf lay bleeding and gasping its last, the pelt peeled off again and he was just as he had been, years ago, when he ran away from his marriage bed, so that she wept and her second husband beat her.

They say there's an ointment the Devil gives you that turns you into a wolf the minute you rub it on. Or, that he was born feet first and had a wolf for his father and his torso is a man's but his legs and genitals are a wolf's. And he has a wolf's heart.

Seven years is a werewolf's natural span but if you burn his human clothes you condemn him to wolfishness for the rest of his life, so old wives hereabouts think it some protection to throw a hat or an apron at the werewolf, as if clothes made the man. Yet by the eyes, those phosphorescent eyes, you know him in all his shapes; the eyes alone unchanged by metamorphosis.

Before he can become a wolf, the lycanthrope strips stark naked. If you spy a naked man among the pines, you must run as if the Devil were after you.

It is midwinter and the robin, the friend of man, sits on the handle of the gardener's spade and sings. It is the worst time in all the year for wolves but this strong-minded child insists she will go off through the wood. She is quite sure the wild beasts cannot harm her although, well-warned, she lays a carving knife in the basket her mother has packed with cheeses. There is a bottle of harsh liquor distilled from brambles; a batch of flat oatcakes baked on the heathstone;

a pot or two of jam. The girl will take these delicious gifts to a reclusive grandmother so old the burden of her years is crushing her to death. Granny lives two hours' trudge through the winter woods; the child wraps herself up in her thick shawl, draws it over her head. She steps into her stout wooden shoes; she is dressed and ready and it is Christmas Eve. The malign door of the solstice still swings upon its hinges but she has been too much loved ever to feel scared.

Children do not stay young for long in this savage country. There are no toys for them to play with so they work hard and grow wise but this one, so pretty and the youngest of her family, a little late-comer, had been indulged by her mother and the grandmother who'd knitted her the red shawl that, today, has the ominous if brilliant look of blood on snow. Her breasts have just begun to swell; her hair is like lint, so fair it hardly makes a shadow on her pale forehead; her cheeks are an emblematic scarlet and white and she has just started her woman's bleeding, the clock inside her that will strike, henceforward, once a month.

She stands and moves within the invisible pentacle of her own virginity. She is an unbroken egg; she is a sealed vessel; she has inside her a magic space the entrance to which is shut tight with a plug of membrane; she is a closed system; she does not know how to shiver. She has her knife and she is afraid of nothing.

Her father might forbid her, if he were home, but he is away in the forest, gathering wood, and her mother cannot deny her.

The forest closed upon her like a pair of jaws.

There is always something to look at in the forest, even in the middle of winter – the huddled mounds of birds, succumbed to the lethargy of the season, heaped on the creaking boughs and too forlorn to sing; the bright frills of the winter fungi on the blotched trunks of the trees; the cuneiform slots of rabbits and deer, the herringbone tracks of the birds, a hare as lean as a rasher of bacon streaking across the path where the thin sunlight dapples the russet brakes of last year's bracken.

When she heard the freezing howl of a distant wolf, her practised hand sprang to the handle of her knife, but she saw no sign of a wolf at all, nor of a naked man, neither, but then she heard a clattering among the brushwood and there sprang on to the path a fully clothed one, a very handsome young one, in the green coat and wide-awake hat of a hunter, laden with carcasses of game birds. She had her hand on her knife at the first rustle of twigs but he laughed with a flash of white teeth when he saw her and made her a comic yet flattering little bow; she'd never seen such a fine fellow before, not among the rustic clowns of her native village. So on they went, through the thickening light of the afternoon.

Soon they were laughing and joking like old friends. When he offered to carry her basket, she gave it to him although her knife was in it because he told her his rifle would protect them. As the day darkened, it began to snow again; she felt the first flakes settle on her eyelashes but now there was only half a mile to go and there would be a fire, and hot tea, and a welcome, a warm one surely, for the dashing huntsman as well as for herself.

This young man had a remarkable object in his pocket. It was a compass. She looked at the little round glassface in the palm of his hand and watched the wavering needle with a vague wonder. He assured her this compass had taken him safely through the wood on his hunting trip because the needle always told him with perfect accuracy where the north was. She did not believe it; she knew she should never leave the path on the way through the wood or else she would be lost instantly. He laughed at her again; gleaming trails of spittle clung to his teeth. He said, if he plunged off the path into the forest that surrounded them, he would guarantee to arrive at her grandmother's house a good quarter of an hour before she did, plotting his way through the undergrowth with his compass, while she trudged the long way, along the winding path.

I don't believe you. Besides, aren't you afraid of the wolves?

He only tapped the gleaming butt of his rifle and grinned.

Is it a bet? he asked her. Shall we make a game of it? What will you give me if I get to your grandmother's house before you?

What would you like? she asked disingenuously.

A kiss.

Commonplaces of a rustic seduction; she lowered her eyes and blushed.

He went through the undergrowth and took her basket with him but she forgot to be afraid of the beasts, although now the moon was rising, for she wanted to dawdle on her way to make sure the handsome gentleman would win his wager.

Grandmother's house stood by itself a little way out of the village. The freshly falling snow blew in eddies about the kitchen garden and the young man stepped delicately up the snowy path to the door as if he were reluctant to get his feet wet, swinging his bundle of game and the girl's basket and humming a little tune to himself.

There is a faint trace of blood on his chin; he has been snacking on his catch.

He rapped upon the panels with his knuckles.

Aged and frail, granny is three-quarters succumbed to the mortality the ache in her bones promises her and almost ready to give in entirely. A boy came out from the village to build up her hearth for the night an hour ago and the kitchen crackles with busy firelight. She has her Bible for company, she is a pious old woman. She is propped up on several pillows in the bed set into the wall peasant-fashion, wrapped up in the patchwork quilt she made before she was married, more years ago than she cares to remember. Two china spaniels with liver-coloured blotches on their coats and black noses sit on either side of the fireplace. There is a bright rug of woven rags on the pantiles. The grandfather clock ticks away her eroding time.

We keep the wolves outside by living well.

He rapped upon the panels with his hairy knuckles.

It is your granddaughter, he mimicked in a high soprano.

Lift up the latch and walk in, my darling.

You can tell them by their eyes, eyes of a beast of prey, nocturnal, devastating eyes as red as a wound; you can hurl your Bible at him and your apron after, granny, you thought that was a sure prophylactic against these infernal vermin . . . now call on Christ and his mother and all the angels in heaven to protect you but it won't do you any good.

His feral muzzle is sharp as a knife; he drops his golden burden of gnawed pheasant on the table and puts down your dear girl's basket, too. Oh, my God, what have you done with her?

Off with his disguise, that coat of forest-coloured cloth, the hat with the feather tucked into the ribbon; his matted hair streams down his white shirt and she can see the lice moving in it. The sticks in the hearth shift and hiss; night and the forest has come into the kitchen with darkness tangled in its hair.

He strips off his shirt. His skin is the colour and texture of vellum. A crisp stripe of hair runs down his belly, his nipples are ripe and dark as poison fruit but he's so thin you could count the ribs under his skin if only he gave you the time. He strips off his trousers and she can see how hairy his legs are. His genitals, huge. Ah! huge.

The last thing the old lady saw in all this world was a young man, eyes like cinders, naked as a stone, approaching her bed.

The wolf is carnivore incarnate.

When he had finished with her, he licked his chops and quickly dressed himself again, until he was just as he had been when he came through her door. He burned the inedible hair in the fireplace and wrapped the bones up in a napkin that he hid away under the bed in the wooden chest in which he found a clean pair of sheets. These he carefully put on the bed instead of the tell-tale stained ones he stowed away in the laundry basket. He plumped up the pillows and shook out the patchwork quilt, he picked up the Bible from the floor, closed it and laid it on the table. All was as it had been before except that grandmother was gone. The sticks twitched in the grate, the clock ticked and the young man sat patiently, deceitfully beside the bed in granny's nightcap.

Rat-a-tap-tap.

Who's there, he quavers in granny's antique falsetto.

Only your granddaughter.

So she came in, bringing with her a flurry of snow that melted in tears on the tiles, and perhaps she was a little disappointed to see only her grandmother sitting beside the fire. But then he flung off the blanket and sprang to the door, pressing his back against it so that she could not get out again.

The girl looked round the room and saw there was not even the indentation of a head on the smooth cheek of the pillow and how, for the first time she'd seen it so, the Bible lay closed on the table. The tick of the clock cracked like a whip. She wanted her knife from her basket but she did not dare to reach for it because his eyes were fixed upon her – huge eyes that now seemed to shine with a unique, interior light, eyes the size of saucers, saucers full of Greek fire, diabolic phosphorescence.

What big eyes you have.

All the better to see you with.

No trace at all of the old woman except for a tuft of white hair that had caught in the bark of an unburned log. When the girl saw that, she knew she was in danger of death.

Where is my grandmother?

There's nobody here but we two, my darling.

Now a great howling rose up all around them, near, very near as close as the kitchen garden, the howling of a multitude of wolves; she knew the worst wolves are hairy on the inside and she shivered, in spite of the scarlet shawl she pulled more closely round herself as if it could protect her although it was as red as the blood she must spill.

Who has come to sing us carols, she said.

Those are the voices of my brothers, darling; I love the company of wolves. Look out of the window and you'll see them.

Snow half-caked the lattice and she opened it to look into the garden. It was a white night of moon and snow; the blizzard whirled round the gaunt, grey beasts who squatted on their haunches among the rows of winter cabbage, pointing their sharp snouts to the moon and howling as if their hearts would break. Ten wolves; twenty wolves – so many wolves she could not count them, howling in concert as if demented or deranged.

Their eyes reflected the light from the kitchen and shone like a hundred candles.

It is very cold, poor things, she said; no wonder they howl so.

She closed the window on the wolves' threnody and took off her scarlet shawl, the colour of poppies, the colour of sacrifices, the colour of her menses, and, since her fear did her no good, she ceased to be afraid.

What shall I do with my shawl?

Throw it on the fire, dear one. You won't need it again.

She bundled up her shawl and threw it on the blaze, which instantly consumed it. Then she drew her blouse over her head; her small breasts gleamed as if the snow had invaded the room.

What shall I do with my blouse?

Into the fire with it, too, my pet.

The thin muslin went flaring up the chimney like a magic bird and now off came her skirt, her woollen stockings, her shoes, and on to the fire they went, too, and were gone for good. The firelight shone through the edges of her skin; now she was clothed only in her untouched integument of flesh. This dazzling, naked she combed out her hair with her fingers; her hair looked white as the snow outside. Then went directly to the man with red eyes in whose unkempt mane the lice moved; she stood up on tiptoe and unbuttoned the collar of his shirt.

What big arms you have.

All the better to hug you with.

Every wolf in the world now howled a prothalamion outside the window as she freely gave him the kiss she owed him.

What big teeth you have!

She saw how his jaw began to slaver and the room was full of the clamour of the forest's *Liebestod*[1] but the wise child never flinched, even as he answered: All the better to eat you with.

The girl burst out laughing – she knew she was nobody's meat. She laughed at him full in the face, she ripped off his shirt for him and flung it into the fire, in the fiery wake of her own discarded clothing. The flames danced like dead

---

1 *Liebestod*: death song of the beloved.

souls on Walpurisgnacht[1] and the old bones under the bed set up a terrible clattering but she did not pay them any heed.

Carnivore incarnate, only immaculate flesh appeases him.

She will lay his fearful head on her lap and she will pick out the lice from his pelt and perhaps she will put the lice into her mouth and eat them, as he will bid her, as she would do in a savage marriage ceremony.

The blizzard will die down.

The blizzard died down, leaving the mountains as randomly covered with snow as if a blind woman had thrown a sheet over them, the upper branches of the forest pines limed, creaking, swollen with the fall.

Snowlight, moonlight, a confusion of paw-prints.

All silent, all silent.

Midnight; and the clock strikes. It is Christmas day, the werewolves' birthday, the door of the solstice stands wide open; let them all sink through.

See! sweet and sound she sleeps in granny's bed, between the paws of the tender wolf.

JOHN MCGAHERN (1934–)

Born in Dublin, McGahern's novels and short stories reveal the uneasy Irish accommodation between the rural and the urban, past and present. Many of his works focus on the distance between generations, parents and children who nevertheless all feel strongly attached to their local communities. 'High Ground' is the title story of a collection first published in 1985.

High Ground

I let the boat drift on the river beneath the deep arch of the bridge, the keel scraping the gravel as it crossed the shallows out from Walsh's, past the boathouse at the mouth, and out into the lake. It was only the slow growing distance from the ring of reeds round the shore that told that the boat moved at all on the lake. More slowly still, the light was going from the August evening.

I was feeling leaden with tiredness but did not want to sleep. I had gone on the river in order to be alone, the way one goes to a dark room.

The Brothers' Building Fund Dance had been held the night before. A big marquee had been set up in the grounds behind the monastery. Most of the people I had gone to school with were there, awkward in their new estate, and nearly all the Brothers who had taught us: Joseph, Francis, Benedictus, Martin. They stood in a black line beneath the low canvas near the entrance and waited for their old pupils to go up to them. When they were alone, watching us dance, rapid comment passed up and down the line, and often Joseph and Martin doubled up, unable or unwilling to conceal laughter; but by midnight

---

1 **Walpurisgnacht:** the eve of May Day when the witch-world revels.

they had gone, and a night of a sort was ours, the fine dust from the floor rising into the perfume and sweat and hair oil as we danced in the thresh of the music.

There was a full moon as I drove Una to her home in Arigna in the borrowed Prefect, the whole wide water of Allen taking in the wonderful mysteriousness of the light. We sat in the car and kissed and talked, and morning was there before we noticed. After the harshness of growing up, a world of love and beauty, of vague gardens and dresses and laughter, one woman in a gleaming distance seemed to be almost within reach. We would enter this world. We would make it true.

I was home just before the house had risen, and lay on the bed and waited till everybody was up, then changed into old clothes. I was helping my father put up a new roof on the house. Because of the tiredness, I had to concentrate completely on the work, even then nearly losing my footing several times between the stripped beams, sometimes annoying my father by handing him the wrong lath or tool; but when evening came the last thing I wanted was sleep. I wanted to be alone, to go over the night, to try to see clearly, which only meant turning again and again on the wheel of dreaming.

'Hi there! Hi! Do you hear me, young Moran!' The voice came with startling clarity over the water, was taken up by the fields across the lake, echoed back. 'Hi there! Hi! Do you hear me, young Moran!'

I looked all around. The voice came from the road. I couldn't make out the figure at first, leaning in a broken gap of the wall above the lake, but when he called again I knew it was Eddie Reegan, Senator Reegan.

'Hi there, young Moran. Since the mountain can't come to Mahomet, Mahomet will have to come to the mountain. Row over here a minute. I want to have a word with you.'

I rowed slowly, watching each oar-splash slip away from the boat in the mirror of water. I disliked him, having unconsciously, perhaps, picked up my people's dislike. He had come poor to the place, buying Lynch's small farm cheap, and soon afterwards the farmhouse burned down. At once, a bigger house was built with the insurance money, closer to the road, though that in its turn was due to burn down too, to be replaced by the present mansion, the avenue of Lawson cypresses now seven years old. Soon he was buying up other small farms, but no one had ever seen him work with shovel or with spade. He always appeared immaculately dressed. It was as if he understood instinctively that it was only the shortest of short steps from appearance to becoming. 'A man who works never makes any money. He has no time to see how the money is made,' he was fond of boasting. He set up as an auctioneer. He entered politics. He married Kathleen Relihan, the eldest of old Paddy Relihan's daughters, the richest man in the area, Chairman of the County Council. 'Do you see those two girls? I'm going to marry one of those girls,' he was reported to have remarked to a friend. 'Which one?' 'It doesn't matter. They're both Paddy Relihan's daughters'; and when Paddy retired it was Reegan rather than any of his own sons who succeeded Paddy in the Council. Now that he had surpassed Paddy Relihan and become a Senator and it seemed only a matter of time before he was elected to the Dail,[1] he no longer joked about 'the aul effort of a fire', and was gravely concerned about the reluctance of insurance companies to grant cover for fire to dwelling houses in our part of the country. He had bulldozed the hazel and briar from the hills above the lake, and as I turned to see how close the boat had come to the wall I could see behind him the white and black of his Friesians grazing between the electric fences on the far side of the reseeded hill.

I let the boat turn so that I could place my hand on the stone, but the evening was so calm that it would have rested beneath the high wall without any hand. The Senator had seated himself on the wall as I was rowing in, and his shoes hung six or eight feet above the boat.

'It's not the first time I've had to congratulate you, though I'm too high up here to shake your hand. And what I'm certain of is that it won't be the last time either,' he began.

'Thanks. You're very kind,' I answered.

'Have you any idea where you'll go from here?'

'No. I've applied for the grant. It depends on whether I get the grant or not.'

'What'll you do if you get it?'

'Go on, I suppose. Go a bit farther . . .'

'What'll you do then?'

'I don't know. Sooner or later, I suppose, I'll have to look for a job.'

'That's the point I've been coming to. You are qualified to teach, aren't you?'

'Yes. But I've only taught for a few months. Before I got that chance to go to the university.'

'You didn't like teaching?' he asked sharply.

'No.' I was careful. 'I didn't dislike it. It was a job.'

'I like that straightness. And what I'm looking to know is – if you were offered a very good job would you be likely to take it?'

'What job?'

'I won't beat around the bush either. I'm talking of the Principalship of the school here. It's a very fine position for a young man. You'd be among your own people. You'd be doing good where you belong. I hear you're interested in a very attractive young lady not a hundred miles from here. If you decided to marry and settle down I'm in a position to put other advantages your way.'

Master Leddy was the Principal of the school. He had been the Principal as long as I could remember. He had taught me, many before me. I had called to see him just three days before. The very idea of replacing him was shocking. And anyhow, I knew the politicians had nothing to do with the appointment of teachers. It was the priest who ran the school. What he was saying didn't even begin to make sense, but I had been warned about his cunning and was wary 'You must be codding. Isn't Master Leddy the Principal?'

'He is now but he won't be for long more – not if I have anything to do with it.'

'How?' I asked very quietly in the face of the outburst.

'That need be no concern of yours. If you can give me your word that you'll take the job, I can promise you that the job is as good as yours.'

---

1 **Dail**: the Irish Parliament.

'I can't do that. I can't follow anything right. Isn't it Canon Gallagher who appoints the teachers?'

'Listen. There are many people who feel the same way as I do. If I go to the Canon in the name of all those people and say that you're willing to take the job, the job is yours. Even if he didn't want to, he'd have no choice but to appoint you . . .'

'Why should you want to do that for me? Say, even if it is possible.' I was more curious now than alarmed.

'It's more than possible. It's bloody necessary. I'll be plain. I have three sons. They go to that school. They have nothing to fall back on but whatever education they get. And with the education they're getting at that school up there, all they'll ever be fit for is to dig ditches. Now, I've never dug ditches, but even at my age I'd take off my coat and go down into a ditch rather than ever have to watch any of my sons dig. The whole school is a shambles. Someone described it lately as one big bear garden.'

'What makes you think I'd be any better?'

'You're young. You're qualified. You're ambitious. It's a very good job for someone of your age. I'd give you all the backing you'd want. You'd have every reason to make a go of it. With you there, I'd feel my children would still be in with a chance. In another year or two even that'll be gone.'

'I don't see why you want my word at this stage,' I said evasively, hoping to slip away from it all. I saw his face return to its natural look of shrewdness in what was left of the late summer light.

'If I go to the Canon now it'll be just another complaint in a long line of complaints. If I can go to him and say that things can't be allowed to go on as they have been going and we have a young man here, from a good family, a local, more than qualified, who's willing to take the job, who has everyone's backing, it's a different proposition entirely. And I can guarantee you here this very evening that you'll be the Principal of that school when it opens in September.'

For the first time it was all coming clear to me.

'What'll happen to the Master? What'll he do?'

'What I'm more concerned about is what'll my children do if he stays,' he burst out again. 'But you don't have to concern yourself about it. It'll be all taken care of.'

I had called on the Master three evenings before, walking beyond the village to the big ramshackle farmhouse. He was just rising, having taken all his meals of the day in bed, and was shaving and dressing upstairs, one time calling down for a towel, and again for a laundered shirt.

'Is that young Moran?' He must have recognized my voice or name. 'Make him a good cup of tea. And he'll be able to be back up the road with myself.'

A very old mongrel greyhound was routed from the leather armchair one side of the fire, and I was given tea and slices of buttered bread. The Master's wife, who was small and frail with pale skin and lovely brown eyes, kept up a cheerful chatter that required no response as she busied herself about the enormous cluttered kitchen which seemed not to possess a square foot of room.

There were buckets everywhere, all sorts of chairs, basins, bags of meal and flour, cats, the greyhound, pots and pans. The pattern had faded from the bulging wallpaper, a dark ochre, and some of the several calendars that hung around the walls had faded into the paper. It would have been difficult to find space for an extra cup or saucer on the long wooden table. Plainly there were no set meal times. Two of the Master's sons, now grown men, came singly in from the fields while I waited. Plates of food were served at once, bacon and liver, a mug of tea. They took from the plate of bread already on the table, the butter, the sugar, the salt, the bottle of sauce. They spent no more than a few minutes over the meal, blessing themselves at its end, leaving as suddenly as they'd entered, smiling and nodding in a friendly way in my direction but making little attempt at conversation, though Gerald did ask, before he reached for his hat – a hat I recognized as having belonged to the Master back in my school days, a brown hat with a blue teal's feather and a small hole burned in its side – 'Well, how are things getting along in the big smoke?' The whole effect was of a garden and orchard gone completely wild, but happily.

'You couldn't have come at a better time. We'll be able to be up the road together,' the Master said as he came heavily down the stairs in his stockinged feet. He'd shaved, was dressed in a grey suit, with a collar and tie, the old watch-chain crossing a heavy paunch. He had failed since last I'd seen him, the face red and puffy, the white hair thinned, and there was a bruise on the cheekbone where he must have fallen. The old hound went towards him, licking at his hand.

'Good boy! Good boy,' he said as he came towards me, patting the hound. As soon as we shook hands he slipped his feet into shoes which had stood beside the leather chair. He did not bend or sit, and as he talked I saw the small bird-like woman at his feet, tying up the laces.

'It's a very nice thing to see old pupils coming back. Though not many of them bring me laurels like yourself, it's still a very nice thing. Loyalty is a fine quality. A very fine quality.'

'Now,' his wife stood by his side, 'all you need is your hat and stick,' and she went and brought them.

'Thank you. Thank you indeed. I don't know what I'd do but for my dear wife,' he said.

'Do you hear him now! He was never stuck for the charm. Off with you now before you get the back of me hand,' she bantered, and called as we went slowly towards the gate, 'Do you want me to send any of the boys up for you?'

'No. Not unless they have some business of their own to attend to in the village. No,' he said gravely, turning very slowly.

He spoke the whole way on the slow walk to the village. All the time he seemed to lag behind my snail's pace, sometimes standing because he was out of breath, tapping at the road with the cane. Even when the walk slowed to a virtual standstill it seemed to be still far too energetic for him.

'I always refer to you as my star pupil. When the whole enterprise seems to be going more or less askew, I always point to young Moran: that's one good job I turned out. Let the fools prate.'

I walked, stooping by his side, restraining myself within the slow walk, embarrassed, ashamed, confused. I had once looked to him in pure infatuation, would rush to his defence against every careless whisper. He had shone like a clear star. I was in love with what I hardly dared to hope I might become. It seemed horrible now that I might come to this.

'None of my own family were clever,' he confided. 'It was a great disappointment. And yet they may well be happier for it. Life is an extraordinary thing. A very great mystery. Wonderful . . . shocking . . . thing.'

Each halting speech seemed to lead in some haphazard way into the next.

'Now that you're coming out into the world you'll have to be constantly on your guard. You'll have to be on your guard first of all against intellectual pride. That's the worst sin, the sin of Satan. And always be kind to women. Help them. Women are weak. They'll be attracted to you.' I had to smile ruefully, never having noticed much of a stampede in my direction. 'There was this girl I left home from a dance once,' he continued. 'And as we were getting closer to her house I noticed her growing steadily more amorous until I had to say, "None of that now, girl. It is not the proper time!" Later, when we were both old and married, she thanked me. She said I was a true gentleman.'

The short walk seemed to take a deep age, but once outside Ryan's door he took quick leave of me. 'I won't invite you inside. Though I set poor enough of an example, I want to bring no one with me. I say to all my pupils: *Beware of the high stool.* The downward slope from the high stool is longer and steeper than from the top of Everest. God bless and guard you, young Moran. Come and see me again before you head back to the city.' And with that he left me. I stood facing the opaque glass of the door, the small print of the notice above it: *Seven Days Licence to Sell Wine, Beer, Spirits.* How can he know what he knows and still do what he does, I say to the sudden silence before turning away.

'Do you mean the Master'll be out on the road, then?' I asked Senator Reegan from the boat, disturbed by the turn the conversation had taken.

'You need have no fear of that. There's a whole union behind him. In our enlightened day alcoholism is looked upon as just another illness. And they wonder how the country can be so badly off,' he laughed sarcastically. 'No. He'll probably be offered a rest cure on full pay. I doubt if he'd take it. If he did, it'd delay official recognition of your appointment by a few months, that'd be all, a matter of paperwork. The very worst that could happen to him is that he'd be forced to take early retirement, which would probably add years to his life. He'd just have that bit less of a pension with which to drink himself into an early grave. You need have no worries on that score. You'd be doing everybody a favour, including him most of all, if you'd take the job. Well, what do you say? I could still go to the Canon tonight. It's late but not too late. He'd just be addressing himself to his hot toddy. It could be as good a time as any to attack him. Well, what do you say?'

'I'll have to think about it.'

'It's a very fine position for a young man like yourself starting out in life.'

'I know it is. I'm very grateful.'

'To hell with gratitude. Gratitude doesn't matter a damn. It's one of those moves that benefits everybody involved. You'll come to learn that there aren't many moves like that in life.'

'I'll have to think about it.' I was anxious to turn away from any direct confrontation.

'I can't wait for very long. Something has to be done and done soon.'

'I know that but I still have to think about it.'

'Listen. Let's not close on anything this evening. Naturally you have to consider everything. Why don't you drop over to my place tomorrow night? You'll have a chance to meet my lads. And herself has been saying for a long time now that she'd like to meet you. Come about nine. Everything will be out of the way by then.'

I rowed very slowly away, just stroking the boat forward in the deadly silence of the half-darkness. I watched Reegan cross the road, climb the hill, pausing now and then among the white blobs of his Friesians. His figure stood for a while at the top of the hill where he seemed to be looking back towards the boat and water before he disappeared.

When I got back to the house everyone was asleep except a younger sister who had waited up for me. She was reading by the fire, the small black cat on her knee.

'They've all gone to bed,' she explained. 'Since you were on the river, they let me wait up for you. Only there's no tea. I've just found out that there's not a drop of spring water in the house.'

'I'll go to the well, then. Otherwise someone will have to go first thing in the morning. You don't have to wait up for me.' I was too agitated to go straight to bed and glad of the distraction of any activity.

'I'll wait,' she said. 'I'll wait and make the tea when you get back.'

'I'll be less than ten minutes.' The late hour held for her the attractiveness of the stolen.

I walked quickly, swinging the bucket. The whole village seemed dead under a benign moon, but as I passed along the church wall I heard voices. They came from Ryan's Bar. It was shut, the blinds down, but then I noticed cracks of yellow light along the edges of the big blue blind. They were drinking after hours. I paused to see if I could recognize any of the voices, but before I had time Charlie Ryan hissed, 'Will you keep your voices down, will yous? At the rate you're going you'll soon have the Sergeant out of his bed,' and the voices quietened to a whisper. Afraid of being noticed in the silence, I passed on to get the bucket of spring water from the well but the voices were in full song again by the time I returned. I let the bucket softly down in the dust and stood in the shadow of the church wall to listen. I recognized the Master's slurred voice at once, and then voices of some of the men who worked the sawmill in the wood.

'That sixth class in 1933 was a great class, Master.' It was Johnny's Connor's voice, the saw mechanic. 'I was never much good at the Irish, but I was a terror at the maths, especially the Euclid.'

I shivered as I listened under the church wall. Nineteen thirty-three was the year before I was born.

'You were a topper, Johnny. You were a topper at the maths,' I heard the Master's voice. It was full of authority. He seemed to have no sense at all that he was in danger.

'Tommy Morahan that went to England was the best of us all in that class,' another voice took up, a voice I wasn't able to recognize.

'He wasn't half as good as he imagined he was. He suffered from a swelled head,' Johnny Connor said.

'Ye were toppers, now. Ye were all toppers,' the Master said diplomatically.

'One thing sure is that you made a great job of us, Master. You were a powerful teacher. I remember to this day everything you told us about the Orinoco River.'

'It was no trouble. Ye had the brains. There are people in this part of the country digging ditches who could have been engineers or doctors or judges or philosophers had they been given the opportunity. But the opportunity was lacking. That was all that was lacking.' The Master spoke again with great authority.

'The same again all round, Charlie,' a voice ordered. 'And a large brandy for the Master.'

'Still, we kept sailing, didn't we, Master? That's the main thing. We kept sailing.'

'Ye had the brains. The people in this part of the country had powerful brains.'

'If you had to pick one thing, Master, what would you put those brains down to?'

'Will you hush now! The Sergeant wouldn't even have to be passing outside to hear yous. Soon he'll be hearing yous down in the barracks,' Charlie hissed.

There was a lull again in the voices in which a coin fell and seemed to roll across the floor.

'Well, the people with the brains mostly stayed here. They had to. They had no choice. They didn't go to the cities. So the brains was passed on to the next generation. Then there's the trees. There's the water. And we're very high up here. We're practically at the source of the Shannon. If I had to pick on one thing more than another, I'd put it down to that. I'd attribute it to the high ground.'

DEREK MAHON (1941–)

Mahon was born in Belfast and, like Seamus Heaney, first came to prominence as a 'Northern Poet'. His poetry is much influenced by Louis MacNeice.

A Disused Shed in Co. Wexford

> Let them not forget us, the weak souls among the asphodels.
> Seferis, *Mythistorema*
> for J. G. Farrell

Even now there are places where a thought might grow –
Peruvian mines, worked out and abandoned
To a slow clock of condensation,
An echo trapped for ever, and a flutter
5   Of wildflowers in the lift-shaft,
Indian compounds where the wind dances
And a door bangs with diminished confidence
Lime crevices behind rippling rainbarrels,
Dog corners for bone burials;
10   And in a disused shed in Co. Wexford,

Deep in the grounds of a burnt-out hotel,
Among the bathtubs and the washbasins
A thousand mushrooms crowd to a keyhole.
This is the one star in their firmament
15   Or frames a star within a star.
What should they do there but desire?
So many days beyond the rhododendrons
With the world waltzing in its bowl of cloud,
They have learnt patience and silence.
20   Listening to the rooks querulous in the high wood.

They have been waiting for us in a foetor
Of vegetable sweat since civil war days,
Since the gravel-crunching, interminable departure
Of the expropriated mycologist.
25   He never came back, and light since then
Is a keyhole rusting gently after rain.
Spiders have spun, flies dusted to mildew
And once a day, perhaps, they have heard something
A trickle of masonry, a shout from the blue
30   Or a lorry changing gear at the end of the lane.

There have been deaths, the pale flesh flaking
Into the earth that nourished it;

---

21 **foetor**: fetor; a stench.   24 **mycologist**: one who studies mushrooms.

And nightmares, born of these and the grim
Dominion of stale air and rank moisture.
35 Those nearest the door grow strong
'Elbow room! Elbow room!'
The rest, dim in a twilight of crumbling
Utensils and broken flower-pots, groaning
For their deliverance, have been so long
40 Expectant that there is left only the posture.

A half century, without visitors, in the dark
Poor preparation for the cracking lock
And creak of hinges. Magi, moonmen,
Powdery prisoners of the old regime,
45 Web-throated, stalked like triffids, racked by drought
And insomnia, only the ghost of a scream
At the flash-bulb firing squad we wake them with
Shows there is life yet in their feverish forms.
Grown beyond nature now, soft food for worms,
50 They lift frail heads in gravity and good faith.

They are begging us, you see, in their wordless way,
To do something, to speak on their behalf
Or at least not to close the door again.
Lost people of Treblinka and Pompeii!
55 'Save us, save us,' they seem to say,
'Let the god not abandon us
Who have come so far in darkness and in pain.
We too had our lives to live.
You with your light meter and relaxed itinerary,
60 Let not our naive labours have been in vain!'

Courtyards in Delft

Pieter de Hooch, 1659
for Gordon Woods

Oblique light on the trite, on brick and tile –
Immaculate masonry, and everywhere that
Water tap, that broom and wooden pail
To keep it so. House-proud, the wives
5 Of artisans pursue their thrifty lives
Among scrubbed yards, modest but adequate.
Foliage is sparse, and clings. No breeze
Ruffles the trim composure of those trees.

---

54 Treblinka: Nazi death camp. Pompeii: Roman city   Courtyards in Delft Pieter de Hooch: Dutch painter.
destroyed by the volcano Vesuvius.

No spinet-playing emblematic of
10 The harmonies and disharmonies of love;
No lewd fish, no fruit, no wide-eyed bird
About to fly its cage while a virgin
Listens to her seducer, mars the chaste
Precision of the thing and the thing made.
15 Nothing is random, nothing goes to waste:
We miss the dirty dog, the fiery gin.

That girl with her back to us who waits
For her man to come home for his tea
Will wait till the paint disintegrates
20 And ruined dykes admit the esurient sea;
Yet this is life too, and the cracked
Out-house door a verifiable fact
As vividly mnemonic as the sunlit
Railings that front the houses opposite.

25 I lived there as a boy and know the coal
Glittering in its shed, late-afternoon
Lambency informing the deal table,
The ceiling cradled in a radiant spoon.
I must be lying low in a room there,
30 A strange child with a taste for verse,
While my hard-nosed companions dream of war
On parched veldt and fields of rain-swept gorse;

For the pale light of that provincial town
Will spread itself, like ink or oil,
35 Over the not yet accurate linen
Map of the world which occupies one wall
And punish nature in the name of God.
If only, now, the Maenads, as of right,
Came smashing crockery, with fire and sword,
40 We could sleep easier in our beds at night.

---

20 esurient: greedy. 27 lambency: brilliant display of 38 **Maenads**: ecstatic female followers of god Bacchus.
wit.

LIZ LOCHHEAD (1947–)

Born in Motherwell, Lochhead has spent her life in Glasgow and her poetry, drama and television plays reflect the language and sharply satiric perspective of that city.

The Grim Sisters

And for special things
(weddings, school –
concerts) the grown up girls next door
would do my hair.

5   Luxembourg announced *Amami Night.*

I sat at peace passing bobbipins
from a marshmallow pink cosmetic purse
embossed with jazzmen,
girls with pony tails and a November
10   topaz lucky birthstone.
They doused my cow's-lick, rollered
and skewered tightly. I expected that to be lovely
would be worth the hurt.

They read my Stars,
15   tied chiffon scarves to doorhandles,
tried to teach me tight dancesteps
you'd no guarantee
any partner you might find would ever be able to
keep up with as far as I could see.

There were always things to burn
20   before the men came in.

For each disaster
you were meant to know the handy hint.
Soap at a pinch
but better nailvarnish (clear) for ladders.
25   For kisscurls, spit.
Those days womanhood was quite a sticky thing
and that was what these grim sisters came to mean,

'You'll know all about it soon enough.'
But when the clock struck they
30   stood still, stopped dead.
And they were left there
out in the cold with the wrong skirtlength

---

5 **Luxembourg:** Radio Luxembourg, which broadcast   24 **ladders:** runs in stockings or tights.
popular music to Britain.

and bouffant hair,
dressed to kill,

35   who'd been
all the rage in fifty-eight,
a swish of Persianelle
a slosh of perfume.
In those big black mantrap handbags
40   they snapped shut at any hint of *that*
were hedgehog hairbrushes
cottonwool mice and barbed combs to tease.
Their heels spiked bubblegum, dead leaves.

Wasp waist and cone breast, I see them yet.
45   I hope, I hope
there's been a change of more than silhouette.

Bagpipe Muzak, Glasgow 1990

Lochhead's 'Bagpipe Muzak' evokes Louis MacNeice's poem of some 50 years earlier (see p.1436). It is dense in allusions to the popular and political culture of Glasgow in the 1980s.

When A. and R. men hit the street
To sign up every second band they meet
Then marketing men will spill out spiel
About how us Glesca folk are really *real*
5   (Where once they used to fear and pity
These days they glamorise and patronise our city –
Accentwise once they could hear bugger all
That was not low, glottal or guttural,
Now we've 'kudos' incident'ly
10   And the Patter's street-smart, strictly state-of-the-art,
And our oaths are user-friendly).
It's all go the sandblaster, it's all go Tutti Frutti,
All we want is a wally close with Rennie Mackintosh putti.

Malkie Machismo invented a gismo for making whisky oot
        o'girders
15   He tasted it, came back for mair, and soon he was on to his
        thirders.
Rabbie Burns turned in his grave and dunted Hugh
        MacDiarmid,
Said: It's oor National Thorn, John Barleycorn, but I doot we'll
        ever learn it . . .

It's all go the Rotary Club, its ail go 'The Toast Tae The Lassies',
It's all go Holy Willie's Prayer and plunging your dirk in the haggis.

20   Robbie Coltrane flew Caledonian MacBrayne
To Lewis . . . on a Sunday!
Protesting Wee Frees fed him antifreeze
(Why God knows) till he was comatose
And didnae wake up till the Monday.

25   Aye it's Retro Time for Northern Soul and the whoop and the
        skirl o' the saxes.
All they'll score's more groundglass heroin and venison filofaxes.
The rent-boys preen on Buchanan Street, their boas are made of
        vulture,
It's all go the January sales in the Metropolis of Culture.

It's all go the PR campaign and a radical change of image
30   Write Saatchi and Saatchi a blank cheque to pay them for the
        damage.
Tam o'Shanter fell asleep
To the sound of fairy laughter
Woke up on the cold-heather hillside
To find it was ten years after
35   And it's all go (again) the Devolution Debate and pro . . . pro . . .
        proportional representation.
Over pasta and pesto in a Byres Road bistro, Scotland declares
        hersel' a nation.

Margo McDonald spruced up her spouse for thon Govan By-
        Election
The voters they selectit him in a sideyways *left* defection,
The Labour man was awfy hurt, he'd dependit on the X-fillers
40   And the so-and-sos had betrayed him for thirty pieces of Sillars!

Once it was no go the SNP, they were sneered at as 'Tory' and
        tartan
And thought to be very little to do with the price of Spam in
        Dumbarton.
Now it's all go the Nationalists, the toast of the folk and the
        famous
– Of Billy Connolly, Muriel Gray and the Auchtermuchty
        Proclaimers.

45   It's all go L.A. Iager, it's all go the Campaign for an Assembly,
It's all go Suas Alba and winning ten-nil at Wembley.
Are there separatist dreams in the glens and the schemes?
Well . . . it doesny take Taggart to detect it!
Or to jalouse we hate the Government
50   And we patently didnae elect it.
So – watch out Margaret Thatcher, and tak' tent Neil Kinnock
Or we'll tak' the United Kingdom and brekk it like a bannock.

CAROL ANN DUFFY (1955–)

Born in Glasgow and now living in London, Duffy is becoming established as a leading British poet.

In Your Mind

The other country, is it anticipated or half-remembered?
Its language is muffled by the rain which falls all afternoon
one autumn in England, and in your mind
you put aside your work and head for the airport
5   with a credit card and a warm coat you will leave
on the plane. The past fades like newsprint in the sun.
You know people there. Their faces are photographs
on the wrong side of your eyes. A beautiful boy
in the bar on the harbour serves you a drink – what? –
10   asks you if men could possibly land on the moon.
A moon like an orange drawn by a child. No.
Never. You watch it peel itself into the sea.

Sleep. The rasp of carpentry wakes you. On the wall,
a painting lost for thirty years renders the room yours.
15   *Of course.* You go to your job, right at the old hotel, left,
then left again. You love this job. Apt sounds
mark the passing of the hours. Seagulls. Bells. A flute
practising scales. You swap a coin for a fish on the way home.

Then suddenly you are lost but not lost, dawdling
20   on the blue bridge, watching six swans vanish
under your feet. The certainty of place turns on the lights
all over town, turns up the scent on the air. For a moment
you are there, in the other country, knowing its name.
And then a desk. A newspaper. A window. English rain.

Stealing

The most unusual thing I ever stole? A snowman.
Midnight. He looked magnificent; a tall, white mute
beneath the winter moon. I wanted him, a mate
with a mind as cold as the slice of ice
5   within my own brain. I started with the head.

Better off dead than giving in, not taking
what you want. He weighed a ton; his torso,
frozen stiff, hugged to my chest, a fierce chill
piercing my gut. Part of the thrill was knowing
10   that children would cry in the morning. Life's tough.

> Sometimes I steal things I don't need. I joy-ride cars
> to nowhere, break into houses just to have a look.
> I'm a mucky ghost, leave a mess, maybe pinch a camera.
> I watch my gloved hand twisting the doorknob.
> 15   A stranger's bedroom. Mirrors. I sigh like this – *Aah.*
>
> It took some time. Reassembled in the yard,
> he didn't look the same. I took a run
> and booted him. Again. Again. My breath ripped out
> in rags. It seems daft now. Then I was standing
> 20   alone amongst lumps of snow, sick of the world.
>
> Boredom. Mostly I'm so bored I could eat myself.
> One time, I stole a guitar and thought I might
> learn to play. I nicked a bust of Shakespeare once,
> flogged it, but the snowman was strangest.
> 25   You don't understand a word I'm saying, do you?

ROBERT CRAWFORD (1959–)

Poet and academic, Crawford was born in Glasgow and teaches at the University of St Andrew's. One of the most vivid of the younger Scottish poets, his interest in Scot's writing is also the focus of his academic work, notably *Devolving English Literature.*

Rain

> A motorbike breaks down near Sanna in torrential rain,
> Pouring loud enough to perforate limousines, long enough
> To wash us to Belize. Partick's
> Fish-scaled with wetness. Drips shower from foliage, cobbles,
>   tourists
> 5   From New York and Dusseldorf at the tideline
> Shoes lost in hogs, soaked in potholes, clarted with glaur.
> An old woman is splashed by a bus. A gash
> In cloud. Indians
> Arrived this week to join their families and who do not feel
> 10   Scottish one inch push onwards into a drizzle
> That gets heavy and vertical. Golf umbrellas
> Come up like orchids on fast-forward film; exotic
> Cagoules fluoresce nowhere, speckling a hillside, and plump.
>
> Off dykes and gutters, overflowing
> 15   Ditches, a granary of water drenches the shoulders
> Of Goatfell and Schiehallion. Maps under perspex go bleary,
> Spectacles clog, Strathclyde, Tayside, Dundee

---

6 **clarted with glaur:** smeared with mud.

Catch it, fingers spilling with water, oil-stained
As it comes down in sheets, blows
20 Where there are no trees, snow-wet, without thought of the
        morrow.
Weddings, prunes, abattoirs, strippers, Glen Nevis, snails
Blur in its democracy, down your back, on your breasts.
In Kilmarnock a child walks naked. A woman laughs.
In cars, in Tiree bedrooms, in caravans and tenements,
25 Couples sleeved in love, the gibbous Govan rain.

LINTON KWESI JOHNSON (1952–)

Born in Jamica, Kwesi Johnson came to London in 1963. A leading figure in the black
writing and music scene, he has expounded 'dub' poetry, work designed to be recited to
reggae music and his work has been recorded for performance.

Inglan Is a Bitch

w'en mi jus' come to Landan toun
mi use to work pan di andahgroun
but workin' pan di andahgroun
y'u don't get fi know your way aroun'

5   Inglan is a bitch
dere's no escapin' it
Inglan is a bitch
dere's no runnin' whey fram it

mi get a lickle jab in a big 'otell
10 an' awftah a while, mi woz doin' quite well
dem staat mi aaf as a dish-washah
but w'en mi tek a stack, mi noh tun clack-watchah!

Inglan is a bitch
dere's no escapin it
15 Inglan is a bitch
noh baddah try fi hide fram it

w'en dem gi' yu di lickle wage packit
fus dem rab it wid dem big tax racket
y'u haffi struggle fi mek en's meet
20 an' w'en y'u goh a y'u bed y'u jus' cant sleep

Inglan is a bitch
dere's no escapin' it

---

25 **gibbous**: convex, rounded.

Inglan is a bitch fi true
a noh lie mi a tell, a true

25   mi use to work dig ditch w'en it cowl noh bitch
mi did strang like a mule, but, bwoy, mi did fool
den awftah a while mi jus' stap dhu ovahtime
den awftah a while mi jus' phu dung mi tool

Inglan is a bitch
30   dere's no escapin' it
Inglan is a bitch
y'u haffi know how fi suvvive in it

well mi dhu day wok an' mi dhu nite wok
mi dhu clean wok an' mi dhu dutty wok
35   dem seh dat black man is very lazy
but if y'u si how mi wok y'u woulda seh mi crazy

Inglan is a bitch
dere's no escapin' it
Inglan is a bitch
40   y'u bettah face up to it

dem have a lickle facktri up inna Brackly
inna disya facktri all dem dhu is pack crackry
fi di laas fifteen years dem get mi laybah
now awftah fifteen years mi fall out a fayvah

45   Inglan is a bitch
dere's no escapin' it
Inglan is a bitch
dere's no runnin' whey fram it

mi know dem have work, work in abundant
50   yet still, dem mek mi redundant
now, at fifty-five mi gettin' quite ol'
yet still, dem sen' mi fi goh draw dole

Inglan is a bitch
dere's no escapin' it
55   Inglan is a bitch fi true
is whey wi a goh dhu 'bout it?

JACKIE KAY (1961–)

Born in Edinburgh, Jackie Kay grew up in Glasgow, and is now based in London. As well as a poet, she is also a dramatist and screenplay writer.

Pounding Rain

News of us spreads like a storm.
The top of our town to the bottom.
We stand behind curtains
parted like hoods; watch each other's eyes

5   We talk of moving to the west end,
this bit has always been a shoe box
tied with string; but then again
your father still lives in that house
where we warmed up spaghetti bolognese

10   in lunch hours and danced to Louis Armstrong,
his gramophone loud as our two heart beats
going boom diddy boom diddy boom.

Did you know then? I started dating Davy;
when I bumped into you I'd just say Hi.

15   I tucked his photo booth smile into my satchel
brought him out for my pals in the intervals.

A while later I heard you married Trevor Campbell.
Each night I walked into the school dinner hall
stark naked, till I woke to Miss, Miss Miss

20   every minute. Then, I bumped into you at the Cross.

You haven't changed you said; that reassurance.
Nor you; your laugh still crosses the street.
I trace you back, beaming, till –
Why don't you come round, Trevor would love it.

25   He wasn't in. I don't know how it happened.
We didn't bother with a string of do you remembers.
I ran my fingers through the beads in your hair.
Your hair's nice I said stupidly, nice, suits you.

We sat and stared till our eyes filled

30   like a glass of wine. I did it, the thing
I'd dreamt a million times. I undressed you
slowly, each item of clothing fell
with a sigh. I stroked your silk skin
until we were back in the Campsies, running

35   down the hills in the pounding rain,
screaming and laughing; soaked right through.

Author Index

Title Index